D1592104

Britain in the Hanoverian Age 1714–1837

Garland Reference Library of the Humanities (Vol. 1481)

Britain in the Hanoverian Age 1714–1837

An Encyclopedia

Editor
Gerald Newman
Kent State University

Associate Editors

Leslie Ellen Brown
Alma College
Music, Painting, the Arts

Jack Fruchtman, Jr.
Towson State University
Politics, Religion, Philosophy

A.J.G. Cummings
University of Strathclyde
History, Politics, Business, Education

Peter Tasch
Temple University
Literature

Garland Publishing, Inc. New York & London, 1997

Library of Congress Cataloging-in-Publication Data

Britain in the Hanoverian age, 1714-1837 : an encyclopedia / editor, Gerald Newman ; associate editors, Leslie Ellen Brown . . . [et al.].
p. cm. — (Garland reference library of the humanities ; vol. 1481)
Includes bibliographical references (p.) and index.
ISBN 0-8153-0396-3 (alk. paper)
1. Great Britain—History—1714-1837—Encyclopedias. 2. Hanover, House of—Encyclopedias. I. Newman, Gerald. II. Brown, Leslie Ellen. III. Series.
DA480.B75 1997
941.07—DC21

97–16840
CIP

Cover art: Hogarth "Beer Street," 1751. Courtesy of the New York Public Library Picture Collection.
Cover design: Lawrence Wolfson Design, New York.

Printed on acid-free, 250-year-life paper
Manufactured in the United States of America

Contents

Preface

Who the Hanoverians were, how this book was made, and how to use it

During the entire period 1714–1837, a span of 123 years, the rulers of Britain were in the unusual position of being rulers also of the German state of Hanover. After the death of Queen Anne in 1714, a German who barely spoke English came over from Germany and governed until 1727 as King George I. His intentions were not unworthy, but according to one story, the applause line in his first speech was not well received—"I heff come for your goots." Though derided as a corpulent oaf, the king in his thirteen-year reign inaugurated a long period of stability and expansion.

In 1727 he was succeeded by George II. The younger George heartily participated in the national dislike of his father, but he shared also the family affection for military glory and the ancestral seat in Germany. Learning English as well as German and the French he often used with his cultured wife Caroline, he settled down to rule for thirty-three years, from 1727 to 1760, during a period of international combat but domestic peace. He was something of a war hero, and a more sympathetic figure than George I. When he died in 1760, halfway through Britain's most profitable war in history, his grandson came to power as George III.

George III, twenty-two years old, in his first public speech proclaimed his love for the new family homeland and said he was proud to be a Briton; he scorned Hanover, that "howwid Electorate," though he continued to rule it. His reign over Britain and her empire extended for a long time—sixty years—from 1760 to 1820. He was, chronologically and otherwise, the central royal figure in the history of Hanoverian Britain.

George III was hardworking, sober, and faithful to his wife. He discovered the key to royal popularity in Britain and became a respectable bore. But he had to contend with three momentous Revolutions during his reign: the American Revolution, the French Revolution, and the Industrial Revolution. His difficulties helped drive him mad during the last decade of his life, thus limiting his enjoyment of the period known as the Regency (1811–1820). He died a pathetic figure.

His son, George IV, a plump connoisseur and patron of the arts and sciences, survived him and ruled from 1820 to 1830. The Industrial Revolution was now in full swing. George IV and his countrymen saw Britain's amazing economic development as a source of great national pride but also of social concern. When in turn he died in 1830, not very much lamented, his brother, William IV, whose contemporaries noticed he "had a head like a pineapple," took over. Thus ended the unbroken line of Hanoverian kings named George. William ruled from 1830 to 1837, barely hanging on during a period of breakneck political modernization but exhibiting excellent sense at important moments. His popular nickname—"Silly Billy"—was not quite fair.

A problem arose when he died, however. Because William was childless, his niece, young Victoria, eighteen years old, inherited the British title (1837). But German law prevented her from governing Hanover. Therefore the German state, originally the family home, became separated as an entirely different kingdom under one of Victoria's relatives, an uncle. As Michael Fry, the author in this encyclopedia of all the articles on these kings, and also of that on Hanover, neatly puts it, "Hanover ceased to be British when Britain ceased to be Hanoverian." After five kings and 123 years, Britain in 1837 became "Victorian." Germany was less lucky.

An earlier Garland publication, *Victorian Britain: An Encyclopedia* (1988), edited by Professor Sally Mitchell, provides an excellent reference work for Queen Victoria's reign, the period 1837–1901. Another Garland volume, *Twentieth-Century Britain: An Encyclopedia* (1995), edited by Professor F.M. Leventhal, covers the period after that, the most recent period of British history. Still in preparation are other volumes on Medieval England and Tudor Britain. The purpose of the volume presented here is to provide another stepping-stone in this pathway of Garland reference works, a comprehensive guide to British civilization during the period 1714–1837, named in reference to the kings mentioned above.

But the Hanoverian period was not only longer than most of these others, it was also one of tremendous energy and change. It was a period which has deeply affected our modern ideas and styles, for the main architects of modern capitalism, industry, democracy, literature, and even architecture lived in that era. More than that, Hanoverian civilization also decisively influenced conditions in many of today's non–European English-speaking countries such as Canada, the United States, Australia, New Zealand, and India, countries which during much of the Hanoverian period were parts of the British Empire. The editors realized when they began this work that it would have to include something substantial about all those areas, as well as about the central aspects of civilization in the British Isles. They realized too that they were going to need a lot of help.

At the beginning of the project the five editors, each from a different broad area of historical specialization, prepared a long list of names, terms, and topics they deemed essential for inclusion. The idea was to provide basic information, alphabetically organized, on nearly every conceivable subject while still observing fundamental limits of space and accessibility. The main limit on space was the need to stay within the covers of a single volume that could be lifted without mechanical assistance. The main control on accessibility was the desire to satisfy a broad readership that might possibly range from intelligent schoolchildren seeking basic information all the way through browsing general readers, college undergraduates, graduate researchers, and even professional academics seeking recent information or references within familiar fields of reading and expertise.

The editorial group determined from the beginning that this reference work would not only address the main facts of English politics, economics, the arts, the sciences, and so on, but that it would also make a very serious effort to bring the main features of rural and urban life in Scotland, Wales, and Ireland fully into the picture as well; and moreover that while basically traditional in scope, and intended to answer traditional sorts of historical questions, the encyclopedia would not neglect newer areas of interest such as the development of Hanoverian business, education, child-rearing, sexuality, women's work and achievements, consumerism, and so on.

Having built up an article list of more than 1,000 items—people, groups, events, processes, terms, institutions—the editors began making hard choices about the lengths of the various articles required. They then sent invitations to many friends and associates, scholars in many fields of British studies, inviting them to participate in the project. Although from one standpoint it would have been desirable to enlist the help of as many specialists as there were proposed articles, thus sparing each writer from excessive exertion, the editors thought it best instead to farm out the work in interrelated bundles of half a dozen or so articles per scholar so as to economize in space, eliminate duplication of information and, above all, save the time and eyesight of users of the encyclopedia. Another advantage of the "putting-out system" employed was that oftentimes a specialist contributor, in addition to writing a bundle of interrelated articles, might suggest alterations to the article list, so that the final collection of articles presented here is in fact the result of elaborate consultations by many people trained in the study of the Hanoverian Age.

This large book is the product of all this activity. Its text and accompanying bibliographies, running to more than 600,000 words, were produced by 250 authors living throughout the British Isles, Canada, the United States, Australia, and even Japan. The encyclopedia contains 1,121 articles, of which 561 are on single individuals and 17 on family groups. Thousands of other individuals, most with their birth- and death dates provided, are discussed in the volume, and hundreds of associations are commented on. The book also includes an unusually generous selection of high-quality illustrations, mostly reproduced from contemporary engravings. Although many of the 396 pictures and illustrations are of people, most of the encyclopedia's articles are not biographical. Rather, most focus on British government, religion, politics, events, societies, business, the economy, scientific and intellectual activity, social phenomena, the arts, foreign relations, the empire, cultural trends, and wars. In the bibliographies presented here, more than six thousand books and articles are recommended for further reading and research.

To understand how this reference work was made should help in using it as a tool, or rather set of tools, depending on the specific purpose contemplated. The essential point to grasp is that large patterns of interrelated information have been converted into discrete topics, long and short, for easy alphabetical reference. The second is that if the reader so desires, these larger patterns can be reassembled by following the clues and signposts deliberately laid out by the editors. "William Bligh," the notorious sea captain, can be studied as an interesting object in himself; but cross-references to other articles on the Navy, Mutinies, Captain Cook, Australia, the Royal Society, the West Indies, and the Empire all help to exhibit his place in larger contexts of Hanoverian British civilization. Which way a reader might go will depend entirely on the direction of research intended. Following are some suggestions on how to use this encyclopedia most efficiently.

1. For *quick reference,* simply turn alphabetically to the words with which you might expect an article to begin, e.g., "Johnson, Samuel."
2. For *other facts on the same topic,* check the Index at the back of the book.
3. For *clarification or in-depth elaboration of a particular point* mentioned (a) in **boldface type** in the body of an article, or (b) at the end of it with the words *See also,* simply turn alphabetically to the articles indicated thereby. Note: neither of these two forms of signaling is intended to seem more important than the other—they are of equal value, and often the *See also* was simply added by the editors to accommodate terms that could not be conveniently edited into the main text of an article. The purpose in both cases was only to direct attention to other information of possibly related interest.
4. For *extended reading in an entire general area of study,* such as "Wars" or "Business" or "Religion," the reader should turn first to the **Table of Main Topics and Articles** that follows this Preface. The editors' purpose there is to assist the reader to see at a glance the linkages between various items in this volume, the better to furnish linear

pathways for research, parallel objects for comparison, or alternative perspectives onto the same personality, phenomenon, or event.

5. For a *single article generally surveying an entire field and mentioning most of the important people and concepts associated with it,* look in the same Table for those articles specially identified with an asterisk, such as Graphic Arts* or Medicine.* The reader should keep in mind also that although biographical articles have been omitted from this Table, *the biographies of important people often constitute additional valuable surveys* of substantial areas of endeavor.

Editing this collection of articles entailed, in addition to modifications connected with length, clarity, inside knowledge of the contents of other articles, and expectations about readers, occasionally the changing-about of some terms so as to strengthen the network of cross-referencing. The editors also made one other attempt, beyond the Index, the boldface references, the *See also*'s, and the **Table of Main Topics and Articles**, to assist the reader's reading and research. In the body of the collection itself, interrelated articles have been grouped together wherever possible by assigning similar titles (several titles beginning with "Education," for example, or "Welsh"), even though this sometimes meant removing them from other parts of the collection where they might have fit equally well. "Welsh Education," for example, appears with other "Welsh" articles, though it might just as well have appeared with other education articles as "Education, Welsh." The editors attempted, by erecting signposts in the likeliest places, to alert readers to such circumstances and point them in the right direction; but readers should always be prepared to consult the Index when encountering any apparent shortage of information.

The editors, in preparing this work, constantly kept in mind the need to make it easy to use—to anticipate readers' needs, to minimize the duplication of information, and to make the most of the space available by whittling down materials, substituting shorthand terms like "18th" for "eighteenth," and pruning from bibliographical lists those references which seemed most easily dispensable. Generally omitted are details on specific editions of the poems, plays, tracts, books, or collected works of Hanoverian-era authors, on the theory that readers can easily acquire this information for themselves by employing author searches, and that the space thus saved is better employed in referencing less obvious secondary materials known to the specialists who wrote the articles. Much care has been taken, with both the individual bibliographies appended to each article and the excellent **Guide to Further Research on Hanoverian Britain** that follows the entire collection, to present the most up-to-date information available.

The editors, after six years of work on this collaborative project, wish to salute all the contributors to it. We thank them for generously sharing their information and expertise, and sincerely hope they will be pleased with the result. We have considered it a pleasure and an honor to work with them. Their names will be found accompanying the various articles in the collection and on the full list of contributors presented in the back of this book. The editors also wish to extend particular thanks to Dr. Stanley B. Nash of Alexander Library, Rutgers University, for compiling the **Guide to Further Research**, to Mr. Peng Jiang of Kent State University for preparing the maps, and to Rebekkah Tanner, Jay Vissers, and Arthur Williams of New York for their valuable help in selecting the illustrations provided by courtesy of the Picture Collection, The Branch Libraries, The New York Public Library. Thanks are due also to Gary Kuris, Marianne Lown, Phyllis Korper, and Helga McCue of Garland Publishing for their unfailing support for this project.

Gerald Newman

Table of Main Topics and Articles

Usage Note:

1. These lists are not all-inclusive. They identify only the *main* articles connected with each topic.
2. Each article marked with an *asterisk* is a particularly long and full survey, providing a complete overview of a given field and the names and activities of important persons connected with it.
3. In the interest of conserving space, none of the encyclopedia's nearly 600 biographical articles are listed here. However, it should be noted that many of them also contain useful general surveys—of groups, genres, regional patterns, fields of endeavor, historical evolution, and so on.

List of Illustrations

A Chronology, 1714–1837

1714: George of Brunswick-Lüneburg, Elector of Hanover, proclaimed King of Great Britain
1715: Jacobite Rebellion erupts in Scotland and northeast England
1716: Alexander Pope finishes translation of Homer's *Iliad*
1717: Freemasons form Grand Lodge of London
1718: *Leeds Mercury* begins publication
1719: Whigs repeal Occasional Conformity Act
1720: Thousands of investors ruined in South Sea stock crash
1721: Lady Mary Wortley Montagu orders first English smallpox inoculation
1722: Daniel Defoe publishes *Moll Flanders*
1723: Black Act creates 50 new capital crimes
1724: Jonathan Swift's *Drapier's Letters* force policy change on Ireland
1725: Malt Tax Riots shake Glasgow
1726: Faculty of Medicine established at Edinburgh University
1727: Coronation of King George II
1728: John Gay's *The Beggar's Opera* opens in London
1729: John Wesley forms "Methodists" at Oxford University
1730: Philip Doddridge becomes Congregationalist pastor at Castle Hill, Northampton
1731: Edward Cave founds *The Gentleman's Magazine*
1732: Sir Francis Dashwood and others begin Society of Dilettanti
1733: Excise Crisis results in humiliating defeat for Sir Robert Walpole
1734: Nicholas Hawksmoor designs west towers of Westminster Abbey in Gothic Revival style
1735: "Hogarth's Act" passed to stop engravers from pirating artists' work
1736: Porteous Riots threaten Edinburgh
1737: Playhouse Act shuts down London theaters and imposes government control over content of plays
1738: Ironmaster Abraham Darby II takes over Coalbrookdale Company
1739: David Hume publishes *Treatise of Human Nature*
1740: Thomas Arne writes "Rule, Britannia!"
1741: Thomas Coram's Foundling Hospital opens in London
1742: George Frideric Handel's *Messiah* premiers in Dublin
1743: King George II's hat shot off at Battle of Dettingen
1744: Broad-Bottom ministry begins
1745: "Forty-five" Rebellion in Scotland
1746: Sir William Watson fires electric spark across River Thames
1747: Admiral George Anson smashes French fleet off Cape Finisterre
1748: Treaty of Aix-la-Chapelle concludes War of Austrian Succession
1749: Henry Fielding starts Bow Street Runners
1750: Bristol's first bank established
1751: Parliament shortens the year and attacks drunkenness with Calendar Reform and Gin Act

1752: Charlotte Lennox publishes *The Female Quixote*
1753: City of Liverpool builds Salthouse Docks
1754: Thomas Chippendale issues *The Gentleman & Cabinet-Maker's Director*
1755: Samuel Johnson publishes *Dictionary of the English Language*
1756: Black Hole of Calcutta
1757: Admiral Byng executed
1758: Halley's Comet returns as predicted
1759: General James Wolfe dies in capture of Quebec
1760: Coronation of King George III
1761: James Brindley's Bridgewater Canal opens and inaugurates Canal Age
1762: "John Bull" makes first appearance by name in a political cartoon
1763: Peace of Paris registers British successes in Seven Years' War
1764: James Hargreaves revolutionizes textile industry with "Spinning Jenny"
1765: Stamp Act precipitates crisis in North American colonies
1766: Oliver Goldsmith publishes *The Vicar of Wakefield*
1767: Sir George Baker identifies "Devonshire colic" as lead poisoning induced by cider-drinking
1768: John Wilkes stirs tumultuous Middlesex election dispute
1769: James Watt patents steam engine
1770: Lord North becomes Prime Minister
1771: Richard Arkwright's industrial empire begins at Cromford
1772: Feathers Tavern Petition demands modification of clerical requirements
1773: Boston Tea Party
1774: Lord Chesterfield's *Letters to His Son* published
1775: War of American Independence begins with Battles of Lexington, Concord, Bunker Hill
1776: Adam Smith publishes *The Wealth of Nations*
1777: John Howard publishes survey of prison conditions in England and Wales
1778: France declares war on side of American rebels
1779: Abraham Darby III completes world's first cast-iron bridge near Coalbrookdale
1780: Gordon Riots result in 800 Londoners killed or injured
1781: William Herschel discovers planet Uranus
1782: Irish Parliament gains legislative independence
1783: Treaty of Paris acknowledges American independence
1784: India Act establishes parliamentary jurisdiction over East India Company's rule in India
1785: Edmund Cartwright produces world's first steam-driven loom
1786: Robert Burns publishes *Poems, Chiefly in the Scottish Dialect*
1787: Founding of the Society for the Abolition of the Slave Trade
1788: First permanent European settlement of Australia begins under Governor Arthur Phillip
1789: Charles Burney completes his *General History of Music*
1790: Edmund Burke publishes *Reflections on the Revolution in France*
1791: Thomas Paine replies in *The Rights of Man*
1792: Mary Wollstonecraft publishes *A Vindication of the Rights of Woman*
1793: Board of Agriculture established
1794: Thomas Hardy, John Horne Tooke, and John Thelwall acquitted of treason charges
1795: Speenhamland System of welfare supplements begun
1796: Edward Jenner carries out first successful vaccination
1797: Naval mutinies at Spithead and the Nore suppressed
1798: Irish Rebellion crushed
1799: Royal Institution founded to promote technical education among the poor and unemployed
1800: Passage of Irish Act of Union
1801: Census shows 9 million (m.) people living in England and Wales, 5.2 m. in Ireland, 1.6 m. in Scotland
1802: Society for the Suppression of Vice mounts campaign against blasphemy and immorality
1803: Lord Selkirk, pioneer of Canadian development, plants colony of Highlanders on Prince Edward Island
1804: William Blake publishes first volume of *Jerusalem*
1805: Battle of Trafalgar thwarts French invasion plans and ensures British naval supremacy
1806: James Mill begins his *History of British India*
1807: Ministry of All the Talents abolishes British slave trade
1808: Richard Trevithick demonstrates model railway at 12 miles per hour

1809: Duel between William Canning and Viscount Castlereagh
1810: William Cobbett imprisoned for antigovernment writings in *Political Register*
1811: Regency begins under George, Prince of Wales
1812: Sarah Siddons, retiring from London stage, brings the house down one last time
1813: Millenarian prophet Joanna Southcott announces herself with child by Holy Ghost
1814: Walter Scott publishes his first novel, *Waverley*
1815: Battle of Waterloo
1816: Jane Marcet publishes *Conversations on Political Economy*
1817: Elizabeth Fry forms Ladies Association for Improvement of Female Prisoners in Newgate Prison
1818: Stamford Raffles acquires authorization to construct fort at Singapore
1819: Peterloo Massacre leaves 11 people dead and 400 wounded
1820: Coronation of King George IV
1821: Founding of *The Manchester Guardian*
1822: Caledonian Canal opened to link eastern to western Scotland
1823: Thomas Wakley founds *The Lancet,* the first medical journal
1824: Combination Acts of 1799 and 1800 repealed
1825: Stockton and Darlington Railway opens
1826: Explorer Alexander Laing dies in Timbuktu
1827: John Loudon McAdam becomes Surveyor General of Roads
1828: Repeal of Test and Corporation Acts
1829: Daniel O'Connell forces passage of Catholic Emancipation
1830: Coronation of King William IV
1831: Michael Faraday demonstrates electromagnetic induction
1832: Parliamentary Reform Act modernizes national government
1833: Abolition of Slavery in British Empire
1834: Passage of New Poor Law
1835: Municipal Corporations Act modernizes local government
1836: John Fielden publishes *The Curse of the Factory System*
1837: John Ramsay McCulloch publishes *Statistical Account of the British Empire*

Britain in the Hanoverian Age 1714–1837

Actors and the Acting Profession

Actors in the Hanoverian age still suffered from that Puritan disapproval of drama which had closed theaters in the 17th century and identified performers with vagrancy and degeneracy. The profession's respectability improved a little after the Restoration (1660), but this stemmed more from social relaxation of morals than moral reformation by performers. The period 1690–1714 saw strenuous new complaints from writers such as **Jeremy Collier** and **Daniel Defoe**, who attacked theaters as "nurseries of crime" and "universities of the devil." But partly because playwrighting (as distinguished from acting) was now an occupation of people as respectable as **Sir John Vanbrugh**, **Joseph Addison**, **Delarivière Manley**, **Susanna Centlivre**, and **George Lillo**, early Hanoverian moralists wanting to force actors into unemployment were disappointed until they received unexpected help from **Sir Robert Walpole**. There was nothing puritanical about him, but the **Prime Minister**, pelted from the stage by political criticism, engineered passage of the **Playhouse Act** (1737) to muzzle his enemies in the literati.

The Act's ulterior purpose was to censor the content of dramatic productions, but it also had the effect of restricting (down to the year 1843) the number of places of legitimate employment open to actors. In 1736 there were six theaters in London; after 1737, "legitimate drama" in London was confined to the Drury Lane, Covent Garden, and (after 1766) Haymarket theatres, and, similarly, in **provincial towns**, to only those theaters under royal patent and control. Of course, from the 1740s, ways were found for getting around these restrictions, for example, by granting 60-day licenses for occasional performances or by slyly redefining theatrical events as musical or pantomimical ones. Some "strolling" or touring companies also carried royal letters patent, and outside the capital, acting companies often came to town when fairs or other special events drew crowds. They played not in permanent licensed theaters but in churches, barns, or rooms at the local inn. The establishment of circuits for these touring companies led to parliamentary bills for the building of approved playhouses in places like **Bath**, **Bristol**, **Dublin**, **Edinburgh**, and **York**. By 1800 there were over 280 theaters in circuits throughout Great Britain, though some existed under potential threat of official action in case of complaints.

Originally, many of the touring companies were "sharing" companies, sometimes actually run by players themselves, but these were succeeded by companies in which an organizing **entrepreneur** paid contracted salaries to his players and managed the behind-the-scenes business affairs. Tate Wilkinson (1739–1803), whose troupe was based in Yorkshire and whose *Memoirs* (1791) are indispensable for understanding Hanoverian theater, was one of the most respected of these managers. Most actors received their early training in the provincial theaters. Wilkinson used his theater to develop new talent and to bring the stars of Drury Lane and Covent Garden to perform in the summer season for regional audiences.

An actor's life was varied but not easy. The uncertainty of employment and income led to intense rivalries, obsequiousness to rich patrons, irregular habits, and unstable personal lives. Many thespians lived down to public expectations of them. In fact, respect for performers was so low during the earlier Hanoverian period that oafish spectators might shower even great actresses with orange peel or, worse, toss the backless (and nonreservable) benches upon which everyone was forced to sit. The unusually democratic character of theatrical entertainment, which brought together servants, tradesmen, apprentices, and dukes, had its disadvantages.

Conditions improved somewhat after 1750 with the success of **David Garrick**, who helped bring social distinction to performers in the London theaters—though among famous contemporary actors he was flanked on one side by **Charles Macklin**, a convicted killer, and **Samuel Foote**, a performer whose excellence made it impossible to take him seriously. Of course, intelligence and good diction, which all three had, were important to success. By the later 18th century, actors came mostly from the **middle class**, and some actresses, such as Elizabeth Farren and Lavinia Fenton, married aristocrats after having been their mistresses. Many actors were well-

Actors' Benefit Performance at Covent Garden

educated, having attended good public schools, universities, or the Inns of Court. Some, like **Colley** and **Charlotte Cibber** and **Arthur Murphy**, wrote plays in addition to acting in them, and others published **novels**, **poetry**, and **essays**. But despite these accomplishments, public distrust of the theater and moral disapproval of actors persisted into Victorian times.

An actor was typically hired for a stated period, usually 1 or 2 years, at a specified salary, with the additional guarantee of one or more benefit performances each year. Benefits for actors dated from the reign of James II (1685–1688); those for playwrights were still older. After deduction of operating expenses, the proceeds of a benefit performance, amounting perhaps to £50 in 1750, would go to an actor, playwright, or perhaps a charitable group. Less important actors would often have to share their benefits with one or more fellow actors. Though benefits provided actors with increased income, managers often used them as an excuse to pay actors smaller salaries. Benefits could also prove embarrassing if attendance was small, and costly if receipts did not cover operating expenses.

There was a gradual modernization of acting technique, with increasing stress on preserving the dramatic illusion before the audience. Early in the period, the emphasis was on acting as speech-making, with little serious regard to the appropriateness of action, costume, or scenery. An actor playing Julius Caesar, dressed like an 18th-century king in buckled shoes and bag-wig, might wander to the apron, deliver a speech (which might be applauded then and there), and then, while awaiting his next speech, drop his character, stare about the house, and wink at a friend in the gallery, oblivious to notions of artistic teamwork and dramatic naturalism that are routinely in force today. The latter Hanoverian period saw the emergence of more professional attitudes, assisted partly by corresponding changes in theater design and staging, which removed spectators from the stage itself, and in greatly improved sets, lighting, and scenery by mechanical wizards such as **Philippe Jacques de Loutherbourg**.

The profession's progress may be charted in the succession of great stage performers. In the 1730s, James Quin (1692–1766) was considered Britain's best tragic actor; but his declamatory style fell out of popularity with the advent of the more "natural" presentations of Garrick. Garrick tried to reveal character more subtly, rather than merely strut and fret, and to speak intelligently and articulately rather than bombastically. He was, of course, especially renowned for his performance of Shakespearean roles. He was not only the most acclaimed actor on the English stage between 1741 and 1776, he was also manager of Drury Lane, the leading theater, during much of this time. His aim was to get audiences to take drama seriously as art, rather than as spectacle or social gathering. He planned his seasons carefully, introduced new interpretations of familiar characters, and prepared and revised old and new plays, though often with little respect for the original scripts.

The redoubtable Macklin acted for almost 70 years and, like Garrick, with whom he was often compared, strove for a certain realism. Especially known for his portrayal of irascible old men, he triumphed in his impersonation of Shylock as tragic character rather than buffoon. His sensational appearance as Macbeth in Scots clothing (1773) alongside other actors similarly dressed marked the growing interest in dramatic naturalism and authenticity. Macklin also pioneered in drama training, offering instruction in both "schools" and a crude apprentice system.

After these giants, English theater was dominated by great theatrical families, first the Kembles, then the Keans. The Kembles—**Sarah Kemble Siddons** (1755–1831) and her brother John Philip Kemble (1757–1823), an actor as well as theater manager—popularized a classical style of acting, strong on grace and grandeur. Siddons shunned stage tricks and artificial behavior to make her characters psychologically believable. She helped her brother rise to prominence, and the two acted together, though Kemble said he never forgot her technical superiority. He managed Drury Lane from 1788 to 1802 but left because of disagreements with **Richard Brinsley Sheridan**, patentee of the theater. He then became manager of Covent Garden, which he caused to be rebuilt after it was destroyed by fire (1808). His youngest brother, **Charles Kemble**, a very successful actor also, managed Covent Garden (1822–1832, 1842).

By 1820, **Edmund Kean** was challenging the Kembles' decorous style with his own combination of **Romanticism** and realism. Most famous for his Shakespearean roles, he emphasized spontaneity and intense emotion rather than beauty and dignity. Sometimes he "fudged" the quieter moments of a play, his voice becoming inaudible. **Coleridge** remarked on Kean's combination of intensity and indifference: seeing Kean act, he said, was like reading Shakespeare by the light of lightning flashes. Kean magnetized audiences and inspired younger actors such as George Vandenhoff, Samuel Phelp, the Americans Junius Brutus Booth and Edwin Forrest, and his own son, Charles Kean (1811–1868). Charles and his wife, Ellen Tree (1806–1880), carried on the family tradition and strengthened the growing emphasis on historical accuracy in setting, costume, and properties.

The period ended in the age of William Charles Macready (1793–1873), another actor-manager, who debuted in 1810 and acted for over 40 years. His style combined the best of the Kembles and the Keans, dignity with intensity. Each detail of his characterizations was carefully planned. As manager he insisted on painstaking rehearsals, and was the first to bring back Shakespeare unadulterated with changes or additions like those made by Cibber, Garrick, and many others. Unfortunately he was never as popular as Kemble or Kean, or as financially successful.

In sum, the Hanoverian period brought increased realism and concentration on character in acting style, and greatly increased the social standing of actors. Both developments helped to foster the cult of the individual actor, the growth of theater criticism, and modern interest in the history of the acting profession.

Ann W. Engar

Bibliography

Booth, Michael, et al., eds. *The Revels History of Drama in English (1750–1880).* Vol. 6. 1975.

Donohue, Joseph. *Theatre in the Age of Kean.* 1975.

Hume, Robert D., ed. *The London Theatre World, 1660–1800.* 1980.

Kelly, Linda. *The Kemble Era: John Philip Kemble, Sarah Siddons and the London Stage.* 1980.

Manvell, Roger. *Sarah Siddons: Portrait of an Actress.* 1970.

Nicoll, Allardyce. *The Garrick Stage: Theatres and Audience in the Eighteenth Century.* 1980.

Playfair, Giles. *The Flash of Lightning: A Portrait of Edmund Kean.* 1983.

Stephens, John Russell. *The Profession of the Playwright: British Theatre, 1800–1900.* 1992.

Trussler, Simon. *The Cambridge Illustrated History of British Theatre.* 1994.

See also Dramatic Arts; Dramatic Criticism; Shakespeare Industry; Theaters and Staging

Acts of Union

See Union, Act of

Adam Family

The Adam family of architects began with William Adam (1689–1748), who has been called the first classical architect of **Scotland**. He is best known for his remodeling of Hopetoun House, West Lothian (1721–1754), in which he combined elements drawn from **Wren**, **Vanbrugh**, and **Gibbs**. His four sons all became architects: John (1721–1792) with the help of his brother Robert designed the gate at Fort George (*c.* 1753), Inverness-shire, and then abandoned architecture; Robert (1728–1792), the most ambitious and talented of the family, became one of the nation's most active and original architects after spending the years 1754–1758 drawing the ruins and architecture of Italy under the tutelage of the French architect and draftsman Charles-Louis Clérisseau (1721–1820) and the Italian etcher Giovanni Battista Piranesi; James (1730–1794) followed Robert's example by studying with Clérisseau in Italy (1760–1763) and became his brother's collaborator on many projects; and William (1738–1822) was more concerned with the business side of the creation and diffusion of what became known as the Adam style.

Robert brought back to England a new version of **neoclassical** architecture and decoration (inspired by classical and Renaissance sources) which revolutionized English domestic architecture and replaced the Neopalladian style. A prime instrument of his influence was his publication *The Ruins of the Palace of the Emperor Diocletian at Spalatro* (1764), which helped establish his authority as an expert on classical domestic architecture. An important example of his work was Syon

Robert Adam

House, Middlesex (1762–1769), which he extensively remodeled for the Duke of Northumberland. This showed Adam's willingness to combine and synthesize very appealingly and unpedantically architectural motifs drawn not only from ancient sources but also from **Palladian**, Neoclassical, Renaissance, and French sources as well. For example, the House's raised stucco and painted wall and ceiling decorations suggest ancient Roman painted and sculptured sources, as well as those of the Renaissance, but Adam's creations were in fact more delicate and graceful than the originals. The same qualities may be viewed in other **interior designs** such as that of the Marble Hall at Kedleston Hall, Derbyshire (1765–1770). Other rooms, such as the Etruscan Dressing Room at Osterley Park, Middlesex (*c.* 1775–1776), were inspired by the etchings of Piranesi and by ancient vase-painting. Some Adam exteriors, for all Robert's claims of originality and authenticity, were often Neopalladian in inspiration with added Roman decoration (Register House, Edinburgh, 1774–1792).

Robert and James and their innumerable assistants created rich interiors—including wall and ceiling paintings of classical scenes, tapestries, carpets, and other home furnishings—for a total effect. Their interests also extended to **city** planning, with the creation of the Adelphi overlooking the Thames (1768–1772), a complex of public and private buildings that created an enclave of varied yet related architectural forms within a harmonious cityscape. Other examples of Adam architecture on a large scale included part of Fitzroy Square (constructed in 1790–1800) and Portland Place (1776) in **London**, and Charlotte Square (1792–1807), **Edinburgh**, all designed as individual residences but treated as part of overall architectural compositions.

The Adam brothers, never modest, began to publicize their architectural accomplishments in *The Works in Architecture of Robert and James Adam* (1773, 1779, 1822). These richly illustrated volumes pictured their major works in detail, including furniture. The books did not include Robert's romantic **Gothic** designs, such as Culzean Castle (*c.* 1777–1780), nor the Croome Church interiors (1763).

James Adam was made a member of the Society of Arts in 1758 (he later designed its headquarters in the Adelphi) and a fellow of the **Royal Academy** (1761); Robert never became a member because of opposition by other architects. The Adam brothers, while ambitious and at times ruthless and publicity-seeking, were wonderfully talented designers who created a new and influential style based on their broad knowledge of the past. Contemporaries such as **James Wyatt** were influenced by them, as was the next generation of architects.

Thomas J. McCormick

Bibliography

Adam, Robert, and James Adam. *Works in Architecture.* 3 vols. 1773–1822.
Beard, Geoffrey. *The Work of Robert Adam.* 1978.
Fleming, John. *Robert Adam and His Circle in Edinburgh and Rome.* 1962.
Gifford, John. *William Adam, 1689–1748.* 1989.
Harris, Eileen, and Nicholas Savage. *British Architectural Books and Writers, 1556–1785.* 1990.
King, David. *The Complete Works of Robert and James Adam.* 1991.
Rowan, Alistair, and Robert Adam. *Catalogue of Architectural Drawings in the Victoria and Albert Museum.* 1988.
Stillman, Damie. *The Decorative Work of Robert Adam.* 1967.

See also Architects and Architecture; Home Furnishings and Decoration; Housebuilding and Housing

Addington

See Sidmouth, Viscount

Addison, Joseph (1672–1719)

Addison was a leading **Augustan** essayist and literary critic. Educated at Oxford, he shaped the taste of the growing reading public by increasing its awareness of classical and Continental literatures. His **essays** are considered among the greatest in English literature—beautifully organized, sophisticated but familiar, harmoniously pleasing; the "middle style" that he popularized helped to establish prose as a literary medium equal to **poetry**. Moreover, as a fervent supporter of the **Glorious Revolution** and the **Whig** party, he played various political roles in the same era. He received his first political appointment in 1704 and eventually rose to become Secretary of State in 1717 for his support of the **Hanoverian Succession**.

Addison's first publications were Latin and English poems praising King William III. Prominent Whig politicians supported the young author by financially helping him undertake the European grand tour, 1699–1704. His poem "A Letter from Italy" (1701), and a prose account of his travels (1705), depicted the inferiority of Europe's absolute monarchies to the English parliamentary system. "The Campaign" (1704), a heroic poem on **Marlborough**'s victories over the French, brought him popular recognition and a **patronage** appointment as Commissioner of Appeals.

Prompted by writers and politicians at the Kit Cat Club, Addison wrote an opera in 1707. Seeking to counter London's taste for Italian **opera**, *Rosamond* is sung in English and tells a story from British history. Though the topic was timely, the music was uneven; the opera failed. Through the same **club**, Addison also renewed acquaintance with **Richard Steele**, whom he had met at Charterhouse School in 1686, and was influenced by Steele's interest in drama giving moral and political instruction. In 1709 Addison contributed several numbers to Steele's *Tatler*, Addison showing an unexpected flair for humor and "noble discourses" on moral topics.

In 1711 the two men began a new **periodical**, *The Spectator*, which was published 6 times a week and lasted 555 issues. While Steele concentrated on politics and manners, Addison attended to literature and morality. His major contributions were essay series on opera, tragedy, the pleasures of the imagination, and *Paradise Lost*. His aesthetic ideas remained influential throughout the century, as so did *The Spectator* itself, reprinted (in bound editions) more than 50 times by 1800. Addison also authored many "Saturday sermons" on moral topics.

In 1713, with Whigs and **Tories** battling over the succession question, Addison wrote *Cato*, a classical tragedy offering Roman republicanism as a model for Whigs. Although immediately popular, it retained a reputation afterward only as a "closet drama" that read well but acted poorly.

Joseph Addison

After **Queen Anne**'s death (1714), Addison supported the Hanoverian succession. He began two periodical journals, *The Freeholder* and a revived *Spectator*, to provide entertainment and public relations for the new monarch, **George I**. He was rewarded with government positions and married into the **aristocracy** in 1716.

Addison's lasting contribution was the sense of artistry he brought to periodical **journalism**. His important legacy was a vision of cultivated, cultured citizenship that lasted into the 20th century. Explaining the purpose of *The Spectator* (No. 10), he unconsciously wrote his own epitaph:

> I shall be ambitious to have it said of me, that I have brought Philosophy out of the Closets and Libraries, Schools and Colleges, to dwell in Clubs and Assemblies, at Tea-Tables and in Coffee-Houses.

Robert M. Otten

Bibliography

Bloom, Edward A., and Lillian D. Bloom. *Joseph Addison's Sociable Animal: In the Market Place, on the Hustings, in the Pulpit.* 1971.
Bond, Donald F., ed. *The Spectator.* 1965.
———, ed. *The Tatler.* 1987.
Kay, Donald. *Short Fiction in the "Spectator."* 1975.
Ketcham, Michael G. *Transparent Designs: Reading, Performance, and Form in the "Spectator" Papers.* 1985.
Knight, Charles. *Addison and Steele: A Reference Guide.* 1994.
McCrea, Brian. *Addison and Steele Are Dead.* 1990.
Otten, Robert. *Joseph Addison.* 1982.
Smithers, Peter. *The Life of Joseph Addison.* 1968.

Adultery

During the 16th and 17th centuries, adultery in England was dealt with primarily by the Church courts. The penalty for offenders was to stand before the congregation on Sunday or before a crowd at the marketplace on market day wearing a white sheet and holding a candle. By the early 18th century this practice, along with the power of the Church courts themselves, was in decline. It was more common now for the secular state in the form of Justices of the Peace to punish adulterers by sentencing them to fines, the stocks, or a whipping. However, with one exception, by the second half of the 18th century even the English secular courts were largely ignoring adultery.

The exception was the so-called crim-con cases brought before the Court of the King's Bench. The legal classification of adultery as "criminal conversation" resulted from suits brought by husbands against men accused of seducing their wives. Such cases usually involved people of considerable property. They received much publicity from the popular press, and the fines levied on those convicted were often extremely punitive, running to as much as £15,000—enough to financially ruin many an adulterer.

The notoriety of crim-con cases and their significant increase between the 1770s and 1820s has bolstered a belief that in fact adultery was on the rise among upper-class women. There are some grounds for this in contemporary gossip. The Earl of Pembroke (1734–1794) commented (in French) in 1780 that upper-class women were then as promiscuous as sheep, permitting "anyone to board them." Such testimony may be worth little in itself, but some cases were conspicuous. The Devonshires kept two separate nurseries: William **Cavendish**, 5th Duke of Devonshire, had 2 children by Lady Elizabeth Foster and 3 by his wife the Duchess Georgiana, who had one child by Lord Grey (1737–1819). Though no academic theories are required to explain such things, some modern historians consider that the growth of an ideal of marital companionship might have stirred upper-class women to seek love and affection elsewhere if these were unavailable within marriage.

As to the general level of adultery, it remains unclear how different the Hanoverian age was from earlier ones. Researchers know that the sexual "double standard" gave gentlemen much latitude in forming sexual liasons outside marriage, and 18th-century moralists lost no opportunity to flay the upper-class male as licentious. At the other end of the social register, the erosion of religious and legal sanctions made it easier for adultery to take place amongst the poorer classes; in general it seems to have been tolerated if kept sufficiently discreet. However, between 1790 and 1810 a combination of factors, including the growth of **Evangelicalism**, the rise in the number of crim-con cases, and the fear generated by the **French Revolution**—often linked in the British mind with moral laxity—fostered a new conservative moral attitude among many members of the **middle classes**, something that gradually affected the other classes above and below them. It was during this period that bills were introduced in Parliament for the criminalization of adultery and for barring divorced wives from marrying their lovers. Though not passed, these bills reflected the growth of what was to be called (anachronistically) the Victorian morality of the late Hanoverian period.

Stanley D. Nash

Bibliography

Gillis, John R. *For Better, for Worse: British Marriages, 1600 to the Present.* 1985.

Porter, Roy, and Lesley Hall. *The Facts of Life: The Creation of Sexual Knowledge in Britain, 1650–1950.* 1995.

Staves, Susan. "Money for Honor: Damages for Criminal Conversation." *Studies in Eighteenth-Century Culture.* Vol. 11, pp. 279–297.

Stone, Lawrence. *The Family, Sex and Marriage in England, 1500–1800.* 1977.

———. *Road to Divorce: England, 1530–1987.* 1990.

———. *Uncertain Unions and Broken Lives.* 1992.

See also Divorce; Manners and Morals; Marriage; Punishment

Africa

British interest in Africa was triggered by the dramatic growth of the **slave trade**. Yet paradoxically it was the **antislavery movement** that brought the establishment of British colonies in Africa. During the **French Revolutionary and Napoleonic Wars**, the acquisition of the Cape Colony (1806) presaged future imperial ambitions.

Until the 1760s the link with Africa was purely commercial, with Britain taking the European lead in the slave trade; this had now expanded beyond the Gold Coast to Angola and Mozambique. But Britain also sought lesser trades that included at one time or another gold dust, ivory, pepper, and palm kernels. An interest in gum (used for glazing textiles) was one reason for the British seizure from the French of Gorée and annexation of Senegal, creating the Crown Colony of Senegambia, in 1763. But France regained these in 1783, ending Britain's first African colony.

After the **War of American Independence** (1783), and especially after the abolition of the slave trade (1807), the influence of abolitionists and **missionary societies** transformed British African policy. **Granville Sharp** organized the establishment of a colony in Sierra Leone (1787) for ex-slaves (rewarded for their support of Britain during the American War). These were later joined by others, including Maroons deported from Jamaica for their revolt in 1795. Then in 1808 Sierra Leone became a Crown Colony and henceforth the base of British efforts to suppress the slave trade. In 1816 Britain also occupied St. Mary's (Banjul) Island, which, as the Gambia Colony, acted as a base against illicit slave traders and as a source of gum. Efforts to suppress illegal slavery thus helped to plant a string of colonies.

The abolitionists also encouraged **exploration** of the African interior, about which Europe knew almost nothing. In 1788 they helped set up the African Association to fund exploration of Africa in anticipation of future evangelizing activity. After several setbacks, the Association sent out (1795) the expedition of Mungo Park (1771–1806), whose published journal, *Travels in the Interior Districts of Africa* (1797), did much to stimulate further interest.

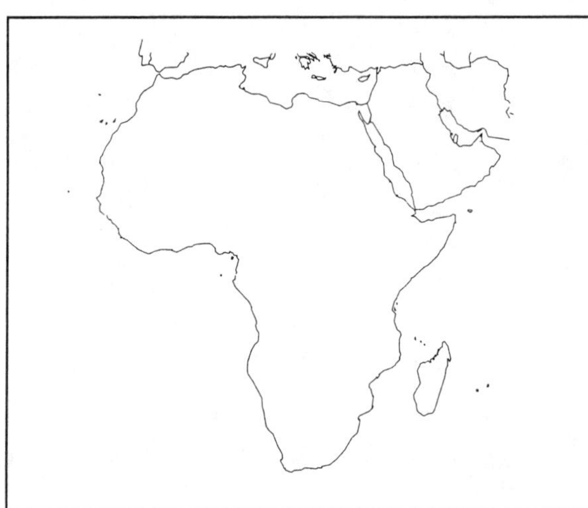

Africa

Interior exploration meant penetrating the center from several coastal locations: Britain's posts on the West African coast, the Cape Colony, and the Arabian Sea soon became the major points of departure. Explorers sought to map the great river systems, notably the Niger, whose route was at last traced by the Lander brothers in 1830. After the 1790s the government took a leading part in funding many of these expeditions.

Acquisition of the Cape Colony (1806) began a new phase of territorial expansion. The Cape was retained as a crucial strategic post in British trade with **India**. But its possession, and the spread of white settlement within it, brought Britain into frontier disputes with indigenous peoples, and also into conflict with the Dutch Boer farmers who had arrived in the 17th century. One result was a series of wars with the Xhosas (1818–1819, 1834–1835); another was the secession of the Boers in the Great Trek north beyond British control (1837). The Hanoverian period thus laid the groundwork for future colonial expansion and for Britain's role in the famous "scramble for Africa" of the late 19th century.

Andrew J. O'Shaughnessy

Bibliography

Ajayi, J.F.A., and M. Crowder, eds. *History of West Africa.* Vols. 1 and 2. 1971.

Curtin, Philip. *The Image of Africa: British Ideas and Action, 1780–1830.* 1965.

Flint, John, ed. *Cambridge History of Africa: From c. 1790–c. 1870.* Vol. 5. 1976.

Fyfe, Christopher A. *The History of Sierra Leone.* 1962.

Gray, Richard, ed. *Cambridge History of Africa: From c. 1600–c. 1790.* Vol. 4. 1977.

Hopkins, A.G. *Economic History of West Africa.* 1973.

Rotberg, R.I. *Africa and Its Explorers.* 1970.

Walvin, James. *Black Ivory: A History of British Slavery.* 1994.

See also Empire and Imperialism

Agricultural Improvers

Traditionally regarded as the instigators of an "Agricultural Revolution," which accompanied or perhaps helped to cause the **Industrial Revolution** in Britain, improvers such as **Robert Bakewell**, **Jethro Tull**, and **Andrew Meikle** are now recognized by historians as participants in a process of agricultural change that actually spanned a much longer period. Improvement, however, was indeed a keynote of 18th-century Britain, and in response to **population** pressure and price changes, agricultural development increased in scale and pace. It had many facets: more efficient estate management; enclosure of open fields; drainage of fen lands; cultivation of soil-enriching or fodder crops; more elaborate crop rotation; more scientific breeding of animals; the application of marl, lime, and appropriate manures; and adoption of new machinery. Many of the techniques and even crops were not new, but their use was vigorously promoted and became more widespread as improvement became fashionable.

The attitude of **aristocracy and gentry**, and of lesser **farmers**, was crucial. In many parts of England and Scotland, enlightened landowners such as **Lord Charles Townshend**, **Thomas Coke of Holkham**, **John Cockburn of Ormiston**, and **Sir Archibald Grant of Monymusk** carried out improvement on their own estates and encouraged tenant farmers by their example and by granting longer leases. They also supported many farming **clubs** that sprang up throughout Britain, and some sat in Parliament, which passed nearly 4,000 Enclosure Acts between 1750 and 1810. Another important role was played by inventors such as Meikle, **James Small**, and **Patrick Bell**, who provided new agricultural machinery. Still another was played by popularizers and propagandists such as **Arthur Young** and **Sir John Sinclair of Ulbster**, whose writings helped to spread improving ideas much more widely and rapidly. It had taken over two centuries for cultivation of the turnip to become widespread in Britain; but so strong was the new spirit of agricultural improvement that the larger, frost-resistant Swedish turnip, introduced in the 1790s, was being grown throughout England and Scotland within a decade.

C.J. Davey

Bibliography

Chambers, J.D., and G.E. Mingay. *The Agricultural Revolution.* 1966.

Jones, E.L. *Agriculture and Economic Growth in England.* 1967.

Kerridge, E. *The Agricultural Revolution.* 1967.

Neeson, J.M. *Commoners: Common Right, Enclosure and Social Change in England, 1700–1820.* 1993.

Phillipson, N.T., and R. Mitchison, eds. *Scotland in the Age of Improvement.* 1970.

Thompson, F.M.L., ed. *Landowners, Capitalists, and Entrepreneurs.* 1994.

See also Agricultural Societies; Agriculture; Finance and Investment; Irish Agriculture; Scottish Agriculture; Welsh Agriculture

Agricultural Laborers

See Farmers and Agricultural Laborers

Agricultural Societies

Improvement Societies or Farming Clubs were formed by landowners interested in promoting **agricultural improvement** by spreading information about the best practices. The typical society included local landowners and their tenants who met fairly regularly to discuss enthusiastically what they thought were "new" improved farming methods—even though some of these had been described by the poet and agricultural experimenter Thomas Tusser (*c.* 1524–1580) centuries earlier. The first societies were inspired by members of the **Royal Society of London**, which formed a Georgical Committee in 1664, and the Royal Society of Arts, which by the 1750s was offering gold medals for reports on improving farming methods.

Most societies appeared after 1750. Many had but few members, did not last long, and left few records—e.g., as at Aberdeen, **Liverpool**, **Manchester**, **Norwich**, **York**, and

Salford. Others continued to flourish, including the **Bath** Society, formed in 1777 for the encouragement and improvement of agriculture, manufactures, commerce and the fine arts, and the Highland Society of Scotland, founded in 1784 with the object of looking into the state of the Highlands, the condition of their inhabitants, and the means of their improvement. In 1810 the Bath Society produced a list of over 80 British Agricultural Societies, some surviving to become involved in the era of scientific farming in the 19th century.

C.J. Davey

Bibliography

Chambers, J.D., and G.E. Mingay. *The Agricultural Revolution.* 1966.

Hudson, K. *Patriotism with Profit.* 1972.

Neeson, J.M. *Commoners: Common Right, Enclosure and Social Change in England, 1700–1820.* 1993.

Smith, J.H. *The Gordon Mills Farming Club.* 1962.

Smout, T.C. *A History of the Scottish People.* 1969.

Thompson, F.M.L., ed. *Landowners, Capitalists, and Entrepreneurs.* 1994.

See also Agriculture; Farmers and Agricultural Laborers

Agriculture

Former generations of historians viewed agrarian developments in the Hanoverian period as revolutionary; indeed, an "Agricultural Revolution" was thought to have occurred between 1750 and 1830. But this view, particularly with regard to England and **Wales**, has been abandoned in favor of one that sees agrarian change as a much more protracted process, stretching back into the 17th century and forward into the later 19th.

A **population** survey in the late 17th century showed that England and Wales were dominated by agriculture, that at least half the population earned a living from or had some connection with the land, and that three-quarters of it lived in hamlets or villages. But England in particular was socially more complex than this suggests. England's social structure, despite its three main tiers, was characterized by a flexibility that allowed for social mobility between them. Primogeniture pushed younger sons of the nobility into the professions, while mercantile and other wealth bought its way into agriculture and its privileges.

The landowning class stretched along a wide spectrum of income and status, from the **aristocracy** or "temporal lords" at the pinnacle down through the **gentry** to the yeomanry and peasantry. Below these in status, but often as wealthy as the lesser sort of landowners, were members of a middle class of tenant **farmers**—the core of the agricultural economy—who in turn employed the **agricultural laborers** and cottagers at the bottom. These latter formed the third component of 18th-century rural society; its small size is an indication that the subsistence sector of the British economy, small by comparison with the market sector, was also relatively small by comparison with the subsistence sectors in other European countries at that time.

Trade had long been important to Britain, and England especially had traditionally been an exporter of grain, even in the lean years of the late 17th century and during the poor harvests of the early 18th. It was not unusual that, in the year 1750, almost one-quarter of the wheat crop was exported. But the poor harvests of 1764–1775 led to a fundamental change in the grain trade, and Britain began to import grain by the 1780s. **Corn Laws**, introduced to protect home producers, imposed duties on this imported grain and awarded bounties to exporters. But, in fact, the proportion of imported grain to home production was never large in Hanoverian Britain, even though the quantities imported increased rapidly in the 1820s and 1830s.

Agrarian change was spurred by a number of factors, but above all by an unprecedented expansion of the home market in the 18th and early 19th centuries. **Population** more than doubled in this period, creating obvious demands. The market became much more pervasive as developments in transport by **road**, river, **canal**, and **coastal shipping** enabled more farmers to take advantage of new commercial opportunities. Agricultural markets also became more concentrated; **London** grew by massive proportion, and other ports, together with rising industrial **cities**, created new centers of demand.

The social composition of the landowning class was also changing. Large estates grew at the expense of lesser proprietors (a group which included the smaller gentry, along with freeholders)—a decline that was only temporarily reversed in the agriculturally very profitable wartime years 1793–1815. Moreover, during 1730–1750, falling agricultural prices increased rent arrears, turning the screw tighter on small landowners and precipitating still more downward social mobility.

However, from around 1750, agricultural prices began to rise, which accelerated agrarian change. The enclosure of open fields (that is, a formal procedure under which compact plots of privately owned fenced-off farmland were made to replace strips of open field over which animals formerly had roved) had begun before the Hanoverian period, but the rate of change increased under the stimulus of price rises, with over 7 million acres being enclosed by Acts of Parliament during 1760–1815 and more than 1,000 Enclosure Acts being passed in the final 40 years of the 18th century. Enclosure, it was said, might double rental income in a generation through gains in efficiency as the scattered holdings of the common fields were consolidated, limitations on land use were lifted, and common grazings were abolished. Commons and wastes were also enclosed, and substantial areas were reshaped, especially in the Midlands and the north. Increased investment in agriculture also manifested itself in new, well-built farmhouses and buildings, which now stood separate from the villages in their own systems of neatly divided fields.

Despite such radical change, rural depopulation was not truly great. Indeed, the number of agricultural workers continued to rise because the task of enclosing and working the expanded cultivable area demanded more labor. Only in relative terms, by comparison with workers employed in other expanding industries, did the agricultural workforce decline. The migration of individuals to industrial and mining centers

Machine used in making hay, 1797

and to ports was compensated in rural areas by the general rise in the population. However, those smaller agricultural producers who had survived on the margins of subsistence and who had depended on the commons and wastes for a living, were now more ruthlessly eliminated.

As smaller producers were squeezed out, landlords sought to replace them with more efficient tenant farmers. In consequence, output increased due mainly to three factors: land-use changes which utilized the soil to better advantage; higher arable and pasture yields as a result of improved **technology** and fertilizers (and, later, drainage); and a modest but real increase in labor productivity, due to the use of more efficient hand tools.

Such advances, however, were far from universal. Many tenants were hamstrung by landlords unable or unwilling to provide the necessary capital investment, and not all farmers, of course, were sufficiently well-informed or receptive to the new ideas. This, together with limitations of topography and soil, made for an unevenness of progress throughout the country. Overall agricultural improvement was modest by comparison with the growth of output in the later 19th and 20th centuries.

Great landlords such as **Coke of Holkham** did play an important role as **agricultural improvers** by creating an environment in which agrarian change could take place. Such men worked to provide security of tenure, and helped tenants acquire fixed capital investments like buildings and drainage. Moreover, large estates did facilitate the diffusion of new agricultural techniques and implements, albeit slowly.

But the key group of agricultural improvers was that of the "great farmers"—the landed gentry, large owner-occupiers, and tenant farmers who held 200 to 500 acres of land. These men made great strides in the selective breeding of livestock in this period. For example, **Robert Bakewell** of Dishley worked on the development of sheep, cattle, and horses. His fame arose from the diffusion of his methods not only in breeding but also in the watering and irrigation of meadows. Though Bakewell is perhaps the most famous of the genre, another score of farmers, including Webster of Canley, Joseph Allom, the Colling brothers, the Booths, and Thomas Bates, all made contributions to progress in this branch of husbandry. These men laid the foundations for the important industry of raising pedigree livestock—one that had become well established by 1800.

Peter Clapham

Bibliography

Chambers, J.D., and G.E. Mingay. *The Agricultural Revolution, 1750–1880.* 1966.

Jones, E.L. *Agriculture & Economic Growth in England, 1650–1815.* 1967.

———. *Agriculture & the Industrial Revolution.* 1974.

Mingay, G.E., ed. *The Agricultural Revolution, Changes in Agriculture, 1650–1880.* 1977.

———, ed. *The Agrarian History of England & Wales, Vol. VI, 1750–1850.* 1989.

Neeson, J.M. *Commoners: Common Right, Enclosure and Social Change in England, 1700–1820.* 1993.

Rule, John. *The Vital Century: England's Developing Economy, 1714–1815.* 1991.

Thirsk, J., ed. *The Agrarian History of England and Wales.* Vol. 5: 1640–1750. Vol. 6: 1750–1850. 1985, 1989.

Thompson, F.M.L., ed. *Landowners, Capitalists, and Entrepreneurs.* 1994.

See also Agricultural Societies; Cities and Urban Life; Finance and Investment; Irish Agriculture; Scottish Agriculture; Tull, Jethro; Welsh Agriculture

Akenside, Mark (1721–1770)

Poet and physician, Akenside contributed to the ongoing discussion of the aesthetic and moral principles of the **sublime** with his extremely well received *The Pleasures of the Imagination* (1744), the revised version of which was published posthumously in *The Poems of Mark Akenside, M.D.* (1772).

Akenside's poetic genius surfaced when he was only 16, with publications of his poems in the *Gentleman's Magazine.* Of humble origins, born at Newcastle-upon-Tyne, he attended college in **Edinburgh** to prepare to be a minister. He changed plans in mid-study and pursued **medicine**, ultimately with much success. But he also attained considerable fame with his **poetry**. His *Pleasures* was influenced by the ideas of Anthony Ashley Cooper, Earl of Shaftesbury (1671–1713), and by **Joseph Addison**'s similarly titled series of essays in *The Spectator.* However, he leaned more toward the moral perspective stressed by Shaftesbury than toward purely aesthetic concerns. In his *Pleasures* can also be found early manifestations of the organic theory of art that saw fuller development later in **Romanticism**.

Mahasveta Barua

Bibliography

Jump, Harriet. "Two New Akenside Manuscripts." *The Review of English Studies.* Vol. 39, pp. 217–230.

Houpt, Charles Theodore. *Mark Akenside: A Biographical and Critical Study.* 1944.

Monk, Samuel H. *The Sublime: A Study of Critical Theories in Eighteenth-Century England.* 1960.

Almanacs

Designed to lay out the astronomical year, and usually replete with a calendar of saints' days, church festivals, and other data, these ubiquitous annual publications served to tell the **farmer** when to plant and when to pray. They formed part of the basic domestic **library**, along with the Bible, the Prayer Book, and Foxe's *Book of Martyrs.* Taken in their aggregate, hundreds of thousands of almanacs were sold annually, and thus outstripped all other titles. One popular publication was *The Ladies' Diary* (1704–*c.* 1840). Another perennial best-seller was Philip Moore's *Vox Stellarum,* which sold a record 82,000 copies annually by 1761, 107,000 copies in 1768, 230,000 in 1789, 365,000 in 1802, and peaked at 560,000 copies in 1839. In **North America**, *Poor Richard's Almanac,* full of homely proverbs on industry and honesty, helped its editor, **Benjamin Franklin**, to grow healthy, wealthy, and wise. Indeed the sale of almanacs was so lucrative that the Company of Stationers attempted to exercise its monopoly control over their production long after it had lost control over most other forms of publication.

Through much of the 18th century, almanacs were produced in two formats—as single broadsheets intended to be affixed to a wall (forerunners of modern wall calendars), and as pocket-sized volumes. The latter traditionally contained a table of the year's astronomical events (such as eclipses); a calendar of days, weeks, and months; and a section devoted to prognostications (which invariably reflected the political and religious controversies of the day). Almanacs owed their origin to the popular belief in astrology, and much of their appeal to the casting of horoscopes; but as belief in astrology began to erode during the 18th century, it lost its centrality in almanacs. An example of the newer sort of almanac was the *Gentleman's Diary; or the Mathematical Repository* (begun in 1747).

The political and religious partisanship that had characterized almanacs of earlier eras also waned. Compilers then focused their prognostications more exclusively on things like the weather and harvests, and compiled lists and tables of more generally useful data, while providing the consumer with a convenient pocket diary and calendar.

N. Merrill Distad

Bibliography

Capp, Bernard. *Astrology and the Popular Press: English Almanacs, 1500–1800.* 1979.

Thomas, Keith. *Religion and the Decline of Magic: Studies in Popular Beliefs in Sixteenth- and Seventeenth-Century England.* 1971.

Wright, Lawrence. *Clockwork Man: The Story of Time, Its Origins, Its Uses, Its Tyranny.* 1968.

See also Reference Works

American Revolution

This term has traditionally referred to the events leading up to the successful effort in the later 18th century by colonists in **North America** to break their political connection with Britain.

Distance, time, European problems, and British domestic crises during the 17th century all combined to make a loosely structured affair of the English colonial system. However, partly because of the prevailing theory of indivisible sovereignty, and partly because of the centralizing logic of mercantilist **economic thought**, British officials maintained throughout the colonial period that central authority over colonial possessions was limited only by voluntary concessions of power. In practice, having failed in efforts to assert greater actual control in the late 17th century (the collapse of the "Dominion of New England" in 1689), the government thereafter followed a policy of "salutary neglect"—a strong theoretical assertion of power, but little exercise of it.

Consequently, as the North American colonies experienced rapid demographic and economic growth, and as colonial legislatures increased their day-to-day authority, the divergence between theory and practice grew wider. Agencies in the government, particularly the Board of Trade, periodically expressed concern about this, but wartime conditions during the reign of **George II** (1727–1760) blunted efforts to reverse the trend.

At the close of the **Seven Years' War** (1763) the government, headed by **George Grenville**, felt compelled to reduce the national debt, which was alarmingly large by the standards of the time, and to do so at a time when military triumphs had created a much enlarged, more administratively expensive **empire**. Efforts to alleviate these financial problems included imposing direct **taxes** upon the colonies, an unprecedented action that produced a spiral of resistance and coercion.

The **Plantation Act** (1764), imposing new duties and expanding the list of "enumerated goods" regulated under the **navigation laws**, initiated the policy, but opposition focused upon the more farreaching **Stamp Act** (1765), which levied taxes on legal documents, advertisements, and newspapers. Colonial resistance to this included theoretical arguments ("no taxation without representation"), effective economic boycotts against British-made imports, and violent reprisals against officials and their supporters. The government repealed this act (1766), at the same time uncompromisingly reaffirming central authority over the colonies with the **Declaratory Act** (1766). This effectively closed off the possibility of recasting the mother country-colonial relationship into a form more amenable to compromises.

Another round of taxation in 1767 (the Townshend Duties, named after **Charles Townshend**), renewed and broadened resistance. Troops transferred into urban areas to assist civilian officials only exacerbated tensions, as in the **Boston Massacre** (1770), in which five colonists were killed. Discontentment subsided temporarily with the repeal of most duties at the outset of **Lord North**'s administration (1770), but the **Tea Act** of 1773, a misguided effort to provide greater revenues to the nearly bankrupted **East India Company**, brought renewed violence (the **Boston Tea Party**) and property destruction. The government's Coercive ("Intolerable") Acts (1774), designed primarily to punish Bostonian resisters and reassert authority, produced instead the Continental Congress (September 1774), an intercolonial meeting that rejected parliamentary authority and orchestrated a thorough boycott of British goods.

In July 1775 a second Congress met to issue a "Declaration of the Causes and Necessity of Taking Up Arms" and to coordinate military resistance. Radicals, most prominently **Thomas Paine** in his influential pamphlet *Common Sense* (January 1776), began questioning the desirability of any imperial connection whatever; on 4 July 1776, with full-scale rebellion already well under way, Congress ended hopes for reconciliation by accepting the *Declaration of Independence,* a call for separation that went beyond earlier concerns about charter rights, or the rights of Englishmen, to anchor the movement exclusively in the natural rights philosophy then current in **Enlightenment** intellectual circles.

David Sloan

Bibliography

Bailyn, Bernard. *The Ideological Origins of the American Revolution.* Enlarged ed., 1992.

Countryman, Edward. *The American Revolution.* 1985.

Egnal, Mark. *A Mighty Empire: The Origins of the American Revolution.* 1988.

Maier, Pauline. *From Resistance to Revolution: Colonial Radicals and the Development of American Opposition to Britain, 1765–1776.* 1972, 1991.

Middlekauff, Robert. *The Glorious Cause: The American Revolution, 1763–1789.* 1982.

Murrin, John M. "The Great Inversion, or Court vs. Country," in J.G.A. Pocock, ed., *Three British Revolutions, 1641, 1688, 1776.* 1980.

Nash, Gary B. *The Urban Crucible: Social Change, Political Consciousness, and the Origins of the American Revolution.* 1979.

Shy, John. "The Spectrum of Imperial Possibilities: Henry Ellis and Thomas Pownall, 1763–1775," in John Shy, *A People Numerous and Armed: Reflections on the Military Struggle for American Independence.* Rev. ed., 1990.

Thomas, P.D.G. *British Politics and the Stamp Act Crisis: The First Phase of the American Revolution, 1767–1773.* 1975.

———. *The Townshend Duties Crisis: The Second Phase of the American Revolution, 1767–1773.* 1987.

———. *Tea Party to Independence: The Third Phase of the American Revolution, 1773–1776.* 1991.

Tucker, Robert W., and David C. Hendrickson. *The Fall of the First British Empire: Origins of the War of American Independence.* 1982.

Ward, Harry M. *The American Revolution: Nationhood Achieved, 1763–1788.* 1995.

White, Morton. *The Philosophy of the American Revolution.* 1978.

See also War of American Independence

Amherst, Jeffrey, 1st Baron (1717–1797)

Amherst commanded British forces in the capture of New France (**Canada**) during the **Seven Years' War** and served as supreme commander of the **army** during much of the later 18th century. At age 14 he obtained an ensigncy in the Guards and by 1756, due to his exceptional abilities as a commander, had risen to lieutenant-colonel of the 15th Regiment of Foot. In 1758 Prime Minister **William Pitt the Elder**, faced with the failure to dislodge French forces occupying the Great Lakes and Allegheny regions of British **North America**, appointed Amherst as major-general in command of an expedition to recapture upstate New York and eliminate French strongholds in New France (1758). Pitt needed a strong-willed, self-disciplined commander such as Amherst to control his more fiery subordinate officers such as **James Wolfe**.

The island of Louisburg, captured on 26 July 1758, provided a base from which to launch subsequent operations. Amherst, now known for prudence and judgment, became commander-in-chief of all British and colonial forces, and personally led the successful recapture of Fort Ticonderoga (July 1759). Further operations under subordinates captured Fort Niagara (July 1759), Quebec (September 1759), and Montreal (September 1760), putting New France firmly under British control.

General Jeffrey Amherst

Knighted (1761) and made Governor-General of British North America (until 1763), Amherst proved less successful in dealing with the Indians, particularly the revolt led by Chief Pontiac. Considering them barbaric, he erred by underestimating their abilities. He nonetheless returned to England a popular hero (1763).

In 1768 he became (briefly) Governor of Virginia. He firmly supported the crown during the **War of American Independence**, was created Baron Amherst (1776), played a role in suppressing the **Gordon Riots**, and was made Field-Marshal (1796). During his long period of leadership he unfortunately failed to check many abuses then current in the army.

Stanley D.M. Carpenter

Bibliography

Amherst, Jeffrey. *Official Papers, 1740–1783.* (Microfilm) 1979.

Parkman, Francis. *Montcalm and Wolfe.* 1962.

Rogers, H.C.B. *The British Army of the Eighteenth Century.* 1977.

See also War and Military Engagements

Amiens, Peace of (1802)

This marked a brief interlude during the **French Revolutionary and Napoleonic Wars** (1792–1815). Both sides were exhausted. In the somewhat lopsided peace treaty, signed (27 March) by **Lord Cornwallis** and Joseph Bonaparte (1768–1844), Britain relinquished her ancient claim to the French throne and returned nearly all her recent imperial conquests except Trinidad and Ceylon to their former possessors (chiefly **France**, Spain, and Holland); France agreed to give up southern Italy, return Egypt to the Porte, and recognize Portugal's integrity. **Richard Sheridan** characterized the deal—negotiated by the ministry of the peace-loving Henry Addington (later **Lord Sidmouth**)—as something "which all men are glad of, but no man could be proud of." Britain terminated the peace and again declared war (17 May 1803) when it became clear that Napoleon, busily acquiring Louisiana, Parma, Piedmont, and Elba, and intervening in Dutch and Spanish affairs, was still bent on large-scale expansion.

Stanley D.M. Carpenter

Bibliography

Rodgers, A.B. *The War of the Second Coalition.* 1964.

Ross, Steven. *European Diplomatic History, 1789–1815.* 1969.

See also Diplomats and Diplomacy

Amusements and Recreation

Hanoverian Britain's slow but steady change from rural to urban and industrial conditions brought with it an undermining of popular recreations. There was a slow disintegration of the robust and somewhat ritualized (though often cruel and violent) popular amusements. As early as 1807, **Robert Southey** could note that "all persons . . . speak of old ceremonies and old festivities as things which are obsolete." By the 1850s, the recreational void was being filled by such diverse developments as modern sport, music halls, and seaside holidays.

Outdoor "diversions" (as popular recreations were called in the 18th century) took place in the locations of everyday life: the marketplace, churchyard, public thoroughfares, and on common land. They had an important social dimension, providing opportunities for feasts, festivals, and seasonal ceremonies, as well as respite from labor. The traditional Christmas, Easter, Whitsun, and May Day festivities all involved eating, **drinking**, and **dancing**. Sword-dancing, ceremonial dancing, mumming, and morris dancing were all enjoyed on such occasions. Guy Fawkes' and New Year's Day also provided opportunities for recreation. Such occasions were supplemented by annual parish feasts or "wakes." In many cases, wakes and fairs, and particularly hiring or "mop" fairs, corresponded with the agricultural and trade calendars, so that recreation accompanied trade. Fairs also provided opportunities for sexual adventure and indulgence, particularly among the young and unmarried. Here again, dancing played a significant role and helped make these both opportunities for, and occasions of, courtship.

Young men were provided opportunities for personal displays of courage and gallantry in the traditional Shrove Tuesday football games that took place throughout the country. Each holiday match had its own special customs and rules, which reflected both the site or context and the degree of organization involved. Football was played widely as a common recreational pursuit, but was also, on occasion, used as a camouflage for popular protest. During the latter 18th century, football was played in the public schools and even at **Cambridge University** but, because of its violent nature, was often regarded by the upper classes as a rough, uncivil game, "fit only for farmboys and butcherboys."

Cricket, by contrast, was more quickly absorbed into

polite society because, as a foreign visitor observed, it could more "readily accommodate the common people and also men of rank." While **clubs** for the wealthy were formed and matches often played on rented grounds or even at country houses, **gambling** and the making of matches helped promote the game for rich and poor alike. Unlike other forms of **sport** such as horse-racing, hunting, and shooting, genteel society had no monopoly on the game. Nevertheless, through the efforts of its aristocratic patrons, cricket developed a formal organizing body, the Marylebone Cricket Club, which ensured the game's diffusion. Cricket's spread and growing popularity can be measured in part by the crowds it attracted—as many as 10,000 spectators watched matches in London in 1750. Nor were such large crowds at sporting matches very unusual. A wrestling contest in Berkshire in 1737 drew 10,000 people.

Pugilism and cock-fighting, like cricket, cut across class lines. Yet all these activities relied on influential patrons who provided purses, fostered interest, and occasionally deterred others in authority who might have restricted amusements in deference to public opposition to gambling, cruelty to animals, and large public gatherings. There were other ways, too, in which economic and class advantages affected the shape of people's recreations and amusements. In *The Deserted Village* (1770), **Oliver Goldsmith** complained of how the rich were depriving the poor of their land and thus their amusements: "The man of wealth and pride / Takes up a space that many poor supplied; / Space for his lake, his park's extended bounds, / Space for his horses, equipage, and hounds. . . ."

Blood sports, shooting, and **fishing** were the chief outdoor rural pursuits for the wealthy. The increasing organization of these activities, and their growing detachment from the rural community, were sources of resentment. Among the necessary amenities of a country seat was a good shoot. The introduction of game birds, such as partridges and pheasants, attracted **poachers**, who in turn furthered the role of the gamekeeper and the passing of very divisive game laws such as the **Black Act** (1723). Hunting also became more organized with the development of "name" and "subscription" hunts, the use of carefully bred hounds, and the improvement of double-barreled hunting **weapons**.

As with hunting, horse-racing's development also depended on the leadership of wealthy patrons. The **Dukes** of **Cumberland** and **Grafton** were typical of those who devoted time and capital to the turf. The importance of established courses such as Newmarket and Epsom, and the influence of the Jockey Club as the controlling body ("jockey" being at this time the term used for an owner as well as a rider), both played a part in the spread of strictly organized meets. This in turn led to the demise of some of the more traditional recreations because the race meeting increasingly took over from the local fair or "wake" as the annual merrymaking festival. By the 1780s, racing was an organized sport with roots already deep in the commercial world, boasting courses all over the country.

The **public house**, as one of the fundamental social centers of the community, was as important as patronage in providing significant social support for popular diversions. The publican himself often acted as patron, providing facilities, equipment, food, and drink; often even acting as stakeholder and bookmaker. Drinking beer and playing skittles became common amusements for working people as other activities became curtailed, and as the more traditional rural structure and pastimes declined.

With urbanization and industrialization came a need for effective labor discipline. Idleness, levity, and pleasure-seeking were among the enemies to be overcome; regularity, orderliness, sobriety, and industry were the virtues promoted. The traditional culture of popular recreations was generally antithetical to these values. The result was that economic and social development forced a steady decline in this traditional culture even while it was already, from the 1790s, under attack from the side of the **Evangelical** movement promoting its neo–Puritan version of the same values of sobriety and industry. Evangelicals often attacked the rougher popular recreations on the grounds of cruelty or vulgarity, but some historians have questioned whether these earnest **middle-class** reformers were not also pursuing, if unconsciously, a strategy of social power which entailed breaking the hold of the landed classes on popular deference, a hold routinely maintained at boxing matches, cock-fights, cricket matches, and the like. It is certain that traditional amusements were being undermined also by other factors: systematic attacks on the traditional blood sports from the angle of **humanitarian** values and the ethic of **sensibility**; the limiting of public space following the agricultural enclosure movement; a weakening of local customs brought about by economic change; and, throughout the Hanoverian period, a deep-seated fear of how large crowds might generate **riots and popular disturbances**.

While none of these changes took place without tension, and many of the traditional recreations continued (albeit in changed form), there was a breaking down of rural insularity and an increasing adoption of urban pastimes among working people. The distinction between the gentleman's life of leisure in the country and the working man's life of labor in the **provincial town** or **city** was etched more deeply by such changes. The recreations prescribed for working people in the late Hanoverian era were "rational" and moral, preparing mind and body for work. The forces of specialization and professionalization also moved on apace, ever revising and modernizing the possibilities for "diversion."

Timothy J.L. Chandler

Bibliography

Altham, Harry, and E.W. Swanton. *A History of Cricket.* 1948.

Clark, Peter. *The English Alehouse, 1200–1830.* 1983.

Cunningham, Hugh. *Leisure in the Industrial Revolution.* 1980.

Hole, Christina. *English Sports and Pastimes.* 1968.

Horn, Pamela. *The Rural World.* 1980.

Itzkowitz, David. *Peculiar Privilege.* 1977.

Malcolmson, Robert. *Popular Recreations in English Society, 1700–1850.* 1981.

Mingay, G.E. *English Landed Society in the Eighteenth Century.* 1970.

Reid, J.C. *Bucks and Bruisers: Pierce Egan and Regency England.* 1981.

Thompson, F.M.L., ed. *The Cambridge Social History of Britain, 1750–1950.* 3 vols. 1990.

Vamplew, Wray. *The Turf: A Social and Economic History of Horseracing.* 1976.

See also Manners and Morals; Music; Pleasure Gardens; Toys and Games; Travel and Tourism

Analytical Society

This society was formed at **Cambridge University** in 1812 by three mathematics' undergraduates, George Peacock (1791–1858), Charles Babbage (1792–1871), and John Herschel (1792–1871), who met for breakfast every Sunday morning to discuss the practical application of analytical mathematical methods, especially of differential calculus. These students, soon joined by four others, are regarded as mathematics reformers because they foresaw the general usefulness of abstract mathematical principles.

They all later had distinguished careers in **science** and mathematics. Peacock in 1836 became the Lowndean professor of mathematics, and (1839) dean of Ely, Cambridge. Babbage, who actually gave its name to the Analytical Society, was a founder of the Astronomical Society (1820), and later (1828) was named Lucasian Professor. Herschel, son of the astronomer **William Herschel**, focused primarily on astronomy. In addition to discussing mathematical notation, the group also debated such historical questions as whether Sir Isaac Newton (1642–1727) or G.W. Leibniz (1646–1716) first discovered calculus. In 1816, after publishing an English edition of Lacroix's *Elementary Differential Calculus,* the society was attacked by conservative mathematicians who refused to accept the new notational language; but by 1830 its methods had generally triumphed.

Jack Fruchtman, Jr.

Bibliography

Ball, W.W. Rouse. *A History of the Study of Mathematics at Cambridge.* 1889.

See also Science, Technology, and Invention

Ancients vs. Moderns Quarrel

European humanism, based on the revival and assimilation of classical authors, generated a centuries-long series of disagreements referred to as the quarrel between the ancients and moderns. In essence, those who valued primarily the lessons which the Renaissance had recovered from Greek and Roman cultures were "ancients," whereas those who valued primarily the means through which those values were recovered were "moderns." Both sides generally agreed that human nature was universal, but moderns felt that cumulative progress had made contemporary achievements superior to those of antiquity, particularly in **science** but increasingly in philosophy and the arts.

The quarrel flared in England when Sir William Temple's "Essay upon Ancient and Modern Learning" (1690) dismissed claims of modern superiority lately advanced in such works as Thomas Burnet's *Sacred Theory of the Earth* (1684–1690) and Pierre Fontenelle's *Conversations on the Plurality of Worlds* (1686). The literary incident known as the "Battle of the Books" erupted when William Wotton (1666–1727) replied with ponderous scholarship to Temple's casual essay. Wotton's *Reflections upon Ancient and Modern Learning* (1694), to which Cambridge philologist **Richard Bentley** added a preface (1697), not only endorsed modern scholarly technique as the vehicle of progress but demonstrated that progress by discrediting the "ancient" texts Temple had praised, the *Epistles* of Phalaris and the *Fables* of Aesop. Temple was defended by an Oxford group, the "Christ Church wits," most particularly **Francis Atterbury** and William King (1663–1712), whose clever ad hominum ridicule, largely of Bentley, seemed to overwhelm the moderns.

The best-known works related to the quarrel are **Jonathan Swift**'s *The Battle of the Books* and *A Tale of a Tub* (both 1704), though the quarrel informed numerous others: Swift's *Gulliver's Travels* (1726) satirized its protagonist as a modern, and **Alexander Pope** attacked modernism as Dullness in *The Dunciad* (1728); **Daniel Defoe**'s *Robinson Crusoe* (1719) suggests support for modernism, and many nonliterary works, for example, Thomas Madox's (1666–1727) *History of the Exchequer of the King of England* (1711), confirm modern doctrine in their scholarly approach.

Ancients and moderns alike studied **classicism**, though ancients saw in this a guide to conduct whereas moderns more often considered it in terms of artifacts to verify, date, and classify. Individuals, of course, were never purely ancient or modern. Thus if the quarrel appears to have been the ancients' swan song before their cause was overwhelmed by the **Industrial Revolution**, it may equally be seen as a step toward integrating taste and scholarship. **Samuel Johnson**, for example, may appear as both classical humanist and contemporary lexicographer, **Edward Gibbon** as modern historian lamenting the decline of classical values.

Richard N. Ramsey

Bibliography

Levine, Joseph M. *The Battle of the Books: History and Literature in the Augustan Age.* 1991.

Spadafora, David. *The Idea of Progress in Eighteenth-Century Britain.* 1990.

See also Classicism; Satire; Translation

Anderson, John (1726–1796)

Anderson had a long and distinguished career at **Glasgow** University. Appointed Professor of Oriental Languages in 1754, he moved to the Chair of Natural Philosophy in 1757. A friend of **Joseph Black** and **Adam Smith**, host to **Benjamin Franklin** and **Samuel Johnson**, Anderson exemplified the liberal ideas of the **Enlightenment** and developed a wide-ranging interest in **science** and **technology**. His model **Newcomen** engine was repaired by **James Watt** and probably stimulated Watt to improve it. Dissatisfied with Glasgow University, he left most of his property—and an elaborate constitution—to found the **Andersonian Institution** (1796), now the University of Strathclyde.

John Butt

Bibliography

Butt, John. *The Good of Mankind and the Improvement of Science.* 1989.

Muir, James. *John Anderson and the College That He Founded.* 1947.

Nolan, J. Bennett. *Benjamin Franklin in Scotland and Ireland.* 1938.

Andersonian Institution

Founded in 1796 in consequence of Professor **John Anderson**'s will, this educational venture was financed and developed by **Glasgow** citizens. Anderson's executors collected subscriptions and began teaching with a staff of one professor, Thomas Garnett (1796–1799), who lectured on Natural Philosophy. Instruction was open to both sexes, and classes were popular, attracting some mechanics and artisans. **George Birkbeck** so admired this format that he later based the **Mechanics Institute** movement in England on it. Later professors included Andrew Ure (1804–1830) and Thomas Graham (1830–1837), both national figures. By 1837 the Andersonian had grown significantly, providing training in **medicine**, **science**, and **technology**.

John Butt

Bibliography

Butt, John. *The Good of Mankind and the Improvement of Science.* 1989.

Lythe, S.G. Edgar. *Thomas Garnett.* 1984.

Muir, James. *John Anderson and the College That He Founded.* 1947.

Anglo-Irish Protestant Ascendancy

By 1603, Ireland had been conquered and brought under effective English control. Thereafter there were several more waves of migration from England and **Scotland**, those from England primarily Anglican in religion, those from Scotland primarily **Presbyterian**. "Protestant Ascendancy" was a term identifying the mainly English immigrant group by its religious affiliation with the Protestant Episcopalian Church of Ireland (twin sister of the **Church of England**), and also indicating its dominant political and social position over not only the Irish **Catholics** but also the immigrant Presbyterian **dissenters**, whose political disabilities were the same as in England. With the defeat of James II at the **Battle of the Boyne** (1690), the ascendancy was confirmed in imposing its regime while developing for itself a distinctive outlook and culture that was neither English nor Irish. Its control of the land was reflected in the pattern of **Irish Land Settlement** that continued to develop.

Despite emerging victorious in 1690, the ascendancy still had much to fear from the Catholic **population**, which comprised more than two-thirds of the total inhabitants. Catholic landed interests had retained some political power, but the ascendancy was determined to break this. This was achieved through the **penal laws**, which excluded Catholics from the **Irish Parliament** and the franchise, restricted their holdings of land, encouraged their heirs to convert to Protestantism, prevented them from taking positions in the **army**, the militia, any branch of the civil service or the legal profession, and forbade them from keeping schools or sending their children abroad. Many of these laws were annuled progressively after 1778. Some Catholics could vote after 1793, but could not seek election to the Irish Parliament.

The 18th century, the period of the Irish Parliament, is considered the high point of the power of the Protestant Ascendancy. It developed a particular brand of radical Irish nationalism and was determined to secure its own rights and independence against English intervention, but it also had to control the Catholic majority. This left it in a precarious position, as its leaders had to rely on English military power to defend its rights and customs in Ireland. Nevertheless it did force concessions from the British Parliament, and in 1782 Westminster's right to legislate over Irish issues was removed. There followed a period of nominal independence from then until the **Act of Union** was passed in 1800—which the ascendancy initially resisted, then finally supported, partly due to fears of Catholic insurrection. Thereafter the influence of the ascendancy was weakened, but it was only after **Catholic emancipation** (1829) that its power was finally broken.

William Kenefick

Bibliography

Beckett, J.C. *The Making of Modern Ireland, 1603–1923.* 1966.

———. *A Short History of Ireland.* 1971.

Lecky, W.E.H. *History of Ireland in the Eighteenth Century.* 1892.

Farrell, B., ed. *The Irish Parliamentary Tradition.* 1973.

See also Ireland and Irish Politics

Anne, Queen (1665–1714)

Anne, the last Stuart monarch, came to the throne in 1702. The younger daughter of James II and Anne Hyde, her succession was the result of the **Glorious Revolution** of 1688, the childlessness of William and Mary, and her own Protestantism. Married to Prince George of Denmark in 1683, she endured several unsuccessful pregnancies. Her only surviving child, William, born in 1689, died in 1701, necessitating the **Act of Settlement** (1701) to secure the Protestant succession.

Anne's reign marked the final phase of revolution politics, with both **Whigs** and **Tories** jockeying for position to influence the inevitable change in dynasty. A devout high church Anglican, Anne refused to countenance any move to substitute her **Catholic** half-brother for the **Hanoverian succession**. She preferred the moderate Toryism of **Robert Harley**, but was not always able to stand against the intense Whiggism of her close friend the Duchess of Marlborough or the more radical Tory machinations of **Henry St. John**. The

Queen Anne

disgrace of both radical factions between 1710 and 1714 brought a growing recognition that ruling politicians should all belong to one party, and meant also that at the queen's death, her successor, **George I**, had no long-standing commitments to senior politicians. His reign saw the emergence of new leaders as well as new issues.

Anne's reign was virtually coterminous with the **War of the Spanish Succession**. Britain and her allies under the leadership of the **Duke of Marlborough** ended Louis XIV's domination of the Continent. The Treaty of Utrecht (1713) confirmed English conquests of Gibraltar, Port Mahon, Nova Scotia, and **Newfoundland**. Anne's successors did not have to face the threat of **France** for many years. The other great success of the reign was the **Act of Union** (1707); England and **Scotland** were united into the Kingdom of Great Britain, a parliamentary, not a personal, union.

As the last sovereign with any direct hereditary claim to the throne, Anne embodied the shift from personal to parliamentary monarchy. She was the last sovereign to touch for the king's evil and the last to veto an act of Parliament. In 1713 she created 12 new peers to ensure approval of the peace terms, a precedent for forcing parliamentary action that would influence politics during later crises in **national government**, most notably at the time of the 1832 **Reform Act**.

Barbara Brandon Schnorrenberg

Bibliography

Green, Edward. *Queen Anne.* 1980.
Gregg, David B. *Queen Anne.* 1971.
Holmes, Geoffrey. *British Politics in the Age of Anne.* 1967.
Jones, J.R. *Marlborough.* 1993.
Robertson, John, ed. *A Union for Empire: Political Thought and the British Union of 1707.* 1995.

Anson, George, 1st Baron (1697–1762)

Anson was the best-known admiral of the early Hanoverian period. Although mainly remembered for an epic circumnavigation of the world, as a naval administrator ashore he helped give Britain the most powerful **navy** in the world by the time of the **Seven Years' War**.

After service in the Baltic, Mediterranean, **West Indies**, and along the Carolina coast, Anson was sent around Cape Horn (1740) to attack Spain's American possessions from the Pacific side. Despite extreme hardships he crossed the Pacific, captured the Manila-Acapulco galleon with its cargo worth more than £1 million, and returned to England in 1744 via the Indian Ocean. A complete victory over the French off Cape Finisterre (1747) brought him a peerage and the dominant role in naval policy. With but one short break (1756–1757) he served as First Lord of the Admiralty from 1751 until his death; his tactical, strategic, and administrative reforms shaped the conduct of naval affairs for the remainder of the century. Averting attempts by the **Duke of Newcastle** and others to politicize the officer corps, he set rigorous standards for training and conduct that influenced a generation of younger officers.

John A. Hutcheson, Jr.

Bibliography

Anson, W.V. *The Life of Admiral Lord Anson.* 1912.
Baugh, Daniel A. *British Naval Administration in the Age of Walpole.* 1965.
Rodger, N.A.M. *The Wooden World: An Anatomy of the Georgian Navy.* 1986.
Syrett, David, and R.L. DiNardo, eds. *The Commissioned Sea Officers of the Royal Navy, 1660–1815.* 1994.
Williams, Glyndwr, ed. *A Voyage Around the World by George Anson.* 1974.

See also War and Military Engagements

Anstey, Christopher (1724–1805)

Anstey, educated at Eton and King's College, Cambridge, was a country squire turned writer, best known for one poem, his comedy of manners, *The New Bath Guide* (1766). Immensely popular, drawing admiring comment from **Thomas Gray** and **Horace Walpole**, this was a **satire** conducted through a series of family letters describing the flirtations, junketings, and vapid conversations of the famous **spa**'s fashionable society. Post–Augustan satire had by 1766 lost its earlier abrasiveness and moral seriousness, but Anstey's tolerant **irony** and occasional wry improprieties capture the spirit of the age. His less memorable poems include *The Patriot* (1767), *An Election Ball* (1776), and *Speculation: or a Defence of Mankind* (1780).

Michael Bruce

Bibliography

Powell, W.C. *Christopher Anstey: Bath Laureate.* 1944.

See also Bath; Poetry and Poetics

Christopher Anstey

Antarctica, Discovery of

Speculation about a large, fertile continent at the southern extremity of the globe began in ancient Greece, but not until the Hanoverian era was there revealed more than 5 million square miles of uninhabitable continent, surrounded by up to 7 million more of pack ice. Storms and fog, which hinder all approaches to the continent and its low-lying continental shelf, delayed its identification as a genuine land mass.

A few Dutch and French explorers had made approaches before England's **James Cook** circumnavigated Antarctica on his second voyage (1772–1775), several times coming within 100 miles of the coast, but going no further than 71°10′ South Latitude (S.Lat.) because of pack ice. Russia's Thaddeus von Bellingshausen duplicated Cook's feat in 1820–1821; he almost certainly sighted land at 69°37′ S.Lat., but was too conservative to assert his claim.

Cook's account of abundant wildlife attracted American and British sealers, and several made notable discoveries while annihilating the seal population. England's Edward Bransfield sighted Trinity Land in January 1820; America's Nathaniel Palmer sighted land in November of the same year; John Davis, another American, recorded the first Antarctic landing in February 1821; England's James Weddell reached 74°15′ S.Lat., 200 miles closer to the pole than Cook (1822).

Almost two decades elapsed before further expeditions from three nations set out to establish the existence of the south magnetic pole. France's Jules Dumont D'Urville (1837–1840), Britain's **James Clark Ross**, and America's Charles Wilkes (1838–1842) each conducted lengthy and successful **explorations**. More decades passed before interest in this inhospitable land revived and exploration resumed.

N. Merrill Distad

Bibliography

Beaglehole, John C., and Raleigh A. Skelton, eds. *The Journals of Captain James Cook on His Voyages of Discovery.* 3 vols. in 4, plus portfolio. 1955–1974.

Christie, E.W. Hunter. *The Antarctic Problem: An Historical and Political Study.* 1951.

Dodge, Ernest Stanley. *The Polar Rosses: John and James Clark Ross and Their Explorations.* 1973.

Fogg, Gordon Elliott, and David Smith. *The Explorations of Antarctica: The Last Unspoilt Continent.* 1990.

***Anti-Jacobin;* or *Weekly Examiner* (1797–1798)**

With this publication **George Canning** launched a weekly **newspaper** war in **London** during parliamentary sessions from November 1797 to July 1798. The paper's mission was to expose the viciousness of the French Revolution's doctrines and castigate French sympathizers and **radical** reformers in England. Canning's prospectus stated these intentions, but did not mention the **poetry** section for which the newspaper would become famous. His three collaborators were John Hookham Frere (1769–1846), George Ellis (1770–1827), and **William Gifford**, the last serving as editor. John Wright (?1770–1844) in Piccadilly Street was the **publisher**.

The most famous items from the *Anti-Jacobin* included *The Loves of the Triangles,* a parody of **Erasmus Darwin**'s *Loves of the Plants;* "The Friend of Humanity and the Knife Grinder," a parody of **Robert Southey**'s "The Widow"; *The Rovers,* a parody of Friedrich von Schiller's (1759–1805) *Robbers;* and *New Morality,* a fulminating farewell to readers.

In the end, Gifford's trenchant editorials so alarmed **Tory** moderates that **William Pitt the Younger** was persuaded to intervene. The paper's 36th and final issue numbered subscribers at 2,500 while estimating circulation to be substantially higher. Such impact attests to the attraction of literary warfare in an age of controversy.

Elizabeth Wilkens Manus

Bibliography

Adams, M. Ray. *Studies in the Literary Backgrounds of English Radicalism.* 1968.

Aspinall, A. *Politics and the Press c. 1780–1850.* 1949.

Bourne, H.R. Fox. *English Newspapers: Chapters in the History of Journalism.* Vol. 1. 1887.

Edmonds, Charles. *Poetry of the* Anti-Jacobin. 1854.

Seccombe, Thomas. *The Age of Johnson (1748–1798).* 1909.

See also French Revolution; Loyalist Associations; Tories and Toryism

Antiquities and Ruins

British interest in Greek and Roman antiquities, while significant in the early Hanoverian period, grew into a fascination that affected not only collecting and academic study but archaeology, travel, landscape architecture, and the arts. By 1837, ruins from many periods of classical and British history loomed on the mental landscape, evoking among contemporaries a nostalgia for the past, a sense of temporal transience, and also new pride in the national inheritance.

In Stuart times, souvenirs from the **Grand Tour** usually amounted to little more than small collections of bronzes, gems, and coins. Rome and Greece represented sites for moral and intellectual improvement, with the monuments of antiquity serving as reminders of a golden age of good government and humanistic learning. The Hanoverians added to these antiquarian interests a new aesthetic appreciation as well as systematic archaeological study. Statuary, reliefs, paintings, and other objects acquired on tour filled many British private collections, including those of **George III**, whose love of ancient art helped facilitate the acquisition of antiquities from the Papal States.

The Society of Dilettanti (founded in 1732) sponsored the excavation and study of archaeological remains. At first mainly a travelers' eating **club** ("for which the nominal qualification is having been in Italy, and the real one, being drunk," **Horace Walpole** wrote in 1743), the dilettanti were especially active in Greek archaeology, publishing reports filled with illustrative **engravings**. Other images of classical **architecture** came from the **Earl of Burlington**'s publications championing the Renaissance classicism of Andrea Palladio (1508–1580), reports of the excavations of Herculaneum (1738) and Pompeii (1748) and, after 1750, volumes of Giambattista Piranesi's etchings of ancient remains.

The burgeoning collections of engravings stimulated Georgian imaginations. **Aristocrats** set about **housebuilding** and **landscape design** that demonstrated their reverence for the classical heritage. Burlington's **Palladian** villa at Chiswick (1725), the Colosseum-inspired Circus and Palladian terraces at **Bath** (after 1754) by John Wood (1704–1754) and his son John Wood II (1728–1781), and the classical grandeur of the gardens and "follies" (eccentric garden buildings) at Blenheim (1720s) are some of the more famous monuments to the authority of Rome. Robert and James **Adam** adapted the public architecture of the Palladian style to colors and ornamentation drawn from the domestic architecture of Pompeii and Herculaneum. The Adam style in **interior design** (1770s) was also reflected in the "antiqued" ceramics of **Josiah Wedgwood**.

For artists, the images of shattered columns and ruined temples stimulated a nostalgia for the lost grandeur of antiquity. Contemporary writers, comparing modern Romans with their ancestors, somberly pondered the decline and fall of the Roman Empire, something which also moved **Edward Gibbon** to write his famous 6-volume **history** (1776–1788). In **painting**, the ruin-strewn Italian landscapes of Claude Lorrain and Nicholas Poussin were highly admired and imitated, especially by the painter **Richard Wilson**. The poem "Liberty" (1736) by **James Thomson** began and ended in Rome, the "Tomb of Empire," and gave way in the latter 18th century to efforts by other versifiers whose fascination with ruins earned them the name "**Graveyard Poets**." By the time of **Romanticism** the theme of decay was sounded often, as in **Shelley**'s "Ozymandias" (1818) and **Byron**'s *Childe Harold's Pilgrimage* (1812), where the hero himself is "a ruin amidst ruins."

Landscape gardens were laid out to incorporate ruins of abbeys or ancient castles, and where ruins were lacking, they were sometimes erected. **Alexander Pope** suggested a sham castle at Cirencester Park in the 1720s, and the first deliberately built ruin was perhaps at Hagley in 1745. The great gardens of Stowe (redesigned by **William Kent** in the 1730s) and Stourhead (in the 1740s) are filled with classical temples and statuary, but also with ruined arches and **Gothic** follies.

Ruin sentiment at the end of the Hanoverian period contained a paradox, in that something new was being made from something dead. An appreciation for antiquity both foreign and domestic helped to substantiate and legitimize a sense of national identity rooted not only in contemporary war and industry but also in the learning and art of the Greeks, Romans, Anglo-Saxons, and Goths.

Jan Widmayer

Bibliography

Burke, Joseph. "The Grand Tour and the Rule of Taste," in R.F. Brissenden, ed., *Studies in the Eighteenth Century.* 1968.

Fleming, Laurence, and Alan Gore. *The English Garden.* 1979.

Janowitz, Anne F. *England's Ruins: Poetic Purpose and the National Landscape.* 1990.

Macaulay, Rose. *Pleasure of Ruins.* 2nd ed., 1966.

Sambrook, James. *The Eighteenth Century: The Intellectual and Cultural Context of English Literature, 1700–1789.* 1986.

Stern, Bernard Herbert. *The Rise of Romantic Hellenism in English Literature 1732–1786.* 2nd ed., 1969.

Woodbridge, Kenneth. *Landscape and Antiquity: Aspects of English Culture at Stourhead, 1718 to 1838.* 1970.

———. *The Stourhead Landscape.* 1982.

See also Ancients vs. Moderns Quarrel; Classicism; Elgin Marbles; Hellenism, Romantic; Neoclassical Style; Translation

Antislavery Movement

Emerging in the late 18th century, the British antislavery movement drew upon **Enlightenment** concepts of natural rights and human freedom, philanthropic efforts, economic arguments, and **humanitarianism**, but most important upon the religious impetus provided by the **Quakers** and **Evangelicals**, who equated slavery with sin and sought to redeem slaves from physical bondage. The movement exerted moral pressure on government officials, M.P.s, slave traders, plantation owners, and the public to sever all British connections with slavery.

The judicial ruling by **Lord Mansfield** in the Somerset case (1772), that West Indian slave owners could not forcibly remove their slaves from England, resulted in the quick dissolution of slavery as an institution in the British Isles. Encouraged by their American counterparts and motivated by the acquittal of the captain of the slave ship *Zong* for throwing sick slaves overboard, a group of British Quakers in 1783 formed a committee to petition Parliament to abolish the **slave trade**. This committee became the core of the Society for the Abolition of the Slave Trade formed in 1787.

Creation of such a national lobbying group was unprecedented, though it borrowed certain tactics from the **associa-**

Slave "Emancipation," 1834

tion movement. It made use of provincial and national committees, printed pamphlets, petitioning, the exacting from M.P.s of pledges for abolition, and boycotts of slave-grown sugar. As a result of such pressure, Parliament in 1788 formed a special committee to take evidence concerning the slave trade and passed the Dolben Act, which regulated conditions on slave-carrying ships.

Although vigorous leadership was provided by **Thomas Clarkson**, **Granville Sharp**, **William Grenville**, **James Stephen**, and **William Wilberforce**, initial attempts at ending British participation in the trade were unsuccessful because of the desire for cabinet unanimity, fear of reforms in general because of the upheaval of the **French Revolution**, the outbreak of a slave rebellion in the French colony of Haiti (1791), and the belief that the sugar plantations and slavery in the **West Indies** were still vital parts of Britain's economy.

The first successful antislavery measure, an order issued by **Pitt the Younger** in 1805, involved a ban on the slave trade in newly acquired territories and a restriction that limited the introduction of slaves in those areas to 3% of the existing slave population. This action was based on national interest rather than moral considerations, essentially because the territories in question might have to be returned after the war. After the death of Pitt, the **Ministry of all the Talents** supported passage of a bill (1806) confirming and extending Pitt's alterations, ending the supply of slaves to conquered territories and foreign colonies, thus in effect cutting off approximately 70% of the British slave trade. In 1807 Parliament outlawed slave-trading by British subjects altogether, and in 1811 participation in the slave trade was made a felony.

Britain used its powerful position to exert pressure on Portugal in 1810 to restrict the slave trade to certain areas and to work for gradual abolition. British **diplomats** at the Congress of Vienna convinced the other countries represented there to agree to a vague statement against the trade (1815). In 1817 a British-Portuguese treaty limited the Portuguese-Brazilian slave trade to south of the equator (though Brazilian independence later undercut the treaty's provisions). A British-Spanish treaty (1817) contained the same terms.

In 1823 Sir Thomas Fowell Buxton (1786–1845), Wilberforce's successor as leader of the campaign in the **Commons**, moved that because slavery was against the British constitution and the Christian religion, it ought to be abolished. Formation of the Anti–Slavery Society (1823) was designed to make the final push for complete abolition through increased use of petitions, pamphlets, lobbying M.P.s, presentation of statistical studies on the mortality rates of slaves, and requests that voters support only candidates pledged for abolition. The end of slavery in Britain's colonies came in 1833 when resistance by the **West India Interest** was overcome by the inclusion of a compensation plan and by arrangements for former slaves to have a period of apprenticeship following emancipation.

Mark C. Herman

Bibliography

Anstey, Roger. *The Atlantic Slave Trade and British Abolition, 1760–1810.* 1975.

———. "The Pattern of British Abolitionism in the Eighteenth and Nineteenth Centuries," in Christine Bolt and Seymour Drescher, eds., *Anti-Slavery, Religion and Reform: Essays in Memory of Roger Anstey.* 1980.

Davis, David Brion. *The Problem of Slavery in Western Culture.* 1966.

———. *The Problem of Slavery in the Age of Revolution, 1770–1823.* 1975.

Drescher, Seymour. *Econocide: British Slavery in the Era of Abolition.* 1977.

Eltis, David. *Economic Growth and the Ending of the Transatlantic Slave Trade.* 1987.

Turley, David. *The Culture of English Antislavery, 1780–1860.* 1991.

Ward, J.R. *British West Indian Slavery, 1750–1834: The Process of Amelioration.* 1988.

Arbuthnot, John (1667–1735)

A man of many interests, Arbuthnot was a physician, scientist, and political and social satirist. His medical and scientific expertise led to his election as Fellow of the **Royal Society** (1704) and appointment as Physician Ordinary to Queen Anne (1709).

He met **Jonathan Swift** in 1711, and through their friendship was introduced to the leading **Tory** politicians and satirists. He wrote (1712) five "John Bull" pamphlets to defend the Tory peace initiatives of **Harley** and **Bolingbroke** to bring the unpopular **War of the Spanish Succession** (1701–1713) to an end with the Treaty of Utrecht. The collected pamphlets were published as *The History of John Bull* (1727);

John Arbuthnot, M.D.

through them, Arbuthnot created the well-known personification of the spirit of the English people, John Bull. He also satirized the **Whigs** in *The Art of Political Lying* (1712).

In 1713 he became a member of the Scriblerus Club, a literary group that included Swift, Harley, **Pope**, **Gay**, Thomas Parnell (1679–1718), and William Congreve (1670–1729). Arbuthnot was the guiding force of the group's effort to satirize "false tastes in learning" through the activities of the fictional dilettante Martinus Scriblerus. *The Memoirs of Martinus Scriblerus,* though not published until 1741, probably influenced Swift in his creation of Lemuel Gulliver.

Writing treatises on politics, **science**, **medicine**, mathematics, and numismatics, Arbuthnot reflected the intellectual spirit and versatility of the early 18th century. His intelligence, kindness, and wit endeared him to the leading Tory writers. In his "Epistle to Dr. Arbuthnot," Pope thanks the physician for his friendship, "Art and Care."

John F. Sena

Bibliography

Beattie, Lester M. *John Arbuthnot, Mathematician and Satirist.* 1935.

Knoepflmacher, U.C. "The Poet as Physician: Pope's Epistle to Dr. Arbuthnot." *Modern Language Quarterly.* Vol. 31, pp. 440–449.

Sherburn, George. "The Fortunes and Misfortunes of *Three Hours after Marriage.*" *Modern Philology.* Vol. 24, pp. 91–109.

Steensma, Robert C. *Dr. John Arbuthnot.* 1979.

See also Clubs

Architects and Architecture

The beginning the Hanoverian age (1714) coincided with the last acts in the extraordinary careers of the great baroque architects **Sir Christopher Wren** and **Sir John Vanbrugh**. While Wren's last years were plagued by controversies regarding the completion of his masterpiece, new St. Paul's Cathedral, Vanbrugh was at the peak of his powers, having just completed Castle Howard in Yorkshire and with Blenheim Palace still under construction. Vanbrugh, the most impressive of English architects in terms of the sheer monumentality of his structures, was equally capable in the manipulation of mass and detail. His later commissions, such as Grimsthorpe Castle for the Duke of Ancaster (begun in 1722), reveal the vastness of his invention and, with his earlier works, remain among the worthiest examples of balanced classical and baroque elements on a grand scale outside of Italy.

Initially embracing the example of Vanbrugh but later recanting were the English **Palladians**, led by Colen Campbell (1676–1729), the first volume of whose enormously influential *Vitruvius Brittanicus* appeared in 1715. Campbell, the builder of Wanstead House in Essex (begun in 1713, now demolished) and, for Prime Minister **Sir Robert Walpole**, of Houghton Hall in Norfolk (begun in 1722), was at least a partial follower of Vanbrugh, deriving from him his general conception of the great house as a centralized structure with wings and pavilions. At Mereworth and Stourhead, however, this sprawling plan was reined in and became a compact and precise homage to Palladio's centralized villas. In fact, in his original plans and engravings for the *Vitruvius,* Campbell was at once the representative and progenitor of a widespread revival of interest in "the English Palladio," Inigo Jones (1573–1652), as well as in the 16th-century Italian architect himself.

Perhaps the most perfect expression of this enthusiasm is to be found in Chiswick House (begun in 1725), designed by its owner, **Richard Boyle, Earl of Burlington**. Burlington had patronized Campbell in the construction of his London house (now housing the **Royal Academy**), and the two of them, together with Burlington's protégé and friend **William Kent**, form a kind of triumvirate of architectural taste-makers at the outset of the Hanoverian era, whose influence lasted well into the latter half of the century. As **Horace Walpole** suggested, Burlington was the "Apollo" of Palladianism, Kent his "high priest." Palladianism itself was at the core of what is sometimes confusingly described as **Georgian** architectural style. The designation *Georgian* roughly marks an historic period, rather than a distinct architectural style. It was applied in the early 20th century by an English preservation movement concerned about the destruction of 18th-century buildings and by an attempt in America to define a high style during the colonial period that corresponded with practice in England. But in actuality, the Hanoverian period was an age of architectural revivals that encompassed many other styles beside the Palladian, such as the Neoclassical, Gothic, exotic, Greek Revival, and Regency.

Among the contemporaries of Burlington and Kent, but one who never wholly espoused their increasingly popular Palladian tenets, was **James Gibbs**. A **Catholic** and a Scot, receiving his early training in Rome, Gibbs necessarily remained a somewhat isolated figure. The two works for which he is best known are the London church of St. Martin-in-the-Fields (begun in 1721) and the Radcliffe Camera at Oxford (1739–1749); both demonstrate that his contribution to British architecture was great and that it was made in consultation not with Palladio or Jones but with the ancient Rome of the Pantheon and the baroque Rome of Bernini. In this he was the true heir to Wren and, with him, he provided prototypes for a great number of buildings in the American colonies throughout the 18th century.

The two architectural giants during the latter 18th century were, like Gibbs, both Scots: **William Chambers**, though born in Sweden, was the son of a Scottish merchant. Robert **Adam** was the son of William Adam, Scotland's chief architect during the period of the first Palladian heyday. Both men were well-traveled, ambitious, and lionized by their own large circles of wealthy patrons. Together, their styles represent a sophisticated blending of earlier trends and original approaches, and mark an enlightened silver age in the history of British architecture.

Chambers was still in his twenties when he entered court circles and began designing for his royal patrons ornamental buildings such as the famous Pagoda in the gardens at Kew. At the same time, he undertook numerous aristocratic commissions for country houses and villas, most of which when viewed now attest to his firsthand knowledge of ancient and modern Italian structures. By far his most important undertaking was the erection of Somerset House, a massive Thames-side governmental office building begun in 1775 and completed after his death. The riverfront facade of this vast and on the whole far from successful *opus architectorum* nevertheless evinces a remarkable diversity of sources—from Michelangelo's Capitoline palaces and the Palazzo Farnese to the works of Inigo Jones—is, despite its absurdly small dome, often pleasing in detail. Chambers, as official architect to **George III**, was also partly responsible for the founding of the **Royal Academy of Arts** (1768), and served as its first treasurer.

If an intellectual ponderousness characterizes much of Chambers's architecture, the same cannot be said of the **Neoclassical** work of his rival, Robert Adam, whose exteriors and interiors alike are marked by infinite variety and movement. To be sure, Adam's exterior features are neither without gravity, as in the hexastyle portico at Osterley (begun in 1761), nor are they devoid of intellectual quotation, as in the exactly contemporary south front of Kedleston Hall, modeled on the ancient Roman triumphal arches with which Adam was intimately familiar.

But it is in Adam's interior designs that the blend of classical (first and foremost, imperial Roman) richness with the lightness of touch and sureness of palette of an expert in **watercolor** defines what is uniquely the "Adam style." This style was widely dispersed by its inventor with the help of his younger brother and assistant, James (1732–1794), and a host of followers and imitators. From his earliest interiors, for example at Hatchlands, through the extraordinary suites of rooms at Syon House (begun in 1692), Landsdowne House (begun in 1762, now dismantled), and Kenwood (1767–1768)—in fact, at any of the myriad country and urban dwellings he designed (or, more often, remodeled) and in the drawing rooms and halls of his large-scale London housing project, the Adelphi (begun in 1768, now destroyed), Adam's personal,

Wansted House, designed by C. Campbell

highly decorative transformation of classical Roman motifs prevailed. Whether for ceiling ornamentation, or the disposition of columnar screens, or the patterns for wood inlays or carpets, Adam provided a seemingly infinite variety of new models, transforming and renewing the organic component of their often very distant ancient sources. Although he continued to undertake important building commissions, among them the facade of Edinburgh University (begun in 1789) and Charlotte Square (also in **Edinburgh**, begun in 1791), it is the harmonious interiors of the 1760s and 1770s for which he is best remembered and rightly considered the first architect of his age.

It is clear from the work of both Chambers and Adam that the Hanoverian period was one of large-scale urban planning. In fact, the **spa** resort of **Bath** introduces one of the more dramatic innovations in civic architecture—the curved terrace. John Wood I (1704–1754), with his so-called Circus (begun in 1754), followed by his son, John Wood II (1728–1781), who built the equally famous Royal Crescent (begun in 1767), abandoned the standard rectilinear conception of the street or square front, creating a new public architecture capable of unprecedented plasticity without sacrifice of monumentality or grandeur. This revolution provided an important precedent for the transformation of **London** under the direction of the last "star" architect of the Hanoverian period, **John Nash**.

After financial difficulties that temporarily slowed his career as a London builder, Nash returned to architecture and, in partnership with **Humphry Repton**, designed numerous **picturesque** villas in a variety of styles, from the Italianate to the increasingly popular "gothick." His most famous work of this sort was commissioned by his most illustrious patron, the Prince of Wales and future king, **George IV**. This was the Royal Pavilion at Brighton, a (formerly humble and nondescript) symmetrical house which Nash completely remodeled in a fabulous Indian style (begun in 1815). More impressive by far than this now crumbling royal caprice were Nash's improvements (only partially executed) of a huge area of London, from Regents Park to St. James, including the Park Crescent (begun in 1812) and Carlton House Terrace (begun in 1827). These magniloquent edifices, with their colossal columnar screens and sweeping, curved arcades, sound the recessional of English **neoclassical** architecture as well as of the Hanoverian period itself.

Every discussion of Hanoverian architecture naturally returns to the central thread of **classicism** that runs through 18th-century European accomplishments. But also throughout this epoch, in ecclesiastical buildings and the scholastic buildings of **Oxford** and **Cambridge** as well as in the picturesque novelties of Horace Walpole's Strawberry Hill (begun 1748) and **James Wyatt**'s Fonthill Abbey (begun for **William Beckford** in 1795, now demolished), a strong tradition of interest in, if not a profound understanding of, medieval forms and motifs manifested itself. This **Gothic Revival** tradition gathered momentum as it gained intelligent support by Victorian luminaries such as A.N.W. Pugin (1812–1852) and John Ruskin (1819–1900), and it came at last to characterize post–Hanoverian architectural style in general. Finally, outside both of these great tendencies, there were also a few thoroughly individual builders of the early 19th century. Perhaps the most notable of these was Sir John Soane (1753–1837), whose own house (begun in 1792, now the Soane Museum) reflects a genius somewhat isolated from its own late–Hanoverian era but intriguing to our own.

David D. Nolta

Bibliography

Archer, John. *The Literature of British Domestic Architecture.* 1985.

Beard, Geoffrey. *The Work of Robert Adam.* 1978.

Clark, Sir Kenneth. *The Gothic Revival.* 2nd ed., 1950.

Cruickshank, D. *A Guide to the Georgian Buildings of Britain and Ireland.* 1985.

Friedman, T. *James Gibbs.* 1984.

Gerrmann, Georg. *The Gothic Revival in Europe and Britain: Sources, Influences, and Ideas.* 1973.

Girouard, M. *Life in the English Country House.* 1978.

Summerson, J. *Architecture in Britain, 1530 to 1830.* Rev. ed., 1983.

Watkin, David. *The Rise of Architectural History.* 1980.

Wiebenson, Dora. *The Sources of the Greek Revival.* 1969.

See also Antiquities and Ruins; Home Furnishings and Decoration; Housebuilding and Housing; Interior Design; Landscape Architecture and Design; Sculpture

Argyll, Dukes of

John Campbell, 2nd duke (1678–1743), politician and soldier, succeeded his father in December 1703. He was known among his clansmen by his Gaelic nickname as "Red John of the Battles." In 1705 **Queen Anne** appointed him Scottish High Commissioner, with the task of preparing the way for parliamentary union between **Scotland** and England. In this he proved to be a more competent politician than his predecessors Queensbury and Tweedsdale, successful in his dealings with both English and Scottish politicians, and demanding more patronage from the queen, which he then used to acquire support in the Scottish Parliament. As a reward he was made an English peer, Baron of Chatham and Earl of Greenwich.

During the **War of Spanish Succession** he served with distinction under **Marlborough** in Flanders, becoming a lieutenant general. A committed **Whig**, he was responsible for the defeat of **Mar**'s Jacobite forces at Sheriffmuir near Stirling during the **Fifteen** rebellion. Together with his brother, the Earl of Islay, he dominated Scottish politics by the early 1720s. Increasingly the actual management fell to Islay while Argyll's temperament caused him various frictions with his **London** political masters, particularly in 1740 when he raised his voice in protest at the punitive measures taken against the city of **Edinburgh** as a result of the **Porteous Riots**. Thereafter, his influence waned.

Archibald Campbell (1682–1761), 1st earl of Islay, succeeded his brother as 3rd duke of Argyll, but is more commonly referred to simply as Islay. He was the first great political manager of Scotland. By using **patronage** he was able to build

John Campbell, 2nd Duke of Argyll

a dominant position in Scottish politics and an important influence in British; he could guarantee disciplined followers, and this was crucially important. As few Scotsmen had the franchise, skillful management ensured that when he died in 1761 he virtually was indeed "the absolute governor of one of his majesty's kingdoms."

Richard Finlay

Bibliography

Ferguson, W. *Scotland, 1689 to the Present.* 1968.

Lenman, B. *Integration, Enlightenment and Industrialisation.* 1981.

Murdoch, A. *The People Above.* 1980.

Shaw, John Stuart. *The Management of Scottish Society, 1707–1764.* 1983.

Simpson, John M. "Who Steered the Gravy Train, 1707–1766?" in N.T. Phillipson and R. Mitchison, eds., *Scotland in the Age of Improvement, Essays in Scottish History in the Eighteenth Century.* 1970.

See also Dundas, Henry

Aristocracy and Gentry

The British aristocracy, though small by comparison with those on the Continent, retained a degree of wealth and political power that distinguished it from the other European elites. Its approximately 13,500 families included the entire hereditary nobility (dukes at the top, then marquesses, earls, viscounts, barons), most knights and baronets (hereditary knights), and innumerable landowners enjoying gentle status, though without title. By 1800 the greatest of the nobility enjoyed incomes that exceeded £100,000; country gentlemen needed at least £1,000 a year to sustain their rank in the 19th century, though an 18th-century squire maintained his with less. The estates of the 200 or so families at the top ranged from 5,000 to 50,000 acres and accounted for more than 20% of the cultivable land; those of the gentry ranged from 500 to 5,000 acres and covered more than 50% of the cultivable land. Despite divergences in wealth and sometimes bitter political divisions, the aristocracy and gentry remained a coherent group, united by a common dependence on land as the basis for income and influence, by a style of living that revolved around estates and country houses, and by a shared assumption of authority.

The group remained open to newcomers, though mainly at its lower levels. Most of Britain's great estates were in place by 1700, and a peerage which grew from 171 members in 1714 to 358 in 1837 recruited new members largely from those already connected to the nobility or, after 1782, from the peerages of **Scotland** and then **Ireland**. Marriage, education, and a background in **government** facilitated movement into an elite that ultimately derived its status from the ownership of land. The cost of accumulating a substantial property and the availability of more remunerative investments meant that landed property became a social, rather than an economic, investment. New entrants, including lawyers, officeholders, and businessmen from **London** and provincial centers, acquired properties piecemeal and over several generations. Few new purchasers established themselves on large estates in a lifetime and, overall, the rate of entry into the group was probably lower than it had been during the previous two centuries.

Between 1714 and 1837 the aristocracy extended its ownership of land. The trend to larger holdings did not occur evenly throughout the country. However, rising incomes and a growing mortgage market enabled landowners to round out estates by buying properties of smaller owners who lacked resources to adapt to changing technical and market conditions. Also, partly as a result of the demographic crisis that gripped the group in the late 17th and early 18th centuries, some surviving aristocratic families enlarged their properties through marriage and inheritance.

Aristocratic estates generally flourished in the Hanoverian period. Between 1715 and 1770, land values rose from around 17 times to around 30 times their annual rental value. Mounting property values reflected an increase in rents which rose from the 1760s until the end of the **French Revolutionary and Napoleonic Wars**; gains of 80% or more were common between 1790 and 1813. Rents and land values slumped for two decades after the war, then resumed their upward climb in the 1830s.

Some members of the landowning elite were **agricultural improvers**, fostering changes that made **agriculture** more productive. Generally, they provided a farm's fixed capital, though the already low level of landlord investment diminished in prosperous times. Their most notable 18th-century investment was in land enclosures that offered an immediate return in higher rents. Landlords also pressed for a consolidation of small tenancies and, sometimes, for improved animal husbandry, the latter through covenants in leases, model home farms, and the sponsorship of agricultural shows and **agricultural societies**. Their increasing reliance on land stewards meant that estate management became more professional, but, generally, advances in husbandry came as a result of experiments made by large tenant farmers, owner–occupiers, and small country gentlemen.

The economic sway of aristocracy extended beyond agriculture. In the northeast, Lancashire, **Wales**, and the Black Country, aristocrats were prominent proprietors of **coal** and **iron** mines and of foundries. Elsewhere, they mined lead and copper. Aristocratic mineowners were among the pioneers of the **canal** network, and later promoted **railways**. Landlords were active in the development of London, of **provincial towns**, of middle-class suburbs, and of **spas** and **seaside resorts**. While large proprietors such as the Dudleys, Fitzwilliams, and Londonderrys retained management of their enterprises, the trend was to lease mineral and industrial properties to outsiders who oversaw their management. For most of the elite, industrial or urban investments supplemented revenue derived from agricultural rents.

The aristocracy required the enormous resources it commanded to sustain their lavish lifestyles. **Housebuilding**, provision for younger children and widows, the expense of managing **elections** and nurturing an electoral interest, and **gambling** all took their financial toll. Indebtedness was a financial reality among noble and gentry families, many of whom sustained a high level of debt by mortgaging their properties. Instances of aristocratic bankruptcy, though spectacular, were rare. However, the size of the aristocratic debt suggests that the group may have absorbed more capital than it invested in agriculture, industry, **transport**, or urban development.

The British aristocracy was a governing class that governed. Nobles dominated cabinets down to 1837; 43 of 65 cabinet members between 1782 and 1832 sat in the **House of Lords**. The **House of Commons** also remained a bastion of the aristocracy and gentry: about two-thirds of its members between 1660 and 1832 came from only 484 families, but after 1832, representation from this core of parliamentary families declined. Though the majority of recruits to the judiciary after 1760 came from the middle class, many judges purchased estates, and representatives of landed families continued to dominate the **army** and **navy**, and to hold the more important posts in **diplomacy**. The aristocracy's control of local government was just as pervasive: of 294 18th-century Lord Lieutenants, 255 were peers or their sons; all the others were large landowners. National government and the lieutenancies remained the province of the nobility and substantial gentry. Lesser gentry were traditionally active at the local level as Justices of the Peace. Gentry families carried great weight in rural society, and were deeply interested in the maintenance of peace, order, and the status quo. The 18th century saw a decline in landowners' participation in the business of the bench, but in the 19th, nobles and gentlemen again were active Justices.

In Parliament, members of landed families advanced the needs of their localities, thus overcoming some of the inequities in the distribution of parliamentary seats. The latter 18th century saw a new breed of aristocratic minister—the man of business, professional in his orientation, and pragmatic in his assessment of issues and situations. On the benches of the **judicial system**, justices of the late 18th and early 19th centuries also manifested a new interest in administration and a concern for good government. At all levels, landed governors pursued their own interests on a host of matters, including enclosure, enforcement of the **Game Laws**, and so on, but the **French Revolution**, **Evangelicalism**, and growing **middle-class** influence in differing ways reinforced aristocratic public-spiritedness by the later Hanoverian era.

Aristocratic culture grew more cosmopolitan and international in the 18th century, and though these extended sentiments contracted somewhat after 1789, that later period saw a compensating new expansiveness toward the middle classes below. The enormous vogue of 18th-century housebuilding testifies to the importance landowners attached to their estates and localities, yet gentry and noble families increasingly migrated for part of the year to town, and from the 1750s on, some foreign travel was considered indispensable also for the young gentleman. Horizons also expanded intellectually and socially as provincial towns and resorts provided the assembly rooms, lending **libraries**, and **learned societies** that became new venues of an urban culture embracing both middle class and aristocracy. Upper-class self-consciousness and even arrogance were stimulated by many new challenges launched by middle-class traders, industrialists, journalists, and professional men. But, over time, this consciousness was also modified to encompass the idea that aristocratic values actually benefited from attitudes and institutions that were middle class in origin.

Michael W. McCahill

Bibliography

Beckett, J.V. *The Aristocracy in England, 1660–1914.* 1986.

———. "Landownership and Estate Management," in J. Thirsk, ed., *The Agrarian History of England and Wales.* Vol. 6: 1750–1850. 1989.

Bush, M.L. *The English Aristocracy.* 1984.

Cannon, John. *Aristocratic Century.* 1984.

Clark, J.C.D. *English Society, 1688–1832: Ideology, Social Structure and Political Practice During the Ancient Regime.* 1985.

Clay, Christopher. "Landlords and Estate Management in England," in J. Thirsk, ed., *The Agrarian History of England and Wales.* Vol. 5: 1640–1750, II. 1985.

Girouard, Mark, *Life in the English Country House.* 1978.

Habbakuk, Sir John. *Marriage, Debt, and the Estates System: English Landownership, 1650–1950.* 1994.

Lewis, Judith Schneid. *In the Family Way: Childbearing in the British Aristocracy, 1760–1860.* 1986.

Mingay, G.E., *English Landed Society in the Eighteenth Century.* 1963.

Thompson, F.M.L., *English Landed Society in the Nineteenth Century.* 1963.

See also Blood Sports; Clubs; Dueling; Government, Local and County; Government, National; Lords, House of; Manners and Morals; Prime Minister; Whigs

Arkwright, Sir Richard (1732–1792)

The story of Arkwright, born in Preston to poor parents, one of 13 children, is the classic success story of the **Industrial Revolution**. Self-taught, he was apprenticed to a barber, then accumulated enough capital to launch his own business in Bolton. While traveling the northern industrial districts to buy hair for making **wigs**, he came into contact with many skilled workers intent upon devising technical improvements for the growing **cotton industry**. Thus began his acquaintance with John Kay, a watchmaker involved in improving roller spinning machines. Arkwright lured him away from his employer and together they produced the water frame, a machine capable of spinning a vast number of threads of any hardness required and able to be driven by horse power or, as Arkwright soon demonstrated, a waterwheel (hence the name). This machine made Arkwright's fortune.

The shortage of good yarns for the Midlands hosiery industry led him to establish his first factory in Nottingham (1769), backed by Samuel Need, the wealthiest hosier in that town, and by **Jedediah Strutt**, a leader in the trade in Derby. From there he moved to Cromford (1771), the center of what would become a major industrial empire and the prime example of the early cotton factory community. In the Midlands, Arkwright was responsible for building 10 mills, and the Strutts built at least five others. By the mid 1770s, with factories capable of handling every aspect of cotton cloth production, he had gone far to establish this as a leading English industry. After the first legal decision against his **patent** (1781) he traveled extensively, seeking partners either to accept his machine as his financial contribution to a partnership or to pay him royalties for its use. Mills were built in Yorkshire, Lancashire and **Scotland** on these terms, though Lancashire cottonmasters were intent on breaking the patent and achieved success in 1785. By that time, however, Arkwright, employing 5,000 **factory workers**, was a very formidable competitor.

Sir Richard Arkwright

Arkwright's contribution to the development of the cotton industry has been the subject of historical controversy. He was no mechanic, but that is not to say that he had no understanding of mechanical principles; he was clearly a very effective **entrepreneur** and one of the fathers of the **factory system**. Knighted in 1786 and High Sheriff of Derbyshire in 1787, his ascent also illustrates the relative flexibility of the contemporary British social structure.

John Butt

Bibliography

Chapman, Stanley D. *The Early Factory Masters.* 1967.
English, Walter. *The Textile Industry.* 1969.
Fitton, Robert S. *The Arkwrights, Spinners of Fortune.* 1989.
Fitton, Robert S., and A.P. Wadsworth. *The Strutts and the Arkwrights.* 1958.

See also Crompton, Samuel; Science, Technology, and Invention; Spinning and Weaving; Textile Industries

Army

Few organizations have had such great impact on a nation's development and yet have been so vilified as this one. The 18th-century public viewed the common soldier as drunken, unreliable, prone to **crime**; a threat to freedom, property, and women. The British Army was a necessary evil. The public wanted it "on the cheap," with as few troops as possible, to be maintained on low pay with minimal standards of food, housing, and health care. **Military education** for much of the Hanoverian period was bought too dearly on the battlefield itself.

Officers came from the ranks of gentlemen, a practice held over from the feudal levy and the Tudor–Stuart militia. Their troops' low pay and lack of a professional ethic, together with the lingering notion of them as essentially private armed retainers, led to officers with independent attitudes, resentful of higher authority, given to long absences from their units, and often indifferent to their men's welfare as individuals. This was not always true, however, of some of the better-known commanders of the Hanoverian era, such as **Marlborough**, **Cumberland**, **Amherst**, **Wolfe**, **Carleton**, **Gage**, **Howe**, **Burgoyne**, **Cornwallis**, **Moore**, **Wellington**, and **Frederick, Duke of York**.

In many respects a regiment was indeed the private property of the colonel possessing a royal warrant to raise it, periodic "beating orders" authorizing recruitment. The government supplied some money for horses, uniforms, recruiting expenses, and basic equipment (arms were issued directly from the royal armories, notably the Tower of London), but the colonel usually had to supplement this privately. Proceeds from the sale of commissions went directly to him, and he selected his own subordinate officers; upon retirement, he sold the warrant to recoup his investment. Regimental agents, representing the Secretary for War, disbursed pay and funds, thus ensuring some governmental control over essentially private battle contractors.

The Death of General Braddock, 1755

Despite its peculiarities, the Army performed as well as, or better than, its adversaries. Typically it suffered at the outset of hostilities from peacetime neglect, but with few exceptions it emerged ultimately victorious. A German observer commented (1748) that British soldiers possessed "an unquenchable spirit, great stubbornness in defence, [and] bravery amounting often to recklessness in the attack," but were "difficult to discipline, quarrelsome in quarters, [and] haughty in their attitude to other troops."

Relations between officers and troops were conditioned by aristocratic paternalism and the soldier's habit of deference to authority. Troops resented cowardice and cruelty more than incompetence. The fundamental duty of a junior officer (subaltern) was to ensure that his men were fed, clothed, and housed, and their grievances promptly addressed. Only at the higher field ranks were officers expected to display tactical acumen.

Annual **mutiny** acts after 1689 placed the military command structure under the king, but Parliament controlled finance, administration, and supply. The Secretary for War served as the chief administrative officer. A captain-general, later the commander-in-chief of the army, represented the monarch and directed the home and theater commanders-in-chief. An adjutant general oversaw discipline, arms, clothing, regulations, and orders; a quartermaster-general directed troop movements, operations, and quartering. The Board of Ordnance, under the Master-General of the Ordnance (a political appointee), regulated the artillery and engineers, neither of them part of the army establishment: the creation of a Corps of Engineers (1788) and the Horse Artillery (1793) gradually brought these branches under the army command structure.

Up through the rank of lieutenant-colonel, officers purchased commissions by money payments, thus preserving the social exclusiveness of the officer corps. Members of the landed **aristocracy** supported the purchase system, which gave them a vested interest in the forces as well as a hedge against royal abuse of power; kings generally disliked it. An ensigncy in a line regiment typically cost £400, while a lieutenant-colonelcy (and command of a battalion) could cost £5,200. Blatant abuses, such as commissions for infants, ultimately led to regulations (1809) governing minimum age (16) and time in grade. The seniority system was rigidly enforced. Promotion for merit was rare, and battlefield promotions by seniority occurred only to fill vacancies created by combat death.

The Army, always voluntary, continually struggled against adverse public perceptions at a time before patriotism and national service emerged as recruiting factors. Soldiers enlisted for life, but gradually, 7-, 10-, and 12-year terms had to be offered. Recruitment occurred at fairs, races, and **public houses**. For **agricultural laborers** and **craftsmen**, enlistment was sometimes the only solution to **poverty**, debt, or legal problems. The army rarely used impressment except with debtors and felons in **prison**, the unemployed, or the "chronically idle." Wartime brought shorter enlistment terms, generally for the duration or for five years, which made both recruitment and postwar demobilization easier. Many recruits came from **Scotland** and **Ireland**, where grinding poverty and a military ethic made service attractive and honorable. In wartime the caliber of recruits rose, particularly during threats of invasion as in 1759 and 1803.

Promotion within the ranks depended on merit and literacy. Most regiments provided basic reading, writing, and arithmetic instruction to those privates identified as potential noncommissioned officers. The rank of serjeant-major (created in 1797), to which every soldier could aspire, earned extraordinary respect and influence in the regiments.

Infantry regiments were organized into battalions of 500 men, subdivided into ten 50-man companies (including one of grenadiers, and another of light infantry after 1770). After 1756 many regiments employed paired battalions, one staying on home service and serving as a training, recruitment, and replacement depot for the other deployed battalion. The platoon (two per company on war service) formed the basic tactical subunit, while the company acted as the principal administrative organ.

Early in the Hanoverian period, cavalry regiments were either "horse" or "dragoon." Horse regiments, composed of large men mounted on heavy horses, acted as shock troops and struck an enemy's line in a headlong charge at full gallop. Dragoons rode into combat, dismounted, and fought as infantry. Light cavalry regiments (formed after 1759 and eventually called "dragoon guards") maintained the charge as the basic tactic, but were more mobile, quicker, and lighter than the old horse cavalry. Dragoons gradually replaced the horse regiments. Several cavalry regiments wore the showy Hungarian or "Hussar" uniform (after 1806), whereas others adopted the lance as their primary weapon, thus becoming "lancers." Cavalry regiments gradually increased from six troops of 36 men (1783) to ten troops of 90 men (1803).

Artillery, organized into "brigades of guns" with 12 pieces each, was distributed among the infantry battalions (two guns per battalion). The unit's contract civilian drivers were replaced by a Driver's Corps as it became integrated into the Army establishment.

Logistical difficulties often limited a soldier's diet, particularly while campaigning. The daily ration consisted of a pound of meat; a pound of bread, flour, or biscuits; and a pint of wine or one-third pint of spirits. Vegetables and fruits, if available, supplemented the ration. A camp kettle was issued for cooking, the lid being used for frying and the pot for boiling and stewing. On the march, each man received 3 days' rations. British forces preferred to subsist on established magazines and protected supply routes, rather than "live off the land," as did most European armies. Of a private's 8-pence-per-day pay, 2 pence was withheld for clothing and expenses (called "off reckonings"); the balance, called "subsistence pay," usually paid for food, drink, and necessities.

Army discipline varied considerably, depending on local conditions. The military machines of the earlier Hanoverian kings suffered from corruption, officer insubordination, desertion, fraudulent enlistment, and poor relations between officers and troops. Conditions improved, but the post–1815 Army deteriorated in consequence of poor discipline, neglected training, and low morale. Commanders believed that only severe corporal **punishment** (or death) would maintain order and discipline; regimental court martials imposed flogging by the "cat o'nine tails." Lesser infractions brought bread-and-water diets, extra duty, public reprimands, or humiliation by being made to wear the regimental coat inside-out. Convictions for mutiny, sedition, or "misbehaviour before the enemy" carried the death penalty for all ranks. For lesser offenses, officers were cashiered and NCOs reduced in rank.

Normal peacetime army strength ranged from 12,000 to 20,000 men, never really adequate for home and colonial duties. Wartime strength exceeded 200,000 regulars and militia. Attempts to draw replacements for the regular army from the militia (raised by ballot in each parish) were opposed by local interests, but the militia gradually evolved into a permanent reserve for the regular Army and was organized into second battalions of line regiments by 1804; by 1815, 40% of regular army recruits volunteered from the militia. Fencible regiments provided home defense during the **French Revolutionary and Napoleonic Wars**; though regulars, their service was limited to the British Isles and for the duration of the war only.

Stanley D.M. Carpenter

Bibliography

Barnett, Correlli. *Britain and Her Army, 1509–1970.* 1970.

Dietz, Peter. *The Last of the Regiments: Their Rise and Fall.* 1990.

Fortescue, J.W. *A History of the British Army.* Vols. 2–10. 1920.

Rogers, H.C.B. *The British Army in the Eighteenth Century.* 1977.

Savory, Reginald. *His Brittanic Majesty's Army in Germany During the Seven Years' War.* 1966.

Sheppard, Eric. *A Short History of the British Army.* 4th ed., 1959.

See also Highland Regiments; War and Military Engagements

Arne, Thomas (1710–1778)

Arne (D. Mus., Oxford, 1759) was a leading composer of theatrical music. His most successful early works were the masques *Comus* (1738) and *Alfred* (1740), which included the patriotic anthem "Rule Britannia." In the 1730s he tried to establish an English equivalent of Italian **opera**, finally succeeding with *Artexerxes* (1762). His pastiche *Love in a Village* (1762) began a trend toward English dialogue opera.

Arne's gift for melody is evident throughout his works, vocal and instrumental. He played a significant role in making English operatic genres prominent in the **London** theatrical world.

Jane Girdham

Bibliography

Cudworth, Charles. "Boyce and Arne: 'The Generation of 1710'." *Music and Letters.* Vol. 41, pp. 136–145.

Fiske, Roger. *English Theatre Music in the Eighteenth Century.* 1986.

Parkinson, John A. *An Index to the Vocal Works of Thomas Augustine Arne and Michael Arne.* 1972.

Walsh, T.J. *Opera in Dublin 1705–1797: The Social Scene.* 1973.

See also Music

Thomas Arne

Artisans

See Craftsmen

Ascendancy

See Anglo–Irish Protestant Ascendancy

Association for the Preservation of Liberty and Property

See Loyalist Associations

Association Movement

The Association Movement, known also as the Petitioning Movement or County Movement, originated in late 1779 in the atmosphere of antigovernment criticism that marked that last phase of the disastrous **War of American Independence**. The movement, which has been described as "an energizing of squires," began in Yorkshire and spread to other counties under the leadership of **Christopher Wyvill**. Its supporters were largely rural men of property, though it gained support from more radical groups. Its activities and program were influenced somewhat by the **Society for Supporters of the Bill of Rights**, founded in 1769 amidst the **Wilkes** disturbances of that period.

The mistakes and cost of the American war inspired Wyvill, an Anglican minister and large landowner, to organize meetings of Yorkshire freeholders and to channel their discontent into a petitioning campaign to influence the **House of Commons** in the direction of making it both more responsible and also more genuinely representative of the independent families of the gentry. The result was the Yorkshire Association, which in 1780 not only sent its own reformist petition to Parliament (bearing 5,800 names) but inspired and concerted the surprisingly lively petitioning activities of other county associations formed in its image. Employing petitioning meetings and making great use of propaganda in such **newspapers** as the *York Chronicle, Leeds Mercury,* and *Newcastle Hue and Cry,* the movement demanded **economical reforms**, the addition of 100 more independent county M.P.s to Parliament and, sharing a few of the more radical ideas of the **Society for Constitutional Information** (founded in 1780), annual elections. In the spring of 1780, representatives from 12 counties and four cities met in London as a sort of general assembly to guide and coordinate the associations' activities.

The movement attempted to steer clear of the parliamentary politicians of the **Rockingham** Opposition who wanted to co-opt it in order to strengthen themselves, and also of the urban **radicals** and dissenters who wanted it to invest more fully in the **Cartwright** program of annual elections, universal suffrage, secret ballot, equal electoral districts, salaries for M.P.s, and abolition of the property qualification for membership in Commons. In the short term, the movement's greatest significance, even though it fizzled out by 1784, was that it saw the engagement of substantial propertied men in the growing movement for parliamentary reform, employing a powerful extraparliamentary pressure group and modern propaganda techniques. More important in the long term, "Association" furnished the prototype for many later agitations.

Frank M. Baglione

Bibliography

Black, E.C. *The Association: British Extraparliamentary Political Organisations.* 1963.

Christie, Ian R. *Wilkes, Wyvill and Reform: The Parliamentary Reform Movement in British Politics, 1760–1785.* 1972.

Cone, Carl B. *The English Jacobins: Reformers in Late 18th Century England.* 1968.

Goodwin, Albert. *The Friends of Liberty: The English Democratic Movement in the Age of the French Revolution.* 1979.

Royle, Edward, and James Walvin. *English Radicals and Reformers, 1760–1848.* 1982.

Astell, Mary (1666–1731)

Astell, England's first published feminist polemicist, came to **London** alone in 1688. She engaged John Norris in epistolary dialogue which he later published as *Letters Concerning the Love of God* (1695), and penned three feminist treatises before 1700: *A Serious Proposal to the Ladies for the Advancement of Their True and Greatest Interest. By a Lover of Her Sex* (1694); *A Serious Proposal to the Ladies Part II Wherein a Method Is Offer'd for the Improvement of Their Minds* (1696); and *Some Reflections upon Marriage, Occasion'd by the Duke & Duchess of Mazarine's Case* (1700).

Entering into political controversy, she upheld the conservative **Tory** position on **occasional conformity** in *Moderation Truly Stated* (1704) and *A Fair Way with Dissenters and Their Patrons* (1704)—replying to **Daniel Defoe** (a dissenter), among others; and on the divine right of kings in *An Impartial Enquiry into the Causes of Rebellion and Civil War* (1704).

A self-taught philosopher, her religious manifesto *The Christian Religion, as Profess'd by a Daughter of the Church of England* (1705) attacked the materialist position of **Locke**. *Bart'lemy Fair; or, an Enquiry after Wit* (1709) replied to Lord Shaftesbury's (1671–1713) sophisticated tolerance. Admired by such intellectuals as **Lady Mary Wortley Montagu** and Elizabeth Elstob (1683–1756), Astell was supported by several wealthy aristocratic women. In 1729 she opened a school for the daughters of pensioners in Chelsea's Royal Hospital. In 1731 she had a cancerous breast removed but did not long survive the operation. Her feminist writings created the prototype for the **Bluestockings** of the next generation, and were the inspiration for many intellectuals, among them Elizabeth Thomas, Lady Chudleigh, and Sarah Chapone.

Ruth Perry

Bibliography

Perry, Ruth. *The Celebrated Mary Astell.* 1986.

See also Women in Literature

Atterbury, Francis (1663–1732)

Atterbury, bishop of Rochester and dean of Westminster (1713), a renowned **Tory** orator, mistrusted by the first Hanoverian king **George I**, was accused of plotting a **Jacobite** restoration and was exiled by Parliament (1722). He died in **France** after years of service to **James Edward** Stuart, **the Old Pretender**.

Bishop Francis Atterbury

A graduate of Christ Church, Oxford (D.D. in 1701), Atterbury took holy orders in 1687. He became an influential High churchman and served in various ecclesiastical posts. He was chaplain to King William and Queen Mary, and later to **Queen Anne**, also archdeacon of Totnes (1701), dean of Carlisle (1704), and dean of Christ Church (1711). He was a political ally of **Robert Harley, Earl of Oxford**, and **Henry St. John, Lord Bolingbroke**, and a friend and commentator on some of the works of **Pope**, **Swift**, Isaac Newton (1642–1727), **Arbuthnot**, **Gay**, and Matthew Prior (1664–1721). As a writer, Atterbury is best known for his eloquent defense of the Anglican church against **Latitudinarianism** in "A Letter Concerning . . . Rights and Privileges of an English Convocation" (1697) and "Representation of the Present State of Religion" (1711).

Laura B. Kennelly

Bibliography

Barrell, Rex A., ed. *Francis Atterbury (1662–1732), Bishop of Rochester, and His French Correspondents.* 1990.

Bennett, Gareth Vaughan. *The Tory Crisis in Church and State, 1688–1730: The Career of Francis Atterbury, Bishop of Rochester.* 1975.

See also Church of England

Attwood, Thomas (1783–1856)

Birmingham banker, monetary theorist, political activist, and M.P., Attwood lobbied in London (1812) on behalf of Birmingham's manufacturing interests against the **Orders in Council**. After 1815 he wrote frequently against the resumption of specie payments and the view of **David Ricardo** that the value of currency should be tied to that of gold, instead arguing in favor of continuous and moderate expansion of a regulated paper currency; inflation, he thought, would bring prosperity and full employment in an organically ordered society.

Branded a crank, Attwood turned from economic to political remedies and organized (1830) the Birmingham Political Union, which agitated in favor of changes soon enacted in the parliamentary **Reform Act** (1832). Celebrated for his efforts, he was elected (1832) M.P. for Birmingham (which formerly had been unrepresented in **Commons**); but, returning unsuccessfully to his obsession with currency reform, he then in disappointment took up "moral force" Chartism, reviving the Political Union (1837) for that purpose. In June 1839 he presented the national Chartist petition to the House of Commons; later that year he unhappily resigned his seat and withdrew from public life.

David Levy

Bibliography

Moss, David J. *Thomas Attwood.* 1990.

See also Economic Thought

Augustan

"Augustan" is an attractive term, the longer used the less understood. When John Dryden (1631–1700) dedicated his play *The Assignation* (1673), he favorably compared the Restoration court with that of the Roman Emperor Augustus and the flourishing patronage system he envisioned under his rule. Dryden and other Restoration artists hoped that under Charles II, Augusta (the old name for London, Dryden elsewhere explained) and England would become a second Rome. Until the end of **Queen Anne**'s reign (1714), occasionally writers urged a renewal of an age of Augustan literary patronage. But after her death, that aspiration yielded to disillusionment among **Tory** conservative writers such as **Jonathan Swift** (who scoffed, "King Charles the Second's Reign . . . is reckoned, though very absurdly, our Augustan Age"). Opponents of Hanoverian rule satirically depicted the first two Georges in light of Caesar's despotic actions or attacked their failure to patronize the arts.

On the other hand, supporters of the **Hanoverian Succession**, mostly **Whigs** such as **Joseph Addison** and Thomas Tickell (1686–1740), generally saw a *Great* Britain rising on mercantilist shoulders, and continued to praise their country as a second Rome. Rome and things Roman, but not necessarily Augustan—Palladian architecture, Italian opera, civic virtue—permeated English culture. At its perimeter, therefore, "Augustan" has been used loosely and incorrectly as a synonym for "classical" and "neoclassical."

Although Tickell eulogized Addison in 1721 "as one of the best authors since the [Latin] Augustan Age," during the 1730s Tory writers continually found the term opprobrious. Otherwise dissimilar figures such as **John Hervey** and **Henry Fielding** denied that their own era was Augustan, the latter calling it a "Gothick Leaden Age" (1754).

In 1759, however, **Oliver Goldsmith** fondly praised an Augustan era when he published in *The Bee* his **essay**, "An Account of the Augustan Age of England." He roughly dated the period from "some years before" the reign of Queen Anne (when "taste was united to genius" and writers shone "like stars lost in each other's brightness") to around 1740. Including both Tories and Whigs, he extolled their prose for its clarity of diction and "manliness." About **Lord Bolingbroke** he wrote that his antipathy toward his political adversary **Sir Robert Walpole** "gave a glow to his style, and an edge to his manner, that never yet have been equalled in political writing." The Roman Augustan Age was for Goldsmith a time when the arts flourished because of **patronage**. In contrast, the poet in his own time is victimized by **newspapers**: "He finds himself . . . at the mercy of men who have neither abilities nor learning to distinguish his merit."

After Goldsmith, the term lay quietly until the end of the 19th century. But in the 20th, British critics began evoking it: George Saintsbury, in *The Peace of the Augustans* (1916); John Butt, in *The Augustan Age* (1950); and British and Americans both use it now as a convenience. Literary historians disagree, however, on the length of the age and whom to consider. David Daiches, for example (*A Critical History of English Literature,* 1960), calls his chapter on the period "The Augustan Age: Defoe, Swift, Pope," but excludes their contemporary **James Thomson**. Butt omits **Daniel Defoe**, and includes both Thomson and **Samuel Johnson** by tenuously arguing that if Thomson was an Augustan, then so too was Johnson. One might better urge that Augustanism was a temperament, or an arrangement of intellectual furniture, and welcome congenial authors from Dryden on.

More than a temperament was the conviction among early 18th-century authors, Whig and Tory, that, as **John Dennis** averred in 1701, "As Nature is Order and Rule, and Harmony in the visible World, so Reason is the very same throughout the invisible Creation." "A mighty Maze!" **Alexander Pope** exclaimed, "but not without a Plan." This belief was strengthened by discoveries in the natural sciences that supported the idea of order in the universe. Language itself was to be lauded for its clarity and accuracy ("clearness of diction," in Goldsmith's phrase), rather than for decorative efflorescence. To that end the **Royal Society** in 1664 appointed a committee "for improving the English language." With that motive Pope "versified" two **satires** by John Donne, and Swift mocked the slang and clichés of his time.

Economically, Augustan literature existed as long as Maecenas survived in multiple numbers. As patronage and subscription editions decreased during the 18th century, however, the distance between artist and audience widened; and into that space stepped the booksellers with their fiscal concerns. **Grub Street** was both a location and a metaphor for the new **publishing** industry. There the poet of genius found his work "mixed with the sordid trash of every daily scribbler" (Goldsmith). Without a patron he substitutes profit for fame and "enrolls himself in the lists of dullness and of avarice for life." Goldsmith's sentimental vision is not that far from Pope's nightmare of contamination in *The Dunciad* (1743).

Authors labeled Augustan tended to cultivate explicit or implied coteries. Addison and **Richard Steele** corresponded with readers of their periodicals; **John Gay** hungered for court approval; Pope solicited for subscribers to his *Iliad.* Defoe, by contrast, aimed for a mass audience. A whiff of snobbery and nostalgia clings to "Augustan"; Swift and Pope, for instance, questioned the idea of progress as they sought to correct the ways of their readers in the cause of a *good* rather than a *great* Britain. Even in the 18th century, "Augustan" was less a style than a hope. For writers such as Dryden and Goldsmith, artistic fame through patronage encouraged by a ruler was the hallmark of an Augustan, utopian, age. "Augustan" continues to be used as a shorthand identification of 18th-century writers, but it is a term that now has the value of a dead metaphor.

Peter A. Tasch

Bibliography

Erskine-Hill, Howard. "Augustans on Augustanism: England, 1655–1759." *Renaissance and Modern Studies.* Vol. 11, pp. 55–83.

Johnson, James William. *The Formation of English Neo-Classical Thought.* 1967.

Weinbrot, Howard D. *Augustus Caesar in "Augustan" England.* 1978.

See also Classicism; Language and Linguistics; Neoclassical Style; Romanticism and Romantic Style

Austen, Jane (1775–1817)

Author of six novels published between 1811 and 1818, Austen had an important impact on the development of the British novel. Eschewing the improbable **gothic** and **sentimental** conventions of contemporary novels, she made ordinary domestic life into a compelling subject for fiction.

The daughter of a clergyman, she lived first at Steventon in Hampshire, then in **Bath** beginning in 1801, and in Southampton after the death of her father (1805). In 1809 she settled in a cottage at Chawton with her mother, sister, and a friend, Martha Lloyd. She resided there until 1817, the year in which she died probably of Addison's disease. Although she made several trips to **London** during her lifetime, her novels represent social relationships and tensions within the group she knew best—the families of landed **gentry** and professional men dwelling in or near a country village.

Her parents and several of her seven siblings enjoyed literature and dabbled in writing. For their entertainment, the 11-year-old girl began composing parodies, most of which mocked 18th-century **novel** conventions. Her juvenilia (1787–1793) gradually moved away from brief parodic pieces and toward sustained attempts at comic novels. She was prolific in the latter 1790s, drafting "Elinor and Marianne" (1795, 1797); "First Impressions" (1796–1797); and "Susan" (1798–1799). That she was now coming to see writing as a vocation is clear from her desire to publish her work. In 1797 her father tried, unsuccessfully, to interest the **publisher** Cadell in "First Impressions." In 1803 her brother Henry helped her sell "Susan" to Crosby & Co., though Crosby did not release the novel.

Perhaps because of these disappointments, she apparently produced only one fragment of a novel in the following few years, "The Watsons" (1804–1805). In 1809, however, she

Jane Austen

began revising old manuscripts and writing new ones. She encountered rapid success, publishing *Sense and Sensibility* (formerly "Elinor and Marianne") in 1811, *Pride and Prejudice* (formerly "First Impressions") in 1813, *Mansfield Park* (1814), and *Emma* (1816). *Persuasion* appeared posthumously (1818) along with *Northanger Abbey* (titled "Susan" in the late 1790s). Austen died before completing her seventh novel, "Sanditon."

In Austen's day, women who made a profession of writing were often considered unladylike and even immodest, selfish, and vulgar. In contacting publishers for her, Austen's father and brother evinced unusual tolerance for their female relative's literary endeavors. But she cultivated that tolerance by putting her family duties first and keeping her work and the labor it required out of their sight. She hid her confidence about her writing from male relatives and most acquaintances, behaving with the deference and humility expected by the times, though to a small circle of female kin and friends she revealed ambition, authority, and pride in her accomplishments. These women encouraged her to discuss her work and opinions candidly, and their companionship also enabled her to remain single. She received at least one marriage proposal from a suitable gentleman, Harris Bigg-Wither, but she chose the lifestyle more compatible with a writing career.

Although Austen did not marry, she provided husbands for her heroines. Indeed, romance figured centrally in the realistic social worlds she constructed, and she made many of her heroes highly desirable. Still, in the playfully aggressive wit of some of her heroines and in some of their female friendships, she recorded her strong ties to women and the more assertive views she expressed in their company. As a result, her representations convey much of the rounded complexity of life itself.

Austen's achievement lies in the creation of an apparently seamless portrait out of diverse attitudes and experiences, which, consequently, have appealed to diverse readers. For many generations the novels have been cherished as a celebration of romantic love and marriage; in recent years, feminist readers have seen in them a subtle challenge to **marriage** as a patriarchal institution and as a diversion of human gifts better employed otherwise. Austen has been hailed as a formative influence on both literary realism and a subversive tradition of British women's writing. To historians and general readers she furnishes the best guide to gentry life in the early 19th century.

Deborah Kaplan

Bibliography

Chapman, R.W. *Jane Austen: Facts and Problems.* 1948.

———, ed. *Jane Austen's Letters to Her Sister Cassandra and Others.* 2nd ed. 1952.

Gilson, David. *A Bibliography of Jane Austen.* 1982.

Honan, Park. *Jane Austen: Her Life.* 1987.

Johnson, Claudia. *Jane Austen: Women, Politics, and the Novel.* 1988.

———. *Equivocal Beings: Politics, Gender, and Sentimentality in the 1790's—Wollstonecraft, Radcliffe, Burney, Austen.* 1995.

Southam, B.C. *Jane Austen's Literary Manuscripts: A Study of the Novelist's Development through the Surviving Papers.* 1964.

See also Women in Literature; Women's Employment

Australia

Development of Australia was an important Hanoverian accomplishment. The opportunity had first gone to the Dutch, who made several landfalls upon the coasts (1606–1644). The last Dutchman, Abel Janszoon Tasman (1603–*c.* 1659), sailed around Australia and Van Diemen's Land (Tasmania), sighting **New Zealand**, but failed to interest further the Dutch East India Company.

England's **Captain Cook**, on his first voyage (1768–1771), explored and charted Australia's east coast, naming it all New South Wales and claiming it for the British crown. **Sir Joseph Banks** testified in 1779 before a parliamentary Select Committee on the salubrious advantages of Botany Bay (near present-day Sydney) for a convict settlement, and James Matra (*c.* 1745–1806), the American-born midshipman on Cook's first voyage, in 1783 argued the advantages of establishing a naval base and place of settlement there for displaced American loyalists.

Simultaneously, American independence was creating a backlog of convicts in England. The government instituted **transportation** to New South Wales as a regular **punishment** under the penal code in 1787. **Arthur Phillip** was dispatched in command of the memorable "first fleet" of convicts, which landed at Sydney Cove in January 1788; a second fleet arrived in 1790, a third in 1791. The colony's first settlers were

Australia

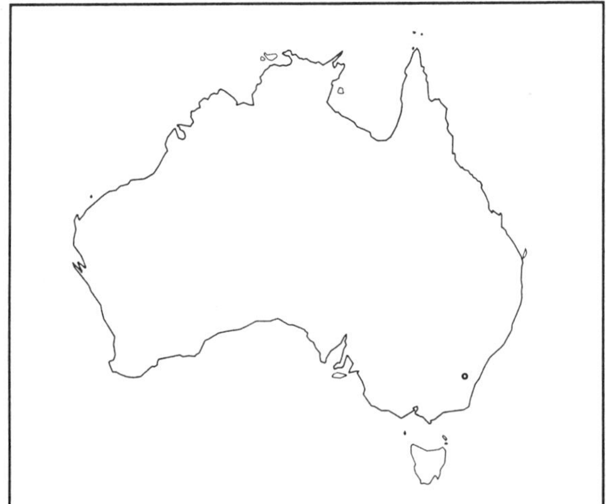

convicts (except for 200 soldiers sent to guard them), and it remained a penal colony for 50 years. Transportation, during its peak (1820–1840), brought 80,000 convicts to Australia, where they provided much-needed labor. Satisfactory completion of half of one's sentence could result in a "ticket-of-leave" (a form of parole) and the opportunity to earn wages and accumulate property. Few ex-convicts ever returned home.

The colony was remote and ill equipped to survive, but giving land grants to soldiers and officials, and employing convict labor, helped to establish grazing and cultivation. But the colony's early military governors were inept at economic management, and a clique of soldiers formed a monopoly to control the sale of imported supplies and domestic crops. Attempts to break this by Governor **William Bligh** prompted his overthrow in the "Rum Rebellion" (1808). Royal authority was restored by Governor **Lachlan Macquarie**, whose administration (1810–1821) witnessed numerous changes, including the beginnings of successful **exploration** and exploitation of the interior.

George Bass, Nicolas Baudin, and Matthew Flinders virtually completed charting Australia's 12,000 miles of coastline by 1803, but exploration of the nearly 3-million-square-mile landmass proceeded more slowly. Despite Sydney's admirable harbor, the nearly impenetrable Blue Mountains hemmed in the colony on the west. From 1798 to 1813, repeated attempts to penetrate the mountain barrier failed. However, drought, the need for more arable land, and fear of rival French claims impelled further efforts. In succeeding decades, numerous explorers filled in the map. They discovered new regions capable of settlement, and vast deserts, but no freshwater lakes or network of reliably navigable rivers.

If explorers and settlers were sorely tried by the inhospitable terrain and fickle climate, they at least found Australia's aboriginal people ("abos") unthreatening. These, in almost 30,000 years, had developed a complex nomadic culture, but one so bereft of material goods (including clothing) that the newcomers dismissed abos as mere beasts. Despite the government's humane pronouncements, atrocities were common, at least until 1838 when seven whites were hanged for killing 28 abos in the Myall Creek Massacre. Cruelties and injustices against natives were endemic.

In 1831 the British government ended free land grants—as **Edward Gibbon Wakefield** had recommended in *A Letter from Sydney* (1829)—and set a price of 5 shillings an acre, which quadrupled to £1 over the next decade. The land sale revenue was used to subsidize free immigrants, another of Wakefield's suggestions. Whereas only 20 free settlers arrived prior to 1801, 200,000 landed between 1825 and 1850. The last reform urged by Wakefield, ending transportation, was effected in 1840 in New South Wales, in 1850 in Tasmania, and in 1868 in Western Australia.

Meanwhile the search for an economic staple produced a success story. Sheep originally imported as food were crossed with purebred Merino stock to produce a very fine wool, and by the 1850s Australia was shipping 20,000 tons of wool—half of Britain's annual import. A prosperous economy grew on the backs of sheep.

N. Merrill Distad

Bibliography

Blainey, Geoffrey. *The Tyranny of Distance: How Distance Shaped Australia's History.* 1966; 2nd ed., 1975.

———. *Triumph of the Nomads: A History of Aboriginal Australia.* 1976.

Clark, Charles Manning Hope. *A History of Australia.* 6 vols. 1962–1987.

Hughes, Robert. *The Fatal Shore.* 1987.

Rudé, George. *Protest and Punishment: The Story of the Social and Political Protesters Transported to Australia, 1788–1868.* 1978.

Scott, Ernest, ed. *Australian Discovery by Sea and . . . by Land.* 2 vols. 1929; rpt. 1966.

Sharp, Andrew. *The Discovery of Australia.* 1963.

Shaw, Alan George Lewers. *Convicts and the Colonies: A Study of Penal Transportation from Great Britain and Ireland to Australia and Other Parts of the British Empire.* 1966.

———. *A Short History of Australia.* 1955; 2nd ed., 1967.

Stockdale, John, ed. *The Voyage of Governor Phillip to Botany Bay.* 1789; facs. rpt. 1950, 1968, 1982.

See also Emigration and Immigration

Autobiography and Confession

The 18th century is not usually reckoned one of the great ages for autobiography. It had no formal model of autobiography to match the spiritual confessions and hagiography of the 17th century. **Edward Gibbon**'s autobiography (1796) illustrates the dilemma, its apparent unity a creation not of Gibbon himself, who died leaving six drafts of his memoirs, but of his executor, Lord Sheffield (1735–1821); Sheffield's "harmony" is the "Gibbon's autobiography" which the reading public knows and admires. While Rousseau's *Confessions* (1782) and **William Wordsworth**'s *Prelude* (1850) were to provide for later times fit models for prose and poetic autobiographies, 18th-century autobiography was relatively improvisational, with collections of **letters**, journals, memoirs, and diaries substituting for more conventionally structured models of self-revelation.

But the lack of a formal model was no deterrent to self-revealing nonfiction. Indeed there was an increasing appetite for personal histories, probably enhanced by **Daniel Defoe**'s numerous pseudo-autobiographical fictions. Readers could choose from a range of writings by different social types, from upper-class clergy and country parsons to well-placed **aristocrats** of both sexes; from travelers and adventurers to artists, inventors, and actresses. The best known of the 18th-century works that might be called "autobiographical" are **James Boswell**'s *Life of Johnson* (1791), which is as revealing of Boswell as of his subject; also Boswell's journals, particularly his *London Journal* (1762–1763, 1950); and his *Journal of a Tour of the Hebrides with Samuel Johnson, LL.D.* (1773, 1785). Johnson also provided his own autobiographical fragment (published in *Diaries, Prayers and Annals, The Works of Samuel Johnson,* I. Yale, 1958). Other autobiographical works were *The Correspondence of* ***Horace Walpole****, The Letters of* ***Lady Mary Wortley Montagu,*** and *The Diaries of* ***Fanny Burney****.* Equally compelling is *My Own Life,* a self-described "funeral oration" by Scottish philosopher–historian **David Hume**. **John Wesley**'s *Journal* (1808) is a kind of spiritual autobiography, full of anecdotes and observations and personal encounters. The versatile natural scientist **Thomas Pennant** produced his *Literary Life of the Late Thomas Pennant, Esq., by Himself* (1793).

In the 19th century, in the wake of Rousseau's influential *Confessions* (1766–1770), autobiography became the dominant mode of **Romantic** literature. Many leading writers produced poetic self-revelations in confessional or conversational poems and odes—Wordsworth's "Tintern Abbey" (1798) and "Immortality" (1802–1804); **Coleridge**'s "conversation poems" (1795–1802); **Keats**'s odes (1819); **Shelley**'s *Epipsychidion* (1821) and the odes "West Wind" (1819) and "Skylark" (1820). Wordsworth's *The Prelude, or Growth of a Poet's Mind* (1805, 1850) has emerged as the representative poem of the age, combining the secular approach of Rousseau with a religious quest for the sources of his imaginative power in the peak experiences or "spots of time" of his early years.

Among prose works, **Dorothy Wordsworth**'s *Alfoxden Journal* (1798) and *Grasmere Journals* (1800–1803), with their wonderfully precise and minute observations of nature, present a contrast to *The Prelude*'s masculine rhetoric of the autonomous self and furnish a female version of Romantic autobiography. **Mary Shelley**'s *Journals* (1814–1844) are worth noting, though they offer only a perfunctory record of the Shelley circle's daily activities. Coleridge's *Biographia Literaria* (1817), which he also called his "Autobiographia Literaria," is a history of the "literary life and opinions" of the leading Romantic critic. The period's major prose remains **De Quincey**'s *Confessions of an English Opium Eater* (1822, 1856), which takes the reader from the outer world into De Quincey's dreams and achieves an unparalleled hallucinatory intensity in the "Pains of Sleep" section. The sequel, *Suspiria de Profundis* (1845), shows similar fuguelike internalizations of external reality. **William Hazlitt**'s *Liber Amoris* (1823) is the memoir of his frustrated love for a younger woman. **Charles Lamb**'s *Essays of Elia* (1823, 1833) is an important work in which the author manipulates the title persona as a confessional lens of his own quirky view of the world. The intimate and loosely structured "familiar" essay developed by Hazlitt, De Quincey, and Lamb is also a significant form of Romantic autobiography.

Romantic fictional confessions include **Hogg**'s Gothic narrative, *The Private Memoirs and Confessions of a Justified Sinner* (1824), as well as **Byron**'s literary alter egos in a sensational poetry that put his imprint on the legend of the **Byronic hero** (*Childe Harold's Pilgrimage,* 1812–1818; *Manfred,* 1817). For contemporaries, however, Byron's satiric masterpiece *Don Juan* (1819–1822) was more revealing. At the end of the period, Thomas Carlyle's extraordinary *Sartor Resartus* (1833) offered a fictionalized search for a faith beyond an outworn Christianity that anticipated the spiritual struggles of the later Victorians.

Richard D. Beards
Eugene Stelzig

Bibliography

Abrams, Meyer H. *Natural Supernaturalism: Tradition and Revolution in Romantic Literature.* 1971.

Greene, Donald. "The Uses of Autobiography in the Eighteenth Century," in P.B. Daghlian, ed., *Essays in Eighteenth-Century Biography.* 1968a.

———. "A Reading Course in Autobiography," in P.B. Daghlian, ed., *Essays in Eighteenth-Century Biography.* 1968b.

McConnell, Frank. *The Confessional Imagination: A Reading of Wordsworth's* Prelude. 1974.

Monsman, Gerald. *Confessions of a Prosaic Dreamer: Charles Lamb's Art of Autobiography.* 1984.

Pascal, Roy. *Design and Truth in Autobiography.* 1960.

Rzepka, Charles. *The Self as Mind: Vision and Identity in Wordsworth, Coleridge, and Keats.* 1986.

Spengemann, William C. *The Forms of Autobiography.* 1980.

B

Bach, Johann Christian (1735–1782)

Bach was a leader of **London** musical life for 20 years. Born in Leipzig, the youngest son of Johann Sebastian Bach (1685–1750), he completed his musical training in Italy (1754–1762). In 1762 he was engaged to compose Italian **operas** for the King's Theatre, London, and in the following year was appointed music master to Queen Charlotte.

Bach, in collaboration with Carl Friedrich Abel (1735–1787), founded an important annual concert series (beginning in 1775). He also pioneered the newly popular pianoforte in both printed sheet music (Six Sonatas, Op. 5, 1766) and in public performance (1768). As a composer, his greatest renown sprang from his symphonies and concertos, and from serious Italian operas of the Metastasian type, most notably *Carattaco* [Caractacus] (1767), on a suitably British topic, and *La Clemenza di Scipione* (1775). More widely appreciated today are his compositions in more modest forms: chamber music, in many instrumental combinations; English songs (many of them written for Vauxhall Gardens); and keyboard sonatas. His idiom resembles that of W.A. Mozart (1756–1791), with whom he developed a close friendship during the latter's stay in London (1764–1765).

Bach's music may be seen as a reaction against his father's learning and profundity, and as catering to the new desire for elegance and "air." Finely crafted and polished, it suffered almost total eclipse in the 19th century, but is currently enjoying a revival of interest. In Bach's time, Italian music was at the height of fashion, and there is no hint of English influence in his style even when set amidst English words or subject matter.

Nicholas Temperley

Bibliography

Terry, Charles S. *John Christian Bach*. 2nd ed., 1967.

See also London Pianoforte School; Music; Musical Concerts and Concert Life

Bacon, Anthony (*c.* 1717–1786)

Bacon was one of those businesspeople always in the right place at the right time. Born in the Isle of Man, as a boy he went to Maryland and ran a store; then around 1740 he bought a ship, learned to captain it himself, and before long began a partnership to victual West African troops, carry government officials and supplies to the **West Indies**, and supply **slaves** to North Carolina. Acquiring interests in the Cumberland coal trade, he moved from these into the **iron industry** in Glamorgan (1755), building a furnace to smelt local ore and adding a forge 10 years later, at the same time leasing the minerals under some 200 square miles centered on **Merthyr Tydfil** to create what was enviously called "Bacon's Mineral Kingdom."

He became a leading munitions-maker during the **Seven Years' War**. Afterward he paused only briefly (1764) to diversify into Canadian coal mining before entering Parliament the same year for Aylesbury (1764–1784), his opponents charging that he had paid five guineas a vote to the electors, far more than the going rate. In his maiden speech Bacon introduced a bill to make M.P.s liable for bankruptcy. Although he opposed **Grenville**'s attempts to tax the Americans (1764–1765), he reversed his position to support the government soon afterward and, during the **War of American Independence**, piled up contracts for the supply of shot and cannon produced using the new "bored from the solid" technique. Bacon retired a very wealthy man in 1782.

R.D. Corrins

Bibliography

Namier, L.B. "Anthony Bacon MP, an Eighteenth Century Merchant." *Journal of Economic and Business History*. Vol. 2, pp. 20–70.

See also Commerce, Overseas; Welsh Industry

Bage, Robert (1728–1801)

Bage, a Midlands papermaker-turned-novelist, authored controversial works, unusual in their varied discussion of social issues. As the early **Industrial Revolution** progressed, he produced novels that were both entertaining and serious, laced with witty **radicalism**.

The son of a Derby papermaker, Bage spent most of his life in the Staffordshire village of Elford, where he operated a papermill. Intellectually curious, he exhibited a brand of provincial radicalism closely associated with the Midlands' industrial development. He shared the interests of his contemporaries, including industrialists **Matthew Boulton** and **Josiah Wedgwood**, scientist **Joseph Priestley**, and writer **Erasmus Darwin**—all members of the **Lunar Society**.

Bage wrote to distract himself from financial loss. His **novels**, *Mount Henneth* (1782), *Barham Downs* (1784), *The Fair Syrian* (1787), *James Wallace* (1788), *Man as He Is* (1792), and *Hermsprong, Or Man as He Is Not* (1796), include serious themes loosely woven into plot and character development. *Hermsprong* is perhaps his most successful novel, exhibiting his sympathy with American political institutions, feminism, and religious freedom. **Sir Walter Scott** included three of Bage's novels in Ballantyne's Novelist's Library (1824).

Although influenced by the **French Revolution**, Bage endorsed the values of the commercial **middle class** while he expressed radical social views in a uniquely comic mode.

Robin Nilon

Bibliography

Faulkner, Peter. *Robert Bage.* 1979.

Scott, Sir Walter. "Prefatory Memoir to Bage," in *Ballantyne's Novelist's Library.* Vol. IX (Novels of Swift, Bage, and Cumberland). 1824.

Tompkins, J.M.S. *The Popular Novel in England: 1770–1800.* 1932.

Baillie, Joanna (1762–1851)

Baillie, Scottish poet and dramatist, grew up near **Glasgow**. Though a bright child, she did not learn to read until age 10; she soon afterward attended boarding school. Moving to Hampstead, near London (1783), her prolific literary output began with her anonymously published *Poems: Wherein It Is Attempted to Describe Certain Views of Nature and Rustic Manners* (1790). This went largely unnoticed, although a review praising the naturalism of her style appeared in the *Monthly Review.*

In 1798 Baillie published (again anonymously) the first volume of a *Series of Plays, in which It Is Attempted to Delineate the Stronger Passions of the Mind,* the work that brought her celebrity and caused some controversy when her gender was revealed. In her preface she explained her plan: to trace, in both comedy and tragedy, the progress of specific emotional states such as hatred, love, jealousy, and fear. Though written "for the closet," the plays attracted the notice of some noted artists, including **Sir Walter Scott** (who compared Baillie to **Shakespeare**) and the actor John Kemble (1757–1823). With Kemble's help a production of *De Monfort,* a tragedy exploring hatred, was performed at Drury Lane in 1800, Kemble and (his sister) **Sarah Siddons** taking leading roles.

Joanna Baillie

Two further volumes of *Plays on the Passions* appeared in 1802 and 1812. Baillie continued to write plays throughout her life, not all based on her original plan. Only seven of her 28 dramas were ever staged. Most successful was *The Family Legend,* which ran to much acclaim in Edinburgh (1810).

Baillie's *Metrical Legends of Exalted Characters* (1821) used the old **ballad** form to recount the histories of important figures such as William Wallace, Christopher Columbus, and Lady Grisell Baillie. She edited an anthology of verse (1823), published "A View of the General Tenor of the New Testament Regarding the Nature and Dignity of Jesus Christ" (1831), wrote another volume of plays (1836), and continued to compose **poetry** until her death in 1851. Her *Dramatic and Poetical Works* appeared that same year.

Though her celebrity declined, Baillie was well regarded by her contemporaries throughout her career. Intelligent and humorous, she maintained lifelong friendships with Scott, **Samuel Rogers, Maria Edgeworth, Hannah More,** and **Anna Letitia Barbauld.** Her importance for the **Romantic** period, particularly her anticipation of **Wordsworth**'s ideas on style, has only recently been recognized.

Samantha Webb

Bibliography

Baillie, Joanna. *Dramatic and Poetical Works.* 1851; facs. 1976.

Brewer, William. "The Prefaces of Joanna Baillie and William Wordsworth." *Friend: Commentary on Romanticism.* Vol. 1, pp. 34–47.

Carhart, Margaret. *The Life and Work of Joanna Baillie.* 1923.

Purinton, Marjean D. *Romantic Ideology Unmasked: The Mentally Constructed Tyrannies in Drama of William*

Wordsworth, Lord Byron, Percy Shelley, and Joanna Baillie. 1994.

See also Dramatic Criticism; Women in Literature

Bairds of Gartsherrie

The business ascent of the Baird family provides an illustration of the chain of modernization that transformed **Scotland** in the later Hanoverian period. Alexander (1765–1823) sprang from a long line of tenant farmers in the Monklands district near **Glasgow**. An enthusiastic **agricultural improver**, he seized the opportunity presented by the agricultural boom during the period 1790–1815 to lay the foundations of the family's fortune. He enclosed the runrig fields, introduced the latest methods, and extended into large-scale processing. He eagerly exploited the new **canal** linking the Monklands with the rapidly growing city of Glasgow, whose hunger for coal offered fresh opportunities to assist the upward mobility of his sizable family of two daughters and eight sons.

In 1816 two sons, William (1796–1864) and Alexander (1799–1862), extended the family's activities into **coal mining**. This grew significantly as canals, then **railways**, opened up the Lanarkshire mineral field. **J.B. Neilson**'s patenting of the hot-blast process (1828) made possible the exploitation of local blackband ore. The Gartsherrie Ironworks put its first furnace on stream in 1830 and within 7 years expanded to seven furnaces producing 26,500 tons. In the Victorian era, William Baird and Company entered the front ranks of world producers and realized large fortunes for the seven brothers who made up the partnership.

R.D. Corrins

Bibliography

Campbell, R.H. "Investment in the Scottish Pig Iron Trade 1830–1843." *Scottish Journal of Political Economy.* Vol. 1, pp. 233–249.

Corrins, R.D. "The Scottish Business Elite in the 19th Century: The Case of William Baird and Co," in A.J.G. Cummings and T.M. Devine, eds., *Industry, Business and Society in Scotland Since 1700.* 1994.

Slaven, A. *The Development of the West of Scotland, 1750–1960.* 1975.

See also Iron Industry

Bakewell, Robert (1725–1795)

Bakewell, often called the "father of animal husbandry," is best known for his revolutionary work in breeding sheep, cattle, and horses. While running his own farm at Dishley he studied breeding methods throughout Britain and Europe. His efforts were designed chiefly to improve meat production; to him, a sheep was "a machine for turning grass into mutton." His Leicestershire sheep doubled the amount of mutton normally provided by such animals, though he cared little about fleece quality. His Dishley cattle were low-set and blocky, and matured quickly. His breed of black horses proved strong enough for both farmwork and military service.

Bakewell laid the foundation for purebred farm animals. His innovations included the careful keeping of performance records, sire testing, and the maintenance of museums of skeletons for comparative purposes. He pioneered stud-farming, and his sires earned hefty sums (though experimentation costs often exceeded profits). His watchword, "breed the best to the best," led him toward successful inbreeding and culling. His work was copied widely by other **agricultural improvers**.

Thomas D. Veve

Bibliography

Pawson, H.C. *Robert Bakewell.* 1957.

Trow-Smith, Robert. *A History of British Livestock Husbandry, 1700–1900.* 1959.

See also Agricultural Societies; Agriculture

Ballad

A ballad is a song that tells a story, or a story told as a song. In Hanoverian Britain, ballads circulated among people of all socioeconomic groupings and constituted one of the many bonds of national society. The Hanoverians did not distinguish between traditional ballads circulating orally, printed broadside ballads that might be topical narratives composed for an immediate commercial audience, and printed literary ballads that began with 18th-century attempts by educated poets to achieve the evocative power and verbal economy of traditional ballads. All three types circulated both orally and in print. Literary interest in the texts of traditional ballads began in the reign of the Stuarts, reached adolescence under the Hanoverians, and attained scholarly maturity in the Victorian era and the early 20th century. The musical aspect was largely ignored until the Victorian era, and not treated seriously until the mid 20th century.

Traditional or folk ballads were folksongs which told stories of historical or legendary figures and events, of domestic tragedy and comedy, and of supernatural happenings. They are composed in stanzas, typically of four lines rhyming *xaxa* (the first and third lines may or may not rhyme), with the lines measured (according to strong beats only) 4/3/4/3 or composed in two-line stanzas of four strong beats in which are alternated refrain lines of three strong beats. Traditional ballads frequently begin *in media res* and proceed through a mixture of narrative and dialogue, often abruptly leaping from one scene to another and then lingering for several stanzas on a particular event or scene. Although some performances may be fairly lengthy, others may not, preferring instead to reduce the ballad text to its "emotional core." The language is usually simple, direct, popular, and highly stylized, incorporating commonplace phrases ("go saddle my horse," or "looked over his left shoulder") with well-worn epithets ("blood-red wine," "wee penknife," and "milk-white steed"). Transmitted primarily through oral tradition, folk ballads are differentiated from their popular and literary counterparts by their infinite textual variation. In folk tradition there is no one definitive text.

Broadside ballads (texts printed on one side of single sheets of cheap paper, sold whole or cut in half lengthwise to make broadslips) were new songs on any topic of current public interest (politics, religion, war, sport, love, sex, marriage, contemporary fads, crime, poverty, etc.), usually sung to old tunes. Traditional folk ballads were also printed as broadsides and, in addition, frequently appeared in chapbooks (printed on single sheets of cheap paper, folded and cut into eight- or sixteen-page booklets), for example, "Barbara Allen's Cruelty," "Children in the Wood," and "Chevy Chase." Broadside ballads developed their narratives in a more evenly linear manner than did folk ballads; their language was a mixture of folk vernacular, contemporary street talk, and literary diction and, because their medium of transmission was print, they tended toward textual standardization. Broadsides, broadslips, and chapbooks were sold cheaply in city streets and at country fairs, thus making available a printed literature to the lower classes (though there are many signs that all classes heard and bought them).

The Hanoverian era marks the first period of wide literary interest in traditional ballads, but a few commentaries preceded it. The fame of the ballad "Chevy Chase" began with a comment by Sir Philip Sidney in his *Apology of Poesie* (1595) in which he expressed his admiration for the old martial song that began "God prosper long our noble king. . . ." **Joseph Addison** added to the reputation of "Chevy Chase" with his much longer discussion of the ballad in *The Spectator* (1711), arguing that such old ballads were worthy of serious study and even emulation by poets. Throughout the Hanoverian period, British intellectuals felt a certain ambivalence toward these products of popular culture, one which, however, was ultimately resolved in their favor. In **poetry** the argument was reshaped and intensified by **Wordsworth** nearly a century later in his "Preface" to the ***Lyrical Ballads*** (1798), and meanwhile British playwrights and poets appropriated subjects, diction, and structural elements from folk and broadside tradition for their ballad operas and their literary ballads. One of the earliest examples of this was David Mallet's (1705–1765) reworking of a broadside ballad about a dead woman and her faithless lover to produce a literary ballad called "William and Margaret" (1723), which became an instant success, going back into broadside circulation and holding its popularity for the remainder of the century. And then there were **Gay**'s *The Beggar's Opera* (1728), **Lillo**'s *The London Merchant; or, the History of George Barnwell* (1731), **Goldsmith**'s "Edwin and Angelina" (1764), **Thomas Percy**'s "The Friar of Orders Gray" (1765), and **Coleridge**'s "The Rime of the Ancient Mariner" (1798).

Despite changes in taste there was also serious and growing interest in the collection of authentic ballads from the past, from the early efforts signaled by Thomas d'Urfey's collected *Wit and Mirth or Pills to Purge Melancholy* (1719–1720), down through the anonymously edited *A Collection of Old Ballads* (1723–1725), Percy's *Reliques of Ancient English Poetry* (1765), and the numerous editions of ballads that were to follow (among them those by David Herd, 1769 and 1776; by Joseph Ritson, 1783, 1790, 1791, and 1795; and by William Motherwell, 1827). Percy's *Reliques,* in particular, was a major inspiration for several generations of poets, scholars, and a new kind of collector who would actually take the words of ballads from the lips of living singers. Perhaps the collection best known among literary scholars today is **Sir Walter Scott**'s *Minstrelsy of the Scottish Border* (1802–1803), a large collection of authentic historical and romantic ballads along with Scott's own efforts in imitation of them.

Cathy Lynn Preston
Arthur F. Schrader

Bibliography

Anderson, Flemming G. *Commonplace and Creativity: The Role of Formulaic Diction in Anglo-Scottish Traditional Balladry.* 1985.
Bronson, Bertrand. *The Singing Tradition of Child's Popular Ballads.* 1976.
Buchan, David. *The Ballad and the Folk.* 1972.
Child, Francis James, ed. *The English and Scottish Popular Ballads.* 5 vols. 1882–1898; rpt. 1965.
Dugaw, Dianne. *Warrior Women and Popular Balladry, 1650–1850.* 1989.
Friedman, Albert B. *The Ballad Revival: Studies in the Influence of Sophisticated Poetry.* 1961.
Holloway, John, and Joan Black, eds. *Later English Broadside Ballads.* 1975.
Laws, G. Malcolm. *The British Literary Ballad.* 1972.
Shephard, Leslie. *The History of Street Literature.* 1973.
Simpson, Clause M. *The British Broadside Ballad and Its Music.* 1966.

See also Ballad Opera; Folksong

Ballad Opera

Ballad opera was a British genre that flourished for about a decade after 1728, when **John Gay**'s *The Beggar's Opera* first appeared. In ballad opera, spoken dialogue was interspersed with songs set to preexisting tunes, both traditional and composed.

The precursors of ballad opera included the English theatrical **burlesque**, popular since the previous century, and the *comédie en vaudeville,* in which new words were set to familiar tunes. Allan Ramsay's (1686–1758) pastoral *The Gentle Shepherd* (1725) was an early staged work in a similar form but with only four songs; Ramsay later revised it as a true ballad opera (1729), adding 18 songs.

Before 1728, the only kind of **opera** regularly available in **London** was Italian opera, performed by the Royal Academy of Music. When *The Beggar's Opera* opened to instant success at Lincoln's Inn Fields in January 1728, it was not in direct competition with the Italian company, which played for an **aristocratic** audience; the Royal Academy's imminent failure was therefore unrelated to the success of *The Beggar's Opera.* Even so, one of the main reasons for the popularity of this work was its **satire** on what the English considered the more ridiculous aspects of *opera seria:* castrati, weak plots, recitative, and the rigid structure dictated by the singers. In his text for *The Beggar's Opera,* Gay satirized Italian opera in London, the **legal profession**, and the government of **Sir Robert Walpole**.

The story revolves around characters from the London underworld: robbers, **highwaymen**, and **prostitutes**. Gay selected the 69 tunes to which he wrote new words. Some originated as **folksongs**, others as popular works by composers such as **George Frideric Handel** and Henry Purcell (1659–1695). Johann Christoph Pepusch (1667–1752) added basses to the tunes and composed an overture. Gay's sequel, *Polly* (1729), incidentally, was banned.

Almost 100 ballad operas were produced in the following decade. Most were comic, and some treated themes similar to *The Beggar's Opera.* Others were based on historical and patriotic subjects. One of the most successful was Charles Coffey's *The Devil to Pay* (1731), which, when performed in German translation in the 1740s with music adapted by a Mr. Seedo, became influential in the formation of the German opera genre *Singspiel.* **Henry Fielding** was also a popular author of ballad operas, writing, for example, *The Lottery* (1732). Not all ballad operas were performed in London. Some were staged regularly in **Ireland** and America, where works on local themes using native folksongs were also produced. Coffey's *The Beggar's Wedding* (Dublin, 1729) was particularly successful.

Ballad opera declined rapidly in popularity in the late 1730s. However, its influence was still felt in the 1760s, when English composers led by **Thomas Arne** and Samuel Arnold (1740–1802) began to develop a new form of English dialogue opera. Although such operas were partly newly composed, many of the first used borrowed music. The plot of Arne's *Love in a Village* (1762) was based on a ballad opera—Charles Johnson's *The Village Opera* (1729).

Ballad opera was the first genre of English opera. Although its popularity was short-lived, it offered a dramatic and musical form that appealed to the London theater audience, provided an alternative musical entertainment to the limited attractions of Italian opera, and demonstrated to later composers that there was a place for an English operatic form.

Jane Girdham

Bibliography

Berger, Arthur V. "The Beggar's Opera, the Burlesque, and Italian Opera." *Music and Letters.* Vol. 17, pp. 93–105.

Bronson, Bertrand H. "The Beggar's Opera." *University of California Publications in English.* Vol. 8, pp. 197–231.

Fiske, Roger. *English Theatre Music in the Eighteenth Century.* 1986.

Gagey, Edmond McAdoo. *Ballad Opera.* 1937.

Goberman, Max. "Mr. John Gay's *The Beggar's Opera.*" *Music Review.* Vol. 24, pp. 3–12.

Guerinot, J.V., and Rodney D. Jilg. *The Beggar's Opera.* 1976.

Morrissey, L.J. "Henry Fielding and the Ballad Opera." *Eighteenth-Century Studies.* Vol. 4, pp. 386–402.

Bamford, Samuel (1788–1872)

Bamford was a weaver, poet, and **radical** organizer whose autobiographical *Passages in the Life of a Radical* (1841–1843) and *Early Days* (1849) provide rare firsthand insight into working-class life and political activity in the later Hanoverian era. Born in Middleton near rapidly industrializing **Manchester**, the son of a **Methodist** weaver, he went to grammar school and **Sunday school**, educated himself by reading **Shakespeare**, **Milton**, and national history, and tried a series of rough jobs ranging from **agricultural labor** to bookselling to working in **coastal trade** as a **seaman** transporting coal from South Shields to London. After marrying (1812), he and his wife settled down as weavers.

Becoming an admirer of **Cobbett**, Bamford helped found a local **Hampden Club** (1816) and attended the January 1817 London convention of club delegates where he met **Cartwright**, **Hunt**, and other radical leaders. Though he refused to join the ill-conceived Manchester **Blanketeer March** two months later, his agitation nonetheless caused him to be arrested and tried for treason (March 1817) (though he was acquitted for lack of evidence). Two years later he was one of the main organizers of the ill-fated Manchester reform meeting that ended in the **Peterloo Massacre** (1819); he served a year in jail afterward for conspiracy to incite to riot.

Bamford then retreated from radical agitation, but continued to support reform. In the 1830s he worried about the growing split between **middle-class** and working-class progressives and, hoping to prevent violence during the Chartist agitations, served as a constable on the side of law and order.

Thomas D. Veve

Bibliography

Baylen, Joseph O., and Norbert J. Gossman. *Biographical Dictionary of Modern British Radicals.* Vol. 1. 1979.

Dictionary of National Biography, s.v. "Bamford, Samuel."

Maccoby, S. *English Radicalism.* Vol. 2, 1786–1832. 6 vols. 1935–1961.

Royle, Edward, and James Walvin. *English Radicals and Reformers, 1760–1848.* 1982.

Thompson, E.P. *The Making of the English Working Class.* 1963.

White, R.J. *Waterloo to Peterloo.* 1957.

Bangorian Controversy

This controversy in the **Church of England** resulted from a sermon delivered in 1717 by **Benjamin Hoadly**, Bishop of Bangor, who questioned whether Jesus Christ had delegated any authority to any religious institutions such as the Anglican Church. A very influential **Latitudinarian Whig** churchman, Hoadly maintained not only that Christ was the sole judge and lawgiver for all Christians but that Christians' loyalty was to Him, not the organized body of the visible church. Religious opinion was not state business, and the church needed no props of secular law and temporal rewards. Hoadly recommended supplanting ecclesiastical authority with private conscience; the hallmark of true belief was not orthodoxy, but the sincerity of the believer.

This set off a storm of controversy. Hoadly's views struck **Tory** churchmen such as **William Law** as nothing short of a sweeping repudiation of the foundations upon which the

Anglican Church was built. Law argued that Hoadly's reliance on sincerity as a test of religious belief was insufficient; not only would this make established churches superfluous, but any Christian society based on common principles would be impossible. A paper snowstorm comprising over 200 pamphlets by more than 50 writers descended on the bishop. The Lower House of Convocation (the Council of the Church of England) attacked his writings (and the Whig principles connected with them), with the result that the Whig government ordered the Convocation prorogued; it was not reconvened until 1852.

K.J.H. Berland

Bibliography

Dickinson, H.T. "Benjamin Hoadley, 1676–1761: An Unorthodox Bishop." *History Today.* Vol. 25, pp. 348–355.

Hearnshaw, F.J.C., ed., *The Social and Political Ideas of Some English Thinkers of the Augustan Age, AD 1650–1750.* 1928.

Stephen, Leslie. *History of English Thought in the Eighteenth Century.* 2 vols. 2nd ed., 1881.

Sykes, Norman. *Church and State in the XVIIIth Century.* 1934; 1975.

———. *From Sheldon to Secker: Aspects of English Church History, 1660–1768.* 1959.

See also Hare, Francis; Potter, John

Bank of England

In 1694 the need of the English government to raise money led to the foundation of the Bank of England. It was formed as a **joint-stock company** for a period of 21 years with a capital of £1.2 million, which was loaned to the government. The bank was permitted to receive deposits on which it could make further, short-term advances. It quickly came to handle government payments to armies abroad, and bills issued to pay governmental debts. In 1708 it was granted a monopoly of joint-stock **banking** in England, a measure that affected the development of English banking until the 19th century.

The bank's influence over government borrowing was highlighted in 1715. It then agreed to handle the annual supply loan, on condition that this was issued as transferable stock, and that the bank would not be dissolved until this, and any such future loans, were repaid. The unlikelihood of the latter ensured the bank's permanency. The bank was also involved in the **South Sea Bubble** crisis of 1720, advancing proposals to fund the national debt. These were rejected, but when the boom collapsed, **Sir Robert Walpole** asked the bank to help resolve the situation.

During the 18th century, the bank began to display the characteristics of a central bank, although it did not formally admit to such a role. In addition to acting as the government's banker, by advancing money to other bankers through rediscounting bills of exchange, it became, in effect, a banker's banker. As the main source of gold to the mint, the bank could influence, but not directly control, the money supply—a circumstance also underlined by its importance as the largest note issuer in the country. Because such notes were convertible to gold, the amount of credit banks could advance was limited to the level of their deposits. Weaknesses in the system surfaced in 1797, when wartime problems forced the British government to suspend large payments in cash, thus increasing the issuance of notes overall. This measure was not revoked until 1821, when the country effectively established the gold standard.

Bank of England, London

Throughout the period, the Bank of England continued to act as a private bank, operating accounts for its customers. Economic growth and the rise of provincial banks led to pressure to remove its monopoly of joint-stock banking. In 1826 this was restricted to a radius of 65 miles from London and, in 1833, it was revoked altogether. In 1826 the bank was permitted to open branch offices outside London, increasing its ability to issue notes. As its private functions declined, its public role increased, ensuring that, by the end of the Hanoverian era, the bank was secure at the apex of the country's banking system.

A.J.G. Cummings

Bibliography
Clapham, Sir John. *The Bank of England.* 2 vols. 1944.
Collins, M. *Money and Banking in the U.K.: A History.* 1988.
Dickson, P.G.M. *The Financial Revolution: A Study in the Development in Public Credit 1688–1756.* 1967.
Neal, Larry. *The Rise of Finance Capitalism: International Capital Markets in the Age of Reason.* 1990.

See also Economic Thought; Finance and Investment

Bank of Scotland

Founded in 1695 by an act of the Scottish Parliament as a **joint-stock company**, the Bank of Scotland was dependent on private capital and was formed for the purpose of creating **banking** as a trade. A substantial share of its capital was raised in **London**, and it issued its own notes based on pounds sterling.

The bank faced competition from the Darien Company in the late 17th century, and a liquidity crisis developed in 1696 as many investors, believing Darien more profitable, presented Bank of Scotland notes for payment. General economic crises compounded the bank's problems, though Darien's failure did remove some of the pressure. Despite further liquidity crises in 1704–1705 and 1708 (the latter resulting from rumors of French invasion), management was tightened and greater access was gained to the London money market. Although established to improve credit, the bank was extremely conservative; it was only in 1704 that it issued a note as low as £1 sterling.

Tainted with **Jacobitism**, however, it lost its monopoly in 1716. An expansion of credit facilities occurred with the establishment of the **Royal Bank of Scotland** in 1727. Initially fierce rivals, the two banks learned to live together, unsuccessfully trying to retain a duopoly as additional new banking organizations came into existence.

Richard Finlay

Bibliography
Checkland, S.G. *Scottish Banking: A History, 1695–1973.* 1975.

See also Finance and Investment

Banking and Bankers

During the Hanoverian period, the development of banking was essential for both **commerce** and industry. Two distinct strands in banking had developed by the late 17th century—public and private. Public banking dealt with the needs of the government and the management of the national debt, private banking with the needs of individuals and the business community.

Concern over the mounting costs of **war** with **France** and the government's need to borrow money had led to the formation of the **Bank of England** in 1694. During the Hanoverian period the Bank of England acted as banker to the government as well as handling issues of government stock, issuing notes, and discounting (i.e., advancing cash against) bills of exchange presented by other banks. At the height of the **South Sea Bubble** crisis in 1720, the bank assisted **Walpole** in rescuing the **South Sea Company** from total collapse. The bank also acted as a commercial bank for private customers in **London**. A parliamentary act of 1708 confirming its monopoly of **joint-stock** banking in England also stated that the maximum number of partners in other banks should be six. Thus, although such firms could accept deposits, issue notes,

Bank of Scotland, Edinburgh, 1830

make loans, discount bills of exchange, and transfer money by cheque, their activities were limited by the amount of capital they could raise. Because these organizations did not have limited liability, much of the confidence in them lay in the extent of the partners' private assets. Private bank note issues were only a fraction of those of the Bank of England.

In the early 18th century, the bulk of private banking activity took place in London. At the time of the Restoration (1660), much banking was done by goldsmiths, who had secure premises in which to keep deposits, and whose receipts became recognized as instruments of exchange. Goldsmiths also quickly realized that only a portion of their funds needed to be kept on hand, and thus that the remainder could be loaned at interest. To encourage deposits they also paid interest to clients.

By the early 18th century the goldsmiths had given way to two distinct types of bank—West End banks and City banks—each with a distinct type of business. West End bankers, such as Hoares and Coutts, were basically gentlemen banking for other gentlemen. Their customers were the landed **gentry**, the **aristocracy**, and royalty. Their business included dealing in rents remitted from customers' country estates, settling customers' debts in London, and arranging loans on the security of estates. Some, such as Hoares, had goldsmith origins, some came from other professions; Goslings, for example, came from bookselling and printing. Later in the century, much of Goslings' business was with wealthy men returning from **India** such as **Clive** and **Warren Hastings**.

City bankers were different. Often coming from a merchant or trade background, they specialized in discounting bills of exchange, although they also issued notes and handled investments for merchants. Thus they were more significant in the general mobilization of credit. As the 18th century progressed, some acted as agents for country banks, thus assisting the movement of funds between regions, their discounting facilities providing a necessary part of the capital required by nascent manufacturing firms during the **Industrial Revolution**.

The number of London bankers multiplied during the 18th century from 25 in 1725 to 70 in 1800, much of this increase coming in the latter decades, a sure indication that this was a period of steady economic growth. This growth is confirmed also by the development of a network of country banks in the second half of the century. These necessarily developed later because London, as a sophisticated financial center, required specialist bankers before the provinces. The gap was filled by people acting as bankers in a part-time capacity. In Lancashire, attorneys mobilized funds and put potential borrowers in touch with potential lenders. Grain merchants, maltsters, and others acted as bankers, sometimes as a sideline, sometimes as their main activity. **Domestic production** and nascent manufacturing industry, with their links with both internal and external trade, were also important recruiting grounds for country bankers, many of whom engaged in more than one field of activity. By the end of the 18th century there were approximately 350 country banks.

Some industrialists, working in areas where financial services were lacking, became bankers. The issue of notes, circulation of drafts, and acceptance of deposits from the public not only provided a local means of payment, but often provided capital for industrialists, some using advances from their own banks to finance industrial ventures. The first bank in **Birmingham**, founded by the **Lloyd Family**, started in the iron trade, and **Wilkinson** became a partner in a Shrewsbury bank in 1793. In textiles, **Arkwright** and the elder **Robert Peel** had banking connections. **Brewing**, a big business in the 18th century with high demands for capital and credit, also produced a crop of bankers. However, a partner's banking and other activities could become so intermingled that the collapse of one could lead to the collapse of the other: for example, Benjamin Roebuck's Sheffield bank is said to have collapsed in 1778 because of his involvement with the crisis-hit **Carron Ironworks**.

Lawyers also entered banking, but rarely in a full-time capacity. Their function was to draw business into the bank through their clients and their savings. They were invaluable to banks because of their knowledge of local people and resources. Traders were also of importance in country banking. Shopkeepers might indulge in a little discounting, but rarely went much further. The main candidates for recruitment in this sphere were the commodity dealer, the general merchant, and the overseas trader: in inland centers, commodity dealers were important; in seaports, general **merchants**. In **Liverpool**, of 14 banks of importance, 10 came from merchant houses.

Links with the London money market drew country banks into a loosely knit national system. Rural banks with a surplus of funds looked to London for profitable investment. Banks in industrial areas, where funds tended to be short, looked to London to discount bills of exchange to provide short-term credit. Thus it was essential for the country bank to have a London agent. Most employed city bankers, as these better suited their purposes, but some also had links with West End bankers. Such business was very profitable for the London bankers. In some cases too there was interconnection in partnerships between banks in London and in the country. The Lloyds of Birmingham and the Smiths of Nottingham both had London connections. The London agent could be a bank's lifeline in times of crisis or panic. Additional credit could keep a bank open; but the refusal by a London agent or the Bank of England to continue accepting a firm's drafts could often lead to collapse.

In England it was not possible, because of the limitations on the size of banks, to develop a branch system such as that in **Scottish banking**. Also, the economic uncertainties caused by the French wars (1792–1815) and their aftermath, together with the lack of a clear set of regulatory measures on the issue of notes, combined to ruin many private banks in the early 19th century. A particularly severe crisis in 1825 resulted in a rash of bankruptcies and the restriction of the Bank of England's monopoly of joint-stock banking to within 65 miles of London (1826). This, together with the abolition of the monopoly altogether in 1833, allowed for the growth in the Victorian era of larger, more secure joint-stock banks with branch networks.

A.J.G. Cummings

Bibliography

Clapham, Sir John. *The Bank of England. A History.* 2 vols. 1944.

Collins, M. *Money and Banking in the U.K.: A History.* 1988.

———. *Banks and Industrial Finance in Britain 1800–1939.* 1991.

Crouzet, F., ed. *Capital Formation in the Industrial Revolution.* 1972.

Joslin, D.M. "The London Private Bankers, 1720–1785." *Economic History Review.* Vol. 7, pp. 167–186.

Pressnell, L.S. *Country Banking in the Industrial Revolution.* 1956.

See also Finance and Investment

Banks, Sir Joseph (1743–1820)

Banks, the son of a wealthy Lincolnshire landowner, was educated at Harrow, Eton, and Christ Church, Oxford, where he developed early that interest in botany which would make him a leading scientist. His subsequent **explorations** and long presidency of the **Royal Society** provided opportunities to sponsor and revitalize scientific work, and encourage practical use of scientific discoveries.

His father's death (1761) left him a substantial inheritance, which he used to further his interests. In 1766 he made his first overseas expedition, traveling to **Newfoundland** and Labrador, where he collected many specimens of plants and insects. The reputation he gained from this, together with maneuvering by his friend **Lord Sandwich**, smoothed the way for his inclusion aboard **Captain James Cook**'s first Pacific voyage in 1768–1771. Preparing carefully, he brought along Daniel Solander, a former student of the Swedish botanist Linnaeus (1707–1778), and also an artist to draw specimens impracticable to collect. In three years' labor he greatly enlarged his collections. His contact with **Australia** became the source of new European knowledge about plants (the shrub called "Banksia" was first discovered in Botany Bay) and animals (Banks was the first to show that marsupials were more ancient than placental mammals). In 1772 he financed another expedition, to Iceland, again accompanied by Solander and other assistants, this time bringing back not only more items for his burgeoning collection but many Icelandic books and manuscripts, which he added to his vast library.

Considered an expert botanist, and favored personally by the king, Banks was made President of the Royal Society (1778), a post he held for more than 40 years until his death. It was in this capacity that he made his most important contributions. He encouraged the renewal of interest in the natural sciences, which had been suffering from the Newtonian emphasis on mathematics; promoted the collection of specimens of all types of plants, animals, and minerals; and through his many contacts facilitated international cooperation between scientists. He recognized the importance of classifying specimens to make possible accurate identifications, and supported first the Linnean system of classification, then the new system of plant classification developed by the French botanist Antoine-Laurent de Jussieu (1748–1836).

A doer as much as a thinker, Banks also promoted applied science. He helped improve minting, manufacturing, and **agriculture** through his position as scientific advisor to the government, and was particularly interested in the transfer and cultivation of economically useful plants to strengthen the **empire**—a famous example being the transfer of breadfruit from Tahiti to the **West Indies** aboard **Captain Bligh**'s ill-fated ship the *Bounty* (1789).

Named botanical advisor to **George III**, Banks planned the royal gardens at Kew as a botanical laboratory and pleasure garden. In 1788, at George's request, he smuggled several Spanish merino sheep into England, and for several years oversaw the enlargement of the king's flock in hopes of eventually eliminating imports of fine Spanish wool. Rewarding him for loyal service, George made Banks a baronet (1781) and later invested him with the Order of the Bath (1795). Banks bequeathed his herbarium and large collection of books and periodicals to the **British Museum**.

Anne Thompson

Bibliography

Carter, Harold B. *His Majesty's Spanish Flock: Sir Joseph Banks and the Merinos of George III of England.* 1964.

———. *Sir Joseph Banks, 1743–1820.* 1988.

Gascoigne, John. *Joseph Banks and the English Enlightenment.* 1994.

O'Brian, Patrick. *Joseph Banks: A Life.* 1993.

See also Pennant, Thomas; Science, Technology, and Invention; White, Gilbert

Baptists

The Baptists, a denomination of Protestant **dissenters**, believe in spiritual regeneration through adult baptism by immersion. With their origins in **Congregationalism** they reflected two strands of Augustinian theology: Arminianism and Calvinism. The Arminian (or General) Baptists believed Christ's atonement was general for all persons. The Calvinistic (Particular or "Strict") Baptists believed that atonement applied exclusively to the elect. General Baptists were Separatists; Particular Baptists were non-Separatist independents. Both groups gained a foothold in England during the first quarter of the 17th century and grew significantly before 1660, though the Particular group had the greater gains, as the General lost members to the **Quakers**. The works and examples of two outstanding 17th-century Baptists, John Bunyan (1628–1688) and Benjamin Keach (1640–1704), left a legacy to the Hanoverian period. Keach, a pioneer author of religious books for children, introduced congregational hymn-singing, whereas Bunyan's towering narrative genius and vigorous style made *Pilgrim's Progress* (1678) the expression of a spiritual radicalism that affected not only 18th-century Baptists but the entire English working class.

In the religious apathy following the **Toleration Act** (1689), the General Baptists continued to suffer severe losses. Over the next 50 years, many of their churches disappeared as members of their congregations became Socinian or **Uni-**

tarian. The Particular Baptists reacted by developing a rigid system of quietistic hyper-Calvinism and by drawing in upon themselves, engaging in few evangelical or missionary efforts. They did, however, encourage hymn-singing, and produced several fine hymnists, including Anne Steele (1717–1778), the most distinguished woman hymn writer of the age.

Ignored by or excluded from "polite" society, suspicious of education and formal learning, the Baptists rarely touched and scarcely influenced the course of national history during the Hanoverian period. The Baptist who became Mayor of Coventry in the 1770s is remarkable only for the lonely singularity of his achievement. Apart from a handful of **merchants** and physicians, the Baptists remained anonymous outsiders.

Yet after 1750, **religious revivalism** and **Evangelicalism** heralded a period of growth for them as for many other Nonconformist sects. Between 1750 and 1790 the membership of Baptist congregations nearly doubled. The New Connection General Baptists, influenced by the theology of **John Wesley** and the Methodist revival, were founded in 1770 by Dan Taylor (1738–1816) and grew rapidly in the emerging industrial areas of Yorkshire. Among Particular Baptists, Andrew Fuller's (1754–1815) *The Gospel of Christ Worthy of All Acceptation* (1785), which drew heavily on the works of the American divine Jonathan Edwards (1703–1758), stimulator of the Great Awakening, stressed the missionary implications of Calvinist theology. Fuller became the first secretary of the Baptist Missionary Society (1792), which began the modern foreign **missionary** movement and influenced all branches of the Christian church. The Missionary Society's many-talented founder was William Carey (1761–1834), a botanist and horticulturist who was also an outstanding missionary statesman, unsurpassed translator of the Bible, and the society's first missionary to **India**. Baptist missions spread to many parts of the **empire**, competing with Anglican establishments.

In theology, rapid Baptist growth raised questions about the terms of membership in a Baptist church, centering around the conditions for admission to Holy Communion. Robert Hall (1764–1831), one of the most influential and respected preachers of his day, argued for a spirit of ecumenical cooperation. The Particular Baptists, aware of the advantages of denominational unity, formed the General Baptist Union (1813), which began efforts to merge with the New Connection General Baptists (though union was not completed until 1891).

In British **North America**, Baptist churches were an indigenous product of left-wing Puritanism. Roger Williams (*c.* 1604–1683) established the first Baptist church in Providence (1639) after he was banished from the Massachusetts Bay Colony, but the General Baptists never gained real strength, even in Rhode Island; most of their churches were eventually reorganized as Particular Baptist. Particular Baptists were most active in the Middle colonies, Philadelphia becoming the center of colonial Baptist life. The Philadelphia Baptist Association (formed in 1707) vigorously promoted missionary activity and sponsored new churches. Baptist growth in colonial America, however, was largely a product of the Great Awakening, which also influenced American Baptist doctrine by replacing much of the traditional theology with the views of the leaders of the Evangelical revival.

William Edward Morris

Bibliography

Davies, Horton. *Worship and Theology in England: From Watts and Wesley to Maurice, 1690–1850.* 1961.

Payne, E.A. *Fellowship of Believers: Baptist Thought and Practice Yesterday and Today.* 1944.

Rupp, Gordon. *Religion in England, 1688–1791.* 1986.

Whitley, W.T. *A History of British Baptists.* 1923.

Barbauld, Anna Laetitia (1743–1825)

Sometimes unfairly remembered only because she rebuked **Coleridge** for not providing his *Rime of the Ancient Mariner* (1798) with a moral, Barbauld was a serious poet and essayist. After her first volume of **poetry** (1773) she was painted by Richard Samuel (*fl.* 1770–1786) as one of the "Nine Living Muses of Great Britain."

Barbauld wrote several works for children. The most popular, *Hymns in Prose for Children* (1781), was translated into five languages and frequently reprinted in the 19th century. In 1804 she edited both the six-volume *Correspondence of Samuel Richardson* (with an introductory essay) and a three-volume *Selections from the Spectator, Tatler, Guardian and Freeholder.* Her *The British Novelists, with an Essay and Prefaces Biographical and Critical,* a 50-volume anthology, helped the novel to be considered a respectable genre. A literary collection for girls, *The Female Speaker,* appeared in 1811.

Although politically liberal—she supported the **French Revolution** and the **antislavery movement**—and fluent in French, Italian, Latin, and Greek, Barbauld was conservative about **women's rights** and concerned about women becoming overeducated. Her poem "The Rights of Woman" (*c.* 1797) was an ironic rejoinder to **Mary Wollstonecraft**. However, she was friends with numerous **Bluestockings** and other intellectuals, as well as with **Wordsworth**. The hostile reception accorded her *Eighteen Hundred and Eleven* (1812), a poem expressing despair about English society, discouraged her from further publication. Nevertheless, in 1816 she was judged to have "employed her excellent genius to the noblest ends, in exciting infancy to virtue, and maturer age to a love of freedom."

Peter A. Tasch

Bibliography

Aikin, Lucy. *The Works of Anna Laetitia Barbauld.* 1825.

Rodgers, Betsy. *Georgian Chronicle.* 1958.

Rogers, Katharine M. *Feminism in Eighteenth-Century England.* 1982.

Todd, Janet, ed. *A Dictionary of British and American Women Writers 1660–1800.* 1987.

See also Children's Literature; Essay; Novel

Barrington, Shute (1734–1826)

Barrington, one of the more aristocratic of Hanoverian prelates, was the son of an Irish peer. Educated at Eton and Merton College, Oxford, he was ordained in 1757. Though a pillar of the Anglican establishment, he developed closer ties with **Evangelicalism** than other prelates and sympathized with **Wilberforce** and the **antislavery movement**. He was consecrated Bishop of Llandaff in 1769; though he did not speak Welsh, he attempted to stock some of his parishes with Welsh-speaking clergymen. Concerned with orthodoxy and public morality, in the **House of Lords** he sought unsuccessfully (1771) to make remarriage after **divorce** illegal, and amidst the general discussion of relaxing restrictions on **dissenters** he fulminated (1772) against the subversive views of **Priestley**. He was later translated to the sees of Salisbury (1782–1791) and Durham (1791–1826), the latter one of the richest in the realm. His 1809 tract, *The Grounds on which the Church of England Separated from the Church of Rome Reconsidered,* was regarded as one of the major statements against granting **Catholics** more privileges.

Donald W. Nichol

Bibliography

Clark, J.C.D. *English Society, 1688–1832.* 1985.
Hole, Robert. *Pulpits, Politics and Public Order in England, 1760–1832.* 1989.
Mather, F.C. *High Church Prophet: Bishop Samuel Horsley (1733–1806) and the Caroline Tradition in the Later Georgian Church.* 1992.
Sykes, Norman. *Church and State in the XVIIIth Century.* 1934, 1975.

See also Church of England; Manners and Morals

Bath

The Somerset **spa** of Bath was the most fashionable resort town of the 18th century. Its initial attraction rested on its medicinal waters. Invalids, imaginary and real, flocked to the spa to immerse themselves in the several baths and to swallow drafts of spa water. But Bath's importance as a seasonal social center for the polite classes soon overshadowed its healing powers.

The town's importance as a watering place reaches back to Roman times, but it burgeoned in the course of the 18th century, its population increasing tenfold. Its transformation into a focal point of Georgian **fashion** has often been attributed to Richard "Beau" Nash (1674–1761), master of ceremonies for the town's numerous polite **amusements** from 1705 until his death. This is an exaggeration, though Nash did stamp his personality on the town's highly structured social life, which featured assemblies, balls, teas, promenades, **concerts**, and excursions. Bath's lively social life made it an important **marriage** market, and the stress placed on easy **manners** and relatively egalitarian intercourse made it something of a melting pot for the elite. Bath enjoyed easy accessibility, with increasingly frequent **coach** service as the 18th century passed, and the town's governors took great pains to provide the amenities necessary to attract a fashionable clientele.

John Wood the Elder (*d.* 1754), followed by his son of the same name, undertook an ambitious program of building that made Bath the architectural showpiece of the British Isles. Queen Square, North and South Parades, King's Circus, Royal Crescent, and Lansdown Crescent are among the greatest urban achievements of the Hanoverian age, and exemplify Bath's unique balance between rural and urban environments. Public and private spaces were carefully planned for both social function and formal appeal. The Pump Room was opened in 1706 and enlarged in 1751; the first of several assembly rooms was completed in 1708; and a ballroom was opened in 1720. Despite continued investment in public venues, however, private entertaining became increasingly the mode in the second half of the 18th century.

The relative social openness of Bath contributed to the gradual withdrawal of the elite as the **aristocracy and gentry** found themselves joined by **nabobs**, newly rich industrialists, **merchants**, and colonial adventurers. Permanent residents multiplied. Bath's dominance as a leisure center was affected also by the growing popularity of **seaside resorts**. Social change, the general development of **transport**, and changes in the character of the community of Bath led, by the early 19th century, to its declining popularity and the end of its supremacy among British resort towns.

Daniel Statt

Bibliography

Borsay, Peter. *The English Urban Renaissance.* 1989.
Corfield, P.J. *The Impact of English Towns, 1700–1800.* 1982.
Gadd, D. *Georgian Summer: Bath in the Eighteenth Century.* 1971.
Girouard, Mark. *The English Town.* 1990.
McIntyre, Sylvia. "Bath: The Rise of a Resort Town, 1660–1800," in Peter Clark, ed., *Country Towns in Pre-Industrial England.* 1981.
Neale, R.S. *Bath: A Social History, 1680–1850.* 1981.
Wood, John. *An Essay towards a Description of Bath.* 2nd ed., 1765.

See also Anstey, Christopher; Architects and Architecture; Provincial Towns and Society

Beattie, James (1735–1803)

Beattie, Professor of Moral Philosophy at Marischal College, Aberdeen, was rewarded with royal **patronage** for his orthodox opposition to the skepticism of **David Hume** in his *Essay on Truth* (1770). His more enduring legacy was an unfinished poem, "The Minstrel" (1771–1774), which, in tracing the growth of a poet's mind, anticipated **Wordsworth**'s *Prelude* (1799–1805). Written in Spenserian stanzas, though largely free of **Gothicism**, *The Minstrel* describes the **sentimental** education of Edwin, a "love enthusiast." The nostalgia, the atmosphere of melancholic solitude, and the exploration of individual genius provide a barometer of changing sensibilities,

James Beattie

which would later catch the attention of such poets as **Byron**, **Keats**, and **Clare**.

Michael Bruce

Bibliography

Forbes, M. *Beattie and His Friends.* 1904.
Land, Stephen K. "James Beattie." *Philological Quarterly.* Vol. 51, pp. 887–904.
Walker, R.S. *James Beattie's London Diary, 1773.* 1946.

See also Romanticism and Romantic Style

Beckford, William (1760–1844)

Beckford was one of the most unusual characters and writers of the Hanoverian Age. Heir to immense wealth, he spent much of his life in escape from the conventional political and social career contemplated for him by his father, the **radical** Lord Mayor of **London**, William Beckford (1709–1770). Privately educated at Fonthill, the family estate in Wiltshire, Beckford was prompted by his drawing master, Alexander Cozens, to explore the alternative worlds of Eastern literature Beckford had encountered in the *Arabian Nights' Entertainments,* which had entered Europe in French translation (1704–1717). In 1777, in Geneva, Beckford composed *The Long Story,* a prose tale eventually published in 1930 as *The Vision.* Its landscape of dreams is a characteristically autobiographical exploration, while additional passages containing images of sexual transgression and guilty pleasures foreshadow the gloomy ambivalences of Beckford's novel *Vathek.*

After he returned from the Grand Tour in 1781, two homosexual flirtations (one in Italy, one at home) intensified his and society's perception of him as a fated outcast while also severely threatening his social position. *Dreams, Waking Thoughts and Incidents* (1783) was a subjective rendering of

William Beckford

his **travels**; the confessional tone probably led to his suppressing publication shortly before his arranged marriage to Lady Margaret Gordon. *Dreams* would appear in 1834 as the revised first volume of *Italy; with Sketches of Spain and Portugal.* Beckford spent the next 15 years in exile on the Continent before returning to his famous "abbey" at Fonthill (a remarkable example of **Gothic revival** taste in **architecture**), where he lived much of the rest of his life apart from society.

In 1786 Beckford published *Vathek* in French, some months after Samuel Henley prematurely published his English translation. The Caliph of the title is a man of Faustian aspirations who pursues his demonic appetites to Eblis, a subterranean world of the damned. The narrative is often wayward in tone; ironic, farcical, yet discernibly serious in its sympathy for Vathek's unfettered sensuality. In a sequel, *Episodes of Vathek* (1912), Beckford roamed through images of equivocal sexuality, incest, necrophilia, and murder. As a satirist, however, he burlesqued the contemporary vogue for **Gothic fiction** and **sentimental** experience in *Modern Novel Writing; or, The Elegant Enthusiast* (1796) and in *Azemia: A Descriptive and Sentimental Novel* (1797). Yet his distinction as a novelist lies in his fascination with the ego's aspirations after the bizarre and the illicit. In this he anticipated the **Romantic** concerns of **Byron**, Edgar Allen Poe (1809–1849), and Algernon Swinburne (1837–1909).

Michael Bruce

Bibliography

Alexander, Boyd. *England's Wealthiest Son: A Study of William Beckford.* 1962.
Fothergill, B. *Beckford of Fonthill.* 1979.
Gemmett, Robert J. *William Beckford.* 1977.

See also Orientalism

Bedford, Dukes of

See Russell Family (and Dukes of Bedford)

Beer

See Brewing and Public Houses

Bell, Andrew (1753–1832)

A Scottish clergyman and educator, Bell emerged reluctantly from retirement in 1806 to help coordinate the **Church of England**'s response to the rapid spread of nondenominational schools for poor children organized by the **Quaker** educator **Joseph Lancaster**. Bell, whose own system of cheap instruction Lancaster had copied and extended, had himself partly copied his model of mutual instruction from Indian practices he observed while serving as the first superintendent of the Madras Male Orphan Asylum (1789–1796). Alarmed by Lancaster's successes, Bell in 1811 was appointed superintendent of the National Society for Promoting the Education of the Poor in the Principles of the Established Church. He oversaw the establishment of over 1,200 **charity schools** and a model **teacher's education** center in London. He bequeathed the fortune he amassed from his chaplaincies in India, and his **pension** from the **East India Company**, to several educational causes, including endowed lectureships that would lead to the establishment of university chairs of education at **Edinburgh** and St. Andrews.

Kim P. Sebaly

Bibliography

Jones, M.G. *The Charity School Movement: A Study of Eighteenth Century Puritanism in Action.* 1938.

Soloway, R.A. *Prelates and People: Ecclesiastical Social Thought in England, 1783–1852.* 1969.

Wilhelm, Albert E. "Andrew Bell," in Laura Dabundo, ed., *Encyclopedia of Romanticism: Culture in Britain, 1780's–1830's.* 1992.

See also Education, Elementary; National Society for the Education of the Poor

Bell, Henry (1767–1830)

Bell, a pioneer of steamships, served under various engineers before going to **London** as an apprentice to the young civil engineer John Rennie (1761–1821), later famed for his Waterloo, Southwark, and New London bridges over the Thames. In 1790 Bell settled in **Glasgow**, which was already becoming an engineering and **shipbuilding** center. He began his experiments with steam navigation around 1798, and in 1800 equipped a small vessel with a **steam engine**. Unable to gain government assistance, he also had to face the challenge of William Symington (1763–1831), who sailed his *Charlotte Dundas* on the Forth and Clyde **Canal** (1803), and Robert Fulton (1765–1815), the American who sailed his *Steamboat* on the Hudson River (1807). In 1812 Bell's *Comet*, a 30-ton vessel, began the first commercial service on the River Clyde; this continued until 1820, when the vessel was wrecked. Although not the first to build a steamship, Bell was important in finding practical solutions to many of the problems involved.

Ian Donnachie

Bibliography

Williamson, J. *The Clyde Passenger Steamer, 1812–1901.* 1904.

Bell, Patrick (1799–1869)

Bell, an **agricultural improver**, the son of a tenant **farmer**, was the inventor of one of the first reapers. While still a divinity student at St. Andrews University he developed his machine, first demonstrating it in 1826 on the Perthshire farm of his brother, George. It used a scissor-clipping action and was pushed, rather than pulled, by horses. Bell received a prize of £50 for his invention but did not patent it. It was, indeed, rather badly made by local blacksmiths, and it was only through improvements made by Americans in the 1830s that a commercially viable reaper was developed.

Ordained in 1843, Bell spent the remainder of his life in pastoral duties near Arbroath. In 1868, in recognition of his achievements, the Highland Society awarded him £1,000 and a plate donated by the farmers of **Scotland**.

A.J.G. Cummings

Bibliography

Derry, T.K., and T.I. Williams. *A Short History of Technology.* 1960.

Singer, C., et al. *A History of Technology, Vol. 4: The Industrial Revolution, c.1750–1850.* 1958.

See also Scottish Agriculture

Benevolence

A Christian concept of benevolence flourished in the writings of the 17th-century **Cambridge Platonists** and then the Anglican **Latitudinarians**. Archbishop John Tillotson (1630–1694) preached, "He that is charitable to others provides a supply and retreat for himself in the days of distress . . . all our pains and expence in doing good for a few days will be recompensed and crowned with joys and glories of eternity."

This noble idea underwent partial secularization in the Hanoverian period, helped along by the many rationalistic and humanitarian forces at work alongside religious forces. The influential philosopher Anthony Ashley Cooper, 3rd Earl of Shaftesbury (1671–1713), maintained in *An Inquiry Concerning Virtue or Merit* (1711) that to have "generous affections . . . towards the good of the public, is to have the chief means and power of self-enjoyment." Private betterment was included in the public good, and the individual had a "moral sense" by which he or she might distinguish right from wrong. Shaftesbury's followers, such as **Francis Hutcheson**, increasingly emphasized enlightened self-interest as a motive for benevolence. **David Hume** believed that "nothing can bestow more merit on any human creature than the sentiment of benevolence." Part of its merit "arises from its tendency to promote the interests of our species and bestow happiness on human society." By the end of the century, **Jeremy Bentham**'s utilitarianism completed the process of secularizing this virtue.

Literary ideas naturally followed the trend. Throughout the 18th century, literature insisted that benevolence be part of the good-natured, virtuous person. As **Joseph Addison** reflected in the *Spectator*, No. 169 (1711), "Half the Misery of Human Life might be extinguished would Men alleviate the general Curse they lie under, by mutual Offices of Compassion, Benevolence and Humanity." Following Shaftesbury's lead, **Alexander Pope** rhymed in *An Essay on Man* (1733–1734), "Grasp the whole worlds of Reason, Life, and Sense, / In one close system of Benevolence." In plays such as **Richard Steele**'s *The Conscious Lovers* (1722) and **George Lillo**'s *The London Merchant* (1731), fatherly merchants demonstrated their benevolence. In **novels**, **Henry Fielding**'s Squire Allworthy (*Tom Jones*, 1749) and **Samuel Richardson**'s Sir Charles Grandison (*Sir Charles Grandison*, 1753) good-naturedly indulged in "the glorious Lust of doing Good," as Fielding termed the activity. Benevolence and good nature were not only inseparable—as in **Laurence Sterne**'s Uncle Toby (*Tristram Shandy*, 1760–1767) and **Henry Mackenzie**'s Harley (*The Man of Feeling*, 1771)—the virtue also could be salutary.

Oliver Goldsmith, in *The Vicar of Wakefield* (1766), coupled Sir William Thornhill's benevolence with **sensibility**—a mental anguish he felt whenever he discovered the "slightest distress" in others. He thus relieved his pain as he aided the unfortunate. Similarly, **Tobias Smollett**'s Matthew Bramble (*Humphry Clinker*, 1771) regained his health as he helped others.

By the century's close, benevolence was less frequently singled out as a commanding virtue (although Hermsprong, in **Robert Bage**'s *Hermsprong*, 1796, has a "soul of benevolence"). **Jane Austen** did not use the word to describe Elizabeth Bennet's Darcy (*Pride and Prejudice*, 1813); he embodies it. Good-natured, "affable to the poor," and unselfish, he is "the best landlord and the best master that ever lived." In such manner, the divines, philosophers, poets, and novelists of the age conspired to coach ordinary folk in the pleasures of doing good.

Peter A. Tasch

Bibliography

Roberts, Tom Aerwyn. *The Concept of Benevolence*. 1973.
Sheriff, John K. *The Good-Natured Man*. 1982.
Todd, Janet. *Sensibility*. 1986.

See also Enthusiasm; Humanitarianism

Bentham, Jeremy (1748–1832), and Benthamites

The terms *Utilitarianism, Benthamism,* and *Philosophic Radicalism* refer to the philosophy, followers, and political stance taken by Jeremy Bentham—philosopher, jurist, and political theorist. Described in 1948 by the *Times* as one of "the greatest Englishmen of all ages," he was one of the most influential thinkers of his era, an honorary citizen of the first French Republic (1792), revered by progressives in Europe and in North and South America.

A precocious child, born in **London**, where he lived all his life, he read Latin and Greek at age 4 and began to learn French at 6. Tiny in stature, so weak as a child that he climbed stairs carefully and one at a time, he felt a lifelong sympathy with the underdog, writing in favor of prisoners, slaves, prostitutes, and other unfortunates; and attacked war, dueling, and religious fanaticism. His father, a wealthy lawyer-turned-land-speculator, sent him to Oxford (B.A. 1763) and later (1792) left an inheritance which allowed Bentham to devote himself to philosophy. In 1823 he contributed a large sum to help start the *Westminster Review*, a **periodical** designed to promote his ideas and those of his first "Benthamite" or "utilitarian" followers, **James Mill**, whom he had met in 1808, and Mill's son, **John Stuart Mill**. The latter founded a "Utilitarian Society" (1823), which studied the works of Bentham, **Thomas Malthus**, **David Ricardo**, and others, but utilitarianism was to become much better known generally than its coterie of hard-core Benthamite supporters, and to influence people as dissimilar as **Major John Cartwright** and **Robert Peel**, **Francis Place** and **Henry Brougham**.

An indefatigable worker, Bentham produced thousands of pages of manuscript in his lifetime but published only two principal works. His thought was influenced by the ideas of **David Hume**, **Dugald Stewart**, **David Hartley**, and **Joseph Priestley**. *A Fragment on Government* (1776), an excerpt from his exhaustive *Comment on Blackstone's Commentaries*, rejected his Oxford professor **William Blackstone**'s claim to have provided a comprehensive and factual picture of the English law and constitution, and condemned Blackstone's eulogistic treatment of the **Glorious Constitution**'s balances between branches of government. Bentham scorned Blackstone's justification of the status quo and his antipathy to political and social reform, ridiculing him as a weathercock who blew with the wind—"the dupe of every prejudice, and the abettor of every abuse," as he commented privately in his *Commonplace Book*. Aided by men like Blackstone, the judicial branch, Bentham believed, had invaded the legislative. Common-law judges, steeped in obsolete ideas, had actually become legislators because English statute law lagged far behind events. Bentham, a non-practicing lawyer, declared that lawyers were "the only persons in whom ignorance of the law was not punished."

His major work on utilitarianism was *An Introduction to the Principles of Morals and Legislation* (1789). Here he argued that morality was based on the French philosopher Helvétius's (1715–1771) essentially democratic principle that the greatest happiness of the greatest number was the highest good. He reinforced this by devising a quantitative measure of individual pleasure and pain (ridiculed by **William Cobbett** as a "felicific calculus"), and concluded that the pursuit of personal happiness led society toward a state of general harmony and welfare (another idea later attacked as harmfully selfish in tendency). From this foundation of personal ethics and social philosophy, based on what he considered obvious principles of human nature, Bentham projected an entire vision of political, social and legal reform.

But Bentham "had grown old before he had any followers," as the younger Mill recalled. He and his disciples, who included the Mills, Brougham, Ricardo, lawyers such as **Samuel Romilly** and John Austin (1790–1859), and other reformers such as **Francis Place, Edward Gibbon Wakefield,** and **Edwin Chadwick,** were often called "philosophic radicals" because they paired a scientific outlook with extreme impatience with the status quo. Their outlook and program foreshadowed the whole subsequent history of Victorian reformism. They favored, among other things, reform of **elections and the franchise**, expansion of the electorate, reform of the **prisons** and criminal laws, alleviation of the condition of the poor, Malthusianism, contraception, **law reform**, codification of the laws, and reduction of the **Church of England**'s political influence. To achieve these goals they advocated the accumulation of hard facts to convince parliamentarians who, they maintained, too often acted on the basis of mere sentiments and emotions. The Benthamites, always posing as tough empiricists unmoved by mere "feelings" not listed in their felicific tables, also supported laissez-faire capitalism because in their view the facts proved that businessmen took better care of their enterprises than government functionaries, the result being greater efficiency, productivity, and general happiness. Karl Marx (1818–1883) later reluctantly acknowledged Bentham's general influence when castigating him as "that insipid, pedantic, leather-tongued oracle of the ordinary bourgeois intelligence of the nineteenth century."

As part of their "scientific" claims, the Benthamites, though truly children of the **Enlightenment** (Bentham as a young man greatly admired and translated writings by Voltaire), rejected the universalist concepts of natural law and natural rights that had descended from **John Locke**. Rights did not precede positive law; in fact, positive law created rights. The Benthamites' insistence on this, and their seemingly hardheaded and scientific approach to reform (an approach recommended by the apparent failure after 1789 of reforms based on natural-rights philosophy), attracted an increasing number of 19th-century reformers, though sentimental radicals like Charles Dickens (1812–1870) and Thomas Carlyle (1795–1881) would follow Cobbett in detesting their "hardhearted" reliance on numbers, statistics, rationality, and self-interest. After 1830 the younger Mill helped to moderate and lend sophistication to the utilitarian philosophy when he argued that human pleasures could be measured qualitatively as well as quantitatively.

Benthamism, along with **Evangelicalism**, was one of the major intellectual forces of the latter Hanoverian period, shaping the Victorian. Strangely enough, despite the Benthamites' pronounced religious skepticism (which they tried to conceal from public view), the two impulses often worked together in the same individual. Even Bentham, though an atheist, once commented that he would have been "a methodist . . . had I not been what I am." The Evangelicals and the Benthamites cooperated in **humanitarian** causes and the **antislavery movement**, and beyond that, they both inspired seriousness, public spirit, and a very pronounced emphasis on the civic importance of individual responsibility—some of the key elements of Victorian liberalism. **Wilberforce** died in 1833 still disapproving of the **Reform Act** (1832), whereas Bentham died lamenting that it did not go far enough.

Constantinos G. Athanasopoulos
Robert Gibson Robinson III

Bibliography

Costigan, Giovanni. *Makers of Modern England: The Force of Individual Genius in History.* 1967.

Crimmins, James E. *Secular Utilitarianism: Social Science and the Critique of Religion in the Thought of Jeremy Bentham.* 1990.

Dinwiddy, John. *Bentham.* 1989.

Halévy, Elie. *The Growth of Philosophic Radicalism.* 1928, 1972.

Hamburger, J. *Intellectuals in Politics: J.S. Mill and the Philosophical Radicals.* 1965.

Harrison, Ross. *Bentham.* 1985.

Kelly, P.J. *Utilitarianism and Distributive Justice: Jeremy Bentham and the Civil Law.* 1990.

Postema, Gerald J. *Bentham and the Common Law Tradition.* 1986.

Rosenblum, Nancy L. *Bentham's Theory of the Modern State.* 1978.

See also Law Reform; Radicalism and Radical Politics

Bentinck, Lord (William Cavendish-Bentinck) (1774–1839)

Bentinck is most noted for his reforms in **India** during his term as governor-general (1827–1835). The second son of the 3rd Duke of Portland, he first pursued a career in politics and the **Army**. In 1803 he became governor of Madras, but his mishandling of the Vellore mutiny (1806) forced him to resign. He reestablished his reputation while commanding British forces in Sicily, where he engineered the downfall of the local Bourbon monarchy and the creation of a liberal constitution. From 1816 to 1827 he served as a **Whig** M.P., associating with various extraparliamentary **radicals**. It was as a practitioner of **Benthamite** philosophy in India that he made his greatest mark.

As governor-general, Bentinck was an able administrator. He transformed the Indian government's deficit of £1.5 million into a surplus of £2 million. Most of his reforms, however, were social. Bentinck believed that Indians could assume greater responsibility in their government if they followed Britain's lead. He therefore allowed them greater access to administrative positions while replacing Persian with English as the language of government, the courts, and higher education. In 1829 he challenged Indian custom by abolishing *sati* (widow burning) and suppressing infanticide. Similarly, he was willing to ignore caste barriers in appointing Indians to administrative positions. Less controversial was his suppression of the *thagi* (thuggee) cult, whose members murdered travelers as a sacrifice to the goddess Kali.

Although Bentinck's reforms emerged from liberal idealism, they came to be regarded as flagrant examples of cultural imperialism when implemented in India. Nevertheless, by encouraging the development of an intellectual English-speaking elite throughout the British *raj*, Bentinck hastened the development of Indian nationalism and the end of British rule.

A. Martin Wainwright

Bibliography

Ahmad, Manazir. *Lord William Bentinck.* 1977.

Gupta, Maya. *Lord William Bentinck in Madras and the Vellore Mutiny, 1803–1807.* 1986.

Joshi, J.C. *Lord William Bentinck: His Economic, Administrative, Social, and Educational Reforms.* 1988.

Rosselli, John. *Lord William Bentinck: The Making of a Liberal Imperialist, 1774–1839.* 1974.

See also East India Company; Empire and Imperialism

Bentley, Richard (1662–1742)

Probably the most brilliant classical scholar of his time, Bentley was Master of Trinity College, Cambridge, for nearly 40 years, and vice-chancellor of the University. Yet he is chiefly remembered today as the butt of **satires** by **Swift, Arbuthnot,** and **Pope.** His literary feuding began with his "Dissertation upon the Epistles of Phalaris . . . and the Fables of Aesop" (1697, with a much enlarged edition in 1699). In criticizing Sir William Temple (1628–1699) and Charles Boyle (1676–1731), the latter of whom had edited Phalaris (whose letters Bentley found spurious), he joined the Moderns in the European intellectual **Ancients vs. Moderns** quarrels, which pitted classical achievements against post–Renaissance creativity. Although rhetorically routed by Swift for the Ancients in *The Battle of the Books* (1704), Bentley was eventually acknowledged as the victorious scholar. He forcefully demonstrated the value of what was then a new criticism, one in which accurate philological knowledge supplemented historical research.

Richard Bentley

This same painstaking labor can be found in his scholarly editions of Menander and Philemon (1710), Horace (1711), Terence (1726), and Manilius (1739), but it worked against him in his edition of *Paradise Lost* (1732). Bentley not only assumed that the blind Milton's amanuensis had made numerous clerical errors, but also that in the hands of an editor, the epic was "*twice lost.*" Over 800 emendations—most of them unacceptable—reflect Bentley's learning rather than Milton's poetry.

Bentley numbered among his friends William Wotton (1666–1727), Bishop Edward Stillingfleet (1635–1699), Isaac Newton 1642–1727), and **Samuel Clarke.** Under his stewardship as Master, beginning in 1700, Trinity College strengthened its reputation for high standards of scholarship, expanded its scientific work in astronomy and chemistry, and broadened its interest in oriental studies. Yet his endeavors were frequently—and acrimoniously—opposed: during his tenure, the fellows sought unsuccessfully three times to deprive him of his mastership.

Bentley deserves great credit for helping to restore classical learning and enhance philological scholarship. **Samuel Johnson**'s concluding lines on Milton could be applied appropriately to Bentley: although not a genius of "original invention . . . he was naturally a thinker for himself . . . he was born for whatever is arduous."

Wight Martindale, Jr.

Bibliography

Brink, C.O. *English Classical Scholarship; Historical Reflections on Bentley, Porson, and Housman.* 1986.

Levine, Joseph M. *The Battle of the Books: History and Literature in the Augustan Age.* 1991.

White, Reginald J. *Dr. Bentley: A Study in Academic Scarlett.* 1965.

See also Church of England; Milton, John, in Hanoverian Memory

Berkeley, George (1685–1753)

Bishop Berkeley, history's only advocate for "immaterialism," enlarged on the empiricists' interest in the mental representation of experience. Even more than **John Locke**'s, Berkeley's is the philosophy of *ideas.* From his early *Treatise Concerning the Principles of Human Knowledge* (1710) and *Three Dialogues between Hylas and Philonous* (1713) to his climactic *Alciphron: Or the Minute Philosopher* (1732) and *Siris: A Chain of Philosophical Reflections and Inquiries Concerning the Virtue of Tar-water* (1744), Berkeley steadily cultivated a radical **empiricism.** In his works, ontology and epistemology converge, while the empiricist watchword, *experience,* often acquires extravagant meaning.

Berkeley's career reflects the interplay of English, British, and colonial culture. Born in **Ireland** near Kilkenny, he graduated from **Trinity College, Dublin,** in 1702. By 1713 he had entered the English literary scene. **Pope, Swift, Arbuthnot,**

Bishop Berkeley

Addison, and the Scriblerian **Club** relished his acquaintance. After rising through assorted church and university offices, he masterminded an abortive scheme to establish a Christian College in Bermuda (1722–1728). This awkward plan left him stranded for three years in Rhode Island (1728–1731) without material means. But 1734 brought him the bishopric of Cloyne, where he remained, content and useful, until his retirement in 1752.

Berkeley's early philosophy expounds "immaterialism," the theory that notions about "material" or "extended" substance are superfluous when explaining the origin of human knowledge. Enlarging on Locke, Berkeley argued that we perceive experience not *through* but *in* "ideas." Unlike "extended material substance," ideas are mental entities. For Berkeley, it made far more sense to say that one intelligent mind presents mental ideas to another than to claim, as did Locke, that inert, mindless, and passive objects can represent themselves to a thinking being. Qualities like "hot" or "cold" or "red" or "hard" are experiential and intellectual, not ontological. Berkeley referred to the ultimate source of ideas as "The Author of Nature." His readers were invited to identify this "Author" with God. The world as he saw it was thus far more than a tissue of subjectivities. "Objects," that is to say clusters of "ideas," continued to exist even when human observers did not, for God always perceives them.

Berkeley's later works, poems, and **journalism** enlarged on the subtle spiritual side of immaterialism. Part philosophical dialogue and part **satire**, *The Analyst* (1734) and *Alciphron* attack atheistic tendencies in assorted contemporary philosophies, from post–Cartesian materialism to Leibnizian optimism to simple libertinism. Berkeley found materialism or "mechanism" particularly offensive because of its emphasis on "dull" and "stupid" matter. He went to great lengths to defend his *esse is percipi* (to be is to be perceived) formula. He elucidated God's activities as described in the book of Genesis by arguing that God did indeed create a universe—of an immaterialist variety. The corps of angels was on hand to perceive the process of creation, even before the advent of perceiving humans. Berkeley's most extravagant production, *Siris,* begins with a practical treatment of tar-water (turpentine), a home remedy, and culminates in a paean to neo–Platonic mysticism and Christian enthusiasm. Ancient lore is reconciled with modern immaterialism as Berkeley argues that Aristotle and others prepared the way for his own interpretation of reality.

Berkeley's significance for the Hanoverian era extended well beyond his philosophical speculations. A master of witty dialogue as well as a hardheaded empiricist, he epitomizes the Hanoverian man of letters. He combined unusual social interests with rare philosophical originality and considerable skill in the simple expression of rarefied ideas. Today his continuing appeal to both technical philosophers and neoclassical poets is perhaps the best demonstration of his belief that the world is "a congery of ideas."

Kevin L. Cope

Bibliography

Atherton, Margaret. *Berkeley's Revolution in Vision.* 1990.
Browne, Joseph W. *Berkeley's Intellectualism.* 1975.
Foster, John, and Howard Robinson, eds. *Essays on Berkeley: A Tercentenary Celebration.* 1985.
Sosa, Ernest, ed. *Essays on the Philosophy of George Berkeley.* 1987.
Tipton, I.C. *Berkeley: The Philosophy of Immaterialism.* 1974.
Urmson, J.O. *Berkeley.* 1982.
Walmsley, Peter. *The Rhetoric of Berkeley's Philosophy.* 1990.
Winkler, Kenneth P. *Berkeley: An Introduction* 1989.

Berridge, John (1716–1793)

Berridge, Anglican clergyman and miscellaneous writer, exemplifies the attraction felt by some parish priests to the Hanoverian **religious revival**. Born the son of a rich Nottinghamshire **farmer**, he attended Cambridge (B.A. 1738, M.A. 1742) and in 1755 became vicar of the isolated rural parish of Everton (Bedfordshire). Becoming acquainted (1758) with **Wesley** and **Whitefield**, who both preached in his church, he himself began preaching outdoor (1759), attracting large crowds. His circle of friends enlarged to include **Lady Huntingdon**, **John Newton**, **Henry Venn**, and **Charles Simeon**.

His charm and erudition earned him friendships with several politicians as well, including **Pitt the Elder**. His letters were collected under the title, *Cheerful Piety, or Religion Without Gloom* (1792), but his most popular work was a simple testament of faith, *The Christian World Unmasked: Come Pray and Weep* (1773 and many later eds.).

Richard M. Riss

Bibliography

Pibworth, Nigel R. *The Gospel Pedlar.* 1987.
Rupp, Gordon. *Religion in England, 1688–1791.* 1987.
Ryle, J.C. *Five Christian Leaders of the Eighteenth Century.* 1960.

See also Church of England; Evangelicalism; Methodism

Bewick, Thomas (1753–1828)

In Bewick's **book illustrations** of animals, birds, and nature, the art of wood-engraving reached new heights in both precision and accuracy. Bewick inspired the production of many later works in British **graphic arts**, and influenced engravers, artists, and naturalists in Europe and America until the 1880s, when photographic methods became more popular.

Thomas Bewick

Bewick's strong interest in educating youth first led him to encourage reading by illustrating books for children, including **Gay**'s *Fables* (1779), *Select Fables* (1784), and *Fables of Aesop* (1818). Both his *General History of Quadrupeds* (1790) and his two-volume masterpiece *A History of British Birds* (1797–1804) went through multiple editions. Most of his books contain oval-shaped tailpieces and vignettes depicting life in the Tyne Valley in the late 18th century, and include social satire, humor, and some moralizing. During his last 6 years he wrote his memoirs (published posthumously in 1862), in which he detailed his life and described his **engraving** techniques. Bewick is considered one of Britain's most talented engravers and observant naturalists.

Sylvia Patterson Iskander

Bibliography

Bewick, Thomas. *A Memoir of Thomas Bewick, Written by Himself.* Ed. Iain Bain. 1975.
Stone, Reynolds, ed. *Wood Engravings of Thomas Bewick.* 1953.
Weekley, Montague. *Thomas Bewick.* 1953.

See also Children's Literature; Fable; Reference Works

Biblical Criticism

Historical criticism of the Bible in the Hanoverian era grew out of the rise of rationalism and the application of the scientific method to the study of history. On the Continent, Richard Simon (1638–1712), Hermann Reimarius (1694–1768), Johann David Michaelis (1717–1791), and Jean Astruc (1684–1766) were among the great progenitors of the historical–critical method of biblical analysis. English scholars took the lead in textual research. John Mills (1645–1717) and Benjamin Kennicott (1718–1783) studied, respectively, variants in ancient manuscripts of the Greek New Testament and Hebrew Old Testament. **Robert Lowth**, in his *Lectures on the Sacred Poetry of the Hebrews* (Latin, 1753; English trans., 1787), stressed the beauty and sophistication of biblical verse forms, and consequently inaugurated modern aesthetic considerations of the Scriptures. While many biblical handbooks and commentaries from the 17th century were popular, a host of more historically informed and critically sophisticated works quickly came into widespread use in the 18th century.

Two of the most important handbooks originated in **France**: Augustin Calmet's *Historical, Geographical, Critical, Chronological, and Etymological Dictionary of the Holy Bible* (English, 1732) and Claude Fleury's *The Customs of the Israelites* (English, 1750). The most well-known survey of Jewish antiquity was *The Old and New Testaments Connected in the History of the Jews* (1716–1718) by Humphrey Prideaux (1648–1724), dean of Norwich. **Philip Doddridge** produced the most popular biblical commentary of the 18th century, *The Family Expositor* (1738–1755). Although his work was written for the common reader and not for a scholarly audience, Doddridge nevertheless made extensive use of recent philological studies of New Testament Greek to explain grammatical difficulties in the sacred text. Not all biblical criticism led to an increase in devotion, however. The conclusions of Thomas Hobbes (1588–1679) and Baruch Spinoza (1632–1677)—that the Scriptures were a purely historical production and not a vehicle of divine revelation—continued to influence scholarship throughout the Hanoverian period.

Michael F. Suarez, S.J.

Bibliography

Cragg, Gerald R. *Reason and Authority in the Eighteenth Century.* 1964.
Drury, John, ed. *Critics of the Bible, 1724–1873.* 1989.

Frei, Hans, W. *The Eclipse of Biblical Narrative: A Study in Eighteenth and Nineteenth Century Hermeneutics.* 1974.

Preston, Thomas R. "Biblical Criticism, Literature, and the Eighteenth-Century Reader," in *Books and Their Readers in Eighteenth-Century England.* 1982.

Reventlow, Henning G. *The Authority of the Bible and the Rise of the Modern World.* 1984.

See also History Writing and Historians; Language and Linguistics; Reference Works; Theology

Bickerstaff, Isaac (1733–1808?)

Bickerstaff, playwright and librettist, gave permanent shape to the English comic **opera** with his production of *Love in a Village* (1762). After serving in the Marines (1745–1755) he turned to the theater. *Thomas and Sally* (1760), with music by **Thomas Arne**, and *Judith* (1761), an **oratorio** composed by Samuel Arnold (1740–1802), established his reputation.

Bickerstaff's contribution to comic opera in *Love in a Village* was solidified by his collaboration with Arnold on *The Maid of the Mill* (1765). Perhaps his most fruitful musical partnership was with **Charles Dibdin**, with whom he developed *The Ephesian Matron* (1769); *The Padlock* (1768); *Love in the City* (1767); *Lionel and Clarissa* (1768); *The Recruiting Sergeant* (1770); and, from Giovanni Battista Pergolessi's (1710–1736) *La Serva Padrona, He Wou'd If He Cou'd* (1771).

Among Bickerstaff's adaptations were German François Poullain de Saint-Foix's (1698–1776) *L'Oracle* as *Daphne and Amintor* (1765), Pedro Calderón de la Barca's (1600–1681) *El Escondido y la Topada* as *'Tis Well It's No Worse* (1770), and William Wycherley's (1641–1715) comedy *The Plain Dealer.*

Bickerstaff's career was brought to an early end when, accused of homosexuality, he left England to live in France for the remainder of his life on a **pension** earned from service in the Marines. He received his last pension payment in 1808, the probable year of his death.

Richard J. Dircks

Bibliography

Tasch, Peter A. *The Dramatic Cobbler.* 1971.

See also Dramatic Arts; Homosexuality in Literature

Billingsley, Case (*d.* 1747)

Billingsley was representative of a new type of man operating in the growing financial markets of early 18th-century **London**. Originally a purser in the **navy**, he became a London businessman. Made bankrupt in 1716, he reemerged during the **South Sea Bubble** to play a leading part in the flotation of the **Royal Exchange Assurance** and the **York Buildings Company**. Billingsley was also interested in the practical application of new scientific knowledge, and proposed schemes for coinage, lotteries, and water engines as well as a method for calculating **longitude**. Always hoping to make a fortune, he tried in vain to interest famous patrons in his projects. Remaining constantly on the verge of bankruptcy, Billingsley died without achieving any lasting success.

A.J.G. Cummings

Bibliography

Cummings, A.J.G., and Larry Stewart, "The Case of the Eighteenth Century Projector," in Bruce Moran, ed., *Patronage and Institutions: Science, Technology and Medicine at the European Court, 1500–1750.* 1991.

Stewart, Larry. *The Rise of Public Science: Rhetoric, Technology, and Natural Philosophy in Newtonian Britain, 1660–1750.* 1992.

Biography

The English **novel**, the periodical **essay**, **history writing**, and biography took modern shape and prospered in the 18th century. Causality remains debatable, but all four genres interacted and appealed to a new public who preferred realism to romance, gossip to gospel; the older panegyrics, "Lives" as vehicles of ethical instruction, and Theophrastian characters no longer sufficed. While biographies of classical figures continued to be written (Conyers Middleton's Life of *Cicero,* 1741, for example), readers wanted to know about famous contemporary villains such as Jonathan Wild, the gangland boss who for 15 years fronted as a respectable thief-taker until he was hanged in 1725. Hack writers responded with realistic fictions like **Daniel Defoe**'s *Moll Flanders* (1722) and with real rogues' lives, such as that of Jack Sheppard, again by Defoe (1724; Sheppard had in fact been apprehended by Wild).

Specialized biographical encyclopedias began to satisfy curiosity about theatrical figures, and anthologies of villainy such as Captain Alexander Smith's *Lives . . . of the Most Notorious Highwaymen* (1714) and various cautionary versions of the *Newgate Calendar* (1764–1824) outsold translations of Plutarch's and Suetonius's *Lives.*

The Hanoverian period witnessed the impressive growth of biographical encyclopedias which judiciously celebrated lives other than those of **pirates** and **highwaymen**. They include the 10-folio-volume *General Dictionary, Historical and Critical* (1734–1741): based on Pierre Bayle's French *Dictionary* (1697–1706), this was largely the work of **Thomas Birch**, aided by John Peter Bernard (*d.* 1750) and John Lockman (1698–1771). The 7-volume *Biographia Britannica* (1747–1766) was compiled by John Campbell (1708–1775), Thomas Broughton (1704–1774), and the antiquarian William Oldys (1696–1761), who also edited the *Harleian Miscellany* (1744–1746) with **Samuel Johnson**. The 11-volume *New and General Biographical Dictionary* (1761–1767) evolved into Alexander Chalmers's 32-volume *Biographical Dictionary* (1812–1817). **Mary Hays** produced a 6-volume *Female Biography* (1802), highlighting the lives of many women from many countries.

The century also saw the burgeoning of serious lengthy biographies such as those by Roger North (1653–1734), Samuel Johnson, William Mason (1724–1797), and **James Boswell**. Published posthumously in 1740 and 1742, but written by 1715, were North's remembrances of his three brothers: *The Lives of Baron Guilford . . . Sir Dudley North and the Honourable and Reverend Doctor John North.* In recording the private, trivial moments as well as the public aspects of his brothers' lives (the "lilies and roses" and the "scars and blemishes"), he practiced his belief that if "the history of a life hangs altogether upon great importances," it may be a good "history . . . but of anything rather than that person's life."

When Johnson told Boswell that "he did not know of any literary man's life in England well written" (1773), he should have excepted his own *Life of Richard Savage* (1744). That work supported Johnson's assertion that "nobody can write the life of a man, but those who have eat and drunk and lived in social intercourse with him." Johnson included this portrait as one of the 52 lives which comprise his *Prefaces Biographical and Critical to the Works of the English Poets* (1779–1781), a collection of essays that combined biographical facts, character analysis, and **literary criticism**. There was precedent for this undertaking (Theophilus Cibber's *Lives of the Poets,* 1753), but no equal.

Mason's *Life and Letters of Thomas Gray* (1774) was the result of a long friendship with the poet. Mason changed the nature of biography by allowing Gray's **letters** to reveal his character. "In a word, Mr. Gray will become his own biographer," Mason declared, and he would be Gray's annotator.

Boswell's *Life of Samuel Johnson* (1791) is the first great English biography and still may be the greatest (though modern detractors would say that Boswell's *Johnson* should be *Boswell's* Johnson). "The great art of biography," Boswell asserted, "is to keep the person whose life we are giving always in the reader's view." He built upon the principles of earlier biographers, singling out Mason, but he did so more thoroughly and substantially than did his predecessors.

Biographical encyclopedias, full-length popular biographies, and scholarly works like Edmund Malone's *Life of Dryden* (1800) continued to be published in the early 19th century. **Robert Southey**'s *Life of Nelson* (1813) and John Gibson Lockhart's lives of *Burns* (1828) and *Scott* (1838) burnished their heroes. Having established its legitimacy in the 18th century, biography increased its stately respectability in the 19th.

Peter A. Tasch

Bibliography

Browning, J.D., ed. *Biography in the 18th Century.* 1980.

Cockshut, A.O.J. *Truth to Life.* 1974.

Longaker, Mark. *English Biography in the Eighteenth Century.* 1931.

Rawlings, Philip. *Drunks, Whores and Idle Apprentices.* 1992.

Stauffer, Donald A. *The Art of Biography in Eighteenth Century England.* 2 vols. 1941.

See also Periodicals; Reference Works

Birch, Thomas (1705–1766)

Historian, antiquarian, biographer, and priest, Birch was best known for his literary accomplishments, chiefly his contributions to the 10-volume *General Dictionary, Historical and Critical* (1734–1741). A **translation** and expansion upon Pierre Bayle's (1647–1706) French production, this *Dictionary* featured 889 new biographies of Englishmen, 618 of them by Birch. The work was in effect the ancestor of *The Dictionary of National Biography.* While those entries establish his place in history, Birch also wrote the first **biography** of the Restoration dramatist Catherine Trotter (1679–1749), and reintroduced numerous primary documents of antiquity—**letters**, treatises, and memoirs—into the 18th-century consciousness. Though the quality of his work did not match its quantity, Birch contributed significantly to the renewal of interest in the past that marked the **Gothic Revival**.

Elizabeth Wilkens Manus

Bibliography

Dictionary of National Biography, s.v. "Birch, Thomas."

Osborn, James Marshall. "Thomas Birch and the General Dictionary (1734–41)." *Modern Philology.* Vol. 36, pp. 25–46.

Ruhe, Edward L. "Birch, Johnson and Elizabeth Carter: An Episode of 1738–39." *Publications of the Modern Language Association.* Vol. 73, No. 5, pp. 491–500.

Seccombe, Thomas. *The Age of Johnson (1748–1798).* 1909.

Stauffer, Donald A. *The Art of Biography in Eighteenth Century England.* 2 vols. 1941.

See also Reference Works

Birkbeck, George (1799–1841)

Birkbeck pioneered the education of workingmen. After receiving his M.D. from the University of Edinburgh (1799) he became professor of natural philosophy at the **Andersonian Institution** in **Glasgow**. The following year he established a lecture program to educate workers. Though he soon afterward established a medical practice in **London**, he maintained an interest in vocational education and in 1823 became a founder and first president of the London Mechanics' Institution (later renamed Birkbeck College). The intention was to bring scientific and technical knowledge cheaply to workers, and to provide them with libraries. Within a year, Birkbeck's school had 1,887 students. Similar schools quickly spread throughout the country and numbered more than a thousand by the early 1830s. Birkbeck remained president of the London Mechanics' Institution until 1840 and was also active in helping found the **University of London**.

David B. Mock

Bibliography

Gorland, J.G. *Life of Dr. Birkbeck.* 1884.

See also Education, Technical; Mechanics' Institutes

Birmingham

The town of Birmingham in the West Midlands became one of the major centers of Britain's expanding manufacturing industries in the course of the 18th century. Building on a long tradition of **metalworking**, and benefiting from the absence of a corporate structure of local economic regulation, Birmingham developed into one of the focal points of the **Industrial Revolution**.

Birmingham was a center of the "toy" (small inexpensive goods) trade until methods of **transport** changed in the 1760s and 1770s. The creation of **canal** links with the **coal** fields of south Staffordshire ensured a ready and cheap supply of fuel. The Soho manufactory, established (1762) by the partnership of **Matthew Boulton** and **James Watt**, was the best known of the burgeoning industrial enterprises undertaken in Birmingham.

The town enjoyed a wealth of talent—technical and **entrepreneurial**. **Population** growth accompanied economic expansion. From a population of about 15,000 in 1700, and still only about 24,000 around 1750, Birmingham grew to over 70,000 by 1801. Cultural and intellectual life blossomed as well. Members of the **Lunar Society**, including **Erasmus Darwin**, **Josiah Wedgwood**, and **Sir William Herschel**, met to discuss philosophical and scientific questions, and schools, theaters, and other amenities appeared. The *Birmingham Gazette,* the town's first **newspaper**, commenced publication in 1741, and a circulating **library** opened in 1763. Birmingham was also a center of **dissent**, and played an important part in the growth of **Methodism**.

By the second half of the 18th century the rudimentary form of Birmingham's **local government** under the lord of the manor was showing the strain of the city's growth. A body of street commissioners was established in 1769, the visible results of which were a town hall and considerable physical improvements, though complaints were voiced that the commissioners were not held accountable to the inhabitants. Successive acts in 1772, 1784, 1801, 1812, and 1828 extended the powers of the street commissioners, though improvements could not keep pace with demographic and industrial growth. Public services remained hopelessly inadequate. Various proposals were put forward to obtain a charter over the course of the 18th century, but Birmingham was incorporated and acquired a city government only in 1838. By that time it was one of the foremost industrial cities of the world.

Daniel Statt

Bibliography

Gill, Conrad. *History of Birmingham, Vol. I: Manor and Borough to 1865.* 1952.

Money, John. *Experience and Identity: Birmingham and the West Midlands, 1760–1800.* 1977.

See also Cities and Urban Life; Provincial Towns and Society

Bishop, Henry (1786–1855)

Bishop held a dominant position in the world of English musical **theater** from about 1810 to 1834, though he is now known only for a handful of songs, most notably "Home, Sweet Home" (from *Clari,* 1823), and two regimental marches.

Bishop contributed music to over 100 theater pieces. But even those termed **operas** were worked out dramatically in spoken dialogue, the music being largely ornamental. His most ambitious efforts were *The Maniac* (1810), *Aladdin* (1826), and *Manfred* (1834, after **Byron**). He also set several dramatizations of **Sir Walter Scott's novels** and provided incidental music to five **Shakespeare** plays. His melodrama *The Miller and His Men* (1813) seems to have outlasted all his other theatrical works.

Nicholas Temperley

Bibliography

Carr, Bruce. "Theatre Music: 1800–1834," in Nicholas Temperley, ed., *The Blackwell History of Music in Britain.* Vol. 5. 1988.

Northcott, Richard. *The Life of Sir Henry R. Bishop.* 1920.

See also Music

Black, Joseph (1728–1799)

A noted chemist and professor of **medicine**, Black was one of the leaders of the **Scottish Enlightenment**. He entered Glasgow University (1746) to study medicine but also studied chemistry under **William Cullen**. Cullen's removal to **Edinburgh** (1756) led to Black's appointment as Professor of Anatomy and Chemistry at **Glasgow**. Despite the demands of teaching and practicing medicine in the ensuing decade, Black maintained his interest in chemistry and physics, undertaking pioneering research into latent heat (heat radiated or absorbed during a change of phase at constant pressure and temperature). Heating different substances to the same temperature he also, in the 1760s, laid the foundations for the theory of specific heats. These investigations, in addition to advancing thermal science, also fortified **James Watt's** work on improving **steam engines** through separate condensation chambers, and the two men maintained regular contact. Black

Joseph Black, M.D.

meanwhile joined Cullen at Edinburgh, where he was appointed Professor of Medicine and Chemistry (1766). His reputation was now international, acknowledged in honors from **France** and Russia. His friends included **Adam Smith**, **David Hume**, and **Adam Ferguson**.

Ian Donnachie

Bibliography

Crowther, J.G. *Scientists of the Industrial Revolution.* 1962.

Robinson, E., and D. McKie, eds. *Partners in Science: The Letters of James Watt and Joseph Black.* 1970.

See also Science, Technology, and Invention

Black Act (1723)

Also known as the "Waltham Black Act," this piece of legislation recognized some 50 new capital crimes and was directed primarily against **poaching** and related offenses which had formerly been misdemeanors. It was at once the major precedent for, and largest part of, the so-called Bloody Code of the 18th century, which saw the increase of capital offenses from 50 to over 200 between 1688 and 1820.

Specifically, the act detailed a list of property offenses which, if committed while armed or with blackened or otherwise disguised faces, in the king's forests or in any forest, park, or the like where game were kept, would carry the death penalty. The act was in fact interpreted by judges to mean that being armed or disguised by blackening one's face could be considered a capital crime in and of itself. The property offenses were enumerated very specifically. These included hunting, wounding, killing, or stealing red or fallow deer in the king's forest; the poaching of hares; breaking the head or mound of a fish pond; killing or maiming cattle; cutting down trees in a garden, orchard, or plantation; arson involving a house or barn; anonymous letters attempting to extort money or venison; and the rescue by force of an offender against this statute. The act also provided that sworn statements given to the Privy Council could be sufficient grounds for judging an offender guilty and sentencing him or her to death without trial, if he or she failed to surrender.

This act was directed against the often violent and destructive activities of gangs of poachers and **smugglers** operating in Windsor Forest and Waltham Chase (Hampshire) in the early 1720s; these resulted in the deaths of several officials in 1723. Some close students of the Black Act maintain that the perceived need for such a draconian law was the general threat to order, authority, and property posed by the "Waltham Blacks" and that the main objective underlying its passage was the desire to replace ineffectual past modes of **punishment**, such as whipping, with a sort of official terror. Other writers have emphasized the political motivation of **Sir Robert Walpole** in pressing for an act to strengthen the **Whig** government. One historian suggests that the act was used to "control" **Jacobitism**, with which the "Blacks" were associated. The act was not fully repealed until 1823.

Stanley D. Nash

Bibliography

Broad, John. "Whigs and Deer-Stealers in Other Guises: A Return to the Origins of the Black Act." *Past and Present.* No. 119, pp. 56–72.

Cruickshanks, Eveline, and Howard Erskine-Hill. "The Waltham Black Act and Jacobitism." *Journal of British Studies.* Vol. 24, pp. 358–365.

Radzinowicz, Leon. *A History of English Criminal Law and Its Administration from 1750,* vol. I. 4 vols. 1948–1968.

Thompson, E.P. *Whigs and Hunters: The Origin of the Black Act.* 1975.

See also Crime; Judicial System

Black Book

See Wade, John

Black Hole of Calcutta (1756)

This was a detention cell at Fort William in Calcutta, Bengal. It earned its epithet as the scene of a much-publicized incident involving the deaths by neglect of British prisoners of war during the **Seven Years' War**.

In early 1756 the British **East India Company** added fortifications to its trading post at Fort William. This action outraged Siraj-ud-daula, the *nawab* (chief tax collector) of Bengal and the province's *de facto* independent ruler, whose permission the company had not sought. Siraj responded by occupying the fort on 20 June.

According to the commander of the surrendering garrison, Bengali soldiers, on invading the fort, forced 146 British prisoners, including a woman and several wounded officers, into a poorly ventilated subterranean cell which measured only 14 by 18 feet; the following morning, only 23 emerged alive.

THE BRITISH REINFORCEMENTS WELCOMED BY THE FUGITIVES AT FULTA.

Arrival of Reinforcements after the Calcutta Outrage

Recent scholarship, however, indicates that only 64 spent the night in the "black hole," and that 21 survived.

Although Siraj did not order the incarceration, news of the event evoked outrage and prompted swift retaliation that ended with the company's conquest of Bengal the following year. The British subsequently cited the incident as an example of the "barbarity" that supposedly justified their occupation of **India**.

A. Martin Wainwright

Bibliography

Barber, Noel. *The Black Hole of Calcutta: A Reconstruction.* 1966.

Gupta, Brijen K. *Sirajuddaullah and the East India Company, 1756–1757.* 1966.

Moorehouse, Geoffrey. *Calcutta.* 1971.

Blackburne, Francis (1705–1787)

Blackburne, Archdeacon of Cleveland, was a theologian and controversialist whose liberal views on **religious toleration** and church authority sparked a heated debate of the 1760s, known as the subscription controversy, over whether tests of religious orthodoxy should be required of Anglican clergymen. Blackburne set forth his position in *The Confessional, Or a Full and Free Inquiry Into the Right, Utility, and Success of Establishing Confessions of Faith and Doctrine in Protestant Churches* (1766). Here he maintained that the Bible should be the sole source of authority in Protestant churches, and that the practice of compelling clergy to subscribe to the Thirty-nine Articles of Faith, Anglicanism's official creed, was wrong. The agitation encouraged by this book resulted in the abortive Feathers Tavern Petition (1772), which requested that Parliament abolish clerical subscription to the Thirty-nine Articles. The request, converted into a parliamentary motion, was, however, easily defeated in the **House of Commons**.

Eric K. Heavner

Bibliography

Bradley, James E. *Religion, Revolution and English Radicalism: Nonconformity in Eighteenth Century Politics and Society.* 1990.

Clark, J.C.D. *The Language of Liberty, 1660–1832: Political Discourse and Social Dynamics in the Anglo-American World.* 1994.

Gascoigne, John. *Cambridge in the Age of Enlightenment: Science, Religion and Politics from the Restoration to the French Revolution.* 1989.

Lincoln, Anthony. *Some Political and Social Ideas of English Dissent: 1763–1800.* 1938, 1971.

Robbins, Caroline. *The Eighteenth-Century Commonwealthman.* 1961.

See also Church of England; Jebb, John; Lindsey, Theophilus

Blackstone, William (1723–1780)

Blackstone, English jurist and statesman, was the first Vinerian professor of law at **Oxford** (1758). His monumental *Commentaries on the Laws of England* (4 vols., 1765–1769) was the first successful attempt to make the whole structure of English law comprehensible and accessible to laymen. As a result, this work enjoyed tremendous influence in both Britain and **North America**, shaping legal education as well as more general attitudes toward the English Constitution.

William Blackstone

In 1746, following his legal education at the Middle Temple, Blackstone became a barrister, but his practice was unsuccessful. Turning to scholarship and teaching the subject of English law, he published his lectures (1756) as *An Analysis of the Laws of England.* After election to the Oxford professorship in 1758 he further worked these into the *Commentaries.* Meanwhile, in 1761 he was elected to Parliament, where he served until 1770, progressively giving up academic activity. As an M.P., Blackstone supported the expulsion of **John Wilkes** from the **House of Commons** (1769); the following year, he was appointed judge of the Court of Common Pleas.

Blackstone's reputation rests upon the *Commentaries.* Written very attractively, these attempted to describe and explain the structure of 18th-century law within grander frameworks of history, society, natural law, and divine order. Thus to a certain degree Blackstone figured as a constitutional propagandist, a judicial interpreter and expositor of the **Glorious Constitution**. But it is untrue to say that he took an entirely uncritical view of contemporary political conditions. Blackstone expressed some discontent, for example, with the role of wealth and influence in contaminating **elections and the franchise**. Notwithstanding, he was indeed vulnerable to the charge of glorifying the status quo. **Joseph Priestley** was one of many prominent reformers who took issue with Blackstone's attack on **rational dissent** as an offense against the Church. **Jeremy Bentham**, his most powerful critic, excoriated him as an opponent of reform, claiming that his writings were full of sycophantic "nebulosities" that shored up the power structure and frustrated legal and constitutional reform. Ironically, Blackstone's elegant tableau of English law, a model of exposition, furnished a purchase for its critics, a body that grew rapidly after 1800.

Jack Fruchtman, Jr.

Bibliography

Liberman, David. *The Province of Legislation Determined: Legal Theory in Eighteenth-Century Britain.* 1989.
Lockmiller, David A. *Sir William Blackstone.* 1970.
Milsom, S.F.C. *The Nature of Blackstone's Achievement.* 1981.

See also Judicial System; Law Reform; Legal Profession

Blair, Hugh (1718–1800)

Blair, famed both as a preacher and teacher of rhetoric, was a leading figure in the **Scottish Enlightenment**. His five volumes of *Sermons* (1777–1801) and his *Lectures on Rhetoric and Belles Lettres* (1783) were for many years some of the most popular writings in the English language, and did much to shape British and American conceptions of polite preaching and **literary criticism**. In both the Church of Scotland and the University of Edinburgh, Blair was closely associated with **William Robertson**'s circle of Moderate party clergymen, with whom he shared a commitment to polite learning and moderate religion, along with a conservative outlook on political issues such as the **American** and **French** revolutions.

Born in **Edinburgh**, Blair was educated at the high school and university there. After briefly serving as a private **tutor** and minister of the country parish of Collessie, he was called to the Canongate Church near Edinburgh (1743) and then to Lady Yester's Church in Edinburgh proper (1754). From 1758, Blair served as one of the ministers of the prestigious New or High Kirk in St. Giles Church, Edinburgh, where he preached to great acclaim before the most eminent congregation in **Scotland**. He began delivering his course of lectures on rhetoric in 1759, first informally, then with a nonsalaried professorial appointment at the University of Edinburgh (1760), and finally as the Regius Professor of Rhetoric and Belles Lettres (1762–1784).

Hugh Blair

Blair was largely responsible for encouraging and promoting the Ossianic poetry of **James Macpherson**, which he praised in his first major publication, *A Critical Dissertation on the Poems of Ossian* (1763). That work earned him the scorn of **Samuel Johnson** who, more than a decade later, nonetheless helped to bring about the publication of the first volume of Blair's *Sermons.* Blair was also a patron of **Robert Burns**, whose somewhat belittling comment that Blair was "merely an astonishing proof of what industry and application can do" is perhaps more typical of modern than of contemporary assessments of his abilities.

Richard B. Sher

Bibliography

Dwyer, John. *Virtuous Discourse: Sensibility and Community in Late Eighteenth-Century Scotland.* 1987.
Schmitz, Robert Morrell. *Hugh Blair.* 1948.
Sher, Richard B. *Church and University in the Scottish Enlightenment: The Moderate Literati of Edinburgh.* 1985.

See also Church of Scotland; Sermons

Blair, Robert (1701–1746)

Born in **Edinburgh**, Blair published little beside *The Grave* (1743), a long and dramatic **graveyard** poem begun before he became a minister in East Lothia in 1731. The elegy *A Poem Dedicated to the Memory of Mr. William Lee* (*c.* 1728), on his father-in-law, and some verses in *The Edinburgh Miscellany* (1720), are also ascribed to him.

Like **Edward Young**'s *The Complaint; or, Night Thoughts* (1742–1746), *The Grave* evokes melancholy and horror through descriptions of tombs and a nocturnal churchyard, while recommending reformation through meditations on the brevity and vanity of life and the horrors of death. Reprinted in **London** and Edinburgh soon after publication, *The Grave* became immensely popular later in the century, helping to foster **Romantic** sensibilities.

James E. May

Bibliography

Anderson, Robert, ed. *The Poetical Works of Robert Blair. Containing The Grave; and a Poem to the Memory of Mr. Lee.* 1794.
Dictionary of National Biography, s.v. "Blair, Robert."
Gilfillan, Rev. George, ed. *The Poetical Works of Beattie, Blair, and Falconer.* 1854.
Means, James A. "The Composition of *The Grave.*" *Studies in Scottish Literature.* Vol. 10, pp. 3–9.
———, ed. *The Grave.* Augustan Reprint Society, no. 161. 1973.

Blake, William (1757–1827)

Blake was an extraordinarily gifted engraver, painter, and Romantic poet. His major works were published by Blake himself from copper plates on which he engraved both text and illumination. Of his 22 illuminated works, the more important include *Songs of Innocence* (1789), *The Book of Thel* (1789), *The Marriage of Heaven and Hell* (*c.* 1790), *Visions of the Daughters of Albion* (1793), *America: A Prophecy* (1793), *Songs of Innocence and of Experience* (1794; *Experience* was never printed separately), *Europe: A Prophecy* (1794), *The [First] Book of Urizen* (1794), *Milton* (1815), and *Jerusalem the Emanation of the Giant Albion* (1818–1820). One important illuminated work, *The Four Zoas* (*c.* 1800–1803), was never set in final form or engraved.

Blake, born in London, was educated at home. In 1772 he was apprenticed to James Basire and assigned to make **drawings** of the statues in Gothic Westminster Abbey, a task that influenced his work throughout his career. He also studied briefly at the **Royal Academy** (1779–1780), the effect of which was mostly negative. In 1782 he married Catherine Boucher (1762–1831), whom he taught to read, write, and make prints; her impact on Blake's work, though significant, is not entirely understood. The death of his favorite brother, Robert (1767–1787), affected him greatly, and Blake claimed to have learned his technique of relief etching from his dead brother in a dream.

Blake's career is marked by an opposition between his trade as an engraver and his calling as a divinely inspired poet and prophet. His **engravings** appeared in works as diverse as John Stedman's *Narrative, of a Five Years' Expedition, against the Revolted Negroes in Surinam, in Guiana, on the Wild Coast of South America* (1796), Josiah Wedgwood the Younger's pottery catalogues (1815–1816), and a commercial broadside for "Moore & Co's Manufactory & Warehouse of Carpeting and Hosiery" (*c.* 1797–1798). As a businessman, Blake was not generally successful because of his ill temper. When provoked by clients he considered unimaginative or insensitive, he often spoke or wrote in offensive tones. He believed that invention and execution should be inseparable, and was impatient with the copying often required of an engraver.

Blake was easily distracted from commissioned work by his own imaginative visions. This tension reached a climax in 1800–1803, when Blake lived in Felpham and worked under the patronage of William Hayley (1745–1820). A poet himself, Hayley recognized Blake's talent as an engraver and **painter**, but had little patience with his visionary poetry. Their conflict marked a turning point in Blake's career, and its history (and much else) is recorded in a transformed fashion in the "**sublime** allegory" of *Milton* and *Jerusalem,* his last and most ambitious poems.

The shape of Blake's poetic career resembles the Virgilian model of Edmund Spenser and **John Milton**. His early work is mainly **pastoral**, including elegies and **satires**; his later work is visionary and **epic**. Blake connected the line of British poets with the line of biblical prophets, and despite his regard for the achievement of Homer, came to believe that the chief problem with English history was the erroneous tracing of its origin to Troy—through Brutus—rather than to Jerusalem through Jesus. His critique of England's ruling myth of origin sought to address the injustices he saw daily in **London**'s streets, and included his criticism of the **Enlightenment**, of the materialist progress of Baconian science, of the mathematical form of the Newtonian universe, and of the passivity of the Lockean mind.

Relatively unknown in his own time, Blake's importance in English literary studies has increased steadily. He is recognized as one of the most insightful—and daring—readers of Milton and of 18th-century **poetry** and philosophy. His influence is evident in the writing of Dante Gabriel Rossetti, William Butler Yeats, James Joyce, and Allen Ginsberg, and in the theories of critics such as Northrop Frye and Harold Bloom.

R. Paul Yoder

Bibliography

Damon, S. Foster. *A Blake Dictionary: The Ideas and Symbols of William Blake.* Rev. ed., 1988.

Erdman, David V. *Blake: Prophet against Empire.* 3rd ed., 1977.

———, ed. *The Complete Poetry and Prose of William Blake.* Rev. ed., 1988.

Essick, Robert N. *William Blake and the Language of Adam.* 1989.

Frye, Northrop. *Fearful Symmetry: A Study of William Blake.* 1947.

Gleckner, Robert F. *The Piper and the Bard: A Study of William Blake.* 1957.

Hilton, Nelson. *Literal Imagination: Blake's Vision of Words.* 1983.

Mitchell, W.J.T. *Blake's Composite Art: A Study of the Illuminated Poetry.* 1978.

Natoli, Joseph P. *Twentieth-Century Blake Criticism: Northrop Frye to the Present.* 1982.

Tannenbaum, Leslie. *Biblical Tradition in Blake's Early Prophecies: The Great Code of Art.* 1982.

See also Romanticism and Romantic Style

Blanketeer March (1817)

This march, apparently more an economic than a political manifestation of unrest, was organized to call attention to and find remedies for the economic distress of the industrial Lancashire area after 1815. The event, organized by the **dissenting** intellectual William Benbow (1784–1841) and others, chiefly involved rural weavers, though other working groups were also represented. The marchers gathered in **Manchester** on St. Peter's Fields (10 March), carrying petitions they hoped to present to the Prince Regent in London; they carried a few provisions and some blankets, planning to sleep on the ground en route and pick up support along the way. The magistrates, however, read the **Riot Act** and rounded up many of the marchers before they could start. Another 200 or so were soon arrested. Only one individual ever reached London to present his petition. Most of those arrested were released after expressing their contriteness, others after submitting a petition written in jail, while the last stubborn eight prisoners were released after 5 months' incarceration without benefit of trial.

Thomas D. Veve

Bibliography

Hammond, J.L., and Barbara Hammond. *The Skilled Labourer 1760–1832.* 1919.

Thompson, E.P. *The Making of the English Working Class.* 1963.

White, R.J. *Waterloo to Peterloo.* 1957.

Worrall, David. *Radical Culture: Discourse, Resistance and Surveillance, 1790–1820.* 1992.

See also Radicalism and Radical Politics; Riots and Popular Disturbances

Blessington, Marguerite (Power), Countess of (1789–1849)

Though a journalist, novelist, poet, and literary hostess, Blessington is better known for her adventurous life than for any of her literary productions; and this despite the fact that after the death of her second husband, Charles John Gardiner, first Earl of Blessington, she wrote constantly in order to provide for her family and to sustain her luxurious lifestyle.

Marguerite Power was born in Tipperary, the daughter of a small landowner. She married at age 15 Captain Maurice St. Leger Farmer, an unfortunate drunk who died in a debtor's prison a dozen year later (1817). She then married Blessington (1818), and spent much of the next decade touring the Continent with him. After his death (1829), she and Alfred Count D'Orsay took up residence in Mayfair. At Seamore Place, where she was known for her beauty and wit, she and D'Orsay entertained some of the most prominent literary and political figures of the day, enlarging a salon that continued until bankruptcy forced them in 1849 to flee to Paris, where she died of a heart seizure.

Countess of Blessington

The first of her many **novels**, *Grace Cassidy, or the Repealers* (1833), gave way quickly to her most significant production, *Conversations of Lord Byron* (1834), based on a four-months' visit with **Byron** in Genoa in 1823. She also edited and contributed to two Annuals, *The Keepsake* (1841–1848) and the *Book of Beauty* (1834), both of which included poems by well-known authors of the day. Blessington's **travel book**, *The Idler in Italy* (1839), full of gossip and anecdote, was her most lucrative publication; an *Idler in France* followed (1841).

Mary Tiryak

Bibliography

Lovell, Ernest J., ed. *Lady Blessington's Conversations of Lord Byron.* 1969.

Madden, R.R. *The Literary Life and Correspondence of the Countess of Blessington.* 1855.

Molloy, J. Fitzgerald. *The Most Gorgeous Lady Blessington.* 1897.

Bligh, William (1754–1817)

Sea captain, botanist, and colonial administrator, Bligh was one of the colorful characters of the age. Born in Cornwall and taken to the sea at age 7, he joined the **navy** (1770) and sailed on **Captain Cook's** second voyage (1772–1774) to the Pacific, during which he discovered breadfruit on Tahiti. Due to his familiarity with the Pacific and botanical credentials he received command of H.M.S. *Bounty* (1787) with orders to transport breadfruit trees from Tahiti to the **West Indies**, to provide a new food staple for **slaves**. But the ship's crew, softened by half a year's idyllic stay on the island and led by Lieutenant Fletcher Christian, mutinied and cast Bligh adrift in an open boat along with several loyal men.

The captain, without a map or much food, in a remarkable feat of courage and **navigation** sailed 3,500 miles to reach Timor in the Dutch East Indies. After arranging punishment for the mutineers he successfully completed his mission (1792), for which he received the Gold Medal of the Society of the Arts (1794) and election to the **Royal Society** (1805); Jamaica's slaves, who preferred bananas and plantains, were not polled.

During the **French Revolutionary and Napoleonic Wars** Bligh experienced a second **mutiny** when his crew, putting him ashore, joined the "Floating Republic" of the Nore (1797). He demonstrated tactical skill in naval actions at Ushant (1794), Camperdown (1797), and Copenhagen (1801). But as Captain-General of New South Wales (1805–1808), the first British colony in **Australia**, his harsh exercise of authority sparked still another mutiny that resulted in his imprisonment for 2 years by the mutineers.

Despite promotion to flag rank, Admiral Bligh held no

William Bligh

subsequent commands. His achievements in navigation, naval command, and science were marred by leadership failures rooted in his irascibility, abuse of subordinate officers, and often vindictive treatment of inferiors.

Stanley D.M. Carpenter

Bibliography

Dening, Greg. *Mr Bligh's Bad Language: Passion, Power, and Theater on the* Bounty. 1992.

Kennedy, Gavin. *Bligh*. 1978.

———. *Captain Bligh: The Man and His Mutinies*. 1989.

Mackaness, George. *The Life of Vice-Admiral Bligh*. 1951.

Syrett, David, and R.L. DiNardo, eds. *The Commissioned Sea Officers of the Royal Navy, 1660–1815*. 1994.

Blood Sports

Many sports of the early 18th century had bloodshed and the infliction of pain as integral parts of their performance: hunting, shooting, bear-, bull-, and badger-baiting; dog- and cock-fighting, and prizefighting. All these activities were physically violent but were not yet widely considered cruel. Such violence was, of course, evident elsewhere, as in public hangings.

With both rich and poor alike, cock-fighting was the most popular blood sport of the day. It usually involved **gambling** and, like other blood sports, flourished until the passing of the Cruelty to Animals Act of 1835. There appear to have been several reasons behind the growing desire to halt blood sports. Opponents maintained that all such "sport" was cruel and inhumane. Others complained that it drew together "idle and disorderly persons." It also distracted working people from their occupations, particularly those earning only subsistence wages, who could ill afford gambling losses. The fact that many blood sports took place in pubs and grog shops, where cheap spirits were readily available for sale, also condemned such activities in the eyes of reformers.

From the middle of the 18th century on, many blood sports came under attack. Their persistence was a cause for considerable concern in respectable society generally, but especially among **Evangelical** Christians and many people affected by the cultivation of **sensibility**. Attempts at their suppression were not uniformly successful. Working class in character, blood sports were often merely driven underground; when enjoyed by the rich, their glamor as well as the law could be relied on for protection.

The best example of this is perhaps **fox-hunting**. Transformed in the 18th century from a private, informal recreation of a few country squires to a highly organized public institution, fox-hunting became the consuming sporting passion of the outdoorsman/woman. As a social activity it became imbued with a significance beyond its role as mere sport. Originally, fox-hunting was an extension of hare-hunting, where the hounds were harriers (slow animals with well-developed scenting powers), and where hunting was protracted, often lasting many hours and even entire days. But all this changed in 1753, when Hugo Meynell (1735–1808), a young gambler and racing man, rented Quornden Hall in Leicestershire and began to hunt with hounds specially bred for speed. The speed of his hounds made fox-hunting more exciting and greatly increased its appeal, while Meynell, soon considered the best foxhunter in the country, went on to become M.P., Sheriff of Derbyshire, and Master of the Royal Staghounds.

Meynell's success prompted outsiders to visit "The Quorn," and the neighborhood became a center of hunting and **fashion**. Fox-hunting attracted the attention of the elite and was seen as an interesting contrast to the softer, more urban and effeminate amusements of the assembly and card table—and as excellent training for **war**. What particularly attracted sportsmen was the opportunity for hard and exhilarating riding. The countryside, although enclosed, provided long, fast runs. The cooperation of landowners, graziers, and farmers was vital, and thus their presence in the field was the best way to ensure such cooperation. It may be noted that women hunted, although they were not particularly encouraged to. Lady Salisbury was Master of the Hatfield Hounds in 1793, and continued participating as a septuagenarian. In the 19th century, the mythology of the hunt was spread by the writings of "Nimrod" (C.J. Apperley) and R.S. Surtees.

Timothy J. Chandler

Bibliography

Holt, Richard. *Sport and the British: A Modern History*. 1989.

Itzkowitz, David. *Peculiar Privilege*. 1977.

Malcolmson, Robert. *Popular Recreations in English Society, 1700–1850*. 1981.

Thompson, F.M.L., ed. *The Cambridge Social History of Britain, 1750–1950.* 3 vols. 1990.

See also Amusements and Recreation; Sport

Bluestockings

In the latter 18th century, *Bluestockings* was the name assumed by a group of women, mostly Londoners, who shared intellectual interests, provided mutual support for intellectual development, and indirectly helped to spread the idea of the virtuous intellectual woman. The principal early members were Elizabeth Carter (1717–1806), **Elizabeth Robinson Montagu**, Catherine Talbot (1721–1770), **Hester Mulso Chapone**, and Elizabeth Vesey (1715?–1791). Second-generation Bluestockings included Hester Lynch Thrale Piozzi (1741–1821), **Hannah More**, and **Fanny Burney**. Most were either aristocratic or socially well connected.

The term Bluestocking suggested a party centered on literary conversation rather than cards or mere gossip. It first appeared in 1756, in Montagu's correspondence, in humorous reference to the erudite but socially unadapted Benjamin Stillingfleet who, with perhaps a deliberate show of plainness, wore blue worsted stockings to gatherings where white or black silk would be expected. In the **letters** of Montagu and her friends the term later referred to men with intellectual interests, "bluestocking philosophers," whose conversation and letters had contributed to their own intellectual development. By the mid 1770s the term designated a circle of men and women and their intellectual conversations ("rational entertainment"); eventually it referred to women only and, by the end of the century, in a disparaging sense, to women with pretensions to learning.

The original Bluestockings came together to share interests in serious reading and study. Virtually all benefited from the encouragement of men in their families and from friends such as **Samuel Johnson** and **George Lyttelton**, but the psychological and emotional as well as practical support they received from other women appears to have been vital to their accomplishments. They recommended books to each other and exchanged thoughts on them as equals, encouraged each other to write and publish, and gave each other a sympathetic ear as they attempted to balance the domestic with the intellectual life. Although some works of the early Bluestockings were published—Montagu's attack on Voltaire (1769) would have made any contemporary best-seller list—the extent of their intellectual activity is best seen in their correspondence, much of it still unfortunately unpublished. The second generation were more widely published and have been more thoroughly attended to by modern critics.

Monica Letzring

Bibliography

Bodek, Evelyn Gorden. "Salonières and Bluestockings: Educated Obsolescence and Germinating Feminism." *Feminist Studies.* Vol. 3, pp. 185–199.

Myers, Sylvia H. *The Blustocking Circle: Women, Friendship and the Life of the Mind in Eighteenth-Century England.* 1990.

Tinker, Chauncey Brewster. *The Salon and English Letters: Chapters on the Interrelations of Literature and Society in the Age of Johnson.* 1915.

Wheeler, Ethel Rolt. *Famous Blue-Stockings.* 1910.

Williamson, Marilyn L. "Who's Afraid of Mrs. Barbauld? The Blue Stockings and Feminism." *International Journal of Women's Studies.* Vol. 3, pp. 89–102.

See also Women in Literature

Bolingbroke, Viscount (Henry St. John) (1678–1751)

Statesman, philosopher, historian, and pamphleteer, Bolingbroke organized the opposition to **Sir Robert Walpole** into a coherent force that appealed to **Whig** and **Tory** alike. His journal, ***The Craftsman,*** made landmark contributions to political **journalism** for its criticisms of Walpole and his ministry.

As Henry St. John, he began in Parliament in 1700 as a High Church Tory, but later aligned with the moderate **Robert Harley.** A Secretary of State from 1710, he became Viscount Bolingbroke (1712). By this time he had emerged as a rival to Harley, using his own terms for the Treaty of Utrecht (1713) and his leadership in favor of the antinonconformist **Schism Act** (1714) to win over Tory support. Although he claimed to support the **Hanoverian succession** after **Queen Anne**'s death (1714), he feared the backlash against Tories and fled to France, remaining there for 10 years after briefly accepting a secretaryship with **James Edward, the Old Pretender** and supporting the **Fifteen**—acts which resulted in his outlawry and loss of rank and property in England.

Pardoned in 1723 (but never restored in his peerage), Bolingbroke on his return joined with Sir William Wyndham (1687–1740) and **William Pulteney** to concert biparty opposition against Walpole (1726) and, with Pulteney, to found *The Craftsman* (1727) as the organ of the **Opposition.** Bolingbroke's *Remarks on the History of England* (1730–1731) and *Dissertation on Parties* (1734) both appeared there and, with the later *The Idea of a Patriot King* (1739), helped to build up a "Country" ideology against Walpole's "court" politics. With its roots in Machiavellian republican thought, this ideology held that civic virtue was manifested in a patriotic desire to realize the public good, whereas corruption resulted when politicians only sought their own interests. Corruption, especially in its Walpolean form, was discerned in the ministry's support of public credit, central banking, the national debt, and a standing army. Bolingbroke also charged that Walpole's **patronage** system corrupted an independent Parliament. A Patriot King could rid the nation of these corruptions and revive civic virtue through a new sense of public spiritedness.

Bolingbroke's ideas, though they certainly sprang partly from personal animosity against Walpole and frustrated ambition, helped inspire both **Bute** and the young **George III** as well as reformers such as **Christopher Wyvill.** His other publications included *Reflections Concerning Innate Moral Principles* (1724) and *Letters on the Study and the Use of History*

(1735–1736). His **freethinking** views were not fully revealed until their publication posthumously. Though a political opportunist, he was considered by **Chesterfield** one of the most impressive characters of the age.

Carole S. Fungaroli

Bibliography

Biddle, Sheila. *Bolingbroke and Harley.* 1974.

Dickinson, H.T. *Bolingbroke.* 1970.

Gerrard, Christine. *The Patriot Opposition to Walpole: Politics, Poetry, and National Myth, 1725–1742.* 1995.

Harris, Robert. *A Patriot Press: National Politics and the London Press in the 1740s.* 1993.

James, D.G. *The Life of Reason: Hobbes, Locke, Bolingbroke.* 1949.

Kramnick, Isaac. *Bolingbroke and His Circle: The Politics of Nostalgia in the Age of Walpole.* 1968.

Mansfield, Harvey C. *Statesmanship and Party Government: A Study of Burke and Bolingbroke.* 1965.

Varey, Simon. *Henry St. John, Viscount Bolingbroke.* 1974.

See also Political Thought

Book Illustration

Various types of illustrated books were published in England in the 17th century (e.g., emblem books, garden and architectural books, topographical surveys, scientific treatises), but Jacob Tonson's (1656–1737) 1688 edition of **Milton**'s *Paradise Lost,* with 12 copperplate engravings by Brussels-born J.B. Medina, was the first high-quality illustrated edition of a contemporary literary work.

During the next 30 years the enterprising Tonson published many other fine editions of ancient and modern literary works, setting a high standard of design and production that endured well beyond his death. Tonson's most outstanding publications were editions of **Shakespeare** (1709), Beaumont and Fletcher (1711), Ovid (1717), Milton (1720), and a seven-volume folio edition of Bernard Picart's monumental *Religious Ceremonies and Histories of the Known World* (1730s); the plates for them all were executed by a small group of highly skilled French and Dutch émigré artist-engravers. In the absence of trained English artists and engravers, other publishers, following Tonson's example, employed the same émigré artists; Bernard Lintot, for instance, commissioned Louis du Guernier in 1714 to illustrate his edition of Pope's *Rape of the Lock.* Through the 1730s it was the decorative Continental style of **drawing** and **engraving** practiced by these men that dominated British book illustration at all levels.

The first English artists to design literary illustrations were **William Hogarth** and John Vanderbank, both of whom, along with **Francis Hayman**, in 1720 attended Cheron's St. Martin's Academy, established "for the Improvement of Sculptors and Painters by drawing from the Naked." Hogarth's first production was a series of 16 original illustrations for Samuel Butler's **mock-heroic** *Hudibras* (1725), issued (as was to become his regular practice) as a series of single plates. Between

Thomas Bewick, "The Fox and the Goat" in Fables of Aesop, *1818*

1723 and 1729 Vanderbank completed a series of 67 illustrations for an extraordinary scholarly edition of *Don Quixote* that Tonson and John Wood eventually published in 1738. Hogarth, in the mid 1730s, hit upon the idea of the "moral progress," in which a story of his own invention was narrated in a series of single plates and sold separately by subscription.

The French vogue of the elegant engraved book was brought to England by Hubert-François Gravelot (1699–1773) in 1732. Through his association with St. Martin's Academy, Gravelot introduced the spirit of rococo to various English painters. His greater achievement, however, was as a book illustrator, executing in his sophisticated style a number of important literary works, including Tonson's *Dramatic Works of Dryden,* **Theobald**'s Shakespeare, and Knapton's edition of **Gay**'s *Fables.* Gravelot, fascinated with the contemporary scene, was the first to illustrate the new "realistic" **novels** of the 1740s, most notably **Richardson**'s *Pamela* (1742 ed.) and **Fielding**'s *Tom Jones* (1749). The influence of Gravelot, with whom he collaborated on *Pamela* and on Sir Thomas Hammer's Shakespeare, is conspicuous in Hayman's later illustrations, particularly the set of plates he made for the 1753 **Smollett** translation of *Don Quixote.* Perhaps the most sophisticated example of French-inspired rococo book illustration is Richard Bentley's *Designs for Six Poems by Mr. T. Gray* (also 1753). Bentley's images are filled with rococo scrolls, **Gothic** ruins, and echoes of the newly fashionable **chinoiserie**.

Demand for illustrated reading editions increased steadily in the latter half of the 18th century, and the shifts that took place in taste, literary temper, and styles of pictorial representation can be readily traced through illustrated editions of that most popular poem of the century, **James Thomson**'s *Seasons.* New technologies as well as new developments in painting suggested to publishers ambitious undertakings. The rise of **history painting**, for instance, prompted John Boydell to invite a number of artists, including **Benjamin West**, James Barry, **Henry Fuseli**, and **Joshua Reynolds**, to contribute large-scale pictures for a permanent Shakespeare Gallery. The gallery project opened in 1789, and Boydell also issued a portfolio of mezzotints; and following his example, Fuseli founded a Milton Gallery and issued a series of prints in the mode of the "Miltonic **Sublime**." Illustrated Bibles appeared throughout the century, none as ambitious as Thomas Macklin's subscription folio edition of 1789–1800, adorned with 125 vignettes and 71 plates, 21 of which were based on sublime paintings of miraculous events and divinely wrought natural disasters by **Philippe de Loutherbourg**. Earlier, in the 1760s and 1770s, interest in Greek **antiquities**, encouraged by the Society of the Dilettanti, had occasioned some of the most beautifully engraved books of the age, such as Stuart and Revett's *Antiquities of Athens* (1762), Robert **Adam**'s great folio on Spalatro (1764), and Sir William Hamilton's splendid *Ancient Vases* volumes (1791–1795), the last of which inspired **John Flaxman**'s enormously influential illustrations to Homer's *Illiad* and *Odyssey* (1793).

Until the end of the century, paint technology remained relatively constant and unchanging—copperplate engraving for book illustration and the immensely popular **caricatures** and graphic satires of such masters and **James Gillray** and **Thomas Rowlandson**, mezzotint and stipple engraving for larger reproductions. In the late 1770s, however, **Thomas Bewick** perfected a new technique of wood engraving in which the image was cut into the end grain of the block in ways that allowed for exceptional detail and subtle shading and a "white line" tonal effect. He employed this brilliantly in his Gay's *Fables* (1779), and at the height of his career in his *General History of Quadrupeds* (1790), *History of British Birds* (1797 and 1804), and other volumes rich with small-scale illustrations.

Thanks to the onrush of new **technology**, publishers and artists from the 1790s mastered various other techniques, including lithography, etching, steel engraving, and aquatint. This last was used in **travel books** and topographical books, and in tour guides like Gilpin's *Picturesque Travels* (1792), that began to appear in the 1790s. Especially noteworthy are the books issued from the Strand shop of Rudolph Ackermann (1764–1834), particularly his illustrated *Histories* of Oxford and Cambridge and his color aquatints for the *Microcosm of London* (1802); the mezzotints for *Paradise Lost* (1836) by John Martin; and the minute steel engravings by **J.M.W. Turner** for the extraordinarily popular *Italy* (1830) and *Poems* (1838) of **Samuel Rogers**. But few of these works can compare with the unique illuminated books of **William Blake**, which extended from the *Songs of Innocence* (1789) through the *Book of Job* (1825).

The 123 years of Hanoverian book illustration saw many achievements by artists and illustrators, printers, and publishers. These furnished a solid base from which the Victorians, from the early 1840s on, would continue to transform the art, under the impetus of new technical developments in printing processes, a rapid expansion of periodicals and popular journals, increasing demand from an ever-growing world readership of illustrated novels, and further innovations in design and in methods of representation and ornamentation.

Carl A. Peterson

Bibliography

Altick, Richard. *Paintings from Books: Art and Literature in Britain, 1760–1900.* 1985.

Bland, David. *A History of Book Illustration.* 2nd ed., 1969.

Hammelmann, Hans, and T.S.T. Boase. *Book Illustrators in Eighteenth-Century England.* 1975.

Harthan, John. *The History of the Illustrated Book: The Western Tradition.* 1981.

House, Simon. *The Dictionary of British Book Illustrators and Caricaturists: 1800–1914.* Rev. ed., 1981.

Paulson, Ronald. *Book and Painting.* 1982.

Pointon, Marcia. *Milton and English Art.* 1970.

Ray, Gordon. *The Illustrator and the Book in England from 1790 to 1914.* 1976.

Stafford, Barbara Maria. *Art, Science, Nature, and the Illustrated Travel Account, 1760–1840.* 1984.

See also Graphic Arts; Publishers and Booksellers; Reference Works

Booksellers

See Publishers and Booksellers

Boroughs

Boroughs were incorporated towns, with legal, commercial, and political privileges granted by charters. Of Anglo-Saxon origin, borough status in England from the 14th century on included the right of parliamentary representation. Much of the complexity of Hanoverian British administration and politics derived from the wide legal, administrative, and political variations of the 215 boroughs of England and **Wales**. Their Scottish counterparts, the **burghs**, developed differently and had special terms of representation set by the **Act of Union (Scotland)** of 1707. Irish boroughs, however, generally resembled those of England after the **Act of Union (Ireland)** of 1800.

A borough's authority over common property, internal **commerce**, and minor criminal offenses typically reposed in a municipal corporation made up of a mayor, a small group of aldermen, and a larger body of common councilmen. Usually categorized by criteria related to national **elections and the franchise** and to the mechanisms of **local government**, boroughs may be seen broadly as either "open" or "close." In an open borough, the electorate actively decided the membership of the borough's corporation and its parliamentary representation, independent of external influences or pressures from internal interests. In close boroughs—the majority—some form of oligarchic cooptation from within the borough, or influence from outside, selected local officials and parliamentary representatives, who were frequently remote from the needs or wishes of borough inhabitants. This type included most of the notorious "pocket" boroughs.

Borough reform began with repeal in 1828 of the **Test and Corporation Acts**, which had excluded **dissenters** from membership in municipal corporations. The **Reform Act** (1832) deprived 86 underpopulated (or "rotten") boroughs of seats in the **House of Commons** and imposed a standard borough franchise for parliamentary elections throughout the country. Most important, the **Municipal Corporations Act** (1835) replaced 184 corporations with elected councils chosen on a relatively democratic basis, which in turn selected mayors and aldermen who served fixed terms. Boroughs retained their identities in parliamentary politics and local government for another 50 years, but further reforms in the 1880s broke up most into roughly equal electoral districts and vested their adminstrative powers in new county councils.

John A. Hutcheson, Jr.

Bibliography

Halévy, Elie. *England in 1815.* 1913.

Lewis, B. Keith. *The Unreformed Local Government System.* 1980.

Namier, Lewis B. *The Structure of Politics at the Accession of George III.* 2nd ed., 1957.

Phillips, John A. *The Great Reform Bill in the Boroughs: English Electoral Behavior, 1818–1841.* 1992.

Webb, Sidney, and Beatrice Webb. *English Local Government from the Revolution to the Municipal Corporations Act,* Vols. 2 and 3, *The Manor and the Borough.* 1908.

See also Government, National; Patronage; Radicalism and Radical Politics

Boscawen, Edward (1711–1761)

Boscawen, commissioned in the Royal Navy in 1732 and known to his sailors as "Old Dreadnought," earned his first command as captain of H.M.S. *Leopard* (1736) on Mediterranean station. As master of the 20-gun H.M.S. *Shoreham* he took part during the **War of Jenkins' Ear** in the attack on Cartegena (1741), where he successfully led the assault on a formidable Spanish fortification. In 1742 he became M.P. for Truro and married Fanny Glanville, one of the **Bluestockings**; during the **War of Austrian Succession** he ably commanded several warships and, as captain of the *Namur*, participated in **Anson**'s victory off Cape Finisterre (1747), during which a musket ball struck him in the shoulder. Promoted to flag rank and designated commander-in-chief in the East Indies, he tried unsuccessfully to take the French outpost at Pondicherry on the southeast coast of **India** (1748). His performance of duty resulted in his appointment as a Lord of the Admiralty (1751).

In 1755, newly appointed Vice Admiral, Boscawen sailed for **North America** and was there involved in some early hostilities of the **Seven Years' War**, most notably as commander of the fleet that assisted **Jeffrey Amherst** in the important cap-

Admiral Boscawen

ture of the French Canadian island fortress of Louisburg (1758). Returning to Europe, he commanded the squadron patrolling the Straits of Gibraltar and blockading Toulon (1759). When the French squadron stationed at Toulon attempted a break out in order to join forces with the Brest squadron to support an invasion of Britain, Boscawen, risking a court-martial for violating the rigid line formation prescribed by the "Fighting Instructions" and also infringing Portuguese neutrality, ordered a general chase and destroyed five French warships which had taken shelter in Lagos Bay, Portugal (August 1759).

Boscawen died of typhus fever while commanding the British fleet anchored at Quiberon Bay. Throughout his career he initiated efforts to improve the health and comfort of his seamen and marines, and was one of the first commanders to emphasize personal hygiene, lower-deck ventilation, quarantine for the sick, and fresh fruit and vegetables for those in hospital.

Stanley D.M. Carpenter

Bibliography

Creswell, John. *British Admirals of the Eighteenth Century: Tactics in Battle.* 1972.

Mackay, Ruddock F. *Admiral Hawke.* 1965.

Southworth, J.V.D. *The Age of Sails.* 1968.

Boston Massacre (1770)

When a British garrison arrived in Boston in 1768, relations between the residents and the British government began a serious decline. The garrison was sent to help enforce collection of **Charles Townshend**'s Townshend Duties (1767), which taxed imports of tea, glass, lead, paper, and paint. The duties represented a more aggressive governmental initiative to raise revenue from the American colonists. Irritated over the duties, the colonists now protested the presence of a standing army during peacetime.

Worsening relations between the garrison and the Bostonians turned into violence on 5 March 1770 when the "lobsterbacks" fired on a mob harassing and snowballing the Customs House guard, killing five people. The garrison was removed from the city; the troops involved, defended legally by John Adams (1735–1826, later second president of the United States), were acquitted of murder charges. But the event, stigmatized as a "massacre" by patriots and commemorated for a dozen years afterward in Boston, became a defining moment in the drift toward the **American Revolution**.

K.R. Wood

Bibliography

Thomas, P.D.G. *The Townshend Duties Crisis: The Second Phase of the American Revolution, 1767–1773.* 1987.

Zobel, Hiller. *The Boston Massacre.* 1970.

Boston Tea Party (1773)

When **Lord North** in 1770 addressed the unpopular Townshend Duties (which in 1767 had taxed American imports of tea, glass, lead, paper, and paint), he repealed all but the tea tax which assisted the financially strapped **East India Company**. With a new **Tea Act** (1773) he then allowed that company to ship its tea to America, eliminating the payment of English (though not American) duties.

Colonial merchants, organizing intracolonial resistance, called for a boycott against the tea's importation. In Boston, disguised "Sons of Liberty," led by Samuel Adams (1722–1803), their faces daubed to make them look like indians, boarded the company's three tea ships and dumped 340 tea chests into Boston Harbor (16 Dec. 1773). This destruction of property sent to the colonies by legal authority of King and Parliament was the culminating event in a series of acts of revolutionary defiance. North responded with the Coercive (or "Intolerable") Acts (1774), which closed the port of Boston and dissolved the Massachusetts assembly. The colonies responded by forming the First Continental Congress. Not long afterward the **War of American Independence** began in Massachusetts.

K.R. Wood

Bibliography

Labaree, Benjamin W. *The Boston Tea Party.* 1964.

Thomas, P.D.G. *The Townshend Duties Crisis: The Second Phase of the American Revolution, 1767–1773.* 1987.

Ward, Harry M. *The American Revolution: Nationhood Achieved, 1763–1788.* 1995.

Boswell, James (1740–1795)

Long famous for his biography of **Samuel Johnson**, Boswell is now appreciated also for his extensive autobiographical journals, which were not found and published until the 20th century.

Boswell was a proud offspring of the old Scottish family of Auchinleck. He acquired cosmopolitan tastes during his

James Boswell

years in **London** and on the Continent, married his cousin Margaret Montgomery (1738–1789), and practiced law in **Edinburgh**. On frequent visits to London he became friendly with Johnson, **Reynolds**, **Goldsmith**, and Edmond Malone (1741–1812). Increasingly Anglophile, he settled in London in 1786.

Boswell's *Life of Johnson* (1791), far longer than any prior **biography**, combines the depiction of Johnson as stoic Christian hero and consummate Englishman with minute details about his opinions, idiosyncrasies, and relations with contemporaries. Particularly striking are the "conversations"—snatches of dialogue between Boswell, the deliberately naive questioner, and Johnson, the master of common sense and wit. Of special interest also are dramatic scenes such as Boswell's first meeting with Johnson, and Johnson's interview with **George III**. The *Life,* though now criticized for some inaccuracies, quickly achieved the status of a popular classic.

Boswell's private journals reveal his experiences and shifting moods with great frankness, and also record contemporary social and intellectual life. Highlights are his attachment to Johnson, his sexual exploits, his interviews with Rousseau and Voltaire in 1764, his vain pursuit of unwilling heiresses, and his legal efforts on behalf of a certain sheepstealer. The later journals record Boswell's futile attempts to enter politics in the train of the brutal Lord Lonsdale (1736–1802) while struggling, with Malone's support, to finish the *Life.* Boswell mined his journals for matter to include in other publications—*An Account of Corsica* (1768) about his visit to the Corsican freedom-fighter Pasquale Paoli (1725–1807), and *The Journal of a Tour to the Hebrides* (1785) about his visit to **Scotland** with the notoriously anti–Scottish Johnson.

Most of Boswell's writings express his staunch monarchism, hero worship, and patriarchal attitudes. His journals also reveal the ambitions, failings, inconsistencies, and self-absorption of an unheroic sensual man. His intellectual makeup thus combines the political conservatism of the earlier Hanoverian era with the growing individualism and subjectivity of the later.

Marlies K. Danziger

Bibliography

Brady, Frank. *James Boswell: The Later Years.* 1984.

Buchanan, David. *The Treasure of Auchinleck: The Story of the Boswell Papers.* 1974.

Clingham, Greg. *James Boswell: The Life of Johnson.* 1992.

———, ed. *New Light on Boswell: Critical and Historical Essays on the Occasion of the Bicentenary of "The Life of Johnson."* 1991.

Pottle, Frederick A. *James Boswell: The Earlier Years.* 1966.

Simpson, Kenneth. *The Protean Scot: The Crisis of Identity in Eighteenth-Century Scottish Culture.* 1988.

Spacks, Patricia Meyer. *Imagining a Self: Novel and Autobiography in Eighteenth-Century England.* 1976.

Vance, John, ed. *Boswell's "Life of Johnson": New Questions, New Answers.* 1985.

See also Autobiography and Confession

Boulton, Matthew (1728–1809)

Boulton's comment to **James Boswell**, visiting his Soho factory, is famous: "I sell here, sir, what all the world desires to have—*power.*" Boulton, a farseeing industrialist and engineer, was the chief founder of the steam engine industry. Born into a manufacturing family of silver stampers in **Birmingham**, he succeeded his father in business. A judicious marriage and fat dowry enabled him to establish the famous Soho works, which made his name as a producer of high-quality metalworks.

Although he had experimented on steam devices to expand the power sources for the Soho manufactory, his crucial association with **James Watt** was due to fortuitous circumstances. Watt's partner in the steam engine **patent**, **John Roebuck**, was financially desperate by 1773; his ultimate bankruptcy enabled Boulton to buy Roebuck's share in the patent and to move Watt and his family to Birmingham. Through carefully cultivated political connections, Boulton and Watt were able to secure the patent for a period of 30 years, though the flagrant activities of engine pirates, and the infringement of the patent, forced an aggressive suit in the courts.

Both Boulton and Watt were Fellows of the **Royal Society** and active members of the **Lunar Society** of Birmingham. Boulton's remarkable business acumen encompassed an exceedingly wide range of interests, including the construction of engines for pumping, stamping, and manufacturing; the recruitment and control of large numbers of skilled metalworkers; and concerns in milling, **metallurgy**, and chlorine bleaching. Boulton and Watt laid the foundation for a remarkable partnership that by itself was to construct almost 500 steam engines by 1800.

Larry Stewart

Bibliography

Dickinson, H.W. *Matthew Boulton.* 1936.

Hills, Richard L. *Power from Steam: A History of the Stationary Steam Engine.* 1989.

Musson, A.E., and Eric Robinson. *Science and Technology in the Industrial Revolution.* 1969.

Schofield, Robert E. *The Lunar Society of Birmingham: A Social History of Provincial Science and Industry in Eighteenth Century England.* 1963.

See also Chemical Industry; Science, Technology, and Invention; Steam Engines; Wilkinson, John

Bow Street Runners

Britain possessed no effective police force prior to the 19th century. The first step toward the establishment of a public constabulary was taken by the novelist **Henry Fielding**, Justice of the Bow Street Magistrate's Office from 1748, who in 1749 appointed six voluntary "thief-takers," two of whom were always to be on call at his court. These men, who acquired the name of Bow Street Runners only at the end of the century, worked part-time and without uniform, and retained in addition to their modest stipend of a guinea a week a share of the reward money payable for convictions of criminals they helped to detect and apprehend (a **highwayman**, for example, brought a £40 reward).

As officials supplementing the inadequate **law enforcement** provided by the parishes in the persons of constables and watchmen, the Runners quickly achieved success against various gangs, and overcame suspicions aroused by their resemblance to the notorious and corrupt private thief-takers. On the death of Henry Fielding in 1754 his half-brother **John Fielding** succeeded to his post and carried on the promotion and expansion of the Runners both in his court and through published writings.

In 1757 John Fielding acquired a grant of £400 a year from secret service funds and authorization to operate outside the city. His object was to extend foot patrols to include the crime-ridden highways on the capital's outskirts. This was not fully achieved until 1805, however, when the Bow Street horse patrol was established and empowered to patrol up to 20 miles from **London**. With the passage of the Metropolitan Police Act of 1829 the days of the Bow Street Runners were numbered, and their separate existence came to an end in 1839.

Daniel Statt

Bibliography

Beattie, J.M. *Crime and the Courts in England, 1660–1800.* 1986.
Critchey, T.A. *A History of Police in England and Wales, 900–1966.* 1967.
Fielding, Henry. *An Enquiry Into the Causes of the Late Increase of Robbers.* 1751.
Fielding, John. *An Account of the Origin and Effects of a Police.* 1758.
Hay, Douglas, and Francis Snyder, eds. *Policing and Prosecution in Britain, 1750–1850.* 1989.
McLynn, Frank. *Crime and Punishment in Eighteenth-Century England.* 1989.
Radzinowicz, Leon. *History of English Criminal Law and Its Administration from 1750.* 4 vols. 1948–1968.

See also Crime; Judicial System

Bowdler, Thomas (1754–1825)

Bowdler, though an energetic philanthropist and **prison reformer**, is best known for his abridged version of Shakespeare (1818). Born in **Bath**, he studied **medicine** at St. Andrews (1770) and **Edinburgh** (1776), but spent his spare time in literary and political circles. He was a frequenter of **Elizabeth Montagu**'s salon and belonged to the **Proclamation Society**, whose purpose was to campaign against impiety and vice. His rationale for changing Shakespeare's text, as well as biblical Scriptures and his revised version of **Gibbon**'s *Rise and Fall of the Roman Empire* (1826), was that "if any word or expression is of such a nature that the first impression it excites is an impression of obscenity, that word ought not to be spoken nor written or printed; and, if printed, it ought to be erased." He thus expurgated or "bowdlerized" all those phrases he considered offensive. His name, suggesting moral censorship and the aggressive **Evangelical** transformation of **manners and morals** in the early 19th century, has become part of the language.

Elisabeth W. Joyce

Bibliography

Perrin, Noel. *Dr. Bowdler's Legacy: A History of Expurgated Books in England and America.* 1969; rpt. 1992.

See also Censorship; Shakespeare Industry

Bowles, William Lisle (1762–1850)

A poet and critic, Bowles was important as a transitional literary figure between **Neoclassicism** and **Romanticism**. Contemporary reception of his writing illustrates key themes in Romantic notions of poetic genius and the articulation of the **sublime**.

Bowles was born at King's Sutton, Northamptonshire. Before completing his degree (1792) at Trinity College, Oxford, he studied at Winchester as a student of **Joseph Warton**, poet and author of *Essays on the Genius and Writings of Pope* (1756). His career in the church was successful; he became chaplain to the Prince Regent in 1818.

Bowles's most popular volume was his *Fourteen Sonnets Written Chiefly on Picturesque Spots During a Journey* (1789). Eight editions were published by 1805. Influenced by **Cowper**, **Goldsmith**, **Gray**, and Warton, Bowles's **poetry** often evinces a sense of **melancholy** and **sentimental** reflection. Many of his poems are meditations on the transience and isolation of the human condition. Later, more political works display his patriotic feeling for England and his enmity toward **France**.

Reaction to Bowles's poetry varied. His revival of the sonnet form formatively influenced the **Lake School of Poets**; in his *Biographia Literaria* (1817), **Coleridge** hailed Bowles as "the first who combined natural thought with natural diction." Conversely, **Byron** in his *English Bards and Scotch Reviewers* (1809) dubbed him the "maudlin prince of mournful sonneteers."

In 1806 Bowles published a ten-volume edition of the works of **Pope**, its critical preface challenging Pope's poetic merits. He then wrote *The Invariable Principles of Poetry* (1819), which prompted Byron to respond in defense of Pope and his methods. The controversy illustrates the Romantics' concern with the concept of the sublime and with how it is aesthetically achieved. Bowles argued strictly for the supremacy of natural imagery and diction in poetry; Byron and others asserted that in some cases, art and artificial effects can more successfully approach sublimity.

Bowles also wrote *The Battle of the Nile* (1799), *The Sea of Discovery* (1805), *The Missionary* (1822), and *St. John in Patmos* (1833). Though not exemplary, his poetry and **literary criticism** furnish yardsticks by which to examine preferred poetic forms and debated aesthetics in Romantic literature.

Dominique Calapai

Bibliography

Bowles, William Lisle. *Fourteen Sonnets.* 1789; rpt. in Donald H. Reiman, ed., *The Romantic Context: Poetry.* 1978.

Cooper, Howard. "William Lisle Bowles: A Wiltshire Parson and His Place in Literary History." *Hatcher Review.* Vol. 3, pp. 316–322.

Gilfillan, George, ed. *The Poetical Works of William Lisle Bowles with Memoir, Critical Dissertation and Explanatory Notes.* 2 vols. 1855.

Greever, Garland, ed. *A Wiltshire Parson and His Friends: The Correspondence of William Lisle Bowles.* 1926.

Van Rennes, Jacob J. *Bowles, Byron and the Pope Controversy.* 1966.

See also Augustan; Picturesque Movement

Boyce, William (1711–1779)

Boyce was a leading composer and organist. He studied with Maurice Greene (1696–1755) and Johann Christoph Pepusch (1667–1752), and at Cambridge University became a Doctor of Music (1749). In 1757 he succeeded Greene as Master of the King's Musick, and in 1758 also became an organist of the Chapel Royal.

Boyce chiefly composed **vocal music**: anthems, odes, and theatrical music. From 1749 to 1751 he worked for **David Garrick** at the Theatre Royal, Drury Lane. His **operas** include *The Chaplet* (1749) and *The Shepherd's Lottery* (1751). As Master of the King's Musick he composed annual New Year and birthday odes for **George II**. He published some of the overtures to these in his *Eight Symphonies* (1760) and *Twelve Overtures* (1770): the first set was successful, but the second proved too old-fashioned and failed. Boyce also took over Greene's unfinished collection of **church music**, much of it Elizabethan and Jacobean, which he published as *Cathedral Music* (1760–1773).

Boyce's music is vigorous and attractive. His style changed little throughout his life, perhaps partly because of his encroaching deafness. His orchestration is meticulous and conservative; his forms and textures remained essentially baroque.

Jane Girdham

Bibliography

Cudworth, Charles L. "Boyce and Arne: 'The Generation of 1710.'" *Music and Letters.* Vol. 41, pp. 136–145.

———. "The English Symphonists of the Eighteenth Century." *Proceedings of the Royal Musical Association.* Vol. 78, pp. 31–51. Appendix: "Thematic Index of English Eighteenth-Century Overtures and Symphonies." 1953.

Fiske, Roger. *English Theatre Music in the Eighteenth Century.* 1986.

Hawkins, John. "Memoirs of Dr. William Boyce," in William Boyce, ed., *Cathedral Music.* 2nd ed., 1788. Vol. 1, pp. i–xi.

Johnstone, H. Diack. "The Genesis of Boyce's *Cathedral Music.*" *Music and Letters.* Vol. 56, pp. 26–40.

McGuinness, Rosamond. *English Court Odes, 1660–1820.* 1971.

See also Music

Boyne, Battle of the (1690)

This victory near the river Boyne brought the defeat of the Stuart cause in **Ireland**. On 1 July 1690 (later celebrated on 12 July) near Drogheda an army commanded by King William III defeated French and Irish forces led by the deposed King James II. William III's victory secured his Protestant monarchy in England. As to Ireland, **penal laws** greatly restricting the liberties and opportunities of Irish **Catholics** were enacted; for example, not until the passage of **Catholic Relief Acts** in the 1780s could they buy or lease land.

To the victorious Protestants, William III, his ancestral title of Prince of Orange, and "the Boyne" henceforth became watchwords of liberation from despotism; marches, banners, paintings, songs, glassware, and pottery figurines memorialized William's victory. But "the Boyne" was employed not only against Catholics; the men of the **Anglo-Irish Protestant Ascendancy** later often invoked it and the Orange cause to resist English efforts to restrict Irish trade and to limit the independence of the **Irish Parliament**. The **Irish Rebellions** of the 1790s to grant Catholics political and religious liberties provoked among some Protestants the formation of the **Orange Order** (1795), a group that opposed these goals with increasing militancy.

Robert D. McJimsey

Bibliography

Cathcart, Rex. "Ireland and King Billy: Usage and Abusage." *History Today.* Vol. 38, pp. 40–45.

Hill, Jacqueline R. "Popery and Protestantism, Civil and Religious Liberty: The Disputed Lessons of Irish History." *Past and Present.* Vol. 118, pp. 96–129.

Senior, Hereward. *Orangism in Ireland and Britain, 1795–1836.* 1966.

Simms, J.G. *Jacobite Ireland.* 1969.

Bradley, James (1693–1762)

Bradley, "the founder of modern observational astronomy," was born in Sherborne and educated at Oxford where, after a short clerical career, he became professor of astronomy (1721). In 1725, continuing earlier experiments of Robert Hooke (1635–1703), he made one of the most important astronomical discoveries of the 18th century.

Bradley first fixed a large telescope to a chimney stack on the Kew residence of his friend, Samuel Molyneux (1689–1728). With this, carefully measuring the apparent northward and southward wanderings of the star Gamma Draconis, which appears to pass nearly overhead in London's latitude, he discovered the aberration of starlight. This is an illusory optical effect produced by the combined action of the velocity of light from a star and the moving earthly position of the star's observer. By formulating his discovery into the law of the "constant of aberration," Bradley was able to provide the first empirical evidence for the Copernican heliocentric theory that the earth actually did *move* (which hitherto had been supported only by conceptual and mathematical arguments), as well as to confirm the velocity of light at 183,000 miles per second, and to help improve the accuracy of later measurements of star positions.

Bradley communicated his discovery to the **Royal Society** in a letter (1729) to his friend and patron **Edmond Halley**, Royal Astronomer. He was appointed to succeed Halley at his death (1742). In 1748 he published his second great astronomical discovery, scarcely less complicated than the first. This also dealt with apparent oscillations of the stars, an effect he explained to be the result of slight motions of the Earth's axis (nutation), initiated by the stronger pull of the moon at the Earth's poles than at the equator.

At Greenwich, Bradley lavishly refurbished the Observatory and extended its international reputation. His varied work proved useful to his friend the astronomer George Parker, Earl of Macclesfield (1697–1764), in his successful campaign for **calendar reform** (1752). His later years were capped with honors from foreign and domestic scientific societies.

Thomas D. Veve

Bibliography

Abetti, G. *The History of Astronomy.* 1954.

Dictionary of National Biography, s.v. "Bradley, James."

Hall, A.R. *The Scientific Revolution, 1500–1800.* 1954.

Jacob, M.C. *The Newtonians and the English Revolution, 1689–1720.* 1976.

Rigaud, S.P., ed. *Miscellaneous Works and Correspondence of James Bradley, D.D.* 1832.

See also Herschel, William; Science, Technology, and Invention

Brand [Hollis], Thomas (1719–1804)

A central figure in the **radicalism** of the era of George III, Thomas Brand was the son of a prosperous **London** businessman who became a landed gentleman. He studied at **Glasgow** University, where he met his future lifelong friend, Thomas Hollis (1720–1774), a prominent figure in left-wing political circles. Sharing his friend's classical republican or **commonwealthman** ideas and supporting American radicalism, he became a friend of **Benjamin Franklin** as well as of Thomas Jefferson (1743–1826) and John Adams (1735–1826). On Hollis's death (1774), Brand inherited his fortune and adopted his surname.

A sociable man, Brand Hollis kept an open house for his radical friends, among them **John Jebb**, **Major John Cartwright**, **William Godwin**, and John Disney (1746–1816), who eventually inherited his fortune. As a **rational dissenter** he supported **Theophilus Lindsey**'s Essex Street Unitarian Chapel, helped to found Hackney Academy in 1786, and was an active member of the committee for the repeal of the **Test and Corporation Acts** (1787–1791). Equally, he was an inveterate supporter of parliamentary reform, a founder of the **Society for Constitutional Information** (1780) and frequent chairman of its meetings, a committee member of the Westminster Association, and subsequently a member of the **Society of the Friends of the People** (1792–1794) and Society of Friends to the Liberty of the Press (1792–1793). He was also a prominent member of the London Revolution Society. Brand advocated universal male suffrage and annual elections. but in the context of the 1790s he was a moderate reformer, believing in political rather than social equality.

Martin Fitzpatrick

Bibliography

Baylen, Joseph O., and Norbert J. Gossman, eds. *Biographical Dictionary of Modern British Radicals.* Vol. 1. 1979.

Bonwick, Colin. *English Radicals and the American Revolution.* 1977.

Robbins, Caroline. "Thomas Brand Hollis (1719–1804)." *Proceedings of the American Philosophical Society.* Vol. 97, pp. 239–247.

———. *The Eighteenth Century Commonwealthman: Studies in the Transmission, Development and Circumstances of English Liberal Thought from the Restoration of Charles II until the War with the Thirteen Colonies.* 1959.

Brewing and Public Houses

The 18th-century brewing industry was transformed by the emergence of large, competitive, commercial breweries, eager to supply the growing urban populations' demand for beer. **London** became the most important center of mass production. The entrepreneurial firms of **Whitbread**, **Courage**, Barclay, Perkins, Calvert, Bass, Worthington, Allsopp, Charrington, Truman, and Guinness of **Dublin** were all established in this period, some with financial backing from **Quakers**. Several brewers became M.P.s.

In **Scotland**, important firms such as J & R Tennent of **Glasgow**, George Younger of Alloa, and **William Younger** and Archibald Campbell of **Edinburgh**, were also founded. The traditional, semidomestic publican brewers who produced beer for their own consumption or for sale in their taverns coexisted with commercial breweries, particularly in country districts, though their numbers gradually declined by the 19th century.

Brewing had been important economically since the Middle Ages. It consumed a large share of agricultural produce, thereby giving employment to **farmers** and maltsters. It also provided government revenue from **taxes**. In 1805, one-seventh of all national revenue came from duties levied on malt, hops, and beer. Acts of Parliament strictly regulated ingredients, malting, and the beer-related excise duties. Many such laws were unpopular. Introduction of a **malt tax** in Scotland after the **Act of Union** (1707) led to serious riots (1725).

The brewing process is relatively simple, but susceptible to contamination by microorganisms. Ground, malted barley is mixed with hot water. This liquid (liquor) is next boiled with hops to give its bitter flavor; then cooled, injected with yeast to induce fermentation, cleared of sediment, and finally matured in wooden barrels or large vats. In the Hanoverian period, spent malt went for animal feed, whereas excess yeast was sold to bakers and distillers. Strong, pale, and brown ales; porter, stout, and weak table beers were the standard products, often safer to drink than local water. There were also regional variations, such as Scottish "twopenny," which was very weak.

From Hogarth's "Beer Street," 1751

By the 18th century the terms *ale* and *beer* lost their original meanings and were confusingly interchangeable. Ale was originally an unhopped brew; whereas beer, which was hopped, had been introduced by Flemish brewers in the 15th century.

Breweries were situated near sources of good water, normally supplied by deep wells. Their extensive complexes of buildings included maltings (in Scotland), the brewhouse, cooperage, stables, warehouses, and offices. The workforce consisted of brewers, managers, coopers, clerks, delivery men, and laborers. Many horses were required for deliveries; the firm of Samuel Whitbread (1720–1796) kept 100 in 1796.

The introduction of a new beer—porter—by Ralph Harwood of Shoreditch (1722), had a profound effect on the industry. This dark, "black," highly hopped beer became the staple drink in London and spread rapidly throughout the whole country. This led to the expansion of porter breweries, better organization, and larger-scale production, enabling London porter brewers, in particular, to become rich. In 1796 Whitbread's was the first brewery to produce 100,000 barrels of porter in one season. Porter brewing was capital-intensive because the product had to mature for at least six months in huge vats, some capable of holding 20,000 barrels. In 1814 a gigantic vat burst at Meux's Horseshoe Brewery, killing eight people.

The need to produce greater quantities of beer more efficiently and economically led brewers to seek technical innovations to produce beer of consistent quality and taste. The introduction of the brewing thermometer and saccharometer enabled accurate measurements to be taken. Refrigeration and controlled fermentation permitted year-round brewing, instead of from October to May. Isinglass (made from fish bladders) removed the sediment from beer and left it clear. **Steam engines** made by **Boulton** and **Watt** pumped beer through the brewery faster, thus increasing output. By 1800, Whitbread and Barclay-Perkins were each producing 200,000 barrels.

By 1750, Scottish and English beers were being exported to **North America**, the **West Indies**, the Baltic, Ireland, and Europe. Domestic markets, principally public houses within 5 miles were supplied by horse and cart. **Canals** and river transport were used to move beer farther afield.

Alehouses (as they were mostly called in the Hanoverian period), or public houses ("pubs"), had long been an integral part of village and town life. These ranged enormously in quality—from respectable taverns or **coaching** inns providing food and lodgings, to dirty alehouses frequented by criminals and prostitutes. Inns were marked by hanging signs, their names derived from many sources—heraldic devices, the local landowner's name, religious themes, the local countryside. Taverns, the early equivalent of modern restaurants, were not only drinking sites but meeting places used by lawyers, **merchants**, and politicians to conduct business—some parliamentary petitions, such as the Feathers Tavern Petition (1772) requesting parliamentary action concerning the **Church of England**'s articles of faith, took their names from those taverns. They often harbored **clubs**. They served beer, ale, wine, brandy, rum, gin, and whisky. Spirits were often smuggled in from **France**. Claret was popular in Edinburgh, as were raw oysters and porter. Alehouses, by contrast, could not serve spirits. Licences were granted by magistrates, who often could be corrupted by bribes.

By 1800 in England (not Scotland) many pubs were either owned or "tied" to particular breweries by loans on the one side, exclusive agreements to sell specific products on the other. But this practice was considered restrictive and, in an attempt to create more free trade and encourage the drinking of beer instead of cheap gin, the Beer House Act was passed in 1830. This act abolished the duty on beer and allowed any rate-payer to sell beer on his own premises by purchasing a licence for 2 guineas. Within a few years, 40,000 new beer houses had been established, an undesirable outcome curbed by later legislation.

Alma Topen

Bibliography

Bickerdyke, John. *The Curiosities of Ale and Beer.* 1886.

Donnachie, I. *A History of the Brewing Industry in Scotland.* 1979.

Gourvish, T.R., and R.G. Wilson. *The British Brewing Industry, 1830–1980.* 1994.

Haydon, Peter. *The English Pub: A History.* 1994.

Jackson, M.A. *The English Pub.* 1976.

Mathias, P. *The Brewing Industry in England, 1700–1830.* 1959.

Stuart, M.W. *Old Edinburgh Taverns.* 1952.

See also Commerce, Domestic; Drink Industries; Drinking

Bridgewater, 3rd Duke of (Francis Egerton) (1736–1803)

Bridgewater was the "Father of the Canal Age." Frail as a child, he acquired his title when only 12, owing to the death of his brother, John, 2nd duke. He also inherited, along with his place in the **House of Lords**, control of two seats in the **Commons**. In politics Bridgewater generally supported whatever ministry was in office, though he lined up against the more liberal Rockingham **Whigs** when he opposed repeal of the **Stamp Act** (1766) and the **Fox-North Coalition**'s India Bill (1783). After 1783 he steadily supported **Pitt the Younger**.

He is chiefly remembered for his role in economic development. The high cost of transporting bulk **coal** from Bridgewater's estate at Worsley to **Manchester** some 10 miles away led him to employ **James Brindley** to design and build what became known as the Bridgewater **Canal**. At that time, this was a very remarkable and costly engineering project. The canal even carried coal on an aqueduct high over the Irwell valley from Bridgewater's mines to the city, and reduced freight rates by half. No sooner was the canal opened (1761) than Bridgewater embarked upon a much more daunting project—obtaining parliamentary authority (1762) to build a waterway three times as long, over obstacles still more formidable, linking **Liverpool** to Manchester (completed in 1772). Because he personally provided much of the capital for these canals, Bridgewater lived abstemiously until great sums began rolling in from the high volumes of coal, textiles, and **agricultural** products carried on them. Bridgewater thus helped himself as he helped these two great **cities** of southern Lancashire to communicate and prosper.

George F. Clements

Bibliography

Dyos, H.J., and D.H. Aldcroft. *British Transport.* 1974.

Hadfield, Charles. *British Canals.* 1969.

Malet, Hugh. *The Canal Duke: A Biography of Francis, 3rd Duke of Bridgewater.* 1961.

Mather, F.C. *After the Canal Duke: A Study of the Industrial Estates Administered by the Trustees of the Third Duke of Bridgewater in the Age of Railway Building, 1825–1872.* 1970.

Ward, J.R. *The Finance of Canal Building in Eighteenth-Century England.* 1974.

See also Transport, Inland

Brindley, James (1716–1771)

Mistakenly described as illiterate, "Schemer" Brindley ranks among the greatest of the early civil engineers if only because of his versatility. In 1733 he began a 7-year apprenticeship with Abraham Bennett, millwright, in Staffordshire, where he made his reputation as a skilled and ingenious workman on the main tasks of building and maintaining wind- and watermills, and making and repairing farm equipment.

After Bennett died, Brindley established his own business in Leek. But, attracted by the opportunities presented by the industrial development of the Potteries, he later rented a workshop from **Wedgewood** in Burslem and gradually widened his industrial experience—draining **mines**, erecting **steam engines**, and building flint mills.

James Brindley

However, it is as a **canal** engineer that Brindley is most recognized. He was commissioned to survey the Trent and Mersey Canal route linking the Potteries with **Liverpool** and Hull (1757–1758), and was employed by the **Duke of Bridgewater** to construct a canal between Bridgewater's coal mines at Worsley and the **textile industry** in **Manchester** (1759). The Bridgewater Canal, 10 miles long and employing several novel features (a subterranean channel, an aqueduct), brought fame and fortune to Brindley and also inaugurated the "Canal Age." Inland navigation companies and canal promoters flocked to secure his services or to consult him. Thus Brindley, having connections with 22 proposals, in effect masterminded the main pattern of Britain's inland waterways linking the Mersey, the Trent, the Severn, and the Thames. He and his assistants provided the canal-building expertise that industrializing Britain required and, after Brindley's death, provided the continuity with the early **railway** age.

John Butt

Bibliography

Ashton, T.S. *An Economic History of England: The 18th Century.* 1955.

Boucher, Cyril T.G. *James Brindley, Engineer, 1716–1772.* 1968.

Hadfield, Charles, ed. *The Canals of the British Isles.* 8 vols. 1966–1977.

Mullineux, Frank. *The Bridgewater Canal.* 1959.

Smiles, Samuel. *The Lives of the Engineers.* Vol. 1. 1862.

See also Transport, Inland

Bristol

Bristol was one of the chief mercantile and port cities of

Hanoverian Britain. Its prosperity derived from its favorable location for both the European and transatlantic sea trades, although its dominance of those trades was surpassed by the dramatic growth of **Liverpool**.

The **city** underwent dramatic change over the course of the 18th century. Its most dramatic growth came before the accession of **George III** (1760). In 1700, with perhaps 22,000 inhabitants, Bristol was Britain's third largest city after **London** and **Norwich**, but by 1750 it had surpassed Norwich and possessed a **population** of about 50,000. By the early 19th century, however, Bristol had fallen behind the dynamically growing industrial centers farther north. The city expanded to the north and west, though from the 1760s its ancient core underwent extensive rebuilding. Bristol could never lay claim to the elegance in outward appearance of neighboring **provincial towns** such as **Bath**, though Queen Square, completed in 1727, was an early example of **Georgian** refinement. Its inhabitants, in their absorption in trade, were said to be lacking in politeness.

Unrivaled among the provincial ports at the opening of the Hanoverian period, Bristol experienced absolute growth but relative decline as other ports expanded faster in terms of volume of trade and tons of **shipping** owned. The absolute growth was formidable: from about 20,000 tons of merchant shipping in overseas trade to 76,000 over the course of the century. Yet by 1800 Bristol had slipped to eighth among the outports in volume of overseas trade. Bristol is famous for its triangular trade in **slaves** and sugar with America, but in fact the commodities involved in its **overseas commerce** were considerably more diversified, and mostly of high value: **tobacco**, spices, snuff, **textiles**. Moreover, Bristol's trade was varied in its sources and destinations, serving a thriving **coastal** traffic to the ports on the Bristol Channel as well as a very substantial trade with Ireland. In 1764, for example, of 343 ships passing through the port, 85 went to Europe, 53 to the **West Indies**, 52 to North America, 32 to **Africa**, and 107 to Ireland. Nor did Bristol's economy fail to become diversified over the period, as the **domestic commerce** of the city increased, and its role as a service center expanded. The first **bank** in Bristol was established in 1750.

Bristol was notorious for the turbulence of its politics and the chauvinism of its inhabitants. As a close **borough** corporation of 42 members, it was governed by a narrow mercantile oligarchy. The city nevertheless had a vigorous political life, and its large electorate of several thousand freemen was factionalized and influenced by pressure groups.

Daniel Statt

Bibliography

Corfield, P.J. *The Impact of English Towns, 1700–1800.* 1982.
Little, B. *The City and County of Bristol.* 1954.
McGrath, Patrick, ed. *Bristol in the Eighteenth Century.* 1972.
Morgan, Kenneth. *Bristol and the Atlantic Trade in the Eighteenth Century.* 1994.

British and Foreign School Society

In 1808 the **Quaker** chemist William Allen (1770–1843) and his friend Joseph Fox took over **Joseph Lancaster**'s Borough Road School and his campaign to educate masses of poor children. They formed the Institution for Promoting the British System of Education of the Labouring and Manufacturing Classes of Society of Every Religious Persuasion, renamed the British and Foreign School Society in 1814.

In factory towns this organization attempted to establish day schools that would teach basic subjects and assist in the moral regeneration of youth. Although intended to be nonsectarian, with both Anglicans and **dissenters** involved, it was dominated by the latter. The schools used Lancaster's so-called monitorial system, in which older students instructed small groups of younger ones while under the overall supervision of a schoolmaster. The society's successes led to the establishment (1811) of the Anglican **National Society for the Education of the Poor**, a competitor.

In 1833 Parliament responded to a growing demand for popular education by appropriating £20,000 for the construction of new schools. It funneled funds through both these societies to schools which after 1839 were visited by inspectors who reported to the Privy Council Committee on Education. The Newcastle Commission of 1858 reported that one-tenth (150,000) of the 1,566,000 total students then being taught, were educated in British and Foreign School Society schools.

David B. Mock

Bibliography

Armytage, W.H.G. *Four Hundred Years of English Education.* 1964.
McCann, Phillip, ed. *Popular Education and Socialization in the Nineteenth Century.* 1977.

See also Education, Elementary

British Linen Company

The history of this company, established in 1746, illustrates the risky and somewhat predatory character of Hanoverian **banking**. The company was designed to encourage the Scottish linen industry but was also given limited powers to engage in banking. It had the support of the **Royal Bank of Scotland**, some of whose directors served on its board. But as it did not enjoy great success in linens (small businesses proving more in tune with the needs of the trade), the company turned almost wholly to banking in order to survive. In the 1760s a plan was devised to put notes into circulation by giving cash credits to people in the linen industry. Agents were appointed to push the notes, particularly in the northeast of Scotland, though other bankers, encouraged by the **Bank of Scotland**, tried to drive the notes out of circulation. The plan failed, with the Bank of Scotland then recognizing British Linen notes (1771). These two major Scottish banks opposed Linen's plans for extension of its banking activities and managed to keep these in check. By the early 19th century, when both major banks had capital of £1.5 million, that of Linen remained at only £200,000.

A.J.G. Cummings

Bibliography

Checkland, S.G. *Scottish Banking: A History 1695–1973.* 1975.

Malcolm, C.A. *The British Linen Bank 1746–1946.* 1950.

British Museum

Reflecting the **Enlightenment** ideal of universal knowledge as well as the increasing fascination with **antiquities and ruins** that marked the Hanoverian era, the British Museum and Library became Britain's first comprehensive national public research museum. In the modern era it has shed its natural history and library divisions, but remains a preeminent British cultural institution and one of the great **museums and galleries** of the world.

Sir Hans Sloane provided that on his death (which occurred in 1753) the crown and hence the nation could purchase, for £20,000, his vast and varied collection of artifacts and books. The Foundation Act (1753) authorized the purchase, with needed funds to be raised by lottery. Joining the Sloane collection were the Sir Robert Bruce Cotton (1571–1631) collection, owned by the nation since 1700; and the manuscripts collection of Robert Harley, **Earl of Oxford**, and his brother Edward (1689–1741). The act established governance by trustees, among them the Archbishop of Canterbury, the Lord Chancellor, and the Speaker of the House of Commons. In 1756 the Royal Library was added to the collections; with it came the privilege of copyright deposit.

Montagu House, built in Bloomsbury near London in the 1670s, became the museum's first permanent building in 1759. Expansion was undertaken from 1804; a new **neoclassical** museum building, designed by Sir Robert Smirke (1781–1867) and begun in 1824, replaced Montagu House on the site. The famed domed Reading Room dates from 1854–1857.

This rebuilding was necessitated by numerous large additions to the collections throughout the period. Most notable were the Hamilton collection of Greek vases (1772), Egyptian artifacts acquired through the Treaty of Alexandria (1802), sculptures from the Temple of Apollo at Bassae (1815) and from the Parthenon at Athens (the **Elgin Marbles**, 1816); and the book collection of **George III** (1823).

Prior written application was required to visit the museum until 1810; the first unrestricted opening to the general public occurred in 1837.

Ron Rarick

Bibliography

Caygill, Marjorie. *The Story of the British Museum.* 1981.

———. *Treasures of the British Museum.* 1985.

Wilson, David, ed. *The Collections of the British Museum.* 1989.

Broad-Bottom Administration (1744–1754)

This Whig ministry of **Henry Pelham** and his brother the **Duke of Newcastle** was called the broad-bottom administration because it included men from varying political factions. After a 2-year period of instability the brothers gradually won the confidence of **George II** and gave him a stable, supportive government until the death of Pelham (March 1754), at which the agonized king cried, "I shall now have no more peace."

In 1742 **Sir Robert Walpole**'s opponents **William Pulteney** and **John Carteret** had succeeded him in power, but could make few changes, due to the king's dislike of **Tories** and the **Cobham** faction. When Pulteney chose to go to the **Lords** as Earl of Bath, leadership of the **Commons** passed to Pelham, who became first Lord of the Treasury and Chancellor of the Exchequer (1743). The Pelhams began to court the **Opposition**, bringing into their group **Chesterfield**, **Lyttelton**, **Sandwich**, **Anson**, **George Grenville**, **John Russell**, 4th Duke of Bedford, and (later) **Pitt the Elder**, among others. To break finally the influence of Carteret (now 1st Earl of Granville), who still had the king's ear, the brothers resigned (February 1746), as did some 45 others in their administration. When Bath and Granville were unable to form a new ministry because they were little liked or trusted, the king was forced to turn again to the Pelhams. He learned to rely on Henry Pelham almost as much as he had on Walpole.

P.J. Kulisheck

Bibliography

Coxe, William. *Memoirs of the Administration of the Right Honourable Henry Pelham.* 1829.

Owen, John B. *The Rise of the Pelhams.* 1957.

Williams, Basil. *Carteret and Newcastle.* 1966.

See also Whigs and Whiggism

Brooke, Frances (1724–1789)

Dramatist and novelist, Brooke was best known to her contemporaries for her immensely popular comic **operas** *Rosina* (1783) and *Marian* (1788). She was also the author of the first Canadian **novel**, *The History of Emily Montague* (1766), which took the epistolary form and reflected life in **Canada** in the 1760s. Other novels included *The History of Lady Julia Mandeville* (1769), *The Excursion* (1777), and *The History of Charles Mandeville* (a sequel to *Julia Mandeville,* published posthumously in 1790). Brooke also wrote two tragedies, *Virginia* (1756, never produced) and *The Siege of Sinope* (1781), which ran for 10 nights. Contemporary reviewers generally favored her works, praising her **sensibility** and **wit**.

Brooke was born into a clerical family in Lincolnshire. In 1756 she married the Rev. John Brooke, with whom she had a son. She moved to **Quebec** in 1763 but returned to England in 1768. Brooke knew most of the British women writers of her day and maintained friendships with **Fanny Burney**, **Hannah More**, and **Anna Seward**. From 1773 to 1778 she comanaged the Haymarket Opera House with actress Mary Ann Yates (1728–1787). In 1788 she returned to Lincolnshire, staying with her son until her death.

Mary Tiryak

Bibliography

Blaine, Virginia, et al. *Feminist Companion to Literature in*

English: Women Writers from the Middle Ages to the Present. 1990.
McMullen, Lorraine. *Life of Frances Brooke.* 1983.
Todd, Janet. *Dictionary of British and American Women Writers.* 1984.

See also Women in Literature

Brooke, Henry (1703–1783)

Brooke, Irish author and lawyer, though he wrote plays that were praised by **Garrick** and poetry admired by **Pope** and **Swift**, is best remembered as the author of *The Fool of Quality* (1765–1770), a **novel** in 5 volumes which appealed to the contemporary taste for sentimental literature.

Educated at **Trinity College, Dublin**, Brooke was also a political propagandist, for beside writing pamphlets during the 1750s and 1760s on issues of Irish constitutional rights and religious controversy, he penned two plays, a tragedy titled *Gustavus Vasa* (1739), and the satirical **opera** *Jack the Giant-Queller* (1748), which were suppressed by the government for their subversive content.

Rather like the sentimental novels of **Goldsmith**, **Sterne**, and **Mackenzie**, Brooke's *Fool* celebrates the man of "feeling" who combines powerful emotional **sensibility** with religious conviction and the highest moral standards.

Francis P. Wilson

Bibliography

Spacks, Patricia Meyer. *Desire and Truth: Functions of Plot in Eighteenth-Century English Novels.* 1990.
Todd, Janet. *Sensibility: An Introduction.* 1986.
Wright, Walter Francis. *Sensibility in English Prose Fiction, 1760–1814.* 1972.

Henry Brooke

William Broome

Broome, William (1689–1745)

Born of poor Cheshire farmers and educated at Eton and St. Johns, Cambridge, Broome was a polished versifier, scholar, and clergyman who collaborated with **Alexander Pope** and Elijah Fenton (1683–1730) on *The Odyssey* (1725–1726). He translated parts of *The Iliad* into blank verse in a collaboration with William Oldisworth (1680–1734) and John Ozell (*d.* 1743) (1712, 1714). Broome contributed to B.B. Lintot's (1675–1736) *Miscellaneous Poems and Translations* (1712), *Original Poems and Translations* by Aaron Hill (1685–1750), et al. (1714), and *Poems on Several Occasions,* edited by Pope (1717). Having helped Pope with **translations** for the notes to *The Iliad,* he translated eight books of *The Odyssey* and wrote the notes. Broome published two **sermons** (1723, 1737) and contributed translations of Anacreon's odes to the *Gentleman's Magazine* (1739–1740). Conventional and derivative, Broome's lyrical poetry was gathered in *Poems on Several Occasions* (1727), revised with additions in 1739.

James E. May

Bibliography

Barlow, T. Worthington. *Memoir of William Broome, LL.D. The Associate of Pope in the Translation of Homer's* Odyssey. *With Selections from His Works.* 1765.
Mack, Maynard. *Alexander Pope: A Life.* 1985.
Sherburn, George. *The Correspondence of Alexander Pope.* 1956.

Brothers, Richard (1757–1824)

Brothers, **millenarian** prophet of doom and of the second coming of Christ, proclaimed himself the prince of the Hebrews and pronounced **London** the New Jerusalem. In his *Revealed Knowledge of the Prophecies and Times* (1795) he described his visions foretelling the overthrow of the British monarchy by the revolutionary armies of **France**, a prelude to the return of Christ and the onset of the millennium. Born in **Newfoundland**, as a youth Brothers emigrated to England, where he was educated at Woolwich. He served in the **navy** and saw some action during the **War of American Independence**, but left with a **pension** and a devotion to prophecy. Brothers filled his later years with detailed preparations for the arrival of the New Jerusalem, concerning himself even with the design of uniforms, flags, banners, and other decorative touches appropriate to the event.

Jack Fruchtman, Jr.

Bibliography

Garrett, Clarke. *Respectable Folly: Millenarians and the French Revolution in France and England.* 1975.

Harrison, J.F.C. *The Second Coming: Popular Millenarianism, 1780–1850.* 1979.

See also Enthusiasm; Religious Revivalism

Brougham and Vaux, Baron (Henry Peter Brougham) (1778–1868)

Brougham was a leading **Whig** politician who made important contributions to the advancement of **education**, **law reform**, the **antislavery movement**, and political reform. Beginning his career as a lawyer, he later became M.P., Lord Chancellor, and a member of the **Grey** and **Melbourne** ministries (1830–1834).

Born in **Edinburgh** and educated at Edinburgh University, he was called to the bar in 1800. In 1802 he, **Francis Jeffrey**, and others founded the *Edinburgh Review*, one of the great **periodicals** of the age, known for its whiggish bent, seriousness, and literary excellence; Brougham was one of its most prodigious and versatile contributors. He moved to **London** in 1803 and became a member of the English bar in 1808. His political debut was as a pamphleteer and election organizer. Interested in antislavery activity, Brougham first attempted to gain a parliamentary seat as a **Tory** through the influence of **William Wilberforce**; and when he entered Parliament on the Whig side as a protégé of Lord Grey (1810), he forwarded Wilberforce's work by promoting a bill making participation in the **slave trade** punishable by **transportation** (1811).

In 1808 Brougham served as counsel for **Liverpool** merchants in their fight for repeal of the British **Orders in Council**. Though unsuccessful, his arguments before **Commons** established his reputation as an advocate and in 1812 he was able to get a parliamentary committee to investigate the matter, leading **Lord Castlereagh** to withdraw the Orders. In 1811 he built his reputation with contemporary **radicals** by securing the acquittal of John and **Leigh Hunt**, then under prosecution for their article condemning flogging in the military. Brougham later became legal adviser to **Queen Caroline** and helped to defend her in the annulment case tried in the **House of Lords** (1820), delivering a summation of great power and eloquence.

Henry Brougham

Brougham's greatest influence was in educational reform. In 1816 his Charities Inquiry Act established a royal commission to investigate abuses in the administration of educational charities. In 1820 he introduced (but failed to carry) a modified version of **Whitbread**'s earlier bill proposing a national system of elementary education. In 1825 he published *Practical Observations upon the Education of the People,* which sold 50,000 copies in a few weeks and went through 20 editions; here he urged that inexpensive publications be used to bring the new scientific knowledge to the working classes. Taking his own advice, Brougham helped to found (1826) the **Society for the Diffusion of Useful Knowledge** (its first publication in 1827 was his own essay on the "Pleasures and Advantages of Science"), and strongly supported the popular *Penny Magazine* also as a means of educating workers. In 1833 he was influential in the government's important decision to approve an annual grant of £20,000 to two societies that maintained schools for the education of poor children—the **British and Foreign School Society** (founded in 1807 by Anglicans and Nonconformists), and the **National Society** (founded in 1811 by the **Church of England**).

Brougham also played an important role, along with **Lord John Russell** and the poet **Thomas Campbell**, in forming (1825) a public utility company on Benthamite lines to raise money for a college. T.B. Macaulay (1800–1859), George Grote (1794–1871), **James Mill**, and other liberals and radicals supported the scheme, and in 1828 the **University of London** was founded to provide nondenominational and practical higher education for the sons of the industrial and commercial **middle classes**.

Audacious but unpredictable in politics, Brougham mediated between moderate Whigs and radicals. Hoping from 1812 to 1816 to replace **Sir Francis Burdett** as the chief parliamentary spokesman of the radicals, he worked with radical reformer **Francis Place** and the **Benthamites**. But when he returned to Commons in 1816 Brougham failed to promote any of the reforms they wanted, doing more instead for the commercial classes by leading their opposition to the property tax, which the ministry was forced to abandon in March 1816. Raised to the peerage and made Lord Chancellor in 1830, Brougham played an important role in forcing the **Reform Act** (1832) through the **House of Lords**, though he also tried to convince Grey to preserve a few pocket **boroughs**.

As Lord Chancellor (1830–1834), Brougham attacked the long delays (up to 20 years) in chancery court by simplifying procedures, creating new rules for the court, and setting up a new court to deal with bankruptcy. He also created the Central Criminal Court in London, removing some of the worst inefficiencies and confusions of the legal system.

In the 1840s Brougham urged repeal of the **corn laws**, but by this time his age and eccentricity were taking their toll. He spent much of his time in Cannes after 1838, helping to make it a favored seaside resort, driving about in his "brougham," the one-horse, four-wheeled carriage which he had designed.

Frank M. Baglione

Bibliography

Davis, H.W.C. *The Age of Grey and Peel.* 1964.
Dinwiddy, John R. *From Luddism to the First Reform Bill: Reform in England, 1810–1832.* 1986.
Hawes, Francis. *Henry Brougham.* 1957.
Hone, J.A. *For the Cause of Truth: Radicalism in London, 1807–1821.* 1982.
Stewart, Robert. *Henry Brougham.* 1985.
West, E.G. *Education and the Industrial Revolution.* 1975.
Williams, Gwyn. *Artisans and San-Culottes.* 1969.

See also Legal Profession

Brown, Lancelot ("Capability") (1715–1783)

Although many features of the gently serene English landscape garden had been invented and ingeniously employed by other designers, Brown combined them so successfully, and used his formula so widely, that he is now identified with the flourishing of a particularly characteristic style in Hanoverian **landscape architecture and design**.

Nicknamed "Capability" for his enthusiastic assessment of an estate's "capabilities," Brown typically surrounded the park of a country house with an irregular belt of trees, broken occasionally to admit an interesting view. A circuit walk threaded this belt with carefully manipulated views out to distant prospects and also back to the house. Lawns replaced parterres near the house and, dotted with clumps of trees (some the remnants of ancient avenues), ran down to the gently curving banks of a river or lake formed artificially by the damming of a smaller stream.

In the 1740s Brown began his career as a kitchen gardener for Richard Temple, Lord **Cobham**, at Stowe. While there he evidently helped transform the existing geometric pleasure gardens into the more natural style favored by Cobham and the versatile contemporary architect **William Kent**. By the 1750s his talent and affability had procured enough wealthy clients for him to establish his own practice at Hammersmith, near London. There he began to collaborate with master mason Henry Holland on **Palladian** architectural projects. Despite an attack by **Sir William Chambers**, who favored pseudo-Chinese intricacy over Brown's simplicity, he was highly successful both professionally and socially, improving between 120 and 140 estates during his career. One of his most famous landscapes is at Blenheim, where he dammed a small stream to create two lakes large enough to complement **Sir John Vanbrugh**'s massive bridge.

After his death, advocates of the **picturesque**, particularly Richard Payne Knight (1750–1824) and **Uvedale Price**, criticized Brown's "bare and bald" style, particularly his lawns which ran right up to the house, tight clumps of trees and shrubbery, and unadorned river banks. Most aspects of his style were defended by **Humphry Repton**, his greatest successor, who did, however, favor many more plantings of shrubbery and flowers around the house.

Anne Kapler McCallum

Bibliography

Hinde, Thomas. *Capability Brown: The Story of a Master Gardener.* 1987.
Hyams, Edward. *Capability Brown and Humphry Repton.* 1971.
Stoud, Dorothy. *Capability Brown.* 1950; rpt. 1975.
Turner, Roger. *Capability Brown and the Eighteenth Century.* 1985.

Brown, Thomas (1778–1820)

Brown, the last in the genuine line of Scottish common-sense philosophers, was the son of a parish clergyman in Kirkmabreck. He studied law, then **medicine**, gained his M.D. at **Edinburgh** in 1803, and began medical practice in 1806. His philosophical interests developed early. At age 18 he wrote his critical *Observations on the Zoonomia of E. Darwin* (1798). In 1804 he published *An Inquiry Into the Relation of Cause and Effect,* which began as a defense of **David Hume**'s ideas on causation and John Leslie's (1766–1832) espousal of them, and resulted in the enlarged editions of 1806 and 1818 as a detailed account of how Hume's ideas could be reconciled with religious belief and modified so as to answer effectively the caustic criticism of the great Scottish philosopher **Thomas Reid**.

In 1810 Brown became an Associate Professor with **Dugald Stewart** (formerly his teacher) in Moral Philosophy at the University of Edinburgh. He was a stimulating teacher. His popular lectures were published as *Lectures on the Philosophy of the Human Mind* (1820), with many subsequent editions. He was a founding member of the Academy of Physics (1797) and also an early contributor to the *Edinburgh Review,* where he attacked Immanuel Kant (1724–1804) in the **periodical**'s second number. Brown was influenced by the French Ideologues and was particularly interested in metaphysics and the philosophy of mind and science, where his writings were to provide a guiding influence to the "philosophic radicals" **James Mill** and **John Stuart Mill**, as well as other philosophers in the **empiricist** tradition.

Constantinos Athanasopoulos

Bibliography

Gilmour, Peter, ed. *Philosophers of the Enlightenment.* 1989.

Grave, S.A. *The Scottish Philosophy of Common Sense.* 1960.

Mills, John A. "Thomas Brown's Theory of Causation." *Journal of the History of Philosophy.* Vol. 22, pp. 207–227.

Stalley, R.F. "Common Sense and Enlightenment: The Philosophy of Thomas Reid." *Journal of the History of Philosophy.* Vol. 18, pp. 74–90.

Brummell, George Bryan ("Beau") (1778–1840)

Fashionable society during the **Regency** was dominated by the **aristocracy.** One of the characteristic figures of the age was the dandy, epitomized by Beau Brummell, who for a while dominated the London social scene and set the standard for the well-dressed gentleman.

Brummell's father had been private secretary to **Lord North.** In 1790 he sent his son to Eton, where the Prince of Wales (later **George IV**) noticed and befriended him. There he developed the traits of self-confidence, meticulous dress, and quick retort that made him popular. Friendship with the prince soon brought him a cornet's position in the latter's regiment, the 10th Hussars. Then taking army retirement (1798) and receiving his inheritance, he moved into his Mayfair bachelor's home and took up his calling as dictator of **fashion.**

Beau Brummell

His influence in the field of **clothing** extended even to the prince, whose coats he freely criticized. He popularized the double-breasted riding coat, trousers with straps at the bottom to ensure a tight fit, black riding boots, the tall hat, a large bow at the neck, and masses of immaculately clean, white linen. His taste was not foppish or extravagant, but moderate and stylish. It marked a pleasant transition from the elaborate, gentlemanly garb of the 18th century to the dull business wear of the 19th.

Brummell's amusing but impertinent manners and quick tongue were the subject of delicious gossip. He was capable of commanding the prince, 16 years his senior—"Wales! Ring the bell!" At length there was a rupture with the prince (1813), and **gambling** debts caused him to depart England for residence at Calais (1816). Although many old friends visited him there, and although he served as British consul at Caen (1830), his life was never happy again. His creditors encarcerated Brummell in a French jail for a brief period. By 1837 he had begun to show the signs of mental disability which left him unhappily spending his last years in a Caen asylum, ill attended and vilely clad.

Thomas D. Veve

Bibliography

Cole, Hubert. *Beau Brummell.* 1977.

Connely, Willard. *The Reign of Beau Brummell.* 1940.

Tenenbaum, Samuel. *The Incredible Beau Brummell.* 1967.

Woolf, Virginia. *Beau Brummell.* 1930, 1972.

Burdett, Sir Francis (1770–1844)

Burdett was one of the most prominent **radical** politicians of the early 19th century. A well-to-do baronet, he began a long and distinguished parliamentary career in 1796 by purchasing the seat of the rotten **borough** of Boroughbridge, Yorkshire. In 1802 and again in 1804 he ran unsuccessfully for a seat for Middlesex, a liberal **Whig** stronghold, but was returned in 1807 (thanks partly to the efforts of **Francis Place**) in one of the first victories of the reviving radical tradition so severely weakened by the national reaction against the **French Revolution.** He would remain in this seat for 30 years.

Burdett was an advocate of political reform. A champion of free speech, he worked to expose the abuses of power as well as to give voice to popular opposition to excessive **taxes** and the **war** with **France.** He criticized the **army**'s use of corporal **punishment,** investigated the maltreatment of political prisoners, and more than once was fined and jailed for his attacks on the official repression of protesters (e.g., in 1820 after the **Peterloo Massacre**).

In 1825 Burdett began to campaign for **Catholic Emancipation,** a cause that succeeded in 1829. Though he played a small role in the parliamentary **Reform Act** (1832), he was now losing his interest in radical politics, partly because of his intense dislike of **Daniel O'Connell.** From 1837 to his death in 1844 he represented North Wiltshire as a conservative. Because of his consistent support for parliamentary reform and

Sir Francis Burdett

freedom of speech, however, he is rightly associated with the tradition of radical **London** politics.

David B. Mock

Bibliography

Dinwiddy, John R. *From Luddism to the First Reform Bill: Reform in England, 1810–1832.* 1986.

Patterson, M.W. *Sir Francis Burdett and His Times (1770–1844).* 1931.

See also Elections and the Franchise

Burgh, James (1714–1775)

Burgh, a cousin of the historian **William Robertson**, was one of a group of **radical** political writers that included **Richard Price, Joseph Priestley**, and **Major John Cartwright**. He was born in Perthshire and educated at St. Andrews. His poor health prevented him from entering the ministry, and he was a failure in business. In 1747 he opened an academy at Stoke Newington. Burgh remained there for much of his life, writing copiously on education, oratory, morals, and politics. In 1771 he retired to Islington, where he died.

Burgh has been described as first a "moralist in Babylon," then a "moralist politicized." His *Britain's Remembrancer,* a work completed in the wake of the **Jacobite** uprising of 1745, lamented "our degenerate times and corrupt nation," and dwelt upon the moral significance of the **Forty-five**. He then spent some decades trying to enlist the king and other leaders in promoting national moral reformation. Losing faith in the top-down approach, he produced his magnum opus, *Political Disquisitions,* in 1775. In this wide-ranging essay he blasted parliamentary corruption and the evils of a standing **army**, and called for reform of the colonial system. Burgh attacked the severity of criminal **punishments** and the inadequacy of the **poor laws**, and emphasized the importance of sound manners and education. His book, intensely anti-aristocratic in outlook, demanded a "GRAND NATIONAL ASSOCIATION FOR RESTORING THE CONSTITUTION" and vaguely threatened mass action to restore liberty. His patriotic radicalism influenced the **Association movement** a few years later and the founders of the **Society for Constitutional Information** (1780).

Michael L. Oberg

Bibliography

Hay, Carla H. *James Burgh, Spokesman for Reform in Hanoverian England.* 1979.

Kramnick, Isaac. *Republicanism and Bourgeois Radicalism: Political Ideology in Late Eighteenth-Century England and America.* 1990.

Zebrowski, Martha K. "The Corruption of Politics and the Dignity of Human Nature: The Critical and Constructive Radicalism of James Burgh." *Enlightenment and Dissent.* Vol. 10, pp. 78–103.

See also Political Thought

Burghs, Scottish

The mercantile life of **Scotland**, both before and after the **Act of Union** (1707), was concentrated in the burghs or incorporated towns. It was through them that Scotland's import and export trades flowed, and also a large portion of available capital.

Prior to 1707, Scottish trade was based predominantly on the east coast. The access to British imperial markets under the banner of free trade following the union had a profound affect on the balance of power between the burghs. **Edinburgh** had traditionally been the most affluent burgh, reflected in its status as capital. The decades after the union witnessed the rise of the west, particularly **Glasgow**, some 50 miles away. Opportunities for successful **overseas commerce** with **North America** and the **West Indies** were ruthlessly exploited by Glasgow **merchants** and **entrepreneurs**. Transatlantic trade accelerated to unprecedented levels, notably in the **tobacco trade**, which earned successful Glasgow merchants the nickname "Tobacco Lords"; by the 1770s they controlled more of this trade than all other British ports combined. **Daniel Defoe** noted that the union had profited Glasgow's merchants "more than any other part of Scotland, for their trade is new form'd by it."

Glasgow's expansion facilitated the growth of other western ports and burghs, such as Dumbarton. In the east, the markets of the burghs were focused on Europe, particularly Norway, Sweden, the Baltic, and Holland. Linen manufacture and herring **fishing** accounted for a large part of their trade. Defoe concluded that Aberdeen was the dominant burgh on the east and the "third city" in Scotland after Edinburgh and Glasgow.

The internal politics of burghs were controlled by burgh councils. Prior to 1707, each royal burgh was entitled to send one commissioner to the Scottish Parliament, with the exception of Edinburgh (which could send two); the burghs were represented as a separate estate within the Scottish Parliament. After 1707, when Scotland's 33 counties began sending 30 representatives to the British Parliament in London, Edinburgh was allocated one parliamentary seat while the remaining 65 royal burghs were divided into 14 groups with one parliamentary seat apiece. (For example, Glasgow, Dumbarton, Renfrew and Rutherglen formed one such group.) The **Reform Act** (1832) maintained the same principle of 14 districts.

During much of the Hanoverian period, Scotland's burghs, like its counties, had small electorates that were often thoroughly dominated by entrenched elites headed by magnates like the **Dukes of Argyll**, the Earls of **Bute**, and **Henry Dundas**, who employed political **patronage** much as it was employed in England. Contemporary life in the western burgh of Irvine was vividly described by the novelist **John Galt** in *The Provost* (1822).

John Roach Young

Bibliography

Defoe, D. *A Tour Through the Whole Island of Great Britain.* 1724.
Devine, T.M. *The Tobacco Lords.* 1975.
Ferguson, W. *Scotland, 1689 to the Present.* 1977.
Keay, J., and J. Keay, eds. *Collins Encyclopaedia of Scotland.* 1994.
Rait, R.S. *The Parliaments of Scotland.* 1924.
Smout, T.C. *A History of the Scottish People 1560–1830.* 1969.

See also Boroughs; Elections and the Franchise; Municipal Corporations Act (1835)

Burgoyne, John (1722–1792)

Burgoyne was a general, dramatist, and politician chiefly remembered for his disastrous defeat at the **Battle of Saratoga** (1777) during the **War of American Independence**. Born and raised under circumstances that suggest illegitimacy, he failed to improve his reputation when he eloped (1742) with Charlotte Stanley, daughter of the earl of Derby. He distinguished himself during the **Seven Years' War**, particularly by a daringly successful cavalry assault in Portugal (1762), but remained known for flamboyance, financial extravagance, and an unsavory willingness to pull strings to get ahead.

Supporting military action against the Americans, Burgoyne sailed (1775) in the same ship with generals **Howe** and **Clinton**, his superiors. Realizing after the bloody experience at Bunker Hill (June 1775) that the war had to be conducted on a grander scale, he proposed to divide the American opposition through a coordinated campaign to control the Hudson River. His painfully slow drive down the Richelieu River–Lake Champlain invasion route during the summer of 1777 was not supported by an army from the south. Finding himself surrounded by a rebel army that had not existed when he designed the campaign, he surrendered his remaining 5,700 men on October 17.

General Burgoyne

Burgoyne failed to get the court-martial that he was convinced would clear him of responsibility. His military career over, he turned successfully to playwriting. **Horace Walpole** considered one of his plays, *The Heiress* (1786), the best comedy of the time. He was also an M.P. (1761–1792), and, speaking frequently, led parliamentary attacks on **Clive** (1773), **North** (after 1778), and **Hastings** (1787).

David Sloan

Bibliography

Billias, George A. "John Burgoyne, Ambitious General," in George A. Billias, ed., *George Washington's Opponents.* 1969.
Burgoyne, John. *A State of the Expedition from Canada as Laid Before the House of Commons.* 1780.
Hargrove, Richard. *General John Burgoyne.* 1983.
Howson, Gerald. *Burgoyne of Saratoga.* 1979.
Lunt, James. *John Burgoyne of Saratoga.* 1975.
Mintz, Max M. *The Generals of Saratoga.* 1990.

See also Army; Dramatic Arts; War and Military Engagements

Burke, Edmund (1729–1797)

Philosopher, reformer, political theorist, statesman, and orator, Burke is famous as both a liberal supporter of the **North American** colonies and a conservative critic of the **French Revolution**. His father, an Irish lawyer, was (at least nominally) Protestant, his mother **Roman Catholic**. Born in **Dublin**, he studied at **Trinity College** and after receiving his B.A. (1749) went to **London** to study law, but left this uncompleted. He began a literary career in 1756 with *A Vindication of Natural Society* in response to **Bolingbroke**'s rationalistic inquiry into the moral basis of society. His *Philosophical Enquiry Into the Origin of Our Ideas of the Sublime and the Beautiful* (1756), later extremely influential, attempted to reconcile classical rhetorical theories with an empirical approach to the responses evoked by affective experiences. These works helped prepare Burke's acceptance in the literary circle surrounding **Samuel Johnson**.

His political life began in 1759, when he became private secretary to William Gerard Hamilton (1729–1796), chief secretary for Ireland. Breaking with Hamilton over a **pension** the latter had supposedly acquired for him, he became private secretary (1765) to **Lord Rockingham**, First Lord of the Treasury, and was returned as M.P. for Wendover (1766), then **Bristol** (1774), and Malton (1780–1794). Burke served as writer and spokesman for the Rockingham **Whigs**, and in Parliament became famous for his long-winded eloquence. He opposed harsh treatment of the American colonies, the use of military force against Englishmen gathered to protest economic troubles, limitations on popular political rights, and the continued suppression of religious freedom for Roman Catholics in Ireland. Throughout his career he stood for principles outlined in his pamphlet "Thoughts on the Present Discontents" (1770), defending **party politics**, opposing royal encroachments on the independence of the **Commons**, and working to limit royal **patronage**.

Burke's unsuccessful efforts to guide Parliament on American affairs produced several powerful works, particularly "On Conciliation with America" (1775). From 1770 until the outbreak of hostilities he served as parliamentary agent for the Assembly of New York. His 1774 speech opposing the duties imposed by the **Tea Act** was published as "On American Taxation." He spoke against limits imposed on American trade and individual rights, but Parliament rejected every proposal; prophetically Burke warned that "great empires and little minds go ill together." He also led the effort to reform the **East India Company**'s administration of **India**, an effort that fell short of the impeachment of **Warren Hastings** in a trial that lasted from 1788 to 1795.

Edmund Burke

These activities contributed to Burke's contemporary reputation as a reformer. His conservative response to the French Revolution (1789) therefore surprised some observers. Convinced that time-honored social and political institutions preserved the wisdom of the ages, and unpersuaded by **Richard Price** that abstract rights and liberties should dictate radical change and the framework of future governments, Burke argued that society and government developed slowly over long periods of time. Abstract principles like reason, liberty, and rights were ineffective in forming a basis for planning reforms. Burke's doctrine of prescription held that existing institutions have lasted because they have worked; their lasting existence prescribed their continued use. **Radical** or revolutionary changes introduced worse problems than those they supposedly resolved.

Thus, in the burst of controversy surrounding the revolution, Burke predicted that it would soon degenerate into tyranny and dictatorship. To the suggestion that English precedents for French actions could be found in the **Glorious Revolution** of 1688, he countered that the English had reformed a corrupt monarchy and established constitutional government, whereas the French were destroying monarchy itself in a vain attempt to make a completely fresh start. His famous *Reflections on the Revolution in France* (1790), intended to counter the threat that French disorder supposedly posed to British stability, helped destroy his old friendship with **Charles James Fox**, and made him the hated bugbear of **Thomas Paine** and the radicals of the 1790s. The book became a storehouse of weapons to conservatives, and Burke's ticket into the pantheon of a revived **Tory** party after his death.

K.J.H. Berland

Bibliography

Cone, Carl. *Burke and the Nature of Politics.* 2 vols., 1957, 1964.

Copeland, Thomas, ed. *The Correspondence of Edmund Burke.* 10 vols., 1958–1978.

Dreyer, Frederick A. *Burke's Politics: A Study in Whig Orthodoxy.* 1979.

Freeman, Michael. *Edmund Burke and the Critique of Political Radicalism.* 1980.

Furniss, Tom. *Edmund Burke's Aesthetic Ideology: Language, Gender and Political Economy in Revolution.* 1993.

Kramnick, Isaac. *The Rage of Edmund Burke: The Conscience of an Ambivalent Conservative.* 1977.

Lock, F.P. *Burke's Reflections on the Revolution in France.* 1985.

Mansfield, Harvey, Jr. *Statesmanship and Party Government: A Study of Burke and Bolingbroke.* 1965.

O'Brien, Conor Cruise. *The Great Melody: A Thematic Biography of Edmund Burke.* 1992.

See also Irish Literature before the Union; Picturesque Movement; Political Thought; Sublime, The; Whigs and Whiggism

Burlesque

Burlesque has been defined as "an incongruous imitation and deflationary treatment of serious themes for satiric purposes." Burlesques were common in the early Hanoverian period because familiarity with classical genres, especially the **epic**, was widespread, and because authors were normally expected to measure their own achievements and those of their contemporaries against those of their predecessors.

Burlesque may be divided into high and low varieties. Low burlesques, which present dignified and serious subjects as if they were relatively insignificant, were fairly rare during the period. **Henry Fielding**'s *The Tragedy of Tragedies* (1731), which burlesques the conventions of the so-called heroic dramas popular on the Restoration and early-18th-century stage, is a good example because it demonstrates that pretensions to dignified status may be as much a target as high generic status itself. The most famous example of the burlesque of pretentious claims to high seriousness is **John Gay**'s *The Beggar's Opera* (1728), which treats low-life thieves and riffraff in the context of Italian **opera** conventions.

Conversely, high burlesques incongruously treat trivial subjects as if they were worthy of the diction, style, and form associated with great epic heroes and events. The most common high burlesques of the period were often mock-heroic or mock-epic works (or parts of works). Works that as a whole are not mock epics may include mock-epic incidents: An early example is **John Milton**'s comic representation of Satan's mock-heroic pretensions to epic military glory in *Paradise Lost* (1667, 1671). A later example is the churchyard battle between Molly Seagrim and other women in Fielding's *Tom Jones* (1749). The most accomplished **mock-heroic** works of the period were mock-epic poems: Sir Samuel Garth's *The Dispensary* (1699); **Alexander Pope**'s *The Rape of the Lock* (1712, 1714, 1717), and *The Dunciad* (1743); and **Lord Byron**'s *Don Juan* (1819–1824), all of which underscored the triviality of modern pursuits by inviting readers to measure them against the significant actions of the past.

In practice, the mock-heroic is often complex, treating both past and present with some degree of ambivalence, and compelling readers to consider what is being mocked and what is offered as heroic. For example, in both *Paradise Lost* and *The Rape of the Lock,* the past glorification of military valor is criticized as much as are any of the foolish actions of the present. In *Don Juan,* Byron's attitude toward the epic form seems to be as irreverently mocking as his attitude toward his modern characters and their behavior.

Vincent Carretta

Bibliography

Bond, Richmond. *English Burlesque Poetry, 1700–1750.* 1932.

Broich, Ulrich. *The Eighteenth-Century Mock-Heroic Poem.* 1990.

Colomb, Gregory. *Designs on Truth: The Poetics of the Augustan Mock-Epic.* 1992.

Kitchin, George. *A Survey of Burlesque and Parody in English.* 1931.

Rawson, Claude. "Byron Augustan: Mutations of the Mock-Heroic in *Don Juan* and *Peter Bell the Third,*" in A. Rutherford, ed., *Byron: Augustan and Romantic.* 1990.

See also Mock Heroic; Satire; Wit and Ridicule

Burletta

The dramatic term *burletta* outlasted its original form. In 1748 Rinaldo de Capua's *La Comedia in Comedia* was advertised as a "Burletta or Comic Opera . . . the first . . . ever exhibited in England." The burletta depended on a simple, comic plot (*burla*), farce, and lively music to delight an English audience largely ignorant of the Italian language. For the first successful English burletta, the afterpiece *Midas* (Covent Garden, 1764), **Kane O'Hara** adapted the French tradition of burlesquing classical deities by domesticating them into familiar English characters, and (as in **ballad opera**) by setting new words to English and Irish ballads. He again used myth in *The Golden Pippin* (1772), but by then burlettas had begun to shed their classical dress.

A change in the law was the primary reason why "burletta" became a catchall term. To circumvent the **Playhouse Act** (1737), managers of minor theaters took legitimate, full-length plays (which they could not stage), shortened them, added songs, converted prose to verse, and called the product "burletta." By the 1830s, any play of three acts with five or more songs was acceptable as a burletta. In 1843, minor theaters were loosened from the Playhouse Act, and the term was no longer needed. It lingered in the provinces until about 1866.

Peter A. Tasch

Bibliography

Clinton-Baddeley, V.C. *All Right on the Night.* 1954.

Dircks, Phyllis T. "The Eighteenth-Century Burletta." *Restoration and Eighteenth-Century Theatre Research.* Vol. 10, pp. 44–52.

Nicoll, Allardyce. *A History of English Drama, 1660–1900.* Vol. 3, 1961; Vol. 4, 1960.

See also Dramatic Arts

Burlington, 3rd Earl of (Richard Boyle) (1694–1753)

Burlington was the leading evangelist of the **Palladian style** in English architecture. Both patron and practicing architect, he furnishes a classic example of the "gentleman amateur." He made an extensive study of the works of Andrea Palladio (1508–1580), the most influential Italian architect of the 16th century, during a 1719 trip to Italy. When he returned to England he was determined to improve his nation's architecture by publicizing the need for close adherence to classical precedents. Burlington's subsequent designs, characterized by an austere, astylar classicism incorporating elements inspired

Lord Burlington

by Palladio and the English architect Inigo Jones (1573–1652), include Chiswick House (*c.* 1723–1729), his own country seat, and the Assembly Rooms at **York** (1731–1732). Burlington's protégé **William Kent**, the painter, architect, and designer, worked with his patron on several projects.

Kimerly Rorschach

Bibliography

Colvin, Howard. *A Biographical Dictionary of British Architects, 1600–1840.* 1978.

Lees-Milne, James. *Earls of Creation: Five Great Patrons of Eighteenth-Century Art.* 1963.

Wittkower, Rudolf. *Palladio and English Palladianism.* 1974.

See also Antiquities and Ruins; Architects and Architecture; Housebuilding and Housing

Burney, Charles (1726–1814)

Musicologist, organist, teacher, minor composer, and author of *A General History of Music from the Earliest Ages to the Present Period* (1776–1789), Burney is also remembered as father of a large, talented family that included the novelist and diarist **Frances (Fanny) Burney** and Rear-Admiral James Burney (1750–1821), successor to **Captain Cook** as commander of the *Discovery.*

Doctor of music (Oxford, 1769) and protégé of **Thomas Arne**, Burney recounted, often amusingly, his extensive search for materials for his *History* in France, Italy, Germany, the Netherlands, and elsewhere. His recollections appeared in *The Present State of Music* (1771 and 1773) and in his manuscript journal, which was published in 1969 as *Music, Men and Manners in France and Italy (1770).*

A congenial member of "The Club," Burney is closely identified with **Samuel Johnson** and his circle as a man of many interests, notably astronomy, poetry (in which he dabbled), and painting (of which he became a connoisseur). His work in **music scholarship** is often ranked with that of **Sir John Hawkins**, whose five-volume *General History of the Science and Practice of Music* (1776) appeared the same year as Burney's first volume. While both histories continue to be considered authoritative and comprehensive, Burney's makes more agreeable reading.

James Gray

Bibliography

d'Arblay, Madame Frances Burney. *Memoirs of Dr. Burney.* 3 vols. 1832.

Grant, Kerry Scott. *Dr. Burney as Critic and Music Historian.* 1983.

Hemlow, Joyce. *A Catalogue of the Burney Family Correspondence, 1749–1878.* 1971.

Klima, Slava, Gary Bowers, and Kerry Scott Grant, eds. *Memoirs of Dr. Charles Burney, 1726–1769.* 1988.

Lonsdale, Roger. *Dr. Charles Burney, a Literary Biography.* 1965.

Ribeiro, Alvaro, ed. *The Letters of Dr. Burney.* Vol. I (1751–1784). 1991.

Burney, Frances (1752–1840)

Frances (Fanny) Burney was famous as a novelist in her lifetime, and since her death has also been known for her posthumously published journals and **letters**, which present a vivid tableau of her age.

Second daughter of the music historian **Charles Burney**, "the silent, observant Miss Fanny" (as an early acquaintance called her) in 1768 began a secret diary, which she filled with shrewd descriptions of the visitors to her father's London home. Her private writings over the next 15 years contain portraits of many celebrities, among them **Johnson**, **Reynolds**, and **Burke**. In 1778 Burney published a **novel** anonymously, *Evelina,* which became an instant success. A second novel, *Cecilia* (1782), confirmed her popularity as a writer of domestic comedies of **manners**.

Profiting from her good reputation, from 1786 to 1791 she was Second Keeper of the Robes to Queen Charlotte (consort of **George III**); her journals for this period are invaluable records of daily life at court. After marrying the French emigré army officer Alexandre d'Arblay (1793) she published a third novel, *Camilla* (1796); a final novel, *The Wanderer,* appeared in 1814. Widowed in 1818, she spent her last 20 years editing her father's and her own papers. After her death, her niece, Charlotte Barrett, published the *Diary and Letters of Madame*

Fanny Burney, Mme. D'Arblay

D'Arblay (7 vols., 1842–1846), a highly selective and bowdlerized edition that has been supplanted by the modern editions of Hemlow and Troide.

Lars E. Troide

Bibliography

Doody, Margaret Anne. *Frances Burney: The Life in the Works.* 1988.

Grau, Joseph. *Fanny Burney: An Annotated Bibliography.* 1981.

Hemlow, Joyce. *The History of Fanny Burney.* 1958.

———, ed. *The Journals and Letters of Fanny Burney (Madame D'Arblay), 1791–1840.* 12 vols. 1972–1984.

Johnson, Claudia L. *Equivocal Beings: Politics, Gender, and Sentimentality in the 1790's—Wollstonecraft, Radcliffe, Burney, Austen.* 1995.

Troide, Lars E., ed. *The Early Journals and Letters of Fanny Burney, 1768–1791.* 3 vols. and forthcoming. 1988–.

See also Women in Literature

Burns, Robert (1759–1796)

Burns, **Scotland**'s national poet, was a poor, self-educated Scottish farmer who lived outside the literary mainstream but was well-read in contemporary British writing, as well as the classics of **Shakespeare**, **Milton**, and Dryden. His **poetry** is most important perhaps because it successfully integrated the racy, concrete diction and imagery of ordinary Scottish rustic life with contemporary ideas of social, political, aesthetic, and personal freedom.

Burns was born near Ayr, the eldest son of a farmer. His early life was full of hard work, poverty, disappointment over his father's bankruptcy and early death, and rebellion against religious orthodoxy and social conformity. By 1786 he had weathered many romantic affairs, some exceedingly painful, and fathered three illegitimate children. His first volume of poems, published that year at Kilmarnock (to raise money to help him emigrate to Jamaica), *Poems, Chiefly in the Scottish Dialect,* was an immediate success, partly because it jibed with contemporary **sentimental** theories about "heaven-taught" rustic poets, but partly also because it transformed some of his life experiences into the common chords of great poetry.

Burns's poetic diction (combining Scots vernacular and contemporary English) and verse forms (favoring the six-line "Standard Habbie") derived from the Scottish revival poetry of Allan Ramsay (1686–1758) and **Robert Ferguson**. Many of his poems are satiric, expressing anger at economic and social inequality, and religious and intellectual repression. But they suggest that one could live with hardship by enjoying the dignity of ordinary life, by pursuing personal and artistic freedom, and by believing in the essential goodness and brotherhood of man.

The Kilmarnock poetry's distinctiveness comes from the immediacy and sensuousness of its everyday diction and imagery, taken from commonplace experiences of working, eating, drinking, singing, walking in the woods, talking with friends, sitting in church, making love. One famous poem in the collection, "To a Mouse," uses the ordinary experiences of a farmer and a mouse as a metaphor that argues against **Augustan** notions of "nature's social union," substituting a worldview that is harsh, without much sense, but endurable.

Though he earned only £20 from this first publication, Burns overnight became a national celebrity, his poems finding their way onto the lips of professors and plowboys alike. He moved to **Edinburgh** (1786), where he was entertained and flattered by **Dugald Stewart**, **Adam Ferguson**, and other luminaries of the **Scottish Enlightenment**. But discontentment set in again, and he moved, first to a farm in Ellisland, Dumfriesshire (1788), then to Dumfries (1791), where he took a post in the excise service salaried at £70 per annum—which he almost forfeited because of indiscreetly expressed enthusiasm over the **French Revolution**.

Before his death, Burns, though he issued several enlarged editions of his poems, spent much of his time collecting, editing, and reworking old Scottish **folksongs**, often adding songs he wrote himself, usually borrowing the music from popular Scottish airs. Taking little payment for these efforts, dedicating them to his nation, he produced some 200 songs for James Johnson's *Scots Musical Museum* (1787–1803), and 70 others for George Thomson's *Select Collection of Original Scottish Airs* (1793–1818). Among his contributions were the famous "Auld Lang Syne," "A Red, Red Rose," "Comin' thro' the Rye," and "Mary Morison." His songs present as wide a range of ordinary human emotions as can be found in British poetry.

Suspect because of his radical opinions, embittered, and still poor, Burns died in ignorance of the high place reserved for him in the national literature. Late in life he wrote "Tam o'Shanter," perhaps his greatest work, a mock-fable about a drunken peasant who stumbles across a witches' coven, an

Robert Burns

exploration of the conflict between the attraction of lawless pleasures and the inevitability of obligation. Burns was a poet of ideas and feelings, but perhaps more truly one of democracy. His greatest merit was his expression of belief in ordinary people and ordinary responses, conveyed in powerfully emotional and sensuous poetry.

Raymond Bentman

Bibliography

Bentman, Raymond. *Robert Burns.* 1987.
Bold, Alan. *A Burns Companion.* 1991.
Crawford, Thomas. *Burns: A Study of the Poems and the Songs.* 1960.
Daiches, David. *Robert Burns.* 1950.
Jack, R.D.S., and Andrew Noble. *The Art of Robert Burns.* 1982.
Kinsley, James, ed. *The Poems and Songs of Robert Burns.* 1968.
Low, Donald A. *Robert Burns: The Critical Heritage.* 1975.
McGuirk, Carol. *Robert Burns and the Sentimental Era.* 1985.
Roy, G. Ross, ed. *The Letters of Robert Burns.* 1985.
Snyder, Franklin Bliss. *The Life of Robert Burns.* 1968.

See also Romanticism and Romantic Style

Bute, 3rd Earl of (John Stuart) (1713–1792)

In 1737 Bute was appointed one of the lords of the bedchamber to **Frederick, Prince of Wales**, and on his death (1751) became groom of the stole to Frederick's son, the future **George III**. By 1756 Bute had gained the latter's trust and friendship, and was responsible for his education. A pious and upright man, Bute became a sort of father figure to the young prince.

His political career was less enjoyable. The death in 1761 of Islay, 3rd Duke of Argyll, left a gap in Scottish politics that Bute attempted to fill by appointing his own brother, James Stuart Mackenzie (*c.* 1718–1780), as the new Scottish political manager. Bute's ministerial career (1761–1763), first as Secretary of State, then as First Lord of the Treasury (**Prime Minister**), was dogged by unusual resentment because he was both Scottish and a royal favorite. Scotophobia was rampant among English **opposition** M.P.s, who talked about a sinister Highland phalanx controlling British politics. Accusations were also made that Bute's ministry was soft on **Jacobitism**, and there was a vigorous campaign against him in the press. Much of this was unfair, but Bute was not an effective politician, and his counterattacks were weak. He resigned in 1763, but the idea that he manipulated the king from behind the scenes persisted long after he ceased to have any influence.

Richard Finlay

Bibliography

Ferguson, W. *Scotland: 1689 to the Present.* 1968.
Lenman, B. *Integration, Enlightenment and Industrialisation: Scotland, 1746–1832.* 1981.
McKelvey, James Lee. *George III and Lord Bute: The Leicester House Years.* 1973.
Schweizer, Karl W. *Frederick the Great, William Pitt, and Lord Bute: The Anglo-Prussian Alliance, 1756–1763.* 1991.
———, ed. *Lord Bute: Essays in Re-interpretation.* 1988.

See also Wilkes, John

Butler, Joseph (1692–1752)

Butler, Bishop of Durham (1750), a leading English theologian and moralist, the son of a **Presbyterian** tradesman, was educated at Oxford (1718), and benefited from the patronage of **Queen Caroline**. He was noted for his religious writings, especially "Fifteen Sermons" (1726) and *The Analogy of Religion, Natural and Revealed, to the Constitution and Course of Nature* (1736). In this treatise, which succeeding generations considered a definitive answer to skeptical **freethought**, Butler defended Christian faith from the intense deistic attacks of the 1730s by finding confirmation in Nature for its revealed doctrines. The thrust of his argument was that if there are obscure and inexplicable things in Nature, whose Author is God, then it is unreasonable to charge revealed or supernatural religion, emanating from the same Author, with error; the two are analogous, and the latter must be accepted, along with miracles and the afterlife.

Butler was also a distinguished moral philosopher. He countered the views of earlier moralists such as Hobbes and Shaftesbury in "Of the Nature of Virtue" (1736), wherein he argued against hedonism and the notion that self-interest was the foundation of good conduct. He held instead that man's intuition and ability to reason made him a moral agent superior to animals. Later divines such as J.H. Newman (1801–1890) were influenced by Butler's defense of traditional Christian **theology**, but skeptics such as **John Stuart Mill** saw support for their position, and even for atheism, in Butler's powerful rebuttal of deistic optimism.

Barbara Jean Whitehead

Bibliography

Carlsson, Percy. *Butler's Ethics.* 1964.
Cunliffe, Christopher, ed. *Joseph Butler's Moral and Religious Thought: Tercentenary Essays.* 1992.
Mossner, Ernest. *Bishop Butler and the Age of Reason: A Study in the History of Thought.* 1936.
Penelhum, Terence. *Butler.* 1985.

See also Church of England

Byng, John (1704–1757)

Byng, the son of an admiral, rose to become a rear-admiral in the Royal Navy in 1745, but was found incompetent and executed early in the **Seven Years' War**. The execution reflected not only the public's fury at a military loss to **France** but several other contemporary phenomena.

In 1756 Byng took command of a naval squadron charged with the relief of a garrison in Minorca besieged by the French. However, more through insufficient force and tactical errors than lack of aggressiveness, he failed in this and withdrew, leaving the garrison to surrender. This led to a furor of bellicosity in Britain and to a politically motivated court-martial for "neglect of duty." Byng's execution (14 March 1757) on the quarterdeck of H.M.S. *Monarque* in Portsmouth harbor, despite the court's recommendation of mercy, aroused controversy as to the appropriateness of the 12th Article of War (revised in 1749) which made negligence a capital offense. The incident also set off rancorous debate over the government's war policy, with Byng cast as a scapegoat for its mishandling by the **Duke of Newcastle's** administration. Byng's fate also prompted the sardonic remark by the war-hating French philosopher Voltaire (1694–1776) that the English occasionally shot an admiral "pour encourager les autres," (to encourage the others).

Stanley D.M. Carpenter

Admiral Byng

Bibliography

Creswell, John. *British Admirals of the Eighteenth Century: Tactics in Battle.* 1972.
Naval Records Society. *Papers Relating to the Loss of Minorca in 1756.* Vol. 42. 1913.
Pope, Dudley. *At Twelve Mr. Byng Was Shot.* 1962.

See also Navy; War and Military Engagements

Byron, George Gordon, Lord (1788–1824)

The only son of Captain John ("Mad Jack") Byron and Catherine Gordon, Byron was one of the most commercially successful yet controversial poets of the early 19th century. Byron grew up lame (with a clubfoot) and in near poverty in Aberdeen until he unexpectedly inherited a title at age 10. Thereafter he attended Harrow School and, later, Trinity College, Cambridge.

His first volume of verse, the highly conventional *Hours of Idleness* (1807), was savagely attacked in the *Edinburgh Review,* prompting his satirical response, *English Bards and Scotch Reviewers* (1809). Byron attacked his antagonists in the **periodical** press as well as his poetic contemporaries **Wordsworth**, **Coleridge**, and **Southey**, allying himself stylistically with **Pope**, John Dryden (1631–1700), and other **Augustan** writers. Despite his aversion to **Romantic** rusticity of style, however, Byron remained a lifelong supporter of the liberal politics and revolutionary causes that characterized many Romantic writers.

Byron's fame spread suddenly with the publication of the first two cantos of his romance, *Childe Harold's Pilgrimage* (1812). This poem, which earned him the respect of his early *Edinburgh* detractors, loosely follows the travels of its gloomy hero, who has exhausted the pleasures of life through dissolute living; it contains Byron's early experiments with persona that gave his name to the **Byronic Hero**, suffering from *Weltschmerz.* The public's fascination with the poem stemmed partly from a confusion of author with narrator, something Byron both struggled against and exploited later.

In 1813 he followed up this success with a number of hastily written narrative poems based on his own **travels** in Europe and Asia Minor, capitalizing on the current vogue for eastern subjects: *The Bride of Abydos* (1813), *The Corsair* (1814; it sold 10,000 copies on the first day of its release), and *The Giaour* (1814). During the height of his fame, Byron was lionized by **London** society. He engaged in numerous affairs, the most public and acrimonious of which was with **Lady Caroline Lamb**, who famously called him "mad, bad and dangerous to know."

Lord Byron

It was also during this time that he developed an intense attachment to his half-sister, Augusta Leigh, whom he had not seen since childhood. But, like his fictional creation Childe Harold, he apparently became exhausted with dissolute life and, perhaps to gain some stability, married Annabella Milbanke in 1815. The marriage was not a success. Despite the birth of a daughter, the couple separated within a year, following accusations of incest against Byron and his half-sister. The scandal was more than fashionable society could tolerate, and Byron left England in 1816 never to return.

Moving about from Geneva to Venice, Rome, and Pisa, Byron became the focal point of a group of English exiles that included the **Shelleys**, Edward Trelawny (1807–1886), and Edward Williams (*d.* 1822). He produced during this time the much-anticipated last canto of *Childe Harold* (1818), as well as a number of closet dramas, including *Manfred* (1817), *Cain* (1821), and *Marino Faliero* (1821), and began work on his creative tour de force, *Don Juan* (1819–1824). This latter work, a mock-epic in *ottava rima* stanzas, exploits the Byronic narratorial persona in the service of social satire and, beyond that, provides philosophical commentary on man's odyssey in a world without fixed principles. The self-absorbed Byronic hero is here transformed into a witty, self-deprecating narrator, whose sardonic consciousness digresses endlessly on contemporary issues as he passes through shipwrecks, harems, battles, and London high society. Though the poem was heavily criticized in the English press for immorality, Goethe (1749–1832) admired it, a fact that pleased Byron immensely. **Gifford** declared that it placed Byron in the same rank as **Shakespeare** and **Milton**.

After a period of relative domestic calm with a married Italian Countess, Byron left for Greece, intending to lend his support to the Greek struggle against Turkish control. But while stationed in Missolonghi, training troops and enlisting support for the cause, he died of fever. His fascinations with Greece and national liberation, typical of many of his countrymen, were among his more attractive enthusiasms.

Flamboyant, exhibitionistic, famous throughout Europe, Byron stamped himself upon contemporary consciousness as few other writers have done. In many ways, the trajectory of his life (and its perceived close connection to his work) epitomized the Romantic struggle between poetry and action. Unlike the attention paid to his contemporaries Shelley and **Keats**, interest in his work has remained fairly constant since he first burst onto the literary scene. While he had little stylistic influence on his English contemporaries, his life and work became especially significant to the Continental Romantics, including Victor Hugo (1802–1885), George Sand (1804–1876), Heinrich Heine (1797–1856), and the painter Eugene Delacroix (1799–1863).

Samantha Webb

Bibliography

Bloom, Harold, ed. *George Gordon, Lord Byron: Modern Critical Views.* 1986.
Manning, Peter J. *Byron and His Fictions.* 1978.
Marchand, Leslie. *Byron: A Biography.* 1957.
McGann, Jerome, ed. *The Complete Poetical Works.* 1980–.
Rutherford, Andrew, ed. *Byron: The Critical Heritage.* 1970.

See also Epic; Poetry and Poetics

Byronic Hero

This term refers to a stock figure of literary **Romanticism**, derived from the descriptions and circumstances of the protagonists of **Lord Byron**'s drama and poetry. The hero thematically displays aspects of the Romantic engagement with nature, society, and political institutions. Literary sources for Byron's creation included Prometheus, the Wandering Jew, **Milton**'s Satan, the villains of **Gothic fiction**, and Goethe's Faust.

The various dimensions of this complex character type were explored by Byron in *Childe Harold's Pilgrimage* (1812–1818), *Manfred* (1817), *Don Juan* (1819), and *Cain* (1821). The figure stands tragic, solitary, at one time noble and privileged, but later outcast or self-exiled for an obscure but presumably monumental transgression. Throughout, however, the hero remains rebellious and defiant, articulate and self-searching, eliciting sympathy and admiration from other dramatic characters and from Byron's audience.

An essential preoccupation of the Byronic hero is his journey or quest. The questing allows for an articulation of the Romantic Self in relation to the traditions of existing institutions. An attractive and potent nonconformist, the hero can be socially and politically threatening. The restless pursuit of knowledge or self-awareness may take an historical form, as in *Childe Harold's Pilgrimage,* or be the record of a psychological search, as in *Manfred.* Contributing to the Romantic discussion of man in relation to nature, Byron's hero is defiant in the face of both natural and supernatural elements, asserting a **sublime** individualism (both historical and psychological) that can persist even after the protagonist's demise. Other literary creations influenced by the Byronic hero are the Poet of **Percy Bysshe Shelley**'s *Alastor* (1816) and **Mary Wollstonecraft Shelley**'s Dr. Frankenstein (1818). The type resurfaces in Victorian literature in Emily Brontë's Heathcliff in *Wuthering Heights* (1847) and in Captain Ahab of Herman Melville's *Moby-Dick* (1851).

The literary invention and its creator were often considered indistinguishable by Byron's acquaintances and readers. Byron disavowed this intriguing correspondence with little success.

Dominique Calapai

Bibliography

Bloom, Harold, ed. *George Gordon, Lord Byron: Modern Critical Views.* 1986.

Gaull, Marilyn. *English Romanticism: The Human Context.* 1988.

Lovell, Ernest J., Jr. *Byron: The Record of a Quest.* 1966.

Manning, Peter J. *Byron and His Fictions.* 1978.

Marchand, Leslie A. *Byron: A Bibliography.* 3 vols. 1957.

McGann, Jerome J. *Fiery Dust.* 1968.

Railo, Eino. *The Haunted Castle: A Study of the Elements of English Romanticism.* 1964.

Thorslev, Peter. *The Byronic Hero: Types and Prototypes.* 1962.

Calendar Reform (1751)

In 1582 Pope Gregory XIII, acting on advice from astronomers, amended the inaccurate leap-year mechanism of the Julian Calendar and subtracted 10 days from that October, making the vernal equinox coincide with 21 March. **Catholic** Europe adopted the reformed "Gregorian Calendar" immediately; Protestant and Greek Orthodox Europe resisted from doctrinal obstinacy. However, for once the Catholic Church and **science** were on the same side, and the intervention of scientists was needed to overcome religious prejudice. The German Protestant states adopted the reformed calendar in 1699, through the influence of G.W. Leibnitz (1646–1716). In England, the "Bill for Regulating the Commencement of the Year," or "Calendar New Style Act" of 1751, designed to convert 3 September 1752 to the 14th, and move New Year's day from 25 March to 1 January, was the work of astronomer George Parker, Earl of Macclesfield (1697–1764). Its unopposed passage by Parliament (March 1751) was aided by the mellifluous oratory of the **Earl of Chesterfield.** Nonetheless, many denounced it as "popery" and demanded their 11 days back.

N. Merrill Distad

Bibliography

Jones, Sir Harold Spencer. "The Calendar," in Charles Singer, et al., eds., *A History of Technology,* Vol. 3: *From the Renaissance to the Industrial Revolution, c. 1500–c. 1750.* 1957.

O'Neil, William Matthew. *Time and the Calendars.* 1975.

Philip, Alexander. *The Calendar: Its History, Structure, and Improvement.* 1921.

Richmond, B. *Time Measurement and Calendar Construction.* 1956.

Cambridge Platonists

The Cambridge Platonists of the 17th century had wide-ranging influence on Hanoverian thought. As members of Emmanuel and Christ Colleges, **Cambridge University**, they were active in religious and philosophical debates between 1633 and 1688. Their chief leaders were Benjamin Whichcote (1609–1683), the father of the movement, who lectured on ancient philosophy and religious development; Ralph Cudworth (1617–1688), who wrote on metaphysics and was eager to disprove materialism and uphold the freedom of the will; and Nathanael Culverwel (?1618–?1651), a defender of Calvinistic teachings and an exponent of the doctrine that God had given man the light of reason, by which he might know nature.

The group's central tenet was that faith and reason were reconcilable: Without reason, God's natural gift, faith could not attain understanding. The Platonists also maintained that God himself dwelt in all human souls. These ideas and others were drawn upon by **Bishop George Berkeley**, whose concept of one spiritual substance, which was known by reflection on human powers and perceptions, descended directly from their metaphysics. Their belief in eternal beauty, an underlying rational purpose in the world, and the human moral sense all filtered into the ideas of 18th-century moral philosophy and theology, as did their detailed and relentless critique of materialism (as it had been manifested in the writings of Thomas Hobbes and Francis Bacon).

Daniel E. Shannon

Bibliography

Cassirer, Ernst. *The Platonic Renaissance in England,* trans. James Pettegrove. 1953.

Cragg, Gerald, ed. *The Cambridge Platonists.* 1968.

Rodgers, G.A. "Locke, Newton, and the Cambridge Platonists on Innate Ideas." *Journal of the History of Ideas.* Vol. 40, pp. 191–205.

Willey, Basil. *The Seventeenth Century Background: Studies in the Thought of the Age in Relation to Poetry and Religion.* 1942.

See also Theology

Cambridge University

Hanoverian Cambridge saw itself first and foremost as a pillar of the Established Church and of the Constitution of which it was a part. As an integral part of the established order, it reflected the tenor of the age in its opposition to thoroughgoing reform and its emphasis on the virtues of stability. However, like Hanoverian society more generally, behind this facade Cambridge in this period changed in significant ways—most notably in its curriculum and examination system—and this helped prepare it for the more outward and visible upheavals of the Victorian period.

Outwardly, the university continued to be governed by a traditional and increasingly anachronistic constitution. The Elizabethan Statutes of 1570, which had largely regularized and codified long centuries of medieval practice and which, in theory, were not subject to change, governed the university down to the legislative reforms of the 19th century, which began with acts in 1854 and 1856 freeing graduates from the obligation to be members of the **Church of England**. But despite its traditionalism, Cambridge changed in significant ways. The Hanoverian period saw an almost total remodeling of Cambridge's curriculum as the last remnants of the traditional scholastic order were replaced by an increasingly exclusive emphasis on Newtonian natural philosophy—a transformation which owed much to the perceived theological and apologetic uses of Newtonian **science** as an aid to the Argument from Design. In particular, the mathematical aspects of Cambridge's Newtonian heritage came more and more to dominate the undergraduate curriculum, and geometry came to assume the importance as a form of mental training that had formerly been devoted to logic.

Mathematics, moreover, had the advantage that it enabled the university to rank its students ever more precisely in its public examinations. For it was Hanoverian Cambridge which produced, in the form of the Senate House Examination (which, after 1824, became known as the Mathematical Tripos), the model of the competitive examination. This model, over the course of the 19th century, was to be applied to more and more branches of public life as part of the crusade to replace **patronage** by meritocratic selection. The most evident indication that the mathematical examination was, by the mid 18th century, supplanting the traditional means of examining students through participation in public disputations was that in 1783, for the first time, students were placed in three classes: Wranglers, and Senior and Junior Optimes. Thereafter, the examination more and more dominated university life as it became the established route to a fellowship. And as the competition for examination honors intensified, so too the importance of mathematics loomed larger as a means of ever more minutely distinguishing between rival candidates. Some attempt was made to counter this mathematical obsession with the establishment of the classical Tripos in 1824, but this was only open to those who had already taken honors in the Mathematical Tripos.

Movement for other reform was stifled by the mood of general reaction that followed the American and French revolutions of the latter 18th century. In Cambridge this led to a virtual extinguishing of the university's 18th-century traditions of **Whig** political sympathy and **Latitudinarian** theology (evident in the careers of such men as **John Jebb** and **William Paley**), and also to the vigorous growth of **Evangelicalism**, a movement which in its early stages owed much to Cambridge interest and activity. As the shock of the **French Revolution** abated, however, Cambridge showed greater willingness to contemplate change. The **Analytical Society**, founded in 1812, helped to promote a greater attention to Continental methods in the key discipline of mathematics. The Cambridge Philosophical Society, founded in 1819, was linked to an attempt to encourage the study of sciences other than those based on mathematics (though the examination system ensured that mathematics remained supreme). Early-19th-century Cambridge Broad Churchmen such as Adam Sedgwick (1785–1873) and William Whewell (1794–1866) helped to revitalize the 18th-century emphasis on the accord between science and religion by promoting new forms of natural **theology**. Such developments, together with the more fundamental institutional and intellectual transformations wrought over the course of the 18th century, were to provide the foundation for the quickened pace of reform and scientific achievement that characterized Victorian Cambridge.

John Gascoigne

Bibliography

Gascoigne, John. *Cambridge in the Age of the Enlightenment: Science, Religion and Politics from the Restoration to the French Revolution.* 1989.

———. "Mathematics and Meritocracy: The Emergence of the Cambridge Mathematical Tripos." *Social Studies of Science.* Vol. 14, pp. 547–584.

Schneider, B.R. *Wordsworth's Cambridge Education.* 1957.

Winstanley, Denys. *The University of Cambridge in the Eighteenth Century.* 1922.

———. *Unreformed Cambridge.* 1935.

Wordsworth, Christopher. *Scholae Academicae: Some Account of Studies at the English Universities in the Eighteenth Century.* 1877.

Campbell, Thomas (1777–1844)

Campbell, son of a merchant, was educated at Glasgow University and later studied law at Edinburgh. His first publication, *The Pleasures of Hope* (1799), though a considerable success (passing through 10 editions, 1799–1815) brought him no patronage. After a Continental **tour** (1800–1801) and marriage in 1803, Campbell settled in **London** to eke out a living with publishers' hackwork. Little of this is identifiable, although he did edit *The New Monthly Magazine* (1829–1830) and *The Metropolitan* (1831–1832). In *Specimens of the British Poets* (1819) he compiled a popular anthology, notable for its defense of **Alexander Pope** against the **Romantic** strictures of the poet **William Lisle Bowles**.

The Pleasures of Hope continued an established tradition of discursive philosophical verse, yet despite Campbell's allegiance to Pope, and his heroic couplets, the poem's emotional landscapes exhibit anything but **Augustan** poise. Campbell's "plea-

Thomas Campbell

sures" encompass Greek philosophy, **science**, poverty, Polish freedom, the **slave trade**, and other phenomena. The poem has the capaciousness of **James Thomson**'s *Seasons* (1726–1730), but lacks thematic coherence. Its success depended on a series of pathetic cameos held in loose association by sentimentality and an intensity of feeling that occasionally descends into hyperbolic rant. The **Lake School** was hostile to Campbell's "poetical indigestion," but *Pleasures* was the first long romantic poem to achieve popular acclaim, touching a public taste that had failed to respond to the *Lyrical Ballads* a year earlier.

In 1809 Campbell published *Gertrude of Wyoming*. In this idyllic story in Spenserian stanzas his Romantic credentials become more apparent. The heroine is "an enthusiast for the woods," living in what is now Wyoming County, Pennsylvania, where **Coleridge** and **Southey** had planned their pantisocracy. Her tragic death during an indian attack typifies the poem's pathos and sentimentality; but if this was a false note, it was one to which the age returned an echo.

Michael Bruce

Bibliography

Beattie, W. *The Life and Letters of Thomas Campbell.* 1849.

Bierstadt, A.M. "Gertrude of Wyoming." *Journal of English and Germanic Philology.* Vol. 20, pp. 491–501.

Dixon, W.M. *Thomas Campbell: An Oration.* 1928.

Canada

What is called Canada today was, under Hanoverian kings, a growing collection of separate colonies, most of which in 1867 became unified under the British North America Act as the Dominion of Canada. From unpromising beginnings, Canada became the prototype for the evolution of responsible government throughout the **Empire**.

Canada's name, first used by Jacques Cartier (1534), probably comes from the indian word for town or settlement. Its early history reflected the long-standing commercial and imperial struggle between Britain and **France**. The French, after beginning the settlements of Acadia (Novia Scotia) in 1605 and Quebec in 1608, worked to expand the lucrative fur trading operations of the Company of New France, spreading down the St. Lawrence River and as far west as Lake Huron. The British founded the **Hudson's Bay Company**, a typical **chartered trading company**, to counter this (1670), and Canadian history for the next 90 years could be written in terms of the rivalry between the two organizations bent on supplying **overseas commerce** with the raw materials for **hats** and **clothes**. After the French departed (1763), the Hudson's Bay Company found a new rival in the **North West Company**. Still later it played an important role in Canadian westward expansion.

Britain's possessions under the Hanoverians evolved from a few scattered, lightly populated holdings to become the largest imperial property remaining in **North America**. In 1713 after the **War of Spanish Succession**, Nova Scotia and **Newfoundland** (important for its **fishing** industry) were detached from France and absorbed and, in 1763 after the **Seven Years' War**, when British forces drove France entirely off the continent, New France became the colony of Quebec. The **Proclamation of 1763** and **Quebec Act** (1774), drawn up to deal with the results of this, were contributory causes of the **American Revolution**. The subsequent **War of American Independence** (1775–1783) helped cement the Canadian colonies' relation to Britain, as did the **War of 1812**.

British North America, as it was now called, was augmented by the additions of New Brunswick (1784) and Prince Edward Island (1799). Meanwhile the **Nootka Sound** Convention (1790) and **George Vancouver** were strengthening Britain's claims in the Far West, and soon immigration enthusiasts such as **Lord Selkirk** would sponsor settlements in the Great Lakes and Manitoba regions.

There were around 80,000 French speakers in Canada at the time of the American Revolution, and Britain had assumed that Canada would remain predominantly French. But the revolution resulted in some 50,000 English-speaking American loyalists migrating into Canada, some joining the Maritime Colonies but many others settling west of the primarily French-speaking civilization on the lower (i.e., eastern) St. Lawrence River. A large stream of "late loyalists," mostly simple land-seekers, continued to arrive for decades afterward. This led the British government, in the **Constitutional Act** (1791), to divide the colony of Quebec into two parts, Upper Canada (Anglophone) and Lower Canada (Francophone), extending British constitutional rights to each.

This remained the situation, despite ethnic tensions and economic and political discontents, until an abortive rebellion in 1837 underlined the need for constitutional amendments. There was also, from 1830, a rapidly growing wave of British immigrants to consider. Under the British parliamentary Act of Union (1840), the United Province of Canada was created, amending the arrangement of 1791.

The Death of General Wolfe at the Battle of Quebec, 1759

Further unification of nearly all the North American colonies was achieved in 1867. Canada's history, though in some ways similar to that of the American colonies which severed ties with the Empire, provides a counterexample to it, and may furnish one example of how remembering history can avert the tendency to repeat it.

Stuart R. Givens

Bibliography

Craig, G.M. *Upper Canada: The Formative Years, 1784–1841.* 1963.

Finlay, J.L., and D.N. Sprague. *The Structure of Canadian History.* 1984.

Harris, R. Cole, and John Warkentin. *Canada Before Confederation: A Study in Historical Geography.* 1974.

MacNutt, W.S. *The Atlantic Provinces; the Emergence of Colonial Society, 1712–1857.* 1965, 1977.

Smith, Allan. "Metaphor and Nationality in North America." *Canadian Historical Review.* Vol. 5, pp. 247–275.

Warkentin, John, ed. *Canada: A Geographical Interpretation.* 1968.

Canals and Waterways

Development of river navigations and canals was crucial to the process of Hanoverian economic development. River improvements had been pursued from the 16th century, initially to ease the supply of foodstuffs to **London**, but in the 17th century this spread to other regions. It was soon realized that such improvements also reduced the cost of moving other goods, and by the early 18th century such improvements as the Aire and Calder and the Don in the Yorkshire area, and the Mersey and the Weaver in northwest England, were principally motivated by the need to move **coal**. Such developments were usually financed by business groups in the towns affected, often in the form of **joint-stock companies**.

By the 1720s the potential of the inland river system had been almost fully realized, and it was becoming apparent that further progress lay in the development of artificial waterways like those in **France**. But the collapse of the **South Sea Bubble** in 1720 and a period of sluggish trade in ensuing decades meant that investment conditions were not yet right. The first dead-water canal, designed by **James Brindley**, connecting the **Duke of Bridgewater**'s mines in Worsley to Manchester, was not opened until 1761.

The period from 1761 to 1790 saw the second phase of development linking London to the Northwest and Yorkshire by means of canals such as the Grand Junction, Grand Union, and Trent and Mersey. **Birmingham** became the hub of the system, reflecting the fact that the North and the Midlands were the main centers of the **Industrial Revolution**. In **Scotland**, east and west were linked by the Forth and Clyde Canal.

The heyday of the system—1790 to 1830—resulted largely from expansion in economic output and national needs

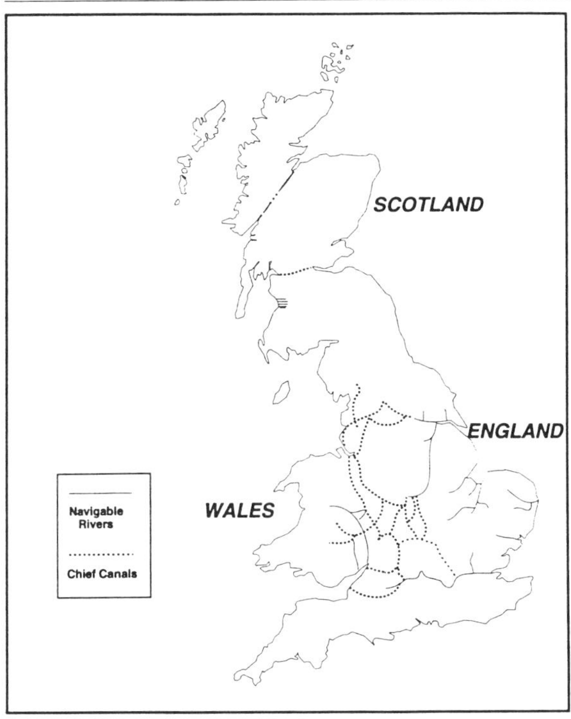

Canals

during the French wars (1793–1815). In this period, east–west links such as the Leeds and Liverpool and Kennet and Avon canals were completed, as well as enterprises serving the agricultural regions of southern England.

Canals were owned and operated by private companies. Investment, particularly in the early stages, came from the locality in which they were to be constructed. Subscribers included bankers, farmers, landowners, merchants, and industrialists. **Josiah Wedgewood** invested in the Trent and Mersey Canal on whose banks his potteries were to be found. Capital was raised by means of share and debenture issues. Preference shares with fixed interest rates were developed to overcome resistance to fluctuating dividends and uncertain returns. Short-term finance could be obtained from banks.

To avoid a monopoly situation, canal companies were forbidden to operate barges—any barge operator paying the required toll could use the canals. As a result, the carrying trade was divided into different organizations. Many small operators sprang up, but large-scale fleets such as Pickford's also emerged. In addition to freight, a considerable passenger trade emerged, such as that between **Glasgow** and **Edinburgh**, a route that carried 200,000 people in 1836.

Canals provided many benefits to the wider economy. Because canal carrying capacity was much greater than that of road vehicles and pack horses, developing industry could depend on regular supplies of raw materials and fuel to larger-scale enterprises. The building of canals gave employment to many and also encouraged the construction of feeder **roads** and **waggonways**. Wherever canals were introduced, lower freight costs for raw materials and foodstuffs resulted. These waterways also helped to move toward a truly national economy: for example, the opening of the Forth and Clyde Canal created a wholly Scottish grain market for the first time. The profession of civil engineering grew out of the canal age, providing such luminaries as Brindley, **John Smeaton**, and **Thomas Telford**.

Toward the end of the Hanoverian period, accusations of overcharging led merchants and industrialists to seek to overcome what was seen as a canal monopoly. The result was a movement toward **railway** construction.

A.J.G. Cummings

Bibliography

Dyos, H.J., and D.H. Aldcroft. *British Transport.* 1974.
Hadfield, Charles. *British Canals.* 1969.
Lindsay, J. *Scottish Canals.* 1968.
Rule, John. *The Vital Century: England's Developing Economy, 1714–1815.* 1991.
Willan, T.S. *River Navigation in England, 1600–1750.* 1936.

See also Finance and Investment

Canning, George (1770–1827)

Canning was one of the most able **Tory** politicians of the decades following 1800, and an important architect of British foreign policy. The son of an impecunious Irish gentleman and an actress who bore many illegitimate children, his career illustrated the old idea that a promising lad could rise to lead the Tories despite severe social disadvantages. Sent by an uncle to Eton and Christ Church, Oxford (B.A. 1790), he won the affections of his aristocratic classmates through his personal charm and intellectual talents. Like his older contemporary **Charles James Fox**, he discovered early how important to political success was the art of cultivating remarkable friends. Yet, also like Fox, while he was greatly loved by some, he was greatly hated by others.

In 1793 Canning was taken into the intimate circle of the Prime Minister, **William Pitt the Younger**, and received a government seat in the **House of Commons**. He helped to begin the ***Anti-Jacobin*** weekly paper (1797), blasting radical and whiggish sympathizers with the **French Revolution**. Canning spent much of the next decade in political skirmishing against other Tories, including **Sidmouth**, **Perceval**, and his arch-rival **Castlereagh**—whom he fought in a duel (1809) that emerged from disputes over strategic failures against Napoleon. He served as Foreign Minister (1807–1809) and, sitting as M.P. for **Liverpool** (1812–1822), became influenced by more progressive commercial and economic ideas than many of his fellow Tories. As President of the Board of Control (1816–1820), responsible for **India**, his arrogance, strong opinions, and biting wit kept him from achieving further heights of leadership in that country. Disapproving of **George IV**'s attempt to divorce **Queen Caroline** (1820), he would have been forced to remain an outsider if Castlereagh had not committed **suicide** in 1822, leaving a vacancy at the top few others could fill.

Canning then became Foreign Minister and leader of the House of Commons (1822–1827), then Prime Minister (1827). His old school friends served as the nucleus of a Canningite group within the Tories in the 1820s, a group of

George Canning

liberals—including **Huskisson** and **Peel**—who challenged the orthodoxies of mercantilism, an exclusive Protestant Constitution, and ultraconservative monarchicalism in foreign affairs. Canning was indeed hated by many in his party (and indulged by some **Whigs**) as a supporter of **Catholic emancipation**, although he was also an opponent of domestic radicalism and parliamentary reform. These alignments precipitated a political crisis in 1827. On the death of **Lord Liverpool**, Canning became leader of a deeply divided Tory party; the strain of governing broke his health, and he died after only four months in office.

It was, however, as Foreign Secretary in the conduct of Britain's foreign relations that Canning accomplished those goals which mark him out as one of the three or four leading British statesmen of the 19th century. His foreign policy combined an intense awareness of England's interest in upholding the European balance of power, a mistrust of the post-1815 Congress system to settle European disputes, and a confidence in his own abilities to create a world, from Rio to Athens, open to British manufacturing goods, naval supremacy, and liberal constitutional ideas. Following lines laid out by Castlereagh, he favored disengagement from conservative states on the Continent, and in fact began working against Britain's former allies in 1823, particularly by recognizing (against opposition by **George IV**, **Eldon**, and **Wellington**) the independence of Spain's rebellious colonies in South America. He also supported the Greek struggle for independence, and sent a fleet and 4,000 troops to Lisbon to support the constitutionalists there against the absolutists (1827). When he died it was widely believed that the South and Central American states, Greece, and Portugal, owed what liberty they possessed, after their own endeavors, to Canning.

James J. Sack

Bibliography

Dixon, Peter. *George Canning: Politician and Statesman.* 1976.
Hinde, Wendy. *George Canning.* 1973.
Marshall, Dorothy. *The Rise of George Canning.* 1938.
Temperley, H. *The Foreign Policy of Canning, 1822–1827.* 1925.

See also Foreign Relations

Cardiff

Cardiff was a borough and county town of Glamorgan, but had only 1,870 residents in 1801, fewer than it had had in the 13th century, when it had been the largest **borough** in **Wales**. It was essentially the trading outlet of the rich agricultural Vale of Glamorgan, a satellite of **Bristol** with a small international **trade** that linked it with Memel in Prussia. A daily mail coach linked it with **London**. Many of Cardiff's inhabitants in the early 18th century were engaged in **agriculture**, though it was clearly distinguished from its surrounding rural area by its trades and professional services. The Englishness of its customs also reflected its urbanity.

Cardiff's fortunes were transformed with the construction of the Glamorganshire **Canal** with its sea lock (completed in 1798). This allowed Cardiff to be the outlet for the **iron** trade of **Merthyr Tydfil** (25 miles in distance and 500 feet in altitude away) to an extent that previous **road** transportation had not allowed. Its population multiplied rapidly, reaching 10,077 in 1831. This new growth was achieved with little physical expansion; infilling of gardens and other open spaces accommodated the population in increasingly overcrowded conditions. The town was in the midst of a gentry heartland: landed families dominated it, with the nonresident earls (marquesses from 1796) of Bute emerging supreme by the late 18th century, controlling the corporation and the parliamentary seat. Occasional challenges by merchant groups, such as in the "spasm of rebellion" of 1818, were largely ineffective, and motivated by factional strife rather than political principle.

The town was part of the Glamorgan boroughs constituency (sharing the seat with seven other boroughs), for which it provided a third of the voters. This was divided in 1832, with Cardiff remaining the chief town in Cardiff boroughs seat, to which Llantrisant and Cowbridge also provided voters. In 1832 the Bute estate began the construction of a **dock**, and (in a separate but related venture) a **railway** link to Merthyr was built at the same time. The opening of these (in 1839 and 1841 respectively) set Cardiff off on an even greater exponential growth.

Neil Evans

Bibliography

Davies, John. *Cardiff and the Marquesses of Bute.* 1981.
Evans, Neil. "Urban Growth, Class Division and Civic Integration: Society 1800–1914," in Phillip Riden, ed., *A History of Cardiff.* Forthcoming.
Hargest, Leighton. "Cardiff's 'Spasm of Rebellion' in 1818." *Morgannwg.* Vol. 21, pp. 69–88.
Jenkins, Philip. "The Tory Tradition in Eighteenth-Century Cardiff." *Welsh History Review.* Vol. 12, pp. 180–196.

Rees, William. *Cardiff: A History of the City.* 2nd ed., 1969.
Williams, Molewyn I. "Cardiff—Its People and Its Trade, 1660–1720." *Morgannwg.* Vol. 7, pp. 74–97.

See also Welsh Agriculture; Welsh Industry; Welsh Mining

Carey, Henry (1687–1743)

With little known about Carey's life it has not been possible to prove or disprove claims that he was an illegitimate son of George Savile, Marquis of Halifax (1633–1695). Poet, dramatist, and musician, he is best known for his **satires** and **burlesques**, such as his poem "Namby Pamby; or, a Panegyric on the New Versification" (1725) and the theatrically successful *The Dragon of Wantley* (1737). He wrote music and lyrics for the theater, and some credit him with having written the British National Anthem. Carey's earliest known publication, *Records of Love; or Weekly Amusements for the Fair Sex* (1710), was one of the first English **periodicals** to publish serial fiction and to include women readers in its audience.

A student of the organist John Reading (1677–1764) and a teacher of Catherine Clive (1711–1785), Carey was well connected to the **music** and **dramatic arts** of **London**. Although he sang professionally for a short time, he made his reputation as composer and librettist. **John Gay** used the tune from his popular **ballad** "Sally in Our Alley" in *The Beggar's Opera* (1728). Carey wrote music and lyrics for other successful plays, including *The Provoked Husband* (1728) by **Colley Cibber** and **Sir John Vanbrugh**.

In 1732, with John Lampe (*c.* 1703–1751) and **Thomas Arne**, he attempted to restore serious **opera** in English. With music by Lampe, Carey's *Amelia* was produced at the Little Theatre in the Haymarket which, some scholars have conjectured, Thomas Arne senior (1682–1736) leased for the 1732 season. Targets for Carey's humor included tragedies, as in his burlesque *Chrononhotonthologos* (1734), and Italian **opera**, as in his own comic opera with music by Lampe, *The Dragon of Wantley*, which outran *The Beggar's Opera* in number of performances.

Janice Broder

Bibliography

Broder, Janice. "Sentiment and Satire in Henry Carey's *Records of Love; or, Weekly Amusements for the Fair Sex.*" *Massachusetts Studies in English.* Vol. 11, pp. 28–41.
Carey, Henry. *Poems for Several Occasions* (1713, 1720, 1729; each edition significantly different from the others).
____. *The Musical Century* (1737, continuation in 1740; 2nd ed., 1743; rpt. 1976).
Lonsdale, Roger, ed. *The New Oxford Book of Eighteenth Century Verse.* 1984.
Macey, Samuel, ed. *The Plays of Henry Carey.* 1980.
Noyes, Robert Gale. "The Contemporary Reception of 'Sally in our Alley.'" *Harvard Studies and Notes in Philology and Literature.* Vol. 18, pp. 165–175.
Scouten, Arthur H. *The London Stage, 1729–1747: A Critical Introduction.* 1968.
Wood, Frederick. T., ed. *The Poems of Henry Carey.* 1930.

Caricature

Originally a product of the Italian Renaissance, caricature became a popular and distinctive English art during the period 1730–1820. The art of caricature, from the Italian verb *caricare* ("to load," as with exaggerated traits), consists in the distorted presentation of an individual's salient features while preserving an identifiable likeness. While sometimes purely comic, Hanoverian caricature was more often satirical, achieving its effect through grotesque exaggeration. Following the tradition of Renaissance painting, where the executioners at Christ's Passion or those individuals committing the Seven Deadly Sins were represented as hideous characters, the satirical caricature's portrayal of outward disfigurement was intended to capture moral deformity within.

When Arthur Pond (1701–1758) produced *Pond's Caricaturas* (1736, 1742), two sets of prints after drawings by Annibale Carracci (1560–1609), Pier Leone Ghezzi (1674–1755), and others, caricature quickly became part of the English printmaker's visual repertoire. One of the earliest works to caricature a public official, *Great Britain and Ireland's Yawn* (1743), by George Bickham the Younger (*c.* 1706–1771), depicts the face of "Prime Minister" **Sir Robert Walpole** disfigured with the tedium of his 21-year administration. It was not until **George Townshend**'s *The Recruiting Serjeant* (1757), however, that personal caricature became a standard weapon in the armory of political **satire**. As such it became a formidable force, peculiarly English perhaps because of the greater openness of English politics in the Hanoverian age and the taste for deflationary **ridicule** fostered not only by **party politics** but also by the social pretense generated by rapid economic expansion.

Henry Fielding, in his preface to *Joseph Andrews* (1742), used the newly popular art of caricature to develop his aesthetic of the comic, suggesting that caricature is closely allied to the **burlesque** in writing. **William Hogarth**, inspired by Fielding (his friend) and reacting against the popularity of Pond's works, produced *Characters and Caricaturas* (1743): the subscription ticket for *Marriage à la Mode* (1745), this etching was intended to distinguish Hogarth's own work from caricature, though it seems not to have had the desired effect. Later in the century, Johann Lavater's *Essays on Physiognomy* (Eng. trans. 1788–1798) likewise sought to distance his "science" from caricature with little success.

Though no less a painter than **Sir Joshua Reynolds** briefly experimented with this genre, the caricature groups of Thomas Patch (1725–1782) represent the finest work of this kind in oils by an English artist. And while Patch was painting England's elite on the **Grand Tour** in Florence, Mary and Matthew Darly, leading printsellers of the day, were popularizing the art of caricature from their print shops in **London**. *A Book of Caricatures . . . With ye Principles of Designing in the . . . Pleasing Manner* (1762) appeared just when the print market was being greatly invigorated by intense political opposition to the **Earl of Bute**. Ironically it was not Bute but rather **John Wilkes**, his opponent, who was leeringly portrayed (by Hogarth) in the most popular political print of the day (1763); it sold out its initial run of 4,000 copies almost immediately, then engaged several presses day and night in order to keep up with the unprecedented demand.

Amateur artists such as George Townshend, Henry William Bunbury (1750–1811), Henry Wigstead (*d.* 1800), John Nixon (*c.* 1750–1818), and James Sayers (1748–1825) made significant contributions to the evolution of English caricature and helped to underscore the notion that this was a truly popular art form open to all, regardless of formal training. Many of their innovations and ideas were taken up by the three greatest masters of the English satirical print, **Thomas Rowlandson**, **James Gillray**, and **George Cruikshank**. The caricatures of Rowlandson, the best draftsman of the group, generally lack the acid quality of Gillray's and Cruikshank's grotesquely distorted personal satires, which often were bitingly aimed at the fads, **fashions**, and fops of high society.

Although the satirical aspects of English caricature would soon be subordinated to the comic designs of the Victorian cartoon, *Rules for Drawing Caricaturas* (1789) by Francis Grose (1731–1791), and J.P. Malcom's *An Historical Sketch of the Art of Caricaturing* (1813) testify to the considerable accessibility, sophistication, and celebrity that caricature enjoyed in Hanoverian Britain. The Victorians, more sentimental, had rather less appetite for satire in general, and caricature faded somewhat among the graphic arts.

Michael F. Suarez, S.J.

Bibliography

Carretta, Vincent. *The Snarling Muse: Verbal and Visual Political Satire from Pope to Churchill.* 1983.
———. *George III and the Satirists from Hogarth to Byron.* 1990.
Dickinson, S.T. *Caricatures and the Constitution, 1760–1832.* 1986.
George, M. Dorothy. *English Political Caricature: A Study of Opinion and Propaganda.* 2 vols. 1959.
Godfrey, Richard. *English Caricature 1620 to the Present.* 1984.
Hofmann, Werner. *Caricature from Leonardo to Picasso.* Eng. ed., 1957.
Riely, John. *The Age of Horace Walpole in Caricature.* 1973.
Wood, Marcus. *Radical Satire and Print Culture, 1790–1822.* 1994.

See also Drawing; Engraving; Graphic Arts; Political Prints

Carleton, Guy, Baron Dorchester (1724–1808)

Carleton was a soldier and high administrator intimately connected with the history of imperial Canada throughout the latter 18th century. In 1759 he accompanied **General James Wolfe** to Quebec and was wounded during the Battle of the Plains of Abraham. In 1766 he was named Lt. Governor of **Quebec**, and in 1768, Governor. He was a primary architect of the **Quebec Act** (1774), by which the British government for the first time legislated that the rights and cultures of non–British peoples within the **Empire** should be recognized.

The **American Revolution** tested Carleton's military talents. He proved a master strategist, but was much weaker as a tactician. In 1775 he successfully defended Quebec City

Guy Carleton, Baron Dorchester

against a concerted American attack, but he too hesitantly handled the pursuit of the American army from the St. Lawrence to Lake Champlain (1776). He fully supported **Burgoyne** as the latter prepared his invasion southward (1777), but disagreements between Carleton and **Lord George Germain**, Secretary of State for the Colonies, led to his resignation and return to England (1778).

Notwithstanding, in 1782 he was named Commander-in-Chief and Commissioner of British forces in America, in which capacity he labored to evacuate Loyalists from New York; many of whom went to Canada. In 1786, just after being created Baron Dorchester, he was named Governor-in-Chief of British North American provinces. He was now asked, as the framer of the Quebec act, to propose a new plan to meet the changed conditions brought about by the influx of Loyalists into Quebec. When he failed, **Baron Grenville**, Secretary of State for Colonies, drew up the **Constitutional Act of 1791**, which split the Canadas in two—a move that Carleton totally opposed. Failing also to secure official support for the indians of the Great Lakes area in the face of American expansionist pressure, Carleton angrily resigned and left for permanent retirement in Britain (1796).

Carleton has been praised for many of his contributions to the development of British North America, though he has also been condemned for his failures and for what his enemies termed his mean-tempered and vindictive behavior. His place in Canadian history, while tarnished, is nonetheless secure.

Stuart R. Givens

Bibliography

Allen, Robert S. *His Majesty's Indian Allies: British Indian Policy in the Defense of Canada, 1774–1815.* 1992.

Burt, A.L. "Guy Carleton, Lord Dorchester, 1724–1808." *The Canadian Historical Association Booklet No. 5.* 1968.
———. *The Old Province of Quebec.* 1993.
Upton, L.F.S., ed. *The Diary and Papers of William Smith.* 1963–1964.

See also Canada; War of American Independence

Carlile, Richard (1790–1843)

Carlile, radical printer and social reformer, was a conspicuous champion of a free press, birth control, free secular education, universal suffrage, and republican government. Born in Devon, he attended a local **charity school** until age 12. For the next 15 years he worked as a tinsmith until moving to **London**, where he encountered poverty and inequality as well as **radical** and republican political ideas. Turning to **journalism**, he became a salesman of *The Black Dwarf,* a radical newspaper, and then publisher of *Sherwin's Weekly Political Register.* He also reissued radical and **deist** works, including those by **Thomas Paine** and **William Hone**. Carlile was attracted to the political style of **Henry Hunt** and the even more radical ideas of the **Society of Spencean Philanthropists**.

In 1819, the year before his admiring *Life of Thomas Paine* appeared, Carlile was, in a famous trial, convicted of blasphemous libel, sentenced to three years in prison, and fined £1,500 for reprinting Paine's *The Age of Reason* and other works. Also in 1819 he took over Sherwin's paper, changed its name to *The Republican,* and operated it for the next 6 years while still in prison. During his lifetime he spent more than 9 years in jail for publishing subversive ideas. These appeared in a variety of pamphlets and **newspapers** such as *The Gorgon* (founded by **John Wade**) and *The Lion* in the 1820s, and the *Gauntlet* and *Carlile's Political Register* in the following decade.

In the latter 1820s, as a **freethinking** preacher, Carlile adopted the language of **millenarianism** to spread his gospel of the liberation of the working class. In the 1830s he "converted" to Christianity (his friends denounced his apostasy) and, suffering illness from his incarcerations and poverty, went on to dabble in vegetarianism and **mesmerism**.

Jack Fruchtman, Jr.

Bibliography

Aldred, Guy A. *Richard Carlile, Agitator: His Life and Times.* 1941.
Wiener, Joel H. *Radicalism and Freethought in Nineteenth-Century Britain: The Life of Richard Carlile.* 1983.

See also Laws of Public Worship, Speech, and the Press

Carlyle, Alexander (1722–1805)

Carlyle, minister of the parish of Inveresk (near Edinburgh) from 1748 until his death, was a prominent clergyman in the Moderate party in the **Church of Scotland** during the second half of the 18th century. Closely associated with **Adam Ferguson** and **John Home**, he was a member of the Select Society, the Poker Club, and other convivial and improving organizations of the **Scottish Enlightenment**. He published more than a dozen pamphlets and occasional **sermons**, and participated in other productions. Most of these writings were polemical and more or less political, promoting causes such as the Scots militia bill, Home's tragedy of *Douglas,* economic improvement and liberal education for the Scottish clergy, and ecclesiastical **patronage**, while opposing others such as the American and French revolutions. Carlyle is best known as a memorialist: His anecdotal memoirs, first published in 1860, constitute one of the liveliest examples of that genre and the most insightful and revealing account of the social life and personalities of the Scottish Enlightenment and the Church of Scotland in his day.

Richard B. Sher

Bibliography

Burton, John Hill, ed. *The Autobiography of Dr. Alexander Carlyle of Inveresk, 1722–1805.* 1910; rpt., with a new introduction by Richard B. Sher, 1990.
Kinsley, James, ed. *Alexander Carlyle's Anecdotes and Characters of the Times.* 1973.
Sher, Richard B. *Church and University in the Scottish Enlightenment: The Moderate Literati of Edinburgh.* 1985.

Caroline, Queen, Wife of George II (1683–1737)

Caroline Wilhelmina of Anspach was the most politically involved of the Hanoverian queens. Orphaned as a girl, she grew up at the courts of Saxony and Prussia. In 1705 she married George Augustus of Hanover. At the Hanoverian court she became a protégé of the Dowager Electress Sophia, and under her tutelage began to study English and British politics in preparation for the anticipated **Hanoverian succession**.

In 1714 Caroline and her husband accompanied **George I** to Britain as Prince and Princess of Wales. Bad relations between the king and the prince culminated in 1717 with George Augustus's banishment from court. He and Caroline moved to **Leicester House**, where they attracted many ambitious politicians as well as literary and social figures. During this period Caroline became friendly with **Robert Walpole**. The royal family formally reconciled in 1720.

Tradition says that Caroline was crucial in George II's retaining Walpole as chief minister after George I's death. Her role has probably been overrated, though both George and Walpole depended on her as a channel of communication. Caroline, a staunch **Whig**, was an active patron of politicians and also of writers, clerics such as **Bishop Hoadly** and **Archbishop Potter**, and such luminaries as Gottfried Wilhelm von Leibnitz (1646–1716), Sir Isaac Newton (1642–1727), and **George Frideric Handel**. Her interest in cultural, religious, and political affairs gave her court more prestige and a better reputation than those of other Hanoverians.

Caroline and George had eight children. She tolerated his mistresses. He trusted her as Regent when he was in Hanover. She was widely mourned at her death from cancer in 1737. Handel wrote an anthem for her funeral.

Barbara Brandon Schnorrenberg

Bibliography
Arkell, Ruby L. *Caroline of Anspach.* 1939.

Queen Caroline, Wife of George IV

Caroline, Queen, Wife of George IV (1768–1821)

When there are warring camps in the royal family, many people will support the anti-establishment figure. It was almost for this reason alone that Caroline became loved. Caroline Amelia of Brunswick married George, Prince of Wales, in 1795. She was his cousin, the niece of his father, **George III**. The prince had agreed to marriage only to salvage his desperate financial position. Caroline was ill-educated, with few pretensions to taste or manners, and possessed few attractions. By the time of their daughter's birth (1796), the two were no longer living together.

Rejected by most of the royal family, Caroline lived in several houses in London. Her choice of companions was indiscreet, and her lifestyle was the subject of unfavorable, though unprovable, gossip. She was often refused access to Charlotte, her daughter, especially after George became Regent (1811).

In 1813 Caroline went to the Continent, where her conduct continued to elicit talk. London wags, condensing gossip about her travels in Italy, referred to her as a "Mother of the Italian People." **George IV**, detested even more than she, on his accession in 1820 ordered her name omitted from the liturgy and insisted that his ministers institute **divorce** proceedings in the **House of Lords**. The effect was to make her a popular heroine. Returning to England, she found herself cheered by the public as a wronged woman and exploited by the **Whigs** to attack the **Tory** ministry. Popular disturbances swirling around her, the Lords passed the divorce bill by only nine votes; it was clear that the **Commons** would reject it altogether.

The government was forced to abandon the bill, but George had his revenge by refusing Caroline a royal lodging and having her locked out of the coronation. On coronation day (19 July), before the ceremony, against friends' advice, she went to each door of Westminster Abbey, demanding to be admitted, but was turned away. She died unexpectedly a year later, of an intestinal obstruction.

Barbara Brandon Schnorrenberg

Bibliography
Holme, Thea. *Caroline: A Biography of Caroline of Brunswick.* 1980.

Carron Company

Carron Ironworks at Carron in Stirlingshire, **Scotland**, was established (1759) to exploit the demand for iron during the **Seven Years' War**. The company's principal partners were William Cadell Sr. (1708–1777), a merchant in the Swedish iron and timber trades; his son, William Cadell Jr. (1737–1819), **Dr. John Roebuck**; and Samuel Garbett (1717–1803)—the last two already being joint partners in several enterprises, including sulphuric acid works in **Birmingham** and at Prestonpans near **Edinburgh** (1749). Cadell Sr. had local knowledge and Roebuck the necessary technical skills, while Garbett provided business expertise. Carron Company had an initial capital of £12,000, with provision for its increase to £24,000, but by a decade later more than £150,000 had been invested in its expensive equipment, making it a very large enterprise even by contemporary standards, well beyond the resources of small-scale operation. In 1773, beset by financial problems, it was relaunched as a **joint-stock company**.

Carron differed from earlier Scottish ironworks in both scale and techniques. It used local iron ores and adopted coke-smelting, the latter developed half a century earlier by **Abraham Darby** at Coalbrookdale, Shropshire. Much of the needed expertise and skilled labor was initially imported from England, with production being concentrated on cannon manufacture. Technical problems associated with casting and boring dogged Carron's fortunes for some years, but in the longer term the "Carronade" (a short cannon of large bore) became the company's most famous product—used, for example, by **Admiral Horatio Nelson** on his flagship *Victory*—and a standard **weapon** in the Royal **Navy**. By 1800, Carron was the largest munitions plant in all Europe.

Carron had also supplied the iron cylinder for an experimental **steam engine** developed in 1765 by **James Watt**. Although historically important, little of the early plant survives today, though parts of the complex water supply system can still be seen. Carron Company provides an interesting case study of business enterprise during the early stages of the **Industrial Revolution**.

Ian Donnachie

Bibliography
Campbell, Roy H. *Carron Company.* 1961.

See also Banking and Bankers; Iron Industry; Metallurgy and Metalworking

Carteret, John (Lord Granville) (1690–1763)

Statesman, classical scholar, and **diplomat**, 1st Earl of Granville from 1744, Carteret's career reflected the political struggles within the **Whig** party between 1715 and 1750. His intelligence, charm, and diplomatic skill won him favor with Hanoverian kings, but his cheerful detachment from the struggles for office left him vulnerable to the skills of political insiders.

After the accession of **George I** (1714), as a member of the **Stanhope** and Sunderland faction of the Whigs, Carteret served as Ambassador Extraordinary to Sweden (1719–1720). During the settlement of the Great Northern War he managed a reconciliation between Sweden and Denmark, and protected the interests of **Hanover**. In 1721 he became Secretary of State, but in 1724 his bungled plan to marry one of the king's mistresses into the French nobility lost him George's confidence and allowed his rival, **Robert Walpole**, to maneuver him into the secondary post of Lord Lieutenant for **Ireland**.

In Ireland Carteret supervised administrative reforms, opened the church and the government to Irishmen, and ended a controversial monopoly of the coinage. In 1730 he resigned and joined the Whig **opposition** to Walpole.

When Walpole fell (1742), Carteret returned as Secretary of State. He focused English diplomacy in the **War of Austrian Succession** on protecting Hanover and keeping Spanish and French influence out of Italy and central Europe. To this end he constructed alliances bringing together Austria, Prussia, and Sardinia. His ministerial rivals, the **Pelhams**, criticized his diplomacy's cost and its weak support of an alliance with Austria. By 1744 Carteret's prospective allies had fallen out, and the Pelhams convinced **George II** that his aggressive policies were losing parliamentary support; in November he had to resign. In 1750 he accepted appointment as President of the Privy Council, an office he held until his death.

Robert D. McJimsey

Bibliography

Browning, Reed. *The Duke of Newcastle.* 1975.
Harris, Robert. *A Patriot Press: National Politics and the London Press in the 1740s.* 1993.
Langford, Paul. *The Eighteenth Century, 1688–1815.* 1976.
Plumb, J.H. *Sir Robert Walpole: The King's Minister.* 1961.
Rogers, Nicholas. *Whigs and Cities: Popular Politics in the Age of Walpole and Pitt.* 1990.
Williams, Basil. *Carteret and Newcastle.* 1966.

See also Broad-Bottom Administration; Foreign Relations

Cartography

Hanoverian Britain witnessed many efforts to produce hydrographic charts and land maps, to reduce distortion in two-dimensional projections, and to develop maps representing data such as tides and currents, climate, geology, mineralogy, soil, agriculture, and demography.

Early land maps were based on estimated distances, whereas sea charts employed rhumb lines based on compass headings between known points of land. Accurate cartography depends on plotting coordinates of latitude and longitude on an imaginary grid projected over the surface of the Earth. These concepts formed the basis of Ptolemy's *Geography,* a 2nd-century book first **translated** into Latin in 1409 which provided the foundation of 18th-century research.

Improvements in measuring latitude and longitude at sea produced more reliable coordinates. The reflecting sextant (1757) replaced earlier devices for the astronomical measurement of latitude, and doubled in making azimuth calculations more accurate than those measured by compass. The problem of determining **longitude** was first solved by "lunars," or observations of the moon's orbit, and later by means of John Harrison's (1693–1776) accurate **chronometers**. The application of spherical trigonometry and logarithms meant that land could be surveyed by triangulation from carefully measured baselines, without pacing off and measuring every foot of ground.

At sea, explorers such as **Captain Cook** filled in blank spaces on world maps by charting previously unknown coastlines and thus establishing newer, more accurate coordinates. England and **France** led in this scientific **exploration**, which paralleled their commercial and military rivalry. In 1795 the Admiralty established a Hydrographic Office under **Dalrymple**, which in 1811 took control of the **navy**'s surveying service; in 1814 it added the first surveying **ships** to the navy's lists. Admiralty charts of the world's seas and coasts set international standards.

On land, England's Deputy Quartermaster General Lt-Col. David Watson (*c.* 1713–1761) set out in 1746 to produce a military map of **Scotland**'s Highlands. William Roy (1726–1790), his assistant, was appointed Surveyor General of Coasts and made responsible for military surveying throughout the United Kingdom in 1765. In 1783, at the invitation of the French, Roy joined a project to triangulate the topography between the Greenwich and Paris observatories. With the sponsorship of the king and **Sir Joseph Banks**, President of the **Royal Society**, Roy laid out a baseline more than 5 miles long on Hounslow Heath and, using instruments by Jesse Ramsden (1735–1800), England's foremost instrumentmaker, began triangulating the southeastern counties.

After Roy's death this work was formalized as the Trigonometric Survey by the Master-General of the Ordnance, and thus became known as the Ordnance Survey. Extended to Scotland, **Ireland**, and **Wales**, the triangulation was completed in 1853; the parallel work of engraving and printing the one-inch-to-one-mile scale maps took longer. Meanwhile, similar national trigonometric surveys were conducted throughout Europe and in **India**, yielding a world map accurate in detail, albeit still incomplete. For the printing of maps, copper **engraving** was the preferred technology; however, the introduction of lithography after 1800, and zincography after 1855, simplified their reproduction.

N. Merrill Distad

Bibliography

Day, Vice-Admiral Sir Archibald. *The Admiralty Hydrographic Service, 1795–1919.* 1967.

Pera, Mary. *Surveys of the Seas: A Brief History of British Hydrography.* 1957.

Ritchie, Rear-Admiral George Stephen. *The Admiralty Chart: British Naval Hydrography in the Nineteenth Century.* 1967.

Skelton, Raleigh Ashlin. "Cartography," in Charles Singer et al., eds., *A History of Technology,* Vol. 4: *The Industrial Revolution, c. 1750–c. 1850.* 1958.

Taylor, Eva G.R. "Cartography, Survey, and Navigation, 1400–1750," in Charles Singer et al., eds., *A History of Technology,* Vol. 3: *From the Renaissance to the Industrial Revolution, c. 1500–c. 1750.* 1957.

Tooley, Ronald Vere. *Maps and Map-Makers.* 1949; 6th ed., 1978.

Cartwright, Edmund (1743–1823)

The inventor of the power loom, a momentous addition to Britain's **textile industries**, the Rev. Dr. Cartwright was born in Nottinghamshire, educated at Wakefield Grammar School and Oxford, and made Vicar of Goadby Marwood in Leicestershire. He was the younger brother of the redoubtable **Major John Cartwright**, leader of **radicalism** for decades.

While on holiday at Matlock in Derbyshire Cartwright met some **Manchester** businessmen who challenged him, after a spirited discussion of current **spinning** technology, to produce a power loom, which they regarded as impracticable. At that time, thanks to **Arkwright**'s water frame, great quantities of fine yarn were available but not the machinery to weave it into cloth; to export the yarn might seriously injure the British textile industry. Cartwright produced a steam-driven loom in 1785, but it was very heavy and extremely complicated, and required two men to work it. Observing its operation carefully, he significantly improved his prototype by 1788. His machine could now be used successfully to weave **cotton** and other textiles.

Edmund Cartwright

In 1787 he established a power-loom **factory** at Doncaster, but this was not successful. In 1791 he managed to interest the Grimshaw brothers of Manchester in his project, but though a large factory was built, it was willfully burned down after various acts of intimidation, deterring other investors. Over time, nonetheless, the improvement and adoption of the power loom proceeded. By 1810, Cartwright's invention had proved itself. There were then some 2,000 power looms in Britain (though there were still a hundred times that many handlooms). With a parliamentary grant of £10,000 (1809) Cartwright purchased a farm in Kent and lived in relative comfort until his death. **Factory workers** meanwhile began organizing their lives around the power loom; handloom weavers organized theirs around growing unemployment.

John Butt

Bibliography

English, Walter. *The Textile Industry.* 1969.

Mantoux, Paul. *The Industrial Revolution in the Eighteenth Century.* 1961.

Cartwright, John (1740–1824)

Major John Cartwright, brother of **Edmund Cartwright**, the inventor of the power loom, was one of the chief spokesmen for radical political reform during the reign of **George III**. Though a member of the landed **gentry**, he was one of the first Englishmen to contend that mere citizenship, not property, should be the basis for political rights, thus anticipating the fundamental idea of modern democracy. Indeed, his main reform ideas were nearly all eventually adopted in the modern democratic parliamentary system.

Cartwright first served in the **navy**, rising to a lieutenancy (1766), but later gained appointment as Major in the Nottinghamshire Militia (1775). He had then just emerged as an early supporter of the American colonists and a severe critic of the entire system of English government, which he considered corrupted by the selfishness and degeneracy of professional politicians. In his *American Independence, the Interest and Glory of Great Britain* (1774), he argued that England should not impose imperial rule but rather be content to reinvigorate and spread her ancient, pre–Norman heritage of individual liberties and to also rely on the common language and culture of Englishmen as the ties by which to bind the Americans.

In his popular pamphlet, *Take Your Choice* (1776), Cartwright argued for drastic domestic reform that would include universal manhood suffrage, salaries and the abolition of property qualifications for M.P.s, annual elections, the secret ballot, and the drawing up of equal electoral districts. Claiming that annual elections and universal manhood suffrage had existed in the historic golden age of Anglo-Saxon England, he insisted that his program was one of restoration, not innovation. Some historians, forgetting how patriotic ideology may invent a past in order to shape the future, have mistakenly portrayed Cartwright as conservative, but in fact

Major John Cartwright

his patriotic **nationalism**, which he shared with **John Horne Tooke** and others, was radical if deceptive. He also borrowed from **James Burgh** the idea, shocking to contemporary politicians, that a national **association** or convention should be formed to restore ancient English liberties if Parliament refused to act. Such alternative "parliaments" were in fact tried several times between the 1770s and the 1850s.

Cartwright advocated universal manhood suffrage and did not, as many radicals did, conceive of limiting the vote to ratepayers. But he was not a notable champion of the working class as such. His program was political, not economic, and his radicalism had an 18th-century cast to it. In calling for the elimination of property qualifications for office, his aim was evidently to have the right to sit in Commons extended to a broad section of the **middle class** who possessed property other than land. His appeal for salaries for M.P.s was calculated more to reduce the **patronage** influence of the government than to induce the working classes to seek election. But Cartwright was broad-minded and interested more in political inclusiveness than exclusion; and the principles he articulated, and the reforms he proposed, became central to British radicalism down to the era of Chartism and beyond.

Cartwright joined with Horne Tooke and others in forming the **Society for Constitutional Information** in 1780. During the period of the **French Revolution** he doggedly continued his agitations, testifying at Tooke's trial (1794), proposing schemes for military reform along the lines of the Anglo-Saxon militia, running repeatedly but unsuccessfully for Parliament, helping to invent and spread **Hampden Clubs** (after 1812), and touring the country, trying to stir up interest in parliamentary reform. Cartwright was on first-name terms with all the important radicals of the era, including **Burdett**, **Cobbett**, **Place**, **Henry Hunt**, and **Thomas Wooler**. In 1820, in the atmosphere of governmental repression that marked that period, he was convicted of sedition, but nonetheless went on with his radical agitations and publications until his death. His persistence for over 50 years, and his centrality to radical leadership, earned him the name "Father of Reform."

Frank M. Baglione

Bibliography

Cone, Carl B. *The English Jacobins: Reformers in Late 18th Century England.* 1968.

Cowie, L.W. *Hanoverian England, 1714–1837.* 1967.

Goodwin, Albert. *The Friends of Liberty: The English Democratic Movement in the Age of the French Revolution.* 1979.

Hone, J. Ann. *For the Cause of Truth: Radicalism in London, 1796–1821.* 1982.

Mee, John. *Dangerous Enthusiasm: William Blake and the Culture of Radicalism in the 1790s.* 1992.

Newman, Gerald. *The Rise of English Nationalism: A Cultural History, 1740–1830.* 1987.

See also Elections and the Franchise; Radicalism and Radical Politics

Castlereagh, Viscount; 2nd Marquess of Londonderry (Robert Stewart) (1769–1822)

Castlereagh was perhaps the most eminent foreign secretary of the Hanoverian period. His reputation as an ultrareactionary in both foreign and domestic policy has been modified lately by a clearer recognition of his accomplishments and aspirations in the period following 1815. Born in **Dublin** of an upwardly mobile Ulster family of Scottish descent, he was elected to the **Irish Parliament** in 1790 as someone who had shown sympathy with the revolutionary ideals of the Americans and the French. By 1794, however, when he was returned to the Westminster Parliament, his earlier enthusiasm for revolution had faded and he had become a devoted admirer of **William Pitt the Younger** and a supporter of the emerging **Tory** party.

The **Irish Rebellion** of 1798 confirmed Castlereagh in this stance and, as Chief Secretary for Ireland (1798–1801), he played a vital role in persuading the Irish Parliament to accept the **Act of Union** (1800) with Britain. Like Pitt, however, he believed that, at the same time, concessions needed to be made to the **Roman Catholic** community in Ireland and, also like Pitt, he resigned at **George III**'s unwillingness to do so (1801). While lacking oratorical skills, he proved an efficient minister. As Secretary of War in 1805 and again in 1807–1809 he made major improvements in the organization of the war office and gave **Wellington** command in the Iberian Peninsula. His standing was undone, however, by the failure of the Walcheren expedition (near Antwerp, 1809) and by a notorious duel (also 1809) in which he wounded **George Canning**, his bitter rival for the mantle of Pitt.

In 1812 Castlereagh took office as Foreign Secretary and was also chief spokesman in the **Commons** for the government of **Lord Liverpool**. As a result, he had to accept much of the opprobrium for an increasingly reactionary domestic policy. With a cool, controlled use of power unimpeded by political idealism, in 1814–1815 he played a central role in

Lord Castlereagh, from a painting by T. Lawrence

arranging a peace settlement across Europe, imposing the will of the great powers on lesser states, gaining most of what Britain wanted from the settlement, and bringing a chastened France back into the world of political respectability.

Castlereagh tried to construct a postwar system of regular conferences of powers to discuss necessary future adjustments as a rational alternative to the Tsar's "sublime mysticism and nonsense" of a "Holy Alliance." But his hopes were never realized, and by 1818 Britain was steadily withdrawing from a central role in European affairs. Castlereagh's commitment to international order did not extend to an endorsement of the despotic politics of Russia, Austria, or Spain, but this did not save him from the bitter hatred of liberal intellectuals such as **Byron** and **Shelley**, not to mention contemporary **radicals** such as **Thistlewood**, **Cobbett**, and **Orator Hunt**, who saw him as the mastermind also of domestic repression. After the failed attempt to push **Queen Caroline**'s divorce through Parliament (1820), Castlereagh had a mental breakdown and committed **suicide** at age 53.

W. Hamish Fraser

Bibliography

Bartlett, C.J. *Castlereagh.* 1966.

Derry, J.W. *Castlereagh.* 1976.

Kissinger, H. *A World Restored.* 1973.

Montgomery Hyde, H. *The Strange Death of Lord Castlereagh.* 1959.

Webster, C. *The Foreign Policy of Castlereagh.* 2 vols. 1963.

See also Foreign Relations

Catholics

See Roman Catholicism

Catholic Committee

"Catholic Committee" was the name taken by several liberal and largely lay-governed **Catholic** groups in the Hanoverian age, but it also designates a single organization founded (1782) to promote better relations between the government and the **Roman Catholic** Church, and to stimulate internal church reform.

This organization's progressive spirit was captured in *The State and Behaviour of the English Catholics from the Reformation to the Year 1780* (1780) by Catholic divine Joseph Berington (1746–1827); who, with his brother the Catholic Bishop Charles Berington (1748–1798), campaigned during the 1780s for relief from discrimination against Catholics and for the liberalization of the Church hierarchy. Led by the older Catholic gentry, and stimulated by shock at the violence of the **Gordon Riots** (1780), the committee urged consideration of an English-language mass and the assertion of greater independence from Rome. Its labors were influential in helping to remove some anti–Catholic prejudices, Parliament passing a second **Catholic Relief Act** in 1791 to enlarge the effects of the earlier act of 1778.

The committee's more sweeping plans for harmony were frustrated by the conservative social climate of the 1790s, when England was at war with **France**, and **Ireland** was in rebellion. Some members of the committee joined the new Cisalpine **Club** (1792), whose aim of achieving cooperation with Anglicanism was, however, opposed by the ultraconservative Roman-Catholic Club (founded 1793). The Catholic Committee, with a membership composed of largely well-to-do and professional persons, continued into the 19th century as a major lobbying force in favor of **Catholic Emancipation**. "The Liberator," **Daniel O'Connell**, had become one of its leaders by 1815.

Timothy Erwin

Bibliography

Aveling, J.C.H. *The Handle and the Axe: The Catholic Recusants in England from Reformation to Emancipation.* 1976.

Machin, G.I.T. *The Catholic Question in English Politics, 1820 to 1830.* 1964.

Catholic Emancipation

Before the Hanoverian period, many restrictions against the political and civil rights of **Catholics** had been laid down in innumerable discriminatory **penal laws**. After the **Forty-five**, in the more expansively liberal atmosphere of the latter 18th century, various **Catholic Relief Acts** ameliorated conditions for Catholics in Great Britain while still largely ignoring those in **Ireland**. The **Act of Union** (1800) had been intended by **Pitt** to combine constitutional merger with complete political enfranchisement so that Irish Catholics, who in 1793 had gained the right to hold land and vote for M.P.s on the same terms as Irish Protestants, would also be permitted to sit in Parliament and hold high office; but Pitt's plan foundered on the obstinacy of **George III** and Catholic Emancipation remained unfulfilled.

To Ireland's Catholics, full political rights seemed a possible deliverance from severe worsening economic and social problems. Absentee landownership, backward **Irish agriculture**, the ever-present danger of **famine**, scarcity of natural resources, the weakness of **Irish industry** (injured by English competition after the Union), political and agrarian violence led by **Defenders** and **Ribbonmen** and a host of other groups, all combined to create an explosive mixture. And there were other reasons why emancipation became the central political question of the 1820s. Not only was it a fond old theme of the **Whigs**, but repeal (1828) of the **Test and Corporation Acts**, giving **dissenters** full political rights, dismantled the old argument for keeping politics an exclusive official preserve of Anglicans.

The question was forced by **Daniel O'Connell**, leader of the Catholic Association founded (1823) to reorganize the Catholic voting power normally trained deferentially toward landlords of the **Anglo-Protestant Irish Ascendancy**. Standing for election to Parliament from County Clare, and supported by priests as well as the forty-shilling Irish tenant–farmers (in Ireland there were close to 200,000), O'Connell's election (1828) as M.P. to a seat, which (as a Catholic) he was forbidden to take, led to a crisis. With Ireland in possibly dangerous excitement, and with opinion in the **Commons** (though not the **Lords**) almost evenly divided on, or perhaps slightly in favor of, emancipation, the government of **Wellington** and **Peel** carried the act of emancipation. By its terms, virtually all remaining restrictions on Catholics were removed; they were permitted to sit in Parliament and hold nearly every office in the country but those of Regent or Lord Chancellor. A separate act (a piece of revenge on O'Connell and his poor followers) altered Irish voting qualifications to favor larger property-holders but the **elections** of 1830 saw 16 Catholics seated notwithstanding.

Timothy Erwin

Bibliography

Machin, G.I.T. *The Catholic Question in English Politics, 1820 to 1830.* 1964.

Norman, Edward. *The English Catholic Church in the Nineteenth Century.* 1984.

O'Ferrall, Fergus. *Catholic Emancipation: Daniel O'Connell and the Birth of Irish Democracy, 1820–30.* 1985.

Scally, Robert. *The End of Hidden Ireland: Rebellion, Famine, and Emigration.* 1995.

Catholic Relief Acts

The Catholic Relief Acts of 1778 and 1791 provided for the repeal of some of the more severe **penal laws** preventing English **Roman Catholics** from inheriting family property, practicing their religion, educating their children within the faith, serving in the military, and holding public office. Similar acts were passed in the **Irish Parliament**, ratifying similar relief to Catholics in **Ireland**.

There was a relaxation of anti–Catholic feeling during the generation after 1745. In 1778 an address was presented to **George III** bearing the signatures of Charles Howard, 11th Duke of Norfolk (1746–1815), and nine other peers and 163 commoners on behalf of the rights of Catholics. Upholding the Hanoverian succession and allegiance to the English constitution, it requested royal indulgence. Passed in Parliament shortly thereafter was the first Catholic Relief Act, introduced by Sir George Savile (1726–1784) and the **Rockingham Whigs**. This repealed certain clauses of an act of 1697 that had placed obstacles in the way of Catholic worship by rewarding anti–Catholic informers, condemning priests and schoolmasters to life imprisonment, and restricting landownership.

The secretary of the **Catholic Committee**, lawyer Charles Butler (1750–1832), wrote that the act's passage was an important step toward full **Catholic emancipation**, and indeed it was partly from suspicion that this was true that **London** witnessed the **Gordon Riots** (1780). Another Catholic Relief Act (April 1791) provided for a lenient oath of allegiance, abolished the double land tax for Catholics, opened certain legal and military posts to Catholics, and legalized the construction of Catholic chapels and schools. The **Irish Parliament** at the insistence of the home government passed its own Catholic Relief Act (1793), giving Catholics voting rights on the same basis as Protestants and allowing them to sit on juries and hold minor civil and junior military posts; these liberties were incorporated into the **Act of Union** (1800).

Timothy Erwin

Bibliography

Reynolds, E.E. *The Roman Catholic Church in England and Wales.* 1973.

Cato Street Conspiracy (1820)

Amidst the **radical** unrest after 1815 a group of plotters led by **Arthur Thistlewood** began planning to overthrow the government. The conspirators, mostly cobblers, met in lodgings on Cato Street to solidify their plans. George Edwards, an *agent provocateur,* encouraged them to attack and kill the assembled Cabinet ministers while they dined at Lord Harrowby's house on 23 February 1820. The rebels planned also to behead the hated lords **Castlereagh** and **Sidmouth** and parade their heads on pikes around **London**, take over key London installations, proclaim a republican "Provisional Government" under Thistlewood, and foment a general uprising throughout the countryside.

Well informed by Edwards, the government used the dinner at Harrowby's to trap the conspirators. A detachment of Cold Stream Guards and the **Bow Street Runners** surprised and promptly arrested them. After the trial that followed, five men, including Thistlewood, were hanged, and five more received **transportation** for life. The **Peterloo Massacre**, the **Six Acts**, and the failure of this desperate plot helped dissuade radicals from countenancing violence in their pursuit of drastic change.

David B. Mock

Bibliography

McCalman, Iain. *Radical Underworld: Prophets, Revolutionaries and Pornographers in London, 1795–1840.* 1988.

Stanhope, John. *The Cato Street Conspiracy.* 1962.

Cato Street conspirators, from a drawing by G. Cruikshank

Wilkinson, George T. *An Authentic History of the Cato Street Conspiracy.* 1820.

Worrall, David. *Radical Culture: Discourse, Resistance and Surveillance, 1790–1820.* 1992.

Cavalry

See Army

Edward Cave

Cave, Edward (1692?–1754)

London printer and **publisher**, Cave ("Sylvanus Urban") founded and edited the *Gentleman's Magazine* (1731–1754), having learned his trade with the *Norwich Courant* (1714–?), and Nathaniel Mist's (*d.* 1737) *Weekly-Journal* (*c.* 1720). A Post Office employee from 1723 to 1745, Cave was incarcerated in 1728 for forwarding parliamentary intelligence to rural newspapers; he was later fined for publishing proceedings against **Lord Lovat** (1747). In 1738 **Samuel Johnson** began writing for and virtually coediting Cave's successful weekly; other contributors included Richard Savage (*c.* 1697–1743), the **Bluestocking** Elizabeth Carter (1717–1806), and **Mark Akenside**. Cave is remembered for popularizing the "news digest" and for being an early publisher of Johnson and **Benjamin Franklin**.

Alexander Pettit

Bibliography

Carlson, C. Lennart. *The First Magazine: A History of the* Gentleman's Magazine. 1938.

Foxon, D.F. Introduction. *The* Gentleman's Magazine *1731–1751.* 1966.

Johnson, Samuel. *Cave. The Works of Samuel Johnson, LL.D.* Vol. 4. 1787.

See also Journalists and Journalism; Periodicals

Cavendish Family (and Dukes of Devonshire)

One of the great **Whig** families and holders of a vast Derbyshire estate, the Cavendishes of Chatsworth, dukes of Devonshire, were granted that title in 1694 as a reward for the 1st Duke's contribution to the **Glorious Revolution**. Although members

Henry Cavendish

of the family rarely held high administrative office, the Cavendishes provided continuous support and advice to the Whig cause throughout the Georgian period. The dukes usually served the monarch as high steward, president of the council, or as a lord justice of regency councils.

William, 2nd Duke (1672–1729), a strong advocate of the **Hanoverian succession**, introduced what became the **Septennial Act** (1716) and was a close friend of **George II** while he was Prince of Wales. William, 3rd Duke (1698–1755), sat in **Commons** while Marquis of Hartington but never sought a leadership role, choosing rather to serve as an adviser and arbitrator for his Whig friends. Although Devonshire proved a popular Lord Lieutenant of **Ireland** (1737–1744), the resignation of his good friend **Sir Robert Walpole** apparently caused him to lose interest in party politics.

Before he succeeded to the title, William, 4th Duke (1720–1764), served in Commons together with his brothers lords George (1727–1794), Frederick (1729–1803), and John Cavendish (1732–1796). Although he often supported the **Pelham** brothers, Devonshire maintained his independence and was known for his integrity and disinterestedness. Out of duty, he reluctantly led a stopgap administration as First Lord of the Treasury (1756–1757). After Devonshire's death, Lord John Cavendish headed the family voting bloc made up of his two brothers, two nephews, and a cousin. The Cavendishes were **Rockingham** Whigs who followed **Charles James Fox** after 1782 but went over to **William Pitt the Younger** in 1794. William, 5th Duke (1748–1811), was not an active politician, but his wife Georgiana (1757–1806), noted for her beauty, promiscuity, and very heavy **gambling** debts, canvassed publicly for Fox and made Devonshire House the center of Whig society in the 1780s.

The scientist Henry Cavendish (1731–1810), a shy, eccentric man who lived only for his research, was a nephew of the 3rd Duke. He determined the densities of hydrogen and carbon dioxide in relation to air (1766), the compound nature of water (1784), and the density of the Earth (1798). His ground-breaking discoveries in electrostatics were not published until 1879. The Cavendish Laboratory, **Cambridge University**, was named in his honor.

P.J. Kulisheck

Bibliography

Berry, Arthur J. *Henry Cavendish: His Life and Scientific Work.* 1960.
Bickley, Francis. *The Cavendish Family.* 1911.
Brown, Peter, and Karl Schweizer, eds. *The Devonshire Diary 1759–1762.* 1982.
Masters, Brian. *Georgiana, Duchess of Devonshire.* 1981.
Namier, Sir Lewis, and John Brooke, eds. *History of Parliament: The House of Commons, 1754–1790.* 3 vols. 1964.
Sedgwick, Romney, ed. *History of Parliament: The House of Commons, 1715–1754.* 2 vols. 1960.
Stokes, Hugh. *The Devonshire House Circle.* 1917.
Thorne, R.G., ed. *History of Parliament: The House of Commons, 1790–1820.* 5 vols. 1986.

See also Aristocracy and Gentry; Whigs and Whiggism

Cemeteries and Monuments

Although Britain's greatest cemeteries (those "cities of the dead" modeled on the Père Lachaise in Paris, such as **London**'s Highgate and **Glasgow**'s Necropolis) were largely created in the Victorian era, their origins lay in the Hanoverian, which left a rich legacy of public monuments and private memorials.

Commemoration of the dead has a long history. Over time, death became overlaid by rituals in which the need to commemorate was almost as important as that to bury. From the 16th century, village churchyards began to acquire an array of local stone monuments, some of excellent craftsmanship. Parish church walls became adorned with ornately carved white marble monuments, their floors with commemorative brasses, while the gentry were laid to rest in elegant side chapels or somber family vaults. There was a growth of burial grounds in urban centers, each a sea of tombstones or more elaborate family lairs and burial chambers, as well as of noble mausolea, placed strategically in the great landscaped gardens of the **aristocracy**. Ultimately, the burial and commemoration of the dead became big business; trades flourished in serving the needs of the bereaved, and commemoration became an art form.

Stone and Marble Mason's advertisement

The 18th century saw the erection of some of the most **sublime** monuments ever created. Contemporary **neoclassicism** resulted in magnificent temple-like structures being built, such as **Hawksmoor**'s mausoleum for the Howards at Castle Howard and **Wyatt**'s Yarborough mausoleum at Brockelsby. **Robert Adam**'s splendid monument to **David Hume** in **Edinburgh**'s Old Calton Cemetery showed that public cemeteries were to acquire works of art as well as sepulchres. Mortuary sculpture flourished in the hands of artists like **Flaxman** and **Chantrey**. The aftermath of the **Napoleonic Wars** provided a particular opportunity to celebrate victory and show patriotic enthusiasm by erecting an abundance of public monuments. The exploits of **Wellington** and **Nelson** were commemorated on a grand scale in many places by towers, obelisks, and statues, but lesser heroes—admirals such as Collingwood (1750–1810) and Hardy (1769–1839), and generals such as Baird (1757–1829) and **Sir John Moore**—acquired impressive memorials that were to become major landmarks due to their prominent hilltop locations. The ladies of Torrington, Devon, erected a pioneering monument for their Waterloo Tower (actually an obelisk) commemorating not simply the victorious generals but all who had fought. Its dedication read: "Peace to the souls of the heroes." Victorian democracy was anticipated in late–Hanoverian churchyards and monuments.

G.T. Bell

Bibliography

Colvin, Howard. *Architecture and the After-Life.* 1991.
Curl, James Steven. *A Celebration of Death.* 1980.
Weaver, Lawrence. *Memorials and Monuments.* 1915.

See also Architects and Architecture; Sculpture

Censorship

Historically, the chief purposes of censorship have been to restrict and punish, in the name of the common good, public pronouncements deemed antigovernment, antireligious, obscene, slanderous or falsely defamatory of persons, or otherwise detrimental to society. Hanoverian Britain, which enjoyed a high reputation as one of the freest states in Europe, saw a general movement toward the removal of formal restrictions on such pronouncements, though processes of religious and moral conformity were also increasingly at work to minimize the effect of this growing liberation. Britons at the accession of Queen Victoria (1837) formally enjoyed more freedoms than previously, but were perhaps less inclined to exercise them openly.

Government censorship of publications reporting parliamentary debates was effectively at an end when the Hanoverian period began, thanks to the lapse in 1695 of a prior licensing act. From this time on, standing orders that parliamentary debates should not be reported were habitually ignored, and the failed attempt by **Lord North** in 1771 to enforce these orders (in the so-called printers' case) confirmed this important freedom of the press. But political censorship could still be conducted indirectly by means of prosecutions for seditious libel. Over the course of the Hanoverian period, convictions on this charge numbered in the hundreds. The most famous trials came during periods of political and social crisis, such as those at the times of the **American Revolution** and **French Revolution**, and of numerous tumults afterward during the period 1815–1820. For example, in 1764 **John Wilkes** was found guilty (in absentia) of seditious libel for criticizing the king's speech in *The North Briton,* and at the same time was convicted of obscene libel for printing Pego Borewell's *Essay on Woman* (the title page pictured an erect penis being measured next to a 10-inch ruler). **William Cobbett** was fined and imprisoned for two years (1810–1812) for condemning military flogging in his *Political Register,* one of the great reform journals of its time. **Radical** journalist and publisher **Richard Carlile** served a total of 112 months in prison for seditious libel for reprinting the works of **Thomas Paine** and for publishing radical ideas in his journal, *The Republican.* These latter prosecutions took place despite the important liberalizing change that took place when **Charles James Fox**'s Libel Act (1792) was passed, giving juries (rather than traditionally conservative judges) greater influence over verdicts in libel cases—a change that came just in time to help many men escape conviction under the tightened treason and sedition acts (1795, 1799) imposed due to fear of revolutionary contagion from **France**.

Other antigovernment criticism, in newspapers for example, was countered during much of this period through the simple expedient of government subsidies to progovernment papers. **Sir Robert Walpole**'s administration handsomely subsidized and freely distributed to **coffeehouses** a number of newspapers such as the *Daily Courant, Free Briton,* and *London Journal* (all three were amalgamated in 1735 as the *Daily Gazeteer*). Walpole dealt successfully with satirical attacks on his administration launched from the **theaters** by pushing through the **Playhouse Act** (1737), which required theaters to submit copies of plays to the Lord Chamberlain for approval before performance. The act hung over subsequent dramatic freedom but as time passed was rarely enforced.

The free discussion of religion was restricted throughout the period by laws against blasphemy after the passage of the Blasphemy Act (1697), which legislated strict adherence to Christian doctrine. Freethinkers stepping beyond the bounds of the Christian tradition, in the written or spoken word, were subject to prosecution, civil disability, jail, and fines. The act prohibited denial of the divinity of the Bible or of any one Person of the Trinity, the assertion of polytheism, and the rejection of Christianity. In an age when Christianity was, thanks to the principles of **John Locke**, considered reasonable, deists, Arians, and Unitarians often went too far. When Thomas Woolston argued in 1729 that miracles were merely allegories, he was jailed for a year and fined £100. Some 70 years later, in 1797, Thomas Williams served a year in jail for reprinting Paine's blasphemous *The Age of Reason.*

One of the more effective forms of censorship operated indirectly through governmental imposition of **taxes** on undesirable criticism. A stamp tax, providing for levies on **newspapers** and pamphlets, advertisements, and even newsprint, was first enacted in 1712, and extended to the displeased American colonists in 1765. The working-class press, consisting mainly of magazines and cheap **periodicals**, was exempt until 1819, when the government, fearing sedition, made it too subject to taxation, setting off the "war of the unstamped." At its height between 1830 and 1836, some 200,000 copies of unstamped publications were sold every week; 800 journalists and editors were arrested. By 1836 the stamp tax had been reduced from fourpence to one penny.

Moral censorship grew during the period. In 1727 a defendant was successfully prosecuted for publication of allegedly obscene and indecent material, and after this such acts of publication became indictable misdemeanors. (It was not until 1857, however, with the Obscene Publications Act, that the publication of **pornography** became illegal.) Particularly with the revival of **Evangelicalism** after 1800, moral criticism became increasingly influential. The interests of moral censorship were promoted by the **Society for the Reformation of Manners** and the **Society for the Suppression of Vice** (active after 1802), and by individuals like **Thomas Bowdler**, who published **Shakespeare**, the Bible, and other writings after expurgating those parts he deemed irreligious and immoral. The Victorian Age was now fast approaching.

Roger D. Lund
Jack Fruchtman, Jr.

Bibliography

Gillett, Charles Ripley. *Burned Books: Neglected Chapters in British History and Literature.* 1932.
Hyland, Paul, and Neil Sammells, eds. *Writing and Censorship in Britain.* 1992.
Myers, Robin, and Michael Harris, eds. *Censorship and the Control of Print in England and France, 1600–1910.* 1992.
Siebert, Fredrick S. *Freedom of the Press in England, 1476–1776.* 1952.
Thomas, Donald S. *A Long Time Burning: The History of Literary Censorship in England.* 1969.
Wiener, Joel H. *The War of the Unstamped: The Movement to Repeal the British Newspaper Tax, 1830–1836.* 1969.

See also Freethinkers and Freethought; Laws of Public Worship, Speech, and the Press; Manners and Morals; Radicalism and Radical Politics

Centlivre, Susanna (1669?–1723)

Centlivre, Hanoverian Britain's most successful female playwright, wrote 19 plays, mostly comedies, from 1700 on. Three were among those most often performed in the 18th century: *The Busie Body* (1709), *The Wonder! A Woman Keeps a Secret* (1714), and *A Bold Stroke for a Wife* (1718). The first of these was staged nearly 500 times, almost annually between 1709 and 1800.

Centlivre's early biography is unknown before her marriage to a Mr. Carroll around 1685. In 1707 she married Joseph Centlivre, cook to **Queen Anne**, then **George I**. Her comedies succeeded because (unlike Restoration comedies) the language and behavior of their characters stayed within the boundaries of bourgeois taste, and because she created parts

Susanna Centlivre

that flattered their performers. Some **actors** enlarged their fame through them. Around 1750, Catherine "Kitty" Clive (1711–1785) was a much-celebrated Anne Lovely (*A Bold Stroke for a Wife*), and appeared as Flora (*The Wonder!*) at her farewell performance. **David Garrick** took up Marplot in *The Busie Body*—the role that was responsible for much of his early renown. He was also responsible for a later run of *The Wonder!*, finishing his career in the role of Don Felix. These two plays survived into the 20th century as parts of British and American repertory companies.

Centlivre drew upon romance and Spanish intrigue plots, and adapted Jonsonian humors characters and Restoration stock types. Marplot, for instance, deviates modestly from the traditional bungler, but early-18th-century audiences would have easily recognized his type even as they applauded Centlivre's particular portrayal. Centlivre's characters were presented more sympathetically than their Restoration forebears. In *A Bold Stroke for a Wife*, the two comic butts, Prim and Periwinkle, are duped by the main character, Fainwell, but they are treated with some compassion, not with rough **satire**.

Centlivre supported the **Whigs** in many of her plays, and championed the **Church of England** and mercantilism over **Catholicism** and **Tory** nostalgia. Probably these affiliations earned her **Alexander Pope**'s wrath in *The Dunciad* (1728). Also apparent in her plays is a conscious positioning of women as responsible beings.

Stephen Hicks

Bibliography

Bowyer, John W. *The Celebrated Mrs. Centlivre.* 1952.
Frushell, Richard C. *The Plays of Susanna Centlivre.* 3 vols. 1982.
Lock, F.P. *Susanna Centlivre.* 1979.
Pearson, Jacqueline. *The Prostituted Muse.* 1988.

See also Dramatic Arts; Women in Literature

Chadwick, Edwin (1800–1890)

Chadwick, English physician and social reformer, was well known for his work on the Royal Commission of Enquiry on the Poor Laws (1832–1834), writing a third of the final report that served as the basis for the **New Poor Law** (1834). Born near **Manchester**, the son of a businessman, he had earlier come to know **James Mill** and served as **Bentham**'s secretary (1830–1832). Imbued with Benthamism as well as the new political economy of **Ricardo**, Chadwick was assisted by **Nassau Senior** in writing the poor law report; in the latter 1830s he was violently condemned for the workhouses it had produced. He nonetheless labored to implement many other Benthamite proposals through public commissions whose reports influenced police, prison, and public health reforms. His *Report on the Sanitary Condition of the Labouring Population* (1842), a masterpiece of meticulous factual analysis, became the basis for modern British public health policy. He retired in 1854, though continuing to write tracts supporting social reform.

William Edward Morris

Bibliography

Finer, S.E. *The Life and Times of Edwin Chadwick.* 1952.
Lewis, R.A. *Edwin Chadwick and the Public Health Movement, 1832–1854.* 1952.
———. "Edwin Chadwick and the Railway Labourers." *Economic History Review.* Vol. 3, pp. 107–118.

Edwin Chadwick

Thomas Chalmers

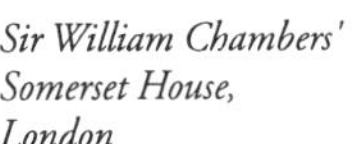
Sir William Chambers' Somerset House, London

Chalmers, Thomas (1780–1847)

Scottish divine and social reformer, Chalmers exemplified the vigorous **Evangelical** approach to urban problems in the early 19th century. Born of merchant stock in Anstruther, Fife, he was educated at the University of St. Andrews and became minister of Kilmeny (1803) in the **Church of Scotland.** Though interested in astronomy, chemistry, mathematics, and commerce, his reading of **Wilberforce**'s *Practical View of Prevailing Religious Systems* (1797) moved him to take up Evangelical preaching. Famous for this (he moved **Canning** to tears and was extolled by **Lockhart** and others), Chalmers moved to **Glasgow** where, emphasizing the need to foster self-help and independence, he worked (1815–1823) in some of the city's poorest areas to combat illiteracy, drunkenness, poverty, and demoralization. He later produced valuable treatises reflecting his experiences, *Christian and Civic Economy of Large Towns* (3 vols., 1821–1826) and *On Political Economy* (1832).

In 1823 Chalmers was appointed Professor of Moral Philosophy at St. Andrews, and 5 years later became Professor of Divinity at the University of Edinburgh; he was a prolific writer on secular as well as religious subjects. In the 1830s his opposition to civil interference in church matters embroiled him in controversies that led ultimately to creation (1843) of the Free Church of Scotland, of which he was a founder. Chalmers's most significant theological work was *On the Adaptation of External Nature to the Moral and Intellectual Constitution of Man* (1833).

Donald W. Nichol

Bibliography

Watt, H. *Thomas Chalmers and the Disruption.* 1943.

See also Humanitarianism; Religious Revivalism

Chambers, Sir William (1723–1796)

Chambers, Swedish-born architect and writer, contributed substantially to the professional development of Hanoverian architecture. His accomplishments included Kew Gardens (1757–1762) and Somerset House (1776–1796), as well as theoretical writings on civil and oriental **landscape architecture.** Knighted in 1770 by Gustav III of Sweden, Chambers was known as "Sir William" throughout the rest of his career in England.

Educated in England, Chambers returned to Sweden in 1739 to join the Swedish East India Company. While traveling in the Orient, he developed an interest in eastern architecture, which he later pursued at J.F. Blondel's École des Arts in Paris. Further study in Rome enabled him to cultivate a method of direct and critical architectural observation that became the foundation for the theories and practices he would develop in England.

In 1755 Chambers settled in **London** and established an architectural practice that prospered under royal **patronage.** His influence with **George III** aided in the founding of the **Royal Academy** (1768) and secured Chambers's appointment as architect of Somerset House (begun in 1775), the huge Thames-side governmental office building which was his greatest achievement. Somerset House embodied the academic theories he formulated and published in a *Treatise on Civil*

Architecture (1759), and served as the capstone to his career.
Mary Ann A. Powers

Bibliography

Harris, John. *Sir William Chambers: Knight of the Polar Star.* 1970.

See also Architects and Architecture

Chandos, 1st Duke of (James Brydges) (1674–1744)

In many ways Chandos represented the changing mood of the late Stuart and early Hanoverian years: the quest for new knowledge going hand in hand with the desire to make money. As Paymaster to the British **Army** in the Netherlands between 1705 and 1713 he "borrowed" funds in his charge to speculate and amassed a considerable fortune. Chandos was heavily involved in the speculation surrounding the **South Sea Bubble** and was one of the few believed to profit from the affair. In the 1720s and 1730s he speculated in the Royal Africa Company and the **York Buildings Company**. There he sustained heavy losses.

Chandos was interested in much more than money, however. He was, among other things, a Fellow of the **Royal Society**, a friend and benefactor of **Pope**, patron of **Handel** and **J.T. Desaguliers**, and Chancellor of the University of St. Andrews. He was deeply interested in the practical applications of Newtonian **science**. He built a great house at Canons near Edgeware, and was actively involved in the development of the town of **Bath**. However, his speculative activities drained his wealth, and after his death, Canons was sold in lots and eventually demolished by the purchaser.
A.J.G. Cummings

Bibliography

Johnson, Joan. *Princely Chandos: James Brydges 1674–1744.* 1984.
Neale, R.S. *Bath, 1680–1850: A Social History.* 1981.
Stewart, Larry. *The Rise of Public Science.* 1992.

Chantrey, Sir Francis (1781–1841)

Chantrey, a **neoclassical** sculptor, ranked with **John Flaxman** as the greatest England has produced. He was considered by contemporaries the finest portrait bust-maker who ever lived, but he also executed public monuments and funerary memorials. His advantages over his older contemporary Flaxman were his sincere simplicity and his ability to render in marble the qualities of flesh and bone.

Largely self-taught, Chantrey was born of a poor family in Sheffield. After an apprenticeship to a local carver he began his artistic career as a **portrait painter**. Soon, however, he became better known for his sculpture in plaster. His first major commission in marble was for a funerary memorial to the Rev. James Wilkinson of Sheffield (1805). Marble would thereafter be his medium of choice, though he often did preparatory work in clay and also created some public monuments in bronze.

Chantrey's first major success was his portrait bust of the Rev. **John Horne Tooke**, exhibited at the **Royal Academy** in 1811. The Tooke commission brought him thousands of pounds and remains one of his greatest masterpieces. This bust captures the rugged character and powerful intelligence of the sitter as well as the differing textures of Tooke's soft cap and firm flesh. In 1820 Chantrey triumphed again with his masterful and popular bust of **Sir Walter Scott**.

In Chantrey's monument works there is an amalgamation of 18th-century neoclassicism, **Romanticism**, and nascent Victorian sentimentality. Although he claimed to despise mawkish sentiment, his memorials frequently played upon the viewer's emotions, for example, *The Sleeping Children* (1817), a touching monument to two sisters who had died young. The babes seem not dead but sleeping, their chemises lying in long, straight folds, their arms entwined, snowdrops clutched in the younger one's hand.

Partly because he was self-educated, Chantrey usually steered clear of classical allusions, allegories, and religious symbolism. Personifications, he believed, never touched the human heart. His monuments frequently depict realistic deathbed scenes, and his figures wear contemporary or simplified garb, displayed in the broad folds he preferred. Among his greatest monuments are the statue of Robert Dundas of Arniston (1824) and the memorial to Anna Maria Graves (1819) in Waterperry, Oxford.

Chantrey was knighted in 1837 by **William IV**. He died suddenly in 1841, a very rich man. He left his fortune of £150,000 to the nation on the death of Lady Chantrey in 1876. The Chantrey bequest was dedicated to the purchase of British works of art; the works acquired are deposited at the Tate Gallery, London. Chantrey's generous gift helped to build the nation's art collections.
Bonita L. Billman

Bibliography

Binfield, Clyde, ed. *Sir Francis Chantrey: Sculptor to an Age, 1781–1841.* 1981.
Holland, John. *Memorials of Sir Francis Chantrey.* 1851.
Potts, Alexander. *Sir Francis Chantrey, 1781–1841.* 1981.
Whinney, Margaret. *Sculpture in Britain, 1530–1830.* 1988.

See also Cemeteries and Monuments; Sculpture

Chapone, Hester Mulso (1727–1801)

Chapone, one of the early **Bluestockings**, was a woman of strong opinions, boldly stated. After the death of her mother she assumed the care of the household and began to educate herself in languages, philosophy, and poetry with the assistance of her three older brothers. She corresponded with the naturalist **Gilbert White**, and to **Samuel Richardson** she sent a series of strong **letters** attacking his ideas on filial duty and female independence in *Clarissa*. These were widely circulated and eventually published. Her *Letters on the Improvement of the Mind* (1773) were frequently reprinted well into the 19th century and used in schools.
Monica Letzring

Bibliography

Chapone, Hester Mulso. *The Posthumous Works of Mrs. Chapone.* 1807.

Myers, Sylvia Harcstark. *The Bluestocking Circle: Women, Friendship, and the Life of the Mind in Eighteenth-Century England.* 1990.

See also Women in Literature; Women's Education

Charitable Corporation Scandal

This was one of the greatest frauds perpetrated in the 18th century. The Charitable Corporation (founded in 1707) was designed to keep the industrious poor out of the hands of rapacious pawnbrokers by advancing money to them on pledges at the maximum legal interest rate of 5%. Following the crisis of the **South Sea Bubble**, the corporation came under the control of a group of directors including **Sir Archibald Grant**, who increased the share capital and then diverted the corporation's funds to their own use to speculate in Charitable Corporation shares. They employed one of their number, George Robinson, a broker, to deal in the shares, but he cheated his partners in crime by diverting shares and funds into his own name. When threatened with discovery (1729), Robinson persuaded the fraudsters to trust him again, this time speculating in **York Buildings Company** stock. Despite stringent attempts to control him, Robinson again defrauded his partners and disappeared, leaving others to face the music. The corporation's shareholders obtained a parliamentary enquiry into the affair which revealed that over £320,000 had been raised by fictitious pledges. Grant and a fellow director, Sir Robert Sutton, were expelled from Parliament, but because of powerful protectors, none of the principals were prosecuted. The paupers, however, were not excused from repayments.

A.J.G. Cummings

Bibliography

Cummings, A.J.G. "Industry and Investment in the Eighteenth Century Highlands: The York Buildings Company of London," in A.J.G. Cummings and T.M. Devine, eds. *Industry, Business and Society in Scotland Since 1700.* 1994.

———. "The Business Affairs of an Eighteenth Century Lowland Laird: Sir Archibald Grant of Monymusk, 1696–1778," in T.M. Devine, ed. *Scottish Elites.* 1994.

Charity Schools

Charity schools, the favorite objects of 18th-century English benevolence, were financed by the generosity of private citizens and also organized and coordinated by organizations such as the **Society for the Promotion of Christian Knowledge**. Charity elementary schools offered the only opportunity for thousands of poor children to become educated. They promoted the catechetical efforts of the **Church of England** and were also intended to combat pauperism and the influences of **freethinking**, **Roman Catholicism**, and **Rational Dissent**.

The Bible, the catechism, and "the three Rs" formed the curriculum. Pupils frequently wore coarse, plain, donated uniforms and attended for six or seven hours a day. Often the schools provided basic training in a craft or trade, and sometimes paid children's apprentice fees. Sponsors wanted the schools to provide an education that would, among other things, maintain social equilibrium by making certain the children were not educated above their station. The most vocal opponents of charity schools were merchants who wanted cheap **child labor** and tradesmen who feared that their own children would be displaced in the ranks of apprentices. Nevertheless, from its origin in 1699 the charity school movement grew steadily, particularly in **London** and a few other large towns such as **Bristol**. In 1729 London had 132 charity schools with 5,225 pupils; 70 years later the numbers increased to 179 and 7,108. By 1818 there were 18,400 such schools, with 333,432 pupils in England and **Wales**.

The charity school movement had important consequences. Despite a purposefully limited curriculum of "Christian and useful education," the schools were the only means of education for the poor. They opened education to girls, prepared many children for a life above poverty and, with the Bible as the central text, fostered religious zeal, New Testament ethics, and a basic appreciation of words and poetry. The movement inspired the establishment of similar schools elsewhere and formed the model for the **Sunday schools** and industrial schools that emerged for British working children in the last quarter of the 18th century.

H. George Hahn

Bibliography

Jones, M.G. *The Charity School Movement: A Study of Eighteenth-Century Puritanism in Action.* 1938.

See also Education, Elementary

Charles, Thomas (1755–1814)

An educator and leading figure in the second wave of Welsh **Methodism**, Charles served the Anglican Church in Somerset for 5 years before marrying Sally Jones of Bala in 1783. Though he was unsuccessful in gaining a curacy because of his **Evangelistic** views, his wife's ownership of a shop allowed him to work outside the church. Methodism, lacking an advocate of sufficient social standing, had not yet become firmly established in North Wales. Charles, beginning in the 1780s, supplied this need, bringing Calvinistic Methodism to the area of Wales where it would ultimately build most vigorously. His interest in catechisms and use of **Sunday schools** solved the Methodists' difficulties with education, which had mounted since the demise of **circulating schools**. His major literary work was a scriptural dictionary (4 vols., 1805–1811), and as a founder of the British and Foreign Bible Society (1804) he did much to standardize the text of the first Welsh Bible. In 1811, after long opposing this step, he ordained Methodist ministers, thereby making the final breach with the Anglican Church and launching a succession of Methodist divines who were to be influential in 19th-century Wales.

Neil Evans

Bibliography

Honourable Society of Cymmrodorion. *The Dictionary of Welsh Biography.* 1959.

Jones, Ieuan Gwynedd. "Thomas Charles, (1755–1814)," in Faculty of Education, University College of Swansea, *Pioneers of Welsh Education.* 1964.

Stephens, Meic, ed. *The Oxford Companion to the Literature of Wales.* 1986.

See also Wales and Welsh Culture; Welsh Religious Revival

Charles Edward, the Young Pretender (1719–1788)

Popularly known as "Bonnie Prince Charlie," Charles Edward Stuart was the son of **James Edward, the Old Pretender**, the **Jacobite** claimant to the throne. It was largely due to Charles's perseverance that the **Forty-five** (1745) uprising took place. He convinced his followers that he had secured French support and that a Jacobite rebellion in England was imminent, when in fact these promises represented his wishes more than actual commitments.

Charles was not a competent military leader, and the initial successes of the uprising, which realized—more or less—his complete capture of **Scotland**, can be credited more to luck than to genius. His forces had to withdraw from Derby in the face of superior Hanoverian forces. The retreat was orderly. At **Culloden**, Charles made his stand. But this was unsound tactically, leading to terrible defeat and to his flight from the field.

This desertion left the Jacobite forces without strategy or leader. Charles's location was discovered by the Hanoverian forces but he made his (now legendary) escape, dressed as a woman and helped by the heroic **Flora MacDonald**. After 1754, drinking excessively, he went into physical and moral decline. In 1760 his Scottish mistress, Clemintina Walkinshaw, who had suffered much at his hands, left him. His subsequent marriage to a minor German princess, Louisa of Stolberg-Gedernin, collapsed by 1780, again due to his violent alcoholism. He was looked after until his death by his daughter, Charlotte. With the death of his brother Henry in 1807, the royal line ended.

Richard Finlay

Charles Edward Stuart

Bibliography

Lenman, B. *The Jacobite Risings in Britain.* 1980.

McLynn, F. *The Jacobites.* 1985.

Chartered Trading Companies

A product of 17th-century mercantilism, chartered trading companies were important in **overseas commerce** and remained active until the early 19th century. Originally endowed with a trade monopoly in a given geographical area, many, such as the **East India Company**, also acquired administrative duties within the **Empire** and significantly helped to advance it in **North America**, **Canada**, and **India**. Indeed, the historiography of the system has been dominated by accounts of the prototypical East India Company. But while all the chartered companies shared some common characteristics in origin and demise, the singularities of their experiences should not be forgotten.

As trade expanded in the early 17th century, so did its risks. Voyages were long, tying up large amounts of capital for considerable periods. Bulky products such as sugar, **tobacco**, spices, and **cottons** required larger **ships**, thus increasing costs. **Joint-stock companies** were formed to reduce some of these risks. By around 1700, such organizations could be extremely profitable, the East India Company, for example, averaging 18% per annum, making its directors among the richest men in England, exercising considerable political power.

The chartered companies were important in the early expansion of British trade as an emerging multilateral system. They figured as key links in this system by providing the produce for re-export to the Continent, thus increasing buying power of goods such as timber, pitch, hemp, and high-grade iron-bar, which had to be sought from Continental Europe and the Baltic. But, from the beginning of the 18th century, chartered companies began to experience difficulties, facing competition as well as growing criticism from manufacturers and economists. The Royal African Company (chartered in 1672), initially conceived as a supplier of **slaves** for the triangular Atlantic trade, was so plagued by interlopers that in 1698 African trade was opened to all who made a contribution to the upkeep of the company's forts; by the 1720s the company was not financially sound. Further, manufacturers demanded duties and import bans on competing goods carried by the overseas companies. Bans on Indian calicos in 1700 and 1721, ostensibly to protect the **woolen industry**, were also designed to aid other nascent **textile industries**. Ironically, this temporarily aided the situation of the Levant Company, which expanded its import of raw silk. But as economists such as **David Hume** and **Adam Smith** criticized the costs of monopolies for the consumer, and manufacturers demanded entry into colonial markets, the fate of chartered companies was sealed, their monopolies being gradually rescinded between 1750 and 1835. Without monopolies, cumbersome business structures made chartered companies unable to compete with individual traders.

With the advent of the **Industrial Revolution**, chartered companies seemed to become a hindrance to the further development of British trade. With a dominant Royal **Navy** and the development of marine **insurance**, and with the capital already brought into Britain by the companies, their success brought their demise. Risks for individual traders were progressively reduced, and gradually these same traders turned to undermining and then achieving removal of chartered companies' exclusive privileges. British **factories** and workshops needed wider markets to maintain their production levels, and manufacturers demanded the cheapest raw materials: Under such circumstances, the system that had excluded British ships from east of the Cape of Good Hope until 1813 had to be abandoned.

Thus gradually there emerged a world in which there was no need for chartered trading companies and their monopolies based on restricted theories of mercantilism. Free trade was to bring about the next expansion of British overseas trade. Ironically, though, the use of the trading company as an agent of colonial expansion was to be utilized once again in the Victorian era, with the chartering of the British South Africa Company (1889).

Patricia Collins

Bibliography

Davies, K.G. *The Royal African Company.* 1957.

Griffiths, Sir Percival. *A Licence to Trade: A History of the English Chartered Companies.* 1974.

Lawson, P. *The East India Company, 1600–1857.* 1994.

See also Economic Thought; Hudson's Bay Company; Northwest Company; South Sea Company

Chatham, Earl of

See Pitt, William, the Elder

Chatterton, Thomas (1752–1770)

Variously known as the "marvelous boy" and the "imposter poet," Chatterton proved in his tragically brief life to be one of the most inventive writers of the 18th century. He created facsimile manuscripts of 12 fictitious antique poets from the medieval period, published posthumously (1777) as "Poems Supposed to Have Been Written at Bristol by Thomas Rowley and Others in the 15th Century." Scholars disputed the authenticity of these for years, arguing in favor of the actual existence of Rowley, the "priest of St. Johan's, Bristowe," out of disbelief that a poorly educated teenager could produce such quantities of gorgeous **poetry**. They now agree that the manuscripts originated with Chatterton and were written by him between ages 12 and 17.

Chatterton was born in **Bristol** to Sarah Young, a seamstress, and Thomas Chatterton, a schoolmaster of the Pyle Street **Charity School**. The father, who died before his son's birth, had also been sexton of the church of St. Mary Redcliffe, inheriting an office that had been in his family from the 15th century. From infancy, the younger Chatterton played among the ancient manuscripts in the care of his family; and by age 9 was beginning to demonstrate intellectual genius. He was writing poetry when he was 11, and at 12 created the masterful figure of Thomas Rowley. At 15 he became a lawyer's apprentice, copying legal documents all day while working on his poetry and studying heraldry, metaphysics, astronomy, medicine, music, mathematics, and antiquities in his after hours.

In 1769 he sent one of his Rowley manuscripts, "The Ryse of Peyncting in Englande," to **Horace Walpole**, who received the work graciously and asked for more. In a second note, Chatterton referred to his **poverty** and his hopes for securing his life as a poet. Inexplicably, Walpole took offense at this request for **patronage** and dismissed Chatterton as a petty forger. Chatterton's lines of August 1769—"To Horace Walpole"—express the disappointment he felt about this rejection. Angry but more determined than ever to succeed, Chatterton left Bristol for **London** (April 1770); but the money he earned from his publications could not keep him from destitution. A few months later he burned all the manuscripts in his room and took his own life.

Posthumous publications of his works yielded the highest praise. Walpole was deeply repentant: "I do not believe there ever existed so masterly a genius." **Samuel Johnson** pronounced Chatterton "the most extraordinary young man that has ever encountered my knowledge." **Keats** dedicated "Endymion" to him, and **Shelley** celebrated him in "Adonais." D.G. Rossetti (1828–1882) believed "the absolutely miraculous Chatterton [to be] as great as any English poet whatever."

Mary Tiryak

Bibliography

Kaplan, Louise. *The Family Romance of the Imposter Poet.* 1988.

Kelly, Linda. *The Marvelous Boy.* 1971.

Taylor, Donald S. *The Complete Works of Thomas Chatterton.* 1971.

See also Gothic Fiction and Gothicism; Tyrwhitt, Thomas

Chemical Industry

Traditionally, the chemical industry had exploited nature for raw materials: salt from the sea and from inland brine wells; bleach from sour milk; dyes from wood and plants; oil from whales and seals; acids and alkali from the distillation of timber. This picture was altered very considerably by the end of the Hanoverian age, under the twin impacts of **science** and industry.

Production costs in a number of industries intimately influenced progress. **Salt** production, for instance, early be came large-scale because of great industrial demand. The saltmasters of the Forth, South Shields and Lymington (Hampshire) regions evaporated seawater using local small coal for fuel; brine wells and rock salt were exploited in Cheshire and Worcestershire. Rock salt eventually triumphed at the expense of imports and seacoast saltpans.

There was an extensive trade in wood ashes and kelp (seaweed ashes), the main sources of alkali until the late 18th century. Products of wood distillation also included charcoal, an essential ingredient in gunpowder; and pitch and tar, used in **shipbuilding**. Demand from soapmakers, bleachers, and **glassmakers** elevated the cost of alkali, and Spanish barilla, another major source, was often excluded from Britain because of **wars**.

The transformation of salt into soda (alkali) was the real beginning of the heavy chemical industry, and underpinning this was the expansion of sulphuric acid production. Joshua Ward (1685–1761) began making this acid in glass vessels in Twickenham (1736), greatly reducing its price. **Birmingham** was a major consumer, and there **John Roebuck** and Samuel Garbett (1717–1805) opened a works (1746) using large lead vessels. This successful partnership established another plant at Prestonpans near **Edinburgh** (1749), in a region where bleaching and soap, pottery, glass, and salt manufacture were well established. As Britain industrialized, more acid plants were opened.

Dilute sulphuric acid replaced sour milk in bleaching from the 1750s and greatly reduced the time taken in the process. Experiments in soda production by James Keir (1735–1820), Lord Dundonald and others were undertaken in the 1760s and 1770s, and others followed by Nicholas Leblanc (1787). Mass production occurred by the 1820s at the St. Rollox works in **Glasgow**, founded by **Charles Tennant**, already committed to producing chlorine bleaching powder—invented by Charles Macintosh (1766–1843), but patented by Tennant (1799). Macintosh's most famous invention was the rubberized coat that still bears his name, and behind that the process of waterproofing (which he accomplished by dissolving india-rubber in naphtha, a by-product of tar).

Fashion changes in the 18th century favored brighter colors, and thus dyeing, quintessentially an empirical craft, responded by using cochineal, indigo, and logwood. Calico printing, forbidden under an act of 1720 so as to favor **East India Company** imports, was allowed in 1774. Production of mordants and dyestuffs greatly developed in the 1780s as the **cotton industry** expanded, but was still dependent on natural substances. Turkey red dyeing (based on madder) was introduced to Britain from Rouen by Papillon (1785) and the Borelle brothers (1786), and quickly took root in the Glasgow area, where it became a specialty. Dyestuffs based on coal tar replaced this craft after 1860.

Coke production from **coal** had many by-products, gas being the most obvious. Town gasworks produced feedstocks for chemical manufacturers from the 1820s. Further revolutionary change occurred in the 1850s with the discovery of oil shales and petroleum.

John Butt

Bibliography

Clow, Archibald. *The Chemical Revolution.* 1952.

Haber, L.F. *The Chemical Industry in the Nineteenth Century.* 1958.

Musson, A.E. *Science, Technology and Economic Growth in the Eighteenth Century.* 1972.

Robinson, Eric, and A.E. Musson. *Science and Technology in the Industrial Revolution.* 1969.

See also Science, Technology, and Invention

Chesterfield, 4th Earl of (Philip Dormer Stanhope) (1694–1773)

His contemporaries knew Chesterfield as a diplomat, politician, and polemical writer. Posterity knows him best for his witty and worldly *Letters* to his natural son and his godson, instructing them in gentlemanly **manners and morals**—letters that are often cited in studies of **aristocratic** society. The letters to his son were published (1774) a year after his death and ran to 11 editions by 1800, despite furious complaints by **middle-class** publicists alleging the immorality of his advice—which, it is true, emphasized unapologetically the great usefulness of always imitating the behavior of "people of the first **fashion**," and of striving ("chameleon-like," his critics said) to please through the study of other people's weaknesses and through a tireless adjustment of appearances.

Chesterfield's intelligence and eloquence never brought him political leadership. He became completely fluent in French in his youth and traveled on the Continent (1714), then returned to enter politics under the wing of his kinsman, **James Stanhope**. During his career in the **Commons** (1715–1723) he vacillated in support of the **Whig** administration but remained a close friend of the Prince of Wales (after 1727 **George II**). Entering the **Lords** (1726), he added his wit to the **opposition** to **Sir Robert Walpole**. George II appointed him Ambassador to The Hague (1728–1732) but later withdrew his favor, perhaps because of Chesterfield's marriage (1733) to the king's natural half-sister (Melusina von der Schulenburg, Countess of Walsingham).

Chesterfield opposed the foreign policy of **Carteret**, particularly as regarded **Hanover**. He wrote newspaper articles and pamphlets that helped him gain a legacy (1745) of £20,000 from Sarah Churchill, Duchess of Marlborough. In the **broad-bottom administration** he served as Lord Lieutenant of **Ireland** (1745–1746) and as Secretary of State for the northern department (1746–1748), but resigned after disagreements with **Newcastle**. He then withdrew from active politics and passed several years in leisurely pursuits and estate improvement. Chesterfield introduced and shepherded through Parliament a bill (1751) authorizing British adoption of the Gregorian **calendar**. After 1753, increasing deafness made reading and writing his chief interests, but politicians still sought his advice and arbitration of their conflicts.

P.J. Kulisheck

Bibliography

Coxon, Roger. *Chesterfield and His Critics.* 1925.

Dobrée, Bonamy, ed. *The Letters of Philip Dormer Stanhope, 4th Earl of Chesterfield.* 1932.
Franklin, Colin. *Lord Chesterfield: His Character and Characters.* 1993.
Gulick, Sidney L. *A Chesterfield Bibliography to 1800.* 2nd ed., 1979.
Sedgwick, Romney, ed. *History of Parliament: The House of Commons 1715–1754.* 2 vols. 1970.
Shellabarger, Samuel. *Lord Chesterfield and His World.* 1951.

See also Diplomats and Diplomacy; Foreign Relations; Letters

Child Labor

Child labor did not begin with the **Industrial Revolution** of the late 18th century, but the intensity and length of children's working day increased so dramatically then that reformers were moved to shorten and ameliorate it. By the 1870s they had made many improvements.

In the pre-industrial age, tasks were assigned to children in **agriculture**, households, and primitive industries. Their work on farms, mostly gender-specific, was essential. They gathered food, fuel, and water; tended babies and livestock; ran errands; helped in household cooking and production; and generally assisted adults. Skills learned in farming and at home in **domestic production** prepared them by age 13 to earn their room and board as apprentices or more often as servants indentured for 7 years. In the late 18th century, perhaps 15% of the country's children were **servants**.

The **hours and working conditions** of children differed little from those of adults. On the positive side, family-based pre-industrial work was mixed with conversation, play, singing, and at least some rest even though, on the negative side, it could be accompanied by excessive corporal punishment or cruelty. Children were affected by cottage crafts (such as cotton-twisting, nail-making, saddling, carpentry, and tailoring) that caused muscle spasms; children were affected too by the sometimes cramped, damp, airless and otherwise unhealthy conditions of cottage industry. Each line of work carried its own special hazards: in needle trades, children suffered from eyestrain and experienced abnormal bone defects from lack of exercise; in **mines** they faced dangers of cave-ins and bad air; chimney-sweepers' assistants (always small head-shaven boys) faced the danger of getting caught in the flues.

As the production of textiles, pottery, **metals**, and paper moved from cottage to **factory**, so did child workers. Historians estimate that by 1840, approximately 28% of British boys and 17% of girls worked in agriculture, while 25% of both girls and boys were in factories or mines. Many poor boys went to sea. Between 1756 and 1862 more than 10,000 children contributed to the strength of the merchant marine and **navy**, according to the Marine Society.

The exploitation of children in **textile industries** between 1760 and 1840 is considered one of the worst aspects of the Industrial Revolution. Orphans had long been exploited even before industrialization, in workhouses and apprenticeships. Foundling hospitals and parishes from 1760 to 1820 shipped orphans in batches of five to 50 children to the first water-driven textile mills to augment local labor. These young urban poor-law wards, often from **London**, provided needed hands in remote countryside mills, contributed to the centralization of production, and were more easily molded than locals with roots nearby. What records exist indicate that many did not survive to finish their indentures.

Legislation was passed in 1747 to protect pauper apprentices, in 1788 to protect chimney sweeps, and in 1802 to regulate apprentices' hours and housing in **cotton** mills. All these laws were ineffectual. The dire working conditions in textile factories from the 1760s in Lancashire, Yorkshire, and Cheshire, coupled with the increasing speed of sometimes dangerous machinery, eventually concentrated reformers' attention on conditions of child labor. In 1833 Parliament passed the first Factory Act with "teeth" in the form of inspectors to ensure compliance with its provisions.

The parliamentary investigations preceding this act revealed much about contemporary conditions. The long working day for child factory operatives (acknowledged by manufacturers who in 1831 indignantly declared that they never worked children over 16 hours a day without paying them overtime) became the focal point of attention. It was revealed that children began working as young as 6, but usually from age 9. Hours were mostly from 6 AM to 7 PM, 6 days a week; overtime and night work were generally compulsory. Air was often polluted, rests infrequent, speed-ups common, and children who did piecing (joining broken threads in **spinning**) were constantly on their feet, some walking 25 miles a day. Job-related disabilities and illnesses were almost as common as disciplinary thrashings. Even modern-day apologists admit that at least 20% of all textile workers in 1835 were age 14 or younger.

During much of the Hanoverian period, child labor was viewed as not only an immutable fact of life but desirable. But a broad **humanitarian** reform movement was gathering strength, and at last affected this as well as many other harsh aspects of existence. After the 1833 act the **factory movement** scored several more important victories, and by the 1870s it was increasingly common for youngsters to experience something of a distinct children's life of play and **elementary education** before plunging into the world of adult labor.

Carolyn Stevens

Bibliography

Bolin-Hort, Per. *Work, Family and the State: Child Labour and the Organization of Production in the British Cotton Industry, 1780–1920.* 1989.
Cunningham, Hugh. "The Employment and Unemployment of Children in England, 1680–1851." *Past and Present.* Vol. 126, pp. 115–150.
Nardinelli, Clark. *Child Labor and the Industrial Revolution.* 1990.
Pinchbeck, Ivy, and Margaret Hewitt. *Children in English Society.* 2 vols. 1969.
Rose, Mary B. "Social Policy and Business: Parish Apprenticeship and the Early Factory System, 1750–1834." *Business History.* Vol. 31, pp. 5–32.

In the nursery

Rule, John. *The Labouring Classes in Early Industrial England, 1750–1850.* 1986.

See also Factory Workers

Child-Rearing

At the beginning of the Hanoverian era, the traditions of paternal dominance, Christianity, and household economics were the primary influences on child-rearing. Throughout the period 1714–1837 the household remained the basic social unit and was structured legally and customarily on patriarchal and hierarchical lines. The law recognized a man as master of his wife, children, and servants. However, a father had a sacred as well as temporal responsibility in raising his children; the family's submission to patriarchal authority stood on religious as well as political foundations. Although patriarchal tradition continued, mothers by the end of the period played a more active role in child-rearing, especially in the middle and upper classes. For working-class children, the **factories** of the **Industrial Revolution** partially replaced familial authority.

In families of the **aristocracy and gentry**, child-rearing could be either harsh or indulgent, depending on parental temperament and familial religious beliefs. Stricter discipline was more common in the early 18th century, parents often using corporal punishment and fear to instill obedience; but the popularity of these methods declined over the century. Among those upper-class parents who inclined to be more indulgent, parent–child relationships were less severe but still often somewhat impersonal because of parents' reliance on **servants** for child-care. Supervised by a nurse (nannie) and taught by a governess or tutor of inferior station, upper-class children often became confident, precocious, and headstrong. Their parents, though formal and distant, typically treated their children fondly and generously. Society claimed much of such parents' time; however, they provided lavish sums for their children's **travel**, dowries, **gambling** debts, and career opportunities. Aristocratic children often grew up copying their parents' lax moral and sexual attitudes.

By the turn of the 19th century, the upper-class family had developed more intimate relationships. The old formality between parents and children diminished. More casual and loving terms such as "mama" and "papa" replaced the more formal "madam" and "sir." Wet-nursing declined after 1750, and by 1780 most mothers nursed their own children, encouraging closer maternal attachment to infants. Parents felt more responsibility to provide a good education. Nevertheless, upper-class children still spent much of their time in the care of servants. In fact, concern began to grow about servants' corrupting influence on children. The decline in wet-nursing partly followed from this. But most worry centered on adolescent children and the dangers of sexual defilement. Parents feared that footmen would seduce their daughters, or that maids would debauch their sons. Actually, in the latter case, maids were more frequently prey than hunters.

Until the end of the 18th century, by which time mothers were making more decisions about upbringing, increasing maternal attachment to children did not substantially alter patriarchal authority. British families were nuclear. Adult, married brothers and sisters did not live together, neither did married children live with their parents except for financial reasons. Married men therefore ran their households without interference. Fathers played important roles in child-rearing decisions, such as how an infant would be fed (by wet-nursing, maternal-nursing, or bringing up "by hand" without breast milk), and when the baby would be weaned. As the child grew older, fathers closely oversaw the education of sons, especially the heir, but mainly left daughters to the mother's care. If the mother died and the father did not remarry quickly, young children were sent to a female relative. Boys often went to school at age 6 or 7, but mothers educated daughters at home with the help of **governesses** and **tutors**.

The **middle classes** developed somewhat closer family relationships. Because they had fewer servants, family members had more contact with each other. Much evidence indicates that parent–child relationships were often loving. As in the upper classes, nursing by mothers replaced wet-nursing and encouraged maternal bonding to infants. If the mother died, an adult or teenage daughter often postponed marriage to manage her father's household and care for him. Brothers and sisters were expected to influence the growth of gender identity in childhood. Sisters were taught to encourage morality in brothers, while the latter were taught to protect the girls.

Parental responsibilities here, as in the upper classes, complemented those of the children. Fathers primarily provided economic support and attention to sons, especially those who would take over the family's business or inherit its wealth. Mothers supervised the moral and spiritual education of all the children and the entire upbringing of daughters. When necessary, teenage or adult daughters managed the household. The youngest or unmarried daughter cared for her elderly parents and nursed any ill family members. Sons' responsibilities were less defined but were usually financial.

For the pre-industrial laboring classes, the family often was not just the primary social unit but also the basic economic unit. In 1714 the typical home included a workshop—the center of production in town and countryside alike. Child-rearing, like marriage, was an aspect of the domestic economy. The family trained children for their economic roles. In these traditional households, infants were swaddled or confined in cradles to protect them from the bustle of daily life. Children performed many simple but necessary tasks, from picking apples to aiding their parents with **domestic production**. For such children, family life was in some respects the reverse of that in the higher classes—very personal, but very work-oriented. Despite the impact of industrialization, this pattern survived the Hanoverian period, reflecting the longevity of rural and agrarian folkways.

For many families of the working class, the late Hanoverian era brought great change. As industrialization expanded and capitalized on inexpensive **child labor**, the **factory** to some extent replaced working-class parents as an authority and educator. Since children's factory work was regimented and repetitive, they were no longer taught a variety of skills, neither was their moral education an everyday affair woven into the texture of family life. The new industrial pedagogy was that of the factory, with its lessons of promptness, industry, and docility. Although **Robert Owen** and other factory reformers attempted to adjust child-rearing to the new economic landscape, there was no immediate improvement in working-class child-rearing practices. If anything, the new age encouraged poor parents to exploit children for their economic power more than they had before. In addition, working mothers had to rely on paid child-minders, relatives, or older children for baby-sitting. Circumstances made them unable to breast-feed, or to afford wet nurses. Since no nutritionally balanced baby foods were available, infants frequently died from malnutrition. Thus in roughly the same period that the wealthier and more comfortable classes were turning to maternal nursing—a safer and more nutritional practice—factory hours forced working women to replace nursing with bringing up "by hand."

Poor parents have been criticized for caring less for their children than the upper classes. However, there is evidence that the need for children's wages, and the high child mortality rate, did not seriously diminish parental affection. Also, poorer parents realized the advantages of education and, if possible, sent their sons to school. A daughter's education in domestic work was her mother's responsibility. Parents tried to secure domestic service jobs for daughters in familiar and safe homes. Alternatively, girls worked at home at such tasks as sewing buttons or finishing lace until they found work at a factory.

As child-rearing evolved, formal theories of parenting also underwent a complicated transformation. Four factors were primarily responsible for this. First, the growth of commercial society fostered increasing parental interest in elementary and secondary **education**. Second, industrialism shifted workplaces from the home to the factory. Third, the growth of other secular and national interests reassigned training responsibilities to agencies outside the home, such as the school and the workplace. And fourth, the rise of **humanitarianism** and **religious revivalism** promoted emphasis on individual development, children's education, and women's special importance as moral educators. From the beginning of the 18th century, moral reform societies such as the **Society for the Reformation of Manners**, the **Society for Promoting Christian Knowledge**, and the **charity schools** movement paved the way for some of these changes. They declared moral education a social issue, not merely a religious or family matter.

The same message emerged in much of the social criticism of the **Enlightenment**, especially in the writings of J-J. Rousseau (1712–1778), whose *Julie* (1761) and *Émile* (1762) were widely discussed in Britain. Rousseau was the first exponent of "the modern child," the founder of child-centered pedagogy. For him, proper child-rearing fostered the good that lay deep in the child's nature until it emerged in moral behavior and intellectual attainments. The regeneration of society depended on the family, and this in turn on mothers, who henceforth were to be moral educators. Child-rearing was thus no longer primarily a battle against original sin; rather, its purpose was to encourage the unfolding of individuality, to the ultimate advantage of society. The "developmental model" of child-rearing and education evolved from Rousseau's work.

These ideas entered British thought from 1760 to 1790, appearing, for example, in the novels of **Henry Brooke** and **Thomas Day**. Like Rousseau, these writers stressed the virtues of practical learning, moral independence, and self-help. They also deemphasized paternal dominance and elevated maternal emotion. The Rousseauist model also influenced middle-class religious propagandists. Writers such as **Mary Sherwood** helped spread the new domesticity, advocating a pivotal role for mothers in the moral regeneration of society. Toward the end of the century, the **Evangelical** movement, especially in the works of **Hannah More**, extolled the distinctly maternal side of moral education. The Evangelicals contributed to the popularization of these ideas by starting **Sunday schools**. But although middle-class children received more thoughtful and individualized care as a result of new ideas, the Industrial Revolution delayed benefits for the working classes. For poor children, the factory, not the home, provided training, and mothers and children separated during the workday.

Although there were many changes between 1714 and 1837, the one that was perhaps most uniform in its social impact was the realization that moral, intellectual, and occupational education was of importance to society as well as the family. To this extent, patriarchal authority lost ground. In the 19th century, Britain increasingly saw previously "domestic" issues such as child labor, education, married women's property, and even family violence as public policy issues. But if patriarchy was weakened, there are those who argue that it only restructured itself and rose again in industrial and post-industrial forms.

Change certainly did not completely revolutionize traditional child-rearing practices, for the nuclear family continued in Britain. Victorian fathers continued to rule their households in law and under society's rules. Typically, throughout the

Hanoverian era, children of the upper and middle classes enjoyed individual attention, reasonably good education, affectionate security, and a prolonged childhood. The children of the working classes had shorter childhoods and greater responsibilities at a young age, both inside and outside the realm of economic production. It may be mentioned also that although methods of family discipline changed, the state continued to treat children accused of crimes with harshness, assuming that severe punishment was the best deterrent to **crime**. Children over age 7were tried as adults responsible for their actions, and sentences included **transportation** and hanging.

Valerie Frith
Anne Thompson

Bibliography

Badinter, Elizabeth. *Mother Love: Myth and Reality.* 1981.

Bayne-Powell, Rosamund. *The English Child in the Eighteenth Century.* 1939.

Davidoff, Lenore, and Catherine Hall. *Family Fortunes: Men and Women of the English Middle Class, 1780–1850.* 1987.

Gillis, J.R. *For Better, for Worse: British Marriages, 1600 to the Present.* 1985.

Legates, Marlene. "The Cult of Womanhood in Eighteenth-Century Thought." *Eighteenth-Century Studies.* Vol. 10, pp. 21–39.

Pinchbeck, Ivy, and Margaret Hewitt. *Children in English Society.* 1969.

Rendall, Jane. *Women in an Industrializing Society: England, 1750–1880.* 1990.

Stone, Lawrence. *The Family, Sex and Marriage in England, 1500–1800.* 1977.

Trumbach, Randolph. *The Rise of the Egalitarian Family: Aristocratic Kinship and Domestic Relations in Eighteenth-Century England.* 1978.

After the Bedtime Story, 1809

See also Children's Literature; Factory Movement and Factory Acts; Manners and Morals; Standard of Living; Women's Employment

Children's Literature

In 1714 children's literature as defined today did not exist. But children were the targets of many books: Latin grammar texts, **charity school** books published by the **Society for Promoting Christian Knowledge**, and religious leisure readings such as James Janeway's *A Token for Children* (1672), John Bunyan's *Pilgrim's Progress* (1678), and **Isaac Watts**'s *Divine Songs for Children* (1715). Less reputable subject matter in chapbooks, broadsheet **ballads**, and tales, was available for general audiences, including children.

By around 1750, however, a new literature with a revised identity and mission was emerging. It went beyond earlier juvenilia designed to "instruct and delight," in usually sugar-coated traditional religious and moral lessons, in three ways. First, because the new authors adopted **Enlightenment** ideals from **John Locke** and others, which championed rational order, their children's books emphasized learning and living in this world while demoting the importance of preparing for the next. Second, the new works appealed to children because of their numerous **book illustrations**, often woodcuts, the finest of which were drawn by John and **Thomas Bewick**. Third, by vigorously advertising their books, **publishers** created a new market that cut across class lines.

John Newbery (1713–1767) established children's literature by publishing *A Little Pretty Pocket-Book* (1744) and thereafter setting the pace for the trade in variety and output. Many genres familiar today were developed by bookseller–printers even though they specialized in adult fare. So great was the demand for novelty by the 1760s that publishers, often short of fresh material, recycled different combinations in their coveted juvenile miscellanies (sixpenny catchalls), or issued singly (some for as little as onepence) familiar materials from many genres such as decorative alphabets, narratives about good children learning to read, and Bible stories. Publishers translated imported fairy tales—French (*Tales of Past Times. By Mother Goose,* 1729; "Beauty and the Beast," 1756), Eastern ("Sinbad" and "Aladdin," 1704–1717), and German (Grimms' *Popular Stories,* 1823). Popular too were traditional home-grown sagas, for example "Tom Thumb," "Guy of Warwick," and "Jack the Giant-Killer." Religious works continued to be readily available: catechisms, "Thumb" (miniature) and hieroglyphic (rebus) Bibles, and new editions of Janeway, Bunyan, and Watts.

There also were conduct books, **fables** from Aesop and others, natural histories, and abridged adult **novels** (*Gulliver's Travels,* 1726, particularly Part I, "Lilliput"; *Robinson Crusoe,* 1719; and *Pamela,* 1740). Novels began to be fashioned specifically for the young—the first was **Sarah Fielding**'s *Governess* (1749); the best-selling **Oliver Goldsmith**'s *Goody Two-Shoes* (1767). Long-popular nursery rhymes, verses, and song games of uncertain origin appeared in book form in Mary Cooper's Lilliputian collection, *Tommy Thumb's Pretty Song Book* (1744), a tiny printed book with cuts and text engraved in red and black. Reissued and augmented, these verses came to be known as *Mother Goose's Melodies* or *Nursery Rhymes.* With modifications, many are the same songs tots may hear today: "Little Boy Blue," "Baa, Baa, Black Sheep," "Hickery, Dickery, Dock," and so on.

Recognizing the trade's influence on popular attitudes, middle- and upper-class writers from the 1770s penned books to encourage class and gender decorum and to uplift **manners and morals.** Whereas **Enlightenment** optimism had inspired the trade at mid century, more conservative ideals prescribed the attitudes proper for young Britons after 1789. Instability due to **radicalism** and the **Industrial Revolution** was countered by inculcating traditional values: religious faith, national solidarity, and social duty and order. Subtle or ponderous, many hundreds of tomes "pointed a moral." The best of them still have a certain charm: **Anna Laetitia Barbauld**'s *Hymns in Prose* (1781), Dorothy Kilner's *Life and Perambulation of a Mouse* (*c.* 1783), **Sarah Kirby Trimmer**'s *History of the Robins* (1786), **Thomas Day**'s *Sandford and Merton* (1783–1789), **Hannah More**'s widely popular *Cheap Repository Tracts* (1795–1798), **Maria Edgeworth**'s superb juvenile stories (from 1795 to 1827), and **Mary Martha Sherwood**'s famed *History of the Fairchild Family* (1818).

In this same period, new whimsical diversions appeared, graceful and witty, some elegantly engraved: William Roscoe's (1753–1831) *Butterfly's Ball and Grasshopper's Feast* (1806); Catherine Ann Dorset's finer imitation, *The Peacock "At Home"* (1807); and John Harris's history of *Sixteen Wonderful Old Women* (1820), forerunner of Edward Lear's nonsense limericks. Children's literature of unparalleled quantity and diversity filled the British market by 1837, helping to provide the large audience and varied taste of the Victorian era.

Mary V. Jackson

Bibliography

Darton, F.J. Harvey. *Children's Books in England.* 3rd ed., rev. Brian Alderson. 1982.

Jackson, Mary V. *Engines of Instruction, Mischief, and Magic: Children's Literature from Its Beginnings to 1839.* 1989.

Neuburg, Victor. *The Penny Histories.* 1968.

Opie, Iona, and Peter Opie, eds. *The Oxford Dictionary of Nursery Rhymes.* 1951.

Pickering, Samuel F., Jr. *John Locke and Children's Books in Eighteenth-Century England.* 1981.

Thwaite, Mary F. *From Primer to Pleasure in Reading.* Rev. ed., 1972.

Whalley, Joyce. *Cobwebs to Catch Flies: Illustrated Books for the Nursery and Schoolroom, 1700–1800.* 1975.

See also Education, Elementary; Engraving; Graphic Arts; Orientalism

Chinoiserie

The term *chinoiserie,* borrowed from the French for "Chinese," describes designs based however loosely on eastern forms and motifs. The English infatuation with the Orient began with the 17th-century importation, by the Dutch and also by the English **East India Company**, of Chinese and Japanese silks, porcelains, hand-painted wallpapers, and lacquerwork. Some families sent to China for furnishings or sets of porcelain dinnerware marked with their own coat of arms; others caused coromandel or lacquered panels to be integrated into their traditional English cabinetry. By the late 17th century, domestic recipes for "lacquer in the manner of Japan" had been patented, and Stalker and Parker's *Treatise of Japanning and Varnishing* (1688) had so popularized lacquerwork techniques that England was transforming items large and small with enamels, a fad that was to continue well into the 19th century. The style soon spread to **home furnishings and decoration**, and even **landscape design**; by the 1750s, few great houses in England lacked a bedroom, drawing room, or garden "in the Chinese manner."

But even as such works as *A New Book of Ornaments* (1752) by Matthias Lock and Henry Copland, and *The Gentleman & Cabinet-Maker's Director* (1754, 1755, 1762) by **Thomas Chippendale**, made the style accessible to **middle-class** homeowners, the **aristocracy** was turning to the **neoclassical style** advanced by **Robert Adam** and others. Chinoiserie did not disappear from the Continent, however, and English patrons welcomed the continuing importation of Chinese taste that would allow Henry Holland (1745–1806) to design the Chinese dairy at Woburn (1787), French decorators to install the Chinese drawing room at Carlton House (1790), and **John Nash** to develop the oriental fantasy of the Royal Pavilion in Brighton (completed *c.* 1820) for the Prince Regent.

English chinoiserie was pure in neither lineage nor expression. Of the many British **architects** working in the style, only **Sir William Chambers** had visited China; and his own work in the Chinese manner, such as the pagoda at Kew Gardens, was heavily anglicized. Further modification of the eastern prototype came as English cabinetmakers interpreted the Continental expressions of it, themselves less than literal, mixing mandarins, monkeys, fretwork, dragons, bamboo, cranes, and pagodas to exuberant if sometimes disconcerting effect. As Chippendale's *Director* reveals, the style could be combined with others—**Gothic**, **Palladian**, or French. The eclectic **Regency style** was equally unorthodox.

There was a whimsical side to this cultural exchange. Unlike the contemporaneous Gothic style, which retained an essential masculinity (even when arches, tracery, and buttresses were reduced to decorative lines), chinoiserie, despite the regulating geometry of its fretwork, was equated with femininity and relaxation. And while the Orient was seen as a home of ancient philosophies and political stability, occidental translations of its basic styles culminated strangely in the fantasies of the Vauxhall and Ranelagh **pleasure gardens**, and in the Royal Pavilion.

Reed Benhamou

Bibliography

Chambers, Sir William. *Designs of Chinese Buildings, Furniture, Dresses, Machines and Utensils.* 1757.

Chippendale, Thomas. *The Gentleman & Cabinet-Maker's Director.* 1754, 1755, 1762.

From Chippendale's The Gentleman & Cabinet-Maker's Director, *1754*

Dinkel, John. *The Royal Pavilion, Brighton.* 1983.
Lock, Matthias, and Henry Copland. *A New Book of Ornaments.* 1752.
Musgrave, Clifford. *Regency Furniture: 1800 to 1830.* 1961.
Whiton, Sherrill. *Interior Design and Decoration.* 1974.

See also Exoticism; Interior Design; Orientalism

Chippendale, Thomas (1718–1779)

It is not certain whether Chippendale was born in Yorkshire or **London**, or from whom he learned his craft of cabinetmaking. By the early 1750s, however, he had opened a shop in London's St. Martin's Lane that eventually employed some 20 journeymen and as many apprentices. On his death, the shop passed to Thomas III, the eldest of his 11 children, who continued the business until his own death in 1822 or 1823.

Chippendale's versatility and business acumen are evident in *The Gentleman & Cabinet-Maker's Director,* first issued in 1754 "to assist the one in the Choice, and the other in the Execution of the Designs," then twice revised and enlarged (1755, 1762). As much sales catalogue as pattern book, the work ranges from chairs to chimneypieces the appearance of which could be adapted to the client's purse and taste: "If any of the small Ornaments should be thought superfluous, they may be left out, without spoiling the Design."

Published too early to include pieces in the **neoclassical style** Chippendale built for architect **Robert Adam**, the second and third editions of the work do demonstrate his mastery of French, Chinese, and Gothic idioms, and his ability to combine these disparate elements into the intricately carved English rococo style that defines the Age of Mahogany (1725–1760). Typical of Chippendale's pieces is the "ribband-back" chair, its back carved to resemble intricately interlaced grosgrain; equally typical is the style now called Chinese Chippendale, ornamented with pagodas, fretwork, and exotic birds, and standing on straight legs shaped to suggest bamboo. Good construction was never sacrificed to fantastic form, however; and it is this blend of creativity and craft that has made Chippendale one of the great figures in the history of British **home furnishings and decoration**.

Reed Benhamou

Bibliography

Chippendale, Thomas. *The Gentleman & Cabinet-Maker's Director.* 1754, 1755, 1762.
Hayward, Helena, ed. *World Furniture.* 1965.
Macquoid, Percy. *A History of English Furniture, III: The Age of Mahogany.* 1905.
Thornton, Peter. *Authentic Decor: The Domestic Interior, 1620–1920.* 1984.
Whiton, Sherrill. *Interior Design and Decoration.* Rev. ed., 1990.

See also Architects and Architecture; Chinoiserie; Hepplewhite, George; Interior Design; Sheraton, Thomas

Chronometers

Hanoverian **cartography** waited on chronometry. Pendulum clocks offered accuracy but lacked portability; spring-driven clocks were portable but inaccurate. Both qualities were essential to determining longitude at sea, and efforts to do so by measuring "lunars," based on the moon's orbit, were problematic. Britain's growing maritime interest in **navigation** led Parliament in 1714 to pass the **Longitude Act** providing a large cash prize for an accurate means of determining longitude. John Harrison (1693–1776), a Yorkshire carpenter and self-taught clockmaker, built five chronometers between 1735 and 1770 that met every seaborne test of accuracy. A copy of his H4, accurate to within one-tenth of a second per day, accompanied **Captain Cook** on his second and third voyages of discovery. Harrison's ingenuity solved the problems posed by friction and temperature variation. Later, Thomas Earnshaw (1749–1829) perfected simpler mechanisms only recently rendered obsolete by quartz movements and navigation satellites.

N. Merrill Distad

Bibliography

Howse, Derek. *Greenwich Time and the Discovery of Longitude.* 1980.

May, William Edward. *A History of Marine Navigation.* 1973.

Quill, Humphrey. *John Harrison: The Man Who Found Longitude.* 1966.

Taylor, Eva G.R. *The Haven-Finding Art: A History of Navigation from Odysseus to Captain Cook.* 1957.

Church of England

In 1714 this was the Established Church, the Anglican Church. On its side in any dispute were tradition, architecture, the weight of numbers, the power of the state. The king, though himself a German Lutheran, was sworn to its protection. The church's superiority was guaranteed by many legal requirements and prohibitions, including the **Test and Corporation Acts** (1661, 1673, 1678), Bill of Rights (1689), and **Act of Settlement** (1701). Its income was ensured by endowments, pensions, landholdings, Queen Anne's Bounty, **tithes**, and church rates. The crown appointed its top functionaries—bishops, deans, canons. Its 26 bishops sat by right in the **House of Lords** and constituted a solid voting bloc on the side of the king's ministers. At the local level, where there were thousands of parishes, each containing one or more churches headed by vicars or vicars' deputies (curates), the clergy were upholders of both church and state; many served in **local government**. These clerics usually owed their appointments not to the crown but rather to the landed classes. Though this meant some dissimilarity in both income and outlook between them and the upper clergy, both groups were essentially conservative, with the interests of the landed classes at heart.

For many people for most of the Hanoverian period, the church was the intellectual and social center of the country. Its membership grew moderately in the earlier 18th century as dissent waned. The church dominated the English universities. A goodly proportion of the nation's scholars and intellectuals were ordained in its service. Its buildings were the largest public meetinghouses with entire communities laid out around them. Its bells tolled the hours of the day and news of national military victories. Its leaders, communicating from their three-decker pulpits, provided information, education,

Clergyman from Hogarth's "Sleeping Congregation," 1736

encouragement, solace, and communion. Clerics' **sermons** and **tracts** were read widely, and they presided over both local and national holidays and ceremonies. The church was the greatest educational force in the British Isles, involved throughout the period 1714–1837 in **education**: religious, secondary, and elementary. It was involved in many philanthropic projects as well. As time passed it became ever more involved in **missionary** work both within the kingdom and abroad in the **Empire** through organs such as the **Society for Promoting Christian Knowledge** and the **Society for the Propagation of the Gospel in Foreign Parts**. Many Anglican priests and university intellectuals cooperated with **dissenters** in the **humanitarian** projects of the latter Hanoverian period, together joining the **antislavery movement** and supporting the **Sunday school** movement.

Because the church was "the praying branch of the State," its history was intimately connected also with political life. In the early 18th century its privileged political position made it sensitive not only to theological controversy from within, as in the **Bangorian controversy** over its temporal authority, but also to the threats represented by **nonjurors** loyal to their oaths to James II, **Jacobites**, **Roman Catholics**, and dissenters. The **Fifteen** and the **Forty-five** threatened not only the **Hanoverian succession** but Anglican supremacy. Ongoing struggles by dissent and by Catholics to gain relief from their disabilities were always aimed indirectly at Anglican privileges. During the reign of **George III** (1760–1820), a liberal movement within the church produced the Feathers Tavern petition (1772), demanding abolition of the Anglican clergy's requirement to subscribe to the Thirty-nine Articles—an attempt to broaden the Protestant communion and reach out to dissenters. Though this failed, the breaking away of American communicants after the **American Revolution**, and the new amalgamation and need for reform resulting from the **union** with Ireland (which produced a single "United Church of England and Ireland"), forced changes in church organization and governance.

The church's identification with the state greatly strengthened it in public estimation during the **French Revolutionary and Napoleonic Wars**, when "Church and King" divines were loud in their patriotic exhortations. But the same identification made it a prime object of **radical** attacks during the 1790s and afterward, aimed particularly at its controls on **laws of public worship, speech, and the press**, and its access through tithes to agricultural income. Agricultural enclosure in the latter 18th century, possible only with the consent of tithe-holders, had often doubled parsons' acreages and incomes, separating them socially from parishioners who suffered from the same process, making the church's efforts to restrict poor relief and reduce rural **crime** far more unpopular. Politicians, hoping to spare Parliament itself from reform, sacrificed major church privileges to appease reform agitation in the latter 1820s, which saw repeal of the Test and Corporation acts, and **Catholic emancipation**. The **Irish Church Act** (1833) reflected the same tendencies, as did the Tithes Commutations acts of the later 1830s. The tumult preceding the **Reform Act** (1832) saw unprecedented violence against all churchmen, including the Archbishop of Canterbury.

Church doctrine, though firmly based on the Thirty-nine Articles, Book of Common Prayer, and Catechism, naturally reflected the evolving intellectual currents of the era. Contributing significantly to contemporary ideas were many Anglican divines—for example, bishops **Atterbury**, **Barrington**, **Butler**, **Hare**, **Hoadly**, **Horne**, **Hurd**, **Horsley**, **Law**, **Potter**, **Sherlock**, **Warburton**, **Watson**, and **Whately**, not to mention the great miscellany of priests that included men as diverse as **Bentley** and **Porson**, **Collier**, **Tucker**, **Blackburne**, **Wesley**, **Berridge**, **Paley**, **Sterne**, and **Toplady**.

The early 18th century saw the continued promotion, especially by Low Church **Whigs** dominant at that time, of liberal theology (**Latitudinarianism**) as religious intellectuals attempted to find a broad doctrinal pathway that would attract moderate dissenters and help to reunite Protestantism. Churchmen, especially those inclined to High-Church emphasis on authority and ritual, always found it necessary to combat anti–Trinitarian doctrines such as Arianism, Socianism, **Unitarianism**, and still freer forms of **freethinking**; but at the same time, interest in **science** helped push Anglican theology itself toward more "reasonable" and "natural" formulations. Yet by 1750 this more sophisticated outlook, which lingered down to 1790 and brought with it growing **religious toleration**, was being challenged from within by a countertendency, a new **religious revivalism** affecting both Europe and America; which, in Britain, manifested itself in Low-Church pietism launched first by **William Law**, the **Wesleys**, and **Methodism**, and later by **Evangelicalism** led by men such as **Wilberforce**, both stressing much more than Latitudinarianism the moral and emotional rather than intellectual character of religious experience, and greatly downplaying doctrine.

The church hierarchy was slow to respond to this challenge, preferring after 1790 rather to wage war against the radical unbelief spreading among literate workers than against the more deeply subversive currents of **enthusiasm** working within the **middle classes** and, by 1815, resulting in the appointment of more zealous men to clerical positions. The Oxford Movement (begun in 1833) would spring from some of these promptings of self-reformation; but when John Keble (1792–1866), John Henry Newman (1801–1890), and others reacted against the Irish Church Act (1833) as "National Apostasy" and called for a reinvigoration of the Catholic tradition within the church, they hardly foresaw how, in the Victorian period, their movement would turn out.

Although the church gave structure, dignity, and decency to the lives of millions, many of its advantages worked to its detriment, as **Bishop Edmund Gibson** discovered when he tried to effect reforms in the early Hanoverian era. By 1837 the church's position was far less secure than in 1714. Afflicted in the latter 18th-century countryside by nonresidence, pluralism, nepotism, and other abuses, and in the cities by the growth of luxury and consumerism, it also was slow to respond to the spiritual challenges represented by the growth of industry and urban problems. While Methodism broke away and began flourishing in the industrial districts, in remote country parishes, in **Wales** and even in **Ireland**, and while dissent found new vigor from the 1790s on, the leadership of the church could think of little more to do after 1815 than build new churches and hope more people would attend them. Many parishioners would be lost and decades pass before it would acquire the vitality it needed in the coming urban and scientific age. However, Evangelicalism, its most dynamic element in the early 19th century, contributed powerfully to the new **manners and morals** that had emerged by 1837.

George F. Clements

Bibliography

Abbey, Charles J., and John H. Overton. *The English Church in the Eighteenth Century.* 2 vols. 1878.
Bennett, G.V., and J.D. Walsh, eds. *Essays in Modern English Church History.* 1966.
Clark, J.C.D. *English Society, 1688–1832.* 1985.
Hole, Robert. *Pulpits, Politics and Public Order in England, 1760–1832.* 1989.
Mather, F.C. *High Church Prophet: Bishop Samuel Horsley (1733–1806) and the Caroline Tradition in the Later Georgian Church.* 1992.
Miller, Peter N. *Defining the Good: Empire, Religion and Philosophy in Eighteenth-Century Britain.* 1994.
Smith, Mark. *Religion in Industrial Society: Oldham and Saddleworth, 1740–1865.* 1994.
Sommerville, C. John. *The Secularization of Early-Modern England: From Religious Culture to Religious Faith.* 1992.
Spellman, W.M. *The Latitudinarians and the Church of England.* 1993.
Sykes, Norman. *Church and State in the XVIIIth Century.* 1934, 1975.
———. *From Sheldon to Secker: Aspects of English Church History, 1660–1768.* 1959.
Ward, W.R. *Religion and Society in England, 1790–1850.* 1973.

See also Clerical Profession; Theology; Welsh Religious Revival

Church of Scotland

Under the terms of the **Act of Union** (1707), Scots lost their separate parliament but gained other advantages while also keeping their own legal system, educational system, and established (i.e., official) church, the Church of Scotland (Presbyterian), or "Kirk." This was strongest in Lowland Scotland, whereas Catholic and Episcopalian tendencies remained, especially in the Gaelic-speaking Highlands, as residues of former times.

Power in the church was determined, in theory at least, by a hierarchy of courts, stretching from the parish kirk session through the district presbytery to the regional synod and then to the annual General Assembly. This made for a "democratic" structure in which lay elders were elected, along with the ministers, to represent the views of the parishes. Bishops and patronage were theologically unacceptable, as the church's identity was molded by the religious wars of the 17th century, which had witnessed popular resistance to the imposition of alien systems of ecclesiastical government, and by the Revolution Settlement and Claim of Right (1688–1690), which had brought the triumph of presbyterianism over the episcopal system supported by the Stuarts.

One of the church's challenges in the 18th century was to penetrate the Highlands, where **Jacobitism** and **Roman Catholicism** reinforced each other; to this end it supported the work of the Scottish **Society for the Propagation of Christian Knowledge**. Another challenge was to control its own tendency to schism; and indeed the Secession Church came into being in 1733. The background of the split lay in Parliament's passage of the **Patronage Act** (1712) which, contrary to the spirit of presbyterianism, had restored laymen's power to appoint ministers to livings in the church. But while, on the one hand, secessionists withdrew from its communion, the Kirk, on the other, gradually shed its puritanical and repressive character and came under the influence of the Moderate party, which rejected much of the Calvinist fundamentalism of the Scottish presbyterian tradition.

Because many appointed ministers shared the intellectual and cultural tastes of the landowners, Moderatism came to dominate the General Assembly by the mid 18th century. Moderatism in some ways resembled the **Latitudinarianism** of the **Church of England** and emphasized a more rational approach to religion; it made possible, and became part of, the **Scottish enlightenment**. Socially conservative, it also provided theological and rational justifications of the status quo—scarcely surprising, since ministers were dependent on their aristocratic superiors for **patronage** and positions. Many leading churchmen, such as **Hugh Blair** and **William Robertson** (the main leader of the Moderate party), were prominent thinkers in the Scottish Enlightenment. Other aspects of the strength, activities, connections with politics, the arts, and **dissent** can be seen in the careers of ministers such as **Alexander Carlyle**, **James Fordyce**, **John Home**, and **Alexander Webster**.

However, by the end of the 18th century, largely due to the development of a **middle class** that was hostile to aristocratic patronage and privilege, the **Evangelical** wing or Popular party began to reassert itself. The Scottish Evangelicals, like the Evangelicals south of the border, emphasized a more fundamentalist interpretation of the Gospels and were passionate in their beliefs, unlike the cool Moderates. In the 1830s, led by **Thomas Chalmers** and still protesting the appointment by lay patrons of ministers, as well as the latitudinarian outlook of appointees, they withdrew and provoked the Disruption of 1843, which split the Kirk in half. The Free Church of Scotland did not reunite with its parent until 1928.

Richard Finlay

Bibliography

Brown, C. *The Social History of Religion in Scotland since 1730.* 1987.
Drummond A.L., and J. Bulloch. *The Scottish Church, 1688–1843.* 1973.

See also Enlightenment, The; Presbyterians

Charles Churchill

Churchill, Charles (1731–1764)

Though his public career was brief, Churchill, an impoverished Westminster cleric, was well known to contemporaries as a poet and polemicist. His literary career began in 1761 with publication of *The Rosciad,* a mock epic poem attacking many contemporary **actors**, and *The Apology,* which attacked playwright **Arthur Murphy**, novelist **Tobias Smollett**, and *The Critical Review.* Shortly thereafter, Churchill became coeditor with **John Wilkes** of *The North Briton* (1762–1763), a **periodical** whose attacks on **George III** helped fire the era's growing **radicalism**. His first political **satire**, *The Prophecy of Famine* (1763), prognosticated the rape of England by George's Prime Minister, **Lord Bute**, and his Scottish minions. When **Hogarth** attacked Wilkes in a famous unflattering caricature, Churchill, who saw Wilkes as a martyr to liberty, counterattacked in *An Epistle to William Hogarth* (1763). He again defended Wilkes in his satirical poems *The Candidate* (1764) and *The Duellist* (1764).

Churchill quickly became notorious for his wit, invective, and hedonistic lifestyle. Hogarth depicted him as "The Bruiser" (1763)—a Russian bear with a club in one hand for bludgeoning his opponents, a tankard of ale in the other. Dissipated and diseased, he died unexpectedly in Boulogne while traveling to visit Wilkes in exile.

John F. Sena

Bibliography

Brown, Wallac Cable. *Charles Churchill: Poet, Rake, and Rebel.* 1953.

Golden, Morris. "Sterility and Eminence in the Poetry of Charles Churchill." *Journal of English and Germanic Philology.* Vol. 66, pp. 333–346.

Lockwood, Thomas. *Post-Augustan Satire.* 1979.

Smith, Raymond. *Charles Churchill.* 1977.

Cibber Family

Important participants in British dramatic arts and the London theatrical community from the 1690s to the 1760s, the chief Cibber family members consisted of patriarch Colley Cibber (1671–1757; **Poet Laureate** in 1730), son Theophilus (1703–1759), daughter Charlotte Cibber Charke (1713–1760), and daughter-in-law Susanna Arne Cibber (1714–1766).

Despite **Alexander Pope**'s infamous portrayal of Colley Cibber as a hack in the *The Dunciad* (1728), he was a highly successful playwright. Taking advantage of theatrical turmoil in 1696 to present the play that successfully launched his playwriting career, *Love's Last Shift,* he thereafter wrote more than 20 plays, of which *Love Makes a Man* (1700), *She Wou'd and She Wou'd Not* (1702), *The Careless Husband* (1704), and *The Provok'd Husband* (1728, with **Sir John Vanbrugh**) became perennial favorites for a century. An astute judge of public taste and a careful craftsman, Colley Cibber had an uncanny knack for creating performance vehicles that allowed the talented members of the resident Drury Lane company to shine. While he did add some inventions to his plays, he excelled at adaptation.

He was also an excellent actor and an effective theatrical manager. Colley Cibber began his career with Thomas Betterton's (1635–1710) United Company in 1690, soon specializing in character types such as the "fop" in comedies,

Theophilus Cibber

the villain in serious plays. In 1710, along with Robert Wilks (*c.* 1665–1732) and **Sir Richard Steele** (later replaced by Barton Booth, 1679?–1733), Colley Cibber became a comanager of Drury Lane Theatre. This management team, known as The Triumvirate, guided Drury Lane through some of its most successful years, ending in 1732.

Other members of the Cibber family achieved varying degrees of success and prominence. Charlotte, the unpredictable daughter, pursued an acting career. She performed in **Henry Fielding**'s company in the 1730s, and wrote a fascinating if treacherously unreliable autobiography, *A Narrative of the Life of Mrs. Charlotte Charke* (1755). Theophilus Cibber appeared to be the heir apparent to his father's theatrical fortunes. By 1723 he was summer manager of the company, but after Colley sold his share in the Drury Lane company (1732), Theophilus's aspirations declined. By far the greatest performer in the family was Susanna, estranged wife of Theophilus, who was identified in the 1730s by her father-in-law as an aspiring talent. By 1750 she was performing regularly with **David Garrick** and was widely acclaimed as one of the premier actresses of her generation.

William J. Burling

Bibliography

Ashley, Leonard. "Colley Cibber: A Bibliography." *Restoration and Eighteenth-Century Theatre Research.* Vol. 6, pp. 14–27, 51–75. Also see Supplement, *RECTR,* Vol. 7; and further update by Timothy J. Viator, *RECTR,* 2nd ser., Vol. 4.

Barker, Richard Hindry. *Mr. Cibber of Drury Lane.* 1939.

Burling, William. "Theophilus Cibber and the Experimental Summer Season of 1723 at Drury Lane." *Theatre History Studies.* Vol. 7, pp. 3–11.

Hume, Robert D. *The Development of English Drama in the Late Seventeenth Century.* 1976.

Koon, Helene. *Colley Cibber: A Biography.* 1986.

See also Actors and the Acting Profession; Dramatic Arts

Circulating Schools

These schools originated in South Wales during the 1730s. **Griffith Jones**, their founder and inspiration, maintained that only moving schools of this type could reach the scattered population of rural **Wales**. His schools operated mainly in the winter months, when farmwork was slow and both children and adults had leisure time to learn. Jones restricted learning to Bible-reading in the Welsh language, something that reflected his **Evangelical** preoccupation with literacy as a means to promoting biblical understanding and saving souls. Exercises in writing and arithmetic would only detract from that objective, given that the schools rarely stayed more than 9 months in the same location. The schools expanded rapidly and by 1760 they had taken root in every Welsh county. Their peripatetic character, coupled with their mission to teach Welsh reading, stimulated Welsh cultural nationalism and the growth of **Methodism**.

Momentum was lost after Jones's death (1761), but the schools revived in the 1790s under the direction of **Thomas Charles**, a Calvinist Methodist from Bala in North Wales. Charles supplemented day schools with **Sunday schools** where possible, but otherwise sought to preserve the system and philosophy inherited from Jones. Charles was also an effective propagandist outside Wales, and in the early 19th century circulating schools spread to **Ireland**, where the Hibernian Society introduced them on the Welsh model (1809) despite protests from Irish priests who feared their potential for spreading Protestantism. Similarly, in 1811 a Gaelic School Society was founded in **Edinburgh**; which, soon joined by similar organizations based in **Glasgow** and Inverness, promoted Highland circulating schools teaching Gaelic reading. Here too the promotion of popular literacy had a markedly Evangelical purpose.

Lawrence Williams

Bibliography

Durkacz, V. *The Decline of the Celtic Languages.* 1983.

Kelly, Thomas. *Griffith Jones, Llanddowror, Pioneer in Adult Education.* 1958.

Jenkins, D.E. *The Life of the Reverend Thomas Charles of Bala.* 1908.

Jones, M.G. *The Charity School Movement in the Eighteenth Century.* 1938.

See also Wales and Welsh Culture; Welsh Education; Welsh Religious Revival

Cities and Urban Life

Rapid urbanization importantly changed Hanoverian life. Between 1714 and 1837 the urban **population** of Britain more than doubled in per-capita terms, from 20% to over 40% of the total population.

London, as Britain's political, legal, and financial center, and as the country's largest port and manufacturing complex, was far and away the most dynamic urban area. In 1700 London contained over a half million inhabitants, whereas the next largest city, **Norwich**, contained less than 30,000. Throughout most of the 18th century, London's share of the total English urban population grew; by 1750, one in 10 lived within the metropolis. By 1800, with nearly a million inhabitants, London was easily the largest city in Europe; its population approached 2 million by the late 1830s. At the same time, however, London from the 1790s experienced a declining share of a growing British urban population as still more rapid urbanization was occurring in commercial and industrial centers in the West Midlands, Northern England, and Central **Scotland**.

The rising productivity of **agriculture** supported this rapid 18th-century urban growth, as a proportionally smaller agricultural labor force was able to support a larger number of urban dwellers. But with deaths predominating over births in the larger urban areas where sanitation was poor and disease transmission rampant, actual urban growth resulted chiefly from internal **immigration**. It took 10,000 migrants per year simply to maintain the population level of London by 1800.

City scene with coaches and sedans, c. 1745

The majority of urban immigrants came from the ranks of the rural poor. **Agricultural improvements**, the intensification of arable production and enclosure, rapid population growth after 1760, and internal migration created a steady flow from countryside to town, dispossessed laborers being drawn to the generally better **wages** and employment opportunities existing in urban areas. Men often took work in semi- and unskilled labor related to small-scale manufacturing or **domestic commerce. Women's employment** often came in the **clothing trade**, in work as **servants**, or in various retailing and victualing occupations. But a significant minority of migrants to cities also came from more elite social groups. The younger sons of prosperous **farmers** were often apprenticed to masters in skilled **crafts** and trades. **Gentry** and **aristocratic** families established residences in London and in provincial centers for the purposes of business, leisure, and civic activity, and their involvement in **overseas commerce**, state **finance**, and the **legal profession** was significant.

Because cities were centers of brisk consumer demand, their inhabitants were generally more material-oriented than their country counterparts. This heightened materialism and acquisitiveness of urban life may have reflected a greater need to acquire and display wealth and status in rapidly changing communities where sounder indicators of personal worth were difficult to discern. Also, people faced with urban density seem to have allocated more time and attention to their persons, dwellings, and furnishings, avoiding the hustle and bustle of street life. Certainly they had a profusion of **clothing** and other goods available for lavish **home furnishing and decoration** from which to choose. The 18th century witnessed a remarkable expansion in shops and **shopping**. By 1760, England had 140,000 retail establishments (exclusive of alehouses); London had one shop for every 30 residents, and a small city such as Durham had one for every 82. Shopkeeping was an important occupation, with shopkeepers and tradesmen making up the largest sector of the middle class.

Urban areas witnessed heightened levels of expenditure on **amusements and recreation**. Demand for legal, administrative, and **medical** services was also concentrated there. Increased spending on eating and **drinking** led to the proliferation of taverns, inns, and **coffeehouses** catering to the tastes of the middle classes and resident gentry. Victualing houses, alehouses, and gin shops expanded to meet the demands of the laboring poor. Commercial entertainment expanded beyond the metropolis to a number of **provincial towns**, where **dramatic arts, music, dance, pantomimes**, and so on were provided to growing audiences. This period witnessed the growth of **spa** towns such as **Bath**, and **seaside resorts** that specialized in providing leisure and entertainment facilities for the middle and landed classes.

However, by the late 18th century the most vigorous urban growth was to be found in industrial towns and the ports that served them. Economic historians believe that 18th-century urbanization, heavily driven originally by agricultural change, played an important role in commercial expansion and the development of a more consumer-oriented society, and that these (essentially "pre-industrial") developments preceded the more intensive industrialization of the early 19th century and the spread of "machinofacture," i.e., mechanized work in factories utilizing inanimate sources of energy. The fastest-growing cities of the early 19th century were the industrial centers of **Manchester**, **Birmingham**, **Leeds**, and Sheffield, and the ports of **Liverpool** and **Glasgow**, all of which experienced decadal growth rates in some cases as large as 50% in the 1820s, and whose populations had surpassed 500,000 by the end of the 1830s. Manchester and eventually Leeds were centers of machinofacture in the early 19th century, but as emergent industrial towns in the 18th century they had grown as finishing and service centers for local rural production of **cotton** and **woolen** textiles, respectively.

Indeed, the expansion of rural manufacturing in the 18th century intensified local population densities, and Lancashire and West Riding industrial "villages" were transformed into manufacturing "towns" during the early 19th century. Hence by the 1830s, "mill towns" such as Bradford and Preston capped a second tier of rapidly growing cities whose population was then approaching or surpassing 100,000. However, independent production by **craftsmen** was still the earmark of the **metalworking** cities of Birmingham and Sheffield and the regional network of smaller industrial towns that surrounded them, where workshops and handtools were more characteristic than **factories** and **steam**-driven machinery. And London was still the nation's largest manufacturing center, though with the exception of **brewing** and refining, it was mostly devoid of machinofacture.

Rapid population growth in early-19th-century industrial cities posed daunting problems of sanitation, housing, and pollution. While wages were generally higher, working **hours** were long, and living conditions generally deteriorated in the 1820s and 1830s, most notably in the factory and port cities. **Factory workers** and factories competed for scarce urban real estate with little or no government intervention, the result being high rents, poor housing facilities, and the growth of slums. The majority of the inhabitants of Liverpool and Manchester in the 1830s lived in cellars, common-lodging houses, or poorly ventilated "back-to-backs," with unhygienic sanitary facilities that often led to the proliferation of dysentery and cholera. The prices of foodstuffs were high and the quality poor; adulteration was commonplace. Infant and child mortality in industrial cities was double the national average, and the overall life expectancy of unskilled workers was about 18 or 19 years—less than half the national average. In the face of dire conditions, the laboring poor developed close kinship relationships; newly arrived migrants sought out kin or neighbors to live nearby, for support. Instrumental kinship in early industrial cities anticipated the creation of neighborliness and communality that would be associated with working-class urban life after 1850.

Tim Keirn

Bibliography

Borsay, Peter. *The English Urban Renaissance: Culture and Society in the Provincial Town, 1660–1770.* 1989.

Corfield, P.J. *The Impact of English Towns: 1700–1800.* 1982.

Dennis, R. *English Industrial Cities in the Nineteenth Century: A Social Geography.* 1984.

Koditschek, Thomas. *Class Formation and Urban-Industrial Society: Bradford, 1750–1850.* 1990.

Rodger, Richard. *Housing in Urban Britain, 1780–1914.* 1991.

Rule, John. *The Labouring Classes in Early Industrial England, 1750–1850.* 1986.

Walvin, J. *English Urban Life, 1776–1851.* 1984.

See also Housebuilding and Housing; Middle Class; Standard of Living

Clanny, William Reid (1776–1850)

Clanny, a pioneer of **mining** safety lamps, was an Irish physician and medical writer. He practiced **medicine** in Sunderland in northeast England, a major **coal-mining** region where many tragedies resulted from colliery explosions. Joining the local Society for Preventing Accidents in Coal Mines, he invented and improved several safety lamps, notably the Clanny lamp and "blast lamp." He read papers to the **Royal Society** on his experiments (1813, 1815) and received the silver and gold medals of the London Society (1816, 1817) for his work. **Humphry Davy** and **George Stephenson** also invented lamps, and controversy raged over which one should take precedence. Clanny's first lamp was developed in 1813, 2 years before Davy's (1815), though Davy's was evidently a conscious improvement of it. In the *Mining Journal* (1844) Clanny explained his pioneering role; shortly before his death, his work was recognized by public testimonial.

Theresa McDonald

Bibliography

Flinn, N.W. *The History of the British Coal Industry, Vol. 2. 1700–1830: The Industrial Revolution.* 1984.

Hardwick, F.W., and L.T. O'Shea. "Notes on the History of the Safety-lamp." *Transactions of the Institute of Mining Engineers.* Vol. 51, pp. 548–699. 1915–1916.

See also Science, Technology, and Invention

Clanship

The survival of vast feudal landholdings in the Scottish Highlands allowed notions of kin-based society to survive longer than was the case in lowland **Scotland**. Clans were reinforced by the notion of mutual obligation and responsibility between a clan chief and his followers, a notion founded on beliefs (however inaccurate in reality) in direct blood connection between the chief and his clan.

Shored up by war and militarism in the 17th century, this structure proved remarkably difficult to dismantle in the early part of the 18th century. The vastness of the Highlands made it difficult to police or govern, and this meant that clan chiefs maintained a quasi-military structure for their own protection and also to further clan interests. The ebbing and flowing of particular clan fortunes, especially in the 17th century, meant that there were winners and losers, each on the lookout to reinforce its own position or reclaim lost territory. More than any other factor, this would determine the particular loyalty of a clan during a **Jacobite** uprising.

Social status was determined by the number of men a chief could call to arms. This meant that the Highland economy was geared toward labor retention by means of subsistence agriculture. The Tacksman, often a relative of the chief, acted as his factor in economic affairs by dividing the land among the chief's clansmen for rental. Also, the Tacksman was responsible for recruitment during military conflict. The ability of Highland families to raise fighting men quickly meant that the region was central to Jacobite fortunes. However, clanship was eroded by commercial factors, as money became an ever more important determinant of social status. Government repression after the **Forty-five** uprising outlawed most of the visible aspects of clanship. The maintenance of an effective fighting force on Highland estates after the 1740s was not only illegal but virtually unaffordable.

Richard Finlay

Bibliography

Devine, T.M. *From Clanship to Crofters.* 1993.
Gray, Malcolm. *The Highland Economy, 1750–1850.* 1957.
Hunter, J. *The Making of the Crofting Community.* 1976.

See also Culloden, Battle of; Forfeited Estates Commission; Highland Clearances; Highland Regiments; Lovat, 11th Baron; MacGregor, Rob Roy

Clapham Sect

The Clapham sect was an Evangelical Anglican group active during 1790–1830, led by **William Wilberforce**, the born-again reformer and M.P. who successfully worked to abolish slavery and accomplish social reform. The group's political, spiritual, and social life centered around **John Venn**'s Anglican church in Clapham, South **London**, after 1792. Venn set up parish schools, started evening services, published hymns, worked with the local poor, and labored to establish African and Eastern missions.

The group included many distinguished individuals. Among its members were **Henry Thornton**, a member of Parliament whose Clapham estate served as an Evangelical base; **Granville Sharp**, who worked for the 1772 legal verdict that abolished slavery in England; **Zachary Macaulay**, governor of the Council in Sierra Leone, later secretary to the Sierra Leone Company, and editor of the Evangelical *Christian Observer* (1802–1838); **James Stephen**, who campaigned against the slave trade after seeing its manifestations in the **West Indies**; and Charles Grant (1746–1823), chairman of directors of the **East India Company**, whose early Bengali mission experiences moved him to assist the formation of the Church Missionary Society in **India**.

These and other Clapham associates also supported **Hannah More**'s schools and the British and Foreign Bible Society. In addition, they worked on behalf of **prison reform**, fought to overthrow **blood sports**, labored collectively in the **antislavery movement**, and engaged in many other struggles intended to improve British society. Their critics attacked them (and the **Methodists**, by whom they had been influenced) as "Saints," pious hypocrites slyly promoting their own economic, religious, and professional interests; but they were nonetheless extremely influential and widely admired in their time.

Laura B. Kennelly

Bibliography

Bradley, Ian. *The Call to Seriousness: The Evangelical Impact on the Victorians.* 1976.
Brown, F.K. *Fathers of the Victorians: The Age of Wilberforce.* 1961.
Hennell, Michael. *John Venn and the Clapham Sect.* 1958.
Hilton, Boyd. *The Age of Atonement: The Influence of Evangelicalism on Social and Economic Thought, 1785–1865.* 1988.
Howse, Ernest Marshall. *Saints in Politics: The "Clapham Sect" and the Growth of Freedom.* 1960.
Meacham, Standish. *Henry Thornton of Clapham, 1760–1815.* 1964.

See also Evangelicalism; Religious Revivalism

Clare, John (1793–1864)

Perhaps the most neglected of all great English poets, Clare, familiarly known in his day as the Northamptonshire peasant poet, was a prolific writer of nature **poetry**, songs, **satire**, sonnets, and religious verse. Works published in his lifetime were *Poems Descriptive of Rural Life and Scenery* (1820), *The Shepherd's Calendar* (1827), and *The Rural Muse* (1835). He also wrote hundreds of other poems, prose **letters** on natural history, **essays** on a variety of subjects, notes on **literary criticism**, and an **autobiography**. Much of his verse first appeared in annuals, **periodicals**, and **newspapers**.

John Clare

Clare was largely self-taught, and his unreliable grammar, spelling, and punctuation have contributed to his neglect. But he read popular literature, and was also quite familiar with English poetry. He appreciated nature, and wrote masterly descriptions of the Fen landscape; his knowledge of its birds, animals, insects, trees, and plants was unparalleled. Though **Tory** in general outlook, Clare was a friend of the poor against the depredations of farmers, enclosers, parish officials, and the clerical magistracy.

He enjoyed a brief fame in **London** in the early 1820s and there met **Coleridge**, **Hazlitt**, and many other notables. Though patronized by several prominent aristocrats and by numerous Evangelicals, Clare never escaped from rural poverty to achieve independence. He went mad and, after a time, was committed to a lunatic asylum, where he lived out his days.

Unfortunately, the attention paid to Clare's unhappy life has overshadowed his literary accomplishments. A reassessment, however, is taking place. He is generously represented in anthologies of 19th-century verse, at least four biographies have been written, and the critical literature is accumulating. Poems like "The Mores," "Summer Images," "To the Snipe," and his many poems on birds, now appeal to a wider audience. At some point he may be hailed as the most authentic poetical voice of the English rural laboring class.

Eric Robinson

Bibliography

Deacon, George. *John Clare and the Folk Tradition.* 1983.

Grainger, Margaret. *Natural History Prose Writings of John Clare.* 1983.

Robinson, Eric. *Autobiographical Writings of John Clare.* 1983.

Robinson, Eric, and David Powell. Oxford Authors *John Clare.* 1984.

Robinson, Eric, David Powell, and Margaret Grainger. *The Later Poems of John Clare.* 2 vols. 1984.

———. *The Early Poems of John Clare.* 2 vols. 1989.

Storey, Mark. *Letters of John Clare.* 1985.

Clarke, Samuel (1675–1729)

Clarke, English philosopher and divine, was an exponent of Newtonian physics and a leading theologian of the early Hanoverian period. He defended rational **theology** against the disciples of Thomas Hobbes (1588–1679), Pierre Gassendi (1592–1655), Baruch Spinoza (1632–1677), and **John Locke**, attempting to prove the existence of God by a form of philosophical argumentation closely approximating scientific proof. He believed that the laws of ethics were as constant as those of mathematics, and therefore could be known to reason, unassisted by revelation or faith.

In his 1715–1716 correspondence with Gottfried Wilhelm von Leibniz (1646–1716) on space and time (published in 1717), Clarke defended the theories of Newton (1642–1727) and argued for the existence of absolute space. Clarke's *Scripture-Doctrine of the Trinity* (1712), which found no basis in Scripture for trinitarian doctrine, stirred great controversy and led many of his adversaries to charge him with Arianism, the heretical belief that Christ was neither fully human nor fully divine. **Samuel Johnson** nevertheless ranked Clarke's *Sermons* (1730–1731) among the great Christian writings of the age.

Samuel Clarke

Michael F. Suarez, S.J.

Bibliography

Alexander, Henry, ed. *The Leibniz–Clarke Correspondence.* 1956.

Ferguson, James P. *The Philosophy of Dr. Samuel Clarke and Its Critics.* 1974.

Jacob, Margaret C. *The Newtonians and the English Revolution, 1689–1720.* 1976.

Perl, M.R. "Physics and Metaphysics in Newton, Leibniz, and Clarke." *Journal of the History of Ideas.* Vol. 30, pp. 507–526.

See also Church of England; Freethinkers and Freethought; Science, Technology, and Invention; Sermons; Whiston, William

Clarkson, Thomas (1760–1846)

A leading **humanitarian**, Clarkson was a stalwart of the **antislavery movement** who dedicated his life to informing the public and mobilizing national support for efforts to abolish the **slave trade** and, later, slavery itself, in British possessions. An Anglican with a powerful sense of duty, many friendships

Thomas Clarkson

among the **Quakers**, and advanced notions of **women's rights**, in his later years he helped forge an Anglo–American antislavery alliance.

In 1785, at **Cambridge University**, Clarkson produced a prize-winning essay on the topic, "Is It Lawful to Make Slaves of Others against Their Will?" His *Essay on the Slavery and Commerce of the Human Species* was published the following year and brought Clarkson into contact with **Granville Sharp** and **William Wilberforce**, who he helped to found (1787) the Society for the Abolition of the Slave Trade. Touring England, he gathered information about slave **ships**, interviewed sailors (especially in **Bristol** and **Liverpool**), purchased handcuffs and leg irons and other grisly implements of the trade, researched customs records, and published his findings in a pamphlet, "A Summary View of the Slave Trade and of the Probable Consequences of Its Abolition" (1787). He also promoted a project in Sierra Leone to relieve ex-slaves, and in 1789 attempted to arouse antislavery sentiment in revolutionary France.

Clarkson's fact finding provided grist for Wilberforce, who brought a call for abolition before Parliament annually. But the cause languished in the latter 1790s. Plagued by ill health, Clarkson retired temporarily. He married and settled in the Lake District, where he became friends with **Wordsworth** and **Coleridge**. Resuming his antislavery activities in 1804, he and his fellow crusaders saw a major victory when **Pitt the Younger** issued orders-in-council banning the slave trade in captured colonies. Subsequent actions by Parliament confirmed these orders, and in 1807 Parliament passed the Abolition Act, outlawing the slave trade.

Clarkson then (1808) published his *History of the Rise, Progress and Accomplishment of the Abolition of the African Slave-Trade by the British Parliament,* the first account of the development of the antislavery movement. By 1815 the British government took over the role diplomatically that Clarke had played earlier, **Castlereagh** obtaining condemnation of the trade from the other European great powers. Clarkson met personally with Alexander I of Russia at the Congress of Vienna (1814–1815) and the Congress of Aix-la-chapelle (1818), trying to enlist further support for abolition. During the 1820s, as a new generation of antislavery crusaders emerged to push for complete emancipation (accomplished in 1833); Clarkson continued his propaganda and organizational efforts, reviving the national network of abolition committees.

Clarkson's latter years were occupied with religious studies and an unpleasant quarrel with Wilberforce's sons over the question of whose leadership had been more important in the antislavery movement. At the convention of the British and Foreign Anti-Slavery Society in London in 1840, he was elected president.

Mark C. Herman

Bibliography

Anstey, Roger. *The Atlantic Slave Trade and British Abolition, 1760–1810.* 1975.

Davis, David Brion. *The Problem of Slavery in the Age of Revolution, 1770–1823.* 1975.

Drescher, Seymour. *Econocide: British Slavery in the Era of Abolition.* 1977.

———. *Capitalism and Antislavery: British Mobilization in Comparative Perspective.* 1987.

Eltis, David. *Economic Growth and the Ending of the Transatlantic Slave Trade.* 1987.

Griggs, Earl Leslie. *Thomas Clarkson: The Friend of Slaves.* 1936.

Turley, David. *The Culture of English Antislavery, 1780–1860.* 1991.

Wilson, Ellen Gibson. *Thomas Clarkson: A Biography.* 1990.

Classicism

"Classicism," defined in the strict sense as knowledge of the Greek and Roman classics, was a limited phenomenon in 18th-century Britain. It existed mostly among a small number of men belonging to the professional and upper classes. Only a few women, such as Elizabeth Carter (1717–1806), who translated Epictetus; Elizabeth Elstob (1683–1756), an Anglo-Saxon scholar who published her *Rudiments of Grammar for the English Saxon Tongue* in 1715; and **Lady Mary Wortley Montagu**, could claim a solid understanding of Latin. Many classicists, including famous ones like **Pope**, **Johnson**, and **Gibbon**, were largely self-taught. Gibbon, in fact, was contemptuous of the classical instruction he received at **Oxford University**, where the dons seemed more interested in drinking than learning. No one, however, could call himself an educated man who did not have some knowledge of the Greek and Latin languages. As Johnson remarked, "those who know them have a very great advantage over those who do not."

The 18th century saw a gradual separation of the gentleman amateur from the professional scholar. An early sign of this divergence was the so-called Phalaris controversy, which pitted Sir William Temple (1628–1699) against the foremost scholar of the age, **Richard Bentley**. In a masterly *Dissertation* (1699), Bentley proved, to the mortification of Temple's defenders (the staunchest of whom was **Jonathan Swift**), that the Aesopian Fables were not the work of Aesop and that the Letters of Phalaris were a forgery of a later age. Bentley was correct, but his pride and arrogance had the unfortunate effect of giving erudition a bad name; he became for many people the archetypal "Pedant," thanks largely to Pope's brilliant caricature in the fourth book of *The Dunciad.* A far more genial figure, though less scholarly than Bentley, was **Henry Fielding**, who wore his classical learning with grace and good humor, most engagingly in *Joseph Andrews* (1742) and *Tom Jones* (1749).

If the general public was ignorant of Latin and Greek, it avidly devoured the many excellent translations produced during this period. The end of the 17th century witnessed a vogue for literary versions of the major Latin poets. John Dryden (1631–1700) did more than anyone else to stimulate and supply this popular demand with his lively renderings of Virgil, Ovid, Horace, Juvenal, and Lucretius. On a grander scale, Pope did for Homer what Dryden did for Virgil, namely, produce in rhymed couplets his translations of the *Iliad* and *Odyssey* (1715–1725)—a work "of matchless talent and ingenuity," as **Coleridge** later remarked. (Pope, however, neither forgot nor forgave the caustic verdict of Bentley: "a very pretty poem, but he must not call it Homer.") The latter 18th century saw the range of Greek writers available in English expand to include nearly all extant poets and dramatists. By 1800, multiple versions of ancient authors were plentiful. Inevitably, much of this vast literature was mediocre, and some of the more imaginative British responses to it came in the forms of parody and imitation, as for example in the modernizations of Horace and Juvenal by Pope and Johnson.

Prompted by the example of Bentley, classical scholars began to write their commentaries and dissertations in English—a startling departure from the older practice of composing learned works in Latin. Professors of Rhetoric such as **Hugh Blair** and **Adam Smith** broke with tradition by giving their lectures in English. Slowly but steadily, recognition grew that few people could master the ancient languages. For every **Lord Chesterfield** able to insist that the "word *illiterate,* in its common acceptation, means a man who is ignorant" of Greek and Latin (as he put it in his *Letters*), there were countless others like **Horace Walpole** who, despite his many gifts, freely admitted his ignorance of Latin and Greek. **Defoe** and **Richardson**, though great novelists, were illiterate in the same way. **Joseph Addison** labored to make the classics fashionable, but was swimming against the tide; many of the playgoers who attended his *Cato* (1713) had no idea who Cato and Caesar were.

Twentieth-century readers should not be overly impressed by the classical quotations adorning the pages of the *Spectator* and *Rambler.* The age could boast many men of genuine learning, such as **Thomas Gray** and **Laurence Sterne**; but it also had its share of dunces like Fielding's Beau Didapper (*Joseph Andrews*) who, on being saluted with a famous line of Horace, answered that "he did not understand Welch."

Taylor Corse

Bibliography

Clark, M.L. *Classical Education in Britain, 1500–1900.* 1959.
Frost, William. *Dryden and the Art of Translation.* 1955.
Hammond, John. *John Oldham and the Renewal of Classical Culture.* 1983.
Highet, Gilbert. *The Classical Tradition.* 1949.
Johnson, James William. "The Classics and John Bull, 1600–1714," in H.T. Swedenberg, Jr., ed., *England in the Restoration and Early Eighteenth Century.* 1972.
Mack, Maynard. *The Garden and the City: Retirement and Politics in the Later Poetry of Pope.* 1969.
Pfeiffer, Rudolf. *History of Classical Scholarship from 1300 to 1850.* 1976.
Stack, Frank. *Pope and Horace.* 1985.
Weinbrot, Howard. *The Formal Strain: Studies in Augustan Imitation and Satire.* 1969.
Wilson, Penelope. "Classical Poetry and the Eighteenth-Century Reader," in Isabel Rivers, ed., *Books and Their Readers in Eighteenth-Century England.* 1982.

See also Ancients vs. Moderns Quarrel; Antiquities and Ruins; Augustan; Epic; Hellenism, Romantic; Mock Heroic; Neoclassical Style; Satire; Translation

Cleland, John (1710–1789)

Cleland was the author of *Memoirs of a Woman of Pleasure* (1748–1749), one of the world's best-known works of erotic fiction. After several business failures in the 1740s he was imprisoned for debt in the Fleet, where he wrote (or perhaps rewrote from an earlier version) the two volumes of his famous pornographic **novel**. From this time on he earned his living primarily as a writer. He published at least two more novels, *Memoirs of a Coxcomb* (1751) and *The Woman of Honour* (1768); several unproduced plays; some hackwork **translations** and compilations; various linguistic pamphlets, medical treatises, and political **tracts**; at least 30 articles for the *Monthly Review;* and more than 200 pseudonymous **letters** to the **newspapers**, especially the *Public Advertiser,* in which he appeared as an established spokesman for ministerial and opposition factions. Stigmatized as a "sodomite" by contemporaries, he seems never to have married.

The *Memoirs,* or more familiarly *Fanny Hill* after its first-person prostitute narrator, was banned soon after its initial appearance but continued to be published surreptitiously in English and other languages until it was legally republished in the 1960s. Remarkable for its convoluted style, which (as Cleland claimed in a deposition) avoids "rank words," *Fanny Hill* has recently been treated as, among other things, a dialogue between Cleland and the work of **Defoe**, **Richardson**, **Henry Fielding** (a pamphlet-war foe), **Smollett** (a friend and journalistic coworker), and **Sterne** (a casual acquaintance), and also as a significant text in the **Enlightenment** discourse on sexual practices and gender roles.

William H. Epstein

Bibliography

Epstein, William H. *John Cleland: Images of a Life.* 1974.

———. "John Cleland," in *Dictionary of Literary Biography.* Vol. 39, Part 1. 1985.
Naumann, Peter. *Keyhole und Candle: John Clelands "Memoirs of a Woman of Pleasure" und die Entstehung des pornographischen Romans in England.* 1976.

See also Pornography

Clementi, Muzio (1752–1832)

Clementi, whose serious music is little known today, was acknowledged by Ludwig van Beethoven (1770–1827) as master and model, and won the title of "Father of the Pianoforte." Born in Rome, he was brought to England by Peter Beckford (1740–1811), who supported him for 7 years at his Dorset mansion. His first appearances as a pianist in London (1779) quickly made him so famous that Emperor Joseph II invited him to Vienna in 1782 for a public contest with Wolfgang Amadeus Mozart (1756–1791). Clementi quickly rose to prominence in London's musical life. A skilled promoter, he combined in himself the roles of pianist, piano manufacturer, music **publisher**, teacher, and composer.

Clementi published over 80 piano sonatas in **London** between 1771 and 1821. These are as remarkable for originality of ideas as for bold exploration of the technical possibilities of the new instrument. In style they range from polished "galanterie" to the classical idiom that had so strongly influenced Beethoven to the brooding **Romanticism** of Clementi's last sonata, Op. 50, No. 3, "Didone abbandonata" (1821). His final testament was a three-volume set of 100 studies, *Gradus ad Parnassum* (1817–1826), virtually a compendium of the language of the piano—a language which he had done more than any other musician to develop.

Nicholas Temperley

Muzio Clementi

Bibliography

Plantinga, Leon. *Clementi: His Life and Music.* 1977.
Temperley, Nicholas, ed. *The London Pianoforte School.* Vols. 1–5: Works for Pianoforte Solo by Muzio Clementi. 1984–1987.

See also London Pianoforte School; Music

Clerical Profession

The Anglican Church was Hanoverian Britain's largest and most comprehensive institution. During the period 1714–1837 there were approximately 10,000 parishes under the control of 26 bishops, and 1,000 higher clerics associated with the cathedrals. The clerical profession was overcrowded. A clerical career, like others in law, **medicine**, and the military, was considered a respectable avenue by which a reasonably intelligent and hardworking young man with the right connections might advance himself. Yet the steady procession of university graduates presenting themselves as candidates for ordination meant that many clergymen were either unemployed or forced to accept the mean income of a curate with little prospect for advancement.

Family influence, wealth, and **patronage** were essential in securing a desirable living. Although a number of the era's outstanding clergymen, including two archbishops of Canterbury, **John Potter** and Thomas Secker (1693–1768), rose from modest backgrounds to positions of considerable influence and power, fewer than 5% of the bishops under **George III** came from the lower class.

Clergymen who did hold livings, known as incumbents, often found that a significant portion of their income came from the collection of **tithes**, a process sometimes fraught with difficulty and corruption. Another important source of funds came from farming the glebe, a plot of land granted to a cleric as part of his benefice, so that many country parsons were chiefly **farmers** during the week and preachers on Sundays. In both city and country, curates, who were ruefully said to rely on "leavings" rather than "livings," were typically paid an annual salary between £20 and £50, and so were often obliged to supplement their meager incomes by teaching, writing, or farming. The practice of undertaking two occupations was especially common among **dissenting** clergy.

Although a government scheme known as Queen Anne's Bounty operated to supplement incomes from the poorest **Church of England** livings and curacies—some of which paid less than £10 per annum—the overall effect of this program was to forestall the comprehensive reformation of an inequitable and mercenary system. An attempt by the **Duke of Newcastle** to control clerical patronage in the 1730s only served to align government and clerical interests more effectively. Increasing the political cachet and monetary value of certain benefices, Newcastle attracted the sons of England's landed gentry to take up clerical positions with incomes and influence befitting their social standing. As England's agricultural prosperity grew, tithes from farmlands rose in value, making many livings far more lucrative than they had been.

Pluralism (the holding of more than one living by a single

clergyman), nonresidence, and the bestowing of livings on lay rectors were common practices that often deprived worthwhile men of advancement and made the institution of poorly paid curates a financial and pastoral necessity. In some cases, however, livings were so meager that fiscal exigencies drove even conscientious rectors to pluralism, especially when the value of fixed livings diminished in the face of mounting inflation. Although it was widely acknowledged that pluralism and nonresidence greatly compromised the quality of pastoral care in the parishes and further entrenched dependence upon the clerical underclass of curates, these abuses became more frequent throughout the 18th century. In Devon, for example, nonresidence rose from 50% in the 1740s to about 70% in 1780.

Government ministers and court officials, colleges, and corporations; noblemen and local squires; eminent clergymen and even bishops—all commonly dealt in tithes and advowsons, the right of presenting a candidate for a benefice to the local bishop for his approval. Nepotism, financial considerations, and political agendas frequently supplanted more spiritual concerns. Around 1750 in Oxfordshire, for example, 89% of advowsons were controlled by individuals and groups outside the institutional church. The appointment of bishops was increasingly inseparable from secular politics. **Samuel Johnson** lamented that a willingness to vote with the government in the **House of Lords**, rather than the possession of learning and piety, seemed to be the chief requirement for receiving an episcopal appointment.

The country parson was an important political force in the community: the people who attended his church service lived dispersed throughout the countryside. Because of their learning and stature in the community, clergymen were frequently magistrates, not only in civil and ecclesiastical courts but as justices of the peace in **local government**. The parish was the basic administrative unit of church and state, and neither **Whig** nor **Tory** hesitated to use clerical influence in determining parliamentary **elections**. Some country livings were quite lucrative, and the caricature of the squire parson or "squarson," whose love of fox-hunting and a well-laid table eclipsed more otherworldly matters, was a commonplace of Hanoverian literature.

The daily life of the clergy is well documented in a rich deposit of diaries by figures as diverse as William Jones (1726–1800), a prominent High-Church Anglican who worked in Kent and Suffolk; the nonconformist **Philip Doddridge**, pastoral theologian and hymn writer; James Clegg (1679–1755), a **Presbyterian** minister and village physician in the Peak district; William Cole (1714–1782), an accomplished Cambridgeshire antiquary and friend of **Horace Walpole**; **George Whitefield**, Calvinistic leader of the **religious revival**; and **James Woodforde**, a rather ordinary country parson in Norfolk whose chief distinction was keeping a highly detailed diary for 43 years.

A clergyman's duties consisted primarily of conducting the service and preaching a sermon on Sundays, baptizing children, presiding at weddings, visiting the sick, burying the dead, and celebrating occasional ecclesiastical and civil feasts. Popular participation in the services of the Anglican Church was low; in 1801, for example, approximately 10% of England's citizens took communion at Easter in the Established Church. At Oxford, 30 parishes had a total of 911 communicants in 1738; by 1802, despite an overall rise in the population, the number of those taking communion had decreased by 25%. Most of the religious vitality and missionary creativity in Hanoverian Britain was to be found in the dissenting congregations and in the **Evangelical** revival.

The contribution of the clergy to scholarly and cultural life was enormous. Among the most outstanding clergymen were scientists **Stephen Hales**, **Gilbert White**, and **Joseph Priestley**; hymn writers **Isaac Watts** and **Charles Wesley**; the classicist **Richard Bentley** and the Hebraist **Robert Lowth**; literary historians and editors **William Warburton**, Joseph and Thomas **Warton**, **Thomas Percy**, and **Richard Hurd**; the novelist **Laurence Sterne**; philosophers **Samuel Clarke**, **George Berkeley**, and **Richard Price**; and a host of antiquaries and theologians too numerous to mention.

Michael F. Suarez, S.J.

Bibliography

Addison, William Wilkinson. *The Country Parson.* 1947.

Best, George. *Temporal Pillars.* 1968.

Cash, Arthur H. *Laurence Sterne: The Early and Middle Years.* 1975.

Hart, A. Tindal. *The Eighteenth-Century Country Parson (c. 1689 to 1830).* 1955.

———. *Clergy and Society, 1600–1830.* 1968.

———. *The Curate's Lot: The Story of the Unbenificed English Clergy.* 1970.

O'Day, R.O., and F. Heal. *Princes and Paupers of the English Church.* 1981.

Rupp, Ernest Gordon. *Religion in England, 1688–1791.* 1986.

Sykes, Norman. *Church and State in England in the Eighteenth Century.* 1934.

———. *From Seldon to Secker: Aspects of English Church History, 1660–1768.* 1959.

Watts, Michael R. *The Dissenters.* 2 vols. 1978, 1995.

Clive, Robert (1725–1774)

Clive, created Baron Clive of Plassey (1762) and Knight of the Bath (1764), was one of the most important figures in the making of British **India**. He first arrived in Madras (1744) as a clerk for the **East India Company**. He obtained an ensign's commission in the company's army and served in the unsuccessful siege of the French garrison of Pondicherry.

Following the Peace of Aix-la-Chapelle (1748), British and French trading companies became embroiled in disputes between rival Indian rulers. Clive received an independent command charged with protecting company interests. His defense of the fortress at Arcot (1751) against numerically overwhelming native and French forces, and his subsequent capture of the French stronghold at Trichinopoly, cemented his reputation as a superior commander.

Clive traveled to England for health reasons (1753), but in an unsuccessful bid for a parliamentary seat, rapidly squandered his fortune in prize money gained from his military conquests. He returned to Madras as Deputy-Governor of Fort St. David just as new difficulties were emerging. Reacting to expanding British economic and military influence, the *nawab* of Bengal, Siraj-ud-daula, captured the British fort in Calcutta and set in motion the outrage of the **Black Hole of Calcutta**. Clive, commanding company and regular **army** troops, and supported by a Royal **Navy** squadron, recaptured Calcutta (January 1757) and defeated the *nawab* at the **Battle of Plassey** (June 1757). During the campaign Clive proved to be a bold, aggressive risk-taker and an adept diplomat who successfully maintained the tenuous coalition of European and native allies.

Displacing the *nawab* and becoming virtual ruler of Bengal (1757–1760), Clive consolidated company control, defeating attempts by the Dutch East India Company and various native princes to overthrow the British position. He firmly established company responsibility for military affairs and revenue collection during his subsequent term as commander of all British and company forces in India (1762–1764). Controversy over **nabobs**' corruption within company administration marred his tenure, but a parliamentary inquiry (at which Clive famously declared himself "astonished at his own moderation") exonerated him of inappropriate behavior. Nonetheless, always temperamental and moody, he committed suicide less than a year later. His administrative and military successes laid the foundations for subsequent British rule in India.

Stanley D.M. Carpenter

Bibliography

Bence-Jones, Mark. *Clive of India.* 1974.
Edwardes, Michael. *Plassey: The Founding of an Empire.* 1969.
Fisher, Michael H., ed. *The Politics of the British Annexation of India, 1757–1857.* 1994.
Lawford, James P. *Clive: Proconsul of India.* 1976.

See also Empire and Imperialism

Clothing

British dress reflected a definable national style. It was influenced by the customs and ideas as well as industrial and commercial vigor that characterized the nation. Initially, among the **aristocracy and gentry** clothing was influenced by French fashion. But style was also shaped by a regional love of the countryside. The seasonal journey from **city** to country **house** defined the year for the upper classes. In manor houses and rural estates in every shire they indulged their tastes for hunting, shooting, and other outdoor **amusements**. This passion for the country life explains notable British fashion innovations: the popularity of informal garments, and the adaptation of particular types of clothing.

Fashionable clothing of 1760

Men's clothing by 1714 already included the essential elements of modern costume: a coat, waistcoat, and pants in the form of knee breeches. The combination of these three pieces was called a suit and worn by men of all social classes. What distinguished the vicar from the viscount were differences in fabric and ornamentation.

Around 1714 the coat was a boxy garment with very full skirts anchored into pleats at the waistline, with long, full sleeves bounded by great, deep cuffs. The front of the coat hung from neck to knee-length hem. The waistcoat, sleeved or sleeveless, extended almost to the knee. Breeches were always close-fitting through the thigh and, early in the century, worn above the knee. Later, the shape of the coat narrowed and the pleats held less material; sleeves were closer, and cuffs shorter. The front line of the coat began a backward slant from chest to hem, ending with a garment that became the 19th-century tailcoat. The waistcoat underwent a similar transformation; whereas its skirt had begun long and straight, it too began to slant away from the waist toward the hips. The skirt became shorter until, in the 1780s, it was eliminated altogether.

The changing waistcoat's length affected the style of the breeches. Early breeches, which were almost totally concealed, fit low around the torso with a fly-front closure. About 1760, as more of the torso was revealed, full-front breeches were introduced, creating a smoother line around the lower abdomen. In the 1780s the waistline rose above the hip line, complete with buttons for braces. Breeches became longer as waistcoats shortened. By the end of the 18th century, breeches extended down the leg to mid-calf and were given a new name, pantaloons.

The habits of country life led to a certain easiness in the attire of gentlemen and gentlewomen. As early as the 1730s, newspapers criticized the rusticity of ladies' garb, suggesting that the style of dress implied an innocence that was lacking. At the same time, young men of noble families emulated the dress of coachmen, grooms, and **servants**, to the dismay of their elders.

Around 1714, British ladies' fashions copied the French. Hooped skirts with elaborate decorations were popular. But during the 1730s and 1740s the hoop petticoat began to fade in popularity as simpler styles competed with the flowered silks and brocades that had been the standard earlier. Taste now ran toward dresses made of brown or plain silk, worn with a lace fichu over a quilted petticoat, enhanced by an apron embroidered in gold. Silk weavers used only the best materials to create this apparel, importing their silk directly from **France** and employing expert needlewomen who were members of the local guild. Their work was precise, exact, and exquisite to a degree that modern tailoring cannot begin to match.

The loose-fitting French *saque,* known as the sack in England, was increasingly popular. The T-shaped garment hung from the shoulders in pleats—both front and back—with full, cuffed sleeves. The gown was worn either open or closed in the front, usually concealing the petticoat. Soon all pleats were relegated to the back of the gown, falling in a graceful sweep from the shoulders into an extended train. The gown's front was fitted to the torso and worn with an ornamented stomacher and a matching or contrasting petticoat. Narrower sleeves were trimmed with flounces, ribbons, and lace. The sack was to remain the most formal gown, and was worn for the better part of the century by all women, with variations only in richness of fabric and trimmings.

But English practicality demanded more rational everyday dress. The back pleats of the sack gown were stitched down to the waist, launching what the French christened the *robe à l'Anglaise* after its inventors. Another, more relaxed gown revealed the petticoat in the front, with the skirts of the gown draped at the sides or looped back. This gown, called the nightgown, was favored by all ranks for all but the most formal occasions.

British women of the latter 18th century also dressed in various jacket-and-petticoat combinations, again suggesting the influence of the laboring classes on the fashionable. One of the distinguishing features of British costume was the common types of clothing found in virtually all classes and regions. Fabrics differed greatly, along with wealth, in this stratified society, and occupational garb also distinguished one group from another; but from lowland Scotland south, there were consistent cross-class standard models of apparel for men, women, and children; regional variations were evident more in accessories and patterns of use.

By 1800, plain white cotton round gowns, sashed around the waist, had come into vogue—a style previously worn only by children. Ladies' fashions were inspired by the classical lines of the French Empire style. Waistlines were located under the newly discovered, naturally shaped uncorseted bosom. Simple gowns of sheer muslins and lawns, shortened jackets, and warm shawls became the vogue. Over time, round gowns were made in heavier fabrics, with long sleeves, fuller skirts, and natural waistlines. This style of gown, with variations, was to remain popular for the next 50 years.

Meanwhile, the *beaux* of **George II**'s reign had begun to change their costume by wearing smaller hats and very short coats and capes, and carrying tall walking sticks. A very British garment, the frock coat, was first worn around 1745. Similar to the coat in style, it fit more loosely and more comfortably. Usually single-breasted, the frock coat was the garment of preference for the active British **sporting** life, an adaptation of the frock worn by laboring men.

The great coat was another important innovation which replaced the draftier cape. Similar in cut to the frock coat, and often with multiple collars or capes, this warm outer garment found favor in all circles. In fact, both frock coat and great coat were probably adaptations of working-class dress. The heavy utilitarian wool garb worn by **coachmen** and **waggonway** drivers found a more elegant expression in the wardrobes of lords and gentlemen.

By the 1820s a significant change had taken place in men's clothing. For centuries, gentlemen's clothes had been just as extravagant as ladies'; no fabric, color, or decoration was worn by the one sex that was not worn by the other. But now, thanks partly to the influence of **Beau Brummell**, silks and satins, lace and ribbons, feathers, **jewelry**, and delicate colors were considered unmanly and ungentlemanly. Men's clothes became steadily more somber, with colorful waistcoats being replaced by dark frock coats; breeches were replaced by long trousers strapped down under the foot.

Aristocratic fashions, here as elsewhere, were being superseded by a style that was **middle class** in its origin. The dark-hued garments of **merchants**, the **Quaker**-like apparel of the trading class, was the accepted national style by the 1830s. Broadcloth and **worsted** for men were matched by printed **cottons**, plain muslins, and linens for women. The ethos of the affluent manufacturing and commercial class blended with that of the traditional leaders of society. And now national dynamism was carrying these British styles throughout the world.

Beverly Lemire
Janice Pence Ryan

Bibliography

Boucher, François. *20,000 Years of Fashion.* 1966; 1987.
Bradfield, Nancy. *900 Years of English Costume.* 1970.
Buck, Ann. *Dress in Eighteenth-Century England.* 1979.
Waugh, Norah. *The Cut of Men's Clothes, 1600–1900.* 1964.
———. *The Cut of Women's Clothes, 1600–1930.* 1968.

See also Clothing-Makers; Clothing Trade; Fashion; Hats and Caps; Manners and Morals; Wigs, Hair, and Hairdressing; Women's Employment

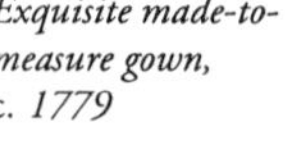

Exquisite made-to-measure gown, c. 1779

Clothing-Makers

How did people obtain their **clothing** in the Hanoverian era? Ready-to-wear garments and accessories, as well as secondhand items, were available in growing quantities from the **clothing trade**. And all family members routinely bequeathed garments to relatives. But for the social elite—the **aristocracy and gentry**, and also the richer urban trading families—clothing was usually made to order by a range of tradesmen and women.

Exquisitely fashioned garments had always been the preserve of the upper classes; the cut, colors, materials, and accessories of their dress demonstrated and reinforced their superior social standing. But they no longer enjoyed a monopoly of such garments. Wealth acquired through trade and industry was displayed by aldermen's wives and prosperous manufacturers alike; each decade, more of them wore facsimiles of the current fashions. To reinforce their standing, those in the upper ranks relied on made-to-measure garments often reflecting the latest French styles with the newest fabrics and embellishments. And just as there was a hierarchy among the fashionable, so too was there a hierarchy of workers who labored to clothe them.

Creating the requisite look required stamina, taste, wealth, and up-to-date information. The process was complex, as clothing goods and services were generally purchased separately. The acquisition of a new garment began with the selection of fabric. **London** furnished both the most fashionable merchandise and the most accomplished fitters. **Provincial towns** were always somewhat out of date, though less so toward 1800 as fashion **magazines** flourished and **travel** improved. Yard goods were available from mercers and drapers who stocked imported silks from France and Italy; English silk brocades produced in Spitalfields; wool fabrics like calimancos, worsted crapes, and broadcloths; and lighter chintzes, muslins, linens, and cottons.

Once the fabric was chosen, it went to a tailor or a mantua-maker—a maker of women's clothes (the mantua was the principal type of gown worn around 1714). The tailoring **craft** was now in the midst of an ongoing transformation. Notoriously labor-intensive, for centuries it had relied on the organized toil of guildsmen. But now it was relying increasingly on the less structured labor of city women. Lower labor costs outside guilds had been encouraging 17th-century manufacturers to restructure production, the effect being the gradual reorganization of the clothing industry itself. By 1714 the making, mending, and selling of clothes (many to the **army** and **navy**) employed more than 20% of London's women. Simultaneously, the new female trade of mantua-maker broke the tailors' monopoly on made-to-measure garments. By 1714, mantua-makers had taken over much of women's employment in dressmaking, only women's riding habits remaining with the tailors. (Staymaking was a separate profession.)

While made-to-measure dressmaking and millinery were genteel occupations for daughters of the middling ranks, women of the lower classes increasingly plied their needles stitching ready-made goods of predetermined sizes—particularly military clothing, aprons, caps, and other accessories—in large workshops, backrooms of retail outlets, and in garrets and lodging-house rooms. The abundance of cheaper, industrially produced **cottons**, linens, and **wools** facilitated the development of more and larger clothing manufacturing companies by the beginning of the 19th century, many springing up near the **textile industries** in Lancashire, Yorkshire, **Ireland**, and various ports outside London. By the 1830s, generations after its inception, the sweated labor of the clothing trade was receiving its first public scrutiny.

Tailors prepared all made-to-measure outer garments for men. Their establishments varied greatly in size and expertise, with master tailors employing journeymen and apprentices. Tailors for the elite supplied current fashion advice and created exquisite suits (three-piece sets consisting of coat, breeches, and waistcoat) in brilliant silk brocades, velvets, and wools for most of the 18th century. The more restrained styles of the early 1800s were largely an English innovation, and English tailoring then came fully into its own. The clothing popularized by fashion innovator and court favorite **Beau Brummell** depended on a perfect line and fit for its elegant appearance, the focus shifting from fabrics and ornaments to form.

Such made-to-order clothing was increasingly in demand. In towns and villages across Britain, tailors, mantua-makers, and seamstresses made and repaired garments for gentry households, yeomen farmers, tradespeople, even laborers. Sewing was routinely taught, and the skills of cutting could be learned; there was no shortage of women or men who could ply a needle. In households where women had neither time nor talent to make up shirts or petticoats, seamstresses were occasionally brought in or commissioned to do the work.

Particularly in the north and in districts geographically isolated from major markets, there seems to have been a broader reliance on made-to-measure garments than in southern and central England. This pattern changed gradually over the second half of the Hanoverian period as retail **shops** increased in number and the distribution of ready-made garments improved. Ready-to-wear clothing was increasingly available. But taste and limited alternatives ensured a continuing role for made-to-order clothing.

Beverly Lemire

Bibliography

Buck, Ann. *Dress in Eighteenth-Century England.* 1979.

Harte, N.B., ed. *Fabrics and Fashions: Studies in the Economic and Social History of Dress.* Special issue of *Textile History.* Vol. 22, No. 2. 1991.

Lemire, Beverly. *Fashion's Favourite: The Cotton Trade and the Consumer in England.* 1991.

———. *Dress, Culture and Commerce: The English Clothing Trades in the Industrious Era, 1660–1800.* Forthcoming.

Sanderson, Elizabeth. "The Edinburgh Milliners, 1720–1820." *Costume.* Vol. 20, pp. 18–28.

Styles, John. "Clothing the North: The Supply of Non-Élite Clothing in the Eighteenth-Century North of England." *Textile History.* Vol. 25, pp. 139–166.

Morning Dress, 1799

Thale, Mary, ed. *The Autobiography of Francis Place.* 1972.

See also Fashion; Women's Employment

Clothing Trade

The energy, skill, and trading acumen of many thousands of people were required to clothe a **population** growing from about 5 million in 1714 to nearly 15 million by the 1830s. As the 18th century opened, the purchase of new garments of all sorts—utilitarian and fashionable—accounted for about one-quarter of all national expenditure; an estimated 15% of all laboring families added to their incomes by knitting stockings for domestic and overseas **commerce.**

Clothing-making was now in the midst of an ongoing transformation, with women moving in large numbers into made-to-measure mantua-making as well as ready-made production. Consumer tastes were also beginning to change markedly: more and different apparel and accessories were becoming necessities. The **navy** and **army** generated an extraordinary demand for apparel; shirting and breeching the armed forces was an administrative imperative during the many **wars** of the period. Huge sums flowed to large and small clothing contractors, representing a major source of profit for **entrepreneurs** as well as channels of political **patronage.**

Simultaneously, lighter, more colorful textiles from Europe and Asia stimulated civilian demand. For their discerning clients, tailors and mantua-makers made bespoke gowns, petticoats, and waistcoats from silk brocades and painted calicoes. Rich materials, imported from **France**, Italy, and Holland, were easily obtained in **London**, as were the gossamer muslins of the East. The New Exchange in the Strand was a center of elegant **shops**, with its covered arcade and several counters displaying the fashionable wares of the day. Here could be bought yards of silver and gold lace, silk stockings, gloves, ribbons, fans made of only the richest materials, scissors, combs, tweezers, and baubles of all types.

The nation's shops offered made-to-measure and ready-to-wear garments in a widening range of fabrics for middling and well-off customers. Ready-made accessories, shirts, petticoats, breeches, waistcoats, and banyans or dressing gowns were soon obtainable from peddlers and retailers throughout the land, accessibility spreading from south to north over the 18th century. New patterns of production assured expanding quantities of both cheap and higher-quality apparel.

Not everyone, of course, could afford new attire. Many people traditionally turned to secondhand goods. Garments of all qualities entered the secondhand market in extraordinary volumes, through specialist traders, peddlers, pawnbrokers, tailors, mantua-makers, and general shopkeepers. Cast-offs from masters and mistresses passed from **servants**' hands to local clothes dealers, to be bought or exchanged at shop counters, street-side stalls, or cellar entries. Men and women from all ranks sold and pawned garments to raise money, or for short-term loans. Respectable tailors accepted trade-ins on last year's suits to encourage wealthier customers to add to their wardrobes, at the same time recycling used merchandise to poorer clients. Poor women, petty salesmen, and recent immigrants bought, mended, and recycled garments acquired from neighbors and transients. As an aspect of **women's employment** this sort of flexible petty enterprise blended well with household duties, transferring the skills consonant with household frugality to the marketplace. **Jews**, by the latter 18th century, were particularly associated with the secondhand clothing trade, though even in London they were just a fraction of it. This trade flourished until cheap ready-to-wear eroded its market, a trend noticeable by the early 19th century.

Clothes, as articles of value, were also linked with **crime**. Professional and amateur thieves presided over the involuntary redistribution of clothing, moving it from past to future owners. Clothing and household textiles were among the most commonly stolen commodities of the period. As a type of currency, clothing could be transformed with little difficulty into goods, services, or cash. For the aspirant to **fashion** of limited means, the cast-off, sold-off, or stolen garment offered value and utility at a fraction of the cost of made-to-measure.

Much changed in the clothing trade during the Hanoverian period. By 1837, men and women of every class altered and augmented wardrobes with greater regularity, reflecting new patterns of consumer behavior. Changes among workers, fabrics, methods of production, and tastes had all transformed the dress trade. In the 1850s, the sewing machine would transform it yet again.

Beverly Lemire

Bibliography

Buck, Anne. *Dress in Eighteenth-Century England.* 1979.

Harte, N.B., ed. *Fabrics and Fashions: Studies in the Economic and Social History of Dress.* 1991.

Lemire, Beverly. *Fashion's Favourite: The Cotton Trade and the Consumer in Britain, 1660–1800.* 1991.

———. *Dress, Culture and Commerce: The English Clothing Trade before the Factory, 1660–1800.* Forthcoming.

Spufford, Margaret. *The Great Reclothing of Rural England: Petty Chapmen and Their Wares in the Seventeenth Century.* 1984.

Styles, John. "Clothing the North: The Supply of Non-Élite Clothing in the Eighteenth-Century North of England." *Textile History.* Vol. 25, pp. 139–166.

Tozer, Jane, and Sarah Levitt. *Fabric of Society: A Century of People and Their Clothes, 1770–1870.* 1983.

Vickery, Amanda. "Women and the World of Goods: A Lancashire Consumer and Her Possessions, 1751–81," in John Brewer and Roy Porter, eds., *Consumption and the World of Goods.* 1993.

See also Clothing; Hours, Wages, and Working Conditions

Clubs

The 18th century was a clubbable age. Male preserves, the clubs encouraged widely varying pleasures: social, artistic, political, dining, literary, sporting, and gambling. At all levels of society, different associations housed like-minded men.

The clubs' genesis was the **coffeehouses** and chocolatehouses of the 17th century; at these "penny universities," patrons of like opinions and tastes came together to read **newspapers**, write **letters**, and exchange ideas. Thus White's, opened in the 1690s as a chocolatehouse, became a customary gathering place for **Tory** friends; by 1736 it had become an exclusive club, a notorious gaming house, and a favorite haunt of gentlemen of fashion, with a distinguished membership including the **Duke of Devonshire**, the Earl of Cholmondeley, and Major-General Churchill. White's was matched by the **Whig** club Brookes's, where as much as £5,000 might be staked on a single card at faro.

Early in the 18th century, 39 Whig nobles, politicians, and artists met at the Kit-Cat Club, among them the Earl of Dorset, **Robert Walpole**, **Joseph Addison**, and William Congreve (1670–1729). The smaller Tory Scriblerus Club, begun by **Jonathan Swift** in 1714, included **Alexander Pope**, **John Gay**, and Thomas Parnell, as well as **Robert Harley** and occasionally **Henry St. John, Lord Bolingbroke**.

Samuel Johnson belonged to several clubs, the most famous being the Literary Club, which he founded with **Sir Joshua Reynolds** (1746). The Dilettanti Society was composed in 1734 of gentlemen who had traveled to Italy and wished to patronize the arts, often as festively as possible. The rake **Sir Francis Dashwood** (who began a **Hell-Fire Club** in the 1740s), Reynolds, **David Garrick**, and **George Colman the Elder** were members. The Cape Club of **Edinburgh** (1774–1841), formed to debate literary matters convivially, met at different taverns, and insisted that its members adopt

Pall-Mall East and University Club House

fanciful titles of knighthood. Thus **Robert Fergusson** became Sir Precenter, and the artist Alexander Runciman (1736–1785) was Sir Brimstone. The Athenaeum Club (founded by **John Wilson Croker** in 1824) brought together scientists, authors, and artists, as well as their patrons. Larger and more diverse than earlier clubs, the Athenaeum's membership reached 1,200 and more with a mix of conservatives and radicals, bishops, and dandies, who rarely spoke to each other.

But clubs were not just an upper- and middle-class phenomenon. Especially during the 1790s, **radical** political groups like the Friends of Universal Peace and Liberty expressed their response to the **French Revolution**. The Scottish poet **Robert Tannahill** belonged to a tradesmen's club whose members critically discussed literature. Lancashire weavers met at spouting clubs to rehearse different dramatic characters; some then joined strolling companies. The **Hampden Clubs** of 1812–1817 were a continuation of the radical **associations** of the period 1780–1795.

Serious women's clubs existed, despite the "cabal" satirized by Kit-Cat Congreve in *The Way of the World* (1700) and the "scandal school" of Brookes's Club member **Richard Brinsley Sheridan** in *The School for Scandal* (1777). The most famous women's group was the **Bluestockings**, which included **Elizabeth Montagu**, **Hannah More**, and **Fanny Burney**. That club lasted for several generations and met at members' homes.

Timothy J.L. Chandler
Peter A. Tasch

Bibliography

Allen, Robert J. *The Clubs of Augustan London.* 1967.
Darwin, Bernard. *British Clubs.* 1943.
LeJeune, Anthony. *The Gentlemen's Clubs of London.* 1984.
Porter, Roy. *English Society in the Eighteenth Century.* 1982.
Timbs, John. *Clubs and Club Life in London.* 1872; rpt. 1967.

See also Amusements and Recreation; Gambling

Coaching

Stagecoaches first made their appearance in the 17th century and, before 1700, were from **London** serving towns and cities at the extremities of England such as Kendal, Newcastle, and Plymouth. The development of **roads**, particularly turnpikes, meant that coaching traffic grew steadily during the 18th century, a boom occurring in the latter decades and lasting into the 19th. Services became ever more frequent, linking London with the provinces and **provincial towns** with one another. On a busy route such as that from London to Brighton there were 50 coaches a day in each direction by the 1830s.

Road improvements also meant a steady reduction in journey times. Whereas in 1754 it had taken 10 days to travel between London and **Edinburgh**, in 1836 the fastest mail coach was completing the journey in just under 2 days. Most other journeys were also considerably reduced. The use of coach travel also accelerated, passenger miles rising from 67,000 in 1715 to 2.4 million by 1840.

Coach construction also improved during the period. The use, from the early 19th century, of elliptical springs made coaches lighter and more comfortable, enabling more outside passengers to be carried; a law of 1806 fixed their maximum number at 12. The number of inside passengers was generally four. Part of the incentive toward better coach construction had come from mail carriers who saw themselves losing out on revenues to other operators.

Most coach journeys began and ended at inns, and it was

The yard of a country inn, from a Hogarth engraving, 1747

from this lodgings trade that many important coach operators of the latter Hanoverian period derived their original capital. The largest coach operator in the early 1830s was W.J. Chaplin, with 64 coaches; his father had been an innkeeper on the Dover Road. Most of the major services out of London at that time were provided by Chaplin and two major rivals.

Inns were also important staging posts, where passengers obtained refreshments and horses were changed. On longer routes, proprietors might only provide horses for the early part of the journey, employing those of subcontractors for the remainder. Journeys could be dangerous, as accidents caused by bad roads or reckless driving were not infrequent; and there was a risk of robbery by **highwaymen** in isolated areas.

Coach fares varied according to the type of service provided and could only be afforded by the better-off. Most expensive was the private hire of a post-chaise. The most expensive public fare was on mail and flying coaches, which charged a premium for speed. Slower services charged a lower price. Travelers prepared to journey on slow goods' wagons paid least. Fares were also determined by the cost of tolls on the roads and by the level of stagecoach **taxes** imposed on the operators by the government, based on capacity, and levied whether or not the coach was full. Rising costs made it difficult for newcomers to enter the industry after the late 18th century.

The development of **railways** from the 1830s provided severe competition for long-distance coaches, and led many operators to oppose the passing of railway acts in Parliament. By the end of the Hanoverian era the great days of coaching were numbered, but traffic in more remote rural areas remained significant well into the Victorian era. Charles Dickens's *Pickwick Papers* (1836) provides an entertaining picture of coaching in its latter days.

A.J.G. Cummings

Bibliography

Bagwell, Philip. *The Transport Revolution from 1770.* 1974.

Chartes, J.A., and G.L. Turnbull. "Road Transport," in D.H. Aldcroft and M. Freeman, eds., *Transport in the Industrial Revolution.* 1983.

Copeland, J. *Roads and Their Traffic, 1750–1850.* 1968.

Dyos, H.J., and D.H. Aldcroft. *British Transport.* 1974.

See also Transport, Inland; Travel and Tourism

Coal Mining and Miners

Coal mining, already a well-established industry in the early 18th century, experienced substantial expansion in the Hanoverian period, with output rising from an estimated 3 million tons in 1700 to 31 million in 1830. There were, however, marked regional variations. Although Tyneside in northeast England remained the single most important producer, its share of production decreased, as did that of **Scotland**. By contrast, both South **Wales** and Lancashire grew considerably in importance. Growth was fastest in Cumberland (which served the Irish market), but only until 1780, when output leveled off. Although markets were important in a region's success, so too were geological conditions and the types of coal available.

In 1700, coal was used mainly as a domestic fuel. **London**, supplied almost entirely by sea from the northeast, was the single most important market, consuming some 15% of British output. Domestic demand continued to rise as **population** and **urbanization** increased. In the early 1700s, coal was used in such manufacturing processes as **saltmaking** and lead and copper smelting, but after 1760 industrial demand largely led the industry's expansion. By far the most important new user was the **iron industry**, which, following innovations by **Abraham Darby** and his son in iron-smelting, could turn from charcoal to coal fuel. Accordingly, production rose in the major iron-making districts, particularly South Wales and Staffordshire. The second major new source of demand was the gas industry, which by the late 1820s was supplying mains gas for lighting in most British towns of over 10,000 people. **Steam engines**, too, consumed vast quantities of coal. From around 1775 they were used in blast furnaces and, after **James Watt**'s development of rotary motion in 1781, for driving **textile** machinery. The invention of steam locomotives in the early 1800s further increased demand.

Steam power also played a critical role in coal production. Virtually every colliery proprietor or lessee faced the problem of how to drain water; the capacity of older methods for removing it—by gravity or the power of wind, water, or horses—was limited, especially at deeper levels. In regions such as the east coast of Scotland and Tyneside, outcrops of coal and the shallower seams had been exhausted by the latter 1600s. The patenting by Thomas Savery (1650?–1715) of his atmospheric steam pump in 1698, although of little practical benefit in itself, was extremely important in providing the model for **Thomas Newcomen**'s more efficient pump, first used in 1712. Newcomen engines spread remarkably quickly, and were used into the 1800s. After 1775, however, these tended to be replaced by the engines made by Watt and **Boulton**, which were cheaper to operate and able to pump water from greater depths.

Removing poisonous and combustible gases was less easily achieved, making explosions and the resultant fatalities commonplace. Over time, however, considerable progress was made in ventilating pits by driving air through them, but it was not till around 1815 that **W.R. Clanny**, **Sir Humphrey Davy**, and **George Stephenson** almost simultaneously invented safety lamps for underground lighting. Methods of cutting and hauling coal below ground were also improved. Traditionally, coal had been cut by the "pillar and stall" system, whereby pillars of coal were left by the hewers to support the roof as they worked along the seam. Thus in deep mines as much as a third of the coal was left unmined. Over time, where conditions allowed, this system was gradually replaced by the longwall method, all the coal being removed and the roof supported temporarily by props. But coal-cutting itself remained little changed, with gunpowder, picks and wedges, and muscle power being the staple equipment of the miner.

Coal was the property of the surface owner, and many landowners adopted the role of colliery proprietor. The proportion of owners who worked their own coal varied from region to region, although the tendency was for them to withdraw in favor of lessees, ranging from small partnerships of working miners to better-capitalized **merchant** partnerships. Many merchants, from the **Glasgow tobacco** trade for example, be-

Workers and a steam engine at the coal pit-head, c. *1820*

came proprietors of coal-bearing estates which they then worked. In parts of South Wales, the Midlands, and Central Scotland, iron company involvement became increasingly common after 1760. Coal mining, however, was fraught with risks, and many enterprises failed or experienced long periods of financial loss, often because of geological problems or marketing difficulties. Nevertheless, high profits could be made, especially by those who could afford to invest heavily in their concerns.

Work in the mining industry took many forms. Face-working hewers or colliers comprised about a third of the workforce. Among the remaining workers were "sinkers" who sank new pits; roadsmen who cleared underground roads and passages; and horse-keepers, enginemen, and "banksmen," who unloaded the coal sent up from below. Although overwhelmingly a male-dominated industry, female labor was used in some regions, almost always at unskilled tasks; females were most common in the east of Scotland, where at some pits in the 18th century there were more female bearers than male hewers. Boys, usually the sons of families from the close-knit mining communities, were more numerous everywhere, doing a variety of heavy underground tasks. This was largely because pit work, and hewing in particular, had to be learned young, while the strength required to cut coal dictated that most colliers be younger adult males.

As the supply of colliers was limited, they were often employed by their masters on long contracts or annual "bonds." The most extreme form occurred in Scotland, where a system of life-binding was in force until finally abolished in 1775 and 1799. Where there were shortages and intense competition for labor between masters, the colliers—especially if they were organized—could exercise considerable bargaining power, even in Scotland, where the deleterious effects of mining "serfdom" have been exaggerated. Indeed the 1799 "Emancipation" act, as it has been called, was actually an anticombination act. Thus, while mining was a dangerous, unpleasant, and unpopular occupation, often requiring long hours of work for 6 days a week, by the end of the 18th century and in the early 19th, collier's **wages** compared very favorably with those of laborers, and were at least comparable with those of many skilled workers.

Christopher A. Whatley

Bibliography

Atkinson, F. *The Great Northern Coalfield, 1700–1900.* 1966.

Benson, John. *British Coalminers in the Nineteenth Century: A Social History.* 1980.

Duckham, Baron F. *A History of the Scottish Coal Industry.* Vol. 1, 1700–1815. 1970.

Flinn, Michael. *The History of the British Coal Industry. Vol. 2: 1700–1830, The Industrial Revolution.* 1984.

Whatley, Christopher. "'The fettering bonds of brotherhood': Combination and Labour Relations in the Scottish Coal-Mining Industry *c.* 1690–1775." *Social History.* Vol. 12, pp. 139–154.

See also Child Labor; Mining and Miners

Coastal Shipping

The British Isles, with a long, indented coastline and many navigable estuaries, are well suited to the movement of goods and people by water, and long before 1700 there was extensive coastal traffic. But this increased significantly during the Hanoverian period. With industrialization and urbanization gathering momentum, coastwise shipping provided a vital link between areas of production and consumption.

The shipment of goods to and from **London** best illustrates this. With a **population** of over 500,000 by 1700, and a range of growing industries, the capital was already a center of mass consumption. Much of London's huge and expanding grain requirement was brought by coasters (coastal transport **ships**); industrial raw materials like timber, stone, slate, and clay were conveyed up the Thames in large quantities; wine and spirits were shipped in from **Bristol** and Southampton; and, above all, there was the flow of **coal** from Newcastle and Sunderland, a trade that accounted for over half of Britain's coal shipments in 1780. In return, London dispatched a large volume of goods coastwise, disseminating foreign luxury items to provincial ports, together with many locally manufactured goods.

Though London remained the leading port in the coastal trade, her predominance declined as the coastwise business of the outports, notably Hull and **Edinburgh** on the east coast and, even more, **Liverpool** and Whitehaven on the west, increased dramatically during the period 1780–1840. Much of this burgeoning traffic was carried in relatively small sailing vessels. The north-east coal trade, however, employed collier brigs able to carry over 300 tons of coal in the 1720s, a very large capacity that was enhanced still more over time. The introduction of steamships after 1812 also greatly augmented the coastal trade; regular services were established between the major ports, with passengers and high-value, low-bulk goods forming a new and profitable line of business. This remained the case until the **railway** boom of the 1830s and 1840s.

David J. Starkey

Bibliography

Aldcroft, D.H., and M.J. Freeman, eds. *Transport in the Industrial Revolution.* 1983.

Clark, E.A.G. *The Ports of the Exe Estuary, 1660–1860: A Study in Historical Geography.* 1960.

Willan, T.S. *The English Coasting Trade, 1660–1760.* 1938.

See also Docks and Harbors; Shipping and Seamen; Transport, Inland

Cobb, James (1756–1818)

Cobb worked for the **East India Company** (he rose to become one of its secretaries in 1814) while writing about 24 emphemeral comedies, farces, and musical pieces for the **London** stage from 1779 (*The Contract, or Female Captain,* which failed) to 1809 *(Sudden Arrival; or Too Busy by Half).* His comic operas were vehicles for composers and performers and, in one instance, for live elephants (*Ramah Droog,* 1798).

In Cobb's musical afterpiece *Doctor and Apothecary*

(1788), London audiences first heard the music of Stephen Storace (1762–1796), who soon produced several popular comic **operas** for Drury Lane. Storace's sister, soprano Anna Selina ("Nancy") Storace (1765–1817), made her London debut in Cobb's comic opera *The Haunted Tower* (1789), for which Storace supplied the music. This was the most successfully staged full-length opera at Drury Lane in the 18th century, with 84 performances in the its first two seasons.

Laura Morrow

Bibliography

Dictionary of National Biography, s.v. "Cobb, James."

Fiske, Roger. *English Theatre Music in the Eighteenth Century.* 1973.

Nicoll, Allardyce. *A History of English Drama, 1660–1900.* Vols. 3 & 4. 1961, 1960.

See also Dramatic Arts

Cobbett, William (1762–1835)

Cobbett, journalist and agriculturalist, was one of the most influential proponents of radicalism for several decades leading up to the great **Reform Act** of 1832. Born at Farnham in Surrey, and throughout his life deeply attached to the land, he combined the outlook of a **Tory** democrat with a fierce sense of the worth of the common Englishman and the need for political reform. Cobbett is perhaps best remembered as the author of *Rural Rides* (1830), a discursive work in which he recorded his tribute to the old ways of life in the English countryside and expressed his abhorrence of the sweeping changes that were then altering the physical landscape.

Though he received little formal education, Cobbett immersed himself in literature during the leisure allowed him in 8 years of military service spent largely in Nova Scotia. In 1792 he emigrated to Philadelphia, where he began his career as a political **journalist**. In many ways his entire career furnishes an interesting contrast to that of **Thomas Paine**, who also took up journalism in America before returning to Britain. Cobbett gained notoriety by his pamphleteering defenses of Great Britain and his espousal of the Federal party in American political debate. In 1797 a prosecution led to his removal to New York, and in 1800 he returned to England.

In **London** he enjoyed a warm reception from **Canning** and the anti–Jacobin party, and founded the *Political Register* in 1802, a weekly **periodical** that continued to be published until his death in 1835. In 1803 he began publication of the *Parliamentary Debates* (a landmark in the history of parliamentary reporting), subsequently edited by Hansard and continuing to this day under that name. But by 1804 Cobbett's political views had led him to the popular side of politics, and he henceforth applied his formidable polemical powers to the cause of reform. This brought him into conflict with the government, and a prosecution for seditious libel in 1810 resulted in 2 years' imprisonment and a fine of £1,000.

Financially ruined by his imprisonment, Cobbett's journalistic agitation for reform grew more vehement after his release, and in 1816 he reduced the price of his journal to

William Cobbett

AUTHOR OF "THE POLITICAL REGISTER".

expand its circulation among the laboring classes. But the tide of repressive measures was rising; Cobbett, fearing another prosecution, in 1817 returned to America. There he developed a new form of writing—social and political criticism expressed in the context of wide-ranging observations on rural ways of life—that eventually bore fruit in *Rural Rides.*

In 1819 Cobbett returned to England, but soon faced bankruptcy, owing to the government's repressive taxation of radical **journals**. Bankruptcy meant the loss of the farm at Botley near Southampton that Cobbett had owned since 1805, but in 1821 he settled in Kensington to pursue his agricultural interests on a small holding that he developed into a seed farm. From the Kensington farm he traveled by horseback across the English countryside in journeys recorded from 1821 and published in collection in 1830 as *Rural Rides.* Like *Cottage Economy* (1822), *Rural Rides* reveals both Cobbett's devotion to the cause of reform and his fiercely nostalgic attachment to the traditional way of life of the English countryside.

Cobbett was intimately involved in the political turmoil that culminated in the passage of the Reform Act of 1832. In 1831 a charge of sedition laid against him was discharged, and after several unsuccessful contests for other seats, he was elected M.P. for Oldham in the newly reformed Parliament. His bellicosity and vituperative language weakened his influence in the **Commons**, though he continued to campaign for a variety of reforms on behalf of the English worker until his death in 1835.

Cobbett was unrelenting in his concern for the welfare of the poor, and if his economic ideas were retrospective and his political views at times inconsistent, the rustic eloquence of his journalism and the evocative power of his descriptions of the rural scene make him one of the most revealing figures of the early years of the 19th century.

Daniel Statt

Bibliography

Briggs, Asa. *William Cobbett.* 1967.
Cole, G.D.H. *The Life of William Cobbett.* 1947.
Dyck, Ian. *William Cobbett and Rural Popular Culture.* 1992.
Green, Daniel. *Great Cobbett: The Noblest Agitator.* 1983.
Osborne, John W. *William Cobbett.* 1966.
Schweizer, Karl W., and John W. Osborne. *Cobbett in His Times.* 1990.
Spater, George. *William Cobbett, the Poor Man's Friend.* 2 vols. 1982.
Williams, Raymond. *Cobbett.* 1983.

See also Radicalism and Radical Politics

Cobham, Viscount (Richard Temple) (1675–1749)

Cobham was a loyal **Whig** supporter of **Sir Robert Walpole** until his opposition to the latter's excise legislation (1733), which Cobham loudly denounced, cost him his office and regiment. In revenge, the wealthy Cobham financed the election of men to oppose Walpole relentlessly in the **House of Commons**, helping to reduce Walpole's majority there between 1734 and 1741 by more than 50 M.P.s. Called "the boy patriots" or "Cobham's cubs," the group was made up of Cobham's nephews by blood—**George Lyttelton**, **George Grenville**, James Grenville (1715–1783), and Richard Temple Grenville (1711–1779)—and by marriage, Thomas Pitt (1707–1761) and **William Pitt the Elder**. Cobham's great estate at Stowe, where he employed the noted architects and landscape gardeners **William Kent** and **Capability Brown** to design things in the classical **Palladian** style, survives as a visual expression of his "patriotism."

P.J. Kulisheck

Bibliography

Gerrard, Christine. *The Patriot Opposition to Walpole: Politics, Poetry, and National Myth, 1725–1742.* 1995.
Lawson, Philip. *George Grenville.* 1984.
Wiggin, L.M. *The Faction of Cousins: A Political Account of the Grenvilles, 1733–1763.* 1958.

See also Elections and the Franchise; Excise Crisis; Opposition

Cockburn, Henry (1779–1854)

Lawyer, politician, and reformer, Cockburn was born and educated in **Edinburgh**, where he was a member of a **radical Whig** group that included Francis Horner (1778–1817), **Henry Brougham**, and **Francis Jeffrey**. A member of the Faculty of Advocates in 1800, he served as Advocate-Deputy from 1806 to 1810. A fine criminal lawyer, particularly for the defense, he was a prominent speaker and prolific pamphleteer in favor of **burgh** and parliamentary reform. As Solicitor-General for **Scotland** in **Lord Grey**'s government, Cockburn was largely responsible for the bill that became the Representation of the People (Scotland) Act (1832). Although appointed to the Court of Session as Lord Cockburn in 1834, he was more prominent as a Lord of Justiciary in criminal cases after 1837. Twice elected Rector of Glasgow University, he contributed regularly to the **Edinburgh Review**, wrote a life of Jeffrey, and two volumes of memoirs.

C.J. Davey

Bibliography

Bell, Allan, ed. *Lord Cockburn: A Bicentenary Commemoration.* 1979.
Fry, M. *Patronage and Principle.* 1987.
Miller, Karl. *Cockburn's Millenium.* 1975.

See also Elections and the Franchise; Reform Act (1832); Scottish Legal System

Cockburn, John, of Ormiston (1679–1758)

A noted early **agricultural improver**, Cockburn served as a member of the last Scottish Parliament before the **Act of Union** (1707), and as a member of the British Parliament until 1741. On taking over the running of his estate (1714), he began introducing new methods such as enclosure and crop rotation while giving tenants longer, renewable leases on condition that they carried out improvements. He also created a **planned village** at Ormiston, actively encouraging the linen industry. Such heavy capital investment left him overextended, forcing him to sell the estate in 1747. His **letters** to his gardener and principal tenants give a fascinating insight into his activities. Despite recent research that shows improving methods developing since the 17th century, the importance to **Scottish agriculture** of Cockburn and other contemporaries such as **Grant of Monymusk** should not be underestimated.

A.J.G. Cummings

Bibliography

Colville, James, ed. *Letters of Sir John Cockburn of Ormiston to His Gardner 1727–1744.* 1904.
Devine, T.M. *The Transformation of Rural Scotland.* 1994.
Smout, T.C. *A History of the Scottish People 1560–1830.* 1969.

See also Agriculture

Coffee and Coffeehouses

Coffee was introduced into Britain in the 17th century. By the beginning of the 18th, the numerous coffeehouses to be found in most towns and cities had become focal points in the spread of ideas and catalysts of social change. They served as relatively democratic social gathering places comparable to the open-air piazzas of southern Europe today.

The earliest coffeehouses of the 1650s and 1660s encountered antagonism from vintners wary of their competition and from the authorities who saw them as potential centers of sedition. However, early attempts at suppression proved futile.

Coffee house politicians

By 1714, fears had subsided and the coffeehouse was an established social institution. Some 2,000 such houses were to be found in **London** alone, and every **provincial town** that aspired to any reputation for polite culture possessed at least one.

The relatively egalitarian atmosphere of the coffeehouses made them vehicles of social change, bringing together for conversation people from a variety of social classes. Coffeehouses nevertheless tended to specialize in their clientele. **Tories** frequented some coffeehouses; **Whigs**, others; and virtuosi, **merchants**, rakes, wits, and beaux all had their favorite houses. Two common features that made them all centers for the exchange and diffusion of ideas were the supply of **newspapers**, pamphlets, **tracts**, and broadsides available there, and the lively political discourse that often animated the atmosphere.

The coffee itself cost a penny and was served in a dish or bowl in the French manner. The drink was thought to have many medicinal properties, and coffeehouse proprietors publicized these in their advertising sheets. Quacks attached themselves to the coffeehouses, rendering diagnoses there and using coffeehouses as business addresses. This led to the coffeehouses' involvement in the development of early **postal services**.

The location of a coffeehouse contributed to its character. **LLoyd's** (the insurance concern) and Garraway's in the City attracted a largely mercantile clientele. In the West End, courtiers and literary men congregated in the coffeehouses. In and around Covent Garden, many coffeehouses carried on a thinly veiled secondary trade in **prostitution**.

In the course of the 18th century the strictly open and public nature of the coffeehouse began to be altered by the proprietors' growing tendency to provide private rooms for meetings of **clubs** and societies, a compromise of the egalitarian principle. After around 1750, directories and street numbering also began making coffeehouses less necessary as clearinghouses of business and postal transactions. In addition, coffee's popularity was gradually supplanted by that of tea, thanks partly to the government's policy of promoting the trade of the **East India Company**; and this shift in drinking habits was only reversed in Britain after World War II. The declining price and growing accessibility of newspapers by the beginning of the 19th century undermined the role of the coffeehouses in the distribution of news. But the most important reason for their decline was the rise of the private club. By the 1830s, most coffeehouses had become taverns or eating-houses, or had simply closed their doors.

Daniel Statt

Bibliography

Albrecht, Peter. "Coffee-Drinking as a Symbol of Social Change in Continental Europe in the Seventeenth and Eighteenth Centuries." *Studies in Eighteenth-Century Culture.* Vol. 18, pp. 91–103.

Ellis, Aytoun. *The Penny Universities: A History of the Coffee-Houses.* 1956.

Lillywhite, Bryant. *London Coffee Houses.* 1963.

Coiffure

See Wigs, Hair, and Hairdressing

Coke of Holkham, Earl of Leicester of Holkham (Thomas William Coke) (1752–1842)

A noted **agricultural improver**, Coke inherited large estates in Norfolk and Derbyshire. He engaged in experimental farming at Park Farm, Holkham, regarded by contemporaries as a model farm. Between 1778 and 1821 some 7,000 visitors attended his "Sheep Shearings"—that is, exchanges between agricultural experts, and practical demonstrations (with prizes) of efficient methods, all important in spreading agricultural ideas.

Coke was a successful and popular landlord who granted long leases to **farmers** but insisted on up-to-date cultivation, including the growing of turnips and sown grasses to improve the soil; he was the first to concentrate on wheat rather than rye in Norfolk. He also encouraged irrigation, underdraining, fertilization, and seed drilling. He carefully planned his livestock, introducing Devon cattle; and, campaigning against Norfolk sheep, brought in **Bakewell**'s breeds such as Leicesters and Merinos. He was a founding member of the Board of Agriculture (1793).

Coke took his father's place as M.P. for Norfolk, representing the county for most of the period 1776–1832. He called himself "a downright **Whig**, trained to hate all **Tories**," and, supporting **Fox**, the American colonists, **Dunning**'s 1780 resolution, and parliamentary reform, vigorously opposed **Pitt the Younger**. Considering **George III** an upstart, when the king enforced an old rule that no one but his majesty himself could drive about **London** in a coach-and-six, Coke drove around in a coach pulled by five horses and a donkey, going repeatedly past the palace. Though he refused earlier offers of a peerage, he was created earl in 1837.

Theresa McDonald

Bibliography

Chambers, J.D., and G.E. Mingay. *The Agricultural Revolution.* 1966.

Mingay, G.E., ed. *The Agrarian History of England and Wales. Vol. VI. 1750–1850.* 1989.

Neeson, J.M. *Commoners: Common Right, Enclosure and Social Change in England, 1700–1820.* 1993.

Parker, R.A.C. "Coke of Norfolk and the Agrarian Revolution." *Economic History Review.* 2nd ser. Vol. 8, pp. 156–166.

———. *Coke of Norfolk: A Financial and Agricultural Study, 1707–1842.* 1975.

See also Agricultural Societies; Agriculture

Samuel Taylor Coleridge

Coleridge, Samuel Taylor (1772–1834)

Poet, critic, lecturer, philosopher, and religious writer, Coleridge was the chief philosopher of English **Romanticism** and one of the most brilliant intellectuals of the Hanoverian era. The youngest of 10 children, he was the son of the vicar of Ottery St. Mary's, Devonshire. In 1781 he went to **London** to study for the clergy, then to Jesus College, Cambridge. However, because of debt, doubt, and a perhaps more immediate interest in politics, he abandoned clerical studies (1794). But he retained a profound religious sense that colored his poetic and critical work.

During these early years Coleridge met **Charles Lamb**, **William Wordsworth**, and **Robert Southey**, all busy establishing their own literary reputations. Like other young intellectuals, he supported the republican principles of the **French Revolution** and the **radical** writings of **William Godwin**. He and Southey planned to start a "pantisocratic" society of equals in Pennsylvania, to which end they became engaged to the Fricker sisters, Sara and Edith. Though the plan came to nothing, Coleridge found himself contracted to Sara, and reluctantly went ahead with the marriage (1795).

By the time he moved to Nether Stowey, Somerset (1796), Coleridge had already produced a volume of **poetry**, *Poems on Various Subjects* (1796), as well a short-lived radical journal, the *Watchman* (1796). Influenced by **William Cowper**, he developed the "conversation poem" or "effusion," a variation on 18th-century reflective verse. This new form, exhibiting an informal, conversational style and unobtrusive imagery, and deploying lyric unity of feeling as epistemological exploration, broke away from more decorous 18th-century practice and initiated "Romantic" techniques of composition. Filtering into this also, Coleridge's admiration for **David Hartley**'s theory of "associationism" found expression in "The Eolian Harp" (1796), in which the wind harp tropes the mind's unity with the natural world and, by the poem's end, with God. In this subgenre of quiet "associational" poetry, Coleridge first began a highly modern exploration of the relationship between epistemology, language, and mind. This concern, which he repeatedly explored later in philosophical meditations attempting to unify the relationships between imagination, intuition, and sensation, permeated other early conversation poems such as "This Lime Tree Bower My Prison" (1797) and "Frost at Midnight" (1798).

Turning away from radical politics, Coleridge began his

intimate association with Wordsworth. Together they published the ***Lyrical Ballads*** (1798), which, with its Preface (1800) by Wordsworth, became a manifesto of revolutionary poetics and a major influence on the next generation of poets. Coleridge's best-remembered contribution, *The Rime of the Ancient Mariner,* opened the volume.

Though he continued to write poetry for the remainder of his life, Coleridge's reputation as a poet derives chiefly from his works of the 1790s. By 1800 he was gaining a reputation also as a philosopher and critic, a career that was unfortunately made uneven by a persistent and exhausting addiction to opium. His "Dejection: An Ode" (1802) captured the pain of that addiction as well as his disillusionment with his own poetic powers in the face of what he saw as Wordsworth's superior talent. He turned more seriously to prose writing and to philosophy, heavily influenced by the German philosophers Johann Schiller (1759–1805), Immanuel Kant (1724–1804), and August Schlegel (1764–1845).

After several years of sporadic writing and traveling, Coleridge separated from his wife, became estranged from Wordsworth, and unhappily moved to London. But his fortunes improved—he was always a mesmerizing talker—when he lectured there to fascinated audiences on **Shakespeare** (1811–1812). His play *Osorio* was produced (as *Remorse,* 1813), and he published *Christabel, Kubla Khan: A Vision,* and *The Pains of Sleep* at the behest of **Lord Byron** in 1816, his last volume of original verse. Written in the 1790s, these poems explore the psychological themes of his earlier work, but recast them from the tranquil musings of the associative mind into a **Gothic** framework of dream vision and nightmare.

In 1817 Coleridge published his most famous critical work, the *Biographia Literaria,* an autobiographical miscellany of recollections and **literary criticism** in which he critiqued, among other things, Wordsworth's poetry. Continuing to publish regularly until his death, he brought forth several collected editions of his poems (*Sybilline Leaves,* 1817; *Poetical Works,* 1828, 1829, 1834). In the 1820s he returned to Christianity as his philosophical lodestone, acquiring new respectability as a defender of Christian faith and as a provocative neoconservative theorist of organic society. His *Aids to Reflection* (1825), a blend of Anglican orthodoxy and neo-Platonism, was his most popular prose work. His philosophical discourse *On the Constitution of the Church and State* (1829), attempting to reconcile utilitarian with **Tory** theories of the national welfare, would influence Victorian Liberals as well as Conservatives.

Samantha Webb

Bibliography

Bate, Walter Jackson. *Coleridge.* 1969.

Haven, Richard, ed. *Bibliography of Criticism and Scholarship.* 1983.

Holmes, Richard. *Coleridge: Early Visions.* 1989.

McFarland, Thomas. *Coleridge and the Pantheist Tradition.* 1969.

Wallace, Catherine Miles. *The Design of Biographia Literaria.* 1983.

See also Exoticism; Lake Poets, School of

Jeremy Collier

Collier, Jeremy (1650–1726)

Collier, English clergyman and writer, distinguished himself during and after the **Glorious Revolution** (1688–1689) as a defender in writing and action of **nonjurors.** Today he is best known for his attack on the theater in *A Short View of the Immorality and Profaneness of the English Stage* (1698), which sparked debate and a flurry of counterattacks from such dramatists as **John Dennis, Sir John Vanbrugh,** and William Congreve (1670–1729). Rather than reform the stage, Collier wanted to close all theaters permanently because of the indecency, profane language, and abuse of the clergy that were common in them, as well as their apparent effects in undermining public morality. Many contemporaries, despite Collier's unpopularity as a nonjuror, agreed with him. **Defoe** sided with him in his poem "The Pacificator" (1700) and elsewhere wrote that theaters were "Nurseries of Crime" and "Universities of the Devil" deserving closure.

Collier was consecrated a nonjuring bishop in 1713; in 1715 he became the leader of this dwindling group separated from the **Church of England**, though before long his insatiable appetite for controversy helped to split it and assist in its eventual demise. Collier's voluminous writings included *Great Historical, Geographical, Genealogical, and Poetical Dictionary* (4 vols., 1701–1721) and *An Ecclesiastical History of Great Britain* (2 vols., 1708–1714).

Donald W. Nichol

Bibliography

Anthony, Sister Rose. *The Jeremy Collier Stage Controversy 1698–1726.* 1937, 1966.

Krutch, Joseph Wood. *Comedy and Conscience after the Restoration.* 1966.

Rupp, Gordon. *Religion in England, 1688–1791.* 1987.

See also Dramatic Arts; Manners and Morals

Collier, Mary (1679?–1762?)

Collier, a washerwoman and poet, came to public notice with *The Woman's Labour* (1739), an angry response to *The Thresher's Labour* (1736) by another working-class poet, **Stephen Duck**. She was possibly the first working-class female poet to publish her work. Her literary labors did not raise her much above her station as a single, poor washerwoman, though later she did become a housekeeper. Toward the end of her life she reprinted her best-known work in *Poems, on Several Occasions* (1762), prefaced by a brief autobiographical sketch. *The Woman's Labour* is significant as a protest against the working woman's hard "double shift" in the labor force and at home. It places Collier among early working-class feminists who challenged traditional aesthetic, social, and sexual norms.

Mahasveta Barua

Bibliography

Hill, Bridget. *Women, Work, and Sexual Politics in Eighteenth-Century England.* 1989.

Landry, Donna. "The Resignation of Mary Collier: Some Problems in Feminist Literary History," in Laura Brown and Felicity Nussbaum, eds., *The New Eighteenth Century: Theory, Politics, English Literature.* 1987.

———. *The Muses of Resistance: Laboring-Class Women's Poetry in Britain, 1739–1796.* 1990.

See also Women in Literature; Women's Employment

Collins, William (1721–1759)

Collins came of age near the end of **Alexander Pope**'s dominant career and strove to invent a new **poetic** idiom and to enlarge the resources available for poetic expression. His verse first appeared pseudonymously in the *Gentleman's Magazine* (1739) as he began work on poems for his *Persian Eclogues* (1742; rev. 1757 as *Oriental Eclogues*), which he pretended to have translated from Persian originals.

Collins's impatience with didacticism was shared by **Joseph Warton**, his fellow poet and school friend from Winchester and **Oxford**. They planned a joint volume of odes, but the idea fell through. Collins published his *Odes on Several Descriptive and Allegoric Subjects* in 1746 (imprint reads 1747). Notable among these 12 poems are the evocative "Ode to Evening," the rhetorically sly "Ode to Fear," and the richly modulated "Passions. An Ode for Music." The "Ode on the Poetical Character"—a complex rendering of allegory, myth, and allusion—explores the nature of poetic inspiration. Five patriotic poems, keenly felt and perceptive, register Collins's response to political crises of the 1740s—the **War of Austrian Succession** and the Jacobite **Forty-five**.

The *Odes* sold poorly. Collins reportedly bought the remaining copies to burn them. His stature rose, however, with a posthumous edition of his works (1765). The "Ode on the Popular Superstitions of the Highlands of Scotland" lay neglected in private hands until mention of the missing work by **Samuel Johnson** (1781) led to its recovery and publication (1788).

Collins might have achieved much more had his creativity not been cut short by illness. Thought "mad" by some, and briefly confined in 1754, he was described by Johnson as suffering no "alienation of mind," but as prey to general "feebleness," or deep depression.

Collins aspired to a **poetry** "attended by Daring, and all-embracing Power" (motto to *Odes,* from Pindar). With Warton he wished to indulge the imagination, and **Thomas Gray**'s crediting him with "a fine Fancy" is a gauge of his success. While innovation was his first concern, his best work also evinces remarkable technical control, with effects ranging from boldness to delicate restraint. His odes, Thomas Warton predicted, "will be remembered while any taste for true poetry remains."

Thomas F. Bonnell

Bibliography

Lonsdale, Roger, ed. *The Poems of Gray, Collins, and Goldsmith.* 1969.

Sigworth, Oliver F. *William Collins.* 1965.

Sitter, John. *Literary Loneliness in Mid-Eighteenth-Century England.* 1982.

Weinbrot, Howard D. "William Collins and the Mid-Century Ode: Poetry, Patriotism, and the Influence of Context," in Maximillian E. Novak, intro., *Context, Influence, and Mid-Eighteenth-Century Poetry.* 1990.

Wendorf, Richard. *William Collins and Eighteenth-Century Poetry.* 1981.

See also Orientalism

Colman, George, the Elder (1732–1794)

Dramatist and theatrical manager, Colman, after briefly practicing law, turned to the theater and wrote the afterpiece *Polly Honeycombe* (1760), followed by the very successful *The Jealous Wife* (1760). When **David Garrick** left Drury Lane for the Continent in 1763, Colman, left in charge of selecting plays, staged his adaptation of *Philaster* (1763) and his comedy *The Deuce Is in Him* (1763).

The two also collaborated on the successful *Clandestine Marriage* (1766). In 1767, in partnership with Thomas Harris (*d.* 1820), John Rutherford (n.d.), and William Powell

(1762–1812), Colman purchased the patent for Covent Garden and began his successful managing of that **theater**, where he produced **Oliver Goldsmith**'s comedies *The Good Natured Man* (1767) and *She Stoops to Conquer* (1773). Selling his share of the Covent Garden patent to Thomas Hull (1728–1808) in 1774, he succeeded **Samuel Foote** as manager of the Haymarket.

Colman made important contributions as a writer and editor of **periodicals** and **newspapers**, working with Bonnell Thornton (1724–1768) on *The Connoisseur,* with Thornton and Garrick on the *Saint James Chronicle,* and contributing to the *London Packet,* the *Public Advertiser,* and *The London Chronicle.* He edited *The English Plays by Samuel Foote* (1778) and *The Dramatic Works of Beaumont and Fletcher* (1778). **George Colman the Younger** was born to Colman when he was living with the actress Sarah Ford (1762); he too became a playwright.

Richard J. Dircks

Bibliography

Page, E.R. *George Colman the Elder.* 1935.

Peake, R.B. *Memoirs of the Colman Family, Including Their Correspondence.* 2 vols. 1841.

See also Dramatic Arts

Colman, George, the Younger (1762–1836)

Colman, dramatist and manager, studied for the law but was destined for the **theater**. His second play, *Two to One* (1784), for which Samuel Arnold (1740–1802) wrote the music, saw 18 performances. His sentimental comic **opera**, *Inkle and Yarico* (1787), also with music by Arnold, was hugely successful.

Colman gradually took over managerial responsibilities from his father, **George Colman the Elder**, at the Haymarket Theatre, and by 1789 was its manager. After producing his *The Battle of Hexham* (1789), which was performed 20 times, he began to create melodramas. *The Surrender of Calais* (1791) ran for 28 performances during its first season. During the rebuilding of Drury Lane Theatre he welcomed its actors to the Haymarket for a successful 1793–1794 season. Colman inherited the Haymarket license on his father's death (1794). His often revived comedy *The Heir at Law* (1797) ran for 28 nights.

Colman prepared lavish melodramas, with music by Michael Kelly (1762–1826), for both major theaters—*Blue-Beard; or Female Curiosity* (1798) running for 64 nights at Drury Lane, and *John Bull; or The Englishman's Fireside* (1803), for 47 at Covent Garden. In 1824 Colman succeeded John Larpent (1741–1824) as Examiner of Plays, a post equivalent to government censor.

Richard J. Dircks

Bibliography

Peake, R.B. *Memoirs of the Colman Family, Including Their Correspondence.* 2 vols. 1841.

See also Dramatic Arts

Patrick Colquhoun

Colonies

See Empire and Imperialism

Colquhoun, Patrick (1745–1820)

Colquhoun exemplifies the spirit of "improvement" in the latter Hanoverian era. He was an energetic writer and reformer of the period 1780–1820, best known today for his efforts in the improvement of **law enforcement** but also very active in various commercial and **humanitarian** causes, including the relief of **poverty** and the provision of cheap **elementary education**.

He was born in Dumbarton and moved to Virginia, engaging successfully in trade until he returned to settle in **Glasgow** (1766), where he quickly made a name for himself as a civic-minded improver and propagandist of the **cotton industry**. In 1783 he helped found the Glasgow Chamber of Commerce and became its first chairman; some authors call him "Father of Glasgow." Moving to **London** (1789), he became a magistrate (1792) through the influence of the Scottish power broker **Henry Dundas.** From his seat on the bench he began publishing his recommendations (often backed with statistics) on a variety of social ills, including **drinking** (1794), poor relief and the creation of soup kitchens (1794–1795, 1798), an interparochial plan for revenue sharing and the employment of the indigent (1799), and "A New and Appropriate System of Education for the Labouring People" (1806). In 1814 he published an economic history of the **Empire**, evaluating colonial resources and recommending **emigration** as an outlet for surplus **population**.

Colquhoun's greatest influence, however, lay in the improvement of public safety and of the methods of **crime** prevention. His most important work was his *Treatise on the Police of the Metropolis* (1795), which went through many editions and helped earn him various honors. He appealed for a rational and many-sided attack on crime, calling for creation of a board of police commissioners for the whole of London, a police gazette to advertise crime statistics and the descriptions of offenders, extension of the jurisdictions of paid magistrates, the use of convict labor, and education of the labor force and the creation of a board of education. His *Treatise on the Commerce and Police of the River Thames* (1800) led to the establishment of an effective Thames police force that greatly reduced thefts from the London **docks**.

Thomas D. Veve

Bibliography

Andrew, Donna T. *Philanthropy and Police: London Charity in the Eighteenth Century.* 1989.

Colquhoun, Patrick. *A Treatise on the Commerce and Police of the River Thames.* 1800; rpt. 1969.

Dictionary of National Biography, s.v. "Colquhoun, Patrick."

Hay, Douglas, and Francis Snyder, eds. *Policing and Prosecution in Britain, 1750–1850.* 1989.

Rumbelow, Donald. *I Spy Blue: The Police and Crime in the City of London from Elizabeth I to Victoria.* 1971.

Combe, William (1741–1823)

Combe was best known for his parodic *Tour of Doctor Syntax in Search of the Picturesque* (1812) and two further Tours in 1820 and 1821, hudibrastic verse narrations of a pedantic, peregrinating clergyman–schoolmaster. Imprisoned for bankruptcy from 1780 to his death, Combe nevertheless produced a large number of satirical, political, literary, journalistic, and edited works. In 1809 Rudolph Ackermann (1764–1827), the **publisher** of the monthly *Poetic Magazine,* arranged for **Thomas Rowlandson** to send an illustration each month for Combe to versify. Without their ever meeting and with no advance planning, they composed the Dr. Syntax volumes and *The English Dance of Death* (1814).

Elisabeth W. Joyce

Bibliography

Hamilton, H.W. *Doctor Syntax: A Silhouette of Combe.* 1969.

Hotten, J.C. *Life of Combe.* 1869.

See also Periodicals; Picturesque Movement

William Combe

Combination Acts (1799, 1800)

Emerging trade unionism met with tightening legal repression, 26 restrictive measures being passed between 1700 and 1825. Prior to 1799, these prohibited trade unionism in specific trades or particular towns, declaring such organizations criminal conspiracies in restraint of trade. Such legislation—at least prior to 1796—did have a positive side insofar as these statutes specifically authorized the regulation of **wages** and conditions by the local authorities (usually the justices of the peace), thus circumscribing unilateral employer power.

The Combination Act of 1799 (39 Geo. III, c.81) was unique in the sense that it made all workmen's combinations unlawful, on pain of up to 3 months' imprisonment. It also omitted any reference to wage regulation. The act of 1800 only modified these draconian clauses slightly, extending the legislation to employers' associations (this proved inoperative) and requiring two magistrates (rather than one) to prosecute. In 1817 the combination acts were extended to incorporate **Scotland** and **Ireland**.

The combination acts have generated much controversy among labor historians. The "pessimistic" interpretation (associated with Marx, the Webbs, the Hammonds, and E.P. Thompson) treats 1799 as a major turning point and the connected legislation as an effective damper on trade **union** development. This view has been countered in the work of George, Prothero, and Musson, who emphasize the precedents of legal repression and the relative ineffectiveness of the combination acts in preventing union growth (especially of the established craft unions) over the period 1799–1824. Recently, Moher and Rule have gone some way to reconcile conflicting arguments, recognizing both the limitations of this legislation and also its intrinsically oppressive and class-based character.

The repeal of this body of legislation was engineered by the **radical Francis Place** in 1824. A wave of strikes and a surge in unionization thereafter led to some revision in the 1825 Amendment Act, which upheld the legality of workers joining trade unions campaigning on wages and **working conditions**, thus recognizing a legitimate role for such bodies in collective bargaining. It also resurrected the common law of conspiracy, whereby acts of violence and intimidation in pursuance of union objectives remained criminal conspiracies. This legal situation remained virtually unchanged until 1871. Legal repression of trade union activities thus remained prevalent after the repeal of the combination acts, though trade unions enjoyed greater legal status in Britain than anywhere else in Europe from 1824 on.

Arthur McIvor

Bibliography

George, M.D. "The Combination Laws." *Economic History Review.* 1st Series, VI. 1935–1936.

Moher, J. "From Suppression to Containment: Roots of Trade Union Law to 1825," in John Rule, ed., *British Trade Unionism, 1750–1850: The Formative Years.* 1988.

Musson, A.E. *British Trade Unions, 1800–1875.* 1972.

Prothero, I. *Artisans and Politics in Early Nineteenth Century London.* 1979.

Rule, John. *The Experience of Labour in Eighteenth Century Industry.* 1981.

Thompson, E.P. *The Making of the English Working Class.* 1968.

Webb, Sidney, and Beatrice Webb. *The History of Trade Unionism.* 1894.

See also Craft Guilds; Hours, Wages, and Working Conditions; Labor Laws, Movements, and Unions

Commerce, Domestic

Internal **trade** during the Hanoverian period was of immense significance for overall economic growth. Although **overseas commerce** stimulated industrialization, this was surpassed in importance by the development of the home market. Increasing levels of activity by **merchants**, the growth of **domestic production**, the beginnings of **factory** production, improvements in the **inland transport** network, and the evolution of a more sophisticated **banking** system all contributed to make more raw material and goods available to producer and consumer alike. It was through the changing patterns of domestic commerce that these activities were coordinated.

Since the Middle Ages, much commerce in the British Isles had revolved around fairs and markets. But by the 18th century, large-scale annual fairs that drew merchants and traders from afar (those at Stourbridge near Cambridge, for example) were beginning to decline. Meanwhile, weekly markets in towns throughout the country were growing in importance. Some, such as those in the cloth halls of Halifax and Bradford, or at major markets in the grain areas, might deal in a single commodity, where the principal customers might likely be, in the first case, merchants from **Leeds**, and in the second, grain dealers, distillers, brewers, and maltsters from **London**.

Indeed, the redistribution of agricultural produce was a leading function of domestic commerce. The continued growth of London and of provincial centers such as **Bristol** and **Norwich**, coupled with the rise of northern commercial and industrial towns such as Leeds, **Liverpool**, and **Manchester**, meant that reconfigurations were necessary in the grain trade. During the second half of the 17th century it had become apparent that old regulations designed to stop speculators from cornering the market and forcing up prices were restrictive. Hence during the 18th century a network of middlemen emerged to move produce from farms to **urban** areas. The rise of commercial **breweries** in many regions also stimulated changes in agricultural trade. Increasing demands

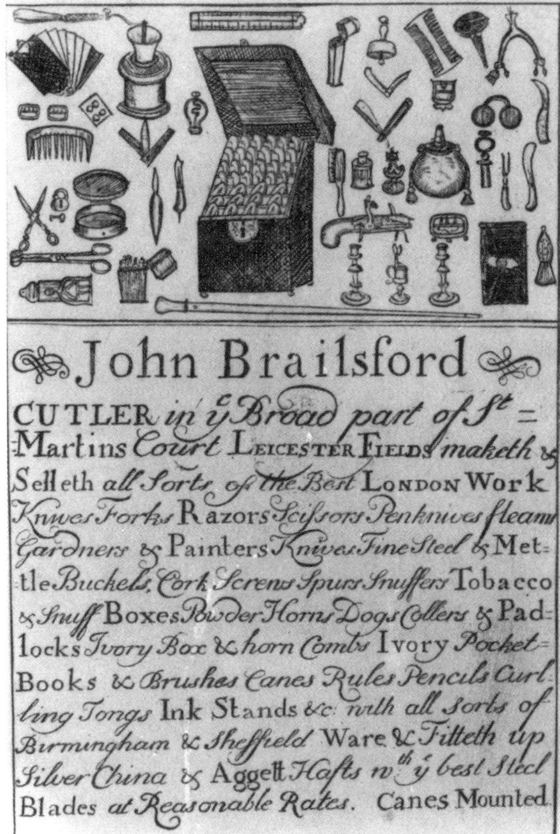

Hardware dealer's advertisement

for meat, and for fuel for domestic and industrial purposes, spurred the rise of middlemen in the livestock and coal trades. Conversely, the urban areas became increasingly important in distributing the manufactured goods demanded by the wealthier **middle** and upper **classes** in both town and country.

Increasing **agricultural** output brought higher income to landlords and **farmers**. More than that, reliable and increasing food supplies also contributed to the growth of **population** apparent from around 1750. Both factors powered climbing demand for manufactured goods. This was chiefly satisfied by increases in the level of domestic manufactures and the number of small workshops. However, in some industries such as **cotton** and **iron**, the nature and volume of growth led to larger-scale units and the spread of **factories**. Although the level of direct selling increased, it was still often the case that manufactures passed through several middlemen before reaching the final customer. The increasing cost of buildings and machinery, and the increasing value of goods circulating within the commercial network, led to more businessmen protecting their interests and hence stimulating an increasing **insurance** market.

Commercial growth would have been impossible without major improvements in transport and an increase in **coastal shipping**. The sea was a natural highway for the bulkier domestic commerce, but important first were river improvements and **canal** works to permit easier riverine access to inland grain-producing areas and coalfields. Also webbing together producers, **waterways**, cities, villages, and harbors were better **roads, streets, and turnpikes**. The growth of carrier businesses freed producers from the need to provide their own freight services, an advantage further underlined by the beginnings of **railway** development in the 1820s. Commercial development was helped along also by advances in commercial intelligence. Improved communication came from speedier **postal services**, and the growth of **newspapers** made commercial information available throughout the country.

The rise of domestic commerce also stimulated changes in **shops and retailing**. In 1714, many people still made most of their retail purchases from market stalls or wandering peddlers and chapmen—who, in rural areas, provided not only goods but contact with the outside world. In towns, open-air weekly general markets were often held, serving both customers and sellers from country and town. But also in urban regions, **craftsmen** and other small producers might maintain tiny retail areas at the front of their workshops. Gradually, more such glass-fronted areas began to appear; the world of peddlers and stalls began to fade, and that of the modern emporium to materialize. Competing retailers attempted to increase business by means of better service and advice to customers and, because they had the facilities to hold larger stocks of goods, were able to offer better prices than itinerant peddlers.

The growth of domestic trade led to an increasing demand for credit to ensure its smooth operation. Merchants and manufacturers, facing delays in receiving payment from their customers, in turn demanded credit from their suppliers. Settlement of commercial debts was often by means of bills of exchange, payable at a future date. To assist in the handling of such paper and to accept deposits from businesses and individuals, a banking system began to emerge in London and **Edinburgh** from the late 17th century, and in the provinces as the 18th century progressed. Because London was the focus of much foreign as well as domestic trade, it became the leading banking center, with other financial intermediaries such as bill brokers and stock jobbers also beginning to emerge.

The 18th century witnessed a considerable degree of regional specialization, as **Daniel Defoe** noticed as early as the 1720s. The economic advances of the 18th and early 19th centuries were based on easier exchange between industrial and agricultural areas and between town and country, allowing specialization to take place that could have considerable cost-saving implications. The fact that Britain had no internal **tariff** barriers also kept costs down and encouraged the growth of commerce. As the Hanoverian age gave way to the Victorian (1837), the call was heard ever more loudly to extend free trade to overseas commerce and to encourage other countries to follow suit. But this should not be allowed to obscure the fact that internal commerce still dwarfed that which passed overseas, and that it had been the main driver earlier of the **Industrial Revolution**.

A.J.G. Cummings

Bibliography

Ashton, T.S. *An Economic History of England: The 18th Century.* 1955.

Daunton, M.J. *Progress and Poverty: An Economic and Social History of Britain, 1700–1850.* 1995.

McKendrick, N., J. Brewer, and J.H. Plumb. *The Birth of Consumer Society: The Commercialization of 18th Century England.* 1982.

Westerfield, R.B. *Middlemen in English Business, 1660–1760.* 1915.

Commerce, Overseas

With the exploitation of its Atlantic and Asian colonies and of the re-export trade to its traditional trade partners in Europe, Britain became the major overseas trading nation of the 18th century. Between 1700 and 1800, British exports grew by 568%, imports by 523%, and re-exports by 906%. While it is still debatable whether international trade fostered the **Industrial Revolution** in Britain or vice versa, the two were inextricably linked.

Overseas trade provided extended market opportunities for finished goods, and supplies of cheap raw material. Its expansion in the 18th century saw the diversification of both markets and products. In 1700 the bulk of English and Scottish foreign trade was still oriented toward Continental Europe and the Baltic region. But by 1800, Europe accounted for only 29% of Britain's imports and 21% of its exports. Europe's decline was compensated by the growing importance of British colonial trade in **North America**, the **West Indies**, and **India**, and in general trade with China.

Britain was increasingly a nexus between European and global trading patterns. The new tropical goods allowed Britain to continue trading with Europe after the saturation of the older **woolen and worsted** markets. North American tobacco, Canadian furs, West Indian tea, Indian calicos and spices, and Chinese tea were exchanged for Baltic timber and tar, Swedish iron and, increasingly from the 1780s, European grain. By the early 19th century the output of Britain's growing **cotton** and **iron** industries was coming to play a significant role also. In fact, by about 1800, Britain had already developed the system of multilateral links that were to govern trade relations until the depression of the 1930s. The importance of the Atlantic trade was such that even after the **American Revolution** the United States remained a major British trading partner.

Initially, a great deal of long-distance overseas commerce had been in the hands of **chartered trading companies** such as the **East India Company**, founded in 1600. These had been launched because individual resources were inadequate for risky long-haul ventures, and to obtain monopolies on potentially lucrative trade routes; and mercantilist governments also rightly saw such companies' activities as a cheap way of acquiring foreign colonies. It was through such activities in North America, **Canada**, and India that Britain began carving out her **Empire**.

But, inevitably, the increase of commerce also damaged the chartered companies even as it transformed the domestic landscape. Even in the 17th century, there were opportunities for the individual merchant or for partnerships; and by 1714 such alternative organizations dominated all branches of trade except that to the East. Their increasing significance in the Atlantic (including the Caribbean colonial trade) accounted for the growth of the western ports of **Liverpool**, Whitehaven,

Bristol, and **Glasgow**. The rise of these **cities** can be measured in the increase of their **populations**, their new domestic communications links (for instance, links between London and Liverpool date only from the 1750s), their grand new **docks** and port facilities, and the rise of their commercial elites.

Profits from overseas trade also aided the development of maritime industries, including the naval engineering centers of the Thames and the Clyde. Further, the new commercial elite also invested in **banks** and **insurance** services, and from around 1750 there were increasing ties between commercial and industrial capital. The sugar barons Tate and Lyle were linked to early cotton manufacturers, and many Glasgow merchants in the **tobacco trade** had industrial interests in the surrounding area.

The impact of overseas commerce can be seen too on Hanoverian **economic thought**. As the 18th century progressed and opportunities for trade expanded, mercantilist theories came under attack from economists such as **Adam Smith** and **David Hume**. High **tariffs** were held to be against consumers' interests despite their necessity to pay for successive **wars**. By around 1800, many British manufacturers were seeking free trade. Chambers of commerce were created in Manchester and Glasgow to lobby for an end of protectionism and the remaining trade monopolies; they claimed that the former stifled the further expansion of industry, the latter the further expansion of trade.

In the 1820s the **Tories** began responding to the free-trade clamor: the **navigation laws** were revised in 1822 and 1825; tariffs were reduced and recodified in 1825–1826; 1824 saw the repeal of the laws preventing the **emigration** of artisans. Free trade did not arrive until the Victorian era, thanks to the continuing importance of agricultural tariffs and governmental reliance on customs duties (which as late as 1830 accounted for 43% of government revenue), but the rise of overseas commerce was critical to its acceptance.

In sum, between 1700 and 1840, overseas commerce was a revolutionary force. It created a demand for the products of British industrialization, allowing the specialization of production. This in turn promoted the development of internal trade links and the expansion of the great industrial conurbations of Manchester, Birmingham, Sheffield, and central Scotland, as well as the development of the west coast ports. The accumulated profits of trade aided the development of banking and insurance institutions, and later commercial and industrial ventures. International trading obligations increasingly came to be settled by bills of exchange drawn on **London**, which made that city the dominant financial center in Europe by the end of the Hanoverian era. The development of trade helped the creation of the first British Empire. Without its rapid increase in the 18th century, the British economy would not have been able to expand and develop as rapidly as it did.

Patricia S. Collins

Bibliography

Chaudhuri, K. *Trade and Civilisation in the Indian Ocean.* 1985.

Davis, R. *The Rise of the Atlantic Economies.* 1973.

Farnie, D.A. *The English Cotton Industry and the World Market, 1815–1896.* 1979.

Minchinton, W., ed. *The Growth of English Overseas Trade in the Seventeenth and Eighteenth Centuries.* 1969.

Thorner, D. *Investment in Empire.* 1950.

See also Shipping and Seamen

Commons, House of

The Glorious Revolution (1689) ensured free speech, regular meetings, and control over taxation to the House of Commons, the elected body of Parliament. The early Hanoverian Commons consisted of 558 men elected for a 7-year term by voters with particular qualifications, usually including landownership. The **Act of Union (Ireland)** (1800) increased membership to 658.

Members of Parliament (M.P.s) received no salary and had to meet property qualifications. Commons met in St. Stephen's Chapel in the Palace of Westminster (until it burned in 1834), for annual sessions that normally lasted from November to May. Members debated and voted on public bills requested by the king's ministers, and on private bills arising from petitions from individuals and local governments. One member was elected Speaker to regulate debate. The work of drawing up and reporting bills was assigned to committees, whose reports were debated and amended before a final vote. Compromise over content and wording had to be worked out with the **House of Lords** before bills became Acts of Parliament. (The structure and functions of the U.S. Congress are based on those of the 18th-century Parliament.)

The most important business of Commons was finance.

House of Commons in the time of Sir Robert Walpole

By custom, Commons had the exclusive right to originate money bills, and Lords had no power to amend them. At the opening of the session, the king's message, written by his ministers, laid out policy for the year and included a request for supply (money). The Committee of Supply then proposed expenditures. The Committee of Ways and Means, guided by the Chancellor of the Exchequer, proposed **taxes**. Commons could influence and modify the actions of a ministry by voting less or no money for a particular project, or by refusing to approve a tax. The majority of members were elected with little or no assistance from the administration, and so had to be persuaded by debate to give their votes. While ministries took great care, often using **patronage**, to ensure safe majorities, they could never stifle criticism of their policies in debate. Commons' right of free speech was a powerful curb on the executive powers of the king and his ministers.

Commons' influence on the administration was greatest when the chief minister, the First Lord of the Treasury, was a member and leader of that house. Through him, Commons had direct access to the head of government, the monarch, because as principal advisor he spoke with the king frequently. This influence was most apparent under such long-serving chief (or prime) ministers as **Sir Robert Walpole**, **Henry Pelham**, **Lord Frederick North**, **William Pitt the Younger**, and **Lord Liverpool**.

Increasing national wealth and **population** made Commons the more important House of Parliament by the early 19th century, and created a demand for parliamentary reform and extension of the franchise (changes enacted in the **Reform Act** of 1832). The establishment of the two-party system and the gradual loss of royal influence on politics toward the end of the Hanoverian age (1837) shifted power to the majority party in Parliament, represented by the Cabinet. Commons, however, would not become the sole source of power and administration until the 20th century.

P.J. Kulisheck

Bibliography

Brewer, John. *The Sinews of Power: War, Money and the English State, 1688–1783.* 1989.

Namier, Sir Lewis, and John Brooke, eds. *The House of Commons: 1754–1790.* Vol. 1, Introductory Survey. 3 vols. 1964.

Sedgwick, Romney, ed. *The House of Commons: 1715–1754.* Vol. 1, Introductory Survey. 2 vols. 1970.

Thomas, P.D.G. *The House of Commons in the Eighteenth Century.* 1971.

Thorne, R.G., ed. *The House of Commons: 1790–1820.* Vol. 1, Introductory Survey. 5 vols. 1986.

See also Constitution, The Glorious; Elections and the Franchise; Government, National; Prime Minister

Commonwealthmen

Commonwealthmen, an assortment of chiefly early-18th-century **opposition** politicians and writers, denounced the corruption and acquisitiveness they saw festering at the heart of the British **Empire**. Unpatriotic politicians, in their view, were corrupting an ever more tainted society; the disease that had infected the **manners and morals** of the governing and business classes was demoralizing those lower on the social ladder. Although admiring the **Glorious Constitution**, they feared the rise of ministerial power, the increasing size of the bureaucracy, and the growth of the standing **army**. To them the ministry of **Sir Robert Walpole** was a dreadful machine threatening to corrupt the very fabric of society.

Their perceptions were colored by 17th-century radicalism and the republicanism of the Puritan Commonwealth. Commonwealthmen drew their inspiration from the writings of **John Milton**, James Harrington (1611–1677), Henry Neville (1620–1694) and **John Locke**. Prominent among them were "Real" or radical **Whigs** such as **Robert Molesworth**, **John Trenchard**, and **Thomas Gordon**, as well as **Bishop Benjamin Hoadly** and the **Tory** Viscount **Bolingbroke**. Their larger following included many **dissenters** and most **freethinkers**. Later figures of commonwealthmen outlook included **Richard Price** and **Joseph Priestley**.

In no sense were the commonwealthmen an organized opposition. Not until after the death of **George II** (1760) were they closely connected with parliamentary politics. Rather, they relied on their voluminous writings, social connections, and domestic and foreign correspondence to disseminate their views. They favored shorter and more frequent parliaments, elimination of the rotten **borough** system and the reform of parliamentary representation, a reduction in the number of **placemen**, the establishment of a national militia in the place of a standing army, and greater **religious toleration**. The more whiggish writers tended to favor institutional amendments similar to those that would be established by the **Reform Act** of 1832. In contrast, Commonwealthmen of a Tory stripe, tending to favor greater central direction under a popular leader, often argued for the necessity of a "Patriot King" who would govern wisely, placing himself above all parties and factions. Both schools shared a belief that unless the spread of corruption could be contained and the morals of the nation uplifted, England would be shackled with a tyranny from which there could be no recovery.

The commonwealthmen, though mostly intellectuals, few in number, and without any other particular achievements, helped to keep alive the radical beliefs of England's "century of revolutions." They themselves were hardly revolutionary, but their arguments, warnings, and dire predictions as well as the stress they laid on the importance of a virtuous citizenry appealed to later radicals and revolutionaries, especially of the period 1750–1790.

Michael L. Oberg

Bibliography

Brewer, John. "English Radicalism in the Age of George III," in J.G.A. Pocock, ed., *Three British Revolutions: 1641, 1689, 1776.* 1980.

Colley, Linda. "Eighteenth-Century English Radicalism before Wilkes." *Transactions of the Royal Historical Society.* Vol. 31, pp. 1–19.

Kramnick, Isaac. *Bolingbroke and His Circle: The Politics of Nostalgia in the Age of Walpole.* 1968.
Pocock, J.G.A. *The Machiavellian Moment: Florentine Political Thought and the Atlantic Republican Tradition.* 1975.
Robbins, Caroline. *The Eighteenth Century Commonwealthman.* 1959.
Rogers, Nicholas. "Popular Protest in Early Hanoverian England." *Past and Present.* Vol. 79, pp. 70–100.
———. "The Urban Opposition to Whig Oligarchy, 1720–1760," in Margaret Jacob and James Jacob, eds., *The Origins of Anglo-American Radicalism.* 1984.

See also Radicalism and Radical Politics; Rational Dissent

Concerts

See Musical Concerts and Concert Life

Congregationalists

The Congregationalists (Independents) were one of the most important **dissenting** denominations in Hanoverian Britain. Emphasizing the universal priesthood of all believers, they advocated a form of church polity rooted in "the gathered church," a voluntary association joined together by the Holy Spirit as an autonomous worshipping community. Having Christ as its sole head, every local church was theoretically independent of external authority and governed at the "church meeting" by the democracy of its "covenanted" members. Congregationalists thus rejected both the territorial basis of the parish system and the episcopal and civil structures of governance found in the **Church of England**. Unlike the **Presbyterians**, they rejected the use of credal formulae.

Congregationalists had been an important force during the age of Cromwell. With the restoration of the monarchy in 1660 and the Act of Uniformity in 1662, however, they, like the Presbyterians and other nonconforming groups, were excluded from mainstream society. Around 1720 there were approximately 230 Independent churches in England and **Wales**, having 67,000 members. Independents were strongest in south Wales and Monmouthshire, and in Essex, Herefordshire, and Northamptonshire.

The period 1720–1750 saw a sharp reduction in membership, despite the efforts of **Philip Doddridge**, who attempted to arrest decline by propagating a lively form of moderate Calvinism against both the old Calvinist orthodoxy and the new religious liberalism. Assisted by his efforts, both as principal of the **dissenting academy** at Northampton and as a devotional writer, the Independent churches resisted the deistic, Arian, and Socinian or **Unitarian** ideas then gaining currency among other dissenting communities. He and his fellow Congregationalist minister **Isaac Watts** (one of England's greatest hymn-writers) advocated a Christian piety that embraced the affections without falling prey to excessive enthusiasm, and recognized the value of intellectual rigor without becoming overly rationalistic.

From the 1740s, **religious revivalism** and the rise of **Methodism** began reinvigorating many Independent churches. New members often sprouted after hearing the **Evangelical** preaching of **John Wesley**, **George Whitefield**, and their fellow Methodists. Whitefield fostered close associations with Congregationalists in England, Wales, and **North America**, and together with another leading figure in the revival, the **Countess of Huntingdon**, founded many churches with strong Congregational connections.

Congregationalism thus began to take on a more distinctly Evangelical quality. The revitalized new spirit was reflected in the founding of the London Missionary Society (1795), the establishment of flourishing Congregational communities in the industrial north of England during the early 19th century, and the doubling of membership in the gathered English churches from 15,000 in 1750 to 35,000 in 1800. Encouraged by the church's social activism and vitality, many members of the working class were now joining. Following repeal of the **Test and Corporation Acts** (1828), the Congregationalist churches joined themselves in an administrative association, the Congregational Union of England and Wales (1832). In 1836 they founded the Colonial Missionary Society. In keeping with their advocacy of the separation of church and state, they strongly opposed state-supported denominational **education** and advocated disestablishment of the Church of England. In the Victorian era, many Congregationalists allied themselves with the Liberal party.

Among the most distinguished laymen of the Hanoverian period was Sir Thomas Abney (1660–1722), an early promotor and founding director of the **Bank of England**, Lord Mayor of London, and President of St. Thomas' Hospital; he was noted for his public service and philanthropy. William Coward (*d.* 1738) became famous in his later life for his prodigal support of Nonconformity; he established a Congregationalist meetinghouse, funded sacred lectures, and at his death left the bulk of his considerable fortune for the training of dissenting ministers. Another Independent, **John Howard**, was so celebrated a **prison reformer** that his statue, erected by public subscription after his death, was the first ever admitted into St. Paul's Cathedral. Among the working class, many Congregationalists, like other dissenters, labored in trades associated with the **textile industry** and **clothing** manufacture. They were often known in the commercial world for strictly maintaining high ethical standards.

Michael F. Suarez, S.J.

Bibliography

Corrigan, John. *The Prism of Piety: Catholick Congregational Clergy at the Beginning of the Enlightenment.* 1991.
Davie, Donald. *A Gathered Church: The Literature of the English Dissenting Interest, 1700–1939.* 1978.
Jones, Robert Tudur. *Congregationalism in England, 1662–1962.* 1962.
Lincoln, Anthony. *Some Political and Social Ideas of English Dissent, 1763–1800.* 1938; rpt. 1963.
Nuttall, Geoffrey Fillingham. *Visible Saints: The Congregational Way, 1640–1660.* 1957.
Rivers, Isabel. *Reason, Grace, and Sentiment: A Study of the*

Language of Religion and Ethics in England, 1660–1780. Vol. 1. 1991.
Watts, Michael. *The Dissenters.* 2 vols. 1978, 1995.

See also Missionary Societies

Constable, John (1776–1837)

Constable's **landscape painting**, though undervalued during his lifetime, represents the highest achievement of English **Romantic** realism and naturalism. His oil sketches, painted outdoors, exhibit a high fidelity to nature through their tone, atmosphere, color, and implied movement. He developed new techniques for recording visual experience and for reproducing light and shade, using rough brush strokes and pure color applied with a palette knife. In tone and intensity, his rendering of skies and clouds is unsurpassed.

Constable was the son of a prosperous miller in East Bergholt, Suffolk, and his early outdoor experience there inspired his lifelong commitment to precise rendition of its vivid beauty. Two patrons, Sir George Beaumont and the Bishop of Salisbury, encouraged his career as a painter in the face of his father's objections. The bishop's son, Archdeacon John Fisher, became the artist's closest friend, correspondent, and supporter. Constable's marriage to Maria Bicknell in 1816 was happy and stable. The couple's seven children inherited most of the artist's paintings; his daughter bequeathed them to the nation in 1888, when they finally became appreciated.

Constable's early paintings were influenced by Claude Lorrain (1600–1682), **Thomas Gainsborough**, Thomas Girtin (1775–1802), and **Benjamin West**, who was President of the **Royal Academy** when Constable exhibited there in 1802. The young artist consciously copied the portraits of **Sir Joshua Reynolds**, thus strengthening his skills and knowledge of structure and preparing for a lucrative career as a portraitist. **Picturesque** theory, with its emphasis on the general and ideal, accounted for Constable's relatively conventional early **watercolor** landscapes.

John Constable

In 1808 Constable's work entered a new stage; he began to sketch scenes of his native Stour Valley in oils. These, rather than the large finished paintings he made from them, are the works on which his reputation rests. *Dedham Vale: Morning* (1811) realistically depicts rural workers and animals in a still atmosphere subtly suggesting a coming storm. Accuracy of figural depiction and almost palpable rendering of atmosphere also characterize *Flatford Mill* (1817) and *A Cottage in a Cornfield* (1815–1816). Constable exhibited these and other East Anglia subjects in successive shows at the Royal Academy. Scenes he painted repeatedly were of Dedham Vale, locks on the Stour River, and cloud formations suggesting imminent atmospheric changes. *The Leaping Horse* (1825), often considered his masterpiece, suggests motion in its figure, landscape, and sky.

Constable's success in France was dramatic. *The Haywain* (1812) was sold there in 1824, exhibited at the Louvre, and awarded a gold medal. In 1825 Constable exhibited *The White Horse* at Lille. His handling of light influenced Barbizon painters and Impressionists.

Constable was well read in English **poetry**, especially that of the late 18th century. He was familiar with, and inspired by, the work of **Goldsmith**, **Gray**, and **Thomson**. He admired **Wordsworth** and shared his belief in the spiritual, revelatory power of nature, seeing in it the source of man's moral sensibility. In his mystical vision of creation, Constable could focus with equal intensity on a poppy or a cloud bank. English critics were slow to recognize his genius, however, and considered his work rough and unfinished. His admission to the Royal Academy came late in his career (1829). Following his death, his work went unnoticed until after the French Impressionists had taught his countrymen to appreciate his vision.

Elise F. Knapp

Bibliography

Beckett, R.B., ed. *John Constable's Correspondence.* 6 vols. 1962–1968.
Cormack, Malcolm. *Constable.* 1986.
Hemingway, Andrew. *Landscape Imagery and Urban Culture in Early Nineteenth-Century Britain.* 1992.
Kroeber, Karl. *Romantic Landscape Vision: Constable and Wordsworth.* 1975.
Parris, Leslie, and Ian Fleming-Williams. *Constable.* 1991.
Reynolds, Graham. *Constable's England.* 1983.
Rosenthal, Michael. *Constable, the Painter and His Landscapes.* 1983.
———. *Constable.* 1987.
Venning, Barry. *Constable.* 1990.

See also Painting

Constitution, The Glorious

The concept of the Glorious Constitution lay at the heart of English political discourse during the Hanoverian period. In essence, this unwritten constitution was considered an inheritance of liberties and institutions derived from ancient times, which had reached fullest expression in 1688–1689 in the **Glorious Revolution**. Yet that was not all, for when **George I** ascended the throne, he inherited a monarchy that had seen a number of limitations placed on its prerogative powers in the turbulent quarter-century since that time. The Bill of Rights of 1689, the Triennial Act of 1694, and the **Act of Settlement** (1701) circumscribed the independence of the crown. By 1714 the King-in-Parliament had finally triumphed over the royal prerogative, and this concept now lay at the core of the idealized notion of the Constitution.

Englishmen regarded the King-in-Parliament as comprising three separate but interdependent agencies: the king, representing the monarchical; the **House of Lords**, representing the aristocratic; and the **House of Commons**, representing the popular or democratic element of the state. The balancing of these three forces supposedly gave the nation the finest of all political systems, for according to classical republican political theory, a pure monarchy would degenerate into tyranny, a pure aristocracy into oligarchy, and a pure democracy into anarchy.

Hanoverian political writing contains countless references to the Glorious Constitution. This, as one admirer, Roger Acherly, wrote in his *Britannic Constitution* (1727),

> equally advances the greatness and power of the crown, at the same time as it secures Britons their private property, freedom, and liberty, by such walls of defense as are not to be found in any other parts of the universe.

Yet that wonderful and heaven-ordained device was fragile, having only narrowly missed dismantlement under Stuart despotism; and observers were always ready to exaggerate the dangers posed by their enemies to its survival. The Glorious Constitution thus became a rhetorical device as well as a nebulous description of the supposedly matchless excellence of balanced national government. **Whigs** and **Tories** engaged in furious yet often contradictory debates about what course of action was required by fidelity to it.

Michael L. Oberg

Bibliography

Dickinson, H.T. "The Eighteenth Century Debate on the 'Glorious Revolution.'" *History.* Vol. 61, pp. 28–45.

Lovejoy, David S. "Two American Revolutions, 1689 and 1776," in J.G.A. Pocock, ed., *Three British Revolutions, 1641, 1688, 1776.* 1980.

Pocock, J.G.A. *Politics, Language and Time: Essays on Political Thought and History.* 1971.

———. *The Ancient Constitution and the Feudal Law: A Study of English Historical Thought.* 1987.

Speck, W.A. *Stability and Strife: England, 1714–1760.* 1977.

Weston, Corinne Comstock. *English Constitutional Theory and the House of Lords.* 1965.

See also Political Thought

Constitutional (Canada) Act (1791)

This was an act by which the British government attempted to resolve a number of issues stemming from the **Quebec Act** (1774) and also to deal with the impact in Canada of the **American Revolution** and the arrival in Quebec of some 10,000 British Loyalists. The act provided for the division of Quebec into two parts—Upper Canada (British) and Lower Canada (French)—each with representative government. In Upper Canada the **Church of England** was established and given one-seventh of the land for the support of its clergy, while the **Roman Catholic Church** was allowed to continue to collect **tithes** in Lower Canada. In Upper Canada a freehold land policy was mandated, whereas the seigneurial system was sustained in Lower Canada. In order to maintain greater imperial control, the governor in each section was granted veto power, and the Crown reserved final assent to all colonial legislation.

The act was not an unmitigated success. It soothed the tensions that had arisen between the British and French residents of **Quebec**, and granted the British merchants the representative government they desired; but in dividing the colony it left most of them as a minority in Lower Canada. Moreover, with the separation of the two societies the long-term British hope of anglicizing all Canada was foredoomed.

Stuart R. Givens

Bibliography

Graham, G.S. *British Policy and Canada, 1774–1791.* 1930.

McInnis, Edgar. *Canada: A Political and Social History.* 1969.

Neatby, Hilda. *Quebec: The Revolutionary Age, 1760–1791.* 1966.

See also Canada, Empire and Imperialism

Cook, James (1728–1779)

Cook's name is synonymous with some of the greatest feats of Hanoverian **navigation**. He was born at Marton-in-Cleveland, North Yorkshire, the son of a Scottish **agricultural laborer**. He rose from humble origins to become a celebrated explorer, renowned for his leadership skills, for placing **exploration** on a firm scientific footing, and for producing charts of supreme accuracy.

After serving as an apprentice **seaman** in the North Sea and Baltic trades, he joined the **Navy** (1755). Cook's performance as pilot and marine surveyor in the Louisbourg and Quebec campaigns brought recognition and promotion. Later he published a respected series of charts and sailing directions to **Newfoundland** and Labrador (1766–1768).

In 1768 several astronomical expeditions sought to observe the transit of Venus between the sun and Earth, to enable calculation of the distance between those two bodies. The **Royal Society** proposed sending **Alexander Dalrymple**, but his insistence upon taking command led the Admiralty to promote Cook to Lieutenant and appoint him instead. On his first voyage (1768-1771) he sailed *Endeavour* to Tahiti to observe the transit on 3 June 1769, circumnavigated and charted the coasts of **New Zealand**, charted the east coast of **Australia**, then made for the Cape of Good Hope and home.

Captain James Cook

While failing to disprove popular theories (promoted by Dalrymple) about a lush southern continent, he had charted more than 5,000 miles of coastline without a longitudinal chronometer, so adept was he at calculating lunar movements. Despite careful attention to the health and diet of his crew, including antiscorbutics to prevent scurvy, 35 of his 85 men died.

Cook's second voyage (1772–1775) again tested theories of a southernmost continent. With two ships (*Resolution* and *Adventure*), Cook, promoted Commander, sailed south in his first of three attempts to penetrate **Antarctica**'s pack ice. During the intervening seasons he revisited New Zealand and Tahiti, exploring and charting numerous islands. His extraordinary feat of circumnavigating Antarctica exploded Dalrymple's vision of a "Great South Land." Harrison's **chronometer** also proved its accuracy on this voyage. Finally, only four of a 118-man company died—none of them of scurvy—a testament to Cook's regimen.

On his third voyage (1776–1779), Cook, promoted Captain, sought the Northwest Passage from the west. Along the way he explored more islands, discovered Hawaii and, with **George Vancouver**, charted the western coast of **North America** from the Columbia River's mouth to Bering's Strait and beyond, until stopped by pack ice. In Hawaii, on 14 February 1779, he was killed by islanders in an altercation over a stolen ship's boat, a fatal lapse in his otherwise exemplary dealings with natives.

Cook's greatest genius lay in painstaking planning, surveying, and **cartography**. He filled in the world map with an accuracy that resisted improvement for nearly two centuries. His conduct as a leader was afterward emulated but seldom equaled.

N. Merrill Distad

Bibliography

Beaglehole, John Cawte. *The Life of Captain James Cook.* 1974.

Beaglehole, John Cawte, and Raleigh Ashlin Skelton, eds. *The Journals of Captain James Cook on His Voyages of Discovery.* 3 vols. in 4, plus portfolio. 1955–1974.

Fry, Howard Tyrrell. *Alexander Dalrymple (1737–1808) and the Expansion of British Trade.* 1970.

Withey, Lynne. *Voyages of Discovery: Captain Cook and the Exploration of the Pacific.* 1987.

Woolf, Harry. *The Transits of Venus: A Study in Eighteenth-Century Science.* 1959.

Cooking and Cuisine

The 18th century is noted for British country cooking at its best, when advances in **agriculture** and **commerce** produced a fairly reliable supply of raw material, and changes in cooking technology combined with generally available cookery books to produce a distinctively British cuisine stressing economy and simplicity. French cooking, which nearly overshadowed native English fare during the Victorian period, was surprisingly unimportant, considering the great impact of other French fashions on Hanoverian culture.

Cookery books, always more plentiful in England than elsewhere in Europe, were distinguished by their appeal not just to courtly feast-givers but to "huswifes" who managed all aspects of a household. **Translations** of French cookbooks were used in only a few of the richest households; the most important English cookbooks were written by women for women and their **servants**. Though the cookbooks extant do not make clear which dishes and menus were everyday fare and which were exotic or reserved for feasting, some clear patterns emerge.

Throughout the period, the working-class breakfast was eaten very early in the day and consisted of cereal pottages,

The Pig Pye Man. *London Food Vendors*

cold meats, fish, cheese, and ale or beer. In former times this menu had been common for all classes, but a lighter breakfast around 11 AM for the leisured classes became increasingly customary (reflecting their very late bedtime), while their main meal of the day moved dramatically from noon to 8 or 10 PM. Since this was the pattern for the upper classes, late dinners came to acquire status, so that social climbers became embarrassed by too early a dinner hour. Toward the turn of the century, the tradition of afternoon tea at 4 or 5 PM began, and a light meal was reinstituted at 1 or 2 PM.

Menus and serving patterns for typical two-course dinners were expressed in diagrams in the cookery books, with the dishes of each course put on the table at the same time in precise symmetrical patterns. In nearly all cookbooks of the period, the two-course meal (only rarely were there three courses) is illustrated, with as many as 21 dishes a course. Record books from the kitchens of **George III** show that what mainly distinguished royal from ordinary fare was the number of dishes in each course. As French cooking grew in popularity during **the Regency**, meals with more courses were served (this was called, however, dining *à la Russe*).

The foods in the sample dinners contain local ingredients, simply prepared. **Fish**, domestic meats, game, vegetables, fruits, and sweets appear in both courses. Few "made dishes" appear, and the cookbooks reveal a general disdain of "kickshaws" (a corruption of *quelque chose*) and other French follies. The days of the Regency and the reign of **George IV**, however, brought the great French chefs to England, especially Alexis Soyer (1809–1858), whose influence changed 19th-century English cooking.

Changes in the Hanoverian diet were mainly the result of advances in agriculture, increased domestic commerce, and the progress of **science, technology and invention**. Adequate winter fodder ended the traditional autumn slaughter and preservation (mainly by pickling and smoking) of meat, whereas scientific breeding doubled the size of some farm animals. Salted fish continued in importance, but fresh fish became even more widely available. Smaller households began to depend on market gardens and local dairies (one effect of the enclosure of common lands), and even the largest estates became less self-sufficient.

Coffee, tea, and chocolate were imported after 1660, changing drinking habits and forming the basis of the men's **club**, alongside early coffee- and chocolatehouses. As the cost came down, tea drinking spread so quickly that by 1714 some observers were worried about the replacement of good, healthful ale with a drink lacking nutritional value. Sugar consumption, ensured by Britain's imperial position in the **West Indies**, quadrupled during the Hanoverian period. The New World potato (accepted first in **Ireland**) became common throughout Britain, but the tomato began to gain acceptance as a food only in the second half of the 18th century.

By the end of that century, food could be preserved in glass bottles by heat processing; it could be "canned" in tinned metal containers after 1813. The biggest revolution in cooking technique came with the invention of the cookstove, at first an enclosed brick oven with iron plates on top, then a cast-iron contraption. "Wet roasting," or slow boiling of food, had traditionally been the dominant cooking method for all but the wealthiest families (who possessed adequate fireplaces for spit-roasting), while public bakehouses had often done the work of cooking breads and meats for poorer families. Such bakehouses had been producing deep-dish meat pies (an English delicacy) for consumption on the street ever since the 14th century. Now the development of the cookstove dramatically increased the cooking options of even the smallest houses.

Jan Widmayer

Bibliography

Glasse, Hannah. *The Art of Cookery Made Plain and Easy.* 1747; rpt. 1971.

Hardyment, Christina. *Home Comfort: A History of Domestic Arrangements.* 1992.

Hope, Annette. *Londoner's Larder: English Cuisine from Chaucer to the Present.* 1990.

Mennell, Stephen. *All Manners of Food: Eating and Taste in England and France from the Middle Ages to the Present.* 1985.

Oddy, Derek, and Derek Miller, eds. *The Making of the Modern British Diet.* 1976.

Raffald, Elizabeth. *The Experienced English Housekeeper.* 1769; rpt. 1970.

Wilson, C. Anne. *Food and Drink in Britain: From the Stone Age to the 19th Century.* 1973; rev. ed., 1991.

———, ed. *"The Appetite and the Eye": Visual Aspects of Food and Its Presentation within Their Historic Context.* 1991.

See also Fashion; Manners and Morals

Cooper, Elizabeth (n.d.)

Cooper was a minor playwright and ambitious literary scholar. Her works began to appear after the death of her husband, Thomas Cooper, in 1735. *The Rival Widows, or Fair Libertine* (1735), a comedy dedicated to Sarah, duchess of Marlborough (1660–1744), was performed at Covent Garden for 9 nights, with Cooper herself in the lead role on at least one occasion. In the play's preface Cooper expressed her hope that women would appreciate the heroine, Lady Bellair, who was "capable of thinking for herself." She also expressed her satisfaction at the regularity and decorum in her play because "'Tis what we Women—Authors, in particular, have been thought greatly deficient in." Cooper's only other play, a tragedy called *The Nobleman, or the Family Quarrel* (1736), ran for one night at the Haymarket; the manuscript has been lost.

A more significant undertaking was her anthology of 400 pages, *The Muses Library, or a Series of English Poetry from the Saxons to the Reign of King Charles II* (1737, reissued 1741), which included verses selected from writers as diverse as Edward the Confessor (*d.* 1066) and Samuel Daniel (1563–1619), together with critical commentary and brief biographies. This was a remarkably early contribution to the national literary scholarship just beginning at this time. Acknowledging, in her preface, the assistance of the antiquarian William Oldys (1696–1761), Cooper looked forward to publishing a second volume, along with a history of English criticism. Neither came to fruition.

Mary Tiryak

Bibliography

Blain, Virginia, et al. *Feminist Companion to Literature in English: Women Writers from the Middle Ages to the Present.* 1990.

Cotton, Nancy. *Women Playwrights in England, 1363–1750.* 1980.

See also Dramatic Arts; Women in Literature

Coote, Sir Eyre (1726–1783)

An **East India Company** military commander, Coote played a major role in the British conquest of **India.** Born the son of an Irish Protestant clergyman, he fought against the **Jacobites** in the **Forty-five** rebellion. He arrived in India as an army captain in 1756, in time to assist **Robert Clive** in operations to retake Calcutta. His advice was important in Clive's decision to confront Bengali and French forces at the momentous and successful **Battle of Plassey** (1757).

From 1759 to 1761, Coote forced the French to withdraw from southern India. His reward was the command of company forces in Bengal. With the virtual elimination of French power, he returned to England in 1762 and won a seat in Parliament; but he returned to Bengal as military commander-in-chief in 1769. He was knighted in 1771. Serving in the latter 1770s under **Warren Hastings**, his successful but arduous campaign against Prince Hyder Ali of Mysore left him ill and prompted his resignation (1781). He died in Madras, having eliminated the most serious military obstacles to the East India Company's domination of India.

A. Martin Wainwright

Sir Eyre Coote

Bibliography

Sheppard, Eric William. *Coote Bahadur: A Life of Lieutenant-General Sir Eyre Coote.* 1956.

Coram, Thomas (1668–1751)

Coram, born in Lyme Regis, founded the London **Foundling Hospital** (1739). This was the first English **joint-stock company** designed for nonprofit, charitable purposes.

Coram settled in **London** after many years as a sea captain and commercial **shipbuilder.** Working as a businessman in Massachusetts (1693–1703), he had gained experience raising money for Anglican schools. Combining his knowledge of business and money-raising with an unusual sensitivity to the plight of children, he began work on the Foundling Hospital (1722) by organizing aristocratic women to petition for the new charity. He overcame much resistance to it, some centered on the fear that an institution for abandoned illegitimate children would encourage sexual misconduct.

Coram had married a **Congregationalist** woman, Eunice Wayte, in 1700. They were happy, but childless. Coram allegedly reacted to every deserted child as if it had been his own. The first two infant waifs accepted by his institution were named Thomas and Eunice Coram. Other causes in which he involved himself were those of unemployed soldiers, women disinherited of property, and American Indians. Liked and respected in his own time, the sense of Coram's importance as

Captain Thomas Coram

an early example of Hanoverian **humanitarianism** has increased in the 20th century.

Carolyn Stevens

Bibliography

Compston, H.F.B. *Thomas Coram: Churchman, Empire Builder and Philanthropist.* 1918.

McClure, Ruth K. *Coram's Children: The London Foundling Hospital in the Eighteenth Century.* 1981.

Cork

Cork's emergence as a major Irish port dates from the 1680s. Its expansion during the Hanoverian era cannot be measured easily, but the fivefold increase in the tonnage invoiced at Cork port between 1700 and 1800, and the rise in **population** from around 17,000 in 1700 to 57,000 in 1796, and to 80,000 in 1841, provide perspectives on its growth.

Cork's development rested on its preeminence in the Atlantic provisions trade. For a time it was the greatest slaughter yard in Western Europe. Profiting from **war**, it benefited from the rivalry of the French and British navies, and also from the need to feed **slaves** on the West Indian sugar plantations. Although America displaced Cork in the important **West Indies** market in the late 18th century, the outbreak of war between Britain and France in 1793 prolonged the life of the provisons industry until 1815.

The enormous wealth this industry brought to the city enabled it to expand beyond its medieval core. It was **merchants**, rather than landowners (as in **Dublin**), who provided money for the reclamation after 1740 of the marshy lands to the west and south of the old city, on which this expansion was initially based. Further developments radiated outward from these heartlands in the period 1780–1820. One of the key figures here was Cooper Penrose, a **Quaker** merchant who developed a thousand feet of river frontage on the northeastern edge of the city.

The contraction of the international provisions trade after 1815 resulted in a sharp downturn in Cork's prosperity. The city retained its dominant position in Munster's economy, but this rested increasingly on such **middle-class** employments as **banking**, the law, and administration. This in turn hastened the spatial differentiation of residential and commercial functions as the middle classes abandoned the maze of bustling streets in the city, leaving these to poorer folk while themselves heading for the more elegant and spacious suburbs growing nearby.

James Kelly

Bibliography

Butel, P., and L.M. Cullen, eds. *Cities and Merchants: Perspectives on Urban Development.* 1986.

O'Sullivan, William. *An Economic History of Cork City.* 1937.

See also Cities and Urban Life; Irish Agriculture

Corn Laws

In 1815 Parliament passed Britain's most notorious Corn Law (cereal grain **tariff**) in an effort to protect British **farmers** from dramatically falling agricultural prices and to limit the country's

Demonstration against 1815 Corn Law

reliance on foreign foodstuffs. The act, which superseded earlier Corn Laws of 1773, 1791, and 1804, prohibited the importation of foreign cereal grains until domestic demand pushed up prices to the level of 80 shillings a quarter (eight bushels). Despite this effort to stabilize prices at a plateau advantageous to farmers and the landed interest, grain prices fluctuated and the rigid requirements of the 1815 statute proved unworkable. In 1828 Parliament revised it and established a sliding scale relating **tariffs** to prices that worked somewhat more predictably and reasonably.

The Corn Law of 1815 was extremely unpopular with urban **factoryowners** and **workers**, and stood as a conspicious symbol of both the domination of politics by the **aristocracy and gentry**, and what increasingly appeared to be the moral unjustifiability of artificial barriers to free trade. Severe **riots and popular disturbances** accompanied its passage. Agitation against it became extremely well organized in the 1830s, particularly by the Anti-Corn Law League established in 1839. This national organization, relying on **middle-class** energies, campaigned effectively for free trade and began to contest parliamentary elections in 1841. In 1842, Parliament altered the corn tariff again, but it was the 1845 potato **famine** in **Ireland** and a crop failure in England that gave Sir **Robert Peel**, Prime Minister and leader of the Conservative party, the emergency he needed to convince Parliament to repeal the Corn Laws altogether. Actually the 1846 "repeal" reduced the sliding scale until 1849, when the tariffs were discontinued. Peel, condemned as a traitor to the landed interest, fell from power, his Conservative party shattered.

David B. Mock

Bibliography

Barnes, Donald G. *A History of the English Corn Laws from 1600 to 1846.* 1930.

Dinwiddy, John R. *From Luddism to the First Reform Bill: Reform in England, 1810–1832.* 1986.

McCord, Norman. *Anti-Corn Law League, 1838–1846.* 1958.

Torrens, R. *An Essay on the External Corn Trade.* 1829; rpt. 1972.

See also Taxes and Tariffs

Cornwallis, 1st Marquess of (Charles Cornwallis) (1738–1805)

General Charles Cornwallis

Cornwallis's defeat at **Yorktown** (1781) ended the **War of American Independence.** A grandson of the 2nd Viscount **Townshend,** he trained for a military career, then took the family seat in the **House of Lords** on succeeding to his father's earldom (1762). Although he opposed taxing the Americans and voted (1766) to repeal the **Stamp Act,** he accepted an American command when resistance turned to rebellion. He was impatient with **North**'s mismanagement of the war. He was nonetheless one of Britain's best field commanders. He failed to wrest full command of the British effort from his excessively cautious commander-in-chief, Henry Clinton (1738–1795).

Controlling British forces in the southern colonies in 1780, Cornwallis smashed the rebels at the Battle of Camden (Aug. 16) but fell short in his efforts in 1781 to counter the guerrilla activities of partisan irregulars and gain a decisive victory over the wily General Nathanael Greene (1742–1786). Having convinced himself that control of Chesapeake Bay could lead eventually to a reversal of fading British fortunes, he removed his army toward the Virginia coast. But the seemingly advantageous position became untenable when the **navy** lost control of its sea approaches. Cornwallis, his supply lines cut and himself unable to break the siege imposed by French and American forces under **George Washington,** surrendered at Yorktown on October 19, 1781.

While the disaster was a permanent setback for the British **Empire,** it barely slowed Cornwallis. The public and the government held Clinton responsible for it. Both men wrote angry self-defenses. Cornwallis, becoming a supporter of **Pitt the Younger** after 1784, went on to gain renown for his success as a reform-minded Governor-General of **India** (1786–1793) and, as Viceroy of **Ireland,** for crushing the **Irish Rebellion** of 1798. In India he established the Cornwallis (or Bengal) Code for cleaning up the civil service, a system with valuable long-term effects. In Ireland he also sought to curb corruption but, supporting the **Act of Union,** resigned in disapproval of the failure to concede political rights to **Catholics.** Next year (1802) he was Britain's chief negotiator of the **Peace of Amiens.** Cornwallis died in India after being reappointed Governor-General.

David Sloan

Bibliography

Mackesy, Piers. *The War for America, 1775–1783.* 1964.

Rankin, Hugh F. "Charles Lord Cornwallis: A Study in Frustration," in George A. Billias, ed., *George Washington's Opponents.* 1969.
Wickwire, Franklin, and Mary Wickwire. *Cornwallis: The American Adventure.* 1970.
———. *Cornwallis: The Imperial Years.* 1980.

See also Army; War and Military Engagements

Corresponding Societies

Since federations of political societies were illegal in Hanoverian Britain, links by correspondence constituted a way around the law. This was a tactic used in both America and Britain during the years of the **American Revolution**. Its use was renewed during the era of the **French Revolution** with the formation of the Sheffield Constitutional Society in December 1791, which began corresponding with other **radical clubs** in Yorkshire and the Midlands. Inspired by these activities, the important **London Corresponding Society** was formed by the Scottish shoemaker **Thomas Hardy** in January 1792. By that summer it had grown to nearly 300 members.

The new societies differed from earlier reform associations in that membership was open to all; they deliberately appealed to **craftsmen** and workmen without the **franchise**. They laid emphasis on democratic structures and, influenced by **Thomas Paine**, called for universal suffrage and annual parliaments. By combining support from craftsmen and middle-ranking professionals they constituted the most broad-based political reform movement of the age. By the end of 1792, between 5,000 and 6,000 people were attending **London** meetings.

During 1793 the London Society corresponded with similar societies in almost all the main **provincial towns**. Far from intimidating the new crop of **radicals**, the sentences of 14 years' **transportation** imposed on Maurice Margarot and Joseph Gerrald, who attended the **Edinburgh** Convention of November 1793 as delegates from the London Society, seem to have stimulated a new spurt of membership and new activists like the young tailor **Francis Place**. **John Thelwall**, a leading radical theorist, talked of "the social compact between the English Nation and their Governors" being dissolved. The government arrested Hardy and other leaders in May 1794, but failed to achieve a conviction for high treason.

Government intimidation led to the demise of many societies during 1794, though many reappeared in 1795. The government responded with two "Gag" acts, tightly restricting public meetings and debate. Habeas corpus was suspended, and government spies were used extensively. Radical organizations began to split between those who were prepared to defy the law and those who wanted to remain on a constitutional path. Links with the Irish involved in the 1798 **Irish Rebellion** led to the formal suppression of the London Society in 1799.

W. Hamish Fraser

Bibliography

Collins, Henry. "The London Corresponding Society," in J. Saville, ed., *Democracy and the Labor Movement.* 1954.
Thale, M., ed. *The Autobiography of Francis Place.* 1972.
———. *Selections from the Papers of the London Corresponding Society.* 1983.
Thompson, E.P. *The Making of the English Working Class.* 1965.
Williams, Gwyn A. *Artisans and Sans-Culottes.* 1968.
Wright, D.G. *Popular Radicalism: The Working-Class Experience, 1780–1880.* 1988.

Cort, Henry (1742–1800)

Born in Lancaster, Cort became involved with iron production when, as a **navy** agent in **London**, he participated in experiments to improve the wrought iron used for naval ordnance. He acquired a forge and slitting mills at Fontley, near Fareham, where his first major contribution to iron production was the invention of grooved rollers, patented in 1783, which largely replaced hammering to change ingots into usable bars and sheets. A year later he patented the puddling process, whereby the molten pig iron in the reverberatory furnace was stirred to promote the decarburizing process. The resultant "loop" of pure metal, after having the slag hammered out, could then be speedily and efficiently finished in his roller mills. The two innovations, neither revolutionary in itself, played a key role in the expansion of the British iron industry by making the production of wrought iron (which, unlike pig iron or cast iron, is purified and hence malleable) much easier and cheaper than before. Unfortunately, Cort's partner's source of funds proved to be money embezzled from the Admiralty, and in the ensuing debacle Cort lost everything, including his **patents**. For the last 6 years of his life he lived on a government **pension** of £200 per year.

R.D. Corrins

Bibliography

Mott, R.A. *The Great Finer: Creator of Puddled Iron.* 1983.

See also Iron Industry; Metallurgy and Metalworking; Science, Technology, and Invention

Cotton Industry

Manufacture of cotton was introduced to Britain from the Netherlands in the 16th century, and by 1720 was established in Lancashire and other counties, notably East Anglia. **London** was important as a market for fustians (linen and cotton mixtures), which were often printed there, and as a supplier of capital and of raw cotton—initially brought from the Levant. **Fashion** was influenced by expensive oriental products, especially those supplied by the **East India Company**; much imitation occurred. Industrial organization was increasingly based on a system of **domestic production**, controlled by merchants.

Merchants based in Manchester, Bolton, Blackburn, **Norwich**, and **Glasgow** developed trade connections with London and overseas markets and distributed materials for spinning and weaving to operatives through local agents who supervised manufacture. Thus experienced labor and a well-developed commercial network existed before the cotton industry began to move into **factories**.

The factory system emerged in the silk industry just after 1700 and was transferred to cotton by **Richard Arkwright**

Crompton's spinning mule, c. *1780*

in the late 1760s. Concentration of production without significant alterations in technology was commonplace from the 1750s, but increasing demand led first to the mechanization of spinning with **Hargreaves**' jenny, Arkwright's water frame, and **Crompton**'s mule, and then to the improvement of preparation machinery, especially carding, before the power loom and factory-based weaving emerged.

The main determinant of the physical location of factories was the availability of power. Horse capstans, windmills, and waterwheels were all used. **James Watt**'s rotary **steam engine** encouraged **entrepreneurs** to locate factories in towns where waterpower was inadequate, unavailable, or controlled by other economic interests. Hand spinning was rapidly displaced; but the progress of the power loom against handloom weaving was slower.

Capital requirements in the early industry were relatively modest, but large mills and factory villages were, of course, more expensive. Working capital was, however, more important than the fixed investment in factories and machinery, and credit was commonly the basis for many early business successes and a major explanation of the rapid growth and wide dispersal of the industry between 1780 and 1840. Most firms specialized in either spinning or weaving, but by 1840, a trend toward integration had slowly established itself.

The **merchant** community responsible for importing raw cotton and exporting yarn and cloth also evolved quickly, but the most important feature on the supply side was the spread of cotton cultivation in the southern states of America and the adoption of Eli Whitney's (1765–1825) cotton gin to clean the increased output. **Liverpool** superseded London as the most important port for the cotton trade soon after 1800, and this gave Lancashire an important cost advantage, as did the growth of the machine-making firms of Oldham and **Manchester**. Thus Manchester became the main center for cotton trading and manufacturing in the dominant region, Lancashire, although the industry survived successfully in **Scotland** and the English Midlands.

Cotton's role in the developing Hanoverian economy can be easily exaggerated; it probably never accounted for more than 8–10% of national income. Its influence was wider, however, than this single statistic might convey: It became the model for the other textile industries to emulate; it stimulated the development of civil and mechanical engineering, and also the growth of the **chemical industry** through the finishing trades' demand for bleaching and dyeing agents. These industries developed their own momentum, but cotton was the catalyst that brought about fundamental change.

John Butt

Bibliography

Bythell, Duncan. *The Handloom Weavers.* 1969.

Chapman, Stanley D. *The Early Factory Masters.* 1967.

———. *The Cotton Industry in the Industrial Revolution.* 2nd ed., 1987.

Edwards, Michael M. *The British Cotton Trade, 1780–1815.* 1967.

Tann, Jennifer. *The Development of the Factory.* 1970.

Wadsworth, A.P., and Julia de L. Mann. *The Cotton Trade and Industrial Lancashire.* 1931.

See also Science, Technology, and Invention; Spinning and Weaving; Textile Industries

Cotton Weavers Massacre (1787)

Hanoverian class conflict and official repression were well illustrated in these events that unfolded in **Glasgow**'s East End. The Calton district was an important **cotton** manufacturing area, where around 10,000 handloom **weavers** plied their trade. The cloth market was volatile, and in response to a sharp recession (1786), weaving merchants slashed wages and went on to propose a further massive cut of 25% in 1787. Around 7,000 weavers stopped work in protest, maintaining their strike for almost 10 weeks, enduring intense deprivation.

The dispute led to violence, incendiarism, and sabotage, particularly directed against the replacement "blackleg" workforce that the employers attempted to recruit. In one incident on 3 September 1787, troops opened fire on stone-throwing strikers, killing three, fatally wounding three more, and injuring many others. This "massacre" prompted **riots** and, subsequently, a drift back to work on the employers' terms. Arrests and victimization of activists ensued, with one leader, James Granger, subjected to a public flogging and banishment for 7 years.

Despite or perhaps because of such autocratic treatment—which included the creation of a permanent **army** barracks in the heart of the Calton weaving community—the Glasgow weavers retained high levels of organization and militancy, and contributed significantly to political **radicalism** in the region up to the 1830s.

Arthur McIvor

Bibliography

Fraser, W.H. *Conflict and Class: Scottish Workers, 1700–1838.* 1988.
King, Elspeth. *The Strike of the Glasgow Weavers, 1787.* 1987.
Smout, T.C. *A History of the Scottish People, 1560–1830.* 1969.

See also French Revolution; Mealmaker, George; Militia Riots; Muir, Thomas of Huntershill; Radical War

Counties

See Government, Local and County

Courage, John (*d.* 1793)

The founder of one of the country's most noted **brewing** firms, Courage, born in Aberdeen, was the younger son of a family descended from French Huguenot exiles. In 1769 he went to **London** as an agent for **Carron Company**, based at Glasgow Wharf on the north bank of the Thames. He diversified into brewing in 1787, purchasing the brewhouse at Horselydown in Southwark, an already established brewing area, for £616.

The site was part of the extensive property formerly belonging to the Knights of St. John of Jerusalem, containing wells that were essential for brewing. Courage's Anchor Brewhouse was in production by 1789, when the first entry in the brewing book was recorded for 51 barrels of beer. He died suddenly in 1793, leaving a widow, Harriot, and four children. Harriot continued the brewery with the assistance of the managing clerk, John Donaldson, until her death in 1797. Donaldson was then in sole charge and became a partner.

Young John Courage entered the brewery at age 14 with a handsome salary of £60 and was made a partner in 1811. During this partnership with Donaldson, the brewery prospered. It expanded along the foreshore of the Thames, acquiring wharves and a fleet of barges for transporting the beer. The brewery remained as a family partnership until 1888, when a limited company was formed.

Alma Topen

Bibliography

Hardinge, G.N. *Courages, 1787–1932.* Privately printed, 1932.
Mathias, P. *The Brewing Industry in England, 1700–1830.* 1959.
Pudney, J. *A Draft of Contentment, the Story of the Courage Group.* 1971.

See also Drink Industries; Drinking

Cowley, Hannah (1743–1809)

Poet and dramatist, Cowley wrote over 13 plays, many of them quite popular well into the 19th century. Her most enduring effort was *The Belle's Stratagem* (1780), a patriotic

Hannah Cowley

comedy of manners that was performed regularly for over a century afterward. Cowley's intellectual mentors were Aphra Behn (1640–1689) and **Susanna Centlivre.**

Cowley was born in Devon, the daughter of the scholarly bookseller Thomas Parkhouse. In 1772 she married Thomas Cowley, a journalist, and moved to **London**, where she lived until 1801, raising three children and living from her literary earnings. Her husband was absent in **India** from 1783 on.

Cowley wrote her first play, *The Runaway* (1776), on a bet with her husband that she could write as financially successful a play as any contemporary dramatist. She experimented with tragedy when writing *Albina, Countess Raimond* (1779)—which incidentally she accused **Hannah More** of plagiarizing in More's play *The Fatal Falsehood* (1779)—and *The Fate of Sparta, or the Rival Kings* (1788). But she excelled in the writing of comedy, especially in *The Runaway* (1776), *Who's the Dupe?* (1779), *The Belle's Stratagem* (1780), and *Which Is the Man?* (1782). Cowley's other works include a **Gothic novel** (*The Italian Marauders,* 1810), several long narrative poems (*Maid of Arragon,* 1780; *Scottish Village,* 1786; *Siege of Acre,* 1801), and the **sentimental** "Anna Mathilda" poems written to "Della Crusca" (Robert Merry) for *The World* in 1788. Eleven plays and most of her **poetry** were published in 1813.

Mary Tiryak

Bibliography

Gagan, Jean. "The Weaker Sex." *The University of Mississippi Studies in English.* Vol. 8, pp. 107–116.

Nicoll, Allardyce. *A History of English Drama, 1660–1900.* Vol. 3. 1961.

Todd, Janet. *Dictionary of British and American Women Writers.* 1984.

See also Dramatic Arts; Women in Literature

Cowper, William (1731–1800)

Poet, satirist, abolitionist, and **Evangelical** hymnist, Cowper was acclaimed by his contemporaries as England's finest living poet, though critical estimates fell afterward. His chief works include the *Olney Hymns* (1779) published with **John Newton**, *Poems* (1782), and *The Task* (1785). Criticism now sees him as a transitional figure between imitative and expressive, Evangelical and natural, **Augustan** and **Romantic poetic** developments.

After an unsuccessful start as a lawyer, and suffering suicidal depressions, Cowper retired from **London** to Huntingdon, where he met Mrs. Mary Unwin, his eventual lifelong companion. They settled in Olney. He had been a sickly and sensitive youth, and for the remainder of his life experienced depressions and nightmarish apprehensions of damnation, frequently attempting **suicide**.

At Olney Cowper wrote 66 of the 348 *Olney Hymns.* Following **Isaac Watts**'s Christian modernizing of the Psalms, Cowper and Newton attempted to assist **dissenters** to broaden church service participation. Expanding the hymns' sources from biblical materials well beyond the Psalms, Cowper

William Cowper

achieved distinction, sometimes shock, through unsoftened images conveying man's dependence on grace: "There is a fountain fill'd with blood / Drawn from Emmanuel's veins." In "Jehovah Our Righteousness," Cowper's Calvinistic sense of human sinfulness before God becomes an expression of each sinner's dilemma even in using a hymn: "Sin twines itself about my praise / And slides into my pray'r."

Some of Cowper's poems, however, were more playful. He wrote many amusing eulogies, laments, and fables. In "On the Death of Mrs. Throckmorton's Bullfinch" (1789), nymphs join the lady in mourning a bird who was "assassin'd" by a cat. On the other hand, in "The Castaway" (1799), Cowper caught the terror of a life ending, cut off from saving grace.

Eight moral **satires** form most of Cowper's 1782 *Poems.* In **Augustan** couplets, his writing moved toward the lyricism that came to undergird his natural descriptions 3 years later in *The Task.* But that great work, full of superb personal observations of the countryside but also of Evangelical doctrine and sometimes scathing political criticism, has defied easy attempts to define its poetic unity. Book I, "The Sofa," unfavorably contrasts the urban, artificial productions of man with the rural sights of nature; this contrast culminates in Books V and VI in the preference for God's creation over man's. Nature becomes the means to an acute **sensibility** that brings intimate and particular joy. But the poem also raises a question as to whether Cowper had come to naturalize his Evangelical Christianity. Foreshadowing **Wordsworth**'s *Prelude,* it provides the first long, "autobiographical," blank verse narrative poem of spiritual salvation in English.

J. Scott Lee

Bibliography

King, James, and Charles Ryskamp, eds. *Letters and Prose Writings of William Cowper.* 4 vols. 1979–1984.

Newey, Vincent. *Cowper's Poetry: A Critical Study and Reassessment.* 1982.

Spacks, Patricia Anne Meyer. *The Poetry of Vision: Five Eighteenth-Century Poets.* 1967.

See also Poetry and Poetics

Crabbe, George (1754–1832)

Crabbe was born poor at Aldeburgh in Suffolk, where the harsh life and bleak landscape were to color his **poetry.** After an unsatisfactory career in **medicine** he moved to **London** (1780) and was befriended by **Edmund Burke,** who encouraged him to publish *The Library* (1781). His first important work, *The Village,* revised by Burke and **Samuel Johnson,** appeared in 1783. Having taken orders (1781), he spent the remaining years of his life as a rural cleric. Despite recognition of his talent, he published nothing between 1785 and 1807. At last he brought forth his *Poems* (1807), which contained *The Parish Register,* and followed this with *The Borough* (1810), *Tales* (1812), and *Tales of the Hall* (1819).

Crabbe has been difficult to classify. His couplet verse tales suggest an **Augustan** survivor in the **Romantic** period, while his narrative emphasis on the rigors of village life has prompted comparison with the **novel. Byron** described him as "nature's sternest painter yet the best," and it is his realistic grasp of provincial existence that marks his distinctiveness. *The Village* and *The Parish Register,* in the genre of rural poetry, contrast starkly with such **sentimental** visions as Oliver Goldsmith's *Deserted Village* (1770). Crabbe in his later works dwelt more on what he called "the middling classes," presenting a gallery of characters in miscellaneous collections of stories, perhaps the most famous being "Peter Grimes" in *The Borough.*

George Crabbe

Michael Bruce

Bibliography

Chamberlain, R.L. *George Crabbe.* 1965.

Cruttwell, P. "The Last Augustan." *Hudson Review.* Vol. 7, pp. 533–554.

Haddakin, L.F. *The Poetry of Crabbe.* 1954.

Craft Guilds

Craftsmen wielded significant power in 18th-century urban society, particularly where they were organized within craft guilds. Such organizations dated back to the early Middle Ages and constituted formal associations of master artisans along craft lines—for example, as blacksmiths, hammermen, tailors, printers, saddlers, and armorers. The members were essentially **entrepreneurs,** providing both capital and labor, buying their own raw material, and selling their product direct to the consumer.

The historic role of the guild was to protect the interests of the constituency of relatively privileged freemen (burgesses) of the English **boroughs** and Scottish **burghs** who were its members against the vagaries of product and labor markets. Guilds restricted the labor market by controlling entry to the craft through a licensing system—endorsed by the town authorities—and via strict apprenticeship regulations, frequently only allowing a ratio of one apprentice to one journeyman. Thus, untrained workers—classed as "outsiders"—could be excluded. The guilds also attempted to fix product prices, often on the pretext of quality control, hounding out interlopers who undercut guild rates. Entry to the guild was restricted to those who had undergone an arduous 12-year apprenticeship and probationary period, and could afford high membership fees. The rewards, however, could be great, with guild affiliation conferring prestige and often public office and power, for example as town councillor or magistrate.

Some historical debate has focused on the relationship between craft guilds and early **trade unions.** Early observers stressed the evolution of the latter from the former, though the Webbs' classic account of trade unionism dismissed this view, arguing unequivocally for the independent development of these two quite distinctive institutions. Recent research has stressed the heterogeneity of trade union antecedents, though the weight of opinion has now swung back to emphasizing the genesis of trade unionism out of the collapsing guild structure of the 18th century. The essential similarity of the two lies in the common interest in membership control; the essential difference lies in the evolution of master craftsmen, owning capital and often employing several workers, toward industrial entrepreneurship.

Much of the ritual and ceremony of the craft guilds was replicated in early trade unions, which consisted predominantly of artisans aiming to retain the restrictive labor market defenses of the guilds (apprenticeship), while agitating for local and central government regulation of the market. This mode of regulation via the craft guilds fitted well with medieval ideas—distrust of competition, exaltation of skill, stress on community interests—but eroded rapidly during the 18th century as industrialization and the concept of laissez-faire gained ground. Indeed, by this period, guild regulation was characterized by inefficiency, poor training, and corruption.

However, the process of guild dissolution was far from uniform across the country, mirroring the variable and localized nature of industrialization. In **Glasgow**, for example, guild restrictions were swept away by the 1750s; they survived longer in **London** and some smaller **provincial towns**. Pragmatic removal of craft guild regulation (as in the case of Glasgow) provided some competitive advantage, hence facilitating economic growth.

Arthur McIvor

Bibliography

Dobson, C.R. *Masters and Journeymen: A Prehistory of Industrial Relations, 1717–1800.* 1980.

Musson, A.E. *British Trade Unions 1800–1875.* 1972.

Rule, J. *The Experience of Labour in Eighteenth Century Industry.* 1981.

Smout, T.C. *A History of the Scottish People, 1560–1830.* 1969.

Webb, S. and B. Webb. *The History of Trade Unionism.* 1894.

See also Craftsmen; Hours, Wages, and Working Conditions; Labor Laws, Movements, and Unions; Standard of Living

Craftsman, The

Begun in December 1727 by **William Pulteney** and Viscount **Bolingbroke**, opponents of the government of **Robert Walpole**, this weekly journal became the most popular source of political commentary during the early 1730s. Its authors used **satire** to present the political **opposition**'s favorite themes: the government's corrupt and authoritarian methods, its misuse of **patronage**, its maintenance of a standing **army**, its sponsorship of **foreign relations** serving the interests of foreign princes, and its toleration of both a national debt and high **taxes**. In 1732 and 1733 *The Craftsman* helped mobilize an outcry that forced Walpole to withdraw his scheme to collect the **excise tax**. Its circulation at that time was over 10,000, subscribers representing all parts of the political spectrum. Walpole acknowledged *The Craftsman*'s influence by subjecting its printer to searches and prosecutions, and by founding rival journals.

By reprinting writings from other sources and by reprinting and binding its own back issues into book-sized volumes, *The Craftsman* influenced themes and styles of English political commentary later in the century. Even its opponents acknowledged its high literary standards. By 1740 its circulation was around 4,000. After the death of its editor, Nicholas Amhurst (1742), it continued until 1753, when its editor changed its title and dropped "Caleb D'Anvers," the pen name under which its authors had written.

Robert D. McJimsey

Bibliography

Battestin, Martin, ed. *New Essays by Henry Fielding: His Contributions to the Craftsman, 1734–1739.* 1989.

Harris, Robert. *A Patriot Press: National Politics and the London Press in the 1740s.* 1993.

Kramnick, Isaac. *Bolingbroke and His Circle.* 1968.

Varey, Simon, ed. *Lord Bolingbroke: Contributions to* The Craftsman. 1982.

See also Hervey of Ickworth, Baron; Periodicals; Political Thought

Craftsmen

Most manufactured goods in the 18th century were produced by skilled workers trained in definite crafts, that is, craftsmen, using hand methods or simple machines. Many produced articles of great intricacy and beauty—technical instruments; watches and clocks; **jewelry, clothing, home furnishings and decoration** of all kinds; agricultural, commercial, industrial and other equipment. The degree of skill required varied greatly from master artisans through journeymen to apprentices, but all skilled workers would have distinguished themselves from those without skill, and generally their wages might be at least 30–40% higher than those of the vast mass of unskilled **agricultural laborers**, **seamen**, **servants**, drovers, watermen, slaughterers, porters, coal heavers, and the like.

Skill came principally through the system of apprenticeship. In traditional crafts, covered by the 1563 Statute of Artificers and Apprentices, a 7-year, indentured apprenticeship was required, though there were other means of entry for exsoldiers and others. A young apprentice worked alongside a skilled man to learn his craft, perhaps even living in the master's house and being provided with food and clothes. During the apprenticeship, the youth not only acquired skills but was introduced to the "mysteries" of the craft, its lore and customs. Having completed the apprenticeship, he became a journeyman, often continuing to expand and refine his skills by working with different masters. Tramping around to gain work was a common means by which new skills were assimilated.

After a time, a journeyman, with a little capital, could expect to be able to set up in business as a master. For a time before employing his own apprentices and journeymen, he might occupy an intermediate stage of small master, buying his own raw material and selling directly to the public when he could, taking work from bigger masters when circumstances dictated. In older towns especially, entry to the ranks of master could be restricted by the controls of the **craft guilds** or incorporations. Journeymen, as much as masters, felt that they had a duty to protect the skills and standing of the craft.

The usual form of industrial organization for the consumer trades (in which the craftsman retailed his own products), such as shoemaking, tailoring, and cabinetmaking, was that of a small workshop, where a master, journeymen, and apprentices might work side by side. Alternatively, groups of independent journeymen would hire work premises. Equally common was that a journeyman would be self-employed, working at home in the system of **domestic production**, helped by wife and family perhaps, taking work from and supplying finished goods to a number of different masters. Journeymen would own or rent tools, but receive raw materials from a master. This often meant weekly journeys to a master's shop, and delay while waiting for the raw material or for payment for the finished product. Payment was by the piece, and related to the quality of the finished product.

The rates paid were shaped by the standing of the craft and its customary relationship to other trades—not by supply and demand—and could occasionally involve payment in kind. **Wages** for **London** journeymen masons and weavers in 1770 ran about 15s. (75p) per week, and many complained that these had been fixed many decades earlier. Payment rates involved concepts of a "fair" or "just" wage, which could sometimes be tested in the courts. The time spent at work was largely the journeyman's own concern, and artisans placed much store on the right to control their own rhythm of work, though all trades were subject to a regular pattern of seasonal fluctuation. Even in those industries capitalized with fixed hours, such as **shipbuilding** or **housebuilding** or other building trades, the journeyman shipwright or mason owned his tools and exercised considerable independent control over the work processes. Possession of a skill was seen as the artisan's property, which brought with it a certain independence and certain rights, including that of passing these on to his children.

Within the craft workplace there were many customary practices controlled by the workmen. Rituals of initiation and of passage, usually accompanied by alcoholic **drinking**, were common excuses for leisure. The so-called Saint Monday day off persisted in some cases well into the 20th century. At the same time, shoemakers' and tailors' workshops had a reputation for self-education and political debate.

There was a steady erosion of these traditional patterns throughout the period. Technical changes were bringing about the displacement of many old crafts and the emergence of new ones, not covered by earlier legislation. The apprenticeship system was weakening: legal indentures gave way to informal agreements; the 1563 statute was not enforced, and many masters used apprentices merely as cheap labor. As the social gap between master and workman widened, there were fewer living-in apprenticeships. Craft guilds were abandoning the effort to control entry into the respective crafts. Expanding demand encouraged the expansion of crafts. Many employers were keen to enlarge their workforce much faster than regular apprenticeship practice would allow. Controlling the number of master craftsmen was no longer realistic; regulating the number of apprentices was abandoned.

Gradually the distinctive tasks associated with producing goods came to be subdivided, with new workers being taught only one part of the job. The term *shoemaker* or *tailor* no longer meant someone who could produce a complete pair of shoes, or a **clothing-maker** of great knowledge and experience, but was applied to a huge number of half-trained, half-skilled workers. Formal controls over prices and wages gave way under competitive pressures, and supply and demand in the labor market increasingly came to determine wage rates. By the end of the 18th century, many crafts had "honorable" and "dishonorable" divisions. The former sought to maintain

A comb-maker, 1805

some semblance of traditional regulation; the latter went for cheapness and division of labor. As markets widened from local to regional and national ones, the distribution of goods fell increasingly into the hands of merchant capitalists or "manufacturers," who were not necessarily themselves working at the trade. This imposed new disciplines on craftsmen. Through their agents, the manufacturers would impose a timetable for delivery and impose tighter control of quality; artisans lost much of their independence. In 1814 the repeal of the Statute of Artificers, removing restrictions on trade entry, formalized a situation that had long existed. Other repealing legislation ensured that the courts could no longer regulate wage rates.

As customary patterns were eroded, journeymen began to develop mutual aid organizations. Initially these were essentially trade funds to provide some resources for widows and orphans, but gradually these expanded into **friendly societies** providing insurance for sickness, tool loss, and old age, and for the all-important decent funeral. Some developed into defensive organizations to protect the customs of the craft and to resist the pressures on **hours, wages, and working conditions**, which the advance of capitalism was bringing. They became a way of trying to regulate entry into the craft and of checking the qualifications of the rapidly expanding labor force. Many craft societies developed houses of call in particular **public houses** where new workers could register for work and have their credentials checked by the society, and where employers, seeking laborers, could find workers.

By the early 19th century, many such societies were developing into **trade unions**. These saw their role as protecting against hostile employers the interests of journeymen who could expect to remain wage-earners throughout their working lives. The sense of a common community of craft had given way to a relationship based on what Thomas Carlyle (1795–1881) called the "cash nexus." With continuing rapid **urbanization**, especially in the 1820s and 1830s, craft unions fought a losing battle against the increased undermining of their skills and status that accompanied expanding capitalism.

W. Hamish Fraser

Bibliography

Fraser, W. Hamish. *Conflict and Class: Scottish Workers, 1700–1838.* 1988.

Prothero, Iorwerth. *Artisans and Politics in Early Nineteenth Century London.* 1979.

Rule, J.G. *The Experience of Labour in Eighteenth Century England.* 1981.

———. *The Labouring Classes in Early Industrial England, 1750–1850.* 1986.

Thompson, E.P. *The Making of the English Working Class.* 1965.

See also Factory Workers; Farmers and Agricultural Laborers; Industrial Revolution; Labor Laws, Movements, and Unions; Servants; Standard of Living

Crawshay Family

The Crawshay family, which rose from obscurity to control the world's largest **iron** manufacturing concern at Cyfartha, South **Wales**, was controlled by a succession of classic industrial "iron barons." Richard (1739–1810), the founder of the dynasty, ran away from Normanton, Yorkshire, for **London** (1755), where, through hard work and marriage to his employer's daughter, he quickly rose to control an iron-trading business. In 1777 he moved into iron manufacturing by setting up a partnership with a rich London merchant, **Anthony Bacon**, who 10 years earlier had built the first furnace at Cyfartha. Although never the sole controller of the works, Crawshay, even while retaining his London iron-trading partnership, was the enduring member of several partnerships that expanded the complex until it occupied a leading place in the industry.

Despite employing very gifted managers, Richard Crawshay was almost obsessive in his concern with every detail of the business. Quick to appreciate the advantage of improved **transport** links, he became the main promoter of the Glamorganshire Canal. Central to his success was his immediate support for **Henry Cort**'s puddling process, developed at Cyfartha to become a practical working technique. Profits, often exceeding 80%, were plowed into expansion, the output of bar-iron rising from 500 tons in 1784 to 10,000 tons in 1809. On Richard's death in 1810, his son William (1764–1834) inherited what was considered the largest iron-producing complex in the world. He continued to develop the business through considerable ingenuity, securing sole control and placing Richard's grandson William II (1788–1867) in charge. He in turn became an archetypal ironmaster and the leading figure in the industry in the closing years of the Hanoverian period.

R.D. Corrins

Bibliography

Addis, J.P. *The Crawshay Dynasty.* 1957.

Birch, A. *The Economic History of the British Iron and Steel Industry 1784–1879.* 1967.

Crouzet, F. *The First Industrialists.* 1985.

Harris, J.R. *The British Iron Industry 1700–1850.* 1988.

See also Entrepreneurs and Entrepreneurship; Metallurgy and Metalworking; Science; Technology, and Invention; Welsh Industry

Crime

Aside from acts of political subversion, most 18th-century crimes fit into two categories: traditional crime, including such transgressions as murder and robbery; and social crime, in which the perpetrator did not often consider a given action a crime.

Social crime, which was very common, included such acts as shipyard workers taking wood and other material ("chips") from the docks, and tailors' apprentices walking off with cloth cuttings ("cabbage") from the shop. The distinction between such acts and ordinary theft rested on the employee's belief that by customary rights he was entitled to such scraps. It was because of this that throughout much of the Hanoverian period, perceived customary rights became the targets of severe punitive legislation. The **Black Act** of 1723, for example, created numerous capital crimes related to **poaching**, even while many poachers continued to consider hunting their natural right. **Smuggling**, often a community effort, may be counted in this category as well. An important theme of Hanoverian social history was this class struggle over customary rights, which time and time again became criminalized by the stroke of the legislator's pen.

When exhibited openly in collective action, the struggle for perceived customary rights might take the form of rioting, which under the **Riot Act** (1715) could be deemed a felony if 12 or more people were involved. Thus **riots** of any substantial size could incur the death penalty. Until relatively recently, historians accepted the judgment of contemporaries that rioting was the work of chaotic and violent crowds. However, some investigators have produced studies indicating that rioters were coherent and rational not only in their purposes but in their behavior. The many food riots, the protests in favor of **John Wilkes** in 1768, and the devastating **Gordon Riots** (1780) have several things in common: The crowd did little physical injury to anyone, it had a fairly definite agenda and purpose, and those involved felt that they were only demanding their "rights" (even though to the upper classes they were perceived as criminals).

A bird in the hand 's worth two in the bush.

Removing the evidence of a crime

The thought of 18th-century traditional crimes conjures up names like those of Dick Turpin, the famous **highwayman**; Jack Sheppard, whose miraculous escapes from the condemned hold at Newgate prison are legendary; and Catherine Hayes, who was burned at the stake (1726) for her part in the gruesome murder of her husband. However, the bulk of traditional crime was much less sensational. It usually involved minor theft, and was closely connected to **poverty**. In the countryside, the level of traditional crime generally reflected economic conditions. Unemployment and rising prices, especially of food, often caused a corresponding sharp increase in crime level, and the objects of theft were often food and **clothing**. In **urban** centers, especially **London**, although a high level of crime existed throughout the period, notable increases in theft occurred during the periods immediately following **wars**. The inability of returning sailors and soldiers to find sufficient employment to sustain themselves and their families seems to have caused many normally law-abiding folk to resort to crime. In short, a considerable amount of contemporary criminal activity may be ascribed to desperate economic need.

Crime was professional only in London. The infamous Johnathan Wild, hanged in 1725, is credited with the founding of "organized crime." Though billing himself attractively as the "Thief-Taker General" of England and **Ireland**, he in fact, until he got caught, ran a gang of thieves which he disciplined by turning over the unruly ones to the authorities for one of the parliamentary rewards established from the 1690s for the capture and conviction of highway robbers and other criminals. Never missing a trick, Wild also fenced many of the stolen goods back to their original owners, who generally asked no questions. It has been suggested that Wild merely expanded and improved on a system of receiving and disposing of stolen property utilized by such artful criminals as Mary Frith ("Moll Cutpurse") in the previous century. At any rate, the gangs that operated in this period, such as the Black Boy Alley Gang and the Gregory Gang (whose membership included Dick Turpin), indicate the continued expansion of the criminal population. Their members communicated with each other in the so-called **London** sanctuaries and "Flash-Houses," protected by the twisted alleys and courts that were the product of the unregulated growth and building of London during the 17th century. While sanctuaries such as the Whitefriars, the Mint, and the Savoy—previously the sites of religious orders and traditionally providing a measure of immunity from arrest—were largely suppressed between 1697 and 1721, many other areas of London, in which few constables would venture forth, existed throughout much of the Hanoverian period.

From the 1750s on, better policing, lighting, and other urban improvements represented the main method of reducing these strongholds of criminal training, association, and refuge. In these strongholds, gangs of footpads, receivers of stolen property, highwaymen, shoplifters, and pickpockets developed their criminal careers and communicated in their own jargon ("cant"). Yet most gangs were in fact loose and usually short-lived, exhibiting little internal cohesion; the only significant exceptions being the gangs of poachers and smugglers, operating in the countryside, who in fact were fairly well organized. Moreover, even in London, despite the steady stream of criminal activity and the most brazen acts of lawlessness (which went largely unchecked in the first half of the century), most crime consisted of minor theft, often from the workplace and often supplementing or temporarily sustaining the livelihoods of the laboring poor.

The overall picture of contemporary crime levels is still unclear and in dispute. Some investigators believe that for Britain as a whole, crime levels were constantly rising. Others suggest that the amount of crime, at least in some areas, declined until about 1750 (the increasing severity of punishment may have had something to do with this), then rose in the last quarter of the 18th century. The bulk crime rate certainly did rise in the latter half of the Hanoverian period, but when the definitional ambiguity of criminal action and also normal **population** increases are taken into account, this may not seem particularly meaningful. In London, where crime levels were always high, it is likely that the entire period 1700–1750 saw a higher proportional number of traditional crimes than the period 1750–1775. But many investigators feel that after the 1780s, London's crime rate began to climb again, and continued to do so through the first quarter of the 19th century.

What seems more clear is the fact that reported criminal *violence* diminished after 1750. Humanitarian changes in attitude toward the family, children, and even animals have been cited as the chief reason for this. Most violence then (as now) evidently took place between persons who knew each other; perhaps some 50% of all murders took place within families, and the greater proportion of murders involved persons with close personal ties of one sort or another. It should also be noted that with the exception of cases involving footpads (armed robbers on foot), there was, throughout the period, a very low incidence of violence and of homicide connected with thefts.

The relative decline after 1750 of reported acts of criminal violence does not necessarily mean that a great deal of casual violence did not take place. There is no question that London, especially in the earlier part of the period, was an extremely violent **city**. And the contemporary acceptance of violence, especially as regarded male abuse of wives and children, undoubtedly conceals from modern research the entire magnitude of the problem. Unless a homicide or very serious injury occurred, many violent acts went unreported. The notorious case of Elizabeth Brownrigg exemplifies how far things might go before the law was called upon to intervene. Brownrigg had literally tortured her servants for several years, but it was not until one of them died as a result that she was brought to justice and hanged (1767). The patriarchal structure of the contemporary **judicial system** contributed to this situation. Few juries would take a servant's word over a master's, or a wife's over a husband's. Moreover, the servant's livelihood and the wife's economic and social welfare were largely dependent on the good graces of their abusers.

Similar conditions surrounded many rapes. The master's position over his female **servants** placed the latter in a very vulnerable position. Children, too, were extremely vulnerable to "legal" rapes, since the age of consent had been set at age 10 in the 16th century; the molesting of 11-year-old servant girls could take place with impunity. Ironically, while child-abuse and wife-abuse seem to have been in decline after 1750, the number of reported rape cases seems to have risen at the same time. Possibly this may be attributed to a greater willingness to prosecute rape during this period of growing **humanitarianism** and **sensibility**. But despite the diminution of violence toward children and women, and an increasing reaction against it by contemporaries, it should be remembered that until the early 19th century, British society and law permitted a great deal of violence: public whippings, executions, and the torture of animals for **sport** continued throughout most of the 18th century. The transition away from a culture of physical violence was a gradual one.

Finally, it may be noted that women made up a very small percentage of those committing traditional crimes. They committed relatively few property crimes or homicides; and in most cases, when a woman did commit homicide, it was in a domestic situation, often involving infanticide. In urban settings, women in desperate economic circumstances were more likely to gravitate toward **prostitution** than thievery, though prostitutes often became involved in property crime as accomplices or as a receivers of stolen goods.

Stanley D. Nash

Bibliography

Beattie, J.M. *Crime and the Courts in England, 1660–1800.* 1986.

Brewer, John, and John Styles, eds. *An Ungovernable People: The English and Their Law in the Seventeenth and Eighteenth Centuries.* 1980.

Cockburn, J.S., ed. *Crime in England, 1550–1800.* 1977.

Emsley, Clive. *Crime and Society in England, 1750–1900.* 1987.

Hay, Douglas, and Francis Snyder, eds. *Policing and Prosecution in Britain, 1750–1850.* 1989.

Innes, Joanna, and John Styles. "The Crime Wave: Recent Writing on Crime and Criminal Justice in Eighteenth-Century England." *Journal of British Studies.* Vol. 25, pp. 380–435.

Linebaugh, Peter. *The London Hanged: Crime and Civil Society in the Eighteenth Century.* 1992.

McLynn, Frank. *Crime and Punishment in Eighteenth-Century England.* 1989.

McMullan, John L. *The Canting Crew: London's Criminal Underworld, 1550–1700.* 1984.

Rudé, George. *The Crowd in History: A Study of Popular Disturbances in France and England, 1730–1848.* 1959; rev. ed., 1981.

Stevenson, John. *Popular Disturbances in England, 1700–1870.* 1979.

Thompson, F.M.L., ed. *The Cambridge Social History of Britain, 1750–1950.* 3 vols. 1990.

See also Criminality in Literature; Law Enforcement; Poverty and Poor Laws; Prisons and Prison Reform; Punishment

Criminality in Literature

Early-18th-century literature delighted readers with the cleverly criminal adventures of **Defoe**'s *Moll Flanders* (1722) and **Henry Fielding**'s *Jonathan Wild* (1743). Specialized dictionaries of criminal language and stories of real criminals in *The Newgate Calendar* (1824) titillated audiences, as did tales of prostitutes and their procurers. Investigation of **crime** took on an urgent social dimension in **Gay**'s *Beggar's Opera* (1728), a sympathetic appreciation of a criminal underworld and, increasingly, **Romantic** literature of the latter 18th century pondered the political and psychological foundations of crime.

Picaresque and **satirical** literature about criminals, specialized in by early novelists such as Defoe, Fielding, and **Smollett**, took on a more thoughtful aspect in the age of **George III**. There was a deeper analysis of the foundations of law itself, and growing **humanitarian** appeals for constitutional and legal reform helped to condition artistic attitudes. As liberty was more deeply examined, tyranny was more willingly perceived to justify retaliation; the boundaries between crime, deeds of protest, and acts of conscience wavered.

In the wake of the **American** and **French revolutions**, John **Milton**'s Satan was reinterpreted as a brave rebel defying tyranny, and hence as a model for literary heroes such as **Blake**'s Los, **Shelley**'s Prometheus, and **Byron**'s Bonnivard in "The Prisoner of Chillon" (1816). **Wordsworth**'s play *The Borderers* (1796) explored the violence which power sometimes seems to necessitate; his prose introduction to this play speculated on the criminal mind. In Byron's dramas and romances, the brooding outlaws (**Byronic Heroes**) Manfred, Cain, and Lara commit crimes in exercising their freedom on the outskirts of a political system far more cruel than their rebelliously individualistic deeds.

Absolute definitions of crime were further called into question by a new **sentimental** stress on environment and circumstance, upbringing and education, variations in culture and **manners**. There was a tendency, particularly strong in the period 1770–1790, for writers to embrace the lower classes and extol them largely as "the people." In "the simple annals of the poor," newly recognized as significant, hunger and **poverty** might explain, if not exonerate, **poaching**, robbery, even infanticide and murder. As **Coleridge** proclaimed in his *Lectures 1795*, a government that neither feeds nor instructs its poor "hangs the victim for crimes, to which its own most sinful omissions had supplied the cause and the temptation."

The hero of **Godwin**'s novel *Caleb Williams* (1794) is one of the first criminals to be pushed to the edge, harried and deprived by his aristocratic doppelganger until he cannot help but strike back. The murders committed by the monster in *Frankenstein* (1818) and the monster's flight to escape punishment may have been modeled by **Mary Shelley** on this novel by Godwin, her father. Women's crimes were similarly pitied as the result of a cruel social system. When the "youthful harlot" "blights with plagues the marriage hearse" in Blake's poem "London" (1795), she does so in the context of a society that degrades all children, chimney sweeps, chamber maids, and juvenile cotton workers.

The Romantic investigation of the political and social roots of crime was reinforced by the empirical probing of the psychologically divided being, an exploration that found in the collision of multiple inner impulses the deep Romantic chasms from which the will to destruction (as well as to creativity) may arise. In Coleridge's *Rime of the Ancient Mariner* (1798) the opening crime is impulsive, the punishment disproportionally cruel and endless—something that suggests this collision and that also probes the foundations of criminal remorse. In his *Confessions of an English Opium Eater* (1821), **De Quincey** sought in dreams of crime the irrationality that imbued the real world with dread. The will to destruction was so fascinating to Romantics that it verged on the admirable, partly for the sole reason that it represented a primal expression of energy, revolutionary impulse, and imaginative power.

All this growing sympathy with the criminal, whether seen as justified, or driven, or even heroic, was paralleled by more concerted efforts in the practical world to control crime, strengthen **law enforcement**, improve **prisons**, and review the system of **punishments**. **Patrick Colquhoun** and **Robert Peel** worked to regulate **public houses** as breeding grounds of crime, and to establish the first metropolitan **police** forces. The reform of prisons was undertaken gradually. There can be little doubt that the greater understanding of crime engendered by Hanoverian fiction and **poetry** played a significant role in these and in many related improvements.

Anya Taylor

Bibliography

Bell, Ian A. *Literature and Crime in Augustan England.* 1991.
Cockburn, J.S., ed. *Crime in England, 1550–1800.* 1977.
Friedland, M.L., ed. *Rough Justice: Essays on Crime in Literature.* 1991.
McGowen, Randall. "The Body and Punishment in Eighteenth-Century England." *Journal of Modern History.* Vol. 59, pp. 651–679.
Taylor, Anya, ed. *Romanticism and Criminal Justice.* Special Edition, *The Wordsworth Circle.* Vol. 19.

Croker, John Wilson (1780–1857)

Croker, one of the leading literary figures of the **Tory** party, was a powerful debater in the **House of Commons** (1807–1830), a chief contributor to the *Quarterly Review* (from 1811), and founder of the Athenaeum Club (1824). In years when party rancor raged, he played an important role in the influential **periodical** literature of the day by writing vigorously in support of traditional institutions and views.

Born in **Ireland** and educated at Trinity College, Dublin, and Lincoln's Inn, he made his parliamentary debut with a speech and subsequent pamphlet, *A Sketch of the State of Ireland, Past and Present* (1808), which led to close alliances with **Canning**, **Perceval**, and the **Duke of Wellington**. Croker's political contacts and acerbic pen made him invaluable at the ultra–Tory *Quarterly*, and he is remembered for his strident criticism of **Keats**'s *Endymion* (1818) and Tennyson's *Poems* (1832). A great admirer of the **classicism** of **Pope**, he disapproved of the **radicalism** of the new school of **poetry** as represented by **Hunt**, **Shelley**, and **Keats**, whom he indicted not only for the subversiveness of their supposed religious and political views but also for their innovations in meter and diction.

Alice D. Fasano

John Wilson Croker

Samuel Crompton

Bibliography

Brighton, Myron F. *John Wilson Croker.* 1940.

Morton, Peter F. *Literary Critics and Reviewers in Early 19th-Century Britain.* 1983.

Pool, Bernard, ed. *The Croker Papers: 1808–1857.* 1884; new ed., 1967.

Shattock, Joanne. *Politics and Reviewers:* The Edinburgh *and* The Quarterly *in the Early Victorian Age.* 1989.

See also Romanticism and Romantic Style

Crompton, Samuel (1753–1827)

Crompton, inventor of the cotton **spinning** mule, was typical of those who benefited little from the technical advances they made possible. Born in 1753 in the then physically isolated community of Bolton-le-Moors, he used **James Hargreaves**'s jenny (with eight spindles) to produce yarn, which he then wove into quilting fabrics. Dissatisfied with the yarn's quality, in 1774 he began construction of his mule, so called because it combined features of the jenny with those of **Richard Arkwright**'s water frame.

This new machine had an innovative spindle carriage that reduced yarn breakage and initially operated with 20 to 30 spindles, but was capable of much greater output capacity and produced very fine yarn. Later developments by others turned this small hand machine into a fully powered giant instrument of **steam** production. Ironically, this technical progress was possible because Crompton did not patent his invention; its secrets were widely known, since for a small charge he displayed his mule in 1780 before representatives of leading **cotton** firms.

From the 1790s on, the mule dominated spinning technology, producing the fine threads required for newly popular fustians, calicoes, and muslins. But Crompton remained a small independent businessman with little capital while others made fortunes. He did not take his opportunities. Large firms offered him attractive partnerships, but he lacked the **entrepreneurial** vision and the will to exploit these chances. His psychology was against him; he was a brooding recluse, more interested at critical moments in Swedenborgian religion and organ music than in his personal fortune. As he grew older he became embittered and, despite a public subscription and a parliamentary grant, died a poor man.

John Butt

Bibliography

Catling, H. *The Spinning Mule.* 1970.

Chapman, S.D. *The Cotton Industry During the Industrial Revolution.* 2nd ed., 1987.

Edwards, M.M. *The Growth of the British Cotton Trade 1780–1815.* 1967.

English, Walter. *The Textile Industry.* 1969.

French, Gilbert J. *Life and Times of Samuel Crompton.* 1970 ed., with intro. by S.D. Chapman.

See also Science, Technology, and Invention

Crowley Family

The Crowley family **iron** business is significant in that it was already a major industrial concern at the beginning of the Hanoverian period, a forerunner of what the **Industrial Revolution** was to bring. The founder was the illiterate nailer Ambrose I (1635–1721), who rose to significance as an iron merchant and ironworks owner. His son, Ambrose II (born in 1658), became a leading wholesale ironmonger who integrated backward, setting up extensive works at Winlaton linked to a **London** headquarters and to warehouses throughout England.

Pioneers in the emerging industrial world, the Crowleys regulated every facet of the business. Their managers used a comprehensive system of regulations in their "Law Book," which governed all commercial and industrial activities in their combined factory and domestic concern, and every aspect of its unusual internal social welfare system.

Wartime demand after 1689, particularly from the **navy**, ensured considerable profits, and Ambrose II became a leading London figure, knighted in 1707, and an M.P. in 1713 (the year of his death). His son John led the firm until his premature death in 1728, but it was John's widow, Theodosia, who became the key figure during the next 54 years. Her sons Ambrose III (who came of age in 1739 but died in 1754) and John II (*d.* 1755) were of secondary importance. Day-to-day control of the largest ironworks in Europe was exercised by professional managers, but Theodosia presided over the iron business and the landed estates, and managed to hold a leading position in London society. After her death, the firm was reorganized as Crowley Millington and Company, Millington being the latest of the managers, but it lost its leading position and went into decline after 1815. The works were eventually sold in 1863.

R.D. Corrins

Bibliography

Flinn, M.W. *Men of Iron: The Crowleys in the Early Iron Industry.* 1962.

Harris, J.R. *The British Iron Industry 1700–1850.* 1988.

Cruikshank, George (1792–1878)

As a **caricaturist** and **book illustrator**, Cruikshank ranks among the most popular and prolific practitioners of his art. He developed his talents under his father, Isaac Cruikshank (1756–1810), himself a popular illustrator and caricaturist. From 1811 on he achieved notoriety for his comic drawings and irreverent social **satires** and **political prints**, which appeared in such publications as the *Scourge,* the *Satirist,* and the *Meteor.* Ridiculing folly wherever he found it, he spared none from his often grotesquely exaggerated caricatures. His dynamic technique helped to establish him as successor to the great **James Gillray**, the leading English caricaturist of his father's generation.

While he continued to publish political satires, Cruikshank in 1820 began illustrating books as well. Some of his best-known etchings accompany Pierce Egan's *Life in London* (1821), Chamisso's *Peter Schlemihl* (1823), Grimm's *German Popular Stories* (1824–1826), and Dickens's *Sketches by Boz* (1836–1837) and *Oliver Twist* (1838). In all, Cruikshank illustrated more than 860 books, and was a pioneer in providing comic scenes for **children's literature**. In addition, he published many books of illustrations himself; his serial *The Comic Almanack* (1835–1853) was especially successful.

Cruikshank's satirical style was often a bizarre mixture of the comic and the grotesque. The borders of his etchings sometimes seem barely able to contain the crowded movement and intensity of the distorted figures within. His genius for more benevolent humor emerges in his later book illustrations.

Michael F. Suarez, S.J.

George Cruikshank

Bibliography

Bryant, Mark, ed. *The Comic Cruikshank.* 1992.

Buchanan-Brown, John. *The Book Illustrations of George Cruikshank.* 1980.

Jones, Michael Wynn. *George Cruikshank: His Life and London.* 1978.

Patten, Robert L. *George Cruikshank's Life, Times and Art. Volume 1: 1792–1835.* 1992.

———, ed. *George Cruikshank: A Revaluation.* 1974.

Wardropper, John. *The Caricatures of George Cruikshank.* 1977.

See also Drawing; Engraving; Graphic Arts

Cullen, William (1710–1790)

Cullen was an eminent medical figure of the **Scottish Enlightenment**. Born in Hamilton, Lanarkshire, he studied **medicine** at Glasgow University, graduating M.D. (1740) and becoming lecturer in medicine and related subjects (1744). In his private practice at Hamilton he instructed **William Hunter**, while **Joseph Black** was one of the students he encouraged at the university. The university's medical curriculum was not yet well organized, and Cullen lectured on botany as well as chemistry and medicine. His unusual lecturing abilities were confirmed by the unauthorized publication of his lectures (1771), which realized many editions.

First appointed professor of medicine at Glasgow in 1751, he soon moved to **Edinburgh** as professor of chemistry (1756), there continuing his private practice and lecturing on clinical medicine at the Royal Infirmary. In 1766 he became the Professor of Medicine and, on the death of John Gregory (1724–1773), the Professor for the Practice of Physic. He published *Institutions of Medicine* (1770), *First Lines of the Practice of Physic* (1774), and *Synopsis Nosologicae Medicae* (1785), in which he set up a fourfold classification of diseases.

Although he made no path-breaking discoveries, Cullen was highly regarded in his own lifetime, and his teaching and publications influenced several generations who helped to keep **Scotland** in the vanguard of later Hanoverian medicine.

Ian Donnachie

Bibliography

Chitnins, Anand. *The Scottish Enlightenment: A Social History.* 1976.

Risse, G.B. "Dr William Cullen, Physician, Edinburgh." *Bulletin of the History of Medicine.* Vol. 48, pp. 338–351.

See also Science, Technology, and Invention

Culloden, Battle of (1746)

The defeat of the Jacobite army near Culloden Moor, 5 miles east of Inverness, on 16 April 1746 by the **Duke of Cumberland**, marked the end of the **Forty-five** and of the Stuarts' claim to the throne. The defeat was both symbolic and military. The site was poorly chosen for the lightly armed **Jacobites**, and tactical errors contributed to their defeat. Cumberland, the government commander, had trained his men to withstand the initial Highland charge, and the rebels were slaughtered by the superior firepower of the Hanoverian army. In 40 minutes a thousand of the 5,000-man Jacobite force were killed, whereas Cumberland lost only 50 of his 9,000 men.

The battle was also noted for the savagery with which Cumberland put down the rebels, earning him the title of the "Butcher." Their leader, **Charles Edward, the Young Pretender**, fled, leaving his men to the mercy of the enemy. Repression of the **clan** system followed, with estates being confiscated, possession of arms forbidden, tartans proscribed, and even the playing of bagpipes outlawed. In later times, Culloden was given a sentimental gloss and treated as the end of a romantic era; the "loyal clans" were extolled for their bravery and devotion, and even Queen Victoria would proclaim herself a Jacobite at heart.

Richard Finlay

Bibliography

Lenman, B. *The Jacobite Cause.* 1985.

Speck, W.A. *The Butcher.* 1980.

See also Forfeited Estates Commission; Highland Regiments; Lovat, 11th Baron

Cumberland, Duke of (1721–1765)

Born William Augustus, the third son of **King George II**, Cumberland had a distinguished military and political career. His military service included campaigns in the Low Countries during the **War of Austrian Succession** and the defeat of the **Jacobite** rebellion at **Culloden** Moor (1746).

Although Cumberland's campaign to pacify the Scottish Highlands after the **Forty-five** earned him the nickname "Butcher," his program of **road** building and surveying secured Britain from the threat of another rebellion. As Captain-General (1745) in the **army** his stern and dutiful atten-

William Augustus, Duke of Cumberland

tion to military discipline, though unfortunate for some undercommanders such as **James Oglethorpe**, helped to prepare the officers who achieved the colonial conquests of the 1750s. Between 1751 and 1757 he often presided over meetings of the Lords Justices who governed during George II's absences overseas. His influence over preparations for the colonial and European struggles with **France** was of great importance.

During the **Seven Years' War**, when Cumberland's father refused to accept the terms of his capitulation to the French at Klosterzeven (1757), he suffered disgrace and retired from public life. He returned in the wake of the **Stamp Act** crisis (1765) to help form the **Rockingham** ministry, holding cabinet meetings at his own house. He thus sponsored a second generation of **Whig** politicians. His **landscaping** of the Great Park at Windsor remains his monument to the cultural taste of his age. Many contemporaries thought him the most able member of the Hanoverian dynasty.

Robert D. McJimsey

Bibliography

Rogers, Nicholas. *Whigs and Cities: Popular Politics in the Age of Walpole and Pitt.* 1990.

Trench, C.C. *George II.* 1973.

Whitworth, Rex. "William Augustus, Duke of Cumberland." *History Today.* Vol. 27, pp. 82–91.

Cumberland, Richard (1732–1813)

Descended from **Richard Bentley** on his mother's side and a family of bishops on his father's, the dramatist left a promising academic career at Cambridge for one of political preferment, first as Private Secretary to Lord Halifax (1716–1771), and later as Secretary of the Board of Trade under **Lord George Germain**.

While serving in these capacities he began writing for the **theater**. His fame was established by the productions of *The Brothers* (1769) at Covent Garden, and *The West Indian* (1771)

Richard Cumberland

and *The Fashionable Lover* (1772) at Drury Lane. These successes led to a close association with **David Garrick**, though Cumberland's other duties sometimes employed him elsewhere. After an undercover mission to Spain (1780) he resumed writing for the stage. The productions of *The Jew* (1794) and *The Wheel of Fortune* (1795) reestablished him as a leading dramatist.

In addition to more than 40 dramas and miscellaneous **poetry** and prose, Cumberland published *Anecdotes of Eminent Painters in Spain* (1782); *The Observer* (1786–1790); three **novels**, *Arundel* (1789), *Henry* (1785), and *John of Lancaster* (1809); *Calvary* (1792), an **epic** poem; and his *Memoirs* (1806–1807).

Richard J. Dircks

Bibliography

Bemis, Samuel Flagg. *The Hussey-Cumberland Mission and American Independence.* 1931.

Dircks, Richard J. *Richard Cumberland.* 1976.

———, ed. *The Letters of Richard Cumberland.* 1988.

———, ed. *The Unpublished Plays of Richard Cumberland.* 2 vols. 1991–1992.

Williams, Stanley. *Richard Cumberland: His Life and Dramatic Works.* 1917.

See also Diplomats and Diplomacy; Dramatic Arts

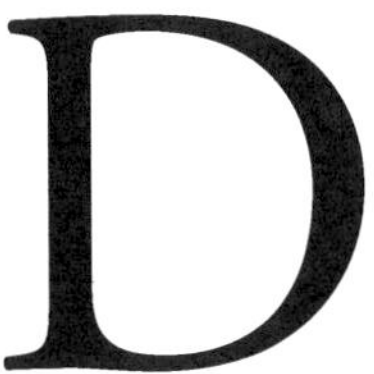

Dale, David (1739–1806)

The son of a general dealer, Dale became a successful **Glasgow** businessman. Apprenticed to a **Paisley** weaver, he gravitated through the "putting out" system to become by 1763 a **textile** merchant. In 1777 he married Ann Caroline Campbell, daughter of a director of the **Royal Bank of Scotland**, and in 1783 became the bank's Glasgow agent. Dale combined banking with **cotton** manufacturing, having many business interests, including mills at **New Lanark**. Genial and philanthropic, he was a Glasgow magistrate and a committed **Evangelical** Christian. He is also remembered as the father-in-law of **Robert Owen**, to whom he sold New Lanark in 1799.

John Butt

Bibliography

Black, William G. *David Dale's House.* 1908.

Butt, John. *Robert Owen, Prince of Cotton Spinners.* 1971.

Donnachie, Ian, and George Hewitt. *Historic New Lanark.* 1993.

McLaren, David J. *David Dale of New Lanark.* 1983.

Dalrymple, Alexander (1737–1808)

Dalrymple's lengthy experience in the **East India Company** made him a tireless promoter of **overseas commerce**. His related interest in **exploration** led the **Royal Society** to propose him to lead the transit of Venus expedition in 1768, but his insistence upon receiving naval command led to his replacement by **Captain Cook**, whose voyages exploded Dalrymple's vision of a populous Antarctic continent ripe for British trade.

Appointed Hydrographer to the East India Company in 1779, and first Hydrographer to the Admiralty in 1795, Dalrymple's talents were well employed in organizing a department to chart the seas. Unfortunately the destruction of his pet theories about **Antarctica** and the Northwest Passage, and his quarrelsome personality and dismissal by the Admiralty in 1808, long overshadowed his considerable contributions to trade, exploration, and hydrography.

N. Merrill Distad

Bibliography

Dalrymple, Sir Alexander. "Memoirs of Alexander Dalrymple, Esq." *European Magazine.* Vol. 42 (1802), pp. 323–328, 421–424; revised and updated as "Biographical Memoir of Alexander Dalrymple, Esq.," in *The Naval Chronicle,* Vol. 35 (1816), pp. 177–204.

Day, Vice-Admiral Sir Archibald. *The Admiralty Hydrographic Service, 1795–1919.* 1967.

Fry, Howard Tyrrell. *Alexander Dalrymple (1737–1808) and the Expansion of British Trade.* 1970.

Ritchie, Rear-Admiral George Stephen. *The Admiralty Chart: British Naval Hydrography in the Nineteenth Century.* 1967.

Dalton, John (1766–1844)

Dalton, "father of modern atomic theory" but known also for many other contributions to chemistry and physics, was born in Eaglesfield, Cumberland, the son of a **Quaker** weaver. He was mostly self-taught. In 1781, when only 15 years old, he moved to Kendal to assist at a school run by his cousin; he and his brother became its proprietors in 1785. Here he completed his own education, studying mathematics, zoology, and botany. In 1787 he commenced a journal of **meteorology** which he maintained throughout his life, recording over 200,000 entries.

Dalton moved to **Manchester** (1793) as Professor of Mathematics at New College, taking private pupils afterward when the college moved to York. An intuitive scientific genius, he was socially reserved, less than outstanding as a lecturer, and so independent-minded that he was apt to scorn or ignore other researchers. Nonetheless, he was president of the Manchester Literary and Philosophical society for 27 years. He revealed his discovery of color-blindness ("Daltonism") in 1794, and made important contributions to the studies of meteorology and aurora, proposing his Law of Partial Pressures in 1801. It was evidently while studying aqueous vapor that he made his most famous contribution to science, proposing his atomic theory (1807), which bridged the speculative at-

John Dalton

omism of the Greeks into modern physical theory by picturing how elements chemically combine at the level of differently weighted atoms to form molecular compounds. He lectured at the **Royal Institution** in 1804 and 1809, and was elected a fellow of the **Royal Society** in 1822. Over 40,000 people attended his funeral in Manchester.

Jim Burton

Bibliography

Cardwell, D.S.L., ed. *John Dalton and the Progress of Science.* 1968.

Golinski, Jan. *Science as Public Culture: Chemistry and Enlightenment in Britain, 1760–1820.* 1992.

Greenaway, F. *John Dalton and the Atom.* 1967.

Patterson, Elizabeth C. *John Dalton and the Atomic Theory.* 1970.

See also Science, Technology, and Invention

Dance

The subject of dance in the Hanoverian age may be divided into two areas, with the understanding that in reality there were many connections between these. On the one side, there was social dancing by amateurs; on the other, there was professional dancing by artists who made a living at it. What both areas had in common throughout the period was a tendency to be influenced greatly by fashions from abroad, and an evolutionary movement toward more fluid, free, emotional, and spectacular forms.

Dancing as a profession included both professional dancing-masters who trained the children of the well-off, and people who danced at various set performances, particularly in the **theater.** It must be remembered that British theaters of the early 18th century presented many different forms of entertainment. Besides comedies and tragedies there were Italian, French, and English **operas**, pantomimes, and other productions. Within these, dance often played an important role. Country dances were sometimes performed as a finale by the principals of a play, and "grotesques," or dances in character, were performed between acts or as entrées within plays and operas. Abstract duos often shared the stage with comic tumblers and Harlequins from the Italian commedia dell'arte tradition, appearing alternately as entrées and entr'actes in plays, operas, and pantomimes. Other duos and solos also appeared, using the classic steps of French noble technique (the famous "noble style" was developed in the court of Louis XIV during the latter 17th century) for such dances as bourrée, canary, chaconne, gavotte, gigue, menuet, passepied, sarabande, and two specifically English genres, the triple-time hornpipe and a duple-time rigadoon.

Professional requirements as well as the scientific bent of the age led to a gradual systematization of knowledge regarding dance. The publication of Raoul Auger Feuillet's *Chorégraphie* (1700) made available a system of notation for preserving and distributing composed dances. The first collection of theatrical dances to appear in print was by Anthony L'Abbé (*fl.* 1698–1737), dancing master to the family of **George I.** The special importance of French dance styles in the early 18th century is underlined by the numerous treatises translated from the French, many in several editions. Translations of Feuillet's works by P. Siris and John Essex appeared (1706–1710); in 1728 Essex published a translation of Pierre Rameau's *Le Maître à Danser* (1725), and in 1735 Kellom Tomlinson's *The Art of Dancing* appeared.

But the most important English contributor to this systematizing trend was **John Weaver**, who staged his first ballet in London in 1702; translated Feuillet's book; and set about placing English dance on a scientific basis, writing works on its history, physiology, and relationship to music. He believed that noble dance lacked feeling and that character dances were merely tricks and posturing. He also believed that dances should tell a story through gesture, facial expressions, and mime. Turning to **classical** Rome for inspiration, he composed *The Loves of Mars and Venus* (1717), a path-breaking piece that has been called the first ballet en action and a forerunner of English pantomime.

In 1734, dancer–choreographer Marie Sallé (1707–1756) produced the ballet *Pygmalion* in **London**, followed soon afterward by *Bacchus & Ariadne.* In these ballets she continued the thrust begun by Weaver, introducing costume reforms and dancing in an expressive style. After 1750, three more important factors influenced dance's development. The first was the branching off of ballet as an independent artform; the second was the rise of centers of innovation other than Paris; the third, corresponding to other cultural trends, was the growing demand for a more natural style of dancing. One of the most important contributors here was Jean Georges Noverre (1727–1810), whose early development was influenced by his contact with Sallé and **David Garrick.** Noverre favored a "dramatic" as opposed to a "mechanical" type of dance. He promoted a vision of ballet en action as music, drama, chore-

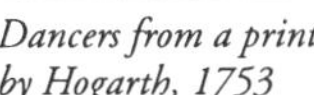

Dancers from a print by Hogarth, 1753

ography, and staging, with all parts subordinated to the general scheme; he also argued for greater variety of dancing styles to suit the various characters, and called for an end to virtuosity for its own sake.

In the 1780s, while demand for dancing at the playhouses gave way to increasing emphasis on singing, dancing at the opera house carried Noverre's ideas forward. Ballet masters arranged dances of every description, from simple Pas Seul to a "grand dramatic ballet in 3 acts in the Scotch style." The decorations and machinery for some of these larger pieces was spectacular, especially toward the close of the century, with dancers, chariots, and sets ascending and descending midair. In 1796, Charles Louis Didelot produced a divertissement using machinery to allow individual dancers to pose on tiptoe, heralding the introduction of pointe technique.

By the early 19th century, dances were being amalgamated into great melodramatic–balletic spectacles at the immense new theaters of Drury Lane and Covent Garden. With less formal dancing, and more processions and combats, these massive productions were devised to include large forces of dancers and supernumeraries. By the 1830s, the transition was complete. Dancing with which the audience felt kinetic familiarity was gone; dance had become a spectacle of fantasy.

Social dancing underwent a similar transition during the 123 years of the Hanoverian period. At the beginning of this period, and for much of its remainder, social dancing existed in three broad genres that corresponded roughly with social position. The lowest classes used dance for recreation as well as sundry employment. Their social dancing featured simple circle or line dances, reels, jigs, clog dances, and solo or duo stepping dances. In some localities, especially in Scotland, various forms of ritual and ceremonial dances flourished, preserved by families who closely guarded their forms. Sword and morris dances functioned as both social recreations and theatrical events. Gifted step dancers, rope dancers, and dance–acrobats found employment at fairs and on local stages.

At court, and at the social functions of the **aristocracy**, minuets and choreographed solo and duo ballroom dances were favored. Based on the French "noble style," the technique of these dances was taut and controlled, yet they were performed without apparent effort. Until the 1790s the minuet provided the ceremonial opening of most formal social gatherings; at court, an entire evening was often occupied with only minuets.

Among the **gentry** and **merchant** classes, dancing was not merely an amusement but rather an indispensable part of a young person's training. Dance for all the upper classes was a social and theatrical art, its outward goal to give pleasure to participants and onlookers, its unannounced effect to reinforce social position and hierarchy. Dancing signified education, breeding, and social eligibility. Pupils learned ballroom minuets, and also progressive longways country dances, at public and private dancing schools, and exhibited their skills at balls, assemblies, and private parties.

Although the minuet was the chief ritual through which social aspirants could exhibit their learned skills, the most popular group dance was in fact the country dance, an urban ballroom dance for any number of couples arranged in lines, men facing women. In response to public demand and a competition between publishers, many new country dances were published between 1715 and 1730 with music by leading composers. Like the minuet, the country dance was a repetitive figure dance that could be performed at many levels of expertise. The chief requirement was good taste in selecting and fitting the dance to its music, using appropriate steps for the company. French technique was used by trained dancers in country dances throughout the century.

Historians of **manners**, politics, and the arts have noted increasing competition in the latter 18th century between middle-class and aristocratic forms, with aristocrats particularly favoring foreign fashions in hopes of underlining their own social superiority. Something similar can be seen in the realm of dance. As the **middle classes** became more adept at minuets and country dances, elite social dancers and the masters who trained them concentrated on the more difficult or exotic dances. In 1772, Giovanni Gallini (1728–1805) affirmed that the dances most in request were the Saraband, Bretagne, Forlana, Passepied, Folie d'Espagne, Rigaudon, Minuet du Dauphin, La Mariée, and "the most pleasing of them all," the Louvre. Also, from the 1760s to the 1820s a nonprogressive square dance, the French cotillon (anglicized to "cotillion"), became fashionable: this employed sophisticated step sequences and required considerable training and practice before it could be performed in public; at last in the 1820s this gave way to the quadrille, a closer relative of the French contredanse. As the middle classes tried to keep up with the trend-setters in performing these complex group dances, prompting became necessary. In the 1780s, Francis Werner boosted his clientele by advertising that he directed the figures from the bandstand.

The German allemande also appeared in ballrooms in the 1760s. This must have come as a relief. The allemande was a less demanding dance for couples, in which the partners joined hands and turned around each other in various ways. The allemande paved the way for the waltz, which began appearing in English ballrooms in the 1790s. While peasant dancing had always involved substantial physical contact, the concept of couples moving in close position was revolutionary to polite society. In the waltz, the dancers turned inward toward each other and were cut off from the throng of similarly close couples. Though vehemently opposed on moral and sanitary grounds because of the closeness of the hold and the lack of control inherent in the spinning motion, the waltz satisfied dancers' desire for freedom of expression, releasing formal inhibitions and signaling the final overthrow of the French noble style of dance.

In retrospect, it can be seen that two forces, one essentially cultural, the other professional, had helped, beyond the normal interplay of scientific progress and social maneuvering, to transform British dancing. On the one hand, sentimentalists and Romantics had sought to make dance more expressive and capable of telling stories without words. On the other, virtuosi simply wanted more scope in which to show off. By the 1820s, dance on the stage and in the ballroom had been revolutionized. On stage, with male roles reduced to lifting and support, female theatrical dancers discarded the mechanical advantage of the low sprung foot for a high rigid pointe and danced in gravity-defying spectacles; themes from the orderly classical world were abandoned for those of the **supernatural**. In the ballroom, dancers were no longer afraid to exhibit emotions in public: freed from constricting **clothing** and heeled shoes, they turned inward as couples in close embrace and danced for their own pleasure.

Kate Van Winkle Keller

Bibliography

Hilton, Wendy. *Dance of the Court & Theater: The French Noble Style 1690–1725.* 1981.

Leppert, Richard. *Music and Image: Domesticity, Ideology and Socio-Cultural Formation in Eighteenth-Century England.* 1988.

Marsh, Carol. "French Court Dance in England, 1706–1740: A Study of the Sources." Ph.D. diss. 1985.

Quirey, Belinda. *May I Have the Pleasure? The Story of Popular Dancing.* 1976.

Sadie, Stanley, ed. *The New Grove Dictionary of Music and Musicians,* s.v. "Dance." 1980.

See also Minuet; Music, Dance; Pantomime; Theaters and Staging

Darby Family

This Bristol **Quaker** family produced a dynasty of ironmasters forever associated with Coalbrookdale (Shropshire) and technical innovation. Abraham Darby I (1678–1717), after an apprenticeship in **Birmingham**, began as a brass-founder in **Bristol** but experimented with casting ironware, for which he took a **patent** in 1707. He then moved to Coalbrookdale, taking over the disused ironworks which he put into blast in 1709. He successfully tried smelting with coke in an attempt to reduce fuel costs, but not until the 1750s did this produce sufficient savings to warrant replacing charcoal smelting. The Coalbrookdale Company began leading the country, specializing in high-quality castings.

Abraham Darby II (1711–1763) took over in 1738 and diversified into bar-iron production, sponsored experiments in "potting" (the prelude to **Henry Cort**'s puddling process), and also applied a **Newcomen** engine (1742) to pump water back into the reservoir to provide constant power. Abraham Darby III (1750–1789) extended the works into the 1770s, built possibly the first iron bridge in 1779 (consisting of 378.5 tons of cast iron), made cast iron rails for **waggonways**, and greatly widened the firm's markets and reputation by a long and profitable association with **Matthew Boulton** and **James Watt**.

The later Darbys faced volatile markets and deflation in the aftermath of the French **Wars** (1792–1815), and severe competition from the South **Wales** industry. They responded by maintaining a reputation for structural and architectural iron, and the specialist equipping of sugar mills. Throughout the period 1709–1840 the Darby family and their relatives were a major innovative force in British ironworking.

John Butt

Bibliography

Harris, J.R. *The British Iron Industry 1700–1850.* 1988.

Hyde, Charles K. *Technological Change and the British Iron Industry, 1700–1870.* 1977.

Raistrick, Arthur. *Dynasty of Iron-Founders: The Darbys of Coalbrookdale.* 1970.

Smiles, Samuel. *Industrial Biography: Iron Workers and Tool Makers.* Rpt. 1970.

See also Iron Industry; Metallurgy and Metalworking; Science, Technology, and Invention

Darwall, Mary Whateley (1738–1825)

Darwall's poems illustrate both patriarchal constraint on women's writing and changing tastes in 18th-century **poetry**. Her first collection (1764), written before her marriage and under the mentorship of **William Shenstone**, consists mainly of decorous **pastorals**, but also contains strong feminist expressions of her sense of vocation and her frustrations as a woman poet. Her second book (1794), published after the death of her clergyman husband, collected 30 years of work in a full range of genres, from musical drama to an imitation of Ossian, and bears witness to her greater freedom as a respected widow and to the century's changing sensibilities.

Ann Messenger

Bibliography

Messenger, Ann. "'Like—but oh, how different!': William Shenstone and Mary Whateley Darwall," in A. Messenger, ed., *Gender at Work.* 1990.

———. *Woman and Poet in the Eighteenth Century: The Life of Mary Whateley Darwall.* 1993.

See also Women in Literature

Darwin, Erasmus (1731–1802)

Darwin was highly esteemed in his own time as a writer, social critic, and scientist. His reputation since has suffered, however, because as a writer of sparkling Popean couplets in the early **Romantic** period he was too old-fashioned, and as a scientist he was too innovative, anticipating by half a century the ideas of his grandson, Charles Darwin. On reform, his published ideas attacking the **slave trade** and supporting **women's education** were fully in tune with the **radicalism** of the early Romantics.

As an innovative physician and one of the founders of the **Lunar Society** of **Birmingham**, Darwin speculated early on matters of biology, geology, chemistry, and botany, so that when his elaborate couplet poems appeared, most notably *The Botanic Garden* (1791) and *The Temple of Nature* (1803), both with extensive prose notes, the effect was equally literary and scientific. He also published prose treatises full of innovative ideas during the energetic final decade of his life; *The Zoonomia* (1794–1796), for example, clearly influenced his grandson's theory of evolution. Even though Darwin's poetic style offended the more experimental Romantics, his ideas and wit deserve appreciation as distinctly modern and productive.

Erasmus Darwin

Donald M. Hassler

Bibliography

Hassler, Donald M. *The Comedian as the Letter D: Erasmus Darwin's Comic Materialism.* 1973.

———. *Erasmus Darwin.* 1974.

King-Hele, Desmond. *Doctor of Revolution.* 1977.

Dashwood, Sir Francis (1708–1781)

Dashwood was a politician known for his aesthetic interests, especially as a founder of the Society of Dilettanti (1732), a group of wealthy gentlemen devoted to promoting the arts. Elected (1741) to the **House of Commons**, Dashwood considered himself one of its independent members, those who did not vote along party lines. He was most active in the 1750s, when he supported the militia bills and defended **Admiral John Byng**. He accepted his only major office, Chancellor of the Exchequer (1762), in the **Bute** administration and was made 15th Baron le Despenser (1763). Dashwood took an interest in theological questions and published his own abridgement of the Book of Common Prayer (1773). He is called in popular histories the organizer of a **Hell-Fire Club** that practiced debauchery and even devil worship at Medmenham Abbey; his biographer finds the charge an exaggeration and says it originated in the **newspaper** *North Briton* (1763), as part of attacks on the Bute administration written by **John Wilkes** and **Charles Churchill**.

P.J. Kulisheck

Bibliography

Kemp, Betty. *Sir Francis Dashwood: An Eighteenth-Century Independent.* 1967.

Namier, Sir Lewis, and John Brooke, eds. *History of Parliament: The House of Commons, 1754–1790.* 3 vols. 1964.

Nobbe, George. *The North Briton: A Study in Political Propaganda.* 1939.

Sedgwick, Romney, ed. *History of Parliament: The House of Commons, 1715–1754.* 2 vols. 1970.

See also Antiquities and Ruins; Learned Societies

Davy, Sir Humphry (1778–1829)

Davy, one of the great Hanoverian scientists, was born in Penzance, the son of a poor wood-carver. Though apprenticed to a surgeon, he abandoned **medicine** to pursue **science**. Employed as a laboratory assistant (1798) by Thomas Beddoes (1760–1808) of the Medical Pneumatic Institution in **Bristol**, he experimented with nitrous oxide and, discovering that its inhalation could alleviate pain, published *Researches, Chemical and Physical* (1799). Appointed assistant chemistry lecturer at the **Royal Institution** in London, his presentations were so popular that they constituted social events. He became Professor of Chemistry (1802) and was elected a fellow of the **Royal Society** (1803).

Davy began a series of electrochemical investigations that resulted in the discovery of potassium, sodium, magnesium, calcium, barium, strontium, and chlorine—discoveries which he explained in the five Bakerian Lectures he gave from 1806 to 1810. His lectures at the Royal Institution and in **Dublin** (1810–1811) attracted thousands; Trinity College awarded him an honorary LL.D., his only university distinction. During a Continental tour with his assistant **Michael Faraday** (1813) he pursued his theory of volcanic action, burning diamonds in oxygen to prove that they were made of carbon. On another tour he investigated the **electricity** of the torpedo-fish. In 1815 he invented a safety lamp for use in **coal mines**; later, he said he valued this more than anything else he had done.

Sir Humphry Davy

From boyhood Davy had cherished a passion for **fishing** and made a scientific study of it; confined by illness, he produced *Salmonia* (1828). Throughout his life he wrote **poetry**; when young, he had been encouraged by **Southey** and **Coleridge**. His contribution to science was recognized by a knighthood (1812), a baronetcy (1818), and election to the presidency of the Royal Society (1820).

Theresa McDonald

Bibliography

Golinski, Jan. *Science as Public Culture: Chemistry and Enlightenment in Britain, 1760–1820.* 1992.

Hamilton, Sir H. *Humphry Davy.* 1966.

Musson, A.E., and E. Robinson. *Science and Technology in the Industrial Revolution.* 1969.

Watkins, D. "Sir Humphry Davy—The Miner's Friend." *Colliery Guardian.* November 1978, pp. 648–649.

See also Chemical Industry; Clanny, William Reid

Day, Thomas (1748–1789)

Day was a **radical** novelist, philosopher, and activist. Some contemporaries considered him ridiculous because of his naive insistence on living life according to a system—specifically, that set forth by Jean Jacques Rousseau (1712–1778). Two prospective brides he tutored failed his tests, and he died when a horse he tried to train by his own humane doctrines threw him. Yet in life he was a benevolent, eccentric liberal **humanitarian**; a friend of **Erasmus Darwin**, **Sir William Jones**, and the **Edgeworth** family; a spokesman of the **antislavery movement**; and a champion of **moral** education for children.

His first publication was *The Dying Negro* (1773), a poem in heroic couplets that included many lines by his friend John Bicknell, a lawyer who later married one of Day's failed bridal candidates. The poem was occasioned by a newspaper account of a runaway slave who, after being caught, shot himself. Day also wrote a *Fragment of an Original Letter on the Slavery of the Negroes* (1776), unpublished until 1784 because he favored the **American Revolution** even as he abhorred the revolutionaries' acceptance of slavery.

In 1783 Day (with a wife) retired to Anningsley in Surrey, where he wrote *The History of Sandford and Merton: A Work Intended for the Use of Children* (3 vols., 1783–1789) and *The History of Little Jack* (1789). Here he borrowed from **Henry Brooke**'s *The Fool of Quality* (1765–1770), itself indebted to Rousseau's *Émile, ou l'Éducation* (1762). In *Sandford* the spoiled Tommy Merton learns how to be a good English boy from Harry Sandford, the virtuous son of an honest farmer, and from Mr. Barlow, a cleryman much given to fables and learning by doing. The book attacks aristocratic heartlessness and exalts **middle-class** virtues. Its tremendous 19th-

Thomas Day

century popularity outlasted its Victorian parodies, and like its manly English descendant, *Tom Brown's School Days* (1857), remains readable—in measured portions.

Peter A. Tasch

Bibliography

Gignilliat, Jr., George Warren. *The Author of "Sandford and Merton": A Life of Thomas Day, Esq.* 1932.

Sypher, Wylie. *Guinea's Captive Kings: British Anti-Slavery Literature of the XVIIIth Century.* 1942.

See also Children's Literature; Sensibility and Sentimentalism

De Quincey, Thomas (1785–1859)

Upon the serial publication of *Confessions of an English Opium-Eater* in the *London Magazine* (1821–1822), De Quincey gained both instant notoriety and an enduring eponym. Earlier he had been primarily an unheralded and self-effacing disciple of **Wordsworth**; subsequently, the "Opium-Eater" became a prolific writer of literary **journalism** which, in its sheer diversity of coverage and genre, defies easy categorization. De Quincey himself described this work as "impassioned prose," a term that comes as close as any to capturing his remarkably rhythmic, ornate, complicated, and memorable style.

By his own admission, the key fact about De Quincey's life was his addiction to opium. Shortly before embarking on 3 years of intensive but uncompleted study at Worcester College, Oxford, he first experimented with it (1804) as both anodyne and tranquillizer; however, it was not until 1813 that he began taking opium daily in the form of laudanum. Despite this dependency throughout a career haunted by financial need, De Quincey composed a stunning range of work for the **periodical** press. Omitting from the account his **Gothic** novel, *Klosterheim* (1832), and several shorter tales in the same vein, his best imaginative writing included "On the Knocking at the Gate in *Macbeth*" (1823), "Murder Considered as One of the Fine Arts" (1827), *Suspiria de Profundis* (1845), *The English Mail-Coach* (1849), and, arguably, the revised *Confessions* (1856).

But De Quincey was a self-described polymath whose encyclopedic *oeuvre* spans a gamut of other topics, many related to contemporary events and history. Often exhibiting his formidable intellect as well as his very conservative **Tory** bias, he wrote on subjects as diverse as astronomy, economics, psychology, politics, economics, history, rhetoric, and German philosophy. He was even more "interdisciplinary" in interests than most 19th-century men of letters were routinely expected to be. Like **Coleridge**, whose personal afflictions were similar to his own, De Quincey remains a revealing index to the multifaceted developments of late–Hanoverian thought and history.

Robert Lance Snyder

Bibliography

Barrell, John. *The Infection of Thomas De Quincey: A Psychopathology of Imperialism.* 1991.

De Luca, V.A. *Thomas De Quincey: The Prose of Vision.* 1980.

Dendurent, H.O. *Thomas De Quincey: A Reference Guide.* 1978.

De Quincey, Thomas. *The Posthumous Works of Thomas De Quincey.* Ed. Alexander H. Japp. 2 vols. 1891.

———. *The Collected Writings of Thomas De Quincey.* Ed. David Masson. 14 vols. 1896–1897.

Lindop, Grevel. *The Opium-Eater: A Life of Thomas De Quincey.* 1985.

Maniquis, Robert M. "Lonely Empires: Personal and Public Visions of Thomas De Quincey." *Literary Monographs.* Vol. 8. Eds. Eric Rothstein and Joseph Anthony Wittreich, Jr. 1976.

McDonagh, Josephine. *De Quincey's Disciplines.* 1994.

Miller, J. Hillis. *The Disappearance of God: Five Nineteenth-Century Writers.* 1963.

Thomas De Quincey

Snyder, Robert Lance, ed. *Thomas De Quincey: Bicentenary Studies.* 1985.

See also Essay

Declaratory Act (1766)

In response to tumultuous colonial protest, Prime Minister **Rockingham** repealed the **Stamp Act** of 1765. However, not wanting to give the appearance of caving in to pressure, and following the advice of his Attorney-General, Charles Yorke (1722–1770), he paired the repeal with a new act asserting Parliament's legislative jurisdiction over the colonies "in all cases whatsoever." The precedent for this was the Irish Dependency Act (1719, repealed in 1782) that confirmed Parliament's legislative sovereignty over **Ireland**. The colonists, celebrating repeal of the Stamp Act, at first took little notice of the Declaratory Act. Soon it would harden positions on both sides of the deepening dispute over **taxes**.

K.R. Wood

Bibliography

Christie, I.R. *Crisis of Empire.* 1976.
Thomas, P.D.G. *British Politics and the Stamp Act Crisis: The First Phase of the American Revolution, 1763–1767.* 1975.

See also American Revolution; North America

Defenderism

Defenderism marked a new phase in Irish rural protest, exhibiting greater sophistication in organization and ideology than the agrarian secret societies that had preceded it in the 1760s.

The movement began in Armagh in the 1780s, originally as a nondenominational attempt to defend **Catholics** from attacks by Protestant fighting societies. As it spread southeastward in 1792, assisted by a highly mobile rural labor force, it became more militantly Catholic yet also mixed with French revolutionary ideas and claims for land redistribution. The "Defender War" in Cavan, Monaghan, Kildare, and Dublin brought Defenderism to the notice of authorities, but its cellular structure made it impervious to penetration. The Defenders received a further boost from the attacks on Catholics in Armagh in 1795 (the "Armagh outrages"), which again promoted violent and sectarian tendencies within the movement.

The development of Defenderism's cohesive nationwide structure attracted the attention of the radicalized **United Irishmen**'s leaders. By 1796 informal coalescence had begun between the two bodies, with the common aim of promoting a French invasion. Defenders proceeded to form the rank-and-file of the **Irish Rebellion** (1798) in many parts of **Ireland**.

The Defenders proved more enduring than the United Irishmen after the rebellion was crushed. After a brief lull, there were signs of regrouping in Ulster from the summer of 1803 on. By 1811, Defenderism had shaded into **Ribbonism**, more urban and artisan in character, but still belligerently championing Catholic nationalism.

E.W. McFarland

Bibliography

Beames, M.R. "Peasant Movements: Ireland 1785–1795." *Journal of Peasant Studies.* Vol. 2, pp. 502–506.
Elliot, M. "The Origins and Transformations of Early Irish Republicanism." *International Review of Social History.* Vol. 23, pp. 405–428.
Smyth, J. *Men of No Property: Irish Radicals and Popular Politics in the Late Eighteenth Century.* 1992.
Williams, T.D., ed. *Secret Societies in Ireland.* 1973.

See also Hearts of Oak; Irish Agriculture; Irish Land Settlement; Radicalism and Radical Politics; Whiteboys

Defoe, Daniel (1660?–1731)

Defoe was well into his fifties when **King George I** assumed the throne (1714). Born a **dissenter** of Flemish ancestry, educated at the **Dissenting Academy** at Stoke Newington, a failed businessman, inveterate traveler, and skillful polemicist both for and against the succession of governments that ran from the **Glorious Revolution** through the **War of Spanish Succession**, his greatest importance to the early Hanoverian era was as a voice of the rising bourgeois **middle class**.

Although he is probably best known to posterity for his prose fiction, over 500 different publications—pamphlets, periodicals, poems—have been attributed to Defoe. He began writing on political and religious subjects around 1697, defending William III against English xenophobia in his best-selling poem, *The True-Born Englishman* (1701). After William's death, however, he was pilloried and imprisoned for writing a seditious libel, *The Shortest Way with the Dissenters* (1702), a fine **satire** carrying to absurd lengths the **Tories**' distaste for religious nonconformists just as **Swift** in his *Modest Proposal* (1729) would caricature the English oppression of **Ireland**. Rescued from Newgate **Prison** through the intervention of Robert Harley (later **Earl of Oxford**), Defoe became a government propagandist and intelligence agent, writing, among other things, the thrice-weekly **periodical** *The Review* (1704–1713), an important forerunner of *The Spectator* begun by **Steele** and **Addison**. His most important prose work after 1714 was his *Tour through the Whole Island of Great Britain* (3 vols., 1721–1726), still considered the best primary source for the general picture of British economic and social life during that period. The book focuses on trade, the keys to prosperity, middle-class virtues, and the need for improvements in **education**, transportation, and the humane treatment of the poor.

Though he spent much of his life as a **journalist**, Defoe is, however, most frequently studied today as an author of prose fiction. He is widely recognized as a major pioneer of the **novel**. His narratives have been studied as **travel literature**, as Puritan spiritual **autobiography**, and as part of the exploration of **criminality in literature**. His most famous book, translated into many languages and admired by critics everywhere, was

Daniel Defoe

Robinson Crusoe (1719), the archetypal tale of a resourceful castaway on a desert island—and an idealization, it has been said, of the English middle-class virtues of industry, practicality, endurance, and simple faith. J-J. Rousseau (1712–1778) later called the book "the finest of treatises on education according to nature."

After attempting unsuccessfully to follow up this success with two sequels also about "Crusoe," Defoe published an imaginative account of 17th-century warfare, *Memoirs of a Cavalier* (1720), and a story about a fictitious pirate, *Captain Singleton* (1720). Three impressive works appeared in 1722: *Moll Flanders* is a vivid tale of one woman's attempt to avoid destitution in the grim world of 17th-century England; *A Journal of the Plague Year* is a spurious chronicle of the events of 1665; and *Colonel Jack* begins with an outstanding imaginative re-creation of a boy's struggle to survive on the streets of **London**. Defoe's final long works of prose fiction were published in 1724. In *Roxana* he returned to the problems unprotected women faced at the time, whereas *A New Voyage Round the World* offered a convincing narrative of an entirely imaginative trip.

Defoe's narratives are all written in the first person, retrospectively, so that they profess to relate adventures which have already taken place. In each case, the main characters not only tell the reader what happened during each episode in their careers, they reconsider their previous conduct from the perspective provided by the passing of time. As a consequence, Defoe's narratives seem to convey psychological depth because a careful reader often learns to distinguish between what he or she is being told by the narrator, and what, by implication, he or she suspects actually happened. This discrepancy sometimes tends to assume the ironic character associated with the "unreliable narrator" of modern fiction. Defoe's intentions may have been rather different, however, and the works most often read today, *Robinson Crusoe, Moll Flanders,* and *Roxana,* can also be interpreted as convincing attempts to dramatize ambiguous issues at the heart of Calvinist salvation theory.

J.A. Downie

Bibliography

Backscheider, Paula. *Daniel Defoe: His Life.* 1989.

Earle, Peter. *The World of Defoe.* 1977.

Furbank, P.N., and W.R. Owens. *The Canonisation of Daniel Defoe.* 1988.

Healey, George Harris, ed. *The Letters of Daniel Defoe.* 1955.

Moore, John Robert. *Daniel Defoe: Citizen of the Modern World.* 1958.

———. *A Checklist of the Writings of Daniel Defoe.* 1960; rev. ed., 1971.

Novak, Maximillian E. *Realism, Myth, and History in Defoe's Fiction.* 1983.

Peterson, Spiro. *Daniel Defoe: A Reference Guide 1731–1924.* 1987.

Schonhorn, Manuel. *Defoe's Politics: Parliament, Power, Kingship and Robinson Crusoe.* 1991.

Stoler, John A. *Daniel Defoe: An Annotated Bibliography of Modern Criticism, 1900–1980.* 1984.

Sutherland, James. *Defoe.* 1937.

Deism

See Freethinkers and Freethought

de Loutherbourg, Philippe Jacques (1740–1812)

An experimental artist from Strasbourg, de Loutherbourg moved to Paris in his teens and rose to fame as a painter of historical, mythological, and religious scenes; landscapes; portraits; and theater backdrops. Denied proper recognition by the French Academy, he left Paris for **London** (1771) and was hired by **David Garrick** to become Drury Lane's set designer and "machinist," specializing in innovative scenography with an eye to lavish spectacles assisted by elaborate machinery. He invented, among other things, the *Eidophusikon* (1781), a miniature sound-and-sight theater that imitated sunrises, sunsets, thunderstorms, waterfalls, battle scenes, and naval actions. Admired by royalty as well as by fellow artists such as **Reynolds** and **Gainsborough**, he was elected to the **Royal Academy** in 1781. Between 1801 and 1805 he published two aquatint series depicting the **picturesque** scenery of England and **Wales**.

James Gray

Bibliography

Allen, Ralph Gilmore. "The Stage Spectacles of Philip James de Loutherbourg." Ph.D. diss. 1960.

Joppien, Rüdiger. *Die Szenenbilder Philippe Jacques de*

Loutherbourgs: Eine Untersuchung zu ihrer Stellung zwischen Malerei und Theater. 1972.

———. Introduction to *Philippe Jacques de Loutherbourg. R.A.* Exhibition catalogue. 1973.

See also Painting; Theaters and Staging

Dennis, John (1658–1734)

It is the misfortune of some to be remembered mainly through misrepresentations made of them by their enemies. Such was the fate of Dennis, whose stare, "Tremendous! with a threatening Eye" was satirized by **Alexander Pope** in the *Essay on Criticism* (1711). But despite Pope's jibes, Dennis made major contributions to English **literary criticism**, and wrote important defenses of the morality and utility of modern drama.

A Cambridge graduate (1683), he joined the circle of wits that surrounded John Dryden (1631–1700), whom he defended in his first lengthy works of criticism, *The Impartial Critick* (1693), and *Remarks on a Book Entitul'd Prince Arthur* (1696). Here he advocated a criticism based on the religious, social, and political conditions in which the work criticized was produced—aligning himself with the moderns in the **ancients vs. moderns quarrel**. The attacks of **Jeremy Collier** on Restoration dramatists, including Dryden, led Dennis to publish *The Usefulness of the Stage, to the Happiness of Mankind, to Government, and to Religion* (1698), in which he argued that the pleasure afforded by plays is not immoral, but rather is the instrument through which they calm and reform the passions.

The effect of literature on the passions soon became Dennis's main theme in such works as *The Advancement and Reformation of Modern Poetry* (1701) and *The Grounds of Criticism in Poetry* (1704), in which he defined **poetry** as an art that excites passion "to delight and reform the mind," and shifted the focus of criticism from the work itself to its effect on the reader. Some literary historians credit Dennis with having invented the psychological basis for the later **Graveyard poetry** of **Edward Young**, **William Collins**, and **Thomas Gray**, and for the interest in the **sublime** at the century's close.

Geoffrey M. Sill

John Dennis

Bibliography

Albrecht, W.P. *The Sublime Pleasures of Tragedy: A Study of Critical Theory from Dennis to Kant.* 1975.

Grace, Joan C. *Tragic Theory in the Critical Works of Thomas Rymer, John Dennis, and John Dryden.* 1975.

Hooker, Edward Niles, ed. *The Critical Works of John Dennis.* 2 vols. 1939.

Johnson, J.W., ed. *The Plays of John Dennis.* 1980.

Murphy, Avon Jack. *John Dennis.* 1984.

Paul, H.G. *John Dennis: His Life and Criticism.* 1911.

See also Dramatic Criticism

Desaguliers, John Theophilius (1683–1744)

The son of a Huguenot refugee, Desaguliers was educated at Oxford under the natural philosopher John Keill. Although he took holy orders, he was primarily concerned with scientific pursuits and, late in the reign of **Queen Anne**, went to **London**, where he soon received the patronage of the wealthy **Duke of Chandos**. Made a fellow of the **Royal Society** (1714), Desaguliers's reputation was fundamentally as an **experimental lecturer** on Newton's science. His lectures were intended to bridge the gap between theory and practice. He is known to have taken a particular interest in early **steam-engine** technology and was employed on a variety of water-supply ventures, including the **York Buildings Company** in London.

Larry Stewart

Bibliography

Rowbottom, Margaret E. "John Theophilius Desaguliers (1683–1744)." *Proceedings of the Huguenot Society of London.* Vol. 21, pp. 196–218.

Stewart, Larry. *The Rise of Public Science: Rhetoric, Technology and Natural Philosophy in Newtonian Britain, 1660–1750.* 1992.

See also Science, Technology, and Invention

Devonshire, Dukes of

See Cavendish Family (and Dukes of Devonshire)

Dibdin, Charles (1745–1814)

Without formal training, Dibdin became an **actor**, singer, librettist, and composer. With John Rich (1692?–1761) of Covent Garden guiding his early career, Dibdin provided the words and music for the afterpiece *The Shepherd's Artifice* (1764), and worked with **Thomas Arne** on **David Garrick's** *A Fairy Tale* (1763).

Charles Dibdin

Dibdin's collaboration with **Isaac Bickerstaff** was most successful. At Covent Garden he acted and sang in Bickerstaff's *The Maid of the Mill* (1765) and contributed two-thirds of the music for *Lionel and Clarissa* (1768). After Rich's death he joined Bickerstaff at Drury Lane, where they collaborated on *The Padlock* (1768) and *Damon and Phillida* (1768). They also worked together for pieces at the **pleasure gardens** and the Haymarket.

Dibdin contributed music for Garrick's *Stratford Jubilee* and set his masque *The Institution of the Garter* (1771–1772). Later he entered into a fruitful relationship with Thomas Harris (*d.* 1820) at Covent Garden, producing *The Seraglio* (1776) and a number of afterpieces. From 1791 to 1808 Dibdin offered his material at the small San Souci theaters which he controlled. He also published *A Complete History of the English Stage* (5 vols., 1800) and wrote a novel, *Henry Hooka* (1800).

Richard J. Dircks

Bibliography

Highfill, Philip, Kalman Burnim, and Edward Langhans, eds. *A Biographical Dictionary of Actors, Actresses, Musicians, Dancers, Managers, and Other Stage Personnel in London, 1660–1800,* vol. 4, s.v. "Charles Dibdin."

See also Dramatic Arts; Music, Popular; Shakespeare Industry

Dibdin, Charles Isaac Mungo (1768–1833)

Eldest son of dramatist and songwriter **Charles Dibdin** and father of musician Henry Edward Dibdin (1813–1866), Dibdin was often referred to as "Charles the younger" in deference to his famous father. He was proprietor and acting manager of Sadler's Wells Theatre, where he presented many of his own works. He was well known for **burlesques** and comic **operas**. Along with his brother Thomas (1771–1841), Joseph Grimaldi (1779–1837), and Charles Farley (1771–1859), he created the classic 19th-century form of **pantomime**. Among Dibdin's better-known works are *Claudine* (1801) and *The Great Devil* (1801). Also worthy of note is his *History of the London Theatres* (1826).

Samuel Lyndon Gladden

Bibliography

Dibdin, Charles. Selected Works in *English and American Drama of the Nineteenth Century.* G. Freedley and A. Nicoll, eds., 1965–1975; J. Ellis and J. Donohue, eds., 1975–.

Meyer, David. *Harlequin in His Element: The English Pantomime, 1806–1836.* 1969.

See also Dramatic Arts

Dictionaries

See Reference Works

Diplomatic Revolution (1756)

This was a major international realignment that greatly affected British **foreign relations**. In 1754, Anglo–French hostilities began in **North America**. Fearing that **France** and her ally, Frederick the Great of Prussia, would attack **Hanover** and the Low Countries, the British turned to their Dutch and Austrian allies. But neither of those countries desired **war** with France. Continued concern about Hanover led then to the beginning of Anglo–Prussian negotiations in August 1755. These were spurred forward by an Anglo–Russian agreement of 30 September 1755. Frederick, offered the opportunity to join an apparently powerful diplomatic alignment, guaranteed Hanoverian neutrality by the Convention of Westminster (16 January 1756). Anger at this led Austria and France to sign the First Treaty of Versailles (1 May 1756).

These agreements were less important for their detailed provisions than for the revolutionary new alignments they created. The "Old Alliances" of Britain, Austria, and the Dutch that had resisted France for most of the period since 1689 were overturned. Anglo–Austrian relations were not to improve until 1793, when both powers found themselves at war with revolutionary France. The Diplomatic Revolution therefore left Britain in a weaker international position, although maritime and colonial successes during the **Seven Years' War** were to disguise this.

Jeremy Black

Bibliography

Black, Jeremy. *The Rise of the European Powers, 1679–1793.* 1990.

———. *A System of Ambition? British Foreign Policy, 1660–1793.* 1991.

Diplomats and Diplomacy

The art of negotiation was not in this period a taught skill. Though the foundation of the Regius Chairs of History at **Cambridge** and **Oxford** universities in 1724 was designed to facilitate the training of diplomats, the scheme had little practical effect. The principal schools of British diplomats continued to be the court in **London**, and the households of other diplomats.

A diplomat was the personal representative of the sovereign, and in a prestige-conscious age the ability of a man to discharge an office was believed to reflect in part his social rank. Honor was a crucial concept in diplomatic representation, and the rank of the official appointed, whether ambassador, envoy extraordinary, minister resident, secretary, or some other less common designation, was apt to correspond with his social rank, and both of these with the level of respect and trust he could rely upon.

The most prestigious postings for British diplomats were Paris, Madrid, The Hague, and Vienna. With the addition of Rome, this list was a common European one, and at these centers the diplomatic world was an intensely aristocratic one. It would be wrong to suggest that high-born diplomats were mediocre simply because many of them lacked previous on-the-job experience. Several of the most impressive diplomats, such as **Lord Chesterfield** (who served at The Hague, 1728–1732, 1745), were men from the **aristocracy**.

Far from being a sinecure, diplomacy was not well paid. Most diplomats complained about inadequate and late payment. Cost was a particular problem at the more expensive and prestigious courts, where diplomats were expected to maintain a showy appearance, and was an additional reason to appoint wealthy men.

Aside from becoming Secretary of State, there were few promotion prospects that could not be better obtained by remaining in Britain, and many diplomats complained bitterly that absence from London hindered their careers and the pursuit of other interests. Although a few embassies left plenty of time for leisure, as Sir Horace Mann at Florence (1738–1786) and Sir William Hamilton at Naples (1764–1800) discovered, diplomats could be criticized severely if they failed to write sufficiently often or comprehensively, or if they were absent from their posts.

Apart from a disproportionate number of Scots (who benefited from the career opportunities presented by the **union** of 1707), it is difficult to see other patterns among those who followed diplomacy as a career. Some had acquired experience through posts on the staffs of envoys, though others had not. As French increasingly became the diplomatic *lingua franca,* language became less of a problem; many British diplomats were insufficiently familiar with other languages.

The choice of envoy was not always easy. Royal approval was generally necessary, and those who fell foul of the monarch generally lost their posts. Connections were crucial in appointments. And of course the pool of available talent was drastically limited by restrictive attitudes toward **women's employment**.

Many diplomats complained about the infrequency or quality of their instructions, but even when these were frequent, fast, and comprehensive, there was considerable room for initiative. The shifting nature of court factions made the diplomatic task a difficult one, and when mistakes and misunderstandings arose, the potential damage was worsened by the difficulties of securing supplementary lines of communication that could provide a check on diplomats. Distance and protocol kept most sovereigns from engaging in personal diplomacy.

British diplomats did not enjoy the high reputation of their French counterparts, and their diligence and competence were often criticized. However, in view of the difficulties of the job and the resources available, too much criticism would be inappropriate. Learning on the job could have unfortunate consequences, but it was a feature of the semiprofessional nature of much British administration in the period.

Jeremy Black

Bibliography

Black, Jeremy. *A System of Ambition? British Foreign Policy, 1660–1793.* 1991.

———. *British Foreign Policy in an Age of Revolutions, 1783–1793.* 1993.

Cobban, Albert. *Ambassadors and Secret Agents: The Diplomacy of the First Earl of Malmesbury at The Hague.* 1954.

Doran, Patrick F. *Andrew Mitchell and Anglo–Prussian Relations during the Seven Years' War.* 1986.

Horn, Donald B. *Sir Charles Hanbury-Williams and European Diplomacy, 1747–58.* 1930.

———. *The British Diplomatic Service, 1689–1789.* 1961.

Roberts, Michael. *British Diplomacy and Swedish Politics, 1758–1773.* 1980.

See also Foreign Relations

D'Israeli, Isaac (1766–1848)

D'Israeli was the father of Prime Minister and novelist Benjamin Disraeli (1804–1881). A scholar and bibliophile, his *Curiosities of Literature* (1791–1834), a 6-volume compilation of literary and historical **essays** and miscellaneous anecdotes, was so popular that it was printed 12 times before his death. D'Israeli also made one of the earliest attempts at literary history in his 3-volume *Amenities of Literature* (1840). With *Essays on the Literary Character* (1795), *Calamities of Authors* (1813), and *Quarrels of Authors* (1814), he explored the **melancholy** temperament of literary men. His historical works included *An Inquiry into the Literary and Political Character of James I* (1816) and *Commentaries on the Life and Reign of Charles I* (1828–1831). He was a member of the literary circle that met at the home of **publisher** John Murray (1778–1843), and an enthusiastic patron of **William Blake**'s illuminated works.

Steve Patterson

Bibliography

Ogden, James. *Isaac D'Israeli.* 1969.

Dissenters

Dissenters (nonconformists), in the most general sense, were members of Protestant religious sects, notably the **Presbyterians, Baptists, Congregationalists, Quakers,** and **Unitarians** (also the **Methodists** after 1795), who refused to conform to the liturgy and rites of the **Church of England.** Their unpopularity with Anglicans stemmed from their originally republican and **radical** ideas, and a continuing fear that, once empowered, they might disestablish the church. They rejected the church's Thirty-nine Articles of Faith (1563), rejected the Act of Uniformity (1662), and for most of the Hanoverian period lay under the official sanctions of the **Test and Corporation acts,** which limited their civil and political rights. By virtue of the **Toleration Act** (1689), most of these groups were permitted to worship in their chapels, and by the hypocritical practice of **occasional conformity** some might even take up legal careers or hold public office, but discrimination remained a source of deep irritation and loss.

Dissenters had to pay in various ways for the support of the Anglican Church and to be married and buried according to its rites. Discrimination made it difficult for them to take up careers in the military, and impossible to graduate from the universities. Many, thanks to this, attended their own **dissenting academies** (which were the best schools in Britain) and then found work in industrial and commercial enterprises that did not rely on the government or the **aristocracy.** Many scientists, academics, intellectuals, and inventors, especially in Presbyterian **Scotland,** were dissenters.

Their numbers varied. In 1714 there were around 180,000 Presbyterians, 60,000 each of Baptists and Congregationalists, and less than 40,000 Quakers. Dissenters made up some 8% of the **population** in 1715 (there were then more than a quarter-million dissenters in England and **Wales,** and some 5.25 million Anglicans), and perhaps 20% in 1815 (some of this growth attributable to the later inclusion of Methodists, some attributable to internal religious revival). Dissenters tended to congregate in the Midlands, where they had been influential in the 17th century, and in large cities elsewhere, such as **London** and of course **Edinburgh** and **Glasgow.**

The dissenters' central quarrel with the established Church was over its official connection with the state. Throughout the 18th century they agitated for separation of the two, seeing the first step as being a repeal of the detested Test and Corporation acts. United by persecution and a reformist perspective, always on the political Left, allied with the **Whigs,** descending from a radical tradition passed down from the 17th century, led by various groups—**Protestant dissenting deputies, commonwealthmen, rational dissenters**—they became especially prone to political radicalism after the **American Revolution** galvanized supporters of religious toleration and more perfect political representation. By the 1770s two of their most influential spokesmen were the dissenting ministers **Richard Price** and **Joseph Priestley:** Their reformist activism and support of the **French Revolution** led to renewed though totally unjustified Anglican suspicion of the loyalty of nonconformity as a whole during the period 1790–1800.

Over the 18th century the religious beliefs of dissenters tended to gravitate from strict Calvinism toward **Latitudinarianism** and then (especially amongst Presbyterians) toward Arianism, Socinianism, and Unitarianism, denying the essential divinity of Christ altogether. By the time of Priestley's death (1804), dissent was associated less with concerns of salvation, baptism, and communion than with Unitarian political activism. Dissenters were heavily involved in **antislavery** agitation and **prison reform** as well as parliamentary reform. They were active in **banking,** and many were important industrialists of the new age, such as potter and china-maker **Josiah Wedgwood,** textile manufacturers Thomas Walker (1784–1836) and **Jedediah Strutt,** engineers **James Watt** and **Matthew Boulton,** and **iron** industrialists **John Wilkinson** and the **Darby** family. Sometimes, wealthy second- and third-generation dissenters tended to drift into the church. Dissenting intellectuals included novelist **Daniel Defoe,** hymnist **Isaac Watts,** and political theorists **William Godwin** and **Thomas Paine.**

By the 1820s the **Industrial Revolution** and the remarkable progress made by many dissenting families and industrial dynasties had so greatly changed the economic bases of politics that political alteration was inevitable. The dissenters came into their own with repeal of the Test and Corporation Acts (1828) and the **Reform Act** (1832) that included assignment of parliamentary representation to many dissenting population centers that had been without it. Nonconformity went on to greater strength in the Victorian age, lending its energy to the Liberal and ultimately Labour parties.

Carole S. Fungaroli

Bibliography

Armstrong, Anthony. *The Church of England, the Methodists and Society 1700–1850.* 1973.

Bradley, James E. *Religion, Revolution and English Radicalism: Nonconformity in Eighteenth Century Politics and Society.* 1990.

Clark, J.C.D. *English Society, 1688–1832: Ideology, Social Structure and Political Practice during the Ancien Regime.* 1985.

Fruchtman, Jack, Jr. *The Apocalyptic Politics of Richard Price and Joseph Priestley: A Study in Late Eighteenth-Century English Republican Millennialism.* 1983.

Kramnick, Isaac. *Republicanism and Bourgeois Radicalism: Political Ideology in Late Eighteenth-Century England and America.* 1990.

Lincoln, Anthony. *Some Political and Social Ideas of English Dissent, 1763–1800.* 1938, 1971.

Pocock, J.G.A. *Virtue, Commerce and History: Essays on Political Thought and History, Chiefly in the Eighteenth Century.* 1985.

Robbins, Caroline. *The Eighteenth-Century Commonwealthman.* 1959.

Vann, Richard T., and David Eversley. *Friends in Life and Death: British and Irish Quakers, 1650–1900.* 1992.

Watts, Michael R. *The Dissenters.* 2 vols. 1978, 1995.

See also Religious Revivalism

Dissenting Academies

The **dissenters**' schools, like their churches, date principally from the Restoration, when Charles II (1630–1685) moved to check Puritanism. Legislation ensuring religious conformity, especially the Clarendon Code, effectively closed formal education at the universities of **Oxford** and **Cambridge** to dissenters, and further made them subject to Anglican **theology** in the country's grammar schools. This legislation effectively prompted the founding of dissenting education; **Presbyterians** and **Congregationalists**, **Baptists** and **Quakers** began to establish their own institutions.

The dissenting school was a charity foundation, but the dissenting academy had university standing. Three periods mark the history of the dissenting academies. During the first period (1663–1690), they were "private," each founded and staffed by a single minister and organized along university lines in a 3- to 5-year program. Such programs were designed to educate clergy for the orthodox dissenting ministry, though some also trained laymen for other professions. It was not uncommon for these academies to expire with the death of their founders.

Dissenting academies of the second period (1691–1750) were increasingly "public," founded and governed "publicly," that is, by a group of ministers who hired several tutors, each a specialist. In this second period the academies admitted large numbers of students who sought nonclerical education; the Northampton Academy of **Philip Doddridge** was one of the most notable. While its Calvinism was tempered—one evidence of this being Doddridge's "comparative" divinity lectures—it became, through his *Lectures on Divinity* (1763), the source for courses in theology, psychology, and ethics in many other academies. Doddridge's curriculum was basically classical, but leaned heavily toward modern subjects such as algebra, optics, civil law, and geography. Moreover, instruction was in English, a practice of only 1 academy before 1689. Doddridge also incorporated certain ideas popularized in the books of **Isaac Watts**, *Logic; or the Right Use of Reason* (1725) and *Improvement of the Mind* (1741), this second work expounding "radical" Lockean principles. Although Doddridge and his disciples at other academies held a middle ground between orthodoxy and **Unitarianism**, his encouragement of nonclerical and rational education produced mixed blessings in the next period.

During the third period (beginning in 1750) orthodox academies—for example, Wellclose Square and Gosport—continued to attract students, as did the new Baptist academies such as Trowbridge and Bristol. Many academies, influenced by Doddridge, however, encouraged the most radical freedom of inquiry. In those at Warrington and Hackney, **Joseph Priestley** introduced not only chemistry and other sciences but also set the study of history at the center of the curriculum. His promotion of the study of the past and of nature yielded further opportunity for **freethought**, comparative reasoning, and intellectual challenges to authority. He saw the academies as places where young people might learn the most liberal principles in religion and politics. **Edmund Burke** accused Hackney of fomenting sedition as "the new arsenal in which subversive doctrines and arguments were forged." Church elders in the era of the **French Revolution** closed Warrington, Hackney, and Hoxton for propagating theological anarchy. Begun as universities for dissenting clerics, the academies had become seminaries of freethinking laymen. **William Hazlitt** typified the intellectual output of the 1790s before the academies were closed.

The significance of the dissenting academy is that it kept alive dissenting religion and gave to it an intellectual voice. It opened higher education to dissenters and promoted modern education by bringing "practical" subjects into the curriculum long before Oxford and Cambridge. Its distinguished faculty produced many fine students such as **Robert Harley**, **Daniel Defoe**, **Joseph Butler**, **Richard Price**, and **William Godwin**, as well as Watts, Priestley, and Hazlitt. The academy ultimately undermined orthodox dissenting theology, rejected Calvinism, and opened the way to Unitarianism, Socinianism, and freethought. Nevertheless, it was the flower of Puritan culture and the seed of modern education in method and matter.

H. George Hahn

Bibliography

Parker, Irene. *Dissenting Academies in England.* 1914.

Smith, J.W.A. *The Birth of Modern Education: The Contribution of the Dissenting Academies.* 1954.

See also Education, Secondary

Divorce

The most notorious divorce case in Hanoverian Britain was unsuccessful, as **George IV** was forced to drop his attempt to rid himself of **Queen Caroline** (1820). But until the Divorce Reform Act of 1857 there was no legal means of divorce with the right to remarry available in England to any but the very wealthy. Such divorce was rare because each action necessitated (from the 1690s on) a special act of Parliament. The primary justification for divorce was **adultery**. Parliamentary divorce was a long and arduous process, often preceded by a lawsuit pursued in one of the 26 Church Consistory courts. If the church courts found cruelty, the endangering of life, or adultery, they would grant a separation, but not permission to remarry. The brutal treatment of wives by husbands was often the reason for seeking a divorce; however, this kind of brutality diminished during the 18th century.

For the people of the **middle** and upper **classes** who could afford it, a more common legal procedure for dissolving a marriage was a "private separation," verified by a legal deed that included an agreement on property distribution between the wife and husband. (Legal rights to children belonged to the father until 1857.) Although not recognized by the church, the general acceptance of this procedure by the civil government afforded some opportunity for women to obtain independence. Private separations were not, however, divorces, and carried no permission for legal remarriage.

For the lower classes, several avenues were open for dissolving a marriage. None was recognized by the church or civil government, but all were acceptable to the local community.

Some rural communities recognized what were in effect "trial" marriages in which both partners agreed to divorce after 1 year if the marriage proved barren or if the couple found that they were incompatible: both were then free to remarry. Also, it was commonly believed that one could remarry if the spouse were dead, missing for 7 years, repeatedly adulterous, or had committed bigamy. Other quaint divorce practices persisted in many areas well into the 19th century. For example, those who had entered marriage by "jumping the broom" could divorce by jumping backwards over the broom. And there are documented cases of "wife sale," which included the ceremony of a husband leading his wife by a halter to the market center to be sold at auction to the highest bidder. Some, if not most, of these sales probably emerged from agreements between the wife and the husband, the wife being conveyed to the man she actually wanted to be with. However, interpretations of this ritual have been a source of debate among historians.

Still simpler avenues existed. Many individuals simply deserted their spouses and remarried. It has been estimated that some 6% of all women applying for poor relief in southeast England were abandoned wives, a fact suggesting that desertion was not too uncommon. Husbands and wives who deserted their spouses and married again were in fact committing bigamy—a felony technically punishable by death. However, prosecutions were rare, and when they did take place, the sentence was reduced to burning the thumb of the offender; by the end of the 18th century this was often done symbolically.

Stanley D. Nash

Bibliography

Gillis, John R. *For Better, for Worse: British Marriages, 1600 to the Present.* 1985.

Menefee, Samuel Pyeatt. *Wives for Sale: An Ethnographic Study of British Popular Divorce.* 1981.

Stone, Lawrence. *Road to Divorce: England, 1530–1987.* 1990.

———. *Broken Lives: Separation and Divorce in England, 1660–1857.* 1993.

Thompson, E.P. "The Sale of Wives," in E.P. Thompson, ed., *Customs in Common.* 1991.

See also Manners and Morals

Dixon, Sarah (1671–1765)

Dixon's **poetry** is both representative of the 18th century and vividly individual. She published one book, *Poems on Several Occasions* (1740); a few additional manuscript poems survive. An impoverished spinster, born in Rochester but living near Canterbury, she probably knew the **bluestocking** Elizabeth Carter (1717–1806). Dixon wrote in a wide range of genres, from **pastoral** to hymn. One poem, "To the Muse," explains that she used writing as therapy for the tragedy of her life, which she does not directly identify, and many autobiographical poems express deep anguish. Some of her work, however, is refreshingly comic and satiric.

Ann Messenger

Bibliography

[Dixon, Sarah.] *Poems on Several Occasions.* 1740.

See also Women in Literature

Docks and Harbors

The Hanoverian era's steadily rising volume of **coastal shipping** and **overseas commerce** exerted growing pressure on the facilities of British ports. Those whose merchants and municipal authorities were unable to respond to such growing demand, like Blakeney and Rye, tended to lose business and decline. Elsewhere, successful adaptations to changing circumstances occurred, and increases in trade and shipping were facilitated or, in some cases, stimulated.

Though such responses varied according to a port's particular physical features and commercial interests, two main lines of development emerged. First, the access to, and amenities offered by, many ports were improved. River ports such as Boston, Stockton, Ipswich, and Lynn benefited from the widening, deepening, or straightening of approach channels. On the coast, piers were constructed or strengthened; some were designed to provide harbors of refuge (as at Scarborough and Bridlington in Yorkshire, and Ramsgate in Kent), whereas others were erected by landowners seeking outlets for the **mining** products of their estates. In Cornwall, the harbors at Portreath, Hayle, Charlestown, and Pentewan were built or enhanced between 1760 and 1820 to service interior mines and clay works. Likewise, piers were constructed or extended at Seaton Sluice and Seaham in Northumberland and, most notably, at Whitehaven in Cumberland, though in these cases the shipment of **coal** was the reason for improvements.

The second type of port development was dock construction. This response to trade expansion, and the shipping congestion it entailed, was largely restricted to the major ports. Though wet docks (enclosed areas of tide-free water) had already been built on the Thames to fit out and lay up vessels, Britain's first commercial dock was opened in **Liverpool** in 1715. Permitting vessels to load and discharge beyond the tidal race of the Mersey, this innovative facility was followed by the construction of a second dock as trade mushroomed after 1750. At Hull, a nine-acre dock, much larger than its Liverpool predecessors, and funded by a private company rather than town authorities, was constructed in the 1770s to alleviate overcrowding.

A similar motive underlay the creation of the first docks in **London**, though here the elimination of pilfering was another objective. Comparatively late in the field, London was nevertheless equipped with a range of docks by 1812, all established and operated by private companies concerned with particular branches of trade. Accordingly, West Indiamen and East Indiamen were handled at the **West India** and **East India** docks respectively, whereas vessels engaged in the northern European trades were accommodated at the Baltic, Norway, and East Country docks on the Surrey side of the river.

With further docks constructed in the major ports and elsewhere, and a variety of improvements implemented in numerous harbors, Britain's capacity to handle a growing vol-

St. Catherine Docks, London

ume of trade was greatly enhanced in the early 19th century. However, even before the advent of the **steam railway** and the steamship, these provisions were already proving inadequate.

David J. Starkey

Bibliography

Aldcroft, D.H., and M.J. Freeman. *Transport in the Industrial Revolution.* 1983.

Bird, J. *The Major Seaports of the United Kingdom.* 1963.

Capper, C. *The Port and Trade of London.* 1862.

Jackson, G. *The History and Archaeology of Ports.* 1983.

See also Lighthouses; Shipping and Seamen; Ships and Shipbuilding

Doddridge, Philip (1702–1751)

Doddridge, **Congregationalist** minister, author, and hymnist, was a great proponent of **religious toleration** and one of the most widely respected **dissenting** writers of the early Hanoverian period. Educated at John Jennings's **dissenting academy** at Kibworth, Leicestershire, an especially liberal-minded institution, he became minister there when Jennings died (1723). In 1730 he became president of the academy and pastor of the Congregationalist Church at Castle Hill, Northampton, serving there until his death. His great ambition was to promote unity among dissenters and improve relations between them and the **Church of England**. His writings included **sermons**, scriptural commentaries, pastoral **theology**, and an extensive correspondence. His principal work, *The Rise and Progress of Religion in the Soul* (1745), was dedicated to **Isaac Watts**, whose writings and hymns profoundly influenced his own. Among Doddridge's most popular hymns were "My God, and Is Thy Table Spread," "O God of Bethel, by Whose Hand," and "Ye Servants of the Lord."

Michael F. Suarez, S.J.

Bibliography

Deacon, Malcom. *Philip Doddridge of Northampton.* 1980.

Gordon, Alexander. *Philip Doddridge and the Catholicity of the Old Dissent.* 1951.

Greenall, R.L., ed. *Philip Doddridge, Nonconformity and Northampton.* 1981.

Nuttall, Geoffrey F. *Richard Baxter and Philip Doddridge: A Study in Tradition.* 1951.

Rivers, Isabel. *Reason, Grace, and Sentiment: A Study of the Language of Religion and Ethics in England, 1660–1780.* 1991.

Dodington, George Bubb (1691–1762)

Dodington's political career in both government and **opposition** from 1720 to 1760 illustrates central aspects of early Hanoverian politics. The **patronage** of his uncle gained him a seat in Parliament (1715) and a diplomatic post in Spain (1715–1717), where he helped negotiate valuable commercial treaties. His uncle's death (1720) left him in control of four parliamentary seats. Personally ambitious, he parlayed his social, financial, and political assets into a variety of offices in **local** and **national government**. Dodington became Lord Lieutenant of Somerset (1720–1744), Lord of the Treasury (1724–1740), Treasurer of the **Navy** (1744–1749), and Treasurer of the Chamber to the Prince of Wales (1749–1751). His knowledge of parliamentary procedures, skill in debate, and folksy style of dress and speech aided his usefulness as a government spokesman who could appeal to the politically independent country gentlemen. Dodington courted such interests by opposing the maintenance of a standing **army** and supporting a foreign policy promoting **commerce** and colonization.

Despite holding office under **Robert Walpole** until 1740, Dodington's ambitions made him gamble on political opportunities. He cultivated Walpole's rumored successor Sir Spencer Compton (*d.* 1743) and briefly acted as political adviser (1732–1734) to **Frederick, Prince of Wales**. This lost him the favor of **King George II**, however, and he only held office after 1740 because the **Pelhams** needed broad-based support for their **war** ministry. In 1749 he rejoined the Prince of Wales's household, hoping the prince would soon become king. Frederick's death (1751) dashed these hopes. Dodington's final achievement was his "Political Journal," which he began in 1757 and which remains a most valuable portrait of his age.

Robert D. McJimsey

Bibliography

Carswell, John. *The Old Cause: Three Biographical Studies in Whiggism.* 1954.
Carswell, John, and Lewis Arnold Dralle. *The Political Journal of George Bubb Dodington.* 1965.
Gerrard, Christine. *The Patriot Opposition to Walpole: Politics, Poetry, and National Myth, 1725–1742.* 1995.

Dodsley, Robert (1703–1764)

Dodsley began as a footman and ended as an influential **publisher**. His early **poetical** works (*Servitude,* 1729; *The Muse in Livery,* 1732) were sponsored by his employers and their circle. He wrote several comedies, including *The Toyshop* (1735), a dramatic moral **satire**, often reprinted. He set up a bookshop (1735) that developed into a major publishing business, later shared with his brother James. The firm published **Pope**, Paul Whitehead, **Johnson**, Young, **Akenside**, **Shenstone**, **Gray**, **Goldsmith**, and also three major anthologies: *A Select Collection of Old Plays* (12 volumes, 1744), *A Collection of Poems, by Several Hands* (6 vols., 1748–1758), and Bishop Percy's *Reliques of Ancient English Poetry* (3 vols., 1765).

Dodsley suggested the idea of an English Dictionary to **Johnson**; his innovative self-instructor, *The Preceptor* (1755), has a preface by Johnson. He was also connected with the **periodicals** *The Museum* (1746–1747), *The World* (1753–1757), and *The Annual Register,* edited by **Burke** (from 1758 on). *Trifles* (2 vols., 1745); *The Economy of Human Life,* often attributed to **Chesterfield** (1750); *Public Virtue* (1753); a tragedy, *Cleone* (1758); and *Select Fables of Esop* (3 vols., 1761), are by Dodsley. His personal charm, extensive connections, wide-ranging interests, and commercial acumen enabled him to play an important role in the Hanoverian emergence of the publisher as a key figure promoting cultural tastes and consumption.

Phyllis J. Guskin

Bibliography

Strauss, R. *Dodsley: Poet, Publisher and Playwright.* 1910.

Doherty, John (1798–1854)

Doherty, an Irish-born **trade union** organizer, **journalist**, Owenite sympathizer and political **radical**, is best known for his involvement in the "general unionism" movement during the economic recession of 1829–1832. He led the **Manchester** cotton spinners in the 1820s and instigated the formation of the first federation of British cotton spinners in 1829. In 1830 he formed, and became the first General Secretary of, the National Association for the Protection of Labour (NAPL). Some historians dismiss the NAPL as sectional and fairly localized, but recent research has revised this overly negative interpretation; in fact the NAPL, consisting of 150 trade unions, was more broadly based and survived longer than the better-known experiment in general unionism by **Robert Owen** in 1834, the Grand National Consolidated Trades' Union (GNCTU). Leaving the NAPL in 1832, Doherty became more closely involved in political movements, particularly **factory** reform.

Arthur McIvor

Bibliography

Kirby, R.G., and A.E. Musson. *The Voice of the People: John Doherty.* 1975.
Musson, A.E. *British Trade Unions, 1800–1875.* 1972.
Sykes, R. "Trade Unionism and Class Consciousness: The 'Revolutionary' Period of General Unionism, 1829–1834," in John Rule, ed., *British Trade Unionism, 1750–1850: The Formative Years.* 1988.
Webb, S., and B. Webb. *History of British Trade Unionism.* 1894.

See also Cotton Industry; Factory Movement and Factory Acts; Labor Laws, Movements, and Unions; Spinning and Weaving

Domestic Production

Domestic production, or putting-out, the major means of manufacture before the **Industrial Revolution**, was well established by the early 18th century. In essence, a single man or perhaps firm came to control all the processes in an industry, from the acquisition of raw materials, through manufacture, to the sale and distribution of the final product. This type of operation was to be found in almost all industries producing goods for wholesale distribution, particularly in **textiles** and **metalworking**, methods varying from industry to industry and even within different organizations in the same trade. The capitalist organizer, often a **merchant**, was dependent at each stage on groups of **craftsmen** or other operatives, working in their own homes or workshops, who were, in theory, self-employed. Raw materials and manufactures were moved to and from the operatives either by the organizer himself, or, more likely, by an agent acting on his behalf.

Domestic production represented a primitive stage of capital accumulation. The machinery, equipment, and tools

Woman spinning at home

used, such as looms and anvils, generally cost very little, allowing growth to take place in small units with only minimal demand on capital resources. Production was labor- rather than capital-intensive, and was flexible if the **population** expanded and more people could be recruited. It ran into difficulties if demand outstripped productive capacity, leading to pressures on **wages**, which could affect profit margins.

Domestic production allowed some division of capital, combined with a degree of stability. Often the merchant required little capital for buildings or machinery, but needed money on credit for raw materials, wages, and to finance the sale of the finished article. The craftsman could provide fixed capital in the form of machines, tools, and workshops (usually his own house), but did not require trading capital.

The system also allowed for social mobility. Craftsmen could eventually enter the ranks of merchants, and some merchants would perhaps move down, possibly becoming agents for larger ones. Merchants were the cornerstone of the system, selling the finished goods and usually providing credit, perhaps even advancing money to the operatives to acquire the basic tools to enter their trade. Such merchants had a hold over the tools as security, and eventually some acquired fixed capital themselves, renting it to operatives.

At the apex of the system was a group of rich merchants centered in **London**, **Norwich**, **Leeds**, **Glasgow**, and Hull, many in the export trades, who were ultimately responsible for its growth during the 18th century. Encouraged by many landowners, they spread their activities to the countryside, providing employment to **agricultural laborers** only required at peak planting or harvesting periods. In **Scotland** it was a feature of the **planned-village** movement that facilities were provided for the types of occupations usually associated with the putting-out system. In the long term, putting-out led to regional specialization, and to competition both within and between regions. Cost levels became a major factor in the development or decline of an area.

As the 18th century progressed, the system began to be subjected to violent fluctuations in wages and prices, and so became less stable. It was satisfactory only within certain limits, as merchants found it impossible to recruit the necessary skilled labor over the short term. As demand expanded, the putter-out began to control the system more tightly by bringing groups of outworkers together in one place. This was the first step in the transition to the **factory system**. Some industrial processes remained outside the factories, for example, **cotton** weaving until the advent of the power loom, and some aspects of **metalworking** (particularly nailmaking) until well into the Victorian period. Thus the two systems existed side by side until the end of the Hanoverian era, often under the control of the same firm. In the Sheffield cutlery trades, a sort of halfway house existed where craftsmen shared workplaces.

Domestic production was an important base for later change. Many industrial **entrepreneurs** such as the **Crowleys** in **iron** and the **Peels** in cotton began their careers in the domestic system, and it was they who decided to change it. It generated employment, stimulating the market and increasing the **middle class**, thus raising **standards of living** in some areas, leading to further increases in demand. This boosted local and then regional markets, finally creating a national market. Much of this was stimulated by, and indeed encouraged developments in, **transport**; the effect was bigger and better outlets for the individual firm. But domestic production, by encouraging diversification, which in turn led to innovation, ironically but inevitably set up the overthrow of the system itself.

A.J.G. Cummings

Bibliography

Ashton, T.S. *An Economic History of England: The 18th Century.* 1955.
Berg, Maxine. *The Age of Manufactures, 1700–1820: Industry, Innovation and Work in Britain.* 2nd ed., 1994.
Hamilton, Henry. *An Economic History of Scotland in the Eighteenth Century.* 1963.
Pollard, Sidney. *The Genesis of Modern Management.* 1965.
Wadsworth, A.P., and J. de L. Mann. *The Cotton Trade and Industrial Lancashire, 1600–1780.* 1931.

See also Commerce, Domestic; Commerce, Overseas

Doyle, James Warren (1786–1834)

Bishop Doyle, a notable Catholic reformer and defender of the Irish faith, was born in county Wexford. At age 14 he entered the seminary in New Ross, passing on to attend the University of Coimbra in Portugal (1806–1808). His studies were disrupted when Napoleon invaded that country; he then joined the British **Army** there, acting as an interpreter. After returning to **Ireland** he was ordained (1809), then moved to Carlow College in southeastern Ireland to teach rhetoric and theology (1813). Elected Bishop of Kildare and Leighlin (1819), he gained a reputation as a vigorous reformer, establishing schools, assisting the poor, and conciliating the masses affected by **Ribbonism**.

In the 1820s Doyle became famous for his attacks on the Anglican hierarchy in Ireland, publishing over the initials J.K.L. such works as his *Vindication of the Religious and Civil Principles of the Irish Catholics* (1824) and *Letters on the State of Ireland* (1824, 1825). What **O'Connell** was to the cause of **Catholic emancipation**, Doyle was to the ouster of the United Church of England and Ireland from its privileged position. Though disliked (and glorified) as a slashing polemicist, his demeanor and abilities in interviews by parliamentary committees on the state of Ireland (1825, 1830, 1832) earned him accolades from **Wellington** and others.

Donald W. Nichol

Bibliography

Fitzpatrick, W.J. *Life, Times and Correspondence of Dr. Doyle.* 1861; rev. ed., 1880.
MacDonald, Michael. *Bishop Doyle, "J.K.L.": A Biographical and Historical Study.* 1896.

See also Irish Church Act; Roman Catholicism

Dramatic Arts

After a raucous adolescence during the Restoration, British **theater** came of age in the Hanoverian period. Though perhaps less vital in some ways than its Restoration predecessor, the stage after 1714 broadened its audience to include a bourgeois **middle class**, diversified its genres beyond heroic tragedy and comedies of **manners**, and fostered the production of some of the most frequently revived plays in the history of British dramatic arts. Under the influence of **David Garrick** of the Drury Lane company and John Rich (1682?–1761) at Covent Garden, the theaters stabilized, improved their scenic designs, withdrew the actors behind the proscenium arch, and formalized acting styles. The enlarged theaters, seating up to 2,000 people by the last decades of the century, relied increasingly on **music**, spectacle, and melodrama, driving the English genius for comedy off the stage.

The direction taken by British drama in this period cannot be understood without some reference to the forces that brought Restoration drama to a close. **Jeremy Collier**'s 1698 essay, *A Short View of the Immorality and Profaneness of the English Stage,* was the best known of several attacks on the stage for the failure of its playwrights "to recommend virtue and discountenance vice" and to distinguish between "mirth and madness." Collier's views were supported from without the dramatic community by societies of reform led by King William and Queen Mary, and from within by **Richard Steele** and Colley **Cibber**, who may not have shared Collier's tastes, but saw in reform the opportunity to produce a new kind of comedy, now called "**sentimental**." Such comedy, whose touchstone is Steele's *The Conscious Lovers* (1722), featured moral speeches between lovers, disapproval of **duels**, tearful family reunions, and **ridicule** of foppish men or lewd women; but it also included laughter as well, sometimes mixed with tears, precluding any simple dichotomy between sentimental and "laughing" comedy.

The effect for which sentimental comedy reached was the calling forth of "tears of exquisite joy," opening the observer to instruction by example. This, however, depends on an audience response that may no longer be available; the excessive sensibility of Steele's character John Bevil Jr. strikes modern readers of *The Conscious Lovers* as pathetic and hypocritical, rather than worthy of emulation. Frank Ellis, in recent scholarship, has sought to identify a list of subjects which, when treated with "cosmic optimism," render a play sentimental. Thus Cibber's *Love's Last Shift* (1696) is sentimental in its insistence on the goodness of human nature, but Edward Moore's *The Foundling* (1748), which was thought by many in its own time to be a sentimental comedy, appears by Ellis's tests to lack the "essentials" of this subgenre. Richard W. Bevis,

"Garrick between Tragedy & Comedy"

however, rejects such intrinsic tests, preferring to rely on "common sense and sensibility" to distinguish in a play, considered as an artistic whole, "an intent to sentimentalize," which he finds abundantly present in *The Foundling.*

Though pervasive, sentimentality did not dominate drama in this period. Traditional comic elements, including ridicule of the follies and vices of the lower social orders, continued to appear even in plays that were otherwise sentimental, and survived in the farces and afterpieces that provided comic relief for an evening of moral drama. **John Gay** satirized both the taste for Italian **opera** and the political establishment of **Sir Robert Walpole** in his "Newgate Pastoral," *The Beggar's Opera,* in 1728. **Henry Fielding** followed his example with *The Author's Farce* in 1730, in which an impoverished author turns his play into a puppet show to satisfy the taste of the town, and with *Tom Thumb* (later *The Tragedy of Tragedies*) in 1731, a **burlesque** of heroic tragedy. Such "irregular" productions provided a refuge for the laughing tradition of comedy in a moralistic age.

Fielding's exploitation of the other dimension of Gay's success—political **satire**—led to the successful *Pasquin* in 1736, *The Historical Register for 1736* and *Eurydice Hiss'd* in 1737, and finally to the passing of the **Playhouse Act** of 1737, which required that all new plays be approved by the lord chamberlain, and that they be produced only in patented playhouses. The effect of this was not only to restrict political expression but also to confine new drama to the Drury Lane and Covent Garden theaters, something that discouraged the writing of new plays. Henceforth, burlesques, musicals, and farces, which did not require official approval, dominated the theater in **London**, though a few comedies continued to appear, and serious drama survived in the suburbs and **provincial towns.** Not until the 1760s did English drama, under Garrick's tutelage, begin to challenge the expectations of its audience. Such plays as **George Colman the Elder**'s *The Clandestine Marriage* (1766), in which he collaborated with Garrick, and **Frances Sheridan**'s *The Discovery* (1763) were still heavily flavored with sentimentality, but **Richard Cumberland**'s *The West Indian* (1771) sought to achieve its uplifting effects through laughter rather than tears.

The tide distinctly turned in 1773 with **Oliver Goldsmith**'s *She Stoops to Conquer,* which exposed the weaknesses of sentimentalism while maintaining the benevolent outlook on which such comedy was based. In this play, the roguish antics of Tony Lumpkin contrast with the sentimental attitudes of Charles Marlow, while Kate Hardcastle's masquerade shows how inhibited her lover's sensibilities really are. In a comic subplot, the inflamed passions of George Hastings are cooled into a more restrained sensibility by his inamorata, Constance Neville. The resolution of the play balances wit with understanding, passion with social constraint, and sentiment with affection, leading many to see it as harmonizing the Restoration tradition of comedy with late Georgian values. Goldsmith himself encouraged this view in his "Essay on the Theatre; or, A Comparison between Laughing and Sentimental Comedy" (1773), which, though it has long been taken as a serious critical manifesto, is now also seen as Goldsmith's effort to prepare the public for the satire of sentimentality that is a crucial element in his play.

The only talent that equaled, and perhaps exceeded, Goldsmith's in the second half of the century was that of **Richard Brinsley Sheridan**. Sheridan was influential as a producer as well as an author and actor. In *The Rivals* (1775) he continued Goldsmith's satire of sentimental comedy through the excesses of Lydia and Faulkland, but hedged his bets by rewarding the barely reformed Faulkland with his beloved Julia at play's end. *The School for Scandal* (1777) endeavors to resolve the question of sentiment by contrasting two brothers, Joseph Surface, who represents falsity of sentiment, and Charles Surface, whom Richard Bevis calls an "imprudent benevolist." The resulting adventures between false and true **wit** remind some audiences of Restoration comedy, but the wit that succeeds in the play is not the repartee of Wycherley or Congreve—it is rather an accord between language and feeling. On the other hand, while there are sentimental touches in the play, it lacks the reforming agenda that is essential to sentimental comedy. In *The School for Scandal* Sheridan laid the foundation for a new comic tradition on the bedrock of both sentimental and "laughing" comedy, but nearly a century was to pass before British dramatists—overwhelmed by the public taste for spectacles, musicals, and romantic melodramas—could take advantage of it.

Geoffrey M. Sill

Bibliography

Bevis, Richard W. *The Laughing Tradition: Stage Comedy in Garrick's Day.* 1980.
———. *English Drama: Restoration and Eighteenth Century, 1660–1789.* 1988.
Ellis, Frank H. *Sentimental Comedy: Theory & Practice.* 1991.
Hume, R.D. *The Rakish Stage.* 1983.
———, ed. *The London Theatre World, 1660–1800.* 1980.
Nicoll, Allardyce. *British Drama.* 1925.
———. *A History of Early Eighteenth Century Drama, 1700–1750.* 1925.
Sherbo, Arthur. *English Sentimental Comedy.* 1957.
Stephens, John Russell. *The Profession of the Playwright: British Theatre, 1800–1900.* 1992.

See also Actors and the Acting Profession; Addison, Joseph; Bickerstaff, Isaac; Burgoyne, John; Dramatic Criticism; Home, John; Kelly, Hugh; Macklin, Charles; Murphy, Arthur; O'Hara, Kane; Theaters and Staging; Thomson, James; Vanbrugh, Sir John; Women in Literature; Young, Edward

Dramatic Criticism

British dramatic criticism evolved into an astonishingly rich and prolific activity during the Hanoverian years, engaging nearly every major writer from **Alexander Pope** to **William Hazlitt**. The staggering variety of its outlets—in **newspaper** notices, pamphlets, **periodical** reviews, editorial prefaces, books, chapters in broader historical and philosophical studies, lecture series, prologues and epilogues to plays, and even entire stage productions like **Richard Brinsley Sheridan**'s *The Critic* (1779)—suggests the wide range of its interests, engagements, and cultural impact.

Surrey Theatre, Blackfriars Road, 1828

Much of the dramatic criticism of the early 18th century was occasioned by the persisting controversy over drama's social value, first provoked by **Jeremy Collier**'s *Short View of the Immorality and Profaneness of the English Stage* (1698), and still hotly continuing in 1726 when **William Law** published *Absolute Unlawfulness of the Stage* and **John Dennis** issued *The Stage Defended.* The sociopolitical ground of this debate helped establish a political center for dramatic criticism that would become increasingly important throughout the next hundred years.

Contributing to a different kind of precedent, **Pope**'s edition of **Shakespeare**'s works and its theoretical preface (1725) reinforced a new and steadily developing scholarly tradition of sustained critical commentary on the drama. The most important innovations in dramatic criticism of this time, however, were the beginning of newspaper notices of theatrical events (in such papers as the *Daily Courant,* the *Evening Post,* and the *Examiner*); and the first periodical criticism of British drama, by **Richard Steele** in the *Tatler, Town-Talk,* and the *Theatre;* **Joseph Addison** in *The Spectator;* and **Lewis Theobald** in the *Censor.* This periodical criticism, to which other dramatic critics like Dennis often replied in separate pamphlets, offered reviews of new stage productions—Steele's main strength—and theoretical discussions of the morality of dramatic writing and the applicability of **neoclassical** theory to British drama.

The work of Steele, Addison, and Theobald established an important foundation for the outpouring of periodical dramatic criticism when the first periodicals fully devoted to the theater appeared—*Cote's Weekly Journal; or The English Stage Player* (1734) and Aaron Hill's the *Prompter* (1734–1736). Meanwhile, emerging to offer frequent commentary on theatrical activity were numerous journals such as the *Monthly Review, Universal Magazine, Gentleman's Magazine, London Chronicle, Critical Review,* and the *Trifler.* The 1740s also witnessed a great advance in scholarly editions of Shakespeare and other earlier dramatists. Editors established new standards of textual correctness and provided a massive amount of critical commentary, which was augmented by numerous treatises and books on classical and British drama such as **David Hume**'s *Essay on Tragedy* (1742), John Upton's *Critical Observations on Shakespeare* (1746), William Guthrie's *An Essay Upon English Tragedy* (1747), **Richard Hurd**'s *A Dissertation on the Provinces of the Drama* (1757), and the anonymous *An Essay upon the Present State of the Theatre* (1760).

Such a marked increase in dramatic criticism developed out of the new surge of the **middle class** into literary activity, which moved the drama out of its aristocratic Restoration contexts and toward a more democratic audience eager for critical discussion of it. Predictably, this criticism tended to stress **middle-class** moral values—most famously in **Samuel Johnson**'s *Preface to Shakespeare* (1765), and perhaps most infamously in Elizabeth Griffith's pious *The Morality of Shakespeare's Dramas* (1775). It also championed the presentation of nonaristocratic characters in central dramatic roles, an issue raised in **George Lillo**'s play *The London Merchant* (1731) and critically elaborated in Thomas Franklyn's *A Dissertation on Ancient Tragedy* (1760) and Edward Taylor's *Cursory Remarks on Tragedy* (1774).

The voluminous production of dramatic and other types of **literary criticism** during these years helped fashion in the latter 18th century a new consciousness of national artistic traditions, particularly of Britain's rich dramatic history. That engagement with the past generated the first major anthologies of British drama up through the 18th century—an example was *Bell's British Theatre* (1776)—and numerous histories of British drama, beginning as early as Colley **Cibber**'s *An Apology for the Life of Mr. Colley Cibber* (1740), and fully developing with Benjamin Victor's *History of the Theatres of London and Dublin* (1771), Thomas Hawkins's *The Origins of the English Drama* (1773), and **George Colman the Elder**'s *Critical Reflections on the Old English Dramatic Writers* (1787). In addition to this historical emphasis, one of the major theoretical preoccupations of late-18th-century dramatic criticism involved the more detailed evaluation of character portraiture—the main subject of William Richardson's *A Philosophical Analysis and Illustration of Some of Shakespeare's Remarkable Characters* (1777), Maurice Morgann's *Essay on the Dramatic Character of Sir John Falstaff* (1777), and Thomas Whatley's *Remarks on Some of the Characters of Shakespeare* (1785).

These concerns with history and character were developed in important new directions throughout the **Romantic** era, which witnessed an unprecedented explosion of dramatic writing occasioned by a substantial revival of Renaissance drama and the volatile influence of the **French Revolution** on British dramatic writing and periodical reviewing. At least 160 newpapers and journals were devoted exclusively to the theater between 1800–1837, among which **Thomas Holcroft**'s *The Theatrical Recorder* (1805) provided one of the most incisive accounts of the teeming theatrical world of the early 19th century. Major periodicals like *Blackwood's Edinburgh Magazine, Edinburgh Review, Quarterly Review, Analytical Review,* the *London Magazine,* and **Leigh Hunt**'s *Examiner* all featured regular sections on contemporary theater and dramatic theory. Many new dramatic histories, dictionaries, and anthologies appeared, with the numerous critical prefaces of **Elizabeth Inchbald**'s 25-volume *British Theatre* (1808) comprising one of the period's most substantial investigations of past and present drama.

And what is arguably the most richly condensed production of dramatic criticism in British history emerged in a group of major theoretical works—Hazlitt's *Characters of Shakespeare's Plays* (1817), *Lectures on the Dramatic Literature of the Age of Elizabeth* (1820), and his many theatrical reviews for **London** newspapers and periodicals; **Samuel Taylor Coleridge**'s lectures on Shakespeare and Renaissance drama (1818–1819); **Walter Scott**'s *An Essay on the Drama* (1827); **Charles Lamb**'s *Specimens of English Dramatic Poets Who Lived about the Time of Shakespeare* (1808) and "On the Tragedies of Shakespeare Considered With Reference to Their Fitness for Stage Representation" (1811); **Joanna Baillie**'s *Introductory Discourse* to her plays on the passions (1798); and some 600 theatrical reviews and papers by Hunt.

This impressive body of theatrical writing took the history and character issues of late-18th-century criticism into a new depth of inquiry that set the agenda of dramatic criticism for generations to come. Coleridge, Hazlitt, and Baillie intensified earlier discussions of dramatic character by elevating psychological interiority as the chief object of dramatic writing. This emphasis on mental theater led Scott and Lamb, among others, to extol the act of reading drama for psychological substance over the experience of watching it for the spectacle of its stage representation. Meanwhile, dramatic consciousness was often colored by the era's political debates and resulted in indirect efforts to fend off Jacobin threats, as Coleridge sought to do in his Shakespeare criticism, or to support political reform, as Hazlitt did in his Elizabethan lectures.

In fact, one of the greatest interests of Hanoverian dramatic criticism may lie in study of its relationships to contemporary ideology. Some of its most striking characteristics arose in response, however obliquely, to the ideological dislocations of the time. Of course one must be analytically careful in this, for the psychological emphases so characteristic of Romantic criticism, for example, are at least discernible in the earlier criticism of Steele and Pope. On the other hand, there are compelling arguments in favor of treating Romantic endorsements of nonrepresentational drama and psychological interiority as so many efforts to resist the sociopolitical instabilities of the revolutionary era after 1789 by withdrawing into the private, more secure regions of mental theater.

Greg Kucich

Bibliography

Bevis, Richard. *English Drama: Restoration and Eighteenth Century, 1660–1789.* 1988.

Burwick, Frederick. *Illusion and the Drama: Critical Theory of the Enlightenment and Romantic Era.* 1991.

Cox, Jeffrey. *In the Shadows of Romance: Romantic Tragic Drama in Germany, England, and France.* 1987.

Gaull, Marilyn. "The Theater," in *English Romanticism: The Human Context.* 1988.

Gray, Charles. *Theatrical Criticism in London to 1795.* 1931.

Heller, Janet. *Coleridge, Lamb, Hazlitt, and the Reader of Drama.* 1990.

Hoagwood, Terence, and Daniel Watkins. *Romantic Drama: Historical and Critical Essays.* Special issue of *The Wordsworth Circle.* Vol. 23.

Loftis, John, et al. *The Revels History of Drama in England.* Vols. 5, 6. 1976.

Nicoll, Allardyce. *A History of English Drama: 1660–1900.* Vols. 2–4. 1955.

Stratman, Carl. *A Bibliography of Britain's Dramatic Periodicals: 1720–1960.* 1962.

See also Actors and the Acting Profession; Dramatic Arts; Women in Literature

Drawing

Drawing was a very common accomplishment in the Hanoverian era, partly because accurate drawings before the days of photography were the simplest method of recording and transmitting visual data. The flourishing of Hanoverian **architecture, interior design, book illustration,** and **science, technology, and invention** all favored emphasis on drawing as well, to such an extent even that machines were invented to reproduce drawings automatically. And while nearly all educated people were capable of at least some drawing, accomplished travelers were often extremely good at it. Drawing also held pride of place in the world of 18th-century art, and was especially favored by portraitists such as **Sir Joshua Reynolds,** the foremost **portrait painter** of the era. Drawings more elaborate than portraiture, such as serial drawings that told a moral tale, took form most successfully in the engraved work of the satirical moralist **William Hogarth,** with his biting **caricatures** and talent for seeing the grotesque.

Reynolds encouraged young artists at the **Royal Academy** (in his *Discourses on Art,* a series of lectures given between 1769 and 1790) to begin their artistic careers by learning how to draw correctly. In this they employed such standard books as Jacob Cats's *Book of Emblems* (1637), Padre Pozzo's *The Jesuit's Perspective* (1707), and an English translation of André Felibien's *Tent of Darius* (1707). These books, which contained black-and-white illustrations as models for imitation, dealt with subject matter typical for the age: Cats concerned himself with the portrayal of the universal through the particular, Pozzo with the technical aspects of perspective, and Felibien with architecture. Also influential was the Frenchman Jean Antoine Watteau (1684–1721), whose example helped British artists begin to develop new styles of drawing by scorning the inanimate objects used in the past and drawing from life.

But 18th-century artists were always, as Reynolds urged in his *Discourses,* to avoid the "accidental discriminations" of nature, and to focus instead on a distinct, precise exhibition of the *general forms* of things. This emphasis, an aspect of the **neoclassical style** so influential after 1750, was on drawing things as they *were,* not necessarily as they appeared. The idea was to draw, for example, a great hero as a great hero, not as a mere man. Yet **Thomas Gainsborough,** one of Reynolds's chief rivals, succeeded in creating a distinct style of his own, marked by cool elegance and fluid, translucent technique. Gainsborough was interested only in reproducing reality as accurately as he could, in contrast to the neoclassical mandate of portraying general forms through the particular. The slightly later drawings of **Thomas Rowlandson** reveal a stronger emotional attachment, bordering on affection, especially in those scenes where the subjects consisted of crowded streets and the interiors of **London** townhouses. Rowlandson's soft-line style was one of pleasant narrative, an incisive but gentle caricature of his surroundings, in contrast to Hogarth's often harsh and savage line. To emphasize the softness of his work, Rowlandson often enhanced his drawings with **watercolor.**

For many graphic artists of the **Romantic** era (1790–1830), the characteristic striving for perfection of form and emphasis on aesthetic and emotional values inevitably led to

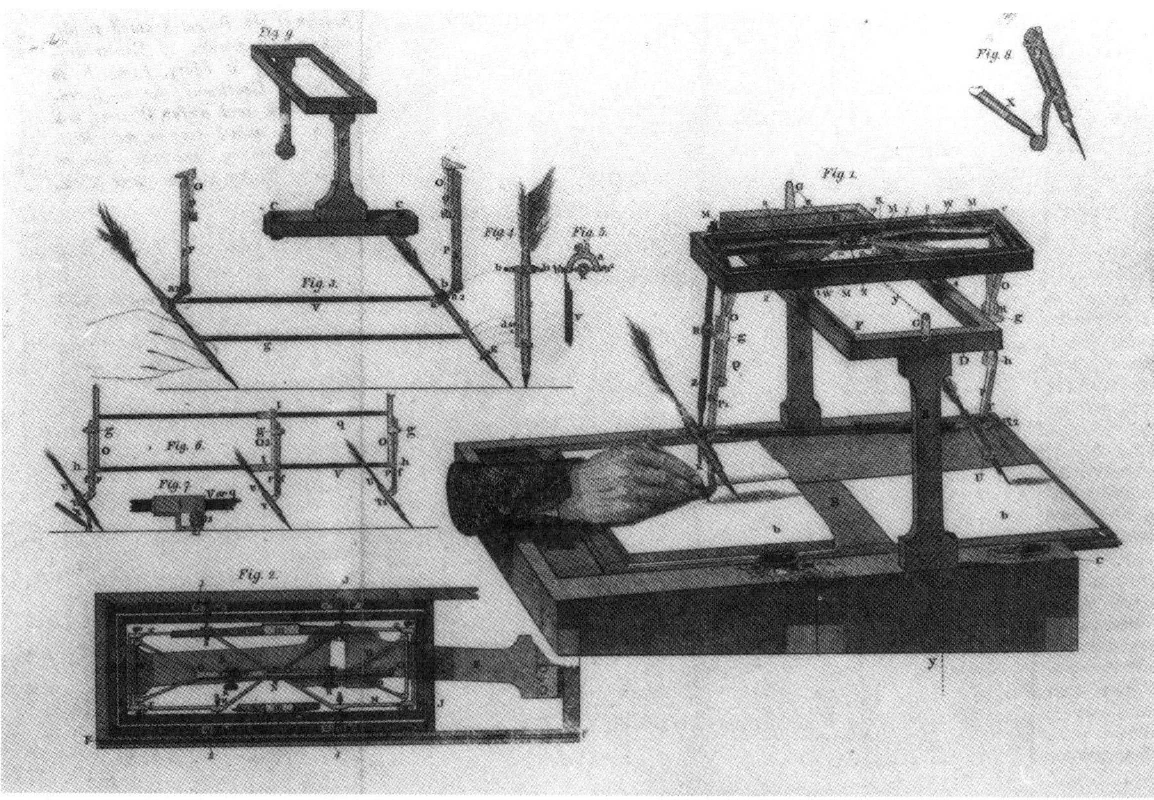

Machine for copying drawings, 1800

a dampening of artistic creativity. Drawing, however, took on a renewed importance during the same period and tended to become a haven for the **poetic** imagination. Line was often favored, almost as if to bear out the contention that pure outline is the most effective means of artistic expression. The most original draftsman of the day, one who outspokenly defended line above every other aesthetic element, was the poet and artist **William Blake**, who devoted himself mainly to book illustration. In his productions he gloried in dramatic tension, defining character and movement in flowing lines, and used watercolor not to soften his line as Rowlandson had done, but rather to heighten emotional response to it. **Henry Fuseli**, with whom Blake did much of his work, and with whom he shared a deep respect for the great Renaissance draftsman **Michelangelo**, probably encouraged him in this. Fuseli was the creator of hand-colored drawings that frequently bordered on surrealistic extravagance or ambiguous eroticism. An explorer of **the supernatural**, he painted his subjects on watercolored disks with a plain background, a technique enabling him to produce some weird effects.

The style of the drawings of **J.M.W. Turner** is also linear, but it is easier to recognize a poetic feeling in them through the soft atmospheric effects achieved by means of a complex handling of watercolor. **John Constable**, on the other hand, remained faithful to the 18th-century tradition; even in his landscape drawings there is a masterly treatment of light, which is sensitively realistic. Thus the British school of drawing, fluctuating between ideal and naturalistic approaches, entered the Victorian Age still divided.

Matthew S. Novak

Bibliography

Hipple, Jr., Walter J. *The Beautiful, the Sublime, and the Picturesque in Eighteenth-Century British Aesthetic Theory.* 1957.

Lewine, J. *Bibliography of Eighteenth-Century Art and Illustrated Books.* 1969.

Oppe, Adolf. *English Drawings, Stuart and Georgian Periods.* 1950.

Reynolds, Sir Joshua. *Discourses on Art.* Ed. Robert R. Wark. 1966.

Stainton, Lindsay. *Drawing in England from Hilliard to Hogarth.* 1987.

Watrous, James. *The Craft of Old-Master Drawings.* 1967.

See also Caricature; Engraving; Painting; Political Prints

Drink Industries

The Hanoverian alcoholic drink industries were centered in the activities of **brewers** and distillers, together with their distributors and retailers. Of the two, brewers were far more important. Breweries were everywhere; beer was the most common drink throughout the British Isles except in Highland **Scotland** and **Ireland**, where whiskey took its place. Every village and hamlet had its brewhouse; larger households might have their own. Though the production process was relatively simple, the product itself was delicate and did not travel well, and in any case tended to spoil quickly. It was bulky and cumbersome, too. Given the insuffiency of **transport** facilities before the great **canal**-building boom of the latter 18th century, brewing was almost exclusively a local industry.

A partial exception to this existed in **London**, where even before the 18th century some Southwark brewers supplied home counties publicans and gentry families. It was there that the first breakthrough in production methods occurred, spurred by the invention of a new type of beer. First brewed in 1722 by Ralph Harwood, a partner in the Bell Brewhouse in Shoreditch, the publicans he sold it to called it by the not-very-lip-smacking name, "entire butt." It soon came to be known as porter, after the men who became its great customers and champions, for they believed that it gave them the strength and stamina they needed to work 12 or more hours unloading ships or hauling cargoes daily through the streets.

Though an unintended consequence of its discovery, this rich, dark beer was chemically more stable and robust than the fine ale it replaced. It was able to withstand excessive heat during the various stages of production, as well as changes in temperature, and it stored well, which meant that producers could expand their plants and distribution networks. By 1760, five London breweries made over 50,000 barrels annually; 20 years later, six made over 80,000 barrels each year. Truman and Barclay, two famous names that survive in the trade today, were among them, as was **Whitbread**. In 1796 the founder of that firm, Samuel Whitbread (1720–1796), became the first brewer to top the 200,000 barrel mark. His plant, including stocks, was worth over half a million pounds, and included over 100 horses. He supplied more than 500 publicans, and perhaps another 1,000 customers besides.

In the provinces, these "power loom" brewers were the envy of many small **entrepreneurs** who tried to emulate them. Burton-on-Trent would become a new haven for brewers because of its gypsum-flavored water, especially after the opening of the **railway** from Derby (1839). By that time, tastes had changed: porter was out, and pale ale back in; but not before a Scottish brewer, Arthur Guinness (*d.* 1855), had established his porter brewery in **Dublin**. This would become the largest industry in Ireland, and is famous today for its porter or stout, a beer that made the great revolution in brewing possible.

By comparison, the distillation of alcoholic beverages was a small business, at least until the introduction of Geneva or "Gin" from the Continent in the 1720s. A parliamentary act of 1689 had prohibited the importation of French brandies and all other spirits, laying the foundation for 18th-century expansion of British licensed distilleries, but in England their products were generally too expensive for ordinary people until gin and gin shops changed everything. It is now usual to say that the mania for gin and the resulting social problems of the age of **George II** (1727–1760) were much exaggerated by contemporaries, but the contrast drawn by **William Hogarth** in his two prints of 1751, *Beer Street* and *Gin Lane,* the first reflecting the pleasant sociability of ordinary folk and the other the deadening effects of alcoholic addiction, is telling. The quantities of high-proof alcoholic spirits distilled in Britain speaks for itself: in 1714, about 2 million gallons were distilled; by 1735 the figure was more than 5 million, of which the great bulk was gin; by 1742, more than 7 million gallons were produced; by 1751, more than 11 million were consumed annually. Naturally the craze for gin put a real dent in beer sales, and these did not recover until the **Pelham** ministry (1751, 1753) prohibited distillers from retailing spirits themselves or selling them to unlicensed retailers, and unlicensed retailers were made subject to drastic **punishments** of imprisonment, whipping, and (for the third offense) **transportation**.

Complaints against gin were heard from Scottish and Irish brewers, also. But in Scotland and Ireland, beer was a good deal less popular, and distilleries rather than breweries were prevalent. These were often both modest and illegal, and the distilling industry was a good deal more fragmented than brewing. In Ireland, itinerant distillers could be seen on the roads with small pot stills strapped to their backs well into the 19th century. In both countries, malted grains were used nearly exclusively, which, together with the peat fire used to fuel the still and the peat-flavored water, gave the whiskey its distinctive taste. Unless adulterated, it was quite high in alcoholic content and, since it was always aged briefly, quite harsh and fiery. Like the "white lightning" of Appalachia, it was colorless but extremely potent. Called "poteen" in Ireland, it was much preferred to the more expensive product made in licensed distilleries and known as "parliament whiskey."

Whiskey drinking increased at both ends of the social scale in Scotland in the latter 18th century. But **wars**, the resulting need for revenue, and rising duties on legitimate distillers had the effect of diverting more and more production to the small, untaxed stills supposedly for domestic production. Illicit distilling burgeoned until the Excise Act of 1823 was passed, deliberately lowering duties by over 50% on legitimate distilleries and thus eroding the advantage of illegal competitors. Parliament distilleries then began to prosper in both Scotland and Ireland, though illegal operations continued for decades in Ireland. By the middle years of the 19th century, when even some Englishmen took to it, a softer, more mature whiskey was preferred. It became usual to blend malted whiskey with neutral grain spirits, and to age it in sherry casks. The casks gave it the color now associated with Scotch and other whiskeys, but today it is caramel coloring that is used to give whiskey its characteristic tint.

Viniculture was also ancient in Britain, but during the Hanoverian period the domestic wine industry was small and stagnant. Some wine was produced in the south, and **James Oglethorpe** had an interest in reviving viniculture in both England and his colony of Georgia; the greatest share of wine was, however, imported. Wine was in fact the preferred drink among the upper classes, though beer drinking in wine glasses was a fad, and beer was socially shared by men from all social classes at **blood sports**. French claret was very popular until it was displaced by port in the early 18th century; port in turn was challenged but not overthrown by sherry from the 1780s on. French wines did not make a great comeback until the 1860s.

The chief remaining alcoholic beverage of Hanoverian Britain was apple cider (some perry was also made), produced as a domestic industry in country houses and by **farmers** for personal consumption and provision to **agricultural laborers**. A medical breakthrough occurred in 1767 when Sir George

Baker (1722–1809), a physician, traced "Devonshire colic" to the lead presses, pipes, and containers used in cider production, thus discovering lead poisoning.

George Bretherton

Bibliography

Clark, Peter. *The English Alehouse: A Social History, 1200–1830.* 1983.

Connell, K.H. *Irish Peasant Society.* 1968.

Harrison, Brian. *Drink and the Victorians: The Temperance Question in England, 1815–72.* 1971.

Mathias, Peter. *The Brewing Industry in England, 1700–1830.* 1959.

———. *The First Industrial Nation: An Economic History of Britain, 1700–1914.* 1969.

McGuire, E.B. *Irish Whiskey: A History of Distilling in Ireland.* 1973.

Smout, T.C. *A Century of the Scottish People: 1830–1950.* 1980.

Weir, Ronald B. "Brewing and Distilling," in John Langton and R.J. Morris, eds., *The Atlas of Industrializing Britain, 1780–1914.* 1986.

See also Brewing and Public Houses; Drinking; Gin Acts

Drinking

The first thing to be said about drinking during the Hanoverian period is that there was a great deal of it. As religion became less rigorous, and **manners** lost something of their severity, so, too, attitudes toward heavy drinking and even drunkenness began to soften. Moreover, a run of good harvests during the first two-thirds of the 18th century, and technological changes improving **transport**, encouraged people to drink more. Plentiful grain harvests lowered prices for the brewer, which were passed on in the form of cheap beer to the public. "Pudding Time," as this era of prosperity was called, was also "Porter Time."

Of course, Britons could have spent their money on other things beside alcoholic beverages. Though many foreign visitors thought the climate drove them to drink, others considered that more healthy recreations had been denied them by the puritanical restrictions that left them with only their beer on Sundays. The Swiss traveler Cesar de Saussure, who visited **London** in the 1720s, was amazed to find that little water was drunk, despite the relative purity of the water supply.

Neither sex nor class set limits on drink. Women drank in public, and drunken women were a common sight in London. **Pitt the Younger** was a tippler, and so was his nemesis, **Thomas Paine**. The expression "drunk as a lord" is telling, for lords could afford frequent intoxication, thus easily joining the bishops, academics, parsons, and professional men who spent years in an alcoholic haze; and in this if in little else, many commoners could emulate them, once cheap gin was invented. Toasts were drunk in many a stately home from round-bottomed glasses: These could not be set down until they were emptied of their content, and once emptied, they were quickly refilled by a ready attendant.

However, food was often taken along with drink, and the upper classes, at least, did not stint. A London physician, George Cheney, habitually ate one large meal each day, "consisting of a bottle of port, a quarter bottle of brandy, a tankard of ale, a trifle of broiled fowl or plate of fish, and a 1 1/2 pound rump steak." It took him about one and one-half hours to finish. As **Addison** said in *The Spectator* when commenting on the "Medley of Intemperance" that was typical of the dietary habits of 1712, "I fancy that I see Gouts and Dropsies, Feavers and Lethargies, with other innumerable Distempers lying in Ambuscade among the Dishes."

Feasting among the lower orders was not so elaborate. Beer, it must be remembered, is nutritious—"liquid bread." Frequently, little more than bread, cheese, and beer was available at the chandlers' shops, but there was in pudding time plenty of beer. **Benjamin Franklin**, who worked as a printer in London in 1725, reported on his "companion at press," who, like the other journeymen, drank "every day a pint before breakfast, a pint at breakfast . . . a pint between breakfast and dinner, a pint in the afternoon about 6 o'clock, and another pint when he had done his day's work." After work, there was always the pub.

It was, however, at this point, in the 1720s, that the dram shop, selling hard liquor, was becoming a greater concern. Whereas beer was the drink of **artisans** and people engaged in heavy labor, the new drink, gin, was the favorite of women, workingmen in sedentary trades (weavers, particularly), and of the destitute, the imprisoned, and hopeless, for whom spirits were both effect and cause of misery. Although alehouses were routinely licensed, the first gin shops were not; and amidst the furor over gin drinking it was discovered in 1725 that around London (where gin drinking was almost exclusively centered), more than 6,000 establishments were selling it, and this was not counting all the peddlers, tobacconists, chandlers, and other casual back-alley retailers. The "gin mania" became so serious, and created such a spectacle in the streets and such danger of **crime**, that in the period 1736–1751 a series of **gin acts** were passed that sharply limited dram shops and imposed heavy penalties on illegal retailers. Consumption in the 1750s fell by 75%, gratifying reformers like **Jonas Hanway**, who wrote (1759) that "the people themselves seem at length to have discovered, that health and pleasure, food and raiment, are better than sickness and pain, want and wretchedness."

The consumption of spirits declined from around 11 million gallons annually in 1751 to a little over 2 million annually in the 1760s and 1770s, and to less than that in the 1780s and 1790s, thanks to poor harvests, rising corn prices, higher taxes on spirits, and an absolute prohibition on distilling that occurred in 1795. A decade later, an American visitor commented that "the common people in England drink but little ardent spirits, because its excessive dearness places it almost beyond their reach."

People did their best to compensate by flocking to **public houses**. A growing **population** and a lack of alternative gathering places made pubs very popular. At one time it had been remarked that Englishmen met either in churches or in pubs, but by the 18th century's end it was a commonplace that the former were never open and the latter never closed. Friendly and trade societies held their meetings in pubs, as did political and professional groups. Pubs were centers of **gambling**, **sport**, and other **amusements and recreation**. These also served as houses of call, that is, as labor exchanges, with the publican in a position to trade drinks for work: when the job was done, the workers would be paid in the pub and encouraged to drink up their wages.

Not surprisingly, the new moral reformers—**Evangelicals** and various working-class self-help movements—launched their attacks against both beer drinking and spirits drinking. One result was the founding of the British Association for the Promotion of Temperance (1834), the first step in the Victorian temperance campaign that followed. But a particular worry over the recrudescence of gin drinking, and even fear of a new "gin age," resulted in the Beer House Act (1830) of the **Wellington** ministry, which sought again to shift drinking from spirits to beer by reducing pub license fees. The regulation of drinking hours began in 1838, with a requirement that pubs close from midnight Saturday to noon on Sunday.

George Bretherton

Bibliography

Clark, Peter. *The English Alehouse, 1200–1830.* 1983.

———. "The Gin Mania and Official Controls in Early Hanoverian England," in Susanna Barrows, et al., eds., *The Social History of Alcohol: Drinking and Culture in Modern Society.* 1987.

———. "The 'Mother Gin' Controversy in Early Eighteenth Century England." *Transactions of the Royal Historical Society.* Vol. 38, pp. 63–84.

George, M. Dorothy. *London Life in the Eighteenth Century.* 1965.

Harrison, Brian. *Drink and the Victorians: The Temperance Question in England, 1815–72.* 1971.

Schwartz, Richard B. *Daily Life in Johnson's London.* 1983.

See also Brewing and Public Houses; Drink Industries; Manners and Morals

Dublin

Dublin was by far the most populous and dynamic **city** in Hanoverian **Ireland**. It had grown rapidly in the 17th century as a consequence of an influx of thousands of English and European Protestants (mainly Huguenots); a majority of the city's 60,000 **population** around 1714 was Protestant. This religious mix changed greatly in the 18th century because the city's strong demographic growth, which saw its population rise to 100,000 by 1730 and to 182,000 by 1798, was propelled primarily by the immigration of **Roman Catholics** from the surrounding countryside. This pattern was intensified in the early 19th century. The population reached a quarter of a million by the end of the Hanoverian era (1837).

The growth in population stimulated economic activity. As Ireland's capital, center of government, and main commercial and entertainment center in the 18th century, Dublin was ideally placed to profit from the growth in population that

The Four Law Courts, Dublin, c. 1837

took place, and it is no coincidence that it consolidated its position as the country's main port during this period. It was through its harbor that Ireland's main export commodities, including linen, were shipped, and its main imports, manufactured goods, admitted. Moreover, the presence of a large volume of indigenous and imported goods meshed with the vital political and administrative functions conducted in the city to provide stimuli and outlets for a whole range of commercial, industrial, and luxury activities.

Dublin had a large **textile industry**, based in the Liberties (an area long outside city jurisdiction), dating back to the 17th century. Textiles continued to be produced in great volume into the 19th century, though the emergence of newer fabrics like **cotton** hastened the demise of luxury fabrics such as silk, while sustained English competition before and after the **Act of Union** (1800) caused the contraction of other sectors. Luxury manufactures in gold and silver, printing, bookbinding, coachbuilding, and fine furniture manufacturing, all of which flourished in the 18th century, also contracted sharply in the early 19th century. So too did the ambitious physical remodeling of the city's heartland that was one of the greatest achievements of the earlier Hanoverian era.

The construction of new Houses of Parliament on College Green in the 1720s and 1730s symbolized the desire of the ruling **Anglo–Irish Protestant Ascendancy** to possess a capital that mirrored its own dominance. The splendid new parliamentary building stimulated landowners such as Luke Gardiner and Earl Fitzwilliam into similarly ambitious undertakings and led to a massive program of development and construction that resulted in the creation of an elegant **Georgian** city, characterized by broad vistas, impressive public buildings, spacious squares, and delightfully appointed townhouses. This world contrasted severely with the **poverty** of those at the bottom of the **urban** social pyramid, but neither the political elite that came to Dublin for parliamentary sessions nor the city's municipal elite was unsolicitous of their welfare. Relief programs were set up to combat distress, and though the initial impact of these was modest, they were tangibly more effective by the early 19th century, when a network of hospitals and dispensaries, a House of Industry, and private and parish organizations to provide a safety net were in place.

Dublin corporation, too, played its part, though municipal politics were largely the preserve of a small elite. The challenge that the **radical** physician and pamphleteer Charles Lucas (1713–1771) offered in the 1740s to the aldermanic oligarchy did prompt some reforms in the 1760s, but the corporation offered little to disfranchised artisans or the Catholic **middle classes** who were the most enthusiastic advocates of radical change in the last quarter of the century. During the 1790s, indeed, the corporation was firmly under the control of conservative Protestants who were determined to preserve the political status quo. Events, including the **Act of Union**, rendered this impossible, but they continued to exercise disproportionate influence in the less prosperous, less consensual, and less expansionary post-union era.

James Kelly

Bibliography

Dickson, D. "The Place of Dublin in the Eighteenth-Century Irish Economy," in D. Dickson and T. Devine, eds., *Ireland and Scotland, 1600–1850.* 1983.
———. "The Demographic Implications of Dublin's Growth, 1650–1850," in R. Lawton and R. Lee, eds., *Urban Population Development in Western Europe.* 1989.
Fagan, Patrick. *The Second City: Portrait of Dublin, 1700–60.* 1986.
Murphy, S. "The Corporation of Dublin, 1660–1760." *Dublin Historical Record.* Vol. 38, pp. 22–35.

Duck, Stephen (1705–1756)

"Born in a cot and bred to till the earth," the "Thresher Poet" Duck wrote of himself; but because of the friendship of Joseph Spence (1699–1768) and others, **Queen Caroline** awarded him an annuity and a house in 1730. That year an unauthorized edition of his poems helped transform the hitherto unknown bard into a candidate for the **poet laureateship**.

His sudden fame evoked imitators, including **Mary Collier**, the literary washerwoman, who vigorously protested in "The Woman's Labour" (1739) Duck's picture of women in "The Thresher's Labour" (1730), his best poem. But neither criticism nor **patronage** nor his ordination (1746) improved his **poetry**. Though he had philosophically rejected **suicide** in "To Death" (1738), Duck drowned himself (1756).

Peter A. Tasch

Bibliography

Davis, Rose Mary. *Stephen Duck, the Thresher-Poet.* 1926.
Ferguson, Moira, introd. *The Thresher's Labour and The Woman's Labour.* 1985.

Dueling

The Hanoverian period was the last in which dueling was a realistic choice for gentlemen, not merely a Romantic anachronism. Fragmentary evidence suggests that the frequency of dueling varied during the period, increasing during the reign of **George I** after a period of relative decline, dipping for a while after 1750, then increasing again around the time of the **French Revolution**—partly due perhaps to the argumentative temper and martial spirit provoked in Britain by that event, perhaps also in some way to the self-dramatizing impulses of **Romanticism**.

While some historians suggest that dueling on the Continent was practiced chiefly by idle aristocrats, in Britain some of the most prominent public men fought duels: **George Canning** with **Lord Castlereagh**; the Duke of **Bedford** with the Duke of Buckingham; **William Pitt the Younger**, **John Wilkes**, **Charles James Fox**, the **Duke of Wellington**, Lord **Townshend**, the Duke of York, **Richard Brinsley Sheridan**, numerous naval and army officers, and even some clergymen. Duels also played a central role in the literature of the time: **Defoe**, **Fielding**, **Richardson**, **Smollett**, **Scott**, and **Austen** all depicted characters dueling, threatening duels, fearing duels, or fleeing from them.

Hanoverian duels tended to be more formal affairs than

earlier. More were fought with pistols than swords, a change which may have reduced mortality rates (pistols were not very accurate before 1800). Pistols also allowed older men (like the 60-year-old Duke of Wellington) to take part. In addition, since pistols, unlike swords, were never a part of the daily costume, there was an enforced delay between provocation and actual combat. Thus the use of pistols may have contributed to the transition from duels as brawls to duels as ritualized affairs of honor.

Dueling was against the law, condemned by both churches and the sages of the **Enlightenment**, but a certain tolerance toward it existed throughout the entire period. Duels could be deadly—one analysis, of 172 duels in the reign of **George III**, reveals 69 deaths and 96 woundings. Certainly the duelist was in much more danger from his opponent than from the law: those same 172 duels led to only two criminal executions and eight imprisonments. Indeed, if one observed all the proper rituals—a delay between challenge and duel, proper seconds—there was almost no chance of legal penalty. While a pauper could be hanged for petty theft, a gentleman could blow another's brains out with impunity.

The duel is unintelligible without some understanding of the **aristocracy** and its code of honor, which celebrated physical courage, coolness under fire, and the sacredness of a man's word. For the aristocracy and landed **gentry**, the duel was the ultimate proof of honor; not only the honor of the duelist himself as a man, but also the honor of the landed class. The willingness to face an opponent calmly on the field of honor proclaimed something about the man, and also about the class to which he belonged. Duelists were, in their own eyes at least, a class apart, temporarily above the laws of church and state. Observance of this was a sign of class solidarity. By the same token, men would duel only with equals; inferiors were not worthy of this attention.

Defenders of dueling argued that it bred courage and gave England a brave **army**, channeled violence into an acceptable form, and gave rise to greater delicacy and refinement of manners. Certainly the cool and arrogant courage displayed by so many leading figures in duels contributed to the belief in their innate moral superiority and their felt right to command other classes and other races. This was perhaps the same show of authority that allowed Britain to win and maintain the **Empire** with a relative handful of men.

On the other hand, dueling was often linked to the excesses, especially heavy **drinking** and **gambling**, of the landholding elite. Lives were risked not only over betrayal in love or politics, or profound disagreements in principle, but also for frivolous reasons—a drunken jest, a gambling debt. In one especially ludicrous instance, a duel between two gentlemen was provoked by a fight between their dogs.

Throughout the period, opponents of the duel attacked it as a perversion of true honor, an insult to law and reason, and an affront to God akin to **suicide**. **Jeremy Bentham** addressed an indignant letter to Wellington about dueling, beginning with the admonition: "Misguided Man!" For a long time the duel withstood all such challenges, but a number of factors contributed to its demise: the rise of **Evangelical** Christianity, with its more rigorous moral code; a new **middle class** with far more faith in material progress than in old notions of honor, lineage, and gallantry; and the gradual loss of power and wealth by the landed classes. Men willing to die over an insult or a point of **manners** began to be viewed not as heroic, but as ridiculous.

Kevin Mulcahy

Bibliography

Andrew, Donna T. "The Code of Honour and Its Critics: The Opposition to Duelling in England, 1700–1850." *Social History*. Vol. 5, pp. 409–434.

Kiernan, V.G. *The Duel in European History: Honour and the Reign of Aristocracy*. 1988.

Millingen, J.G. *The History of Duelling: Including Narratives of the Most Remarkable Personal Encounters That Have Taken Place from the Earliest Period to the Present Time*. 1841.

Thompson, F.M.L., ed. *The Cambridge Social History of Britain, 1750–1950*. 3 vols. 1990.

Dundas, Henry (Viscount Melville) (1741–1811)

Known as "Harry the Ninth, uncrowned King of Scotland," Dundas became the most powerful man in **Scotland** and a major force in British government. Born in **Edinburgh**, he entered the Faculty of Advocates in 1763. After 1774, first as M.P. for Midlothian and a supporter of **Lord North**, later as a friend of **Pitt the Younger** and power broker in his own right, he built up his political connections through dispensation of government **patronage**. He led Scotland's M.P.s and determined more than anyone else their nomination for election to the **Commons**; he also determined the selection of repre-

Henry Dundas

sentative peers for the **Lords**. In 1780 the government won 41 out of 45 parliamentary seats, Dundas controlling 12 of them; by 1784 he controlled over 22 M.P.s.

Dundas was patronage broker also for jobs in the Scottish churches and universities; he displayed an even hand in dealing with the Moderates and Evangelicals, avoiding making enemies. He was industrious, lucid, and strong willed. The fact that he was Pitt's indispensable ally was reflected in the seniority of the positions he held. As Treasurer of the Navy from 1782 he furthered his own interests, and on the Board of Control from 1784 he used his position to promote sons of the Scottish gentry to positions in **India**. As Secretary for War (1794–1801) and First Lord of the Admiralty (1804–1806) he planned and supervised Britain's struggles in the **French Revolutionary and Napoleonic Wars**. Though soldiers died like flies in the **West Indies** and froze to death in the Low Countries, his management of the **Navy** produced significant improvements.

Yet military failings and political wranglings sapped his influence. Forced to resign from the cabinet after a report revealed improper use of Navy funds for private speculation, he was impeached but acquitted by one vote (1806). Pitt's death the same year finished any chance of his return to politics. He was created 1st Viscount Melville and Baron Dunira in 1802.

Richard Finlay

Bibliography

Christie, Ian R. *Wars and Revolutions: Britain 1760–1815.* 1982.

Fry, M. *Henry Dundas.* 1993.

Lenman, B. *Integration, Enlightenment and Industrialization: Scotland 1746–1832.* 1981.

Dunning, John (1731–1783)

A member of the **Shelburne** faction in the **House of Commons**, Dunning introduced on 6 April 1780 a motion that "the influence of the Crown has increased, is increasing, and ought to be diminished," which passed 233–218. Dunning's victory marked one of the high points of the **radical** and **economical reform** movements then pressing the North administration and, indirectly, **George III**. Dunning's later motion, that Parliament not be prorogued until steps were taken to reduce the influence of the Crown, was defeated. Dunning (created 1st Baron Ashburton in 1782) was a noted barrister, and served as Solicitor-General (1768–1770). He was especially opposed to **Lord North**'s policies in dealing with the revolt of the American colonies.

P.J. Kulisheck

Bibliography

Namier, Sir Lewis, and John Brooke, eds. *History of Parliament: The House of Commons, 1754–1790.* 3 vols. 1964.

Norris, John. *Shelburne and Reform.* 1963.

O'Gorman, Frank. *The Rise of Party in England: The Rockingham Whigs 1760–82.* 1975.

See also Pension and Place Bills

E

Earbery, Matthias (1688?–1740)

Earbery, **Jacobite**, **nonjuror**, and polemicist, assailed equally the Hanoverian government and its genteel and sometimes anti–episcopalian critics such as **Lord Bolingbroke** (1678–1751) and his journal, the ***Craftsman***. As incautious a writer as the period produced, Earbery was prosecuted by the government for writing *The History of the Clemency of Our English Monarchs* (1717), an attack on the treatment by **George I** of the leaders of the Jacobite rebellion of 1715. He was again prosecuted for writing the *Universal Spy* (1732), a Jacobitical newspaper hostile to both progovernment and **opposition** apologists for the Revolution Settlement (1689) and the parliamentary monarchy it authorized. Broken by legal problems, Earbery finally swore allegiance to Hanover in the late 1730s, declaring himself "a conquered person, reduced by an Enemy, to the utmost extremity of suffering, and forced to yield, not by choice but by necessity." He died destitute. His career illustrated the ferocity of the government's persecution of critics unprotected by officeholding or powerful friends. His writing also serves as a reminder of the ideological diversity of the opposition to **Sir Robert Walpole**.

Alexander Pettit

Bibliography

Harris, Michael. *London Newspapers in the Age of Walpole: A Study of the Origins of the Modern English Press.* 1987.

East India Company

This company was chartered in 1600 to compete with Dutch traders in the East Indies. Early ventures laid the foundations of trade to Asia and hence of the company's monopoly of British **trade** to **India** and China. It would also act as the agent of British imperialism on the Indian subcontinent.

Sir Thomas Roe, English Ambassador to the court of Jehangir, negotiated the company's first trading post in 1615. By 1628 it had 23 posts, all located on the coast, relying on Indian middlemen in the interior. As the Mughal Empire weakened, European rivalry in India increased. By the 1740s the company faced severe competition from the French Compagnie des Indes. Anglo–French rivalry in Europe spread to India, but the French failed to perceive the value of their colonial possessions there, and increasingly their forces were starved of funds. Victory at **Plassey** in 1757 assured British preeminence over both indigenous and foreign rivals.

The 1760s witnessed a boom period for company servants as they compensated for low wages by private trading (estimated at £500,000 in Bengal by 1763), creating the leg-

Cornwallis receiving the Sons of Tippoo Saib as Hostages 1792

end of the **nabobs**. As British control widened, the paradox of the company's governmental role became more obvious. Directors criticized the impact of expansion on profits, while British liberals criticized "abuses" of power.

Administrative costs rose sharply while the company's Indian exports declined because of competition from the British **cotton industry** and **war** in Europe. Private traders in India and Britain demanded that Parliament abolish the company monopolies, arguing that Indian profits were being lost by an unwieldy, conservative company. Relations between the company and domestic manufacturers were almost always tense. In 1700, imports of Indian calicoes were banned to protect English woolen manufacturers.

The 1698 charter granted the company its Indian and Chinese monopolies, and Parliament the right to scrutinize company policy. By 1770, with the company facing financial crisis, Parliament should have initiated major reform, but failed to do so. The Regulating Act of 1773 reduced company privileges, but failed to impose Crown control.

The career of **Warren Hastings**, the first Governor-General of India (1774–1784), highlighted such problems. Territorial expansion, and the adoption of English law and language, cemented British rule; however, Hastings found himself enmeshed in both company and domestic politics. Increased concern about abuses of power, expressed by **Edmund Burke** and **Henry Dundas**, provided the rationale for **Pitt's India Act** of 1784. Under this, the board of directors was counterbalanced by a board of control consisting of a secretary of state and five privy councillors. Henceforth, the company controlled only trade policy, other aspects being decided by the British cabinet. Yet the pretense of company rule was maintained, the directors continuing to enforce government decisions. Critical reports of the 1780s resulted in Hastings's impeachment in 1788, but it became evident that he was a scapegoat; he was acquitted in 1795.

The costs of the company's governmental role in India were significant. Between 1792 and 1809 its total deficit there equaled £8 million. This was in contrast to its other trade ventures in Asia, above all its Chinese tea monopoly, a purely commercial venture operating through a network of officially recognized Chinese merchants. Between 1793 and 1810 the Chinese trade made a profit of £17 million. However, the company's rule in India was vital to the continued success of its Chinese operations, supplying the opium traded for China's tea. Independent British **merchants** clamored to enjoy such lucrative trade, and the government eventually bowed to relentless campaigns, removing the company's Indian and Chinese monopolies in 1813 and 1834 respectively.

As the company's trading interests in India declined, its employees became salaried civil servants with career paths fashioned by **Charles Cornwallis**, Governor-General from 1785 to 1793. While the British government was still reluctant to assume political control, through the Board of Control it dominated policy decisions, overturning earlier restrictions on the activities of **missionaries** and demanding cash payments for land revenue. The façade finally broke in the Indian Mutiny (1857); the government was then forced to assume full responsibility for governing India. Though shorn of its power, the company continued its trading activities until 1873.

Patricia S. Collins

Bibliography

Bayley, C. *Indian Society and the Making of the British Empire.* 1988.

Bowen, H.V. *Revenue and Reform: The Indian Problem in British Politics, 1757–1773.* 1991.

Fisher, Michael H., ed. *The Politics of the British Annexation of India, 1757–1857.* 1994.

Furber, H. *John Company at Work.* 1948.

Lawson, P. *The East India Company 1600–1857.* 1993.

Marshall, P.J. *East Indian Fortunes: The British in Bengal in the Eighteenth Century.* 1976.

See also Chartered Trading Companies; Commerce, Overseas; Empire and Imperialism; Finlay, Kirkman

Economic Thought

Though initially dominated by **mercantilism**, Hanoverian economic thought gradually evolved until the doctrines of laissez-faire capitalism prevailed. Mercantilism held that the nation enhanced its power by increasing its wealth through the accumulation of bullion (gold and silver) and by a favorable balance of **trade**. The route to prosperity was through the maximization of foreign—not domestic—trade, and through manufacturing and processing, not **agriculture** or extractive industries. Accordingly, the British government entered into trade agreements to obtain exclusive trading privileges, set **wage** and price controls, created monopolies, and felt few inhibitions against restrictive practices. Britain's restrictive **navigation laws** and monopolistic **chartered trading companies**, both dating from before the Hanoverian period began (1714), were monuments to the mercantilist system of thought and practice.

But economic thought was closely geared to basic philosophic and scientific understanding. The first substantial challenge to mercantilism came when the philosopher **John Locke** argued in his *Second Treatise of Government* (1689) that whereas God had given mankind the Earth to own in common, later, with the invention of money, a man's labor, when "mixed with" the land, gave him title to property, or landed estates. Man, while in a natural state, could only use as much land as he needed; but with the invention of coinage, he could accumulate as much individual wealth as he wished.

While Locke's "labor theory of value" implicitly challenged the mercantilist philosophy of state controls, it had no impact on government policy until augmented by basic economic developments (most notably the **Industrial Revolution**) and complemented by theoretical ideas expounded by later thinkers such as **Bernard de Mandeville**, **David Hume**, and especially **Adam Smith**. Mandeville argued in *The Fable of the Bees* (1714) that man's most enduring characteristic was his selfish nature; religion and morality were only fictions that rulers and the clergy promoted in attempts to dominate him.

But private vice led to public virtue: the pursuit of self-interest by the individual created jobs, stimulated the economy, and generally benefited society—an idea akin to Smith's later notion (though Smith condemned Mandeville) that private interests promoted the production of public goods.

Hume, with the growth of commerce, industry, and **Empire** by the 1740s and 1750s, further prepared the way for Smith's great inauguration of "classical" capitalist economics. Hume never published a tract on economic doctrine, but in many essays he attacked mercantilist concepts. He decried the emphasis on bullion and argued that the appropriate yardsticks of an economy were its labor and its production of commodities. He condemned as absurd the mercantilist fear that an unbalanced trade always leads to wealth draining away from the country; more important were the productive energies of the people themselves. When these were abundant, international trade would flourish and all would prosper.

Josiah Tucker, an influential and tireless pamphleteer, concerned himself especially with free trade. Like his predecessors he challenged the mercantilist principle that national wealth should be gauged by accumulation of precious metals (1749, 1755). Labor was the source of wealth; society achieved prosperity when the economy rested on the division of labor and on free markets. These allowed individuals to pursue their own self-interests without state intervention and restrictive trade practices.

Building on all this, Smith, the most influential economic thinker of the Hanoverian age, in *The Wealth of Nations* (1776) powerfully argued on behalf of laissez-faire capitalism. He set forth two essential principles, both repudiating mercantilism; one brilliantly expounding the advantages of the division of labor, the other providing the intellectual underpinnings of a free market economy. Like Locke he emphasized that the value of goods increased by the labor used in their production, and like Mandeville he argued that individual self-interest was a natural human characteristic. But he added that this would inexorably lead to the accumulation of wealth for the entire nation because, like Hume, he argued also that when manufacturers prospered, everyone else did as well. Smith was certain, therefore, like Tucker, that government should neither intervene in the economy nor rely exclusively on specie as the means of exchange. Other implications included the idea that both the old navigation laws and the great chartered companies would have to go.

However, as the economy expanded in the latter 18th century, the **population** increased. Economics, always sensitive to new scientific information, was thus diverted from its rosy visions and optimistic outlook to become the "dismal science" when **Thomas Malthus** concluded that with population inevitably destined to outstrip food production, one result would be the growing starvation of the poor (1798). The poor, unless their multiplication could be checked, were doomed to lives of misery. Malthus also argued that the existing system of poor relief, no matter how well intended to help the indigent, actually increased **poverty** by encouraging unchecked population growth.

Malthusian concepts had great impact on subsequent economic thought, helping to invest it with qualities of moral didacticism hitherto undeveloped. **David Ricardo**, deeply influenced by Smith and convinced that Malthus's views of overpopulation were correct and that free trade was essential, synthesized the main doctrines of laissez-faire capitalism and helped turn them into the new "science" of political economy. Ricardo's two major concerns were the **Bank of England**'s overissuance of paper money—thus causing inflation and holding down the value of the currency—and the duties on the importation of grain, which he thought raised rents, raised corn prices, and decreased non-agricultural profits. His hopes for an end to duties on grain were dashed in 1815 when Parliament passed the most prohibitive **Corn Law** ever enacted. Ricardo was prompted by the venerable philosopher **Jeremy Bentham** to publish his work in a full-scale exposition (1817) and to enter Parliament, which he did in 1819.

Ricardo and Bentham's other followers, the **Benthamites**, helped in many other ways to propagate the new economic doctrines and associate them with their own spirit of practical, scientific rationalism. For them, the facts clearly proved that manufacturers took care of their enterprises better than governmental officials did, and that the result was the increased good (and happiness) of the people. **James Mill**, advised by Bentham and Ricardo, helped to spread the new economic doctrine in his influential *Elements of Political Economy* (1821).

By the end of the Hanoverian period the main doctrines of Smith, Malthus, and Ricardo were widely accepted, though there were hot debates over their application to governmental policy and over various details. The gospel of the "Manchester School," a somewhat simplified and vulgarized version of free-trade doctrine, emphasized, as **Manchester**'s manufacturers naturally would do, the great advantages to be expected from repeal of the corn laws. **John Ramsay McCulloch**, an admirer of Smith and Ricardo, was perhaps the first professional economist in the sense that he was able to support himself by literary and editorial activity in the field. **Robert Torrens** meanwhile argued that wealth resulted from the interworkings of land, labor, and capital; and as a follower of Ricardo he favored the Bank of England's broad authority to issue paper money. **Jane Marcet**, in her highly readable *Conversations on Political Economy* (1816), brought the economic gospel to the masses.

The economists were far from unanimous. Unlike Malthus, **Nassau Senior**, who held the first chair of economics at Oxford (beginning in 1825), favored adjustment of poor relief as a means to ameliorate the condition of the poor, and played a key role in passage of the **New Poor Law** (1834). In opposition to the gold standard was **Thomas Attwood** who, unlike Ricardo but somewhat in line with the banker–economist **Henry Thornton**, believed that continuous expansion of credit and paper money would benefit not only manufacturers but everyone. Attwood, like many others, was not only an economic innovator but a political reformer because, given the inertia of the past, the two usually went together.

Thomas Hodgskin, initially a follower of Ricardo, took economic thought in a more **radical** direction: he was one of the first British socialist theorists to argue that because labor was the sole source of wealth in society, wage-earners were routinely deprived of their true share of the wealth they produced. In some ways his views complemented the earlier economic radicalism of **Thomas Spence**, who from about 1790 to 1814 had advocated confiscation and collective ownership of national agricultural lands. The **utopian** socialist **Robert Owen** had some impact also on late Hanoverian economic thought, as did **John Stuart Mill**, helping to sensitize it anew to the responsibilities of the state in economic management.

All in all, Hanoverian economic thought reveals in outline the whole gamut of economic ideas characteristic of a society moving as Britain did from state paternalism, protectionism, and monopoly, to industrial development, international commercial dominance, free trade, paper currency, and more democratic ideas about the freedom and rights of labor. Not surprisingly, by the end of the period, all the old navigation laws and chartered trading companies were nearly dead.

George F. Clements

Bibliography

Gray, Alexander. *The Development of Economic Doctrine.* 1931.
Heimann, Eduard. *History of Economic Doctrines.* 1964.
Hollander, Samuel. *The Economics of Adam Smith.* 1973.
———. *The Economics of David Ricardo.* 1979.
———. *Classical Economics.* 1987.
Langer, Gary F. *The Coming of Age of Political Economy, 1815–1825.* 1987.
Winch, Donald. *Riches and Poverty: An Intellectual History of Political Economy in Britain, 1750–1834.* 1996.

Economical Reform

The **Rockingham Whigs** undertook their program of economical reform (1779–1782) to lessen what they perceived as the secret and undue influence of the Crown in **Commons**. From the time of his accession (1760), **George III** had been accused of unconstitutional meddling in parliamentary elections and in the dispensation of political **patronage**. The early stage of the reform program gained strength from the Petitioning Movement begun in Yorkshire by **Christopher Wyvill**. Three reform bills were passed in 1782. Clerke's Act barred men holding government contracts from sitting in Commons. Crewe's Act disfranchised Crown revenue officers, who were believed to have too much influence in some constituencies. **Edmund Burke**'s Establishment Act abolished a number of appointments to the royal household and government posts considered sinecures, some of which could be held by M.P.s and were thought to be the means by which the king's chosen ministers maintained a majority in Commons. The act affirmed parliamentary control of the civil list, a fund granted to the monarch out of public money.

P.J. Kulisheck

Bibliography

Christie, Ian. *Wilkes, Wyvill and Reform.* 1962.
O'Gorman, Frank. *The Rise of Party in England: The Rockingham Whigs, 1760–82.* 1975.

See also Pension and Place Bills

Edgeworth, Maria (1767?–1849)

Edgeworth is famous for her **novels** of **manners**, many of which are set in the Irish countryside and sympathetically reflect Irish customs, language, and character. Her works won the admiration of **Sir Walter Scott** ("the great Maria," he called her), **Jane Austen**, William Makepeace Thackeray (1811–1863), and John Ruskin (1819–1900).

Edgeworth was one of the most commercially successful women writers during the height of her literary production (*c.* 1800–1814). Her novels include *Castle Rackrent* (1800), which influenced Scott's *Waverley* (1814); *Belinda* (1801); *Vivian* (1812); *The Absentee* (1812); *Patronage* (1814); and *Ormond* (1817). She also cowrote with her father, the educator Richard Lovell Edgeworth (1744–1817), an influential multivolumed instructional manual for educating children, *Practical Education* (1798), and an *Essay on Irish Bulls* (1802), a study of popular Irish humor. In addition, she wrote children's stories (*The Parent's Assistant,* 1796) and tales.

Edgeworth was born in Oxfordshire, the second of 21 children. Her mother died in 1773. Richard Edgeworth remarried three times afterward but Maria never married. After a troublesome childhood spent living away from home, she moved at age 15 with her father, his wife Elizabeth (Sneyd), and all his other children to Edgeworthstown in the Irish Midlands where, as the eldest daughter, Edgeworth served as her father's amanuensis and managerial assistant, and contrib-

Maria Edgeworth

uted to his studies in child education. After her father's death she completed and published his *Memoirs* (1820) and traveled extensively throughout England and Continental Europe. She continued to manage the Edgeworthstown estate until her death, when, despite the fading of her powers, she still enjoyed a wide European reputation.

Mary Tiryak

Bibliography

Butler, Marilyn. *Maria Edgeworth.* 1971.

Colvin, Christina, ed. *Letters from England, 1813–1844.* 1971.

Luria, Gina. "Introduction," in *Letters for Literary Ladies.* 1974.

Newcomer, James. *Maria Edgeworth.* 1973.

Todd, Janet. *A Dictionary of British and American Women Writers.* 1984.

See also Children's Literature; Education, Elementary; Irish Literature

Edinburgh

Following the **Act of Union** (1707), Edinburgh lost its status as the capital city of an ancient and independent kingdom. The city nevertheless continued to develop and, during the Hanoverian period, a **population** numbering around 40,000 in 1700 grew to 162,403 in 1831. This was due partly to the fact that the union had recognized the distinct ecclesiastical and legal identity of Scotland. The city remained the center of administration of the **Church of Scotland** and the **Scottish legal system**, both of which brought it many visitors and much business.

Edinburgh also became an important social center, many aristocratic and other landed families maintaining townhouses and spending part of every year in the city. Although **commerce** and industry were not as essential to Edinburgh as to **Glasgow**, the city's **merchants** catered to local needs, imported merchandise from England and the Continent through its adjacent port of Leith, and distributed goods throughout a wide hinterland. The lively market life of the city was observed by **Daniel Defoe**, while **Sir Walter Scott** in *The Heart of Midlothian* described the infamous **Porteous Riots** (1736), a noteworthy example of the civil unrest and disobedience to which the Old Town had been prone over the centuries.

The cramped and dirty nature of the Old Town meant that expansion was necessary. Southward development included the building of George Square near the university, but the draining of the Nor'Loch in 1759 and its bridging in 1765, which had previously contained urban development, allowed the construction of the New Town to the north as planned by James Craig (1744–1795) and approved by the council in 1767. This, particularly Charlotte Square, conceived by **Robert Adam**, remains one of the finest examples of the **Neoclassical** style in **architecture**.

Edinburgh witnessed an unprecedented flourishing of cultural growth in the 18th century, to such an extent that "Auld Reekie" became the "Athens of the North." The **Scottish Enlightenment** was identified with the city, which was truly at the forefront of the European **Enlightenment**, including among its luminaries **David Hume** and the painter **Allan Ramsay**. At the same time, the university came to be regarded as an international center of excellence in **medicine**, **science**, and the arts, numbering among its professors the Monro fam-

Part of the New Town, Edinburgh

ily in medicine, the chemist **Joseph Black**, and the historian **William Robertson**.

By the end of the Hanoverian era, Edinburgh had been supplanted as Scotland's largest city by **Glasgow**. But it still remained of paramount importance in Scotland's cultural, legal, and religious life.

John Roach Young

Bibliography

Campbell, R.H., and A.S. Skinner, eds. *The Origins and Nature of the Scottish Enlightenment.* 1982.

Ferguson, W. *Scotland, 1689 to the Present.* 1977.

Keay, J., and J. Keay, eds. *Collins Encyclopaedia of Scotland.* 1994.

Massie, A. *Edinburgh.* 1994.

Scott, Sir W. *Waverley.* 1814.

———. *The Heart of Midlothian.* 1818.

See also Scotland and Scottish Culture

Education, Elementary

Elementary education was very spotty and haphazard for much of the Hanoverian age. Education was the concern of voluntary religious activity or private enterprise or of philanthropy, but not of the government.

One form of elementary education continuously available was at the lower ranks of the endowed grammar school, inherited from previous centuries. Ordinarily such schools, together with the handful of still more elite public boarding schools, were the preserve of the **middle** and upper **classes**, but occasionally a poor child might be assisted to find a place reserved for him and, passing up through the grades of this preparatory education, go on perhaps even to university.

The second main form of elementary education was that found in private day schools. Typically these were run by a female or, less commonly, male schoolmaster, or perhaps simply a disabled workman, receiving a small fee from each pupil. Such teachers' incomes were often very meager, though sometimes made up partly from parish funds—for example, in 1807 a Cornish parish paid a crippled miner £12 a year to educate "ten or twelve scholars" and any other fee-paying children he could secure. One man recalled that "any shattered being wrecked in the mill or the mine, if he could read John Bunyan, count to 50 backwards, and scribble the squire's name was considered good enough for a pedagogue; and when he could do nothing else was established behind a low desk in a school." Small, poorly equipped, and informally organized, these private schools typically began when teachers well known in their communities opened rooms in their homes and attempted to teach reading and, occasionally, some writing and arithmetic. Derisively called "dames' schools" or "common day" and "ordinary" schools by 19th-century educational reformers, these schools were in fact usually known by the name of the teacher or trade in the communities they served. The pupils were children who usually attended irregularly for 2–4 years (most heavily in winter, when work demands were less), typically before going to work to supplement the family income.

"The Dunce Disgraced"

The third general form of elementary schooling was that in the free **charity schools**, many of which were founded in a burst of educational enthusiasm in the period 1700–1730. These schools were rooted in English Poor Law traditions and originally encouraged by the **Society for Promoting Christian Knowledge** (founded in 1698). Unlike the older endowed schools set up by large bequests, these were supported by smaller subscriptions from social ranks running down into the level of tradesmen, hence "broadening the base of charity." The charity schools were often meticulously organized, strong on discipline, more interested in religious than secular training, and inexpensive; though without prestige, and centered mostly in **London** and a few other big cities, they succeeded in bringing some education in the catechism and the Bible to hundreds of thousands of children before they were apprenticed.

There was a lull in the founding of charity schools after 1730, then a new surge after 1780. This reflected deepening upper-class concern over social and political turmoil, and a recognition of the potential of schooling to regulate the poor in a rapidly changing society. Renewed subscriptions and endowments for cheap education for the poor became a major focus of **humanitarian** social reform. Infant schools for children age 3 to 6, inspired by **Robert Owen**'s model school at **New Lanark** (1816) and developed by Samuel Wilderspin (1792–1866) after 1818, launched a movement for elementary education for the youngest poor. The far more important **Sunday school** movement after 1780 was also driven by humanitarian impulses, though here children attended for only a few hours on Sundays, and writing was generally not taught in such schools after the 1790s. Sunday schools were complements to day schools, helping to check the generally negative effects of early industrialization, which drew heavily on **child labor**. (The ratio between population and literacy probably descended to its nadir around 1820, then began to improve.) Some authorities believe that perhaps three-fourths of all working-class children attended Sunday schools by 1850.

The new charity schools of 1780–1790, oriented toward factory-like discipline and religious indoctrination, attracted enough children to compete with the more popular common day or dames' schools (though these latter evolved also, some becoming bigger and better organized). They also influenced the great new wave of elementary schooling initiated after 1800. **Joseph Lancaster**'s success in educating (or at least forcing memorization upon) hundreds of students in the same room at the same time provided school supporters with new techniques for organizing and financing mass instruction. The success of Lancaster's schools and the formation (1808) of the originally nonsectarian **British and Foreign School Society** to promote them sparked Anglican supporters to create a rival **National Society for the Education of the Poor** (1811) and to recruit **Andrew Bell** to oversee its work and promote in it his own system of monitorial instruction. The **Evangelical** and **missionary** energies of the revolutionary era thus found its way into basic schooling.

Intense competition between rival sponsors of inexpensive schooling shifted national debates about whether the poor should receive education to the question of whether voluntary or state effort was needed to fund it. Theorists such as **Adam Smith**, **Thomas Malthus**, and **Thomas Paine** had proposed state organization of elementary schooling. The state took a first step with the Health and Morals of Apprentices Act (1802), which required employers to educate apprentices in the **textile industries** in mathematics, writing, and reading—though this had little effect until the 1830s, when inspectors and enforcement began. **Samuel Whitbread**'s (1807) and **Henry Brougham**'s (1820) bills for state involvement in education were based on statistics and testimony drawn from common day and charity school provisions; but sectarian rivalries delayed action. The first government building grant (£20,000) for education (1833) was divided between the two denominational societies, and the **Factory Act** (1833), with its age restrictions on child labor, made school attendance by poor children more feasible. In 1839 the Privy Council set up a committee to oversee such grants (which had now become annual) and to inspect the voluntary schools that received them. The committee soon became a small department, and later still the Ministry of Education.

Britain was one of the last Western European states to evolve a national system of education. There was by 1850 a public system for elementary education, but it was still patchy and grossly inadequate. Every literacy measurement is debatable (for example, reading ability, which was gained first, did not necessarily translate into the ability to write), but whereas one study has found that in 1850 perhaps 70% of males and 55% of females were at least minimally literate; another study finds that in 1839 a third of the men and half the women married in church could not sign their own names in the church registers. It was only in 1870, with Forster's Education Act, that the formation of local tax-supported public elementary schools was encouraged, as a supplement to the patchwork of private and state-subsidized sectarian schools. Elementary education was made compulsory in 1876.

Kim P. Sebaly

Bibliography

Gardner, Phil. *The Lost Elementary Schools of Victorian England.* 1984.

Jones, M.G. *The Charity School Movement, a Study of Eighteenth Century Puritanism in Action.* 1938.

Laqueur, Thomas W. "Working Class Demand and the Growth of English Elementary Education, 1750–1850," in Lawrence Stone, ed., *Schooling and Society: Studies in the History of Education.* 1976.

McCann, Philip, and Francis A. Young. *Samuel Wilderspin and the Infant School Movement.* 1982.

Rule, John. *The Labouring Classes in Early Industrial England, 1750–1850.* 1986.

Thompson, F.M.L., ed. *The Cambridge Social History of Britain, 1750–1850.* Vol. 3. 1990.

See also Education, Secondary; Irish Education; Scottish Education; Tutors and the Teaching Profession; Welsh Education; Women's Education

Education, Irish

See Irish Education

Education, Military

In 18th-century **war**, the ability to maneuver troop formations quickly and efficiently required arduous training in close-order drill. Officers, relying on such drill guides as *The Exercise of the Horse, Dragoon, and Foot Forces* (1728), learned to execute complicated troop movements; soldiers, it was hoped, would subordinate all actions and instincts to duty and carry out orders without hesitation.

The multistep priming, loading, and discharge of firelocks in volleys required precision, speed, and efficiency, but not much in the way of accuracy or aiming. The **army** allotted only 30 musket balls and 60 blank cartridges per year per man for live-fire training. Units conducted surprisingly little bayonet training, despite the British propensity for bayonet charges.

Formal, inflexible, Prussian-style procedures dominated the reigns of **George I** and **George II**, but after 1760 the experience of North American warfare began altering these. Colonel Henry Bouquet of the 60th Royal Americans, who developed a training system designed to produce troops capable of fighting effectively in the wilderness, laid the foundation of the light infantry system. In 1792 Colonel David Dundas produced the *Rules and Regulations for the Formations, Field Exercises, and Movements of His Majesty's Forces,* the first official manual, which established a standard drill applicable to the open-terrain battlefields of Europe. Dundas patterned his system on Prussian practices, but it proved effective in the European battles of the **French Revolutionary and Napoleonic Wars**.

Cavalry training emphasized horsemanship, often polished at a riding school. Surprisingly, prior to the French wars at the end of the century, little sword training was conducted, a situation corrected by adoption of Colonel Le Marchant's *The Rules and Regulations for the Attainment and Practice of the Sword Exercise* (1797).

Until 1800, officers received nearly all their training either at drill or on the battlefield. When at war, ensigns, the two most junior officers in each infantry regiment, carried the regimental colors, thus learning the art of command without actually directing formations in the field. But **Frederick, Duke of York**, Commander-in-Chief during the critical period 1798–1809, established as part of a general tightening of the Army the Royal Military College (1799), the first formal center of military education for infantry and cavalry officers. (For artillery officers the Royal Military Academy at Woolwich had provided formal training since 1741.) From this, and from the 95th Regiment (the Rifle Brigade) he also created (1800), there emanated a new spirit of efficiency, discipline, knowledge, and military science.

The post–Waterloo period, however, saw a decline. Annual maneuvers ceased, as did training in formations larger than battalions. Systematic education in military science was revived only in the late Victorian era. As for private soldiers, never during the Hanoverian age did they receive training in any but the most basic requirements of drill, weaponry, and tactical formations.

Stanley D.M. Carpenter

Bibliography

Barnett, Correlli. *Britain and Her Army, 1509–1970.* 1970.
Dietz, Peter. *The Last of the Regiments: Their Rise and Fall.* 1990.
Prest, Wilfrid R., ed. *The Professions in Early Modern England.* 1987.
Rogers, H.C.B. *The British Army of the Eighteenth Century.* 1977.
Screen, J.E.O. "The 'Royal Military Academy' of Lewis Lochee." *Journal of the Society for Army Historical Research.* Vol. 70, pp. 143–156.

See also War and Military Engagements; Weapons

Education, Religious

Almost all education in Hanoverian Britain was in some respect religious. **Oxford** and **Cambridge** universities were always the principal institutions for training candidates for the Anglican clergy. In **Scotland** the universities at **Edinburgh**, **Glasgow**, St. Andrews, and Aberdeen were dominated by members of the **Church of Scotland**, though unlike their English counterparts they accepted students of all denominations. At the level of **secondary education**, Scotland's excellent parish and **burgh** schools concentrated on both Latin and the reading of Scripture; England's many grammar schools and boarding schools concentrated on Latin but also prepared young men for religious training in the universities. The **dissenting academies**, begun mainly by **Congregationalists** and **Presbyterians** in the late 17th century, modernized their curricula to include sciences, modern languages, and history; although they did prepare ministers for the dissenting chapels, they also provided the best secondary education available during the period. Many **dissenters** went abroad for university education until the **University of London** was founded (1826) to educate students ineligible for the other English universities, where Anglican religious tests persisted until 1871.

At the level of **elementary education** the various denominations, assisted by philanthropic individuals and societies, promoted religious education among the lower classes in England and **Wales**. Endowed **charity schools**, begun in 1699, taught "Christian education" and the principles of the **Church of England** to hundreds of thousands of poor children during the Hanoverian era. **John Wesley** began the first school for the children of **Methodist** preachers at Kingswood in the 1780s, his aim being to rescue them from corrupting passions and willfulness. In Wales, **Griffith Jones** established **circulating schools** for adults and children where traveling teachers instructed their pupils in reading the Welsh Bible and learning the church catechism; by 1760, with help from the **Society for Promoting Christian Knowledge**, as many as 3,000 such schools were operating.

The latter 18th century saw the launching of interdenominational **Sunday schools** where poor children were taught to read and study the Bible. The **British and Foreign School Society**, founded (1808) by dissenters to educate older children and using the reading of Scripture as the principal means to teach literacy, stimulated the church to open the **National Society for the Education of the Poor** (1811) for similar purposes.

Interdenominational conflicts and lingering worries about **radicalism** in an educated working class delayed the spread of state-supported education. In 1837, as one of a series of annual appropriations begun in 1833, the government voted £20,000 toward education, at the same time providing £50,000 for rebuilding the royal stables.

Samuel J. Rogal

Bibliography

Burgess, H.J. *Enterprise in Education: The Story of the Work of the Established Church in the Education of the People Prior to 1870.* 1958.
Cross, F.L., and E.A. Livingstone, eds. *The Oxford Dictionary of the Christian Church.* 2nd ed., 1983.
Rogal, Samuel J. *The Education of the British Literati: A Guide to Their Schools and Colleges.* 1992.

Education, Scottish

See Scottish Education

Education, Secondary

Hanoverian Britain's oldest secondary schools were the endowed grammar schools that had been widely established earlier by the church or by wealthy philanthropists. Although a few of these, by increasing their staffs and taking in boarders, had become "public" schools especially favored by the better-off **gentry** and **aristocracy**, the vast majority were located in market towns or large villages, and were attended by the sons of farmers, the clergy, and the lesser gentry.

All the grammar schools employed clergymen as teachers and provided learning suited to keeping Britain Protestant, but they too often failed to equip their upper-class and **middle-class** students with the modern and scientific understanding necessary to the evolving culture. Many schools were legally

Eton College

chained to earlier statutes that required them to teach Latin and Greek grammar and literature, and their staffs were wedded to teaching methods that favored a type of backward learning—rote memorization in fear of a caning from behind. The theory was that "construing" Latin texts encouraged analytical ability and broad habits of mind; and that mathematics, taught in smaller doses, developed reasoning powers. Though some schools charged extra fees for adding classes in modern subjects, most simply resisted reformist attempts to alter their curricula, and continued by law (until passage of the Grammar School Act of 1840) to focus on the classical humanistic subjects and "gentlemanly education" required for entrance to **Oxford**, **Cambridge**, and the Inns of Court, and for training for careers in the church and the law.

The "public" schools were at the top of the pyramid. Of the nearly 700 endowed grammar schools in existence by 1815, about 100 were designated "public"; of these only a select few continued to provide most of Britain's leaders, as they had done already for over a century. Nine "great" schools, led by Westminster in **London** (the oldest, founded in the 11th century) and Eton in Eton, Berkshire (1440), which together supplied nearly three-fourths of all ministers of state, and then by Winchester (1382) and Harrow (1571), dominated and helped solidify Britain's social class system. These public grammar schools, which drew students from wider localities and distinguished themselves from smaller unendowed private boarding schools, attracted such severe criticisms—chiefly on the score of their antiquated curricula but also on that of their often unnecessarily brutal and insalubrious environment—that enrollment fluctuations threatened their continuation. The public schools were notorious for violence, and it has been remarked that when **Wellington** spoke of the **Battle of Waterloo** as having been won "on the playing fields of Eton," he did not refer to cricket but to fighting. Bullying, birching, insubordination, the destruction of furniture, mutinies, attacking masters, and even **riots** occurred with such frequency that when **George III** met a young Etonian, he queried: "Have you had a rebellion lately?"

Reforms designed to meet criticism would continue to shape the public school tradition into the 20th century. It took considerable force of will and character to effect changes in old school habits. Samuel Butler at Shrewsbury (1798–1836) and Thomas Arnold at Rugby (1828–1842) were the two headmasters most famous for introducing reforms in teaching (exams, tutorials, games) and organization (prefects, houses, improved teachers' salaries) that helped modernize the existing schools and encourage new Victorian foundations. The reforming headmasters introduced a more serious and more religious atmosphere, and encouraged responsibility among the older pupils in some ways reminiscent of the "monitorial system" introduced into **elementary education** at about the same time by **Joseph Lancaster**.

Greatly helping to encourage reform within the grammar schools were developments from outside. On the one hand, the **dissenting academies** taught more advanced subjects and, since they received the sons of Anglicans willing to send them, furnished a point of comparison and source of competition. On the other, the latter 18th century, experiencing an unprecedented surge in **population**, saw the establishment of new unendowed classical schools and academies that forced Britain's oldest secondary institutions to reappraise their offerings and the atmosphere in which they were presented. Outstanding private teachers organized their own establishments for the teaching not only of classical and linguistic studies but also of foreign languages, English literature, mathematics, surveying, **navigation**, and other **scientific** subjects. Without degrees and church affiliation, they organized integrated studies to fill the demand for specially skilled people in the country's expanding military services, private industry, and public works. Although many such academies were short-lived, their teaching expanded the market for secondary education and forced grammar schools to integrate classical and scientific studies.

Such schools, teaching perhaps 20 to 80 students, some of them boarders, were not run by clergymen as much as by men (and in some cases their wives) who had been trained in more practical and useful subjects—accounts, mathematics, mensuration, perhaps even experimental philosophy. In the competition for students they had many of the forces of general modernization on their side—not only population increases but industrialization, foreign competition, the growth of science, and the beginnings of political democratization. Nevertheless, official confidence in the adequacy of the grammar school tradition, with its heavy emphasis on Latin and Greek, did not really decline until after the Great Exhibition (1851).

Kim P. Sebaly

Bibliography

Armytage, W.H.G. *Four Hundred Years of English Education.* 1970.

Clark, M.L. *Classical Education in Britain, 1500–1900.* 1959.

Gathorne-Hardy, Jonathan. *The Old School Tie: The Phenomenon of the English Public School.* 1977.

Hans, Nicholas. *New Trends in Education in the Eighteenth Century.* 1951.

Sutherland, Gillian. "Education," in F.M.L. Thompson, ed., *The Cambridge Social History of Britain, 1750–1850.* Vol. 3. 1990.

Tomson, Richard S. *Classics or Charity? The Dilemma of the 18th Century Grammar School.* 1971.

See also Governesses; Irish Education; Scottish Education; Tutors and the Teaching Profession; Welsh Education

Education, Teachers'

Despite their frequency, few proposals for systematic teachers' education were implemented before 1800. It was the introduction of practical schemes for charity-based **elementary education** for the poor that initiated the view that teaching should be a vocation and trained profession. It was discovered that pupil–teachers, or monitors, on whom the growing network of **charity schools** depended, needed to learn the principles and procedures of the system in which they worked. **Joseph Lancaster** established the first course for training senior monitors at his Borough Road center in **London** (1805). Guided by **Andrew Bell**, the **National Society for the Education of the Poor** then attached a training department to its model school at Baldwin's Gardens (1812) to train monitors and school organizers for its church-supported schools. By 1839, when state grants for teacher education were finally distributed to upgrade each society's training schools, support for the charity-based system was eroding and new schemes for teacher education were proliferating.

Reports about European and American systems after 1815 alerted British educational reformers to the speed with which state-sponsored universal education, including normal schools for teachers, was developing abroad. They consequently worked to circulate criticisms of both monitorial and grammar school teaching, and to highlight practical steps by which teachers might become better prepared to run pupil-involved instruction in broadened curricula. David Stow (1793–1869), a Scottish silk **merchant** and infant school founder, developed Britain's first normal school in **Glasgow** in 1824. His training center, described in his book *The Training System* (1836), offered a 9-month course for elementary teachers, including teacher observations and criticism of model lessons. Deputations of school sponsors, including supporters of both the Bell and Lancasterian developments, fueled demands for Stow's "trainers" and plans for new teacher-training institutions to increase their numbers.

Grammar school teachers, although far removed from elementary education, were not immune to sharp criticisms of the quality of their work or to proposals for reform. Intense public scrutiny and competition from educational academies, private schools, and home tutors, forced endowed grammar schools to reform teachers' procedures and working conditions. Reports from early-19th-century school surveys, and visits to experimental schools in Europe and Britain, provided the storehouse of ideas about teaching methods from which James Kay-Shuttleworth (1804–1877) organized nondenominational teacher training colleges throughout Britain after 1839.

Kim P. Sebaly

Bibliography

Armytage, W.H.G. *Four Hundred Years of English Education.* 1970.

Horn, Pamela. *Education in Rural England 1800–1914.* 1978.

Troop, Asher. *The School Teachers: The Growth of the Teaching Profession in England and Wales from 1800 to the Present Day.* 1957.

See also Tutors and the Teaching Profession

Education, Technical

Established resistance to **science, technology, and invention** in Britain's universities did not prevent activity in these important areas from being impressed on schooling. Practical training and technical studies developed from a variety of locations throughout the Hanoverian period. Whereas craft training and **mechanics' institutes** promoted vocational skills for workers and their children, new private technical academies, and a variety of technical societies, advanced modern studies for an increasingly diversified **middle class**.

Traditionally, the great bulk of technical education was provided through the process of apprenticing **craftsmen**, through the education of children in the cottage workshops of **domestic production**, and through the actual work experience of innumerable self-made inventors and engineers such as **Telford**, **Watt**, and **Trevithick**. There were also workingmen's **clubs**, where information was exchanged, and paternalistic organizations like the **Royal Institution**, established to help the poor learn useful skills. The early Hanoverian period also saw the establishment for children of "schools of industry," often connected with textile concentrations, knitting works, and the like. However, producing more efficient manual labor, rather than more fully developing individual technical skills, was the primary motive for the establishment of such schools.

Revived at the end of the 18th century by **Sunday schools** and growing provisions for **elementary education**, **charity schools** of industry and private work schools evolved to help meet the demand for disciplined **child labor** in **textile**, printing, and other developing industries. The decline of apprenticeship as a vehicle for acquiring skills needed by new manufacturers, and restrictions on child labor, encouraged experiments with integrated reading and vocational teaching. **Robert Owen**'s "Institution for the Formation of Character" at **New Lanark** (1816) stimulated the development of child and adult vocational and general education in rapidly emerging cooperative industrial communities. Mechanics' institutes, initially created for assisting skilled mechanics to teach other mechanics, grew quickly in all industrial areas after the establishment of the flagship London Institute in 1823.

As to the middle and upper classes, while grammar school traditions prohibited the development of technical education, recognition of its value was nonetheless rising in the early 19th century. Challenged by private and **dissenting academies** that offered vocational and science-based technical instruction, grammar schools slowly began to supplement their core of classical teaching. To promote Britain's commercial interests, traveling lecturers in mathematics and **science**, and provincial **agricultural societies**, supplemented the prizes and exhibitions sponsored by the **Royal Society** from 1754 on. Middle-class supporters of practical applications of science assumed leadership of the mechanics' institutes and established the **Society for the Diffusion of Useful Knowledge** in 1826 to compete with the growing working-class press in disseminating technical advice and political opinion. The founding of the **University of London** (opened in 1828), with its emphasis on applications from all fields of modern knowledge, and separation from any religious teaching, represented the culmination of Hanoverian attempts to link education with spreading demands for technical progress.

Kim P. Sebaly

Bibliography

Armytage, W.H.G. *Four Hundred Years of English Education.* 1970.
Caldwell, D.S.L. *The Organisation of Science in England; a Retrospect.* 1957.
Roderick, Gordon, and Michael D. Stephens. *Education and Industry in the Nineteenth Century.* 1978.
Simon, Brian. *The Two Nations and the Educational Structure, 1780–1870.* 1974.

Education, University

See Cambridge University; Oxford University; Scottish Universities; Trinity College, Dublin; University of London

Education, Welsh

See Welsh Education

Education, Women's

See Women's Education

Egan, Pierce (1774–1849)

The leading sports **journalist** of Regency England, Egan is most remembered for his *Life in London* (1821), the archetypal urban **novel** of the early 19th century. He was an important influence on the early work of Charles Dickens, especially his *Sketches by Boz* (1836) and *Pickwick Papers* (1836–1837).

Egan's output of **satires**, **biographies**, novels, and lively **journalism** on **crime** and **sport** demonstrates the variety of popular **publishing** activity in the early 19th century. His *Boxiana* (1812), a comprehensive history of boxing and an "inside" account of the fight game, established him as the acknowledged spokesman of pugilism, England's most popular sport.

An expatriate Irishman, Egan also authored the first **London** novel. In *Life in London* (or *Tom and Jerry*), serially published (1821–1828), he made London the central character, exploring the great variety of **urban life** both high and low, with its diversity of **manners and morals**, slang, and speech patterns. He also inaugurated the literary tradition of the working-class urban novel, charting the topographical divisions of London's social classes and faithfully portraying the Cockney, a tradition carried on by Dickens and Rudyard Kipling. The novel's sensational popularity helped establish serial publication as a staple of Victorian publishing. Egan's other novels include *The Life of an Actor* (1825), *The Finish to the Adventures of Tom, Jerry and Logic* (1828), and *The Pilgrims of the Thames* (1838).

Kenneth Daley

Bibliography

Keating, P.J. *The Working Classes in Victorian Fiction.* 1971.
Reid, J.C. *Bucks and Bruisers: Pierce Egan and Regency England.* 1971.

Eldon, Earl of (John Scott) (1751–1838)

Eldon stood at the controls of government for almost the entire latter Hanoverian age and typified "ultra" **Tory** conser-

John Scott, Lord Eldon

vatism. He served as Lord Chancellor (chief government law officer and Speaker of the **House of Lords**) from 1801 through 1827 except for a 14-month break, 1806–1807.

The son of a Newcastle **merchant**, distinguished in youth by a strong memory and a taste for pranks, he was educated at **Oxford** and the Middle Temple, **London**, called to the bar (1776), and entered the **House of Commons** in 1783 for a pocket **borough**, serving until 1799. Eldon served as Solicitor General (1788–1793), Attorney General (1793–1799), and as Lord Chief Justice for the Court of Common Pleas (1801). In 1799 he was created Baron Eldon of Eldon and entered the Lords. **Prime Minister Henry Addington (Lord Sidmouth)** insured his appointment as Lord Chancellor (1801), a post he continued to occupy until 1827. **George IV** created him 1st Earl of Eldon in 1821.

Eldon was a leader of the most conservative Tories and an opponent of virtually every species of political reform, except perhaps in his 1783 maiden speeches against **Fox**'s India bill and in support of **Pitt the Younger**. In the **Regency Crisis** (1788–1789) he drew up Pitt's bill. As Attorney General during the **French Revolution** he was largely responsible for the measures used to suppress political meetings and halt the flow of seditious literature, and he managed the prosecutions of **Horne Tooke** and the other **radicals**. Eldon also fiercely opposed the abolition of imprisonment for debtors, the abolition of the **slave trade**, and parliamentary reform. An extreme critic of **Catholic emancipation**, he resigned (1827) over his opposition to the emancipation plans of **Canning**'s ministry.

Hated by the political left, Eldon was always quick to defend authority. As a judge, however, he was criticized even by friends for his protracted delays of important matters—he had a habit of minutely examining cases before him. He successfully settled the rules for the use of the injunction as a remedy, and helped fully develop trademark laws by serving injunctions against merchants selling goods bearing the names of others. His career provides an interesting contrast to that of **Thomas Erskine**, whom he opposed not only in the divorce case of **Queen Caroline** (1820) but in much else.

Thomas D. Veve

Bibliography

Duman, David. *The Judicial Bar in England, 1727–1875: The Reshaping of a Professional Elite.* 1982.

O'Gorman, Frank. *The Emergence of the British Two-Party System.* 1982.

Sack, James J. *From Jacobite to Conservative: Reaction and Orthodoxy in Britain, c.1760–1832.* 1993.

Surtees, W.S. *A Sketch of the Lives of Lords Stowell and Eldon.* 1846.

Twiss, Horace. *The Public and Private Life of Lord Chancellor Eldon, with Selections from His Correspondence.* 2 vols. 1844.

See also Judicial System; Legal Profession

Elections and the Franchise

By guaranteeing the powers of frequent and freely elected parliaments, the Bill of Rights (1689) ensured that general elections for the House of Commons, and the franchises by which they were conducted, became central concerns in British politics. Electoral seats in the Commons were the building blocks of power by which royal ministers, dispensing patronage, maintained themselves in office and conducted the country's business. The struggle for parliamentary reform and representative government therefore centered upon the elections and franchises by which these seats were legally held. Only at the end of the Hanoverian era, however, was there significant alteration of the patterns and practices that had come down from the Middle Ages.

The frequency of general elections was established first by the Triennial Act (1694), which provided that they be held at intervals no longer than 3 years, and later by the **Septennial Act** (1716), which extended the maximum length of a parliament to 7 years. Primarily because of the expense of elections, the majority of Hanoverian parliaments ran all or most of their statutory course. Even uncontested seats could require significant expenditures by candidates, patrons, or local organizations, and contested seats might demand outlays of £10,000 or more if the constituency had a large electorate. Only in 1722 were as many as half of the English and Welsh seats contested; in other Hanoverian elections prior to 1832 the proportion was commonly between a quarter and a third. While some funds were raised by subscription, most came from candidates or their patrons, whether local aristocratic and gentry landlords or outsiders (including such government departments as the treasury or the admiralty), who dominated the local economy of a constituency by land ownership, government contracts, and other means. The money supported every means of evoking enthusiasm for particular candidates or cementing closer ties between electors and their parliamentary representatives—"treating" in taverns and inns, donating to local charities and philanthropies, providing fees to officials and payments for local services, and indulging in some outright bribery (although less than commonly supposed).

General elections after 1714 often had greater local than national significance, for nearly all the dynamics directly affecting the outcome—personalities, financing, and issues—were tied to the local setting. So too were most of the ritual and drama surrounding an election. Once the writs of summons for a new parliament had arrived from Westminster, local returning officers—typically the sheriffs in **counties** and the mayors or bailiffs in **boroughs**—set the date, time, and place of the polling, within broad statutory limits. An act of 1696 set a maximum duration of 40 days for voting; in practice, polls usually stayed open as long as electors remained to vote. After the 1784 election in Westminster lasted a scandalous 47 days, the maximum polling period was set at 15 days, excluding Sundays. The act of voting was oral, performed on the hustings—raised platforms from which candidates were nominated, speeches were delivered, and results were proclaimed—or in nearby polling booths. No attempt was made to assure privacy. Candidates' supporters kept running totals, and if these were not satisfactory, they resorted to various strategems such as challenging opposing voters' qualifications or arranging the carefully timed appearance of friendly electors, previously canvassed and held in reserve for critical moments.

The tactics used in a particular constituency depended on its type and the character of the franchise there. The most basic distinction was between the county, borough, and university constituencies, but important differences also existed between England, **Wales**, **Scotland**, and (especially) **Ireland**. (In Ireland, **penal laws** prohibited **Catholics** and those married to them from voting until 1793.) The county franchise was straightforward; except for some minor variations in Scotland, county members throughout the United Kingdom were elected on a uniform franchise, which went to all who held freehold property producing a land tax revenue of at least 40 shillings a year. The borough franchises, on the other hand, manifested an extraordinary diversity.

Prior to 1832, the 203 English boroughs elected 405 of the 658 members of the House of Commons (558 before 1801 and the Irish Union, which added 100 more). Their franchises fell into five general categories. The widest was that of the 12 householder or "potwalloper" boroughs, where all inhabitant householders not on poor relief and thus able "to dress their own meat and keep their pot boiling" were enfranchised. Almost as inclusive were the 37 scot and lot boroughs, where the franchise rested on payment of an ancient levy that amounted to a poor rate—a provision that excluded the poorest segment of the population. The third category, covering the 92 freeman boroughs, was the most numerous and most diverse. In these the vote belonged to all who by birth, apprenticeship, marriage, or purchase claimed the legal status of freeman, but the qualifications varied wildly, being determined by the borough's corporation or the provisions of borough charters. Ambiguity abounded, making it possible to influence contests by expansion or contraction of the number of freemen as circumstances demanded. Politics in the freeman boroughs tended to be very contentious, and in some of them, especially around **London**, radicalism and the movement for reform of Parliament sank their earliest roots.

In the remaining two classes of boroughs were many examples of what outraged the reformers. The 27 corporation boroughs confined the vote to members of their governing bodies. Finally, there were the 35 burgage boroughs, where the vote belonged to those who were owners or tenants of particular pieces of property called burgages. Since whoever controlled a majority of the burgages in a borough controlled its parliamentary representation as well, these were most likely to become "pocket" or "rotten" boroughs, completely under the control of a single patron and regarded as heritable property.

The university franchise belonged to doctors and masters of arts from the universities in **Oxford**, **Cambridge**, and (after 1800) **Dublin**. Combined with the county or borough franchises, the university vote was a basis for plural voting, whereby a single elector could cast multiple votes. In this context, however, it was not so important as the property qualification, which underlay the county and burgage franchises. Although an act of 1413 required electors to reside in the counties where they voted, this soon went unenforced and a man could vote in any county or borough where he held sufficient property to meet the franchise qualifications. In 1773 the residency requirement for electors was repealed, thus legitimizing a practice that had been conventional for over three centuries. Plural voting survived the reforms of the 19th century, and its last vestiges, the university franchises, were not abolished until 1948.

Demands for franchise reform began during the agitation surrounding **John Wilkes** and the Middlesex election dispute in 1768–1769 and gathered strength from the economic distress and political disillusionment caused by the **War of American Independence**. Along with the removal of **placemen** from Parliament and a redistribution of seats, franchise reform, demanded particularly by the **Society for Constitutional Information** (founded in 1780) and other **middle-class** elements as well as the **gentry** connected with the **Association Movement**, became a principal objective of a growing opposition to the existing structure of politics in the 1780s, both within and outside Parliament. Reform attracted some cautious sympathy in high places, and became extremely popular after 1789 in the **London Corresponding Society** and other working-class associations, but this enthusiasm disappeared amid fears aroused by the **French Revolution** and the repression of political dissent adopted by the **Pitt** administration in the 1790s.

During the wartime period 1793–1815 the idea of reform was sustained mainly by the activities of extraparliamentary working-class and middle-class organizations whose members' lives the **Industrial Revolution** was changing in new and unanticipated ways. The commitment of affluent, middle-class industrialists to reform attracted the attention of a new cohort of **Whig** leaders, such as **Henry Brougham** and **Lord John Russell**. In the 1820s, with repeal of the **Test and Corporation acts** and with younger **Tories** taking over the old Whig cause of **Catholic emancipation**, parliamentary and franchise reform became the vehicle of Whig hopes to regain power for the first time in a generation. The fall of **Wellington**'s Tory ministry in 1830 and the return of the Whigs under **Grey** set in motion events that finally led to the **Reform Act of 1832**.

The franchise clauses of the 1832 measure were a mixed bag. The county franchise was considerably more complicated after the act; it retained the old 40-shilling freehold qualification (except in Ireland, where it had been abolished in 1829 as a condition of Catholic emancipation), but it now included copyholders and long-term leaseholders whose land produced "clear yearly value" of £10, and short-term leaseholders and tenants-at-will whose land generated a minimum value of £50. The borough franchise, on the other hand, was greatly simplified. All occupiers, whether owners or tenants, of property having a yearly value of £10 received the vote. Existing franchises were retained for those who held them prior to 1832, but all voters were required to register and to be residents of their constituencies.

In general, the electorate after 1832 was about 50% larger than before, but because the reformed franchises were still tied to property, general elections for another 35 years retained much of their 18th-century character and produced parliaments that hardly differed from their predecessors. Yet the very fact that the array of franchises, heretofore the illogical products of specific historical circumstances, had now been systematized by applying universal criteria arising from design, was a momentous precedent. As many of reform's Tory opponents lamented in 1832, no one could know where the process might end.

John A. Hutcheson, Jr.

Bibliography

Brock, Michael. *The Great Reform Act.* 1973.

Cannon, J.A. *Parliamentary Reform, 1640–1832.* Rev. ed., 1982.

Halévy, Elie. *England in 1815.* 1913.

Hanham, H.J. *The Nineteenth-Century Constitution, 1815–1914.* 1969.

Namier, Lewis B. *The Structure of Politics at the Accession of George III.* 2nd ed., 1957.

O'Gorman, Frank. *Voters, Patrons, and Parties: The Unreformed Electoral System of Hanoverian England, 1734–1832.* 1989.

Owen, John B. *The Eighteenth Century, 1714–1815.* 1974.

Phillips, John A. *The Great Reform Bill in the Boroughs: English Electoral Behavior, 1818–1841.* 1992.

Stevenson, John. *Popular Disturbances in England, 1700–1832.* 2nd ed., 1992.

Williams, E.N. *The Eighteenth-Century Constitution, 1688–1815.* 1960.

See also Commons, House of; Government, National; Patronage; Political Thought; Radicalism and Radical Politics

Electricity

Electricity fascinated the Hanoverians, though intelligence of new experiments often came as shocking news. Electrical forces were, of course, recognized by the ancient Greeks. The founder of British electrical understanding was William Gilbert (1544–1603), the most famous scientist of the Elizabethan era, who postulated that a body became electrified when a fluid was removed from it by friction, leaving it surrounded by an "effluvium" or atmosphere (electrical field). By the early 18th century this theory had been revised to feature two fluids, one supposedly positive, the other negative, to account for the observed phenomena of attraction and repulsion. However, electrical knowledge was still confined largely to static electricity and such atmospheric manifestations as St. Elmo's fire.

Early Hanoverian scientists experimented by rubbing glass rods with leather or wool pads, and machines were used to rotate globes in contact with cushions of leather; but no practical applications emerged until the storage and conduction of electricity were better understood. In 1745 the Dutch scientist Pieter van Musschenbroek (1692–1761) invented the Leyden jar: a glass receptacle partly filled with water, equipped with a wire leading out of it, and charged with energy by conducting into it electricity generated from a friction device. In the following year, Sir William Watson (1715–1787), borrowing both the principle of the Leyden jar and the earlier discovery by Stephen Gray (1696–1736) that electricity will flow down a thread or a wire (1729), built an improved apparatus and shot an electrical spark over a wire spanning the River Thames at Westminster Bridge. Soon, not only scientists but quacks and miscellaneous entertainers everywhere were electrifying unsuspecting volunteers and killing birds. Electricity was at first novel, then fashionable, then a craze.

In Philadelphia, **Benjamin Franklin** temporarily gave up other activities to study electricity. He first saw a Leyden jar in 1746 and soon began making his own improvements to it. By 1749 he had postulated that lightning was an electrical phenomenon, and in 1752 during a thunderstorm he proved it by collecting electricity by means of wet twine attached on one end to a kite, on the other end to a metal key running from a Leyden jar. He soon rejected the two-fluid theory, postulating instead that electricity exists in two states of the same fluid, one positive, the other negative, both adhering to or inhering in matter, flows between them being natural attempts to equalize the "Electrical Fire" they contained.

Joseph Priestley made a few modifications to Franklin's ideas in his *History and Present State of Electricity* (1767), theorizing additionally that electrical and gravitational forces must obey similar laws. His ideas were later taken up by **Michael Faraday**. Another British scientist, **Henry Cavendish**, began precisely measuring the quantity, velocity, and distance of electrical flows, but unfortunately published little of his data. The next important development was the discovery in the 1790s that electricity might be generated not only by friction but also by chemical action. This was the work of Alessandro Volta (1745–1827), an Italian. Volta discovered that electricity could be generated by placing pairs of certain dissimilar metals in juxtaposition and in contact with a liquid conductor; and that the effect was multiplied by arranging several pairs in series.

Electrical experiment, 1753

His apparatus, known as the Voltaic pile, was the first electric battery, demonstrated in 1800. It was immediately improved upon by W. Cruikshank (1745–1800), who built a battery with 60 pairs of zinc and copper plates soldered together in a trough filled with brine. **Sir Humphry Davy** later constructed another with 2,000 pairs at the **Royal Institution**.

A battery provided continuous current. One consequent early discovery was electrolysis and the development of electroplating, another the realization that electrical currents give rise to magnetic fields. The great physicist Faraday showed these forces to be circular, and demonstrated (1832) how electrical currents could be used to force mechanical rotation. The repercussions were enormous, leading eventually to development of today's electrical industry.

Jim Burton

Bibliography

Derry, T.K, and T.I. Williams. *A Short History of Technology.* 1970.

Heilbron, J.L. *Electricity in the 17th and 18th Centuries.* 1979.

Sharlin, Harold I. *The Making of the Electrical Age.* 1963.

Whittaker, E.T. *A History of the Theories of Aether and Electricity.* 2 vols. 1960.

Williams, L.P. *Michael Faraday.* 1965.

Elgin Marbles

The array of Greek sculpture, vases, and coins now in the **British Museum** and known as the Elgin Marbles was collected by Thomas Bruce (1766–1841), 7th earl of Elgin and 11th earl of Kincardine. Elgin, a representative peer of **Scotland**, was appointed British Ambassador Extraordinary and Minister Plenipotentiary to the Sublime Porte at Constantinople from 1799 to 1803. While there he employed artists to draw and make plaster casts of the antiquities of Athens; the artists were supervised by Giovanni Battista Lusieri, an Italian painter whose surviving drawings record many of the Athenian sculptures *in situ.*

Elgin, recognizing the extensive deterioration of the architectural sculpture of the Acropolis, secured permission (or so he later claimed) from the Turks to buy and remove the sculptures from the metopes, frieze, and pediments of the Parthenon. The sculptures, brought to England between 1803 and 1812, elicited a variety of responses. Painters such as **B.R. Haydon** and **Thomas Lawrence** championed them whereas others, including Richard Payne Knight (1750–1824) and the Society of Dilettanti, unaccustomed to their naturalism of style and the pitted condition of their surfaces, questioned their quality.

In 1810, Elgin, out of public office and with reduced finances, tried to sell the marbles to the government, issuing a *Memorandum* in defense of the antiquities and of his motives in acquiring them. Despite the public attack on Elgin by **Lord Byron** in *Childe Harold's Pilgrimage,* the marbles were purchased in 1816 for the nation on the recommendation of a select parliamentary committee. At £35,000, the price was little more than half Elgin's estimated costs. Elgin's act saved from destruction and brought to world attention works of art that mark a high point of human endeavor, and that provided a standard of art for many 19th-century artists. Today a British Committee for the Restitution of the Parthenon Marbles continues to push for a return of the marbles to Greece.

Joan K. Stemmler

Bibliography

Andrew Ballantyne. "Knight, Haydon and the Elgin Marbles." *Apollo.* Vol. 128, pp. 155–159ff.

Hitchens, Christopher. *Imperial Spoils: The Curious Case of the Elgin Marbles.* 1987.

Jenkins, Ian. "George Frederic Watts and the Elgin Marbles." *Apollo.* Vol. 120, pp. 176–181.

Liscombe, R.W. "Richard Payne Knight: Some Unpublished Correspondence." *The Art Bulletin.* Vol. 61, pp. 604–611.

St. Clair, William. *Lord Elgin and the Marbles.* 1983.

Smith, A.H. "Lord Elgin and His Collection." *Journal of Hellenic Studies.* Vol. 36, pp. 163–372.

See also Antiquities and Ruins; Classicism; Sculpture

Emigration and Immigration

Overseas emigration from Britain, mainly to North American destinations, was much less extensive during the Hanoverian era than in Victorian and Edwardian times. Nonetheless, especially after the 1770s, it was becoming substantial, and within 50 years would widen to include destinations as remote as Tasmania off the southeast coast of **Australia**.

The British Settlement at Hobart, Tasmania, 1821

Between 1630 and 1700, England lost an estimated 300,000 people on balance of migration with **North America** and the **West Indies**; and roughly 378,000 when all overseas destinations, including **Ireland**, are taken into account. In the course of the 18th century England's net loss of **population** rose to around 519,000. It reached even higher levels in the period 1815–1850, when a further 500,000 departed. Losses were heaviest in the 1720s, 1750s, 1760s, early 1790s, and after 1815—particularly in 1819, 1827, and the early 1830s.

Emigration from **Scotland** to the countries of the New World did not become significant until after the **Act of Union** (1707), and remained relatively moderate in scale until the end of the **Seven Years' War** (1763). Between 1763 and 1775, approximately 25,000 people left Scottish ports for overseas destinations. A further 27,000 are estimated to have departed between 1783 and 1825, most in 1783–1793 and 1801–1802. Prior to 1815, the yearly number of departures rarely exceeded 2,000. But between 1825 and 1837 the volume of emigration increased dramatically: the total number of emigrants rose to over 92,000. Although the proportion of all emigrants from the Lowland counties rose during the latter years of the Hanoverian period, the bulk of Scotland's overseas emigration continued to emanate from the populations of the western Highlands and Islands.

Why Hanoverian Britain lost so many of its inhabitants to the countries of the New World is a question that has attracted considerable scholarly attention. To some extent, the exodus reflected a desire to escape from **poverty** and restricted employment opportunities at home. The push of economic deprivation was especially noticeable in the motives of Scottish emigrants. In the western Highlands and Islands, where the problems caused by the pressure of population growth on a primitive system of **Scottish agriculture**—rising rents, a decline in the status of tacksmen (lessees), and the spread of cattle and sheep farming—were aggravated after 1815 by the collapse of the kelp industry and the decay of the **fishing** and linen industries in the face of Lowland competition, the need to consider emigration was particularly pronounced. Emigrants from Lowland Scotland included large numbers of handloom **weavers** whose livelihoods were destroyed by new **technology**, and small **farmers** whose subtenancies disappeared with the trend toward larger, consolidated farm holdings.

At the same time, the influence of push factors should not be exaggerated. Significantly, only a minority of those who emigrated from England were drawn from the ranks of those worst afflicted by poverty. Most were farmers or skilled industrial workers with adequate means to meet the cost of emigration and for whom migration to the New World was not a flight from poverty but rather an escape from the possibility of future destitution or a desire to improve their current socioeconomic status.

Emigrants from Scotland, particularly in the period immediately following the **Napoleonic Wars**, were often responding to the push of actual unemployment and poverty. But even here, many (and in areas like northeast Scotland perhaps most) people were reacting primarily to the pull of the greater opportunities offered in England or the New World for personal advancement, or for maintaining traditional ways of life that were rapidly disappearing in their homeland.

Together, the twin forces of push and pull created a sufficient divergence of opportunity between the Old and New Worlds to convince large and ever-growing numbers of people that the risks of an ocean crossing were worthwhile. By the early 19th century, facilitated by improvements in methods of **transport**, more abundant information on prospects overseas, and financial assistance provided by earlier emigrants, what had once been a relative trickle of emigration was fast approaching a flood.

Despite the almost complete absence of data on numbers of immigrants, it is probably safe to assume that, relative to the size of population, net losses on balance of in- and out-migration were greater for Scotland than England. The number of Scots leaving to settle in England always exceeded the number of English moving to Scotland, while emigration from Ireland (the main source of Scottish immigration) was negligible before the 1750s. As late as 1787, the number of Irish-born residents in the whole of mainland Britain totaled just 20,000. By 1821 this had risen to 182,000; and by 1841 to over 415,000, of whom perhaps 126,000 (nearly 5% of the total population) were resident in Scotland. Many of these, however, were temporary, not permanent, immigrants. Not even the arrival of a further 110,000 migrants from Ireland to Scotland in the 1840s was sufficient to make up the number of Scots who left.

Neil L. Tranter

Bibliography

Bailyn, B. *Voyagers to the West.* 1986.
Baines, Dudley. *Migration in a Mature Economy: Emigration and Internal Migration in England and Wales, 1861–1900.* 1985.
Bumstead, J.M. *The People's Clearance: Highland Emigration to British North America, 1770–1815.* 1982.
Cowan, H.I. *British Emigration to North America: The First Hundred Years.* 1961.
Donaldson, G. *The Scots Overseas.* 1966.
Flinn, Michael. *Scottish Population History from the Seventeenth Century to the 1930s.* 1977.
Graham, I.C.C. *Colonists from Scotland: Emigration to North America, 1707–1783.* 1956.
Gray, Malcom. *Scots on the Move: Scots Migrants, 1750–1914.* 1990.
Harper, Marjory. *Emigration from North-East Scotland.* Vol. 1. 1988.
Scally, Robert. *The End of Hidden Ireland: Rebellion, Famine, and Emigration.* 1995.
Wrigley, E.A., and R.S. Schofield. *The Population History of England, 1541–1871: A Reconstruction.* 1981.

See also Irish Emigration

Emmet, Robert (1778–1803)

Emmet was born of a wealthy **Dublin** family linked to the **Anglo–Irish Ascendancy**. During his education at Trinity College he first made his mark as an orator, but by April 1798 had come under suspicion as the leader of the **United Irishmen** in the university. A warrant being issued for his arrest in 1799, he escaped to **France**, where he made contact with exiles from the failed Irish Rebellion of the previous summer.

Robert Emmet

Questioning Irish **radicalism**'s continuing dependence on France, he returned to Ireland in 1802 with plans for a military insurrection. Originally the uprising was to concide with Napoleon's expected invasion of England in August 1803, but premature discovery forced Emmet's hand a month earlier. The result was a confused and abortive skirmish, after which he was forced to flee. He was arrested, tried for treason, and, after a passionate speech from the dock, hanged in Dublin on 20 September.

In death, however, Emmet proceeded to achieve cult-like status. His image as a Romantic visionary, embracing the ideal of heroic self-sacrifice, was powerfully transmitted to successive generations of Irish nationalists.

E.W. McFarland

Bibliography

Elliot, M. *Partners in Revolution: The United Irishmen and France.* 1982.

Madden, R.R. *The Life and Times of Robert Emmet.* 1856.

See also Irish Rebellions; Tone, Wolfe

Empire and Imperialism

The Hanoverian period witnessed the rise of Britain as the world's preeminent imperial power, with the Empire embracing about a quarter of the global population by the 1820s. The loss of the American colonies in the **War of American Independence** did not herald the end of the Empire but only the beginnings of a new empire centered elsewhere, in the East.

The imperial dimension became increasingly important in 18th-century history, inaugurating what some historians have termed the first world wars. For Britain, the defeat of **France** in the **Seven Years' War** resulted in the acquisition (1763) of **Canada**, the "neutral" islands of the **West Indies** (Grenada, St. Vincent, Dominica, and Tobago), and the Ohio territories of **North America**; it also laid the foundation for later mastery of **India**. The American war that followed seemed to many contemporaries the beginning of the end of British imperialism because Britain not only lost the 13 mainland colonies and Ohio territories but also came close to defeat everywhere else as well. This was the only war of the Hanoverian period where British naval power was inferior to the combined strength of her opponents. **Edward Gibbon**'s *Decline and Fall of the Roman Empire* (1776–1788), whose publication coincided with this defeat, evoked fears of a similar British collapse.

Heroes of Empire: Wolfe, Clive, Cook, Boscawen

But these proved unfounded. Britain built a much larger Empire after 1783, "the second British Empire," whose focus lay to the east. The **East India Company** purchased Penang, off the Malay peninsula, from the Sultan of Kedah (1786). Abolitionists funded the settlement of exslaves in Sierra Leone in **Africa** after 1787. **James Cook**'s voyages to the South Pacific established claims to vast territories, including **Australia**, where penal colonies were established in New South Wales (1788), Van Diemen's Land—later Tasmania (1804), and Norfolk Island (1825).

The expansion of the second Empire gained great momentum during the **French Revolutionary and Napoleonic Wars**, when Britain acquired Sri Lanka (Ceylon, 1796), Trinidad (1797), Malta (1799), the three provinces of Dutch Guiana (1803), Tobago (1810), St. Lucia (1805), the Cape Colony (1806), Heligoland (1808), the Ionian Islands (Cephalonia and Zante in 1809, Corfu in 1814), Mauritius, and the Seychelles (1810), which were officially ceded to Britain in the resulting peace treaties.

The British subsequently obtained Singapore, through **Sir Stamford Raffles**'s purchase from the Sultan of Johore (1819), and nearby Malacca, from the Dutch (1824). They annexed the Falkland Islands (1832–1833), where they had long disputed a title. They claimed the entire continent of Australia (1829), where they established a new colony in the south (1836). While Canada expanded westward into Alberta, Manitoba, and British Columbia, the East India Company extended its power and territories within India—the new "jewel" of the British Empire. Indeed, the trade of India largely dictated the choice of colonial acquisitions, requiring strategic naval posts to defend its avenues with England, and entrepots in East Asia for its increasingly important connection with China.

Mixed motives were behind this burst of expansion and imperial activity. Economic interests always remained prominent, even though Britain did conduct most of her **overseas commerce** outside her Empire. Other influences were important, and sometimes took priority. Anglo–French rivalry, later spurred by fear of the spread of Jacobin ideology, led to European **wars**, and it was these which resulted in the largest colonial gains. Strategic interests explain British imperialism in the Mediterranean and the Baltic, where colonies brought little direct economic reward but were considered critical to British naval supremacy and the security the **navy** provided, as well as protecting the arteries of **trade**. The influence of **Evangelicals**, **missionary societies**, and abolitionists played a significant role in British involvement in Africa and also produced innovations in imperial government. Scientific inquiry and the challenge of **exploration** also laid the foundation for territorial claims. Other influences included the "subimperialism" of colonial officials acting on their own initiative, and the insistence of native allies seeking protection against local enemies.

This new eastern Empire was much more authoritarian than its predecessor. It was pieced together from predominantly non–European, non-white, and non–Christian populations, even while Britain was becoming more militantly anti–Catholic, nationalistic, and reactionary during the period 1790–1820. The conservative backlash to the **French Revolution**, so apparent in domestic politics and in relation to **Ireland**, was also reflected in the Empire. Attempts to rationalize and centralize imperial government, which after 1763 had helped to trigger the American war, became even more pronounced after 1790. That new era saw the establishment of the Colonial Office, masterminded by **James Stephen**; the gradual creation of a more professional salaried civil service, pioneered by **Lord Charles Cornwallis** in India; larger military garrisons; police forces; and much more powerful colonial executives. The elected legislatures of the old colonial system were retained in the older colonies and were gradually extended to new white settler colonies (as in the **Constitutional [Canada] Act**, 1791), but did not appear in the new Crown colonies, which chiefly comprised non-white populations.

Additionally, British imperial agrarian policies discouraged communal land tenure in favor of private property, and this was to have revolutionary effects in Asia and Africa. Imperial agriculturalists, working from English models, sought to create societies of "improving" paternal landowners and industrious peasants, thereby reinforcing local hierarchies and even creating new privileged elites. The movements of nomadic peoples were also discouraged, as for example by the notorious pass laws of the Cape Colony (1809–1828). Missionaries meanwhile sought to spread Christianity and the English language as part of a "civilizing" mission. The British Empire bore an increasingly close resemblance to a neo-absolutist European state.

Imperial apologists have traditionally emphasized the liberalism and supposed benevolence of this second empire, tendencies they attribute to the influence of **humanitarians**, Evangelicals, utilitarian philosophers, and classical economists. They point to the trial of **Warren Hastings** in the 1780s as a sign of improving administrative behavior and responsibility. The colonial governments of conquered territories did often try to incorporate precolonial legal systems and customs (thereby creating a vast array of differing law codes and constitutions). **Lord Bentinck's** reforms in India, and the successes of the **antislavery movement**, were triumphs of humanitarian agitation. The direct government of the Crown colonies was often more sensitive to the interests of the majority than the former ruling oligarchies of the Irish Protestants, Dutch Boers, and white West Indian sugar planters.

But although this emphasis on British determination to rule "beneficently" has contributed to a legend of a uniquely enlightened Empire, British rule was in fact essentially authoritarian, exploitative, and racist in character. Throughout the Hanoverian period the political power of the imperial government was supreme, and coercion remained always a very real option. Britain encountered resistance everywhere—from slaves, maroons, Irish Catholics, French Canadians, Native Americans, and Africans. Everywhere, the economic interests of the colonists were subordinated to those of the Mother Country. Despite notable victories for free-trade interests, like the East India Company's loss of its monopolies, restrictive trade and **Navigation laws** remained largely intact. Coercive forms of labor continued even after the eradication of slavery (1833), which itself survived through most of the Hanoverian era.

The bigotry of the second Empire was evident in discrimination against Catholics in Ireland and in Lower Canada, where separatist movements developed from the late 1820s. A new wave of British **emigration** to the colonies after 1815, encouraged by parliamentary grants and the theories of **Edward Gibbon Wakefield**, ensured white Protestant English-speaking majorities in Canada, Australia, and the Cape. Racism, accentuated by pseudoscientific theories, was overt. The imperial civil service was closed to non-whites except at the lowest echelons. The British **army**, although increasingly dependent on indigenous peoples, was officered by whites. A stratified racial hierarchy emerged throughout the colonial societies. An invidious distinction arose between the governments of the white settler colonies (Canada, the Cape Colony, and Australia), which gradually moved toward greater autonomy in the 1830s, and the "direct" governments of the non–European populations. The vaunted reforms and self-imposed restraints of the second Empire were, furthermore, not simply a product of British altruism but were often necessitated by colonial resistance, a changing world economy, and the problem of maintaining obedience.

Sir John Seeley (1834–1895), writing in the latter 19th century, urged that a knowledge of the British Empire was vital to an understanding of Hanoverian Britain. His sentiments have found an increasingly appreciative audience among modern historians, who emphasize the centrality of the empire in the economic expansion of Britain, the rise of the British state, Anglo–French rivalry, **foreign relations**, the emergence of the British Navy, and the growth of British **nationalism**.

Andrew J. O'Shaughnessy

Bibliography

Bayly, C.A. *Imperial Meridian: The British Empire and the World, 1780–1830.* 1989.

Canny, Nicholas P. *Kingdom and Colony: Ireland in the Atlantic World, 1560–1800.* 1988.

Colley, Linda. *Britons: Forging the Nation 1707–1837.* 1992.

Gascoigne, John. *Joseph Banks and the English Enlightenment: Useful Knowledge and Polite Culture.* 1994.

Greene, Jack P. *Peripheries and Center: Constitutional Development in the Extended Polities of the British Empire and the United States, 1607–1788.* 1986.

———. *Pursuits of Happiness: The Social Development of Early Modern British Colonies and the Formation of American Culture.* 1988.

Harlow, Vincent T. *The Founding of the Second British Empire, 1763–1793.* 2 vols. 1952, 1964.

Knorr, Klaus E. *British Colonial Theories, 1570–1850.* 1944.
Lawson, Philip. "The Missing Link: The Imperial Dimension in Understanding Hanoverian Britain." *Historical Journal.* Vol. 29, pp. 747–791.
Mackay, David. *In the Wake of Cook: Exploration, Science & Empire, 1780–1801.* 1985.
Robertson, John, ed. *A Union for Empire: Political Thought and the British Union of 1707.* 1995.
Seeley, Sir John R. *The Expansion of England.* 1883.
Tucker, Robert W., and David C. Hendrickson. *The Fall of the First British Empire: Origins of the War of American Independence.* 1982.

Empiricism

Empiricism, the philosophical doctrine that all genuine knowledge is acquired from human observation and experience through sense perceptions, made important advances during the Hanoverian period. Broadly speaking, the empirical outlook is the scientific outlook; it advanced just as **science** advanced in the 18th and 19th centuries. There were several different branches of British empiricism, but they all generally held that people do not possess innate ideas, "inborn" notions of things, but rather that they acquire knowledge by reflecting on particular experiences. Information collected through the senses is formed by the mind's operations into ideas. Because human beings are unable to go beyond sensory data and these ideas formed about such data, ultimate certainty in most areas is not possible. The boundaries of probable knowledge, however, are very wide.

The dominant strain in Hanoverian philosophy was English empiricism. Its founder, **John Locke**, writing in the latter 17th century, held that the human mind was a "tabula rasa," a blank slate on which sense perceptions impinged, and that the mind developed, through reflection, first simple, then increasingly complex, ideas. But a generation later, the empiricism of **George Berkeley**, Bishop of Cloyne, was far more spiritual than that of Locke. Berkeley held that because God was the source of all knowledge, human experience could be perceived in ideas, and not merely through them, as Locke had contended. Perception was the key. Berkeley even argued that matter did not exist apart from human perception of it. But God perceived everything and hence ensured continuity and order in the world, and made it possible for human beings to achieve knowledge.

David Hume, writing around the middle of the 18th century, agreed with Locke in taking a position far removed from theological suggestion, but also contradicted Locke's assumptions about the ultimate knowability of anything. Hume, though helping to move empiricism from epistemology to the more modern plane of psychology, held that human knowledge could never be achieved with certainty because data collected through sensory perception were mere impressions on the mind. No person could be certain that causality existed, for its existence could not be proven, or even really perceived. For example, a person could collect impressions that one billiard ball, after being struck by another, moved, but could never truly know in an absolute sense that the one action caused the other, however many repetitions of the event were watched. Hume demoted knowledge to mere probability—though an experimental scientist of today, comfortable with the idea of Truth as something which we merely approximate as best we can, would certainly tend to see this as a step up, rather than a step down.

Meanwhile **David Hartley**, the associationist psychologist, pursuing another implication of Locke's teachings, chipped away at the ancient distinction between mind and body. Through the mind's physical functioning, human beings acquired knowledge and understanding; they then combined ideas about the universe through the psychological process of the association of ideas. These universal processes of "knowing" were seated in the physiology of the brain and spinal cord. Hartley thus helped bridge the gap between early "natural philosophy" and modern neurobiology.

Scottish philosophy included a branch of empiricism heavily blended with moral philosophy, a development that flourished during the latter half of the Hanoverian period in the ideas of **Francis Hutcheson**, **Thomas Reid**, and **Dugald Stewart**. Hutcheson elaborated the idea that humans have, in addition to 5 external senses, a moral sense that leads instinctively, when evaluating conduct, to making moral judgments that refer to whether or not mankind will be bettered by a given action. Somewhat similarly, Reid, rejecting Hume's empiricist approach as too subjective, argued that social and political moral principles were immediately knowable by the mind through experience. Stewart, a student of Reid's, went even further and proposed that through empirical understanding of the universe and its laws, and through an innate love of excellence, human beings themselves were perfectible. He also believed that elected officials, through experience, could understand and use the norms of equity and justice in their day-to-day affairs.

Finally, in the 19th century, **John Stuart Mill**, maintaining like his predecessors that empirical knowledge was the only human knowledge, held that human beings could develop generalizations from particular experience, but took another step by including for the first time generalizations in logic and mathematics.

Jack Fruchtman, Jr.

Bibliography

Priest, Stephen. *The British Empiricists: Hobbes to Ayer.* 1990.
Thomas, Keith. *The British Empiricists.* 1990.
Woolhouse, R.S. *The Empiricists.* 1988.

See also Enlightenment, The; Political Thought; Scottish Enlightenment

Enclosures

See Agriculture

Encyclopedias

See Reference Works

Engraving

English engraving was long dominated by foreign influences. French engravers excelled in amplitude and variety of stroke; Italians produced balanced compositions with lightness of touch and fancy. Even in the 18th century, many English etchers imitated Rembrandt. Where they did innovate and excel was in the art of graphic **satire**.

George Vertue (1684–1756), though revealed to be a mediocre engraver in such works as his *Oxford Almanacks* (1723–1756), produced notebooks which today are a valuable source of information about early-18th-century British art. In them he emphasized how hard and unrewarding was the life of a line engraver. His greatest contemporary in that field was **William Hogarth**—great not because he was a master engraver or etcher (his work was functional and emphatic, rather than delicate and graceful), but because of his extraordinary invention and imagination.

Hogarth's earliest large engraving, *South Sea Bubble* (1721), marks the beginning of the English tradition of satiric engraving. Soon afterward came his *Masquerades and Operas* (1724), attacking false foreign tastes and reproving the neglect of native artistic genius (the print shows **Shakespeare**'s works being hauled away to be pulped). *A Harlot's Progress* (1731), with its serious moral purpose, carefully wrought details, and variety of pose and expression established Hogarth as a great original force in English art. Though he later branched out into **history painting** and **portrait painting**, social criticism, political action, philanthropy, and aesthetic controversy, Hogarth remained all his life a master of the engraved print, as revealed in his *Rake's Progress* (1735), *Marriage à la Mode* (1745), in which his style approached the grace of French engraving; and *Gin Lane* and *Beer Street* (1750–1751)—which, blunt in style, gained him a wide audience. Always discontented, his work reveals a pessimistic outlook: Hogarth's last engraving, *Tailpiece, or the Bathos* (1764), is a scene of desolation and decay depicting Time clutching in his hand a will appointing Chaos his sole executor.

Hogarth deserves mention also for his attempt to improve the financial status of engravers by originating and piloting through Parliament (with the help of influential friends) the Engraver's Copyright Act of 1735 ("the Hogarth Act"), which for the first time protected the rights of graphic artists and guaranteed them the proceeds of the sales of their work.

Two important satirists who followed Hogarth were **Thomas Rowlandson** and **James Gillray**. Rowlandson, the son of a **middle-class** tradesman, trained in academy schools and studied for 2 years in Paris. More facile than Hogarth (perhaps because he was also a **watercolor** artist), his engravings good-humoredly caricatured everyday life and sought to capture the ridiculous in expression, dress, manners, customs, and politics. Rowlandson's work has been praised for its rotundity of form and charm of curve. Much of it appeared in the magazines *Repository of Arts* (1809–1828) and *Poetical Magazine* (1809–1812). Other productions included his *Tour of Dr. Syntax in Search of the Picturesque* (1812) and *Dance of Life* and *Dance of Death* (1816).

Gillray, more draftsman than painter, was much more venomous than other contemporary caricaturists. He lam-

Hogarth's "Masquerades and Operas," 1724

pooned not only dangerous foreigners such as Bonaparte but the English royal family and many politicians. Gillray was a closer and wittier observer than Rowlandson, though he avoided coarse humor and easy tricks. His most famous works (nearly all from the period 1790–1810) include *French Liberty. British Slavery, The Gradual Abolition of the Slave Trade,* and *The Zenith of French Glory.*

English engraving in the age of **George III** also produced a great innovator, **William Blake.** After attending drawing school, Blake was apprenticed for 7 years to James Basire (1769–1822), a famous antiquarian engraver from whom he learned the intaglio engraving technique. During his lifetime he produced over 1,200 illustrations, including 800 separate designs on copperplate. His greatest innovation was to engrave simultaneously text he had composed and the illustration he had designed for works such as *Songs of Innocence* (1789). This led to a harmonious interweaving of text and image, with color used to accentuate important parts. Blake himself colored the pages, of which only a few copies were printed.

Color was always a problem. Since 1660, printmakers had been trying to compete with painters by attempting to color prints with mezzotint. Mezzotint engraving was especially popular in England; its most successful employment was by the Irishmen John Brooks (*fl.* 1730–1755) and James MacArdell (*c.* 1729–1765), and later the Englishmen Valentine Green (1739–1813) and J.R. Smith (1752–1812). After 1750 at least 700 mezzotint engravings were produced in England after paintings by **Sir Joshua Reynolds.** Most were done under the aegis of the **publishers** John and Josiah Boydell. Experiments in color were also done with chiaroscuro woodcuts. Elisha Kirkall (*c.* 1682–1742) imitated certain drawings of Italian masters by using the mezzotint rocker for etching and modeling, and then overprinting the result with color from woodblocks.

Engraving in the Hanoverian period thus developed in both subject matter and technique. Engravers were able to improve their financial stability and social status. They also broke away from Continental influences and achieved greatness in satire and novelty in bookmaking, and successfully explored the use of color in printmaking.

Ann W. Engar

Bibliography

Adhemar, Jean. *Graphic Art of the 18th Century.* 1964.

Essick, Robert N. *William Blake: Printmaker.* 1980.

Godfrey, Richard T. *Printmaking in Britain: A General History from Its Beginnings to the Present Day.* 1978.

Hind, Arthur M. *A History of Engraving and Etching from the 15th Century to the Year 1914.* 1963.

Paulson, Ronald. *Hogarth, Volume 1: The Modern Moral Subject, 1697–1732.* 1991.

See also Book Illustration; Caricature; Graphic Arts

Enlightenment, The (1689–1789)

The Enlightenment, the dominant European intellectual movement of the 18th century, was built on the inherited rational and optimistic principles of the 17th-century intellectual revolution. Enlightenment thinkers aimed at a thorough revamping of institutions for the sake of liberty and the improvement of the material conditions of life. Many were French, although Germans and Italians were represented as well, but the movement had some of its deepest roots in Britain, and took hold not only there but in the **North American** colonies.

The bedrock of Enlightenment faith was a belief in the ability of human reason to address all governmental, religious, and societal abuses effectively, and to design ways in which life in general could be improved for everyone. This belief had been encouraged in the ideas of Francis Bacon (1561–1626), Isaac Newton (1642–1727), and **John Locke.** Bacon and Newton had fostered the optimistic assumption that the world operated under demonstrable and unchanging laws; Locke's theory of knowledge implied that because all minds begin with the same sort of data and data-processing operations, people might arrive without great difficulty at common understandings. Combined, these theories helped to inculcate relativism, toleration, expectations of progress, faith in science, and beliefs that ordinary people might ultimately be trusted with their own governance.

The new emphasis on reason deeply affected **theology** and led to an unprecedented growth of **freethinking.** Belief in a rationally ordered universe promoted the conception of a rational caretaker God, very different from the deity portrayed in Scripture. This belief, generally known as deism, emphasizing God but drawing away from the traditional Trinity, consisted of both constructive philosophical arguments—as seen, for example, in **John Toland**'s *Christianity Not Mysterious* (1696) and **Matthew Tindal**'s *Christianity as Old as the Creation* (1730)—and negative attacks on the traditions and institutions of Christianity, focusing on the clergy and the Bible. Open attacks were more frequent on the Continent than in Britain, where **religious toleration** was better established, but anticlerical criticism was not only produced in Britain, it was also imported and widely read. Analysis of the sales catalogues of more than 200 private libraries belonging to British gentlemen show, for example, that Voltaire's works were more heavily represented (in 78% of the libraries) than those of anyone else, including all English authors; an English periodical reviewer wrote in 1759 that "the writings of Mr. Voltaire are as much in fashion among the English as Chinese furniture." **Edward Gibbon,** one of Voltaire's many British visitors and admirers, reflected deist and anticlerical opinion in his *Decline and Fall of the Roman Empire* (1776–1788), snidely chuckling at miracles and the credulity of early Christian converts. Within organized religion, there was a steady gravitation of **Presbyterians** and other **dissenters** toward **Unitarian** rationalist theology. In the **Church of England,** beliefs in natural religion and **Latitudinarian** tolerance at last brought the rationalistic Christian apologetics of **William Paley** toward the end of the 18th century. With the **French Revolution** and the publication of **Thomas Paine**'s *Age of Reason* (1794, 1796), Hanoverian freethinking was far from over, though the Enlightenment itself was now finished.

Any consideration of 18th-century activity in **biblical criticism**, **literary criticism**, **history** and **biography** writing, **classical** studies, **music scholarship**, and the compilation of **reference works** (to take only a few examples), reveals how strong was the thrust of the British wing of the Enlightenment. The same might be said of other intellectual phenomena, such as the proliferation of **learned societies** and the enormous strides taken in **science**. But the Enlightenment was also partly responsible (though **religious revivalism**'s part should not be minimized) for the **humanitarianism** that increasingly marked the age and that resulted in the **antislavery movement**, attempts at **prison** and **law reform**, and the like. The general flowering of practical programs of improvement, including the entire campaign for the extension of personal liberty that resulted in the French and **American** revolutions and the rise of **radicalism** in England, **Scotland**, and **Ireland**, sprang partly from it as well. The broad intellectual movement known as **rational dissent**, which flourished in the period 1750–1790, was roughly equivalent to the culture of the philosophers and writers in Paris. British **political thought** responded to the Enlightenment, particularly in the areas of rights, administrative reform, and electoral entitlement.

Although Enlightenment thinkers in **France** were more numerous and no less distinguished than those in Britain, Englishmen and Scots played an important role not only in originating the movement but also, by 1800, in ending it. The **Scottish Enlightenment**, centered in **Edinburgh**, an entire division within the larger movement and better organized than any activities in **London** or **Birmingham**, saw a remarkable outburst of analytical thought in the realms of history, ethics, economics, psychology, and natural science in the latter 18th century. But it was **David Hume**, Scotland's greatest philosopher, who publicized the ideas that were to bring it to a close. Exploring human reasoning powers in his *Enquiry Concerning Human Understanding* (1748), Hume concluded that man's reason was incapable of reaching objective knowledge of any kind. Reacting to Locke's empiricism, he showed that human beings possessed no immediate knowledge of causes, nature's laws, or even their own moral power. Enlightened rationalism, at last questioning even its own assumptions, thus ironically opened the door to pessimism, skepticism, and that countervailing faith in the emotions which emerged toward the end of the 18th century with the rise of **Romanticism**.

Barbara Jean Whitehead

Bibliography

Becker, Carl. *The Heavenly City of the Eighteenth-Century Philosophers.* 1932.

Bradley, James E. *Religion, Revolution and English Radicalism: Nonconformity in Eighteenth Century Politics and Society.* 1990.

Cassirer, Ernst. *The Philosophy of the Enlightenment.* 1951.

Fruchtman, Jack, Jr. *Thomas Paine: Apostle of Freedom.* 1994.

Gascoigne, John. *Cambridge in the Age of Enlightenment: Science, Religion and Politics from the Restoration to the French Revolution.* 1989.

———. *Joseph Banks and the English Enlightenment.* 1994.

Gay, Peter. *The Enlightenment: An Interpretation.* 2 vols. 1966.

Haakonssen, Knud, ed. *Enlightenment and Religion: Rational Dissent in Eighteenth-Century Britain.* 1996.

Hampson, Norman. *The Enlightenment.* 1968.

Spadafora, D. *The Idea of Progress in Eighteenth-Century Britain.* 1990.

Entertainment

See Amusements and Recreation

Enthusiasm

Eighteenth-century changes in the meaning of the word *enthusiasm* mirror the rising value placed on individual personal experience, a development reflected also in the emergence of **Evangelicalism** and **Romanticism**. Conversely, these changes accompanied the decline of **neoclassicism** and its associated ideals of moderation, reasonableness, and consensus.

Enthusiast in much of the 18th century was a derogatory term applied generally to the religious fanatic, impostor, or zealot, but more specifically to someone who was deluded or pretending to be divinely inspired. Derived from the Greek word meaning "possessed by God," the term was used to stigmatize unpopular religious groups, especially **Quakers**, **Roman Catholics**, Puritans, and **Methodists**. Wild behavior and outlandish doctrines were the symptoms of enthusiasm.

Because of the violent sectarian strife of the 17th century, public opinion well into the 18th century was highly suspicious of extreme or unusual outbursts of religious emotion, commonly dismissing these as delusions or counterfeits. Enthusiasm was detected in religious mania, frenzy, credulity, extravagantly or excessively pious behavior, states of ecstasy, and conversion experiences. **Jonathan Swift** ridiculed it in his *Tale of a Tub* (1704) and *The Mechanical Operation of the Spirit* (1710). **David Hume** linked it to superstition in his philosophical essays of the period 1740–1780. **William Hogarth** vigorously and crudely caricatured it in his engraving *Enthusiasm Delineated* (*c.* 1760).

This older and more negative distrust of enthusiasm lingered into the 19th century, but before 1800 the word was being employed much more positively in the areas of literature and the arts. Critics were more willing by the 1770s to praise enthusiasm in **poetry**, where wildness, exuberance, and passion seemed less alarming than in religion. To poets and painters, it was increasingly good and even necessary to be divinely inspired. As early as 1747, **William Collins**, in his "Ode on the Poetical Character," extolled the inspired poet as a "loved enthusiast." As Methodism rose after 1750, personal inspiration even in the religious sphere became more widely approved. Thus in his "Sermon on Enthusiasm" (1750) **John Wesley** sought to shift the values carried in this "dark ambiguous word."

In the early 19th century, **Samuel Taylor Coleridge** made a point of distinguishing enthusiasm from fanaticism, whereas a century earlier, the two conditions had been considered interconnected. Coleridge himself often used the word *enthu-*

siasm positively and in nonreligious contexts, and indeed by the 1830s it had taken on its general modern sense: deep and excited intensity of feeling for a person, subject, or cause; an absorbing interest.

The history of enthusiasm as a described mental state captures an important cultural development in the Hanoverian era, the growing prestige of personal and rapturous experience. What had earlier been denounced as dangerous instability came to be esteemed as a sign of emotional or aesthetic sensitivity. These changes made for greater tolerance of unusual experiences and perceptions, but also encouraged extreme individualism and moral subjectivism. The same developments can be traced in the 18th-century history of such terms as ***sensibility*** and ***sentimentalism***.

R.D. Stock

Bibliography

Knox, Ronald. *Enthusiasm.* 1950.

Stock, R.D. *The Holy and the Daemonic from Sir Thomas Browne to William Blake.* 1982.

Tucker, Susie I. *Enthusiasm: A Study in Semantic Change.* 1972.

Whelan, Sister M. Kevin. *Enthusiasm in English Poetry of the Eighteenth Century (1700–1774).* 1935.

See also Benevolence; Humanitarianism; Manners and Morals; Millenarianism

Entrepreneurs and Entrepreneurship

The idea of entrepreneurship in the **Industrial Revolution** labors under various difficulties. For example, the term has often been used loosely to describe the aggregate activity of persons who made money quickly. But technically speaking, *entrepreneurship* concerns the taking of strategic decisions, whereas *management* is more concerned with tactics. Thus an ability to see the wider picture, and to assess the means necessary to further the business, is better proof of entrepreneurship than mere success in business.

Josiah Wedgwood

Entrepreneurship has always existed. In the Middle Ages it was not considered respectable by the authorities. The church held out strongly for the "just price," frowned on monopolies, and banned usury. **Craft guild** regulations stifled those who tried to place individual advancement before the common good. Society needed to be more open if entrepreneurship was to flourish. In Britain, society became more secular after the Reformation, a trend accelerated during the **Enlightenment**. People became a little more concerned with the present and less with the hereafter, regulation of interest rates passed into government hands, and economic needs rather than religious ideals took precedence.

Other obstacles were removed. Businessmen moved some stages of industrial processes from the town to the country, as rural labor could be used more efficiently on a part-time basis, and strict guild regulation could be avoided. Also, the ending of the **trade** monopolies of **chartered companies** allowed more people to deal directly in foreign markets. All of this encouraged enterprise to flourish.

Some historians have given fairly broad definitions of entrepreneurship, but others have refined these by looking not just at its scope but also at its links with, and differences from, management. One writer (Pollard) sees the entrepreneur as a risk-taker who makes decisions about two particular strategic areas: the general direction the firm should take, and its objectives. His ideal entrepreneur decided the kind of business to be started and developed, where to seek finance, the goods and services to be offered, the level of production, and the market to be targeted; other functions were the preserve of management.

Such clear-cut divisions could be difficult in the Hanoverian era. Early management was often carried on by entrepreneurs. Many early entrepreneurs were production managers and could also be concerned with coordinating stocks of raw material and finished goods; such decisions could be crucial for cash flow and hence the progress of the organization. Some entrepreneurs supervised labor and, like **Robert Owen**, made themselves responsible for providing community services in company villages. Some were particularly concerned with accountancy and with costing to determine prices. Some were drawn into problems of transport. Some, such as **Josiah Wedgwood**, who turned a small Staffordshire pottery into a world enterprise, were skillful at all these aspects of entrepreneurship. The entrepreneur coordinated many functions essential to the operation of a successful business.

No accurate statistics exist for the recruitment patterns or success rates of entrepreneurs. Qualitative generalizations can be made about their origins, and bankruptcy figures can give some idea of how many failed. Some, like **David Dale**, had mercantile origins. The **Lloyds** had a landowning background. Others, such as **Jedediah Strutt**, came from the yeoman farmer class, and a number were in textiles—for example, the **Peels**. Weavers and skilled **craftsmen** provided a few entrepreneurs. Some who began as technical men or managers also rose to enter the entrepreneurial class. A significant number were **dissenters** who were barred by law from English universities and many public offices.

Merchants were important because they were significant providers of capital. New businesses in the 18th century, especially in the **textile industries**, were generally small, consisting of one man or a partnership, often of merchants and artisans, the knowledge of both being required to found a business. The amount of fixed capital involved could be small, but even in industries such as **iron** and **brewing**, where larger amounts of capital were required, entrepreneurs generally favored partnerships, the law making it difficult to form **joint-stock companies**.

Entrepreneurs established **factories** to achieve control over production, for as the economy grew, the preexisting system of **domestic production** did not always allow the degree of control necessary to satisfy growing demand. It also required a host of agents, making it difficult to control the supply and quality of output, as operatives could work for several different masters, each striving to have his work finished first. Embezzlement of raw material was also a problem. In some circumstances, therefore, factory organization seemed a lesser evil.

On the other hand, where the domestic system was flexible, for example in the **weaving** sector of the textile industry and the production of small ironware, it would be maintained. Entrepreneurs moved into the domestic system in a piecemeal fashion, but the profits they achieved soon made it apparent that they had become a significant force. They shared risks and saved complicated cost calculations by introducing fixed piece rates, thus bringing a degree of security into the system. They also saw disadvantages, such as middlemen's profits and subcontracting, which they tried, not always successfully, to curtail.

Down to around 1820, therefore, many entrepreneurs operated in a mixed economy of factories and outworkers, often employing both. Sometimes, outwork techniques were used in factories; powered and hand machines in the same complex were not uncommon. Thus at the same time as they were moving into factories, entrepreneurs were also keeping more and more people employed at home. It was not until the 1830s, following the development of the power loom, that weavers moved into factories. Many aspects of **metalworking** remained in the domestic system into the Victorian era.

Although it can no longer be held that entrepreneurs were the prime movers of the Industrial Revolution, their contribution to the development of the economy in the Hanoverian era was immense.

A.J.G. Cummings

Bibliography

Crouzet, François, ed. *Capital Formation in the Industrial Revolution.* 1972.

Flinn, M.W. *The Origins of the Industrial Revolution.* 1966.

Payne, P.L. *British Entrepreneurship in the Nineteenth Century.* 1974.

Pollard, Sidney. *The Genesis of Modern Management.* 1965.

Wilson, C. "The Entrepreneur in the Industrial Revolution in Britain," in *Explorations in Entrepreneurial History.* Vol. 7. 1955.

Epic

Epic **poetry** is that which, like the "Aeneid" of Virgil, celebrates the achievements of heroes usually in a continuous narrative. Yet in the 18th century there were surprisingly few English epics or heroic poems. Perhaps that high place which the epic occupied in critics' minds daunted poets. For instance, *A New and Complete Dictionary of Arts and Sciences* (1754) warned the epic aspirant that

> there must be a judgement so solid, a discernment so exquisite, such perfect knowledge of the language . . . such obstinate study, profound meditation, and vast capacity, that scarce whole ages can produce one genius fit for an epic poet.

Then too, perhaps heroism itself was less credible in the rationalistic 18th century. No successful epic celebrated the exploits of **Marlborough**, **Cook**, **Boscawen**, or **Wellington**.

The dearth of great British epics seems the more surprising in view of how promisingly the century began, with Richard Blackmore's (*c.* 1655–1729) *Prince Arthur* (1695), *King Arthur* (1700), *Eliza* (1705), and *Alfred* (1723). Richard Glover's (1712–1785) *Leonidas* (1737, revised 1770) was extravagantly praised for its **whiggish** attacks against **Sir Robert Walpole**, but its popularity barely extended beyond Walpole's political demise. William Wilkie's (1721–1772) *The Epigoniad* (1753) was lauded by his Scottish contemporaries, who called Wilkie "the Scottish Homer." Another Scot, **James Macpherson**, had great success on the Continent—particularly in Germany and France—with the purported works of *Ossian* (1762–1763), though his work suffered in England from charges of fraud leveled by **Samuel Johnson** and others. Notwithstanding, in scope if not form, *Ossian* resembles an epic; and if the term was applied to any large, ambitious undertaking, then such works as **Blake**'s prophetic poems (*Vala,* 1804; *Milton,* 1815; and *Jerusalem,* 1820), **Wordsworth**'s *The Prelude* (1850), and **Byron**'s *Don Juan* (1819–1824) would be epics.

If great epics were scarce, the period was a golden age for **mock-heroic** works and serious translations. **Pope**'s *The Rape of the Lock* (1714) was not the first but is the most famous mock epic, and **Henry Fielding** defined his novel *Tom Jones* (1749) as a "comic epic in prose." Nicholas Rowe (1674–1718) **translated** Lucan's *Pharsalia* (1716); and Pope's version of *The Iliad* (1715–1716) has been called an epic in its own right. Its financial success encouraged other translations, including Christopher Pitt's (1699–1748) *Aeneid* (1740) and William Mickle's (1734–1788) *The Lusiad* (1755). Henry F. Cary's (1772–1844) *Divine Comedy* (1805, 1812) has been often reprinted.

Although poets continued to attempt epics—**John Keats**'s fragmentary *Hyperion* (1818) and *The Fall of Hyperion* (1819), for instance, and **Robert Southey**'s early epics about which **Richard Porson** predicted, "they would be remembered when Homer and Virgil are forgotten—and not until then"—**novels**, such as William Thackeray's *Vanity Fair* (1847–1848), became the preferred form in the 19th century.

Peter A. Tasch

Bibliography

Merchant, Paul. *The Epic.* 1971.

Swedenberg, H.T., Jr. *Theory of the Epic in England, 1650–1800.* 1944.

Tillyard, E.M.W. *English Epic and Its Background.* 1954.

See also Classicism

Epistle

The epistle as a literary form in Hanoverian Britain must be defined by and divided into two categories: **poetry** and prose. The verse epistle, one of the **neoclassical** forms of familiar and complimentary poetry, often after the model of Horace, falls under the first heading; and **essays** and **novels** cast into the epistolary form, under the second.

Alexander Pope was instrumental in popularizing both forms of the literary epistle: in poetry, in his *Imitations of Horace* (1733–1737) and *Moral Essays* (1731–1735; or *Epistles to Several Persons,* as they were originally known); and in prose, in the letters to his friends he contrived to have published in his lifetime, in surreptitiously edited form, supposedly without his knowledge or consent.

The verse epistle, based on imitation of Horace's *Satires* and *Epistles,* furnished Pope with a conveniently ready-made stance as a satirical poet. Its style was characterized by a blend of informality and civility, what Pope would call a "graceful negligence"; its subject commonly concerned a celebration of pastoral retreat, of the pleasures and virtues of friendship, of the importance of self-knowledge and integrity.

In the four *Moral Essays,* comprising the *Epistle to Burlington* (1731), the *Epistle to Bathurst* (1733), the *Epistle to Cobham* (1734), and the *Epistle to a Lady* (1735), Pope attacked, by means of symbolic portraiture and ironical antithesis, such targets as bad taste, pride, egocentricity, and greed, which he associated with the burgeoning capitalism of the age.

Pope carefully selected the recipients of his verse epistles as a means of defining the context of the targets he satirized. The *Epistle to Dr. Arbuthnot* (1735), for example, derives much of its didactic impact through being addressed to an individual famed for his kindliness and probity; as **John Arbuthnot**'s friend, the "I" of the poem, Pope gains in moral stature over the enemies he attacks within it.

In Pope's purportedly genuine personal letters to his friends (published in 1735, 1737, and 1741), he returned to the theme of the good man and the good poet in a celebration of virtue and friendship. In preparing his letters for publication, he modeled them on Seneca's moral essays cast into epistolary form which, with the letters of Cicero and Pliny, were immensely popular throughout the 18th century as exercises in Latin grammar, composition, and translation. Pope's own letters enjoyed great popularity throughout the 18th century, promoting the idea of the personal letter as literature, although of a type only admissible when composed without apparent intention of publication.

With its potential as the most flexible, versatile, and amorphous of literary forms, the epistle naturally adapted itself to a wide range of purposes; it was not only used to teach Latin. More significantly, philosophical and theological arguments, political propaganda, and **travel** accounts (real or imaginary) often were cast into the congenial letter form. Three of Pope's closest friends furnish examples: **Jonathan Swift** preached a powerful political polemic in the *Drapier's Letters* (1724); **Lord Bolingbroke** analyzed the paucity of good English historical literature in *Letters on the Study and Use of History* (1752); and **Lady Mary Wortley Montagu** cast a sociological travelogue into epistolary form in her "Turkish Embassy Letters" (1763).

Other important examples of the essay cast into the epistolary form include Courtney Melmoth's (S.J. Pratt, 1749–1814) *Letters of Sir Thomas Fitzosborne on Several Subjects* (1742–1749), Bolingbroke's *Letters on the Spirit of Patriotism* (1749), **Richard Hurd**'s *Letters on Chivalry and Romance* (1762), Richard Watson's (1737–1816) *An Apology for Christianity, in a Series of Letters, Addressed to Edward Gibbon, Esq.* (1776), and **Edmund Burke**'s *Letter to the Sheriffs of Bristol on the Affairs of America* (1777).

The prose epistle as a literary form was instrumental in the development of the **periodical** journals of the 18th century, with the *Tatler* and *Spectator* combined, including more than 800 imaginary letters to the editor. Social and epistolary decorum were taught together in homely utilitarian formularies such as **Samuel Richardson**'s *Familiar Letters on Important Occasions* (1741), from which *Pamela* (1740–1742) evolved, thus serving an important function as the forerunner of the **novel**.

Richardson cast subsequent novels—*Clarissa* (1747–1748) and *Sir Charles Grandison* (1753–1754)—in the epistolary form. It was a literary convention that followed naturally from his initial approach to the novel as a writer of model letters, and it was one that inspired a new direction for the novel, profoundly influenced by Richardson's delicate exploration of the subjective consciousness under the pretense of realism. The epistolary mode also served the purposes of **Tobias Smollett** in *Humphry Clinker* (1771), **Fanny Burney** in *Evelina* (1778) and, in an early version, **Jane Austen** in *Sense and Sensibility* (1811).

The epistle as a literary genre imparted a sense of immediacy, intimacy, and authenticity, whether in poetry or in prose. With its flexible diversity of usage, the epistle was one of the most widely employed literary forms of the Hanoverian period, although its popularity was on the wane by the early 19th century.

Wendy Jones Nakanishi

Bibliography

Brower, Reuben. *Pope: The Poetry of Allusion.* 1959.

Butt, John. *English Literature in the Mid-Eighteenth Century.* Edited and completed by Geoffrey Carnall. 1979.

Jones, Wendy L. *Talking on Paper: Alexander Pope's Letters.* 1990.
Probyn, Clive T. *English Fiction of the Eighteenth Century, 1700–1789.* 1987.
Winn, James. *A Window in the Bosom: The Letters of Alexander Pope.* 1977.

See also Letters

Erskine (of Restormel), Baron (Thomas Erskine) (1750–1823)

Erskine was a jurist best remembered for his skill as a trial lawyer defending the political **radicals** of the 1790s and the principles of free speech and freedom of the press.

The son of a Scottish earl, he served as a midshipman in the **West Indies** and as an **army** officer in Minorca before being admitted to the bar (1778). Establishing a reputation for fearlessness and eloquence, he successfully defended the strongly whiggish Admiral Augustus Keppel (1725–1786) at his politically colored court martial for indecisive naval action off Ushant (1779), then Lord George Gordon (1781), the man charged with inciting the **Gordon Riots**.

An intimate friend of prominent **Whigs** such as **Sheridan** and **Fox** (whose 1783 India Bill he unwisely supported as an M.P. from Portsmouth), Erskine continued in the 1790s to defend radicals who, like the Manchester **cotton merchant** and agitator Thomas Walker (1749–1817), and **United Irishman** Arthur O'Connor (1763–1852), were being prosecuted by the government for seditious libel. In a series of famous treason trials in 1794 he secured the acquittal of **Thomas Hardy**, founder of the **London Corresponding Society**; Hardy's associate in the society, **John Thelwall**; and **Horne Tooke** of the **Society for Constitutional Information**.

Thomas Erskine

His best-known client was **Thomas Paine**, whom he defended unsuccessfully in 1792 against a charge of seditious libel for publication of his *Rights of Man.* Equally famous and unsuccessful was his defense of Dr. W.D. Shipley, the Dean of St. Asaph, on a charge of criminal libel in 1784. Erskine's argument, though rejected by the court, was that it was for the jury, not the judge, to determine if a publication was libelous; but this view became law in Fox's Libel Act of 1792. Erskine's last notable case was his successful defense of **Queen Caroline**, the estranged wife of **King George IV**, who was being tried for adultery before the **House of Lords** (1820).

Erskine served in Parliament from 1783 to 1784 and from 1790 to 1806, when he was elevated to the peerage and became Lord Chancellor in the **Ministry of all the Talents**. He also made major contributions to English commercial law. His personal vanity was notorious, but his legal work made him an important figure in the development of civil liberties.

Frank M. Baglione

Bibliography

Goodwin, Albert. *The Friends of Liberty: The English Democratic Movement in the Age of the French Revolution.* 1979.
Stryker, L.P. *For the Defense, Thomas Erskine.* 1947.

See also Censorship; Legal Profession

Essay

Samuel Johnson's *Dictionary* (1755) defined *essay* as "a loose sally of the mind; an irregular indigested piece; not a regular and orderly composition." The characteristics of the Hanoverian "informal essay" are indeed ease, digression, topicality, and reflection. Such essays may appear casual, conversational, and experiential, yet they also lent themselves to didacticism, irony, **satire**, and reflections on morality and aesthetics. The essay form looks back to Montaigne, but its development in 18th-century Britain was intimately connected with profound changes in the production and consumption of writing.

Many interrelated phenomena shaped this development: for example, the increase in printing presses and an upswing in literacy, particularly in the urban **middle class** and among women; a gradual shift from a system of **patronage** to a literary market economy controlled by **publishers and booksellers** served by hired writers; and the emergence of a periodical press, which was beginning to organize an audience increasingly enlarged by readers from the middle and lower classes. The essay was closely associated with periodical publication, and assumed one of two principal forms: the single-essay periodical, usually consisting of one page containing a single (albeit often loosely structured) essay; and the serial essay, a continuing feature contained within a larger context, usually a magazine. After their initial appearance, periodical essays were typically collected and published in bound volumes.

The 18th-century model was established by the *Tatler* (1709–1711) and *Spectator* (1711–1713), single-essay periodicals written by **Richard Steele** and **Joseph Addison**. Published in a period of great political turmoil, these shunned overt engagement with politics, declaring themselves "censors" of "**manners and morals**"; their personae, "Isaac Bickerstaff" and "Mr. Spectator," offered corrective commentary on the **London** scene. Their style was generally relaxed, informal, humorous, and mildly **satirical**; they incorporated fiction and **letters** ostensibly from readers. *The Spectator,* in particular, became the model of correct essayistic style for subsequent generations.

Periodicals, many imitating this, proliferated during the Hanoverian era, with titles such as the *Free-Thinker* (1718–1719), *Plain Dealer* (1724–1725), *World* (1753–1756), and *Mirror* (1779–1780). **Henry Fielding, Charlotte Lennox, Henry Mackenzie, James Boswell,** and **Oliver Goldsmith** all at some point in their careers wrote periodical essays. **Samuel Johnson** brought gravity and stylistic elegance to the genre. His influential essay periodical the *Rambler* (1750–1752) was less informal and topical than most; its dominant mode was meditative, moral, and literary, though it did employ fictional narrative letters and the character of the observer.

Many male essay writers sought to expand their audience by addressing "the fair sex," treating "women's topics" such as love and marriage, and prescribing ideals of domestic femininity. But this also opened the door for women writers. **Eliza Haywood**'s *Female Spectator* (1744–1745) and **Frances Brooke**'s *Old Maid* (1755–1756) were early examples of women-authored essay periodicals directed toward predominantly female audiences.

By 1800 the single-essay periodical had virtually disappeared, replaced by the serial essay published in **magazines** and journals. Yet in many respects the work of the early-19th-century "familiar essayists" reinvigorated the Addisonian essay tradition, though emphasizing eclecticism, flexibility, and experientiality. **Charles Lamb**, in his serial *Essays of Elia* (published in the *London Magazine* during the 1820s), intensified the self-expressiveness of the experiential essayistic voice. **Thomas De Quincey**'s periodical essays blended **autobiography** and literary criticism, and **William Hazlitt** sought in his periodical essays to combine "the literary and the conversational."

As the periodical essay developed over time, one factor remained constant: the appearance of direct engagement with a reading public, which itself was expanding to include new social groups. Women, the lower levels of the middle class, and later the working class, began to participate in print culture first as consumers, then producers, of writing; the essay either specialized or expanded its general appeal in relation to these demographic changes. Its informality and versatility, its emphasis on experience, and its construction of a rhetorical identification with its readers made the essay a genre highly adaptive to changes in the social practices of reading and writing.

Kathryn Shevelow

Bibliography

Bond, Richmond P. *The Tatler: The Making of a Literary Journal.* 1971.

Kernin, Alvin. *Samuel Johnson and the Impact of Print.* 1987.

Klancher, Jon P. *The Making of English Reading Audiences, 1790–1832.* 1987.

Randel, Fred V. *The World of Elia.* 1975.

Shevelow, Kathryn. *Women and Print Culture: The Construction of Femininity in the Early Periodical.* 1989.

See also Literary Criticism; Periodicals

Evangelicalism

Evangelicalism, as an historical term, has two related but distinct meanings. It refers to a general school of Protestant belief, emphasizing God's free offer of salvation through faith in the atoning death and resurrection of Christ, rather than by the efficacy of good works or sacraments; and also to a particular historical group of so-called Low Church Anglicans subscribing to Evangelical beliefs and promoting religious and social renewal from within the **Church of England** roughly during the period 1770–1850. A similar group rose in the **Church of Scotland** at about the same time, in the early 19th century.

Evangelicalism in its general sense stresses the authority and inspiration of the Bible, the depravity of fallen human nature, the necessity of personal conversion and moral earnestness, and a piety recognizing the centrality of the affections and the legitimacy of personal religious experience. Closely associated in British history with the rise of the **Methodists** and the preaching of **John Wesley** and **George Whitefield**, this Evangelicalism was arguably the single most important religious development in Hanoverian Britain. Although it began as a movement within the Established Church, it quickly gained remarkable popularity among the nonconformist churches, infusing them with a new vitality and religious rigor. Evangelical worship emphasized public proclamation of the Word and the importance of preaching by both ordained ministers and the laity.

Wesley did not envision a separatist church, but rather sought to reinvigorate Anglicanism. Nevertheless, the great success of **religious revivalism** among many **dissenting** churches sometimes obscures the fact that many Anglican clergymen became strong advocates of Evangelicalism while remaining lay members of the Church of England. Most conspicuous among these "Evangelicals" in the narrow but more specific sense was **John Newton**, pastor at Olney in Buckinghamshire and subsequently in Lombard Street, **London**, where he led many in the established church to embrace Evangelical ideas. While at Olney, Newton converted Thomas Scott (1747–1821), an Anglican divine whose highly popular *The Force of Truth* (1779) sought to prove that Evangelical **theology** and piety were linked with the most legitimate interpretations of the gospel. Newton also profoundly influenced **William Cowper**, one of the greatest writers of the century, whose **poetry** and hymns were among the age's most eloquent expressions of Evangelical ideas.

Another famous Anglican Evangelical was **William Wilberforce**, who for some 40 years used his considerable political and social influence to promote Evangelical programs in education and social welfare. His most outstanding contribution was successfully leading the opposition to the **slave trade**. He was a member of the **Clapham Sect**, a wealthy and influential group that worked for abolition of the slave trade, promotion of **Sunday schools**, the extension of **missionary societies**, **humanitarian** relief of the poor, and the reform of morality. National reaction during the period 1790–1810 against the **French Revolution**, with all its supposed atheism and lasciviousness, helped tremendously to put wind into the Evangelicals' sails.

Although the Claphamites included such well-known figures as **Zachary Macaulay**, **Granville Sharp**, **Henry Thornton**, Lord Teignmouth (1751–1834), and **Henry Venn**, the most famous of these activists was the celebrated **Bluestocking** and author **Hannah More**. Closely associated with Newton and Wilberforce, she established schools for the poor, and philanthropic societies for the relief and education of adults. Because many wealthy Evangelicals sought the extinction of vice and the establishment of a new respectability—an improved system of **manners and morals**—they were (and are) sometimes accused of an elitist neo-Puritanism; though the value of many Evangelical programs seemed beyond dispute. The Evangelicals' participation in the **Society for the Suppression of Vice** exposed them to hostility and ridicule from whiggish and **radical** spokesmen after 1804.

Other important Anglican Evangelical efforts included founding (in cooperation with **dissenters**) the Religious **Tract** Society (1799) and then the British and Foreign Bible Society (1804) for dissemination of Scripture at home and abroad, and also founding the Society for the Missions in Africa and the East (later called the Church Missionary Society) in 1799, which helped to launch the church on overseas missionary activity. **Charles Simeon**, Anglican clergyman at **Cambridge** and a compelling Evangelical leader, took an especially active role in these foundations.

Evangelicalism never did gain broad acceptance within the Established Church. Many Anglicans were suspicious of Evangelical **enthusiasm** (or emotional excess), could not endorse its Low Church theological tenets, and saw the neglect of ritual as contrary to the dominant Anglican tradition of worship. Much the same was true within the Church of Scotland, where bitter disputes between the Evangelical party, led by **Thomas Chalmers**, and the established Kirk led to the Disruption of 1843. Although disruptive wherever it took root, Evangelicalism indisputably made highly significant contributions to Hanoverian social and religious life.

Michael F. Suarez, S.J.

Bibliography

Balleine, George R. *A History of the Evangelical Party in the Church of England.* New ed., 1951.

Brown, Ford K. *The Fathers of the Victorians: The Age of Wilberforce.* 1961.

Hilton, Boyd. *The Age of Atonement: The Influence of Evangelicalism on Social and Economic Thought, 1785–1865.* 1988.

Hylson-Smith, Kenneth. *Evangelicals in the Church of England, 1734–1984.* 1989.

Kiernan, V. "Evangelicalism and the French Revolution." *Past and Present.* Vol. 1, pp. 44–56.

Noll, Mark A., David W. Bebbington, and George A. Rawlyk, eds. *Evangelicalism: Comparative Studies of Popular Protestantism in North America, the British Isles, and Beyond, 1700–1990.* 1994.

Thompson, David Michael. *Denominationalism and Dissent, 1795–1835: A Question of Identity.* 1985.

Excise Crisis (1733)

An excise bill proposed in 1733 by **Sir Robert Walpole** was designed to reform the assessment and collection of **taxes** on wine and **tobacco**, with an eye to curbing **smuggling**. The **opposition** seized on the issue as a means of attacking him, and the resulting furor, in which the whole country rang with the cries of "No slavery, no excise, no wooden shoes," forced Walpole to withdraw the measure.

In retrospect, the crisis seems to harbinger Walpole's fall (1742). In pamphlets and **newspapers**, particularly the ***Craftsman***, the opposition hammered at three points, all untrue. They claimed that Walpole actually planned to introduce a general excise; that, to collect this, he planned to appoint many new excise officers, giving him more scope for **patronage** and political corruption; and that these officers would be given extensive powers to search for contraband, even in private homes. Great country-wide public agitation resulted. Many voters, convinced that their liberties were threatened, instructed their M.P.s to oppose the excise bill, with the result that Walpole was eventually forced to drop it.

P.J. Kulisheck

Bibliography

Langford, Paul. *The Excise Crisis: Society and Politics in the Age of Walpole.* 1975.

Plumb, J.H. *Sir Robert Walpole: The King's Minister.* 1960.

Vaucher, Paul. *La Crise du Ministère Walpole en 1733–1734.* 1924.

Exoticism

Hanoverian England defined itself largely in relation to the non-English world it came to know through imported goods, people, and information. The details included in **travel books** and in theological, scientific, and literary works, as well as in **periodicals** and the growing number of **reference works**, helped create a sense of difference between what was English and what was not; what was familiar and what was essentially foreign and culturally, racially, or sexually strange. It made little difference if seemingly factual writings were actually fictional. George Psalmanazor's (*c.* 1679–1763) *Description of Formosa* (1704) and Robert Paltock's (1697–1767) *The Life and Adventures of Peter Wilkins, a Cornish Man* (1751), with its flying women and men, were, respectively, fraudulent and fantastic; **Daniel Defoe**'s *Robinson Crusoe* (1721) and **Jona-**

than Swift's *Gulliver's Travels* (1726) were edifying and **satirical**. But the notions of difference through which the English came to understand the world and themselves were by no means unitary or homogeneous.

Interest in the exotic was shaped in part by contemporary **exploration**; contacts with China; encounters with Africa and the Americas; experience with different religions, drugs, and insanity; antique revivals; and a growing fascination with **Gothic** art. Sometimes the interest was deeply appreciative, as in **Sir William Jones**'s study of Indian literature and **Sir William Chambers**'s borrowings from Chinese architecture and decoration, but often it was translated into political convenience. For example, the English presence in **India** promoted study of Indian history and culture, yet the knowledge gained by this was often simply assimilated unthinkingly to preexisting views of English superiority. British colonists found Native Americans exotic in their apparently unconstrained daily activity and social organization, yet their lack of recognizable "culture" justified the conquest of the Americas. Stories of Turkish harems fulfilled English desire for transgressive eroticism while fueling condemnation of the Turks' treatment of women. A similar complex of desire and denial operated on narratives from the South Pacific: accounts of native sexuality aroused some English writers and readers, whereas others merely incorporated them into a more general view of human corruption.

More than anything else, English literature brought together the many strands of exoticism, its interests and aversions, fascinations, justifications, and compulsions, into a single continuous medium of entertainment and instruction for contemporaries. The *Arabian Nights' Entertainment: Consisting of One Thousand and One Stories*, translated into French by Antoine Galland (1646–1715) in 1704 and immediately thereafter into English, followed by *Persian and Turkish Tales* (translated by 1714), began the thirst for "eastern" or "oriental" stories still unslaked in the 19th century. Works as widely varied as **Samuel Johnson**'s *Rasselas* (1759), **William Beckford**'s *Vathek* (1786), **Thomas Moore**'s narrative poem *Lallah Rookh* (1817) and James J. Morier's (1780?–1849) *The Adventures of Hajji Baba of Ispahan* (1824) owe their origin to the continuing enthusiasm for Arabian tales. **Lord Byron** capitalized on the allure of alien locales for his verse Turkish narratives, *The Giaour* and *The Bride of Abydos* (both 1813).

Although the exotic was usually defined as *foreign*—from a distant land—it also could arrive from a distant time. For instance, **James Macpherson** claimed to be translating the Gaelic poems of the 3rd century warrior–bard Ossian (1763). **Thomas Chatterton** created the medieval poems of Thomas Rowley (1778). And in addition to *Reliques of Ancient English Poetry* (1765), **Thomas Percy** published "Five Pieces of Runic Poetry" from the Icelandic. Percy's efforts were based on genuine "Reliques," but all three poets were contributors to the exotic movement called the Gothic, as were **Samuel Taylor Coleridge** (*Christabel*, 1816) and **John Keats** (*The Eve of Saint Agnes*, 1820). While the Gothic withstood naturalization by **Clara Reeve** and **Ann Radcliffe**, another form of exotic fiction did not. **Sir Walter Scott** domesticated the exotic by sentimentalizing it into the historical **novel** (*Ivanhoe* [1820], for instance), transforming the alien past into a near neighbor of the present. Romantics such as Coleridge (*Kubla Khan*, 1816), **Thomas De Quincey** (*Confessions of an English Opium-Eater*, 1821), and **James Hogg** (*The Private Memoirs and Confessions of a Justified Sinner*, 1824) explored the most exotic of lands, the human mind.

Exoticism was not limited to literature; it also shaped Hanoverian colonial policy, helped direct the **Society for Promoting Christian Knowledge** (SPCK), and framed the emerging fields of anthropology and linguistics.

Joel Reed

Bibliography

Barrell, John. *Painting and the Politics of Culture: New Essays on British Art, 1700–1850.* 1992.

Dabydeen, David. *Hogarth's Blacks: Images of Blacks in Eighteenth Century English Art.* 1987.

Marshall, P.J., and Glyndwr Williams. *The Great Map of Mankind: Perceptions of New Worlds in the Age of Enlightenment.* 1982.

Pailin, David A. *Attitudes to Other Religions: Comparative Religion in Seventeenth- and Eighteenth-Century Britain.* 1984.

Rousseau, G.S., and Roy Porter, eds. *Exoticism in the Enlightenment.* 1990.

See also Orientalism; Romanticism and Romantic Style

Experimental Lectures

The practice of providing public lectures on **science** was an outgrowth of mathematical lectures given in **London** in the late 17th century. Initially given gratis by the Newtonian John Harris (1666–1719) "for the public good," pressure from other scientists led to the rapid expansion of public lectures on natural philosophy during the reign of **Queen Anne**. At the succession of **George I** there were numerous Newtonians lecturing on experimental science in London, including William Whiston (1667–1752), Humphrey Ditton (1675–1715), and the prolific **John Theophilius Desaguliers**. These men increasingly relied on a vast array of apparatus by which mechanical principles and the experimental method could be demonstrated to a public willing to spend the considerable sums of two or three guineas to attend a course. It was not long before Newton's first generation of disciples was being challenged for the field by younger lecturers, such as the mathematician James Stirling (1692–1770).

The experimental lecturers increasingly sold their expertise as essential to the success of the mechanical ventures with which Britain was then inundated. This was the theme advanced by Desaguliers in his lecture courses, but, soon taken up by promoters such as the financier Thomas Watts, whose academy in London promoted natural and experimental philosophy for commercial purposes, its acceptance led to the widespread expansion of lecturers into the countryside and into **Scotland**. Desaguliers went as far afield as Holland, but more common were lecturers like Benjamin Martin (1705–

1782) who, keeping a boarding school at Chichester in the 1730s, then combined publishing works on mathematics and natural philosophy with itinerant lecturing until he retired to London in the 1750s.

By the middle of the 18th century the craze of experimental lecturing had apparently declined somewhat, challenged by new interest in practical medical lectures, and inhibited by the growing expense of developing and maintaining apparatus that had to be carted from town to town. Even in London, such popular lecturers as the astronomer and mechanician James Ferguson (1710–1776), and Desagulier's pupil, Stephen Demainbray (1710–1782), found that the audience was not as easily enticed as had once been the case. Lecturers soon learned that the establishment of more formal settings, such as those provided by the formation of the Royal Society for the Encouragement of Arts, Manufactures, and Commerce (1754), meant that audiences might no longer require private **entrepreneurs**. The rage for public lecturing was not revived until it was promoted by the **middle class**, and artisan, scientific societies of the 1790s.

Larry Stewart

Bibliography

Stewart, Larry. *The Rise of Public Science: Rhetoric, Technology and Natural Philosophy in Newtonian Britain, 1660–1750.* 1992.

See also Mechanics' Institutes; Royal Institution

Exploration

The Hanoverian era, coming after the Renaissance Age of Discovery, brought a second great wave of geographical **exploration** after which few regions remained uncharted. A new impetus from **science** combined with older national rivalries of **commerce** and colonization; the **Royal Society** joined with **chartered trading companies** to press for government-subsidized expeditions in search of scientific knowledge, as well as new sources of raw material and markets. Religious **missionary societies** proliferated, intensifying the competition for empire with foreign rivals, particularly the French and Dutch. Moreover, England had the advantages of much experience in **navigation**, a vast **navy** unemployed between **wars**, and large reserves of skilled **seamen** willing to undertake risks in pursuit of fortune and adventure.

While much motivation for exploration was commercial and strategic, science was served too by the gathering of geographic and hydrographic data and by the work of naturalists who recorded the flora and fauna they encountered. The most fateful expedition of the era was Robert Fitzroy's second hydrographic voyage, in command of H.M.S. *Beagle* (1831–1836), on which Charles Darwin served as naturalist, gathering materials that would lead to his theory of evolution.

At the beginning of the 18th century the Pacific basin was imperfectly known from the exploits of Portuguese, Spanish, and Dutch mariners. The early voyages by English circumnavigators—Sir Francis Drake (1577–1580), William Dampier (1679–1691), Woodes Rogers (1708–1711), and **George Anson**—were for plunder rather than for exploration. However, the voyages of **Captain Cook** (1768–1771, 1772–1775, and 1776–1779) and Louis-Antoine de Bougainville (1766–1769) inaugurated an era of truly scientific exploration. Cook's skill as a navigator and surveyor produced charts of exceptional accuracy for much of the Pacific, from the Arctic to the **Antarctic**.

Cook's search on his third voyage for the western end of the Northwest Passage through the **North American** continent had suggested that ice rendered the route of little practical value. Nonetheless, a Grail-like quest for the Northwest Passage continued, luring Christopher Middleton (1741–1742), William Moor (1746–1747), and William Coats (1749) into the recesses of Hudson's Bay. In the latter Hanoverian era they were followed by **John Ross** (1818, 1829–1833), **William Edward Parry** (1819–1820, 1821–1823, 1824–1825), and **John Franklin**, whose searches, by land (1819–1822, 1825–1827) and by sea (1845–1848), eventually proved tragically fatal. Meanwhile, **George Vancouver** carried on where Cook left off on the Pacific coast (1792–1794); and the interior of British North America was further revealed by the overland explorations of Jonathan Carver on the upper Mississippi (1766–1778); Samuel Hearne to the Arctic Ocean (1771–1772); and Alexander Mackenzie (1793), Simon Fraser (1805–1808), and David Thompson (1807–1811) to the Pacific.

Meanwhile in **Africa** James Bruce searched for the source of the Nile (1769–1772) and another Scot, Mungo Park, died leading his second expedition on the River Niger (1805); the brothers Richard and John Lander finally resolved the riddle of the Niger's course and outlet (1830–1832). Hugh Clapperton and Dixon Denham crossed the Sahara and explored much of the territory between Timbuktu and Lake Chad (1822–1825); Alexander Laing crossed the Sahara and also reached Timbuktu (1825–1826), where he died.

Cook had circumnavigated **New Zealand** and charted the east coast of **Australia**, where British settlement began at the end of the 18th century, but the bulk of the new continent and its coasts invited further exploration. Matthew Flinders's (1774–1814) circumnavigation (1802–1803) proved Australia was a continent, bereft of any straits or other navigable passages. The further surveys of Philip King (1817–1822), and the Frenchmen Nicolas Baudin and Louis-Claude de Freycinet (1801–1803), all but completed the mapping of the coasts. Between 1813 and 1847 Gregory Blaxland, George Evans, John Oxley, Allan Cunningham, Charles Sturt, and Thomas Mitchell led more than a score of separate expeditions to explore Australia's interior, a process that continued into the Victorian era.

In Central Asia, Russian and British imperial interests converged. The British feared that Russian annexations would ultimately pose a threat to **India**, which prompted a series of travelers—some with official sanction of the **East India Company**—to venture north and west as secret agents, usually disguised as Muslims. Charles Christie and Henry Pottinger visited Herat in western Afghanistan (1809–1811); Thomas Manning became the first Englishman to reach Lhasa (1811–

1812); William Moorcroft reached Lake Manasarowar in western Tibet (1812), explored Kashmir and the Punjab (1822–1823), and visited Bokhara in Turkestan (1825); Alexander Burnes visited Kabul and Bokhara (1832).

Collectively, these efforts by Britain's explorers extended the boundaries of **science**, colonization, and commerce, and established the basis of a second—and much vaster—British **Empire**.

N. Merrill Distad

Bibliography

Baker, John N.L. *A History of Geographical Discovery and Exploration.* 1931; 2nd ed., 1937; rpt. 1967.

Brose, Jacques. *Great Voyages of Discovery: Circumnavigators and Scientists, 1764–1843.* 1985.

Day, Vice-Admiral Sir Archibald. *The Admiralty Hydrographic Service, 1795–1919.* 1967.

Friendly, Alfred. *Beaufort of the Admiralty: The Life of Sir Francis Beaufort, 1774–1857.* 1977.

Hopkirk, Peter. *The Great Game: The Struggle for Empire in Central Asia.* 1992.

Newby, Eric. *Mitchell Beazley World Atlas of Exploration.* 1975.

Ritchie, Rear-Admiral George Stephen. *The Admiralty Chart: British Naval Hydrography in the Nineteenth Century.* 1967.

Stafford, Barbara. *Voyage into Substance: Art, Science, Nature, and the Illustrated Travel Account, 1760–1840.* 1984.

Sykes, Percy. *A History of Exploration from the Earliest Times to the Present Day.* 1934 and later eds.; reissued 1961.

Eyles, Sir John (1683–1745)

A **London** businessman and son of a former governor of the **Bank of England**, Eyles became sub-governor of the **South Sea Company** in 1721 to try to rescue it from its difficulties following the **South Sea Bubble**. He seemed right for the job, having been a director of the Bank of England and of the **East India Company**. By 1729 Eyles had helped convert the company from a trading to a financial concern. As M.P. and Alderman he was also **Sir Robert Walpole**'s political manager in the City of London. However, he was involved in some of the more dubious concerns of the time, such as the fraudulent Harburgh Lottery of 1723, quashed by Parliament. In the Derwentwater scandal he profited from the fraudulent sale of the estate of a forfeited **Jacobite**, despite being a member of the commission set up to sell it for the public benefit; but Eyles was saved by Walpole's intervention. In 1732 he was accused, with others, of private deals within the South Sea Company, and resigned in 1733. He typified the corruption for which Walpole's administration was criticized.

A.J.G. Cummings

Bibliography

Black, Jeremy, ed. *Britain in the Age of Walpole.* 1984.

Dickson, P.G.M. *The Financial Revolution in England: A Study in the Development of Public Credit, 1688–1736.* 1967.

Sedgewick, Romney. *History of Parliament: The House of Commons, 1715–1774.* 2 vols. 1970.

Fable

The 18th century was probably the only time in English literary history when the fable was considered a legitimate literary genre. Contemporary interest embraced not only the standard Aesopian and classical collections but original fables by contemporary writers, and allegorical works of didactic and moralistic intent.

The single most important work in establishing the fable's popularity was the Frenchman Jean de La Fontaine's (1621–1695) *Fables* (1668), which reworked and embellished the Aesopian collection with wit and humor, using its seemingly innocuous form for social commentary. La Fontaine's English popularity was attested to by **Joseph Addison**, who referred in *The Spectator* No. 183 (1711) to "*La Fontaine,* who by this way of Writing is come more into vogue than any other Author of our times." Addison himself published his own collection of Aesop's fables.

The fable's 18th-century acceptance was also a carry-over from the Stuart era, when fabulists had been impelled by sometimes hidden philosophical, political, and social concerns. Late-17th-century fables often reflected the political turbulence of that era and served to disguise political opinions through the genre's shielding capacities. Roger L'Estrange's (1616–1704) *Fables of Aesop and Other Eminent Mythologists* (first published in 1692) was nominally aimed at children but resonated with **Tory** political suggestions.

George I's succession (1714) marked a change. The fables of his reign reflect relative political calm. Fables supporting the status quo abounded, such as Samuel Croxall's *Fables of Aesop* (1722), the **Whig** answer to L'Estrange's collection; but contemporary practice was also very greatly influenced by **John Gay**, whose *Fables* (1727) became what is now probably the best-known collection in English literature, laden with satiric commentary on social vices and incorporating human characters.

However, at some point during the age of **George II** (1727–1760) the fable began a long decline. Possibly this might have been predicted from the angry reaction to **Bernard de Mandeville**'s satiric *Fable of the Bees* (1714), attacked by moralists as revolting to religion and fellow-feeling. As the 18th century passed, fables, **satire**, and **wit and ridicule** all seemed increasingly offensive, contrary to the optimistic and sentimental spirit of the age of **George III** (1760–1820). The altered and usually happy endings of **William Godwin**'s *Fables Ancient and Modern* (1805) reflect this. Changes in literary fashion played a part also, working against imitation of the classics and of the artificial **pastoral** forms associated with them, and also in favor of realism—as symbolized, for example, in the flourishing of Hanoverian **biography**. Gradually, fables either merged into folklore or received a new lease on life in the form of **children's literature**.

Mahasveta Barua

Bibliography

Blackham, H.J. *The Fable as Literature.* 1985.

Noel, Thomas. *Theories of the Fable in the Eighteenth Century.* 1975.

Patterson, Annabel. *Fables of Power: Aesopian Writing and Political History.* 1991.

Factories and the Factory System

The emergence of the factory, where production in the **textile industries** moved from small domestic workshops to large single units with centralized power sources, has long been considered one of the most important characteristics of the **Industrial Revolution** centered in the Hanoverian period. In the 19th and early 20th centuries, historians placed much emphasis on the apparent suddenness of change; but in recent years a more gradualist view of the transition to factory production has emerged.

Even in the 18th century, the idea of concentrating scattered production under a single roof was not new. The gathering together of 200 looms in a single shed in the early 16th century by legendary "Jack of Newbury" may not have existed outside the imagination of the Elizabethan writer Thomas Edlin, who described it, but the idea must have come from

Spinning in the 19th-century factory

somewhere. However, the age of the modern factory can be said to have definitively begun with the development in the early 18th century of silk mills in Derbyshire, where concentrated groups of workers operated machinery powered by flowing water.

The most significant developments in the evolution of the factory, however, came in the **cotton industry**, initially in the **spinning** sector. Gradually, **merchant**-manufacturers in **domestic production** began to gather groups of operatives together under a single roof. Several reasons have been advanced for this, including attempts to control labor (which, in the domestic system, was sometimes unreliable), a desire to save on **transport** costs and losses from embezzlement that came with a scattered labor force, and the possibility of greater quality control that came from increased concentration. Initially, hand-operated machinery was employed, often in converted premises. However, with the technical developments pioneered by innovators such as **James Hargreaves**, **Samuel Crompton**, and **Sir Richard Arkwright** from the 1760s, the use of water power became widespread by the latter years of the 18th century.

The new spinning mills required good sources of fast-flowing water, and thus considerable development took place in the hilly Peak District bordering on the East Midlands, the Pennines of Lancashire, and in West and Central **Scotland**. As some of the sites selected were in relatively remote areas, factoryowners such as Arkwright and **David Dale** were often obliged to build whole communities in order to attract a labor force. But as weaving initially remained in the domestic sector, proximity to a pool of suitably skilled labor in that and in the cloth finishing trades was also a determinant in factory location. These factors, together with the growing application of power from newly developing **steam engines** (which allowed production to be moved away from swift streams), allowed more widespread location, and by favoring Lancashire, with a considerable pool of labor in the weaving and finishing trades and an adequate supply of coal and other raw material, assisted that county to dominate the cotton industry.

Although **Edmund Cartwright** had developed a power loom as early as 1785, large-scale factory weaving was not widespread until after 1830, partly because machines were not yet capable of producing finer cloths, and partly because many weavers were willing to work for lower returns in order to maintain their independence. The **woolen and worsted** industries concentrated in Yorkshire developed at a similar pace for comparable reasons, though factories in these branches of textiles were less numerous than in cotton production.

In the main, early factoryowners were drawn from the **middle classes**. Many were merchants and traders, already involved in domestic industry; others came from the ranks of yeoman **farmers**. Only rarely were they drawn from the working classes. All this resulted from the fact that in the early stages, the need of most firms was access to funds for working capital; and to obtain this, a local reputation and known credit-worthiness were essential. Thus those with technical skills but no access to the necessary funds might seek partners with capital to establish a factory. As mill size and fixed capital requirements grew from the latter 18th century, factoryowners were more likely to come from an industrial background. The history of the cotton-spinning firm of McConnell and Kennedy, where the two technically trained men first of all combined with sleeping financial partners, then later established a larger operation on their own out of their accumulated profits, illustrates this type of progression.

New patterns of work evolved for **factory workers**. Instead of the freedom to work at their own pace as in the domestic system, workers were forced to adapt to the pace of the machinery and attend the factory during the hours specified by the factoryowners. Discipline, including strict time-keeping, was rigidly enforced, and systems of fines were established for breaches of regulations. Because of the nature of the work, there were often more jobs for women and children than for adult males. The latter, if unable to find factory work, often sought employment in allied or other trades in the region. Another source of recruitment for young factory employees was the pauper orphan, provided by the workhouse. Gradually, society began looking into the growing abuse of **child labor**.

The use of a single power source meant that all machines were connected to it by means of a system of gears, belts, and pulleys. Switching off one machine meant closing down the entire factory and losing production. Reluctance to do so, and the fact that machines were unguarded, meant that accidents were common. In the early years of the 19th century this, together with the effects of long hours—especially on children—gave social commentators increasing cause for concern. Traditionally, the policy of government had been one of nonintervention; but with the growth of the **factory movement** and passage of the Factory Act of 1833, which also created an inspectorate to enforce itself, the role of the government as a regulatory body was clearly established.

Although large-scale, capital-intensive works existed in other industries such as **iron** and **brewing**, it was really only in textiles that factory production emerged during the Hanoverian era. Even by the end of the period, much of the industrial output of Britain was still coming from small workshops such as those in the **metalworking** trades of the West Midlands and the cutlery trades in Sheffield, though such trades did contain numerous large operators. It was only during the Victorian era that many other trades adopted factory production.

A.J.G. Cummings

Bibliography

Berg, M. *The Age of Manufactures, 1700–1820: Industry, Innovation and Work in Britain.* 2nd ed., 1994.

Chapman, S.D. *The Early Factory Masters: The Transition to the Factory System in the Midlands Textile Industry.* 1967.

Crouzet, F. *The First Industrialists: The Problem of Origins.* 1983.

Daunton, M.J. *Progress and Poverty: An Economic and Social History of Britain, 1700–1850.* 1995.

Lee, C.H. *A Cotton Enterprise, 1795–1840: A History of McConnell and Kennedy, Fine Cotton Spinners.* 1972.

Pollard, S. *The Genesis of Modern Management: A Study of the Industrial Revolution in Britain.* 1965.

See also Entrepreneurs and Entrepreneurship; Hours, Wages, and Working Conditions; Science, Technology, and Invention

Factory Movement and Factory Acts

The factory movement of the 19th century consisted of loose alliances of workers, clergymen, philanthropists, and employers interested in reforming factory conditions. Members of the movement pressured Parliament to regulate hours and conditions of factory work, especially in the **textile industry**. The most important Factory Act (1833) was the first to enforce the regulation of **child labor**; further legislation in the 1840s and 1850s marked other important victories for the reformers.

Sir **Robert Peel the Elder** (1750–1830) promoted the first factory act, which regulated the working hours and hygiene of pauper apprentices (1802). **Robert Owen** joined Peel to press for the Factory Act of 1819, which forbade the employment of children under age 9 and restricted to 69 hours the work week of youngsters age 9–18. Factory acts restricting Saturday hours (1825), and restricting anyone below age 21 from night work (1831), followed. But these laws, opposed by some manufacturers and economic theorists as costly and damaging, were only sporadically enforced. Something stronger was needed.

Thus **humanitarian** reformers and local Short Time Committees of northern workingmen launched the "Ten Hours Movement," which from 1831 to 1874 was the most organized aspect of the factory movement. In it, **Tory Evangelicals** and unenfranchised factory operatives aimed to impose more effective limits on the working hours of children and, indirectly, adults. **Richard Oastler**'s oratory and **Michael Sadler**'s writings influenced public opinion in the early 1830s. Sadler presented the first Ten Hours Bill in Parliament in 1832, but it failed; the nationally prominent Evangelical, **Lord Shaftesbury**, together with Lord Althorp (1782–1845), leader of the **House of Commons**, then shepherded through Parliament the Factory Act of 1833. This was important because it affected nearly all textile mills, limited children's working hours (even calling for 2 hours' schooling for some), and initiated regular and responsible inspection of conditions—momentous changes for a decidedly laissez-faire age. Later, Shaftesbury sponsored an act (1844) that extended protection to women on the same basis as to "young persons," and the **Unitarian** M.P. **John Fielden** helped to bring about at last a 10-hour day for women and children with the passage of the Ten Hours Act (1847). In the 1850s, further factory legislation met the earlier goal of limiting hours not only for children and women but also for men.

Carolyn Stevens

Bibliography

Bartrip, P.W.J., and P.T. Fenn. "The Evolution of Regulatory Style in the Nineteenth Century British Factory Inspectorate." *Journal of Law and Society.* Vol. 10, pp. 201–222.

Cowherd, Raymond G. *The Humanitarians and the Ten Hour Movement in England.* 1956.

Driver, Cecil. *Tory Radical: The Life of Richard Oastler.* 1946.

Ward, J.T. *The Factory Movement, 1830–1855.* 1962.

See also Factory Workers; Hours, Wages, and Working Conditions; Industrial Revolution; Standard of Living

Factory Workers

Only a small number of workers were employed in factories before the end of the 18th century. Factories emerged either where machines became too large to be accommodated in a back room or a small workshop, or where power was being applied to the machinery. The emergence of these factories began among sectors of the **textile industry**, first in silk throwing, then in the **spinning of cotton, wool, and worsted**; which meant that they were geographically confined at first to only a few regions in Lancashire, Yorkshire, and West Central **Scotland**. And even in these areas, factories spread but slowly and unevenly as the spinning jenny got larger and as mule spinning gradually replaced it. Not until the 1820s did the improved power loom bring weaving into the factories.

Since many of the early textile mills depended on ample water power, they were located in relatively remote areas. The problem of attracting labor could be a difficult one; hence the development of factory villages, such as Styal and **New Lanark**, that offered housing as well as work to entire families. Women and children were the largest part of the early factory labor force, and, until their use was restricted by legislation in 1802 and 1819, the largest millowners made extensive use of pauper children from city workhouses. The coming of **steam** power by 1800 allowed the locating of mills in towns and a reliance on "free" labor (again predominantly women and children) as carders, reelers, and piecers.

Factory work involved a quite different rhythm of work from that of domestic labor. At 12 to 16 hours a day, actual working hours were probably no longer in the factories than was usual in **domestic production**, but factory workers had to accept a new clock-regulated discipline. Great emphasis was placed on good time-keeping, and regularity was enforced often by heavy fines and the threat of dismissal. Workers could no longer set their own patterns of work, but were required to begin and end work at fixed hours, and to follow formal work rules. Discipline was imposed with considerable harshness, including occasional physical violence by overseers. Increased use of piece-rate payments further intensified labor, with little or no concern for safety or health.

Within the early factories a number of tasks began to be demarcated as requiring particular skills. This was the case, for example, with mule spinning which, partly because considerable physical strength was required to move the mule carriage, became the preserve of an elite of adult men who thus displaced women from what had traditionally been their dominance in spinning. Similarly, spinners began to import into the factory the more formal attitudes and practices of traditional **craftsmen** attempting to control entry into the trade, seeking privileged admission for their own children, and asserting the right of largely regulating their own work patterns. Spinners took responsibility for providing and paying their own piecers, the children who assisted them by crawling under the machines to fix threads, and for finding replacement workers to keep their machines running when they wanted to take time off. Not surprisingly, from the 1820s there were increasing struggles over the issue of management authority in the mills.

W. Hamish Fraser

Bibliography

Butt, J., and K. Ponting, eds. *Scottish Textile History.* 1987.

Collier, Francis. *The Family Economy of the Working Classes in the Cotton Industry, 1784–1833.* 1964.

Pollard, Sidney. *The Genesis of Modern Management.* 1965.

Thompson, E.P. "Time, Work-Discipline and Industrial Capitalism." *Past & Present.* No. 38, pp. 56–97.

See also Child Labor; Factory Movement and Factory Acts; Hours, Wages, and Working Conditions; Industrial Revolution; Women's Employment

Falconer, William (1732–1769)

Falconer was one of the most articulate **seamen** of the Hanoverian era. Born the son of a poor **Edinburgh** barber, he put to sea and took a pen with him. His long poem, *The Shipwreck* (1762), is a realistic portrayal in formal couplets of the sea and of a mariner's life. Dedicated to the Duke of York (1739–1767), then a rear-admiral, Falconer's poem gained him the Duke's **patronage**, who procured him a midshipman's situation. At about the same time he also wrote a **satire**, *Demagogue* (1764), against **John Wilkes**.

Falconer based *The Shipwreck* on his own experience in the shipwreck of the *Britannia* (1750) off Cape Colonna, Greece, from which he was one of only three to survive. The exciting subject and his evocation of a deeply felt experience may compensate for the poem's imitative **classicism**. But in its vivid and original pictures of the sea, *The Shipwreck* contributed to the Scottish tradition of nature **poetry** and anticipated the **Romantic** poets. **Byron** turned to it as material for the storm scene in *Don Juan* (1819–1824).

Falconer also found time for scientific writing. His *Universal Marine Dictionary* (1769), copious, orderly, and accurate, begun at the suggestion of a friend, George Lewis Scott (1708–1780, a barrister and respected mathematician), superseded all previous efforts and was adopted by the **navy**. Unfortunately, Falconer drowned at sea in the sinking of the *Aurora,* somewhere east of the Cape of Good Hope.

Kenneth Daley

Bibliography

Joseph, Michael Kennedy. "William Falconer." *Studies in Philology.* Vol. 47, pp. 72–101.

Walker, Hugh. *Three Centuries of Scottish Literature.* Vol. 2. 1893.

Famines (Scotland and Ireland)

The last famine to have a serious effect on the whole of Scotland occurred in the 1690s. Food shortages were experienced in 1740, 1751, 1756, 1782–1783, 1806–1807, 1811, and 1816–1817, and starvation was experienced during 1836–1837, but these events tended to be more regional and less widespread than before. Subsistence crises became rarer and mostly confined to the Highlands of Scotland; and, until the Great Highland Famine of 1845–1848, did not involve many deaths. By contrast, death by starvation was literally unheard of in England after the early 17th century.

The situation in Ireland was potentially much more calamitous. The economic structure was more susceptible to subsistence crises than that of the rest of the British Isles, with more people living near or below the margin of subsistence. This was compounded by a **population** growth that was the highest in Europe. The south experienced severe and widespread famine in 1727–1730, 1740–1741, and 1769–1770, while near-famine conditions in 1745, 1757, and 1783–1784 had a greater effect on the country as a whole. Later, famine was to be more problematic in western Ireland, and a considerable degree of distress was experienced in 1800–1801, 1816–1819, 1822, and 1826. In 1831, excess deaths were recorded in the west.

The Irish economy was less well developed than that of England and Lowland Scotland, and during the 19th century Ireland experienced high levels of underemployment which caused much distress, particularly in the west and southwest. The Scottish Highland economy had similar economic problems, with population expanding, the economy contracting, and more people remaining on the land, surviving on potato cultivation. The wet climate of both of these regions made survival on the potato possible, but also left people vulnerable. Overreliance on a single crop spelled danger when it failed, and during the early 19th century, localized famine began to increase in frequency and intensity.

The increasing regionality of subsistence failure meant that famine was no longer a threat to the entire population. But where it did occur, it showed up the weaknesses of narrow and fragile economies dependent on land and the potato for survival. Increasing intervention by the state meant that few people would die as a direct result of famine, but the threat still remained; and this was realized during the tragic Great Famine of the 1840s.

William Kenefick

Bibliography

Cullen, L.M. "Population Growth and Diet, 1603–1850," in J.M. Goldstrom and L.A. Clarkson, eds., *Essays in Honour of the Late K.H. Conceal.* 1981.

Daly, Mary E. *The Famine in Ireland.* 1986.

Devine, T.M. *The Great Highland Famine.* 1988.

Gibson, A.J.S., and T.C. Smout. *Prices, Food and Wages in Scotland, 1550–1780.* 1994.

O'Grada, Cormac. *The Great Irish Famine.* 1989.

See also Highland Clearances; Irish Agriculture; Irish Emigration; Scottish Agriculture

Faraday, Michael (1791–1867)

Faraday was one of the greatest scientists of the 19th century. The son of a poor blacksmith, he was apprenticed to a **London** bookbinder; his initial enthusiasm for science was aroused by the books he bound. In 1813 he was appointed assistant to **Humphry Davy** at the **Royal Institution**, there acquiring laboratory skills, chiefly in chemical manipulation. His discovery in 1821 of electromagnetic rotations—the principle of the electric motor—gained him an international reputation and election to the **Royal Society** in 1824. Other important discoveries soon followed: he discovered benzene in 1825,

Faraday with heavy glass used in electrical experiments

electromagnetic induction in 1831, and the laws of electrolysis a few years later. Although remembered for these and other discoveries, Faraday was also an original speculative thinker, propounding his own ideas about matter, forces, and fields, but opposing prevailing views on atomism.

A skilled lecturer who attracted crowds to his courses at the Royal Institution, Faraday also helped popularize science and added to the institution's prestige and finances by founding the Friday evening discourses (1826) and the Juvenile Christmas Lectures (1827). He served as scientific advisor to the Admiralty, Trinity House (responsible for **lighthouses**), and other bodies. A devout Christian, he was a Sandemanian, a member of a small but extremely rigorous sect that had once numbered **William Godwin** among its devotees.

Geoffrey Cantor

Bibliography

Cantor, Geoffrey, David Gooding, James Gooding, and A.J.L. Frank. *Faraday.* 1991.

Golinski, Jan. *Science as Public Culture: Chemistry and Enlightenment in Britain, 1760–1820.* 1992.

Gooding, David, and A.J.L. Frank, eds. *Faraday Rediscovered.* 1985.

Thomas, John Meurig. *Michael Faraday and the Royal Institution.* 1991.

See also Electricity; Franklin, Benjamin

Farmers and Agricultural Laborers

The early Hanoverian years were not generally prosperous for agriculture. Harvests were usually abundant, and with **population** growing only slowly, home demand for food was easily met. Grain prices, and hence profits, were low. Many landowners found it difficult to find tenants. **Daniel Defoe** in

"Mowers," by W.H. Pyne

1709 placed farmers "who fare indifferently" only just above the poor, "who fare hard." To him, *farmer* described the small landholders, owners or tenants, whom he elsewhere described as "mere husbandmen."

In 1696 the early analyst and demographer Gregory King (1648–1712) enumerated 180,000 freeholders and 150,000 tenant farmers, and considered the former group to be better off. By 1751, according to the statistician Joseph Massie, tenants had become the better-off group, although still slightly less in number. By 1800, around three-quarters of England's farmland was rented, and tenants equaled owner–occupiers in number, farmed larger acreages, and were significantly richer.

The second half of the 18th century, with poorer harvests and rapidly rising population, brought higher grain prices and bigger profits. The big **agricultural improvers** consolidated their lands and leased them as larger farms. In this era, the farmer came into his own; the term "Farmer" (as in "Farmer Giles") became a title, as much as an occupational description. The large tenant farmers could afford the investment that had become critical—it was the investment of farmers, more than that of landowners, which propelled English agriculture to levels of output per head unequaled in Europe and which allowed it to feed a dramatically increased population.

As a social group, farmers achieved status in agricultural communities. As well as being the most important employers, in **local government** they enjoyed extra power in key parish offices as churchwardens and overseers of the poor. At their top was a class of rich farmers who had profited steadily from rising food prices over the latter 18th century and spectacularly from soaring prices during the **French Revolutionary and Napoleonic Wars** (1792–1815). Their pretensions were satirized in the symbols of "the piano in the parlour" and in tales of the farmer's wife and daughter becoming too proud to work or to dine at the same table as the farm **servants**. Yet despite such **satires**, and although the income of farmers as a whole was undoubtedly increasing, most farmers aspired to comfortable, rather than luxurious, lifestyles; they were the solid **middle class** of the countryside. As the *Times* put it in 1800, a year when high grain prices were causing widespread hunger among the poor, "A farmer ought not to be a rich man."

Although peasant farming persisted in several parts of Britain, notably in **Wales**, **Scotland**, and **Ireland**, and although family labor still sustained many smaller farms, the rise of the tenant–farmer was accompanied by the proliferation of hired, landless farm laborers. Older forms of agricultural labor were declining over the period, although the rate of decline differed by region. This was especially true of living-in farm service. This practice of boarding young men and women in the farmhouse on a yearly hiring was proving less attractive to farmers whose status was rising, while higher food prices and, following enclosures, a reduction in the need for labor, combined to remove its economic advantage.

Over the second half of the 18th century, a major divide

developed between agricultural **wages** in northern England, where growing industrial employment affected the labor market, and significantly lower wages in the south. Except around **London**, by the 1790s the laborer's standard of living had been declining for 30 years. In some areas, dairying increased the demand for **women's employment**, but in general the changing methods of farming reduced the need for women in cereal production, and family incomes suffered accordingly.

The wartime prosperity from 1793 to 1815, with the male labor supply reduced by the needs of **war**, brought a temporary reversal, but the ending of war brought from 1816 a decline again to the point where the southern farm laborer was to become the very symbol of desperate **poverty**, living on wages that only allowed the barest of subsistence even when full-time regular employment was available. In Wiltshire, wages of 6–7 shillings (30–35p in 1794) rose through 8 shillings (40p in 1804) to 12 shillings (60p in 1812). By 1817 wages had reverted to 7 or 8 shillings, and were to remain at that desperate level for at least another 30 years. Some specialized workers, such as shepherds or carters, could earn a little more than this, but in general the life of the southern farm laborer from the 1790s was one of miserable poverty, endured in a hovel of a cottage on a diet in which meat was hardly ever consumed.

It was this desperate poverty and the demand for work at a living wage which, more than the simple resentment of threshing-machines, drove the southern laborers to join the **Swing Riots** of 1830. They accomplished nothing because the landed ruling class would not tolerate such insubordination in the countryside. The last laborer's uprising was firmly suppressed and its leaders cruelly punished.

John Rule

Bibliography

Chambers, J.D., and G.E. Mingay. *The Agricultural Revolution, 1750–1880.* 1966.

Gibson, A.J.S., and T.C. Smout. *Prices, Food and Wages in Scotland, 1550–1780.* 1994.

Hobsbawm, E.J., and G. Rudé. *Captain Swing.* 1969.

Horn, Pamela. *The Rural World, 1780–1850: Social Change in the English Countryside.* 1980.

Malcolmson, R.W. *Life and Labour in England, 1700–1780.* 1981.

Neeson, J.M. *Commoners: Common Right, Enclosure and Social Change in England, 1700–1820.* 1993.

O'Grada, Cormac. *Ireland: A New Economic History, 1780–1939.* 1994.

Reed, Mick, and Roger Well. *Class, Conflict and Protest in the English Countryside, 1700–1880.* 1990.

Rule, John. *Albion's People: English Society, 1714–1815.* 1992.

Snell, K.D.M. *Annals of the Labouring Poor: Social Change and Agrarian England, 1660–1900.* 1985.

See also Corn Laws; Hours, Wages, and Working Conditions; Irish Agriculture; Poverty and Poor Laws; Scottish Agriculture; Welsh Agriculture

Fashion

Fashion in Hanoverian Britain was much more than simply a yearly transformation of dress or furnishings by the elite. It was a social, cultural, and economic phenomenon that touched many ranks. Goods and pastimes defined as fashionable emerged from both ends of the social spectrum. Not all began among the upper classes—though many did—helping to preserve superior rank against encroaching inferiors. But increasingly the display of fashionable goods was no longer the exclusive preserve of the **aristocracy and gentry**. Economic dynamism and social mutability engendered desire for stylish goods and fashionable activities across an ever-broadening social spectrum.

During the course of the period 1714–1837, fashion moved in fits and starts from the more elaborate imitation of the French court of Louis XIV to simpler tastes reflecting, first, the sober German heritage of the Hanoverian monarchs, and then later the trends of a more **Romantic** and egalitarian era. At the same time, again somewhat under French sponsorship, a "universal" Western European look began to take hold, with some variations due to regional affections.

In **clothing** (as in **architecture** and **home furnishings and decoration**), fashions evolved generally from heavier and boxier forms to lighter and more comfortable ones. Male as well as female dress lost many of the frills of Stuart times, although, perhaps predictably, among the very elite a contrary tendency also began with the emergence of the youthful *beau*, fop, or dandy. For such persons, looking fashionable was expensive and time-consuming. **James Boswell**, though not quite a dandy, in 1762 felt compelled to budget fully one-fourth of his income for clothes. A well-made **wig** of natural hair, curled à la mode, might cost £300. True *beaux* also used gold or silver snuff boxes with small mirrors inside for adjusting appearances. **London** shop assistants became expert at mimicking this look and demeanor.

Farther down, there was literal significance to "putting one's best foot forward"; a good leg was considered irresistible to women. Skinny calves could be enhanced by padding, and fortunes were spent on silk stockings and buckled shoes with elevated heels. The dandy often hired a sedan chair, at the rate of a shilling a mile, to carry him about over the city's muck and mire. Of course, ladies of high fashion also dressed to excite interest. Their gowns were cut low, and under the guise of demureness a "modesty piece" called a "tucker" was worn between the breasts, attracting more gazes than it averted.

But fashion connoted much more than clothes and personal appearance. It signified the entire upper social set—"people of fashion"—and also the current craze: something popular was "in the fashion." One of the most fashionable activities among fashionable women was visiting, with the sedan-chair serving as the favored mode of conveyance. Visitors enjoyed playing cards and gossiping while consuming light meals of tea, pastries, and sweets. New social rituals evolved around newly popular hot beverages like **coffee**, tea and chocolate; by around 1750 the drinking of such beverages was customary within the middling ranks where novelty, comfort, and style enjoyed increasing cachet. Whole new in-

"The Tide of Fashion in the Park," c. 1810

dustries developed in the hands of a **Wedgwood** or **Spode** to serve the demand for decorative porcelain and pottery accessories for the tea table.

Fashionable life for men in London often centered on the chocolatehouses and coffeehouses. Two of the most famous **clubs** were White's and the Cocoa-Tree, both patronized by the **Tories**, as was Ozinda's Coffee House; the **Whigs**' principal establishment was the St. James Coffee House, located in St. James Street.

Travel also was "in the fashion." For much of the period, Paris was considered the center of international fashion. The Grand Tour, primarily of France and Italy, was considered *de rigueur* among the wealthy and was esteemed the hallmark of an aristocratic education. Often the well-to-do young traveler would be accompanied by a **tutor** or "bear-leader" who served as his guide to Europe's sights and society. If he traveled as far as Naples he would acquire a taste for Italian pasta and thus distinguish himself as a "macaroni" by ordering noodles when returning to London. In Europe he gained not only an appreciation for foreign cooking and society but an amateur's education in the masterpieces of European **painting** and **sculpture**. The collecting of **antiquities** and foreign art thus became fashionable activities among cultivated noblemen. For others, domestic **spas** and **seaside resorts** like **Bath**, Scarborough, and Brighton flourished as centers of fashionable excess and recuperation.

These are only a few of the spheres dominated by fashion. And of course fashion was also influenced by political and economic change. It is particularly clear in the realm of dress that by the 1790s, pushed first by **sensibility** and then the **French Revolution**, fashion was becoming simpler and somewhat less hierarchical. Men were more inclined to wear plain fabrics; and women, simple printed cottons. Even children's clothes became more comfortable. Both sexes began dressing their hair more naturally. By the 1820s, fashion was coming increasingly under the influence of **middle-class** respectability and the tastes of the new men of business.

Matthew S. Novak
Beverly Lemire

Bibliography

Burton, Elizabeth. *The Georgians at Home, 1714–1830.* 1967.

Earle, Peter. *The Making of the English Middle Class.* 1989.

Ede, Mary. *Arts and Society in England under William and Mary.* 1979.

George, M. Dorothy. *London Life in the Eighteenth Century.* 1965.

Hart, Roger. *English Life in the Eighteenth Century.* 1970.

Langford, Paul. *A Polite and Commercial People: England 1727–1783.* 1989.

Lemire, Beverly. *Fashion's Favourite: The Cotton Trade and the Consumer in Britain, 1660–1800.* 1992.

McKendrick, Neil, et al. *The Birth of a Consumer Society: The Commercialization of Eighteenth-Century England.* 1983.

Parreaux, André. *Daily Life in England in the Reign of George III.* 1969.

Weatherill, Lorna. *Consumer Behaviour and Material Culture in Britain, 1660–1760.* 1988.

See also France; Manners and Morals

Ferguson, Adam (1723–1816)

Ferguson, moral philosopher and historian, was a leader of the **Scottish Enlightenment**. His most successful book, *An Essay on the History of Civil Society* (1767), was published over the objections of his close friend **David Hume**, but drew critical acclaim for its emphasis on morality and its sociological perspective on the human condition. Ferguson then published an outline of his moral philosophy lectures at the University of **Edinburgh**, *Institutes of Moral Philosophy* (1769), and a revision of the same lectures into a 2-volume work, *Principles of Moral and Political Science* (1792). He also published *The History of the Progress and Termination of the Roman Republic* (1783), which was intended as a warning against the corruption that he perceived in his own day. Among his minor works were pamphlets written in support of militias and stage plays, and against the **American Revolution**. On these and other

Adam Ferguson

issues, such as the controversy surrounding **James Macpherson**'s Ossianic **poetry**, Ferguson's views were usually the same as those of the wider circle of Moderate party ministers and men of letters with whom he was closely connected in both ecclesiastical and academic affairs.

Ferguson was born and raised in Logierait, Perthshire, then considered part of the Highlands. He was educated in arts and divinity at St. Andrews University and the University of Edinburgh. After serving a decade as chaplain to a **Highland regiment**, he returned to Edinburgh in the mid 1750s, eventually becoming Professor of Natural Philosophy (1759–1764) and Moral Philosophy (1764–1785) at the university there. He was a popular lecturer and an active participant in Edinburgh **clubs** and societies, such as the Select Society, Poker Club, and **Royal Society of Edinburgh**. During the American Revolution Ferguson **traveled** to America as secretary to the unsuccessful Carlisle commission, and continued to play the role of unofficial advisor to **Henry Dundas** and other politicians. As a moral philosopher, Ferguson was distinguished for his commitment to a stoic emphasis on actively striving to attain virtue with a minimal regard for consequences, which he considered ultimately beyond human control. His political ideology was that of a civic-minded conservative **Whig** who valued participatory citizenship in defense of the status quo, and believed that the greatest threat to the British constitution came from growing moral corruption in government.

Richard B. Sher

Bibliography

Anderson, Robert D. *Education and the Scottish People, 1750–1918.* 1995.

Bryson, Gladys. *Man and Society: The Scottish Inquiry of the Eighteenth Century.* 1945.

Kettler, David. *The Social and Political Thought of Adam Ferguson.* 1965.

Kidd, Colin. *Subverting Scotland's Past: Scottish Whig Historians and the Creation of an Anglo-British Identity, 1689–c.1820.* 1993.

Robertson, John. *The Scottish Enlightenment and the Militia Issue.* 1985.

Sher, Richard B. *Church and University in the Scottish Enlightenment: The Moderate Literati of Edinburgh.* 1985.

See also Church of Scotland

Fergusson, Robert (1750–1774)

Fergusson, whom **Robert Burns** called "by far, my elder brother in the Muses," celebrated in his poetry the **Tory** ideal of a hierarchically organized cosmos and society. While a student at the University of St. Andrews, he began writing **satiric** poems, but was forced to leave (1768) to support his family. Dividing his time between poetry and work as a legal clerk, he began contributing poems to Walter Ruddiman's *Weekly Magazine* (1771). In style, these exercises in **pastoral**, ode, and **mock heroic** mimicked a hackneyed English **neoclassicism**, but early in 1772 Fergusson suddenly turned to his native Scottish tradition with "The Daft Days." There followed a series in Scots dialect, among them "Caller Oysters," "Hallow Fair," and "Leith Races," which captured the energy, color, and bustle of the city's street life. The poems brought immediate celebrity, and a collected edition was published (1773).

Fergusson, who had extended the vernacular idiom beyond the comic and domestic, was now acclaimed as a successor to Allan Ramsay (1686–1758), who had attempted to reassert **Scotland**'s cultural identity earlier in the century. The measure of his achievement is found in the modified Spenserian stanzas of "The Fariner's Ingle," an affectionate and unsentimental evocation of Scottish rural life that inspired and arguably surpassed Burns's "The Cotter's Saturday Night." Unfortunately, in 1774, following illness and an accident, Fergusson was committed to **Edinburgh**'s Bedlam, where he died almost immediately.

Michael Bruce

Bibliography

Freeman, F.W. "Robert Fergusson: Pastoral and Politics at Mid Century," in A. Hook, ed., *The History of Scottish Literature.* Vol. 2: 1660–1800. 1987.

McDiarmid, Matthew P., ed., with a critical life. *The Poems of Robert Fergusson.* 2 vols. 1954, 1956.

Smith, S.G., ed. *Robert Fergusson 1750–1774: Essays by Various Hands.* 1952.

Wittig, Kurt. *The Scottish Tradition in Literature.* 1958.

See also Poetry and Poetics; Romanticism and Romantic Style

Ferrier, Susan (1782–1854)

Along with her contemporaries **Walter Scott** and **John Galt**,

Ferrier originated the Scottish **novel** of **manners** and ordinary parochial life. *Marriage, a Novel* (1818), *The Inheritance* (1824), and *Destiny, or, the Chief's Daughter* (1831) convey her belief that a good moral could not be dispensed with in fiction. The first two (both published anonymously) taught the importance of a young woman's upbringing in her ability to choose the right husband, while *Destiny*'s moral is clear: no one can escape fate.

Ferrier was influenced by **Jane Austen**, but while Austen's **irony** is delicate, Ferrier's is hard-hitting. Her **caricatures** of the Scottish scene, from the peasantry to English lords, elicited praise from George Saintsbury (1845–1933), who thought they ranked with the best in English fiction. Scott saluted *Marriage* as evidence of the literary promise that representations of everyday life held for the Scots.

Ferrier was born in **Edinburgh**, the youngest of 10 children. Her father managed the estates of the 5th **Duke of Argyll**. After her mother died (1797), she at age 15 assumed responsibility for her father and the household. James Ferrier disapproved of women writing, but while he was ailing, Susan read *Marriage* aloud to him. Only after he expressed his delight in the novel did she reveal its authorship. Her successes made her a popular figure, and contemporaries considered her a most gifted conversationalist. For several years after her father's death (1829) she continued to enjoy society, but growing blindness and infirmity forced her to retire after the publication of *Destiny*, which she dedicated to Scott.

Mary Tiryak

Bibliography

Ashton, Rosemary. Introduction to *Marriage*. 1986.

Cullinan, Mary. *Susan Ferrier*. 1984.

Doyle, John A., ed. *Memoir and Correspondence of Susan Ferrier . . . by Her Grandnephew John Ferrier*. 1898, reissued 1929.

Grant, Aline. *Susan Ferrier of Edinburgh, a Biography*. 1957.

See also Women in Literature

Field, John (1782–1837)

Irish composer and pianist, Field originated the nocturne for piano, which epitomized lyrical **Romantic** piano music. Born in Dublin, he moved to **London**, where he was apprenticed to **Muzio Clementi**, the composer, pianist, instrument-maker, and **publisher**. In 1802 they toured Europe together, until Field parted from Clementi in St. Petersburg and found success there as a pianist and teacher. He later moved to Moscow, where he remained until his death.

Field's piano compositions include about 16 nocturnes and seven concertos. His early London works include variations, rondos, and three sonatas. They exhibit Clementi's influence and reveal few hints of the style Field later developed in St. Petersburg. There he created the nocturne, a dreamy character piece for solo piano in one movement, in which virtuosity was used to expressive ends. His nocturnes have lyrical, ornamental melodies with accompaniments of widely

John Field

spaced broken chords that require the sustaining pedal in a manner particularly suited to the early piano.

As a pianist and the originator of the nocturne, Field influenced those later Romantic composers and pianists for whom virtuosity was the servant of artistic sensitivity. Frédéric Chopin (1810–1849), in particular, owed a debt to him.

Jane Girdham

Bibliography

Branson, David. *John Field and Chopin*. 1972.

Hopkinson, Cecil. *A Bibliographical Thematic Catalogue of the Works of John Field*. 1961.

Nikolayev, Aleksandr A. *John Field*. Trans. Harold M. Cardello. 1973.

Piggott, Patrick. *The Life and Music of John Field, 1782–1837: Creator of the Nocturne*. 1973.

Temperley, Nicholas, ed. *The London Pianoforte School*. Vols. 12, 13. 1985, 1986.

See also London Pianoforte School; Music

Fielden, John (1784–1849)

A major Lancashire **cotton manufacturer** who began life working in the mills, Fielden was a noted **Unitarian** who took **radically** democratic positions as M.P. from Oldham (1832–1847) and played an important role in the **factory movement**. He was unusual as a rich and successful businessman who not only called himself a radical but favored parliamentary regulation of manufacturing establishments. To give workers political power he supported a wider **franchise** than that permitted by the **Reform Act** of 1832, and was sympathetic to Chartism. He also opposed the **New Poor Law** (1834), favored government intervention to help hand-loom weavers displaced by machinery, and fought for a shorter workday.

Frequently but persistently voting in tiny parliamentary minorities, he was nicknamed the "self-acting mule." In 1836 Fielden published *The Curse of the Factory System*, condemning **child labor** and recommending parliamentary intervention to restrict it. His greatest parliamentary achievement was his successful sponsorship of the "Ten Hours" Act (1847), which crowned the effort to shorten the workday of children and women in textile factories.

Carolyn Stevens

Bibliography

Fielden, John. *The Curse of the Factory System.* 2nd ed., with Intro. by J.T. Ward. 1969.

Weaver, Stewart A. *John Fielden and the Politics of Popular Radicalism, 1832–1847.* 1987.

See also Factory Workers; Shaftesbury, 7th Earl of

Fielding, Henry (1707–1754)

Henry Fielding

Fielding was one of the pioneers of the English **novel**, yet before writing any of his 4 novels he had established himself as one of the leading playwrights of his day. In only 8 years he wrote 33 plays—mostly sentimental comedies or **satirical** farces—from *Love in Several Masques* (1729) to *The Historical Register for the Year 1736* (1737). Most of his plays were commercial and popular successes and many are hilarious but, apart from *Tom Thumb* (1730), none are performed today.

The **Playhouse Act** (1737), which in effect permitted **censorship** of plays, was probably not—as was once thought—intended specifically to silence Fielding, but he did give up the theater for a career in the law, and also founded a **newspaper**, the *Champion* (1739–1741), in which he began to experiment with authorial voices in the leading articles. He now began to assemble his *Miscellanies* (1743), a ramshackle collection that included the incomplete *Journey from This World to the Next* and the most obviously **ironic** English novel ever written, *Jonathan Wild*—a sustained attack on politics, politicians, and their corruption. The authentic historical Wild was a criminal, a **highwayman**, but Fielding turned him into an ironic hero, a "great man" whose greatness consists of bombast, cowardice, cheating, and lying.

Jonathan Wild was written before, but published after, *Joseph Andrews* (1742), which grew from Fielding's response to *Pamela* (1740), the first novel by **Samuel Richardson**. Fielding and Richardson, the two chief English novelists of the 1740s, developed differing ways of narrating novels, became rivals in the public eye, and have been treated as opposites ever since. Fielding's initial response to *Pamela* was his outrageously funny pamphlet, *Shamela* (1741), but his measured response, *Joseph Andrews,* was his first major exploration of his own philosophy of writing fiction. This comic romance, loosely based on *Don Quixote,* involves low-life characters who exemplify generosity and goodwill in contrast to the people they meet. It is also the first novel to develop seriously the intrusive narrator, who controls the narrative and reminds readers, by addressing them directly, that this is what he is doing.

Fielding's masterpiece, *Tom Jones* (1749), is a carefully structured comic **epic**, rigorously moral without ever being solemn, with an incredibly complicated plot and another cheerfully intrusive narrator. The characterization tends to be schematic, as the good-natured but wayward Tom Jones, an orphan, is adopted by the aptly named Allworthy, falls in love with the fair Sophia, but is turned out of his home because his half-brother has told lies about him. When Jones takes to the road in pursuit of Sophia, he symbolically pursues wisdom as he meets a series of adventures that teach him to control his youthful spirits. He turns out to be the son of a gentleman and marries Sophia, and the novel, never truly realistic, ends in the formula of a romance.

Fielding had finished *Tom Jones* late in 1748, about the time he became a magistrate in **London**. Plagued by ill health and dispirited by the wretched people who passed through his courtroom, he wrote his last novel, *Amelia* (1752), in which he abandoned his intrusive narrator and some of his breezy style. Where *Tom Jones* is more morally serious than it looks, *Amelia* is uncompromising in its condemnation of an unfair **judicial system** and the contemporary culture that allowed decent people to be continually cheated and threatened. The glum realism of this novel is relieved by another improbably happy ending.

Fielding was a versatile writer—of plays, political essays, newspaper articles (he edited 4 newspapers in all), legal pamphlets, a few poems, and novels. His reputation rests on *Jonathan Wild, Joseph Andrews,* and *Tom Jones,* the last being recognized as one of the finest achievements in the comic writing of the time, and as one of the great English novels.

Simon Varey

Bibliography

Battestin, Martin C., with Ruthe R. Battestin. *Henry Fielding: A Life.* 1989.

Cleary, Thomas R. *Henry Fielding: Political Writer.* 1984.

Hahn, H. George. *Henry Fielding: An Annotated Bibliography.* 1979.

Varey, Simon. *Henry Fielding.* 1986.

———. *Joseph Andrews: A Satire of Modern Times.* 1990.

See also Dramatic Arts; Fielding, Sarah; Irony; Law Enforcement

Fielding, Sir John (1721–1780)

Fielding was a pioneer of modern professional **law enforcement**. Though blind from age 19, he succeeded his half-brother, **Henry Fielding**, as Justice of the Peace ("beak," in contemporary slang) for Westminster (1754), and continued the work that both had begun with the founding (1749) of the **Bow Street Runners**. Among thieves he soon became famous as "the Blind Beak" who reputedly could recognize the voices of 3,000 criminals as they pleaded in his dock.

Fielding acquired governmental support for expansion of his Bow Street force (1757) and worked to professionalize its operations, beginning a program to circulate descriptions of criminals. Like his half-brother, he believed in strict discipline to maintain order, and the use of the gallows for convicted felons; also like him, he was accused of corruption, especially of inspiring, then entrapping, criminals for the reward—though nothing was proven against him. He sought to change the treatment of juvenile offenders by analyzing and attacking the root causes of crime—for example, promoting the employment of distressed youths as **servants** or as **seamen** in the **navy** or in **overseas commerce**. He published several treatises on law, **police**, and **crime** prevention, and was knighted (1761) for his services.

Thomas D. Veve

Bibliography

Andrew, Donna T. *Philanthropy and Police: London Charity in the Eighteenth Century.* 1989.

Beattie, J.M. *Crime and the Courts in England, 1660–1800.* 1986.

Browne, Douglas. *The Rise of Scotland Yard: A History of the Metropolitan Police.* 1956.

Dictionary of National Biography, s.v. "Fielding, Sir John."

Hay, Douglas, and Francis Snyder, eds. *Policing and Prosecution in Britain, 1750–1850.* 1989.

McLynn, Frank. *Crime and Punishment in Eighteenth-Century England.* 1989.

See also Crime; Humanitarianism; Punishment

Fielding, Sarah (1710–1768)

Fielding, whose talents are still overshadowed by her more illustrious brother **Henry Fielding**, was a competent novelist who edited and sometimes rewrote parts of her early books. Her first **novel**, *The Adventures of David Simple* (1744), is a romance laced with **satire**, about a man who searches to find anyone with the simple qualities of a true friend, but who discovers that scarcely anyone measures up to his hopes. This gentle, melancholy, slightly **sentimental** book enjoyed only modest success.

An apparent but not a genuine sequel, *Familiar Letters between the Characters of David Simple,* is a novel in letters—a form Fielding probably learned from her friend **Samuel Richardson**, who praised the psychological perception found in all her writing. The real sequel (*Volume the Last*) appeared in 1753. Meanwhile, she wrote the first school story for girls, *The Governess* (1749).

Fielding's six novels are allegories that use character types and make much of the virtues of being honest and straightforward. Her unusual psychological study, *The Lives of Cleopatra and Octavia* (1757), and her excellent **translation** of Xenophon (1762) from the Greek both deserve more acclaim.

Simon Varey

Bibliography

Barker, Gerard A. "*David Simple:* The Novel of Sensibility in Embryo." *Modern Language Studies.* Vol. 12, pp. 69–80.

Sabor, Peter. Introduction to *Remarks on Clarissa.* Augustan Reprint Society, nos. 231–232. 1985.

Fifteen, The

This was an uprising in 1715 in favor of **James Edward, the Old Pretender**. Its origins lay in continued adherence to **Jacobitism**, post–**Union** discontent, and opposition to the **Hanoverian Succession** (1714). It was led by the **Earl of Mar**, known as "Bobbing John" for his inconstancy and opportunism. Under the pretense of assembling Highland **clans** for a hunting expedition, Mar raised the standard of the Old Pretender at Braemar in late summer 1715 and proclaimed himself James's commander-in-chief in **Scotland**.

Despite strong backing in the northeast and from a majority of Highland clans, the uprising failed due to the military incompetence of Mar himself. Government forces were led by **John Campbell, 2nd Duke of Argyll**. Mar initially took Perth with 10,000 clansmen, but failed to build on this advantage. He failed to secure Stirling when Argyll had only 2,000 men, and later allowed Argyll to strengthen his forces. The two sides eventually clashed in November at the Battle of Sheriffmuir. The result was indecisive, despite Mar's superior forces of four to one. Jacobite clans snatched what booty they could and returned to their homelands, but rallied again in 1716. Mar retreated, however, and attempts at renewed rebellion collapsed. The Old Pretender himself had landed at Peterhead in 1715 (after the Sheriffmuir disppointment), but returned to **France** early in February 1716. The rebellion had failed.

John Roach Young

Bibliography

Baynes, J. *The Jacobite Rising of 1715.* 1970.

Ferguson, W. *Scotland, 1689 to the Present.* 1977.

Keay, J., and J. Keay, eds. *Collins Encyclopaedia of Scotland.* 1994.

Lenman, B. *The Jacobite Risings in Britain.* 1980.

McLynn, F. *The Jacobites.* 1985.

Monod, Paul Kleber. *Jacobitism and the English People, 1688–1788.* 1993.

See also Forty-five, The; George I

Finance and Investment

During the Hanoverian period, the developing role of finance and investment was crucial not only for the progress of **commerce** and industry, but also for managing the national debt and mobilizing the savings of the **aristocracy and gentry** and growing **middle classes**.

The latter years of the 17th century had witnessed severe problems in financing governmental expenditures. This was partly resolved by the formation of the **Bank of England** (1694). During the course of the following half century, the bank came to dominate and regularize the management of the national debt by issuing and redeeming government securities, thus providing greater security for investors. Government stocks, together with the bank's own stock and that of the other monied companies—the **East India Company** and the **South Sea Company**—came to be regarded as safe havens for surplus funds, providing a steady income for an increasing *rentier* class as well as widows and orphans.

Throughout the period, **entrepreneurs** raised much capital for business by reinvesting profits of an existing enterprise or by raising money from friends and acquaintances. This was true of both those engaged in **domestic production** and the early factory masters of the **Industrial Revolution**. Connections could come through membership of a religious group such as the **Quakers**, or through technical men inducing sleeping partners with funds to invest in their ideas. In some areas, Lancashire for example, men of the **legal profession** could act as middlemen, putting clients with surplus funds in touch with those who required capital. Business was usually carried on by sole traders or partnerships with unlimited liability, although some partners could negotiate agreements that limited their liability. The Bubble Act of 1720 restricted the formation of **joint-stock companies** without government permission, but it is now generally agreed that the small-scale nature of many early industrial and commercial enterprises made such organizations generally inappropriate.

After 1750, the rise of country **banking** brought a new dimension to industrial finance. Its principal role appears to have been the provision of short-term funds. The reason for this was liquidity. If a long-term loan was granted, it could not be called in at times of crisis; and, given the relatively limited nature of many country banks' resources, this was a very important factor. Thus their principal contribution was to advance cash against bills of exchange (discounting) and make funds available by means of overdraft. However, by means of renewing bills or continuing overdrafts, some short-term lending could, in effect, become long-term. The growth of business in bills of exchange led to the development of a new intermediary, the bill broker, most of whose customers were banks. In turn, the bill brokers could rediscount bills with the Bank of England, making the latter the lender of last resort. The use of **London** agents to settle transactions between regions, and indeed to settle international obligations, increased London's importance in the financial system.

Evidence from the **metal** and **textile** industries seems to back up the theory that finance was generally short term. In file making, for example, Peter Stubs (1756–1806) of Warrington in Lancashire made use of overdraft facilities when converting from domestic production to **factory** operations in the early years of the 19th century. **Arkwright** and **Oldknow** both had recourse to bankers for short-term finance in textiles. The extent of country bankers' involvement in **agriculture** is altogether a more thorny problem. The relatively limited size of country banks' funds meant that they would be unlikely to grant loans to the large landowner; the landowner would more likely raise money by mortgaging his property with London banks. However, if any landowners were connected with a bank, things could be different. Also, agriculture did tend to benefit from banking sources during the **French Revolutionary and Napoleonic Wars**, but this receded when peace returned.

As in previous centuries, a major investment of those who made money in **trade** and industry during the Hanoverian period was in the purchase of landed estates. As well as providing security against economic downturns, landowning could also bring increased social prestige and a basis from which to enter politics. Such new landowners often sought to increase the value of their investments by becoming **agricultural improvers**.

As time progressed, new sources of investment became available. The development of the **canal** system after 1760 and the **railway** network after 1825 demanded finance on a scale hitherto unseen outside government. Thus canal and railway companies sought, and usually obtained, acts of Parliament allowing them to become incorporated. Such was the interest aroused by the potential returns on such stocks that in the 1790s a "canal mania" and in 1836–1837 a "railway mania" occurred, leading to overspeculation and financial panic. Investors in canals and railways were often local people who realized the advantages such improvements could bring to their area, although outsiders were also involved. **Insurance** companies with surplus funds also contributed to the growing financial network by lending on the security of life policies or providing mortgages to landowners on the security of their property.

Much financial activity was centered on London as the seat of government, the hub of the nation's international trade, and the apex of its banking system. It was here that the major financial and stock markets were located. Thus, by the close of the Hanoverian period, much of the financial system, which was to underpin the Victorian era, was already in place.

A.J.G. Cummings

Bibliography

Cottrell, P.L. *Industrial Finance 1830–1914: The Finance and Organization of English Manufacturing Industry.* 1980.

Crouzet, François, ed. *Capital Formation in the Industrial Revolution.* 1972.

Dickson, P.G.M. *The Financial Revolution: A Study in the Development of Public Credit, 1688–1756.* 1967.

Floud, Roderick, and Donald McCloskey, eds. *The Economic History of Britain since 1700.* Vol. 1: 1700–1860. 2nd ed., 1994.

Neal, Larry. *The Rise of Financial Capitalism: International Capital Markets in the Age of Reason.* 1990.

See also Scottish Banking

Finch, Anne (1661–1720)

Recognized as the foremost English woman poet of her age, Finch was one of the earliest women to commit herself seriously to **poetry**. Yet much of her work remained unpublished during her lifetime, and in fact it was not until shortly before her death that her *Miscellany Poems, on Several Occasions* (1713) appeared in print.

Finch had begun writing in the literary environment of the court wits while serving as Maid of Honor (1683–1684) to Mary of Modena, consort of the future James II. Her marriage to Heneage Finch, a courtier and soldier (1684), was fortunate for literature, for he took upon himself the lifelong role of editor, transcriber, and muse for his wife's poetry. After the **Glorious Revolution** (1688) the Finches were exiled from court for their loyalty to the Stuart cause, and for the remainder of their lives they endured the threat of political retaliation for their steadfast **Jacobite** and **nonjuring** commitments.

Nonetheless, in the 1690s Finch began to publish anonymously some songs and religious verse, and in 1701 "The Spleen," her most frequently anthologized poem, appeared. She developed her poetic identity in part by defining her relationship to other women writers, including Katherine Philips (1631–1664) and Aphra Behn (1640–1689). In her later years she formed friendships with **Swift** and **Pope**, who encouraged her to publish. Her work contains **satire**, verse **epistles** to friends, elegies, love lyrics, panegyrics, **fables**, religious verse, and 2 verse plays.

Finch's reputation rested long upon **Wordsworth**'s remarks in an essay prefacing the *Lyrical Ballads,* praising her poetry for its images of "external nature." Recently, however, she has gained admiration for the richness and diversity of her poetry and for the perspective she provides onto the experience of the woman writer in the early 18th century.

Barbara McGovern

Bibliography

Barash, Carol. "The Political Origins of Anne Finch's Poetry." *Huntington Library Quarterly.* Vol. 54, pp. 327–351.

Finch, Anne, Countess of Winchilsea. *The Poems of Anne Countess of Winchilsea.* Ed. Myra Reynolds. 1903.

McGovern, Barbara. *Anne Finch and Her Poetry: A Critical Biography.* 1992.

Messenger, Ann. "Publishing Without Perishing: Lady Winchilsea's *Miscellany Poems* of 1713." *Restoration: Studies in English Literary Culture, 1660–1700.* Vol. 5, pp. 27–37.

See also Women in Literature

Finlay, Kirkman (1773–1842)

The younger son of the founder of the company of James Finlay and Sons, Kirkman Finlay was one of **Scotland**'s most noted **cotton** manufacturers, with a reputation for innovation and boldness. His purchase of modern mills made him the largest cotton manufacturer in the West of Scotland and ended his company's dependence on Lancashire.

Between 1812 and 1819, as M.P. and Lord Provost of **Glasgow**, he campaigned tirelessly against the **East India Company**'s monopoly of British trade with **India**. When this ended (1813), Kirkman laid the foundations of Finlay's great business empire in India. Later he attacked one of the last vestiges of the company's power—its China monopoly—sending agents from Calcutta to Canton for another successful campaign. He also expanded business westward into **West Indian** sugar and American cotton.

Finlay's business success led to many municipal honors, including the presidency of the Glasgow Chamber of Commerce, a post he held for 8 terms. While many of his campaigns benefited the Glasgow commercial community as well as himself, Finlay was not afraid to court unpopularity, most memorably causing a **riot** in Glasgow's Queen Street in March 1815 after voting for "Prosperity" Robinson's Corn Bill. In 1816 he was partly responsible for establishing a network of government agents to penetrate **radical** groups.

Patricia S. Collins

Bibliography

Anonymous. *James Finlay and Company, Ltd.: Manufacturers and East India Merchants, 1750–1950.* 1951.

Gourley, J., ed. *The Provosts of Glasgow from 1609 to 1832.* 1942.

Stewart, G.S. *Curiosities of Old Glasgow Citizenship.* 1881.

Firearms

See Weapons

Fishing

Hanoverian fishermen not only exploited home waters, but also harvested fish from grounds as distant as the Icelandic and **Newfoundland** coasts. These catches formed the basis of an extremely diverse and sophisticated trade.

The herring fisheries were among the most important. Herring shoaled off different coasts at different seasons of the year, and were usually taken by boat by different fleets of nets. The various fisheries were exploited with differing degrees of intensity. In Norfolk, the Yarmouth autumn season supported a large fleet of local and visiting craft. Part of the catch was consumed locally or immediately shipped off to nearby towns and villages; the remainder was cured as white or red herring.

White (i.e., salt-cured) herring were split, salted, and packed in barrels between layers of salt, whereas reds were smoked over a fire of wood shavings in a smokehouse for up to 21 days. After either process, the cured fish remained edible indefinitely. White herring were sent to **Ireland**; reds were often exported to the Mediterranean. Both products were shipped to the **West Indies** to provide food for plantation **slaves**, and this trade continued almost to the end of the Hanoverian period. However, 18th-century British curing

"Fishermen," by W.H. Pyne

standards could not match those of the Dutch, who fished the same North Sea grounds and serviced the most lucrative markets. When English standards rose in the 19th century, exports expanded markedly.

Liverpool became an important base for the west coast herring fisheries. Fast cutters and sloops left the Mersey for grounds off the Isle of Man, Cornwall, **Wales**, and the west coast of **Scotland**. Some craft purchased the fresh fish from local boats and shipped them back to Liverpool, where the herring were either smoked or salted, according to demand. In 1786 the British Fisheries Society was founded. It soon developed a number of fishing villages and harbors along the Western Highlands and islands of Scotland. Other herring seasons included those on the Firth of Forth and the Northumbrian, Yorkshire, and eastern Channel fisheries, but some were of little more than local importance. In Cornwall, St. Ives and district fishermen followed the herring and pilchard fisheries.

White fish were mainly harvested using a baited hook. Fishing gear varied from hand lines to long and great lines deploying numerous hooks. A number of other less important means were also used; turbots, for example, were sometimes harvested using stationary nets; a limited amount of trawling also took place. By the latter half of the 18th century, trawling was concentrated on coastal waters off Brixham in Devon and on the approaches to the Thames, which were worked by trawling smacks from Barking in Essex. By the 1790s a few trawlers also worked from Ramsgate in Kent, and elsewhere. The French Wars (1792–1815) stimulated this activity and encouraged a movement farther afield, with fishing grounds being worked in the Southern Bight of the North Sea as far north as Smith's Knoll and almost across to Holland. During the 1820s and 1830s, smacks began trawling along the Channel and also commenced seasonal fishing from the Yorkshire ports of Hull and Scarborough.

London's Billingsgate was the most important market for white fish; it was mainly supplied from Essex by Barking, Gravesend, and Harwich lining boats. These vessels often had large flooded holds or wells in which the catch was kept alive until it was unloaded at Billingsgate. If not sold fresh, white fish was either salt-cured in barrels, or smoked and dried.

Despite difficulties caused by relatively poor **inland transport**, the fish trade built up a considerable range of trading links during the Hanoverian era. In Scotland, **Edinburgh** provided an important market for fresh white fish from boats that had landed at villages and towns on the Fife coast. Fish sent from ports farther north were often smoke cured, and by 1800 a number of villages, including Findhorn on the Moray Firth, had established reputations for haddock curing. By the 1770s, inland towns provided the most important markets for the Yorkshire coast industry, with consignments of fish being sent by pannier pony from villages such as Staithes as far as **Manchester** by the 1780s. In the English Midlands, **Birmingham** had a well-established market, and catches from the southwest were sold not only in **Bristol**, **Bath**, and Exeter but also at Billingsgate. Turnpike **roads** assisted the development of longer-distance trade, and in 1761 Parliament granted London fish vans freedom from post horse duties and exemption from turnpike fees on their empty return journey.

Though the evidence suggests overall growth in the fishing industry in the Hanoverian era, this was not dramatic when compared to the changes being wrought in **agriculture** as it adapted to the growing **population**'s demand for food. The high cost and slow pace of contemporary transport restricted trade in perishable commodities like fish. Pannier ponies and fish vans could transport catches, but only limited amounts could be carried swiftly. These high costs limited inland trade in fresh fish to prime varieties destined for the wealthier end of the market. Cured fish also increased in price. The resident inland poor could not usually afford to buy fresh fish: fish came into their price range only when its quality had deteriorated. Herring were an exception; these were transported by the cartload to London during the East Anglian season. But being an oily fish, they deteriorated rapidly without curing and can scarcely have remained attractive for long. It would take the arrival of the **railways** to provide a cheap, fast means of overcoming this transport bottleneck and allowing fish to become an item for cheap mass consumption.

Robb Robinson

Bibliography

Chaloner, W.H. "Trends in Fish Consumption," in T.C. Barker, J.C. MacKenzie, and J. Yudkin, eds., *Our Changing Fare.* 1966.

Gray, M. *The Fishing Industries of Scotland, 1790–1914.* 1979.

Robinson, R. "The Rise of Trawling on the Dogger Bank Grounds: The Diffusion of an Innovation." *Mariner's Mirror.* Vol. 75, pp. 79–88.

———. "The Fish Trade in the Pre-Railway Era: The Yorkshire Coast, 1780–1914." *Northern History.* Vol. 25, pp. 222–234.

Flaxman, John (1755–1826)

Flaxman, the son of a commercial plaster cast-maker, was one of the greatest and most prolific **neoclassical** artists of the Hanoverian era. Born in **York**, he had little formal schooling but was already studying at the **Royal Academy** at age 15 and working for **Josiah Wedgwood** as a pottery designer by age 20.

John Flaxman

He was also now beginning his extensive study of classical Greek vases, incorporating much of what he learned into his compositions as sculptor and as **book illustrator**.

A subsidy from Wedgwood enabled Flaxman to travel to Rome (1787), where he was able to absorb additional classical art. He achieved great repute on the Continent, becoming better known there by 1800 than any previous British artist, owing in part to his many influential illustrations of Homer (73) and of Dante (109). His **sculptures** vary in quality, from splendid funeral pieces such as his **Nelson** Memorial in St. Paul's (begun in 1808) and his monument for Lady Fitzharris (1815), to stiff productions in the heroic mode. Flaxman became a full member of the Royal Academy in 1800 and Professor of Sculpture in 1810; his friends included **William Blake** who, in 1817, engraved a series of Flaxman's illustrations of Hesiod.

Flaxman's visual style rejected pictorialism, opting instead for classical simplicity and purity of line. His visual work became particularly influential again in the mid-Victorian period.

Stephen C. Behrendt

Bibliography

Bindman, David, ed. *John Flaxman.* 1979.

Irwin, D. *John Flaxman, 1755–1826: Sculptor, Illustrator, Designer.* 1979.

Symmons, Sarah. *Flaxman and Europe: The Outline Illustrations and Their Influence.* 1984.

See also Antiquities and Ruins; Cemeteries and Monuments; Classicism; Elgin Marbles

Flood, Henry (1732–1791)

With **Henry Grattan**, Flood is the best known of the "Irish **Patriots**" who contended that because **Ireland** was an equal kingdom with England under the crown, it deserved to be treated equally both constitutionally and commercially.

Flood, the illegitimate son of Lord Chief Justice Warden Flood, followed his father into politics in 1759, but after supporting for several years the Dublin Castle interest (i.e., the direct will of the **London** government) in the House of Commons of the **Irish Parliament**, he gravitated toward the Patriot grouping. His oratorical prowess and command of parliamentary procedure impressed many, but Flood was not content with opposition; he was attracted by the possibilities of power.

The failure of his initial negotiations with the government (1767) left him free to attack what he called the despotic policies of the Castle during the viceroyalty of Lord George Townshend (1767–1772), but following the appointment of Lord Simon Harcourt (1772–1777) he accepted office, after protracted negotiations, in 1775. This proved unwise; and he was only rescued from his predicament when he was dismissed from office (1781) for opposing the administration in the Commons.

Flood played an active role in the agitation that produced legislative independence (1782), and subsequently displaced Grattan in the affections of the Patriot masses by supporting their demand that London should renounce its claim to legislate for Ireland (1782–1783) and their campaign for parliamentary reform (1783–1785).

This did not, however, signal the beginning of a glorious new phase in Flood's political career. He was elected to the **House of Commons** at Westminster in 1783, and though he aspired to eminence in both the Irish and British parliaments, his was a lone and largely uninfluential voice.

James Kelly

Bibliography

Dickson, David. "Henry Flood," in C. Brady, ed. *Worsted in the Game: Losers in Irish History.* 1989.

Kelly, James. *Henry Flood.* Forthcoming.

Fog's Weekly Journal (1728–1737)

With the ***Craftsman***, the livelier and less narrow *Fog's Weekly Journal* led the newspaper press' attack on **Sir Robert Walpole**. Its principal writer was the **Jacobite** and minor dramatist Charles Molloy (*d.* 1767), who later founded *Common Sense* (1737). **Henry Fielding** may have contributed an anti–Walpole **satire** in 1730; **Lord Chesterfield** provided 3 essays in 1734. *Fog's* was a continuation of *The Weekly-Journal: or, Saturday's-Post* (1716–1725) and the extremist *Mist's Weekly Journal* (1725–1728), both of which had been printed by the Jacobite Nathaniel Mist (*d.* 1737), who had fled to **France** to escape prosecution for publishing Jacobite material in *Mist's* (1728). The abandonment by *Fog's* of political writing was apparently a condition of the government's decision to allow Mist to return from exile (1736); a series of essays by John Kelly (1680–1751), published after Mist's death, briefly revived the paper's antigovernment program.

Alexander Pettit

Bibliography

Crane, R.S., and F.B. Kaye. *A Census of British Newspapers and Periodicals, 1620–1800.* 1966.

Gerrard, Christine. *The Patriot Opposition to Walpole: Politics, Poetry, and National Myth, 1725–1742.* 1995.

Goldgar, Bertrand A. *Walpole and the Wits: The Relation of Politics to Literature, 1722–1742.* 1976.

Harris, Michael. *London Newspapers in the Age of Walpole: A Study of the Origins of the Modern English Press.* 1987.

Stewart, Powell. *British Newspapers and Periodicals.* 1950.

See also Newspaper Press; Periodicals

Folksong

Folksongs are poems that are sung, usually remembered and transmitted by a process of oral tradition. Written documentation of oral texts was haphazard until the very end of the Hanoverian era; the documentation of tunes even rarer. Systematic collection of folksong texts was not common until well into the 19th century, and transcription of folktunes was quite rare until the 20th century. But it was during the 18th century that British intellectuals became interested in the old traditional folksongs. The **popular music** of British folksong had by that time developed the characteristics that remain today.

There are a limited number of "tune families" to which a larger number of song texts can be sung. Folksong texts generally cannot stand alone, and so must fit poetically the meter, line, and stanza of the **music**. The melodies, as in British instrumental folk music, often reflect a different tonal sensibility than that of the diatonic scale common in formal music. Some folktunes have larger intervals between tones, creating the sound of "gapped scales." Tunes with only 5 tones (pentatonic) are common. It has proven useful to think of folk music not in terms of major or minor "keys" but as "modal," like the church modes of the Middle Ages.

The 18th century was the great age of British broadside balladry. Until 1800, ***ballad***, the term we now use for traditional narrative folksong, referred almost exclusively to hackneyed popular **poetry** sold in the form of "broadsides"—single sheets of cheaply produced text. Since the Renaissance, broadside ballads had been sold by book dealers and "balladmongers," street singers employed to put on "pitches" in streets, fairs, and pubs. After 1690, musical notes or references to familiar tunes were occasionally included in a text, though most broadsides still consisted of only the lyrics of any sort of song or poem—mostly topical ditties that were never absorbed into oral tradition, but also occasionally "old ballads" and newer songs that were.

In 1711, **Joseph Addison**, writing as "Mr. Spectator," initiated ballad criticism by publishing his "Chevy Chase" papers. In these he referred to "Chevy Chase," a folksong well known to his readers, as a "ballad" that he recommended for its "extreme natural and poetical" sentiment and "majestic simplicity." In a later **essay** he expanded his praise of ballads to include another "old song" known as "The Two Children in the Wood." After Addison's time, *ballad* could refer to either an antique traditional song or a newly composed broadside.

Before long, amateur antiquarians began extending to these earlier products their interest in "reliques" from an ancient and vaguely defined British past. The Hanoverians delighted in tangible **antiquities and ruins**, and expressed this enthusiasm by visiting ruins from medieval, Roman, and even pre–Roman times. In rather the same way, the conviction of folksong enthusiasts was that the survival of ancient songs on the lips of peasant singers connected the present to a rich cultural past.

Thomas Percy's *Reliques of Ancient Poetry* (1765) contributed significantly to the growing fascination with old ballads as a type of literature—not merely crude, hackneyed verse but a "natural" form of poetry. Percy was not the first to think oral poetry in the form of song worth preserving. The Scottish poet and bookseller Allan Ramsay's (1686–1758) *Evergreen* (1724) and *The Tea Table Miscellany* (1724–1732) included old folksongs as well as broadsides. Individual broadsides of such old ballads as "Gill Nourice," "Young Waters," and "Edom o Gordon," were published in **Glasgow** in 1755. But it was Percy's *Reliques* that marked the beginning of an intense period of national interest in folksong. Later,

Wordsworth saw in Percy's collection the beginnings of the **Romantic** movement in English literature.

The Hanoverian attitude toward folksong, conditioned by **neoclassical** literary ideas but affected by an increasingly popular primitivism, was somewhat ambivalent at the beginning. Percy himself had found the ancient songs he had discovered somewhat crude and in need of rewriting to transform them into "literature." Such conflicting regard for folksong continued throughout the era. **Samuel Johnson** knew many ballads but refused to regard them as "literature." **Scott**, **Wordsworth**, and **Coleridge** all found in folksongs—ballads, specifically—the pure spirit of a better, earlier age, but nonetheless tended to treat them chiefly as mere inspiration for their own polished art. The collector and editor Joseph Ritson (1752–1803), who criticized Ramsay, published a *Select Collection of English Songs* (1783), and also exposed various Scottish and Irish antiquarian forgeries, stood nearly alone in this era as a defender of folksongs in their raw, untouched form as the products of an authentic voice of the British "folk."

Continental theories about the importance of folksongs as expressions of the pure voice of a people or "race" came to influence British thought late in the Hanoverian era and helped to condition the Romantic preoccupations of the 19th century. These theories helped to validate the preservation of authentic folksong texts by the great collectors of the Victorian age.

Kenneth A. Thigpen

Bibliography

Bayard, Samuel P. "Prolegomena to a Study of the Principal Melodic Families of Folk Song." *Journal of American Folklore.* Vol. 63, pp. 1–44.

Bronson, Bertrand Harris. *The Ballad as Song.* 1969.

Child, Francis J. *The English and Scottish Popular Ballads.* 5 vols. 1882–1898.

Friedman, Albert B. *The Ballad Revival.* 1961.

Hodgart, M.J.C. *The Ballads.* 1962.

Leach, MacEdward, and T.P. Coffin. *The Critics and the Ballad.* 1961.

See also Ballad; Music, Vocal

Foote, Samuel (1721–1777)

Nicknamed the "English Aristophanes," Foote delighted in mimicking almost anyone on or off the stage (except **Samuel Johnson**, who threatened to beat him with an oak stick). As an epitaph put it, "Death *took him off*, who *took off* all the world." This satiric bent served Foote well in some 25 farces from 1747 to 1776, plays which he insisted were comedies because, he said, they ridiculed the "Follies and Absurdities of Men."

Foote began his theatrical career by playing Othello at the Haymarket (6 February 1744), a **theater** he rented in 1747 to stage his first foray into mimicry, *The Diversions of the Morning; or, a Dish of Chocolate.* He usually lost friends and associ-

Interior of the Little Theatre, Haymarket, 1815

ates because of his **satires**, but **Arthur Murphy** charged betrayal. After the success of Foote's *The Englishman in Paris* (1753), Murphy volunteered to write a sequel, *The Englishman from Paris.* Without telling him, Foote produced his own *The Englishman Returned from Paris* (3 February 1756), 1 month before Murphy's version.

Foote spent money as quickly as he angered friends; thus, when he was not performing in **London**, he frequently acted in **Dublin**, and occasionally in **Edinburgh**. In his most famous play, *The Minor* (Haymarket, June 1760; revised from a two- to a three-act comedy after it failed at Dublin's Crow Street Theatre), Foote caricatured the Methodist evangelist **George Whitefield** in the Epilogue. He also cross-dressed to play Mother Cole (based on Jennie Davis, a London procuress), a convert to **Methodism** who quotes Whitefield as she tries to corrupt the play's hero. *The Minor's* 35 summer performances encouraged **David Garrick** to produce it at Drury Lane beginning in November 1760, but only after the Lord Chamberlain forbade the epilogue.

As a result of being thrown from a horse (February 1766), Foote had to have his leg amputated; depeditated, he was an easy target for jokes: "A Foot too little now you are; / Before a Foote too much." But he was also granted a royal patent to run the Haymarket as a summer theater, and by July 1766 he was again acting and managing. In 1767 he purchased and refurbished the Haymarket. He continued to write topical **satires**, including one that began as a puppet show, *The Handsome Housemaid; or, Piety in Pattens* (15 February 1773). It spoofed Methodism, and *Pattens* attacked **sentimentalism** by parodying **Isaac Bickerstaff's** comic **opera**, *The Maid of the Mill* (1765).

Foote was a master at creating theatrical characters who came to life on the stage rather than in print. His rhythm of hard work and expensive vacations left no room for a wife. He had married Mary Hickes (1741), "a young lady of a good family," spent her fortune, abused and probably deserted her when he was young. As a contemporary noted, "a perfect harmony did not long subsist between them." Enemies used this unharmonious marriage to accuse him of homosexuality. Had he not been so charged in court—and acquitted—he probably would not have sold his interest in the Haymarket to **George Colman the Elder** in 1777. Within a year after the trial, Foote died on his way to recuperate in southern **France**.

Peter A. Tasch

Bibliography

Chatten, Elizabeth N. *Samuel Foote.* 1980.

Highfill, Philip H., Jr., Kalman A. Burnim, and Edward A. Langhans, eds. *A Biographical Dictionary of Actors, Actresses, Musicians, Dancers, Managers, and Other Stage Personnel in London, 1660–1800.* Vol. 5. 1978.

Trefman, Simon. *Sam. Foote, Comedian.* 1971.

See also Dramatic Arts; Wit and Ridicule

Fordyce, James (1720–1796)

Fordyce was a Scottish **Presbyterian** minister who established himself in a **dissenting** congregation in Monkwell Street, **London**, and became one of the 18th century's most successful writers of popular moral and religious advice books, especially for young people. His most important works, *Sermons to Young Women* (1765) and *Addresses to Young Men* (1777), were widely reprinted in Britain, **Ireland**, and America. He also published *Addresses to the Deity* (1785), *Poems* (1786), and several occasional **sermons** and pamphlets.

Born into a prominent Aberdeen family, Fordyce was educated for the ministry at Marischal College, where he earned an M.A. He served as minister of Brechin (1745–1753) and Alloa (1753–1760), but left **Scotland** for London in 1760 soon after preaching a celebrated sermon against "unlawful pleasure" before the general assembly of the **Church of Scotland**. Although his eloquence initially attracted a large following to his Sunday afternoon sermons in Monkwell Street, in the mid-1770s the congregation was divided by his dispute with the junior minister; Fordyce's following declined, and he finally resigned (1782). The decline of his preaching career, however, did not affect the extraordinary success of his published sermons and addresses to young men and women, which today remain mirrors of late-18th-century views about youth, gender, and sociability.

Richard B. Sher

Bibliography

Dwyer, John. *Virtuous Discourse: Sensibility and Community in Late Eighteenth-Century Scotland.* 1987.

———. "Enlightened Spectators and Classical Moralists: Sympathetic Relations in Eighteenth-Century Scotland." *Eighteenth-Century Life.* Vol. 15, pp. 96–118.

See also Manners and Morals

Foreign Relations

Britain between 1714 and 1837 became the most powerful state in the world, best able to project its strength around the world; the leading maritime, colonial, and economic force in world affairs. This was essentially achieved by war, and foreign relations have to be understood in high terms of war and peace, though relevant of course also are the historically specific decisions of foreign-policy architects such as **Stanhope**, **Carteret**, **Viscount Townshend**, **Sir Robert Walpole**, **Pulteney**, **Newcastle**, both **Pitts**, **Shelburne**, **Castlereagh**, and **Canning**.

The development to Britain's admired position in 1837 had been far from inevitable. Indeed, for much of the period down to the **Battle of Trafalgar** (1805), the overall picture is as much one of military and diplomatic problems as of successes. There had been major invasion fears in 1744–1746, 1756, 1759, and 1779. These all sprang from war with **France**, and that enmity was central to Britain's foreign relations. The two powers were formally at war in 1744–1748, 1756–1763, 1778–1783, 1793–1802, 1803–1814, and 1815; while conflict was also in progress in 1743 and 1754–1755, and the two powers were close to war on a number of other occasions, including 1731 and 1787. France was Britain's principal maritime and colonial rival, and this rivalry interacted with their differing views on European power politics. Differing views could neither prevent an alliance in 1716–1731, nor tentative attempts toward cooperation thereafter on a number of occasions (particularly in 1772–1773 and 1786), but this rivalry was central to British diplomacy and strategic thought.

Spain, ruled from 1700 by a Bourbon, generally supported France, although the unwillingness of Ferdinand VI to help France during the **Seven Years' War** helped to give Britain a crucial margin of naval superiority for much of that conflict; and the French navy was destroyed in 1759, before war broke out between Britain and Spain (then under Charles III) in 1762. Spain backed France in the **War of American Independence** and for part of the **French Revolutionary and Napoleonic Wars** (1792–1815)—Trafalgar was also a Spanish defeat; but the Spanish revolt against Napoleon (1808) gave British forces under the **Duke of Wellington** a crucial opportunity to challenge France successfully on the Continent of Europe.

Britain's relations with other powers were subordinate to the Anglo–Bourbon struggle. Austria was seen as a vital ally against France in 1741–1755, but the Austro–French reconciliation in 1756 led to cooler relations until the two powers found themselves at war with Revolutionary France in 1793. The Dutch were seen in a similar light, their naval and commercial importance being such that the British sought to keep them out of the French sphere. The rise of Russia under Peter the Great was a source of concern, and **George I** organized an opposing coalition, while in 1791 the government of **Pitt the Younger** came close to war with Catherine the Great in the so-called Ochakov Crisis; but, in general, Britain accepted Russian domination of Eastern Europe, and in the Napoleonic period saw Russia as a vital ally against French expansionism.

Under George I and **George II** the interests of the Electorate of **Hanover** played a major role in British foreign policy, often leading to antiministerial criticism, but they played a far smaller role under **George III**, who had never been to Hanover. The dynastic link continued until 1837, but Hanover was not of much significance in British foreign policy in the early 19th century.

The lack of a large **army** greatly affected British capabilities, but so also did the essentially passive and reactive British stance in Europe. Britain was a "satisfied" power, not interested in territorial gain on the mainland of Europe, and chiefly concerned to prevent significant changes in the territorial situation. In contrast, Britain followed a much more expansive policy outside Europe. There the balance of advantage lay with her naval strength, while the goal was commercial opportunity and strategic strength. Victory over the French in the 1750s left Britain as the leading European power in **India** and **North America** and, although the loss of the Thirteen Colonies was a very serious blow in 1783, the bulk of the rest of the **Empire** was retained intact after the American war.

Naval expenditure in the 1780s ensured that Britain was well placed to extend her maritime and colonial power when war resumed in 1793. Her gains by 1815 included Malta, St. Lucia, Tobago, Trinidad, Ascension, Tristan de Cunha, Mauritius, the Seychelles, the Maldives, and Ceylon—all islands—and Cape Colony. Additionally, significant gains had been made from non–European powers. In 1786 at Penang, the first British establishment in Malaya was made; 2 years later it was **Australia**'s turn. The Third and Fourth Mysore Wars (1790–1792, 1799), the Second Maratha War (1803), and the war with Jaswant Rao Holkar (1804–1805) led to significant territorial gains in India.

The net effect of these changes was considerable. The 4 decades from 1775 to the Congress of Vienna in 1815 helped to give the British Empire and the English-speaking world a very different shape. The latter was no longer exclusively part of the former, and the former now included a far greater number of non–English speakers who were neither Christian nor of European descent, and who moreover were ruled instead of being largely self-governed. This situation would be accentuated by further colonial expansion in the latter decades of the 19th century so that, in sum, the Victorian imperial experience would become quite unlike that of the Hanoverians.

Jeremy Black

Bibliography

Black, Jeremy. *Natural and Necessary Enemies: Anglo–French Relations in the Eighteenth Century.* 1986.

———. *A System of Ambition? British Foreign Policy, 1660–1793.* 1991.

———. *British Foreign Policy in an Age of Revolutions, 1783–1793.* 1993.

Brewer, John. *The Sinews of Power: War, Money and the English State, 1688–1783.* 1989.

Jones, Jim. *Britain and the World, 1649–1815.* 1980.

Middleton, Charles. *The Administration of British Foreign Policy, 1782–1846.* 1977.

Scott, Hamish. *British Foreign Policy in the Age of the American Revolution.* 1990.

See also Commerce, Overseas; Diplomats and Diplomacy; Empire and Imperialism; War and Military Engagements

Forfeited Estates Commission (Scotland)

Following the **Fifteen** and **Forty-five Jacobite** uprisings, the lands of Stuart followers throughout the Highlands and islands of Scotland were forfeited to the government. Many of the estates were sold (to the **York Buildings Company** and others), while a Board of Annexed Estates administered the remaining 13 (ranging in size from tiny Monaltie in Aberdeenshire to the huge Perth estate), all "inalienably" annexed to the British government in 1752. The unpaid commissioners—drawn primarily from loyal Scottish gentry—were to manage the estates and apply the income from rents "for civilizing the inhabitants on the said estates, and other parts of the Highlands and Islands of Scotland, and promoting amongst them the Protestant religion, good government, industry and manufactures, and the principles of duty and loyalty to His Majesty, his heirs and successors." They tried, but to limited effect.

The main concerns of the commission were **agricultural improvement**, the development of the linen industry, **fishing**, and communications. Only in communications were they particularly successful. Much of the income from the estates helped in the construction of **roads**, bridges, and harbors, notably those built in the Highlands by the famous Scottish civil engineer **Thomas Telford**. Even the estates' losses tended to the same effect, since a substantial injection of capital was made into Scotland by the payment of debts on the estates by the treasury and by public spending of the capital repaid by owners resuming possession. Much of this capital was spent on public works, notably the Forth and Clyde **Canal**, and harbor improvements along the east coast.

The estates were returned to the original owners (or their heirs) in 1784, although one estate, that of **Lovat**, was returned as early as 1774. Thereafter the Highland and Agricultural Society and the British Fisheries Society became important forces for improvement in the north of Scotland, led by progressive landowners like the redoubtable enthusiast **Sir John Sinclair of Ulbster**.

Ian Donnachie

Bibliography

Smith, Annette M. *Jacobite Estates of the Forty-five.* 1982.

See also Agricultural Societies; Culloden, Battle of; Highland Regiments; Planned Villages; Society for Promoting Christian Knowledge

Return of Charles Edward to Scotland, 1745

Forty-five, The

The rebellion of 1745 was the last sustained effort by the **Jacobites** to reclaim the crown. Ironically, it was the venture which, on paper, had the least chance of succeeding, yet the one that produced the greatest military result. It was largely engineered by **Charles Edward Stuart** who persuaded his followers into believing that he enjoyed the support of the French and of many elements in England. The moment seemed opportune, as the British government's heavy contemporaneous involvement in the **War of Austrian Succession** meant that its military forces were largely committed outside the country.

Plans in 1744 for an invasion by **France** floundered after a storm in Dunkirk wrecked their fleet. However, although the French abandoned the project to concentrate their war effort in Flanders, Charles was convinced that should an invasion force of Jacobites strike from the north, a French invasion of the English coast would be ordered. Accordingly, he raised his standard at Glenfinnan (15 miles west of Fort William, near the North West Highlands) in August 1745, hoping to force the French hand. Support was weak to begin with, though a number of clans rallied to him, and it was only when the prince reached Perth, north of **Edinburgh**, that his force grew. Inexperienced government forces under General John Cope (*d.* 1760) were defeated at Prestonpans in September. Charles took Edinburgh and, after a month of building up forces, decided to march south.

The lack of support in England dismayed Charles's generals. However, they encountered little or no resistance and—marching south through Carlisle, Preston, and Manchester—on 4 December reached Derby, 127 miles from **London**. Little stood between the Jacobite army and the capital, though they did not know this, and even though the hoped-for French invasion had not occurred. Charles decided to conduct an orderly retreat. This, however, alerted government forces to the fact that there was no pincer movement afoot, hence no French invasion to deal with, which left them free to dispatch troops in pursuit. The Jacobite victory at Falkirk on 17 January 1746 showed that the rebel army was still a force to be reckoned with, though it was chronically short of firepower, and increasingly its leadership was losing coherence as disputes over strategy became more bitter. Further, the Jacobites failed to mobilize support among the lowland population, and were finally forced to retreat into the Highlands.

The royal forces, now better organized under the command of the **Duke of Cumberland** who had returned from Flanders, moved northward and defeated the rebels close to where they had begun, far to the north at **Culloden** in April 1746. The government moved swiftly to stamp out resistance. Cumberland pursued the fleeing rebels and earned the nickname of the "Butcher." Some of the captured rebels were tried and executed in England; others were **transported** to the colonies. The Highland chieftains, most of them supporters of the rebellion, were punished by the removal of various powers and privileges, including the wearing of the tartan and the carrying of firearms. All this had the effect of hastening the end of the **clanship** system.

Richard Finlay

Bibliography

Lenman, B. *The Jacobite Risings in Britain.* 1980.

McLynn, F. *The Jacobites.* 1985.

———. *Bonnie Prince Charlie: Charles Edward Stuart.* 1991.

See also Forfeited Estates Commission; Lovat, 11th Baron

Foulis Brothers

Noted **publishers and booksellers,** the Foulis brothers were the sons of a **Glasgow** maltman. Robert (1707–1776) trained as a barber, and Andrew (1712–1775), after studying at Glasgow University, taught languages. In 1738–1739 they toured England and Europe, amassing many books, which they profitably resold. Robert became a bookseller in 1741 and then a publisher; appointed University Printer in 1743, he published the first Greek book in Glasgow the same year, following this with many fine editions of the classics, including an immaculate edition of Horace.

Robert, though assisting with the evening book auctions and other aspects of the business, devoted himself to establishing an Academy of Fine Arts in Glasgow. The institution lacked sufficient popular support, and after 20 years' precarious existence Robert was obliged to sell its picture collection at a great loss and close its doors. The brothers' book business itself declined sadly after Andrew's death in 1775.

Theresa McDonald

Bibliography

Murray, D. *Robert and Andrew Foulis and the Glasgow Press.* 1913.

———. *Some Letters of Robert Foulis.* 1917.

Foundling Hospital

The Hospital for the Maintenance and Education of Exposed and Deserted Young Children, more simply known as the Foundling Hospital, was chartered in 1739 and opened its doors to destitute and illegitimate infants in **London** in 1741. Founded by an imaginative retired sea captain, **Thomas Coram,** it was England's first incorporated charity.

Historians estimate that over two-thirds of the children born in London in the early 18th century died as infants. Originally, the babies accepted at the Foundling Hospital had to pass a health inspection and be under 2 months old, a policy that led to a relatively low death rate, compared to that of infants in workhouses. Nonetheless, so great was infant mortality at that time that from 1741 to 1760, of 16,326 infants admitted, 61.2% died. Those who survived usually became productive as apprentices in industry.

Finances were another problem. Coram encouraged upper-class supporters to follow the Continental example of caring for abandoned and illegitimate infants. He solicited the philanthropic support of aristocratic women, and also raised money by utilizing the hospital building to stage **musical concerts** and display **paintings:** works of **Handel** and **Hogarth** were among those exhibited at these fund-raising events. Government subsidies were added in 1756, on the understanding that the hospital's services should be opened to the public; the result was that on 2 June 1756, the first day of this new arrangement, 117 babies were deposited on the doorstep—a convincing illustration of the acute need for the hospital. In 1760, however, after an unsuccessful 4-year experiment with this arrangement, the institution reestablished its funding base in private philanthropy, the basis for infant admission becoming a £100 fee raised by subscriptions.

The Foundling Hospital, still operating today, represented an important early channel for the growing **humanitarianism** of the latter 18th century, though historically the demand for its services frequently outpaced its capacity.

Carolyn Stevens

Bibliography

McClure, Ruth K. *Coram's Children: The London Foundling Hospital in the Eighteenth Century.* 1981.

Nichols, R.H., and E.A. Wray. *The History of the Foundling Hospital.* 1935.

Pinchbeck, Ivy, and Margaret Hewitt. *Children in English Society.* 2 vols. 1969.

Fox Family

Members of the Fox family were prominent figures in **Whig** politics throughout the Hanoverian era. Henry Fox (1705–1774) and his son Charles James (1749–1806) were the best known, partly because of their rivalries with **William Pitt the Elder** and then his son **Pitt the Younger.** Henry Fox's skill in debate and political maneuvering gained him a long career in **Commons,** many administrative appointments and, eventually, the title 1st Baron Holland (1763). Yet the highest office eluded him, possibly because his contemporaries thought him vastly ambitious but dedicated to his own narrow interests. Charles James Fox's support of liberal causes and inveterate hostility to **George III** made him a leader of the Whigs until his part in the **Fox–North coalition** damaged his credibility.

The grandfather, Sir Stephen Fox (1627–1716), made a great fortune as paymaster of the forces for Charles II. Henry, his son, gambled away his inheritance but recovered his fortune through a rich mistress. He entered Parliament (1735) and held a succession of lesser posts considered preliminary to the office of first minister. When that office fell vacant in 1754, Fox faced opposition not only from Lord Chancellor **Hardwicke** because of their quarrel over the Clandestine **Marriages Act** (1753), but also from the Prince of Wales's faction because of Fox's alliance with the **Duke of Cumberland.** Fox accepted leadership of the Commons in 1762 but declined the office of chief minister, perhaps because he was unwilling to fight his many enemies. As Paymaster General (1757–1765) he amassed a large fortune, much of it later gambled away by his sons.

Fox brought his spoiled but very likable son Charles James into Parliament when he was just 19 years old (1768), and the younger Fox soon proved a self-assured speaker. He held several junior appointments but, lacking the self-discipline to apply himself to routine work, was dismissed from the Treasury Board (1774). That same year, he declared his oppo-

Charles James Fox

sition to the **North** administration's policies toward the American colonies and thereafter supported the Americans' right to choose their own form of government. The competition between Fox and **Lord Shelburne** for leadership of the Whigs may have been a factor in Fox's decision to join his former opponent Lord North in the Fox–North coalition ministry (1783).

A self-centered man, Fox never anticipated the coalition's extremely adverse effect on public opinion. The enduring hostility of George III kept him from office for the next 20 years, which Fox spent as the chief opponent of the policies of Pitt the Younger. Fox's sympathy for the **French Revolution** cost him the friendship of **Edmund Burke** but did not extend to Napoleon, whom Fox opposed while he was Foreign Secretary (1806). Just before his death, Fox secured a resolution of Commons to abolish the **slave trade**, his last liberal cause.

Fox had great influence over his nephew, Henry Richard Fox, 3rd Baron Holland (1773–1840), who had lost his father while an infant. Holland devoted himself to continuing his uncle's policies and made his **London** home, **Holland House**, the intellectual center for the Whig party, a gathering place for up-and-coming men like **Brougham** and **Sydney Smith** as well as natural Whig successors like **Grey** and young **Lord John Russell**. Holland's writings provide the Whig view of the political events of his time.

P.J. Kulisheck

Bibliography

Holland, Henry Richard Fox, Baron. *Memoirs of the Whig Party during My Time.* 1852.
———. *Further Memoirs of the Whig Party.* 1905.
Ilchester, Earl of. *Henry Fox, First Lord Holland.* 1920.
Kriegel, Abraham, ed. *The Holland House Diaries, 1831–1840.* 1977.
Mitchell, Leslie G. *Charles James Fox and the Disintegration of the Whig Party 1782–1794.* 1971.
———. *Holland House.* 1980.
———. *Charles James Fox.* 1992.
Namier, Sir Lewis, and John Brooke, eds. *History of Parliament: The House of Commons, 1754–1790.* 3 vols. 1964.
Schweitzer, David. *Charles James Fox 1749–1806: A Bibliography.* 1991.
Sedgwick, Romney, ed. *History of Parliament: The House of Commons, 1715–1754.* 2 vols. 1970.
Thorne, R.G., ed. *History of Parliament: The House of Commons, 1790–1820.* 5 vols. 1986.

Fox-North Coalition

By allying their followings, former antagonists **Charles James Fox** and **Lord North** gained the majority in the **House of Commons** and ended the unpopular **Shelburne** ministry (April 1783). But the public and many politicians considered the resulting coalition administration unnatural, untrustworthy, and bound to fall. Previously, Fox, as leader of the **Rockingham** faction, had gained a reputation as a "man of the people" by severely criticizing North's policies, in particular those dealing with the revolt of the American colonies; but this new alliance with his former enemy made him seem completely unprincipled. **George III**'s intense personal dislike of Fox, and the opposition of **William Pitt the Younger**, led to the coalition's fall on the question of the **East India Company** bill (Dec. 1783).

P.J. Kulisheck

Bibliography

Cannon, John. *The Fox–North Coalition: Crisis of the Constitution, 1782–4.* 1969.
Mitchell, L.G. *Charles James Fox and the Disintegration of the Whig Party, 1782–1794.* 1971.
Valentine, Alan. *Lord North.* 1967.

Foxhunting

See Blood Sports

France

Textbooks on Europe's history from 1700 to 1850 identify two great contests that governed many lesser circumstances of that era. First, there was a protracted struggle between the 5 European great powers—France, Britain, Prussia, Austria, and Russia. France was at the middle of this contest, aggressively challenging her neighbors. Typically in 1756 one Englishman described France as "this ambitious, perfidious, restless, bigoted, persecuting, plundering Power, which has long been the common Disturber of the western World, and as long struggled for Universal Monarchy." France's powerful armies made her the greatest land power of the age, the only one able to take on all her enemies simultaneously. Allied with Bour-

Lord Uxbridge's regiment charging the French, 1815

bon Spain, she was also able to command the largest naval forces in Europe. Moreover, she was, with the exception of Russia, the largest and most populous of the great powers, with a citizenry and domestic market three times larger than Britain's, and in 1750 an empire larger, too.

France also had very important intangible strengths. French was the accepted language of **diplomacy**. The productions of French intellectuals and artists were admired everywhere. French literary standards were imported into every country. France's philosophers generated an attractive francophilic cosmopolitanism that few educated foreigners could resist. Beside all this, as the German historian Leopold von Ranke (1795–1886) observed, lay the cultural prestige of the French capital:

> Paris was the capital of Europe. She wielded a dominion as did no other city, over language, over custom, and particularly over the world of fashion and the ruling classes. Here was the center of the community of Europe.

Whether or not France's arms triumphed, there was always her allure and cultural glamor to sap foreign resistance. It is no exaggeration to say that French culture colonized Europe and threatened the identities and independent development of many smaller nations. One English traveler remarked in 1781 that "few nations in Europe have retained their original characters. They have almost all adopted the French fashions and customs."

England, after a hesitant start, increasingly played the spoiler, emerging as France's inveterate foe. Earlier she had been more submissive. In the 17th century her kings, the later Stuarts, cousins of the French King Louis XIV (1638–1715), had been his paid supporters. But from 1689 on, when William III, Louis's most implacable European foe, took charge of English military policy, the two powers went into battle head-to-head. They were at **war** with each other nearly half the time between 1689 and 1815. The wars raged not only in Europe but in the imperial dominions of the two nations—in the **West Indies**, **North America**, and **India**. For the English there was another geographic frontier in this long struggle, one which deeply affected the national consciousness. England, with an insignificant **army**, was no threat to French power in France. But the reverse was not true. France repeatedly threatened the English homeland. There were invasion scares and actual French launchings of invasions in 1744–1746, 1759, 1779, 1796–1798, and 1803–1805. France continually conspired with disaffected men in **Scotland**, **Ireland**, and even England itself to overthrow English dominance there. Moreover, France was a serious economic threat. In the first half of the 18th century she out-produced Britain not only in luxury goods, a French specialty, but in basic products such as **iron** and **cotton**. In 1756 French international dominance seemed secure and destined to grow greater every year. Yet its very magnitude was beginning to provoke unprecedented British efforts of competition, self-definition, and achievement.

The second great historic contest of the period was apparently unrelated to this long military, economic, imperial, and cultural struggle for supremacy. It was a social contest, operating not between nations but between classes within them. The period 1700–1850 saw a great historic process of modernization at work in which an essentially rural, agrarian, and aristocratic European society gave way to an increasingly urban, industrial, and democratic one. In many ways the scene of 1850 marked a complete transformation of that of 1700. This transformation advanced more speedily in England than anywhere else. In France and other countries, "absolutist" kings during the period 1600–1750 had negotiated deals with their **aristocracies**, receiving from them obeisance and official service in return for greater authority over everyone else. In France the 18th century was still overwhelmingly the age of aristocracy. There, until at least the 1780s, the "bourgeois gentleman" was still nearly an impossibility and an object of ridicule. In England, however, the merchants, professionals, and artist–intellectuals of the **middle class** began shedding their inhibitions from as early as the 1740s. While the English aristocracy was just as effective as those on the Continent, indeed richer, more concentrated, and hardly less determined to preserve its exclusiveness and privileges, the English middle classes were increasingly aggressive in demanding change.

Hence already by 1760 a struggle that would ultimately become not only social and economic but cultural and political had begun to form in England. It was natural for noblemen and "people of fashion" to look to France for cultural support in this struggle, to emulate elegant French **manners**, and to hold up France as a cultural and intellectual model to their countrymen. It was just as natural for England's bourgeois intellectuals, slowly and ambivalently discarding the francophilic cosmopolitanism of the era, to become increasingly anti–French and, as time passed, unapologetically chauvinistic. The social differentiation of cultural opinion and growing clash in domestic values was captured in a comment in the *Gentleman's Magazine* of 1766:

> Those who have conversed with persons of different ranks, that have been in France, will find the account favourable, in proportion as their rank is high. The man of fashion is always captivated with his journey to France; the man who moves in a lower sphere always disgusted.

Thus gradually the two great contests of the era became merged in the powerful nationalist ideologies that began to flourish everywhere. With aristocratic supremacy linked to cosmopolitan and French cultural values, bourgeois self-assertion became allied to intense nationalist sentiment and rhetoric. Students of modernization in Germany, Russia, and elsewhere have noted these convergences, but it was English artist–intellectuals who fashioned the great ideological prototype employed in them all. In essence, a domestic "smear campaign" was employed, calculated to repudiate aristocratic authority by associating it with submission to foreign (French) standards. The mixture of anti–French with anti–aristocratic moral and social criticism, evident in English **novels**, **sermons**, **tracts**, **travel books**, and various manifestations of **political thought**, grew steadily until it became formulaic and engrained by the 1780s. A Gallic stereotype, a travestied profile of "the French Character," was generated, which became an instrument of condemnation directed against the **fashions**, **morals**, tastes, and political authority of the English upper classes. According to this, the esteemed French values were nothing but dishonesty, moral corruption, intellectual imitativeness, insincerity, and artificiality of manner. It did not matter that this stereotype was a mean **caricature** of "Frenchness," or that some supposedly "French" characteristics were no less English than French. All that mattered was that the device was successful.

This stereotype became an important component in a comprehensive critique of the English upper classes. What formerly had helped to underline their aristocratic exclusiveness and superiority was now employed against them—their proficiency in French, their love of Paris, their infection by "French" deism and irreligion, their decadent "French" manners and superficial "French" intellectual pursuits, their alleged descent from the dreadful French "Normans" rather than the hardy and bluff Germanic Anglo-Saxons. In the period 1760–1790 the supposedly conspicuous decadence of a few notorious Francophiles such as the **Earl of Chesterfield** and **Charles James Fox** simply confirmed the stereotype.

Modern history exhibits many such smear campaigns. The Pope, the Spanish, the **Jacobites**, and others had all taken their turn in the dock, until the smears were no longer useful or believable. The smear, the "big lie," is a cannon in the armory of propaganda tricks. But until 1789 the anti–Gallic campaign, though well-rounded, was not really very influential because of the continuing dominance of aristocratic cultural leadership. Its most evident practical effects were simply to help reform and correct the education of upper-class boys and to influence national moral tastes and political preferences. And then came the **French Revolution**. What gave tremendous force and permanent significance to the anti–Gallic smear campaign was completely unexpected—the revolutionary events in France and their military aftermath, the **French Revolutionary and Napoleonic Wars**. These events not only ratified the earlier anti–French campaign but guaranteed 25 more years of it under extremely emotional circumstances—circumstances of national emergency. Examination of English propaganda during this long period reveals that the French Revolution was blamed, however irrationally, on the decadent French aristocracy and its "soulless" philosophy of reason and unbelief, that Jacobin popular excesses were traced back to the same source, and that a wholesale transformation of English thought, morality, and social manners was demanded *in England* as a decontaminant before the same dreadful influences "from a neighbouring country" should cause disaster in Britain as well.

The propaganda campaign, always recommending what was presented as an English (but also bourgeois) set of values in contrast to a French (but also aristocratic) one, continued long after 1815 and the period of war that gave it such immediacy and force. **Evangelicals** aiming to reform Christian faith found it of inestimable value. **Romantic** writers aiming to reshape national literary attitudes framed their ideas as a national liberation from "the yoke of French taste." Most important of all, moral condemnation of a travestied "France" became the prime tool in transforming domestic manners and morals. Magazine articles for many years after 1815 still contained the sharpened pairs of moral antithesis between "English" and "French" traits—"A woman who swerves from her sex's point of honour in England, is aware that she has committed an unpardonable offense. . . . But it is very different in France. A female there . . . experiences little, if any alteration, in consequence of the violation of her person." "The French act from feeling, and the British from principle," and so on. If it was true, as Edward Bulwer-Lytton (1803–1873) remarked in his *England and the English* (1833), that "*we no longer hate the French,*" then it was only because 50 years of anti-French propaganda had so greatly helped to transform the domestic value system that it was no longer needed any more than Jacobitism was. In 1833, Victorian values were already in place. The Age of Mr. Podsnap, when a thing could be flatly dismissed because it was "Not English," had already begun. It was now the turn not of the French aristocracy but of the English middle class to dictate international fashions and ideas.

Gerald Newman

Bibliography

Andrews, John. *A Comparative View of the French and English Nations, in Their Manners, Politics, and Literature.* 1785.

Brown, John. *An Estimate of the Manners and Principles of the Times.* 2 vols. 6th ed., 1757.

Chartier, Roger. "Intellectual History or Sociocultural History? The French Trajectories," in Dominick LaCapra and Steven L. Kaplan, eds., *Modern European Intellectual History: Reappraisals and New Perspectives.* 1982.

Crouzet, F. "England and France in the Eighteenth Century: A Comparative Analysis of Two Economic Growths," in R.M. Hartwell, ed., *The Causes of the Industrial Revolution in England.* 1967.

Faber, Richard. *French and English.* 1975.

Kiernan, V. "Nationalist Movements and Social Classes," in A.D. Smith, ed., *Nationalist Movements.* 1976.

Labatut, Jean-Pierre. *Les noblesses Européenes: de la fin du XVe siècle à la fin du XVIIe siècle.* 1978.

Newman, Gerald. *The Rise of English Nationalism: A Cultural History, 1740–1830.* 1987.

Porter, Roy, and Mikulas Teich, eds. *The Enlightenment in National Context.* 1981.

Texte, Joseph. *Jean-Jacques Rousseau and the Cosmopolitan Spirit in Literature: A Study of the Literary Relations between France and England during the Eighteenth Century.* Trans. J.S. Matthews. 1899.

See also Fashion; Nationalism and Patriotism

Franchise

See Elections and the Franchise

Franklin, Benjamin (1706–1790)

Before the **War of American Independence** made **George Washington** famous, Franklin was the best-known citizen of the British **Empire**. Printer, publisher, author, inventor, scientist, politician, **diplomat**, and quintessential representative of the **Enlightenment**, he knew many of the great men of Britain, **France**, and America, and in England was particularly intimate with reform-minded **commonwealthmen** in **London** and the progressive **Lunar Society** of Birmingham.

He was born in Boston, Massachusetts, the tenth son in a family of 17 children, his father an immigrant from Ecton (Northamptonshire). Largely self-educated, Franklin was apprenticed at age 12 to his brother James, a printer. In this profession he gained wealth and reputation. He followed this profession until 1723 in Boston, in 1724–1726 in London, and then until 1748 in Philadelphia, where he published the *Pennsylvania Gazette* and *Poor Richard's Almanac.* He also demonstrated his enthusiasm for civic improvement and the spread of knowledge, founding the Library Company of Philadelphia (1731), the Union Fire Company (1736), and the American Philosophical Society (1744).

Retiring from business at age 42, Franklin devoted himself to scientific investigation. His interest in "electrical fire" produced the series of experiments (including that of capturing electrical energy from clouds during a thunderstorm through the use of a kite) that resulted in his book, *Experiments*

Benjamin Franklin

and Observations on Electricity (1751). In this he laid out the theory of positive and negative charges that gained him respect as a scientist on both sides of the Atlantic. His interests remained practical, however, and he gained equal fame for his inventions, including the "Franklin" stove, bifocal spectacles, and the lightning rod.

From the 1750s to the 1770s Franklin played an important role as a go-between, linking colonial opinion with British governmental thinking, and even finding himself accused by extremists on one side of colluding with the other. His activities were many. He attempted unsuccessfully to organize a defensive "Plan of Union" between the colonies and the central government to deal with French and Indian difficulties on the colonies' borders (1754). He represented the Pennsylvania legislature in London (1757–1762, 1764) in attempts to negotiate changes in taxation and in that colony's charter. In 1760–1763 he was important in recommending British acquisition of **Canada** at the close of the **Seven Years' War**. He made a dramatic appearance in the **Commons** to call for repeal of the **Stamp Act**, "the mother of mischief" as he called it, urging England instead to pursue a union with the colonies similar to that forged earlier with **Scotland** (1766). During 1765–1775 he lived mostly in London, acting as agent for not only Pennsylvania but three other colonies as well, all the while appealing in private and in public (he wrote more than 100 **newspaper** articles) for more understanding and conciliatory policies to avert an **American Revolution**.

Embittered by the turn of events, in 1775 he departed London for Philadelphia, changing entirely from peacemaker to colonial patriot. Franklin played an important role in the independence struggle, serving as a member of the Second Continental Congress, as the head of the American delegation to France, and finally as a negotiator of the **Treaty of Paris** (1783). To the end of his life he remained an influential public figure, serving at age 81 as a member of the Constitutional Convention of 1787.

David Sloan

Bibliography

Ketcham, Ralph. *Benjamin Franklin.* 1966.

Labaree, Leonard W., et al., eds. *The Papers of Benjamin Franklin.* 1959–.

Lopez, Claude-Anne, and Eugenia W. Herbert. *The Private Franklin: The Man and His Family.* 1975.

Van Doren, Carl. *Benjamin Franklin.* 1938.

Wright, Esmond. *Franklin of Philadelphia.* 1986.

Wright, Esmond, et al. "Benjamin Franklin: A Reassessment." *Pennsylvania Magazine of History and Biography.* Vol. 111, pp. 435–560.

See also Electricity

Franklin, Sir John (1786–1847)

Later famous as an explorer, Franklin when young saw naval action at Copenhagen, Trafalgar, and New Orleans during the **Napoleonic Wars**. He then assisted his cousin, Matthew Flinders (1774–1814), in surveying the coasts of **Australia**,

Sir John Franklin

where he displayed great skill as a navigator. Accompanying an abortive expedition to reach the North Pole via Spitsbergen (1818) instilled in him a fascination with the Arctic; he led two overland expeditions to chart the cold northern coastline of **North America** (1819–1822, 1825–1827).

Despite great hardships on the first expedition, including being reduced to eating his frozen boots, he gained success and fame. Following his distinguished lieutenant governorship of Van Diemen's Land (Tasmania) in 1837–1843, he volunteered to lead yet another Arctic attempt by sea to discover the Northwest Passage (1845). The mysterious disappearance (and, as it turned out, icy death) of his entire 138-man crew inspired more than two dozen international relief expeditions afterward and became the leading mystery and tragic emblem of Arctic **exploration**.

N. Merrill Distad

Bibliography

Beattie, Owen, and John Geiger. *Frozen in Time: Unlocking the Secrets of the Franklin Expedition.* 1988.

Berton, Pierre. *Arctic Grail: The Quest for the North West Passage and the North Pole, 1818–1909.* 1988.

Franklin, Sir John. *Narrative of a Journey to the Shores of the Polar Sea, in the Years 1819–20–21–22.* 1824.

———. *Narrative of a Second Expedition to the Shores of the Polar Sea, in the Years 1825, 1826, and 1827.* 1828.

Neatby, Leslie H. *The Search for Franklin.* 1970.

Owen, Roderick. *The Fate of Franklin.* 1978.

Woodman, David C. *Unravelling the Franklin Mystery: Inuit Testimony.* 1991.

See also Cartography; Parry, William Edward; Ross, Sir James Clark; Ross, Sir John

Frederick, Duke of York

Frederick, Duke of York (1763–1827)

The second son of **King George III**, York was commander-in-chief of the **army** and organizer of army reforms. His command of British forces in Flanders at the beginning of the **French Revolutionary and Napoleonic Wars** (1792–1795) ended in retreat and withdrawal. His generalship showed him adept at making the best out of adverse circumstances, but only fair at creating good ones.

After becoming Field-Marshall (1795) and Commander-in-Chief (1798), York set regulations requiring parliamentarians to appoint experienced soldiers to commissions. He established the schools that later became the Royal Military College and the Staff College. In 1809, facing accusations that he supplied commissions on the advice of a former lover, Mrs. Mary Ann Clarke, he resigned his office. Shortly before his death he joined the political struggle against **Catholic emancipation.**

Robert D. McJimsey

Bibliography

Burne, Alfred H. *The Noble Duke of York.* 1949.
Fulford, Roger. *The Royal Dukes.* 1949.
Sullivan, A.E. "The Duke of York and Major Hogan." *Army Quarterly.* Vol. 91, pp. 244–251.

See also Education, Military

Frederick, Prince of Wales (1707–1751)

The eldest son of **King George II** became a patron of the arts and a sponsor of **Whig** politicians opposing his father's ministers. A final break with his father resulted from personality conflicts, his father's refusal to sanction his marriage to the Princess Royal of Prussia (1730), and the refusal of the king and his prime minister, **Robert Walpole**, whom Frederick despised, to increase financial support for Frederick's household (1737), a hothouse of **opposition** politics.

Frederick struck back by publishing *The History of Prince Titi* (1736). Detailing his alleged misfortunes and accusing his parents of seeking to disinherit him, this work caused a publishing sensation. Opposition politicians even sponsored a stage production of it. To those who joined his "**Leicester House**" faction the prince offered the respectability of service to the royal heir and the prospect of government office under the future monarch. Frederick, however, preceded his father to the grave by 9 years.

The prince's circle of patronage included **William Kent, Thomas Gainsborough, George Frideric Handel, Jonathan Swift,** and **Alexander Pope.** His collections of **paintings, sculpture,** and decorative objects marked him as one of the most significant patrons of his age. Yet ironically his most significant historical legacy might have been the sheer detestation of George II which he handed on to his own son, **George III** who, when he took power in 1760, set out to repudiate his dead grandfather's ministers and policies.

Robert D. McJimsey

Bibliography

Edwards, Averyl. *Frederick Louis: Prince of Wales.* 1947.
Harris, Robert. *A Patriot Press: National Politics and the London Press in the 1740s.* 1993.

Frederick, Prince of Wales

Jones, Stephen. "Frederick, Prince of Wales: A Patron of the Rococo," in Charles Hind, ed., *Rococo in England: A Symposium.* 1986.

Newman, A.N. "Communication: The Political Patronage of Frederick Lewis, Prince of Wales." *The Historical Journal.* Vol. 1, pp. 68–75.

Shipley, John B. "James Ralph, Prince Titi, and the Black Box of Frederick, Prince of Wales." *Bulletin of the New York Public Library.* Vol. 71, pp. 143–157.

Freemasons

Freemasons originated with organizations of working masons, who actually designed and constructed buildings. Speculative masonry began in early-18th-century England in a private fraternal organization concerned with the intellectual construction of God's master plan as revealed in the Bible and the "mysteries" of antiquity. Its goal was to create a society which realized the ideals of freedom, justice, and **religious toleration**.

The Freemasons formed a secret society whose most intimate documents were protected from outsiders. Their history began in 1717 when four separate Masonic units ("lodges") united to form the Grand Lodge of London, the parent of all subsequent Masonic groups. Grand Lodges in **Ireland** (1725) and **Scotland** (1736) soon followed, and the organization spread quickly to the Continent. The term *Free and Accepted Mason* soon referred only to those members who adhered to the *Old Charges* (1723), or articles of belief and ritual, that the Grand Lodge of London had proclaimed.

The masons claimed ancestry among the ancient Egyptians and Greeks, and even maintained that the *Book of Constitutions* (1723) of the original London Grand Lodge had a biblical forerunner, unhappily lost. Their claims reflected a desire to establish their legitimacy and significance. So did their symbols, taken from sources both secular and religious. For example, from the secular, the three levels of membership reflect the medieval working-class guild structure—a mason is, in turn, apprentice, journeyman, and master; and from the religious, frequent references, for example, to the construction of Solomon's Temple, point to the first temple built for the one God of Christianity.

Freemasonry's greatest contribution to Hanoverian culture was in its social openness and tendency toward unrestricted thought. Although membership was limited to men (women were later consigned to "Lodges of Adoption"), participation was theoretically restricted neither by religious belief nor class standing. Members included noted intellectuals such as **J.T. Desaguliers**, members of the nobility such as the **Duke of Cumberland** and **Frederick, Prince of Wales**, many wealthy **merchants**, and a number of artists.

Part of the "work" freemasons assigned themselves was the creation of a climate of religious and personal tolerance in which hate and injustice would cease to exist. Lodge meetings included discussions of practical philosophy, ethics, politics, and, especially, religious matters. This earned masonry its most ardent enemy, the **Church of England**, which looked with alarm on such independent gatherings of open-minded **freethinkers**.

Joseph T. Malloy

Bibliography

Baigent, Michael, and Richard Leigh. *The Temple and the Lodge.* 1989.

Clawson, Mary Ann. *Constructing Brotherhood: Class, Gender, and Fraternalism.* 1989.

Haywood, Harry Le Roy. *Freemasonry and Catholicism.* 1943.

Hellmuth, Eckhart, ed. *The Transformation of Political Culture: England and Germany in the Late-Eighteenth Century.* 1990.

Jacob, Margaret C. *The Radical Enlightenment: Pantheists, Freemasons and Republicans.* 1981.

———. *Living the Enlightenment: Freemasonry and Politics in Eighteenth-Century Europe.* 1991.

Lemay, J.A. Leo, ed. *Deism, Masonry, and the Enlightenment.* 1987.

Stevenson, David. *The Origins of Freemasonry: Scotland's Century, 1590–1710.* 1988.

Freethinkers and Freethought

Freethinkers referred primarily to all those who departed from the official doctrines of the **Church of England**, and secondarily to those who believed in autonomous reason rather than faith alone to discern religious and moral truths. There were many of these in the Hanoverian age, which coincided with the Age of Reason in Europe.

In the early 18th century the most influential freethinkers were the Deists, who rejected revelation, relied on natural religion, and professed belief in general principles uniting all religions. After a period of vigor, **deism** went into decline by the 1740s, giving way to various forms of Arianism and Socinianism, including **Unitarianism**. All three of these, unlike the major dissenting sects, were anti–Trinitarian: Arianism treated Christ as subordinate to the Father; Socinianism and Unitarianism essentially denied His divinity altogether, treating Him chiefly as a moral exemplar. All these doctrines were deemed subversive because they repudiated Anglican belief in Christ's Atonement, the accessibility to all of salvation, and Christ's institution of a priesthood.

Though greatly in the minority, and sharing condemnation from Anglicans and some **dissenters** as well, freethinkers did not often agree with each other, either. Arians such as **Samuel Clarke** and **William Whiston**, believing in revelation, were fierce opponents of deists such as **John Toland** and **Matthew Tindal**.

Freethinking implied anticlericalism and thus, in a country with an established church, suggested treason. England's Blasphemy Act (1697) silenced many writers, encouraging freethinkers to publish anonymously. Their numbers were never large, and many were linked by marriage, social ties, dissenting affiliations, radical **commonwealthmen** political views, and understandably strong feelings in favor of **religious toleration**. Some publications of the early 18th century expounding their position were Anthony Collins's (1676–1729) *Discourse of Free-Thinking* (1713), and *The Freethinker,* a **periodical** attributed to Ambrose Philips (1675–1749).

By 1714, writers were waging a fierce, albeit mostly anonymous, printed debate against revelation. **Bernard de Mandeville** wrote *Free Thoughts on Religion* (1720), Thomas Woolston (1670–1733) the popular *Discourses on Miracles* (1726–1728), and Matthew Tindal *Christianity as Old as Creation* (1730), "the deists' Bible." Most of these books sold in the tens of thousands and elicited impassioned responses. Many freethinking publications were banned when discovered, and authors who signed their works were imprisoned. Woolston, convicted of blasphemy (1729), was imprisoned, and in 1763 Peter Annet (1693–1769), a deist, was imprisoned for criticizing Old Testament history. In 1736 **Bishop George Berkeley** called (unsuccessfully) for the death penalty against freethinkers and blasphemers, including members of secret societies as well as deists in his definition of intellectual subversives.

Freethinkers considered secret societies necessary because freethought could lead to ostracism, the pillory, or imprisonment. The **freemasons** revived their secret society, building a Grand Lodge in **London** in 1717. Though not a religious group as such, they believed in a pattern of universal truth that was compatible with the tenets of freethought. Another group, which included some **Latitudinarians** and deists, was more conventionally religious, insisting that Christianity should be based on Christ's teachings rather than dogma; some even called themselves Christian deists.

The list of British freethinkers, in the broadest sense of the word, includes the names of such eminent writers as **John Locke, Lord Bolingbroke, Edward Gibbon, David Hume,** and **Percy Bysshe Shelley.** Their theological opponents included **Joseph Addison, Richard Steele, Jonathan Swift, Alexander Pope,** and **William Warburton.** While Low Church **Whigs** sought to rehabilitate the term *freethinker* and render it acceptable to churchmen as distinguishable from *deist,* others flatly argued that Christianity and freethought were incompatible.

While the latter 18th century saw fewer contributions to freethinking theory, the rationalistic influences of the **Enlightenment,** together with the growth of more assertive attitudes by dissenters and by **rational dissent,** were disposing more people toward its general outlook—though at the same time provoking a **religious revival** among believers. By the 1790s many freethinkers, inspired partly by the **French Revolution,** were inclined to embrace agnosticism, political radicalism, and even revolution. The most influential writer here was **Thomas Paine,** whose deistic *The Age of Reason* (1794, 1796), written in a plain English style easily understood by the common man, violently attacked the Christian scheme of salvation and the Bible. For this he, as well as his **publishers and booksellers,** were prosecuted.

Paine's publishers, including **Richard Carlile,** continued to face persecution and imprisonment as late as 1819. The strong connection between freethought and **radicalism** can be seen in the Blasphemous and Seditious Libels Act (1820), aimed at silencing the radical press. During the remainder of the 19th century such Victorian secularists as Charles Bradlaugh (1833–1891) developed the social consciousness of freethinkers to include women's suffrage, national education, and trade unionism.

Carole S. Fungaroli

Bibliography

Armstrong, Anthony. *The Church of England, the Methodists and Society 1700–1850.* 1973.

Blanshard, Paul, ed. *Classics of Free Thought.* 1977.

Byrne, Peter. *Natural Religion and the Nature of Religion: The Legacy of Deism.* 1989.

LeMay, J.A.L., ed. *Deism, Masonry, and the Enlightenment.* 1987.

Royle, Edward, ed. *The Infidel Tradition from Paine to Bradlaugh.* 1976.

Tribe, David. *One Hundred Years of Freethought.* 1967.

See also Censorship

French and Indian War

See Seven Years' War

French Revolution (1789)

The French Revolution was one of the defining events of modern world civilization, whose effects in even China and Latin America have been detailed. Though it began in Paris, it also became one of the central events shaping British civilization at home and in the **Empire.** Among the English, who greeted it with some enthusiasm before turning to wage **war** for 22 years in an attempt to undo it, its impact was all-pervasive but complicated.

Initial reactions were favorable to the fall of the Bastille (July 1789) and the French National Assembly's proclamations of human rights, religious toleration, the abolition of feudalism, and the advent of popular self-government. In 1789–1792 idealistic young writers like **Wordsworth** crossed the Channel to witness the revolution firsthand and came home filled with democratic and republican ideas. Older **radicals** such as **Horne Tooke** and **Major John Cartwright,** veterans of the parliamentary reform battles of 1769–1783, hopefully restarted the **Society for Constitutional Information** and redoubled their efforts of **nationalist** organization and propaganda. The radical **dissenters,** their erstwhile friends and collaborators, such men as **Richard Price** and **Joseph Priestley,** also intensified their efforts to remove dissenters' civil disabilities, signed petitions, and applauded the more universalist prorevolutionary propaganda produced by **Tom Paine, Mary Wollstonecraft,** and **William Godwin;** dissenting businessmen like **Josiah Wedgwood** expected good things from "the French example" also.

Antislavery stalwarts like **Granville Sharp** and **Thomas Clarkson** saw new opportunities for freedom in general. In Parliament, aristocratic **Whigs** applauded the revolution, pronounced it the French version of the **Glorious Revolution,** and began a **Society of Friends of the People** (1792) to convert enthusiasm for it into new political strength for themselves. Artisans, **craftsmen**, and workingmen formed the **London Corresponding Society** (LCS) to educate the lower classes and agitate in favor of radical reform of **elections and the franchise**. There was a flurry of patriotic celebrations of liberty, congratulatory addresses to the French, and "association" between local societies that sprang up in **cities** and **provincial towns**. Young men in **Dublin** like **Wolfe Tone** and in **Edinburgh** like **Thomas Muir** founded societies of "Friends of the People" and corresponded with like-minded enthusiasts in Britain, **France**, and elsewhere. Every domestic movement for progressive change was given new impetus but also an odd new twist. For whereas reformers earlier had always vaunted their patriotism, making it a moral platform from which to bombard their enemies in government, they now relinquished that advantage and sang incautiously the praises of France, Britain's historic enemy.

The revolution had taken everyone off guard. **Edward Gibbon**, an expert on historical decline, had just invested in French government bonds. Antirevolutionary feeling thus began slowly. **Edmund Burke**, though a lonely voice in 1790, invoked patriotic sentiment *against* political reform in his *Reflections on the Revolution in France* and provided an interpretative context within which the revolution appeared to be a denial not only of normal intellectual, **moral**, and political virtues but of civilization itself. The Whig party began to split, Burke and **Portland** leading the majority away from the Francophile **Fox** and **Grey** in support of the tougher line taken by the government of **Pitt the Younger**.

Strange things happened in the confusion. Developments that might have taken decades were telescoped into a few years. The **Tory** party, armed with Burke's rhetoric purloined from the older patriotic radicalism, began its long, slow revival. Life became more exciting but also more dangerous. Anglican magistrates fomented hostility against the dissenters, terrible **riots** erupted in July 1791 against celebrations of Bastille Day, the government counseled local magistrates to be less restrained in controlling meetings (May 1792); Paine and others were condemned as seditious libelers; **publishers** were arrested. When, beginning in September 1792, the French massacred more than 1,000 aristocrats in a week, deposed their king, proclaimed a republic, announced their intention to help peoples everywhere overthrow tyranny, executed Louis XVI (January 1793), and went to war with Britain (February 1793), the die was cast.

Pitt's government in 1793–1794, its hand strengthened by war against the Jacobin power and alarmed by the domestic meeting of a radical "British Convention" seemingly designed to bypass Parliament itself (Edinburgh, October 1793), prosecuted Muir and the leaders of the LCS, tightened the definition of sedition in a traitorous correspondence act, and suspended Habeas Corpus to permit indefinite detention of political prisoners. The country became polarized. Strong-minded men on both sides became more extreme, while the fainthearted retreated; the undoctrinaire headed for the closet. Wordsworth cheered the fall of Robespierre (1794) and traded his Francophilism for English patriotism. **Hardy**, the shoemaker founder of the LCS, though acquitted of treason, shrank from agitation. **Place**, another London radical, deplored large meetings and threatening tactics.

Yet in 1795, fueled by poor harvests and increasing wartime dislocation of **trade**, furious food riots erupted in Nottingham and Coventry, and monster demonstrations in London—the crowds, numbering 100,000 or more people, crying "No war! No famine! No Pitt! No King!" **George III**'s coach was stoned, 10 Downing Street's windows were attacked. Anticlerical **freethinking** began to color radical literature. In the cabinet the belief grew that radical organizations were conspiring to assist a French invasion of England. Parliament passed the "Two Acts" (December 1795), landmarks of repression, which bound and gagged its critics: one redefined the law of treason to criminalize criticism of the **Constitution** and coercion of Parliament as well as the aiding of invaders or conspirers against the king; the other prohibited for 3 years any unlicensed political lectures or gatherings of more than 50 people. In effect, reformers were required to shut down or move operations underground.

These drastic measures had the desired effect, paired as they were with a continuing fear of French invasion, the basic conservatism of the propertied classes, the natural recrudescence of Gallophobia, and the predictable flourishing of **loyalist** associations throughout the country—and, springing from them, volunteer military associations that burgeoned in nearly every county and town. Repressed, intimidated, ideologically outmaneuvered, and hugely outnumbered by their progovernment opponents from 1796 on, the reform organizations disintegrated; reform could now be discussed only in Parliament. Although Grey unsuccessfully introduced a reform bill in 1797, naval **mutinies** the same year and the **Irish Rebellion** (1798) helped pave the way for a complete outlawing of organized radical politics. This was finally accomplished by a Newspaper Publication Act (1798) imposing closer supervision of the press, a Corresponding Societies Act (1799) under which all such societies throughout the British Isles were "hereby utterly suppressed and prohibited, as being unlawful Combinations and Confederacies against the Government of our Sovereign Lord the King," and the two famous **Combination Acts** (1799, 1800) that criminalized societies working to secure better **hours, wages and working conditions**.

The political side of the revolution's impact thus became increasingly contingent upon the French Revolutionary and **Napoleonic Wars** that lasted until 1815. Britain found herself in a long crusade that was both antirevolutionary and anti-French. The legacy of this confused double effort (naturally exploited as long as possible to keep patriotism on the side of oligarchical rule) was the derailment of political reform until the latter 1820s, the country continuing under the same ultraconservative rulers who won the war. The liberal Whigs, friends of civil rights though not of fundamental constitutional change, remained in the wilderness until 1830. But, compared to the situation before 1789, there was at least a new seriousness and public-spiritedness about aristocratic political leadership. There was also an artificial prolongation lasting up to the early 1820s of **middle-class** support for the unreformed Constitution, and an advancement of working-class self-consciousness. Other political effects included the Irish **Act of Union** (1800) with all its unhappy consequences.

The revolution and the war to defeat it imposed derailments, detours, and distortional patterns on all aspects of national life from 1789 to 1830. It cost the country an estimated £1,650,000,000 and brought overhaul of the **tax** system. It resulted in expansions of the **army** and **navy** by multipliers of 6 and 8, respectively. It enlarged the Empire and solidified national pride through France's defeat. It helped to forge closer bonds between the ethnic constituents of the United Kingdom. In **agriculture** it led to rapid expansion and rising prices, followed by the unpopular **Corn Laws** (1815) to preserve agricultural gains. Economically it greatly stimulated the **Industrial Revolution** while permitting **entrepreneurs** to exploit repressive legislation for their own ends against industrial combinations. It affected domestic life by stimulating demands for **Sunday schools** and more effective **elementary education**. It impacted social welfare by prompting adoption of the **Speenhamland System**. In religion it provided a springboard for the rise of **Evangelicalism** by enabling its propagandists, who churned out cheap **tracts**, to terrify respectable people over the supposed political consequences "in a neighbouring country" of unbelief, and hence to ensure acceptance of the severe new manners and morals they grimly handed down while climbing to new positions of influence.

Today, the main avenue to the revolution's impact on British life is through the study of literature and **biography**. In literature the revolution famously energized **poetry** by stimulating Britain's **Romantics** to find ways to combine their "French" universalism with their "English" patriotic localism, and after 1800 it also gave tremendous new sophistication and bite to **literary criticism** by involving it, in the new **periodical** literature, in political and social animosities bred under these tangled political and intellectual conditions. The revolution affected people deeply and personally. To read the biographies and **letters** of many who lived then is to become impressed with the unusual excitement, danger, **travel**, risk, contradictoriness, and richness of their human experiences. It was an unusual era; many lived very unusual lives. Wordworth, looking back, remembered it so: "Bliss was it in that dawn to be alive, / But to be young was very heaven!"

Gerald Newman

Bibliography

Christie, Ian R. *Stress and Stability in Late Eighteenth-Century Britain: Reflections on the British Avoidance of Revolution.* 1986.

Colley, Linda. *Britons: Forging the Nation 1707–1837.* 1992.

Cone, Carl B. *The English Jacobins: Reformers in Late 18th Century England.* 1968.

Crossely, Ceri, and Ian Small, eds. *The French Revolution and British Culture.* 1989.

Dickinson, H.T. *British Radicalism and the French Revolution, 1789–1815.* 1985.

Dickinson, H.T., ed. *Britain and the French Revolution, 1789–1815.* 1989.

Elliott, Marianne. *Partners in Revolution: The United Irishmen and France.* 1982.

Goodwin, Albert. *The Friends of Liberty: The English Democratic Movement in the Age of the French Revolution.* 1979.

Hone, J. Ann. *For the Cause of Truth: Radicalism in London, 1796–1821.* 1982.

Kelly, Gary. *Women, Writing, and Revolution: 1790–1827.* 1993.

Kiernan, V. "Evangelicalism and the French Revolution." *Past and Present.* Vol. 1, pp. 44–56.

Mee, Jon. *Dangerous Enthusiasm: William Blake and the Culture of Radicalism in the 1790s.* 1992.

Meikle, Henry W. *Scotland and the French Revolution.* 1969.

Newman, Gerald. *The Rise of English Nationalism: A Cultural History, 1740–1830.* 1987.

Olsen, Gerald Wayne, ed. *Religion and Revolution in Early-Industrial England: The Halévy Thesis and Its Critics.* 1990.

Pakenham, Frank. *The Story of the Great Irish Rebellion of 1798.* 1969.

Philp, Mark. *The French Revolution and British Popular Politics.* 1991.

Stevenson, John. *Popular Disturbances in England, 1700–1832.* 2nd ed. 1992.

Thompson, E.P. *The Making of the English Working Class.* 1963.

Williams, Gwyn A. *Artisans and Sans-Culottes.* 1968.

French Revolutionary and Napoleonic Wars (1792–1815)

Europe experienced 23 years of war set in motion by the French Revolution when France's new government, repelling an Austro–Prussian attack (1792), went on to invade the Austrian Netherlands. Britain hesitantly joined the First Coalition of antirevolutionary European states (February 1793), focusing chiefly on seizing French **West Indian** possessions. This costly colonial campaign required most of Britain's regular **army**, leaving few troops available for Continental service and contributing to the defeat of the Duke of York's Low Countries Campaign (1794–1795), loss of the captured port of Toulon (1793), and the disintegration of the coalition (1797). France thus won the first round, spreading her ideas and control into the Low Countries, Switzerland, Italy, and the Rhineland.

With **France** victorious and her revolutionary fervor hardening into old-style thirst for conquest and annexation, Britain in the late 1790s faced the threat of invasion and also of **Irish rebellions** assisted by France. Unable to strike the foe on land, the **navy** combined defensive tactics with offense by tightly blockading France's ports, interdicting her maritime **trade**, and continuing to chip away at her overseas colonies. Napoleon's visionary Egyptian expedition finally offered an opportunity to strike back: Admiral **Horatio Nelson** cornered Napoleon's naval escort and destroyed it at Aboukir Bay (Battle of the Nile, 1798). With renewed vigor and hope, a Second Coalition formed (1798–1802), with Austria, a major partner, hoping to recover Northern Italy. But Napoleon's victory

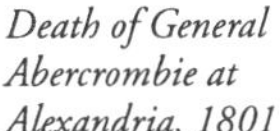

Death of General Abercrombie at Alexandria, 1801

at Marengo (1800) unhinged the coalition and led to a humiliating treaty (1801). Britain, fighting on alone, agreed to the **Peace of Amiens** (1802)—unpopular because it left France the dominant power in Europe and returned recent British colonial acquisitions.

Despite defeats on the Continent, efforts on the periphery yielded positive results. Sir Ralph Abercrombie (1734–1801) successfully disposed of the French army marooned in Egypt (1801), though he died of his wounds. The **Duke of Wellington** was among those who by 1804 destroyed French influence in **India**. British war planners discovered the strategic use of naval forces to land and support troops at selected sites, which provided the ability to attack French weak points selectively. Meanwhile the army, under the new Commander-in-Chief the Duke of York, underwent considerable reformation; this included intensified training, officer education, light infantry tactics development, improved cavalry field discipline, and establishment of a rifle corps.

Napoleon's plan to invade Britain with 100,000 men and 2,000 transports launched from Bologne foundered on the superiority of the British Navy, proven decisively at the **Battle of Trafalgar** (1805). He then turned his forces east against the Austrians and Russians in the War of the Third Coalition (formed in 1805). Britain did not commit troops to the Continent, opting instead to fund the Allied effort. With overwhelming victories against Austria and Russia at Ulm and Austerlitz (1805), and against Prussia at Jena-Auerstadt (1806), Napoleon shattered the coalition. Only a successful British occupation of Copenhagen and capture of the Danish fleet (1807) checked the amazing tide of French victories.

The ideological and military struggle was also economic, with France bent on destroying British trade and credit, and Britain attempting not only to enlarge her **Empire** but to bring as much seaborne trade with Europe as possible under her own control. The economic battle was most intense in 1806–1812. Napoleon, recognizing the impossibility of defeating Britain at sea, constructed his Continental System with a series of decrees (1806–1810) aimed at closing the entire European coastline against British trade. Britain responded with **Orders in Council** (1807) aimed at controlling and **taxing** the substantial trade being carried on by neutral ships. Some of the effects of this counterpoint were, on the one hand, to propel continuing French coastal expansion, which ultimately stretched Napoleon's empire too thinly and, on the other, to intensify British domestic hardship and war weariness (severe by 1811) and fuel the **War of 1812** with America.

French intervention in Spain (1807) and deposition of the Spanish Bourbon monarchy in favor of Joseph Bonaparte (1808) provided Britain a favorable opportunity at last to conduct Continental operations. The Peninsular Campaign (1808–1814) under **Sir John Moore** and then Wellington was intended to protect Portugal (Britain's ally), exploit Iberian hatred of French tyranny, and expel the French from Spain. It ultimately cost Napoleon thousands of troops and also undercut his ability in the east to defend his empire against a resurgent Prussia, Russia, and Austria, as well as to force compliance with the anti–British Continental System. Spain was Napoleon's "bleeding ulcer."

His constant warfare against Austria and the disastrous Russian campaign (1812) also drained his resources. Wellington's victory at Vittoria (1813) invigorated the Alliance and led to British invasion of southern France. Meanwhile at Leipzig (1814) the Allies defeated Napoleon and compelled his abdication. His return to Paris from exile in Elba ended in final defeat at the **Battle of Waterloo** (1815), which concluded the Anglo–French struggle that had lasted more than a century and established Britain's global political, economic, and imperial dominance for the next hundred years.

In Britain the wars caused huge enlargements of governmental expenditure (estimated at £1,500,000,000) and of military manpower (the army and navy expanded tremendously, to approximately 250,000 and 150,000 men respectively, while at the height of the invasion scare there were nearly 400,000 men acting as home volunteers). There was also a sharp increase in **radicalism** and in accompanying government repression. On the other side of the ledger, the wars hugely stimulated the British economy, resulted in the annexation of some 20 additional overseas colonies, and provided an unshakable foundation for national pride in the century after 1815.

Stanley D.M. Carpenter

Bibliography

Chandler, David. *Dictionary of the Napoleonic Wars.* 1979.

———. *Waterloo: The Hundred Days.* 1980.

Connelly, Owen. *Blundering to Glory: Napoleon's Military Campaigns.* 1987.

Herold, J. Christopher. *The Age of Napoleon.* 1984.

Marcus, G.J. *The Royal Navy in the Age of Nelson, 1793–1815.* 1971.

Quimby, Robert S. *The Background of Napoleonic Warfare.* 1957.

Ross, Steven. *From Flintlock to Rifle Infantry: Tactics, 1740–1866.* 1979.

Rothenburg, Gunther. *The Art of Warfare in the Age of Napoleon.* 1978.

See also French Revolution; War and Military Engagements

Friendly Societies

Friendly societies, also known as "benefit societies" and "box clubs," collected a small subscription from their usually poor members and in return guaranteed certain benefits, for example, a respectable burial, sick pay, cattle insurance, widows' and orphans' pensions, distress grants, and free medical treatment. Although their main purpose was to guarantee mutual benefits, they also spread, as the name implies, a spirit of fraternity and fellowship. They often employed secret rituals and passwords, but attempted to avoid allegations of sedition by prohibiting political and religious debates. They encouraged workers' self-improvement by teaching the virtues of thrift, honesty, hard work, and sobriety. They fined members for misbehavior, drunkenness, and swearing, and even for singing political songs.

Friendly societies originated in the 16th century, with purposes combining some objectives of **craft guilds** with others of general relief. Although primarily local, there were by the late Hanoverian period some national friendly societies such as the Oddfellows (reorganized in 1833), the Ancient Order of Foresters (reorganized in 1834), Hearts of Oak, and the Loyal Order of Ancient Shepherdesses, a women's society. By 1850, local groups tended to merge into national organizations, something that permitted improved benefits.

The government first recognized friendly societies (1793) when Parliament passed an Act for the Encouragement and Relief of Friendly Societies, also known as the "Rose Act" in honor of M.P. George Rose (1744–1814), its initiator. Its purpose was to protect societies' funds from unscrupulous officers, grant them exemption from **taxes**, and establish procedures under which they would report to local authorities. In the **radical** atmosphere of the 1790s, the upper classes felt that friendly societies were respectable and deserved protection; and obviously these would also reduce burdens on taxpayers. Legislation in the Victorian period (1842, 1855) continued this benevolent governmental assistance to the societies. Trade unions attempted, though often unsuccessfully, to shelter themselves under the protections extended to the friendly societies.

Membership in these societies increased over the course of the 19th century. In 1793 their members numbered 648,000 in some 7,200 clubs. By 1803 there were 704,350 members. By 1872 about 4 million people were enrolled. In 1900, membership was estimated at over 5.5 million. Some 191 clubs that had begun in the 18th century were still meeting in 1905. Although friendly societies remain in existence today, their membership has declined sharply since the National Health Insurance Act of 1911.

David B. Mock

Bibliography

Beveridge, William, Lord. *Voluntary Action: A Report on Methods of Social Action.* 1948.

Gosden, P.H.J.H. *The Friendly Societies in England, 1815–1875.* 1961.

See also Clubs; Combination Acts; Freemasons; Labor Laws, Movements, and Unions

Fry, Elizabeth (1780–1845)

Fry took up the cause of **prison reform** where **John Howard** left off, and in the early 19th century became one of its chief international promoters. A member of a wealthy, worldly **Quaker** family, the Gurneys of Norwich, Elizabeth became a strict Friend in her late teens. Married to Joseph Fry, a **London merchant** (1800), she settled down to domestic life. Her call as a minister, however, could not be silenced. In 1811 she was recognized as a "minister" by her Meeting, in tribute to her earnestness, intelligence, and goodheartedness. In 1817, after bearing 10 children, she began her work to improve the conditions in prisons, especially those for women and children.

Under her leadership a Ladies Association for the Improvement of the Female Prisoners in Newgate Prison was formed (1817), which established some of the basic principles later adopted everywhere—the separation of the sexes, classification

Elizabeth Fry

of criminals, institution of visitor practices, a school, a laundry, a matron. In 1818 she visited Scottish prisons, in 1827 Irish ones, and in the period 1838–1840 she took extensive working tours of **France**, Switzerland, and Germany. Her reports on these experiences were recognized in the **House of Commons** and among influential authorities and correspondents abroad, and led to many improvements in hospitals and asylums as well as prisons. Although her notions of prison reform were rejected as too paternalistic by later reformers, she did much in her day to improve life for the most unfortunate.

Barbara Brandon Schnorrenberg

Bibliography

Fry, Elizabeth. *Observations on the Visiting, Superintendence, and Government of Female Prisoners.* 1827.

Fry, Katharine, and Rachel Cresswell, eds. *Memoirs of the Life of Elizabeth Fry with Extracts from Her Journal and Letters.* 1847.

Johnson, R. Brimley, ed. *Elizabeth Fry's Journeys on the Continent.* 1931.

Kent, John. *Elizabeth Fry.* 1963.

Rose, June. *Elizabeth Fry.* 1980.

See also Humanitarianism

Furniture

See Home Furnishings and Decoration

Fuseli, Henry (1741–1825)

Johann Heinrich Füssli, who changed his name to Henry Fuseli after he settled in England, was a **history painter** of heroic, literary, and bizarre themes, and is also known for his dramatic **drawing**. He was born in Zurich, the son of the artist and aesthetician Johann Caspar Füssli. His father's circle included Johann Kaspar Lavater (1741–1801), whose interest in "magnetic" trances and writings on facial expressions and physiognomy were to have a great influence on him. His broad classical education included the study of **Milton** and **Shakespeare** (when still young he **translated** *Macbeth* into German), whose works would provide major themes for his paintings and drawings.

Fuseli went to England in 1764, the next year publishing the first English translation of Johann Joachim Winckelmann's (1717–1768) *Reflections on the Painting and Sculpture of the Greeks.* Encouraged to paint by **Sir Joshua Reynolds**, he spent the years 1770–1778 in Italy, mainly in Rome, where he was stimulated by antiquity, Michelangelo, and mannerism. Borrowing elements from all of these, he developed a **Romantic** neoclassical style that he would put to use in illustrating dramatic scenes from Shakespeare, Milton, Ossian, Wieland, and others from northern legends.

Fuseli exhibited at the Society of Artists in 1775, 1778, and 1783, and at the **Royal Academy of Arts** on several occasions down to 1820. He was the largest contributor to John Boydell's (1719–1804) *Shakespeare Gallery* from 1786 on, and created his own Milton Gallery of 49 pictures in 1799. Famous for his renditions of nudes in emotional or violent scenes, he exerted great influence on other artists, particularly **William Blake** who in turn influenced Fuseli. Fuseli's best-known and most influential work is *The Nightmare* (1782). Like many of his works, its meaning is not entirely clear; but Sigmund Freud (1856–1939) thought it sufficiently interesting to hang an engraving of it above his desk. Fuseli's Shake-

Henry Fuseli

speare pictures included *Lear Sending away Cordelia* (1785–1790), *The Three Witches* from *Macbeth* (1783), and *Titania and Bottom* (1786–1789). Today, his drawings are even more appreciated than his paintings. Two of his finest are *The Death of Cardinal Beaufort (Henry VI pt. 2)* (1772) and *The Artist in Despair Over the Magnitude of Antique Fragments* (1778–1780).

Fuseli was made associate of the Royal Academy in 1788, a full member in 1790, Professor of Painting in 1799, and keeper of the Royal Academy in 1804. His academy lectures were later published (1831) by John Knowles (1781–1841). His position, lectures, writings, and unusual art made him one of the most influential artists of his time.

Thomas J. McCormick

Bibliography

Antal, Frederick. *Fuseli Studies.* 1956.
Friedman, Winifred. *Boydell's Shakespeare Gallery.* 1976.
Knowles, John. *The Life and Writings of Henry Fuseli, M.A., R.A.* 3 vols. 1831.
Powell, Nicolas. *The Drawings of Henry Fuseli.* 1951.
———. *Fuseli: The Nightmare.* 1972.
Presley, Nancy. *The Fuseli Circle in Rome.* Exhibition catalogue, British Art Center, Yale University. 1979.
Schiff, Gert. *Johann Heinrich Füssli's Milton-Galerie.* 1963.
———. *Johann Heinrich Füssli (1741–1825).* 2 vols. 1972.
———. *Henry Fuseli, 1741–1825.* Exhibition catalogue, Tate Gallery. 1975.
Tomory, Peter. *Life and Art of Henry Fuseli.* 1972.

G

Gage, Thomas (1721–1787)

General Gage, a leading figure in the American colonies at the time of the **American Revolution**, entered the military in 1741. After gaining experience at **Culloden**, in Flanders, and under General Braddock near Fort Duquesne (1754), he served under **Amherst** in the capture of French **Canada**. Appointed Commander-in-Chief of British forces in North America (1763–1773), operating from New York, he skillfully administered the 50-odd posts under his far-flung command but misjudged the strength of the independence movement, sending hard-line recommendations back to **London**. It was his job to implement these in Massachusetts when he became military governor there (1774).

Unpopular already for having brought troops to Boston in 1768, he became more so as he attempted to cope with mushrooming resistance to **Lord North**'s Coercive Acts (1774) closing the port and modifying local law. In April 1775 his effort to seize rebel arms at Lexington and Concord backfired, leaving him besieged in Boston. Neither his declaration of martial law nor his costly frontal assault on entrenched rebel forces (Battle of Bunker Hill, June 1775) improved his situation. Under heavy criticism on both sides of the Atlantic, he resigned his position and sailed home. Though uninvolved thereafter in important duties, he became a full general in 1782.

David Sloan

Bibliography

Alden, John R. *General Gage in America.* 1948.

Carter, Clarence E., ed. *The Correspondence of General Thomas Gage, 1763–1775.* 2 vols. 1931–33.

Shy, John. "The Empire Militant: Thomas Gage and the Coming of War," in John Shy, ed., *A People Numerous and Armed: Reflections on the Military Struggle for American Independence.* Rev. ed., 1990.

See also Army; North America; War of American Independence

Gainsborough, Thomas (1727–1788)

Gainsborough was, along with **Richard Wilson**, one of the founding fathers of the British landscape school and one of the greatest and most original **portrait painters** of his day. Unlike Wilson, he did not adhere consciously to the classical tradition typified in the work of Nicolas Poussin (1594–1655) and Claude Lorrain (1600–1682), but created works of a new delicacy and poetic **sensibility** that profoundly moved contemporary critics and fellow artists.

Raised in Sudbury in rural Suffolk, Gainsborough went to **London** in about 1739 to study with the French illustrator Hubert Gravelot (1699–1773), who brought him into the circle of the St. Martin's Lane Academy. There he absorbed much of the French rococo style of Gravelot, the elegance of

Thomas Gainsborough

Francis Hayman, and the directness of **William Hogarth**. By 1745 he had his own London studio.

Gainsborough returned to Sudbury (1748), remaining there until he moved to Ipswich (1752). The masterpiece of the Sudbury period is *Mr. and Mrs. Andrews* (*c.* 1750), in which he combined the geniality of Hayman with a landscape of a naturalism he was never to surpass. This was a complex group portrait in which allusions to pride in landownership are as dominant as the portrait elements. Gainsborough's Suffolk paintings at first derived most closely from the Dutch 17th-century tradition, notably the landscapes of Jacob van Ruisdael (1628?–1682), but by the 1750s he was moving toward a more French pastoral in which rustic lovers are seen within a warmer, more sympathetic setting.

Gainsborough began to throw off the vestiges of the provincial artist with his arrival in the **spa** town of **Bath** in 1759. There he earned a reputation as a portrait painter of ease and grace, working for more sophisticated patrons. At the same time, in country houses near Bath, he became acquainted with the work of great predecessors such as Peter Paul Rubens (1577–1640) and, most significantly, Sir Anthony Van Dyck (1599–1641). Van Dyck's influence on him was powerful, beginning with his *Mrs. Philip Thicknesse* (1760), with its remarkable virtuoso drapery painting.

Although he had difficulty selling the result, Gainsborough continued his **landscape painting** throughout this period, seeking an intense poetic rendering based not so much on direct observation as on contemplation of his own feelings for nature. His insistence on self-expression led him to disassociate himself from topographical painting. His handling of landscape became increasingly lucid and free, the subjects more nostalgic and removed from commonplace reality, and the compositions broader and more sweeping.

Gainsborough's portraits and landscapes from his London period (from 1774 to his death in 1788) consciously challenged the great masters of the past with their expansiveness and monumentality. *The Watering Place* (1777) was a direct response to Rubens, whereas *Mrs. Graham* (1777) is more elegant than even Van Dyck while remaining true to Gainsborough's light palette. But Gainsborough was more intimate and compelling when painting members of his own circle. His portrait of the composer Johann Christian Fischer (1780), for example, remains a sophisticated yet lively picture recalling the artist's own delight in listening to and performing **music**.

In his last great works, Gainsborough often attempted to integrate portraiture with landscape in paintings, so-called fancy pictures, which combined imaginary rustic figures, usually children, with idealized rural settings. Most notably in the *Cottage Door* paintings (e.g., of 1788), these late pictures, quite unlike Gainsborough's earlier and more elegant town portraits, conjure up the imagined delights of rustic life at the heart of Gainsborough's own feelings (he treasured his rural roots) while neglecting the hard facts of rural poverty. These fancy pictures, painted with Gainsborough's loosest brushstroke, were lauded by **Sir Joshua Reynolds** in his Discourse XIV to the **Royal Academy** for being formed "in the same manner as nature creates her works."

J.C. Steward

Bibliography

Barrell, John. *Painting and the Politics of Culture: New Essays on British Art, 1700–1850.* 1992.

Hayes, John. *The Drawings of Thomas Gainsborough.* 2 vols. 1972.

———. *Gainsborough's Landscape Paintings.* 1982.

Levey, Michael. *Gainsborough: The Painter's Daughters Chasing a Butterfly.* 1975.

Pointon, Marcia. *Hanging the Head: Portraiture and Social Formation in Eighteenth-Century England.* 1993.

Solkin, David. *Painting for Money: The Visual Arts and the Public Sphere in Eighteenth-Century England.* 1993.

Thicknesse, Philip. *A Sketch of the Life and Paintings of Thomas Gainsborough, Esq.* 1788.

Waterhouse, Ellis K. *Gainsborough.* 1958.

Wendorf, Richard. *The Elements of Life: Biography and Portrait-Painting in Stuart and Georgian England.* 1990.

Woodall, Mary. *Thomas Gainsborough: His Life and Work.* 1949.

See also Painting

Galt, John (1779–1839)

Galt, a prolific writer, significantly helped, along with **Susan Ferrier** and **Walter Scott**, to develop the Scottish **novel of manners** and parochial life. His most important contribution to the Scottish novel and to the novel generally was his skillful use of dialect—especially West Scotland dialect—to establish character, class, and locale. He is best known for three novels that he intended to be read as local theoretical histories of the economic development of West Scotland: *Annals of the Parish* (1821), *The Provost* (1822), and *The Entail* (1823). These were all successes, eliciting high praise from Scott, **Byron**, and **Coleridge**. Along with many other novels and a quantity of published poems, dramas, travelogues, and textbooks, Galt wrote **biographies** of Cardinal Wolsey (1812), **Benjamin West** (1820), and Byron (1830), as well as two **autobiographies** (1833, 1834).

He was born in Irvine, West Scotland, the son of a shipmaster in the **West Indies** trade. He left school at age 16 to work in a customs house, then rose to become a trading agent and **traveled** throughout the Near East (where he met Byron), and also to France, Holland, and **Canada**. As an official of the Canada Land Company (1825–1829) Galt helped with Canadian settlement and founded the town of Guelph in upper Canada (1827). In 1829 he was forced to resign from the company; bankruptcy and a brief imprisonment diminished his health and productivity, though he spent his last years in Greenock, writing furiously to the end.

Mary Tiryak

John Galt

Bibliography
Aldrich, Ruth. *John Galt.* 1978.
Gordon, Ian. *John Galt: The Life of a Writer.* 1972.
Waterston, Elizabeth, ed. *John Galt: Reappraisals.* 1985.

See also Scotland and Scottish Culture

Gambling

Gambling was classless, indulged in by all manner of men and women, but it was particularly popular amongst the highest and the lowest. As a writer in *The World* noted in 1754, "My lord and the [sedan] chairman are upon a level in their amusements, except that his lordship is losing his estate with great temper and good breeding in White's and the chairman beggaring his family with oaths and curses in a night-cellar."

The oldest statute on gaming still in force at the beginning of the 18th century dated from 1542. With a stated intention to promote industry, it prohibited the lower classes from playing at tennis, gaming tables, cards, dice, and all other games. But Hanoverian Britain, despite further laws to limit losses to £10 (1712), to suppress the games of faro, basset, and hazard (1739), and to prevent gambling in public houses (1750), was unable to stop gambling by legislation. Such laws were impossible to enforce, and further, since gambling was intertangled with **sport**, and sport was a favorite pursuit of lawmakers, one may doubt whether the laws were in any way enacted very seriously. In fact, since state lotteries were legal from 1709 on, and private lotteries were suppressed by a parliamentary act in 1745, the state profited from the general passion for gambling.

The idea of sport as a "rational recreation" or "relaxation" did not gain wide acceptance until around 1850. Before then, it was not the love of exercise but rather gambling that spurred games and sports. From this gambling passion there did, however, come a kind of revolution in sporting life. During the 18th century, rules, organizations, and clubs all flourished, motivated by the practical impulse to prevent unfair advantage in the placing of bets. Rules made the betting odds more even; organizations and clubs provided additional opportunities for those who wished to participate in sport and to gamble with like-minded individuals.

The traditional **blood sports** of cock-fighting and bull- and bear-baiting were all wager sports. Both the owners of the animals and the spectators would bet on the results. These events often took place in alehouses, and could be as simple as one man pitting his animal against another's for a sum of money. Cricket matches were often played for high stakes and, since some teams were clearly better than others, it became necessary either to add men to one team or to offer very long odds if a "match" was to be held; village games were also usually played for a stake, such as 2 shillings and sixpence per man.

The race course furnished another natural center for sporting and gambling activities. Cock-fights were often held on the mornings of race meetings, and a prizefight might occur after the last race. The founding of the Jockey **Club** (1750) was for the particular purpose of settling disputes and acting as arbiter among owners and stakeholders. Because large sums of money were often involved, unfair and even criminal practices were not uncommon. "Blacklegs" (bookmakers, so named because of the black leather top-boots they wore) were known to persuade cricketers, jockeys, and prizefighters to "throw" a game or contest for personal gain.

Gambling linked all strata of society with a common compulsion, and stimulated sports such as prizefighting, pigeon-shooting, and pedestrianism. In village pubs, quoits, skittles, shuffleboard, and nine-pin bowling were all diversions available for petty gaming, and publicans ranged from passive presiders over gaming to active **entrepreneurs** of such activities. By contrast, in exclusive clubs such as White's, Boodle's, Crockford's, and Brooks's, members sat down in palatial premises, out of the reach of undesirables, to gamble at cards throughout the night. Superstitious gamblers often wore their coats inside out for good luck. Others wore leather aprons to protect their lace ruffles—and, after **Lord Sandwich**'s memorable culinary discovery, their laps. High **Whig** society during the early reign of **George III** (1760–1820) was notorious for its high rollers. Georgiana **Cavendish**, Duchess of Devonshire, lost a million pounds in gambling; her good friend **Charles James Fox** by age 18 had lost a hundred thousand.

The general popularity of gaming is evidenced by the demand for Richard Seymour's book of gaming rules, *The*

Compleat Gamester (1734), which went through seven editions by 1750. Naturally, from the beginning of the period to its end, philanthropists, clergymen, and **humanitarians** urged an end to gambling, especially to protect the poor from the workhouse, and debtors from debtors' **prisons**. Helping to strengthen their appeal was the spirit of moral earnestness that developed toward the end of the 18th century, and which countributed to the founding of such organizations as the **Society for the Suppression of Vice** (1802). While never stamping out gambling completely, the new spirit of moral improvement greatly curtailed its influence and prevalence.

Timothy J.L. Chandler

Bibliography

LeJeune, Anthony. *The Gentlemen's Clubs of London.* 1984.
Malcolmson, Robert. *Popular Recreations in English Society, 1700–1850.* 1981.
Thompson, F.M.L., ed. *The Cambridge Social History of Britain, 1750–1950.* 3 vols. 1990.
Vamplew, Wray. *The Turf: A Social and Economic History of Horseracing.* 1976.

See also Amusements and Recreation; Drinking; Manners and Morals; Toys and Games

Game Laws

See Poaching and Game Laws

Games

See Sport; Toys and Games

Gardens

See Landscape Architecture and Design

Garrick, David (1717–1779)

Generally considered in both his own time and ours to have been the greatest **actor** of 18th-century England—even of Europe—Garrick also wrote a large number of plays and managed Drury Lane Theatre (1747–1776), of which he was part owner. He was indeed the quintessential "Homme de Théâtre."

Garrick was precocious. In Lichfield he produced a comedy, starring himself, at age 11, and began acting professionally in **London** at age 24. His success was immediate, broad, and lasting. Anecdotes of his powers are legion. The playwright **Richard Cumberland** remembered him "bounding on the stage," "young and light and alive in every muscle," opposite old James Quin (1693–1766), and "it seemed as if a whole century had been stept over." Even deaf admirers, and foreign visitors who could not understand him, were moved by his "expressive features" and "speaking eyes." Garrick staged a "naturalistic" revolution based on close analysis of texts and amazing muscular control; one observer said he could mime every emotion without moving. "Damn him!" exclaimed an actress, moved despite herself by his King Lear, "I believe he could act a gridiron." In effect, "the English Roscius" taught audiences a new aesthetic in which the rhythm of the verse

Garrick as Richard III

was subordinated to passion and meaning. Said Quin, "If this young fellow be right, then we have been all wrong."

Garrick was only 23 when his first play was produced at Drury Lane. He wrote easily, taking note of what worked for other writers and giving audiences a fresh-seeming yet vaguely familiar version of it. So *Lethe* (1740) and *Lilliput* (1756) are reruns of Fieldingesque and Swiftian satires, while *The Lying Valet* (1741) and *Miss in Her Teens* (1747) are short comedies filled with echoes of Farquhar and **Shakespeare**. Most of Garrick's plays are farces, **satires**, and *petites comédies* designed as "afterpieces" to the main play. His most successful and significant five-act comedy was *The Clandestine Marriage* (1766), a collaboration with **George Colman the Elder**. He also altered or extracted material from earlier plays, such as *The Country Girl* (1766) from Wycherley's *The Country Wife,* and *Florizel and Perdita* from *The Winter's Tale.*

Garrick's record as manager of England's principal playhouse is mixed. He considered Drury Lane "the house of Shakespeare" and stated his opposition to **pantomimes** and circus acts, but made frequent concessions on these points. His most popular afterpieces were pantomimes, and he regaled audiences with spectacles such as *The Chinese Festival* (1755) and *The Jubilee* (1769). Garrick's interest in new scenic and lighting technologies from the Continent furthered the **theater**'s drift into "special effects": he outspent the rival theater on lights, scenes, and costumes. In order to coax the audience off the stage, he doubled the seating capacity of the house, creating a less intimate space; that the lighting was better upstage also tended to increase the distance between actors and spectators. Garrick revived several of Shakespeare's plays—in altered versions; his Romeo, for example, has not sighed for Rosaline. He staged 85 new full-length plays in his 29-year career, but rejected authors complained that their judge was a rival playwright.

When Garrick retired, however, the audience wept and refused to see the afterpiece. When he died, **Johnson**, **Burke**, **Sheridan** and other friends escorted him to Poets' Corner. His contemporaries credited him with raising the reputation of both dramatic **poetry** and the **acting profession**, and noted a sharp decline in the quality of English theater after his death.

Richard W. Bevis

Bibliography

Berkowitz, Gerald M. *David Garrick: A Reference Guide.* 1980.

Burnim, Kalman A. *David Garrick, Director.* 1961.

Dircks, Phyllis T. *David Garrick.* 1985.

Kendall, Alan. *David Garrick.* 1985.

Little, David M., and George M. Kahrl. *The Letters of David Garrick.* 1963.

Pedicord, Harry W., and Frederick L. Bergmann. *The Plays of David Garrick.* 1980–1982.

Perrin, Michael. *David Garrick: Homme de Théâtre.* 1978.

Stein, Elizabeth P. *David Garrick, Dramatist.* 1938.

Stone, George W., Jr., and George M. Kahrl. *David Garrick: A Critical Biography.* 1979.

See also Dramatic Arts; Dramatic Criticism; Theaters and Staging

Gay, John (1685–1732)

John Gay

Gay was, along with **Defoe**, one of the most versatile literary observers of early Hanoverian **London**. In **poetry** and plays alike, he found ways of commenting on the affairs of his day. Presenting himself typically as a naive observer—walker of the city's streets, teller of beast stories, unsophisticated beggar—he acutely noted human corruption and self-deception.

Born in the west of England, he came to London first as apprentice to a silk mercer. He soon discovered the literary scene and became friendly with **Swift** and **Pope**. *Wine,* his first published poem, appeared in 1708, followed quickly by others and by a series of plays, beginning with *The Mohocks* (1712). In the **South Sea Bubble**, the stock market crash of 1720, he lost much of the considerable wealth he had earned from his poems. Afterward he failed in attempts to win court preferment, but he retained loyal friends, notably the Duke and Duchess of Queensberry, with whom he resided in his last years.

The Beggar's Opera (1726) was Gay's most successful work. It represents a **criminal** society composed of **highwaymen**, **entrepreneurs** who profit from distributing their gains, and women who compete for male affections and wealth. Depicting a precisely structured class system that parodied England's, Gay employed animal imagery and insistent references to money to suggest the scandal of existing social arrangements. Yet his use of rollicking traditional tunes, the insouciance and wit of his dialogue, and the inconsequence of the play's ending (the highwayman Macheath escapes hanging because the audience prefers a cheerier resolution) lent comic relief to what might have been a more severe satiric indictment.

Although less familiar to modern readers, Gay's poetry shows comparable verve and complexity. Particularly entertaining are *Trivia* (1716), a record of walking through London's streets that captures a countryman's excitement at the city's multifariousness; and *Fables* (1727, 1738), which allows elephants, rabbits, snails, butterflies, and monkeys to comment on the human scene. Charming and apparently innocuous, the animals dwell on humanity's inveterate self-deception and inability to achieve self-knowledge.

Gay wrote in many of his century's poetic modes—Georgic, verse **epistle**, mock-**pastoral**, town eclogue, **satire**, versified narrative—and in dramatic forms ranging from farce (e.g., *Three Hours After Marriage,* 1717) through pastoral **opera** (*Acis and Galatea,* for which **Handel** wrote the music, 1732) to tragedy (*The Captives,* 1724). His versatility, vigor, and creativity make him lastingly attractive.

Patricia Meyer Spacks

Bibliography

Armens, Sven M. *John Gay, Social Critic.* 1954.

Irving, William Henry. *John Gay, Favorite of the Wits.* 1940.

Klein, Julie Thompson. *John Gay: An Annotated Checklist of Criticism.* 1974.

Noble, Yvonne, ed. *Twentieth Century Interpretations of* The Beggar's Opera. 1975.

Spacks, Patricia Meyer. *John Gay.* 1965.
Winton, Calhoun. *John Gay and the London Theatre.* 1993.

See also Dramatic Arts; Fable; Mock-Heroic

General Warrants

A General Warrant, one of the varied instruments of **censorship** still employed in Hanoverian Britain, was a process issued from the Secretary of State's office directing the arrest of the author, printer, and publisher of materials deemed to constitute seditious or obscene libel. The warrant's name emerged from the fact that, acting as a sort of dragnet, it did not specifically name the person or persons to be arrested.

The use and legality of such warrants was challenged in 1763 after Secretary of State Lord Halifax (1716–1771) issued one for the arrest of the authors, printers, and publishers of issue No. 45 of the *North Briton* for its criticism of the government. Among those arrested was **John Wilkes**, the paper's owner but also a member of the **House of Commons**. On 6 May 1763 the Chief Justice of the Court of Common Pleas, Sir Charles Pratt (later Lord Camden, 1714–1794), released Wilkes on the grounds of his parliamentary privilege against arrest. In a related case, Pratt ruled that the warrant was invalid for failure to name the persons to be arrested. The Commons adopted this reasoning and declared General Warrants illegal on 22 April 1766, thus completing another page in the history of liberty.

Frank M. Baglione

Bibliography

Anonymous. *Libels, Warrants, and Seizures: Three Tracts, 1764–1771.* 1974.
Cone, Carl B. *The English Jacobins: Reformers in Late 18th Century England.* 1968.
Rudé, George. *Wilkes and Liberty: A Social Study of 1763 to 1774.* 1983.

See also Judicial System; Legal Profession; Radicalism and Radical Politics

Gentry

See Aristocracy and Gentry

George I, King (1660–1727)

George was born the son of Ernest Augustus, Elector of **Hanover.** His mother, Sophia (1630–1714), was the daughter of Frederick, Elector Palatine, and of Elizabeth, daughter of James I of England and VI of Scotland. Through this descent he came to stand, after deposition of the Stuarts, in line of succession to the thrones of Great Britain and **Ireland.** In 1682 he married Sophia of Celle (1666–1726), but in 1694 divorced her and imprisoned her for life on grounds of **adultery.** His interests were military: he became a soldier at age 15 and led Hanoverian forces in the anti–French alliances of the day.

The English Parliament passed in 1701 the **Act of Settlement**, making the Electress Sophia heir to the throne. She died in June 1714, followed by **Queen Anne** in August. Despite

King George I

efforts by **Tories** to prevent it, George I was at once proclaimed, and arrived in September. His inability to speak English and reluctance to step outside his Hanoverian entourage brought major constitutional and political developments. Since he could not preside over councils of his ministers, the system of cabinet government began to evolve.

The **Whigs** began their long supremacy by winning the first election of the reign, then consolidated it by passing the **Septennial Act** (1716) to extend the life of the Parliament to 7 years. George's acquiescence was reinforced by the abortive **Jacobite** uprising of 1715. He serenely returned to Hanover, leaving the Prince of Wales—the future **George II**—as Guardian of the Realm. Returning in 1717 he expressed himself displeased with the state of affairs and tried to place his son under house arrest, only to be thwarted by the English law of habeas corpus. The heir to the throne thus became the focus of **opposition**, something which turned into a Hanoverian tradition.

By ably dealing with all the elements of a new political

order, **Sir Robert Walpole** rose to undisputed personal power from 1721. George was content to leave everything to him. Not popular with his people, who called him "King Log" and "that corpulent oaf," he remained disinterested in his new kingdom and spent as much time as possible in Hanover. He was on his way there when he died.

Michael Fry

Bibliography

Beattie, J.M. *The English Court in the Reign of George I.* 1967.
Hatton, Ragnhild. *George I, Elector and King.* 1978.
Marlow, J. *George I, His Life and Times.* 1973.
Plumb, J.H. *The First Four Georges.* 1956.

See also Fifteen, The; Government, National; Hanoverian Succession; Prime Minister

George II, King (1683–1760)

George was born to the then heir to the duchy of Brunswick-Lüneburg, later King **George I**, and his wife Sophia. He grew up to become a soldier, and commanded the Hanoverian cavalry in the Allies' **wars** against **France**. In 1705 he married **Caroline** of Ansbach, whom he loved sincerely, despite his many mistresses.

George accompanied his father to Britain in 1714 and was created Prince of Wales. But the two disliked each other; this dislike turned into a political problem for their new homeland. Arriving back from a visit to **Hanover** in 1717, the king tried to put his son under house arrest for misconduct, desisting only when his ministers told him that the law of the land did not allow it. The prince had taken the trouble to learn English and was, with his wife, a patron of the arts and performed many public duties. His court at **Leicester House**, more inviting than the king's grimly teutonic court, attracted **opposition** politicians hoping to improve their prospects by cultivating the heir to the throne.

Even **Sir Robert Walpole** frequented Leicester House, striking up a friendship with Princess Caroline that survived his rising in the king's favor. Though the prince never trusted him, Walpole helped to restore correct, if hardly cordial, relations within the royal family. On ascending the throne in 1727, George reappointed him **prime minister**. The situation remained stable until Queen Caroline's death 10 years later. After that, Walpole's influence declined, and he fell in 1742.

The country was now fighting the **War of the Austrian Succession**. The rising parliamentary star, **William Pitt the Elder**, charged that it was being waged in Hanoverian rather than British interests. Certainly concern for "my German business" weighed heavily with the king when he came to choose Walpole's successors. He traveled to Germany in 1743, where he was the last monarch to take personal command of British forces at the Battle of Dettingen that year—leading the redcoats into battle with the cry: "Now fight for de honour of England, charge!" Though his hat was shot off, he remained until 1745, when he heard of Prince **Charles Edward Stuart**'s landing in **Scotland**. Returning to **London**, George helped to maintain calm when the Highland army advanced to Derby. When it retreated, he sent his favorite son, the **Duke of Cumberland**, in pursuit.

King George II

George's last years were taken up with efforts to contain the growing popularity of Pitt, whom he nevertheless had to admit as Secretary of State in 1756. This occurred soon after the outbreak of the **Seven Years' War**, when Pitt again brought his charges about excessive official care for Hanover. The war, and disputes over its conduct, continued until the king's death in 1760. He ordered his coffin to be placed next to Queen Caroline's, and the sides to be removed so that their dust could mingle.

Michael Fry

Bibliography

Owen, J.B. "George II Reconsidered," in A. Whiteman, J. Bromley, and P.G.M. Dickson, eds., *Statesmen, Scholars and Merchants.* 1973.
Plumb, J.H. *The First Four Georges.* 1956.
Rogers, Nicholas. *Whigs and Cities: Popular Politics in the Age of Walpole and Pitt.* 1990.
Trench, C.C. *George II.* 1973.

See also Forty-five, The; Government, National; Hanoverian Succession; Jacobitism

George III, King (1738–1820)

George was the eldest son of **Frederick, Prince of Wales**, and Princess Augusta of Saxe-Gotha (1719–1792). His father died in 1751, and his mother appointed the **Earl of Bute** his tutor. He succeeded his grandfather, **George II**, in 1760. The following year, he married Princess Charlotte of Mecklenburg-Strelitz (1744–1818), to whom he was unswervingly faithful. They had 15 children.

At Bute's hands, George had developed a high if self-righteous sense of duty, directed at the corrupt **Whig** politicians whom George II had allowed to run the country. He came to the throne determined to regain the part in government which he considered the monarch's due. Even so, he continued to rely heavily on Bute for advice, whom he appointed a Secretary of State, then **Prime Minister** (1762). He also purged large numbers of office-holding **placemen** in order to bring in new men. This was the beginning of his troubles. The Whigs pilloried him as a tyrant misusing royal **patronage**, a slur that stuck through his inflexible handling of the ensuing crises, though it merely masked the Whigs' own greed for power.

The crises passed through several stages. The initial stage ended in 1763 when Bute, unable to withstand the furious attacks against him, resigned. George then appointed **George Grenville**. Together they annoyed the Americans with the **Stamp Act** (1765), and the British as well by botching the affair of **John Wilkes**. The king turned in desperation back to the Whigs under the **Marquess of Rockingham**, but they played false with him. He next appointed **William Pitt the Elder**, who had waited in the wings since leaving office in 1761. Able and popular though he had always been, Pitt was now entering into his decline. George leaned rather on Pitt's associate, the **Duke of Grafton**. They staggered only from calamity to calamity, in **North America**, in **India**, and then in another prolonged fight with Wilkes (1768–1769).

King George III

In 1770 the king thought he had found a strong man in **Lord North**, effective enough as a parliamentary manager but unequal to the struggle soon unfolding across the Atlantic in the **American Revolution** and then the **War of American Independence**, which brought North down in 1782. With the loss of the American colonies and a further rapid succession of weak governments, the condition of the state looked dire indeed. But salvation was at hand in the shape of **William Pitt the Younger**. Though a political novice, he had the great advantage of clean hands. A few months after George appointed him Prime Minister at the end of 1783, he went to the country and learned that voters shared their sovereign's judgment. They returned Pitt's government with a comfortable majority.

From then on, George III took relatively little part in policy-making. Pitt and his lieutenants could be relied on for everything; by the time the **French Revolution** broke out (1789), followed by the **French Revolutionary and Napoleonic Wars** (1792–1815), George had lost any desire to personally direct a global struggle. He did, however, continue to intervene at crucial points, notably by his refusal to grant **Catholic emancipation** after the **Act of Union** with **Ireland** in 1801, which brought about Pitt's resignation. Otherwise he was content to play the part of "Farmer George," living in the country with his boring family. This made him far more popular than he had ever been while trying to rule, rather than reign.

Unfortunately, his life was increasingly clouded by illness, diagnosed in modern times as porphyria, which brought repeated bouts of madness. The first onset came as early as 1762, and a severe attack again in 1788; arrangements had been made for a regency when George suddenly recovered, bringing this **regency crisis** to an end. But further attacks followed, until George descended into permanent insanity in 1810. He was cruelly treated by his custodians, and died a pitiful figure in 1820.

Michael Fry

Bibliography

Ayling, S. *George the Third.* 1972.

Brooke, J. *King George III.* 1972.

Macalpine, I., and R. Hunter. *George III and the Mad Business.* 1969.

Pares, R. *George III and the Politicians.* 1953.

Sedgwick, R.R., ed. *The Letters from George III to Lord Bute, 1757–1766.* 1939.

See also Government, National

George IV, King (1762–1830)

George was the eldest child of **George III** and Queen Charlotte (1744–1818). A strict upbringing made him rebel. By the time he came of age, he had debts of £30,000; by 1796 his debts had mounted to £630,000. He had his first love affair at age 17, and his love life soon caused problems. He became infatuated with Mrs. Fitzherbert (1756–1837), a widowed

King George IV

Catholic. He wedded her secretly in 1785 in defiance of the **Act of Settlement** and the Royal Marriage Act (1772), which prevented members of the royal family from marrying without the sovereign's consent. Not until 1795 did he agree to make a legal marriage, with Princess **Caroline** of Brunswick.

That marriage was disastrous. As soon as Caroline bore a daughter (1796), they separated. George took up again with Mrs. Fitzherbert, while the princess too gained a scandalous reputation, living abroad after 1815 in adulterous liaison with an Italian. Meanwhile (in 1810) George III suffered permanent insanity, his son became Prince Regent (1811), and the **Regency** (1811–1820) began. The prince had always consorted with the **Whig** opposition, including **Fox**, **Burke**, and **Sheridan**, but he now abandoned his friends and retained the **Tory** ministry, appointing **Lord Liverpool** its head (1812). Eight years of turbulence followed: the decade was full of **riots**, assassination attempts on governmental officials, and governmental repression.

George assumed the throne and took full power as king in 1820. There was an immediate crisis over Queen Caroline who, returning from Europe and assuming the somewhat ludicrous role of the injured woman, was cheered by crowds stirred up by Whigs and **radicals** inflamed against the king and his government. The people, as **Coleridge** suggested, were not so much "Queenite" as "anti-Kingite." George attempted to divorce Caroline, but could not get the divorce bill through Parliament. Caroline came to his coronation but was refused admission to Westminster Abbey; soon afterward she died.

George took little interest in politics, except to sustain the Tories. He tried to restore the monarchy's reputation. He visited **Ireland** and **Scotland**, the latter trip orchestrated by **Sir Walter Scott**. He patronized the arts and sciences, bequeathing the **Regency style**. His favorite architect, **John Nash**, completed the Brighton Pavilion, restored Windsor Castle, and drew up ambitious plans for buildings in **London**, including Buckingham Palace (begun in 1825). The king donated his father's library of 70,000 books to the nation (1821), assisted with construction of the **British Museum** to house them (1823–1847), and also helped establish (1824) the National Gallery (built in 1832–1838).

The end of George's reign was marked by his resistance to reforms. It saw instability after Liverpool's retirement in 1827. A run of weak ministries ended in that of the **Duke of Wellington** and **Sir Robert Peel**, which passed **Catholic emancipation** over the threat of the king's veto.

Michael Fry

Bibliography

Fulford, R. *George the Fourth.* 1949.
Hibbert, C. *George IV, Regent and King.* 1973.
Leslie, S. *George IV.* 1926.
Margetson, Stella. *Regency London.* 1971.
Palmer, A. *The Life and Times of George IV.* 1972.
Priestley, J.B. *The Prince of Pleasure and His Regency, 1811–20.* 1969.
Wood, Marcus. *Radical Satire and Print Culture, 1790–1822.* 1994.

See also Government, National; Regency Crisis

Georgian Style

See Architects and Architecture

Germain, Lord (George Sackville Germain, Viscount Sackville) (1716–1785)

Germain (as George Sackville called himself after 1770, when he inherited from Lady Betty Germain), responsible for British military action during the **War of American Independence**, was born the third son of the Duke of Dorset and educated at Westminster School and Trinity College, Dublin. Entering the **army** in 1737, he gained distinction in the **War of Austrian Succession** and helped **Cumberland** crush the **Jacobites** in the **Forty-five**. But, prone to criticize other commanders, during the **Seven Years' War** he was himself accused of cowardice, court-martialed, and disgraced after refusing an order to advance his forces at the Battle of Minden (1759).

His political isolation ended (1774) with his appointment as Secretary of State for the colonies in the administration of **Lord North**, a position that gave Germain supervision of military operations against the American rebels. A hardliner, his opposition to all conciliation and peace talks alienated his generals. His critics also held him responsible for the lack of clarity that characterized British strategy. Criticized for the loss at **Saratoga** (1777), he became the butt of antiwar politicians. His modern supporters emphasize the difficulties that he faced in working with commanders of greater social prestige and better political connections, and also stress his success in organizing the campaign of 1776, which was the greatest land–sea action in British history up to that time.

Unlike other members of North's ministry, Germain did not see the surrender at **Yorktown** as fatal to the British war effort. He was nonetheless forced to resign in 1782, taking his viscountcy (to much irritated protest in the House of Lords) as a reward for doing so.

David Sloan

Bibliography

Brown, Gerald S. *The American Secretary: The Colonial Policy of Lord George Germain, 1775–1778.* 1963.
Mackesy, Piers. *The War for America, 1775–1783.* 1964.
———. *The Coward of Minden: The Affair of Lord George Sackville.* 1979.
Pancake, John S. *1777: The Year of the Hangman.* 1977.
Valentine, Alan. *Lord George Germain.* 1962.

Gibbon, Edward (1737–1794)

Gibbon was perhaps the greatest historian of the Hanoverian age. His *History of the Decline and Fall of the Roman Empire* (vol. 1, 1776; vols. 2–3, 1781; vols. 4–6, 1788) contained many of the prime virtues of 18th-century British **history writing**—philosophic breadth, critical use of sources, an appreciation of the elements of gradual historical change, and great skill in the telling of a great story. It remains today one of the classics of world historical literature.

Gibbon's life was uneventful. He was raised in Putney by an indulgent father, an affluent **Tory**. He was the eldest of seven children; small in stature and of indifferent health, he was the only child to survive infancy. His father sent him to Westminster School, private **tutors**, and **Oxford University**, but he learned more from reading. This led him to convert to **Catholicism** at age 16 (1753), but his strong-willed father reacted by sending him to Lausanne (1753–1758) to live with a strict Calvinist minister. Gibbon reconverted to Protestantism; became proficient in Latin and French; joined other

Edward Gibbon

British visitors in habituating the drawing room of the greatest French historian and philosopher of the era, Voltaire (1694–1778); and fell in love with Suzanne Curchod (1739–1794; afterward Madame Necker)—to the dismay of his father, who again overrode his will and recalled him to England.

Gibbon, much influenced by the **Enlightenment**, was now so Francophile that he published his first essay in French (1761) even while drilling in the Hampshire militia (1759–1763) to defend England against French invasion. He toured Europe in 1763–1765 and met other *philosophes.* From 1774 to 1784 he sat in Parliament, speaking little but supporting **Lord North**. For his services Gibbon received a **patronage** sinecure at the Board of Trade and Plantations (1779–1782) worth £800 a year. Perhaps strangely, he showed less historical insight in his attitude toward the **American Revolution** (and the **French Revolution** later, deeply disapproving of both) than other parliamentarians, and for his apparent political indifference and lack of idealism was later reviled by critics as "the elector of Hanover's slave." He was an intimate of **Samuel Johnson** and his circle, though **Boswell** detested him. In later life he again lived in Lausanne and then with his friend and literary executor the Earl of Sheffield (1735–1821).

Gibbon published the first part of his masterpiece in 1776 to initial praise, but before long found himself attacked by many religious writers incensed at his ironic and "sneering" treatment of Christianity in his famous chapters 15 and 16. This was not quite fair. Gibbon greatly admired the intelligence, toleration, and pagan virtues of the Rome of the Antonines, and saw its decline as an epic tragedy; he also believed that the same forces that had assisted the rise of Christianity had caused Rome's downfall: "I have described the triumph of barbarism and religion." But although he was a suavely ironic **freethinker**, his attempts to examine Christianity purely as an historical phenomenon were bound to be misunderstood because he was virtually the first English historian to do so. He paused in 1779 to defend himself, publishing *A Vindication of Some Passages in the Fifteenth and Sixteenth Chapters.*

Gibbon's greatest impact came through people's willingness, in that age when the British **Empire** was being dismembered, to read contemporary lessons in past history. True to his classical sensibilities, he saw historical decline ultimately as a question of hubris:

> The decline of Rome was the natural and inevitable effect of immoderate greatness. Prosperity ripened the principle of decay; the causes of destruction multiplied with the extent of conquest; and as soon as time or accident had removed the artificial supports, the stupendous fabric yielded to the pressure of its own weight.

This seemed frighteningly relevant in the 1780s.

George F. Clements

Bibliography

Black, J.B. *The Art of History: A Study of Four Great Historians of the Eighteenth Century.* 1926.

Bowerstock, G.W., John Clive, and Stephen R. Graubard, eds. *Edward Gibbon and the Decline and Fall of the Roman Empire.* 1977.

Burrow, J.W. *Gibbon.* 1985.

Carnochan, W.B. *Gibbon's Solitude: The Inward World of the Historian.* 1987.

Craddock, Patricia B. *Young Edward Gibbon, Gentleman of Letters.* 1982.

———. *Luminous Historian, 1772–1794.* 1989.

De Beer, Gavin, Sir. *Gibbon and His World.* 1968.

Fuglum, Per. *Edward Gibbon: His View of Life and Conception of History.* 1973.

Gibbon, Edward. *Autobiography.* 1962.

Porter, Roy. *Gibbon: Making History.* 1988.

Wedgwood, C.V. *Edward Gibbon.* 1969.

Gibbs, James (1682–1754)

Gibbs, one of the most successful **architects** of his time, was born in Aberdeen and raised a **Catholic.** After 1700 he **traveled** through Europe and remained in Rome for 6 years, attending the Pontifical Scots College and working for Carlo Fontana, surveyor to Pope Clement XI. In 1709 he returned to England, where he enjoyed the **patronage** of the **Tory** nobility, including Edward Harley, earl of Oxford, who in 1713 gave him a post on a commission to build 50 new churches in **London.** Gibbs's first creation was St. Mary-le-Strand (1714–1717), a building that reveals his indebtedness to the Italian baroque. His most famous church, later often copied in Britain and America, was St. Martin-in-the-Fields (1720–1726), a work that again combined Italian and English baroque sources in the **Palladian style.**

Model of James Gibbs's St. Martin-in-the-Fields, 1720s

Another outstanding example of Gibbs's work is the Radcliffe Camera, Oxford (1727–1747), which shows some indebtedness to his rival **Nicholas Hawksmoor**, a former employee of **Sir Christopher Wren.** At Cambridge, Gibbs designed the Senate House (1721–1730) and the Fellows Building at Kings College (1724–1731) in a more conservative Neopalladian style. Among his country houses, Dilchley Park, Oxfordshire (1720–1727), is his best known; its great hall is particularly fine. Gibbs also designed numerous monuments for Westminster Abbey and other churches, as well as a garden pavilion at Stowe (1738–1742). His general fame and influence sprang chiefly from his publications on architecture (notably *A Book of Architecture,* 1728), which inspired numerous buildings throughout England and the east coast of America.

Thomas J. McCormick

Bibliography

Colvin, H.M. *A Biographical Dictionary of British Architects 1660–1840.* 2nd ed., 1978.

Friedman, Terry. *James Gibbs.* 1984.

Summerson, John. *Architecture in Britain, 1530–1830.* 5th ed., 1970.

Gibson, Edmund (1669–1748)

Bishop Gibson's career illustrates some of the drawbacks of the officially established and protected status of the **Church of England** in the early Hanoverian age. Gibson was educated at Oxford, where he acquired a taste for Anglo-Saxon studies. He graduated with a B.A. (1691), then became chaplain to Archbishop Thomas Tenison (1636–1715) and librarian at Lambeth. After being consecrated Bishop of Lincoln (1716), then of London (1720), Gibson became (1723) **Sir Robert Walpole**'s chief adviser on ecclesiastical **patronage** and affairs until 1736 (when disagreement over Walpole's plan to ease the tithe burdens of **Quakers** led to a break between them).

Gibson, an instrument of the "Whig Ascendancy," had no doubt that all bishops should be good **Whigs** and advised Walpole accordingly. But his experience also made him aware of many of the church's shortcomings—notorious differences in the sizes of episcopal sees and of incomes, failure of pastoral provision, pluralism, the inadequacy of support to colonial branches of the church. His wide-ranging ideas for reform, however, were all defeated by inertia and the church's entanglement in establishment politics.

Like many men of the higher clergy, Gibson produced several substantial literary works. His first effort (1691) was an edition of macaronic **poetry.** Best known today for his monumental work on church law, *Codex Juris Ecclesiastici Anglicani* (1713), he also edited the *Anglo-Saxon Chronicle.* In 1695 he **translated** (with the help of Bishop William Lloyd, 1637–1710) *Britannia* by William Camden (1551–1623). He first attained public prominence in debates with Bishop **Francis Atterbury.** Offered the Archbishopric of Canterbury in 1747, he declined because of age and died the following year.

Donald W. Nichol

Bibliography

Sykes, Norman. *Life of Edmund Gibson.* 1927.
———. *Church and State in the XVIIIth Century.* 1934, 1975.
———. *From Sheldon to Secker: Aspects of English Church History, 1660–1768.* 1959.

Gifford, William (1756–1826)

A classical scholar, satiric poet, and early editor of 17th-century playwrights, Gifford published the works of Phillip Massinger (1813), John Ford (1827), and Ben Jonson (1816). He is best remembered, however, as the first editor of the *Quarterly Review* (1809–1824), a **Tory** journal founded in 1809 to counter the **Whig** partisanship of the *Edinburgh Review.*

Gifford was born in Ashburton, Devonshire. A cobbler's apprentice, he became the protégé of William Cokesley, who sponsored him at Exeter College, Oxford. There he began his **translation** of the *Satires of Juvenal* (published in 1802). In 1791 he published the *Baviad* and in 1795 the *Maviad,* **satires** directed against the expatriate English poetasters known as the Della Cruscans, for which he was unsuccessfully sued for libel. In 1800 he published *An Epistle to Peter Pindar,* a satire attacking **John Wolcot**, the foremost political satirist of the day.

After serving as **George Canning**'s hand-picked editor of ***The Anti-Jacobin*** (1797–1798), Gifford became editor of the *Quarterly Review* (1809) when **Sir Walter Scott** declined the position. He was energetic, eliciting **Southey**'s protests at his "mutilations," and a choleric partisan, prompting **Hazlitt**'s vitriolic portrait in *The Spirit of the Age* (1825).

James Held

Bibliography

Clark, Roy Benjamin. *William Gifford: Tory Satirist, Critic, and Editor.* 1930.
Shattock, Joanne. *Politics and Reviewers.* 1989.

See also Periodicals

Gillray, James (1756–1815)

Gillray, a lesser giant among the Hanoverian **graphic arts**, is generally considered the greatest English master of **caricature**. Largely self-taught, he studied at the **Royal Academy of Arts** beginning in 1778 and worked initially as a conventional reproductive engraver. Strongly influenced by **Hogarth**, he devoted himself after 1782 primarily to topical and political subjects. His first really great works date from the late 1780s and early 1790s. Patriotic and conservative in tone, these initially attacked **Whig** and **Tory** politicians alike as well as the royal family, whose pretensions Gillray delighted in lampooning. **Political prints** like *The Anti-Saccharrites* (1792) and *A Voluptuary Under the Horrors of Digestion* (1792, attacking the Prince of Wales) exposed to public ridicule the vices of the royal establishment.

By 1790 Gillray had come to ally himself with **William Pitt the Younger** and the Tories, securing an annual **pension** for his services (beginning in 1797). He worked at that time with the Tory editors of ***The Anti-Jacobin,*** which sought to marshal public opinion against the **French Revolution**'s English supporters. His works reflect this allegiance, attacking **Fox** and his whiggish circle in prints like *The Tree of Liberty* (1798) and *Stealing Off* (1798). Gillray increasingly portrayed the French, in prints like *French-Taylor Fitting John Bull with a "Jean de Bry"* (1799), with a xenophobic savagery that was remarkable even for the time. Coarse and oafish but steadfast, Gillray's **John Bull**, in prints like *John Bull's Progress* (1793), responds to the follies of his own government and the assaults of the French with long-suffering endurance.

Gillray completed many prints satirizing not only political targets but the vanity of contemporary society. Solitary and relatively unsocial, he became insane in 1810 and enjoyed only occasional lucid spells until his death. His artistic achievement, however, was as great as his influence was profound. He completed perhaps more than 1,500 prints, an enormous achievement, and finished many of them brightly with hand-coloring. His work is characterized by its great energy and inventiveness, its often coarse humor, and Gillray's ability to deploy great numbers of figures in visually dramatic (even if comically absurd) scenes.

Stephen C. Behrendt

Bibliography

Hill, Draper. *Mr. Gillray the Caricaturist.* 1965.
———, ed. *The Satirical Etchings of James Gillray.* 1976.
Wood, Marcus. *Radical Satire and Print Culture, 1790–1822.* 1994.
Wright, Thomas, ed. *The Works of James Gillray, the Caricaturist: With the History of His Life and Times.* 1873; rpt. 1970.

See also Drawing; Engraving; Watercolor

Gin

See Drinking

Gin Acts (1736, 1751)

After about 1724 a "gin mania" began in **London**, fueled by extremely inexpensive, locally distilled, spirits. Gin was sold in unlicensed dram shops, on the street, in chandlers' shops (small provisions stores), and in certain haunts, where, the floor covered with straw, patrons could become "drunk for a penny, dead drunk for tuppence." Many contemporaries, seeing the results of this in what appeared to be a rapidly accelerating growth of **crime**, homelessness, indigence, and the neglect of children, became convinced that gin-drinking threatened public order, and persuaded Parliament to enact legislation to restrict its retail sale.

The 1730s and 1740s saw a number of parliamentary acts, many amending those just recently passed, as the results of legislation were empirically tested and as political and other forces contended in Parliament. Legislators were torn between issues of public health and safety on one side, and land rents and corn profits on the other; and popular unrest and **riots** complicated things further. Although Parliament adopted its first regulatory bill in 1729 (repealing it 4 years later), the most famous Gin Act became law in 1736. It taxed spirits heavily, ordered retailers to pay £50 for a license, and outlawed the innumerable street vendors. Resented as discriminating against the poor, the act grew in unpopularity when the government paid informers in order to prosecute lawbreakers. Retreating in 1743, Parliament reduced the license fee to £1. But finally, in 1751, after renewed concern over gin-drinking, Parliament doubled the spirits license and increased the spirits tax.

By general admission, these last actions were remarkably successful. Gin consumption in the decade that followed declined by perhaps as much as 80%, though it is also true that by this time a new kind of beer, known as porter, had become the most popular alcoholic drink. Some historians today believe that contemporaries greatly exaggerated gin-induced drunkenness and the impact of spirits-drinking on crime and death rates; gin, they contend, was the scapegoat for the ills of a modernizing and urbanizing society. Undisputed is the fact that the antigin agitation foreshadowed the better-known attacks upon alcoholic drink of the 19th century.

David M. Fahey

Bibliography

Clark, Peter. "The Gin Mania and Official Controls in Early Hanoverian England," in Susanna Barrows et al., eds., *The Social History of Alcohol: Drinking and Culture in Modern Society.* 1987.

———. "The 'Mother Gin' Controversy in Early Eighteenth-Century England." *Transactions of the Royal Historical Society.* 5th ser. Vol. 38, pp. 63–84.

George, M. Dorothy. *London Life in the Eighteenth Century.* 1925.

See also Brewing and Public Houses; Drink Industries; Drinking

Glasgow

At the outset of the Hanoverian period (1714), Glasgow, long a leading regional center, with a **population** of around 12,000, was **Scotland**'s second largest city. A census of 1755 indicated a population of 31,000. By 1801, the figure was 83,000. By 1831, with 202,000 inhabitants, Glasgow had overtaken **Edinburgh** to become the largest city in Scotland.

Several factors account for this growth. During the 17th century, Glasgow's **merchants** had developed trading links with the western Highlands and Islands, with **Ireland**, with Continental Europe, and even with the English colonies in **North America**—mainly through English ports such as Whitehaven, as direct trade was illegal before 1707. These links continued to be developed in the 18th century, the **tobacco** trade becoming increasingly significant as a re-export sector after 1740. And as the American colonists required manufactured goods in return, this brought special stimulation to the workshops of Glasgow and surrounding areas. The tobacco trade became smaller and less significant with the rupture that accompanied the **War of American Independence**, but it nonetheless continued until the early 19th century. In addition, Glasgow was also a center of craft workshops, and moreover there is evidence that by the early 18th

18th-century view of Glasgow

century some larger-scale "manufactories" had been established. Expansion in the **textile** and **metalworking** sectors, the presence of **coal** and the development of a **banking** sector, ensured that Glasgow's economic growth would be based on both **commerce** and industry.

Economic growth accelerated after 1780. The completion of the Forth and Clyde, Union and Monklands **canals**, as well as the deepening of the River Clyde, made the **city** more accessible to its own hinterland as well as to the east coast and to points overseas. Increasing contact with the **West Indies** ensured a supply of **cotton** for **steam**-driven spinning mills that began to emerge, and their output fed an ever-increasing supply of handloom weavers within the city and the wider region. Capital raised in Glasgow was also largely responsible for the establishment of several **ironworks** in the area, laying the basis for the city's later reputation as a center of engineering excellence. The increasing pool of unskilled and semiskilled labor that was needed to ensure the smooth operation of this burgeoning industry and commerce was drawn from outlying areas, other parts of Scotland, and Ireland.

Glasgow was also an educational center and a home of the **Scottish Enlightenment**. The university counted **Adam Smith** and **Joseph Black** among its faculty. **John Anderson** left provision in his will for the founding of the **Andersonian Institution** as a "place of useful learning," stressing the practical aspects of education. Links between the academic and business communities were forged in societies such as the Political Economy **Club**.

The pace of change importantly affected the physical layout of the city. Economic success led to the creation of new luxury housing for the wealthy, beyond existing boundaries, in areas such as Buchanan Street. However, the speed of change meant that for many newcomers, **housebuilding** could not keep up with demand. The result was that overcrowding and unsanitary conditions became serious problems for the city's poorer inhabitants.

Primarily because of its energetic trade and industry, Glasgow's history was linked unusually closely to that of the **Empire**. By the end of the Hanoverian period, Glasgow had begun to assume the characteristics that were to make it the "second city of the Empire" during the Victorian era.

A.J.G. Cummings

Bibliography

Devine, T.M. *The Tobacco Lords.* 2nd ed., 1990.
Devine, T.M., and G. Jackson, eds. *Glasgow.* Vol 1: *Beginnings to 1830.* 1995.
Gibb, A. *Glasgow.* 1983.

Glassford Family

The economic history of the Glassfords illustrates that of 18th-century **Glasgow**. John Glassford (1715–1783) and his sons-in-law, Henry Riddell and James Gordon, were Glasgwegian merchants. They traded through six companies, forming the second largest group of the city's **tobacco** merchants. Glassford was thus one of Glasgow's great "Virginian Dons." At its height the family owned 25 ships and a network of stores throughout America valued at £500,000.

Glassford, like many of his contemporaries, was also heavily involved in local industries, though his interests were diversified to an unusual degree and included the **Carron Company** and the Prestonpans Vitriol Works. Yet despite his success as a businessman, he left £93,000 of debt at his death. Gambling and high living were partly responsible, but Glassford, who condemned what he called the "English quarrel with America," lost much of his fortune in consequence of problems connected with the **American Revolution**. His trading firm weathered the war but was, in effect, one of its economic casualties.

Patricia S. Collins

Bibliography

Devine, T.M. *The Tobacco Lords.* 1975.
Gourlay, J. *A Glasgow Miscellany: The Tobacco Period in Glasgow 1707–1775.* n.d.
Stewart, G. *Curiosities of Glasgow Citizenship.* 1881.

See also Commerce, Overseas

Glassmaking

Glass has been produced in Britain since Roman times. In 1714, **coal** was the main fuel used by the glassmaker. By the end of the 18th century, glassmaking was established at ports such as **Liverpool**, **Glasgow**, **Bristol**, **Dublin**, **London**, and Newcastle, and in inland centers such as Stourbridge in Worcestershire, **Birmingham**, and St. Helens and Warrington in Lancashire. All these centers had access by water **transport** to their markets and to sources of raw material not available locally.

The glassmaker's products fell into three main classes: tableware, window glass, and bottles. A typical glassmaking house would be in the form of a truncated cone, 60 to 80 feet high, with a diameter at the base of 40 to 60 feet. The coal was burned in a furnace within the cone, the pots in which the glass was melted being placed around the fire on a raised platform through arches supported by a brick dome or crown which directed the heat onto the pots. Except for working holes, the arches were sealed once the pots were in place. In addition to a supply of coal, the glassmaker required sand, alkali, and clay for pots.

There were some technical improvements during the 18th century, the most significant being the introduction of the lehr or annealing oven. Glass, when formed into products, must be cooled at a rate that will not create surface stresses by uneven cooling. By 1750, cooling was being carried out by passing the finished glass very slowly through a tunnel, one end of which was near the working heat of the glass and the other at room temperature. In addition, by 1780 the cutting of lead crystal glass had become an in-house operation, giving added value to the glassmaker. Steam-powered cutting, introduced about 1790, was in general use by 1810. The manufacture of plate glass, using French technology transferred to England around 1773, had become a profitable operation at St. Helens by the 1790s. By 1832, Birmingham glassmakers, again using French technology, were producing window glass in sheets as large as 10 square feet in area by blowing large cylinders, which after cooling were slit and then made into flat sheets of glass by reheating and smoothing them out.

Despite these innovations, the existence of a heavy excise duty on glass militated to some extent against experimentation. The first such measure in 1745 **taxed** raw material, but this did not include the cullet, or waste, glass. Glassmakers reduced the tax's impact by using as much as one-half of the batch of raw material as cullet. In 1777 the tax was doubled, and was increased again in 1781 and 1787. In 1825 it became related to the weight of the contents of the pot. Meanwhile, there was an immense increase in the production of bottles. In 1714 the amount of glass charged to duty (not including bottles) was 1,400 tons; by 1837, when the Hanoverian age ended, the glass industry was paying duty on about 23,000 tons of glass, of which about 12,000 tons was in bottles.

T.V. Jackson

Bibliography

Barker, T.C. *The Glassmakers: Pilkington 1826–1976.* 1977.
Derry, T.K, and T.I. Williams. *A Short History of Technology.* 1960.
Lattimore, C.R. *English Nineteenth-Century Press Moulded Glass.* 1979.
Thorpe, W.A. *English Glass.* 3rd ed., 1961.
Wilkinson, O.N. *Old Glass: Manufacture, Styles, Uses.* 1968.

See also Chemical Industry; Coal Mining and Miners; Saltmaking and Salters; Steam Engines; Tinplate Industry

Glorious Revolution (1688–1689)

The "glorious" overthrow of King James II (1688) and his replacement by William III and Mary II (1689) led to a redefinition of the monarchy's constitutional powers and its relationship with Parliament. A Bill of Rights (1689) decreed that the monarch must be a Protestant who could neither limit the power of law beyond the right to pardon, nor maintain an **army** in peacetime, nor raise revenue without the approval of Parliament. The bill also prohibited tampering with jurors, forbade cruel and unusual **punishments**, defended the subject's right to petition the monarch, and protected the charters of local communities. Subsequently, Parliament asserted the right to maintain army discipline, granted **toleration** to non–Anglican Protestants, authorized triennial **elections** to Parliament, granted judges tenure for life, and allowed press publication without **censorship**.

These acts confirmed the cardinal "revolution principles" of a balanced constitution (king, **Lords** and **Commons**), and of (limited) religious liberty and individual rights. Until the final suppression of the **Jacobite** heirs of James II (1745), British statesmen made defense of these principles the cornerstone of their foreign policy. Their successes caused European intellectuals to praise the English constitution and its principles of liberty. The same successes satisfied Britain's governing elite that further constitutional change was unnecessary. Thus, ironically, the Glorious Revolution became the **Glorious Constitution**, a shibboleth not to be questioned.

The revolution of 1688 and its legal aftermath (the "Revolution Settlement") reformed neither parliamentary representation nor the organization of **local government**. By 1770, in America as well as England, political **radicals** were challenging the control of the monarchy and the **aristocracy** over the unreformed electoral system. Not unreasonably, they maintained that the principles of the revolution needed to be carried forward. From these demands the reform movements of the latter Hanoverian period drew significant support. By the Victorian era it was popularly believed that the Glorious Revolution expressed a national tradition of personal liberty, representative government, and peaceful reform.

Robert D. McJimsey

Bibliography

Bailyn, Bernard. *The Ideological Origins of the American Revolution.* 1967.
Clark, J.C.D. *The Language of Liberty, 1660–1832: Political Discourse and Social Dynamics in the Anglo-American World.* 1994.
Holmes, Geoffrey, ed. *Britain after the Glorious Revolution, 1689–1714.* 1969.
Jones, J.R., ed. *Liberty Secured? Britain Before and After 1688.* 1992.
Pocock, J.G.A. *Three British Revolutions, 1641, 1688, 1776.* 1980.
Pocock, J.G.A., Gordon J. Schochet, and Lois G. Schwoerer, eds. *The Varieties of British Political Thought, 1500–1800.* 1993.
Sack, James J. *From Jacobite to Conservative: Reaction and Orthodoxy in Britain, c. 1760–1832.* 1993.
Schwoerer, Lois G. *The Declaration of Rights, 1689.* 1981.
———, ed. *The Revolution of 1688–89: Changing Perspectives.* 1992.
Wilson, Kathleen. "Inventing Revolution: 1688 and Eighteenth-Century Popular Politics." *Journal of British Studies.* Vol. 28, pp. 349–386.

See also Political Thought

Godwin, William (1756–1836)

Godwin was, next to **Thomas Paine**, the most **radical** English philosopher in the era of the **French Revolution**. He was a social critic, political **journalist**, novelist, husband of Mary Wollstonecraft, and father of **Mary Wollstonecraft Shelley**. His chief philosophical work was *An Enquiry Concerning Political Justice and Its Influence on General Virtue and Happiness* (1793), an incendiary document espousing rational anarchism, of which **William Hazlitt** wrote: "No work in our time gave such a blow to the philosophical mind of the country." Godwin's **novel** *The Adventures of Caleb Williams, or Things as They Are* (1794) presented the same philosophy in a narrative whose **sentimentalism** enhanced the impact of its political ideas on contemporary readers.

Godwin was born in Wisbeach, Cambridgeshire, the son

William Godwin

of a **dissenting** minister. Groomed for the pulpit, he had difficulty finding a congregation because of his attraction to the Sandemanians, an anti-establishmentarian sect modeling itself on the egalitarian primitive Christian church. Godwin's early politics were **Tory**, but he became much more radical in 1780s, influenced by, among others, the French philosophers Rousseau, D'Holbach, and Helvetius. He became a deist, and under the influence of **Joseph Priestley** he briefly embraced Socinianism, a proto–**Unitarian** creed. After flirting with atheism, he emerged a Coleridgean theist.

Godwin's political ideas, full of the exalted and abstract spirit of 1789, left little room for human frailty and error. Man is perfectible; reason is the instrument of self-perfection; truth, ascertained by reason, is omnipotent; vice is merely a correctable error in judgment. Marriage, a form of property-holding, is evil. Government is, too, for though it restrains the worst in men, it usurps individual freedom of conscience and judgment. As humanity grows toward perfection, government will fade away; for the time being, government should be based not on constraint but on the deliberations of the governed.

Pitt the Younger thought of suppressing Godwin's *Political Justice* when it came out, but concluded that it could do little harm because it cost 3 guineas. The philosopher continued to philosophize, producing a collection of essays, *The Enquirer: Reflections on Education, Manners, and Literature* (1797). Godwin's novels include *Imogen* (1784), *St. Leon* (1799), *Mandeville* (1817), and *Cloudesley* (1830). He also produced numerous historical and biographical works. His radical thought and unconventional marriage made him notorious in the 1790s, and his work influenced the ideology of **Romanticism**, the English socialist tradition and, through **William Thompson** and the Saint-Simonians, his ideas passed on to Marx. He, however, mellowed and became more conservative as he aged, even taking a government sinecure (1833).

James Held

Bibliography

Clark, John P. *The Philosophical Anarchism of William Godwin.* 1977.

Locke, Don. *A Fantasy of Reason: The Life and Thought of William Godwin.* 1980.

Marshall, Peter H. *William Godwin.* 1984.

Tysdahl, B.J. *William Godwin as Novelist.* 1981.

See also Political Thought; Wollstonecraft, Mary

Goldsmith, Oliver (1730?–1774)

Goldsmith was one of the most brilliant lights in the intellectual circle of **Samuel Johnson**. His writing career extended for only 16 years (1758–1774), but he published in virtually every genre and was as much a writer of nonfictional prose as a poet, dramatist, and novelist. Three of his works—a short comic novel, *The Vicar of Wakefield* (1766); a philosophical poem, *The Deserted Village* (1770); and a comedy of **manners**, *She Stoops to Conquer* (1773)—retain an enduring place in literature.

Born in **Ireland**, Goldsmith took a B.A. at **Trinity College, Dublin** (1750), and studied **medicine** at Edinburgh University (1752–1753). After **traveling** for 2 years on the

Oliver Goldsmith

Continent he settled in **London** (1756), never again returning to Ireland. Always in financial difficulties, he supported himself as a **periodical** editor, **journalist**, and miscellaneous writer. He became a founding member of Johnson's **Club** in 1764, and was a close friend of both Johnson, who made significant contributions to some of his writings, and **Sir Joshua Reynolds**.

Among Goldsmith's many nonfictional works are treatises such as the *Inquiry into the Present State of Polite Learning in Europe* (1759); histories of England, ancient Greece, and ancient Rome; scientific writings, such as *An History of the Earth and Animated Nature* (1774); memoirs, **translations**, anthologies, **biographies**, and **literary criticism**. His poem *The Traveller* (1764) grew out of his travels in Europe; written in graceful rhyming couplets, it dwells on the national characteristics of Italy, Switzerland, France, and Holland, before turning to Britain. Goldsmith's "Chinese Letters," collected as *The Citizen of the World* (1762), satirize contemporary manners by depicting English life from the perspective of a naive Oriental traveler. Goldsmith's first comedy, *The Good-Natured Man* (1768), met with some success, but was eclipsed by *She Stoops to Conquer,* a brilliant "laughing comedy" written in opposition to the fashionable "weeping sentimental comedy" that Goldsmith had recently condemned in a provocative critical essay.

The Vicar of Wakefield, Goldsmith's only **novel**, is still read and enjoyed today. Both humorous and pathetic, the eponymous vicar, who recounts the story of the fall and rise of his family, evokes laughter as well as pity. But while the sufferings of this family are removed in a comic conclusion, no such ending alleviates the depiction of destruction wrought on the countryside depicted in Goldsmith's finest poem, *The Deserted Village.* Intensely nostalgic, the poem evokes the lost beauties of English village life and deplores the displacement of small **farmers** by powerful landowners, **agricultural improvers** whose desire for luxury comes at the expense of "rural virtues."

Goldsmith's social ineptitude, vividly characterized by **Boswell** in his *Life of Johnson* (1791), is also evoked by **David Garrick**'s gibe that he "wrote like an angel but talked like poor Poll." Johnson, however, in his epitaph on Goldsmith's monument in Westminster Abbey, generously observed that there was scarcely any literary genre that Goldsmith did not touch, and none that he did not adorn.

Peter Sabor

Bibliography

Balderston, Katharine C., ed. *The Collected Letters of Oliver Goldsmith.* 1928.

Dixon, Peter. *Oliver Goldsmith Revisited.* 1991.

Friedman, Arthur, ed. *The Collected Works of Oliver Goldsmith.* 5 vols. 1966.

Quintana, Ricardo. *Oliver Goldsmith: A Georgian Study.* 1967.

Woods, Samuel H. *Oliver Goldsmith: A Reference Guide.* 1982.

See also Irish Literature before the Union

Gordon Riots (1780)

Beginning as an anti-**Catholic** demonstration, the Gordon Riots became a 6-day orgy of plunder and arson over a large portion of **London**. The event takes its name from Lord

Gordon Rioters burning furniture near Newgate Gaol, 6 June 1780

George Gordon (1751–1793), son of a Scottish nobleman and leader of the Protestant Association formed to oppose the easing of political restrictions on Catholics.

On 2 June 1780 a huge crowd led by Gordon descended on Westminster to demand the repeal of the **Catholic Relief Act** of 1778, which had removed some of the disabilities imposed on Catholics. Raising the cry of "No Popery," Gordon and the group attempted to present their petition for repeal. Some in the mob began handling members of Parliament roughly, and attempted to burst into the **Commons**. Failing that, they moved into the streets.

At first, the rioters sacked and burned religious buildings, including the chapels of ambassadors from Roman Catholic countries. They then turned to less sectarian pursuits, invading and burning Newgate **Prison** and releasing its inmates (June 6), and attacking the houses of magistrates. The remaining days of the riot were spent in looting and burning throughout the city. The government was forced to employ the **army** to end the riot's destruction.

Approximately 800 people were killed or injured during the violence. Many of the rioters were arrested; 21 were executed. Gordon, however, was acquitted, due largely to the skillful maneuvering of his attorney, **Thomas Erskine**.

The riots tended to discredit the extraparliamentary **associations** that were currently agitating for political reform. Their fearful reputation was used also to argue against calls for extension of the suffrage to elements that seemed unable to participate in the political process in a restrained manner. Save for open rebellions such as the **Fifteen**, the **Forty-five**, and the **Irish rebellions** at the turn of the century, the Gordon outrages constituted the worst **riots and popular disturbances** of the Hanoverian period.

Frank M. Baglione

Bibliography

Hayter, A.J. *The Army and the Crowd in Mid-Georgian England.* 1978.

Hibbert, Christopher. *King Mob: The Story of Lord George Gordon and the London Riots of 1780.* 1958.

Holcroft, Thomas. *A Plain and Succinct Narrative of the Gordon Riots.* 1944.

Stevenson, J. *Popular Disturbances in England, 1700–1870.* 1979.

Gordon, Thomas (*d.* 1750)

Little is known about the early life of this political writer and classicist. Born in **Scotland** late in the 17th century, he was admitted to the Scottish Bar in 1716. As a young man he moved to **London** and began to teach languages. With his partner **John Trenchard**, whom he met in 1719, he became one of the most widely read of the **radical** Whig **commonwealthmen** writing during the reign of **George I**.

Gordon apparently became convinced of the degenerate state of British society through the collapse of the **South Sea Bubble**. His **essays** in the *Independent Whig* and *Cato's Letters,* which began to appear in 1720, were harshly anticlerical. He was a strong supporter of the commonwealthmen tradition, opposing the ostentation, display, and political corruption he descried in his age. His writings show him to have been consistently opposed to all forms of artificial inequality. An admirer of Roman virtues, his **translations** of Tacitus and Sallust appeared in 1728 and 1744, respectively. His works, attacking the ministries of **Sir Robert Walpole**, were enormously popular in the **North American** colonies, where he enjoyed a large following. Late in life he slackened his complaints and entered government service as First Commissioner of the wine licenses, a position he held until his death.

Michael L. Oberg

Bibliography

Clark, J.C.D. *English Society, 1688–1832: Ideology, Social Structure and Political Practice During the Ancien Regime.* 1985.

———. *The Language of Liberty, 1660–1832: Political Discourse and Social Dynamics in the Anglo-American World.* 1994.

Robbins, Caroline. *The Eighteenth Century Commonwealthman.* 1959.

Gothic Fiction and Gothicism

The word *Gothic,* before the latter 18th century, designated the medieval, the unsophisticated, the uncouth. This was before **Horace Walpole** helped make the **Gothic revival** a literary as well as an architectural phenomenon. Pseudomedieval architecture characterized Strawberry Hill, Walpole's country estate; his **novel**, *The Castle of Otranto* (1764), inaugurated Gothic fiction. Marked by vaguely medieval settings intended to establish an atmosphere of fantasy, and by a stress on terror (often induced by **supernatural** appearances), the highly charged imaginative mode of Gothic allowed novelists to explore new aspects of inner experience, family life, and even politics.

Edmund Burke had established for the 18th century the aesthetic and philosophic importance of the **sublime** in his early *Philosophical Enquiry into the Origin of Our Ideas of the Sublime and Beautiful* (1757). Associated with terror, obscurity, vastness, and power, sublimity (in **landscape painting**, for example) generated strong emotions in the beholder. Thunderstorms, great forests, mountains: such natural manifestations, Burke suggested, produced the aesthetic effect characteristic of the sublime.

Writers of Gothic novels often tried to produce comparable effects. The events in such works typically occurred in grand natural settings or in half-ruined castles surviving from the distant past. But the notion of the sublime extended to character as well as to landscape. Male figures of obscure purpose and terrifying power populated these novels, often exercising tyrannic force over women (associated, in Burke's scheme, with the appealing category of the beautiful). Such "sublime" characters helped to elicit emotion that attested to the importance of the experience producing it.

In its efforts to evoke the sublime, the Gothic novel relied on supernatural effects. Sometimes the supernatural figures as a genuine power: thus **Matthew Gregory Lewis**'s *The Monk* (1797) provides a demon in the guise of a beautiful young woman who lures the central character to destruction; *The Castle of Otranto* opens with the crash of a giant helmet of no apparent provenance that kills the castle's heir; the protagonist of **William Beckford's** *Vathek* (1786) sells his soul to the devil. In other novels, supernatural appearances turn out to issue from inflamed imaginations rather than otherworldly sources. In **Ann Radcliffe's** *The Italian* (1797), for example, a young man repeatedly sees ghostly apparitions that derive from his habit of overinterpretation.

Supernatural effects supplied a way to suggest psychological mystery. The demon that tempts Ambrosio in *The Monk* is "real," within the narrative's context, but it might equally well dwell within the monk's sexually tinged imagination. The demonic figure provides terms for discussing a sexual disorder existing at first only in Ambrosio's inner life.

False appearances of the otherworldly can also reveal the psychic disturbance of beleaguered young heroes and heroines. As in contemporaneous and earlier novels of **sensibility**, concerned with glorifying the operations of human sympathy and the importance of tender feeling, in Gothic novels the life of emotion provides a narrative center. Such works, though, add to the celebration of feeling, vague intimations of its dangers. Because the protagonists of many Gothic novels respond with deep feeling to every experience, they make themselves vulnerable to emotion's ravages as well as its delights. The supernatural gives shape and unmistakable meaning to the potential for self-destructiveness in the responsive consciousness.

The dynamics of the disordered family, investigated in often lurid symbolic fashion, supplied a central subject for Gothic novels. Apparent incest or near-incest or symbolic incest between fathers and daughters occurs frequently. Fathers express murderous impulses toward their children. Mothers are monstrous, helpless, or missing. Often orphaned or mysteriously cast off, girls wander through sinister environments in search of new parental figures—who, when found, may prove as threatening as their predecessors. In *The Castle of Otranto* and in works by Radcliffe and her followers, a series of chaotic adventures typically resolves itself in the establishment of new familes and new harmonies; but an alternative tradition, begun by Lewis in *The Monk,* follows plot actions into death rather than marriage, insisting to the end on the impossibilities of the family.

Some Gothic novels convey disorders of sexual politics. Often, young women, vividly oppressed by older men, serve as their protagonists. Such women faint and weep in response to their victimization, but the plots they inhabit allow them also to resist and to escape. Moreover, symbolic structures, centered on supernatural appearances, elaborate scenery, architectural detail, and hidden depths (most Gothic novels contain fearsome and lovingly depicted cellars, often including dungeons and corpses), enabled the indirect expression of female sexual fears and fantasies.

The Gothic structures also facilitated covert celebration of the politics of resistance and even of **radicalism**. The **French Revolution** coincided with Gothic's efflorescence, and the **American Revolution** preceded it. Awareness of these great events lent special emphasis to the novels' stress on oppression and defiance, both overt and hidden. It seems no accident that Charlotte Smith (1749–1806), for instance, in *The Old Manor House* (1793), sends her male protagonist to **war** in America and allows him to comment on the political exploitation of the poor, while her heroine, back in England, suffers from more personal forms of oppression, symbolized partly in the mysterious terrors of an ancient building.

The Gothic tradition survived vigorously into the 19th century, mingling with other influences to produce such works as **Mary Shelley's** *Frankenstein* (1818). Debased, it still may survive today in supermarket romances, even now providing release to feelings of oppression and a will to resist.

Patricia Meyer Spacks

Bibliography

Day, William Patrick. *In the Circles of Fear and Desire: A Study of Gothic Fantasy.* 1985.

Duncan, Ian. *Modern Romance and Transformations of the Novel: The Gothic, Scott and Dickens.* 1992.

Ellis, Kate. *The Contested Castle: Gothic Novels and the Subversion of Domestic Ideology.* 1989.

Fleenor, Juliann E., ed. *The Female Gothic.* 1983.

Johnson, Claudia L. *Equivocal Beings: Politics, Gender, and Sentimentality in the 1790's—Wollstonecraft, Radcliffe, Burney, Austen.* 1995.

MacAndrew, Elizabeth. *The Gothic Tradition in Fiction.* 1979.

Punter, David. *The Literature of Terror.* 1980.

Summers, Montague. *The Gothic Quest.* 1930.

Thompson, G.R., ed. *The Gothic Imagination: Essays in Dark Romanticism.* 1974.

Gothic Revival

The Gothic Revival in the visual arts (especially architecture) paralleled a growth in English cultural **nationalism**, drew on an emerging interest in the **picturesque** and **sublime**, helped to condition literary **Romanticism**, and ultimately did much to shape Victorian conceptions of beauty.

Although Gothic style had been used in England since the Middle Ages, it was attacked in the 17th century by proponents of classical architecture who saw it as representative of a medieval "barbarous age." This criticism had become conventional by 1729, when Ephraim Chambers stated in his *Cyclopedia* that Gothic's lack of classical proportions illustrated the ignorance of the Goths. But such disparagement actually helped rally support for the Gothic by antiquarians who saw it as an attack on the national heritage; to them, the argument against Gothic became a reason to study and support it. Their case was encapsulated in an anonymous **tract** titled *Common Sense* (1739), which defended Gothic style as a reminder of England's golden age, when the nation's political institutions had taken shape. The tract also saluted Gothic's absence of classical proportions and symmetry as indicative of England's untrammeled liberty and genius, and called for the preservation of medieval buildings as a warning to would-be tyrants.

Fonthill Abbey, from an engraving by J. Wyatt

Although the Gothic Revival was much affected by literary theory (particularly that which emanated from **literary critics** such as **Richard Hurd** and **Thomas Warton**), elements of Gothic mediaevalizing may in fact be seen in some of the architecture of such great early Hanoverian builders as **Nicholas Hawksmoor**, **Sir John Vanbrugh**, and **William Kent**. The style was employed chiefly in smaller buildings and villas, while the **Palladian** and then (after around 1750) **Neoclassical** styles continued to dominate large public buildings. Vanbrugh's Castle at Greenwich (*c.* 1717), and Castle Howard in Yorkshire (upon which he and Hawksmoor collaborated in the 1720s) employ castellated and picturesque elements from medieval military architecture; and Kent's work at Westminster Hall and at **Henry Pelham**'s villa at Esher reveal a rococo Gothic interest. Esher was the first complete Gothic revival house erected in the 18th century, preceding by several years **Horace Walpole**'s Strawberry Hill (begun in 1748).

By 1742, when Batty Langley prefaced his architectural pattern book on *Gothic Architecture Improved by Rules and Proportions* with an "Historical Essay" tracing the style to the "ideal age" of the Saxons, the argument for preserving Gothic buildings was actually being employed to promote the style in new construction and **housebuilding**. How strong the revival had become by 1780 can be judged from the fact that **Robert Adam**, whose name seems almost synonymous with Georgian neoclassicism and elegance, in fact produced designs for some 40 buildings in the Gothic manner.

All these influences affected Walpole, whose Strawberry Hill, built in the Romantic castle style with several circular towers, became one of the best-known Gothic Revival buildings of the century. Strawberry Hill represented two themes generally identified with Gothic style. Its asymmetric form was believed to be sympathetic to nature (which "abhors a straight line"), and its capacity to evoke **melancholy** feelings provided a showcase for the family history which Walpole celebrated throughout the house. Walpole indulged his Gothicizing impulse also by writing what has been called the first Gothic **novel**, *The Castle of Otranto* (1764). Related literary tendencies were beginning to appear in contemporaneous studies of Chaucer, Spenser, and others.

Walpole saw Strawberry Hill as a prime example of modern Gothic and considered himself the "**Lord Burlington**" of the movement, just as Burlington had been the central figure in English Palladianism 50 years earlier. To establish the case for it in the history of English art he gave an account of its development in *Anecdotes of Painting in England* (1762–1780). He also promoted the careers of architects who worked in Gothic, including **James Wyatt**, the designer of **William Beckford**'s Fonthill Abbey (1795–1805), another famous example of the style. However, though at first Walpole's interest was more playful than serious, ultimately his most significant contribution was to help introduce a more assiduous and "archaeological" approach to the understanding of Gothic that influenced the researches of later critics such as John Carter (*The Ancient Architecture of*

England, 1795, 1807), and helped shape Thomas Rickman's *Attempt to Discriminate the Styles of English Architecture* (1817) and Augustus Charles Pugin's *Specimens of Gothic Architecture* (1821).

While these essentially antiquarian writers emphasized the Gothic style's relation to the past, other people pondered its kinship with the landscape. The architect and painter Richard Payne Knight's (1750–1824) Downton Castle (1772) in Herefordshire, which combined a castle-like exterior with a classical interior and set the pattern for many other buildings, is considered the link between Strawberry Hill and the 19th-century picturesque movement. Knight and **Uvedale Price** defined the relationship of the Gothic to nature and directly influenced the architects **Humphry Repton** and **John Nash**, whose work, spreading over the country in the early 19th century, helped to create the picturesque as an architectural movement independent of the Gothic style. John Britton's two monumental series of books on Britain's *Architectural Antiquities* and *Cathedral Churches* (published 1807–1835) accompanied a widespread building frenzy which, so far as the Hanoverian age was concerned, culminated in 1836 with the acceptance (after much revealing argument) of a Gothic design for the rebuilding of the Houses of Parliament.

David D. McKinney

Bibliography

Clark, Kenneth. *The Gothic Revival: An Essay in the History of Taste.* 1928.

Davis, Terence. *The Gothick Taste.* 1975.

Kliger, Samuel. *The Goths in England: A Study in Seventeenth and Eighteenth Century Thought.* 1952.

McKinney, David. "The Castle of My Ancestors: Horace Walpole and Strawberry Hill." *British Journal for Eighteenth-Century Studies.* Vol. 13, pp. 199–214.

See also Antiquities and Ruins; Architects and Architecture; Gothic Fiction and Gothicism; Landscape Architecture and Design

Governesses

Governess, as it is usually defined, is a woman living with a family who is responsible for the education of its children. This profession developed fully in the second half of the 18th century. (The term governess was also applied to any female teacher, though this became less common usage by the 19th century.) Governesses were increasingly employed by the upper and **middle classes**, and reached their point of greatest importance and desirability in the period 1840–1880.

Governesses existed before the middle of the 18th century but were usually employed only under special circumstances. The education of children was, until that time, regarded as a family responsibility. Mothers bore most of the burden, but many fathers, older siblings, aunts, and other members of the extended family also participated in the education of the young. A governess was employed only if the mother died and the father did not remarry, or if the mother was an invalid. Families of **diplomats** or of officers in the **navy** and **army** might employ a governess if both parents were abroad or frequently away from home. Courtiers also might use the services of a governess.

Changes in society and in the economic structure, together with the influence of new **Evangelical** definitions of the family and of gender roles, were, by the latter 18th century, affecting the ways in which families dealt with educating their children. Home and work were increasingly separated; males moved out of the domestic environment for most of their working hours. Boys were sent to school to be socialized and prepared for the male world; girls, destined first to be wives and then mothers, were more and more trained for these roles by governesses. Many parents of the new **entrepreneurial** middle class hired governesses also to reinforce the social requirements of their new wealth and status.

The governess was preferably a gentleman's daughter. Clergymen's daughters, such as Charlotte, Emily, and Anne Brontë (born, respectively, in 1816, 1818, and 1820) were obvious candidates, though many governesses (**Mary Wollstonecraft**, for example) came from the lower middle class. Being a governess was a respectable employment for a lady; writers on **women's employment** always listed it as one of the preferred occupations. The governess received room, board, and sometimes services (such as having her laundry done) in addition to an annual salary. **Wages** varied widely, depending on the income of the family and the experience, accomplishments, and sophistication of the governess. Some families in metropolitan areas hired governesses as day workers whose wages were usually lower than those of women who lived in.

A governess's duties varied with the children in her charge. She usually superintended the **elementary education** of the younger children of both sexes. Sons were sent to a school or given a tutor at about age 7; the governess continued to be responsible for the education of daughters. Her duties included instruction in English literature, composition, French, Italian, Scripture, **history**, geography, botany, elementary arithmetic, and sewing. If the governess was accomplished in **drawing**, **music**, or **dancing**, she taught these as well. The governess was also expected to instruct her charges in **manners** and proper behavior.

There were no institutions or standardized qualifications for training governesses. Most women who became governesses were themselves educated at home, and then attended a school for a few years. Many young women began their careers at age 18 or younger. It is little wonder that many were not very effective, and that parental complaints and bad childhood memories of governesses were often heard. The governess, too, had reasons for dissatisfaction. She was usually more than a **servant** but less than the family's social equal, so could suffer slights from both sides. There was always the possibility of sexual harassment from male employers; a governess who lost her virtue could not keep her job or get a new situation. A governess was, by definition, single.

Barbara Brandon Schnorrenberg

Bibliography

Peterson, M. Jeanne. "The Victorian Governess: Status Incongruence in Family and Society," in Martha Vicinus, ed., *Suffer and Be Still: Women in the Victorian Age.* 1972.

Schnorrenberg, Barbara Brandon. "Education for Women in Eighteenth Century England: An Annotated Bibliography." *Women & Literature.* Vol. 4, pp. 49–55.

West, Katharine Leaf. *A Chapter of Governesses: A Study of the Governess in English Fiction, 1800–1949.* 1949.

See also Tutors and the Teaching Profession

Government, Local and County

A conglomerate of officials, their offices created over the centuries by custom or royal edict, performed the functions of local government in Hanoverian Britain. Local government was like **national government** in that it was generally under the control of the **aristocracy** and landed classes, though otherwise the two were almost entirely separate. Officials were mainly amateurs, usually unpaid, in the three main administrative units—counties, boroughs, and parishes. There were 40 English, 12 Welsh, and 33 Scottish counties; 215 English and Welsh **boroughs** and (their Scottish counterpart) 66 **burghs**; and, in England alone, more than 9,000 parishes. The ecclesiastical parish, the smallest geographic unit, was in relative decline in the 18th century, though parish councils (often dominated by country clergy) retained some functions of local control.

County government was surmounted by a great nobleman, the Lord-Lieutenant. His office was both military and civil, but though he was responsible for the county's defense in case of invasion or rebellion, and responsible also for nominating for crown appointment the real county overlords—the justices of the peace—his real importance lay in the social and political influence he exerted as a great magnate and landowner; a fact always kept in mind by, for example, the **Duke of Newcastle**, who retained the lord-lieutenancies of Middlesex, Nottinghamshire, and Sussex as his parliamentary power base, through **patronage** granting local offices to electors who then returned him and his nominees to Parliament.

The real mainstays of county authority were the justices of the peace, responsible not only for **law enforcement** and the administration of the **judicial system** but also for government administration. Unpaid but highly respected, frequently landowners of the **gentry** class, often untrained in the law (though advised on legal matters by the clerk of the peace), justices were, until the emergence of professional law enforcement in the 19th century, the first line of defense against **riot** and disorder, after 1715 reading the **Riot Act** before forcibly dispersing crowds. Lesser questions of day-to-day criminal adjudication, such as judging and punishing drunkards and **poachers**, were handled by a single justice sitting in his own locality, whereas two or three justices might meet in petty sessions to deal with more serious offenses; more serious cases were judged by all the justices of the county (sometimes using juries), sitting together four times a year at quarter sessions. At all three levels, justices also performed administrative functions: at the lowest, the parish, which was nominally still in charge of preserving the peace, maintaining **roads**, and caring for the **poor**, justices—whose power over parishes had continued to grow since Tudor times—appointed constables and other officials, and fixed the local rates (**taxes**) for these purposes, often working with local churchwardens and vestrymen. At higher levels, justices had responsibility for many local appointments and local duties connected with the poor rates, other taxes, the highways, **prisons**, licensing, **wages**, and the like. In fact, by all these means as well as their authority to proclaim anything they disliked a "common nuisance" and then as judges to suppress it, Hanoverian justices of the peace held extraordinary powers.

A Justice of the Peace at work, 1742

Over 200 municipal boroughs, some mere villages and others **cities** as large as **Bristol** and **Norwich**, dotted the British countryside in the 18th century, each with its own government. Here, in a system much less uniform than in the counties, the top officials—mayors and aldermen (or, as they were called in various places, councilmen, or burgesses)—shared (and too often evaded) responsibility for addressing the challenges of rising **population**, industrialization, and **urbanization**. Mayors were generally chosen for 1-year terms by councilmen from the pool of the council itself, which, depending on the size of the town, might even be (as in Louth) coextensive with the entire body of borough electors. Standing behind the mayor, the town clerk, usually a barrister, brought continuity to town government as the clerk of the peace did to the county; a clerk might remain in office for 30 or 40 years. Councilmen were typically property-owners or professional men (though in Malmesbury they were all workingmen). Due to the **Test and Corporation acts**, only members of the **Church of England** could be councilmen (until 1828), though in some cases (Nottingham, for example) special exemptions were granted so that **dissenters** would be allowed to sit. One of the chief functions of aldermen was hearing cases in petty and quarter sessions, like the justices. Larger cities had independent courts, whereas smaller towns either shared courts with county and municipal officials sitting together on the bench, or sent their cases to the county for adjudication.

The governments of these boroughs, royally chartered entities, were not responsible to their residents but rather to the corporation holding the charter. Like the counties, they tended to be oligarchic and self-perpetuating, though exceptions existed. Toward the end of the 18th century a philosophical shift occurred toward more civic-minded, responsible government, especially in larger cities such as **Liverpool** and **London**, though many borough governments remained notoriously corrupt, incompetent, and unresponsive to the increasingly pressing needs of an industrializing society. The final result of this was a pressure for reform leading to the **Municipal Corporations Act** (1835), which, following upon repeal of the Test and Corporation acts (1828), provided the foundation of modern borough government. A similar bill (1831) had provided a foundation for the modernization and democratization of the vestries, the parish assemblies, but county government remained the unreformed preserve of justices of the peace until much later.

Scotland generally maintained autonomous local government after the Union (1707). The Scottish counties and burghs were dominated by small oligarchic elites headed by great noblemen such as the Dukes of **Argyll** and the Earls of **Bute**. Scottish managers, centered in **Edinburgh**, controlled affairs, sometimes working (as after the **Forty-five** uprising) in tandem with the government in London. Elections, education, and other social matters remained in Scottish hands, though with some modifications based on English models. During the **Napoleonic Wars**, Scottish reformers, like English ones, pressed for improvements in policing, public lighting, and the provision of safe water supplies.

In **Ireland** the **Anglo-Irish Protestant Ascendancy** continued its absorption of Irish aristocratic power by importing the English county system. Early in the 18th century this system was secure only around **Dublin**. Slowly the system of justices and municipal magistrates crept its way over the island, so that by 1800 the English system dominated Irish local government, with offices monopolized by Protestant landowners and their agents. But, also from around 1800, the conservative Protestants dominating the Dublin corporation found themselves increasingly challenged by **middle-class Catholic** reformers demanding greater control of education, policing, poor relief, and public works. In some respects Ireland served as an experimental laboratory; innovations in civil administration there, such as the creation of short-term constabulary forces in the 1780s, often found their way to England.

K.R. Wood

Bibliography

Aylmer, G.E. "From Office-Holding to Civil Service: The Genesis of Modern Bureaucracy." *Transactions of the Royal Historical Society.* 5th ser. Vol. 30, pp. 91–108.

Eastwood, David. *Governing Rural England: Tradition and Transformation in Local Government, 1780–1840.* 1994.

Jones, C., ed. *Britain in the First Age of Party, 1680–1750.* 1987.

Keith-Lucas, B. *The Unreformed Local Government System.* 1980.

Landau, Norma. *The Justices of the Peace, 1679–1760.* 1984.

Langford, Paul. *A Polite and Commercial People: England, 1727–1783.* 1989.

Lewis, B. Keith. *The Unreformed Local Government System.* 1980.

Moir, E. *Local Government in Gloucestershire, 1775–1800.* 1969.

Smellie, K.B. *A History of Local Government.* 4th ed., 1968.

Webb, B., and S. Webb. *The Development of English Local Government, 1689–1835.* Rpt. 1963.

Williams, E.N. *The Eighteenth Century Constitution: Documents and Commentary.* 1960.

See also Aristocracy and Gentry; Legal Profession

Government, National

Throughout the period 1714–1837, the national government's role was conceived minimally—to provide order and **law enforcement**, to foster economic prosperity and the welfare of Protestantism within the country, and to conduct **foreign relations** by both **diplomacy** and **war**. Although economic and military affairs prompted much bureaucratic growth and accumulation of power, especially in fiscal matters, the regime itself remained a patchwork of authorities inherited from much earlier times. **Local government** carried out much of the actual administration of the country, with important variations between England, **Wales**, **Scotland**, and **Ireland**.

Compounding the complexity of all this was a divergence between theory and practice. Theoretically, the country was governed by the separate powers of king, **Lords**, and **Commons** under the **Glorious Constitution**; Hanoverian **political thought** held that stability depended on preserving the balance struck between them by the **Glorious Revolution** (1688–1689). But in practice, Hanoverian government was a contest for administrative control between the executive authority of the Crown and the legislative power of Parliament. The Revolution Settlement left much unsettled in the relationship between these two primary organs of the national government, and while the general tendency after 1714 was for

British Sovereigns of the 18th and 19th centuries

Parliament to gain influence at the expense of the Crown, each of the Hanoverian sovereigns was a major political force. Although there were no royal vetoes after 1707, persons or policies that did not enjoy at least the acquiescence of the monarch had little hope of success, regardless of their support in Parliament.

The Crown's influence grew from the monarch's position as chief executive and the highest source of honors and privileges. The central government conducted all its administrative business in the name of the Crown, and the royal family stood atop the social pyramid. Besides retaining the power to create peers and confer knighthoods and other chivalric honors, the sovereign controlled a **patronage** consisting of hundreds of positions and **pensions** in the royal service. He also dominated several dozen seats or "places" in the House of Commons because of the importance of government business to the constituencies they represented.

For advice and assistance in the conduct of government, the monarch theoretically relied on the Privy Council, a body that had emerged in the 16th century, composed of the great officers of state and the household. By the 1680s, however, this had become so large and unwieldy that the king instead consulted a smaller group of especially trusted advisors who usually held the most important ministerial offices. Given the restraints on royal power after the Glorious Revolution, if the business of government was to be accomplished, this group needed the support of a parliamentary majority as well as the approval of the monarch. By the reign of **Queen Anne** it was referred to as the cabinet, especially when it met in the sovereign's presence. His inability to understand English and his preference for staying in **Hanover** rather than in England led **George I** to cease attending meetings of the cabinet, thereby setting a precedent for his successors. Withdrawal of the monarch from its regular deliberations gave the cabinet much more autonomy and began the process whereby it became increasingly accountable to Parliament in fact, though remaining an adjunct of the Crown in theory.

Cabinet membership fluctuated, depending on a delicate interplay of political personalities and circumstances that reflected issues facing the country and Parliament, particularly the House of Commons. By far the most important cabinet members were the First Lord of the Treasury and the two secretaries of state; between them, these officials oversaw virtually all the Crown's administrative business. After 1714 a board of commissioners supervised the treasury and all collection and expenditure of government revenue; its head, the First Lord, therefore held a uniquely influential position. Between 1721 and 1742 **Sir Robert Walpole** made this indisputably the dominant ministerial post, so that he and most of its subsequent occupants came to be regarded informally but functionally as **prime ministers.**

The influence of the two secretaries of state arose from their extraordinarily broad responsibilities for all foreign relations and all domestic affairs except those directly concerned with financial and judicial matters. The division of labor between them ostensibly reflected their diplomatic involvement with different parts of Europe; hence one was Secretary of State for the Northern Department and the other for the Southern Department. Each, however, had full authority to act on the other's behalf, and no formal distinction existed between them regarding domestic business. Occasionally there were additional secretaries of state, for Scotland and for the colonies. When the colonial secretaryship was abolished in 1782, its duties were assigned to the southern secretary, who also assumed full responsibility for domestic and Irish administration and thus established the foundations of the Home Office. The northern secretary received exclusive responsibility for foreign affairs and became head of the Foreign Office. These reforms set a precedent for the later creation of additional specialized offices whose heads became recognized as members of the cabinet.

The evolution of cabinet government was the principal constitutional development of the Hanoverian era, but the process was neither steady nor always clear. That the cabinet became the mediator between the influence of the Crown and the power of Parliament—and thus the central organ of government—resulted not only from the characteristics of the Hanoverian monarchy but also from changes affecting Parliament.

Parliament remained structurally unaltered throughout the Hanoverian period, but its representative character changed significantly between 1714 and 1837. The **House of Lords** nearly doubled in size over the next century, when the **Peerage Bill** (1719) failed to limit its numbers. It remained the very embodiment of the landed interest, but the political complexion of the Lords changed from **Whig** to **Tory** because most of the increase in size comprised the new peerages created by **George III** as he and his ministers tried to counterbalance the Whig ascendancy of the reigns of George I and **George II**. In the House of Commons, 100 new members for Irish seats appeared in 1801 after the **Act of Union (Ireland)**, but until the **Reform Act** of 1832 the system of **elections and the franchise** was largely unchanged. Although occasional **pension and place bills** attempted to reduce royal influence by prohibiting holders of government or court offices from sitting in the Commons, these proved fairly easy to circumvent.

Three developments most strongly affected the place of the House of Commons during the reign of George III—acceptance of the principle of loyal **opposition**, increasing pressure on the Commons after 1760 from **radicalism** and other outside movements demanding reforms to make the House more broadly representative and accountable, and the intensification of **party politics** during the second half of the reign. All three were influenced by George III's assertive use of Crown influence and by the repercussions of the **American** and **French revolutions**. The king's political activism alone was sufficient to unsettle the relationship between Crown and Parliament that had matured under George I and George II; beyond that, the democratic implications of what unfolded in America and **France** reopened questions about the balance between king, Lords, and Commons that had not been directly addressed for nearly a century and were now more volatile than ever.

That Britain's government escaped revolutionary upheaval after 1790 was due to patriotic enthusiasm aroused by the wars with revolutionary and Napoleonic France and to the repression of domestic political dissent by the administrations of **William Pitt the Younger** and his successors. After 1815, however, the prewar issues of opposition, representation, and the role of parties resurfaced, with social and economic tensions generated by the **Industrial Revolution** increasing their urgency. Two specific questions—**Catholic emancipation** and parliamentary reform—brought matters to a head and led to the reforms of the late 1820s and 1830s. The former grew out of the union with Ireland; the latter had been agitated for more than 50 years. Both evoked broad-based popular movements that eventually forced the hands of the Crown and of each major party.

The government of the United Kingdom in 1837 bore many outward resemblances to the regime of 1714 and, as late as 1834, **William IV** could succeed in dismissing an administration holding a majority in Commons. But the resulting public outcry damaged the influence of the monarchy, just as resistance to passage of parliamentary reform in 1831–1832 had undermined the prestige of the Lords. It was still possible to speak of a government balanced between king, Lords, and Commons, but clearly the balance was now weighted toward the Commons as an arena where a new political element—public opinion—increasingly found expression. As the Hanoverian era ended, parties and politicians contemplated ways to harness this newly potent force.

John A. Hutcheson, Jr.

Bibliography

Brewer, John. *The Sinews of Power: War, Money, and the English State, 1688–1783.* 1988.

Cannon, J.A. *Parliamentary Reform, 1640–1832.* Rev. ed., 1982.

Halévy, Elie. *England in 1815.* 1913.

Hill, B.W. *British Parliamentary Parties, 1742–1832.* 1985.

Kemp, B. *King and Commons, 1660–1832.* 1957.

Namier, Lewis B. *The Structure of Politics at the Accession of George III.* 2nd ed., 1957.

O'Gorman, Frank. *The Emergence of the British Two-Party System, 1760–1832.* 1982.

Owen, John B. *The Eighteenth Century, 1714–1815.* 1974.

Pares, Richard. *King George III and the Politicians.* 1953.

Phillips, John A. *The Great Reform Bill in the Boroughs: English Electoral Behavior, 1818–1841.* 1992.

Plumb, J.H. *The Growth of Political Stability in England, 1675–1725.* 1967.

Thomas, P.D.G. *The House of Commons in the Eighteenth Century.* 1971.

Williams, E.N. *The Eighteenth-Century Constitution: Documents and Commentary.* 1960.

Grafton, 3rd Duke of (Augustus Henry Fitzroy) (1735–1811)

Grafton was First Lord of the Treasury when the leader of his administration, **William Pitt the Elder** (Earl of Chatham from 1766), fell ill and resigned (1767–1768). The reluctant Grafton then became Prime Minister, even though he lacked the authority and ability the post required. His ministry suffered from internal dissension and formed no coherent plans to deal with parliamentary **opposition** or the problems surrounding **John Wilkes**; misjudging Continental relations, it made no determined opposition when **France** purchased Corsica (1769); and it failed to implement its own policy to reconcile the American colonists.

Abused by nearly all the press and most viciously in the "**Junius" letters**, the unhappy Grafton resigned in January 1770. He had first held office in 1765, as Secretary of State for the Northern Department, but resigned the following year when his leader, **Rockingham**, refused to bring Pitt into the ministry. In later years Grafton twice served as Lord Privy Seal (1771–1775 and 1782–1783).

P.J. Kulisheck

Bibliography

Anson, Sir William, ed. *The Autobiography of the Third Duke of Grafton.* 1898.

O'Gorman, Frank. *The Rise of Party in England: The Rockingham Whigs, 1760–82.* 1975.

See also Whigs and Whiggism

Grand Tour

See Travel and Tourism

Grant, Sir Archibald, of Monymusk (1696–1778)

Son of a Scottish judge, Grant was himself trained to the law and practiced in **Edinburgh** from 1717 until his election as M.P. for Aberdeenshire in 1722. He was given the estate of Monymusk by his father in 1717 and began the work which made him one of the most noted **agricultural improvers** in **Scotland.** In **London** he became involved with speculative ventures such as the Harburgh Lottery and the **York Buildings Company.** He leased estates as well as **coal** and salt works from the latter and operated them in conjunction with his family and associates. In 1729, along with the **Duke of Chandos** and others, he helped found the Scotch Mines Company.

In 1725, Grant became a director of the **Charitable Corporation** and a leading figure in its notorious downfall. A parliamentary investigation revealed massive fraud, resulting in Grant's expulsion from the **House of Commons**, but he escaped prosecution and later avoided total financial ruin by civil action because the chief witness was ruled ineligible to testify against his former associates. Grant returned to Scotland and continued the improvement work in forestry and **enclosure** for which he is noted, but because of his very spotty reputation he failed to gain any significant public office.

A.J.G. Cummings

Bibliography

Cummings, A.J.G. "The Business Affairs of a Lowland Laird: Sir Archibald Grant of Monymusk, 1696–1788," in T.M. Devine, ed., *Scottish Elites.* 1994.

Sedgewick, Romney, ed. *The History of Parliament: The House of Commons, 1715–1754.* 2 vols. 1970.

Simpson, I.J. "Sir Archibald Grant and the Charitable Corporation." *Scottish Historical Review.* Vol. 44, pp. 52–62.

See also Scottish Agriculture

Graphic Arts

The Hanoverian period witnessed remarkable advances in the graphic arts as a result of three main developments: the emergence of a group of highly talented pictorial artists including **Sir Godfrey Kneller, Sir Joshua Reynolds, Thomas Gainsborough, George Romney,** and **Joseph M.W. Turner;** the establishment of several bodies to stimulate artistic activity, such as the Academy of Painting, of which Kneller was the first governor (1711), the Society for the Encouragement of Arts, Manufactures, and Commerce (1754), the Society of Artists of Great Britain (1765), and the **Royal Academy of Arts** of **London** (1768); and the rapid expansion of **printing and bookmaking** throughout the country, with a consequent increase in the quantity and quality of **book illustrations** desired. In addition, the sale of prints, **engravings**, etchings, and woodcuts, in individual copies and collections, became widespread, and there was also a vogue for **portraits** and **caricatures.** Demand stimulated supply, and painters who were also engravers, from **William Hogarth** to **William Blake,** flourished.

Much of the work of the foremost graphic artists involved an amalgamation of two or more arts. Hogarth's six *Beggar's Opera* paintings (1729) were based on his direct experience with stage settings, and he used the proscenium as a compositional unit for many later engravings such as his *Garrick as Richard III* (1746). **William Kent**, the famous **landscape architect**, was also the illustrator of Thomson's *Seasons* (1730). The architectural drawings of Augustus Pugin (1762–1832) and the caricatures of **Thomas Rowlandson** were combined with the color-plate lithography of Rudolph Ackerman (1764–1834) to produce *The Microcosm of London* (1808–1811), a series of vignettes of London city life, its buildings, its institutions, and its people.

Although Reynolds, in his *Discourses* (1769–1790) given as President of the Royal Academy, tended to discount the "mechanical" aspects of art reproduction, others acknowledged that the creative element was as much involved in line **drawing**, engraving, aquatint, and etching as in painting itself. Hogarth's celebrated graphic-narrative series, such as *The Harlot's Progress* (1733) and *Marriage à la Mode* (1745), enjoyed (and continue to enjoy) a reputation greater than the paintings from which they evolved. His group portraits, showing lively interaction against dramatic backgrounds, inspired followers like Joseph Highmore (1692–1780), Arthur Devis (1711–1787), and Johann Zoffany (1734–1810), who all learned how to crowd drama into a moment and to imitate stage lighting in heightening facial expressions.

As the 18th century progressed, the energies of graphic artists turned more and more to book illustration, which, with the advent of the **novel** and the growth of **periodical** literature, had become a profitable pursuit. Cooperation between artist–designer and craftsman–engraver was, of course, essential, though a number of artists, most notably **Francis Hayman** and William Blake could sign their work *inv. et del.* or *fec. et sculp.* to show that both the creation and the execution were their own.

Of the many graphic artists who excelled in book illustration, only a fraction can be mentioned here: **Thomas Bewick**, whose forte, end-grain engraving on wood, is best seen in his books for children, such as *A Pretty Book of Pictures* (1779) and his *History of British Birds* (1797 and 1804); Francesco Bartolozzi (1725–1815), who popularized the stipple method of engraving and went on to experiment with color printings; Lady Diana Beauclerk (1734–1808), who illustrated Dryden's *Fables Ancient and Modern* (1797) with pencil drawings, engraved by Bartolozzi and others; the Swiss-born **Henry Fuseli**, whose imaginative illustrations of the plays of **Shakespeare** and of **Milton**'s *Paradise Lost* are less known now than his **Gothic** fantasies and nightmarish scenes; Francis Hayman, whose first important commission was to design 11 plates for the sixth edition of **Samuel Richardson**'s *Pamela* (1742), with engravings by Hubert Gravelot (1699–1773), and who, with the same engraver, produced 36 plates for Sir Thomas Hammer's six-volume Oxford *Shakespeare* (1743–1744); Angelica Kaufman (1740–1807), whose paintings were very popular and who prepared designs for Thomas Stothard (1755–1834), one of the earliest illustrators of the works of

Scott and **Byron**; and George Vertue (1684–1756), prolific engraver of frontispiece portraits.

Several British graphic artists excelled in the production of sporting and animal illustrations. Among these were John Wootton (1678–1765), George Morland (1763–1804), and **George Stubbs**. Stubbs's sporting prints, depicting horses of every description, became favorite decorations in **clubs** and inns throughout the British Isles. The work of **landscape painters** such as **Richard Wilson**, **John Constable**, and Turner was frequently reproduced. Turner, who made nearly a thousand drawings for copper engravings, graced *The Collected Poems of Sir Walter Scott* (1834) with engravings of his visionary landscapes and stormy seascapes. Like some other graphic artists, he had begun as a topographical draftsman, apprenticed to a mezzotint engraver, and developed the art of **watercolor** to perfection.

In the field of graphic comedy and **satire**, Hogarth's acknowledged successors included Isaac Cruikshank (1756–1810) and his son **George Cruikshank**, **James Gillray**, who deployed his wicked satirical weapons to the discomfiture of politicians and royalty alike, and Thomas Rowlandson, who brought the art of the hilarious-grotesque to its peak at the beginning of the 19th century. All four adeptly depicted crowd scenes revealing the ridiculous antics of humanity, but Rowlandson, who enjoyed a life of indulgence himself, was especially talented in caricaturing similarly indulgent sybarites. Of his book illustrations, his best appear in **William Combe**'s *Tours of Dr. Syntax* (1809–1826), a verse satire of William Gilpin's *Tours* (1783–1789) which Rowlandson thought over-idealized, and in *The English Dance of Death* (1815–1816), which treads the precarious borderland between the comic and the macabre.

For many, the greatest graphic artist of the period was William Blake, whose intense spirituality and **poetic** fervor were combined with a perfectionist commitment to craftsmanship. For him the essential component of all art was the living line: "He who draws best must be the best Artist." His most important original work began with his *Songs of Innocence* (1789), in which both text and illustrations were etched in relief and hand-painted. That volume set the pattern of a series of illuminated books illustrating the **poetry** of Milton, **Young**, **Gray**, and **Blair**, as well as parts of the Bible, most notably *The Book of Job* (1825). Blake's *Jerusalem* (1804–1820), both text and illustrations again his own, is considered by modern scholars to be the most significant example of his experiments in illuminated poetry.

James Gray

Bibliography

George, M. Dorothy. *Hogarth to Cruikshank: Social Change in Graphic Satire.* 1967.

Hammelmann, Hanns, and T.R. Boase. *Book Illustrators in Eighteenth-Century England.* 1975.

Hayes, John. *Rowlandson: Watercolours and Drawings.* 1972.

Keynes, Sir Geoffrey, ed. *Drawings of William Blake.* 1970.

Lipking, Lawrence. *The Ordering of the Arts in Eighteenth-Century England.* 1970.

Paulson, Ronald. *Hogarth: His Life, Art, and Times.* 2 vols. 1971.

Ray, Gordon N. *The Illustrator and the Book in England from 1790 to 1914.* 1976.

Rosenblum, Robert. *Transformations in Late Eighteenth-Century Art.* 1967.

Russell, Ronald. *Guide to British Topographical Prints.* 1979.

Wilton, Andrew. *Turner and the Sublime.* 1980.

Wood, Marcus. *Radical Satire and Print Culture, 1790–1822.* 1994.

See also Caricature; Painting; Political Prints

Grattan, Henry (1746–1820)

Grattan, "the greatest of Irish orators," was a leading figure in Irish politics during the latter 18th century. Under **George I** and **George II** the kingdom of **Ireland** was governed like a colony, with legislation first sanctioned in **London** by the king and his Privy Council, then normally approved in **Dublin** by the colonial-type **Irish Parliament**. This Parliament, overseen from Dublin Castle by a viceroy, was managed by bribery and **patronage** among the electors, all of whom were members of the **Anglo-Irish Protestant Ascendancy**—the "occupying force" of landowners and other families originally from Great Britain.

The members of this Parliament in Grattan's time have been described as "Protestant Episcopalians who were anti–English because they regarded themselves as an English garrison in Ireland who were not paid enough for their garrison duties." This is cynical, but Grattan, a Protestant educated at **Trinity College** and called to the Irish bar in 1772, entered the Irish Parliament (1775) in the interest of James Caulfield, Earl of Charlemont (1728–1799), and, skilled in oratory, quickly became the leader of the **patriot** group. The patriots, sensitive to Ireland's colonial status, demanded Irish parliamentary independence from the Privy Council and the Westminster Parliament. Britain was now locked in the **War of American Independence**, which both stimulated Irish nationalism and made **Lord North** and the British government less reluctant to placate it. Accordingly, in 1779 Grattan and his colleagues succeeded in having most of the home government's restraints on Irish **trade** repealed and, in 1782, backed by the Irish **volunteers**—dressed in Irish wool, commanded by Charlemont, and stationed throughout the country—they gained its acceptance of the proposition that only the Irish Parliament had the power to legislate for Ireland.

Grattan was the hero of the hour, and the Irish Parliament of 1782–1800 was known as "Grattan's Parliament." But Grattan, unlike Charlemont and **Henry Flood**, favored complete freedom of worship and the admission of propertied **Catholics** to Parliament. "The Irish Protestant," he declared, "could never be free till the Irish Catholic had ceased to be a slave." He thus moved again toward an oppositional position, working in the period 1782–1796 for **Catholic emancipation** and a more thorough reform of the rotten **borough** system that still made the Irish legislature unrepresentative even of the Protestant minority permitted to vote for it. Some of his efforts bore fruit in the early 1790s.

Yet **Wolfe Tone** and the **United Irishmen** condemned Grattan's caution and sought to go well beyond him in creating an Irish republican government and ecumenical state completely severed from the remaining viceregal control. When they failed (1798) and **Pitt the Younger** subsequently drew up plans for a legislative union of the two Parliaments, Grattan reacted with implacable hostility, emerging from retirement to address the Irish House of Commons in a volunteer uniform, "deathly pale and hardly able to walk." But the heavily bribed House endorsed the **Act of Union** anyway, and Grattan soon became one of the 100 Irish M.P.s to sit in Westminster, representing Malton (1805–1806) and Dublin City (1806–1820). A supporter of the **Whigs**, he was invited to join the **Ministry of All the Talents** but refused. He continued to support Catholic emancipation, though a more radical group connected with the **Catholic Committee** and **Daniel O'Connell** came to lead that cause by 1815. Grattan was just preparing to again introduce the Catholic question when he died in 1820. He was buried in Westminster Abbey near the tombs of Pitt and **Fox**.

George F. Clements

Bibliography

Lecky, W.E.H. *Leaders of Public Opinion in Ireland.* 2 vols. 1903; rpt. 1973.

McHugh, Roger Joseph. *Henry Grattan.* 1937.

O'Brien, Gerard. *Anglo-Irish Politics in the Age of Grattan and Pitt.* 1987.

Graveyard School of Poetry

This nickname, which gained currency in the 1920s, refers to poems, mainly written around 1750, that affect **melancholy** and horror through descriptions of graveyards and meditations on mortality. In content, graveyard poems continued earlier lyrical and homiletic traditions, but they also represented a new development in being characteristically longer than earlier works, preceding their meditations with more extended descriptions, dramatizing the speaker's feelings and, in some cases, seeking secular consolations. Since similar graveyard meditations were written in prose, and the principal authors belonged to no formal school, we might more properly speak of "graveyard literature."

The truest and most influential examples of the form are **Edward Young**'s *The Complaint; or, Night Thoughts on Life, Death and Immortality* (1742–1746) and **Robert Blair**'s *The Grave* (1743), largely composed before 1742. To them must be joined James Hervey's (1714–1758) prose *Meditations among the Tombs in a Letter to a Lady* (1746) and, although more secular, **Thomas Gray**'s *Elegy Written in a Country Church-yard* (1751). Early precursors often reprinted with the others are Thomas Parnell's (1679–1718) *Night-Piece on Death* (1722) and Young's *A Poem on the Last Day* (1713), the former with all the essential topics in short compass and the latter with most motifs in a long narrative. All these works passed through scores of editions by 1800, their popularity peaking from 1775 to 1810, with shorter poems like Blair's *Grave* and Gray's *Elegy* regularly reprinted together (there were over 45 joint editions by 1800). Thus enjoying extraordinary influence, they gave rise to imitations, sometimes reprinted with the major exemplars, such as Bishop Beilby Porteus's (1731–1808) *Death* (1759); Reverend Moore's (n.d.) *Night Thoughts among the Tombs* (1794); and George Wright's (n.d.) *Pleasing Melancholy, or a Walk Through the Tombs* (1793).

In most graveyard literature, a speaker stirred with emotion, addressing the reader with dramatic immediacy in a style shifting between the conversational and the oratorical **sublime**, describes a moonlit churchyard animated with the calls of owls and ravens. George Vertue's (1681–1756) frontispiece for Young's fifth *Night* illustrates these descriptive motifs and might as easily preface Blair's *The Grave* or Parnell's *Night-Piece on Death:* a man alone in a churchyard reads a tomb under a full moon. This setting provokes thoughts about the transience and vanity of life, the imperial sway of death, the last judgment, and the hereafter.

Applying critical tenets of **John Dennis** and **Joseph Addison** in a style indebted to John Milton, **James Thomson**, and the dramatists from **Shakespeare** to Thomas Otway (1652–1685), graveyard literature exploits religious material to produce sublime and pathetic effects. Like the sentimental **novel**, it reflects a shift in taste toward **sensibility**, emotional display, and, in literature, the **Romantic style**.

James E. May

Bibliography

Draper, John W. *The Funeral Elegy and the Rise of English Romanticism.* 1929.

Reed, Amy. *The Background of Gray's 'Elegy': A Study in the Tastes for Melancholy Poetry, 1700–1751.* 1924.

Van Tieghem, Paul. *La Poésie de la nuit des Tombeaux.* Rpt. as *Le Préromantisme d'Histoire.* 1930.

Gray, Thomas (1716–1771)

Gray, a reclusive man, lived much of his life apart from the public scene, but his *Elegy Written in a Country Church-yard* (1751) was the most popular poem of his time and remains one of the most anthologized and quoted. The greatness of Gray's work comes from his ability to combine important general truths, stated in the abstract style of his time, with an intense, subtly implied passion.

Gray was born in **London** and educated at Eton and **Cambridge**. After **traveling** in Europe with his Eton classmate **Horace Walpole**, he settled in Cambridge and took his B.A. (1744). Two of his poems of the 1740s were *Ode on a Distant Prospect of Eton College,* and *Sonnet [on the Death of Mr. Richard West].* The former expressed eloquently the contrast between the excitement and innocence of childhood play, stated with nervous, vivid imagery, and adult sorrow, stated with powerful abstractions; its strength lies in "that interplay of the subjective and objective which distinguishes Gray's **poetry**" (Lonsdale). The sonnet on West (whom Gray had also met at Eton) was his most personal poem in English (he wrote some more openly emotional poems to West in Latin); his emotions give it an unusual intensity.

Thomas Gray

Gray wrote his masterpiece, the supreme achievement of the **Graveyard School of Poetry**, *Elegy Written in a Country Church-yard,* during the years of self-imposed isolation after West's death. Again the poem pulsates between a distant, abstract style and a subtle passion. Its narrator, a lonely young man, wanders the churchyard without apparent purpose, isolated from the vigorous life of the nearby village and the ambitious bustle of the city. His musings express the poem's themes: the inevitability of death, the certainty of suffering, the contrast of rural and city life, the arbitrariness of fame, the aimlessness of contemporary life.

Gray declined the **poet laureateship** (1757) but received appointment (1768) as Professor of Modern History and Languages at Cambridge. One of the most learned men in Britain, he affected an aristocratic aloofness and deliberately wrote for an intellectually select audience. The two most important poems he wrote in the 1750s were "The Progress of Poetry: A Pindaric Ode," and "The Bard: A Pindaric Ode." In them he covered historical and aesthetic subjects in a form and meter that he adapted from the Greek ode. That they were regarded as obscure by many contemporaries perversely pleased him: "Nobody understands me, & I am perfectly satisfied." His **biography** was written by his friend William Mason (1775), and later by Samuel Johnson.

Raymond Bentman

Bibliography

Downey, James, and Ben Jones, eds. *Fearful Joy: Papers from the Thomas Gray Bicentenary Conference at Carleton University.* 1974.

Golden, Morris. *Thomas Gray.* 1964.

Ketton-Cremer, R.W. *Thomas Gray: A Biography.* 1955.

Lonsdale, Roger, ed. *The Poems of Gray, Collins, and Goldsmith.* 1969.

Toynbee, Paget, and Leonard Whibley. *Correspondence of Thomas Gray.* 1935.

Weinfield, Henry. *The Poet Without a Name: Gray's "Elegy" and the Problem of History.* 1991.

See also Sensibility and Sentimentalism

Greg, Samuel (1758–1834)

A noted figure in the **cotton industry**, Greg, the son of a Belfast shipowner with interests in the linen and **chemical** industries, founded a family firm which survived for three generations after his death. He came to **Manchester** and established a merchant-manufacturing business in linens and fustians before entering the cotton industry. A single-minded paternalist, he then established the factory village at Styal (Cheshire) between 1784 and 1787. The Quarry Bank Mills were built on the River Bollin. Local farm buildings were converted to accommodate incoming skilled **factory workers**, and additional housing for **spinners** was provided, but the mills were heavily reliant on pauper apprentices until the prohibition of **child labor**.

From 1798 to 1814, Peter Ewart (1767–1842), previously an employee of **Boulton** and **Watt**, was Greg's partner. Greg prospered during and after the French **wars** (1792–1815), acquiring additional mills in Lancashire. At his death he left an industrial empire to his sons.

John Butt

Bibliography

Butt, J., and I.L. Donnachie. *Industrial Archaeology in the British Isles.* 1979.

Collier, Frances. *The Family Economy of the Working Classes in the Cotton Industry, 1784–1833.* 1965.

Edwards M.M. *The Growth of the British Cotton Trade, 1780–1815.* 1967.

Rose, Mary. *The Gregs of Quarry Bank Mill.* 1986.

Grenville, Baron (William Wyndham Grenville) (1759–1834)

Grenville was one of only two men in British history (the other was his first cousin, **William Pitt the Younger**) to follow his father (**George Grenville**) to the premiership. Educated at Eton and Christ Church, Oxford, a protégé of Pitt, he held at one time or another most of the important offices of state: Speaker of the House of Commons (1789); Home Secretary (1789–1791); Foreign Secretary (1791–1801); and **Prime Minister** (1806–1807). Yet despite these distinctions he was perhaps most proud of being Chancellor of **Oxford University** (1809–1834).

Grenville was in charge of **foreign relations** during some of the darkest days of **French Revolutionary and Napoleonic Wars**. He was a proponent of the traditional British policy of alliances with and subsidies of Prussia, Russia, and Austria, as the most effective means of countering French power. As Prime Minister immediately after Pitt's death during the coalition **Ministry of All the Talents** (1806–1807), he superintended the successful bill for the abolition of the **slave trade**

Lord Grenville

in the British **Empire**. During the first three decades of the 19th century he was also one of the most influential proponents of complete **Catholic emancipation** for Irish and British **Roman Catholics**.

James J. Sack

Bibliography

Jupp, Peter. *Lord Grenville, 1759–1834.* 1985.
Sack, James J. *The Grenvillites, 1801–1829.* 1979.

Grenville, George (1712–1770)

Scion of a leading Buckinghamshire **gentry** family, educated at Eton and Oxford, Grenville sat in the **House of Commons** (1741–1770) throughout his distinguished political career. As a follower of **Lord Bute** and **George III** he served as First Lord of the Admiralty (1762–1763) during the closing months of the **Seven Years' War**, then as **Prime Minister** (1763–1765). Grenville was the patriarch of a notable political dynasty, his eldest son becoming a marquess, his youngest (**William Wyndham Grenville**) a baron and prime minister; his eldest Grenville grandson became first duke of Buckingham and Chandos in 1822.

Although Grenville was an able man of business and a noted factional leader for many years, his short administration will always be judged by its prosecution of **John Wilkes** for seditious libel (1763) and its passage of the **Stamp Act** (1765). The latter, in view of its unfortunate results in alienating American colonists, has been regarded as a monumental blunder, but a case could be made that Grenville's American policy was both necessary and prudent. Certainly from the government's point of view the Stamp Act seemed to make good sense both financially and morally. But the fall of Grenville's ministry in July 1765 owed less to the act than to Grenville's unpleasant habit of lecturing the king. Out of power, he kept up his campaign to **tax** the Americans and so assisted **Charles Townshend** in the passage of new revenue measures (1767) that worsened the colonial crisis.

James J. Sack

Bibliography

Christie, I.R. *Crisis of Empire: Great Britain and the American Colonies, 1754–1783.* 1966.
Lawson, Philip. *George Grenville: A Political Life.* 1984.
Thomas, P.D.G. *British Politics and the Stamp Act Crisis.* 1975.

See also American Revolution; Plantation Act

Grey, 2nd Earl of (Charles Grey) (1764–1845)

While **Prime Minister** (1830–1834), Grey secured passage of the first **Reform Act** (1832), which reallocated electoral constituencies and initiated the 19th-century extension of the franchise. A traditional **aristocratic Whig**, Grey saw reform as a means of preserving a balanced constitution, not the beginning of universal suffrage. Even when, early in his career, he helped found the **Society of the Friends of the People** (1792) and introduced an unsuccessful parliamentary reform bill (1797), his goal was to defuse class conflict and protect the Whig interest.

During his service in the **House of Commons** (1786–1807), Grey, an excellent debater, joined his friend **Charles James Fox** in opposing **Pitt the Younger**'s policies, and became

Lord Grey

Foreign Secretary after Fox's death (1806). A few months before Grey succeeded to the earldom (1807), he resigned from the **Ministry of All the Talents** over the issue of Catholic relief, presaging his vigorous support of the 1829 **Catholic emancipation** bill. Grey, like all Whigs, spent a long period out of office but finally saw his opportunity in the **Wellington** administration's mishandling of foreign affairs.

When Grey did become head of government (1830), he recruited a cabinet dominated by aristocrats, some not as committed to reform as their leader. After his first reform bill was defeated (March 1831), Grey called a general election that confirmed his policies. His second bill was voted down in the **House of Lords** (October 1831). A third bill was delayed in Lords until Grey obtained **William IV**'s promise (May 1832) to create enough new peers to force the bill through, the threat of which finally secured its passage. Another major achievement was the abolition of slavery in all British-controlled territories (1833). Disagreements among the members of the cabinet increased, especially over Irish questions, leading the 70-year-old Grey to resign (1834) and retire from politics.

P.J. Kulisheck

Bibliography

Derry, John W. *Charles, Earl Grey: Aristocratic Reformer.* 1992.

Smith, E.A. *Lord Grey, 1764–1845.* 1990.

Thorne, R.G. *History of Parliament: The House of Commons, 1790–1820.* 5 vols. 1986.

See also Antislavery Movement; Elections and the Franchise

Grub Street

Samuel Johnson defined Grub Street in his *Dictionary* in this way: "Originally the name of a street in Moorfields in London, much inhabited by writers of small histories, dictionaries and temporary poems; whence any mean production is called *grubstreet.*" There was playful self-reference here, but the definition is accurate. The term applies strictly only to **London**, although scholarship on the literary underground in 18th-century Paris has recently appropriated it.

The concept came to be used in the Restoration, and it was John Dryden's *Mac Flecknoe* (1682) which filled out its implications by associating bad and venal writing with the squalid outlying districts of London. **Alexander Pope** developed this topographical metaphor in the later version of his *Dunciad* (1743), which situates "the cave of poverty and poetry" in a hidden "cell" near the madhouse of Bedlam, again in conformity with the real-life layout of the city. Pope's creation may be read as a full-blown epic of Grub Street, in which the new class of professional authors (including **journalists**, compilers, abridgers, popular novelists and the like) stands accused of flooding the nation with a deluge of print. This evolved as the century progressed into a sustained mythology of Grub Street, in which the writers of hack literature were portrayed as producing an endless flow of unwanted works from their seedy quarters in London garrets and back alleys. The classic embodiment of this myth in **graphic art** is

"Dr. Johnson Rescuing Oliver Goldsmith from His Landlady"

Hogarth's *Distressed Poet* (1735); its most durable literary treatment is the depiction of Richard Savage (*c.* 1697–1743) in Johnson's *Life* of his friend (1744). A later **caricature** of it appeared in T.B. Macaulay's (1800–1859) **essay** on Johnson (1831).

The myth was based on a genuine reality, but it heightened the truth. It was the case that a growing number of authors, not all highly educated, were now able to make a living by writing for an ever-expanding readership. Their works helped to fill the **newspapers** and **periodicals** that proliferated after the suspension of official **censorship** in 1695. Their social origins were not strictly plebeian; indeed, few of them had as humble a background as **Daniel Defoe**, who emerged from a literary environment close to that of the mythical Grub Street and made a brief appearance in *The Dunciad.* They lost caste because of the rather miscellaneous nature of their productions, as viewed by the more successful and secure writers such as Pope, **Swift**, and **Fielding**. It is also true that (as the myth asserted) their activities were often organized and orchestrated by a small number of prominent **publishers and booksellers**, the audacious Edmund Curll (1683–1747), for example, whose long battle with Pope helped to disseminate the idea of a grasping publisher managing the flow of cheap, salacious, and unauthorized books.

Most professional writers led more humdrum lives than the myth suggests, and some made valuable contributions to forms such as the emergent **novel**, social reportage, and popular **biography**. It would be sentimental to see their work as a deliberate critique of the polite world of letters, since most were only too anxious to achieve security, fame, and public admiration. But insofar as the myth served to present them as marginal and deviant, they could be enlisted in an anti-establishment cult of the writer as outsider. There was an actual Grub Street of day-to-day popular literature, but more lastingly there was a Grub Street created in the poems of Pope and the novels of Fielding, which dramatized an increasing split between the noble aspirations of authorship and the commercial pressures of writing in the marketplace.

Pat Rogers

Bibliography

Gerrard, Christine. *The Patriot Opposition to Walpole: Politics, Poetry, and National Myth, 1725–1742.* 1995.
Pinkus, Philip. *Grub Street Laid Bare.* 1967.
Raven, James. *Judging New Wealth: Popular Publishing and Responses to Commerce in England, 1750–1800.* 1992.
Rogers, Pat. *Grub Street: Studies in a Subculture.* 1972.

See also Russel, Richard

Guest, Sir Josiah John (1785–1852)

A leading figure in the **iron industry**, Guest was born in **Merthyr Tydfil**, South **Wales**, where his father was part owner of the Dowlais ironworks. He went from grammar school straight into the works whose development was to be his life's great achievement. A progressive and innovative manager, he was ever alert for practical improvements. Dowlais became a center of continuous incremental advance, notably through the adoption of **coal** in place of coke, and improvements in the blast system that included the adoption of **James Neilson**'s hot-blast method. In 1815 Guest became sole manager: between then and 1849, when he finally became sole owner, he presided over his firm's expansion from an output of 5,000 tons in 1806 to 100,000 tons at "the largest manufactory in the world," with profits estimated at £50,000 per annum. He was the archetypal iron baron, firm but charitable as he presided over the entire community as employer, M.P. (1832–1852), and Baronet. A fellow of the **Royal Society** and the Geological Society, he died at Dowlais in 1852.

R.D. Corrins

Bibliography

Birch, A.M. *The Economic History of the British Iron and Steel Industry, 1784–1879.* 1967.
Harris, J.R. *The British Iron Industry 1700–1850.* 1988.

See also Entrepreneurs and Entrepreneurship; Metallurgy and Metalworking; Welsh Industry

H

Hair Styles

See Wigs, Hair, and Hairdressing

Haldane Brothers

Robert Haldane (1764–1842) and his younger brother James (1768–1851) furnish noteworthy examples of the impact of the late-18th-century **religious revival** on **Scotland**. Born into the Scottish gentry, they studied at Edinburgh University and in the 1780s joined the **navy** under the protection of their uncle, Viscount Duncan. They **traveled** widely (James making four voyages to **India** and China) and then at some point came under the influence of David Bogue (1750–1825), **Congregationalist** minister at Gosport and later a founder of the London Missionary Society (1795).

Both increasingly felt the impulse of religious enthusiasm and began to preach. Influenced by the evangelistic Rev. Rowland Hill (1744–1833) and ceasing communication with the conservatively respectable **Church of Scotland** (1799), they began their own Congregational Church in **Edinburgh** (the first in Scotland). James became its first pastor (1799) and, refusing to accept a salary, devoted the church's income to support of the nonsectarian Society for Propagating the Gospel at Home, which he had founded (1797). Meanwhile Robert, expending huge sums (perhaps more than £70,000 in 1798–1810), labored to build a network of allied congregations in surrounding **population** centers and to provide seminaries to staff them. Both found it necessary to defend themselves against charges leveled at their excessively democratic religious and political views.

Like many others, the Haldanes also burned to carry the gospel to foreign lands. They worked closely with **missionary societies** devoted to international distribution of the Bible. In 1796 Robert almost rashly sold off his estates and headed to India with only Bogue, a few others, and a printing press; in 1798 he helped hatch a plan, actually implemented, for bringing 24 African children to Edinburgh, to inject them with Christianity and send them back to evangelize others; and in 1816–1819 he toured Geneva and parts of **France**, stirring up *le Réveil,* a significant awakening sometimes known as "Haldane's Revival."

The brothers shocked their co-religionists and set off more general argument when they moved over to the **Baptist** persuasion in 1808. They were able controversialists, as they proved by writing on dozens of questions both religious and educational. Representative works were Robert's *Evidences and Authority of Divine Revelation* (1816) and *The Books of the Old and New Testaments Canonical and Inspired* (1840), and James's *Duty of Christian Forbearance in Regard to Points of Church Order* (1811) and *Man's Responsibility; the Nature and Extent of the Atonement* (1842). By their efforts the Haldanes brought a new fervor, seriousness, and philanthropic spirit to many Scottish communities during the first half of the 19th century.

Richard M. Riss

Bibliography

Haldane, Alexander. *Memoirs of the Lives of Robert Haldane of Airthrey and of His Brother, James Alexander Haldane.* 1852.

Kirk, Edward Norris. *Lectures on Revivals.* 1875.

Lloyd-Jones, D. Martyn. "An Introduction to the Author of This Commentary" and "Foreword," in Haldane, Robert, *An Exposition of the Epistle to the Romans.* 1958.

Montgomery, John W. "Believing the Bible Breeds Revival." *Christianity Today.* Vol. 25, pp. 689–690.

Stunt, Timothy. "Geneva and British Evangelicals in the Early Nineteenth Century." *Journal of Ecclesiastical History.* Vol. 32, pp. 35–46.

Hales, Stephen (1677–1761)

Botanist, physiologist, inventor, and clergyman, Hales pioneered quantitative experimentation in plant and animal physiology. Educated at **Cambridge**, he studied botany and chemistry, and accompanied his friend **William Stukeley** on archaeological tours. Ordained in 1703, he served as minister to a parish at Teddington from 1709 until his death. A

Stephen Hales

member of many scientific societies, including the **Royal Society** (1718) and the French Academy (1753), Hales also earned a doctorate in divinity from **Oxford** (1733). Among his friends and admirers were **Frederick, Prince of Wales** and **Alexander Pope**. Though cheerful and good-natured, he wrote several pamphlets protesting the heavy **drinking** of the 1730s.

Hales is best known for three great scientific accomplishments, all connected with pressures, flows, and circulations of natural substances. In plant physiology he extensively studied plant transpiration, sap flow, and pressure. In animal physiology he quantified the measurement of blood pressure. His major written work was *Statical Essays* (1733): volume one, *Vegetable Staticks,* covered his botany discoveries; volume two, *Haemastaticks,* described his studies of circulation. His experiments stimulated **Joseph Black, Henry Cavendish,** and **Joseph Priestley.** As an inventor, he produced an artificial ventilator that reduced mortality rates when used to provide fresh air in **prisons** and **ships**' holds. He also experimented with distilling fresh water out of saltwater, meat preservation, and various methods of measuring depths and temperatures.

Thomas D. Veve

Bibliography

Darwin, Sir Francis. *Rustic Sounds and Other Studies in Literature and Natural History.* 1917.

Dictionary of Scientific Biography, s.v. "Hales, Stephen."

Gascoigne, John. *Joseph Banks and the English Enlightenment: Useful Knowledge and Polite Culture.* 1994.

Golinski, Jan. *Science as Public Culture: Chemistry and Enlightenment in Britain, 1760–1820.* 1992.

Stewart, Larry. *The Rise of Public Science: Rhetoric, Technology and Natural Philosophy in Newtonian Britain, 1660–1750.* 1992.

See also Science, Technology, and Invention

Halley, Edmond (1656–1742)

Halley, astronomer and mathematician, is best known for his prediction that the great comet of 1531, 1607, and 1682 would reappear in December 1758. He was born in **London** and educated at **Oxford.** Influenced by John Flamsteed (1646–1719), first Astronomer Royal, Halley went to St. Helena in the South Atlantic (1676) and mapped the stars of the southern sky (complementing Flamsteed's work on the northern), a project which earned him an M.A. from **Oxford** and membership in the **Royal Society.** Halley met Isaac Newton (1642–1727) at Cambridge and urged him to complete his gravitational calculations, afterward editing and bearing the costs of publishing Newton's *Principia Mathematica* (1687).

Halley's scientific interests ranged widely. In his lifetime he pioneered the publication of meteorological charts, lunar tables, mortality tables, and magnetic studies of great use to the science of **navigation.** He calculated Earth's distance from the sun, and like many others labored to determine **longitude** accurately. But his most famous achievement was his *Synopsis of the Astronomy of Comets* (1705), which included his prediction of the return of the great comet. He asked his associates to remember his prophecy after his death; and when the comet returned on Christmas Day 1758, Halley's fame was insured and the comet was given his name. He became the nation's second Royal Astronomer (1720) and held the post until his death, re-equipping the Royal Observatory and spending most of his tenure studying the moon. His handpicked replacement, **James Bradley,** was a worthy successor.

Thomas D. Veve

Bibliography

Armitage, A. *Edmond Halley.* 1966.

Ronan, Colin A. *Edmond Halley—Genius in Eclipse.* 1969.

See also Science, Technology, and Invention; William Herschel

Hampden Clubs

These clubs, named after John Hampden (1594–1643), the 17th-century parliamentary foe of Charles I, constituted a network of local organizations designed to raise the level of **radical** political awareness and promote parliamentary reform as a cure for popular grievances in the period 1812–1817. Organized as reading and discussion **associations** similar to those which had flourished from 1780 to 1795, they were especially successful in the northern industrial regions of Yorkshire, Leicester, Lancashire, and Birmingham. **Major John Cartwright** founded the first club in 1812, but the larger affiliation of groups enjoyed greatest growth in 1816. Besides Cartwright, the clubs' leadership included **Samuel Bamford, Henry Hunt,** and, briefly, Hunt's rival **William Cobbett** (though he also condemned them for playing into the hands of extremists). The government, not without reason, considered them connected to **Luddism.**

Their high point was the open convention arranged by Cartwright, attended by some 70 delegates, and held in **London** at the Crown and Anchor Tavern, beginning on 22 January 1817. The delegates circumvented the ban against meetings of "seditious" groups imposed by the Corresponding Societies Act (1799) by presenting themselves as individuals gathered to petition Parliament. The gathering, backed by petitions signed by many hundreds of thousands of people, called for annual parliaments, universal manhood suffrage, and vote by ballot; Cartwright arranged their presentation to Parliament at the end of January.

The government did not interrupt the convention, but it was held in a turbulent time. Ever since passage of the **Corn Law** (1815) there had been **riots** and unrest, including the **Spa Fields Riot** just one month earlier (December 1816). After the convention came an attack on the Prince Regent's carriage (January 28, 1817); the **Blanketeer March** (March 1817); and the Pentrich Rising (June 1817), a sad attempt by 100 misguided Derbyshire villagers to overthrow the regime. The government acted by repressing popular meetings, suspending habeas corpus, and rounding up radical leaders. The radical movement fragmented, some leaders urging moderation, others resistance by force. The clubs, much weakened, continued to disseminate political reform information through the 1820s via permanent newsrooms called "reading societies."

Thomas D. Veve

Bibliography

Royle, Edward, and James Walvin. *English Radicals and Reformers, 1760–1848.* 1982.

Sack, James J. *From Jacobite to Conservative: Reaction and Orthodoxy in Britain, c.1760–1832.* 1993.

Thompson, E.P. *The Making of the English Working Class.* 1963.

White, R.J. *Waterloo to Peterloo.* 1957.

Handel, George Frideric (1685–1759)

Handel, an exact contemporary of Johann Sebastian Bach (1685–1750), far excelled him in fame and critical repute until well into the Victorian period. He settled permanently in England in 1713, built a formidable reputation, and eventually through his oratorios acquired posthumous acclaim as "Britain's national composer" and the master of the religious sublime. It is only in comparatively recent times that a balanced view of his genius has been attained.

Handel was born at Halle in Saxony, and after early training as an organist went to Hamburg (1703) as a violinist and then harpsichordist in the city opera house, for which he wrote his first **operas** (1705). From 1706 to 1710 he resided in Italy, where he mastered the current idioms in music for the church, the chamber, and the **theater**. In 1710 he became Kapellmeister to the Elector of Hanover (later **George I** of England) and made his first visit to **London**, where he scored a stunning success with his Italian opera *Rinaldo* (1711). His second visit, begun in 1712, became permanent. In 1713 he composed works in honor of **Queen Anne**'s birthday and the peace of Utrecht, and under George I and **George II** wrote other ceremonial music: the Water Music (1717), coronation anthems (1727), Dettingen Te Deum (1743), and Royal Fireworks Music (1749). Handel was appointed a composer to the

George Frideric Handel

Chapel Royal in 1723; from then until his death he resided at 25 Brook Street, becoming a well-known figure in London society. He was naturalized in 1727.

From 1717 to 1719 Handel was employed at Cannons, Middlesex, by the Earl of Caernarvon (later **Duke of Chandos**), for whom he wrote the charming masque *Acis and Galatea* and the 11 "Chandos anthems." Returning to London, he became one of three composers attached to the **Royal Academy of Music** (1719–1729), which, despite its name, was a commercial opera company of the most ambitious kind. He produced a series of masterpieces of Italian heroic *opera seria,* most notably *Radamisto* (1720), *Giulio Cesare* (1723), and *Rodelinda* (1725). When the academy failed because of enormous overexpenditures, Handel continued to compose for various opera ventures, losing much of his own fortune in the process. In 1741 he was forced to conclude that Italian opera, however well suited to his dramatic and musical gifts, could not provide him a secure living.

Meanwhile he had been developing a genre that had a wider and more immediate appeal to the English. He turned seriously to the composition of **oratorio** in 1733, when he embarked on a long series of works designed in part to assert the truth of the Anglican religion in the face of deist attack. With masterly skill he turned the triumphal late-baroque idiom, originally developed to celebrate absolute monarchy, into an assertion of the authority of the British church and state. Above all, his *Messiah* (premiered at **Dublin** in 1742), with words directly compiled from the King James Bible, exercised a profound appeal for the **middle-class** public. In a series of gigantic Handel festivals at Westminster Abbey (1784–1791), the choral and orchestral forces were gradually increased, giving the oratorios a ritual grandeur undreamed of by Handel.

Handel also excelled on a more modest scale in his many

cantatas for solo voice, his chamber duets, trio sonatas, and keyboard suites. His Twelve Grand Concertos, Op. 6, for string orchestra (1739), offer grandeur offset by intimacy and dramatic surprise. He was the inventor of a uniquely English genre, the organ concerto (with orchestra), which grew out of his improvisations between the acts of oratorios in the theater.

Handel does not match the learning and perfection of Bach, but he is more accessible, with an unerring instinct for the dramatic, and an unsurpassed melodic gift. He is the first composer in musical history whose music never left the canon.

Nicholas Temperley

Bibliography

Abraham, Gerald, ed. *Handel: A Symposium.* 1954.

Chrysander, Friedrich, ed. *Georg Friedrich Händels Werke.* 97 vols. 1859–1894.

Dean, Winton. *Handel's Dramatic Oratorios and Masques.* 1959.

Johnstone, H. Diack, and Roger Fiske, eds. *The Blackwell History of Music in Britain.* Vol. 4: *The Eighteenth Century.* 1990.

Lang, Paul Henry. *George Frideric Handel.* 1966.

Myers, Rollo H. *Handel's "Messiah": A Touchstone of Taste.* 1948.

Smith, Ruth. *Handel's Oratorios and Eighteenth-Century Thought.* 1995.

Temperley, Nicholas. "Handel's Influence on English Music." *Monthly Musical Record.* Vol. 90, pp. 163–174.

See also Music

Hanover

By the accession of **George I** in 1714, Hanover, a German electorate of the Holy Roman Empire, came into personal union with Great Britain. George I and his son **George II** considered themselves German, spent much time in their homeland in northwestern Germany, and took close interest in its security. Its link with a major European power helped expand its territory. But Britain's commitments became increasingly imperial, therefore maritime. The process by which Britain would give up military intervention in Continental wars to concentrate on her **navy** was inhibited by these Hanoverian sovereigns. Several politicians, notably **William Pitt the Elder**, publicly disapproved of the tie and fell out of royal favor as a consequence.

Hanover's problem lay in its strategic position between two other powers: **France** and Prussia. In 1743, George II personally went to defend the electorate, and at the Battle of Dettingen (1743) was the last monarch to lead the British **Army** into battle. In 1757 he entrusted the same task to his son, the **Duke of Cumberland**, who could not prevent the French from overrunning the electorate and occupying it for a year. Under **George III**, the first Hanoverian to identify himself as British, Hanover became less of a burden, even though he, like the two kings both before and after him, continued to rule it. From 1793 the two countries fought together against revolutionary France, but in 1795 Hanover dropped out of the war and became neutral, whereas Britain carried on. The electorate was occupied alternately by Prussians and French until 1807 when Napoleon partitioned it. It was restored with extended frontiers in 1815.

George III never visited Hanover; **George IV** and **William IV** each visited once. It became a kingdom in 1814, still ruled by the British sovereigns. The British connection ended in 1837, on the accession of Queen Victoria, because only males could succeed to the throne of Hanover. The throne went to Victoria's uncle, Ernest Augustus (1771–1851). Thus Hanover ceased to be British when Britain ceased to be Hanoverian.

Michael Fry

Bibliography

Blanning, T.C.W. "'That Horrid Electorate' or 'Ma Patrie Germanique'? George III, Hanover, and the Fürstenbund of 1785." *Historical Journal.* Vol. 20, pp. 311–344.

Brewer, J. *The Sinews of Power: War, Money and the English State, 1688–1783.* 1988.

See also Foreign Relations

Hanoverian Succession

In July 1700, William, Duke of Gloucester, the last surviving child of Princess **Anne**, the heir to the thrones of England and Scotland, died, inevitably raising the question as to who would ultimately succeed her. The **Act of Settlement** (1701) excluded **Roman Catholics** from the throne of England, and this measure was extended to Great Britain after the **Act of Union** with Scotland (1707).

Catholicism thus ruled out the senior male line of the Stuarts, deposed by the **Glorious Revolution** of 1688 and after 1701 represented by **James Edward, the Old Pretender**, son of James II and VII (1633–1701). The nearest Protestant claimants were Sophia (1630–1714), widow of Ernest Augustus, Elector of Hanover (1629–1698), and her heirs. Sophia's right rested on descent from James I and VI (1566–1625), her parents being James I's daughter Elizabeth (1596–1662), and Frederick V, Elector Palatine (1596–1632). Though she greatly looked forward to sitting on the British throne, Sophia had to contend with the machinations of her son; and as she died only 3 months before Anne in 1714, it was he who succeeded the latter as **George I.**

The first half of the 18th century witnessed several rebellions aimed at restoring the Stuarts, but the threat to the Hanoverian succession from **Jacobitism** was finally ended at the Battle of **Culloden** (1746).

Michael Fry

Bibliography

Hatton, Ragnhild. *George I, Elector and King.* 1978.

Monod, Paul Kleber. *Jacobitism and the English People, 1688–1788.* 1993.

Ward, A.W. *The Electress Sophia and the Hanoverian Succession.* 1909.

See also Fifteen, The; Forty-five, The

Hanway, Jonas (1712–1786)

Destined to fame as a humanitarian, Hanway was born at Portsmouth, the son of a navy victualer. He began his career as a **merchant** in Lisbon, where he was apprenticed in 1729. In 1743 he obtained a partnership with another merchant in St. Petersburg, and that same year conducted a shipment of goods to Persia. He recounted his extraordinary adventures on this trip in *An Historical Account of British Trade Over the Caspian Sea* (1753). Hanway returned to England to claim an inheritance in 1750, then devoted the remainder of his life to promotion of **humanitarian** causes. A prolific writer, he produced more than 70 books and pamphlets to promote these; their titles read like a catalogue of Hanoverian philanthropies.

Hanway was the principal founder of the Marine Society, established in 1756 to equip landsmen for service at sea. More than 10,000 recruits to the **navy** were thus furnished during the **Seven Years' War**; the society continues its work to this day. He was also instrumental in creating the Society for the Encouragement of British Troops, which supplied the **army** in **North America** with books and warm clothing, and he was active in promoting the Stepney Society, founded in 1674 to apprentice young men to the sea.

In addition to his work on behalf of the Misericordia Hospital for venereal patients, in 1758 Hanway helped establish the Magdalene Hospital to rehabilitate **prostitutes**. In that same year he became a governor (and later served as Vice-President) of the celebrated **Foundling Hospital**. Indeed, Hanway's active lobbying on behalf of foundlings and orphans led to two parliamentary acts: one requiring parishes to keep records of all parish infants, the other directing **London** parishes to put infants out to nurse in the country rather than housing them in parish workhouses, where the mortality rate of infants often approached 100%.

Jonas Hanway

Hanway's concern for the young also prompted him to campaign on behalf of chimney sweeps' climbing boys. However, this was one of his less successful campaigns, as was his proposal to establish county naval free schools, his attack upon tea consumption (which elicited a rebuke from **Samuel Johnson**), and his pioneering practice of carrying an umbrella—which made enemies of the chairmen and cabmen of London.

Hanway's prolific and didactic writings are suffused with a blend of religious fervor and mercantile **nationalism**. Thus, rescuing foundlings would yield more good citizens and soldiers; curtailing prostitution would force men into marriage; reducing **drinking** would increase grain exports; and substituting indigenous herbal beverages for imported tea would reduce a trade deficit. Nearly all Hanway's worthy causes served practical and patriotic purposes. Seeing Christian devotion as another source of national strength, he campaigned for repeal of the so-called **Jew Act** (1753).

Hanway's tireless moralizing and campaigning set a humanitarian example that was much honored in an otherwise callous era, and argued that national prosperity could march hand in hand with Christian charity.

N. Merrill Distad

Bibliography

Andrew, Donna T. *Philanthropy and Police: London Charity in the Eighteenth Century.* 1989.

Crawford, T.S. *A History of the Umbrella.* 1970.

Hutchins, John H. *Jonas Hanway, 1712–1786.* 1940.

Jayne, Roland Everett. *Jonas Hanway: Philanthropist, Politician, and Author, 1712–1786.* 1929.

Taylor, James Stephen. *Jonas Hanway, Founder of the Marine Society: Charity and Policy in Eighteenth-Century Britain.* 1985.

See also Manners and Morals

Hardwicke, Earl of (Philip Yorke) (1690–1764)

Hardwicke was a **Whig** politician and distinguished jurist noted for loyalty to his patrons and support of executive authority. Trained in the law, he gained the **patronage** of the **Duke of Newcastle**, who sponsored his entry into Parliament (1719). He refused to manage the impeachment of Lord Macclesfield (1725), supported **Robert Walpole's** maintenance of a standing army (1732), and proposed **excise tax** (1733). His judicial preferments attested to his talents and political connections: he became Solicitor-General (1720), Attorney-General (1724), Chief Justice of the King's Bench (1733), and Lord Chancellor (1737).

Hardwicke was long one of Newcastle's most trusted advisers. He followed him into opposition against Walpole (1742), but honored a pledge not to prosecute Walpole on charges of corruption (1744). He advised Newcastle on the formation of the **Broad-Bottom administration**. After the **Jacobite** rising of 1745, he championed the abolition of the

Lord Hardwicke

judicial powers of the Highland clans and the banning of the wearing of the **clan** tartans. He helped reform marriage law in the **Marriage Act** of 1753. Perhaps his greatest achievement was facilitating the alliance between Newcastle and **William Pitt the Elder** (1757). He joined Newcastle's opposition to the **Peace of Paris** (1763) and defended **John Wilkes**'s opposition to the use of **general warrants**, though he opposed Wilkes's proposal to have the proceedings of Parliament printed.

As Lord Chancellor, Hardwicke's respect for precedent and his desire to promote uniformity between the common law and equity inspired several rulings defining and clarifying the principles of equity within the **judicial system**. His constitutional writings supported the ideals of the **Glorious Constitution**, while stressing the importance of the monarchy as a check on the popular will.

Robert D. McJimsey

Bibliography

Browning, Reed. *The Duke of Newcastle.* 1975.

———. *The Political and Constitutional Ideas of the Court Whigs.* 1982.

Holdsworth, Sir William. *Some Makers of the English Law: The Tagore Lectures, 1937–38.* 1938.

Yorke, Philip C. *The Life and Correspondence of Philip Yorke, Earl of Hardwicke, Lord High Chancellor of Great Britain.* 3 vols. 1913.

See also Legal Profession

Hardy, Thomas (1752–1832)

Hardy was the founder of the **London Corresponding Society** (LCS), the chief organization of English **radicals** in the 1790s. Born in **Scotland**, he moved to **London** (1774), worked as a shoemaker, married the daughter of a carpenter, and in 1791 opened his own shoemaker's shop in Piccadilly. Having absorbed various political writings, including **Price**'s *Observations on the Nature of Civil Liberty* (1776) and various tracts of the **Society for Constitutional Information** (SCI), and sharing the reformist hopes which many people felt in contemplating the early phase of the **French Revolution**, he formed the idea of the LCS as an organization to work for parliamentary reform and the restoration of English liberties. After meeting with **Horne Tooke**, Secretary of the SCI (now reviving after several years of dormancy), he and seven others launched the LCS in late January 1792.

As Secretary and Treasurer, Hardy was responsible for correspondence with the rapidly growing network of like-minded radical societies emerging not just in London but throughout the country, which turned increasingly to his group for leadership. His prominence ensured that when the government decided to crack down, he would be a target. In May 1794 he was arrested, charged with high treason, and committed to the Tower of London. His week-long trial, in which he was prosecuted by **Lord Eldon** and brilliantly defended by **Thomas Erskine**, resulted in his acquittal (5 November 1794). But his incarceration had been long and expensive, and during it his wife died in a miscarriage. After the trial, though still sympathetic to radical principles, he retired from political activity. In later years he was helped financially by **Sir Francis Burdett** and **Francis Place**.

Frank M. Baglione

Bibliography

Cone, Carl B. *The English Jacobins: Reformers in Late 18th Century England.* 1968.

Goodwin, Albert. *The Friends of Liberty: The English Democratic Movement in the Age of the French Revolution.* 1979.

Hardy, Thomas. *Memoir of Thomas Hardy.* 1832.

Williams, Gwyn. *Artisans and Sans-Culottes.* 1969.

Thomas Hardy

Hare, Francis (1671–1740)

Hare, **Whig** polemicist and Bishop of St. Asaph (1727–1731) and Chichester (1731–1740), rose to prominence under the **patronage** of the **Duke of Marlborough**, **Queen Caroline**, and **Sir Robert Walpole**. At **Cambridge**, where he earned the Doctor of Divinity (1708), Hare tutored Marlborough's son and the young Robert Walpole. He was Marlborough's chaplain during the Flanders campaign (1704) and his biographer afterward (1705). He remained loyal to Marlborough after the latter's dismissal (1711), publishing many pamphlets on his behalf and defending him against attacks by **Jonathan Swift** and **Delarivière Manley**, among others. His antideistic *Difficulties and Discouragements Which Attend the Study of the Scriptures* (1714) was often reprinted, and during the **Bangorian Controversy** he became embroiled in controversy with **Benjamin Hoadly** and **Richard Steele**. He opposed repeal of the **Test and Corporation acts**, and his **antidissent** sermon before the **Lords** in 1732 enraged **Thomas Gordon** and other Low-Church polemicists. Walpole, still faithful, unsuccessfully nominated Hare for the archbishopric of Canterbury in 1736. His professional ascent helps to suggest the importance of **patronage** in the early Hanoverian church, and his publications record some of the period's most fervid controversies while illustrating the diversity of opinion even within whiggery about church and secular politics.

Alexander Pettit

Bibliography

Horn, Robert D. "Marlborough's First Biographer: Dr. Francis Hare." *Huntington Library Quarterly.* Vol. 20, pp. 145–162.

Pettit, Alexander. "The Francis Hare Controversy of 1732." *British Journal of Eighteenth-Century Studies.* Vol. 17, pp. 41–53.

See also Church of England

Hargreaves, James (*c.* 1719–1778)

A pioneer in the **cotton industry**, Hargreaves, inventor of the **spinning** jenny, became a handloom weaver near Blackburn, Lancashire. A man of technical skill, he improved methods of carding and was noticed by the great cotton manufacturer, Robert **Peel**. The growth of demand, following the widespread adoption of **Kay**'s flying shuttle, spurred experiments to improve spinning. Hargreaves developed (1764) the "jenny," a hand-operated machine, relatively cheap to make, and very easy to use. Instead of working one spindle as the ordinary wheel did, his jenny worked eight, and before long this was increased to 16 and ultimately 120.

At first Hargreaves kept his invention secret, but gradually he supplied relatives and friends with jennies, which they used in their cottages. As knowledge of them spread, fear of unemployment grew, and in 1758 Hargreaves' house and jennies under construction were attacked. He moved to Nottingham, where he entered into partnership with Thomas James to supply jenny yarns to local hosiers. Their business was successful, but the quality of their yarn could not match the strength of those supplied by **Arkwright**'s water frame, or the fineness of those from **Crompton**'s mule, and so they became licensees of Arkwright's frame. Despite his unsuccessful attempt to **patent** his invention in 1770, a move which the Nottingham hosiers opposed, Hargreaves remained a successful cottonspinner during his lifetime.

John Butt

Bibliography

Aspin, Christopher, and Stanley D. Chapman. *James Hargreaves and the Spinning Jenny.* 1964.

Chapman, Stanley D. *The Early Factory Masters.* 1967.

English, Walter. *The Textile Industry.* 1969.

Harley, Robert

See Oxford (and Mortimer), Earl of

Harris, Howel (1714–1773)

Harris, an itinerant lay preacher, founded Welsh Calvinistic **Methodism** with **Daniel Rowland**. After experiencing a religious awakening (1735), he began to preach, then formed a society for mutual support in living the Christian life. The people who followed him soon could not be contained in the houses at which he preached, and he lost his place as a schoolmaster in an Anglican school because of his **enthusiasm**. By 1739 he had founded 30 evangelical societies in South Wales and, amidst persecution, began expanding his efforts into North Wales.

George Whitefield, impressed by Harris's open-air preaching, began following this practice and influenced the **Wesleys** to do the same. Harris helped form an alliance between the Welsh and English Methodist groups in 1742. After a falling-out with Rowland in 1750 (dividing Welsh Methodism in two), he founded an alms house and school at Trevecca. This was later frequented by leaders of the **Evangelical** movement, including the **Countess of Huntingdon**, who in 1768 built a seminary there for Evangelical ministers.

Harris, also an **agricultural improver**, helped found the Brecknockshire **Agricultural Society** (1755). His published works are all in Welsh.

Richard M. Riss

Bibliography

Bennett, Richard. *Howell Harris and the Dawn of Revival.* 1987.

Evans, Eifion. *Howel Harris, Evangelist, 1714–1773.* 1974.

Luff, Alan. "250 Years of the Welsh Revival: The Two Leaders." *The Expository Times.* Vol. 97, pp. 364–368.

Nuttall, Geoffrey F. "Howel Harris and 'The Grand Table:' A Note on Religion and Politics 1744–50." *Journal of Ecclesiastical History.* Vol. 39, pp. 531–544.

———. *Howel Harris, 1714–1773: The Last Enthusiast.* 1965.

Williams, R.R. *Flames from the Altar: Howell Harris and His Contemporaries.* 1962.

See also Wales and Welsh Culture; Welsh Religious Revival

Hartley, David (1705–1757)

English physician, clergyman, and philosopher, Hartley was the founder of a system of psychology called "associationism," which has become an enduring component of psychological theory. He is credited with formulating his theory on the basis of human physical characteristics, rather than metaphysics.

Educated at **Cambridge University**, Hartley refused to assent to all Thirty-nine Articles of Faith of the **Church of England**. Objecting to the doctrine of eternal damnation in Article IX because of his commitment to **religious toleration** and his belief in universal salvation, he decided to devote his life to philosophical inquiry and medical science. Hartley practiced **medicine** in several English cities, including **London** and **Bath**.

In his important treatise, *Observations of Man, His Frame, His Duty, and His Expectations* (2 vols., 1749), he set forth his belief in the oneness of body and mind. In this work he developed the principle of the association of ideas, which he had initially adopted from **John Locke**, into a general psychology of understanding. He argued that God, loving all human beings, had made them physically and psychologically the same. Their mental processes operated identically as a result of the vibrations of the white medullary substance in the spinal cord and the brain. It was through the association of simple sensations, a purely physical process lodged in the nervous system, that the mind acquired all knowledge and understanding. Hartley's work profoundly influenced the scientific work of **Joseph Priestley** (who printed his own edition of the *Observations* in 1772) and affected the later history of British **empiricism**.

Jack Fruchtman, Jr.

Bibliography

Feig, Stephen. "Two Early Works by David Hartley." *Journal of the History of Philosophy.* Vol. 19, pp. 173–189.

Fruchtman, Jack, Jr. "Late Latitudinarianism: The Case of David Hartley." *Enlightenment and Dissent.* Vol. 11, pp. 3–22.

Leslie, Margaret. "Mysticism Misunderstood: David Hartley and the Idea of Progress." *Journal of the History of Ideas.* Vol. 33, pp. 625–632.

Oberg, Barbara Bowen. "David Hartley and the Association of Ideas." *Journal of the History of Ideas.* Vol. 38, pp. 441–453.

Willey, Basil. *The Eighteenth-Century Background: Studies on the Idea of Nature in the Thought of the Period.* 1961.

Hastings, Selina

See Huntingdon, Countess of

Hastings, Warren (1732–1818)

The first Governor-General of **India**, Hastings consolidated British rule there. But the controversy surrounding his administration made him the target of an impeachment trial in England.

The son of an Anglican clergyman, Hastings attended Westminster School, then sailed (1750) for Bengal, where he became a writer (junior clerk) for the **East India Company**. In 1757 he became the company's resident in Murshidabad. From 1761 to 1764 he served on the Calcutta Council, the company's governing body in Bengal. The corruption of fellow administrators ("**nabobs**") so disgusted him that he returned to England (1765); financial need, however, forced him to reoccupy his seat on the council in 1769, and in 1772 he became Governor of Bengal.

Warren Hastings

From 1772 to 1774 Hastings extended the company's control over Indian local administrators and restored order to the province's judicial system. His attempts to eliminate corruption raised the ire of many company agents. The Regulating Act (1773) placed the three Indian presidencies under a single governor-general, a position filled by Hastings from 1774 until 1784. His rivalry with Sir Philip Francis (1740–1818), a member of his Supreme Council, tarnished his career and, in one instance, led to accusations of his participation in a judicial murder.

Hastings's foreign and military policy extended British power in India, but sometimes used extortion and mercenary tactics. After his return to England he faced impeachment charges initiated by **Edmund Burke**. Hastings was acquitted, but the inordinate length of the trial (1788–1795) damaged his reputation. He spent the remainder of his retirement pursuing scholarly activities and living the life of a country gentleman.

Although Hastings extended the territorial scope and social depth of British rule in India, he reaffirmed indigenous practices and institutions. His consolidation of company rule enabled his successors to introduce further reforms, but his failures encouraged them to attempt a still more thorough imposition of control.

A. Martin Wainwright

Bibliography

Bowen, H.V. *Revenue and Reform: The Indian Problem in British Politics, 1757–1773.* 1991.

Feiling, Keith. *Warren Hastings.* 1954.

Fisher, Michael H., ed. *The Politics of the British Annexation of India, 1757–1857.* 1994.

Forrest, G.W. *India under Hastings.* 1984.

Marshall, P.J. *The Impeachment of Warren Hastings.* 1965.

Turnbull, Patrick. *Warren Hastings.* 1975.

See also India Act

Hats and Caps

Hanoverian head coverings were more than just barriers against the elements. Men's headgear reflected social standing and sometimes political and religious inclinations; whereas for women, rank and marital status were both suggested by the articles covering and decorating the head. The need for such objects was so unquestioned that governments routinely **taxed** them, legislated against foreign imports, and barred colonies from competitive manufacturing.

Two gentlemen in hats, c. 1785

The lucrative beaver hat industry, a cause of many armed conflicts, sustained the colonial fur trade with **North America**, and the extensive manufacture of felted hats in South London and, later, the provincial northwest, supplied British and foreign markets. English-made hats and caps were an export staple, with over 700,000 hats exported in 1736. Domestic haberdashers, hatters, milliners, and general shopkeepers sold a wide range of head coverings—felted, knitted, or stitched—to meet the needs of adults and children of every occupation and social standing.

Men's hats, whether felted, laced, trimmed, feathered, or banded, came only in a few basic shapes. Most common was the felted three-cornered hat with a high, cocked brim rolled above the crown. Popular also was the round-crowned, flat-brimmed hat, worn not only by men in the **legal** and **clerical professions** but also by many in the laboring classes. However, whatever the shape, hats were key counters in social interplay. Public acknowledgment of an equal was marked by doffing the hat; the elegance of the gesture, as much as the article, proclaimed the gentleman. Deference to superiors also demanded the timely removal of headgear—though saucy defiance by apprentices and urban youth could be signaled by a round hat "fiercely cocked" or by wearing "the nab or trenched hat with the brim flapping over their eyes" (as **Fielding** commented in *Jonathan Wild,* 1743). It is significant in the evolution of **manners and morals** that "hat honor" gradually declined. Larger **cities**, more complex and egalitarian social ideas, and less explicit relationships of dependency reduced its frequency among men, though gentlemen continued to doff hats before ladies.

Beyond courtesy, a piece of headgear might reflect awareness of fashionable trends or even a statement of political sentiments; its color, shape, and angle gave contemporaries clues about its wearer. Prominent individuals frequently adopted distinctive headgear—**Charles James Fox**, for example, often wore an unusual black top hat. Some Londoners wore "American-style" hats in the era of the **American Revolution**; **Benjamin Franklin**'s archaic round Quaker hat was appreciated as a statement of sturdy principles; and in the 1820s the white hat was a symbol of **radicalism**.

Women's attention to head coverings was just as assiduous as men's. Soft, gathered fabric caps, such as the pinner, the coif, and the mob cap, were staples of female dress. These were worn indoors habitually, and women of the laboring classes donned clean white mob caps on Sundays to mark the day. The size, trimmings, and fabric of a cap reflected the age, marital status, and social standing of the woman wearing it. Outdoors, no respectable woman would be seen without a headcovering, whether a hat, cap, hood, or bonnet—though at points during the 18th century, bits of lace and ribbons assumed the same function. Caps evolved and varied; they were worn under hats and instead of hats, padded, ruffled, and trimmed with lace. At night, both sexes wore nightcaps; and for men, caps were a comfortable alternative when hats and **wigs** were removed at home.

Head coverings offered great scope for creative millinery, a trade that offered a genteel occupation for women adept with a needle and inventive with materials. The flat bergère hats of the 1750s were followed by the wide-brimmed, high-crowned, plain and colored straws of the 1780s; deep-brimmed bonnets swathed in ribbons followed, as the evolution of styles continued. Straw plaiting by the poor expanded with the development of the straw hat industry which, by the early 19th century, employed women and girls throughout the southern and Midlands **agricultural** districts.

Beverly Lemire

Bibliography

Amphlett, H. *Hats: A History of Fashion in Headgear.* 1974.

Corfield, Penelope J. "Dress for Deference and Dissent: Hats and the Decline of Hat Honour." *Costume: The Journal of the Costume Society.* Vol. 23, pp. 64–79.

Corner, David. "The Tyranny of Fashion: The Case of the Felt-Hatting Trade in the Late Seventeenth and Eighteenth Centuries," in N.B. Harte, ed., *Fabrics & Fashions: Studies in the Social and Economic History of Dress.* Special issue of *Textile History.* Vol. 22, No. 2. 1991.

Ginsburg, Madeleine. *The Hat: Trends and Traditions.* 1990.

See also Clothing; Clothing-Makers; Clothing Trade; Fashion; Women's Employment

Hawke, Edward (1705–1781)

Hawke's defeat of the French at **Quiberon Bay** was a key victory in the **Seven Years' War.** He entered the **navy** as a volunteer (1719), later attaining a commission (1725). He first commanded the sloop H.M.S. *Wolf* (1733) on West Indian station. During the **War of Austrian Succession** his aggressive action as Captain of the *Berwick* against the French at the Battle of Toulon (1744) won him promotion to Rear-Admiral. Due to his superior's illness Hawke assumed command of the Channel Fleet and promptly devastated a French convoy off La Rochelle, which earned him promotion to Vice-Admiral and a Knighthood of the Bath (1748).

A decade later, while blockading Brest (May to November, 1759), Hawke introduced revolutionary changes in the practices of resupplying, refitting, maintaining, and periodically relieving British ships and crews, enabling his force to remain continuously on blockade station. His defeat of the Brest squadron at the famous Battle of Quiberon Bay (20 November 1759), the decisive naval action of the Seven Years' War, devastated French naval power and ended the threat of an invasion of **Ireland;** no French squadron put to sea for the remainder of the war.

Admiral Edward Hawke

The victory earned Hawke promotion to Admiral, appointment as First Lord of the Admiralty (1766–1771), and the title Baron Hawke of Towton (1776). Although his success has been attributed to good fortune rather than tactical genius, Hawke's attention to careful planning and execution, and his concern for the health and comfort of his sailors and marines, were quite advanced for the era. Perhaps his most enduring legacy, however, was his establishment of high professional standards for naval officers.

Stanley D.M. Carpenter

Bibliography

Mackay, Ruddock F. *Admiral Hawke.* 1965.

———, ed. *The Hawke Papers: A Selection, 1743–1771.* 1990.

Marcus, Geoffrey. *Quiberon Bay: The Campaign in Home Waters, 1759.* 1960.

See also War and Military Engagements

Hawkins, Sir John (1719–1789)

Lawyer, magistrate, musicologist, and biographer, Hawkins is best known as author of a pioneering five-volume *General History of the Science and Practice of Music* (1776) and a *Life of Samuel Johnson, LL.D.* (1787). The former is still considered authoritative, though for readability it is often compared unfavorably to **Charles Burney**'s three-volume *General History of Music from the Earliest Ages to the Present Period* (1776–1789). Hawkins's biography of **Johnson,** prefixed to his edition of the latter's *Works,* was eclipsed by that of **Boswell** (1791), but Hawkins had the advantage of a much earlier acquaintance with Johnson, dating back more than 20 years before Boswell met him.

James Gray

Bibliography

Davis, Bertram H. *A Proof of Eminence: The Life of Sir John Hawkins.* 1973.

Hawkins, Laetitia-Matilda. *Memoires, Anecdotes, Facts, and Opinions.* 1824.

Scholes, Percy A. *The Life and Activities of Sir John Hawkins.* 1953.

See also Music Education; Music Scholarship

Hawksmoor, Nicholas (1661–1739)

Hawksmoor was probably the most original and creative English baroque architect of his time. Born in Nottinghamshire, he was first a clerk to **Sir Christopher Wren,** assisting on the Chelsea Hospital (1682) and on Winchester Palace (1683), and then on several **London** churches, including St. Paul's.

Hawksmoor's own work, stately and impressive and in some ways more inventive than Wren's, reflects this early training.

In 1698 Hawksmoor was named clerk of the works at Wren's Greenwich Hospital, where he met **Sir John Vanbrugh**, comptroller of the works. Hawksmoor became Vanbrugh's assistant at Greenwich and later helped him (the share of each is still not completely clear) with the building of Castle Howard for the earl of Carlisle (1699–1726), and of Blenheim Palace for the duke of Marlborough (1704–1725). Hawksmoor succeeded Vanbrugh at Blenheim and designed the majestic mausoleum at Castle Howard (1729–1736). More original were the London churches he built, the finest of which was St. Anne's Limehouse (1714–1724). In 1723 he was made Wren's successor as surveyor of Westminster Abbey, and designed the west towers in the Gothic style (1734). He also worked in the Gothic mode at All Soul's College, Oxford (1715–1740). Only in recent years have Hawksmoor's true originality and genius been appreciated.

Thomas J. McCormick

Bibliography

Downes, Kerry. *Hawksmoor.* 2nd ed., 1979.

Saumurez Smith, Charles. *The Building of Castle Howard.* 1990.

Summerson, John. *Architecture in Britain, 1530–1830.* 5th ed., 1969.

See also Architects and Architecture; Gothic Revival

Haydn, Joseph (1732–1809)

Haydn was one of the greatest composers of his age. His triumphant appearances in **London** in the 1790s were a climax in the development of the capital's concert life. Born in Austria, trained in Vienna, Haydn spent the greater part of his professional career (1766–1790) in relative isolation as Kapellmeister (director of music) to Prince Nikolaus Esterházy. It was in the prince's splendid palace at Esterház (Hungary) that he slowly developed his mastery of the classical forms of the symphony, sonata, and string quartet, as well as of **church music** and **opera**. Gradually his reputation spread abroad. Many of his works were published and performed in London during the 1780s.

On the death of Prince Nikolaus in 1790, Haydn was free to accept a tempting invitation from Johann Peter Salomon (1745–1815), an energetic impresario, to visit London (1791–1792) as the crowning attraction of Salomon's new subscription **musical concerts**. The composer was lionized on all sides, favored by nobility and royalty, and awarded an honorary doctorate at **Oxford University**. An equally successful second visit followed in 1793–1794.

The great monument to these visits is the 12 "London" symphonies, Nos. 93–104. Haydn adapted his Esterházy idiom to the more formal setting of great public concerts, often adding a ceremonial or military flavor by means of trumpets and drums. For England he also composed his last opera, *L'Anima del filosofo* (not performed), his last three sonatas, a number of piano trios and occasional works, and 12 "canzonets" (songs with English texts and piano accompaniment).

Shortly before Haydn's final departure, Salomon commissioned him to compose an **oratorio** in the Handelian tradition, and provided for it a text of unknown authorship. In Vienna, Haydn had Baron Gottfried van Swieten translate the text into German in a way such as to fit the English. He completed *Die Schöpfung/The Creation* in 1797, performed it in 1798, and published the score bilingually in Vienna in 1800: it had its London premiere in March 1800. A second oratorio soon followed, *The Seasons* (after **James Thomson**'s poem). These are regarded by many as Haydn's greatest compositions. *The Creation,* with its universal theme and its lyrical treatment of the works of nature, soon won its way into the permanent repertory of English choral performances, hitherto reserved almost exclusively for the oratorios of **Handel**.

Nicholas Temperley

Bibliography

Landon, H.C. Robbins. *Haydn: Chronicle and Works,* especially vol. 3, *Haydn in England 1791–1795;* vol. 4, *Haydn: The Years of "The Creation" 1796–1800.* 5 vols. 1976–1980.

Rosen, Charles. *The Classical Style: Haydn, Mozart, Beethoven.* 1972.

Temperley, Nicholas. *Haydn: The Creation.* 1991.

See also Music; Music, Choral

Haydon, Benjamin Robert (1786–1846)

Haydon was a more ambitious than successful **history painter**, lecturer, and apostle of British art whose **autobiography** (three volumes, 1853) furnishes many insights into the condition of early-19th-century artists.

Born in Plymouth, the only son of a prosperous printer, he studied painting under **Henry Fuseli** at the **Royal Academy** and exhibited his first painting there in 1807. Proud and opinionated, Haydon played an important part in the struggle to bring the **Elgin Marbles** to England, hoping their arrival (1816) would help elevate public taste. Alienated through controversies from the Royal Academy, he visited Paris with his friend **David Wilkie**, studied at the Louvre, then produced his remarkable *Christ's Entry into Jerusalem* (1820), which included portraits of his friends **Keats**, **Wordsworth**, and other "great spirits" of the age (Voltaire, for example) looking on. Marriage followed (1821), together with pecuniary difficulties and imprisonments for bankruptcy (1823, 1827), a number of epic paintings of historical figures (Napoleon, Xenophon), and large group portraits of contemporaries (for example, Haydon's *Reform Banquet* of 1834, painted for Lord **Grey**, contains 197 portraits).

In 1835 Haydon began lecture tours of England and Scotland, attempting to earn a little money while elevating aesthetic understanding and a national appreciation of the "high art" of historical painting. Yet though he had influential friends, the painter, overcome by debt and disappointment, committed **suicide** in 1846. He is remembered now mostly for introducing revolutionary **drawing** methods, for **genre paintings** like *May Day* (1829) which he himself viewed as not of the highest order, and for his broodingly **Romantic** *Wordsworth on Helvellyn* (1842); but his grandest monument may in fact be his voluminous *Autobiography* and *Diary*, and his writings on art theory.

Joan K. Stemmler

Bibliography

Ballantyne, Andrew. "Knight, Haydon and the Elgin Marbles." *Apollo*. Vol. 128, pp. 155–159.

Barrell, John. *Painting and the Politics of Culture: New Essays on British Art, 1700–1850*. 1992.

Cummings, Frederick, and Allen Staley. *Romantic Art in Britain: Paintings and Drawings, 1780–1860*. 1968.

George, Eric. *The Life and Death of Benjamin Haydon*. 1967.

Jenkins, Ian. "George Frederic Watts and the Elgin Marbles." *Apollo*. Vol. 120, pp. 176–181.

Jolliffe, John, ed. *Neglected Genius: The Diaries of Benjamin Robert Haydon. 1808–1846*. 1990.

Taylor, Tom, ed. *The Autobiography and Memoirs of Benjamin Robert Haydon (1786–1846)*. 1853.

Woolf, Virginia. "Genius," in her *The Moment, and Other Essays*. 1947.

See also Painting

Hayman, Francis (1708–1776)

Hayman, a friend and contemporary of **William Hogarth**, was one of the leading painters of his day. He was immensely versatile, excelling in the fields of portraiture, **history painting**, and decorative painting as well as **book illustration**.

Like **Sir James Thornhill** earlier, Hayman began his career as a theatrical scene painter. By the 1740s, his most prolific decade, he was painting **portraits**, conversation pieces, and theatrical genre scenes. He also designed over 50 large paintings as decorations for the open-air supper-boxes at Vauxhall Gardens, the **London pleasure gardens**. He was a leading teacher at the St. Martin's Lane Academy and was instrumental in the founding of the Society of Artists in 1759.

Kimerly Rorschach

Bibliography

Allen, Brian. *Francis Hayman*. 1987.

Hays, Mary (1760–1843)

Hays was a sturdy feminist writer and novelist, and a member of the **radical London** group that also included the **publisher** Joseph Johnson (1739–1809), **William Godwin**, **Thomas Paine**, and **Mary Wollstonecraft**.

An ardent supporter of **women's rights**, she sought out Wollstonecraft's criticism and friendship. When Wollstonecraft died, Hays produced two important obituaries for the *Monthly Magazine* (1797) and *Annual Necrology, 1797–1798* (1800), defending her views. Hays's main feminist works were *Letters and Essays, Oral and Miscellaneous* (1793) and *Appeal to the Men of Great Britain on Behalf of Women* (1798), which differed from Wollstonecraft's feminism only in its emphasis on Christianity as a basis for women's equality. Hays's **novels**, especially *Memoirs of Emma Courtney* (1796), which shocked contemporaries because of its frank portrayal of a heroine declaring her passion, and *The Victim of Prejudice* (1799), also dwelt upon women's plight.

In 1802 Hays published *Female Biography* (six volumes), incorporating the lives of women from all countries and peri-

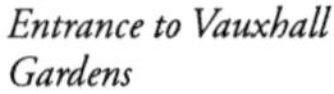
Entrance to Vauxhall Gardens

ods. Though she suffered conservative attacks in the late 1790s and was repeatedly ridiculed in the ***Anti-Jacobin Review***, Hays never retreated from her feminist views, though her later writing became somewhat more conventionally moral and **Evangelical**.

Barbara Brandon Schnorrenberg

Bibliography

Adams, M. Ray. *Studies in the Literary Backgrounds of English Radicalism with Special Reference to the French Revolution.* 1947.

Kelly, Gary. *Women, Writing, and Revolution: 1790–1827.* 1993.

Luria, Gina. "Mary Hays's Letters and Manuscripts." *Signs.* Vol. 3, pp. 524–530.

Pollin, Burton R. "Mary Hays on Women's Rights in the *Monthly Magazine.*" *Études Anglaises.* Vol. 24, pp. 271–282.

Wedd, A.F., ed. *The Love Letters of Mary Hays (1779–1780).* 1925.

———. *The Fate of the Fenwicks: Letters to Mary Hays (1798–1828).* 1927.

See also Women in Literature

Haywood, Eliza (?1693–1756)

Haywood was one of the most popular and prolific writers of the early 18th century. She made her name as an author of scandal **novels**, but also wrote plays, **essays** (including some for her own **periodicals**), **poetry**, **translations**, and conduct books. Occasionally she acted onstage.

Haywood's first novel, *Love in Excess* (three parts, 1719–1720), was one of the three fiction bestsellers of the era, alongside *Robinson Crusoe* (1719) and *Gulliver's Travels* (1726). During the 1720s she wrote three plays and many **Romance** novels, as well as *romans à clefs,* including *Memoirs of a Certain Island* (1725), in which she lampooned the Duchess of Marlborough. In the 1730s, though she acted in **Henry Fielding**'s New Theatre in the Haymarket until the **Playhouse Act** (1737) closed it, she made only rare appearances in print. Possibly she suffered from **Pope**'s attack in *The Dunciad* (1728), satirizing her as a hack novelist. A famous 18th-century illustration to *The Dunciad* depicts her novels on the back of an ass.

Haywood reappeared in the 1740s as a **journalist** professing a desire to provide **moral** guidance. Her *Female Spectator* (1744–1746), an imitation of **Addison** and **Steele**'s *Spectator,* offered moral discussions and advice on conduct, and went through eight editions before 1778. She also wrote three conduct books during the 1740s and 1750s, and though she attacked **Richardson**'s *Pamela* (1741), her late novels reveal his moral influence. In *Betsy Thoughtless* (1751), for example, Haywood weds realism with morality.

Haywood's biography and bibliography remain unclear. The facts of her birth and marital status are still debated. She has been credited with over 90 works, but more may have been published pseudonymously or anonymously.

Stephen Hicks

Bibliography

Blouch, Christine. "Eliza Haywood and the Romance of Obscurity." *Studies in English Literature.* Vol. 31, pp. 535–552.

Firmager, Gabrielle M., ed. *The Female Spectator.* 1992.

Schofield, Mary Anne. *Eliza Haywood.* 1985.

Whicher, G.F. *The Life and Romances of Mrs. Eliza Haywood.* 1915.

See also Actors and the Acting Profession; Women in Literature

Hazlitt, William (1778–1830)

A distinguished literary and cultural critic, and a major figure of the **London** literary scene during the **Regency**, Hazlitt made important contributions in the areas of moral philosophy, **literary criticism**, and political analysis. Among his most notable works are: *Essay on the Principles of Human Action* (1805), *A Reply to the Essay on Population* (1807), *Characters of Shakespear's Plays* (1817), *Lectures on the English Comic Writers* (1819), *Political Essays* (1819), *Table-Talk* (1821), and *The Spirit of the Age* (1825). Notable too in its own way is *Liber Amoris* (1823), Hazlitt's emotional account of his infatuation for a teenage girl.

Born into a **dissenting** family (his father was an itinerant **Unitarian** minister), Hazlitt, much like his father, thrived on controversy and hence found little stability in his life. Without uncritically admiring many 18th-century literary forms, he was also apt to be uncomplimentary toward the literary innovations and products of his sometime friends **Wordsworth**, **Coleridge**, and **Scott**. Self-consciously presenting himself as a child of the **French Revolution**, he liked to bludgeon writers who fell short of his political standards, measuring them according to their proximity either to "legitimacy" (perpetuation of the status quo) or "liberty" (meaning any activity tending to promote freedom and institutional reform).

After unsuccessfully studying painting, Hazlitt married (1808), and a few years later established himself as a popular critic, lecturer, and miscellaneous writer, publishing much of his work in journals and **newspapers**. He loved the **theater**, and his numerous reviews, often superior to the plays they discussed, began in 1813, appearing in the *Times, London Magazine,* and *Examiner.* His brilliant descriptions of such performers as **Edmund Kean** and **Sarah Siddons** are still worth reading. His subsequent Shakespearean criticism and commentaries on Elizabethan drama were admired by contemporaries for their psychological insight, but his forceful judgment, combative character, and powerfully incisive style are best revealed in the 25 pen-portraits of his contemporaries presented in *The Spirit of the Age.*

Hazlitt's greatest commitment was to the imagination, understood in its widest sense. For him, this manifested itself in moral and political, as well as literary, dimensions. Imagination as he saw it was the origin and agent of "sympathy"—that is, the human capacity to go beyond the narrow bounds of self-interest to a wider concern for the human community. He employed this conception in many ways, for example to challenge the egocentric reliance on abstract reason that he saw expressed in **Godwin**'s *Enquiry Concerning Political Justice* (1793), and to counter **Locke**'s contention that the mind was a *tabula rasa*—himself asserting that there are innate principles of knowledge that reveal themselves through exercise of the imagination. Hazlitt's commitment to the sympathetic imagination was but one of many marks of his profound idealism, humanity, and attachment to truth. To his great credit, his works met the standard he set for other writers, namely, "to say as an author what he felt as a man."

Robert W. Uphaus

Bibliography

Baker, Herschel. *William Hazlitt.* 1962.
Bromwich, David. *Hazlitt: The Mind of a Critic.* 1984.
Houck, James A., ed. *William Hazlitt: A Reference Guide.* 1977.
Jones, Stanley. *Hazlitt: A Life.* 1989.
Uphaus, Robert W. *William Hazlitt.* 1985.

See also Autobiography and Confession; Dramatic Criticism; Romanticism and Romantic Style

Hearne, Thomas (1678–1735)

Antiquarian, **nonjuror**, and **Jacobite**, Hearne took his B.A. (1699) and M.A. (1703) from **Oxford University**. He was assistant keeper (1701–1712) and second keeper (1712–1716) of the Bodleian Library, but in 1716 was stripped of his position and denied access to the **library** for refusing to swear loyalty to the Hanoverian monarchy.

Cast in **Alexander Pope**'s *Dunciad* (1728) as the pedant Wormius, Hearne edited and contributed to numerous editions of English historical and antiquarian works. His original *Ductor Historicus* (1698, 1704) and his 9-volume edition of John Leland's *Itinerary* (1710–1712) were reprinted several times during the century. Following his dismissal from the Bodleian, Hearne retired to Edmund Hall, Oxford. He repeatedly turned down offers of prestigious employment—including two invitations to assume the head librarianship of the Bodleian (1719, 1729)—that would have required him to take the oaths or to leave Oxford.

The Oxford University Press edition of Hearne's diaries and correspondence (1885–1921) reproduces much of his profuse (and often acerbic) commentary on Oxford and Oxonians in the early 18th century and on the second generation of Jacobites and nonjurors and their detractors.

Alexander Pettit

Bibliography

Hearne, Thomas. *Remarks and Collections.* 11 vols. 1885–1921.
———. *The Remains of Thomas Hearne.* 1966.
Macray, William Dunn. *Annals of the Bodleian Library.* 2nd ed., 1890.

Hearts of Oak

Agrarian secret societies, sometimes violent, dominated 18th-century peasant life in **Ireland**. Typical was the hearts of Oak or "Oakboys" movement, so-called for the sprig of oak that adorned their caps. Appearing in Ulster in 1763, their main grievance was the **taxes** levied for **road** building, particularly when it was perceived that these proceeds often went into the coffers of landlords. The movement also fought successfully to keep the price of land down, forcing landowners to promise on oath not to raise rents above 7 shillings (35p) an acre.

Described by contemporaries as "absolute masters" in Armagh, Cavan, and other northern counties, the Oakboys movement stood out from others such as the **Hearts of Steel** in that it attempted to mobilize **Catholics**, Anglicans, and **Presbyterians** in often spectacular disturbances. It mainly appealed to small **farmers** and to **weavers**, a group seen here in their most aggressive mood.

E. W. McFarland

Bibliography

Donnelly, J.S. "Hearts of Oak, Hearts of Steel." *Studia Hibernica.* Vol. 31, pp. 7–73.
Senior, H. *Orangeism in Ireland and Britain, 1795–1836.* 1966.

See also Irish Land Settlement; Peep O' Day Boys; Whiteboys

Hearts of Steel

The Hearts of Steel or "Steelboy" agitation began in south Antrim in the 1770s, originally as a rebellion against the imposition of fines for the renewal of leases on the 5th Earl of Donegall's (1739–1799) estates. But soon the agitation developed into a more general protest against high rents and **tithes**, and began displaying a clear sectarian dimension, emphasizing the principles of **Presbyterian** egalitarianism and loyalty to the crown. The movement articulated popular Protestant resentment at land being let to **Catholics** who were able to pay inflated rents.

The Steelboys developed a sophisticated organization which was able to intimidate the **gentry**. Yet the economic grievances of small tenants was the prime focus of the movement, rather than principled antilandlordism. Like the **Whiteboys**, their counterparts in the South, the Hearts of Steel represented the popular notion of fair rent levels and a desire to regulate **wages** and prices in accordance with the traditional "moral economy."

E. W. McFarland

Bibliography

Donnelly, J.S. "Hearts of Oak, Hearts of Steel." *Studia Hibernica.* Vol. 31, pp. 7–73.
Maguire, W.A. "Lord Donegall and the Hearts of Steel." *Irish Historical Studies.* Vol. 21, pp. 351–376.
Senior, H. *Orangeism in Ireland and Britain, 1795–1836.* 1966.

See also Hearts of Oak; Irish Land Settlement; Peep O'Day Boys

Hedge Schools

Roman Catholic elementary schools for peasants had flourished in **Ireland** since Cromwellian times. But because of the **penal laws** that outlawed Roman Catholic education and teachers, such schools often convened unobtrusively outdoors "'neath the sheltering hedge" or in barns or other outbuildings to escape notice. Although their expenses were sometimes defrayed by Catholic country **gentry** and priests, it more often was parents who footed the bill for their children's instruction. This always included the three Rs and Latin; in some schools, Greek and Hebrew were also taught, but history was ruled out because it was thought to breed discontent. Teachers were usually young priests in training, and many instilled interest that was augmented by chapbooks and the Latin classics.

By 1824 there were 8,000 such schools with religious teachers, and 7,600 independent pay schools with lay teachers. The hedge school, the most vital force in Irish popular education, became the common school in Ireland after piecemeal dismantlement of the penal laws between 1782 and 1829.

H. George Hahn

Bibliography

Dowling, P.J. *The Hedge Schools of Ireland.* 1935.

See also Irish Education

Hell-Fire Club

There were actually several "Hell-Fire" clubs founded in the 18th century. The first was organized by the Earl of Wharton in 1719. This brought together a group of wits, rakes, and gamblers who met at the Greyhound tavern on Bury Street in **London** near St. James' Square. Apart from **gambling**, they liked to poke fun at religion by eating something called "Holy Ghost" pie. Legend has it that satanic rituals and sex orgies figured in their observances.

The most famous Hell-Fire club was started by **Sir Francis Dashwood** and others in the 1750s. Its activities paralleled those of its predecessor. The club included politicians such as George Selwyn (1719–1791), who earlier had been expelled from **Oxford** for preparing the sacrament at a drinking rout; and **Bubb Dodington**, another job-hunting parliamentarian; and well-known personalities such as the 3rd Duke of Queensberry (1726–1756), the **Earl of Sandwich**, **William Hogarth**, and **John Wilkes**. Its activities were sometimes written up disapprovingly in the popular press, for example, in the *Public Advertiser* (June 1763) and in *Town and Country* magazine (1769). Claims were made that in addition to their formal meetings held in Medmenham Abbey (a former Cistercian monastery), the "monks" of the club met in caves in West Wycombe to perform sex acts with prostitutes from the brothels of famous madams, such as Charlotte Hayes.

Probably very few of these charges were true. Their chief source—hardly a reliable one—seems to have been certain allegations made by Wilkes during the course of his attacks on **Lord Bute**'s ministry in 1763, when Dashwood was Chancellor of the Exchequer.

Stanley D. Nash

Bibliography

Blackett-Ord, Mark. *Hell-Fire Duke: The Life of the Duke of Wharton.* 1982.
Chancellor, E. Beresford. *The Hell Fire Club.* 1926.
Jones, Louis C. *The Clubs of the Georgian Rakes.* 1942.
Kemp, Betty. *Sir Francis Dashwood, an Eighteenth-Century Independent.* 1967.

See also Clubs; Prostitution

Hellenism, Romantic

British Romantic Hellenism, an enthusiasm for the art, **architecture**, style, mythology, philosophy, and literature of ancient Greece, began, ironically, in Naples, in 1738, with the excavations of Pompeii and Herculaneum, two Greco–Roman villages destroyed in 79 A.D. by the eruption of Mt. Vesuvius. Based on the bits and shards of pottery, mosaics, and domestic life, scholars and artists invented a golden age when, as **Shelley** wrote later, "The human form and human mind attained to a perfection in Greece . . . whose very fragments are the despair of modern art" (*Hellas,* Preface, 1822).

The initial expressions of Hellenism were formal. Starting in 1751, the Dilettanti Society (founded in 1732 by **Sir Francis Dashwood**) sponsored expeditions to Greece itself; from 1762 it published *The Antiquities of Athens,* the architectural drawings of James "Athenian" Stuart (a close friend of **Robert Adam** and the recognized authority on pure Greek architectural style) and Nicholas Rivett (1720–1804). This collection announced the triumph of Greek style in architecture and greatly influenced the design of British public buildings (courts, libraries, banks, and even churches). Meanwhile, **Josiah Wedgwood** at his pottery works ("Etruria") in Staffordshire interpreted and popularized the Hellenic in pottery designs.

Those who could, however, traveled to Greece to collect authentic treasures. It was these scavengers—"marble mongerers" as **Byron** called them in "The Curse of Minerva" (1815)—who brought back the monumental fragments, the broken limbs and horses' heads—the **Elgin Marbles**—that Lord Elgin (1766–1841) acquired for the British government and that were ultimately displayed in the **British Museum**, supposedly to initiate a national school of public art. (At the very least, they inspired **Keats** in a rhapsodic sonnet on the mingling of "Grecian grandeur with the rude / Wasting of old time.")

Another strain of equally idealizing Hellenism, the philosophical, intellectual, and heroic, began with **sculpture**. It originated with Johann Winckelmann (*Reflections on the Painting and Sculpture of the Greeks,* 1755; translated by **Henry Fuseli**, 1765), who studied the weathered and bleached collection of statues in the Vatican and concluded that the greatness of Greek art was its simplicity, spirituality, and approximation of Platonic ideals, and that it represented the greatness of the Greeks themselves. At the same time, German scholars, "mythogogues," looking for a unified myth behind biblical Genesis, stimulated an interest in ancient Greek religion. In England, the paucity of Greek scholars and texts inhibited the study of myth and of Plato. Handbooks such as that by John Lamprière (1788), commentaries such as that (1790) by John Bell (1745–1831), even an illustrated text for children by **William Godwin** (1806), helped remedy the deficiency and popularized Greek myths. In 1802, Thomas Taylor (1768–1835) published the first **translation** of Plato in 200 years, but it was inaccessible to most people because it was very expensive and, as even the brilliant **Coleridge** complained, it turned "difficult Greek into incomprehensible English." But among poets, the Platonic strain of Hellenism found expression in Shelley and in **Wordsworth**'s "Ode: Intimations of Immortality" (1807), where the Platonic myth of preexistence explained the loss of vision that he believed accompanies maturity.

Naked statues, evocative drapery, and procreation myths promoted another strain of Hellenism, a hedonistic, sensual, and erotic one that appeared variously in the priapic re-creations of Dashwood's **Hell-Fire Club** and its descendants, the dampened muslin gowns of **Regency** ladies, and the versified biology of **Erasmus Darwin**, whose *Botanic Garden* (1791) treated all of contemporary natural history as a vast seduction ritual. The strain was summed up in what Keats called in "Sleep and Poetry" (1817) the realm of "Flora and old Pan."

Finally, there was a political dimension to English Hellenism. Unlike the aristocratic and elitist Roman neoclassicism, the Hellenic supposedly affirmed an ancient democracy, a pastoral economy, a unity of belief that English Romantics liked to believe survived in their northern and industrializing island. "We are all Greeks," Shelley proclaimed in his preface to *Hellas,* "our laws, our literature, our religion, our arts have their roots in Greece."

But for all its appeal, Hellenism became increasingly alien to the cultural climate of the 1830s—pious, economically driven, morally earnest. In 1834, a century after the excavation of Pompeii, Bulwer-Lytton (1803–1873) in *The Last Days of Pompeii* buried Pompeii again, a fit retribution for what he saw as the lascivious, greedy, violent society that had rejected Christianity. That was not the last chapter of the story, however. Matthew Arnold (1822–1888) opened another when he cried in *Culture and Anarchy* (1869): "Now it is time to Hellenise, and to praise *knowing.*"

Marilyn Gaull

Bibliography

Bush, Douglas. *Mythology and the Romantic Tradition.* 1937.

Buxton, John. *Grecian Taste, 1740–1820.* 1978.

Crook, J.M. *The Greek Revival.* 1972.

Gaull, Marilyn. *English Romanticism: The Human Context.* 1987.

Hungerford, Edward. *Shores of Darkness: A Study of the Influence of Mythology on the Romantic Movement in Poetry.* 1941.

Muller, Herbert J. *The Uses of the Past: Profiles of Former Societies.* 1952.

Newsome, David. *Two Classes of Men: Platonism and English Romantic Thought.* 1972.

Stern, Bernard. *The Rise of Romantic Hellenism in English Literature, 1732–86.* 1940.

Webb, Timothy. *English Romantic Hellenism, 1700–1824.* 1982.

See also Antiquities and Ruins; Classicism; Neoclassical Style; Romanticism and Romantic Style

Hemans, Felicia (1793–1835)

A popular poet, Hemans, née Browne, was celebrated in Britain and America in the 1820s and 1830s. She was born in **Liverpool** but raised in a mountainous coastal area of **Wales**, a landscape reflected in much of her later **poetry**. In 1812 she married Captain Alfred Brown, a soldier, but he abandoned her in 1818, leaving her with five sons. Before moving to Dublin (1831) she became friends with **Scott** and **Wordsworth**. The latter tenderly eulogized her in his "Extempore Effusion upon the Death of James Hogg" (1835).

Her earlier poetry was written mostly in an heroic mode on historical and pseudohistorical subjects; her later, more on domestic themes and religious sentiments. Hemans's work included *The Domestic Affections, and Other Poems* (1812), *The Restoration of the Works of Art to Italy* (1819), *Tales and Historic Scenes* (1819), *The Sceptic* (1820), *Welsh Melodies* (1822), *Lays of Many Lands* (1826), *Records of Woman* (1828), *Songs of the Affections* (1830), *Hymns for Childhood* (1827, 1834), *National Lyrics* (1834), and *Scenes and Hymns of Life* (1835). She also completed two plays, *The Vespers of Palermo* (1823) and *The Siege of Valencia* (1823), which were less well received than her poetry; and contributed prose **essays** on foreign literature to the *Edinburgh Monthly Magazine.*

Felicia Hemans

Modern readers may find Hemans's expression bombastic, her characters unreal, her lengthy narratives tedious. But contemporaries were charmed. Schoolchildren memorized and declaimed "The boy stood on the burning deck" ("Casabianca") and "The breaking waves dash'd high / On a stern and rock-bound coast" ("The Landing of the Pilgrim Fathers in New England"). Many of Hemans's patriotic poems, frequently mediating between military duty to country and familial love, became British classics ("England's Dead," "The Homes of England," and "The Graves of a Household").

Glen A. Omans

Bibliography

Chorley, Henry F. *Memorials of Mrs. Hemans, with Illustrations of Her Literary Character from Her Private Correspondence.* 2 vols. 1836.

Clarke, Norma. *Ambitious Heights: Writing, Friendship, Love—The Jewsbury Sisters, Felicia Hemans, and Jane Welsh Carlyle.* 1990.

Jeffrey, Francis. "Felicia Hemans." *Edinburgh Review.* Vol. 50, pp. 32–47.

Lootens, Tricia. "Hemans and Home: Victorianism, Feminine 'Internal Enemies,' and the Domestication of National Identity." *Publications of the Modern Language Association.* Vol. 109, pp. 238–253.

Memoir of the Life and Writings of Felicia Hemans: By Her Sister, in *The Works of Mrs. Hemans.* 7 vols. 1839.

See also Women in Literature

Hepplewhite, George (1726–1786)

Very little is known about the personal life of this cabinetmaker who, alongside his younger rival **Thomas Sheraton**, did much to popularize the **neoclassical style of home furnishings and decoration**. Hepplewhite is thought to have begun his career around 1760, working in Lancaster with Gillow and Company before setting up on his own in **London**. His designs are a restrained version of the neoclassical style associated with **Robert Adam**, with whom he often collaborated. He is credited with popularizing the use of painted motifs and inlaid satinwood veneers in his furniture, and he made frequent use of the serpentine curve. No authenticated examples of his delicately proportioned, even fragile, furnishings are thought to exist today. His pattern book, *The Cabinet-Maker's and Upholsterer's Guide,* containing more than 250 designs, was published posthumously by his wife Alice in three editions (1788, 1789, 1794); this was less a catalogue than a recapitulation of the fashions prevailing in the Age of Satinwood (1765–1810).

Reed Benhamou

Bibliography

Aronson, Joseph. *The New Encyclopedia of Furniture.* 1967.

Hayward, Helena, ed. *World Furniture.* 1965.

Macquoid, Percy. *A History of English Furniture.* Vol. 4: *The Age of Satin Wood.* 1905.

Whiton, Sherrill. *Interior Design and Decoration.* 1974.

See also Architects and Architecture; Chippendale, Thomas; Housebuilding and Housing; Interior Design

Herschel, William (1738–1822)

On 13 March 1781, Herschel, then an amateur astronomer, observed through his telescope what he thought to be a comet. The object was later identified as a planet, which at first was dubbed "Georgium Sidus," after **George III**, but later renamed Uranus. This planetary discovery was but one of Herschel's important contributions to astronomy. His four complete sweeps of the night sky produced one of the first models of the universe based on observational data, as well as catalogues of nebulae and double star systems. He is also credited with discovering two satellites of Saturn, infrared "heat" radiation, and the 595-million-kilometers-per-year motion of the sun through space, relative to the local neighborhood of stars.

Herschel came from a musical family. His father, Isaac (1707–1767), was an oboist in the **Hanover** *Hofkapelle* and military band; several of his brothers were also trained in music. He came to England in 1756 as a member of the Hanoverian regimental band, then decided to stay, supporting himself as a performer, music copyist, itinerant music teacher, and composer. His earliest compositions—chamber music and oboe and violin concertos—date from this period; many were probably first performed at private musical gatherings in the homes of his pupils. In 1761 he was appointed Director of the **Leeds** Concert series, for which he composed his later symphonies. He began writing a textbook (unfinished) on music composition, left Leeds (1766), and soon afterward moved to **Bath**.

Herschel's activities at Bath provide an index to the vitality of local musical life at that time. He served as organist and choir director for the Octagon Chapel, violinist in sev-

William Herschel

eral area ensembles, teacher of various musical instruments, and conductor of **oratorio** performances in both Bath and nearby **Bristol**. During these years he also continued to compose, producing substantial chamber music, including many solo compositions for violin and harpsichord, some organ compositions, and miscellaneous vocal works. In 1769 his *Sei Sonate per il Cembalo* was published in Bath by Thomas Baker.

But Herschel's interests changed, gravitating toward science and away from music. In 1772 his sister, Caroline Lucretia (1750–1848), came to live with and assist him, recording the data of her brother's systematic sweeps of the night sky through giant telescopes. She later reduced these observations to produce the important *Catalogue of Nebulae in Zones,* a task that earned her a Gold Medal and Honorary membership in England's Royal Astronomical Society. She was an astronomer in her own right, having discovered eight comets and several of the nebulae listed in the catalogue.

After discovering Uranus in 1781, scientific observation became Herschel's full-time occupation. In 1782, appointed Royal Astronomer, he moved to the vicinity of Windsor. The king provided money to build larger telescopes and to devote Herschel's time entirely to scientific astronomical surveys; in return, Herschel received the king and his guests as weather conditions and interest dictated. He was knighted in 1817 and elected First President of the Royal Astronomical Society the same year.

George F. Reed
Sterling E. Murray

Bibliography

Armitage, Angus. *William Herschel.* 1962.

Hoskin, M.A. *William Herschel and the Construction of the Heavens.* 1963.

Murray, Sterling E., ed. *William Herschel (1738–1822): The Symphonies. The Symphony 1720–1840.* 1983.

Woodfield, Ian. *The Celebrated Quarrel between Thomas Linley (Senior) and William Herschel: An Episode in the Musical Life of 18th Century Bath.* 1977.

See also Bradley, James; Halley, Edmond; Music; Musical Concerts and Concert Life; Science, Technology, and Invention

Hervey of Ickworth, Baron (John Hervey) (1696–1743)

Hervey's political career as a **Whig** courtier began when he visited Hanover (1715) and became friendly with **Frederick**, later Prince of Wales. He continued this association in England and entered the **House of Commons** (1725) allied to the Whig opponents of **Robert Walpole**. Under **George II**, who took the throne in 1727, he remained a favorite of **Queen Caroline**, a position which gave him office and influence. By 1730 he had become a faithful adherent of Walpole (and his go-between with the queen) and, a skillful political writer, he attacked Walpole's enemies **Bolingbroke**, **Pulteney**, and their publication ***The Craftsman;*** the quarrel resulted in a duel with his former friend Pulteney, from which Hervey barely escaped with his life. Political animosity also resulted in **Alexander Pope**'s savage satires of Hervey as Sporus, Lord Fanny, Adonis, and Narcissus. Walpole's fall (1742) and **Newcastle**'s enmity forced him out of office.

Hervey's political writings celebrated the **Glorious Constitution**'s liberty and "balance" and the role of the **aristocracy** in maintaining that balance, yet in private he honored the monarchy as the protector of the state. His career, admirably illustrated in his posthumously published (1848) *Memoirs*—a major source for historians studying this period and a brutally frank account of both George II and his son Frederick—reveals the reconciliation made by Whig politicians between their heritage as defenders of constitutional liberty, and their early Hanoverian role as servants of the monarchy.

Robert D. McJimsey

Bibliography

Browning, Reed. *The Political and Constitutional Ideas of the Court Whigs.* 1982.

Halsband, Robert. *Lord Hervey: Eighteenth Century Courtier.* 1974.

Sedgwick, Romney, ed. *Some Materials Towards Memoirs of the Reign of George II, by John Hervey.* 3 vols. 1931; rev. 1963

Highland Clearances

By 1750, Highland landowners were forced to adapt to the increasingly commercial values of society. Estates had to be made profitable, and there is evidence that even before the rising of **Forty-five** some estates, most notably the **Argyll** estates, were adopting commercial values whereby rentals were given to the highest bidder rather than to a kinsman under the system of **clanship**.

The commercial exploitation of Highland estates was not without its social consequences, as traditional notions of clan loyalty were replaced with market relations. Often this involved social displacement as crofters were "cleared" or moved from their traditional holdings to make way for new enterprises, or simply moved to other areas of economic activity. The Highland crofter had no guarantee of tenure, and could be evicted or moved at will.

The desire for commercial return induced many landowners to subdivide the land into uneconomic holdings. This had the effect of prodding tenants to bring wasteland into cultivation, and also to seek alternative employment in rural industries such as kelp harvesting, **fishing**, quarrying, and illicit whiskey-making, which were considerably more profitable for the landowner. The limited introduction of sheep also meant displacement for some tenants, who were often moved to less fertile ground.

The kelp boom of the Napoleonic era (kelp was seaweed processed as a substitute for barilla, an alkaline product used in **glassmaking** and soap manufacture whose importation was disrupted by war) encouraged many landlords to move their tenants to the coastline, onto small plots of land so that they could work in the industry. This had the effect of limiting the amount of land available for subsistence (though the problem was initially offset somewhat by introduction of the potato). Crofters received little benefit from this relocation, many lived on the edge of starvation, and when the price of kelp collapsed at the end of the war, the crofting community was left in a precarious position.

Richard Finlay

Bibliography

Devine, T.M. *From Clanship to Crofters.* 1993.

Gray, Malcolm. *The Highland Economy.* 1957.

Hunter, J. *The Making of the Crofting Community.* 1976.

Richards, E. *A History of the Highland Clearances: Agrarian Transformation and the Evictions 1746–1886.* 1982.

See also Highland Regiments; Planned Villages; Sellar, Patrick

Highland Regiments

One of the most enduring legacies of the Scottish Highlands has been its contribution of fighting personnel for the British **Army** and **Empire**. Historically, Highland regiments have enjoyed an awesome military reputation, often instilling fear into the hearts of their opponents.

Military recruitment from the Highlands must be seen in the context of the crisis of the Highland economy in the aftermath of the failed rebellion of the **Forty-five**. Military service permitted the absorption of many Highlanders who otherwise would have been underemployed. Poverty, feelings of traditional **clan** loyalty, and coercion from clan chieftains requiring military service in return for land, all helped boost Highland recruitment. In addition, military service was beneficial to the Highlands in that it provided injections of capital and helped remedy the problem of overpopulation. Britain benefited by partially solving the "Highland problem" while raising cannon fodder for imperial warfare.

Between 1759 and 1793, 20 regiments were raised from the Highlands. These were not only employed in the **Seven Years' War** and the **Napoleonic Wars**, but also in colonial service in many parts of **North America**, **India**, and **South Africa**. Out of a **population** of 300,000 it has been calculated that around 74,000 Highlanders fought during the contemporary wars against **France**, while expatriate Highland regiments such as the 84th Royal Highland Emigrants and the North Carolina Highlanders also fought for the British Crown in the **War of American Independence**.

John Roach Young

Bibliography

Keay, J., and J. Keay, eds. *Collins Encyclopaedia of Scotland.* 1994.

Richards, E. *A History of the Highland Clearances: Agrarian Transformation and the Evictions 1746–1886.* 1982.

Watson, F. *The Story of Highland Regiments, 1725–1925.* 1925.

See also Forfeited Estates Commission; Highland Clearances; War and Military Engagements

Highland Scotland

See Scotland and Scottish Culture

Highwaymen

Highwaymen were mounted robbers, often brandishing pistols, who held up coaches and other vehicles on public **roads** leading in and out of **London** (and, to a lesser extent, **provincial towns**). They flourished especially in the first half of the 18th century, beginning to decline in numbers thereafter. By the 1830s, improvements in **law enforcement** and lighting, coupled with the clearing of natural wooded hiding places around London, led to their complete demise.

The highwayman has been depicted in popular fiction, motion pictures, and television as an heroic and romantic knight of the road who displayed the manners of a gentleman and the heart of a Robin Hood. A mythology of the highwayman has developed, based on fictional works such as **John Gay**'s *Beggar's Opera* (1726) and William Harrison Ainsworth's (1805–1882) **novel**, *Rookwood* (1834). While the myths contain some truth, historians have shown that highwaymen were hardly the "merry rogues" found in popular works.

In reality, many of them were brutal in their treatment of their victims. Some combined rape with theft, and many were members of gangs notorious for cruelty in the commission of an assortment of crimes much broader than highway robbery. Their social origins were usually unglamorous, despite the popular belief that many were upper-class men who had fallen on hard times. The fashion-conscious Jack Rann (hanged in 1774), known as "sixteen-string Jack" for the silk

Dick Turpin

strings attached to his breeches, was a former footman and coachman. James MacLaine (hanged in 1750), admired by many fashionable ladies of the time—his upper-class victims, incidentally, included the elegant **Horace Walpole**—had been a grocer. And a fair number of highwaymen apparently got their start either as butchers or as other **artisans** connected with the meat trade, thus becoming particularly knowledgeable about the roads and the movement of money and goods in and out of London. In fact, one of the most famous highwayman, Dick Turpin (hanged in 1739), was a butcher's apprentice (as well as a cattle rustler, **smuggler**, and member of the Gregory gang, a brutal band of housebreakers). Despite the gallant demeanor of men like Rann and MacLaine, and the magnanimous gestures of Benjamin Child (who used stolen money to free all the debtors in Salisbury gaol in the 1720s), most highwaymen were unattractive characters.

Stanley D. Nash

Bibliography

Hibbert, Christopher. *Highwaymen.* 1967.

Linebaugh, Peter. *The London Hanged: Crime and Civil Society in the Eighteenth Century.* 1992.

McLynn, Frank. *Crime and Punishment in Eighteenth-Century England.* 1989.

Pringle, Patrick. *Stand and Deliver: The Story of Highwaymen.* 1951.

See also Crime

History Writing and Historians

The Hanoverian period saw several significant shifts in history writing. The main development was that historiography changed from chronicle, personal narrative, or party polemic to a more reflective, though still often partisan, account. By the early 19th century, historians had established a more careful approach to their material that would be dominant throughout the Victorian era.

The 18th century saw an increased interest in the raw material of history. Public documents, pamphlets, private **letters**, and memoirs were not only consulted by historians but published and more widely read than ever before. Other changes came from the influence of secular and rational ideas deriving from the **Enlightenment**. Historians wrote for a public who were not only curious about the past but philosophically interested in its implications for the present and future.

To most Hanoverian Britons, history meant an account of their own country's past. Naturally the 17th century, when so many events of political and religious importance had occurred, was of special interest. In the first half of the 18th century, virtually all histories endorsed the **Glorious Revolution** and the victories of Parliament, the **Whigs**, and broad church principles. The most comprehensive and widely read work of this sort was Paul de Rapin-Thoyras's (1661–1725) *Histoire de l'Angleterre* (15 volumes, 1723–1725), **translated** and continued by Nicholas Tindal as *Rapin-Thoyras's History of England* (1726–1731). The historian was a Huguenot refugee who had served under William III; his biases, appropriate to the age, were anti-French and anti-**Catholic.**

By 1750, most **Tories** as well as Whigs had accepted the idea of the **Glorious Constitution** and the rightness of mixed monarchy. Historical interest shifted away then from whether Charles I, Cromwell, or the Revolution of 1688 had been right or wrong, to investigations of how people had interacted with each other in building national society and its political structure. History writing took on a somewhat more objective and scientific tone, at least in outward appearance. Philosophers, meanwhile, looked increasingly to history instead of to an hypothetical state of nature to explain society.

David Hume, today remembered chiefly for his **Empiricist** philosophy, was more widely known by his contemporaries for his *History of England* (6 volumes, 1754–1762). His work, judicious in tone, was considerably more favorable to the Stuart kings, and less sympathetic to the **Presbyterians**, than that of his predecessors. Hume was variously condemned as a Tory and an atheist, and was resented also as a Scotsman who had presumed to write English history. His account was nonetheless influential. Another (transplanted) Scot, **Tobias Smollett**, published an expanded and popularized version of Hume as *A Complete History of England* (9 volumes, 1757–1765). **Oliver Goldsmith**'s *History of England* (4 volumes, 1771) presented Hume in simplified form for school use.

The History of England from the Accession of James I (8 volumes, 1763–1783) by **Catharine Macaulay** was in part an answer to Hume. Her first volumes countered his strictures on the Puritans and the parliamentary cause, and rebutted his defense of the Stuarts. In her later volumes, though she never tempered her defense of individual liberty and the rights of citizens, she attempted, like Hume, to write secular, critical history in a reasonably objective spirit. Her republican views, however, led her to condemn the corrupt results of the Glorious Revolution as heartily as she did the acts of Charles I.

Macaulay and Hume both used documents and other material from the 17th century, and both were somewhat selective in their use of evidence, though Macaulay offered long excerpts from and frequent citations of her sources. A new kind of history writing was now emerging from a more concentrated interest in historical documents, one that paralleled the increasingly patriotic tone of literature in general. Publication of volumes from the *Clarendon State Papers* (1767), the *Somers Tracts* (16 volumes, 1748–1751), and *Hardwicke's Miscellaneous State Papers* (2 volumes, 1778), as well as of many treaties, statutes, and parliamentary proceedings, fed the demand for historical documents and for a more detailed and intimate acquaintance with the national past. Much of the parliamentary material was collected in the 36 volumes of *The Parliamentary History of England from 1066* (1806–1820), edited by **William Cobbett** and others.

The private or semiprivate papers of individuals were also popular historical reading. Such works as William Coxe's (1747–1828) *Memoirs of the Life and Administration of Robert Walpole* (3 volumes, 1798) and *Memoirs of the Duke of Marlborough* (3 volumes, 1818–1819) have proven indispensable to later historians. The letters of people who were not political or military figures were popular, too; publication of these included *The Correspondence of Samuel Richardson* (6 volumes, 1804), *Letters from Mrs. Elizabeth Carter to Mrs. Montagu* (3 volumes, 1811), and the *Memoirs of the Life and Correspondence of Mrs. Hannah More* (4 volumes, 1834).

Biography as a form of history came increasingly into vogue. In some cases this took the shape later known as "life and letters" (as in Coxe's various works); but simple narrative accounts of the lives of famous and not-so-famous persons were also well received. The lives of individuals were considered instructive for the young as well as interesting to adults, and biographies, according to many contemporary experts, had the additional attraction of being much safer than **novels** for the reading needs of women. The greatest Hanoverian biography was **James Boswell**'s famous *Life of Samuel Johnson* (2 volumes, 1791). Popular also were biographical collections such as **Johnson**'s own *Lives of the English Poets* (10 volumes, 1779–1781), George Ballard's (1706–1755) *Memoirs of Several Ladies of Great Britain* (1752), **Horace Walpole**'s *A Catalogue of the Royal and Noble Authors* (1806), and **Mary Hays**'s *Female Biography* (1802). **Robert Southey**'s *Life of Nelson* (1813) and *Life of Wesley* (1820) are still worth reading.

Most historians focused narrowly on English politics; **Scotland** and **Ireland** were examined only as they affected English events. **William Robertson** of Edinburgh—he was, like his friend Hume, a leader of the **Scottish Enlightenment**—provided some corrective to this. He published *The History of Scotland* (2 volumes, 1759) as well as *A History of the Reign of the Emperor Charles V* (3 volumes, 1769), and *The History of America* (2 volumes, 1777). His works stressed progress, tolerance, and moderation, values that more or less permeated all contemporary British historiography.

Perhaps the greatest of all Hanoverian historians, **Edward Gibbon**, turned even farther away from England. His *Decline and Fall of the Roman Empire* (6 volumes, 1776–1788) is probably the most important work of philosophical history in English. Gibbon instructed his readers not so much about Rome as about man and his works. Sophisticated Britons already knew much about the Eternal City; they read Gibbon partly through an interest in "man-in-general," and partly in an attempt to understand more about their own society and their own **Empire**.

Henry Hallam's (1777–1859) *View of the State of Europe during the Middle Ages* (2 volumes, 1818), 10 years in preparation, a survey of the formation of the main European states from the 5th to the 15th centuries, was the greatest historical work after Gibbon's and a pioneering study of medievalism. Hallam followed this with his *Constitutional History of England* (2 volumes, 1827); though he ended his account at the accession of **George III**, neither this restraint nor his attitude of objectivity saved him from charges by Southey and others of partisanship, and the work was in fact instrumental in establishing "the Whig view of history."

Hallam, and the Roman Catholic John Lingard (1771–1851) in his *History of England* (8 volumes, 1818–1830), owed much to Robertson and the increasingly accepted view

Illustration for edition of Hume's History of England, *1793*

that history should be based very carefully on the sources. They also reflected the increasing interest in English history before the 17th century and in local history, another tendency manifesting itself after 1770 in such works as E. Hasted's *Kent* (4 volumes, 1778–1799), T. Nash's *Worcestershire* (2 volumes, 1781–1782), and W. Hutchinson's *Durham* (3 volumes, 1785–1794). **John Millar**'s *Historical View of the English Government* (1787), like John Whitaker's (1735–1808) *Genuine History of the Britons Asserted* (1772) and John Pinkerton's *Dissertation on the Origin of the Scythians or Goths* (1787), patriotically explored the ancient origins of national liberty. A similar medievalizing or Gothicizing tendency appears in the very different work of Thomas Carlyle (1795–1881). Carlyle, though often thought of as a Victorian, was in fact 42 years old when Victoria ascended the throne, ending the Hanoverian era (1837). That same year he published the most remarkable example of British **Romantic** historiography, his *French Revolution,* which combined poetic sweep with magnificent portraiture in a style distinctively his own.

None of these authors was an historian in the modern sense, making a living by writing and teaching history. They were men and women of letters who wrote history as well as other sorts of literature. History was not a separate subject to be taught and left in the classroom; it was literature to be read, enjoyed, and understood by all educated people.

Barbara Brandon Schnorrenberg

Bibliography

Black, John Bennett. *The Art of History: A Study of Four Great Historians of the Eighteenth Century.* 1926.

Kenyon, John. *The History Men: The Historical Profession in England since the Renaissance.* 1983.

Kidd, Colin. *Subverting Scotland's Past: Scottish Whig Historians and the Creation of an Anglo–British Identity, 1689–c.1820.* 1993.

Okie, Laird. *Augustan Historical Writing: Histories of England in the English Enlightenment.* 1991.

Peardon, Thomas Preston. *The Transformation in English Historical Writing, 1760–1830.* 1933.

Phillipson, Nicholas. *Hume.* 1989.

Pocock, J.G.A. *Politics, Language, and Time: Essays on Political Thought and History.* 1971.

———. *Virtue, Commerce, and History: Essays on Political Thought and History, Chiefly in the Eighteenth Century.* 1985.

Porter, Roy. *Gibbon: Making History.* 1988.

See also Literary Criticism; Music Scholarship; Party Politics; Reference Works

Hoadly, Benjamin (1676–1761)

Hoadly, Bishop of Bangor, Hereford, Salisbury, and Winchester (1723–1734), was the most powerful **Latitudinarian** divine of his time. He supported the **Whig** and Hanoverian establishment and was a leader of Low-Church divines, preaching a rational, deistic **theology.** The High-Church party opposed him after he preached the doctrine that inspired the **Bangorian controversy** (1717).

Hoadly graduated M.A. from **Cambridge University** in 1699. After receiving holy orders he became a lecturer and soon afterward a rector (1704). He opposed the bill against **occasional conformity** (1703) and expressed himself in several notable treatises, including "A Defense of the Reasonableness of Conformity to the Church of England" (1707).

In Hoadly's sermon (1717) on "The Nature of the Kingdom, or the Church, of Christ," he called the whole community of believers the true Church of Christ, and attacked the church's power over individual conscience. This prompted the war of pamphlets known as the "Bangorian controversy" that same year.

Hoadly later wrote another controversial **tract** on the Eucharist, *A Plain Account of the Nature and End of the Sacrament,* in which he denied the scriptural and theological foundations of the Sacramental Test Act (1735), again outraging the orthodox, High-Church party. Hoadly regarded the Eucharist as a simple memorial to Christ's sacrifice and an opportunity for Christian unity and fellowship. His tract was considered whiggish heresy, and many divines attacked his views. **Jonathan Swift** at one point ridiculed his faith as amounting to nothing less than the abolition of Christianity.

Carole S. Fungaroli

Bibliography

Dickinson, H.T. "Benjamin Hoadly, 1676–1761: An Unorthodox Bishop." *History Today.* Vol. 25, pp. 348–355.

Rack, H.D. "'Christ's Kingdom Not of This World': The Case of Benjamin Hoadly versus William Law Reconsidered." *Studies in Church History.* Vol. 12, pp. 275–291.

Sykes, Norman. "Benjamin Hoadly, Bishop of Bangor," in J.F.C. Hearnshaw, ed., *The Social and Political Ideas of Some English Thinkers of the Augustan Age, AD 1650–1750.* 1928.

See also Church of England; Hare, Francis; Law, William

Hoare, Prince (1755–1834)

A distinguished member of the **Royal Academy of Arts** (where he studied **painting** and later exhibited in 1781–1782), the Society of Antiquaries, and the Royal Society of Literature, Hoare was an influential artist and playwright. Although he stopped exhibiting after 1785, he became the honorary foreign secretary to the Academy in 1799, and in that capacity published three volumes of correspondence and related material.

The first of his 20 dramas was *Such Things Were* (1788), a tragedy that was revived as *Julia* (1796) as a benefit for **Sarah Siddons.** His greatest contribution to the **theater** was the popular musical farce, *No Song, No Supper* (1790), with **music** by Stephen Storace (1762–1796).

In 1820 Hoare edited the posthumous memoirs of **Granville Sharp,** the abolitionist and biblical scholar, but most of his writing concerned British art, **poetry, opera,** and comedy.

Laura Morrow

Bibliography

Craik, Thomas Wallace, and Clifford Leech, eds. *The Revels History of Drama in English.* Vol. 4. 1978.

Fiske, Roger. *English Theatre Music in the Eighteenth Century.* 1973.

Hughes, Leo. *A Century of English Farce.* 1950.

Nicoll, Allardyce. *A History of English Drama, 1660–1900.* Vol. 3, 1961; Vol. 4, 1960.

Hodgskin, Thomas (1787–1869)

Hodgskin, English educator and **radical** economic theorist, the son of a shopowner in a **navy** dockyard, was, along with **William Thompson,** one of a small group of late-Hanoverian economic thinkers who drew socialist conclusions from the labor theory of value.

With little formal education, Hodgskin was basically self-taught. He came to believe, after studying **Ricardo,** that labor was the sole source of wealth and that capitalism deprived workers of their true share of the wealth they produced. Friendships with **Place, Bentham, Godwin,** and **James Mill** influenced his economic thinking. His support of the movement to repeal the **combination acts** led to his most famous work, *Labour Defended against the Claims of Capital* (1825), followed by his *Popular Political Economy* (1827), in which he rejected the theory—accepted by orthodox economic thinkers—that owners of land and capital were entitled to shares in the fruits of labor. Free-market distribution was acceptable, but production should be cooperative, and the Malthusian **population** principles advanced by **McCulloch** and others were distractions from correct economic analysis. These two books, along with Hodgskin's *The Natural and Artificial Right of Property Contrasted* (1832), established him as one of the major anticapitalist writers of the early 19th century. Hodgskin also had a hand in the opening of the London **Mechanics' Institute** (1824).

William Edward Morris

Bibliography

Halévy, E. *Thomas Hodgskin.* 1956.
Thompson, N.W. *The People's Science: The Popular Political Economy of Exploitation and Crisis, 1816–1834.* 1984.

See also Economic Thought

William Hogarth

Hogarth, William (1697–1764)

Hogarth was the first English-born artist of international repute. He created in native **painting**, **engraving**, and art theory a new species of narrative social **satire** by wedding the exuberance and naturalism of English drama to techniques from Continental painting.

After completing his apprenticeship to a silverplate engraver (1720), Hogarth gained a modest reputation for his copperplate satirical prints and **book illustrations**—notably, *Masquerades and Operas* (1724), which ridiculed the false taste of **London**'s theatrical and artistic establishment; and 12 large plates (1726) for Samuel Butler's *Hudibras,* which juxtaposed the heroic and grotesque with great success. He attended St. Martin's Lane Academy and subsequently took instruction from **Sir James Thornhill**, Serjeant Painter to the King, whose daughter he married in 1729; he also helped Thornhill with a group portrait of members of the **House of Commons**. Hogarth was soon in great demand as a painter of "conversation pieces," informal portrait groups rendered "in small" and often emphasizing social interaction. These playful yet realistic productions prepared him for the great narrative series he was to undertake.

The six engravings of *A Harlot's Progress* (1732), depicting the gradual ruin and death of a young woman who descends to **prostitution**, reflect the artist's maturing sense of dramatic narrative, his fondness for realistic scenes from everyday life, and his commitment to the **moral** function of art. Characteristically, Hogarth not only condemned the bawd but also indicted the rest of society for its indifference and complicity in her fate. The harlot, like the protagonists of Hogarth's other moral narratives, is blamed mainly for embracing the folly and licentious values of fashionable society. The central figure in *A Rake's Progress* (1732, 1735) likewise chooses according to **fashion** with disastrous consequences. *Marriage à la Mode* (1743, 1745), the most sophisticated and intimate of Hogarth's "progresses," is his narrative masterpiece. Other series include *Industry and Idleness* (1747), *Four Stages of Cruelty* (1751), and *Four Prints of an Election* (1755–1758). Also among Hogarth's most memorable engravings are *Southwark Fair* (1733), *The Sleeping Congregation* (1736), *The Strolling Actresses Dressing in a Barn* (1738), *The March to Finchley* (1751), *Beer Street* and *Gin Lane* (1751), and *The Cockpit* (1759).

Although Hogarth never achieved the success he sought as a **history painter**, his portraits of *Captain Coram* (1740) and *The Shrimp Girl* (*c.* 1756) are two masterpieces of British painting. In the first of these—the portrayal of **Coram**, father of the **Foundling Hospital**—the tired conventions of the baroque are invigorated by Hogarth's compelling frankness and psychological realism.

A dedicated activist, Hogarth so vigorously promoted the Copyright Act for Engravers that it was known as "Hogarth's Act" when it passed (1735). He refounded St. Martin's Lane Academy, developing new ideas for the training of painters and for promoting artistic interchange and innovation. He was also a governor of St. Bartholomew's Hospital and of the Foundling Hospital, where he organized the first public exhibition of contemporary English art (1745).

Hogarth's *Analysis of Beauty* (1753), the first European aesthetic treatise based entirely on formal critique, is the great manifesto of his art. Here he championed his own brand of the rococo while attacking the Renaissance canons of simplicity, symmetry, harmony, and regularity. He proposed rather intricacy, variety, movement, and exaggeration, emphasizing the importance of expressive over formal qualities. His assault on traditionalism took as its primary target the serpentine "Line of Beauty, which leads the eye and mind a wanton kind of chase." His account of the comic, reflecting his own practice, still stands as an important contribution to aesthetics.

Although Hogarth's originality and importance were not recognized by the London connoisseurs he routinely excoriated, J.A. Ronquet, **Henry Fielding**, **Tobias Smollett**, and **Horace Walpole** all acknowledged his genius during his own lifetime. Championed by the **Romantics**, many of whose ideas he anticipated, Hogarth was the subject of insightful and sympathetic essays by **Charles Lamb** and **William Hazlitt**. Today he is seen as a central figure in the emergence and modern history of British art.

Michael F. Suarez, S.J.

Bibliography

Bindman, David. *Hogarth.* 1981.
Cowley, Robert L. *Marriage à la Mode: A Re-View of Hogarth's Narrative Art.* 1983.
Hogarth, William. *The Analysis of Beauty.* Ed. Joseph Burke. 1955.
Paulson, Ronald. *Hogarth: His Life, Art, and Times.* 1971; abr. ed., 1974.
———. *The Art of Hogarth.* 1975.
———. *Hogarth's Graphic Works.* 3rd rev. ed., 1989.
———. *Hogarth.* 3 vols. 1991.
Quennell, Peter. *Hogarth's Progresses.* 2nd ed., 1973.
Shesgreen, Sean. *Engravings by Hogarth.* 1973.
———. *Hogarth and the Times-of-the-Day Tradition.* 1983.

Hogg, James (1770–1835)

Though best known for his **novel**, *The Private Memoirs and Confessions of a Justified Sinner* (1824), Hogg was prolific in many genres and is considered a major figure in the Scottish literary tradition.

Born in the Scottish Border Country and mostly self-educated, the "Ettrick Shepherd" began his literary career as a rural poet, publishing two early collections: *Scottish Pastorals* (1801) and *The Mountain Bard* (1807). In 1802 he formed a friendship with **Sir Walter Scott**, but it was not until he moved to **Edinburgh** (1810) and published *The Queen's Wake* (1813) that his **poetry** was praised throughout **Scotland** and England. Soon after, Hogg became a major contributor to *Blackwood's Edinburgh Magazine* and published his first novel, *The Brownie of Bodsbeck* (1818). Acquiring a farm in Yarrow in 1816, he returned to rural life, where he wrote poetry, fiction, and nonfiction, including his novel *The Three Perils of Man* (1822), and *Familiar Anecdotes of Sir Walter Scott* (1834).

James Hogg

Despite a mixed reception by contemporaries such as **Wordsworth** and **Byron**, Hogg is now viewed as an important link between Scottish and English **Romanticism**.

Lauren Fitzgerald

Bibliography

Batho, Edith C. *The Ettrick Shepherd.* 1927.
Gifford, Douglas. *James Hogg.* 1976.
Groves, David. *James Hogg: The Growth of a Writer.* 1988.
Murphy, Peter T. *Poetry as an Occupation and an Art in Britain, 1760–1830.* 1993.
Smith, Nelson C. *James Hogg.* 1980.

Holcroft, Thomas (1745–1809)

Novelist, playwright, translator, and **radical** intellectual, Holcroft was a prolific writer whose most interesting work perhaps is his *Memoirs* (1816), edited by his friend **William Hazlitt**. His other publications include the dramas *Duplicity* (1781), *The Road to Ruin* (1792), and *The Deserted Daughter* (1795); the **novels** *Alwyn, or the Gentleman Comedian* (1780), *Anna St. Ives* (1792), *The Adventures of Hugh Trevor* (1794, 1797); and his **translations** from German of the life of Baron Frederic Trenck (1792).

Holcroft was born in **London**, the son of a poor shoemaker. Working by day, he studied music and languages at night. He tried teaching as well as shoemaking, but found his true calling in the **theater**, first as an **actor**, then as a playwright. In the 1780s his interests were less political than literary, though he met the radical **Godwin** in 1786 and would later meet **Coleridge**, **Lamb**, **Wollstonecraft**, and **Paine**, whom he resembled philosophically.

In the 1790s, ardently supporting the **French Revolution**, he associated himself with the **Society for Constitutional Information** and hence found himself indicted for high treason in 1794 (though he was discharged without a trial). His political ideas were essentially **middle class** and Godwinian, in favor of general reform through individual intellectual and **moral** transformation. His affairs deteriorated in the latter 1790s and, after attempting various literary and business adventures in Hamburg and Paris, he returned to London, where he died leaving his *Memoirs*—a touching story of his life, times, and struggles—incomplete.

Mary Tiryak

Bibliography

Baine, R.M. *Thomas Holcroft and the Revolutionary Novel.* 1965.

Hazlitt, William. *The Life of Thomas Holcroft.* Eldridge Colby, ed. 2 vols. 1925.

See also Dramatic Arts; Dramatic Criticism

Holland House

Situated not far west of Hyde Park, Holland House was the home of Henry Richard Fox, 3rd Baron Holland (1773–1840), and the popular meeting place for **Whig** society in the period 1800–1840. Holland's wife, the autocratic and formidable Elizabeth, Lady Holland, modeled her gatherings on the Parisian salon and entertained persons of talent and distinction. Guests were chosen to represent an interesting mixture of science, literature, art, and politics. This social setting also provided a coherent center for the Whig Party, which was out of office until 1830. Dinner parties devoted to discussions of prearranged topics exposed traditional Whig thinking to ideas from the **Scottish Enlightenment** and Continental nationalism. The death of Lord Holland (1840) put an end to the entertaining. Holland House was destroyed during a bombing raid in 1941.

P.J. Kulisheck

Bibliography

Hudson, Derek. *Holland House in Kensington.* 1967.
Ilchester, Giles Stephen Holland Fox-Strangeways, 6th Earl of. *The Chronicles of Holland House, 1820–1900.* 1937.
Mitchell, Leslie G. *Holland House.* 1980.
Sanders, Lloyd C. *The Holland House Circle.* 1908.

See also Fox Family

Hollis, Brand

See Brand Hollis, Thomas

Home, John (1722–1808)

Minister of the **Church of Scotland** (1746–1757), volunteer soldier in the **Forty-five** rebellion, secretary to British Prime Minister **Lord Bute** of **Scotland** (1757–1767), and **tutor** of the Prince of Wales (later **George III**), Home is also considered to be one of the few significant 18th-century British tragedians and the first from Scotland.

Home was born at Leith, the son of a town clerk. He attended grammar school there and received his M.A. from the University of Edinburgh in 1742. His most important and successful work, *Douglas* (1757) was produced at Edinburgh's Canongate Theatre through the efforts of Home's friends, including **David Hume**. The play was enthusiastically received by audiences but was opposed by authorities within the Church of Scotland, which led to pamphlet wars in **Edinburgh** and **London**, and to Home's resignation from the ministry. *Douglas* was followed by productions of *Agis* (1758), *The Siege of Aquileia* (1760), *The Fatal Discovery* (1769), *Alonzo* (1773), and *Alfred* (1778). Home went on to write a **history** concerning the Forty-five rebellion. In addition to his published works, he wrote two unpublished plays and a fragment of a third. He died in Merchiston, near Edinburgh.

Grace Rusk Kerr

Bibliography

Gipson, Alice Edna. *John Home: A Study of His Life and Works.* 1916.
Home, John. *The Plays of John Home.* James S. Malek, ed. 1980.
Mackenzie, Henry. *An Account of the Life and Writings of John Home, Esq.* 1822.

See also Dramatic Arts

Home Furnishings and Decoration

The decorative styles of Hanoverian Britain are divided into four periods and three "ages," the periods denoting chronology, and the ages the predominant material. Design historians thus speak of the Early Georgian (1714–1750), Middle Georgian (1750–1765), Late Georgian (1765–1800), and **Regency** (1800–1837) periods; and of the ages of Walnut (1690–1725), Mahogany (1725–1760), and Satinwood (1760–1800). Using decorative sources and designers as additional indicators, they also associate the Neopalladian Early Georgian period with **William Kent** (1685–1748); the rococo Middle Georgian with **Thomas Chippendale** (1718–1779); the neoclassical Late Georgian with **Robert Adam** (1728–1792), **George Hepplewhite** (1726–1786), and **Thomas Sheraton** (1751–1806); and the eclectic Regency with Thomas Hope (1770–1831).

Soon after the accession of **George I** (1714), the restrained and sturdy Queen Anne style was challenged by Kent's **Palladianism**. Furnishings, inspired by baroque Rome and Florence, grew in scale and complexity; tables and seating pieces were elaborately sculpted and gilded; heavy satin damasks in saturated colors were used for upholstery and, occasionally, on the walls. Eagles, cartouches, chimeras, and other oversized classical ornaments were applied to overdoors and chimney breasts, and walls were hung with similarly oversized paintings. But with the exception of a *sgabello*-like chair that dominated hall furniture well into the 19th century, Kent's approach had little influence on later designers. Responding to the emerging desire for domestic ease, less theoretical craftsmen had been working from the Queen Anne prototype, keeping its comfortable and efficient forms but replacing pad feet with the ball-and-claw, opening up solid backsplats with carving, emphasizing with decorative brackets the join of leg to rail, and developing such new furniture types as the breakfront and a variety of expandable cardtables.

Among these craftsmen was Chippendale, who converted Kent's baroque into an appealing rococo, and then, profiting from popular enthusiasms, added **Chinoiserie** and **Gothic** to his repertoire. Under the arches, scrolls, frets, and pagodas used to convey a sometimes mixed decorative heritage, his furnishings exhibited the strong outlines and superb craft of traditional English cabinetry. Kent facilitated decoration in the various modes by offering a variety of railings, accessory pieces, and wallpaper borders to complement the client's scheme. The draw-up window covers that had replaced the split curtain in the early years of the century continued in use; floors were covered with rugs and carpets, either imported

Design of a chest of drawers by Batty Langley, 1750

or domestic. Few rooms, with the exception of eating areas, were yet dedicated to specific functions and because most homes were sparsely furnished, many pieces of furniture were carried from place to place to accommodate the company and activity.

The rococo disappeared around 1760, replaced by the refined **neoclassicism** ushered in by Adam on his return from Italy. Taking his decorative vocabulary from Pompeii, Adam introduced coffered half-domed ceilings, and reintroduced the architectural orders, into interior space. He decorated strongly colored flat surfaces with dainty stucco swags, arabesques, and palmettes picked out in white. To ensure unity, he designed furnishings and equipment for each installation. His Chippendale-built consoles and tables were characterized by intricate satinwood marquetry; pieces by other cabinetmakers were often gilded or painted in clear colors. Nearly all were semicircular or elliptical in form, echoing the patera that was one of his signature motifs. Adam is credited with the invention of the one-piece sideboard, and with reviving *scagliola,* a marble-like substance made from tinted plasters.

Adam's severe style, developed for a select group of discriminating and wealthy patrons, was popularized by Hepplewhite and Sheraton, who kept his straight lines and delicate scale but simplified his decoration. Hepplewhite is best known for the variety of his chairbacks, the most original of which was a draped heart. Sheraton favored mechanical and dual-purpose furnishings, such as table–stepstools, cribs that automatically rocked the baby, and extendable dining tables.

Sheraton continued designing into the Regency period and although his average interior was as pleasant as it was modest, the dangers inherent in so eclectic a period are apparent in the increasing clumsiness of his work. Furniture was often painted in black and gilt, or constructed of dark rosewood, zebrawood, or mahogany. Hope proposed furnishings based on Greek vase paintings, Roman sarcophagi, and Egyptian tomb decorations. Plinth-based consoles and especially sidechairs modeled on the graceful *klismos* of classical Greece, became popular. Tabletops resting on single pedestals rather than four legs appeared, but this minimalist support soon ballooned into the pillar-and-claw. Gothic and Chinese styles were enthusiastically revived, the latter becoming especially popular with the Prince of Wales. Around 1830, mechanization reached the furniture industry, and products began to be adapted to the simplified forms and decoration that could be produced using a machine lathe.

There was both revolution and evolution in the furnishings and decoration of Hanoverian Britain. The shifts from walnut to mahogany and from mahogany to satinwood, were readily and cleanly accomplished; the Regency adoption of rosewood and zebrawood was less abrupt. The neoclassical designs of Adam, Hepplewhite, and Sheraton quickly supplanted the rococo popularized by Chippendale, just as Chippendale's styles had deposed those of Kent; the dissolution of Adam's coherent elegance into the eclecticism of the Regency style was gradual but steady.

Three things may be said of the period as a whole. First, its furniture was primarily the product of the joiner: the meeting of horizontal and vertical elements was emphasized; the natural grain of the material was more often enhanced by shellac and stain than hidden with gilt, lacquer, or paint; and upholstery was subordinated to a wooden frame. Second, styles were literally superficial, denoted through motifs applied to traditional forms. Third, decoration and design were generated not by artist–craftsmen but by artisan–**entrepreneurs** who sought to stimulate demand and develop market share with pattern books; it is our good fortune that, with few exceptions, the process resulted in attractive spaces and handsome furnishings.

Reed Benhamou

Bibliography

Aronson, Joseph. *The New Encyclopedia of Furniture.* 1967.

Chippendale, Thomas. *The Gentleman & Cabinet-Maker's Director.* 1754; 1755; 1762.

Heyward, Helena, ed. *World Furniture.* 1965.

Macquoid, Percy. *A History of English Furniture.* 1905.

Rybczynski, Witold. *Home: A Short History of an Idea.* 1986.

Sheraton, Thomas. *The Cabinet-Maker and Upholsterer's Drawing Book.* 1791–1794; 1802.

Thornton, Peter. *Authentic Decor: The Domestic Interior, 1620–1920.* 1984.

Whiton, Sherrill. *Interior Design and Decoration.* 1974.

See also Architects and Architecture; Housebuilding and Housing; Interior Design

Homosexuality in Literature

Historians believe that before *c.* 1700 in England, homosexual behavior was considered immoral and illegal but not necessarily dishonorable, since men took the active role and were rarely effeminate. Men—some men, at least—were considered sexually omnivorous and capable of homosexual desires without this necessarily compromising their sexual relations with women. But by the beginning of the 18th century, homosexual desire, because of a growing association with effeminacy, was considered increasingly dishonorable and therefore appropriate for concealment. The difference can be seen in the contrasted lives and writings of two poets: Rochester (1648–1680), and **Byron**. Rochester had sexual relations with boys as well as women, and wrote of both as sexual alternatives without suffering any loss of manly status. Byron, however, could openly pursue males only when he was abroad. He seems to have suffered great anguish over his repressed feelings, and the poetic expression of his last passion for a Greek boy was tortured and full of his own disapproval.

This may help to explain why, in the early Hanoverian era, homosexual desire could no longer be as openly expressed in literature as it had occasionally been earlier. Its treatment before 1750 became increasingly satirical. **Pope**, for example, excoriated **Lord Hervey** as an effeminate hermaphrodite, and **Charles Churchill** in the *Times* (1764) charged that many men married women or took mistresses only to hide their exclusive desire for men. Homosexual men were also **satirized** in **novels**. In the *Love Letters between a Certain Late Nobleman and the Famous Mr. Wilson* (1723), an early anonymous epistolary novel, male transvestism and a complete misogyny were presented as their characteristics. **Smollett** also painted a discreditable image in his novels and poems. **John Cleland** in *Fanny Hill* (1748–1749) described anal intercourse between two males in detail, but followed it with a denunciation of their effeminacy; his publisher was nevertheless prosecuted for printing the passage.

It is worth noting that Cleland, who himself was later accused of being homosexual, described lesbian relations without condemnation. Charlotte Charke (1713–1760) denounced effeminate men in a novel, but in her memoirs described her own flirtations with women without apology. The discrediting of sexual relations between men changed the nature of 18th-century writing, but women's same-sex involvements seem to have escaped the same degree of critical scrutiny.

A similar evolution appeared in the **dramatic arts**. On the stage during the Restoration and in the 1690s, woman-chasing men were also shown with boys. But they were not effeminate: effeminacy was a characteristic of fops who were sexually interested in women. In the early Hanoverian era, all effeminate males on stage were presumed to be exclusively homosexual. **David Garrick**'s character of Fribble in *Miss in Her Teens* (1747) set the final stamp upon this conception. At the same time, a homosexual playwright such as **Isaac Bickerstaff** would entirely avoid homosexuality in his plays as too personally compromising. Hester Thrale Piozzi (1741–1821) could presume, however, that the playwright **Richard Cumberland** was secretly homosexual because he dwelt on male beauty in the same way as did a known homosexual, **Beckford**.

It is clear that an important element in this cultural evolution was the rising insistence on a linkage between homosexuality and effeminacy. In a society still bound by military and chivalric aristocratic codes, a society moreover which from the 1740s was increasingly asserting its opposition to **France** and to everything self-consciously denigrated as "French," and was engaged in prolonged warfare, this was perhaps inevitable. But whatever the cause, writers after 1750 such as **Walpole**, **Gray**, and Beckford either covertly expressed homosexual desires within traditional forms or allowed their sensibilities to surface in new forms like the **Gothic novel**.

Randolph Trumbach

Bibliography

Crompton, Louis. *Byron and Greek Love: Homophobia in Nineteenth-Century England.* 1985.

Fothergill, Brian. *Beckford of Fonthill.* 1979.

Kimmel, Michael S., ed. *Love Letters between a Certain Late Nobleman and the Famous Mr. Wilson.* 1990.

Rousseau, G.S. *Perilous Enlightenment.* 1991.

Straub, Kristina. *Sexual Suspects: Eighteenth-Century Players and Sexual Ideology.* 1992.

Hone, William (1780–1842)

Hone was a satirical writer and advocate of the freedom of the press best known perhaps for his acquittal of blasphemy charges in December 1817. Born in **Bath** of **dissenting** stock, he was largely self-educated. In 1796 he was briefly a member of the **London Corresponding Society** and afterward held advanced political views, though his somewhat vacillating temperament and humorous outlook kept him away from the more extreme forms of **radicalism**.

A bibliophile, Hone tried to make a living as a **London** bookseller and writer after 1800. In 1810 he helped organize demonstrations in favor of the parliamentary radical **Sir Francis Burdett**, and after 1815, failing in various attempts at **newspaper** publishing, emerged as a clever satirist of the contemporary guardians of church and state. Three productions of 1817, *The Late John Wilkes's Catechism, The Sinecurist's Creed,* and *The Political Litany Diligently Revised,* combined political criticism with religious parody to such popular effect that the government decided to punish him by prosecution. He defended himself with three days of speech in court (December 1817), but the most effective defense may have been simply the reading aloud of his more offensive passages, which produced unseemly laughter and irritated complaints from the prosecution.

Hone's acquittal was a victory against the government's attempts to restrain the press. His best-known work, the *Political House that Jack Built* (1819), enjoyed a release of over 50 editions. His other writings were numerous. Charles Dickens (1812–1870) attended his funeral, as did the **caricaturist George Cruikshank**, with whom he had frequently collaborated.

Thomas D. Veve

Bibliography

Baylen, Joseph, and Norbert J. Gossman. *Biographical Dictionary of Modern British Radicals.* Vol. 1. 1979.

Hone, J. Ann. *For the Cause of Truth: Radicalism in London, 1796–1821.* 1982.
Royle, Edward, and James Walvin. *English Radicals and Reformers, 1760–1848.* 1982.
Wickwar, William Hardy. *The Struggle for Freedom of the Press, 1819–1832.* 1928.

See also Laws of Public Worship, Speech, and the Press; Satire

Hood, Samuel (1724–1816)

Hood was a prominent naval commander during all Britain's **wars** of the latter 18th century. The son (like many other well-known sea captains) of an obscure clergyman, he entered the **navy** as a captain's servant (1741) and soon attained a commission (1746). He first commanded the sloop H.M.S. *Jamaica,* patrolling the North American coast. During the trial of Admiral **Byng** (1757) he aggressively volunteered to take temporary command of any ship whose captain attended the court-martial, and as an interim captain he bagged a French warship and two privateers, earning himself command of H.M.S. *Bideford.*

Subsequent success in the Channel and the Mediterranean during the **Seven Years' War** earned Hood a baronetcy, promotion to flag rank and, during the **War of American Independence**, command of a large squadron sent to the **West Indies** to reinforce Admiral **Rodney** (1781). Following the disastrous British defeat at the Battle of the Capes off Chesapeake Bay (1781), caused primarily by overly rigid adherence to the tactics prescribed by the navy's "Fighting Instructions," Hood, who had commanded the rear of the line, was instrumental in changing tactical doctrine to permit greater flexibility—an important improvement that paved the way for **Horatio Nelson**'s successes later.

Successful operations against the French in the Caribbean earned Hood the title Viscount Hood of Catherington (1782) and a seat on the Admiralty Board. Elected M.P. in 1785, he served until 1796, acting as **Pitt**'s spokesman. At the renewed outbreak of war with **France** (1793) he became supreme commander in the Mediterranean. Despite his initial success in the siege of Toulon (1793) and the capture of Corsica, the Admiralty recalled him (1794), citing his ill-health, though it is more likely that strategic disagreements prompted the recall. The indignant reaction of his officers showed the esteem in which they held him; Nelson described him as the best officer in the navy. Relatively humane in the treatment of his men, he also inspired awe with his aggressiveness, physical courage, and tactical acumen.

Stanley D.M. Carpenter

Bibliography

Creswell, John. *British Admirals of the Eighteenth Century: Tactics in Battle.* 1972.
Macintyre, Donald. *Admiral Rodney.* 1962.
Rose, J. Holland. *Lord Hood and the Defence of Toulon.* 1922.

Hood, Thomas (1799–1845)

Hood was a comic poet who matured into a social critic late in life. He was always in financial distress; he handled his money badly, and was not lucky. As a young man he worked as an engraver and later as an editor on the *London Magazine* (1821–1823), through which he met **Charles Lamb**, J.H. Reynolds (1796–1852), **De Quincey**, **Hazlitt**, and **Wordsworth**. His earliest verse was indebted to the **Romantics**, but in 1826 he published *Whims and Oddities,* a volume of comic **poetry** that found great success. Until the end of his life he would publish similar works of parody and punning, using the **ballad** stanza form in *Whims and Oddities: 2* (1827); *Comic Annual* (1830–1839, 1842); *Hood's Own,* a monthly magazine (1838); *Whimsicalities* (1844); and *Hood's Monthly Magazine and Comic Miscellany* (1844).

Hood often illustrated his own work with grotesque **drawings**, many of which contained their own visual puns. His verse is highly skillful parody with an underlying **moral** and social concern, but black humor, combined with a refined notion of the grotesque, often takes it over. In "Faithless Nelly Gray," Nelly addresses her lover, who has lost a leg: "Before you had those timber toes, / Your love I did allow, / But then, you know, you stand upon / Another footing now." Hood also had success with his late social protest poems, "The Song of the Shirt" (1843), "The Lay of the Labourer" (1844), and "The Bridge of Sighs" (1844). These often responded to actual events—the first of them, for example, sympathetically described an arrested sweatshop seamstress who had pawned stolen articles as endlessly sewing "Till over the buttons I fall asleep, / And sew them on in a dream." The naturalness of his language tied Hood to the Romantics; his moral tone places him with the Victorians.

Elisabeth W. Joyce

Bibliography

Hood, Thomas, Jr., and Frances Freeling Broderip, eds. *Thomas Hood: The Works.* Rpt. 1970.
Morgan, Peter F., ed. *The Letters of Thomas Hood.* 1973.
Reid, J.C. *Thomas Hood.* 1963.

Hook, Theodore Edward (1788–1841)

Born in **London**, educated at Harrow (**Byron** was his classmate), Hook began his career writing melodrama and farce. He helped introduce melodrama into English with his loose **translation** of two of Guilbert Pixericourt's (1773–1844) plays: *Tekeli, or the Siege of Montgatz* (1806), and *The Fortress* (1807). His most successful farce, notorious for its attack on **Methodism**, was *Killing No Murder* (1809).

In 1812 he was appointed Accountant General to the Island of Mauritius, but 6 years later he was dismissed and sent home because of £12,000 missing from the treasury, a retirement he later attributed to "a disorder in the chest." He then helped to found and anonymously edit the **Tory** *John Bull* (1820–1841), a **newspaper** which bitterly attacked **Queen Caroline** and prominent **Whigs**.

Among **novels**, Hook published his *Sayings and Doings* in 1824. His *Love and Pride* (1833) and *Jack Brag* (1837) are

Theodore Edward Hook

fine examples of **satirical** but thin treatment of social mores. *Gilbert Gurney* (1816) is his most stylistically complex novel. He also was the ghost-writer of the tenor Michael Kelly's (1764?–1826) *Reminiscences* (1826), a valuable source of theatrical material still in print.

Chat Ewing

Bibliography

Brightfield, Myron. *Theodore Hook and His Novels.* 1928.

See also Dramatic Arts; John Bull

Horne, George (1730–1792)

Horne, Bishop of Norwich (1790–1792), was known in his time as a sturdy defender of High-Church Anglicanism. He vigorously questioned the authority and conclusions of Isaac Newton (1642–1727), **David Hume**, **Adam Smith**, and **William Law** in pamphlets published between 1753 and 1784. He also protested the **theology** of **George Whitefield** and **John Wesley**'s disciples, though his refusal to prohibit Wesley's preaching suggests he sympathized with the **Methodists**. An Oxford graduate of University College (1749) and then Magdalen College (1752), of which he was later elected president (1768), Horne was influenced in part by John Hutchinson (1674–1737), the father of a sect that opposed Newtonian mechanics and upheld the scientific authority of the Bible. Horne is mainly remembered for his "Commentary on the Psalms" (1771), an exposition of the Messianic idea, and was respected in his own time as a great preacher and earnest scholar.

Laura B. Kennelly

Bibliography

Sykes, Norman. *Church and State in the XVIIIth Century.* 1934; 1975.

———. *From Sheldon to Secker: Aspects of English Church History, 1660–1768.* 1959.

Ward, R.D. *Georgian Oxford, University Politics in the Eighteenth Century.* 1958.

Horsley, Samuel (1733–1806)

Bishop of St. David's (1788), Rochester (1793), St. Asaph's (1802), and dean of Westminster (1793), Horsley (L.L.B. Cambridge, 1758) was one of the ablest Anglican writers of the period of **George III** on behalf of conservative High-Church Anglican values. A supporter of **William Pitt the Younger**, he dabbled in astronomy and geometry, was elected to the **Royal Society** (1767), became a member of **Samuel Johnson**'s club (1783), and was known as a conscientious bishop, a forceful preacher, and an outstanding scholar.

Horsley's published works in **science**, **theology**, philology, and politics include a reconstruction of a treatise of Apollonius of Perga (1770), an edition of Sir Isaac Newton's works (1779–1785), and *Theological Works: Sermons, Charges, Psalms, and Biblical Criticism* (8 vols., n.d.). In a 1778 sermon he launched a fierce controversy with **Joseph Priestley**, attacking the latter's view that the primitive church had not held the doctrine of the Trinity. His *Review of the Case of the Protestant Dissenters; with Reference to the Corporation and Test Acts* (1790) argued that lowering the barriers to **dissenters** would lead to the destruction of the Constitution. In politics as in religion, he was a vigorous champion of orthodoxy and of a patriotic response to the **French Revolution**.

Laura B. Kennelly

Bibliography

Hole, Robert. *Pulpits, Politics and Public Order in England: 1760–1832.* 1989.

Mather, F.C. *High Church Prophet: Bishop Samuel Horsley (1733–1806) and the Caroline Tradition in the Later Georgian Church.* 1992.

See also Church of England

Hospitals

At the beginning of the 18th century, few hospitals in Britain had survived the suppression and neglect of the previous two centuries. In **London** only two ancient institutions, St. Thomas's and St. Bartholomew's, along with the lunatic asylum, Bedlam, remained. However, the 18th century was a period of rapid growth in the provision of medical care.

The intellectual climate of the **Enlightenment**, which emphasized **humanitarianism** and philanthropy, provoked an unprecedented spate of donations to medical charities. A clear manifestation of this was the foundation of voluntary hospitals and later of public dispensaries. These institutions were intended chiefly for the "deserving poor," and often imposed restrictions on entry; more affluent members of society continued to prefer receiving treatment in their own homes.

Five general hospitals were opened in London in the earlier 18th century, all founded by private individuals: the Westminster (1720), Guy's (1724), St. George's (1733), the London (1740), and the Middlesex (1745). Hospital development was not confined to London. A survey of 1719 showed 23 English counties with no such provision, but by 1799 every county and many of the larger cities boasted their own hospitals or "infirmaries," bringing the total to 38 by 1800; by 1840 there were 114. A similar pattern arose in **Scotland**, the Royal Infirmary of Edinburgh (1729) being the first such establishment in Hanoverian times.

In England the management of new hospitals remained largely in lay hands. Funding was provided by numerous donors, and long-term subscribers were encouraged; bequests were also welcomed. Regular subscription entitled the donor to privileges, ranging from the right to admit patients to a seat on the board of governors in exchange for more substantial donations. Each hospital had at least one medical appointment, usually an honorary position whose acceptance was seen as a favorable career move by more ambitious medical practitioners because they could derive publicity for their skills and make advantageous connections among the well-connected hospital governors. But this position became more substantial as time passed. From about 1750, London hospital doctors lectured on anatomy and other aspects of practical medicine, and began regular examinations of patients while making the ward rounds. At the same time, medical students' fees formed an increasingly important part of hospital revenue.

Gradually, English doctors—particularly surgeons—became more involved in daily administration, creating the hospital environment that ultimately would nurture the scientific advances of the mid 19th century. In Scottish hospitals, however, doctors were often involved in administration early on; this included drawing up duty rotas comprising local physicians and surgeons. Patient care was undertaken not only by these qualified visiting doctors but by live-in apothecaries or medical students attending hospital training courses. Later, hospital work was undertaken by trainees according to seniority; this was the forerunner of **medical education** in the modern teaching hospital. Already in **Edinburgh** and **Glasgow** hospitals provided teaching facilities for the respective universities' medical schools.

Although this was not the case in **Scotland**, the new English hospital foundations tended to exclude certain patient categories such as fever victims because of the risk of hospital epidemics. In England, specialized fever hospitals were opened—in London, for example, in 1801. Such hospitals could do little to cure disease, but by isolating victims they could at least inhibit the spread of infection.

A parallel development brought the rise of the dispensary. Dispensaries were founded to supplement hospitals and provide outpatient services. They also promoted domiciliary services in which physicians visited the poor. The first London dispensary was established in 1773; the first in Scotland (in Edinburgh) in 1776. Other British towns and cities gradually followed suit. One by-product of domiciliary visits by eminent physicians was that they highlighted the living conditions among the poor and hence gradually led to agitation for sanitary and housing improvements in the Victorian period.

Hanoverian philanthropy also extended to provision for the insane. St. Luke's Hospital, the first public lunatic asylum apart from Bedlam, was opened in London in 1751; by 1800, many of the larger towns had followed suit. In Scotland, provision was more patchy, often being met within existing infirmaries. Other specialized institutions also arose, such as London's Lock Hospital (1746), which treated venereal disease. In the mid-18th century, three lying-in hospitals were also opened. These institutions provided a few days' respite for working-class women giving birth, and trained midwives as well as the newer male midwives. Males' training ultimately evolved into the medical field of obstetrics.

The expansion of hospitals in the Hanoverian era perhaps represented a change in philosophy more than an indisputable medical advance. Mortality rates remained very high in all hospitals. A lack of knowledge of hygiene prevented the curing of disease and impeded the successful performance of surgery. The greatest medical breakthroughs occurred only after scientific advances such as anaesthesia and antiseptic surgical techniques were developed in the mid-19th century.

C.E. Hivey

Bibliography

Cartwright, F.F. *A Social History of Medicine.* 1977.

Cunningham, A., and R. French, eds. *The Medical Enlightenment of the Eighteenth Century.* 1990.

Granshaw, L., and R. Porter, eds. *The Hospital in History.* 1989.

Hamilton, David. *The Healers: A History of Medicine in Scotland.* 1981.

Porter, Roy. *Disease, Medicine and Society in England, 1550–1860.* 2nd ed., 1993.

See also Foundling Hospital; Hunter Brothers; Medicine

Houldsworth, Henry (1774–1853)

Born near Nottingham, the third son of a yeoman farmer, Houldsworth served a brief apprenticeship to a grocer and then entered the **cotton** trade in **Manchester** in 1793. He and his brothers quickly built up a considerable business. Observing the rapid growth of the Scottish cotton trade, in 1799 he left the Manchester business to his brothers and set up as a **spinner** at **Glasgow**. His firm, centered on Anderston, soon became the second largest in **Scotland**, with 45,096 spindles. His mechanic's shop blossomed into a business in its own right as the Anderston Foundry; and Houldsworth's search for the requisite **iron** alerted him to the potential of the Lanarkshire mineral field. At age 62 he made his third career switch by acquiring the Coltness Iron Company, and between 1839 and 1845 he built five furnaces. In 1849 he and his three sons expanded into Ayrshire, where they set up the Dalmellington Iron Company. This became the third largest iron producer in Scotland. Houldsworth's career was remarkable for its range, variety, and success.

R.D. Corrins

Bibliography

Carvel, J.L. *The Coltness Iron Company.* 1948.

See also Entrepreneurs and Entrepreneurship

Hours, Wages, and Working Conditions

Before the **Industrial Revolution** labor force hours were characteristically irregular. Workers tended to alternate periods of intense activity with periods of leisure. This was true of unsupervised outworkers such as **weavers** or cutlers who worked at home; and also of many craftsmen in small workshops, whose irregularity did not pose too many problems for employers with little investment in fixed capital. "Saint Monday" was widely kept as a holiday by artisans and **miners**, who consequently had to work harder as the end of the week approached. Workers who could support their customary living standard from 5 days of work preferred leisure to working a sixth day.

The **factory system** made workers "clock in" to a more regular rhythm of work, but until this was well developed, any reference to a "normal" work day or work week needs qualification. Not all periods of idleness were matters of choice. For example, in outdoor work the weather or the length of daylight played an important part. However, a pattern can be detected for most urban journeymen. An act of 1721 required **London** tailors to work from 6 A.M. to 8 P.M. In 1752 tailors petitioned for a reduction on the grounds that 12 hours from 6 A.M. to 6 P.M. was by then usual in "most handicraft trades." By 1827 this was described as the "English system" and usually meant 10 hours of actual work with 2 hours for meal breaks. A general pattern had been established. But again, there were many exceptions: miners worked in shifts of 8 hours typically; whereas at the other extreme, in the early **textile** factories of the period 1790–1815, workdays were of 14, 16, and even 18 hours in length—not only for adult males, but also for most women and children.

Concerning wage levels, there was a gap between those who were skilled and those who were unskilled; and also between the wages of men and women. Much of **women's employment** was subsumed in the family wage paid to a manufacturing household, but even in trades specific to them, women's wages were low. As regards regional differences, London wages were higher than provincial wages throughout the 18th century, and especially so before 1770. **Adam Smith**, writing in 1776, thought the wages of London's building craftsmen to be from 50% to 100% higher than those of building laborers: 15 shillings to 18 shillings (75–90p), compared to 9s. to 10s. (45–50p). Provincial wages were around a third less. Generally speaking, a wage difference of around a third between skilled and unskilled wages seems to have been typical throughout the period. Skilled trades were categorized as "honourable" and "dishonourable." The former included coachmakers, engravers, compositors, and cutlers; the latter covered the larger trades like shoemaking or tailoring, which tended to be glutted with labor. In the great **metalworking** towns of **Birmingham** and Sheffield, wages for some craftsmen were comparable to London wages. Included among the better-paid laborers were miners and male **spinners** in the **cotton industry**. Workers employed under the "putting-out" system of **domestic production** were paid piece rates, which remained unchanged for most of the 18th century. By the third quarter of the 18th century, wages in northern England were beginning to show a more favorable aspect than those in the provincial south and west, reflecting the impact of an increasing demand for manufacturing labor.

The most evident general trend in wages over the period was the rapid rise of money wages during the wartime inflation from 1793 to 1815, although only the better-organized workers secured the rise of around two-thirds needed to keep real wages from falling against soaring prices. These are, of course, generalizations; individual trades had their ups and downs. Several trades had already enjoyed their "golden age" and were forced to look back bitterly from the 19th century to better times, when earnings were high and work more plentiful. For cotton handloom weavers this had been the case from 1788 to 1803: at that time, machine-spun yarn gave to handloom weavers in cotton and, a little later, in **wool**, a period of prosperity before the arrival of power looms from the 1820s. The framework knitters of the East Midlands, who as the original **Luddites** began to smash stocking-frames in 1811, had only just emerged from a golden period, which had lasted from the 1790s until 1809.

Generally speaking, the Industrial Revolution only slowly improved the **standard of living**. Few historians now support the extremely pessimistic view of its impact, except in the case of particular groups like the handloom weavers, but no universal upward trend in living standards occurred before 1820.

By the beginning of the 19th century the increasing importance of the factory system seemed to point toward more supervised labor and hourly wages. In fact, most factory masters preferred to pay piece rates, believing this an incentive for greater productivity. As early as 1776, Adam Smith, however, suggested that intense labor in response to piece rates often wrecked the health of manufacturing workers causing "the peculiar infirmity of the trade"; there is little doubt that even before the coming of the factory, many industrial workers suffered sickness, injury, and shortened lives. Some—like miners, grinders, and cotton workers—suffered lung disease from dust in the air; others—like potters, plumbers, painters, and hatters—were poisoned by the lead or mercury they used; while even those safe from the injuries inherent in dangerous occupations like mining nevertheless wrecked their constitutions or their eyesight through life-long strain.

It is clear that the problem of industrial workers' health did not begin with the cotton mills, but it was in this context that it first became a matter of public notice and then a matter of legislative concern. Debate centered on the health of women and, especially, of children. **Child labor** was widespread in 18th-century manufacturing and mining, but the factory separated child labor from the family, systematized it, and placed it in a more intolerable environment. The early water-powered rural spinning mills depended on bringing child pauper apprentices from distant parishes—an unfree source of labor. Long and regimented hours, more formal discipline involving the infliction of corporal **punishment**, and the dangers to tired children from unfenced machinery, all justify the heinous reputation of the early textile mills for their exploitation of child labor. In 1802 work hours for apprentices were restricted and other aspects of their employment regulated. However, **steam** power enabled factories to be built in towns where child labor could be drawn from the local population. The unfree pauper child gave way to the "free" child, placed in a factory from age 8 or sometimes younger by his or her own parents.

In 1815 the long struggle to extend protection to these children began. An act of 1819 helped some way, but it was not until the Factory Act of 1833 that much was achieved. This act restricted the hours of persons under age 13 to 48 a week, and those age 13–18 to a weekly 65. It also required factory owners to provide 2 hours of schooling daily. The setting up of a factory inspectorate was a milestone in the history of state regulation of industry, but it should be remembered that its scope was limited to textile mills, and that most child workers across the economy enjoyed no more protection than did the adults with whom they worked.

John Rule

Bibliography

Berg, M. *The Age of Manufactures.* 1994.

Hill, B. *Women, Work and Sexual Politics in Eighteenth-Century England.* 1989.

Malcolmson, R.W. *Life and Labour in England 1700–1815.* 1981.

Porter, R. *English Society in the Eighteenth Century.* 1990.

Randall, A. *Before the Luddites: Custom, Community and Machinery in the English Woollen Industry 1776–1809.* 1991.

Rule, John. *The Labouring Classes in Early Industrial England, 1750–1850.* 1986.

———. *Albion's People. English Society 1714–1815.* 1992.

See also Craft Guilds; Craftsmen; Factory Movement and Factory Acts; Friendly Societies; Labor Laws, Movements, and Unions

House of Commons

See Commons, House of

House of Lords

See Lords, House of

Housebuilding and Housing

During the Hanoverian period a number of important changes affecting all ranks of society took place in the design, layout, and function of houses. Some of these arrived because of general improvements in the economy. For example, until the opening of **canals** lowered **transport** costs, houses of every kind were usually built of local materials including stone, flint, tile, and slate. Even the largest country houses were built with bricks made from clay found and baked on the estate. Much building was carried out by masons, carpenters, and bricklayers, often self-employed and on a small scale, with the ever-present threat of bankruptcy. Architecture as a full-time profession was only beginning to emerge at the very end of the 18th century, though many country gentlemen had a genuine knowledge of the principles of classical architecture and were delighted to be able to display it in their buildings and **landscape architecture.**

The **aristocracy and gentry** spent prodigious sums building and rebuilding both town and country houses during this period. The tradition of building "prodigy" houses, established in the 16th century and resumed after the disruption caused by the civil wars, continued on a grand scale throughout the 18th century. Wanstead House, Essex, built for a wealthy East India **merchant** by Colen Campbell (1676–1729), had a front 260 feet long. Hopetoun House, rebuilt for the Duke of Hamilton by William **Adam**, was on a similar scale; but the grandest of all must have been Wentworth Woodhouse in Yorkshire, measuring 606 feet from end to end when finished.

In these elaborate constructions for the wealthy, the principles of classical architecture, well understood by the last decades of the 17th century, were developed by a series of architects who stamped their own personalities upon them, from **Sir Christopher Wren** (whose direct connection with country-house building was minimal), through **Sir John Vanbrugh** (responsible for the Baroque splendors of Blenheim), William Adam and Sir William Bruce (*d.* 1710) in Scotland, and the **Earl of Burlington**, whose interpretation of the **Palladian style** swept all before it in the first decades of the 18th century, to **Robert Adam**, whose marvelous fertility of invention is to be found at Osterley Park, Syon (Sion) House, and Kedleston Hall (Derbyshire). In the last half of the century, however, new themes began to appear; the **Gothic Revival** at Strawberry House, the **picturesque** at Downham Castle, Chinese themes or architectural **chinoiserie** in garden buildings such as the Pagoda at Kew, and the dazzling confection of oriental themes in the Royal Pavilion at Brighton.

These new houses both hastened and are evidence of significant social changes. **Servants** were relegated either to garrets or basements. The great hall, once the center of every activity in the house, became instead an imposing entrance room, its most prominent feature an elaborate staircase leading to the principal rooms on the first floor. Domestic life, even in great country houses, became more private as the tradition of open-handed hospitality rapidly declined. Splendid public apartments for lavish entertainment were still required, but family rooms (including a nursery and a schoolroom) became more common, privacy being greatly helped by the introduction of the "double-pile" house, where rooms opened into corridors rather than into each other. Visiting great houses became increasingly popular during the 18th century, but the family rooms were never open to the public. A separate dining room appeared, and with it the practice of ladies retiring after dessert to brew tea and coffee, leaving gentlemen to their port. Consequently, a drawing room became essential.

Where the rich led, the well-to-do **middle classes** followed. Building and rebuilding in town and country swept Britain, driven by successive waves of economic prosperity and

View of Alexander Pope's house on the Thames at Twickenham

slump, the greatest boom of all beginning in 1783 and collapsing around 1797. In **provincial towns**, houses were invariably built, rebuilt, or at least refaced, in **neoclassical** style. Brick and tile replaced timber and thatch, save in towns like Stamford in Lincolnshire, Chipping Camden in Oxfordshire, and many Scottish towns, where stone prevailed. Townhouses were given regular façades, with pediments supported on Tuscan columns, vertical sash windows becoming standard. Pattern books were published and widely read. Thus in a town such as Beverley in Yorkshire, it is possible to recognize the source of some specific decorative motifs. Many townhouses had outhouses and gardens, a sign that the self-sufficiency so characteristic of 16th-century households had by no means entirely disappeared.

The enclosure movement in **agriculture** led to the building of large farmhouses set in the midst of new consolidated farms away from villages. These shared the same classical themes as townhouses, and by the end of the 18th century some architects were specializing in the design and layout of new farms and farmhouses. Unmarried **farm laborers** ceased to live-in, leading, it was said, to "an increased neglect of the Sabbath and looseness of morals."

Individual landlords made some attempt to rebuild cottages for their laborers. Timber-framed and thatched cottages were replaced with more substantially built cottages. Two bedrooms—one for parents and one for children—became increasingly regarded, on **moral** grounds, as the essential minimum. This rural rebuilding had reached some of the most remote parts of Britain by 1800, but it depended on individuals and particularly on the efforts of landlords.

The distinction between home and work was by no means firm and certain in an era when **domestic production** was still dominant. Middle-class townhouses could incorporate a counting-house or a **banking** parlor. Technological innovation, especially in **textiles**, gave rise to houses incorporating a workshop where a loom could be installed. Rows of terraced cottages, 3-stories high, with only one room on each floor, that on the top given up to a loom, were erected in many parts of the Pennines. These were sometimes built into the hillside, so that a "taking-in" door at the back led straight into the workshop. As **spinning** became mechanized and **factories** emerged in the countryside to exploit water power, so **cotton** mill proprietors built rows of terraced cottages to house their workers, sometimes, as with **Arkwright** at Cromford, providing church and inn as well.

In industrializing **cities** like **Liverpool**, Nottingham, **Leeds**, and **Glasgow**, housing conditions for the working poor deteriorated catastrophically as **immigration** led to gross overcrowding. Cellar dwellings in Liverpool and back-to-back houses in Nottingham and Leeds appeared by the 1780s. Nottingham back-to-backs had cellar, living room, bedroom, and workshop stacked one on top of the other and built in rows around a central courtyard. In Leeds, much of this building was done by small-scale proprietors, profoundly influenced by the pattern of small fields created by preparliamentary enclosure. Some houses were built by building **clubs**, from which building societies later emerged. Very little attention was paid to drainage and sanitation.

Housing is, of course, an important factor in judging a **standard of living.** Much housing became undoubtedly more comfortable, convenient, and private than it had been at the beginning of the Hanoverian period. However, even by contemporary standards, more people dwelled in inferior housing in 1837 than in 1714. Improvements in the design and layout of housing reflected economic, social, and cultural developments. Nevertheless, there was no fundamental change either in construction techniques or in domestic conveniences. Large-scale building contractors began to emerge at the end of the 18th century, but it was well into the 19th when gas lighting became widely available, and nearly the 20th when electricity and central heating began to make their appearance.

Michael Reed

Bibliography

Barley, M.W. *The English Farmhouse and Cottage.* 1961.

Chalklin, C.W. *The Provincial Towns of Georgian England.* 1974.

Chapman, S.D., ed. *The History of Working Class Housing.* 1971.

Dunbar, J.G. *The Historic Architecture of Scotland.* 1966.

Fenton, A., and B. Walker. *The Rural Architecture of Scotland.* 1981.

Hussey, C. *English Country Houses: Early Georgian, 1715–1760.* 1955.

———. *English Country Houses: Mid-Georgian, 1760–1800.* 1955.

Reed, M. *The Georgian Triumph.* 1983.

Summerson, J. *Georgian London.* 1945.

See also Architects and Architecture; Home Furnishings and Decoration; Interior Design

Howard, John (1726–1790)

Howard became one of the most important early advocates of **prison reform** at age 47 when he was appointed High Sheriff of Bedfordshire. Discovering the deplorable conditions of local jails, he began investigating the general conditions of prisons in Britain, then elsewhere. He spent many years on tour, compiling data drawn from his prison inspections. Ultimately he **traveled** some 50,000 exhausting miles, exposing himself to disease that was rife in 18th-century prisons and spending huge sums of his own money in the process. His last trip was to Russia, where, visiting military hospitals, he contracted a fatal fever.

Howard's inspections revealed many abuses in prisons, including inadequate food, improper sanitation, and endemic disease. In England he was particularly shocked by the system of jail fees by which even an acquitted prisoner remained incarcerated until he paid the jailor a stipend. Influenced by his strong religious principles, certain Continental practices, and the growing **humanitarianism** of the age, he became a champion of highly structured penitentiaries in which uniformed prisoners would be contained in solitary cells at night but kept busy with a strict regimen of work and prayer during the day.

John Howard

Although it was not until the 1840s, when national penitentiaries began to be built, that large-scale prison reform took place, Howard's ideas had laid the groundwork for it. In his own lifetime his influence was felt in many ways. His published writings, most notably *The State of the Prisons in England and Wales* (1777), were widely read. His testimony before Parliament resulted in the passage of three acts which, despite their proving ineffectual, marked a new departure in prison reform. The first two (both passed in 1774) dealt with improving health conditions and abolishing jailors' fees. The third (1779), drafted by Howard, William Eden (1744–1814), and **William Blackstone,** authorized construction of two model penitentiaries. This project failed, and Howard's reputation has suffered from some complaints that the structured prison penitentiary replaced a physically brutal regimen with one equally brutal in mental punishment. However, contemporaries considered him a dedicated and sincere philanthropist.

Stanley B. Nash

Bibliography

Howard, Derek Lionel. *John Howard: Prison Reformer.* 1958.

Ignatieff, Michael. *A Just Measure of Pain: The Penitentiary in the Industrial Revolution, 1750–1850.* 1978.

Morgan, Rod. "Divine Philanthropy: John Howard Reconsidered." *History.* Vol. 62, pp. 388–410.

See also Fry, Elizabeth; Punishment

Howe, William (1729–1814)

General Howe was commander-in-chief of British forces in **North America** after the resignation of **General Gage.** He had established his military reputation in America earlier, fighting

General William Howe

in many engagements during the **Seven Years' War**, including (under **General Wolfe**) the successful siege of Quebec (1759). He succeeded Gage in October 1775 after the disastrous Battle of Bunker Hill.

Howe retired from besieged Boston to Nova Scotia, then returned in June 1776 to conduct a joint land–sea action against New York with naval forces commanded by his brother, Admiral Richard Howe (1726–1799). Failing first to prevent General **Washington**'s army from escaping to the mainland, and then to overtake Washington as he retreated through New Jersey, Howe lost the chance to deliver a decisive blow early in the war. He moved his forces to Philadelphia, overcoming the rebels' effort to block him at Brandywine, but found himself severely criticized for failing to assist **Burgoyne** at the disastrous **Battle of Saratoga** (1777).

Piqued by what he considered inadequate parliamentary support for the war effort, he resigned his command (1778) and was replaced by General Henry Clinton (*c.* 1738–1795). In 1779 he and his brother, who had also resigned, successfully defended his record before Parliament, instead attacking **Germain**, **Sandwich**, and the **North** ministry for the war's conduct. In 1780 he published a *Narrative* to much the same purpose—one in a series of self-defensive literary forays by Britain's commanders; Clinton wrote his own after surrendering at **Yorktown** (1783).

David Sloan

Bibliography

Anderson, Troyer S. *The Command of the Howe Brothers during the American Revolution.* 1936.

Conway, Stephen. "To Subdue America: British Army Officers and the Conduct of the Revolutionary War." *William and Mary Quarterly.* Vol. 43, pp. 380–407.

Gruber, Ira D. *The Howe Brothers and the American Revolution.* 1972.

Jones, Maldyn A. "Sir William Howe, Conventional Strategist," in George A. Billias, ed., *George Washington's Opponents.* 1969.

Pancake, John S. *1777: The Year of the Hangman.* 1977.

See also Army; War and Military Engagements; War of American Independence

Hudson's Bay Company

Furs were in great demand in Europe, particularly those used in beaver felt **hats**. So common was the fur trade in northern **North America** that beaver pelts were used as the medium of exchange. The Hudson's Bay Company Charter, granted in 1670, gave the English company the monopoly of the fur trade with Indians in the drainage basin of the Hudson Bay. The French colony of New France, however, depended on the trade for its viability, and violent hostilities between the two interests continued into the 18th century, even after the Treaty of Utrecht (1713) returned several French-captured trading posts to the British.

Despite many advantages, including direct passage for British **ships** to Hudson Bay, the company's difficulties were worsening by the 1730s. In 1738–1748 the number of furs brought to the company's forts fell by one-half. The French traded directly with Indian hunters, unlike the British, who tended to wait for the hunters to come to them. The company's cumbersome management structure also created problems. Run from **London** by proliferating committees that sent out orders infrequently by supply ship, and that commanded company agents to divide their time between trading and foraging for their own food, timber, and fuel, the company was at a serious competitive disadvantage.

After French defeat in the **Seven Years' War**, which left the British in control of all **Canada** (1763), poor management remained the company's chief problem when faced with new competition from the **North West Company**, established (1783) as a loose partnership of Scots–Canadian fur traders based in Montreal. Within 5 years the British lost most of their Indian middlemen to the Canadians, thanks again to cheeseparing by the London directorship, and the inferior stores and trading goods (chiefly guns and tobacco) they dispatched. With morale plummeting and trade being lost to the Canadians, the company suspended dividends in 1808.

Within a decade the position was being reversed. Management practices in Canada and London were restuctured thanks to **Lord Selkirk**, who had used the company's financial weakness to purchase a controlling interest. Canadian operations were concentrated in the York Factory, giving greater latitude to men on the spot. But Selkirk's creation after 1810 of the Red River Valley settlement (in present-day Manitoba) cut across the supply lines of the Canadian traders, leading to bloody territorial disputes. After the massacre of Seven Oaks (1816), in which 20 Hudson's Bay people were killed by their rivals, the Colonial Office intervened to promote a merger (1821) which marked the effective victory of the older company over its Canadian rival.

The company was then given a trading monopoly over western lands until pressure from American interests forced a division of the Oregon Country between Britain and the United States (1846), leaving the company in control (until 1858) of the British portion. Withstanding all later changes, it remains today a major Canadian firm.

Patricia S. Collins

Bibliography

Innes, H.A. *The Fur Trade in Canada.* 1956.
Newman, Peter C. *Company of Adventurers.* 1987–1988.
Rich, E.E. *The History of the Hudson's Bay Company, 1670–1870.* 1958–1959.

See also Chartered Trading Companies; Commerce, Overseas

Humanitarianism

In a **sermon** delivered shortly before his death (1791), **John Wesley** happily observed that "benevolence and compassion toward all forms of human woe" had increased during his lifetime "in a manner not known before, from the earliest ages of the world." Although precedents certainly existed—charitable expenditure on behalf of the poor and other sufferers had long been viewed as Christian duty, and society had accepted responsibility for the relief of **poverty** since 1600—philanthropic outreach in Britain did change dramatically in scope and purpose during the Hanoverian period.

This new humanitarianism, particularly influential after around 1770, was manifested in such activities as the establishment of **charity schools** by the Rev. Thomas Bray (1656–1730) and Robert Nelson (1656–1715), of orphanages by **Thomas Coram**, and of hospitals by Thomas Guy (?1645–1724). There were new "Magdalene" societies, organizations designed by **Jonas Hanway** and others to relieve the working conditions of seamen and to provide humane alternatives to impressment. There were efforts to reform the code of **punishment** by such men as **Samuel Romilly**, to alleviate the brutal conditions prevailing in **prisons** and asylums by such figures as **John Howard** and James Neild (1744–1814) and, perhaps most dramatically, there was the campaign mounted by **William Wilberforce** and **Thomas Clarkson** for abolition of the **slave trade** and eventually of slavery itself.

These initiatives were the product of a number of overlapping cultural, socioeconomic, and political developments. The **religious revival** of the 18th century, of which Wesley's own **Methodist** movement formed a part, encouraged the ardent sense of personal responsibility that characterized contemporary philanthropists. The **Enlightenment** contributed its own distinctive confidence in the malleability of human nature and the possibility of social perfectibility, and the **Scottish Enlightenment** contributed its own practical spirit of improvement. Poverty, suffering, and sin were increasingly viewed as rectifiable evils, and their rectification as civic responsibility. Whereas charity had earlier reflected piety and the giver's aspirations to salvation, the new humanitarian philanthropy was distinguished more by its attempts to effect positive changes in this world.

The development of philanthropy in these increasingly utilitarian directions took place during the onset of industrialization, an historic coincidence that has attracted much scholarly interest. Admiring interpretations featuring notions of humanity's progressive moral development have now been displaced by scholarly skepticism emphasizing the "interested" character of humanitarian activity, and especially its relationship to the economic, political, and social forces that were transforming Hanoverian life. Doubts have even been raised as to whether this humanitarianism impulse was essentially moral at all. Many of the institutional initiatives most closely associated with its emergence, especially in such realms as prison reform and the reform of punishment, are often now quite unsentimentally characterized as merely refinements in the state's capacity to control, manage, and manipulate its citizenry for political and economic advantage. Even what is presumably that least "interested" of all humanitarian endeavors, the **antislavery movement**, is now sometimes attributed to **middle-class** interests in legitimizing "free" wage labor and casting an attractive mantle over the new industrial and commercial greed.

Yet the important fact remains that Wesley was right in lauding the remarkable and growing number and intensity of humanitarian projects in the Hanoverian age. While various abuses continued to multiply, there was also a deepening sense of humanity's responsibility to correct and abolish them.

Susan Thorne

Bibliography

Andrew, Donna T. *Philanthropy and Police: London Charity in the Eighteenth Century.* 1989.
Bender, Thomas, ed. *The Antislavery Debate: Capitalism and Abolitionism as a Problem in Historical Interpretation.* 1992.
Foucault, Michel. *Discipline and Punish: The Birth of the Prison.* 1977.
Owen, David. *English Philanthropy, 1660–1960.* 1964.
Thompson, E.P. *The Making of the English Working Class.* 1963.

See also Manners and Morals

Hume, David (1711–1776)

Scottish influences dominated latter 18th-century British philosophy; Hume dominated Scottish philosophy. A diplomat, *bon vivant,* and historian as well as the most renowned figure connected with the British empiricist movement, Hume is widely remembered for his essay on miracles (in his *Enquiry Concerning Human Understanding*) and is hailed among specialist philosophers for his precise analysis of the question of causality. He has also secured a place in literary history, thanks to his elegantly spare late-neoclassical prose style.

Hume's career took many more turns than did those of the other empiricists. Born into a family of moderate means, he proceeded through a normal course of education, leaving Edinburgh University when he was about 15. He applied himself to his studies with such energy that he nearly destroyed his health (1729), at last retreating to **France** in search of a simple, healthy life (1734). After recovering he returned to Britain (1737), carrying a draft of his *Treatise of Human Nature* (1739). Settling near **Edinburgh**, he promptly produced his *Essays, Moral and Political* (1741–1742). After working as **tutor** and secretary he became (1752) keeper of the Library of the Faculty of Advocates and, by 1763, assistant and chargé d'affaires of the British embassy in Paris.

During the 1750s he produced a vast body of philosophical literature, including assorted works later collated under the title *An Enquiry Concerning Human Understanding.* As he rose through the university and the ranks of diplomacy, his salary and waistline expanded. He proclaimed himself "opulent." After his philosophical outburst of the 1750s, he passed the remainder of his literary days preparing several installments of his *History of England* (1754–1762). In 1766 he tried, in a curious episode, to rescue Jean-Jacques Rousseau (1712–1778) from political persecution, bringing him to Britain only to find himself embarrassed by Rousseau's conduct. Hume passed the last 10 years of his life in **London**. He died in peace, but was hounded to the grave by crowds fearful of the spiritual consequences of burying **freethinkers** in hallowed ground.

Hume's philosophical writings cover myriad topics. Those most central to his place in the history of **empiricism** are those pertaining to causality, miracles, the passions, and philosophical scholasticism in its relation to empiricism. Hume's notions concerning the idea of causality modified the airy empiricism of **George Berkeley**. Whereas Berkeley argued that only minds could convey ideas—that nonmental "substance" could not make itself known to a perceiving mind—Hume acknowledged nonmental reality. Yet material substance quickly receded into the background. Hume subdivided human knowledge into "impressions" delivered to the mind by experience and "ideas" manufactured by the mind as it cogitates impressions. Objects give us "impressions" of such qualities as *purple* and *cold*; minds correlate these "impressions" into more complex ideas. Consideration of the nature of reality thus resolves itself into a question of the management of perceptions. When impressions of *wet, cold,* and *blue-green* appear together regularly and consistently, chances are high that percipients are looking at and thinking about water. Such consistent "conjunctions" or "associations" supported Hume's epistemological model of cause and effect. Whenever one event consistently followed another, percipients could call the consistent conjunction between the two "causal." The phrase "gravity makes men fall" really meant only that "it has been regularly observed that falls dependably follow upon a step over a cliff," *gravity* being "the name for this consistent conjunction."

Hume's famous critique of miracles displayed a similarly skeptical outlook. Calling an event a "miracle" amounted to postulating a miraculous cause for it. But causes could be known only through a consistent conjunction of ideas. If a supernatural event occurred frequently, viewers would associate it with other events, thus postulating a cause. They would discover a putatively supernatural cause in the very same way that they went about finding a natural cause for any other natural event.

David Hume

Miracles or supernatural events were thus a species of illusion, produced by the same imperfect psychological and linguistic mechanisms as those we apply to natural events. Miracles could indeed occur, but the nature of human cognition prevents us from identifying them. And as to the larger question of religious faith itself, neither arguments from experience, revelation, design, nor nature could give it adequate support. No proof of God's existence was in fact possible.

Hume's fascination with cognitive processes underlay his lifelong preoccupation with the passions. Perception was itself passionate. Impressions moved the mind as it formed ideas. Passions contributed to the formation of societies, both by fostering fellow-feeling and by propelling the intellectual processes that produced political theory. Hume's scorching critique of neo–Aristotelian "scholasticism" was one aspect of his attack on any ontology that undervalues sensibility. If any theoretical work contained no "experimental reasoning concerning matter of fact and existence," Hume growled, "commit it then to the flames."

Hume's *History of England,* which when completed covered much of the period from the Middle Ages up to his own time, incorporated a sustained antiwhiggish reading of political history and a vindication of **Scotland** with a novel attempt to present literary and social history within the larger context of national evolution. His numerous short **essays** are valuable for their contributions to psychologically based dramatic theory and to the cultivation of the English essay. As a **diplomat**, Hume was known for his cheerful sociability and unaffected kindness. In recent years, scholars have investigated the charm of his conversation and the complexity of his public life, areas of inquiry that will continue to flourish as we learn more about "le bon David."

Kevin L. Cope

Bibliography

Flew, Anthony. *David Hume, Philosopher of Moral Science.* 1986.
Livingston, Donald W. *Hume's Philosophy of Common Life.* 1984.
Mackie, John L. *Hume's Moral Theory.* 1980.
Mossner, E.C. *The Life of David Hume.* 2nd ed., 1980.
Penelhum, Terence. *David Hume: An Introduction to His Philosophical System.* 1991.
Stewart, John B. *Opinion and Reform in Hume's Political Philosophy.* 1992.

See also History Writing and Historians; Scottish Enlightenment

Hunt, Henry ("Orator") (1773–1835)

Though an agitator for **radical** parliamentary reform, Hunt was born into a solid Wiltshire family. His success as a gentleman farmer made him admired, though his relationship with a married woman did not. In **Bristol** he unsuccessfully attempted brewing. Turning to politics as a critic of **William Pitt's** leadership, he stood for Parliament (1812) but finished last among four candidates.

Moving to **London**, Hunt immersed himself in politics, fighting the property tax, renewal of the **war** against Napoleon, and the **corn laws**. He earned the sobriquet "Orator" for his great speaking ability, which was best demonstrated when addressing large outdoor public meetings, where he urged the standard radical program for universal manhood suffrage, the secret ballot, and annual parliaments. Always seeking to promote the interests of the working class, he was critical of high **taxes**, the public debt, wasteful spending, and the impact of industrialization.

In 1816–1817 Hunt addressed three meetings held at Spa Fields in London by the **Society of Spencean Philanthropists**, even though he did not subscribe to Spencean land-reform schemes and was not involved in the **Spa Fields riot** (1816). Hunt's object was to bring pressure on the government to enact reform, but his speeches caused a break with moderate reformers less zealous to mobilize the masses. He is credited with developing new tactics of mass protest by fully engaging the working class in rallies and petitioning.

After running unsuccessfully again for Parliament (1818), Hunt accepted an invitation to address a mass rally in **Manchester** (August 1819). His arrest that afternoon was the central event in the military riot known as the **Peterloo masssacre**, after which he was unfairly convicted for unlawful and seditious assembling. He spent two and a half years in an Ilchester jail, writing his memoirs.

After his release Hunt again dabbled in business. One venture entailed manufacture of a breakfast powder from roast

Henry "Orator" Hunt

corn. Returning to politics, in 1830 he won a by-election at Preston, defeating Edward George Stanley (1799–1869), the future earl of Derby and Prime Minister. In Parliament his opposition to the **Reform Act** of 1832 (because it failed to provide for universal manhood suffrage) caused a breach with other parliamentary radicals who accused him of working with the **Tories** to defeat the bill. He supported women's suffrage, and worked to promote working-class interests until his electoral defeat in December 1832. He spent the last years of his life criticizing the Reform Act. His efforts to develop working-class radicalism set the stage for the promotion of political reform and working-class interests by the Chartist Movement.

Mark C. Herman

Bibliography

Belchem, John. "Henry Hunt and the Evolution of the Mass Platform." *English Historical Review.* Vol. 93, pp. 739–773.

———. *"Orator" Hunt: Henry Hunt and English Working-Class Radicalism.* 1985.

Hunt, Henry. *Memoirs of Henry Hunt, Esq.: Written by Himself in His Majesty's Jail at Ilchester.* 3 vols. 1820–1822.

Osborne, John W. "Henry Hunt's Career in Parliament." *Historian.* Vol. 39, pp. 24–39.

———. "Henry Hunt, 1815–1830: The Politically Formative Years of a Radical M.P." *Red River Valley Historical Journal of World History.* Vol. 5, pp. 177–194.

Thompson, E.P. *The Making of the English Working Class.* 1968.

See also Cato Street Conspiracy; Riots and Popular Disturbances

Hunt, Leigh (1784–1859)

As editor of the radical weekly *Examiner* and a succession of periodicals, Hunt played a prominent role in **London**'s literary and political affairs in the early 19th century. Himself a prolific writer of **poetry**, **literary criticism**, **journalism**, and **essays**, he published important works by **Byron**, **Hazlitt**, and **Lamb**, among others, and was an early friend and encourager of **Keats** and **Shelley**.

Born near London to expatriate Loyalist American parents, Hunt entered the literary world with the publication of his precocious *Juvenilia* (1801). In 1808 he established the *Examiner* with his brother John, and with him was convicted (1813) on charges of libel (for an article pillorying the Prince Regent) and sentenced to 2 years in prison. In 1816 he published "O Solitude," Keats's first poem to appear in print. The **radical** opinions expressed in Hunt's **newspaper**, and his association with Keats and Hazlitt, led *Blackwood's Magazine,* generally **Tory** in outlook, to name him the leading member of the "Cockney School" in a series of harsh attacks beginning in 1817.

Notable among Hunt's other **periodical** publications are the quarterly *Reflector* (1810–1811), which included important essays by Lamb; the weekly *Indicator* (1819–1821), in which Keats's "La Belle Dame sans Merci" (1820) and many of Hunt's own familiar essays appeared; the *Liberal* (1822–1824), a journal, established with Byron in Italy, which included Byron's *The Vision of Judgement* (1822) and work by Shelley, Hazlitt, and Hunt; the weekly *Companion* (1828); the daily *Tatler* (1830–1832); and the popular eponymous miscellany *Leigh Hunt's London Journal* (1834–1835).

Hunt's poetry, though uneven, importantly influenced second-generation **Romantic** poets, especially Keats, who learned from his experiments in relaxing the **neoclassical** couplet. *The Story of Rimini* (1816), retelling Dante's incestuous tale of Paolo and Francesca, was controversial upon publication and remains Hunt's best-known poem. In 1818 he published his verses in *Foliage;* in 1819 appeared *Bacchus and Ariadne,* and *Hero and Leander.* "Abou Ben Adhem" and "Jenny Kissed Me," two popular short poems, appeared in 1838; *Poetical Works,* in 1844.

Covent Garden successfully produced Hunt's 5-act play *A Legend of Florence* in 1840. Other important texts published late in life include *Imagination and Fancy* (1844), *Men, Women, and Books* (1847), *Table Talk* (1848), a famous *Autobiography* (1850), *The Religion of the Heart* (1855), and *The Old Court Suburb* (1855).

Leigh Hunt

Mike Wiley

Bibliography

Blainey, Ann. *Immortal Boy: A Portrait of Leigh Hunt.* 1985.

Blunden, Edmund. *Leigh Hunt's Examiner Examined.* 1928.

———. *Leigh Hunt.* 1930.

Fenner, Theodore. *Leigh Hunt and Opera Criticism.* 1972.

Houtchens, L.H., and C.W. Houtchens. *Leigh Hunt's Literary Criticism.* 1956.

Hunt, Leigh. *Leigh Hunt's Works.* 1859.

———. *The Correspondence of Leigh Hunt.* 1862.

Hunter Brothers

The Hunter brothers made important contributions to 18th-century **medicine**. William (1718–1783), entering Glasgow University to study for the church, transferred to medicine in 1737, becoming **William Cullen**'s resident pupil. After a spell in **Edinburgh** he went to **London** (1741), training in anatomy at St. George's Hospital. After 1748 William concentrated his attention especially on midwifery and published significant work on the uterus. A noted lecturer, he founded a private anatomy school and taught a range of medical subjects; as London had no university, such institutions were a major provider

John Hunter, M.D.

of medical education. Hunter made great use of practical illustrations and amassed an important collection of anatomical specimens (later willed to Glasgow University). In 1770 he built a house with an amphitheater for lectures, a dissecting room, and a museum for his collection. In 1768 he was appointed first Professor of Anatomy at the **Royal Academy**.

John (1728–1793), a pioneer of surgery, spent some time as a cabinetmaker before joining his brother in London (1748) to work as an assistant in William's dissecting room. He studied surgery and became house surgeon at St. George's (1756), but during the **Seven Years' War** John signed on as a military surgeon and gained considerable knowledge of gunshot wounds in the Portuguese campaign (1762). On returning to London he established his own surgical practice. Among his many achievements were the development of a method for treating aneurysms, and pioneering research into veneral disease, blood inflammation, and aspects of dentistry. John lacked his brother's talent as a lecturer but took private pupils, including **Edward Jenner**. His skill as a dissector led to his becoming the most noted surgeon of the day, this in turn helping to raise the image of the profession above that of the barber–surgeon. His most important appointments were to the post of Surgeon Extraordinary to **George III** (1776) and Surgeon-General to the **Army** (1790).

The brothers parted unpleasantly in 1760, the breach becoming serious in 1780 when William claimed credit for discoveries made by John. Both were elected Fellows of the **Royal Society** in 1767.

C.E. Hivey

Bibliography

Bynum, W.F., and Roy Porter, eds. *William Hunter and the Eighteenth Century Medical World.* 1985.

De Moulin, Daniel. *A History of Surgery.* 1988.

Hunting

See Blood Sports; Weapons

Huntingdon, Countess of (Selina Hastings) (1707–1791)

A central figure in the Hanoverian **religious revival**, Hastings was the daughter of the 2nd Earl Ferrers and married Theolphilus Hastings, 9th Earl of Huntingdon. Soon after her conversion to **Methodism** (1739) she regularly attended the **Wesleys'** Methodist Society, and in 1740 began to spread its influence (and protect clergymen suspected of Methodism) by virtue of her right as a peeress to appoint Anglican clergymen as household chaplains and assign their duties, and to purchase presentation rights to chapels. **George Whitefield** was among the many chaplains she appointed and continued to finance for many decades.

Huntingdon's husband, who sympathized with her enthusiasm, died in 1746. Among the chapels she built was one in Brighton, which she financed by selling her jewels (1761); then others in fashionable places such as **Bath**, where she hoped to attract other members of the **aristocracy and gentry**. In 1779, with 60 chapels functioning under her auspices, this practice was disallowed by a consistory court of **London**. Under the **Toleration Act** she henceforth registered her chapels as **dissenting** places of worship, known as "The Countess of Huntingdon's Connexion," or Calvinistic Methodists.

Huntingdon frequently invited members of the aristocracy to her home to hear the preaching of the Wesleys, Whitefield, **Isaac Watts**, **Philip Doddridge**, **John Berridge**, **Henry Venn**, and others. She even lobbied **George III** and Queen Charlotte for church reform. The resistance she faced may be

Selina, Countess of Huntingdon

gauged from a letter she received from another peeress, the Duchess of Buckingham:

> It is monstrous to be told you have a heart as sinful as the common wretches who crawl upon the earth. This is highly offensive and insulting, and I cannot but wonder that your Ladyship should relish any sentiments so much at variance with high rank and good-breeding.

Persisting nonetheless, she founded, on property adjoining the home of **Howel Harris** in North **Wales**, Trevecca House, a seminary for the training of Evangelical ministers. Whitefield preached the inaugural sermon when it opened in 1768.

Richard M. Riss

Bibliography

Barker, Esther T. *Lady Huntingdon, Whitefield and the Wesleys.* 1984.

Davis, Mollie C. "The Countess of Huntingdon," in Hilah F. Thomas and Rosemary Skinner Keller, eds., *Women in New Worlds: Historical Perspectives on the Wesleyan Tradition.* 1981.

Williams, R.R. *Flames from the Altar.* 1962.

See also Evangelicalism; Religious Revivalism

Huntsman, Benjamin (1704–1776)

One of the many pioneers of the **Industrial Revolution**, Huntsman, a clockmaker of Dutch descent, was born at Barton-on-Humber, Lincolnshire. In business at Doncaster from 1725, his attempts to devise better clockmaking tools were hampered by the poor quality of the (blister) steel available. His research into steelmaking prompted a move to Sheffield (1742), where he conducted extensive secret experiments, varying the fuel, flux, and crucible in his efforts to produce material of higher quality and consistency. In about 1751 he succeeded, only to find local manufacturers rejecting his new steel as too hard to work. When he then began supplying his output to the French, whose finished products found a ready market in England, Sheffield's cutlers tried to have a ban placed on the export. Huntsman's security was eventually breached and his process copied by others entering the expanding and highly lucrative steel market, but his reputation for quality secured him a competitive advantage and his own firm continued to prosper and grow.

R.D. Corrins

Bibliography

Ashton, T.S. *Iron and Steel in the Industrial Revolution.* 3rd ed., 1963.

See also Iron Industry; Metallurgy and Metalworking

Hurd, Richard (1720–1808)

Essayist, editor, and bishop, Hurd was born in Congreve, Staffordshire, and educated at **Cambridge University**. His commentary on the *Ars Poetica* of Horace (1749) gained him the **patronage** of **William Warburton**, with whom he remained allied, and whose works he edited (1788). Warburton ensured his appointment as Whitehall preacher in 1750, but it was his *Moral and Political Dialogues* (unpublished until 1759) which, **George III** reportedly said, "made Hurd a bishop" (1755). **Samuel Johnson** deplored their "woefully whiggish cast," but Hurd is usually accounted a moderate **Tory**.

Hurd's *Letters on Chivalry and Romance* (1762) was a sympathetic evocation of knight errantry and a vindication of **Gothic** (including Elizabethan) literature and art. "Shakespeare," he wrote, was "the first to break through the bondage of classical superstition." A bishop first for Lichfield and Coventry, Hurd was translated to Worcester in 1781. There, after Warburton's death, he bought his patron's books and built a valuable **library** at Hartlebury Castle. He edited Abraham Cowley's works (1772), and those of **Joseph Addison** (posthumously published, 1811).

Hurd is best remembered for his *Letters,* in which he upheld the role of imagination in **poetry**: "The poet has a world of his own, where experience has less to do, than consistent imagination." His lament at the triumph of reason is frequently quoted:

> What we have gotten by this revolution, you will say, is a great deal of good sense. What we have lost, is a world of fine fabling; the illusion of which is . . . grateful to the *charmed spirit.*

His sentiment anticipates the **Romantic** movement and poets such as John Keats.

Ronald Rompkey

Bibliography

Hurd, Richard. *Works.* 1811; rpt. 1967.

Kilvert, Francis. *Memoirs of the Life and Writings of the Right Rev. Richard Hurd, D.D.* 1860.

See also Shakespeare Industry

Huskisson, William (1770–1830)

Born near Wolverhampton, Staffordshire, son of a minor country gentleman, Huskisson attended no major **public school** or any university. His entrance into public life—as private secretary to the British ambassador to Paris during the early years of the **French Revolution**—was even more accidental than most such events. Huskisson, as a special follower of **George Canning**, held generally minor political offices: Under-Secretary of State for War (1795–1801); Joint Secretary to the Treasury (1804–1806; 1807–1809); Treasurer of the **Navy** and President of the Board of Trade (1823–1827); and Secretary of State for the Colonies (1827–1828). Huskisson became the leader of the Canningite **Tories** after the death of Canning (1827). Yet, more than any other statesman of his day, Huskisson at the Board of Trade led the attack on mercantilist doctrine and propagated the principles

William Huskisson

of **Adam Smith, Ricardo,** and other political economists in several reciprocal treaties with other nations. In the long run, his influence was greater than that of many prime ministers and foreign secretaries. Unfortunately this apostle of modernity and progress was run over and killed by a train at the opening of that **Liverpool and Manchester Railway** (September 1830) in which his expansive mind had taken such a keen interest.

James J. Sack

Bibliography

Brady, Alexander. *William Huskisson and Liberal Reform.* 1928.
Fay, C.R. *Huskisson and His Age.* 1951.
Melville, Lewis. *The Huskisson Papers.* 1931.

See also Commerce, Overseas; Economic Thought

Hutcheson, Francis (1694–1746)

Moral philosopher and moderate **Presbyterian** academic, Francis Hutcheson's sentimentalist ethics made human sociability and benevolence the source of all virtuous behavior. His thought provided critical impetus to the **empiricist** school of Scottish philosophy of the second half of the 18th century, particularly to the ideas of **David Hume** and **Adam Smith.** His reputation during his own lifetime rested on two works: *An Inquiry into the Original of Our Ideas of Beauty and Virtue* (1725), and *An Essay on the Nature and Conduct of the Passions and Affections* (1728). His most comprehensive and important work was the posthumously published *System of Moral Philosophy* (1755).

Born in **Dublin,** Hutcheson was educated at Glasgow University, where he served as Professor of Moral Philosophy from 1730 to 1746. An eclectic and elusive thinker, Hutcheson is recognized chiefly for his "moral sense theory," according to which moral judgments represent real and empirically ascertainable features of human nature. Taking his lead from the moral insights of the 3rd Earl of Shaftesbury (1671–1713), he intended to show that moral behavior was not, as Thomas Hobbes (1588–1679) and **Bernard de Mandeville** had argued, a species of self-love or self-interest, but rather a product of disinterested **benevolence.**

Peter J. Diamond

Bibliography

Campbell, T.D. "Francis Hutcheson: 'Father' of the Scottish Enlightenment," in R.H. Campbell and Andrew S. Skinner, eds., *The Origins and Nature of the Scottish Enlightenment.* 1982.
Moore, James. "The Two Systems of Francis Hutcheson: On the Origins of the Scottish Enlightenment," in M.A. Stewart, ed., *Studies in the Philosophy of the Scottish Enlightenment.* 1990.
Purviance, Susan M. "Intersubjectivity and Sociable Relations in the Philosophy of Francis Hutcheson." *Eighteenth-Century Life.* Vol. 15, pp. 23–38.

See also Church of Scotland; Scotland and Scottish Culture; Scottish Enlightenment

Hutton, James (1726–1797)

A Scottish geologist, closely associated with the men of the **Scottish Enlightenment,** Hutton was an avid **agricultural improver,** a shrewd industrialist, a **freethinker** in religion, and a contributor to the debates of the **Royal Society of Edinburgh.** His great contribution to geology was to propose that Earth's history can be reconstructed by reference to forces presently observable; that no miracles or unrepeatable geological events need be invoked. The geologist, in Hutton's famous dictum, sees "no vestige of a beginning—no prospect of an end." The Earth's surface, he believed, is continuously modified by the perpetual action of two balanced sets of forces: erosion and renewal. Continents come and go, but the process is so slow that habitable environments are always plentiful; and catastrophies have not eradicated life.

Hutton's views obviously conflicted with Old Testament accounts, but they were perfectly in line with the coolly skeptical and scientific temper of the **Enlightenment.** Hutton presented his view of Earth's history and of geological methodology in his *Theory of the Earth* (2 volumes, Edinburgh, 1795).

Michael Bartholomew

Bibliography

Daiches, D., P. Jones, and J. Jones, eds. *A Hotbed of Genius.* 1986.
Dean, D.R. *James Hutton and the History of Geology.* 1992.

I

Inchbald, Elizabeth (1753–1821)

Mrs. Inchbald (née Simpson), novelist and dramatist, defied both convention and a speech impediment when she set out to become an **actress** (1772). After several rejections, then an acceptance conditional on becoming the manager's mistress, she married Joseph Inchbald, an established **actor** who helped advance her career until his death (1779).

Inchbald appeared regularly in plays throughout England, debuting as Cordelia in *King Lear.* But, knowing her own acting limitations, she began work on her first **novel**, *A Simple Story* (completed 1779, accepted and published 1791), followed by her second, *Nature and Art* (1796). Comic drama, however, became her specialty; her first success, *A Mogul Tale* (1784), encouraged her to continue writing even though she remained an actress until 1789.

Inchbald's aim was to entertain but also to make a **moral** statement, and in most of her plays to bring about a happy ending in which characters reform or reconcile. Even her sole tragedy, *The Massacre* (1792), a closet drama set during the **French Revolution**, reveals the extent of her commitment to drama as a conduit of ethical values. Following *Massacre,* she wrote her most popular comedies: *Everyone Has His Fault* (1793), *The Wedding Day* (1794), *Wives as They Were* (1797), *Lovers' Vows* (1798), and *To Marry or Not to Marry* (1805).

Inchbald also wrote biographical and critical prefaces for the *British Theater* (25 volumes, 1806–1809, a collection of British plays from Shakespeare's time on); an anthology, *The Modern Theater* (10 volumes, 1809); and her 7-volume *Collection of Farces and After-Farces* (1809). Her years of practical experience as actress and writer informed her critical judgments. Well acquainted with the tastes and demands of her audience, her **sentimental** moral focus reflected the public distaste for the bawdiness of Restoration comedy. Even so, as a woman she occupied a rare position in contemporary criticism, and her forthright critiques of her male contemporaries brought her strictures as "unfeminine."

Diane McManus

Elizabeth Inchbald

Bibliography

Manvell, Roger. *Elizabeth Inchbald: A Biographical Study.* 1987.

See also Dramatic Arts; Women in Literature

Indemnity Acts

The Indemnity acts of 1727 and afterward reduced the penalties for refusing to obey the **Test and Corporation Acts**. The **Hanoverian Succession** had warmed the climate for **dissenters** during the reign of **George I**. Although the harsh restraints of the Test and Corporation acts still applied, enforcement was exceedingly lax. Dissenters often tried to satisfy the sacramental test by **occasional conformity**, though what they really wanted was repeal. **Sir Robert Walpole**, in the first year of George I's reign, realizing that it might be possible to allay

Anglican fears by letting the old statutes stand even while minimizing their impact on dissenters (friendly to Walpole's administration), introduced a Bill of Indemnity which in effect excused dissenters even from failing to practice occasional conformity. Similar acts were passed quite often during the period 1728–1756, and annually after that, enabling dissenters to hold many public offices even though the Anglican church's monopoly officially existed up to 1828, when the Test and Corporation acts were finally repealed.

William Edward Morris

Bibliography

Nevill, E. William. *The Eighteenth-Century Constitution, 1688–1815: Documents and Commentary.* 1968.

Webb, R.K. "From Toleration to Religious Liberty," in J.R. Jones, ed., *Liberty Secured? Britain Before and After 1688.* 1992.

See also Church of England; Toleration, Religious

India

When **George I** ascended the throne, British interests in India were almost entirely commercial. But by the beginning of Victoria's reign (1837), Britain indirectly ruled most of India and was reshaping the subcontinent's political and social structures.

Two major factors contributed to the rise of Britain's Indian empire. One was the collapse of the Mughal empire and the inability of any Asian power to replace it. The other was the assertiveness of the British **East India Company** toward its French competitors and the indigenous rulers of the subcontinent.

The 17th century saw the apogee of the Mughal empire. Building on the interethnic consensus developed by Akbar (*r.* 1556–1605), his successors presided over a golden age of artistic creation and relative political stability. However, under the reign of Aurangzeb (*r.* 1658–1707), an othodox Muslim, communal harmony disintegrated, and powerful noble families, most notably the Hindu Marathas, rebelled against the imperial center.

Aurangzeb's death inaugurated a period of chaos in the Mughal court that culminated in the Afghan sack of the royal palace in Delhi (1739). Operating from independent, regional bases, provincial *nawabs* (governors) paid formal tribute to the Mughal throne, but turned on one another in a series of often self-destructive wars that rendered the subcontinent vulnerable to European intervention. The most spectacular of these episodes ended in the Second Battle of Panipat (1761), which nearly annihilated Maratha military power.

The forces tearing apart the Mughal empire embroiled the East India Company in Indian politics. In order to defend its commercial connections against European rivals, the company maintained its own armed forces, consisting mainly of Indian soldiers. During the **War of Austrian Succession** and the **Seven Years' War** the British and French East India companies raided each others' centers and used Indian political upheavals to expand their influence among states now independent of Mughal rule. In 1750 the French became kingmakers in Hyderabad. The following year, British forces under the leadership of **Robert Clive** installed a pro–British *nawab* in the Carnatic, a dependency of Hyderabad, and French influence declined.

The Seven Years' War propelled the British East India Company to dominance. In 1756, Siraj-ud-daula (1732–1757), *nawab* of Bengal, occupied the British trading center of Calcutta. The resulting **black hole** incident inflamed British opinion and encouraged Clive to reoccupy the city. The **Battle of Plassey** (1757) confirmed the company's supremacy in Bengal, and Clive's political maneuvering after the battle laid the foundations for Britain's Indian empire.

Clive installed a pro–British *nawab,* but the arrangement failed because nobody could find the money to administer Bengal. The new *nawab* was heavily in debt. The company, however, faced its own financial crisis because its own servants, whom the British disparagingly called "**nabobs**," were trading independently, extorting money from local officials and tax farmers, and embezzling payments due to the company. In 1765, in an attempt to gain additional sources of funding, Clive had the almost powerless Mughal emperor make the company his *diwan* (chief revenue collector) of Bengal. This act added legitimacy to the company's existing military control but did not solve its financial problems, because nabobs interfered with revenue collection.

When crops failed in 1769, governmental paralysis intensified the resulting famine, which killed a third of Bengal's population. As appalling as this mismanagement was, it was ultimately less injurious than Britain's **Industrial Revolution**, which enabled the company to sell **cotton** cloth in India below the cost of local production. By the 1830s, India's cottage textile industry had virtually disappeared.

It was, however, the East India Company's drift toward bankruptcy that forced the British government to intervene. Parliament made the company solvent but reorganized its government through the Regulating Act (1773). Under the new arrangement the company's directors appointed a governor–general and supreme council who jointly governed the company's territories. But the governor–general lacked veto power, and **Warren Hastings**, who occupied the office from 1774 to 1784, experienced perpetual friction with his rivals on the council.

These tensions, and the scandals that accompanied them, forced Hastings to return to England (1785) to face impeachment charges and spurred Prime Minister **William Pitt the Younger** to author the **India Act** (1784). This created a Board of Control, which supervised the company's government in India and was directly responsible to the Crown. The British government could now appoint and recall company administrators on a regular basis. But the governor–general also gained a veto power over his council, thus ending the standoff that had plagued Hastings' administration.

The India Act was a watershed in Indo–British relations. From 1757 to 1784 the company often exploited India economically, but did not attempt to transplant British values or institutions to Indian society. Hastings, as Governor of Bengal

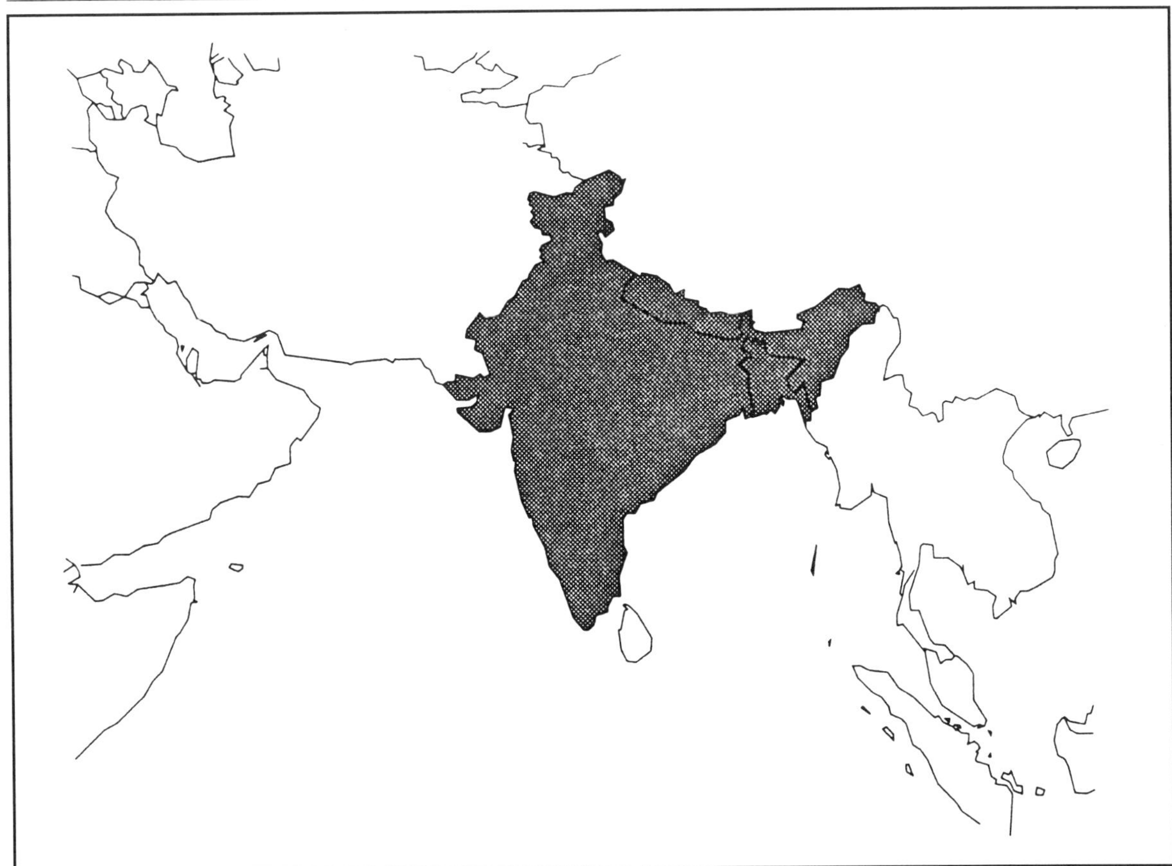

India

(1772–1774), drew on Indian models to rebuild the province's administrative institutions. Further, the company forbade Christian **missionary** activities in its territories but embraced orientalists, such as Sir **William Jones**, who admired and publicized India's cultural heritage. The India Act did not alter these policies overnight. But by placing the company under the Crown's close supervision, it better enabled special interests within Britain, such as free traders and Protestant **Evangelicals**, to influence India's political and social development.

In order to improve Bengal's administration, **Lord Cornwallis**, Governor-General from 1785 to 1793, enacted the Zamindari Settlement (1793), which encouraged *zamindars* (tax farmers) to buy property with the help of the company and Bengali merchants. This practice soon established a class of absentee landlords and businessmen, who remained loyal to the company during the Sepoy Rebellion (1857–1858) even as they developed into the westernized Indian middle class which would one day form the country's nationalist movement. But Cornwallis also diminished Indian participation in the judicial system, and this policy gradually spread to other institutions.

As the new century unfolded, India soon felt the zeal of British reformers. The Charter Act (1813) opened the subcontinent to Christian missionaries, but perhaps the most ambitious social reforms occurred under **Lord Bentinck**, Governor-General from 1828 to 1835. Influenced by utilitarian philosophy and assisted by British intellectuals such as **John Stuart Mill** and T.B. Macaulay (1800–1859), Bentinck abolished certain inhumane practices such as *sati* (widow-burning) and *thagi* (robbery and ritual murder in the name of the goddess Kali). Through the Charter Act (1833) he also made employment in the company open to all, regardless of caste. British liberal reformers believed they could educate Indians into adopting European manners and culture.

Many Indians regarded British reforms as cultural imperialism. But some, most notably Rammohan Roy (1774–1833), drew on Western culture while reviving awareness of their own heritage. The Hindu Renaissance of the early 19th century signaled the fusion of cultures that was already resulting from Britain's occupation of India. A century later, this fusion enabled Indians to express their opposition to British rule effectively.

A. Martin Wainwright

Bibliography

Bowen, H.V. *Revenue and Reform: The Indian Problem in British Politics, 1757–1773.* 1991.

Chaudhuri, K.N. *The Trading World of Asia and the English East India Company, 1660–1760.* 1978.

Fisher, Michael H., ed. *The Politics of the British Annexation of India, 1757–1857.* 1994.

Frykenberg, Robert E. *Land Control and Social Structure in Indian History.* 1969.

Ghosh, S.C. *The Social Condition of the British Community in Bengal, 1757–1800.* 1970.

Gopal, Ram. *How the British Occupied Bengal.* 1962.

Ingham, K. *Reformers in India, 1793–1833.* 1956.

Mason, Philip. *The Men Who Ruled India.* 1954.

Philips, Cyril Henry. *The East India Company, 1784–1834.* 1961.
Spear, T.G.P. *Twilight of the Mughals.* 1951.
———. *The Nabobs.* 1963.

See also Chartered Trading Companies; Commerce, Overseas; Empire and Imperialism

India Act (1784)

The India Act established Parliament's jurisdiction over the **East India Company**'s government in **India**. It marked the end of a quarter century in which the company's rule over Bengal became increasingly controversial.

Although throughout the 18th century the company held a monopoly charter from the Crown, Parliament rarely interfered with its internal affairs—until 1772, when it faced bankruptcy because of its employees' misappropriation of funds. **Lord North**'s government agreed to loan the company £1.4 million to keep it solvent. But Parliament also passed the Regulating Act (1773), coordinating the company presidencies under a governor-general and a supreme council. Despite **Warren Hastings**' reforms, the tension between him and the supreme council led to a further reassessment in the early 1780s.

The resulting act was **Pitt the Younger**'s first major piece of legislation. It was a compromise between allowing the existing system to continue, and supplanting the company with direct rule from **London**. It left the directors in charge of **commerce**, but created a Board of Control who supervised the company's government in India and was directly responsible to the Crown. The British government could now appoint and recall company administrators on a regular basis. The governor–general also gained veto power over his council, thus ending the standoff that plagued Hastings' administration.

Legislation in 1833 and 1853 further eroded the company's power. But the Act of 1784 remained the basis of the relationship between the British government and the company until the Sepoy Rebellion (1857–1858).

A. Martin Wainwright

Bibliography

Bowen, H.V. *Revenue and Reform: The Indian Problem in British Politics, 1757–1773.* 1991.
Fisher, Michael H., ed. *The Politics of the British Annexation of India, 1757–1857.* 1994.
Sutherland, Lucy. *The East India Company in Eighteenth Century Politics.* 1952.

Industrial Revolution

This is a term applied to the changes that occurred both in industry and in the wider economy and society during the latter 18th and early 19th centuries. Historians generally stress the spread of machinery and of water and steam power, and the use of new and more abundant raw material, particularly the substitution of mineral for vegetable or animal substances. These developments were accompanied by a sustained and unprecedented **population** growth, rapid **urbanization**, and a shift in the distribution of population away from agricultural employments. Looking back from a later perspective and using the analogy of the French political revolution, many commentators (including most notably Karl Marx, Arnold Toynbee, the Hammonds, and the Webbs) saw the Industrial Revolution as radical, cataclysmic, and socially divisive. They emphasized change in **agriculture**, **commerce**, and property rights as well as in manufacturing, and pointed to the deleterious impact of early industrialization on the **standard of living** of the masses, calling in their own times for increased state involvement to ameliorate the worst effects of the new economic order.

The rise of new industries and technologies in the 20th century, shifting views of the nature of economic development, and different approaches to research in economic and social history have resulted in much debate about the pace and nature of change in the Industrial Revolution; and the use of the term itself has been frequently challenged. J.H. Clapham, writing in the 1920s, was an early critic. He correctly argued that no single British industry had experienced a complete technical revolution before 1830, and that England in the mid-19th century still abounded in ancient types of industrial organization and in nonmechanized industries. Even in **cotton**, the sector at the forefront of technological change and **factory** development, the machine operative was not the most representative worker in 1850, the **steam engine** had not been generally introduced until after 1830, and typical firm size remained small. Clapham also attacked the notion that living standards declined in these years except for those in the dying trades and in handloom **weaving**.

In the 1950s, W.W. Rostow revived the notion of fundamental economic discontinuity in the process of English economic growth. He identified a take-off into self-sustaining economic growth in England in the period 1783–1802, marked by a rise in the investment ratio and the emergence of a succession of high-growth sectors of the economy, initially cotton. He argued that all other countries would eventually experience the pattern set by "the first industrial nation." Other historians of the same period continued to stress the gradual nature of change and its long antecedents. Alexander Gerschenkron (writing during the 1960s) placed England's experience in a European context, arguing that the nature and speed of industrialization in a country varied according to its timing: England industrialized slowly, but others benefited from imported technology and from greater state involvement in the drive to compete in world markets.

By the late 1960s, the experience of underdeveloped (Third-World) countries was highlighting a need to place British and West European industrialization into a world perspective, and more stress came to be placed on the adverse effects of **imperialism** and external economic domination. Persistent underdevelopment in the Third World thus came to be seen largely as a product of industrial revolutions elsewhere, and it was no longer acceptable to view the English experience as a path down which others would inevitably follow.

Recent historiography retains a gradualist perspective. New estimates of capital formation, industrial output, and national income growth (building on those provided by Phyllis

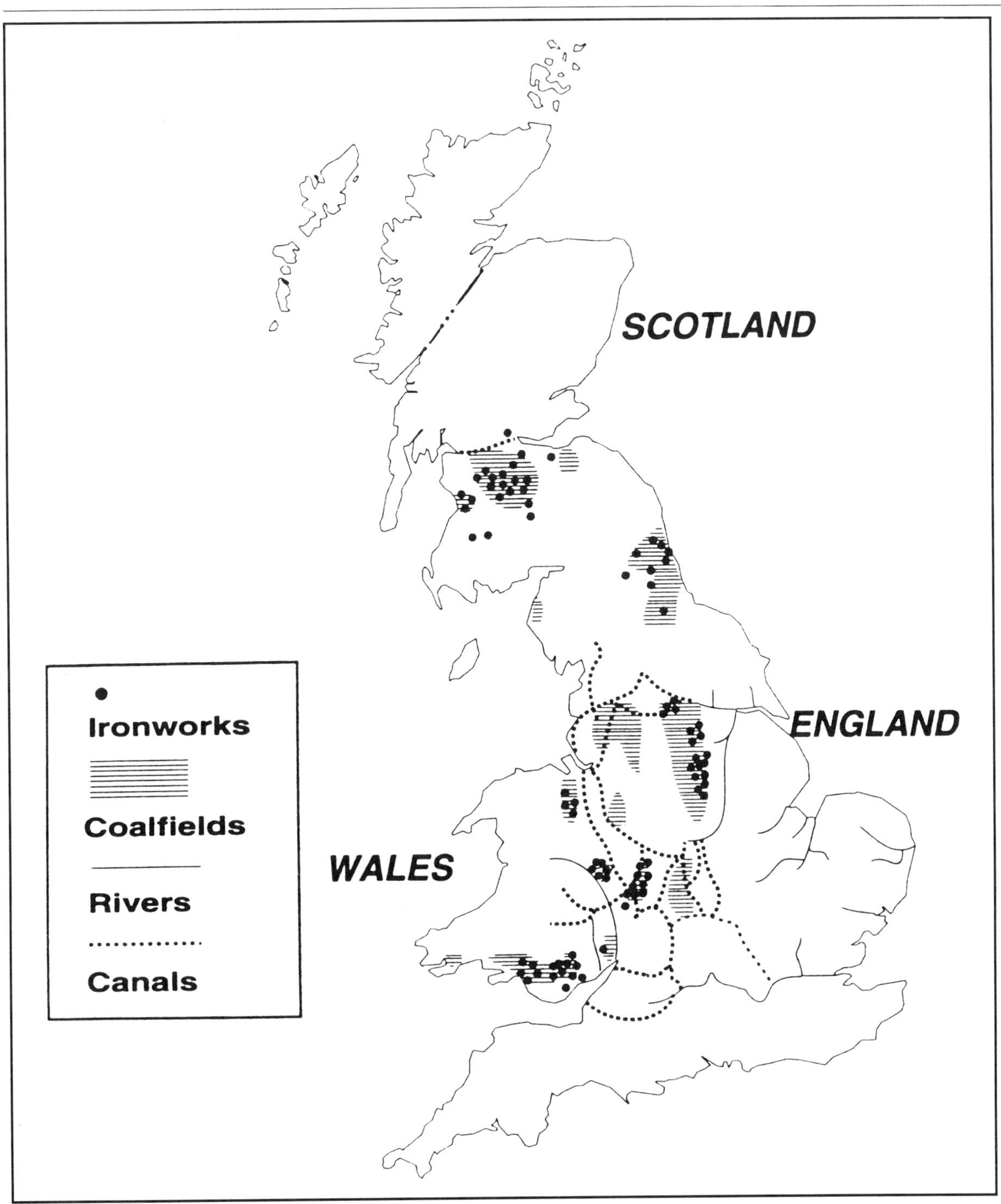

Sinews of Industry

Deane and W.A. Cole in the 1960s) have shown that English growth began earlier and was a great deal slower than was previously thought. These new indices, such as those discussed by N.F.R. Crafts (1985), suggest that the Industrial Revolution period has no greater claim to a decisive discontinuity in economic growth than many others. The weight of the nonmechanized, low-productivity sectors in the economy is seen to have acted as a brake on growth rates. It has also been argued that England never achieved a fully-fledged industrial revolution, preferring a gentlemanly form of capitalism: the state and the economic and cultural elite were always more concerned with international trade and **finance** than with the promotion of manufacturing, a fact that explains many of the weaknesses of the British manufacturing economy of the late 20th century.

In social history, the emergence of a new class society and of class antagonisms has been regarded as a hallmark of the Industrial Revolution. Proletarianization, loss of common rights, regressive **taxation**, unemployment, **poverty**, radical changes in working and living environments, and increasingly collective struggles of ordinary people to improve their position, have been seen as contributing to the making of the working class, while the rise of manufacturing has been associated with the rise to economic and (at least local) political power of **middle-class entrepreneurs**. In recent years, however, more stress has been placed on the continuing power of the older landed and financial elites in the British class and political structure, and increasing interest in social identities other than class (local, national, familial, sexual) have contributed to the currently dominant view that the Industrial Revolution saw much less in the way of radical social changes or **radical** oppositional politics than the flowering of research in the 1960s and 1970s (most notably in the work of E.P. Thompson) had suggested. Post-structuralist approaches have also pointed to continuities in the nature of politics and society in the 18th and 19th centuries, to the enduring language of a (limited) **dissent**, and to the weight and importance of long-embedded beliefs and practices regarding such matters as gender and social distance.

There are, however, some weaknesses in the current view that England's Industrial Revolution was slower and much less radical than was once believed. Rates of growth of industry and of national income may not have accelerated markedly in the period, but the shift was sufficient to increase the pace of per capita income growth thereafter in an unprecedented manner. It is also important to note that rates of growth of output or productivity are not good indicators of innovativeness. In fact, because of the capital required, the rapid obsolescence of older technologies, and the time taken for workers and employers to learn to operate with new skills, technologies and organizations, one would expect that a period of revolutionary change in the economy would be accompanied by slower rather than faster growth, at least in the short term. The period was marked by a large increase in **women's employment** and **child labor** in many manufacturing sectors; by new methods of organizing and disciplining labor; by new ways of buying, selling, and using credit instruments; and by innovations not only in technologies but in product design and marketing. These innovations had little effect on productivity growth or output in the short term, and have therefore been underplayed.

Additionally, the macroeconomic perspective of much recent literature may be misleading because industrialization was a regional phenomenon. Some regions industrialized, adopted new methods and technologies, and came increasingly to dominate the national production of key commodities (cotton in South Lancashire, **woolens and worsteds** in the West Riding of Yorkshire, **metalworking** in the Black Country and in south Yorkshire, **iron** and **shipbuilding** in the Northeast and in South Wales, smallwares in the Birmingham area). This sectoral concentration by region, enabling industries to benefit from the associated concentration of marketing and banking services and **transport** links, lay at the heart of industrialization. Other regions, such as East Anglia, the East Midlands, and the Lake Counties, de-industrialized or grew much more slowly, contributing to the slow growth of indices overall.

New work has rightly pointed to the great variety of experience of social and economic change according to region and sector, gender and ethnicity, as well as class. Notwithstanding, the regional concentration of similarities of experience advanced class formation sufficiently to produce distinctive and new forms of middle-class culture and politics; whereas social protest and conflict occurred on an unprecedented scale in strikes, machine-wrecking, factory reform, antipoor law agitation, and Chartism. These involved the development of an anticapitalist critique in **economic thought**. The factory may never have dominated in any sector, but we are left with explaining its force as a symbol of change and a focus of protest against radically changing methods of production and ways of life. Waves of major innovation in the 20th century, and the social and cultural changes that these have wrought in their train, may appear to make the achievements of the 1760s to 1830s pale into insignificance. But the point to emphasize is that the potentialities of later developments, and their social and ecological dangers, stem essentially from the nature of the phenomenon classically interpreted as revolutionary.

Pat Hudson

Bibliography

Berg, Maxine. *The Age of Manufactures, 1700–1820: Industry, Innovation and Work in Britain.* 1994.

Crafts, N.F.R. *British Economic Growth during the Industrial Revolution.* 1985.

Floud, R., and D. McCloskey. *The Economic History of Britain since 1700.* Vol. 1: *1700–1860.* 1994.

Hudson, Pat. *The Industrial Revolution.* 1992.

O'Brien, P.K., and R. Quinault. *The Industrial Revolution and British Society.* 1993.

See also Domestic Production; Hours, Wages, and Working Conditions; Labor Laws, Movements, and Unions; Science, Technology, and Invention

Insurance

In Elizabethan England, marine insurance and life term assurance took root. Fire insurance developed after the Great Fire of London (1666), which reputedly damaged property valued at over £10.5 million. The industry made only slow progress despite many schemes to float companies: there were but six of these by 1720; the most important was **Sun Fire** (1710), which slowly created provincial agencies. In **Scotland**, the first fire insurance office, the "Friendly Society," was founded in **Edinburgh** about 1719.

There had been a gradual increase in life underwriting from the 1670s, but as late as the 1750s it was still largely a **gambling** activity centered on **Lloyd's coffeehouse**. The industry lacked certain fundamentals: there was no sound actuarial base, no comprehensive mortality statistics, no concept of average likely liabilities, no premium policy, and only the most rudimentary awareness of the importance of probability theory. Early life companies thus rarely lasted long; the oldest survivor was the Amicable Society for a Perpetual Assurance, established by charter in 1706. (It was absorbed by Norwich Union in 1866.)

As the 18th century progressed, life insurance acquired a scientific base and lost its disreputable association with gambling. Probability theory was made more scientific in a series

Fire and Life Insurance Offices, Regent Street, London, 1827

of papers by Abraham de Moivre (1667–1754), a Huguenot refugee and friend of Sir Isaac Newton (1642–1727). The Gambling Act (1774) specified that an insurer must have a proper interest in the life or death of an insured. By that date, three proprietary offices dominated the life business—the **Royal Exchange**, the Amicable, and London Assurance—and they attempted to eliminate competition.

Yet the Equitable, a mutual office founded in 1762, had become very significant by 1800. Its adviser, **Richard Price**, produced two important publications, *Observations on Reversionary Payments* (1771) and the *Nofe Table* (1781), which became the working guides for most life companies. But assessing mortality remained a difficult problem until after 1850 (by which time the life business was worth about £150 million).

Industrialization created greater wealth and many more fire risks. Insurance grew in **London** but spread very rapidly to the provinces after 1790. Phoenix Assurance, a fire office created in 1782 by **sugar** refiners dissatisfied with the premiums charged them, developed from its London base at home and abroad to become one of the most substantial firms by 1840. Its associated life company was the Pelican, founded in 1797. But London had to meet provincial competition, especially from Scottish firms (such as Scottish Widows and Standard Life) usually based in Edinburgh but also in other towns and cities. Many followed the London companies in covering life and fire risks.

The collection of premiums produced large aggregate sums that were at first invested mostly in gilts and other fixed-interest securities. Gradually, companies diversified their portfolios into mortgages on the security of landed estates, and many made loans to policyholders against prospective surrender values. By 1837 a major industry had emerged, with considerable potential for expansion at home and abroad.

John Butt

Bibliography

Dickson, P.G.M. *The Sun Insurance Office 1710–1960.* 1960.

Raynes, H.E. *A History of British Insurance.* Rpt. 1968.

Supple, B.S. *The Royal Exchange Assurance 1720–1970.* 1970.

Trebilcock, Clive. *Phoenix Assurance and the Development of British Insurance.* Vol. 1: *1782–1870.* 1985.

See also Finance and Investment

Interior Design

The character of interior space in Hanoverian Britain varied in time and by designer. The architect-dominated early (1714–1750) and late (1765–1800) **Georgian** periods reflected classical prototypes and subordinated furnishings to the architectural space or "envelope." The middle Georgian (1750–1765) and **Regency** (1800–1837) periods extended greater influence to cabinetmakers and upholsterers, who tempted the public with exotic styles; the latter years of the Regency period were unabashedly eclectic.

Early Georgian designers such as architect **William Kent** took their inspiration from the great 16th-century Italian architect Andrea Palladio (1508–1580), proportioning formal rooms on the cube and double cube, and projecting a feeling of stability and grandeur with intense color, bold pattern, and suites of heavily decorated furniture. Eagles, cartouches, and similar motifs of classical antiquity embellished furnishings,

Fireplace in Kedleston Hall, Derbyshire, by Robert Adam, c. 1768

doorways, and fireplace walls; geometric plasterwork ornamented flat, high ceilings. Paneling was reduced to dado and cornice board, the space between them filled with stretched fabric or wallpaper.

Furniture, wallcovers, and accessories became the basic elements of interior design in the middle Georgian period, as cabinetmakers and upholsterers such as **Thomas Chippendale** and John Linnell (active 1720–1763) experimented with various styles. **Gothic** was popular for libraries and other masculine retreats, rococo and **chinoiserie** for areas controlled by women. Lower ceilings provided a more human scale. Fireplaces and doorways were emphasized with moldings, particularly the squared "Georgian ear." The wall treatment of the previous period was retained, but soft colors, curving forms, playful motifs, and fluid furniture arrangements diminished somewhat the earlier formality.

Architect **Robert Adam** revived formality and classicism in the late Georgian period but, entry halls excepted, retained a small scale. Furnishings were designed to complement specific installations, and furniture once again lined walls. Rooms were sometimes octagonal or elliptical; apsoidal ends and semicircular alcoves with half-domed ceilings expanded rectangular spaces. Decorative elements were fixed in place: walls were embellished with delicate stucco ornament painted to contrast with intense pastel backgrounds; ceiling patterns, often borrowed from Roman and Pompeiian sources, were echoed in floor treatments.

The Regency style established no consistent mood. Until around 1820, most installations were pleasant and comfortable, warmed by striped or sprigged wallpapers and fabrics, mirrors, wall-to-wall carpeting, and flexible furniture arrangements. Connoisseur and collector Thomas Hope (1760–1831) advanced a severe antiquarianism based on Greek, Roman, and Egyptian prototypes, however; and architects Henry Holland (1745–1806) and **John Nash** produced **oriental** fantasies for the Prince of Wales at Carlton House and the Royal Pavilion. Pattern books written by Hope and **Thomas Sheraton** brought these approaches to public attention.

The late Regency style was much more diverse, but since most popular styles were only ornamental veneers applied to traditional architectural shells, this affected interior decoration more than interior design. Two of the most coherent approaches taken in the period—French (not English) rococo, and neo-Gothic—brought a political dimension to design, being inspired by eras and societies in which everyone supposedly knew his or her place. The first, greatly favored by upholsterers, created rooms and furnishings covered with heavy fabrics, providing a cushioned comfort. The second emphasized architectural elements, restoring the Tudor arch to fireplace openings, and translating the plasterwork of Jacobean ceilings into wood or even papier-mâché.

While character varied throughout the period, other aspects of interior design changed little. Most rooms received relatively little natural light, in part because of their depth and in part because houses were sited to take advantage of view rather than sun. Fireplaces could be placed on any inside wall, but were usually perpendicular to the windows. Connecting corridors evolved late; and until the 19th century, most public rooms were arranged linearly along window walls that acted as thoroughfares, their connecting doors left open to emphasize the sweep of the house. There was a change in the number and type of spaces, however. State apartments disappeared from all but the grandest homes and were replaced by areas in which friends and family could be entertained with dinner, cards, **music**, tea, **dancing**, and conversation. The tension between dignity and domesticity was ultimately resolved in favor of the latter.

Reed Benhamou

Bibliography

Fletcher, Sir Banister. *A History of Architecture on the Comparative Method.* 1989.

Harrison, Molly. *People and Furniture: A Social Background to the English Home.* 1971.

Thornton, Peter. *Authentic Decor: The Domestic Interior, 1620–1920.* 1984.

Whiton, Sherrill. *Interior Design and Decoration.* 1974.

See also Home Furnishings and Decoration; Housebuilding and Housing

Ireland and Irish Politics

Ireland in the earlier Hanoverian period is often spoken of as Georgian Ireland, a term that suggests a compact civilization bound together under clear chronological and other limits. Paralleling that term is the idea of "the Hidden Ireland," which in a colonial context implies that the dominant civilization lay over another one, ruling but not subduing it. Beginning with the poet William Butler Yeats (1865–1939), there was also increasing stress on the Big House as the central point of the political and cultural life of Georgian Ireland, the citadel of a society controlled by the **Anglo–Irish Protestant Ascendancy**.

The story of 18th-century Ireland was marked at the outset by two features: (1) consolidation of the Anglo–Irish interest, and (2) systematic subjugation of the **Catholics**. From one point of view the society that emerged from the **wars** of 1689–1691 was homogeneous. No new landowners from England emerged in the land redistribution of the defeated in the 1690s after the **Battle of the Boyne**: the result was that the friction which had existed in the past between older settlers and new arrivals did not occur on this occasion. Neither, for the same reason, did absenteeism increase. In fact, absenteeism was a structural feature, arising from the fact that some people held land in both islands; the absence of a new incoming settler interest meant that absenteeism did not grow afresh, and hence Protestant landed society emerged out of the cauldron of the early 1690s with an unprecedented common purpose and a novel sense of confidence.

One consequence was that Protestants were acutely conscious of their political rights, and 18th-century Irish political society was capable of commanding an impressive unity when its rights appeared challenged by England: the dropping of **William Wood**'s half-pence project at the end of a protracted struggle in 1722–1725, unfettered disposal by the **Commons** of the revenue surplus in 1753–1754, free trade in 1779, and legislative independence in 1782 were secured because the political interests that normally supported the central government at Dublin Castle made common cause with opposition politicians and public opinion; and adamant opposition from England would have resulted not only in the perpetuation of politically unsustainable crises but, from the 1770s, perhaps even worse.

Such a determined political class could only be made amenable to political management by local political magnates, not by **London**-appointed politicians. This in turn ensured the emergence of two great managing interests in the island: the Connolly interest, which on the death of Speaker Connolly in 1728 passed to the Ponsonby group; and the County Cork interest, which at first revolved around the Broderick family and afterward the Boyle family, headed by Richard Boyle, 2nd Earl of Shannon (1728–1807). The Cork interest, which was cohesively based on Cork Protestant society, commanded the largest phalanx of seats in the Irish House of Commons. It was held together by blood and marriage ties and, through politically cultivated memories of 17th-century religious outrages, by collective consciousness of an heroic Protestant past. Although prepared to oppose the government in defense of Protestant prerogatives, the dominant desire was always to return to allegiance. The Cork interest firmly opposed **Catholic relief**.

Ireland

The Ponsonby interest inherited the mantle and supporters of the Connolly network. William Connolly had been a self-made man who did well in the Williamite Plantation out of the enforced disposal of rebel land. In contrast to his rival Alan Broderick, head of the Cork grouping, Connolly was less identified with an established or Protestant interest or with the emerging **penal laws**. The Ponsonbys, as political inheritors of the Connolly interest, repeated the pattern and drew their support from the counties in which a significant part of the political interest had converted. Less anchored to the Protestant constitution and to the paramount importance of a close English connection, when they passed into political opposition in 1769 they were destined (unlike the Cork interest, likewise rebels in 1769) to remain almost permanently in opposition. Links with the more tolerant English **Whigs** reinforced this pattern in the latter age of **George III**, and the crisis of the Fitzwilliamite viceroyalty in 1795, in essence the final confrontation of the two interests, occurred precisely because the issue at stake was the Catholic question.

This amalgamated controlling society with its semi-independent landed class hardly pleased English governments in the age following the **Seven Years' War**, when imperial pretensions grew and the arrogance of power produced the **American Revolution**. From 1767 a new central policy emerged of dispensing with the services of Irish politicians of established status, and of building up instead a cohort of promising and more cooperative politicians. In the case of the Shannon family, opposition to them in their bailiwick of County Cork was encouraged. Thus by 1772 the two old dominant interests, despite their power bases, were pushed aside and Irish political management gradually centered on a coterie of rising politicians subservient to government, such as John Foster (later Speaker of the Irish House of Commons), with an interest in a single county (Louth); and John Fitzgibbon, who failed to command an effective interest even in his home county (Limerick). The group based in County Cork, though remaining in support of a Protestant constitution and an English connection, was replaced in political weight by a northern interest with the contiguous counties of Louth, Armagh, and Down and Derry. This explains why this region was so agitated politically in the 1780s and 1790s. The dominant individual subgroups within the northeast were the Beresford and Hill (Hillsborough or Downshire) families. The Whig magnates could assert themselves only fleetingly in 1782 and more disastrously in 1794–1795.

Such a society had been to some extent at ease with itself into the early 1770s on its political prerogatives. Division began to emerge as Dublin Castle created a new support base, and it widened further and more bitterly on the Catholic question. From the 1750s, the question of softening the penal laws became a live issue, and acquired real impetus from 1762. The anti–Catholic stance of the Cork group was taken up in turn by the Beresford and Downshire groups who, along with John Foster, and using the weight of their Castle support, were able to turn the Protestant interest of the northeast into a live force. They were able to deploy in favor of their aims the support of the Castle, and were also concerned with neutralizing the rising Presbyterian interest.

It is clear that Irish political life never belonged to a monolithic Ascendancy. It was deeply divided. Some counties, like Kerry, Limerick, Clare, Tipperary, Galway, Mayo, and Kildare had a real Catholic interest, but there was also a Protestant interest sometimes aligned with this. Others like Cork—and an interconnected interest running through Louth, Armagh, Down, and Derry—supported a Protestant constitution that excluded **Presbyterians** as well as Catholics. A long fringe of counties along North Leinster and North Connaught created a political frontier, and was both a literal and figurative battleground. Presbyterian and Catholic opinion was important, though in a more restricted region. Antrim was dominated by the Presbyterian interest, and the county's Anglican establishment was subservient to it; Down was deeply divided between the Downshire interest and an opposition supported by Presbyterians; and Derry was divided between the Connolly interest, famously sensitive to Presbyterians, and the Beresford interest, Anglican and later destined to provide from its own sons, pillars of the Established Church.

Because a Catholic and Presbyterian alliance was feared by the government, it became an aim of the **United Irishmen** in the 1790s. Afterward, Presbyterian and Catholic districts tended to support the **Union** (1800); on the other hand, Dublin interests and the Protestant politicians of the Armagh-Louth-Down triangle, seeing themselves betrayed by England, were the most inveterate opponents of the Union. But the **Irish Rebellion** of 1798 did not really change life—that came later from **Evangelicalism** in the Protestant churches, the flood of ultramontanism in the Catholic Church, and the reassertion of the Protestant interest around the inept Castle administration. The divisive Tory and Whig Irish politics followed old lines, and gradually ended as the more assertive and anti-landlord politics emerged in the 1870s and 1880s.

As a society, Ireland was more modern than many commentators have assumed. In some respects it had too much politics, not too little. The Irish were also harnessed, to a greater degree perhaps than the English and Scots, to national interests, and local politics responded. Neither was the country wholly poor, or its condition worsening. While **textile** industrialization retreated to the northeast, **Irish agriculture** increased its output. However, though agriculture from the 1760s gave a handsome surplus to farmers (and their landlords), its productivity depended heavily on potatoes as a root rotation crop. There was a sharp economic division between the well-off (who were beneficiaries of this surplus) and the less-well-off (who lived or depended on the produce of potato plots). This in turn helps to explain the pattern of the Great Famine of the 1840s that killed one million of the **population** but in varying degrees left many of the remaining people relatively unscathed.

Seen as a catalyst of changes in political outlook the famine's role has in fact been greatly exaggerated. Politicization was already growing rapidly in the 1830s and 1840s in the wake of **Catholic emancipation** (1829). The outcome of the famine, and the issues of the management and financing of famine relief, could, however, become further grievances of political society. Such grievances were broad based, and some initial inspiration even came from supporters of the landed class, who drew the same conclusions about the limits of England's commitment to Ireland's welfare.

Louis Cullen

Bibliography

Bartlett, T., and D.W. Hayton. *Penal Era and Golden Age: Essays in Irish History, 1690–1800.* 1979.

Becket, J.C. *The Making of Modern Ireland, 1603–1923.* New ed., 1981.

Cullen, L.M. *Anglo–Irish Trade, 1660–1800.* 1968.

———. *An Economic History of Ireland since 1660.* 1972.

———. *The Emergence of Modern Ireland, 1600–1900.* 1981.

James, F.G. *Ireland in the Empire, 1688–1770.* 1973.

Johnston, E.M. *Ireland in the Eighteenth Century.* 1974.

Lecky, W.E.M. *History of Ireland in the Eighteenth Century.* 1892.

McDowell, R.B. *Ireland in the Age of Imperialism and Revolution, 1760–1801.* 1980.

McFarland, E.W. *Ireland and Scotland in the Age of Revolution: Planting the Green Bough.* 1994.

Moody, T.W., and W.E. Vaughan, eds. *A New History of Ireland.* Vol. 4: *Eighteenth Century Ireland.* 1986.

See also Hedge Schools; Irish Church Act; Irish Education; Irish Industry; Irish Land Settlement; Irish Literature before the Union; Roman Catholicism; Volunteering Movement

Irish Agriculture

Irish agricultural practice underwent fundamental change between 1550 and 1700 as a consequence of the transfer of the control of land to a new Anglophone elite, the **Anglo–Irish Protestant Ascendancy**. This resulted in the replacement of the hitherto dominant lineage society, which operated along traditional clientalist lines, with an essentially cash-based nexus involving landlords and tenants. It became easier to introduce new breeds of livestock and new techniques of land management and utilization. Irish **farmers** and their landlords became increasingly conscious of the necessity of producing commodities for sale, and Irish agriculture became markedly more dependent on external markets. This was furthered, despite complaints, by the ban on the export of Irish **woolens** imposed by the British Parliament in 1698, and the restrictions (dating from the 1660s) imposed on live cattle exports that were not lifted until 1758.

Irish agriculture was in reasonably good shape at the commencement of the Hanoverian era in 1714. The country had escaped the worst ravages of the famines that had racked Europe during the previous 20 years, and enjoyed four particularly good years (1710–1714) when export demand for Irish goods was strong and prices were high. However, agriculture, like the Irish economy in general, was susceptible to crisis because of its narrow range of products and its vulnerability in periods of bad weather. This was manifest in the late 1720s when a series of poor harvests, precipitated by bad weather, plunged the country into **famine**, resulting in many deaths. The crisis in these years was acute, and those dependent on the country's two staple foodstuffs—the potato and oatmeal—struggled to pay the inflated prices demanded for foodstuffs. Their vulnerability was even more apparent in 1740–1741, when bad weather and harvests so damaged the staple foodstuffs that most of southern Ireland was thrown into a severe famine costing tens of thousands of lives.

Matters then improved, and agriculture embarked on a period of sustained growth in the 1740s that lasted until 1815. This resulted partly from the rise of flax cultivation (which fed the rapidly expanding linen industry based in northern Ireland) and the buoyant Atlantic provisions export **trade** based at **Cork**. This trade stimulated large graziers in Munster, who specialized in fattening cattle brought south from the midlands and the west, and also dairy farmers, who provided large volumes of butter for export.

The decline in the Atlantic provisions trade that began in the late 18th century forced Irish agriculture to readjust, but the loss of Atlantic business was compensated for by a strong and ever-growing demand in industrializing Britain for Irish cattle and flour. The increasing volume of Irish agricultural exports helped sustain the fourfold increase in **population**, from 2 to nearly 8 million, that took place between 1750 and 1831. This rise presented no major problems when the economy was buoyant and prices were high. But in the deflationary economic environment after 1815 there was a surplus of labor, with the result that while the commercial farming sector continued to perform reasonably well, hundreds of thousands of laborers and small tenant–farmers were consigned to the increasingly precarious existence of relying on the potato to survive. **Ribbonism** and other agrarian violence stemmed partly from these conditions.

James Kelly

Bibliography

Cullen, L.M. *An Economic History of Ireland since 1660.* 1972.

O'Grada, Cormac. *Ireland: A New Economic History, 1780–1939.* 1994.

Power, Thomas P. *Land, Politics, and Society in Eighteenth-Century Tipperary.* 1993.

See also Agriculture; Irish Emigration; Irish Industry; Irish Land Settlement; Scottish Agriculture

Irish Church Act (1833)

The **Act of Union** (1800) unified not only political institutions but created one unified established church, the "United Church of England and Ireland." Growing agitation for removal of Catholic disabilities resulted in **Catholic emancipation** (1829), but Catholic resentment continued (indeed intensified) against the **tithes** and church cess (**taxes** used to pay for church maintenance) collected by the Established Church. Unpopular and alien, the church, supported by little more than 10% of the population, owned some 5 million acres of Irish land; and many Protestant bishops in Ireland were considerably richer than their counterparts in England, some receiving as much as £15,000 per annum.

In 1833 the **Whig** government, acknowledging the injustice of this and supported by parliamentary **radicals** and Irish M.P.s, attempted to improve Irish relations by passing the Church Temporalities bill, which abolished cess, eliminated 10 out of 22 Irish bishoprics and numerous sparsely populated parishes, levied a tax on the remainder, and established a commission to expend the estimated £300,000 that the act would save. The act encountered heavy going in **Commons** and revealed deep divisions in the Whig cabinet. One of its effects was to help inspire the Oxford Movement, which began at **Oxford University** with the Reverend John Keble (1792–1866) angrily denouncing the act as an intolerable secular invasion of church privileges and property (1833). It also left the more serious injustice of tithes unrectified (until 1838, when the Tithe Rentcharge Act somewhat ameliorated that problem by transferring the payment of tithes from occupiers of land to landowners). Irish grievances continued nonetheless, and the church in Ireland was finally disestablished in 1869.

David B. Mock

Bibliography

Bentley, Michael. *Politics Without Democracy.* 1984.

Cornish, Patrick J., ed. *A History of Irish Catholicism.* 1970–1971.

Foster, R.F. *Modern Ireland, 1600–1972.* 1988.

See also Doyle, James Warren

Irish Education

Ireland had two educational systems during the Hanoverian period. There was an "official" system of schools created by legislation, and an unofficial system of "**hedge schools**" created by the **Catholic** Irish.

The first official schools were the parochial schools first established in 1537. These hoped to encourage the use of the English language and the Protestant religion among the Irish peasantry. The poverty of the Protestant clergy and the opposition of the mass of the Catholic population ensured that the spread of parish schools was slow and incomplete. A report of 1792 revealed that only 361 parochial benefices out of a recorded total of 838 contained operative parish schools.

The English government also attempted to establish schools for the Irish **middle class** during the 16th century. These "diocesan" schools were intended to be like English grammar schools, teaching classical languages as well as elementary subjects. However, the diocesan schools made scarcely any impact on Ireland, and there were only 17 in existence by 1809. "Royal" schools, erected in the early 17th century, had a comparable struggle to survive. These were academically the best of the Irish schools and were intended to cater to the sons of the Irish **gentry**. Understandably, they aspired to be like the English public schools, but operated in a much less favorable climate both economically and culturally. In 1791 the six royal schools (at Armagh, Banagher, Cavan, Dungannon, Enniskillen, and Raphoe) had only 211 pupils between them, and it was evident that the bulk of the Irish upper-class children went to England for their education.

Parish, diocesan, and royal schools were all products of 16th- and 17th-century English legislation. The main Protestant educational initiative of the next century came from the **Evangelical charity school** movement. In 1717 Dr. Henry Mauala founded the "Society in Dublin for Promoting Christian Knowledge," whose purpose was to create a network of charity schools similar to those spreading at the same time in England. These schools supplemented parish schools and taught a similar elementary curriculum including, inevitably, the **Church of England**'s catechism. This naturally deterred Catholic parents, and by the late 18th century it became apparent that a more liberal approach was needed. The Kildare Place Society was founded in 1811 in an attempt to win over Catholic parents and their priests. The society's schools were conducted along nondenominational lines, and provided Bible reading without note or comment. The British government soon recognized the value of this conciliatory approach and gave the Kildare Place Society an annual grant of £7,000 in 1814. There were signs of early cooperation from Catholic parents, but this did not last; and by the late 1820s the society had come to be seen as a proselytizing agency despite its nondenominational credentials.

The only Irish schools to thrive during this period were the hedge schools, established by the Catholic peasantry in close association with their priests. Their pupils often met, literally, under a hedge, with one pupil acting as a "look out" in case any legal officer encroached upon their illegal Catholic proceedings. Hedge schools tried to offer a varied curriculum with as many higher subjects as possible in order that selected pupils could be given a solid educational background before entering a seminary to train for the priesthood. By 1824 there were an estimated 400,000 Catholic children attending hedge schools and, apart from their educational value, these schools played a vital role in the cultivation and preservation of a national cultural and religious identity in Ireland.

Irish higher education also reflected Anglican supremacy. Until 1793, Catholics were barred from attending the country's only university, **Trinity College** in **Dublin**. The college, however, remained a bastion of the Church of England, and its traditions and prevailing ethos did not encourage Catholic entrants. A more significant contemporary development was the founding in 1795 of a Catholic seminary for training priests at Maynooth. Maynooth College and the hedge schools were the cornerstones of Irish Catholic education in a country still dominated by the Anglican establishment.

Lawrence Williams

Bibliography

Akenson, Donald. *The Irish Educational Experiment—The National System of Education in the Nineteenth Century.* 1970.

McDowell, R.B., and D.A. Webb. *Trinity College, Dublin, 1592–1952.* 1982.

Vaughan, Moody, ed. *A New History of Ireland.* Vols. 4, 5. 1989.

Irish Emigration

Increasingly in Hanoverian Britain, **Ireland**'s chief export was people. Ireland was virtually unique among European countries in this long-term exodus. By the beginning of Queen Victoria's reign (1837), the Irish were coming to look upon emigration as almost a natural part of the human life cycle. Even before the **famine** of the 1840s, the Irish provided a narrow majority of United Kingdom emigrants, about three Irishmen leaving home for every two Scots or Englishmen. Emigration reached a peak during the Great Hunger of the 1840s, when 1 million out of a total of 8.2 million Irish inhabitants emigrated, another 1.5 million dying in their homeland. Needless to say, in-bound migration was relatively insignificant during the Hanoverian period.

The first factor promoting the accelerating flight abroad was **population** growth. Statistics are sketchy for the period before 1821 when the first Irish census was taken, but it is believed that Ireland's population at the beginning of the Hanoverian period (1714) was around 2 million, that it was 2.3 million in 1754, nearly 2.9 million in 1785, 5.3 million in 1803, more than 6.8 million in 1821, and 8.3 million by 1845 when the Great Famine struck. Connected with this high demographic growth, which obviously was especially rapid after 1780, were high marital birth and declining death rates, both the result of a number of causes such as modest agricultural prosperity during the **wars** of the period 1793–1815 and growing frequency of **smallpox** inoculation.

The second factor promoting emigration was the country's economic inability to support its burgeoning population.

During the period 1750–1815, Britain's industrialization, population growth, imperial expansion, and involvement in costly wars stimulated **Irish agriculture**, which produced grain, beef, pork, and linen yarns and cloth with which to feed and clothe British troops, people in overseas possessions, and the population in Great Britain. However, Ireland's arable land was overwhelmingly owned by the **Anglo–Irish Protestant Ascendancy**, fewer than 10,000 Protestant families, who, though they sincerely cared about **agricultural improvement** and the ongoing commercialization of agriculture, cared less for the welfare of the Irish peasantry; and the same was true of the **Irish Parliament** which reflected the will of this landlord class. The peasantry could not find alternative means of subsistence in **Irish industry**, which England's commercial and political domination left vulnerable throughout the period, and more so after the **Union** (1800) than before. Irish industry was suppressed, subjected to overwhelming English competition, and generally treated as a colonial appendage whose purpose was to export a few highly specialized industrial goods along with raw material to the English and Scottish markets. The result was that Ireland's growing population, instead of becoming urbanized workers relying on industrial wages, remained overwhelmingly rural, sometimes employed on large estates producing goods for export, sometimes not employed at all, but in either case living on ever tinier potato plots as parents subdivided their holdings among their sons. Ireland's peculiarity in remaining rural during Britain's industrializing age is reflected in the fact that between the beginning and the end of the Hanoverian period, the proportion of Irishmen living in towns of 1,500 inhabitants or more rose from 7% to only 14%, even while the population quadrupled.

Even in the early 18th century, economic factors were probably more important than religious or political ones in Irish emigration. In years of famine, the Irish either starved or emigrated. In the famine period 1726–1729, while thousands starved, thousands more emigrated to the **West Indies**. Another proof that economic motives were paramount lies in the fact that before about 1820, the main Irish emigrants were not **Catholics** but Protestants, members of the ruling religious minority. Something on the order of half a million people emigrated during the 18th century, of whom about three-fifths were Scots–Irish from Ulster—many of them leaving (especially during the earlier 18th century) because of pressures to convert tillage to pasturage, which brought agricultural unemployment even in the North. Another fifth of the emigrants were Anglican, another fifth Catholic. But beginning around 1818, and linked to the economic depression that began in 1816, there was a very significant jump in Catholic emigration. Up to this point, and throughout the 18th century, no more than 4,000 people or so had emigrated per year (and it must be remembered that during some periods, **wars** made all migration impossible). But more than 20,000 departed in 1818, and this was just the beginning of a flood that saw more than a million people leave Ireland before 1845.

About two-thirds of these emigrants were relatively young adults, under age 35. Many were single, especially those who went to Canada or America. Compared to other European migrant groups, in which males always predominated, there was an unusual parity in the sexes of Irish emigrants. In accordance with their poor and rural backgrounds, very few took with them any particular skills. They often found work in their adoptive regions as servants or laborers. Having had enough of villages, the vast majority moved to cities rather than to rural communities. Following a pattern established early in the 18th century, they often practiced "chain migration," the first to arrive encouraging others to join them. Those intending to cross the Atlantic also practiced "step migration," walking or begging their way to an Irish **seaport**, somehow finding their way across the Irish Sea, working for a while in a Scottish or English city to raise the money for steerage passage to **North America** (for most of the 19th century ranging from £2 to £6) or Australia (between £10 and £15).

Liverpool was nearly always the first leg in emigration. In the 1830s, two-thirds of all Irish emigrants passed through Liverpool, whether going on then to the other three favored destinations in the United Kingdom—**Glasgow**, **Manchester**, and **London** (which, respectively, contained the largest proportions of Irish immigrants after Liverpool)—or to New York, Quebec, or Australia. Although the percentages are debated, one estimate is that by 1850 about 35% of Irish men and women were migrating into mainland Britain (chiefly into industrial slums), about 40% into the United States, and about 10% into Canada.

The effects of the exodus were many. Violence in Ireland grew rife during the last decades of the Hanoverian period—the authorities executed three times as many convicted murderers, and recorded twice as many criminal offenses per capita, as in England—and emigration served as a safety valve for growing tension. However, it also greatly intensified national consciousness, encouraged a bitter sense of victimization, and fed the longing for national independence. In recipient countries overseas, especially the United States, Irish emigration negatively affected subsequent relations with Britain. In mainland Britain, Irish immigrants often encountered social and religious hostility. In the railway construction force, for example, where Irishmen constituted about 10% of the navvies, the 1840s saw something approaching tribal wars. Anti–Irish feeling brought a proliferation of **Orange Order** lodges among resentful Englishmen to such a degree that legislation was written to control them in 1825 and 1836. This hostility would only grow in the Victorian period.

Mary Margaret O'Reilly

Bibliography

Adams, W.F. *Ireland and Irish Emigration to the New World from 1815 to the Famine.* 1932.

Connell, K.H. *The Population of Ireland, 1750–1845.* 1950.

Ferenczi, I., and W.F. Willcox. *International Migrations.* 2 vols. 1929, 1931.

Fitzpatrick, D. *Irish Emigration, 1801–1921.* 1984.

Hansen, M.L. *The Atlantic Migration, 1607–1860.* 1940.

Mokyr, J., and C. O'Grada. "Emigration and Poverty in

Pre-Famine Ireland." *Explorations in Economic History.* Vol. 19, pp. 360–384.
Scally, R.J. *The End of Hidden Ireland: Rebellion, Famine, and Emigration.* 1995.

See also Emigration and Immigration

Irish Industry

Hanoverian Ireland was overwhelmingly agricultural and rural. Even much of what passed for industry took place in a rural, domestic setting. This is not to say that there was no urban-based industry. Most of the kingdom's county and market towns performed some economic and commercial functions, and many of the dozens of planned urban settlements established by landowners during this period sustained linen, **cotton**, and other enterprises at some time or other.

Established **urban** centers (mostly ports) provided more permanent homes for enterprise. In **Dublin**, whose industrial emergence dates from the latter 17th century, **textile** production was most important; the populous Liberties area provided employment in textiles throughout the Hanoverian period. Dublin also sustained a dynamic book-printing industry, second only to **London**'s until the end of the 18th century. There were, in addition, many luxury crafts and trades catering to the Irish **aristocracy**, food and victualing services providing for the city's general **population**, and diverse activities connected with the city's port. The pattern in other centers was comparable, though the range of employments and core businesses varied. In **Cork** the provisions **trade** was the mainspring of activity; in Belfast, which grew rapidly from 1780, it was linen and cotton; in inland towns like Bandon and Carrick-on-Suir it was **woolens**.

Reliable data do not exist, but undoubtedly many more people worked in rural **domestic production** than in urban workshops. Both woolens (mainly for home consumption) and linen (much of it exported) were made primarily in this way. Linen production dominated the industrial economy of northern **Ireland**. It was so profitable that the **spinning** of linen yarn spread from its Ulster homeland into North Leinster and North Connacht. Such was linen's contribution to Ulster's prosperity (linen exports rose from 4 million yards in 1730 to 38 million in 1795) that landlords in other provinces sought to foster its production in **planned villages**. Many of these, however, failed with the downturn in international demand in the early 1770s.

By this date, linen had to withstand competition from the new fabrics of the **Industrial Revolution**. Encouraged by British successes, attempts were made near Dublin, Belfast, and Cork to establish cotton enterprises. The best known is that of Robert Brooke at Prosperous, County Kildare, which collapsed spectacularly in the mid-1780s. Brooke's was a special case, but claims that the cotton industry employed 50,000 people around Belfast are exaggerations. Cotton briefly flourished in Ireland's protected environment, but it proved less competitive in the less sheltered post–**Union** context after 1800, succumbing to English competition in the 1820s and yielding regional primacy again to linen production.

Though linen, like **brewing** and distilling, successfully negotiated the transition from proto- to full-fledged industry, its future seemed in doubt at one stage at the beginning of the 19th century. But technological innovation, which allowed fine linens to be produced in factories, and the unique qualities of the product itself, were its salvation; the establishment of 64 linen mills in 1828–1838 showed its viability.

The same was not true of the thousands of rural **spinners** and **weavers** who lost their jobs to industrialization. Many chose to **emigrate** rather than live (and die) in Ireland penuriously. The fact that the number of people engaged in **trade** and manufacture fell by 15% between 1820 and 1840 attests vividly to Ireland's failure to experience an industrial revolution parallel to Great Britain's, and suggests the magnitude of Ireland's approaching difficulties.

James Kelly

Bibliography

Cullen, L.M. *An Economic History of Ireland since 1660.* 1972.
Gill, Conrad. *Rise of the Irish Linen Industry.* 1925.
Kelly, James. "Prosperous and Irish Industrialization 1780–90." *Journal of the Kildare Archaeological Society.* Vol. 16, pp. 441–467.
O'Grada, Cormac. *Ireland: A New Economic History, 1780–1939.* 1994.

See also Irish Agriculture; Irish Emigration

Irish Land Settlement

From the 12th century **Ireland**'s takeover by the English meant the confiscation of Irish land and its transfer to the invaders. By the beginning of the Hanoverian period (1714), Irish landowners held only about one-seventh of the land, Scottish immigrants and the English Episcopalians of the **Anglo–Irish Protestant Ascendancy** controlling the remainder. **Penal laws** restricted Irish landholding rights even more. The basic features of the resulting system of land settlement dated from the 17th century, when the landlord–tenant axis, centering on the cash payment of rent for designated portions of land, was introduced over most of the island. It was then also that many forests were cleared, the **enclosure** of much of the countryside begun, and the familiar pattern of medium-sized fields surrounded by hedgerows laid down.

This pattern of field enclosure was accelerated in the 18th century as landlords intensified their efforts to shape the countryside, patterning land use and settlement according to English models. Their ruling ambition was to construct suitably imposing residences surrounded by elegantly landscaped demesnes; and throughout the Hanoverian era successive landowners replaced the increasingly ramshackle dwellings of their forebears with the fine **Palladian** and **neoclassical** edifices that are their most enduring legacy. They also orchestrated the building of **roads** linking their residences with nearby towns, constructed estate villages and, as **Arthur Young** testified, as **agricultural improvers** did their utmost to introduce improved strains of livestock and crops, and to update agricultural practices. Not all, of course, were equally motivated by the enthusiasm for improvement, but throughout most of Leinster, Ulster, and Munster the available productive land was enclosed and brought into use.

There were some areas with markedly different patterns, notably along the western seaboard, where traditional rundale practices (which involved the periodic redistribution of fragmented holdings) persisted. This region was commercially detached and thinly populated until the end of the 18th century.

In those areas where the high quality of land encouraged investment, traditional commonage was brought under private control in the teeth of bitter resistance, as the **Whiteboy** agrarian movement of the 1760s amply attests. The enclosure of commonage was a matter of enormous consequence for those (usually smaller) tenants and laborers who relied on it, as was demonstrated in the later agrarian violence of such groups as the **Rightboys, Defenders, Ribbonmen, Terry Alts,** and **Shanavests.**

The larger farmers who worked most of the good land in Munster and Leinster had less cause for anxiety, but accelerating **population** growth after the 1770s brought increased tension to their relationship with the smallholders and landless whom they engaged as **agricultural laborers**, and frequently paid by letting them small plots of land on insecure tenure for potato cultivation. The rise in population also produced a fragmentation of landholdings (especially in those areas where middlemen were active), and growing agricultural utilization of hitherto uneconomical hillsides and boggy land.

In 18th-century Ulster, to which many Scots had immigrated, many tenants lived comfortably on small farms producing oats, potatoes, and flax, because linen manufacture provided them supplementary cash income. By the early 19th century their proliferating small holdings promised less security, but now the occupier faced more tangible hazards, particularly the potato's susceptibility to disease, and the threat of eviction as landlords turned to clearance as the most effective way to liquidate the multiplicity of uneconomic holdings.

James Kelly

Bibliography

Cullen, L.M. *The Emergence of Modern Ireland, 1600–1900.* 1981.

Graham, B.J., and L.J. Proudfoot, eds. *An Historical Geography of Ireland.* 1993.

See also Anglo–Irish Protestant Ascendancy; Irish Agriculture; Irish Industry

Irish Literature before the Union (1800)

Any appreciation of 18th-century Irish literature should begin by noting the main consequence of the **Battle of the Boyne** (1690), when **Catholic** Ireland, led by James II, was defeated by William of Orange: the domination of **Ireland** for the next century by an alien ruling class known as the **Anglo–Irish Protestant Ascendancy**, employing the **penal laws** to hold down the native **population.** Irish literature during this period was marked by a constant sense of political anxiety and frustration, whether produced by members of the ruling Protestant minority who clung uneasily to the protective power of the British state, or by writers from the Catholic majority, who for many decades yearned for a Stuart restoration. Ireland was ruled as a colony, a country divided by political, religious, cultural, and linguistic loyalties.

The most important literary figure of the century was **Jonathan Swift** who, as a member of the Ascendancy, supported the **Hanoverian succession** but rejected Ireland's acceptance of inferior colonial status. Swift became Dean of St. Patrick's cathedral in **Dublin** just as **George I** was acceding to the British throne (1714). In 1720 he published *A Proposal for the Universal Use of Irish Manufacture,* the first of over 50 pamphlets on Irish affairs he was to produce (usually anonymously) over the next two decades. He here revealed his distinctive brand of practical patriotism, calling for a boycott of English imports and an end to legislative discrimination from **London.** A few years later Swift produced his famous *The Drapier's Letters,* a series of pamphlets (1724–1725) wherein he adopted the fictive persona of a Dublin tradesman to protest a move by London to allow **William Wood** to mulct Ireland through an issuance of copper coinage. This was as much a political as a literary achievement, for in these *Letters* he appealed to "The Whole People of Ireland" to assert the justice and reason of complete legislative independence from the British Parliament in Westminster. Dismissing the 1719 Declaratory Act of George I, which had defined Ireland as a "dependent Kingdom," the "drapier" aroused a new sense of defiance and pride in his audience. Such sentiments were declared seditious and treasonable, but London nevertheless withdrew Wood's patent. For decades afterward, Swift was fondly known as "the Hibernian Patriot."

Despite this, he always identified his art with English literary culture and tradition. *Gulliver's Travels* (1726), for example, although composed in Ireland, was always intended to appear in England, partly because its allusions depended on an audience familiar with contemporary English history. After *Gulliver,* Swift continued, in pamphlets and verse, to project his increasingly bitter image of Ireland's unnatural and unnecessary poverty and dependence, drawing attention to the evils of absentee landlords, **famine**, Protestant **emigration** (especially to the American colonies), and the misery of the **Catholic** peasantry. His rage and frustration over the general crisis inspired his most famous pamphlet, *A Modest Proposal* (1729), in which he ironically advocated the eating of Irish children as the most logical remedy for a situation nearly beyond repair. After this he withdrew from political writing, devoting himself instead to the defense of the Established Church of Ireland; one of his last and best poems, *A Character, Panegyric, and Description of the Legion Club* (1736), attacked Irish politicians who sought to undermine its authority. In the last analysis, although Swift might be criticized as merely a maverick among the whole class of men then engaged in the rape of Ireland, this would lack historical understanding. His ultimate legacy lies in the way he articulated an identity for Ireland that connected it with government by consent and even with Irish independence.

If Ireland's colonial status helps to explain Swift, it also helps to explain why so many literary talents migrated toward London, often trying to conceal, sometimes to exploit, their Irish background. This was particularly true of several dramatists, of whom the most noteworthy were **Richard Steele**, **Thomas Sheridan**, **Richard Brinsley Sheridan**, and **Oliver Goldsmith**—the latter two being among the most celebrated "English" dramatists of the latter 18th century. One of their contributions to London **theater** was their popularization of "the stage Irishman," usually a figure of fun, distinguished by his "brogue." This stereotype began in the earliest years of the century with the work of another Irish emigré, George Farquhar (1678–1707), author of *The Recruiting Officer* (1706) and *The Beaux' Stratagem* (1707).

The writings of **Edmund Burke** have traditionally been regarded as important documents of British political and constitutional history, though they are now often valued as much for their rhetoric as for their perspective onto 18th-century Ireland. Burke's career followed a familiar pattern. After graduating from Trinity College, **Dublin**, he achieved a successful political career in England. Despite his conversion to Protestantism, his Catholic background seems to have given him a special appreciation of, and sensitivity to, the plight of the majority in "penal Ireland." Like Swift, he passionately defended the virtues of tradition; unlike Swift, he abhorred the humiliation of the native population. Conciliation, in the interests of authority and survival, was the theme of many of his writings and speeches on imperial responsibility, whether the issue was Ireland, **India**, or the American colonies. His views on the venality of the Protestant Ascendancy are most forcefully expressed in his two *Letters to Sir Hercules Langrishe* (1792, 1795). His fear that French Jacobins would encourage Irish republicans and deepen the cleavage of Irish society lay behind his *Reflections on the Revolution in France* (1790), a remarkable tribute to aristocratic civilization.

The literature of Gaelic-speaking Ireland during this period represents a very different, and almost completely separate, social and political order. Gaelic verse could boast of the oldest vernacular literature in Europe, a tradition reaching back a thousand years, preserved and circulated in manuscript form by a dwindling band. After 1690 the bardic schools of **poetry** and their scholars lost their traditional support from the Gaelic aristocracy, and the surviving poets, often reduced to poverty, lamented the disappearance of the older way of life. Their favorite poetical form was the *Aisling*, a "vision" poem, usually an elaborate allegory in which Ireland was represented as a beautiful woman who appears in a dream to a young man, pleading for release from a tyrannical suitor. The subtext of these fantasies was the hope that the Pretender would return from **France**, avenge Catholic Ireland, and be restored to his rightful throne.

The finest exponents of the *Aisling* include Aogán ó Rathaille (*c.* 1675–1729) and Eoghan Rua ó Suilleabháin (1748–1784). Two other poets deserve special mention: Eibhlín Dhubh Ní Chonaill (*fl.* 1770), who wrote one of the greatest poems of the century, *Caoineadh Airt Uí Laoghaire* (*Lament for Art O'Leary*), about the murder by English officials of her beloved husband who had returned from service in the Austro–Hungarian army; and Brian Merriman (1749–1805), who composed *Cúirt an Mheán Oíche* (*The Midnight Court*), a satirical parody of the *Aisling* in which the women of Ireland curse men for the country's misfortunes and proclaim a new female order. Both of these classic poems turned on themes of injustice.

The two literary cultures remained almost mutually incomprehensible until the end of the century, when **translations** of Gaelic verse began to appear, revealing a rich oral tradition. Charlotte Brooke (*c.* 1740–1793) pioneered some of this work in her *Reliques of Irish Poetry* (1789), a bilingual model of Celtic revivalism. A growing interest in the native tradition is also reflected in the fiction of **Maria Edgeworth**, especially in *Castle Rackrent* (1800), Ireland's first **novel**, an ironic exposure of the moral and political bankruptcy of the landlord class. Edgeworth's tale appeared in the same year as the **Act of Union**, which dissolved the **Irish Parliament** and ended the hegemony of the Protestant Ascendancy.

In sum, Ireland before the Union, or certainly before the failed experiment of the **United Irishmen** in the 1790s, was a deeply divided society, without any shared sense of nationhood. Writers who served the Protestant interest, like Swift and Burke, wrote out of a deep concern for order and stability in a country which promised neither. Gaelic literature clung to a dream of recovery, based on a nostalgic sense of lost community.

Joseph McMinn

Bibliography

Craig, Maurice. *Dublin, 1660–1860.* 1992.

Cruise O'Brien, Conor. *The Great Melody: A Thematic Biography of Edmund Burke.* 1992.

Deane, Seamus, ed. *The Field Day Anthology of Irish Writing.* 3 vols. 1991.

Ehrenpreis, Irvin. *Swift: The Man, His Works and the Age.* 3 vols. 1962–1983.

McDowell, R.B., ed. *The Writings and Speeches of Edmund Burke.* 1991.

McMinn, Joseph, ed. *Swift's Irish Pamphlets: An Introductory Selection.* 1991.

Moody, T.W., and W.E. Vaughan, eds. *A New History of Ireland.* Vol. 4: *Eighteenth Century Ireland.* 1986.

Irish Parliament

Although the Irish Parliament dated back to the Middle Ages, its only continuous history ran from 1692 to 1800. It consisted of a House of Lords and a House of Commons, similar to the British Parliament in Westminster. It was a Protestant-controlled assembly, speaking largely for the Irish landed class and the interests of the Protestant, chiefly Anglican, minority (less than one-third of the **population**) who are generally referred to as the **Anglo–Irish Protestant Ascendancy. Catholics** were excluded throughout the 18th century, and between 1728 and 1793 no Catholics or their spouses were allowed to vote. Protestant **dissenters** could vote (they were more numerous in Scots-settled Ulster than elsewhere), though none sat in Lords and only a handful sat in Commons. The Parliament met for about 6 months, every 2 years.

"A Prospect of Dublin, the Capital of Ireland"

The assembly was only nominally independent, and after 1719 the British Parliament claimed the right to legislate entirely for **Ireland**. However, in the aftermath of the **War of American Independence** came a campaign for legislative autonomy, and in 1782 this was partly achieved when Westminster relinquished the right to legislate for Ireland (although it retained the right of veto, a power it never exercised). The assembly between 1782 and 1800 is generally called "Grattan's Parliament"—referring to **Henry Grattan**, one of its most eloquent and best-known leaders. Grattan believed that the Irish assembly, despite all its imperfections, was a positive force because it sat in **Dublin**.

Throughout the Parliament's last 11 years its activities were continually overshadowed by the **French Revolution**. Fear of French interference in Ireland was the main reason why **Pitt the Younger** pressured it to pass a bill of **Catholic Relief** (1793) giving voting rights at last to Catholics (contrary to the earlier **penal laws**), and why more generally he wished to reorganize political relations between **London** and Dublin. Such fears were warranted, as seen in the failed attempt by the French to land an expedition in 1796, and were heightened after the **Irish Rebellion** led by the **United Irishmen** (1798). It was felt that Ireland was sliding into chaos and that this could worsen problems in Britain. Pitt thus began to push for the union of the two parliaments. After several failed attempts this was finally achieved on 1 January 1801, when the **Act of Union** came into effect. This marked the end of the Irish Parliament. Thereafter, all decisions affecting Ireland were formulated in London.

William Kenefick

Bibliography

Beckett, J.C. *The Making of Modern Ireland, 1603–1923.* 1981.

Farrell, Brian, ed. *The Irish Parliamentary Tradition.* 1973.

Lecky, W.E.M. *History of Ireland in the Eighteenth Century.* 1892.

McCraken, J.L. *The Irish Parliament in the Eighteenth Century.* 1971.

McDowell, R.B. *Ireland in the Age of Imperialism and Revolution, 1760–1801.* 1980.

See also Ireland and Irish Politics

Irish Rebellions (1798, 1803)

The **United Irishmen**'s Rebellion of 1798 and **Robert Emmet**'s Rebellion of 1803 marked the climax of tensions that had been developing in **Ireland** over the course of the 18th century. Sectarian polarization, agrarian unrest, and economic crisis intensified during the 1780s and 1790s amidst conditions of general international dislocation.

The impact of the **American Revolution** and the **French Revolution** also helped to ensure the take off of political **radicalism** and **nationalism** among the northern Irish Protestant community, rather than the disaffected **Catholic** majority. Political consciousness had initially been raised by the gentry-led **Volunteering Movement** in the 1780s, but the main engine for reform agitation became the cross-sectarian **United Irishmen**, founded in Belfast in 1791. After an initial period of constitutionalist activity, this group developed into an underground military movement (1795); an informal alliance with **defenderism** allowed it to tap traditional Catholic rural protest and transform it into a nationwide mass movement with over 120,000 sworn members.

Diplomatic negotiations by United Irish agents in Paris brought a narrowly unsuccessful French invasion attempt in 1796, but chronic internal splits over the nature and timing of any future rising, coupled with a governmental military onslaught, drove the radicals back onto the defensive during 1797. By the beginning of 1798 a wave of officially sanctioned terror was in full swing in the Irish countryside.

The rebellion that resulted was a spontaneous and chaotic grassroots response to government repression and rumored French invasion, very unlike the carefully planned struggle for national liberation that United Irish leaders had initially envisaged. It broke out around **Dublin** on 23 May 1798 and lasted a ferocious 10 weeks. The arrest of their Leinster leadership the previous spring compromised the society's ability to control events. In many areas the rising degenerated into sectarian slaughter and mass atrocities, which were to live on in popular memory.

Neither Dublin, the southwest, nor Ulster, rose, thanks mainly to arms raids and faltering rank-and-file confidence; but the rebels met with more success in Wexford and Wicklow, in the southeast. Their military tactics were unsophisticated but savage, tending to involve bands of pikemen under improvised local leadership, and the speed of events was in their favor. They attacked and captured Enniscorthy on 28 May, defeated several contingents of inexperienced government troops, then pressed into Munster, where their effort stalled after the failure to capture New Ross in County Kilkenny. Government forces took the initiative and broke the back of the insurgents' strength at the rout of Vinegar Hill on 21 June. Those bands who regrouped were extinguished in the savage mopping-up operation that lasted the rest of the summer.

The final hope for the rebels was French assistance. Partly due to the efforts of **Wolfe Tone**, three small expeditions eventually set out, but these had little hope of snatching back a United victory. Only General Humbert's landing in Connacht in August brought troops in any force. After defeating Crown troops at Castlebar, he was eventually surrounded and captured on 8 September.

The 1798 rebellion has been described as probably the most concentrated episode of violence in Irish history. The death toll on both sides has been estimated at 30,000. The security risk it exposed also helped to win support for the constitutional **Act of Union** of the British and Irish Parliaments, achieved in 1801. But for the United Irishmen, the rebellion was a massive defeat. The movement adopted a new elitist military structure, and leadership passed to a new generation. Of these new United leaders, Robert Emmet stood out in terms of inspirational ability. After abortive negotiations with Talleyrand and Napoleon, he became convinced of the need for a more independent insurrectionary strategy, drawing on the Irish rebels' own resources. Secrecy and professionalism were to be its hallmarks.

Emmet returned to Ireland in 1803 with careful plans for his rebellion. An attack by Dublin tradesmen and artisans on the center of government was to be the signal for the rest of the country to rise, and would attract French support. In the event, the discovery of one of the rebels' arms depots prompted their leaders to set the attempt in motion before preparations for coordinated external assistance, or even for that matter broad-based support within Ireland, were satisfactorily completed. They issued last-minute instructions to their supporters and moved on 23 July, but confusion and indecision caused the uprising to stall almost at once. Emmet and the Dublin leaders launched an attack on foot but, after a series of misadventures, this was easily defeated. The attempts of Emmet's associate Thomas Russell (1767–1803) to raise Ulster similarly failed.

Emmet's rebellion was the last armed uprising in Ireland for 45 years, but this did not mean the disappearance of the disaffection which had fueled it. In the absence of formal political leadership, this increasingly found expression in the early 19th century in the proliferation of agrarian protest movements like **Ribbonism**. The most enduring legacy of the two rebellions, however, was the intensified religious polarization of Irish life. The sectarian attacks of the 1798 rebellion prompted a wave of loyalist hysteria and drove Protestants increasingly into support for the Union with Great Britain. Political battlelines were thus drawn for the new century, with Irish nationalism destined to become almost exclusively a Catholic preserve.

E. W. McFarland

Bibliography

Curtin, Nancy J. *The United Irishmen: Popular Politics in Ulster and Dublin, 1791–1798.* 1994.

Dickson, D., D. Keogh, and K. Whelan, eds. *The United Irishmen: Republicanism, Radicalism and Rebellion.* 1993.

Elliot, M. *Partners in Revolution: The United Irishmen and France.* 1982.

Foster, R.F. *Modern Ireland, 1600–1972.* 1989.

McDowell, R.B. *Ireland in the Age of Imperialism and Revolution, 1760–1801.* 1980.

McFarland, E.W. *Ireland and Scotland in the Age of Revolution: Planting the Green Bough.* 1994.

Pakenham, T. *The Year of Liberty.* 1972.

Iron Industry

Iron was the revolutionary all-purpose building material, the plastic, of industrializing Britain. It became the sinew of the **Industrial Revolution**. Iron is one of the cheapest, most abundant, strongest, hardest, versatile, and magnetic substances known. British industry and leisure both proceeded on its girders, wheels, cranks, rails, drills, springs, pistons, polishers, and cylinders. Yet little could have gone forward until iron could be supplied in great quantities and varied qualities so that designers and engineers could think of it as just another building material—as available for use as wood, leather, stone, paper, or cloth.

Although iron is one of the oldest human discoveries,

production had not proceeded very far by 1714. It had changed little since the furnace and forge had replaced the bloomery industry (hearth smelting) at the beginning of the 16th century. While the total number of furnaces varied little throughout the 17th century, ranging from 70 to 80, productivity per furnace rose by one-third to reach about 340 tons. Hence in 1720 national production stood at 25,000 tons from 74 charcoal furnaces scattered across the country, often in remote timber-rich locations. Usually these were chosen because it was easier to take the ore to the charcoal than vice versa. But despite rich deposits of native ore, remote location and higher costs led to steadily rising imports of foreign ore and bar iron. Over the next 30 years, productivity continued to rise but the industry stagnated, with the average number of furnaces drifting downward, and the total annual output of pig iron hovering around 28,000 tons. Rising demand was met by increased imports, mainly from the Baltic states of Sweden and Russia; domestic prospects seemed dim.

Bar iron, the main product in use, was produced in two stages. This was chiefly because ore, to be heated, had to be mixed with fuel which, though it burned off some impurities, also had the effect of carburizing the product (virtually all fuels contain carbon) and hence making it unmalleable. First was the furnace stage, which produced pig iron in a red-hot furnace by smelting (heating), deoxidizing (burning the oxygen out of), and carburizing (chemically uniting with carbon from the fuel) the ore (iron oxide), pouring ("casting") this molten product then into "pigs" (ingots) or simple castings of some particular design. If something more than cast iron was wanted, then bar iron had to be produced in a second stage. This stage was performed in a forge (a special fireplace): it reheated, decarburized, and refined the brittle, unworkable, high-carbon pigs so as to provide bars of medium-carbon steel or low-carbon "wrought iron" suitable for working into implements. The two sectors—furnaces and forges—were organizationally and geographically distinct: two stages, as it were, on the road to the village blacksmith and the industrial engineer.

Although contemporaries and many later historians attributed the Hanoverian iron industry's initially poor performance to the exhaustion of timber needed for charcoal (which produced the high temperatures required for smelting), this was only one factor. Inadequate **transport** links and water shortages also imposed severe constraints. But the experiments of the **Darby family** at Coalbrookdale, west of **Birmingham** in Shropshire, did result in the first successful use of coke (distilled **coal**) in place of charcoal in smelting. This was a crucial step forward because it enabled a changeover from costly and limited natural fuel to cheap and plentiful mineral fuel. The new process was not generally adopted before the 1750s, when Abraham Darby II improved on his father's process, and when certain advances in blowing engines produced iron better suited to the forge. Even then, the use of coal in the forge advanced only slowly. It replaced charcoal in some of the later stages, but the key refining processes remained entirely dependent on charcoal.

The solution lay not in modifying but in replacing the process. The first significant advance was achieved by the Wood brothers, who introduced their potting process in the early 1760s. Their coke-based system was soon replaced by a coal-fired version, and in 1788 this accounted for one-half of the production of bar iron. This vital improvement on the refining side coincided with the numerical advance of coke-smelting furnaces from 4 out of 72 furnaces in 1750 to 72 out of 96 in 1785. In the same period, the annual output of pig iron rose sharply from 28,000 to 80,000 tons; and of bar iron from 13,350 to 32,000 tons. High **tariffs** led to a reduction in imports.

In 1784 **Henry Cort** developed the puddling process. This used a "reverberatory" furnace, which greatly simplified the conversion from cast to wrought iron by heating the charge in a chamber separate from the fuel (sucking heat over it from the fuel chamber) and hence minimizing recarburization. This, and the often neglected but equally important rolling technique that Cort developed, permitted a fifteenfold increase in production of wrought iron bars and sheets, and the growth of a cheap mass-production system based on coal. Moreover, the furnace and forge could now be geographically reintegrated. But although Cort's inventions were sound he, like **James Watt** with his **steam engine** at about the same time, needed the heavy backing of a big ironmaster to ensure their practical implementation. This was mainly achieved at **Crawshay**'s Cyfartha works in the 1790s, and, following the end of Cort's patents, the puddling process rapidly spread. Thus the second half of the 18th century, in contrast to the first, witnessed a dramatic transformation in the industry, principally by **technological** changes that allowed the adoption of coke in the furnace, and coal in the forge.

Demand grew rapidly during the French **wars** (1792–1815), and after the shock of postwar depression, picked up again in the 1820s. Despite faltering briefly in the depressions of 1826 and 1831, annual pig iron production, which stood at only 180,000 tons in 1800, reached 1 million tons by the end of the Hanoverian period. By the 1840s, which saw Europeans and North Americans still typically operating small charcoal furnaces, Britain was producing half the world's pig iron; and by the 1870s she was producing three times more than that.

Advances in engineering, which assisted the progress of the iron industry and to which the ironmasters themselves contributed, also ensured this long-term growth despite short-term fluctuations. Such advances, plentiful in the period 1760–1825, included introduction of the steam engine in all its variants, and of the **railway** at last in 1825—a massive consumer of iron. Hall's "wet" puddling process was also introduced in the 1820s, and the last of the decisive Hanoverian innovations came in 1828 when **James Neilson** patented the "hot-blast" process for firing the blast furnace (which formerly had simply blown unheated air), increasing temperatures and production while greatly lessening fuel consumption. Although of general benefit to the industry, this technique was particularly important to the rise of the Scottish pig-iron sector: a large, integrated, technologically progressive works had been built at Carron near Falkirk in 1759 and prospered after a shaky start, but the cluster of smaller works built in the West of **Scotland** struggled to survive until Neilson's invention transformed the industry's fortunes there.

The geography of the industry altered substantially as coal replaced both timber and water for fuel and power. The traditional centers of Sussex and the Forest of Dean declined as the industry expanded in the Midlands, South **Wales**, and Central Scotland. For a time, government conservatism meant that the virtual monopoly of gunfounding held by Sussex continued, but this collapsed rapidly in the last quarter of the century in the face of **John Wilkinson**'s invention of his boring machine and the development of **Carron Company's** carronade, which transformed naval gunnery.

R.D. Corrins

Bibliography

Birch, A. *The Economic History of the British Iron and Steel Industry, 1784–1879.* 1967.

Gale, W.K.V. *The British Iron and Steel Industry, a Technical History.* 1967.

Harris, J.R. *The British Iron Industry, 1700–1850.* 1988.

Hyde, C.K. *Technological Change and the British Iron Industry, 1700–1870.* 1977.

See also Metallurgy and Metalworking; Science, Technology, and Invention

Irony

Samuel Johnson unsurprisingly defined *irony* in his *Dictionary* (1755) as a rhetorical term: "A mode of speech in which the meaning is contrary to the words." But irony not only utilizes direct contradiction, it also employs appreciative understatement and other forms of slanted language to create a disjunction between the statement and its implication.

Irony's success depends on an audience's awareness of this separation. Hating **dissenters**, unsophisticated Anglican readers of **Defoe**'s satirical *The Shortest-Way with the Dissenters* (1702) applauded what he wrote; the government, seeing that Anglican bigotry was his true target, punished him for what he meant. In contrast, few readers have misunderstood **Swift**'s *A Modest Proposal* (1729), though whether Swift found hypocrisy acceptable in his *Argument against the Abolishment of Christianity in England* (1711) can still be debated.

Irony and its bedfellow, **satire**, found a congenial home in the **periodical** essays of the early 18th century, in the *Tatler* and *Spectator* where, in the latter, **Addison** turned Sir Roger de Coverley into an example of anachronistic **Toryism** and excelled in what **Pope** characterized as damning with faint praise. Pope's *Moral Essays* (1731–1735) and *Imitations of Horace* (1733, 1737) explored the discordances between the good and the new.

When irony is more than a rhetorical device, it is a view of life that denies any closure between what is and what should be. **Gay**'s *The Beggar's Opera* (1782) contains many instances of rhetorical and situational irony (where a character's expectations and actuality remain unreconciled), and in its refusal to reconcile opposites is itself an ironic work. But **Goldsmith**'s *The Vicar of Wakefield* (1766), because of its concluding reconciliation, is not itself ironic, although that **novel** has many effective ironic moments. The most thoroughgoing ironic novelist in the Hanoverian period was **Jane Austen**, a master of the technique.

Generally speaking, the ironies of 18th-century works, such as **Henry Fielding**'s *Jonathan Wild* (1743) and **Gibbon**'s *The Decline and Fall of the Roman Empire* (1776–1788), remained within broadly accepted moral and sociopolitical frameworks. True, as **Sterne**'s *Tristram Shandy* (1760–1767) testifies, order is always breaking down; but still it is the illusion we use to shut out chaos. Mainstream 18th-century artists strengthened that illusion because, in their view, society depended on it. In *Rasselas* (1759), however, Johnson began to ask difficult questions whose answers might be unknowable; and starting with **William Blake**, the **Romantics** gloried in attacking received reality. Even before the **French Revolution**, other authors identified order with repression and began treating the individual as his own (but not always her own) denominator. **Gothic** novelists enthusiastically wielded irony to shock readers from their conventional expectations. **Matthew Lewis**'s *The Monk* (1796) displayed the vulnerability of virtue; **Mary Shelley**'s *Frankenstein* (1818) emphasized the awful consequences of irresponsible creation.

Unlike earlier authors who shared with their audience widely held beliefs in what was right and real, alienated Romantics such as **Shelley** and the **Byron** of *Don Juan* (1819–1824) knew better what was wrong and false. The Romantic ironists' belief in the instability of reality enabled them to deconstruct their age's pieties without feeling the necessity to posit new ones. Their self-absorption created ironies which, as in **Keats**'s "Ode to a Nightingale" (1819), spiraled inward to reflect their own private plight. But unlike *Tristram Shandy*, which wittily enshrined solipsism and its attendant ironies, Romantic ironists usually were more stern than comic, and more cosmic than stern.

Peter A. Tasch

Bibliography

Conrad, Peter. *Shandyism.* 1978.

Mellor, Anne K. *English Romantic Irony.* 1980.

Muecke, D.C. *The Compass of Irony.* 1969.

Simpson, David. *Irony and Authority in Romantic Poetry.* 1979.

Test, George A. *Satire: Spirit and Art.* 1991.

See also Mock Heroic; Wit and Ridicule

J

Jacobitism

Jacobites were the followers of the Stuart claimants to the Scottish and English thrones. The term is derived from the Latin word *Jacobus*, meaning James. Ideologically, Jacobitism was based on the notion of the indefeasible right of hereditary succession: The Stuarts were the lawful monarchs of Scotland and England. Jacobites rejected the settlement following the **Glorious Revolution** (1688–1689), believing that it violated this right, which they claimed lay at the heart of civilized society. Jacobites believed that the usurpation of the Stuarts' throne went against both civil and religious law, and they drew comparisons with the upheavals of the mid-17th century which, they claimed, represented divine judgment against a society that had unlawfully deposed its king. Jacobitism, centered in **Scotland**, was able to draw support from the **Catholic** and, more prominently, Episcopalian communities which were hostile to the Presbyterian religious settlement of the **Church of Scotland**. They felt that their religion would be safeguarded by a Stuart monarch who was Catholic and more favorable to their religious beliefs.

Expediency was another factor that accounted for Jacobite support in Scotland. Disgruntled politicians who felt that they had been mistreated, such as the **Earl of Mar**, or disaffected **clans**, such as the MacDonalds, believed that their position would be improved if a Stuart restoration occurred. The fluid nature of Scottish politics, particularly in the early 18th century, encouraged opportunism as politicians and clan leaders threw in their lot with Jacobitism when it appeared to have a chance of success. Being on the right side was, for many, more important than ideological considerations. The key Jacobite rebellions were in 1715 (**The Fifteen**) and 1745 (**The Forty-five**), with an abortive attempt in 1719.

The role of Jacobitism in England is more ambiguous, the one certain generalization being the fact that it was continually held up as a menace by ambitious **Whig** politicians of the reigns of **George I** and **George II**, and hence used as an instrument to tar their political enemies, no matter how unfairly. Jacobitism faded in importance after 1745.

Richard Finlay

Bibliography

Dickinson, H.T. *Liberty and Property: Political Ideology in Eighteenth Century Britain.* 1977.

Lenman, B. *The Jacobite Risings in Britain.* 1980.

———. *The Jacobite Cause.* 1986.

Macinnes, Allan I. "Jacobitism," in Jenny Wormald, ed., *Scotland Revisited.* 1991.

Monod, Paul Kleber. *Jacobitism and the English People, 1688–1788.* 1993.

See also Charles Edward, the Young Pretender; Culloden, Battle of; James Edward, the Old Pretender; Lovat, 11th Baron

James Edward, the Old Pretender (1688–1766)

The only surviving son of James VII and II, who was deposed by the **Glorious Revolution** (1688–1689), James Edward was born during the midst of his father's troubles. He was educated

James Edward Stuart

in **France** and named Prince of Wales by his father. When the latter died (1701), James was proclaimed King, and recognized as such by France and Spain. Attempts on his part for a **Jacobite** rising following the **Act of Union** (1707) failed in 1708. He served briefly in the French armed forces but returned to **Scotland** for the ill-fated **Fifteen** rebellion. After this he returned to the Continent and was involved in another failed rebellion in 1719. Backed by the papacy, James Edward eventually settled in Rome, married Clementina Sobieski (granddaughter of the Polish king), and had two sons: **Charles Edward, the Young Pretender**, and Prince Henry (Henry IX). He took no part in the **Forty-five** rebellion, though the standard was raised by his son in his name. He died in Rome. The royal Stuart line ended when Henry died in 1807.

John Roach Young

Bibliography

Ferguson, W. *Scotland, 1689 to the Present.* 1977.
Keay, J., and J. Keay, eds. *Collins Encyclopaedia of Scotland.* 1994.
Lenman, B. *The Jacobite Risings in Britain.* 1980.
McLynn, F. *The Jacobites.* 1985.
Monod, Paul Kleber. *Jacobitism and the English People, 1688–1788.* 1993.

See also Foreign Relations; Hanoverian Succession

Jebb, John (1736–1786)

Jebb was a close friend of **Major John Cartwright** and a leading figure in the **radical** reformism of the latter 18th century. Born in **London** of an Irish cleric, he studied in Dublin and Cambridge (B.A. 1757, M.A. 1760), was ordained (1763), and continued at Cambridge to teach and study mathematics and ancient languages (**Capell Lofft** was a disciple) until 1775, when he left the church, moved to London, and, after 2 years' study, began to practice medicine. By this time Jebb had already marked out his path by agitating for university reform and, alongside his friend **Theophilus Lindsey**, participating in the radical movement within the church that produced the Feathers Tavern Petition (1772) demanding parliamentary abolition of the requirement that Anglican clergy subscribe to the Thirty-nine Articles.

In 1779, the environment heated over the **War of American Independence** and the governmental corruption that supposedly had caused and prolonged it, Jebb plunged into pamphleteering. Like Cartwright, **Tooke**, **Sawbridge**, **Brand**, **Day**, and other radicals, he wholeheartedly supported the colonial revolutionaries, condemned the corrupting influences of electoral **patronage**, and was a founder of the important **Society for Constitutional Information** (1780). Jebb supported **Wyvill's Association movement** and was an important theorist of national associationism, although, standing for what he called "Major Cartwright's Plan," he went much further than Wyvill and demanded equal electoral constituencies, the ballot, universal manhood suffrage, and annual parliaments, in addition to **economical reform** and the exclusion of **placemen** from Commons. In Westminster he worked briefly with **Fox** around 1780, but stood aghast at the **Fox–North Coalition** (1783). He worked for Irish political reform, **law reform**, and **prison reform**, influencing **John Howard** with his *Thoughts on the Construction and Polity of Prisons* (1786). In **medicine** Jebb proposed the instructional use of medical case histories, and wrote a treatise on paralysis (1782).

George F. Clements

Bibliography

Baylen, Joseph, and Norbert J. Gossman. *Biographical Dictionary of Modern British Radicals.* Vol. 1. 1979.
Jebb, John. *Works, Theological and Political, with Memoirs of the Life of the Author.* Ed. by John Disney. 3 vols. 1787.
Robbins, Caroline. *The Eighteenth-Century Commonwealthman.* 1959, 1968.
Royle, Edward, and James Walvin. *English Radicals and Reformers, 1760–1848.* 1982.

Jeffrey, Francis, Lord (1773–1850)

Co-founder of the influential Whiggish quarterly the *Edinburgh Review,* Jeffrey served as its first editor (1802–1829) and became its most rigorous literary reviewer. Championing literary authorities of the past, he was a formidable antagonist of **Wordsworth**, **Coleridge**, and **Southey**, whose unconventionally inelegant diction, emphasis on the poetic self, and selection of characters from lower social classes he found objectionable.

Born in a high **Tory Edinburgh** household and coming of age under a Tory Scottish government, Jeffrey himself held fast to liberal **Whig** principles. Along with his critical endeavors, he practiced law and, after the Whigs rose to power in 1830, was elected to Parliament (1832). In 1834 he became a judge and a lord. He was a reformer and a longtime associate of **Henry Brougham**.

His role as an arbiter of literary taste, however, has established his lasting reputation. While notoriously misassessing

Francis Jeffrey

Wordsworth and his circle, whom he disparagingly called the "**Lake School**," Jeffrey was a sympathetic reviewer of **Byron** and **Keats**. For all his critical harshness and political bigotry, he attempted to maintain a balance of opinions in his periodical. **Hazlitt** mirrored the opinion of many when he called Jeffrey both the "severest of critics" and the "best-natured of men."

Mike Wiley

Bibliography

Cockburn, Henry, Lord. *Life of Lord Jeffrey, with a Selection from His Correspondence.* 1852.

Greig, James A. *Francis Jeffrey of the* Edinburgh Review. 1948.

Morgan, Peter F., ed. *Jeffrey's Criticism: A Selection.* 1983.

See also Literary Criticism; Periodicals

Jenner, Edward (1749–1823)

An important pioneer in the prevention of smallpox, Jenner was interested in natural history from boyhood. He was apprenticed to a Gloucestershire surgeon, then completed his training in **London** under **John Hunter** while also being employed by **Sir Joseph Banks** to help arrange the zoological specimens he had brought back from the South Pacific. In 1773 he returned to Gloucestershire as a country doctor. His continued interest in natural history kept him in contact with Hunter and Banks, and this led to a paper on cuckoos (1788) and a Fellowship in the **Royal Society** (1789). Soon afterward he acquired the M.D. degree from St. Andrews (1792).

Dr. Jenner, pioneer of vaccination

Dissatisfied with variolation as a means of preventing smallpox, he began research into cowpox, a milder form of the disease, according to country lore, which brought immunity against the greater. Jenner carried out his first successful vaccination with cowpox (1796–1797) and published his findings in his *Inquiry into the Cause and Effects of the Variolae Vaccinae* (1798). As his discovery threatened the earnings of many medical professionals engaged in providing inoculation, he initially aroused great hostility and had difficulty in getting anyone to be vaccinated. However, his cause was helped by powerful friends, a Royal Jennerian Society was established (1802–1808), and vaccination quickly became widespread (although its efficacy in parts of the world has since been questioned).

Jenner's work brought him European fame and many honors at home, and marked the beginning of attempts to control infection by immunization. Nevertheless, more than a decade after his famous discovery the College of Physicians refused to admit him until he could pass an examination in classics. His response was caustic: "I would not do it for a diadem. That indeed would be a bauble; I would not do it for John Hunter's museum."

C.E. Hivey

Bibliography

Sunders, Paul. *Edward Jenner: The Cheltenham Years 1795–1823.* 1982.

See also Smallpox

Jenyns, Soame (1704–1787)

Jenyns wrote occasional verse, satirical **poetry** and prose, political pamphlets, and metaphysical tracts. A **Whig** M.P. (1741–1780), he received after 1754 a yearly secret service **pension** of £600. A master of unexceptional, witty, **neoclassical** verse populated with Chloes and Cupids, his "Modern Fine Gentleman" (1746) and "Modern Fine Lady" (1750) are competently composed in seemingly familiar satirical couplets. His poems appeared extensively in **Dodsley**'s influential *Collection of Poems* (1748), and his contemporaries praised his Addisonian prose.

Because **Samuel Johnson** attacked Jenyns's *Free Inquiry into the Nature and Origin of Evil* (1757) in a brilliant review for the *Literary Magazine* (1757), it has become Jenyns's most well-known **essay**. He replied that he wished to "reconcile the numerous evils so conspicuous in the creation, with the wisdom, power, and goodness of the Creator." His other major essay was the popular "View of the Internal Evidence of the Christian Religion" (1776), which Johnson condescendingly termed "a pretty book." But Jenyns, in his epitaph on Johnson, had the last word: "Religious, moral, generous, and humane / [Johnson] was . . . / Fond of, and overbearing in dispute, / A Christian, and a scholar—but a Brute."

Ronald Rompkey

Bibliography

Jenyns, Soame. *The Works of Soame Jenyns, Esq., in Four Volumes.* 1790; rpt. 1969.

Rompkey, Ronald. *Soame Jenyns.* 1984.

Jerrold, Douglas (1803–1857)

Jerrold was a **journalist**, novelist, early contributor to *Punch,* prolific playwright, and longtime friend of Charles Dickens (1812–1870). His plays *The Devil's Ducat* (1830), *Rent Day* (1832), *Doves in a Cage* (1835), and in particular *Black-Eyed Susan or "All in the Downs"* (1829), were notable successes.

Born in Sheerness, the son of a theater manager, he was precocious. At age 15 he wrote *The Duelists,* which was produced (1821) with modest success as *More Frightened than Hurt.* Hired as a playwright for the Coburg Theater, and later for the Surrey, he then produced a flood of melodramas and farces. In 1829 *Black-Eyed Susan,* a nautical drama, won him fame if little money.

His great obsession was to restore native drama to a stage dominated by **translations** of French plays, and to that end he wrote *Thomas à Becket* (1829), an historical drama. But he soon reverted to the congenial genres of melodrama and farce, using English settings. In 1835 he had 13 plays produced in London.

Jerrold wrote **radical** critiques of society for the *Athenaeum* and humorous pieces for such journals as the abortive *Punch in London* and *Blackwood's.* In 1841 he began a long and productive association with *Punch,* where his most popular work was *Mrs. Caudle's Curtain Lectures* (1845); the comic scold Mrs. Margaret Caudle and her long-suffering husband John became household names. Jerrold's plays have not aged well, but they provide insight into popular tastes. The influence of his nondramatic work is apparent in William Thackeray's (1811–1863) *Titmarsh Papers* and in Dickens's *Sketches by Boz* (1836–1837) and *A Christmas Carol* (1843).

James Held

Bibliography

Jerrold, Douglas. *The Writings of Douglas Jerrold.* 8 vols. 1851–1858.

Jerrold, Walter. *Douglas Jerrold, Dramatist and Wit.* 2 vols. 1914.

Kelley, Richard M. *The Best of Mr. Punch: The Humorous Writings of Douglas Jerrold.* 1970.

———. *Douglas Jerrold.* 1972.

See also Dramatic Arts; Periodicals

Jew Act (1753)

The Jew Act, properly the Jewish Naturalisation Act, intended to relieve Jews of some legal disabilities, was passed by Parliament in 1753 but repealed the same year. Its author was the **Duke of Newcastle**, manager of the **Whig** party, motivated by gratitude to the **London** Jewish financial community, which, at a crucial moment in the **Jacobite** rebellion of 1745, secured the government's precarious credit. By allowing them to omit the words "on the true faith of a Christian" from the oaths of supremacy and allegiance, the act aided foreign-born Jews to become naturalized citizens and to acquire all the rights enjoyed by their native-born children. However, it caused a large though not violent outcry, which radical opponents of the ministry sought to exploit. Newcastle, facing a general election in 1754, was sufficiently impressed by the reaction to decide that the law ought not to remain in effect, and himself had it withdrawn.

Michael Fry

Bibliography

Engleman, Todd M. *The Jews of Georgian England, 1714–1830: Tradition and Change in a Liberal Society.* 1979.

Roth, Cecil. *A History of the Jews in England.* 3rd ed., rev. 1964.

See also Jewry

Jewelry

France led **fashion** in the early 18th century, and British pattern books for jewelry were reprinted from French sources. In this manner the *rocaille* style was introduced, but it soon took on a distinctly English character, sometimes combining rococo scrollwork or shellwork with classical figures. Jewelry for women included gold chains, diamond necklaces, strands of pearls (usually worn with matching earrings), and gold hairpins. Rings were not commonly worn, and wedding bands are absent in portraits of married women. Women also favored lockets, pendants, crosses, and girdle buckles of gold or silver, set with precious stones; and they wore watches suspended from stay hooks attached to the corset, or from a chain around the neck. The watch, usually enclosed in a case of gold or tortoiseshell, was the most important article of men's jewelry, and was hung from a fob or chatelaine. Precious gems were used sparingly in men's buckles; diamond rings were flaunted by the *beaux.*

From 1750 to 1800, miniatures painted on enamel were worn by both men and women; they eventually became more popular than goldwork. Women often wore black velvet ribbon neckbands suspending a cross, heart, or pendant. Floral motifs were used around 1750 to decorate watches with jewels of many colors, but in the 1770s, more severe **neoclassical styles** replaced the asymmetrical motifs of the rococo. **Josiah Wedgwood** had enormous success reproducing classical subjects (found mostly on ancient gems and Roman plasterwork) for adornment of jewels, beads, earrings, and plaques. At the same time, jewelry was increasingly manufactured by machinery, and the fabrication of paste, or false, gems became a lucrative enterprise. Cut steel (an English innovation) and marcasites were increasingly used as substitutes for diamonds. By the end of the 18th century, British jewelry-making was almost completely industrialized.

Well before that time, the influences of **sensibility** and of the **Gothic Revival** had begun to compete with neoclassicism as major influences on style. In England, memorial rings and brooches containing plaited hair or initials, and decorated with symbols of mourning, were immensely popular. Memorial jewelry and other English trends, made affordable by mass production, quickly spread to France where, after 1789, political tumult abolished the craftsmen's guilds that had been the leaders of European fashion and decorative arts for two centuries. Napoleon eventually recovered most of the French crown jewels, bringing neoclassical cameos and jewelry set with rubies, diamonds, and emeralds back into fashion. But the tough economic times following his fall (1815) prompted French jewelers to look across the Channel for inspiration, where jewelry made of semiprecious stones, such as amethysts, topaz, and opals (and, in **Scotland**, cairngorms and freshwater pearls), was being produced at lower cost through industrialized techniques. In the 1820s and 1830s, the growing prosperity of the **middle classes** made popular taste an important arbiter of fashion, and **Romantic** motifs from the literature of that period dominated jewelry design.

Deidre Dawson

Bibliography

Cunnington, C. Willett, and Phillis Cunnington. *Handbook of English Costume in the Eighteenth Century.* 2nd ed., 1964.

Evans, Joan. *English Jewelry from the Fifth Century A.D. to 1800.* 1921.

———. *A History of Jewelry 1100–1870.* 1953.

See also Clothing

Jewry

In 1700, British Jews were concentrated in **London**, where a Sephardim community, originally from Spain and Portugal, had lived since being readmitted to the country by Oliver Cromwell. They engaged in **banking** and **commerce**, and grew wealthy. The early decades of the 18th century also saw the formation of an Ashkenazim community, worshipping in separate synagogues. These immigrants from Germany and Holland were generally less affluent. Many earned their living from traveling salesmanship, and the Jewish peddler became a familiar figure in the more distant parts of Britain. Over the course of time, some moved to **provincial towns**, especially ports such as **Bristol**, **Liverpool**, Portsmouth, and Plymouth. There was another community in **Dublin**, but the numbers residing in **Scotland** were very small. From these new homes the peddlers could wander the countryside selling their wares, and return to spend the Sabbath with their own people.

The Jews enjoyed freedom of worship, but suffered disabilities under two heads. A large proportion of them had been born abroad, and there was no procedure for their becoming British citizens except by a special, individual act of Parliament, an undertaking far too invidious and costly for any of them. As noncitizens, they were restricted in the extent of real property they could own, and this had an effect on both their economic and their religious position. They were forbidden to buy landed estates, and in 1743 the courts abrogated the provision of a will leaving a bequest for the foundation of a Jewish seminary. The government tried to offer some remedies under the terms of the "**Jew Act**" (1753), but opposition in the country at large caused the measure to be rescinded. While native-born children of immigrants did acquire the right to own property freely, they were still subject to the disability of exclusion from any public office, a plight not relieved until Lionel de Rothschild (1808–1879) took a seat in the **Commons** in 1858.

Meanwhile, the need to safeguard common interests prompted leading members from the Sephardim and Ashkenazim communities to start meeting together intermittently from about 1760 to discuss matters of concern. Later, men from the provincial towns were also called in. This was the origin of the Board of Deputies, the representative body of British Jewry formally constituted in 1859.

Even without the help of the law, the Jews' condition improved. They became less unpopular, to judge by literary portrayals of them. At the beginning of the 18th century, **Daniel Defoe** had depicted Jews as being vicious and corrupt; later authors did the same. But in mid century the Scottish novelist **Tobias Smollett** showed his audience a virtuous Jew, more moral than the Christians around him, as did the playwright **Richard Sheridan**. In **Sir Walter Scott's** *Ivanhoe* (1819) the Jews appear as a people who have nobly endured terrible persecution without compromising their fine qualities.

The community in any event continued to prosper. Families such as the Goldsmids and Rothschilds had risen to be among the most influential in the City of London. In contrast to their earlier position, most Jews were now native. Some, such as **Isaac D'Israeli**, had their children baptized as Christians so that they could avoid the religious disabilities, Benjamin Disraeli (1804–1881) being baptized in 1817. But among the majority unwilling to take that course, the desire for emancipation grew, stimulated by the example of revolutionary **France** and of other countries. No public move was made until after the relief of **Roman Catholics** in 1829. Even then, it was Christian politicians who took the lead: Robert Grant, M.P. for Inverness, and Thomas Babington Macaulay (1800–1859), the **Whig** historian, supported in the **House of Lords** by the Duke of Sussex, a son of **George III** and a Hebrew scholar. In 1833, the year after the first **reform act**, the Commons passed a Jewish Emancipation Bill, but it was thrown out by the Lords. There matters rested until the reign of Queen Victoria.

Michael Fry

Bibliography

Engleman, Todd M. *The Jews of Georgian England, 1714–1830: Tradition and Change in a Liberal Society.* 1979.

Roth, Cecil. *A History of the Jews in England.* 3rd ed., rev. 1964.

John Bull

This enduring **caricature** of English traits was created by a Scot, **John Arbuthnot**, in his *Law Is a Bottomless Pit* (1712), the first of a series of five pamphlets reprinted together in 1727 as *The History of John Bull.* Arising from Aesopian beast **fables**, Arbuthnot's Bull, a clothier, was "plain-dealing . . .

John Bull eating French ships, from a print by Gillray, 1798

cholerick, Bold and of a very inconstant Temper." Originally "ruddy," "plump," and a "boon companion," he grew on the drawing boards of **Gillray**, **Rowlandson**, and Isaac (1756?–1811) and **George Cruikshank** into a coarse, stout bully, defying Napoleon but often succumbing to domestic tyranny and taxation.

Both **Whigs** and **Tories** deployed the Bull figure for their own **party politics**, and gradually, as in the cartoons of John Doyle (1797–1868) during the 1820s, he matured into the conservative squire and urban citizen portrayed by John Leech (1817–1864) and later John Tenniel (1820–1914) in *Punch.* Bull was sometimes accompanied by another icon of Englishness, the bulldog; occasionally he was punningly portrayed as a bull; but conspicuously absent was Mrs. Bull. ("Goody Bull, or the Second Part of the [Stamp Act] Repeal," *c.* 1766, was a rare exception.)

By name, he first appeared in a political cartoon of 1762 attacking Scottish perfidy ("A Poor Man Loaded with Mischief, or John Bull and His Sister Peg"). That same year, John Bull died from "inadvertently swallowing a *thistle,*" the anti–Scottish print of the **periodical** the *North Briton* reported, and was butchered by **Lord Bute** in the "Caledonian Slaughter-House." But cartoon characters are immortal, and though burdened by taxes (as in "The Free-Born Briton or a Perspective of Taxation," 1788) and Scottish politicians, Bull survived to the 1790s when Gillray first portrayed him as a country bumpkin ("Alecto and Her Train, at the Gate of Pandaemonium:—or—The Recruiting Sarjeant enlisting John Bull, into the Revolution Service"). Gillray's anti–Jacobin Bull resisted the **French Revolution**; earlier (1779) he had been enlisted in the anti–**Catholic** cause and would oppose (in the 1820s) **Catholic emancipation**. Most of the time, however, Bull was portrayed as simply wanting to be left alone.

The 19th century began with **Colman the Younger**'s stage comedy *John Bull; or The Englishman's Fireside* (1803), in which Job Thornberry, an idealized mercantile Bull, recognizes the legitimacy of social classes but also demands the observance of English rights, irrespective of class; he also warns despots at home and abroad to leave him at his fireside. Bull's image was now too widely accepted for either party to relinquish claims to him. Thus he appeared simultaneously in the Tory **newspaper** *John Bull* (edited by **Theodore Hook**) and the Whigs' *Real John Bull* in 1821, to champion the causes both for and against **Queen Caroline**. Rather than representing a faction, Bull increasingly came in the early 19th century to embody the grievances of those many Englishmen who still felt politically powerless. By the time of the **Reform Act** (1832), prints and squibs signifying **middle-class** consciousness transformed him into a squire and an enfranchised citizen. Thus Arbuthnot's clothier spiraled into the Victorian man of substance.

Peter A. Tasch

Bibliography

Atherton, Herbert M. *Political Prints in the Age of Hogarth.* 1974.

Mellini, Peter, and Roy T. Matthews. "John Bull's Family Arises." *History Today.* Vol. 37, pp. 17–23.

Taylor, Miles. "John Bull and the Iconography of Public Opinion in England c. 1712–1929." *Past & Present.* No. 134, pp. 93–128.

Johnson, Samuel (1709–1784)

Journalist, critic, poet, lexicographer, biographer, translator, and conversationalist, Johnson is the most famous English writer of the Hanoverian age, so central to its spirit that the period 1740–1800 has often been called "The Age of Johnson." Despite self-accusations of indolence, his productivity was vast and various; he left scarcely any genre of writing untouched. He was lionized in his own time and, after his death, as the hero of the first modern literary **biography**, **James Boswell**'s landmark *Life of Johnson* (1791).

The brilliant but ungainly son of a Lichfield bookseller, scarred by illness and afflicted with nervous tics, Johnson fought poverty, disease, and recurrent depression throughout much of his life. Forced by lack of funds to withdraw from Pembroke College, Oxford, after only 14 months (1729), he tried schoolteaching before turning to writing in the 1730s, producing a **translation** of Father Lobo's *Voyage to Abysinnia* (1735) and moving to **London** (1737) to begin 16 years of prolific but low-paid writing for the *Gentleman's Magazine.*

Two long poems, both imitations of Juvenal, established his reputation: *London* (1738), an angry poem that attracted **Alexander Pope**'s approval; and *The Vanity of Human Wishes* (1749), more mature and accomplished, in which Johnson set

At the club: Goldsmith, Boswell, and Johnson

out a vision of human desire and discontent. Had he written nothing else, according to T.S. Eliot, he would still rank as a major English poet. Ironically, Johnson attached his highest hopes to his verse tragedy, *Irene,* which, although staged (1749), proved a disappointment.

Despite the deaths of his wife Tetty (1752) and his mother (1759), the 1750s were Johnson's most productive decade. In 1750–1752 his twice-weekly *Rambler* **essays** included short fiction (both realistic first-person narratives and **oriental** tales), critical discussions (of **Milton**, Shakespeare, **poetics**, and the **novel**), and psychologically insightful pieces on everyday life and human problems (marriage, adolescence, avocations, boredom, self-delusion). Often considered his masterpiece, the *Rambler* has been reprinted in hundreds of editions and excerpted in innumerable schoolbooks and anthologies.

Johnson's *Dictionary of the English Language* (1755), the culmination of 8-years' work, transformed lexicography. Noted particularly for its illustrative quotations, the *Dictionary* held sway for more than a century and exerted enormous influence on both Noah Webster's (1758–1843) American dictionaries and James Murray's (1837–1915) *Oxford English Dictionary.* By contrast, Johnson wrote his oriental tale about the search for happiness, *Rasselas* (1759), in a week. For its transcendent questioning and unsentimental wisdom, *Rasselas,* which has been translated into more than 100 languages, has been popular across cultures and over time. Johnson in the 1750s produced other **periodical** writing, including contributions to the *Adventurer* (1753–1754), the *Literary Magazine* (1756–1757), and all of the *Idler* (1758–1760).

Johnson's edition of *The Works of Shakespeare* (1765) marked a new era in Shakespeare criticism and a new step in the **Shakespeare industry**, helping to rehabilitate the national bard. His Preface not only urged common sense and audience-centered criticism over such abstract formalist standards as the three unities, it also encouraged first-time readers to ignore the footnotes as they read. Meanwhile a royal **pension**, awarded for services to literature, eased his financial exigencies (1762). Honorary doctoral degrees followed, from **Trinity College, Dublin** (1765), and **Oxford** (1775). Apart from such provocative political pamphlets as *The False Alarm* (1770) and *Taxation No Tyranny* (1775), which indicted the hypocrisy of Americans "yelping" for freedom while still holding slaves, Johnson's next major work was *A Journey to the Western Isles of Scotland* (1775), which, despite its mixture of appreciation and criticism, offended many Scots.

The Lives of the Poets (1779–1781), originally conceived as "prefaces biographical and critical" to the works of 52 English poets in a commercial anthology, crowned Johnson's achievements. Overshadowing the texts they were meant to complement, these prefaces contained some of Johnson's greatest **literary criticism**, established literary biography as a genre, and set a mark against which criticism has measured itself from **Coleridge** up to the present.

The central figure in Hanoverian literary life, Johnson

included among his friends **Goldsmith**, **Burke**, **Reynolds**, **Richardson**, **Garrick**, the **Burneys**, **Charlotte Lennox**, **Arthur Murphy**, **John Hawkins**, and Hester Thrale Piozzi (1741–1821)—the last three of whom also wrote biographies of him. He was notorious for his contradictoriness: his rudeness and his kindness, his ferocity in conversation and charity to the unfortunate, his critical authoritarianism and alliance with the common reader, his purported misogyny and support of women's causes, his **Tory** conservatism and opposition to **slavery**. It was partly because of his penetration and intellectual courage, even if he contradicted himself, that he became legendary and perhaps ultimately incorporated somehow into the great national myth of **John Bull**. His influence continues to be felt in the shape of our language and literary canon, our practices in journalism, criticism, and biography, and our reflections on human nature.

James G. Basker

Bibliography

Bate, W.J. *The Achievement of Samuel Johnson.* 1955.
———. *Samuel Johnson.* 1977.
Boswell, James. *The Life of Johnson.* G.B. Hill and L.F. Powell, eds. 6 vols. 1934–1964.
Cannon, John. *Samuel Johnson and the Politics of Hanoverian England.* 1995.
Clark, J.C.D. *Samuel Johnson: Literature, Religion and English Cultural Politics from the Restoration to Romanticism.* 1995.
Clifford, J.L., and D.J. Greene. *Samuel Johnson: A Survey and Bibliography of Critical Studies.* 1970. Suppl. by D.J. Greene and J.A. Vance. *A Bibliography of Johnsonian Studies 1970–85.* 1987.
Courtney, W.P., and D. Nichol Smith. *A Bibliography of Samuel Johnson.* 1915; rpt. 1968.
Gerrard, Christine. *The Patriot Opposition to Walpole: Politics, Poetry, and National Myth, 1725–1742.* 1995.
Greene, D.J. *Samuel Johnson.* 1989.
Johnson, Samuel. *The Letters.* B. Redford, ed. 5 vols. 1992–1994.
———. *The Yale Edition of the Works of Johnson.* 1958–.
Korshin, P.J., ed. *The Age of Johnson: A Scholarly Annual.* 1988–.
Sherman, Stuart, ed. *The Johnsonian Newsletter.* 1941–.

See also Language and Linguistics; Reference Works

Joint-Stock Companies

A joint-stock company is one in which the capital is divided into units known as stock, or shares, which are easily transferable from one owner to another. Such organizations have become essential in business concerns where the amount of capital required is too great for a single trader or small partnership to raise. Historically, such organizations began to emerge in Britain with the formation of **chartered trading companies** such as the **East India Company** in the early 17th century, when the length of voyages and the complexity of the trade began requiring a spreading of risks. The need by the government to mobilize significant amounts of capital led also to the formation of monied joint-stock companies such as the **Bank of England** (1694) and the **South Sea Company** (1711), both of which lent much of their capital to the government.

Other business concerns began to consider the possibilities of joint-stock organization, but a promotional boom in the 1690s soon petered out. In the years following the end of the **War of Spanish Succession** (1713), a reduction in government debt and borrowing released a flow of funds into the economy. The relatively limited outlets for such monies contributed to an upsurge in the promotion of speculative ventures of all kinds after 1718, culminating in the **South Sea Bubble**. In this financial disaster, the South Sea Company in 1720 submitted proposals to the government to convert a considerable part of the national debt into company stock. In June of that year, however, fearful that other ventures were draining capital away from its scheme, the company persuaded the government to pass the Bubble Act, which suppressed all unauthorized companies floated since 1718. Henceforth all such organizations would require official approval. This, together with the collapse of the Bubble later the same year—which ruined many investors—left joint-stock companies with a somewhat dubious reputation.

Some historians have claimed that failure to repeal the Bubble Act until 1825 hindered the development of the British business corporation in the latter 18th century. But in fact, many of the innovations that occurred in **textiles** and other industries during the Hanoverian period were far better suited to investment by individuals and small groups in the traditional manner, without benefit of joint-stock organization. Where large-scale investment, beyond the capacities of the individual businessman or partnership, was needed, for example in **canals**, companies successfully petitioned the government, and joint-stock incorporation was granted. However, each individual application had to be approved in the form of a private act of Parliament, and this could be a costly business; hence the reluctance of smaller concerns to seek this form of organization. But the success of canal companies led to **railway** companies proceeding in the same manner, and shares in both, together with those in chartered and monied companies and government securities, formed the basis of nascent stock exchanges. However, it was only later in the Victorian era that joint-stock organization became widespread in British industry.

A.J.G. Cummings

Bibliography

Du Bois, A.B. *The English Business Company after the Bubble Act 1720–1800.* Rpt. 1971.
Scott, W.R. *The Constitution and Finance of English, Scottish and Irish Joint Stock Companies to 1720.* 3 vols. Rpt. 1968.

Jones, Griffith (1683–1761)

Jones made a major contribution to the development of **Welsh education** and the propagation of the Welsh language. His interest in education dated from 1713, when he became a Welsh corresponding member of the **Society for Promoting**

Christian Knowledge (SPCK). In 1716 he was appointed Rector of the parish of Llanddowror in South **Wales**, and from this base he developed his **radical** and controversial policies.

Jones's ideas took a more concrete shape during the 1730s when he introduced a system of **circulating schools** teaching Welsh reading only. This attempt to inculcate mass literacy in the people's native tongue was, for him, a means to an end: the evangelization of the Welsh population. His intention to extend his schools to the whole of rural Wales was hampered at the outset by a lack of suitable books in the Welsh language. In response to this need, the SPCK published 15,000 Welsh Bibles in 1746. By the time of Jones's death (1761), the circulating school movement had penetrated every Welsh county and helped educate some 158,000 Welsh readers. Jones's itinerant preaching and teaching, and his identification with the Welsh language, made him a very important figure also in the **Welsh religious revival**.

Lawrence Williams

Bibliography

Clement, Mary. *The S.P.C.K. and Wales, 1699–1740.* 1954.

Jones, M.G. *The Charity School Movement in the Eighteenth Century.* 1938.

Kelly, Thomas. *Griffith Jones, Llanddowror, Pioneer in Adult Education.* 1950.

See also Education, Elementary

Jones, Sir William (1746–1794)

Jones was a scholar and jurist who encouraged the study of Asian cultures and helped to revolutionize the science of linguistics. Born the son of a Welsh mathematician living in **London**, he studied at Harrow and **Oxford**. He became a classical scholar and learned French, Italian, Hebrew, Arabic, and Persian. In 1774 he became a barrister; in 1783 he received a knighthood and became a justice of Calcutta's supreme court.

Jones spent the remainder of his life in India. In 1784 he founded the Royal Asiatic Society of Bengal in order to encourage **oriental** studies. He continued to study languages, of which he had learned 28 by his death. In 1786 he proposed the common ancestry of Sanskrit and Europe's classical languages.

Jones's publications influenced the studies of both law and language. His *Essay on the Law of Bailments* (1781) was used in Britain and America; his *Institutes of Hindu Law* (1794) provided valuable insights for British rulers in India. His *Grammar of the Persian Language* (1771) remained an authority for decades. But his greatest contributions were the worldwide attention that he brought to Asian cultures, and his participation in the foundation of comparative linguistics.

A. Martin Wainwright

Bibliography

Cannon, Garland Hampton. *The Life and Mind of Oriental Jones: Sir William Jones, the Father of Modern Linguistics.* 1990.

Kopf, David. *British Orientalism and the Bengal Renaissance: The Dynamics of Indian Modernization, 1773–1834.* 1969.

Mukherjee, S.N. *Sir William Jones: A Study in Eighteenth Century British Attitudes to India.* 1968.

Singh, Jenarden. *Sir William Jones: His Mind and Art.* 1982.

See also India; Language and Linguistics; Learned Societies

Journalists and Journalism

During the 18th century, journalism as a profession struggled for identity, respect, and maturity that it would not achieve until the middle of the 19th century. Such literary figures as **Smollett**, **Henry Fielding**, **Johnson**, **Garrick**, **Goldsmith**, **Chesterfield**, **Horace Walpole**, **Hazlitt**, **Charles Lamb**, and **Leigh Hunt** plentifully contributed to **newspapers** and **periodical** magazines, and a number of them even spent time as paid "staffers" of those publications. However, none would have desired to be considered journalists or what **William Pulteney** termed "contemptible scribblers" and "low drudges of scurrility."

Though most journalists were indeed obscure inhabitants of **Grub Street**, they worked hard, often receiving subsidies from the political parties, to popularize information and reduce important issues to terms understandable by unsophisticated readers. But in the face of **censorship** and **party politics**, some journalism, such as the reporting of parliamentary debates, was forced to become a creative exercise. In the 1750s both the *London Magazine* and the *Gentleman's Magazine,* for example, fictionalized their reports from Westminster by portraying them as discussions and "reprinted" reports from mythical **clubs** and governing bodies.

Journalism as a profession was not yet well defined. It still embraced more highbrow literary activity. Johnson's first tenure (1737–1739) with **Edward Cave** at the *Gentleman's Magazine* illustrates the multifarious roles of a periodical magazine journalist at that time. He judged verse submitted to **poetry** competitions, selected extracts from books for reprinting, composed Latin verse to adorn the magazine with a classical motif, wrote prefaces for its collected volume (1738), prepared a four-installment **biography** of the Dutch physician Hermann Boerhaave, and wrote biographies and prepared **translations** that Cave published in the *Magazine* or separately under his own imprint.

If literary and political news were primary, the stage was not far behind. In the words of one historian of the **theater**, "Newspaper puffery of every possible kind was advanced long before organized **dramatic criticism** secured a foothold." Players and managers plied journalists with money in one hand, and, in the other, their own favorable advertisements and reviews, hoping to attract audiences, extend runs, and increase profits. Thus **Horace Walpole** never seriously considered newspaper praise of **David Garrick**'s roles or productions, knowing that the actor had very probably written the copy himself. The press did perform a service by printing playbills, particularly those of Drury Lane and Covent Garden, but it was not until late in the 18th century that journalists began publishing their own critical accounts, objective notices of new productions and important revivals, and evaluations of actors' performances. Magazines like the *Universal Museum* and the *London Magazine* joined such newspapers as the *Public Advertiser* in offering more reliable reviews. By the time of **the Regency**, the dramatic criticism of a journalist such as Hazlitt was a thoroughly professional undertaking.

Despite social contempt, political attacks, and official attempts to influence, **tax**, or suppress them, journalists managed to survive and to sustain a relatively high degree of independence. Their numbers multiplied tremendously during the period. In 1724, professional journalists worked for three daily, 10 thrice-weekly, and five weekly newspapers in **London** alone. An advertisement in the initial number of the *Gentleman's Magazine* (1731) maintained that "no less than 200 half-sheets per month are thrown from the press, only in London, and about as many as printed elsewhere in the three kingdoms." By 1760, nearly every major **provincial town** published one paper. By the early 19th century, many cities published more than one, and newspapers had generally become very large and very full of diverse information. Thus, wrote the Victorian historian W.E.H. Lecky, "without any great change in education, any display of extraordinary genius, any real enthusiasm for knowledge," journalism eventually contributed to expanding the "circle of intelligence."

Samuel J. Rogal

Bibliography

Black, Jeremy. *The English Press in the Eighteenth Century.* 1987.

Harris, Michael, and Alan J. Lee. *The Press in English Society from the Seventeenth Century to the Nineteenth Century.* 1986.

Smith, David Nichol. "The Newspaper," in A.S. Turberville, ed., *Johnson's England.* Vol. 2. 1933.

See also Laws of Public Worship, Speech, and the Press; Newspaper Press

Judicial System

The judicial system of Hanoverian Britain has attracted considerable scholarly attention since the 1970s as a test case for examination of the ways in which law and the courts contributed to the political stability so characteristic of the 18th century after the upheavals of the Stuart period.

Was stability achieved, in part, by a judicial system that acted as an instrument of social control? Some scholars have argued that the tremendous 18th-century increase in capital **punishment**, especially for crimes against property, indicated the fear that separated the governing elite from the great mass of ordinary citizens. Yet the actual frequency of capital punishment under this harsh code was comparatively rare: control emanated more from the prospect than the actual infliction of judicial punishment. This does not diminish the fact that the judicial system derived its legitimacy ultimately from a monopoly on coercion. But interest in these problems should not obscure the role played by the judiciary in the area of private law.

The Hanoverian system of criminal justice differed in substantial respects from other systems in use today. For example, it was usually the victim of a **crime**, not a representative of the state, who brought about the indictment and prosecution of an alleged culprit. What crimes were punished often depended on the resources available to the victim. Thus the notion that social control rested on fear must be qualified by recognition that the state rarely intervened on its own. Moreover, statistics on criminal prosecutions indicate that few cases arose from incidents involving conflict between upper-class individuals and persons from other social groups. The preponderance of victims who chose to prosecute their tormentors rose from the "middling sort" and even poorer classes. Trials rarely lasted for more than a few hours, and often were over within an hour. There was no general right of a defendant to counsel, and the rules of evidence usually barred testimony from anyone familiar with the case.

In other respects, however, the criminal justice system functioned in familiar ways. Serious crimes, which carried the death penalty, were tried at county assizes by royal judges twice a year. Offenses in this category included homicide, rape, robbery, and arson. Lesser offenses were heard at the quarter sessions, which met four times a year under presiding justices of the peace. At these proceedings such crimes as assault, fraud, **riot**, and petty larceny were tried. If judged by the ability to deter crime, the Hanoverian criminal justice system may be regarded as a distinct failure. Concerns about the high incidence of crime, especially of crimes against property, were a major theme of public policy debate. The failure to ensure social stability gave rise to incremental changes in the criminal law, and the philosophy of punishment evolved. Substitution of incarceration in **prisons** for capital punishment had made significant progress by 1837. Recognition of the inefficacy of capital punishment gave rise to acceptance of alternative methods of punishment and the securing of public safety. The certainty of punishment, not its harshness, became the prevailing principle behind the criminal code.

In the area of private law, fundamental changes in the law resulted from judges operating within the traditional framework of judicial legislation. It might be argued, therefore, that civil litigation remained more in harmony with Hanoverian social change than the criminal justice system. Hanoverian economic evolution necessitated many changes affecting **banking, insurance, patents, finance and investment**, and the like. Perhaps the most famous example of a creative judge was **Lord Mansfield**, whose contributions to commercial and maritime law modernized those sectors of the law and shaped legal doctrines for many decades. Mansfield epitomized a judicial flexibility that adapted customary doctrines to new social and economic requirements by thoughtful reinterpretation of the law. In contract and tort law, Mansfield left an indelible impression upon the law's future evolution.

Other parts of the law such as equity and the civilian jurisdictions of maritime, probate, and matrimonial law languished in relative unimportance except during special periods that touched them closely. The **French Revolutionary and Napoleonic Wars**, for example, saw prize law become a major topic of legal discussion. Whatever conclusions might be drawn about the operation of the Hanoverian judicial system, it must be remembered that the ordinary citizen had no doubts about the validity, and indeed superiority, of the constitutional tradition in which he or she lived. The judicial system, despite questions about its administration, constituted a significant part of the **Glorious Constitution** that was the envy of many Continental observers. And whatever its defects, the system was strengthened by the reaction against the **French Revolution**; it survived in substantial form until the impact of Victorian legal reform changed many of its elements.

Richard A. Cosgrove

Bibliography

Beattie, J.M. *Crime and the Courts in England, 1660–1800.* 1986.

Brewer, John, and John Styles, eds. *An Ungovernable People: The English and Their Law in the Seventeenth and Eighteenth Centuries.* 1980.

Cockburn, J.S., ed. *Crime in England, 1550–1800.* 1977.

Gatrell, V.A.C. *The Hanging Tree: Execution and the English People, 1770–1868.* 1994.

Hay, Douglas, Peter Linebaugh, and E.P. Thompson, eds. *Albion's Fatal Tree: Crime and Society in Eighteenth-Century England.* 1975.

Landau, Norma. *The Justices of the Peace, 1679–1760.* 1984.

Linebaugh, Peter. *The London Hanged: Crime and Civil Society in the Eighteenth Century.* 1992.

McLynn, Frank. *Crime and Punishment in Eighteenth-Century England.* 1991.

Thompson, E.P. *Whigs and Hunters: The Origin of the Black Act.* 1975.

See also Aristocracy and Gentry; Black Act; Cockburn, Henry; Erskine, Baron; Government, Local and County; Hardwicke, Earl of; Legal Profession; Lords, House of; Macqueen, Robert, Lord Braxfield; Romilly, Sir Samuel; Scottish Legal System

Junius

Junius (a pseudonym) was the author of a series of satirical letters, written from the **Whig** standpoint, that appeared in the **London newspaper** the *Public Advertiser* between 1769 and 1772, and that helped to bring down the **Grafton** administration (January 1770). The letters attacked many members of the government as well as **George III**, the subject of Junius's unflinching invective, and avidly supported **John Wilkes**, a key reformer and the central figure in contemporary political controversy.

Junius was probably Sir Philip Francis (1740–1818), despite his denials. The son of a schoolmaster, he clerked in the War Office from 1762 to 1772, then was appointed one of four councillors to help rule British **India** under **Warren Hastings**, the Governor-General. Francis disagreed with Hastings on many issues and was at last wounded by him in a duel (1780), after which he left India, wrote still more anonymous pamphlets, entered Parliament (1784), and assisted **Edmund Burke** in preparing the charges that eventually led to Hastings's impeachment (1788).

The search for Junius's identity—which recently has included computer-assisted stylistic analysis—has yet to be resolved definitively. Whoever he was, Junius was a satirist of unusual power.

Robin Nilon

Bibliography

Cordasco, Francesco. *A Junius Bibliography.* 1974.

Ellegard, Alvar. *Who Was Junius?* 1962.

McCracken, David. *Junius and Philip Francis.* 1979.

Justices of the Peace

See Government, Local and County

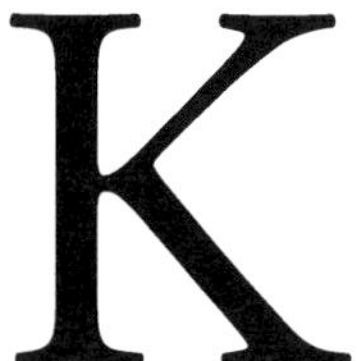

Kames, Lord (Henry Home) (1696–1782)

Home, philosopher and judge, was a prolific writer whose publications ranged into epistemology, **moral** philosophy, aesthetics, jurisprudence, and **agricultural improvement**. He was not a philosopher of the first rank, yet he epitomized the aggressive and wide-ranging intellectual culture that has come to be termed the **Scottish Enlightenment**. His most notable publications include *Essays on the Principles of Morality and Natural Religion* (1751), *Historical Law Tracts* (1758), *Principles of Equity* (1760), and *Sketches of the History of Man* (1774). His lengthy *Elements of Criticism* (1762), which contains a philosophy of aesthetics defining beauty in terms of simple visual and aural pleasure, received greatest contemporary acclaim and continues to sustain critical scrutiny.

Born in Eccles, a parish in the eastern Scottish borders, he was educated first at home and then in **Edinburgh** for the Scottish bar. In 1752 he was appointed to the Court of Session and assumed the title, Lord Kames. In 1763 he was appointed to the High Court of Justiciary, **Scotland**'s highest criminal court. Most of his writings were devoted to the problem of rationalizing Scots law, which he believed had become inadequate to the social needs of a commercial society. A philosophical optimist, he invariably considered humanity's moral and social nature in terms of the operation and advancement of civil society.

Peter J. Diamond

Lord Kames

Bibliography

Lehmann, William C. *Henry Home, Lord Kames, and the Scottish Enlightenment.* 1971.

Lieberman, David. "The Legal Needs of a Commercial Society: The Jurisprudence of Lord Kames," in Istvan Hont and Michael Ignatieff, eds., *Wealth and Virtue: The Shaping of Political Economy in the Scottish Enlightenment.* 1983.

McGuinness, Arthur E. *Henry Home, Lord Kames.* 1970.

Ross, Ian Simpson. *Lord Kames and the Scotland of His Day.* 1972.

Wokkler, Robert. "Apes and Race in the Scottish Enlightenment: Monboddo and Kames on the Nature of Man," in Peter Jones, ed., *Philosophy and Science in the Scottish Enlightenment.* 1988.

See also Law Reform; Scottish Legal System

Kay, John (1704–1781)

Kay, a mechanical genius, was an unappreciated revolutionary of the **textile industry**. He was the inventor of the fly (or "flying") shuttle, for centuries the most significant improvement to the handloom. He served an apprenticeship to a reed maker at Bury in Lancashire, later establishing his own business. While working in Colchester he enrolled **patents** for carding and roving mohair and **worsted** (1730), and for the fly shuttle (1733), which enabled the weaver to shoot the shuttle back and forth with only one hand. Although this doubled productivity with no more expenditure of energy, it was only slowly adopted because of weavers' resistance to paying the small royalty Kay asked.

Disappointed, in 1747 he went to **France**, patenting the fly shuttle and the fixed cone bobbin with government support. However, French weavers treated him no differently than English. He made several trips back to Bury, but in 1753 a machine-breaking mob entered his Bury home and smashed his furniture and loom, causing him to settle permanently in France, where he died a poor man. Few labor-saving devices have been received with such bad grace as Kay's shuttle.

John Butt

Bibliography

English, Walter. *The Textile Industry.* 1969.

Lord, John. *Memoir of John Kay.* 1903.

Wadsworth, A.P., and Julia de L. Mann. *The Cotton Trade and Industrial Lancashire, 1600–1780.* 1931.

See also Spinning and Weaving

Kean, Edmund (1787?–1833)

Kean was the most influential actor of his day. Although he claimed that his father was the duke of Norfolk and that he had attended Eton, he actually was illegitimate, and was raised by his uncle's mistress. He performed a number of small parts and played Harlequin in the provinces before making a triumphant appearance as Shylock at Drury Lane (1814), after which he established himself as the greatest actor of the time. He eventually ruined his career through irresponsibility, alcoholism, and sexual escapades.

Kean's greatest accomplishment was his influence on acting styles. In the 1740s **David Garrick** had introduced a naturalistic acting style, but another actor, John Philip Kemble (1757–1823), had helped turn practices back toward the stiffer and more formal style that had been in vogue earlier. Kean reversed this by giving performances that radiated emotional energy. He gave a sense of actually being the character and feeling the character's emotions, rather than performing in the declamatory tradition. He portrayed Shakespearean figures such as Hamlet, Macbeth, and Richard III in such a way that commentators believed he was bringing them to life for the first time. **Coleridge** reported that seeing Kean act was "like reading Shakespeare by flashes of lightning."

Edmund Kean as Richard III

Kean was also one of a growing number of British actors who toured America. He was popular during his first tour (1820–1821), but his refusal to perform to a small audience in Boston caused the first recorded theater riot in the United States; undismayed, he undertook a second tour in 1825. His influence on acting in general and the interpretation of Shakespearean characters in particular was immense. He was also important because people saw in his life a pattern for the myth of the misunderstood genius and social misfit.

Brent Chesley

Bibliography

Fitzsimons, Raymund. *Edmund Kean.* 1976.

Playfair, Giles. *Kean.* 1939.

Taylor, Gary. *Reinventing Shakespeare.* 1989.

Woods, Leigh. "Actors' Biography and Mythmaking: The Example of Edmund Kean," in Thomas Postlewait and Bruce A. McConachie, eds., *Interpreting the Theatrical Past.* 1989.

See also Actors and the Acting Profession; Shakespeare Industry

Keats, John (1795–1821)

Many readers have been attracted to Keats's poetry by the pathos of the life that produced it. Born in **London** and orphaned early on, he trained for the medical profession but soon decided to devote himself entirely to **poetry**. Because of his humble birth, the weakness of his early verse, and his championing of **radical** poet and **journalist Leigh Hunt**, his early poems were savaged by the **Tory** critics of the **Regency** (1818). Falling madly in love with Fanny Brawne but desponding over the onset of his tuberculosis, and hoping vainly to retrieve his health in a warmer climate, he **traveled** to Italy (1820) but died a few months later. He was buried in Rome, under a stone bearing the legend, "Here lies one whose name was writ in water."

Keats's first volume, *Poems* (1817), mainly contained unremarkable exercises in traditional forms: sonnets, verse epistles, declamatory odes, meditations, and fragmentary attempts at verse romance. But "Sleep and Poetry," a meditation on poetry itself, announced a program of disciplined self-development intended to culminate in a noble poetry on "the agonies, the strife / Of human hearts"; and the sonnet "On First Looking into Chapman's Homer" startlingly foreshadowed the rich associational compression of his brief **poetic** maturity.

Keats's second volume, *Endymion* (1818), was a 4,000-line verse romance concerning the shepherd of Greek mythology who was loved by the moon goddess. Although clearly intended to portray some scheme of human values, the poem's meaning is uncertain, and while brilliant in brief passages, it suffers from diffuseness and a problematic ending. Keats's final volume, *Lamia, Isabella, The Eve of St. Agnes, and other Poems* (1820), contains almost all the poems by which his name still lives. Notable were the richly wrought verse romances named in the volume's title; the two epic "Hyperion" fragments, no doubt originally intended to fulfill the program announced in "Sleep and Poetry"; and the six "great odes," in which Keats hauntingly explored the farthest reaches of experience and understanding. About 250 of his **letters** also survive, providing one of the fullest revelations of personal character and commitment that we have from any poet.

Despite Keats's liberal humanism, earlier criticism praised his poetry for its craftsmanship while often dismissing its content as escapist. There was a tendency to think of him only as the great pioneer of "art for art's sake," teaching (as he did in the "Ode on a Grecian Urn") that "Beauty is truth, truth beauty,—that is all ye know on earth, and all ye need to know." He did believe that everyday affections "proved upon our pulses" were the surest guides to happiness, but modern criticism also finds in his exotic and mythic poetry an imaginative displacement of real social and political concerns whose inner relations can be contemplated more justly *because* of their removal from contemporary associations. This may help to explain why his sumptuous imagery, imaginative intensity, unwavering libertarianism, and unassuming decency have made him one of the most universally loved English poets.

Walter H. Evert

Bibliography

Evert, Walter H., and Jack W. Rhodes, eds. *Approaches to Teaching Keats's Poetry.* 1991.

Gittings, Robert. *John Keats.* 1968.

Rollins, Hyder Edward, ed. *The Letters of John Keats, 1814–1821.* 1958.

Sperry, Stuart M. *Keats the Poet.* 1973.

Stillinger, Jack, ed. *The Poems of John Keats.* 1978.

Waldoff, Leon. *Keats and the Silent Work of Imagination.* 1985.

Watkins, Daniel P. *Keats's Poetry and the Politics of the Imagination.* 1989.

Wolfson, Susan J. *The Questioning Presence: Wordsworth, Keats, and the Interrogative Mode in Romantic Poetry.* 1986.

See also Literary Criticism; Lockhart, John Gibson; Romanticism and Romantic Style

Kelly, Hugh (1739–1777)

Kelly, a popular dramatist, came to **London** from **Ireland** in 1760. He became clerk to an attorney before becoming a **journalist** writing for **Lord North** (and thereby incurring the enmity of the supporters of **John Wilkes**). He also published a popular **novel**, *Memoirs of a Magdalen, or the History of Louisa Mildmay* (1767).

Kelly achieved early theatrical fame through the production of the sentimental comedy *The False Delicacy* (1768) at Drury Lane. The play, produced also in Paris and Lisbon, brought him an international reputation. His next comedy, *A Word to the Wise* (1770), sparked rioting by the supporters of Wilkes, who succeeded in halting its production on the second night. Kelly palmed off subsequent plays as the work of others, and in that way received a fair hearing for them. *The School for Wives* (1773), purporting to be by a Captain William Addington, was markedly successful.

Kelly's satiric poem *Thespis; or, A Critical Examination into the Merits of All the Principal Performers Belonging to Drury Lane Theatre* (1766), and a sequel examining Covent Garden, brought him many theatrical enemies. He turned unsuccessfully to a legal career before his death.

Richard J. Dircks

Bibliography

Bevis, Richard W. *The Laughing Tradition.* 1980.

Carrer, L., ed. *The Plays of Hugh Kelly.* 1980.

Rawson, C.J. "Some Remarks on Eighteenth-Century Delicacy." *Journal of English and Germanic Philology.* Vol. 61, pp. 1–13.

Schorer, M. "Hugh Kelly: His Place in the Sentimental School." *Philological Quarterly.* Vol. 12, pp. 398–401.

See also Dramatic Arts

Kemble, Charles (1775–1854)

Actor, theater manager, and minor playwright, Kemble was the eleventh child of a remarkable theatrical family. Youngest brother of **Sarah Kemble Siddons** and John Philip Kemble (1757–1823), he served a long apprenticeship in their shadow before achieving recognition as a leading actor in both Britain and the United States. He excelled in youthful or supporting roles—Benedick, Mercutio, Faulconbridge, Mirabell, Jaffier, Charles Surface among them—but received less favorable reviews for his Hamlet and Romeo, partly because of vocal inadequacy and excessive formality. His daughter, Frances Anne (Fanny) Kemble (1809–1893), played Juliet to his Mercutio at Covent Garden (1829) and appeared with him in a variety of other parts. Her *Records of a Later Life* (1882) show her discernment of his weaknesses as well as her loyalty and appreciation of his strengths.

As manager of Covent Garden Theatre (1822–1832 and 1842), Kemble encountered legal and financial difficulties yet managed to mount spectacular performances of such classics as Shakespeare's *King John* (1823) and *The Tempest* (1842), in which he even utilized a real ship for the storm scene. He wrote 10 plays, mainly **translations** or adaptations, of which *The Point of Honour* (1800), based on Louis Sébastien Mercier's (1740–1814) *Le Déserteur,* was the most acclaimed.

James Gray

Bibliography

Donne, William Bodham. *Essays on the Drama.* 1858.

Doran, [John]. *"Their Majesties' Servants": Annals of the English Stage from Thomas Betterton to Edmund Kean,* ed. Robert W. Lowe. 3 vols. 1888.

Williamson, Jane. *Charles Kemble, Man of the Theatre.* 1970.

See also Actors and the Acting Profession; Shakespeare Industry

Kent, William (1685–1748)

Kent's varied career covered a wide range of artistic activity. He was not only an accomplished architect in the **Palladian style** but also one of the first architects to undertake **interior design** in order to achieve unified effects. He was also a designer and **painter** of landscapes and history scenes, a **book illustrator**, a stage designer, and one of the most outstanding garden designers and **landscape architects** of his age. He was involved in creating such famous gardens as Rousham (in Oxfordshire, 1738–1741) for Lt. General James Dormer, and Stowe (in Buckinghamshire, 1730s) for Richard Temple, **Lord Cobham**.

Born in Yorkshire, Kent traveled to Italy in 1709, where he studied painting for 10 years and exhibited remarkable abilities. While there he met many traveling gentlemen who later became his **patrons**, such as Thomas Coke (*d.* 1759), the future earl of Leicester, and **Richard Boyle, Earl of Burlington**, with whom he returned to England in 1719.

In **London**, Kent first worked at Burlington House, completing the mythological cycle left unfinished by Sebastiano Ricci, and later worked at Chiswick House, Middlesex, the exterior of which had been designed by Burlington himself in 1725. From about 1727 the interior and much of the furniture was the work of Kent. He also designed parts of the gardens as well as the structures in them, including an obelisk and a gateway.

Through Burlington's influence Kent obtained a post in the Office of Works, and decorated major rooms for **George I** at Kensington Palace (1721–1727), including a *trompe l'oeil* coffered dome ceiling in the Cupola Room, a brightly colored grotteschi ceiling inspired by ancient and Renaissance examples in the Presence Chamber, and the walls and ceiling of the King's Staircase. In 1727 he was made inspector of paintings at the Royal Palace and restored P.P. Rubens's (1577–1640) ceiling in the Banqueting House of Whitehall Palace. For Hampton Court Palace he designed in 1732 the East Range of the Clock Court in a Tudor Gothic style, a change from his usual Palladian mode, no doubt to harmonize with the earlier parts of the palace. That same year he designed an elaborate royal barge for **Frederick, Prince of Wales**. Later in 1739 he was made portrait painter to the king, succeeding Charles Jervas. Other aristocratic commissions followed.

As at Chiswick, Kent was asked to design the interiors and much of the furniture at **Sir Robert Walpole**'s country house, Houghton Hall, Norfolk (1726–1731), which had recently been built by Colen Campbell (1676–1729). Even more impressive was Holkham Hall, Norfolk, for Thomas Coke, now Earl of Leicester. Here Kent, with the collaboration of the earl and Lord Burlington, designed the house and its elaborate interiors, as well as garden pavilions and monu-

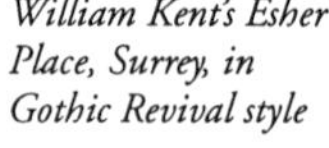

William Kent's Esher Place, Surrey, in Gothic Revival style

ments. Most of these were executed with modifications by Matthew Brettingham (1699–1769), beginning in 1734.

Kent's design for the Treasury (London, 1734–1736) was only partly executed, and perhaps his most impressive building, the Horse Guards, London, was not built until 1750–1758 by John Vardy (*d.* 1765), after Kent's death. Both Holkham and the Horse Guards, while neo-Palladian in style, have little of the dryness and dullness associated with that movement. Perhaps Kent's background as a theatrical designer accounts for this, just as **John Vanbrugh**'s experience as a dramatist may have influenced his architecture also. Kent's Worcester Lodge at Badminton House (in Gloucestershire, 1740s), for the earl of Beaufort is even more vigorous in its composition and juxtaposition of rusticated and smooth stone.

Kent designed outstanding gardens, which included a variety of monuments and pavilions, all inspired to some extent by ancient and modern Italian precedents, and by more recent Italian and French painters. Kent also designed funerary monuments in Westminster Abbey and found time to work on various book illustrations. In 1727 his edition of the *Designs of Inigo Jones* was published, and his illustrations appeared in two volumes of **John Gay**'s *Poems* (1720), and *Fables* (1727). His illustrations for Spencer's *Faerie Queene* were published in 1751 after his death.

Though extraordinary for the variety of his artistic activities, Kent is best remembered and had his greatest contemporary influence as a designer of rich interiors and **home furnishings**, and as the creator of idyllic gardens filled with architectural points of interest.

Thomas J. McCormick

Bibliography

Clarke, G.B., ed. *Descriptions of Lord Cobham's Gardens at Stowe (1700–1750).* 1990.

Colvin, H.M. *A Biographical Dictionary of English Architects, 1660–1840.* 2nd ed., 1978.

Croft-Murray, Edward. *Decorative Painting in England, 1537–1837.* 2 vols. 1962–1970.

Hunt, John Dixon. *William Kent, Landscape Designer.* 1987.

Jourdain, Margaret. *The Work of William Kent, Artist, Painter, Designer and Landscape Gardener.* 1945.

Wilson, Michael I. *William Kent, Architect, Designer, Painter, Gardener 1685–1748.* 1984.

See also Architects and Architecture

King George's War

See War of the Austrian Succession

Kneller, Sir Godfrey (1646/9–1723)

Kneller was the dominant and most prolific **portrait painter** of late Stuart England. His innovative format (the "kit-cat") and painterly style greatly influenced his Hanoverian successors. Born Gottfried Kniller in Lübeck of a well-to-do family, he studied in Amsterdam with Ferdinand Bol (1616–1680), a student of Rembrandt (1606–1669), and possibly with Rembrandt himself. Further study in Rome and Venice contributed to the growth of his own sober and sincere portrait style.

Kneller arrived in England around 1676, already an experienced painter. He quickly established a court career and managed to retain royal favor through five English reigns, including that of **George I**, who bestowed a baronetcy upon him in 1715. (He was knighted by William III in 1692.) His great gift was his ability to capture a likeness. His experience abroad, artistic style, personal charm, and industry also contributed to his success.

Success had disadvantages, however: The demand for his portraits was greater than he could supply. Like other overworked portraitists, he formed a studio of assistants—drapery painters, wig painters, background painters—to churn out copies. He frequently painted only the face of his sitter, assistants filling in all the rest. The existence of too many mediocre copies has sullied Kneller's reputation as an inventive, insightful portrait painter. His best works, however, demonstrate a brilliant portrayal of character and an innovative sense of design. He reveled in the full-length portrait. Examples of the best of these include *Louise de Keroualle, Duchess of Portsmouth* (1684) and *The Chinese Convert* (1687).

Kneller's most famous works are the *Hampton Court Beauties* series (full-length portraits of aristocratic ladies painted for Queen Mary in 1691 in answer to Lely's *Windsor Beauties*) and his group of portraits of members of the Kit-Cat Club, a **Whig** social group. These 42 male life-scale "Kit-Cats" are of head, torso, and (at least) one hand. The paintings are identical in size—36 by 28 inches. This new format—called the kit-cat—was adopted as a standard size for 18th-century portraits. Among the best of the simple yet varied Kit-Cats are *Sir John Vanbrugh* (*c.* 1704), *Sir Richard Steele* (1711), and *Jacob Tonson* (1717); Tonson was club secretary and owner of the portraits. The series occupied Kneller for 20 years.

Kneller died while still active and popular, but without a clear successor. He was the last great foreign painter to dominate English art. Thereafter, native sons **William Hogarth**, **Joshua Reynolds**, and **Thomas Gainsborough** held sway.

Bonita L. Billman

Bibliography

Killanin, Lord. *Sir Godfrey Kneller and His Times, 1646–1723.* 1948.

Stewart, J. Douglas. *Sir Godfrey Kneller.* Exhibition catalog. 1971.

———. *Sir Godfrey Kneller and the English Baroque Portrait.* 1983.

See also Clubs

Knight, Ellis Cornelia (1758–1837)

Knight, a miscellaneous writer, is particularly interesting for the conclusive sequel, *Dinarbas* (1790), she produced for **Samuel Johnson**'s essentially unfinished *Rasselas* (1759). She also wrote two other **novels**, *Marcus Flaminius* (1793) and *Sir*

Guy de Lusignan (1833); a **travel book**, *A Description of Latium* (1805), which she illustrated with her own drawings; histories; poems; prayers; and **translations** from German.

In *Dinarbas,* picking up exactly where Johnson had left off, Knight invented numerous adventures for his major characters, introduced new ones, and ended with Rasselas married and on the throne of Abyssinia. Her sequel complemented rather than contradicted Johnson's view of the impossibility of happiness, concluding that although earthly happiness is not permanent, it is nevertheless real. She also anchored her novel in concrete history and geography, unlike Johnson's more abstract practice. Her book, with its developed characters, illustrates differences between apologue and novel as well as between male and female points of view.

Ann Messenger

Bibliography

Luttrell, Barbara. *The Prim Romantic: A Biography of Ellis Cornelia Knight.* 1965.

Messenger, Ann. "Choices of Life: Samuel Johnson and Ellis Cornelia Knight," in A. Messenger, *His and Hers: Essays in Restoration and 18th-Century Literature.* 1986.

———, ed. *Dinarbas.* 1993.

Uphaus, Robert W. "Cornelia Knight's *Dinarbas:* A Sequel to *Rasselas.*" *Philological Quarterly.* Vol. 65, pp. 433–446.

See also Women in Literature

Knowles, James Sheridan (1784–1862)

Playwright, poet, **actor**, schoolmaster, minister, lecturer, and literary critic, Knowles is perhaps best known for his drama *Virginius* (1820), though he wrote 20 other plays, such as *Leo, or the Gypsy* (1810), *William Tell* (1825), and *The Hunchback* (1832), all reasonably well received. His writings in other genres were less successful, but his **poetry**, in *Fugitive Pieces* (1810), and his fiction, *The Magdalen and Other Tales* (1832), are worth studying for their historical value, as is his instructional manual of rhetoric *The Elocutionist* (1823), used in English and American classrooms throughout the 19th century.

Knowles was born in **Cork** to a lexicographer, James Knowles, a cousin of the dramatist **Richard Brinsley Sheridan.** In 1793 his family moved to **London**, where he became friends with **Hazlitt**, **Lamb**, and **Coleridge**. He served in the **army**, studied **medicine**, and began acting in the **theater**, where he met and married actress Maria Charteris (1809). To provide for his family, he opened a grammar school in Belfast, then moved to **Glasgow** (1816), where he continued to teach, and finally to **Edinburgh** (1830). In 1834–1835 he conducted a popular lecture tour of the United States. He continued to write plays until 1843, when he became a **Baptist** minister. In 1850 he was nominated for the **poet laureateship**, but lost the award to Tennyson.

Mary Tiryak

Bibliography

Meeks, Leslie Howard. *Sheridan Knowles and the Theatre of His Time.* 1933.

See also Dramatic Arts

L

Labor Laws, Movements, and Unions

The history of early **trade** unionism has been receiving overdue attention. The century-old history by Sidney and Beatrice Webb, *History of Trade Unionism* (1894). long provided the research agenda. Although the Webbs recognized that trade unionism predated the **Industrial Revolution**, they insisted that only permanent organizations formed to protect or advance the interests of labor could be regarded as trade unions. Realizing that, given the nature of the 18th-century economy, this is an anachronistic definition; historians have recently shown that collective labor action was widespread, significant, and, in some respects, successful.

By 1700, combinations of journeymen exercising trade union functions already existed among a number of skilled workers, including woolen **weavers** and combers, tailors, printers, and hatters. In his *Wealth of Nations* (1776), **Adam Smith** considered it normal in manufacturing for combinations of workmen to come into conflict with their employers. Trade union activity can be found across a range of waged-workers from **textile** and **clothing** workers, through printers, papermakers, cabinetmakers, shipwrights, and building **craftsmen**, to sailors and **miners**. By the end of the century the Lancashire **cotton spinners** had formed the first true **factory** trade union, which was to play an important part in securing the **factory acts** of the 1830s and 1840s.

The first known use of the word *strike* in its modern sense was during a dispute in the **London** tailoring trade in 1765. A count has been made of 383 recorded instances of industrial disputes in Britain between 1717 and 1800. The real figure is indeterminable and, clearly, industrial action was far from uncommon in Hanoverian Britain.

"Combinations" of skilled workers (for unskilled labor and practically all working women remained unorganized) often fought to protect their perceived "rights" as members of a trade. Such an attitude underlay attacks on machinery. The best known of such attacks, which took place in 1811–1813 in the East Midlands, the West Riding of Yorkshire, and in Lancashire, gave the word ***Luddite*** to the language. In fact, this episode was more complex than simple reaction against machines that threatened livelihoods, and may even have had a political dimension. But more generally, craft unions sought to maintain apprenticeship as a means of controlling entry and securing a closed shop. They sought too to preserve "customary" work hours, **standards of living**, and working practices.

The enduring characteristics of craft-based British trade unionism have a long history. However, unions also took action to improve their conditions. They often deployed effective strategies, building up strike funds, choosing times when their employers were most vulnerable to lost orders, and in some cases employing the sophisticated technique of the "rolling strike" against one employer at a time. In the long run, the sides were hardly equal, and employers held distinct advantages; but, from time to time, in the more localized and segmented labor market of the period, unions could be successful.

Even before the passing of the notorious **combination acts** of 1799 and 1800, laws inhibited trade unions. The common law of conspiracy could be used against workers who combined to take action against their employers, while rapid summary redress was made available to employers not only through long-established master and servant legislation, which prevented workers leaving their contracted employer's work unfinished, but through a number of statutes specific to particular trades. Among workers affected by these were woolen workers, tailors, hatters, and papermakers, while an act intended originally to be specific to the millwrights (engineers) was turned by the government in 1799 into a general prohibition of trade unionism, which was to remain in force for 25 years.

The combination acts have been the subject of historical controversy. Among labor historians from the Webbs through the Hammonds to E.P. Thompson, they were considered a political act by a ruling class alarmed by the **French Revolution** into hardening its attitude toward the lower orders and seeking to limit the spread of political disaffection to their organizations. This is part of the explanation of the acts of 1799 and 1800, but there is also evidence that the government was in any case concerned that trade unionism should not spread to the newly industrializing districts of the Midlands and North. Historians have also disagreed over the effect of the acts. If they succeeded in constraining trade union activity, they did so more as intimidation than through the number of actual prosecutions that were undertaken. It is apparent too that with a moderate degree of circumspection, the long-established craft unions, especially in **London** and other large centers of **urban** manufacturing, could continue to operate much as before. However, the acts do seem to have made things more difficult for emerging unions in the North and Midlands.

Arguing that the combination acts had been a dead letter against the powerful craft unions was the main strength of the campaign organized by the adroit politician **Francis Place**, which led to their repeal in 1824. With liberal economists increasingly convinced that the acts were a form of interference in the labor market which made conflict more, rather than less, likely, and with the political dangers now seen as over, repeal was in the event achieved with little opposition. With the new Act of 1824, tidied by another in 1825, unions achieved a degree of legal recognition that allowed them at least to exist. This coincided with an economic boom and released an upsurge of union activity on the part of some newly formed unions, some of which had survived under the cover of representing themselves as **friendly societies**, and others which had continued to operate much as usual despite the acts. Alarmed manufacturers began to press for some measure of reinstatement, but this did not happen. However, there were still various restraining laws that could be used: master and **servant** laws could discipline individuals; actions like picketing or intimidation of fellow workers were still offenses; and, as the **Tolpuddle Martyrs** (six Dorset farm laborers **transported** to Australia for forming a union in 1834) were to discover, laws could still be found by a determined judiciary—in this case, a law against the administering of oaths.

Nevertheless, the legal situation had sufficiently changed after 1825 for a trade union movement to develop. A trade union press emerged. Local unions began to federate into regional and even national organizations, for example among cotton spinners, printworkers, and stone masons. More exciting at the time, but ultimately short-lived and less significant for the future, was the movement for general union, aiming at uniting the different trades. This movement, led by the socialist **Robert Owen**, peaked in 1834 with the Grand National Consolidated Trades Union. Given its brief career, historians have tended to regard the period that followed the repeal of the combination acts as one of only limited success for trade unionism. Yet in those years a language of labor emerged, closely allied to a critique of classical economic orthodoxy, which was an important input not only into the later strength of the trade union movement but also into Victorian working-class political movements like Chartism.

John Rule

Bibliography

Hammond, J.L., and B. Hammond. *The Skilled Labourer.* 1919; rpt. 1979.

Orth, John V. *Combination and Conspiracy: A Legal History of Trade Unionism, 1721–1906.* 1991.

Rule, John. *The Labouring Classes in Early Industrial England, 1750–1850.* 1986.

———, ed. *British Trade Unionism, 1750–1850: The Formative Years.* 1988.

Schwarz, L.D. *London in the Age of Industrialisation: Entrepreneurs, Labour Force and Living Conditions, 1700–1850.* 1992.

Thompson, E.P. *The Making of the English Working-Class.* 1968.

Webb, Sidney, and Beatrice Webb. *History of Trade Unionism.* 1894; rev. ed., 1911.

See also Hours, Wages, and Working Conditions; Women's Employment

Lake School, Poets of the

This is the term employed by early-19th-century literary reviewers referring to **William Wordsworth, Samuel Taylor Coleridge**, and **Robert Southey**. Although the three poets, who lived in Northern England's Lake District, denied that they shared literary theories and practices to such a degree as to constitute a school, the name became popular; and it still remains a useful if inexact description of these men who so strongly influenced each other and collectively affected the course of literary history.

Francis Jeffrey seems to have invented the term while reviewing Coleridge's *Biographia Literaria* in the *Edinburgh Review* (August 1817). But much earlier, in an October 1802 review of Southey's *Thalaba,* he had described a new "sect of poets" that clearly included the three; and in an October 1807 review of Wordsworth's *Poems in Two Volumes* he commented on a "certain brotherhood of poets, who have haunted for some years about the Lakes of Cumberland." Jeffrey, like most other early reviewers, used the term derisively, censuring the group for rejecting established canons of **poetry**, for making claims to poetic originality (he believed these simply masked a dependence on French and German poetic and social doctrines), and for selecting inelegant diction and characters from the lower social orders.

William Hazlitt in his essay "On the Living Poets" (1818) suggested that the Lake School had originated from the same impulse as the **French Revolution** and that its diction and characters reflected the revolution's leveling ideals. **Lord Byron**, charging Southey especially with eventually betraying his **radical** ideals, made the most famous reference to the school in his "Dedication to *Don Juan*" (1819), where he satirized "all the Lakers, in and out of place."

Coleridge maintained in *Biographia Literaria* that all assumptions that he, Wordsworth, and Southey ever thought of themselves as a poetic school were baseless. **De Quincey**, in *Recollections of the Lake Poets* (1834–1839), noted that the three poets' phraseology derived from a shared veneration of biblical language, but observed also that there never had been a well-defined school and reported that in 1812 Southey too had denied the existence of a single outlook by distancing himself from what he had called the error of much of Wordsworth's poetic method. But of course De Quincey's own references to the school, even as he denied its existence, indicate that the term had become a recognized critical concept in the analysis of literary **Romanticism**.

Mike Wiley

Bibliography

Abrams, Meyer Howard. *Natural Supernaturalism: Tradition and Revolution in Romantic Literature.* 1971.

Langbaum, Robert Woodrow. *The Poetry of Experience: The Dramatic Monologue in Modern Literary Tradition.* 1975.

Metzger, Lore. *One Foot in Eden: Modes of Pastoral in Romantic Poetry.* 1986.

Lamb, Charles (1775–1834)

Charles Lamb

Lamb was one of the great essayists of the early 19th century, alongside **Hazlitt**, **De Quincey**, **Leigh Hunt**, and a few others. He was born in **London** of the lower middle class, studied at Christ's Hospital where he first met Hunt and **Coleridge**, became an associate of the other **Lake Poets** and a familiar figure in London intellectual circles, and worked as a clerk for the **East India Company** during most of his life from 1792 to 1825. After 1796 Lamb lived with and looked after his unbalanced sister **Mary Lamb**, collaborating with her in the publication of various works of **children's literature**, including *Tales from Shakespear* (1807), *The Adventures of Ulysses* (1808), and *Mrs. Leicester's School* (1809). Before this, he published a few poems in the 1790s, a tragedy, *John Woodvil* (1802), and an unsuccessful farce (1806). During the period 1808–1820 he produced various writings on Shakespeare, Hogarth, Wordsworth, and other topics (collected and published in 1818), often writing in **periodicals** owned by Hunt such as the *Reflector* and *Examiner.*

In the 1820s Lamb wrote his greatest essays under the pseudonym Elia for the *London Magazine,* collecting them for separate publication in 1823 and 1833. Though he is grouped in time and by association with the **Romantics**, Lamb's outlook constituted a Romanticism not of nature and exotic locations, such as that of his friends Coleridge and **Wordsworth**, or of moralistic reform, which he distrusted, but rather of the sense of history, and of time, and of the variegated atmosphere of London. He seldom left the city, declared his indifference to mountains, and was genuinely conservative, an observer of quaint habits and a lover of old books. His fascination with the Elizabethan and Jacobean periods, and conservative relish of **city** life, perhaps even made him somewhat hesitant about his own identity. He always spoke in what his friends and sister remembered as a "pleasant little stammer," and part of the great effectiveness of his essay writing lies in his simple modesty and charm. In both his **letters** and his journalistic essays he painted wonderful pictures of the London scene, reminiscent of those provided earlier by **Addison**'s "Mr. Spectator" and **Johnson**'s moody "Rambler." The difference was that Lamb, sharing the subjective perspective common to the Romantic era, projected himself much more fully into his writings, making them charmingly personal revelations of thought and feeling.

Donald M. Hassler

Bibliography

Blunden, Edmund. *Charles Lamb and His Contemporaries.* 1933.

Johnson, Edith C. *Lamb always Elia.* 1935.

Lucas, E.V. *The Life of Charles Lamb.* Rev. ed., 1921.

Morley, F.V. *Lamb before Elia.* 1932.

See also Periodicals

Lamb, Lady Caroline (1785–1828)

Romantic writer and glittering ornament of **Regency** society, Lamb is associated in memory with two famous men of her time: **Byron** the poet and **Melbourne** the Victorian **prime minister**. Although her **novels** and poems are forgotten, her personality lives on in literary history.

In June 1805 she married the young and studious William Lamb, who was to become 2nd Viscount Melbourne; he taught her classics and philosophy. Then with Byron she continued her literary development, eventually writing three novels, *Glenarvon* (1816), *Graham Hamilton* (1822), and *Ada Reis* (1823). The first, along with mock-Gothic pastiche, contains a celebrated caricature of Byron, whom Lamb memora-

Lady Caroline Lamb

bly characterized also in her diary as "mad, bad, and dangerous to know." She also published **poetry** and was known for her sparkling conversation. Despite a legal separation, her husband was at her side when she died; and at his death 20 years later, he was buried beside her.

Donald M. Hassler

Bibliography

Cecil, David. *Melbourne.* 1954.
Jenkins, Elizabeth. *Lady Caroline Lamb.* 1932.
Quennell, Peter. *Byron: The Years of Fame.* 1935.

Lamb, Mary Ann (1764–1847)

During the time when **bluestocking** literary ladies would show off their reading by publishing epistolary **novels**, Mary Ann Lamb's program of self-study with her well-educated brother, **Charles Lamb**, and their collaboration on writing projects for children, added new dimensions to both female expression and **Romantic** sensibility.

Mary Ann suffered from episodes of insanity. In fact, her periodic madness was the reality that drove her studies with her brother and shaped the particularity and innovation of their writing for children. This mental instability was evidently inherited, since Charles and other members of the family suffered similar seizures. Nonetheless, in 1796, her mind temporarily overthrown, Mary Ann killed her mother with a knife and wounded her father. Letters between the Lambs and their friend **Coleridge** recount the sad story of coming to terms with this dreadful event over the ensuing years. Charles took responsibility for his sister, and they read and worked together, helping each other through recurring episodes of mania.

Through his poetry, Charles had gotten to know **William Godwin**, who was, among other things, at the center of **radical** ideas on **women's education** and **children's literature**. Mary then, with Charles's encouragement and help, wrote the majority of entries for their *Tales from Shakespear Designed for the Use of Young Persons* (1807), published by Godwin. She also wrote most of the Preface, which tied the work to female education. Later, she wrote much of *Mrs. Leicester's School* (1809), a collection of short stories. Well acquainted with her brother's friends—Romantic poets and essayists—Lamb carried her genuine insight into the potential horror of childhood into writings that conveyed this knowledge, though very discreetly.

Donald M. Hassler

Bibliography

Gilchrist, Anne. *Life of Mary Lamb.* 1883.
Lucas, E.V. *The Letters of Charles Lamb, to Which Are Added Those of His Sister, Mary Lamb.* 3 vols. 1935.
Ross, Ernest C. *The Ordeal of Bridget Elia.* 1940.

See also Women in Literature

Lancaster, Joseph (1778–1838)

Lancaster, a **Quaker** schoolmaster, organized and promoted school instruction so successfully that by 1806 his system for educating poor children was the most widely emulated in the world. His Borough Road school, opened in South London in 1801, focused on nonsectarian educational training. His "monitorial system" became a means of systematic instruction by which a single schoolmaster used his pupils to teach one another. From 200 to 1,000 children would be gathered in a single room, often in rows of 10; the adult teacher taught the older pupils, the monitors, each of whom then taught his row. Other monitors were used to take attendance, give examinations, and the like. The classroom emphasis was on discipline and memorization, and of course the noise was deafening. The monitors themselves had but limited opportunity to learn advanced skills in writing, grammar, geography, or arithmetic, being preoccupied with teaching. But however poor the education provided, the system's student–teacher ratios would have been the envy of many school administrators and taxpayers today.

Lancaster's success in cheaply providing **elementary education** for large numbers forced the **Church of England** to renew its interest in inexpensive schooling and to adopt **Andrew Bell**'s monitorial system for its provision. Parliament's first grant for education (1833) was divided between the societies organized to implement Bell and Lancasterian schools. As to Lancaster himself, his perpetual indebtedness and declining role in developing new schools forced him to leave England for the United States in 1818. There, as in Britain and elsewhere in the world, the adoption (and eventual rejection) of his methods helped spur the demand for free nonsectarian education.

Kim P. Sebaly

Bibliography

Dickson, Mora. *Teacher Extraordinary: Joseph Lancaster, 1778–1838.* 1986.

Dabundo, Laura, ed. *Encyclopedia of Romanticism: Culture in Britain, 1780's–1830's,* s.v. "Lancaster, Joseph." 1992.

Landscape Architecture and Design

Hanoverian landscape gardening has been called England's greatest contribution to the arts. Around 1700, English gardens, imitating French and Dutch models, were formal in style, with geometrically shaped beds, straight walks and terraces, and regularly placed fountains and statues. As time passed, however, and as great landlords indulged their taste for lavish **housebuilding**, the creators of large gardens and parks designed increasingly naturalistic landscapes, based on evolving ideas about the ideal relationship between art and nature. It was felt that a garden should imitate nature more closely, though strategies for doing this changed radically as the century advanced.

Earlier literary descriptions of gardens and their relationship to nature, in the works of Bacon, Milton, John Evelyn, and Anthony Ashley Cooper, 3rd earl of Shaftesbury, were studied with interest in the early 18th century. One of the most important proponents of a new gardening strategy, **Alexander Pope**, advocated a closer adherence to nature; a greater variety of design elements; and a painterly attention to principles of perspective, color, light, and shade. Pope's own garden at Twickenham, despite the deceptive regularity of its plan, exemplified his new gardening principles. In line with the **classicism** of the early 18th century and the growing interest in **antiquities and ruins**, he and his contemporaries were also interested in ancient Roman gardens as models for contemporary ones. For example, the gardens at Chiswick (from *c.* 1716), the **Palladian** villa erected by the **Earl of Burlington**, were inspired in part by contemporary descriptions of classical gardens.

In the early Hanoverian age the two most important professional garden designers were Charles Bridgeman (*d.* 1738) and **William Kent**. Bridgeman created grand axial layouts, still semiformal in style but brilliantly adapted to the irregularities of his sites. He was one of the first in England to make use of the ha-ha, a sunken fence which served as a barrier to livestock without being visible in the landscape. His most important works were at Blenheim (from 1709), Claremont (from *c.* 1725), and Stowe (1715–1726), which was later embellished by Kent. Kent's designs were more those of a painter than an architect; he provided views of the landscapes he wanted improved, rather than architectural plans for them. His landscape sketches convey a pastoral vision reflecting the influence of the much-admired 17th-century landscape painters Poussin, Dughet, Rosa, and Claude. His most completely realized landscape, still well preserved, is at Rousham (from 1738) in Oxfordshire.

English gardens at this time were often adorned with temples and decorated with **sculpture**, with statues and inscriptions meant to convey specific messages to knowledgeable visitors. The quintessential example is at Stowe, whose nu-

Duke of Newcastle's Claremont House by Vanbrugh, Bridgeman

merous temples and monuments spelled out the political philosophy of its owner, Richard Temple, **Viscount Cobham**. During the second half of the century, however, gardenmakers generally eschewed such detailed and specific iconography; the ever-more-naturalistic landscape itself was the main feature. The visitor's thoughts, instead of being directed into specific channels, were invited to wander more freely among various meanings or associations brought to mind by the landscape and by any monuments it contained.

The primary proponent of this less "emblematic," more "expressive" landscape was **Lancelot ("Capability") Brown**. Brown introduced a radically simplified style, involving extensive smooth grass lawns, belts and clumps of trees, and large artificial lakes. He suppressed the more formal elements still admired in **France**, such as straight walks, beds, and terracing. His majestic landscapes, such as those at Petworth (from *c.* 1750) and Blenheim (from 1763), embody what is still the standard idea of the English landscape in its "natural" state, even though Brown's landscapes were achieved by means no less artificial—plentiful digging, heaping-up, grading, channeling, planting—than those used earlier in more formal gardens.

After Brown's death (1783), **Humphry Repton** became the country's leading landscape designer. His creations were superficially similar to Brown's, with spreading lawns encircled by belts of trees, but Repton emphasized practical convenience as well as visual effect, and reintroduced formal terraces, flower beds, and even covered walks near the house in an effort to make his gardens more pleasant and convenient for their owners. A failed but still clever businessman, Repton presented his landscaping plans in the form of his famous "red books"—handwritten volumes, bound in red morocco, containing discussions of proposed improvements, illustrated by **watercolor** views. These views incorporated what Repton called "slides," flaps that could be lifted to show the later effects of proposed improvements.

Meanwhile, British aesthetics in the second half of the 18th century saw the development of an extended debate concerning the nature of beauty; and because this was often expressed in terms of natural beauty as observed in a landscape, the debate naturally had consequences for landscaping. **Edmund Burke**'s book on the sublime and the beautiful (1757) introduced the notion (or, rather, elaborated a notion present in the earlier writings of **Addison**) that aesthetic value could be found in something not conventionally beautiful but rather wild and irregular, capable of inspiring feelings of terror and awe. The debate was further continued in the writings of **Uvedale Price**, Richard Payne Knight (1750–1824), and others, who pondered the nature of the **picturesque** and its relationship to the beautiful and the **sublime**.

The term "picturesque" itself already had a confused history; in Pope's time it had signified principles of landscape composition such as those used in **painting**. But by the latter 18th century it had come to mean a landscape worthy of consideration as if it were a picture—a landscape full of varied and visually pleasing incident, but not necessarily beautiful in a regular or conventional way. Advocates of the picturesque were especially critical of Brown, whose landscapes were felt to lack this quality (or absence of a quality). Although this notion of the picturesque influenced many late-18th-century gardenmakers, leading to the introduction of grottoes, false ruins, and other curiosities, Repton, who represented the mainstream tradition, never embraced it fully because he could not reconcile the notion of "picture-making" in this sense to his own requirements for neatness, order, and formality in certain parts of the garden. His most notable gardens include Woburn Abbey (from 1802) and Sheringham Hall (from 1812).

With Repton's death (1818), the great age of the English landscape garden came to a close. Grand landscape design in the architectural sense now gradually gave way to smaller-scale, more horticulturally centered gardening.

Kimerly Rorschach

Bibliography

Chambers, Douglas. *The Planters of the English Landscape Garden: Botany, Trees, and the Georgics.* 1993.
Desmond, Ray. *Bibliography of British Gardens.* 1984.
Hadfield, Miles. *A History of British Gardening.* 1969.
Hemingway, Andrew. *Landscape Imagery and Urban Culture in Early Nineteenth-Century Britain.* 1992.
Hunt, John Dixon. *Gardens and the Picturesque.* 1992.
Hunt, John Dixon, and Peter Willis, eds. *The Genius of the Place.* 1975; rev. ed., 1989.
Jacques, David. *Georgian Gardens: The Reign of Nature.* 1983.

See also Architects and Architecture; Painting, Landscape

Language and Linguistics

The Hanoverian era was marked by a desire to codify and regulate the English language. Inspired by the model of the Italian and French academies, **Daniel Defoe** had in 1697 called for an academy of 36 "gentlemen" to dictate English usage; **Jonathan Swift** in 1712 had argued for the establishment of an English academy "to correct, improve, and ascertain" the language. They and other intellectuals felt, the need for an adequate dictionary, a sensible grammar, and a native system of metrical structure and versification in English.

Remembering that no dictionaries as authorities on meaning or grammar books as authorities on usage existed for quick reference during this fertile literary period may help to explain these standardizing desires. Other proponents of an academy were John Dryden (1631–1700), John Evelyn (1620–1706), and Thomas Cooke (1703–1756). The sole dissenter was John Oldmixon (?1673–1742), who ridiculed the idea that anything could keep languages from changing; yet his objection may have sprung as much from dislike of Swift as linguistic philosophy. Ultimately the movement failed because of a growing sense of the futility of the proposed academy's broad purpose.

Nathaniel Bailey (*d.* 1742) published his *Universal Etymological English Dictionary* in 1721. This provided a beginning for 18th-century lexicography and for the first time featured etymology, syllabification, usage, illustrations, and pronunciation. **Samuel Johnson** published his two-volume *Dictionary of the English Language* in 1755: expanding Bailey's crude etymologies, this established a standard for spelling, used quotations to illustrate usage, provided definitions, and showed the breadth of the English vocabulary. Of course, in some ways Johnson's work was sorely lacking. Sometimes he expressed his own prejudices and provided amusing though inexact definitions: "Lexicographer: A writer of dictionaries, a harmless drudge"; "Oats: A grain given in England to horses and in Scotland to the people." The value of his *Dictionary,* however, greatly transcended such flaws, and with its publication, Johnson became the great arbiter of taste in language. His dictionary's influence was so great that it remained in use until about 1900.

Several grammarians attempted to do for grammar what Johnson did for lexicography. Their goal was to prescribe and proscribe language. Most important was **Robert Lowth**, whose *Short Introduction to English Grammar* appeared in 1762 and went through 21 more editions in the 18th century. Meanwhile, Noah Webster (1758–1843) published the second part of *A Grammatical Institute of the English Language* (1784), which was very popular in England as well as in his native America.

To these and other grammarians of this period goes the credit (or blame) for many of the prescriptive grammatical rules that have been the bane of schoolchildren ever since. One outlawed the double negative: sentences such as "She didn't go neither" and Hamlet's "Be not too tame neither" were declared ungrammatical. Two negatives make a positive, it was decided, thereby condemning a common idiom to doom. Which pronoun should precede a gerund was debated: eventually Webster prevailed, and constructions such as "I worry about his becoming bored with his job" were accepted as grammatically correct. The distinction between *shall* and *will* originated during this time, as did the rules against splitting infinitives and ending sentences with prepositions.

In sum, Hanoverian scholars established the idea that English was a language worth studying and improving. The desire to "freeze" the language in a form considered pure and ideal emanated from a worthy—but misguided—purpose, which failed to recognize that a living language, one that is spoken, constantly changes.

L. Ben Crane

Bibliography

Baugh, Albert C., and Thomas Cable. *The History of the English Language.* 3rd ed., 1978.

Crane, L. Ben, Edward Yeager, and Randal Whitman. *An Introduction to Linguistics.* 1981.

Myers, L.M. *The Roots of Modern English.* 1966.

Nist, John. *A Structural History of English.* 1966.

Pyles, Thomas. *The Origins and Development of the English Language.* 1964.

See also Reference Works

Latitudinarianism

Latitudinarianism, a term suggesting theological moderation and breadth in the **Church of England**, was commonly used in the 1660s and thereafter to describe a group of Anglican divines who advocated a nondogmatic, comprehensive Protestant communion that would include, rather than exclude, moderate **dissenters**. Latitudinarians promoted science as an ally of religious belief and developed a "plain" style of preaching to reach the new commercial classes in **London**. They emphasized the centrality of the moral life in the practice of Christianity and reasserted the importance of reason in biblical interpretation and theological discourse. In addition, they urged an end to Protestant infighting over doctrine, founded parish schools, and sought to educate the clergy by their numerous publications.

In the aftermath of the Civil War and the failed Puritan experiment of the Cromwellian Interregnum, the latitudemen saw the Church of England as the structure best suited to secure Protestant unity, a unity they believed essential to combat **Roman Catholicism** and to maintain a stable sociopolitical and ecclesiastical order. In the reign of William III (1689–1702) the Latitudinarians became the most powerful group in the church. Many of them, such as Thomas Burnet (1635?–1715), Simon Patrick (1626–1707), and Edward Stillingfleet (1635–1699), were made bishops, and John Tillotson (1630–1694) became Archbishop of Canterbury (1691–1694). But despite their prominence, the Latitudinarians' agenda of comprehension for moderate dissenters was never realized.

In the 18th century, Latitudinarianism continued to exercise a significant influence, largely through the ongoing alliance between Newtonian natural philosophy and theology, the reading of Tillotson's sermons, and the association of latitude with **Whig** politics. The Feathers Tavern Petition of 1772, which sought to remove the clergy's obligation to subscribe to the Thirty-nine Articles of Faith, was a notable example of the Latitudinarian inheritance. The true nature of Latitudinarianism has been obscured by subsequent **deist** claims. Needing to legitimate their own **radical** and unsettling ideas, **John Toland** and other deists argued that their rationalistic natural theology was a logical product of the rational methods of latitudemen warmly embraced. It would perhaps be more true to say that although the English deists were influenced by their Latitudinarian forebears, they differed with them over the concept of human reason. Deism exalted reason as all-sufficient, whereas Latitudinarians reclaimed common-sense reason as a tool for the conduct of Christian **theology**.

Michael F. Suarez, S.J.

Bibliography

Gasgoigne, John. *Cambridge in the Age of Enlightenment: Science, Religion and Politics from the Restoration to the French Revolution.* 1989.

Griffin, Martin I.J. *Latitudinarianism in the Seventeenth-Century Church of England.* 1992.

Jacob, Margaret C. *The Newtonians and the English Revolution, 1689–1720.* 1976.

Rivers, Isabel. *Reason, Grace, and Sentiment: A Study of the Language of Religion and Ethics in England, 1660–1780.* 1991.

Rupp, Gordon, *Religion in England, 1688–1791.* 1986.

Spellman, W.A. *The Latitudinarians and the Church of England, 1660–1700.* 1992.

Law, Edmund (1703–1787)

Law, Bishop of Carlisle, exemplified the intellectual and humane side of Hanoverian Anglican **Latitudinarianism.** Born in Lancashire, the only son of a curate, he studied at St. John's College, Cambridge, becoming Master of Peterhouse (1756) and Professor of Moral Philosophy (1764) before attaining his bishopric (1769). **Whiggish** in politics and reasonable in philosophy, he produced, among other works, his popular *Considerations on the Theory of Religion* (1745), which by 1784 had gone to seven editions. Beginning with **Locke**'s ideas on the incompleteness of revealed truth, he argued that humanity had undergone progressive divine education through natural and revealed religion, both keeping pace with all other knowledge.

Law's Christianity, like that of younger theologians such as **Richard Watson** and (Law's friend and biographer) **William Paley**, combined revelation with natural philosophy. Although some of his theories, such as his belief that the soul passes into a state of sleep between death and resurrection, were considered eccentric; this may have made him more supportive of **religious toleration**, which he defended anonymously in a much-condemned pamphlet (1774) interpreting broadly the need for clerical faithfulness to the Thirty-nine Articles. (The pamphlet indirectly supported **Francis Blackburne** and the **dissenters**' Feathers Tavern petition of 1772.) In 1777 Law published an edition of Locke's works, with an admiring preface and life of the philosopher; next year he spoke in the **Lords** against government policy in America.

Samuel J. Rogal

Bibliography

Hole, Robert. *Pulpits, Politics and Public Order in England, 1760–1832.* 1989.

McAdoo, H.R. *The Spirit of Anglicanism.* 1965.

Rupp, Gordon. *Religion in England, 1688–1791.* 1987.

Law, John (1671–1729)

Law, a noted financier of the era of the **South Sea Bubble**, was born in **Edinburgh**, the son of a goldsmith and banker. In his youth he showed considerable mathematical talent. Following a riotous spell in **London** he fled after killing a man in a **duel**, traveling to Amsterdam, where he began studying the workings of the **banking** system. After other travels he finally settled in **France** in 1714.

Following the death of Louis XIV, Law gained considerable influence over the Regent, the Duke of Orleans, under whose **patronage** he planned to solve the financial plight France faced after Louis's wars. In 1716 he founded the Banque Générale, whose initial success led him to form the Compagnie de l'Occident the following year. Like the British **South Sea Company**, this gained commercial privileges in return for taking over part of the national debt. Law's design seemed to flourish, his bank becoming the Banque Royale (1718) and his extended trading operation the Compagnie des Indes (1719). He proposed to take over the national debt and manage it on terms favorable to the state, but the company's stock could not sustain the high prices necessary for debt holders to realize a profit. A collapse ensued in the early summer of 1720, the first of a series of financial crises that were to engulf European markets that year. Law fled to Venice, where he died in poverty in 1729.

John Law

A.J.G. Cummings

Bibliography

Hyde, H.M. *John Law: The History of an Honest Adventurer.* 1969.

Minton, Robert. *John Law: The Father of Paper Money.* 1975.

Neale, Larry. *The Rise of Financial Capitalism: International Capital Markets in the Age of Reason.* 1990.

Law, William (1686–1761)

Law, a **nonjuring** divine, wrote controversial works directed against **Benjamin Hoadly** in the **Bangorian controversy** and against stage plays, **Quakers, Catholics, Bernard Mandeville, Matthew Tindal,** and **William Warburton.** Stripped of his Cambridge fellowship as a nonjuror unwilling to swear allegiance to **George I** after the latter's accession in 1714, Law was unable to advance in the Anglican Church. In 1729 he published his most important work, *A Serious Call to a Devout and Holy Life,* a dialogue that redefined devotion as a moral discipline going well beyond mere prayer: devotion involved the entirety of life and required an intention to please God in everything.

Law's devotional works greatly influenced **John Wesley** and hence **Methodism**. Wesley praised Law's *Call* as virtually unmatched in English for beauty of expression and depth of thought, and **Samuel Johnson** credited Law with arousing his own religious interests. Law's later writings, such as *The Way to Divine Knowledge* (1752), touched with more mystical ideas about personal union with the Divine, found less favor. His personal life, however—characterized by piety, self-denial, and good works—was fully consistent with his teaching. Together with a small community of friends he founded schools and almshouses, and when not engaged in controversy lived a quiet, ascetic life in King's Cliffe, Northamptonshire.

K.J.H. Berland

Bibliography

Rack, H.D. "'Christ's Kingdom Not of This World': The Case of Benjamin Hoadly versus William Law Reconsidered." *Studies in Church History.* Vol. 12, pp. 275–291.

Rudolph, Erwin Paul. *William Law.* 1980.

Talon, Henri Antoine. *William Law: A Study in Literary Craftsmanship.* 1948.

See also Dramatic Criticism

Law Enforcement

Policing in the early 18th century was still an essentially amateur function carried on by the local community, but as the **crime** rate rose, pleas for a reform of the traditional system increased. Particularly in **London**, the ancient system of watchmen and constables was glaringly inadequate. Official thief-takers were established around 1750, but a professional police force was created only in 1829, and then only for London. Provincial centers followed the lead of the capital only in the Victorian period.

The policing regime of early modern England remained in essence that established in 1285 by the Statute of Winchester, which laid down a system by which all male adults were made responsible for keeping the peace in their communities, and constables, sometimes aided by watchmen, were appointed to present criminals in court. All rate-payers were obligated to assume the office of constable or watchman in rotation, but by the 18th century, most people hired substitutes for this disagreeable and unpaid responsibility. In consequence, the ranks of the constables and watchmen were generally composed of the elderly, the unemployable, and the alcoholic. Their incompetence was proverbial.

The watchmen formed the front line in the defense of public order and were responsible for apprehending criminals and raising the hue and cry when they discovered a crime in progress. They patrolled a defined area from a watch-house, were generally on duty from dusk to dawn, and were usually armed with a lantern and a cudgel. Watchmen brought apprehended malefactors to the constable on duty, who in turn either presented the suspect to a magistrate (a justice of the peace) or held him in jail until a justice was available. The magistrates possessed wide-reaching powers of examination, incarceration, and sentencing.

At all three levels of the system of enforcement—watchman, constable, and magistrate—corruption was rife. Moreover, the criminal justice system was based on private prosecution by aggrieved parties, so that detection was left in the hands of the victims of crime, and prosecution depended on the financial ability of victims to bring an action at law. Rising rates of crime in the 18th century led to the grafting of a rewards system onto the ancient policing arrangements, and this in turn promoted the rise of professional thief-takers. The most notorious of these was Jonathan Wild (1682–1725), who styled himself "Thief-taker-General of Great Britain and Ireland" while concealing his own wrongdoing. He had made himself, by the time he was found out and hanged at Tyburn (1725), the leader of a large gang of criminals in a system that exploited the considerable rewards paid for criminal convictions.

The first substantial reforms in the system of law enforcement were put in place by **Henry Fielding**, magistrate at Bow Street from 1748. Fielding established a group of official thief-takers, later called the **Bow Street Runners**, whose efforts contributed to a modest improvement in enforcement and detection in the capital. Half a century later (1805), the Bow Street horse patrol was empowered to police the highways to a distance of 20 miles from London.

The system of the watch was incapable of responding to

Thief-takers attacking smugglers

large-scale **riots** or public disturbances, and thus militia and military forces were called out to deal with demonstrations of the "mob," for example when the **Gordon riots** of 1780 spread looting and destruction through London. The fear excited by such riots helped to break down public opposition to the establishment of a professional police force. Yet the use of military forces could end in chaos and the loss of innocent life, as at the **Peterloo massacre** (1819).

Anxiety that a police system would become an instrument of tyranny and a corrosive of cherished British liberty began declining toward the end of the 18th century. Reformers urged the separation of policing and judicial functions, and the establishment of a professional force. The most influential amongst them was **Patrick Colquhoun**, whose *Treatise on the Police of the Metropolis* appeared in successive revised editions from 1797 to 1806. **Piracy** on the Thames presented another acute policing problem to which Colquhoun and others drew attention, and in 1798 the Thames police force was formed as a private venture by the **merchants** of the **West India interest**; the success of its 80 officers in patrolling the port of London encouraged the government to take over the force under the Thames Police Bill of 1800.

The early years of the 19th century witnessed repeated parliamentary enquiries on police reform for the metropolis. Recommendations for a professional force were presented by parliamentary committees in 1812, 1816, and again in 1818. Home Secretary **Robert Peel** vigorously promoted, from the early 1820s, a general act for a police force for the capital. His efforts bore fruit in the Metropolitan Police Act of 1829. Under its terms, two commissioners—the Waterloo veteran Charles Rowan (1782?–1852) and the barrister Richard Mayne (1796–1868)—were given command of the force, which consisted of nearly 3,000 men, divided among 17 districts. The commissioners' headquarters was entered from Scotland Yard, Whitehall, and the name was soon applied to the central police station there.

The constables wore blue uniforms and top hats, and the hostility felt toward them was registered in their nickname of "Blue devils," an appellation far more common at first than the affectionate "bobbies" that recalled Sir Robert Peel. Gradually, however, the metropolitan police earned the respect of the public, though professional police forces outside the capital developed more slowly. The **Municipal Corporations Act** (1835) enabled **boroughs** to establish their own police forces, but the creation of a uniform system throughout the country required many decades more.

Daniel Statt

Bibliography

Andrew, Donna T. *Philanthropy and Police: London Charity in the Eighteenth Century.* 1989.

Beattie, J.M. *Crime and the Courts in England, 1660–1800.* 1986.

Browne, Douglas. *The Rise of Scotland Yard: A History of the Metropolitan Police.* 1956.

Critchey, T.A. *A History of Police in England and Wales, 1900–1966.* 1967.

Hay, Douglas, and Francis Snyder, eds. *Policing and Prosecution in Britain, 1750–1850.* 1989.

McLynn, Frank. *Crime and Punishment in Eighteenth-Century England.* 1989.

Radzinowicz, Leon. *History of English Criminal Law and Its Administration from 1750.* 4 vols. 1948–1968.

Thompson, F.M.L., ed. *The Cambridge Social History of Britain, 1750–1950.* 3 vols. 1990.

See also Judicial System; Prisons and Prison Reform; Punishment

Law Reform

It was remarked by **Jeremy Bentham** that under the Hanoverian legal system, justice was denied to nine-tenths of the people and sold too dearly to the rest. The law was indeed a maze through which members of the **legal profession** attempted to guide their clients' affairs, taking care to observe technicalities and to take advantage of their adversaries' failures to do so. And there was profit in it. Bentham cynically commented that it was "as impossible to a lawyer to wish men out of litigation, as for a physician to wish them in health." It was not in the lawyers' interest to reform, simplify, or rationalize the law.

But there were greater obstacles to law reform than lawyers' self-interest. The immensity of the ancient structure and the innate conservatism that went with it ensured that practices which were two, three, or even more centuries old remained in use, so that "peine fort et dure," burning at the stake, benefit of the clergy, drawing and quartering, and even trial by battle were still legal in the 18th century. Civil law was even more chaotic, encrusted with involved formulae, procedural subterfuges, and legal fictions, of which the theory of "virtual representation" (under which people who were voteless were considered adquately represented) was but the most notorious.

Large-scale law reform did not occur until the 1870s, but two important steps toward it were taken in the Hanoverian age. Ironically, the first was by a man considered a judicial conservative, **William Blackstone.** Starting in 1753 the first course in law ever taught at an English university, he began writing for his students' guidance a series of lectures soon published as *An Analysis of the Laws of England* (1756); these, in turn, he expanded into his monumental *Commentaries on the Laws of England* (1765–1769). These commentaries were extremely influential because they seemed to make systematic, rational, and intelligible to laymen the whole structure of the law as it had evolved since the Middle Ages. Though they have been heavily criticized by modern writers as vague, incorrect, and excessively reverential toward the **Glorious Constitution**, that is beside the point here. By treating English law as a continuous and coherent system, the outcome of divine processes and a replica of natural law, Blackstone created the ideal that would inspire later reformers: to make the law regular and to purge it of its fictions, anachronisms, and barbarities.

The second step was taken by Bentham, Blackstone's very disenchanted student at Oxford. Bentham rejected

Blackstone's theoretical assumptions in almost every respect. In *A Fragment on Government* (1776) he emphasized that Blackstone's reverence for the common law was misplaced. Centuries of development had encrusted the legal system with doctrines and procedures that offended human reason and were alien to an efficient jurisprudence. Bentham dismissed the doctrine of natural rights as "nonsense upon stilts." He based his own analysis on the principle of utility; each statute and legal rule must work for the greatest good of the greatest number. By the relentless application of this principle, Bentham dissected the problems he attributed to a legal system badly misshapen by judicial precedent. He argued strongly for the primacy of legislation, of law made by statute, under which reason as he defined it—the principle of utility—would eliminate legal archaisms and introduce reforms on a sound philosophical basis.

Bentham's ideas, stressing results-based analysis and legislative initiative, though destined to prevail in the Victorian age, had little effect before his death (1832). His disciples made only a little progress. **Samuel Romilly** succeeded in reforming the dreadful criminal code in a small way by gaining parliamentary support for a bill substituting **transportation** for death as the punishment for pickpockets (1808), but he accomplished little more in the face of determined opposition from the **House of Lords**. Sir James Mackintosh (1765–1832), also influenced by Bentham, carried on Romilly's work after the latter's death (1818) by having a commission appointed to look into the large number of capital offenses on the books, but though this recommended repeal for some of the more ridiculous offenses such as damaging Westminster Bridge, the Lords continued to block reform. However, between 1823 and 1828 the liberal **Tories** led by **Peel** and **Canning** succeeded in removing about a hundred lesser felonies from the death penalty, and in 1832 counterfeiting, horse-stealing, sheep-stealing, and housebreaking also ceased to be capital crimes. A few more capital offenses were abolished in 1837 and 1841, and after 1838 no one was executed except for murder or (until 1861) attempted murder.

Reform of the civil law was even slower, thanks in part to the adamant opposition of **Lord Eldon**, Lord Chancellor (chief government law officer) for virtually the entire period 1801–1827. But in 1828 **Henry Brougham**, also influenced by Bentham, delivered in the **Commons** a remarkable speech of 6-hours' duration analyzing, enumerating, and attacking abuses in every part of the existing system of judicature. Himself becoming Lord Chancellor for 4 years (1830–1834), he initiated the long-overdue reform of the court of chancery (equity), abolishing sinecure posts, laying down more streamlined rules, and creating a much-needed new court for bankruptcy cases (though imprisonment for debt remained in force until several enactments in 1844, 1861, and 1869 abolished it). A start, at least, had been made in legal reform, which mounting public irritation would at last bring to a spectacular climax in the Judicature Act (1873), a sweeping reform that resulted in the system still essentially in place today.

Richard A. Cosgrove

Bibliography

Beattie, J.M. *Crime and the Courts in England 1660–1800.* 1986.

Dinwiddy, John. *Bentham.* 1989.

Hart, Herbert L.A. *Essays on Bentham: Studies in Jurisprudence and Political Theory.* 1982.

Kelly, Paul. *Utilitarianism and Distributive Justice: Jeremy Bentham and the Civil Law.* 1990.

Lieberman, David. *The Province of Legislation Determined: Legal Theory in Eighteenth-Century Britain.* 1989.

Lobban, Michael. *Common Law and English Jurisprudence 1760–1850.* 1991.

Postema, Gerald. *Bentham and the Common Law Tradition.* 1986.

Radzinowitz, Leon. *A History of English Criminal Law.* 4 vols. 1948–1968.

Thomas, William. *The Philosophic Radicals: Nine Studies in Theory and Practice, 1817–1841.* 1979.

See also Judicial System; Punishment

Lawrence, Stringer (1697–1775)

Lawrence is considered the founder of the Indian army. He rose through the British **Army** while serving in Gibraltar and in the **Forty-five** rebellion. Early in 1748 the **East India Company** appointed him commander of its troops at Madras. He organized his European and Indian soldiers into regiments that repelled a French attack the following June. In 1761, after several years of successful campaigns against the French, he became a major-general and commander-in-chief of all company forces. He retired in 1766. By partially centralizing the administration of the company's forces, Lawrence enabled them to conquer and hold **India** for generations.

A. Martin Wainwright

Bibliography

Cambridge, R.O. *Account of the War in India.* 1761.

Dictionary of National Biography, s.v. "Lawrence, Stringer."

Orme, R. *History of Military Transactions in Indostan.* 1803.

Lawrence, Sir Thomas (1769–1830)

Beginning as a child prodigy with little formal training, the gifted Lawrence became the successor of **Sir Joshua Reynolds** as Britain's greatest **portrait painter**. He was born in **Bristol**, the son of an innkeeper; while still a child he could capture in pencil the likenesses of his father's guests. As a young draftsman of portraits in pastel, and with access in **Bath** to the art collections of his patrons, he had an early introduction to original works and **engravings** of the antique and of old masters from which he copied. Admitted as a student at the **Royal Academy** (1787), he was encouraged to work in oil and achieved rapid success as a portrait painter, exhibiting in the Royal Academy (1790) 12 paintings, including two of *Queen Charlotte.*

Lawrence was not only talented but handsome, charming, a good talker, and a careful observer. In the **romantic** portraits of *Eliza Farren* (1790) and *Arthur Atherly as an Etonian*

Sir Thomas Lawrence

(1790–1791) his psychological insight into character, technically dazzling brushwork, and choice of full, singing color show the insight and virtuosity that led later critics to call him "the English Titian." He became an associate of the Royal Academy in 1791, and painter to the Dilettanti Society and painter-in-ordinary to the king in 1792 at the death of Reynolds. He joined his friends Richard Westall (1765–1836) and William Hamilton (1751–1801) in their interest in **Milton**, following the "Romantic Horrific" tradition of another friend, **Henry Fuseli**, and painting the monumental *Satan Calling Up His Legions* (1797).

The landscape artist Joseph Farington (1747–1821), friend of **John Constable** and father-figure to Lawrence, left in his diary a detailed record of the troubled years that followed, when Lawrence, a poor businessman, became entangled financially. Keeping neither sitter books nor dated correspondence, and constantly in debt even though fully employed, he frequently abandoned works midway or left them for assistants to finish. But the end of the **Napoleonic Wars** marked a new phase for him. Knighted by the Prince Regent in 1815, he was sent (1818) to Aix-la-Chapelle and Vienna to paint full-length portraits of two dozen men involved in Napoleon's overthrow, including Prince Metternich, Pope Pius VII, and Cardinal Consalvi—a signal honor that established his superiority in the eyes of contemporaries everywhere. These works now hang in the Waterloo Chamber at Windsor Castle.

In 1820 Lawrence became President of the Royal Academy, succeeding **Benjamin West**. Passionately devoted to his art, he valued the notion that good portrait painters ought to preserve a resemblance yet make the subject appear more beautiful. His late paintings of *George IV* (1822) and *Lady Peel* (1827) show his breadth and talent in the last decade of his life. A connoisseur, Lawrence had advocated the purchase of the **Elgin Marbles** for the nation, was influential in founding the National Gallery of Art (1824), and assembled one of the largest drawing collections of Michelangelo and Raphael of the age.

Joan K. Stemmler

Bibliography

Garlick, Kenneth. *Sir Thomas Lawrence: A Complete Catalogue of the Oil Paintings.* 1989.

———. *Sir Thomas Lawrence: Portraits of an Age, 1790–1830.* 1993.

Levey, Michael. *Sir Thomas Lawrence, 1769–1830.* 1979.

Millar, Sir Oliver. *Later Georgian Pictures in the Collection of Her Majesty the Queen.* 1969.

Solkin, David. *Painting for Money: The Visual Arts and the Public Sphere in Eighteenth-Century England.* 1993.

Wendorf, Richard. *The Elements of Life: Biography and Portrait-Painting in Stuart and Georgian England.* 1990.

Williams, D.E. *The Life and Correspondence of Sir Thomas Lawrence, Kt.* 2 vols. 1831.

See also Painting

Laws of Public Worship, Speech, and the Press

Laws relating to worship, speech, and the press were, in comparison to modern times, highly restrictive during most of the Hanoverian period. The **Toleration Act** (1689) supported limited freedom of worship by allowing **dissenting** ministers to hold services in licensed meetinghouses. But by the 1750s, **Evangelical** preachers were forming chapels that were rarely licensed because those who preached in them were either Anglicans or not ordained at all. Laws were nonetheless employed to discourage their followers: The government invoked various statutes to harass the field preachers. In **Wales**, the **Riot Act** (1715) was used repeatedly throughout the period against **Methodist** revivals, though many of these attempts failed, as the law of riot could not be convincingly applied to religious meetings. A thin but widely accepted idea of **religious toleration** made it difficult to enforce the laws that were available to authorities.

The scope of tolerance narrowed as the century progressed and the targets became political associations. Political agitation, economic depression, and public reaction to the **French Revolution** produced violent outbreaks of petitioning, conspiracies, and riots. Prosecution under existing statutes was generally unsuccessful, and the government of **Pitt the Younger** resorted to restrictive legislation. The Habeas Corpus Act (1679) was suspended in 1794. Treason and sedition acts (1795, 1799) extended the definition of treason and limited the right of public meeting, while the **combination acts** (1799, 1800) banned societies with secret committees or members.

But the most significant developments concerned laws regulating the press. The Licensing Act, designed to prevent the publication of seditious writings, lapsed in 1695, though opposition to its renewal was due more to failures in the licensing system than to enthusiasm for extending the liberty of the press. The stamp acts of 1712, 1725, and 1765 were partly intended to muffle **newspaper** criticisms of government, but legal loopholes made them easy to evade. Writers were nonetheless subject to severe existing laws of libel, and these were construed broadly by judges generally supportive of established authority. Yet public sentiment against seditious libel prosecutions grew. After the Special Juries Act of 1729, which reinforced a popular belief that juries could be packed to government benefit, juries began to refuse to convict in libel cases. The courts also objected to executive interference with the press, as several decisions surrounding **general warrants** and the prosecutions of **John Wilkes**, Henry Woodfall (publisher of the *Public Advertiser* in which **Junius's satires** appeared), and others showed in the period 1763–1772.

These cases, followed by various well-publicized cases of criminal libel and treason fought by the liberal **Whig** lawyer **Thomas Erskine** in the 1780s, helped set the stage for libel law reform. **Charles James Fox**'s Libel Act (1792) gave juries, rather than judges, the right to decide whether accused publications were in fact libelous. The act came just in time to help many individuals accused of violating the new treason and sedition acts of the latter 1790s. However, printers and **publishers** were still being convicted of blasphemous libel as late as 1819, which saw the jailing of **Richard Carlile** for publishing the works of **Thomas Paine**. Carlile eventually served more than 9 years in jail for printing **radical** works. Recognition of the public's right to discuss politics without any restraint whatsoever came as slowly as the advance of democracy itself.

William Edward Morris

Bibliography

Armstrong, A. *The Church of England, the Methodists and Society, 1700–1850.* 1973.

Black, Jeremy. *The English Press in the Eighteenth Century.* 1987.

Hanson, L. *The Government and the Press, 1695–1763.* 1936.

Williams, E. Neville. *The Eighteenth-Century Constitution, 1688–1815: Documents and Commentary.* 1960.

See also Censorship; Pornography

Learned Societies

Wide-ranging scientific, historical, and philosophical interests prompted the establishment of several learned societies during the Hanoverian period. Most were centered in **London**, though a few, such as the Royal Society of Arts (1754) and the **Lunar Society** of Birmingham (1766), extended more widely; some, such as the Royal Asiatic Society of Bengal (founded by **Sir William Jones**), were even founded outside the country.

At the beginning of the 18th century there were only two British societies of any importance: the **Royal Society of London** and the Royal College of Physicians. The study of science, originally conceived as "natural philosophy," was formally organized in 1660 with the creation of the former. (Its counterpart in **Scotland**, the **Royal Society of Edinburgh**, after its founding in 1783 offered its audiences the opportunity to hear lectures and read its publications, which included treatises by such leading Scots scholars as geologist **James Hutton**, historian **Adam Ferguson**, and chemist **Joseph Black**.) The College of Physicians consisted only of medical graduates of the universities of **Oxford** and **Cambridge**, and excluded many well-trained physicians from the universities in Edinburgh and **Glasgow**.

As knowledge became more specialized, societies were formed to cater to particular interests and specific disciplines. The Society of Dilettanti was formed (1732) by **Sir Francis Dashwood** and others to sponsor archaeological study in Italy. Another group interested in **antiquities and ruins**, The Society of Antiquaries (*f.* 1717), became incorporated in 1751, and stimulated interest in historical study. The Society Instituted at London for the Promotion of Arts, Manufactures, and Commerce (or, simply, the Society of Arts) was designed to promote practical improvements, offering awards for the application of scientific discoveries to everyday life; through book publications and public exhibitions, and later its system of examinations, the society encouraged improvements in the mechanical arts, chemistry, manufactures, and **agriculture**. Many **agricultural societies** formed, particularly after 1750, to disseminate information and stimulate **agricultural improvement**. The Society for Promoting Natural History, and the British Mineralogical Society, focused on the study of particular scientific areas.

In the arts, the **Royal Academy of Arts** was founded (1768) under the **patronage** of **George III**, specifically to help artists; its first president was **Sir Joshua Reynolds**. The chief musical societies, which accomplished at least some scholarship alongside their music-making, were the Academy of Ancient Music (founded in 1710), the Madrigal Society (1741), the Nobleman and Gentlemen's Catch Club (1761), the Anacreontic Society (1766), the Concert of Antient Music (1776–1848), the Philharmonic Society (founded in 1813), and the **Royal Academy of Music** (1823).

In mathematics, the **Analytical Society** was formed at Cambridge (1812) to advance the practical applications of mathematics and the new notational system in calculus. Increased discoveries in **science, technology and invention** in the latter Hanoverian period also spurred the creation of several new organizations. The Linnaean Society, founded (1788) with the help of the great landowner and president of the Royal Society, **Sir Joseph Banks**, acquired the vast collection of specimens of the founder of modern biological classification, Carl Linnaeus (1707–1778). Banks and fuel scientist Benjamin Thompson, Count Rumford (1753–1814), pooled resources in 1799 to create the **Royal Institution**, a training center for young mechanics. Other scientific associations with special interests included the Royal Horticultural Society (1804), Geological Society (1807), Astronomical Society (1820), Meteorological Society of London (1823), Entomological Society (1833), and Statistical Society (1834).

These organizations were designed to promote progress not only in the highest intellectual circles but also among the working classes. In 1826 the **Society for the Diffusion of Useful Knowledge**, an accompaniment to **Mechanics' Insti-**

tutes, was founded to provide lectures and cheap publications or "penny booklets" for workers. A culminating point in the creation of learned societies occurred in 1831 with the formation of the British Association for the Advancement of Science, which promoted scientific investigation and discourse throughout the **Empire**.

Jack Fruchtman, Jr.

Bibliography

Harrison, J.F.C. *Living and Learning, 1790–1960.* 1961.

Inkster, Ian, and Jack Morrell, eds. *Metropolis and Province: Science in British Culture, 1780–1850.* 1983.

McKie, Douglas. "Scientific Societies to the End of the Eighteenth Century." *The Philosophical Magazine.* No. 150, pp. 133–143.

Russell, Colin. *Science and Social Change, 1700–1900.* 1983.

Lee Sisters

Born into a theatrical family, the sisters Sophia (1750–1824) and Harriet (1757–1851) Lee were both novelists and dramatists. Together they ran a private school in **Bath**. Sophia's play *The Chapter of Accidents* (1780) was an early success; her historical **novel**, *The Recess* (1783–1785), was a tale of the daughters of Mary Queen of Scots by the Duke of Norfolk—"the first English romance," according to Harriet, "that blended interesting fiction with historical events and characters, embellishing both by picturesque description."

Harriet herself, though she too wrote for the stage, was successful primarily as a novelist. Her first novel, *The Errors of Innocence* (5 vols., 1786), is about the consequences of a hasty marriage. *Clara Lenox: or, The Distressed Widow* (1797) concerns lovers who have been divided by disapproving parents. The Lee sisters are remembered most for their frequently reprinted collection of stories, *The Canterbury Tales,* which first appeared in 1797 and comprised five volumes by 1805. The 12 stories (10 by Harriet) are on various themes—political, sentimental and **Gothic**; **Byron** adapted his *Werner* (1822) from one of them (the "German's Tale, Kruitzner"), which Harriet also dramatized (1825). To modern scholars the Lees are perhaps most important for their exploration of the combinations possible among the **Romantic**, Gothic, and historical literary traditions.

Howard A. Mayer

Bibliography

Roberts, Bette B. *The Gothic Romance: Its Appeal to Women Writers and Readers in Late Eighteenth-Century England.* 1980.

See also Dramatic Arts; Dramatic Criticism; Sensibility and Sentimentalism; Women in Literature

Leeds

The city of Leeds was an incorporated **borough** known for its **textile** manufacture. Traditionally a broadcloth town, Leeds's linen manufacture was briefly important after its introduction in the last decade of the 18th century, but this was eclipsed by the burgeoning of the **cotton industry** in the 19th century.

Located on the border of the West Riding textile region to the west and south, and the pastoral region to the north and east, Leeds was strategically placed for development as an industrial center. The city nevertheless remained relatively small until the latter half of the 18th century. Its **population** increased from about 7,000 around the year 1700, to perhaps 30,000 in 1775, to 53,000 at the time of the first census in 1801.

The construction of a great **canal** between Leeds and **Liverpool** was authorized by Act of Parliament in 1769, and this contributed to the growth of the town, though the project was not fully completed until 1816. An improvement act for lighting and paving was obtained in 1755, and by 1791 the town was lighted by oil lamps. The Leeds Infirmary opened in 1767. Leeds's first **newspaper**, the *Leeds Mercury,* began publication in 1718, and by the 1850s had become one of the leading liberal publications in England. The chapels of **dissenters** proliferated in the 18th century. The city's heyday, however, came in the Victorian period.

Daniel Statt

Bibliography

Beresford, M.W. *East End, West End: The Face of Leeds during Urbanisation, 1684–1842.* 1988.

Rimmer, W.G. "The Industrial Profile of Leeds, 1740–1840." *Thoresby Society Miscellany.* Vol. 14, pp. 130–157.

Wilson, R.G. *Gentlemen Merchants: The Merchant Community in Leeds, 1700–1830.* 1971.

See also Cities and Urban Life; Provincial Towns and Society

Legal Profession

Between 1714 and 1837 the modern form of the British legal profession emerged in the basic divisions of the judiciary between barristers and attorneys (solicitors). Another important development was the first tentative step to place the law on a professional basis in order to overcome the prejudices of popular culture. Major improvements included new levels of educational attainment, qualifying examinations, and new emphasis on strict adherence to an internal professional culture. By 1837, lawyers had made substantial progress that became the foundation of a more complete professionalization in the Victorian period.

There were many general similarities between the Hanoverian legal profession and the **clerical profession**, at least so far as Anglicans were concerned. Both professions were particularly respected because they were in a sense "established" by virtue of their connections with the constitution and church, the law and official faith of the land. Both were closely connected also with fundamentals—landowning, property, inheritance, birth, death, **crime**, and **punishment**. Both were professions of "gentlemen." This meant also that in both cases, professional training at the upper ranks for a long while amounted to little more than a liberal education in the classics and mathematics, acquisition of professionally useful con-

Judges on the bench, from a print by Hogarth, 1758

tacts, and certification without much in the way of competency examinations. Legal careers, however, were less dependent on **patronage** and family contacts than clerical careers, and so offered greater opportunities for penetration by upwardly mobile elements in the **middle class**. Law in this respect was more similar to **medicine**, the third of the "liberal professions" of the Hanoverian era; and it also resembled medicine in the sense that both careers were only then developing regular systems of training to ensure some uniform levels of competence.

The legal profession was divided into two branches. The upper, the bar, commanded much social respect and could often lead to high careers in politics, just as bishops of the church might become important public figures. Usually the crucial stepping-stone up was from barrister to judge, and for many barristers that was enough. Unlike Continental legal systems, where judges trained specifically for their duties, most judges in Hanoverian Britain were selected from the ranks of practicing barristers. The judge dominated everything in the courtroom, including the other barristers who practiced before him. He examined witnesses, evaluated evidence, and delivered instructions to juries so forcefully that they often returned verdicts in minutes. The impartial, detached demeanor of the modern judge did not apply in the hectic world of Georgian trials. Judges were often the sole representative of authority in a situation that frequently degenerated into a shouting match between two aggrieved parties.

The social composition of the judiciary, like that of the legal profession in general, evolved. By 1837 its composition reflected the more general social transformation wrought by the **Industrial Revolution**, inasmuch as there were growing numbers of judges drawn from the middle class at the expense of former links to the landed classes. In **Scotland**, where the **Act of Union** (1707) safeguarded the **Scottish legal system** (still fundamentally depending on principles drawn from Roman law), the legal profession underwent many of the same processes as in England and **Wales**, yet retained the distinctive markings of different historical antecedents. Many Scots were called to the English bar, some, like **Boswell**, merely dilettantes; others, like **Mansfield**, judges of great learning and accomplishments.

English barristers' legal education continued along the traditional pathway, the candidate attending one of the four Inns of Court in **London**: Lincoln's Inn, Gray's Inn, Inner Temple, or Middle Temple. These alone determined who should be considered fit to practice. But training at the inns during the Hanoverian period declined to such a low point that requirements amounted to little more than paying fees and attending dinners, so that an aspiring barrister often had to learn the law afterward by reading privately and by attaching himself to a successful practitioner. For this reason among others, **William Blackstone** gave the course of lectures in 1753 that anticipated his *Commentaries* (1765–1769). He hoped to make the law into a scholastic discipline, one that would reward intensive study at the universities, but he achieved little in this. The creation of an academic culture for the law in the universities would not occur until the later Victorian era. Educational standards did rise in general because the acquisition of a B.A. degree prior to reading for the bar became routine (though not required).

Theoretically, the higher knowledge of the law belonged only to judges and to the barristers who performed as advocates before them (and who also, for a fee, provided learned counsel). They looked down their noses at attorneys (solicitors), who stood in roughly the same inferior relation to barristers that surgeons and apothecaries did to physicians in the medical profession. Attorneys in the age of **Samuel Johnson** were disliked and ridiculed for their sharp practices—Johnson himself commented of a certain individual that though he, Johnson, hated to speak ill of anyone, he believed him an attorney. Yet the numbers and importance of attorneys evolved greatly during the era, partly because of the impact of the economic revolution upon such things as land management, **patents**, contracts, partnerships, **mining** rights, **canal**-building, turnpike trusts, insurance, and so on. The attorney was a middleman. He might not aspire to the legal heights, but he stood to make a decent living through his expertise, which he acquired, like a **craftsman**, from an apprenticeship rather than through liberal education. His training system was founded in an act of 1729 which required 5 years' legal apprenticeship and an examination by judges (apparently rarely observed) before a candidate might be sworn in as an attorney. In 1739 a professional association or Law Society was founded in London to encourage attorneys' education and interests, and other such societies were founded between 1770 and 1800 in **Bristol**, Yorkshire, Somerset, and Sunderland.

Equally important to attorneys' advancement was the fact that they increasingly stood as gatekeepers between the ordinary individual, perhaps living in the **provinces**, who needed legal services, and the barristers (centered in London except when they went on circuit) who could provide specialized information and formal advocacy. The division of labor was specifically defined. By about 1800 the fixed requirement that attorneys would meet initially with those needing legal counsel, and later contact a barrister on behalf of the client, formed a cornerstone of practice. Barristers turned into legal specialists, whereas attorneys became responsible for the provision of routine legal services. This gave attorneys a boost in prestige and income because they thereby gained a virtual monopoly over many areas of practice, particularly the new areas connected with economic development. Nor could barristers seek business from attorneys without diminishing their own higher status. In addition, courts held that barristers could not sue for their fees because such payments were honoraria, a view that suited the rising prestige of the barristers.

Few individuals became wealthy in practice of the law. The bar was intensely competitive; substantial fees were commanded only by a handful of titans. Of them, Lloyd Kenyon, Baron Kenyon (1732–1802), furnishes an example. After being articled to a solicitor in Nantwich he enrolled at the Middle Temple (1750), became a barrister (1756), then became law secretary for his friend and fellow student Edward Thurlow (1731–1806), succeeding him as king's counsel (1780) and attorney general (1782–1783). At this point his income from legal opinions alone was 2,578 guineas in 1780, 2,936 guineas in 1781, and 3,020 guineas in 1782. On the other hand, many called to the bar with less ability or fewer well-placed friends did not attract the attention of solicitors, and thus received no briefs at all. A career at the bar was a major gamble, with a small number of winners but many more failures. For solicitors, routine legal work brought growing rewards, though few achieved considerable incomes. Some compensation did emerge in the growing acceptance of their place within the legal profession itself.

Helped along by the law societies, the definition of what constituted appropriate professional behavior expanded gradually. For example, increasing recognition that an individual accused of a felony might profit from legal counsel led to what was considered an acceptable commercialization of practice, so that such counsel had become commonplace by 1780. Intervention of this sort brought significant alterations in the conduct of trials, as well as specific changes in the standards of evidence. Thus the modern adversarial system of the common law, joining counsel for each party in legal combat, was largely a product of Hanoverian development.

Outside the legal system, the bar was an avenue to, among other things, authorship. Writers as diverse as **Henry Fielding**, **Lord Kames**, **Lord Monboddo**, **Edward Young**, **Samuel Romilly**, **John Wilson**, and **Henry Crabbe Robinson** were trained in the law. Legal training was ideal preparation also for a political career. Many prominent political figures were trained in the law, for example, **Hardwicke**, **Burke**, **Dunning**, **Erskine**, **Perceval**, and **Eldon**. Of course, legal training did not necessarily produce political compatibility. The long list of Hanoverian lawyers includes people as **radical** as **Thomas Muir**, founder of the Scottish Association of the Friends of the People, and **Robert Macqueen, Lord Braxfield**, who sentenced Muir to 14 years' **transportation** in what has been called a classic abuse of judicial power.

Richard A. Cosgrove

Bibliography

Beattie, J.M. *Crime and the Courts in England, 1660–1800.* 1986.

Cocks, Raymond. *Foundations of the Modern Bar.* 1983.

Duman, David. *The Judicial Bar in England, 1727–1875: The Reshaping of a Professional Elite.* 1982.

Holdsworth, Sir William S. *A History of English Law.* 17 vols. 1903–1967.

Lemmings, David. *Gentlemen and Barristers: The Inns of Court and the English Bar, 1680–1730.* 1990.

Prest, Wilfrid R., ed. *The Professions in Early Modern England.* 1987.

Robson, Robert. *The Attorney in Eighteenth-Century England.* 1959.

See also Judicial System; Law Reform

Legal System

See Judicial System

Legge, Henry Bilson (1708–1764)

The fourth son of the 1st Earl of Dartmouth, Legge epitomized three phenomena not uncommon in the early Hanoverian age: the younger son seeking his fortune, the **Tory** offspring turned **Whig**, and the hard-working junior government official. Legge's good humor and intelligence so pleased **Sir Robert Walpole** that he made Legge his personal secretary (1735–1739) and brought him into Parliament (1740). He was rarely out of office thereafter, his most important appointments being to the Admiralty Board (1745–1746), Treasury Board (1746–1749), and Exchequer (1754–1755, 1756–1761). He was an able speaker in **Commons** on financial matters but lacked the charisma of his sometime friend **William Pitt the Elder**. Legge's fortune was made when he inherited an estate in reversion (1754), requiring the addition of the name Bilson. His family's social status was secured when his wife was granted the revival of her father's barony (1760). Although removed from office (1761), Legge remained a member of Commons up to his death.

P.J. Kulisheck

Bibliography

Kulisheck, P.J. "'The Favourite Child of the Whigs': The Life and Career of Henry Bilson Legge, 1708–1764." Unpubl. Ph.D. diss. 1995.

Leicester House

Built during the 1630s on the north side of present-day Leicester Square, Leicester House became under the Hanoverians "the pouting place of princes." **George I**'s son bought the house (1717), and until his succession as **George II** (1727), he there entertained **William Pulteney** and other members of the parliamentary **opposition**. In 1741 his own son, **Frederick, Prince of Wales**, moved in and restored Leicester House as a haven for the opposition. Frederick's entertainments and collections made it a center for **painting**, **music**, and letters. On his death (1751), his own son George lived there, imbibing the opinions of the opposition until his coronation as **George III**. Royalty vacated in 1766, and in 1790 this symbol of partisan politics was demolished.

Robert D. McJimsey

Bibliography

Cowie, Leonard W. "Leicester House." *History Today.* Vol. 23, pp. 30–37.

Jones, Stephen. "Frederick, Prince of Wales: A Patron of the Rococo," in Charles Hind, ed., *Rococo in England: A Symposium.* 1986.

McKelvey, James Lee. *George III and Lord Bute: The Leicester House Years.* 1973.

Roscoe, Ingrid. "Andien de Clermont: Decorative Painter to the Leicester House Set." *Apollo: The Magazine of the Arts.* Vol. 123, pp. 92–101.

Sedgwick, Romney, ed. *Letters from George III to Lord Bute.* 1939.

———. *Some Materials towards Memoirs of the Reign of George II, by John Hervey.* 3 vols. 1931; rev. ed., 1963.

Charlotte Lennox

Lennox, Charlotte (1729?–1804)

Best known for her **novel** *The Female Quixote* (1752), Lennox was also a poet, playwright, **translator**, and critic. Her other works included the novels based on her American experiences, *The Life of Harriot Stuart* (1751) and *Euphemia* (1790); and *Shakespear Illustrated* (1753–1754), one of the first comparative studies of Shakespeare's sources.

Lennox was born Charlotte Ramsay, possibly in **North America**, and spent her early life there. She married Alexander Lennox in 1747, and with her writing supported him and their children throughout their married life. She was admired and encouraged by **Samuel Richardson** and **Samuel Johnson**, though she was never a part of the **bluestocking** group they associated with. Her *Female Quixote,* which examined the comic and heroic possibilities of a quixotic woman, generated critical praise, but despite this and her varied literary efforts to support herself, she died in poverty. Her one masterwork nevertheless established her reputation as a witty novelist and influenced later women writers, including **Jane Austen**.

Mahasveta Barua

Bibliography

Doody, Margaret Anne. "Shakespeare's Novels: Charlotte Lennox Illustrated." *Studies in the Novel.* Vol. 19, pp. 296–310.

Small, Miriam Rossiter. *Charlotte Ramsay Lennox: An Eighteenth Century Lady of Letters.* 1935.

Spencer, Jane. *The Rise of the Woman Novelist.* 1986.

See also Women in Literature

Leslie, Charles (1650–1722)

Leslie, born in **Dublin** and educated at **Trinity College** and the Temple, was perhaps the best-known writer among the **nonjurors**, defending the independence of the **Church of England** and launching vigorous attacks on **Quakers**, **free-thinkers**, **Latitudinarians**, and republicans. Critics such as **Matthew Tindal** charged him with seeking to introduce a new form of Anglican popery. A fierce opponent of **occasional conformity** and an ardent defender of Dr. Henry Sacheverell (1674–1724), he also provided inspiration for the mocking *The Shortest Way with Dissenters* of **Daniel Defoe**. Charged with open **Jacobitism**, Leslie fled to **France**, where he attempted without success to convert **James Edward, the Old Pretender**, to Anglicanism. In 1721 he returned to **Ireland**, where he died the following year.

Roger D. Lund

Bibliography

Frank, Bruce. "The Excellent Rehearser: Charles Leslie," in J.D. Browning, ed., *Biography in the Eighteenth Century.* 1980.

Lathbury, Thomas. *A History of the Nonjurors.* 1845.

Letters

That Hanoverian Britain has been dubbed the "age of the great English Letter Writers" can be attributed to four factors: the development of the **postal service** and founding of the penny post in the late 17th century, accompanied by a dramatic increase in the quantity of letters carried to all parts of the country; a rise in literacy, with a new class of shopkeepers and their wives swelling the size of the writing public; a contemporary emphasis on sociability, as expressed in conversation and letters; and a peculiar rhetorical self-consciousness, which could mold even the most informal message into an expression of literary artistry.

Three types of letter in Hanoverian Britain have been identified: the intimate message intended only for its recipient, the more formal "public" letter designed for a wider audience, and the fictitious letter used as a literary device (as in all the novels of **Samuel Richardson**).

Although familiar letter writing probably consumed more paper than any other literary enterprise of the period, and conveyed as much useful information, very little of it was intended for publication. Indeed, the publication of personal letters was frowned upon as a breach of privacy and propriety. But the great letter writers found ways to get around this. **Alexander Pope** followed the example of Erasmus and pretended that his letters had been stolen from him, publishing a surreptitiously revised edition of his correspondence in 1735. **Lady Mary Wortley Montagu**'s "Turkish Embassy Letters," published posthumously to great acclaim (1763), apparently consist of 52 genuine letters sent by Montagu to friends and relations as she accompanied her husband's embassy to Constantinople in 1718; but recent research has shown that the letters were fabricated from a journal she had kept while in Turkey. **Horace Walpole** carefully fashioned a vast personal correspondence, including thousands of letters, into a social chronicle of his age that he intended ultimately to be published, deliberately choosing a wide spectrum of correspondents to participate unwittingly in this enterprise.

Conyers Middleton's (1683–1750) use of Cicero's letters in his *Life* (1741) promoted the idea of the personal letter as an invaluable form of **autobiography**. His method was adopted by William Mason (1724–1797) in the "Memoirs," including many letters, which he prefixed to his edition of **Thomas Gray**'s *Poems* (1775). Gray and **William Cowper** rank among the age's greatest epistolary artists who wrote their letters without thought of publication. The same was true of the **Earl of Chesterfield**, though his posthumously published *Letters to His Son* (1774) aroused public indignation by their cynical advice on the art of pleasing for personal advancement.

Lord Byron too was an exceptionally witty and conversational correspondent, but the finest letters of the late Hanoverian period were those by **John Keats**. These have been ranked among the treasures of English literature. Filled with insights into the nature of **poetry**, they vividly describe Keats's quest for a poetic identity, and rival in importance and interest the poetry itself.

Wendy Jones Nakanishi

Bibliography

Anderson, Howard, Philip B. Daghlian, and Irvin Ehrenpreis, eds. *The Familiar Letter in the Eighteenth Century.* 1966.

Bond, Richmond. "Eighteenth-Century Correspondence: A Survey." *Studies in Philology.* Vol. 33, pp. 572–586.

Halsband, Robert, ed. *The Complete Letters of Lady Mary Wortley Montagu.* 1965–1967.

Irving, William. *The Providence of Wit in the English Letter Writers.* 1955.

Lewis, W.S., ed. *The Yale Edition of Horace Walpole's Correspondence.* 1937–1983.

Trilling, Lionel, ed. *The Selected Letters of John Keats.* 1951.

See also Epistle

Levellers' Rising (1724)

Beginning in March 1724, a series of dykes or stone fences, some several miles long, was pulled down in parts of Galloway in southwest **Scotland** by large, well-organized bands of men and women, opposed to the creation by local landowners of large enclosed parks for cattle grazing. The "Levellers," as these bands were called, were sometimes armed with guns as well as with "kents," the long poles used to level the dykes; sometimes they also maimed cattle, the object of their desperation.

The livestock trade to England had been growing in the 17th century, but the immediate post–**Union** years saw even further expansion. As grazing became increasingly important to Galloway's agricultural economy, landowners evicted many of their smaller peasant tenants in favor of grassland, and began putting up fences. The "Levellers," for their part, owed much to the region's Covenanting religious tradition, which in the latter 17th century had seen popular violence used against the state-imposed Episcopalian clergy. The same parish-based, anti-authoritarian tradition was tapped by the Levellers' leaders, some of whom were closely connected with Covenant-supporting churchmen.

Military force was brought in, and despite strong popular support, the movement was effectively crushed by midsummer 1724, though sporadic outbreaks did occur thereafter. Heavy fines for damages were imposed, and the established **Church of Scotland** made clear its disapproval. Enclosure carried on apace.

Christopher A. Whatley

Bibliography

Leopold, John. "The Levellers Revolt in Galloway in 1724." *Scottish Labour History Society Journal.* Vol. 4, pp. 4–23.

See also Radicalism and Radical Politics; Scottish Agriculture

Lewis, Matthew "Monk" Gregory (1775–1818)

Lewis, among the "kindest and best creatures that ever lived" (according to **Sir Walter Scott**), at age 19 wrote one of the most sensational of **Gothic novels**, *The Monk* (1796). Treating topics such as necrophilia, incest, homosexuality, rape, murder, revenge, demonology, religion, and damnation, the novel resembles a grand horror comic book without illustrations. Its power ensured its outlasting all adverse criticism, such as that which points out its clumsy plotting, stereotypical characters, and secondhand material.

The Monk was Lewis's first published work; an earlier play, *The Epistolary Lady,* a farce, was not produced; and a comedy, *The East Indian,* was not staged until 1799. He had mastered German in Weimar (1792–1793), where he was influenced by German Romanticism. But **Horace Walpole**'s *The Castle of Otranto* (1764) and **Ann Radcliffe**'s *The Mysteries of Udolpho* (1794) were major inspirations for *The Monk,* which, Lewis told his mother, he had written in 10 weeks. The novel went through five editions by 1800, with changes to soothe an outraged public.

Although an M.P. from 1796 to 1802, Lewis preferred literature to politics and in 1797 he wrote *The Castle Spectre,* a dramatic romance produced successfully at Drury Lane (December 14). Perhaps remembering the charges of plagiarism brought against *The Monk,* he appended his sources to the printed version of the play. In 1797 he also **translated** German plays by Friedrich Schiller (1759–1805) and August von Kotzebue (1761–1819). Two years later he translated Juvenal's thirteenth satire, and in 1801 he published *Tales of Wonder,* a collection of his own **ballads**. Two more of his plays were produced that same year (1801). His translation of *Abällino* (1794), a "robber" novel by J.H.D. Zschokke (1771–1848), appeared as *The Bravo of Venice* in 1805; both it and his two-act melodramatic adaptation, *Rugantino; or, The Bravo of Venice* (1805), were successful. Drury Lane spectacularly staged *The Wood Daemon; or The Clock Has Struck,* a Gothic extravaganza, in 1807; it ran for 34 nights. Even more popular was *Timour the Tartar* (1811), staged at Covent Garden for 44 nights, complete with onstage horses.

Lewis's posthumously published *Journal of a West Indian Proprietor, Kept during a Residence in the Island of Jamaica* (1834) reveals a man very much concerned about the well-being of his slaves, but one who regretted that the slavery "system is now so incorporated with the welfare of Great Britain as well as of Jamaica as to make its extirpation an absolute impossibility." The *Journal* contains poems by Lewis and Jamaican folktales; the straightforward narrative of his two trips to Jamaica (he died returning home from the second) and plantation life there won **Coleridge**'s praise as "by far his best work."

Although Lewis's Gothic plays were popular, and he wrote comedies and tragedies as well as poems and translations, and though his *Journal* reveals a humane and sensitive side to his character, justifiably, Lewis's fame rests with *The Monk.*

Peter A. Tasch

Bibliography

Baron-Wilson, Mrs. Cornwell. *The Life and Correspondence of M.G. Lewis, Author of "The Monk," "Castle Spectre," & with Many Pieces in Prose and Verse Never Before Published.* 1839.

Conger, Syndy M. *Matthew G. Lewis, Charles Robert Maturin and the Germans: An Interpretative Study of the Influence of German Literature on Two Gothic Novels.* 1977.

Evans, Bertrand. *Gothic Drama from Walpole to Shelley.* 1947.

Irwin, James Joseph. *M.G. "Monk" Lewis.* 1976.

See also Dramatic Arts; Gothic Fiction and Gothicism; Romanticism and Romantic Style; West Indies

Libraries and Librarianship

Although publicly funded libraries open to all did not emerge in the Hanoverian period, books became available to more readers and in more varied ways. In 1714, private libraries belonged to royalty, the peerage, and many professionals; to the universities of **Oxford** and **Cambridge** and their colleges; to the four **Scottish universities** and **Trinity College, Dublin**; to many schools and academies; to the Inns of Court and the Faculty of Advocates, **Edinburgh**; to numerous cathedrals and parishes; and to a few municipalities, such as **Bristol**, **Norwich**, and **Manchester**. But such institutions severely restricted borrowing. More widely accessible were books in **coffee-houses**, the newly emerging book **clubs**, and circulating or rental libraries. The age saw dramatic increases in research collections, the working libraries of writers and professionals, and small outreach and mid-sized subscription libraries.

University collections were accessible to faculty, graduates, upper-level students, and scholarly or noble visitors, while other institutions served clergy and professionals. Increased literacy and religious **enthusiasm** called for new distribution systems, such as book clubs and circulating libraries. A greater awareness of the progress of knowledge and its economic and civic value fueled improvements in research libraries, and

Circulating library advertisement, c. 1750

many of these purchased more and more books for more specialized fields. New libraries were built for Cambridge and Trinity College, and at Oxford the Radcliffe Camera was built and endowed for All Souls, Christ Church, and Worcester Colleges (1749). Cataloguing grew more exacting, shelving more systematic and subject-related, and acquisitions more diverse. This greater complexity and orientation toward service would eventually create a need for librarianship as a separate discipline, but contemporary librarians were usually only professors exceptionally experienced in textual scholarship.

University collections grew slowly through copyright deposits, author donations, and acquisitions, but they moved dramatically forward with large bequests. The stipulation of the 1710 Copyright Act that fine-paper copies be deposited at nine libraries dissuaded many from registering books, especially those sought by faculty. Librarians and janitors appealed to authors for copies, but the Bodleian in 1727 received only 27 deposit copies and 10 works donated by authors. Even with small funds collected from readers' fees, rental property, and the sale of duplicates, the Bodleian and Cambridge libraries had little money for collection development until late in the century, when they received funding from student fees; only then could they address the needs of faculty and students in modern fields. However, large private collections were donated or bequeathed to universities, such as the antiquarian Richard Rawlinson's to the Bodleian (1755), and Bishop Moore's to Cambridge (1715). The mere shelving of these donations partly prevented the librarian and his small staff of one or two sublibrarians and janitors from producing revised general catalogues. Thus the Bodleian's 1738 catalogue, the first since 1674, had to serve the library for over a hundred years.

Faced with inexpensive acquisition of **Sir Hans Sloane**'s enormous collection, Parliament in 1753 established the **British Museum** "for publick use to all Posterity." To Sloane's 50,000 volumes were joined the Harleian Manuscripts, the Royal Library (given by **George II** in 1757), and the Thomason Tracts (purchased by **George III** in 1762). The British Museum opened in Montague House in 1759, and its first catalogue appeared in 1787. Later the library acquired **Charles Burney**'s collection with its wealth of English **newspapers** (1828), **Sir Joseph Banks**'s natural history library (1820), and George III's library (1823).

Of some significance were the mushrooming book clubs and subscription libraries. By around 1750, scores of circulating libraries were renting hundreds and sometimes thousands of catalogued books and magazines from bookshops and stalls. To serve and expand the reading public, religious organizations, such as the Associates of Reverend Thomas Bray (1656–1730), established parochial libraries throughout England. Educated **dissenters**, barred from Anglican collections, had a special need to form book clubs and subscription libraries with scholarly collections. By the end of the Hanoverian era, hundreds of book clubs, with 10 to 20 members each, met monthly to exchange books, collect dues, fine absentees, and select acquisitions. Club collections were often housed in coffeehouses or public rooms, and sold at annual auctions. In many cities, subscription libraries emerged; in these, proprietors built up large holdings, with published catalogues, for indefinite continuation. Later in the 19th century, this expansion of services would help promote **Mechanics' Institutes** and tax-supported public libraries.

James E. May

Bibliography

Harris, Michael H. *History of Libraries in the Western World.* Rev. 3rd ed., 1984.

Kaufman, Paul. *Libraries and Their Users: Collected Papers in Library History.* 1969.

Kelly, Thomas. *Early Public Libraries: A History of Libraries in Great Britain before 1850.* 1966.

McKitterick, David. *Cambridge University Library, a History: The Eighteenth and Nineteenth Centuries.* 1986.

Olle, James G. *Library History: An Examination Guidebook.* 1967.

Philip, Ian. *The Bodleian Library in the Seventeenth and Eighteenth Centuries.* 1983.

See also Museums and Galleries; Newspaper Press; Periodicals; Publishers and Booksellers; Reference Works

Licensing Act

See Playhouse Act

Lighthouses

The lighthouse is the most important of the fixed marks used by the navigator to check his ship's position. While it is unlikely that such shipping aids appeared in Britain before the Norman Conquest, an increasing number were brought into operation as **trade** expanded from early medieval times. By the early 18th century, over 40 lights were located on the coasts of the British Isles, their greatest concentration occurring on the east coast of England to serve the extensive trade in **coal** from the Northeast to **London**. However, as the **commerce** of **Bristol**, **Liverpool**, **Glasgow** and other west-coast ports increased, new lighthouses were constructed at western locations such as St. Anns Head (1714), the Skerries (1714), and St. Bees (1717).

Various authorities were responsible for lighthouse administration. Of leading importance was the Corporation of Trinity House, a medieval guild of mariners that had been granted (in 1566) the power to erect beacons at its own expense and to charge dues on shipping passing its lights. There were also private lighthouse owners, their rights to operate lights and to levy tolls being granted in perpetuity by Act of Parliament or held under lease from Trinity House.

While the corporation dispensed its income in alms to distressed seafarers and their families, the private operators were motivated largely by profit. Complaints about the excessive charges imposed for often inadequate services reached a peak in the early 19th century. After a series of Select Committee reports, legislation was passed (1836) empowering Trinity House to purchase the rights of the remaining dozen or so private lighthouse owners. With authority over Scottish beacons vested in the Commissioners of Northern Lighthouses in 1786, and control over Irish lights exercised by a succession of statutory bodies from 1767, lighthouse provision in Britain was consolidated and in large measure made publicly accountable by the time of Queen Victoria's accession (1837).

Lighthouses of various designs and materials were constructed in the 18th century. Many were rudimentary buildings, though some have been justly praised as significant feats of engineering. Among the most celebrated are the Eddystone Lighthouse, a stone tower built by **John Smeaton** on an exposed rock off Plymouth, in service from 1759 to 1882; and Henry Whiteside's wooden pile lighthouse, built on the Smalls (off Pembrokeshire) in 1776 and operational for 85 years. In these multifarious structures, coal, wood, candles, oil, and gas fueled the lights that rendered safer the burgeoning traffic using the seas around the British Isles during the Hanoverian period.

David J. Starkey

Bibliography

Cotter, C.H. *The Complete Coastal Navigator.* 1964.

Hague, D.B., and R. Christie. *Lighthouses: Their Architecture, History and Archaeology.* 1975.

See also Coastal Shipping; Shipping and Seamen

Lillo, George (1693–1739)

Lillo broke with Restoration forms and popularized moralistic domestic bourgeois tragedy, commencing a new and more sentimental era on the stage. Reared as a **dissenter**, he was originally a jeweller. His best plays, though declamatory and exaggerated in sentiment, present **middle-class** characters beset by tragic circumstances.

The opening-night success of *The London Merchant, or The History of George Barnwell* (1730) was one of the greatest and least expected events in English dramatic history. Before the play was to open, wits planning to attend ridiculed Lillo's source, a **ballad** later printed in **Thomas Percy**'s *Reliques of Ancient English Poetry* (1765). But the critical audience was deeply moved by the play, which even **Alexander Pope** praised. London **merchants** sent their apprentices to see this drama of an apprentice, led by a courtesan to commit murder, who afterward expiates his sin; it was performed regularly for over a century.

After an unremarkable masque, *Britannia and Batavia* (1734), and an unsuccessful tragedy, *The Christian Hero* (1735)—whose plot he appropriated from deceased playwright Thomas Whincop—Lillo presented a companion masterpiece, *Fatal Curiosity* (1736). **Henry Fielding**, manager of the Haymarket Theatre, wrote a prologue for and successfully promoted this play, whose source was, again, a 17th-century ballad.

George Colman the Elder (1783) and **Henry Mackenzie** (1784) both wrote adaptations of *Fatal Curiosity,* as did German playwrights, most notably Gotthold Ephraim Lessing (1729–1781); but Lillo's domestic tragedy ultimately influenced novelists, especially Denis Diderot (1713–1784), more than dramatists.

Laura Morrow

Bibliography

Burgess, C.F. "Further Notes for a Biography of George Lillo." *Philological Quarterly.* Vol. 46, pp. 424–428.

Dictionary of National Biography, s.v. "Lillo, George."

Nolte, F.O. *Early Middle-Class Drama, 1696–1774.* 1935.

Palette, D.B. "Notes for a Biography of George Lillo." *Philological Quarterly.* Vol. 19, pp. 261–267.

Rothstein, Eric. *Restoration Tragedy.* 1967.

Sherbo, Arthur. *English Sentimental Drama.* 1957.

Steffensen, James L., ed. *The Dramatic Works of George Lillo.* 1993.

See also Dramatic Arts

Lindsey, Theophilus (1723–1808)

Lindsey was educated at St. John's College, Cambridge. From 1746 to 1773 he enjoyed a modest career as a cleric in the **Church of England**. Influenced by Archdeacon **Francis Blackburne** of Cleveland, whose stepdaughter he married in 1760, he was an energetic supporter of the Feathers Tavern Association, formed in July 1770 to obtain relief from clerical subscription to the church's Thirty-nine Articles of Faith and create a more comprehensive Protestant-established church. The petitions of the association were decisively defeated in the **House of Commons** in 1772 and 1774.

Lindsey, by 1773 a convinced **Unitarian**, left the church then and with the aid of friends such as **Richard Price** and

Joseph Priestley set up the first avowedly Unitarian chapel in England (1774), in Essex Street, **London**. He spent the remainder of his career encouraging the Unitarian movement. Though fiercely attacked by orthodox clerics and **dissenters**, Lindsey kept an equable temper, defending his views with mildness and dignity. If he failed in his intention to create a reformed Church of England, he succeeded in institutionalizing liberal heterodox dissent.

Martin Fitzpatrick

Bibliography

Baylen, Joseph O., and Norbert J. Gossman, eds. *Biographical Dictionary of Modern British Radicals.* Vol. 1. 1979.

Bradley, James E. *Religion, Revolution and English Radicalism: Nonconformity in Eighteenth Century Politics and Society.* 1990.

Gascoigne, John. *Cambridge in the Age of the Enlightenment: Science, Religion and Politics from the Restoration to the French Revolution.* 1989.

Mather, F.C. *High Church Prophet: Bishop Samuel Horsley (1733–1806) and the Caroline Tradition in the Later Georgian Church.* 1992.

Robbins, Caroline. *The Eighteenth Century Commonwealthman.* 1959.

See also Rational Dissent

Liquor

See Drink Industries

Literary Criticism

There were heroes before Homer and critics before Dryden (1631–1700), but Dryden, in his essays (prefaced to his plays and **translations**), raised English criticism to a status that approached, if not always appropriated, literature. Criticism would have remained a privileged preserve, however, if the **middle class** had not begun its overwhelming growth during Dryden's time. Contrasted to the upper class, which at least pretended to know the criteria for judging **poetry** and drama, the newly literate class, which included women, was a large audience determined to learn what properly to admire. And the new industry of print **journalism** was delighted to bring the teachings of self-anointed critics to the task.

Most of the literary criticism during the Hanoverian period was journalistic—practical, not theoretical, appearing first in **essays** in **newspapers** and in hundreds of journals for an immediate reading, and only secondarily for a "collected works" or subscription edition. Countless reviews concentrated on the plot (or **fable**), characters, language, and **morality** of the works. The largest number of critical essays reviewed plays as drama (tragedy or comedy) or as **theater** (judging the performers and production). Toward the end of the 18th century, **publishers** increasingly discovered profit in multivolume anthologies of poetry, plays, and **novels**, and **Samuel Johnson**, **Elizabeth Inchbald**, and **Anna Laetitia Barbauld** (among others) helped form their readers' tastes with their often moralistic and conservative biographical and critical introductions. But however important these forms of journalistic criticism, some of the most influential opinions did appear in book form or as independent essays.

From classical writers such as Horace, Virgil, and the author called Longinus, and from French critics, among them Nicholas Boileau (1628–1702), René Rapin (1621–1687), and André Dacier (1651–1722) and his wife Anne (1654–1720), English critics such as Dryden, Thomas Rymer (1641–1713), **John Dennis** and others derived and adapted tenets of **neoclassicism**. But, as William Congreve (1670–1729) observed, "He that will have a May Pole shall have a May Pole"; thus Dennis, who argued strongly for poetic justice (a term coined by Rymer) and neoclassical rules, also championed **enthusiasm** (heightened emotion), by way of Longinus, as a basis for poetry. The stock rule-bound partisan of neoclassicism is largely a straw man built by the **Romantics**. Nevertheless, many 18th-century critics upheld the validity of genre expectations, and many of their judgments relied on how well works met the criteria for such recognized kinds of literature as odes, tragedies, and **pastorals**.

When it came to the novel, however, which had no recognized classical authority, authors such as **Henry Fielding** created their own heritage and criteria, or reshaped a rule to fit the occasion. In prefaces and postscripts, novelists defended and defined the new genre. **Clara Reeve** devoted two volumes to *The Progress of Romance* (1785), in which she authoritatively distinguished between romances and novels, the former describing "what never happened nor is likely to happen"; the latter, a "familiar relation of such things as pass every day before our eyes."

The most important critic between Dryden and Johnson was **Joseph Addison**, who succeeded in synthesizing classical precepts, French rules, and philosophical principles mainly by **John Locke** into popular *Spectator* essays. Although **Alexander Pope**'s poetic *Essay on Criticism* (1711) was a witty recapitulation of "what oft was thought but ne'er so well expressed," it was Addison who judiciously explained how to appreciate **Milton**, and analyzed the pleasure of the imagination. Not a pioneer in critical thought, he guided his middle-class audience's perceptions of literature.

Although reason and correctness (based on readings of classical authorities) were hallmarks of neoclassicism, early-18th-century critics and philosophers such as Addison and the 3rd Earl of Shaftesbury (1671–1713) emphasized emotional and aesthetic responses. The term "taste," which denoted a combination of **sensibility** and imagination—and also, in the second half of the century, judgment—came into play, sometimes against **wit**. Occasionally late-century critics wielded it to club authors who, lacking the sublimity of Homer or Milton, rose no higher than to good taste; others used it to laud those who appreciated the **picturesque**.

Addison defined taste as the discriminating "faculty of the soul." This "enthusiasm" helped facilitate the growing acceptance of the **sublime** into English criticism. Longinus's doctrine considered sublimity as the "echo of greatness of spirit" without regard to genre. It became one of the routes to **Gothi-**

A literary party at Sir Joshua Reynolds's: (from left to right) Boswell, Johnson, Reynolds, Garrick, Burke, Paoli, Burney, Warton, Goldsmith

cism with its attempts at awe and terror, and to Romanticism with its recollection of emotion evoked by the grandeur of nature. Two of the major landmarks are **Edmund Burke**'s *The Origin of Our Ideas of the Sublime and the Beautiful* (1756) and **Edward Young**'s *Conjectures on Original Composition* (1759).

However conservative Johnson may now seem, he warred with contemporary critical doctrines. Neoclassicism and the "tyranny of prescription" he rejected along with taste (an unreliable guide since it preferred beauty to reason as a basis for judgment). The critic should go beyond "partial representation," Johnson advised, "to hold out the light of reason whatever it might discover." As for poets, the power which invigorates them is "genius" (that energy which animates); so he preferred Dryden, who "often surpassed expectation," to Pope, who "never fell below it." In his *Idler* and *Rambler* essays, his preface to the *Lives of the Poets,* and his edition of **Shakespeare** (which very much fed the growing popularity throughout the period of native authors), Johnson earned the title, wryly bestowed by **Tobias Smollett**, of The Great Cham of Literature.

In a **letter** (April 1742), **Thomas Gray** stated: "The language of the age is never the language of poetry." That Gray felt compelled to emphasize what was then a truism makes 1742 a convenient date to mark the gradual decline of neoclassical poetry, and with it Pope's reputation. **William Wordsworth**'s rejoinder (almost 60 years later, in 1800), that poetry is the "language really spoken by men," is but one of many voices in the dispute which often declared Pope its point man.

The argument over Pope's poetic stature was part of the larger issue about the source of poetic strength. In the *Essay on Pope* (1782), **Joseph Warton** argued that because Pope relied on art rather than nature, he was in the rank of poets second to Spenser, Shakespeare, and Milton. Similarly, **William Cowper** rejected Pope's polished couplets for the "manly, rough line with a deal of meaning in it" (1791). The poetic ground had been prepared by the time Wordsworth wrote his *Preface to the Lyrical Ballads* (quoted above). Pope's last hurrah came in the "Bowles-Pope" controversy (1819–1826), after **William Lisle Bowles**, in his edition of Pope's works (1806), pronounced the early Hanoverian giant merely second-rate. Bowles made the by-then familiar argument (fathered by Joseph Warton) that "images drawn from what is beautiful or sublime in nature are more sublime and beautiful than images drawn from art, and that they are therefore *per se* more adapted to poetry than manners." Some of the most famous Romantic writers took part in the debate: **William Hazlitt** and the editors of *Blackwood's Magazine* supported Bowles, while **William Gifford**, **Thomas Campbell**, **Isaac D'Israeli**, and **Lord Byron** were among Pope's partisans.

Neoclassicism did not die by proclamation. Generic assumptions continued to inform much criticism; but (as it were) "Who or what is Hamlet?" increasingly yielded to "I am Hamlet." Psychologically based criticism, and with it empathy, became a standard of Romanticism. The reader, **Thomas De Quincey** exhorted, should "never . . . pay any attention to his understanding ['the meanest faculty'] when it stands in opposition to any other faculty of his mind."

The third great artist–critic during the Hanoverian era was **Samuel Taylor Coleridge**, "a man of grand and original genius," as **John Lockhart** called him. He did not reject generic identity, but in contrast to neoclassical critics, he viewed each work as unique and the parent of laws governing it. He elicited both the discreetness and the universality of a work, but unlike neoclassicists, he began with the particular. Imagination for him was the great mediator of opposites. With his theory of organic unity he narrowed the gap that neoclassicism only observed, between art and nature, genius and judgment (Pope's "grace beyond the reach of art"). Coleridge's reliance on a psychological awareness of character and his belief that form results from the energy of the particular work (rather than being imposed upon it), helped maintain his important critical influence, and that of Romanticism, throughout the Victorian and modern periods.

Peter A. Tasch

Bibliography

Atkins, J.W.H. *English Literary Criticism: 17th and 18th Centuries.* 1951.

Bate, Walter Jackson. *Samuel Johnson.* 1975.

Clark, J.C.D. *Samuel Johnson: Literature, Religion and English Cultural Politics from the Restoration to Romanticism.* 1995.

Elioseff, Lee Andrew. *The Cultural Milieu of Addison's Literary Criticism.* 1963.

Elledge, Scott, ed. *Eighteenth-Century Critical Essays.* 2 vols. 1961.

Fogle, Richard Harter. *The Idea of Coleridge's Criticism.* 1962.

Hoffman, Daniel G., and Samuel Hynes. *English Literary Criticism: Romantic and Victorian.* 1963.

Hooker, Edward Niles. *The Critical Works of John Dennis.* 2 vols. 1939.

Humer, Robert D. *Dryden's Criticism.* 1970.

Needham, H.A. *Taste and Criticism in the Eighteenth Century.* 1952.

Pocock, Gordon. *Boileau and the Nature of Neo-Classicism.* 1980.

Van Rennes, J.J. *Bowles, Byron and the Pope Controversy.* 1927.

Wimsatt, Jr., William K., and Cleanth Brooks. *Literary Criticism.* 1964.

See also Dramatic Criticism; *Lyrical Ballads*; Periodicals; Poetry and Poetics

Liverpool

Liverpool, a borough town on the estuary of the Mersey River, became in the Hanoverian period the principal British port on the west coast. Its thriving **overseas commerce** led to a phenomenal expansion in **population** that made it Britain's third largest **city** by 1801.

It rose from humble origins. It probably had no more than 1,000 inhabitants at the Restoration. But from that time forward its growth was rapid, driven by the flourishing **trade** that passed through its expanding port. By around 1700, Liverpool's population had increased to perhaps 5,000, owing to the increasing importance of the manufacturing industries of south Lancashire and the burgeoning trade to the **West Indies** and America. **Salt** was exported from Liverpool, and the chief imported goods were sugar and Chesapeake **tobacco**. Increasing demand for these luxury commodities, as well as improvements in **inland transport**, contributed to the city's expansion between 1714 and 1760.

By 1750 the value and volume of Liverpool's Anglo–American trade was surpassed only by **London**'s. New **docks** were constructed from the beginning of the 18th century to accommodate and encourage this trade. The original port was expanded into the Old Dock in 1715, followed by Salthouse Docks (1753), George's Dock (1771), King's Dock (1788), and Queen's Dock (1796). Liverpool **merchants**' entry into the lucrative **slave trade** contributed to the dramatic rise of the city as a port. By 1750, Liverpool's eclipse of **Bristol** as the chief western port was apparent. Liverpool thus became one of the points on the triangle of trade between **Africa**, the West Indies, and England, sending ships to Africa for slaves that were traded for sugar and rum that was in turn imported to England. On the eve of the abolition of the slave trade in 1807, 185 Liverpool ships were engaged in a trade that trafficked in some 50,000 slaves a year. But abolition did not bring the feared collapse of Liverpool's commercial economy, as trade with **North America** was by then growing rapidly.

The town suffered only a temporary setback on account of the loss of the American colonies. The close connections that Liverpool enjoyed with the nearby Midland counties then undergoing rapid industrial development ensured its continuing success and expansion in the late Hanoverian period. The digging of **canals** and the improvement of **roads** contributed to its role as the outlet for the industrial manufactures of the industrial centers and the inlet for colonial merchandise. Liverpool's merchants prided themselves on the part they had played in the **Napoleonic wars**, and the port's facilities, by the 1820s constructed in **iron** rather than wood, continued to be expanded on both sides of the Mersey. Liverpool's dominance of the Atlantic trade continued unabated into the Victorian period. Yet the problems brought about by the city's economic success, deficient public services, inadequate **housing**, and grinding **poverty** remained largely unaddressed.

Daniel Statt

Bibliography

Clemens, Paul G.E. "The Rise of Liverpool, 1665–1750." *Economic History Review.* 2nd ser. Vol. 29, pp. 211–225.

Corfield, P.J. *The Impact of English Towns, 1700–1800.* 1982.

Hyde, F.E., ed. *Liverpool and the Mersey: An Economic History of the Port, 1700–1970.* 1971.

Vigier, F. *Change and Apathy: Liverpool and Manchester during the Industrial Revolution.* 1970.

See also Irish Emigration; Provincial Towns and Society

Liverpool, 2nd Earl of (Robert Banks Jenkinson) (1770–1828)

Liverpool was the son of Charles Jenkinson, **George III**'s leading "Friend," and the heir to his earldom (to which he succeeded in 1808). Educated at Charterhouse and Christ

Church, Oxford, he went on to hold many of the greatest positions of state: Foreign Secretary (1801–1804); Home Secretary (1804–1806, 1807–1809); Secretary for War and the Colonies (1809–1812); and **Prime Minister** (1812–1827).

Liverpool was the epitome of the slow starter in politics. Widely believed to have advanced far beyond his merits, ridiculed by his more talented political contemporaries as "poor Jenky," he nonetheless lived to produce one of the most successful premierships in British history. During his long hold on power, Napoleon was defeated, domestic **radicalism** was tamed, and the foundations of economic liberalism and of the Victorian Pax Britannica were laid. Liverpool skillfully juggled interest groups and managed powerful men in his cabinets—**Lord Castlereagh**, **George Canning**, the **Duke of Wellington**—and retained their support for many years.

He was a good politician as well as a successful conciliator. Of the 50 British prime ministers, only **Sir Robert Walpole** and the **Pitt the Younger** surpassed him in the number of years they consecutively held office. Along with William E. Gladstone (1809–1898) and Harold Wilson (1916–1995), he won as many general elections as any prime minister in British history (four, in 1812, 1818, 1820, and 1826).

James J. Sack

Bibliography

Brock, W.R. *Lord Liverpool and Liberal Toryism.* 1967.
Cookson, J.H. *Lord Liverpool's Administration, 1815–1822.* 1975.
Gash, Norman. *Lord Liverpool.* 1984.
Hilton, Boyd. *Corn, Cash, Commerce: The Economic Policies of the Tory Government, 1815–1830.* 1977.
Sack, James J. *From Jacobite to Conservative: Reaction and Orthodoxy in Britain,* c. *1760–1832.* 1993.

Liverpool and Manchester Railway

The first major railway in Britain to rely solely on steam power and to serve two major centers of **population**, this is considered the first modern **railway**. It was devised by local businessmen who were frustrated by the stranglehold enjoyed by **canal** and river navigation over the transportation of bulky goods, particularly **cotton**, between the two cities, and by the length of time it took to move such cargoes on the congested waterways. Plans for a railway were published as early as 1824, but parliamentary consent was necessary for this type of enterprise; and before this could be obtained, opposition from local landowners as well as canal proprietors had to be overcome.

The railway's construction was accomplished by civil engineering triumphs such as the cutting at Olive Mount in Liverpool and the crossing of the marshy Chat Moss near Manchester. By 1829 the proprietors had decided on the steam locomotive (rather than fixed engines) as the means of propulsion, and held trials at Rainhill near Liverpool (1829) that resulted in victory for the "Rocket" designed by Robert and **George Stephenson**. The latter had already established his credentials as the designer of the "Locomotion," the locomotive that had opened the **Stockton and Darlington Railway** (1825).

The Liverpool and Manchester railway opened on 15 September 1830, though rejoicing was dimmed by the fatal injury to the politician **William Huskisson**. From the beginning, passenger traffic was considered to be as important as freight—a new direction in the development of inland **transport**. The railway's financial success meant that by end of the Hanoverian era, plans were laid and construction was underway for more intercity railways, signifying the beginning of the end for the long-distance **coaching** industry.

A.J.G. Cummings

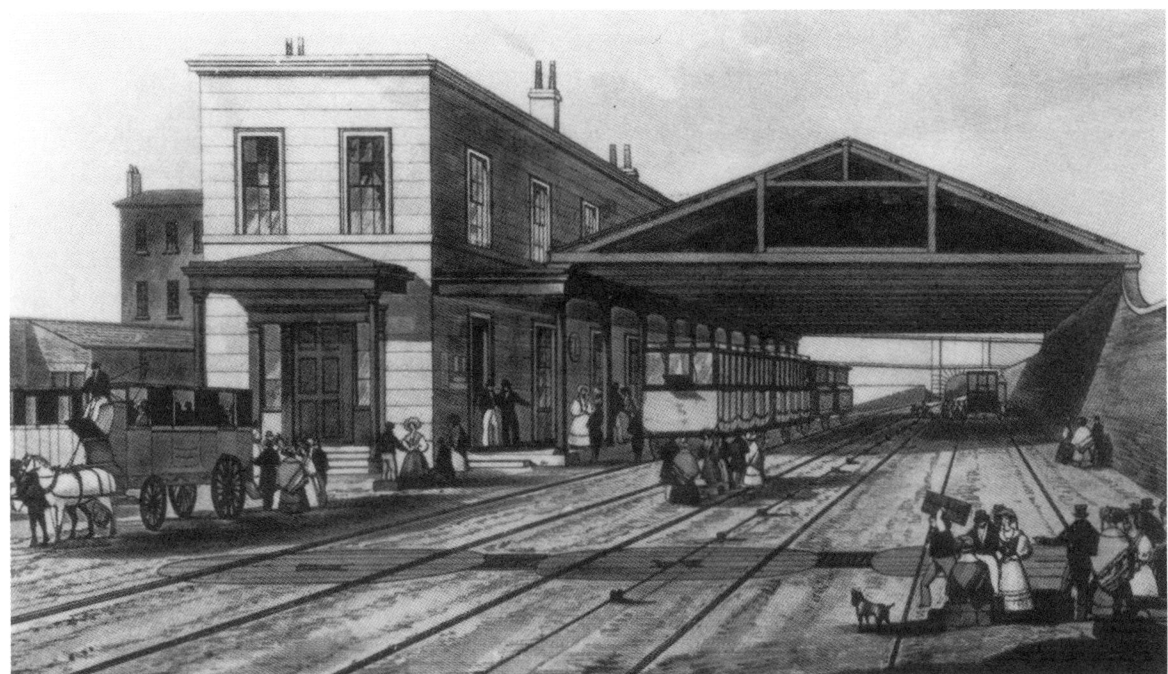

Liverpool railway office, 1831

Bibliography

Bagwell, Philip. *The Transport Revolution from 1770.* 1974.

Dendy-Marshall, C.F. *The Centenary History of the Liverpool and Manchester Railway.* 1930.

Dyos, H.J., and D.H. Aldcroft. *British Transport.* 1974.

Lloyd Family

The Lloyds, who became prominent in the **iron** trade and in **banking**, sprang from an old Montgomeryshire family who also provided a deputy governor and a chief justice to Pennsylvania. Sampson Lloyd (1664–1724), younger son of Charles, the first of the **Quaker** Lloyds, migrated to **Birmingham** (1698), where his sister had married John Pemberton, a leading iron **merchant**. Sampson set up as an iron merchant and soon went into production also. His older brother, Charles (1662–1747), who had set up a forge in **Wales** and as early as 1721 experimented with the **Darby family**'s coke-smelting technique, sold iron through Sampson but became bankrupt in 1727 and also moved to Birmingham. His son and grandsons failed to reestablish the senior line's position, and it fell to Sampson's descendants to restore the family's fortunes.

Sampson II (1699–1779) and his sons Sampson III (1728–1807), Nehemiah (1745–1801), and Charles (1748–1828), extended business interests further, acquiring a slitting mill and later forges at Burton-on-Trent and Worcestershire. Like many industrialists they were virtually forced by the deficiencies of the existing provincial system to undertake banking activities. From this came Birmingham's first bank, formed (1765) in partnership with a prominent button manufacturer, John Taylor. This, true to its industrial origins, played a significant part in financing the industrialization of the Midlands. The partners were quick to set up a sister bank in **London** (1770), but Birmingham remained the principal center of activity. From a low point at which Sampson II was a widower with one sickly son and the Lloyd name on the verge of extinction, the family went from strength to strength, boasting 120 descendants three generations later, closely linked into the Quaker elite of the Midlands and from their prominent position in industry and **finance** playing a leading role in public life.

R.D. Corrins

Bibliography

Flinn, M.W. "The Lloyds in the Early English Iron Industry." *Business History.* Vol. 2, pp. 21–31.

Lloyd, H. *The Quaker Lloyds in the Industrial Revolution.* 1975.

Lloyd's of London

Today, Lloyd's is the most famous high-risk insurance marketing concern in the world, with more than 25,000 associated but independent underwriters insuring everything from lives in war zones to movie stars' legs. It began as a mere **coffeehouse** at about the time of the **Glorious Revolution**, involved in the risky business of insuring seagoing **ships**.

In common with many other sectors of commerce in **London** in the late 17th and early 18th centuries, much of the marine insurance business took place in coffeehouses. Gradually, Edward Lloyd's Coffeehouse became associated with marine insurance ventures, though even by 1720 it was by no means singular in its activities. However, by 1750 its position as the leading place for such insurance was certain, and Lloyd's List was being published. It is probable that by 1760 a register was being kept, to which only members who paid a subscription had access.

Ships were classified according to information received on seaworthiness, state of repair, destination, and any other intelligence that could be gleaned. The best category with minimum risk was assigned an A-1 rating. Business was booming in the mid-18th century because of the succession of **wars**, and it was important to secure a degree of privacy for the business. Thus a new Lloyd's was established, eventually moving into the Royal Exchange (1774). Although essentially still a coffeehouse, it was effectively becoming institutionalized into a vast syndicate of individual underwriters, each assuming unlimited liability, the corporation itself assuming none. The speed and despatch with which they and the **joint-stock companies** such as the **Royal Exchange Assurance** organized their business and dealt with claims led to a fair degree of foreign business coming into London. This was to be an important part of Britain's invisible exports in the Victorian age, and was one important example of the increasing sophistication of the London financial markets during the Hanoverian era.

A.J.G. Cummings

Bibliography

Raynes, H.E. *A History of British Insurance.* Rpt. 1968.

See also Banking and Bankers; Finance and Investment; Insurance; Shipping and Seamen

Local Government

See Government, Local and County

Locke, John (1632–1704)

"O Locke!" exclaimed young **Jeremy Bentham**, "First master of intellectual truth! without whom those who have taught *me* would have been as nothing!" Locke, the chief intellectual precursor of the Hanoverian age, produced the political philosophy that would sustain its secular state and worked out the epistemology that would stimulate its foremost philosophers and poets. His bumpy career as scholar, propagandist, exile, surgeon, and philosopher expressed itself in the astonishing range of his work, which included tracts on **education**, **government**, **theology**, **language**, philosophy, and psychology.

Locke's own political fortunes were spotty. His service to his patron Anthony Ashley Cooper, Earl of Shaftesbury (1621–1683), culminated in 5 years of exile. But his political thought, expressed in his *Two Treatises on Government* (1690), consolidated and enhanced the "social contract" theory of Hugo Grotius (1583–1645), Samuel Pufendorf (1632–1694), Thomas Hobbes (1588–1679), and several others. Reacting against Robert Filmer's (*c.* 1588–1653) affirmations of monar-

John Locke

chical divine right, Locke vested the authority of government in consensual agreements between citizens. His notion that political power derives less from God than from consenting citizens helped to smooth the introduction of constitutional monarchy and to justify the choosing of German kings to guide the British nation. All subsequent writers on human rights, popular sovereignty, and the right to revolution are in his debt.

Lockean philosophy focuses on epistemology, the study of knowledge and of knowing. Locke's renowned *Essay Concerning Human Understanding* (1690) investigated the means by which persons come to know the world of ordinary experience. It devoted little space to nonnatural sources of information such as revelation and church teaching, and was therefore viewed with suspicion by religious authorities. Locke's philosophy, one of the first thorough explorations of the cognitive process, has long been mistaken for subjectivism or relativism. For him, however, it was the interaction of the mind with experience—the "ideas" and "qualities" of objects as they manifested themselves to percipients—that was the chief topic of philosophical study. His concern with the richness of nature and the additive powers of perception helped to inspire the huge quantity of descriptive **poetry** that graced the Hanoverian age.

Locke's theological and educational theories have fared less well than his political and philosophical theories. But his *Letters Concerning Toleration* (1689, 1690, 1692) and essay on *The Reasonableness of Christianity* (1695), which attempted to found faith on reason, fortified Hanoverian **Latitudinarianism** and provided ideas for later natural rights theories of conscience and belief. Locke has been called (by Harold Laski) the first great secular philosopher of Western society, and the description is not far off. His ideas were permanent fixtures of the Hanoverian age.

Kevin L. Cope

Bibliography

Ashcraft, Richard. *Revolutionary Politics and Locke's Two Treatises of Government.* 1986.

Clark, J.C.D. *The Language of Liberty, 1660–1832: Political Discourse and Social Dynamics in the Anglo-American World.* 1994.

Fox, Christopher. *Locke and the Scriblerians.* 1988.

Tipton, I.C., ed. *Locke on Human Understanding.* 1977.

Wood, Neal. *The Politics of Locke's Philosophy: A Social Study of "An Essay Concerning Human Understanding."* 1983.

———. *John Locke and Agrarian Capitalism.* 1984.

Yolton, John. *John Locke and the Way of Ideas.* 1968.

———. *Locke: An Introduction.* 1985.

See also Constitution, The Glorious; Empiricism; Political Thought

Lockhart, John Gibson (1794–1854)

Journalist, poet, novelist, translator, and editor, Lockhart, "the scorpion," was a central figure in late-Hanoverian letters. He was also, among other things, an accomplished biographer. His **biography** of his father-in-law **Sir Walter Scott** (seven volumes, 1838) was long considered second only to **Boswell**'s *Johnson*. Lockhart also wrote lives of **Robert Burns** (1828) and Napoleon Bonaparte (1829).

After receiving a first in classics at Oxford (Balliol) and a law degree from **Edinburgh**, Lockhart joined *Blackwood's Edinburgh Magazine* ("Maga") in April 1817, along with **John Wilson** and **James Hogg** ("The Ettrick Shepherd") to counter successfully the **Whig** *Edinburgh Review*. Maga's October 1817 issue is memorable for its collaborative, exuberant, sophomoric, biblically styled **satire** of Edinburgh's publishing scene, "The Chaldee Manuscript." Lockhart is also probably responsible for the series, "On the Cockney School of Poetry," in which he damned **John Keats**'s *Endymion* (1818) as "calm, settled, imperturbable drivelling idiocy."

Lockhart's **essays** appeared under a variety of pseudonyms, including Z, Baron von Laurerwinkel, Peter Morris, M.D., William Wastle, and Dr. James Scott ("the Odontist"). Between 1821 and 1826, when he left Maga for John Murray's (1778–1843) conservative *Quarterly Review* (London), Lockhart was constantly writing; among other efforts, he published four **novels** and **translated** *Ancient Spanish Ballads* (1823). With Wilson, Hogg, and William Maginn (1793–1843) he contributed to the *Noctes Ambrosianae,* a long-running series of fictional conversations in Maga (1822–1835) supposedly held at Ambrose's tavern.

As editor of the *Quarterly Review* until 1853, he maintained an uneasy friendship with **John Wilson Croker**, who had opposed his appointment. Lockhart found more congenial colleagues at *Fraser's Magazine,* which Maginn managed beginning in 1830. Under the name Pierce Pungent, the two continued the satiric partnership begun at Maga.

Disproving the fable about the scorpion and the frog, however, Lockhart left most of his satiric nature behind and successfully shaped the *Review* to reflect an "unlimited sympathy with society [and] to be a running panorama of English life and thought and manners." The son of a clergyman, the **Tory** Lockhart found his readers among "the clergy and country gentry."

Peter A. Tasch

Bibliography

Hart, Francis Russell. *Lockhart as Romantic Biographer.* 1971.

Hildyard, Margaret Clive. *Lockhart's Literary Criticism.* 1931.

Lockhead, Marion. *John Gibson Lockhart.* 1954.

Oliphant, Margaret. *William Blackwood and His Sons.* 3 vols. 1897.

Sullivan, Alvin, ed. *British Literary Magazines.* Vol. 2. 1983.

Thrall, Miriam M.H. *Rebellious Fraser's.* 1934.

See also Literary Criticism; Periodicals

Lofft, Capell (1751–1824)

Poetaster, lawyer, astronomer, and classical scholar, Lofft agitated against the **slave trade** and supported the rebels in the **War of American Independence.** A liberal **Whig** in the **commonwealthman** tradition, acquainted with many of the London **radicals** of the latter 18th century, he fought against judicial injustice at the cost of his name being struck from the roll of magistrates (1800). A prolific author of political, critical, and **poetic** works, he charitably oversaw the publication of *The Farmer's Boy* (1799) by Robert Bloomfield (1766–1823) and wrote its Preface; **Byron** joked that he was "preface-writer-general to distressed versemen." Lofft's second wife, Sara Watson, contributed to his five-volume anthology of sonnets, *Laura* (1814), which anticipated **Leigh Hunt**'s collection of 1816.

Peter A. Tasch

Bibliography

Dictionary of National Biography, s.v. "Lofft, Capell."

London

London was the center of British government, the focal point of political activity, and the fountainhead of social and cultural change. A major center for trade, the country's chief port, and a site of manufacture, it was also the chief consumer's market in the kingdom. More than ten times the size of the next largest British city, the capital exemplified for contemporaries the best and worst features of urban life. Though it grew less quickly than industrial centers such as **Manchester** and **Liverpool**, it nevertheless astounded by its size. With perhaps 650,000 inhabitants in 1700 and about 1 million at the time of the first census in 1801, London was the largest city in Western Europe, and was rivaled only by Constantinople and Tokyo. London contained more than 10% of the total **population** of England and **Wales**.

From **Defoe**'s image of London as a whale at the beginning of the period to **Cobbett**'s denunciations of the "great Wen" at its end, the scale of the metropolis and the pace of its growth excited constant comment. Fashionable suburbs marched westward and, more slowly, northward. To the east, **housing** for the laboring classes and commercial building also expanded greatly. The areas south of the river, made more accessible by the building of Westminster Bridge (1750) and Blackfriars Bridge (1769), were rebuilt in the second half of the century. Much of the physical growth—the march of brick and mortar—came about through a system of speculative building within large, aristocratically owned estates, with properties held on leaseholds of 99 or fewer years. One consequence was a high degree of uniformity in the built fabric of the city, encouraged still more by the various building acts passed during the period.

The growth of London's population proceeded despite the notorious excess of number of deaths over births. The continual flow of inward migration, numbering at least 8,000 individuals per year, made up the demographic deficit and provided the surplus necessary for growth. Migrants were mostly from southern England, although a growing number of Scots and Irish made London their home, and a modest but not negligible stream of foreigners settled in the capital. Attempts were repeatedly made to stanch the immigration of population. The foundation of hospitals arose partly from this motive. The Foundling (1739), and the general hospitals like the Westminster (1720), the London (1740), and the Middlesex (1745), sought to reduce the social costs of high mortality. Their total effect on the death rate was probably negligible, but they reveal the growing **humanitarian** sentiment of the period.

The magnetic pull for migrants was London's thriving and increasingly diversified economy. Within the domestic economy, London was by far the largest outlet for the burgeoning market in consumer goods and in commercialized forms of leisure and entertainment. As the seat of government and the venue of law and the courts, London was the point of rendezvous in the annual social season that embraced parliamentary sessions. Thus the nation's elite also spent much of its increasing wealth in the capital. A substantial segment of London's economy catered to the growing social class seeking to indulge and demonstrate its taste and politeness at **operas**, assemblies, **coffeehouses**, **concerts**, and **pleasure gardens**.

Satisfying the cravings for **shopping** of the fashionable provided a lively trade for London's shopkeepers. Supplying the capital with food and other necessaries represented a major segment of the metropolitan economy, and by the end of the 18th century the city's wholesale food markets were suffering from severe congestion. The retail trades became less and less dominated by the traditional guilds as London expanded physically beyond the jurisdiction of the corporation of London. The city came increasingly to be a mercantile and commercial center, as **merchants** began to take up residence in outlying districts. Indeed, London's role as a center of international **banking**, **insurance**, and **finance** evolved rapidly as the city adapted to Britain's new strength in **overseas commerce**.

Thus the port of London retained its predominance, and a vast overseas trade flowed through the city. The lucrative re-export trade flourished as the valuable commodities of the East Indian and West Indian trades flowed to the imperial capital.

Cornhill, the Exchange, and Lombard Street, London, c. 1780

The construction of a series of new **docks** to the east of the old and inadequate Pool of London in the early 19th century bears testimony to the continuing importance of London as a port.

Although London was never an industrial center in the same sense as Manchester or **Birmingham**, much manufacturing existed in the capital. Many London manufactures were connected with the international trade of the port, and involved colonial goods or raw material. Also important were skilled trades in high-quality goods, from compasses and telescopes to watches and furniture. These manufactures were almost uniformly small in scale, and the most notable large-scale manufacture, the silk-weaving industry of Spitalfields, suffered continuing decline despite protective legislation.

Poverty was a ubiquitous problem in Hanoverian London, despite the city's vibrant economy. Beggars were to be seen in nearly every street, and the growing cost of relieving the poor was a continual vexation. Poverty and **crime** were often conjoined, and the poorest quarters of St. Giles were notorious as "rookeries" of criminals. Housing and sanitary conditions were often appalling, and the pattern of casual employment alternating with periods of cyclical or seasonal unemployment made survival itself precarious at times for London's poor. Yet on the whole, conditions were probably better at the end of the period than at its beginning. Although London exemplified the problems of the early modern urban environment and embraced the extremes of wealth and poverty, that diversity was in many respects its strength; and the social fabric, though often stretched, proved remarkably resilient.

Daniel Statt

Bibliography

George, M. Dorothy. *London Life in the Eighteenth Century.* 1925.

Landers, John. *Death and the Metropolis: Studies in the Demographic History of London, 1670–1830.* 1993.

Linebaugh, Peter. *The London Hanged: Crime and Civil Society in the Eighteenth Century.* 1992.

Olsen, Donald. *Town Planning in London: The Eighteenth and Nineteenth Centuries.* 1964.

Rasmussen, Steen Eiler. *London: The Unique City.* 1937.

Rudé, George. *Hanoverian London, 1714–1808.* 1971.

Schwarz, L.D. *London in the Age of Industrialisation: Entrepreneurs, Labour Force and Living Conditions, 1700–1850.* 1992.

Sheppard, Francis. *London, 1808–1870: The Infernal Wen.* 1971.

Summerson, John. *Georgian London.* 1945.

Wrigley, E.A. "A Simple Model of London's Importance in Changing English Society and Economy 1650–1750." *Past and Present.* Vol. 37, pp. 44–70.

London Corresponding Society (LCS)

The London Corresponding Society (LCS) was founded in January 1792 by **Thomas Hardy**, a London shoemaker, and a small group of reformers inspired by the **French Revolution**. Its political objectives were universal manhood suffrage and annual parliaments—the same two democratic objectives that had been pursued since the latter days of the **American Revolution** by many **radicals** and by the venerable **Society for Constitutional Information** (SCI), itself revived in 1791 by **Horne Tooke** and others.

LCS's membership was much larger and more plebeian than SCI's, though in the 1790s many of the leaders of both groups were members of both organizations. LCS was predominantly a working-class organization, its membership made up of small-scale employers, **craftsmen** and mechanics, even porters and laborers, contributing a penny a week. Its membership grew very rapidly, from a mere eight men to several thousand within a matter of months. In its earliest months it was extremely suspicious of co-optation by parliamentary politicians or even **middle-class** reformers, though two of its top officials, Joseph Gerrald (1760–1796) and Maurice Margarot (1745–1815), were propertied lawyers. (Hardy was its secretary–treasurer.) Its main activities were to discuss political questions both within itself and with other groups by correspondence, but naturally as the reform situation evolved in the early 1790s, changing from optimism to aggressive, then increasingly desperate, confrontation, it expanded into other spheres.

Thus it printed pamphlets, circulated the ideas of **Tom Paine**, sent congratulatory addresses to the French National Convention (e.g., in September 1792), collected some 6,000 signatures with which to petition Parliament (May 1793) for political reform, sent delegates to successive "British Conventions" in **Scotland** (December 1792, October 1793), and organized increasingly huge mass meetings in the **London** area (April 1794, May and June 1795); in October and November 1795 LCS twice attracted crowds numbering more than 100,000 to hear **John Thelwall** voice their anger over the **war**, economic hardships, and food prices, and denounce the constitutional system, which LCS saw as responsible.

LCS was at the center of radical agitation, and government authorities, reacting to this, convinced themselves that its rhetoric in the spring of 1794 implied both violent resistance to authority and support for a French invasion of Britain. Beginning on 12 May 1794, government officers seized the papers of LCS and SCI, and arrested Hardy, Thelwall, Horne Tooke, and some 30 others on charges of treason. Although all were acquitted at trial or simply released, the trials were expensive for LCS and reduced its membership. Other blows came with the suspension of Habeas Corpus from 1794 to 1801, which meant that political prisoners could be jailed without trial; then the passage of the Treasonable Practices Act and the Seditious Meetings Act (the Two Acts, 1795), which proscribed, among other things, denunciation of the British **constitution**, and unlicensed meetings of more than 50 people.

These repressive measures, together with the unfavorable position forced upon radicals by the war against France, spelled the end of LCS. It had dwindled to a few dozen members by 1797. It managed to survive until 1799, when Parliament passed the Corresponding Societies Act, which finally suppressed it and similar organizations. The **Combination Acts** of 1799 and 1800 enlarged the ban to all societies organized for political or economic reform. Yet LCS had performed an historic function. It had served as a vehicle for the political education of the working class, promoting serious political activity and serving as a stepping-stone in the gradual but inevitable advance of democracy.

Frank M. Baglione

Bibliography

Cone, Carl B. *The English Jacobins: Reformers in Late 18th Century England.* 1968.

Dickinson, H.T. *British Radicalism and the French Revolution, 1789–1815.* 1985.

Goodwin, Albert. *The Friends of Liberty: The English Democratic Movement in the Age of the French Revolution.* 1979.

Hone, J. Ann. *For the Cause of Truth: Radicalism in London, 1796–1821.* 1982.

Wright, D.G. *Popular Radicalism: The Working-Class Experience, 1780–1880.* 1988.

See also Anti-Jacobin; Association Movement; Corresponding Societies; Loyalist Associations; Society for Supporters of the Bill of Rights

London Debating Society

An informal discussion-group, founded primarily by **John Stuart Mill**, the London Debating Society existed from 1825 to 1830. Mill wished to engage it in debates on important social, political, and economic issues of the day. Its membership, which included T.B. Macaulay (1800–1859), Connop Thirlwall (1797–1875), George Villiers (1800–1870), and John Austin (1790–1859), ordinarily met fortnightly in the Freemason's Tavern in **London**. Early participants included debaters from Oxford and Cambridge, M.P.s, and such notable figures as the novelist George Edward Bulwer-Lytton (1803–1873) and his brother the diplomat William Henry Bulwer-Lytton (1801–1872). The first debate, though well attended, was, according to Mill, a fiasco because the discussants—all being liberals—found little to fight about. This was remedied by the 1828–1829 season, when followers of **Coleridge** debated **Benthamites**. The disputes contrasting **Byron** with **Wordsworth** caused Mill to question his utilitarian beliefs, and in 1829 he withdrew from the society.

Cynthia Guidici

Bibliography

Britton, Karl. *John Stuart Mill: Life and Philosophy.* 1969.

Packe, Michael St. John. *The Life of John Stuart Mill.* 1954.

London Pianoforte School

This term refers somewhat loosely to the manufacturers, performers, and composers, both British and foreign, who made **London** the world capital of piano music during the decades on either side of 1800.

The piano was invented by Italians and developed by Germans. It was introduced to London by the German maker Johannes Zumpe in about 1760, and quickly gained enormous popularity. Soon English pianos became the most advanced in the world. By superior **technology**, mass production, and aggressive marketing techniques, leading London manufacturers such as Stodart, Broadwood, and Clementi dominated the European piano market from the 1780s until the 1820s. It was during this period that the piano, with its capacity for expressive dynamics and its sustaining pedal, decisively replaced the harpsichord on the concert platform and in the home. It became the favorite medium both for the spectacular display of virtuosity and for Romantic expression. Beethoven was but one of many Continental composers who desired an English piano.

Simultaneously, a brilliant school of pianist–composers came forward to exploit the possibilities of the new instrument. Though the first London edition of music for the piano was by **Johann Christian Bach** (Op. 5, 1766), the seminal figure was **Muzio Clementi**, who surpassed all Europe in the brilliance of his playing technique in the late 1770s and 1780s, and began to publish a long series of influential sonatas. In following decades, new forms of pianistic expression were developed by Clementi's London pupils John Baptist Cramer (1771–1858), pioneer of the *étude* (study), and **John Field**, inventor of the nocturne (which, however, he developed after emigrating to Russia in 1802). Other prominent members of the school were the expatriate Bohemian Jan Ladislav Dussek (1760–1812) and native composers such as **Samuel Wesley**, George Frederick Pinto (1785–1806), and Philip Cipriani Hambly Potter (1792–1871). London continued to attract foreign pianist–composers in the early decades of the 19th century, notably Ferdinand Ries (1784–1838), Friedrich Kalkbrenner (1788–1849), and Ignaz Moscheles (1794–1870).

Although the leading exponents of the London Pianoforte School were male professionals, they composed predominantly for female amateurs, a fact often reflected in the dedications of their published works. In a time when a great deal of trivial piano music was printed for drawing-room use, the leaders of the school generally maintained high standards. They showed how the piano could provide variety of emotional expression, imagery, and intellectual challenge far beyond the demands of fashionable prettiness. Several generations of Continental composers, from **Haydn** to Chopin (1810–1849), were deeply influenced by the London Pianoforte School, a fact that has been fully appreciated only in recent times.

Nicholas Temperley

Bibliography

Caldwell, John. *English Keyboard Music Before the Nineteenth Century.* 1973.

Good, Edwin M. *Giraffes, Black Dragons, and Other Pianos.* 1982.

Loesser, Arthur. *Men, Women and Pianos: A Social History.* 1954.

Newman, William S. *The Sonata in the Classic Era.* 1963.

Ringer, Alexander L. "Beethoven and the London Pianoforte School." *The Musical Quarterly.* Vol. 66, pp. 742–758.

Rosenblum, Sandra, ed. *Clementi's Introduction to the Art of Fingering on the Piano Forte.* 1801.

Temperley, Nicholas, ed. *The London Pianoforte School, 1766–1860.* 20 vols. 1984–1987.

———. "London and the Piano, 1760–1860." *The Musical Times.* Vol. 129, pp. 289–293.

London University

See University of London

Longitude Act (1714)

Establishment of exact longitudinal reckoning had preoccupied astronomers and mathematicians for decades before the Hanoverian period; it had been one reason for the establishment of the Royal Observatory in the 17th century. The initiative of Humphrey Ditton (1675–1715) and **William Whiston**, disciples of Sir Isaac Newton (1643–1727), convinced the Crown in 1713 that it should provide an inducement to research.

The act passed by Parliament in 1714 provided a reward of £10,000 for a method of discovering the longitude at sea within 1 degree or 60 miles (or £20,000 for within 30 miles) and established a Board of Commissioners to vet the proposals. Ditton and Whiston had one; there were many others, some utterly fanciful, including that by the wheeler-dealer **Case Billingsley**.

None satisfied the commissioners. Newton disparaged the many efforts, which he believed doomed to failure, maintaining that only astronomers could possibly solve the riddle. He was wrong. The reward was ultimately won, more than a generation later, by the carpenter John Harrison (1693–1776) for his invention of the marine **chronometer**.

Larry Stewart

Bibliography

Stewart, Larry. *The Rise of Public Science: Rhetoric, Technology and Natural Philosophy in Newtonian Britain, 1660–1750.* 1992.

Taylor, E.G.R. *The Mathematical Practitioners of Hanoverian England.* 1966.

See also Navigation

Lords, House of

The House of Lords in 1714 consisted of 213 members: 171 peers of Britain, 26 bishops, and 16 representative Scots peers. Membership remained constant until 1780 but then increased as a result of creations and the addition of 32 Irish representative peers and bishops at the time of the **Act of Union (Ireland)** (1800). The 439 members in 1837 included most of the great landed proprietors of the United Kingdom, along with many political, judicial, military, and imperial leaders.

During the 18th century it was believed that the Lords

was the body "where the great support of Government should naturally lie." This belief reflected the economic outlook of the age, which was still agrarian and still dominated by the vision of great landowners conducting the country's business. Waning partisan rivalries enabled **Sir Robert Walpole** to build a "party of the crown" in the Lords that included noble pensioners, courtiers, Scots, and bishops. With officeholders, these groups ensured consistent ministrial majorities in the Lords. The peers' support was not entirely unquestioning, but they only threatened governments when the latter were at odds with their sovereign (as **Rockingham**'s first administration and then later the **Fox–North Coalition** were with **George III**), or when court politicians divided among themselves. Reinvigorated **oppositions** created by such divisions made it impossible for Walpole to carry his **excise** bill in 1733, threatened the Chatham (**Pitt the Elder**) Administration in 1767, and destroyed Addington's (**Sidmouth**'s) credibility as a minister in 1804.

Though few peers participated regularly in its business, the House of Lords was an effective legislative chamber. By 1717 it was customary for one peer to serve as its leader, securing attendances and speakers, and overseeing the passage of bills. The presence of leading judges enhanced the Lords' stature as a revising chamber. Peers attended at major divisions and to oversee business that affected their localities. Most 18th-century legislation was private or local; by 1800 the Chairman of the Lords Committees had established control over this business and even dictated some of the contents of private bills still in the **House of Commons**.

Until 1832 the Lords rarely challenged the House of Commons, which of course was the more active and less conservative of the two parliamentary bodies. Walpole relied on the Lords to defeat a succession of **place bills**; **Lord North** looked to it to reject **dissenters**' bills in 1772–1773. However, during the 18th century there was little controversial legislation to divide the two legislative bodies. Also, the inclination of peers to settle difficult issues privately with a minister or through a dependent M.P. in the Commons contributed to harmonious relations with a Commons whose members' return was in fact increasingly dominated by noblemen: in 1714 they controlled 105 seats; by 1807 the number had risen to 234.

Relations between the two houses began changing after 1820 due largely to the more democratic impulses then growing in the country. Even before 1832 there was a sense that the Lords should not stand in the way of the reiterated will of a House of Commons backed by public opinion, but **Lord Grey**'s ministry only overcame the conservative Lords' obstruction of the **Reform Act** (1832) by forcing **William IV** to promise a creation of new peers sufficient to carry the measure. According to the **Duke of Wellington**, the Reform Act left the Lords "an assembly still powerful in legislation but without influence." Lacking their former influence with ministers and in the Commons, and confronted by reforming legislation, the Lords between 1835 and 1837 defeated or amended several bills. Even before Wellington and Sir Robert **Peel** brought their Conservative colleagues under control, the government had resolved that a vote of the Commons could counteract a defeat in the Lords on a matter of confidence. This shift in opinion reflected many interrelated changes in the economic and social system as a whole.

Michael W. McCahill

Bibliography

Jones, C., ed. *A Pillar of the Constitution: The House of Lords in British Politics, 1640–1784.* 1989.

Jones, C., and D.L. Jones, eds. *Peers, Politics and Power: The House of Lords, 1603–1911.* 1986.

McCahill, Michael. *Order and Equipoise: The Peerage and the House of Lords, 1783–1806.* 1978.

Turberville, A.S. *The House of Lords in the XVIIIth Century.* 1927.

———. *The House of Lords in the Age of Reform, 1784–1837.* 1958.

See also Aristocracy and Gentry; Constitution, The Glorious; Elections and the Franchise; Government, National; Prime Minister

Lovat, 11th Baron (Simon Fraser) (1667–1747)

Lovat, a prominent Scottish **Jacobite**, was an opportunist often willing to trade his allegiance for personal advancement. Obsessed with the disputed succession to the chieftainship of his clan, he foolishly kidnapped and then forcibly married the widowed Lady Lovat, daughter of the Marquis of Atholl, in an attempt to bolster his claim. As a result he was outlawed, and though he became 11th Lord Lovat (1699), he was left without an estate. He then aligned himself with the exiled Jacobite court in **France** and swore allegiance to **James Edward, the Old Pretender**.

Returning to **Scotland** as a Jacobite spy (1703), he changed colors again and was the prime mover behind the Queensberry plot, which betrayed Jacobite plans for a French invasion of Scotland to the loyal 2nd Duke of Queensberry (1662–1711). With the collapse of this plot, Lovat fled to France, where he was arrested and imprisoned for 10 years. Deciding to bring his followers onto the side of the Hanoverians during **the Fifteen** uprising, he received a pardon (1716) and in 1725 took command of a Highland company faithful to **George I**. But, dismissed for embezzlement and still hoping for gains from a Stuart restoration, in 1739 he again changed colors and helped to found a group known as the Jacobite Association.

Predictably, at the outset of **Forty-five** he did not openly support **Charles Edward, the Young Pretender** (though he forced his son to) until the Jacobite victory at Prestonpans (September 1745); after which, following the unanticipated collapse of the Jacobite cause, he was imprisoned in London and executed for treason.

John Roach Young

Bibliography

Keay, J., and J. Keay, eds. *Collins Encyclopaedia of Scotland.* 1994.

Lenman, B. *The Jacobite Risings in Britain.* 1980.
McLynn, F. *The Jacobites.* 1985.

See also Clanship; Culloden, Battle of

Lowth, Robert (1710–1787)

Lowth, the most influential Hebrew scholar of 18th-century England, was educated at Winchester and Oxford. He became professor of **Poetry** at Oxford (1741–1750); then Bishop of St. David's (1766), of Oxford (1766–1777), and of London (1777–1787). His *Lectures on the Sacred Poetry of the Hebrews* (Latin, 1753; English translation, 1787) stimulated new appreciation of the beauty and structural elegance of Old Testament verse in both England and Europe. His erudite biblical interpretations and discussions of Hebrew **poetic** forms, and of parallelism as a prominent poetic technique in the Psalms, profoundly affected the compositions of **Christopher Smart**. A grammarian also, his *Short Introduction to English Grammar* (1762) was highly regarded and went through many editions. Esteemed as a scholar and pastor, Lowth was offered the primacy of the **Church of England** (1783), but declined due to ill health.

Michael F. Suarez, S.J.

Bibliography

Hepworth, Brian. *Robert Lowth.* 1978.
Lowth, Robert. *Lectures on the Sacred Poetry of the Hebrews.* 1969.
Prickett, Stephen. *Words and "The Word": Language, Poetics, and Biblical Interpretation.* 1986.

See also Biblical Criticism; Language and Linguistics

Loyalist Associations

Known also as Reeves Societies or Reeves Associations, these organizations sprang up in the early years of the **French Revolution** to defend the monarchy and Constitution against threats of domestic **radicalism** and French invasion.

Early 1792 saw the founding of the **London Corresponding Society** and the rapid proliferation of other ardently reform-minded societies in both the wider **London** area and other cities such as **Manchester**, Cambridge, and **Edinburgh**. The government, alarmed by this and by the radicals' unconcealed admiration for the events in **France**, issued a "Proclamation against Seditious Writings" and simultaneously indicted **Tom Paine** for treason (May 1792). But the government still lacked political support for taking more drastic measures.

With tacit government approval if not direct support, John Reeves (1752?–1829), a legal writer and former Chief Justice of **Newfoundland**, came to the rescue by founding (November 1792) an "Association for the Preservation of Liberty and Property against Republicans and Levellers." This proliferated, divided, replicated itself, and spread into the provinces even more rapidly than the radical associations, gaining some 15,000 activist adherents by February 1793. Reeves claimed that it included 2,000 branches in cities and towns; this was probably not too great an exaggeration. Its chief activists came from the **middle classes**—merchants and professional men in the **cities**, substantial landowners and yeomen farmers in the countryside—with the Anglican clergy playing a key role. They published pro-government tracts for the masses; countered the influence of the radicals by providing an alternative patriotic line of thinking; harassed and sometimes inspired violence against radicals, and worked to turn local innkeepers, printers, and attorneys against them; burned countless effigies of Paine; and provided the political support needed by the government for more drastic measures of repression.

Though strongest and most effective in the critical period 1793–1794, the loyalist associations lingered on. But with the beginning of the **French Revolutionary and Napoleonic Wars**, loyal men increasingly drifted toward military defense of the realm. The loyalist associations thus furnished the grass-roots contacts and machinery for the remarkable spread after March 1794 of a nationwide volunteer force of cavalry and infantry units, rooted in nearly every county and town, which by 1800 numbered some 300,000 men.

Martin Fitzpatrick

Bibliography

Dozier, R.R. *For King, Constitution, and Country: The English Loyalists and the French Revolution.* 1983.
Emsley, Clive. *British Society and the French Wars, 1793–1815.* 1979.
Philp, Mark, ed. *The French Revolution and British Popular Politics.* 1991.
Sack, James J. *From Jacobite to Conservative: Reaction and Orthodoxy in Britain, c.1760–1832.* 1993.

See also Anti-Jacobin; Association Movement

Luddism

Luddism was probably something more than mere attacks on modern machinery by unsophisticated workers. Some historians have argued that it was a quasirevolutionary movement that was concerned with **radical** political reform; a more conventional view is that it was a symptom of technological change and extreme temporary distress, which did, however, have some positive effects on contemporary attitudes and reform legislation.

In 1811, during the last phase of the long **French Revolutionary and Napoleonic War**, widespread **famine** and trade depression severely threatened many factory workers, especially in **textile industries** where newly introduced machines were making handworkers redundant. Their violent response began in Nottinghamshire in March. Led by "King Ludd" (or "General Ludd"), a mythical figure supposedly headquartered in Sherwood Forest, disciplined bands attacked carefully selected factories at different locations on a given evening, destroying the knitting frames that threatened workers' livelihoods. In January 1812 the attacks spread to Cheshire, Lancashire, and the West Riding of Yorkshire, where violence was less coordinated and where Luddite attacks often camouflaged criminal activity.

In February 1812 the cabinet dispatched 3,000 troops to stop the destruction and threats to social order. The number of soldiers grew to 12,000 after an unsuccessful attack on a mill at Rawfolds and the murder of William Horsfall, a Midlands factory owner. Special constables and watch patrols reinforced the **army**. Accompanying these repressive measures, Parliament also made frame-breaking a capital offense (1813) and increased the **police** authority of local magistrates.

The government finally restored order in early 1813, following its execution of 17 Luddites at **York** and the **transportation** of six others. Repeal of the **Orders in Council** and an improving economy also removed some of the causes of unrest, though there were further outbreaks in 1816 and later.

David B. Mock

Bibliography

Beaumont, G., et al. *The Luddites: Three Pamphlets, 1812–1839.* 1813, 1839; rpt. 1972.

Hammond, J.B., and B. Hammond. *The Skilled Labourer.* 1919.

Reid, Robert William. *Land of Lost Content: The Luddite Revolt, 1812.* 1986.

Sale, Kirkpatrick. *Rebels against the Future: The Luddites and Their War on the Industrial Revolution.* 1995.

Thomis, Malcolm I. *The Luddites: Machine-Breaking in Regency England.* 1970.

Thompson, E.P. *The Making of the English Working Class.* 1966.

Wright, D.G. *Popular Radicalism: The Working-Class Experience, 1780–1880.* 1988.

See also Crime; Law Enforcement; Riots and Popular Disturbances

Lunar Society

The Lunar Society of Birmingham, founded in 1766, provided an opportunity to scientists, industrialists, and interested laymen to discuss the practical applications of **science** to industry. Especially active during the 1780s, the same 14 members met informally each Monday afternoon at the time of the full moon (hence the name).

One of several **learned societies** of its type, the group included many of the greatest medical, scientific, and industrial figures of the age of **George III**. Its members included industrialist **Matthew Boulton**, physician **Erasmus Darwin**, chemist **Joseph Priestley**, engineer **James Watt**, and chinamaker **Josiah Wedgwood**. In addition to their monthly meetings, the men conversed daily and often corresponded with each other. Watt's ideas concerning the **steam engine** and many of Priestley's theories of chemistry were mulled over at its meetings.

All these men were **dissenters**, most were **Whigs**, and some counted themselves **radical**. Politically, they generally supported the **American Revolution** and the principles of the **French Revolution**. As its members began to die off or depart **Birmingham**, the society's meetings became more infrequent. It had faded from view by 1800, though a few members continued to meet for another decade.

Jack Fruchtman, Jr.

Bibliography

Cadbury, Paul S. *The Lunar Society of Birmingham Bicentary.* 1966.

Musson, Albert Edward. *Science, Technology, and Economic Growth in the Eighteenth Century.* 1972.

Schofield, Robert E. *The Lunar Society of Birmingham: A Social History of Provincial Science and Industry in Eighteenth-Century England.* 1963.

Lyrical Ballads (1798)

The anonymous *Lyrical Ballads, with a Few Other Poems* originally contained 19 poems, including "Tintern Abbey" by **William Wordsworth**; and four, including "The Ancient Mariner," by **Samuel Taylor Coleridge**. The two-volume second edition (1801, dated 1800), with Wordsworth's name on the title page, included additional poems and a Preface by him. The poems and Preface constitute a landmark of English Romanticism, proclaiming new aims and language for **poetry** against those espoused earlier by **Pope**, **Gray**, and **Johnson**.

The volume grew out of the walks and visits of Wordsworth, Coleridge, and Wordsworth's sister **Dorothy Wordsworth** when they lived as neighbors near **Bristol**. In *Biographia Literaria* (1817) Coleridge wrote that his contributions were intended to be poems involving "persons and characters supernatural, or at least romantic," whereas Wordsworth's were to be on "subjects . . . chosen from ordinary life."

Wordsworth described the poems as "experiments"—not traditional lyrics, **ballads**, or street-ballads, but poems on subjects often from the margins of normal society (e.g., beggars, a convict, a mad woman, an idiot boy), speaking the "language of conversation" rather than conventional poetic diction, in a variety of metrical forms. The aim of the experiment was to present "a natural delineation of human passions, human characters, and human incidents" in a way that might give pleasure.

This "natural delineation" was achieved through a variety of voices (for example, a wedding guest; a sea captain; a healthy, full-grown shepherd in tears; an uncomprehending adult and a confident child talking about death; a female vagrant), uttering thoughts and feelings in states of excitement. The **poetic** voices are made to interact, producing a volume that Coleridge considered to be "one work . . . as an Ode is one work." Although initially received with some bafflement and negative reviews, *Lyrical Ballads* has come to be recognized as seminal and pivotal.

David McCracken

Bibliography

Bialostosky, Don. *Making Tales: The Poetics of Wordsworth's Narrative Experiments.* 1984.

Butler, James, and Karen Green, eds. *Lyrical Ballads, & Other Poems, 1797–1800.* 1993.

Glen, Heather. *Vision and Disenchantment: Blake's Songs and Wordsworth's Lyrical Ballads.* 1983.

Jacobus, Mary. *Tradition and Experiment in Wordsworth's Lyrical Ballads.* 1976.

Jordan, John E. *Why the Lyrical Ballads?* 1976.

Mason, Michael, ed. *Lyrical Ballads.* 1992.

Parrish, Stephen M. *The Art of the Lyrical Ballads.* 1973.

Sheats, Paul D. *The Making of Wordsworth's Poetry, 1785–98.* 1973.

See also Lake School, Poets of the; Literary Criticism; Romanticism and Romantic Style

Lyttelton, Baron (George Lyttelton) (1709–1773)

Family connections brought Lyttelton a career in politics, but he preferred to be known as an author, poet, and literary critic. Although once popular, his writings are now seldom read. He was the patron and friend of **Henry Fielding**, who dedicated *Tom Jones* (1749) to him and may have modeled "Squire Allworthy" on him; and also of the poet **James Thomson**. An amateur **landscape architect**, he designed the much-admired garden at his estate, Hagley Hall.

Lyttelton entered Parliament (1735) as a member of his family's political group, "**Cobham**'s cubs," and wrote pieces for **newspapers** promoted by the **opposition**. When his faction joined the **Broad-Bottom Administration** he became a junior Lord of the Treasury (1744–1754). But after declining to follow **Pitt the Elder** into opposition (1755) he was abused by his former friends for accepting the post of Chancellor of the Exchequer (1755–1756), and in fact proved unequal to the demands of the office. He accepted a barony (1756) and made up with his cousins the **Grenvilles** and Pitt in the 1760s. Two of his brothers, Richard (1718–1770) and William (1724–1808), also served in the **House of Commons** but were not considered part of the cousinhood.

P.J. Kulisheck

Bibliography

Davis, Rose Mary. *The Good Lord Lyttelton: A Study in Eighteenth Century Politics and Culture.* 1939.

Dickins, Lilian, and Mary Stanton. *An Eighteenth Century Correspondence.* 1910.

Namier, Sir Lewis, and John Brooke, eds. *History of Parliament: The House of Commons, 1754–1790.* 3 vols. 1964.

Phillimore, Robert. *Memoirs and Correspondence of George, Lord Lyttelton.* 1845.

Sedgwick, Romney, ed. *History of Parliament: The House of Commons, 1715–1754.* 2 vols. 1970.

Wyndham, Maud. *Chronicles of the Eighteenth Century.* 1924.

M

Macaulay, Catharine (1731–1791)

Catharine Sawbridge Macaulay Graham was a prominent **radical** author and the first Englishwoman to write serious **history**. In her multivolume history of 17th-century England and her pamphlets she advocated such reforms as manhood suffrage, frequent elections, and the reduction of executive power. Her works represent a final statement of the Old Whig or **Commonwealth** political philosophy.

Living in **London** after marrying Dr. George Macaulay in 1760, she joined the republican circle of Thomas Hollis (1720–1774) and his friend **Thomas Brand** (Hollis). Through her brother, the radical politician **John Sawbridge**, she became associated with **John Wilkes**. She published the first volume of *The History of England from the Accession of James I* in 1763; the eighth appeared in 1783. W.E.H. Lecky (1838–1903) called her the ablest of the radical writers then at work; her *History* was regarded by contemporaries as the **Whig** answer to **David Hume**'s *History of England.* In it she attacked the abuse of political power, whether by the Stuarts, Cromwell, bishops, or Puritans, and tried to show how past liberties might have been better defended. A friend of **Benjamin Franklin**, she also published pamphlets supporting American radicals; later, visiting America, she stayed with **George Washington** at Mount Vernon. Her last publication was a tract (1790) attacking **Edmund Burke** and defending the **French Revolution.**

Macaulay was attractive in appearance and never short of new ideas. After her husband's death in 1766, she lived mostly in **Bath** with the radical Anglican parson Dr. Thomas Wilson (1703–1784). In 1778, the 47-year-old Macaulay eloped with 21-year-old William Graham. This had a negative effect on her social position and credibility. Her reputation survived longer in the United States, where several revolutionaries were among her correspondents.

Macaulay's last major work, *Letters on Education* (1790), contained her ideas on education for a virtuous and free society. Although she had always acted with scant regard for contemporary prejudices, this work flatly put on record her conviction that, the only difference between the sexes being physical, girls and boys should have the same education. For this she has been honored by later feminists.

Barbara Brandon Schnorrenberg

Catharine Macaulay "In the Character of a Roman Matron"

Bibliography

Hill, Bridget. *The Republican Virago: The Life and Times of Catharine Macaulay, Historian.* 1992.

Robbins, Caroline. *The Eighteenth Century Commonwealthman.* 1959, 1968.

See also Women's Education; Women's Rights

Macaulay, Zachary (1768–1838)

Macaulay, a member of the **Clapham Sect** and the father of historian Thomas Babington Macaulay (1800–1859), worked to abolish slavery and the **slave trade**. In 1784 his father, a Scots minister, sent him to Jamaica to work as a bookkeeper and manager of a plantation. Appalled by the treatment of the slaves there, he returned to England in 1792, and the following year became Governor of the Sierra Leone Company, which had been founded in 1791 by **William Wilberforce**, **Granville Sharp**, and **Henry Thornton** to form a colony for liberated slaves in **Africa**. After several years of work in the colony, during which his marriage failed, Macaulay remarried, settled in Clapham, and entered into the African goods trade with a nephew. From 1802 to 1816 he edited the *Christian Observer,* the organ of the Clapham Sect, and tried to abolish both the slave trade and slavery. With the demise of the trade he became secretary of the African Institute (1807–1812) and a founder of the Anti-Slavery Society (1823). He promoted church missionary work, infant and **Sunday schools**, and the **University of London**.

Samuel J. Rogal

Bibliography

Annan, Noel. *Leslie Stephen, the Godless Victorian.* 1984.
Knutsford, Lady Catherine, ed. *The Life and Letters of Zachary Macaulay.* 1900.
Stephen, Sir James. *Essays in Ecclesiastical Biography.* 1849.

See also Antislavery Movement; Humanitarianism; West Indies

MacDonald, Flora (1722–1790)

One of the most famous women in Highland history, Flora is notorious for her involvement with "Bonnie Prince Charlie"—**Charles Edward, the Young Pretender**—after the defeat of his **Jacobite** army at **Culloden** in 1746. She helped smuggle the prince from the Outer Hebrides to the Island of Skye and out of the reach of government forces hot on his trail. With Charles disguised as a young Irish girl ("Betty Burke"), the plan succeeded; Charles reached safety at Portree on Skye.

The heroic Flora, however, was imprisoned in the Tower of London. Released in 1747, she returned to Skye and married Allan MacDonald of Kingsburgh. The couple emigrated to America in 1751 and, ironically, Allan fought on the side of the British imperial government in the **War of American Independence**. Following her husband's capture in 1776, Flora returned to Skye in poor health. Allan returned, penniless, in 1785.

In a strange twist of fate, Flora MacDonald died in the very bed that Bonnie Prince Charlie had occupied on the way to Portree in 1746. At her funeral, 300 gallons of Scotch whiskey were consumed; 12 pipers played a lament over her body. Her reputation surviving, she has become immortalized in Scottish folklore in the well-known "Skye Boat Song."

John Roach Young

Bibliography

Keay, J., and J. Keay, eds. *Collins Encyclopaedia of Scotland.* 1994.

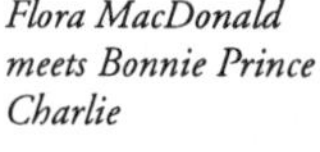

Flora MacDonald meets Bonnie Prince Charlie

Lenman, B. *The Jacobite Risings in Britain.* 1980.
McLynn, F. *The Jacobites.* 1985.
———. *Bonnie Prince Charlie: Charles Edward Stuart.* 1991.

See also Forty-five, The

MacGregor, Rob Roy (1671–1734)

Like **Flora MacDonald**, MacGregor occupies a fond position in Scottish folklore. An infamous cattle thief and outlaw, he was a man of intimidating physical presence. Local belief around the Loch Lomond area maintains that he swam the length of the loch. He also enjoys a reputation as a formidable fighter in hand-to-hand combat.

The real-life MacGregor fought for the **Jacobite** cause at the Battle of Killiecrankie (1689) under Viscount Dundee (1649?–1718). He was also a member of the Lennox Watch, a group of Highlanders who offered protection in the Lowlands in return for blackmail. He became a cattle dealer in 1708, became embroiled in a failed business transaction with the Duke of Montrose (*d.* 1742), and was declared an outlaw in 1712. Based in the Trossachs, he subsequently raided the Lowlands, stealing sheep and cattle. Charged with high treason after leading the Clan Gregor for the Jacobites in the **Fifteen**, he twice escaped from imprisonment. Finally surrendering in 1725, he received a royal pardon. His remains now lie in the village of Callander in the Trossachs. His life was romanticized by **Sir Walter Scott** in the novel *Rob Roy* (1817) and in a modern film of the same name (1995).

John Roach Young

Bibliography

Keay, J., and J. Keay, eds. *Collins Encyclopaedia of Scotland.* 1994.
Murray, H. *Rob Roy.* 1982.
Scott, Sir Walter. *Rob Roy.* 1817.

See also Clanship; Highland Regiments

Mackenzie, Henry (1745–1831)

Mackenzie, a Scottish lawyer who became Comptroller of the Taxes for Scotland (1799), is best known for *The Man of Feeling* (1771), perhaps the most influential sentimental **novel** in English. He published other novels, *The Man of the World* (1773) and the epistolary *Julia de Roubigné* (1777), political writings such as *An Answer to Paine's Rights of Man* (1796), and a tragedy called *Virginia; or, The Roman Father* (1824?), as well as editing the **periodicals** *Mirror* (1779–1780) and *Lounger* (1785–1787).

From the 1740s on, the literature of **sensibility** was increasingly popular. Stock characters, and scenes of virtue in distress, were employed in novels and onstage to arouse the "finer feelings" and to release tearful responses. *The Man of Feeling* was written when the cult was at its height. Mackenzie reminisced: "I was somehow led to think of introducing a Man of Sensibility into different Scenes where his Feelings might be seen in their Effects." This could serve as a description of his story, which parades its hero, Harley, through cruel **gambling** dens, a brothel, and a lunatic asylum, exhibits his anger against the depredations of the **East India Company**, and at last kills him off as a victim of unrequited love.

The Man of Feeling enjoyed a tremendous vogue until literary taste changed in the 19th century. Mackenzie's reputation remained high for many years, and he became a friend and advisor of **Sir Walter Scott**, who dedicated his first novel, *Waverley* (1814), to Mackenzie, "Our Scottish Addison."

J.A. Downie

Bibliography

Barker, Gerard A. *Henry Mackenzie.* 1975.
Drescher, Horst W., ed. *Letters to Elizabeth Rose of Kilravock, on Literature, Events and People, 1768–1815.* 1967.
Thompson, Harold W. *A Scottish Man of Feeling.* 1931.

See also Manners and Morals; Scotland and Scottish Culture

Macklin, Charles (1699–1797)

Born in Inishowen, **Ireland**, as Cathal MacLaughlin, of old Irish gentry, Macklin probably arrived in **London** in 1725, but he did not establish himself until 1733 when he joined the Drury Lane Company. As an actor he was most often compared with **David Garrick**, 18 years his junior, who likewise opposed the then-prevalent declamatory style popularized by James Quin (1693–1766). Although deprived of a serious formal education, he was, in his acting style, both intellectual and intense. Noting his powerful build, jutting chin, and aquiline nose, Quin once said of him, "If God Almighty writes a legible hand, that man must be a villain."

Macklin's bad reputation was not improved by his conviction of manslaughter in 1735, when he killed a fellow actor in a backstage brawl. He continued to act until 1789, playing over 200 roles. But he is best remembered for his portrayal of Shylock; indeed, he single-handedly restored Shakespeare's play to the stage, pushing aside an adaptation, George Granville's (1667–1735) *The Jew of Venice* (1701), in which Shylock was a villainous buffoon, generally played by comedians.

Macklin wrote 11 plays and was admired by fellow authors for his aggressive insistence on controlling his material and getting paid for all uses of it. His first success as a playwright came in 1759 when Drury Lane performed *Love à la Mode*, a farce in which four suitors—an Irishman, a Scotsman, an Englishman, and a Jew—compete for a lady, with the Irishman winning because only he cares for her, with or without her money. Macklin himself played the Scot, Sir Archibald McSarcasm. His last play, *The Man of the World* (1764, Dublin; 1781, London), is perhaps his best. It was not granted a license in England because of its political **satire** until Macklin was 81, but after he twice revised it, the comedy was performed successfully at Covent Garden with Macklin in the leading role of Sir Pertinax Macsycophant, a part in which he had to memorize some 9,000 lines. His friend **Arthur Murphy** helped to support him in his last years; he was buried in St. Paul's, Covent Garden.

Wight Martindale, Jr.

Bibliography

Appleton, W.W. *Charles Macklin: An Actor's Life.* 1960.
Bartley, J.O. *Four Comedies by Charles Macklin.* 1968.
Bevis, R.W. *The Laughing Tradition.* 1980.

See also Actors and the Acting Profession; Dramatic Arts; Shakespeare Industry

Macpherson, James (1736–1796)

Macpherson, the son of a Scottish farmer, educated at Aberdeen and Edinburgh universities, initiated one of the period's greatest literary controversies. Was he the creator, or merely the **translator** (as he claimed), of the epics of Ossian? A skilled writer and student of Gaelic poetry, he published three volumes attributed to the 3rd-century Celtic bard: *Fragments of Ancient Poetry* (1760), *Fingal* (1762), and *Temora* (1763). These prose narratives enjoyed immense popularity in Britain and on the Continent, feeding the cults of primitivism and **sensibility**.

But Macpherson, challenged by **Samuel Johnson** to produce the manuscripts he had supposedly translated, refused, and was denounced as a fraud. Many scholars today believe that the "poems of Ossian" were Macpherson's compilation of authentic, traditional, orally transmitted material, shaped into coherent narratives but supplemented increasingly with his own inventions. Apparently his motivation was the wish to establish in his homeland a literary tradition comparable to that of ancient Greece and Rome.

Macpherson's Ossian narratives display in germ the Romantic themes of nostalgia for a simpler past, the sublimity of nature, *mal de siècle* or *Weltschmerz,* and the conception of the poet as a secular prophet. Their significance for **Romanticism** was suggested by **William Hazlitt**'s list of "four of the principal works of poetry in the world, at different periods of history—Homer, the Bible, Dante, and let me add Ossian."

Laura Pieringer

Bibliography

Gaskill, Howard, ed. *Ossian Revisited.* 1991.
Stafford, Fiona J. *The Sublime Savage: A Study of James Macpherson and the Poems of Ossian.* 1988.

See also Literary Criticism; Scotland and Scottish Culture

Macquarie, Lachlan (1762–1824)

Macquarie, the most prominent and successful of the early governors of New South Wales, **Australia**, was born in **Scotland**. Both his parents were related to **clan** chiefs—connections that later proved valuable. He entered military service (1776) and was given an ensigncy (1777) in the 84th Regiment, the Royal Highland Emigrants, commanded by a cousin, Colonel (later General) Maclean.

During the **War of American Independence** he served in Nova Scotia, New York, and Charleston. He was posted to Jamaica, returned to Scotland (1784), and retired on half-pay. Thanks again to Maclean he became senior lieutenant in the 77th Regiment for service in **India** (1787). His years in the East brought further promotion, administrative experience, and marriage (which fizzled but swelled his finances). Paymaster General of troops and Military Secretary to the governor of Bombay, he was ultimately promoted to lieutenant colonel; he left India in 1807.

In 1808 Macquarie learned that he would be sent with his regiment to New South Wales, where one of his superiors was to be made governor. Ever greedy for promotion, he not only asked to be made a colonel but wrote to **Castlereagh**, then Secretary of State for the Colonies, asking to be made lieutenant-governor. Soon afterward he moved from this office to the governorship.

Macquarie was under explicit instructions stating that "The Great Objects of attention are to improve the Morals of the Colonists, to encourage Marriage, to provide for Education, to prohibit the use of Spiritous Liquors, to increase the Agriculture and Stock, so as to ensure the certainty of a full supply to the Inhabitants under all Circumstances"—and these he followed as far as possible. He was both pragmatic and visionary, promoting new towns, public works, and public morality. He reformed the forces that had overthrown governor **William Bligh**, established educational and charitable institutions, and attempted a humanitarian policy toward the Aborigines, recalling that of the first governor, **Arthur Phillip**. He encouraged emancipists (exconvicts) by giving them public offices and land grants, much to the indignation of immigrant settlers and the military.

This last brought his administration under scrutiny by J.G. Bigge (1780–1843), who was appointed to enquire into the affairs of the colony. By the time Macquarie had quit office and returned home (1822), his reputation—thanks to the biased Bigge report, which took an unfavorable view of the emancipist policy and the "absurd" public works—was already tarnished. He ultimately obtained a **pension** but died before he could collect it. Macquarie can be regarded as a controversial champion of the emancipists whose term of office, though it ended unhappily, marked a turning point in Australian history.

Ian Donnachie

Bibliography

Ritchie, J. *Lachlan Macquarie: A Biography.* 1986.

Macqueen, Robert, Lord Braxfield (1722–1799)

Macqueen was born at Braxfield (later the home of **Robert Owen**) near Lanark, in which county his father acted as a sheriff-substitute. He was educated at the University of Edinburgh, being admitted as an advocate in 1744. He acted as a counsel for the Crown on issues connected with the **Forfeited Estates** following the **Forty-five**, and later gained a considerable reputation as an expert on feudal law. Coincident with the rise to power of **Henry Dundas**, Macqueen became in turn a Lord of Session, with the title of Lord Braxfield (1776), a Lord of Justiciary (1780), and ultimately Lord-Justice Clerk (1788).

Macqueen enjoyed a formidable reputation as a judge, and in the 1790s presided over the trials of **Thomas Muir** and other Scottish **radicals**. The harsh sentences he handed down were the subject of parliamentary criticism, though Dundas, for one, supported him. Despite his vigorous defense of law and order, Macqueen himself seems to have been an idiosyncratic character. Whether he was as extreme in his manners and speech as Lord **Cockburn** and others later maintained is hard to assess, since he lacks a modern biographer.

Ian Donnachie

Bibliography

Cockburn, Henry Thomas. *Memorials of His Times.* 2 vols. 1856.

McFarland, E.W. *Ireland and Scotland in the Age of Revolution: Planting the Green Bough.* 1994.

Magazines

See Periodicals

Mallet, David (?1705–1765)

Born David Malloch, of a Perthshire farming family, Mallet, a miscellaneous writer, anglicized his name after leaving **Scotland** (1723) to become a **tutor** and author; his popular **ballad** "William and Margaret" appeared the same year. *The Excursion* (1728) shows the influence of his friend **James Thomson** in its blank-verse survey of the cosmos. His *Of Verbal Criticism* (1733), addressed to **Alexander Pope**, attacked **Lewis Theobald's** *Shakespeare Restored* (1726) and **Richard Bentley's** edition of Milton (1732). Through Pope he met **Lord Bolingbroke**, whose *Works* he edited (1754). Under **Prince Frederick's patronage** he and Thomson wrote the masque *Alfred* with the song "Rule Britannia" (1740), set by **Thomas Arne**. Mallet also wrote three tragedies, a **biography** of Francis Bacon (1561–1626) noted for its detailed examination of Jacobean politics (1740), and much **poetry**, all forgotten except the narrative *Amyntor and Theodora, or the Hermit* (1747) and the ballad *Edwin and Emma* (1760).

James E. May

Bibliography

Dinsdale, Frederick, ed. *Ballads and Songs [by David Mallet]: A New Edition with a Memoir of the Author.* 1857.

Foxon, David F. *English Verse 1700–1750.* 1975.

Nussbaum, Felicity. *The Plays of David Mallet.* Facs. rpt. with intro. by Nussbaum. 1980.

Malt Tax Riots (1725)

In the aftermath of the **Act of Union** in 1707 the British Parliament sought to equalize taxation between **Scotland** and England. However, one of several concessions gained by the Scots was temporary freedom from duty on malt (set at 6d [2.5p] per bushel in England) for the duration of the **War of Spanish Succession**. Accordingly, amid much clamor from Scottish M.P.s and Representative Peers the malt tax was ultimately extended to Scotland in 1713, the duty being set at a lower rate of 3d (1.25p) per bushel.

But collection was apparently so inefficient and the resulting revenue so modest that the government decided to tighten the excise system and extend the duty levied on malt to ale and beer at 6d per barrel. Despite a deluge of petitions from landowners and innkeepers all over Scotland, this took effect in June 1725. Popular protest was immediate and widespread. In **Glasgow** the house of Donald Campbell of Shawfield (*c.* 1671–1753), the local M.P., was wrecked, and troops fired on the mob; while in the capital, **Edinburgh**, there was a brewers' strike.

Similar protests against shortages caused by failure of the grain harvest and by the rising cost of living recurred often during the 18th century, mainly as Meal Mobs and food riots, and typically involved raids on mills, granaries, and ships loading or carrying grain. A number of riots occurred during the **French Revolutionary and Napoleonic Wars**, when imports were restricted by limitations on shipping causing high prices and inflation.

Ian Donnachie

Bibliography

Campbell, R.H. *Scotland since 1707: The Rise of an Industrial Society.* 2nd ed., 1985.

Devine, T.M., and Mitchison, R., eds. *People and Society in Scotland. Vol. 1: 1760–1830.* 1988.

See also Riots and Popular Disturbances; Taxes and Tariffs

Malthus, Thomas Robert (1763–1834)

Malthus's ideas dominated social policy debates concerning **poverty** in the latter Hanoverian period. An Anglican clergyman, demographer, and economist best known for his principle of **population**, Malthus laid the foundations for scientific population studies and provided classical political economy with some of its central tenets. During the period 1798–1834 he was one of the most respected economic writers in Europe, honored by the **Royal Society** (1819) and its equivalents in Paris and Berlin (1833).

Malthus was an unknown curate when he anonymously published his *Essay on the Principle of Population* (1798) in reply to the optimistic **radicalism** of **William Godwin** and the Marquis de Condorcet (1743–1794). His book ushered in a new age of economic pessimism. Progressive legislation, he believed, would never succeed in bringing general happiness because poverty and its attendant evils would always remain: poverty was an irremovable consequence of natural laws that will always govern population growth. His theory was that since human reproduction, when unchecked, increased in geometrical ratios (2, 4, 16, 256, . . .) while food production increased in arithmetic ratios (2, 4, 8, 16, . . .), population would always outrun the means of subsistence. There would always be many more mouths than food to put into them unless war, disease, or chastity came to the rescue. Either way, misery awaited mankind, especially the poorer classes of it.

Although Malthus qualified this pessimistic conclusion in subsequent editions of his book, the controversies he started have never ended. He challenged the assumptions of 18th-century social theory, which associated populousness with prosperity and national power, but he also vexed friends of the poor who resented his critique of the **Poor Laws**, Britain's traditional system of parish relief. According to Malthusian doctrine, the Poor Laws, rather than helping poor people, in fact misguidedly increased their misery by providing doles which encouraged procreation, larger families, and hence still more pressure on food and subsistence goods already in short supply. Traditional charity was a boomerang. One effect of Malthusianism then was to divide reformers between those who continued to favor charity and those who, like the **Benthamites**, earnestly opposed it on grounds considered up to date and scientific.

Malthusianism affected contemporary thought in many other ways, inspiring schemes to boost **emigration** and attempts to reform welfare through the **New Poor Law** (1834). Opposition to it was extremely emotional by many populist writers such as **Cobbett**, who scorned it, and the early socialist theorist **William Thompson** who, though calling it pernicious, thought enough of it to recommend birth control and women's emancipation as partial remedies to the disasters it predicted. To such writers Malthusianism seemed particularly hardhearted because it not only discouraged traditional charity but tended to redefine the exemplary employer as someone who on principle paid the lowest "subsistence" minimum wages (thus helping to avert the global calamities that would arise from happy workers indulging themselves), and, on top of all that, recommended "moral restraint" and sexual abstinence to the very people whose alternative enjoyments were most limited. It was not without reason that economics after Malthus was called "the dismal science."

His political economy was no less controversial. Malthus's unique view of **agriculture**, set forth in the *Principles of Political Economy* (1820) and other works, separated him from the mainstream **economic thought** of the Ricardian school (though theorists such as **Robert Torrens** attempted to reconcile the two). Unlike the followers of **David Ricardo**, Malthus saw agriculture as intrinsically more productive and of greater moral value than manufactures. The capacity of the land to feed more people than are needed to work it, and the life-sustaining properties of agriculture, provided the basis for Malthus's theory of rent, his defense of Britain's system of agricultural protection (the **Corn Laws**), and his criticism of the alleged self-adjusting mechanism of the marketplace known as Say's Law.

Eric K. Heavner

Bibliography

Gilbert, Geoffrey. "Economic Growth and the Poor in Malthus' *Essay on Population*." *History of Political Economy*. Vol. 12, pp. 83–96.

James, Patricia. *Population Malthus: His Life and Times*. 1979.

Petersen, William. *Malthus*. 1979.

Poynter, J.R. *Society and Pauperism: English Ideas on Poor Relief, 1795–1834*. 1969.

Winch, Donald. *Malthus*. 1987.

———. *Riches and Poverty: An Intellectual History of Political Economy in Britain, 1750–1834*. 1996.

Manchester

The town of Manchester in Lancashire became in the course of the 18th century one of the chief centers of the **Industrial Revolution**. Its phenomenal growth, fueled by its rapid economic expansion, made it the second-largest city in Britain at the time of the first census in 1801.

Around 1700, Manchester was a town of perhaps 8,000 inhabitants, governed by the lord of the manor. But it was already an important regional **trade** center. In the 1720s, **Daniel Defoe** ironically referred to it as a "mere village" which, despite its growing manufacturing economy and its 12,000 inhabitants, had no urban government. Most 18th-century commentators saw the city's freedom from guild and corporate restrictions and controls as a source of its success, although its nonincorporation is now thought to have played only a minor role in its growth.

By 1758, Manchester's **population** had reached perhaps 20,000. The second half of the century witnessed dramatic

Manchester from Kersall Moor, 1857

growth, so that Manchester and the adjoining city of Salford together possessed over 80,000 inhabitants by 1801, excelled in size only by **London**.

The manufacture with which Manchester was associated at the beginning of the period was linen. The linen drapers of Manchester acted as **entrepreneurs**, buying and selling, and putting out linen yarn to be spun, wound, warped, and woven in a typical manifestation of the system of **domestic production**. Cotton played a part in the manufacture of Manchester linen cloth, and this eventually evolved into the burgeoning **cotton industry** of the area. A class of **merchant** capitalists, many from **dissenting** backgrounds, emerged in the course of the century to lead the city's transformation into a thriving industrial center.

The building of a **canal** in 1761 to supply Manchester with coal, in addition to more general improvements in **transport**, set the stage for the mechanization of cotton manufacture that can be dated symbolically to 1789 when the first **steam engine** for **spinning** cotton was erected. Despite the hardships of the **French Revolutionary and Napoleonic Wars**, Manchester's rise as the "metropolis of manufactures" continued in the early 19th century, reinforced with the arrival of the steam **railway** in 1830.

Rapid growth and **radical** political agitation led to the notorious **Peterloo massacre** in 1819, and in the **Reform Act** (1832) Manchester obtained three seats in Parliament. In 1838, by which time the city contained scores of cotton factories and some of the most appalling slums in Britain, Manchester attained municipal **borough** status.

Daniel Statt

Bibliography

Chapman, S.D. *The Cotton Industry in the Industrial Revolution.* 1972.

Deane, Phyllis. *The First Industrial Revolution.* 2nd ed., 1982.

Engels, F. *The Condition of the Working Class in England.* 1844.

Thornton, W.H. *History of Manchester to 1852.* 1967.

Vigier, F. *Change and Apathy: Liverpool and Manchester during the Industrial Revolution.* 1970.

See also Provincial Towns and Society

Mandeville, Bernard de (1670–1733)

Mandeville (he dropped the "de" in 1715) was an eccentric but insightful and prolific author whose ethical and religious ideas provoked great controversy but helped clear the way for **Jeremy Bentham**'s utilitarian philosophy later. Born near Rotterdam, he took a degree in **medicine** from Leyden in 1691, and a few years later **traveled** to England, where he married an Englishwoman (1698). We know little about his life, but **Benjamin Franklin** called him an "entertaining, facetious companion," and **Joseph Addison** described him as "a parson in a tye-wig." He probably did not build a large medical practice, but in 1703 he began to publish in his adopted language, producing "The Pamphleteers," a poem that defended the memory of William III (also a Dutchman) and sympathized with his difficulties opposing the French abroad while "striving to Appease / A grumbling Nation that was ne'er at ease" at home.

In 1705 Mandeville published a 433-line doggerel poem, "The Grumbling Hive, or Knaves turned Honest," intended as a political **satire** on the state of the country, which in 1714 was reprinted along with some 20 "Remarks" as *The Fable of the Bees.* Although the poem was now buried beneath its commentary, the work was still less than half its eventual size. By 1723 he had added "An Enquiry into the Origin of Moral Virtue," "An Essay on Charity and Charity-Schools," "A Search into the Nature of Society," and two more remarks, bringing the work near to its final form. The *Fable* sold well and was reprinted five times from 1724 to 1732.

Although Mandeville claimed that he wished only to divert his readers, his *Fable* was vigorously denounced by **William Law**, **Isaac Watts**, **John Dennis**, **John Wesley**, **Edward Gibbon**, and many others, most of whom deemed it an attack on **morality** and religion, and a defense of vice and luxury. **Adam Smith** in his *Theory of Moral Sentiments* (1759) attacked Mandeville's "licentious systems" as "wholly pernicious," although, ironically, some modern writers conclude with M.M. Goldsmith that Mandeville was in fact a "theorist of the spirit of capitalism."

Mandeville philosophically aligned himself with Thomas Hobbes (1588–1679) in finding virtue in selfish instincts, and opposed the 3rd Earl of Shaftesbury's (1671–1713) tender claims about man's "moral sense" or conscience, whose existence he denied. His famous belief that "private vices produce public benefits" held that self-love and self-regarding actions stimulate action, invention, accumulation, and progress; and that virtue (other-regarding actions aimed at the benefit of others or the control of one's own passions), which rulers and philosophers attempt to inculcate in society, is in fact detrimental to intellectual and commercial progress. His *Fable* pictures a society full of virtue, security, and contentedness, but drifting into collapse. In economics, his position was that prosperity was increased more by expenditure than by saving.

Mandeville's other works include *The Virgin Unmask'd: Or, Female Dialogues Betwixt an Elderly Maiden Lady and Her Niece* (1709), 10 dialogues which hint at **pornography** but evolve into discussions of **marriage**, politics, and **foreign relations**; numerous contributions to the *Female Tatler* (1710), which include satirical thrusts at **Richard Steele** and his priggish Squire Bickerstaff; *Free Thoughts on Religion, the Church and National Happiness* (1720), which argues against the state's enforcing any particular form of Christian orthodoxy, and counsels toleration of atheism; *A Modest Defense of Publick Stews: Or an Essay on Whoring as It Is Now Practiced in These Kingdoms* (1724); "Fable of the Bees, Part II" (1729), which continues his cynical view of society and politics; and *An Enquiry into the Origin of Honour, and the Usefulness of Christianity in War* (1732).

Wight Martindale, Jr.

Bibliography
Cook, Richard. *Bernard Mandeville.* 1974.
Goldsmith, M.M. *Private Vices, Public Benefits.* 1985.
Harth, Philip, ed. *The Fable of the Bees.* 1989.
Horne, Thomas A. *The Social Thought of Bernard Mandeville.* 1978.
Kaye, F.B., ed. *The Fable of the Bees.* 1988.
Monro, Hector. *The Ambivalence of Bernard Mandeville.* 1975.
Primer, Irwin. *Mandeville Studies.* 1975.

See also Economic Thought

Manley, Delarivière (1672?–1724)

Dramatist, fiction-writer, political editor, and satirist, Manley, whose reputation was once negligible, is currently being reassessed. As a playwright she created one comedy and three tragedies, most notably *The Royal Mischief* (1696). Along with Mary Pix (1666–1709), Catherine Trotter (1679–1749), and **Susanna Centlivre**, she helped open the playwriting profession to women and explored issues they confronted. Her comedy *The Lost Lover* (1696) turned on the consequences resulting from romantic decisions, while her tragedies explored women's victimization by marriage or the general misogyny of the social order.

Manley was also an innovator in prose fiction and a political propagandist. Her *Secret History of Queen Zarah* (1705), an attack on Sarah Churchill, Duchess of Marlborough (1660–1744), is now recognized as one of the first *romans à clef* written in English. She is perhaps best known, however, for the *New Atalantis* (1709) and *Memoirs from Europe* (1710), "secret histories" containing thinly veiled accounts of contemporary people and affairs. As a contributor to the **Tory** *Examiner* she participated in the political fray of the volatile last years of **Queen Anne**'s reign, also writing *The D. of M[arlborough]h's Vindication* (1711), which earned the praise of **Jonathan Swift**.

William J. Burling

Bibliography
Burling, William. "'Their Empire Disjoyn'd': Serious Plays by Women, 1660–1737," in Cecilia Macheski and Mary Anne Schofield, eds., *Curtain Calls.* 1991.
Cotton, Nancy. *Women Playwrights in England, c.1362–1750.* 1980.
Morgan, Fidelis. *A Woman of No Character: An Autobiography of Mrs. Manley.* 1986.

See also Dramatic Arts; Novel; Satire; Women in Literature

Manners and Morals

It is always hazardous to generalize about moral evolution, though few moralists have ever thought so. Social manners—the characteristic ways in which people behave toward one another—reflect deeper attitudes toward morality. Such attitudes emerge from historical forces composed of such things as events, economic and social trends, religious beliefs, patterns of socialization, levels of education, and the impact of current ideas and personalities. These represent patterns of great magnitude and complexity. But one oversimplified way to conceptualize the morals and manners of the period 1714–1837 would be to think of them as evolving through four stages corresponding to the ascendancy, excess, reformation, and reestablishment of ruling-class respectability. In other words, the social transformation from aristocratic to bourgeois society involved four stages of what might be called composure, unbuttoning, buttoning-up, and then a new composure.

Morally, the period 1714–1750 exhibits a certain equilibrium. For many, it was "Pudding Time." Harvests were generally good, **population** growth was very slow, politics were stable, and the **Glorious Constitution** was admired and secure. The Court was still firmly at the center of things, the **aristocracy and gentry** still a little behind. The **middle classes** were small and overawed; social deference was still very strong. Literature remained predominantly aristocratic and modeled on classical forms; **ridicule, satire,** and classical allusion excluded plebeians and reinforced elite solidarity. Religion supported morality, but its voice was divided. On the one side there were prophetic voices which, still condemning the licentiousness and frivolity of the Restoration, demanded a more thorough reformation of morality; on the other, rationalistic and **freethinking** influences were penetrating religion and eroding religious **enthusiasm.** Overall, the result was a condition of equilibrium, as close to a rural "Merrie Old England" as the Hanoverians would come. This also meant that life was dirtier and more brutal than it would be later. If superstition, routine cruelty to animals, and callous treatment of the weak are reliable indicators, morality and the impulses of fellow-feeling were low.

The period 1750–1790 saw a general unbuttoning. This occurred despite increasingly aggressive complaints from middle-class intellectuals. Among the landed classes, agricultural profitability gave rise to a flood of elite consumerism in the forms of **housebuilding, travel, gambling,** and other conspicuous consumption. The bulk of the middle classes, still trained to imitate their betters, unthinkingly followed, purchasing and displaying whatever they could. For most people, religion became even more a secondary and merely social interest; for others, it was less than that. The **Earl of Chesterfield** advised his godson that "religion is by no means a proper subject of conversation in a mixed company," and some companies jettisoned not only its discussion but also its practice. Meanwhile, **fox-hunting, pleasure gardens,** musical entertainments, and theater-going saw many new patrons. Droves of middle-class social climbers began joining "the Ton" in trips to Paris, much to the dismay of bourgeois moralists. Illegitimacy rates began climbing. Parents in all social registers experienced less control over the behavior—sexual and other—of the young. Yet the same conditions favored innovation and release from tradition. Agronomists experimented. The government's **patent** office became busier and busier. Some people in the upper classes, to the dismay of others, began marrying for love. Child-rearing began to loosen up. Travel increased markedly. Scientific, artistic, philanthropic, and educational activities and **learned societies** proliferated, all giving enhancement to new respect for individuality, genius, and invention among the more "productive" classes, yet providing motivations and foot soldiers for more extensive **humanitarian** inquiries into the conditions of all those left behind—**prisoners**, **prostitutes**, **slaves**, the agriculturally dispossessed, dumb animals. Satire faded in light literature as the cult of bourgeois "**sensibility**" peaked in the 1770s. At the same time, politics saw innovations in the form of growing demands for middle-class enfranchisement. New campaigns for the relief of **Catholics** and **dissenters** were launched. Morality, if measured by the standards above, was improving significantly.

The **French Revolution** was the omnibus cause of a buttoning-up that lasted more than a quarter of a century. Religious laxity and indifference during the two earlier periods had reactively produced an increasingly influential **religious revival** by the 1780s, but the revivalists could scarcely have attained a fraction of the influence they enjoyed during the period 1790–1815 without sidelong reinforcement from fear of the supposed contagiousness of the revolutionary diseases of "French" atheism, slaughter, and democracy. The upper classes led Britain into the **French Revolutionary and Napoleonic Wars**, greatly restoring themselves in the eyes of middle-class critics who well before the 1780s had begun to denounce their moral influence over everyone else. Moreover, the upper classes began making a great show of church-going. In an historic change, the upper classes were, for once, not leaders but followers of opinion; it was middle-class religious and philanthropic leaders who, having found a new voice and now more strenuously bent than ever upon instructing both poor and rich in Christian conduct, dispensed the leading moral ideas. They called for a new Puritanism. They were listened to not only because of French evils but also because the population was now multiplying rapidly, with no one sure of how to control its behavior. They were also listened to because the old sobriety and new importance of middle-class traders and manufacturers stood behind them. Public men and women became more careful about what they said and did. In 1812 even the Prime Minister, **Perceval**, was a fervent **Evangelical**. Bibles were distributed everywhere, at home and abroad. Major improvements in secular as well as **religious education** began. There was new rigor and discipline in this age, which its critics castigated as neo–Puritanical. With so many political and religious crusaders on the loose, it was an age of tremendous excitement and energy. While slavery, cruelty, and licentiousness were repressed, political anger and a new class-consciousness rose alongside the old-time religion. Polite literature, now **Romantic**, reflected all these cross-currents while still further elevating the value of individuality.

The period 1815–1837 saw a restoration of balance—a balance much more inclusive than that of 1714–1750. Although class division continued along the one central fault line between landed and urban, aristocratic and commercial, upper-class and middle-class attitudes, the most important conditioning agent was that other, sharper fault line, below which lay the growing, proletarianized labor force. Though no longer so **radical** after the dangerous period 1815–1820, and benefiting from sponsored educational and other self-help programs, this labor force, by its very existence, helped to ensure the continued maintenance of a "respectable" morality by the dispensers of moral standards. Within that new association of leadership, both upper and middle classes found subsidiary accommodations in shared ideas of civility, morality, and public service. The value of duty began to rise while that of individuality began to decline. Among the better-off, a new spirit of optimism, energy, and strength began to take hold. The nation's successes against the French, the expansion of the **Empire**, and the new opportunities for hard work and enterprise, all helped to buttress the new moral climate handed on to young Queen Victoria (1837). The late-Hanoverian morality—conveyed, for example, in Dickens's *Pickwick Papers*, with which the period closed (1836–1837)—combined energetic philanthropy and fellow-feeling with disgust at cruelty and religious humbug, and required, more than earlier, a fuller moral accounting from the whole population. The tone was more "earnest," "strenuous," and "manly" than that of the 18th century, but some children religiously trained in the 1830s later complained bitterly about the spiritual tortures and intellectual inelasticity of the new moral discipline. A distinctive new national character type had been created—highly repressed, full of nervous tension, prone to self-righteousness,

A family breakfast, 1740s

yet also imbued with new seriousness, gravity, a noble rejection of baseness and compromise, a new sensitivity to the value of fair play.

The manners dispensed during this long period, the forms of address and social presentation, evolved along lines reflecting many of these changes in moral ideas and leadership. The stages of manners may be distinguished under four corresponding headings: Courtesy, Politeness, Conduct, and Etiquette. This progression also reflects the general societal transformation from aristocratic, rural, and religious to more democratic, urban, and secular.

Early Hanoverian society was aristocratic. The social center was the Court, where the civilizing of behavior was highly valued by such figures as **Caroline, Queen of George II**. A code of Courtesy accompanied this. "Courtesy books," dispensing the language and arts of courtesy, were written primarily by and for men, and were popular down to the late 18th century. Characteristic was Chesterfield's *Letters to His Son* (1774), often considered the last Courtesy book. This and similar works addressed the aristocratic gentleman whose privileged place in the world was taken for granted, rather than the upwardly mobile individual seeking acceptance by the elite. Courtesy books offered behavioral equipment for life, and were comprehensive in content. For example, a man was always to make himself agreeable to his superiors; he was to identify the weaknesses and exploit the *amour-propre* of associates; he was to pretend to treat women's minds with respect, but never to follow their advice. Pointers on ceremony, particular to time and place, were mixed with discussions of religion, moral virtues, and universal principles of good taste.

By the middle of the 18th century there had been a considerable growth of trade, science, and the professions. A more "polite and commercial" society was emerging. Court remained the apex of society, but the locus of elite sociability was shifting to the urban environments of West End **London** and the **provincial towns** and **spas**. With their new **coffeehouses**, gardens, theaters, and assembly rooms, these environments were more accessible than the Court. In such settings, both aristocrats and aspiring members of the middle class displayed increasing surplus wealth, intermingling but also waging status contests using tokens of **fashion**, manners, conversation, and learning. A code of Politeness began to replace Courtesy in these more public arenas for self-display and social sparring. Politeness was more all-encompassing than Courtesy. It lay at the heart of a new public culture in which the adjective "polite" was being increasingly applied to arts, letters, learning, behavior, and conversation. In reference to intellectual and literary activities, polite denoted that which was general and amateurish, as opposed to specialist and pedantic. The word "**bluestocking**," which referred to some centers of this new Politeness, affirmed the intellectuality of these centers while humorously denying it. Polite learning was central to gentle conversation, defined as the pleasing exchange of opinions and feelings. But Politeness was not entirely secular. Although it did stress the importance of being socially pleasing and agreeable, it also required the cultivation of Christian moral character.

British reaction against the French Revolution gave a tremendous opening to the new moral intensity that had been building up in the **Methodist** and Evangelical movements. This was also reflected in the new code of Conduct introduced by writers such as **Hester Chapone**, **James Fordyce**, **Hannah More**, and **William Wilberforce**, who, especially after 1789, flooded the country with conduct books and cheap **tracts** for the masses. Like earlier courtesy books, these works dispensed the new prescriptions for Conduct and dealt with all aspects and stages of life. Advice on matters of ceremony and fashion mingled with admonitions concerning the importance of moral behavior, and particularly praised benevolence, perseverance, self-examination, and integrity. Considered the highest virtues were sincerity, frankness, modesty, and honesty. The attention given to Conduct far outweighed that given to dress and manners, reflecting a subordination of manners to religiously informed social morality that had not characterized the codes of Courtesy or Politeness. In addition, Conduct was an identity-establishing mechanism for an emerging middle class, rather than the aristocratic elite. Conduct books addressed mostly middle-class readers and defined behavioral norms in opposition to aristocratic manners, which arbiters of conduct viewed as frivolous and insincere. Moreover, Conduct was not a male-dominated behavioral idiom. Conduct books addressed both sexes equally, as titles such as *The Character and Conduct of the Female Sex* (1776) and *An Enquiry Into the Duties of Men* (1797) suggest. The emergence of Conduct thus reflected a growing collective consciousness among the middling sorts, as well as women's rising prominence in both print and society.

The combination of such reforming agents as conduct books, cheap tracts for the masses, antivice societies, factory supervisors, vital religion, and **Sunday schools** worked to transform manners and morals at all levels of society. Contemporaries commented on the transformation. **Francis Place**, for example, noted how the drunkenness, uncleanliness, coarseness, and promiscuity present in his youth had disappeared from most of the population by 1830. Similarly, some of the grosser 18th-century **blood sports** such as cock-fighting and bull-baiting declined in popular acceptance. What was emerging as a favorite pastime was reading aloud in the family circle. Expurgators like **Thomas Bowdler** labored to eliminate objectionable passages from **Shakespeare** and other earlier authors to render them fit for family readings. In short, earnest, respectable Victorians were in the making at least 30 years before Victoria came to the throne in 1837.

But although conduct-book writers attacked aristocratic manners as superficial, they failed to quell demand for knowledge of them among social climbers. In fact, such demand was steadily intensifying as a result of industrialization, the increase of wealth, and middle-class expansion. The **Industrial Revolution** enriched a new group of manufacturers who, by the 1820s and 1830s, possessed the economic but not the behavioral requisites for mixing in polite social and political circles. **Publishers** capitalized on this desire for instruction in fine aristocratic manners by producing pocket manuals about Etiquette—the code of behavior prevailing in aristocratic circles by the end of the Hanoverian period.

The emergence of Etiquette reflected the decline of both the Court and of urban public space as venues for aristocratic sociability. Etiquette governed behavior in "Society"—a term first used in the early 19th century to designate the social circles of the aristocratic elite, and particularly denoting the drawing rooms of London-based aristocrats. To appease the appetite for knowledge about what went on in those drawing rooms, publishers began dispensing in the early 1830s such etiquette books as *Hints on Etiquette and the Usages of Society* (1834), and *Etiquette for the Ladies* (1836). The content of these very popular works reveals that the new conception of manners differed significantly from earlier concepts. Etiquette writers, unlike the Christian moral writers whom they superseded, left Christian moral principles out of the picture, focusing instead on ceremonious forms particular to time and place. Etiquette was grounded much less in religion than in fashion and in social ethics requiring a concern for others so as not to offend. Its growing popularity as a code signified the rise again of more secular standards as the basis of approved behavior.

It is an oversimplification to say, but the picture at the end of the Hanoverian period, though it still included elements of old-fashioned courtesy and politeness, is one featuring the gradual accommodation to each other of the new middle-class conduct and an updated aristocratic etiquette. The product of this merger, more appropriately called late Hanoverianism than early Victorianism (Victoria had nothing to do with it), was a behavioral code calculated to support the more democratic, urban society that was emerging. Its precise behavioral rules were easy to acquire, and this helped to support a more broadly based elite. Its rules also engendered the sort of ritualized, predictable behaviors essential for efficient and harmonious human relations in urban environments. A new respectability, or as the historian G.M. Young (1882–1959) sensitively put it, a new "Code," had emerged.

Gerald Newman
Marjorie Morgan

Bibliography

Bradley, I. *The Call to Seriousness.* 1976.

Bristow, E. *Vice and Vigilance: Purity Movements in Britain Since 1700.* 1977.

Brown, Ford K. *Fathers of the Victorians: The Age of Wilberforce.* 1961.

Curtin, M. *Propriety and Position: A Study of Victorian Manners.* 1987.

Davidoff, L. *The Best Circles.* 1973.

Hemlow, J. "Fanny Burney and the Courtesy Books." *Publication of the Modern Language Association of America.* Vol. 65, pp. 732–761.

Jaeger, Muriel. *Before Victoria: Changing Standards and Behaviour, 1787–1837.* 1956.

Klein, L. *Shaftesbury and the Culture of Politeness.* 1994.

Langford, P. *A Polite and Commercial People: England, 1727–1783.* 1989.

Mason, J. *Gentlefolk in the Making, 1531–1774.* 1935.

McKendrick, Neil, John Brewer, and J.H. Plumb. *The Birth of a Consumer Society: The Commercialization of Eighteenth-Century England.* 1982.

Morgan, M. *Manners, Morals and Class in England, 1774–1858.* 1994.

Newman, G. *The Rise of English Nationalism: A Cultural History, 1740–1830.* 1987.

Prest, Wilfrid R., ed. *The Professions in Early Modern England.* 1987.

Quinlan, M. *Victorian Prelude, 1700–1830.* 1941.

Wahrman, Dror. *Imagining the Middle Class: The Political Representation of Class in Britain, c.1780–1840.* 1995.

Wildeblood, J., and P. Brinson. *The Polite World.* 1965.

Young, G.M. *Victorian England: Portrait of an Age.* 1936; rpt. 1977.

See also Adultery; Child-Rearing; Crime; Divorce; Drinking; Dueling; France; Law Enforcement; Marriage; Pornography; Punishment; Society for the Promoting of Christian Knowledge; Society for the Reformation of Manners; Society for the Suppression of Vice; Sport; Suicide; Witchcraft

Mansfield, Earl of (William Murray) (1705–1793)

Although Murray, the son of a Scottish peer, was considered as good a speaker in the **House of Commons** as **Pitt the Elder**, his family's **Jacobite** connections stifled his political career. His legal career flourished, however, and with his title of 1st Earl of Mansfield (conferred in 1776) he served as Lord Chief Justice of King's Bench (1756–1788) and founded English commercial law.

Mansfield established his reputation in the 1730s, gaining attention by his ability as a parliamentary speaker. The **Duke of Newcastle** brought him into Commons as Solicitor General (1742) and made him Attorney General (1754). But because of his connections, and because **Horace Walpole** had included him in a slander circulated anonymously (1752), some people were prepared to believe him a Jacobite. His reputation was too damaged for him to be considered a successor to **Henry Pelham** in 1754, and he returned to law.

Although Mansfield made major contributions to the **judicial system**, helping to reshape and modernize the understanding of contract, tort, maritime, and commercial law for many decades, he was in most other respects extremely cautious and conservative. Indeed, T.B. Macaulay (1800–1859) went so far as to call him "the father of modern **Toryism**." He oversaw several famous cases while Lord Chief Justice. In 1768 he found a legal technicality that allowed him to reverse a decree of outlawry against **John Wilkes**. In 1770, in a decision attacked by the **Whigs**, he ruled to limit the functions of juries and to enlarge those of judges in libel cases. In 1772 he ruled that English law did not recognize the institution of **slavery**, the first small step toward abolition. In 1781, presiding at the treason trial of Lord George Gordon, Mansfield mentioned every point favorable to the prisoner, even though his own house had been attacked during the **Gordon riots** the previous year.

P.J. Kulisheck

Bibliography
Fifoot, C.H.S. *Lord Mansfield.* 1936.
Heward, Edmund. *Lord Mansfield.* 1979.
Namier, Sir Lewis, and John Brooke. *History of Parliament: The House of Commons, 1754–1790.* 3 vols. 1964.
Sedgwick, Romney. *History of Parliament: The House of Commons, 1715–1754.* 2 vols. 1970.

See also Law Reform

Manufacturing

See Factories and the Factory System

Maps

See Cartography

Mar, 11th Earl of (John Erskine) (1675–1732)

Known as "Bobbing John" for his tendency to change his mind and switch sides, Mar, a Scottish noble, led the disastrous **Fifteen.** An architect of the **Act of Union** (1707) and a government official under **Queen Anne**, he expected to retain favor after 1714 under **George I**. The latter, however, snubbed him at a reception. Mar, a supreme opportunist, knew that he faced political oblivion and that a leading role in a Stuart restoration would redeem his political fortunes. Relying on the unpopularity of the Hanoverian regime in **Scotland**, in late summer 1715 he raised a rebellion in the name of **James Edward, the Old Pretender**, promising restoration of the traditional Scottish constitution. But though his procrastination worked to his advantage in politics, as a military leader it led to his downfall. He failed to defeat the loyal **Duke of Argyll**'s inferior forces at Sheriffmuir in November, effectively sealing the fate of the 1715 uprising. Fleeing to the Continent, Mar enjoyed the Pretender's friendship and favors for a decade until his love of intrigue made him an object of suspicion there as well.

Richard Finlay

Bibliography
Cruickshanks, Eveline, ed. *Ideology and Conspiracy: Aspects of Jacobitism, 1689–1759.* 1982.
Lenman, B. *The Jacobite Rebellions in Britain, 1689–1746.* 1980.
———. *The Jacobite Cause.* 1986.
Monod, Paul Kleber. *Jacobitism and the English People, 1688–1788.* 1993.

Marcet, Jane (1769–1858)

Marcet wrote several popular books for children on scientific and economic subjects when simple scientific textbooks were virtually unknown. The only daughter of Francis Haldiman, a Swiss merchant and banker living in **London**, she was educated at home by a **governess**. In 1799 she married the physician Alexander Marcet. Becoming a close friend of **David Ricardo**, she eventually wrote some eight "conversations" books between 1806 and 1844 for children. Her first, *Conversations on Chemistry* (1806) in 26 lessons "intended especially for the Female sex," was an immediate and enormous success. Although all her books went rapidly through many editions, the most famous was *Conversations on Political Economy* (1816), about which T.B. Macaulay (1800–1859) is said to have noted that "every girl who has read Mrs. Marcet's little dialogues on political economy could teach Montagu or Walpole many lessons in finance." Marcet's simplification anticipated Ricardo's own *Principles of Political Economy and Taxation* (1817); subsequent editions influenced 19th-century **economic thought** considerably by helping to form the first impressions of budding economists.

William Edward Morris

Bibliography
Thomson, Dorothy Lampen. *Adam Smith's Daughters.* 1973.

See also Children's Literature; Education, Secondary; Women in Literature

Marlborough, Duke of (John Churchill) (1650–1722)

Statesman and leader of the coalition armies in the **War of Spanish Succession** (1702–1713), Marlborough was one of the great men of his age. His victories sustained the strategy of the Grand Alliance, prepared the way for the advantageous terms Britain gained by the Treaty of Utrecht (1713), and ushered in Britain's prominence as a great European power. Dismissed from his command (1711) by a **Tory** government anxious to make peace, Marlborough (created Duke, 1702) lived abroad (1712–1714), returning to authority under **George I**, for whom he helped organize resistance to the **Fifteen** rebellion (1715).

Although a series of strokes (1716) forced him to surrender active participation in public affairs, his support of his son-in-law the Earl of Sunderland (1674–1722) contributed to the "Whig Schism" of 1717. A proponent of Continental, as opposed to "blue-water," warfare, Marlborough was this concept's most illustrious advocate. He combined a mastery of strategy, tactics, and administration with personal popularity among his troops. His ranking among Britain's greatest soldiers remains unchallenged.

Robert D. McJimsey

Bibliography
Chandler, David. *Marlborough as military commander.* 1973.
Churchill, Winston. *Marlborough: His Life and Times.* 6 vols. 1938.
Speck, W.A. "The Whig Schism under George I." *The Huntington Library Quarterly.* Vol. 40, pp. 171–179.

See also Anne, Queen; Army; War and Military Engagements

Marriage

Prior to the 11th century, jurisdiction over English marriage was local and very irregular. In the competition for authority that dominated the politics of the late Middle Ages, the church and the emerging church courts gained legal control over marriage, ultimately defining its minimum requirement as the "exchange" of consent at the church door. This quaint rule was extended by canon law in 1604 to include requirements that the couple obtain parental permission if either party were under 21 years of age, that either banns be announced 3 consecutive weeks before the wedding or a bishop's license be obtained, and that church weddings take place between eight A.M. and noon. While other marriage rites were in fact recognized, only these procedures were deemed valid for purposes of inheritance of land and other property. In essence, the regulations of 1604 were accepted into civil law by Parliament in 1753 in the **Marriage Act** sponsored by **Lord Hardwicke**, which, among other things, bolstered the central government's authority over marriage. However, the **Church of England**'s legal monopoly on the rites of marriage was not ended until the advent of civil marriage in 1836.

Among the lower classes, prior to the Marriage Act, two fundamental types of marriage were dominant—the "little" and "big" weddings. The former (known also as betrothal) was in effect a precontract, and allowed couples to get to know one another intimately. If sexual intercourse took place, the community considered that a marriage had occurred, and the man was now considered responsible for the woman and her new children. Betrothal was the main socially accepted vehicle by which young men and women were permitted to move out of the single state. Betrothals were not marriages in terms of property law, but in many cases couples would in fact have a "big wedding" later in order to fulfill the requirements of the church and the common law with regard to property.

Big weddings involved much ritual and revelry, and were very public affairs. Discouraged by the upper classes as disturbances of the peace, their popularity declined in the late 18th century. But the lower classes of England, **Scotland**, and **Wales** also practiced, well into the 19th century, a colorful variety of marriage rites and customs, which were accepted as legitimate by their local communities. These included "broomstick" or "besom" weddings in which the couple jumped over a broom placed at the doorway of a house; "handfasting," (joining hands before witnesses) and "smock weddings," where the bride wore only a simple dress, symbolizing that she brought nothing else to her marriage in the way of personal property. The extent to which these marriage rites were practiced has been a subject of historical debate.

Before 1750, most British people lived in rural settings, where the family was an economic team that was part of the greater economic team of the community. The choice of a marriage partner was critical to the economy of all concerned. Equally critical was the need to deter young couples from having sexual relations outside marriage, since illegitimate children would become the financial responsibility of the community. To evade parental and community controls, many couples, poor as well as rich, resorted to secret or "clandestine marriages." Performed by impoverished clergymen for a fee, these were reluctantly accepted as legal by the church. There was a sharp increase in such marriages between 1690 and 1753

Wedding procession at the village church, 1742

(when Hardwicke's Marriage Act was passed in an attempt to abolish them among the upper classes), and in the 1740s perhaps one in five English marriages was "clandestine." Many of these were performed in the Fleet **prison** in **London** (hence the term "Fleet marriage"); then, from 1754 on (until 1856, when the law was changed), many eloping couples headed for Gretna Green, the nearest village on the Scottish side of the border, where a marriage was considered executed if the parties declared their vows before witnesses—a blacksmith, tollkeeper, or ferryman would do, and some blacksmiths lived handsomely on gratuities provided by the 200-odd couples a year up from England.

Greater freedom for young men and women in choosing a marriage partner was increasingly fostered after the Marriage Act by the emergence of a **wage** economy that afforded young adults the opportunity to break free of their economic dependence on the community. Growing **urbanization** and industrialization also brought increased economic opportunities that permitted couples to marry a little earlier. Between 1700 and 1750, the mean age of marriage was 27.5 years for men and 26.2 for women. Between 1750 and 1800, the figures were 26.4 for men and 24.9 for women.

For the upper classes, the arrangement of marriages was a formal matter that carried serious consequences for the preservation of landed property and hence of political and social power. Yet as 18th-century individualism grew, the desire for freedom of choice came into conflict with arranged marriages. The 1753 Marriage Act, with its provision for the need for parental consent if either prospective marriage partner were under age 21, gave parents the legal control they desired, but this ran counter to the growing tendency for couples to marry for love or at least personal compatibility. Both tendencies were reconciled somewhat by the growth of mobility, leisure, and organized social opportunities for young men and women of the same class to meet and get to know each other (for example, at balls and dances). Parents, while still holding the reins, could now countenance a larger selection of suitable candidates for marriage. While women—in terms of property and children—still remained under the legal control of their husbands, the greater freedom of choice in partners and the consequent emergence of marriages based, at least in part, on mutual affection, did mean some improvement in the quality of the lives of upper-class women.

Stanley D. Nash

Bibliography

Gillis, John R. *For Better, for Worse: British Marriages, 1600 to the Present.* 1985.

McFarland, Alan. *Marriage and Love in England: Modes of Reproduction, 1300–1840.* 1986.

Parker, Stephen. *Informal Marriages, Cohabitation and the Law, 1750–1989.* 1990.

Stone, Lawrence. *The Family, Sex and Marriage in England, 1500–1800.* 1977.

———. *Road to Divorce: England, 1530–1987.* 1990.

———. *Uncertain Unions and Broken Lives.* 1992.

See also Adultery; Child-Rearing; Divorce; Manners and Morals; Women's Employment; Women's Rights

Marriage Act (1753)

Introduced by the Lord Chancellor, the **Earl of Hardwicke**, this "Act for the Better Preventing of Clandestine Marriages" went into effect on 25 March 1754. It decreed that all marriages performed in England or **Wales**, which did not take place in a church or "public" chapel, or by authority of a Bishop's license, would be considered "null and void." In addition, it was now required that banns be publicized on the three consecutive Sundays before the wedding took place. Furthermore, marriages under license required parental consent if either principal were under 21 years of age. Those performing marriages not in accord with the act's provisions were liable to 14 years **transportation**. The act did not apply to **Jews** or **Quakers**.

The act was precipitated by the upper-class parental concern over clandestine marriages, most notoriously the so-called Fleet marriages performed in or near the Fleet debtors' **prison**. It was feared that these were often part of fraudulent schemes exploiting young upper-class men and women and creating a potential danger of bigamy, thus jeopardizing both immediate wealth and the legal transfer of property. The act's underlying cause lay in the desire of upper-class parents to control the marital choices of their young. In the process, however, the act attacked lower-class informal marriage customs. Its provisions were evaded by some young couples by eloping to Gretna Green in **Scotland**, where the act was not valid and where legal marriages could be quickly enacted solely upon personal declarations before witnesses.

Stanley D. Nash

Bibliography

Gally, Henry, et al. *The Marriage Act of 1753: Four Tracts.* Rpt. of works originally published 1750–1755. 1984.

Gillis, John R. *For Better, for Worse: British Marriages, 1600 to the Present.* 1985.

Parker, Stephen. *Informal Marriage, Cohabitation and the Law, 1750–1989.* 1990.

See also Divorce; Marriage

Maturin, Charles Robert (1780–1824)

An Anglican Church of Ireland clergyman, in his **novels** and plays the French-descended Maturin vigorously supported Irish nationalism, attacked **Roman Catholicism**, satirized Calvinists, and utilized Gothicism. Supplementing their sensational **Gothic** elements, Maturin brought to his works a psychological dimension that perhaps reflected his own awareness of alienation.

His most popular efforts were the drama *Bertram; or, The Castle of St. Aldobrand* (1816), assisted into print by **Sir Walter Scott**, and the Gothic novel, *Melmoth the Wanderer* (1820). In both, the eponymous characters are outcasts and hero–villains. *Bertram,* a contemporary predicted, would rank with *Faust* and *Manfred,* but only *Melmoth,* which particularly enthralled French writers such as Balzac (1799–1850), Hugo (1802–1885), and Baudelaire (1821–1867), came close to fulfilling the prophecy.

Charles Robert Maturin

Although Maturin strove to describe "scenes of actual life," his efforts were seemingly thwarted by his confessed fascination with the "obscure recesses of the human heart." This is particularly evident in his novel *Women: Pour et Contre* (1818), in which Maturin mixed his religious biases with his sexual uncertainties in a story appropriate for **opera**. Nevertheless, of Maturin's six novels, *Women* and *Melmoth* (with its Chinese box construction of six stories exemplifying the contest between hope and despair) deserve scholarly editions.

Peter A. Tasch

Bibliography

Kramer, Dale. *Charles Robert Maturin*. 1973.

Lougy, Robert E. *Charles Robert Maturin*. 1975.

Rafroidi, Patrick. *Irish Literature in English: The Romantic Period*. 2 vols. 1980.

See also Byronic Hero

McAdam, John Loudon (1756–1836)

McAdam **traveled** over 30,000 miles of Britain's unimproved highways and earned his nickname, "Colossus of Roads." He was born into the lesser landed **gentry** of Ayrshire, the youngest of 10 children. He went to America at age 14 to join an uncle, a New York merchant in the colonial trade and a prominent Loyalist. They both helped to establish the New York Chamber of Commerce, and McAdam enlisted in the **War of American Independence** as a Loyalist volunteer. A better career choice was marriage (1778) to a rich landowner's daughter, as McAdam was able to return to **Scotland** with a fortune (1783).

Settling in Ayrshire (1785), McAdam set himself up as a country gentleman. He worked in local affairs as a roads trustee, became deputy lieutenant for the county, and raised a group of volunteers when French invasion threatened. In 1798 he was appointed naval agent for victualing and supplies in the West of England, and moved to remote Falmouth, where he continued his expensive private road-making experiments. These led toward a much-improved road surface.

McAdam's building method depended on the creation of good drainage on a uniform surface by elevating the road above adjacent ground with successive courses of crushed and ever smaller stones and gravel. (In later times, the surface was also often oiled, tarred, or asphalted.) He unfolded his ideas while giving evidence to the Select Committee on the Turnpike Acts in 1811; and in 1816, having been appointed Surveyor General of the Bristol roads, began putting these ideas into effect on a large scale. He advised other turnpike trusts on his road-building method, and published *Remarks on the Present System of Road-Making* (1816) and a *Practical Essay on the Scientific Repair and Preservation of Roads* (1819).

In 1827, McAdam became Surveyor General of Roads. His sons became partners in a consultancy that ultimately became a world-class business, advising 70 road trusts in 28 countries. "Macadamization" of roads contributed substantially to improved **transport** before the **railway** age.

Ian Donnachie

Bibliography

Reader. W.J. *Macadam: The McAdam Family and the Turnpike Roads*. 1980.

See also Coaching; Roads, Streets, and Turnpikes; Science, Technology, and Invention; Telford, Thomas

McCulloch, John Ramsay (1789–1864)

McCulloch, a Scottish-born economist and statistician, was the first systematic historian of economics. He was also the first economist to support himself by **journalism**. His published output included 78 articles in the *Edinburgh Review* (1818–1837), an historical *Discourse on the Rise, Progress, Peculiar Objects and Importance of Political Economy* (1824), a dictionary of commerce and navigation (1832), and a *Statistical Account of the British Empire* (1837). In 1818 he lauded *The Principles of Political Economy* of **David Ricardo** in a review for the *Edinburgh Review;* his effusive praise serves to justify his label as Ricardo's disciple, though he was not uncritical in this. He labored to dovetail Ricardo's insights with the framework of **economic thought** provided first by **Adam Smith**, and his annotated editions of Smith's *Wealth of Nations* (1828) and Ricardo's *Works* (1846) helped greatly to publicize as well as synthesize some of the classics of the new economic doctrines.

David M. Levy

Bibliography

O'Brien, D.P.J.R. *McCulloch*. 1970.

See also Marcet, Jane; Periodicals; Torrens, Robert

Mealmaker, George (1768–1808)

Mealmaker, like many Scottish working-class **radicals** of the 1790s, was a handloom weaver. In Dundee, where he lived, there was strong support in the early 1790s for the **French Revolution** and for British parliamentary reform. Suspected of disloyalty, he went underground, managing to avoid the fate of his fellow radical Thomas Fysche Palmer (1747-1802), one of the five famous "Political Martyrs" of 1793–1794 who was **transported**—the others were **Thomas Muir**, William Skirving (*d.* 1796), Maurice Margarot (1745–1815), and Joseph Gerrald (1760–1796). Mealmaker reemerged in 1796 and 1797 as a leader of the Society of **United Scotsmen**. Charged with sedition for this involvement and for writing his *Moral and Political Catechism of Man* (1797), which demanded annual parliaments and universal manhood suffrage, Mealmaker was tried in **Edinburgh** in 1798 and sentenced to transportation. He died in Botany Bay, Australia.

Christopher A. Whatley

Bibliography

Logue, Kenneth. *Popular Disturbances in Scotland, 1780–1815*. 1979.

McFarland, E.W. *Ireland and Scotland in the Age of Revolution: Planting the Green Bough*. 1994.

Murray, Norman. *The Scottish Hand Loom Weavers, 1790–1815*. 1978.

Mechanics

See Craftsmen

Mechanics' Institutes

An important component of the working-class self-help movement of the early 19th century, this Hanoverian invention had its background in the 18th century. In 1760 **John Anderson** established an institute in **Glasgow** that offered evening classes in technical subjects to adult workers. On his death, his bequest endowed the "**Andersonian Institution,**" which continued his work with adult students by employing **George Birkbeck** as its first professor (1799). In 1804 Birkbeck left Glasgow for **London** to be a physician but, retaining his educational interest, in 1823 he founded the London Mechanics' Institute with the support of **Thomas Hodgskin, Lord Brougham,** and **Francis Place.**

Companion institutes soon followed in Coventry, **Manchester**, Sheffield, **Leeds, Liverpool,** and other cities. By 1860 there were 610 institutes with some 102,050 members. Their purpose was to provide practical economic, scientific, and technical education to adult students; ideally, students would be able to apply their new knowledge directly to their work. Instruction was provided through public lectures, museums, reading rooms, and **libraries** holding technical manuals and books.

But the institutes had problems. Lectures were not always easily digestible by men who had worked a day's shift, and workers' educational limitations narrowed the program's success as time often had to be spent on preliminary instruction in reading and writing. Sponsors from the **middle class** were essential to the institutes' support. When subscriptions failed to defray the cost of lecturers, middle-class sponsors stepped forward to provide funds. As the libraries did not initially contain literary works, middle-class sponsors founded accompanying literary and philosophical societies that eventually became merged with the institutes. In fact, the middle classes gradually took over many of the institutes. The curriculum also changed, becoming less formal and less technical as it began providing general education and literary studies.

The educational significance of the Mechanics' Institutes began to decline by the 1850s as their premises became the sites of dances, debates, and other informal social functions. Yet they had been an important part of the self-help movement that was reflected also in the creation of atheneums, **Sunday schools,** and organizations like the **Society for the Diffusion of Useful Knowledge** and the **British and Foreign School Society.**

David B. Mock

Bibliography

Curtis, S.J. *History of Education in Great Britain.* 1967.

Roach, John. *A History of Secondary Education in England, 1800–1870.* 1986.

Vaughan, Michael, and Margaret Scotford Archer. *Social Conflict and Educational Change in England and France, 1789–1848.* 1971.

See also Education, Technical

Medical Education

At the beginning of the Hanoverian period the practice of medicine was prescribed by a handful of legislative measures dating from the 16th century. Medicine today is handled largely by physicians (who are trained in medical diagnosis, the prescription of drugs, and surgery), apothecaries (druggists or chemists), surgeons (specialists in healing through manual operations), and also dentists. But in the 18th century these professions were still partly jumbled together and not as yet fully articulated. For example, "physicians" were gentlemen–amateurs often with little hands-on training. It was not until 1745 that "surgeons" split away from "barbers" fully (who thereafter were confined to pulling teeth and supplying **wigs** and dentures), allowing subsequent independent evolution of surgery and dentistry. Apothecaries had only secured their separation from grocers in 1617 (the one ran establishments stocking imperishable items, the other, perishables), but by the 18th century, apothecaries were general medical practitioners who were evolving up from the level of craftsman–trader.

Training in these fields was, by today's standards, extremely haphazard. Surgeons and apothecaries entered their professions by practical apprenticeships, whereas members of the more genteel group of physicians were required by the Royal College of Physicians only to hold a university degree—which meant that most of them started out knowing more about Cicero than about taking a pulse or analyzing a urine specimen. It was perhaps fortunate that since the universities at **Oxford** and **Cambridge** proscribed student **dissenters** and **Catholics** as much as they shunned modern practical education, many would-be British medical students went instead to Continental universities such as Leyden, which had no religious restrictions and taught in Latin, the common tongue of educated men.

Leyden became an important center for medical education with the appointment of Hermann Boerhaave (1668–1738) as Professor of Botany and Medicine. Boerhaave was allocated 12 beds in the town **hospital**, which he used for teaching purposes. He there introduced "bedside medicine" into the training of physicians and became the leading European medical educator of his age. It was after his death that British students became more attracted to the medical school in **Edinburgh**, modeled on his principles.

Medical education in Edinburgh was much influenced by that in Leyden, though local roots also played a part. There was a strong tradition in the city for surgeons to train by apprenticeship, and they had held dissecting rights there since medieval times. By 1704, six physic gardens had been established in Edinburgh for the training of surgeons and apothecaries. A key figure in the development of the medical school was John Monro (1670–1740). After training as a surgeon apprentice and studying at Leyden and Padua, he became Deacon of the Surgeons' Corporation. In 1726 he had a hand in setting up a school that would teach "medicine in all its branches." Four professors were appointed, and a group of teachers. No religious tests were required of students, and lectures, given in

English, were first delivered by Alexander Monro (1697–1767), whom his father had groomed for the post and sent to study under Boerhaave. (Three more generations of Alexander Monros were to teach anatomy at Edinburgh University.) The school was a success and, becoming Britain's leading academic medical center, increasingly drew students from England and **Ireland** as well as **Scotland**. Its professors were unpaid or received only a small salary, and augmented their incomes by charging fees to students and by collecting royalties for their published lecture notes. The popularity of Edinburgh's medical education can be judged by the fact that in 1728 Robert Knox lectured to an anatomy class of over 500.

Crucial to Edinburgh's success was the building of Edinburgh Royal Infirmary, which opened in 1741. It had 228 beds, sufficient to meet local needs and teaching requirements. Clinical teaching became established in 1748, when John Rutherford was appointed to give formal patient-based lectures. Unfortunately in **Glasgow**, political pressures, the lack of a hospital, and opposition from the faculty of Physicians and Surgeons spoiled the possibility of a similar development.

The 18th-century boom in English hospital foundations led to the establishment of small teaching centers. Many doctors, particularly younger ones, were prepared to accept unpaid hospital appointments in return for practical experience with sick patients. There was also a pool of students willing to pay fees to "walk the wards," or, like **Edward Jenner**, to become "house pupils" of eminent consultants. However, systematic teaching, even in hospitals, was impossible because, while anatomical studies required dissection, the Company of Barber-Surgeons still jealously controlled a monopoly of dissection rights. The Royal College of Physicians was able to give some anatomy demonstrations, but this was totally inadequate to fill the need. Improvement came in 1745, when the split between barbers and surgeons was achieved because the College of Surgeons was thereby freed to organize a teaching center that included dissection. This plan was avidly pursued by another Scottish doctor and teacher of anatomy, **William Hunter**, who in 1746 began private anatomy classes in Covent Garden. In 1767 Hunter began bringing to his school other lecturers on a profit-sharing basis. His school, increasingly noted for its collection of specimens, produced a number of famous doctors and provided courses in chemistry, surgery, and medicine until 1833. Its success prompted other private foundations of varying quality.

Throughout the period the universities at Oxford and Cambridge continued to award degrees and issue licenses, but offered no vocational or practical training. A small medical school attached to the Radcliffe Hospital was opened in Oxford in 1767, but it only functioned for a few years. Possession of a university doctorate was still the necessary qualification for fellowship of the Royal College of Physicians. The college refused to admit Jenner, one of the most famous doctors of the Hanoverian era, because he refused to take a Latin examination. However, most serious students passed on from the English universities to additional course work at Edinburgh and then to training in a London hospital.

In the early years of the 19th century there was a demand to produce some order within the medical profession. **Sir Joseph Banks**, president of the **Royal Society** and former manager of the Apothecaries Physic garden at Chelsea, instituted an inquiry into medical education that resulted in the important Apothecaries Act of 1815. This established that all apothecaries in England had to be examined and licensed by the Society of Apothecaries after a 5-year apprenticeship. This was the beginning of the modern licensing system. The act gave the society control over all medical practitioners by virtue of its authority to prosecute unlicensed men. The society also received power to demand certificates of attendance at lecture courses in anatomy, physiology and theory, and the practice of medicine, as well as proof of 6-months' hospital experience.

From Hogarth's "Anatomy Lesson" 1751

In a parallel development, in 1800 the Company of Surgeons was transformed into the Royal College of Surgeons. The **French Revolutionary and Napoleonic Wars** was producing a number of surgeons from the armed services with improved practical skills and, anxious for equality with the apothecaries, surgeons were forced to raise the status of their own qualifications. Hence it soon became customary for young doctors to seek membership in the Royal College of Surgeons (thereupon becoming entitled to designate themselves MRCS) as well as the Licence of the Society of Apothecaries (LSA), thus nurturing the idea of the general practitioner as an individual qualified as both surgeon and physician. The British general medical practitioner today is usually described as "Physician and Surgeon."

The 1815 act was successful in enhancing the status of qualified medical practitioners. However, its drawbacks included the proliferation of private schools which, with little medical supervision, were basically crammers for the apothecaries' examinations. This in turn led to abuses like that caricatured by Charles Dickens (1812–1870) in his portrayal of drunken medical students in *Pickwick Papers* (1836–1837). Additionally, the act failed to deal with the objectionable system under which eminent surgeons and physicians still maintained house pupils by charging expensive fees.

Other important late-Hanoverian developments included the Anatomy Act (1832), which at last empowered the Home Secretary to issue licenses for the lawful acquisition of cadavers for dissection. This measure was prompted by the illegal activities of grave robbers or "resurrection men," which had culminated in the infamous trial of William Burke and William Hare in 1829. These men, motivated by profits originating in the growing interest in anatomical study, and undeterred by old laws forbidding the dissection of cadavers other than those of criminals, had gone beyond body-snatching to the actual murder of poor people for the sale of their corpses.

By the end of the Hanoverian period, medical education had produced a body of respectable and reasonably educated medical practitioners. It had evolved up from apprenticeships through hands-on hospital experience and university training to professional certification. It was a sign of the times when in 1823 Thomas Wakley (1795–1862) founded *The Lancet,* the first medical journal. Small local medical societies also proliferated. However, full-scale regulation of medical education was only achieved after the Medical Act of 1858 founded what is now known as the General Medical Council.

C.E. Hivey

Bibliography

Cartwright, F.F. *A Social History of Medicine.* 1977.

Hamilton, D. *The Healers: A History of Medicine in Scotland.* 1981.

Nutton, V., and R. Porter, eds. *History of Medical Education in Britain.* 1993.

Porter, R. *Disease, Medicine and Society in England, 1550–1860.* 2nd ed., 1993.

Poynter, F.N.L., ed. *The Evolution of Medical Education in Britain.* 1966.

See also Medicine; Scottish Universities

Medicine

In 1746 it was said of Dundee doctors that they "dangled goldheaded canes . . . and looked wise: and according to the strength or weakness of their natural constitution, the patient survived or died." This was fair comment. But the Hanoverian period did see genuine improvements in the healing arts and in medical practice by the growing professionalization of medical education; the spread of **hospitals,** and of ever more sophisticated anatomical knowledge; the evolution of obstetrics, and the development of inoculation and vaccination; and the discovery of new and very effective drugs.

Some of the most effective prescriptions developed during this period included iron used for anemia; a bark extract containing quinine and antimony for fevers; and the plant extract, digitalis, for heart complaints. Opium and its derivative, laudanum, were effectively employed as analgesics and soporific drugs (though misuse was common, as was testified to by **Thomas De Quincey** and **Samuel Taylor Coleridge**). All these drugs were widely available into the 19th century without legislation or control. They were prescribed by licensed and unlicensed practitioners alike, and formed the basis of many patent medicines available from traveling salesmen and by post.

Surgery also saw technical advances. The **Hunter brothers** were famous practitioners. John Hunter gained military experience during the **Seven Years' War** and used his knowledge to advance the art of dissection and the comparative understanding of anatomy, while his brother William was a pioneer of obstetrics. Another Scots-born doctor, William Smellie (1698–1763), opened the first lying-in hospital for pregnant women in London (1749) and soon afterward began publishing his important *Treatise on the Theory and Practice of Midwifery* (3 volumes, 1752–1764), in which he not only explained the use of his leather-covered metal obstetrical forceps but broadened the foundations of modern obstetrics. The **French Revolutionary and Napoleonic Wars** produced a further generation of experienced surgeons. Operations to remove bladder stones became successful and highly lucrative. Caesarian sections were performed (though no woman survived this procedure before the end of the 18th century). The greatest medical success story of the period was that of the growing war on **smallpox** with which the name of **Edward Jenner** is imperishably linked, though no cure or prevention was found for such scourges as typhus fever, tuberculosis, or venereal disease.

Medicine was practiced in many settings and locations and, until the late Hanoverian period, under very different licensing systems or under none at all. Universities, hospitals, and corporate groups of apothecaries, surgeons, and physicians all had a hand in establishing the regulations of practice, with the effect that rules varied tremendously, depending especially on geographic location and the economic status of the patient. Naturally it was in the **cities** that medical practice was most sophisticated as well as most varied. In **London,** while distinguished physicians such as **Sir Hans Sloane** and **John Arbuthnot** served royalty and the nobility, voluntary hospitals became available for the poorer working classes from the 1720s, and from 1770 a network of dispensaries with domiciliary services also became available. Much the same was true of many other large cities in both England and **Scotland,** especially in **Edinburgh,** the leading center of medical education in Britain. Also, in some of the new industrial areas, enlightened employers such as **Josiah Wedgwood** set up sickness insurance schemes for their employees. It was not uncommon also for employers of domestic **servants** to contribute to hospital charities to guarantee admittance for their employees.

Outside urban areas, popular contact with medicine was somewhat different. Major medical events such as childbirth were often in the hands of local surgeon–apothecaries who, if successful, were then consulted on other medical matters. More routine matters were generally handled, in the case of upper- or middle-class patients, through house calls, while doctors also often kept special quarters ("surgeries") in their own residences for callers. Some **friendly societies** and other fraternal groups contracted for medical services from a private physician just as some village corporations might contract with a local schoolmaster to educate a given number of pupils at a fixed cost per head. In the most rural areas, in parts of **Ireland**, northern **Wales**, and the Scottish Islands, there were no qualified medical practitioners as late as 1790. Medicine in such areas was administered by local healers, ministers or priests, or the **gentry**. Often such men were also vaccinators and blood-letters, and held regular "surgeries." Women, outside midwifery, had no recognized right to practice medicine until the mid–Victorian period (1865).

The London medical elite included not only men like Sloane and Arbuthnot but highly respected figures like the Hunter brothers, the surgeon William Cheselden (1688–1752), and Mathew Baillie (1761–1823). Such men commanded high fees and moved easily in society alongside those two other essentially middle-class professional groups that circulated throughout the ranks of the "respectable," the men of the **legal profession** and those of the **clerical profession**. Outside London and a few other cities, the best-paid medical practitioners tended to congregate near **spa** towns such as **Bath**, Buxton, and Scarborough in England; and Moffat and St. Fergus in Scotland. Some doctors combined practical medicine with advanced medical research and teaching, such as **Joseph Black** and **William Cullen**. Others combined it with high literary achievement—**Bernard de Mandeville**, **John Wolcot**, and **Tobias Smollett**, for example—and some of their writings present interesting pictures of contemporary medical practice. Other writers who studied medicine were **George Crabbe**, **Robert Southey**, **Oliver Goldsmith**, and **Mark Akenside**. Philosophers adept in medicine included **Thomas Brown** and of course **David Hartley**, who began the fusion of neurology with psychology. Political agitators who practiced medicine included **John Jebb** and **John Thelwall**. Other individuals better known for their work in entirely different fields, such as **Thomas Bowdler**, **James Sheridan Knowles**, **John Roebuck**, **W.R. Clanny**, **Sir Humphry Davy**, and **William Williams** took training in medicine.

The 18th century has been called the "golden age of quackery," partly because there was then a very great imbalance between medical knowledge and the desire to purchase its benefits. The distinction between quackery and serious medicine was, of course, harder to sustain in an era when medicine itself was still fairly primitive and when governments did nothing to test or regulate medicines. Nonetheless, the quack doctor was a stock figure on the theatrical stage. Contemporary quackery encompassed a wide range of irregular medical treatments available in town and country for all classes. Quack practitioners were invariably travelers who elicited custom by spectacular publicity, making profits by selling miracle potions and then moving on before results became clear. Though some quack practitioners had basic orthodox medical training, the character of Dr. Dulcamara as depicted in Gaetano Donizetti's (1797–1848) comic **opera** *L'Elisir d'Amore* (1832) was by no means an exaggeration. Many quacks earned a good deal of money with dubious remedies. Some sufferers thought it well to keep plenty of Solomon's "Balm of Gilead," which claimed to cure the ill effects of masturbation, on hand; another group anxiously awaited the outcome of "Hooper's Female Pills," supposedly an abortifacient. **Robert Raikes**, the newspaper publisher and promoter of **Sunday schools**, made a fortune from "Dr. Bateman's Pectoral Drops." Even bona fide medical practitioners were not above profiting from patent medicine sales. "Dr. Jane's Fever Powders" were made by a qualified doctor, a medical author and friend of **Samuel Johnson**.

Throughout the period, perceptions of health needs changed and diversified. Growing general prosperity freed resources to be spent on health care. Medicine became a "consumer product." The medical profession became more lucrative for qualified doctors, who began to rise in social status. However, there was little state involvement in these changes, and few doctors held state employment before 1837. Medicine was a private enterprise. Medical practitioners were largely dependent on their patients. And then as now, patients tended to trust more to results than to wise looks and "goldheaded canes."

C.E. Hivey

Bibliography

Hembry, P. *The English Spa, 1560–1815: A Social History.* 1990.

Loudon, I.S. *Medical Care and the General Practitioner, 1750–1850.* 1987.

Porter, R. *Health for Sale: Quackery in England, 1650–1850.* 1989.

———. *Disease, Medicine and Society in England, 1550–1860.* 2nd ed., 1993.

Williams, G. *The Age of Agony: The Art of Healing, c.1700–1800.* 1975.

See also Medical Education; Middle Class

Meikle, Andrew (1719–1811)

Meikle was the son of a millwright who worked mainly in East Lothian, the center of agricultural improvement in **Scotland**. After working as a millwright, he developed some of his father's ideas in the construction of mills and milling machinery. Meikle concentrated mainly on the threshing mill, in which there was considerable interest because of its labor-saving potential. His design of a rotary thresher in 1786 was widely adopted and improved upon, but his failure to secure a **patent** meant that he derived little profit from his invention. **Sir John Sinclair**, the great **agricultural improver** and propagandist, later raised £1,500 for Meikle's benefit in his old age.

Ian Donnachie

Bibliography

Devine, T.M. *The Transformation of Rural Scotland.* 1994.

See also Agriculture; Science, Technology, and Invention; Scottish Agriculture

Melancholy

In 1712 **Joseph Addison** turned from approving cheerfulness in *The Spectator*, No. 387, to lament that "melancholy is a kind of demon that haunts our island, and often conveys herself to us in an easterly wind." Melancholy fascinated English authors, and by around 1750, **graveyard** poets were fast in her embrace. In celebrating melancholy as a woman, poets such as John Dyer (1699–1757), **William Collins**, and **Thomas Warton the Younger** were continuing a centuries-old tradition.

Significantly, Dyer wrote of the "kindly mood of melancholy that wings the soul, and points her to the skies," in *The Ruins of Rome* (1740); for her outward sign was often **antiquities and ruins**, medieval and classical, reminders that the "paths of glory lead but to the grave" (**Thomas Gray**, *Elegy Written in a Country Church-yard,* 1751). An elegaic appreciation of ruins was a test of one's **sensibility**. There was a painful pleasure for those who yielded to melancholy; they achieved "that elegance of soul refin'd, / Whose soft sensation feels a quicker joy / From Melancholy's scenes, than the dull pride / Of tasteless splendor and magnificence / Can e'er afford" (Warton, *The Pleasures of Melancholy,* 1747). That particular joy arose from the contemplation of eternity through the ruins of the finite, a joy alloyed with melancholy recognition of one's own mortality, and strengthened by the particular creativity melancholy inspired: "Our sweetest songs are those that tell of saddest thought" (**Percy Shelley**, *To a Sky-Lark,* 1824).

Romantic poets such as **Wordsworth** and **Keats** needed no ruins to prompt their melancholy—to hear the "still, sad music of humanity" (*Tintern Abbey,* 1798), or to see rain hide "the green hill in an April shroud" (*Ode on Melancholy,* 1820). Romantic melancholy differed from the traditional physiological description, which in a medical dictionary (1787) still cited both the humors doctrine that melancholy proceeded

> "from a redundance of black bile" and the theory that too heavy and too viscid a blood . . . permits not a sufficiency of spirits . . . to animate and invigorate the nerves and muscles. Its cure is in evacuation, nervous medicines, and powerful stimuli.

Although melancholy was feminine—"She dwells with Beauty" (Keats's *Melancholy*)—in less **poetic** moods the condition was commonly called "blue devils," as in the farce of that name by **George Colman the Younger** (1798). Most Romantics treated melancholy with respect; the brilliant satirical exception was *Nightmare Abbey* (1818) by **Thomas Love Peacock.**

Peter A. Tasch

Bibliography

Gaull, Marilyn. *English Romanticism.* 1988.
Goldstein, Laurence. *Ruins and Empire.* 1977.
Klibanski, Raymond, Erwin Panofsky, and Fritz Saxl. *Saturn and Melancholy.* 1964.
Kuhn, Reinhard. *The Demon of Noontide.* 1976.
Quincy, John. *Lexicon Physico-Medicum; or, a New Medicinal Dictionary.* 1787.

See also Gothic Fiction and Gothicism; Spleen

Melbourne, 2nd Viscount (William Lamb) (1779–1848)

Melbourne was **Whig** Prime Minister when the 18-year-old Victoria succeeded to the throne (1837), and he became her closest advisor, helping her form opinions on many subjects. His handsome appearance, intelligence, sympathy, and graceful manners charmed the young queen. His influence waned after she married Prince Albert (1840), and he left office the following year.

Melbourne's marriage (1805) to Caroline Ponsonby (**Lady Caroline Lamb**) proved unhappy and was marred by her affair (1812) with **Lord Byron**; the Melbournes separated legally in 1825. Despite long service in the **House of Commons** (1806–1828), Melbourne did not hold office until 1827, when he was appointed Chief Secretary for **Ireland**. His second office was as Home Secretary (1830–1834). As such he became responsible for public safety in the midst of the **Swing riots**, which he handled with firmness but restraint, reprieving eight of 11 men sentenced to death. Supporters of working-class rights denounced him for his savage handling of the Dorset laborers known as **Tolpuddle Martyrs** (1834).

Melbourne reluctantly supported the **Reform Act** (1832), but, like most aristocrats, defended the **Corn laws**. Two constitutional issues arose while he was **Prime Minister** (1834, 1835–1841). **King William IV** disliked a proposed appointment and dismissed Melbourne after only 4 months in office; but the public disapproved, and for the first time, the principle that ministers were responsible to the House of Commons, not the monarch, became obvious. A coalition of Whigs, **Radicals**, and Irish members outvoted the minority ministry of **Sir Robert Peel**, and Melbourne was recalled in April 1835. In the "Bedchamber Crisis" (1839), Melbourne

William Lamb, Viscount Melbourne

lost a vote in Commons, which forced Victoria to send for Peel. When the queen refused to show confidence in the latter by replacing her Whig ladies of the bedchamber with the Conservatives Peel recommended (which was Peel's political right), Peel declined to force the issue and withdrew, allowing Melbourne's return.

P.J. Kulisheck

Bibliography

Cecil, David. *Melbourne.* 1965.
Thorne, R.G. *History of Parliament: The House of Commons, 1790–1820.* 5 vols. 1986.
Torrens, W.M. *Memoirs of the Right Honourable William Second Viscount Melbourne.* 1878.
Ziegler, Philip. *Melbourne.* 1976.

Mercantilism

See Economic Thought

Merchants

The simple definition of a merchant as one who buys and sells things cannot convey the vast differences in status and wealth that existed among merchants in Hanoverian Britain. Such individuals ranged in status from the mercantile princes of **London** to the humble local trader not far removed from the peddler.

At the pinnacle of the structure were the great merchants of the City of London. Many came from long-established families and dominated **overseas commerce**. In addition to trading on their own account, some were involved in **chartered trading companies** such as the **East India Company** and in financial institutions such as the **Bank of England**. This group of powerful individuals often had the ear of government, which sought their advice and used them to raise money in times of **war** and other national emergencies. Their privileges were often resented by lesser merchants in London and the provinces who were excluded from this circle. As the 18th century progressed, however, the growth of European and Atlantic trade led to the increasing importance of merchant communities in towns such as **Bristol**, **Liverpool**, **Glasgow**, and Hull. The functions of these merchants differed, for whereas many London merchants catered for the luxurious demands of London's wealthy classes, many provincial merchants tended to deal in agricultural produce, raw material, and, as the Hanoverian period progressed, the products of the developing **Industrial Revolution**.

Entry to the mercantile profession was often by way of an apprenticeship for which a premium was payable. Those trained in a top London merchant house could expect to pay more than those in the provinces. Many recruits were the sons of merchants, but leading houses might also attract younger sons of the landed **gentry**. Often this led to intermarriage between the groups; for example, there were strong links between Glasgow merchants in the **tobacco trade** and the landed classes of the west of **Scotland**. According to the economic writer Malachy Postlethwayt (1707?–1767), commenting in 1750, overseas merchants needed to acquire a knowledge of commodities, foreign languages, bookkeeping, foreign customs, and business methods as well as an understanding of stock and commodity markets. Needless to say, few could command expertise in all these fields. The qualities and capital required to conduct overseas trade meant that in both London and provincial towns it was dominated by a small group who also constituted the urban political elite.

In addition to native merchants, Britain had long attracted foreign merchants. Some, including Sephardic Jews and French Huguenots, had come in earlier times to avoid persecution. In Hanoverian Britain, the emergence of London as the leading international financial center led others, particularly the Dutch, to join them. Because of their international connections, immigrant businesses came to dominate the finance of foreign trade. Migration, however, was a two-way process, and where appropriate, British merchants established foreign branch houses or used trusted foreign houses as agents, residency in either of which might play a significant part in the training of the young merchant. Increasing international contacts were thus essential for the survival of the merchant.

Being a merchant was a risky business. In addition to economic fluctuations, changing demand or the failure to adapt to new trends could lead to bankruptcy. In the latter Hanoverian period, the tendency of some industrialists to sell goods direct to foreign customers reduced the need for merchants and led some to seek new sources of activity. This accelerated a trend that had been under way for some time. **Insurance** companies such as the **Royal Exchange Assurance** and the **Sun Fire Office** included many merchants among their directors. Merchants, who were accustomed to transferring funds for trading purposes, also began to transfer funds for loans and investment. For some, this gradually became the major part of their business—leading, in the later years of the period, to the evolution of merchant **banks**, which came to dominate this field after 1815. One such bank was Baring Brothers, founded by Francis Baring (1740–1810), "the first merchant of Europe," who was among other things a director of the East India Company and a **Whig** M.P. between 1784 and 1806; another was N.M. Rothschild and Sons, founded by Baron Nathan de Rothschild (1777–1836), a bank that became a major creditor of the government and which helped reimburse West Indian slave owners upon the abolition of **slavery** (1834), helped finance relief for the Irish **famine** of the 1840s, and assisted with purchase of the Suez Canal (1875). Meanwhile, other merchants gradually evolved to the more specialist profession of bill-broker. Country merchants used their London counterparts as agents, and had considerable dealings with London bankers. As a result, many country merchants themselves became bankers in their own areas as such institutions developed in the provinces after 1750.

Merchants involved in **domestic commerce** outnumbered their counterparts in foreign trade and were responsible for a greater amount of business. Such men were to be found not only in the major ports but also in **provincial towns** and **cities** all over the country. Some, such as grain merchants and coal merchants, were highly specialized. These were trades that grew significantly in the 18th century, bringing increasing wealth to their participants. Relaxation of the rules for dealing in grain not only created a more national market in grain for foodstuffs, which increased the role of the merchant, but also assisted the rise of commercial **brewing**, which gave merchants a boost. Those dealing in coal, especially in northeast England, saw a considerable growth in coastwise trade to London and other growing cities. Other merchants were in business in a much smaller way, dealing in a greater variety of goods, supplying a variety of local customers, perhaps even supplying peddlers who hawked goods and news around rural communities. Some merchants might combine wholesaling and **retailing** functions, selling to affluent customers as well as supplying smaller local retailers. As the economy grew, the functions of merchants changed and broadened.

Merchants were also closely involved in the process of industrialization. Industrialists such as **Boulton**, **Darby**, and **Wedgwood** often included merchants among their partners, using them to raise finance capital or to find markets for their output. In some areas such as Glasgow, merchants invested in industry in order to provide goods to satisfy the demands of overseas customers. In the developing **textile industries**, merchants involved in **domestic production** such as **David Dale** and **Samuel Greg** gradually invested in **factories**.

The profits from merchant businesses were an important factor in economic growth. Many merchants sought to enhance their social status by acquiring landed estates, which were looked upon also as a safe investment. Thus merchants helped to encourage a continuously active land market. Such men also saw the advantages of improved **transport** and were leading investors in **turnpikes**, **canals**, and, later, **railways**. Many merchants also invested directly in the developing industries. The increasing range of their activities, particularly their expansion into financial services, meant that by the mid-19th century, the mercantile profession had a distinctly different profile from that prevailing in 1714.

A.J.G. Cummings

Bibliography

Ashton, T.S. *An Economic History of England: The 18th Century.* 1955.

Chapman, Stanley. *The Rise of Merchant Banking.* 1984.

———. *Merchant Enterprise in Britain: From the Industrial Revolution to the First World War.* 1992.

Daunton, M.J. *Progress and Poverty: An Economic and Social History of Britain, 1700–1850.* 1995.

Westerfield, R.B. *Middlemen in English Business, 1660–1750.* 1915.

See also Finance and Investment

Merthyr Rising (1831)

The Merthyr rising of June 1831 was one of a series of popular disturbances in the late Hanoverian period, which included the Scottish **Radical War** and the English **Swing riots**. Starting in **Merthyr Tydfil** in connection with the out-of-doors agitation in favor of the first parliamentary reform bill, the protest became intertwined with threatened **wage** cuts at the Cyfarthfa Ironworks and anger at the operation of the local debtors' court, the Court of Requests.

Riots against the court escalated when troops were dispatched from Brecon, 15 miles away, to quell the disturbances. They confronted an angry crowd outside the Castle Inn. When the troops opened fire, the workers fired back. At least 16 people died, and many others were buried in secret. Armed camps were set up around the town to repel further troops, and a cloth was dipped in lamb's blood to produce a red flag. Eventually the uprising collapsed and many fled from the town, fearing reprisals. In the aftermath, two men were condemned to death, though the real leader, Lewis Lewis ("Lewsyn Y Heliwer") escaped hanging and was **transported**. Richard Lewis ("Dic Penderyn"), far less prominent in the uprising, was hanged at **Cardiff** and became the first martyr of the Welsh working class.

There were two major consequences of the uprising: first, a major strike at the ironworks, involving the National Association for the Protection of Labour, which marked the emergence of organized working-class action—it was defeated in November 1831. Second, Merthyr acquired an M.P. as part of the **Reform Act** (1832). This had not been contemplated prior to the Merthyr rising.

Neil Evans

Bibliography

Jones, David. *Before Rebecca: Studies in Popular Protest in Wales, 1790–1835.* 1973.

Williams, Gwyn A. *The Merthyr Rising.* 1978.

See also Riots and Popular Disturbances

Merthyr Tydfil

In the early 18th century, Merthyr was a small rural community on the road from Brecon to **Cardiff**, with a population of perhaps 500. **Daniel Defoe** found it beautifully situated, a welcome relief after the terrors of the Brecon Beacons, the range of hills nearby. A pastoral community, it also had small **iron** works and **coal** workings, and had been a leading area of **dissent** in South **Wales** since the civil wars of the mid-17th century.

The use of coal for iron smelting transformed the area into a leading center of **Welsh industry**. From 1759 four huge ironworks were established and the road to Cardiff improved. The Dowlais Works (1759), later the largest ironworks in the world, was followed by **Anthony Bacon**'s Cyfartha (1765, sold to **Richard Crawshay** in 1794), as well as Penydarren and Plymouth. The invention of iron puddling in the 1780s (the "Welsh method," developed at Cyfarthfa) and the construction of the Glamorgan **Canal** (completed in 1794), which resolved the difficulties over **transport**, enhanced the growth of production. The canal required 16 locks to climb the 500 feet from Cardiff, including a spectacular step ladder at Abercynon. All this made Merthyr into the largest town in Wales when recorded **population** reached 7,705 in 1801. Most of them turned out to watch the world's first **steam** locomotive in operation (1804), built by **Richard Trevithick**. The

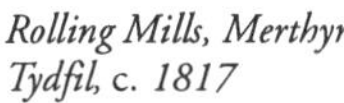

Rolling Mills, Merthyr Tydfil, c. 1817

population was scattered over a vast parish, though most gathered around the four ironworking communities associated with the major works. The village was off center from these, and visitors were dismayed at the lack of anything approaching a recognizable focus. The situation symbolized the lack of any civic government in the town. In 1850, Merthyr was still described as being "as destitute of civic government as the smallest village in the empire." Yet by the 1830s there were over 30,000 inhabitants.

The people paid a price for this slowness of civic modernization. The town was overwhelmingly Welsh-speaking, and dissent formed the seed-bed for a **radical** tradition; **Baptists** and Independents (**Congregationalists**) shaded into **Unitarians** and **deists**. Radical **craftsmen** from the Vale of Glamorgan were attracted by the burgeoning economy. The Cyfarthfa Philosophical Society, established in 1807, drew in both ironmasters and shopkeepers, adding to the radical leaven. Working-class turbulence was stirred into the mixture. In 1800 there was a major food **riot** in the town, and in 1816 Merthyr was the storm center of the first coalfield-wide strike in South Wales, causing troops to be dispatched to the area. Yet events in 1831 eclipsed all this when workers occupied the town for 4 days and repelled troops sent to restore order. This **Merthyr rising** was quelled, but in the aftermath the town obtained parliamentary representation under the **Reform Act** (1832)—a development not envisaged in the original bill. The ironmaster **Sir Josiah John Guest** was elected to the seat, which he held (often dependent on working-class and radical support) until his death (1852).

Neil Evans

Bibliography

Evans, Neil. "The Urbanisation of Welsh Society," in Trevor Herbert and Gareth Elwyn Jones, eds., *People and Protest: Wales, 1815–1880.* 1988.

Jones, David. *Before Rebecca: Studies in Popular Protest in Wales, 1790–1835.* 1973.

Merthyr Teacher's Centre. *Merthyr Tydfil: The Growth of a Community.* 1981.

Williams, Gwyn A. *The Merthyr Rising.* 1978.

See also Bacon, Anthony; Metallurgy and Metalworking

Mesmerism

The remarkable success of 18th-century science inspired several doubtful medical specialties, including phrenology and electrical medicine. Mesmerism, the most spectacular "pseudoscience" of all, came to prominence as a technique for treating nervous illnesses. Though rejected by contemporary **medicine** as quackery, it was nonetheless the forerunner of modern hypnotism and one source of the scientific study of psychopathology.

It was invented by Franz Anton Mesmer (1734–1815), a Viennese physician whose Paris practice became notorious. Mesmer held that illnesses were due to imbalances in the body of a subtle physical fluid ("animal magnetism"), caused by blockages impeding the fluid's flow. He claimed that he could remove these by channeling his own animal magnetism into the patient, and that he could control the flow by stroking the patient's body. This treatment produced a convulsive "crisis" and, frequently, a trance-like state in his patients, supposedly indicating that the flow of animal magnetism was no longer restricted and that balance had been restored.

Mesmer's practices aroused the ire of the medical establishment, which resented his popularity and begrudged him his fat fees. Louis XVI appointed a Royal Commission to investigate. Chaired by **Benjamin Franklin** and directed by other leading scientists, the commission condemned Mesmerism and attributed its results to "imagination." Mesmer, ridiculed in satirical plays and cartoons, left Paris (1785), but two disciples continued to mesmerize. The Marquis de Puysegur (1751–1825) is credited with inducing the first case of "somnambulism through hypnosis," in which the subject remembers nothing of the events when awakened; Nicholas Bergasse (1750–1832) extended Mesmer's model to the social sphere, justifying revolution as political mesmerism.

Several practitioners emigrated to America and England. In America they lectured widely to enthusiastic audiences. In England their reception was mixed, though their philosophical views interested **Coleridge** and their practice significantly affected Harriet Martineau (1802–1876), who attributed her liberation from an invalid's life to her female mesmeric healers. Radical physician John Elliotson (1791–1868) of University College, London, defended the use of mesmerism in treating functional nervous disorders, though he met great hostility in the medical community. Mesmerism was also touted as a practical anesthetic, again to great resistance, which led James Braid (1795–1860) to coin the term "hypnosis" in hopes of reducing its spiritualist associations.

William Edward Morris

Bibliography

Buranelli, V. *The Wizard from Vienna.* 1975.

Darnton, Robert. *Mesmerism and the End of the Enlightenment in France.* 1968.

Ellenberger, Henri. *The Discovery of the Unconscious.* 1970.

Weyant, Robert G. "Protoscience, Pseudoscience, Metaphors and Animal Magnetism," in Marsha Hanen et al., eds., *Science, Pseudoscience, and Society.* 1980.

See also Science, Technology, and Invention

Metallurgy and Metalworking

Hanoverian advances in **iron** production were particularly significant and have tended to overshadow other branches of metallurgy in the production of steel, tin, lead, copper, brass, and zinc, and advances in metal finishing. However, there were important developments, often interrelated, in these other sectors.

Given that the extraction and processing of the still limited range of commercially significant nonprecious metals involved similar processes, it is not surprising that cross-fertilization often took place. Moreover, the leaders of iron production were frequently involved in the production of other metals, or related to men who were. It was during this period that metallurgy progressed from an art to a **science** involving growing knowledge of the principles underlying the behavior of metals, and pointing toward a technology grounded in chemistry and physics.

In contrast with iron production, the critical breakthrough to mass production of its subspecies, steel, did not occur until Victorian times. But an important interim development was achieved in the Midlands. **Birmingham** and Sheffield (especially) were the centers of steel processing for specialist usage, particularly cutlery. However, they were dependent on limited production of steel by traditional cementation methods using imported Swedish iron. In 1740 **Benjamin Huntsman**, a clockmaker, came to Sheffield from Doncaster, where he had been struggling to improve the quality of the steel used for watch springs. A decade of experiments led to a high-quality process involving smelting in sealed fireclay crucibles with charcoal and ground glass added as reagents. Initial opposition by the Sheffield cutlers collapsed in the face of the threat posed by the adoption of the new steel in Birmingham and **France**. Thus Huntsman's works at Attercliffe, the first true steelworks, prospered. He relied on secrecy rather than **patents**, but his process was eventually copied, and crucible steel output rose. By the 1830s, British output was 8,400 tons while only small amounts were being produced on the Continent. Britain also accounted for 20,000 tons of the world's output of 53,500 tons of steel produced by older methods.

Despite having been a center of tin mining as early as 1100 BC, Britain had to import expertise from Saxony in the 17th century to develop the production of **tinplate**, though tin was also used in the production of solder, pewter, bronze, and type. Building on this imported knowledge, Britain became a center of innovation. Smelting progressed from the 17th-century reverberatory furnace to improved **coal**-firing in the 18th century, and from this developed the Cornish furnace that was copied throughout the world in the 19th century. The first successful tinplate manufacturing center was begun at Pontypool in the 1720s, and **Wales** became the heartland of the industry. It gave its name to the Welsh dipping process (introduced in 1745), involving the use of a separate grease pot to prepare the plate. By 1800, when there were 11 works (mainly in South Wales and Monmouthshire), Britain had become the world's leading supplier, producing 4,000 tons (of which 2,500 went for export), stimulated by the rise of the canned food industry.

Although there were lead deposits scattered down the western side of Britain, it was again Wales that became the main smelting center, following the work of Edward Wright, who developed the Cupola furnace in 1701. During the 18th century the adoption of coke and the consequent need for a stronger blast were problems common to all branches of metallurgy, and there was much cross-fertilization, particularly in the design of furnaces and associated equipment. As demand grew, the aggregate impact of numerous minor innovations improved the production of lead from 28,000 tons in 1706 to 57,000 tons in 1759. An example of linkage at the level of personalities was the patenting of a process for the production of lead pipe by extrusion taken out by **John Wilkinson**, the great ironmaster, in 1790. He built a lead-pipe works at Rotherhithe to supply the expanding water system of **London**.

The copper industry and the associated brass industry,

which had been in difficulty in the 17th century, began to revive with the introduction of the reverberatory furnace originally adapted to copper smelting at **Bristol**. The Champion family was prominent among the innovators who streamlined the process. The revival of brass production was assisted at first by using German and Dutch workers. Here, too, local developments were important. Coal was adopted as the preferred fuel, and Nehemiah Champion developed coal-fired annealing and granulation. The relative transport costs of fuel versus ore, and the advantages of mixing ores, led to the growth of the copper-smelting industry around **Swansea**, using Cornish ore shipped from Bristol and the Anglesy ores of **Thomas Williams**, the "Copper King." The Bristol reverberatory furnace became the basis of the "Welsh Process." A carefully balanced variety of ores, each with distinctive impurities to act as reagents, was smelted in a coal-fired furnace, thus minimizing input costs and maximizing control over output quality. By 1800, Swansea was the world's leading producer. British output, which had been less than 600 tons at the beginning of the 17th century, had risen to 12,000 tons by the middle of the 19th century. The Welsh lead in copper-smelting technique was so secure that as ore deposits were opened in Latin America and elsewhere, Swansea remained the focus of a world trade, and Wales retained its lead until the last quarter of the 19th century.

The last of the major nonferrous metals of the period was zinc. Calamine (zinc oxide), mined in the Mendip Hills, was used from the 17th century in brass production, but direct reduction from the ore, long known in India, was only introduced into Europe at the beginning of the 18th century. William Champion, a member of the **Quaker** network of ironmasters, which included the **Lloyds**, at age 20 returned from studying European practices in 1730 and began experiments at Bristol, where his father was manager of the Brassworks. (This had been established by another Quaker, **Abraham Darby**, in 1702, using German workers.) He patented his process (1738), and built a works for copper zinc and brass production (1746). This large-scale distillation plant, operating at temperatures above 900 degrees, prevented reoxidizing.

By the close of the Hanoverian period, Britain was responsible for the production of 50% of the lead, 60% of the tin, and 75% of the copper in the world, in addition to half the pig iron. Increases in volume were accompanied by steady growth in the scale of production as the new capitalist metal masters and merchants grappled with the novel problems of creating gigantic integrated industrial enterprises, a leading example being "Copper King" Williams's £800,000 business.

By contrast, the finishing trades, which absorbed the expanding production of metals, remained overwhelmingly small in scale until Victorian times, in consequence of extreme specialization and the almost complete absence of standardization. The oft-cited examples of large-scale production such as **Crowley**'s nailworks and **Boulton**'s Soho buttonworks were exceptions, and in any event these consisted simply of large numbers of highly specialized handicraft workers under one roof. Geographical specialization did emerge, notably in the cutlery and edge-tool trades of Sheffield and the small-arms trades of Birmingham, and indeed each district in the Black Country around Birmingham was said to produce its own distinctive nail. London, whose large market compensated for its lack of coal, also became a leading center of metalware manufacture. As late as the 1851 census, the typical firm had less than six employees (and many were sole employee concerns), yet the scale of the sector as a whole is shown by the fact that the aggregate employment was 250,000.

R.D. Corrins

A Marlborough blacksmith, 1794

Bibliography

Barton, D.B. *A History of Tin Mining and Smelting in Cornwall.* 1967.

Day, J., and R.F. Tylecote. *The Industrial Revolution in Metals.* 1991.

Hamilton, H. *The English Brass and Copper Industries to 1800.* 2nd ed., 1966.

Minchinton, W.E. *The British Tinplate Industry: A History.* 1957.

Rowlands, M.B. *Masters and Men in the West Midlands Metalware Trades before the Industrial Revolution.* 1975.

Meteorology

The study of atmospheric phenomena has a long history, and many meteorological instruments had been invented before the Hanoverian period. Meteorology after 1714 attracted many prominent scientists, among them the versatile **Erasmus Darwin**, whose speculations on human weather control led him to suggest towing icebergs to tropical regions to lower temperatures there. Less fanciful were many solid contributions to the understanding of cloud, atmospheric circulation, and the strength and direction of winds.

The systematic recording of weather elements was a particular concern at the beginning of the period. The **Royal Society** became involved when James Jurin (1684–1750), its secretary, invited weather observers to submit records (1723). Unfortunately this initiative soon faded, but observers' networks were formed. The theory of weather elements tended to follow discoveries in other fields. Chemical theories of weather emerged alongside the identification of different gases by **Joseph Black**, **Henry Cavendish**, **Joseph Priestley**, Antoine Lavoisier (1743–1794), and others, while physical ideas about electrical influences followed the discoveries by **Benjamin Franklin** in America and Alessandro Volta (1745–1827) in Italy. Continuing research pointed to the physical nature of atmospheric changes; **John Dalton**, whose meteorological work preceded his famous contributions to chemistry, never accepted the chemical theories.

Fundamental to later understanding of atmospheric circulation was the theory of George Hadley (1735). Extending a proposal by **Edmond Halley** to explain the pattern of the trade winds, Hadley suggested that heated air rises over the Equator, spreads poleward at high levels, and sinks back to Earth in higher latitudes—thence flowing Equatorward along the surface to form the trade winds. This circulation, known as the Hadley cell, furnished a valuable model to later scientists.

Study of cloud formations was a particular interest of Darwin's, but was carried further by Luke Howard (1772–1864), a **Quaker** manufacturing chemist. In 1804 Howard presented a classification consisting of four basic types—stratus, cumulus, cirrus, and nimbus—and, with these and their combinations, classified all clouds that occur in the atmosphere. This formulation has stood the test of time; the present-day system is based on Howard's classifications.

The growth of **travel**, and the dependence of sailing **ships** on wind, also brought an increasing understanding of weather patterns. It became evident, for example, that winds blow in a circular manner around storms. A scale for describing wind strength and its effect on sailing vessels was proposed by the Hydrographer to the **navy**, Francis Beaufort (1774–1857), in 1806. Although Beaufort related wind strength to sail patterns carried by now obsolete men-of-war, his scale remains in common use.

Celestial theories enjoyed some vogue, ranging from pure astrology to the concept that planet and star motion could influence weather. But such hypotheses gradually became less influential, and a sign of growing interest in scientific meteorology was the formation of the Meteorological Society of London (1823).

Jim Burton

Bibliography

Frisinger, Howard. *The History of Meteorology to 1800.* 1977.

Middleton, W.E.K. *A History of the Theories of Rain.* 1965.

Shaw, Sir Napier. *Manual of Meteorology.* Vol. 1. 1932.

See also Science, Technology, and Invention

Methodism

Methodism was the greatest British religious invention of the 18th century. Beginning in the late 1730s as a tiny revival movement, a century later it was an enormous new Protestant denomination embracing people throughout the British Isles, the British **Empire**, and the world.

Several circumstances contributed to this. The first was the vulnerable condition of the **Church of England**, whose ministers sometimes yielded not only to the rationalistic and **Latitudinarian** tendencies of the 18th century but also to affluence, worldliness, and neglect of their flocks. The second was the steady growth of **population** after 1750, which had the effect of worsening the effects of this neglect and also creating more urban centers needing religious care. A third was the **religious revival** that spread across the Western world in the 18th century, inspiring people to find new energy in Bible reading, religious conversion, and emotional experiences not easily defined or restricted by existing doctrines or denominations. A fourth was the remarkable talent, energy, and charisma of a handful of individuals, notably **John Wesley**, his brother **Charles Wesley**, and their associate **George Whitefield**.

Methodism actually began at **Oxford** in 1729 as a small fellowship of earnest young men committed to Bible study, frequent attendance at Holy Communion, and **prison** visitation. It began more formally when the Wesleys and several others formed an Anglican religious society (1738) in Fetter Lane, **London**. The following year, John preached at Methodism's first chapel, the King's Foundery, Moorfields. The same year (1739) saw the beginning of open-air or "field" preaching when he and his friend Whitefield, another Anglican priest, began ministering to the masses in **Bristol**. Whitefield was a passionate speaker, capable, it was said, of moving his audiences to tears simply at his wondrous pronunciation of the word *Mesopotamia.* Such was the inauguration of a technique that would soon become a hallmark of the Methodist movement and a key to its success. Before long, the horrified clergy of many parishes would find themselves unwilling to open their churches to any revivalist preachers, Anglican or other.

As the movement spread in the 1740s and 1750s, other earnest Anglicans such as **John Berridge**, **John Newton**, and the **Countess of Huntingdon** began to adjust their ideas and activities to promote its success. Wesley, always keeping just within the correct boundaries of Anglican ecclesiastical organization, began a lifetime career of itinerant preaching and organization to bind together the many far-flung communities of the new movement. A skillful administrator, he divided these into smaller units: bands (which met regularly for prayer, fellowship, and mutual exhortation), then classes, then societies, which began in 1744 to send representatives to annual conferences presided over by Wesley himself. Gradually there emerged a network of lay preachers appointed by Wesley, moving annually from one circuit to another. The number of Methodist communicants roughly tripled between 1767 and 1797 (by which time there were about 77,000). In 1784, seeing the need to cut free the tightly knit organization from his own life and leadership, Wesley established it as a corporate body, even though, following his lifelong insistence, it remained officially a society within the church. Soon after his death (1791) the conference broke away entirely (1795), ending Anglican ordination and beginning Methodist administration of all the sacraments. Methodism henceforth was essentially a **dissenting** organization.

Before this, by affecting respectable elements within the church, it had helped give rise to **Evangelicalism**. But its impact was much greater among the urban working classes of such places as **Bristol**, London, **Manchester**, and Newcastle-upon-Tyne; and also in **Wales**, where, in this region Calvinist rather than Arminian in doctrine, it flourished under leaders such as **Howel Harris** and **Daniel Rowland**. The rise of Methodism brought a revival of popular Christianity that could scarcely have been anticipated in the 18th century, the century of **Enlightenment**; and it powerfully affected the **manners and morals** of the following era. Its success must be attributed not only to the failures of Anglicanism but also to its own appealing teachings of salvation by simple faith, rigid and relentless personal discipline, self-help, charitable activity, and political conservatism. It was indeed partly because of this last that Wesleyan Methodism fragmented after its authoritarian leader's death, giving rise to the Methodist New Connexion (1797), the populist Primitive Methodists (1811), and Bible Christians (1815). These smaller groups were more deeply rooted than Wesleyan Methodism in the late-Hanoverian working class and often provided leadership disproportionate to their numbers.

George F. Clements

Bibliography

Armstrong, A. *The Church of England, the Methodists and Society, 1700–1850.* 1973.

Bradley, James E. *Religion, Revolution and English Radicalism: Nonconformity in Eighteenth Century Politics and Society.* 1990.

Currie, Robert. *Methodism Divided.* 1968.

Davies, R.E. *Methodism.* 1976.

Langford, Thomas. *Practical Divinity: Theology in the Wesleyan Tradition.* 1983.

Olsen, Gerald Wayne, ed. *Religion and Revolution in Early-Industrial England: The Halévy Thesis and Its Critics.* 1990.

Rupp, Gordon. *Religion in England, 1688–1791.* 1987.

Wakefield, Gordon S. *Methodist Devotion: The Spiritual Life in the Methodist Tradition.* 1966.

Wearmouth, F.R. *Methodism and the Common People of the Eighteenth Century.* 1945.

See also Welsh Religious Revival

Metropolitan Police Act

See Law Enforcement

Middle Class

The British middle class (or classes) experienced growing economic prosperity, social authority, and political power during the Hanoverian period. From 1700 to the 1830s this class so expanded in membership that by the latter date some 20% of the total British **population** was "middle-class"; and of course the figure was significantly higher in urban areas.

Middle-class expansion also took place in the sense that a broadening spectrum of urban middle-class occupational groups emerged, prompted by major sectorial shifts in the economy as agriculture ceased to be the principal employer of labor and contributor of wealth to the economy. The growing importance of manufacturing, mining, and the commercial and service sectors coincided with the relative growth of the urban population at the expense of the rural, as enhanced agricultural productivity facilitated both rapid demographic expansion and the growth of the nonagricultural economy.

It was commercial **farmers** who made up the bulk of the rural middle class, directly employing labor on farms that grew larger as the period progressed. However, the urban middle classes were the chief beneficiaries of demographic and economic change. These classes were generally divided between those involved in the "professions" and those involved entrepreneurially in **commerce** and manufacturing.

Traditionally, the upper ranks of the older professions in the **army**, **navy**, and **Church of England** had been reserved for the younger sons of the **aristocracy and gentry**. The growth of the state in the 18th century increased career opportunities in these areas, but primogeniture, strict settlement, and growth in the size of landed families helped to force many such men into emergent professions, particularly **medicine** and the **legal profession**. These, by 1800, were twin pillars of middle-class wealth in most towns; and, because lawyers and doctors ranged freely through high and low society, of middle-class prestige, also. Many attorneys came from propertied backgrounds, and profited from the growing volume of civil and business litigation and transactions. Medicine experienced significant restructuring in the 18th century, and medical men, though they often originated lower in the social scale, also grew in number to serve the health needs of the landed and middle classes. And while M.D.'s like **David Hartley**, **Edward Jenner**, and **Tobias Smollett** came from the middle class, the upper ranks of the profession, embracing such figures as **John Arbuthnot** and **Sir Hans Sloane**, attained sufficient status and financial reward to attract the younger sons of the gentry. This involvement of the landed in the professions (and to a lesser extent in trade) was characteristic of the fluidity of Hanoverian society, though this was more conspicuous in the downward mobility of the landed classes' younger sons than in their reciprocal openness to middle-class ascent.

Not all professional people, of course, were in the upper ranks of the middle class. Clergymen, the third pillar of the professional middle class, had the status of attorneys and doctors, but often less pay. The **clerical profession** then faded off easily into the **teaching profession** (it was assumed that anyone ordained could teach), which, being notoriously ill-paid too, and also more open to **women's employment**, stood still lower down. Another group, growing in tune with the growth of the state and significantly augmenting the ranks of the lower middle class, comprised the clerks and "revenue men" in government service.

But the bulk of the Hanoverian middle class was involved directly in commerce and manufacturing. During the 18th century, traders in **overseas commerce** stood near the top of the commercial middle class—though the wealthiest of them, particularly those in **London**, might indeed be considered members of the nation's ruling elite. The high costs of training and of entry into established overseas trading operations restricted membership to men of relative wealth, a group that included some sons of the landed, but more typically the sons of **nabobs** and prosperous mercantile families. As for **domestic commerce**, as a consequence of **transport** improvements and expanding consumerism, the 18th century witnessed the growth of much domestic and wholesale trading, expanding the ranks of inland **merchants**. While the profits of domestic commerce generally paled in comparison to those generated in overseas activity, domestic traders far outnumbered overseas merchants.

Shopkeepers and tradesmen made up the bulk of the Hanoverian middle class, albeit within its bottom ranks. Heightened materialism and acquisitiveness, going hand in hand with urban growth, stimulated a remarkable expansion in **retailing** and shopkeeping. It is estimated that in 1750, London had one shop per 30 inhabitants, and 16,000 drinking establishments; smaller urban areas had proportional numbers of both. The wealth of the proprietors of these concerns varied greatly. In small towns and villages, retailing was dominated by the local grocer, involved in general merchandising. However, in London and larger towns, retailing was quite specialized, with specialty shops that dealt, for example, in books, footwear, **jewelry**, fabrics for **clothing**, and imported foodstuffs. As to **drinking** establishments, while the vast majority were gin shops and **public houses**, a significant number were respectable **coffeehouses**, inns, and taverns. The owners of the former were not much richer than the poor they served, yet the retailers of food and alcohol in inns and taverns, and the purveyors of coffee, were substantial people, sometimes involved also in the promotion of **sport** and politics.

Like shopkeepers, tradesmen (i.e., those who retailed the commodities they themselves made) were expanding in numbers but were often quite dissimilar in wealth and scale of operation. On the one hand, master tailors (**Francis Place** was an example), makers of **home furnishings** such as **Thomas Chippendale**, and others who catered to elite consumers lived comfortably, whereas village and urban **clothing-makers** and shoemakers lived and worked much closer to **poverty**.

Some of the wealthiest members of the urban middle class who engaged in both manufacturing and trading in the 18th century were the **entrepreneurs** or "protoindustrialists" or "putting-out capitalists" who controlled the movement of raw material and organization of **domestic production** in cottage industries. This was most notable in **textile** production, in the career of such a man as **David Dale**. **Woolen** clothiers, in particular, were men of substantial wealth and local standing. Yet despite their wealth, such people were "middle class" because of their direct exploitation of labor. Such individuals became joined socially with the organizers of heavy industry—of **mining**, for example (like the Welsh "Copper King" **Thomas Williams**), and of **iron** production (a notable example being the **Darby family**). In the latter 18th century the **Industrial Revolution** promoted the rise of "factory masters" who employed labor and organized production at one central location—**Richard Arkwright**, for example, in the bellwether **cotton industry**. The numbers and prosperity of these nascent "industrialists" (the modern usage of the term was not current until the 1860s) rose with the spread of **factory** organization to more manufacturing processes during the 1820s and 1830s. These new industrialists were middle class in origin, social status, and consciousness. Over 80% came from middle-class backgrounds, and virtually none earned incomes like those of the nabobs and metropolitan traders whose wealth gained them entry into the ranks of the landed and ruling elite.

During the early Hanoverian period, the English middle classes were pluralist and culturally heterogeneous. The formation of a middle-class consciousness lagged behind the expansion of middle-class economic power. Although the middle classes were politically active at the local level in connection with municipal governance and parish affairs, they did not directly challenge the political authority of the landed elite at the national level. In the period 1768–1769 they showed a capacity for independent political action in those few constituencies with substantial middle-class representation (in London and Middlesex, particularly), and in 1779–1780 they worked to forge a program and cooperative networks to promote it. But the creation of a distinct middle-class political identity and platform for electoral reform was drastically sidetracked by the impact of the **French Revolution** and by shared fears of proletarian **radicalism**.

As another factor helping to explain this, it should also be noted that the unreformed Parliament was not insensitive to middle-class pressures. As with the passage and then repeal of the **Stamp Act** (1765, 1766), to take an early example, the middle classes formed commercial and manufacturing lobbies, and utilized petitioning, personal contacts, and the press to influence economic and social legislation; such pressures were quite well organized by 1820. Though most M.P.s came from landed backgrounds, there was a general acceptance in Parliament of market values, and a common recognition that the fortunes of land and trade were interwoven. If the middle classes accepted higher levels of indirect **taxation** without direct political representation, they did so mainly because the state worked to promote commercial and manufacturing interests.

In the decades following 1815, the middle class developed a more uniform political identity and consciousness. This had roots in 18th-century cultural and political **nationalism**, but it also emerged from a more recent and frustrated sense that the middle classes had borne the brunt of financial sacrifice during the French wars, due both to **Pitt**'s income tax and to the **Orders in Council**. Middle-class opposition to the **Corn laws** after 1815 helped solidify a sense of separate, reform-minded political identity, one which found expression in the **Reform Act** (1832) and **Municipal Corporations Act** (1835). More generally, notions of free trade, belief in the dictates of the market, and other aspects of new laissez-faire **economic thought** were characteristically middle class, and were manifest in, for example, the development the Anti-Corn Law League in the late 1830s.

Another element of middle-class consciousness and sensibility emerged from religious experience. In the 18th century, **dissent** was largely concentrated in urban areas and often connected with new industrial enterprise. Dissenters' opposition to the Anglican religious establishment dovetailed with opposition to landed interests and landed political dominance. Further, the sense of legal, political, and educational discrimination felt by dissenters helped to imbue them with a common seriousness about work and achievement. The growth of militant nonconformity in the late 18th century, and with it the influence of a vigorous **Evangelical** movement within the church, cooperative in its attitudes toward dissenters, helped to produce an emergent middle-class morality, a pattern of manners and morals, that emphasized seriousness, sobriety, discipline, and personal responsibility, as against what were felt to be the frivolity, laxity, and religious slackness of the aristocratic elite.

Some commentators have gone on to argue that these stringent moral notions played a role in the "gendering" of "public" and "private" that were associated with the emergent middle-class identity. According to this theory, middle-class men displayed their social identity in public functions of business and civic responsibility, and also by relegating middle-class women to the subordinate spheres of domesticity and family functions. The exaltation of chastity and motherhood, and the pairing of these with concepts of male competitiveness and hardheaded self-interest, further suggest that transformations of morality and socialization had gone hand in hand with economic and social change.

Tim Keirn

Bibliography

Borsay, Peter. *The English Urban Renaissance: Culture and Society in the Provincial Town, 1660–1770.* 1991.

Crouzet, F. *The First Industrialists.* 1985.

Davidoff, L., and C. Hall. *Family Fortunes: Women and Men of the English Middle Class, 1780–1850.* 1987.

Davison, L., T. Hitchcock, T. Keirn, and R.B. Shoemaker, eds. *Stilling the Grumbling Hive: The Response to Economic and Social Problems in England, 1689–1750.* 1992.

Earle, Peter. *The Making of the English Middle Class: Business, Society and Family Life in London, 1660–1730.* 1987.

Holmes, Geoffrey. *Augustan England: Professions, State and Society, 1680–1730.* 1982.

Koditscheck, Theodore. *Class Formation and Urban Industrial Society: Bradford, 1750–1850.* 1990.

Langford, Paul. *Public Life and Propertied Englishmen, 1689–1798.* 1991.

McKendrick, Neil, John Brewer, and J.H. Plumb. *The Birth of a Consumer Society: The Commercialization of Eighteenth-Century England.* 1982.

Mui, Hoh-Cheung, and Lorna H. Mui. *Shops and Shopkeeping in Eighteenth-Century England.* 1989.

O'Brien, Patrick, and Roland Quinalt, eds. *The Industrial Revolution and British Society.* 1993.

Perkin, H.J. *The Origins of Modern British Society, 1780–1880.* 1969.

Prest, Wilfrid R., ed. *The Professions in Early Modern England.* 1987.

Rule, John. *Albion's People: English Society, 1714–1815.* 1992.

Schwarz, L.D. *London in the Age of Industrialization: Entrepreneurs, Labour Force and Living Conditions, 1700–1850.* 1992.

Wahrman, Dror. *Imagining the Middle Class: The Political Representation of Class in Britain, c.1780–1840.* 1995.

See also Cities and Urban Life; Manners and Morals; Standard of Living

Middlesex Election Dispute

See Wilkes, John

Military Education

See Education, Military

Militia Riots (1797)

The Scottish Militia Act (1797) was part of the government's attempt to increase the number and flexibility of its home defense forces in response to the dangers posed by the **French Revolutionary and Napoleonic Wars** and a perceived threat of invasion. It was widely resented because it enforced compulsory military service, possibly abroad. Especially objectionable was the fact that it took no account of an individual's particular circumstances and often had ruinous economic consequences on families. Rioting became widespread, and at one point it seemed as if the act would have to be abandoned, as alarm grew in government circles and among the local gentry. Scottish military resources were so stretched by the rioting that reinforcements had to be brought in from England.

Richard Finlay

Bibliography

Logue, Kenneth. *Popular Disturbances in Scotland 1780–1815.*

See also French Revolution; Riots and Popular Disturbances; United Scotsmen

Mill, James (1773–1836)

Mill, a Scottish-born historian, economist, philosopher, and official in the **East India Company**, was the father of **John**

Stuart Mill and a close associate of **Jeremy Bentham**. He was a powerful advocate of social and economic reform, and stood near the center of the group of Benthamite reforming intellectuals known as "philosophic radicals." With a classics degree from **Edinburgh**, Mill became a licensed **Presbyterian** preacher, then a **tutor**. In 1802 he moved to **London**, entered **journalism** as a freelance writer and editor, and soon afterward began writing on political and economic issues in the *St. James's Chronicle*. In 1805 he married Harriet Burrow; they had nine children. In 1806 Mill began his important *History of British India,* a very critical account of British conquest and administration whose publication (1817) nevertheless resulted in his appointment to a series of posts in the company, culminating in that of Chief Examiner (1830).

In 1808 Mill met Bentham, whose ideas he embraced and helped to publicize in many contributions to **periodicals** such as the *British Review, Edinburgh Review,* and *Westminster Review* (which he helped to found in 1823); in articles on government, politics, education, and so on, which became authoritative in contemporary editions of the *Encyclopaedia Britannica;* and also in his own *Elements of Political Economy* (1821), a reform-minded synthesis of Benthamism, Malthusianism, and Ricardian economic theory.

Besides acting as a synthesist of progressive political and economic ideas, Mill attempted to found a school based on his pragmatic educational ideas (1820), involved himself in the founding of the **University of London** in the 1820s, and increasingly devoted himself to psychological studies. One ambition here, as revealed in his *Analysis of the Phenomena of the Human Mind* (1829) and *Fragment on Mackintosh* (1835), was to draw together the associationist ideas of **David Hartley** and **David Hume** so as to provide a fuller psychological foundation for Benthamism.

Mill was known by his enemies for unusual arrogance and self-conceit, something that does perhaps filter through in his famous son's autobiographical account of his own education. He was, however, as determined a foe of ignorant prejudices as anyone in the age, and did much to help modernize the outlook of less well-informed contemporaries. Although ill for most of his last year of life, he continued to write for the *London Review* almost to the end. He died following a bout of bronchitis.

Robert Gibson Robinson III

Bibliography

Burston, W.H. *James Mill on Philosophy and Education.* 1973.
Mazlish, Bruce. *James and John Stuart Mill: Father and Son in the Nineteenth Century.* 1975.
Robson, John M., and Michael Laine. *James and John Stuart Mill: Papers on the Centenary Conference.* 1976.

See also Economic Thought; India; Radicalism and Radical Politics; Ricardo, David

Mill, John Stuart (to 1837)

Mill, the most famous English philosopher of the Victorian age, spent his youth during the Hanoverian period as a proponent of Benthamite philosophic **radicalism** and of social and political reform. Born in 1806 in **London**, the first child of **James Mill**, he underwent a rigid educational program designed by his father and Jeremy Bentham. At an early age he learned Greek and Latin, logic, mathematics, and natural science, together with history, literature, and political economy. He helped revise his father's *History of British India* (1817). He never received a formal university education because his father feared this would stifle his intellectual development.

In 1822 Mill began organizing the Utilitarian Society of young philosophical radicals, which met at Bentham's house until 1826. At age 17 he became, under his father's supervision, a junior clerk in the **East India Company**, a position that gave him time to write his philosophical works. In 1823 he helped organize the **London Debating Society**, another association of philosophic radicals. From 1822 to 1826 he published articles in several reform **periodicals**, especially the *Westminster Review,* which Bentham had established as an outlet for his ideas; and in the 1830s he helped to edit the reform-minded *London Review* (merged in 1836 with the *Westminster*).

In 1826 Mill suffered a serious mental crisis and depression, which occurred in conjunction with an intellectual transition away from the utilitarian position he had acquired from his father. The first literary fruit of this was a series of seven articles titled "The Spirit of the Age," which appeared in 1831 in *The Examiner.* A year earlier Mill had met Harriet Taylor, who deeply influenced his political principles, especially those connected with **women's rights**. At his father's death (1836), Mill abandoned the latter's utilitarianism to develop his own mature social–democratic ideas concerning the reform of British society and politics. For a full discussion of his career from the accession of Queen Victoria (1837) to his death (1873), see the *Victorian Britain* volume in this series.

Mitchel Gerber

Bibliography

Carlisle, Janice. *John Stuart Mill and the Writing of Character.* 1991.
Donner, Wendy. *John Stuart Mill's Moral and Political Philosophy.* 1991.
Gray, John. *Mill on Liberty: A Defense.* 1983.
Halliday, John. *John Stuart Mill.* 1976.
Himmelfarb, Gertrude. *On Liberty and Liberalism: The Case of John Stuart Mill.* 1974.
McCloskey, H.J. *John Stuart Mill: A Critical Study.* 1971.
Ryan, Alan. *The Philosophy of John Stuart Mill.* 1970.

See also Bentham, Jeremy, and Benthamites

Millar, John (1735–1801)

Millar, one of the luminaries of the **Scottish Enlightenment**, was an influential teacher, a pioneer contributor to sociological theory, and an outspoken advocate of social and political reform. He was born near **Glasgow**, the son of a minister in the **Church of Scotland**. He studied at the University of Glasgow and there came under the influence of **Adam Smith** who, after Millar was admitted to the bar (1760), helped him briefly become **tutor** to the son of **Lord Kames** and then (with additional help from **Lord Bute**) Professor of Civil Law at the university. During the next 40 years of teaching he injected his reformist views into many individuals who were to distinguish themselves later on the liberal side of politics, including James Maitland, 8th earl of Lauderdale (1759–1839), David Erskine, 11th earl of Buchan (1742–1829), the poet **Thomas Campbell**, and **William Lamb, 2nd Viscount Melbourne**.

Millar's chief contribution to sociological theory came with his authorship of a book (1771) published in revised and enlarged form (1779) as *The Origin of the Distinction of Ranks: or, An Enquiry into the Circumstances which Give Rise to Influence and Authority in the Different Members of Society.* Distinguishing between political and civil society, and defining the latter in such terms as property-holding, economic activity, and social status, he explored the nonpolitical foundations of the "distribution of power." His *Historical View of the English Government* from the Saxons to the Stuarts (1787), followed by a posthumously published supplement (1803), unsystematically applied these concepts in a constitutional history noteworthy for its emphasis on original popular liberties and the ominous long-term growth of the military, the national debt, and the power of the Crown.

Unlike other leaders of the Scottish Enlightenment, Millar condemned Britain's handling of the **American Revolution** and was an unrepenting defender of the **French Revolution**. Like **Charles James Fox**, whom he admired, he blamed **Pitt** for the **war** with revolutionary **France** and demanded parliamentary reform as a remedy for Britain's ills. His anonymous *Letters of Sydney on Inequality of Property* and *Letters of Crito,* strongly attacking the government, appeared in the *Scots Chronicle* (1796) and were then reissued as pamphlets.

George F. Clements

Bibliography

Lehmann, William C. *John Millar of Glasgow, 1735–1801: His Life and Thought and His Contribution to Sociological Analysis.* 1960.

Sher, Richard B. *Church and University in the Scottish Enlightenment.* 1985.

See also Scottish Universities

Millenarianism

Millenarianism, a powerful theological idea with considerable influence in the latter Hanoverian period, envisioned a coming age of perfection when corruption, depravity, and sin on Earth would be swept away and replaced by the paradisiacal kingdom of Christ. This was an eschatological system, which held literally true the dream-visions of the book of Daniel and St. John's Revelation, and which foretold a time when Satan would be bound and Christ would reign on Earth for a thousand years.

Historians distinguish pre- from post-millenarianism. The first held that before the thousand-year reign of Christ, several catastrophes would occur, followed by divine peaceful rule until the final unleashing of Satan, the final struggle with evil, the raising of the dead, and then final salvation. Post-millenarianism suggested that the age of perfection could be achieved only by human, not divine, action, either through social progress or, if necessary, war and revolution. In this sense, the reign of Christ was a figurative vision of the future.

All these ideas were rooted in a desire for the redivinization of society, first clearly expressed by the Abbot Joachim of Fiore in the 12th century. In his theory, which influenced Hanoverian millenarians, history was a series of dispensations corresponding to the three persons of the Trinity. Each age saw an increase in spiritual fulfillment and had its own internal structure, calculable length, and inspired leader.

The 17th-century English Revolution had reinvigorated millenarianism as a response to the crises surrounding the execution of Charles I (1649) and the civil war that followed. At that time, millenarian thinkers, though immersed in biblical prophecy, tended toward anticlericalism and anti-intellectualism. The Hanoverian reign of reason, **religious toleration**, and **Latitudinarianism** reduced the energy of such movements, but millenarian sectarianism remained dormant in groups such as the **Quakers**.

The growth of **Methodist enthusiasm** led by 1750 to occasional apocalyptic preachers such as the Methodist George Bell, who predicted the coming of the millennium in 1763 (much to the embarrassment of **John Wesley**). A few decades later, the hopes and fears raised by the **French Revolution** were accompanied by a post-millenarian revival fed even by rationalistic scholar–divines such as **Joseph Priestley**, who was tempted to see in Napoleon Bonaparte a divinely inspired prophet heralding the coming new age of perfection. (Napoleon's **wars** against Europe's old nations and his descent into Egypt perhaps promised the last days foretold in Revelations and Daniel.) Pre-millenarian enthusiasts also began now to count the days before the return of Christ. Swedenborgianism, begun around 1750, increased in popularity, and there was a proliferation of other sects anxiously awaiting a New Jerusalem. Popular prophets such as **Richard Brothers** and **Joanna Southcott** reinterpreted Babylon, once identified as Rome, as London in the coming age, and there were millenarian overtones in some of the **sermons** of various **Evangelical** preachers. Two other groups besides the Southcottians—namely the Buchanites and the Shakers—were heavily under the inspiration of women.

Many members of these small groups, energized partly also by discontents arising from the **Industrial Revolution**, were interested in the ideas of **Robert Owen** and the quasi-socialist reform movements of the early 19th century. Today the most highly regarded (though hardly typical) millenarian of that age was the poet **William Blake**, whose writings and drawings convey some of the intensity of this complicated movement often focusing (as Blake did in his longest poem, 1804–1808) on Albion united with Jerusalem.

Linda Robinson
Jack Fruchtman, Jr.

Bibliography

Cohn, Norman. *The Pursuit of the Millennium.* 1981.

Fruchtman, Jack, Jr. *The Apocalyptic Politics of Richard Price and Joseph Priestley: A Study in Late-Eighteenth-Century English Republican Millennialism.* 1983.

Garrett, Clarke. *Respectable Folly: Millenarians and the French Revolution in France and England.* 1975.

Harrison, J.F.C. *The Second Coming: Popular Millenarianism 1780–1850.* 1979.

Reeves, Marjorie, and Warwick Gould. *Joachim of Fiore and the Myth of the Eternal Evangel in the Nineteenth Century.* 1987.

Tuveson, Ernest Lee. *Millennium and Utopia: A Study in the Background of Progress.* 1949, 1972.

Williams, Ann, ed. *Prophecy and Millenarianism: Essays in Honour of Marjorie Reeves.* 1980.

See also Religious Revivalism

Miller, Patrick (1731–1815)

Miller was one of those many-sided individuals who contributed to the **Industrial Revolution.** Born in **Glasgow,** the son of a lawyer, he became a merchant in **Edinburgh** and ultimately a large shareholder in the **Carron Ironworks.** In 1785 he purchased the estate of Dalswinton in Dumfriesshire, reduced his business activities, and became an **agricultural improver.** But, still interested in technical development, during the 1780s he also experimented with hand-propelled double- and triple-hulled paddle vessels on the River Forth. In 1788, together with James Taylor (1757–1825) and William Symington (1763–1831), he developed a **steam**-driven paddle boat whose trials on Dalswinton Loch were allegedly witnessed by the poet **Robert Burns.** Miller then commissioned Symington to build a larger engine at Carron, which, successfully tried out on the Forth and Clyde Canal the following year, helped lead ultimately to the development of the world's first regular steamship runs, between Glasgow and **Liverpool** (1815).

A.J.G. Cummings

Bibliography

Macleod, I., and J. Neil. *The Dalswinton Steamboat, 1788–1988.* 1988.

See also Bell, Henry; Coastal Shipping; Napier, Robert; Ships and Shipbuilding

Millinery

See Hats and Caps

Milner, Isaac (1750–1820)

Milner was the man who converted **William Wilberforce** to vital religion, and was also the first **Evangelical** appointed (through Wilberforce's influence) to an important living (as Dean of Carlisle, 1791). As a young boy he became a weaver, but in 1768 he returned to Hull grammar school, beginning a distinguished career in mathematics, chemistry, natural philosophy, and religion. In 1770 he entered Queen's College, Cambridge, where he won many academic honors; he became President (1788), then Vice-Chancellor (1792) of Queen's, where he worked to promote Evangelical beliefs. A **Royal Society** member and an energetic and gregarious **Tory,** Milner edited his brother Joseph's *History of the Church of Christ* (1816) and was known for his own writings and controversies, for example with the Rev. William Frend (about **Unitarian** reform), Dr. Thomas Haweis (about Lutheran teachings), and Dr. Herbert Marsh (about the Bible Society).

Laura B. Kennelly

Bibliography

Elliot-Binns, E. *The Early Evangelicals.* 1953.

Hylson-Smith, Kenneth. *Evangelicals in the Church of England.* 1988.

Milner, Mary. *The Life of Isaac Milner, Dean of Carlisle . . . Comprising a Portion of His Correspondence and Other Writings Hitherto Unpublished.* 1842.

See also Cambridge University

Milton, John, in Hanoverian Memory

The evolving reputation of the great 17th-century poet Milton (1608–1674) reveals much about changing tastes and assumptions in the literary arts of the Hanoverian age, as does the growth of the **Shakespeare industry.** Milton inspired Hanoverian artists, musicians, and writers with both his life and his work; his style and literary forms attracted many followers, including **Pope** and **Keats.**

In 1714 Milton was seen by many critics as a larger-than-life figure whose heroic poems had placed England on a literary plane equal to Greece and Rome (despite a few lapses into the Spenserian and Ariostan modes). While some continued to see Milton as a regicide and hypocrite (**Samuel Johnson**'s criticisms of 1779 stand at the end of this tradition), the majority saw him, in this era of praise for the **Glorious Constitution,** as a sincere "lover of liberty." He received his monument in Poets' Corner in 1737, a sure sign of acceptance. A few went so far as to claim him as a modern-day Cato or **radical** reformer. **William Blake**'s Satanist reading of *Paradise Lost* (1667) would grow from this position, which gained popularity with several of the **Romantics.**

Biographies of Milton and notes to editions of his work disclose little distinction made between the poet and his **poetry.** His poetry, especially *Samson Agonistes* (1671), was often read as a gloss on his life, and he was admired for his cheerfulness in adversity and clear conscience. Despite his many flaws Milton seemed a model of Christian piety.

Yet tastes continually evolved. By 1750, Milton's image was becoming that of a great relic of England's literary tradition and the last of an imaginative line that had developed from Spenser and the Romance writers. Instead of "classical," he was now "**sublime.**" Yet some decades later, by the early 19th century, writers such as **Hazlitt** and **Byron** had begun to admire instead of sublimity his steadfast constancy in the face of opposition and his noble critical mind, whereas others were following Blake's line in revering him as a revolutionary artist with a prophetic voice. **Augustans** saw him as a great poet and sincere Christian, whereas Romantics saw him as the epitome of an ideal, a great poet who was also a rebellious thinker.

Some of Milton's **poetic** works flourished in metamorphosed forms. Three performances of an **opera** pasticcio arranged by Paul Rolli called *Sabrina* (1737) ran at the King's Theater. John Dalton revised *A Masque Presented at Ludlow* and renamed it *Comus* (1738) for performance at Drury Lane; the composer **Arne** made his reputation on this work. **Garrick** arranged a 1750 performance to benefit Elizabeth Foster, Milton's sole surviving grandchild; and Johnson, who had arranged the benefit, wrote a prologue for the occasion. In 1772 **George Colman the Elder** reduced the Dalton *Comus* to an afterpiece for Covent Garden, retaining most of Arne's 1738 music and about 20% of Milton's text. By 1800 *Comus* had been performed in **London** 388 times; it saw several more performances after 1815 with new music by **Henry Bishop**.

Hanoverian Britain's greatest composer, **Handel**, based one of his most frequently performed oratorios, *Samson* (1743), on Newburgh Hamilton's (*fl.* 1712–1759) adaptation of *Samson Agonistes*. Handel also set "L'Allegro" and "Il Penseroso" (words arranged by Charles Jennens) for **musical concerts** at Lincoln's Inn Fields (1740), and some incidental songs for a private performance of *Comus* (1745). Portions of Handel's "L'Allegro" often found their way into various productions of Dalton's *Comus* after 1742. Handel also recycled some of his own music for *Comus* to set Milton's **translations** of the psalms (1745).

Linda Veronika Troost

Bibliography

Brisman, Leslie. *Milton's Poetry of Choice and Its Romantic Heirs*. 1973.

DiSalvo, Jackie. *Founder of Titans: Blake's Critique of Milton and the Politics of Religion*. 1983.

Griffin, Dustin. *Regaining Paradise: Milton and the Eighteenth Century*. 1986.

Jarvis, Robin. *Wordsworth, Milton, and the Theory of Poetic Relations*. 1991.

Sherwin, Paul. *Precious Bane: Collins and the Miltonic Legacy*. 1977.

Wittreich, Joseph. *Angel of Apocalypse: Blake's Idea of Milton*. 1975.

———, ed. *The Romantics on Milton: Formal Essays and Critical Asides*. 1970.

See also Byronic Hero; Epic; Literary Criticism; Poetry and Poetics

Milton, Lord (Andrew Fletcher of Saltoun) (1692–1766)

Advocate and agent of Islay, 3rd duke of **Argyll** (1682–1761), **Robert Walpole**'s political manager in **Scotland**, Milton had a brilliant legal career. Admitted advocate in 1717, he became a Lord of Session in 1724, Lord Justice Clerk in 1735, and Keeper of the Signet in 1748. This was partly a result of his close relationship with Islay, whose affairs he administered in Scotland while the latter was in London. Milton was an extremely competent bureaucrat who handled the day-to-day business of the Argyll family, including applications for preferment. He displayed a cool head during the **Jacobite** occupation of **Edinburgh** (1745) and remained a valuable agent of the government. Milton was also devoted to the pursuit of commercial and **agricultural improvement** in Scotland.

Richard Finlay

Bibliography

Shaw, John Stuart. *The Management of Scottish Society, 1707–1764*. 1983.

Mime

See Pantomime

Mining and Miners

In the Hanoverian period, mining, like so many other enterprises, benefited from increasing market opportunities. **Domestic commerce** was growing, and rising incomes among the upper classes stimulated demand for nonferrous metals for many products made of silver and brass. Changes in heavy industry greatly intensified demand for **coal and iron**.

In the early 18th century, a fair number of minerals were mined. Cornwall yielded tin, Derbyshire and **Wales** lead, and the Lake District copper. In **Scotland**, projects in silver and lead mines were established. There were some small yields of gold, and it was an old tradition that English queens should receive wedding rings made of Welsh gold. Coal, the most prominent mineral, was to be found in many areas of mainland Britain; its production rose from 3 million tons in 1700 to over 30 million tons in 1830.

Sometimes mining ventures could be widespread, yet actual production fairly small, as in Cornish tin mining. Not until pewter became commonplace in the 1780s was growth stimulated in this particular sector. Likewise, demand for copper increased significantly after 1760, when it became widely used as sheathing for ships' bottoms. Such trends show that mining could be a very speculative concern. A few people, such as the copper magnate **Thomas Williams**, did make fortunes, but often mining, particularly of nonferrous metals, could be a temporary speculation by landowners, and spectacular failures were not unknown.

In the early 18th century the coal industry had to overcome the serious disadvantage of high **transport** costs. Thus landowners and coal owners (the **Duke of Bridgewater** was both) were a major force in many early river and **canal** developments, and later in waggonways and **railways**. Technical problems, such as draining and ventilation, were also tackled as increasing demand necessitated deeper mining.

Many 18th-century mines were relatively small, and in the case of coal were sometimes allied to other enterprises, such as lime burning and **salt** boiling. Integration could also be seen in **glassmaking** and in the iron industry, where firms such as **Carron Ironworks** integrated backward into raw materials.

However, larger mines were being excavated, particularly near developing industrial centers, or, as in the case of northeast England, where the London market was important.

Mining was usually carried on in family groups—the use of kinship groups as the paying unit was commonplace—the miner receiving the pay for the group, and distributing it among them. In theory, such groups were self-employed; the reality was somewhat different. In general, miners were the dregs of the labor force. Lead miners were the exception, partly due to the remote location of lead works, which necessitated recruitment from afar. Others were badly paid, and working conditions were notoriously poor. Miners and salt boilers in Scotland often lived as serfs; their emancipation did not finally occur until 1799. And even when nominally free, miners could be kept down by coal owners colluding in the exclusion of troublemakers. Also, miners often had little choice of occupation, as mining communities frequently were isolated. Partly because miners inspired fear as well as contempt in their neighbors, such communities could become very introspective.

Mining was dangerous even by contemporary standards, making it difficult to recruit labor beyond existing communities. Fatal accidents were common. Yet this did not strengthen miners' hands in bargaining for significantly higher **wages**. Often, owners operated the truck system and conspired to keep people in debt, making it impossible for them to leave the community. Long periods between pay were the norm. Much worked to the advantage of the owner against his labor force.

A.J.G. Cummings

Bibliography

Barton, D.B. *A History of Tin Mining and Smelting in Cornwall.* 1967.

Flinn, M.W. *The History of the British Coal Industry.* Vol 2: *1700–1830, The Industrial Revolution.* 1984.

Hamilton, Henry. *The English Brass and Copper Industries to 1800.* 2nd ed., 1967.

Harris, J.R. *The Copper King: A Biography of Thomas Williams of Llanidan.* 1964.

Hunt, C.J. *The Lead Miners of the Northern Pennines in the Eighteenth and Nineteenth Centuries.* 1970.

Lewis, W.J. *Lead Mining in Wales.* 1967.

See also Coal Mining and Miners; Welsh Mining

Ministry of All the Talents (1806–1807)

After the death of **Pitt the Younger** (January 1806), **George III** was forced to turn to the opposition. **Baron Grenville** drew men from various factions to form the so-called Ministry of All the Talents, which included **Charles James Fox, Spencer Perceval,** and Henry Addington, 1st Viscount **Sidmouth.** The ministry proved ineffectual in curbing Napoleon's Continental expansionism. In domestic policy, its major achievement was the final abolition of the British **slave trade** (1807).

Insecure from the beginning, the ministry was shaken by the death of Fox (September 1806) and splintered over an Irish question (1807). Without fully informing the king of their plans, the ministers introduced bills allowing **Catholics** to serve in the armed forces in Britain (as was the case in **Ireland**), and to be admitted to the ranks of admiral and staff general. Faced with George III's opposition, the ministry refused to promise to never again raise the question of Catholic relief, and was dismissed.

P.J. Kulisheck

Bibliography

Harvey, A.D. "The Ministry of All the Talents." *Historical Journal.* Vol. 15, pp. 619–648.

Mitchell, L.G. *Charles James Fox.* 1992.

Sack, James J. *The Grenvillites, 1801–1829: Party Politics and Factionalism in the Age of Pitt and Liverpool.* 1979.

Minuet

Developed at the court of Louis XIV during the 1660s, the ballroom minuet, or *menuet ordinaire,* was originally a dance performed by one couple alone. From the late 17th century until the 1790s, minuets were performed at the beginning of Court and public balls, providing a ceremonial opening that helped reinforce a sense of social hierarchy among those in attendance.

The minuet's track and basic movements remained virtually unchanged over the period, and dancers could perform it without previous practice together. The gentleman leads the dance, signaling his partner with his arm movements and the management of his hat. After opening honors to the company and partner, a lead-in pattern brings the dancers to the opposite corners of a square, facing each other. From the corners, the dancers trace a Z on the floor, moving sideways to the other corner, then forward diagonally though the center, and past each other to the opposite corner, then sideways to complete the Z. As each Z-track is performed, the dancers may either pass each other without touching, or take hands in the center and turn by the right, the left, and finally, both hands. The dance is completed as it began, with honors to the company and partner. The basic movement pattern consists of four steps taken to six notes (two bars in $^3/_4$ or $^3/_8$ time), beginning always on the right foot. The minuet step is made up of combinations of demi-coupé (in which one rises from a previous bend during transfer of weight from foot to foot), plain steps onto the ball of the foot, and small leaps from foot to foot.

Kate Van Winkle Keller

Bibliography

Cobau, Judith. "The Preferred *Pas de Menuet.*" *Dance Research Journal.* Vol. 16 (no. 2), pp. 13–17.

Hilton, Wendy. *Dance of the Court & Theater: The French Noble Style, 1690–1725.* 1981.

See also Dance; Music, Dance

Missionary Societies

The **Society for the Propagation of the Gospel in Foreign Parts** (SPG) was founded in 1701 as the missionary arm of the **Society for Promoting Christian Knowledge** (SPCK) (1698),

Minuet

whose work was more particularly educational. Both groups labored especially in **North America** and the **West Indies**. The SPG made progress among the Native Americans of the Carolinas and New England—Dartmouth College was originally founded (1749) to educate the sons of chiefs—while the SPCK distributed Bibles in Indian languages. The missionaries also worked to protect Indians against the rum trade.

Foreign missionary activity was relatively weak, however, until the rise of that later-18th-century **humanitarianism** that concentrated increasingly on the evils of the **slave trade**. The stalwarts of the **antislavery movement** saw many connections between the bondage imposed by the planters of the Caribbean and the economic, social and political evils at home. Their leadership included many **Evangelicals** whose energies and religious feelings spilled over from the battles against African slavery to broader ideas of civilizing and carrying the gospel to people of every race and color, especially those subject to the British crown.

The **Methodist** Missionary Society (founded in 1786) was a harbinger of this new era of expansion. In 1792 the **Baptist** Missionary Society for Propagating the Gospel among the Heathen appeared; its first secretary was Andrew Fuller (1754–1815), its first missionary William Carey (1761–1834), the author of *An Enquiry into the Obligations of Christians to Use Means for the Conversion of the Heathen* (1792). Carey went to **India** (1793) and later published letters, which stimulated further missionary endeavors. Indefatigable, he eventually supervised the **translation** of the Bible, in whole or in part, into 36 languages and dialects.

Though the London Missionary Society was founded in 1795 by some Anglicans, **Presbyterians**, and Wesleyan Methodists working together, it drew its support primarily from **Congregationalists**. Its founders were David Bogue (1750–1825), a Congregational minister in Gosport, and Thomas Haweis (1734–1820), rector of Aldwinkle. Its first 29 missionaries went to Tahiti in 1796; it carried out extensive work in China, India, Southeast Asia, and south and east **Africa**, as well as the South Sea Islands.

The Scottish Missionary Society and Glasgow Missionary Society both originated in 1796. In England, the powerful Church Missionary Society (CMS), originally known as the Society for Missions in Africa and the East, was founded in 1799 by prominent Evangelicals within the **Church of England**, including many in the **Clapham Sect**. **John Venn** was instrumental in its formation; its first secretary was Thomas Scott (1747–1821), who succeeded **John Newton** in the curacy at Olney, Buckinghamshire, in 1781. CMS pioneered missions in Northwest **Canada**, **New Zealand**, the Middle East, west and east Africa, Persia, and parts of India, Pakistan, Ceylon, South China, and Japan.

The Religious Tract Society was also founded in 1799, with a committee of an equal number of Anglicans and **dissenters**, for the publication and dissemination of Christian Evangelical literature. It published in 200 languages for missionary purposes, and established societies in India and China. Bogue was one of its first writers.

Two groups were established in London in 1804: the London Hibernian Society, founded by Irish Protestants for evangelism among **Roman Catholics**; and the larger and more influential British and Foreign Bible Society, founded partly through the efforts of **Thomas Charles**, a Calvinistic Methodist pastor in **Wales**. This, endorsed by the Claphamites, was strictly interdenominational, intended to "encourage the wider circulation of the Holy Scriptures, without note or comment." This society supported nearly all the others, which became dependent upon it to provide Scriptures in the vernacular of their converts. Its simple object explains its extraordinary success; by 1825 it had issued some 4.25 million bibles.

Another important point of interdenominational unity and collective power came in the annual May meetings of religious representatives at Exeter Hall in the Strand, where foreign missionary work was discussed and information transmitted back to the constituencies of the various denominations. The political power of "Exeter Hall" was at its height in the 1830s and dominated the Colonial Office, where missionary interests established a stronghold during the secretaryship of Lord Glenelg (1835–1839) and his permanent Under-Secretary, **James Stephen**.

Richard M. Riss

Bibliography

Allen, W.O.B., and Edmund McClure. *Two Hundred Years: The History of the Society for Promoting Christian Knowledge: 1698–1898.* 1898.

Bennett, Elizabeth. *Guide: Methodist Missionary Society Archives, London.* 1980–1982.

Gidney, William Thomas. *The History of the London Society for Promoting Christianity amongst the Jews: From 1809 to 1908.* 1908.

Horne, Charles Silvester. *The Story of the LMS, 1795–1895.* 1895.

Ingham, Kenneth. *Reformers in India, 1793–1833: An Account of the Work of Christian Missionaries on Behalf of Social Reform.* 1956.

Stock, Eugene. *The History of the Church Missionary Society.* 4 vols. 1899–1916.

Webb, Pauline. *Women of Our Company.* 1958.

See also Empire and Imperialism

Mitford, Mary Russell (1787–1855)

Mitford is best known for the informal sketches she wrote for the *Ladies' Magazine* of the local characters and environs of her village, Three Mile Cross. Compiled (1824–1832) into five volumes titled *Our Village,* these won a wide readership. Their uniqueness lies in their spontaneity (written "on the spot and at the moment," Mitford remarked), extraordinary detail, and fresh, unlabored style. Later writers credited Mitford with inventing the graphically descriptive **essay**. Since most of these sketches predated the first **railways** and the **Reform Act** (1832), the Victorians saw in them one of the last panoramic views of pre-industrial England.

Mary Russell Mitford

Mitford began her writing career with *Miscellaneous Poems* (1810). Three of her tragedies were produced in **London** during the 1820s: *Julian* (1823), *Foscari* (1826), and *Rienzi* (1828). She followed up *Our Village* with *Belford Regis* (1834), *Country Houses* (1837), and *Atherton and Other Tales* (1854).

Mitford corresponded prolifically with Elizabeth Barrett Browning (1806–1861) and John Ruskin (1819–1900), among others. Her memoirs, *Recollections of a Literary Life,* appeared in 1852; *The Life of Miss Mary Russell Mitford. Told in Her Letters* appeared posthumously (1870).

Lauren D. McKinney

Bibliography

Edwards, P.D. *Idyllic Realism from Mary Russell Mitford to Hardy.* 1988.

Keith, W.J. *The Rural Tradition: A Study of the Non-Fiction Prose Writers of the English Countryside.* 1974.

Watson, Vera. *Mary Russell Mitford.* 1949.

See also Women in Literature

Mock-Heroic

Mock-heroic or mock-epic is a subset of the larger class of the *burlesque,* not treating great subjects as trivial (as high burlesque does), but rather the reverse—treating trivial subjects as though they were heroic. Classical Greece had its *Batrachomymachia* (*The Battle of the Frogs and Mice*), and the medieval period enjoyed beast epics and **fables** such as "The Nun's Priest's Tale" by Geoffrey Chaucer (1343?–1400). During the Renaissance, Edmund Spenser (1552–1599) celebrated the fate of a butterfly (*Muiopotmos,* 1591) and Alessandro Tassoni (1565–1635) mocked war in *La Secchia Rapita* (*The Rape of the Bucket,* 1624). In **France**, *Le Lutrin* (1683) by Nicholas Boileau (1636–1711) greatly helped legitimate the mock-heroic for English writers in the Restoration and Hanoverian periods. **Addison** was apparently the first to use the term in print in his *Spectator,* no. 273, 1712.

John Dryden (1631–1700), who admired *Le Lutrin,* wrote the first influential English mock-heroic, *Mac Flecknoe* (1682), a poem in heroic couplets (the favorite verse form for satirists), which ridiculed the plays and person of Thomas Shadwell (*c.* 1642–1692). Like the mock-heroics which followed it, the poem elevated the trivial—ostensibly to praise but actually to accentuate the triviality, ineptitude and dullness of its subject. Celebrating the coronation of a "King of Dulness," *Mac Flecknoe* thereby set the form for a number of 18th-century **satires**, among them **Pope**'s *The Dunciad* (1743) and **Charles Churchill**'s *The Rosciad* (1761). Over 200 "-iad" poems were published during the century.

The finest English mock-heroic poem is Pope's *The Rape of the Lock* (1714), which drew upon *The Iliad* and *Paradise Lost,* among other works, for its epic treatment of a private squabble, and in the process elegantly set forth the deficiencies of the English ruling classes. Not all mock-heroics were poems, however; **Swift**'s *The Battle of the Books* (1704) pitted **ancients vs. moderns**, and the **ballad opera** *The Beggar's Opera* by **John Gay** equated **London**'s underworld to society's upper ranks. The best sustained prose mock heroic may be Part I of Swift's *Gulliver's Travels,* "A Voyage to Lilliput" (1726).

Henry Fielding attempted the mode in three genres: in his **novel** *Tom Jones* (1749), his poem *The Vernoniad* (1741), and his burlesque play *The Tragedy of Tragedies; or, The Life and Death of Tom Thumb the Great* (1730). *Tom Jones* was indebted to *Don Quixote* (1605, 1615), whose author, Cervantes (1547–1616), **Joseph Warton** called the father of the mock-heroic.

Mock-heroics crowded the bookshelf during the early 18th century. **Henry Carey** briefly characterized the mode in his Prologue to *Chrononhotonthologos* (1734): his comic Muse "gives her self no small Romantic Airs; / Struts in Heroics, and in pompous Verse, / Does the minutest Incidents rehearse. . . ."

When the mock-heroic technique ridicules a genre, as in Carey's and Fielding's satires of tragedies and heroic plays, the result is *burlesque.* But often when the same method aims at nonliterary targets (**George III**'s reaction to a louse, for instance, in **John Wolcot**'s *The Lousiad,* 1785), the result may also properly be called mock-heroic. In both cases, however, ridicule diminishes the subject. A work may mock the heroic attitude—for example, *The Recruiting Serjeant* (1770), a serenata by **Isaac Bickerstaff**, with its song, "What a charming thing's a battle!"—but it is not therefore mock-heroic. However, whether the mock-heroic (such as *The Rape of the Lock*) intentionally mocks its heroic models remains unsettled.

The mock-heroic prospered when **wit** was paramount. When that yielded after 1750 to sentiment, and satire to **sensibility**, the mock-heroic lost its voice in the new damp climate. As Joseph Warton put it, "Wit and Satire are transitory and perishable, but Nature and Passion are eternal" (1782). Then too, by its allusiveness, the mock-heroic appealed to an educated upper class, but a democratizing force was reforming **poetry** to speak the "very language of men" (**Wordsworth**). Warton notwithstanding, satire survived, but by leveling, not by heroic measures.

Peter A. Tasch

Bibliography

Bond, Richmond. *English Burlesque Poetry, 1700–1750.* 1932.

Fuchs, Jacob. "Knowing and Remembering: The Resources of Mock-Epic." *Philological Quarterly.* Vol. 69, pp. 319–336.

Highet, Gilbert. *The Anatomy of Satire.* 1962.

Jack, Ian. *Augustan Satire: Intention and Idiom in English Poetry, 1660–1750.* 1952.

Kinsley, James, and James T. Boulton, eds. *English Satiric Poetry, Dryden to Byron.* Introduction. 1966.

Kitchin, George. *A Survey of Burlesque and Parody in English.* 1931.

See also Burlesque; Classicism; Poetry and Poetics; Satire

Molasses Act (1733)

To reduce competition from the French sugar trade, British planters in the **West Indies** persuaded the **London** government to place a heavy duty on foreign sugar, molasses, and rum entering British colonial ports (1733). Molasses was especially important in **North America**, where it was distilled into rum and used in trade. But the act had little effect because the American colonists were skillful at evasion, and the Admiralty lacked the resources to enforce it. The act would prove more contentious when it was revivified as part of the **Plantation Act** of 1764.

P.J. Kulisheck

Bibliography

McCusker, John J., and Russell R. Menard. *The Economy of British America, 1607–1789.* 1985.

Rogers, Nicholas. *Whigs and Cities: Popular Politics in the Age of Walpole and Pitt.* 1990.

Sheridan, Richard B. "The Molasses Act and the Market Strategy of the British Sugar Planters." *Journal of Economic History.* Vol. 17, pp. 62–83.

See also Navigation Laws

Molesworth, Viscount (Robert Molesworth) (1656–1725)

Molesworth sought to secure the constitutional reforms of the **Glorious Revolution**. It was this concern that lay at the heart of his most famous historical work, *An Account of Denmark* (1694), which explored the process through which a free state could succumb to absolutism. Both history and polemic, the *Account* made explicit the argument that the preservation of liberty ultimately rested upon the vigilance and moral stamina of the people in maintaining effective checks on those who held power. Molesworth celebrated England's ancient constitution, and saw Parliament as responsible for preserving popular liberties. These ideas helped inspire the reform-minded group known as 18th-century **Commonwealthmen**.

Molesworth was born in Dublin and lived an active public life. A firm partisan of the Prince of Orange in the struggle that accompanied the Glorious Revolution in **Ireland**, he was attainted in 1689 by James II and fled to England to join the circle around Anne of Denmark. In 1692 he was sent to Denmark as Envoy Extraordinary to that country, but was dismissed in 1694 for giving offense to the Danish Court.

Molesworth returned to Ireland in 1695 and served as a member for **Dublin** in the Irish Parliament. In 1697 he became privy councillor for Ireland, a position he held until 1712–1713, when he fell out of favor. On the accession of **George I** he obtained a seat in the English Parliament and soon was renamed a privy councillor for Ireland and named Commissioner for Trade and Plantations. In July 1719 he was created Baron Molesworth of Philipstown and Viscount Molesworth of Swords. Molesworth died at his home in Brackenstown, near Dublin.

Michael L. Oberg

Bibliography

Clark, J.C.D. *English Society, 1688–1832: Ideology, Social Structure and Political Practice during the Ancien Regime.* 1985.

———. *The Language of Liberty, 1660–1832: Political Discourse and Social Dynamics in the Anglo-American World.* 1994.

Robbins, Caroline. *The Eighteenth Century Commonwealthman.* 1959.

Monboddo, Lord (James Burnett) (1714–1799)

Scottish judge, philosopher, and anthropologist, Monboddo was born in Monboddo, Kincardineshire. After studying Greek philosophy at Aberdeen University he pursued law at **Edinburgh** and Groningen (1733–1736). He excelled at the Scottish bar and gained his title on becoming a Lord of Session (1767). Though as a judge he gained a reputation for independent thinking, it was as an eccentric if intuitive early scientist and philosopher of the **Scottish Enlightenment** that he is remembered today.

His first work on human origins, *Of the Origin and Progress of Language* (6 volumes), appeared between 1773 and 1792. Having heard reports that the inhabitants of the Nicobar Islands possessed tails, Monboddo argued that the orangutan and the human race were connected as part of the same family. This outrageous pre–Darwinian assumption sparked mirth and controversy. Monboddo also delved into the natural history of **language**, seeing its development as a function of human social needs rather than divine origins. His *Antient Metaphysics* (6 volumes, 1779–1799) presented man as ascending naturally from an animal condition to one of higher thought and creativity.

At home in Kincardineshire, Monboddo worked alongside his tenant **farmers** and refused to raise their rents despite his meager inheritance. **Samuel Johnson** and **James Boswell** stopped to visit him on their trip to the Hebrides in 1773, enjoying his amiable conversation in spite of Johnson's pious disregard for his host's belief in "men having tails." Monboddo was known for other quirks, such as his preference for visiting **London** on horseback rather than comfortably in a **coach**.

Donald W. Nichol

Bibliography

Cloyd, E.L. *James Burnett, Lord Monboddo.* 1972.

Wokkler, Robert. "Apes and Race in the Scottish Enlightenment: Monboddo and Kames on the Nature of Man," in Peter Jones, ed., *Philosophy and Science in the Scottish Enlightenment.* 1988.

See also Science, Technology, and Invention; Scottish Legal System

Montagu, Elizabeth Robinson (1720–1800)

Though an essayist and prolific letter-writer, Montagu was best known for holding lavish gatherings of intellectual men and women who described themselves as "**bluestockings**," thus earning her **Samuel Johnson**'s title, "Queen of the Blues."

She developed her conversational gifts and perhaps also her penchant for hostessing during her girlhood under the tutelage of her step-grandfather, Conyers Middleton (1683–1750), university librarian at Cambridge. Middleton had urged her to mingle among his guests and provide him accounts of their conversation. Attractive in appearance, she had many suitors but in 1742 married mathematician Edward Montagu, 30 years her senior. Though apparently more an amicable marriage of convenience than of love, it was long lasting, with husband and wife often living separately and pursuing their own interests. Montagu, losing her only child in infancy (1744), turned her attention to her intellectual friends and her writing.

For almost 50 years beginning in 1750, her home in Hill Street, Mayfair, was a leading **London** center for literary and intellectual conversations. Her evening assemblies—"conversation parties"—regularly attracted **David Garrick**, **Horace Walpole**, and **Edmund Burke**, among others; and she numbered among many friends **Elizabeth Carter**, **Hannah More**, and **William Cowper**. **Richard Price** and **James Beattie** were among her protégés; **William Wilberforce** was a young admirer.

Montagu contributed three dialogues anonymously (XXVI, XXVII, and XXVIII) to **George Lyttleton**'s *Dialogues of the Dead* (1760). Her *Essay on the Writings and Genius of*

Elizabeth Montagu, "Queen of the Blues"

Shakespear (1769), written to refute the dramatic strictures of Voltaire (who had, among other things, characterized Shakespeare's plays as "a few pearls on a dung hill"), earned her a reputation as an "English Minerva." Her essay, as Johnson commented, was very superficial, but it was an important landmark in the rise of English literary **nationalism** and helped fuel the growing **Shakespeare industry**. There are signs that as late as 1760 it was not Shakespeare but rather **Pope** whom Englishmen unhesitatingly thought of as their "favourite British bard," but reaction against Shakespeare's French detractor figured importantly in the realignment of taste.

Diane McManus

Bibliography

Blunt, Reginald, ed. *Mrs. Montagu, "Queen of the Blues": Her Letters and Friendships from 1762 to 1800.* 2 vols. n.d.

Busse, John. *Mrs. Montagu: Queen of the Blues.* 1928.

Climenson, Emily J., ed. *Elizabeth Montagu, the Queen of the Bluestockings: Her Correspondence from 1720 to 1761.* 2 vols. 1906.

Maison, Margaret. "Elizabeth Montagu," in Janet Todd, ed., *British Women Writers: A Critical Reference Guide.* 1989.

Myers, Sylvia Harcstark. *The Bluestocking Circle: Women, Friendship, and the Life of the Mind in Eighteenth-Century England.* 1990.

Montagu, Lady Mary Wortley (1689–1762)

Montagu, *née* Pierrepont, an intellectual noblewoman, wrote in most genres of **poetry** and prose. Her **travel** letters, especially those from Turkey, are considered among the greatest of the 18th century. She was instrumental in establishing **smallpox** inoculation (not vaccination) in England. **Alexander Pope** made her notorious in **satire**.

Daughter of a duke, she educated herself in his library. Notable among her **letters** are those of 1710–1712 to Edward Wortley Montagu (with whom she eloped, evading forced marriage to another); those from Europe and Turkey, 1716–1718 (surviving in her transcript, a draft **travel book**, published in 1763); those including some dazzling satire from the 1720s; love letters of 1736–1741 to the savant Francesco Algarotti (1712–1764); and letters to her daughter from North Italy, 1746–1756, distilling a lifetime's thinking on literature and the human mind.

Montagu's first publications were anonymous. In 1714 **Joseph Addison** admitted her to *The Spectator* (she was its only female contributor). In 1716 Edmund Curll (1675–1747) illicitly printed three of her "town eclogues," which mocked the contemporary with Virgilian parallels. Many of her poems were feminist critiques of **marriage**; some replied to poems by Pope or **Swift**. Her prose included fictionalized **autobiography**, an "Account of the Court of George I," and *The Nonsense of Common-Sense* (1737–1738), a periodical that supported the ministry of **Robert Walpole** and discussed interest rates, political morality, and antifeminism. Her comedy, *Simplicity,* adapted from Pierre Marivaux (1688–1763), remained unproduced until 1967.

Montagu accompanied her husband to Constantinople upon his appointment as ambassador (1716). Having witnessed inoculation there (and herself having been scarred by smallpox just a year or two earlier), she caused both of her children to be inoculated. Her daughter's was the first such

Lady Mary Wortley Montagu

procedure in Britain (1721), and she vigorously championed it in print.

Vilified (as "Sappho") by Pope from about 1728, she left England in 1739, planning a rendezvous with Algarotti. Disappointed in this, she remained abroad until 1761, after her husband's death. In Italy and southern **France** she participated in intellectual life in several languages, but left few written traces. Her daughter later destroyed her life-long diary; she herself, unfortunately, destroyed her "History of [Her] Own Time." Nonetheless, as a sophisticated, clever, well-traveled and careful observer and correspondent, she still furnishes excellent guidance to early Hanoverian civilization.

Isobel Grundy

Bibliography

Halsband, Robert. *The Life of Lady Mary Wortley Montagu.* 1956.

Montagu, Lady Mary Wortley. *Complete Letters.* Robert Halsband, ed. 3 vols. 1965–1967.

See also Women in Literature

Moore, Sir John (1761–1809)

Moore, an ingenious and extremely popular military commander, is best known for his efforts in Portugal and Spain during the **French Revolutionary and Napoleonic Wars** (1792–1815). He entered the **army** as an ensign of the 51st Regiment of Foot (1776) and served in **Canada** during the **War of American Independence**. During the struggle against revolutionary France his efficient performance in the Corsican Campaign (1794–1795) resulted in promotion to brigadier. Under Sir Ralph Abercrombie (1734–1801), a mentor who greatly aided his career, he commanded brigades in the Caribbean, in **Ireland** against the rebels (1797–1799), and in the Netherlands, where he was twice wounded at the Battle of Egmont-op-Zee (1799). He served as a division commander in Abercromby's Egyptian expedition (1800–1801).

Sir John Moore

Moore took charge of army training at Shorncliffe Camp (1803), where he created a light infantry corps skilled in skirmishing and mobile tactics, emphasizing the rapid battlefield movement that would characterize the Light Division in the Peninsular War (1809–1814). He drew upon light infantry experience gained from the North American wars as well as the writings of various light infantry tacticians. Some of his ideas were later adapted for use by Britain's first **police** forces.

Moore's reputation for efficiency, gallantry, excellent subordinate relations, the superior training and discipline of his troops, and tactical acumen resulted in his promotion to Lieutenant–General, a knighthood (1804), and the command of British and Spanish forces in Iberia (1808–1809). However, he lacked experience in managing the administrative, diplomatic, and financial complexities of a multinational command and never successfully molded the disparate Spanish units into an effective fighting force.

Facing over 300,000 French troops, Moore aborted his northern Spanish expedition (1809) and commenced an arduous mid-winter retreat to Corunna for evacuation by sea. During the embarkation, his forces successfully repulsed a French attack, but he died of grapeshot wounds. His year-long delay of the French conquest of Spain was a noteworthy achievement.

Stanley D.M. Carpenter

Bibliography

Fortescue, J.W. *A History of the British Army.* 13 vols. Vol. 6. 1910.

Fuller, John F.C. *Sir John Moore's System of Training.* 1925.

Glover, Richard. *Peninsular Preparation: The Reform of the British Army, 1799–1809.* 1963.

Oman, Carola. *Sir John Moore.* 1953.

Oman, C.W.C. *A History of the Peninsular War.* 5 vols. 1902–1930.

See also War and Military Engagements

Moore, Thomas (1779–1852)

Moore is remembered mainly as the composer of such enduring Irish airs as "The Last Rose of Summer" and "The Harp that Once through Tara's Halls." In his own day he was an enormously successful composer, poet, biographer, and satirist. The son of a **Dublin** grocer, educated in law in **London**, he first achieved fame for his collection of songs (with words and music) in his 10-installment *Irish Melodies* (1807–1834); two other volumes, *National Airs* (1815) and *Sacred Songs* (1816), secured his reputation as national lyricist of **Ireland**, comparable to **Robert Burns** of **Scotland**.

By this time, Moore, patronized by the **Whigs** and critical of contemporary **Tory** governments, was publishing occasional political **satires** in *The Morning Chronicle.* A collection of his pieces lampooning the Prince Regent's circle appeared

Thomas Moore

as *Intercepted Letters; or, The Twopenny Post-bag* (1813); and under the pseudonym Thomas Brown the Younger, he wrote *The Fudge Family in Paris* (1818), a satire on the Englishman abroad. Later, true to his patriotic roots, he also wrote a four-volume *History of Ireland* (1834–1846).

In 1817 Moore published a narrative poem in the style already made famous by his friend and fellow-poet, **Lord Byron**. *Lalla Rookh,* a mysterious and exotic romance set in the East, was instantly successful. **Translated** into many languages, the poem earned Moore an international reputation; its subject matter did much to encourage the vogue of **Orientalism**. Today the poem, over 5,000 lines long, seems virtually unreadable, but its success during Moore's lifetime rivaled that of any work published by Byron or **Scott**.

Moore also wrote three exemplary literary **biographies**, still useful today—of **Richard Brinsley Sheridan** (1825), Byron (1830), and Lord Edward Fitzgerald (1763–1798) in 1831. Given his penchant for biography, it is ironic that Moore and **publisher** John Murray (1778–1843) honored Byron's request that his memoirs, entrusted to Moore in Venice, be destroyed. Moore's own diaries and memoirs remain informative and entertaining.

Steve Patterson

Bibliography

Clifford, Brendan. *The Life and Poems of Thomas Moore.* 2nd rev. ed., 1993.

Dowden, Wilfred S., ed. *The Journal of Thomas Moore.* 6 vols. 1983.

Jones, Howard Mumford. *The Harp That Once—; A Chronicle of the Life of Thomas Moore.* 1937.

Jordan, Hoover H. *Bolt Upright: The Life of Thomas Moore.* 2 vols. 1975.

Sharafuddin, Mohammed. *Islam and Romantic Orientalism: Literary Encounters with the Orient.* 1994.

Tessier, Therese. *The Bard of Erin: A Study of Moore's Irish Melodies.* 1981.

White, Terence de Vere. *Tom Moore: The Irish Poet.* 1977.

See also Irish Literature before the Union

Morals

See Manners and Morals

More, Hannah (1745–1833)

More—poet, playwright, moral reformer and activist—was one of the most influential women of the early 19th century. She was born at Stapleton near Bristol, the fourth of five daughters, her father a schoolmaster. After writing a few pastoral plays she went to **London** (1772) and soon met **Johnson**, **Garrick**, and **Elizabeth Montagu**, impressing them with her **wit** and conversation. As a **Bluestocking** she enjoyed an early dramatic triumph with her tragedy *Percy* (1777), for which Garrick wrote both prologue and epilogue; *The Fatal Falsehood* (1779) was less successful and gave rise to charges of borrowing from a play written the same year by **Hannah Cowley**.

More turned after 1779 to the serious and religiously uplifting activities for which she was later best remembered. Becoming acquainted with **Wilberforce**, **Macaulay**, and other **Evangelical** luminaries of the **Clapham sect**, she began penning treatises and stories critical of the moral laxity then prevalent in high and low society. Her *Thoughts on the Importance of the Manners of the Great to General Society* (1788) and *An Estimate of the Religion of the Fashionable World* (1790) were both unflattering to the world of "**fashion**" with which she was well acquainted. In the 1790s, with England recoiling from the **French Revolution** and seeking in **religious revival** some security against domestic tumult, More began churning out didactic works such as *Strictures on the Modern System of Female Education* (1799) and *Hints towards Forming the Character of a Young Princess* (1805). Tremendously popular was her **novel** descriptive of the proper woman and of proper home life, *Coelebs in Search of a Wife* (1808). Her tale *Village Politics* (1792) was a direct reply to **Tom Paine**'s doctrines in plain words, put into the mouths of rustics. Most influential of all were the "Cheap Repository Tracts," produced with great rapidity for 3 years by More and her sisters; these sold for a penny, reached millions of people, and sought both to attach the poor to their betters and to reform the latter by emphasizing sobriety, industry, religion, and pride in the British Constitution. More was very important to the contemporary realignment of manners and morals. She also supported the crusade against the **slave trade** and took a determined part in the **Sunday school** movement.

More's work, attacked as priggish by some contemporaries and as morally rigid by some critics today, failed to call for the kind of reform of **women's rights** that contemporaries such as **Mary Wollstonecraft** advocated. Recent scholars have, however, presented an interesting reevaluation of More's attempts to create for women a separate sphere of action within religious and moral movements—an option she saw as a viable alternative to women's rights.

Shawn E. Carleton

Bibliography

Hopkins, Mary Alden. *Hannah More and Her Circle.* 1947.

Jones, M.G. *Hannah More.* 1952.

Kowaleski-Wallace, Elizabeth. *Their Fathers' Daughters: Hannah More, Maria Edgeworth, and Patriarchal Complicity.* 1991.

Roberts, William, ed. *Memoirs of the Life and Correspondence of Mrs. Hannah More.* 2 vols. 1834.

Yonge, Charlotte M. *Hannah More.* 1888.

See also Children's Literature; Manners and Morals; Women in Literature

Morton, Thomas (1764–1838)

Morton, a playwright, penned 25 works, chiefly comedies and musical dramas. *Columbus* (1792), an historical drama, successfully initiated his career and was followed by the immensely popular **opera** *The Children in the Wood* (1793). With *The Way to Get Married* (1796) he revised his style in the mode of the "blue-coat-and-white-waistcoat" contemporary comedies popular at Thomas Harris's Covent Garden Theatre. He created the unseen but pervasive "Mrs. Grundy," a symbol of conventional propriety, in *Speed the Plough* (1798). In about 1828 he became the Covent Garden Reader of Plays; he later occupied the same post at Drury Lane (1831–1833). Morton's trademark blending of tragic and comic modes, and his apt mirroring of the audience's taste, ensured a healthy income—£1000 for *Town and Country* (1807)—and popularity in the era of the newly enlarged **London** playhouses.

Susan Bolet Egenolf

Thomas Morton

Bibliography

Sutcliffe, Barry, ed. *Plays by George Colman the Younger and Thomas Morton.* 1983.

See also Dramatic Arts; Theaters and Staging

Muir, Thomas, of Huntershill (1765–1799)

Muir was a prominent **radical** and "Scottish Martyr" at the time of the **French Revolution**. Born and educated in **Glasgow**, he became a high-principled young lawyer and a vociferous opponent of aristocratic privilege. In July 1792 he, William Skirving (*d.* 1796), and others began the Scottish Association of the Friends of the People. Its membership grew quickly, and Muir, its Vice-President, called for a General Convention of the many reform societies recently established.

At this "National" or "General Convention" (which met in **Edinburgh** in December 1792, receiving addresses and delegations from such groups as the **London Corresponding Society** [LCS] and the **United Irishmen**), Muir, who advocated a united campaign of Scotsmen and Irishmen for reform and ultimate national independence, declared that "We do not, we cannot consider ourselves as mowed and melted down into another country." This led to his arrest in January 1793 on a charge of sedition and, in August, to his trial before **Robert Macqueen, Lord Braxfield** in what has been called "a classic example of the abuse of the judicial process for political ends." After being sentenced to 14 years' **transportation** and sent to **Australia** along with Skirving and Maurice Margarot (1745–1815), the LCS leader, he escaped (1796) but died in **France**, where he had been welcomed as a hero of the Revolution.

Richard Finlay

Bibliography

Baylen, Joseph O., and Norbert J. Gossman, eds. *Biographical Dictionary of Modern British Radicals.* Vol. 1. 1979.

Bewley, C. *Muir of Huntershill.* 1981.

Lenman, B. *Integration, Enlightenment and Industrialisation: Scotland 1746–1832.* 1981.

McFarland, E.W. *Ireland and Scotland in the Age of Revolution: Planting the Green Bough.* 1994.

Meikle, W.H. *Scotland and the French Revolution.* 1912.

See also Corresponding Societies

Mulready, William (1786–1863)

Mulready was an Irish-born **genre painter** of great technical accomplishment and emotive power. In his early years, following on his association with the landscape painters John Varley (1778–1842), John Linnell (1798–1882), and William Henry Hunt (1790–1864), he painted local views of remarkable vividness, such as *An Old Gable* (1809)—works which were not well received because of their extreme, informal realism. After 1809 Mulready turned to more anecdotal rural and domestic scenes in which the influence of the Scotsman **Sir David Wilkie** is clear. In the 1820s he began to develop a more individual style, the result partly of his great precision of draftsmanship, and partly of his distinctive use of a light palette over white ground. In some works, such as *The Sonnet* (1839), the poetic intensity and literary subject matter look forward to the pre–Raphaelites of the Victorian period.

Mulready's most powerful paintings, like Wilkie's, were closely related to social conditions and events of his time such as the abolition of slavery (see, e.g., *The Toyseller,* 1835) and the British colonial experience. His paintings of children, notably *The Wolf and the Lamb* (1820) and *Giving a Bite* (1834), grew closely out of 19th-century attitudes toward childhood and sexuality. They also expressed his profoundly pessimistic view of human nature.

J.C. Steward

Bibliography

Heleniak, Kathryn Moore. *William Mulready.* 1980.

See also Painting; Painting, Landscape

Municipal Corporations Act (1835)

This act brought the first major reform of government in the towns of England and **Wales**. In some ways it gave effect more importantly than the parliamentary **Reform Act** of 1832 to the growing influence of the **middle classes**.

Prior to 1835, town government was carried out by bodies that were often unrepresentative, cautious, unimaginative, self-perpetuating, and not infrequently corrupt (being responsible only to themselves). Some towns, especially new ones like **Manchester** and **Birmingham**, legally only parishes, were, despite their burgeoning **populations**, still governed like villages by justices of the peace and parish vestries; some 200 others, being ancient **boroughs** with rights to parliamentary representation and self-government, were corporations governed in many cases (though not all—**Liverpool** and Oxford, for example, were exceptions) by local oligarchs too prone to abuse the corporate income and charities, or by national politicians interested in them chiefly for the **patronage** they yielded. The result was that problems caused by Hanoverian urban growth were often left unattended to, or else were dealt with by a welter of new authorities performing specialized functions: improvement commissions, turnpike trusts, corporations for administration of the poor law, and the like.

The act of 1835 followed upon the report of a royal commission inspired by the reformed **Commons** and headed by the **radical Benthamite** Joseph Parkes (1796–1865). Under this act, a uniform system of directly elected town councils (councilmen would hold office for 3 years) and indirectly elected aldermen (holding office for 6 years) and mayors (with 1-year terms), responsible to the local community, was imposed on 178 of the old borough corporations. The act's remarkably democratic franchise (open to all local rate-payers) and radically reformist implications brought stiff opposition in the **Lords**, but after passage it provided the basic structure of Victorian local government. Within a few years it was extended to towns such as Manchester and Birmingham, which had not had corporations earlier, and following decades saw the new elective corporations taking over many of the separate functions formerly directed by improvement commissioners, and many new functions besides. **London**, considered too huge and complicated to fall under the act, was declared exempt (London's government was not reformed until 1888), but **Scotland** and **Ireland** saw somewhat similar municipal reforms in 1833 and 1840, respectively.

K.R. Wood

Bibliography

Eastwood, David. *Governing Rural England: Tradition and Transformation in Local Government, 1780–1840.* 1994.

Fraser, Derek. *Power and Authority in the Victorian City.* 1979.

Redlich, Joseph, and Francis W. Hirst. *The History of Local Government in England.* 2nd ed., 1970.

See also Cities and Urban Life; Government, Local and County; Government, National; Provincial Towns and Society

Murphy, Arthur (1727–1805)

The finest British comic dramatists in the second half of the 18th century were Irish: **Sheridan**, **Goldsmith**, and Murphy. Unlike the others, Murphy also wrote tragedies and was an accomplished actor, journalist, biographer, translator, and lawyer.

Murphy was the son of a **Dublin** merchant. He studied on the Continent and worked in a **Cork** counting-house, but found his way to **London** by 1752, where he began writing and acting. Of his more than 20 plays (many of them adaptations from the French), his best comedies are *The Way to Keep Him* (1760) and *Know Your Own Mind* (1777). Sheridan drew upon the latter for his *School for Scandal* (1777) and beat Murphy at his own game. *The Grecian Daughter* (1772) is his most well-known tragedy. *The Apprentice* (1756; his first play) and *The Upholsterer* (1758) were popular farces.

Arthur Murphy

Between 1752 and 1755, Murphy wrote about 104 **essays** for **Henry Fielding**'s *Covent Garden Journal,* the ***Craftsman,*** and *Gray's Inn Journal.* In 1756–1757 he published a weekly paper, the *Test,* in support of the politician **Henry Fox,** and contributed to **Samuel Johnson**'s *Literary Magazine.* In 1757–1758 he wrote about 50 essays of perceptive **dramatic criticism** for **Robert Dodsley**'s **newspaper** the *London Chronicle.* Murphy wrote Fielding's **biography** and edited his works in 1762, and did the same for Johnson in 1792. His two-volume *Life of Garrick* (1801) remains an important source of theatrical history. His **translation,** *The Works of Cornelius Tacitus* (1793), was the standard until the 20th century.

Peter A. Tasch

Bibliography

Dunbar, Howard Hunter. *The Dramatic Career of Arthur Murphy.* 1946.

Emery, John P. *Arthur Murphy.* 1946.

Highfill, Philip H., Jr., Kalman A. Burnim, and Edward A. Langhans. *A Biographical Dictionary of Actors, Actresses, Musicians, Dancers, Managers & Other Stage Personnel in London, 1660–1800.* Vol. 10. 1984.

Spector, Robert Donald. *Arthur Murphy.* 1979.

See also Dramatic Arts; Periodicals

Murray, James (1721–1794)

Murray, born into a Scottish baronial family, entered the **army** at age 15. During the **Seven Years' War** he commanded as a colonel the left wing at the Battle of the Plains of Abraham (1759). Following this he was rapidly promoted from Governor of the captured garrison to first British Governor of the Province of **Quebec** (1763).

As the first Governor of this predominantly non–Anglo-Saxon territory, Murray influenced the way it emerged as a British colony. Through his efforts a satisfactory relationship was forged with the already well established seigneurial and clerical leadership of Quebec. This was accomplished primarily, however, by limiting the political rights claimed by the small but powerful British business community; and after only 2 years as Governor, he was recalled largely because of their protests.

While Murray's tenure as Governor was brief, his awareness of the need to accommodate the francophone **population** clearly influenced his successor, **Sir Guy Carleton,** and the latter's thinking in drafting the **Quebec Act** (1774).

Stuart R. Givens

Bibliography

Browne, G.P. "James Murray." *Dictionary of Canadian Biography.* Vol. 4, 1771–1800. 1979.

Maheux, Arthur. *France, Canada and Britain: A New Interpretation.* 1942.

Mahon, R.H. *Life of General the Honorable James Murray, a Builder of Canada.* 1921.

McCulloch, Ian. "With Wolfe at Quebec: Who Fought on the Plains of Abraham?" *The Beaver.* April–May, 1992.

See also Canada

Museums and Galleries

The 17th-century "cabinet of curiosities" became in the next century a more ordered, scholarly, and public institution—the museum. The Hanoverian age, marked by expanding scientific and artistic concerns, and by a growing citizenry both interested and prosperous enough to patronize permanent collections, popularized museums and art galleries as places of enlightenment and recreation.

While the Ashmolean at Oxford holds pride of place as the first British museum to open to the gentility (1683), many similar institutions followed it. For example, the Fitzwilliam Museum of the University of Cambridge was founded (1816) in direct emulation of the Ashmolean; Richard, 7th Viscount Fitzwilliam (1745–1816), gave his entire collection of paintings, **sculpture,** and Rembrandt prints, as well as £100,000 to house it in a suitable building. Of course, the greatest such institution established during the Hanoverian age was the **British Museum.** Created by Act of Parliament (1753), it had as its nucleus the eclectic collection of **Sir Hans Sloane.** To his books, manuscripts, coins, and natural history specimens there were afterward added the manuscript collections of **Robert Harley, Earl of Oxford** and Sir Robert Bruce Cotton (1571–1631); the **Royal Society**'s ill-kept natural history objects; Sir William Hamilton's Greek vases (1772); Charles Towneley's (1737–1805) collection of Graeco–Roman marbles, bronzes, coins and gems (1805); the **Elgin Marbles** (1816); and **George III**'s library (1823). By the early 19th century the museum had outgrown its original location at Montague House; the present Greek Revival structure was erected on the site, and currently houses collections of drawings, paintings, sculpture, antiquities, coins, medals, jewelry, ceramics, and natural history objects.

A common pattern was for private collections to become converted to public or institutional use. **Dr. John Hunter**'s anatomical museum (1763–1793), for example, located in his home, later became the collection of the Royal College of Surgeons. But the concept of scientific and historical museums evolved more rapidly than that of public art exhibitions and galleries. The first two of these were opened in the 1730s at Jonathan Tyers' Vauxhall **pleasure gardens** (1732) and Captain **Thomas Coram's Foundling Hospital** (1739); their purposes, respectively, were commercial and philanthropic. Tyers (*d.* 1767) commissioned artists such as **Hogarth** and **Hayman** to paint historical and social subjects for his customers' enjoyment. The chief interest of philanthropist Coram was the care of **London** orphans. He persuaded his friend Hogarth and other artists to donate pictures to his collection on view to the public, hoping thereby to gain support for his charity; **history paintings, portraits,** and **landscapes** soon graced a public gallery at the hospital.

The great vogue of Shakespearean and other national revivals played a role, too. Alderman and London printseller John Boydell (1719–1804) commissioned dozens of artists to paint Shakespearean subjects for his **Shakespeare** Gallery (1786–1805). The paintings, by **Reynolds, Fuseli, West,** and others, were also **engraved** and sold as prints. Bower's Historic

Gallery, the Poet Gallery, a Milton Gallery, and other short-lived enterprises followed. But so few venues for exhibiting contemporary artwork existed that artists were nonetheless forced to open their homes and studios to interested parties as galleries. They often gained commissions based on this practice, for buyers otherwise had few opportunities to view painters' pictures and judge their abilities. And lacking galleries, the latter often had to rely excessively on contacts and personal recommendations to achieve success.

While there had been a succession of private educational art academies in London, founded by such men as **Kneller** and Hogarth, these institutions had emphasized teaching over exhibiting. The founding of the **Royal Academy of Arts** (1768) created both an art school and an exhibition venue. The academy formed its own collection through donations, and in particular from the diploma work required of each elected artist. Old Master art, however, was on view only in private collections and auction houses, though some owners permitted public viewings of their pieces. Dr. Richard Mead (1673–1754), for example, was well known for his generosity toward art students. In a **provincial town** such as **Bath** it was only through similar generous hospitality by a private collector that an individual such as **Thomas Lawrence**, as a humble but talented youngster, could improve his techniques. In the capital, auction houses constituted another sort of gallery: Sotheby's (founded in 1744) was a book and print house; James Christie (1730–1803) opened his art auction house in 1766. At auction, the public, and artists especially, could view many works; **Thomas Gainsborough**, for example, frequented Christie's.

At the picture gallery, 1821

The sale of the great art collection of **Sir Robert Walpole** to Catherine the Great in 1777 and the threat of the loss of the paintings of John Julius Angerstein (1735–1823) served as the catalyst for the founding of a national collection of art. The National Gallery was created (1824) with the encouragement of **George IV**, the 38 Angerstein pictures becoming its first acquisition. Eventually the idea of a national collection evolved into the formation of three distinct institutions: the National Gallery (concentrating on Old Masters), the National Portrait Gallery, and the Tate Gallery (holding British and modern art). Later in the 19th century, national galleries and museums in **Edinburgh**, **Dublin**, and **Cardiff** were established in emulation of the National Gallery and the British Museum. By the time of the accession of Queen Victoria (1837), museums and art galleries were a standard feature of British civilization.

Bonita L. Billman

Bibliography

Caygill, Marjorie. *The Story of the British Museum.* 1981.

Gaunt, William. *The Great Century of British Painting: Hogarth to Turner.* 1971.

Hutchinson, S.C. *The History of the Royal Academy.* 1968.

Shawe-Taylor, Desmond. *The Georgians: Eighteenth-Century Portraiture and Society.* 1990.

Strong, Sir Roy. *Recreating the Past.* 1978.

Strong, Sir Roy, et al. *The British Portrait: 1660–1960.* 1991.

Wilson, David, ed. *The Collections of the British Museum.* 1989.

See also Libraries and Librarianship

Music

As in any other time or place, Britain in the Hanoverian age saw the cultivation of music by all classes of the population. Rural **folksong**; country **dance music** with fiddle, harp, and bagpipe; street **ballads**, and popular hymnody all flourished, and this music has enjoyed both survival and revival in the present age. Amateur music-making was also widespread in upper- and middle-class circles, and this helped to stimulate **music publishing**, **music education**, and **music scholarship**. At the same time, there was a dynamic development of elite or **classical music** provided by professional musicians, supported by many new institutions, and dominated in large part by Italian styles and genres; though it was in this period also that a British canon or permanent musical repertory was first developed, with **Handel** as its first major figure. Creative achievement by British-born composers, though relatively modest, was far from negligible.

The tunes of both the British and American national anthems first appeared in Georgian England. These, together with the much-loved carol tunes "Adeste fideles" (by John Francis Wade, *c.* 1740) and "Joy to the world" (anonymous, *c.* 1830), and the Scottish fiddle reel now sung as "Auld lang syne" (*c.* 1765), may well be the most widely known specimens of **popular music** originating in Hanoverian Britain, exceeding even the "Hallelujah Chorus" from Handel's *Messiah* in their penetration of musical consciousness around the world. Many other well-known traditional songs also date from this period, together with scores of hymn tunes still deeply valued by countless congregations.

Cultivated domestic music, both **vocal** and **instrumental**, was a field in which women increasingly predominated. Their usual role was to play a keyboard instrument (first the harpsichord, spinet, or chamber organ; later the piano), harp, or English guitar, and to sing—in English or Italian. Melodic instruments such as the violin, cello, oboe, and flute were played in higher social circles only by men, but after about 1770 these tended to be relegated to an accompanying role. The more serious musical genres were the dance suite (up to about 1740), the sonata (first for one or two melodic instruments and keyboard, after 1750 for keyboard with or without "accompaniment" for flute, or violin, and cello), the solo song (sometimes called a "canzonet" or a "ballad"), the vocal or instrumental duet and, after 1800, the piano study (étude). In some circles (generally male), chamber music for larger combinations of instruments was cultivated.

A great deal of this music was imported, or composed by Italian or German composers resident in Britain. Lighter musical entertainment often took the form of variations or fantasias based on fashionable tunes of the day, or simplified forms of ballroom **dances**—typically the **minuet** or polonaise in the 18th century, gradually replaced by the waltz in the 19th.

Gentlemen's **clubs**, meeting in taverns, **coffeehouses**, or private mansions, existed in many towns for eating, drinking, and convivial music. Often the gentlemen amateurs would be backed up by paid professional singers, in songs harmonized in three to five vocal parts. When the music included a part for treble voices, it was most often sung by boys. Two characteristically English genres of partsong, the "catch" and the "glee," reached their zenith in the reign of **George III**, and even the much older madrigal enjoyed revival in this period.

Professional **musicians** had long relied on Court, church, or municipal appointments for their livelihood, and this remained true on the Continent during most of this period. Royal **patronage** played its part in Britain, and the **Church of England** continued to maintain choirs and organs in cathedrals and other foundations. But the chief progressive development of the age, in which Britain undoubtedly led the way to modern musical life, was in the public **operas**, **musical concerts**, and **choral musical** festivals, where the decisive element was the support provided by increasingly large and wealthy **middle-class** audiences. Commercial opera companies, subscription concert series, and provincial musical festivals followed in close succession throughout the era. By the 1790s, opera and concert managers were in a position to offer enormous rewards to both performers and composers, with the result that many of the most famous and talented musicians from all over Europe either moved permanently to Britain or paid long and frequent visits. **Dublin** and **Edinburgh**, as well as London, housed colonies of Italian, German, and Bohemian musicians.

Under these circumstances the greatest opportunities for British-born composers lay in fields where they were relatively protected from foreign competition. In Anglican cathedral music, ancient traditions were maintained, and the leading composers to the Chapel Royal in particular kept up a respectable artistic standard of **church music** at a time of declining support for most choral foundations. The English organ in this period differed in design from those on the Continent; among the best native writers of organ voluntaries were John Stanley (1713–1789) and **Samuel Wesley**. In the English theaters (as opposed to the King's Theatre, which was the home of Italian opera) the brilliant success of **John Gay**'s *The Beggar's Opera* (1728) was never equaled, but **Thomas Augustine Arne**, Samuel Arnold (1740–1802), and **Henry Rowley Bishop**, among many others, catered to a vigorous kind of musical theater in which the music was prominent and popular, but largely incidental to the drama.

Among the most accomplished composers of glees, Samuel Webbe (1740–1816) and John Wall Callcott (1766–1821) should be mentioned, while Robert Lucas Pearsall (1795–1856) achieved a remarkable revival of the madrigal. In chamber music, keyboard music, and songs for home consumption, a group of excellent native-born composers quietly developed their art. The only one to achieve international fame was the **Dublin**-born **John Field** who, after his training in London under **Muzio Clementi** and emigration to Russia in 1802, invented a new kind of Romantic piano piece—the nocturne—the first three of which were published at St. Petersburg in 1812 and proved a seminal influence on Frédéric Chopin and his successors.

Nicholas Temperley

Bibliography

Blackwell History of Music in Britain, The. Vol. 4: *The Eighteenth Century.* Ed. H. Diack Johnstone and Roger Fiske. 1990. Vol. 5: *The Romantic Age, 1800–1914.* Ed. Nicholas Temperley. 1988.

Brown, James D., and Stephen S. Stratton. *British Musical Biography.* 1897.

Ehrlich, Cyril. *The Music Profession in Britain since the Eighteenth Century: A Social History.* 1985.

Fiske, Roger. *Scotland in Music.* 1983.

Hogwood, Christopher, and Richard Luckett, eds. *Music in Eighteenth-Century England: Essays in Memory of Charles Cudworth.* 1983.

Leppert, Richard. *Music and Image: Domesticity, Ideology and Sociocultural Formation in Eighteenth-Century England.* 1993.

Mackerness, E.D. *A Social History of English Music.* 1964.

Musica Britannica: A National Collection of Music. 1951–.

Smith, Ruth. *Handel's Oratorios and Eighteenth-Century Thought.* 1995.

Weber, William G. *The Rise of Musical Classics in Eighteenth-Century England.* 1992.

Music, Choral

Ceremonial music for massed choirs with orchestral accompaniment was a feature of the Hanoverian period and was peculiarly English; both **Haydn** and Hector Berlioz (1803–1869) commented admiringly on it during their visits to **London**. It was exploited, above all, in the oratorios of **Handel**, which in later years took on the character of patriotic ritual.

The choral tradition probably originated in such customs as the annual Festival of the Sons of the Clergy (from 1655), where a ceremonial Te Deum was performed by an unusually large choir, in the odes composed for annual observances of St. Cecilia's Day in the latter 17th century, and in celebrations of royal occasions and military victories. Early in the 18th century a number of **provincial towns** began to stage choral festivals to promote local charities, usually hospitals. Especially prominent were the Three Choirs Festival (held in turn at Gloucester, Hereford, and Worcester, possibly from as early as 1713) and those at **Birmingham**, **Leeds**, **Liverpool**, **Manchester**, **Norwich**, and Salisbury. At first these were merely special services in the cathedral or principal parish church, and for many years Henry Purcell's (1659–1695) or Handel's Te Deum was the central work. But in time they also included secular **concerts** in assembly rooms or theaters, and generally concluded with a ball. In many towns, permanent musical societies were formed to meet for the performance of choral music.

Handel's **oratorios** were originally designed for use in the London theaters in seasons when **operas** were not permitted, but his fund-raising performances of *Messiah* at the **Foundling Hospital** were soon imitated at festivals around the country. The choruses were at first formed from combined or enlarged cathedral choirs, with boy sopranos and male counter-tenors, but by the 1770s, women began to sing the high voice parts; during the same period, choirs in congregations of religious **dissenters** were introduced. The choral societies of Yorkshire and Lancashire became particularly famous for their knowledge of Handel's works and for the quality of their singing. When in 1784 the first triumphal Handel Festival was held in Westminster Abbey under the **patronage** of **George III**, the organizer, Joah Bates, himself a Halifax man, drew heavily on the northern choirs to build his chorus, which reached the unprecedented number of 274 voices of a total of 525 performers; by the time of the 1791 festival, that number had doubled. In the early 19th century there was strong competition among **cities** to promote bigger and better festivals (and to capture the revenue that large and wealthy audiences brought).

The ceremonial ode typical of the early years was eclipsed by Handel's oratorios, which dominated the field well into the Victorian period. Among choral works by English composers that enjoyed a more modest success were **William Boyce**'s *Solomon* (1742), **Thomas Arne**'s *Judith* (1761), and William Crotch's *Palestine* (1812).

Nicholas Temperley

Bibliography

Johnstone, H. Diack, and Roger Fiske, eds. *The Blackwell History of Music in Britain.* Vol. 4: *The Eighteenth Century.* 1990.

Myers, Rollo H. *Handel's Messiah: A Touchstone of Taste.* 1948.

Reid, Douglas J., and Brian Pritchard. "Some Festival Programmes of the Eighteenth and Nineteenth Centuries." *The Royal Musical Association Research Chronicle.* Vol. 5, pp. 51–79; Vol. 6, pp. 3–23; Vol. 7, pp. 1–27; Vol. 8, pp. 1–33.

Shaw, H. Watkins. *The Three Choirs Festival.* 1954.

Smith, Ruth. *Handel's Oratorios and Eighteenth-Century Thought.* 1995.

Weber, William. "The 1784 Handel Commemoration as Political Ritual." *Journal of British Studies.* Vol. 28, pp. 43–69.

See also Music, Church

Music, Church

Three distinct musical practices coexisted in the **Church of England**. In cathedrals and choral foundations, endowed choirs sang the daily liturgy to almost empty buildings for the greater glory of God. In urban parish churches, the tradition of congregational singing was increasingly taken over by choirs of **charity school** children accompanied by the organ. Country churches were filled with rough but spirited sounds put forth by volunteer choirs and bands.

In the cathedrals, the Hanoverian period saw a long but very slow decline in the great tradition of choral singing that had survived the Reformation. Resources intended to support the choirs had been diverted by deans and chapters to less exalted purposes. No new choral foundation dates from this period. Nevertheless, most foundations kept up at least a semblance of daily choral performance of the liturgy. Prayers were intoned by the officiating clergyman, responses and psalms were chanted, canticles were often sung to composed settings.

The most elaborate music, the anthem, was not part of the liturgy, but could be on any text from the Bible or Book of Common Prayer. A surprisingly large number of anthems were composed during this period, many by organists of the three **London** foundations—the Chapel Royal, Westminster Abbey, and St. Paul's Cathedral. This includes the work of William Croft (1678–1727), Maurice Greene (1695–1755), **William Boyce**, Samuel Arnold (1740–1802), and Thomas Attwood (1765–1838). Increasingly, the preference was for anthems in which the solo voice predominated, often with independent organ accompaniment and interludes; the full choir played an increasingly perfunctory role.

In town churches, a sustained effort had been initiated in **Queen Anne**'s time to reform the dismal effects of congregationally sung metrical psalms. The charity schools founded in most of the wealthier parishes provided children who were taught to sing and lead the congregation in the psalms sung from the organ gallery. Occasionally these children sang a special hymn or anthem also for the annual charity sermon. Organ voluntaries were regularly played in town churches as well as cathedrals.

Country parishes, even if they could have afforded an organ, could not have maintained an organist; so the conduct of singing was entrusted to groups of voluntary singers, often taught by self-appointed itinerant "psalmodists." By 1750 a small band of stringed and wind instruments was to be found in many parishes, taking its place with the singers in the west gallery or a special pew. The elaborate "fuging tunes" and anthems they performed were despised by **gentry** and the **clerical profession**, and until recently by historians and scholars, but their fresh and vigorous sounds have today won some respect and appreciation. The heyday of the church bands was perhaps at the turn of the century; gradually, they were replaced by barrel organs or, later, harmoniums.

Congregationalist and **Baptist** churches later joined in the country psalmody movement, while the **Church of Scotland** and other **Presbyterian** churches tended to continue in the "old way of singing"—that is, in extremely slow, unaccompanied congregational singing of the old psalm tunes. The **Methodist** and **Evangelical** movements, on the other hand, encouraged a much heartier style of singing, adapting the most popular and fashionable secular tunes of the day for use with the emotional hymn texts of **Charles Wesley**, **John Newton**, and their colleagues. Another innovation of Methodist meetings was to encourage women to sing, sometimes in dialogue with men.

Roman Catholics were compelled to worship quietly during much of this period, but under **George III** the Catholic embassy chapels in London became the focus of new musical developments: Gregorian chant was revived, masses and motets by leading Continental composers were performed, and new music was commissioned from English composers such as Samuel Webbe (1740–1816) and **Samuel Wesley**. The excellence of both Methodist and Catholic music seems to have stimulated improvements in the music of Anglican churches in the years leading up to the Victorian period.

Nicholas Temperley

Bibliography

Bumpus, John S. *A History of English Cathedral Music.* 1908; rpt. 1972.

Knight, Gerald H., and William L. Reed. *The Treasury of English Church Music.* Vols. 3 and 4. 1965.

Lightwood, James T. *Methodist Music in the Eighteenth Century.* 1927.

Long, Kenneth R. *The Music of the English Church.* 1972.

Temperley, Nicholas. *The Music of the English Parish Church.* 1979.

———. "Music in Church," in *The Athlone History of Music in Britain.* Vol. 4: *The Eighteenth Century.* 1990. Also see "Cathedral Music" in Vol. 5: *The Romantic Age, 1800–1914.* 1981.

See also Music, Choral

Music, Classical

Today, this term suggests full-scale orchestral music of a secular character, but in the early Hanoverian age it suggested Italian operatic music. Italian **opera** was introduced early in the 18th century and was enthusiastically cultivated, but only by aristocratic and intellectual audiences. Fat remunerations attracted spectacular Italian singers as well as distinguished operatic composers such as **Handel**, who settled in England and soon became acknowledged as the master of the genre. **London** became the major center for Italian opera outside Italy, and it remained so, with its splendid productions of both serious and comic operas at the King's Theatre.

The **middle classes** had little interest in such exotic entertainment and favored lighter works in English, preferably with the dialogue spoken rather than sung. The most successful early endeavor in this line was *The Beggar's Opera* (1728), a **ballad opera** written by **John Gay**, with the music mainly from popular melodies; it inspired many imitations. Later theatrical presentations ranged from full-length serious and comic English operas to short theater pieces with either original or borrowed music. **Thomas Arne** and **Charles Dibdin** were among their most prominent composers.

Although Handel's Italian operas did not have widespread appeal, his **oratorios**, written in English and based on biblical subjects, were admired by all classes and led to his recognition as the most beloved of "English" composers. His popularity soared, especially after his death, when Handel festivals were held throughout Britain, and *Messiah* and other oratorios were frequently performed by both professional and amateur choirs. The Handel festivals thus brought music of superior quality to a vast audience.

A number of people wished to preserve not only the music of Handel but also the great music of the national past, including the compositions of Henry Purcell (1659–1695) and the madrigals and sacred repertoire of the 16th and 17th centuries. Such works might have fallen into oblivion had not concert organizations such as the Academy of Ancient Music (1710–1792) and the Concert of Ancient Music (1776–1848) been established; the latter was strongly supported by **George III** and the **aristocracy**. There was also a body of chamber music inherited from the 17th century, which still figured importantly in domestic music-making, and which was nourished in the Hanoverian tradition of instrumental music.

In the early 18th century, musical concerts were held mainly in taverns and **clubs**. It was especially after 1750 that concert life began to flourish in London and in **provincial towns**. Elegant concert halls began to be erected from the 1730s on, and concert-going rivaled the theater in attendance. The premier London concert hall was in Hanover Square Rooms, which opened in 1775; it had excellent acoustics and accommodated nearly 900 people. The prestigious Bach–Abel subscriptions concerts (arranged by **Johann Christian Bach** and Carl Friedrich Abel, 1725–1787) were performed there until 1782, as were the Professional Concerts (1783–1793). Perhaps the most significant series of concerts were those directed by Johann Salomon (1745–1815), sponsor of **Joseph Haydn**'s two visits to London in the 1790s. Haydn enjoyed phenomenal success, and his dozen "London" symphonies set exceptionally high standards for orchestral music.

Meanwhile, another instrument was joining the repertoire of classical music. Audiences relished novelties, and the new pianoforte, introduced around 1760, captured their imagination. London became a major center for piano manufacturing, and the instruments produced by the Broadwood, Stodart, Erard, and Clementi firms were unmatched in quality. Further, Bach, who settled in London in 1762, championed the instrument. Later in the century, major contributions to the repertoire were made by the so-called **London Pianoforte School**, an international group of pianists that included **Muzio Clementi** from Italy, Jan Ladislav Dussek (1760–1812) from Bohemia, Johann Baptist Cramer (1771–1858) from Germany, and **John Field** from **Ireland**. The group developed a distinctive style of piano composition that anticipated the expressive Romantic keyboard idiom.

In orchestral music proper, England did not assume a leading role until 1813, when the Philharmonic Society, the first fully professional permanent symphony orchestra in Europe, was founded. Symphonies until this time were usually introductory; the mainstays of most programs were concertos and solo compositions, principally songs. But now the large audiences of the Philharmonic were treated to fine performances of the great symphonies of Haydn, Mozart, and Beethoven. Britain did not produce composers of equal stature; notwithstanding, the public was rewarded with a rich musical life that was unrivaled in Europe.

Eve R. Meyer

Bibliography

Fiske, Roger. *English Theatre Music in the Eighteenth Century.* 1973.

Sachs, Joel. "London: The Professionalization of Music," in Alex Ringer, ed., *Music and Society: The Early Romantic Era.* 1990.

Temperley, Nicholas, ed. *The Athlone History of Music in Britain: The Romantic Age, 1800–1914.* 1981.

Temperley, Nicholas, et al. "London," in *The New Grove Dictionary of Music and Musicians.* Vol. 11, pp. 142–217. 1980.

Walker, Ernest. *A History of Music in England.* 1952.

Weber, William. "London: A City of Unrivalled Riches," in Neal Zaslaw, ed., *Man and Music: The Classical Era.* 1989.

———. *The Rise of Musical Classics in Eighteenth-Century England: A Study in Canon, Ritual, and Ideology.* 1992.

Young, Percy M. *A History of British Music.* 1967.

See also Music, Instrumental; Musical Concerts and Concert Life

Music, Dance

Music for social and theatrical dancing in Hanoverian Britain came from many sources and composers. Marches, **minuets**, hornpipes, and arias by Henry Purcell (1659–1695), Jeremiah Clarke (?1669–1707), and **George Frideric Handel**; patriotic songs by **Thomas Arne** and William Shield (1748–1829); fiddle variation sets by Niel Gow; **pantomime** tunes by James Oswald—these and many other composers' works were quickly taken up by dancing masters and stage choreographers anxious to give their patrons the latest and most fashionable music for their recreational activities. Most of the older tunes found in John (1623–?1686) and Henry (*b.* 1657) Playford's pathbreaking editions of the *Dancing Master,* issued between 1651 and 1703, were discarded. In 1706, when John Young took over this highly successful series, a new kind of music was in favor.

Eighteenth-century dances for the stage and the ballroom were composed of short phrases of 8, 10, or 12 measures, each often repeated. The music mirrored the symmetrical dance forms, usually falling into an AABB or AABA structure. Until about 1750, composers found a rich market for minuets in 3/4 time, bourrées and rigadoons in duple time, and hornpipes in 3/2. After 1750, duple hornpipes, marches in 4/4, and lively quicksteps in 6/8 and 2/4 were favored, while the minuet continued in strong demand.

The quality of English dance music in general peaked between 1715 and 1730 with John Walsh's (*c.* 1665–1736) publications of court ballroom dances by a Mr. Isaac, set to music by James Paisible (1626–1721), and of country dances and minuets set to fine theater tunes by Purcell, Handel,

Musicians and dancers

Giovanni Bononcini (1677–1726), John Galliard (1687?–1749), Charles Fairbank, and others. At first, tunes were relatively long, voguish, and artful, fitting their dances well. The 3/2 hornpipe is probably the most striking of all the dance music of the early period, and was a distinctly English form. Characteristics include two-bar phrases, some syncopated rhythms chiefly in the second and fourth measures, and a point of arrival on the third beat of the cadential measure.

In the second half of the 18th century a new class of dance tune with patriotic motifs became popular. Many such tunes took the name of the dancer for whom they were composed, as in "Aldridge's," "Miss Baker's," and so on. These fiddle tunes were in quick duple time. Rhythmically they were like older Scottish measures, with a distinctive phrase ending, and some in double tonic tonalities derived from bagpipe tuning. These energetic tunes were soon adopted for social dancing. They proved very enduring, and continued in the repertory of traditional musicians until the 20th century.

The commercial market for dance music throughout the period was large and varied. Every year from 1700 to 1830, the tunes of "the latest dances" appeared in instrumental tutors and pocket companions for the recreational instrumentalist, with and without dance choreographs, and usually without attribution. John Walsh succeeded John Playford as the major **music publisher** of the day. Issuing annual collections from the late 1690s through 1766, the Walsh firm set new standards for dance publications, featuring easy-to-read engraved music, complete with dance notation. Annual collections of 24 pieces were periodically gathered into large volumes of 200 to 300 dances.

With economic growth and growing leisure for the **middle classes**, the demand for dance music soon outstripped the supply. There was a deluge of mass-produced tunes intended to meet and spur on public demand for novelty as the minuet and country dance fad spread to the middle classes, and as dance performances moved to larger social settings such as public assemblies and **pleasure gardens**. These tunes were usually short, two-reprise forms with clearly defined rhythms and accessible melodies. Responding to the growing demand for dances and dance music in the 1740s, John Rutherford, John Johnson, and Peter Thompson all began annual dance publications that competed with those of John Walsh. By the 1770s the market had grown so large that several more **publishers** joined the list. Longman and Broderip, Thomas Preston, and Thomas Cahusac began series that lasted into the 1810s, and these publishers were joined by Button and Whittaker, William Campbell, George Goulding, and many others.

In the early 19th century, London dancing master Thomas Wilson tried to keep English dances and dance music in the repertory with several significant publications that culminated in *The Complete System of English Country Dancing* (1820). But **fashion** soon swept these dances from the urban ballroom. European dance music flooded the country. French cotillions and German waltzes were danced to their own tunes, and quadrilles were often set to suites from popular Italian or German **operas**.

Kate Van Winkle Keller

Bibliography

Emmerson, George S. *Rantin' Pipe and Tremblin' String: A History of Scottish Dance Music.* 1971.

MacPherson, William Alan. "The Music of the English Country Dance, 1651–1728: With Indexes of the Printed Sources." Ph.D. diss. 1984.

Marsh, Carol. "French Court Dance in England, 1706–1740: A Study of the Sources." Ph.D. diss. 1985.

See also Dance

Music Education

Education in music during the 18th century was very often a household affair for both upper and middle classes. Regular music masters served on the staffs of many large households, and with the growth of **music publishing**, driven by the wishes of amateurs and dilettantes as well as professionals, there was a greater sharing of pedagogy on technique and composition. Musical literacy gradually became a way of life among the educated, reflecting the growth of a cultured and affluent leisured class.

Pedagogical materials were deemed successful according to their soundness and usefulness, a tradition first begun with Thomas Morley's *A Plaine and Easie Introduction to Practicall Musicke* (1597) and continued in the 18th century with Peter Prelleur's *The Modern Musick-master or the Universal Musician* (1730–1731). Recognized for its ease and brevity, Prelleur's book included an introduction to singing, directions for playing various instruments (recorder, flute, oboe, violin, and harpsichord), instruction in thorough bass, a brief history of music, and a musical dictionary. Eighteenth-century thorough bass treatises also received their impetus from an early model, John Coprario's *Rules How to Compose* (1610), as well as an abundance of publications combining figured bass techniques with instruction on composition in general; by around 1750 these were often augmented with more discussion on the composition of melody.

Some of the most influential pedagogical publications from this period were **translations** of prominent European treatises on performance, particularly Pier Francesco Tosi's *Observations on the Florid Song* (1742) and Francesco Geminiani's *The Art of Playing the Violin* (1751). Various publications of music also suggested a pedagogical purpose; Anthony Young's six *Suits of Lessons* (1719) was typical in that loosely ordered suites were often called "lessons" or "setts of lessons."

Professional education in music took a major turn during the close of the 18th century with the importation from revolutionary **France** of the idea of a national state conservatory. Based on the notion of music as a practical rather than theoretical art, the conservatory movement also recognized the social and educational merits of formalized training in music-making. The impetus in Britain emerged in 1822 with the publication of F.W. Horncastle's "Plan for the Foundation of an English Conservatorio" in the *Quarterly Music Magazine.* Supporters were gathered and an endowment was announced for a **Royal Academy of Music**, which opened in **London** in 1823. Under the direction of William Crotch (1775–1847), both male and female students received instruction from a faculty of mostly foreign instructors in general education, harmony and composition, singing and sightsinging, and instrumental performance. In 1832 the new academy director, Cipriani Potter (1792–1871), began leading the way to curricular improvement in the piano program, orchestration and symphonic analysis, and extended composition.

Music education in the schools was a part of the 19th-century reform movement to improve British schools in general. **Robert Owen**, for instance, founded in 1816 an experimental school for the children of **cotton** millworkers in Lanark, **Scotland**, the curriculum of which included singing, dance, and musical literacy. Before long, the first textbooks designed for the teaching of music in schools were published. John Turner's *Manual of Vocal Instruction* (1833) and Sarah Anna Glover's *Scheme to Render Psalmody Congregational* (1836) were designed to improve congregational singing but were also used in schools to teach the rudiments of music. Also of note was W.E. Hickson's *Singing Master* (1835), which included a number of children's songs.

Leslie Ellen Brown

Bibliography

Johnstone, H. Diack, and Roger Fiske, eds. *Music in Britain: The Eighteenth Century.* 1990.

Sadie, Stanley, ed. *The New Grove Dictionary of Music and Musicians,* s.v. "Education in music." 1980.

Temperley, Nicholas, ed. *The Athlone History of Music in Britain: The Romantic Age.* 1981.

See also Music Scholarship; Musicians

Music, Instrumental

Instrumental music has been used from time immemorial to accompany dancing, marching, banquets, and other activities. In Britain there was also a strong tradition of playing chamber music for its own sake, especially in affluent circles where often a professional master would lead and direct a group of amateur players. By the time of **George I** the older "consort of viols" had been replaced by groups of instruments supported by a *basso continuo* (figured bass), performed on a lute or keyboard, together with a viola da gamba (a surviving member of the viol family) or cello.

The two main types of piece were the trio sonata, for two violins and continuo (one of the violins might be replaced by a flute or oboe), and the "solo" for flute, oboe, or violin and continuo. Both were sonatas in several movements, often including one or two **dance** movements such as a **minuet** or jig. They had originated in Italy, chiefly under the influence of Arcangelo Corelli (1653–1713), and continued to be popular in Britain after their demise on the Continent, as is proved by the large output of published sets until about 1770. Subscriber lists show that most of the amateur players of this music were male.

Women played chiefly keyboard instruments: the harpsichord, spinet, or chamber organ, and later the piano. The harp and guitar were also regarded as appropriate for women, but throughout the Hanoverian period, women rarely wielded

The Paine family at the Keyboard

bows or blew wind instruments. As the piano became fashionable after 1770, piano-led combinations began to replace the older string-dominated forms; and in this case the majority of subscribers were female. The piano trio (with optional or at best subordinate parts for violin and cello) was the prevailing form of chamber music in the reign of **George III**; Vienna and Paris now replaced Italy as the chief sources of musical style and fashion. Typically, the piano would be played by one of the daughters of the family, while the string parts would be taken by young men.

Thus in the field of domestic music-making—increasingly a social, rather than a spiritual or intellectual pursuit—women were becoming dominant. The situation was not unlike that in the realm of **painting**, in which amateurism, new **technology**, and women's interest were bringing **watercolor** new attention and importance. And although much of the music thus performed was superficial in character, composers of serious sonatas also began more often to dedicate their works to female piano pupils.

Types of chamber music without keyboard, such as the flute duet, violin duet, and string quartet, were still seriously cultivated by groups of men, often a mixture of amateurs and professionals; a remarkable example was the group led by William Gardiner (1770–1853), a wealthy hosier, who claimed to have given at his Leicester house in 1793 the first performance in England of any work by Beethoven: the String Trio, Op. 3.

In all these areas, British-born composers were active, but won only a small share of the market. The most popular composers were, successively, Corelli, **Handel**, **Johann Christian Bach**, **Haydn**, Mozart (1756–1791), and Beethoven (1770–1827).

Nicholas Temperley

Bibliography

Gardiner, William. *Music and Friends: Or, Pleasant Recollections of a Dilettante.* 1838–1853.

Johnstone, H. Diack, and Roger Fiske, eds. *The Blackwell History of Music in Britain.* Vol. 4: *The Eighteenth Century.* 1990.

Newman, William S. *The Sonata in the Baroque Era.* 1959.

———. *The Sonata in the Classic Era.* 1963.

Temperley, Nicholas. "Domestic Music in England, 1800–1860." *Proceedings of the Royal Musical Association.* Vol. 85, pp. 31–47.

See also Musical Concerts and Concert Life; Women in Art

Music, Military

From earliest times, music has been associated with military ceremonies and activities. This association changed significantly during the Hanoverian period, resulting in the emergence of new and more specialized musical groups (for example, the field music); the standardization of military beats, calls, and signals; and the establishment of new traditions, customs, and attitudes that persist to the present.

Central to military music was the drummer. The practice of using the snare drum to maintain the cadence of marching infantry, and the trumpet to sound signals for mounted troops, was firmly established by Elizabethan times. The drum also signaled commands, and fifes were added to provide melodic interest. Drums, trumpets, and fifes likewise provided music for ceremonies, such as escorting the colors, reviews, tattoo, retreat, and funeral parades.

Drummers, who learned their office by rote, were responsible for beating the camp duties (the general, assembly, reveille, retreat, tattoo, to arms, and the parley) and signals (facing motions; calls for adjutants, sergeants, and corporals; to go for wood, water, or provisions; and for the front of the column to march quicker or slower). Because of his importance as a signalman, the drummer was clothed in reversed facings (the ground of his coat was the color of the regiment's facings). In addition to their musical duties, drummers served as messengers and were also required to carry out court-martial sentences. Drummers were company musicians and were ranked and paid as corporals. An appointed drum major performed as a drummer but was also responsible for all the musicians when massed. He also received some extra pay from the officers and boys under his instruction.

By the close of the 17th century the fife had fallen into disuse, but it reappeared on the scene around 1745 when a German Hanoverian colonel gave a young fifer to his British counterpart. Soon afterward, each regiment's grenadier company was authorized two fifers. No longer content with only the drummers, the other companies evaded the regulations by training boys—especially soldiers' sons—to serve as fifers. The many fife tutors published between 1756 and 1815 attest to the popularity of the instrument. Pipers were used instead of fifers in Scottish **highland regiments.** The drummers and fifers or pipers of the regiment formed the field music, a new organization separate and distinct from that referred to as the band of music.

The latter had come into existence when Charles II, influenced by his years in **France,** granted six hautboys to the regiment of Horse Grenadiers in 1678. Thus the term "hautboys" was used to designate the musicians as well as the instrumentation, a combination of oboes and bassoons. At their own expense officers of a regiment engaged these musicians to provide music for social occasions and military ceremonies. Unlike field musicians, these bandsmen were professionals who were expected to play the standard instruments much in the manner of the old waits or *Stadtpfeifer* (town musicians, usually wind players). Employing wind instruments on the parade ground or outdoors, bandsmen also played winds and strings indoors at the consolidated officers' mess or in church. They were also engaged for special occasions, as was the case when massed regimental bands performed **Handel's** *Fireworks Musik* in 1749. By this time the original hautboys instrumentation had changed to the European *Harmoniemusik* (wind bands) of pairs of oboes, clarinets, horns, and bassoons. The size of the band was determined by the wealth of the regiment, since the officers' fund continued to provide instruments, special uniforms, music, and extra pay for the musicians. Besides the necessary slow and quick marches, many serenades, nocturnes, cassations, parthias, and divertimenti were written for the five- to eight-piece combination.

Attempts were made in 1749 to have all bandsmen enlisted as soldiers and placed under military discipline, but many regiments continued to hire civilian musicians and bandmasters. The Guard regiments in **London,** for example, until 1783 engaged musicians from the major theaters to play at the daily changing of the guard. Even when the bandsmen were enlisted, the bandmaster often remained a civilian. In 1803, regulations allowed for one soldier from each company to be trained as a musician and for a sergeant to act as bandmaster, but many regiments exceeded the authorization with the addition of boys and blackamoors, the latter playing the Janissary instruments (fifes, shawms, triangle, cymbals, kettledrums, Turkish crescent, and bass drum) that had become popular by the end of the 18th century. Despite regulations (1823) that restricted bands to a sergeant (master) and 14 musicians, bands were usually augmented to 25 or 30.

The latter Hanoverian period saw many changes in the *Harmoniemusik.* The Janissary instruments were balanced by the addition of flutes, piccolos, bass clarinets, contrabassoons, trumpets, trombones, and serpents. Halliday's keyed bugle of 1810 quickly led to keyed bass horns and ophicleides. Valved brass instruments soon replaced the keyed ones, leading to the development of all-brass bands, beginning in 1833. Because of the constantly changing instrumentation, bandmasters had to write their own arrangements of music that ranged from simple marches and hymns for ceremonial use to symphonies, overtures, solo concertos, and selections from **operas** and **oratorios.** Many regiments also adopted their distinctive slow and quick marches during this period.

The roots of many traditions and customs, such as trooping the color, changing the guard, tattoo, and the last post, may be found in the Hanoverian period. It is a heritage that should be treated with respect.

Raoul F. Camus

Bibliography

Camus, Raoul F. *Military Music of the American Revolution.* 1975.

Farmer, Henry George. *History of the Royal Artillery Band, 1762–1953.* 1954.

———. *Handel's Kettledrums and Other Papers on Military Music.* 1965.

———. "The Martial Music of the Georges." *Journal of the Society for Army Historical Research.* Vol. 42, pp. 203–206.

See also Army; Musicians; War and Military Engagements

Music, Popular

The British tradition of vernacular song took on a new significance during the Hanoverian period. It was during this time that truly "popular" music reached its full evolution in the form of songs written by professional songwriters, targeted at the largest possible audiences, and specifically intended for amateur performance. The period saw too few serious composers of distinction, but the vigorous rise of popular music compensated for this deficiency.

By the Hanoverian period the oral tradition had fallen into such decay that the young **Sir Walter Scott** took it upon himself in 1802 to memorialize this fading art form in his *Minstrelsy of the Scottish Border.* The anonymous bard of ages past had, already by the time of the Restoration, long given way to the professional writer of broadside **ballads** who either composed his own settings and entrusted the accompaniment to a musician, or (most often) fitted his lyrics to some familiar tune, time-honored or current. The most prominent early songwriter in this vein, much admired by the Hanoverians, was Thomas Durfey (1653–1723), whose six-volume compendium of his own and others' popular songs, *Wit and Mirth, or Pills to Purge Melancholy* (1719–1720), was an unequaled trove of everything from courtly love ballads to bawdy rustic ditties. Much imitated but unsurpassed in his time, Durfey was succeeded by **Charles Dibdin,** his son Thomas Dibdin (1771–1841), and **Thomas Moore.** On a more artistic but fully as popular level were **Robert Burns,** and Scott. Many other songwriters now forgotten participated in making Hanoverian popular song the distinct and flavorful musical form that it was, its best works still surviving today.

The Hanoverian period saw momentous changes wrought by such events as the **American Revolution, Industrial Revolution,** and **French Revolutionary and Napoleonic Wars,** and popular song copiously recorded these events with varying degrees of seriousness. The common man's love for the "right little, tight little island" of Thomas Dibdin's patriotic panegyric is even more abundantly represented. The political climate of intense change seems to have drawn the British Isles together in spirit, if song is any indication. A strong sense of national unity shows itself in the enthusiastic welcome given to Scottish, Welsh, and Irish songs written in dialect and set to suitably folklike tunes.

Hanoverian popular song evolved in both expression and content with the passage of time, but a strong sense of optimism, energy, and experiment endured throughout the period. The Italian **opera** enjoyed by the upper classes was burlesqued in the **ballad opera,** an unabashedly proletarian musical form that began with **John Gay**'s wildly successful *Beggar's Opera* (1728) and continued until the 1740s. As Britain became increasingly industrialized and urbanized, nostalgia for country life showed in songs concerning the amours, chaste or otherwise, of rustic swains and lasses; and as England grew in military strength and sea power, song took on a decidedly patriotic tone. The "jolly Jack tar"—the British ordinary **seaman** of the **navy**—became a hero idealized and extolled in innumerable ballads, as was his invariably faithful sweetheart—both of them the favorite subjects of **Henry Carey** and Charles Dibdin. Dibdin's son, Thomas, perpetuated his father's patriotic fervor, most notably in the famous vernacular paean mentioned earlier, "The Snug Little Island." By the end of the Hanoverian period, insular **nationalism** confronted by a rapidly changing world inspired a reactionary nostalgia resulting in a penchant for things medieval and chivalric, creating a vogue for the rousing ballads woven into Scott's epics and novels (e.g., "Young Lochinvar"). At the same time, the Romantic high-mindedness of the Southron ballad was liberally offset by a craze for comic ditties, whether bitingly satirical or merely silly, which in later years would become the staple fare of the music hall.

The national fondness for popular music, ever a part of the British spirit, found new objects, especially after the onset of the Industrial Revolution. The street-corner singer and vendor of broadside ballads continued to flourish, and his wares exhibited constant innovation in form and content. As literacy increased, so did the demand for printed music and lyrics. **Music publishing** flourished. Popular music in such forms as playhouse songs, ballads, and **dances** was published in extraordinary amounts during this time, and many new magazines featured songs. During the reigns of **George I** and **George II** the public stage became a type of musical concert hall, with increasingly elaborate musical entertainments given as interludes and after-pieces to the plays; vernacular song and dance played a prominent role in these diversions. The concert hall proper, which had come into being by the first decade of the 18th century, featured musical works of a more elevated nature, a situation that was not to change until the early Victorian period and the rise of the music hall. However, other venues for popular song rapidly arose. At the **London pleasure gardens** the populace gathered and took enjoyment from musical entertainments. These were designed to appeal to every class, and popular songs could be heard along with operatic arias, cantatas, and symphonic works. The prolific James Hook (1746–1827) composed over 2,000 popular songs, which were performed in concert halls, theaters, and pleasure gardens.

More accessible, however, to the tastes and incomes of the working class were the evening gatherings variously designated as "harmonious meetings," "chanting **clubs**," or "singing saloons," most often held in taverns. Here the conviviality centered on popular songs rendered in glee-style choruses, or sometimes solo performances by the patrons themselves, of songs that predictably became ever more bawdy as the night wore on and drunkenness became general. (Some proprietors excluded women for this reason.) More select were the "supper rooms" or "night houses" that catered to a **middle-class** semi-bohemian male audience, entertaining it with witty, risqué, and topical songs generally delivered by paid professional singers. Mixed company enjoyed more decorous performances in middle-class drawing rooms, where marriageable young ladies might exhibit their musical accomplishments to prospective suitors by warbling the latest sentimental favorites, accompanying themselves on the piano. Outside the urban orbit, provincial music festivals became widely popular from the early 1800s on. Virtually every village had its singing society and band. The rise of **Methodism** made a great contribution to popular music also in the form of tuneful hymns sung by countless congregations throughout Britain.

Hanoverian popular song bridges two vernacular musical cultures: that of the late 17th and early 18th centuries, grounded in oral tradition and the broadside ballad; and the thoroughly commercial music hall entertainment of the Victorian period. In Hanoverian song, the concerns and values of the British common man are presented with robust and unself-conscious conviction, as is natural in a musical form essentially middle class in origin and amateur in performance. The rise of the Victorian music hall, with its paid professional entertainers, would produce new song forms well calculated to tug an audience's purse strings as much as its heart strings. But the Hanoverian popular song portrayed the average Briton more simply, and also assumed him or her to be a singer as much as an observer offstage.

Carolyn Kephart

Bibliography

Bratton, J.S., ed. *Music Hall: Performance and Style.* 1986.
Mackerness, E.D. *A Social History of English Music.* 1964.
Nettel, Reginald. *A Social History of Traditional Song.* 1969.
Rudé, George. *Hanoverian London, 1714–1808.* 1971.
Vincent, David. "The Decline of the Oral Tradition in Popular Culture," in Robert D. Storch, ed., *Popular Culture and Custom in Nineteenth-Century England.* 1982.
Young, Percy M. *A History of British Music.* 1967.

See also Folksong; Music Vocal

Music Publishing

English music publishers were among the most active in early-18th-century Europe, and their numbers and output increased throughout the century. **Vocal music** was their most profitable product, particularly the song sheet. Some music publishers did their own printing; others contracted outside printers. Printing techniques remained relatively unchanged throughout the Hanoverian period, with metal (normally copper or pewter) plates engraved by hand or partly punched.

John Walsh (*c.* 1665–1736) set the tone for publishers when he began to publish song sheets in the late 17th century. He later expanded his range to **instrumental music**, including works by Arcangelo Corelli (1653–1713). He also became principal publisher to **George Frideric Handel**. Walsh became the most successful publisher of his generation by exploiting the popularity of the song sheet, and also by employing such shady but common practices as publishing unauthorized editions.

In fact, music publishers often sold works copied without permission from other publishers' editions. Such publications were not strictly illegal until the latter 18th century. Music was not effectively protected by copyright law until Carl Friedrich Abel (1725–1787) won a court case against the music publisher James Longman in the 1770s. By the late 1780s the smattering of copyright entries for music increased dramatically and, by 1798, music comprised two-thirds of all copyright entries at Stationers' Hall. Publishers usually paid composers a lump sum for the rights to a composition; royalties were not paid until the mid-19th century. Also, some composers, especially amateurs, published works at their own expense. Large projects were often funded by subscription.

Music publishers played other related roles. They sold music, sold and rented instruments, acted as ticket agents, ran music libraries, and invented "improvements" for musical instruments. A few were professional composers and performers, notably **Muzio Clementi** and Johann Baptist Cramer (1771–1858).

Publishing firms often included several family members, women as well as men. Walsh passed his business to his son John in 1736; the Thompson business, founded by Peter Thompson in 1746, remained in the family until 1805 and involved at least seven family members. Changes in partnership occurred fairly often, and firms sometimes sold their engraved plates to other publishers. Although the majority of music publishers operated in **London**, there was an active provincial trade within England. **Edinburgh** and **Dublin** were also minor centers.

Song sheets remained one of the most profitable items throughout the Hanoverian period. By the mid-18th century, publishers had expanded their size, sometimes including a decorated title page and instrumental arrangements. Most songs originated in **operas**, or in **musical concerts** at the **pleasure gardens**. Operas were also published in their entirety.

Orchestral music was published as sets of parts without a comprehensive score. The most adventuresome series was Robert Bremner's "Periodical Overtures" (1763–1783), 60 symphonies that introduced the English public to the new Mannheim style of orchestral music. Other publishers also reached abroad for material. George Thomson of Edinburgh, for instance, made his reputation by commissioning **folksong** arrangements from Beethoven, **Haydn**, and others.

The domination of the large English publishing market by vocal music indicates an active tradition of domestic amateur music-making and **popular music**. Publishers were obviously important for local composers, few of whom were published outside Britain, while at the same time they brought foreign music before the British public.

Jane Girdham

Bibliography

Fiske, Roger. *Scotland in Music: A European Enthusiasm.* 1983.

Humphries, Charles, and William C. Smith. *Music Publishing in the British Isles.* 1954.

Hunter, David. "Music Copyright in Britain to 1800." *Music and Letters.* Vol. 67, pp. 269–282.

Jones, David Wyn. "Robert Bremner and *The Periodical Overture.*" *Soundings.* Vol. 7, pp. 62–84.

Krummel, D.W., and Stanley Sadie, eds. *Music Printing and Publishing.* 1990.

Maxted, Ian. *The London Book Trades, 1775–1800: A Preliminary Checklist of Members* 1977.

Neighbour, O.W., and Alan Tyson. *English Music Publishers' Plate Numbers in the First Half of the Nineteenth Century.* 1965.

See also Music, Dance; Music, Instrumental; Music, Popular; Publishers and Booksellers

Music Scholarship

The theory of music, seeking to explain the nature of musical sound and harmony by speculative inquiry, has a history going back to the ancient Greeks. But the scholarly study of music history, now termed musicology, first arose in Hanoverian Britain.

The main new development under the Hanoverian kings was a self-conscious desire to preserve, and then to revive, music of the recent and then the more remote past. Some authorities attribute this to **Tory** politics and High Churchmanship, which began to associate old, severe, and well-established music, especially that of cathedral choirs, with the authority of church and king. Already by 1700 a number of collectors of old music prints and manuscripts had emerged. The volumes of old cathedral music copied by Thomas Tudway (1656–1726) for Edward Harley, 2nd Earl of Oxford, in 1714 to 1720 (British Library, Harley MSS. 7337–7342), probably represent the first major antiquarian edition of music in existence. Three generations of this activity culminated in the publication of **William Boyce**'s *Cathedral Music* in three volumes (London, 1760–1778).

Outside the **Church of England**, the developing interest in performing "ancient" music, which meant primarily that of the 16th and early 17th centuries, can be traced through several **London** institutions: the Academy of Ancient Music (1725–1792), the Madrigal Society (1741, still exisiting), and the Concert of Antient Music (1776–1848). The parallel desire to learn about music history was met by two monumental books, the first of their kind in the world: one by the austere **Sir John Hawkins**, the other by the more urbane **Charles Burney**.

Other activities of a kind that would later be called musicological include the world's first scholarly edition of a composer's collected works, Samuel Arnold's of **Handel** (1787–1797); the first scholarly collections of **folksongs** and of non–Western music; and the first published historical anthology of music, John Stafford Smith's *Musica Antiqua* (1812). The music monthly *The Harmonicon* (1823–1833) contained many substantial scholarly articles.

Nicholas Temperley

Bibliography

Burney, Charles. *A General History of Music, from the Earliest Ages to the Present Period.* 4 vols. 1776–1789; rpt., ed. F. Mercer, 1957.

Duckles, Vincent. "Musicology," in Nicholas Temperley, ed., *The Blackwell History of Music.* Vol. 5. 1988.

Hawkins, John. *A General History of the Science and Practice of Music.* 5 vols. 1776; rpt. 1963, intro. Charles Cudworth.

Kassler, Jamie Croy. *The Science of Music in Britain, 1714–1830: A Catalogue.* 1979.

King, A. Hyatt. *Some British Collectors of Music.* 1963.

McGeary, Thomas. "Music Literature," in H. Diack Johnstone and Roger Fiske, eds., *The Blackwell History of Music in Britain.* Vol. 4. 1990.

Weber, William. *The Rise of Musical Classics in Eighteenth-Century England.* 1992.

See also History Writing and Historians; Music Education; Music Publishing; Reference Works

Music, Vocal

Hanoverian composers and publishers collaborated to produce a great amount of vocal music. This fed a growing appetite for music in both English and Italian that could be sung in the home. Italian vocal music consisted chiefly of songs from the currently popular **operas** of the day, and was published in short score soon after first performances of the operas. Numerous Italian composers residing in Britain, such as Felice Giardini (1716–1796), Tommaso Giordani (*c.* 1730–1806), and Venanzio Rauzzini (1746–1810), were active in this endeavor, as were some English and German composers writing both part music and songs in Italian.

Similarly, songs in English derived from operas then in vogue, and their publication, in collections referred to as "favourite songs," enabled the public to remain in touch with contemporary music. Of particular importance were songs emanating from productions at the **pleasure gardens**; **Thomas Arne**, Samuel Arnold (1740–1802), William Bates (*fl.*1750–1780), and James Hook (1746–1827) were some of the composers connected with this transfer from professional entertainments to domestic music-making.

Further, there existed a large body of published vocal music composed specifically for the amateur music-maker in the home. Usually written for women, this was presented in the soprano or mezzo soprano range, with figured bass keyboard accompaniments and brief instrumental interludes between lines simple enough to be performed by the singer herself. Such publications, appearing in sheet-long form, also included a version of the melody transposed for unaccompanied flute or guitar.

Amidst this tradition, it is hardly surprising that well into the 19th century, songwriting was considered a purely commercial enterprise. Composers at the close of the Hanoverian era tended to select texts not for their excellent literary quality but for their adaptability to melodic setting. Some of the composers possessing a good command of an expressive melodic line, and who were also sensitive to the texts they chose, were Mozart's pupil Thomas Atwood (1765–1838), who often borrowed texts from **Sir Walter Scott** and **Thomas Moore**; John Clarke (1770–1836), who borrowed from **Byron**; and George Frederick Pinto (1785–1806), who borrowed from **Pope**.

Works for part-singing were also important in domestic music-making. Glee, madrigal, and part-song were the dominant forms. Glees, however, were also favored by social **clubs**. Consisting usually of four (sometimes five) parts, these works were sung one to a part and unaccompanied. The traditional influence of the English madrigalists remained intact, with a certain emphasis on word imagery and mixtures of homophonic and polyphonic textures. Composers intentionally avoided the extremes of textual bawdiness associated with the catch (or "round") tradition, instead preferring to work with themes considered appropriate for mixed company, namely amatory, convivial, picturesque, pastoral, patriotic, and elegiac themes. The repertoire for glees was huge, with many publications appearing often in series, such as the annual publications (1763–1794) edited by Edmund Thomas Warren, titled *A Collection of Catches, Canons and Glees.*

Leslie Ellen Brown

Bibliography

Johnstone, H. Diack, and Roger Fiske, eds. *The Blackwell History of Music in Britain: The Eighteenth Century.* 1990.

Temperley, Nicholas, ed. *The Athlone History of Music in Britain: The Romantic Age.* 1981.

See also Folksong; Music, Choral; Music, Popular

Musical Concerts and Concert Life

The public concert, in which auditors paid to listen to **music**, was a British invention. The pioneer was John Banister (1630–1679), who organized performances by leading professional **musicians** at the George Tavern, **London**, beginning in 1672. Thomas Britton (1644–1714) established a famous series of concerts, which lasted from 1678 until his death, in a long room above his Clerkenwell coal warehouse. By 1700, public concerts were widespread in the taverns and **coffeehouses** of London and **provincial towns**, and were attended by those engaged in trade and manufacture. The Stationers' Hall and other livery halls were also used for musical entertainments for the rich men of the city. Thus the Hanoverian period inherited a well-established activity that had already found a new **middle-class** audience.

The pooled wealth of the new public allowed concert managers to compete with aristocratic patrons in securing the best musicians, and the standard of performance was high. Social distinctions began to be observed: private and semiprivate concert societies were formed, such as the Castle Society, founded by violinist Talbot Young (1699–1758), which met at the Castle Tavern, Paternoster Row, from about 1724 to 1783. Large-scale concerts were sometimes given in the public theaters. Soon, purpose-built concert halls appeared, the most important of which was Hickford's Room, which moved to the West End (Brewer Street) in 1738. The world's oldest purpose-built concert hall still surviving is the Holywell Music Room, Oxford, erected in 1748. A still larger and more brilliant complex was the Hanover Square Concert Rooms (1773), which housed both the subscription series offered by **Johann Christian Bach** and Carl Friedrich Abel (1725–1787) beginning in 1775, and the still more famous series conducted by Johann Peter Salomon (1745–1815) in the last decade of the century, at which **Joseph Haydn** was the star performer. A rival venue during the **Regency** period was the fashionable Argyll Rooms (1806–1830). For more popular concerts the **pleasure gardens** at Vauxhall, Marylebone, and Ranelagh were favored.

The prevailing types of concert were the subscription series, for which an independent manager hired musicians and reaped any profits himself; and the single "benefit," where the beneficiary acted as **entrepreneur** and principal performer, often obtaining the services of fellow musicians free in return for similar services later. (**Actors** followed a similar practice.) Prices generally ranged from a shilling to half a guinea. Throughout the Hanoverian period, most concert programs were long by modern standards, and were mixed in their musical fare. There was always an orchestra, which would play concertos, overtures, or symphonies, and accompany solo singers or instrumentalists between selections. Later in the period, chamber music or the occasional harp or piano solo might also be featured. A peculiarly English form was the organ concerto (for organ and orchestra), first introduced by **Handel** between the acts of **oratorios** performed at Covent Garden Theatre.

Handel's oratorio performances, customarily given on Wednesdays and Fridays during Lent (when **opera** productions were forbidden), survived his death in 1759 by at least 70 years, but soon degenerated into mere selections from his and other composers' works, with concertos interspersed between the "acts." More specialized concerts were offered by the Academy of Ancient Music (founded in 1710), the Madrigal Society (1741), the Nobleman and Gentlemen's Catch **Club** (1761), and the Anacreontic Society (1766); these existed as much for the participants as for audiences.

A more important landmark was the foundation of the Concert of Antient Music (1776–1848), in which a board of aristocratic directors provided music of an earlier era (primarily Handel's), sung and played by the best available performers for the edification of an exclusive invited audience. In contrast to this, the Philharmonic Society was a forward-looking organization, established in 1813 by a committee of professional musicians who agreed to share the direction of its concerts. The repertoire was dominated by recent music of Haydn,

Concert in the Shire-Hall, Gloucester, c. 1840

Mozart, and Beethoven, and in its early, prosperous decades new works were commissioned, including Beethoven's Ninth Symphony. But its programs were still a mixture of orchestra, vocal, chamber, and solo music. The orchestra was still directed from the pianoforte. Purely orchestral concerts, with baton conductors directing permanent orchestras, did not appear until the Victorian era, whereas the first series of classical chamber concerts dated from 1835 and the first solo piano recitals from 1840.

Although London remained overwhelmingly the center of concert music, **Edinburgh**, **Dublin**, and **Bath** all had distinguished concert series on a smaller scale, and few **provincial** towns lacked a concert society by the early 19th century.

Nicholas Temperley

Bibliography

Busby, Thomas. *Concert Room and Orchestra Anecdotes.* 1825.

Foster, Myles Birket. *The History of the Philharmonic Society of London, 1813–1912.* 1912.

Johnstone, H. Diack, and Roger Fiske, eds. *The Blackwell History of Music in Britain.* Vol. 4: *The Eighteenth Century.* 1990.

Sadie, Stanley. "Concert Life in Eighteenth-Century England." *Proceedings of the Royal Musical Association.* Vol. 85, pp. 17–30.

Temperley, Nicholas. "Beethoven in London Concert Life, 1800–1850." *The Music Review.* Vol. 21, pp. 207–214.

Tilmouth, Michael. "Some Early London Concerts and Music Clubs, 1670–1720." *Proceedings of the Royal Musical Association.* Vol. 84, pp. 13–26.

See also Music; Theaters and Staging

Musicians

Because **London** had a richer and more varied musical life than almost any other European **city** and offered greater opportunities for financial reward, it became a musical Mecca that attracted the most talented composers, singers, and instrumentalists from the Continent, especially from Italy and Germany. Foreign-born artists thus dominated the musical profession during the Hanoverian era and largely overshadowed native musicians.

The central figure was **Handel**, of German heritage, who settled permanently in London (1712) as organist and composer of Italian **opera** and of music for the English Court and church. It was his English **oratorios**, however, that brought him lasting fame, so that by the late 18th century, Handel festivals were held in London and elsewhere with hundreds of performers, and Handel's music formed the core of countless programs.

The public's enthusiastic support of music, which escalated during the latter part of the century, led energetic musician–**entrepreneurs** to compose and **publish** vast quantities of **music**, manufacture instruments, give lessons, and construct music halls. Eminent musicians such as **Bach** and Carl Friedrich Abel (1725–1787) established successful subscription **musical concerts** that introduced the finest performers and the latest symphonies, concertos, and solo works to an eager audience. Another versatile musician was virtuoso pianist **Clementi**, who performed, composed, conducted, manufactured pianos, and also contributed to **music education** and music publishing.

Both royalty and the public avidly welcomed distinguished musicians from abroad, for example Mozart (1756–1791), who arrived in 1764 as an 8-year-old prodigy. In the 1790s **Haydn** attained unprecedented success during his two

"The Enraged Musician," from a print by Hogarth

trips to London, where he composed his final 12 symphonies. Felix Mendelssohn (1809–1847) made 10 journeys to Britain as a pianist, conductor, and composer, and was inspired to write his overture *The Hebrides* (1830) by his **travels**.

Most English-born musicians were professional organists and church musicians like **William Boyce** and **Samuel Wesley**, or composers of songs, operas, and theatrical works like William Shield (1748–1829) and **Thomas Arne**, best remembered for "Rule, Britannia" (1740). Musicians flourished not only in London but in **provincial towns**, where over 100 musical societies, mostly amateur, were founded under professional leadership. By the early 19th century the public's love of music was so deeply rooted that Britain was regarded as one of the most musical of all European countries.

Eve R. Meyer

Bibliography

Ehrlich, Cyril. *The Music Profession in Britain since the Eighteenth Century: A Social History.* 1985.

Kelly, Michael. *The Reminiscences of Michael Kelly, of the King's Theatre, and Theatre Royal, Drury Lane.* 1826; rpt. 1975.

Temperley, Nicholas, et al. "London," in *The New Grove Dictionary of Music and Musicians.* Vol. 11, pp. 142–217. 1980.

Walker, Ernest. *A History of Music in England.* 1952.

Young, Percy M. *A History of British Music.* 1967.

See also Music

Mutinies

All states require regulations for the control of their armed forces. Down to 1688, such regulations were issued under royal prerogative as Articles of War. The **Glorious Revolution** (1688–1689) saw the beginning of a peacetime standing **army** over which Parliament gained control by passing mutiny acts that superseded the prerogative articles. These controlled military discipline up to 1879.

The first Mutiny Act (1689) was passed to punish mutineers in the Royal Scots Regiment during its transfer to the United Provinces. Reenacted nearly annually afterward, similar mutiny acts regulated virtually all activities connected with military discipline, including mutiny, desertion, sedition, enlistment, leave of absence, civil offenses, damage by neglect, inebriation, and misbehavior before the enemy. The acts also established the office of judge advocate general to oversee their enforcement and provide legal advice to army commanders.

By sanctioning courts-martial to deal with disciplinary problems during peacetime, the acts legalized the existence of a standing army, yet by necessitating regular parliamentary renewal they also helped ensure continuous parliamentary meetings and popular control of the armed services. An act of 1717 reauthorized the crown to draw up Articles of War, while this and other acts of 1757 and 1803 extended the range of courts-martial to include militia forces and troops both inside and outside the crown's dominions.

The discipline of these acts was invoked typically to deal with large-scale outbreaks resulting from violations of the terms of military service—for example, when the 76th MacDonald's Highlanders refused to embark for **North America** until they received delinquent enlistment bounties (1779), and when the 77th Athole Highlanders, raised for 3-years' service only (or the duration of the American War), mutinied over orders to embark for **India** (1783). But harsh conditions also caused sporadic mutinies, as in the famous case of the *Bounty* mutiny against **Captain William Bligh** (1789).

During the **French Revolutionary and Napoleonic Wars** a far more serious case occurred at Spithead in the Channel Fleet (17 April 1797) when the government ignored sailors' petitions for changes in discipline, better pay, food, clothing, medical care, and liberty in port. In effect the fleet went on strike, refusing to return to its station off Brest. Lord Richard Howe (1726–1799), Admiral of the Fleet, the government's representative, trusted on the "lower decks" for his concern for the average sailor, offered the mutineers a royal pardon (15 May), and Parliament granted many of the petitioners' requests, applying the reforms to the entire **navy**. Howe received the king's gratitude and the Order of the Garter. This ended the Spithead mutiny, but the excitement had already spread to the North Sea Fleet at the Nore, on the Thames (12 May). Here, in a more clearly political spirit, all but three ships issued demands and began dubbing themselves "The Floating Republic." The mutineers were soon overcome (14 June); 28 of their leaders were hanged.

A conviction of mutiny by courts-martial generally meant death by hanging for ringleaders. Those troops or sailors who simply followed along usually received severe corporal punishment, typically multiple lashes administered by the "cat o' nine tails."

Stanley D.M. Carpenter

Bibliography

Barnett, Correlli. *Britain and Her Army, 1509–1970.* 1970.

Marcus, G.J. *Heart of Oak: A Survey of British Seapower in the Georgian Era.* 1975.

Rogers, H.C.B. *The British Army in the Eighteenth Century.* 1977.

Southworth, John V. *The Age of Sails.* 1968.

Nabobs

These were **East India Company** servants who acquired vast wealth through dubious practices. The term *nabob* originated as a 17th-century English corruption of the Mughal title *nawab,* which was itself derived from the Arabic *na'ib.* All three terms referred to a governor. But with the company's conquest of Bengal in 1757, "nabob" became an epithet used to stigmatize corrupt company administrators who became wealthy by withholding money that rightfully belonged either to their employer or to India's peasantry.

Although from 1757 to 1765 an Indian *nawab* officially ruled Bengal, the company held the effective regional military power. Its agents used this to extort money acquired by Indian tax farmers who collected revenues in accordance with the established Mughal land system. Nabobs also took advantage of their tax-exempt trading status in territories occupied by the company. These abuses increased when in 1765 the company became *diwan* (the Mughal emperor's chief revenue collector) of Bengal. Whereas earlier *diwans* had used revenues at least partly to administer their territories, the company used these almost exclusively to finance its own operations.

During his second governorship of the company's Bengal operations, **Robert Clive**, though himself perhaps the greatest nabob of all, tried to curb corruption among company agents. Few of them heeded his policy, and when in 1769 the monsoon failed, the nabobs' behavior intensified the ensuing famine.

As a commoner class of *nouveaux riches,* the nabobs' public displays of wealth in England offended the upper echelons of British society. But it was their misappropriation of funds intended for the company that finally led Parliament to pass the Regulating Act (1773) and assume a greater responsibility over company affairs. As governor of Bengal from 1772 to 1774, **Warren Hastings** curbed the nabobs' activities; their importance soon diminished.

A. Martin Wainwright

Bibliography

Mason [pseudonym Woodruff], Philip. *The Men Who Ruled India.* 1954.

Spear, T.G.P. *The Nabobs: A Study of the Social Life of the English in Eighteenth Century India.* 1963.

See also India

Napier, Robert (1791–1876)

Napier began the great tradition of Clyde steamship builders. Born in Dumbarton, he established his own business in **Glasgow** with a £50 loan from his father, built his first marine engine in 1824, and turned to shipbuilding in the 1830s. Regular British steamship service had begun in 1815 on the Liverpool–Glasgow route. Further services were established in the 1820s, for example between **Edinburgh** and **London**, this **coastal shipping** being relatively more important before the coming of the **railways** than later. By the 1830s, Napier was attempting to solve the greater problem of ocean **navigation** by **steam** (though there had been isolated Atlantic passages since the Americans' *Savannah* run of 1819). The rewards were sweetened when the government made known its desire to substitute steam vessels for sailing ships in carrying the transatlantic mail. Samuel Cunard (1787–1865) of Nova Scotia won the contract, undertaking to run a regular service with four steamships of identical size and power. Napier built and designed these, and also fronted the consortium of predominantly Glaswegian investors who founded what was to become the famous Cunard Line. The first voyage was on the *Britannia* from **Liverpool** to Boston; it took just over 2 weeks (4–19 July 1840).

Napier also broke the English monopoly of Admiralty contracts (1838) and built the paddle sloops *Vesuvius* and *Stromboli.* His yards supplied many of the navies of the Continent, as well. His other achievements included construction of the world's first train ferry (1849). His reputation lay not only in his ships but in the excellent training available at his yards, which produced, among other things, the first certificate in steam navigation for the British **Navy**.

Patricia S. Collins

Bibliography

Napier, J. *Life of Robert Napier.* 1904.

Osborne, B.D. *Robert Napier, 1791–1876: The Father of Clyde Shipbuilding.* 1991.

Shields, J. *Clyde Built.* 1949.

See also Bell, Henry; Miller, Patrick; Ships and Shipbuilding

Napoleonic Wars

See French Revolutionary and Napoleonic Wars

Nash, John (1752–1835)

Nash not only changed the face of central **London** with his **neoclassical** creations of Regent Street and Regents Park but also designed major buildings in a variety of other styles, the **Gothic**, Italian villa, picturesque, and Oriental. No other **architect** of his time was more varied.

Born in Lambeth, Nash first worked in the office of the architect Sir Robert Taylor (1714–1788), but by 1777 was on his own as an architect and speculative builder. After several early failures he moved to **Wales**, where he designed jails and country houses. He returned to London in 1796, forming a partnership with the **landscape designer Humphrey Repton**. Luscombe Castle, Devon (1800–1804), is the first of his Gothic castle designs in England, while Southgate Grove, Middlesex (1797), reflects his interest in the neoclassical style. Cronkhill, near Shrewsbury (*c.* 1802), is the first of the new Italian villas that combine classical and Renaissance details with the freer and more **picturesque** outline of the Gothic. Nash's interest in the picturesque reached its highest point in a group of rustic thatched and tiled cottages with Gothic and other details, which he built at Blaise Hamlet, outside Bristol, for John Scandrett Harford (1811).

In 1806 Nash was named architect to the Department of Woods and Forests, and in 1813 Surveyor General (in succession to **James Wyatt**); in effect he became the Prince Regent's architect. The term **Regency style** is more frequently applied to interiors than exteriors, but insofar as it pertains to external architecture, it is almost synonymous with the name of Nash. His appointments resulted in the creation of Regent Street and Regents Park (1812–1828), connecting Carleton House Terrace on the south with the new Regents Park on the north by means of a new street; the street was flanked by Nash's buildings, many with arcades, quadrant in shape at one part and with a variety of Greek and Egyptian details. Before reaching Regents Park, the street changed to a crescent shape. The park itself was rimmed with neoclassical terraces, large groups of row houses treated as one architectural unit. There were also individual houses in two park villages. Further royal commissions for Nash included Buckingham Palace (1815–1823) and the completion of the Royal Pavilion at Brighton (1815–1823) with a fantastic Indian domed exterior and Chinese interior.

Nash worked in a variety of styles in all parts of England and **Ireland**, but he is best remembered for designing compositions on a large scale. He had little interest in the finer points of design or the correct use of orders. The sweeping, coordi-

The Royal Pavilion, Brighton

nated design of Regent Street and the creation of Regents Park with its housing were his greatest achievements.

Thomas J. McCormick

Bibliography

Colvin, H.M. *A Biographical Dictionary of English Architects, 1660–1840.* 2nd ed., 1978.

Davis, Terrence. *The Architecture of John Nash.* 1960.

———. *John Nash: The Prince Regent's Architect.* 1960.

Mansbridge, Michael. *John Nash, a Complete Catalogue.* 1991.

Summerson, John. *The Life and Work of John Nash.* 1980.

Temple, Nigel. *John Nash and the Village Picturesque.* 1979.

National Government

See Government, National

National Society for the Education of the Poor

Formed in 1811 by the **Church of England**, this was designed primarily to combat inroads in education among the poor and working classes being made by schools operated by **dissenters**. By the end of the 18th century, **Sunday schools** and **charity schools** were the only institutions attempting to educate poor children, and they were hopelessly inadequate. Around 1800 **Joseph Lancaster**, a **Quaker**, opened a school for working-class children using the "monitorial system," in which a teacher taught older children who in turn taught younger ones. The Lancasterian schools, propagated by dissenters, became the foundation for the Royal Lancasterian Society, which, in 1808, became the **British and Foreign School Society**.

It was to counteract this that the National Society for Promoting the Education of the Poor in the Principles of the Established Church was formed. Its first superintendent, coaxed from retirement, was **Andrew Bell**. But both societies, though they represented a step forward in national education, were unable to deal with the large number of working-class children who received no institutional instruction at all. Those who did attend were not taught very much—little more than the basic skills necessary for reading the Bible. Gross misappropriation of the voluntary contributions upon which both societies relied was also common.

Despite the efforts of **Henry Brougham**, who headed a commission to investigate the educational charities, a bill proposing a national system of education failed to carry in 1820. Denominational antagonism and mutual suspicion between Anglicans and dissenters, together with a residual distrust of educating the poor, continued for decades afterward to frustrate attempts to create a national system.

William Edward Morris

Bibliography

Burgess, Henry James. *Enterprise in Education: The Story of the Work of the Established Church in the Education of the People Prior to 1870.* 1958.

James Murphy. *Church, State, and Schools in Britain.* 1971.

See also Education, Elementary

Nationalism and Patriotism

Patriotism is probably the oldest group sentiment on record. Scholarship has traced it even in ancient Egypt. In its simplest forms it is little more than an elaboration of sentiments of family and kinship, a sense of "we-ness," which is often pricked into being by confrontation with strangers, an alien "they." Signs of patriotism are evident from the earliest history of the British Isles. In Saxon times, English patriotism was awakened in the age of King Alfred in opposition to the invading Danes. It was fired again by the Norman Conquest, the last successful invasion in English history. After 1066 it was kept alive in Norman England by being allied to a sense among the English of being a conquered people, and this was reinforced by the condescension, exclusiveness, and continuing French connections of the upper classes. One result of this was the "theory of the Norman Yoke," the idea that some day the oppressed "Saxon" English would rise up to reclaim their land from their alien francophile rulers and renew their ancient freedom—a theory of "national renewal," which has had a surprisingly long history, partly because it is so adaptable. After World War II some English propagandists even treated the Americans as new imposers of the foreign "yoke."

English patriotism vigorously unfolded in the age of Shakespeare, and it was now fortified also by a distinctive national religious faith, that of English Protestantism, which altered concepts of national freedom and also contributed greatly to the sense of distinctive national identity. Nonetheless, in the 17th century the sense of alien domination and the theory of the Norman Yoke resurfaced among English **radicals**. This was partly a reaction to the renewed sense of Bourbon France as alien predator, but it also worked off a continuing uneasy sense of French influence operating *within* the country. The alienness of the Stuart kings, and their affiliations with the French court which bankrolled and subsidized them—and which in the end took them in and honored them—helped to keep this sense alive.

Thus when the Hanoverian kings took over in 1714, a very solid and well-developed sense of English patriotism existed. England's German kings suffered from it themselves, but they were far less objectionable than the popery, authoritarianism, and Frenchness of the Stuarts. By the time of **George II**, the country was becoming accustomed to the German kings. **George III** took care at his accession (1760) to announce that he "gloried in the name of Briton," and this was a sign of the times. For the struggle between England and France was now reaching a climax. There was much at stake, including the possession of spreading global empires. The "Second Hundred Years' War" stretched from 1689 to 1815, and, the whole period being punctuated by battles, crises, and invasion scares, the patriotic sentiment was continually aggravated. Indeed it was now being ignited into something else, nationalism.

Patriotism is an essentially conservative sentiment, connected particularly with a protective attachment to the nation's honor in a military context, and with loyalty to the visible carriers of that honor—king, **army**, **navy**, flag. Nationalism, though it may sometimes resemble patriotism in flag-waving enthusiasm, is actually much more complicated. While the patriot is often aggressively proud of his or her country and loyal to its leaders, the nationalist is just as likely to be angry about its condition and contemptuous of its leaders. The soldier is likely to be a patriot, but the scholar is more likely to be a nationalist, perhaps even a radical nationalist. An important distinction is that between the flag as the object of patriotism, and the people themselves as the object of nationalism. This is one reason why another distinguishing mark of nationalism, though not of patriotism, is a deep interest in the language, poetry, history, ancient morality, ancient political rights, and ancient culture of the people. The desire to "repossess" these things in their imagined "ancient purity" leads to scholarly research, and then, almost inevitably, to the formation of an ideology and a political program the whole point of which is to give authentic expression to the supposedly suppressed voice and will of the culture itself. Nationalism thus often develops toward an essentially populist and democratic political program. And because nationalism idealizes the state as a moral community, *every* citizen is held to possess natural political rights in it—not by virtue of rank or property but simply by ascription, simply by virtue of participating in its moral essence as an Englishman, German, Italian, or whatever.

It would be foolish to imagine that patriotic and nationalistic impulses cannot coexist within the same breast, or that whole populations cannot be moved at least partially from one pattern to the other, depending on circumstances. Confusing analytical problems may thus arise when a populist and nationalist group faces off against another, patriotic but intensely traditionalist and conservative group, still holding power. The key distinction then to remember is that nationalism is essentially secular and modern, connected with the whole process of modernization, whereas patriotism is not. Nationalism may *appear* to be a reactionary call for a revival of ancient forms, but the "ancient forms" themselves often tend to be self-serving inventions, and the analyst must look carefully into "traditionalist" packagings and disguise to see whether or not they conceal revolutionary substance. Nationalism, by most scholars' definitions, never existed before the 18th century. Though there may be important religious notes in it, at its core it is about people, land, cultural wholeness, and popular political sovereignty. Historically it accompanies growing literacy, economic development, and, most important, the new idea of the individual as a full participant in the state. Much of its force lies in its ability to stigmatize, undermine, discredit, and revolutionize existing institutions and forms under the claim that they do not truly represent the authentic "spirit of the people." This is why nationalism finds it so important and convenient to personify and demonize as alien those national characteristics that are deemed least favorable to wholesale modernization ("renewal").

Nationalism in the British Isles received very little scholarly attention before the 1980s. Now, however, English nationalism and various questions raised by it—questions of identity, ethnicity, class, and so on—constitute a leading area of scholarly research. By many historians the English nationalist movement is reckoned the "flagship" movement in Europe, one that (like the **Industrial Revolution** with which it was linked) got under way before the French, German, Irish, or Italian. It is recognized that England in the Hanoverian period witnessed a transition from early stirrings of cultural nationalism to a mature nationalist program with a nationalist philosophy and political agenda. Some of its greatest shaping spirits were **Hogarth**, **Handel**, **Pitt the Elder**, **Johnson**, **Wilkes**, **Horne Tooke**, **Cartwright**, and **Wordsworth**. Abstractly, the movement progressed from a cultural critique to an exploration of "ancient native virtues" to a literary renaissance to a moral attack on the "alien" characteristics of the upper classes to a political program featuring "renewal and repossession" of the country by its supposedly despised and oppressed masses. More specifically, its development may be traced from the 1740s, in the creation of what were regarded as distinctively authentic and native forms of **music**, national anthems, **painting**, theater, and **landscape** gardening; the 1750s, in the establishment of new **learned societies** and academies honoring the native arts, and preparation of **reference works** extolling and attempting to fix the native **language**; the 1760s, which saw new schools of national **historical writing** and the beginnings of literary research into older linguistic forms and cultural origins, and the spread of deeply held opinions on the moral corruption of the nation and its need for wholesale renewal; and the 1770s and 1780s, which saw the renovation of old heroes (King Alfred, **Shakespeare**) and the creation of new ones (Pitt, Johnson), and, more important, the formation of a populist, radical, and implicitly democratic line of **political thought** centered on universal suffrage like that which allegedly had existed "in Saxon times." Throughout this period, the sense of France as external enemy, threatening England deeply, served as a foil to the elaboration of nationalist ideology, which again revived the old Norman Yoke idea and worked to de-legitimize the English ruling class as alien and excessively francophile (which in fact it was). Against a manufactured "French" negative stereotype there was set up a counterethic, a personality profile, of the true-born Englishman, as (all the things "the French" were not) honest, morally pure, blunt, frank, forthright, "natural," and full of "original genius."

The 18th century ended climactically with the greatest Anglo–French military struggle of all, the **French Revolutionary and Napoleonic Wars**. This struggle, lasting 22 years, ensured the success of the English nationalist movement. The **French Revolution** itself was treated as confirmation of the nationalist ideology, and the struggle against it as a warrant for wholesale national decontamination from "French influences." Few historical events have been more serendipitous. While the war boosted native patriotism, it also furnished perfect cover for nationalistic elements in the **middle class**, most notably the **Evangelicals** of the **Church of England**, to revamp the nation's **manners and morals** and remake them into what was usefully described as an anti–French, but in fact inwardly a deeply anti-aristocratic, mold. The basic mechanisms of contemporary propaganda may be examined in two published comments from the late 1790s. The first, inculcating patriotism, appeared

Hogarth's "Gate of Calais, O the Roast Beef of Old England," 1749

in the ***Anti-Jacobin:*** "To cherish an Anti-Gallican spirit has, in all times, been deemed an effort of genuine patriotism, a mark of love for one's country, which distinguishes the true-born Englishman from the mongrel cosmopolite." The other, slyly carrying this over into the de-legitimation of aristocratic leadership, was a statement by **Hannah More** in her *Strictures on the Modern System of Female Education* (1799), in which, condemning existing patterns by smearing them as "French," she attacked "that levity of manners, that contempt of the sabbath, that fatal familiarity with loose principles, and those relaxed notions of conjugal fidelity, which have often been transplanted into this country by women of fashion, as a too common effect of a long residence in a neighbouring country." By the end of the Hanoverian period (1837), after decades of this sort of propaganda, English nationalism was thoroughly entrenched. It had assisted the massive transformation of the country's economy, morality, institutions, and even of the "national character" by glorifying a profile—a role model—of personal traits supposedly descended from England's "Saxon ancestors."

This swelling tide of English nationalism naturally affected relations between "Saxon" England and its Celtic neighbors in **Wales**, **Scotland**, and **Ireland**. Increasingly the English took the superiority of their culture as self-evident. Their neighbors, not without misgivings but increasingly overwhelmed politically and economically, began to agree. Developments in the British Isles during the entire period 1714–1837 may be seen in one way as an advancing English political, economic, and cultural imperialism transforming and homogenizing life within the kingdom even as the British **Empire** advanced abroad. Of course the English attitude toward the Welsh, Scottish, and Irish varied according to historical circumstances. All three, being different in lineage and language, much smaller in **population**, poorer and more visibly backward in culture, were considered inferior and in varying degrees barbaric. But there were important differences. For example, the Welsh and Irish had been beaten in battle and, geographically at least, absorbed, whereas the Scots had not.

It is easy enough to catalog the English prejudices of the period. There was a tendency to see the Welsh as harmless and amusing, though inclined to pilferage and unnecessarily prone to religious fanaticism. Scotland, at least up to 1800, was seen by the English in a more threatening light as the staging base of **Jacobite** threats to the state, a potential ally of France, a bastion of the **Earl of Bute**'s supposedly insidious influences, and as the nursery of innumerable well-trained **legal**, **medical**, scientific and engineering **professionals** who, coming for economic reasons to London, benefited English civilization but also constituted a threat to jobs and livelihoods. Ireland, being more remote, **Catholic**, another potential staging base for French designs, and increasingly violent as Irish secret societies proliferated, received that growing hatred which conquering peoples usually reserve for those whom they have ruined. But the "Irish Question" did not emerge until the end of the Hanoverian era.

Looking at matters from another direction, English political and cultural dominance gradually inspired nationalist awakenings in Wales, Scotland, and Ireland just as French international dominance up to the 1780s had spurred English nationalist development. But these regional movements, except for the Irish, were far less powerful. And now, of course, the shoe was on the other foot. Now it was England, not France, which was stereotyped and condemned as the alien, dominating, corrupting power—the evil "neighbouring country." And again, since all these movements dealt with national origins as their stock in trade, racial terms were drawn into the pairs of antitheses through which the nationalist ideologies operated—though now the cultural and political threat was "Saxon," not "Norman."

Welsh nationalism grew significantly but had little impact. Its origins have been traced in early-18th-century London, in the reactions of Welshmen who found themselves, their language, and their culture ridiculed by Englishmen assuming cultural superiority. By the middle of the 18th century these Welshmen were founding societies whose purpose was to revive the Welsh language and bardic culture—the "aboriginal" Cymmrodorion Society, for example, dated from 1751—and they made a particular point of claiming for themselves a moral superiority as well as historical precedence in the British Isles, treating the "Saxon" English as invaders and bearers of cultural imperialism. The **poetic** productions of Goronwy Owen (1723–1769) and literary forgeries of **Edward Williams (Iolo Morganwg)** were symptomatic and influential. Yet for all that, Welsh nationalism remained unimportant until the 20th century.

Scottish nationalism was of stronger growth, but it was all but killed by Scotland's remarkable economic, educational, and technical success. In Scotland the initial results of the **Union** were disappointing. Unlike Wales, Scotland had not been conquered, but rather voluntarily gave up her parliament as a trade-off for preserving the Kirk, the **Scottish legal system**, and **Scottish education**, and for promoting economic progress in alliance with England. It was not until after the **Forty-five** rebellion and the suppression of the Highland clans that economic improvement began to accelerate. After 1750, Lowland Scotland entered wholeheartedly into the "age of improvement," joining England in this and at the same time leading the attack on the separateness and backwardness of Highland culture. **Glasgow** and the west coast became increasingly prosperous through Atlantic trade, while **Edinburgh** experienced a building boom and even **Highland regiments** found increasing employment in the **wars** of the latter 18th century. By the 1780s, economic integration was proceeding at high speed. Scottish landlords emulated English ones in improving their estates and in building **planned villages**, and it was not only in this that an "Anglomania" began affecting the region. Sophisticated Scotsmen labored to eliminate the burrs from their speech and the Scotticisms from their expressions. The Scottish upper classes, like the Welsh, set up **fox-hunting clubs** and imported other English fashions.

Yet it would be wrong to conclude that Scotsmen forgot their identity in this rush to succeed within the framework laid out by the English. In fact, while Scotsmen were assimilating themselves to English culture, their own culture was also reaching a high point of development. Scotland, particularly in her institutions of learning, was esteemed throughout the Western world, and this more than anything else shielded her from disorientation under the growing cultural prestige of England to the south. The **Scottish Enlightenment** had been spurred into being in the early 18th century by the sense of loss and cultural humiliation that followed the Union, but after decades of development in the **Scottish universities** and **cities** it fortified Scotsmen even as many took the high road to English jobs and professional advancement. The Scottish intelligentsia's outlook was always a blend of the cosmopolitan and the local. Even **Robert Burns** was ambivalent in his attitude toward Scottish nationalism. Before him, the Scots had pioneered in experiments of cultural nationalism by being among the first to collect their old folk **ballads** and to attempt reconstruction of Scottish bardic literature. But their painters and philosophers, who traveled everywhere and created many of the forms now considered "English," gained them respect throughout Europe, and they moved with increasing ease into English society.

The pattern of Scottish politics was even more favorable to assimilation. Scottish reformers saw in English progressivism a valuable counterweight to provincial authoritarianism and reaction. Just as Scotland's "Friends of the People" showed solidarity with English radicals at their "British Convention" (1793), **Francis Jeffrey** and the Scottish reformers at the *Edinburgh Review* extolled the virtues of English liberal **Whig** reformism and saw the important political changes of the early 1830s, which constituted a much greater liberation of the Scottish masses than of the English, as a welcome destruction of Scottish political separateness. Scotland thus entered the Victorian period as a valued partner in overall British development, and it was not until the 1960s that truly significant developments appeared in the area of Scottish nationalism.

Ireland, again, presents a very different case. Irish nationalism began late, but by the end of the Hanoverian period was already becoming extremely important to the subsequent course of British history. Its fundamental materials were very old and deeply laid. There was, of course, an ancient sense of locale, of the island and its land. As with Wales and Scotland, there were communal cultural elements—in this case the Gaelic Irish language, Ireland's history, customs, lore, and folklore. In the 18th century there continued to be bardic poets, itinerant ballad singers, religious festivals such as that at Gouganebarra in Cork, and ancient Celtic beliefs such as those in witches and fairies. On top of all this, there was the Roman Catholicism that bound some 82% of the population (as determined in 1831 when the first religious census was taken). And of course the main mechanism of nationalist transformation was "a given" of the situation: There was in full measure a sense of the oppressive foreign overlords, the *Sasanaigh* (Saxons), the usurping Englishmen with their confiscations, **penal laws**, and multifarious discrimination. These common elements of consciousness would eventually become combined to take precedence over all other relationships between Irish peasantry, clergy, gentry, and middle classes, and to fuse the population together in concerted feeling and action.

However, many aspects of 18th-century Irish history were unfavorable to such an outcome. Nationalist development depends very much on literacy and communications, yet the mass of the Irish people were nearly illiterate (before the 1830s less than 40% received any education) and regionally isolated from each other. Political domination by the **Anglo-Irish Protestant Ascendancy** and by London had also brought such demoralization among Catholics that few had the heart to organize resistance. There was also the growing power, prestige, cultural imperialism, and economic dynamism of England to contend with, particularly (as in Scotland) after 1760. As in Scotland also, this produced internal Irish cultural differentiation along class lines that impeded the growth of common nationalist sentiment. Further, the natural leadership of the Catholic masses was divided and ineffectual, thanks to the same overshadowing influence from "a neighbouring country." The Catholic clergy, instead of stirring up popular resistance, sought accommodation with England and found its efforts rewarded between 1778 and 1793 in the removal of many of the penal laws and the granting of the franchise to Catholics. The clergy also assisted the Anglicization of the country, furthering schemes to depress the use of Irish and spread that of English as the language of progress, modernity, and opportunity. A homogenized "west British" culture was increasingly an ideal. The same ideal was so cultivated by the bilingual or simply English-speaking Catholic gentry and middle classes that social and economic fissures began to deepen between them and the Irish-speaking rural masses. This fragmentation of the Catholic population was evident in the growth of secret societies which, in the period 1760–1790, assaulted priests as well as modernizing Catholic farmers. Rural laborers and smallholders felt less allegiance than ever before to their natural leaders busily abandoning the common language and customs.

Irish nationalism was also prevented from forming before 1800 by the continuing Irish Protestant dominance and exclusivity. Yet the Protestants too were divided, not only socially but also between Establishment Churchmen and dissenters, particularly Scots–Irish **Presbyterians**. In the **Irish Parliament** a **Patriot** group representing the Protestant gentry emerged in the early reign of George III and succeeded in gaining legislative autonomy in 1782. **Henry Grattan** and a few others were friendly to religious toleration and political emancipation of the Catholics, and it is possible that over time, without the tragic effects of the French Revolution in Ireland, they might have created an ecumenical Irish state. As it was, deep social as well as sectarian divisions remained within the Protestant ruling class, and anti–Catholic feeling continued to divide it as well, as the abortive **Irish Rebellion** of 1798 revealed by splitting Ulster between ecumenical **United Irish** rebels and loyalist Orangemen. Before 1800 neither Protestants nor Catholics could have organized a strong sectarian nationalist movement, nor, beyond **Wolfe Tone** and a few others, did anyone aspire to organize a nonsectarian one.

After 1800 the picture began to alter rapidly, and a nationalist movement, which was both Catholic and socially inclusive, began to emerge. One obviously important factor here was disappointment over the failed promise of the **Act of Union** (1800). The Catholic clergy had supported this in the continuing expectation that political moderation and a cooperative attitude would bring tangible benefits and full Catholic rights. When they found they had been mistaken, they changed tack and began actively throwing their support to **Daniel O'Connell** and the campaign for **Catholic Emancipation**, at the same time mending relations with the Catholic peasantry and reasserting leadership over the masses. Catholic nationalism, despite the Anglicization discussed above, also appealed increasingly to middle-class elements politically frustrated and economically depressed after 1814, and, equally important, it helped to cover over major economic differences within the Catholic community. The Protestant community negatively helped this process by also dressing ranks, solidifying in favor of the Union, and elaborating the anti–Catholic ideology of the **Orange Order**. Two distinct Irish "nations" began forming, their identities colored by religion, reinforcing each other by antipathy and opposition.

By the 1820s, O'Connell and his lieutenants were preaching an ideology indiscriminately attributing all Ireland's evils and sufferings to the *Sasanaigh* (this racial term neatly lumped together and rejected both Englishmen and Irish-born Protestants as oppressive foreigners) and holding out a promise of national redemption, unity, and fellowship to be achieved through the securing of political rights and ultimately through repeal of the Union. O'Connell rhetorically asked,

> Who is to blame . . . if we are poor, and cannot clothe and feed ourselves better than we do? . . . Yes, the Saxons! the English! despotic England is to blame [for oppressing] our beautiful, much to be pitied Ireland!

Irish literature was now assisting the movement by beginning to generate an image of pre–Conquest Irish purity—just as, half a century earlier, English literature and political ideology had glorified the pre–Norman paradise when Saxons had all been pure, strong, and free.

The Irish nationalist movement was well under way by 1830. It made important preliminary political gains in the period 1828–1838 (with Catholic Emancipation, the **Irish Church Act** of 1833, and the **Tithe** Commutation Act of 1838), and received useful literary and intellectual support in the 1840s from Thomas Osborne Davis (1814–1845), Charles Gavan Duffy (1816–1903), John Blake Dillon (1816–1866), and other members of the "Young Ireland" group. This in turn helped to inspire the Fenians and Sinn Fein as well as the Gaelic revival and Irish literary renaissance of the latter 19th century.

It becomes clear in all this that nationalism, the most powerful ideology in the modern world, can be either a solvent or a glue, depending on the entity upon which it works.

It can build up, or break down. English nationalism prospered, and in its wake "colonized" the other subcultures of the British Isles (though of course it would be absurd to deny that some important influences operated in the other direction). These subcultures were, however, by the same dynamics prodded into wakefulness, resistance, and the formation of programs to dismantle the English-dominated confederated state, the United Kingdom of Great Britain and Ireland. None of these secondary programs has yet been realized except that marked by the departure in 1921 of the Irish Free State.

Finally, some historians have argued that "Britain" had its own nationalism, something *apart from* English nationalism, something entirely separate from the obvious expansion of English cultural hegemony; and that the resultant British entity was "forged" during the period 1790–1820. There is something to be said for this theory. Certainly many individuals—Scots, Welsh, and Irish—stood to benefit from attachment to an amalgamated British state with a unified economy, a common British peerage, a British Empire, and so on, and there were assorted Irish, Scottish, and Welsh intellectuals who helped to promote the idea of a common British homeland—**Tobias Smollett**, for example, in his *Expedition of Humphry Clinker* (1771). And of course the successes of the Empire, particularly in the latter 19th century, furnished a common point of identification. However, some historians continue to doubt the strength of British nationalism as an embracing sentiment, or else tend to think of it as something that did not really flourish until the later Victorian period, and then chiefly in the context of imperial warfare and the international struggles of the earlier 20th century—in which case, they suggest, it was perhaps not nationalism at all but rather a form of conservative "state patriotism," designed not to revolutionize but to consolidate attachment to state authority. Thus the picture here remains somewhat clouded. So far, writers on British nationalism have not given very clear accounts of it as an ideology or shown how it might be classified alongside the other varieties of nationalism delineated by political science.

Gerald Newman

Bibliography

Arac, Jonathan, and Harriet Ritvo, eds. *Macropolitics of Nineteenth-Century Literature: Nationalism, Exoticism, Imperialism.* 1991.

Colley, Linda. *Britons: Forging the Nation, 1707–1837.* 1992.

Coupland, Reginald. *Welsh and Scottish Nationalism.* 1954.

Dozier, R.R. *For King, Constitution, and Country: The English Loyalists and the French Revolution.* 1983.

Emsley, Clive. *British Society and the French Wars, 1793–1815.* 1979.

Finn, Margot. "An Elect Nation? Nation, State, and Class in Modern British History." *Journal of British Studies.* Vol. 28, pp. 181–191.

Greenberg, William. *The Flags of the Forgotten: Nationalism on the Celtic Fringe.* 1969.

Greenfeld, Liah. *Nationalism: Five Roads to Modernity.* 1992.

Harvie, Christopher. *Scotland and Nationalism: Scottish Society and Politics, 1707–1977.* 1977.

Hechter, Michael. *Internal Colonialism: The Celtic Fringe in British National Development, 1536–1966.* 1975.

Jenkins, Philip. *The Making of a Ruling Class: The Glamorgan Gentry, 1640–1790.* 1983.

Kearney, Hugh. *The British Isles: A History of Four Nations.* 1989.

Kidd, Colin. *Subverting Scotland's Past: Scottish Whig Historians and the Creation of an Anglo-British Identity, 1689–c.1830.* 1993.

Nairn, Tom. *The Break-Up of Britain: Crisis and Neo-Nationalism.* 1977.

Newman, Gerald. *The Rise of English Nationalism: A Cultural History, 1740–1830.* 1987.

———. "Anti-French Propaganda and British Liberal Nationalism in the Early Nineteenth Century: Suggestions toward a General Interpretation." *Victorian Studies.* Vol. 18, pp. 385–418.

———. "Nationalism Revisited." *Journal of British Studies.* Vol. 35, pp. 118–127.

Philp, Mark, ed. *The French Revolution and British Popular Politics.* 1991.

Philpin, C.H.E., ed. *Nationalism and Popular Protest in Ireland.* 1987.

Porter, Roy, ed. *Myths of the English.* 1992.

Robbins, Keith. *Nineteenth-Century Britain: Integration and Diversity.* 1988.

Robertson, John, ed. *A Union for Empire: Political Thought and the British Union of 1707.* 1995.

Samuel, Raphael, ed. *Patriotism: The Making and Unmaking of British National Identity.* Vol. 1: *History and Politics.* Vol. 2: *Minorities and Outsiders.* Vol. 3: *National Fictions.* 1989.

Smith, Anthony, and John Hutchinson, eds. *Nationalism.* 1995.

Strauss, Erich. *Irish Nationalism and British Democracy.* 1975.

Teich, Mikulas, and Roy Porter, eds. *The National Question in Europe in Historical Context.* 1993.

Weinbrot, Howard. *Britannia's Issue: The Rise of British Literature from Dryden to Ossian.* 1993.

Wingfield-Stratford, Esme Cecil. *The History of English Patriotism.* 2 vols. 1913.

See also France

Navigation

By the 16th century the development of astronomical and mathematical principles, and the skill of instrument makers, had made it possible for **seamen** to find their way to and from all corners of the known world. Using the sun and stars as fixing points, to gauge their position, mariners deployed the magnetic compass (invented in the 12th century) and more recent instruments such as the astronomical quadrant, the mariner's astrolabe, and the cross-staff.

Then, for over two centuries, there was little improvement in instruments or techniques. In practice, **ships** sought the approximate latitude of their destination, from which point they sailed east or west, "running down the latitude" until land was sighted. But the calculation of longitude remained elusive, even though the first Astronomer Royal, John Flamsteed (1646–1719), was directed in 1675 to "apply himself with the utmost care and diligence" to rectify this last major navigational problem.

With the **Longitude Act** (1714) an enormous prize was offered to the inventor of any method of determining a ship's longitude to within half a degree. Some of the ideas forwarded to the Board of Longitude were ludicrous, but the competition did foster the quadrant (1731) by John Hadley (1682–1744) and the series of sea clocks developed by John Harrison (1693–1776) that eventually took the prize. Refined versions of these **chronometers** proved highly effective in determining longitude during **Cook's** exploratory voyages to the Pacific, though it was not until 1818 that chronometers were fully adopted by the **navy**.

Further developments such as the refinement of the magnetic compass by Knight (1750s), Walker (1790s) and Phillips (1825), and the development by Foxon (1772) and Massey (1802) of mechanical logs to estimate a ship's speed, added precision to navigational methods. With improvements in **cartography** and the accurate charts published by the Admiralty Hydrographic Department from 1795, travel by sea was much safer in 1837 than it had been in 1714.

David J. Starkey

Bibliography

Cotter, C.H. *The Complete Coastal Navigator.* 1964.

Quill, H. *John Harrison, the Man Who Found Longitude.* 1966.

Stimson, A.N. *The Mariner's Astrolabe.* 1993.

Waters, D.W. *The Art of Navigation in England in Elizabethan and Early Stuart Times.* 1958.

Navigation Laws

A series of measures passed by Parliament and supplemented by Orders in Council, navigation laws were designed to enlarge **overseas commerce**, protect **shipbuilding**, extend **shipping**, promote the training of British **seamen**, and strengthen the British Empire. Based on the belief that national power derived from control of the sea, and originating as attempts to limit the Dutch carrying trade with England, these laws became part of the mercantilist system that set national economic policy and regulated trade from the 1650s to the 1820s.

The laws' basic provisions were set forth in Navigation and Trade Acts of 1650, 1651, 1660, 1662, 1663, and 1696. These (1) banned foreign traders from British colonial ports; (2) required that European products entering Britain be brought only in British ships or in those of the country producing (or first importing) the goods; and (3) required that Asian, African, and American products entering Britain or her colonies be brought only in British or colonial **ships** of which the master and the majority of the crew were British. "English ships with English crews" was the basic principle; British colony ports were barred to foreign ships, and a monopoly of intra-imperial shipping was secured for British and colonial interests.

Also, the carrying of certain specific items, known as "enumerated goods," was regulated with particular care; these could be carried only to Great Britain, whence the surplus might be sold (re-exported) to the Continent or elsewhere (customs duties then usually being refunded), English merchants reaping the extra profits. These goods included timber and naval stores from the Baltic; fruits, oils, and wines from the Mediterranean; and sugar, **tobacco**, rice, indigo, ginger, molasses, naval stores, and cotton wool from the American colonies. Colonial enumerated goods at first came chiefly from the islands, but by 1760 they had proliferated to include 63% of the total value of American colonial exports. However, if this was discriminatory, Americans benefited from the stipulation that European products bound for America had to be carried in British-built ships by crews that were predominantly British. One-third of British merchant ships were built in the American colonies by 1760.

Temporary exceptions to these elaborate restrictions might be made in wartime, but their routine enforcement, and imposition of the **taxes** (customs and excise duties) connected with them, aroused the opposition of American colonists and was an important cause of **smuggling** and other evasion of their provisions.

The coming of the **Industrial Revolution** promoted gradual but important modifications in these laws. Ships from the United States, and from Portuguese and Spanish possessions in South America, were allowed to transport materials from those areas to Great Britain. In the 1820s a policy of reciprocity with regard to imports and customs duties was adopted. Beginning in 1822, Britain gradually abandoned the concept of enumerated goods altogether and moved toward free trade.

Mark C. Herman

Bibliography

Dickerson, Oliver M. *The Navigation Acts and the American Revolution.* 1951; rpt. 1978.

Harper, Lawrence A. *The English Navigation Laws: A Seventeenth-Century Experiment in Social Engineering.* 1939; rpt. 1973.

Wilson, Charles. *England's Apprenticeship, 1603–1763.* 1965.

See also Empire and Imperialism

Navy

Hanoverian military, economic, and political power ultimately rested on the "wooden walls" of the Royal Navy. From modest Tudor beginnings, the navy emerged by 1815 as the unchallenged master of the oceans. During the Hanoverian period it grew considerably in size; between 1720 and 1783 alone, the number of ships of the line (i.e., great fighting ships, exclusive of frigates and lighter craft) grew from 124 to 174; the total number of **seamen** grew from around 20,000 to around 85,000; and the number of admirals grew from 6 to 57. Throughout the entire period also, except on a few disastrous occasions when the navy faced the combined French and Spanish fleets—as in the latter years of the **War of American Independence**—it was the largest naval force in the world. The navy was charged not only with defending Britain itself, and the worldwide system of British trade, but also with providing the leading thrust of Britain's offensive war-making capability. Britain's admirals—men such as **Anson**, **Hawke**, **Boscawen**, **Hood**, **Rodney**, and **Nelson**—were among the nation's greatest heroes; and many of her captains, such as **Cook**, **Vancouver**, and **Franklin**, were illustrious explorers as well.

Situated in Whitehall, a largely civilian Board of Admiralty, led by the First Lord of the Admiralty (generally a successful flag officer), oversaw all administrative and tactical operations. The Navy Board supervised **ship** construction, maintenance, supply, **dockyards**, and repair facilities. The 17th-century organization of the fleet into three squadrons—red (center), white (van), and blue (rear)—evolved in the 18th century into a much larger fleet divided into battle squadrons, each composed of three divisions—the van, center, and rear. A flag officer whose color indicated his seniority—red to white to blue in descending order—commanded each division.

British **shipbuilders** preferred to construct sound, seaworthy ships that relied on skillful handling and superior gunnery for battle effectiveness, whereas the French and Spanish, who usually built superior and often bigger vessels (envied by British commanders), typically sought constant improvements in naval architecture. Captured ships, commissioned into the navy, often served as models for improved British shipbuilding methods. Britain's addition of copper sheathing on hulls from the early 1760s (pioneered by the Welsh industrialist **Thomas Williams**) increased speed and gave a short-term advantage by preventing marine growth and shipworm damage.

Warships were classified by "rate," from first to sixth, depending on the number of guns. A "first rate ship-of-the-line" mounted 100 or more guns, carried on three gundecks. Only the top three rates (all with over 70 guns) formed the Line of Battle and were designated "ships." A typical first-rate ship required a crew of 800 officers, sailors, and marines. Frigates, brigs, and smaller vessels acted as cruisers, commerce raiders, and scouts.

Naval cannon was classified by the weight of the shot, with 32-pounders mounted on the lowest gun deck, 24-pounders on the second deck, and 18-pounders on the main or upperdeck. "Carronades" (from **Carron Company**), with wider bores firing heavier shots, were added (1799) to the forecastle and quarterdeck (highest decks fore and aft) for short-range engagements. The hazards of accidental powder explosions, which often accounted for 25% of battle casualties, were ameliorated by gradual safety improvements such as a flintlock firing system. The addition of block and tackle, and steel recoil springs, to hold a gun in position after firing, allowed for limited oblique fire. Due to constant drilling, a British crew could fire a round every 90 seconds—an extraordinary rate! During the **French Revolutionary and Napoleonic Wars**, Congreve rockets, with explosive charges in the nose, were shot off the main deck from chutes, though they did little damage.

Officers came from the **gentry** class, with many, like Nelson, the sons of clergymen. But commissions were not for sale in the navy (as they were in the **army**). For the lower classes, the opportunity to rise to warrant ranks such as masters, pursers, and gunners was open to men of talent, and in wartime there were even some (rare) promotions to commissioned officer. The most important element in officer promotion and posting was "interest," or **patronage**. Service "interest" meant assistance from high-ranking serving officers; political "interest" meant help from parliamentary or ministerial patrons.

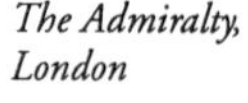

The Admiralty, London

The navy's greatest weaknesses, and the battle losses that marked the beginning of many wars, arose from the tendency of British politicians, worried about expenses, to let the navy disintegrate between wars; also, chronic political indifference to the pay and conditions of ordinary seamen was an additional weakening factor. In peacetime, there were enough volunteers to fill the navy's depleted ranks. In wartime, however, involuntary impressment, regarded as a necessary evil, was employed. This was limited legally to seamen between 18 and 45 years of age—presumably, merchant sailors and fishermen. Illegally, many "landsmen" were also impressed. Periodic quota acts, based on **population**, sought to assess cities and counties, which invariably resulted in the dumping of undesirables and outcasts into the navy. The scarcity of seamen typically resulted in the impressment of vagrants, debtors, fugitives, and felons. The establishment of the Impress Service in the late 18th century improved the effectiveness and quality of the pressed crews, and relieved ship captains of the responsibility for manning their vessels. The shilling-a-day pay attracted few volunteers, but in wartime the possibility of prize money, divided among commanders, officers, and crew, attracted many recruits.

Seamen had no official uniform until the 19th century. However, tradition dictated the wearing of a blue jacket, white trousers, and canvas hat (straw in summer). A black silk handkerchief was worn around the head during quarters (duty at battle stations). The crew was divided into divisions and placed under the administration of an officer charged with ensuring the men's health, welfare, and cleanliness. Sailors lived in eight-man "messes" and berthed between guns in hammocks strung from the overhead deck. Their food was laid out on large, suspended tables.

The food allowance of a pound of biscuit per day, four pounds of preserved meat, and a gallon of beer per week, was supplemented by peas, oatmeal, butter, and cheese as available. Lime or other citrus fruit juice, mixed with sugar and distributed daily, was intended to prevent diseases such as scurvy, ulcers, and fevers, though appalling losses from disease (much greater than those from battle injuries) were recorded throughout the period. Rum, spirits, and wine were thought to have a curative effect on the digestive and health problems caused by the poor sea diet, particularly in hot climates. After 1740, grog, or rum diluted with water, was a daily dole. Hand-operated bellows, called "ship's lungs," provided below-deck ventilation.

Basic tactical doctrine was laid down in the sets of "Fighting Instructions" issued periodically throughout the Hanoverian period. The *King's Regulations and Admiralty Instructions* (1731) provided the navy's permanent disciplinary code. Apart from the death penalty applied to cases of **mutiny**, the most severe corporal **punishment** was flogging, administered aboard a sailor's own ship, or "around the fleet" for severe infractions such as desertion. (Desertions occurred most frequently with experienced seamen rather than fresh recruits, and often followed a trip to hospital.) Commanders who enjoyed success and the admiration of their crews rarely experienced severe disciplinary problems, even among impressed men. The better-run ship became a sailor's home and family, engendering pride of association and thereby largely averting problems of discipline and morale.

Stanley D.M. Carpenter

Bibliography

Creswell, John. *British Admirals of the Eighteenth Century: Tactics in Battle.* 1972.

Dening, Greg. *Mr. Bligh's Bad Language: Passion, Power, and Theater on the* Bounty. 1992.

Fowler, William M., Jr. *Jack Tars and Commodores.* 1984.

Kennedy, Paul M. *The Rise and Fall of British Naval Mastery.* 1983.

Lewis, M. *The History of the British Navy.* 1957.

Lloyd, Christopher, ed. *The Health of Seamen.* 1965.

Marcus, G.J. *A Naval History of England.* 1971.

———. *Heart of Oak: A Survey of British Sea Power in the Georgian Era.* 1975.

Rediker, Marcus. *Between the Devil and the Deep Blue Sea: Merchant Seamen, Pirates, and the Anglo-American Maritime World, 1700–1750.* 1993.

Southworth, J.V.D. *The Age of Sails.* 1968.

Syrett, David, and R.L. DiNardo, eds. *The Commissioned Sea Officers of the Royal Navy, 1660–1815.* 1994.

See also War and Military Engagements

Neilson, James Beaumont (1792–1865)

Neilson, born near **Glasgow**, acquired engineering knowledge in apprenticeship to his elder brother, later supplementing this with classes at the **Andersonian Institution**. In his twenties he became foreman and then manager of the Glasgow Gas Works. A bright innovator, Neilson became involved in the search for ways to improve the performance of blast furnaces in the local iron industry. The critical breakthrough was his realization of the need to reverse the existing practice of cooling the blast. He patented his "hot-blast" idea in 1828. Although **patent** disputes dogged him later, the hot-blast was highly significant in the expansion of the British iron industry, and particularly influential in boosting **Scotland**'s prominence in it. Neilson's contribution was recognized by his election to a fellowship of the **Royal Society**.

R.D. Corrins

Bibliography

Harris, J.R. *The British Iron Industry, 1700–1850.* 1988.

Hyde, C.K. "The Adoption of the Hot Blast by the British Iron Industry: a Re-interpretation." *Explorations in Economic History.* Vol. 10, pp. 397–418.

See also Iron Industry; Metallurgy and Metalworking; Science, Technology, and Invention

Nelson, Horatio (1758–1805)

Nelson, his name inextricably connected with British victory in the **French Revolutionary and Napoleonic Wars**, was one of the nation's greatest naval commanders and military heroes.

Though born the fifth son of a humble clergyman, he enjoyed the influence of his uncle, Captain Maurice Suckling (Comptroller of the Navy, 1775–1778). Nelson began his naval career as a captain's servant on H.M.S. *Raisonnable* (1770) and rose quickly, serving in the East Indies, the Mediterranean, and the Caribbean. He held several posts during the **War of American Independence**, displaying exceptional tactical knowledge for a junior officer and also a tendency to disobey senior officers' orders. Characteristically, when sent after the war to patrol the Leeward Isles, he violated the station commander's order to permit American commerce to continue unhampered, and instead suppressed the trade and seized American vessels (1785).

The onset of renewed war with **France** (1793) brought him command of the 64-gun H.M.S. *Agamemnon* and service in Admiral **Hood**'s fleet patrolling the Mediterranean. During operations in Corsica Nelson took part in a marine assault (July 1794) that left him blinded in the right eye. However, his service brought promotion to Commodore and command of a small frigate squadron patrolling the Gulf of Genoa to disrupt French maritime commerce (1796). Nelson later claimed with characteristic bravado that had he been given sufficient forces, the French invasion of northern Italy might have been stopped.

With the strategic situation shifting, the British were forced to withdraw from the Mediterannean and take on a new enemy: Spain. During a confrontation with a Spanish fleet off Cape St. Vincent (14 February 1797), Nelson again exhibited that mixture of insubordination and improvisation that marked his genius. By departing from the line of battle without orders from his commander (Jervis), he managed to thwart a Spanish attack and turn what might have been a serious defeat into a British victory. The battle earned him a knighthood and promotion to Rear-Admiral.

A few months later (3 July 1797), while bombarding Cadiz, Nelson, standing in his launch, was narrowly saved from being killed in hand-to-hand fighting by his coxswain. A few weeks afterward, while personally leading a landing assault on Santa Cruz in an attempt to capture treasure ships in port, he received a bullet wound in his right elbow that necessitated the arm's amputation. Ever undaunted, he assumed command of the squadron covering Toulon. His ships blown off station by a gale, he failed to intercept the departing force carrying Napoleon's Egyptian Expedition troops (20 May 1798); but after deducing that the French had sailed for Egypt, Nelson made for Alexandria, where he surprised the enemy at anchor at Aboukir Bay (1 August 1798). Again revealing his genius, he devastated the French fleet by passing

Commodore Nelson in a desperate encounter, 1797

down their line on the shore side rather than on the seaward side as expected. This extraordinary action, which put an end to French hopes for Eastern conquest, earned him yet another promotion: Baron Nelson of the Nile and Burnham-Thorpe.

While in the Mediterranean, Nelson became romantically involved with Lady Emma Hamilton, wife of the British envoy to the King of Naples. Despite attempts to keep the affair secret, it cost Nelson his marriage, but not his career. Emma bore him a daughter, Horatia, shortly before he sailed on an expedition against the "Armed Neutrality" of Baltic states, in which he won still another remarkable victory at the Battle of Copenhagen (1 April 1801), again exhibiting "the Nelson touch" of courage, audacity, seamanship, and insubordination. As Nelson's ships entered the harbor, Sir Hyde Parker, his commander-in-chief, fearing the shore batteries' heavy fire, prudently signaled a withdrawal. Nelson, however, putting his telescope to his blind eye, declared he could see no signal and pressed on into the harbor, where he proceeded to demolish Danish fortifications. The incident enhanced the legend that already surrounded his name and led to another elevation: viscount.

With the renewal of war (May 1803) following the **Peace of Amiens**, Nelson returned to the Mediterranean as Commander-in-Chief aboard his flagship H.M.S. *Victory* with the mission of preventing the Toulon squadron from joining the Brest squadron in support of an invasion of Britain. When the French successfully departed Toulon, Nelson chased them to the **West Indies**, then back to Cadiz, Spain. Their unsuccessful attempt to elude him and sail to Brest resulted in the famous **Battle of Trafalgar** (21 October 1805), an action that insulated Britain against invasion, solidified Nelson's reputation as the country's greatest naval commander, and, thanks to a French sniper's bullets through his shoulder and chest, cost Nelson his life. Before expiring, and learning of the historic victory, he exclaimed, "Thank God, I have done my duty." His funeral at St. Paul's was the occasion of a great outpouring of **patriotic** national feeling.

Stanley D.M. Carpenter

Bibliography

Creswell, John. *British Admirals of the Eighteenth Century: Tactics in Battle.* 1972.
Howarth, David, and Stephen Howarth. *Lord Nelson.* 1989.
Lloyd, G. *Nelson and Sea-Power.* 1973.
Marcus, G.J. *A Naval History of England.* Vol. 2. 1971.
Oman, Carola. *Nelson.* 1946, 1970.
Syrett, David, and R.L. DiNardo, eds. *The Commissioned Sea Officers of the Royal Navy, 1660–1815.* 1994.
Terraine, J. *Trafalgar.* 1976.

See also Navy; War and Military Engagements

Neoclassical Style

Combining the revival of classical antiquity with both rationalism and refinement, the neoclassical movement dominated British art and **architecture** during the reign of **George III**. Although the defining term seems only to have gained currency in the late 19th century, and then with a negative connotation, it is now generally accepted as perhaps the most fitting characterization for the art of this era, more fitting perhaps than "Georgian style," not only in Britain but throughout Europe and in the new United States.

The neoclassical style was most evident in architecture. Arising partly from a growing fascination with archaeological remains in Italy, Greece, and Asia Minor, which British amateurs often helped to unearth, the new architectural approach combined a certain dissatisfaction with Renaissance forms with a new and stronger taste for elegance, refinement, and rationalism. As a result of various expeditions and publications such as those of Robert Wood (*Ruins of Palmyra,* 1753; *Ruins of Balbec,* 1757); James Stuart and Nicholas Revett (*Antiquities of Athens,* 1762–1816); Robert Adam (*Ruins of the Palace of the Emperor Diocletian at Spalatro in Dalmatia,* 1764); and Richard Chandler, Nicholas Revett, and William Pars (*Ionian Antiquities,* 1769–1797), architects were now able to seek out sources much more broadly through antiquity. They combined these with the existing Burlingtonian **Palladian style**, tempering it with delicacy, elegance, restraint, and a more rational symmetry. Inspired by exciting developments in Rome, three younger British architects, James Stuart (1713–1788), **Sir William Chambers**, and Robert **Adam**, developed this neoclassical style after their return to **London** in the last half of the 1750s. It flourished in country and townhouses, churches, and a wide range of public buildings until the end of the 18th century. In the 1780s and 1790s, as well as the early part of the 19th century, the style was modified toward stronger and more powerful forms in the work of George Dance the Younger (1741–1825), Sir John Soane (1753–1837), and others.

In **painting**, a related neoclassical style utilizing classical influence and details was characteristic of those artists who had **traveled** to Rome in the 1750s, especially Gavin Hamilton (1723–1798) and **Benjamin West** as well as **Allan Ramsay** and **Sir Joshua Reynolds**. But the term is often applied generically to most British painting of the latter 18th century, including the works of such artists as **Thomas Gainsborough**, whose refined and delicate style paralleled the spirit of Robert Adam's architecture.

In **sculpture**, the neoclassical taste was especially evident in the work of **John Flaxman**, though it was also characteristic of many of his contemporaries, including **Sir Francis Chantrey**. It was the dominant style in the decorative arts, a fact epitomized in the extremely popular jasperware of **Josiah Wedgwood**. Silver, ormolu (gilt bronze), **textiles**, and furniture all shared in this ethos, which was particularly manifested in the furniture designs of **George Hepplewhite** and **Thomas Sheraton**. The neoclassical style had its heyday during the last four decades of the 18th century, but left its mark on the whole extended image of late Hanoverian Britain.

In terms of literary form, the neoclassical model could suggest works on the **epic** scale of *Paradise Lost* (1667), but rather than compete with **Milton**, the age more generally preferred to treat classical genres (except the ode) analogically. In terms of subject, the idea that art embodies universal truth had favored since the 17th century the development of criticism as public instruction. Together, these tendencies fostered the satirical **mock-heroic** mode, seen for example in John Dryden's (1631–1700) *Mac Flecknoe* (1682). **Jonathan Swift** never worked directly in classical genres, but his ubiquitous classical references provide a standard against which to measure the specious modern values **satirized** in such works as *A Tale of a Tub* (1704) and *Gulliver's Travels* (1726). **Alexander Pope** used classical references similarly, for example in *The Dunciad* (1728–1742). **Henry Fielding** called *Tom Jones* (1749) a "comic epic in prose," suggesting, through reference to a form he did not use, the classical values that did inform his relatively new genre. Neoclassical authors often called on readers' knowledge of the classics in close "imitations" of specific works. For example, **Samuel Johnson**'s "London" (1738) juxtaposes an ironic view of contemporary vice and virtue with Juvenal's third satire (first century AD).

Neoclassical authors were often in fact somewhat ambivalent toward the ancient period, which they saw as their model, and against which they measured themselves. They seemed to acknowledge the impossibility—or modern arrogance—of attempting to improve on classical forms, but if they thought of themselves as pygmies building on the shoulders of giants, they nevertheless built. Their outlook was typified in **Edward Gibbon**'s *The Decline and Fall of the Roman Empire* (1776–1788), which at once venerates and anatomizes its subject.

Neoclassicism, despite its evocation of reason and control, had a markedly pessimistic streak, rooted perhaps in fear that refinement and imitation, even of Nature, were inadequate springs for originality, perhaps also in knowledge that antiquity's classical ideals had failed to prevent the decay of the ancient world. But if we do see in Gibbon's great history of the classical era an emblem of the neoclassical idea itself, we find, alongside scholarship that truly has been superseded, a style that is still powerful and aesthetically pleasing.

Damie Stillman
Richard N. Ramsey

Bibliography

Adam, Robert, and James Adam. *The Works in Architecture.* 1773–1779, 1822; rpt. 1976.

Arts Council of Great Britain. *The Age of Neo-Classicism.* 1972.

Bate, Walter Jackson. *The Burden of the Past and the English Poet.* 1970.

Bredvold, Louis I. "The Gloom of the Tory Satirists," in James L. Clifford and Louis A. Landa, eds., *Pope and His Contemporaries: Essays Presented to George Sherburn.* 1949.

Burke, Joseph. *English Art, 1714–1800.* 1976.

Honour, Hugh. *Neo-Classicism.* 1968.

Irwin, David. *English Neoclassical Art: Studies in Inspiration and Taste.* 1966.

Musgrave, Clifford. *Adam and Hepplewhite and Other Neo-Classical Furniture.* 1966.

Stillman, Damie. *English Neo-Classical Architecture.* 1988.

Summerson, John. *Architecture in Britain, 1530 to 1830.* 6th ed., 1977.

Thomson, J.A.K. *The Classical Background of English Literature.* 1948.

Waterhouse, Ellis K. *Painting in Britain, 1530 to 1790.* 4th ed., 1978.

Weinbrot, H.D. *Augustus Caesar in "Augustan" England: The Decline of a Classical Norm.* 1978.

See also Antiquities and Ruins; Augustan; Classicism; House-building and Housing

New Lanark

The building of this cotton factory village was begun in 1784 by **David Dale** to exploit the water power of the Falls of Clyde, near Lanark in **Scotland**, on land leased from **Robert Macqueen, Lord Braxfield** and from the Incorporation of Shoemakers in Lanark. **Richard Arkwright** was Dale's partner

New Lanark, 1820s

until his waterframe patent was quashed. Dale erected four mills by 1793, and provided housing nearby for over 200 families. The labor force consisted of highlanders and pauper apprentices mainly from the **Edinburgh** and **Glasgow** workhouses.

The **population** of nearly 1,800 people formed a healthy and happy community because Dale was concerned with providing them a good diet, hygienic accommodations, and proper education. He naturally acquired a reputation as an enlightened employer, and New Lanark was visited by about 3,000 people between 1795 and 1799.

In 1799 Dale sold the village to his son-in-law, **Robert Owen**, managing partner of the Chorlton Twist Company, and it was under Owen that New Lanark acquired its special reputation as a profitable but humanely managed enterprise. Owen ran the mills for two other partnerships between 1810 and 1825, and continued to make substantial profits. Yet he built a new school and an Institution for the Formation of Character, both intended to improve the lot of his workers and demonstrate his commitment to environmental psychology. Owen gradually withdrew his shares in New Lanark from 1824, and the Walkers, a **Quaker** family, assumed control. They continued to operate New Lanark profitably and humanely until 1881.

John Butt

Bibliography

Butt, John, ed. *Robert Owen, Prince of Cotton Spinners.* 1971.

Donnachie, Ian, and George Hewitt. *Historic New Lanark.* 1993.

McLaren, David J. *David Dale of New Lanark.* 1983.

Owen, Robert. *Life of Robert Owen by Himself.* Rpt., 1971.

See also Child Labor; Factory Movement and Factory Acts; Hours, Wages, and Working Conditions; Humanitarianism

New Poor Law (1834)

The rapid expansion of poor rates since the beginning of the 19th century was one of the factors influencing the **Whig** government's attitudes toward **poverty and poor laws** in 1832 when it established a commission to investigate the operation of the system of charitable relief. This commission, headed up by **Edwin Chadwick** and **Nassau Senior**, made recommendations that became the basis of the New Poor Law or Poor Law Amendment Act of 1834.

This revolutionary legislation consolidated over 15,000 units of the old parochial system into 643 unions, each with its own workhouse. "Impotent" paupers—children, the aged, sick, and insane—could continue to receive "outdoor" relief (without taking up residence in a workhouse), but "able-bodied" paupers, if they wanted assistance, were required to move into workhouses with living standards deliberately intended to be Spartan. Strict discipline, hard work, bland food, the absence of alcoholic **drink** and **tobacco**, and rigid separation of the sexes to minimize the still greater growth of a dependent pauper class, were all calculated to encourage the unemployed to seek work outside the workhouses rather than accept relief within them. Three new Poor Law Commissioners made national policy and imposed it on local authorities, reversing the old tradition of local poor relief inherited from the Elizabethan Poor Law and the **Speenhamland System**.

The new system of welfare, criticized as an abandonment of the traditional rights of the poor and as a heartless attack on the less fortunate, especially on children (most notably by Charles Dickens in his **novel** *Oliver Twist,* 1837–1838), was defended by reformers and many taxpayers of the new **middle classes**. Critics called attention to the suffering it caused; supporters responded that it actually reduced total suffering by removing incentives to dependence. Critics condemned it as uncharitable; supporters replied that it replaced an older system that was not, as its defenders believed, a public charity but rather a public evil which accustomed people to be dependent on the charity of others.

One-year extensions of the act in 1839 and 1840, and a 5-year continuation in 1842, prolonged its life. Its results are still debated. Within the first 5 years, poor rates did fall by £3 million and the percentage of paupers also declined, though some of this was attributable to good harvests and energetic railway-building. Historians believe that the law's impact was much less beneficial in the industrial north (where cyclical trade unemployment affected many more workers) than in the agrarian south. Its great unpopularity among industrial workers, along with that engendered by the **Reform Act** of 1832, encouraged popular support of Chartism.

David B. Mock

Bibliography

Blaug, Mark. "The Myth of the Old Poor Law and the Making of the New." *Journal of Economic History.* Vol. 23, pp. 151–184.

Digby, A. *The Poor Law in Nineteenth Century England and Wales.* 1982.

Himmelfarb, Gertrude. *The Idea of Poverty: England in the Early Industrial Age.* 1983.

See also Malthus, Thomas Robert; Scottish Poor Law

New South Wales

See Australia

New Zealand

The native Maori had arrived in New Zealand from eastern Polynesia by the 8th century. The first European contact came in 1642, when Abel Janszoon Tasman (1603–*c.* 1659) sailed from Batavia in the Dutch East Indies in search of Terra Australis Incognita. The next recorded contact was by **Captain Cook** on his first voyage (1769), when he spent 6 months charting the islands and studying the flora and fauna. He formed a favorable impression of the Maori, despite their warfare and cannibalism.

Cook introduced pigs, potatoes, and iron implements. His three visits were succeeded by those of Christian **missionaries**—**Methodist** and **Catholic** as well as Anglican—who

New Zealand

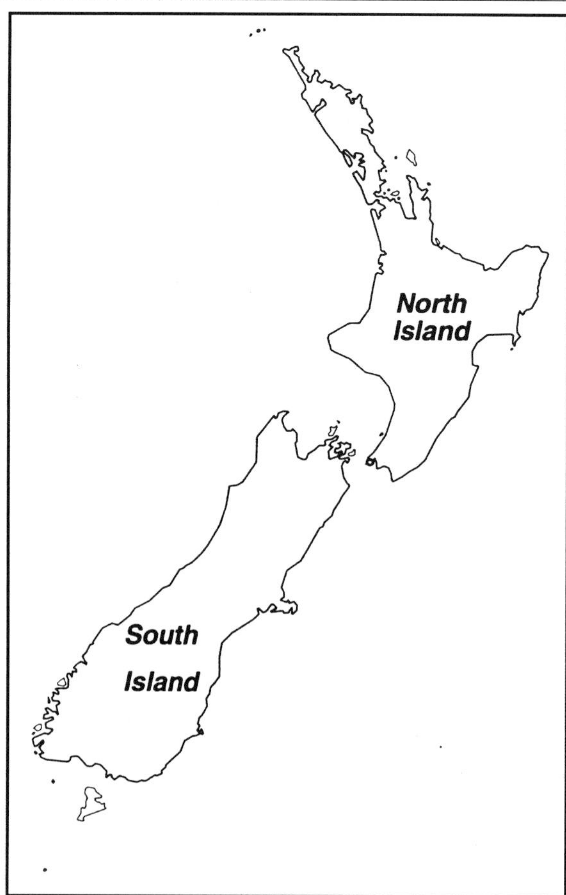

labored without much success to convert the natives. Whalers, sealers, and traders from **Australia** appeared, and gradually Australian companies, mainly whaling, built small trading and provisions bases on the coasts of the two main islands.

The visitors introduced guns, liquor, European disease, and new concepts such as prostitution. Maoris were recruited as sailors and laborers, and the newcomers traded for Maori products and ship's provisions. Potatoes soon replaced fernroot and kumara as staple crops.

The Maori adopted firearms with enthusiasm, employing them in their vendetta-ridden internecine warfare in which tens of thousands were slaughtered. So many others died of introduced disease that their cultural self-confidence was undermined. By the end of the 1830s they were converting en masse to Christianity, which they had formerly scorned as unseemly for warriors. The Maori were not conquered by Europeans but rather co-opted, first by technology and money, then by religion.

Their country was meanwhile becoming the object of British social thinkers intent on releasing domestic tensions by starting programs of systematic **emigration**. In 1839 **Edward Gibbon Wakefield**'s New Zealand Company sent out the first shipload of colonists, who joined the 2,000 non-natives already there. The British government then annexed New Zealand, primarily to protect Maori interests, in the Treaty of Waitangi (1840); this asserted the sovereignty of Queen Victoria, and was signed by more than 50 Maori chiefs. By 1856 there were 45,000 white settlers, many engaged in land wars with the natives.

N. Merrill Distad

Bibliography

Beaglehole, John Cawte. *The Discovery of New Zealand.* 2nd ed., 1961.

Sinclair, Keith. *A History of New Zealand.* 1959; 3rd ed., 1980.

———, ed. *The Oxford Illustrated History of New Zealand.* 1990.

Taylor, Nancy M., ed. *Early Travellers in New Zealand.* 1959.

Wright, Harrison M. *New Zealand, 1769–1840: Early Years of Western Contact.* 1959.

Newcastle, Duke of (Thomas Pelham-Holles) (1693–1768)

Despite the quirks that made him a figure of fun to some of his contemporaries, Thomas Pelham-Holles, 1st Duke of Newcastle, was a leader of the **Whig** Party for 20 years and an influential politician all his adult life. He was rarely out of office, being Lord Chamberlain (1717–1724), Secretary of State (1724–1754), and First Lord of the Treasury (1754–1756, 1757–1762). His power had three bases: the great landed estates he inherited, giving him control of seven and sometimes nine seats in the **House of Commons**; the political sagacity of his younger brother **Henry Pelham** (*d.* 1754); and Newcastle's understanding of, and ability to work with, **George II**.

Newcastle increased his power by working hard at his posts and by accumulating "friends," persons obliged to him for favors. His electoral activities also built up a network of **patronage** (which was strongest in Sussex). In 1736 **Sir Robert Walpole** gave Newcastle, a genuinely devout man, control of the government's ecclesiastical patronage; later, as head of the treasury, he gained control over even more appointments. But despite success he was emotionally insecure, and throughout his career relied on his friend Philip Yorke, 1st Earl of **Hardwicke**, for advice and support.

During the Pelham administration (1746–1754), Newcastle concentrated on foreign affairs, negotiating peace with **France** in 1748. At his brother's death he became chief minister, but was unable to maintain from his place in the **Lords** the tight control Pelham had exercised while sitting in Commons. After conflict in **North America** made another **war** with France inevitable, Newcastle was forced to exchange (1756) the Austrian alliance for one with Prussia in a **diplomatic revolution**.

Although **William Pitt the Elder** often is given credit for Britain's success in the **Seven Years' War**, the outcome rested on Newcastle's ability to raise the vast sums of money needed to finance the war. However, his indefatigable service never outweighed **George III**'s dislike of him, and Newcastle was pushed out of office along with many of his followers in the "purge of the Pelhamite Innocents" (1762).

P.J. Kulisheck

Bibliography

Browning, Reed. *The Duke of Newcastle.* 1975.

Clark, J.C.D. *The Dynamics of Change: The Crisis of the 1750s and English Party Systems.* 1982.

Kelch, Ray. *Newcastle: A Duke Without Money.* 1974.

O'Gorman, Frank. *Voters, Patrons, and Parties: The Unreformed Electoral System of Hanoverian England, 1734–1832.* 1989.

Owen, John B. *The Rise of the Pelhams.* 1957.

Sykes, Norman. "The Duke of Newcastle as Ecclesiastical Minister." *The English Historical Review.* Vol. 57, pp. 59–84.

See also Government, National

Newcomen, Thomas (1664–1729)

Famous for his work on the steam engine, Newcomen was born into a substantial **Baptist** family in Dartmouth, Devon. After serving an apprenticeship in engineering and business he entered into a partnership with John Calley, a glazier, and apparently went into ironmongering. Although the genesis of his invention is unclear, at some point he discovered that the atmospheric engine of Thomas Savery (1650?–1715), patented in 1698, did not operate effectively in **mines** flooded with water. In 1712 he constructed, for use at Dudley Castle, a beam engine, the first to employ a cylinder. The engine's piston worked up and down—by steam injection, then condensation, then injection. Although Savery died in 1715, his **patent** had been extended until 1733; but Newcomen and his associates were able to take advantage of its security by entering into an agreement with the patentees, and thus constructed engines as the "Committee of Proprietors of the Invention for Raising Water by Fire." By 1769 there were 100 Newcomen engines draining mines in the area. That was when **James Watt** became to Newcomen what Newcomen had been to Savery.

Larry Stewart

Newcomen's "Engine for Raising Water by Fire," 1717

Bibliography

Allen, John S. "Thomas Newcomen (1663/4–1729) and His Family." *Transactions of the Newcomen Society.* Vol. 51, pp. 11–24.

Hills, Richard L. *Power from Steam: A History of the Stationary Steam Engine.* 1989.

Rolt, L.T.C., and J.S. Allen. *The Steam Engine of Thomas Newcomen.* 1977.

Smith, Alan. "Steam and the City: The Committee of Proprietors of the Invention for Raising Water by Fire, 1715–1735." *Transactions of the Newcomen Society.* Vol. 49, pp. 5–20.

See also Science, Technology, and Invention; Steam Engines

Newfoundland

Newfoundland consists of the 43,359-square-mile triangular island at the eastern edge of the Gulf of St. Lawrence. It has a deeply indented coastline, and in the 18th century was heavily forested. In the Hanoverian period it was known for its seal grounds, but was even more important to the British **fishing** industry. West Country fishermen regularly worked its cod fisheries themselves, while rival fish merchants in **London** and **Bristol** hired resident settlers to make the catch.

Newfoundland became British under the Treaty of Utrecht (1713), though Frenchmen were allowed to continue drying fish on the north and eastern shores. The island was under the jurisdiction of the colony of Nova Scotia until 1729, then placed under the **navy**. French drying rights were diminished by the 1763 **Peace of Paris** (though French possession of Miguelon and St. Pierre off the south coast was granted), and following the **Treaty of Paris** (1783), American as well as French fishing privileges were acknowledged.

Britain, interested in preserving fishing for domestic markets, discouraged colonial settlement. Nevertheless, in 1824 Newfoundland was finally recognized by Parliament as a colony. In 1832, with a growing **population** of 50,000 (later swollen by Irish immigrants), it was granted representative government, and in 1855 responsible government. Newfoundland later annexed Labrador (1927) but did not join **Canada** until 1949.

Stuart R. Givens

Bibliography

Hiller, J.K. "Utrecht Revisited: The Origins of French Fishing Rights in Newfoundland Waters." *Newfoundland Studies.* Vol. 7(1), pp. 23–39.

Innis, Harold. *The Cod Fisheries: The History of an International Economy.* 1954.

McLintock, A.H. *The Establishment of Constitutional Government in Newfoundland, 1783–1832.* 1941.

Rose, J. Holland, et al., eds. *The Cambridge History of the British Empire.* Vol. VI: *Canada and Newfoundland.* 1930.

Newspaper Press

British papers of news began in the 17th century but came

partly of age in the 18th century. These papers began to flourish first in the **London coffeehouse**, an institution intended to meet the needs of the emerging commercial and professional classes. From the first English daily paper, the *Daily Courant* (1702–1735), to *The Times* (founded in 1785) and the Sunday *Observer* (founded in 1791), the daily and weekly press—in the provinces as well as the capital—carried accounts of current happenings while also helping powerfully to shape political thought and national ideas.

The growth of newspaper reading also reflects the development of communication throughout Britain. In 1690, nine weekly papers served the public; in 1709, one could count the *Courant* and 18 weeklies; during the reign of **George I**, London claimed three daily papers, six weeklies, and 10 tri-weeklies. By 1750, 7.5 million copies of newspapers were sold throughout England; that figure rose to 12 million in 1808. In 1800 alone, 278 newspapers and journals found their way to the reading public of London, while at least 150 English provincial newspapers came and went between 1700 and 1765.

By the 1780s, virtually all the sizable **cities** in the nation had at least one newspaper, and many had two or more. The most influential papers, however, were those of London. And whereas in the reigns of George I and **George II** politicians had often bribed or even routinely subsidized these newspapers to cast a particular political light on events, the reign of **George III** saw papers expanding in their general news coverage and often making some effort to conceal editorial biases in order to attract greater numbers of more sophisticated readers.

One of the leading London papers of George III's reign was the *Public Advertiser*, begun in 1752 as *The London Daily Post and General Advertiser*. It published news both domestic and foreign, political correspondence reflecting a range of opinion, commercial information and, as the title suggests, much advertising. Its accounts and those of other papers powerfully helped to condition national responses to many contemporary events. For example, the press, receiving accounts from special correspondents in the North American colonies and from sea captains engaged in Atlantic trade, published a wealth of information featuring the commercial value of the colonies, voicing warnings about the evil designs of the French and the unruly behavior of the Bostonians, and so on, thus conditioning the English in the early reign of George III to see little distinction between homeland and **Empire**, and to experience colonial unrest as deeply threatening to the fabric of English life itself. As regards America, many papers also exploited public interest in the **exotic** and in tales of blood and sex by supplying much information on American Indians, slaves, immigrants, convicts, "Natural Curiosities," and the like.

Rustics reading the news

The newspapers were also a venue of literary production. During the editorship (1758–1793) of Henry Sampson Woodfall (1739–1805) the *Advertiser* published such literary gems as the "Letters of **Junius**" (1769–1771) and **William Cowper**'s poem, "The Diverting History of John Gilpin" (1785). Another notable publisher, **Robert Dodsley**, founded in 1757 *The London Chronicle, or Universal Evening Post,* a thrice-weekly evening paper, which began free of advertising and political bias, included reports of corn and stock prices, carried regular marriage and death notices, and featured a literary section with book reviews. The introductory article in the first number (1 January 1757) by **Samuel Johnson** provides a perceptive account of the state of journalism at that date. Another important paper, *The Public Ledger*, founded in 1760 by John Newbery (1713–1767), came forth as a commercial daily, with its own advertisements and with abstracts of advertisements from rival papers, yet it also included domestic news, political **essays**, and **literary criticism** of some quality (it was, among other things, the vehicle of **Oliver Goldsmith**'s "Chinese Letters").

The 1760s saw growing complaints in connection with the activities of **John Wilkes**, over parliamentary restrictions on the right of the press to publish parliamentary proceedings. This right was finally granted in 1771, giving newspapers thereafter a firmer claim on political reporting and commentary. William Woodfall's (1746–1803) *Morning Chronicle* (1769–1862) became a mouthpiece of **Whig** politics, operating sometimes through James Perry's (1756–1821) efforts to gather a staff from among the liberal *literati* (contributors included **R.B. Sheridan**, **Charles Lamb**, **David Ricardo**, **Thomas Moore**, and **Thomas Campbell**). Another eminent paper, *The Morning Post* (1772–1937), began as a highly successful commercial paper less concerned with politics; under Daniel Stuart (1766–1846), the *Post* published pieces by **Robert Southey**, **Arthur Young**, and **William Wordsworth**. Its rival, *The Morning Herald and Daily Advertiser* (1780–1869), featured reports of police cases illustrated by **George Cruikshank**. *The Morning Advertiser* (1794–), founded by the Society of Licensed Victuallers of London, catered to economic and trading interests.

The launching of *The Times* must stand out as the principal journalistic event of the latter Hanoverian period. Beginning in 1785 as *The Daily Universal Register,* its name change occurred in 1788. By 1795, circulation stood at about 4,800 copies. Founded by John Walter (1739–1812), the paper included news, advertisements, essays, and correspondence; it employed **Henry Crabb Robinson** as a special correspondent to Germany and published pieces by **Leigh Hunt**. It was also one of the first London papers to provide extensive coverage of events outside the capital. It exhibited its objectivity and freedom from government control in its coverage of such events as the **Peterloo massacre** (1819), and was a steady supporter of moderately reformist causes until the end of the Hanoverian period. It was joined in this by the *Leeds Mercury,* taken over in 1801 by the liberal reformer Edward Baines (1774–1848), and the *Manchester Guardian,* founded in 1821 by John Taylor (1791–1844), both of which symbolized the growth of progressive provincial journalism and played important roles in the reform era 1828–1835.

Samuel J. Rogal

Bibliography

Crane, R.S., and F.B. Kaye. *A Census of British Newspapers and Periodicals, 1620–1800.* 1966.

Cranfield, G.A. *The Development of the Provincial Newspaper, 1700–1760.* 1962, 1978.

Harris, Robert. *A Patriot Press: National Politics and the London Press in the 1740s.* 1993.

Linton, David, and Ray Boston. *The Newspaper Press in Britain.* 1987.

Morison, Stanley. *The English Newspaper: Some Account of the Physical Development of Journals Printed in London between 1622 and the Present Day.* 1932.

Rudé, George. *Hanoverian London: 1714–1808.* 1971.

Smith, David Nicholl. "The Newspaper," in A.S. Turberville, ed., *Johnson's England.* Vol. 2. 1933.

Tercentenary Handlist of English and Welsh Newspapers, Magazines, and Reviews. 1920.

Wiles, Roy M. *Freshest Advice: Early Provincial Newspapers in England.* 1965.

See also Censorship; Journalists and Journalism; Laws of Public Worship, Speech, and the Press; Periodicals

Newton, John (1725–1807)

The life of Newton—**slave trader**, Anglican clergyman, and hymn-writer—reveals much about the rise of **Evangelicalism**. He spent the better part of his early life at sea. In 1743 he entered the service of a slaver bound for Sierra Leone. Having, as he later said, lost all sense of morality and religion, he experienced a dramatic religious conversion when he was nearly drowned in a storm (1748). Newton later bitterly repented the fact that he then made three more slave-trading voyages to **Africa**, though he did make some effort to repress swearing and profligacy, and to encourage religious exercises by the crew. After becoming ill in 1754 he gave up the sea, met the charismatic preachers **Whitefield** and **Wesley**, and, after some indecision about whether to become an Anglican or **dissenting** clergyman, began preparing for the cloth. He educated himself in Greek, Hebrew, and theology, was ordained priest (1764), took up a curacy at Olney, and simultaneously published an account of his seafaring and religious experiences.

Newton became a close friend of the poet **William Cowper**, who collaborated with him on a book of hymns; one of these was "Amazing Grace," whose sincerity and intensity convey something of the man. An effective preacher, he became rector of St. Mary Woolnoth in **London** (1779), one of the earliest Evangelical ministers to work there. He became a friend of **William Wilberforce** and assisted him in his campaigns against the abolition of the **slave trade**. Newton's *Thoughts upon the African Slave Trade* (1788), based on his personal experiences, an eye-opening recital of the trade's horrors, became an important part of this effort.

Richard M. Riss

Bibliography

Cropper, Margaret. *Sparks among the Stubble.* 1955.

Demaray, Donald E. *The Innovation of John Newton (1725–1807): Synergism of Word and Music in Eighteenth-Century Evangelism.* 1988.

Martin, Bernard. *John Newton: A Biography.* 1950.

Pollock, John Charles. *Amazing Grace: John Newton's Story.* 1981.

See also Music, Church

Nichols, John (1745–1826)

Like many 18th-century printers and publishers, Nichols had literary, historical and **antiquarian** interests. He edited the important monthly, the *Gentleman's Magazine,* from 1778 until his death, and produced numerous collections and editions that preserved valuable archival material. At age 12 he was apprenticed to printer William Bowyer the younger (1699–1777), became his partner in 1766, and in 1777 his heir. He edited works by **Jonathan Swift**, William King (1663–1712), **Francis Atterbury**, and Leonard Welsted (1688–1747), as well as **Richard Steele**'s correspondence and *The Tatler.* He printed **Samuel Johnson**'s *Lives of the English Poets* (1779–1781), and provided Johnson with biographical information; he also contributed to the revision of Alexander Chalmers's (1759–1834) *Biographical Dictionary* (1784 and 1812–1817).

Nichols's *Biographical Anecdotes of Mr. Hogarth* appeared in 1781 and *Biographical and Literary Anecdotes of William Bowyer* in 1782. His *Progresses and Public Processions of Queen Elizabeth, Illustrated with Historical Notes* (4 volumes, 1788–1821) preserved useful historical material. His own *History and Antiquities of the Town and County of Leicester* (8 volumes, 1795–1815) involved him in considerable financial loss, compounded by a disastrous fire at his printing office in 1808. His *Literary Anecdotes of the Eighteenth Century* (9 volumes, 1812–1815) and *Illustrations of the Literary History of the Eighteenth Century* (6 volumes, 1817–1831; volumes 7 and 8 added by John Bowyer Nichols, 1848, 1858) are still valuable to scholars. Nichols also produced a major anthology conserving mid-18th-century taste in *A Select Collection of Miscellaneous Poems* (volumes 1–4, 1780; volumes 5–8, 1782).

Phyllis J. Guskin

Bibliography

Nichols, John. *Minor Lives.* Ed. and introd. by Edward L. Hart. 1971.

See also Publishers and Booksellers; Reference Works

Nonconformists

See Dissenters

Nonjurors

Clergy and laymen of the **Church of England** became nonjurors when they refused to take the oaths of Supremacy and Allegiance, as set forth in the Bill of Rights and the Toleration Act (both 1689). The offensive passage read, "I . . . do sincerely promise and swear that I will be faithful and bear true allegiance to their majesties King William and Queen Mary. So help me God." Nonjurors maintained that to swear this oath would void their earlier oaths to King James II and to his exiled successors. They saw William of Orange as a pretender to the Crown, and they also based their position on the spiritual independence of the church.

The original nonjurors included the Archbishop of Canterbury, William Sancroft (1617–1693), and nine bishops: Thomas Ken (1637–1711), of Bath and Wells; John Lake (1624–1689), Chichester; Francis Turner (1638?–1700), Ely; Thomas White (1628–1698), Peterborough; Robert Frampton (1622–1708), Gloucester; William Lloyd (1637–1710), Norwich; William Thomas (1613–1689), Worcester; and Thomas Cartwright (1634–1689), Chester. Although conceding that William and Mary should retain their crowns, the bishops would neither attend their sovereigns nor include state prayers in their services. For this they were suspended in 1689, and in 1690 they were deprived of their sees; in 1691, William consecrated new bishops to replace them.

The unhappy nonjurors, thus alienated from the Establishment, condemned the new archbishop John Tillotson (1630–1694) and his bishops as intruders who occupied sees not canonically vacated. In 1694 they consecrated the former dean of Worcester, George Hickes (1642–1715), as titular Bishop of Thetford, and he rose to become their leader. Hickes, in turn, consecrated three bishops in 1713. A nonjuring tradition lived on into the Hanoverian period. One of its strongest early defenders was **Charles Leslie**.

In his comedy *The Non-Juror* (1717; dedicated to **King George I**), **Colley Cibber** included a prologue by Nicholas Rowe (1674–1718) that ridiculed the nonjurors' intransigence:

> Like bawds, each lurking pastor seeks the dark,
> And fears the Justice's enquiring clerk.
> In close back rooms his routed flocks he rallies,
> And reigns the patriarch of blind lanes and allies.
> There safe, he lets his thundering censures fly,
> Unchristians, damns us, gives our laws the lie
> And excommunicates three-stories high.

The nonjurors' "war" with the Established Church declined as time passed. By the late 18th century the tradition had nearly disappeared.

Samuel J. Rogal

Bibliography

Broxap, Harold. *The Later Nonjurors.* 1924.
Lathbury, Thomas. *History of the Nonjurors.* 1845.
Livingstone, Elizabeth A. *The Concise Oxford Dictionary of the Christian Church.* 1977.
Overton, John H. *The Nonjurors.* 1902.
Sykes, Norman. *Church and State in England in the Eighteenth Century.* 1934.
———. *From Sheldon to Secker: Aspects of English Church History, 1660–1768.* 1959.

Nootka Sound Controversy (1790)

This dispute was between Britain and Spain over territorial rights on the Pacific coast of northwestern **North America**. The point of contact was Nootka Sound, at 49° 40′ N. Lat. on the rugged west coast of Vancouver Island.

Although both Spanish and British explorers had sailed along the Pacific Northwest, it was not until the arrival of **Captain Cook** (1778) that any landed. He put in at Nootka Sound, claimed the area for Britain, and traded with the Indians, obtaining seal and sea otter furs that were later sold in China at great profit.

Included in Cook's party was John Meares (1756–1809), who 11 years later returned to establish a fur business. This trade and that of the Russians in Alaska led Spain in 1789 to dispatch Estevan José Martinez to establish a settlement at Nootka Sound and assert's Spain ancient claim to the entire northwest coast, founded on the papal Treaty of Tordesillas (1493). Martinez's seizure of Meares's vessels and goods led to a British threat of **war** and demands that Spain surrender exclusive-ownership claims to the region. Spain yielded by signing the Nootka Sound Convention (28 October 1790). Ultimately, this made possible the expansion of **Canada** to the Pacific.

Stuart R. Givens

Bibliography

Manning, W.R. "The Nootka Sound Controversy." *Annual Reports of the American Historical Association.* 1904.
Ricard, T.A. *Historic Backgrounds of British Columbia.* 1948.
Tovell, Freeman M. "The Other Side of the Coin: The Viceroy Bodega y Quadra, Vancouver, and the Nootka Crisis." *B.C. Studies.* Vol. 93, pp. 3–29.

See also Foreign Relations; Vancouver, George

North, Frederick, Lord (1732–1792)

It was North's misfortune to be Prime Minister during the **American Revolution** and **War of American Independence**. Educated at Eton and Oxford, he entered Parliament at age

Lord North

22 as a protégé of the **Duke of Newcastle**. He was appointed Lord of the Treasury (1759) and continued in that office in the 1760s under the administrations of **Bute** and **George Grenville**. He became Chancellor of the Exchequer on the death of **Charles Townshend** in 1767. In 1770 he replaced **Grafton** as First Minister to the king.

North opened his administration with the repeal of the Townshend Duties of 1767 (excepting that on tea), a step that temporarily reduced transatlantic tensions. But his more fundamental problems—to reduce the national debt and to redefine the nature of the imperial relationship—remained unresolved, and with the passage of the **Tea Act** of 1773, colonial **radicals** resumed their campaign of defying authority and destroying property in the **Boston Tea Party** (1773). North, an affable but indecisive leader, himself uncertain about how to deal with the radicals (and underestimating their determination) but sensitive to **George III**'s conviction that compromise would mean imperial collapse, supported passage of the Coercive Acts (1774), punishing Massachusetts and attempting to regain control there.

His subsequent efforts to find a balance between firmness and conciliation failed to prevent rebellion, leaving him with the task of conducting a war he neither fully understood nor firmly supported. As it dragged on he became increasingly discouraged, continuing in office only because the king begged him to. News of the disastrous surrender at **Yorktown** (1781) convinced him that victory was impossible, and in March 1782 he resigned the position he had held for 12 difficult years.

Yet in April 1783 he entered into an extraordinary coalition with **Charles James Fox**, his nemesis throughout the war, briefly becoming Secretary of State until this very unpopular **Fox–North Coalition** collapsed in December. North opposed young **Pitt** but retired from politics 3 years later and became 2nd Earl of Guildford in 1790.

David Sloan

Bibliography

Butterfield, Herbert. *George III, Lord North, and the People, 1779–1780.* 1949.
Christie, Ian. *The End of North's Ministry, 1780–1782.* 1958.
Donne, W. Bodham, ed. *The Correspondence of King George the Third with Lord North 1768 to 1783.* 1971.
Smith, Charles Daniel. *The Early Career of Lord North.* 1979.
Thomas, P.D.G. *Lord North.* 1976.
Valentine, Alan. *Lord North.* 1967.

North America

When the Hanoverian era began (1714), North America was in the hands of three European powers and of the Native Americans (Indians) living there. Spain held bases in Florida and the Southwest. **France** controlled the interior—the St. Lawrence Valley, the Great Lakes, and the length of the Mississippi River. The English controlled Hudson's Bay and an 1,800-mile strip of the eastern seaboard between present-day Canada and Florida, flanked narrowly on the west by the Appalachian Mountains.

The colony of Virginia began with the founding of Jamestown (1607) by a **joint-stock company**, and became a royal colony in 1624. Such sponsorship also lay behind the Puritan founding of Plymouth (1620) and Massachusetts Bay (1630). New Englanders established Rhode Island (1636) and Connecticut (1637). New Hampshire began as a privately chartered proprietorship, but became a royal colony (1679). The Crown consolidated Plymouth, Massachusetts Bay, and Maine into the royal colony of Massachusetts in 1691. In 1624, the Dutch settled New York, but the English took control in 1664 under the proprietorship of James, Duke of York (afterward King James II, 1633–1701), who also controlled Jersey and Delaware, which he granted to his supporters in 1664 and 1682 respectively. The remaining colonies were proprietorships: Maryland (1634), Carolina (1663), Pennsylvania (1681), and Georgia (1733). Three became royal colonies: South Carolina (1619), North Carolina (1629), and Georgia (1753).

The **population** of British North America burgeoned from 275,000 in 1700 to over 2 million by 1770. In 1770, Englishmen represented a little less than half the total, with Scots and Scots–Irish accounting for a little more than a tenth; thus three colonists in five were British. One in five was of African descent, with the remainder coming from Continental Europe, Germans leading the way.

To Europeans, North America represented both escape and opportunity. Dutch traders and farmers settled the Hudson River valley in the 1620s. Religious **wars** drove waves of German farmers to Pennsylvania in the 1680s. Huguenots came after 1685, establishing themselves in cities as **merchants** and artisans; a small number of Jews did the same. Irish,

North America

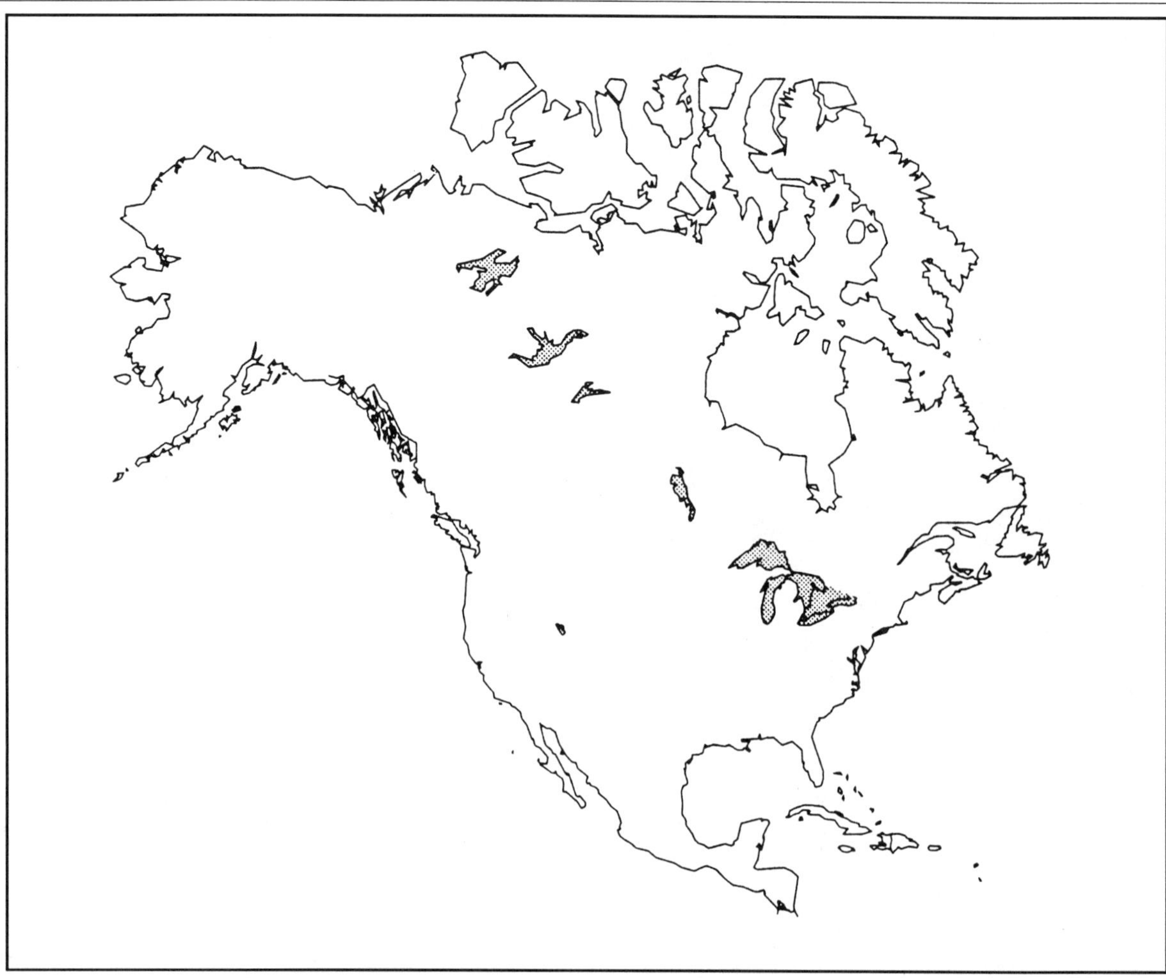

Scots–Irish, and Scots fleeing English pressure began arriving in the 1710s, and in larger numbers after 1763. The Scots–Irish headed for Pennsylvania and, along with many Germans, migrated south to settle in the Carolina backcountry. Only about 10% of all African slaves ended up in North America; most slaves were sent to the **West Indies**. They toiled on Southern **tobacco**, rice, and indigo plantations, but artisans and merchants in cities to the north utilized slaves as well. The **slave trade** in North America began to grow in the late 17th century and accelerated in the middle decades of the 18th century. Rich and respected colonial planters—for example, **George Washington**—owned slaves, but many, like him, took reasonably good care of them. Washington fed and clothed his slaves well, had their health looked after, and refused to sell them. On the other hand, **James Oglethorpe**, when founding Georgia, banned slavery altogether.

Congregational churches flourished in New England, whereas the **Church of England** exerted most influence in Virginia and Maryland. The middle colonies contained the greatest number of non–English Europeans and the greatest range of Protestant denominations, including **Quakers**, Lutherans, Dunkards, and Moravians. The **Presbyterian Church** arrived with the Scots–Irish. By the 1730s, colonists began to fear they did not have the faith of their fathers and found themselves moving westward without religious leadership. A wave of revivals, the "Great Awakening," emphasized emotional conversions and individual policing of one's relationship with God, rather than deference to traditional church leaders. With this increased emphasis on personal faith and discipline, religious toleration and a more egalitarian spirit spread.

In many ways, British North America was an experimental laboratory for home-based British philanthropists, evangelists, and traders such as Oglethorpe, **George Whitefield**, and **John Loudon McAdam**. Some colonials, such as **Benjamin Franklin**, were respected in Britain and on the Continent as much as at home on the western fringe of the **Empire**. But mercantilist **economic thought** dictated that the colonies existed to benefit the mother country, and the **navigation laws** of the 17th century were designed to ensure that they did. The northern colonies exported fish, furs, and timber; the middle colonies exported meat, grain, and flour; the Chesapeake colonies exported tobacco; and the colonies of the lower south exported rice and indigo. Nearly half of the colonies' exports found their way to the West Indies, southern Europe, and Africa. Before the 18th century, the colonies were too small and poor to import many goods, but this changed after 1700. By the 1770s the colonies received about a third of England's exports. The bulk of goods consumed were **textiles**, followed by metal tools and housewares. But colonists disliked the unfavorable trade balance, and preferred selling their produce in the non–English West Indies. **Smuggling** became common even among respectable social elements, who thus routinely broke the law long before fundamental constitutional questions rose to the surface. England attempted to administer the colonies through the Board of Trade and Plantations, and the office of the Secretary of State of the Southern Department, but with its attention focused elsewhere, the government failed to enforce its own regulations.

During the wars of the period 1690–1748, England commanded the colonists to make war, too, but did not supply much aid. War in the colonies consisted mostly of small engagements. It was the **Seven Years' War** that brought large numbers of British regulars and colonists together for the first time. Though fighting on the same side, the impressions received were often unfavorable, the British officers viewing the colonists as rabble, the colonists viewing the British commanders as martinets. Still, the colonists rejoiced that the **Peace of Paris** (1763) removed **France** from the scene, expecting to see their own settlements spread into the western wilderness. But with the accession of **George III** (1760), the doubling of England's colonial territory, a colossal war debt, and a Native American revolt at Detroit, English policy shifted toward stricter control and a new tax policy designed to make colonists pay for the troops and bureaucracy needed to control a North American empire. The **Proclamation of 1763**, **Plantation Act** (1764), and **Stamp Act** (1765), together with colonial resistance to them, became the first steps leading to the **American Revolution** and subsequent **War of American Independence**.

The colonial willingness to fight over political principles had been historically strengthened not only by official neglect but by long experience within the colonial assemblies of an unusual measure of popular control. These assemblies, like the **House of Commons** itself, had many powers, including the power to levy taxes. But the relative weakness of the executive arm of government, represented by royally appointed colonial governors, and the more democratic makeup of the assemblies (a high proportion of colonists owned land and voted), meant that the assemblies actually did represent a broad spectrum of the population. More ominous still, they accepted **John Locke**'s contract theory of government, and contemporary English **radicalism**'s extremely hostile portrayal of the corruption of the metropolitan government. When the English moved to enforce policy and tax the colonists directly, they stood upon their tradition of self-government and revolted.

During the war (1775–1783), loyalists accounted for a quarter of the colonial population. They were often from urban areas, or were government officials or large landowners, although loyalists did exist at all levels of society. About 50,000 loyalists joined the imperial forces, many fought in local actions, while others lay low. After the war, following land confiscations, nearly 100,000 loyalists left the American colonies, some for the West Indies, others for England, but most for Canada, which now became the only sizable remaining constituent of British North America. Many loyalists returned to America later, when attitudes toward them relaxed.

In the years that followed, the new United States attempted to remain neutral in the Anglo–French conflict of 1793–1815, but went to war with England in the **War of 1812**. However, each side realized that the other might be an important trading partner and ally, and commerce between the two countries enriched both during the 19th century. Another legacy of the rupture was Britain's new wariness of establishing more colonies of Englishmen abroad, which, it was assumed, would only break away ultimately as the Americans had done. That, and world shortages of uninhabited real estate, led the later Hanoverians to redirect energies toward **Australia** and still more toward **India**.

Kim M. Gruenwald

Bibliography

Anderson, Fred. *A People's Army: Massachusetts Soldiers and Society in the Seven Years' War.* 1984.

Bailyn, Bernard. *The Ideological Origins of the American Revolution.* 1967.

———. *The Peopling of British North America: An Introduction.* 1986.

Bonomi, Patricia U. *Under the Cope of Heaven: Religion, Society and Politics in Colonial America.* 1986.

Greene, Jack P. *Pursuits of Happiness: The Social Development of Early Modern British Colonies and the Formation of American Culture.* 1988.

Kulikoff, Allan. *Tobacco and Slaves: The Development of Southern Cultures in the Chesapeake, 1680–1800.* 1986.

McCusker, John J., and Russell Menard. *The Economy of British North America, 1607–1789.* 1985.

Nash, Gary B. *Red, White & Black: The Peoples of Early North America.* 1992.

Smith, Paul H. *Loyalists and Redcoats: A Study in British Revolutionary Politics.* 1964.

Spivak, Burton. *Jefferson's English Crisis: Commerce, the Embargo, and the Republican Revolution.* 1979.

See also Canada; Quebec

North West Company

France's expulsion from North America (1763) after the **Seven Years' War** left the extensive French fur-trading operations uncertain. In opposition to the legal monopoly of the **Hudson's Bay Company** a group of Montreal-based Canadians, Scots-born Simon McTavish and Yorkshire-born Joseph and Benjamin Frobisher, formed the North West Company (1783), which employed the experienced French *voyageurs* and aggressively pressed its operations into the interior wilderness. The "Montrealers" not only worked the entire central region of lakes Superior and Winnipeg but forged westward, establishing posts even in the areas of present-day Washington and Idaho states. They prospered from the high fur prices brought by production of **hats** and other **clothing**.

Yet the company's loose structure created problems. The latter 1790s saw several partners withdraw and create a "New North West Company." Although the two reunited after McTavish's death (1804), the Montrealers now faced intensifying competition from the Hudson's Bay Company, which, worried by the spread of the Canadian company, reformed its administration and practices. Open conflict ignited in 1816, the Nor'Westers breaking up **Lord Selkirk**'s Red River Settlement and the Hudson's Bay men retaliating by destroying Fort Gibraltar (both near modern Winnipeg). The British government then forced a merger under the name and charter of the Hudson's Bay Company (1821), putting an end to its rival.

Patricia S. Collins

Bibliography

Innis, H.A. *The Fur Trade in Canada.* 1956.

Reid, W. Stanford, ed. *The Scottish Tradition in Canada.* 1976.

Rich, E.E. *The History of the Hudson's Bay Company.* 1959.

Norwich

In 1714, the city of Norwich in the county of Norfolk was the second largest city in Britain. Its prosperity rested on a cloth trade that was in the course of the 18th century eclipsed by the expanding manufacturing power of the industrial **cities**, and Norwich increasingly became a regional rather than a national commercial and cultural center.

Norwich, with a **population** of perhaps 30,000 in 1700, was then the largest **provincial town**. Yet it scarcely grew at all, as its population at the time of the 1801 census was slightly less than 37,000. The city's preeminence, both demographically and economically, was lost first to **Bristol**, then to the new manufacturing centers of **Liverpool**, **Manchester**, and **Birmingham**. Its eclipse was not complete, however, and it remained a **textile** center as well as a regional trade center throughout the 18th century and beyond. The **worsted** weaving manufacture of "Norwich stuffs" continued, though the industry entered into difficulties in the late 18th century, owing to the disruption of markets and competition from the Yorkshire industry.

The troubles of the textile industry contributed to the general political agitation of the 1790s. Although the **borough** corporation was closed and generally conservative, a wide municipal franchise meant that Norwich's urban political life had a distinctly popular bent. Yet the role of Norwich politics as a barometer of a wider public opinion faded with the city's increasing drift to the margins of economic life, and Norwich settled into a comfortable place as regional and cultural center.

Daniel Statt

Bibliography

Borsay, Peter. *The English Urban Renaissance.* 1989.

Corfield, P.J. *The Impact of English Towns, 1700–1800.* 1982.

Girouard, Mark. *The English Town: A History of Urban Life.* 1990.

Novel

The emergence of the English novel as a form distinct from other types of narrative was largely a Hanoverian phenomenon; by 1837 the conventions that came to govern it were firmly and finally in place. Although explanations have been offered to account for "the rise of the novel," linking its emergence to the rise of the bourgeoisie and the growth of the reading public, even to epistemological changes that had taken place in the 17th century, no explanation is entirely convincing.

There were a number of precursors of the novel, such as novellae, Romances, picaresque tales, Cervantes's *Don Quixote,* and **travel books**. What appears to have been distinctive about the new form was its avowed "realism," its determination to "copy nature" instead of allowing imagination free rein. "The Romance is an heroic fable, which treats of fabulous persons and things," **Clara Reeve** explained: "The Novel is a picture of real life and manners, and of the times in which it is written."

Traditional histories of the novel tend to focus on the five "great" 18th-century writers whose works are thought principally to have influenced its development, **Daniel Defoe**, **Samuel Richardson**, **Henry Fielding**, **Tobias Smollett**, and **Laurence Sterne**, before leaping forward to the fully-fledged novels of **Jane Austen** and **Sir Walter Scott**. But this can give a distorted picture. In fact, of prose fiction first published in the early 18th century, the following three very different works outsold all others:

1. Defoe's *Robinson Crusoe* (1719) is the archetypal tale of a castaway on a desert island. Informed by travelers' tales as well as Puritan spiritual **autobiography**, it is a curious hybrid—as are all Defoe's other narratives. *Moll Flanders* (1722) and *Roxana* (1724), for instance, marry the conventions of the picaresque with those of Puritan literature, whereas *A Journal of the Plague Year* (1722) masquerades as a true account of the events of 1665 to offer both spiritual and practical guidance at a time when the plague had once again broken out on the Continent.
2. *Love in Excess* (1719–1720), by **Eliza Haywood**, differs markedly from Defoe's "novels." Haywood's characters are little more than types lifted from Restoration theater, while the form of her story—full of passionate intrigue until the obligatory happy ending—is a cross between French Romance and a *chronique scandaleuse.* It differs from Haywood's later works, such as *The History of Betsy Thoughtless* (1751), in that it looks back to earlier forms of prose fiction rather than to future developments.
3. Included in 18th-century lists of novels, *Gulliver's Travels* (1726) by **Jonathan Swift** is usually classified as a prose **satire** and not a novel. Essentially a spurious traveler's tale in which Gulliver, the first-person narrator, journeys to several "remote nations" in order to satirize contemporary British (and European) society, *Gulliver's Travels* remains outside the mainstream of the form's development.

There were other popular writers of prose fiction contemporary with Defoe, Haywood, and Swift, but it was only in the 1740s that new, distinctive voices began writing, and theorizing, about the novel.

Richardson's *Pamela* (1740) introduced a new method of "writing to the moment" through a narrative made up of **letters**. Epistolary novels were to be in vogue throughout the rest of the 18th century both in Britain and on the Continent. Although the plot retains aspects of the fairy tale—the virtuous virgin threatened by her dangerous but attractive master whom she marries in the end—*Pamela* influenced the new fashion in sentimental literature as well as anticipating elements of the **Gothic**. Richardson's next novel, *Clarissa* (1747–1748), was a much more rounded work, with multiple narrators offering multiple viewpoints on events.

Fielding also claimed to have invented a "new species of writing" while linking *Joseph Andrews* (1742) and *Tom Jones* (1749) to the classical **epic**. He insisted that his fictions were in fact "true histories," vehicles for moral instruction, rather than old-fashioned romantic narratives. The characteristic tone of these novels is one of massive irony, controlled by a third-person narrator who remorselessly and self-consciously manipulates the reader for satiric effect as Fielding's complex plots unfold.

Richardson and Fielding had many imitators, as did Sterne, whose *Life and Opinions of Tristram Shandy, Gentleman* (1760–1767) became an instant bestseller on the appearance of the first two volumes in 1760. The seeming inability of Sterne's first-person narrator to keep his narrative under control is at the heart of the novel's success, and has led to comparisons with modern stream-of-consciousness techniques. Sterne wrote within the newly fashionable sentimental vein, yet his own artistic concerns were firmly rooted in an earlier tradition of "learned **wit**," and he regarded himself as the heir of a satiric tradition leading back not only to the Scriblerian satirists, but beyond to Robert Burton, Cervantes, and Lucian.

The cult of **sensibility** (which Austen satirized in *Sense and Sensibility*, 1811) markedly influenced the novel, as well as **poetry** and drama. Both **Oliver Goldsmith** in *The Vicar of Wakefield* (1766) and Smollett in *The Expedition of Humphry Clinker* (1771) exploited its central concepts for comic effect. However, perhaps the most typical sentimental novel is *The Man of Feeling* (1771), by **Henry Mackenzie**, in which the central character is introduced "into different Scenes where his Feelings might be seen in their Effects."

Linked to the sentimental in various ways was the Gothic novel (also satirized by Austen in *Northanger Abbey*, 1818). *The Castle of Otranto* (1764), by **Horace Walpole**, effectively subverted the novel's claim to be a realistic medium, different from the old Romance. In the Preface to the second edition, Walpole argued that, in modern prose fiction, "the great resources of fancy have been dammed up, by a strict adherence to common life." He wanted instead "to blend the two kinds of romance, the ancient and modern." His contribution to the novel's development reintroduced elements of the **supernatural**. Some novels, such as *Frankenstein* (1818) by **Mary Wollstonecraft Shelley**, and *Melmoth the Wanderer* (1820) by **Charles Maturin**, followed Walpole's lead; while others, *The Mysteries of Udolfo* (1794) by **Ann Radcliffe**, for instance, exploited the appeal of the supernatural in the course of the narrative before providing a resolution that offered a natural explanation for an apparently inexplicable series of events.

The **French Revolution** supplied the stimulus for novels like **William Godwin**'s *Things as They Are; or The Adventures of Caleb Williams* (1794), which probed the ideological bases of Hanoverian society; **Robert Bage**'s *Hermsprong, or Man as He Is Not* (1796), which told of a "natural" man who did not share European social conventions; and **Maria Edgeworth**'s *Castle Rackrent* (1800), which explored the political and social upheavals in **Ireland** occasioned by the troubles of 1798.

The fiction of Austen and Scott, on the other hand, seems largely unaffected by the politics of the revolutionary era. Instead, both writers looked back to the stability of the previous period. Austen succeeds in delineating convincing characters through an ironic but conventional third-person narrator, rather than exploiting epistolary or first-person forms, while, through satire, exposing the way in which early-19th-century society has deviated from her **Augustan** ideal. Only in the posthumously published *Persuasion* (1818), set in the aftermath of **Waterloo**, does Austen appear to question the old ways themselves. Scott's fiction, especially *Waverley* (1814), which deals with the **Jacobite** rebellion of the **Forty-five**, *Old Mortality* (1817), and *Rob Roy* (1818), proved seminal to the development of the "historical novel."

But of equal significance perhaps was Scott's contribution to the sense that there was a tradition of "great novelists." He was involved in the publication of *Ballantyne's Novelists Library* (1824), which reprinted works by Defoe, Richardson, Fielding, Smollett, and Sterne, each prefaced by a critical **essay** by Scott himself. At the same time, Ballantyne's series chose to discount or ignore the output of a number of writers, particularly women, who had been immensely popular earlier in the Hanoverian period. In this way, Scott might be said to have been instrumental in the creation of a canon of early novels and early novelists—a canon that has only recently fallen under critical scrutiny.

J.A. Downie

Bibliography

Battestin, Martin C., ed. *British Novelists, 1660–1800.* 1985.

Duncan, Ian. *Modern Romance and Transformations of the Novel: The Gothic, Scott and Dickens.* 1992.

Kelly, Gary. *English Fiction of the Romantic Period, 1789–1830.* 1989.

McKeon, Michael. *The Origins of the English Novel, 1600–1740.* 1987.

Probyn, Clive T. *English Fiction of the Eighteenth Century, 1700–1789.* 1987.

Spencer, Jane. *The Rise of the Woman Novelist from Aphra Behn to Jane Austen.* 1986.

Watson, Nicola J. *Revolution and the Form of the British Novel, 1790–1825.* 1994.

Watt, Ian. *The Rise of the Novel: Studies in Defoe, Richardson and Fielding.* 1957.

Oastler, Richard (1789–1861)

Known as "the Factory King" for the role he played in inproving the lives of workers and children, Oastler was a central figure in the **factory movement** of the 1830s and 1840s. A Yorkshire country estate manager, happily married though childless, he was motivated by **Evangelical** pity to help restrict **child labor** in the **textile** mills. His six famous "Yorkshire Slavery" **letters** to **Leeds newspapers** (1830–1831) started the groundswell that resulted in the Factory Act of 1833, and its progressive revisions.

A staunch **Tory**, dedicated to social reconstruction, Oastler helped organize Short Time Committees among workers. By Leeds businessmen of his own class and some later historians he was labeled a demagogue as well as a **radical**. At many open-air meetings during the 1830s his speeches could move people to tears or frenzy, and with his extraordinary energy and constant letter-writing he motivated such leaders in Parliament as **Michael Sadler** to carry on factory reform. Of all contemporary reformers he was the most talented publicist to oppose children's overwork at a time when cruelty and laissez-faire exploitation were normal.

Carolyn Stevens

Bibliography

Cowherd, Raymond G. *The Humanitarians and the Ten Hour Movement in England.* 1956.

Driver, Cecil. *Tory Radical: The Life of Richard Oastler.* 1946.

Oastler, Richard. *Richard Oastler: King of Factory Children; Six Pamphlets, 1835–1861.* 1972.

Ward, J.T. "Richard Oastler on Politics and Factory Reform, 1832–1833." *Northern History.* Vol. 24, pp. 124–145.

Occasional Conformity

Suspected for their assumed disloyalty to the later Stuarts yet taking advantage of certain "freedoms" within the Corporation Act (1661) and Test Act (1673), a number of ambitious **dissenters** (particularly **Presbyterians** and **Congregationalists**) embraced the practice of receiving Anglican communion once a year for no reason other than to qualify for government posts. Soldiers, sheriffs, customs officials, and mayors alike practiced this hypocritical custom, attending Anglican service in the morning and a dissenting chapel later in the day.

The **Tories**' Occasional Conformity Act (1711), designed to end this practice, stipulated that civil and military officers who engaged in it would be fined and deprived of their offices. The Hanoverian **Whigs**, more positively responsive to dissenting influences, repealed the bill in 1719, urging dissenters to protect their civil rights by refraining from attending *any* church. The more affluent dissenting officials therefore began to hold private worship services in their own homes. From 1727, however, annual **indemnity acts** protected dissenters from prosecution, largely eliminating the need for occasional conformity.

Samuel J. Rogal

Bibliography

Flaningham, John. "The Occasional Conformity Controversy: Ideology and Party Politics." *Journal of British Studies.* Vol. 17, pp. 38–62.

Thomas, Richard. "Presbyterians, Congregationals, and the Test and Corporation Acts." *Transactions of the Unitarian Historical Society.* Vol. 11, pp. 120–136.

Watts, Michael R. *The Dissenters.* 2 vols. 1978, 1995.

See also Church of England

O'Connell, Daniel (1775–1847)

O'Connell, "the Liberator," was the most prominent Irish politician of the late Hanoverian age and a contributor to Irish **nationalism**. Born in Cahirciveen (County Kerry), his father a landlord, O'Connell was one of the first **Catholics** permitted to practice law (1798), prohibitions having been removed in 1792. Although inspired by **Enlightenment** ideas and democratic idealism, and enrolled in the **United Irishmen**, he

Daniel O'Connell

shrank from the **Irish rebellions** (1798, 1803) and remained permanently opposed to Irish revolutionary violence. He joined the **Catholic Committee** (1805), combining with other **middle-** and upper-**class** Catholics to lobby for **Catholic emancipation**, which had been left incomplete under the terms of the **Act of Union** (1800).

This, by the early 1820s, was becoming the central issue of British politics. Several emancipation bills had been only narrowly defeated in Parliament. In 1823 O'Connell and Richard Lalor Sheil (1791–1851) founded the Catholic Association, their purpose being to raise and coordinate mass opinion behind a campaign to force constitutional revisions that in fact went well beyond emancipation, even to a democratic suffrage, repeal of the Union, and the abolition of **tithes**. O'Connell, emboldened by the association's success, stood for election to Parliament (1828) and, being elected (though as a Catholic being unable to take his seat in **Commons**), presented the **Tory** government with the dilemma of combating what might soon be civil war in **Ireland**, or emancipating the Catholics—that is, repealing statutory limitations on their eligibility to hold parliamentary seats and other high offices. Bitterly the Tories passed the Act of Emancipation (1829), repudiating one of their own most sacred principles, unqualified support for the constitutional position of the **Church of England**.

O'Connell was now not only the hero of the hour in Ireland but a key figure in Parliament. He and his fellow Irish M.P.s (his "tail"), whose numbers had grown to over 70 by the mid-1830s, were a swing group helping other **radical** politicians to pass the **Reform Act** (1832), the abolition of **slavery** (1833), **municipal** reform (1835), and other improvements. Though always favoring repeal of the Union because he believed a restored **Irish Parliament** would be the best guarantor of Ireland, he dropped this during the period 1835–1841 in favor of helping to keep **Melbourne**'s weak **Whig** government, which promised reforms, in office. Disappointed and faced by his old opponent **Peel** (1841), O'Connell returned to his earlier and more radical cause: organizing a repeal association and further mass agitations in Ireland. This time his strategy of provoking unrest or reform did not work. He was jailed briefly (1844) for seditious conspiracy and died a few years later while on a pilgrimage to Rome.

George F. Clements

Bibliography

Chevenix Trench, Charles. *The Great Dan: A Biography of Daniel O'Connell.* 1984.
Machin, G.I.T. *The Catholic Question in English Politics, 1820–1830.* 1964.
McCaffrey, Lawrence J. *Daniel O'Connell and the Repeal Year.* 1966.
O'Ferall, Fergus. *Catholic Emancipation: Daniel O'Connell and the Birth of Irish Democracy, 1820–30.* 1985.
Reynolds, J.A. *The Catholic Emancipation Crisis in Ireland, 1823–1829.* 1954.

Oglethorpe, James (1696–1785)

Oglethorpe, soldier and philanthropist, is best known as the founder of the colony of Georgia in 1732. The son of a gentleman, he attended Eton and Oxford, received a commission in the **army** and, after the deaths of both his elder brothers, inherited the family estate and took a seat in Parliament (1722). The death of a friend from **smallpox** contracted in the Fleet **prison** while incarcerated for debt led to his interest in the barbaric conditions endured by such prisoners. Oglethorpe was able to act on this through his work on a parliamentary committee (1729) to investigate the harsh treatment of inmates of debtor's prisons. It was these circumstances that led to his scheme to establish a colony in **North America** for debtors.

The colony, chartered by **George II** (after whom it was named), was planned as a haven for the English poor, who

General James Oglethorpe

would form a network of sturdy yeoman communities (slavery and rum were prohibited) to produce wines, silks, and spices to relieve the homeland of foreign economic dependencies. Georgia's settlement absorbed Oglethorpe during most of the 1730s. He led not only in the formation of its government but in military operations against the Spanish and Indians in nearby Florida, and he also worked (not entirely harmoniously) with **Whitefield** and the **Wesley** brothers in their evangelism.

Returning to Britain, he was promoted to Major-General (1745). His military career was tarnished by a court-martial over what the **Duke of Cumberland** stigmatized as his "softness" against the Scottish rebels of the **Forty-five**; his family's **Tory** background undoubtedly figured here. Though acquitted, he withdrew from military service and politics, coming out of retirement only to fight in the **Seven Years' War**. He was a member of the **Royal Society** and a friend of **Samuel Johnson**.

Stanley D. Nash

Bibliography

Ettinger, Amos Aschbach. *James Oglethorpe: Imperial Idealist.* 1936.

Garrison, Webb. *Oglethorpe's Folly: The Birth of Georgia.* 1982.

Spalding, Phinizy, and Harvey H. Jackson, eds. *Oglethorpe in Perspective: Georgia's Founder after Two Hundred Years.* 1989.

See also Humanitarianism

O'Hara, Kane (*c.* 1712–1782)

O'Hara's **burlettas** satirized contemporary theatrical fads. The Irish-born O'Hara received his B.A. (1732) and M.A. (1735) from **Trinity College**, **Dublin**, where he spent most of his adult life. His *Midas,* the first English burletta, satirized the then fashionable Italian form. This musical **burlesque** of a classical myth opened in Dublin (1761), then in **London** (1764), and was frequently revived into the next century. Another noteworthy example of this form is his *The Golden Pippin* (1772).

O'Hara was blind at the time he wrote an operatic version of **Henry Fielding**'s *Tom Thumb* (1780). He also helped found the musical academy in Dublin (in 1758).

Laura Morrow

Bibliography

Craik, Thomas Wallace, and Clifford Leech, eds. *The Revels History of Drama in English.* 1975–1983.

Dictionary of National Biography, s.v. "O'Hara, Kane."

Fiske, Roger. *English Theatre Music in the Eighteenth Century.* 1973.

Gagey, E.M. *Ballad Opera.* 1937.

Nicoll, Allardyce. *A History of English Drama, 1660–1900.* 1952–1959.

Stanley Sadie, ed. *The New Grove Dictionary of Music and Musicians.* 1980.

See also Dramatic Arts

O'Keeffe, John (1747–1820)

O'Keeffe, like several other 18th-century dramatists, began as a strolling **actor** in **Ireland**, migrated to **London** (1781), and began writing for the stage. His best-known play is *Wild Oats* (1791), several times revived in the latter 20th century; but in his own day he was best known for a succession of two- and three-act comic **operas**, in which spoken dialogue is interspersed with songs. The best of the two-act afterpieces are *The Son-in-Law* (1779), *The Agreeable Surprise* (1781), *The Poor Soldier* (1783), *Peeping Tom of Coventry* (1784), and *The Farmer* (1786). The best known of his three-act mainpieces are *The Castle of Andalusia* (1782) and *The Highland Reel* (1788). In addition to **pantomimes** and adaptations, O'Keeffe produced several other nonmusical plays, of which *The Young Quaker* (1783) joins *The Wild Oats* (both with five acts) as particularly noteworthy.

O'Keeffe was essentially a house dramatist for Covent Garden, working with house composers like Samuel Arnold (1740–1802) and William Shield (1748–1829) on works for a wide audience, and taking maximum advantage of the strengths of the company, especially those of the great comedian John Edwin (1749–1790). The comic operas usually present a romanticized, bucolic England; they are full of singable tunes with simple lyrics and farcical action, and celebrate country virtues, **patriotism**, and generosity.

Over his career, O'Keeffe had some 20 successes and only six clear failures; his 10 most successful pieces had received close to 1,200 performances in London alone before 1801. With **Isaac Bickerstaff** he formed part of the tradition that led to 20th-century musical comedy.

Frederick M. Link

Bibliography

Fiske, Roger. *English Theatre Music in the Eighteenth Century.* 1973.

Link, F.M. *John O'Keeffe: A Bibliography.* 1983.

———, ed. *The Plays of John O'Keeffe.* 4 vols. 1981.

O'Keeffe, Adelaide, ed. *O'Keeffe's Legacy to His Daughter.* 1834.

O'Keeffe, John. *Recollections* . . . . 2 vols. 1826.

See also Dramatic Arts; Music, Popular

Oldknow, Samuel (1756–1828)

A pioneer in the **cotton industry**, Oldknow was born in Lancashire. Apprenticed to his uncle, a Nottingham draper, he became his partner in 1781. Yarns from **Samuel Crompton**'s mule enabled the fine weavers of the Stockport–Anderton area of Cheshire to produce Indian-type muslins, and in 1783 Oldknow entered this trade. Very few other manufacturers had done so; he made very substantial profits until competition developed.

Demand for his fine goods grew rapidly. He became friendly with the **Arkwrights**, who, along with Derby and Nottingham **banks**, provided capital for expansion. Among other activities, he built a **spinning** mill at Mellor, added limekilns and **coal** pits, promoted the Peak Forest **Canal**, and improved local farming. Entering financial difficulties in 1793, Oldknow sold off his interests in Lancashire and concentrated on his factory estate at Mellor where, organizing the feeding of his workers, he kept a gardener at work on three acres, producing vegetables and fruits. But after his death the Arkwright family were the true beneficiaries of his efforts.

John Butt

Bibliography

Edwards, Michael M. *The Growth of the British Cotton Trade 1780–1815.* 1967.
Pollard, Sidney. *The Genesis of Modern Management.* 1965.
Unwin, George. *Samuel Oldknow and the Arkwrights.* Rev. ed., 1968.

See also Entrepreneurs and Entrepreneurship; Textile Industries

O'Neill, Eliza (Lady Becher) (1791–1872)

O'Neill, a leading actress who retired while still in her twenties and at the height of her fame, was the daughter of a stage manager in Drogheda, **Ireland**. Following a brief apprenticeship there and in Belfast and **Dublin**, she quickly won celebrity as Juliet to W.A. Conway's Romeo at Covent Garden Theatre (1814). For the next 5 years she was hailed as "a younger and better Mrs. Siddons," though important critics like **William Hazlitt** were at times displeased by her excessive histrionics and penetrating voice. Yet it was Hazlitt who rated her "the greatest tragic performer" next to **Edmund Kean**, "unsurpassable in tenderness of susceptibility and the simple force of passion."

O'Neill was particularly popular in such comedic roles as those of Lady Teazle, Mrs. Oakley, Lady Townley, and Widow Cheerly; and in the tragic roles of Belvider and Monimia. Her final stage appearance (July 1819) was as Mrs. Haller in Kotzebue's *The Stranger.* In that same year she married William Wrioxon Becher, an Irish M.P. who was later raised to a baronetcy. Among her admirers were playwright **Richard Brinsley Sheridan** and poet **Perch Bysshe Shelley**. Shelley thought the character of Beatrice, in his controversial tragedy *The Cenci,* "precisely fitted" for O'Neill, but the play remained unstaged until 1868.

James Gray

Bibliography

Agate, James. *These Were Actors.* 1969.
Booth, Michael. *Theatre in the Victorian Age.* 1991.
Hazlitt, William. *Dramatic Essays.* 1851.
Jones, Charles I. *Memoires of Miss O.* 1816.
Mullin, Donald. *Victorian Actors and Actresses in Review.* 1983.

See also Actors and the Acting Profession; Sarah Kemble Siddons

Opera

Like most European countries, Hanoverian Britain supported two coexisting operatic traditions: English and Italian. Italian opera was already established in **London** by 1714, while English composers were still only experimenting with operatic forms. In the Italian tradition, by around 1750 *opera seria* was beginning to lose its place to *opera buffa,* which in turn was replaced by early Romantic opera. In English opera, **ballad opera** flourished during the second quarter of the 18th century. Dialogue opera emerged in the 1760s and reached its peak in the 1790s, but after that, English opera in the early 19th century had little new to offer.

Attempts by English composers during the reign of **Queen Anne** to meld Italian operatic forms with the English language had been ineffectual. In 1711, **Handel** firmly established Italian opera in London with *Rinaldo,* and he dominated that form for over 20 years. Handel hired Italian singers, and English **musicians** were rarely involved. In 1728, **John Gay** ridiculed the conventions of *opera seria* in *The Beggar's Opera,* which became the biggest operatic success of the century. Gay alternated spoken dialogue with songs set to familiar tunes. *The Beggar's Opera* stimulated nearly 100 other ballad operas over the next decade.

After this ballad opera form lost popularity, English operas continued to be written occasionally by composers such as **Thomas Augustine Arne**, **William Boyce**, and John Frederick Lampe (*c.* 1703–1751). Their works included operas with spoken dialogue, all-vocal operas, masques, and burlesques; no single form was dominant. **The Playhouse Act** (1737) limited speech (and therefore most English operas) to the Theatres Royal at Covent Garden and Drury Lane, and confined Italian opera to the King's Theatre. During the summer, operas were also produced at London's Little Theatre, in **provincial towns**, and in **Dublin**.

In 1762, Arne found a successful model when he wrote *Love in a Village,* a pastiche for which he borrowed **music** from various English and Italian sources, and also composed a few numbers of his own. Samuel Arnold (1740–1802) then produced a similar work, *The Maid of the Mill* (1765), for which he borrowed almost entirely from Italian and French operas. Over the next few decades, composers wrote many of these dialogue operas, which used spoken dialogue and comic plots. Later works contained more original material than the earlier ones. Other composers included Thomas Linley (1756–1778) and **Charles Dibdin**.

The 1780s and 1790s were active decades for English dialogue opera. Composers included William Shield (1748–1829) and Stephen Storace (1762–1796). Shield's operas are tuneful, with many solo airs and short choruses, including glees. Storace achieved some of Drury Lane's biggest financial successes with *The Haunted Tower* (1789) and *The Siege of Belgrade* (1790). He had studied in Italy, and incorporated dramatic elements from *opera buffa* into his ensembles. However, Storace's innovations had no influence on later generations. The most prolific composer of the early 19th century, **Henry Bishop**, kept to a tuneful musical style similar to Shield's. The most important musical event of the early 19th century was the commissioning by Covent Garden of Carl Maria von Weber's *Oberon* (1826).

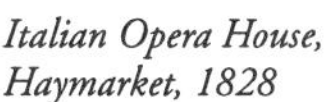

Italian Opera House, Haymarket, 1828

In the latter 18th century the King's Theatre was one of the leading Italian opera houses of Europe. In the 1760s, *pasticcios* were popular, as were operas by Baldassare Galuppi and **Johann Christian Bach**. Toward the end of the century, Giovanni Paisiello and Domenico Cimarosa were frequently performed. Surprisingly, no operas by Mozart were staged in London until 1806. However, between 1810 and 1840, operas by Mozart, Gioachino Rossini, Vincenzo Bellini, and Gaetano Donizetti dominated the stage. Operatic development in Britain paralleled that in other European countries: A national genre with spoken dialogue had emerged and was performed in separate theaters from Italian opera (which continued to be the one truly international medium). English opera was performed in other English-speaking countries, but only rarely in Continental Europe. It was not particularly innovative, and seems most interesting for its place in London's active theatrical life.

Jane Girdham

Bibliography

Bauman, Thomas, and Marita Petzoldt McClymonds, eds. *Opera and the Enlightenment.* 1995.

Burney, Charles. *A General History of Music from the Earliest Ages to the Present Period.* 2nd ed., 1789; rpt. 1957, ed. Frank Mercer.

Ebers, John. *Seven Years of the King's Theatre.* 1828.

Fenner, Theodore. *Opera in London: Views of the Press, 1785–1830.* 1993.

Fiske, Roger. *English Theatre Music in the Eighteenth Century.* 1986.

Hogarth, George. *Memoirs of the Musical Drama.* 2 vols. 1838.

Kelly, Michael. *Reminiscences of Michael Kelly of the King's Theatre and Theatre Royal Drury Lane.* 2 vols. 1826.

Mount-Edgcumbe, Richard Edgcumbe, second earl of. *Musical Reminiscences, Chiefly Respecting the Italian Opera in England, from the Year 1773 to the Present Time.* 3rd ed., 1828.

Nalbach, Daniel. *The King's Theatre, 1704–1867: London's First Italian Opera House.* 1972.

Petty, Frederick C. *Italian Opera in London, 1760–1800.* 1980.

Smith, Ruth. *Handel's Oratorios and Eighteenth-Century Thought.* 1995.

Walsh, T.J. *Opera in Dublin, 1705–1797: The Social Scene.* 1973.

White, Eric Walter. *A History of English Opera.* 1983.

See also Music, Vocal; Oratorio; Theaters and Staging

Opposition

In the early Hanoverian period, no faction could form an administration solely on the basis of a majority in Parliament because ministers were appointed by the head of government—the king—as individuals and as his own choices. Although two parties did exist in 1714, **George I**'s dislike of **Tories** diminished their number and weakened their ability to provide an alternative to the **Whigs**. Opposition in Parliament to governmental policies was regarded as **Jacobitism** at worst and, at best, opportunism. The concept of a loyal and principled opposition centering itself on a program of alternative policies gained favor after the defeat of Jacobitism in 1745 but did not become a reality for another 80 years. In the meantime, opposition within Parliament provided a safe outlet for public discontent and a check on ministerial excesses.

Even though the Whigs continued to flourish after the accession of **George II** (1727), disgruntled politicians such as **Pulteney** and **Carteret** opposed the **Walpole** administration, sometimes over policy, sometimes out of sheer thirst for office, but most often through apparently public-minded assaults on the formidable system of **patronage** Walpole built up through his distribution of **places** and **pensions**. Intraparty conflict over the conduct of the two major **wars** of the period 1740–1760 created opposition based more clearly on policy differences, but also a frequent reshuffling of ministries to silence it. Debate centered on whether British war efforts should be directed primarily toward America or the Continent. Politicians often used the press as a means of gaining public support for their positions.

The accession of **George III** (1760) increased the hopes and numbers of Tories sufficiently to make them an effective party again by the end of the century, while the Whigs splintered and went into decline. The Whigs of the **Rockingham** and **Fox** connections added significantly during the period of the **War of American Independence** (1775–1783) to the idea of loyal opposition, articulating a theory of parties as groups united by "measures, not men"—principles, not lust for office. The revived Tories' monopoly of power under **Pitt the Younger** and their conduct of the **French Revolutionary and Napoleonic Wars** forced politicians who differed from them to unite, and a revived Whig Party was able to take office at last (1830) on a platform of specific policies. The phrase "His Majesty's Opposition" was first used in 1826 to designate the Whigs at that time, as the second-largest party in Parliament.

When the Tories lost the 1830 election, their ministers resigned together as a party, not individually. Thereafter, the end of royal influence, the beginning of responsible cabinet government, electoral reform, and disciplined party organization all contributed to the formation of a true Opposition, ready to provide an administration whenever the party in power lost its majority.

P.J. Kulisheck

Bibliography

Baugh, Daniel. "Great Britain's 'Blue-Water' Policy, 1689–1815." *The International History Review.* Vol. 10, pp. 33–58.

Foord, Archibald. *His Majesty's Opposition, 1714–1830.* 1964.

Harris, Robert. *A Patriot Press: National Politics and the London Press in the 1740s.* 1993.

Pares, Richard. "American versus Continental Warfare, 1739–63." *The English Historical Review.* Vol. 51, pp. 429–465.

Schweizer, Karl, and Jeremy Black, eds. *Politics and the Press in Hanoverian Britain.* 1990.

See also Government, National; Party Politics

Orange Order

The Loyal Orange Institution (Orange Order) was founded in the aftermath of the battle of the Diamond, near Loughgall, County Armagh, on 21 September 1795. Despite being rooted in local circumstances of land hunger and sectarian rivalry in the border counties of Ulster, this vehicle for strident anti–**Catholic** and Protestant **patriotism** spread rapidly in tandem with the process of emigration from Ulster. By the end of the century, Orange outposts were to be found in British cities such as **Manchester**; by the 1820s, the order had spread to America and **Canada**.

In **Ireland** itself, the highly unsettled political conditions of the 1790s also favored the movement. The foundation of a controlling Grand Lodge in July 1797 marked the beginning of a process whereby the order became a national phenomenon, organized in an hierarchical system of lodges. The service of Orangemen in the Militia and Yeomanry against the **Irish Rebellions** of 1798 and 1803 further helped to secure aristocratic **patronage** and win over the authorities who had previously been suspicious of the order's unruly populist overtones. This favored position in Irish politics was only eroded with the end of the **Napoleonic Wars** and the **famine** of 1817. At this point, the Orange Order entered into a period of internal disputes and conflict with the government over issues of public order.

The order was revived in the 1830s in the face of the threats of church disestablishment and **Catholic emancipation**. It also gained strength from the support of the ultra **Tory** faction in Britain, led by the dukes of York and Cumberland. The publication of a hostile Parliamentary Report in 1836, which suggested that the lodges were involved in a dangerous conspiracy, brought this latest phase of activity to an abrupt close.

E.W. McFarland

Bibliography

Connolly, S.J. *Religion, Law, and Power: The Making of Protestant Ireland, 1660–1760.* 1992.

Curtin, Nancy J. *The United Irishmen: Popular Politics in Ulster and Dublin, 1791–1798.* 1994.

Gibbon, P. "The Origins of the Orange Order and the United Irishmen." *Economy and Society.* Vol. 1, pp. 135–163.

Senior, H. *Orangeism in Ireland and Britain 1795–1836.* 1966.

See also Boyne, Battle of the

Oratorio

The English oratorio arose in the 1730s. It was originally a sacred drama, performed in theaters without action or costume, on days when secular plays were forbidden (primarily, Wednesdays and Fridays in Lent). Over the course of time, performances in church became more and more frequent, especially when associated with charity.

Oratorio first took root in the oratory attached to the church of St. Philip Neri in 16th-century Rome. English oratorio stemmed directly from this Italian tradition, brought to **London** by **Handel**. During his 4-year stay in Italy (1706–1710), Handel had mastered the oratorio along with other forms. His own principal contribution, *La Resurrezione* (1708), had been performed in the palace of the Marchese Francesco Ruspoli, with leading operatic singers, a large orchestra under the direction of Arcangelo Corelli (1653–1713), and a sumptuously decorated stage.

A precursor of the main English development was Handel's sacred masque *Esther,* performed privately at Cannons, Middlesex, the mansion of the earl of Caernarvon (later **Duke of Chandos**), probably in 1718. A pirated staging of this work in London in 1732 provoked Handel into producing a hastily revised version at the King's Theatre, Haymarket. He had planned a staged production, but this was vetoed by the Bishop of London, so he was compelled to resort to a concert performance against a pictorial backdrop. The unexpected success of this performance encouraged Handel to compose a succession of new oratorios performed in the same manner, most notably *Athalia* (performed in 1733), *Saul* (1739), *Israel in Egypt* (1739), *Samson* (1743), *Messiah* (**Dublin**, 1742), *Belshazzar* (1745), *Judas Maccabaeus* (1747), *Solomon* (1749), *Theodora* (1750), and *Jephtha* (1752).

Typically, each work was based on a sacred poem inspired by an Old Testament story, with named characters and imagined action. The exceptions are *Israel in Egypt* and *Messiah,* which have no named characters and are compiled directly from the Authorized Version of the Bible; and *Theodora,* founded on the legend of an early Christian saint. Handel's oratorios were fundamentally operatic, but were distinguished from both opera and Italian oratorio by the prominence of the chorus, which he used in a great variety of dramatic functions and musical styles. Here he drew on English models, such as the anthem and the ceremonial ode. His confident grasp of the English language (despite occasional infelicities) was remarkable for a non-native speaker. His ability to enhance the majestic prose of the English Bible was unsurpassed.

Modern scholarship has demonstrated the theatrical power of Handel's dramatic oratorios, and these have often been staged in recent years. There was also, however, a religious and political side to the works: scholars have shown how their texts served as an Anglican rebuttal to **deist** attacks, and their **patriotic** overtones have also attracted much attention.

Throughout the remainder of the Hanoverian period, Handel's oratorios occupied an unrivaled position. They were performed with ever-increasing pomp and grandeur, especially at festivals in Westminster Abbey and in **provincial** cathedrals. In the course of time *Messiah* drew far ahead of all the others, as the preeminent legacy of "Britain's national composer." Handel's chorus of a few dozen singers grew to hundreds and then thousands, while his orchestra was augmented proportionally; and audiences grew apace as well. In the 19th century, even **dissenters** gave up their opposition to oratorio, and became its staunchest champions.

But the fact remains that few oratorios other than Handel's gained more than an occasional hearing. **Thomas Arne**'s *Judith* (1761) and William Crotch's *Palestine* (1812) enjoyed a modest success, but the only non–Handel works that had a lasting impact on the repertory were of foreign origin: **Joseph Haydn**'s *The Creation* (1798, British premiere 1800), Louis Spohr's *Die letzen Dinge* (1826, British premiere as "The Last Judgment," 1830), and Sigismund Neukomm's *David* (commissioned for the Birmingham Festival, 1834).

Nicholas Temperley

Bibliography

Dean, Winton. *Handel's Dramatic Oratorios and Masques.* 1959.
Myers, Robert Manson. *Handel's "Messiah": A Touchstone of Taste.* 1948.
Shaw, Watkins. *The Three Choirs Festival.* 1954.
Smith, Ruth. *Handel's Oratorios and Eighteenth-Century Thought.* 1995.
Smither, Howard. *A History of the Oratorio.* Vol. 2: *The Oratorio in the Baroque Era: Protestant Germany and England.* 1977. Vol. 3: *The Oratorio in the Classical Era.* 1987.
Weber, William. *The Rise of Musical Classics in Eighteenth-Century England.* 1992.

See also Music, Choral; Opera

Orders in Council (1807)

These were executive orders issued on the advice of the Privy Council. The most famous such orders of Hanoverian Britain were those connected with Britain's economic warfare against **France**. By decrees in 1806–1807 Napoleon erected a "Continental System" designed to close all European ports under his control to goods coming from Britain and her colonies. The British responded with Orders in Council (November 1807) that required all neutral ships entering or leaving European ports to call at British ports to purchase licenses and pay customs **duties**. Napoleon replied with equal determination in his Milan Decree (December 1807), which declared that all neutral ships submitting to the orders would be confiscated.

The economic battle ultimately faded as Napoleon lost power after 1812. But it had nonetheless caused shortages in Europe and widespread resentment against France and, for its maintenance, had tended to drive French expansion into Spain and other coastal areas. In Britain it also caused economic difficulties especially severe in 1808 and 1811, and, by aggravating Anglo–American relations, helped cause the **War of 1812**.

Stanley D.M. Carpenter

Bibliography

Horsman, R. *The Causes of the War of 1812.* 1962.
Herold, J. Christopher. *The Age of Napoleon.* 1963.
Kennedy, Paul M. *The Rise and Fall of British Naval Mastery.* 1983.
Ross, Steven. *European Diplomatic History, 1789–1815.* 1969.

See also French Revolutionary and Napoleonic Wars

Orientalism

As antagonism between the Ottoman Turks of the Muslim world and Christian Europe waned in the 18th century, a variety of Eastern cultural influences were felt in European fiction, scholarship, furniture, comparative literature, and even theories of language. The most significant impact occurred with the French **translation** of *Les Mille et une Nuits* (1704–1717) by Antoine Galland (1646–1715), which was immediately translated into English as *The Arabian Nights* by an unknown **Grub Street** writer. This work's British popularity may be sensed from the number of genuine and pseudo–Eastern tales that began appearing, beginning with *Turkish Tales* (1708), *Persian Tales* (1714), *Chinese Tales* (1725), *Mogul Tales* (1736), and *Oriental Tales* (1745).

These were only the first in a succession of **novels** or Romances with exotic Arabic settings and an enriched mixture of magic, enchantments, and talismans; populated with caliphs, Circassian slaves, black eunuchs, genii, and demons. John Hawkesworth's (1715–1773) *Almoran and Hamet* (1761), **Frances Sheridan**'s *Nourjahad* (1767), **Clara Reeve**'s *Charoba, Queen of Egypt* (1785), **William Beckford**'s *Vathek* (1786), **Maria Edgeworth**'s *Murad the Unlucky* (1804), and James Morier's (?1780–1849) *Hajji Baba* (1824)—to cite the best known—contributed to the vogue of exotic Eastern adventure.

At the same time, a diverse group of writers—both French and British—exploited the Eastern milieu and imagery as a vehicle for new **Enlightenment** doctrines and philosophy. Their productions occasionally took the form of pseudo-**letters**—for example, Baron Montesquieu's (1689–1755) *Persian Letters* (1721, English translation 1730), **George Lyttelton**'s *Letters from a Persian in England* (1735), and **Oliver Goldsmith**'s "Chinese Letters" or *Citizen of the World* (1762). In the form of philosophic Romance with a Levantine setting, one must count Voltaire's (1694–1778) *Zadig* (1749) and *Babouc* (1754), and **Samuel Johnson**'s somber work of genius, *Rasselas* (1759).

Travel writers, scholars, and religious thinkers were also busy discovering the Middle East and Asia as they supplied a curious public with information, some accurate, some quite fraudulent, as in George Psalmanazor's (*c.* 1679–1763) *Description of Formosa* (1704), which is entirely the product of his imagination. More genuine as well as critical of inaccuracies by previous travel-writers were **Lady Mary Wortley Montagu**'s delightful *Embassy Letters* (published posthumously, 1763), written while she visited Turkey in 1717–1718. A few Arabists emerged in an academic setting in the 17th century, mostly developing dictionaries and grammar books. In the early 18th century the Koran was translated (1734) by George Sale (1680–1736), and scholars introduced the history of Islam and Asia to more tolerant readers in, for example, Barthélemy d'Herbelot's (1625–1697) *Bibliothèque orientale* (1697) and Simon Ockley's (1678–1720) *History of the Saracens* (1708). Oriental language study soon reached such sophistication that **Sir William Jones** in **India** was able to discover the Indo–European family of languages while working with Sanskrit.

Artifacts from the East, especially Chinese porcelain, were highly prized and collected as **chinoiserie**, while **landscape** styles were also influenced by Chinese examples. Orientalized **home furnishings** and **interior design**—Chinese rooms—as well as pagodas and palaces like the Indian-inspired Royal Pavilion designed by **John Nash** in Brighton, became the vogue in the new century. After Napoleon's conquest of the Middle East, furniture in ancient Egyptian style competed in the **Regency** period with Chinese and Japanese.

Orientalism as a branch of study has come under some suspicion and revisionism thanks to Edward Said's epochal *Orientalism* (1978), which claimed that the study of the East that began in the 18th century created an image of the "other," which made it easier psychologically and ideologically for the West to dominate and colonize the Eastern world, thus justifying imperialism. Recent investigators have begun to question this formulation, though the term "orientalist" remains pejorative for most scholars in the field.

Arthur J. Weitzman

Bibliography

Allen, B. Sprague. *Tides in English Taste, 1619–1800.* 1937.

Appleton, William W. *A Cycle of Cathay.* 1951.

Caracciolo, Peter L., ed. *The Arabian Nights in English Literature.* 1988.

Conant, Martha P. *The Oriental Tale in England.* 1908; rpt. 1966.

Mack, Robert L., ed. *Oriental Tales.* 1992.

Rousseau, G.S., and Roy Porter, eds. *Exoticism in the Enlightenment.* 1990.

Sharafuddin, Mohammed. *Islam and Romantic Orientalism: Literary Encounters with the Orient.* 1994.

Wahba, Magdi, ed. *Bicentenary Essays on* Rasselas. 1959.

Webber, Henry, ed. *Tales of the East.* 3 vols. 1812.

See also Exoticism; Gothic Fiction and Gothicism Movement; Picturesque

Ossian

See Macpherson, James

Overseas Commerce

See Commerce, Overseas

Owen, Robert (1771–1858), and Owenism

Owen was the preeminent philosopher of British socialism, cooperationism, trade unionism, and educational reform. He was born in Newtown, Montgomeryshire, and sent off by his family as a boy of 10 to make his way in the world. Aided by his elder brother, William, he gained experience in **retailing** at Stamford, **London**, and **Manchester**, with different social groups as his customers in each place. He was an effective salesman but decided to apply his talents to the **cotton industry** at a time of rapid expansion in Manchester. Owen formed a partnership with another young Welshman, John Jones, a skilled mechanic, operating from rented premises with £100 borrowed from William Owen and with raw material supplied on credit.

Within a few years Owen dissolved this partnership, taking a post as manager at Peter Drinkwater's Bank Top Mill, the first cotton factory in Manchester to be powered by a **Boulton** and **Watt** rotary **steam engine**. Keen to obtain a partnership, he moved to the Chorlton Twist Company, a very large firm marketing its yarns over a wide area. To promote sales in **Scotland**, Owen went to **Glasgow** and there met and married in 1799 the daughter of **David Dale**, the leading Scottish cottonmaster.

On behalf of his partners, Owen purchased the mill and village of **New Lanark** from Dale for £60,000. In 1800 Owen became managing partner there, an enterprise he operated very profitably until 1825. Following Dale's example, he was an enlightened employer, claiming that his humane type of management was most profitable. His partners did not always appreciate this, and his secretive financial dealings also alienated them. By 1825 he had been involved with three partnerships at New Lanark and made considerable capital gains as well as taking his share in the profits.

Owen's reputation was founded on his paternalistic management of New Lanark, which was widely publicized. However, it should not be forgotten that he was a very successful businessman who commanded attention for that reason. His ability to make profits and at the same time improve the lot of his workers—in particular, to provide them with very good community and education facilities—attracted many visitors to New Lanark. His success in achieving social harmony at a time of widespread popular unrest drew him into a habit of generalizing about his experience. His beliefs were that character was generally formed by environment, that large industrial towns were not the best form of social and economic organization, and that the condition of the working classes could be much improved without any long-term loss of profitability. He saw a national system of **elementary education**, staffed by properly trained **teachers**, as central to the **moral** improvement of society. His utopian vision of a new society rested also on organization in "villages of cooperation."

These tenets, coupled with his idea that labor was the most important factor in production, and therefore should be adequately rewarded and protected during trade depressions, came to be known as Owenism. Owen became a proponent of many social and economic reforms. He favored factory reform, the recognition of trade unions (in the 1830s he formed that grandiose failure, the Grand National Consolidated Trade Union), shorter working hours, cooperation, and a national education system. However, he regarded parliamentary reform as irrelevant to the condition of the people.

Owen's ideas appeared in his main writings, *A New View of Society* (1813–1814) and *Report to the County of Lanark* (1820), and these and his other works influenced at least two generations of working people in Britain and America (which he visited in 1825). His followers responded to his attack on Gradgrind or classical **economic thought** and his alternative vision to unregulated industrial capitalism. They recognized that he had given up a successful business career to improve on the condition of the working classes. Hence he has been described as the "Father of British Socialism," but it could be equally argued that he made a significant contribution to the practice of scientific management.

John Butt

Bibliography

Butt, John, ed. *Robert Owen, Prince of Cotton Spinners.* 1971.

Harrison, John F.C. *Robert Owen and the Owenites in Britain and America.* 1969.

Owen, Robert. *Life by Himself.* Rpt. 1971.

———. *A New View of Society.* Everyman ed. 1973.

Pollard, Sidney, and John Salt, eds. *Robert Owen, Prophet of the Poor.* 1971.

See also Entrepreneurs and Entrepreneurship; Factory Movement and Factory Acts; Factory Workers; Radicalism and Radical Politics

Oxford (and Mortimer), Earl of (Robert Harley) (1661–1724)

An important politician during the reigns of William III and **Queen Anne**, Harley led a "New Country Party," criticizing administrative mismanagement and political corruption, and advocating a foreign policy defending England's particular interests. Preferring a middle course between partisan **Whigs** and **Tories**, he formed (1710) a ministry, which he tried to convert into a "Court" party dominated by moderates. Although his ministry rested ultimately upon Tory support, Harley (Earl of Oxford, 1711) stayed with his middle course, presiding over England's withdrawal from the **War of the Spanish Succession** while supporting the **Hanoverian succession** against **Bolingbroke**'s efforts to restore the Pretender. His dismissal by **George I** (1714) led to imprisonment and Whig efforts to impeach him for treason, but he exploited divisions within the Whigs and his own past good relations with **Robert Walpole** to defeat the impeachment. His taste for patriotic political ideals and shrewd parliamentary maneuvering became standard with 18th-century **opposition** politicians.

Robert D. McJimsey

Robert Harley, Earl of Oxford

Bibliography

Hayton, David. "Robert Harley's 'Middle Way': The Puritan Heritage in Augustan Politics." *British Library Journal.* Vol. 15, pp. 158–172.

Hill, Brian. *Robert Harley, Speaker, Secretary of State, and Premier Minister.* 1988.

Jones, Clyve. "The Impeachment of the Earl of Oxford and the Whig Schism of 1717: Four New Lists." *The Bulletin of the Institute of Historical Research.* Vol. 55, pp. 66–87.

McInnes, Angus. *Robert Harley, Puritan Politician.* 1970.

Oxford University

In contrast to **Cambridge University**, Oxford in the period up to the accession of **George III** (1760) never fully made its peace with the Hanoverian dynasty and so kept alive some of the religious and political traditions of the Stuart period, transmittting these to 18th-century culture.

The beginnings of Oxford's reputation as a center of opposition to the prevailing political influences of the day date from the reign of William III (*r.* 1689–1702) as the consequences of the **Glorious Revolution** and **Toleration Act** (1688–1689) undermined the privileges of the Anglican Church and left it competing with **dissent** for the religious loyalties of the nation. The sense of grievance resulting from this was heightened by the coming of the Hanoverians (1714), with their lukewarm regard for Anglican ways and their affinity with **Whig** politicians who made no secret of their anticlerical sentiments. So strong was Oxford's lingering nostalgia for the Stuarts and their conception of the union of Throne and Altar that during the **Jacobite** uprising of 1715 (**the Fifteen**) it was thought necessary to send troops to garrison the city. By the time of the Jacobite **Forty-five** such precautions were no longer necessary, but there was still sufficient evidence of lingering Jacobite sympathies to prompt a proposal for a parliamentary visitation of the universities—a proposal that proved as abortive as the plans for university reform that surfaced in the wake of the 1717 uprising.

Linked to this High Toryism—which could, on occasion, spill over into open Jacobitism—was a traditional conception of the character of the **Church of England** harking back to the 17th century before the Whig politicians had captured it for their own ends and subverted its apostolic character and the close association between Throne and Altar. This conception owed much to Archbishop William Laud (1573–1645), who had left a deep imprint on his alma mater—most notably in the form of the Laudian Statutes of 1636, which remained in force throughout the 18th century. Here was a style of religiosity that helped nurture the determination of the young **John Wesley** to revitalize the Established Church, even though ironically he was eventually to travel far from the High-Church traditions to which he was exposed while at Oxford from 1720 to 1735. Oxford's conservative religious traditions also provided the seedbed in which the Tractarian movement of the 1830s and 1840s would germinate.

With the accession of George III (1760), who valued his relationship to the Established Church and sought to distance himself from "the dirty arts" of Whig politicians, Oxford's conservative traditions began to be a source of harmony rather than division in its relations with the monarchy. This reconciliation was reflected in the election of George's loyal servant, **Lord North**, as Chancellor in 1772. The fact that, by the end of the century, Oxford no longer felt so besieged by the government of the day may help to explain why, in 1800, it introduced a major reform in the form of the New Examination Statute. By thus introducing a system of competitive examinations the university increased the rigor of the undergraduate curriculum and provided the possibility of a more meritocratic means of selecting candidates for fellowships. Intelligent men had long recognized the need for reforms. **Jeremy Bentham**, though extreme in his condemnation, was by no means alone in declaring that "mendacity and insincerity" were "the sure and only effects of an English university education" in the 18th century. He also commented that "the genius [of Oxford was] a compound of orthodoxy and corruption."

Unlike Cambridge, however, Oxford's curriculum did not change fundamentally over the course of that century. Logic, albeit of a modernized variety, continued to be a basic staple of undergraduate instruction as it had since medieval times, and the classics were given even more attention as the traditional scholastic curriculum decayed. Since the study of the classics could extend to the Greek New Testament and the Fathers of the Church, this was a study that had a natural affinity with an institution that stressed the historical foundations of the Established Church of which it was an integral part.

Oxford, then, emerged from the 18th century with its 17th-century traditions only partially modified. While the beginnings of a competitive examination system had been established, its curriculum had made little concession to **science** and modern learning. Its deepest loyalties were still attached to a conception of the union of church and state, which was to prove more and more elusive as the 19th century progressed.

John Gascoigne

Bibliography

Gascoigne, John. "Church and State Allied: The Failure of Parliamentary Reform of the Universities, 1688–1800," in A.L. Beier, David Cannadine, and James Rosenheim, eds., *The First Modern Society: Essays in English History in Honour of Lawrence Stone.* 1989.

Godley, A.D. *Oxford in the Eighteenth Century.* 1908.

Rothblatt, Sheldon. "The Student Sub-Culture and the Examination System in Early 19th Century Oxbridge," in Lawrence Stone, ed., *The University in Society.* Vol. 1: *Oxford and Cambridge from the 14th to the Early 19th Century.* 1974.

Sutherland, Lucy, and Lesley Mitchell, eds. *The History of the University of Oxford.* Vol. 5: *The Eighteenth Century.* 1986.

Ward, W.R. *Georgian Oxford.* 1958.

See also Scottish Universities; Trinity College, Dublin

P

Paine, Thomas (1737–1809)

Paine, revolutionary writer and propagandist, profoundly influenced the development of 18th-century **radical** thought and modern liberal democratic political theory. Throughout his life he acknowledged the influence of his father's **Quaker** beliefs on his own intellectual and **moral** convictions. Born in Thetford, at age 14 he became, like his father, a maker of stays for women's corsets. In the period 1757–1774 he had two unsuccessful marriages and was involved in a variety of unprofitable ventures and occupations. In 1774 he departed for **North America**. Settling in Philadelphia, he soon became editor of the *Pennsylvania Magazine*.

With the encouragement of Benjamin Rush (1745–1813), **Benjamin Franklin**, and others, Paine publicly advocated American separation from Britain in his pamphlet *Common Sense*. This pamphlet, which appeared in January 1776, articulated the colonies' historical and moral justifications for independence. It sold some 120,000 copies within the first 3 months; Paine donated his share of the profits to the American cause. Between 1776 and 1783 he further helped to shape American opinion in a series of papers called *The American Crisis*. The first of these (December 1776) opened with the memorable words, "These are the times that try men's souls."

During the **War of American Independence** Paine publicly criticized Silas Deane (1737–1789), the American Commissioner to **France**, concerning the costs of French war material delivered to the American colonies. His premature release of information about America's dealings with France led to his resignation as secretary to the Committee on Foreign Affairs of the Congress. After the war and despite charges that he was a hired pen, Paine helped Robert Morris (1734–1806) establish the Bank of North America, believing that this would become an important vehicle for national unity and prosperity. His attachment to the ideal of strong federal union manifested itself also in a series of **letters** disputing Rhode Island's refusal to pay a nationally imposed **tax** on imports.

In 1787 Paine returned to **London** to sell his design of an iron bridge. He became the friend of **Edmund Burke**, **Charles James Fox**, and other **Whig** politicians and radical intellectuals, and actively corresponded with Thomas Jefferson (1743–1826). An enthusiastic supporter of the **French Revolution**, in 1791 he published the first part of his famous *Rights of Man* in response to Burke's 1790 critique, *Reflections on the Revolution in France*. Paine, in contrast to Burke, argued not only the justifiability but the necessity of radical revolution in France and made a persuasive case for limited government, natural rights, written constitutions, and active political participation on a broad popular base. In 1792, on being made a citizen of France, he was in fact elected to the French National Convention, where he worked on a new constitution. That same year he published his most radical production yet, the second part of his *Rights of Man,* which argued in favor of government

Thomas Paine

subsidies to the working poor, old age insurance, and death benefits. The work has been seen as an anticipation of social–democratic ideas widely shared in the latter 19th century.

Paine, notorious for his radical activities in America, England, and France, had many admirers, but also many detractors. He outlined his religious principles in a critique of organized religion (especially Christianity) titled *The Age of Reason* (1794, 1796), wherein he censured and ridiculed "priestcraft" for blinding people with superstitions and mythologies. It was largely because he voted against the execution of Louis XVI (1754–1793) that the French revolutionary government in 1793 sent him to prison for 10 months. After his release he openly criticized President **George Washington** for failing to come to his aid. His last great work, *Agrarian Justice* (1796), advocated the imposition of a large inheritance tax to help the poor. Returning to America in 1802, Paine lived out the remainder of his life in bitterness. To many critics his apparent atheism, uncompromising radicalism, and conduct as a rebellious agitator tainted his intellectual standing. On the other hand, it is doubtful whether a single radical living in the 19th century escaped his influence. His conceptions of natural rights and prescriptions for an ideal political community, founded on rational, scientific, and secular criteria, profoundly influenced many subsequent reform movements, not all of which were British.

Mitchel Gerber

Bibliography

Aldridge, Alfred Owen. *Thomas Paine's American Ideology.* 1984.

Claeys, Gregory. *Thomas Paine: Social and Political Thought.* 1989.

Foner, Eric. *Tom Paine and Revolutionary America.* 1976.

Fruchtman, Jack, Jr. *Thomas Paine and the Religion of Nature.* 1993.

———. *Thomas Paine: Apostle of Freedom.* 1994.

Hawke, David Freeman. *Paine.* 1974.

See also American Revolution; Political Thought; Radicalism and Radical Politics

Painting

The Hanoverian age, though it started unimpressively in this, became a golden age for British painting. It produced many giants in art, and the range of subject matter expanded considerably. For the first time, native-born artists dominated painting. Art institutions were founded for both art education and exhibitions. The general energy and prosperity of the era drove art as it did so many other things—including **science**, **Empire**, **commerce**, and **education**.

The first two Hanoverian kings spent little money patronizing art, leaving artists to seek patrons from the **aristocracy** and **middle class**. But after 1760, royalty was far more artistically involved. For example, **George III** encouraged the founding of the **Royal Academy of Arts** in 1768. **George IV**, as regent and then king, was a great connoisseur and taste-maker; he supported the founding of the National Gallery (1824).

The founding of the Royal Academy was a turning point because it offered the first formal salon setting for the exhibition and teaching of art in Britain. Within the academy, the 18th-century hierarchy of genres in painting prevailed. The highest genre was **history painting**, which included religious, mythological, allegorical, and historical subjects. **Sir James Thornhill**, Gavin Hamilton (1723–1798) of **Scotland**, the American immigrant **Benjamin West**, and the Irishman James Barry (1741–1806) were some of the better-known exponents of this vaunted style. Theirs was a difficult genre in which to be successful. **William Hogarth** and **Sir Joshua Reynolds**, among others, were frustrated history painters, forced to take up other, more lucrative, genres.

Below the grand standard set by history painting were the genres considered less imaginative: portraiture, **landscape**, **genre painting**, sporting art, and still life. It was in these areas that home-grown British artists excelled. Most 18th-century commissions were for **portraits**. The two most brilliant practitioners in this field were Reynolds and his contemporary, **Thomas Gainsborough**. They were succeeded in the first quarter of the 19th century by the wonderfully talented **Sir Thomas Lawrence**. These three artists did not work alone in the genre; they had able competition from **Francis Hayman**, John Hoppner (1758–1810), **George Romney**, **Allan Ramsay**, and Henry Raeburn (1756–1823).

Reynolds—genial, immensely learned, and nearly deaf—was the most famous portrait painter of his day. Compared to his rival Gainsborough he was the more pedantic, formal, classically influenced, and academic painter. He often couched his sitters in classically derived poses and swathed them in classical rather than contemporary clothes as a solution to the "datability" of portraits. His best works are his more informal pictures, such as *Lady Caroline Scott as Winter* (1777), but more typical of his *oeuvre* is *The Montgomery Sisters Decorating a Term of Hymen* (1773). Reynolds's pictures have unfortunately suffered from faulty materials; many faded even during his lifetime.

Suffolk-born Gainsborough was a more naturalistic painter, noted then and now for his lightness of touch with paint, his superb technical ability, and his virtuosity. It has been said that whereas Reynolds set his portraits in the context of history, Gainsborough set them in the context of landscape. He thought classical dress for sitters preposterous, contending that togas and drapes diminished the likeness of the sitter. He turned to Anthony Van Dyck's (1599–1641) portraits instead of **antiquity** for his costumes, impressions of movement, and fluid, painterly style. His most famous picture, *The Blue Boy* (*c.* 1770), borrowed from Van Dyck both fancy dress and pose; the fluid, feathery paint and the daring color were Gainsborough's own. He also painted landscapes and genre paintings. In fact he began his career as a landscapist, turned to "face-painting" for the money in it, and then, late in life, returned to landscape as an escape from the mobs of prospective sitters. He drew on his memories of Suffolk to paint what he called "fancy pictures" of peasants and woodlands. Two fine examples are *The Harvest Wagon* (1784–1785) and *A Peasant Girl Gathering Faggots* (1782).

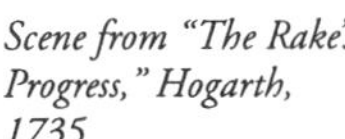

Scene from "The Rake's Progress," Hogarth, 1735

Painting's "minor" genres were not as lucrative as portraiture; painters of landscape and still life, of animals and peasants, had a tougher row to hoe. While there were always one or two buyers interested in Welsh landscapes or peasant cottage scenes, there were rarely enough. But among the masters of minor genres were Hogarth, Hayman, and **David Wilkie**. The greatest of these, Hogarth, was multifariously accomplished, painting histories, theatrical pieces, conversation groups, and satirical genre scenes. Frustrated at the ignorance of British collectors who appreciated only foreign art, he painted modern history pictures, satirizing the **manners and morals** particularly of the upper classes. Like his contemporary **Henry Fielding**, Hogarth launched social criticism through his art, especially through the wide distribution of prints from such paintings as *Marriage à la Mode* (1745) and *The Rake's Progress* (1735). **Joseph Wright of Derby**, the greatest provincial painter of the century, painted both portraits and wonderful tenebristic genre scenes of contemporary science, such as *Experiment with an Airpump* (1768).

George Stubbs painted a very special kind of portrait featuring the beloved dogs and horses of the **aristocracy**. In landscape settings he also combined people and animals in so-called conversation pieces, a very English style of group portrait. Among other practitioners of conversation pieces were Hogarth, Hayman, and Arthur Devis (*c.* 1711–1787). The conversation piece was a new kind of group portrait, featuring a private rather than public gathering of people and animals in a place particularly important to them. It bore French origins in the work of Jean Antoine Watteau (1684–1721), was brought to England by Philip Mercier (1689–1760), and was made an English specialty.

English conversation groups represented persons related by blood or common interests, caught in an activity or simply in conversation. Sometimes the activity took place indoors, as in Johann Zoffany's (1733–1810) charming *Tribuna of the Uffizi* (1772–1776), which features a roomful of artworks and of connoisseurs engaged in discussing them; but more often outdoors with a pastoral setting (and often the family manse) behind the figures. Middle-class status-climbing made the conversation piece a popular device for recording worldly success. Examples include Devis's *Sir Joshua Vanneck and His Family* (1752) and Stubbs' *The Milbanke and Melbourne Families* (1770s). Joseph Highmore (1692–1780) combined the genre-based storytelling of Hogarth with the conversation piece to produce 12 paintings illustrating scenes from Richardson's *Pamela* (1745), and Hayman painted literary scenes for **book illustrations** as well as 50 large decorative paintings for the open-air supper-boxes at Vauxhall Gardens.

Landscape, as suggested above, was, at the beginning of the Hanoverian period, perhaps the least appreciated genre of all. It is ironic that at a time when British tourists were returning from the Continent with landscapes by Claude, Poussin,

Canaletto, and Rosa, Britons neglected similar art by native artists, chief among them **Richard Wilson**. The great Victorian art critic John Ruskin declared that the history of "sincere" landscape painting in fact began with Wilson. Prior to the 18th century, most British landscape painting was topographical; that is, it merely recorded a particular scene. During the 18th century, landscapes came to be classified as historic or epic, pastoral or topographic—categories found in the much-admired works of the Italians. Wilson, although esteemed by his colleagues of the Royal Academy, was frustrated by a lack of interest in his pictures. Though he **traveled** to Italy to acquire for his Welsh and English landscapes an Italianate feeling, still they found little demand. Posterity, however, has elevated him to the station of founder of the English school of landscape, a school that culminated brilliantly in the success of **John Constable** and **J.M.W. Turner**.

Constable painted scenes of his native Suffolk countryside, limiting himself to places he knew well. His special interest in capturing a place on a particular day and time heralded the beginning of Impressionism; his broken color and interest in light were to make his work appealing to Delacroix (1798–1863) and his French successors. But Constable's accurate depiction of the river Stour and of Dedham Vale were far less flamboyant than the landscapes of his contemporary, Turner. Turner's chief interests were light and its qualities in air. Painting in all weather and in romantic places, he eliminated the narrative element, leaving only his impression of something—a fire, a snowstorm, a flood. Tiny figures and literary-sounding titles were the only remnants of history painting in his later works. Some of his critics did not see what the artist saw—"Pictures of nothing, and very like it," one complained. Fortunately, Turner had an influential apologist in Ruskin, whose book *Modern Painters* (1843), though it embarrassed Turner himself, clarified and established the nature of his genius.

The Hanoverian age thus saw a great success story in British painting. During that century and a quarter, Britain produced five giants: Reynolds, Gainsborough, Constable, Turner, and Lawrence. They, with the company of a dozen or more other painters of superb abilities (not to mention a flood of often extremely able satirists, engravers, caricaturists, amateur watercolorists, and book illustrators), also created many new forms in painting such as the conversation piece portrait, and freed landscape from its topographical ties. **Museums and galleries** were opened, private collections were expanded by travelers returned from the **Grand Tour**, and the Royal Academy provided a secure source of art education and art exhibition that would help to smooth the path of the Victorians.

Bonita L. Billman

Bibliography

Barrell, John. *Painting and the Politics of Culture: New Essays on British Art, 1700–1850.* 1992.

Gaunt, William. *The Great Century of British Painting: Hogarth to Turner.* 1971.

———. *Court Painting in England from Tudor to Victorian Times.* 1980.

Hemingway, Andrew. *Landscape Imagery and Urban Culture in Early Nineteenth-Century Britain.* 1992.

Hermann, Luke. *British Landscape Painting of the Eighteenth Century.* 1973.

Johnson, E.D.H. *Paintings of the British Social Scene from Hogarth to Sickert.* 1986.

MacMillan, Duncan. *Painting in Scotland—The Golden Age.* 1986.

Piper, David. *The Genius of British Painting.* 1975.

Shawe-Taylor, Desmond. *The Georgians: Eighteenth-Century Portraiture and Society.* 1990.

Solkin, David. *Painting for Money: The Visual Arts and the Public Sphere in Eighteenth-Century England.* 1993.

Strong, Sir Roy, et al. *The British Portrait: 1660–1960.* 1991.

Waterhouse, Ellis. *Painting in Britain, 1530 to 1790.* 1953.

Wendorf, Richard. *The Elements of Life: Biography and Portrait-Painting in Stuart and Georgian England.* 1990.

See also Graphic Arts; Watercolor

Painting, Genre

The discovery of genre, the painting of (at least purportedly) realistic scenes of daily life, was one of the great advances of 18th-century British painting. The technique was adapted from various 17th-century Dutch and French sources such as the interior family scenes of Pieter de Hooch (1629–1684) and the peasant scenes of the Le Nain brothers. **William Hogarth**, however, modifying the model for British tastes, thought of his subjects (in series such as *Marriage à la Mode,* 1745) as "modern moral scenes," conveying social and political criticism of contemporary life. The prints he made from these paintings were popular and lucrative.

Other painters of Hogarth's generation discovered other markets for genre painting. **Francis Hayman** put his work before the public largely through his decorations (1741–1761) of the supper-boxes and other pavilions at Vauxhall Gardens, the London **pleasure garden**. His images of rural life were a new kind of picture, seen perhaps by more people in London than any other paintings. The French expatriate Philip Mercier (1689?–1760) helped bring French taste to Britain, but failed to find an urban market for his genre pictures of childhood.

The possibilities of genre painting were more fully exploited by the generation that followed and included the most successful artists of that time: **Sir Joshua Reynolds** and **Thomas Gainsborough**. Their invention of the so-called fancy picture—an imaginary scene often containing idealized rustic children—found ready patrons, some of whom may have responded to subtly sexual suggestions in scenes of rural tranquility (e.g., Gainsborough's *Cottage Girl with Dog and Pitcher,* 1785). Gainsborough took his inspiration largely from the Spanish painter Bartolome Murillo (1618–1682), whose works he evidently saw in London.

Paintings of domestic and rural subjects proliferated at century's end in the works of such artists as **David Wilkie**, George Morland (1763–1804), and Francis Wheatley (1747–

1801). Wilkie specialized at first in Scottish village scenes before moving on to his great *The Chelsea Pensioners Reading the Waterloo Dispatch* (1822) and his later career in **history painting**. Morland was in many ways the archetypal figure of a new age of painting; he refused commissions from any patron—noble or commoner—and instead offered his very popular rural genre scenes on the open art market. He had learned his trade by copying (indeed forging) Dutch landscapes by 17th-century masters. Most of his enormous output, first the sentimental family and childhood scenes of the 1780s and then the larger rustic scenes of the 1790s, was sketched from imagination, without specific recourse to nature. These scenes of domestic harmony in rural surroundings appealed to an increasing and nostalgic market for rural life, recoiling from the everyday realities of agrarian **enclosure** and **poverty**.

Wheatley's work also combined sentimental literary themes with domestic genre for a largely **middle-class** audience. Culminating in his *Cries of London* (shown at the **Royal Academy** in 1793–1795 and enormously popular in **engravings**), his genre studies lacked the social piquancy of Morland's work and aimed at something more self-consciously genteel and **picturesque**.

J.C. Steward

Bibliography

Barrell, John. *The Dark Side of the Landscape: The Rural Poor in English Painting, 1730–1840.* 1980.

Johnson, E.D.H. *Paintings of the British Social Scene from Hogarth to Sickert.* 1986.

Waterhouse, Ellis K. *Painting in Britain, 1530 to 1790.* 1978.

Webster, Mary. *Francis Wheatley.* 1970.

Winter, David E. "George Morland." Ph.D. diss. 1978.

See also Painting

Painting, History

A native school of history painting developed later in Britain than on the Continent, due to political and religious tensions. **France** and Italy had been home for the exiled Stuart sovereigns, and few British artists made the **Grand Tour** to study classical art and architecture until after the 1750s for fear of being labeled sympathetic to **Catholicism** and **Jacobitism**. The decorative painter **James Thornhill** was named "History Painter to His Majesty" in 1718, 2 years after completing *Stories from the Life of Saint Paul* in the cupola of Saint Paul's cathedral, but religious history paintings were still considered idolatrous by many Anglican clergyman, and Protestant art connoisseurs in general still preferred portraits, landscapes, and genre paintings. The most popular Court painters of **Queen Anne**'s time, Swedish-born Michael Dahl (1659–1743) and German-born **Sir Godfrey Kneller**, were primarily portraitists.

The lack of a strong royal **patronage** of history painting indirectly encouraged the founding of numerous private academies (Kneller, for example, founded one), but these were unable to arrive at a consensus on the direction British art should take. Recognizing the need for royal patronage, the Scottish architect **Sir William Chambers** petitioned **George III** to sponsor a **Royal Academy of Arts** in 1768. **Sir Joshua Reynolds** was named its president; its first 40 members included two women, Angelica Kauffmann (1740–1807) and Mary Moser (1744–1819).

The academy was a great boon to British history painters, but they did not all emulate the grand style promoted by Reynolds, who exhorted painters to be true to nature but to seek their inspiration in the art of classical **antiquity** and the Italian Renaissance. Artists representative of the grand style were the Irishman James Barry (1741–1806), the Scotsman Gavin Hamilton (1723–1798), and Swiss-born Angelica Kauffmann. Hamilton spent most of his career in Rome and became a leader in the **neoclassical style** with his monumental paintings based on the *Iliad.* Kauffmann also spent several years studying the art of the Italian masters and became famous for her paintings and decorative panels depicting both mythological and historical themes, such as *Cleopatra at the Tomb of Marc Antony* (1770) and *Venus Persuading Helen to Love Paris* (1793).

A modern school of history painting, which tended to depict contemporary heroic subjects in modern, not classical, costumes was initiated by the American-born artists John Singleton Copley (1738–1815) and **Benjamin West**. West's painting *The Death of Wolfe* (1771) and Copley's *Brooke Watson and the Shark* (1778), in which popular heroes were represented in a dramatic, anecdotal manner, sparked a revolution in the genre. John Opie (1761–1807) and James Northcote (1746–1831) were part of yet another school of history painters who modeled themselves stylistically after the Dutch masters of the 17th century and executed paintings based on Elizabethan and Restoration subjects for John Boydell's **Shakespeare** Gallery, founded in 1786. Medievalism also saw a rise in popularity, as evidenced by Alexander Runciman's (1736–1785) Ossian ceiling at Penicuik house.

By the beginning of the 19th century the modern school had succeeded in redefining history painting to incorporate characteristics of narrative and **genre painting**. **Sir David Wilkie** of **Scotland** was the outstanding painter of this era. His *Chelsea Pensioners Reading the Gazette of the Battle of Waterloo* (1822), depicting the common people's reaction to **Wellington**'s victory, won praise from both British art connoisseurs and French painter Théodore Géricault (1791–1824), whose *Raft of the Medusa* had been exhibited in England in 1820. The religious and mythological paintings of William Etty (1787–1849) and **Benjamin Robert Haydon** met with some success in the 1820s, but by the 1830s **neoclassicism** had run its course, and painters were looking to contemporary literature for inspiration.

Deidre Dawson

Bibliography

Boase, T.S.R. *English Art, 1800–1870.* 1959.

Cannon-Brookes, Peter. *The Painted Word: British History Painting, 1750–1830.* 1991.

Irwin, David. *English Neoclassical Art.* 1966.
Monod, Paul. "Painters and Party Politics in England, 1714–1760." *Eighteenth-Century Studies.* Vol. 26, pp. 367–398.
Reynolds, Sir Joshua. *Discourses.* Ed. and intro. by Pat Rogers. 1992.
Solkin, David. *Painting for Money: The Visual Arts and the Public Sphere in Eighteenth-Century England.* 1993.
Waterhouse, Ellis. *Painting in Britain, 1530 to 1790.* 1953.

See also Museums and Galleries; Painting

Painting, Landscape

Before 1700, English landscape art was almost entirely limited to background settings for **history paintings** and **portraits.** But by the end of the 18th century, in an unprecedented development, landscape painting had become a primary expression of the nation's cultural values.

Several interrelated developments contributed to the rise of landscape art: the growth of industrialism and consequent nostalgia for a disappearing rural way of life; the accelerating pace of agricultural **enclosure** between 1750 and 1815, with accompanying displacement and impoverishment of rural workers; growing **nationalism** and critical reaction to the **French Revolution**; scientific discoveries in geology, botany, and geography, with landscape painting anticipating the role of photography; and, finally, the **Romantic** movement in aesthetics, which brought painting, **poetry**, and philosophy together to celebrate the individual's free response to physical nature as a source of spiritual, moral, and aesthetic inspiration.

Touching up a landscape, 1804

Artists' responses to these developments were personal and often conflicting. The harsh life of **agricultural laborers** was accurately depicted by George Morland (1763–1804), while **George Stubbs** idealized them and their contribution to national life. **Richard Wilson** substituted English landscape and history for earlier classical Italian models. **Joseph Wright of Derby** recorded scientific phenomena with scrupulous accuracy in his studies of volcanoes.

After 1750, three influential and related aesthetic theories helped to promote landscape painting: the **picturesque, sublime,** and Romantic. All were linked to contemporary aesthetic ideas, especially to **Edmund Burke**'s *Philosophical Enquiry into the Origins of Our Ideas of the Sublime and the Beautiful* (1757). Burke's theory of the sublime explored the viewer's moral and psychological responses to awe-inspiring scenery. Picturesque theory, also based on individual aesthetic response to wild landscape, promoted artistic creation of ideal scenes from observable elements. **J.M.W. Turner**'s art illustrates both picturesque and sublime theory, and also the link between landscape art and **sentimental** literature. His *Picturesque Views in England and Wales* (1825–1837) rely on picturesque theory and derive inspiration also from **James Thomson**'s influential poem on nature, *The Seasons* (1726–1730). In a sublime painting evoking the fury of an Alpine storm, Turner compelled his viewers' awe in *Snowstorm: Hannibal and His Army Crossing the Alps* (1812). **Thomas Gainsborough**, a consummate portraitist, also created rustic, Romantic landscapes like *The Market Cart* (1786), portraying scenes of his native Suffolk. **John Constable**, inspired by Gainsborough, followed his practice of sketching in the open air and passed his own rough painting techniques down to the French Barbizon painters and Impressionists of the 19th century.

Technological advances provided landscape artists with new options for experiments in printmaking, mezzotint, etching, lithography, and aquatint. Meanwhile, in a related art, **landscape architecture** rose to great eminence. Vast new landscape gardens were first created by designers hired by their owners and then painted and engraved by artists. By the end of the Hanoverian period, the portrayal of the British landscape had become a language variously expressing both man's attachments to his land and his power over it.

Elise F. Knapp

Bibliography

Barrell, John. *The Dark Side of the Landscape: The Rural Poor in English Painting, 1730–1840.* 1980.
Bermingham, Ann. *Landscape and Ideology: The English Rustic Tradition, 1740–1860.* 1986.
Hemingway, Andrew. *Landscape Imagery and Urban Culture in Early Nineteenth-Century Britain.* 1992.
Hemming, Charles. *British Landscape Painters: A History and Gazette.* 1989.
Humphreys, Richard. *The British Landscape through the Eyes of the Great Artists.* 1989.
Rosenthal, Michael. *British Landscape Painting.* 1982.

Painting, Portrait

The 18th century was the great age of portrait painting in Britain, although it began unpromisingly. While the 17th century had seen many flamboyant, courtly portraits, produced chiefly by foreign-born artists (e.g., Anthony Van Dyck, 1599–1641), by 1700 British portrait painting was moribund. Dominated by **Sir Godfrey Kneller**, principal painter to the king, and his chief rival, the Swede Michael Dahl (*c.* 1659–1743), its conventions were standardized to the taste of the age and molded to "the Augustan mask," which denied the quest for individual character or likeness. As Jonathan Richardson wrote in his *Theory of Painting* (1715), likeness was not enough: the portrait must be ennobling and "must raise the Character." When appropriate, the object of a painting was "to divest an Unbred Person of his Rusticity, and give him something at least of a Gentleman."

By the 1730s this tradition was fading. The arrival in **London** of the French painter Jean-Baptiste Van Loo (1684–1745) in 1737 brought him immediate success for his technique in rendering facial features, a great advance over the mask-like work of his native rivals. Van Loo's success also attests to the prevailing taste for the curvilinear grace of the French rococo, which influenced most British portraitists of the 1730s, including **William Hogarth**.

Hogarth was the exception to the mediocrity of British portraitists of his generation. His success as a portraitist in the 1740s owed much to the challenge provided by French competitors, but ultimately rested in his fresh, direct, and solid appreciation of the personalities of his sitters. Although Hogarth repeatedly made attempts to gain patrons from the upper classes, his most consistent support came from the **middle class**, which tolerated and even encouraged his direct, unpretentious portrait style. Only Joseph Highmore (1692–1780) could match Hogarth's informality.

Informality was also the most distinguishing characteristic of the "conversation piece," a group portrait of figures, usually on a small scale, emphasizing the social context. This became increasingly popular from the 1720s, with the work of Hogarth and of regional artists such as Arthur Devis (*c.* 1711–1787); and later **Joseph Wright of Derby**; and the more cosmopolitan, German-born Johann Zoffany (1733–1810). Zoffany, after arriving in England around 1758, began by following Hogarth's lead in painting theatrical scenes (several, such as *The Farmer's Return,* 1762, featuring **David Garrick**), but then, exploiting his almost photographic technique, with patronage received from **George III** traveled to Italy in the 1770s and **India** in the 1780s, painting portraits and conversation pieces; his *Tribuna of the Uffizi* (1772–1776) is a charming example, featuring a roomful of sculptures and old masters hanging in the Florentine museum, under discussion by a score of prominent connoisseurs and travelers on the **Grand Tour**.

Around 1750, fashionable portraiture was dominated by the prolific Thomas Hudson (1701–1779) and by the Scotsman **Allan Ramsay**. Ramsay, with his Italian training, could, at his most accomplished, rival the best Continental portraitists, combining simplicity and elegance with sophisticated brushwork. His supremacy went unchallenged until the return from Italy in 1753 of the young **Joshua Reynolds**.

Reynolds, despite his technical shortcomings and unfortunate use of unstable pigments (causing his paintings to deteriorate with age), was the most original and creative portrait painter of the century. A friend of many of the age's great intellectuals, it is through his eyes that we now usually see them. He attempted to elevate portraiture from the ignoble level of "face painting," derided as an inferior artform in Britain for centuries, to the more esteemed and "timeless" academic genre of **history painting**, largely through the incorporation of references to mythology, classical history, and the old masters. Although in his own work Reynolds often failed to practice what he preached in his regular *Discourses* to the **Royal Academy**, he used his knowledge of the old masters, breadth of learning, and psychological insight into his sitters to achieve such enormous variety that his rival **Thomas Gainsborough** exclaimed enviously, "Damn him, how various he is!"

Unlike Reynolds, who used studio assistants to paint drapery and landscape backgrounds for his enormous output, Gainsborough himself reveled in painting sumptuous drapery and shimmering reflections on richly varied surface textures—all with a delicacy and ease of handling previously unknown in British portraiture. If Reynolds favored intellect, substance, and pose, Gainsborough favored feelings, light, and movement. His soft line, loose brushwork, and light palette were premonitions of the future. And if his mature style looked back to the Flemish example of Van Dyck (1599–1641), Gainsborough incorporated a native-born love for nature and the English countryside that was to mark the work of the following generation of artists.

Late in the 1770s a number of rivals stepped forward who would ultimately succeed Gainsborough and Reynolds. Chief among these was **George Romney** who modeled his style on the casual nonchalance of the Italian Pompeo Batoni (1708–1787), a painter with a taste for flamboyant poses and settings. Sir Henry Raeburn (1756–1823), while remaining in **Edinburgh**, emerged as the heir to Ramsay, with soft, evocative portraits of the Scottish aristocracy, painted with technical bravura. Raeburn threatened for a time to set up in London as a rival to Reynolds and, later, **Sir Thomas Lawrence**, but was convinced by others that his market lay in the north. Sir William Beechey (1753–1839), trained by Zoffany, and John Hoppner (1758–1810), working in the later style of Reynolds, also achieved prominence, until the dazzling and energetic talent of Lawrence eclipsed his rivals in the last years of the century. With his first major royal commission in 1789, and first great success at the Royal Academy in 1790 with his glittering portrait of *Miss Farren,* Lawrence dominated portrait painting idiosyncratically with his bravura style in a time when the increasingly sentimental taste for **Romanticism** was on the rise.

J.C. Steward

Bibliography

Greater London Council. *The Conversation Piece in Georgian England: Catalog of an Exhibition.* Iveagh Bequest, Kenwood. 1965.

Kerslake, John. *Early Georgian Portraits.* 2 vols. 1977.
Pointon, Marcia. *Hanging the Head: Portraiture and Social Formation in Eighteenth-Century England.* 1993.
Shawe-Taylor, Desmond. *The Georgians.* 1990.
Sitwell, Sacheverell. *Conversation Pieces: A Survey of British Domestic Portraits and Their Painters.* 1936.
Waterhouse, Ellis K. *Painting in Britain, 1530 to 1790.* 1978.
Wendorf, Richard. *The Elements of Life: Biography and Portrait-Painting in Stuart and Georgian England.* 1990.
Whitley, W.T. *Artists and Their Friends in England, 1700–1799.* 1928; rpt. 1963.

See also Painting

Paisley

Paisley, a town neighboring **Glasgow**, was one of the principal centers of **textile** production in the West of **Scotland** during the 18th century. Its most famous product was its shawls, modeled on the patterns of Indian fine muslins. Such was the volume of business that the town's **population** increased fivefold over the century. Until the 1820s, production was divided into factory-manufactured yarns and hand-woven, high-quality cloth. The industry also employed tens of thousands of women in nearby rural districts in tambouring, the hand embroidery of the muslins and crepes.

The trade, subject to the vagaries of **fashion**, was precarious, marked by cycles of boom and recession. This helped to radicalize the Paisley weavers, many of whom joined political **clubs** such as the **Friends of the People** and the **United Scotsmen**. Paisley men took a leading role in both the weavers' strikes of 1812 and the **Radical War** of 1819–1820. During the latter there were mass arrests of weavers who were, however, later acquitted by sympathetic local magistrates. Paisley weavers were also famous, apart from **radicalism**, for their literary talents. It was rumored that every third Paisleyman was a poet. Most local verse originated in songs sung to the rhythms of the loom. The most famous of the Paisley poets were **Robert Tannahill**, Alexander Wilson (1766–1813), and William McLean.

Patricia S. Collins

Bibliography

Gilmour, D. *Reminiscences of the "Pen" Folk.* 1871.
McLean, A. *Local Industries of Glasgow and the West of Scotland.* 1901.
Murray, Norman. *The Scottish Hand Loom Weavers, 1790–1815.* 1978.
Slaven, A. *The Development of the West of Scotland, 1750–1960.* 1975.
Smout, T.C. *A History of the Scottish People, 1560–1830.* 1969.

See also Factory Workers; Provincial Towns and Society; Spinning and Weaving

Paley, William (1743–1805)

Archdeacon of Carlisle, theologian and Christian apologist, Paley summed up and synthesized the beliefs of the liberal wing of the **Church of England**. His work constitutes a systematic rational defense of the Christian religion and the British social order. It epitomizes the alliance of religion, **science**, and utilitarian **moral** theory that characterized late-18th-century **Latitudinarianism**.

Paley, born at Peterborough, was the son of the headmaster of Giggleswick school. After taking holy orders and serving as a curate for a brief period, he was elected fellow of Christ's College, Cambridge (1766), where he lectured on **Locke**, **Bishop Butler**, and moral philosophy. Like **John Jebb**, also teaching at **Cambridge University** then, he became involved in the subscription controversy over the Thirty-nine Articles, producing an anonymous publication in favor of their relaxation, though he did not not sign the Feathers Tavern petition of 1772.

After becoming archdeacon, Paley produced his *Principles of Moral and Political Philosophy* (1785), which was almost immediately adopted as a textbook at Cambridge. His central argument was that happiness is the motive of individual conduct, and that God, willing the general happiness, brings individual conduct into line with this through providing the incentives, sanctions, rewards, and punishments of the Christian religion. The individual, acting in his own interest, acts prudently when he judges by gains and losses in this world; but he acts virtuously when he also considers the rewards and losses of the afterlife. From this utilitarian base Paley also vindicated the political system and attacked the **slave trade**.

William Paley

In the realm of **biblical criticism**, Paley's *Horae Paulinae: or, The Truth of the Scripture History of St. Paul Evinced* (1790) and *A View of the Evidences of Christianity* (1794) sought to demonstrate the historical authenticity of the scriptures and the veracity of the miracles recorded in them, against the objections of **deists** and skeptics. His final work, *Natural Theology* (1802), was a restatement of the old argument from design in which, using analogies of the human body and the watch, he marshaled voluminous evidence to prove that the order and purpose evident in natural phenomena imply the necessity of "an intelligent designing mind"—a theory weakened later by evolutionism, though Paley's book strongly influenced Charles Darwin (1809–1882).

Eric K. Heavner

Bibliography

Clarke, M.L. *Paley: Evidences for the Man.* 1974.

LeMahieu, D.L. *The Mind of William Paley.* 1976.

See also Law, Edmund

Palladian Style

The Palladian (or Neopalladian) movement was an attempt to distance England's architecture from the Continental baroque and create a national style that would surpass the architecture of the ancients. Capitalizing on a contemporary enthusiasm for classical archeology, the proponents of the movement sought to rethink classical architecture as filtered through the work of the 16th-century Italian architectural giant Andrea Palladio (1508–1580) and his English disciple Inigo Jones (1573–1652). Although the roots of Palladianism can be traced to John Evelyn's English **translation** of the *Parallel of Architecture of the Ancient and the Modern* (1665) by the French theorist Roland Fréart du Chambray, the impetus for the movement came in 1715 with the publication of Colen Campbell's (1676–1729) extremely influential *Vitruvius Britannicus* and the English translation of Palladio's *Four Books of Architecture.* In *Vitruvius Britannicus* Campbell advocated the adaptation of Palladio's and Jones' architecture to create a modern standard of design, while both publications introduced Vitruvius' 1st-century B.C. *De Architectura* to the contemporary English audience. Importantly, Campbell also secured the support of the English **gentry** by dedicating designs to prominent persons like **Sir Robert Walpole.**

Campbell's work spurred the interest of the **Earl of Burlington**, who became the great apostle of the movement. After a pilgrimage to Vicenza in 1717, where he visited Palladio's buildings, Burlington began collecting the drawings of both Palladio and Jones. He also sponsored research and publications on these architects as well as on ancient architecture. An amateur architect himself, Burlington designed Chiswick as an essay in English Palladianism and collaborated on other buildings with his protégé **William Kent**, the best-known designer of the movement.

While Burlington and Kent popularized Palladianism, the writer Robert Morris (1701–1754) provided the theoretical basis for the movement. His *Essay in Defence of Ancient Architecture* (1728) and *Lectures on Architecture* (1734) explained the nature and use of the classical orders, advocated harmonic proportions, and related architectural design to the building site. These writings represent the first attempt in England to tie architectural practice to theory, and their in-

Lord Burlington's Chiswick House, begun in 1725

fluence continued after the Palladian movement subsided around 1750.

David D. McKinney

Bibliography

Archer, John. *The Literature of British Domestic Architecture, 1715–1842.* 1985.

Rykwert, Joseph. *The First Moderns: The Architects of the Eighteenth Century.* 1980.

Wittkower, Rudolf. *Palladio and the English Palladianism.* 1974.

See also Antiquities and Ruins; Architects and Architecture; Housebuilding and Housing

Pantomime

In a successful bid to attract crowds, 18th-century theaters presented controversial dramas known as pantomimes or afterpieces—plays less than an hour long that followed the main show of the evening. This practice caused some curious pairings, for example between **Shakespeare**'s *Richard III* and **David Garrick**'s *Harlequin's Invasion; or, A Christmas Gambol* (1759). So popular were these entertainments that critics complained about how they were taking over the stage.

Pantomimes were spectacular entertainments that combined slapstick, stage magic, acrobatics, trained animals, singing, **popular music**, and **dance**. In the 18th century the usual format involved juxtaposing a silent Harlequin and other characters from the Italian *commedia dell'arte* with characters from classical mythology. Pantomime arrangers modeled Harlequin's adventures loosely on the story of Faustus: typically, the trickster made a pact with a devil or other magical being and received a wooden sword with which he could cause upsetting transformations, such as changing a character into an animal, a man into a woman, or a house into a prison. When his adventures ended, Harlequin either went to Hell or found a way out of his pact.

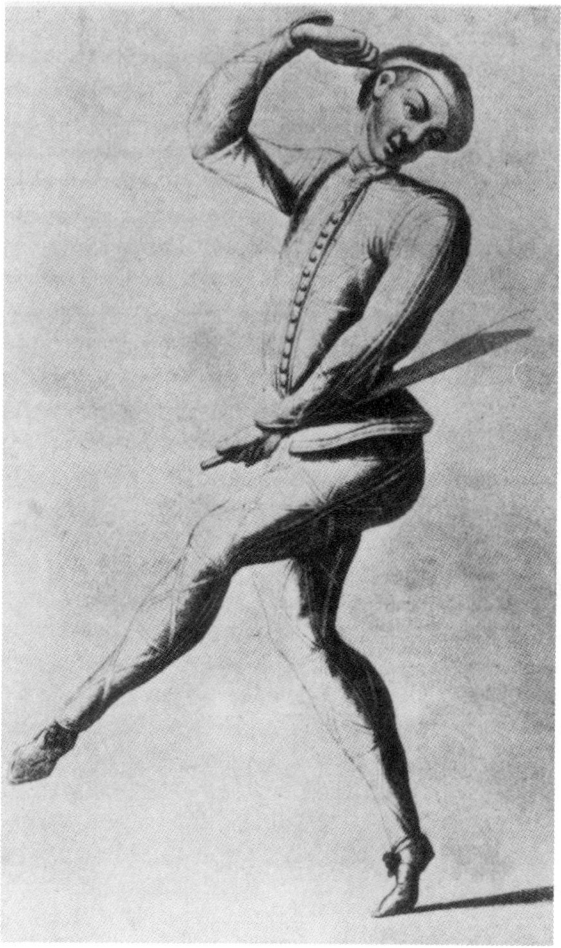

John Rich as Harlequin

Along with Harlequin there were also stories from classical mythology. In this portion of the pantomime, characters such as Apollo and Daphne sang and, in general, went through their adventures in an operatic fashion. Titles such as *Harlequin Doctor Faustus with the Masque of the Deities* and *Harlequin Sorcerer: With the Loves of Pluto and Proserpine* reflect the disparity between the elements in this entertainment.

The person most commonly associated with pantomime during the early Hanoverian period was John Rich (1692–1761), manager of Covent Garden Theatre. Rich arranged many pantomimes and also performed the part of the trickster under the stage name "Lun." As Lun, he would delight the crowds by scratching his ear with his foot, or emphasize his rage by taking scores of tiny steps in rapid succession while moving only a few yards. His pantomimes also featured fantastic creatures such as dragons and mechanical serpents.

In the final decades of the 18th century, three major changes occurred. First, although pantomimes had always depended on spectacles, pantomime arrangers came to depend increasingly on elaborate scenery to fill the burgeoning theaters with spectators. Second, James Messink (1721–1789) created a reformed Harlequin in pantomimes such as *The Choice of Harlequin; or, The Indian Chief* (1781). This character no longer performed the same amoral pranks, and thus became rather less interesting and important to the entertainment; the character Clown took over the role of agent of amoral activity. Finally, various fairy tales and also stories such as those of Robinson Crusoe, Dick Whittington (the poor boy who becomes Lord Mayor of London), and Aladdin replaced Faustus and the classical characters as sources for plots.

The name most closely associated with pantomime after these changes occurred is that of Joseph Grimaldi (1778–1837), who usually played the part of Clown. Clown, though he never made a pact with a **supernatural** agent to gain magical powers, resembled the unreformed Harlequin. For example, he was greedy: He would find ways to distract other characters, then steal them blind. Similarly, he was voracious: One famous routine involved eating a whole string of sausages without pausing. Whereas Rich and others had portrayed Harlequin in mime, Grimaldi as Clown both spoke and sang, and was especially gifted as a punster.

Before Harlequin's reform, commentators had expressed dismay over pantomime for a number of reasons. Many, including **Pope**, **Henry Fielding**, and **Johnson**, worried that this popular entertainment might debase the stage and bring an end to the performance of Shakespeare. A related concern involved the power of pantomime to corrupt audiences. **Samuel Richardson** fretted that it would drive out good taste, and even imagined that it would cause impressionable apprentices to turn to **crime**. These complaints had some effect, but after Harlequin's reform, pantomime's critics tended to dismiss them as silly.

Brent Chesley

Bibliography

Chesley, Brent. "Messink's Moral Pantomime." *Restoration and 18th Century Theatre Research.* 2nd ser. Vol. 4, no. 1, pp. 52–61.
Disher, M. Willson. *Clowns and Pantomimes.* 1925.
Sawyer, Paul. "The Popularity of Pantomime on the London Stage, 1720–1760." *Restoration and 18th Century Theatre Research.* 2nd ser. Vol. 5, no. 2, pp. 1–16.
———. "Smorgasbord on the Stage: John Rich and the Development of Eighteenth Century English Pantomime." *Theatre Annual.* Vol. 34, pp. 37–65.

See also Actors and the Acting Profession; Theaters and Staging

Paris, Peace of (1763)

The treaty that ended the Anglo–Bourbon aspect of the **Seven Years' War** was signed in Paris on 10 February 1763. Its terms registered Britain's success in the conflict. **France** yielded Senegal, **Canada**, and, in the **West Indies**, Grenada, Tobago, Dominica, and St. Vincent, and accepted the British position in **India**. Spain ceded Florida to Britain, recognized the British right to cut wood at Belize, and restored Minorca. The restoration to France of the British conquests of Guadeloupe, Martinique, St. Lucia, and Goree; and to Spain of Havana and Manila, was, however, bitterly criticized, as was the French retention of fishing rights off **Newfoundland**. **Pitt the Elder** told the Commons that the government of **George III** and **Lord Bute** was giving to France "the means of recovering her prodigious losses, and of once more becoming formidable to us at sea." The abandonment of Britain's ally Frederick the Great of Prussia was also criticized. The Bourbons were to seek revenge for their losses in the **War of American Independence**.

Jeremy Black

Bibliography

Black, Jeremy. *Pitt the Elder.* 1992.
Rashed, Zenab. *The Peace of Paris.* 1951.

See also Foreign Relations

Paris, Treaty of (1783)

This peace treaty, signed at Versailles on 3 September 1783, brought to an end the **War of American Independence**. It was unpopular in Britain and helped to bring down the **Shelburne** ministry (1783) which negotiated it because it seemed, among other things, an unnecessary giveaway of the American continental interior to the revolutionaries. It acknowledged American independence, and though Britain retained **Canada**, her reasonable claims to the "Old North West," the area south of the Great Lakes, were relinquished. **France** won minor territorial gains from Britain, including Tobago and Senegal, and consent to the fortification of Dunkirk. Britain ceded Minorca, which Spain had conquered in 1782, and East and West Florida, to Spain. The treaty with the Dutch, who had suffered badly in the war with Britain, was not signed until May 1784; the Dutch lost Negapatam, an Indian trading station, and conceded the right to "navigate" in the Dutch East Indies, which had hitherto been maintained as a monopolistic trading preserve.

The peace settlement as a whole formalized the schism in the English-speaking world, but also indicated that the Bourbons were not powerful enough to destroy the British **Empire**.

Jeremy Black

Bibliography

Dull, John R. *A Diplomatic History of the American Revolution.* 1985.

See also American Revolution

Parliamentary Reform

See Elections and the Franchise

Parry, Sir William Edward (1790–1855)

After accompanying the abortive first Arctic expedition (1818) of **Sir John Ross**, Parry led four expeditions himself. Three were in search of the Northwest Passage (1819–1820, 1821–1823, 1824–1825); the fourth was a failed attempt to reach the North Pole from Spitsbergen over the pack ice (1827). The first was a very considerable achievement; Parry sailed west through Lancaster Sound and reached Melville Island at a point 112°51′ West Longitude. Though best known for these Arctic **explorations**, Rear-Admiral Parry enjoyed a long and varied career, including service as the Admiralty's Hydrographer (1825–1829) and Controller of Steam Machinery (1837–1846), and in **Australia** as Commissioner of the Australian Agricultural Company (1830–1834).

N. Merrill Distad

Bibliography

Berton, Pierre. *The Arctic Grail: The Quest for the Northwest Passage and the North Pole, 1818–1909.* 1988.
Parry, Ann. *Parry of the Arctic: The Life Story of Admiral Sir Edward Parry, 1790–1855.* 1963.

Party Politics

In the long run of history, it is certainly arguable that one of the most important contributions made by English civilization to the modern world of democracy, mass participatory politics, and liberty, was the development after 1679 of a definite party culture. Individuals have, of course, often acted together politically in groups large and small, but what was distinctive about the English party experience was its longevity, its geographical dispersion throughout the country, and its presence throughout nearly all ranks of society.

The longevity itself is remarkable. A Whig party was in existence and usually flourishing in England (and often in **Scotland** and **Ireland**) from the great Exclusion crisis of 1679–1681 (over whether a **Roman Catholic** could inherit the throne) through at least the Irish Home Rule Crisis of 1885–1886. The Tory party proved itself even more resilient, lasting from 1689 to around 1762 and then, after languishing a while, again from around 1812 to the present.

Party politics in the Hanoverian age differed markedly from party politics after the mid-Victorian period. After around 1870, party political activity involved, beyond its parliamentary functions, centralized bureaucracies, yearly conferences, annual manifestoes, and mass membership lists. During the Hanoverian period, when **elections and the franchise** were much more limited, such techniques were unknown, and party was based upon some mixture of principle and political allegiance. The problem was that party combinations operating in **opposition** to the government were apt to be looked on as disloyal and hence illegitimate, as "factions" working against the king.

It was during the 1760s and 1770s (the reign of **George III**) when powerful Whig groupings found themselves denied power, that party activity began to be held up more clearly as an honorable activity and contrasted with mere *faction* or *connection. Party* came to imply a certain political ideology, honestly and openly expressed, and a bidding for public support for certain parliamentary activities. It usually involved a commitment to particular views on issues such as the Royal Prerogative, the **dissenting** churches, the **unions** with **Scotland** and **Ireland**, domestic **radicalism**, **Catholic emancipation**, peace or **war** in Europe and the **Empire**, and parliamentary reform. In other words, *party* came to connote a rather grand and consistent way of looking at political issues, while *faction* continued to imply a rather narrow, self-interested egoism, using politics in an unprincipled search for **patronage** or jobs, and in the process often giving uncritical loyalty to an automatically functioning family or kinship grouping. Thus the country came to see Whigs and Tories (and in the 19th century, Conservatives and Liberals) as altogether more respectable and honorable groupings than the factional Grenvillites, Foxites, Canningites, and so on.

Party strife in late Stuart and Hanoverian England led to a completely new way of perceiving and practicing politics. Tory and Whig social and political **clubs** dotted the capital and the countryside. In the early 19th century such clubs were often given the names of national political heroes: there were **Fox** clubs, **Pitt** clubs, **Canning** clubs, **Wellington** clubs, **Eldon** clubs. Such institutions served as vehicles for linking together national and local party politics, as well as for training local elites in the skills of public speaking and organization.

It is difficult also to divorce party politics entirely from the contemporary media explosion. Party politics shaded off into a literary realm of **satires**, **poetry**, **sermons**, pamphlets, petitions, and (thanks to the lifting of **censorship** in 1695) **newspapers**. **London**, **Edinburgh**, **Dublin**, many **provincial towns**, and most shires boasted newspapers adhering to one or another political party. The **political prints** of Hanoverian Britain—graphic satires, often powerful, savage, grotesque—are today still one of its greatest monuments. Through such agencies, party politics came to envelop the nation.

Party politics also led to sometimes raucous general elections in shires and (especially) **boroughs**. Each party had its own candidates, its own colors, its own methods for propagandizing and "treating" the electors. "Treating" was ubiquitous: for their votes, the electorate expected party representatives to provide elaborate breakfasts, fireworks displays, ample beer and spirits, and even bribes of money. Even the unenfranchised were sometimes allowed to partake of this treating in order to whip up enthusiasm in a borough or to ward off disruptions concocted by political enemies.

Two classic ages of party politics were 1679–1715, which saw 16 general elections (or one every 2.25 years); and 1802–1837, which saw 12 general elections (or one every 2.9 years). The destabilizing electoral excitement surrounding such frequent expressions of the "popular will" led in the earlier period to the **Septennial Act** (1716), changing from 3 years to 7 the necessary time interval between general elections, and in the later period to calls for substantial parliamentary reform.

James J. Sack

Bibliography

Harris, Tim. *Politics Under the Later Stuarts: Party Conflict in a Divided Society, 1660–1715.* 1993.

Hill, B.W. *The Growth of Parliamentary Parties, 1689–1742.* 1976.

———. *British Parliamentary Parties, 1742–1832.* 1985.

Namier, L.B. *The Structure of Politics at the Accession of George III.* 1929.

O'Gorman, Frank. *Voters, Patrons, and Parties: The Unreformed Electorate of Hanoverian England, 1734–1832.* 1989.

Plumb, J.H. *The Growth of Political Stability in England, 1675–1725.* 1967.

See also Government, National; Political Thought; Tories and Toryism; Whigs and Whiggism

Pastoral

Pastoral originates with the *Idylls* of Theocritus (*c.* 270 BC), writing of rural life in his native Sicily, and with the *Eclogues* of Vergil (70–19 BC), set in an imaginary Arcadia. Together these provided the acknowledged models for **neoclassical** poets.

The pastoral world of Golden Age innocence, which had much in common with Christian notions of Eden, was, paradoxically, a self-consciously artificial expression of sophisticated urban societies. In England the tradition retained something of its original provenance in the two collections of *Pastorals* (1704 and 1708, respectively) of **Alexander Pope** and Ambrose Philips (*c.* 1675–1749), although the conventions extended into various Georgic, elegiac, dramatic, and topographical forms.

But a schism developed when Philips took issue with Pope's perceptive recipe for a pastoral of Arcadian myth.

Philips's poems introduced an English landscape, folklore, and dialect, and were championed by **Joseph Addison** and his circle of "Modern" critics in a series of *Guardian* papers (1713) which ridiculed the bucolic clichés of classical imitation. Pope exposed Philips's mediocrity in an ironic tribute in *Guardian* No. 40, while **John Gay** burlesqued the taste for Anglicized pastoral in *The Shepherds' Week* (1714). However, despite Gay's **satirical** intent, this poem exhibits a sympathetic delight in English country customs, and its effectiveness as an anti-idyll is ambiguous.

Pope's defense of the Golden Age shepherds was partly born of a nostalgic conservatism, and proved to be a rearguard action. The idealized motifs of classical pastoralism were giving way to a demand for a more realistic domestic countryside. They would recur in Georgic poems like *The Fleece* (1757) by John Dyer (1699–1758) and *The Seasons* (1726–1730) by **James Thomson**. Now, however, they were complicated by nationalistic themes of **mercantile** progress.

Pastoralism became a storehouse of material to which many genres had access. It provided a congenial environment for poems of gentlemanly retirement, as well as a backdrop for pastoral drama. There were eclogues from Persia and **Africa**, while in the melancholic tones of his *Elegy Written in a Country Church-yard* (1750), **Thomas Gray** recaptured the original strain of lament for lost innocence. The new realism, however, was endorsed by **Samuel Johnson** in *Rambler* No. 37 (1750), and toward the end of the 18th century, rural life is refracted through an increasingly pessimistic lens. In 1770 **Oliver Goldsmith** published *The Deserted Village,* in which nostalgia for a Golden Age of pastoral harmony clashes discordantly with certain hard facts of what was called **agricultural improvement**. Even more sensitive to the brutalities of agricultural life was **George Crabbe**, who painted in *The Village* (1783) an uncompromising picture of rural **poverty**. **William Wordsworth**'s 1800 Preface to the ***Lyrical Ballads*** proclaimed a shift in **sensibility**. His celebration of the unrefined moral strength of his lakeland rustics took account of the arduousness of their work, but also insisted that this lent them dignity. In "Michael," provocatively subtitled "A Pastoral Poem," Wordsworth described the tragic reality of subsistence living on a hill farm, yet idealized that existence in ways that invoke the origins of the pastoral. Here again was a landscape where the inhabitants achieved a harmony by working in cooperation with nature.

Michael Bruce

Bibliography

Congleton, J.E. *Theories of Pastoral Poetry in England, 1684–1798.* 1952.

Empson, W. *Some Versions of Pastoral.* 1935.

Feingold, R. *Nature and Society: Late Eighteenth Century Uses of the Pastoral and Georgic.* 1978.

Greg, W.W. *Pastoral Poetry and Pastoral Drama.* 1906.

Patterson, Annabel. *Pastoral and Ideology: Virgil to Valéry.* 1988.

Williams, R. *The Country and the City.* 1976.

Patents and Patent Laws

Patents of monopoly stem from the royal prerogative and date from at least 1449, when the Patent Rolls began, though precedent can be found in a grant by Edward III (1331). Tudor–Stuart policy used them to promote importation of new industries and skills. Though Parliament objected to the enforcement powers allowed monopoly holders, the Crown's persistence nonetheless in granting patents led to many grievances and culminated in Sir Edward Coke's Statute of Monopolies (1624), prohibiting all patents but those for inventions, imposing a 14-year limit, and directing the common law courts to adjudicate disputes. In practice, however, the Crown was only prevented from granting "illegal" monopolies by legislation limiting its power after 1688.

The labyrinthine procedures for obtaining a patent dated from the Clerk's Act of 1535, which was designed to compensate unsalaried government clerks. In 1829 a Select Committee of the **Commons** ascertained that 10 major stages involved 30 separate steps—including obtaining the sovereign's signature twice—and aggregate fees of more than £100, all of which had to be repeated for patent protection in **Scotland**, and again for **Ireland**. Charles Dickens (1812–1870) found this situation ripe for **satire** in both "A Poor Man's Tale of a Patent" (*Household Words,* 1850) and *Little Dorrit* (1855–1857).

Nonetheless, the impetus provided by the development of **science, technology and invention** during the **Industrial Revolution** caused this unreformed and cumbersome bureaucracy to grant patent applications as never before. From the decade of the 1790s the total number of patents granted each decade prior to reform rose as follows: 647, 924, 1,124, 1,462, 2,452, and 4,581. This is in contrast to a decadal average of 80 granted in the middle of the 18th century. Yet, even in that early period there was pressure for reform from rival manufacturers seeking an end to all patents. Petitions to Parliament to reform the procedures were numerous from 1819 on. Half-hearted reform attempts were made in 1835 and 1839, but substantial reform, including creation of a central patent office and unified protection throughout the United Kingdom, came only with the Patent Act of 1852.

N. Merrill Distad

Bibliography

Armitage, Edward. "Two Hundred Years of English Patent Law," in *Two Hundred Years of English and American Patent, Trademark, and Copyright Law: Papers.* 1977.

Boehm, Klaus, and Aubrey Silberston. *The British Patent System.* Vol. 1: *Administration.* 1967.

Fox, Harold George. *Monopolies and Patents: A Study of the History and Future of the Patent Monopoly.* 1947.

Gomme, Arthur Allan. *Patents of Invention: Origin and Growth of the Patent System in Britain.* 1946.

Patriots (Irish)

"Patriotism" is the term loosely applied to the ideology of the Irish **gentry** of the latter 1770s and 1780s. Though the term itself was first used in the 1720s, the patriotic movement drew its real strength from the example of the **American Revolu-**

tion and had strong affinities with American colonial nationalism. The leading Patriots were **Henry Grattan** and **Henry Flood.** They asserted **Ireland's** right to constitutional independence from the Westminster Parliament, and, using the military threat implied by the **volunteering movement,** were able to boost Irish legislative rights during the constitutional crisis of 1782. Patriotism, however, remained an exclusive movement, limited to the enlightened elite among Irish Protestants; in 1783–1784, Patriots split over how far reform should also accommodate the demands of Irish **Catholics.**

The high-flown rhetoric of Patriot politicians and the movement's use of the press were instrumental in raising Irish political expectations, which the **United Irishmen** attempted to fulfill in the next decade.

E.W. McFarland

Bibliography

Bartlett, T., and D. Hayton. *Penal Era and Golden Age: Essays in Irish History, 1690–1800.* 1979.

Foster, R.F. *Modern Ireland, 1600–1972.* 1988.

Malcolmson, A.P.W., and J. Foster. *The Politics of the Anglo-Irish Ascendency.* 1978.

See also Irish Parliament

Patronage

In the Hanoverian era, patronage might mean a wealthy person's financial support of an architect, writer, or artist, but the term was more likely to be used in its political sense. Political patronage was the system by which royal ministers managed Parliament and, in particular, maintained the majority in **Commons** necessary "to do the King's business." Because patronage was financed by the Crown, **opposition** politicians called it corruption and undue influence. However, patronage never provided the monolithic power often attributed to first ministers (**prime ministers**).

Within the **Glorious Constitution** the Crown was the executive branch, responsible for all administrative expenses and salaries and the upkeep of buildings, in addition to the costs of the Court. These funds came out of the Crown's hereditary revenues and the Civil List, an annual sum voted for life to the monarch at the beginning of each reign. While politicians agreed that the Crown needed financial independence to maintain its position in the constitution, they also feared that the Crown bought control of Parliament.

The ministers influenced appointments to public offices, both efficient and sinecure, to the **army,** the **navy,** and to many **Church of England** livings, and also suggested persons to be granted titles, **pensions,** or contracts. Members of Parliament who supported the ministers could be rewarded with these benefits for themselves or for their friends and relatives. Because all government finance flowed through the treasury, its first lord became the most powerful minister early in the 18th century. **Sir Robert Walpole,** helped by advisors such as **Bishop Edmund Gibson,** perfected the art of patronage during his term as First Lord, especially through appointments to the Customs and Excise services.

Elections of M.P.s were usually influenced by patronage. Wealthy landowners often gained control over **boroughs** and induced the electors to choose a particular candidate. Even in county **elections,** a candidate needed the support of the major landowners to succeed. These political patrons among the **aristocracy and gentry** were wooed by Crown ministers to return men who would vote with the administration. The ministers also were able to name candidates in towns where the government had a large financial interest, such as the naval dockyards at Portsmouth.

The system of patronage was gradually dismantled over the period 1780–1830. In consequence, the Crown's ability to influence Parliament was destroyed, and the new system of cabinet government, political parties, and **party politics** emerged. The greatest blow to patronage was the Establishment Act (1782), which affirmed Parliament's right to oversee the Civil List, set spending limits, and require written accounts. Other acts abolished **places** and sinecures, barred government contractors from Commons, and curtailed pensions. Contracts and loans were opened to competitive bidding. The Bribery Act (1809) curbed government dealings with borough proprietors.

Opposition political pressure and government debt forced ongoing reforms. Public opinion increasingly condemned the influence of politics in church appointments, and deterred ministers from ordering politically motivated dismissals in the military and the civil service. The result was that by 1830, ministers had little royal patronage at their disposal other than the granting of honors and peerages.

P.J. Kulisheck

Bibliography

Foord, Archibald S. *His Majesty's Opposition, 1714–1830.* 1964.

———. "The Waning of 'The Influence of the Crown,'" in Rosalind Mitcheson, ed., *Essays in Eighteenth-Century History.* 1966.

Owen, J.B. "Political Patronage in 18th Century England," in Paul Fritz and David Williams, eds., *The Triumph of Culture: 18th Century Perspectives.* 1972.

Reitan, E.A. "The Civil List in Eighteenth-Century British Politics: Parliamentary Supremacy versus the Independence of the Crown." *The Historical Journal.* Vol. 9, pp. 318–337.

Thomas, P.D.G. *The House of Commons in the Eighteenth Century.* 1971.

See also Economical Reform; Government, Local and County; Government, National; Pension and Place Bills

Patronage Act (1712)

This act was introduced in 1712 against the explicit terms of the **Act of Union** with **Scotland.** It allowed the heritors or landowners of a particular parish to impose their own choice of minister on a congregation, in so doing removing one of the provisions of the 1690 Claim of Right. Patronage strengthened the hand of the Scottish **gentry** by giving them greater authority in the local community. It led by reaction to the creation of the breakaway Secession Church in 1733, whose ministers believed that the imposition of unpopular clergy went against the principles of the **Church of Scotland.** The idea that the minister had to be popularly endorsed by the laity, as expressed through the views of the elders, was deeply rooted in Scottish society. Imposed ministers could often expect a hostile reception, particularly in rural areas, where they might find the church boarded up and the locals even threatening physical abuse.

Richard Finlay

Bibliography

Drummond, A.L., and J. Bulloch. *The Scottish Church, 1688–1843.* 1973.

Galt, John. *Annals of the Parish.* Ed. with intro. by James Kinsley. 1967 ed.

Peace of Paris

See Paris, Peace of

Peacock, Thomas Love (1785–1866)

English poet, novelist, and friend of **Shelley**, Peacock, an only son, was born in Weymouth. In 1819 he began service with the **East India Company**, first under, then succeeding, **James Mill** as examiner. After publishing several youthful poems such as *Palmyra* (1806) and *The Genius of the Thames* (1810), he turned to **novel** writing.

The first of what was to become a series of "conversation novels" was his *Headlong Hall* (1816). This was a **satire** adopting the Socratic dialogue to comment on contemporary political and philosophical trends. Mr. Foster, the novel's optimist, and Mr. Escot, the pessimist, portray to some extent the contemporary conflict between the optimism of a **William Godwin** and the pessimism of a **Thomas Malthus**. In *Melincourt* (1817), the longest and most serious of Peacock's novels, Anthelia Melincourt, "mistress of herself and of ten thousand a year," is abducted and saved by Sir Oran Haut-ton, an orangutan who holds a seat in Parliament; paper currency, rotten **boroughs**, slavery, and the **Lake Poets** are all topics with which the novel is concerned.

In *Nightmare Abbey* (1818), which further satirizes the Romantics and **Romantic** attitudes, **Byron**, **Coleridge**, and Shelley are playfully mocked. *Maid Marian* (1822) and *The Misfortunes of Elphin* (1829) both employ historical settings. The former, which was later turned into a popular operetta, satirizes the church and monarchy; the latter, set in **Wales**, is a satire on contemporary debates about **elections and the franchise.** *Crotchet Castle* (1831) is again a conversation novel in which guests assembled at a country house represent various political and social views. *Gryll Grange* (1860–1861), a dual-plotted novel, presents a variety of amusing characters representative of many mid-Victorian attitudes.

It may be that despite all these creations, Peacock is best remembered for his *Four Ages of Poetry* (1820), not because of his argument (namely, that as humankind progresses, **poetry** deteriorates) but because of Shelley's more famous response to it (*Defense of Poetry*, 1840). In addition to this and his early poetry and novels, Peacock wrote *Rhododaphne: or The Thessalian Spell* (1818), a narrative poem (reminiscent of **Keats**'s *Lamia*) about a shepherd boy, Anthemion, torn between the love of the mortal Calliroe, and Rhododaphne, who contrives to carry him to an enchanted palace. Peacock's pseudonymously published *Sir Proteus: A Satirical Ballad* (1814) was an attack on **Southey**. He also produced a popular grammar for children, *Sir Hornbook* (1814). All in all, Peacock was an unusual writer who, while parodying many Romantic attitudes, shared the ideologies and emotions of the early 19th century.

Howard A. Mayer

Bibliography

Brett-Smith, H.F.B., and C.E. Jones, eds. *The Works of Thomas Love Peacock.* 10 vols. 1924–1934.

Butler, Marilyn. *Peacock Displayed: A Satirist in His Context.* 1979.

Mulvihill, James. *Thomas Love Peacock.* 1987.

Van Doren, Carl. *The Life of Thomas Love Peacock.* 1911.

Peake, Richard Brinsley (1792–1847)

A prolific writer of some 40 melodramas, **burlettas**, musical entertainments, and extravaganzas, as well as the treasurer of the Lyceum Theatre (1837–1847), Peake was the first dramatist to stage **Mary Wollstonecraft Shelley**'s *Frankenstein.* His *Presumption; or, The Fate of Frankenstein* (English Opera House, 1823) set the pattern for later dramatic and cinematic representations of *Frankenstein* by robbing the creature of speech, turning him into an "automaton," introducing a comic servant, and converting the story into a melodrama of ungodly science challenging domestic tranquility.

Born the son of Richard Peake, Drury Lane Theatre's treasurer for 40 years, Peake served as a clerk at Drury Lane (1806–1809) and was then apprenticed to the engraver James Heath (1809–1817). However, he soon began writing for the theater, offering such works as the dramatic sketch "The Bridge That Carries Us Safe Over" (1817), the operatic farce *Amateurs and Actors* (1818), the melodrama *The Haunted Inn* (1828), and the comedy derived from **Richard Steele** and **Frances Sheridan**, *Court and City* (1828). Among his nondramatic works was his *Memoirs of the Colman Family* (1841). Despite some success, Peake left his large family in difficult circumstances on his death.

Jeffrey N. Cox

Bibliography

Cox, Jeffrey N. *Seven Gothic Dramas, 1789–1825.* 1992.

Forrey, Steven Earl. *Hideous Progenies: Dramatizations of* Frankenstein *from Mary Shelley to the Present.* 1990.

Nitchie, Elizabeth. *Mary Shelley, Author of* Frankenstein. 1953.

Peake, Richard Brinsley. Selected works available in *English and American Drama of the Nineteenth Century.* G. Freedley and A. Nicoll, eds., 1965–1975; J. Ellis and J. Donohue, eds., 1975–.

See also Dramatic Arts

Peel Family

The Peels of Staffordshire were one of the great economic and political success stories of Hanoverian Britain. Within three generations, they passed from yeoman farmer status to wealth abounding to the prime ministership of the kingdom.

The family's antecedents cannot be traced with any certainty prior to **George II**'s reign. Robert Peel I (1750–1830), a great **cotton** manufacturer and M.P., died a multimillionaire some 40 years after purchasing the Tamworth estate of the first Marquess of Bath. But the elder Peel had no wish to see his sons follow him in business, however profitable. Instead, he educated them at Harrow, Oxford, and Cambridge, paving the way for them to pursue careers in the **army** and in Parliament. Treading a path later followed by many other British industrialists, the Peels became country gentlemen.

The patriarch was in his political views generally a reactionary: he opposed parliamentary reform and **Catholic emancipation**, supported slavery, and, like many High **Tories**, was paternalistic in outlook. His distinguished and talented eldest son, Robert Peel II (1788–1850), who entered the **House of Commons** in 1809, marched to a slightly different drummer. He was known as "Orange Peel" to denote his sympathy for Irish Protestantism during his period in **Ireland** as Chief Secretary (1812–1818)—a job in which he succeeded **Castlereagh** and **Wellington**.

Yet Peel gradually, as Home Secretary (1822–1827, 1828–1830), liberalized his position on Ireland and on other matters. He split with the High Tory tradition in 1829 to take the lead in the House of Commons in support of Catholic emancipation. This turned out to be but a prelude to his apostasy as **Prime Minister** in 1846, when he endorsed the end of agricultural protection and the repeal of the **Corn laws**, and, once again, split the Tory party. It was during his first term as Prime Minister (1834–1835) that Peel issued his famous political call to arms, the Tamworth Manifesto, which, on behalf of the Conservative party, accepted the **Reform Bill** of 1832 but reaffirmed the traditional Tory support for the monarchy, the church, and the **House of Lords**.

James J. Sack

Robert Peel the Younger

Bibliography

Clark, G. Kitson. *Peel and the Conservative Party.* 1929.

Gash, Norman. *Mr. Secretary Peel: The Life of Sir Robert Peel to 1830.* 1961.

———. *Sir Robert Peel: The Life of Sir Robert Peel after 1830.* 1972.

Sack, James J. *From Jacobite to Conservative: Reaction and Orthodoxy in Britain, c.1760–1832.* 1993.

Thorne, R.G. *The History of Parliament: The House of Commons, 1790–1820.* 5 vols. 1986.

Peep O' Day Boys

This was a militant Protestant society, which emerged in Armagh in the 1780s amid intense economic competition between Protestant and **Catholic**. The specific issue that sparked the movement was Catholic access to weapons. The nonenforcement of the **penal laws** had allowed Catholics to acquire arms during the preceding period, the era of the **volunteering movement**. This had symbolic and practical implications, being perceived generally to strengthen the Catholic position in **Ireland**. In response, the Peep O' Day Boys began a series of dawn arms raids against Catholic homes—hence the dawn's light appellation.

These activities stimulated the growth of the Catholic protection organization known as the **Defenders**. Its federated cell-structure soon proved superior to the loosely organized Peep O' Day Boys. Clashes between the two groups continued intermittently during the 1780s and 1790s, culminating in the Battle of the Diamond, near Loughall, County Armagh, on 21 September 1795. It was in the aftermath of this conflict that the **Orange Order** emerged, intended as a more disciplined and cohesive alternative to the Peep O' Day Boys. The latter inevitably gravitated to the new lodge structure, despite being officially denied membership, and were active in the wave of attacks on Catholics in 1795 known as the "Armagh outrages."

E.W. McFarland

Bibliography

Gibbon, P. "The Origins of the Orange Order and the United Irishmen." *Economy and Society.* Vol. 1, pp. 135–163.

Miller, D.W. *Peep O' Day Boys and Defenders: Selected Documents on the County Armagh Disturbances, 1784–1796.* 1990.

Senior, H. *Orangeism in Ireland and Britain 1795–1836.* 1966.

See also Anglo–Irish Protestant Ascendancy; Catholic Relief Acts

Peerage

See Aristocracy and Gentry

Peerage Bill (1719)

In this the **House of Lords** proposed to limit the Crown's authority to establish new peerages. The bill was partly a posthumous swipe at **Queen Anne** for her politically motivated creation of 12 peerages in 1712. The objective in 1719 was to bolster the government's Court-based **Whig** majority against the growing influence of **Robert Walpole**'s country-based opposition Whigs in the **Commons**. Walpole and his supporters saw the bill as an attempt to close the **Lords** against them, and defeated it. The controversy revealed the internal rifts in Whig politics, especially the Court-versus-country rivalry.

K.R. Wood

Bibliography

Foord, A.S. *His Majesty's Opposition, 1714–1830.* 1964.
Naylor, John F., ed. *The British Aristocracy and the Peerage Bill of 1719.* 1968.
Rogers, Nicholas. *Whigs and Cities: Popular Politics in the Age of Walpole and Pitt.* 1990.

See also Political Thought

Pelham, Henry (1696–1754)

Pelham was the next great **Whig** Prime Minister after **Sir Robert Walpole**. His true stature as a politician has been obscured by the much longer career of his elder brother, Thomas Pelham-Holles, **Duke of Newcastle**. Yet, while Pelham headed their administration as First Lord of the Treasury and Chancellor of the Exchequer (1743–1754), he rationalized finances, maintained a safe majority in the **House of Commons**, won over members of the **opposition**, and earned the confidence of **George II**. As First Minister, he was honest, efficient, and skillful in getting his colleagues to work together. When the king learned of his death (6 March 1754), he moaned, "Now I shall have no more peace!"

Pelham entered the Commons in 1717 and held a succession of responsible posts: Junior Lord of the Treasury (1721–1724), Secretary at War (1724–1730), and Paymaster General (1730–1743). His good friend Walpole made him his deputy in Commons and his political heir-apparent. After Walpole's fall (1742), Pelham and Newcastle set about winning the king's support and control of the government. Eventually they succeeded (1746) in consolidating their **broad-bottom administration**.

Pelham took pride in his chief financial accomplishment, the consolidation of the national debt at the lower interest rate of 3%. He also pleased the king by reducing secret service expenditure to less than half of what Walpole had spent each year. Pelham's contemporaries admired his integrity and applauded the fact that he made no personal gain from holding offices that others had used to enrich themselves.

P.J. Kulisheck

Bibliography

Coxe, William. *Memoirs of the Administration of the Right Honourable Henry Pelham.* 1829.
Owen, John B. *The Rise of the Pelhams.* 1957.
Sedgwick, Romney. *History of Parliament: The House of Commons, 1715–1754.* 2 vols. 1970.
Wilkes, John. *A Whig in Power: The Political Career of Henry Pelham.* 1964.

Penal Laws

Protestants in **Ireland**, in the aftermath of the **Glorious Revolution** and the **Battle of the Boyne** (1690), were determined to safeguard their position against a recrudescence of Catholic power. The result was the penal laws, a body of legislation, enacted in a fairly piecemeal manner between 1697 and 1728, aimed at undermining the influence of the **Roman Catholic** Church and the wealth, social standing, and political weight of the Irish Catholic **population** at large. These laws were much more severe than those against Catholics in England.

Regulations were ratified that prevented Catholics from voting and sitting in the **Irish Parliament**, restricted their rights to inherit and to lease land, and to prosper in trade and industry. Catholics were excluded from military, legal, and educational professions, and a sustained attempt was made between 1697 and 1709 to undermine the capacity of the Catholic Church to minister, both by banishing the regular clergy and those who exercised ecclesiastical jurisdiction, and by providing for the registration and nonreplacement of the secular clergy who were allowed to remain.

In practice, these laws were only fitfully enforced. They were appealed to during the **Jacobite** invasion scares of 1715, 1719, and 1745, and on a number of other occasions when the anxieties of the **Anglo-Irish Protestant Ascendancy** were acute. Otherwise, Catholic clergy were largely left free to minister, provided they did so discreetly. The laws against Catholic landownership proved more effective; the percentage of land in Catholic ownership fell because of some landowners' conversion to Protestantism, but many Catholics neutralized the legislation against them (using the tactic of collusive discoveries).

Evasionary tactics were less feasible in circumventing the laws against Catholic participation in politics, which successfully secured Protestants in exclusive political control until the late 18th century. Then a combination of Catholic assertiveness and British conciliatoriness was responsible for **Catholic relief acts**, which repealed many of the penal laws. The main exception was the right to sit in Parliament; this remained prohibited until **Catholic emancipation** (1829).

James Kelly

Bibliography

Bartlett, Thomas. *The Fall and Rise of the Irish Nation: The Catholic Question, 1690–1830.* 1992.
Connolly, S.J. *Religion, Law and Power: The Making of Protestant Ireland, 1660–1760.* 1992.

Peninsular Campaign

See French Revolutionary and Napoleonic Wars

Pennant, Thomas (1726–1798)

Pennant, naturalist and antiquary, a leader of Hanoverian **science**, was born in Downing, Flintshire. A boyhood present of Willoughby's *Ornithology* encouraged him to study natural history. His early nature studies included fossils and other minerals in Cornwall. He **traveled** extensively, visiting not only various parts of England and **Wales** but **Ireland**, **Scotland**, the Isle of Man, and the Continent, where he met Voltaire (1694–1778), the naturalist Buffon (1707–1788), and other luminaries. He liked to travel on horseback, and kept elaborate journals of his observations. His frequent traveling companion, Moses Griffith, made sketches and drawings afterward reproduced in Pennant's various *Tours*. His principal work on zoology, *British Zoology*, appeared in four volumes between 1761 and 1777; his own favorite work, the *History of Quadrupeds*, in 1781.

Pennant's works on natural history did much to popularize the subject. *Outlines of the Globe*, in 22 manuscript volumes, was his most ambitious literary undertaking. He also produced works on local **history**, militia laws, and mail **coaches**. He received numerous honors, becoming a Fellow of the Society of Antiquaries and of the **Royal Society**. He was given the freedom of **Edinburgh**, and was High Sheriff of Flintshire. He regarded his election to the Royal Society of Upsala, on the nomination of Linnaeus (1707–1778), as his greatest literary honor. In 1793 he wrote his *Literary Life of the Late Thomas Pennant, Esq., by Himself.*

Theresa McDonald

Bibliography

Darwin, Sir Francis. *Rustic Sounds and Other Studies in Literature and Natural History.* 1917.

Dictionary of Welsh Biography Down to 1940. 1959.

Gascoigne, John. *Joseph Banks and the English Enlightenment: Useful Knowledge and Polite Culture.* 1994.

Pennant, Thomas. *The Literary Life of the Late Thomas Pennant, Esq., By Himself.* 1793.

Stewart, Larry. *The Rise of Public Science: Rhetoric, Technology and Natural Philosophy in Newtonian Britain, 1660–1750.* 1992.

See also Autobiography and Confession; Banks, Sir Joseph; White, Gilbert

Pension

As employed by historians of 18th-century Britain, *pension* normally refers to fixed amounts paid regularly by the government to nominees or their dependants. Pensions were paid by the Crown out of its Civil List income from the revenues, chiefly customs and excise, granted to the monarch for life. **Opposition** politicians regarded Crown pensions as a source of corruption when used by royal ministers in a system of patronage, especially pensions granted to M.P.s.

Sinecures (public offices that required no work but paid a good salary) and offices that could be filled by a deputy were given as a form of public pension, ostensibly as a reward for service to the state. Total cost of all Civil List pensions was on average £95,000 a year during the period 1721–1780. The recipients and number of private pensions awarded by the Crown during this period are unknown because the secret service books listing them are lost. Surviving random lists indicate that many went to persons in poor health or reduced circumstances; some went to needy writers and artists.

The revenues of **Ireland**, a separate kingdom to 1800, produced at least as large a sum for royal pensions, some granted to foreigners and English M.P.s. The Crown also received the annual surplus of the Scottish government (less than £10,000), which provided pensions for widows of Scots politicians and the genuinely impecunious Scots peers.

At his accession (1760), **George III** turned over the Civil List revenues to Parliament in exchange for a fixed sum of £800,000 a year, a measure devised by his father. His grandfather **George II**'s revenues had grown with national prosperity, but George III's fixed sum quickly proved inadequate. On several occasions his ministers were forced to ask Parliament to pay the king's arrears, which allowed opposition politicians to question Civil List expenditures and demand an accounting. At length the Establishment Act (1782) brought the Civil List under parliamentary control. One provision limited the pension list to £95,000 a year and required public payment and listing of names. The Irish pension fund was reduced in 1793, the Scots in 1810, and their lists published. In 1830, **William IV** was allowed a maximum of £75,000 from any source for pensions.

P.J. Kulisheck

Bibliography

Foord, Archibald S. "'The Waning of "'The Influence of the Crown,'" in Rosalind Mitcheson, ed. *Essays in Eighteenth-Century History.* 1966.

Namier, Sir Lewis B., and John Brooke. *History of Parliament: The House of Commons, 1754–1790.* 3 vols. 1964.

Reitan, E.A. "The Civil List in Eighteenth-Century British Politics: Parliamentary Supremacy versus the Independence of the Crown." *The Historical Journal.* Vol. 9, pp. 318–337.

Sedgwick, Romney. *History of Parliament: The House of Commons, 1715–1754.* 2 vols. 1970.

Thorne, R.G. *History of Parliament: The House of Commons, 1790–1820.* 5 vols. 1986.

See also Patronage; Pension and Place Bills

Pension and Place Bills

"Places" were offices of profit held under the Crown, a category that embraced Cabinet ministers, other civil officials, **army** and **navy** officers, members of the royal household, members of statutory commissions, and others. "Placemen" referred more narrowly to members of Parliament, particularly backbenchers in the **House of Commons**, who also held appointments such as these (and sometimes royal **pensions** as well), and who hence, through the Crown's ongoing patronage, were believed to be especially susceptible to its political influence. Much of 18th-century politics turned on the attempts by **opposition** politicians, through place bills and pension bills, to reduce or eradicate this influence (at least until they could enjoy its fruits themselves); which they and more sincerely **radical** propagandists denounced as systematic "corruption" of the body politic.

The number of placemen grew at the end of the 17th century from the contemporary expansion of the armed forces, treasury, and revenue offices. In the next century, when the civil service alone grew to employ some 16,000 officials by around 1800, 100 placemen on average sat in Parliament (roughly one-fifth of the total membership) during the period 1720–1780. The stipulation in the **Act of Settlement** (1701) that all placemen were to be removed from the House of Commons at the **Hanoverian succession** was circumvented, but many removal bills were introduced subsequently. From 1730 through 1742 the opposition to **Sir Robert Walpole** introduced five pension bills and six place bills in unsuccessful efforts to curtail Crown influence. In 1782 their successors, the **Rockingham Whigs**, in what they called **economical reform**, obtained passage of the Establishment Act, which confirmed Parliament's control of the Civil List and abolished 134 sinecures, salaried offices that required no duties. Over the next 40 years, various acts and administrative reforms removed some 3,500 sinecures; only 55 remained and were abolished in 1834.

Other acts that removed placemen were Clerke's Act (1782), which excluded government contractors from seats in Commons, and Crewe's Act (1782), which disfranchised most revenue officers on the assumption that the treasury influenced elections in port cities through the votes of customs and excise employees. Historians disagree on the efficacy of Crewe's Act, but not on the fact that all these acts, combined with Commons' oversight of the Civil List, greatly diminished the influence of the Crown by the end of the Georgian era.

P.J. Kulisheck

Bibliography

Foord, Archibald S. "The Waning of 'The Influence of the Crown,'" in Rosalind Mitcheson, ed., *Essays in Eighteenth-Century History.* 1966.

Kemp, Betty. "Crewe's Act, 1782," in Mitcheson op. cit.

Reitan, E.A. "The Civil List in Eighteenth-Century British Politics: Parliamentary Supremacy versus the Independence of the Crown." *The Historical Journal.* Vol. 9, pp. 318–337.

See also Dunning, John; Government, National; Patronage; Political Thought

Perceval, Spencer (1762–1812)

Son of the second Earl of Egmont (1711–1770), Perceval was educated at Harrow and Trinity College, Cambridge. A lawyer, first elected to the **House of Commons** in 1796, he held a series of public legal positions. Perceval quickly established himself as one of the leading **Tory** debaters in the House. He became Chancellor of the Exchequer under the **Duke of Portland** and **Prime Minister** from 1809 to his death in 1812.

Spencer Perceval

Perceval's premiership coincided with the greatest upsurge in domestic **radicalism** since the 1790s, but he nonetheless stalwartly opposed all attempts to reform Parliament or to extend the suffrage. He continued to oppose, as he had done throughout his career, any attempt to allow **Roman Catholics** to sit in Parliament. In **foreign relations** he maintained the policy of providing substantial British support to Portugal and Spain in their attempts to defeat Napoleon. A fervent **Evangelical**, his extensive study of biblical prophecy convinced him that the world would end in 1926. He was murdered in the lobby of the House of Commons by John Bellingham, a disappointed claimant for government compensation, and thus became the only assassinated British Prime Minister in history.

James J. Sack

Bibliography

Gray, Denis. *Spencer: The Evangelical Prime Minister, 1762–1812.* 1963.

Walpole, Spencer. *The Life of the Right Honourable Spencer Perceval.* 1874.

See also Regency, The

Percy, Thomas (1729–1811)

Translator, editor, and bishop, Percy was born at Bridgnorth, Shropshire, and educated at Oxford. He became Bishop of Dromore in 1782. Eclectic in his interests, he **translated** Chinese, involved himself in study of Gaelic and Erse, and in 1765 published three very influential volumes of **ballads**, *Reliques of Ancient English Poetry,* thus contributing much to the revival of the ballad tradition and to **antiquarian** literary scholarship. By giving new life to the lyrical ballad and the ballad stanza, he also helped generate an interest in English medieval culture. The sheer force of the ballad revival may be observed in the works of poets who followed him, notably **William Wordsworth**.

Ronald Rompkey

Bibliography

Davis, Bertram H. *Thomas Percy: A Scholar–Cleric in the Age of Johnson*. 1989.

Percy, Thomas. *The Percy Letters*. Eds. David Nichol Smith, Cleanth Brooks, and A.F. Falconer. 1944–1949.

See also Ballad

Periodicals (Magazines)

The Hanoverian periodical magazine, one of the era's great inventions, emerged from a thin, mixed parentage of 17th-century learned journals, book catalogs, monthly compilations of court news and the talk of the town, and ephemeral experiments in **poetry**, storytelling, and commentary on contemporary topics. The main fruits of this in the early decades of the 18th century were *The Review* (1704–1713), started by **Daniel Defoe**, *The Tatler* (1709–1711), begun by **Sir Richard Steele**, and *The Spectator* (1711–1712, 1714), begun by Steele and **Joseph Addison**. These all carried short essays along with serial narratives—often fictional—on contemporary topics, and did much to shape contemporary opinion on many things, including the proper content of periodicals themselves. The American **publisher** and polymath **Benjamin Franklin** later recounted how he had labored to imitate the prose style of *The Spectator* when he was a youth in Boston.

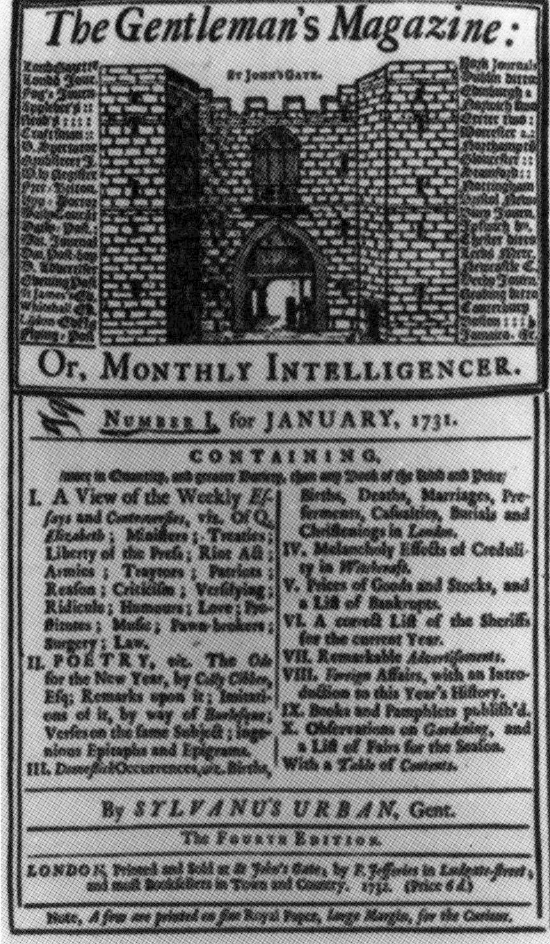

The Gentleman's Magazine:

ST JOHN'S GATE.

Or, MONTHLY INTELLIGENCER.

NUMBER I. for JANUARY, 1731.

CONTAINING,

more in Quantity, and greater Variety, than any Book of the Kind and Price

I. A View of the Weekly *Essays* and *Controversies*, viz. Of Q. *Elizabeth*; Ministers; Treaties; Liberty of the Press; Riot Act; Armies; Traytors; Patriots; Reason; Criticism; Versifying; Ridicule; Humours; Love; Prostitutes; Musick; Pawn-brokers; Surgery; Law.

II. POETRY, viz. The *Ode* for the New Year, by *Colly Cibber*, Esq; Remarks upon it; Imitations of it, by way of *Burlesque*; Verses on the same Subject; ingenious Epitaphs and Epigrams.

III. *Domestick* Occurrences, viz. Births, Deaths, Marriages, Preferments, Casualties, Burials and Christenings in *London*.

IV. Melancholy Effects of Credulity in *Witchcraft*.

V. Prices of Goods and Stocks, and a List of Bankrupts.

VI. A correct List of the Sheriffs for the current Year.

VII. Remarkable *Advertisements*.

VIII. *Foreign* Affairs, with an Introduction to this Year's History.

IX. Books and Pamphlets publish'd.

X. Observations on *Gardening*, and a List of Fairs for the Season.

With a *Table of Contents*.

By *SYLVANUS URBAN*, Gent.

The FOURTH EDITION.

LONDON: Printed and Sold at *St John's Gate*, by *F. Jefferies* in *Ludgate-street*, and most Booksellers in Town and Country. 1732. (Price 6 d.)

Note, *A few are printed on fine* Royal Paper, *large Margin, for the Curious*.

First Issue of The Gentleman's Magazine, *1731*

The most successful offspring of these early beginnings was *The Gentleman's Magazine*, founded by **Edward Cave** in 1731. Cave, behind his pen name "Sylvanus Urban," began the *Gentleman's* by reprinting news items, miscellaneous essays, and pieces of general interest, which he borrowed from his competition. The publication was one of many popular in **coffeehouses**. Within 8 years, partly at the instigation of his young assistant **Samuel Johnson**, Cave determined to increase the quantity of original material and intensify his magazine's appeal to serious, informed readers. He began to include maps; foreign literary intelligence; book announcements; letters to the editor; memoirs, essays on **antiquity**, verse, even **music**; birth, marriage, and death notices; current stock prices; and general data on British commerce and trade. The magazine even contained scientific notices; parts of **Benjamin Franklin**'s important *Experiments and Observations on Electricity* (1751) had been published there earlier in the form of letters.

All this, together with the inevitable advertisements, was to be the staple of many later periodicals. The *Gentleman's* itself remained a fixture of British culture down to 1907, and even today its volumes, preserved in many libraries, may be read with interest. It was, of course, imitated. Among its most successful 18th-century stepchildren were Ralph Griffiths' *The Monthly Review* (1749–1845), a serious and reform-minded monthly often expressing **dissenting** opinions, and Archibald Hamilton's *The Critical Review* (1756–1817), stringent, conservative, and Anglican in outlook. There were hundreds of less long-lived competitors. To name only a few from the period around 1750, there were the *Champion* (1739–1741), *Covent Garden Journal* (1752), *Female Spectator* (1744–1746), *Parrot* (1746), *World* (1753–1756), *Rambler* (1750–1754), *Literary Magazine* (1756–1758), *Idler* (1758–1759), and *Bee* (1759).

The number of periodicals continually expanded, in line with the absolute expansion of the British **population** and also the spread of literacy at lower social levels. By the time of Queen Victoria, publishers were aiming inexpensive weeklies such as the *Penny Magazine* (begun in 1832) at the broadest mass of consumers. The total number of periodicals begun during the Hanoverian age is difficult to estimate, but must have been in the neighborhood of 400. Its magnitude is suggested in the *Tercentenary Handlist of English and Welsh Newspapers, Magazines, and Reviews* (1920), which identifies, for the period 1715–1830, 1,321 titles published in **London** and its suburbs, and another 479 published in English counties and **Wales**. The volume does not even consider **Scotland**, where many of the most eminent periodicals were published, or **Ireland**, which in the 18th century had the largest book-printing industry in the world outside London.

To their readers, periodicals offered regular entertainment, enlightenment, and informed opinion. But to the intellectuals who produced them, they provided excellent opportunities for self-expression, the guidance and improvement of the public, and the ripping up of their literary enemies. Virtually every major writer of the period contributed to periodicals, and many, such as Addison, Steele, Johnson, Defoe, **Lady Mary Wortly Montagu**, **Henry Fielding**, **Eliza Haywood**, **Tobias Smollett**, **Francis Jeffrey**, **Leigh Hunt**, **John Wilson Croker**, **Sir Walter Scott**, **James Mill**, **James Hogg**, and **John Wilson**, had a hand in founding or regularly editing them. Filtering their learning into their writings, the intellectuals offered creative descriptions of and critical commentaries on the events, politics, personalities, and especially the literature of the age.

It was in this last respect that periodicals had their most enduring impact. Though the *Monthly* and the *Critical* were important pioneers, it was only in the first decade of the 19th century that there emerged the truly literary periodical, the ancestor of those well known today, whose editor vigorously competed with others to publish verse, prose criticism, political and biographical essays, and even fiction of the very highest caliber, paying authors so well that a literary profession actually began to come into being. The first new journal of the period, the *Edinburgh Review*, founded and edited by Francis Jeffrey (1802), proved that critics could be both aggressive and independent in defense of literary conservatism, as in their condemnation of the literary renegades **Wordsworth** and **Coleridge** and their slighting comments on **Byron**. The *Edinburgh* ignored contemporary events and focused on literature, paying its authors handsomely and encouraging essays worthy of lasting admiration. The satirist **William Gifford** founded the *Quarterly Review* in 1809, as **Tory** in outlook as the *Edinburgh* was **Whiggish**. While men of stature like Jeffrey, **Sydney Smith**, **Henry Brougham**, and **Thomas Malthus** wrote behind the anonymity of the one, Gifford paid **Scott**, Croker, and **William Lamb** to thunder away anonymously in the other.

The *Edinburgh* and the *Quarterly* dominated and divided opinion, having a greater influence than any earlier and most later periodicals. It is estimated that they were selling around 14,000 copies apiece by 1818, with readerships five or six times that large. The whole story of the reception of and bitter controversies surrounding **Romantic** literature, from the time of *Lyrical Ballads* (1798) on down through that of the deaths in the 1820s of **Shelley** and Byron, can be read in their pages and in those of their well-known imitators, the *Examiner* (*f.* 1808), *New Monthly* (*f.* 1814), *Blackwood's Edinburgh Magazine* (*f.* 1817), *London Magazine* (*f.* 1819), *New Monthly Magazine and Literary Journal* (*f.* 1820), the *Liberal* (*f.* 1822), and *Westminster Review* (*f.* 1824).

Of course there was more in the pages of these publications than literary and political warfare. Lamb, **Hazlitt**, and **De Quincey** wrote as much about life as about literature. Lamb's *Essays of Elia* appeared initially in the *London Magazine* between 1820 and 1823; there the book-lover and city-dweller proved to his wide reading audience that the English essay could again be both informative and winningly quaint, humorous, and tender, as in the great days of *The Spectator* a century earlier. Hazlitt, one of the greatest essayists of the Hanoverian age, contributed articles on art and criticism to the *New Monthly Magazine* and *Edinburgh Review*, whereas De Quincey's two most anthologized pieces—"Confessions of an English Opium Eater" and "On Murder as One of the Fine Arts"—appeared in *Blackwood's Magazine*. Some scholars have maintained that these Romantic essayists guided periodical literature back to its **Augustan** parentage. But literary assumptions themselves had changed, and the periodicals of the early 19th century permitted prose writers to exercise their own individual voices with far greater freedom than did their predecessors during the age of Queen Anne.

Samuel J. Rogal

Bibliography

Anderson, Patricia. *The Printed Image and the Transformation of Popular Culture, 1790–1860*. 1991.

Crane, R.S., and F.B. Kaye. *A Census of British Newspapers and Periodicals, 1620–1800*. 1966.

Goldgar, Bernard. "Fielding's Periodicals and the Idea of Literary Fame." *Journal of Newspaper and Periodical History*. Vol. 2, pp. 2–9.

Graham, Walter. *The Beginnings of English Literary Periodicals*. 1926.

Klancher, Jon P. *The Making of English Reading Audiences, 1790–1832*. 1987.

Law, Marie H. *The English Familiar Essay in the Early Nineteenth Century*. 1934.

Reitan, Earl R. *The Best of the* Gentleman's Magazine, *1731–1754*. 1987.

Sullivan, Alvin, ed. *British Literary Magazines*. 2 vols. 1983.

Tercentenary Handlist of English and Welsh Newspapers, Magazines, and Reviews. 1920.

See also Essay; Journalists and Journalism; Literary Criticism; Newspaper Press; Russel, Richard

Peterloo Massacre (1819)

This was the bloodiest popular disturbance of the **Regency**, one of several confrontations after 1815 between workers hurt by economic dislocation, radicals desirous of political and economic reform, and conservative authorities relying on force to resolve problems much more complicated than anyone understood.

On the afternoon of Monday, August 16, 1819, more than 60,000 people, most of them workers, a few of them armed, and some displaying flags, banners, and Caps of Liberty, gathered at St. Peter's Field, **Manchester**, to hear radical reformer **Henry ("Orator") Hunt** deliver a speech calling for reform of the **House of Commons**. This meeting, possibly the largest English political gathering ever held up to that time, was also one of the first to which the press sent reporters to cover an out-of-town political event, as **newspapers** from **Leeds**, **Liverpool**, and **London** covered the rally.

The crowd, organized by an extensive radical network in northwestern England—**Samuel Bamford** was a typical local activist—formed in surrounding towns and entered Manchester that morning in colorful processions. The pathetic **Blanketeer March** (1817) had begun earlier from the same point. Local magistrates, fearing some destruction of property, had prepared an assemblage of mounted yeomanry, constables, and dragoons to observe the activities. Shortly after Hunt's arrival, but apparently before he began to speak, they read the **Riot Act** (1715) from a point far away, ordering his arrest and the dispersal of the gathering. The yeomanry and constables, using staves and the backs of sabres, plunged into the crowd, attempting to arrest him. Not all of them went berserk: one officer was heard to shout, "Gentlemen, gentlemen, for shame, forbear! The people cannot get away!" In the confusion as they cleared the area, 11 people were killed and more than 400 were wounded.

The aftermath might have been predicted. The troop commanders praised themselves (one glorying in how "the instant they saw ten or a dozen Mobbites together [his men] rode at them and *leathered* them properly"). Conservatives throughout the country rallied around the authorities. Parliament passed the repressive **Six Acts** (1819). The victims were blamed. Hunt, arrested along with 40 others, had to post a heavy bail and was subsequently convicted of unlawful and seditious assembling; he spent 2.5 years in Ilchester jail. Among radicals, the military riot was soon in bitter derision labeled "Peterloo" after the British victory against French forces at Waterloo (1815).

Afterward, repression, improving economic conditions, and division within the ranks of radical reformers caused a temporary decline in the radical movement. At the same time, Manchester's **cotton** manufacturers, **journalists**, and other respectable elements, largely quiescent before Peterloo, were spurred into political action. They started relief committees for the victims and produced an important Declaration and Protest, signed by 5,000 citizens, which vindicated the crowd as "*perfectly peaceable*" and condemned the "*unexpected and unnecessary Violence by which the Assembly were dispersed.*" The *Manchester Guardian* was founded (1821) by John Edward Taylor (1791–1844), one of the organizers of this protest. Peterloo, a proving ground of all the forces at work in 1819, thus helped to startle the **middle classes** into reformist activity after three decades of submission to extreme official conservatism and reaction.

Mark C. Herman

Bibliography

Belchem, John. *"Orator" Hunt: Henry Hunt and English Working-Class Radicalism.* 1985.

Hunt, Henry. *Memoirs of Henry Hunt, Esq. Written by Himself in His Majesty's Jail at Ilchester.* 3 vols. 1820–1822.

Lawson, Philip. "Reassessing Peterloo." *History Today.* Vol. 38, pp. 24–29.

Marlow, Joyce. *The Peterloo Massacre.* 1969.

Read, Donald. *Peterloo: The "Massacre" and Its Background.* 1959; rpt. 1973.

Reid, Robert. *The Peterloo Massacre.* 1989.

Walmsley, Robert. *Peterloo: The Case Reopened.* 1969.

See also French Revolution; Radical War; Radicalism and Radical Politics; Riots and Popular Disturbances

Petitioning Movement

See Association Movement

Phillip, Arthur (1738–1814)

Phillip is best known as the first governor of the penal colony founded in New South Wales in 1788, the first permanent European settlement in **Australia**, but his life was spent chiefly as a sailor. Completing his apprenticeship in the merchant marine (1755), he served in the **navy** until 1763. After farming for a while he again went to sea, and between 1774 and 1778, with permission from the British government, served as Captain in the Portuguese navy. He rejoined the British navy from 1778 to 1784 and was soon afterward appointed governor of the penal colony planned for convicted British felons, to be established in New South Wales.

Governor Arthur Phillip

He and his 11 ships (the "first fleet") landed in Botany Bay in January 1788, carrying some 736 convicts and several hundred marines and civil servants. He remained governor of the colony until 1792. Biographers credit him with much humanity in dealing with the convicts, and courage and resourcefulness in overcoming the difficulties of starting an agricultural economy and coping with the Aborigines. His later career saw his promotion to Admiral during the **Napoleonic Wars**.

Stanley D. Nash

Bibliography

Australian Dictionary of Biography, s.v. "Phillip, Arthur."

Frost, Alan. *Arthur Phillip, 1738–1814: His Voyaging.* 1987.
Mackaness, George. *Admiral Arthur Phillip.* 1937.
Phillip, Arthur. *The Voyage of Governor Phillip to Botany Bay.* 1789.

See also Transportation, Penal

Philosophical Radicalism

See Bentham, Jeremy, and Benthamites

Picturesque Movement

This aesthetic movement stretched from the 1780s down to the end of the Hanoverian period. Earlier, public interest in the idea of the picturesque had been prepared by **Edmund Burke**'s influential treatise *A Philosophical Enquiry into the Origins of Our Ideas of the Sublime and the Beautiful* (1756), which defined *beauty* in terms of smoothness and regularity, and *sublimity* in terms of the awe inspired in viewers as they looked upon scenes of natural grandeur.

The concept of the picturesque grew up between these two categories, the beautiful and the **sublime**—and emphasized the aesthetic quality of scenery that was rough, irregular, and in some way surprising or unexpected. Stressing the importance of Britain's natural history, and encouraging **travel** into remote and wild parts of the country, it became a powerful shaping force in late-18th-century aesthetics, particularly affecting **landscape painters**, **landscape gardeners**, travelers, and **architects**, as well as the general reading public.

The Rev. William Gilpin (1724–1804) was probably the most influential theorist of the picturesque, which he discussed in his eight travel journals, especially in *Three Essays: On Picturesque Beauty, on Picturesque Travel, and on Sketching Landscape* (1792). In these lively books, illustrated by his own aquatints, he gave his readers clear instructions on how to judge prospects in nature and, when sketching, how to improve what they saw by combining elements of actual landscapes into ideal imaginary scenes. Travelers, following Gilpin, sought out places he recommended for their particular historic, aesthetic, or spiritual significance; thus Tintern Abbey and the Wye Valley became widely celebrated by "picturesque" artists and writers.

A second influential theorist was **Sir Uvedale Price**, whose treatise, *An Essay on the Picturesque, as Compared with the Sublime and the Beautiful, and on the Use of Studying Pictures for the Purpose of Improving Real Landscape* (1794), stressed the broken lines and rough texture necessary for picturesque effects. Richard Payne Knight's (1750–1824) poem *The Landscape* (1794) completed the definition of the popular theory; and hence before long, naturally, a satirical reaction grew up against it. **William Combe** parodied it (and Gilpin too) in a long verse parody, one of the most popular publications of its time, *The Tour of Dr. Syntax in Search of the Picturesque* (1809–1811). Here Dr. Syntax, a caricature of Gilpin, is a pedantic bumbler rigidly bound by absurd rules, which prevent him from seeing the real world. **Thomas Rowlandson**, the **caricaturist**, illustrated Combe's verses with amusing and imaginative **watercolor** pictures, which exemplify picturesque theory even while spoofing it.

In literature as well as art, the influence of picturesque theory was pervasive. **Wordsworth**, **Austen**, **Fanny Burney**, **J.M.W. Turner**, and **John Constable**, and the Americans Henry David Thoreau (1817–1862) and Oliver Wendell Holmes (1809–1894), felt its power and reinforced its aesthetic values. It seems clear in retrospect that the growing appreciation of the picturesque signaled important underlying shifts, often interrelated, not only in the progressive acceptance of **Romantic** aesthetics but in nostalgic attitudes toward nature and quasi-egalitarian attitudes toward the political community.

Elise F. Knapp
Timothy Morton

Bibliography

Andrew, Malcolm. *The Search for the Picturesque: Landscape Aesthetics and Tourism in Britain, 1760–1800.* 1989.
Brennon, M. *Wordsworth, Turner, and the Romantic Landscape.* 1987.
Hipple, Walter J., Jr. *The Beautiful, the Sublime and the Picturesque in Eighteenth-Century British Aesthetic Theory.* 1957.
Howard, Peter. *Landscapes: The Artists' Vision.* 1991.
Hussey, Christopher. *The Picturesque: Studies in a Point of View.* 1927; rpt. 1967.
Manwaring, Elizabeth Wheeler. *Italian Landscape in Eighteenth-Century England: A Study Chiefly of the Influence of Claude Lorrain and Salvator Rosa on English Taste, 1700–1800.* 1925.
Pugh, S., ed. *Reading Landscape: Country, City, Capital.* 1990.
Robinson, S.K. *Inquiry into the Picturesque.* 1991.

Pirates and Piracy

Although piracy has existed since ancient times and Elizabethan "sea dogs" such as Francis Drake (*c.* 1540–1596) and John Hawkins (1532–1595) had preyed on Spanish shipping, and 17th-century buccaneers like Sir Henry Morgan (*c.* 1635–1688) had prowled the Caribbean, Britain's "golden age of piracy" came during the period 1680–1730.

There was little piracy around the British Isles, but perhaps as many as 2,000 British pirates operated in the waters off **North America** and **Africa**, in the Indian Ocean, and especially in the Caribbean, where treasure-laden Spanish galleons were the traditional target. Many pirates were privateersmen (i.e., men from privately owned warships, employed during wartime by governments as mercenary fighters) whose letters of marque had expired; others were former merchant sailors, or men of the **navy** who were unemployed because of peace, or escaped indentured servants.

Pirates, who averaged 25 years of age and came mostly from **Wales** and western England, operated on the collective authority of the crew, which drew up articles to govern their behavior, distribute spoils, and provide compensation for injuries. The captain, who functioned only as the vessel's military leader, was elected by the crew, as was the quartermaster, who was in charge of discipline on board ship. Many buccaneers and pirates formed homosexual unions called *matelotage,* which provided for the holding of property in common, with inheritance rights for the surviving partner. Pirate attacks depended on swiftly overtaking the prize, boarding it, and forcing its crew to surrender or subduing it through the use of pistols and cutlasses in hand-to-hand fighting.

The Romantic image of pirates in modern film bears little resemblance to reality. Most pirates spent their loot on drinking, women, and carousing; few ever buried their treasure, and apparently only one pirate captain made his victims walk the plank. Pirates did fly the "Jolly Roger," with its fearsome skull and crossbones.

The best-known Hanoverian pirate was Edward Teach or Thatch (?–1718) better known as "Blackbeard." A huge and violent character, born in **Bristol**, Teach and his men (and his 14 wives) had his headquarters at New Providence in the Bahamas. Teach had a long black beard, which he split and tied up around his ears in colored ribbons. Sailing his 40-gun warship *Queen Anne's Revenge,* he would often light smoking matches in his hair to create the image of a hellish fiend when he attacked his prey. After a ferocious battle with government naval vessels in Ocracoke Inlet, North Carolina (1718), he was killed, his severed head then triumphantly displayed from a government bowsprit.

Major Stede Bonnet (?–1718), a retired army officer and successful Barbados planter who purchased his own ship and set out as a pirate after domestic troubles, worked with Blackbeard for a time and was eventually hanged at Charleston, South Carolina, in 1718. Bartholomew "Black Bart" Roberts (1682–1722), a strict Sabbatarian and teetotaler, took more than 400 prizes until he was killed fighting a government vessel off the coast of West Africa in 1722. Apparently the only exceptions to the all-male world of piracy were Anne Bonney and Mary Read, who were part of a pirate crew that operated in the Caribbean; both escaped the gallows in 1720 because they were pregnant.

The fates of Blackbeard, Bonnet, and Roberts were emblematic of general changes occurring in the age of **George I**. The government's crackdown on pirates through a strong naval campaign, its establishment of admiralty commissioners in chartered colonies and royal provinces to deal with piracy, the issuance of amnesty, the criminalization of contact with pirates, and the use of publicity to brand pirates as outlaws, were bringing piracy to an end.

Changing economic conditions in North America and the **West Indies**, which depended on the safety of **overseas commerce**, together with the organizing of convoys, better naval patrols, harshly repressive policies, ongoing 18th-century warfare which attracted the glut of seamen toward privateers or the navy, and a shift among outlaws from piracy to the safer and more lucrative activity of **smuggling**, were also taking a heavy toll on this particular branch of **crime**. After the European and Latin American **wars** of the early 19th century there was a brief increase in piracy as more sailors were thrown out of work, but it never reached its former levels. Privateering, from which historically it had originated, was outlawed in 1856 in the Declaration of Paris that followed the Crimean War.

Mark C. Herman

Bibliography

Dow, George Francis, and John Henry Edmonds. *The Pirates of the New England Coast, 1630–1730.* 1923.

Gosse, Philip. *The Pirates' Who's Who.* 1924; rpt. 1968.

———. *The History of Piracy.* 1932; rpt. 1968.

Lucie-Smith, Edward. *Outcasts of the Sea: Pirates and Piracy.* 1978.

Marx, Jennifer. *Pirates and Privateers of the Caribbean.* 1992.

Rediker, Marcus. *Between the Devil and the Deep Blue Sea: Merchant Seamen, Pirates, and the Anglo-American Maritime World, 1700–1750.* 1987.

Williams, Neville. *Captains Outrageous: Seven Centuries of Piracy.* 1961.

Woodbury, George. *The Great Days of Piracy in the West Indies.* 1951.

See also Shipping and Seamen

Pitt, William, the Elder (1708–1778)

Pitt was a political outsider who rose to direct British policy in the **Seven Years' War**, a crucial struggle with the Bourbons for oceanic and **North American** hegemony. A loud critic of domestic corruption, he was subsequently a champion of American liberties. His achievements were all the more remarkable for a politician who, for much of his life, was dogged by poor physical health and considerable mental stress.

Pitt's position as an outsider was crucial: it helped to make his reputation, and to render him an unpredictable and unsettling figure in British politics. It caused certain problems when he gained office, but it bolstered his reputation as a man to whom the national interest might be entrusted, for he seemed apart from the world of Court and connection. Pitt was a Hanoverian hero, tarnished by the compromises of politics, but a hero for a country that wished to hear the bells of victory. To many people he seemed for a while the embodiment of contemporary **nationalism**.

Ironically, Pitt entered politics as M.P. for Old Sarum (1735–1747), one of the most rotten **boroughs** in England. Initially an **opposition** critic of **Sir Robert Walpole** and his use of **patronage**, Pitt continued his attacks on Walpole's successor, **John Carteret**, castigating his foreign policy and the payment of Hanoverian troops. Pitt's effectiveness was such that he was brought into office as Paymaster General in 1746. However, having failed to succeed **Henry Pelham** as head of the ministry in 1754, he returned to opposition. The government collapsed, and in December 1756 Pitt became Secretary of State for the Southern Department. **George II's** hostility and the exclusion of the powerful **Duke of Newcastle** crippled this ministry, however, and in July 1757 a new ministry, based on Pitt and Newcastle, was formed.

This government, fortified by Pitt's confident and domineering spirit, his great parliamentary eloquence, and his char-

William Pitt the Elder

acteristic willingness to break the rules—in this case, the rules of military seniority, for he put the **army** and **navy** under new, young commanders and ordered them to concert strategy as never before—took Britain to victory over **France** (1763). Nevertheless, **George III**'s accession in the middle of the conflict (1760) weakened Pitt, popular though he was now as "the Great Commoner." His warlike policy had alienated young George, and relations deteriorated further as a result of George's promotion of his favorite, the **Earl of Bute**. Pitt resigned in September 1761, when his demand for war with Spain was rejected by the cabinet.

Pitt was without office for the final 17 years of his life, with the exception of his tenure as Lord Privy Seal (1766–1768). He remained a figure of considerable importance until effectively incapacitated by ill-health in early 1767, but his role was largely that of a spoiler. He was often unwilling either to support ministries or to help create a united opposition, and as a disgruntled former leader with only a smallish parliamentary following he adopted an excessively peremptory tone in negotiations. His unhappy experience of the policies of George III and Bute led him to reject thoughts of taking office again unless assured of royal favor and the absence of a favorite.

Pitt benefited from the chronic weakness of the ministries of the 1760s, and the fall of the brief **Rockingham** ministry (1766) allowed him to form an administration; but it was a failure. His aim of governing "patriotically" without faction proved unrealistic, while his health lured him to take the peerage that would weaken his hold on the **House of Commons** (he became Earl of Chatham in 1766). He did not succeed in finding a reliable Commons manager, and his hopes for rescuing Britain from isolation by alliances with Prussia and Russia were never realized. Relinquishing power as a consequence of poor health, he attempted a return in 1769–1771, but his opposition to the **Grafton** and **North** ministries had little effect. His last political cause was the conciliation of the American colonists, whose security from France he had regarded as such an important goal in the Seven Years' War; but he lived long enough to see them break from British control and turn to France for support. Rising to speak in the **House of Lords** on 7 April 1778, he collapsed and died on 11 May. He had no opportunity to witness the meteoric rise in politics a few years later of his son, **William Pitt the Younger**.

Jeremy Black

Bibliography

Ayling, Stanley. *The Elder Pitt, Earl of Chatham.* 1976.

Black, Jeremy. *Pitt the Elder.* 1992.

Brown, Peter. *William Pitt, Earl of Chatham: The Great Commoner.* 1978.

Middleton, Richard. *The Bells of Victory: The Pitt–Newcastle Ministry and the Conduct of the Seven Years' War.* 1985.

Peters, Marie. *Pitt and Popularity: The Patriot Minister and London Opinion during the Seven Years' War.* 1980.

Pitt, William, the Younger (1759–1806)

The second son of **William Pitt the Elder** (later Earl of Chatham), Pitt was born in the year of his father's greatest military and administrative triumphs during the **Seven Years' War**. As T.B. Macaulay (1800–1859) put it, "the child inherited a name which, at the time of his birth, was the most illustrious in the civilized world, and was pronounced by every Englishman with pride, and by every enemy of England with mingled admiration and terror." The importance of this to Pitt's career can scarcely be exaggerated. Not only did it ease his path to

William Pitt the Younger

become the youngest **prime minister** in history, but it also encouraged expectations of success in his later career, during further wars against **France**, that never materialized.

A sickly child, he was not educated at a great public school, but at home. He was precocious. In 1773 (at age 14) he went to **Cambridge University**, where he remained until 1779. In 1781 he entered Parliament; in 1783, when 24 years old, he became Prime Minister. Pitt served in this office until 1801, slightly over 17 years, and then again (1804–1806) until his death. His tenure was longer than that of any prime minister in history, with the one exception of **Sir Robert Walpole**.

Beyond the important fact of his distinguished parentage, the sources of Pitt's power were threefold. First, he nearly always enjoyed the support of **George III**. When this was withdrawn in 1801 over Pitt's plan in the Irish Act of Union—to place England's and **Ireland's Catholics** on an equal footing with Protestants—Pitt's government quickly fell. Second, in an age when a magnificent group of orators shone in Parliament, Pitt, with his "silver-toned" voice, his logical, factual, reasoned speeches, and his supreme ability to ferret out the weaknesses in his opponents' arguments, dominated the **House of Commons**. And third, through his reputation of virtue and proven ability to manage the nation's financial establishment, he appealed more than any other contemporary politician to the body of public opinion, largely **middle class**, of an increasingly urbanized and capitalistic kingdom.

Pitt's premiership can be divided into two periods. The first period, from 1783 to 1792, was one of nearly unalloyed triumph. Pitt restored respect for the government after the political and military disasters of the 1770s, and dealt effectively with a number of pressing financial and imperial problems. His **India Act** (1784) established government control over the **East India Company**; his **Constitutional (Canada) Act** (1791) dealt comprehensively with Canadian problems; his reduction of customs duties deterred **smuggling** and won domestic approval, as did his introduction of a new **sinking fund** (1786) to cope with the gigantic debt of some £250 million inherited from the American war. Even in those instances where he failed to gain immediate political success—for example, his goals of moderately reforming the conditions of **elections and the franchise** (defeated in 1785) and of abolishing the **slave trade**—his efforts were credited as moral accomplishments. He was the personal acquaintance and *Wunderkind* of many **radicals** in the 1780s, who saw in him both virtue and effective political power.

Pitt reacted cautiously but not with immediate hostility at the beginning of the **French Revolution** (1789), and the **French Revolutionary and Napoleonic Wars**. But between 1793 (when France declared war) and his death 13 years later, he became the defender not only of the nation but of propertied conservatism, cracking down on **radicals**, suspending habeas corpus and supporting treason trials (1794), and leading the three European coalitions formed to counter French power. All three coalitions were complete failures. Pitt was not a decisive war leader. Neither a Chatham nor a Churchill, he had little background or even serious interest in military and naval affairs. When he died, Napoleon was in control of most of Europe.

As his woes mounted, Pitt, a bachelor, increasingly sought solace in drink. He had never possessed an iron constitution, and some recent studies suggest that he was suffering from cancer. In any case, his **drinking** was excessive. Macaulay wrote that "two bottles of port were little more to him than two dishes of tea." Like his distant successor during World War I, Herbert Asquith (1852–1928), Pitt not infrequently appeared drunk in public and sometimes even in the House of Commons. He died in his leased home at age 46, reportedly lamenting: "Oh, my country! How I leave my country."

James J. Sack

Biography

Ehrman, John. *The Younger Pitt: The Years of Acclaim.* 1969.
———. *The Younger Pitt: The Reluctant Transition.* 1983.
Reilly, Robin. *William Pitt the Younger.* 1978.
Sack, James J. *From Jacobite to Conservative: Reaction and Orthodoxy in Britain, c.1760–1832.* 1993.

See also Grenville, Baron; London Corresponding Society; Loyalist Associations; Regency Crisis; Tories and Toryism; Union, Act of (Ireland, 1800)

Place, Francis (1771–1854)

Place was for many years one of the most influential **radical** reformers in late Hanoverian Britain. Born in **London**, Place, who was self-educated, began work as a journeyman leather-worker, became a master tailor, and opened his own shop at 16 Charing Cross in 1799. His early radical activity included organizing a strike of London leather-workers in 1793 and joining the **London Corresponding Society** (LCS) in 1794.

Always more a backstage organizer than an agitator, Place valued education over public demonstrations, tirelessly emphasizing the material and moral benefits of education for workingmen. As a member of the LCS he opposed large public meetings and violent tactics. After passage (1795) of the two acts suppressing large meetings, he refused to be reelected as chairman of the LCS' General Committee, gave up his office as division delegate, and finally resigned from the LCS in June 1797.

Place's shop, piled high with his ever-growing collection of pamphlets and books (today an invaluable resource held in the **British Museum**), became a gathering place of reformers. He became a spokesman for the English workers and a bridge between them and the **middle-class** radicals, especially those around **Jeremy Bentham**, his own "venerable preceptor." In 1807 Place managed the campaign in Westminster that elected **Sir Francis Burdett**, a wealthy radical and disciple of **Horne Tooke**. Several years later he helped the educational reformer **Joseph Lancaster** to set up nonsectarian schools in London. Concerning himself with problems of **population** and working-class education, he published his only book, *Illustrations and Proofs of the Principles of Population* (1822), in which he agreed with **Malthus** on the deleterious moral effects of overpopula-

Francis Place

tion but cautiously proposed contraception as the remedy for this.

Place's political skills were most evident in his long campaign for repeal of the **combination acts**, his greatest achievement. He believed that the anti-union acts of 1799 and 1800 were ineffectual because the more workers' combinations were prohibited, the more desirable they seemed to the workers. He rather naively believed that combinations would naturally disappear in a free economy because wages would find their own level as a result of the operation of the laws of supply and demand, workers thenceforth concluding reasonably that no combination could defeat these economic laws.

He worked for repeal with the economist **J.R. McCulloch** and the radical M.P. Joseph Hume (1777–1855). At his suggestion, Hume called for a select committee to look into the combination acts and managed to pack the committee with repeal-minded M.P.s. Place then managed the hearings, producing a succession of expert witnesses expertly coached by himself. The committee produced legislation that gave workers the right to organize **trade unions** and bargain collectively, and that repealed the common law doctrine of conspiracy in restraint of trade so far as unions were concerned (1824). But when the unions (to Place's dismay) then promptly used these rights to organize strikes, break contracts, and intimidate other workers; and when outraged employers called for a new committee to undo the legislation, Place helped (1825) to stem the panic and save the right to organize and bargain collectively (though contract-breaking was limited and the unions were once again made subject to the common law of conspiracy).

A few years later, Place was again a key popular player in politics. He and other radicals, including **John Thelwall**, a veteran of the 1790s reform movement, founded the National Political Union to organize support for the **Reform Act** (1832). With legislation stalled in the **House of Lords**, Place suggested a run on the **banks** to create a financial panic, and placarded London with the slogan, "To stop the Duke, go for gold." A few years later, again working from voluminous documents and statistics, he helped the Benthamite Joseph Parkes (1796–1865) prepare the **Municipal Corporations Act** (1835). He also helped with the initial phase of the Chartist movement, though he always maintained that the political fortunes of the working class were tied to popular education and to cooperation with middle-class radicals. Working-class solidarity was unthinkable to him.

Frank M. Baglione

Bibliography

Baylen, Joseph O., and Norbert J. Gossman. *Biographical Dictionary of Modern British Radicals.* Vol. 1. 1979.

Cone, Carl B. *The English Jacobins: Reformers in Late 18th Century England.* 1968.

Dinwiddy, John R. *From Luddism to the First Reform Bill: Reform in England, 1810–1832.* 1986.

Goodwin, Albert. *The Friends of Liberty: The English Democratic Movement in the Age of the French Revolution.* 1979.

Hone, J.A. *For the Cause of Truth. Radicalism in London, 1807–1821.* 1982.

Thompson, W.S. "Francis Place and Working-Class History." *Historical Journal.* Vol. 5, pp. 61–70.

Wallas, Graham. *The Life of Francis Place.* 1925.

West, E.G. *Education and the Industrial Revolution.* 1975.

Wright, D.G. *Popular Radicalism: The Working-Class Experience, 1780–1880.* 1988.

Places, Place Acts, Placemen

See Pension and Place Bills

Planché, James Robinson (1796–1880)

Playwright, campaigner for theatrical causes, antiquarian, and scholar, Planché helped direct English theater toward realism by encouraging historical accuracy in costuming and design. He was elected to the Society of Antiquaries (1829) and helped found the British Archaeological Association (1843). Priding himself on remaining true to sources as diverse as Shakespeare and the French *féerie,* he tempered his antiquarianism to make works accessible to new audiences and to conform the originals to contemporary **moral** codes.

In his earlier years, Planché wrote more than 160 plays; he completed only a dozen in the last 25 years of his life. His **burlesques** and Christmas pieces established his theatrical reputation, but he is best remembered for his fairy extravaganzas, such as *Puss in Boots* (1837), which retold fairy tales with humor and visual excitement. These productions also made use of **satires** and allusions to literary works, historical events, and contemporary theatrical and social concerns. Fairy extravaganzas took advantage of advanced theatrical **technology** while poking fun at theater in general. Planché's comedies, such as *Orpheus in the Haymarket* (1865), comment on such popular theatrical forms as dioramas, animal shows, and minstrel troupes; his social satires included *Hold Your Tongue* (1849). Planché ardently supported regulation of copyright control and royalty fees.

Samuel Lyndon Gladden

Bibliography

Planché, James Robinson. *Recollections and Reflections: A Professional Autobiography.* 1901.

———. *Plays by James Robinson Planché.* Donald Roy, ed. 1986.

See also Dramatic Arts; Theaters and Staging

Planned Villages

The planned village was essentially a feature of Scottish society in the age of **agricultural improvement** and **industrial revolution**, although some English examples may be found, including Nuneham Courtney in Oxfordshire, Milton Abbas in Dorset, and New Houghton in Norfolk. Improving landowners who wished to have their estates redesigned by such landscaping experts as **Lancelot "Capability" Brown** or **Humphry Repton** sometimes found existing village communities to be unsightly obstacles to the development of a park or garden, and so the village would be rebuilt in a fresh position—out of sight.

Most English planned villages were more ornamental than useful. Their more utilitarian counterparts in **Scotland**, where over 150 appeared in the century after 1730, were usually associated with **agriculture**, **fishing**, or industry. Some communities in the Lowlands were resettled as a result of agricultural enclosures, while in the North, others were evicted during the **Highland clearances** to make way for sheep and deer. The new village of Ormiston in East Lothian was designed by the improver **John Cockburn**, and included a bleachfield, brewery, distillery, and a market for the increased yields of agricultural produce. Other planned villages included the **Duke of Argyll**'s Inverary, the 3rd Duke of Buccleuch's (1746–1812) Newcastelton, and the Duke of Perth's Crieff and Callendar.

The **Forfeited Estates Commission** developed some new villages after 1752, and the British Fisheries Society, founded in 1768 to aid improvements in the Highlands, was responsible for others, including Helmsdale in Sutherland, Pultneytown in Caithness, Tobermory on the Isle of Mull, and Ullapool in Wester Ross. There were also the industrial communities based on **coal**, **iron**, or **cotton**, such as the Duke of Atholl's Stanley in Perthshire; the best example is **New Lanark**, developed by **David Dale** and **Robert Owen**, and a tourist attraction by the 1820s.

C.J. Davey

Bibliography

Dunlop, J. *The British Fisheries Society.* 1978.

Donnachie, I., and G. Hewitt. *Historic New Lanark.* 1993.

Phillipson, N.T., and R. Mitchison, eds. *Scotland in the Age of Improvement.* 1970.

Smith, A.M. *Jacobite Estates of the Forty-five.* 1982.

Plantation Act (1764)

The great debt incurred during the **Seven Years' War** led the government to search for new revenue, particularly for the support of defense and administration in **North America.** A scheme to tighten the collection of customs, long evaded by American colonists, was embodied in the Plantation Act (popularly called the Sugar Act), part of a package of revenue legislation presented by **George Grenville**'s ministry. The act reduced the duty on foreign molasses to 3d. per gallon (formerly 6d. per gallon under the **Molasses Act** of 1733) but imposed excessively high duties on foreign refined sugar; prohibited the entry of foreign rum; and increased duties on wines, coffee, silks, and linens. The act stated in its preamble that its purpose was to increase revenue; other purposes were to stop the **smuggling** of French **West Indian** molasses and balance the interests of the West Indian planters with those of New England distillers by giving them both monopolies.

Molasses was economically important to New England, where it was distilled into rum. This was shipped to Europe for sale or used in frontier barter and the **African** trade, especially for **slaves**. Grenville intended the trade laws to be enforced with new vigor but assumed that the colonists would recover the cost of the molasses duty by raising prices on goods sold to French planters, who were dependent on America for supplies. And since large quantities of molasses would be required, more than those obtainable from the British islands, substantial revenue would be generated for the crown.

However, the act's complicated administrative provisions and strict enforcement proved a serious impediment to intercolonial trade. Some colonists began complaining about "taxation without representation"; but since this was difficult to do without appearing to defend smuggling, a better cause was found the following year in Grenville's **Stamp Act**.

P.J. Kulisheck

Bibliography

Barrow, Thomas C. *Trade and Empire: The British Customs Service in Colonial America 1660–1775.* 1967.

Johnson, Allen S. "The Passage of the Sugar Act." *William and Mary Quarterly.* Vol. 16, pp. 507–514.

Lawson, Philip. *George Grenville: A Political Life.* 1984.

See also American Revolution; Navigation Laws; North America

Plassey, Battle of (1757)

Fearful of expanding British military and economic domination, the *nawab* (chief tax collector and virtual provincial ruler) of Bengal, Siraj-ud-daula, in 1756 captured Calcutta, a principal trading center of the British **East India Company**. In charge of the company's effort to recover Calcutta and reestablish its trading privileges was Colonel **Robert Clive**. With company and regular **army** troops, supported by a royal naval squadron, Clive recaptured Calcutta (January 1757) and subsequently destroyed French influence in Bengal with the capture of the fortress of Chandernagore.

The confrontation at Plassey followed from these events. Opponents of the (Muslim) *nawab*, led by Hindu merchants, conspired to depose him, and Clive joined the conspiracy in the expectation of a more advantageous arrangement from the future *nawab*, Mir Jafar. On 13 June he marched against Siraj-ud-daula with 613 European infantry, 171 artillerymen equipped with 10 guns, and over 2,000 (native) sepoy troops. He established a defensive position at Plassey around a mango grove, with his line anchored by a brick hunting lodge. At dawn on 23 June the *nawab*'s army of 50,000 troops, supported by a French contingent, advanced across the open ground toward Clive.

Clive, while French artillery pounded his men, nonetheless was able to cover his army's ammunition with tarpaulins as a soaking rain began. The rain wet the *nawab*'s powder, and after losing several captains and suffering heavily from devastating musketry and artillery fire, his attack faltered. Seizing the moment, Clive charged and routed the panicked enemy. The *nawab* lost 500 to Clive's 18 dead, and Plassey became a milestone not only in Clive's career but in the history of Britain's takeover of **India**.

Stanley D.M. Carpenter

Bibliography

Bence-Jones, Mark. *Clive of India.* 1974.
Edwardes, Michael. *Plassey: The Founding of an Empire.* 1969.
Fisher, Michael H., ed. *The Politics of the British Annexation of India, 1757–1857.* 1994.
Lawford, James P. *Clive: Proconsul of India.* 1976.

Playhouse Act (1737)

The Playhouse Act, known also as the Licensing Act and the Stage Licensing Act, was the most successful governmental attempt to control drama in the early Hanoverian period. The act shut down playhouses within the city limits of **London**, which were in competition with the **theaters** at Drury Lane and Covent Garden. These latter operated under patents granted by Charles II, while other theaters could not claim royal endorsement. In addition, the act required theaters to submit copies of plays to the Lord Chamberlain for approval before performance. The act's dual purpose was to keep obscene plays from corrupting audiences, and seditious plays from encouraging a rebellion that might topple the government of **Sir Robert Walpole** and possibly undermine the monarchy itself. The act also had unintended effects. Among these were a decline in the number of new plays performed at Drury Lane and Covent Garden, and an increase in the number of theatrical offerings—especially **pantomimes** and other less literary fare—outside the city limits.

Brent Chesley

Bibliography

Bevis, Richard W. *English Drama: Restoration and Eighteenth Century, 1660–1798.* 1988.
Liesenfeld, Vincent J. *The Licensing Act of 1737.* 1984.

Pleasure Gardens

Much of the leisure time of Hanoverian Londoners was spent in relatively simple open-air **amusements and recreation**. Ranking high among the places favored for such activities were pleasure gardens. These were a particular feature of **London** life from the late Stuart period to the beginning of the 19th century, and were among the earliest of the Hanoverian and Victorian pleasure resorts.

The Spring Gardens, opened at Lambeth in 1661, were

Drury Lane Theatre

View of the Rotunda at Ranelagh

the forerunner of the most famous of the 18th-century gardens, Vauxhall. Situated on the south side of the Thames, Vauxhall could be reached by water. There, visitors could enjoy the beautiful walks, grottoes, statues, temples, **paintings**, and waterfalls by day; and **music**, brilliant lights, balls, masquerades, and fireworks at night. Acquired in 1728 by Jonathan Tyers, Vauxhall was reorganized and reopened in 1732. Admission was 1 shilling, and during its heyday (1750–1790), Vauxhall was a favorite summer meeting place for Londoners from all social strata. Becoming steadily less select, however, it began to decline at the end of the century; it survived until 1859.

Ranelagh was more aristocratic. Opened in Chelsea in 1742, it boasted an enormous rotunda, which could accommodate both summer and winter festivities. By 1744, **Horace Walpole** could remark that "nobody goes anywhere else—everybody goes there." In fact, it became so popular that at the height of the season the **roads** to Ranelagh were often completely blocked by coaches. The cost of admission was as much as 2s.6d. on nights when masquerades or fireworks' displays were held. Unlike Vauxhall, Ranelagh never became a purely popular resort. Yet it too gradually declined and was finally closed in 1803.

Other pleasure gardens of the period, such as Marylebone, Bagnigge Wells, Bermondsey, and Sadler's Wells, flourished because of their **spas** but never achieved the status of either Vauxhall or Ranelagh.

Timothy J.L. Chandler

Bibliography

George, M. Dorothy. *London Life in the Eighteenth Century.* 1930.

Sands, Mollie. *Invitation to Ranelagh.* 1930.

Wroth, William. *Cremorne and the Later London Gardens.* 1907.

See also Seaside Resorts; Spas

Poaching and Game Laws

The right to hunt game on royal hunting preserves was restricted as early as 1217, and in 1389 it was decreed by Richard II that hunting could only be carried on by landowners. A further restriction was established by a statute (1603) which made it illegal to sell pheasants, partridges, and hares. However, it was with the Game Act of 1671, which permitted hunting only for those who owned land worth £100 per year or leased property worth £150 per year, that an era began that defined hunting as the singular right of only the most powerful landed gentlemen in England.

The penalties attached to these and subsequent laws grew harsher during the Hanoverian period as a more concerted attack gathered against **crime** of all kinds. In response, poachers—often poor cottagers motivated by the need to provide food for their families—became increasingly organized in gangs, sometimes armed and ready to do battle with the landlord's agents (gamekeepers). Landlords, to strengthen their position, formed local associations for the prosecution of poachers. One historian has described the resulting protracted and often violent struggle as the longest and bloodiest rural war in English history.

From the beginning of the 18th century a succession of **punishments**, including heavy fines (as high as £30), **prison**, whipping, **transportation**, and even death, were legislated in order to cover every aspect of poaching and close any loopholes that might sanction it. The severest penalties were laid down in the **Black Act** (1723), which created some 50 new capital offenses. Some statutes, such as the Night Poaching Act of 1770, permitted easier prosecutions by authorizing summary justice before a single magistrate. Others, such as an act passed in 1800, permitted gamekeepers to arrest without a warrant individuals suspected of poaching. Other legislation became even more punitive in response to fears generated by the **French Revolution** and by rural disturbances during the first 30 years of the 19th century. Such legislation continued as a symbol of class conflict well into the 20th century.

Stanley D. Nash

Hunter and Gamekeeper

Bibliography

Archer, John E. *By a Flash and a Scare: Incendiarism, Animal Maiming, and Poaching in East Anglia, 1815–1870.* 1990.

Hay, Douglas, et al. *Albion's Fatal Tree: Crime and Society in Eighteenth-Century England.* 1975.

Hopkins, Harry. *The Long Affray: The Poaching Wars, 1760–1914.* 1985.

Thompson, E.P. *Whigs and Hunters: The Origin of the Black Act.* 1975.

Walsh, E.G. *The Poacher's Companion.* 1983.

Poet Laureates

The poet laureateship was less than a livelihood, but more than the mere joke its detractors tried to make it. After the Elector of Hanover became **George I** (1714), Nahum Tate (1652–1715), the third offical Laureate (after John Dryden, 1631–1700, and Thomas Shadwell, 1642?–1692), celebrated the new king's birthday in forgettable verse and died 2 months later. He was succeeded by Nicholas Rowe (1674–1718, Laureate from 1715), who produced the expected New Year and birthday odes. As Peter Pindar explained, "Know, reader, that the Laureate's post sublime, / Is destined to record in tuneful rhyme, / The deeds of British monarchs, twice a year. . . ." The Laureate received £100 annually and a butt or pipe of Canary wine every Christmas.

Laurence Eusden (1688–1730, Laureate from 1718) has "by few been read, by fewer prais'd," his contemporary Thomas "Hesiod" Cook (1703–1756) versified; but **Colley Cibber** (Laureate, 1730–1757), age 59 when appointed (the other candidates were **Lewis Theobald** and **Stephen Duck**), already had a successful career as an actor, dramatist, and theater manager. His laureate poems confirmed **Alexander Pope**'s choice of Cibber as prince of Dulness in *The Dunciad* (1743).

William Whitehead (1715–1785, Laureate from 1757) sometimes attempted **patriotic** sentimentalism as in *Verses to the People of England* (1758), where he hoped to rally the country against **France** during the **Seven Years' War**. An Oxford scholar, **Thomas Warton** (1728–1790, Laureate from 1785) began his tenure with a birthday ode that resulted in the literary joke, *Probationary Odes for the Laureateship* (1785): his was the only poem of 22 included, which was not a deliberate **burlesque**. He was a better poet than the **satire** suggested, but Henry James Pye (1745–1813, Laureate from 1790) was—declared **Sir Walter Scott**—"eminently respectable in everything but his poetry." He traded in the annual Canary wine for £27.

Robert Southey (Laureate, 1813–1843) objected to writing the obligatory poems, but it was not until **George III** died in 1820 that the custom ended. The king's death occasioned Southey's *A Vision of Judgement,* which called forth **Lord Byron**'s *The Vision of Judgement* (1822). Southey thus became the third Laureate—after Shadwell (as Dryden's *Mac Flecknoe*) and Cibber—to be the hero of a satiric masterpiece greater than any of the works by laureates.

Peter A. Tasch

Bibliography

Broadus, Edmund Kemper. *The Laureateship.* 1921.

Hopkins, Kenneth. *The Poets Laureate.* 1973.

Russel, Nick. *Poets by Appointment.* 1981.

Poetry and Poetics

Poetry in the Hanoverian age encompassed a range of poetic styles and practices, from **Neoclassical** to **Romantic**. In the early part of the period and for much of the 18th century, the dominant poetic mode was termed Neoclassical or **Augustan** because of the aesthetic authority accorded to the ancient Roman poets, particularly Horace (65–8 BC) and Vergil (70–19 BC) and to the poetic theories of Aristotle and Longinus. By 1714 these had been made familiar by such influential French writers as Nicolas Boileau (1636–1711), René Rapin (1621–1687), and Pierre Corneille (1606–1684); and by English authors John Dryden (1631–1700), **John Dennis**, and Thomas Rymer (1641–1713).

Broadly speaking, this Neoclassicism had begun as a reaction against a certain indiscipline in the use of poetic language by both English and Continental Renaissance poets. Theorists pointed back to the poetics of Aristotle, Longinus, and the others who had "discovered" the universal, transhistorical principles of composition and poetic excellence. For example, where Jacobean metaphysical poetic practice had incorporated sometimes obscure metaphors and overdetermined conceits, the Neoclassical impulse was to regularize poetic language by stressing restraint, decorum, and metrical rules, all of which were seen as concordant with the universal laws of nature. Poetry at its best was thought to derive from and to imitate natural processes, and in so doing to narrow the gap between art and Nature.

Thomas Chatterton, the "Marvelous Boy," with early manuscripts

This, however, is not to imply that Neoclassical poetry stagnated as mere imitation of earlier forms. A new awareness of distinctly local and national literary traditions, the growth of popular forms such as the **novel** and the **periodical** press, the emergence of a literate **middle class**, and a sense of the socially corrective role of poetry helped to diversify 18th-century poetic practice. Most critics and poets even agreed on a notion of genius or *je ne sais quoi*—an undefinable quality of excellence (sometimes likened to the Longinian sublime) that distinguished the transcendent from the merely imitative and mundane.

Thus, while **Alexander Pope**'s *Essay on Criticism* (1711) contains perhaps the best-known and most definitive statements about Neoclassical poetics, his theories were indebted to Boileau's *L'Art Poetique* (1674), which had been **translated** by a largely sympathetic Dryden, as well as to Horace. Pope's own poetry certainly exemplifies the paradox between an adherence to ancient convention and the spark of original "**wit**": his practice was to assimilate old forms and ideas, and to craft them in new and fresh ways that suited his own time and purposes—"What oft was thought, but ne'er so well expressed."

The view of poetry as a system based on empirical principles found strong support in the **Enlightenment** interest in **science**, and this manifested itself in varying formal ways in 18th-century poetry and in debates about affective response. Neoclassical poetry is often characterized by its use of the heroic couplet, two rhyming iambic pentameter lines containing within themselves a complete thought or statement, creating a taut, controlled and balanced rhetorical effect. (This poetic unit was later derided by Keats as a mere "rocking horse.") Moreover, while personification was a frequent device, poetic language was refined of the excessive ornamentation characteristic of Renaissance poetry, which was felt to depart from the standard of Nature.

Hewing to their poetic theory, the Neoclassicists breathed new life into poetic forms such as the ode, the **pastoral**, the tragedy, and the **epic**, always adhering to generic boundaries, and with a view of poetry as a social discourse that circulated as a corrective within a community of learned individuals. Most of the major poets of the early 18th century attempted imitations of classical authors by adapting their works to contemporary issues and audiences. **John Gay** imitated Vergil in "The Birth of the Squire. An Eclogue" (1720), **Samuel Johnson**'s *The Vanity of Human Wishes* (1749) explicitly recalled Juvenal's (*c.* 60–140) Tenth Satire, while **Anne Finch** produced a Pindaric ode titled *The Spleen* (1713).

Further, because of the occasional and public importance granted to poetry by the **ancients**, and because most of the age's literati were fiercely partisan in their politics, **satire** flourished—and became a powerful political weapon—in the Neoclassical period. **Jonathan Swift**'s *Verses on the Death of Dr. Swift* (1739) is an example of Neoclassical verse satire, as is **Lady Mary Wortley Montagu**'s *Epistle from Mrs. Yonge to Her Husband* (1724; 1977), which was based on an acrimonious **divorce** case. The interest in satire led to the perfection of a form now seen as typically Neoclassical: the **mock-heroic**. This deployed epic loftiness and style to lampoon trivial subjects and political or literary rivals. Pope's *The Rape of the Lock* (1712, 1714) comically turns a feud between local families into an epic struggle, whereas his *The Dunciad* (1728, 1743) more cynically presents the "Triumph of Dullness" (the **Grub Street** hacks and Pope's critics) over the literary scene and, indeed, over the entire social order.

The death of Swift (1745) is generally taken to mark the beginning of the decline of Neoclassical poetry. The period 1745–1784 can be termed "pre–Romantic" because of the revival, through **Thomas Gray**, **William Collins**, and **William Cowper**, of the lyric, which had suffered earlier in the century for its more reflective, individualist bent. Gray's much-admired "Elegy Written in a Country Church-yard" (1751) is an early example of Romantic lyric in its sustained meditation on death. Cowper's *The Task* (1785) incorporates both Neoclassical and Romantic modes; for while it begins as a mock-epic tribute to a sofa, it incorporates Romantic affinities for natural description and the pleasures of rural life.

The **French Revolution** and its bloody aftermath generally mark the beginning of the Romantic movement. Attracted by the individualist ideologies of Jean-Jacques Rousseau (1712–1778) and **William Godwin**, but disillusioned at the revolution's political failures, poets deployed their craft as an expression of self and of the transcendent, socially transformative possibilities of the individual imagination. Consequently, although poetry retained its socially corrective aims, Romantic "sincerity" came to replace Neoclassical "decorum" as a means to that end.

With **William Wordsworth**'s and **Samuel Taylor Coleridge**'s *Lyrical Ballads* (1798), along with its Preface of 1800, Romantic poetics found its first theoretical expression, although these poets in fact only represented a part of the movement that came to be known as Romanticism. ***Lyrical Ballads*** was intended as a radical break from 18th-century poetic practice, especially in terms of genre (both the lyric and the **ballad** had fallen out of favor in the 18th century) and poetic diction. Wordsworth insisted that the language of poetry must not differ from that of prose, and that the rural lower classes were more appropriate than fashionable people as subjects for poetry because their language was closer to "the language really spoken by men." He felt that he was redefining the very basis of good poetry and poetic language, but he was mercilessly attacked for banality and rudeness in the periodical press. Later, Coleridge mounted a more philosophical, if similarly critical, attack on Wordsworth's theories in his *Biographia Literaria* (1817).

Despite their revolutionary tone and their influence on later poets, Wordsworth and Coleridge were not the most popular poets of their day. That honor belonged to **Sir Walter Scott**, whose verse Romances, *Lay of the Last Minstrel* (1805), *Marmion* (1808), and *The Lady of the Lake* (1810) were influenced by Coleridge's as yet unpublished *Christabel.* Later, **Lord Byron**, who adapted the Romance form to suit contemporary interest in individual subjective experience, achieved such commercial success that he reputedly caused Scott to abandon poetry for novel writing. Moreover—and against Wordsworth's dictates—Byron, **Thomas Moore**, and **Felicia Hemans** added to a growing public appetite for narrative poems set in **exotic** lands.

Because of this new interest in the individual mind, the lyric flourished in the form of odes and sonnets, with **Percy Bysshe Shelley** and **John Keats** producing some of the finest of these. The sonnet's revival was aided by Charlotte Smith's (1749–1806) *Elegiac Sonnets* (1784–1800), which expanded through nine editions by 1800. With the exception of Byron's *Don Juan* (1818–1824), the **epic** again became a serious venture, as poets attempted (sometimes uneasily) to access a national poetic tradition identified with **Milton**. The Romantic epic *par excellence,* however, Wordsworth's autobiographical *The Prelude,* was not published until after the poet's death in 1850.

With the passage of the **Reform Act** in 1832, much of the political urgency of the Romantic movement ended; further, much of its idealism now seemed untenable, especially the potentially solipsistic search for self. It remained for Thomas Carlyle (1795–1881) to sound its end with his admonishment to the readers of his *Sartor Resartus* (1833–1834) to "Close thy Byron; open thy Goethe."

Samantha Webb

Bibliography

Abrams, M.H. *The Mirror and the Lamp: Romantic Theory and the Critical Tradition.* 1953.

Colomb, Gregory. *Designs on Truth: The Poetics of the Augustan Mock-Epic.* 1992.

Curran, Stuart. *Poetic Form and British Romanticism.* 1986.

Edinger, William. *Samuel Johnson and Poetic Style.* 1977.

Gerrard, Christine. *The Patriot Opposition to Walpole: Politics, Poetry, and National Myth, 1725–1742.* 1995.

Johnson, James William. *The Formation of English Neoclassical Thought.* 1967.

Murphy, Peter T. *Poetry as an Occupation and an Art in Britain, 1760–1830.* 1993.

Sherbo, Arthur. *English Poetic Diction from Chaucer to Wordsworth.* 1975.

See also Literary Criticism

Police

See Law Enforcement

Political Economy

See Economic Thought

Political Prints

The English political print has its roots in Reformation anti–Catholic satires and in 17th-century Dutch prints. **William Hogarth**'s satire *The South Sea Scheme* (1721) typifies a continuing indebtedness to these sources in the early 18th century. The 1730s and 1740s saw dramatic gains in the sophistication and popularity of the graphic political satire. The long premiership (1721–1742) of **Walpole** occasioned many powerful attacks along the lines of *Idol-Worship or The Way to Pre-*

ferment (1740), a clever mixture of classical, biblical, and scurrilous.

During the first half of the century, emblems dominated the satirical print. For example, animal imagery to represent England and foreign nations became an established convention. When Arthur Pond (1701–1758) produced two sets of prints (1736, 1742) after caricatures by Annibale Carracci (1560–1609) and Pier Leone Ghezzi (1674–1755), distorted drawings exaggerating the features of individuals soon became part of the English visual vocabulary. It was not until George Townshend's (1724–1807) *The Recruiting Serjeant* (1757), however, that personal **caricature** became a standard weapon in the political satirist's armory.

The **Seven Years' War** and the controversies surrounding the administration (1761–1763) of **Bute** engendered a flurry of prints. Hogarth's *The Times. Plate I* (1762), a defense of Bute and **George III**, made him the object of great scorn, especially in the satires of Paul Sandby (1730–1809); Hogarth's revenge, the satirical portrait of Bute's critic *John Wilkes* (1763), was a best-seller.

The successful assault on Bute's ministry led many observers to recognize graphic satire's potency as a political weapon. Quickly and inexpensively produced, the satirical print's visual **ridicule** and simple message were readily intelligible to the common citizen; its popular impact was formidable, as thousands of shopkeepers and tradesmen could read the latest political "editorials" in **London**'s printshop windows. Moreover, unlike the printed word, political prints were virtually immune from **censorship**.

The political print also helped to crystallize English self-consciousness. English xenophobia is evident throughout the century; from the 1760s on, **John Bull**, often pictured with English roast beef, became an emblem of the pugnacious English patriot, frequently contrasted with the effete Frenchman and the impoverished Scotsman. Students of English **nationalism** as well as of **party politics** have found in prints a treasure house of information, some of it going to "the collective unconscious."

In the 1770s, social satires—especially prints ridiculing the extremes of Macaroni **fashions**—helped to make prints a staple of London culture. Replacing the laborious engraving technique with the faster method of etching further invigorated the market for satirical prints.

The period 1775–1825 was the "Golden Age" of the English political print. The **American Revolution**, the detested **Fox–North Coalition**, the even more detested **French Revolution**, and the outlandish conduct of the Prince Regent and **Queen Caroline** provided ideal subjects for the three acknowledged masters of the medium: **Thomas Rowlandson**, **James Gillray**, and **George Cruikshank**. It could be argued that Britain offered the most fertile territory in Europe for savage political satire at this time because of the greater openness and popularity of political debate and the taste for deflationary ridicule fostered by contemporary political conditions. Certainly the prints of these great masters—hilarious, grotesque, enormous in power—are one of the most distinctive marks of the life and vitality of Hanoverian Britain.

But by the time of the death of **George IV** in 1830, the virulently satirical flavor of English political prints had died, too; the comic "cartoon" would soon replace graphic political satire.

Michael F. Suarez, S.J.

Bibliography

Carretta, Vincent. *The Snarling Muse: Verbal and Visual Political Satire from Pope to Churchill.* 1983.

———. *George III and the Satirists from Hogarth to Byron.* 1990.

Dickinson, H.T. *Caricatures and the Constitution, 1760–1832.* 1986.

Duffy, Michael. *The Englishman and the Foreigner.* 1986.

George, M. Dorothy. *English Political Caricature: A Study of Opinion and Propaganda.* 2 vols. 1959.

———. *Hogarth to Cruikshank: Social Change in Graphic Satire.* 1967.

Langford, Paul. *Walpole and the Robinocracy.* 1986.

Miller, John. *Religion in the Popular Prints, 1600–1832.* 1986.

Wood, Marcus. *Radical Satire and Print Culture, 1790–1822.* 1994.

See also Drawing; Engraving; Graphic Arts

Political Thought

Hanoverian political thought developed chiefly in response to the rapid modernization of society presided over by the oligarchic regime that arose after the **Glorious Revolution**, and particularly after the succession of **George I** of **Hanover** in 1714. It ended with the **Reform Act** of 1832.

At its bottom was the idea, generally accepted by the 1720s, of the **Glorious Constitution**. This was essentially a moderate theory of individual and group rights, which was grounded in the notion of a national inheritance of laws and institutions (the most important of these reaffirmed in the Glorious Revolution); and of an ongoing constitutional balance or equilibrium between legitimate forces working sometimes together, sometimes marginally at cross-purposes with one another, as represented in Crown, **Lords**, and **Commons**. All rights, under this theory, were protected by virtue of being represented in the constitutional balance of the King-in-Parliament.

Beyond this there were several lines of contending thought, upon which, as the decades passed, variations were introduced. One basic debate pitted proponents of the classical-republican tradition against defenders of the **Whig** ascendancy. On one side, representatives of the so-called **Commonwealthman** or "Country" tradition argued that a political system based on royal **patronage** and public credit was destroying the constitutional balance between Crown, Lords, and Commons, and with it the freedom and independence of the citizenry. On the other side, the proponents of a "Court" ideology defended the methods used to make the delicately balanced constitution work in a commercial society.

Complicating this discussion was another theme inherited from the 17th century. **John Locke** had set forth a vision of politics framed in the social contract theory of the state, with its accompanying insistence on rights and liberties, including even the right of revolution. This vision, particularly popular with **dissenting** theorists, stimulated demands for the reformation and later democratization of British politics and society, and in the early reign of **George III** gave theoretical sanction to American politicians determined to break the bonds that held overseas colonies within the **Empire**.

In addition, the absolutist theories of the 17th century did not disappear, as **nonjurors**, **Jacobites**, and several other groups proved. But the religiously grounded doctrines associated with the **Tories** of the reign of **Queen Anne**—of strong monarchy, divine right, indefeasible hereditary succession, nonresistance, and passive obedience—became less influential as society accepted the political and religious arrangements of the **Hanoverian succession** and the **Church of England** under the Whigs and their patrons George I and **George II**.

A moral thread connected many debates, as one of the central questions was whether or not the financial, administrative, and military policies of the government, related as they were to the accumulation of wealth in an increasingly commercial society, corrupted society's governors and their subjects. This question was framed early in the period by a group of **opposition** intellectuals led by Henry Neville (1620–1694), Walter Moyle (1672–1721), Andrew Fletcher of Saltoun (1653–1716), **Viscount Molesworth**, **John Toland**, **John Trenchard**, **Thomas Gordon**, and **Lord Bolingbroke**. They believed that the independent and virtuous citizenry of the balanced and stable state, which supposedly had existed in earlier times, was being corrupted by individuals pursuing private, selfish ends. Their perspective was lodged in the widely held idea that the exercise of citizenship proceeded best from the possession of landed property, and that collective welfare resulted from propertied individuals reasoning with authority to concert policy as well as preserve rights. Now, as it seemed to them, the Court was corrupting this process by helping to introduce a new ruling elite (or "monied interest") of stockbrokers and officeholders who depended for their influence not on land but upon the Court, and to whom the government was indebted.

Borrowing from this stock of ideas, Whig and Tory opponents of the Court denounced its increasing influence and the growth of standing armies, which allowed the king to rule by spending money on professional soldiers instead of relying on the support of free armed proprietors. They objected to the government's growing capacity to bring the members of the legislature, and those they represented, into relationships of personal, political, and economic dependence, and frequently suggested that behind this lay a growing depravity of **morals** at the highest levels.

The defenders of central power responded to this challenge on several theoretical fronts. One line of defense, cultivated by urban essayists such as **Daniel Defoe**, **Joseph Addison**, and the third Earl of Shaftesbury (1671–1713), reached its greatest expression in the more systematic writings of Baron de Montesquieu (1689–1755), **David Hume**, and **Adam Smith**. These men abandoned the classical ideal of citizenship as unworkable and dangerous, while conceding that patronage and the commercial society on which it rested damaged civic virtue. They also asserted that the mainsprings of human behavior—imagination, passion, and self-interest—and the conditions of social existence were such that the classical ideal could never be fully realized, and that an alternative theory of political society must be found. They proposed to rely on a strong executive within a balanced constitution to preserve order, leaving men free to become progressively more involved in economic and cultural affairs. They thus arrived at a more thoroughly modern political morality, valuing the consequences of men's actions rather than their motives.

Other theorists, uncomfortable with pragmatic arguments, attempted to justify the established Whig order by appealing to immutable principles. Some, such as **Benjamin Hoadly**, invoked Locke's theory of natural rights, claiming that the government was based on consent and the protection of civil liberties. Others, such as Thomas Herring (1693–1757), Samuel Squire (1714–1766), and **Lord Hardwicke** tried to legitimate governmental authority by revising natural law theory. They argued that the moral and political order was governed by a natural law independent of human will but accessible to human reason. Such law imposed divinely ordained limits on both government and citizen, though valuing the good of the community over that of the individual. Court Whigs argued that Britain's constitutional balance was legitimated by its existence: it was part of God's plan.

More intense criticism of the Whig regime began to emerge after 1760, as the policies of George III and his ministers came to be seen as repressive and corrupt. Whigs of the **Rockingham** faction, led by **Edmund Burke**, maintained that the king's actions were contrary to the spirit of the Constitution, and laid out new lines of thought defending united opposition on grounds of principle—that is, a theory of **party politics**—as well as new measures of **economical reform** and the reduction of crown influence through **places** and **pensions**.

Outside Parliament and beyond the Whigs, a new **radicalism** also began to form. Prior to 1776, few radicals believed that the constitution was beyond repair. Commonwealth republicanism remained a source of protest for dissenters such as **James Burgh**, **Richard Price**, and **Joseph Priestley**. But they combined their appeals to civic virtue, stability, and constitutional balance with Lockean invocations of the popular right of resistance and the need for government to secure natural rights. The **American Revolution** and then the **French Revolution** hastened the death of classical conceptions of politics, simultaneously helping to usher in two appreciably new developments of political thought.

One of these new developments, though never widely popular, derived from the influence after 1760 of Jean-Jacques Rousseau's (1712–1778) social-contract theory, which resembled Locke's theory except for the significant omission of property qualifications, thus resulting in a considerably more radical philosophy of popular sovereignty and democracy: the most influential exponent of these ideas was **William Godwin**, who had some following in radical circles after 1793.

The other new development was an essentially **nationalist** and nativist strain of political thought that had been brewing and coexisting with radicalism since 1760. Political thought in the earlier Hanoverian period had always risen from fixed assumptions about the relevance of religion and property; but after 1760, new assumptions about the secular state, the historic nation, and the rights of all national citizens—regardless of property—began to supplant these. This new tendency of thinking, anchored in anti–French and anti-**aristocratic** feeling as well as in the early Commonwealthman tradition, and powered by resentment over national military and cultural embarrassments as well as by pride over triumphs and achievements, was to give increasing coloration to political thought, left and right, in the 19th century. In the reign of George III, two of its most influential promoters were **John Horne Tooke** and **Major John Cartwright**.

Yet the older traditions were not yet dead. The Lockean and Commonwealthman tradition was revived in the opening years of the French Revolution by **Thomas Paine**, who took it further than earlier Hanoverian theorists had dared with his call for the abandonment of monarchy and aristocracy as useless archaisms, his radical demands for parliamentary reform, and his cry for social and educational reform as well; Paine helped move this tradition into the 19th century and modernize it to the needs of propertyless workingmen. The final statement of the old agricultural and commercial order was articulated by **Edmund Burke**, who emphasized the many virtues of hierarchical society but did so in a new context of organic social thought, which ironically rendered him a pioneer of late-Victorian "Tory Democracy." At the same time, the old contract theory was moving onto a new level better suited to the times when **Jeremy Bentham** and later **John Stuart Mill** began to justify civil liberties and legal and constitutional reform not on the grounds of rights at all, but on those of "utility," efficiency, and general happiness. **Robert Owen** and his followers, meanwhile, were proceeding even further with a theory that deemphasized property as the basis of individual rights, instead stressing communal harmony and social welfare within a democratically organized polity.

Peter J. Diamond

Bibliography

Browning, Reed. *Political and Constitutional Ideas of the Court Whigs.* 1982.

Clark, J.C.D. *English Society, 1688–1832: Ideology. Social Structure and Political Practice during the Ancien Regime.* 1985.

———. *The Language of Liberty, 1660–1832: Political Discourse and Social Dynamics in the Anglo-American World.* 1994.

Dickinson, H.T. *Liberty and Property: Political Ideologies in Eighteenth-Century Britain.* 1977.

Forbes, Duncan. *Hume's Philosophical Politics.* 1975.

Gunn, J.A.W. *Beyond Liberty and Property: The Process of Self-Recognition in Eighteenth-Century Political Thought.* 1983.

Jacob, Margaret, and James Jacob, eds. *The Origins of Anglo-American Radicalism.* 1984.

Kramnick, Isaac. *Republicanism and Bourgeois Radicalism: Political Ideology in Late Eighteenth-Century England and America.* 1990.

Newman, Gerald. *The Rise of English Nationalism: A Cultural History, 1740–1830.* 1987.

Plumb, J.H. *The Growth of Political Stability in England, 1660–1730.* 1967.

Pocock, J.G.A. *The Machiavellian Moment: Florentine Political Thought in the Atlantic Republic Tradition.* 1975.

———. *Virtue, Commerce, and History: Essays on Political Thought and History, Chiefly in the Eighteenth Century.* 1985.

———, ed., with the assistance of Gordon J. Schochet and Lois G. Schwoerer. *The Varieties of British Political Thought, 1500–1800.* 1993.

Robbins, Caroline A. *The Eighteenth-Century Commonwealthman: Studies in the Transmission, Development and Circumstance of English Liberal Thought from the Restoration of Charles II until the War with the Thirteen Colonies.* 1959.

See also Elections and the Franchise; Government, National

Poor Laws

See Poverty and Poor Laws

Pope, Alexander (1688–1744)

Pope, recognized with **Jonathan Swift** as one of the two premier satirists of his age, lived during a period when literary careers were undergoing radical changes due to the development of a print culture, the decline of traditional **patronage**, and the growth of a **middle-class** readership. While often identifying himself with an older, more aristocratic mode of cultural production, Pope proved a master at exploiting these changed circumstances in order to become an admired poet who was also an astute businessman, able to amass a small fortune by taking control of his work's publication and successfully marketing it for an audience that was both elite and popular.

Born in **London** to **Roman Catholic** parents in the year of the **Glorious Revolution**, Pope was immediately marginalized from a society about to restore its monarchy to Protestant hands and enact anti–Catholic legislation. He was further marginalized by a youthful illness, which stunted his growth, deformed his body, and made him a near-invalid in later years. It has been thought that all this made Pope peculiarly sympathetic to the plight of women, enabling him, for example, to identify with the long-suffering Eloisa in his **epistle** *Eloisa to Abelard* (1717), though it can be argued equally that these circumstances stimulated Pope's aggressive striving to take center-stage by making himself heir to a classical literary tradition, by speaking as arbiter of taste in *An Essay on Criticism* (1711), and by placing himself in the line of true

British patriots who, through his poetry, "pleas'd by manly ways."

Following the Vergilian model, Pope began his poetic career by writing *Pastorals* (1709), later incorporating **pastoral** elements into his topographical poem, *Windsor-Forest* (1713), which celebrates the Peace of Utrecht engineered by the **Tory** ministry under **Queen Anne**. His brilliant **mock-heroic** *The Rape of the Lock* (1712), expanded into a five-canto poem (1714) complete with the **epic** machinery of the sylphs, combines a conservative sexual ideology with a witty critique of a fashionable but morally hollow society whose frivolous pursuits travesty the epic actions of a more heroic past. His Homeric **translations**—the *Iliad* (1715–1720) and, with collaborative assistance, the *Odyssey* (1725–1726)—were successful projects, which invested him with a cultural authority that partially compensated for his political powerlessness in the now Whig-dominated society of his day, while simultaneously giving him an economic independence virtually unknown among contemporary writers.

Inspired by the **satiric** schemes of the Scriblerus Club, Pope published his "heroic poem," *The Dunciad,* in 1728. In its revised and expanded four-book version (1743), the **Poet Laureate** Colley **Cibber** replaces **Lewis Theobald**, critic of Pope's *Shakespeare* (1725), as the King of the Dunces. Loosely following the Lord Mayor's Day procession from the city of **London** to Westminster, and concluding with a mock-apocalypse reducing Western civilization to "Universal Darkness" and chaos, *The Dunciad* satirically exploits the dilapidated environs of **Grub Street**, home to working-class professional writers, and the popular entertainments of Bartholomew Fair, to symbolize a perceived vulgarization of taste and all-encompassing degeneration of values. A fascinating study in ideological contradiction, the poem simultaneously satirizes and embodies popular culture, and attacks the new age of print by masterfully exploiting the print medium for its own ends.

During the 1730s Pope labored on his never-finished "Magnum Opus," which included the *Epistles to Several Persons,* the so-called *Moral Essays* (1731–1735), and *An Essay on Man* (1733–1734), dedicated to Pope's **deist** friend, **Lord Bolingbroke**, and noted for its celebration of the Great Chain of Being and its affirmation of a cosmically conceived status quo ("Whatever Is, is Right"). At the same time, Pope's *Imitations of Horace* (1733–1738) expressed dissatisfaction with the political status quo, deriding the **Whig** government's practices under Prime Minister **Robert Walpole** and the court of the mock-Augustus, King **George II**. They also contain memorable satiric portraits of Pope's erstwhile friend and fellow writer **Lady Mary Wortley Montagu** as the venomous Sappho, and the Court favorite **Lord Hervey** as Sporus, "that mere white Curd of Ass's milk." Transforming his diminutive suburban villa at Twickenham into an embodiment of the country house ideal, Pope, despite his family's mercantile connections, criticized the commercialism of urban society and upheld an aristocratic way of life, and called for an **opposition** party composed of "Chiefs, out of War, and Statesmen, out of Place"—his alienation assuming particular intensity in the *Epilogue to the Satires* (1738), which rejects the moderation of

Alexander Pope

Horace (65–8 BC), here portrayed as a Court flatterer, for Juvenal's (*c.* 60–140) savage indignation.

Pope's achievements, along with his distinctive contributions to 18th-century verse, included his success in creating a carefully crafted self-image for posterity and in helping to construct definitions of high and low culture, of literature and the canon, which have greatly influenced traditional views (only recently challenged) of literary history.

Carole Fabricant

Bibliography

Ault, Norman, ed. *The Prose Works of Alexander Pope.* Vol. 1. 1936, 1968.

Barnard, John, ed. *Pope: The Critical Heritage.* 1973.

Brown, Laura. *Alexander Pope.* 1985.

Butt, John, et al., eds. *The Poems of Alexander Pope.* (The Twickenham Edition.) 11 vols. 1938–1968.

Cowler, Rosemary, ed. *The Prose Works of Alexander Pope.* Vol. 2. 1986.

Damrosch, Leopold, Jr. *The Imaginative World of Alexander Pope.* 1987.

Gerrard, Christine. *The Patriot Opposition to Walpole: Politics, Poetry, and National Myth, 1725–1742.* 1995.

Hammond, Brean. *Pope.* 1986.

Mack, Maynard. *Alexander Pope: A Life.* 1985.

Morris, David B. *Alexander Pope: The Genius of Sense.* 1984.

Rogers, Pat. *Essays on Pope.* 1993.

Sherburn, George, ed. *The Correspondence of Alexander Pope.* 5 vols. 1956.

See also Augustan; Clubs; Neoclassical Style; Poetry and Poetics; Satire; Wit and Ridicule

Population and Demographics

At the opening of the Hanoverian period the population of

mainland Britain was in the middle of a long phase of relative stagnation. With about 1.1 million inhabitants, the population of **Scotland** was probably no larger than it had been 100 years or so earlier; as late as 1755, it remained as low as 1.3 million. In England, where the number of inhabitants rose from 5 million in 1670 to just 5.7 million in 1750, the population was growing at an average rate of no more than 0.2% per year.

Around 1750, the pace of population increase began to accelerate. In Scotland, average annual rates of population growth rose from 0.25% in the half century before 1755 to 0.6% between 1755 and 1801, and 1.5% between 1801 and 1831. By the end of the Hanoverian era, the population of Scotland numbered around 2.5 million, two and a half times larger than that of 1714. In England, from an annual average of 0.6% during the 1750s and 1760s, rates of population growth soared to 1% between 1771 and 1801 and to almost 2% between 1801 and 1831. By 1837, England's population at around 14 million was nearly three times larger than at the beginning of the 18th century.

This "revolution" in rates of population increase was accompanied by an equally dramatic change in the geography of human residence. As late as the 1770s, only about one-quarter of the inhabitants of England and **Wales**, and less than one-fifth of those of Scotland, lived in urban communities. By 1841 the respective proportions had risen to almost one-half and around one-third. Between the late 18th and mid 19th centuries, Britain emerged as the world's first extensively urbanized society. At the same time, the spatial distribution of its population began to shift away from the more peripheral, rural parts of the country toward a relatively small number of more central, commercialized or industrialized locations in southeast, northeast, and northwest England, south Wales, and southwest Scotland.

In the case of Scotland, as in the countries of Continental Europe, it is assumed that a decline in mortality rates was the mechanism chiefly responsible for the acceleration in rates of population growth during the later Hanoverian period. The almost total absence of reliable information on numbers of births and deaths, however, makes it impossible to test the validity of this assumption. In the case of England, though declining death rates certainly contributed, it is now clear that the main mechanism of population growth was an increase in fertility.

Between roughly 1750 and 1850, English crude death rates fell from 25 (or 26) to 22 deaths per 1,000 population, and death rates in infancy from over 200 to 150 deaths per 1,000 live births; while the average life expectancy at birth rose from 36 (or 37) to about 40 years.

Before around 1825, the increase in fertility (both inside and outside marriage) was more pronounced. English illegitimacy ratios increased from under two illegitimacies per 100 live births around 1700 to over six by 1850, the increase beginning in the 1730s. A similar increase in bastardy occurred in Scotland, where illegitimacy ratios rose from around four throughout the first half of the 1700s to between 9 and 10 by the 1850s. Crude birthrates in England increased from 34.2 births per 1,000 population in 1751 to 40.9 per 1,000 in 1821, before falling to 35.2 in 1831 and 36.0 in 1841. At their peak in the quinquennium around 1816, English gross reproduction rates (defined as the mean number of female children the average newborn female will bear during her lifetime) were 30% higher than in 1751, and nearly 50% higher than in 1711.

So far as we can tell from the admittedly scanty evidence derived from parish register family reconstruction procedures, the increase in levels of legitimate fertility in England owed little to any increase in the frequency of childbearing within **marriage**. Overwhelmingly, increasing fertility levels was the combined result of declining average age at marriage and a reduction in the proportion of males and females who remained unmarried throughout their lifetimes. Comparing the period 1700–1749 to 1800–1849, mean age at first marriage fell from 27.5 years to 25.3 years for men, and from 26.2 years to 23.4 years for women. In 1751, as many as 107 in every 1,000 men and women age 40–44 had never married. By 1831, that figure had fallen to 75.

Far from clear are the factors responsible for the declining mortality, increasing illegitimacy, and the increase in nuptiality, all of which caused levels of legitimate fertility to increase. The decline in mortality was probably a consequence of a variety of influences, the most important being autonomous changes in the virulence of infectious disease viruses or in human resistance toward them, medical innovations such as the introduction of inoculation and vaccination against **smallpox**, and better standards of nutrition made possible by improvements in **agriculture** and real incomes. The increase in illegitimacy stemmed largely from the weakening of parental and communal control over the sexual behavior of the young, itself a product of the process of economic growth. Rising levels of nuptiality seem to be due mostly to a combination of greater opportunities for employment and (on the assumption that wage-earners marry earlier and in greater proportions than the self-employed) a trend toward a more proletarianized labor force.

Much more work needs to be done, however, before we have a clear understanding of the nature of the forces that underlay the striking changes that occurred in Britain's demographic structure between the beginning and the end of the Hanoverian period.

Neil L. Tranter

Bibliography

Flinn, Michael. *British Population Growth, 1770–1850.* 1970.

———, ed. *Scottish Population History from the Seventeenth Century to the 1930s.* 1977.

Tranter, Neil L. *Population and Society, 1750–1940: Contrasts in Population Growth.* 1985.

Wrigley, E.A., and R.S. Schofield. The *Population History of England, 1541–1871: A Reconstruction.* 1981.

See also Cities; Emigration and Immigration; Famines; Irish Emigration

Pornography

Although erotic literature can be traced back to Anglo-Saxon times, modern British pornography originated largely in the 18th century. Explicit sexual writing meant to amuse or arouse the reader became increasingly available from the 1650s when works imitating the 16th-century writer Pietro Aretino (1492–1556) began to appear. Aretino's main text, translated as *Postures*, incorporated erotic illustrations by Giulio Romano (*c.* 1499–1546). English writers produced their own versions of Aretino such as *The Crafty Whore* (1658), a fictional dialogue between a bawd and a prostitute. Similar productions such as *The Wandering Whore* (1660–1663) and *The Whore's Rhetorick* (1683) were written in imitation of other old pornographic works.

While foreign erotic texts, largely of French origin, were increasingly imported, **translated**, and imitated, by the early 1700s English writers were beginning to find a market for pornographic inventions of their own. The growth of this native literature culminated in the "classic" pornographic novel by **John Cleland**, *Fanny Hill, or The Memoirs of a Woman of Pleasure* (1748). In the second half of the 18th century, partially pornographic **periodicals** such as *Covent Garden Magazine, List of Covent-Garden Ladies,* and *Ranger's* magazine appeared, advertising expensive prostitutes whose anatomy and sexual prowess were often described graphically.

Between 1640 and 1727 the church courts had sole jurisdiction over obscene and pornographic literature. The **punishments** they could impose were excommunication or some form of public humiliation. But these courts were in decline. Slowly eroding at the same time were the licensing laws of the 16th century that gave some control to the Stationers Company to block the publication of works not deemed proper. The result was that virtually the only licensing of fiction in the 18th century pertained to plays, which under the **Playhouse Act** (1737) had to be approved 7 days before a public performance. However, pornography began to come under the jurisdiction of civil law though a court precedent set in 1727, when it was determined that the **publisher** Edmund Curll (1683–1747) was guilty of "obscene libel" for publishing a work titled *Venus in the Cloister or The Nun in Her Smock.* The court determined that Curll's offense came under the common law as a breach of the king's peace, since it undermined the morals of the king's subjects. But the truth is that very few cases were prosecuted, and that pornography remained largely unchecked throughout the 18th century. While Cleland was prosecuted for *Fanny Hill,* he was ultimately given a government **pension** for agreeing not to write any more such works. And the well-known prosecution of **John Wilkes** for the pornographic poem *Essay on Woman* (1763) had more to do with politics than taste.

The liberal atmosphere of the 18th century began to end with the emergence of the **Evangelical** movement in the 1780s and 1790s. Its **Society for the Suppression of Vice** (founded in 1802) was very active in prosecuting publishers and sellers of pornography up to the 1850s. Fear of the excesses of the **French Revolution** contributed to the growing worry over public immorality, there was a felt need to impose tighter social discipline on the masses toiling in new mines and mills, and there are many signs also that a **middle-class** social revolution was in progress against the former aristocratic laxity. In 1857 the Obscene Publications Act was passed, authorizing magistrates to destroy books deemed obscene, capping the shift from an era of sexual freedom to one of much sexual anxiety, vigilance, and repression.

Stanley D. Nash

Bibliography

Foxon, David. *Libertine Literature in England, 1660–1745.* 1965.

Kendrick, Walter. *The Secret Museum: Pornography in Modern Culture.* 1987.

Porter, Roy, and Lesley Hall. *The Facts of Life: The Creation of Sexual Knowledge in Britain, 1650–1950.* 1995.

St. John-Stevas, Norman. *Obscenity and the Law.* 1956.

Stone, Lawrence. *The Family, Sex and Marriage in England, 1500–1800.* 1977.

Thompson, Roger. *Unfit for Modest Ears: A Study of Pornographic, Obscene and Bawdy Works, Written or Published in England in the Second Half of the Seventeenth Century.* 1979.

See also Censorship; Crime; Laws of Public Worship, Speech, and the Press; Manners and Morals; Prostitution

Porson, Richard (1759–1808)

Porson, the Greek scholar whom A.E. Housman (1859–1936) placed second only to **Richard Bentley** among the English classicists, is remembered primarily as a textual critic and metrist whose emendations of ancient texts and illustrations of rules of meter did much to advance the standards of Greek scholarship.

Richard Porson

Born in Norfolk to a family of **artisans**, a child prodigy gifted with an encyclopedic memory and phenomenal grasp of mathematics as well as language, Porson was sent to Eton by a wealthy benefactor and later attended Trinity College, Cambridge, where he became a Fellow in 1782; in 1792 he was appointed to the Regius Professorship of Greek. His first important work was the *Letters to Travis* (1790), his only contribution to **biblical criticism**, which also contains his defense of **Edward Gibbon**'s scholarship, if not his style. Porson is best known, however, for his work with the Greek drama, especially his notes and emendations to four plays by Euripides: *Hecuba* (1797), *Orestes* (1798), *Phoenissae* (1799), and *Medea* (1801). The important Supplement to the Preface to the second edition of the *Hecuba* (1802) discusses the laws of iambic and trochaic verse in both tragedy and comedy, and includes Porson's rule about the pause ("Canon Porsonianus").

Alice D. Fasano

Bibliography

Brink, C.O. *English Classical Scholarship: Historical Reflections on Bentley, Porson, and Housman.* 1986.

Clarke, M.L. *Richard Porson: A Biographical Essay.* 1937.

Porteous Riots (1736)

The trigger of these **Edinburgh** riots was the judicial hanging of a **smuggler**, but their underlying cause was popular resentment against the British government's collection of indirect **taxes**. The captain of the town guard, "Black Jock" Porteous, and his men, being threatened by an angry mob after the smuggler's execution, opened fire on the crowd and killed several people. Porteous was then tried and condemed, but received from **London** an official respite for 6 weeks; upon which a well-organized mob rose up in fury, forced the tollbooth, and hanged him on the day originally appointed. Government officials were furious and believed that the incident could not have taken place without the cooperation of the city officials. Harsh measures were adopted, such as the destruction of the Nether Bow port so that troops could be brought in quickly, and the punishment of city magistrates.

Although punishments were moderated by the influence of the **2nd Duke of Argyll**, the provost was deposed and disqualified for life, and the city was fined. A political consequence was that these events opened a breach between the **Walpole** government and its important Scottish supporters of the Argyll faction. **Sir Walter Scott** retold the Porteous story in *The Heart of Midlothian* (1818).

Richard Finlay

Bibliography

Kidd, Colin. *Subverting Scotland's Past: Scottish Whig Historians and the Creation of an Anglo-British Identity, 1689–c.1820.* 1993.

Mitchison, Rosalind. *Lordship to Patronage: Scotland 1603–1745.* 1983.

Scott, Sir Walter. *The Heart of Midlothian.* 1818.

See also Riots and Popular Disturbances

Portland, 3rd Duke of (William Henry Cavendish Bentinck) (1738–1809)

Twice **Prime Minister**, Portland exemplifed the background, outlook, and many characteristics of the liberal Whig **aristocrat** of the latter 18th century. He attended Westminster (1747–1754), Oxford (1755–1757), and took the **Grand Tour** (1757–1761), then entered politics as M.P. for Weobly in 1761. Inheritance and marriage brought him a very substantial income, and his friendship with the **Marquess of Rockingham** added political weight. He formed predictably whiggish opinions on the main issues of the 1760s and 1770s—standing up for parliamentary privileges, supporting **Wilkes**, opposing **Lord North**'s American policy and the continuation of the **War of American Independence**, supporting **economical reform**.

A solid, steady, and conscientious administrator, Portland became nominal head of Rockingham's parliamentary faction after the latter's death (1782), and then of the **Fox–North coalition** (1783), while actually following the lead of **Charles James Fox**. Reacting to the **French Revolution**, he eventually (1794) transferred his allegiance and that of his followers to **Pitt the Younger**, and became Home Secretary (1794–1801). During his second ministry (1807–1809), the ailing duke again was the figurehead, trying to reconcile discordant ministers. His ministry pressed the trade war with Napoleon and opened the Peninsular Campaign (1808).

Portland was also, among other things, a Fellow of the Society of Antiquaries and the **Royal Society**, trustee of the **British Museum**, and Chancellor of **Oxford University** (1792–1809).

P.J. Kulisheck

Bibliography

Namier, Sir Lewis, and John Brooke. *History of Parliament: The House of Commons, 1754–1790.* 3 vols. 1964.

O'Gorman, Frank. *The Rise of Party in England: The Rockingham Whigs, 1760–82.* 1975.

Smith, E.A. "The Duke of Portland," in Herbert van Thal, ed., *The Prime Ministers.* 1975.

See also Whigs and Whiggism

Postal Services

The Royal Post was established by Henry VIII for government use. Public use developed during the 17th century, with **coffeehouses** often figuring as centers of business and postal communication. Postage was assessed by distance and the number of letter sheets conveyed, and payment was made by the recipient. A penny post service was established in **London** for local mail (1680), a service later copied in other **cities**. The Post Office Act of 1711 unified postal services and set rates for the several kingdoms and overseas.

Postage in the 18th century was expensive because the Crown used the Post Office as a cash cow. It also burdened it with practices that invited abuse. For example, numerous government **pensions** were charged against its revenues. A franking privilege, allowing officials and M.P.s to receive mail without paying postage, was widely abused; estimates of this franked mail range as high as half the total volume. Government tampering—opening letters, reading, and resealing them—was also routine, excused on the grounds of detecting **crime** and subversion.

Improvements in service resulted from contractors' initiatives, not those of government. Thus Ralph Allen of Bath (1694–1764) developed cross-posts, which extended service to areas far removed from the six main post **roads** radiating from London. In 1785 John Palmer (1742–1818) inaugurated mail **coaches**, which cut delivery time in half. The post was further accelerated in the 19th century by the application of **steam** propulsion to packet ships and the new **railways**. Technologically, the stage was set for administrative overhaul and cheaper rates when in 1837 Rowland Hill (1795–1879), father of the penny adhesive postage stamp, published his seminal pamphlet titled "Post Office Reform."

N. Merrill Distad

Bibliography

Ellis, Kenneth. *The Post Office in the Eighteenth Century: A Study in Administrative History.* 1958.

Robinson, Howard. *The British Post Office: A History.* 1948.

———. *Carrying British Mails Overseas.* 1964.

Staff, Frank. *The Penny Post, 1680–1918.* 1964.

Potter, John (1674?–1747)

Potter, Archbishop of Canterbury, was born the son of a linen draper in Wakefield (Yorkshire) and educated at Oxford, where he later became Regius Professor of Divinity (1707). Assisted by **Marlborough**, he became Bishop of Oxford (1715), and was translated to Canterbury in 1737 with help from **Queen Caroline**. A supporter of the **Whigs** though a High Churchman, he is best known for *A Discourse of Church Government: Wherein the Rights of the Church and the Supremacy of Christian Princes are Vindicated and Adjusted* (1707; 3rd ed., 1724), where he insisted on the authority of the church through the bishops as direct descendants of the Apostles. He also, among other things, wrote against **Hoadly** in the **Bangorian controversy** and expounded on classical archaeology and early Christianity. Late in life he disinherited his eldest son for marrying a **servant**; his second son, Thomas (1718–1759), was rumored to have cuckolded **William Warburton**, Bishop of Gloucester, and sired Ralph Allen Warburton in 1764.

Donald W. Nichol

Bibliography

Clark, J.C.D. *English Society, 1688–1832.* 1985.

Sykes, Norman. *Church and State in the XVIIIth Century.* 1934; 1975.

———. *From Sheldon to Secker: Aspects of English Church History, 1660–1768.* 1959.

See also Church of England

Poverty and Poor Laws

Tudor England experienced a rise in vagrancy and crime that was linked to land **enclosures**, the disbanding of feudal militias, and the dissolution of the monasteries. These both increased the number of unemployed and eliminated a major source of charity. Early Tudor legislation directed that the impotent or deserving poor be licensed to beg within their parishes, and that the able-bodied poor be punished. Famines and bread riots in the 1590s forced the government to provide more systematic relief for the impotent poor by a tax, rather than relying entirely on private charity, and by putting the able-bodied to work, rather than merely punishing them.

Three statutes codifying previous legislation were passed by the Parliament of 1597–1598. Parish officials were directed to apprentice pauper children; to build houses for paupers; to commit to jail any who remained idle or begged for more than food; to return vagrants to the parish of their birth or last residence (with or without a salutary whipping); and to raise a local poor rate (or tax) to buy raw materials for work for the able-bodied. Initially viewed as temporary, this legislation formed the basis of the "Elizabethan Poor Law Code" and was renewed several times in the 17th century.

The parish remained the basic administrative unit for the poor laws for more than two centuries. An officer created for this purpose, the Overseer of the Poor, was elected to a 1-year term by either the parish churchwardens or justices of the peace. The job was not popular with the men of substance who were usually elected, so many paid a stiff fine instead of serving. In some few parishes, private charity and casual doles sufficed to meet local need, so poor rates and overseers were unknown there. Richer parishes were liable to "rates-in-aid" levied against them by neighboring parishes with insufficient means to cope in times of widespread distress.

Charitable gifts continued to provide significant revenue, particularly for the relief of the impotent poor, such as the elderly, children, the sick, the maimed, and the insane. Most of

Children relieving a young beggar

these were provided with "outdoor" relief, though the insane might be confined in the new county houses of correction known as "Bridewells," after their London prototype. The Elizabethan system laid particular emphasis on the apprenticing of pauper children, and on the need to set the able-bodied to work. After 1660, however, few parishes seriously attempted to put the able-bodied poor to work, and the impracticality of employing them at a profit in workhouses led to the common practice of contracting out their labor (a variant of the medieval "roundsman" system, when farmers employed pauper laborers). Under the terms of the 1662 Act of Settlements, greater energy was exerted by parish overseers to eject vagrants and other potential relief claimants, especially if pregnant. This rendered laborers prisoners in their parishes of birth or official settlement, a restriction on the free movement of labor with serious implications for later industrialization.

By the early Hanoverian period, public attitudes toward the poor had shifted from the more typical Elizabethan view that poverty was the result of misfortune, to the notion that it resulted from vice and improvidence. Harsh treatment prevailed during much of the 18th century. Paupers were sometimes stigmatized by the enforced wearing of badges, to prevent those receiving parish relief from further begging. Improvements during the age of **George III** resulted partly from new **humanitarian** currents expressed in the work of philanthropists and reformers such as **Jonas Hanway**, Joseph Townsend (1739–1816), and Sir Frederick Eden (1766–1809), all of whom made important efforts to quantify and analyze the problems of poverty and to propose practical solutions. The motives of these reformers ranged from the religious to the mercantilist and patriotic.

Despite occasional legislative attempts as early as 1693 to place the overseers more tightly under the control of the justices of the peace, a form of parochial laissez-faire prevailed in which corruption and peculation by parish officials were rife. Another ardent poor law reformer, Thomas Gilbert (1720–1798), secured parliamentary passage of an act (1782) that sought to limit the authority of parish overseers by creating larger administrative units called "unions." Where implemented, this led to more scrupulous administration and a decline in poor rates, but this trend was short-lived.

In the 1790s, when agricultural workers' wages proved inadequate in the face of rising wartime food prices, a group of Berkshire magistrates, meeting at Speenhamland in 1795, chose to make up the shortfall in wages by "allowances" from the poor rates, rather than by prevailing upon farmers to raise wages. As the "**Speenhamland System**" of outdoor relief spread across much of the country, its effects on wages were predictable—they remained below the subsistence level. With the return of peace in 1815, Parliament kept grain prices artificially high by imposing the **corn laws**, which were designed to provide agricultural price protection. As a result, poverty and outdoor relief spread further, while poor rates rose to higher and higher levels.

The resultant burdensome rise in poor rates led to calls for reform of the poor laws, fueling a movement that had begun decades earlier in the 18th century. The movement for reform, however, gained both a new impetus and a sinister twist from the theories of **Thomas Malthus** and **David Ricardo** that population growth would always eclipse the food supply and that real wages therefore would always tend to sink to subsistence levels, the bare minimum to keep people alive and working. There was widespread concurrence that outdoor relief to workers distorted not only the agricultural economy but also that of Britain's burgeoning industrial sector.

Scottish and Irish poor relief were governed by different statutes and traditions before the 1830s. The Irish peasant lived close to destitution, yet **Ireland** long lacked any statute directly providing for poor relief. Scottish law never acknowledged the right of able-bodied paupers to relief, and thus comparatively little was expended on those able to work. On the other hand, the Scottish Law of Settlement did not allow parishes to expel outsiders who might later claim relief.

Reform, slow in coming, took the form of the **New Poor Law** of 1834, primarily the handiwork of **Nassau Senior** and **Edwin Chadwick**. It enshrined the principle of "less eligibility," that is, that the condition of those receiving relief must be rendered considerably less attractive than that of the gainfully employed. This was achieved by abolishing most forms of outdoor relief, by confining paupers in large workhouses where even married couples were separated by sex, and by providing inmates with drab uniforms and a barely adequate and thoroughly unappetizing diet. Run by a central poor law commission acting through local boards of guardians, this harsh new system, destined to last a century, offered paupers (in Charles Dickens's critical assessment) the choice between starving slowly within the workhouse or more rapidly outside it. The imposition of this rigid system upon Ireland in 1838 later proved untenable in the face of widespread **famine**.

N. Merrill Distad

Bibliography

Brundage, Anthony. *The Making of the New Poor Law: The Politics of Inquiry, Enactment, and Implementation, 1832–1839.* 1978.

Eden, Sir Frederick Morton. *The State of the Poor: or, A History of the Labouring Classes in England . . . with Parochial Reports.* 1797; facs. rpt. 1966; abridgement by A.G.L. Rogers, 1929; rpt. 1971.

Himmelfarb, Gertrude. *The Idea of Poverty: England in the Early Industrial Age.* 1984.

Marshall, Dorothy. *The English Poor in the Eighteenth Century: A Study in Social and Administrative History.* 1926; rpt. 1969.

Nicholls, Sir George. *A History of the English Poor Law.* 1854; rev. ed., 1898; rpt. 1967.

———. *A History of the Irish Poor Law.* 1856; rpt. 1967.

———. *A History of the Scotch Poor Law.* 1856; rpt. 1967.

Poynter, John Riddoch. *Society and Pauperism: English Ideas on Poor Relief, 1795–1834.* 1969.

Townsend, Joseph. *A Dissertation on the Poor Laws by a Well-Wisher to Mankind.* 1786; rpt. 1971.

Webb, Sidney, and Beatrice Webb. *English Poor Law Policy.* 1910; rpt. 1963.

———. *English Poor Law History, Part I: The Old Poor Law; Part II: The Last Hundred Years.* 1927–1929; rpt. 1963.

See also Hours, Wages, and Working Conditions; Scottish Poor Law; Standard of Living

Presbyterians

Presbyterians, a Protestant **dissenting** sect, are followers of the English-speaking reformed church with its nonhierarchical governance structure. Standing at some point between Anglicans (governed by bishops) and **Congregationalists** (governed by congregations), Presbyterians believe that all church members are equal in the sight of God. Their congregations are governed by lay and clerical elders, or presbyters, chosen by the congregations themselves but subject to higher control by diocesan synods and a national assembly.

The stronghold of British Presbyterianism has always been **Scotland**. There the **Church of Scotland**, founded in 1557 by John Knox (?1514–1572), was the only Presbyterian church established by law in Great Britain (1690). During the 17th century the main conflict in Scotland was between Evangelical Calvinists and Moderates over the Westminster Confession and catechism. After 1712 the Moderates were in control, thanks to their support by English landowners in Scotland. With the advent of **religious revivalism** by the 1750s, Scottish Presbyterianism increasingly took on Evangelical and revivalist overtones.

In **Ireland**, Presbyterianism emerged after James I took control of Ulster (1610) and Scottish immigrants carried it in in the 1640s; it was aided there by Crown grants until 1870, though its success was limited by the fact that many Scotch–Irish Presbyterians left for **North America** during the 18th century. In **Wales**, however, Presbyterianism grew substantially under the influence of religious revivalism in the Hanoverian period. In the 1730s **Howel Harris** and **Daniel Rowland**, an Anglican minister, inspired the Welsh Calvinistic Methodists, as Presbyterians were called there. This group subscribed to the free grace doctrine of **George Whitefield**, a critic in this respect of the predestinarian position of **John Wesley**. The inevitable break with Anglicanism and **Methodism** occurred in 1811 when the Rev. **Thomas Charles** ordained nine clergymen, after which two Presbyterian synods were created in North and South Wales.

English Presbyterianism dates from the 17th-century Puritan revolution. It suffered repression during the Restoration but nonetheless benefited from the **Toleration Act** (1689) and the growing **religious toleration** of the 18th century. There were more than 200 congregations in the 1720s, though they were badly organized and there was a tendency for members to drift toward **latitudinarian** and even **Unitarian** beliefs, and **rational dissent**. England's Presbyterians arguably had their greatest influence in the **dissenting academies** with luminaries such as **Joseph Priestley** teaching at Warrington and **Richard Price** at Hackney. By 1800, following a struggle over the doctrine of the Trinity, English Presbyterianism was in decline, many members having become **Congregationalists** or, more frequently, Unitarians. But Scottish settlers helped to make up the difference and at length organized the Presbyterian Church of England (1876), which still later (1972) became part of the United Reformed Church in England and Wales.

Hanoverian Presbyterians were active in politics and business. Many of those who served in Parliament advocated the repeal of the **Test and Corporation acts**. William Plumer, an M.P. who moved for the repeal of the acts, was expelled from Commons in 1723 after his association with the Harbury lottery was exposed. Samuel Holden, M.P. from Cornwall and a **London** banker and merchant, from 1732 to 1736 chaired the Committee of **Protestant Dissenting Deputies** to Repeal the Test and Corporation Acts, and Sir Henry Hoghton, who was educated at the Warrington Academy and served in Commons for nearly 30 years, seconded motions to terminate the acts in 1787, 1789, and 1790.

Presbyterians were represented in the hosiery, **textile**, **shipping**, netting, and **brewing** industries. Among these were Samuel Fellows of Nottingham (hosiery), Thomas Touchet and James Bayley (textiles), and Ralph Carr (shipowner and broker). The Gundries of Bridport were famous for the two branches of their family, which were successful in the fishnetting and brewing industries. The brothers Joseph and John Gundry operated both sides of the business. Their sons, Joseph and Samuel, later ran the netting and brewing concerns, respectively.

Jack Fruchtman, Jr.

Bibliography

Bolam, C.G., Jeremy Goring, H.L. Short, and Roger Thomas. *The English Presbyterians: From Elizabethan Puritanism to Modern Unitarianism.* 1968.

Davies, Horton. *Worship and Theology in England, from Watts and Wesley to Maurice, 1690–1850.* 1961.

Henderson, George D. *Presbyterianism.* 1955.

Hunt, N.C. *Two Early Political Associations: The Quakers and the Dissenting Deputies in the Age of Sir Robert Walpole.* 1961.

Kidd, Colin. *Subverting Scotland's Past: Scottish Whig Historians and the Creation of an Anglo–British Identity, 1689–1830.* 1993.

Leith, John H. *Introduction to the Reformed Tradition: A Way of Being the Christian Community.* 1981.

Loetscher, Lefferts A. *A Brief History of the Presbyterians.* 1984.

Rupp, E. Gordon. *Religion in England, 1688–1791.* 1986.

Seed, John. "Gentlemen Dissenters: The Social and Political Meanings of Rational Dissent in the 1770s and 1780s." *The Historical Journal.* Vol. 28, pp. 299–325.

Short, Basil. *A Respectable Society: Bridport 1593–1835.* 1976.

Watts, Michael. *The Dissenters.* 1978.

Price, Richard (1723–1791)

A moral philosopher, dissenting minister, mathematician, economist, and **Royal Society** member, Price defended rationalism against empiricist attacks by **Francis Hutcheson** and **David Hume.** As one of Britain's leading **dissenters,** he championed freedom of worship and passionately defended the **American** and **French revolutions.** He drew political fire from **Edmund Burke** and, with his friend **Joseph Priestley,** left his mark on the history of British **radicalism.**

Price was born into a leading Welsh dissenting family. Raised a High Calvinist, he read **Locke's** *The Reasonableness of Christianity* (1695) and **Samuel Clarke's** *The Scripture Doctrine of the Trinity* (1719), and turned to the **Latitudinarian**-influenced nonconformist tradition. After completing his education at the dissenting Academy at Tenter Alley, he became family chaplain under an English patron, George Streatfield. He studied moral philosophy, **theology,** and mathematics, and wrote his *Review of the Principal Questions in Morals* (1758), an attempted refutation of Hutcheson's "moral sense" theories and a classic statement of the rational and utilitarian foundations of ethics.

In 1757 Price married Sarah Blundell, remaining tolerant of her Anglicanism throughout their marriage. He became a preacher at the **Presbyterian** Chapel in Newington Green, 3 miles north of **London** (1758), a congregation of prosperous Latitudinarian **Whigs** and other well-to-do dissenters. His idea of self-government had radical implications for American independence—he outlined these in his *Observations on the Nature of Civil Liberty, the Principles of Government, and the Justice and Policy of the War with America* (1776)—and for French liberation from monarchy, which he indirectly encouraged in his "Discourse on the Love of Our Country" (1789). In line with his ethical theories, he always defended the rights of individual worship, freedom of inquiry, and the "principle of the convinced conscience," maintaining that each individual must do what he or she believes to be fundamentally right.

Price's dissenting viewpoint stood to the left in British politics; he enthusiastically welcomed all sorts of reform. It was in response to Price's "Discourse on the Love of Our Country" (1789) that Burke wrote his *Reflections on the Revolution in France* (1790), permanently casting Price in the popular mind as an unstable radical. Among his defenders were **Mary Wollstonecraft** and **Thomas Paine,** both of whom wrote in his defense. He was venerated by Priestley, and the two have gone down in history together as outspoken friends of the French Revolution.

Carole S. Fungaroli

Bibliography

Bradley, James E. *Religion, Revolution and English Radicalism: Nonconformity in Eighteenth Century Politics and Society.* 1990.

Cone, Carl B. *Torchbearer of Freedom: The Influence of Richard Price on Eighteenth-Century Thought.* 1952.

Fitzpatrick, Martin. "Richard Price and the London Revolution Society." *Enlightenment and Dissent.* Vol. 10, pp. 35–50.

Fruchtman, Jack, Jr. *The Apocalyptic Politics of Richard Price and Joseph Priestley: A Study in Late-Eighteenth-Century English Republican Millennialism.* 1983.

Peach, Bernard, and D.O. Thomas. *The Correspondence of Richard Price.* 2 vols. 1983, 1991.

Peterson, Susan R. "Richard Price's Politics and His Ethics." *Journal of the History of Ideas.* Vol. 45, pp. 537–547.

Thomas, D.O. *The Honest Mind: The Thought and Work of Richard Price.* 1977.

Thomas, Roland. *Richard Price, Apostle of Liberty and Philosopher.* 1924.

See also Rational Dissent

Price, Sir Uvedale (1747–1829)

Price was the chief theorist of the **picturesque movement** and a leading advocate of its application to **landscape architecture.** Following William Gilpin's (1724–1804) popularization of the term *picturesque,* Price defined it as a distinct aesthetic category much as **Edmund Burke** had defined the beautiful and the **sublime.** He believed that the qualities which made an object picturesque were "roughness and sudden variation joined to irregularity." He and Richard Payne Knight (1750–1824) attacked the serene but "bare and bald" gardens of the famous **Lancelot ("Capability") Brown,** suggesting that gardeners should instead imitate the dramatic effects of the great landscape painters rather than the harmonies and unities of **neoclassical** taste. Brown's successor, **Humphry Repton,** at first agreed with these critics but later balked at surrounding wealthy clients with antiquated cottages and untrimmed vegetation.

Anne Kapler McCallum

Bibliography

Allentuck, Marcia. "Sir Uvedale Price and the Picturesque Garden: The Evidence of the Coleorton Papers," in Nikolaus Pevsner, ed., *The Picturesque Garden and Its Influence Outside the British Isles.* 1974.

Hussey, Christopher. *The Picturesque: Studies in a Point of View.* 1927; rpt. 1967.

Price, Uvedale. *An Essay on the Picturesque, as Compared with the Sublime and the Beautiful: And on the Use of Studying Pictures for the Purpose of Improving Real Landscape.* 1794; rpt. 1971.

Priestley, Joseph (1733–1804)

Priestley was a dissenting **Unitarian** minister, eminent scientist, and outspoken radical of the latter 18th century. Born into a Yorkshire family of **dissenters** and educated at the Daventry Academy, he became **Presbyterian** minister at Needham Market (1755), but raised hackles with his liberal views. He became a tutor at the **dissenting academy** at Warrington (1761), teaching languages and performing scientific experiments. A member of the **Royal Society** from 1766, he befriended **Benjamin Franklin,** and, with his encouragement, wrote *The History and Present State of Electricity* (1767). Under **Lord Shelburne's patronage** he improved techniques for isolating and studying gases. His discoveries included oxygen, nitrogen, nitrous oxide (laughing gas), nitrogen dioxide, ammonia, hydrogen chloride, sulfur dioxide, carbon monoxide, and the principle of carbonation.

Joseph Priestley

Priestley became minister of the New Meeting Society, a large dissenting congregation in Birmingham (1779). He joined the **Lunar Society** of **Birmingham**, which included among its members **James Watt**, **Josiah Wedgwood**, **Erasmus Darwin**, and **Matthew Boulton**. Some doubted his Christianity after the publication of *Disquisitions Relating to Matter and Spirit* (1777), where he described the soul as part of the corporeal form, which expires at death. He went on to deny free will in his *Doctrine of Philosophical Necessity Illustrated,* and in *A History of the Corruption of Christianity* (1782) he further denied miracles as well as the Fall of Man, the Atonement, and the Trinity, maintaining that none of these were founded in Christ's teaching. Priestley did believe in God, supporting his belief with arguments from design (the evidence of divine handiwork in creation). **Utopian** in outlook, he hoped science would lead to a heaven on Earth.

Priestley, like many **radicals**, hailed the **French Revolution** when it began (1789). Utilitarian in outlook, he believed that the state should promote the happiness of the majority; the overthrow of an unjust government was consistent with Christian moral philosophy. **Edmund Burke**, on the other hand, reflecting conservative horror at cataclysmic constitutional change, attacked Priestley as a danger to society, inveighing against him in Parliament (1791). A reactionary mob then burned Priestley's house, laboratory, and many of his papers. Although he was awarded damages, he became generally shunned by all, including members of the Royal Society.

Offered asylum in France, he chose instead to emigrate to Northumberland, Pennsylvania (1794), to be near his friend Franklin. His presentations before the Universalists of Philadelphia on "The Evidences of Christianity" (1796) led to the formation of a Unitarian Society. Although he was nearly deported under the Adams administration, his friend Thomas Jefferson (1743–1826) supported him, and he remained in America for the remainder of his life. Jefferson wrote him that "yours is one of the few lives precious to mankind" (1801) and, like **Jeremy Bentham**, acknowledged Priestley's influence on his own conceptions of liberty, happiness, education, and **science**. Priestley's *Essay on the First Principles of Government, and on the Nature of Political, Civil and Religious Liberty* (1769) contains the core of his democratic and liberal views.

Carole S. Fungaroli

Bibliography

Anderson, R.G.W., et al. *Science, Medicine and Dissent: Joseph Priestley.* 1987.

Bradley, James E. *Religion, Revolution and English Radicalism: Nonconformity in Eighteenth Century Politics and Society.* 1990.

Fruchtman, Jack, Jr. *The Apocalyptic Politics of Richard Price and Joseph Priestley: A Study in Late-Eighteenth-Century English Republican Millennialism.* 1983.

Gibbs, F.W. *Joseph Priestley: Revolutions of the Eighteenth Century.* 1967.

Kieft, Lester, and Bennett R. Willeford, Jr., eds. *Joseph Priestley: Scientist, Theologian, and Metaphysician.* 1980.

Kramnick, Isaac. "Joseph Priestley's Scientific Liberalism," in Isaac Kramnick, ed., *Republicanism and Bourgeois Radicalism: Political Ideology in Late Eighteenth-Century England and America.* 1990.

See also Rational Dissent; Riots and Popular Disturbances; Theology

Prime Minister

To about 1800, the Hanoverian king was clearly the head of his government. As **George II** often said, the office of prime minister did not exist. The king appointed the heads of all administrative departments as equals who reported directly to him, but he usually chose one man sympathetic to his policies to be his chief adviser or minister. He needed a man with sufficient skill and influence to secure passage of acts of Parliament to support royal policies, and this meant raising money for them as well. Since all money bills originated in the **House of Commons**, the king needed a man able to maintain a majority there.

Sir Robert Walpole was the first chief adviser to fulfill all these requirements so well that he was called prime minister by the public and his opponents. His success was attributed to his office, head of the Treasury Board, through which he managed the budget and the levying of **taxes**, and influenced Commons elections. Consequently, all but one of the 23 subsequent Hanoverian chief ministers were appointed First Lord of the Treasury and, if a member of Commons, Chancellor of the Exchequer. All were popularly called prime minister, even though they lacked the powers now associated with that office.

The chief minister served at the pleasure of the king, though the monarch was sometimes forced to dismiss his choice because that man had lost his majority in Parliament. While some fellow ministers might choose to resign when a chief minister was dismissed, they were not obliged to because they were appointed individually by the king.

The first three Georges were strong-willed rulers who attempted to control government through their favorite ministers. However, the several periods of incapacitating illness suffered by **George III** gave Parliament and his chief ministers greater freedom and responsibility. This increase, together with the formation of two more clearly distinct political parties in the early 1800s, made his principal ministers more powerful than their predecessors. The **Regency** (1811–1820) and subsequent reign of **George IV** further diminished the influence of the Crown, and the 1832 **Reform Act** curtailed its intervention in elections. When **William IV** then proved powerless to impose his choice for chief minister on Parliament, the groundwork was laid which would allow Parliament to impose its own choice of a prime minister on the monarch in the next reign.

P.J. Kulisheck

Bibliography

Carter, Byrum. *The Office of Prime Minister.* 1956.
Van Thal, Herbert, ed. *The Prime Ministers.* 1975.

See also Government, National; Party Politics; Patronage

Prince Regent

See George IV

Prints and Printmaking

See Graphic Arts

Prisons and Prison Reform

Throughout the 18th century the main punishments for felonious crimes were death or forced transportation to the colonies. On the whole, long-term imprisonment did not become a standard penalty until the 1840s. However, there were four major categories of incarceration employed during the Hanoverian era.

(1) Debtors' prisons, including in **London** the Fleet, Ludgate, King's Bench, and Marshalsea, held individuals and their families until creditors were satisfied or an act of Parliament confirmed the debtor's insolvency—a practice not totally abandoned until 1869.

(2) Houses of Correction, often called Bridewells (after the first of such institutions, founded in London in the 1550s), held vagrants, prostitutes, and other idle and disorderly people, usually for short terms (typically, 30 days). These institutions were meant to teach industry through hard work. Textile and rope manufacturers supplied materials and contracted with the local justices of the peace for the labor of these inmates. Physical punishment, such as whipping, often accompanied a sentence to a Bridewell.

(3) Jails (gaols) existed on the county and **borough** levels but were used mostly to hold prisoners before sentencing or while awaiting execution or transportation. The largest and most famous jail was London's notorious Newgate, which could house some 200 prisoners; other jails might range from a single room in a shop to a dungeon of an old castle.

(4) Another form of incarceration originated in the practice (begun in 1717) of transporting convicted felons to the colonies. The Hulks, old and decaying ships moored at London **docks**, began to be used in 1776 as a temporary method for holding such prisoners until transportation could be arranged. However, the interruption of transportation caused by the **War of American Independence** led to the Hulks becoming virtual prisons, in which inmates were kept by night and taken out during the day for work on the docks or on dredging the Thames River. Despite the resumption of transportation in 1787 (now using **Australia** rather than America as the main destination), penitentiary reliance on the Hulks as well as on transportation itself continued throughout the early 1830s and only ended in the 1850s.

During the second half of the 18th century, alternatives to capital punishment began to be proposed. These were often accompanied by **humanitarian** criticism of the terrible conditions at existing institutions of incarceration. Complaints were directed against their unsanitary conditions; the physical brutality inflicted upon inmates; and the mixing together of old and young, women and men, and experienced and neophyte offenders. Another target was the system of jail fees. Jailors, whose compensation consisted largely of money made from prisoners, charged for the basic necessities of life, for certain extras (most jails, for example, had "tap" rooms that featured alcoholic beverages), and even for a prisoner's release after his time was served.

A major impetus for reform came from the publication (1774) in Italy of a book by the **Enlightenment** thinker Cesare Beccaria (1738–1794), **translated** into English (1767) as *Essay on Crimes and Punishments.* Beccaria stressed the superior efficacy of humane but certain punishment over corporal and capital punishment. Partly due to his influence, a number of parliamentary investigations began looking into prison conditions in the 1770s. Further impetus came with **John Howard**'s *State of Prisons in England and Wales* (1777), a detailed enumeration of abuse and disease existing in prisons. In 1779 a Penitentiary Act was passed, authorizing a model prison to be built along the lines that Howard called for, and recommending implementation of his novel prescriptions of solitary confinement, hard work, and guilt-inducing religious instruction.

Despite the fact that Howard's prison was never built, the Act of 1779 marked the formal introduction of the concept of reform and rehabilitation, rather than mere punishment, into the budding prison reform movement. This latter was advanced further by the publication of **Jeremy Bentham**'s *Panopticon* in 1791, the utilitarian manifesto that proposed building a prison to be run as a money-making, high-security enterprise—a "mill for grinding rogues honest and idle men industrious," as Bentham put it. Although Parliament autho-

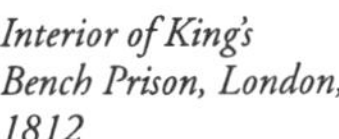

Interior of King's Bench Prison, London, 1812

rized construction, Bentham's Panopticon never materialized, either—one reason being the habit of relying on transportation and the Hulks to deal with felons.

Thus, while private efforts at prison reform were initiated as experiments in several local jurisdictions, it was not until 1816 that the first national penitentiary, Millbank, was built. Several decades then passed, during which much debate was held over the question of whether the so-called silent system (literally forbidding prisoners to speak to one another) or their (more costly) separation in solitary cells was superior as a punishment. Meanwhile, **Elizabeth Fry**, like Howard, took up a roving commission over the British Isles and much of Europe, collecting information particularly on the treatment of women and children in prisons, which, transformed into improvements nearly everywhere, made conditions for them less brutal and more bearable.

The modern prison penitentiary system was really launched in 1842 with the opening of Pentonville, the first of over 50 new penitentiaries built along the same lines. These all instituted a degree of separation of prisoners, strict discipline aided by surveillance, and hard work—often not productive but very punishing (for example, on treadmills). By the 1840s, capital punishment had been reduced to only a few offenses, while incarceration had thus become the dominant method of punishing criminal activities. Traditional historians regarded this as a victory for humane reformers, but some recent writers have suggested that the prison was instead a model for "carceral" institutions, which served to demonstrate the power of the state, and impose fuller social control over the lower classes. One author (Foucault) maintains that the punishment of the body had been replaced by punishment of the "soul."

Stanley B. Nash

Bibliography

Bender, John B. *Imagining the Penitentiary: Fiction and the Architecture of Mind in Eighteenth-Century England.* 1987.

De Lacy, Margaret. *Prison Reform in Lancashire, 1700–1850: A Study in Local Administration.* 1986.

Foucault, Michel. *Discipline and Punish: The Birth of the Prison.* 1977.

Ignatieff, Michael. *A Just Measure of Pain: The Penitentiary in the Industrial Revolution.* 1978.

Radzinowicz, Leon. *A History of English Criminal Law and Its Administration from 1750.* 4 vols. 1948–1968.

Thompson, F.M.L., ed. *The Cambridge Social History of Britain, 1750–1950.* 3 vols. 1990.

Webb, Sidney, and Beatrice Webb. *English Prisons under Local Government.* 1922.

See also Crime; Judicial System; Punishment; Transportation, Penal

Proclamation of 1763

The intent of this royal proclamation (issued on 7 October 1763) was to deal with issues that had arisen in **North America** as a result of Britain's victory in the **Seven Years' War**. The government's aims were to prescribe the boundaries of the new (formerly French) colony of **Quebec** and provide a suitable governance structure for it; establish a policy toward the Indians west of the St. Lawrence River and south of the Great Lakes; and encourage British settlement in Quebec. Hence the boundaries of Quebec were limited to the St. Lawrence Valley; trade and settlement in the area north of the Ohio River and west of the Appalachians and the St. Lawrence was prohibited; and limited British government and laws were provided for Quebec. The policy worked temporarily, but by 1773 its restrictions on civil rights, trade, and especially western settlement had alienated British merchants in Quebec and many would-be American settlers. The **Quebec Act** (1774), which modified it, helped provoke the **American Revolution**.

Stuart R. Givens

Bibliography

Alvord, Clarence W. "The Genesis of the Proclamation of 1763." *Michigan Pioneer and Historical Collections.* Vol. 36 (1908), pp. 20–52.

Smith, Dwight L. "A North American Neutral Indian Zone: Persistence of a British Idea." *Northwest Ohio Quarterly.* Vol. 61, pp. 46–63.

Sosin, Jack M. *Whitehall and the Wilderness: The Middle-West in British Colonial Policy, 1760–1775.* 1961.

See also Canada; Empire and Imperialism

Proclamation Society against Vice and Immorality (1787–1808)

The intention of this society was to ensure the more rigorous enforcement of existing laws concerning morality and to encourage persons of influence in the community to set an example of upright living. As its guiding spirit, the Rev. **Christopher Wyvill** encouraged **George III** to issue a proclamation against vice and immorality (1787). **William Wilberforce**, who helped found the society, believed that in the absence of a public regulator of morals as in ancient states, citizens themselves had to act as guardians of the moral law. The society in 1787 claimed fewer than 50 members but listed many very prominent churchmen (including the Archbishop of Canterbury) and such eminent **aristocrats** as the **Duke of Grafton** and **Lord North**, both former **prime ministers**.

The society remained small and select until its demise. Its work was mainly conducted by a small committee dominated by Wilberforce and Beilby Porteus (1731–1808), who later became Bishop of London. In 1790 it arranged a convention of magistrates in **London** to consider **prison** conditions and vagrancy, and eventually succeeded in having relevant legislation enacted. It generally found Parliament sympathetic to its aims, except as regarded the passing of laws prohibiting labor on Sunday. In 1796 its activities related to **poverty** and vagrancy were taken over by another organization begun by Wilberforce: the Society for the Bettering the Condition of the Poor. With the death of Porteus, who had served as its president since 1793, the society died too. A few of its more energetic members had already turned to the new **Society for the Suppression of Vice**, founded in 1802.

Martin Fitzpatrick

Bibliography

Innes, Joanna. "Politics and Morals: The Reformation of Manners Movement in Later Eighteenth-Century England," in Eckhart Hellmuth, ed., *The Transformation of Political Culture: England and Germany in the Late Eighteenth Century.* 1990.

Roberts, M.J.D. "The Society for the Suppression of Vice and Its Early Critics, 1802–1812." *Historical Journal.* Vol. 26, pp. 159–176.

See also Manners and Morals; Society for the Reformation of Manners

Prostitution

In 1762 **James Boswell** observed that **London**'s prostitutes ranged "from the splendid Madam at fifty guineas a night, down to the civil nymph . . . who tramps along the Strand and will resign her engaging person to your honour for a pint of wine and a shilling." Prostitution indeed operated on all levels during the 18th century, and until the advent of industrial urbanization its main locale was London.

High-class prostitutes who could earn £50 or more per night did exist. The most famous was Kitty Fisher, whose clients included a prince, and whose acceptance by high society is registered in her portraits by **Reynolds** and others. Just below this rank were the women who worked in the fashionable brothels of London's West End, particularly in Saint James's and the Pall Mall. The far less elegant bagnios (ostensibly, Turkish baths) which offered prostitution in Covent Garden were also frequented by many upper-class young men.

Most prostitutes, however, worked in shabby conditions in the many brothels in the East End along the Thames, in Goodman's Fields, and in Wapping. Many **coffeehouses, public houses** (licensed bars), **pleasure gardens**, and other such places were also points of solicitation. The Strand was notorious for streetwalkers. Common prostitutes gratified their clients in taverns or lodging houses, others simply in parks or alleys.

Several things distinguished Hanoverian prostitution from that of other eras. First, it was the bawd (brothel keeper), often an ex-prostitute, who was the most powerful figure in the profession; she, rather than the pimp, exploited and often abused the prostitute. Until the 19th century the pimp was a minor figure, typically involved in arranging liaisons between what today would be described as call girls and upper-class clients. Second, while it is unclear whether there were in the Hanoverian period more prostitutes in proportion to the population than later, it can be said that prostitution was then more open, boisterous, and multifariously connected with other criminal activities. Many prostitutes were pickpockets, and many brothels were receivers of stolen goods. London brothels and prostitutes even figured in the Penlez **riots** of 1749 (when sailors angry at the mugging of shipmates pulled down brothels), and in other riots in 1763.

A significant shift in attitude began in the 1740s, when an intense dialogue propagated in the press about how to reduce the numbers of London prostitutes. From this emerged the first secular charity for prostitutes, the Magdalen Hospital, founded (1758) by **Jonas Hanway** and others for their reform and rehabilitation. Comment on this event reflected a new sympathy for the prostitute's plight, and foreshadowed later thinking about why women turned to prostitution. Three similar institutions, all stressing the rehabilitative effects of religious teaching and hard work, were formed in London between 1787 and 1813, and still more such institutions proliferated later in Britain's burgeoning **cities**.

Much of this is traceable to the new **humanitarianism** of the latter 18th century. But a severe determination to restrict prostitution was also growing in various antivice societies. The **Society for the Reformation of Manners** (1691–1738) claimed to have sponsored the legal prosecution of some 100,000 individuals for immoral behavior; various **Methodists** took up the same cause in the 1750s. In 1787 a **Proclamation Society** was formed; this merged into the **Society for the Suppression of Vice** (founded in 1802), which continued activities well into the 19th century. The charity movement and the antivice societies were both signs of an increasing concern about prostitution and its impact on the family, public health, and the moral fiber of the country.

Yet the law, surprisingly enough, was virtually silent on the question. The void left by the decline of the church courts during the 17th century was not filled by opponents of prostitution until the 1880s, and the result was that prostitution itself was not illegal in Hanoverian times. True, in 1752 the first parliamentary statute specifically directed against brothelkeeping was passed; and it is true also that pubs, often involved with prostitution, were under the jurisdiction of local justices of the peace who had the power to revoke as well as grant licenses. But the expense of prosecution and the corruption attendant upon licensing worked to ensure that little was done. Moreover, while streetwalkers and other prostitutes could receive **punishments** of hard labor and whipping in one of the houses of correction, technically this could be inflicted only if the offender had been "disorderly." It was not until an Act of 1824 that even vagrancy laws could be clearly used against prostitutes; and it was not until the 1860s, when venereal disease became a great concern, that Parliament imposed regulations on prostitution. Only in the 1880s did London **police** begin attempts to suppress brothels.

Modern scholars have tended to view prostitutes as helpless victims who led horrible lives and often died prematurely. However, some maintain that many women, propelled by economic necessity, chose prostitution (sometimes only on a temporary basis) over other low-quality jobs, acting rationally in pursuit of a better condition than was otherwise in store for them in an age still deaf to **women's rights** and larger conceptions of **women's employment**.

Stanley D. Nash

Bridewell prison scene from Hogarth's "Harlot's Progress," 1732

Bibliography

Bullough, Vern L. "Prostitution and Reform in Eighteenth Century England." *Eighteenth-Century Life.* Vol. 9, pp. 61–74.

Nash, Stanley D. "Prostitution and Charity: The Magdalen Hospital, a Case Study." *Journal of Social History.* Vol. 17, pp. 617–628.

———. *Social Attitudes towards Prostitution in London from 1752 to 1829.* Ph.D. diss. 1980.

Porter, Roy, and Lesley Hall. *The Facts of Life: The Creation of Sexual Knowledge in Britain, 1650–1950.* 1995.

Walkowitz, Judith R. *Prostitution and Victorian Society: Women, Class, and the State.* 1980.

Webb, Sidney, and Beatrice Webb. *The History of Liquor Licensing in England Principally from 1700 to 1830.* 1903.

Wooton, Nancy Anne. *Temporary Favours: Women, Prostitution, and Choice in Eighteenth-Century London.* Ph.D. diss. 1987.

See also Manners and Morals

Protestant Dissenting Deputies

Formed in 1732, this was a formal organization of **London**-area **dissenters.** Formally known as the Committee of Deputies of the Three Denominations—their members being elected by the **Presbyterians, Baptists,** and **Congregationalist**—it first came together to work cooperatively with the General Body of Dissenting Ministers to persuade **Sir Robert Walpole** to rescind the **test and corporation acts.** Although this effort ended in failure in 1739, the deputies remained active in this cause until repeal was finally achieved (1828). Other goals included securing rights guaranteed to dissenters by the **Toleration Act** (1689), the elimination of the Anglican church rates which they were obliged to pay, and protection against **riots** and violence directed at dissenters. In addition, the deputies fought to secure official recognition of dissenting **marriages,** rights to register their own births and deaths, and rights to own property in trust. In the 19th century they advocated universal education and were instrumental in the establishment of the **University of London** (1827). The best-known member of the deputies was Sir William Smith, M.P. (1756–1835), chairman from 1805 to 1832.

Jack Fruchtman, Jr.

Bibliography

Hunt, N.C. *Sir Robert Walpole, Samuel Holden, and the Dissenting Deputies.* 1957.

———. *Two Early Political Associations: The Quakers and the Dissenting Deputies in the Age of Sir Robert Walpole.* 1961.

Manning, Bernard Lord. *The Protestant Dissenting Deputies.* 1952.

Watts, Michael R. *The Dissenters.* 2 vols. 1978, 1995.

See also Indemnity Acts; Occasional Conformity; Toleration, Religions

Provincial Towns and Society

The notion of "the provinces" as something in opposition to the metropolis of **London** came into its own in the Hanoverian period. Provincial towns and provincial society, however strongly influenced by the capital, enjoyed increasing importance and influence in the period. Although London remained more than 10 times the size of any provincial town, its relative dominance declined as the urban world of Britain became increasingly multinodal.

Many provincial towns enjoyed considerable growth, and on the whole could claim an increasing share of the nation's **population.** Viewed as a proportion of all urban dwellers, provincial towns increased importantly and dramatically. The proportion of the urban population living in towns of between 10,000 and 100,000 inhabitants rose from about 10% to about 40% between 1700 and 1800. Moreover, there was a marked shift of urban population from the south of England to the industrial centers of the North and Midlands. Growth was very uneven, so that old provincial centers such as **Norwich** and **York** grew scarcely at all, while industrial towns such as **Liverpool** and **Manchester** underwent demographic explosions. The differing fates of provincial towns over the period arose largely from their varied economic circumstances and functions.

Market towns continued to fulfill important local and regional functions in acting as distribution points for mostly regionally produced goods. This function naturally centered on the old market square and often took place in the shadow of a medieval market cross. But newer methods of **retailing** redrew the maps of many provincial towns over the course of the 18th century as shops multiplied, often endowed with bow windows to better display their commodities. In all but the most stagnant provincial centers, retailing became a more conspicuous part of provincial society as the wealth of new consumer goods reached nearly every corner of the country. The vibrant circulation of goods was made possible in part by improved **transport,** but this also tended to undermine some of the smallest provincial centers. The least important markets tended to decline into purely local trade as a process of economic concentration advanced. Seasonal fairs also suffered a general decline.

Provincial centers, above the level of market towns, can best be treated in terms of their function. Perhaps the towns most closely associated with the Georgian age are those that became centers for the fashionable, particularly the **spas** and resort towns such as **Bath.** These towns, along with administrative and regional centers such as York, succeeded in attracting a class of propertied persons eager to partake of refined urban culture in an environment perhaps more congenial and certainly less expensive than the West End of London. In such towns the local **gentry** often mingled with a growing class of urban professionals and businessmen to form a loosely knit provincial urban elite. The energetic construction of assembly rooms, promenades, parades, bowling greens, **pleasure gardens,** ballrooms, and other venues for the fashionable attest to the eagerness with which many towns sought to make themselves focal points of provincial culture. Much of the private stock of **housing** in provincial towns was rebuilt as well, as vernacular-style houses in timber and tile gave way to more classical styles constructed of brick or stone.

While some towns tended to cater to the growing consumption market, others became specialized manufacturing centers, and represented perhaps the most novel development in the urban world. Manchester and **Birmingham** astounded contemporaries by their growth rates and economic vitality and creativity, as well as by their tendencies toward industrial specialization. Provincial **ports** also generally prospered in the period, most notably Liverpool and Newcastle, both of which profited from the growth of industry in the North and Midlands. Foreign trade burgeoned, and the provincial ports, though vulnerable to fluctuations in **overseas commerce**, grew both in absolute and relative terms to the port of London. The **dockyard** towns of Plymouth, Portsmouth, and Chatham all grew considerably, though they too were vulnerable to fluctuations, especially **war**-related ones, on account of their specialized economies.

Provincial towns were as diverse in their political experience as in their economic fortunes. The process of urban growth and change posed new political problems in the towns, and the picture of a placid oligarchic indifference suddenly transformed under the **radicalism** of the 1790s is a misleading simplification of the complexities of urban politics. Parliamentary representation varied widely before the **Reform Act** of 1832. Some boroughs, such as Norwich and **Bristol**, had a broad franchise and a large electorate; others had very narrow **franchises**, while new industrial towns had no representation at Westminster.

Local government also varied greatly. Again, the largest of the industrial centers stood apart. Neither Manchester nor Birmingham possessed a municipal government until the end of the period, and local administration, such as it was, was carried on through the manorial court. The governments of the incorporated towns took a variety of forms, although a major distinction is to be drawn between "open" and "close" corporations. Open corporations were relatively free in their admission of freemen, who chose the city's governors, usually a council and a mayor. However, freemen even in open corporations seldom accounted for more than perhaps one-third of the adult male inhabitants. The close corporations were narrow oligarchies with virtually no democratic element, although the precise constitutional arrangements varied greatly. Even in the open corporations, however, the substantial costs of holding office meant that the wealthy and influential tended to dominate local government. The same could be said for the lowest level of local administration—the parish vestry. On the whole, local government was limited in scope, although the numerous improvement acts of the second half of the 18th century enabled local government to assume many new powers over the infrastructure of the towns. The reform of local government was one of the major political achievements of the 19th century.

Daniel Statt

Bibliography

Borsay, Peter. *The English Urban Renaissance.* 1989.

Chalklin, C.W. *The Provincial Towns of Georgian England.* 1974.

Corfield, P.J. *The Impact of English Towns, 1700–1800.* 1982.

Cranfield, G.A. *The Development of the Provincial Newspaper, 1700–1760.* 1962, 1978.

Girouard, Mark. *The English Town: A History of Urban Life.* 1990.

McInnes, Angus. *The English Town, 1660–1760.* 1980.

Rogers, Nicholas. *Whigs and Cities: Popular Politics in the Age of Walpole and Pitt.* 1989.

See also Boroughs; Burghs, Scottish; Cardiff; Cities and Urban Life; Cork; Dublin; Edinburgh; Glasgow; Government, Local and County; Leeds; Merthyr Tydfil; Municipal Corporations Act; Swansea

Public Houses

See Brewing and Public Houses

Public Schools

See Education, Secondary

Publishers and Booksellers

The publishing and marketing of books underwent evolutionary, rather than revolutionary, change in the Hanoverian era. There were no fundamental alterations in printing and production until the very end of the period, and the essential structure of the book trade remained what it had been. But there was a huge expansion in activity, as measured by the number of titles issued and the number of outlets. In particular, the period saw the emergence of a widespread provincial book trade, although this was essentially a retailing phenomenon rather than a publishing development. New modes of publication, such as part-books and serials, came to the fore. Multivolume ventures such as encyclopedias and collections of the classics became more viable, owing to innovations such as joint financing by groups of booksellers. But the staple of the trade still lay in single volumes, small pamphlets, and collections of **sermons**, along with special markets supplied by the publishers of **almanacs** and chapbooks.

It is important to get the nomenclature straight. Booksellers, as defined in the period, fulfilled three major functions: as publishers in the modern sense, as wholesalers, and as retailers. The basic content of a title page in a Hanoverian book was: "London: Printed by X for Y and sold by Z." In this formula, X is the printer, hired by the principal party (Y) and paid for the job at a standard rate. (That would be true of a binder also, if a book was bound prior to publication, but books were mostly sold in sheets, especially in the earlier part of the period; the purchaser would arrange for his or her own binding.) Y would today be called the publisher, the one who bought the rights of the work from its author, financed publication, reaped the main profit, and stood any losses. It was his business to comply with the formalities of publication. Z was the main distributor; normally he had a retail store and books would be available there, but more important, he was the

Jacob Tonson

agent through whom other retailers, especially those outside **London**, could obtain copies.

Complications surround this basic pattern. Occasionally a bookseller might also be a printer who handled the production himself, but this was very much the exception. A group confusingly known as trade publishers, or just publishers, was in fact wholesalers. Sometimes it is their name which appears in the imprint, perhaps because the real agent wished to remain anonymous—he had most to lose if prosecutions or other governmental action was feared. Thus many of **Jonathan Swift**'s political pamphlets carry the name of John Morphew (*d.* 1720) on the title page, but it was the unnamed Benjamin Tooke (*d.* 1723) with whom Swift dealt and who really instigated proceedings. Some of these trade publishers crop up with astonishing regularity in the first half of the 18th century (examples are Abigail Baldwin [*d.* 1713]; James Roberts [*c.* 1670–1754]; and Mary Cooper [*d.* 1761]), but they did not own the copyrights generally and were known chiefly for shifting large quantities of topical works, often through unorthodox channels such as "mercuries" who organized distribution by means of street-hawkers.

An unusually prominent role was taken by women, who (like Mrs. Baldwin) often inherited the business of a husband after his death, then passed it on within the family (as from Baldwin to her son-in-law, Roberts). This tendency was perhaps less apparent later in the period. There also was specialization within the trade. For example, the factories of chapbook distribution centered on Bow and Aldermary churchyards continued to send out hundreds of thousands of cheap, simple, and crudely printed booklets, to be sold by itinerant peddlers along the length and breadth of the country. The Dicey family was especially well known in this branch of the industry.

The trade remained under the domination of the London-based Company of Stationers, deriving from a medieval guild and incorporated by means of a Royal charter in 1557. As time went on, the company began to exercise quasi-official powers and acted as licensers (in effect censors, too) to the entire national trade in the 17th century. During the Hanoverian era the stranglehold of the company was relaxed in some areas, but it continued to exercise a large degree of influence through the operation of its Court or executive committee. Various factors contributed to the sway of the company: the continuing obligation for recruits to the trade to be apprenticed to freemen of the guild and the established link with government were both important, along with custom and reputation. Moreover, the company had distributed among its members the valuable rights of the English Stock; that is, the sole right to publish certain categories of works such as statutes of the realm, primers, prayer-books, and (most valuable of all) the numerous annual **almanacs** that served as handbooks, diaries and astrological guides. Printers, though they formed a key part of the original company, steadily lost ground; by the 18th century it was above all the booksellers who specialized in what we call publishing, who constituted its heart.

The two major events affecting the course of affairs in the Hanoverian epoch both chanced to occur just before it began. In 1695 the government failed to renew the tight licensing act, which had been in operation since early in the reign of Charles II. This meant that something much more like an open market for books could develop, with some of the hereditary constraints removed. The company was forced to devise its own machinery to protect its interests, and came up with a wholesaling "Conger," or group of separate traders acting in common, and an internal system of "trade sales," by which members of the trade bought and sold at auction the rights to existing books. Outsiders were not admitted, and so the shares in all valuable literary property were kept within the orbit of the large London firms. This system began around the time of the Hanoverian accession, and lasted well into the Victorian era.

The second important development was the emergence of copyright legislation under **Queen Anne**, which resulted in the famous Copyright Act taking effect in 1710. This provided copyright protection for a period of up to 28 years for all future English books. It has always been recognized that the act was designed to protect booksellers (i.e., publishers) rather than authors, and the battles that were to rage around its provisions had more to do with the valuable monopoly powers of copyright owners, rather than with the intellectual property inhering in a work of the mind. A series of challenges was made to the system by those outside the charmed circle. Both Scottish and Irish booksellers attempted to circumvent the provisions of the act, and indeed it was not illegal for the latter to reprint English books (as they did in large quantities), so long as the copies were not exported to England. A pirate industry flourished, which involved the use of false overseas imprints, commonly "The Hague," even though the book in question was really produced in Britain and intended for the home market. False imprints were one of the commonest devices used at the less respectable end of the trade: "J. Tomson," suggesting Jacob Tonson (1656–1737), one of the most highly respected figures in publishing, was a typical example. And many clandestine offerings came out under the name of "A. Moore," that is A.N. Other.

Matters came to a head in the 1770s. The London trade had maintained all along that the Copyright Act served merely to define particular penalties for copyright infringements within the specified periods following publication. It was argued that beyond this there was a fundamental right in common law that had not been affected by the new act, under which publishers owned perpetual property in the books whose rights they had bought. Thus Tonson could be said to own the rights in **Shakespeare** in perpetuity, as the publisher of a major edition. The courts supported this view for some time, but a Scottish bookseller named Alexander Donaldson (*d.* 1794) challenged this interpretation of the law by reprinting English publications, for example **Thomson**'s *Seasons,* after the expiration of the 28-year period defined in the act. The case went to trial first in **Edinburgh** and then on appeal to the **House of Lords** in London. The judgment went for Donaldson and against the London booksellers (1774). The long monopoly of the great London houses was broken, and an era of more open competition began.

As noted earlier, one of the main developments in the early Hanoverian age lay in the development of provincial bookselling. Booksellers set up shop in small towns around the nation, and larger **cities** generally had a number of competing firms. Often this trade was associated with running a local **newspaper**, an important advertising medium rather than a source of genuinely local news (the editorial matter came from the London papers). In addition, it was common for booksellers to engage in the profitable side activity of selling patent **medicine**, as well as handling stationery and small goods. It was rare for the provincial trade to extend to publishing in any large way, though isolated examples are found in places like Salisbury and **York**. There was not a very large indigenous trade in **Scotland**, even though Edinburgh was a crucible of the **Enlightenment**—the majority of classic **Scottish Enlightenment** texts were published in London. **Dublin** operated on a more independent basis, but the Irish industry was tiny compared to that of London.

The most famous publisher at the beginning of the period was Tonson, renowned for his links with leading **Whig** politicians in the Kit Cat **Club**: Tonson bought the rights to *Paradise Lost* (1667) and issued several editions; did much to foster the career of John Dryden (1631–1700), as well as issue works by **Addison, Pope** and Matthew Prior (1664–1721); and brought out Nicholas Rowe's (1674–1718) edition of Shakespeare, the first attempt at a serious collection after the early folios in the 17th century. At the other end of the scale, in terms of respectability, stood Edmund Curll (1683–1747), famous for his scandalously **pornographic** and bawdy books, his instant **biographies** of the lately dead, and his battles with Pope. Major figures in the middle of the 18th century included Thomas Longman (1699–1755), who founded a long-lived publishing dynasty, and **Robert Dodsley**, associated with Pope, **Warburton**, **Gray**, **Garrick**, **Shenstone**, and **Johnson**. Late in the century came firms like those of the Dilly brothers (Edward [*d.* 1779], and Charles [*d.* 1807]—he published **Boswell**'s *Life of Johnson*), William Strahan (1715–1785) (**Gibbon**'s *Decline and Fall,* **Smith**'s *Wealth of Nations*), and the radical Joseph Johnson (1738–1809) who issued works by **Blake**, **Wollstonecraft**, and **Paine** among others. William Lane (1745?–1814) capitalized on popular taste with his Minerva Press and established circulating **libraries**, which stocked his books in country towns.

At the end of the era came the foundation of important houses like that of John Murray (1778–1843), which was in time to publish **Byron**; and that of John Taylor (1781–1864), who published **Keats**. But it says something that the ***Lyrical Ballads*** (1798) were issued by a small Bristol operator, Joseph Cottle (1770–1853), who had few connections with the captains of the London book industry. By this time, too, Edinburgh had developed its own strong base with Archibald Constable (1776–1826) and David Blackie (*d.* 1832) in the van. A significant development in the latter part of the period was the issuing of large series of, for example, *English Poets,* helping to establish a canon of vernacular classics: a leading pioneer here was John Bell (1745–1831).

Meanwhile, bookselling had followed a quieter and more conservative course. One challenge to these staid habits was provided by the emergence of subscription libraries and reading clubs. Another jolt was supplied by James Lackington (1746–1815), the first remainder bookseller of note, who bought stock in large quantities and sold it off cheap. But books remained relatively expensive and near luxury items (the three-decker **novel** continued to sell at £1.11.6; that is, £1.57, up to the late 19th century), and until major advances were made in printing **technology** there were few important innovations in the ways that books were produced and disseminated. The Hanoverian age saw a widening of the reading public, a growth of the print media, and a broadening of the publishing base, but **Jane Austen**'s books were produced and distributed in ways that would have occasioned little surprise 100 years earlier.

Pat Rogers

Bibliography

Anderson, Patricia. *The Printed Image and the Transformation of Popular Culture, 1790–1860.* 1991.

Feather, John. *The Provincial Book Trade in Eighteenth-Century England.* 1985.

———. *A History of British Publishing.* 1988.

Howsam, Leslie. *Cheap Bibles: Nineteenth-Century Publishing and the British and Foreign Bible Society.* 1991.

Myers, Robin, and Michael Harris, eds. *Author/Publisher Relations during the Eighteenth and Nineteenth Centuries.* 1983.

Raven, James. *Judging New Wealth: Popular Publishing and Responses to Commerce in England, 1750–1800.* 1992.

See also Children's Literature; Periodicals

Pulteney, William (1684–1764)

Pulteney, a **Whig** politician, organized and defined the parliamentary **opposition** during the 1720s and 1730s. Earlier he had championed the **Hanoverian succession**, condemned the **Tory** peace of Utrecht, and served **George I** as Secretary at War (1714–1717). He left office with his ally **Robert Walpole** to protest the government's foreign policy in the Baltic, but ultimately broke with Walpole when the latter refused to appoint him secretary of state (1724). In 1726 he joined **Viscount Bolingbroke** and his cousin Daniel to found the opposition periodical ***The Craftsman,*** and in 1730 he organized a Whig–Tory opposition known as the Patriots. He also united with the group of ministerial opponents who headquartered in the household of **Frederick, Prince of Wales**.

Under Pulteney's leadership the opposition harassed Walpole with charges of corruption, mismanagement, misappropriation of funds, the subversion of Parliament's constitutional rights, the employment of a standing **army**, and the promotion of **foreign relations** favoring the interests of **Hanover**, Spain, and **France** at the expense of Britain's traditional alliance with Austria. Although Pulteney often debated with hot rhetoric rather than reasoned argument, he and his colleagues were able to menace Walpole on issues such as France's restoration of Dunkirk's harbor (1730), and Walpole's abortive scheme for an **excise** tax (1733). By forcing Walpole into a patriotic war with Spain (1739) they finally drove him from power (1742).

Pulteney failed to secure a majority in the new ministry for his parliamentary colleagues. His decision to accept a peerage (Earl of Bath, 1742) ended his influence in the **Commons** and reduced his credibility. He failed to form a ministry in 1746, and thereafter made only occasional excursions into political **journalism**.

Robert D. McJimsey

Bibliography

Browning, Reed. *The Duke of Newcastle.* 1975.

Foord, Archibald. *His Majesty's Opposition, 1714–1830.* 1964.

Gerrard, Christine. *The Patriot Opposition to Walpole: Politics, Poetry, and National Myth, 1725–1742.* 1995.

Harris, Robert. *A Patriot Press: National Politics and the London Press in the 1740s.* 1993.

Plumb, J.H. *Sir Robert Walpole: The King's Minister.* 1961.

Sedgwick, Romney, ed. *Some Materials towards Memoirs of the Reign of George II, by John Hervey.* 3 vols. 1931; rev. 1963.

See also Pension and Place Bills

Punishment

Until the 1840s, physical punishment was the preferred means of dealing with violators of the law. While there was increasing sentiment against corporal punishments from 1760 on, a variety of corporal penalties—especially for minor crimes and socially unacceptable behavior—persisted throughout much of the Hanoverian period. The ducking stool was used until 1809 to quiet nagging and gossiping women; and until the 1820s, public whipping was prescribed for vagrants (women as well as men), **adulterers**, **prostitutes**, petty thieves, and drunkards. The pillory (which restricted the head and arms), sometimes used in combination with whipping, and the stocks (restricting the legs), were typical punishments for tradesmen who cheated their customers, individuals who uttered obscene remarks, prostitutes, ruffians, and a host of others who offended contemporary law and decency.

Moreover, more severe forms of physical punishment such as mutilation, drowning, and various tortures applied to prisoners, were by no means extinct (though they greatly diminished during the period). For example, thieves who refused to enter a plea of guilty or not guilty, thus exempting their stolen property from official confiscation, still had to undergo a medieval ordeal known as "peine forte et dure" (torment strong and hard), which consisted of piling heavy stones on their chest until they entered a plea, or died: this practice was finally stopped in 1772. In addition, the horrible penalties for treason—drawing and quartering for men, and burning at the stake for women—did not disappear until nearly the end of the Hanoverian era. The last woman to suffer this fate was Phoebe Harris, who was burned at the stake in 1786 for coining (counterfeiting)—supposedly treasonable since it involved an "attack" on the king's image. And as late as 1803 there was the case of Col. Edward Marcus Despard (1751–1803), a **radical** "friend to truth, to liberty and to justice" (as he described himself on the scaffold) who was hanged, drawn and quartered for an alleged assassination plot against **George III**. For women, petty treason, which included murdering their husbands or masters, also carried the penalty of burning at the stake.

The most notorious form of physical punishment in the period was hanging. Its notoriety stems not from the number of executions, which in fact was far smaller than during the Tudor and Stuart periods, but rather from the enormous increase in the number of **crimes** that became capital offenses. In 1688 there were some 50 crimes punishable by death; by 1800 there were over 200. Many of the new laws converted minor thefts (e.g., from shops, warehouses, and the pockets of individuals) into felonies, which carried the death penalty. This new "Bloody Code," as historians have called it, represented, among other things, a concerted tightening of the rights of property owners at the expense of the poor; it was perhaps best epitomized in the **Black Act** (1723), which created some 50 new capital crimes. The Bloody Code was dramatically reinforced in **London** by the "Tyburn Procession," the carting of condemned individuals from Newgate **prison**, accompanied by throngs of boisterous people, to Tyburn gallows. The banker–poet **Samuel Rogers** described his vision one morning of "a cartload of young girls, in dresses of various colours, on their way to be executed at Tyburn." Such sights were not uncommon.

It is true that despite the large number of capital offenses, historians have found that, around 1750, only about 50% of those sentenced to death were actually executed, and that this rate diminished to around 10% by 1800. The main reason was that Royal pardons or commutations to **transportation** to the

The Tyburn procession, from a print by Hogarth, 1747

colonies were liberally applied. Moreover, except as regarded **highwaymen**, burglars, and forgers, juries were either reluctant to convict (in which case they were dubbed "pious" juries), or they exercised their right to set the amount of the stolen property below the rate that would make the crime a felony (this was called a "partial verdict" or "down-charging").

Historians have debated the reasons for this violent code of punishment, especially since it was by no means enforced systematically. Some have argued that the laws and the ceremony of the trial, and a goodly number of death sentences, were means of gaining respect for and compliance with the political system (based on property), and that the ruling class had not yet developed other means (**police**, education, prisons, etc.) to discipline the lower classes. Others have argued that the felony laws operated to protect the chief victims of property crimes—the **middle classes**—and it has also been noted that it was from this same social stratum that the jurors came who played a key role in the enforcement of these laws.

In any event, by the 1780s the Tyburn procession had disappeared, and between 1800 and 1827 the entire number of capital offenses was reduced to eight. By that time, the country's prison system had largely replaced physical punishment as the chief means of coercing citizens into obeying the laws of the land, while the growth of **humanitarianism** was helping also to diminish the brutality of punishment. Some would maintain that the ideas of the **Enlightenment**, as embodied in Cesare Beccaria's *Essay on Crime and Punishment* (1764, **translated** into English in 1767 and widely read in England), which stressed the certainty of punishment over the pain of it, had finally won out. Others would place more emphasis on the idea that the state had simply found new means of social control and discipline in the country's reinvigorated economic, cultural, and religious systems.

Stanley D. Nash

Bibliography

Burford, E.J., and Sandra Shulman. *Of Bridles and Burnings: The Punishment of Women.* 1992.

Foucault, Michel. *Discipline and Punish: The Birth of the Prison.* 1977.

Gatrell, V.A.C. *The Hanging Tree: Execution and the English People, 1770–1868.* 1994.

Hay, Douglas, et al. *Albion's Fatal Tree: Crime and Society in Eighteenth-Century England.* 1975.

Jenkins, Philip. "From Gallows to Prison? The Execution Rate in Early Modern England." *Criminal Justice History, an International Annual.* Vol. 7, pp. 51–70.

Langbein, John H. "Albion's Fatal Flaws." *Past and Present.* Number 98, pp. 96–120.

Linebaugh, Peter. *The London Hanged: Crime and Civil Society in the Eighteenth Century.* 1992.

McLynn, Frank. *Crime and Punishment in Eighteenth-Century England.* 1989.

See also Judicial System; Law Reform; Romilly, Sir Samuel

Quakers (Society of Friends)

The Society of Friends emerged in the 17th century as the extreme left wing of the Puritan movement. The "Quaker" nickname derived from the admonition of George Fox (1624–1691), the society's founder, that Parliament should "tremble before the Lord," but it caught on because of the enthusiastic exhilaration or "quaking" that Friends sometimes experienced during meetings. Fox, a talented organizer, constructed systems of registration, poor relief, and education that helped make the group a social power. Under his leadership it spread rapidly in England, **Scotland**, **Ireland**, and, eventually, **North America**.

Rejecting creeds, clergy, and formal sacraments, Friends held that each believer could directly apprehend God's revelations by attending to an "inner light." Early services eschewed liturgy and sermons. Worship began in silence, in the belief that God might use any person present as a minister. Stressing plainness in speech and dress, Friends tried to live in humility, simplicity, and honesty. They practiced sexual equality, renounced the taking of oaths, and refused to pay tithes. They refused to recognize the pagan god Woden by speaking of Wednesday, to flatter a single person by addressing him with a plural pronoun, or to doff their hats in salutation. Their emphasis on pacific nonviolence remains a distinguishing characteristic to this day.

Their **radical** views made the Friends natural targets of persecution. They particularly suffered from the **penal laws** set forth in the Quaker Act (1662), but their hardships diminished somewhat after passage of the **Toleration Act** of 1689. Nonetheless, as **dissenters**, Quakers were excluded in the 18th century from universities, the church, the military, law, and Parliament, either by statute or by their own convictions. They therefore tended to channel their intelligence and initiative into trade and industry. With their reputation for honesty, they succeeded in business and **banking**. They founded several banks, including Barclay's and **Lloyd's**. Their schools emphasized science, producing a number of Fellows of the **Royal Society of London**, including chemist **John Dalton**. They figured importantly in the **iron industry** (the **Darby family** was Quaker), invented the safety match, and promoted the first English **railway** line. In politics, the Quaker **Thomas Paine** must be judged the most influential radical theorist of the Hanoverian age.

Religious toleration in the 18th century coincided with, and no doubt helped produce, a quietist phase in Quakerism. Quietist Friends practiced self-denial and passivity in deference to divine direction, trusting solely in the inner light. Though seemingly self-absorbed, Quietist Friends intensified the society's traditional **humanitarian** concerns. They were among the first to oppose slavery and to campaign against the **slave trade**. Cooperation with other Christians in the **antislavery movement** led Friends out of their seclusion and exposed them to **Evangelical** impulses which stimulated and influenced Quaker worship.

Evangelical Friends emphasized the Bible, the atonement of Christ, and other characteristic Protestant doctrines. Their regional meetings featured revivalist methods, hymns, set **sermons**, and paid pastors. Traditionalists opposed these Evangelical intrusions, and the resulting tension precipitated several separations within the society. But despite divisions, the humanitarian goals of the Friends remained strong. In the early 19th century **Elizabeth Fry** formed an association for the improvement of **prison** conditions, helped raise standards for British hospitals, and founded hostels for the homeless. Quakers worked for the education and training of the poor as well as for **prison reform**, and continued to practice conscientious objection and other forms of nonviolent opposition to **war**.

William Edward Morris

Bibliography

Braithwaite, William C. *The Beginnings of Quakerism.* 1955.

Dalglish, Doris N. *The People Called Quakers.* 1969.

Davies, Horton. *Worship and Theology in England: From Watts and Wesley to Maurice, 1690–1850.* 1961.

Raistrick, Arthur. *Quakers in Science and Industry.* 1968.

Rupp, Gordon. *Religion in England, 1688–1791.* 1986.
Russell, Elbert. *The History of Quakerism.* 1979.
Vann, Richard T., and David Eversley. *Friends in Life and Death: British and Irish Quakers, 1650–1900.* 1992.

See also Gibson, Edmund

Quarantine Act (1721)

The apparent outbreak of plague at Marseilles in 1719 alarmed the British government and produced a 3-year plague scare because **France** proved incapable of containing it. By February 1721 the government of **George I** had begun implementing a system of quarantine of foreign vessels in order to prevent the spread of disease into Britain. Enacted on the advice of **Royal Society** Fellows and leading physicians Richard Mead (1673–1754) and **Hans Sloane**, the Quarantine Act became politically controversial. To curtail trade was damaging, especially in the aftermath of the **South Sea Bubble**, but outbreaks of **smallpox** were hardly more welcome. There is some belief now that the menace was a particularly virulent form of smallpox.

Larry Stewart

Bibliography

Mullett, Charles. "The English Plague Scare of 1720–23." Osiris. Vol. 11, pp. 487–491.
Oratz, R. "The Plague. Changing Notions of Contagion: London 1665–Marseilles 1720." *Synthesis.* Vol. 4, pp. 4–27.
Stewart, Larry. "The Edge of Utility: Slaves and Smallpox in the Early Eighteenth Century." *Medical History.* Vol. 29, pp. 54–70.

Quebec

Quebec was the name used historically to refer to predominantly French-settled areas of **North America** from the Atlantic Ocean west to the upper Mississippi River. Since confederation in 1867, it has referred specifically to a province in the eastern part of Canada.

The first permanent French settlement occurred in 1608 at what is today Quebec City. As French **Roman Catholic** civilization developed along the St. Lawrence River, the larger colony of New France emerged. The British, with **General Wolfe** capturing the area during the **Seven Years' War**, renamed it Quebec; and then, for half a century after 1791, it was known as Lower Canada. From 1841 to 1867 it was called the district of Canada East in the Province of Canada.

From 1760 to 1837 the British government by a series of laws attempted to accommodate and, at times, integrate this partially alien and residually hostile francophone society into the **Empire**. The chief of these enactments were the **Proclamation of 1763**, the **Quebec Act** (1774), and the **Constitutional (Canada) Act** (1791). Just as the Hanoverian period ended, the area erupted in an uprising known as the Rebellion of 1837.

Stuart R. Givens

Bibliography

Brunet, Michel. *Les Canadiens après la Conquête, 1759–1775.* 1969.

View of the Battle of Quebec, 1759

Creighton, D.G. *The Empire of the St. Lawrence.* 1956.
Eccles, W.J. *The Canadian Frontier: 1534–1760.* 1969.
Manning, H.T. *The Revolt of French Canada, 1800–1835: A Chapter in the History of the British Commonwealth.* 1962.
Neatby, Hilda. *Quebec: The Revolutionary Age, 1760–1791.* 1966.
Oullet, Fernand. *Lower Canada, 1791–1841: Social Change and Nationalism.* 1979.
Stanley, George F.G. *New France: The Last Phase, 1744–1760.* 1968.

See also Canada

Quebec Act (1774)

This was a parliamentary act aimed at resolving various problems still outstanding from Britain's takeover (1763) of French-speaking and **Roman Catholic Quebec**. Its passage was the first occasion on which imperial policy was made by statute rather than by Royal decree. Its most salient features were: acceptance of the Catholic Church in Quebec; continued use there of Roman civil law (though British criminal law was to be used); formation of a colonial government with an appointed governor and advisory council (the **Test Act** was waived to permit Catholics swearing allegiance to hold office); and modification of the boundaries set forth in the **Proclamation of 1763** to incorporate within Quebec the entire trans–Appalachian west, from the Ohio and Mississippi rivers up through the Great Lakes to Hudson's Bay. This last, whose purpose was to provide government for French settlements and Indian affairs in the interior, caused the legislation to be viewed by many American colonists as a virtual renewal of the old French empire. The act hence became one of the "Intolerable Acts" that precipitated the **American Revolution**.

Stuart R. Givens

Bibliography

Lawson, Philip. *The Imperial Challenge: Quebec and Britain in the Age of the American Revolution.* 1989.
Neatby, Hilda. *The Quebec Act: Protest and Policy.* 1972.

See also Canada; Empire and Imperialism

Quiberon Bay, Battle of (1759)

This most decisive naval engagement of the **Seven Years' War** ended the threat of a French invasion of the British Isles. On 14 November 1759 the French admiral de Conflans attempted to move the Brest Squadron to Quiberon Bay on the coast of Brittany in order to launch an invasion army while a strong gale was forcing off station the British close-blockading squadron under Admiral **Hawke**. Conflans put to sea with 21 ships of the line in three divisions. Despite a substantial lead over Hawke's fleet of 23 ships, inefficiency dissipated his advantage in the race for Quiberon Bay. Hawke, a skillful commander, sighted the French as they arrived at the bay's mouth and attacked (20 November).

Conflans declined to stand and made for the safety of the restricted bay, but Hawke aggressively ordered a general chase despite close shoal water and a rising gale. A sudden wind change forced the French to turn and face their pursuers; Conflans struggled to place his vessels in a line of battle. The action turned into a general melee, ship on ship, with the more skilled British outmaneuvering the enemy and also firing more effectively by uncovering lower gun ports in the heavy swells. They sank or captured seven French ships; Hawke lost only two, both victims of grounding. The victory destroyed French seapower. **France** put no squadrons to sea for the remainder of the **war**.

Stanley D.M. Carpenter

Bibliography

Mackay, Ruddock F. *Admiral Hawke.* 1965.
Marcus, Geoffrey. *Quiberon Bay: The Campaign in Home Waters, 1759.* 1960.

See also Navy; War and Military Engagements

R

Radcliffe, Ann (1764–1823)

Radcliffe was one of the most imaginative and popular novelists of the Hanoverian period. With her complicated plots and mysterious atmospheres she helped to usher in the **Romantic** sense of the **supernatural** without ever really departing from the standards of 18th-century reason. She wrote the **Gothic novels** *A Sicilian Romance* (1790); *An Italian Romance* (1791); *The Romance of the Forest* (1791); *The Mysteries of Udolpho* (1794), her most popular work; and *The Italian, or The Confessional of the Black Penitents* (1797). Her characterization of the melancholic villain Monk Schedoni in *The Italian* contributed directly to the formation of the literary type of the **Byronic Hero.** Her last two novels were widely praised by critics, extraordinarily popular, and **translated** into French and Italian during her lifetime.

Deeply influenced by **Shakespeare**, Radcliffe was also well schooled in the writings of her contemporaries **Horace Walpole, Clara Reeve**, and **Matthew "Monk" Lewis.** Both Lewis and **Sir Walter Scott** praised her work, as did most of the Romantic poets; **Byron** acknowledged her influence in *Childe Harold's Pilgrimage* IV (1818). Despite **Jane Austen**'s **satire** of the effects on the naive reader of *The Mysteries of Udolpho* in *Northanger Abbey* (1803, 1818), Radcliffe's influence extended down through the works of **Mary Wollstonecraft Shelley**, Emily Brontë (1818–1848), Charlotte Brontë (1816–1855), and Charles Dickens (1812–1870).

Radcliffe was born in London to a merchant family. She grew up in **Bath**, an only child with wealthy connections but an average education. At age 23 she married William Radcliffe, a **journalist** and the editor of the *English Chronicle.* She used **travel books** and painted landscapes as the sources for the fantastic descriptions of France, Switzerland, and Italy that appear in her novels, for, in fact, she traveled abroad only once, recording her adventure in a journal published in 1795. Though still hailed as "the Great Enchantress" by contemporaries, Radcliffe ceased to publish after 1797 and spent the remainder of her life crippled by asthma, to which she at last succumbed.

Mary Tiryak

Ann Radcliffe

Bibliography

Grant, Aline. *Ann Radcliffe: A Biography.* 1951.

Johnson, Claudia L. *Equivocal Beings: Politics, Gender, and Sentimentality in the 1790's—Wollstonecraft, Radcliffe, Burney, Austen.* 1995.

Murray, E.B. *Ann Radcliffe.* 1972.

Todd, Janet. *A Dictionary of British and American Women Writers.* 1984.

Radical War (1820)

This extended series of disturbances originated in the vigorous response of Scottish radicals to the **Peterloo massacre** in Manchester in 1819, though unrest had been growing beforehand, especially in the west of **Scotland**, as economic conditions worsened. Radical groups had been growing since 1815.

In them, handloom weavers, who were experiencing savage **wage** cuts, were prominent. Taxation was foremost among their many grievances, and their aims centered on parliamentary reform. Government repression drove them underground. The disturbances culminated in April 1820 in a march by a small number of men who aimed to seize the **Carron** Works near Falkirk, but who were easily defeated by the military at the "Battle of Bonnymuir." Bands of armed insurrectionaries gathered elsewhere in the west, but the anticipated general rising failed to materialize. Three of the leaders, John Baird (1789?–1820), James Wilson, and Andrew Hartdie, were hanged; Baird after a remarkable scaffold speech urging prayer and Bible-reading upon his hearers.

Historians disagree about the significance of the Radical War, with some dismissing it as a rather pathetic and inconsequential affair, serious only in the fevered imaginations of the authorities, while others judge it to have posed a serious threat to the state in Scotland. There seems no doubt that radicals in and around **Glasgow** had planned, with their counterparts in Lancashire, a simultaneous uprising for 1 April 1820, although most of the Scottish leaders were arrested in February. There is evidence too of military-style preparation in some working-class communities. However, while some 60,000 people in the west of Scotland did briefly strike in sympathy, the bulk of the Scottish working class appears to have had little appetite for an armed uprising.

Christopher A. Whatley

Bibliography

Ellis, Peter B., and Seamus Mac a'Ghobhainn. *The Scottish Insurrection of 1820.* 1970.

Fraser, W. Hamish. *Conflict and Class: Scottish Workers, 1700–1838.* 1988.

Young, J.D. *The Rousing of the Scottish Working Class.* 1979.

See also Radicalism and Radical Politics

Radicalism and Radical Politics

Political radicalism arises from intense desires for general improvement and the conviction that only drastic modification of political institutions will bring them to fulfillment. Britain in the 17th century had seen extreme radicalism in such groups as the Levellers, who advocated republicanism, manhood suffrage, and the abolition of the **House of Lords**; and the Diggers, who espoused land redistribution as well as political transformation. But these movements brought a reaction against extreme ideas and tactics of change. The reaction lasted through the **Glorious Revolution**, noteworthy for its respectability and lack of bloodshed, and was still alive when the Hanoverian era began (1714). Attempts in the rebellions of the **Fifteen** and the **Forty-five** to alter politics radically helped to keep anti-radical feelings dominant.

The early Hanoverian period of "**Whig** Ascendancy" therefore saw little organized radicalism. Yet ideas from the 17th century were maintained in diluted form by a band of critics of ministerial power, corruption, and religious intolerance. They called themselves "Real" Whigs (distinguishing themselves from complacent supporters of the Whig-dominated governments of 1714–1760), or **Commonwealthmen**. Though of diverse backgrounds, many were intellectuals, often of deist or **dissenting** outlook in religion. Their program was essentially political, but connected with religious and moral complaints, and anxiety over national decay. Their ideas on limiting ministerial **patronage** and broadening the franchise went beyond the reform ideas of ordinary "Country" opponents of government—they also wanted more frequent elections, greater popular control of the armed forces, and virtually complete **religious toleration**. Most believed in theories of natural rights laid down earlier by **John Locke**.

From these origins a revived radicalism began to emerge in the 1760s and became ever more forceful up to about 1795. Its proponents did not call themselves radicals, but reformers—the term *radical* dates from the intensely political environment of the 1790s and originates in *radix,* the Latin term for "root," as in "root-and-branch" change. The period after 1760 was one of growing **nationalism** everywhere in Europe, and some historians suggest that English radicalism was now connected very little with religious ideas but rather was reactivated as part of the larger rise of an English nationalist movement that demanded a "repossession" by the people not only of the national political culture but of language, art, and literature from an excessively francophile elite. Other historians, emphasizing continuity with 17th-century and Commonwealthman forms, argue for the continuing dominance of religious perspectives and point particularly to the increasingly unrestrained demands of dissenters after 1760, calling attention to their growing assertiveness once the threat of **Jacobite** restoration was over. Many contemporaries believed that the new radicalism was born (or reborn) defensively as a reflex action against **George III**'s determination to reassert the Royal prerogative as soon as he could after his coronation (1760).

The large and occasionally bloody demonstrations in favor of **John Wilkes** during the period 1768–1771 clearly signified a change. This is because of their sheer size and composition, for they comprised large **middle-** and **working-class** elements, and also because of the loose formation around Wilkes of a long-term coalition of passionate antigovernment critics ready to question the basic distribution of political power. There had been **riots and popular disturbances** earlier, but intended to redress immediate grievances in traditional ways: an angry crowd might demand fairness in prices from food merchants, or equitable rents from landlords, but it would not go on—as radicals did after 1760—to question the very existence of **aristocratic** landlords or to attack their grip on the national political system.

Radicalism's prime supporters—again, as in the earlier 18th century, mainly disaffected clerics and intellectuals, but now joined by some farmers and traders—are credited with setting in motion a continuous radical tradition, which saw the creation of specific organizations to mobilize public opinion, and efforts to influence Parliament by massive petitioning. Beneath this leadership Wilkes noted that he had many supporters of "the inferior set," notably **craftsmen**, laborers, **servants**, petty employers, and small tradesmen. Most radicals at this time still resided in **London** and its immediate vicinity.

The enthusiasm for "Wilkes and Liberty" led to the formation of the **Society for Supporters of the Bill of Rights** (1769), which laid out a program of radical demands including drastic reform of the systems of patronage and **places** and **pensions** by which the ruling elite maintained itself, and establishment of annual parliamentary elections on the basis of what Wilkes called "a full and equal representation of the people in Parliament." The demand for purified and more representative government was taken up by others more radical than Wilkes, such as his erstwhile disciple **John Horne Tooke**, a central figure. Outside London (and Middlesex), in Yorkshire around 1780 an Anglican clergyman, **Christopher Wyvill**, put together remarkably well-linked organizations of property-holders to petition Parliament for some of the radical goals. **Major John Cartwright**, who many radicals called the "Father of Reform," was another influential figure. He, like Wyvill, sought to bring back the glories of old England; and he, like Tooke and **Thomas Spence** later, dabbled in Old English linguistics, suggesting a link to passionate nationalist motivations. But the means Cartwright advocated through the important **Society for Constitutional Information** (SCI, 1780) foreshadowed the radically democratic program of the Chartists in the Victorian era: universal manhood suffrage, annual elections, equal electoral constituencies, the secret ballot, abolition of the property qualification for membership in the **Commons**, and payment of M.P.s.

The radical movement now had a gifted female historian in **Catharine Macaulay** and a foothold in Parliament through her brother, **John Sawbridge**, who annually proposed reforms on the floor of the **Commons**; Sawbridge was also a President of the SCI. **John Jebb**, another founder of the SCI, exhibits the further radical linkage to dissenting and **Unitarian** circles, which embraced people like **Theophilus Lindsey** and such **rational dissenters** as **Richard Price** and **Joseph Priestley**, as well as American radicals like **Benjamin Franklin. Novels** of the 1780s by writers like **Robert Bage** and **Thomas Day** reveal the percolation of extremely anti-aristocratic and quasi-republican ideas into light literature.

Two great external events were deepening and strengthening British radicalism: the **American Revolution** of 1775, then the **French Revolution** of 1789. Both drew on theories of natural rights long cherished by radicals, and were also tinged with idealized historical visions of simpler, more democratic times in the national past. With increasing impatience, radicals throughout the Western world saw corrupt and inefficient governments, and religious systems arranged to shield them, as thwarting the attainment of political rights. While the American rebels fought, their radical sympathizers in Britain redoubled their protests and petitions to reform the House of Commons. They ecstatically hailed the outbreak of the French Revolution in 1789, not only because it might regenerate **France** but also because it provided an argument for purifying British institutions before it was too late.

Though workers had participated sporadically in the Wilkite phenomenon, it was now, after 1789, that substantial numbers of British workers were converted to radicalism, a development encouraged by such groups as the **London Corresponding Society**, founded in 1792 by **Thomas Hardy**. It and its affiliates carried on a serious pursuit of political goals through propaganda utilizing French rhetoric and forms, thereby alarming the propertied classes out of all proportion to the number of radicals involved. Feeble attempts by parliamentary Whigs in such groups as the **Society of Friends of the People** (1792) to capture radical support were unavailing. The workingmen's favorite author was the propagandist of genius and lasting fame, **Thomas Paine**, whose *Common Sense* (1776) had already helped push the Americans to revolution. His *Rights of Man* (1791–1792) stated the extreme radical case, arguing for a republican egalitarian democracy that would be attentive to mass education, work, and welfare, and that would be funded by progressive income taxes. Although not all radicals agreed with Paine—some, such as Tooke and Cartwright, wanted to keep the movement clear of him—he was now undoubtedly the single most influential propagandist of radical ideas. A few other propagandists in the 1790s (there were many) were **Mary Wollstonecraft**, who wrote her pioneering manifesto *A Vindication of the Rights of Woman* in 1791, thus joining **women's rights** to the radical cause, and some of the best-known **Romantic** writers, notably young **Wordsworth** and **Southey**.

Radicalism nonetheless faltered in that decade, though there were **Irish rebellions** (1798, 1803), and dangerous radical disturbances in **Scotland**, where a Scottish Association of Friends of the People was formed (1792) and where **United Scotsmen** demanded wholesale change. A mood of conservative reaction set in, typified in the growth of **Loyalist associations** and government repression exercised through treason trials (1794), gag rules against criticism of the Constitution (1795), restrictions on **newspapers** (1798) and **Corresponding Societies** (1799), and prohibitions of workmen's unions (**combinations**) in 1799 and 1800. For many years later, those who hailed the French Revolution were regarded as traitors, "Jacobins" (the name was taken from that of French radicalism), and many arrests were made; some radicals, **William Cobbett** among them, were frequently on the run.

Driven underground in the latter 1790s, radicalism nonetheless reemerged, somewhat changed, after 1810, when it became an extremely serious problem for the political authorities. Riots and machine-breaking by workers called **Luddites** took place from 1811 to 1813; the government responded by making machine-breaking an offense punishable by hanging. In the postwar era after 1815, the radical movement continued to grow diversely as new individuals and groups pursued radical causes. **Hampden Clubs** enrolled new activists. New men like **Arthur Thistlewood** carried the agrarian communist ideas of Spence into violent plots in the **Spa Fields Riot** (1816) and **Cato Street Conspiracy** (1820). Cobbett emerged as the radical movement's greatest propagandist, **Henry ("Orator") Hunt** as its most effective speaker, **John Wade** as its leading research specialist, and **Richard Carlile** as its most frequently jailed publisher.

The radicals gained martyrs and a moral victory at the

Peterloo massacre (1819), and a bitter rallying cry. Although they were outraged at the class economic legislation embodied in the **Corn Law** of 1815, their program still remained essentially political and geared to Cartwright's program announced in the 1770s—the drastic reform of the system of **elections and the franchise**; though this was still augmented by demands for religious toleration and civil liberties, including freedom of speech and of the press. A diverse and vigorous unstamped press continued attacks on the government and promoted radicalism among the lower classes.

As in the periods of "Wilkes and Liberty" (the 1760s and 1770s) and of "The Rights of Man" (the 1790s), radical agitation in the period of "Peterloo" (1811–1822) provoked governmental crackdowns, and these led to still more desperate radical acts and governmental reprisals. To the upper classes, radicals represented presumptuous egalitarianism, violence, and the ignorance of the masses. The **Tory** governments of the period used spies, provocateurs, and informers against them; suspended civil liberties; and when necessary employed lethal force. Legislated repression came with the passage of the **Six Acts** (1819) to curtail radical political activity. The **Radical War** (1820) in **Scotland** ended with three hangings.

Although repressed by the government, divided internally by this repression and by substantive issues, and still mistrusted by most parliamentary politicians, radicals saw reform struggles they inspired win significant victories in the 1820s and 1830s; and a group of men openly calling themselves Radicals entered Parliament after the passage of the **Reform Act** (1832). One reason for this is that radicalism was made more respectable by the "Philosophic Radicals" in the 1820s. When this group's chief philosopher, **Jeremy Bentham**, a highly learned man enjoying international respect, publicized a formula for legislation that called for laws to provide "the greatest good for the greatest number," he proclaimed the creed of the modern democratic state. Bentham brilliantly redirected debate over political reform from the topic of "rights" to that of "usefulness," thereby releasing it from its imprisonment in the rhetoric and memories of the 1790s. More and more middle-class progressives, especially in the industrial **cities**, began to think of themselves as radical. The radical *Westminster Review,* founded by Bentham and **James Mill** in 1824, and contributed to by young **John Stuart Mill**, helped to enlarge this radicalism in the direction of the new economic ideas of free trade and "political economy." Among newspapers, the weekly *Spectator* presented radical views. London dissenters and radicals helped to found the **University of London** in 1828.

Radical leaders of both the middle class and the working class, considering themselves men of "the People," joined to put pressure on Parliament in the 1820s. Some notable victories were achieved, including the repeal of the **Test and Corporation Acts** (1828), **Catholic Emancipation** (1829), and, symbolically most important of all, passage of the Reform Act (1832), in which radical agitation played a vital part—though radicals were not happy with the act's final provisions, which fell far short of the venerable Cartwright program. The **Merthyr Rising** in **Wales** (1831) was but one of the more bloody episodes connected with the act's passage. But the 1830s saw the fulfillment of other radical dreams in the abolition of British slavery (1833) and the reform of local government in the **Municipal Corporations Act** (1835).

Radicalism by this time had broadened its program beyond political purification and civil liberty. Increasingly it had become connected with economic issues resulting from the **Industrial Revolution**. In the 1820s, individual groups of workers formed "combinations," the first modern trade unions, organizations that were highly receptive to radical opinions. Eminent among their intellectual guides was **Robert Owen**, a successful factory owner who surprisingly went on to become Britain's first Socialist. Taking a page from Paine, he proclaimed that humanity could be regenerated by improving economic, social, and educational conditions; his movement became very influential in the 1820s among workers who were as concerned about new issues of employment and working conditions as about legislation and political rights. His disciple **William Thompson** carried the discussion further into realms of quasi-Communist theory, at the same time reaching out as Spence and a few other men had done to the whole allied subject of women's rights.

The Hanoverian "left," like the "right," was always renewing itself, and the complexity of British radicalism grew along with its numbers and with the rapid evolution after 1780 of the British economic system. Though radicalism during the Hanoverian period should be thought of as always essentially political in its special attention to matters connected with elections and the franchise, the complication of economic life increasingly opened up economic and social questions never entertained by Wilkes and his friends, much less by the earlier Commonwealthmen. Religious, geographic, and economic differences had always created subdivisions among radicals, but with the partial enactment of radicalism's political agenda in 1832 a socioeconomic division between middle-class and working-class radicals began to affect it adversely. In the struggle for the reform bill, working-class radicals had joined middle-class radicals in one extended mass still calling itself "the People." But since the property qualification for voting enacted in 1832 denied most workers the right to vote, their dissatisfaction led directly in the early Victorian era to the Chartist drive for democracy, a movement almost exclusively proletarian and working class. In the Victorian era, radicalism was always more deeply affected than in the Hanoverian by this central class division, an inheritance of Britain's industrialization.

Henry Weisser

Bibliography

Adelman, Paul. *Victorian Radicalism: The Middle-Class Experience, 1830–1914.* 1984.

Bonwick, Colin. *English Radicals and the American Revolution.* 1977.

Bradley, James E. *Religion, Revolution and English Radicalism: Nonconformity in Eighteenth Century Politics and Society.* 1990.

Brewer, John. "English Radicalism in the Age of George

III," in J.G.A. Pocock, ed., *Three British Revolutions: 1641, 1689, 1776.* 1980.
Chase, Malcolm. *"The People's Farm: English Radical Agrarianism, 1775–1840.* 1988.
Clark, J.C.D. *English Society, 1688–1832: Ideology, Social Structure and Political Practice during the Ancien Regime.* 1985.
———. *The Language of Liberty, 1660–1832: Political Discourse and Social Dynamics in the Anglo-American World.* 1994.
Cone, Carl B. *The English Jacobins.* 1968.
Derry, John. *The Radical Tradition.* 1967.
Fruchtman, Jack, Jr. *Thomas Paine: Apostle of Freedom.* 1994.
Goodwin, Albert. *The Friends of Liberty: The English Democratic Movement in the Age of the French Revolution.* 1979.
Hill, Bridget. *The Republican Virago: The Life and Times of Catharine Macaulay, Historian.* 1992.
Jacob, Margaret, and James Jacob, eds. *The Origins of Anglo-American Radicalism.* 1984.
Lorch, Jennifer. *Mary Wollstonecraft: The Making of a Radical Feminist.* 1990.
McFarland, E.W. *Ireland and Scotland in the Age of Revolution: Planting the Green Bough.* 1994.
Mee, Jon. *Dangerous Enthusiasm: William Blake and the Culture of Radicalism in the 1790s.* 1992.
Newman, Gerald. *The Rise of English Nationalism: A Cultural History, 1740–1830.* 1987.
Roe, Nicholas. *Wordsworth and Coleridge: The Radical Years.* 1988.
Royle, Edward. *The Infidel Tradition from Paine to Bradlaugh.* 1976.
Rudé, George. *Wilkes and Liberty.* 1962.
Thomas, William. *The Philosophic Radicals: Nine Studies in Theory and Practice, 1817–1841.* 1979.
Thomis, Malcolm I., and Peter Holt. *Threats of Revolution in Britain, 1789–1848.* 1977.
Thompson, Edward P. *The Making of the English Working Class.* 1963.
Wood, Marcus. *Radical Satire and Print Culture, 1790–1822.* 1994.
Wright, D.G. *Popular Radicalism: The Working-Class Experience, 1780–1880.* 1988.

See also French Revolution; Government, National; Regency, The

Raeburn, Sir Henry (1756–1823)

Raeburn, alongside his countryman **Allan Ramsay**, was one of **Scotland**'s greatest **portrait painters**. Having served his apprenticeship as a goldsmith and jeweller, he began to paint miniatures, but at age 22 he married a wealthy widow and was thus able to devote himself to full-time **painting**. Although never formally trained, he developed a style peculiarly and superbly his own. He painted directly onto the canvas without preliminary drawings or underpaintings, thus making his work unusually positive and vigorous. Bold brushwork and contrasting colors seem to add to the vitality, freshness, and honesty of his approach. Often the faces in his portraits are reduced to a series of planes and simplified shapes, with dramatic use of light and shade.

In portrait painting, Raeburn had few rivals. He painted all the leading Scottish figures of his age, such as **Sir Walter Scott**, **David Hume**, and **John Wilson**, but is chiefly remembered for his innumerable portraits of law lords and of the rugged splendors of his Highland Chieftains. His paintings of aristocratic ladies reveal that he also had a delicate touch, capturing their feminine grace and charm.

Raeburn lived in **Edinburgh** all his life, but his election to the **Royal Academy** in 1815 justly recognized his importance in a British context, even if he was unjustly labeled "the Scottish Reynolds." He was certainly preeminent among the Scottish artists of his day, and was knighted by **George IV** in 1822. This, and his appointment as King's Limner in Scotland, a little before his death, crowned his distinguished career.

G.T. Bell

Bibliography

Macmillan, Duncan. *Painting in Scotland: The Golden Age.* 1986.
———. *Scottish Art 1460–1990.* 1990.

See also Wilkie, Sir David

Raffles, Sir Thomas Stamford (1781–1826)

Raffles was the man most responsible for the creation of Britain's **Empire** in East and Southeast Asia. At age 14 he became a clerk for the **East India Company**. He excelled in Asian languages, and in 1805 became assistant secretary to the government of Penang. In 1811 Lord Minto (1751–1814), Governor-General of **India**, made him Lieutenant-Governor of Java as a reward for his supervision of Java's conquest. But in 1816 his ill health, and remorse over his wife's death, forced his return to England.

Although he was knighted in 1817, his opposition to Britain's restoration of the East Indies to the Netherlands relegated him to the minor lieutenant-governorship of Bengkulu in Sumatra. Nevertheless, in 1818 he persuaded Lord Hastings (1754–1826), India's Governor-General, to authorize the construction of a fort east of the Malacca Strait. Raffles chose the island of Singapore and from 1822 to 1824 developed it into an active commercial port. In 1824, illness again forced his return to England. But his development of Singapore secured Britain's position in Southeast Asia and created a port that remains a major center of international commerce. The Raffles Hotel, a famous Singaporean landmark, perpetuates his memory still.

A. Martin Wainwright

Bibliography

Alatas, Hussein Syed. *Thomas Stamford Raffles, 1781–1826: Schemer or Reformer?* 1971.
Bastin, John Sturgis. *The Native Policies of Sir Stamford Raffles in Java and Sumatra.* 1957.

Collis, Maurice. *Raffles.* 1968.
Hahn, Emily. *Raffles of Singapore.* 1946.

Raikes, Robert (1735–1811)

Raikes, businessman, philanthropist, and editor of the *Gloucester Journal* from 1757 to 1802, is widely (but mistakenly) regarded as the originator of **Sunday schools.** Interested in **prison reform** and believing that religious education for poor children might help deter **crime,** he and others began several schools in Gloucester, beginning in 1780. Publicizing these in his newspaper, which he had inherited from his father, he was instrumental in the spreading popularity of such schools; and it has been estimated that at the time of Raikes's death, half a million British children were attending Sunday schools.

Under Raikes's editorship his *Journal* became one of the most successful county **newspapers** in England. Raikes used its distributors to promote the sale of patent **medicines,** especially the popular "Dr. Bateman's Pectoral Drops," a concoction first put out by his father and others in 1730. By 1761, Raikes and John Newbery (1713–1767), a publisher of **children's literature,** owned the rights to these wonder-working drops. The fortune he amassed from their sale permitted Raikes to provide for numerous charities and also a comfortable retirement after his sale of the family paper in 1802.

Kim P. Sebaly

Bibliography

Austin, Roland. "Gloucester Journal, 1722–1922." *Notes and Queries.* Vol. 12 S.X., pp. 283–285.
Cranfield, Geoffrey A. *The Development of Provincial Newspapers, 1700–1922.* 1962.
Laqueur, Thomas W. *Religion and Respectability: Sunday Schools and Working Class Culture, 1780–1850.* 1976.

See also Humanitarianism

Railways and Waggonways

Waggonways, a precursor of railways, first appeared in the early 17th century. They represented an improvement over unassisted packhorses and carts for carrying **coal** from mines to nearby rivers. By around 1660 these were to be found by the rivers Trent, Severn, Tyne, and Wear. Their waggons, with a capacity of around 2 tons, ran on wooden rails; they could be pulled by horses, operated by means of gravity, or simply pushed.

The development of the **steam engine** by **Thomas Newcomen** from about 1715 enabled more efficient draining of mines, and resulted in deeper shafts and a significant increase in coal output. Hence the number of colliery waggonways and the level of traffic on them increased considerably, and the thrust of this, combined with a shortage of timber, led to the development of **iron** rails. Waggonways thus took another step toward railways. A combination of wood and cast iron was first used at **Darby**'s Coalbrookdale ironworks in 1767, and whole systems of cast-iron rails began to appear in the 1790s. Despite the use of the more durable wrought iron from around 1808, it was not until 1820 that a method for rolling it was developed; which ultimately led to the production of the familiar edge rail.

Waggonways and railways spread to many parts of the country, from Cornwall to **Scotland.** By 1800 there were some 300 miles of railway in existence, most still serving short distances between mines and local **canals** or riverbanks, but an

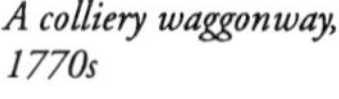
A colliery waggonway, 1770s

increasing number were covering longer distances and handling more diverse businesses. For example, the Kilmarnock and Troon Railway, opened in Ayrshire (1812) to carry coal from the inland town of Kilmarnock to the port of Troon on the coast 10 miles away, carried passengers and general freight from its outset. Such railways still relied on horsepower, but soon the ending of **James Watt's** steam patent led to experiments with steam locomotives such as those pioneered by **Richard Trevithick** in **London** and South **Wales**. The question of whether steam or horse power should prevail remained unresolved at the time of the opening of the **Stockton and Darlington Railway** (1825), both being used in its early days. Even where steam power was employed, stationary engines and moving locomotives were both under consideration. The issue was finally settled in favor of the steam locomotive with the triumph of Robert Stephenson's "Rocket" at the Rainhill trials in 1829, which led to its adoption on the **Liverpool and Manchester Railway** that opened the following year.

The 1830s witnessed the development of the first railway boom. The London and Birmingham Railway, authorized in 1833 and completed 5 years later, was the first mainline out of London. Like the Liverpool and Manchester, it had to overcome hostility from vested interests, including existing transport services such as canal and **coach** operators; but these were overcome, and by the end of the Hanoverian period, other intercity lines were authorized and under construction. By 1844, 2,000 miles of railway had been built at a cost of £54 million. The basis for the great expansion of railways in the Victorian era had been well and truly laid.

A.J.G. Cummings

Bibliography

Baxter, B. *Stone Blocks and Iron Rails.* 1966.
Dyos, H.J., and D.H. Aldcroft. *British Transport.* 1974.
Lewis, M.J.T. *Early Wooden Railways.* 1970.
Reed, M.C. *Investment in Railways in Britain, 1820–1844.* 1975.

See also Finance and Investment; Merthyr Tydfil; Science, Technology, and Invention; Transport, Inland

Ramsay, Allan (1713–1784)

Ramsay was the eldest son of the Scottish poet of the same name (1686–1758), whose bookshop was the hub of the **Edinburgh** literati. The younger Ramsay stood in a similar position to intellectual society, and hence if any artist could claim to be "**portrait painter** to the **Scottish Enlightenment**," it would surely be he. **David Hume** was not only a friend and confidant but the subject of one of his finest canvases.

Having studied both at home and abroad, Ramsay increasingly spent his time in **London**, where his style developed steadily and his reputation grew. The "naturalness" of his portraits became his hallmark, and his portraits of women were especially fine, marked by delicacy, sensitivity, and simplicity. His portrait of the imposing figure of Islay, **3rd Duke of Argyll**, however, amply demonstrated that masculinity and power could also be captured in oils. **Dr. William Hunter**, a close friend, was also the subject of one of Ramsay's most exquisite works.

Ramsay became not only the outstanding portrait painter of his day but also Court Painter to **George III**. By the late 1760s, however, his ever-increasing social activities and growing literary and scholarly interests curtailed his artistic output.

G.T. Bell

Bibliography

Macmillan, Duncan. *Painting in Scotland: The Golden Age.* 1986.
Smart, Alistair. *Allan Ramsay, 1713–1784.* 1992.
———. *Allan Ramsay—Poet, Essayist and Man of the Enlightenment.* 1992.

Rational Dissent

Rational dissent was formed when the liberal wing of the Old Protestant dissent, which had lost its way by the middle of the 18th century, was revived by the emergence of a new generation of leaders from outside the mainstream of **Presbyterianism**, notably (from Calvinist backgrounds) **Richard Price** and **Joseph Priestley**, and (from the **Church of England**) **Theophilus Lindsey**. What these men had in common was a belief in the value of free inquiry, the sufficiency of Scripture, and the importance of toleration for rival opinions.

The movement was marked by lively and often radical rethinking in almost all areas of belief, and by active participation in reform politics. Besides the luminaries mentioned above, it produced a host of thinkers, reformers, and publicists such as the **Unitarian** Samuel Heywood, the famous minister Abraham Rees (1743–1825), Andrew Kippis (1725–1795), **John Jebb**, Joseph Towers (1739–1799), Ralph Griffiths (1720–1803, editor of the *Monthly Review*), and the radical **publisher** Joseph Johnson (1738–1809). These men formed the nucleus of a much wider circle of associates and sympathizers that included **Catharine Macaulay**, **William Godwin**, and **Mary Wollstonecraft**. Rational dissent was also sustained by **dissenting academies**, educational institutions advanced for their day in their range of subjects and for their integration of **science** and the humanities, the most important being the Warrington Academy (1758–1783).

The freewheeling, experimental character of rational dissent could not survive the extremely conservative national reaction to the **French Revolution**. Indeed, its own lack of caution, its attacks on religious orthodoxy and the Anglican church, and its association with political **radicalism** helped to provoke that reaction, which was most manifest in the **Birmingham** riots of July 1791. Those **riots** left Priestley's chapel, house, and laboratory in ruins, and his library and papers destroyed. With his emigration to America in 1794, and the earlier death of Price (April 1791), rational dissent lost its most eminent leaders. Yet it left an important legacy in the subsequent development of British Unitarianism as well as in its advocacy of toleration for **Roman Catholics** and in its contribution to the liberal Christian political tradition.

Martin Fitzpatrick

Bibliography

Elliot, C.M. "The Political Economy of English Dissent, 1780–1840," in R.M. Hartwell, ed., *The Industrial Revolution.* 1970.

Fitzpatrick, Martin. "Rational Dissent and the Enlightenment." *Faith and Freedom.* Vol. 38, pp. 83–101.

Fruchtman, Jack, Jr. *The Apocalyptic Politics of Richard Price and Joseph Priestley: A Study in Late-Eighteenth-Century English Republican Millennialism.* 1983.

Haakonssen, Knud, ed. *Enlightenment and Religion: Rational Dissent in Eighteenth-Century Britain.* 1996.

Lincoln, Anthony. *Some Political and Social Ideas of English Dissent, 1763–1800.* 1938, 1971.

Richey, R.C. "The Origins of British Radicalism: The Changing Rationale for Dissent." *Eighteenth-Century Studies.* Vol. 7, pp. 179–192.

Thomas, D.O. *The Honest Mind: The Thought and Work of Richard Price.* 1977.

Watts, M.R. *The Dissenters.* 2 vols. 1978, 1995.

See also Dissenters; Enlightenment, The

Reeve, Clara (1729–1807)

Although Reeve's reputation rests with *The Old English Baron: A Gothic Story* (1778) and *The Progress of Romance* (1785), she also published **poetry**, a **translation** of John Barclay's *Argenia* (1621) from the Latin as *The Phoenix* (1772), and wrote several other **novels**—as she explained, "to support the cause of morality." Reeve acknowledged her own *Baron* to be the "literary offspring" of **Horace Walpole**'s *The Castle of Otranto* (1764), but Walpole dismissed it as "totally void of imagination and interest." Her design, she explained in her Preface, was to tame Walpole's **supernatural** excesses but still gain the reader's attention while creating an air of probability by portraying the **manners** of real life and dramatizing the pathetic "to engage the heart in its behalf." Her effort prepared readers for rational **Gothic** novels such as **Ann Radcliffe**'s *The Mysteries of Udolpho* (1794).

Reeve's *The Progress of Romance,* the first lengthy history of English fiction, was written as a three-way critical conversation, thus allowing her to comment variously on many writers, including Aphra Behn (*c.* 1640–1689), **Delarivière Manley**, **Eliza Haywood**, and **Sarah Fielding**. Though this was an innovation, Reeve's politically and morally conservative beliefs kept her from sympathizing with the new ideas of the 1790s and limited her creativity in the very genre she helped to make popular.

Peter A. Tasch

Bibliography

Reeve, Clara. *The Progress of Romance.* Rpt. 1930.

———. *The Old English Baron.* Ed. James Trainer. 1967.

Todd, Janet. *A Dictionary of British and American Women Writers, 1660–1800.* 1987.

Tompkins, J.M.S. *The Popular Novel in England, 1770–1800.* 1932.

Reeves Societies

See Loyalist Associations

Reference Works

The 18th-century impulse to make books useful—and to advance knowledge by disseminating it—is revealed in the production of reference works. The word *reference* was not commonly used to signify a distinct class of book or a library division until the latter 1800s, but one can trace the major kinds of reference books (those designed to be consulted for items of information rather than to be read consecutively) to innovative, and often audacious, 18th-century British models.

The foremost contribution was in the form of the dictionary. **Samuel Johnson**'s *Dictionary of the English Language* (1755) has eclipsed the period's "divers wordbooks," which ranged in subject from the technical to the commonplace, from the learned to the low. Once as familiar as Johnson's were the dictionaries of a boarding-school teacher, Nathan Bailey (*d.* 1742). His *Universal Etymological Dictionary* (1721) and *Dictionarium Britannicum* (1730), regularly reprinted, set the standard and conventions for subsequent dictionaries of language. Bailey also wrote a "compleat household dictionary," *Dictionarium Domesticum* (1736). The Latin title is a bit misleading, as this was a handy book of quotidian tips and recipes, including directions for pickling vegetables and purging bedbugs.

For every lexicon of law, medicine, science, spelling, or pronunciation to be studied, a dictionary for delight was published. **Thomas Sheridan** wrote a *General Dictionary of the English Language* (1780) to improve his native tongue; and when **James Beattie** wrote his *Scoticisms* (1787), he sought to "correct improprieties of speech and writing." Less edifying perhaps was *A New Canting Dictionary* (1725), anonymously compiled, of "all the terms, ancient and modern, used in the several tribes of gypsies, beggars, shoplifters, highwaymen, foot-pads, and all other clans of cheats and villains," complete with an appendix of "songs in the canting dialect." The most valuable slang dictionary of the era is Francis Grose's (*c.* 1731–1791) *A Classical Dictionary of the Vulgar Tongue,* a fifth edition of which was edited by **Pierce Egan** in 1823. Another entertaining specimen was *A Poetical Dictionary* (1761), probably by Samuel Derrick (1724–1769), an alphabetical catalog of "beauties of the English poets" under headings such as "chastity" and "street walker."

But it was Johnson's *Dictionary* that stood tallest, for it was at once a dictionary of words, quotations, etymologies, and slang. While it was not the first English dictionary, it was, in two large volumes, the most magnificent. It marked a high point in the career of Johnson, who so often initiated and improved reference books. His output in this line was impressive. He recorded for reference legal and political proceedings, as well as lectures; wrote an informative **travel book**; collected fugitive tracts; introduced an important textbook, *The Preceptor* (1748); an Italian-English dictionary, and a dictionary of trade. He annotated a scholarly edition of **Shakespeare**; his *Prefaces* (1779), a remarkable series of literary biographies, was one of his final monuments.

The second major kind of reference work was the encyclopedia, or cyclopedia, a word which Johnson defined simply as "a circle of knowledge." Three specimens considered most influential historically are John Harris's (1666?–1719) *Lexicon Technicum; or, An Universal Dictionary of the Arts and Sciences* (1704), Ephraim Chambers's (1680?–1740) *Cyclopedia; or, The Universal Dictionary of Arts and Sciences* (1728), and the *Encyclopedia Britannica* (1768–1771), written by a team of Scotsmen. Not as inclusive or general as later editions (the 1775–1789 *Encyclopedia Britannica* was nevertheless the first to include introductory information on a wide range of topics), the first encyclopedias provided advanced scientific information; they are still difficult to read.

Harris, an Oxford scholar and divine, was employed by a group of **London** commercial **booksellers** to write his encyclopedia; this appears to have been a common way for reference works to get written in England, where government did not support such endeavors. What distinguished Harris's *Lexicon* was not its scope—it omitted **theology**, **biography**, and **poetry**—but its format. Harris used alphabetical headings, solicited contributions of experts (a treatise on acids, for example, by Sir Isaac Newton), and included simple bibliographies. Chambers, self-taught but curious and enterprising, arrived in London with a project to expand Harris's *Lexicon.* This he did, adding the great practical advantage of cross-references. After his death, his influence continued. A projected French **translation** of the *Cyclopedia* was the basis for Denis Diderot (1713–1784) and Jean Le Rond D'Alembert's (1717–1783) magisterial *Encyclopédie* (1771). And Abraham Rees (1743–1825) revised and enlarged Chambers's book, making it widely known as *Rees's Cyclopedia* in the early 19th century. The *Encyclopedia Britannica,* which first appeared in 100 installments, was published as a book in the same year as the *Encyclopédie.* Incorporated were 160 copper **engravings** and, as general editor William Smellie (1740–1795) insisted, no short or superficial entries. Its audience was limited to scholars; it did not sell well.

By the turn of the century, later editions of these books, designed for wider audiences, found readers, and new encyclopedias were published. The *Encyclopedia Perthensis,* which appeared in 23 volumes in 1796–1806, was "intended to supersede all other English books of reference." Other encyclopedias were directed to the emerging female audience: *The Ladies Encyclopedia* (1788) and *The Ladies Library* (1790).

Early encyclopedias, imitating Aristotle, Pliny, and Varro, contained little history or biography; this was to be found in the biographical dictionary. A forerunner of the *Dictionary of National Biography,* this form became popular when Louis Moreri's (1643–1680) *Le Grand Dictionnaire Historique* (1676) was translated by **Jeremy Collier** as *The Great Historical, Geographical, Geneological, and Poetical Dictionary* (1701). Throughout the 1700s there appeared biographical dictionaries of impressive scope and beauty. **Thomas Birch** improved on Pierre Bayle (1647–1706) in *A General Dictionary, Historical and Critical* (1734–1741); his *Heads of the Illustrious Persons of Great Britain* (1747), with engraved portraits and large type, is indeed a lovely folio. At mid century two others of note were published: *Biographia Britannica* (1747–1766), edited by William Oldys (1696–1761) and John Towers (1737–1799), and Thomas Tanner's (1674–1735) *Bibliotheca Britanico-Hibernica* (1748). Biographical dictionaries of poets were capacious. Giles Jacob (1686–1744), following efforts of Edward Phillips (1630–1696?) and William Winstanly (1628?–1698), edited *The Poetical Register* (1719–1720); Theophilus **Cibber** (1703–1758) and Robert Shiels (*d.* 1753) put together *The Lives of the Poets of Great Britain and Ireland to the Time of Dean Swift* (1753).

Similar to the biographical dictionary was the collection of anecdotes. Such volumes of miscellaneous information, much of it boring, were crucial to early biographical research, and are still used. Joseph Spence's (1699–1768) anecdotes on **Alexander Pope**, anecdotes of the art world by **Horace Walpole**, and literary anecdotes by printer **John Nichols** (none too painstakingly researched), remain important sources for gleaning information on the times.

Another important reference work was the manual or assistant. This was a guide for behavior or for a skill such as letter-writing, conversation, love-making, shorthand, seamanship, or whist. Other references vital in Hanoverian Britain included the annotated edition, the collection, the scholarly history, the **almanac** and atlas, the cookbook, and the courtesy book.

One of the great weaknesses of 18th-century reference works was the lack of bibliographic information. Before Robert Watts's (1774–1819) *Bibliographica Britannica* (1824), bibliography content was scanty and unscientific. As every modern researcher knows, indexes of magazines, newspapers, books, and manuscripts were inadequate; library, sale, and union catalogs, occasionally making their way into print, were often rather carelessly drawn lists of books.

Matthew Rusnak

Bibliography

Alston, R.C. *Bibliography of Books on the English Language from the Invention of Printing to the Year 1800.* 1965–.

DeMaria, Robert. *Samuel Johnson and the Language of Learning.* 1986.

Fussell, Paul. *Samuel Johnson and the Life of Writing.* 1971.

Heltzel, Virgil B. *A Checklist of Courtesy Books in the Newberry Library.* 1942.

Kafker, Frank A., ed. "Notable Encyclopedias of the Seventeenth and Eighteenth Centuries: Nine Predecessors to the Encyclopédie." *Studies in Voltaire and the Eighteenth Century.* 1981.

Lipking, Lawrence. *The Ordering of the Arts in Eighteenth-Century England.* 1970.

Munby, A.N.L. *Sale Catalogues of Libraries of Eminent Persons.* 1971–1975.

Starmes, D.T., and G.E. Noyes. *The English Dictionary from Czuldrey to Johnson, 1604–1755.* 1945.

Tonelli, Giorgio. *A Short-Title List of the Subject Dictionaries of the Sixteenth, Seventeenth, and Eighteenth Centuries as Aids to the History of Ideas.* 1971.

See also Language and Linguistics

Reform Act (1832)

From the 1760s on, the existing terms of parliamentary elections and the franchise were criticized and attacked by an ever-growing body of political reformers both inside and outside Parliament. The **radical** movement, initiated during **John Wilkes**'s political struggles at that time, a movement that focused tightly on attempts to expand greatly the electorate and make government more clearly accountable to it, picked up growing strength from **middle-class** groups increasingly alienated by a system still dominated by the **aristocracy and gentry**. It was becoming clear by 1815, after the long struggle against the **French Revolution**, that the **Industrial Revolution** in Britain was helping to compound discontentment to dangerous levels. The **riots and popular disturbances** of the period 1815–1820 registered this growing tension. Although repeal of the **Test and Corporation Acts** (1828) and the achievement of **Catholic Emancipation** (1829) helped to release some of this, these parliamentary initiatives also helped prepare the ground for one of the greatest parliamentary battles in history, the culmination of the struggle for political reform during the Hanoverian period.

The **Whigs**, kept out of power for decades, at last came into office in November 1830 under **Lord Grey**, whose name since the 1790s had been linked with parliamentary reform. Another revolution had just occurred in **France**, while in Britain the **Swing riots** were sweeping through the south and east of England. Grey, though no less aristocratic than the **Duke of Wellington** who headed the **Tories**, was convinced that reform was the only way to avert revolution. He told **King William IV** that "it was the spirit of the age which was triumphing; that to resist it was certain destruction." Wellington and the Tory peers in the **Lords** were adamantly opposed to any constitutional alteration.

The Reform Bill's passage was far from easy. **Lord John Russell** introduced the Whigs' bill on 1 March 1831, to mounting jeers and shouts in **Commons** as astonished Tory M.P.s comprehended the revolutionary changes contemplated—among them the complete disfranchisement of 56 two-M.P. **boroughs** and semi-disfranchisement of 30 others, paired with the redistribution of most of these seats to 42 hitherto unrepresented boroughs, including **cities like Manchester, Birmingham,** and **Leeds**. The defeat of Russell's bill in April led to a sharply partisan general election, which produced sufficient parliamentary support to pass it in June. This sent the bill to the Lords, which again defeated it by 41 votes in October, precipitating a nationwide uproar accompanied by extraordinary violence and demonstrations against authority and the upper classes.

The crisis continued into May 1832, when Grey resigned at the king's refusal to create 50 peers to ensure the bill's passage in Lords. But with Wellington unable to form a government, the king had little choice but to consent; and with his backing and the Tories' withdrawal of **opposition** the bill was passed on 4 June and signed into law 3 days later. Separate bills were soon passed also for **Scotland** and **Ireland**.

The act's terms regarding elections and the franchise were complicated. Apart from the borough disfranchisements and electoral redistributions mentioned above, regional distributions also occurred; England lost 18 M.P.s while **Wales** gained five, Ireland five, and Scotland eight. The scot and lot and potwalloper franchises were abolished, while the county franchise was retained by 40-shilling freeholders and extended to £10 copyholders and £50 leaseholders, including farmer tenants-at-will. The new borough franchise, greatly simplified, embraced all owners or occupiers of property valued at £10 or more a year. The entire electorate of the United Kingdom was enlarged from 409,000 (in 1831) to 814,000.

Historians disagree about how radical the Reform Act was, and about whether or not it averted revolution. Early writers praised it as a great historical landmark, a fundamental reorientation of politics, which put an end to the corruption and venality of 18th-century practices, and ushered in an essentially modern and quasi-democratic electoral system. Then, revisionist scholars, led by Norman Gash, were prompted to emphasize just the reverse—the survival after 1832 of some 50 pocket boroughs, the nonrepresentation of some towns with **populations** over 10,000, the continuing absence of voting privileges after 1832 for more than 80% of all adult males, and the continued political dominance of the landed classes. Today's writers come closer to the older view. Some emphasize the act's tremendous symbolic significance to contemporaries as the inauguration of middle-class power and the overthrow of traditional assumptions and prerogatives; others point to its severance of the arrangements by which both Crown and Lords had kept the Commons under control, and still others stress the long-term importance of the crisis itself, of 1830–1832, in "polarizing" and "politicizing" everyone, both Whig and Tory, for decades afterward.

David B. Mock

Bibliography

Bradley, James. *Religion, Revolution, and English Radicalism: Nonconformity in Eighteenth-Century Politics and Society.* 1990.

Brock, Michael. *The Great Reform Act.* 1973.

Cannon, John. *Parliamentary Reform, 1640–1832.* 1972.

Dinwiddy, John R. *From Luddism to the First Reform Bill: Reform in England, 1810–1832.* 1986.

Gash, Norman. *Politics in the Age of Peel: A Study in the Technique of Parliamentary Representation, 1830–1850.* 1953.

———. *Reaction and Reconstruction in English Politics, 1832–1852.* 1965.

O'Gorman, Frank. *Voters, Patrons, and Parties: The Unreformed Electoral System of Hanoverian England, 1734–1832.* 1989.

Phillips, John A. *Electoral Behavior in Unreformed England: Plumpers, Splitters, and Straights.* 1982.

———. *The Great Reform Bill in the Boroughs: English Electoral Behaviour, 1818–1841.* 1992.

Smith, E.A. *Reform or Revolution? A Diary of Reform in England, 1830–32.* 1992.

See also Elections and the Franchise; Merthyr Rising

Regency, The

Spanning the period from February 1811, when George, Prince of Wales, took the oath as Prince Regent, to January 1820, when **George III** died and the prince ascended the throne as **George IV**, the Regency was marked by **war** with and defeat of Napoleon; popular disturbances; economic difficulties; industrialization; and distinctive styles in **fashion**, social behavior, decorating, the fine arts, **architecture**, and literature. The term *Regency* refers to political arrangements and to the decade when they obtained. But it is also, therefore, an atmospheric historical concept embracing particularly the pleasure-seeking world of the Regent himself and of the **aristocracy**, yet also summoning "an age and a society of wild extremes" in which **Evangelical** moralizing, working-class misery and anger **radical** agitation and conspiracy, **Tory** governmental reaction and repression, and a remarkable flowering of styles, intellectual controversy, and artistic genius took place.

The Regency Act (1811), necessitated by George III's final period of mental illness, gave his son limited powers for the first 12 months. The prince kicked off the period with a huge party at Carlton House on 19 June 1811, which was attended by a number of exiled European royalty. He and the other sons of George III set the hedonistic tone of the era with lavish expenditures on fashion, **home furnishings**, art, celebrations, **homebuilding**, and especially **gambling**, through which fortunes were often lost. The royal dukes were unpopular and morally corrupt, and the Regent's failed marriage to Princess **Caroline** and his relationships with his mistresses constituted an ongoing national scandal. Ordinary folk expressed moral indignation as well as political disaffection by taking Caroline's part at the end of the decade when she returned to England (1820) and attempted to assume the throne alongside her husband.

The Regency saw great political turmoil, especially in the period after 1815 beginning with the passage of the extremely unpopular **Corn Law**. Rapid demobilization of soldiers and sailors caused economic hardship, and the ranks of the unemployed swelled greatly. This unemployment, together with industrialization and the economic strains that accompanied it, as well as the desire for political reform, helped spark several significant breaches of public order: the machine-breaking activities of the **Luddites** (1811, 1812), the **Spa Fields riot** (1816), the Pentrich rising (1817), and the **Peterloo massacre** (1819). The year 1820 saw the **Cato Street conspiracy** to assassinate the entire Cabinet. Eight years earlier there occurred the only assassination of a **prime minister** in English history, when **Spencer Perceval** was shot and killed. **Lord Liverpool** succeeded him and held office from 1812 to 1827. Although the Regent had been connected with the **Whig** opposition when he was Prince of Wales, he did not remove the Tories from office; indeed, his own politics were now more in line with theirs, especially concerning opposition to reform and **Catholic Emancipation**.

In the international arena, the Regency's first 4 years overlapped the final phase of the **French Revolutionary and Napoleonic Wars**. (Britain had also fought the United States in the **War of 1812**.) After the allied coalition defeated Napoleon at the **Battle of Waterloo** (1815), the **Duke of Wellington** was elevated to the status of national hero. The juxtaposition of national pride with furious popular unrest was one of the striking contrasts of 1815–1820, and indeed helped give rise to the bitterly ironic sobriquet "Peterloo Massacre," which combined the ideas of military achievement at Waterloo with the slaughter of defenseless Englishmen.

Fashionable society was dominated by the nobility, and one of the characteristic figures of the Regency was the dandy, epitomized by **Beau Brummell**, who dominated the **London** social scene and set the standard for the well-dressed gentleman. Women's fashions also underwent change—petticoats replaced corsets, low-cut dresses became the rage, and sandals or boots were worn. Brilliant colors and shorter hairstyles were also adopted. Social life for the well-to-do flourished. **Sporting** events, gentleman's **clubs**, the **theater**, **opera**, **dance**, masquerades, parties, and **travel** by **coach** within the British Isles and on the Continent occupied the attention of the fashionable. The introduction of gas lighting stimulated nightlife. In some quarters the use of alcohol, snuff, and opium was widespread.

The "Regency Style" that dominated architecture and **interior decoration** was best exemplified in the work of **John Nash**, who was responsible for giving shape to the Regent's ideas in such creations as Regent Street, the terraces of Regent's Park, the Regency Arch, and especially the Royal Pavilion at Brighton—extravagant, brash, and frivolous, with **neoclassical** and **Oriental** influences.

The rapidly growing power of Evangelicalism, morally uplifting if also notoriously censorious not only of the laxity and self-indulgence but even the harmless pleasures of the age, was evidenced in an increase in puritanical religious publications, a proliferation of philanthropic activities (many rooted in **antislavery** agitation), and the remarkable personal dedication of such activists as **Wilberforce**, **Hannah More**, **Zachary Macaulay**, **Henry Thornton**, **James Stephen**, and others. **Utilitarianism** also reinforced philanthropic efforts, the reform of **manners and morals**, and the growing sentiment for reform of **elections and the franchise**. Social reformers such as the factory owner **Robert Owen** labored to improve **hours, wages, and working conditions** for **factory workers** and to improve the lot of workers in general. A flourishing underworld of **crime** existed in Regency London before the creation of the Metropolitan Police Force in 1829 brought important changes in **law enforcement**.

Artistic and literary achievements were in many cases spectacular. **John Constable** (though his talent was not recognized until later) and **J.M.W. Turner** produced great breakthroughs in **landscape painting**. Improvements in printing allowed for the rapid expansion of **newspapers**, and the British Isles were well served by literary **periodicals**. Some of England's most brilliant **Romantic** poets flourished and were at the peak of their creative powers during the Regency—**Wordsworth**, **Coleridge**, **Byron**, **Shelley**, and **Keats**. Byron's *Don Juan* and *Childe Harold's Pilgrimage* are especially noteworthy for their comments on Regency social life and mores.

The **novels** of **Scott** and **Austen** were widely read, and the tradition of **Gothic fiction** survived in the classic horror novel *Frankenstein* by **Mary Shelley**.

Mark C. Herman

Bibliography

Dabundo, Laura, ed. *Encyclopedia of Romanticism: Culture in Britain, 1780s–1830s.* 1992.

Erickson, Carolly. *Our Tempestuous Day: A History of Regency England.* 1986.

Hibbert, Christopher. *George IV: Regent and King.* 1973.

Laudermilk, Sharon, and Teresa Hamlin. *The Regency Companion.* 1989.

Low, Donald A. *Thieves' Kitchen: The Regency Underworld.* 1982.

Margetson, Stella. *Regency London.* 1971.

Priestley, J.B. *The Prince of Pleasure and His Regency, 1811–20.* 1969.

White, R.J. *Life in Regency England.* 1963.

Wood, Marcus. *Radical Satire and Print Culture, 1790–1822.* 1994.

See also Regency Crisis; Regency Style

Regency Crisis (1788–1789)

In the summer and autumn of 1788 **George III** lapsed into periods of physical pain, bizarre behavior, and a confused mental state caused by the hereditary metabolic disorder, porphyria. Although physicians predicted his eventual recovery, alignments in the political landscape caused a major crisis. The Prime Minister, **Pitt the Younger**, enjoyed George's support, but the king's son and heir, the Prince of Wales (later **George IV**), greatly preferred his own political friends in the **opposition**, especially **Charles James Fox**, whom the father detested. Pitt thus foresaw his own fall from power if George III remained incapacitated and the prince acquired full power as Regent.

There had been recent precedents for temporary delegation of Royal powers to individuals and councils standing in for kings unable to perform their duties. A precautionary Regency Act was passed in 1751 on the death of **Frederick, Prince of Wales**, giving Royal powers, in the event of **George II**'s death before his grandson (then 13 years old) came of age, to the Princess of Wales and a specially appointed council. The grandson, after assuming power as George III, signed another Regency Act (1765) slightly modifying these general arrangements.

In the 3-month crisis that began in November 1788, Pitt proposed that the Prince of Wales should be Regent, but under conditions designed to protect the king's rights in the event of his recovery. Parliament should have the power to choose the regent and to restrict, for at least 12 months, his powers, particularly those of appointment to offices and peerages (which Pitt anticipated would be used to entrench Fox and his friends in power). Fox (and **Burke**), straining for power, opposed Pitt's measure and urged that the prince be immediately appointed Regent and given full powers as a matter of his inherent right. Their position, like Pitt's, seemed a reversal of principle, for from the time of the ouster of the **Fox–North Coalition** (1783) Fox had upheld the rights of Parliament and Pitt supported those of the sovereign.

George III at home, wearing a soft cap

The struggle, like that of 1783–1784 between Pitt and Fox, went beyond Parliament as addresses from the country were presented for, as well as against, the Regency bill. Cries of treason were loudly voiced on both sides. But Pitt's bill passed the **House of Commons** and was in the **House of Lords** in February 1789 when the king recovered, promptly thanking his ministers for their loyalty. Throughout the crisis the Prince of Wales had supported the opposition, much to his mother the queen's dismay. Events of the **French Revolution** soon pushed the whole matter to the background, but the provisions of Pitt's Regency bill were followed in 1811 when another Regency act was passed after George III lapsed into his final period of illness.

Mark C. Herman

Bibliography

Derry, John W. *The Regency Crisis and the Whigs, 1788–9.* 1963.

———. *Charles James Fox.* 1972.

Ehrman, John. *The Younger Pitt.* 1969.

Macalpine, Ida, and Richard Hunter. *George III and the Mad Business.* 1969.

Regency Style

The Regency style (1800–1837) of interior design and **home furnishing and decoration**, a narrow subdivision of Hanoverian style, bracketed the political Regency (1811–1820) of George, Prince of Wales, the future **George IV** (1820–1830), from which it takes its name.

Its immediate antecedent was English and French **neoclassicism.** Other stylistic factors and aesthetic theories influenced its development, however. It revived the motifs of **Gothic** and **Chinoiserie** used throughout the Middle Georgian period (1750–1765); borrowed from the French Empire style developed for Napoleon Bonaparte by Charles Percier (1764–1838) and Pierre Fontaine (1762–1853); translated English military and naval victories into decorative elements; and relied increasingly on the "Greek revival" forms and motifs depicted on Greek vases, a source that owed its new importance to growing familiarity with the views of Johann Winckelmann (1717–1768) on the primacy of Greek art. The Regency style differed from most preceding styles in that it responded not only to market forces but to the perception that design, like art, could affect private behavior and should contribute to the public good.

One of the first designers in this style was **Thomas Sheraton**, whose *Cabinet Dictionary* (1803) substituted a rather ponderous Greco–Romanism for the delicate neoclassicism of his earlier *Drawing Book* (1791–1794). In adding Chinese, Gothic, and Egyptian elements in *The Cabinet-Maker, Upholsterer, and General Artist's Encyclopaedia* (1804–1806), Sheraton demonstrated both the rapid evolution of the Regency style and the incongruities to which its disparate sources disposed it.

A connoisseur who tried to counter caprice and turn art to a socially useful end was Thomas Hope (1769–1831). The son of a wealthy banker, his 8-year **Grand Tour** took him to several European and Middle Eastern countries, where he studied architecture, design, and costume, and collected **antiquities.** In 1799 he furnished a **London townhouse** with designs drawn from Greek, Roman, and Egyptian prototypes. In 1804 he in effect made the house a gallery, sending out calling invitations to members of the **Royal Academy of Arts.** The painter **Benjamin West** and architects George Dance (1741–1825) and Sir John Soane (1753–1837) were among those who praised the installation because of the positive effect they expected it to have on public taste.

Hope himself expressed confidence that his designs, published in his *Household Furniture and Interior Decoration* (1807), would assist both the craftsmen who made them and the consumers who purchased them—that they would give "new food to the industry of the poor" and also "new decorum to the expenditure of the rich." But the Oriental extravagance of the Royal Pavilion in Brighton, completed by **John Nash** around 1820, reveals that the Prince of Wales, at least, resisted this argument. After 1812, furnishings grew still more bulbous and clumsy; this tendency increased in the 1830s, when furniture production became mechanized.

The Regency style was affected as much by social change as stylistic concerns. There was a modernizing thrust toward the creation of cozy, clean, and comfortable environments: small rooms visually enlarged with mirrors, flat ceilings, walls treated with paper or paint, fitted carpets, simple window treatments, and washable fabrics. Furniture was pulled informally into the room, rather than lining the walls as in preceding periods. Coffee- and game-tables were placed in front of sofas, and chairs were scattered around them in casual groupings. Argand and Carcel oil lamps provided better illumination than candles.

Furnishings responded to several influences, especially the Greek. The arms of the lyre became the curving shape of sofas and daybeds, and legs were formed into cornucopias and curules. Cabinets followed the French model, with plinth bases and overhanging aprons supported by Greek- or Egyptian-headed herms ending in two tiny feet, but their doors featured brass grilles (sometimes backed by pleated silk) rather than glass or wooden panels. The dolphin returned to the decorative lexicon to recall the successes of **Admiral Nelson.**

Andrew's Place, Regent's Park, designed by Nash

Nelson's last battle (1805) gave its name to the **Trafalgar** chair, modeled on the armless *klismos* of Greek vase paintings.

Such restrained elegance was difficult to maintain, however, perhaps because furniture-making was becoming an industry rather than a craft. The best of the Regency style had in fact disappeared before the political Regency began in 1811.

Reed Benhamou

Bibliography

Dinkel, John. *The Royal Pavilion, Brighton.* 1983.
Musgrave, Clifford. *Regency Furniture: 1800 to 1830.* 1961.
Thornton, Peter. *Authentic Decor: The Domestic Interior, 1620–1920.* 1984.
Watkin, David. *Thomas Hope, 1769–1831, and the Neo-Classical Idea.* 1968.

See also Interior Design

Reid, Thomas (1710–1796)

Reid was an epistemologist and moral philosopher whose efforts to discern the nature and limits of knowledge produced what became widely known as the Scottish philosophy of Common Sense. His best-known work, *An Inquiry into the Human Mind, on the Principles of Common Sense* (1764), attempted to refute the epistemological skepticism of **David Hume** by overthrowing his profoundly disturbing notion, which in Reid's view ran contrary to the evidence of common sense, that ideas themselves, not the objects of ideas, were the immediate objects of the mind's apprehension. Reid went on to apply his own theory to an investigation of the human mind and came up with a two-volume systematic analysis published near the end of his life: *Essays on the Intellectual Powers of Man* (1785), and *Essays on the Active Powers of Man* (1788).

Born and educated in the northeast of **Scotland**, Reid served as the **Presbyterian** minister of New Machar (1737–1751) and Regent in Philosophy at King's College, Aberdeen (1751–1764). During this period he embarked on his lifelong project of placing the study of human nature on a properly scientific footing by adopting a rigorous experimental and inductive program. He believed that revealing the laws governing human behavior would enable moralists to perfect the teaching of virtue. In 1764 he succeeded **Adam Smith** in the chair of Moral Philosophy at Glasgow University, where his concentration on the interrelationships between psychological, ethical, and political phenomena made a considerable impact. Retiring from teaching in 1780, he prepared his *Essays* for publication and devoted the remainder of his days to **Whig** social and political causes. He is remembered for the scientific approach to problems of human improvement that became the cornerstone of the Scottish "Common Sense" school of philosophy.

Peter J. Diamond

Bibliography

Dalgarno, Melvin, and Matthews, Eric, eds. *The Philosophy of Thomas Reid.* 1989.
Lehrer, Keith. *Thomas Reid.* 1989.
Marcil-Lacoste, Louise. *Claude Buffier and Thomas Reid.* 1982.
Rowe, William L. *Thomas Reid on Freedom and Morality.* 1991.

See also Empiricism; Scottish Enlightenment; Scottish Universities

Religious Revivalism

The religious revival in the 18th century was an international Evangelical phenomenon that included America, **Wales, Scotland,** and England. The revival emphasized personal conversion, the authority of the Bible, the centrality of the affections in religious experience, justification by faith alone, and the renewal of piety and religious fervor.

In England the revival was inaugurated by Methodists **John Wesley, Charles Wesley,** and **George Whitefield.** Although the revival movement was begun as an attempt to "awaken" members of the **Church of England** to the gospel, it quickly gained popularity among the **dissenting** congregations, whose leaders were less suspicious of "**enthusiasm**" than were most Anglican clergymen. Within the Church of England some of the more outstanding proponents of the "Evangelical Revival" were **John Newton,** the biblical commentator Thomas Scott (1747–1821), the London preacher Richard Cecil (1748–1810), the church historian Joseph Milner (1744–1797), and the poet **William Cowper.** Most influential of all was the **Clapham Sect,** a group of wealthy and socially prominent Anglican Evangelicals who worked for cultural, religious, and moral reform. The success of the religious revival in England led to the founding of several organizations to promote foreign **missionary** efforts, most notably the Church Missionary Society (1799) and the British and Foreign Bible Society (1804).

In British **North America** the revival began during the 1720s in New Jersey with the Evangelical preaching of the Dutch Reformed pastor Theodorus Frelinghuysen (1692–1747) and the **Presbyterian** minister Gilbert Tennent (1703–1764). Soon afterward Jonathan Edwards (1703–1758), a **Congregationalist** pastor in Massachusetts, became the chief figure of the religious revival in America (the "Great Awakening"). The missions of the Wesleys and especially of Whitefield to the American colonies were instrumental in its dissemination. A similar American Evangelical revival at the end of the 18th century and continuing into the first decades of the 19th century is sometimes called the Second Great Awakening.

The **Welsh religious revival,** which began in the 1730s, had a more distinctly Calvinistic coloring than the others. Its most notable leaders were **Griffith Jones** of Llanddowror, **Howel Harris** of Trevecca, **Daniel Rowland** of Llangeitho, and **William Williams, Pantycelyn,** though again the itinerant Whitefield was also a powerful influence. The Welsh Calvinistic Methodists were sometimes derisively called "Jumpers" because of their enthusiastic leaping for joy at revival meetings.

The revivals in **Scotland** were typically linked to large sacramental services under tents and in open fields. The height of the Scottish revival came in 1742 in the small village of Cambuslang, outside **Glasgow**, where thousands gathered to hear the preaching of William McCulloch (*fl.*1740) and to receive communion, which sometimes took almost the whole day to distribute, so great were the crowds. Here again the indefatigable Whitefield was influential; he made mission visits to Scotland on 14 separate occasions.

Millenarianism, the belief in the imminent second coming of Christ to inaugurate a 1,000-year reign of divine rule on Earth, was a significant aspect of the revival for many groups, including Anabaptists, Moravians, and Pietists. Among the more renowned millenarians of the period were **Joanna Southcott**, who believed she was the woman of Revelation 12, **Richard Brothers**, self-proclaimed "nephew of the Almighty," and **Joseph Priestley**, who expected the Second Coming not later than 1814.

Michael F. Suarez, S.J.

Bibliography

Cairns, Earle Edwin. *Saints and Society: The Social Impact of Eighteenth-Century English Revivals and Its Contemporary Relevance.* 1960.
Carnett, Jane, and Colin Matthews, eds. *Revival and Religion Since 1700.* 1993.
Crawford, Michael J. *Seasons of Grace: Colonial New England's Revival Tradition in Its British Context.* 1991.
Lambert, Frank. *"Pedlar in Divinity": George Whitfield and the Transatlantic Revivals, 1737–1770.* 1994.
Ward, William Reginald. *The Protestant Evangelical Awakening.* 1992.

See also Evangelicalism; Manners and Morals; Methodism

Religious Toleration

See Toleration, Religious

Repton, Humphry (1752–1818)

Coining the term "landscape gardening" to describe his profession, Repton synthesized the serene landscaping ideas of **Lancelot ("Capability") Brown** with the more intricate requirements of the **picturesque**. Although not always a coherent theorist, Repton had a keen awareness of the optical effects of landscape elements, using them effectively in his designs and incorporating them into several popular books on **landscape architecture**, which firmly established him as the foremost man in his field from the 1790s until his death.

After several unsuccessful attempts at careers in business and government, Repton decided in 1798 upon his profession, calling Brown his master. His practice henceforth included presenting potential clients elegant "Red Books" with descriptions and delicate illustrations with removable flaps to show the before-and-after effects of specific proposals.

Though at first agreeing with **Uvedale Price** and Richard Payne Knight (1750–1824) about the value of using sentimental **landscape paintings** as guides to landscape gardening, Repton soon saw the inappropriateness of this; moldering cottages were not, after all, "suitable habitations for affluence." He did, however, begin to diversify the areas adjacent to houses with trellises and flower gardens. This "gardenesque" tendency intensified after a carriage accident in 1811 limited his mobility, and it reached its zenith at Ashridge (*c.* 1814), where he designed 15 small, interconnected gardens, each devoted to a different plant or theme.

Like Brown, Repton developed an interest in **architecture** to complement his gardening, contributing to the popularization of the **Gothic revival** style. His interest in architecture led him and two sons, John Adey and George, into collaboration with **John Nash** from 1796 to 1799. The extent of his work and influence was enormous. His Red Books, his work on hundreds of sites, and his many published books popularized his ideas well into the 19th century.

Anne Kapler McCallum

Bibliography

Hyams, Edward S. *Capability Brown and Humphry Repton.* 1971.
Loudon, J.C., ed. *The Landscape Gardening and Landscape Architecture of the Late Humphry Repton, Esq., Being His Entire Works on These Subjects.* 1840; rpt. 1969.
Stroud, Dorothy. *Humphry Repton.* 1962.

Retailing

See Shopping and Retailing

Reynolds, Frederick (1764–1841)

Known mainly as a writer of comedies, Reynolds successfully began his playwriting career in 1785 with a **sentimental** drama, *Werter,* an adaptation of Johann Goethe's (1749–1832) **novel** *Werthers* (1774). The first of his many comedies was *The Dramatist: or, Stop Him Who Can!* (1789): Vapid, the dramatist of the title, provided a model for later playwrights. The very popular *How to Grow Rich* (1793) helped Reynolds grow rich. With Peter Miles Andrews (*d.* 1814)—and inspired by **Ann Radcliffe**—he wrote the melodrama *Mysteries of the Castle* (1795).

Reynolds adroitly combined the comedy of **manners** with sentiment and **satire** in plays such as *The Rage* (1794), but was not above bringing a dog on stage as the hero in *The Caravan* (1802). He wrote almost 100 comedies, melodramas, and tragedies. The comedies mirror the social life of the age of **George III**, and Reynolds has been called, despite his sentimentalism, the Thomas Shadwell of his age. His two-volume autobiography, *Life and Times of Frederick Reynolds* (1827), surprising for its almost merry perspective on the **French Revolution**, offers the most authoritative source on his life and work.

Chat Ewing

Bibliography

Nicoll, Allardyce. *A History of English Drama, 1660–1900.* Vol. 3, 1961. Vol. 4, 1960.
Reynolds, Frederick. *Life and Times of Frederick Reynolds.* 2 vols. 1827.

See also Dramatic Arts

Reynolds, Sir Joshua (1723–1792)

Reynolds's accomplishments as **portrait painter**, President of the **Royal Academy of Arts**, and author of the *Discourses Delivered at the Royal Academy* (1769–1791) rank him among the preeminent figures of Hanoverian Britain. Born in Plympton, he was educated by his father, then briefly apprenticed to Thomas Hudson, a **London** portrait painter, after which he returned home to practice conventional portrait painting in the style of his early three-quarter-length portrait of *Captain John Hamilton* (1746). In 1749 he embarked on the **Grand Tour** to strengthen his technique and study the ancient and modern masters. His Italian sketchbooks show him much absorbed by ancient sculpture as well as by works of the Venetian Renaissance painters Titian (*c.* 1477–1576), Tinoretto (1518–1594), and Veronese (1528–1588). While in Rome he completed a caricature parodying Raphael's (1483–1520) *School of Athens;* by replacing the figures in Raphael's *School* with prominent British lords and connoisseurs, he illustrated the friendly social relations and future **patronage** that **travel and tourism** were then providing young artists.

Reynolds returned to London in 1752 and immediately became a painter favored by the **aristocracy**. Scores of distinguished individuals sat for him. Borrowing poses and gestures from ancient and modern masters, he created a grand style of historical portrait painting, which presented his sitters in dignity and grace, and which often subtly linked their images to those of great men and women in history. Visual allusions were important in establishing this association with the heroic past. To the educated eye, the portrait *Commodore Keppel* (1752) presented Augustus Keppel ([1725–1786] naval commander, ultimately painted six times by Reynolds) in the stance of Apollo Belvedere, while the portrait *Mrs. Bouverie and Child* (1770) cast Harriet Bouverie (wife of the 1st earl of Radnor) in a Michelangelesque pose borrowed from the Sistine ceiling.

Sir Joshua Reynolds

As Reynolds's career prospered, his circle of associates widened to include many literary and political figures, some of whom were members of **Samuel Johnson**'s Literary **Club** (1764). He immortalized many of these friends in a collection of 13 portraits painted for the library of Henry Thrale (*d.* 1781). Included in the collection are *Giuseppe Baretti* (1773), *Edmund Burke* (1774), and *Samuel Johnson* (1778). These paintings reflect a shift in Reynolds's style from something deliberately grand and stately to more fluid and personal studies of character.

By frequenting societies that promoted the welfare of the arts, Reynolds established many lasting and influential relationships with other English artists. Through his involvement with the Society of Artists he became a founding member of the **Royal Academy** in 1768. His international success as a painter, as well as the diplomatic position he assumed during difficult moments in the academy's founding, resulted in his election as its first president. During a presidency that lasted 20 years he strengthened its reputation through his discourses, delivered at the annual distribution of prizes. Addressing the central issue of the relationship between theory and practice, he used these writings to analyze past art as well as to shape future thinking.

Reynolds, though much respected and admired throughout his career, had to wait rather long to receive Royal patronage. Although knighted (1769) by **George III** for his election as president of the Royal Academy, it was not until 1784, after the death of **Allan Ramsay**, that he was appointed painter to the king. By this time his eyesight and health were failing, and he had already been deaf for many years. He delivered his last discourse to the Royal Academy in 1790 and exhibited his final painting, *Lord Rawdon,* that same year. At his death he left behind a legacy of ideas as well as images that had brought new vitality to the tradition of British portrait painting.

Mary Ann A. Powers

Bibliography

Hilles, Frederick, ed. *Letters of Sir Joshua Reynolds.* 1929.

Hudson, Derek. *Sir Joshua Reynolds: A Personal Study.* 1958.

Penny, Nicholas, ed. *Reynolds.* 1986.

Pointon, Marcia. *Hanging the Head: Portraiture and Social Formation in Eighteenth-Century England.* 1993.

Reynolds, Sir Joshua. *Discourses on Art.* Ed. Robert R. Warks. 1975.

Solkin, David. *Painting for Money: The Visual Arts and the Public Sphere in Eighteenth-Century England.* 1993.

Wendorf, Richard. *The Elements of Life: Biography and Portrait-Painting in Stuart and Georgian England.* 1990.

See also Painting

Ribbonmen and Ribbonism

The period following the 1798 **Irish Rebellion** was characterized by intense economic competition and sectarian conflict in **Ireland**. Agrarian violence became chronic, and various movements such as the **Terry Alts** and **Shanavests**, which had begun life as faction groups, became the outlet for a mass of popular grievances. Ribbonism was the ultimate product, a movement that mobilized discontent behind the goals of **Catholic** nationalism.

Activity by Ribbonmen can be found as early as 1811, when they began to revitalize the surviving remnants of the **United Irish** and **Defender** movements. They drew in urban **craftsmen** and clerks, but also recruited heavily from **agricultural laborers** and cottiers in the countryside, especially from the 1820s on.

Although Ribbonism marked a vital stage in the politicization of the rural poor, economic issues were decisive in shaping the pace of activity. There were three major outbreaks of violence (1814–1816, 1821–1823, and 1831–1834), all with direct economic roots. The agitation of 1814 followed a severe winter and falling grain prices, and was directed against evictions and **wage** cuts in several counties. The immediate cause of the next episode of unrest was evictions in Limerick, but disruption rapidly became more widespread with poor potato crops and falls in agricultural prices. The outbreaks of the 1830s drew on similar economic distress and were exacerbated by anti-**tithe** activity. The movement displayed impressive longevity, with sporadic outbreaks as late as the 1850s, when elements of Ribbonism merged with Fenianism.

Although lacking the leadership and centralization of the United Irishmen, the movement was remarkable for its efficiency, foresight, and sophistication. Violent activity was carefully targeted, and outrages were usually concerned with a specific local issue. These tactics could bring considerable success, holding rents below market values and blunting the threat of eviction. The threat of mass disobedience implied by Ribbonism inevitably attracted the attention of the authorities, resulting in the Peace Preservation Act of 1833, which introduced courts of military justice for offenders.

E. W. McFarland

Bibliography

Beames, M.R. "Rural Conflict in Pre-famine Ireland." *Past and Present.* Vol. 81, pp. 75–91.

Cornewall, Lewis G. *On Local Disturbances in Ireland.* 1836.

Philipin, C.H.E. *Nationalism and Popular Protest in Ireland.* 1987.

Williams, T.D., ed. *Secret Societies in Ireland.* 1973.

See also Irish Land Settlement; Merthyr Rising; Radical War; Swing Riots; Whiteboys

Ricardo, David (1772–1823)

Ricardo, one of the great figures of early "political economy," applied strict standards of the scientific method to the study of finance and economics, and hence is considered the father of scientific **economic thought**. Born into a Jewish family which had immigrated from Holland, he lacked a classical education but was educated for a career in international **finance**. He married a beautiful **Quaker** girl and converted to **Unitarianism**; by age 30 he was a wealthy man, having followed his father into the **London** stock exchange. After 1815, with a fortune of £1 million, he retired to a country estate to write full time. In 1819 he was elected to Parliament and became an effective speaker for **radical** causes, including **religious toleration** and parliamentary reform.

Ricardo's first contribution to economics, *The High Price of Bullion* (1809), an important contribution to central **banking** theory, was in response to the controversy raging over the **Bank of England**'s decision to issue large numbers of bank notes to pay its debts. Ricardo argued that reliance on paper currency as a monetary standard, rather than gold, resulted in inflation, and explained that an economy based on the international gold standard responded more accurately to random economic shocks in the international market. To minimize the cost of supporting the gold standard he later proposed that when gold was converted to paper, government should restrict the new currency to large-denomination notes to avoid inflation.

Ricardo's major work, *The Principles of Political Economy and Taxation* (1817), set forth his argument on how social products were distributed among the three great social classes: landlords, workers, and owners of capital. Partly following **Adam Smith** and **Malthus**, he maintained that the value of commodities emerged from the amount of labor invested in them, that profits varied inversely with wages, that wages would always stay at workers' mere subsistence level because any pay increases would lead to **population** growth and hence downward pressure again on wages (the "iron law of wages"), that capitalists' fortunes too were limited by mutual competition, the constant need to invest, the pressure of wages, and hence the rising cost of land rents (rising according to population growth and ever more marginal cultivation), and thus that landowners (receivers of "unearned income") were the only clear beneficiaries of an expanding economy.

Ricardo's most important theorem pertained to international trade (his "law of comparative advantage" is still accepted as valid), but the translation of his principles into practical understanding had a greater contemporary impact. His theoretical postulation of "economic man" motivated solely by calculations of profit and loss was to inspire hardheaded liberal politicians and economists but horrify critics of capitalist economics. His claim that free trade in grain increased the productivity of labor and capital and thus sped growth and raised living standards, was unwelcome to landowners but acclaimed by opponents of the **Corn laws**, while his apprehensions about population growth cast him as an ally of Malthus, who indeed was his personal friend.

Ricardo was close to **James Mill** and **Jeremy Bentham**, and influenced their economic thought. A great popularizer of his ideas was his friend **Jane Marcet**. His style of economic analysis—spare, rigorous, and difficult—continues to influence economic theorizing today. His main contribution to economics was in the systematic application of the principle of competitive market equilibrium, though his approach to political theory, which viewed political differences as extensions of competing economic interests, has recently drawn specialists' attention.

David M. Levy

Bibliography

Hollander, Samuel. *The Economics of David Ricardo.* 1979.

Levy, David. "Ricardo and the Iron Law." *History of Political Economy.* Vol. 8, pp. 235–251.

Milgate, Murray, and Shannon C. Stimson. *Ricardian Politics.* 1991.

O'Driscoll, Gerald P. "The Ricardian Nonequivalence Theorem." *Journal of Political Economy.* Vol. 85, pp. 207–210.

Samuelson, Paul A. "The Canonical Classical Model of Political Economy." *Journal of Economic Literature.* Vol. 18, pp. 1415–1434.

Winch, Donald. *Riches and Poverty: An Intellectual History of Political Economy in Britain, 1750–1834.* 1996.

See also Entrepreneurs and Entrepreneurship; Hours, Wages, and Working Conditions; Torrens, Robert

Richardson, Samuel (1689–1761)

Richardson was one of the first major English novelists. His second novel, *Clarissa,* belongs among the masterpieces of world literature. A joiner's son, he was apprenticed to a printer and from 1721 on ran his own **London** printing firm. His early miscellaneous writings include *The Apprentice's Vade Mecum* (1732), written for the Stationers' Company; a much expanded and revised edition of **Daniel Defoe**'s *Tour thro'... Great Britain* (1738); and a revision of Sir Roger L'Estrange's (1616–1704) 1692 version of Aesop's *Fables* (1739).

Samuel Richardson

Unlike his great rival **Henry Fielding**, who is celebrated for his power and range, Richardson wrote all three of his novels in epistolary form, allowing his characters to speak for themselves through their **letters** and journals. His first novel, *Pamela* (1740), composed in 2 months when he was 50, grew out of a manual on letter writing he was then compiling (published in 1741 as *Letters Written to and for Particular Friends on the Most Important Occasions*). The novel describes the attempted seduction of a 15-year-old **servant** by her employer, her indignant resistance, and their eventual marriage, crossing class barriers. It was immensely popular. Spurious continuations written by others prompted Richardson to write his own sequel, depicting Pamela as wife and mother; both parts of the novel were published together in 1741.

A few years later, consulting with friends such as Aaron Hill (1685–1750) and **Edward Young**, Richardson began working on *Clarissa.* Among the longest novels in English, and employing a highly complex epistolary technique, this was published in 1747–1748. Its heroine, resisting pressure to accept an unpleasant but wealthy suitor, is abducted and raped by the brilliant and duplicitous libertine, Robert Lovelace; though he repents, she defies his attempts at reconciliation, and both eventually die tragically.

In his final novel, *Sir Charles Grandison,* published also in several installments (1753–1754), Richardson created an exemplary Christian hero beloved by two women, Harriet Byron and the Italian Clementina della Porretta, who ultimately gives way to the Englishwoman. Though much admired by later novelists such as **Jane Austen** and George Eliot (1819–1880), and containing many memorable examples of Richardson's "writing to the moment" technique, this vast work never acquired the following of *Pamela* and *Clarissa.* Richardson published no more fiction, though in 1755 he issued a *Collection of the Moral and Instructive Sentiments* compiled from his novels. His extensive contributions to Young's *Conjectures on Original Composition* (1759) made him virtually coauthor of this critical treatise also.

Richardson's fiction has long been celebrated for its realism, its minute attention to physical details of all kinds. It is equally known for its psychological depth, for carrying the torch, as Denis Diderot (1713–1784) commented, to the depths of the cave. Perhaps more than any other Hanoverian male author, Richardson was concerned with feminist issues. Recent critics have drawn attention to the unusual sympathy he displayed for the condition of women, and to the remarkable self-consciousness of his art. His novels were repeatedly revised; his correspondence gives insight into their composition and revision.

Peter Sabor

Bibliography

Carroll, John, ed. *Selected Letters of Samuel Richardson.* 1964.

Doody, Margaret Anne. *A Natural Passion: A Study of the Novels of Samuel Richardson.* 1974.

Eaves, T.C. Duncan, and Ben D. Kimpel. *Samuel Richardson: A Biography.* 1971.

Flynn, Carol Houlihan. *Samuel Richardson: A Man of Letters.* 1982.
Harris, Jocelyn. *Samuel Richardson.* 1987.
Keymer, Tom. *Richardson's* Clarissa *and the Eighteenth-Century Reader.* 1992.
Kinkead-Weekes, Mark. *Samuel Richardson: Dramatic Novelist.* 1973.
Sale, William M., Jr. *Samuel Richardson: A Bibliographical Record of His Literary Career.* 1936.
———. *Samuel Richardson: Master Printer.* 1950.
Smith, Sarah W. *Samuel Richardson: A Reference Guide.* 1974.

See also Novel; Publishers and Booksellers

Richmond, 3rd Duke of (Charles Lennox) (1735–1806)

Richmond entered **Whig** political life with the advantages of wealth, intelligence, speaking ability, and excellent connections. He was the competent and trusted deputy of the **Marquess of Rockingham**, yet he never became a political leader. Naturally aloof, often tactless and, for a duke, uncharacteristically susceptible to the growing **radicalism** of the age, Richmond offended many contemporaries (including **George III**) and even alienated his own nephew, **Charles James Fox**.

Richmond entered the **army** soon after succeeding to the dukedom (1750) and served with distinction in the **Seven Years' War**. He then turned to politics and angered the king with questions about the Regency Bill (1765). Joining the Rockingham Whigs, he pleased his leader with his frankness and honesty. For 10 years (1770–1780) the hard-working Richmond was a loyal but not uncritical deputy to Rockingham, until they disagreed over Richmond's radical plan for parliamentary reform. Richmond then became part of the **Shelburne** faction.

Richmond's refusal to follow Fox out of office (1782) created a rift and helped turn his interest to military reform. He served as Master-General of Ordnance (1782–1794) but lost his interest and effectiveness after the defeat (1786) of his bill for the fortification of naval dockyards. A confusion in the dispatch of artillery (1793) for the **French Revolutionary War** led to his dismissal.

P.J. Kulisheck

Bibliography

O'Gorman, Frank. *The Rise of Party in England: The Rockingham Whigs 1760–82.* 1975.
Olson, Alison Gilbert. *The Radical Duke: Career and Correspondence of Charles Lennox, Third Duke of Richmond.* 1961.

See also Whigs and Whiggism

Ridicule

See Wit and Ridicule

Rightboys

The Rightboy movement was part of a much larger wave of social and agrarian protest in **Ireland**, which began with the **Whiteboy** agitation of the 1760s, and persisted into Victorian times. The movement grew out of economic discontent on the borders of Cork and Kerry in 1785. By 1786 it had spread throughout Munster and neighboring Leinster counties. Like many rural secret societies of the period, its mode of operation was to act in the name of a fictitious and symbolic figure—in this case "Captain Right," who personified traditional notions of community solidarity and tenants' rights. The Rightboys' chief aim was the regulation and reduction of **tithes**, which had increased with the expansion of tillage after the passage of Foster's Corn Act (1784). This was an issue that transcended social class and encouraged the involvement of "Gentlemen White Boys" in the early stages of the movement. Nevertheless, recruitment was mainly from the small cottier and wage-earning classes.

With little sustained government opposition in the first 6 months of their existence, the Rightboys extended their agenda to include opposition to excessive priests' dues and the regulation of laborers' **wages**. As their agitation became more violently assertive in 1786, upper-class involvement ceased and the government was forced onto the offensive with a wave of repressive statutes. These met with limited success, however, and Rightboy disturbances continued in 1787 and early 1788. Although the movement subsequently faded, it may be credited with laying the ground for more sophisticated protest movements such as the **Defenders** and **Ribbonmen**.

E.W. McFarland

Bibliography

Bric, M. "Priest, Parson and Politics: The Rightboy Movement in County Cork, 1785–8." *Past and Present.* Vol. 100, pp. 75–173.
Cornewall, Lewis G. *On Local Disturbances in Ireland.* 1836.
Donnelly, J.S. "The Rightboy Movement, 1785–8." *Studia Hibernica.* Vol. 17–18, pp. 120–122.
Williams, T.D., ed. *Secret Societies in Ireland.* 1973.

See also Irish Land Settlement; Shanavests; Swing Riots; Terry Alts

Riot Act (1715)

Popular disturbances were endemic in the British Isles, and because of the absence, except in rare cases, of any local **police** forces capable of maintaining public order, they were apt to get out of control, requiring suppression then by force of arms. In the English legal system, riots tended to be dealt with as treasonable offenses. Late in the reign of **Queen Anne** there were unusually serious disorders in **London** accompanying the trial of Dr. Henry Sacheverell (1710) and the ratification of the Treaty of Utrecht (1713); then the High-Church riots and the **Jacobite** rebellion (1715) further demonstrated the problem of keeping public order. The result was the Riot Act, enacted by Parliament in 1715.

According to its provisions, unlawful assemblages of 12 or more persons could be dispersed by a proclamation from a local magistrate. If the people did not disperse within 1 hour, their disturbance would then be treated as a felony and therefore as a capital crime (though local riots were no longer to be dealt with under the treason law). Local authorities would not be held responsible if any rioters were injured or killed while being apprehended.

Despite these provisions, confusion remained as to whether "reading the Riot Act" had to precede any use of force. The first executions under the act's provisions came in 1716, and throughout the Hanoverian period it was read to disperse demonstrators. Among these occasions were disturbances connected with the **South Sea Bubble**, the **excise crisis**, the **Jew bill** (1753), the **Wilkes** protests (1763–1774), and, with most disastrous effect, the reform meeting in Manchester which concluded bloodily as the **Peterloo massacre**. Authorities in London during the **Gordon riots** were reluctant to read the Riot Act for fear of reprisals from the rioters. The act was amended in 1769 to make attacks on mills a felony, and it remained in effect until 1967.

Mark C. Herman

Bibliography

Quinault, R., and J. Stevenson, eds. *Popular Protest and Public Order.* 1974.

Stevenson, John. *Popular Disturbances in England, 1700–1870.* 1979.

See also Riots and Popular Disturbances

Riots and Popular Disturbances

Riots and popular disturbances were very frequent during the Hanoverian period. In a single year, such as 1740, 1756, or 1766, there might be riots in one or two dozen counties. A visiting American colonist remarked (1769) that within a year he had seen "riots in the country, about coin; riots about elections; riots about workhouses; riots of colliers, riots of weavers, riots of coal-heavers."

Such events took different forms and were sparked by different causes. *Riot* is defined as a violent disruption of the peace, typically caused by local circumstances such as high food prices, **game laws**, or a denial of traditional rights to common land; whereas *popular disturbances* sometimes had wider economic or political implications, were occasionally stirred up by self-interested politicians, and sometimes included large-scale political demonstrations and even armed combat. One element, however, that tied many such events together was their common tendency to represent an attempt by "the crowd" to enforce traditional and customary standards of fair dealing. Rioters tended to be traditionalists rather than revolutionaries, interested in maintaining the ties of paternalist society more than in discarding them.

The first two decades of the 18th century were particularly full of riots and political violence. In an effort to deal more effectively with such disorders, Parliament passed the **Riot Act** (1715), which made a felony, and hence a capital crime, of the failure of a group of 12 or more persons to disperse within 1 hour after being ordered to do so, and also prohibited attempts to prevent the issuing of orders to disperse, as well as any attempt to destroy registered chapels, churches, places of worship, houses, dwellings, barns, or stables.

Despite this, subsequent political **elections** and rivalries between **Whig** and **Tory**, Hanoverian and **Jacobite**, often produced disturbances, as did religious tensions that resulted in physical attacks on **dissenters** or **Catholics** and their property. Festivals and public celebrations of political anniversaries frequently got out of hand, as did fights and quarrels. Recruiting for the armed services often produced disorders, and protests against the Militia Act (1757) resulted in a full-scale riot. Strikes for higher **wages**, labor disputes characterized as "collective bargaining by riot," and machine-breaking were frequently met by the reading of the Riot Act. Agrarian protests, pulling down **enclosures**, and food riots were common occurrences. Demonstrations against **taxes** could degenerate into large-scale disturbances, which caused physical injuries and property damage. Attempts to combat **smuggling** and **poaching** sometimes produced what amounted to pitched battles with authorities. **Mutinies** in the military, and attempts to overthrow the government such as those involved in the **Fifteen** and **Forty-five**, can also be classified as large-scale popular disturbances, though it is less confusing to define these last simply as out-and-out rebellions.

Many protests were successful, the authorities lacking the means and sometimes the will to put them down, and believing also that it was perhaps better to do nothing than make an open display of weakness. Also, for the most part, violence perpetrated against persons and property was selective, focusing on those who were felt to be centrally responsible for the distress or particular grievance. As noted earlier, most disorders involved attempts to preserve the status quo in the face of changes that adversely affected those who became participants. In general, most participants were lower-class or working-class people, sometimes led by skilled artisans or a small number of professional people. Although in some instances abuse was heaped on the wealthy who also were sometimes forced to join in the action, there were few fatal episodes; but the longer a disturbance lasted, the more likely it was to become violent. Some political riots tended to be supportive of church and king, and involved appeals to **patriotism**, though the Jacobite rebellions of 1715 and 1745 were again notable exceptions.

Despite a gradual growth of more organized and peaceful means of expressing concerns, disturbances in the early 19th century grew larger in scope and hence more threatening as the events of the **French Revolution** emboldened those who tried to emulate revolutionaries in **France**. But although, as in the **Spa Fields riot** or the **Cato Street conspiracy**, some **radicals** might plot to seize important buildings or to kill national leaders, their leaders (**Henry Hunt**, for example) often failed to support such desperate measures, and government spies also played a role in defeating them.

Over the whole period, the most serious disturbances in England before 1789 were the Jacobite rebellions mentioned above, the **Wilkes** riots (1763–1774), and the **Gordon riots**. The early 1790s saw several huge demonstrations each numbering 100,000 people, which occurred in London and were organized by the **London Corresponding Society**. Later came the actions of the **Luddites** (1811, 1812), the Spa Fields riot, the Pentrich rising (1817), the **Peterloo massacre**, demonstrations during the **Queen Caroline** affair (1820), the very widespread agrarian **Swing riots**, large spontaneous outbreaks during the **Reform act** crisis of 1831–1832, and the actions that mark the beginning of the Chartist movement (1837). Attacks on cholera hospitals, protests against the **New Poor Law**, and resistance to the Metropolitan Police in London were disturbances that spilled over into the Victorian Era.

In **Ireland**, riots tended to be about land rather than food, and rural unrest often involved action by Catholic tenants against Protestant landlords. A secret society operating at night, the **Whiteboys**, sent threatening letters and demonstrated against increases in rent and evictions in 1761–1765. The **Rightboys** of the 1780s protested against **tithes**, rents, and low **wages**. **Defenderism**, anti-Protestant in character, was a later form of agrarian protest, which had links with the **United Irishmen** and supported plans for a French invasion during the **French Revolution**. Scholars argue that the Irish militia riots (1793) marked a new phase of peasant protest because of the greater instance of widespread violence. The **Irish rebellion** (1798), spurred by harsh government measures and a prospective French invasion, resulted in the deaths of 30,000 people; another ill-fated rebellion failed in 1803. **Ribbonism** joined together discontented urban and rural elements which, driven by economic hardship, fomented mass disobedience and acts of violence throughout the period 1814–1834.

Scottish riots and disturbances typically stemmed from protests against taxes and grain shortages. The **Malt Tax riots** (1725) were precipitated by a 3-pence tax on a bushel of malt. In **Edinburgh** the **Porteous riots** (1736), triggered by the execution of a smuggler and by resentment over indirect taxes, resulted in the deaths of innocent bystanders. As in England, forced service in the military could spark **militia riots** such as those in reaction to the Scottish Militia Act (1797). Anti-Catholic riots, similar to the Gordon riots (1780), broke out in 1779, while the 1790s experienced large demonstrations for political reform, rivaling those in London. Deteriorating economic conditions during and immediately after the **Napoleonic Wars** prompted handloom weavers to attempt a general uprising in western Scotland, the **Radical war** (1820), which authorities defeated in the so-called Battle of Bonnymuir. Although workers in **Glasgow** staged a strike in support, nothing else materialized. Food riots were numerous, and the **Highland clearances** of land produced agricultural riots periodically. The **Merthyr rising** in **Wales** (1831) was a bloody event partly political and partly industrial in its origins.

Mark C. Herman

Bibliography

Darvall, Frank Ongley. *Popular Disturbances and Public Disorder in Regency England.* 1934.

Dunbabin, J.P.D. *Rural Discontent in Nineteenth-Century Britain.* 1974.

Ellis, Peter B., and Seamus Mac a'Ghobhainn. *The Scottish Insurrection of 1820.* 1970.

Logue, Kenneth J. *Popular Disturbances in Scotland, 1780–1815.* 1979.

Philpin, C.H.E., ed. *Nationalism and Popular Protest in Ireland.* 1987.

Rudé, George. *The Crowd in History, 1730–1848.* 1964.

Stevenson, John. *Popular Disturbances in England, 1700–1870.* 2nd ed., 1992.

Thomis, Malcolm I., and Peter Holt. *Threats of Revolution in Britain, 1789–1848.* 1977.

Roads, Streets, and Turnpikes

Around 1700, Britain's roads provoked much grumbling by contemporaries. The poorness of the road system was partly due to the fact that maintenance was the responsibility of the parish; in many cases it was difficult to get local people to fulfill their statutory obligations or to find the necessary skilled labor to oversee operations. So rutted, muddy, and unsatisfactory were the roads that in order to protect them, an Act of Parliament (1753) stated that wheel rims on waggons had to be at least 9-inches wide. If this spared roads, it could not have pleased horses.

The rise of the turnpikes signified an attempt to overcome these problems. The aim of turnpike trusts was to raise money to repair and improve stretches of road, and provide funds for future maintenance, through tolls paid by road users. Originally conceived in the 17th century, the idea was developed considerably during the 18th century and was adopted in many parts of the country where commercial traffic was significantly expanding. Before 1750, investors tended to be landowners and gentlemen, but these were soon joined by **merchants**, manufacturers, artisans, and shopkeepers, a reflection of changing economic conditions. Despite their increasing popularity, however, turnpikes never amounted to even one-fifth of the nation's total road network.

The techniques of road building were also improved. John Metcalfe (1717–1810) paid particular attention to foundations and camber, whereas **John Loudon McAdam** was more concerned with drainage. **Thomas Telford**, builder of the Holyhead Road, used stone to make a smooth, hard surface. Road building was also important for strategic reasons. As a result of the **Jacobite** rebellions of 1715 and 1745, a program of road and bridge building was carried out in the Scottish Highlands to assist the movement of troops. After the Irish **Act of Union**, major public funding was invested in the Holyhead Road to assist military and civil communications with **Ireland**.

Increasing economic activity was reflected in the developing nature of road transport. In the late 17th century there was a network carrying **domestic commerce** to and from **London**, but during the 18th century this was extended to include links between many **provincial towns**. Over long distances, freight tended to consist of valuable goods because high road-hauling costs made it uneconomical to move cheap,

A turnpike entrance

heavy items such as **coal**, grain, and industrial raw material (often carried long distance by **coastal shipping**). Many scheduled services operated on a regular basis, even daily on the busiest routes. Contemporaries often complained of the volume of such traffic on the popular main roads, particularly around London (where danger from **highwaymen** was also a problem). In areas where roads were poor, or carts impractical, strings of pack horses were used to move goods. These were popular in upland areas such as the Benzine towns of Yorkshire and Lancashire, where many people were employed in the **domestic production** of **textiles**.

The improvement of roads led to better **coaching** services, and journey times declined between important centers. In the 1750s it took 10 days to travel from London to **Edinburgh**; by 1836 it took two. Time saving such as this also greatly improved **postal services**. The heyday of the stagecoach lasted from the 1770s to the 1830s; then competition from the emerging **railway** system began to be felt.

Many urban streets were every bit as poor as the worst of roads—indeed poorer, when the added hazard of piles of rubbish is considered. In expanding **cities** such as **Liverpool** and **Glasgow**, civic improvement trusts were established, and some streets, often in the better areas, were properly paved. In London the construction of various bridges over the Thames meant that nearby streets had to be improved and widened to cope with the increase in traffic. With the development of piped-in gas to towns in the early 19th century it became possible to provide better street lighting, considerably improving the safety of urban residents at night.

A.J.G. Cummings

Bibliography

Albert, W. *The Turnpike Road System in England, 1663–1840.* 1972.

Bagwell, Philip. *The Transport Revolution from 1770.* 1974.

Dyos, H.J., and D.H. Aldcroft. *British Transport.* 1974.

Pawson, Eric. *Transport and Economy: The Turnpike Roads of 18th Century Britain.* 1977.

Robertson, William (1721–1793)

Robertson, a prominent **Edinburgh** historian, academician, and man of letters, was closely connected with **David Hume** and other luminaries of the **Scottish Enlightenment**. He also played a major role in the **Church of Scotland** by virtue of his position as the acknowledged leader of the ecclesiastical party known as the Moderates. Robertson earned considerable fame and income from his three major historical works: *The History of Scotland* (1759), *The History of Charles V* (1769), and *The History of America* (1777); and in his last years he published an *Historical Disquisition* on ancient India (1791). Thanks to the **patronage** of **Lord Bute**, Robertson was from 1762 until his death the principal of the University of Edinburgh. Throughout this period he also served as one of the ministers of Old Greyfriars Church in Edinburgh, and he actively participated in Edinburgh's rich **club** life by taking part in organizations such as the Select Society and the **Royal Society of Edinburgh**, which he helped to found.

The son of a Presbyterian minister, Robertson was educated at the University of Edinburgh, where he took both the arts and divinity courses and made the acquaintance of **Hugh Blair**, **Alexander Carlyle**, **Adam Ferguson**, **John Home**, and other young men with whom he would remain closely affiliated. Under Robertson's leadership, these "Moderate literati" greatly enhanced the reputation of Edinburgh as a center of polite learning, and their commitment to the values of **religious toleration**, freedom of expression, and polite preaching did much to transform the Church of Scotland into an **Enlightenment** institution. In 1779, however, Robertson's attempts to liberalize the harsh laws against **Roman Catholics** provoked death threats, and this trying experience was probably one of the reasons for his stepping down as the leader of the dominant Moderate party in the church in 1780. Though culturally liberal, Robertson was a conservative **Whig** in politics, supportive of Britain in the **War of American Independence** and of the right of patrons to nominate ministers to vacant churches.

In his own time, Robertson's enormous popularity as an historian rested mostly on his clear and polite writing style, the thoroughness of his narrative accounts, and his commitment to a balanced, evenhanded approach to controversial issues and figures such as Mary, Queen of Scots (1542–1587) and John Knox (1505–1572). If these attributes have lost much of their appeal today, the sweeping introduction to the *History of Charles V,* "A View of the Progress of Society in Europe," and the sociological discussion of native American culture in book four of the *History of America* remain distinguished achievements of the Scottish Enlightenment. When his accomplishments as historian and man of letters are considered along with his activities as the foremost academic and ecclesiastical leader in late-18th-century Scotland, Robertson emerges as one of the intellectual luminaries of the age.

Richard B. Sher

Bibliography

Black, J.B. *The Art of History: A Study of Four Great Historians of the Eighteenth Century.* 1926.

Fearnley-Sander, Mary. "Philosophical History and the Scottish Reformation: William Robertson and the Knoxian Tradition." *Historical Journal.* Vol. 33, pp. 323–338.

Kidd, Colin. *Subverting Scotland's Past: Scottish Whig Historians and the Creation of an Anglo–British Identity, 1689–c. 1820.* 1993.

Sher, Richard B. *Church and University in the Scottish Enlightenment: The Moderate Literati of Edinburgh.* 1985.

Smitten, Jeffrey. "William Robertson," in *The Dictionary of Literary Biography.* Vol. 104, pp. 260–268.

———. "Impartiality in Robertson's *History of America.*" *Eighteenth-Century Studies.* Vol. 19, pp. 56–77.

Womersley, David J. "The Historical Writings of William Robertson." *Journal of the History of Ideas.* Vol. 47, pp. 497–506.

See also History Writing and Historians; Scotland and Scottish Culture; Scottish Universities

Robinson, Henry Crabbe (1775–1867)

A prolific diarist and engaging conversationalist, Robinson is best remembered for the company he kept. Maintaining extensive private records of his encounters and correspondence with **Wordsworth**, **Coleridge**, **Lamb**, and other leading literary figures, and painting detailed portraits of social and literary life, he significantly contributed to our picture of the **Romantic** period.

Born in Bury St. Edmunds, Robinson attended private school. He entered a **London** solicitor's office (1796); resided in Germany (1800–1805), where he became acquainted with Goethe (1749–1832) and Schiller (1759–1805); became a foreign correspondent for *The Times* and covered **Sir John Moore**'s military adventures in Spain; was called to the bar (1813); and practiced law for 15 years before retiring. He was a founding member of the Athenaeum **Club** (1824) and of University College, London. His breakfast parties, like those of **Samuel Rogers**, were known for their brilliant company.

Unfortunately, Robinson never organized or cataloged his observations. The documents that remained after his death (35 volumes of diaries, 32 of letters, 30 of **travel** journals, four of reminiscences, and one of anecdotes) are now housed at Dr. Williams's Library, London. Dr. Thomas Sadler selected excerpts from these and published them as the *Diary, Reminiscences, and Correspondences of Henry Crabbe Robinson* (1869).

Lisa Altomari

Bibliography

Hudson, Derek, ed. *The Diary of Henry Crabbe Robinson: An Abridgement.* 1967.

Morley, Edith J. *The Life and Times of Henry Crabbe Robinson.* 1935.

———, ed. *Blake, Coleridge, Wordsworth, Lamb, etc.: Being Selections from the Remains of Henry Crabbe Robinson.* 1932.

Sadler, Thomas, ed. *Diary, Reminiscences and Correspondences of Henry Crabbe Robinson.* 1869, 1872.

Rockingham, 2nd Marquess of (Charles Watson-Wentworth) (1730–1782)

Rockingham was the patron of **Edmund Burke**, but Burke's political concepts were based on Rockingham's principles about the corrupting influences of the Court. Rockingham was the first British politician to put commitment to party leadership above desire for office, and to hold to a consistent policy while in office as well as in **opposition**. His refusal to court **George III**'s favor while he was First Lord of the Treasury (1765–1766 and 1782) enhanced his reputation but shortened his time in office.

Rockingham's political experience as an independent country **Whig** in Yorkshire colored his attitude toward the Court. His alliance with the **Newcastle** Whigs left him permanently suspicious of any adherents of the **Bute** faction. He proved a poor administrator. He had never held a ministerial post before his appointment to the treasury, and his inefficiency and poor showing in debate added to the problems created by his inexperience.

Rockingham emphasized the importance of public opinion in forming his policies, and obtained repeal (1766) of the **Stamp Act** because of complaints from British **merchants** and manufacturers. Although he favored conciliation toward America, his administration passed the **Declaratory Act** (1766), which asserted British sovereignty over the colonies. The program of **economical reform** his party pushed through Parliament (1782) reflected his constitutional principles and began the steady decline in Royal political power. The Rockingham Whigs are regarded as the foundation of the Victorian Whig party.

P.J. Kulisheck

Bibliography

Albemarle, George Thomas Keppel, Earl of. *Memoirs of the Marquis of Rockingham and His Contemporaries.* 1852.
Guttridge, G.H. *The Early Career of Lord Rockingham.* 1952.
Hoffman, Ross. *The Marquis: A Study of Lord Rockingham, 1730–1782.* 1973.
Langford, Paul. *The First Rockingham Administration, 1765–1766.* 1973.
O'Gorman, Frank. *The Rise of Party in England: The Rockingham Whigs, 1760–82.* 1975.

See also Party Politics

Rockites and Rockism

The Rockites were part of the proliferation of rural protest movements in **Ireland** in the decades immediately following the **Act of Union** (1800); even public officials and participants found it difficult to separate and identify these groups. Though less politicized than the **Ribbonmen**—their contemporaries in the 1820s—the Rockites nevertheless shared their alternative view of law and government, aiming to maintain tenant rights, fair rents, and the traditional "moral economy" in the countryside. These aims were to be accomplished by the tactics of nocturnal mass meetings and the often violent intimidation of individuals perceived to have broken the code of the peasant community.

Like the **Terry Alts**, the Rockites assumed the name of a mythical leader, "Captain Rock" (sometimes "General Rock"), such symbolism serving to bind members in their common cause. The Rockites gained particular notoriety through their literary use by **Thomas Moore** in his *Memoirs of Captain Rock* (1824), a work that satirized the literary form of family **biography** to lay bare real reasons for Irish disaffection.

E.W. McFarland

Bibliography

Clark, S., and J.S. Donnelly, Jr. *Irish Peasants: Violence and Political Unrest, 1780–1914.* 1983.
Cornewall, Lewis G. *On Local Disturbances in Ireland.* 1836.

See also Rightboys; Shanavests; Whiteboys

Rodney, George (1719–1792)

Rodney has been described as one of the most colorful, brash, flamboyant yet intolerable sea captains of the 18th century. He entered the Royal **Navy** in 1732 and rose rapidly, receiving his first command as Captain of the 60-gun frigate H.M.S. *Plymouth* at age 23 (1742). Distinguishing himself in the **War of Austrian Succession**, he was afterward made Governor of **Newfoundland** (until 1752). During the **Seven Years' War** he wrought havoc on the French, destroying many French flat-bottomed boats gathered at Le Havre for the invasion of Britain (1759), and then, as Commander in Chief of the Leeward Islands station, captured Martinique and several other French **West Indies** islands (1762), feats that earned him promotion to Vice-Admiral and a baronetcy (1764).

Rodney sat in the **House of Commons** from 1751, representing several pocket **boroughs** under the control of the **Duke of Newcastle**. In 1768 he was, however, nearly ruined in a contest over a seat for Northampton (paying some £30,000 to win it), and was plagued thereafter by severe financial problems. He commanded the Jamaica station in 1771–1774 ("a complete slave to women and to play," according to W.E.H. Lecky), and was again given the Leeward Islands command (1779) during the **War of American Independence**. His greatest victories were against the Spanish off Cape Finisterre and off Cape Vincent in January 1780 (relieving the siege of Gibraltar), and against the French off Dominica in the Battle of the Saints (12 April 1782), when, employing novel tactics later used by **Admiral Nelson** (viz., breaking the enemy line and fighting a general action rather than firing in line), he trapped and devastated a force under Admiral de Grasse.

Unfortunately, Rodney, aged and unwell, failed to pursue the fleeing survivors, which sparked criticism from **Admiral Hood** and others. But the Saints victory, though it did little to reverse the shifting balance of naval power, did prevent an invasion of Jamaica (the jewel of the British West Indies), left

Admiral George Rodney

Britain in a better position at the **Treaty of Paris** (1783), and earned the retiring Rodney a barony and a considerable pension (£2,000 a year).

Stanley D.M. Carpenter

Bibliography

Creswell, John. *British Admirals of the Eighteenth Century: Tactics in Battle.* 1972.

Macintyre, Donald. *Admiral Rodney.* 1962.

Spinney, David. *Rodney.* 1969.

Syrett, David, and R.L. DiNardo, eds. *The Commissioned Sea Officers of the Royal Navy, 1660–1815.* 1994.

See also Navy; War and Military Engagements

Roebuck, John (1718–1794)

A physician, scientist, and **entrepreneur**, Roebuck, whose friends included **David Hume** and **Adam Smith**, was a typical product of the **Scottish Enlightenment**. Born in Sheffield, he studied **medicine** at Edinburgh University and Leyden in the Netherlands. As a student he became fascinated by science and its practical application to industry. Setting up as a physician in **Birmingham**, Roebuck established a chemistry laboratory and entered into partnership with Samuel Garbett (1717–1803) to refine gold and silver, establishing a works to produce the required sulphuric acid by an improved process (1746) using lead instead of glass vessels. In 1749, together with William Caddell (1708–1777), he and Garbett opened the first such plant in **Scotland** at Prestonpans, near **Edinburgh**. Sulphuric acid proved of great value to industry, being used in cleaning wool, bleaching textiles, and making soap and glass.

In 1759 the three partners founded **Carron Ironworks** near Falkirk, based largely on a plan by Roebuck. While at Carron, Roebuck assisted **James Watt** in the development of his ideas for the **steam engine**. He also established a coal company at nearby Bo'ness to supply Carron. Pushed out of Carron in 1766, he was bankrupted in 1773 but given an allowance by his trustees, who allowed him to manage the coalworks. A restless and excitable man, his scientific talents exceeded his entrepreneurial skills, the former bringing him fellowships of the **Royal Society** and the **Royal Society of Edinburgh**.

A.J.G. Cummings

Bibliography

Butt, John. *The Industrial Archaeology of Scotland.* 1967.

Campbell, R.H. *Carron Company.* 1961.

See also Chemical Industry; Iron Industry; Science, Technology, and Invention

Rogers, Samuel (1763–1855)

Rogers is today considered more important to social than to literary history. His recollections (*Table-Talk,* 1856) of actors, authors, artists, politicians, and other **London** luminaries whom he met and entertained during his long life are of more interest than his once popular poems such as *The Pleasures of*

Samuel Rogers

Memory (1792) and *Italy* (1822; revised 1830). After reading *Pleasures,* **Lord Byron** dubbed the author "melodious Rogers" in *English Bards and Scotch Reviewers* (1809), dedicated *The Giaour* to him (1813), and published *Lara* with Rogers's *Jacqueline* (a tale about a runaway bride with a forgiving father) in 1814. But others were less generous. **Hazlitt** commented (1818) that "there is no other fault to be found in *The Pleasures of Memory* than a want of taste and genius."

A poet of the 18th century rather than a **Romantic**, Rogers, a banker, was financially secure. He composed when he pleased. He filled his house with artists and their art, and was well known for generosity and sharp **wit**. Though Byron recognized that he did not belong "in the higher fields of Parnassus," he remarked that "he has, at least, cultivated a very pretty flower-garden at its base." Rogers refused the **poet laureateship** which Alfred Tennyson (1809–1892) accepted in 1850.

Peter A. Tasch

Bibliography

Powell, G.H. *Reminiscences and Table-Talk of Samuel Rogers.* 1903.

Renwick, W.L. *Oxford History of English Literature.* Vol. 9. 1963.

Weeks, Donald. "Samuel Rogers: Man of Taste," *Publications of the Modern Language Association.* Vol. 62, pp. 472–486.

Roman Catholicism

In **Scotland**, Roman Catholicism, while proscribed since the Reformation, survived in scattered groups, particularly among some Highland clans. Governance was exercised by vicars apostolic appointed by the pope (down to 1878, at which time the church hierarchy was restored under two archbishops and four bishops). Apart from the strength it seemed to lend to

Jacobitism, Scottish Catholicism was of negligible significance in the Hanoverian period.

In **Ireland**, by contrast, Roman Catholicism was the religion of the masses—the Irish natives. This was the only country in Western Europe in which a majority was persecuted by a minority. In 1714 the Catholics owned little more than 10% of the land, primarily in Mayo and Galway in the west, Antrim in the northeast, and in **Dublin** county on the east. The great majority of Catholics were tenants on the large estates previously confiscated by the **Anglo–Irish Protestant ascendancy**, which had spread over the country in the course of **Irish land settlement**. Often, Catholic tenants were supervised by brutal agents working for absentee landlords. A major grievance was the **tithe** they were forced to pay to the established Church of Ireland, the church of the English minority. **Penal laws** had the effect of further impoverishing them by keeping them out of public affairs and working against their acquisition of any additional land. These laws, which remained in effect until 1778, prohibited Catholics from purchasing or inheriting land, and subjected landowning Catholics to an annual double land tax. They also excluded Catholics from any rank in the armed forces and from the bar. This legislation struck hard at property-owners, and by encouraging conformity, effectively thinned the ranks of the Catholic **gentry**. Not surprisingly, some Catholic landlords and a number of **middle-class** Catholics converted to the established church as time went by, so that by 1778 scarcely 5% of Irish land remained in Catholic hands.

Under such circumstances as these, the more salient aspects of Irish–Catholic history in the 18th century largely come down, on the one hand, to exotic tales about individual priests and soldiers who left Ireland for the Continent (an estimated 450,000 emigrated between 1691 and 1745), and, on the other, to the criminal activities of the oppressed and faceless masses, for example the **smugglers** who attempted to evade the unfair restraints imposed on Irish industry and trade, and the attacks by shadowy agrarian secret societies such as the **Whiteboys** and **Hearts of Oak** on landlords, tithes, and the various schemes of "improvement" directed against customary Irish rights.

Hundreds of regular Catholic clergy and many bishops were banished from the country in the 1690s in the wake of the **Battle of the Boyne**, but despite the savage laws ostensibly designed to eradicate Catholic worship, and confiscation by the established church of all the old Catholic church buildings, cathedrals, and monasteries, worship was in fact permitted in stables and storehouses, and increasingly after around 1730 in modest chapels. The priesthood went unmolested and were permitted to reorganize so long as they taught obedience to the government and respect for property; and there were few openly antigovernment priests until after the **Act of Union** (1800).

Nonetheless, the condition of Irish Catholics improved in the latter 18th century. Attempts were made from the 1760s to relax the penal laws, but this had little effect until the **War of American Independence**. The **London** government then desired to conciliate Ireland's Catholics in order to immunize England against a French invasion, and also wished to drop the penal code's prohibitions against Catholics bearing arms so as to recruit Irishmen for military service. The result was the **Catholic Relief Act** of 1778, passed in both London and Dublin (despite opposition in the **Irish Parliament**, which was composed exclusively of Irish Protestants). This act repealed the prohibition on Catholic purchase and inheritance of land (requiring, in exchange, oaths of loyalty to the Crown), and opened the lower ranks of the military to Catholics. It was followed by another Catholic Relief Bill in 1791, which granted Catholics limited access to commissioned service, abolished the double land tax, and explicitly permitted the saying and hearing of mass, which for over 200 years had in theory been prohibited under penalty of death. In 1793, when foreign intervention was again a threat, the Irish Parliament provided further relief by giving Catholics at last the franchise for elections to the Irish Parliament (though they were not permitted to sit in it), and admission to most civil offices.

The late Hanoverian period saw a downturn again in Irish Catholic fortunes. The **United Irishmen** attempted to unite Catholic with Protestant **radicals** in a common cause of radical reform, but this collapsed with the crushing of the **Irish rebellion** of 1798. The Act of Union which followed was disastrous from the Catholic point of view because it abolished the Irish Parliament and submerged Irish Catholic political rights again in the larger British polity. **Emmet**'s insurrection was the first reaction against the union. The struggle for political rights and **Catholic emancipation** followed (achieved in 1829), and in 1838 the hated tithes were commuted. This all resulted in a much stronger and more exclusive identification between Irish Catholicism and Irish **nationalism** than in the 1780s, when Protestants had been the chief Irish **patriots** and had also defied London. In the meantime, the Irish **population** grew enormously, from 2.8 million in 1785 to 5.3 million in 1803 to around 8 million by 1837, and though Catholics led other Irishmen in **emigration** because of their relative **poverty**, the disastrous economic effects of the union kept most of them in conditions not far removed from serfdom.

In England, the Catholic Church in the first half of the 18th century experienced a period of modest progress and consolidation. This set the stage for its very marked expansion between 1770, when English Catholics numbered 80,000; and 1850, when they numbered 750,000. Two significant changes accompanied these developments. First, the number of urban, middle-class and working-class Catholics increased at the expense of the previously dominant rural population under the control of Catholic gentry. Second, and related to this, the balance of power within the Catholic Church shifted from the secular **aristocracy** to the clergy.

Growth and consolidation during the early Hanoverian period was made possible by several factors. Perhaps most important was the discrepancy, in England as in Ireland, between the passage and the full enforcement of anti–Catholic statutes. This pattern was evident from early in the century, even when the Catholic community still lay under the shadow of the penal laws and the Jacobite **Fifteen**. For the harshness of the anti–Catholic code was softened by a variety of positive factors. The **Toleration Act** (1689) virtually eliminated the offense of recusancy (refusing to attend services in the **Church of England**), and other developments favorable to Catholics occurred during the 1690s, including passage of the Treason Act (1696), which gave Catholics a reasonable chance for a fair trial when accused of printing their (officially illegal) books. Moreover, a variety of lucrative opportunities in trade remained open to middle-class urban Catholics, and their numbers and wealth increased. Urban Catholics further benefited from the thriving mid-century economic climate, which offset to some extent the burden of the double land tax imposed on their rural coreligionists.

The number of English Catholics swelled as a result of Irish immigration, which also expanded the numbers of working-class Catholics in industrial areas, particularly in London and on the west coast. Despite occasional manifestations of anti–Catholic feeling in such laws as the **Marriage Act** of 1753 (which denied validity to all marriages not conducted in Anglican churches and according to Anglican rites) and the **Gordon riots** of 1780 (which exploded partly in response to the passage of the first Catholic Relief Act in 1778), Catholics also benefited from the increasingly tolerant climate of the **Enlightenment**. For the most part, they repudiated Jacobitism after 1715: in 1719 the Vicar-Apostolic John Stonor publicly advocated a break with the Stuarts and a Catholic declaration of loyalty to the house of Hanover. By the time of the **Forty-five**, few Catholics retained faith in the Stuart cause. A corresponding moderation in Protestant attitudes manifested itself in the willingness of many Protestants to act for Catholics in the purchase of property, enabling them to buy land with impunity despite laws to the contrary. Even **George III** smiled upon the Catholics when in the 1770s he visited the estates of two of the oldest and wealthiest English Catholic families.

This relaxation of denominational tensions prepared the way for the dismantling of Catholic penal legislation, which began with parliamentary passage of the first Catholic Relief Act (1778) and the Relief Bill of 1791. Only with Catholic emancipation, however, were Catholics, freed at last from the restrictions imposed by the **Test Acts** of the 1670s, allowed to hold public office and participate fully in the political life of the country.

From 1770 to 1830 the cumulative effect of many changes in the membership and structure of the English Catholic community became fully apparent. In the 1770s and 1780s the continuing predominance of the secular aristocracy at the expense of the clergy, and the growing size of the Catholic population itself (nearly 25,000 Catholics now lived in London), were reflected in the **Catholic committees** which promoted the relief acts (and their offshoots, the Cisalpine **Club** and the Catholic Board). The anticlerical magnates on these committees favored lay control of church policy and urged a strong lay voice in the selection of Catholic bishops. Antipapist, antihierarchical, and passionately loyal to England, they favored minimal ties to Rome and hoped to create an English Catholicism cleansed of its counterreformation accretions.

In the wake of the **French Revolution**, however, liberal reformism fell from favor. This permitted growing clerical ascendancy. The same development was fostered by other long-term factors such as the decline of traditional rural Catholicism (with its congregations centered on the estates of local gentry and subject to their control), and the corresponding growth of a secure congregational structure centered on the mass house or chapel in town and countryside. These trends gave the clergy a new confidence and enabled them by 1830 to forge ahead with significant control over a much more diverse Catholic population.

Susan E. Rosa

Bibliography

Aveling, J.C.H. *The Handle and the Axe: The Catholic Recusants in England from Reformation to Emancipation.* 1976.

Bossy, John. "Catholic Lancashire in the Eighteenth Century," in J. Bossy and P.J. Jupp, eds., *Essays Presented to Michael Roberts.* 1976a.

———. *The English Catholic Community 1570–1850.* 1976b.

———. "English Catholics after 1688," in O.P. Grell, J.I. Israel, and N. Tyacke, eds., *From Persecution to Toleration: The Glorious Revolution and Religion in England.* 1991.

Connell, Joan. *The Roman Catholic Church in England, 1780–1850: A Study in Internal Politics.* 1984.

Connolly, Sean J. *Religion, Law, and Power: The Making of Protestant Ireland, 1660–1760.* 1992.

Corish, Patrick J. *The Catholic Community in the Seventeenth and Eighteenth Centuries.* 1981.

———. *The Irish Catholic Experience: A Historical Survey.* 1985.

Leys, M.D.R. *Catholics in England, 1559–1829: A Social History.* 1961.

See also Irish Church Act

Romanticism and Romantic Style

It was once generally believed that English literary Romanticism was a more or less definite style of emotional writing, thinking, and feeling that characterized the era 1790–1830 and that represented in some manner an inversion or repudiation of the "cool" **Augustan** literary values of the age of Queen Anne earlier. But today much controversy surrounds this theory. The very idea of the coherence or underlying unity of Romantic literature has been undermined by theories emphasizing its fragmentation and internal contradictions. Perhaps all one can say now is that there was no single literary style at all during the Romantic period, but rather a multistyle, whose varied threads expressed the literary and intellectual heritage of Britain, the leading tendencies of a changing and expanding society, and the unusually rich but turbulent lives of the greatest writers of that age.

The first generation of "Romantic" writers (active in the 1790s) reacted against the literary ideas of several previous generations, but a still younger group of writers (born around 1790) who are also designated "Romantic" reacted against *them* even while absorbing some of their ideas. Further, new economic classes, social roles, occupations, literacy, and systems of transportation and communication were altering the ways in which people expressed themselves, related to each other, and spent their time and money. The development of a market economy, concentrated in large urban centers, created a new popular culture and style along with the traditional elitist one. Moreover, the **French Revolution** and the long **war** it entailed cut off Britain from foreign sources of taste and style, encouraging the development of a self-consciously *national* literature, culture, and identity, and also unleashing new "French" radical ideas. But **exploration**, colonization, and war also brought new foreign influences—Italian, Egyptian, and Asian—to the evolving native style. All these influences helped to produce the eclectic or assimilative quality and the experimentalism that is characteristic of Romantic literary style.

While no single quality was common to all literary works of the Romantic era, nonetheless a short list of some of their most common elements is possible. Originating in the **architecture** and fiction of the 18th century, the **Gothic** is perhaps the style most commonly associated with Romanticism. Newly built stone castles or chapels with pointed arches; stained-glass windows, artificially aged to suggest an idealized past; a fictional medieval period of chivalry, spirituality, mystery, and evil, appeared in the English countryside and became the setting for **novels** and Gothic melodramas. In **poetry**, Gothic appeared in Spenserian Romances (**Keats**'s *Eve of Saint Agnes,* 1820), in **ballads** recounting popular tales of heroism or unrequited love (**Scott**'s *Lay of the Last Minstrel,* 1805) or mystery and superstition (**Coleridge**'s *Rime of the Ancient Mariner,* 1798), and in totally original tales (**Byron**'s *Childe Harold's Pilgrimage,* 1812, 1816, 1818), where the juxtaposition of Gothic elements with contemporary events became a means of measuring the decline of heroism, the loss of the chivalric ideal. Inevitably the Gothic appeared also in parodies such as **Peacock**'s *Nightmare Abbey* (1818) and **Austen**'s *Northanger Abbey* (1818), ridiculing the excesses of Gothic taste.

Another aspect of Romantic style, allied to this multifarious idealization of the Gothic Middle Ages and the **supernatural** but also connected with the democratic motifs of the era of revolution, was its tendency to exalt the "natural" against the "artificial"; the rural against the urban; the lowborn against the high and mighty; the illiterate against the sophisticated; the cloudy, disordered, and electric against the orderly, accurate, and static. The **pastoral** theme in literature, evolving through the 18th century but greatly modified in the era 1790–1830, found enhancement and new importance as a key aspect of Romantic style. Though the upper classes were still able to enjoy the pastoral life, this was in fact fading along with the rural economy, threatened by agricultural enclosure and the spread of industrial centers. Apart from strictly aesthetic influences passing through the literature of **sensibility**, the **picturesque**, and the critical and poetical influences of such figures as **Beattie**, **Macpherson**, the **Warton** brothers, and others, that Romantic pastoral literature not only took on an elegiac tone (as in **Wordsworth**'s *Michael* [1800], *The Ruined Cottage* [1814], and **Crabbe**'s *The Village* [1783]) but invested the rural lower classes especially with a new level of **moral** strength and dignity, as in the ***Lyrical Ballads*** (1798) by Wordsworth and Coleridge. As part of a larger interest in vernacular literature, collected by antiquarians and folklorists, rural life itself became identified with moral purity, the locus of idealized customs and rituals, which many believed survived unspoiled in the countryside and in the voices of untutored genius.

The emphasis on what was medieval, natural, folkish, and **sublime** was significant for the religious content of Romantic literature. The Bible retained an enormous influence; Bible societies and **Sunday schools** were now teaching nearly everyone how to read it. Its diction and narratives were universally familiar. **Religious revivalism** and **millenarianism** proliferated, and even many working-class political pamphlets were composed in the language and apocalyptic imagery of the Bible. For visual artists, biblical illustrations were especially marketable to the newly enriched and literate **middle classes**. And while censors forbade biblical material to be staged, playwrights and the creators of the **dramatic arts** not withstanding presented evil monks and nuns as the symbols of a perverted Christianity—something that appealed to the anticlerical **freethinking** and **radicalism** which flourished alongside the energetic new **Evangelicalism** of the time. New **translations** of Dante and new editions of Milton, some illustrated by **Blake**, created a new biblical iconography in which Satan instead of Christ was prominent and the landscapes resembled England. Indeed, a revival of legends relating England to biblical stories claimed that the Druids and other ancient Britons were descended from some patriarch or one of the lost tribes of Israel. All this may help explain why much Romantic literature resembles inspired prophecy, the writer loftily recounting tales of innocence, fall, redemption, and return to paradise.

Some of these tendencies, however, helped to stimulate in the "second-generation" Romantics (most notably Byron) a reactive literary countertendency, a throwback in some respects to the earlier 18th century, a combative new willingness to laud Augustan order, clarity, and accuracy in opposition to these new, more emotional, folkish, disorderly, and self-consciously irrational fashions. One sign of this was a revived literary **classicism**, but this, like so many other revivals, also bore the unmistakable imprint of the new Romantic age. The renewed appreciation of Hellenic influence, the idealization of ancient Greece and Rome, was partly influenced by the court of Napoleon, and partly by the archaeological digs at Pompeii and Herculaneum: recovered artifacts were translated into styles in furniture, decorations, mass-produced pottery (including that by **Josiah Wedgwood**), even into the dampened muslin gowns of Regency coquettes. Drawings of ruined temples sent back from Greece became the basis for the design of little temple-like banks and churches in England, and incidentally helped promote the ongoing search for **antiquities**. The **Elgin marbles**, dismembered limbs of giant statues rescued from the Turks, became the impetus for the first school of public **sculpture**. "Romantic Hellenism" was expressed by a revival of interest in ancient Greek myths, especially nature myths as used by **Darwin**, or those relating human beings to the gods: the Prometheus, Endymion, and Orpheus myths were consummately represented in such poems as **Shelley**'s *Prometheus Unbound* (1820) and Keats's *Ode on a Grecian Urn* (1820). Artists found such myths more inspiring than the Christian tradition, which among some writers at least was losing its force in an increasingly secular age.

On the other hand, there was a distinctly patriotic and **nationalist** side to Romanticism, extolling in particular what was considered the distinctly English genius in literature. The history of English **literary criticism** before the Romantic era was in one respect a progressive liberation, then exaltation, of the native genius as represented by Chaucer, Spenser, **Milton**, and especially Shakespeare, to such an extent indeed that one may speak of a **Shakespeare industry**. But this elevation of national literary heroes was interwoven with ideas of the genius of the language and of the common people from which it had mysteriously sprung, so that whereas Romantic poets emphasized the importance to poetry of the "spontaneous" diction of "real men," they often wrote in fact in styles deliberately borrowed from Milton, Spenser, and other predecessors far from ordinary. The result was that many wrote in two styles: one a literary adaptation of a Renaissance English poet, the other some imitation of the real, colloquial language of the men and women actually living around 1800. One result of this (and of other things) was an unusual self-consciousness, an emotionality, a psychological self-awareness that probably could not have been attained but for the tremendous clash of opinions, telescoping of dramatic events, and deliberate consultation of models that marked this age.

The Romantic multistyle, the product of an age of immense drama and energy, was omnivorous in its ability to draw in and assimilate material from every direction, including the contemporary English social scene. Although polar opposites, the **Byronic hero** and the dandy both greatly influenced style in literature as well as in society and fashion. Originally a fictional character invented by Byron as the protagonist in *Childe Harold* and his Eastern tales, the Byronic hero gradually became identified with its creator: a cerebral, passionate, sullen, brooding, solitary adventurer haunted by a nameless sin and pursued by insatiable appetites. But while some, like Shelley, imitated Byron's open collar, black cape, ill manners, and foolish histrionics, others copied **Beau Brummell**, the ultimate Dandy, a type as conventionally amiable and polished as the other was "mad, bad, and dangerous to know," like Byron himself. Brummell, a friend of the Prince Regent, without any visible means of support, spent his days grooming himself and lounging around the **coffeehouses** and **clubs** of **London**, a socially aloof, emotionally detached, anti-intellectual snob and social parasite whose value lay in nothing but his style. Romantic style found room for fribbles as well as titans.

The most subtle but wide-ranging influence on Romantic style in art and life came from the new **technologies**. Outside literature, **Turner**'s and **Constable**'s landscapes and cloudscapes, for example, were made possible by chemical improvements in paint, allowing these amazing artists to leave their studios and sketch in oil or watercolor wherever they chose. The **London Pianoforte School** produced pianos which, rapidly replacing harpsichords, were the envy of the European world, while British-trained pianists such as **Clementi**, whom Beethoven called his own master and model, composed some of the finest Romantic sonatas of the era. In architecture, reinforced concrete and ornamental metalwork lay behind the Regency style townhouses designed by **Nash**, the absurd **Orientalism** of the Pavilion at Brighton, and the enormous **theaters** and **pleasure gardens** that created new kinds of space for public activity, celebration, and a new style of communal behavior.

In literature, the technological equivalent of paint, pianos, and metalwork was the explosion in the Romantic era of **periodicals** and **newspapers**, the phenomenal growth of British print culture. Even now, its impact on literature is not yet fully understood. But what is very surprising on a long historical view is that something as multifarious and indefinite as Romantic style could lead to something as definite as Victorian style, which somehow is felt to be full of certainties even at its most uncertain. The Victorians seem to have known who they were, while their predecessors the Romantics were much more likely to emphasize what they were *not*. The second and third decades of the 19th century saw, in addition to the publication of Romantic writings, an unusually large number of critical **essays** and also a remarkable number of quasi-sociological attempts to describe the "spirit of the age." Newspapers, periodicals, and books, influenced by these speculations, helped to filter and transmit to the nation an ever more integrated view of aesthetics and literary values. Out of the diversity, greatness, silliness, and multiplicity of Romantic styles the evolving print culture helped to produce that more homogeneous style (despite its own variations) which is recognized as Victorian.

Marilyn Gaull

Bibliography

Abrams, M.H. *Natural Supernaturalism: Tradition and Revolution in Romantic Literature.* 1971.

Altick, Richard. *The English Common Reader.* 1957.

———. *The Shows of London.* 1978.

Curran, Stuart, ed. *The Cambridge Companion to British Romanticism.* 1993.

Fenner, Theodore. *Opera in London: Views of the Press, 1785–1830.* 1993.

Gaull, Marilyn. *English Romanticism: The Human Context.* 1987.

Lipking, Lawrence, ed. *High Romantic Argument: Essays for M.H. Abrams.* 1981.

Low, Donald A. *The Sunny Dome: A Portrait of Regency England.* 1977.

McGann, Jerome J. *The Romantic Ideology: A Critical Investigation.* 1983.

Mellor, Anne K. *English Romantic Irony.* 1980.

Newman, Gerald. *The Rise of English Nationalism: A Cultural History, 1740–1830.* 1987.

Peckham, Morse. *The Triumph of Romanticism.* 1970.
Rajan, Tilottama. *Dark Interpreter: The Discourse of Romanticism.* 1980.
Thompson, G.R., ed. *The Gothic Imagination: Essays in Dark Romanticism.* 1974.
Watson, Nicola J. *Revolution and the Form of the British Novel, 1790–1825.* 1994.
White, R.J. *The Age of George III.* 1969.
———. *From Waterloo to Peterloo.* 1957.
Williams, Raymond. *Culture and Society, 1780–1850.* Rpt. 1966.
———. *The Long Revolution.* 1961.
Wood, Marcus. *Radical Satire and Print Culture, 1790–1822.* 1994.

See also Hellenism, Romantic

Romilly, Sir Samuel (1757–1818)

Romilly, the son of a **London** watchmaker, came from an immigrant French Protestant family. He became a barrister (1783), published his approving *Thoughts on the Probable Influence of the Late Revolution in France upon Great Britain* (1790), occupied several important legal posts (including that of Solicitor General, 1806–1807) and, knighted (1806), then for the next decade set about reforming the cruel and illogical system of **punishment** inherited from the 18th century. Central to this was the huge number of drastic punishments for petty offenses—death for stealing a handkerchief or impersonating a Chelsea pensioner, for example. This led to cruel injustices, abuses, and favoritism, and made a mockery of the criminal law itself. Romilly, sitting in the **Commons** and battling entrenched resistance in the **Lords**, was instrumental in getting bills passed that removed the death penalty from a number of minor crimes, including private theft from a person, vagrancy committed by soldiers and sailors without passes, and stealing from bleaching grounds. But his greatest influence, upon public opinion, was posthumous.

Sir Samuel Romilly

Romilly was influenced by J.-J. Rousseau (1712–1778), Cesare Beccaria (1738–1794), his close friend **Jeremy Bentham**, and the **humanitarian** movement of the latter 18th century. Like other progressive **Whigs** he supported **Catholic emancipation** and the **antislavery movement**. His life and numerous writings were colored (as Bentham's were also) by his rejection of formal religion and dry embrace of **deism**. But his emotions got the better of him anyway. Crazed by his beloved wife's death, he rashly took his own life by cutting his throat with a razor.

Stanley B. Nash

Bibliography

Medd, Patrick. *Romilly: A Life of Sir Samuel Romilly, Lawyer and Reformer.* 1968.
Oakes, Cecil George. *Sir Samuel Romilly, 1757–1818, "The Friend of the Oppressed": His Life and Times—His Work—His Family and His Friends.* 1935.
Phillipson, Coleman. *Three Criminal Law Reformers: Beccaria, Bentham, Romilly.* 1970.
Romilly, Samuel. *Memoirs of the Life of Sir Samuel Romilly.* 1841.

See also Crime; Judicial System; Suicide

Romney, George (1734–1802)

Romney's reputation as a **portrait painter** rivaled that of **Reynolds** and **Gainsborough**. He aspired to the stature of **history painter**, and to that end he prepared thousands of sketches for dramatic, monumental works that were never painted. He was especially interested in painting scenes from **Milton** and **Shakespeare**, designing (but not completing) a great number of subjects from *Paradise Lost* and Shakespeare's tragedies.

Born in Lancashire, Romney worked as a youth with his father, a cabinetmaker, developing a talent for **drawing** and **painting**. He began study at about age 20 with a minor artist, Christopher Steele, wandered about doing portraits for a few guineas apiece, and in 1762 traveled to **London**, where he found immediate success as a society portrait painter even though the Society of Arts awarded him a prize for his history painting *The Death of Wolfe* (1763). A falling out with Sir Joshua Reynolds resulted in his severing all ties with the **Royal Academy**. He visited Paris, where he developed a sentimental interest in antique subjects, with the result that many of his works from this period (e.g., *Mrs. Yates as the Tragic Muse,* 1771) are suffused with a somewhat artificially classical flavor.

Visiting Italy in 1773–1775, Romney was further affected by the work of Raphael (1483–1520) and Titian (*c.* 1477–1576), whose influence is apparent in his paintings from this period such as *The Gower Children* (1776) and *Earl Grey* (1784). Romney was subsequently befriended by the poet and critic William Hayley (1745–1820), who encouraged his schemes for idealized pictures on historical subjects and wrote

George Romney

a laudatory critical **biography** after the painter's death. Romney also became involved with the beautiful Emma Hart (the future Lady Hamilton and, still later, the lover of **Horatio Nelson**), whom he portrayed as many classical, mythical, and historical characters in more than 50 paintings.

After 1785, Romney's production and talent both declined, and in his final years he felt a sense of failure. In 1799 he returned to the site of his youthful happiness, Kendal, and to the wife he had abandoned nearly 40 years earlier. His mental state deteriorated rapidly, and he died insane. Romney's best work is characterized by its graceful, lively classicism and its energy of line and of color.

Stephen C. Behrendt

Bibliography

Dixon, Yvonne R. *The Drawings of George Romney in the Folger Shakespeare Library.* 1977.
Henderson, Patricia M. *Romney.* 1966.
Jaffé, Patricia. *Drawings by George Romney.* 1977.
Pointon, Marcia. *Hanging the Head: Portraiture and Social Formation in Eighteenth-Century England.* 1993.
Solkin, David. *Painting for Money: The Visual Arts and the Public Sphere in Eighteenth-Century England.* 1993.
Wendorf, Richard. *The Elements of Life: Biography and Portrait-Painting in Stuart and Georgian England.* 1990.

Ross, Sir James Clark (1800–1862)

Ross entered the **navy** in 1812 through the sponsorship of his uncle, **John Ross**, and served under him on two expeditions devoted to searching for the Northwest Passage (1819, 1829–1833). He also accompanied **Parry** on his four Arctic voyages (1819–1827), the first three devoted to the same goal. During the 1829–1833 expedition Ross mapped hundreds of miles of coastline and discovered the north magnetic pole. His later feats included command of a magnetic survey of Great Britain (1838), a successful **Antarctic** expedition (1839–1843), and one of several unhappy attempts to find **Sir John Franklin** (1848–1849). Rear-Admiral Ross was one of the most experienced and successful figures of British polar **exploration**.

N. Merrill Distad

Bibliography

Berton, Pierre. *The Arctic Grail: The Quest for the Northwest Passage and the North Pole, 1818–1909.* 1988.
Dodge, Ernest Stanley. *The Polar Rosses: John and James Clark Ross and Their Explorations.* 1973.
Ross, M.J. *Polar Pioneers: John Ross and James Clark Ross.* 1994.
Wallace, Hugh N. *The Navy, the Company, and Richard King: British Exploration in the Canadian Arctic, 1829–1860.* 1980.

Ross, Sir John (1777–1856)

Despite his brilliant naval career during the **Napoleonic Wars** and later diplomatic service in Sweden, Rear-Admiral Sir John Ross is best remembered for leading three Arctic voyages: two (1818, 1829–1833) in search of the Northwest Passage, one (1850–1851) in search of the unfortunate **Sir John Franklin**. Mistrusted by the Admiralty after a humiliating error in which he described mirages as impenetrable mountains, his later **explorations** were sponsored by **gin** distiller Sir Felix Booth (1775–1850), whose name Ross spattered about on the Arctic map.

The 1829–1833 voyage produced important surveys and discovery of the north magnetic pole by Ross's nephew and second-in-command, **James Clark Ross**. It also showed how important was the Inuit diet, rich in fats and oils, for sustaining life in the Arctic—though the Admiralty ignored the lesson and many British voyagers died of scurvy.

N. Merrill Distad

Bibliography

Berton, Pierre. *The Arctic Grail: The Quest for the Northwest Passage and the North Pole, 1818–1909.* 1988.
Dodge, Ernest Stanley. *The Polar Rosses: John and James Clark Ross and Their Explorations.* 1973.
Markham, Sir Clements Robert. *The Lands of Silence: A History of Arctic and Antarctic Exploration.* 1921.
Ross, M.J. *Polar Pioneers: John Ross and James Clark Ross.* 1994.

Rowland, Daniel (1713–1790)

The most effective preacher of the **Methodist** revival in **Wales**, Rowland was the son of a clergyman in Llangeitho, Cardiganshire. Ordained a priest (1735), he was at about the same time awakened by the preaching of **Griffith Jones**. Initially his own preaching emphasized fire and brimstone, but under the influence of Philip Pugh he tempered this with new stress on grace. On his preaching tours he met **Howel Harris** (1737) and cooperated with him for some time in evangelism, but Rowland, like most Welsh Methodists, was a Calvinist, and hence in the late 1740s parted company with Harris (who refused to reject **Wesley's** Arminianism). People came from all over Wales to hear him preach on Communion Sunday, and Llangeitho became the Mecca of the **Welsh religious revival**. Rowland stayed in the parish despite the offer of the comfortable living of Newport (Pembrokeshire) in 1769. He published volumes of **sermons**, hymns, and Welsh **translations** of religious works, including one by John Bunyan.

Neil Evans

Bibliography

Honourable Society of Cymmrodorion. *The Dictionary of Welsh Biography.* 1959.

Stephens, Meic, ed. *The Oxford Companion to the Literature of Wales.* 1986.

Rowlandson, Thomas (1756–1827)

Painter, **book illustrator**, and caricaturist, Rowlandson was a master draftsman, famous for his comic depiction of scenes from English social life. Among his most important productions were *The Loyal Volunteers of London and Environs* (1799), *The Microcosm of London* (1808–1810) with Augustus Pugin (1812–1852), *The Three Tours of Doctor Syntax* (1812–1821), *The English Dance of Death* (1815–1816), and *The Dance of Life* (1816–1817), all issued by the **publisher** and printseller Rudolph Ackerman (1764–1834) from his shop on the Strand. Rowlandson also illustrated editions of **Goldsmith**, **Smollett**, and **Sterne**.

Born in **London**, the son of a tradesman, educated at the **Royal Academy** and in Paris, Rowlandson was equally adept at rendering the **picturesque** landscape and the caricatured human figure. He worked typically with pen and ink, then a delicate color wash, then engraved the design on copperplate for reproduction and final coloring by hand. Though his later work was often of inferior quality, he is best remembered in the history of **graphic arts** for his comic invention and energy, the spontaneity and fluid quality of his **drawing**, and the spiritedness and often ribald jocularity of his social commentary.

Michael F. Suarez, S.J.

Bibliography

Basket, John, and Dudley Snelgrove. *The Drawings of Thomas Rowlandson in the Paul Mellon Collection.* 1977.

Falk, Bernard. *Thomas Rowlandson: His Life and Art.* 1949.

Hayes, John T. *Rowlandson: Watercolours and Drawings.* 1972.

———. *The Art of Thomas Rowlandson.* 1990.

Paulson, Ronald. *Rowlandson: A New Interpretation.* 1972.

Wood, Marcus. *Radical Satire and Print Culture, 1790–1822.* 1994.

See also Caricature; Engraving; Watercolor

Royal Academy of Arts

The struggle by British artists to develop public support for the encouragement of domestic art reached a critical turning point when **George III** accepted the Instrument of Foundation for a Royal Academy of Arts on December 10, 1768. This document outlined all facets of the academy's existence and promised that its members would constitute a self-governing and self-supporting association endeavoring to promote the arts in England, while providing academic training for young artists.

From among the 36 original academicians, **Joshua Reynolds** was elected President, George Moser (1707–1783) Keeper, and Francis Newton (*fl.* 1760) Secretary. The architect **William Chambers** was appointed Treasurer, and an eight-member council oversaw the daily business of the academy. All academicians were required to submit what was called a diploma work for admission, and one work for the annual exhibition. Students seeking admission were required to submit a drawing or model demonstrating their abilities.

The Royal Academy offered life drawing classes as well as lectures on **painting**, anatomy, **sculpture**, perspective, **architecture**, and chemistry. Students pursued an education comparable to the academic training Continental artists had been receiving since the Renaissance, yet at the same time they were granted greater liberty in selecting subjects for their exhibition pieces and were encouraged to engage actively in critical study of works of the past.

Not all artists and critics immediately accepted the academy as the primary institution for the arts in England. But largely due to Reynolds's successful presidency, the spirit of the academy began to dominate artistic life at home and influence it abroad. Of particular importance were Reynolds's annual discourses (1769–1791), which received international acclaim. These addresses focused on traditional questions concerning the relationship between artistic theory and practice, and challenged young artists to examine broader issues facing them as artists in the modern world.

By the end of the 18th century the Royal Academy was the country's primary institution for the arts, its member, able to sign R.A. after his name, assured of respect. From a permanent home in Somerset House it boasted financial stability and full enrollment in its Schools of Design. **London periodicals** regularly printed news about it and its annual exhibition, and its students and academicians received **patronage** at home and abroad. Under the guidance of Reynolds and Chambers it entered the 19th century well established in its efforts at educating young artists and strengthening the role of the arts in Britain.

In 1792 the American-born painter **Benjamin West** succeeded Reynolds as President of the academy. Himself a founding member, he adhered closely to its aims as expressed in its charter. He continued to focus its attention on improving the Schools of Design and the exhibition program, while also encouraging new pension plans for academicians and grants for students to study abroad. West served as president for 17 years before his death (1820), and was succeeded by **Sir Thomas Lawrence**, who at that time was recognized as Europe's foremost **portrait painter**.

Under the special interest and patronage of **George IV**, crowned in 1820, the academy continued to grow and to maintain its role as the primary institution of the arts. But it was not without criticism. In particular, its limited membership (restricted to 40 people) weakened its teaching effectiveness, opened it fairly to a charge of oligarchical exclusiveness and conservatism (**William Blake** was one of its more heated critics), and compromised its ability to educate young students in applied arts such as ornamental **metalworking**, plastering, and porcelain manufacture. Such criticism led to the establishment (1837) of a separate government School of Design.

Mary Ann A. Powers

Bibliography

Graves, Algernon. *The Royal Academy of Arts: A Complete Dictionary of Contributors and Their Works from Its Foundation in 1769 to 1904.* 1905–1906.

Hutchison, Sidney C. *The History of the Royal Academy.* 1986.

Sandby, William. *The History of the Royal Academy of Arts.* 2 vols. 1862.

Solkin, David. *Painting for Money: The Visual Arts and the Public Sphere in Eighteenth-Century England.* 1993.

See also Learned Societies

Royal Academy of Music

In the 18th century, only Naples, Venice, and then Paris (1795) had well-established public conservatories for the training of musicians. In 1774 **Charles Burney** and Felice Giardini (1716–1796) had proposed to the governors of the **Foundling Hospital** that their institution should be converted into a musical conservatory on the Neapolitan model, but the suggestion was denied. Equally unsuccessful was a proposal by Thomas Forbes Walmisley (1783–1866) to found a national music school in association with the Philharmonic Society soon after its foundation in 1813.

Eventually, in 1822, Lord Burghersh ([1784–1859], later earl of Westmorland), an accomplished amateur musician, assembled a committee of aristocratic music lovers to found and endow a Royal Academy of Music, under the **patronage** of **George IV**. The original plan was ambitious: free board, residence, and training were to be provided for 40 boys and 40 girls. But in the end only 10 students of each sex were accommodated in an unpretentious house on Tenterden Street, and each had to pay 10 guineas a year. The academy was opened on 24 March 1823 with Dr. William Crotch (1775–1847) as principal, aided by a clerical headmaster, a governess, and a part-time staff of some 18 professional **musicians**, many of them foreigners living in **London**.

In the early years the pupils were between 10 and 14 years old, so their general education (including "religious and moral instruction") was undertaken, with special emphasis on Italian, still the international language of music. The sexes were strictly segregated. **Music education** included harmony and composition, singing and sight-singing, the piano, and various orchestral instruments. In a remarkable contrast to modern ideas, but following Italian precedent, all students practiced their instruments simultaneously in a large room, under the supervision of an usher.

Until a government grant was voted in 1864, the academy was constantly plagued by financial problems. Nevertheless, a successful period opened in 1832 when Crotch was succeeded by Philip Cipriani Hambly Potter (1792–1871), a distinguished pianist and composer who happened also to be a gifted administrator with some educational vision. Potter not only established a new school of piano playing but pioneered in the exposition of systematic principles of symphonic analysis, orchestration, and extended composition. Among his pupils were several of the most distinguished Victorian composers, including George Alexander Macfarren (1813–1887) and William Sterndale Bennett (1814–1875), each of whom later became principal of the academy. Macfarren declared that Potter had accomplished more for the advancement of music in England than anyone else of his time.

It should be mentioned that another institution, also titled the Royal Academy of Music, was founded in 1719. This was in effect an **opera** company, run by a committee of noblemen, to promote and manage the performance of Italian operas at the King's Theatre, Haymarket. It failed in 1729 but was briefly revived from 1730 to 1732.

Nicholas Temperley

Bibliography

Cazalet, William W. *A History of the Royal Academy of Music.* 1854.

Corder, Frederick. *A History of the Royal Academy of Music from 1822 to 1922.* 1922.

Macfarren, George A. *Addresses and Lectures.* 1888.

Rainbow, Bernarr. "Music in Education," in Nicholas Temperley, ed., *The Blackwell History of Music in Britain.* Vol. 5. 1988.

See also Learned Societies; Royal Academy of Arts

Royal Bank of Scotland

This bank's charter was granted on 31 May 1727. The **Argyll** faction believed that **Scotland** should have a second bank, especially if it was one over which they would have considerable control. The **Bank of Scotland**, founded in 1695, had been tainted with **Jacobitism**, and **Walpole**, the **prime minister**, was persuaded that a second bank would be an effective means of furthering his political sway in Scotland.

The Royal Bank had better access than the Bank of Scotland to the **London** money market. Its credit facilities greatly expanded and were crucial in the development of the Scottish economy. It quickly developed particularly close links with the **tobacco trade** and was willing to grant credit on the basis of two adequate guarantors. The expansion of credit encouraged the formation of other banks, though the ease with which money could be borrowed weakened the system. The latter part of the 18th century witnessed some spectacular bank failures, such as that of the Ayr Bank in 1772.

Richard Finlay

Bibliography

Checkland, S.G. *Scottish Banking: A History, 1695–1973.* 1975.

Munro, Neil. *The History of the Royal Bank of Scotland.* 1928.

Royal Exchange Assurance

Before the Hanoverian period, marine **insurance** underwriting was carried on by individual businessmen, usually in association with other businesses. In 1718 a group claiming to offer lower rates applied for incorporation, claiming that unless it received a charter, merchants would acquire cheaper insurance in Amsterdam. Individual underwriters objected, however, fearing a monopoly, and blocked the move. But when a syndicate led by **Case Billingsley**, a noted company promoter, acquired the charter of a semidefunct mining company and refloated it to include marine insurance, corporate underwriting began (March 1719) and soon proved successful.

During the speculative mania of the **South Sea Bubble**, the company acquired its own charter by promising £300,000 to the government, and became the Royal Exchange Assurance. Caught up in the "Bubble" crisis, the company almost failed but survived and succeeded in having its powers extended to include fire and life assurance (1721). During the course of the 18th century it grew steadily, rather than spectacularly. Marine insurance fluctuated with the incidence of **wars**, and fire premium income tended to grow later in the period, due to wartime inflation and the growth of industrialization. Life assurance developed only moderately, although the company was a leader in this sector. The company was to remain one of the giants of the insurance industry.

A.J.G. Cummings

Bibliography

Raynes, H.E. *A History of British Insurance.* Rpt. 1968.

Supple, B.E. *The Royal Exchange Assurance: A History of British Insurance, 1720–1970.* 1970.

See also Finance and Investment; York Buildings Company

Royal Institution

Situated in Albemarle Street, **London**, the Royal Institution has long been a center of scientific interests. Its initial purpose was to aid London's destitute in the aftermath of the **French Revolution**. In 1796 Benjamin Thompson, Count Rumford (1753–1814), an American, suggested that an institution be formed to provide the necessary skills for poor people working in an industrializing society; it should offer lectures on practical subjects, and displays illustrating the best domestic, agricultural, and industrial **technologies**. The Royal Institution was the result, founded (1799) with the help of eminent patrons and philanthropists.

Its functions changed rapidly. Rumford departed, poor people stayed away, and further plans for aiding them failed to materialize. The institution became a meeting place for the comfortable and educated, especially industrialists and landowners. It did retain a strong connection with practical matters, many of its lecturers stressing the importance of agricultural and industrial innovations.

Michael Faraday experimenting at the Royal Institution

Because income depended on subscriptions which often proved inadequate, finances were shaky. Additional revenue was generated through lectures delivered on a wide range of scientific subjects. The appointment of **Humphry Davy** (1801) proved a masterstroke; his lectures on chemistry and agricultural chemistry were very popular. Davy conducted his innovative chemical researches in the institution's laboratory, a unique facility that made it a major center for scientific research.

By around 1815, while Davy was increasingly involved in **Regency** social life, his assistant, **Michael Faraday**, was taking on more of the routine chemical analysis, another source of income. Faraday's researches added to the institution's national and international scientific reputation. He also assisted with lecturing, becoming a major public attraction and drawing great crowds. He founded the prestigious and lucrative Friday evening discourses in 1826, and the Juvenile Christmas lectures in 1827.

By the close of the Hanoverian period the Royal Institution had become not only an established center for scientific research but also the locus for polite London **science**. Its lectures were attended by practicing scientists and also by large numbers of nonscientists, of whom a perhaps surprisingly large number were women.

Geoffrey Cantor

Bibliography

Berman, Morris. *Social Change and Scientific Organization: The Royal Institution, 1799–1844.* 1978.

Gooding, David, and A.J.L. Frank, eds. *Faraday Rediscovered.* 1985.

Thomas, John Meurig. *Michael Faraday and the Royal Institution.* 1991.

See also Dalton, John; Experimental Lectures; Mechanics' Institutes; Royal Society

Royal Scottish Academy

The **Scottish Enlightenment** spawned many new institutions and learned societies, and in **painting** certainly revealed an artistic dimension. But attempts to form a lasting arts body in **Edinburgh** only came to fruition after a few unpromising steps. One of the earlier attempts had been in 1797, when the painter Alexander Nasmyth (1758–1840) tried to form a Society of Artists. In 1808 the successor of this group managed to hold the first public art exhibition in Edinburgh. Progress seemed assured when in 1812 **Henry Raeburn** became the society's president, but in 1813 it faded again from existence. On 27 May 1826, however, the Scottish Academy, largely modeled on its **London** counterpart, the **Royal Academy**, was inaugurated for the "advancement of the Fine Arts in Scotland," and began uniting distinguished artists from Edinburgh into a well-organized professional body.

Another organization, the Institution for Encouragement of Fine Arts in Scotland, had begun in 1819. This had been founded by laymen, its principal aim being to exhibit works by the masters, borrowed from members' homes for the duration of the exhibition; but increasingly, due to a shortage of material, it exhibited contemporary works. Ultimately it joined other organizations to build a Greek-temple-like exhibition hall in Edinburgh at the foot of the Mound. Designed by William Playfair (1789–1857), this was erected in 1822 and enlarged in 1833; it is one of the key buildings that transformed "Auld reekie" into the "Athens of the North."

After a period of uneasy coexistence, the two bodies—the academy and the institution—saw the benefit of alliance and joined forces (1829). Most of the major artists were to become members, and to this day, the Royal Institution building serves as the gallery of the Royal Scottish Academy.

G.T. Bell

Bibliography

Gordon, Esmé. *The Royal Scottish Academy of Painting, Sculpture and Architecture: 1826–1976.* 1976.

Royal Scottish Academy. *The Royal Scottish Academy 150th Anniversary Exhibition, 1826–1976.* 1976.

See also Painting

Royal Society of Edinburgh

This society was founded in 1783, largely at the instigation of **William Robertson**, principal of Edinburgh University, who just earlier had presented the idea at a joint meeting of the *senatus academicus* of the university and the Philosophical Society of Edinburgh. His plan was for an intellectual forum with wider interests than the Philosophical Society, which, like the **Royal Society of London**, devoted itself primarily to **science**. Hoping to stimulate local intellectual life generally, Robertson looked to the example of the academies of **France** and other Continental countries, which cultivated all forms of humane learning. The new society would embrace a "physical class," extending the work of the Philosophical Society, and a larger "literary class" for the study of history, literature, philosophy, and humanities.

At meetings of the new society, papers were read, the best of them afterward published in a series of *Transactions* (from 1788). Speakers were drawn widely from the Edinburgh literati, but especially from younger university men and ministers in the **Church of Scotland**. Membership was wide, the largest single segment, more than 40% of the whole, comprising landowners. The project played some part in institutionalizing the values and work of the **Scottish Enlightenment**.

But it did not prove entirely durable. The literary class failed to sustain itself; by the 1790s it was already meeting less frequently, and by the end of the century it had ceased to function. The society itself continued, but became a predominantly scientific organization. This may have reflected a growing preoccupation with science all over Britain and Europe. It may also reflect a slackening in the general momentum of the Scottish Enlightenment, and a failure by its senior figures to carry it broadly into the new era.

Michael Fry

Bibliography

Chitnis, A. *The Scottish Enlightenment.* 1976.

Sher, R. *Church and University in the Scottish Enlightenment.* 1985.

See also Edinburgh

Royal Society of London

Dedicated to the advancement of **science**, this is one of the most prestigious scientific organizations in the world. Founded in 1660, its presidents in the early 18th century were Sir Isaac Newton (1642–1727) and the physician and naturalist **Sir Hans Sloane**. By the time of Sloane's death (1758), its membership was expanding to include philosophers, literary men, and other nonscientists interested in the application of scientific principles to the improvement of everyday life. By 1780 nearly three-fourths of its members were nonscientists, though notable figures such as chemist **Joseph Priestley**, physicist **Henry Cavendish**, actuary **Richard Price**, engine manufacturer **James Watt**, and inventor **Benjamin Franklin** were still entering its ranks.

The society was involved in many important scientific endeavors. Notable among its accomplishments were the 1743 study of the standard yard, the 1758 inquiry into standard weights and measurements (though Parliament did not act on standardization until 1814), and its work (1752) at **calendar reform**, replacing the Julian (Old Style) with the new Gregorian (New Style) calendar. Other activities included its inauguration (1785) of the manufacture of the largest reflecting telescope ever constructed (finished in 1789), and its inquiry (1801) into the explosion of the gasworks at Westminster and subsequent recommendations concerning gas manufacture, storage, and proximity to residential housing.

The society's long interest in overseas **exploration** began in 1768 with its sponsorship of the voyages of **James Cook**,

A meeting of the Royal Society at Somerset House

who studied the transit of Venus and the flora and fauna of **Australia**. The society also sponsored his exploration of the southern latitudes (1771) and the Arctic region (1773). Accompanying Cook on his first voyage was **Sir Joseph Banks**, the wealthy Lincolnshire landowner, who collected great quantities of botanical specimens, many hitherto unclassified. Banks, later influential in creating Kew Gardens as a botanical center, served as the society's president from 1778 to 1820—though he was criticized by **Samuel Horsley**, himself a Fellow, for overemphasizing biological science at the expense of mathematics, astronomy, and physics.

By the end of the Hanoverian period, notwithstanding the fact that the chemist and physicist **Sir Humphry Davy** had succeeded Banks as president and that in 1825 the society awarded its first gold medal to **John Dalton** for his work on atomic theory, the society was still being reproached for the same shortcomings. Others criticized the continued influence of nonscientists, which left unqualified individuals voting on the acceptance of scholarly papers and presentations. Attempts made later to rectify these weaknesses included a thorough revision of the society's procedures and the publication of the new *Proceedings.*

Jack Fruchtman, Jr.

Bibliography

Andrade, E.N.daC. *A Brief History of the Royal Society.* 1960.

Gascoigne, John. *Joseph Banks and the English Enlightenment: Useful Knowledge and Polite Culture.* 1994.

Gleason, Mary Louise. *The Royal Society of London: Years of Reform, 1827–1847.* 1991.

Hunter, Michael. *Establishing the New Science: The Experience of the Early Royal Society.* 1989.

Hartley, Harold, ed. *The Royal Society: Its Origins and Founders.* 1960.

Lyons, Sir Henry. *The Royal Society, 1660–1940: A History of Its Administration Under Its Charters.* 1968.

See also Learned Societies

Ruins

See Antiquities and Ruins

Russel, Richard (*c.* 1686–?1768)

Russel, a **Jacobite**, **nonjuror**, and classicist, was editor and primary author of the immensely popular *Grub-street Journal* (1730–1737), a weekly **newspaper** erroneously thought for many years to have been supervised by **Alexander Pope**. Awarded the M.A. from Oxford (1705), Russel cofounded the journal in 1730 with fellow nonjuror and future **Royal Society** botanist John Martyn (1699–1768), who abandoned the project 2 years later. Contributors included **Robert Dodsley**, James Miller (1706–1744), Richard Savage (1697–1743), Joseph Trapp (1679–1747), and Pope, who provided some epigrams. Publishing mostly original **essays** on literary, political, ecclesiastical, and miscellaneous topics, Russel introduced the "news digest" format adopted successfully by **periodicals** like the *Gentleman's Magazine,* which followed the *Journal* in printing weekly publication lists. Although critical of **Walpole**'s administration, the *Journal* eschewed ***The Craftsman***'s party line by subordinating its interest in **opposition** politics to its militant high Anglicanism.

Alexander Pettit

Bibliography

Goldgar, Bertrand A. "The Grub-street Journal," in Alvin Sullivan, ed., *British Literary Magazines: The Augustan Age and the Age of Johnson, 1698–1788.* 1983.

———. "Pope and the *Grub-street Journal*." *Modern Philology.* Vol. 74, pp. 366–380.

Hillhouse, James. *The Grub-street Journal.* 1928.

Pettit, Alexander. "The *Grub-street Journal* and the Politics of Anachronism." *Philological Quarterly.* Vol. 69, pp. 437–453.

Russell Family (and Dukes of Bedford)

The Russell family, which was granted the dukedom of Bedford in 1694, owed its political influence primarily to the wealth provided by its great landholdings, in particular the Bloomsbury estate in **London** and the Woburn estate in Bedfordshire. In addition, the Russells had the prestige of being one of the great Whig families, based on the 1st duke's early support of William of Orange and his son's martyrdom for the Rye House plot. The 2nd and 3rd dukes were short-lived.

John Russell, 4th Duke (1710–1771), was an active politician, but his own personality and choice of political supporters kept him from leadership. He was part of the Whig **opposition** that forced the resignation of **Sir Robert Walpole** in 1742. He entered the **Pelham** brothers' **broad-bottom administration** as first lord of the Admiralty (1744). Although the Pelhams disliked Bedford, his control of many seats in **Commons** made him a valuable ally, and they had him promoted to Secretary of State for the Southern Department (1748). Bedford devoted much of his time and money to rebuilding Woburn Abbey, and his frequent absences from London infuriated his governmental colleagues, particularly the elder Pelham, the **Duke of Newcastle**. Bedford also served as Lord Lieutenant of Ireland (1757–1761), where he managed to curb the rival factions in the **Irish Parliament**. His initial cooperation with **John Stuart, 3rd Earl of Bute**, deteriorated to hostility, and he demanded Bute's retirement as a condition for giving his name (1763) to the ministry actually headed by **George Grenville**.

John Russell, 4th Duke of Bedford

Bedford's grandson, Francis Russell, 5th Duke (1765–1802), was a close friend of George, Prince of Wales (later **George IV**), and an effective speaker in the **House of Lords**; but he died before he could establish a political career. The 6th Duke, Francis's brother John (1766–1839), being a firm Whig, had little opportunity to hold government office and devoted himself to **agricultural improvement** and the scientific breeding of sheep. His son, **Lord John Russell**, carried on the family tradition of Whig politics.

P.J. Kulisheck

Bibliography

Bedford, Herbrand Russell, Duke of. *The Story of a Great Agricultural Estate.* 1897.

Thomson, Gladys Scott. *The Russells in Bloomsbury, 1669–1771.* 1949.

Trent, Christopher. *The Russells.* 1966.

See also Aristocracy and Gentry; Whigs and Whiggism

Russell, Lord John (1792–1878)

Russell twice served as **Prime Minister** in the Victorian era, but the major achievement of his early career in the Hanoverian period was to assist passage of the parliamentary Reform Act (1832) under his leader, **Earl Grey**. A member of the **Russell family** of the dukes of Bedford, he entered the **House of Commons** in 1813. In 1817 he attacked the **Tory** government's suspension of the Habeas Corpus Act, and in 1819 adopted the cause of parliamentary reform, interesting himself particularly in disfranchisement of the rotten Cornish **borough** of Grampound (achieving success in 1821). In the 1820s Russell helped to convert his party to the larger cause, and also led the attack on the **Test Acts**, helping to secure their repeal in 1828; his party prevented him from moving **Catholic emancipation**, which he also supported.

Made paymaster-general under the Grey ministry formed in November 1830, he was chosen to present and explain the provisions of the Reform bill. After its passage in 1832, he was hailed as a man of the people. Despite his chronic poor health, he held many offices afterward and served in Commons until 1861, when he was created Earl Russell. For a politician, he wrote copiously—several tales, tragedies, and **essays** (chiefly

Lord John Russell

in the 1820s), and some quite substantial historical works, including seven volumes of memorials, correspondence, and biographical information on **Charles James Fox** and the Hanoverian Whig party (1853–1866). He also edited the *Memoirs, Journal and Correspondence of Thomas Moore* (8 vols., 1853–1856).

P.J. Kulisheck

Bibliography

Prest, John. *Lord John Russell.* 1972.
Trent, Christopher. *The Russells.* 1966.
Walpole, Sir Spencer. *The Life of Lord John Russell.* 1889.

See also Reform Act

S

Sackville, Viscount

See Germain, Lord

Sadler, Michael (1780–1835)

Sadler was a **Tory** linen merchant and M.P. (1829–1832) from **Leeds** who worked closely with **Richard Oastler** and Lord Ashley (afterward **Lord Shaftesbury**) in the **factory movement** to shorten workdays and improve conditions in the **factories.** He chaired the 1832 parliamentary Select Committee on the Bill for the Regulation of Factories, which paved the way for the Factory Act of 1833. An articulate **humanitarian** and reformer, he was considered the most selfless of a number of socially dedicated Tories of his generation.

Sadler was also a vigorous opponent of **Malthus**'s doctrines. In 1830–1831 the *Edinburgh Review* printed a spirited debate between him and the **Whig** historian T.B. Macaulay (1800–1859) regarding Sadler's two books, *Ireland: Its Evils and Their Remedies* (1828) and *Law of Population* (1830), both anti–Malthusian in theme. Macauley unseated him in the 1832 parliamentary election. Not long afterward Sadler died, his health impaired by his reforming exertions.

Carolyn Stevens

Bibliography

Driver, Cecil. *Tory Radical: The Life of Richard Oastler.* 1946.

Ward, J.T. *The Factory Movement, 1830–1855.* 1962.

Saltmaking and Salters

Salt played a much bigger role in the economy and society of Hanoverian Britain than in later times. It was required as a mild abrasive by tanners, as a glaze by potters, and to flavor and preserve certain foodstuffs. From around 1800 it played an increasingly important role in the **chemical industry**, being used to make alkali and bleaching powder.

Around 1700, British salt was manufactured in three main ways: by evaporating seawater in large coal-fired iron pans; by pumping brine from underground springs and then evaporating it; and by processing rock salt, which was mined, mixed with brine, and evaporated. The first method produced a poorer product and required about seven times as much coal (for heat evaporation) as the others. Because of this, most of the sea-salt industry was located along the coast of northeast England and on the banks of the River Forth and its estuary in **Scotland.** The quantities of coal used were so great (around 10% of all the British coal mined in 1700) and of such importance for the profitability of the **coal-mining** industry in these regions that the two were often closely integrated.

Increasingly during the 18th century, sea-salt production was overshadowed by the brine and rock-salt industries of Merseyside. Rock salt, first discovered at Marbury in Cheshire in 1670 and mined intensively from the 1690s, was an excellent substitute for imported "Bay" salt, and was soon exported. The brine-salt industry, centered on the Cheshire towns of Middlewich, Nantwich, and Northwich, labored under the high costs of transporting coal over the Mersey from South Lancashire, whereas rock salt could be carried nearer to the source of the coal, a journey made still easier and cheaper with the completion of the River Weaver (1733) and Sankey Brook (1757) navigations. Both industries expanded spectacularly during the 18th century, and by 1830 were producing some 350,000 tons of salt. As a result, the Tyneside sea-salt industry was virtually eradicated. The Scottish producers managed to survive until 1825, protected by geography and a preferential rate of salt **tax** agreed upon at the time of the **Act of Union** (1707) but abolished in 1825.

Although the nature of the work varied according to the type of salt being made, the job of saltmaking was physically arduous, dirty, and dangerous. Skill was required to keep the brine at a steady temperature for several hours. Conditions in the dank, steam-filled panhouses were miserable, and it was not unusual for workers—men, women, and children—to sleep inside these panhouses during production. As in the coal industry, salt workers were prepared to take collective action, particularly in 18th-century Scotland, even though the salters there, like the colliers, were legally bound serfs. But the first recorded **trade union** of saltworkers was not formed until 1845 (in Winsford, Cheshire).

Christopher A. Whatley

Bibliography

Barker, Theo. "Lancashire Coal, Cheshire Salt and the Rise of Liverpool." *Transactions of the Historic Society of Lancashire and Cheshire.* Vol. 103, pp. 83–101.

Ellis, Joyce. "The Decline and Fall of the Tyneside Salt Industry, 1660–1790: A Re-examination." *Economic History Review.* Vol. 33, pp. 45–58.

Samuel, Raphael. *Miners, Quarrymen and Saltworkers.* 1977.

Whatley, Christopher. *The Scottish Salt Industry: An Economic and Social History.* 1987.

Sandwich, 4th Earl of (John Montagu) (1718–1792)

Politician and naval administrator, Sandwich was Lord of the Admiralty during the **War of American Independence**. Educated at Eton and Cambridge, he entered the **House of Lords** (1739), married Dorothy Fane, a sister of **Lord Stanhope** (1740), and rose through many positions, including Postmaster General (1768–1770) and Secretary of State for the Northern Department (1763–1765, 1770–1771), before returning in 1771 to the Admiralty position he had held earlier (1748–1751).

Sandwich was pleasant and industrious, good-humored and popular. But the cost-cutting policies of **Lord North**'s administration, together with his own unfortunate decision to use inferior German oak in construction and repair, left the British **Navy** poorly prepared for the conflict with America—a condition often attributed by his critics to corruption and the demands of his undisciplined lifestyle. (The sandwich, supposedly his sole sustenance in round-the-clock **gambling**, is named after him, as were the Sandwich or Hawaiian Islands).

Sandwich and **Germain**, who was responsible for conduct of the **army**, became the objects of heated criticism. As the colonial uprising turned into a general European **war** (1778), Sandwich concentrated on the threat of a cross-channel invasion (an event narrowly averted in 1779) and backed a strategy that emphasized reserving much of Britain's naval strength in the waters near home; a policy that, according to his critics, made possible the temporary French naval preponderance that resulted in the surrender at **Yorktown**. He resigned (as did Germain) under parliamentary pressure in 1782.

David Sloan

Bibliography

Barnes, G.R., and J.H. Owen, eds. *The Private Papers of the Earl of Sandwich, First Lord of the Admiralty, 1771–1782.* 4 vols. 1932–1938.

Gardiner, Leslie. *The British Admiralty.* 1968.

Mackesy, Piers. *The War for America, 1775–1783.* 1964.

Martelli, George L. *Jemmy Twitcher: A Life of the Fourth Earl of Sandwich, 1718–1792.* 1962.

Saratoga, Battle of (1777)

The interconnected engagements near Saratoga in present-day New York State are considered a critical turning point of the **War of American Independence**. Having determined that the British **Army**, by gaining control of the Lake Champlain–Hudson River waterway, could isolate the New England colonies, thus splitting the independence movement and bringing about its eventual collapse, Secretary **George Germain** authorized a pincer movement. **General John Burgoyne** was to lead an army of 8,000 men south from the St. Lawrence River; **General William Howe** was to send a force north up the Hudson to meet him. For reasons still unclear, Howe instead moved most of his men in the opposite direction to occupy Philadelphia. Meanwhile, Burgoyne's plodding march allowed the Americans to amass an army of 20,000 on the Hudson above Albany.

At the Battle of Freeman's Farm (September 19), Burgoyne failed to break through the American lines. A second encounter, the Battle of Bemis Heights (October 7), weakened his position further. Surrounded and without hope of reinforcement, Burgoyne surrendered his remaining force of 5,700 men (October 17). These fateful actions near Saratoga forced a complete revision of British strategy and are also credited with having convinced the French to expand their secret aid into an open alliance (1778) with the United States, thus transforming the colonial conflict into a European **war**.

David Sloan

Bibliography

Furneaux, Rupert. *Saratoga: The Decisive Battle.* 1971.

Mintz, Max M. *The Generals of Saratoga.* 1990.

Pancake, John S. *1777: The Year of the Hangman.* 1977.

Satire

Satire might generally be defined as the use of an obvious fiction to attack identifiable targets, be they persons or ideas, by representing them in distorted or exaggerated ways. Satirists do not try to be fair. A satirical spirit may appear as an incidental element in any type of literature, whether drama, **poetry**, or prose; or a satirist may choose any normally nonsatiric form, such as the **epic** poem, **essay**, **novel**, or panegyric poem, and use it as a vehicle for satire.

But satire may also be a specific kind of literature with its own definable formal qualities. What distinguishes Hanoverian satire from that earlier and later is the frequency with which it appeared as the organizing principle of works and the degree to which its practitioners saw themselves as writing within a tradition of satire as a distinct genre. Satire is a rhetorical form of literature; that is, a form marked by a speaker who intends somehow to persuade an audience, causing it to alter its thinking. To be able to judge the satirist's success, the audience must be able to recognize his or her intent.

Between 1660 and 1837, satire was certainly understood in its general sense, though as **Samuel Johnson**'s definition in his *Dictionary* (1755) indicates, satire had a more specific meaning as well:

> A poem in which wickedness or folly is censured. Proper *satire* is distinguished, by the generality of the reflections, from a *lampoon* which is aimed against a particular person; but they are too frequently confounded.

The early Hanoverian period marked the Golden Age of verbal satire, for several reasons: (1) Literature was still considered a type of rhetoric, intended to instruct or persuade as well as please an audience, and hence satire was still generally accepted as literature. (2) Satirists and their audiences shared enough cultural values to enable satirists to offer themselves plausibly as spokespersons of that shared culture. (3) The publicly supported values were increasingly challenged by private actions or arguments for alternative values, and thus seemed to need defending. (4) An almost universally held belief that humankind, because of the Fall of Man, was a sinful species, justified the need for identification and punishment of vice; and the general belief that one's actions were deliberate and fully conscious meant that satirists could legitimately hold their targets responsible for their behavior. (5) Widespread familiarity with and respect for classical—especially Roman—literature enabled satirists to invoke the authority of classical models by creating recognizable imitations of the works of Horace (65–8 BC), Juvenal (*c.* 60–140), and Persius (34–62). (6) **Censorship**—especially of political and religious subjects—encouraged authors to use indirect means, under the cover of recognizable fictions, to attack those in positions of power.

The most influential theory of satire during the Hanoverian period was in John Dryden's (1631–1700) "Origin and Progress of Satire" (1693), which distinguished between Horatian and Juvenalian approaches to writing formal, or direct, verse satire. Direct satire was that in which an author addressed himself as an "I" to either the audience outside the poem or to someone, called the *adversarius,* within it. Since the satirist and the audience shared assumptions as to the uniformity of "human nature," the satirist could appropriate the authority of his or her classical model if the satirist applied his or her predecessor's comments about ancient Rome to 18th-century Britain. Because satire was rhetorical, to be effective, the satirist had to establish an authoritative *ethos,* or character, or otherwise possibly stand accused of attacking others merely out of personal spite. Consequently, satirists would often at some point in their careers write an *apologia,* like those of **Pope** (*Epistle to Dr. Arbuthnot,* 1735) or **Jonathan Swift** (*Verses on the Death of Dr. Swift,* 1731), in which they presented themselves as good people motivated by virtue, upholding the nobility of satire as a means to identify and punish wrongdoers.

The works of the Roman writer Horace were not really satirical in today's sense of the word, but rather amusing, chatty, and full of homely wisdom. Hanoverian Horatian satire, popularized by the success of **Edward Young**'s *Love of Fame, the Universal Passion* (1725–1728), is relatively lighthearted, attacking follies that usually cause more harm to the fool than to others, and the persona of the satirist is normally that of a clever, sophisticated, and somewhat disinterested observer more likely to laugh than scold. When Pope began his series of satires on the political culture under the administration of **Sir Robert Walpole**, he chose to do so as an imitator of Horace.

On the other hand, the Roman writer Juvenal had been a bitterly sharp-tongued moralist, a critic of the vices of his times. Johnson's *London* (1738) and *The Vanity of Human Wishes* (1749) were two famous imitations of Juvenal's satires. As Pope became increasingly disillusioned about national reformation, he used a more Juvenalian persona in his *Epilogue to the Satires* (1738).

The tonal distinction between Horatian and Juvenalian satire could also be applied to works that did not imitate the forms of classical satire. For example, the relatively comic tone of Pope's *Rape of the Lock* (1712, 1714, 1717) might be called Horatian, although in form the poem is **mock-heroic**; **John Gay**'s *The Beggar's Opera* (1728), a dramatic **burlesque**, is generally Horatian. Pope's *Dunciad in Four Books* (1743), an apocalyptic poem on the regress of humankind, is more Juvenalian; so too is **Henry Fielding**'s satiric novel, *Jonathan Wild* (1743). And Swift's prose *Gulliver's Travels* (1726), which could be seen as a very loose formal imitation of the works of the Greek Menippus (3rd century BC) or of his Roman imitator Varro (116?–27 B.C.), is a combination: Horatian in Part 1, Juvenalian in Part 2.

Several factors contributed to the decline of satire after the death of Swift (1745). First, its often political content in the 1730s made it seem a partisan genre; **poetry** increasingly was expected to be more expressive than referential, to be about the poet rather than others or events (hence, in his *Essay on the Genius and Writings of Pope* [1756, 1782], **Joseph Warton** demoted Pope from the first to the second rank of poets because of his satires). Second, writers after 1745 could not assume almost universally shared values with their audience and eventually, as in the cases of **Charles Churchill** during the 1760s, **William Blake** ("An Island in the Moon" [*c.* 1785]; *The Marriage of Heaven and Hell* [1793]), and **Lord Byron** (*The Vision of Judgement* [1822]; *Don Juan* [1819–1824]), satirists wrote from outside rather than inside cultural and political norms; a growing number of people believed that humankind was basically good and that ridicule of others was both unfair and in poor taste. And third, while their potential audience grew rapidly during the period, writers could no longer assume the audience's familiarity with classical models.

Since satire exposed the gap between values and actions, pretenses and practices, satirists frequently relied on **irony** as a way to reflect or represent such gaps. In the last half of the Hanoverian period, Friedrich Schlegel (1772–1829) and other Germans introduced the concept of Romantic irony to identify the gap caused by an author's interrupting the illusion of a consistent fiction to remind the reader of his presence as the controlling force behind the fiction. In satires like **Laurence Sterne**'s *Tristram Shandy* (1759–1767) and Byron's *Don Juan,* the presence of Romantic irony often indicated the satirist's recognition that his or her values might appear idiosyncratic or counterconventional to large parts of the audience.

Vincent Carretta

Bibliography

Bloom, Edward, and Lillian Bloom. *Satire's Persuasive Voice.* 1979.

Booth, Wayne. *A Rhetoric of Irony.* 1974.

Carretta, Vincent. *"The Snarling Muse": Verbal and Visual Political Satire from Pope to Churchill.* 1983.

Guilhamet, Leon. *Satire and the Transformation of Genre.* 1987.

Knox, Norman. *The Word* Irony *and Its Context, 1500–1755.* 1961.

Lockwood, Thomas. *Post-Augustan Satire.* 1979.

Mellor, Anne. *English Romantic Irony.* 1980.

Paulson, Ronald, ed. *Satire: Modern Essays in Criticism.* 1971.

Rawson, Claude. *Satire and Sentiment, 1660–1830.* 1993.

Weinbrot, Howard. *Alexander Pope and the Traditions of Formal Verse Satire.* 1982.

———. *Eighteenth-Century Satire: Essays on Text and Context from Dryden to Peter Pindar.* 1988.

See also Classicism; Literary Criticism

Sawbridge, John (1732–1795)

Sawbridge, an associate of **John Wilkes**, **John Horne Tooke**, and **John Cartwright**, was closely identified with the **radical** cause in company with his sister, **Catharine Macaulay**. First elected to Parliament in 1768 for Hythe, he became a member for **London** in 1774, a seat he held until his death. He also served as Sheriff (1769–1770) and Lord Mayor of London (1775–1776). He is perhaps best known for introducing (1771) the first motion for parliamentary reform, an exercise that he took up annually afterward. In 1787 he was elected President of the **Society for Constitutional Information**. Despite disagreements with conservatives and other radicals, Sawbridge never wavered in his dedication to shorter parliamentary terms, manhood suffrage, and limited executive power.

Barbara Brandon Schnorrenberg

Bibliography

Christie, Ian R. *British "Non-Élite" MPs, 1715–1820.* 1995.

Valentine, Alan. *The British Establishment, 1760–1784: An Eighteenth-Century Biographical Dictionary.* 2 vols. 1970.

See also Elections and the Franchise

Schism Act (1714)

This act required tutors, schoolmasters, and keepers of public and private schools and seminaries to present certificates attesting that they had taken Anglican communion in the past year. It also required that they sign the declaration against transubstantiation and subscribe to the oaths of allegiance, supremacy, and abjuration. The act was chiefly designed to prevent **dissenters** from teaching or keeping schools. **Tory** leaders, disturbed by the growth of dissent following passage of the **Toleration Act** (1689), introduced this measure to stifle nonconformity. The death of **Queen Anne** on the eve of the bill's passage and the accession of **George I**, together with **Whig** opposition to the act, virtually insured that it would be ineffective. It was repealed in 1719.

William Edward Morris

Bibliography

Bradley, James E. *Religion, Revolution and English Radicalism: Nonconformity in Eighteenth Century Politics and Society.* 1990.

Williams, E. Neville. *The Eighteenth-Century Constitution, 1688–1815: Documents and Commentary.* 1960.

See also Bolingbroke, Viscount

Science, Technology, and Invention

The relationships between science, technology, and invention excited the early modern mercantilists, who emphasized science's practical applications. They regarded skilled workmen as an important national asset, an elite responsible for applying science to production. Enlightened despots such as Frederick the Great of Prussia (1712–1786) encouraged the immigration of scientific and technical specialists, whatever their nationality or religion. Science-based technology represented the main route to increasing national wealth and national power, a fact which all governments in the age of **Enlightenment** recognized.

The combinations within this triadic relationship, however, were complex. Scientific inquiry led to the testing of hypotheses and the extension of knowledge, an aspect calculated to appeal most purely to Hanoverian members of the **Royal societies** of **London** and **Edinburgh**, members of the many **learned societies**, and individuals such as Sir Isaac Newton (1642–1727), whose conception of the physical universe dominated 18th-century science. Newton's successors in scientific theory included **Joseph Black**, who established the theory of latent heat; **Benjamin Franklin**, who pioneered in theories of electricity; **John Dalton**, the founder of modern atomic theory; and many others: the astronomers **Edmond Halley**, **William Herschel**, and **James Bradley**; naturalists and archaeologists such as **Hans Sloane**, **Stephen Hales**, **Joseph Banks**, **Thomas Pennant**, **William Stukeley**, and **Gilbert White**; chemists such as **Humphry Davy**, **William Cullen**, **Charles Tennant**, **Joseph Priestley**, and Henry **Cavendish**; physicists such as **J.T. Desaguliers** and **Michael Faraday**; and medical scientists such as John and William **Hunter** and **Edward Jenner**.

The application of science to production through invention saw vast development in the Hanoverian period. The **patents** issued in Britain furnish a crude index. Around 1700, these amounted to only a trickle; in the 1760s they averaged over 20 per year; in the 1780s, over 51; in the first decade of the 19th century, about 84 a year; in the 1820s, nearly 155. Patents, however, do not necessarily mean successful innovation. Innovation was the critical stage, and often occurred after a considerable time lag, as in the case, for example, of **Abraham Darby**'s coke-smelting process, which took decades to spread.

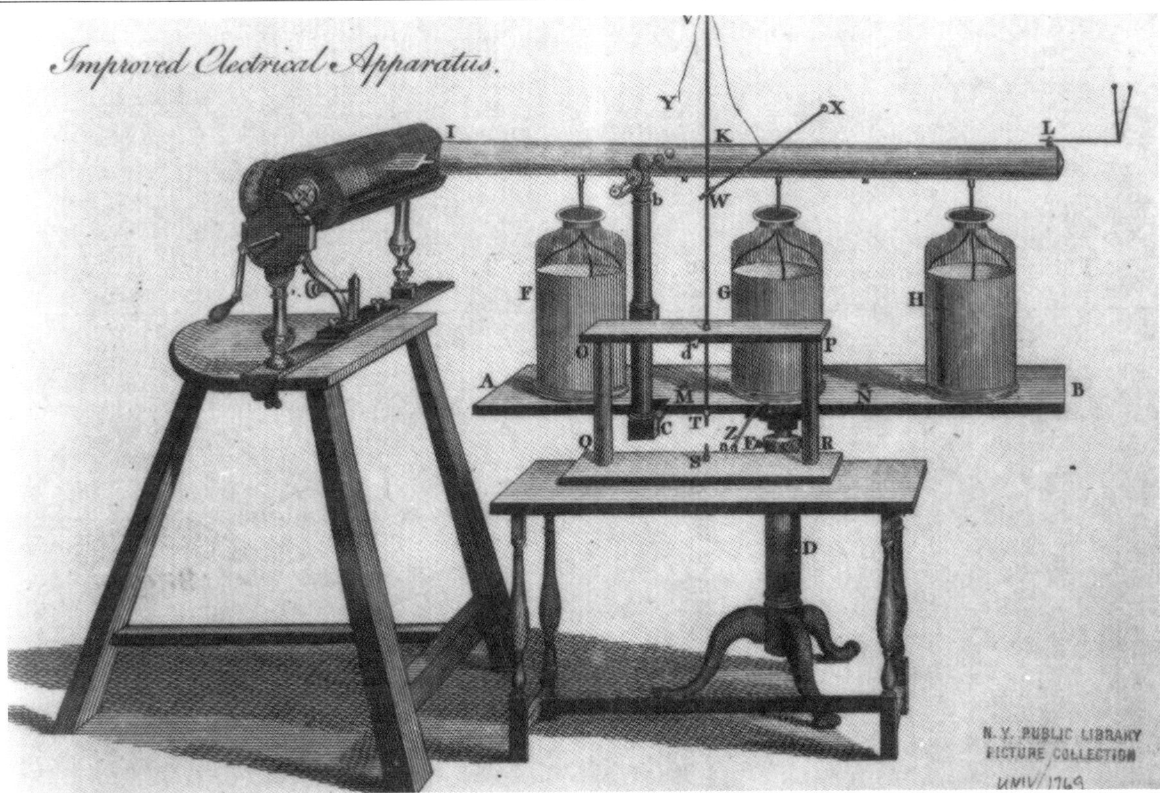

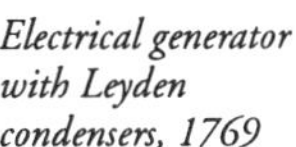
Electrical generator with Leyden condensers, 1769

Similarly, although Leonardo da Vinci (1452–1519) had thought of a screw-cutting lathe (the foundation of precision engineering), the idea was lost for centuries before the engineer Henry Maudslay (1771–1831) put it into practice. Again, the poundlock, vital in **canal** engineering, was used by the Dutch from the 15th century but only applied in Britain in the 18th century.

Sometimes one innovation led to another because of the economic disequilibrium induced by the first invention. Nowhere is this better demonstrated than in the case of the **cotton industry**. **John Kay's** flying shuttle of the 1730s so raised the productivity of handloom weavers that improvements in **spinning** became imperative. In turn, these advances in spinning (many centered in the 1750s and 1760s) altered the cost structure of **weaving**, which could only be cheapened by the power loom (developed in the 1770s and 1780s).

Many inventions have an evolutionary history, initial innovation leading to a period of confused competitive activity before further improvements emerge. **Samuel Crompton's** spinning mule (1779) developed from the milieu just mentioned, in which the improvement of spinning was a clear desideratum, and there were competing claims by other inventors and occasionally complementarity. But another 45 years passed before the versatile Welsh inventor Richard Roberts (1789–1864) produced an automatic spinning mule (1825). Obstruction by workers and from competitors, patent piracy, willful destruction of equipment, and unscrupulous exploitation by others affected such inventors as **Edmund Cartwright**, **J.B. Neilson**, **William Clanny**, **Andrew Meikle**, **Henry Bell**, **James Small**, **Henry Cort**, and **Benjamin Huntsman**. **Richard Trevithick** and Crompton himself epitomized many inventors—technical geniuses but entrepreneurial failures.

Thus, while scientific discovery and basic invention were supply stages on the way to innovation, innovation itself and later improvements also belonged to a commercial world in which **entrepreneurs**, enterprise, capital investment, and market forces assumed priority. The supply stages depended on human intellect and the culture and values of Hanoverian society—attitudes to profit, labor mobility, and consumer satisfaction, for example. But lack of evidence often prevents a proper understanding of the relationship between those supply stages and that commercial world of innovation. Hanoverian businessmen were often technically literate, while some Hanoverian inventors at least were not slow to perceive the economic potential of scientific discovery. **James Watt** discovered independently of Joseph Black the principle of latent heat, but his attempt to apply it was clearly worldly wise; the real problem was finding a partner with capital and access to precision engineering—**Matthew Boulton**. There were many individuals with scientific and technical aptitude who themselves went on to establish important businesses—for example, **John Roebuck**, **Jedediah Strutt**, **John Wilkinson**, **Henry Houldsworth**, **David Dale**, **Samuel Oldknow**, and **Robert Owen**. A classic example was **Richard Arkwright**, with his water-powered spinning machine (the water frame, 1769). The family histories of the **Darbys**, **Crawshays**, and **Crowleys** reveal similar progressions from small beginnings to industrial empires.

Among the products of technology, the **steam engine**, imperishably linked to the name of Watt, provides the classic story of evolutionary change during the entire epoch of the five Hanoverian kings (1714–1837). Early pioneers in steam such as Denis Papin (1647–1712), Captain Thomas Savery (1650?–1715), and **Thomas Newcomen** were not so concerned with the theory of the steam engine as with its practice; scientific curiosity had been turned into practical invention but still awaited economic opportunity to produce widespread innovation. Newcomen developed his revolutionary engine just before **George I** arrived from **Hanover**, but soon still better pumping and draining engines were wanted. At last in the 1760s, Watt became interested in steam power and its applications as an instrument-maker at Glasgow University; **Professor John Anderson** asked him to repair a model Newcomen engine used for demonstrations. But improvement on this model depended upon precise accuracy in working metal, especially in the making of cylinders and piston seals. Having accomplished this, Boulton and Watt turned the steam engine into a multipurpose machine for use in powering all sorts of mills, **breweries**, and distilleries, for winding and draining in **mines**, for providing the blast for **iron** furnaces and foundries, and hammer-power in forges and engineering workshops. The steam engine descended into an empirical world of erectors, local engineers, and patent pirates, whose numbers were legion. There, after expiry of Watt's patent (1800), Trevithick produced efficient high-pressure engines, and **George Stephenson** and his contemporaries further applied them to locomotion on land and water. Between 1800 and 1840 the use of steam engines continued to diversify during the **transport** revolution, and their working efficiency probably quadrupled. **Patrick Miller** and then Henry Bell employed them on water; while James Nasmyth (1808–1890), besides making a huge number of locomotives, presses, and pumps, patented one of the most important **metalworking** tools of the 19th century in the steam hammer (1842).

Of course, science includes general attitudes as well as specific knowledge. Favorable attitudes had become widely diffused by the reign of **George III**, as is evidenced in the great popularity of such bodies as the **Royal Institution**. In many areas there developed **libraries** containing scientific books, technical manuals, and compendious **reference works**. **Technical education** was advanced in the early 19th century by traveling lectures and the establishment of sponsoring groups like the **Society for the Diffusion of Useful Knowledge**. There was also a considerable process of self-education; for instance, most millwrights understood some mathematics and practical mechanics, could produce and work to drawings, and calculate velocity and horsepower of waterwheels. **John Loudon McAdam** arrived at his scientific understanding of road building through trial and error. Sometimes, traditional **craftsmen**—woodworkers, masons, and blacksmiths—found new challenges to test their older skills: the first iron bridge in Coalbrookdale (1779), for example, looks as if it were erected by men skilled in building wooden structures. Craft skills were transferred to millwrighting and early civil engineering. **Thomas Telford** began as a stonemason and, entranced by science, became the greatest of the civil engineers and first President of the Institution of Civil Engineers (1818).

British science was diffused by many channels; the pathways to knowledge were many. Apart from the numerous direct connections between businessmen and scientists based on mutual interest in industrial fields such as **metallurgy**, there was the world of **clubs** and learned societies to which both belonged. At least 30 towns had groups like the **Lunar Society** in **Birmingham**, or the **Manchester** or **Swansea** Literary and Philosophical Societies, and this local institutionalization of science was most prevalent in the new industrial centers. Chambers of commerce like that in **Glasgow** were also very active in stimulating technical improvements such as John Austin's power loom (1789). The Scottish schools and **Scottish universities**, the **dissenting academies** and **Unitarian** and **Quaker** congregations in England, recognized the importance of science and its economic possibilities. **Experimental lectures** and **mechanics' institutes** spread science further.

Moreover, science had become international by the 18th century. Most theories crossed frontiers; for instance, discovery of chlorine by the Swedes greatly stimulated the British **chemical industry**, while advances by the Dutch and Italians were crucial to the important British exploration of **electricity**. Maritime and imperial needs spurred investigations in **navigation**, **chronometers**, **longitude**, **weapons**, and **meteorology**. Other factors, such as low interest rates and relative political stability, were significant advantages also to exchange and innovation. British businessmen knew enough science or were willing to listen to others who might recognize the merits of an invention. **Josiah Wedgwood** employed scientists like Priestley to assist him; he was naturally interested in the composition of clays, the quality of glazes and paints; his concern for accurate temperature control in the pottery kiln led to the development of the ceramic pyrometer.

Of course, throughout all of this, there were complex relationships between scientific curiosity, engineering, immediate applications, and cash value. Mathematics was central to land, canal, and **road** surveying; navigation; and accountancy: Motivation to add a modicum of mathematical understanding to an existing empirical tradition was, therefore, strong. It is significant that scientists like Priestley, Dalton, and Davy undertook commissions from mineowners concerned about gases and ventilation in their pits. Engineers like **James Brindley**, Telford, John Rennie (1760–1821), and William Fairbairn (1789–1874) were not lacking in scientific curiosity or knowledge. **John Smeaton**'s notebooks reveal beyond all doubt the technical understanding and abilities of this great engineer. Telford's fascination with chemistry had some practical utility: he analyzed mortar so that he could use different compositions for different tasks. He joined engineers, academics, instrument-makers, industrial chemists, ironmasters, and manufacturers when he became a Fellow of the Royal Society.

Many engineers, self-educated like Telford, combined scientific knowledge with practical experience, and the greater their experience, the more wary they were of some science. When scientific knowledge appeared to contradict their practical experience, they rightly preferred to err on the side of safety. They knew there was the problem of bogus science or misconceptions, the most famous example outside **mesmerism** being **Jethro Tull**'s belief that air was the best manure; hence his commitment to horse-hoeing husbandry. Technical changes, even ill-advised ones, pushed new scientific questions to the fore, for science is a continuing process, never an end game. Although inventions multiplied, changes in the British economy occurred slowly, and so did the general advance of science.

John Butt

Bibliography

Derry, T.K., and T.I. Williams. *A Short History of Technology.* 1960.

Gascoigne, John. *Joseph Banks and the English Enlightenment: Useful Knowledge and Polite Culture.* 1994.

Golinski, Jan. *Science as Public Culture: Chemistry and Enlightenment in Britain, 1760–1820.* 1992.

Hall, A. Rupert. *The Scientific Revolution, 1500–1800.* 1954.

Macleod, Christine. *Inventing the Industrial Revolution: The English Patent System, 1660–1800.* 1988.

Mathias, Peter. *Science and Society, 1600–1900.* 1972.

Musson, A.E. *Science and Technology in the Industrial Revolution.* 1969.

Russell, Colin. *Science and Social Change.* 1983.

Stewart, Larry. *The Rise of Public Science: Rhetoric, Technology and Natural Philosophy in Newtonian Britain, 1660–1750.* 1992.

Scotland and Scottish Culture

Following the **Act of Union** in 1707, the major center of political activity in Scotland shifted ever more clearly from **Edinburgh** toward **London**. However, the preservation of the distinctive **Scottish legal system**, the **Church of Scotland**, and **Scottish education** meant that in many areas, Scottish development was distinctly different from that elsewhere in Britain.

During the early years of the Hanoverian dynasty the threat of **Jacobitism** was far greater in Scotland than in England, but fear of **Roman Catholicism** and the placing of extensive **patronage** in the hands of **Walpole**'s Scottish managers, the **Duke of Argyll** and his agent **Lord Milton**, ensured that most Scots accepted the new regime. The Jacobite rebellions ended in failure, and following defeat at **Culloden** in 1746, the cause of the Stewart (Stuart) dynasty was effectively ended. In the second half of the 18th century, Scotsmen such as the **Earl of Bute** and **Henry Dundas** were to play a significant role in British, as opposed to purely Scottish, politics. Also in Scotland as in other parts of Britain, the years following the **French Revolution** were marked by the development of **radicalism**, which caused considerable consternation and reaction in government circles.

The Hanoverian period witnessed significant growth in the Scottish economy. In the years before 1740 its performance was sluggish, but the ensuing decades witnessed the rise of **Glasgow** in the **tobacco trade**, which had the effect of giving some stimulation to Scottish industry, including the development of **Carron Ironworks**. In the east, continuing trading links with Europe and developments in the linen industry were notable. But the most significant development in textiles came with the rise of the **cotton industry** after 1770. Initially

Scotland

established in rural areas, this soon spread to growing towns such as Glasgow and **Paisley**. Further developments in **coal** and **iron** underlined Scotland's large contribution to the **Industrial Revolution**.

Scottish agriculture also improved considerably. This was given a boost in the first half of the 18th century by **agricultural improvers** such as **John Cockburn of Ormiston** and **Sir Archibald Grant of Monymusk**. The major changes, however, came after 1750 in both the Highlands and Lowlands. Both agriculture and industry were greatly assisted by the opening of the Forth and Clyde **Canal** (1790), which created a national market in Scotland for the first time. By the 1830s, Scotland was one of Europe's leading agricultural areas.

From the middle of the 18th century there was a remarkable surge in cultural developments, which greatly influenced the Scottish elite but also touched other social groups. These occurred primarily—but by no means exclusively—in high culture associated with the **Enlightenment** and the later rise of **Romanticism**. Romantic works in all forms drew on stories and legends from Scottish history as well as from contemporary rural life as perceived by men of letters. At the same time, a powerful folk tradition, embracing **ballads** and **folksong**, blossomed through the medium of Lallans or Lowland Scots, while in the Highlands the Gaelic (Erse) oral and written tradition was sustained despite increased anglicization and migration.

The **Scottish Enlightenment** closely mirrored its European counterpart but had its own distinctive features, embracing philosophy, the new "social sciences" (notably economics), literature, art, **architecture**, and **music**. There were also significant developments in **medicine** and **science and technology**, seen in the work of **Joseph Black**, **James Watt**, and others. It has been argued that Scotland provided a particularly sympathetic environment in which the new ideas of Reason became established, its roots lying deep in the nation's history, especially in the law, the educational system, and the kirk (all preserved under the union), institutions that had developed along Continental rather than English lines. Strong links had long been established with European centers of learning in the Netherlands, Germany, and **France**.

Scots law was grounded in social law and social philosophy, and the **legal profession** was dominant in politics and economic affairs, as well as playing a significant role in the arts—witness the careers of **Sir Walter Scott**, **Francis Jeffrey**, and **Henry Brougham**, to name only a few. Scottish education perceived the arts as distinctly philosophical. The social sciences, which derived much from law, included economics, history, politics, and sociology, and sprang from the same philosophical tradition that prevailed in the arts. The Church of Scotland dominated the social (and to some extent cultural) affairs of the nation, yet at the same time, **theology** was probably the original social science, paving the way for the secular sciences and thought of the 18th century. Many churchmen were distinguished men of letters, and this remained so well into the 19th century, the Rev. Henry Duncan (1774–1846) being one of many writers who bridged the Ages of Reason and Romanticism.

In philosophy the major figure, **David Hume**, was greatly influenced by the Continental writers of the age, as were his near contemporaries, **Francis Hutcheson**, **Thomas Reid**, **Dugald Stewart**, and George Campbell (1719–1796). Together they represented an important school of Scottish philosophy. The leading social scientists also had a sound grounding in the arts, philosophy, or theology, notably **Adam Smith**, who established political economy as one of the leading social sciences, **Adam Ferguson**, **John Millar**, and the historian **William Robertson**.

Scottish literature enjoyed a golden age in the Hanoverian era. In poetry the earlier period witnessed the pastoral style of Allan Ramsay (1686–1758), whereas the era of **George III** saw the real rise of Scottish vernacular **poetry** through **Robert Fergusson**, who in turn provided the inspiration for **Robert Burns**. In prose fiction, the work of **Tobias Smollett** relied much on the picaresque tradition, but the **novels** of Scott created a Romantic picture of Scotland and Scottish history, which inspired the work not only of European writers but of composers and artists as well. **John Galt**, on the other hand, wittily addressed current religious and political issues such as **patronage** and corruption.

Painting was at first dominated by **classicism** and ultimately by Romanticism, trends reflected in both portrait and landscape works of the period. In **portrait painting** the most prominent artist of his generation was **Allan Ramsay, Jr.**, the Scottish counterpart of **Gainsborough** and **Reynolds**, who was appointed painter to George III. Later, **Sir Henry Raeburn** recorded the personalities associated with the "Athens of the North," the Edinburgh elite and scholars, as well as Highland lairds in their tartan finery, much of it sheer invention. Alexander (1758–1840) and Patrick (1787–1831) Nasmyth were leading **landscape** artists, the former also executing one of the best likenesses of Burns. **Sir David Wilkie** was the greatest exponent of **genre painting**; his *Pitlessie Fair* (1804) began a successful career as limner to "palace and people." As it happened, Wilkie later painted *The Entry of George IV to the Palace of Holyrood House* (1830): this commemorated the visit (1822) of the last but one of the Hanoverian sovereigns (the event was orchestrated by Sir Walter Scott), and contributed much to the subsequent popular appeal of Highland dress and culture, as well as to widespread nostalgia for a disappearing way of life in both Highlands and Lowlands—feelings which contrasted markedly with the reality of the **Highland clearances** and the individuals like **Patrick Sellar** who effected them.

In **architecture**, the work started by Sir William Bruce (*d.* 1710) was carried on by a long line of successors, particularly William and Robert Adam—the latter undoubtedly the greatest Scottish architect of the 18th century. Much of the **Adam family**'s work was in **housebuilding**, the building or rebuilding of country houses for the **gentry** in either **Palladian** or **Gothic Revival** styles, an outstanding example being Culzean Castle (1777–1790), though commissions also embraced humbler structures such as churches, civic buildings, and bridges. In urban planning and architecture, remarkable strides were made, ranging from the classical grandeur of the New Town of Edinburgh, including Robert Adam's Charlotte Square, to more modest estates and **planned villages** built all over the Lowlands such as Gatehouse-of-Fleet in Galloway, and **David Dale**'s cotton spinning community of **New Lanark** on the River Clyde.

Musically, the 18th century was one of vitality and growth as Scotland absorbed European developments. Public **musical concerts** began, music societies were established, **dance** came back into fashion, organs were reintroduced into Episcopal churches, and many parish church choirs formed after 1755. Scotland produced its own reputable classical composers, including William McGibbon (1695–1756), James Oswald (1711–1769), and the Earl of Kelly (1732–1781), while many Continental composers settled and worked in Edinburgh. Fiddle music was also important and the folkmusic tradition was strongly maintained, greatly affecting musical output for both dancing and singing. Like literature, some of the more **popular music** and song was touched by nostalgia for lost nationhood and the Jacobite cause, notably the works of Lady Nairne (1766–1845). Important collections of **ballads** and songs from both Lowlands and Highlands were made by Burns and Scott.

Paradoxically, while the political and economic bonds of union with England tightened during the Hanoverian period, there was a parallel flowering of national sentiment, which found expression in a dazzlingly rich culture, drawing partly on Scottish history and popular tradition and partly on contemporary fashion for the Classical and Romantic. Major questions arise about the origins and nature of the cultural revival during the Scottish Enlightenment and about the influence, if any, of the apparently higher levels (compared to English) of literacy prevailing in Scotland at the time.

Ian Donnachie

Bibliography

Campbell, R.H. *Scotland since 1707: The Rise of an Industrial Society.* 2nd ed., 1985.

Chitnis, Anand. *The Scottish Enlightenment: A Social History.* 1976.

Daiches, David, ed. *The New Companion to Scottish Culture.* 1993.

Davie, George. *The Scottish Enlightenment.* 1981.

Devine, T.M., and R. Mitchison, eds. *People and Society in Scotland.* Vol. 1: *1760–1830.* 1988.

Kidd, Colin. *Subverting Scotland's Past: Scottish Whig Historians and the Creation of an Anglo-British Identity, 1689–c.1820.* 1993.

Lenman, Bruce. *Integration, Enlightenment and Industrialisation.* 1981.

Royle, Trevor. *The Macmillan Companion to Scottish Literature.* 1984.

Scott, John

See Eldon, Earl of

Scott, Sir Walter (1771–1832)

In a remarkably busy literary career, Scott distinguished himself as an editor, poet, historian, critic, and biographer. But his great importance rests upon the **novels** he wrote in the last phase of that career. His Waverley novels expressed an historical sensibility that forcefully synthesized elements of the **Scottish Enlightenment** with **Romantic** notions of **nationalism**, the folk, and nature.

Scott's interests in history were developed in his work as editor of *Minstrelsy of the Scottish Border* (1802), and his contributions to the *Edinburgh Review* and the **Tory** *Quarterly Review* (which he helped found in 1809). He achieved wide recognition as a poet with the publication of *The Lay of the Last Minstrel* (1805), and enjoyed both critical and popular success with *Marmion* (1808) and *The Lady of the Lake* (1810). In 1813 he refused the **poet laureateship** and recommended **Robert Southey** for the honor. *Waverley* (1814), his first novel, marked the start of an unprecedented commercial and cultural ascent. The then anonymous (but hardly unknown) "Author of Waverley" produced in rapid succession historical novels that were extraordinarily well received.

The early novels took as their subject the **Scotland** of the fairly recent past. Scott's formula was to set a domestic romance into a context of historical crisis. For example, *Waverley* concerns the rebellion of the **Forty-five**; *Old Mortality* (1816) is set amidst the bloody skirmishes between Royalists and Presbyterians in 1679; *Rob Roy* (1818) unfolds in 1715 against the backdrop of a still tenuous Hanoverian authority; and *The Heart of Midlothian* (1818) makes the **Porteous riots** (1736) crucial to the main action of the novel. *The Bride of Lammermoor* (1819), though built around no clearly marked historical event, also projects a sense of the complex social and political tensions that constitute historical movement.

With *Ivanhoe* (1819), Scott, perhaps fearing his audience would tire of Scottish scenes, moved to more ancient and distant settings. **Francis Jeffrey** saw this as a shift from historical

Sir Walter Scott

realism to a kind of extravagant pageantry, but there were important continuities, too: Scott always envisioned history as a process impelled by competing styles, ideas, and interests. In any case, the shift of scenes did nothing to diminish his popularity. Such works as *Kenilworth* (1821), *The Fortunes of Nigel* (1822), and *Quentin Durward* (1823) continued to command large audiences. And as is evident in *Redgauntlet* (1824) and the short tales "The Two Drovers" and "The Highland Widow" (both 1827), Scott never abandoned his more familiar Scottish locales.

Despite his novels' tremendous sales, Scott labored under debts resulting from the constant expansion, decoration, and maintenance of his estate, Abbotsford. His silent interest in the **publishing** firm of Constable and Company proved disastrous. When the firm collapsed (1826), Scott was left bankrupt. From that time on he worked to free himself from debt and the shame he felt was attached to it. He was also determined to save Abbotsford, which had become since its original purchase a symbol of great personal importance. After 1826 Scott dropped the pretense of anonymity and wrote feverishly in hopes that future profits would pay creditors. In this final, sad ambition, he was successful. This stage of Scott's life, as revealed by his son-in-law **John Gibson Lockhart**, became an idealized tale of integrity and discipline for many Victorians who sought a model of the morally and socially responsible artist.

Both Scott's broad readership and his high critical reputation began to diminish late in the 19th century. But the international influence of his novels can be seen in major works of Alessandro Manzoni (1785–1873), James Fenimore Cooper (1789–1851), Victor Hugo (1802–1885), George Eliot (1819–1880), and Lev Nikolaevich Tolstoy (1828–1910). His indirect influence remains considerable still; writers like William Faulkner (1897–1962) and Gabriel Garcia Marquez (1928–), who contextualize their characters historically and geographically, and whose works take up themes of change and tragic loss, have much in common with the "Author of Waverley." Ultimately, Scott contributed to modern thought by making history so explicitly the province of Romantic literary art.

Bruce Beiderwell

Bibliography

Beiderwell, Bruce. *Power and Punishment in Scott's Novels.* 1992.

Brown, David. *Walter Scott and the Historical Imagination.* 1979.

Cottom, Daniel. *The Civilized Imagination: A Study of Ann Radcliffe, Jane Austen, and Sir Walter Scott.* 1985.

Duncan, Ian. *Modern Romance and Transformations of the Novel: The Gothic, Scott and Dickens.* 1992.

Farrell, John P. *Revolution as Tragedy: The Dilemma of the Moderate from Scott to Arnold.* 1980.

Ferris, Ina. *The Achievement of Literary Authority: Gender, History, and the Waverley Novels.* 1991.

Gordon, Robert C. *Under Which King? A Study of the Scottish Waverley Novels.* 1969.

Johnson, Edgar. *Sir Walter Scott: The Great Unknown.* 2 vols. 1970.

Kerr, James. *Fiction against History: Scott as Storyteller.* 1989.

Millgate, Jane. *Walter Scott: The Making of a Novelist.* 1984.

Murphy, Peter T. *Poetry as an Occupation and an Art in Britain, 1760–1830.* 1993.

Welsh, Alexander. *The Hero of the Waverley Novels.* 1963.

See also Exoticism

Scottish Agriculture

Scottish rural society was centered in the fermetouns, or townships, which varied considerably in both **population** size and areal extent. Fermetouns were held in tack (leased) from the landowner either by several individuals (multiple tenancy) or by one individual (single tenancy), the latter becoming increasingly common over the 18th century. Though verbal agreements were more customary in an earlier period, written leases had become widespread by the early 1700s, and the incidence of longer tack lengths of 19 years was increasing. "In kind" rentals (rents paid in agricultural produce), a characteristic feature of a weak market economy, were waning, while money rents grew correspondingly, signaling an evolutionary change in market conditions.

Agricultural labor was done by two broad groups of workers. The first were subtenants, sometimes called cottars, who subleased a part of a tenant's lease and paid rentals to the tenant, often in the form of labor. The second group were farm **servants**, both men and women, who were usually hired for 6 months or 1 year.

Cultivated fields in the early 18th century were largely unenclosed and ploughed in raised strips known as rigs, separated one from the next by furrows. This served as both a drainage system and a means of demarcating the lands possessed by individual tenants in the same fields. The intermixture of tenants' strips was known as "runrig" and was originally devised to ensure that all tenants received lands of equal quality, whatever their quantitative share of the whole possession might be.

The lands of the fermetouns were divided into "infield" and "outfield." The former were usually in closer proximity to the buildings of the settlement and were planted continuously with oats and bere (barley), usually under a 3-year rotation, and kept in good heart by the application of most of the fermetoun's animal manure. Outfield lands tended to be more peripheral geographically, and though cultivated with the same crops, were less intensively worked under a system that often left them fallow for some years, after a period of several years' cropping. This method of working the land remained largely intact until the 1750s and 1760s.

The final intrinsic feature of this system of husbandry was the commonty—a species of common land used for grazing and other purposes but held as an accessory to certain specified possessions, not as a common for all. The open nature of the fermetouns required a communal approach to the major daily and seasonal tasks of farming, such as herding, sowing, and harvesting. Since this tended to prevent individual initiative, late-18th-century **agricultural improvers** viewed the whole system as inimical to agricultural reform. Some improving landowners—**John Cockburn of Ormiston** and **Archibald Grant of Monymusk** among them—had effected changes to their estates prior to 1760, such as the enclosing of fields and the introduction of new crops and rotations. But such examples were exceptional, and the reorganization of agricultural lands in the first half of the century was limited.

In the Highlands too, society and agriculture were based on townships underpinned here by the **clanship** system. The cultivation of traditional, dependable crops was carried on in "lazy beds," a kind of raised sandwich of soil and seaweed, though the economic mainstay of the Highlands was the droving or livestock trade in Black Cattle. This unimproved rearing of cattle exported live animals to the Lowlands and England, bringing capital into the region.

From about 1760 the market context of Scottish agriculture changed more rapidly. Population growth quickened from around 1750 and then accelerated more sharply into the early decades of the 19th century. Scotland's rate of **urbanization** was among the fastest in Western Europe, and this, together with the first phase of the industrializing process, conspired to increase the demands placed on agriculture, requiring it to produce more for the growing proportion of the populace dependent on the market for food. The expansion of the national market was also fostered by improvements in **transport** such as the building of estate **roads**, turnpikes, and **canals**, and by improving river **navigation**.

As the market began to penetrate all aspects of the rural economy, the commutation of "in kind" rentals was completed, single tenancies became all but universal, and new, improving leases—detailed and prescriptive as to the methods of agriculture—became increasingly prevalent. From the 1760s, men of the landed class such as **Lord Kames** began a more general pattern of capital investment in the improvement of their estates. They invested with the clear and calculated expectation of quickly recouping their costs through higher rents, which the radical increases in crop yields, produced through improved rotations, techniques of fallowing, and the application of lime, allowed. The bulk of Scotland's commonties were divided between 1760 and 1815, **enclosure** of fields facilitated the introduction of new crops and rotations, and the infield–outfield system was abandoned. Larger farms began to appear as subtenancies, and smaller possessions were consolidated into more regular, enclosed, single-tenant farms.

Social consequences were inevitable. Farm consolidation and the rise of single tenancies led to the eradication of subtenants and small **farmers**, and the creation of a social gulf between the new single tenants and their labor force, clearly visible in the physical separation of living quarters on the farms. Though hired labor now constituted the entire agricultural work force, a complex hierarchy of social status developed, with the "hinds" or ploughmen at its pinnacle. Technologically, their work was assisted by the development of a new, lighter plow by **James Small**, of the threshing machine by **Andrew Meikle**, and of reaper technology by **Patrick Bell**.

In the Highlands, traditional townships were phased out after 1750 as the increase in wool prices induced landlords to introduce sheep farming on a large scale. The **Highland clearances** occurred when those cleared from these areas were relocated in small subsistence holdings called crofts, usually in coastal areas where they were partly employed in fishing and the manufacture of kelp—an alkali extracted from seaweed for use in the manufacture of soap and glass. Rapid population growth in parts of the Highlands caused widespread problems when Black Cattle prices fell sharply after the end of the **Napoleonic Wars** and the other economic supports of the region collapsed.

Peter Clapham

Bibliography

Devine, T.M. *The Transformation of Rural Scotland.* 1994.

Devine, T.M., and R. Mitchison, eds. *People and Society in Scotland.* Vol. 1: *1760–1830.* 1988.

Dodgshon, R.A. *Land and Society in Early Scotland.* 1981.

Gibson, A.J.S., and T.C. Smout. *Prices, Food and Wages in Scotland, 1550–1780.* 1994.

Handley, J.E. *Scottish Farming in the Eighteenth Century.* 1953.

Smout, T.C. *A History of the Scottish People, 1560–1830.* 1969.

See also Agriculture; Agricultural Societies; Sutherland Family

Scottish Banking

In **Scotland** as in England, the need for a banking system was essential if economic growth was to be obtained. Scottish development differed in many ways from England's, as its starting base and its needs were different; and this played a distinct part in the highly developed system that was to arise in Scotland. Differences in the **Scottish legal system** were also of considerable importance as, unlike their English counterparts, Scottish banks were not restricted to a maximum of six partners, giving them greater flexibility.

At the outset of the Hanoverian period, Scottish banking was dominated by the **Bank of Scotland**, founded in **Edinburgh** in 1695. It survived several early crises, but by the early years of the Hanoverian period it was tainted by **Jacobitism** and a tendency to lend only to its friends. Thus a rival, the **Royal Bank of Scotland**, was founded in 1727. The fact that the supple **Lord Milton** was its first governor suggests that this was part of **Walpole**'s system of political control in Scotland.

Almost immediately the Royal Bank started a war with the older bank, aiming to destroy it or force an amalgamation on favorable terms. The plot was unsuccessful. Despite a degree of hostility, the two banks then settled down to a modicum of coexistence. The vigor of the Royal Bank was reflected in its lending policy. It did not insist on the borrower taking the full amount of his loan in notes, instead guaranteeing to make payments to the limit of the agreed borrowing, charging interest only on the sum outstanding. This cash credit system, begun in 1728, was the forerunner of the overdraft.

Alongside the public banks there had developed a number of private bankers; many operated in conjunction with **merchant** businesses. Such banks did not issue notes, but circulated those of the public banks. In Edinburgh some private bankers were also directors of the public banks. Thus by the middle of the 18th century, Scotland had laid the foundation of a banking system, which was to grow rapidly during subsequent decades.

Competition for the two public banks came when the **British Linen Company** turned to banking. Their attempts to stifle the initial growth of the Linen failed, although they did succeed in curbing its expansion plans. Competition also came from a developing provincial banking sector. By the 1740s, **Glasgow** was becoming rich in the **tobacco trade**. Such growth demanded action, and new banks appeared. At first welcomed by the two public banks, the newcomers soon gave cause for concern; but attempts to smash them failed.

The system did have problems, most notably in its balance of payments. Scotland suffered from a general shortage of cash, which at times became acute; interest rates were thus higher in Scotland. Crises caused by **war** as well as economic cycles exacerbated the situation until the end of the 18th century. However, this shortage of cash actually aided the growth of Scottish banking, so that by the 1770s, **Adam Smith** could comment that the country's business was carried on by means of the paper of the different banking companies. In this sector, Scotland was unique and in many ways ahead of its time.

The Glasgow banks were somewhat limited in their growth, as a financial crisis in 1772 was soon followed by the **War of American Independence**. In 1783, the Royal set up a Glasgow agency under **David Dale**, making it supreme in the city. However, the banking sector as a whole did assist the change in Glasgow's pattern of trade from its emphasis on tobacco to sugar and **cotton** from the **West Indies**. The response of the bank to the challenges facing it had been to set up a network of branches. Apart from the Glasgow agency, the Royal tended to forge links with provincial bankers, and thus extend its influence through the country.

The Scottish banking system was important in stimulating economic growth. **Agriculture**, **commerce**, and industry all benefited. Loans provided finance for **agricultural improvers**, and **housebuilding** and trade benefited considerably also. Many of the new Scottish cotton firms benefited from cash credits as well as normal discounting facilities. Most credit was used to finance purchases of raw material, but, on occasion, to finance buildings as well. **Ironworks** were also large borrowers from the banks, as were **canal** and **road** constructors, often for the payment of **wages**.

There is some evidence that banks transferred money from areas of capital surplus to areas of deficit, their officials fearing that in times of crisis, landowners and farmers would demand the repayment of deposits. However, by the early 19th century, the industrial sector in the west of Scotland was perhaps generating its own funds, becoming less dependent on agricultural areas. As in England, short-term bills were often extended, becoming in effect longer-term loans. Flexibility over the repayment of cash credits also contributed to extended credit.

In the early years of the 19th century, the number of private banks declined; and because the monopoly of the **Bank of England** did not apply to Scotland, several new **joint-stock** banks were formed. The savings bank movement also had its beginnings in Scotland in 1810. All of this activity laid the basis for more aggressive competition in the financial sector in the Victorian era.

A.J.G. Cummings

Bibliography

Campbell, R.H. *Scotland since 1707; The Rise of an Industrial Society.* 2nd ed., 1985.

Checkland, S.G. *Scottish Banking: A History, 1695–1973.* 1975.

Munn, C.W. *Scottish Provincial Banking Companies, 1747–1864.* 1981.

Scottish Education

Scottish education was somewhat more vigorous and accessible than English during the Hanoverian period. The Reformation leaders in Scotland, from John Knox (*c.* 1510–1572) in the 1560s onward, were determined that each Scottish parish should be provided with a suitable school. These "parish schools" would be funded by local dignitaries while the church presbytery would examine, appoint, and subsequently inspect each teacher. Parish schools were expected to cater to all local children, regardless of social background, and ensure that they acquired the capacity and desire to read the Scriptures. A second function was to teach Latin and thereby equip selected boys for a subsequent university education. Parental poverty was not to stand in the way of the able working-class "lad of pairts" from fulfilling his academic potential at school and university. Indeed, the **Church of Scotland** traditionally regarded the rural working lower **middle class** as its main recruiting ground for the ministry. The parish school system was best suited to counties where farming communities became relatively prosperous during the 18th century; parishes were moderate in size, and **population** growth did not normally exceed the capacity of the local school.

These conditions did not prevail in extensive Highland parishes, where a single school might only reach a fraction of the scattered population. Large areas of the Highlands were also **Catholic**, Gaelic-speaking, and **Jacobite**, thus making their educational deficiencies all the more alarming when viewed from **London** or **Edinburgh**. It was hoped that the introduction of Scottish schools affiliated with the **Society for the Promoting of Christian Knowledge** (SPCK) from 1709 on would fill educational gaps in the region and evangelize and pacify its people. By the 1760s the Highlands no longer represented a political or military risk, and the original anti–Gaelic policy of the SSPCK could be relaxed. Schools now taught the reading of Gaelic as well as English, and their work was supplemented after 1811 by peripatetic Gaelic school societies, established on the lines of the **circulating schools** developed in **Wales**.

Scotland's expanding urban areas posed problems of a different kind. Each town had its own parish or "**burgh**" school, offering a mixture of elementary subjects and Latin. Burgh schools tended to be larger than rural parish schools and to have proportionally more boys studying Latin. Unlike England, **Scotland** did not develop many boarding schools, but the expansion of private day schools in the latter 18th century offered a less expensive alternative to the urban middle class. These offered a greater breadth of curriculum than the traditional burgh school, and in Edinburgh the choice of subjects ranged from elocution to Sanskrit.

Working-class children living in Scottish towns might have the opportunity to attend the local burgh school, but were more likely to seek a cheaper and less academic alternative. Private "Adventure Schools" sprang up to meet this demand, but there was mounting concern about the educational and moral quality of these establishments. There was also, of course, even more concern about children who rarely, if ever, attended any kind of school. Such children were perceived as playing a conspicuous part in urban **crime** and, in response to this, the Edinburgh Kirk Sessions established the first "Sessional Schools" in 1812. These taught mainly reading and writing, but also attempted where possible to offer Latin to selected pupils. They spread throughout urban Scotland but did not resolve the problem of urban illiteracy.

The **Scottish universities** of Edinburgh, Glasgow, Aberdeen, and St. Andrews were rather more successful in expanding to meet demand. In contrast to **Oxford** and **Cambridge** they accepted students from all denominational backgrounds, and their noncollegiate character also helped to widen their appeal by reducing student expenses. They all offered, at a modest cost, a core curriculum of classics, together with moral and natural philosophy. These subjects provided a foundation for subsequent professional education in the faculties of Divinity, Law, and Medicine. Noted professors included **John Anderson**, **Joseph Black**, **William Robertson**, and **Adam Smith**.

The upper working and lower middle classes continued to attend Scottish universities in appreciable numbers during the first half of the 19th century, and this wider access forms the basis of Scotland's claim to educational distinctiveness and superiority. However, the bulk of the Scottish working class was unaffected by the lad-of-pairts tradition and was only marginally more literate than its English counterparts. Neither country had as yet the resources or the will to make school attendance compulsory.

Lawrence Williams

Bibliography

Houston, Rab. *Scottish Literacy and the Scottish Identity.* 1985.

Phillipson, Nicholas, and Rosalind Mitchison, eds. *Scotland in the Age of Improvement.* 1970.

Saunders, Laurance. *Scottish Democracy, 1815–1840.* 1950.

Scotland, James. *The History of Scottish Education.* Volume 1. 1969.

See also Education, Elementary; Education, Secondary; Irish Education; Tutors and the Teaching Profession; Welsh Education

Scottish Enlightenment

This was an intellectual movement led by natural and moral philosophers in **Scotland** who self-consciously adopted the experimental method of reasoning in pursuit of the accumulation and diffusion of useful knowledge. A similar philosophical spirit permeated the **Enlightenment** throughout 18th-century Europe, but in Scotland this was both very concentrated and in some ways distinctively different. The greatest achievements of the Scottish Enlightenment were realized in moral philosophy, political economy, and historical sociology, though its characteristically analytic manner of thinking was manifest in all areas of intellectual endeavor and among a wide variety of well-educated and highly literate social groups. The centers of activity were in the **Scottish universities** in **Edinburgh**, **Glasgow**, and Aberdeen.

The movement's origins lay in the latter 17th century, when Scotland's universities and other institutions dedicated to the pursuit of scientific knowledge abandoned the Christianized Aristotelianism that had ordered their world, and began to adopt the methods and discoveries of the scientific revolution. Clarity of thought and reliance on experience were the hallmarks of this approach, which promised progressive control over nature and the improvement of material conditions.

Natural philosophy came increasingly to be valued for revealing the order God had imposed in the natural and moral worlds. Gershom Carmichael (1672–1729), the first occupant of the Chair of Moral Philosophy at the University of Glasgow, was the first Scottish philosopher to place moral philosophy on a rational and natural (rather than religious) foundation by arguing that moral guidance too should be sought from an empirical investigation into the nature of things and of man. Since no individual could either supply or understand all the rapidly accumulating information required by the new science, philosophy increasingly became a collective endeavor. By the 1720s, Scotland's intellectual and cultural institutions—its universities, academies, **learned societies**, professional bodies, improvement societies, and **clubs**—were fostering cooperation and communication along the lines suggested by Carmichael.

Commitment to intellectual inquiry and human improvement was also partly the Scots' response to the poverty and political instability plaguing their kingdom around 1700. They sought to better their condition through the **Act of Union**, by which they gave up their political institutions in exchange for the right of free access to English markets at home and abroad. Although substantial economic and political benefits did not materialize until the 1730s, the union's intangible effect—intensifying the Scots' long-standing interest in their own political and moral identity—was immediate and far-reaching. They increasingly turned to the scientific study of history and law in an attempt to understand, the better to improve, their political and economic situation.

Among the Scottish literati who came to maturity during this springtime era and who attempted to adopt a more scientific approach to the study of man and society were the members of Edinburgh's Rankenian Club, which included such prominent intellectuals as William Wishart (*c.* 1692–1753), George Turnbull (1698–1748), Charles Mackie (1688–1770), Colin MacLaurin (1698–1746), John Stevenson (1695–1775), and Robert Wallace (1697–1771). These men discussed morals, metaphysics, and aesthetics in the hope that their example of rational inquiry would help their countrymen lead happier, more useful and virtuous lives. Emphasis on the cultivation of man's natural sociability was in fact the centerpiece of the philosophy of **Francis Hutcheson**, which set the terms for most Scottish academic moral theory during the second half of the century. As Carmichael's successor in Glasgow's Chair of Moral Philosophy, Hutcheson exemplified the enlightened clergyman–academic for whom philosophy was a didactic and character-building scientific discipline.

The movement reached its apogee during the second half of the 18th century. **David Hume**, **Adam Smith**, **Lord Kames**, **Thomas Reid**, **Adam Ferguson**, **William Robertson**, **John Millar**, and **Dugald Stewart** were perhaps the greatest of the period's students of human society. **James Hutton**, **Joseph Black**, and **William Cullen** were among its most noteworthy natural scientists. They and hundreds of others dedicated themselves to various intellectual and practical endeavors, sharing a common optimism about improving the human condition and making Scotland an intellectual center of international importance.

Peter J. Diamond

Bibliography

Davie, G.E. *The Scottish Enlightenment.* 1981.

Emerson, Roger L. "Natural Philosophy and the Problem of the Scottish Enlightenment." *Studies in Voltaire and the Eighteenth Century.* Vol. 242, pp. 243–291.

Forbes, Duncan. *Hume's Philosophical Politics.* 1975.

Hont, Istvan, and Michael Ignatieff, eds. *Wealth and Virtue: The Shaping of Political Economy in the Scottish Enlightenment.* 1983.

Jones, Peter, ed. *Philosophy and Science in the Scottish Enlightenment.* 1988.

Kidd, Colin. *Subverting Scotland's Past: Scottish Whig Historians and the Creation of an Anglo–British Identity, 1689–c.1820.* 1993.

Phillipson, Nicholas. "The Scottish Enlightenment," in David Daiches, ed., *A Companion to Scottish Culture.* 1981.

Sher, Richard B. *Church and University in the Scottish Enlightenment.* 1985.

Stewart, M.A., ed. *Studies in the Philosophy of the Scottish Enlightenment.* 1990.

See also Church of Scotland; History Writing and Historians; Royal Society of Edinburgh; Science, Technology, and Invention; Scotland and Scottish Culture; Webster, Alexander

Scottish Legal System

Scots law was already a mature system at the time of the **Act of Union**, having been set in order by Lord Stair (1619–1695) in his *Institutions of the Law of Scotland* (1681). The treaty of union voided all statutes contrary to itself, but contained safeguards for the continuing autonomy of Scots law. It provided that no change was to be made in laws concerning "private right . . . except for the evident utility of the subjects within Scotland." The existence of the Court of Session, dealing with civil cases, and the High Court of Justiciary, dealing with criminal cases, was guaranteed. The treaty was held by some to have prohibited appeals from these highest courts to the **House of Lords**, but appeals from the Court of Session became possible from 1711.

The status of the treaty in relation to the doctrine of parliamentary sovereignty has been, and still is, disputed. The English constitutional theorist A.V. Dicey (1835–1922) believed that "neither the Act of Union with Scotland nor the Dentists Act 1878 has more claim than the other to be considered as supreme law." Scottish judges have sometimes taken a different view. Lord Cooper, in a test case, said: "The principle of the unlimited sovereignty of Parliament is a distinctively English principle which has no counterpart in Scottish constitutional law."

In any event, during the 18th century, Parliament seldom interfered with Scots law. The major exception was the Heritable Jurisdictions Act (1748), passed after the last **Jacobite** rebellion, the **Forty-five**. This stripped noblemen of their previous judicial powers, which were thought to give them dangerous power over their feudal dependants. Afterward the whole country was ultimately subject to the central courts in **Edinburgh**, with local justice administered under sheriffs appointed by the state to each county.

It was a rational and efficient system, which ushered in the golden age of Scots law. Members of the **legal profession** made major intellectual contributions, not only to the law itself but also to the wider ideas of the **Scottish Enlightenment**. The courts, left largely to themselves, upheld a coherent framework of basic principles but recognized the need to adapt them to novel circumstances, as **Scotland** developed from a traditional agricultural society into a mercantile and industrial country. Even when Parliament passed new Scottish statutes, it generally did so only on the advice of the judges, so that the integrity of the system was maintained.

For the rest, rulings in the Court of Session, often elaborate statements of principle and application, ensured a smooth evolution. The process was aided by institutional writers, notably John Erskine (1695–1768) and George Bell (1770–1843), who at intervals restated the whole range of civil law, and who could be cited as authorities in the courts. The function of the Court of Session in this era has been compared to that of the Supreme Court of the United States today. The system as a whole made Scotland a well-ordered country, with little popular unrest.

Michael Fry

Bibliography

Kiralfy, A., and H.L. MacQueen, eds. *New Perspectives in Scottish Legal History.* 1984.

Smith, T.B. *Studies Critical and Comparative.* 1962.

Walker, D., ed. *Stair Tercentenary Studies.* 1981.

See also Crime; Judicial System; Punishment

Scottish Poor Law

The Scottish Poor Law was not conceived and developed by careful thought, but evolved from the 16th century as a consequence of piecemeal legislation and changing times and values. An act of 1535 decreed that each parish was responsible for the poor born within it and that paupers, granted a badge or token, could only beg within their native parish. But it was an act of 1579 that was to become the cornerstone of the structure. This authorized the compulsory provision for the support of the poor by local inhabitants and drew a stark contrast between these "pure and impotent" who should be relieved and the "strang and idle beggars" who should be punished.

Lay authorities and local rates were, in varying degrees, involved in the securing of the relief, but increasingly the situation developed into one in which Heritors and Kirk Sessions of the **Church of Scotland** acted as the practical instruments of poor relief. They were unequal to the task. With Kirk Sessions largely responsible for the collection and disbursement of funds, the system increasingly reflected the social mores of the **Presbyterian** elite; and limited funding ensured that there was a clear differentiation between those perceived as the "deserving" poor who, due to abnormal misfortune, needed relief, and "undeserving" vagabonds and ne'er-do-wells.

In the last decade of the 17th century a succession of statutes enforced earlier laws more rigorously. Fines were imposed for begging beyond the parish, and correction houses were built to accommodate beggars and make them work. If the system was admired, it was for its inexpensive aspect rather than for its charity. The Poor Law was in place and so it remained throughout the Hanoverian period, with only minor tinkering to tighten its grip. In the 1750s, Court of Session decisions meant that control of the funds came to rest in the hands of the property-owning Heritors rather than the Kirk Sessions.

As the **Industrial Revolution** developed in the late 18th and early 19th centuries, the system proved increasingly inadequate in coping with periodic unemployment. In 1819 there were attempts to exclude the unemployed from relief, and in the 1820s **Thomas Chalmers** sought to ensure that the system would remain voluntary. Full-scale reform did not come until the Poor Law Amendment Act of 1845, and even then it was not yet accepted (as it was in England and **Wales** under the 1834 **New Poor Law**) that able-bodied paupers had any claim on public assistance. The 1845 act did, however, begin the process of weakening the church's control of poor relief and placing it in secular hands.

G.T. Bell

Bibliography

Ferguson, Thomas. *The Dawn of Scottish Social Welfare.* 1948.

Lindsay, Jean. *The Scottish Poor Law.* 1975.

Mitchison, Rosalind. "The Making of the Old Scottish Poor Law." *Past and Present.* Vol. 63, pp. 58–93.

Saunders, L.J. *Scottish Democracy, 1815–1840.* 1950.

See also Poverty and Poor Laws

Scottish Universities

In the years before 1714, winds of change swept through the five Scottish universities. New chairs or lectureships in subjects ranging from Greek to mathematics were founded, while innovative ideas drawn from the texts of Sir Isaac Newton (1642–1727), Samuel Pufendorf (1632–1694), and **John Locke** superseded those of Aristotle. The use of experiments gradually transformed lecturing on natural philosophy, and by the 1740s English replaced Latin as the language of instruction. Scholastic pedagogical practices, such as the teaching of an entire 3-year philosophy course by one instructor known as a regent, also began to disappear. The first Scottish university to switch from regenting to the professorial system was the University of Edinburgh (1707), followed by Glasgow (1727), St. Andrews (1747), Marischal College, Aberdeen (1753), and, last, King's College, Aberdeen (1800).

Moreover, the political world in which the universities operated changed dramatically. The **Fifteen** rising revealed that considerable support remained for the Pretender at Aberdeen and St. Andrews. The Hanoverian regime responded by establishing a Royal Commission of Visitation which removed all those tainted with **Jacobitism** from office, and by tightening the Crown's hold on university appointments. Henceforth the Scottish universities were controlled through the **patronage** of **London**-based politicians like the **Duke of Argyll**, which ensured that the colleges served the Hanoverians loyally during the **Forty-five** and the turmoil of the 1790s.

Once order was restored after the disruption of the Fifteen, local power over the Scottish colleges fell largely to a phalanx of **Whigs** associated with the Reverend William Carstares (1649–1715), who was one of the architects of the **Presbyterian** ascendancy following the **Glorious Revolution** and who served as **Edinburgh**'s principal from 1703 until his death in 1715. This group included principals Thomas Blackwell, Sr. (1660–1728) of Marischal College, Aberdeen, and Joseph Drew (*c.* 1663–1738) of St. Andrews, as well as Carstares' successor in Edinburgh, William Wishart *primus* (1660–1729). Wishart took Carstares' efforts to remodel the college a step further by formally establishing a faculty of **medicine** in 1726. Edinburgh soon began to overtake Glasgow as the preeminent university in Scotland.

The 1720s also saw additional educational initiatives. Some of the Scottish universities began to open their natural philosophy classes to members of the community willing to subscribe money for the purchase of scientific instruments, and this innovation helped to foster a strong tradition of public lecturing on science. Nor did the teaching of moral philosophy lag behind. At Marischal College, George Turnbull (1698–1748) told his classes that moralists ought to apply the Newtonian method to the study of human nature and morality, and his call for the methodological reform of the moral sciences later bore fruit in the Common Sense School of philosophy, founded by a circle of Aberdeen savants centered on **Thomas Reid.** The election of **Francis Hutcheson** to the Glasgow chair of moral philosophy in 1729 served to put moral sense on the philosophical agenda in **Scotland**, while Hutcheson's style sparked a protracted debate over the relationship between the anatomy of the mind and practical moralizing.

Building on these foundations, in the years 1750 to 1780 a new generation of professors created a golden age in the Scottish universities. This efflorescence was partly the result of astute management by **Lord Bute** and local figures like **William Robertson**, Principal of Edinburgh. As leader of the dominant Moderate party in the Kirk, Robertson kept clerical interference in academic affairs to a minimum and fostered an atmosphere in the colleges which allowed intellectual life to thrive.

Although Glasgow's fortunes were generally on the wane, the teaching of moral philosophy remained strong, with **Adam Smith** and Thomas Reid successively holding the chair. Instruction in the human sciences received an additional boost through the appointment of Smith's protégé **John Millar** as Professor of Civil Law in 1761. St. Andrews, and King's College, Aberdeen, were less successful than Glasgow at attracting students and notable teachers during the second half of the century, but King's did boast some lively intellects on its staff, and it profited from the proximity of Marischal College, which was a far more dynamic institution. **James Beattie**, one of the most influential exponents of Common Sense philosophy, taught at Marischal from 1760 until 1796, while his colleague Patrick Copland (1749–1822) was one of the most popular scientific lecturers of the day.

Edinburgh, however, was at its zenith. Students from across the Atlantic world packed the lecture halls and filled the pockets of the professors with handsome class fees. The medical school swelled in both size and stature, and its growth nurtured the flowering of allied subjects such as botany, chemistry, and natural history. Consequently, Edinburgh was able to recruit men from the other Scottish colleges such as **William Cullen** and **Joseph Black**, who raised the medical and scientific prestige of the university to unprecedented heights. Edinburgh also excelled in the human sciences, with **Adam Ferguson** and **Dugald Stewart** successively holding the chair of moral philosophy, **Hugh Blair** occupying a Regius Professorship of Rhetoric and Belles Lettres founded in 1762, and Robertson adding further luster by his philosophical histories. In 1789 Thomas Jefferson (1743–1826) commented that "no place in the world can pretend to a competition with Edinburgh."

These years of brilliance began to fade in 1775 as **Henry Dundas**, later Viscount Melville, rose to political prominence as the "absolute dictator" of Scotland. In the process, he constructed a well-oiled **patronage** machine, which remained in operation until the passing of the Scottish Reform Act in 1833. The professors recommended by Dundas and the Melville interest were sometimes **placemen** of little academic distinction. The hitherto efficient working relationship between the Edinburgh Town Council and its college broke down in 1825, precipitating the establishment of the 1826 Royal Commission of Visitation, whose proceedings marked the passing of an era even if they resulted in little immediate practical reform. Before this, William Robertson's resignation as leader of the Moderates in 1780 had heralded equally significant changes in the religious fabric of academe. Robertson was succeeded by George Hill (1750–1819), whose brand of ecclesiastical management was far more intrusive on the universities than Robertson's.

The alliance between the professorate and the Moderates collapsed in 1805 when Hill and his allies crossed swords with members of the Edinburgh faculty over a professorial appointment. Combined with the backlash to the **French Revolution**, the conservatism of Dundas and Hill produced a stultifying climate in academe. The **Evangelical** challenge to the hegemony of the Moderates during the early 19th century also spilled over into the universities, as witnessed by the appointment of the most prominent Scottish spokesman for Evangelicalism of the age, **Thomas Chalmers**, to the St. Andrews chair of moral philosophy (1823).

Finally, new intellectual currents reshaped the curricula of the colleges. Common Sense philosophy was eclipsed by the rise of German idealism, while in the natural sciences the Scots imported mathematical physics championed in Paris and Cambridge. Only the Edinburgh medical school retained a vestige of its earlier vibrancy, although it was increasingly challenged by English rivals. By 1837, therefore, the Scottish universities faced a crisis of identity that was only resolved through a succession of Visitation Commissions in the latter 19th century.

Paul B. Wood

Bibliography

Anderson, Robert D. *Education and the Scottish People, 1750–1918.* 1995.

Cant, R.G. *The University of St. Andrews: A Short History.* Rev. ed., 1970.

Davie, George. *The Democratic Intellect: Scotland and Her Universities in the Nineteenth Century.* 2nd ed., 1964.

Emerson, Roger. *Professors, Patronage and Politics: The Aberdeen Universities in the Eighteenth Century.* 1992.

Sher, Richard B. *Church and University in the Scottish Enlightenment: The Moderate Literati of Edinburgh.* 1985.

Sher, Richard B., and Andrew Hook, eds. *The Glasgow Enlightenment.* 1995.

Wood, Paul B. *The Aberdeen Enlightenment: The Arts Curriculum in the Eighteenth Century.* 1993.

See also Cambridge University; Oxford University; Scottish Education; Scottish Enlightenment; Trinity College, Dublin

Sculpture

The reemergence of the art of sculpture in Britain during the 18th century resulted from an interest in **antiquity**, and the rise of **housebuilding**, **interior design**, and **landscape architecture** in which sculpture figured as a central decorative element. Beginning with the new **Palladian** housebuilding of the 1720s, sculpture became an extension of the decorative schemes of country houses and created a market for sculptors that continued into the early 19th century.

The **Grand Tour** of the Continent was a part of a young man's education and was intended to heighten his interest in the arts and culture. It thus easily became the fashion for travelers, in pursuit of objects of "virtù," to collect actual Roman antique sculpture or to commission copies of famous works to display in British gardens and country houses. The sculptures most commonly commissioned for interiors were bust portraits. Sitters often had themselves portrayed as Romans with natural hair, but sometimes alternatively in their wigs, nightcaps, or unbuttoned shirts, striking informal attitudes.

The sculptor himself, prior to the Hanoverian period, was often considered primarily as an **artisan** and was principally employed as a creator of sepulchral monuments. During the 18th century sculptors came into their own as artists by executing works for garden pavilions and garden views, for busts and statuary for the gentlefolk, and, late in the century, for public celebration of national victories.

The pivotal year in sculpture's rise as an art form was 1714, coinciding with the accession of **George I** to the throne. In that year the **Earl of Burlington** traveled to Rome, where he met the sculptor Giovanni Battista Guelfi (*fl.* 1714–1734) and persuaded him to visit England. Guelfi's arrival marked the first in a series of sculptural immigrations that included another Burlington protégé, John Michael Rysbrack (1694–1770). These men initially established themselves by executing designs by others, principally by **architects**.

The most influential architect of the early Hanoverian period was **James Gibbs**. His *Book of Architecture* (1728) included designs for monuments that were quickly adapted and executed by carvers all across Britain. Gibbs also launched the English career of Rysbrack, who sculpted Gibbs's designs for sepulchral monuments and chimney pieces before moving into Burlington's employ. Even under Burlington, Rysbrack's statues of Andrea Palladio and Inigo Jones at Chiswick (Burlington's country home) followed the drawings of another Burlingtonian architect, **William Kent**. However, Rysbrack soon built up an independent reputation and by the 1750s was designing as well as crafting his commissions. He dominated the scene until the 1760s, along with Peter Scheemakers (1691–1781) and the French immigrant Louis François Roubiliac (1702–1762), who possessed a wonderful ability to capture fleeting expressions—his best works included statues of **Handel** (for Vauxhall Gardens, 1737) and of the **Duke of Argyll** (1746, in Westminster Abbey). Together, all three transformed the creation of sculpture into an art form and separated it from a craft in the minds of 18th-century Britons.

The fuller establishment of sculptors as artists was also recorded in the founding of the **Royal Academy of Arts** in 1768. The founding members included three sculptors: Joseph Wilton (1722–1803), Agostino Carlini (*d.* 1790), and William Tyler (*d.* 1801). Despite this, however, the actual practice of sculpture continued to follow trends in architecture, partly perhaps because of the dominance of the architect **William Chambers** over the Royal Academy (appointed by **George III**, he was its first treasurer), but more certainly due to the persisting conception of sculpture as part of the decoration of houses and gardens.

But English sculpture, like architecture, had its baroque, Palladian (Roman antique), and rococo phases that were supplanted in the mid-18th century by the **Neoclassical style**. Under this, sculptors depended principally on literary sources such as the fantasies on Roman ruins depicted in the work of Antonio Piranesi (1720–1778), and the writings on Greek sculpture by Johann Joachim Winckelmann (1717–1768). **Henry Fuseli's translation** into English of Winckelmann's 1755 work as *Reflections on the Painting and Sculpture of the Greeks* (1765) heavily influenced both sculpture and architecture into the 19th century.

Sculpture's emancipation from architecture owed something also to the rise of **nationalism** during the age of **George III**. Britain's military victories gave rise to public commissions for statuary of parliamentary leaders and military heroes such as **Pitt, Wellington,** and **Nelson,** as well as to schemes to personify Britannia. The most popular sculptor of this period was Joseph Nollekens (1737–1823), who made likenesses of many of its best-known figures, including **Garrick, Sterne, Pitt, Fox, West,** and the king himself. The most ambitious project of the day was to erect a series of monuments in St. Paul's Cathedral that would celebrate British "worthies." This idea was conceived by **Sir Joshua Reynolds** when president of the Royal Academy, and subsequently funded by Parliament. Parliament later transferred authority over the project to a Committee of National Monuments in 1802; this continued until 1825.

Throughout the latter Hanoverian period, neoclassicism continued to dominate commissions sponsored by the Crown and by private clients. These included both small works by (Nollekens's most notable successor) **Sir Francis Chantrey,** such as his busts of **John Horne Tooke** (1811) and **Sir Walter Scott** (1820); and an unexecuted scheme by the great **John Flaxman** for erecting in Greenwich a 200-foot statue of Britannia, based on the Roman goddess Minerva. Interest in Greek precedents was heightened in 1817 by the transfer of the **Elgin marbles** from the Parthenon to the British Museum. Though placed on display too late to influence the St. Paul's project for British worthies, the Elgin marbles influenced work commissioned by **George IV**; a prominent example may be seen in John Henning's (1801–1857) frieze for the screen at Hyde Park Corner (1828), which is based on the Parthenon frieze.

David D. McKinney

Bibliography

Lipking, Lawrence. *The Ordering of the Arts in Eighteenth-Century England.* 1970.

Physick, John. *Designs for English Sculpture, 1680–1860.* 1969.

Whinney, Margaret. *Sculpture in Britain, 1530 to 1830.* 1964.

Seamen

See Shipping and Seamen

Seaside Resorts

As early as the 1760s, seaside towns were capitalizing on the rising popularity of seawater as a medical restorative. Wealthy aristocrats flocked to the seaside carrying physicians' recommendations. The bathing machine, a hut drawn on wheels into the water, appeared in the 1750s. Physicians and **entrepreneurs** built seaside bathing facilities, assembly rooms, **concert** halls, tea rooms, circulating **libraries**, card rooms, inns, and elegant houses. In so doing they transplanted to the coasts the environment of fashionable **spas** such as **Bath**, Scarborough, and Tunbridge Wells. By the early decades of the 19th century many seaside towns, no longer absorbed in fishing, had become playgrounds of the rich and famous.

Much of the fanfare about seawater was the result of a treatise published by Dr. Richard Russell (1700–1771), who joined earlier writers such as Sir John Floyer (1649–1734) in crediting it with power to cure diseases and invigorate the sickly. In particular, Russell's *Dissertation Concerning the Use of Sea-Water in Diseases of the Glands* (1750) credited it with giving relief from symptoms of glandular disease. Once begun, this reliance on brine as a cure-all persisted well into the 19th century.

Russell moved to Brighton and began putting his theories into practice, yet the patrons of seaside resorts were determined to make the bathing ritual only part of a gratifying social experience. The resort "season" extended from July to October. Visitors expected to advance themselves socially by being seen in the right places, and resorts naturally encouraged such expectations. At Brighton, visitors could walk the "parade," a promenade walkway. Other opportunities arose at assemblies, card parties, concerts, evening **theater** performances, and balls. Many resorts

Bathing machines at Scarborough, 1750s

hired a "master of ceremonies" to orchestrate not only group events but personal introductions.

Until the **railway** made **travel** easy for the **middle classes**, seaside resorts were the domain of the upper crust. Early resorts such as Brighton, Margate, and Ramsgate were exclusive settings. Brighton became even more so in the 1780s after the Prince of Wales (later **George IV**) began visiting and patronizing the town. In 1789 his father, **George III**, visited Weymouth and also indulged in the practice of sea bathing. Such highly publicized visits gave seaside resorts a tremendous boost in popularity. By the 1790s, Worthing, Hastings, Broadstairs, Deal, Dover, Southampton, Eastbourne, and Southend all strove to entice sea bathers. Half a century later, these resorts were competing with dozens of others not just for well-born patrons but also for the trade of the country's newly leisured middle and working classes.

Anne St. John-Scott

Bibliography

Clunn, Harold. *Famous South Coast Pleasure Resorts Past and Present: Their Historical Associations, Their Rise to Fame and a Forecast of Their Future Development.* 1929.

Golby, J.M., and A.W. Purdue. *The Civilisation of the Crowd: Popular Culture in England, 1750–1900.* 1985.

Marsden, Christopher. *The English at the Seaside.* 1947.

Musgrave, Clifford. *Life in Brighton: From the Earliest Times to the Present.* 1970.

Walton, John K. *The English Seaside Resort: A Social History, 1750–1914.* 1983.

Walvin, James. *Beside the Seaside: A Social History of the Popular Seaside Holiday.* 1978.

Selkirk, 5th Earl of (Thomas Douglas) (1771–1820)

Selkirk was a Scottish philanthropist and pioneer of Canadian development. He had an interest in **agricultural improvement**, and after a Highland tour in 1792 developed an enthusiasm for **emigration**, planting his first colony of poor Highlanders on Prince Edward Island in 1803. He planted another in Upper Canada, at Baldoon near Lake St Clair, not without resistance from the colonial authorities, who were suspicious of his motives.

In 1805 Selkirk published his *Observations on the Present State of the Highlands of Scotland.* After taking a hand in the **Hudson's Bay Company** and obtaining from it 116,000 square miles he launched (1811) his most ambitious project, the settlement of the vast and fertile Red River Valley in what is now Manitoba. This was the first major settlement in the Canadian Northwest. Successive parties of Scottish and Irish colonists arrived in 1812–1815.

However, the Red River colony was resented by the **North West Company**, which began an angry dispute with it and its protector the Hudson's Bay Company. This led to the Seven Oaks massacre (1816), when 20 colonists were killed, including Robert Semple, Governor of both the colony and the Bay company's territories in North America. Selkirk arrived the following year with a military force and reestablished the colony. The two fur companies settled their differences in 1821, and Selkirk's colony, administered by governors appointed by Selkirk and his heirs, flourished independently until purchased by the Bay company in 1836.

Ian Donnachie

Bibliography

Bumsted, J.M. *The People's Clearance: Highland Emigration to British North America, 1770–1815.* 1982.

Sellar, Patrick (1780–1881)

A sheep farmer and factor for the Countess of **Sutherland**, Sellar became one of the most detested figures of the **Highland clearances**. To make the Sutherland estate more profitable, tenants were to be moved from inland farms, earmarked for sheep ranching, to seaside villages, where industry and **fishing** were being established. Many tenants were reluctant to move, so their houses were burned down to prevent their return. At Strathnaver in 1814, the **population** was given too little time to arrange their removal, but Sellar nonetheless burned their houses and buildings, an act resulting in fatalities. Tried on a charge of culpable homicide, Sellar was acquitted in 1816. Fired from his job as factor, he remained a sheep farmer and outlived nearly all his victims.

A.J.G. Cummings

Bibliography

Grimble, I. *The Trial of Patrick Sellar.* 1962.

Richards, E. *The Leviathan of Wealth.* 1973.

———. *A History of the Highland Clearances.* 1982–1985.

Senior, Nassau (1790–1864)

Senior, an economist best known for his work on England's poor laws, held the first chair of economics at **Oxford University**. As an advisor to the **Whig** government his report to Parliament provided the empirical basis of the 1834 **New Poor Law**'s policy of strict sumptuary controls in a workhouse system as a condition for welfare. In his *Outline of the Science of Political Economy* (1836) Senior argued that capitalists accumulated interest and profit as a result of abstinence ("savings"). His theory that a firm's profit was made in the last hour of the workday also made him an opponent of the **factory movement**, though he did accept restrictions on **child labor** and also wrote against American slavery, attacking its alleged biblical justification. Through his international relationships he linked British and French liberal circles, as did his friend and admirer **John Stuart Mill**.

David M. Levy

Bibliography

Bowley, Marian. *Nassau Senior and Classical Economics.* 1937.

Levy, S. Leon. *Nassau Senior, 1790–1864: Critical Essayist, Classical Economist, and Adviser to Governments.* 1943, 1970.

See also Chadwick, Edwin; Economic Thought; Malthus, Thomas Robert; Poverty and Poor Laws

Sensibility and Sentimentalism

Allied though distinct, sensibility and sentimentalism denote two of the key concepts in the cult of "feeling" which found diverse expression in the **poetry**, drama, prose fiction, moral philosophy, and medical literature of the period roughly 1740–1790. The term "Age of Sensibility" has been applied to that period in an attempt to describe those literary features that distinguish it from the preceding **Augustan** period and the later **Romantic** period. Keeping in mind that such labeling runs many risks of homogenizing disparate and sometimes conflicting literary practices, a few features can nevertheless be meaningfully isolated.

To begin with, the rise of feeling was connected with a long-term evolution of British moral philosophy. In his *Leviathan* (1651), Thomas Hobbes (1588–1679) suggested that human nature was essentially egocentric and that society consequently was held together by mutual fear, rather than fellow-feeling. Responding to this, the 3rd Earl of Shaftesbury (1671–1713) in his *Characterstícks* (1711) posited an innate moral sense which, in its combination of reason and feeling, led people toward benevolence and sociability. This idea, developed by the Scottish moral philosophers **Francis Hutcheson**, **David Hume**, and **Adam Smith**, was at its height in the latter 18th century, before being challenged by the utilitarianism of **Bentham** and his followers, and helped to lend credibility to all the variations of feeling.

These found expression in many genres. For example, in poetry there was a new emphasis on subjective experience and melancholia, and hence a move away from the "public" and largely satirical verse that had dominated the first half of the 18th century. In drama, gentle, sentimental comedy became the norm, burying at last the bawdy and ironic drama of the Restoration. It was, however, in narrative fiction that sentimentalism's impact was most strongly felt, as the recurrent motif of "virtue in distress" became the occasion for an emphasis on the pathetic, which was unprecedented in earlier literature.

The vocabulary of the new cult is instructive. *Sensibility* took on a new meaning at some point during the second third of the century. It denoted the capacity for elevated feeling, and particularly the ability to feel compassion for the suffering of others—a compassion informed by a highly sensitized and sympathetic response as much to the fictional depiction of virtue in distress as to real suffering. Thus *sensibility* described an aesthetic response as well as a moral one, though it was scarcely coincidental that this was also the beginning of a long period in the growth of **humanitarianism**, with interest focusing increasingly on such evils as the **slave trade**, **crime**, and **child labor**. There are many reasons to believe also that the popularity of Jean-Jacques Rousseau's (1712–1778) works of the 1760s helped greatly to popularize "sensibility," while his repudiation in the 1780s and 1790s had a reverse effect.

The other term, *sentiment*, could connote both a considered opinion and, as **Lord Kames** put it (1774), a thought "prompted by passion." Thus when **Samuel Johnson** recommended reading **Samuel Richardson** "for the sentiment," he was alluding both to the novelist's delineation of the feeling heart and to the moral precepts, which inform such novels as *Pamela* (1740) and *Clarissa* (1747–1748). Lady Bradshaigh's famous letter to Richardson (1749), asking for an explanation of "sentimental"—"so much in vogue among the polite"—indicates that the term was the source of semantic confusion even as it was becoming a buzzword. Its connotations in the period 1740–1780 range from "pertaining to sentiment," through an emphasis on feeling rather than reason in a positive sense, to a pejorative connotation of addiction to insincere and mawkish sentiment (the hypocritical Joseph Surface, in *The School for Scandal* [1777], is a man of sentiment). *Sentimentalism* could thus describe neutrally a complex of ideas yet suggest a negative assessment of the emotion connected with them. And in fact, all the key terms of the cult of feeling took on their modern, negative connotations as the ideas that informed the literature of sensibility fell into disrepute in the 1780s and 1790s.

While sentimentalism can be clearly traced in the poetry of **Thomas Gray**, **Edward Young**, and **William Cowper**; and in the drama of **George Lillo**, **Colley Cibber**, **Richard Cumberland**, **Oliver Goldsmith**, and **Richard Brinsley Sheridan**; it was, as mentioned earlier, in narrative fiction that its impact was most profound. The **novel** of sentiment was typified by Richardson's novels, and the novel of sensibility by such texts as **Henry Mackenzie**'s *The Man of Feeling* (1771) and **Laurence Sterne**'s *A Sentimental Journey* (1768). Both types shared a concern with the theme of virtue in distress and tended to pit their heroes and heroines against an alienating world of suffering in which rapacious and selfish characters are a constant threat. Sensibility was initially the prerogative of female characters, but by the 1760s the "Man of Feeling" had become a recognizable type. The language of sentiment was typically nonverbal; its conventional signs were tears and the swoon, both suggesting an alliance between the body and the moral sense, and alluding to connections between **benevolence** and sexual generosity.

By the end of the century, however, some women in particular began protesting the role thrust upon them as avatars of sensibility. **Mary Wollstonecraft** warned (1792) that when women's "senses are inflamed, and their understandings neglected, [they] become the prey of their senses, delicately termed sensibility, and are blown about by every momentary gust of feeling." **Hannah More** found (1799) "no quality in the female character which will be so likely to endanger the peace, and to expose the virtue of the possessor," as sensibility.

J.T. Parnell

Bibliography

Bredvold, L.I. *The Natural History of Sensibility.* 1962.
Brissenden, R.F. *Virtue in Distress: Studies in the Novel of Sentiment from Richardson to Sade.* 1974.
Conger, S. McMillen, ed. *Sensibility in Transformation: Creative Resistance to Sentiment from the Augustans to the Romantics.* 1990.
Crane, R.S. "Suggestions Toward a Genealogy of the 'Man of Feeling,'" in *The Idea of the Humanities.* Vol. 1. 1967.
Ellis, Frank H. *Sentimental Comedy: Theory and Practice.* 1991.
Erametsa, Erik. "A Study of the Word 'Sentimental' and of Other Linguistic Characteristics of Eighteenth Century Sentimentalism in England." *Annales Academiae Scientiarum Fennicae.* Ser. B, Vol. 74, No. 1, pp. 18–54.
Frye, Northrop. "Towards Defining an Age of Sensibility: The Genealogy of the 'Man of Feeling' Reconsidered." *Modern Philology.* Vol. 75, pp. 159–183.
Hagstrum, J.H. *Sex and Sensibility.* 1980.
Johnson, Claudia L. *Equivocal Beings: Politics, Gender, and Sentimentality in the 1790's—Wollstonecraft, Radcliffe, Burney, Austen.* 1995.
Mullan, John. *Sentiment and Sociability: The Language of Feeling in the Eighteenth Century.* 1988.
Okin, Susan Moller. "Women and the Making of the Sentimental Family." *Philosophy and Public Affairs.* Vol. 11, pp. 65–88.
Rawson, Claude. *Satire and Sentiment, 1660–1830.* 1993.
Todd, Janet. *Sensibility: An Introduction.* 1986.

See also Enthusiasm; Manners and Morals

Septennial Act (1716)

As the Parliament elected in 1714 neared the end of its term, it passed this act to postpone until 1721 elections slated for 1717. In effect, the government of the **Earl of Stanhope** extended its own life by 4 years. The act set the maximum duration of future Parliaments at 7 years before new elections were required, and effectively continued the exclusion from office of the discredited **Tory** party.

Some contemporaries truly saw the 3-year term then in effect as too short, and acknowledged Parliament's right to determine the legal length of future parliaments; however, the sitting Parliament's extension of its own term smelled of jobbery. The act became a bone of contention in the contemporary court-versus-country **Whig** schism, but ultimately helped promote the authority of the **Commons**. It governed the legal duration of parliaments until the Parliament Act of 1911 shortened maximum duration to 5 years.

K.R. Wood

Bibliography

Thomas, P.D.G. *The House of Commons in the Eighteenth Century.* 1971.
Thomson, M.A. *A Constitutional History of England, 1640–1801.* 1938.
Williams, E.N. *The Eighteenth-Century Constitution: Documents and Commentary.* 1960.

See also Party Politics

Sermons

The sermon occupied a central place in the life and literature of Hanoverian Britain. Both High and Low Church English Protestants saw it as the nexus of their communal worship. A carefully prepared reflection on a passage from Scripture, the sermon was a principal means for instructing and encouraging the assembled congregation in the practice of their faith. In many churches, sermons were delivered not only on Sundays but on two or more weekdays as well. For the average citizen, then, the most commonly encountered form of public oratory was the sermon. Pulpit oratory was a public performance, and the preacher was expected not only to edify but to entertain.

The sermon's profound influence on popular culture was not restricted to the aural reception of preaching. Throughout the 18th century, sermons were the most widely distributed form of non-biblical spiritual reading. According to Sampson Letsome's *Index to the Sermons, Published since the Restoration* (1751), about 100 new sermons were published each year between 1660 and 1751. By the end of the century, that figure had almost doubled. **Samuel Johnson** viewed the printed sermon as a significant branch of English literature, which contributed greatly to the development of rhetoric, and the beauty of the English **language**. Some historians have noted significant parallels between the evolution of the **essay** and the progress of the sermon.

Hanoverian sermons display a rejection of the baroque pulpit oratory of such "metaphysical" preachers as John Donne (1573–1631) and Lancelot Andrews (1555–1626) in favor of a more simple and direct style. The early **Latitudinarians**, whose most influential preacher was John Tillotson (1630–1694), promoted a new style of preaching, characterized by simple and direct language, appeals to reason rather than emotion, and an emphasis on moral rather than doctrinal instruction. Throughout the early decades of the 18th century the sermons of Tillotson were the single most important model for Anglican pulpit oratory. Preaching manuals or *artes praedicandi* for training prospective clergymen and assisting those already active in the pulpit were also highly influential in forming pastoral practice. The *Discourse of the Pastoral Care* (1692) of Gilbert Burnet (1643–1715), and *Ecclesiastes* (2nd rev. ed., 1693) of John Wilkins (1614–1672), advanced the Latitudinarian program of pulpit reform down into the 1750s.

The accomplished sermons of **Francis Atterbury**, **Joseph Butler**, and Thomas Secker (1693–1768) reveal the continued influence of the Latitudinarian style. But the first half of the 18th century was not an especially inspired era in the history of English preaching. Particularly after the elaborate rhetoric of Jeremy Taylor (1613–1667) and the sometimes satirical eloquence of Robert South (1633–1716), many early Hanoverian preachers seemed to pale in comparison. Three notable exceptions were the mesmerizingly intense **Isaac Watts**, the great doctrinal preacher **Philip Doddridge**, and the fiery controversialist James Foster (1697–1753). Significantly, none of these men embraced the Latitudinarian principles of pulpit oratory.

Around 1740, the open-air preaching of **George Whitefield** and **John Wesley** inaugurated a new style of religious rhetoric, the Evangelical sermon. In contrast with mainstream Latitudinarian preaching, the Evangelical sermons delivered in Low Church Anglican and nascent **Methodist** congregations were more passionate in their appeal and more effusive in their delivery. Biblical texts and conversion narratives, rather than reasoned ethical arguments and well-ordered demonstrations, were the heart of the Evangelical sermon. In addition to Whitefield and Wesley, many of the greatest preachers of the latter 18th century belonged to the Evangelical school, including **Henry Venn**, **Charles Simeon**, Rowland Hill (1744–1833), and, within the Church of England, Richard Cecil (1748–1810).

Michael F. Suarez, S.J.

Bibliography

Downey, James. *The Eighteenth-Century Pulpit: A Study of the Sermons of Berkeley, Secker, Sterne, Whitefield and Wesley.* 1969.

Lessenich, Rolf P. *Elements of Pulpit Oratory in Eighteenth-Century England, 1660–1800.* 1972.

Webber, F.R. *A History of Preaching in Britain and America.* 3 vols. 1952.

See also Church of England; Dissenters; Evangelicalism; Publishers and Booksellers; Roman Catholicism; Theology

Servants

Employment as a servant in the Hanoverian age usually brought a person security in lodgings and meals, and a reasonable hope of security in illness. There was even some chance of security in old age, provided that the master took his obligations seriously.

The servant **population** in the 18th century was not as great as in the 19th century, but it was more concentrated, being employed in fewer households. In general, the number of servants in a household varied with the status and wealth of the family. A noble household might employ 20 to 60 servants; a household belonging to a very wealthy gentleman, 10 to 20; and households of lesser gentry and country families, five to 10. Lawyers and prosperous businessmen maintained establishments comparable in size to those of the **gentry**, whereas small businessmen, tradesmen, and men of the lower **middle class** might employ as many as five servants, or as few as one.

In every household, regardless of size, function determined the servant's status within the servant hierarchy. The main division was between the upper servants, who worked directly under the master or mistress, and the lower servants, who had little personal contact with their employers. Among the former were the lady's maid, house steward, housekeeper, cook, chambermaid, valet, butler, gardener, and clerks of the kitchen and the stables. On large estates the highest position was that of the land steward whose considerable personal responsibility extended to managing his master's estates, leasing farms, collecting rents, settling disputes, and keeping detailed records.

The lower servants performed the relatively unskilled tasks essential to maintenance of the household: coachman, footman, groom, gamekeeper, scullery maid, yard boy, provision boy, and page. Highest in status were the footmen who, wearing their master's livery, were visibly dissociated from physical labor; they served chiefly as evidence of their master's status.

Contemporary observations and extant records of servants' wages and household management indicate that financially, servants could do reasonably well. Their wages rose

"The Servants' Dinner," from a print by Rowlandson, 1806

throughout the 18th century as estates became more magnificent. By 1750, when perhaps £40 a year marked off the bottom of the "middling ranks" from those below, and **legal professionals** at the top of the "middling ranks" might be making £2,000 or more, the best-paid house steward might receive, in addition to room and board, as much as £100 a year; a cook, £40; a housekeeper, £20; and a postilion, £3. By 1800 a land steward could earn several hundred pounds a year; and for the well-to-do household, the annual cost of keeping a full household of servants was over £1,000. Servants also benefited from the custom of vails-giving, whereby guests of the household were expected to show their appreciation for services rendered by giving the servants vails (tips) at the end of each visit. Servants whose expectations were not satisfied could easily retaliate when the guest next visited, but by the 1760s the increasingly extortionate demand for vails caused masters to balk, and the practice began to disappear.

Masters and mistresses, held responsible for the conduct of their servants, often acted not only as their supervisors but as their moral instructors and disciplinarians. Servants were given rules, and were observed to be sure that they followed them. They were reminded of the importance of fulfilling Christian duties. Nevertheless, throughout the century there were many instances of theft and other abuses of privileges. Both **Jonathan Swift** and **Daniel Defoe** complained of servants' immoral and lazy behavior, advising masters to exert stricter control.

Because of the physical closeness of masters and servants, it was expected that no close social relationships should exist between them. Masters were advised to allow no familiarity between the two. The master's children were especially to be protected from language and behavior ill-suited to their social position. Shortly before 1800, the Eclectic Society, an **Evangelical** religious group, publicly advised mothers to be particularly vigilant where there was the possibility of servants criticizing their employers in the children's presence. But despite social distance, masters and mistresses often did develop fond attachments to particular servants, bequeathing them clothes and money in their wills. There were even marriages between the two groups, though rare and considered scandalous. The **radical Duke of Richmond** ceased being radical after his daughter ran off with a pastry cook.

Servants thus occupied an incongruous place in the household. Their place in the national workforce was just as incongruous. Contemporary opinion placed them outside the working class, as appendages of their masters' households; they were neither thought capable of acting of their own accord nor, thanks to their dependence and internal differences, could they organize into groups capable of unified activity. Nevertheless, among his or her fellows a servant could enjoy considerable respect, based largely on the status of the master. A duke's butler was held in infinitely greater esteem than the butler of a small businessman, and might even himself be addressed as "duke" by underlings. But status evaluations of this kind, between individuals holding similar positions in different households, were much easier than those between servants holding dissimilar positions. For example, the valet of a country gentleman might lord it over a duke's groom of stables. There was as much snobbery among servants as elsewhere in society, if not more.

By the close of the 18th century the rising demand for servants by the middle class was giving them somewhat greater independence. Just as their place in society began to change, however, their duties became more numerous. They still functioned as, among other things, tokens of their employers' status, but by the early 1800s only the wealthiest upper- and middle-class employers could still afford to copy the elaborate household staffs of earlier times. Because more and more families were employing fewer and fewer specialized servants, in many households more duties were being performed by fewer people. Yet collectively the servant class continued to grow. In 1811 it stood at approximately 11.8% of the workforce, second only to **agriculture** in numbers of people employed, and it still retained this important position in 1851, the percentage of domestic workers edging up to 13% (and in fact still higher, to more than 15%, by 1881).

Anne St. John-Scott

Bibliography

Hecht, J. Jean. *The Domestic Servant Class in Eighteenth-Century England.* 1956.

Langford, Paul. *A Polite and Commercial People: England, 1722–1783.* 1989.

Mingay, G. *English Landed Society in the Eighteenth Century.* 1963.

Swift, Jonathan. *Directions to Servants.* 1745.

Turner, E.S. *What the Butler Saw: Two Hundred and Fifty Years of the Servant Problem.* 1963.

See also Child-Rearing; Hours, Wages, and Working Conditions; Women's Employment

Settlement, Act of (1701)

William III, near the end of his reign, wanted to name the successor to his own probable successor, his sister-in-law Anne who, then in her late 30s, was unlikely to produce an heir. To guarantee the throne's passage to a Protestant he named Sophia of Hanover (a granddaughter of James I) and her descendants as Anne's heirs. Parliament legalized William's choice with this act, which thus confirmed (what the **Glorious Revolution** had already partially established) that kings were to hold their power by parliamentary consent. The act also required future sovereigns to be members of the **Church of England** and prohibited them from leaving the country or from waging **war** to protect their Continental territories, and it debarred foreigners from office and Parliament. Other clauses sought to protect judges against Royal dismissal, exclude officeholders from the **Commons**, and nullify the Crown's power to pardon persons impeached by the Commons. Under the act's terms, **George I**, Sophia's eldest son, took office on the death of **Queen Anne** (1714), Sophia having died 2 months before Anne.

K.R. Wood

Bibliography

Thomas, P.D.G. *The House of Commons in the Eighteenth Century.* 1971.

Thomson, M.A. *A Constitutional History of England, 1640–1801.* 1938.

Williams, E.N. *The Eighteenth-Century Constitution: Documents and Commentary.* 1960.

See also Hanoverian Succession

Seven Years' War (1756–1763)

This global conflict, Britain's greatest military success of the 18th century, aligned her with Prussia against a coalition that included **France**, Austria, Russia, Sweden, Saxony, and, eventually, Spain. The **War of Austrian Succession** had ended more from mutual financial exhaustion than any decisive military action, leaving an unstable diplomatic situation. Franco–Austrian fears of an increasingly powerful Prussia upsetting the European balance of power produced the **diplomatic revolution**, ending 3 centuries of Bourbon–Hapsburg enmity and moving Britain and Prussia, adversaries in the earlier war, into a mutual assistance pact, the Convention of Westminster (January 1756). Britain and France had been at war since 1754 over rival claims to the Ohio Valley in North America; when Frederick II of Prussia (1712–1786) invaded Saxony (August 1756), the war broadened into a general European conflict.

The war began badly for Britain's side, with Frederick's forces struggling to cope with offensives by French, Austrian, and Russian armies. However, his opponents were unable to coordinate their activities, allowing him to deal with them piecemeal (with timely aid from British-financed **Hanover**); and when Tsarina Elizabeth died (1762), Peter III (1728–1762), her Prussophile successor, pulled Russia out of the war and created a stalemate in Europe.

Meanwhile, Prime Minister **William Pitt the Elder**'s concentration on transoceanic theaters, where British naval superiority could come into play, transformed the conflict into a true world war, with military actions in **North America**, the **West Indies**, West **Africa**, **India**, and the Far East. From 1759 ("miracle year" of victories) through 1762 Britain had remarkable military success, thwarting a cross-channel invasion, defeating the French Atlantic and Mediterranean fleets, capturing Martinique from France, and Havana and Manila from Spain, lifting the siege of Madras, and forcing the surrender of French **Canada**.

The war ended with two peace treaties. The **Peace of Paris** transferred Spanish Florida, together with all French territory east of the Mississippi River except New Orleans, to Britain. France regained lost holdings in the West Indies and India. Spain regained Cuba and the Philippines and (by separate agreement) acquired French claims west of the Mississippi. By the Treaty of Hubertusburg (February 1763), Austria accepted *status quo ante bellum* terms, thereby reconfirming Prussia's ownership of Silesia.

Britain emerged as a big winner, but efforts to meet the stupendous costs of the war (which increased the national debt by some £130 million) and of the greatly enlarged **Empire** would soon complicate relations with her North American colonies to the point of rebellion. The war's outcome signaled the arrival of British imperial greatness. But ironically it intensified conflicts with France and the Ameri-

Wolfe's interview with Pitt before departure to Quebec, 1759

can colonists to the extent that both would soon cooperate to undo its results.

David Sloan

Bibliography

Ayling, Stanley. *The Elder Pitt: Earl of Chatham.* 1976.

Browning, Reed. *The Duke of Newcastle.* 1975.

Dorn, Walter. *Competition for Empire, 1740–1763.* 1940.

Gipson, L.H. *The British Empire before the American Revolution.* Vols. 6, 7, 8. 1946, 1949, 1953.

Middleton, Richard. *The Bells of Victory: The Pitt–Newcastle Ministry and the Conduct of the Seven Years' War, 1757–1762.* 1985.

Peters, Marie. *Pitt and Popularity: The Patriot Minister and London Opinion during the Seven Years' War.* 1980.

Rashed, Z.E. *The Peace of Paris, 1763.* 1951.

West, Jenny. *Gunpowder, Government and War in the Mid-Eighteenth Century.* 1991.

See also American Revolution; Foreign Relations; War and Military Engagements

Seward, Anna (1742–1809)

Known as the "Swan of Lichfield," Seward was a prolific poet and letter writer. Her best works, though flawed by excessive **sentimentalism** and some artificiality of style, included the poems "Monody on the Death of Major Andre" (1780) and "Elegy on Captain Cook" (1780), and the unusual **novel** in verse, *Louisa* (1784).

Seward was born in Eyam, Derbyshire. In 1754 the family moved to Lichfield, where she resided for the remainder of her life. She never married, though she received numerous proposals. Her home became a center for artists, musicians, and writers. She received early support for her poetry from **Erasmus Darwin**, for whom she wrote a memoir in 1804. She was well acquainted with **Samuel Johnson**, but was not fond of him and criticized him publicly; **Sir Walter Scott**, on the

Anna Seward

other hand, received her lavish praise, and it was to him that she bequeathed her literary estate.

Mary Tiryak

Bibliography

Ashmun, Margaret. *The Singing Swan: An Account of Anna Seward and Her Acquaintance with Dr. Johnson, Boswell, and Others of Their Time.* 1931.

Constable, A., ed. *Letters of Anna Seward, Written between the Years 1784 and 1807.* 6 vols. 1811.

Pearson, Hesketh, ed. *The Swan of Lichfield: Being a Selection from the Correspondence of Anna Seward.* 1937.

Scott, Walter, ed. *The Poetical Works of Anna Seward, with Extracts from Her Literary Correspondence.* 3 vols. 1810.

See also Poetry and Poetics; Women in Literature

Shaftesbury, 7th Earl of (Anthony Ashley Cooper) (1801–1885)

Shaftesbury, or Lord Ashley (as he was called until he succeeded to the earldom in 1851), dedicated his distinguished public career in the **Commons** (1826–1851) and **Lords** (1851–1885) to several philanthropic causes. A **Tory radical** and one of the most prominent **Evangelicals** of his day, an opponent of the 1832 **Reform Act** but a friend of **Catholic emancipation** and the repeal of the **corn laws**, he was the right man in the right place when the ten hours movement of **textile** workers in the North (an important aspect of the larger **factory movement**) needed a new parliamentary leader after **Michael Sadler** lost his seat in the reformed Parliament of 1833. Several pieces of factory legislation, most notably the Ten Hours Act (1847), bore his impress. His work in the interests of **coal miners**, overworked children, sanitary living conditions, public education, and the insane helped mitigate many harmful social effects of the **Industrial Revolution**. Due to his social and religious standing as well as his political influence, Shaftesbury was in a unique position to lend prestige and credibility to many movements to improve the lives of workers.

Carolyn Stevens

Lord Shaftesbury

Bibliography

Battiscombe, Georgina. *Shaftesbury, the Great Reformer, 1801–1885.* 1975.

Best, G.F.A. *Shaftesbury.* 1964.

Bready, J. Wesley. *Lord Shaftesbury and Social–Industrial Progress.* 1926.

Finlayson, Geoffrey. *The Seventh Earl of Shaftesbury, 1801–1885.* 1981.

Hammond, J.L., and B. Hammond. *Lord Shaftesbury.* 1936.

See also Child Labor

Shakespeare Industry

This term refers to one of the most interesting and significant phenomena of literature in the Hanoverian age, the critical rehabilitation of the Elizabethan playwright and the massive popularization of his work. Shakespeare died in 1616, but by time of the Restoration (1660) his fame had perished, too. In 1661 John Evelyn (1620–1706) saw *Hamlet* and observed in his *Diary* that "the old playe began to disgust this refined age"; John Dryden (1631–1700) noted that Beaumont and Fletcher were twice as popular as Shakespeare. The rub lay in Shakespeare's obsolete language, and a shift in critical ideology.

The initial solution was to rewrite the plays: language was brought up to date, and plots and characters were made to fit the requirements of justice and decorum. The most successful alteration was Nahum Tate's (1652–1715) *King Lear* (1681), which held the stage throughout the 18th century and was reprinted in 22 editions. Dryden attempted a more radical approach in his adaptation of *Antony and Cleopatra* as *All for Love* (1678). In all, 35 plays were altered or adapted.

If adaptation and alteration had remained the only solutions to the difficulties of Shakespeare, many modern ideas of literary history would scarcely have come into being. There were, however, individuals whose interests centered on what Shakespeare had actually written. Of these, Jacob Tonson (1656–1737), the publisher, was supremely important. In 1707 and 1709, Tonson purchased the copyrights of 23 Shakespearean plays from the descendants of those who had rights in the text of the fourth folio (1685). Subsequently he acquired ownership of the copyrights for almost all the plays. Under the terms of the first English copyright statute (1710), the owners of copyrights in old books had the sole right to publish these works for 21 years. Tonson established his rights by commissioning Nicholas Rowe (1674–1718) to edit the plays, and Rowe's edition appeared in 1709 in a handy octavo format.

Rowe began the laborious process of making Shakespeare accessible to modern readers. His most substantial contribution was a life of Shakespeare, which remained standard un-

Edmund Kean as Gloster in Richard III

til Edmond Malone's (1741–1812) in 1790. Rowe also printed lists of *dramatis personae,* introduced uniformity into the designation of characters in speech headings, added stage directions, improved grammar, and modernized word forms. Since there were no manuscripts, Rowe claimed to have compared the old editions as part of his "Care to redeem [Shakespeare] from the Injuries of former Impressions."

Tonson's next editor, **Alexander Pope**, collected 29 early quartos, but chiefly exercised his taste when establishing the texts by demoting passages he did not like into footnotes, or omitting them entirely, blaming "whole heaps of trash" and "additions of trifling and bombast passages" on Shakespeare's fellow actors. In addition to marking passages and scenes with commas and stars (to indicate approval), Pope also began the process of annotation. This was necessary because, as his friend **Francis Atterbury** remarked, Shakespeare had alluded "to an hundred things, of which I knew nothing, & can guess nothing." Pope's knowledge of Elizabethan manners and customs was, however, minimal, and his edition (1725) did little more than indicate the need for editors to assist readers in these areas. Indeed, Pope's greatest contribution to the Shakespeare industry was a negative one—to drive **Lewis Theobald** to publish the first book devoted to Shakespeare, *Shakespeare Restored: or, A Specimen of the Many Errors, as Well Committed, as Unamended, by Mr. Pope in His Late Edition of this Poet* (1726). By making Theobald the hero of *The Dunciad* (1728), Pope then secured public attention for Theobald's own edition (1733).

Theobald's "restoration" began the determination of Shakespeare's usage and grammar by means of extensive parallel readings. He also suggested a number of brilliant emendations of the text. In addition to citing parallel readings (either from Shakespeare or from his contemporaries and predecessors) to explain difficult passages or to support emendations, Theobald collated early quartos (of which he owned 29) and folios, and generally recognized the line of descent of the printed texts. He speculated intelligently about the nature of manuscript copy for quartos and the first folio; this, together with his knowledge of Elizabethan literature and secretary-script, made him the pioneer of what the 20th century called the New Bibliography.

The next editor, Sir Thomas Hanmer (1677–1746), whose sumptuous edition was printed in 1744, made little contribution to the texts. In 1747 he was followed by **William Warburton**, undoubtedly the worst of Shakespeare's editors, whose pretensions to scholarship were shattered by Thomas Edwards's (1699–1757) *The Canons of Criticism* (first published in 1747 as *A Supplement to Mr. Warburton's Edition of Shakespear*). **Samuel Johnson**'s edition (1765) was distinguished by a magisterial Preface in which he defended Shakespeare's neglect of neo-Aristotelian rules by an appeal to him as the poet of general nature. Johnson's texts derived chiefly from those of Theobald. He began the tradition of the variorum editions by often reprinting the notes of the earlier editors, though he frequently displayed a bias against Theobald.

Johnson's immediate successor, Edward Capell (1713–1781), is far more interesting as an editor, and shared with Theobald a concern with manuscript sources of the earliest printed texts. However, by determining to print his notes (1775, 1779–?1783) separately from his edition (1767), he diminished the impact of his work on the reading public. Useful contributions to the editorial tradition were also made by George Steevens (1736–1800) and Isaac Reed (1742–1807), but the largest additions to information about Shakespeare's life, stage, and the Elizabethan background generally were made by Malone, first in 1790 and then in the "Third Variorum Shakespeare" (1821), a monumental edition taken over after Malone's death and finally seen through the press by James Boswell, Jr. (1778–1822). In these two great works the plays are encrusted with layers of scholarly information, including an extended essay on the chronology of the plays.

With accessible texts, literary criticism involving close reading became possible. In his periodical, the *Censor* (1715–1717), Theobald had set the agenda: as opposed to Thomas Rymer's (1641–1713) neo-Aristotelian condemnation of Shakespeare's irregular plots, lack of decorum, and disregard of poetic justice, Theobald stressed psychology and language. Attention was focused on the poetry and rhetoric of the plays by William Dodd's (1729–1777) frequently reprinted *The Beauties of Shakespear* (1752). Characterization was the concern of William Richardson's (1743–1814) *Philosophical*

Analysis and Illustration of Shakespeare's Remarkable Characters (1774), Maurice Morgann's (1726–1802) *Essay on the Dramatic Character of Sir John Falstaff* (1777), and Thomas Whately's (*d.* 1772) *Remarks on Some of the Characters of Shakespeare* (1785), which led to **Romantic** criticism.

Even as the minor theaters of the Romantic period produced Shakespearean **burlettas**, travesties, melodramas, and musicals, the major theaters, larger than their 18th-century predecessors, hosted extravaganza productions and restored "original" versions such as *King Lear* (finally around 1840 forsaking Tate's sentimental adaptation). Theatrical stars competed in the roles of Hamlet, Macbeth, and Romeo. But Romantic critics like **Coleridge** and **Lamb** idealized Shakespeare as the master of the human psyche. While **Neoclassical** critics had argued over Shakespeare's adherence to dramatic rules and his conceptions of poetic justice, Romantics read his dramas as the geography of human nature. Coleridge pondered Hamlet's apparent procrastination; Lamb emphasized the psychology of Shakespeare's characters, preferring to consider the plays as closet dramas (mental theater) rather than as theatrical productions because the stage fettered the audience's imagination.

The impact of scholarship and criticism on the performance of Shakespeare was gradual and uncertain. Attention was certainly drawn to the controversies of editors by Pope's *Dunciad,* and interest in the texts, once aroused, was sustained. **Freemasons** occasionally promoted performances of plays, as did the Shakespeare Ladies **Club**. By around 1750, bardolatry was firmly established, partly thanks to Johnson's former pupil, **David Garrick**, whose performances as the leading actor of his day contributed to Shakespeare's popularity. Garrick did not, however, demur from altering the plays, and he added to the Shakespearean hype by promoting the Stratford Jubilee (6 September 1769).

By the 1780s even **George III**, who privately objected to Shakespeare's plentiful "stuff," was commenting on how one could be "stoned" for abusing the national bard. Henry Crawford, in **Jane Austen**'s *Mansfield Park* (1819), commented indirectly on the combined efforts of scholars, critics, and actors:

> But Shakespeare one gets acquainted with without knowing how. It is a part of an Englishman's constitution. His thoughts and beauties are so spread abroad that one touches them everywhere; one is intimate with him by instinct.

Peter Seary

Bibliography

McKerrow, R.B. "The Treatment of Shakespeare's Text by His Earlier Editors, 1709–1768." *Proceedings of the British Academy.* 1933.

Seary, Peter. *Lewis Theobald and the Editing of Shakespeare.* 1990.

Sherbo, Arthur. *The Birth of Shakespeare Studies.* 1986.

Van Lennep, William, Emmett L. Avery, Arthur H. Scouten, et al., eds. *The London Stage, 1660–1800: A Calendar of Plays, Entertainments & Afterpieces, Together with Casts, Box-Receipts and Contemporary Comment, Parts 1 to 5.* 11 vols. 1960–1968.

See also Actors and the Acting Profession; Dramatic Arts; Dramatic Criticism; Literary Criticism; Publishers and Booksellers; Theaters and Staging

Shanavests

The Shanavests or "waistcoats" came into existence in Ireland in the autumn of 1806 in east Munster. They were a rural **middle-class** grouping, formed specifically to challenge the Caravats or "cravats," a local **Whiteboy** movement, whose aim was to band together the poor in an attempt to control the local economy. Their own ideology was one of primitive **nationalism**, painting the Caravats as enemies of national unity. Possessing a formal organizational structure, they functioned chiefly as a vigilante group, reflecting a widespread unwillingness among the **Catholic** middle class to trust the British state for protection.

Conflict in 1806–1811 between the Shanavest and Caravat factions seriously disturbed areas of Tipperary, Waterford, Kilkenny, Limerick, and Cork, spreading northward and westward to involve 11 counties. Their feud, which involved firearms and murder, was a great deal more ruthless and violent than traditional Irish faction fights. The government considered declaring martial law, but instead established a special commission in February 1811, which was successful in curtailing the outbreak.

The Shanavest–Caravat rivalry by no means ceased entirely; it persisted well into the 19th century under elaborate local guises, such as in the struggles of "Magpies" and "Black Hens," or "Coffes" and "Ruskavellas."

E.W. McFarland

Bibliography

Clark, S., and J.S. Donnelly, eds. *Irish Peasants: Violence and Political Unrest, 1780–1914.* 1983.

Cornewall, Lewis G. *On Local Disturbances in Ireland.* 1836.

O'Donnell, P. *The Irish Faction Fighters of the Nineteenth Century.* 1975.

See also Defenderism; Rightboys; Terry Alts

Sharp, Granville (1735–1813)

A leader of **humanitarian** causes, Sharp is known for his contributions to the **antislavery movement**, which he almost single-handedly founded. Born in Durham, employed in the government ordnance department, he became outraged when he learned in 1765 that Jonathan Strong, a slave who had accompanied his master to **London** and suffered a beating at his hands, was about to be sent back to the **West Indies**. His *Representation of the Injustice and Dangerous Tendancy of Tolerating Slavery in England* (1769) became an early milestone of the antislavery movement, as did his involvement on be-

Granville Sharp

half of another slave, James Somerset, in the landmark case (decided by **Lord Mansfield** in 1772) that helped establish the principle that by merely setting foot on English soil, a slave became free.

In another famous case (1783), Sharp unsuccessfully tried to obtain justice against a ship's captain who had pitched overboard more than 100 sick Africans transported on the slaver *Zong*. He struggled also to help former American slaves who, having fought alongside Britain in the **War of American Independence**, now found themselves down and out in London; together with **Jonas Hanway** he developed a committee to provide financial aid and eventually a plan to establish free blacks in **Africa**, in Sierra Leone.

The publicity surrounding these events helped to turn slavery into a national issue. In 1787 Sharp, along with **Clarkson** and **Wilberforce**, was one of the founding members of the (otherwise predominantly **Quaker**) Society for the Abolition of the Slave Trade, chairing its abolition committee and pushing to end the institution of slavery itself, not just the **slave trade**. In the 1790s he protested the reestablishment of slavery in reconquered Caribbean islands and urged emancipation as part of British strategy against the French. He lived to see the trade abolished in 1807.

Sharp was interested in a variety of **radical** causes. Although he opposed **Catholic emancipation**, he otherwise championed the plight of the oppressed, whether they were Native Americans, indentured **servants**, poor immigrants in America, **coal miners** and **salters** in **Scotland**, or **agricultural laborers** in England. He supported the American colonists' independence and, as a member of the **Society for Constitutional Information**, urged domestic political reform. He was also active in specifically religious causes, as his work in the British and Foreign Bible Society (1804) and the Society for Conversion of Jews (1808) attests. He wrote many pamphlets, and also a few scholarly works on the Greek language in its relation to **biblical criticism**.

Mark C. Herman

Bibliography

Anstey, Roger. *The Atlantic Slave Trade and British Abolition, 1760–1810.* 1975.

Davis, David Brion. *The Problem of Slavery in the Age of Revolution, 1770–1823.* 1975.

Drescher, Seymour. *Econocide: British Slavery in the Era of Abolition.* 1977.

———. *Capitalism and Antislavery: British Mobilization in Comparative Perspective.* 1987.

Eltis, David. *Economic Growth and the Ending of the Transatlantic Slave Trade.* 1987.

Royle, Edward, and James Walvin. *English Radicals and Reformers, 1760–1848.* 1982.

Turley, David. *The Culture of English Antislavery, 1780–1860.* 1991.

Shelburne, 2nd Earl of (William Petty) (1737–1805)

Ambition lifted Shelburne to the office of Chief Minister for only 9 months (July 1782 to April 1783) before the unpopularity of his **Treaty of Paris** (1783) and the suspicions of his fellow **Whigs** drove him from office. He was intelligent, and the treaty, which generously satisfied American territorial ambitions above the Ohio and in the American West, was part of his plan to establish a long-range special relationship with the Americans in which both peoples would benefit, Britain (not **France**) serving as America's chief trading partner and link to Europe. But Shelburne was distrusted and disliked by many contemporaries who found his personality and behavior too ambiguous.

Lord Shelburne

He first entered politics (1760) as an aide to **George III** and **Lord Bute**, which earned him the distrust of the **Newcastle** Whigs. He inherited the earldom (1761) before he could take his seat in **Commons**, and became Secretary of State for the Southern Department in the Chatham (**William Pitt the Elder**) administration (1766–1768). His adherence to Chatham's principle of "measures not men" ran counter to the contemporary trend toward **party** government and led George III, who approved of it, to appoint him to the **Rockingham** administration (1782) in the hope of dividing the **opposition**. Shelburne's subsequent protection of the king's wishes led to his promotion to First Lord of the Treasury but, to the Rockingham Whigs, damned him as a Court puppet. He was created 1st Marquess of Lansdowne in 1784. Reform interested him, and he was **patron** to three notable reform-minded intellectuals: **Jeremy Bentham**, **Richard Price**, and **Joseph Priestley**.

P.J. Kulisheck

Bibliography

Brown, Peter. *The Chathamites.* 1967.
Norris, John. *Shelburne and Reform.* 1963.
Ritcheson, C.R. "The Earl of Shelburne and Peace with America, 1782–1783: Vision and Reality." *The International History Review.* Vol. 3, pp. 322–345.

See also Foreign Relations

Shelley, Mary Wollstonecraft (1797–1851)

Shelley's first **novel**, *Frankenstein* (1818; rev. ed., 1831), introduced the science-fiction genre into English literature. Juxtaposing technological power and moral responsibility, Frankenstein and his monster reflect the central social, economic, and political dilemmas of the early industrial era. Immediately popular, the novel has increased in relevance and recognition as the world attempts to deal with the benefits and hazards of developments such as nuclear power and genetic engineering.

Mary Wollstonecraft Godwin Shelley's parents were the **radical** writers **William Godwin** and **Mary Wollstonecraft**. The works of both parents, which advocated egalitarian government and equal rights for women, strongly influenced her writing. In 1814 she eloped with the radical, already married, poet–philosopher **Percy Bysshe Shelley**, a disciple of her parents' reformist concepts. In 1816, following the suicide of his estranged wife who was pregnant with an illegitimate child, Mary and Percy married. Of their four children only the last, Percy Florence, survived both parents.

During their 8 years together the Shelleys lived a peripatetic life, primarily in England and Italy, mutually supporting and encouraging each other's writing and sharing an intellectualism that pervaded their daily way of life. When her husband drowned in the Gulf of Spezia (1822), Mary, though left without income, committed her life to raising their son, to her writing, and to preserving and publishing Percy Shelley's works to achieve for him the public recognition not accorded him in his lifetime. She accomplished all three goals.

Her first publication was *Mounseer Nongtongpaw* (1808), published when she was 11 years old. Among her works are five novels after *Frankenstein: Valperga* (1823); *The Last Man* (1826); *Perkin Warbeck* (1830); *Lodore* (1835); *Falkner* (1837); one novella, *Matilda* (1819, published 1959); two **travel** books, *Six Weeks' Tour* (1817) and *Rambles in Germany and Italy* (1844); and five volumes of Lives (1835–1839) of Italian, Spanish, Portuguese, and French writers for the Cabinet Cyclopedia. As Percy Shelley's editor she published his *Posthumous Poems* (1824), *Poetical Works* (1839), and *Essays, Letters* (1839, dated 1840).

Her works were well received during her lifetime. During the Victorian era, however, her reputation was eclipsed by her husband's, leaving her works other than *Frankenstein* unread by scholars and the general public alike. Presently, reconsideration by Romantic and feminist critics has brought her works to new and increasing prominence.

Betty T. Bennett

Bibliography

Bennett, Betty T., ed. *The Letters of Mary Wollstonecraft Shelley.* 3 vols. 1980, 1983, 1988.
Feldman, Paula R., and Diana Scott-Kilvert, eds. *The Journals of Mary Wollstonecraft Shelley, 1814–1844.* 2 vols. 1987.
Lyles, W.H. *Mary Shelley: An Annotated Bibliography.* 1975.
Sunstein, Emily W. *Mary Shelley: Romance and Reality.* 1989.

See also Gothic Fiction and Gothicism; Romanticism and Romantic Style

Shelley, Percy Bysshe (1792–1822)

Shelley is best known as a lyric poet, but he mastered many other styles of **poetry**. He also wrote much prose, including two short **Gothic** novels (*St. Irvyne* and *Zastrossi,* both 1810). His views on morals, politics, and religion were considered **radical** by contemporaries; he believed in individual liberty and the perfection of humanity, and considered his own age a turning point in history. And for him, the role of the poet was both to reflect and lead his age.

He was born well-off, the son of a Sussex M.P. He went to Oxford but was expelled for coauthoring a pamphlet titled *The Necessity of Atheism* (1811). That same year Shelley married Harriet Westbrook. Three years later he met the daughter of **William Godwin** and **Mary Wollstonecraft**, the future **Mary Wollstonecraft Shelley**, with whom he eloped to Europe in 1814, though his wife was still living. After Harriet's suicide (1816), Mary and Percy were married in England. In 1818 they settled in Italy where, in 1822, he drowned in a sailing accident. His close friends included **Thomas Love Peacock**, **Leigh Hunt**, and **Lord Byron**.

Shelley's poetry is remarkable for its range and eclectic sources as well as its many forms and genres. Its subjects are equally diverse, with his questioning and sometimes skeptical bent often showing up not just in his political commentaries, historical critiques, philosophical inquiries, and literary commentaries, but also in his personal poetry. Often

Percy Bysshe Shelley

written in a highly metaphorical style, his major work is marked by intellectual and emotional intensity.

Queen Mab (1813), a long exercise touting radical social change, was Shelley's first major poem. With the publication of *Alastor; or, The Spirit of Solitude, and Other Poems* (1816), however, his poetry significantly matured. The title piece describes an idealistic poet's vain search for an image of his own making; tragically yet heroically he ignores the external world, and dies in solitude. Two other noteworthy poems in the volume, "Mont Blanc" and "Hymn to Intellectual Beauty," confirm in very different ways Shelley's profound commitment to the power of the mind and imagination. In 1817 he wrote *Laon and Cyntha,* revised the following year as *The Revolt of Islam,* in which he overtly challenged the status quo on moral and political grounds.

The year 1819 was extraordinarily productive for him. In *Julian and Maddalo,* based on the relationship between his views and those of Byron, Shelley considered the differing perspectives of skepticism and idealism. *Peter Bell the Third* **satirized** the contemporary scene and the age's leading poet, **William Wordsworth.** The drama *The Cenci* explored evil and oppression, using the situation of a father sexually victimizing his daughter. Perhaps Shelley's greatest work is *Prometheus Unbound,* a "lyrical drama" in which individual will triumphs over oppressive forces. Shelley also wrote "Ode to the West Wind" in 1819 and "To a Sky-Lark" (1820), two of the most famous poems in the English language.

Shelley's poetic accomplishments after 1819 include *Epipsychidion* (1821), an allegorized autobiographical poem in which the speaker professes love for a young woman; *Adonais* (1821), a **pastoral** elegy inspired by the death of **John Keats**; and the unfinished *The Triumph of Life* (1822), which reviews the folly of history and humanity while also commending figures who had stood up against evil and oppression. Shelley's most famous and influential essay is *A Defence of Poetry* (1821), which places poetry and the poet at the center of knowledge and culture.

Shelley wanted to be a spokesman of his age, but his audience was limited. After his death, however, his reputation grew quickly mainly due to his wife's efforts. During the Victorian period he was perhaps the most influential Romantic poet, with writers like Robert Browning (1812–1889), William Michael Rossetti (1829–1919), and Algernon Charles Swinburne (1837–1909) all glorifying his genius.

G. Kim Blank

Bibliography

Blank, G. Kim, ed. *The New Shelley: Later Twentieth-Century Views.* 1991.

Dawson, P.M.S. *The Unacknowledged Legislator: Shelley and Politics.* 1980.

Dunbar, Clement. *A Bibliography of Shelley Studies: 1823–1950.* 1976. (For a bibliography of Shelley studies since 1950, see *The Keats–Shelley Journal,* published annually.)

Gelpi, Barbara. *Shelley's Goddess: Maternity, Language, Subjectivity.* 1992.

Holmes, Richard. *Shelley: The Pursuit.* 1974.

Jones, Frederick L., ed. *The Letters of Percy Bysshe Shelley.* 2 vols. 1964.

Keach, William. *Shelley's Style.* 1984.

Webb, Timothy. *Shelley: A Voice Not Understood.* 1977.

See also Pastoral; Poetry and Poetics; Romanticism and Romantic Style

Shenstone, William (1714–1763)

Shenstone devoted his retiring, rustic life to his twin passions of writing (both poetry and criticism) and **landscape gardening.** His advocacy of the informal and asymmetrical style of garden which existed on the family estate he inherited, the Leasowes, earned him high repute well before he became known as a writer.

Ill for most of his life, Shenstone began writing poetry at an early age. His work includes **neoclassical** poems like the Spenserian **burlesque** *The School-Mistress* (1737, expanded 1742), and the Drydenesque *Judgment of Hercules* (1741), as well as poems rooted in the fashionable melancholy later associated with pre–**Romanticism.** He admired **James Thomson**'s descriptive poetry, and celebrated in his writing, as he did at the Leasowes, what he called odd picturesque description.

Most of Shenstone's prose and some of his unpublished poems were published after his death by his friend **Robert Dodsley.** His **letters** are lively and witty, and his occasional **essays** reflect a sensitive, reflective consciousness equally at home with the epigram and the discursive essay. He is best known for the values of simplicity, informality, rural elegance, **melancholy,** and picturesqueness, which he embraced in his

William Shenstone

writing and in his lifestyle. His poems were much admired by **Robert Burns**.

Stephen C. Behrendt

Bibliography

Humphreys, A.R. *William Shenstone: An Eighteenth-Century Portrait.* 1937.

Purkis, E. Munro. *William Shenstone: Poet and Landscape Gardener.* 1931.

William, Marjorie. *William Shenstone: A Chapter in Eighteenth Century Taste.* 1935.

See also Picturesque Movement; Poetry and Poetics

Sheraton, Thomas (1751–1806)

Sheraton is thought to have learned cabinetmaking in his native Durham. His interest lay more in **interior design** and publishing than the practice of his craft, however; and soon after coming to **London** (1790), he issued the first part of *The Cabinet-Maker and Upholsterer's Drawing Book* (1791–1794, 1802). This work was followed by *The Cabinet Dictionary* (1803), and by 30 of the 125 plates planned for *The Cabinet-Maker, Upholsterer, and General Artists' Encyclopaedia* (1804–1806). To help his destitute widow, friends republished plates from his last two works as *Designs for Household Furniture* (1810).

Although a good deal of Sheraton-inspired furniture was made in both England and America, there are no authentic examples of his work remaining. Unlike other authors of pattern books, he did not produce the pieces he illustrated, or open a shop where he could supervise their production by others.

Those commentators more familiar with Sheraton's plates than his text sometimes overstate his originality. He freely credited others for some of his designs. He noted, for example, that a certain well-known "summer bed in two compartments" (*Drawing Book,* plate 41) originated with a groomsman to the Duke of York; and that the mechanism to raise and lower the drawers of a "harlequin pembroke table" (plate 56) was developed by a friend. On the other hand, he did not admit to the similarities between his own work and that of **George Hepplewhite** or Thomas Shearer (active *c.* 1788), whose pattern books had appeared in 1788; instead, he used his pen to modify their designs and, substituting round legs for square, reeding for fluting, and straight edges for curved, he evolved the style now identified by his name.

In his later works, Sheraton documented **home furnishings and decoration** seen in workrooms and upholsterers' installations, providing the first visual record of the **Regency style**. Under its influence he coarsened some of his earlier designs, filling the *Dictionary* and *Encyclopaedia* with grotesqueries, straightforwardly described. He died of brain fever before he could complete his last project.

Reed Benhamou

Bibliography

Aronson, Joseph. *The New Encyclopedia of Furniture.* 1967.

Hayward, Helena, ed. *World Furniture.* 1965.

Macquoid, Percy. *A History of English Furniture, III: The Age of Satin Wood.* 1905.

Thornton, Peter. *Authentic Decor: The Domestic Interior, 1620–1920.* 1984.

Whiton, Sherrill. *Interior Design and Decoration.* 1974.

See also Architects and Architecture; Chippendale, Thomas; Neoclassical Style

Sheridan, Frances Chamberlaine (1724–1766)

Novelist and dramatist, Sheridan, wife of the **actor** and theater manager **Thomas Sheridan**, and mother of playwright **Richard Brinsley Sheridan**, learned to read and write clandestinely, against her father's wishes. At age 15 she penned a two-volume romance, *Eugenia and Adelaide,* which her daughter Alicia later transformed into a comic **opera** and which her son employed in writing *The Duenna* (1775). With **Samuel Richardson**'s assistance she published the successful *Memoirs of Miss Sidney Bidulph* (1761; sequel, 1767). Her finest play was the **sentimental** comedy *The Discovery* (1763), comparable to the contemporary productions of **Isaac Bickerstaff** and **Richard Cumberland**. Mrs. Twyfort, from *A Journey to Bath* (first published in 1902), is the source for Mrs. Malaprop in R.B. Sheridan's *The Rivals* (1775).

Laura Morrow

Bibliography

Danziger, Marlies. *Goldsmith and Sheridan.* 1978.

Doody, Margaret Anne. "Frances Sheridan: Morality and

Annihilated Time," in Mary Anne Schofield and Cecilia Macheski, eds., *Fetter'd or Free? British Women Novelists, 1670–1815.* 1986.

Sheridan, Frances. *The Plays of Frances Sheridan,* ed. by Robert Hogan and Jerry C. Beasley. 1984.

See also Dramatic Arts; Dramatic Criticism

Sheridan, Richard Brinsley (1751–1816)

The Irish-born Sheridan—playwright, romantic lover, **theater** manager, M.P., and brilliant orator—came from a distinguished literary family. His grandfather, Thomas Sheridan I (1687–1738), classical scholar and close friend of **Swift**; his mother, novelist and playwright **Frances Chamberlaine Sheridan**; and his father, actor–manager and elocutionist **Thomas Sheridan**, all had theatrical interests and connections.

Sheridan's early elopement with the beautiful singer Elizabeth Linley, and his **duels** to defend her honor, presaged a life of risk-taking and reckless spending. During the 1770s, while only in his twenties, he was one of **London**'s foremost playwrights. Five of his productions—*The Rivals* (1775); *St. Patrick's Day,* a farce (1775); *The Duenna,* an operetta (1775); *The School for Scandal* (1777); *A Trip to Scarborough* (1777); and *The Critic,* a rollicking play within a play (1779)—achieved tremendous popularity at Drury Lane. He succeeded **David Garrick** as manager there but actually devoted most of his energy to **Whig** politics for the following 30 years. He served as M.P., Under-Secretary of State for Foreign Affairs, and Secretary of the Treasury, establishing a high reputation for eloquence, particularly in his speeches as manager of the impeachment campaign against **Warren Hastings**, Governor-General of British **India**.

Sheridan's fame today rests mainly on his **satirical** comedies of **manners**, lampooning modish posturing, society gossip, courtship conventions, snobbery, and intrigue. Among his most memorable characters are Mrs. Malaprop (*The Rivals*), Lady Teazle (*The School for Scandal*), and Mr. Puff (*The Critic*), roles much coveted by leading **actors** of the day.

James Gray

Richard Brinsley Sheridan

Bibliography

Bingham, Madeleine (Lady Clanmorris). *Sheridan: The Track of a Comet.* 1972.

Durant, Davis. *Richard Brinsley Sheridan, a Reference Guide.* 1981.

Loftis, John Clyde. *Sheridan and the Drama of Georgian England.* 1977.

Morwood, James. *The Life and Works of Richard Brinsley Sheridan.* 1985.

Price, Cecil, ed. *The Letters of Richard Brinsley Sheridan.* 3 vols. 1966.

See also Dramatic Arts; Irish Literature before the Union

Sheridan, Thomas (1719–1788)

An **actor** and **theater** manager who improved the standard of acting at **Dublin**'s Smock-Alley Theater between 1743 and 1754, Sheridan did so in the hope that "the Theater would become an admirable Assistant to the school of Oratory" he wished to establish. Inspired by his godfather **Jonathan Swift**, he believed that oratory—elocution—was the key to a proper education; and his career was as much devoted to the furtherance of this idea as it was to the theater.

At Sheridan's instigation the Hibernian Society of Dublin was founded (1758), to put into practice his educational ideas. But the society balked at an actor heading its academy, and Sheridan withdrew from the project. Nevertheless, Oxford and Cambridge were sufficiently impressed by his work to award him honorary degrees (1758, 1759), and the government granted him a £200 **pension** (1762). When he was not acting in **London** or Dublin, he was giving public lectures on elocution.

His one original play, a farce featuring a "stage Irishman" complete with malaprops and other targets of ridicule, was *The Brave Irishman; or Captain O'Blunder,* first performed at Smock-Alley in 1743. But his most enduring production was a **reference work**, his *General Dictionary of the English Language* (1780). The twenty-second new dictionary to be published after **Samuel Johnson**'s (1755), this was the first ever to include a fully systematic plan of pronunciation—one which, modified, still remains in use. Between 1780 and 1811, 12 editions were published.

Sheridan also published a *Life of Swift* (1784) to head his 16-volume edition of Swift's works. Part of a notable family, he was married to novelist and playwright **Frances Chamberlaine Sheridan**, and was the father of the dramatist **Richard Brinsley Sheridan**.

Peter A. Tasch

Bibliography

Benzie, W. *The Dublin Orator.* 1972.

Highfill, Philip H., Jr., Kalman A. Burnim, and Edward A. Langhans, eds. *A Biographical Dictionary of Actors, Actresses, Musicians, Dancers, Managers & Other Stage Personnel in London, 1660–1800.* Vol. 13. 1991.
Sheldon, Esther K. *Thomas Sheridan of Smock-Alley.* 1967.

See also Dramatic Arts; Irish Literature

Sherlock, Thomas (1678–1761)

Sherlock, Anglican prelate, stood near the center of ecclesiastical politics during the early Hanoverian era. Son of William Sherlock (1641–1707), dean of St. Paul's (from 1691), he went to **Cambridge University** (B.A. 1697, M.A. 1701, D.D. 1714), became chaplain to **Queen Anne** (1711), and after several intermediate steps became Bishop of Bangor (1728), of Salisbury (1734), and of **London** (1748).

Though accused of **Jacobite** indiscretions, Sherlock proved himself a stalwart defender of the **Hanoverian succession**. He was a friend of **Hervey**, an intimate of **Queen Caroline**, a defender of **Sir Robert Walpole**, and an effective supporter of the government in the **House of Lords**. He anonymously attacked **Hoadly** in the **Bangorian controversy** (1717) and waged war with **deism** in his popular *The Use and Intent of Prophecy* (1725). Broad in sympathy and true to his **Whig** outlook, he favored friendly relations between the church and **dissenters**.

Donald W. Nichol

Bibliography

Carpenter, E.F. *Life of Thomas Sherlock.* 1936.
Clark, J.C.D. *English Society, 1688–1832.* 1985.

See also Church of England

Sherwood, Mary Martha (1775–1851)

A prolific writer of **children's literature**, Sherwood published over 350 popular stories, many of which reflected her pious **Evangelical** outlook. Her most famous book, *The Fairchild Family* (1818, 1842, 1847)—rigid, anti–**Catholic**, devoted to the inculcation of sobriety, self-examination, and hard work—was standard reading for a generation or more of English **middle-class** children. Her other notable works included the stories "Margarita" and "Susan Gray" (1802), and "The Indian Pilgrim" and "Little Henry and His Bearer" (1815).

Sherwood was born in Stanford, Worcester, in an Anglican clerical family. In 1803 she married her cousin Henry Sherwood, an **army** officer; he took her to **India** (1805), where she ran schools, gave birth to several children, and adopted orphans. After the couple returned to England in 1816, she continued to write and teach until her death at Twickenham.

Mary Tiryak

Bibliography

Blaine, Virginia, Patricia Clements, and Isobel Grundy, eds. *Feminist Companion to Literature in English: Women Writers from the Middle Ages to the Present.* 1990.
Dyson, Ketari Kushari. *A Various Universe.* 1978.
Todd, Janet. *Dictionary of British and American Women Writers.* 1984.

Shipbuilding

See Ships and Shipbuilding

Shipping and Seamen

Shipping was one of the major industries of Hanoverian Britain. Much capital was invested in the vessels and equipment required to convey a steadily increasing volume of goods in the coastal, overseas, and carrying trades. This capital was raised and deployed chiefly by **merchants**, to whom shipowning formed at first only a subsidiary part of much broader commercial operations.

Investment in shipping was traditionally a hazardous business, for as well as the physical dangers of the sea, there were financial risks arising out of price fluctuations, volatile political conditions, and poor market information. Merchants therefore tended to spread risks by owning shares in numerous vessels engaged in the carriage of their goods. With one of their number, the ship's husband, elected to organize the shipping operation, the majority of the shareholders were passive partners. However, from the 1770s, this organizational system began to change. Gradually, and at different rates in different ports, shipowning emerged as a separate branch of **entrepreneurship**.

With industrialization proceeding apace, and the government hiring scores of vessels as transports during the 1793–1815 **wars**, the demand for tonnage increased appreciably. Freight rates increased, as did the profitability of vessel operation. In such propitious conditions, some merchants concentrated on the shipowning facet of their business, while enterprising ship's husbands assumed full control of their charges and applied their managerial skills to the operation of multiple vessels. Accordingly, by the 1820s the specialist shipowner had joined the owner–operator, the partnership, the merchant firm, and the **chartered trading company** (e.g., the **East India Company**) in the ranks of agencies that invested capital in the business of shipping.

Such capitalists employed a vast number of seamen. In 1736 an estimated 51,000 men were engaged in a mercantile marine of some 440,000 tons; in 1790 the figures stood at 80,000 men and 1.437 million tons; while in 1837, approximately 140,000 seafarers worked the 2.334 million tons registered in the British Isles. Throughout this period, seafaring employed the nation's largest occupational group, aside from agriculture. Though this workforce was drawn from all parts of the **Empire** and beyond, the great majority of the recruits hailed from the working-class **population** of Britain's ports and coastal districts.

The typical crew structure was hierarchical. The captain and mates formed the managerial rank; the boatswain, carpenter, surgeon, gunner, and other specialists were responsible for particular facets of the ship; and the able seamen, together with the raw landsmen, performed the many arduous tasks that working a vessel entailed.

The able man, though characterized as an awkward,

drunken buffoon ashore, was a skilled laborer afloat, having learned the arts of shiphandling through at least 2 years' experience at sea. He was generally remunerated by a **wage** (paid monthly in the foreign trades, and by a lump sum for coastal runs). Throughout the 18th century, wages remained constant at around 25 shillings (£1.25) per month in peacetime, rising to 40 or 50 shillings (£2–£2.50) per month in the 1840s. In the frequent wars of the period, however, seafarers were in relatively short supply, and wages in the shipping industry increased sharply, reaching 75 shillings (£3.25) per month in the early 1780s.

War and military engagements also provided a seaman the opportunity to serve aboard a private man-of-war, work which offered a share in prizes taken, rather than a wage. But the chief source of demand in the wartime market for seafarers came from the Royal **Navy**. Requiring upwards of 85,000, 107,000, and 142,000 men during the peak years of the 1756–1763, 1776–1783, and 1793–1815 conflicts respectively, the Admiralty, refusing to increase the net wages of 22.5 shillings (£1.12) per lunar month until the 1790s, offered bounties, recruiting landsmen, and using the Impress Service to obtain its manpower. Though impressment was abhorred, it was an effective means of quickly raising an adequate workforce, one moreover that was trained and available for redeployment in the mercantile marine on the resumption of peace.

David J. Starkey

Bibliography

Davis, R. *The Rise of the English Shipping Industry in the Seventeenth and Eighteenth Centuries.* 1962.

Palmer, S. *Politics, Shipping and the Repeal of the Navigation Laws.* 1991.

Rediker, M. *Between the Devil and the Deep Blue Sea: Merchant Seamen, Pirates and the Anglo-American Maritime World, 1700–1750.* 1987.

Rodger, N.A.M. *The Wooden World: An Anatomy of the Georgian Navy.* 1986.

Ville, S. *English Shipowning during the Industrial Revolution: Michael Henley and Son, London Shipowners, 1770–1830.* 1987.

See also Coastal Shipping; Commerce, Overseas; Docks and Harbors; Navigation; Pirates and Piracy; Ships and Shipbuilding

Ships and Shipbuilding

With extensive and expanding interests in **overseas commerce** and coastal trade, a significant **fishing** industry, and a large and powerful **navy**, Britain in the early 18th century relied heavily on sea-going vessels. Most were comparatively small. The fisheries were mainly exploited in craft of less than 20 tons burden; much of the nation's estuarine and **coastal shipping** was conveyed in hulls of limited capacity. Even long-distance shipping might be prosecuted in diminutive vessels, the transatlantic fishery at **Newfoundland**, for instance, being conducted in brigs as small as 40 tons burden.

Much larger vessels were in service. Burthensome colliers of up to 400 tons plied the route from the Northeast to **London**; West Indiamen of 250–300 tons carried goods to and from the **West Indies**; East Indiamen of up to 500 tons sailed to **India** and the Orient. The navy's ships-of-the-line, equipped with 60 or more carriage guns and carrying over 700 **seamen**, protected and extended Britain's commercial and colonial interests.

All these vessels, large or small, were made of wood and driven by wind. In the early 18th century, most were equipped with square sails arranged according to various plans, or rigs. The larger traders and warships were normally ship-rigged—fitted, that is, with three masts (fore, main, and mizzen), each designed to carry at least three sails. Two-masted vessels rigged as brigs or snows were commonly deployed in the transoceanic trades, whereas single-masted cutters, smacks, and sloops were ubiquitous in coastal and inshore waters.

The principles upon which these vessels were built and operated had changed little since the late 15th century, when the development in Europe of the three-masted, fully rigged ship had revolutionized sea transport. Marginal technical improvements had taken place in the interim, a pattern of incremental change that persisted throughout the 18th century. Wooden sailing vessels of all classes tended to increase in size, while the use of stronger sail- and rope-making materials, and innovations in sail plans (notably the diffusion of the schooner rig, which deployed fore and aft rather than square sails), all led to gains in efficiency.

However, the main **technological** changes of the Hanoverian era were the application of **steam** power as a means of propelling vessels and the use of **iron** in hull construction. Experiments in both areas were conducted in the late 18th century, though it was not until 1813 that the first steam-driven vessel, **Henry Bell**'s *Comet,* entered service in British waters, and 1821 that the two components of the shipping revolution of the late 19th century—steam engines and metal hulls—were combined in the *Aaron Manby.* Steam and iron continued to make headway in the 1820s and 1830s, especially in the short-distance trades, but on the accession of Queen Victoria in 1837 the wooden sailing vessel remained overwhelmingly the chief means of sea transport.

The majority of the nation's 18th-century merchant, fishing, and naval vessels were constructed in shipyards in Britain and her **North American** colonies. This was in line with the **navigation laws**, which excluded foreign-built shipping from the domestic market, but it also reflected the capacity of the British shipbuilding industry to meet a substantial, growing, and varied demand. Based on the **craft** skills of the shipwright, wooden shipbuilding was generally a small-scale activity. In 1804 the typical shipyard engaged the services of less than 20 shipwrights and apprentices, though larger enterprises such as Mawdsleys of London, Vospers of Newcastle, and Thorneycroft of **Glasgow** employed over 150 men.

Capital requirements were generally modest. With the shipwright normally owning his tools, the shipbuilder, to commence operation, needed only to invest in a saw pit, a shed for sawn wood, a steam box for bending planks, and land for timber storage and preparation. Many yards, of course, had more

Ships at Limehouse Dock, Regent's Canal, London, c. 1827

than these basic requirements, with forges and, increasingly in the late 18th century, steam-driven equipment evident in larger establishments such as the Thamesside yards that specialized in the construction of East Indiamen, and the Royal dockyards at Chatham, Portsmouth, and Plymouth where many of the navy's larger vessels were built.

Demand for tonnage and repair facilities conditioned the location of shipyards. Accordingly, the industry was widely dispersed, with yards established on sheltered waterfront sites in most parts of the British Isles. Even so, it was on major trading and shipping rivers like the Thames, Tyne, Wear, Mersey, and Clyde that the largest and most productive enterprises developed. Proximity to supplies of timber, pitch, tar, and hemp was less significant as a locational factor because most of these and other essential raw material were imported from North America or the Baltic. However, the supply of timber and naval stores did influence the distribution of shipbuilding activity within the **Empire**; in 1775, on the eve of the **American Revolution**, approximately 40% of British shipping was constructed in colonial North America.

This explains why the newly independent United States emerged as Britain's rival in wooden shipbuilding. The threat intensified after 1800, and by the 1830s there were fears that the Americans were producing more and better ships. By this time, however, the new technologies of steam and iron were already beginning to shift the competitive balance decisively in Britain's favor.

David J. Starkey

Bibliography

Greenhill, B. *The Evolution of the Wooden Ship.* 1988.

———, ed. *Sail's Last Century: The Merchant Sailing Ship, 1830–1930.* 1993.

MacGregor, D. *Merchant Sailing Ships, 1775–1815.* 1985.

Rediker, Marcus. *Between the Devil and the Deep Blue Sea: Merchant Seamen, Pirates, and the Anglo-American Maritime World, 1700–1750.* 1993.

Ville, S., ed. *Shipbuilding in the United Kingdom in the Nineteenth Century: A Regional Approach.* 1993.

See also Navigation

Shopping and Retailing

During the Hanoverian period, shopping and retailing underwent many changes that in some respects were revolutionary. Prior to the 18th century, purchases of most goods beyond a few basic necessities were limited by cost and supply to the better-off. However, by the era of **George III**, with improvements in transport and communications, as well as with an increased demand for consumer items due to **population** growth and rising incomes, shopping and retailing had begun a rapid evolution that still continues today.

The typical retail shop of the early 18th century operated out of a cellar or ground floor location, sometimes a craftsman's workshop, with goods displayed either outside the shop, sometimes on pavement, or just inside the entrance. Lighting was dim, and the shop floor tended to be cramped and uncomfortable. Special attention to consumers' needs, and specialized customer service, were virtually unknown. However, as demand for goods and services grew, linked to expanding ability to spend, shopkeepers recognized the need to draw in business by creating attractive displays of goods and developing attentive service. Early-19th-century shops increasingly included plateglass window displays, gas-lit interior lighting, artful and appealing arrangements of goods, and more intensive and meticulous attention to consumers' needs.

The traditional hours of retail operation were long, generally from 6 AM to 10 PM, in order to give consumers more time to shop. In the late Hanoverian period, shopkeepers began to use **newspaper** advertising to generate more sales, and

A London bookstore, c. 1800

also developed new sales techniques such as price ticketing, thereby establishing set prices for goods on the basis of percentage markups from dealer costs. Moreover, shop locations began to cluster around central retailing districts, often rather specialized, which benefited also from city improvements in paving and lighting. Such changes led to ever better and more convenient shopping environments.

Along with changes in customer service, sales techniques, and shop locations, the interiors of shops also changed. In the early 18th century, most shops contained only a few shelves or drawers to hold goods. Gradually shops expanded in capacity to store and display wares. Depending on the type of shop, the more advanced fittings might include showcases, shelving, cupboards, containers, cash boxes, weights, measures, and other tools related to the trade. If a shop catered to the luxurious tastes of people of **fashion**, it might well contain lounge areas with chairs and other furniture, and the walls might be decorated with mirrors and gilt. Some shops were so tastefully furnished and conveniently located that they became centers for appointments and assignations.

There was often very little distinction, especially in towns and villages, between shop quarters and personal living quarters. The staff of a shop during the early Hanoverian period generally consisted of the shopkeeper and his family members and, if the shop had evolved from one of the traditional artisanal crafts, perhaps also sundry live-in apprentices, journeymen, and domestic **servants**. Toward the end of the period shop staff more often comprised day workers who lived off the premises, but throughout the period, the shop often housed the shopkeeper's family and employees, and usually some space devoted not only to storage but to the production or repair of goods. The gradual separation of retail establishments from dwelling places was a great improvement because, until then, shopkeeper–craftsmen and their employees often worked and lived together in close, damp, and filthy quarters. Conditions could be dangerous as well as unclean and crowded. Workers in shops containing chemicals and heavy metals, for example, were sometimes forced to live in the same area in which they worked, inhaling fumes and living with constant exposure to hazards. Illness and disfigurement were occupational hazards for early shopkeepers. Another disadvantage, from the worker's point of view at least, was that the living-in system also allowed shopkeepers to maintain control over the lives of their employees and to hold them to the very long hours of work often required. Shop assistants during this time increasingly banded together to try to decrease their hours of work, but with little success.

The typical retail customer during the early Hanoverian period, especially the purchaser of goods other than food, was likely to be reasonably well-off. While the poorer classes spent most of their income on food and rent, consumers from the wealthier landed and business classes had the income with which to purchase luxury goods—**home furnishings**, plate, **jewelry**, hardware, and **clothing**. Typically, clothing was a very costly item for people of the working classes; when they purchased it at all (rather than making it themselves), they generally did so from secondhand dealers or rag shops. But the expanding purchase of clothing was an index of national prosperity and technological improvement. By the late 18th century, foreign visitors to **London** often remarked on the respectable store-bought dress of the working class, and sometimes mistook its members for people of the **gentry**. Later still, by the end of the Hanoverian period, many shops involved in the clothing trade were directly targeting the working classes. The retail food trade saw a similar evolution—first expanding, due partly to the rising incomes of the working classes, and then beginning to specialize according to stratified income groups and tastes. However, general stores, which stocked different types of foods as well as other domestic items on their shelves, also became more common toward the end of the period.

The terms of purchase for goods involved both cash and credit. In luxury shops, credit purchases tended to outweigh those involving cash, due mainly to the fact that shopkeepers felt comfortable with the ability of the better-off to pay. However, only retailers with large amounts of capital could afford to provide credit on an extensive scale. By the early 19th century, shops that catered to the working classes were also providing small amounts of credit to their customers. This allowed people of the working class some security during periods of unemployment, and also provided the shopkeeper with a loyal customer base. But shopkeepers did not provide credit indiscriminately; they usually required a history of payment for goods to be already established before offering it. And to encourage payment on credit accounts, they sometimes charged interest on overdue accounts, or offered other inducements for prompt payment. Many offered goods at a lower price to consumers who paid with cash. Some also held customers' personal items as security for payment. The result was that shopping was made increasingly easy for the working classes, and as living standards gradually improved, shopping became a normal part of life for much of society.

Rochelle R. Athey

Bibliography

Alexander, David. *Retailing in England during the Industrial Revolution.* 1970.

George, M. Dorothy. *London Life in the Eighteenth Century.* 1951.

Marshall, Dorothy. *English People in the Eighteenth Century.* 1980.

McKendrick, Neil, ed. *Historical Perspectives: Studies in English Thought and Society in Honour of J.H. Plumb.* 1974.

McKendrick, Neil, John Brewer, and J.H. Plumb. *The Birth of a Consumer Society: The Commercialization of Eighteenth-Century England.* 1982.

Mui, Hoh-Cheung, and Lorna H. Mui. *Shops and Shopkeeping in Eighteenth-Century England.* 1989.

Turberville A.S., ed. *Johnson's England.* 2 vols. 1933; rpt. 1952, 1965, 1967.

See also Clothing Trade; Craftsmen; Hours, Wages, and Working Conditions; Standard of Living

Siddons, Sarah Kemble (1755–1831)

From her debut in 1782 to her farewell in 1812, Siddons dominated the **London** stage; she was perhaps one of the greatest tragic actresses of all time. She came from a theatrical family. Both her parents and her maternal grandfather managed traveling troupes, and while one brother, John Philip Kemble (1757–1823), was actor–manager of Drury Lane Theatre and then Covent Garden, her youngest brother **Charles Kemble** was also a successful actor and theater manager. In 1773, despite her parents' objections, she married William Siddons, a member of her parents' troupe.

Sarah Siddons

In her first major performance at Drury Lane she suffered from stage fright; lightly regarded, she was dismissed after that first season. But after 7 years in regional theaters she returned to triumph at Drury Lane (1782) as Isabella in *The Fatal Marriage,* **Garrick**'s revival of the Thomas Southerne (1659–1746) tragedy. The following year, the theater collected one of its highest receipts, **George III** invited Siddons to read at Windsor, and she was appointed to teach elocution to **aristocrats**.

During her career Siddons played over 70 different roles. She specialized in Shakespeare and even played Hamlet, but her masterpiece was Lady Macbeth. When she retired in 1812, playing that role one last time, she brought down the house, the audience so appreciative of her performance that the play had to be stopped after the sleepwalking scene. Siddons eschewed comedy and, unlike her contemporary **Edmund Kean**, advocated the grand manner of acting: dignified speeches, combined with melodramatic gestures. **Hazlitt** described her impressive performance: "Power was seated on her brow; passion emanated from her breast as from a shrine; she was tragedy personified." With her dark, dramatic beauty and expressive voice she moved her audiences to tears, fainting, and hysteria.

Courting respectability as well as fame, Siddons moved in the aristocratic and literary circles of **Horace Walpole** and **Samuel Johnson**. **Sir Joshua Reynolds** and **Thomas Gainsborough** both painted her portrait.

Ann W. Engar

Bibliography

Boaden, James. *Memoirs of Mrs. Siddons.* 1827.

Campbell, Thomas. *Life of Mrs. Siddons.* 1834.

Kelly, Linda. *The Kemble Era.* 1980.
Manvell, Roger. *Sarah Siddons: Portrait of an Actress.* 1971.
Siddons, Sarah. *The Reminiscences of Sarah Kemble Siddons, 1773–1785.* 1942.

See also Actors and the Acting Profession; Dramatic Arts; Shakespeare Industry

Sidmouth, Viscount (Henry Addington) (1757–1844)

The son of a society doctor of yeoman farmer antecedents, educated at Winchester and Brasenose College, Oxford, Addington proved, like **Canning** and **Peel**, that in Hanoverian England a gentle birth was not a necessary prerequisite for advancement to the highest positions. He held three major offices, becoming Speaker of the **House of Commons** (1789–1801), **Prime Minister** (1801–1804), and Home Secretary (1812–1822).

For the first three decades of the 19th century the name of Addington (or of Viscount Sidmouth, as he became in 1805) was almost synonymous with political reaction. He worked against abolition of the **slave trade** in the British **Empire**. He succeeded **Pitt the Younger** as Prime Minister in 1801 largely on account of his opposition to allowing the **Roman Catholics** of **Ireland** and Great Britain the right to sit in Parliament, but had to endure the jibe that "Pitt is to Addington as London is to Paddington." He helped destroy **Baron Grenville**'s administration in 1807 because of his opposition to allowing Catholics access to the higher officer corps in the **army** and **navy**. As Home Secretary he earned the ire of British left-wing groups for his frequent suspensions of Habeas Corpus and his tolerance for the heavy-handed antiradicalism of local authorities, which resulted in events like the **Peterloo massacre**.

James J. Sack

Lord Sidmouth

Bibliography

Ziegler, Philip. *Addington.* 1965.

See also Tories and Toryism

Simcoe, John Graves (1752–1806)

Simcoe, born at Cotterstock in Northamptonshire, entered the **army** at age 18 after a limited college and legal education. From 1775 to 1781 he fought in the **War of American Independence**, leading from October 1777 a Loyalist corps, the Queen's Rangers. His experience caused him to admire many qualities about Americans but to abhor republicanism.

Following the enactment of the **Constitutional (Canada) Act of 1791**, Simcoe parlayed his **North American** experience and a brief stint in the **House of Commons** into an appointment as the first Lieutenant Governor of Upper Canada. During his tenure he initiated a great deal of lasting importance. His major contributions included the successful encouragement of land settlement in the area west of Kingston (this was facilitated by road building, and by a publicity campaign in the northern United States), and the founding of the cities of London and York (Toronto). After the Battle of Fallen Timbers in 1794 and Jay's Treaty in 1795 Simcoe became a strong advocate for the strengthening of British defenses along the Great Lakes.

Simcoe's settlement policy, support for economic growth, and concern for the protection of Upper Canada were all important factors in the development of British North America. Many writers believe that he and **Sir Guy Carleton** were the two most important British officials in Canadian colonial government prior to Lord Durham's (1792–1840) appointment in 1837.

Stuart R. Givens

Bibliography

Allen, Robert S. *His Majesty's Indian Allies: British Indian Policy in the Defence of Canada, 1774–1815.* 1992.
Mealing, S.R. "John Graves Simcoe." *Dictionary of Canadian Biography.* Vol. 5, 1801–1820. 1983.
Riddell, W.R. *The Life of John Graves Simcoe, First Lieutenant-Governor of the Province of Upper Canada, 1792–96.* 1926.

See also Canada; Empire and Imperialism

Simeon, Charles (1759–1836)

Simeon was a leader of **Evangelicalism** and important in promoting its spread among the clergy. Born in Reading and educated in Cambridge, he came under the influence of the Evangelical **Venn Family** through his friendship with John Venn (1759–1813) and Henry Venn (1725–1797), John's father. Converted in 1779 to "gospel Christianity," he became a leading pulpit preacher and educator. As Fellow of King's and Vicar of Holy Trinity (1782–1836), he used his immense influence on undergraduates to extend the reach of Evangelical ideas and activities in both clerical and lay society. His "sermon classes" and Friday evening "conversation parties" supplied professional training that was then nearly nonexistent, and his use within his own parish of prayer meetings furnished a model for imitation elsewhere. His published **sermons** and sermon outlines were also designed to assist young clergymen prepare pulpit addresses. A wealthy man, he founded the Simeon Trustees, which was responsible for securing and administering church **patronage** in accordance with Evangelical principles.

Although Simeon was eccentric, passionate, and called ill-tempered, his insistence on church order helped to keep Evangelicals within the **Church of England**, unlike the **Methodists**, who left it after the death of **John Wesley** (1791). His efforts on behalf of religious reform helped lead to the founding (1799) of the Church Missionary Society; and he participated in activities of the Society for Promoting Christianity among the Jews, and the London Clerical Education Society. His *Homileticae* (11 vols., 1819–1820) included 2,536 discourses on the Bible.

Samuel J. Rogal

Bibliography

Abbey, Charles J., and John H. Overton. *The English Church in the Eighteenth Century.* 1878.
Downey, James. *The Eighteenth-Century Pulpit.* 1969.
Hylson-Smith, Kenneth. *Evangelicals in the Church of England.* 1988.
Reeve, Ronald. "John Wesley, Charles Simeon, and the Evangelical Revival." *Canadian Journal of Theology.* Vol. 2, pp. 203–214.
Smyth, Charles Hugh Egerton. *Simeon and Church Order: A Study of the Origins of the Evangelical Revival in Cambridge in the Eighteenth Century.* 1940.
Sykes, Norman. *Church and State in England in the Eighteenth Century.* 1934.

See also Missionary Societies

Sinclair, Sir John, of Ulbster (1754–1835)

Politician, **agricultural improver**, and deviser of the **Statistical Account of Scotland**, Sinclair was educated at Edinburgh, Glasgow, and Oxford, becoming a member of the English Bar. An M.P. from 1789 to 1811, when he obtained a government sinecure (the Cashiership of Excise for **Scotland**), he became the first President of the Board of Agriculture in 1793 and encouraged its Reports on the English Counties. He improved his Caithness estates, introduced new breeds of sheep, created **planned villages**, and raised regiments—even designing their uniforms. He wrote on many subjects, including the public revenues and **agriculture** in the northern counties, but his major legacy is the Statistical Account, a survey of the parishes of Scotland written mainly by kirk ministers and published by Sinclair in 21 volumes between 1791 and 1799. His width of inquiry makes the work an unrivaled source for social historians.

C.J. Davey

Bibliography

Donaldson, J.E. *Caithness in the Eighteenth Century.* 1928.
Gray, Malcom. *The Highland Economy.* 1957.
Mitchison, R. *Agricultural Sir John: The Life of Sir John Sinclair of Ulbster, 1754–1835.* 1962.
Sinclair, Sir J. *Analysis of the Statistical Account.* 1831.

See also Scottish Agriculture

Sinking Fund

At the beginning of the Hanoverian era (1714) there was mounting concern over the national debt, which had grown considerably because of costly **wars**. In 1717 the national debt stood at over £50 million, with interest accruing at £3 million per year.

Robert Walpole and officials of the **Bank of England** planned a progressive fund of invested government revenues, the interest from which would be used to pay the interest on the debt plus part of the principal each year. In theory the fund would grow while the debt "sank." This plan was implemented by the **Earl of Stanhope** in 1717. Despite troubles occasioned by the **South Sea Bubble**, the national debt was reduced to £47.5 million by 1727. By 1733 Walpole had reduced it enough to restore confidence, but it was also becoming an unintended slush fund for extraparliamentary finances and augmentation of the king's civil list, from which many **pensions** were paid. **Pitt the Younger** established a new, more independently run sinking fund in 1786, but the high cost of borrowing after 1793 damaged its operation; it was abandoned in 1828.

K.R. Wood

Bibliography

Clapham, Sir John. *The Bank of England: A History.* 2 vols. 1944.
Collins, M. *Money and Banking in the U.K.: A History.* 1988.

Six Acts (1819)

Initiated by the **Tory** government of **Lord Liverpool** in the wake of the **Peterloo massacre** (1819) and passed by Parliament late that year, these were repressive measures designed to prevent **radical** agitation for reform by preventing large meetings and muzzling the radical press.

The Training Prevention Act provided for penal **transportation** for up to 7 years and imprisonment for 2 years for anyone found training or drilling in military fashion. The Seizure of Arms Act gave justices in some counties power to search for arms and to arrest persons found carrying weapons for purposes dangerous to the peace. The Misdemeanors Act prevented delays in legal proceedings by stopping defendants from postponing pleas. To prevent congregations of more than 50 persons from outside a locality at a meeting not called by local authorities, the Seditious Meetings Prevention Act was passed; this act also forbade the possession of arms, flags, and drums, and the marching in military formation at meetings, and allowed authorities to disperse people after 15 minutes. The Blasphemous and Seditious Libels Act provided that copies of seditious and libelous material could be confiscated, and that second-time offenders in this area could be transported. Duties were placed on cheap publications by the Newspaper and Stamp Duties Act.

These very repressive acts, together with improving economic conditions and divisions among radicals as to the best way to approach reform, helped to dissipate some of the strength of the contemporary radical movement.

Mark C. Herman

Bibliography

Cookson, J.E. *Lord Liverpool's Administration: The Crucial Years, 1815–1822.* 1975.

Stevenson, John. *Popular Disturbances in England, 1700–1870.* 1979.

Thompson, Edward P. *The Making of the English Working Class.* 1968; rpt. 1980.

See also Censorship; Punishment; Riots and Popular Disturbances

Slave Trade

Since ancient times, Europeans had accepted the concept of slavery. European involvement in the African slave trade began in the 15th century, when the Portuguese brought back slaves from their southern voyages. Later, with the establishment of European colonies in the New World, providing adequate labor for plantations and mines became a problem because of the lack of Europeans and Native Americans willing or able to perform arduous tasks. To fill the labor gap, African slaves were introduced.

The slave trade became part of a triangular network involving Europe, **Africa**, and the Americas. European products such as metalware, guns, and textiles were exchanged for African slaves as well as gold, pepper, and other tropical products. Slaves were carried across the Middle Passage, usually an 8-week voyage, and sold to plantation and mine owners; American products, especially sugar, tobacco, and cotton, were shipped to Europe.

The slave trade produced tremendous wealth for the Americas and Europe, and shifted African culture westward. Between 8 and 12 million Africans were forcibly transported, with mortality running between 10% and 20%. Slave **ships**, specially designed with decks rather than holds, had crews that were larger than normal because of the need to guard slaves, and saw high mortality rates because of crowding, unsanitary conditions, and tropical disease.

Britain became involved after Captain John Hawkins (1532–1595) in 1562 picked up 300 slaves from Guinea and smuggled them to Spanish colonies. The British later introduced slavery to their **North American** colonies, though the Caribbean **West Indies** became the area most favored. The Treaty of Utrecht (1713) awarded the *asiento de negros,* the contract to supply Spanish colonies with 4,800 slaves per year, to the British, who held this lucrative privilege until 1743 (when the contract was not renewed). In fact the British exceeded this total, becoming Europe's greatest merchants of slaves; the trade steadily increased, yielding profits of about 10%.

Historians believe that these profits did not contribute significantly to financing the **Industrial Revolution**, though **Bristol**, **Liverpool**, and **London** became heavily involved in the trade and in **overseas commerce** with commodities produced by slaves. Around 1800 the British slave trade was still expanding, but attitudes were changing rapidly as the **antislavery movement** developed among **Quakers** and **Evangelicals**. Coming under increasing pressure, Parliament moved to

Medal struck on abolition of the slave trade, 1807

Medal struck on the Abolition of the Slave Trade.

ameliorate some of the trade's most egregious aspects by passing the Dolben Acts of 1788 and 1799, limiting the number of slaves a ship might carry by its size.

Then in 1805 the Prime Minister, **Pitt the Younger**, issued orders-in-council, which prohibited the importation of slaves after 1807 into newly captured territories, and limited the introduction of slaves in the interim to 3% of the number already in such locations. The Foreign Slave Trade Bill (1806) eliminated about 70% of the British slave trade, while the landmark Abolition Act (1807), sponsored by the **Ministry of all the Talents**, banned the importation of slaves by Britain's subjects into its older colonies as well.

After this, Britain negotiated treaties with other countries to limit the scope of the international slave trade, and the British **Navy** patrolled the Atlantic to try to suppress it. The antislavery movement now focused on the abolition of slavery itself. In 1833 Parliament yielded to this pressure, abolishing slavery, freeing 780,000 slaves, and providing £20 million compensation for slave owners and a 6-year apprenticeship period for slaves following emancipation. Public opinion brought an end to this apprenticeship arrangement after 4 years.

Mark C. Herman

Bibliography

Anstey, Roger. *The Atlantic Slave Trade and British Abolition, 1760–1810.* 1975.
Bean, Richard N. *The British Trans-Atlantic Slave Trade, 1650–1775.* 1975.
Curtin, Philip. *The Atlantic Slave Trade: A Census.* 1969.
Davis, David Brion. *The Problem of Slavery in the Age of Revolution, 1770–1823.* 1975.
———. *Slavery and Human Progress.* 1984.
Drescher, Seymour. *Econocide: British Slavery in the Era of Abolition.* 1977.
Eltis, David. *Economic Growth and the Ending of the Transatlantic Slave Trade.* 1987.
Rawley, James A. *The Transatlantic Slave Trade: A History.* 1981.
Shyllon, Folarin. *Black People in Britain, 1555–1833.* 1977.
Ward, J.R. *British West Indian Slavery, 1750–1834: The Process of Amelioration.* 1988.

See also West India Interest

Slavery

See Antislavery Movement

Sloane, Sir Hans (1660–1753)

Born in **Ireland**, Sloane was educated in **France** and took instruction as chemist and apothecary in **London**. His interest in botany was strengthened by a period spent as physician to the Governor of Jamaica. Well connected to distinguished physicians and botanists, including John Ray (1607–1725), Sloane practiced as a physician on his return to London, and was elected Fellow of both the **Royal Society of London** and the Royal College of Physicians. His reputation was such that he became physician to **Queen Anne** during her last years, and later to **George II**. He was elected President of the College of Physicians (1710) and succeeded Sir Isaac Newton (1642–1727) at his death as President of the Royal Society. Sloane founded the botanic garden in Chelsea in 1721 and played an important role in the inoculation for **smallpox** during the reign of **George I**. A noted bibliophile, after his death his collections provided the core of the materials housed in the **British Museum** since 1759.

Larry Stewart

Bibliography

Brooks, E. St. John. *Sir Hans Sloane: The Great Collector and His Circle.* 1954.
De Beer, G.R. *Sir Hans Sloane and the British Museum.* 1953.
Stewart, Larry. "The Edge of Utility: Slaves and Smallpox in the Early Eighteenth Century." *Medical History.* Vol. 29, pp. 54–70.

Small, James (*c.* 1740–1793)

Small helped to revolutionize the plowing **technology** of his time. He was born in Berwickshire, **Scotland**, where, after serving an apprenticeship as a joiner, he established (1764) a "manufactory" of plows and wheel carriages. Here he developed a metal plow, much lighter than the old, cumbersome Scots wooden implement. This greatly reduced both the manpower and animal-power needed in plowing. In 1784 he published his ideas in *A Treatise on Ploughs and Wheel Carriages.*

Unfortunately his fate was all too characteristic of early inventors. Though the adoption of his plow was rapid and had a profound effect on **agriculture**, Small, despite all his original work, died in debt.

Peter Clapham

Bibliography

Fenton, A. *Scottish Country Life.* 1976.
———. *Country Life in Scotland.* 1987.
Robson, M.J.H. *An Ingenious Mechanic of Scotland.* 1989.
Symon, J.A. *Scottish Farming: Past and Present.* 1959.

See also Agricultural Improvers; Scottish Agriculture

Smallpox

Once the plague abated in the mid-17th century, smallpox became the major cause of epidemic illness. The Bills of Mortality from the early 18th century show deaths from smallpox at around 2,000 a year, the disease mainly striking children under age 5. With the growth of urbanization and industrialization, the infection increased.

Attempts at a cure were as old as the disease itself. It was observed that some people escaped or contracted only a mild form of it after associating with someone more severely affected. John Woodward (1665–1728) described to the **Royal Society** the work of Greek physicians in which pus from the lesions of a patient was scratched into a healthy person, a technique known as variolation (smallpox inoculation). This was extensively practiced in Turkey, and in 1717 **Lady Mary Wortley Montagu** returned to England after having her son inoculated at Constantinople; in 1721, during a severe smallpox outbreak, her daughter was inoculated also, under the observation of several physicians. A clinical trial on Newgate **prisoners** followed, and soon inoculation was enthusiastically adopted in England. However, although inoculees seldom died of smallpox, a minority did, and worse, the inoculated person was for some time a contagious carrier. The general mortality rate thus remained a problem, with two or three deaths occurring per hundred inoculations.

Inoculation continued to be practiced even after **Edward Jenner**'s famous discovery of vaccination (1798). Working from the essentially correct folk belief that persons who had suffered from cowpox, which was far milder in its effects, were immune from smallpox, Jenner advocated infecting people with the lesser disease—a procedure that not only immunized the receiver but eliminated the danger of spreading smallpox itself. Initial opposition from inoculators and clergy was overcome, and by 1801, 100,000 people had been vaccinated. Parliament authorized a central institution for the distribution of vaccine (1807), and later banned inoculation altogether (1840). Deaths from smallpox declined between 1810 and 1830, but vaccination was not yet universal; a major epidemic was recorded between 1837 and 1841. The spread of vaccination was important because it marked not only a significant step in controlling infection but the first intervention by government on behalf of the health of the nation.

C.E. Hivey

Bibliography

Cartwright, Frederick E. *A Social History of Medicine.* 1977.

Dixon, Cyril W. *Smallpox.* 1962.

Hopkins, Donald R. *Princes and Peasants: Smallpox and History.* 1983.

Porter, Roy. *Disease, Medicine and Society in England, 1550–1860.* 2nd ed., 1993.

Smart, Christopher (1722–1771)

Smart was a poet well known in his own time. His work falls into two periods, depending on whether it was published before or after his incarceration for madness (1756–1763). That of the first period established his contemporary fame, but that of the second, in particular *A Song to David* (1763) and *Jubilate Agno* (1939, 1954), has now more greatly advanced his reputation as a major poet.

Smart, a precocious child, was notable for Latin verse at Durham Grammar School and then at Cambridge, where he won scholarships, wrote tripos verses, and became a fellow of Pembroke Hall (1745). In 1747, however, deep in debt, he left for **London** to become a professional author under the **patronage** of the **publisher** John Newbery (1713–1767). Frenetically busy from 1747 to 1756, he edited **periodicals**, wrote song lyrics, produced and acted in a popular variety show (1751), published collected *Poems on Several Occasions* (1752) and short works including five Cambridge prize poems on the attributes of God (1750–1756), engaged in paper wars (1752–1753), eloped with Newbery's step daughter Anna Maria Carnan (*c.* 1752), and fathered two daughters (1753, 1754).

In frail health made worse by overwork and drunkenness, Smart collapsed (1756). In his illness he experienced a religious conversion, manifested in a compulsion to pray without ceasing, which incapacitated him. For the following 7 years Smart was kept in St. Luke's Hospital and one or two private madhouses and, though liberated by friends (1763), he never rejoined his family, undertaking instead the role of a prophet.

Jubilate Agno ("Rejoice in the Lamb"), a long private poem, and *A Song to David* were the products of this period, but after his release, Smart's later **poetry** was virtually disregarded until Robert Browning's (1812–1889) reappraisal of the *Song* in 1887. Smart had to be financially supported by friends during his last years, though his considerable output included the *Song,* his verse **translations** of the **fables** of Phaedrus (1764), the psalms (1765), the works of Horace (1767) and the parables of Christ (1768), three short collections of poems (1763, 1764), two **oratorios** (1764, 1768), and *Hymns for the Amusement of Children* (1770). Imprisoned for debt, he died in the King's Bench Prison.

Smart's nephew, Christopher Hunter (1746–1814), and John Newbery's son Francis (1743–1818), in 1791 published an edition of Smart's poetry calculated to repair **Samuel Johnson**'s omission of Smart from *Lives of the English Poets* (1779–1781). The collection emphasized the pre–1756 works, omitting the *Song* and specimens of Smart's other later works, which, Hunter wrote, "bear for the most part melancholy proofs of the recent estrangement of his mind." But it is those later works—strong, authoritative, and strikingly marked by concise, original, energetic diction—which support Smart's still increasing reputation.

Betty Rizzo

Bibliography

Browning, Robert. "With Christopher Smart," in *Parleyings with Certain People of Importance in Their Day.* 1887.

Mahony, Robert, and Betty Rizzo. *Christopher Smart: An Annotated Bibliography, 1743–1983.* 1984.

Rizzo, Betty, and Robert Mahony. *The Annotated Letters of Christopher Smart.* 1991.

Sherbo, Arthur. *Christopher Smart, Scholar of the University.* 1967.

Smeaton, John (1724–1792)

Smeaton, born near **Leeds**, was a leading civil engineer of the 18th century. The son of an attorney, he abandoned a legal career to become a mathematical instrument-maker in **London** (1750). His research into waterwheels and windmills brought him a medal from the **Royal Society** (1759) and acceptance as a Fellow. The range of important civil engineering projects on which he worked was extremely wide. His work on the third Eddystone **lighthouse** (1755–1759) contributed greatly to lighthouse design. He made a significant contribution to inland waterway development and was one of the few engineers to graduate from river improvements to **canal** construction. He worked on the Calder Navigation in Yorkshire and provided a report (1768) which formed the basis for constructing the Forth and Clyde Canal. Smeaton was also involved in designing **docks and harbors**, surmounting enormous engineering difficulties to construct the harbor at Ramsgate in Kent between 1774 and 1791, and providing designs and improvements for many other harbors along the British coast.

Widely consulted on engineering matters, Smeaton in 1771 formed a **club** called The Smeatonians. The club was a predecessor of the Institution of Civil Engineers, founded in 1818, with **Thomas Telford** its first president.

A.J.G. Cummings

Bibliography

Dyos, H.J., and D.H. Aldcroft. *British Transport.* 1974.
Smiles, S. *Lives of the Engineers.* 1861. Rpt. with intro by Thomas Parke Hughes. 1966.

See also Science, Technology, and Invention

Smith, Adam (1723–1790)

Smith, Scottish economist and moral philosopher, is best remembered for his *Inquiry into the Nature and Causes of the Wealth of Nations* (1776), the foundation stone of classical political economy and modern **economic thought**. This book dominated economics for at least a century and is still highly regarded by experts.

Born in Kirkaldy, **Scotland**, Smith attended Oxford University on a scholarship. After delivering a series of public lectures on rhetoric and belles lettres he was appointed Professor of Logic at Glasgow University (1751), and 1 year later became Professor of Moral Philosophy there. In 1764 he **traveled** to **France** as **tutor** to Henry Scott, 3rd Duke of Buccleuch (1746–1812). There he met François Quesnay (1694–1774), the leading exponent of the Physiocratic school of political economy. After publishing his *Wealth of Nations* he became commissioner of customs in **Edinburgh** (1778), a post he held for the remainder of his life.

Smith's first book, *The Theory of Moral Sentiments* (1759), examined the origin of moral judgment. Rejecting theories that based the perception of right and wrong on a moral sense, benevolence, or utility, Smith maintained that moral judgment was grounded in man's capacity for sympathy, wherein he approved or disapproved of others' actions by imagining himself in their place and sharing their motives. Contrariwise, a man judged his own actions by imagining how an "impartial spectator," with a perfect knowledge of motives and circumstances, might judge them. This theory was to underlie Smith's economic thought.

The *Wealth of Nations,* an examination of the causes and development of economic growth, was a radical departure from previous theories. Unlike 17th-century mercantilists, who conceived of wealth as the accumulation of gold and silver, and the 18th-century French physiocrats, who thought of it as the production of agricultural commodities, Smith believed that the production of material goods was the best measure of a nation's wealth. Prosperity was thus best achieved by encouraging the manufacturing sector of the economy, whose growth depended on two things: the division of labor, and the existence of free markets.

The first furthered economic growth by increasing productivity, as illustrated in Smith's famous example of pin manufacture: 10 men, working in a factory that divided the production of pins into 18 steps, daily created about 48,000 pins; whereas one man performing all the tasks himself produced perhaps one. But division of labor depended on the existence of a large and growing market, which in turn depended on the accumulation of capital or the degree to which businessmen invested their profits in productive, rather than consumable, wealth.

The second cause of economic growth was the creation of an environment in which individuals might freely pursue their economic interests, something Smith called the "system of natural liberty." Using supply-and-demand models, he demonstrated that when individuals pursued their personal economic goals, free from government regulation, the aggregate result was not injustice but efficiency, not chaos but a well-ordered system of free enterprise from which everyone benefited. Accordingly, Smith wanted the state limited to those functions not suitable to private enterprise: among other things national defense, law enforcement, and provision of bridges and roads.

Smith's *Wealth of Nations,* described by his friend **David Hume** as a work of "depth, solidity and acuteness," was an immediate success. Soon **translated** into other European languages, it elicited the admiration of such notable politicians as **Edmund Burke** and **William Pitt the Younger**, became the standard by which all later economic thought would be measured, and furnished many arguments for **entrepreneurs**, **Benthamites**, and others seeking to justify the newly emerging British industrial system. Classical political economists after Smith, such as **Thomas Malthus**, **David Ricardo**, **James Mill**, and **John Stuart Mill**, did little more than elaborate, refine, and reorganize Smith's understanding of the awesome productive powers of free markets. Today, Smith's ideas still nourish neoconservative approaches to economics. While it is not clear how strict an adherent of "laissez-faire" Smith would be by modern standards, it could be argued that no British thinker of the Hanoverian period had as powerful and long-lasting an impact on the modern world.

Eric K. Heavner

Bibliography

Blaug, Mark. *Economic Theory in Retrospect.* 1978.
Campbell, R.H., and A.S. Skinner. *Adam Smith.* 1982.
Campbell, T.D. *Adam Smith's Science of Morals.* 1971.
Hollander, Samuel. *The Economics of Adam Smith.* 1973.
Raphael, D.D. *Adam Smith.* 1985.
Skinner, A.S. *A System of Social Science: Papers Relating to Adam Smith.* 1979.
Winch, D. *Adam Smith's Politics.* 1978.
———. *Riches and Poverty: An Intellectual History of Political Economy in Britain, 1750–1834.* 1996.

See also Scottish Enlightenment

Smith, Sydney (1771–1845)

Clergyman, essayist, and celebrated lecturer, Smith is chiefly remembered for his contributions to the *Edinburgh Review,* the independent **Whig** quarterly, which he founded with **Francis Jeffrey** and others in 1802. Smith supervised the production of the first issues and contributed nearly 80 articles over the following 25 years.

Educated at New College, Oxford (1789–1794), Smith took orders in the **Church of England** (1794), rapidly attaining a reputation for his powerful though unconventional **sermons**. In **London**, as an intimate member of the **Holland House** circle, he also became known for his conversational eloquence and **wit**. His reputation was enhanced by his lectures on moral philosophy at the **Royal Institution** (1804–1806). Attracting 600 to 800 listeners, these made him a celebrity.

Sydney Smith

Smith's major publications include *Six Sermons* (1800), the *Peter Plymley Letters* (published anonymously, 1807–1808), and *Elementary Sketches of Moral Philosophy* (1850). Often compared to the **satires** of **Swift** and Voltaire, Smith's works are notable for their wit, erudition, and political courage. He vehemently argued the liberal position on educational reform, **Catholic emancipation**, the **slave trade**, and the Irish question. A fine representative of some of the highest qualities of his age, he can still be read with admiration and enjoyment.

John Kandl

Bibliography

Bell, Alan. *Sydney Smith.* 1980.

Halpern, Sheldon. *Sydney Smith.* 1966.

Holland, Lady. *A Memoir of the Reverend Sydney Smith.* 1855.

Smith, Nowell C., ed. *The Letters of Sydney Smith.* 1953.

Smollett, Tobias (1721–1771)

Although Smollett's reputation rests today primarily on his final **novel**, *The Expedition of Humphry Clinker* (1771), he has long held a place, along with **Defoe**, **Richardson**, **Fielding**, and **Sterne**, as one of the masters of 18th-century fiction.

His first work, *Roderick Random* (1748), is perhaps his best after *Clinker,* but admirers can make substantial arguments in favor of *The Adventures of Peregrine Pickle* (1751), *The Adventures of Ferdinand Count Fathom* (1753), and *The Life and Adventures of Sir Launcelot Greaves* (1760–1762). Smollett had an active literary career in addition to his fiction writing, most notably as editor from 1756 to 1763 of the *Critical Review,* which was rivaled as a literary arbiter only by the older *Monthly Review.* He also authored the *Complete History of England* (1757–1758) and its *Continuation* (1760–1765), *Travels through France and Italy* (1766), and almost certainly *The History and Adventures of an Atom* (1769), a fiercely scatological political **satire**. Finally, his **translation** of Alain Lesage's (1668–1747) *The Adventures of Gil Blas* (1748) is still arguably the best available; less worthy is a translation of *Don Quixote,* his share of which is still disputed.

Smollett was born in Dumbartonshire, **Scotland**, and attended the University of Glasgow, where he studied **medicine**. In 1739 he followed the path of many aspiring authors and migrated to **London** with a tragedy in his pocket and not much else. A year later, driven by **poverty** and failure, he turned his medical training to the use of the **navy**; *Roderick Random* contains a brilliant chronicle of his experiences. Although he later attempted to set up a medical practice in London, his true profession was writing, and after the success of *Roderick* he turned more and more to his pen as a source of profit and pleasure; the remainder of his life was never without literary projects, whether fictions, translations, reviews, histories, or **periodical** essays. His final work, *Humphry Clinker,* filled with autobiographical glimpses in the character of Matt Bramble, was published just 4 months before his death in Leghorn, Italy, where he was traveling—like Bramble—to mend his health.

As a central figure in the development of the realistic novel, Smollett stands out for his free-wheeling command of those fictional modes—Romance and satire, pseudo biography and allegory—against which the novel is usually defined. His forte lies in a style and diction that is consistently unadorned and factual; he gives every indication of reporting only what stands before his eyes, and convinces us that his vision is piercing and unblinking. It is when this mimetic style is put into the service of the improbable and fantastic, the highly exaggerated and grotesque, that one discovers the productive tensions of Smollett's work. Similarly, he combines a harshly satiric and pessimistic (perhaps cynical) power of observation with a moral insistence that the world and its actions are contrived to produce providential examples of virtue rewarded and vice punished. Out of this clash of ultimately incompatible worldviews, a clash mirroring the age in which he lived and his own suspension between Christian and secular outlooks, Smollett produced fictions notable more for their magnificent and violent dislocations—conveyed always with a further disconcerting transparency of style—than for characterization or plotting.

According to the American novelist John Barth, the pleasure of Smollett is that "one swift reading does him"; but Smollett's simplicity is quite complex, and his directness is a well-crafted mask for doubt and division. One may doubt whether a quick reading will suffice.

Melvyn New

Bibliography

Beasley, Jerry C. "Smollett's Art: The Novel As 'Picture,'" in J.M. Armistead, ed., *The First English Novelists: Essays in Understanding.* 1985.

Bold, Alan, ed. *Smollett: Author of the First Distinction.* 1982.

Boucé, Paul-Gabriel. *The Novels of Tobias Smollett.* 1976.

Grant, Damian. *Tobias Smollett: A Study in Style.* 1977.

Knapp, Lewis M. *Tobias Smollett: Doctor of Men and Manners.* 1949.

———. *The Letters of Tobias Smollett.* 1970.

Preston, Thomas. *Not in Timon's Manner: Feeling, Misanthropy, and Satire in Eighteenth-Century England.* 1975.

Rousseau, George S., and Paul-Gabriel Boucé, eds. *Tobias Smollett: Bicentennial Essays Presented to Lewis M. Knapp.* 1971.

Wagoner, Mary. *Tobias Smollett: A Checklist of Editions of His Works and an Annotated Secondary Bibliography.* 1984.

Smuggling

Although smuggling had been perpetrated since the Middle Ages, it increased dramatically during the Hanoverian period. During the early reign of **George III** the smuggling of wool, **tobacco**, tea, wines, spirits, silks, and other commodities became a very serious problem along the coastal regions of the British Isles and **North America**, resulting in losses of millions of pounds in customs duties. Whole fleets of vessels and districts of population connived or concurred in it. Smugglers, or "free traders" as they called themselves, were often assisted by corrupt customs officials and people of all social strata who sought to earn a profit or acquire cheap goods by avoiding the **navigation laws** and heavy customs duties imposed on many articles.

Packet boats, and also large trading **ships**, especially those of the **East India Company**, often engaged in smuggling. Because of the complexity of such operations, much planning was sometimes involved and there was specialization on the part of smugglers. Wealthier men would raise capital for the purchase of goods abroad; **seamen**, guided by signals from land, would transport the goods to shore; and other smugglers would unload the boats and move the goods inland to be sold. Smugglers used especially swift and well-maintained craft to elude customs patrols and the **navy**. Gangs of smugglers such as those at Hawkhurst in Kent, heavily armed with clubs and guns, often fought with officials and **army** detachments to prevent seizure of their goods. An armed attack on the custom house at Poole to retrieve confiscated goods (1747), and the murder of a customs officer and an informer (1748), were among the more egregious outrages perpetrated by smuggling gangs.

"The Smuggler's Boat"

Smuggling was believed to be extremely widespread, though its true amount has been a matter of historical controversy. Not only its extent but the general attitude of defiance and disregard for the law associated with it, and its possible connections with **Jacobitism** and the French, alarmed the authorities. Some smugglers did indeed run munitions and soldiers for Britain's enemies.

Measures employed against smuggling ("owling" if it involved wool) included the use of informants and rewards. **Punishments** included forfeiture of property and the death penalty for wearing disguises, running, landing, or carrying smuggled goods. Localities could even be fined for failure to apprehend smugglers. But in spite of such harsh provisions, magistrates often did not prosecute, and juries were reluctant to convict. Measures were eventually adopted to regulate the construction of certain types of vessels used primarily for smuggling, and to prevent craft from "hovering" within specified distances of the coast.

Smuggling continued to flourish anyway, and the government found it necessary to fortify customs patrols with better and faster ships and to establish the Preventive Waterguard (1809), Coastal Blockade (1817), and Coastguard (1831). It was not until reform of customs rates and excise duties actually reduced the cost of legally obtained goods that the profits of smuggling declined. After the 1820s, smuggling was confined to fewer commodities and became much more elaborately concealed. Smugglers, always playing cat-and-mouse with British **law enforcement**, began making greater use of hidden compartments in boats, the sinking of goods offshore for later retrieval, and even specially designed garments to pass goods under the noses of customs officers.

Mark C. Herman

Bibliography

Carson, Edward. *The Ancient and Rightful Customs: A History of the English Customs Service.* 1972.

Chatterton, Edward Keble. *King's Cutters and Smugglers, 1700–1855.* 1912.

Cole, W.A. "Trends in Eighteenth-Century Smuggling." *Economic History Review.* Vol. 10, pp. 395–409.

———. "The Arithmetic of Eighteenth-Century Smuggling." *Economic History Review.* Vol. 28, pp. 44–49.

Mui, Hoh-Cheung, and Lorna H. Mui. "'Trends in Eighteenth-Century Smuggling' Reconsidered." *Economic History Review.* Vol. 28, pp. 28–43.

Smith, Graham. *King's Cutters: The Revenue Service and the War against Smuggling.* 1983.

Teignmouth, Henry N. Shore, Lord. *Smuggling Days and Smuggling Ways; or, The Story of a Lost Art.* 1892; rpt. 1929.

Winslow, Cal. "Sussex Smugglers," in Douglas Hay, et al., eds., *Albion's Fatal Tree: Crime and Society in Eighteenth-Century England.* 1975.

See also Crime; Porteous Riots; Taxes and Tariffs

Society for Constitutional Information (SCI)

The Society for Constitutional Information (SCI) was founded in April 1780 by a group of **middle-class radicals** who had sought for at least a decade to establish an organization to agitate for parliamentary reform. Its founding occurred in the general atmosphere of anger and antigovernment criticism that accompanied the later years of the **War of American Independence**. The SCI's membership list over the next dozen years was virtually a Who's Who of contemporary radicalism; it included among others, **John Cartwright**, **Horne Tooke**, **Christopher Wyvill**, **John Jebb**, **Capell Lofft**, **John Thelwall**, and **Thomas Paine**. Its primary objectives were to promote universal suffrage and annual elections to Parliament, measures which its members considered restorations of traditional English liberties lost to centuries of corrupt government relying on **patronage**, **placemen**, and unconstitutional methods and information. It spread these ideas of the country's "lost rights" through general meetings, the publication of many cheap or free political pamphlets and petitions, and the support of reform candidates and bills.

The SCI's roots were in the **Society for Supporters of the Bill of Rights** that had arisen from the **Wilkes** controversies earlier. It supported all efforts to increase political liberty, including those to repeal the **Test and Corporation Acts** and to abolish the **slave trade**. Energized by the **French Revolution**, it greatly intensified its activities from 1791 to 1794, its members founding many local branches—a **Manchester** Constitutional Society, a Warwickshire Constitutional Society, and so on. Members of the SCI were prosecuted by the government in 1794 on charges of high treason and were portrayed as directing the activities of other, still more radical organizations such as the **London Corresponding Society**, several of whose members were also indicted for high treason. Although its members were not convicted and the SCI was never formally dissolved, it ceased functioning after May 1794. Its activities were continued after 1811 by the new **Hampden clubs** started also by the redoubtable Cartwright and others.

Frank M. Baglione

Bibliography

Cone, Carl B. *The English Jacobins: Reformers in Late 18th Century England.* 1968.

Fruchtman, Jack, Jr. *Thomas Paine: Apostle of Freedom.* 1994.

Osborne, John. *John Cartwright.* 1972.

Royle, Edward, and James Walvin. *English Radicals and Reformers, 1760–1848.* 1982.

See also Elections and the Franchise; Radicalism and Radical Politics

Society for the Diffusion of Useful Knowledge (SDUK)

The SDUK, part of the self-help movement that flourished in the early 19th century, was established (1826) to help reconcile the working classes to changing labor conditions and to provide them with improving reading matter in natural history, **technology**, political economy, geography, **biography**, and **history**. Its chief founders were **Henry Brougham** and the publisher Charles Knight (1791–1873). According to its prospectus, the society's aims were to impart "useful information to all classes of the community, particularly to such as are unable to avail themselves of experienced teachers, or may prefer learning by themselves." From the outset it leaned in the direction of the utilitarianism of **Jeremy Bentham**, developing programs of adult education in the practical sciences that complemented the **Mechanics' Institutes** supported also by Brougham and like-minded reformers such as **James Mill** and Harriet Martineau (1802–1876).

One of the society's chief activities was the "diffusion" of cheap "improving literature." Early offerings such as its Library of Useful Knowledge and Library of Entertaining Knowledge were more ambitious than successful, but the *Penny Magazine*, founded in 1832, the first mass-circulation **periodical** published in Britain, offered informative nonfiction articles accompanied by illustrations. Edited by Knight, the magazine briefly attained a readership of 200,000. The novelist **Peacock** satirized the SDUK as the "Steam Intellect Society" in his **novel** *Crotchet Castle* (1831). It ceased operations in 1845.

Timothy Erwin

Bibliography

Thomas, William. *The Philosophic Radicals: Nine Studies in Theory and Practice, 1817–1841.* 1979.
Webb, R.K. *The British Working Class Reader, 1790–1848: Literacy and Social Tension.* 1955.

Society for Promoting Christian Knowledge (SPCK)

This society, founded in 1698 by Thomas Bray (1656–1730), rector of Sheldon, and four lay associates, was designed to promote and encourage **charity schools** and workhouses throughout England and **Wales**. Its goal was to protect children from vagrancy and prepare them for employment. Its founders were concerned about vice and debauchery resulting from **poverty** and the ignorance of Christianity. Accordingly, they distributed Bibles, prayer books, and religious **tracts** to promote Christian knowledge, and encouraged parish clergy and laymen to form local charity schools, print Bibles, and distribute catechisms and devotional **essays**. By 1723 the society claimed to serve 23,421 pupils in 1,329 schools under its control.

A Scottish branch of the organization (SSPCK) was founded in 1709 after the English model. Its founders particularly occupied themselves with "civilizing" the Highlands, by which they meant extending **Presbyterian** religious forms and inculcating the English language in place of Gaelic. Supported by the **Church of Scotland**, the SSPCK had founded 176 schools by 1760, most of them in the Highlands. In **Wales**, under the leadership of **Griffith Jones**, the SPCK proved most active in providing books for **circulating schools**. Jones, Anglican rector of Llanddowror, in 1737 began his circulating schools for adults and children, taught by traveling **teachers** who instructed their pupils to read the Welsh Bible. At the time of his death (1761), the SPCK could claim that whereas before 1737 it had served only 95 Welsh schools (31 in Pembrokeshire), it had come to serve 3,498 Welsh schools since then, providing instruction to no less than 158,237 pupils. In the 19th century the SPCK was a stalwart supporter of both the **Methodists** and the established **Church of England**.

Samuel J. Rogal

Bibliography

Allen, W.O.B., and Edmund McClure. *Two Hundred Years: The History of the Society for Promoting Christian Knowledge, 1698–1898.* 1898.
Cavenagh, F.A. *The Life and Work of Griffith Jones.* 1930.
Clement, Mary. *The S.P.C.K. and Wales, 1699–1740.* 1954.
Howsam, Leslie. *Cheap Bibles: Nineteenth-Century Publishing and the British and Foreign Bible Society.* 1991.
Lowther Clark, W.K. *A History of the S.P.C.K.* 1959.
Thompson, H.P. *Thomas Bray.* 1954.
Watts, Michael R. *The Dissenters: From the Reformation to the French Revolution.* 1978.

See also Education, Elementary; Education, Religious

Society for the Propagation of the Gospel in Foreign Parts (SPG)

The SPG was founded in 1701 as the missionary branch of the **Society for Promoting Christian Knowledge** (SPCK). It was created by Thomas Bray (1656–1730), missionary to Maryland and Vicar of St. Botolph Without, Aldgate, who had also founded the parent society. Bray hoped that as an agency of the Anglican Church the SPG would evangelize all non–Christian races within the jurisdiction of the Crown—which meant, in the 18th century, focusing its attention upon **North America** and the **West Indies**. An adjunct organization arose in 1723, "Dr. Bray's Associates for Founding Clerical Libraries and Supporting Negro Schools"; one leader of this was the **Evangelical James Oglethorpe**. When **John Wesley** sailed for Georgia in October 1735, he did so under the sponsorship of the SPG to minister to the Indians (Native Americans) of that colony.

The organization labored also in **Canada** both before and after the **American Revolution**. By 1758 its missionaries had firmly established the Church of England in Nova Scotia, which 20 years later provided a haven for American loyalist **Tories**. In 1787 the church consecrated a bishop for Nova Scotia, with jurisdiction over Bermuda, **Newfoundland**, New Brunswick, Prince Edward Island, and the territories known as Upper and Lower Canada. By the end of the century, 48 of the 61 Anglican clergy in Upper and Lower Canada served as missionaries for the SPG. The missionary group extended its efforts in the 19th century to **India**, the southern and western parts of **Africa**, **Australia**, and the Far East. Its founding and early activities reflect many relationships between the **Church of England** and the **Empire**.

Samuel J. Rogal

Bibliography

Clark, J.C.D. *The Language of Liberty, 1660–1832: Political Discourse and Social Dynamics in the Anglo-American World.* 1994.

Eaton, Arthur Wentworth. *The Church of England in Nova Scotia and the Tory Clergy of the Revolution.* 1891.

Latourette, Kenneth Scott. *Christianity in a Revolutionary Age: A History of Christianity in the Nineteenth and Twentieth Centuries.* 1958, 1961.

Miller, Peter N. *Defining the Good: Empire, Religion and Philosophy in Eighteenth-Century Britain.* 1994.

Pasco, C.F. *Two Hundred Years of the S.P.G., an Historical Account of the Society for the Propagation of the Gospel in Foreign Parts, 1701–1900.* 1901.

Thompson, H.P. *Into All Lands: The History of the Society for the Propagation of the Gospel in Foreign Parts, 1701–1950.* 1951.

———. *Thomas Bray.* 1954.

See also Missionary Societies; Religious Revivalism

Society for the Reformation of Manners

This society and its chapters emerged in the 1690s, following the **Toleration Act**, as the response of lay piety to what many saw as an increasing licentiousness in public morals. Initially Anglican, the society soon welcomed **dissenters** and adopted a whiggish Low-Church character. Its supporters argued that although many people were beyond the reach of organized religion, the society could promote public correction of vices like lewdness, profanity, and public drunkenness, and encourage the regular preaching of sermons exhorting reform. Many prominent Anglican ministers, including Gilbert Burnet (1643–1715), lent their energies to the cause. Among the most tireless was the Rev. Josiah Woodward (1660–1712), author of many reforming **tracts** and **sermons**, and also of an early account of the society.

While High-Church ecclesiastics such as Henry Sacheverell (1674–1724) opposed the society on the grounds that its acceptance of nonconformity undermined the authority of the **Church of England**, others based their opposition on the idea that vice and debauchery were primarily secular concerns. Moreover, laws against vice, wrote **Daniel Defoe**, were only enforced against the lower classes. If by the 1750s the society had ultimately failed to curb public immorality, it did, through its literature and agitation, keep the problem of public morals in the forefront of public awareness. It may also have moved Anglicanism to strengthen its corrective role by aligning more closely with the **Whig** administrations of the early Hanoverian kings.

Timothy Erwin

Bibliography

Bennet, G.V. "Conflict in the Church," in G. Holmes, ed., *Britain After the Glorious Revolution.* 1969.

Burtt, Shelley. *Virtue Transformed: Political Argument in England, 1688–1740.* 1992.

Holmes, G. *Religion and Party in Late Stuart England.* 1975.

Isaacs, Tina. "The Anglican Hierarchy and the Reformation of Manners." *Journal of Ecclesiastical History.* Vol. 33, pp. 391–411.

See also Manners and Morals; Proclamation Society against Vice and Immorality; Society for the Suppression of Vice

Society for Supporters of the Bill of Rights

This was the first and prototypical **radical** organization of the Hanoverian era. It was founded in February 1769 to provide political and financial support to **John Wilkes**, then the radical hero of the hour. Within its first year it raised £20,000 to help pay off his debts. Following the leadership of **John Horne Tooke**, **John Sawbridge**, and others, it demanded parliamentary and municipal reform and a more conciliatory attitude toward the American colonists. In June 1771 it began to advocate shorter parliaments and fairer parliamentary representation, demands soon adopted by other organizations.

However, also in 1771 a division occurred within the organization as members disagreed about the publication of parliamentary debates, the impeachment of **Lord North**, and the use of society funds, which Wilkes wished to reserve for himself and others wanted for the support of liberty in general. This latter issue prompted Sawbridge and Horne to found the Constitutional Society later that year, a forerunner of the more important **Society for Constitutional Information** founded in 1780.

David B. Mock

Bibliography

Cone, Carl B. *English Jacobins: Reformers in Late Eighteenth Century England.* 1968.

Newman, Gerald. *The Rise of English Nationalism: A Cultural History, 1740–1830.* 1987.

Royle, Edward, and James Walvin. *English Radicals and Reformers, 1760–1848.* 1982.

Society for the Suppression of Vice

Known also, more simply, as the "Vice Society," this organization was founded in 1802 to attack blasphemy, **pornography**, **prostitution**, profanation of the Sabbath, and injurious public **amusements** such as **gambling**, excessive **drinking**, cruelty to animals, and selling by false weights and measures. Its links to the past ran back more than a century to the **Society for the Reformation of Manners** of the 1690s and the somewhat more **aristocratic** and lethargic **Proclamation Society against Vice and Immorality** (founded in 1787), of which it was, more clearly in its objectives than its personnel, a continuation. But it was also plainly an offshoot of the feverish contemporary reaction against the **French Revolution**, as evidenced in its members' well-publicized fear that only by a national moral reformation could Britain escape the evils which had befallen **France**, supposedly deep in laxity and immorality before 1789. Historians of Victorian morality see the society also as a precursor of the moralistic national pressure groups of the latter 19th century (though its objectives and methods of operation were much less political, being more in the way of private supplementary **police** work). Students of urbanization see it as a confused attempt to provide moral leadership in an age of primitive **law enforcement** mechanisms.

Unlike the Proclamation Society, the Vice Society aimed at a very wide membership. It embraced some 1,200 members by 1805, having targeted clergymen, businessmen, lawyers, and women (about one-third were women by 1805). Its connections with the **loyalist** impulses and anti–**Jacobin** government propaganda of the 1790s are reflected in the early participation of John Reeves (1752?–1829), founder of the Association for the Preservation of Liberty and Property against Republicans and Levellers (1792), and the early leadership provided by John Bowles (1751–1819), a pamphleteer against **Paine** (1792) and strongly committed conservative propagandist. Some writers have too carelessly identified the society with the **Evangelicals** of the **Clapham sect**, for although **Wilberforce** joined it in 1804 and Lord Teignmouth (1751–1834) in 1805 (as its vice-president), the Claphamites, fairly ecumenical in outlook, shied away from its rule limiting membership to communicants of the **Church of England**. They also, like the society's far more bitter enemies among Foxite **Whigs** and the Whig–**radicals** of the *Edinburgh Review*, disapproved of its use of spies and paid informers to expose and prosecute immorality.

The society's ambitions were too comprehensive to sustain, once anti–Jacobin enthusiasm began wearing thin around 1809. Its main early successes were against trading on the Sabbath and other supposedly vicious pursuits on Sundays, and it remained the main Sabbatarian pressure group until the founding (1831) of the Lord's Day Observance Society. But following internal crisis and reorganization it emerged after 1812 more exclusively but effectively devoted to efforts against blasphemy and obscenity. Its critics always charged it with underhanded methods, religious intolerance and fanaticism, and prurient hypocrisy. Its defenders ascribed this to the "well known fact, that the immoral and unthinking portion of a community form its far greatest proportion; and [that] the vicious incessantly assail an Institution, at open war with their practice and propensities."

George F. Clements

Bibliography

Bradley, I. *The Call to Seriousness: The Evangelical Impact on the Victorians.* 1976.

Bristow, E. *Vice and Vigilance: Purity Movements in Britain since 1700.* 1977.

Curtis, T.C., and W.A. Speck. "The Societies for the Reformation of Manners: A Case Study in the Theory and Practice of Moral Reform." *Literature and History.* Vol. 3, pp. 45–64.

Hone, J. Ann. *For the Cause of Truth: Radicalism in London, 1796–1821.* 1982.

Quinlan, M.J. *Victorian Prelude: A History of English Manners, 1700–1830.* 1965.

Roberts, M.J.D. "The Society for the Suppression of Vice and Its Early Critics, 1801–1812." *Historical Journal.* Vol. 26, pp. 159–176.

See also Censorship; Manners and Morals

Society of Friends

See Quakers

Society of the Friends of the People

This group was organized (1792) in the wake of the **French Revolution** by young Foxite **Whigs**, followers of **Charles James Fox**, who hoped to capture for their party the public support then growing for moderate parliamentary reform. Older and more conservative Whigs took offense at this apparent challenge to their authority, thus providing **William Pitt the Younger** an opportunity to divide and weaken the **opposition** to his government. The execution of the King of **France** (1793) pushed the **Portland** Whigs toward coalition with Pitt.

The young aristocrats who began the society and were led by **Charles Grey** soon found themselves discredited by being lumped with more **radical** groups promoting reform, including the quasi nationalist Scottish Association of the Friends of the People under **Thomas Muir**. The radicals' sympathy for the French Revolution and their enthusiasm for the republican political forms advocated by **Thomas Paine** in his *Rights of Man* (1791–1792) rendered reform profoundly suspect to British loyalists. Despite this, Grey persevered, offering a motion for reform in 1793, which was then rejected overwhelmingly, even by his own party.

P.J. Kulisheck

Bibliography

Derry, John W. *Charles, Earl Grey: Aristocratic Reformer.* 1992.

Smith, E.A. *Whig Principles and Party Politics: Earl Fitzwilliam and the Whig Party 1748–1833.* 1975.

———. *Lord Grey, 1764–1845.* 1990.

See also London Corresponding Society; Loyalist Associations

Society of Spencean Philanthropists

A "Spencean Society" formed in 1811 to promote the land reform program of radical pamphleteer **Thomas Spence** was remodeled and renamed the Society of Spencean Philanthropists by Thomas Evans (*d.* 1826) and others in October 1814 after Spence's death that year. These men considered themselves philanthropists in the contemporary sense of the word—lovers of mankind. Their object was to try to better the lot of the poor and the working class by implementing Spence's program. In this, all land would be owned by the people as a whole and administered and rented out by local parishes; all profits would be distributed to everyone equally after parish and national expenses had been paid.

Meeting regularly in **London** taverns, this society was one indication of a cohesive **radicalism** that was trying in this decade to unite **craftsmen** and unskilled workers. The Spenceans propagated their ideas through pamphlets, **tracts**, broadsides, and discussions in their evening meetings. The question of landownership was particularly embittered after the passage of the hated **corn laws** (1815), and a small group of Spenceans hoped to foment a revolutionary overthrow of the government and to initiate Spence's land reform immediately. These plotters were responsible for the **Spa fields riot** of 2 December 1816, a plan to seize the Tower of London and **Bank of England**. Several of these conspirators, including **Arthur Thistlewood**, were arrested but not subsequently convicted.

The Spenceans were considered dangerous incendiaries, and did little to dispel this reputation. The **Cato Street conspiracy** to assassinate the British cabinet, led by Thistlewood and other Spenceans, resulted in the execution of five plotters. This helped to discredit the Spenceans, though Spence's ideas were kept alive among working-class activists and in the Chartist movement later.

Mark C. Herman

Bibliography

Chase, Malcolm. *"The People's Farm": English Radical Agrarianism, 1775–1840.* 1988.

McCalman, Iain. *Radical Underworld: Prophets, Revolutionaries and Pornographers in London, 1795–1840.* 1988.

Parsinnen, T.M. "The Revolutionary Party in London, 1816–20." *Bulletin of the Institute of Historical Research.* Vol. 45, pp. 266–282.

Rudkin, Olive D. *Thomas Spence and His Connections.* 1927; rpt. 1966.

Worrall, David. *Radical Culture: discourse, Resistance and Surveillance, 1790–1820.* 1992.

See also Regency, The

South Sea Bubble (1720)

This speculative mania gripped Britain and Europe in 1720. It had its origins in the financial climate following the Treaty of Utrecht (1713) and the **Jacobite** rebellion of 1715. Britain emerged from the **War of Spanish Succession** with a high level of national debt, which the government was determined to reduce. The years 1716 and 1717 were ones of good trade, and there was an upswing in building and the construction of turnpike **roads**. The government deliberately ran down the floating part of the national debt by curtailing the amount of Treasury bills in circulation. Thus there was a surplus of funds available for investment, and in 1719 there began to appear a rash of proposals for the formation of **joint-stock companies**, many of dubious origin. It was in this climate that the **South Sea Company** launched an ingenious plan that was tantamount to a privatization of the long-term portion of the British national debt.

The plan was similar to one already launched by **John Law** in Paris. Holders of certain government securities were to exchange them for stock in the company. Issues were made at different times and at different prices, and payment could be made in installments. Thus, in order for investors to make a profit, it was necessary for the market value of South Sea stock to be continually rising. During the spring and early summer of 1720, the price of this stock rose consistently; a rise reflected in other stocks as an investment mania gathered pace, possibly fueled by funds placed on the **London** market after the failure of Law's plans in Paris. But fear grew that the increasing interest by investors in other stock ventures would harm the South Sea scheme. This led in June to the "Bubble" act, which banned the establishment of joint-stock companies without government permission, and, in August, to specific action against a group of companies (operated by **Case Billingsley**) whose price had risen sharply. The result was a dramatic drop in many stock prices, including that of the South Sea Company, which led to the ruin of many investors, particularly inexperienced first-time investors who had been tempted.

Government investigations revealed corruption; the cashier fled, and the company's directors had their property confiscated. The resulting crisis brought **Sir Robert Walpole** to power, and through his intervention the situation was stabilized with the assistance of the **Bank of England**. Many companies crashed, but the South Sea Company survived as a holder of the government stocks outlined in the scheme. Ironically, it was the public purse that came out of the crisis in the best position. Later in 1720, similar crises hit Holland and Germany, bringing to an end the first international stock market crash.

A.J.G. Cummings

Bibliography

Carswell, John. *The South Sea Bubble.* 1960.

Dickson, P.G.M. *The Financial Revolution in England: A Study in the Development of Public Credit, 1688–1756.* 1967.

Kindleberger, Charles P. *Manias, Panics and Crashes.* 1978.

Neal, Larry. *The Rise of Financial Capitalism: International Capital Markets in the Age of Reason.* 1990.

See also Chandos, 1st Duke of; Finance and Investment; York Buildings Company

South Sea Company

Founded in 1711 as a **chartered trading company**, this company's original aim was to take over part of the national debt at a rate of interest lower than the going rate. This takeover, together with a handling fee, was to provide the basis for dividend distribution to stockholders. To boost the company's prospects, it was granted a trade monopoly with considerable parts of Spanish America, including rights to provide **slaves** under the Treaty of Utrecht (1713), but these proved difficult to exercise because of Spanish hostility and were never profitable.

In February 1720 the company received permission to take over that part of the national debt not already held by the **Bank of England** and the **East India Company**, by exchanging government securities for its own South Sea Company stock. Because the exchange price depended on the market value of the latter at the time of the conversion, this, together with a rash of other **joint-stock company** flotations and the activities of **John Law** in **France**, led to a stock market surge that culminated in the **South Sea Bubble**. In trying to curtail the activities of its rivals, the company caused a panic that provoked a financial crisis.

With the assistance of the Bank of England, the government of **Robert Walpole** put together a rescue package under which parts of the national debt were converted into South Sea stock on terms more favorable to the taxpayer than to stockholders. With its financial problems largely resolved, the company settled down as a financial institution, receiving its payments from the government and distributing them to its stockholders as dividends. In 1750 its right to trade in slaves was surrendered, and in 1807 its monopolistic trading privileges were revoked. Its stock was reconverted to government securities and the company ceased operations in 1854.

A.J.G. Cummings

Bibliography

Carswell, John. *The South Sea Bubble.* 1960.

Dickson, P.G.M. *The Financial Revolution in England: A Study in the Development of Public Credit 1688–1756.* 1967.

Neal, Larry. *The Rise of Financial Capitalism: International Capital Markets in the Age of Reason.* 1990.

Scott, W.R. *The Constitution and Finance of English, Scottish and Irish Joint-Stock Companies to 1720.* 3 vols. 1910.

Southcott, Joanna (1750–1814)

Southcott, an English religious visionary, rose from obscurity to lead a sect of thousands, with three chapels in **London** as well as several congregations in the north and the Midlands. Uneducated and nearly illiterate, she earned her living as a **servant** until around 1792, when, attending an Exeter **Methodist** meeting, she claimed to experience visions and the gift of prophesy. In 1801, after publishing a book titled *The Strange Effects of Faith,* she was brought by three London clergymen to Paddington, where she quickly attracted several hundred disciples, united only by faith in her and her mission as "bride of the lamb." In 1805 she opened a chapel in Southwark. At her career's height she had about 7,000 hardcore followers.

In the tradition of other millenarian prophets, Southcott claimed to be God's special means of revelation during perilous times. As her ministry progressed, challenges to her position as chosen messenger forced her into increasingly sensational claims. Tormented by doubts as to the source of her revelations, she left a body of writing which provides insight into the psychology of the visionary. In 1813, age 64, she temporarily silenced her opposition by announcing that she was with child of the Holy Ghost and would bring forth a son, Shiloh, who would usher in the millennium; but her death soon afterward, apparently of brain disease, resulted in fragmentation of the sect. A remnant of it survives today.

Linda R. Robinson

Bibliography

Harrison, J.F.C. *The Second Coming: Popular Millenarianism, 1780–1850.* 1979.

Hopkins, James K. *A Woman to Deliver Her People: Joanna Southcott and English Millenarianism in an Era of Revolution.* 1982.

See also Brothers, Richard; Enthusiasm; Millenarianism; Religious Revivalism

Southey, Robert (1774–1843)

Southey, the **poet laureate** who once described himself as "well pleased to be abused with **Wordsworth** and **Coleridge**; it is the best omen that I shall be remembered with them," is, in fact, remembered chiefly as an associate of these two giants of the **Lake School**. His failed attempt with Coleridge to found a utopia, and **Byron**'s well-known attacks on him, imply that Southey's grand failures are more interesting than his modest successes.

Born a draper's son in **Bristol**, his literary career culminated in his being named Poet Laureate (1813–1843) and encompassed work in a great variety of literary forms: **poetry**, **epic**, prose, drama, and **biography**. His early **radical** sympathies led to his explusion from school (1792) for writing **satirical essays**. He attended Oxford, where he failed at both divinity and **medicine**. But his college years did initiate a significant if troublesome friendship with Coleridge. In 1794 they jointly developed the idea for Pantisocracy, a utopian New World—a collaboration which led to Coleridge's necessary betrothal of Sara Fricker, Southey's sister-in-law. Their subsequent breakup was caused by lack of funds as well as growing ideological incompatibilities.

Southey's interest in mythography is evident in his early works from the period 1795–1805. Having published *Poems* (1795, 1799) and a long **exotic** Romance, *Thalaba* (1801), he wrote his most ambitious and elaborate epic, *Madoc,* in 1805. Linking contemporary interest in American Indians, Welsh **antiquities**, and **utopias**, the poem contributed to the Celtic

Robert Southey

revival and was one of the few works of this period to deal poetically with the Native American.

Reflecting his radical sympathies, Southey's first epic poem, *Joan of Arc* (1796), expressed the poet's disillusion in the aftermath of the **French Revolution**, presenting Joan as an epic heroine of democracy (though Coleridge scoffed at her image as a "Tom Paine in Petticoats"). Southey's play *Wat Tyler* (about the English revolutionary hero), written at the same time, manifests the poet's fullest republican fervor; unpublished until 1817, it was printed surreptitiously by Southey's conservative political enemies.

Despite **Byron**'s quip about Southey's "blank verse and blanker prose," his prose is commonly regarded as superior to his poetry. The 1808 *Letters from England,* combining travelogue, satire, and familiar essay, offer a copious cross-section of contemporary life and manners, with critical commentary, observations on local culture, and anecdotal curiosities. Southey's monumental *Life of Nelson* (1813) is noted for its frank and engaging portrait of England's most celebrated naval hero.

His later achievements include *Roderick* (1814), his best epic, indicative of his later conservatism, and his final epic, the much-lampooned *A Vision of Judgment* (1821), which depicts **King George III** in heaven and which stimulated Byron's satirical *The Vision of Judgment* (1822) in reply.

Lisa Plummer Crafton

Bibliography

Bernhardt-Kabisch, Ernest. *Robert Southey.* 1977.
Carnall, Geoffrey. *Robert Southey and His Age: The Development of a Conservative Mind.* 1960.
Curry, Kenneth. *Southey.* 1975.
———. *Robert Southey: A Reference Guide.* 1977.
Fitzgerald, M.H., ed. *Letters of Robert Southey: A Selection.* 1912.
Madden, Lionel, ed. *Robert Southey: The Critical Heritage.* 1972.
Simmons, Jack. *Southey.* 1945.

Spa Fields Riot (1816)

Three mass meetings addressed by **Henry ("Orator") Hunt** were held at Spa Fields in **London** on 15 November 1816, 2 December 1816, and 10 February 1817. Hunt hoped to use mass support to press the government to accept his program of parliamentary reform. On December 2 a crowd of several thousand gathered to hear him speak and to sign petitions to the government. He was scheduled to speak at 1:00 PM, but about half an hour earlier a group of ultra-**radical** members of the **Society of Spencean Philanthropists** pulled up a wagon and began addressing the crowd. Hoping to take advantage of the multitude Hunt could attract, and motivated by a desire to implement the land reform program of **Thomas Spence** by violence if necessary, these men led a few hundred of the crowd away to seize arms and to attack the Tower of London and **Bank of England**. They desired to establish a Committee of Public Safety of leading radicals, modeled after the French Revolutionary dictatorship of 1793.

Although they managed to hold the area north of the tower for several hours, and although rioting continued throughout the afternoon and into the evening, the plotters were not successful. Their hope that this might be the start of a general uprising did not come to fruition. **Arthur Thistlewood** and three other participants were arrested but were not convicted (though a sailor involved in the riot was hanged). A subsequent meeting at Spa Fields on 10 February 1817 came off with no violence, but the ideas of revolutionary insurrection and political assassination were revived by Thistlewood and others in the **Cato Street conspiracy**.

Mark C. Herman

Bibliography

Calder-Marshall, Arthur. "The Spa Fields Riots, 1816." *History Today.* Vol. 21, pp. 407–415.
Chase, Malcolm. *"The People's Farm": English Radical Agrarianism, 1775–1840.* 1988.
McCalman, Iain. *Radical Underworld: Prophets, Revolutionaries and Pornographers in London, 1795–1840.* 1988.
Stevenson, John. *Popular Disturbances in England, 1700–1870.* 1979.
Thompson, E.P. *The Making of the English Working Class.* 1968; rpt. 1980.
Worrall, David. *Radical Culture: Discourse, Resistance and Surveillance, 1790–1820.* 1992.

See also Riots and Popular Disturbances

Spas

A number of British towns possess thermal or mineral springs or wells. The early-16th-century custom of making pilgrimages to the springs and shrines associated with the saints to take the "healing waters" gained new momentum in the late 17th century. And while some of the shrines, such as that at Walsingham in Norfolk, continued to fulfill this role, visitors were, by the 18th century, increasingly attracted to the spas and springs solely for medicinal purposes. Since many of these were not easy to reach, their patrons were largely the leisured, wealthy, and fashionable.

As a result of physicians increasingly recommending the healing waters to their patients, in the early years of the 18th century, Epsom, Knaresborough, Harrogate, Matlock, and Tunbridge Wells joined the list headed by Buxton and **Bath** as the leading watering places. Tunbridge Wells, which benefited from the **patronage** of King Charles II (1660–1685), had already developed as one of the more fashionable resorts, offering such **amusements** as **gambling** and **dancing** in addition to bathing. Despite its originally rural setting and rustic accommodations, its waters brought it visitors and prosperity. The same thing occurred later at other spa towns such as Leamington, Harrogate, and Cheltenham.

Bath's evolution into the preeminent spa resort began early in the 18th century when Richard Allen, a speculator, began to transform that ancient town into a beautiful and splendidly unified city in the **Palladian** architectural style with the help of the **architects** John Wood I (1704–1754) and John

Wood II (1728–1781). Richard "Beau" Nash (1674–1762), as master of ceremonies, established a disciplined etiquette and an aura of respectability that attracted the fashionable.

The daily timetable at Bath was mirrored at other resorts. It is perhaps useful to keep in mind the fact that during the Hanoverian era, the spa was the only facility that could produce the effects experienced today in ordinary heated baths, showers, swimming pools, jacuzzis, and the like. Bathing began early in the morning, with men and women walking together in the water, dressed in stiff canvas robes, which completely covered them. After bathing came drinking the waters in the Pump Room. As Lord Torrington (1699–1747) noted in his *Diaries,* this was followed by breakfast, at which "every one then looks fresh and happy; the women are more in their natural looks, not disfigured by over dress and paint, and the men are civil and sober."

The day was then devoted to walking, riding, shopping, reading, or just visiting, while the evenings were for balls, parties, gambling, and the **theater**. Until 1745, when gambling was made illegal in Bath, betting on card games and **sports** was very popular. However, gambling almost certainly continued in lodgings and taverns after 1745; Nash managed to ruin himself through gambling debts.

Fashionable though many of the visitors were, and popular as it was as a resort, Bath was still visited for medicinal reasons. To partake of its waters was regarded by many as a healthful duty rather than a pleasure, and there was still an underlying seriousness among those who came "for the cure." Religious observance was considered by some to be a useful complement to exercise in physical restoration, and hence it was still customary around 1750 for some visitors to attend morning service at the Abbey. Similarly, at Tunbridge Wells, the Church of King Charles the Martyr was built close to the spring, by public subscriptions, specifically for the convenience of visitors.

By the late 18th century the inland spas were facing competition from the newly emerging **seaside resorts**. In fact, as early as 1730, Scarborough was offering seabathing as well as a mineral spring. By 1760, bathing in and drinking seawater were being widely recommended as cures. So, when **George III** took to seabathing, the scene was set for the development of seaside resorts; and very quickly the leading summer resort was no longer Bath but Brighton.

Timothy J.L. Chandler

Bibliography

Hart, Roger. *English Life in the Eighteenth Century.* 1970.

Hole, Christina. *English Sports and Pastimes.* 1968.

Plumb, J.H. *The Commersialisation of Leisure in Eighteenth Century England.* 1973.

Turner, E.S. *Taking the Cure.* 1967.

Speenhamland System

Magistrates in Speenhamland (Newbury), Berkshire, concerned about rising wartime food costs, in 1795 agreed to use parish poor rates to supplement the low winter wages of **agricultural laborers**. The price of bread and the number of children in a worker's family, legitimate or illegitimate, established the amount of "allowance" necessary to provide him with a minimal level of subsistence. This paternalistic policy quickly spread throughout **Wales** and England, particularly in the south.

Despite the best intentions of the magistrates, the policy's consequences were tragic: increasing sexual promiscuity and illegitimacy, and falling wages, as employers, aware that the parish would subsidize workers' incomes, exploited the system and cut pay. As the system penalized diligent workers and encouraged shiftlessness, pauperism spread, causing poor rates almost to double from 1801 to 1821. **Thomas Malthus**, not surprisingly, was one of those who criticized the system for encouraging the poor to have more children. Alarmed by the rising expense of relief, the government enacted the **New Poor Law** in 1834, abolishing the system.

David B. Mock

Bibliography

Briggs, Asa. *The Age of Improvement, 1783–1867.* 1979.

Himmelfarb, Gertrude. *The Idea of Poverty: England in the Early Industrial Age.* 1983.

See also Hours, Wages, and Working Conditions; Poverty and Poor Laws

Spence, Thomas (1750–1814)

Spence holds the distinction of being one of the most **radical** thinkers of the Hanoverian era. Essentially an agrarian communist, regarding the land as "the people's farm," he promoted a land reform plan that called for the ownership of all land by the people, with its management to be conducted by local parish committees. The resulting profits would be distributed equally, after parish and national expenses were met. At first, Spence believed this scheme could be implemented by persuasion, but he later came to advocate the use of revolutionary force.

Spence was born in Newcastle and was influenced by Thomas More's (1478–1535) *Utopia* (1516), James Harrington's (1611–1677) *Oceana* (1656), concepts of natural law, and biblical **millenarianism**. His theories originated in his involvement in successful opposition (1772–1774) to the local magistrates' plan to lease Newcastle Town Moor for **enclosure**. In 1775 he joined the Philosophical Society of Newcastle, a debating society, and presented his land plan in a paper, which was later printed cheaply and distributed; this resulted in his expulsion from the society because of his attack on private property. Spence made his living as an English **teacher** and schoolmaster; he developed and promoted a phonetic alphabet, and printed pamphlets advertising his land scheme.

Around 1790 he moved to **London** and became involved in radical politics as a member of the **London Corresponding Society**. He ran a bookstall in central London, published pamphlets promoting his land plan, and produced a weekly publication, "Pig's Meat" (1793–1796), which consisted of extracts from writings of liberal and radical authors. An indefatigable propagandist, he spread his message by creating his own tokens, counterstamping coins, passing out broadsides, and even chalking slogans on walls. He was arrested several times and served 12 months for seditious libel. In his *Rights of Infants* (1797), Spence upheld and promoted the concept of **women's rights**, full political equality for women. Gradually he attracted a group of followers who formed a Spencean Society in 1811—this became the **Society of Spencean Philanthropists** after his death in 1814. The society's members became involved in the **Spa Fields riot** and the **Cato Street conspiracy**, and kept Spence's ideas alive among working-class activists and the Chartist movement of the early Victorian period, providing a connecting link between early radicalism and British socialism.

Mark C. Herman

Bibliography

Chase, Malcolm. *"The People's Farm": English Radical Agrarianism, 1775–1840.* 1988.

Dickinson, H.T., ed. *The Political Works of Thomas Spence.* 1982.

Kemp-Ashraf, Phyliss Mary. *Life and Times of Thomas Spence.* 1984.

Knox, T.R. "Thomas Spence: The Trumpet of Jubilee." *Past and Present.* No. 76, pp. 75–98.

McCalman, Iain. *Radical Underworld: Prophets, Revolutionaries and Pornographers in London, 1795–1840.* 1988.

Parsinnen, T.M. "Thomas Spence and the Origins of English Land Nationalization." *Journal of the History of Ideas.* Vol. 34, pp. 135–141.

Rudkin, Olive D. *Thomas Spence and His Connections.* 1927; rpt. 1966.

Worrall, David. *Radical Culture: Discourse, Resistance and Surveillance, 1790–1820.* 1992.

Spinning and Weaving

In 1714, both of these operations in textile production were family tasks and very ancient. Women and girls specialized in spinning flax and wool by hand, while men, assisted by their sons, were cloth weavers. The processes were relatively simple and conducted with varying skill at slack periods during the farming year.

Cotton was being used in stockings by the 1730s; gradually this industry concentrated around Nottingham and created a significant demand for yarn. Italian silk-throwing (spinning) machinery was introduced to Derby by the Lombe brothers, who operated a water-powered factory on the River Derwent.

Increased output from handlooms and growing demand for yarn stimulated improvements in spinning. Lewis Paul and

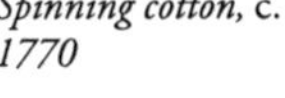

Spinning cotton, c. *1770*

John Wyatt, both skilled artisans, tried to improve wool-spinning by a roller method (patented by Paul in 1738). The Paul machine had some similarities to the silk-throwing machine and was used in several counties, but it was not effective. At length **James Hargreaves** produced the first multispindle machine—the spinning jenny (1762–1764)—which was highly efficient. But, fearing violence, Hargreaves left for Nottingham and established a cotton mill there. His hand machine was widely used and adapted because it was simple, cheap, could be operated by one person in a small space, and was never effectively patented. **Arkwright's** water frame followed, and his warp yarns complemented the weft yarns of the spinning jenny.

The most important development in weaving was **John Kay's** flying shuttle (1733). Kay, a reedmaker, displayed considerable ingenuity. To weavers he sold loom reeds made from wire, instead of split cane; this minor change raised productivity and improved the final quality of the cloth. His flying shuttle greatly accelerated weaving, and raised output further; but it was slow to be adopted. Kay wanted 15 shillings a year from weavers who used it, and in addition, there were legal attacks on his **patent** and personal intimidation, which caused him to settle in **France**.

The early shortage of spinners gave way to a short golden age for weavers, especially after **Crompton**'s mule became available, because it could produce both warp and weft yarns. **Edmund Cartwright** invented the first power loom (1785) able to produce broadcloth; the much earlier Dutch loom could weave tapes and ribbons. Soon afterward, John Austin (1789), J.L. Robertson (1793), and Robert Miller (1796) produced power looms in **Glasgow**, and in 1798 John Monteith of Pollokshaws had 30 **steam**-driven looms at work in his mill. The power loom only slowly replaced handloom weavers after 1830; they were prepared to work for lower and lower piece rates, and the machine was incapable of turning out fancy weaves.

Flax-spinning was mechanized from 1787, and from about 1810 the power loom invaded the linen industry. Meanwhile, Crompton's mule was adopted in the English **woolen industry**; and in worsted spinning, Arkwright's throstle frame was widely applied. Major technical change in Britain was completed by the automatic (self-acting) mule, patented in 1825 by Richard Roberts (1789–1864). After that, the future of textile technology—ring spinning and fully automatic weaving—rested with the United States and with Continental Europe.

John Butt

Bibliography

Aspen, Christopher, and Stanley D. Chapman. *James Hargreaves and the Spinning Jenny.* 1964.

Catling, Harold. *The Spinning Mule.* 1970.

English, Walter. *The Textile Industry.* 1969.

Fitton, Robert S. *The Arkwrights, Spinners of Fortune.* 1989.

French, Gilbert J. *Life and Times of Samuel Crompton.* Rpt. 1970.

Jeremy, David J. *Transatlantic Industrial Revolution.* 1981.

See also Science, Technology, and Invention; Textile Industries

Spleen

Deriving from one of the four humors (black bile) identified in classical Greece, "the spleen" became in the 18th century a common medical affliction and popular personality type. There were, in fact, several terms similar in meaning to *spleen*: *melancholia* and *hypochondria* denoted the condition in men; *hysteria* and *vapours* described the condition in women. A splenetic individual was considered likely to have an irascible temperament, experience depression, and suffer from physical ailments. Thus a splenetic personality easily became a popular guise for satiric narrators or personae.

Spleen, and splenetic characters, abound in 18th-century literature. In "The Spleen" (1713), **Anne Finch**, Countess of Winchilsea described the effects the malady had on her—insomnia and hallucinations; **Alexander Pope** in *The Rape of the Lock* (1714) added that the spleen, while causing physical pain and aberrant behavior, might also inspire artistic creativity. Matthew Bramble, a character in **Tobias Smollett**'s *The Expedition of Humphry Clinker* (1771), was a typical splenetic—brusque with friends, acerbic with strangers, and complaining constantly about his health and surroundings. In his "Epistle to Dr. Arbuthnot" (1735), Pope pictured himself as a splenetic railing against the foolishness and immorality he had observed. He, like Bramble, sought to relieve his splenetic condition by attacking vanity and hypocrisy in society.

John F. Sena

Bibliography

Babb, Lawrence. "The Cave of Spleen." *Review of English Studies.* Vol. 12, pp. 165–176.

Moore, Cecil A. "The English Malady," in C.A. Moore, ed., *Backgrounds of English Literature, 1700–1760.* 1953.

Reed, Amy. *The Background of Gray's Elegy: A Study in the Taste for Melancholy Poetry, 1700–1751.* 1962.

Sena, John. "Belinda's Hysteria: The Medical Context of *The Rape of the Lock*," in Christopher Fox, ed., *Psychology and Literature in the Eighteenth Century.* 1987.

See also Melancholy; Satire

Spode Family

The famous Spode china takes its name from two Hanoverian **entrepreneurs**, Josiah Spode I (1733–1797) and his eldest son Josiah Spode II (1755–1827), who both made significant contributions to the manufacture of earthenware and porcelain.

The elder Spode began his career as a journeyman potter in the factory of potter Thomas Whieldon (1719–1795), where he stayed until **Josiah Wedgwood** became Whieldon's partner (1754). He then entered into partnerships with several other potters, and by 1776 had purchased his own factory in Stoke-on-Trent. He decorated his early pearlware and white stoneware by hand, but in 1784 he introduced the use of a printer's press to make a new line of blue printed earthenware. This innovation made decorated tableware affordable for the general public, and started a trend for blue-and-white that lasted until the end of the century. Spode's factory also produced fine stoneware with white reliefs on chocolate or buff grounds.

By 1785 Josiah Spode II had established a successful warehouse for Spode ware in **London**, and in 1797, on the death of his father, he took over the factory in Stoke. A shrewd businessman as well as an innovative master potter, he began making fine porcelain in addition to the popular Spode earthenware around the year 1800. His greatest contribution to porcelain-making was the perfecting of bone china, a technique which entailed adding calcined bone to fine white burning clay and part-composed granite stone, the classic ingredients of hard paste porcelain. The younger Spode also introduced the method of ornamenting porcelain in raised gold, and succeeded in producing and marketing English bone china that rivaled Sèvres porcelain in quality and beauty, underselling Wedgwood. In 1806 the Prince of Wales, the future **George IV**, named Spode "potter and English porcelain manufacturer to his royal Highness."

The Spode family was directly involved in china-making until the death of Josiah Spode III (1777–1829), who left the business to his partner, William Taylor Copeland; the firm was then run by the Copeland family for over 140 years. Today, Spode china is manufactured at Stoke-on-Trent by Royal China and Porcelain Companies, Inc.

Deidre Dawson

Bibliography

Bedford, John. *Old Spode China.* 1969.

Two Hundred Years of Spode: Catalogue of an Exhibition, 8 August–4 October 1970. 1970.

Whiter, Leonard. *Spode: A History of the Family, Factory and Wares from 1733–1833.* 1970.

Sport

Plenty of sport was played, watched, and paid for in Hanoverian Britain. The most popular sports around the year 1800 were prizefighting, horse-racing, and cricket; golf and boating (both rowing and sailing) were also attracting some devotees. By modern standards, the level of violence tolerated in much 18th-century sport was extraordinary.

Fighting—ranging from boxing and wrestling to cudgeling—was probably the most popular individual sport. Such activity, although not confined to men, was largely a male preserve. The development of prizefighting, as one of the first sports to have a written code of rules, signaled an increasing desire to regulate and organize sport, as well to commercialize and professionalize it. In 1743 the first formal set of rules prohibited hitting opponents who were down, hitting below the belt, and hair-pulling; kicking and butting were outlawed in 1839, and in 1867 the 8th Marquess of Queensberry (1844–1900) laid down the famous rules providing 10-counts, weight classes, and so on. Prizefighting flourished despite its lack of **middle-class** appeal and its association with **gambling**. It did so partly because it was patronized by the highest men in the land. It was also vigorously promoted by publicans, many of whom were retired prizefighters. Popular support for boxing was great, with crowds of up to 10,000 attending the prizefights of such celebrities as the knockout artist John Broughton (*d.* 1787).

John Broughton, "a notorious pugilist"

Similar numbers attended the great horse-races at Epsom and Newmarket. Meetings were often scheduled to coincide with traditional annual wakes or festivals. During the course of the 18th century, horse-racing changed from being casual competition for wagers between noblemen to the most highly organized and regulated sport. It brought all classes together and, over time, the race meetings themselves became traditional social occasions.

Cricket was the one game for teams, rather than single individuals, in which the upper classes exerted themselves. The first written rules were drawn up in 1727 by the 2nd Duke of Richmond (1701–1750, father of the radical peer of the 1770s) for the purpose of determining both the conduct and the outcome of country-house games, where much money was often at stake. The formation of cricket **clubs**, as with other clubs and societies, was largely among like-minded individuals. So, whereas the Jockey Club ruled horse-racing, the Marylebone Cricket Club (MCC) developed as the governing body for cricket. Wager matches gradually gave way to great matches underwritten by wealthy patrons in which "select" teams of gentlemen, supplemented by professionals, played against each other for large sums. This may have developed from the early pattern of village cricket, which also had an aristocrat acting as patron to a team that mixed gentlemen with talented locals. The help of a publican to provide the ground and refreshments, and to act as bookmaker and **entrepreneur**, was again the norm.

The traditional analysis of the history of Hanoverian sport combines, on the one hand, perceptions relating to the slow death of old community-based patterns of play, with, on the other, perceptions recognizing the very limited development of those new mass-based commercial forms that were to dominate the late 19th century. This approach, emphasizing the transitional character of Hanoverian sport, is substantially correct so long as it is understood that Hanoverian forms were being transformed significantly from within by forces such as gambling, and by groups of interested parties such as patrons and publicans, who through many small steps were helping to bring about greater regulation and commercial organization.

Timothy J.L. Chandler

Bibliography

Brailsford, Dennis. "1787: An Eighteenth Century Sporting Year." *Research Quarterly for Exercise and Sport.* Vol. 55, pp. 217–230.

Cunningham, Hugh. *Leisure in the Industrial Revolution.* 1980.

Egan, Pierce. *Book of Sports.* 1832.

Holt, Richard. *Sport and the British: A Modern History.* 1989.

Malcolmson, Robert. *Popular Recreations in English Society, 1700–1850.* 1981.

Plumb, J.H. *The Commercialisation of Leisure in Eighteenth Century England.* 1973.

Reid, J.C. *Bucks and Bruisers: Pierce Egan and Regency England.* 1981.

Strutt, Joseph. *The Sports and Pastimes of the People of England.* 1801.

Vamplew, Wray. *The Turf: A Social and Economic History of Horseracing.* 1976.

See also Blood Sports; Gambling; Toys and Games

St. John, Henry

See Bolingbroke, Viscount

Stage Licensing Act

See Playhouse Act

Stamp Act (1765)

This act was a contributory cause of the **American Revolution**. Prime Minister **George Grenville** proposed and Parliament approved the Stamp Bill (1765) with the intention of partly shifting the financial burden of colonial defense to the colonists themselves by placing a duty on all legal documents, **newspapers**, pamphlets, advertisements, playing cards, and dice sold in the **North American** colonies. Englishmen had paid such duties since 1670. The measure was calculated to raise £60,000 that would be used to support the military establishment in America.

However, in America the act inspired **riots** and a rapidly spreading boycott of British imports, many colonists demanding its repeal on the grounds that it was unconstitutional because the colonies were not represented when Parliament considered the measure. The crisis fell upon the new Prime Minister, **Rockingham**, in 1766. He favored repeal, weighing the views of both colonists and British merchants injured by falling trade. In the **Commons**, **Pitt the Elder**, **Burke**, and **Benjamin Franklin** (who gave evidence) supported repeal. Rockingham repealed the act, but, to avoid the appearance of weakness, asserted Parliament's legislative sovereignty over the colonies with the **Declaratory Act**.

The Stamp Act, because of its effects—uniting all segments of colonial society in resistance and giving rise to radical groups such as the "Sons of Liberty" as well as to growing ideological opposition to central authority itself—must be considered one of the errors that tore the fabric of the **Empire**.

K.R. Wood

Bibliography

Bonwick, C. *English Radicals and the American Revolution.* 1977.

Maier, P. *From Resistance to Revolution: Colonial Radicals and the Development of American Opposition to Britain, 1765–1776.* 1973.

Thomas, P.D.G. *British Politics and the Stamp Act Crisis: The First Phase of the American Revolution, 1763–1767.* 1975.

See also Taxes and Tariffs

Standard of Living

As a consequence of demographic expansion, shifts in agricultural productivity, and urban and industrial growth, British living standards changed significantly during the Hanoverian period.

During the first half of the 18th century, the standard of living generally improved. Prior to the 1760s, **population** growth was moderate at best. The dominant trend, dating from the 17th century, was one of relatively high mortality and low fertility. High mortality resulted partly from the virulence of epidemic disease (notably **smallpox**, influenza, and dysentery) and was unrelated to harvest fluctuations or food supplies. Many diseases—smallpox, especially—were particularly threatening to the young; hence infant and child mortality in the early 18th century hovered around 35% of all births, dragging down overall life expectancy rates to approximately 34 years. Low fertility resulted partly from low rates of nuptiality and rising **marriage** ages (women marrying on average at age 26), both partly caused by growing sex imbalances between nubile men and women seeking employment—young men tending to migrate into rural areas, young women to urban ones.

Slow population growth, together with remarkable gains in the productivity of **agriculture**, significantly enhanced the living standards of laboring people. Historians no longer maintain that an "Agricultural Revolution" was concurrent with industrialization, and instead recognize that the most significant advances in agricultural productivity took place over a long period stretching from the 17th century into the

19th century. In the long run, agricultural prices (cereal prices in particular) declined considerably below expected trends in population. Bread and **beer** were the basic necessities of laboring life (their consumption absorbed the bulk of laboring incomes), and the notable fall in grain prices clearly benefited consumers.

Rising disposable incomes manifested themselves in greater per capita consumption of meat and dairy products, and the growing substitution of wheat for barley bread in all but the most northern parts of England and **Scotland**. Consumption of beer, sugar, tea, and **coffee** rose sharply, and **gin drinking** reached "epidemic" proportions. The consumption of foodstuffs (and indeed of manufactured commodities) was, however, limited by rising levels of indirect taxation as excise **taxes** gradually became more burdensome.

Slow growth in the labor market, combined with significant economic expansion, generally supported and enhanced the **wages** of labor. Declining staple prices contributed significantly to rising real incomes, widening the domestic market for services and manufactured goods. But it was the growing earnings of the **middle classes** and of a few groups of skilled **craftsmen** that had the most positive impact on domestic demand. Even with an increase in real wages, the wages of **agricultural laborers** were still pitifully low, leaving little for the purchase of even cheap and secondhand goods. The wages of manufacturing labor were little better, since manufacturing was still mainly located in the countryside, where the cheap labor of underemployed agricultural workers was exploited in cottage industries. New rural industries in lace and straw-plaiting expanded rapidly, alongside long-established rural production of woolens, and relied almost exclusively on cheap female labor.

Historians have had difficulty reaching a consensus regarding the direction of changing living standards during the period 1760–1830s, the key age traditionally associated with the **Industrial Revolution**. In fact, the "standard-of-living debate" is one of the most lively, long-standing (traceable to the 1920s), and inconclusive controversies connected with the era of industrialization. Traditionally, "optimists" have argued that industrial expansion brought material gain and enriched the majority of British citizens during this period. The "pessimist" school has argued that the Industrial Revolution brought with it immiseration and diminished overall living standards.

The debate has been affected by the now generally accepted notion that the Industrial Revolution was more evolutionary than revolutionary, and was neither unitary nor continuous. Outside regionally specific advanced industrial sectors of the economy (particularly **cotton** textiles, **iron**, and to a lesser extent **coal**), sustained economic growth was gradual until at least the 1820s. Hence, shifts in general living standards may have been a consequence of broader economic and demographic changes, not specifically related to mechanized industrial expansion.

It is true that the period witnessed significant sectorial shifts in employment. In 1750, half of all labor was still employed on the land. By the 1830s, this figure had shrunk to less than one-fourth, though agricultural workers were still the largest occupational group and their numbers had risen in absolute terms. Work in **factories**, **mines**, and **retailing** grew both absolutely and relatively, employing perhaps half of all workers by the 1830s. Yet much of this nonagricultural work still took place in the countryside, as Britain was no more than 40% urban by the late 1830s.

Moreover, the vast majority of workers in manufacturing still used handtools in urban workshops or rural cottages. Despite the growth of factories and **steam** power in rapidly expanding mill towns and industrial **cities** such as **Manchester**, **London** was still the largest manufacturing center in Britain and was virtually untouched by advances in steam power and mechanization. Even many northern industrial cities, such as Sheffield with its **metalworking** and cutlery industry, were essentially unmechanized, with labor characteristically organized on a workshop basis. Hence by the late 1830s, less than 10% of British labor toiled in conditions of "machinofacture" (i.e., in factories with machinery generated by inanimate sources of energy).

Historians now generally agree that material living standards probably worsened between 1760 and 1820, though certain occupational groups benefited from **technological** changes and new commercial opportunities. For example, the Staffordshire potters benefited from an expanding market, and the handloom cotton weavers of Lancashire experienced a "golden age" as beneficiaries of factory-produced yarns before becoming victim by the 1820s to the expansion of their own numbers and ultimately of the power loom.

The general worsening of living standards was less a result of industrial advance than of rapid population growth. The British population tripled between 1750 and 1850 (from 7 to 21 million); in fact, the period 1800–1820 marked the most rapid rate of population growth in British history. Meanwhile, life expectancy rose significantly between 1750 and 1820 (to approximately 40 years), mainly as a result of declining smallpox mortality. Rising fertility, however, contributed most to population growth. Marriage age and celibacy dropped significantly as restraints on marriage weakened from general changes in the nature of employment, as semi- and unskilled wage labor rose and servantry and apprenticeship declined, and as the distribution of employment shifted from agriculture to trade and manufacturing, from country to town, and from overpopulated rural areas in the south to manufacturing areas in the north.

Agricultural productivity failed to keep pace with this rapid demographic expansion, and inflated cereal prices dug deeply into the disposable income of laboring people. Meat consumption fell by over 20%, and barley, turnips and potatoes were increasingly substituted for wheat. The decline in real income was most severe during the **French Revolutionary and Napoleonic Wars**, as wartime expenditure and poor harvests accentuated the underlying rate of inflation, causing real wages to fall by as much as 20%. Only the better-organized workers managed to escape painful cutbacks during this period.

During the 1820s and 1830s, real income for the bulk of British workers generally recovered and perhaps rose as cereal prices fell, thanks to **agricultural improvements** and the continuing low cost of agricultural labor. (Demographic expansion continued to produce "surplus" rural populations.) But while the nominal wages of factory workers rose, those of domestic and agricultural workers, and of artisans, continued to fall. Hence rising real income did not necessarily create significant improvement in living standards. Indeed, while per capita consumption of factory-produced cotton textiles and soap expanded, that of meat, beer, tea, sugar, and **tobacco** fell.

Moreover, as to **hours, wages, and working conditions**, factory and urban workers experienced overcrowding in **housing**, dreadful sanitary conditions, poor and generally unsafe working conditions, and a significant loss of leisure time. Average life expectancy remained essentially static between 1820 and 1860, due to high urban mortality. The 1830s witnessed major cholera outbreaks, and close to 60% of working-class children in industrial cities such as Manchester died before age 5 (compared with 30% in rural districts). Average life expectancy for urban and factory workers was less than 20 years, while that for agricultural labor reached 38 by the end of the 1830s.

Yet, rural workers also suffered from severe overcrowding as the **poverty** of agricultural labor continued in the 1820s and 1830s. Indeed, the ranks of the rural poor were augmented by those artisan groups rendered technologically obsolete by mechanization, notably handloom weavers and wool croppers, who experienced significant loss in earning power and status. In sum, all factors considered, it is hard to say that living standards were clearly on the rise before 1850.

Tim Keirn

Bibliography

Houston, R.A. *The Population History of Britain and Ireland, 1500–1750.* 1992.

Mokyr, Joel, ed. *The Economics of the Industrial Revolution.* 1985.

———, ed. *The British Industrial Revolution: An Economic Perspective.* 1993.

O'Brien, Patrick, and Roland Quinalt, eds. *The Industrial Revolution and British Society.* 1993.

Rule, John. *The Labouring Classes in Early Industrial England, 1750–1850.* 1986.

———. *Albion's People: English Society, 1714–1815.* 1992.

Schwarz, L.D. *London in the Age of Industrialization: Entrepreneurs, Labour Force and Living Conditions, 1700–1850.* 1992.

Snell, K.D.M. *Annals of the Labouring Poor: Social Change and Agrarian England, 1660–1900.* 1985.

Taylor, Arthur J., ed. *The Standard of Living in Britain in the Industrial Revolution.* 1975.

Tranter, N.L. *Population and Society, 1750–1940.* 1985.

See also Friendly Societies; Labor Laws, Movements, and Unions; Servants; Women's Employment

Stanhope, Earl of (James Stanhope) (1673–1721)

A successful military and diplomatic career preceded Stanhope's (1st Earl, 1718) service as Secretary of State (1714–1717 and 1718–1721) and First Lord of the Treasury and Chancellor of the Exchequer (1717–1718). He organized military precautions to secure **George I**'s succession (1714). As Secretary of State his goals in **foreign relations** were to protect the succession, support George's concern with **Hanover**, and settle disputes between Spain and the Holy Roman Emperor in Italy. To pursue these ends he constructed a network of alliances including **France** (1716), the Dutch Republic (1717), and the Emperor (1718); and he used the system to force Spain to settle its Italian claims. To protect Hanover, he employed a naval expedition and the skills of his protégé, **John Carteret**, to force Russia to a settlement ending its Great Northern War with Sweden (1719–1720).

Lord Stanhope

In domestic politics, Stanhope allied with the Earl of Sunderland (1674–1722) against Secretary of State Charles **Townshend** and **Robert Walpole** in defense of Stanhope's northern policy. The scandal of the **South Sea Bubble** brought him under severe parliamentary criticism and apparently led him to a fatal stroke (February 1721). His legacy of diplomatic intervention in European affairs carried on policies begun by King William III in the 1690s and became a point of political contention throughout the 18th century.

Robert D. McJimsey

Bibliography

Browning, Reed. *The Duke of Newcastle.* 1975.

Hatton, Ragnhild. *George I, Elector and King.* 1978.

Michael, Wolfgang. *England under George I.* 2 vols. 1936–1939.

Williams, Basil. *Stanhope: A Study in Eighteenth-Century War and Diplomacy.* 1932.

See also Foreign Relations

Statistical Account of Scotland

This remarkable series of volumes described contemporary society and conditions in the 1790s, and is thus of considerable historical interest and value. The Statistical Account, generally known as the Old Statistical Account, was initiated and compiled by **Sir John Sinclair**, the noted **agricultural improver**, who used his influence to persuade ministers throughout Scotland to submit detailed returns on their parishes. His questionnaire covered all aspects of social and economic life. Those clergy and other contributors who complied with his detailed requests produced invaluable data and descriptions of their localities during an era of dramatic change in agriculture and industry. Not all were as cooperative as he would have liked, so the parish accounts are inevitably quite variable in depth and usefulness.

The production of this massive 21-volume work took nearly a decade (1791–1799), with Sinclair employing a team of editors and clerks to assist with publication. From the standpoint of the researcher, a major weakness arises from the fact that the parish accounts were published as they became available, rather than in county volumes. A modern reprint has corrected this fault. An index was provided in Volume 21 (1799). Sinclair himself later produced the valuable *Analysis of the Statistical Account of Scotland* (1825), which provided an overview of conditions at the time, as well as an update on the original compilation of the 1790s.

The Second (or New) Statistical Account was a comparable exercise undertaken by a committee of the Society for the Benefit of the Sons and Daughters of the Clergy, compilation and revision occurring mainly in the 1830s and early 1840s. A total of 15 volumes resulted, some containing accounts for several counties. The first volume contains an alphabetical list of parishes, and the last a general index to the series.

Ian Donnachie

Bibliography

Mitchison, Rosalind. *Agricultural Sir John: The Life of Sir John Sinclair of Ulbster 1754–1835.* 1962.

See also Scotland and Scottish Culture; Scottish Agriculture

Steam Engines

The first prototype steam engine was the Sphere of Aeolus, built by Hero of Alexandria around 62 AD. In 17th-century Britain the properties of steam—expansion and condensation—were applied primarily to the problem of pumping water. The first practical steam pump was patented (1698) by Thomas Savery (1650?–1715), and the first reliable steam engine was built in 1712 by **Thomas Newcomen**. Low-pressure steam in his "fire-engine" forced a piston to rise, which then was forced downward by atmospheric pressure as the steam condensed and the cylinder enclosing the piston cooled to form a partial vacuum. The reciprocating motion of the piston was transferred to an overhead "walking" beam, which could be employed to pump water. The device found immediate use in coal **mines**, where flooding was a danger and a hindrance. But Newcomen's engine consumed huge quantities of fuel, with a thermal efficiency of about 1%.

After this there was continual improvement in, and widespread application of, steam power to industry, manufacturing, and transportation. Following expiration of Newcomen's **patents** (1733), other inventors produced more efficient designs. Chief among these was **James Watt** who, after repairing a model of a Newcomen engine, set out to redesign it. In 1769 he patented his solution to the problem of the repeated cooling of the cylinder—a separate condensing chamber. In partnership with **Matthew Boulton** of **Birmingham** he manufactured engines that consumed two-thirds less fuel than Newcomen's. However, these were still atmospheric until Watt created the double-action engine (patented in 1782); the innovation of using steam to push the piston alternately, from either side, doubled the power. With still other refinements added, such as a centrifugal governor to control speed, and a flywheel driven on an eccentric to convert reciprocating into rotary action, Watt's engines powered much of the **Industrial Revolution**. By 1800, when his first patents expired, upwards of 1,000 stationary steam engines of all types had been erected throughout Britain, many employed in **textile industries**.

Given these developments, the discovery of steam locomotion was probably inevitable. Moving engines using high-pressure steam became the specialty of Cornish engineer **Richard Trevithick**. Their compact size enabled him to build a steam carriage in 1803 and a tramway locomotive for the Penydarren Ironworks in **Merthyr Tydfil** (1804). In 1808 he offered rides on a working steam train on rails, which he exhibited in **London**. When the first real railway, the **Stockton and Darlington**, debuted in 1825, its locomotives were designed by **George Stephenson**, who had built his first colliery locomotive in 1813. Water-borne applications of steam power began even earlier. While the first small, working steamboats

Watt's design for an oscillating or double-acting engine, 1782

were built by Americans, **ships** of British design employing steam had, by the end of the Hanoverian era, begun to pioneer modern oceanic transport.

British ingenuity made steam power available wherever it was required. Thus wide-scale industrialization, fast and reliable transport, and the transformation of every aspect of material life were made possible.

N. Merrill Distad

Bibliography

Cardwell, Donald Stephen Lowell. *From Watt to Clausius: The Rise of Thermodynamics in the Early Industrial Age.* 1971.

Dickinson, Henry Winram. *Richard Trevithick: The Engineer and the Man.* 1934.

———. *James Watt: Craftsman and Engineer.* 1936; rpt. 1967.

———. *A Short History of the Steam Engine.* 1938; 2nd ed., 1963.

von Tunzelmann, G.N. *Steam Power and British Industrialization to 1860.* 1978.

See also Science, Technology, and Invention

Steele, Richard (1672–1729)

Steele, famous in his own time as an essayist and dramatist, began inauspiciously as an Irish orphan but achieved recognition through his command of the informal **essay** and of **sentimental** drama. His writing served his political beliefs and aspirations as well; in 1714 he was elected M.P., and for his service to the **Whig** cause was knighted (1715) by the newly crowned **George I**.

Steele's early writings included a poem, "The Procession," on the death of Queen Mary (1694), and a prose meditation titled *The Christian Hero* (1701). The latter helped establish his reputation but, seeing the opportunity to achieve fame and possibly fortune in the **theater**, he turned to writing comedies and achieved great success with *The Funeral* (1701). This was neither sentimental nor as witty as the Restoration comedies, which Steele later attacked (for example, in *The Spectator*, No. 65); his moral comedy addressed more contemporary tastes, elevating decorum over bawdiness.

His next play, *The Lying Lover* (1703), a failure, survived only 6 nights. *The Tender Husband* (1705) was more successful, reverting to a comedy of ridicule comparable to Restoration comedy, though without bawdiness. *The Conscious Lovers* (1723), Steele's last and most thoroughly sentimental play, presented exemplary characters for whom **sensibility** was the most reliable guide to moral action. This play, now considered the foundation of sentimental comedy, guaranteed Steele's fame and left a lasting impression on English **dramatic arts**.

In 1709 Steele and his friend **Joseph Addison**, whom he had met at Oxford, began *The Tatler* under the name of Isaac Bickerstaff (a character developed by **Jonathan Swift** in the Partridge papers). They published their paper thrice weekly, using it as a platform for discussing society's faults and foibles in a witty, Horatian manner, and as a pulpit gently urging **benevolence** and moral uplift. After 271 issues they concluded publication by Steele's identifying himself as author; they followed it with another paper, *The Spectator*, in 1711. In this they created the idiosyncratic and reclusive character Mr. Spectator, together with a **club** that included the famous characters Sir Roger de Coverly, Sir Andrew Freeport, and Will Honeycomb. As Steele and Addison slowly and subtly entered into political propagandizing, they used the **Tory** Sir Roger to represent old wealth and the Whig Sir Andrew (Freeport is a hint) to represent mercantilist new wealth. *The Spectator* was a landmark in the development of the **periodical** and of the informal essay. Published 6 days a week for 555 issues, it concluded on 6 December 1712.

The following year, Steele began another journal alone, the *Guardian*, an important mouthpiece of Whig propaganda. He developed other journals later, but none had the success of *The Tatler* or *The Spectator*. After his theatrical success in 1723 with *The Conscious Lovers* he retired to his estate in **Wales**, where he died.

Richard H. Dammers

Bibliography

Blanchard, Rae, ed. *The Christian Hero.* 1932.

———. *The Correspondence of Richard Steele.* 1941.

Bond, Donald F., ed. *The Spectator.* 1965.

———. *The Tatler.* 1987.

Dammers, Richard. *Richard Steele.* 1982.

Kenny, Shirley Strum. "Steele and the 'Pattern of Genteel Comedy.'" *Modern Philology.* Vol. 70, pp. 22–37.

———, ed. *The Plays of Richard Steele.* 1971.

McCrea, Brian. *Addison and Steele Are Dead.* 1990.

Winton, Calhoun. *Captain Steele—The Early Career of Richard Steele.* 1964.

———. *Sir Richard Steele.* 1970.

See also Periodicals

Stephen, Sir James (1789–1859)

Stephen, Colonial Undersecretary, is perhaps best known for his efforts against slavery. He was the nephew of **Wilberforce** and the son of one of the most determined 18th-century **antislavery** activists, also named James Stephen (1758–1832). Raised in the **Clapham sect**, educated at Cambridge and called to the bar, he took an early professional interest in colonial laws and legislatures. He helped Sir Thomas Fowell Buxton (1785–1845) found the Anti-Slavery Society (1823), abandoned private practice to become Legal Adviser to the Colonial Office and the Board of Trade (1825), authored the Slavery Emancipation Act that ended slavery in the **Empire** (1833), and became Assistant Undersecretary for the Colonies (1834) and finally Undersecretary (1837), where he held great power under six secretaries of state until his retirement in 1847.

Stephen was a conscientious public servant, but supervision of some 40 overseas provinces was difficult. His **Evangelical** conscience and determination to protect the "savage races" against exploitation by land-hungry settlers made him the nemesis of colonial reformers and champions of **emigration**. **Edward Gibbon Wakefield** and Charles Buller (1806–1848) ridiculed him as "Mr Mother-country" and "Mr. Over Secretary," attacking his rigidity and unwillingness to provide leadership for colonizing the wildernesses of **Canada**, **Australia**, and **New Zealand**.

Resigning in 1847, Stephen went on to become Regius Professor of Modern History at Cambridge (1849). He wrote several historical works. His children and grandchildren, eminent intellectuals, included Leslie Stephen (1832–1904) and Virginia Woolf (1882–1941).

Thomas D. Veve

Bibliography

Knapland, Paul. *James Stephen and the British Colonial System, 1813–1847.* 1953.

See also Missionary Societies

Stephenson, George (1781–1848)

The "father of the locomotive and the railway" was a practical engineer without formal education. Born at Wylam on Tyneside, Stephenson acquired early experience as an engineman and brakesman on stationary **steam engines** at several collieries. In 1812 he became engine wright at Killingworth, but was allowed to practice independently from 1813, having a retainer of £100 per year. He erected many engines and improved **coal** handling, using tramroads above and below ground. He also invented a miner's safety lamp (1815). He was interested in developing more efficient rails and locomotives, building the Killingworth waggonway and its first locomotive, "Blucher" (1814).

George Stephenson

His only son, Robert, (1803–1859), became his assistant. Engaged by Edward Pease (1767–1858) to build the **Stockton and Darlington Railway**, completed in 1825, the Stephensons had already (1823) opened their locomotive works in Newcastle, where "Locomotion," the first of many railway engines, was built. George's achievement in building the **Liverpool and Manchester Railway** (1830) was matched by the triumph of Robert's "Rocket" at the Rainhill engine trials (1829). These successes left the Stephensons prodigiously busy for the remainder of their lives, consulted at home and abroad by new companies about railway projects of all kinds. Robert, later famous for his railway bridges, sat in the **House of Commons** (1847–1859), became President of the Institution of Civil Engineers (1855), and was buried in Westminster Abbey.

John Butt

Bibliography

Biddle, Gordon, and Oliver S. Nock. *The Railway Heritage of Britain.* 1983.

Nock, Oliver S. *The Railway Engineers.* 1955.

Rolt, L.T.C. *George and Robert Stephenson.* Rpt. 1988.

Simmons, Jack. *The Railways of Britain 1830–1914.* 1978.

Sterne, Laurence (1713–1768)

Sterne's literary reputation rests upon two works: *The Life and Opinions of Tristram Shandy, Gentleman* (1760–1767), and *A Sentimental Journey through France and Italy* (1768). Of all the English 18th-century writers, his influence on modern novelists was the most profound: Diderot, Goethe, Tolstoy, Nietzsche, Woolf, Joyce, and Thomas Mann all recorded their admiration of him.

Sterne, the son of a poor **army** ensign, was born in **Ireland**. When he was 10, his family sent him to England to live with his uncle while attending school. After graduating from Cambridge (1737) he took orders and became Vicar of Sutton-in-the-Forest (in Yorkshire), where he remained until 1759. One outcome of this was 45 surviving sermons, one of which, "The Abuses of Conscience," appears in *Tristram Shandy;* another was a worldview that conflicts significantly with the secular readings that modern critics have often imposed upon him; another may have been too-familiar relations with female parishioners that may have helped to edge his wife toward insanity in 1758.

He began his only novel in 1759. *Tristram Shandy* was published serially over a 7-year period in nine volumes, the first two at Sterne's own expense in 1759. These took **London** by storm, and the **publisher Robert Dodsley** paid Sterne for a second edition, as well as for the next installment (1761). Others followed up to 1767. Whether or not Sterne had completed the work by then is still argued today. In the last phase of his life his attention turned romantically toward a young lady, Eliza Draper, the wife of an **East India Company** official, and to writing about his **travels** in **France**, out of which *A Sentimental Journey* emerged a month before his death.

Tristram Shandy is not easy to describe. It has been called

Laurence Sterne

the first philosophical novel in English, and also the most psychological. Tristram, the narrator, often employing a sort of stream-of-consciousness technique, sketches his own life from its conception on, pausing to describe interesting and often humorous characters of every type—soldiers, lawyers, physicians, parsons, servants, widows, lovers. Sterne's moods are playful, curious, bawdy, thoughtful, and sometimes sentimental. The book is full of curious ideas and self-conscious eccentricities of layout, punctuation, and chapter numbering, so that digression and straight story line become confused—as confused, Sterne seems to say, as real-life illusion and reality themselves.

Contemporary admirers of *Tristram* were divided between those who applauded Sterne's kinship with earlier satiric writers such as **Swift**, and those who ignored or condemned that tradition (with its hallmark of bawdiness) in favor of his warmly sentimental portrayal of domestic characters, Toby Shandy in particular. In the 19th century the latter tendency dominated, and Sterne was seen as a forerunner of Dickens (1812–1870); in the 20th century he was subjected to far more complex readings that projected him first as a proto-existentialist affirming human potential on the brink of (linguistic) despair; then as a proto-phenomenologist recognizing the total coherence of a world within the individual mind; and, more recently, as a proto-postmodernist concerned with differences between signifier and signified, and celebrating the indeterminant, undecidable text.

In short, *Tristram Shandy* has been shaped and reshaped as critical interests evolve, all critics feeling compelled to test their models against this great work. That it continues to resist critical reduction may suggest something about its author's values, particularly his desire to resist interpretation and his satiric treatment of formulaic criticism. In Sterne one finds above all else an interest in portraying worlds and attitudes that defy human pretensions to wisdom. It is a view he might have garnered from classical skepticism or Lockean epistemology, but just as likely it came to him from Ecclesiastes: "Who is as the wise man? and who knoweth the interpretation of a thing?"

Melvyn New

Bibliography

Cash, Arthur H. *Laurence Sterne: The Early and Middle Years,* and *The Later Years.* 2 vols. 1975, 1986.
Curtis, Lewis Perry, ed. *Letters of Laurence Sterne.* 1935.
Howes, Alan B., ed. *Sterne: The Critical Heritage.* 1974.
Lamb, Jonathan. *Sterne's Fiction and the Double Principle.* 1989.
New, Melvyn. *Laurence Sterne as Satirist: A Reading of Tristram Shandy.* 1969.
———, ed. (with Joan New). *The Life and Opinions of Tristram Shandy, Gentleman: The Text,* 1978; (with Richard A. Davies and W.G. Day). *The Notes,* 1984 (vols. I–III of the Florida *Works of Sterne*).
———, ed. *New Casebooks: Tristram Shandy.* 1992.
Stout, Gardner D., ed. *A Sentimental Journey through France and Italy.* 1967.
Swearingen, James E. *Reflexivity in Tristram Shandy: An Essay in Phenomological Criticism.* 1977.
Traugott, John. *Tristram Shandy's World: Sterne's Philosophical Rhetoric.* 1954.

See also Novel; Sensibility and Sentimentalism; Wit and Ridicule

Stewart, Dugald (1753–1828)

Stewart, a celebrated teacher and moral philosopher, developed a perfectibilist moral and political theory based on the belief that a detailed knowledge of the powers of the human mind would enable enlightened legislators to establish precise norms of equity and justice. His reputation rests on his early works: *Elements of the Philosophy of the Human Mind* (1792), *Outlines of Moral Philosophy* (1793), and *Account of the Life and Writings of Adam Smith* (1793). He failed in his ambitious hope to publish a complete account of the principles of moral philosophy, politics, and legislation.

Born in **Edinburgh**, Stewart attended Edinburgh University, where his mentor **Adam Ferguson** taught him to be dissatisfied with the subjectivist ethical theories of **David Hume** and **Adam Smith**. Following Ferguson, Stewart believed that virtue was more than a species of propriety and that its roots lay in a natural love of perfection, possessed by all humans. In 1771 he went to **Glasgow** to study with **Thomas Reid**, who furnished him with a framework within which to organize his science of "human improvement." In 1785 he succeeded Ferguson in the chair of moral philosophy at Edinburgh, remaining there until his retirement in 1810. During those years he earned a reputation as the foremost exponent of Reid's Common Sense philosophy, which he turned into a program for liberal **Whig** political reform.

Peter J. Diamond

Bibliography

Haakonssen, Knud. "From Moral Philosophy to Political Economy: The Contribution of Dugald Stewart," in V. Hope, ed., *Philosophers of the Scottish Enlightenment.* 1984.

Phillipson, Nicholas. "The Pursuit of Virtue in Scottish University Education: Dugald Stewart and Scottish Moral Philosophy in the Enlightenment," in *Universities, Society, and the Future: A Conference Held on the 400th Anniversary of the University of Edinburgh.* 1983.

Winch, Donald. "The System of the North: Dugald Stewart and His Pupils," in Stefan Collini, ed., *That Noble Science of Politics.* 1983.

Stockton and Darlington Railway

Rudimentary 18th-century railway systems operated in many places and served various needs, but chiefly these were used to serve extractive industries such as **coal mining.** Many people saw the potential of developing a more sophisticated system, but in order to make rail a viable and efficient means of transport, it was necessary to harness steam power to strong iron railway track. This was accomplished by engineers such as **Richard Trevithick** who, struggling with technical problems, managed to produce a multitubular boiler, which would increase power without adding to the overall weight of the engine, whereas John Birkinshaw and others found methods of producing wrought-iron, rather than cast-iron, track.

With this accomplished, Edward Pease (1767–1858), a Darlington **entrepreneur,** held discussions in 1822 with **George Stephenson,** a local mining engineer who had already established a considerable reputation as a locomotive engineer. What resulted was the epoch-making Stockton and Darlington, designed to carry coal. Its main line of 27 miles was opened on 27 September 1825. Although the maiden run was a hybrid of horsepower and steampower, Stephenson's engine, "Locomotion," trundled over such a quantity of edge-rail track that the line was hailed as the harbinger of a new age. **Canals** had been the new method of transportation of the early **Industrial Revolution,** but railways would soon become that of the more spectacular second phase of industrialization.

G.T. Bell

Bibliography

Dyos, H.J., and D.H. Aldcroft. *British Transport.* 1974.

Kirby, M.W. *The Stockton and Darlington Railway.* 1994.

See also Liverpool and Manchester Railway; Science, Technology, and Invention; Steam Engines; Transport, Inland

Streets

See Roads, Streets, and Turnpikes

Strutt, Jedediah (1726–1797)

A leading figure in the early **cotton industry,** Strutt, the son of a **dissenting** Derbyshire farmer, trained as a wheelwright. A man of technical ingenuity, he began a revolution in the hosiery industry when, after prolonged experimentation and encouraged by his brother-in-law (William Woollet, a Derby hosier), he took two **patents** for his "ribknitting attachment" to the stocking frame (1758, 1759). His success led to an era of new meshes produced on the frame, and greatly extended the market for Midland hosiery. Woollet and Strutt began a manufacturing business in Derby and successfully resisted two attempts to break their patents, though local knitters gained knowledge of the technology.

Samuel Need, a wealthy Nottingham dissenter and hosier, joined Strutt's firm and, knowing the importance of good cotton warps for their trade, they formed a partnership with **Richard Arkwright** in mills at Nottingham (1769) and Cromford (1771), making a considerable fortune. After dissolving this partnership, Strutt created an independent industrial empire founded on three mills at Belper (1778, 1786, and 1793) and two others at Milford (*c.* 1799) and Derby (1793). His sons continued to consolidate the family's fortunes after his death, his grandson becoming Lord Belper in 1856.

John Butt

Bibliography

Chapman, Stanley D. *The Early Factory Masters.* 1967.

English, Walter. *The Textile Industry.* 1969.

Fitton, Robert. *The Arkwrights, Spinners of Fortune.* 1989.

Fitton, Robert, and A.P. Wadsworth. *The Strutts and the Arkwrights.* 1958.

See also Entrepreneurs and Entrepreneurship; Textile Industries

Stubbs, George (1724–1806)

Stubbs was the leading animal painter of the 18th century. He began as a portraitist in his native **Liverpool,** studied anatomy in **York** in 1750, and visited Rome not long afterward. By 1758 he had begun dissecting horses and drawing them in great detail; this eventually resulted in his great publication, *The Anatomy of the Horse* (1766). He settled in **London** in 1759 and, utilizing his superior knowledge of anatomy, soon became the leading painter of aristocratic horse scenes.

Stubbs's productions, such as *The Duchess of Richmond and Lady Louisa Lennox Watching the Duke's Racehorses at Exercises* (*c.* 1770), were not only correct in detail but possessed a sense of design and mood previously lacking in sporting paintings. He also produced pictures of individual horses, with or without riders, and, most fascinating of all, a series of *Mares and Foals* (1762–1768) against plain brown backgrounds. These provided a stark contrast to his more conversation-like groups of horses and humans, such as *The Melbourne and Milbanke Families* (1769–1770).

In the 1770s, Stubbs painted a series of wild animals, including several versions of *A Lion Attacking a Horse,* and made a rather unsuccessful attempt at **history painting.** The lion-and-horse theme also resulted in a series of ceramic plaques produced in collaboration with **Josiah Wedgwood.** In the 1780s, Stubbs painted poetical scenes of rural life. His proposed comparative anatomy of a human, a tiger, and a fowl was never completed, but his detailed **drawings,** including the depiction of movement, survive at the British Art Center, Yale University. Considered merely a horse painter until recently, Stubbs is now regarded as one of the most talented artists of the period.

Thomas J. McCormick

Bibliography

Egerton, Judy. *George Stubbs, Anatomist and Animal Painter.* 1976.

Solkin, David. *Painting for Money: The Visual Arts and the Public Sphere in Eighteenth-Century England.* 1993.

Tattersall, Bruce. *Stubbs and Wedgwood, Unique Alliance between Artist and Potter.* 1974.

Taylor, Basil. *Stubbs.* 1971.

See also Painting; Sport

Stukeley, William (1687–1765)

A physician passionately concerned with the discovery and recording of **antiquities**, Stukeley traveled the country on archaeological tours (1710–1725), concentrating especially on Avebury and Stonehenge (1719–1724). His fieldwork, surveys, detailed draftsmanship, and observations of monuments, many now damaged or destroyed, remain valuable today. He produced an account of his **travels**, *Itinerarium Curiosum* (1724); manuscripts reveal his intention to publish an objective work on Avebury, Stonehenge, and allied circles in 1725, though his later productions relating the sites to Druids were speculative and fanciful.

In 1727 Stukeley took orders, ending his days as a **London** rector. By encouraging the literary forger Charles Bertram (1723–1765) to publish *De Situ Britannie,* supposedly by Richard of Cirencester (*d.* 1401?), he unwittingly became involved in an audacious and successful literary fraud. A Fellow of the **Royal Society**, he helped establish the Society of Antiquaries (1717).

Theresa McDonald

Bibliography

Piggott, Stuart. *William Stukeley—an Eighteenth-Century Antiquary.* Rev. ed., 1985.

———. "William Stukeley: New Facts and an Old Forgery." *Antiquity.* Vol. 60, pp. 115–122.

See also Learned Societies

Sublime, The

This is a term for awe-inspiring experience, defined according to aesthetic theories developed chiefly in the latter 18th century—for example, in **Edmund Burke**'s *A Philosophical Inquiry into the Origin of Our Ideas of the Sublime and the Beautiful* (1756), and in Immanuel Kant's (1724–1804) *Critique of Judgment* (1790). The **Romantics** were famous for exploring sublimity in art (as in the mountain scenery in **Mary Shelley**'s *Frankenstein* [1818]), but other groups—notably the poets of "sensibility" in the 18th century (**Gray** and **Collins** among them)—pioneered the tendency.

The sublime refers not only to heights and depths, lofty ideas or "deep romantic chasms" (as in **Coleridge**'s *Kubla Khan,* 1816). But certainly such ups and downs often make an appearance, locating the viewer, humbled and horrified, somewhere in the middle. The sublime takes one beyond a limit (Latin, *sub limen*), in order to return to a proper sense of limits. In Kant's *Critique,* the "mathematical sublime," the idea of an infinite number series, establishes a sense both of absolute number and of the proper bounds of limited, mortal thought.

The threat of the sublime may render the subsequent equilibrium "natural." This idea emerges from theories that tried to naturalize or embody moral and political codes. Burke described the political sublime of the **French Revolution** as evoking a proper sense of horror, and his *Reflections* (1790) contain many examples of visceral rhetoric intended to evoke the chastising awe of the sublime.

Rather than attempting to identify specific figures that trigger the sublime, aesthetic philosophy tended to locate it *between* subject and object, reader and text. Thus the sublime could seem rather antirhetorical. In **Wordsworth**'s ***Lyrical Ballads*** (1798) the mundane lives of simple people could be seen as filled with sublimity—something which shocked contemporary reviewers by ignoring classical concepts of decorum. The sublime could become a tool for fashioning a more privatized, "creative" identity. The influential classical author Longinus (213?–273) had associated the sublime with divine creation (and democracy).

The sublimity of creative "genius" built upon earlier formulations. Wordsworth owed a debt to **Mark Akenside**'s *The Pleasures of the Imagination* (1744, 1757), and to John Milton's *Paradise Lost* (1667). **David Hartley**, the associationist philosopher, had shown how ethical impulses could be registered on the body itself (1749), as in the **Gothic** aesthetic of horror. New styles of **landscape architecture** and European **travel** generated a nondecorous sublime aesthetic. **Adam Smith**'s economic theories (1776) showed how the wealth of nations might rise according to abstract mechanisms, and strongly suggested that a sublime "invisible hand" guided and improved the marketplace. In each case, disorder was seen as submitting to a higher ordering principle.

Timothy Morton

Bibliography

De Bolla, Peter. *The Discourse of the Sublime: Readings in History, Aesthetics and the Subject.* 1989.

Deleuze, Gilles. *Kant's Critical Philosophy: The Doctrine of the Faculties.* 1984.

Hamilton, P. *Wordsworth.* 1986.

See also Picturesque; Sensibility and Sentimentalism

Sugar Act

See Plantation Act

Sugar Trade

See West Indies

Suicide

In 1714, at the beginning of the Hanoverian age, suicide was both a **crime** and a grievous sin, punished by the full sanctions of church and state. By law, *felos de se*—those who were judged to have taken their own lives deliberately—were punished by Crown seizure of all goods and property; their bodies, pierced through with stakes, were ordered to be buried in the unhallowed ground of a crossroads; and their souls were doomed, it was believed, to eternal damnation. Suicide was generally regarded as an act of diabolical possession, an eruption of the demonic, which, threatening the entire community, required the harshest deterrents.

Yet during the Hanoverian period a slow shift, begun in the 17th century, gathered momentum. Suicide became a hotly debated topic, and ultimately both popular attitudes and official stances toward it changed radically. In 1823 the law was changed to eliminate the religious penalties for *felo de se*—though the provision mandating forfeiture of goods to the Crown was not repealed until 1870.

Periodic statistics on suicide are fragmentary and inconsistent, and there is little basis for a meaningful comparison with other countries or other periods. There is, however, no evidence to support the contemporary belief that the English were more prone to self-murder than people on the Continent. That belief, espoused by both British and Europeans, was apparently a product of stereotypes about English **melancholy** and dreadful weather, and perhaps also of the relative openness of the British press, so quick to publicize and sensationalize suicides.

Several factors contributed to the changing perception of suicide—what one leading scholar has called its "secularization." Weariness with the religious disputes of the 17th century engendered a growing disbelief in **supernatural** intervention in everyday life. The spread of literacy, **newspapers**, and the **periodical** press allowed the gradual dissemination and acceptance of the scientific and philosophical tenets of the **Enlightenment**, equally hostile to supernatural phenomena. Rationalist philosophers like **David Hume** not only challenged what they saw as the superstitions of the past, but also offered specific defenses of suicide as a justifiable and even a sometimes noble act by a free individual. Some literary figures, like **Joseph Addison**, author of the immensely popular play *Cato* (1713), portrayed suicide as, in certain circumstances, an act of stoic virtue. And the cult of **sensibility**, reflected in the lachrymose response to the tragic death of the impoverished young poet **Thomas Chatterton**, who killed himself at age 17, and to the protagonist's suicide in Goethe's (1749–1832) **novel** *Sorrows of Young Werther* (1774), viewed the suicide as an object of pity, not a criminal defying God and the community.

Another locus of change was the coroner's jury (local citizens charged with determining the cause of death in doubtful circumstances). Available records suggest that juries in 1660 returned a verdict of *non compos mentis* (in essence, a verdict of insanity which spared the deceased and his family from the legal and religious sanctions) in fewer than 5% of the recorded cases; by the early 18th century, *non compos mentis* verdicts were returned nearly 40% of the time; and by 1800 the harsh verdict of *felo de se* was almost never rendered, no matter how clearly willful the death appeared to be. These changes emerged not only from shifts in philosophic attitude but also from aspects of politics and class. Juries were increasingly reluctant to leave the deceased's family destitute and to see property pass from the local community to the Crown; and the very severity of the penalties helped to make the verdict of *felo de se* increasingly unpopular.

Religious conservatives fought against these changes with a full array of theological and moral arguments. The suicide, they claimed, offended against nature, the good order of society, and God Himself. Self-murder, likened to a soldier deserting his God-given post, was condemned as a presumptuous usurpation of God's right to dispose of human lives as He chose. Nonetheless, by the end of the Hanoverian period, when people like **Samuel Whitbread**, **Samuel Romilly**, **Lord Liverpool**, and **Benjamin Haydon** committed suicide, they were much more likely to be pitied as madmen or victims of circumstances, or even celebrated as stoic heroes, than condemned as criminal blasphemers.

Kevin P. Mulcahy

Bibliography

Hume, David. *On Suicide.* 1756.

MacDonald, Michael, and Terence R. Murphy. *Sleepless Souls: Suicide in Early Modern England.* 1990.

Moore, Charles. *A Full Inquiry into the Subject of Suicide: To Which Are Added Two Treatises on Duelling and Gaming.* 1790.

Spratt, S.E. *The English Debate on Suicide from Donne to Hume.* 1961.

Thompson, F.M.L., ed. *The Cambridge Social History of Britain, 1750–1950.* 3 vols. 1990.

Sun Fire Office

The **insurance** of buildings against fire evolved in the latter 17th century. After 1700 this was extended to buildings' contents, the most significant move being the establishment in **London** of the Sun Fire Office by Charles Povey (*c.* 1650–1743) in 1708. Povey created a salvage corps of men to remove goods from buildings on fire; for quick identification, customers were given a fire mark in the form of a sun to display outside their premises.

In 1710 Povey sold out to a group who ran the organization as a copartnership. Surviving the **South Sea Bubble** of 1720, the Sun encountered competition from others, including **joint-stock companies** such as the **Royal Exchange Assurance** in 1721. The Sun responsed by founding agencies in the South of England and later extending these to the Midlands, the north, and **Scotland**: agents, normally small traders and shopkeepers, collected premiums and sent them to London, where policies were written.

As industrialization progressed, the company began to insure factories, warehouses, and mills, though domestic and commercial property still remained the largest source of income during the 18th century. Like other insurance companies, the Sun invested its surplus funds in a variety of ways—in stocks and mortgages, for example—thus contributing to London's growth as a major financial center.

A.J.G. Cummings

Bibliography

Dickson, P.G.M. *The Sun Insurance Office, 1710–1960.* 1960.

Raynes, H.E. *A History of British Insurance.* Rpt. 1968.

See also Finance and Investment

Sunday Schools

These schools, though pioneered a little earlier by people such as **Hannah More** and her sister Martha in Wrington near **Bristol**, and Hannah Ball in High Wycomb, were first organized in Gloucester in 1780 by **Robert Raikes**. They were designed to give poor children an opportunity to spend their Sunday mornings learning how to read and absorb some basic Christian precepts. The impetus of the Sunday school movement lay in the **humanitarianism** of the latter 18th century, the **religious revival**, and the national reaction against the supposed licentiousness and atheism of the **French Revolution**. It succeeded so well that by 1810 an estimated half million British children were attending such schools. In 1818 there were over 5,000 Sunday schools. In 1833 about half the children attending school were going to Sunday schools. Some authorities believe that by 1850, perhaps three-fourths of working-class children were in attendance.

Raikes, a reforming editor of the *Gloucester Journal,* had noticed many poor children, employed in the pin-making trade, who, with no opportunities for formal education, spent their Sundays running about cursing everything in sight. Starting a school for such children and publicizing it in his paper, he watched enthusiasm for such schools spread. **Charity schools**, which had existed for decades, provided the model of education. Children age 6–14 were taught to read, study the Bible, and the catechism. Other subjects were sometimes taught as well. Hannah More and her sister instructed the poor children of **miners** in not only religion and reading but also in personal hygiene.

At first the enthusiasm for Sunday schools was essentially interdenominational. In 1785 William Fox (1736–1826), a **Baptist** merchant, helped set up the Sunday School Society, which provided individual Sunday schools financial support (principally to pay teachers); its trustees numbered equally Anglicans and Nonconformists. **Roman Catholics** also participated, as in **Manchester** under the leadership of the popular priest Rowland Broomhead (*d.* 1820). Another interdenominational organization, the Sunday School Union, was established (1803) to assist in providing **London** Sunday schools with books and materials and in enlisting unpaid teachers for staff. Throughout the growing industrial **cities**, Sunday school auxiliaries arose, encouraged by **Evangelical** and **dissenting** denominations to affiliate with the national union and to spread the growth of the movement.

Tired scholars late for Sunday School

But as time passed there was an opposing tendency toward denominational control: Anglican authorities, for example, worrying about lay teachers and curricula, Wesleyans worrying about the teaching of writing as a violation of the Sabbath (writing instruction was generally discontinued after 1800), and so on. There were also political objections to the schools. Ultra-conservatives opposed any plebeian education as tending toward political instability, some **farmers** opposed it as ruinous to **agriculture**, and, as Hannah More discovered, even some members of the Anglican **clerical profession** opposed it as tending toward **Methodism**. Even so, by 1800 approximately 200,000 children flocked to Sunday schools throughout Britain, and by 1820 nearly every working-class child had, at some time or other, attended a Sunday school. The schools are credited with helping to check the regressive impact of industrialization on literacy rates, a negative influence that peaked about 1820. Another great advantage was that these schools got the children out of the house on Sunday mornings.

Samuel J. Rogal

Bibliography

Booth, Frank. *Robert Raikes of Gloucester.* 1980.

Cliff, Philip B. *The Rise and Development of the Sunday School Movement in England, 1780–1980.* 1986.

Ferguson, John, ed. *Christianity, Society, and Education.* 1981.

Laqueur, T.W. *Religion and Respectability: Sunday Schools and Working Class Culture, 1780–1850.* 1976.

Martin, Christopher. *A Short History of English Schools, 1750–1965.* 1979.

Newby, Catharine R. *The Story of Sunday Schools: Robert Raikes and After.* 1930.

See also Education, Elementary

Supernatural, The

Though an act of Parliament in 1736 declared witches imaginary, **Oliver Goldsmith** some 23 years laters complained that those who had inspired doubt about witches and ghosts had robbed mankind of "a valuable imagination." With increasing intensity after 1760 or so, poets and fiction writers attempted to revive such imagining, pointing to the emotional power of the otherworldly.

The problem of belief, however, troubled them. **William Collins** even made this a poetic subject, unfavorably contrasting his own barren situation to that of his predecessors, who could write under the conviction that ghosts, sprites, and demons actually existed. Some writers attempted to short-circuit the difficulty by locating their evocations of the supernatural in the distant past. **Thomas Gray** relied on Nordic mythology for his cast of otherworldly characters. **James Macpherson,** whose **poetry** abounds in ghosts, claimed that he had **translated** his **epics** from the ancient Gaelic. Imitations of antiquated **ballads** proliferated, familiarizing readers with a tradition of unearthly events and personages.

Given such a tradition, **William Blake** could freely invent supernatural beings who inhabited a timeless realm of the imagination, and **Coleridge** could contribute to ***Lyrical Ballads*** (1798) poems that familiarized the supernatural without depriving it of its strangeness. As early as 1767, the critic William Duff (1732–1815) had declared the invention of supernatural characters the highest effort of original genius. Blake and Coleridge, and **Byron** and **Keats** after them, proved his point.

Novelists, too, relied heavily on the supernatural, particularly in the 1790s, when **Gothic** Romance flowered. Like many poets, these novelists located their fictions in the past or in such exotic realms as a vaguely delineated Orient, where ghosts and demons might seem less implausible. In **novels** and poetry alike, the supernatural often signified the freedom and the dominion of the imagination. Its presence signaled a retreat from realism, an effort to explore psychic rather than literal truth, a determination to create powerful emotional effects. If writers of Gothic fiction did not solicit belief, they nonetheless attempted to evoke responses of pity and terror, and invited imaginative participation in the experience of unforeseeable danger. It remained for the next generation, literary artists such as **Sir Walter Scott**, to merge Romance and history in a way such that the supernatural could coexist with the matter-of-fact.

Patricia Meyer Spacks

Bibliography

Bleiler, Everett. *Guide to Supernatural Fiction.* 1983.
Carter, Margaret. *Spectre or Delusion? The Supernatural in Gothic Fiction.* 1987.
Lea, Sydney. *Gothic to Fantastic: Readings in Supernatural Fiction.* 1973.
Penzoldt, Peter. *The Supernatural in Fiction.* 1952.
Spacks, Patricia Meyer. *The Insistence of Horror: Aspects of the Supernatural in 18th-Century English Poetry.* 1965.

See also Exoticism; Orientalism

Sutherland Family

The marriage in 1785 of Elizabeth Gordon, Countess of Sutherland (1765–1839), to George Leveson Gower (1758–1833) created a union between two ancient Scottish and English families and heralded the family's spectacular economic and social ascendancy in 19th-century Britain. Gower, who became Marquis of Stafford in 1803 and the first Duke of Sutherland in 1833, was one of Europe's wealthiest men. His income came from the family's productive English estates and lucrative investments in parts of Britain's **inland transport** system such as the Bridgewater and Liverpool to Manchester **canals.** By the 1820s the family members were major stockholders in **railways, iron, coal,** and government stocks, while in **Scotland**, rentals from their 1-million-acres estate added to the family's fortunes.

The Sutherlands sought to apply the principles of **agricultural improvement** and investment to their Highland estate in Scotland, but this was to cause considerable social disruption. From 1806 on, tenants were evicted from their traditional lands, often brutally, to make way for sheep. The most infamous episode involved Sutherland's agent and sheep farmer **Patrick Sellar,** who was charged with the death of one elderly tenant, but was acquitted in 1816. To create alternative employments for the displaced **population,** coastal villages with harbors and **fishing** stations were constructed. These did not prove the success the Sutherlands had hoped for, however, as prices for fish, kelp, and cattle collapsed after 1815. To this day, the **Highland clearances** still evoke bitter memories of the Sutherland family and are remembered as events tending toward "the extirpation of the Celtic race" from the Highlands of Scotland.

William Kenefick

Bibliography

Richards, Eric. *The Leviathan of Wealth: The Sutherland Fortune in the Industrial Revolution.* 1973.
———. *A History of the Highland Clearances: Agrarian Transformation and the Evictions, 1746–1866.* 1982.

Swansea

Swansea, an ancient Welsh **borough** on the bridging point of the River Tawe, controlled the rich Gower peninsula and the neighboring uplands. It traded with **Ireland,** mainly in agricultural products, though since Elizabethan times it enjoyed a **coal** trade. Its position near outcropping coal measures and in proximity to Cornish copper deposits caused it to grow in the 18th century as a smelting center. In 1707 its **population** was approximately 2,000; by 1750 it was approximately 3,000, and by 1801, 6,099; population more than doubled to 13,256 in 1831. Swansea became the center of a metal-smelting district, which stretched from Llanelli to Neath, responsible for

90% of all British copper smelting. Most was outside the limits of the borough, in the Tawe Valley, which was navigable to small vessels for 3 miles. Morriston was developed there as a planned industrial settlement in the 1780s.

Until the early 19th century it seemed possible that Swansea's future lay in becoming a major **seaside resort**—"the Brighton of Wales," rather than an industrial town. The outlying village of Oystermouth had some success in attracting tourists; **Thomas Bowdler** came to live (and die) there. Swansea's cultural aspirations were reflected in the launching of the first Welsh **newspaper**, *The Cambrian* (1804–1915), and creation of the Swansea Philosophical and Literary Society (1835). The harbor was poor until trustees were established by the Swansea Harbour Act of 1791, after which there were improvements, but there was no floating harbor until 1852. In the 18th century the High **Tory** Beaufort estate dominated and succeeded in diluting the **radicalism** for which **dissenters** had made the town famous in the 17th century, and were to do again in the 19th. Swansea was part of the Glamorgan Boroughs constituency until 1832, when a Swansea Boroughs seat (including Kenfig, Aberafon, Neath, and Loughor) was created.

Neil Evans

Bibliography

Griffiths, Ralph A., ed. *The City of Swansea: Challenges and Change.* 1990.

Jenkins, Philip. "Tory Industrialism and Town Politics: Swansea in the Eighteenth Century." *Historical Journal.* Vol 24, pp. 103–123.

Williams, Glanmor, ed. *Swansea: An Illustrated History.* 1990.

Williams, Trevor. *The Economic Development of Swansea and the Swansea District to 1921.* 1940.

See also Metallurgy and Metalworking; Wales and Welsh Culture; Welsh Industry; Welsh Mining

Swift, Jonathan (1665–1745)

Swift is recognized as one of the great satirists of the Hanoverian age. A clergyman of the **Church of England**, he eventually became Dean of St. Patrick's Cathedral in **Dublin** (1713). Deeply interested (as his satires show) in contemporary political events, he became a well-known member of the **Tory opposition** to the **Whig** governments of **George I** and **George II**, often satirizing **Sir Robert Walpole**, the king's chief minister from 1721–1742. Swift's literary friends included first the Whigs **Addison** and **Steele**, then later the Tory writers **Pope, Arbuthnot, Bolingbroke**, and **Gay**. During much of his life he was also the guide and friend of Esther Johnson (1681–1728), known to history as Stella; his letters to her, posthumously published (1765), have become known as the *Journal to Stella.*

Swift was recognized as a master of **irony** in his own time, and his satires are still accorded the tribute of allusion and imitation; the adjective "Swiftian" refers to a kind of uncomfortably hostile but also seemingly detached irony. Swift developed his talents as a member of the Scriblerus **Club** (organized in 1713), named after a fictional pedant, which had as its goal the reforming of contemporary cultural and intellectual failings through satirical attacks. Notable in his outlook were his bleak estimates of the prospects for human advancement through **technology** alone, and his critique of **Enlightenment** assumptions about the efficacy of human reason.

Usually numbered among Swift's greatest works were his first important satire, *A Tale of a Tub* (1704), which attacked the "moderns" of the **ancients vs. moderns quarrel**—those who argued that the achievements of recent times had surpassed those of ancient Greece and Rome—and also the religious practices of **Roman Catholics** and 17th-century Protestant **dissenters.** *Travels into Several Remote Nations of the World* (1726), better known as *Gulliver's Travels,* now in edited form still a fixture of **children's literature**, simulates a **travel book** but is also related to **utopian literature**, using utopian motifs to scrutinize and reject beliefs in the possibility of the perfectibility of human societies. Swift's famous *A Modest Proposal* (1729), still considered standard reading, recommends a scheme to bolster **Ireland**'s economy by using babies for meat, thus satirizing Ireland's own self-consuming economic practices and emphasizing the brutality that was fostered by English colonial policies.

As a young man, Swift served for sustained periods as secretary to Sir William Temple (1628–1699), who had earlier been an important **diplomat** and councillor under Charles II. During the last 4 years of **Queen Anne**'s reign (1710–1714) he served the Tory administration as **periodical** writer in *The Examiner* and author of the very influential pamphlet *Conduct of the Allies* (1711), which helped prepare the public for the Tories' conclusion of the **War of Spanish Succession** (1713).

Jonathan Swift

Although Swift supported the **Glorious Revolution**, he was displeased with the **Hanoverian Succession** because after 1714 the kings' Whig supporters encouraged **toleration** for dissenters and hence in his view eroded the dominance of the state church in both England and Ireland. Unlike contemporary whiggish writers like **Defoe**, he vigorously supported the **Test and Corporation Acts**, which discouraged Catholics and dissenters while buttressing Anglican dominance.

Swift took up residence in Ireland in 1714, where he had been born of Anglo–Irish parents and educated at **Trinity College, Dublin** (B.A., 1686). His attitude toward Ireland and the Irish Catholics was a mixture of contempt, pity, and savage indignation. The contempt was conventional among members of the **Anglo–Irish Protestant Ascendancy**, many of whose ancestors had come over to take land and power away from the Irish Catholics, but in Swift's case it was mingled with pity and genuine indignation at the abuse of the Irish by an English administration that acted callously and ignorantly. He produced many **tracts** on Irish issues, the best known an amalgam of satire and argument called the *Drapier's Letters* (1724), which actually forced the London government to reverse itself on the question of **William Wood**'s coinage. Many of Swift's biographers have found the desire that he emphasized in his own Latin epitaph to have been fulfilled: to be remembered and emulated for his championship of liberty.

Everett Zimmerman

Bibliography

Ehrenpreis, Irvin. *Swift: The Man, His Works, the Age.* 3 vols. 1962–1983.

Quintana, Ricardo. *Swift: An Introduction.* 1955.

Rodino, Robert H. *Swift Studies, 1965–1980: An Annotated Bibliography.* 1984.

Rogers, Pat, ed. *Jonathan Swift, the Complete Poetry.* 1983.

Stathis, J.J. *A Bibliography of Swift Studies, 1945–1965.* 1965.

See also Irish Literature; Satire

Swing Riots (1830)

Because of economic dislocation, depressed agricultural prices, and unemployment caused largely by wider use of labor-saving devices in **agriculture** and the introduction of cheap Irish labor, the most widespread agrarian disturbances of early-19th-century England broke out in 1830. Triggered by a poor harvest, revolutions in France and the Netherlands, and calls for reform in England, this "labourers' revolt" is named for "Captain Swing," a name signed to threatening letters received by farmers—apparently the term came from the swinging stick of the flail used in threshing. The riots may also, however, be seen in a larger context, as representing a spontaneous last-ditch protest against the accumulating injuries of the rural poor—pauperization, technologically induced unemployment, and the breakdown of the traditional agrarian community.

Starting in Kent and moving throughout the grain-producing south and east of England from June through December 1830, the disturbance saw more than 1,000 incidents of violence. Events were initiated by relatively young **agricultural laborers** and village artisans or **craftsmen**—blacksmiths, carpenters, wheelwrights—with the craftsmen often acting as leaders. Although no one was killed and the rich were not plundered, the riots did involve arson; destruction of **enclosures**; physical attacks on landlords, parsons, and justices of the peace; demonstrations to increase wages or to exact food and money; the isolated destruction of industrial machinery and farm animals; the sending of threatening letters; and demands for the reduction of rents, **tithes**, and **taxes**. The most widespread and characteristic action undertaken by the Swing rioters was the breaking of threshing machines. The villages that suffered from the riots were above average in size, more dependent than others on agriculture, had higher ratios of rural laborers to farmers, included a number of craftsmen, and experienced some religious friction.

The rioters' demands were economic, not political. They wanted decent wages and an end to unemployment. On occasion the demands of the agricultural laborers and farmers coincided, as when they sought relief from rents, tithes, and taxes. During the riots, subtle divisions in social class, literacy level, and residence in town or countryside appeared, and there were attacks on nonagricultural machinery reminiscent of the earlier **Luddite** disturbances. However, to forestall trouble, many farmers stopped using machines, and increased wages—though this eventually led to decreased use of machinery and a decline in agricultural production.

The rural authorities dealt severely with the riots, and the **Riot Act** was read frequently. Led by the **aristocracy and gentry**, mobile units of volunteer forces, drawn chiefly from shopkeepers, yeomen, and "respectable" laborers, were the main force used against the rioters. In all, 1,976 were arrested and brought to trial in 34 counties. About 500 were **transported** to **Australia** and nearby Tasmania. Of the 252 sentenced to death, 19 were executed; 800 were acquitted.

Because the rioters lacked ideology and organization, the "revolt" neither posed a threat to the government, nor is there evidence that participants were forming unions. The harsh punishments meted out do indicate that the authorities were extremely concerned about the potential threat of upheaval from people who had never previously caused disturbances on such a scale. There were some lingering outbreaks of arson and animal-maiming. Overall, the riots did not result in increased wages or employment, though some contemporaries believed that they had inadvertently helped to influence the passage of the parliamentary **Reform Act** (1832).

Mark C. Herman

Bibliography

Dunbabin, J.P.D. *Rural Discontent in Nineteenth Century Britain.* 1974.

Hammond, J.L., and B. Hammond. *The Village Labourer.* 1948.

Hobsbawm, E.J., and George Rudé. *Captain Swing.* 1968.

Peacock, A.J. *Bread or Blood.* 1965.

Rudé, George. *The Crowd in History.* 1964.

Stevenson, John. *Popular Disturbances in England, 1700–1870.* 1979.

Wright, D.G. *Popular Radicalism: The Working-Class Experience, 1780–1880.* 1988.

See also Farmers and Agricultural Laborers; Hours, Wages, and Working Conditions; Riots and Popular Disturbances

T

Tannahill, Robert (1774–1810)

Critics in the 19th century compared Tannahill, "the prince of **Paisley** poets," to **Robert Burns** for his many sentimental Scottish songs. Some of these are still sung to the music of Robert Archibald Smith (1780–1829), who published the six-volume *The Scottish Minstrel* (1820–1824). Tannahill's poems, however, have found few admirers. While he worked as a Paisley weaver, he composed lyrics about the Scottish countryside and piteous lasses, sometimes (as in "The Dear Highland Laddie," 1807) from the woman's point of view.

With Smith's music, Tannahill's songs—"Jessie the Flower o'Dunblane" and "The Braes o'Balquihither" among them—were sufficiently popular for him to publish *Songs and Poems* in 1807. But when Constable and Company rejected a subsequent collection, the depressed poet destroyed his manuscripts. Tannahill committed **suicide**—drowned himself in 1810. A side of Tannahill not revealed by his lyrical **poetry** was his participation in a Paisley tradesman **club**, where the members closely analyzed literature.

Peter A. Tasch

Bibliography

Royle, Trevor. *Companion to Scottish Literature.* 1983.
Semple, David, ed. *The Poems and Songs and Correspondence of Robert Tannahill, with Life and Notes.* 1873.

See also Scotland and Scottish Culture

Taxes and Tariffs

The rise of Britain as a great power was accompanied by massive increases in state spending, largely on overseas **wars**. Britain was at war nearly half the time between 1700 and 1815. Government expenditure far exceeded tax revenue, creating a national debt so great that by the 1760s there was a general fear of impending national bankruptcy. In the fiscal year ending January 1784, taxes produced altogether only little more than £12.5 million, which was nearly £2 million less than what was required for payment of government services and interest on the funded debt. Such problems preoccupied many Hanoverian ministries, which were often led by men distinguished for their financial acumen. Gradually these ministries decreased the portion of funds necessary to finance government raised by borrowing and increased the portion to be raised through taxation. This became especially significant during the enormously costly **French Revolutionary and Napoleonic Wars**. Whereas only about 25% of the money required to wage the wars of 1702–1713, 1739–1748, 1756–1763, and 1775–1783 was raised through taxation, this increased to about 52% of the money needed in 1792–1815.

Hanoverian governments were forced not only to increase existing tax rates but also to introduce new taxes. They could not rely on economic growth alone, which, though contributing toward higher revenue, never kept pace with the cost of overseas wars and the national debt. The fiscal policies of successive administrations followed three general strategies: the imposition of higher taxes; the employment of a sophisticated public credit system; and the more efficient administration of tax collection. The emergence of a public credit system, facilitated by **Sir Robert Walpole** with the **sinking fund**, made government less immediately dependent on taxation. But the novelty of the system has obscured the role of taxation, which was critical both for paying the interest on the national debt and for creating a climate of confidence among creditors.

Direct taxes were much less significant than indirect taxes in helping to keep the government afloat. The chief form of taxation levied directly on wealth during most of the Hanoverian period was the land tax, based on the value of real estate. This brought in about 75% of all revenue from direct taxes (or about 20% of all revenue from all sources). The land tax was "progressive" in the sense that it fell only upon landowners, not the poorer classes, but it was also unfair and inadequate as an income tax because it left monied men and well-to-do townspeople unaffected. Parliament, which was full of landowners, naturally resisted any increase in the land tax, which yearly remained at 10% on the value of land (except in

London Customs House, 1808

wartime, when it was often increased to around 20%); although because land was not revalued during the century, this meant continually diminishing tax burdens for the landed rich: the real value of land increased but its tax-assessed value remained static.

Whereas the land tax and a few other taxes which today would be considered "luxury taxes" (indirect taxes on nonnecessary goods such as **houses**, **servants**, windows, carriages, **hair** powder, playing cards) generally diminished in relative importance as time passed, the indirect taxes levied on common articles and "the necessities of the poor" proliferated and also increased. The main taxes were those collected by the departments of customs, excise, and stamps. Excise duties, which generally produced nearly 50% of all tax revenue after 1725, were levied on domestic commodities, particularly on malt, hops, **beer** (which was thus taxed several times), nonimported distilled liquor, salt, **glass**, soap, paper, candles, leather, starch, bricks, and printed fabrics. Customs duties, levied on imports, brought in 20–25% of total tax revenue, and were levied chiefly on **tobacco**, imported wines and brandy, tea, **sugar**, timber, **iron** bars, foreign **textiles**, and, occasionally, grain. A tax on stamps was increasingly significant also, by 1800 bringing in nearly 8% of total tax revenue by virtue of the law requiring that stamps be affixed to **newspapers** as well as legal, business, and **insurance** documents.

The government became so dependent on indirect taxes that excise taxes constituted some 55% of revenue at the time of the **excise crisis**. Customs also rose steadily from the 1750s. Custom duties were less favored by governmental policymakers because of their tendency to impede trade and encourage the already widespread **crime** of **smuggling**. Customs were never merely considered a source of revenue; they were also an instrument of governmental **navigation** policy used to regulate trade and reduce foreign competition. Yet, while both excise and customs duties facilitated the extraction of taxes to a much higher degree per capita in Britain than even in prerevolutionary **France**, and at a more decidedly regressive angle, neither was lucrative enough to help sufficiently with the tremendous costs of the wars between 1793 and 1815. It was for this reason that **Pitt the Younger** was forced, at a moment of extreme national danger, to introduce an income tax (1799). Although this temporarily corrected the imbalance between swelling indirect taxes on the entire nation and diminishing direct taxes on the well-to-do (bringing direct taxes up to about 30% of total revenue collected during the period 1800–1810), the original income tax levy was abolished at the first possible opportunity (1802). Then, after being reinstated, the income tax was again abolished in 1816. Historians examining the revenue structures of both France and Britain during the 18th century have been surprised to discover that the British were paying considerably more taxes than the French, and that the taxation rate was more regressive even while there was growing inequality in the distribution of income. It is also evident, however, that the *perception* of unfairness was much less sharp in Britain than in France, and that the receivers of direct and indirect taxes were far less universally detested.

Indeed, in Britain an improved administration of taxes also contributed significantly toward the rise in revenue. The system of tax collection looked absurdly convoluted by the standards of future generations, but later reforms toward greater centralization and efficiency were anticipated under the Hanoverians. The treasury assumed control over all aspects of government finance and promoted greater fiscal responsibility. The excise tax, collected by hordes of state-appointed officials, was a model of successful bureaucracy. Customs was similarly staffed by professional state employees, although it was more encumbered with numerous sinecures. Only the land tax remained the domain of unsalaried genteel amateurs.

The image of the lightly taxed Englishman is a myth, since comparative data shows that tax levels were generally much higher than elsewhere in Europe with the possible exceptions of Prussia and Austria. The tax burden rose sixteenfold between 1660 and 1837. Taxpayers additionally paid local taxes for poor relief in the form of rates levied on buildings and land. The taxation system in Britain nevertheless encountered relatively little opposition, except in the lightly taxed peripheries of **Scotland** and **North America. George Grenville**'s attempt to expand stamp duties to British America with the **Stamp Act**, along with the more indirect **Townshend** duties (1767), provoked tax revolts and became a central issue of the **American Revolution**.

Historians offer several tentative explanations of the relative success of tax increases in Britain as compared to its Continental neighbors. They suggest that the system *appeared* more equitable and fair. The law never extended tax privileges to the **aristocracy** or to individual regions, although in practice there were many discrepancies. While governments could not avoid taxing the necessities of the poor, they were generally careful whenever they did so. Indirect taxes, levied at the source of production and then passed on to consumers as a component of prices, were more difficult to identify than direct taxes, although they were often regressive. Government expenditure was subjected to the scrutiny of Parliament, accounts were increasingly matters of public knowledge, and direct taxes could only be raised with the consent of Parliament. Lastly, one great object of the taxes, foreign wars primarily against France, was popular with a **patriotic** nation.

Andrew J. O'Shaughnessy

Bibliography

Brewer, John. *The Sinews of Power: War, Money and the English State, 1688–1783.* 1989.

Dickinson, P.G.M. *The Financial Revolution in England: A Study of the Development of Public Credit, 1688–1756.* 1967.

Dowell, S. *A History of Taxation and Taxes in England from the Earliest Times to the Present Day.* 1884.

Mathias, Peter, and Patrick O'Brien. "Taxation in Britain and France, 1715–1810: A Comparison of the Social and Economic Incidence of Taxes Collected for the Central Governments." *Journal of European Economic History.* Vol. 5, pp. 601–650.

O'Brien, Patrick. "The Political Economy of British Taxation, 1660–1815." *Economic History Review.* Vol. 41, pp. 1–32.

Ward, W.R. *The English Land Tax in the Eighteenth Century.* 1953.

See also Corn Laws; Poverty and Poor Laws

Tea Act (1773)

To assist the **East India Company** and also to curb tea **smuggling** in the **North American** colonies, **Lord North** devised several bills. One of these, the Tea Act (10 May 1773), allowed the company to distribute its tea from London warehouses without paying re-export duties, and also to establish its own retail stores in the colonies. North's intentions were to reduce colonial tea prices by one-half, allow the company to undersell colonial **smugglers**, provide revenue for colonial defense, and increase colonial acceptance of the Townshend tea tax he had left in force in 1770. But colonial importers, fearing falling profits, seeing a constitutional issue in the implicit reassertion of the right of taxation, and offended by the attempt to undermine constitutional principle by economic inducement, reacted by organizing a boycott to prevent the tea's unloading. This led to the **Boston Tea Party**, another fateful step toward the **American Revolution**.

K.R. Wood

Bibliography

Thomas, P.D.G. *The Townshend Duties Crisis: The Second Phase of the American Revolution, 1767–1773.* 1987.

Ward, Harry M. *The American Revolution: Nationhood Achieved, 1763–1788.* 1995.

Teachers

See Tutors and the Teaching Profession

Technology

See Science, Technology, and Invention

Telford, Thomas (1757–1834)

Telford, **John Smeaton**, and **James Brindley** were perhaps the three greatest civil engineers of the Hanoverian period. Like the others, Telford was a man of prodigious energy and output in the construction of **roads**, bridges, **canals**, and **docks and harbors**. The son of a shepherd, Telford was born in Eskdale and attended the local school until, at age 15, he was apprenticed as a stonemason. The local landowner, the 3rd Duke of Buccleuch (1746–1812), was developing the town of Langholm, and Telford was employed building **housing** there. He apparently spent his leisure hours reading and writing **poetry**. In 1780 he found work as a journeyman mason in **Edinburgh** constructing the New Town, and began to develop an interest in **architecture** and architectural drawing.

It seems probable that his next move, to **London**, was assisted by well-connected individuals in the trade, for he was introduced to both **Robert Adam** and **Sir William Chambers**. The latter was architect of Somerset House, which Telford helped to build (beginning in 1782). He also began to act as

Thomas Telford

consultant to William Pulteney (1729–1805), a wealthy landowner in Dumfriesshire and Northamptonshire, though he spent the mid-1780s at Portsmouth Dockyard, superintending the erection of various buildings, including a chapel. He then went to Shrewsbury at Pulteney's behest, first as his architect, then, until 1792, as Public Surveyor.

The following decade changed the course of Telford's life and earned him a national reputation as an engineer. He worked on the Ellesmere and Shrewsbury canals, the Severn navigation, and the London docks. In 1801 he was appointed engineer to the British Fisheries Society, and in 1802 reported on Highland roads. When the government established Commissions for Highland Roads and Bridges and for the Caledonian Canal, it was to Telford that they turned. He designed and built numerous harbors and bridges throughout the Highlands, notably that at Craigellachie over the River Spey. The Caledonian Canal was begun in 1803 and opened to traffic in 1822. Telford worked on many other roads, including the Holyhead Road and the famous Menai Bridge, then the largest suspension bridge of its type (opened in 1826).

Telford was also responsible for the Gotha Canal in Sweden, begun in 1809 and opened in 1832. Indeed, his canal work continued to be important even on the eve of the **railway** age. His largest canal project was the **Birmingham** and **Liverpool** Junction, constructed in 1826–1835 and completed 6 months after his death. Telford was a Fellow of both of the **Royal Societies** (London and Edinburgh), and was annually elected President of the Institution of Civil Engineers from its birth (1818) and for many years afterward.

Ian Donnachie

Bibliography

Rolt, L.T.C. *Thomas Telford.* 1985.

See also Science, Technology, and Invention

Tennant, Charles (1768–1838)

Tennant, a pioneer of the British **chemical industry**, was born in Ochiltree, Ayrshire. After a local education he was apprenticed to the silk trade in Kilbarchan, Renfrewshire, but soon switched to **textile** finishing and bleaching, which was then receiving particular encouragement. The standard method of bleaching, advocated in Francis Home's *Experiments in Bleaching* (1754), was the use of dilute sulphuric acid, followed by exposure to natural sunlight on the bleachfield. But after chlorine was discovered (1774) by the Swedish chemist C.W. Scheele (1742–1786), and the Frenchman C.L. Berthollet (1748–1822) found it a powerful bleaching agent (1785), Tennant's and several other Scottish bleachworks speedily adopted chlorine bleaching. Tennant himself secured a **patent** for the production of liquid bleach made from chlorine and slaked lime (1789), and another for production of bleaching powder (1799) that could be safely transported. His chemical company settled at St. Rollox, **Glasgow**, to manufacture the product. Tennant soon became a prominent industrialist, and in later years was an active promoter of **railway** development in Glasgow and the West of **Scotland**.

Ian Donnachie

Bibliography

Singer, C., ed. *A History of Technology.* Vol. 4: *The Industrial Revolution, c.1750 to c.1850.* 1958.

Terry Alts

This was an oath-bound peasant society whose agitation in **Ireland** in the counties of Clare and Limerick peaked in the spring of 1831. The movement responded to a range of perceived threats: dispossession, **tithe** collection, the introduction of strangers as workmen, and (in Clare) the lack of potato plots.

Despite these local origins, the society was part of a much broader phenomenon of agrarian discontent. Rural violence in Ireland spiraled in the 1830s through a bewildering array of secret societies such as the White Feet, Black Feet, and Lady Clares, to which the generic names "**Whiteboyism**" and "**Ribbonism**" have been loosely applied. The Terry Alts shared with these groups the central aim of regulating the relationship between landlord and tenant for the benefit of the latter. They had a less **millenarian** focus than some of their contemporaries and displayed a more open and methodical approach, evident in their creation of a "Terry Alt Fund" to support prisoners charged with the **crime** of insurrection.

Their activities led to the establishment of the Clare and Limerick Special Commission (1831), which is the main source of information on the movement. However, the short-lived nature of the Terry Alt disturbances and their geographical exclusiveness have resulted in neglect by historians.

E.W. McFarland

Bibliography

Cornewall Lewis, G. *On Local Disturbances in Ireland.* 1836.

See also Rightboys; Shanavests

Test and Corporation Acts (1661, 1673, 1678)

These acts attempted to compel religious conformity under the **Church of England**, discourage **Roman Catholicism**, and destroy the political power of Protestant **dissenters** in municipal and national government. Though somewhat modified in their effects as time went on, they conditioned many aspects of Hanoverian civilization.

Passed between 1661 and 1665, the acts that constituted the base of this discriminatory program were generally known as the Clarendon Code after the king's chief minister, Edward Hyde, 1st Earl of Clarendon (1609–1674). The Corporation Act (1661), the first of the code to be enacted and the last to be repealed, directed chiefly against dissenters, excluded from municipal office anyone who refused to take communion in the Church of England and required all members of **local governments** to take the Anglican oaths of allegiance, supremacy, and nonresistance.

The restrictions of the Corporation Act were extended to *all* public offices in 1673 with the passage of the Test Act, which excluded Catholics and nonconformists from all civil and military offices. The act, reluctantly signed by the king, required that all persons in Crown employment be recipients of the Anglican communion, take the oaths of allegiance and supremacy, and sign the declaration against transubstantiation. Though aimed primarily at Catholics, the act, followed by a second Test Act in 1678, officially excluded all but Anglicans from public office, including Parliament, for most of the Hanoverian period.

Although these acts were not among the statutes from which nonconformists were exempted by the **Toleration Act**, dissenters evaded their penalties by practicing **occasional conformity**. After 1727 many annual **indemnity acts** suspended the provisions of the acts and the effects of their legal disqualifications. But despite the long-term ill effects of imposing a religious test for secular office, every attempt to win the acts' official repeal failed in **Commons**. They were finally repealed in 1828 (insofar as they required Anglican communion, thus leaving belief in transubstantiation an obstacle to Catholic relief), the lead for repeal being taken by **Unitarians** dissatisfied with the relief afforded by indemnity acts. Dissenters could now hold municipal and national office on equal terms with Anglicans.

William Edward Morris

Bibliography

Kenyon, J.P. *The Stuart Constitution, 1603–1688: Documents and Commentary.* 1986.
Watts, Michael R. *The Dissenters.* 2 vols. 1978, 1995.

See also Catholic Emancipation

Textile Industries

Markets for textiles—woolens, linens, silks, **cotton**, and cotton mixtures—developed considerably in the 18th century. **London** was the center of **fashion**, but production was widely dispersed. Local **clothing-makers** and milliners formed an important group in every town, commonly pursuing trade in surrounding districts; many firms began as packman (peddlers') businesses. In London and the larger towns, two groups supplied the market: guild craftsmen supplying the better-off, and "slop" tailors supplying the remainder.

In the English **woolen industry**, regional specialization emerged. **Worsteds** were produced in the **Norwich** area, the West Country, and Yorkshire, but the coarse cloth trade was initially present in all these regions. Gradually, Yorkshire replaced other areas in coarse woolen production: towns like Halifax, Wakefield, and Huddersfield produced shallons, serges, and kerseys, all cheap durable cloths; later, Bradford and **Leeds** became the main centers. In the East Midlands, woolen stockings, made first by handknitters but increasingly on the frame, were a specialty. In the West Country there were numerous small towns producing flannels and fine cloths; in Devonshire, serges were the chief product, and Exeter was the main market for locally produced woolens and lace.

In most districts, clothiers organized the trade, putting out wool to be spun and yarn to be woven. This elite supplied markets far and wide, but relied upon specialist exporters to consign their goods abroad. The more expensive the raw material, the more likely that concentration of production would occur to prevent waste and embezzlement. **Weaving** produced the first technical advance, "the flying shuttle," which stimulated even further changes.

Silk, the most valuable of textile raw material, was the first to be processed in **factories**, the main centers being Derby and Stockport and Macclesfield in Cheshire. However, silk weaving and garment production became concentrated in east London.

Linen production was widely dispersed in the British Isles, but became increasingly concentrated in Ulster and eastern **Scotland**, though Darlington and Leeds remained important centers up to 1840. Table and bed linen, tapes, ribbons, shirtings, and fine imitations of cotton fabrics, normally imported from **India**, accounted for most of the fine trade, but there were many coarse products as well as medium-value copies of French products such as cambrics, cravats, and lawns.

Linen warps were increasingly woven with cotton wefts, and the growth of the market for mixtures encouraged further experimentation. As the product range widened, the demand for cotton yarns increased, stimulating technical changes in **spinning**. **Entrepreneurs** in the fine linen districts of the Midlands, Lancashire, and West Scotland—**Arkwright**, **Oldknow**, **Dale**, **Owen** and their contemporaries—initiated **technological** changes to factory production.

Pure cotton goods could be made after **Crompton**'s mule became widely available in the 1780s because this flexible machine could produce strong warps and wefts. Home demands for cottons responded vigorously to price reductions, although the upper-class market continued to purchase Indian goods. But it was cheaper cloths that most buyers wanted, and the market for calico was vast by 1840. Demand for cotton clothing and furnishings grew because these were easy to keep clean; women, especially, selected these goods. Male fashions began to succumb to cotton just before 1800, when fine fustians, calicos, and muslins were made into garments. Thus

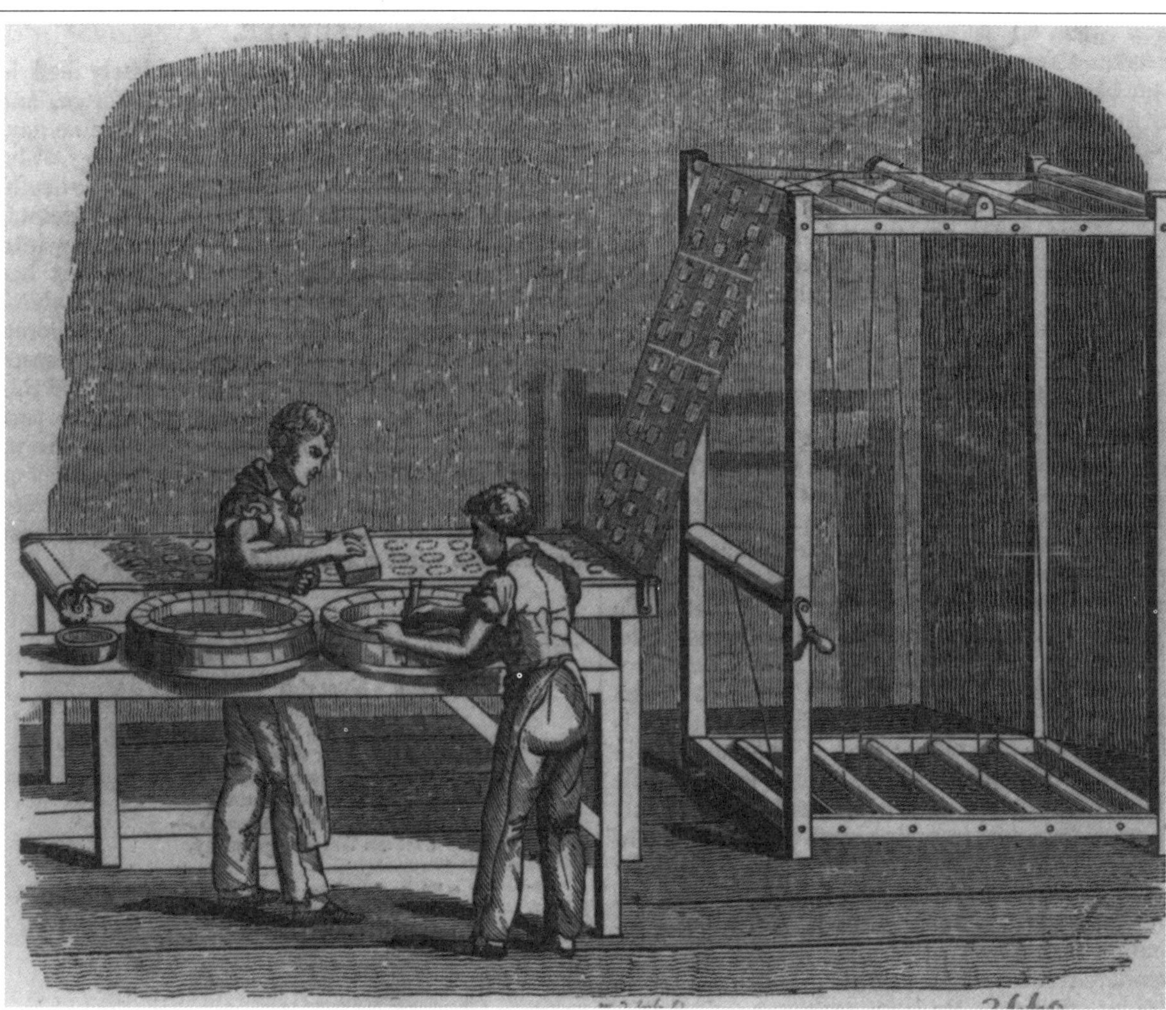
Silk printing

pantaloons, waistcoats, cravats, and handkerchiefs joined ladies' gowns, petticoats, aprons and shawls, and children's clothing as the province of cotton, the king of textiles in the early 19th century.

John Butt

Bibliography

Butt, John, and Ian Donnachie. *The Industrial Archaeology of the British Isles.* 1979.

Butt, John, and Kenneth Ponting, eds. *Scottish Textile History.* 1987.

Chapman, Stanley D. *The Early Factory Masters.* 1967.

Durie, Alistair J. *The Scottish Linen Industry in the Eighteenth Century.* 1979.

Edwards, Michael M. *The Growth of the British Cotton Trade.* 1967.

Hudson, Pat. *The Genesis of Industrial Capital: A Study of the Wool Textile Industry, c. 1750–1850.* 1986.

See also Finance and Investment

Theaters and Staging

The Hanoverian age was one of great performers, but, with only a few exceptions, middling playwrights. British theater did make two important advances: in acting, which became less declamatory and more natural and versatile; and in the building of larger, more sophisticated playhouses.

Although hampered by the **Playhouse Act**, which confined "legitimate" theater to the two **London** houses that held Royal patents (Drury Lane and Covent Garden) and to provincial establishments licensed by the Lord Chamberlain (who also acted as **censor**), nearly every important **city** had its playhouse; and some, like **Dublin**, boasted more than one. In the smaller centers, barns, storage sheds, and church halls were utilized, and temporary booths were also sometimes set up, as at Bartholomew Fair. But more appropriate accommodations for the performances of strolling players and visiting actors from London were gradually provided as time wore on.

In general, significant changes in theater design involved moving from the simple, 20-foot-deep forestage or platform to the proscenium arch or picture-frame stage. Some theaters were quite large, like Crow-Street in Dublin or Drury Lane itself, which in 1794 had a stage 83 feet wide and 92 feet deep, with some flexibility for greater depth (used for parades and pageants), and an auditorium capable of seating 3,000 or more spectators. Unfortunately, acoustic excellence tended to lag behind the enlargement of stages and auditoriums, so that noise, spectacle, and vociferous acting must have often defeated the desire for greater naturalism and more intimate theater.

Proscenium of the English Opera House, 1817

Examination of 18th-century playbills shows that managers, who often were also directors, producers, and actors, did everything possible to provide a large variety of entertainment, including **pantomimes**, farces, fireworks, acrobatics, juggling acts, and lengthy afterpieces. Their purpose was to keep their patrons, seated for the most part on backless benches, amused and under control. They did not always succeed, and the same benches were sometimes picked up and hurled onstage in disapproval of the fare.

Theater design during the 30-year managership of **David Garrick** and afterward had to be adapted to changing demands, sometimes to the detriment of the plays and of individual performances. Unless an actor had the charisma of a Garrick or a **Sarah Siddons**, the audience might become bored at best, infuriated and violent at worst. To ensure peace, the imagination and skills of stage machinists, and what we would now call "special effects" men, were called upon just as much as the efforts of great performers like **Colley Cibber** and James Quin (1693–1766) at the beginning of the Hanoverian period, and Garrick, John Philip Kemble (1757–1823), Mrs. Siddons, her brother **Charles Kemble**, William Macready (1793–1873), and **Edmund Kean** toward its end.

Though all the leading theaters had their machinists and set designers (often called "painters"), it was Drury Lane under Garrick that showed the greatest ingenuity. The new concentration on spectacle, elaborate scenery, and pageant-style costuming promoted the removal of spectators from the stage itself, where the wealthier class had often been seated (sometimes even in privileged boxes). There were other reasons for their removal: in addition to the obstruction of stage exits and the nuisance factor involved, there had also been physical danger from various theatrical contrivances such as fire-breathing dragons and thunder-and-lightning effects. Clearing the stage also enabled the machinist to change sets more rapidly by making use of the groove by which he could alternate as many as six flats or backshutters rapidly, pulling them along the floor channels. The Crow-Street, Dublin, machinest purportedly could shift 20 different views of scenes in less than a minute, though such speed, except for pantomimes, was rarely needed.

Of all Drury Lane's set-designers-cum-machinists, the greatest was **Philippe Jacques de Loutherbourg**, whose virtuosity in mounting over 30 dramatic productions during his 14 years (1771–1785) there paralleled that of Giovanni Servandoni (1695–1766) at Covent Garden, where the wealthier clientele for **opera** and ballet could better afford to pay for lavish scenes and fine costumes.

Drury Lane was fortunate too in its architects, particularly Robert **Adam**, who remodeled the theater in 1775–1776, and Henry Holland (1745–1806), who rebuilt it for **Richard Brinsley Sheridan** in 1791–1794 after a disastrous fire. For his stage machinery, "executed," as he said, "upon the newest and most approved principles," Holland heightened the proscenium area to 108 feet, allowing for flats to be lifted well above the stage; and Drury Lane's machinist, Rudolph Cabanel, who was also an **architect**, inventor, and pyrotechnist, thus managed to make the weird sisters in *Macbeth* fly through the fog and filthy air and then descend, as required, on clouds.

Garrick, helped by his French friend Jean Monnet (1703–1779), also introduced the latest lighting techniques employed by the Opéra Comique and the Comédie Française, including powerful oil lamps set in the wings and footlights, and special reflectors and torches filled with lipcodium. Altogether, the work of many talented machinists and lighting experts helped bring Hanoverian theater to unprecedented effectiveness, with a full combination of **music**, animated scenery, natural prospects, lively action, and visual effects thus enhancing (if sometimes upstaging) the performances of many outstanding actors and actresses.

James Gray

Bibliography

Allen, Ralph Gilmore. "The Stage Spectacles of Philip James de Loutherbourg." Ph.D. diss. 1960.

Craik, T.W., ed. *The Revels History of Drama in English.* Vol. 5 (1660–1750); Vol. 6 (1750–1880). 1975, 1976.

Gray, Charles H. *Theatrical Criticism in London to 1795.* 1931; rpt. 1964.

Highfill, Philip, Kalmin Burnim, and Edward Langhans, eds. *A Biographical Dictionary of Actors, Actresses, Musicians, Dancers, Managers, and Other Stage Personnel in London, 1660–1800.* 1973–.

Leacroft, Richard. *The Development of the English Playhouse.* 1973.

Lynch, J.J. *Box, Pit and Gallery: Stage and Society in Johnson's London.* 1953.

Nicoll, Allardyce. *History of English Drama.* Vols. 2 and 3. 1952, 1959.

Price, Cecil. *Theater in the Age of Garrick.* 1973.

Southern, Richard. *Changeable Scenery: Its Origin and Development in the English Theatre.* 1952.

Van Lennep, W., A.H. Scouten, G.W. Stone, and C.B. Hogan, eds. *The London Stage, 1660–1800: A Calendar of Plays, Entertainments & Afterpieces, Together with Casts, Box-Receipts and Contemporary Comment, Compiled from the Playbills, Newspapers and Theatrical Diaries of the Period.* Parts 2–5. 7 vols. 1960–1968.

See also Actors and the Acting Profession; Dramatic Arts; Dramatic Criticism

Thelwall, John (1764–1834)

Lecturer, **journalist**, and poet, Thelwall was a major **radical** leader of the 1790s. Born the son of a silk mercer, he was mostly self-educated. He tried his hand at law and **medicine** before dedicating himself to politics, which he first entered in 1790, assisting **Horne Tooke**'s unsuccessful Westminster campaign against **Fox**.

In 1791 he joined the Southwark "Friends of the People" and in 1792 the **London Corresponding Society (LCS)**. Thelwall soon became, despite a speech impediment, the society's most effective and powerful speaker, his lectures attracting huge crowds to the radical perspective. He began delivering these almost nightly in late 1793, avowing himself not only an admirer of **Paine** and a proponent of equal political rights but "a Republican" and "the only avowed *sans culottes* in the metropolis." He addressed enormous multitudes—one, at Copenhagen Fields (October 1795), estimated at between 100,000 and 150,000 people; another (a month later) equally large: "If you obtain annual parliaments and universal suffrage it will be no longer in the power of a worthless set of beings to crimp, starve and murder you!"

Thelwall was arrested along with other members of the LCS on charges of high treason in May 1794. Though acquitted, his trial presented a severe test for his attorney, **Thomas Erskine**, because Thelwall's many radical speeches provided the prosecution much documented inflammatory evidence.

In addition to his numerous lectures and speeches on political reform, Thelwall also wrote a number of pamphlets, including *Tribune* (1795) and *Rights of Nature* (1796), which discussed the problems created by industrialization with a sophistication unusual in the 1790s. Thelwall was no socialist, but attacked what he called the unrestrained accumulation of land and capital, and argued that workers' associations and universal education held important keys to future improvement. He played a small role in radical agitation after 1815 with his paper *The Champion* and, though then in his late sixties, joined his old friend **Francis Place** to agitate for the **Reform Act** of 1832.

Frank M. Baglione

Bibliography

Cone, Carl B. *The English Jacobins: Reformers in Late 18th Century England.* 1968.

Dickinson, H.T. *British Radicalism and the French Revolution, 1789–1815.* 1985.

Mee, Jon. *Dangerous Enthusiasm: William Blake and the Culture of Radicalism in the 1790s.* 1992.

Philp, Mark, ed. *The French Revolution and British Popular Politics.* 1991.
Williams, Gwyn. *Artisans and San-Culottes.* 1969.

Theobald, Lewis (1688–1744)

Theobald was an author and Shakespearean scholar whose best efforts as a poet, dramatist, **translator**, and editor have been overshadowed by his feud with **Alexander Pope**. Theobald distinguished himself as an authority on Shakespeare when he published *Shakespeare Restored* (1726), in which he revealed the inadequacies of Pope's edition of 1725, and in return for which the poet made Theobald the butt of the first edition of *The Dunciad* (1728). Despite the lasting impression made by that **satirical** portrait, Theobald's own edition of Shakespeare (1734) continues to form part of the foundation for modern Shakespeare texts. He drew upon his extensive knowledge of Elizabethan drama and its literary contexts, and brought this to bear upon his editorial work. He is credited with being the first to apply the classical scholar's technique of parallel readings—the use of contemporary texts to explicate obscure words or passages—to the study of English literature.

Francis P. Wilson

Bibliography

Jones, R.F. *Lewis Theobald: His Contribution to English Scholarship, with Some Unpublished Letters.* 1919.
Seary, Peter. *Lewis Theobald and the Editing of Shakespeare.* 1990.
Sutherland, James, ed. *The Twickenham Edition of the Poems of Alexander Pope.* Vol. 5. 1963.

See also Literary Criticism; Shakespeare Industry

Theology

Theology in the Hanoverian period was marked by serious divisions in the **Church of England** and by fervent attacks by **freethinkers** on the Anglican establishment. In addition to continuing debate over the doctrine of grace, the primary disagreements within the Anglican communion during these years centered on the nature of the church and the Trinity.

The question of the visible church was argued publicly in the **Bangorian controversy** of 1717, when **Benjamin Hoadly**, Bishop of Bangor, contended that the true church needed no visible organization with distinctive markings, since Christ already knew his sincere servants and subjects. Orthodox Anglican churchmen charged him not only with disparaging the authority of the church but also with questioning the spiritual advantage that any institution of the Christian religion offered to believers. The divisions exposed in this controversy plagued Anglicanism throughout the 18th century. After 1740 the rising **Evangelicalism**, which stressed personal holiness and the religion of sentiment, attracted many who sympathized with Hoadly's emphasis on personal salvation at the expense of doctrinal orthodoxy and external adherence to ritual. Much later, during the 1830s, the Oxford movement, which valued the corporate holiness of the ancient and visible church with its sacramental life and liturgical worship, appealed to those who shared the orthodox position.

A second major doctrine at issue within the church was the Trinity. To those who believed that reason and religion were in harmony, the trinitarian doctrine, reaffirmed in the Thirty-nine Articles of Faith, proved difficult to accept since it appeared contrary to reason. Many opponents of the doctrine of the Trinity who held the **Latitudinarian** view that religious truths were "few and plain" eventually abandoned orthodoxy in favor of **deism**. The most serious challenge to the orthodox position from within the church was brought not on the grounds that the trinitarian doctrine was contrary to reason, but that the New Testament failed to support it, an argument elaborated in 1712 by **Samuel Clarke**, Rector of St. James, Piccadilly, and the foremost metaphysician of his day. Defending himself against charges of Arianism, Clarke claimed that there were no scriptural grounds for the various antitrinitarian positions either, insisting that this was a matter on which each believer might reach his own private conclusion. Opposition to the trinitarian doctrine continued throughout the century; it was vigorously debated in 1750 and again in 1772 when the Socinian **Joseph Priestley** and his friends, many of whom called themselves **Unitarians**, reawakened the controversy. By this time, Unitarian doctrine had spread to the old **dissenting** sects, especially to **Presbyterians**.

The disputes over basic doctrine between mainstream clergymen, who believed that the grounds of Christianity were rational, greatly strengthened the position of those who wanted to shelve those arguments in favor of church teachings derived from miracle, mystery, and authority: **William Law**, **George Berkeley**, **John Wesley**, and **Joseph Butler**, whose *Analogy of Religion* (1736) retained its influence well into the 19th century. Butler, while not abandoning reason, argued that obscurity in religion was not sufficient grounds for rejecting it, and that the investigation of nature revealed not the certainty, but the probability, of religious truth.

On the other hand, deists such as Anthony Collins (1676–1729), **Matthew Tindal**, and **John Toland**, inspired by **John Locke**'s *The Reasonableness of Christianity* (1695), argued that Christianity held no mysteries. Believing in an impersonal God who regulated the universe according to laws accessible to human reason, they denied the possibility of miracles as unnecessary violations of natural order. In *Christianity as Old as the Creation* (1730), Tindal dismissed the necessity of revelation altogether in favor of a natural religion engraved on the hearts of all men. The status of revelation was also threatened by continuing advances in historical **biblical criticism**, which challenged the divine inspiration of the Old and New Testaments, fortified the deist rejection of Christ's divinity, and contributed in the process to the controversy over the nature of atonement and the terms of salvation.

While deist arguments placed rationalist Christianity on the defensive, deism itself, as the arguments of **David Hume** made clear, was weakened by its failure to provide a firm basis for natural religion. In addition, the argument from design, which both deists and rationalist Christians embraced and which implied an orderly, rational universe governed by a benevolent deity, was always subject to question from the standpoint of the problem of evil. These controversies, which remained unresolved, seemed to show that no metaphysical or theological inquiry could produce rationally demonstrable truth.

At the turn of the 19th century **William Paley** revived the argument from design in two works that convinced no unbelievers, but proved reassuring to British Christians. In his *Natural Theology* (1802) he contended that man could know God and His goodness from nature in an immediate and direct manner. In the *Evidences of Christianity* (1794) he argued that this knowledge led indisputably to revelation. Despite Paley's success, however, a real religious revival within Anglicanism appeared only after 1833 with the sudden rise of the Oxford movement.

Susan E. Rosa

Bibliography

Booty, John, and Stephen W. Sykes, eds. *The Study of Anglicanism.* 1988.
Chadwick, Owen. *From Bossuet to Newman.* 1987.
Cunliffe, Christopher, ed. *Joseph Butler's Moral and Religious Thought: Tercentenary Essays.* 1992.
Davies, Horton. *Worship and Theology in England: From Watts and Wesley to Maurice, 1690–1850.* 1961.
Davies, R.E. *Methodism.* 1968.
Harrison, Peter. *"Religion" and the Religions in the English Enlightenment.* 1990.
LeMahieu, D.L. *The Mind of William Paley: A Philosopher and His Age.* 1976.
Miller, Peter N. *Defining the Good: Empire, Religion and Philosophy in Eighteenth-Century Britain.* 1994.
Pelikan, Jaroslav. *Christian Doctrine and Modern Culture.* 1989.
Stephen, Leslie. *History of English Thought in the Eighteenth Century.* 1881.
Stromberg, Roland N. *Religious Liberalism in Eighteenth-Century England.* 1954.

See also Enlightenment, The; Rational Dissent; Religious Revivalism; Roman Catholicism

Thistlewood, Arthur (1770–1820)

Thistlewood was an ultra-**radical** activist during the latter years of **George III**'s reign. Though it was rumored that he had taken part in the Despard conspiracy (Colonel Edward Despard was executed for treason in 1803, having been charged with conspiring to murder the king and overthrow the government in 1802), he is best known for his actions during the **Regency**.

Born the illegitimate son of a land agent, Thistlewood was influenced by the works of **Thomas Paine** and by **travel** in America and **France** during the Reign of Terror in the 1790s. On returning to England, he served in the militia in Yorkshire and Lincolnshire. Becoming active in the **Society of Spencean Philanthropists** (founded to promote the radical land-reform ideas of **Thomas Spence**), he was involved in the **Spa Fields riot** but was acquitted of any wrongdoing. In an attempt to recover his property seized by the government in connection with this event, Thistlewood carried on a bitter correspondence with Home Secretary **Lord Sidmouth**, and was eventually sentenced to a year's imprisonment for challenging the latter to a **duel**.

Departing from more moderate constitutional reformers such as **Henry ("Orator") Hunt**, he continued to plot the government's violent overthrow and headed up the **Cato Street conspiracy** to assassinate the cabinet. This was betrayed by a government agent; Thistlewood was arrested, convicted of treason, and executed, along with four other conspirators. The executions helped bring to a close the period of radical ferment surrounding the end of the **Napoleonic Wars** in 1815.

Mark C. Herman

Bibliography

Johnson, David. *Regency Revolution: The Case of Arthur Thistlewood.* 1974.
McCalman, Iain. *Radical Underwood: Prophets, Revolutionaries and Pornographers in London, 1795–1840.* 1988.
Parsinnen, T.M. "The Revolutionary Party in London, 1816–20." *Bulletin of the Institute of Historical Research.* Vol. 45, pp. 266–282.
Smith, Alan. "Arthur Thistlewood: A Regency Republican." *History Today.* Vol. 3, pp. 846–852.
Worrall, David. *Radical Culture: Discourse, Resistance and Surveillance, 1790–1820.* 1992.

Thompson, William (1775–1833)

Thompson, an Irish landowner, economist, and feminist, was the chief theorist of the cooperative movement, whose philosophy promoted the virtues of communal living. While influenced by the utilitarianism of **Bentham and the Benthamites**, concern with **poverty** and the distribution of wealth led him to the cooperative movement inspired by **Robert Owen**. His association with **Ricardo** led him to conclude that society's wealth was produced by the sweat of labor, not capital investment. Thompson's *Inquiry into the Principles of the Distribution of Wealth Most Conducive to Human Happiness* (1824) was the major work in cooperative political economy. His theme was that the natural laws of distribution maximized human happiness in mutually cooperative communities, where all people drew on the products of cooperative labor and voluntarily renounced personal property rights. Another work, his ringing *Appeal to One Half the Human Race, Women, against the Pretension of the Other Half, Men* (1825), written in collaboration with Anna Wheeler (1785–?), was a powerful statement in favor of **women's rights** and women's suffrage.

William Edward Morris

Bibliography

Pankhurst, Richard Keir Pethick. *William Thompson: Britain's Pioneer Socialist, Feminist and Co-operator.* 1954.
Thompson, N.W. *The People's Science: The Popular Political Economy of Exploitation and Crisis, 1816–1834.* 1984.

Wright, D.G. *Popular Radicalism: The Working-Class Experience, 1780–1880.* 1988.

See also Economic Thought; Malthus, Thomas Robert; Radicalism

Thomson, James (1700–1748)

Thomson was born in Ednam in Roxburghshire, the son of a **Presbyterian** minister. In 1715, after a boyhood spent in the Scottish border regions whose rugged natural beauty he would later celebrate in his **poetry**, he enrolled in the College of **Edinburgh** in preparation for a career in the ministry. Ten years later (1725) he withdrew and repaired to **London** to seek his fortune as a poet.

He succeeded almost immediately with the publication of a blank-verse poem of natural description, *Winter* (1726), followed by *Spring* (1727), *Summer* (1728), and the first collected *The Seasons* (1730), including *Autumn* and *A Hymn on the Seasons;* he spent much of the remainder of his career revising and expanding this poem. His other important works at this point included *A Poem Sacred to the Memory of Sir Isaac Newton* (1727) celebrating the new science, *Britannia* (1729), and a play, *Sophonisba* (1730).

In the early 1730s Thomson **traveled** through Europe as **tutor** to Charles Richard Talbot (1685–1737), later Lord Chancellor. His most political poem, *Liberty,* was the product of his observations (parts I, II and II, 1735; parts IV and V, 1736).

During the late 1730s and early 1740s Thomson revised *The Seasons* and wrote for the stage. His plays included *Agamemnon* (1738); *Edward and Eleonora* (1739); *Alfred* (1740), a coauthored masque for which he wrote the words to *Rule Britannia;* and *Tancred and Sigismunda* (1745). The year 1744 saw the publication of a revised and much-enlarged edition of *The Seasons.* Thomson's last important works were another tragedy, *Coriolanus* (completed by 1747), and a finely wrought neo-Spenserian poem, *The Castle of Indolence* (1748).

James Thomson

Thomson was among the first Scots writers to combine Scottish scenes and traditions with conventional English forms and language in post-**Union** Britain. In *The Seasons,* his most important poem, detailed natural description inspires reflection upon the problem of evil, scientific insight, political commentary, and literary **sublimity**; the poem constitutes an original literary form that was immensely popular in its day. Thomson was deeply engaged in contemporary politics, advancing dissident **Whig** ideology throughout his work, especially in *Liberty,* and the plays. His position at the intersection of the literary, theatrical, and political worlds from the 1720s to the 1740s makes him an important figure for study.

David R. Anderson

Bibliography

Adams, Percy G., introd. *The Plays of James Thomson.* 1979.
Campbell, Hilbert H. *James Thomson.* 1979.
Cohen, Ralph. *The Unfolding of* The Seasons. 1970.
Gerrard, Christine. *The Patriot Opposition to Walpole: Politics, Poetry, and National Myth, 1725–1742.* 1995.
McKillop, Alan Dugald. *The Background of Thomson's* Seasons. 1942.
Sambrook, James. *James Thomson 1700–1748: A Life.* 1991.
———, ed. *The Seasons.* 1981.
———, ed. *Liberty, the Castle of Indolence and Other Poems: James Thomson.* 1986.
Scott, Mary Jane W. *James Thomson, Anglo-Scot.* 1988.

See also Dramatic Arts

Thornhill, Sir James (1675?–1736)

Thornhill was the leading decorative **history painter** of his age. He was born in Dorset and apprenticed to Thomas Highmore (1660–1720), but also learned much from studying with and probably assisting Antonio Verrio (*c.* 1639–1707) and Louis Laguerre (1663–1721). He became a freeman of the Painter-Stainers Company (1704), and in 1720 became the king's serjeant painter and was knighted; he was the first native-born artist to receive this distinction.

After some early work as a painter of theatrical scenery, Thornhill also studied **architecture** and is probably best known today for his painted hall at the Greenwich Royal Naval College (1708–1727), his grisaille paintings of the life of St. Paul in the main dome of St. Paul's, **London** (1714–1719), and his ceiling of the hall at Blenheim Palace (1716). In these and other decorative projects, such as his work at Hanbury Hall (1710), Charborough Park (1718), and the chapel at Wimpole (1724), he depicted allegorical or religious figures in convincing architectural settings.

Thornhill's efforts in art education, both at **Kneller**'s painting academy and at his own **drawing** school, were fail-

Sir James Thornhill

ures. His daughter Jane married **William Hogarth** in 1729, who helped him with a group portrait of members of the **House of Commons**. Though his great accomplishments inspired Hogarth, the latter failed in his attempt to succeed Thornhill as a major history painter. Thornhill also served as M.P. for Weymouth (1722–1734).

Thomas J. McCormick

Bibliography

Allen, B. "Thornhill at Wimpole," *Apollo.* Vol. 122, pp. 204–211.

Croft-Murray, Edward. *Decorative Painting in England, 1537–1837.* 2 vols. 1962–1970.

Fremantle, Katherine, ed. *Sir James Thornhill's Sketchbook Travel Journal of 1711.* 2 vols. 1975.

Waterhouse, Ellis. *The Dictionary of British 18th Century Painters.* 1981.

Thornton, Henry (1760–1815)

Economist, banker, and philanthropist, Thornton was the most acute monetary economist of his period. Having left school at age 18, he first worked for a countinghouse firm, then joined a London **bank** (1784), where he remained until his retirement. He became a central figure of the **Clapham sect**, whose members insisted that public policy should have the same high moral purpose as private life.

Thornton attempted to embody this ideal as a banker, director of the **Bank of England**, and M.P. (from 1782). In Parliament he worked with his closest friend, **Wilberforce**, against the **slave trade**, helping to abolish it in 1807. But his *Enquiry into the Nature and Effects of the Paper Credit of Great Britain* (1802), which argued that inflation was not caused by the Bank of England's issuance of paper currency, was his greatest personal achievement. This brought a level of sophistication to monetary theory that was not surpassed until the end of the 19th century.

Enquiry systematized contemporary economic theory on the subjects of the velocity of monetary circulation, interest rates, prices and employment, and international economic relations. Thornton made three original contributions to monetary theory, all reflecting his deep experience in banking. First, he distinguished between monetary, or actual market, and real, or inflation-corrected, interest rates. Second, he differentiated the market rate (the rate at which funds may be borrowed) from the so-called natural rate (the expected rate of return) of interest. Third, he argued that inflation might increase output and employment through forced saving, even during periods of full employment.

William Edward Morris

Bibliography

Hylson-Smith, Kenneth. *Evangelicals in the Church of England.* 1988.

Meacham, Standish. *Henry Thornton of Clapham.* 1964.

Screpanti, Ernesto, and Stefano Zamagni. *An Outline of Economic Thought.* 1993.

See also Economic Thought

Tickell, Thomas (1685–1740)

The son of a Cumberland minister, educated at Oxford where he was honored as Professor of Poetry (1710–1711), Tickell gained **Joseph Addison**'s confidence, and government employment, on the strength of occasional **poetry** and **translations**. His poetry pleased the polite and offended few. *On the Prospect of Peace* (1712), for instance, ran counter to his fellow **Whigs**' prowar policy without alienating them. *An Epistle from a Lady in England to a Gentleman in Avignon* (1717) was a teasing pro–Hanoverian **satire** against the **Jacobites**. His most controversial work, a competent translation of *The Iliad,* Book I (1715), appeared 2 days after **Alexander Pope**'s version and is generally viewed as part of the paper war against the major poet.

Attributed to Tickell, five anonymous **essays** on **pastoral** poetry were printed in the *Guardian* (1713); they praised Ambrose Philips's (*c.* 1675–1749) *Pastorals* (1710) but ignored Pope's efforts. **Richard Steele** unwittingly printed Pope's ironic response in *Guardian* (No. 40, 1713).

Addison, as Secretary of State, made Tickell Under-Secretary (1717) and also the editor of his own *Works,* wherein appeared Tickell's great elegy, "To the Earl of Warwick on the Death of Mr. Addison" (1721). After becoming Secretary to the Lords Justices of **Ireland** (1724), Tickell published the long-popular **ballad** "Lucy and Colin" (1725). His polished poetry (first collected in 1749) earned him, in **Samuel Johnson**'s words, a "high place among the minor poets of his age."

James E. May

Bibliography

Dobrée, Bonamy. *English Literature in the Early Eighteenth Century, 1700–1740.* 1959.

Foxon, David F. *English Verse, 1700–1750.* 1975.
Johnson, Samuel. "Thomas Tickell," in *The Lives of the Poets.* 1779–1781.
Tickell, R.E. *Thomas Tickell and the Eighteenth-Century Poets.* 1931.
Tickell, Thomas. *The Works of the Most Celebrated Minor Poets.* Vol. 2. 1749.

Tindal, Matthew (1657–1733)

Tindal, one of England's most notable **freethinkers**, published works that became the focus of the **deist** controversy of the early 18th century. His early writings introduced the major themes of his most important work, *Christianity as Old as the Creation* (1730)—anticlerical, rationalistic, tolerant of all but atheists, and intent on proving that positive revelation is superfluous. This work, "the deist's bible," the fundamental 18th-century explanation and defense of natural religion and of the deity as the God of Reason, influenced Voltaire (1694–1778) and elicited more than 150 responses, including the important *Analogy of Religion* (1736) of Bishop **Joseph Butler**. Tindal maintained that because human nature was unalterable, man's reason had led him to a knowledge of God and hence of morality from time immemorial.

Barbara Jean Whitehead

Bibliography

Berman, David. "Censorship and the Displacement of Irreligion." *The Journal of the History of Philosophy.* Vol. 27, pp. 601–605.
Colie, Rosalie. "Spinoza and the Early English Deists." *Journal of the History of Ideas.* Vol. 5, pp. 23–46.
Torrey, Norman L. *Voltaire and the English Deists.* 1930.

See also Clarke, Samuel; Toland, John; Whiston, William

Tinplate Industry

Although Cornwall had an ancient tradition as a tin-mining center, it was unsuited to tin manufacture, and in medieval times the production and trade of tinplate were both virtually monopolized by Germans. But by a curious coincidence, the arrival of the German Hanoverian kings on the British throne (1714) also marked the rise of the British tinplate industry at the expense of the German.

The development of the rolling mill by the ironmaster and M.P. John Hanbury (1664–1734) at Pontypool in the 1690s, which ensured the production of high-quality ironplate, provided the foundation for the manufacture of tinplate in the early 18th century. Although the total market in England remained static to 1750, German products were pushed out: imports collapsed from over 2 million plates in 1710 to a mere 1,600 in 1750. Thereafter, production expanded steadily and Britain began to export tinplate. New works were established throughout the country, but mainly in the west and in south **Wales** in particular, with its abundant water supply and growing **iron** production. Britain became a center of cheap, technically advanced tinplate production. The 14 works in operation in 1805 produced 4,000 tons, of which 2,500 went for export. By 1837, some 9,000 tons went to domestic consumption while the virtual collapse of the industry on the Continent meant another 9,000 tons going to export. Britain had achieved world dominance in the field. The first half of the 19th century saw the erection of 32 new works—19 in south Wales alone—for which the export market was especially important. The industry continued to grow until the protectionist McKinley tariff (1890) closed its major export market in the United States.

R.D. Corrins

Bibliography

Minchinton, W.E. *The British Tinplate Industry: A History.* 1957.

See also Metallurgy and Metalworking

Tithes and Teinds

The history of tithes (teinds in **Scotland**) parallels that of the secularization of politics. Tithes, the tenth part of the natural gain or increase from the land, livestock, or trade and manufacture, were originally voluntary gifts to the church. Made compulsory well before the Norman Conquest, they were in effect taxes in support of the clergy, though after the Reformation they were treated like any other item of monastic property and so very frequently came into lay hands, something which caused mounting resentment. In Scotland, teinds were converted (1633) to a fixed rent charge calculated as a fifth of the rent of the land and payable either in cash or in meal, with provision for the commutation of this rent charge at 9-years' purchase.

By 1714 the payment of tithes had become immensely complex, generating a considerable body of case law, prompted not least by the introduction of new crops and animals such as potatoes, clover, and turkeys. By the 1770s, after a period of religious indifference and with the decline of other customary observances in the countryside, tithes were bitterly resented and widely viewed as a tax levied upon innovation. Tithes increased as the land brought under cultivation increased, though contemporary agricultural reports often declared them to be the single most serious obstacle to **agricultural improvement**; in many cases the tithe system was altered piecemeal by **enclosure** legislation. **Pitt the Younger** even considered (1799) legislation allowing landowners to redeem tithes, with the clergy thenceforth becoming state pensioners paid from the funds.

By 1815, with drastically declining grain prices driving farmers to attack tithes (and **taxes**) as excessive overheads on **agriculture**, these regressive imposts seemed increasingly intolerable. Assisted by the anticlerical **radicalism** of the 1820s (fed by such publications as **John Wade**'s *Black Book* [1819]) and by organized mass protests in **Ireland** in the early 1830s, where tithes were most bitterly resented because they were levied to support an alien church, the question was brought to a head and resolved by the **Whig** governments responsible for the Tithe Commutation Acts of 1836 (England and Scotland) and 1838 (Ireland), which at last made provision for the commutation of tithes into a regular rent charge and their eventual disappearance.

Michael Reed

Bibliography

Burn, R. *Ecclesiastical Law.* 2 vols. 1763.

Reed, M. *The Georgian Triumph, 1700–1830.* 1983.

Whyte, I. *Agriculture and Society in Seventeeth Century Scotland.* 1979.

Tobacco Trade

As tobacco use—snuff and chewed, not just smoked—rapidly spread in the 18th century, the tobacco trade greatly stimulated development of the west coast or Atlantic ports of **Bristol**, **Liverpool**, **Glasgow**, and Whitehaven. This trade benefited greatly from the **navigation acts**, tobacco being one of the commodities which could only be transported by British ships to British ports; the bulk of the trade was then re-exported to Europe. On the eve of the **War of American Independence**, tobacco accounted for fully 50% of American exports.

Initially the trade was conducted on behalf of large planters in Virginia and Maryland by **London** commission houses. However, merchants from west coast English ports began sending factors to America to trade directly with smaller planters. After the **Act of Union**, Glasgow merchants followed suit, their factors successfully challenging the supremacy of their English rivals. In 1738 they purchased only 10% of American tobacco, but by 1768 this had risen to over 50%.

Because the use of factors increased costs, merchants in the west-coast ports tended to belong to larger partnerships than the London commission houses. The rise of the west-coast ports was all the more surprising, given their initial lack of industrial hinterlands to supply goods for America. It was this, added to the need for labor in the plantations, that gave rise to increasing British involvement in the **slave trade**.

There were complaints over the level of indebtedness of American plantation owners. However, because of the fierce competition among factors, it was far easier for small planters to seek new loans than for the large plantation owners to break away from their indebtedness to London houses. The American **war** temporarily disrupted trade, but in the interim many merchants increased their contacts with the **West Indies**. After the war, Glasgow's merchants took an increasing share in directly supplying Europe's growing mania for American tobacco.

Patricia S. Collins

Bibliography

Davies, Ralph. *The Rise of the Atlantic Economies.* 1973.

Devine, T.M. *The Tobacco Lords.* 1975.

See also Commerce, Overseas; Glassford Family

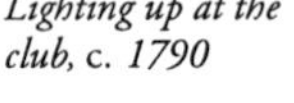

Lighting up at the club, c. *1790*

Toland, John (1670–1722)

Toland was a noted English **deist**, philosopher, diplomat, and political writer. Although some 30 to 100 pamphlets have been credited to him, his most famous work was one of his earliest: "Christianity Not Mysterious" (1696). Here he attempted to prove that reason, without the aid of divine revelation, was sufficient for the understanding of most biblical doctrines. The pamphlet provoked 50 replies and led to his prosecution in both England and **Ireland.** Even **John Locke,** whose *Reasonableness of Christianity* (1695) had influenced Toland, repudiated the man widely believed to be his disciple.

Toland's next controversy came with his *Life of John Milton* (1698), which contained a passage apparently questioning the authenticity of the New Testament. Toland defended his position in *Amyntor, or A Defence of Milton's Life* (1699), in which he included a catalogue of works long considered apocryphal by biblical scholars. Toland's pioneering **biblical criticism** and scholarly writings on religion provoked controversy and forced religious debate, and today remain classics of deist thought. He contributed much to the **free-thinking** tendencies of **Enlightened** belief in the Hanoverian period.

Barbara Jean Whitehead

Bibliography

Daniel, Stephen H. *John Toland, His Methods, Manners and Mind.* 1984.

Sullivan, Robert E. *John Toland and the Deist Controversy: A Study in Adaptations.* 1982.

See also Censorship; Theology; Whiston, William

Toleration, Religious

Although the **Church of England,** by the Act of Supremacy (1534), was the country's established church, several forces converged over the course of the Hanoverian era to promote more tolerant attitudes toward non–Anglican religious groups. These included primarily the Protestant **dissenters (Baptists, Congregationalists, Quakers, Presbyterians, Methodists,** and **Unitarians), Roman Catholics,** and **Jews.** Efforts to extend greater toleration to them resulted in passage of the **"Jew Bill,"** repeal of the **Test and Corporation Acts, Catholic emancipation,** and still broader atmospheric changes in the climate of religious toleration.

The theory underlying state-established churches held that for people to enjoy full citizenship, they had to support and protect the established religious creed—embedded, in England's case, in the Thirty-nine Articles of Faith (issued in 1563). Yet by 1714 the political reliability of certain non–Anglican sects was acknowledged. The **Toleration Act** recognized the legal status of dissenters by permitting them to engage in worship without persecution, and also helped Catholics by virtually eliminating the legal offense of recusancy (refusal to attend Anglican services). Despite this, both groups suffered political and social disabilities: they could not attend the English universities or hold public office, they had to pay for the support of the established church, they had to be married and buried according to its rites, and there were other sources of irritation and grievance. Catholics were further restricted by **penal laws** concerning property ownership and certain professions, and these were not abolished until 1778 and 1791 by **Catholic relief acts.**

One source of more tolerant 18th-century attitudes was the influential philosophy of **John Locke,** who emphasized reason as a principal source of all human knowledge. His *Reasonableness of Christianity* (1695) cleared the way for the rise of **deism**—the belief that humans could use their reason to penetrate natural law, discover moral truth, and improve society. Naturally the church condemned deists, but nonetheless from **John Toland** to **Thomas Paine** these unorthodox thinkers demanded greater toleration and found the general intellectual currents of the European **Enlightenment** working in their favor.

Meanwhile another development, **Latitudinarianism,** was tending toward the same end. Setting forth a **theology** based on reason as well as faith, "Latitudemen" within the church itself proposed a broader doctrine countenancing wider toleration. Dissenters also worked steadily, often with the support of **Whig** politicians (more tolerant than church and state **Tories,** and partially dependent also on the dissenters' growing wealth and prominence), to promote greater toleration and religious liberty. From 1732 a group of **Protestant dissenting deputies** struggled to remove many aspects of official discrimination and especially to repeal the Test and Corporation Acts—though annually from 1727 to 1828, parliamentary **indemnity acts** were passed that at least suspended the penalties for their violation. After 1760, dissenters became more aggressive in their demands. In 1772, moderate Anglican clergymen, in the Feathers Tavern petition, demanded relief for dissenters from subscription to the Thirty-nine Articles; but that project collapsed.

The **French Revolution** brought a temporary backlash against more tolerant attitudes. **Edmund Burke** and conservative clergymen helped incite the church and king riots of 1791 against dissenters, and **Irish rebellions** hardened feelings against Catholics. By the 1820s, however, national pride over the defeat of the French, the growing acceptance of **Evangelicalism,** the increasing respectability of non–Anglican industrial groups, the consistently tolerant attitude of the Whigs who had often supported progressive change, and the political consolidation with Catholic **Ireland** represented by the **Act of Union,** pointed toward the important victories of the latter 1820s, which gave full rights to dissenters and Catholics. Jews waited until 1858 for full political emancipation granted by the Jewish Relief Act.

Jack Fruchtman, Jr.

Bibliography

Endelman, Todd M. *The Jews of Georgian England, 1714–1830: Tradition and Change in a Liberal Society.* 1979.

Henriques, Ursula. *Religious Toleration in England, 1787–1833.* 1961.

Rivers, Isabel. *Reason, Grace, and Sentiment: A Study of the Language of Ethics in England, 1660–1780.* 1991.

Rupp, E. Gordon. *Religion in England, 1688–1791.* 1986.
Stromberg, Roland N. *Religious Liberalism in Eighteenth-Century England.* 1954.
Webb, R.K. "From Toleration to Religious Liberty," in J.R. Jones, ed., *Liberty Secured? Britain Before and After 1688.* 1992.

Toleration Act (1689)

The Toleration Act rewarded nonconformists for supporting the **Glorious Revolution** and granted rights of citizenship to those Protestant **dissenters** who accepted the doctrine of the Trinity, took the oaths of allegiance and supremacy, and subscribed to the declaration against transubstantiation. Dissenters could vote if they met the relevant property requirements; they could carry arms, and were free to worship on premises licensed by Anglican bishops. Their ministers could hold services if they subscribed to those of the Thirty-nine Articles that concerned doctrine, and they were allowed to set up schools and **dissenting academies** with their own instructors.

By 1688, dissenters had achieved significant political influence since the passage of the discriminatory Clarendon Code (1661–1665). But public opinion militated against granting them full equality. The act did not repeal any **penal laws**, though it did exempt dissenters from some of their penalties. Because the **Test and Corporation Acts** were not repealed, dissenters could not legally hold public office; they often qualified, however, by practicing **occasional conformity**. While the Toleration Act gave dissenters statutory security, its mere suspension of penalties was a far cry from the full right of religious toleration that dissenters maintained they should have.

William Edward Morris

Bibliography

Bradley, James E. *Religion, Revolution and English Radicalism: Nonconformity in Eighteenth Century Politics and Society.* 1990.
Clark, J.C.D. *The Language of Liberty, 1660–1832: Political Discourse and Social Dynamics in the Anglo-American World.* 1994.
Williams, E.N. *The Eighteenth-Century Constitution, 1688–1815: Documents and Commentary.* 1960.

See also Toleration, Religious

Tolpuddle Martyrs

The **Whig** government of 1830–1834, though responsible for the **Reform Act**, took a hard line against agitations by the poor and the working class. Indeed, when the Whigs first came to power in November 1830, **Lord Melbourne** as Home Secretary presided over stern repression of the **Swing riots** (1830). In 1834, concerned about the spread of **trade unions**—which had followed repeal of the **combination acts**—and alarmed at a wave of strikes in 1833 and the sudden growth of **Robert Owen**'s umbrella Grand National Consolidated Trades Union (founded earlier in 1834), Melbourne orchestrated the arrest of George Loveless and five other members of the Friendly Society of Agricultural Labourers (affiliated to the "Grand National") in Tolpuddle, Dorset. Convicted under the anticonspiracy legislation of the late 1790s for taking a union oath (which they did not know to be illegal), the men were sentenced to 7-years' **transportation** to Australia—a savage sentence, which Melbourne refused to alter. Two years later, public opinion compelled their release. Their exemplary conviction, however, had slowed enthusiasm for union mergers and served to redirect working-class energies toward the **factory movement**, against the **New Poor Law**, and in favor of a "People's Charter."

David B. Mock

Bibliography

Marlow, J. *The Tolpuddle Martyrs.* 1972.
Wright, D.C. *Popular Radicalism: The Working Class Experience, 1780–1880.* 1988.

See also Friendly Societies

Tone, Wolfe (1763–1798)

Tone, leader of the **United Irishmen**, was the son of a **Dublin** coachmaker. He was educated at **Trinity College**, then the Middle Temple, **London**, and was called to the bar in 1789. Inspired by the **French Revolution**, he wrote a pamphlet, "An Argument on Behalf of the Catholics of Ireland" (1791), very widely circulated, which attacked the constitutional reformism of the Protestant "Patriots" **Grattan** and **Flood** and expounded the novel idea that cooperation between Irish Protestants and Catholics was essential to fundamental Irish reforms. Later that same year he sought to implement this by helping to found the Society of United Irishmen in Belfast, its political program centering on universal suffrage and equal electoral districts.

Disappointed by the lack of government concessions to reformers, Tone soon came to adopt more radical and pro–French positions. He was forced to flee **Ireland** in 1794 after being compromised by contact with a French agent. After a brief sojourn in America he spent the following 3 years in Paris, where his diplomatic overtures to French leaders, accompanied by his exaggerated promises of Irish uprisings to accompany a French landing, resulted in a French military expedition to Ireland of some 43 ships and 14,000 men (December 1796); which, however, failed in a storm off the southwest Irish coast. After news of the **Irish rebellion** broke (May 1798), Tone persuaded the French to launch a second expedition in which he personally participated. This too failed, and Tone was captured and sentenced to death. He cheated the hangman by committing suicide (cutting his own throat) and died 8 days later (19 November 1798). Nonetheless, like **Robert Emmet** he became a powerful role model for later Irish nationalists, not least through the medium of his highly readable *Journals,* published after his death by his son, William Theobald Wolfe Tone (1791–1828), who became a soldier in the French armies under Napoleon.

E.W. McFarland

Bibliography

Curtin, Nancy J. *The United Irishmen: Popular Politics in Ulster and Dublin, 1791–1798.* 1994.

Dunne, T. *Wolfe Tone: Colonial Outsider.* 1984.

Elliot, M. *Wolfe Tone: Prophet of Irish Independence.* 1987.

McFarland, E.W. *Ireland and Scotland in the Age of Revolution: Planting the Green Bough.* 1994.

See also Patriots; Radicalism and Radical Politics

Tooke, John Horne (1736–1812)

Agitator and philologist, Tooke has been treated as the pattern English **radical** of the latter 18th century. A poulterer's son (he liked to cite his connections to a Merchant of Turkey), born John Horne (he later added Tooke to honor a friend and benefactor), he went to Westminster (where he lost an eye in a fight), graduated from Cambridge (1758), and in 1760 became an Anglican vicar at New Brentford in Middlesex, a few miles from **London**. Swept up in support of **John Wilkes** after 1763, he threw himself into Wilkes's turbulent and repeated bids for reelection as M.P. for Middlesex (1768–1769), acting as organizer and all-purpose propagandist against both Royal oppression and aristocratic machinations in Parliament. His excitement was a sign of the times. He now saw the whole political establishment as corrupt, and even Wilkes himself, petted by the **Whig** grandees, was not above suspicion.

John Horne Tooke

To further the central goal of radical parliamentary reform (the *restoration* of the supposed liberties of the pre–Norman era), Tooke, along with **Sawbridge** and a few others, founded the **Society for Supporters of the Bill of Rights** and the Constitutional Society (1771), and helped found the radically democratic **Society for Constitutional Information**. An ardent defender of the American colonists (whom he saw as oppressed kinsmen "faithful to the character of *Englishmen*"), Tooke was imprisoned for a year (1778)—apparently he was the only Englishman so punished for opposing the American war—for characterizing the events at Lexington and Concord in 1775 as the official murder of innocent subjects.

In the 1780s, Tooke, like many other radicals (including Wilkes), was a strong supporter of **Pitt the Younger**, whom he saw as a sincere reformer, against the **aristocratic** Whigs led by **Charles James Fox**, whose character and influence he detested. Tooke failed in his own electoral campaign against Fox for a Westminster parliamentary seat in 1790 and, after being acquitted of treason charges in 1794 (arising from governmental hysteria at **French Revolutionary** contagion), placed third in 1796 behind Fox and another candidate. He did gain a parliamentary seat in 1801 but soon thereafter retired to his home in Wimbledon.

Tooke was an Anglican churchman, not a **dissenter**, and strove to dissociate radicalism from "Paineism" during the 1790s. His radical ideas, always stressing the rights of Englishmen (as compared to those of an abstract "mankind"), were carried into the 19th century by old comrades such as **Major John Cartwright** and younger disciples like **Sir Francis Burdett** and **William Cobbett**. While favoring radical economic and political reform, Tooke also favored property qualifications for the franchise and thus stopped short of some radicals, particularly younger ones.

Tooke, known to some contemporaries as "The Grammarian," was also a noted philologist (Cartwright and **Thomas Spence** shared this interest), and is credited with being the first to encourage the study of the Anglo–Saxon and Gothic roots of the English language.

David B. Mock

Bibliography

Baylen, Joseph O., and Norbert J. Gossman, eds. *Biographical Dictionary of Modern British Radicals.* Vol. 1. 1979.

Newman, Gerald. *The Rise of English Nationalism: A Cultural History, 1740–1830.* 1987.

Yarborough, Minnie C. *John Horne Tooke.* 1926.

See also Chantrey, Sir Francis

Toplady, Augustus Montague (1740–1778)

Toplady, an enthusiastic **Church of England** clergyman and religious polemicist, is now best known as the author of several volumes of hymns and sacred poems. Rector of Blagdon in Somerset, and later of Broadhembury, he was an ardent opponent of **John Wesley** and **Methodism**, and published a number of books defending Calvinist doctrines. His works include *The Doctrine of Absolute Predestination Stated and Asserted* (1769), *The Church of England Vindicated from the Charge of Arminianism* (1769), *Historic Proof of the Doctrinal Calvinism of the Church of England* (1774), *Poems on Sacred Subjects* (1775), and *Psalms and Hymns* (1776). He is well remembered for his moving hymn "Rock of Ages."

Deidre Dawson

Bibliography
Green, V.H.H. *John Wesley.* 1964.

Tories and Toryism

The Tory party is one of the two historic political parties in English history. It originated, like its **Whig** counterpart, in the 1670s, nearly died out (unlike the Whigs) in the early 1760s, revived sometime around 1812, and, outlasting the Whigs of whom little is heard after 1886, is still going strong today. "Tory" was originally a nickname for an Irish bandit, a term of abuse meant to smear the party with a taint of **Roman Catholicism.** Like other nicknames at other times, it stuck and ultimately acquired the luster of age and service.

The political event most responsible for the birth of the Tory party was the exclusion crisis of 1679–1681, occasioned by the Whig desire to exclude James Stuart, Duke of York (later James II), a Roman Catholic convert, from the throne. The Tories, remembering the chaotic civil wars of the 1640s and 1650s, when a previous generation had rebelled against their king, favored no alteration in the line of succession. Paradoxically, because they were in fact the party most attached to the **Church of England**, charges of an excessive tolerance toward Catholicism were to haunt the Tories until their temporary demise around 1762.

The issue of the proper succession to the Crown also haunted them. Although Tories had been as prominent as Whigs in the **Glorious Revolution** (which dethroned James II) and in the **Act of Settlement** (which settled the succession to the throne on the German Protestant **Hanover** family), they sometimes acted as if they had guilty consciences over their part in these acts. There were indeed enough anti–Hanoverian plots by prominent Tories in the 18th century (one of their pet projects was to persuade the Stuart pretenders to adopt Anglicanism) to justify the suspicions that Hanoverian rulers **George I** and **George II** felt toward them. Between 1689 and 1714, under William III, Mary II, and **Queen Anne,** Tories had often aided or taken the lead in the formation of ministries, but after the Hanoverian accession their intercessions ceased.

The most influential Tory thinker and politician of the first part of the Hanoverian era was Henry St. John, **Viscount Bolingbroke.** The first two Georges proscribed him and his party from all offices of church and state: from the county militia; from bishoprics and major benefices in the church; from the cabinet; from **local government**; from **places, pensions,** and **patronage** in the gift of the Crown. From 1714 to 1760 the Tories, who had generally adopted Bolingbrokean or "Country" attitudes such as opposition to foreign **wars,** support for low **taxes,** and parliamentary reform, were still quite popular in shires and **boroughs** with large electorates. Always strong among the landed **gentry,** they continued to form a substantial part of any Parliament. Yet neither George I nor George II would grant them patronage. Talented and ambitious Tory politicians would thus tend to gravitate toward one of the Whig factions rather than remain members of a party that seemed to be going nowhere.

Whether the Tories were **Jacobites** (supporters of the exiled Catholic Stuarts) is a matter of historical debate. What is indisputable is that with the gradual decline of Jacobitism after the defeat of **Charles Edward, the Young Pretender** in the **Forty-five,** Toryism seemed to diminish as well.

When **George III** ascended the throne in 1760, one of his first acts was to end Tory proscription. If there was no Tory party operating under that name in British politics for the half century or so after 1762, that does not mean that Tory ideas had disappeared. George himself was accused of Toryism often by embittered Whig opponents, and during his long reign (1760–1820) there were always those in British factional groupings whose ideological proximity to the old Toryism caused their enemies to term them "Tory." These included **Lord Bute,** the "King's Friends," William Murray, **Earl of Mansfield,** the Northites (followers of **Lord North**), and the Pittites (followers of **William Pitt the Younger**). Such groups often exhibited a marked reverence for the Church of England; a high view of the monarchical prerogative; a complicated but sometimes markedly antagonistic attitude toward the **fashions, manners,** and pretensions of the great landed nobility; an enlarged view of the independence and reliability of the gentry; and a very limited tolerance for democratic stirrings among the masses.

In the latter 18th century the political opponents of the **American Revolution** and the **French Revolution** developed ideological views which seemed, to some observers, suspiciously close to Toryism. But only gradually, in the early 19th century, was the term "Tory" again used self-descriptively by the "Church-and-King" groupings that had recently enrolled in **Loyalist associations** and most vociferously opposed the French Revolution and also Irish and English **radicalism.** And even here, alongside "Tory reactionaries" like **Eldon, Sidmouth, Castlereagh, Liverpool,** and **Wellington,** the picture is complicated by the continued existence of undoubtedly radical Tories, "Tory Radicals" as they are called—the name has been applied to men such as **William Cobbett, William Oastler,** and **Michael Sadler,** among others—who identified strongly with the rural manners and folkways of pre-industrial times, and attempted to defend the lower orders against disenfranchisement and economic exploitation. And, contrarily, there was also emerging in the 1820s a strain of modernized and commercially progressive Toryism in such figures as **Canning, Huskisson,** and **Peel.** Toryism also benefited from the **Evangelical** religious revivalism at work, and the more conservative trend in **manners and morals.**

Right-wing attitudes, like left-wing ones, changed continually under the force of industrialization and with the needs of the day. After 1830, *Conservative* became widely used as a synonym for *Tory,* and the two words still retain some of their original associations, on the one hand with a rural elite's resistance to unwanted changes, on the other with the cautious stance of modern business interests. It was during the Victorian period, not the Hanoverian, that this socioeconomic transformation from a clearly distinguishable Toryism to a clearly distinguishable Conservatism occurred.

James J. Sack

Bibliography

Clark, J.C.D. *English Society, 1688–1832.* 1985.

Colley, Linda. *In Defiance of Oligarchy: The Tory Party, 1714–1760.* 1982.

O'Gorman, Frank. *The Emergence of the British Two-Party System.* 1982.

Sack, James J. *From Jacobite to Conservative.* 1993.

See also Government, National; Whigs and Whiggism

Torrens, Robert (1780–1864)

Torrens, Irish-born soldier and prolific economic writer, was the first to attribute the production of wealth to the joint action of the instruments of production: land, labor, and capital. He was an ally—and in some respects a disciple—of **David Ricardo** in the establishment of scientific political economy and, like Ricardo and **John Ramsay McCulloch**, was connected with **middle-class** reform activity in the early 19th century.

In 1796 Torrens joined the Royal Marines; he retired as a colonel 41 years later, having divided his time between fighting (he was wounded at Anholt in 1811), poring over **Adam Smith**, writing (he even produced two **novels**), and fraternizing with **Whig** and **radical** politicians. Elected to the **Royal Society**, he was a founding member of the Political Economy **Club** (1821). Sitting (not continuously) in the **House of Commons** between 1826 and 1835, he chaired the South Australian Colonization Commissioners in 1835; an Australian lake and a river are named in his honor.

Torrens's first economic writings, *The Economists Refuted* (1808) and *Essay on the External Corn Trade* (1815), were directed against the agricultural interest in the rising controversy over agricultural protection. The latter work first articulated both the law of diminishing returns and the principle of comparative advantage. Torrens's *Essay on the Production of Wealth* (1820) attempted to clarify and reconcile theoretical differences between **Malthus** and Ricardo. Like Ricardo he favored the gold standard and the **Bank of England**'s authority to issue paper money, but he differed from Ricardo on value theory and the question of the resumption of cash payments. Though he opposed agricultural protection, he later speculated (in the early 1840s) that free trade was not necessarily an economic panacea. Torrens is not considered one of the great economic thinkers but rather one of the many competent foot-soldiers and popularizers of the new science.

William Edward Morris

Bibliography

Langer, Gary F. *The Coming of Age of Political Economy, 1815–1825.* 1987.

Robbins, Lionel Charles. *Robert Torrens and the Evolution of Classical Economics.* 1958.

Screpanti, Ernesto, and Stefano Zamagni. *An Outline of the History of Economic Thought.* 1993.

See also Economic Thought

Townhouses

See Housebuilding and Housing

Townshend Family

The Townshend family of Raynham, Norfolk, was active in **Whig** politics throughout the Hanoverian period, but only two members figured prominently. Charles Townshend, 2nd Viscount Townshend (1674–1738), served as Secretary of State (1714–1717 and 1720–1730) and after retirement earned the nickname "Turnip" Townshend for his **agricultural improvements**. His grandson, Charles Townshend (1725–1767), while Chancellor of the Exchequer was responsible for the American Import Duties Act (1767) or "Townshend duties" so much resented by the colonists.

The 2nd Viscount married as his second wife **Sir Robert Walpole**'s favorite sister Dorothy, which created an additional bond between the two Norfolk neighbors. When Townshend was forced out of office (1717), Walpole followed. Townshend negotiated the Treaty of Hanover (1725) and additional alliances to maintain the Continental balance of power in Britain's favor, but the costs involved alarmed Walpole. Townshend was offended by Walpole's increasing engrossment of power, and resigned in 1730. He spent his last years promoting the use of turnips and alfalfa in crop rotations.

By 1820, 17 descendants of the 2nd Viscount bearing the Townshend name had sat in the **House of Commons**. Most had undistinguished careers, and a number held places at Court or served in the **army**. At the end of the 18th century, the Whig affiliation of the family splintered along with the party itself.

Charles Townshend and his brother George (1724–

Charles, 2nd Viscount Townshend

1807) were grandnephews of the Whig leaders the **Pelham** brothers but took up an independent course soon after they entered Commons (1747). George, an army officer, was a keen supporter of militia bills and amused his colleagues by drawing sketches of their political opponents. He is considered the first great English master of **caricature**.

Although Charles Townshend was a brilliant speaker in Commons, his political behavior was too erratic to engender trust. The most memorable example was his speech of 8 May 1767, purportedly made while he was drunk on champagne, in which he attacked the Chatham administration, of which he himself was a member. Afterward his enemies called him "Champagne Charlie." His import duties are often named as a cause of the **American Revolution**, and as an idea Townshend took up on the spur of the moment. In fact, Townshend had suggested plans to reorganize colonial government, a goal to be funded by his duties act, earlier, when he served on the Board of Trade (1749–1754).

P.J. Kulisheck

Bibliography

Black, Jeremy. "Fresh Light on the Fall of Townshend." *The Historical Journal.* Vol. 29, pp. 41–64.

Forster, Cornelius P. *The Uncontrolled Chancellor: Charles Townshend and His American Policy.* 1978.

Namier, Sir Lewis B., and John Brooke. *Charles Townshend.* 1964.

Rosenheim, James M. *The Townshends of Raynham.* 1989.

See also Aristocracy and Gentry; Whigs and Whiggism

Toys and Games

In Europe before the 18th century there was a vague tendency to look upon children as miniature adults, creatures of sin whose souls needed saving. During the Hanoverian period, however, children were increasingly viewed as immature beings whose feelings needed to be understood and whose concerns and interests needed to be cared for and attended to.

Children's books, designed to amuse as well as educate, became very popular. Similarly, instructive board games and card games, enticing to the eye to attract adult buyers, became standard features of **middle-class** households. Self-improvement and self-education were themes connected with many children's amusements. John Spilsbury's jigsaw puzzles, Locke "blocks," and other "improving" toys were widely enjoyed, along with such well-loved games as marbles, battledore, and shuttlecock.

The traditional hoops, hobbyhorses, whips, and tops were supplemented by two other, newer toys: hobbyhorses on wheels, and dollhouses (miniature houses). Puppets and dolls were usually made of either cloth or paper. Cloth dolls with changeable clothing began to be mass-produced toward the end of the 18th century, but seemingly more popular still were

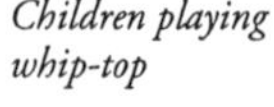

Children playing whip-top

the paper and cardboard dolls and puppets that were housed in the elegant dollhouses. These houses in miniature were created as much for well-heeled adults as children; many were designed by architects mirroring the styles of the time. **Robert Adam**, **Thomas Sheraton**, and **Thomas Chippendale** were all at one time involved in the making of such toys. Obviously these were too expensive for the children of the poor, and so were many toys imported from Germany, **France**, and Switzerland. But cheap mechanical toys (often military or musical in character) were produced in Europe from the late 18th century on, and slowly found their way into increasing numbers of British homes.

While dollhouses were the playthings of the wealthy, the games played by children of all social classes were still the informal, spontaneous, and traditional activities passed on from generation to generation—climbing, hunting, hiding, daring, swimming, cruelty to animals, and, of course, ball games. Football, cricket, rounders, bat and trap, and handball were all popular. A 1765 manuscript, *Nugae Etonenses,* includes the following list as some of the games played by boys at Eton: cricket, fives, football, battledores, pegtop, goals, hoops, marbles, trap ball, and hunt the hare. For most children, games such as these would have been played in the locales of everyday life, such as streets and churchyards. Indeed, the transformation of games such as cricket and football into highly organized sports by the mid–Victorian period was partly aided by the fact that churches were increasingly reluctant to permit their property to be used for games such as fives and football. Other venues had to be found, and for the Victorians these ranged from the **public house** to the country house, and from the public park to the public school.

Timothy J.L. Chandler

Bibliography

Cust, Lionel. *A History of Eton College.* 1899.
Fraser, Lady Antonia. *A History of Toys.* 1967.
King, Constance. *The Encyclopedia of Toys.* 1978.
Malcolmson, Robert. *Popular Recreations in English Society, 1700–1850.* 1981.
Plumb, J.H. "The New World of Children in Eighteenth Century England." *Past and Present.* Vol. 67, pp. 64–95.
Thompson, F.M.L., ed. *The Cambridge Social History of Britain, 1750–1950.* 3 vols. 1990.

See also Amusements and Recreation; Child Labor; Child-Rearing; Children's Literature; Gambling; Sport

Tracts

Tracts, generally speaking, were short pamphlets with limited purposes, usually connected with a current controversy. They developed in the 17th century and figured importantly during the era of the Puritan Commonwealth. In Hanoverian Britain an increasing number of political tracts were written, reflecting the gradual enlargement of public debate to include matters of political reform, colonial policy, trade, **tariffs**, the money supply, and so on. Some of **Samuel Johnson**'s best-known political statements, in *The False Alarm* (1770), *Thoughts on the Late Transactions Respecting Falkland's Islands* (1771), *The Patriot* (1774), and *Taxation No Tyranny* (1775), first appeared in the pamphlet war that preceded the **American Revolution**. Other such flurries of publication occurred in response to the **French Revolution** in the 1790s, the trade depression of the later **Napoleonic Wars**, and the growth of economic controversy following passage of the **Corn Law** of 1815.

Tracts were more important, however, for their role in religious life because they provided information and argument in easily digestible form for millions of people. **John Wesley** as early as 1745 was handing out thousands of tracts to ordinary folk. In 1782 he formed a **Methodist** tract society for the distribution of tracts among the poor; he wrote more than 30 of them himself, presenting his interpretations of Scripture and Christian morality. Other tract societies emerged alongside the development of **Evangelicalism** and **missionary societies** during the period 1790–1815; they disseminated brief, popularly written pamphlets on questions of personal life, attempting to counteract ideas and principles considered dangerous to religion and the social order. The most successful author of such tracts was **Hannah More**. Her "Cheap Repository Tracts," begun in 1795, contained stories, poems, prayers, and other "wholesome fare" extolling the virtues of sobriety, **patriotism**, and trust in God and the British Constitution; the tracts, sold in bulk and handed out free, were circulated by the millions in the late 1790s in response to the dangers apprehended from the French Revolution. As time went on, the subjects treated in tracts began broadening to include such things as the need for **Sunday schools**, encouragement of education, and strictures against rack-renting.

Philanthropic and **humanitarian** projects such as the struggle against the **slave trade** furnished common ground for members of the **Church of England** and **dissenters**, and interdenominationally produced tracts registered this convergence. An important step occurred when George Burder (1752–1832), minister of the Independent Chapel, Fetter Lane, London, and author of *A Collection of Village Sermons* (1799–1812) and a tract titled "Evangelical Truth Defended" (1788), enlisted others to form the Religious Tract Society (1799). This very successful organization published and distributed tracts by dissenters as well as Anglicans; by 1900, its publications could be read in 200 languages, for after 1814 it extended itself far beyond the British Isles. The British and Foreign Bible Society (1804) joined it in external operations. Other major publishers and distributors of religious tracts included the **Society for Promoting Christian Knowledge**, which also provided Christian literature for the home and mission fields, and the Tract and Colportage Society of **Scotland** (founded in 1793), the oldest Bible, tract, and colportage agency in Britain.

The Hanoverian period closed with the Tractarian movement, known also as the Oxford movement, which put an intellectually distinguished end to the great age of religious tracts. High Churchmen at **Oxford University**, buffeted for more than a century by **Latitudinarian** toleration, **Whig**

Erastianism, **Enlightenment** rationalism, and at last the new **enthusiasm** of the **religious revival**, produced 90 famous tracts between 1833 and 1841, attacking their enemies and refining such key points of High-Church doctrine as the value of prayer, liturgy, and good works, and the continuity of the **Catholic** tradition of the Anglican church. The movement halted abruptly when John Henry Newman (1801–1890) published Tract XC (1841), interpreting the Thirty-nine Articles in such a way as to blur distinctions between Anglican and Catholic doctrines.

Samuel J. Rogal

Bibliography

Canton, William. *A History of the British and Foreign Bible Society.* 5 vols. 1904–1910.

Green, S.G. *The Story of the Religious Tract Society for One Hundred Years.* 1899.

Howsam, Leslie. *Cheap Bibles: Nineteenth-Century Publishing and the British and Foreign Bible Society.* 1991.

Latourette, Kenneth Scott. *Christianity in a Revolutionary Age.* 1958.

Lovett, Richard. *The History of the London Missionary Society, 1795–1805.* 1899.

See also Publishers and Booksellers; Sermons

Trade

See Commerce, Domestic; Commerce, Overseas

Trade Unions

See Labor Laws, Movements, and Unions

Trafalgar, Battle of (1805)

This was the decisive naval battle of the **French Revolutionary and Napoleonic Wars**. In early 1805 Napoleon ordered a concentration of French and Spanish fleets for the purpose of escorting an invasion force across the Channel to conquer Britain. To this end the French Admiral Pierre Villeneuve (1763–1806), commanding naval forces at Toulon, during bad weather broke out of the Mediterranean despite a blockade maintained by the English naval hero Vice-Admiral Viscount **Horatio Nelson**, commanding the British Mediterranean station. Nelson pursued Villeneuve to the **West Indies** and back to Cadiz, not far from the British base at Gibraltar, where he reestablished his blockade.

Napoleon, suspending his invasion plans, ordered Villeneuve in late September to slip out and make for Naples to assist French operations there. For his part, Nelson, by maintaining his ships of the line at a discreet distance and relying on frigates to patrol the harbor entrance, hoped to lure Villeneuve into a decisive engagement. Fearing that he would soon be relieved of command, Villeneuve put to sea (19 October) with 33 ships. Nelson formed his 27 ships into two columns (led by himself in his flagship H.M.S. *Victory* and Admiral Cuthbert Collingwood in H.M.S. *Royal Sovereign*) and bore down on the enemy line near Cape Trafalgar as it was hurriedly attempting to retrace its steps back toward Cadiz (21 October).

The death of Nelson, from a painting by J.M.W. Turner

Collingwood's column formed a line on a course perpendicular to the enemy's single-file line of battle. The tactic (carefully planned by Nelson), which contravened the older strategy of fighting line against line, called for breaking through the enemy's line at several points, with each attacking vessel then swinging around and engaging ship on ship. By breaking through the line in the center and rear, Nelson also hoped to destroy a portion of Villeneuve's fleet before its leading ships could reverse course and rejoin the general action.

Collingwood made for the fifteenth ship from the rear and Nelson for the tenth from the head of the column, which proved to be Villeneuve's flagship, *Bucentaure.* Light winds prevented many ships from coming into formation. Undaunted, Nelson ordered a breakthrough of the enemy line at any practical point and engagement, confidently relying on superior British gunnery, initiative, and ship-handling. Although the enemy van slowly came about and joined the action, its efforts proved unimportant.

Early in the engagement a musket ball struck Nelson in the chest; he died shortly before the action ceased. But after the 5-hour battle the enemy had lost nearly 20 ships whereas the British had lost none, and Villeneuve himself was a prisoner. The battle decisively ended French fleet operations and invasion threats for the remainder of the wartime period, and is generally credited with marking a new century of British naval supremacy.

Stanley D.M. Carpenter

Bibliography

Creswell, John. *British Admirals of the Eighteenth Century: Tactics in Battle.* 1972.

Howarth, D. *Trafalgar: The Nelson Touch.* 1969.

Marcus, Geoffrey J. *A Naval History of England: The Age of Nelson.* 1971.

Nicholas, N.H. *The Despatches and Letters of Vice-Admiral Lord Viscount Nelson.* 1846.

Schom, Alan. *Trafalgar: Countdown to Battle, 1803–1805.* 1992.

Warner, O. *The Life and Letters of Vice-Admiral Lord Collingwood.* 1968.

See also Navy; War and Military Engagements

Translation

Translation in the Hanoverian period was distinguished by a remarkable stylistic refinement that assimilated foreign texts to domestic literary canons, but concealed that domestication beneath an illusory effect of transparency—the appearance that the translation was not in fact a translation, but the "original" text. Translators from archaic as well as modern languages aimed for fluent renderings that made the foreign text immediately intelligible while inscribing it with British cultural values.

Alexander Pope's multivolume *Iliad* (1715–1720) and *Odyssey* (1725–1726) consolidated the fluent translation method pioneered by Sir John Denham (1615–1669) and John Dryden (1631–1700), and set the standard for verse translations of classical **poetry**: elegant diction in heroic couplets, executed with great metrical facility. Pope, adhering to current usage, maintained continuous syntax and, fixing precise meanings, producing a translation that read easily and did not call attention to itself as a translation. He not only rendered Homeric hexameters in the dominant verse form in English poetry, but removed passages from the Greek text that contained coarse physical references offensive to an English sense of **moral** propriety.

The enormous success of Pope's Homer, a venture in subscription **publishing** that made him a fortune, shows how well he read his audience. It became fashionable to subscribe years before publication, and the subscribers were both **aristocrats** and **merchants**, landowners and lawyers, **Tories** and **Whigs**. A translating methodology evolved that crossed class and party lines, creating a distinctive critical lexicon that was shared among the **periodicals** even when they were politically at odds with each other. Reviewers, devoting their attention more to style than accuracy, habitually described acceptable translations as "clear," "elegant," "natural," "perspicuous," "smooth," and "unconstrained."

Fluent translating, always stamping its texts with British values, could have amusing results. William Guthrie (*c.* 1708–1770), a reporter of parliamentary debates for the *Gentleman's Magazine,* wrote a version of *The Orations of Marcus Tullius Cicero* (1741) in which Cicero was cast as a Member of Parliament. George Campbell (1719–1796) wanted his version of *The Four Gospels* (1789) to be fluent because he believed that a translation lacking in "simplicity, propriety, and perspicuity" was unchristian, "the superstition, not of the Church, but of the synagogue." **Sir William Jones**, president of the Asiatic Society and an administrator of the **East India Company**, translated the *Institutes of Hindu Law* (1799) to increase the effectiveness of British colonialism, rendering the "Hindus" as unreliable interpreters of their own culture.

Fluent domestication had thus already become the canonical translation method by the end of the 18th century, when it was first systematically formulated in Alexander Tytler's (1747–1813) weighty *Essay on the Principles of Translation* (1791, 1797, 1813). Tytler, a Scottish philosopher, advocated translation that possessed the "ease of original composition" because he found this consistent with **Enlightenment** humanism, the assumption of an essential human nature characterized by universal reason. He praised **Arthur Murphy**'s version of Tacitus (1793) precisely because Murphy's elegantly turned sentences smoothed out the elliptical brevity of the Latin text, and he urged the translator to "prevent that ease from degenerating into licentiousness" by refusing to render classical literature into popular discourses and dialects, "the style of the Evening Post" or "the low cant of the streets."

Essentially the same values operated in John Hookham Frere (1769–1846), a translator of Aristophanes, when he unfavorably reviewed Thomas Mitchell's (1783–1845) versions of *The Acharnians* and *The Knights* (1820); these were filled with Elizabethan archaisms, whereas "the language of translation ought to be a pure, impalpable and invisible element." A translator achieved invisibility not merely by limiting his lexicon to the standard dialect of contemporary English, but by expurgating the grotesque realism of Aristophanic humor, "lines of extreme grossness which have evidently been inserted, for the purpose of pacifying the vulgar part of the audience." Frere's prudish modification of translation theory reflected the growing moral conservatism of the early 19th century and was an apt parallel to the expurgations of **Thomas Bowdler**'s *Family Shakespeare* (1818).

During all this time, alternative theories and practices did in fact exist, even if they were harshly criticized. These alternatives generally aimed to signify, not to elide, the linguistic and cultural differences of the foreign text by experimenting with translation discourses and by choosing to translate literature that was marginalized by dominant domestic values. **William Cowper**'s Homer (1791) was unsuccessful because it was not fluent, written in a Miltonic blank verse with syntactical inversions designed to imitate the Greek text. Dr. John Nott (1751–1825) reformed the canon of foreign literature in English by developing translation projects that focused on the love lyric instead of **epic** or **satire**, the most widely translated genres. He produced versions of Johannes Secundus Nicolaius (1775), Petrarch (1777), Hafiz (1787), Bonefonius (1797), and the first book-length collections of Propertius (1782) and Catullus (1795). Nott rejected the "fastidious regard to delicacy" that might have required him to delete the explicit sexual references in Catullus's poems, because he felt that "history should not be falsified." His translation provoked a moral panic among reviewers who renewed the attack decades later, when expressing their preference for George Lamb's (1784–1834) bowdlerized Catullus (1821).

Thus the canons of Hanoverian translation were fundamentally domesticating, consistent with the cultural values of the elite. Educated people were aware that translation revised the foreign text, but such revision was usually considered necessary, a correction of sense, form, or taste. As **Samuel Johnson** explained in his *Life of Pope* (1779), Pope translated Homer "for his own age and his own nation, [and therefore] he knew that it was necessary to colour the images and point the sentiments of his author." For British translators, a gain in domestic intelligibility and cultural force outweighed any loss suffered by the foreign text.

Lawrence Venuti

Bibliography

Bowers, Fredson, ed. *New Cambridge Bibliography of English Literature.* Vol. 2. 1940.

Foxon, David. *Pope and the Early Eighteenth-Century Book Trade.* 1991.

Hodgart, Matthew. "The Subscription List for Pope's *Iliad,* 1715," in Robert B. White, Jr., ed., *The Dress of Words.* 1978.

Niranjana, Tejaswini. *Siting Translation: History, Poststructuralism, and the Colonial Context.* 1992.

Shankman, Steven. *Pope's* Iliad*: Homer in the Age of Passion.* 1983.

Steiner, T.R., ed. *English Translation Theory, 1650–1800.* 1975.

Tytler, Alexander Fraser, Lord Woodhouselee. *Essay on the Principles of Translation.* 2nd ed., 1797; rpt. 1970.

Venuti, Lawrence. *The Translator's Invisibility: A History of Translation.* 1995.

Williams, Carolyn A. *Pope, Homer, and Manliness: Some Aspects of Eighteenth-Century Classical Learning.* 1992.

Wilson, Penelope. "Classical Poetry and the Eighteenth-Century Reader," in Isabel Rivers, ed., *Books and Their Readers in Eighteenth-Century England.* 1982.

See also Classicism

Transport, Inland

The development of inland transport during the Hanoverian era was of great importance in assisting the expansion of **commerce**, the development of **agriculture**, and the onset of the **Industrial Revolution**. In the early 18th century the poor state of British **roads** led to the growth of **turnpike** trusts, often financed by local business and agricultural interests, and given powers to levy tolls on road users. As a result, road improvements could be carried out and new highways constructed. Traffic increased significantly over the Hanoverian period; by its end (1837) there were some 22,000 miles of turnpikes in England and **Wales**.

Turnpikes were also a feature of road development in Lowland **Scotland**, but in the Highlands, following the **Jacobite** rebellions of 1715 and 1745, the government funded military road building for security purposes. Likewise, in the early 19th century it funded the road to Holyhead in North Wales, to ease communication with **Ireland**.

Most goods transported by road were low bulk and high value because the cost of road transport remained relatively high. Despite this, however, a national network of carrying services developed during the 18th century, and, where roads were unsuitable for carts, pack horses were used. Improved roads also benefited passenger transport and **postal services**, both very useful to commerce, and the late 18th and early 19th centuries witnessed the great era of the **coaching** trade.

In the early years of the 18th century, river improvement schemes greatly assisted the carrying of **coal** and of agricultural produce—commodities extremely costly to move by road. This surge of investment faltered after the collapse of the **South Sea Bubble** in 1720, but not before many important agricultural and potential industrial areas of northern and central England had been opened to traffic. In agriculture this made possible the export of grain in the first half of the century. Profits from this added to the wealth of the nation and later helped to stimulate economic growth.

From the 1760s, **canal** building gave transport development further momentum. In 1761 the opening of the **Bridgewater** Canal from mines at Worsely to nearby **Manchester** reduced transport costs to such an extent that the price of coal in the city was halved. During the following 30 years a network of canals was constructed, often linking existing river navigations (as did the Trent and Mersey Canal), ensuring that the northwest of England and South Yorkshire were connected to the Midlands and **London**. In Scotland, the

"Their Wedding Journey"

Forth and Clyde Canal linked the east and west coasts. Canals were financed through **joint-stock companies** by interest groups such as industrialists, **merchants**, and landowners who stood to benefit by lower transport costs, and by others who simply saw them as a good investment. Coal mine owners, agricultural producers, and industrialists all made extensive use of the canals, leading to lower costs and prices, again providing a stimulus to further economic growth. Canals also carried passengers who often found such journeys cheaper and more comfortable than those by coach.

Wooden **railways**, originally constructed to link coal mines with river staithes and canal banks, also began to grow in importance as the Hanoverian era progressed. Developments in **iron technology** meant that wooden rails could be replaced by metal, and that larger wagons could be used. Ultimately, experiments in the use of steam power led to its replacing horse traction; and with the opening of the **Liverpool and Manchester Railway** in 1830, Britain was on the brink of an entirely new era in internal transportation.

A.J.G. Cummings

Bibliography

Aldcroft, Derek H., and Michael J. Freeman. *Transport in the Industrial Revolution.* 1983.

Bagwell, Philip S. *The Transport Revolution from 1770.* 1974.

Dyos, H.J., and D.H. Aldcroft. *British Transport.* 1974.

Hadfield, Charles. *British Canals.* 1969.

Pawson, E. *Transport and Economy: The Turnpike Roads of Eighteenth Century Britain.* 1977.

See also Coastal Shipping; Science, Technology, and Invention; Steam Engines

Transportation, Penal

Although banishment or transportation of criminals overseas began in England as early as 1597, it was with passage of the Transportation Act of 1718 that this became a systematic policy of **punishment**. By this, offenders could be sent to the American colonies for sentences of 7 years, 14 years, or even life. Over the next half century, 16 other acts were passed, authorizing transportation for a wide range of **crimes**. Between 1718 and 1775 an estimated 50,000 English, Irish, and Scottish convicts were sent to the **West Indies** or one of the **North American** colonies (chiefly Maryland and Virginia).

Transportation to America ended when the **War of American Independence** began. After a decade or so it was reinstituted, **Australia** becoming the main recipient. Between 1788, when the first convicts landed in Botany Bay, and 1868, when the practice was abolished completely, over 150,000 convicts were sent to New South Wales and Van Diemen's Land (Tasmania).

Penal conditions in the colonies varied, depending on the masters to whom convicts were assigned. In the Chesapeake colonies where most convicts ended up during the 18th century, typically doing manual labor in the fields, they usually suffered terrible conditions that differed little from those endured by African **slaves**. Parliamentary investigations in 1837–1838 revealed that convicts sent to Australia fared little better.

The Hanoverian period saw a spectacular expansion in the number of crimes punishable by death. The growing use of penal transportation reflected the dilemma of a society which sought to contain a perceived increase in serious crimes without resorting excessively to the death penalty. The demise of transportation was due primarily to the growing acceptance of long-term imprisonment in British **prisons** after the 1830s.

Stanley D. Nash

Bibliography

Ekirch, A. Roger. *Bound for America: The Transportation of British Convicts to the Colonies, 1718–1775.* 1987.

Robson, Lloyd L. *The Convict Settlers of Australia: An Enquiry into the Origins and Character of the Convicts Transported to New South Wales and Van Diemen's Land, 1787–1852.* 1965.

Shaw, A.G.L. *Convicts and the Colonies: A Study of Penal Transportation from Great Britain and Ireland to Australia and Other Parts of the British Empire.* 1977.

Travel and Tourism

The 18th century witnessed a substantial increase in the number of British men and women traveling, abroad and at home, for pleasure and for other reasons. British domestic travel and tourism boomed. As **roads** were improved, not least by the **turnpike** trusts, journey times shortened dramatically and became more predictable. More frequent **coach** services appeared on major routes, and facilities such as coaching inns spread. Maps and other information for domestic travel appeared in greater quantities, registering the trend. The great stress on health and sociability ensured the triumph of the **spa**. Numerous watering places were founded or expanded in the 18th century, mostly inland, although toward the end of the century **seaside resorts** developed under Royal **patronage**, Weymouth benefiting from the visits of **George III** as Brighton was to benefit from the residence of the Prince Regent. In addition, the development of the leisure facilities of many **provincial towns** made them attractive places to visit.

Domestic tourism, however, was neither unlimited nor without its problems. **Scotland**, **Ireland**, and **Wales** received relatively few tourists and played a smaller role in tourism than leading spas such as **Bath**, Buxton, and Tunbridge Wells. The attitude of royalty was indicative. In the 18th century no monarch visited Scotland, Ireland, Wales, the north of England, or even much of the Midlands. Tourists who did so were struck by the lack of facilities. Domestic tourism increased in popularity with the cult of "natural" **landscape** in the **Romantic** period and the difficulty of Continental travel during wartime (especially 1793–1815), but visiting literary shrines, country houses, and picturesque ruins had not been uncommon earlier.

An increase in tourism was general across much of Europe, and from around 1750 on, much larger numbers of British as well as of French, Germans, Poles, and Russians traveled for pleasure. The famous "Grand Tour" (which included, at a minimum, **France**, Switzerland, and northern Italy) was, however, dominated by British tourists, and the fact of tourism by other nationalities rarely played a part in British debates over tourism—often marked by moralizing over the contaminating influences of foreign (especially French) manners.

But tourism was more varied than is sometimes suggested by the idea of the Grand Tour with its implications of young milords haunting Paris and trotting through Italian **antiquities and ruins**. In fact, British tourists were individuals seeking different objectives and following different routes. The young man keen on a future military career who attended Prussian maneuvers in Silesia, or his counterpart who studied Alpine glaciers, had differing priorities and itineraries from those who chased dancers in Paris or admired paintings in the Uffizi. Of course there was a certain cachet to traveling abroad, and those who traveled farthest often advertised the fact in one way or another, as by ordering pasta in their London **clubs** to display their fondness for Neapolitan cuisine (hence the 1770s nickname "Macaroni" for an ostentatious fop).

Tourists included many of the most intelligent and perceptive people in Britain, and many wrote informed accounts of what interested them: agricultural methods, **opera**, court society, religious ceremonies, and so on. Their accounts were often laced with British national prejudices, but this did not wholly spoil their value. Having a large number of the men of the upper orders abroad during their formative years added much to the general cultural level and carried other useful consequences, not the least of which was travel's service in compensating for the very great contemporary deficiencies of British university education.

It is true that actual exposure to foreign influences was lessened by the employment of traveling **tutors** (the majority of whom were British), the preference for the company of other British tourists, the habit of attending educational establishments patronized by compatriots, and the propensity to cluster in the vicinity of resident British diplomats. Nevertheless, a large number of tourists met and conversed with foreigners as social equals, attended ceremonies (**Catholic** masses, for example), and experienced entertainments (Italian operas, for example) which helped to broaden them. The British upper orders became more aware than ever before of the past and current achievements of Continental society and, until 1789 at least, looked upon themselves as fellow carriers of an **Enlightened** and aristocratic European culture.

Jeremy Black

Bibliography

Andrews, M. *The Search for the Picturesque: Landscape Aesthetics and Tourism in Britain, 1760–1800.* 1989.

Black, Jeremy. *The British Abroad: The Grand Tour in the Eighteenth Century.* 1992.

Newman, Gerald. *The Rise of English Nationalism: A Cultural History, 1740–1830.* 1987.

Ousby, I. *The Englishman's England: Taste, Travel and the Rise of Tourism.* 1990.
Stoye, John. *English Travellers Abroad, 1604–1667.* 1989.

See also Travel Books and Literature

Travel Books and Literature

The expansion of tourism in Hanoverian Britain was part of a more widespread consumerism acting throughout both the social elite and the **middle classes**. There were many aspects to this. There was an increase in the consumption of necessaries, such as foodstuffs, but more obviously of nonessentials such as luxury furniture, souvenirs, and imported art. An information revolution was another aspect of this development, bringing a massive growth in the production of books, **newspapers**, and other printed material.

Authors and **publishers** produced travel literature because they knew there was a market for it among those with the money to buy and the leisure to read it. In fact, travel accounts were an important enhancement of the travel experience as well as a stimulant to the growth of travel itself, as can be inferred from various citations made by travelers along the way. For example, in 1730 the traveler Joseph Atwell cited **Joseph Addison** and François Misson (*d.* 1721) on Mt. Vesuvius; Addison's *Remarks on Several Parts of Italy* (1706) was so popular that it went through 10 editions by 1773 and was referred to by many tourists. Or to take another example, one of the finest travel writers of the latter 18th century was Dr. John Moore (1729–1802), author of *A View of Society and Manners in France, Switzerland, and Germany* (1779), and of a continuation relating to Italy (1781): Hester Thrale Piozzi (1741–1821), in her *Observations and Reflections through France, Italy, and Germany* (1789), cited not only Addison, Patrick Brydone (1741–1819), **Fanny Burney**, **Lord Chesterfield**, John Boyle (1707–1762), Sir William Hamilton (1730–1803), and James Howell (1594?–1666), but also Moore, who had made the rounds just before her.

Travel literature focused chiefly on the European Continent, though as time passed there was increasing interest in **North America**, the **West Indies**, the Levant, and **India**. In tone it showed ambiguity regarding the pleasures of the Continent, and, mixed with praise of **antiquities** and Continental manners, a certain strain of middle-class hostility and moral disapproval. In the 1760s a wave of antiforeigner literature appeared in, for example, the *Letters from Italy* of Samuel Sharp (?1700–1778), and **Tobias Smollett**'s ill-tempered *Travels in France and Italy* (1766)—which earned him the nickname "Smelfungus" from the more amiable **Laurence Sterne**, author of *A Sentimental Journey through France and Italy* (1768).

Travel literature was not uniform. And such literature existed also at some level apart from the experiences of ordinary tourists, not least because, in some cases, it was written to be read as imaginative work, similar to picaresque **novels**, rather than as objective descriptions of the travels of individual tourists. Some late-18th-century travel literature moved from the supposedly objective to the frankly subjective in, for example, the writings of **William Beckford**. And at times, travel literature provided an opportunity for **autobiography** and literary amateurism, not least in the readable context of an heroic or **mock-heroic** journey.

Travel literature, however, had to be concerned with impact and style. There was a major difference between manuscript accounts written for an intimate circle and works produced for a large anonymous market, in which the sole identifiable readers would be publishers and booksellers concerned with commercial appeal. The conventions expected by the market and the reviewers had to be respected. Travel literature could provide political statements or, at least, an ideological slant on what was reported. Writers were not neutral figures. Their works commonly sought to make specific as well as general points for a readership that was political and did not recognize any barrier to partisan viewpoints and political images. There was no more reason why travel literature should be immune to these influences than **history** or **tracts**, both of which were heavily politicized.

Jeremy Black

Bibliography

Adams, Percy. *Travellers and Travel Liars, 1660–1800.* 1962.
———. *Travel Literature and the Evolution of the Novel.* 1983.
Black, Jeremy. *The British Abroad: The Grand Tour in the Eighteenth Century.* 1992.
McVeagh, John, ed. *English Literature and the Wider World.* Vol. 1: *All Before Them, 1660–1780.* 1990.

See also Travel and Tourism

Treaty of Paris

See Paris, Treaty of

Trenchard, John (1662–1723)

Trenchard, a political writer best known for his **freethinking** opposition to religious superstition and political corruption, collaborated with **Thomas Gordon** to produce the *Independent Whig* (1720–1721) and *Cato's Letters* (1720–1723). Born in **Ireland**, Trenchard was educated at **Trinity College, Dublin**. After studying law in **London** he took a government post in Ireland, but an inheritance and a fortunate marriage gave him the financial independence to pursue a career as a political writer. A **Commonwealthman** of radical, even republican, outlook, Trenchard first attracted attention in the 1690s as a vocal opponent of standing armies. With his anonymous publication of *The Natural History of Superstition* (1709) he began a life long battle against what he saw as the persecuting spirit of High-Church Anglicanism and in favor of free expression—an agenda most clearly set out in the *Independent Whig.* Trenchard and Gordon are best known for *Cato's Letters,* a series of **essays** published first in the *London Journal* and then in the *British Journal* (1720–1723). These eloquently defended "old **Whig**" principles, attacked governmental corruption, celebrated liberty, and encouraged civic virtue.

Roger D. Lund

Bibliography

Burtt, Shelley. *Virtue Transformed: Political Argument in England, 1688–1740.* 1992.

Robbins, Caroline. *The Eighteenth-Century Commonwealthman.* 1959.

Sequin, J.A.R. *A Bibliography of John Trenchard* (1662–1723). 1965.

See also Radicalism and Radical Politics

Trevithick, Richard (1771–1833)

A leader in development of the steam locomotive for **railways**, Trevithick, born the son of a Cornish mine manager, trained as a mining engineer. When still in his twenties he was recognized as a worthy rival and successor to **James Watt** in development of the **steam engine**. On 28 December 1801 he demonstrated a steam carriage at Camborne, Cornwall, and in 1803 he drove another model along the Tottenham Court Road in **London**. In 1804 he built for Samuel Homfray a locomotive to run on the railway between Homfray's **coal** mines near **Merthyr Tydfil** and the Glamorgan **Canal** at Abercynon, and shortly thereafter demonstrated still another model at Gateshead on Tyneside.

The major engineering problems Trevithick encountered were the weight of the locomotive, which tended to crush existing rails, and failure to maintain sufficient steam pressure. However, his experiments, spectacularly culminating in "Catch-me-who-Can," the locomotive he demonstrated on a circular track at Euston in London (1808), carrying the public around at 12 or 13 miles an hour, showed that railway steam traction was possible.

Trevithick also employed his engines for dredging and boring, and was well ahead of his time in foreseeing the application of steam to **agriculture** and **shipping**. A man of wide-ranging interests, he lacked the application and business flair to further his ideas, and it was left to later engineers such as **George Stephenson** to come up with solutions to problems identified earlier by Trevithick. From 1816 to 1827 he lived in Peru and Costa Rica, building engines for silver mining. On coming home (1827) he failed to receive a parliamentary reward for his achievements, and died penniless.

A.J.G. Cummings

Bibliography

Bagwell, P. *The Transport Revolution from 1770.* 1974.

Dickinson, H.W., and A. Titley. *Richard Trevithick.* 1934.

See also Science, Technology, and Invention

Trimmer, Sarah (1741–1810)

Trimmer wrote instructional fiction and nonfiction, advancing biblical, ethical, and practical **education**, primarily for children and the disadvantaged. She also established and administered charity **Sunday schools** in Brentford and was consulted in 1786 by Queen Charlotte, who wished to open similar schools at Windsor.

Sarah Trimmer

Inspired by the experience of educating her own 12 children and also by **Anna Laetitia Barbauld**'s writing, Trimmer achieved early success with *An Easy Introduction to the Knowledge of Nature* (1780), containing children's lessons and a sketch of biblical history. In 1786, by then known as an educational activist, she wrote *The Economy of Charity,* dedicated to the queen and intended to promote the development of Sunday schools. Trimmer used fiction in *Fabulous Histories* (1785), *The Servant's Friend,* and *The Two Farmers* (1786) to instruct children and the lower classes in the humane treatment of animals. She edited two **periodicals**, *The Family Magazine* (1788–1789), aimed at **farmers** and **servants**; and *The Guardian of Education* (1802–1806), which evaluated educational children's literature.

Daughter of Sarah Bull and painter John Joshua Kirby, Trimmer was raised in an artistic circle that included **Thomas Gainsborough** and **Samuel Johnson**, whose writing influenced her own. She married James Trimmer in 1762 and resided at Brentford until her death. She is eulogized as a "sister author" by Jane West in "To the Memory of Mrs. Trimmer."

Kathleen Dillon

Bibliography

Chalmers, Alexander, ed. *Chalmers' Biographical Dictionary.* Vol. 30. Rpt. 1969.

Dictionary of National Biography, s.v. "Trimmer, Sarah."

Elwood, Anne Katherine (Curteis). *Memoirs of the Literary Ladies of England.* Vol. 1. 1843.

Séjourné, Philippe. *Aspects généraux du roman féminin en Angleterre de 1740 à 1800.* 1966.

See also Children's Literature

Trinity College, Dublin

Small in size and prestige at the beginning of the Hanoverian period in comparison to Oxford University and Cambridge University, Trinity College, founded in 1592, grew to rival them as a center of learning and scholarship. At the beginning of the 18th century less than 100 students matriculated each year, and the teaching staff consisted of 25 senior and junior Fellows, most on short terms of 3 years. By contrast, 1,750 students were in attendance by 1830, a student population that rivaled Cambridge, and there were then 25 Fellows and 13 endowed Professorships. The college was nominally open to **Catholics** and **dissenters** "in the expectation that they would graduate as good Anglicans," but requirements (which included the denial of transubstantiation and daily attendance at chapel services) made it difficult for them to attend and graduate until at least 1794, when the need to repudiate transubstantiation was repealed. Religious discrimination did not end entirely until 1873.

In the early Georgian era, the college focused on discipline to ensure pupils' attendance in class and their submission to rigorous examinations. Fears of **Jacobite** influences led to the appointment of Provosts partial to the **Whig** Ascendancy. The most notorious Provost, John Hely-Hutchinson (1724–1794), who served from 1774 to 1794, promoted his own political and financial agenda of **patronage** and self-aggrandizement.

The college's course of study covered the traditional disciplines: classics, logic, **science**, and **medicine** (through the School of Physic in association with the College of Physicians), as well as civil and canon law, divinity, oratory, and history. After 1760, endowed professorships were added in more sciences and in mathematics, as well as in Hebrew and Greek, even though Hely-Hutchinson for a while transformed the college into a finishing school for gentlemen with concentrations in riding, fencing, dancing, and foreign languages.

In 1790, partly to throw an obstacle in the way of campus **radicalism**, the college awarded an honorary degree to **Edmund Burke**, its most famous graduate. Nonetheless, the revolutionary ideals of the **United Irishmen** met with sympathy among many students and Junior Fellows, especially after the failed attempt in 1798 to bring off an **Irish rebellion**. The same influences stimulated calls in the college for **Catholic emancipation**, leading to a formal visitation of inquiry to the college to quell radical activity. However, in 1800 the **Act of Union** formalized **Ireland**'s unification with England and cemented the college's subservience to **London**. From 1799 to 1831 a series of four undistinguished Provosts kept revolutionary ideas and French rationalism out of the college.

No major changes in the curriculum took place until after 1831, with the exception of the medical program, which became virtually independent of the College of Physicians. From 1831 to 1837, Bartholomew Lloyd (1727–1837) as Provost reformed the curriculum, terms, and vacations, and added a number of buildings to provide additional lecture halls and residences. Lloyd reorganized the tutorial system, making classes more uniform in size; reduced the number of courses taught by each instructor; revised the course in divinity; and added two new chairs, one in moral philosophy, one in political economy. These reforms carried the college into the Victorian era.

Jack Fruchtman, Jr.

Bibliography

McDowell, R.B., and D.A. Webb. *Trinity College Dublin, 1592–1952: An Academic History.* 1982.

See also Cambridge University; Irish Education; Oxford University; Scottish Universities

Tucker, Josiah (1713–1799)

Anglican clergyman and economist, Tucker was one of the best-known polemical pamphleteers of the Hanoverian age. Writing from the 1740s to the 1790s on everything that interested him, he became embroiled in a number of public controversies, often defending unpopular positions. He wrote in favor of the **Jew Act** but against **Methodism**, the **Seven Years' War**, the **slave trade**, **radical** reform, and religious intolerance (though he also opposed the Feathers Tavern Petition of 1772). He was an early vocal critic of the colonial system—something that earned him the praise of later political economists such as **McCulloch**. In the 1760s Tucker argued that Britain should sever its ties with America and that the economic advantages of colonialism were illusory, and he later maintained that history would consider Britain's war with America as absurd as the crusades. His most enduring contributions were as an economist whose arguments in favor of free trade influenced the Physiocrats and anticipated the doctrines of **Adam Smith**.

The son of a Welsh farmer, Tucker attended **Oxford University**. While serving as a rector in **Bristol**, a thriving commercial center, he became interested in questions of trade. In his *Essay on Trade* (1749), *Elements of Commerce* (1755), and other works, he set forth a remarkably advanced view of economics. He held that the source of wealth was labor, not the accumulation of precious metals (as mercantilists had maintained), and that the key to national and individual prosperity was an economy based on the division of labor and on free markets in which individuals pursued their pecuniary interests without interference from restrictive trade practices. Tucker was a political theorist as well as an economist. His *Treatise Concerning Civil Government* (1781) attacked both divine right and natural rights theories of government; the legitimacy of government depended not on its origin but on its utility in serving the public good.

Eric K. Heavner

Bibliography

Hutchison, T.W. *Before Adam Smith.* 1988.

Pocock, J.G.A. *Virtue, Commerce, and History.* 1985.

Schuyler, J.L. *Josiah Tucker.* 1931.

Shelton, G.W. *Dean Tucker and Eighteenth-Century Economic and Political Thought.* 1981.

See also Economic Thought

Jethro Tull

Tull, Jethro (1674–1741)

A prominent **agricultural improver**, Tull provoked considerable controversy in a period that lacked the scientific knowledge to put his ideas into perspective. Although educated in law and interested in politics, he was forced by ill health to take up farming in his native county of Berkshire. He **traveled** extensively in Italy and **France**, observing agricultural practices as he went, including perhaps the continuous plowing of vineyards in Languedoc.

He devised a seed-drill for the sowing of sainfoin, and later modified it for potatoes, turnips, and wheat, developing ideas for cultivation between the neatly drilled rows, which greatly diminished the need for manure. He published *The New Horse-houghing Husbandry* in 1731; later editions included one in 1822 edited by **William Cobbett**. A practical man prepared to experiment, Tull served as a model for improving farmers.

C.J. Davey

Bibliography

Chambers, J.D., and G.E. Mingay. *The Agricultural Revolution.* 1966.

Fussell, G.E. *More Old English Farming Books.* 1950.

———. *Jethro Tull, His Influence on Mechanised Agriculture.* 1973.

Mingay, G.E., ed. *The Agricultural Revolution.* 1977.

See also Agriculture; Science, Technology, and Invention

Turner, Joseph Mallord William (1775–1851)

Turner was one of England's greatest landscape artists. His extraordinary range of achievement included fine **book illustrations**, superlative **engravings**, expressive **watercolors**, and, most important, late experiments with color and light in visionary **landscape paintings** of exceptional emotional impact.

Turner's early work originated in conscious responses to art and literature. As a young artist he copied the aquatints of **picturesque** theorist William Gilpin (1724–1804) with scrupulous accuracy. He imitated the old masters, especially Claude Lorrain (1600–1682), whose painting stimulated him throughout his career; *Liber Studiorum* (1807–1819), a comprehensive study of English landscape, was a direct response to the French master. Turner was also sensitive to the brilliant watercolor innovations of his friend Thomas Girtin (1775–1802). **Poetry** clearly affected his work too, especially **James Thomson**'s *The Seasons* (1726–1744). Homer, Vergil, **Milton**, **William Shenstone**, and **Alexander Pope** were other inspirations to his brush.

His professional growth began early. In 1789, when only 14, he became a student at the **Royal Academy**, where, between 1790 and 1797, he exhibited **drawings** and watercolors of English towns, cathedrals, bridges, rivers, bays, and seas. In 1798, at age 24, he became an associate of the academy, attaining full membership in 1802. An energetic traveler, Turner found many subjects for his paintings on his journeys. He visited **Wales** in 1792, sketching popular picturesque sites, including Tintern Abbey. In 1797 he traveled to the north of England, and in 1802, for the first time, to the Continent, where he painted Alpine scenes and produced his noteworthy *Calais Pier* (1803). In 1819 and again in 1828 he visited Italy. There the light and color, especially in Venice, brought a radical change to his work: bright color began to replace the soft browns, greens, and grays he had previously favored.

Turner's growth as an artist fell roughly into three periods. The first saw him employing picturesque and **sublime** watercolors to represent idealized but recognizable views of abbeys, **ruins**, and topographical sites. *Llanthony Abbey* (1794) followed the contemporary picturesque formula with its dead tree, torrents of rushing water, and dark foreground. Sublime aesthetics are apparent in *A View in North Wales* (1799); the viewer is awed by dark mountains and threatening clouds, pierced by shafts of sunlight. Sunlight never ceased to fascinate Turner.

His most ambitious period followed a trip to Italy in 1819. He experimented with color, using it in allegorical paintings in which architectural forms seem to dissolve or disappear. In *The Fighting Temeraire Tugged to Her Last Berth* (1839), the splendid old sailing vessel, bare-masted, is towed away by a squat, powerful, steam tug: the old order is giving way to the new. In *Ulysses Deriding Polyphemus* (1829) the hero is escaping the darkness of ignorance. In *Rain, Storm and Speed—The Great Western Railway* (1844), a **steam engine** speeds across a bridge, overtaking a small hare and a man plowing; the painting suggests the speed and power with which industrialization was replacing agrarian life. Color and mist, two of Turner's trademarks, are here dominant.

In 1843 Turner made his last trip to the Continent. In this final period his energy and vision began to weaken. What few paintings he completed treated mythical and epic themes asso-

J.M.W. Turner

ciated with death. Upon his own demise he was buried in St. Paul's Cathedral, leaving £140,000 in trust to benefit indigent painters. All his art—370 oil paintings and 95,950 watercolors, sketches, and engravings—was left to the nation on condition that it be exhibited in a separate gallery. Turner's works are now hung in a building next to the Tate Gallery in London.

Contemporary response to his enormous and revolutionary outpouring was mixed. One illustrious critic who rose to defend him passionately was John Ruskin (1819–1900), whose *Modern Painters* (1843) praised the subtlety and complexity of his work, and helped to establish the immense reputation he enjoyed in the latter 19th century. Turner, like his contemporary **John Constable**, was much admired in **France**, where his originality and experiments with light and color shaped the development of Impressionism.

Elise F. Knapp

Bibliography

Brown, David Blayney. *Oil Sketches from Nature: Turner and His Contemporaries.* 1991.

Cummings, Robert. *Discovering Turner.* 1990.

Gage, John, ed. *Collected Correspondence of J.M.W. Turner.* 1980.

Hemingway, Andrew. *Landscape Imagery and Urban Culture in Early Nineteenth-Century Britain.* 1992.

Herrmann, Luke. *Turner: Paintings, Watercolors, Prints, and Drawings.* 1975.

Lindsay, Jack. *Turner, the Man and His Art.* 1985.

Ruskin, John. *Modern Painters.* 5 vols. 1888.

Wilkinson, Gerald. *Turner on Landscape: The Liber Studiorum.* 1982.

Wilton, Andrew. *J.M.W. Turner: His Art and Life.* 1979.

———. *Turner and the Sublime.* 1980.

See also Painting

Turnpikes

See Roads, Streets, and Turnpikes

Tutors and the Teaching Profession

Teaching in the Hanoverian era was one of the most diversified, unspecialized, and, in general, badly paid of the "liberal professions." Teachers received little respect, and formal teacher training was not available. Teaching posts at the universities, public schools, and grammar schools were held by clergymen, but many of the younger of these men were in transit, looking upon teaching as a step toward preferment and advancement in the church or in government. A broader, inferior level of teachers included many women as well as men, running private educational establishments of differing qualities, usually as "dames' schools" or "common day schools." For many, teaching did not provide a living wage, and only part-time positions could be found. For most of the Hanoverian period, the lower level of teaching consisted of a very broad band of teachers working at a great assortment of jobs in **charity schools**, infant schools, denominational elementary schools, technical training schools, infants' schools, **Sunday schools**, and the like. Some of these jobs were voluntary and unpaid.

As a group, the most influential people in the profession were family tutors, who for most of the period controlled the relatively interesting and important function of educating the elite. The education of young noblemen and the wealthier **gentry** was accomplished mostly on the family estate, the child moving from the care of a governess to a tutor who might then finish his charge's education by accompanying him on the **Grand Tour** of Europe. Some well-off youths, of course, went to the universities as well, in which case tutors were known to follow them there; but many did not, their parents (**Pitt the Elder**, for example) considering the training they provided inferior. However, the tutor himself might well be a young man fresh from the university, no other professional qualifications being necessary since it was assumed that university attendance provided everything essential.

The residential tutor, employed for perhaps 10 or 15 years on an estate if there were several children, might serve as chaplain, physician, librarian, and traveling companion, as well as instructor in classical grammar and literature. Sometimes visiting tutors supplemented the usual run of classical studies with instruction in French and other modern languages, science and mathematics, **music**, **dancing**, and other arts. Through dining and otherwise intimate participation in family activities, tutors extended their teaching to contemporary public affairs and polite manners. There were some households where fathers tutored their own children; in very wealthy families, private libraries and collections of painting and sculpture supplemented formal lessons.

Some of the era's tutors who became famous for other

The parson and his pupils, 1750s

accomplishments were **John Home**, who tutored **George III** when he was still Prince of Wales; **Adam Smith**, who tutored Henry Scott, 3rd Duke of Buccleuch (1746–1812), **Hugh Blair**, **David Hume**, and **Jeremy Bentham**. Many of the era's professional writers had put in time tutoring when young; some tutors never left teaching. Professional, or traveling, tutors provided intermittent instruction for numerous families and often established classes at their own residences to prepare young students for secondary schools. Some teachers employed in grammar schools supplemented their incomes with private tuitions; others left school teaching and opened their own private academies. Often the most prominent tutors were attracted to **dissenting academies** like Warrington and experimental schools like Hazelwood School in **Birmingham** that were challenging the classical curriculum and strict atmosphere of church-controlled grammar and public schools. Exceptional tutors, such as William Jones (1675–1749) and **Joseph Priestley**, were men of science and mathematics who gained national and international reputations for their work. **James Mill** tutored his own son, achieving remarkable if mixed results.

Many distinguished Hanoverian tutors published accounts of their educational experiences in philosophical treatises, **letters**, and fiction. While tutors sought to guide their patrons in procedures for domestic education, they also formulated educational theories and practices that would have much wider influence. Priestley's *Essay on a Course of Liberal Education for Civil and Active Life* (1765) and subsequent abridgment of **David Hartley**'s *Observations on Man* (1749, 1775) encouraged the application of reasoning capacity to utilitarian subjects. **Maria Edgeworth** and her father Richard (1744–1817), a distinguished educator, tested Priestley's theories while tutoring younger members of their own family, and reported their results in their widely read *Practical Education* (1798) and *Essays on Professional Education* (1809). Maria Edgeworth's fictional writings for children and adults popularized the idea that education could become an experimental science, and outlined steps to improve the teaching of all subjects. **Thomas Day**'s influential novel *Sandford and Merton* (1783–1789) was only one of many that lionized educators and propagated educational doctrines through their sayings and examples. In his *Treatise on Education* (1774) and *Lectures on Education* (1789), David Williams (1738–1816), founder of the Royal Literary Fund (1818), discussed new methods of teaching modern subjects and, like most notable Hanoverian tutors, strongly defended home education against school training as the most appropriate setting for initiating these.

The influence of private tutors greatly outweighed their number in the Hanoverian period, but by the end of it, the long-standing preference of the British elite for domestic education was being reversed in favor of outside schooling. The continuing decline of classical studies was moving tutors from private homes into public schools, and pressures from more technically oriented academies were also forcing consideration of entirely new approaches to education.

But formal training of teachers continued to lag. In 1800 it was still assumed that a Christian nation could want nothing more in its finest teachers than skills in the dissection of dead languages in pagan texts. Illumination came as it often does, from the bottom up. The directors of the new **elementary schools** discovered that their monitors and teachers required professional training; between 1812 and 1839 there evolved a literature and several teacher-training institutions that at last provided a core from which the professionalization of work could grow. In 1839 Sir James Kay-Shuttleworth (1804–1877), the secretary of the Privy Council's new Committee of Council on Education, began forging this into a full-fledged system of training colleges. Those who attended and completed these courses were certified and earned higher wages as trained teachers. These innovations followed by decades the founding of such groups as the College of Surgeons and the Institution of Civil Engineers. The nation's educators were in the last **middle-class** profession to think itself in need of education.

Kim P. Sebaly

Bibliography

Beard, Geoffrey. *The Compleat Gentleman: Five Centuries of Aristocratic Life.* 1993.

Butler, Marilyn. *Maria Edgeworth, a Literary Biography.* 1972.

Gordon, Edward E., and Elaine H. Gordon. *Centuries of Tutoring: A History of Alternative Education in America and Western Europe.* 1990.

Hans, Nicholas. *New Trends in Education in the Eighteenth Century.* 1951.

Langford, Paul. *A Polite and Commercial People: England, 1792–1783.* 1989.
Simon, Brian. *The Two Nations and the Educational Structure, 1780–1870.* 1974.
Waddle, David. *The Rise of the Schooled Society: The History of Formal Schooling in England.* 1974.

See also Education, Teachers'; Governesses

Tyrwhitt, Thomas (1730–1786)

Classicist, philologist, and an acknowledged great scholar, Tyrwhitt served as clerk of the **House of Commons** (1762–1768), trustee of the **British Museum** (1784–1786), editor of Geoffrey Chaucer's *Canterbury Tales* (1775), and first editor of **Thomas Chatterton**'s poems (1777)—in his Appendix to the third edition (1778) he argued that Chatterton had written the "medieval" Rowley poems. His Chaucer remained the standard for about a century. In *Observations and Conjectures upon Some Passages of Shakespeare* (1766), though he often judiciously differed with **Samuel Johnson**'s emendations, he ended by exclaiming, "Alas, poor Shakespeare." Contemporaries esteemed him for his generosity as well as for his vast learning.

Peter A. Tasch

Bibliography

Dictionary of National Biography, s.v. "Tyrwhitt, Thomas."
Nichols, John. *Literary Anecdotes of the Eighteenth Century.* Vol. 3. 1812.

See also Shakespeare Industry

Union, Act of (Ireland, 1800)

The Act of Union between Great Britain and **Ireland** received Royal assent in August 1800 and came into effect in January 1801. It consisted of eight articles. The first four concerned political arrangements: Ireland was to send four spiritual and 24 temporal peers to the **Lords**, and 100 representatives to the **Commons** at Westminster. The fifth concerned the union of the **Church of England** and Church of Ireland; the sixth and seventh related to commerce and finance; the last defined all legal procedures and the retention of the Irish courts of law.

The act failed passage several times between 1798 and 1800. Eventually pushed through Westminster by a determined **William Pitt**, it brought to an end the **Irish Parliament**, which had existed for some 500 years; the Irish Parliament in **Dublin**, bribed, intimidated, and also receiving general support in the countryside from Irish Catholic peers and the Irish Catholic hierarchy, followed suit. After 1801, all questions governing Irish politics, society, and economy were to be decided at Westminster. Pitt also intended the act to secure Catholic emancipation, but when he failed in this he resigned over the issue.

To many, the act represented a betrayal of Irish interests. **Lord Cornwallis**, the viceroy who helped to effect it, confided in his private correspondence:

> I despise and hate myself every hour for engaging in such corrupt work, and am supported only by the reflection that without a Union the British Empire must be dissolved.

Lord Byron later called it "the union of a shark with its prey." For Ireland, the effects of the union were almost entirely disastrous; free trade was ruinous for Irish manufactures, removal of the Irish seat of government increased absenteeism among Irish landowners, the union of the two exchequers (1817) resulted in a colossal increase to Irish **tax** burdens, and, perhaps worst of all, the failure to secure the promised Catholic relief promptly led to a growing division between Irish Catholics and Protestants, which boded ill for the future.

William Kenefick

Bibliography

Beckett, J.C. *The Making of Modern Ireland, 1603–1923.* 1981.

Bolton, G.C. *The Passing of the Act of Union.* 1966.

McFarland, E.W. *Ireland and Scotland in the Age of Revolution: Planting the Green Bough.* 1994.

O'Tuathaigh, Geroid. *Ireland before the Famine, 1798–1848.* 1987.

Scally, Robert. *The End of Hidden Ireland: Rebellion, Famine, and Emigration.* 1995.

See also Catholic Emancipation; Grattan, Henry; Roman Catholicism

Union, Act of (Scotland, 1707)

The legislation that abolished the Scottish Parliament in 1707 in favor of a Parliament of Great Britain ensured the survival of the established churches in Scotland and England, and determined the means by which Scottish representatives in the new Parliament would be elected.

The relative importance of the reasons for union are hotly debated. Few disagree that the main impetus came from England, which needed to control its increasingly troublesome northern neighbor. England, at war with **France**, was anxious to secure the border with Scotland and to ensure Scotland's agreement to the **Hanoverian succession**. The Scots' motives are less certain, though the survival of Scottish trade, which the English had threatened to cut off, was a major incentive. Bribery, too, played a part.

Union had looked increasingly likely since 1603 when the Union of the Crowns had taken the Scottish monarch James VI to **London**, to become James I of England (1603–1625). Parliamentary union shifted the political focus even more firmly south toward Westminster. Scotland undoubtedly benefited economically from access to the wider markets of the expanding British **Empire**, but its success within the union was built upon strengths in **commerce** and **agriculture**, which had been evident prior to 1707.

Christopher A. Whatley

Bibliography

Ferguson, William. *Scotland's Relations with England.* 1977.
Riley, P.W.J. *The Union of England and Scotland.* 1978.
Robertson, John, ed. *A Union for Empire: Political Thought and the British Union of 1707.* 1995.
Whatley, Christopher. "Economic Causes and Consequences of the Union of 1707: A survey." *Scottish Historical Review.* Vol. 68, pp. 150–181.

See also Fifteen, the; Jacobitism

Unitarianism

Unitarianism emerged during the Reformation, when certain reforming theologians discovered they could find no warrant for the doctrine of the Trinity in Scripture. Its background lay in Arianism (which held that the Son, though divine, was neither co-equal with the Father, nor eternal) and in the even more heretical Socinianism—named after Faustus Socinus (1539–1604)—which demoted Christ still further to the status of moral exemplar.

The father of English Unitarianism was John Biddle (1615–1662), who published several works disputing the doctrine of the Trinity. It was because they denied the trinity and some of its implications—the doctrine of atonement, the apostolic succession, hence the state establishment of religious institutions—that Unitarians were considered more loathesome than other **dissenters** and excluded from the provisions of the **Toleration Act**; though de facto toleration did exist increasingly in the 18th century.

Unitarian and other antitrinitarian writers, often partially masking their true views, were closely associated with deistic **freethought** and also **Latitudinarianism** within the **Church of England.** After a failed attempt at Salters Hall (1719) by some nonconformist leaders to force trinitarian orthodoxy on all dissenting pastors, there was an increasing gravitation by **Presbyterians** (and to a lesser extent by **Congregationalists** and **Baptists**) toward unitarian rationalist **theology** and the usually accompanying liberal and whiggish politics. Some 223 Unitarian chapels existed in England, **Wales**, and **Scotland** in 1825, 178 of them formerly trinitarian nonconformist.

Unitarianism as a movement began to gain cohesion in the age of **George III.** Drawn toward natural religion and often toward intellectual and scientific pursuits, Unitarians figured prominently in the **radical** intelligentsia of the latter 18th century. There were many in the loose group called **rational dissenters.** The first openly Unitarian congregation was established in 1774 when **Theophilus Lindsey**, leaving the Anglican ministry after the failure of the Feathers Tavern petition to drop the requirement of Anglican clerical subscription to the Thirty-nine Articles (1772), founded the Essex Street Chapel in **London.** He retained Anglican liturgy, adapting it to a worship of God the Father alone. Congregations soon followed throughout the Midlands, mainly in the larger cities, and these attracted several leading industrialists, such as the ceramics-maker **Josiah Wedgwood** and the **iron** manufacturer **John Wilkinson.**

The most conspicuous Unitarian of the revolutionary era was **Joseph Priestley**, who involved himself in many movements for reform. In 1791 he founded the Unitarian Society for Promoting Christian Knowledge and the Practice of Virtue by the Distribution of Books. At its founding the society published documents containing the first public profession of belief in the unity of God, the Father, and the essential humanity of Jesus Christ. Later that same year a **Birmingham** mob, shouting "No philosophers!" and "Church and King!" burned Priestley's house and laboratory after mistakenly identifying his views with those of the French revolutionaries. His friend and fellow minister **Richard Price** helped spread the beliefs of Unitarianism in his chapel at Newington Green in London.

Thomas Belsham (1750–1829) became the leader of the Unitarian movement in England after Priestley emigrated to America in 1794. Belsham published works of **biblical criticism**, and it was also during his leadership that Unitarians, after previous failed attempts to remove their disabilities (as in 1792 under a bill sponsored by **Charles James Fox**), gained relief under the Trinity Bill (1813), which at last legalized Unitarian beliefs and permitted nontrinitarians to vote and hold office. More free now to act as full-fledged citizens, and joined by well-heeled converts from other denominations, in 1825 they formed the British and Foreign Unitarian Association to help spread their doctrine. Unitarians figured importantly in support for repeal in 1828 of the hated **Test and Corporation Acts.** Unitarianism in the Victorian period came under the influence of James Martineau (1805–1900) and his sister Harriet Martineau (1802–1876).

Carole S. Fungaroli

Bibliography

Bolam, C.G., et al. *The English Presbyterians from Elizabethan Puritanism to Modern Unitarianism.* 1968.
Holt, Raymond. *The Unitarian Contribution to Social Progress in England.* 1952.
Wilbur, Earl Morse. *A History of Unitarianism, Socinianism and Its Antecedents.* 1945.
———. *A History of Unitarianism in Transylvania, England and America.* 1952.

United Irishmen

The United Irishmen formed the vanguard of Irish **radicalism** in the 1790s and symbolized a nexus between Irish disaffection and the international crisis born of the **French Revolution.** The society was founded in Belfast in October 1791 by William Drennan (1754–1820), Thomas Russell (1767–1803), Napper Tandy (1740–1803), and **Wolfe Tone.** Influenced by the ideals of **religious toleration** and international brotherhood, as well as an older strain of Ulster **Presbyterian** radicalism, its goal was to unite Irishmen, regardless of religion, in pursuit of advanced democratic political reform. Its early leadership was drawn from the Protestant mercantile and professional classes of Belfast and **Dublin**.

The society operated initially in an open and constitutional manner, but the outbreak of **war** with **France** in 1793 curtailed any possibility of reform and created an extremely unfavorable climate for radicalism. The United Irishmen were formally suppressed in May 1794, just as the **London** government acted also against the **London Corresponding Society** and Scots radicals such as **Thomas Muir**. Repression forced the organization to move fitfully toward a more military format and a more militant republicanism aiming at a separate Irish republic. By 1795, links with **defenderism** brought the **middle-class** radicalism of the United Irishmen in close alliance with rural protest. Through the efforts of Tone, French support for the movement was secured, culminating in a large but unsuccessful invasion attempt off Bantry Bay (December 1796) of some 15,000 Frenchmen, carrying large stores of arms for a rebellion that failed to occur.

By then, however, the United Irishmen were beset by still more difficulties. Penetration by government informers, internal division, and confusion over French intentions paralyzed the movement, and the government was able to regain the initiative with draconian military action. By the summer of 1798, military repression sparked a defensive **Irish rebellion** which United Irish leaders attempted desperately to harness. The rising, however, was crushed, despite further French expeditions.

The United Irishmen subsequently regrouped with a new military structure, but their fortunes were increasingly dependent on the will of the French. **Robert Emmet**'s rebellion in 1803 was an attempt to break free of this situation. After its failure, the dwindling Irish leadership was reduced to lobbying Napoleon for assistance. As a formal organization, the society ceased to exist by 1806.

E. W. McFarland

Bibliography

Curtin, Nancy J. *The United Irishmen: Popular Politics in Ulster and Dublin, 1791–1798.* 1994.

Dickson, D., D. Keogh, and K. Whelan, eds. *The United Irishmen: Republicanism, Radicalism and Rebellion.* 1993.

Elliot, M. *Partners in Revolution: The United Irishmen and France.* 1982.

McDowell, R.B. *Ireland in the Age of Imperialism and Revolution.* 1979.

McFarland, E.W. *Ireland and Scotland in the Age of Revolution: Planting the Green Bough.* 1994.

Smyth, J. *Men of No Property: Irish Radicals and Popular Politics in the Late Eighteenth Century.* 1992.

United Scotsmen

This shadowy underground organization of militant radicals was consciously modeled on the **United Irishmen**. By late 1794, Scottish constitutional **radicalism** had nearly been extinguished by official persecution. When delegates of the Irish group arrived in **Scotland** in the summer of 1796, advocating covert tactics and a new style of military organization, their ideas were seized upon by Scots like **George Mealmaker**, whose pamphlet "The Moral and Political Catechism of Man" set out the United Scotsmen's goals of universal suffrage and annual parliaments.

By the spring of 1797 the group was spreading through west and central Scotland. Weavers and **artisans** formed the backbone of its membership. A further boost came from the widespread **militia riots** in August and September, but recruitment was never on the scale of the United Irishmen, and the organization failed to secure a mass base. By late 1797 the government successfully rounded up leaders such as Mealmaker.

The failure of the **Irish Rebellion** of 1798 was another blow to the morale of the United Scotsmen, but for a time the organization struggled on, doggedly attempting to capitalize on economic distress. There were reports of regrouping and of attempts to link with **Emmet**'s rebellion in Ireland in 1803, but the organization eventually faded from view.

E. W. McFarland

Bibliography

Logue, K.J. *Popular Disturbances in Scotland.* 1979.

McFarland, E.W. *Ireland and Scotland in the Age of Revolution: Planting the Green Bough.* 1994.

Meikle, H.W. *Scotland and the French Revolution.* 1969.

See also Corresponding Societies; French Revolution

University of London

The University of London was founded specifically to educate **dissenters** excluded for religious reasons from **Oxford** and **Cambridge** universities. The two latter institutions, beside admitting only Anglicans, were costly and served chiefly the interests of landed society; by 1825 the growth and concentration of trade and dissent in London required something new. The university's founders—**Henry Brougham**, **Thomas Campbell**, and the Jewish financier and philanthropist Isaac Goldsmid (1778–1859), among others—experienced delays in authorization by the Crown and **Lords**, and objections by Oxford and Cambridge and by London's medical schools. In 1828, when the University of London's College opened, it granted its own certificate of proficiency, but awarded no degrees. It was organized on the Scottish pattern, with lectures by a distinguished faculty, nonresident students, admission to single courses, and a "modern" curriculum that included languages, mathematics, physics, political economy, history, English law, and **medicine**.

When some Anglican advocates of the college questioned its separation from the **Church of England**, a second institution—King's College, London—was incorporated in 1829. This opened in 1831 to include in the curriculum "the doctrines and duties of Christianity as the same as are inculcated by the United Church of England and Ireland." Among the founders and benefactors of King's College were **King George IV**, the **Duke of Wellington**, **Sir Robert Peel**, and Archbishop Charles Manners Sutton (1755–1828). In 1836 the original university, renamed University College, and King's College were united in a new University of London, an examining and degree-awarding institution for both colleges (and for many others which have since become attached to it).

The University of London is important for being the first metropolitan university in England; the first to provide a university education for the **middle class**; for institutionalizing in England the modern or "practical" disciplines, the professorial system, and a democratic approach to higher education; and for providing "usefully" educated manpower to serve both the state and the **Empire**.

H. George Hahn

Bibliography

Bellot, H. Hale. *The University of London: A History.* 1969.

Harte, Negley. *The University of London 1836–1986.* 1986.

Harte, Negley, and John North. *The World of University College London 1828–1978.* 1978.

Heulin, Gordon. *King's College London 1828–1978.* 1978.

Tempest, N.R. "An Early Scheme for an Undenominational University." *Universities Review.* Vol. 32, pp. 45–49.

See also Scottish Universities; Trinity College, Dublin

Urbanization

See Cities and Urban Life

Utilitarianism

See Bentham, Jeremy, and Benthamites

Utopian Literature

The Hanoverian period produced at least 118 examples of utopian literature, exclusive of **translations**, and marked an historic transition between the satiric criticism of Thomas More's *Utopia* (1516) and the great utopian systems of the 19th and 20th centuries. At one end of the Hanoverian literary spectrum lay the best-known piece of 18th-century utopian literature, **Jonathan Swift**'s *Gulliver's Travels* (1726). In part a satirical redaction of **Daniel Defoe**'s *Robinson Crusoe* (1719), *Gulliver* satirized the excesses of early-18th-century society in a manner reminiscent of More. Through **satire**, utopian writers like Swift could simultaneously critique contemporary culture and present an imaginary utopian foil to it.

On the other hand, much Hanoverian literary utopianism was not satirical. In contrast to 16th- and 17th-century utopias like Sir Philip Sidney's *Arcadia* (1590), which place their idealized visions of society outside the confines of human time and space, much Hanoverian utopian literature presented the ideal society as something closer to earthly realization. This may have been partly due to the influence of 17th-century millenarian thought, revived in the 18th century by such groups as the Shakers, a splinter group of the **Quakers**. But there was also the influence of **science** and the **Enlightenment**. Though few poets or novelists shared the apocalyptic ideas of the Shakers, many were at least closet meliorists, believing that massive improvement, even the perfectibility of human society, was a real possibility. Beginning with Defoe's *Robinson Crusoe* (1719), a novel that itself spawned a significant subgenre of utopian literature ("the Robinsonade"), and intensifying in the enthusiastic atmosphere of the **French Revolution**, **novels** such as **William Godwin**'s *Caleb Williams* (1794) and poems such as **Percy Bysshe Shelley**'s *Revolt of Islam* (1819) embraced at least the principle of human perfectibility through reason, humanity, love, strict attachment to the truth as revealed in Nature, and **education**, seen increasingly as a panacea.

The purifying effect of education was an especially prominent feature of feminist utopian literature. Drawing on **Mary Astell**'s plan for a female utopia in *A Serious Proposal to the Ladies; For the Advancement of Their True and Greatest Interest* (1694), narratives like Sarah Scott's (1723–1795) *Millenium Hall* (1756), which presented a celibate community of women devoted to learning and mutual support and respect, and **Mary Wollstonecraft**'s *A Vindication of the Rights of Woman* (1792) expressed the belief that women would best achieve the most perfect society for themselves by education and enlightenment.

Melissa M. Mowry

Bibliography

Elliot, Robert C. *The Shape of Utopia: Studies in a Literary Genre.* 1970.

Harrison, J.F.C. *The Second Coming: Popular Millenarianism, 1780–1850.* 1979.

Manuel, E. Frank, and Fritzie P. Manuel. *Utopian Thought in the Western World.* 1979.

Sargent, Lyman T. *British and American Utopian Literature, 1516–1985.* 1988.

See also Millenarianism; Romanticism and Romantic Style; Women in Literature

Vanbrugh, Sir John (1664–1726)

Vanbrugh was first a soldier, then a leading Restoration playwright, then one of the great baroque architects of England. He was commissioned an ensign in the earl of Huntingdon's Foot Regiment in 1686; imprisoned in Calais, Vincennes, and the Bastille until 1692; commissioned a captain in the marines, where he served until 1698; and then rejoined to the earl of Huntingdon's regiment, resigning in 1702 when named comptroller of the works.

Inspired by the plays of **Colley Cibber**, Vanbrugh turned to playwriting. His first work, *The Relapse, or Virtue in Danger* (1697), was written as a sequel to Cibber's *Love's Last Shift* and proved a great success, as did *The Provok'd Wife* (1698). He continued writing plays until 1705, although his later ones never attained the success or notoriety of his early works. His last play, *Journey to London,* was completed after his death by Cibber as *The Provok'd Husband* (1728). Vanbrugh also worked several years as theatrical manager of the Haymarket Theatre.

In 1699 his interests also turned to architecture, and he was commissioned by the earl of Carlisle to help build Castle Howard in Yorkshire (1699–1726). This first commission established Vanbrugh as a leading architect for the **aristocracy**. His highly personal style, based on both the breaking of classical architectural rules and on the baroque, may have been inspired in part by his experience with theatrical scenery: the impression of great size and bulk, the contrast of recessions and projections, and the use of false perspective all suggest connections with set designs. There is no doubt that he learned a great deal from his fully trained draftsman and clerk of the works, **Nicholas Hawksmoor**, who had worked for **Sir Christopher Wren**. Hawksmoor's influence is much in evidence in the design of Castle Howard. The enormous composition of the dramatic and domed building that moves forward into space and creates a courtyard with contrasts, blocks of stone, and curving forms was carried even further in the design of Blenheim Palace (1704–1725), paid for by **Queen Anne** and the government as a gift to the **Duke of Marlborough** in gratitude for his military victories against Louis XIV. The structure had a long and acrimonious building history.

Vanbrugh became the favored architect of the **Whig** aristocracy, designing Kings Weston (1711–1714) for the Honorable Edward Southwell; Claremont House, (1715–1720) for the **Duke of Newcastle**; Seaton Delaval (*c.* 1720–1729) for Admiral Francis Delaval; and Grimsthorpe (1722–1724) for the Duke of Ancaster. The architect's own house, Vanbrugh Castle, Greenwich (*c.* 1717), included the castellated and **picturesque** massing elements typical of many of his works. Vanbrugh was knighted in 1714 and was one of 48 members of the Kit Kat **Club**. Among his friends were Cibber and William Congreve (1670–1729). His patent as comptroller of works was terminated by the **Tories** in 1713 but was restored in 1715, the year he was made surveyor of gardens and waters. In 1716 he succeeded the aged Wren as architect of the Greenwich Hospital and went on to complete the Great Hall (painted by **Sir James Thornhill**) and the King William Block (designed in great part by Hawksmoor). Vanbrugh had the most varied career of any artist of his time, producing two major plays and two of the finest examples of English baroque country houses.

Thomas J. McCormick

Bibliography

Beard, Geoffrey. *The Work of John Vanbrugh.* 1986.

Downes, Kerry. *Vanbrugh.* 1977.

———. *Sir John Vanbrugh, a Biography.* 1987.

McCormick, Frank. *Sir John Vanbrugh, the Playwright as Architect.* 1991.

Saumurez-Smith, Charles. *The Building of Castle Howard.* 1990.

Whistler, Lawrence. *The Imagination of Sir John Vanbrugh and His Fellow Artists.* 1954.

See also Architects and Architecture; Dramatic Arts; House-building and Housing

Vancouver, George (1757–1797)

Vancouver was best known for his coastal surveying of southwestern **Australia**, northern **New Zealand**, the Sandwich (Hawaiian) Islands, and, especially, the coastline of **North America** from California to British Columbia.

Born in King's Lynn, he entered the **navy** as an able seaman at age 13. In the 1770s he accompanied **Captain Cook** on his second and third voyages; in the 1780s he served in the **West Indies**. In 1791 he received orders to survey the Pacific coast of North America between 30° and 60° N. Lat., take possession of the **Nootka Sound** area, and search for a possible Northwest Passage. En route he was to complete Cook's survey of the Sandwich Islands.

Setting sail on 1 April 1791 in two vessels, he reached the Pacific coast (1792) after rounding the Cape of Good Hope and doing some coastal surveying in Australia and New Zealand. Between June 1792 and August 1794 he minutely charted the Pacific Northwest coast, naming Puget Sound, the Gulf of Georgia, and other markers, and proceeded all the way to Cook's Inlet in the Gulf of Alaska, assuring himself that no Northwest Passage could be found. Vancouver completed the charting of the Sandwich Islands, gained from King Kamehameha the cession to Britain of the island of Hawaii (1794), then headed home via Cape Horn and St. Helena, arriving in October 1795 after traveling some 65,000 miles circumnavigating the Earth.

He spent the last 3 years of his life editing his journals (published posthumously). Captain Vancouver stands next to Cook as Britain's greatest oceanic surveyor. Vancouver Island and two cities—one Canadian and the other in Washington state—are named after him.

Stuart R. Givens

Bibliography

Anderson, Bern. *Surveyor of the Sea: The Life and Voyages of Captain George Vancouver.* 1960.

Fisher, Robin. *Vancouver's Voyage: Charting the Northwest Coast, 1791–1795.* 1992.

Vancouver, George. *A Voyage of Discovery to the North Pacific Ocean and Round the World, 1791–1795.* Edited by W. Kaye Lamb. 4 vols. 1984.

Venn Family

The Venns were a particularly influential family of Anglican clergymen. Henry Venn (1725–1797) was a prominent leader of the Evangelical awakening in the **Church of England**; his son John (1759–1813) was rector of Clapham when the **Clapham sect** rose to the height of its involvement in public life.

Henry Venn was educated at Cambridge and ordained a priest in 1749. At some point in the 1750s, after undertaking a preaching tour with **George Whitefield**, he experienced a conversion, afterward stating that he could no longer preach his past sermons. As Vicar of Huddersfield, Yorkshire (1759–1771), his preaching was so effective that the church became too small to hold all who wished to hear his **sermons**. Holding "kitchen meetings" in his parsonage, he set an example of piety and seriousness that soon drew to him other leaders of the **religious revival** then underway, including **John Berridge**, **Lady Huntingdon**, and **Charles Simeon**. Henry Venn was in considerable demand as a speaker outside of his own parish, and his published correspondence was widely read. His *Compleat Duty of Man* (1763) was reprinted many times.

John Venn was born in Clapham while his father briefly served as curate there, and later became rector there himself (1792–1813). Clapham, not far from **London**, became the home of an informal network of about 12 powerful Evangelical Anglicans who, full of religious enthusiasm, labored in many social causes, including abolition of the **slave trade**, improvement of the conditions of the poor, the extension of Evangelical missions, and the improvement of moral standards. Some of them, including **William Wilberforce**, were M.P.s. John Venn was not only a member of this group but in some sense its leader because they worshipped in his church. He was a founding member of the Church Missionary Society (1799) and served as its administrator until 1808.

Richard M. Riss

Bibliography

Hennell, M. *John Venn and the Clapham Sect.* 1958.

Hilton, Boyd. *The Age of Atonement: The Influence of Evangelicalism on Social and Economic Thought, 1785–1865.* 1988.

Howse, E.M. *Saints in Politics: The "Clapham Sect" and the Growth of Freedom.* 1953.

Hylson-Smith, Kenneth. *Evangelicals in the Church of England.* 1988.

Ryle, J.C. *Five Christian Leaders of the Eighteenth Century.* 1960.

See also Evangelicalism; Missionary Societies

Volunteering Movement (Ireland)

The volunteering movement in **Ireland** developed as a response to the imperial crisis of 1778–1779 and grew to become the "battering ram" of reformers the following decade. During the **War of American Independence**, fears of an attempted French invasion of Ireland grew. Loyal military volunteering represented a spontaneous reaction to this immediate danger. Largely Protestant, the volunteer corps were led by the **gentry** and professional classes, with tradesmen and artisans forming the rank and file. By 1780 they numbered almost 40,000 men, forcing the authorities to incorporate them into defense plans.

But the volunteers represented more than a military force. They embodied progressive ideals of citizenship and **patriotism**, and their political potential was quickly seized upon by reform-minded politicians. The political influence of the corps grew rapidly after 1780, and at the great Volunteer Convention at Dungannon in February 1782, resolutions were adopted calling for the repeal of legislation that limited the powers of the **Irish Parliament**.

The movement reached its high point in the summer of 1782 when its military demonstrations helped persuade the

British government to modify Ireland's constitutional dependence on **London** and drop the British Parliament's claim (ensconced in Poynings' Law and affirmed in the Declaratory Act of 1719) to legislate for Ireland. However, over the next 2 years the volunteers overstretched themselves in campaigning for parliamentary reform, splitting badly over the question of **Catholic emancipation**.

Toward the end of 1792 a radicalized and regenerated volunteering movement seemed to be taking off, stimulated by the example of the **French Revolution** and infiltrated by members of the **United Irishmen**. But again, internal divisions over the extent of reform and the **Catholic** question were constraining factors. The revival slowly collapsed from early 1793 on.

E.W. McFarland

Bibliography

McDowell, R.B. *Ireland in the Age of Imperialism and Revolution.* 1979.

Stewart, A.T.Q. *A Deeper Silence: The Hidden Origins of the United Irishmen.* 1993.

See also Flood, Henry; Grattan, Henry; Patriots (Irish)

Wade, John (1788–1875)

Wade was a prominent **radical** propagandist in the period 1815–1840, whose well-researched publications provided heavy ammunition for reformers. He came from a **London** working-class family and was a journeyman wool sorter by trade. Befriended by the **radical** tailor **Francis Place** and assisted by **Jeremy Bentham**, he started a penny **newspaper**, the *Gorgon* (1818–1819), which, among other things, blasted the **corn laws** of the "vile oligarchy" and demanded universal suffrage to remedy the grievances of the "productive classes."

Wade was best known, however, for his comprehensive attack on what he regarded as the entire system of aristocratic tyranny, expropriation, and misrule, *The Black Book: or Corruption Unmasked,* published first in twopenny sheets (1819), then as a book (1820), with a *Supplement* (1823). Here, with painstaking research, examining **patronage, pensions, places,** and **taxes,** he catalogued the means by which the **middle class** and working class were penalized by the Crown, **aristocracy, clerical profession, legal profession, East India Company,** and so on. Some of his most effective material involved critical comparisons of the expenses of the British Crown and the U.S. government. The work sold 50,000 copies and, because of its explosive content, almost made its author the object of libel proceedings; but its depth of detail made it the favorite reference work of radicals into the 1830s.

Wade, like Place, was a hard-bitten radical of a newer breed, half contemptuous of **Cartwright** with his mythical ideas of the Anglo–Saxon past, of **Paine** with his delusive ideas of natural rights, and of demagogues like **Orator Hunt** (although like all of them he deeply mistrusted the **Whigs**). An educated **Benthamite,** he favored practical reforms—a greatly expanded franchise, extensive **law reform,** free nonsectarian **education,** and a revised tax code. He accepted political economy and Malthusianism. After the **Reform Act** he labored to maintain a united front between workers and the middle class with such works as his *History of the Middle and Working Classes* (1833) and *Glances at the Times, and Reform Government* (1840).

Thomas D. Veve

Bibliography

Baylen, Joseph O., and Norbert J. Gossman, eds. *Biographical Dictionary of Modern British Radicals.* Vol. 1. 1979.

Dinwiddy, John R. *From Luddism to the First Reform Bill: Reform in England, 1810–1832.* 1986.

Hone, J. Ann. *For the Cause of Truth: Radicalism in London, 1796–1821.* 1982.

Royle, Edward, and James Walvin. *English Radicals and Reformers, 1760–1848.* 1982.

Stevenson, John. *Popular Disturbances in England, 1700–1832.* 2nd ed., 1992.

Wages

See Hours, Wages, and Working Conditions

Waggonways

See Railways and Waggonways

Wakefield, Edward Gibbon (1796–1862)

Wakefield was the leading theorist of systematic overseas colonization and an architect of colonial self-government. His career as an expert on **population** exchange began while serving a 3-year **prison** term for abducting an heiress. Resolved to emigrate, he buried himself in literature on **Australia** and colonization. In the year of his release (1829) he published anonymously, in the guise of a settler, a series of articles (reissued later that year as a book, *A Letter from Sydney*) which diagnosed the socioeconomic woes of Britain's Australian colonies. He recommended an end to the **transportation** of convicts and to the free granting of Crown lands, proposing instead that the land be sold in small parcels to free immigrant couples who would build a proper society.

Wakefield then formed a series of organizations, beginning with the National Colonization Society (1830) and the South Australian Association (1834), to promote a new colony in Australia. In 1831 the British government ended free land grants in New South Wales and applied the revenue to an

Sydney, New South Wales, c. *1810*

immigration fund. In 1836 Parliament chartered the new South Australian colony, and Wakefield then founded the New Zealand Society (1837) to lobby for annexation and colonization of those islands. This brought him into contact with Lord Durham (1792–1840), who echoed his enlightened ideas about colonial self-government in his landmark *Report on the Affairs of British North America* (1839), which Wakefield helped to draft.

Wakefield lobbied on behalf of the New Zealand Land Company (1839), whose schemes were opposed by **James Stephen** of the Colonial Office and the Church Missionary Society. A shipload of settlers was nonetheless dispatched to **New Zealand**, which prompted the government to annex the country and grant a formal charter to the new colony (1841). Wakefield worked to promote the interests of British colonists abroad until he sailed for New Zealand (1853) and helped found the Canterbury settlement there. He died in Wellington.

N. Merrill Distad

Bibliography

Bloomfield, Paul. *Edward Gibbon Wakefield: Builder of the British Commonwealth.* 1961.

Garnett, Richard. *Edward Gibbon Wakefield: The Colonization of South Australia and New Zealand.* 1898.

Lloyd Prichard, Muriel F., ed. *The Collected Works of Edward Gibbon Wakefield.* 1968.

Norman, John. *Edward Gibbon Wakefield: A Reappraisal.* 1963

Stuart, Peter Allan. *Edward Gibbon Wakefield in New Zealand: His Political Career, 1853–1854.* 1971.

See also Emigration and Immigration; Empire and Imperialism

Wales and Welsh Culture

Hanoverian Wales saw many major transformations. Economically, while **Welsh agriculture** remained relatively backward—only in the most fertile areas were the techniques of **agricultural improvement** adopted—**Welsh industry** fared better. In the early 18th century, **woolen** textiles, mainly centered in north Wales, were the principal manufacture, but this became increasingly squeezed as the West Riding of Yorkshire came to dominate the industry. However, the gradual development of the **iron** and **tin-plate** industries across the south made Wales one of Britain's most important industrial regions, a fact reflected in the growth of new urban areas such as **Merthyr Tydfil. Welsh mining** also grew significantly. Lead had long been locally worked, and from around 1750, Anglesey's copper reserves began to be mined extensively. **Coal** mining also grew to serve the **metallurgical** industries, output increasing significantly in the later years of the period.

The **Tory** party dominated **Welsh politics** in the early 18th century, although the **Whig** government took steps to ensure that its interests were looked after and its parliamentary representation increased. Some Tories turned to **Jacobitism**, but this was never a serious force in Wales. Tory influence revived during the reign of **George III** while large-scale landowners strengthened their domination of many parliamentary seats, their power monopoly only being broken by changes effected in the 1832 **Reform Act**. In common with many other parts of Britain, Wales witnessed an upsurge of **radicalism** in the late 18th and early 19th centuries. This had its roots partly in popular protest and partly in religious **dissent**. The period saw food **riots**, strikes, and rural unrest, culminating in the **Merthyr rising** of 1831.

In the Cromwellian period, Wales had been regarded as one of the "dark corners of the land" in religion, and its ancient oral culture, based on spoken **poetry** and regulated by a guild of bards, was uncultivated and unadapted to literacy and learning. The growth of **circulating schools**, developed by the **Rev. Griffith Jones**, helped spread the Welsh language in print, and, by making religious literature more accessible, contributed significantly to the Hanoverian **Welsh religious revival**. Centered initially in the **middle classes**, this was stimulated from the latter 1730s by the preaching of evangelists such as **Howel Harris, Daniel Rowland**, and **William Williams (Pantycelyn)**. Welsh **Methodism** led this revival: the break with its parent body, the **Church of England**, coming in 1811 with the ordination of the first Methodist ministers. By the end of the Hanoverian period (1837), the majority of Welsh worshippers were nonconformist. Here as in politics, traditions nurtured in Hanoverian developments were to govern Welsh life long after the last Hanoverian king, **William IV**, died.

Wales

The transformation wrought by the development of a literate culture was almost as great. Ever since 1536 and the "Union" with England, increasing numbers of Welsh people went to **London** only to find themselves, their language, and their alleged lack of literature derided. Reaction against this helped inspire the founding of such cultural groups as the Society of Ancient Britons (1715) and the Honourable Society of Cymmrodorion (1751). *Cymmrodorion* is the Welsh word for *aborigines,* the idea being that Welshmen had descended directly from the island's original inhabitants and thus held special claims on history and cultural respect; the society encouraged **poetic** efforts, publication of manuscripts, and revival of the eisteddfod (an annual assembly of Welsh poets and musicians), which had fallen into disuse. Slowly the eisteddfod, once an institution that had created the rules of the bardic order, reemerged as a competition between poets, while Welsh literature was unlocked from its oral-based repositories and brought into print. Knowledge of past styles allowed Goronwy Owen (1723–1769) to emerge as a classical Welsh poet, fully conversant with the strict metrical patterns of the Middle Ages, while **Edward Williams (Iolo Morganwg)** learned the technique so well that his forgeries of the poems of the greatest Welsh poet, Dafydd ap Gwylim, (*fl.* 1334–1370), went undetected for decades. These forgeries were important to the cultural revival. Iolo invented the Gorsedd ("throne" or assembly) of bards (1792), claiming to be the last survivor of the bardic order, preserving its ceremonies in his head; it was grafted onto the eisteddfod and still survives.

The cultural revival was marked also by historical and prose writing, Ellis Wynne (1671–1734) anticipating the mood of the Methodist revival in his *Gweledigiaethau Y Bardd Cwsg—the Visions of the Sleeping Bard* (1703), which produced images of corruption on Earth and of Heaven and Hell in splendid prose. Theophius Evans (1693–1767) produced a largely mythical but very popular Welsh history, full of tales of Saxon perfidy, in his *Drych Y Prif Oesoedd—the Mirror of Past Ages* (1716; rev. 1740). More serious history came in the work of Edward Lhyud (*c.* 1660–1709), who prepared the way for a scientific archaeology and established the ancient origins of the Celtic languages. Others produced grammars and **dictionaries**, basic tools for a literate culture. Particularly significant was the *Geiriadur Cymraeg a Saesneg—Welsh and English Dictionary* (1803) of William Owen Pughe (1759–1835); Pughe was also a notable editor of ancient literary manuscripts.

The result of the cultural revival was an enhanced sense of the worth of Wales and a pride in its culture and history. With the founding of the Gwyneddigion (Men of Gwynedd) Society in London (1770) and the work of Iolo Morganwg the revival developed a popular and more democratic dimension. One expression of this was the revival of the idea that America had been discovered by Prince Madoc in the 12th century. Some enthusiasts crossed the Atlantic to find his alleged descendants, the Mandan Indians; John Evans (1770–1799) of Wanfawr in Caernarfonshire died in the search, whereas Morgan John Rhys (1760–1804) established a model Welsh community at Beulah, Pennsylvania.

The unprofitable quest for Welsh Indians represented an admiring backward fixation upon Welsh freedom, akin in many respects to the mythic invocation by English radicals of the "Norman Yoke" idea (which implied a Saxon golden age before 1066 and the imposition of an alien rule). It summoned up an idea of Wales independent and glorious, before imposition of the Saxon yoke. But there was also a rural–conservative dimension to Welsh cultural **nationalism**. Angharad Llwyd (1780–1866) won the competition at the Beaumaris eisteddfod (1832) with an antiradical view of the **history** of Anglesey. Augusta Hall, Lady Llanover (1802–1896), concocted Welsh national costume out of regional variants of

Welsh peasant dress and also held eisteddfodau at Abergavenny. Lady Charlotte Guest (1812–1895) participated in the **translation** of Welsh folk tales (and of major strands in the Arthurian legend) into English as *The Mabinogion* (1846).

The impact of all this was less than some apostles had hoped. In the late 1840s an official report on **Welsh education** commented disapprovingly on the condition of the Welsh people, much to the annoyance of this nation of religious nonconformists. The report was quickly dubbed "The Treason of the Blue Books" and treated as the latest stage in Saxon treachery. But this missed an important point. Religious revivalism and **antiquarian** cultural enthusiasm were in many ways deeply opposed to each other; and nonconformity, thrusting aside bards and Gwyneddigions, was enveloping the Welsh way of life. Iolo died in 1826, but already south Wales had become, as he unappreciatively put it, "Methodistical as hell." By the 1850s the eisteddfod had migrated from the pub to the chapel, and Wales had become (in Dylan Thomas's phrase) "Bible black."

Neil Evans

Bibliography

Jenkins, Geraint H. *The Foundations of Modern Wales, 1642–1780.* 1987.

Jenkins, Philip. *A History of Modern Wales, 1536–1990.* 1992.

Jones, David. *Before Rebecca: Popular Protest in Wales, 1790–1835.* 1973.

Moore, Donald, ed. *Wales in the Eighteenth Century.* 1976.

Stephens, Meic, ed. *The Oxford Companion to the Literature of Wales.* 1986.

Williams, Glanmor. *Language, Religion and Nationality in Wales.* 1979.

Walpole, Horace (1717–1797)

Walpole, a most informative and entertaining writer, **wit**, and connoisseur, is best remembered for his letters, which offer an incomparable panorama of his age, and for his popularization of the **Gothic** style in **architecture**, exemplified by Strawberry Hill, his house in Twickenham outside **London**.

Youngest son of the **Prime Minister, Sir Robert Walpole**, he was educated at Eton and Cambridge. After taking the **Grand Tour** (1739–1741) he served as a strong **Whig** M.P. (1741–1768) while holding a variety of sinecure offices. Important literary products of these years were his posthumously published *Memoirs of the Last Ten Years of the Reign of George the Second* and his *Memoirs of the Reign of King George the Third,* which describe the personalities and backroom maneuverings of contemporary politics.

The sinecures bestowed by his father enabled Walpole to devote most of his time to literary, artistic, and antiquarian pursuits. An important result of these "gentleman amateur" studies was his four-volume *Anecdotes of Painting* (1762–1771), the first detailed and systematic account of **painting** in England. Also noteworthy is his only **novel**, *The Castle of Otranto* (1765), generally credited with inaugurating the rise of **Gothic fiction** and the horror tale.

Horace Walpole

Walpole bought Strawberry Hill in 1748. His interest in the medieval past led him over the years to alter the house in the direction of **Gothic revival** style, with pointed arches, battlements, the addition of a round tower, and so on. It became a "tourist attraction," and its popularity was a major factor in promoting changes in architecture, which subsequently spread throughout England and the world.

Walpole's letters, of which some 4,000 survive, assure his reputation as perhaps the foremost chronicler of his times. Elegant and witty, with shrewd insights into human nature and a characteristic tone of light irony, they are both a literary achievement and an historical record of the first importance. Almost the whole range of 18th-century life is found in his various correspondences, which crystallize around specific themes: politics in the letters to Sir Horace Mann (1701–1786), the British envoy at Florence; literature in the letters to the poets **Thomas Gray** and William Mason (1725–1797); antiquarianism in the exchange with the Rev. William Cole (1714–1782); social gossip in the missives to George Montagu (1773–1780) and Anne Liddell (Countess of Upper Ossory [*c.* 1738–1804]); and so on. The definitive 48-volume *Yale Edition of Horace Walpole's Correspondence* (1937–1983), edited by W.S. Lewis and others with copious annotations and indexes, constitutes a veritable encyclopedia of 18th-century England.

Lars E. Troide

Bibliography

Ketton-Cremer, R.W. *Horace Walpole.* 1940; 4th ed., 1966.

Lewis, W.S. *Horace Walpole.* 1960.
Sabor, Peter. *Horace Walpole: A Reference Guide.* 1984.

See also Antiquities and Ruins; Letters

Walpole, Sir Robert (1676–1745)

Walpole was arguably the greatest politician of the Hanoverian age. He was called "The Great Man" by friends and enemies alike, and, while he had the support of both the monarchy and a majority in the **House of Commons** (1721–1742), he was a very powerful chief minister, although never the equivalent of a modern prime minister. In his lifetime and afterward he was called corrupt because he grew rich from holding office and because he constructed an extensive system of **patronage** to secure his power; yet, during his period of leadership, Britain enjoyed the stable government and finance it needed.

The son of a Norfolk squire, he sat in Commons some 40 years (1701–1712, 1713–1742) and held a succession of offices, culminating in that of First Lord of the Treasury. His success rose from his skill in managing Parliament, the king, and administrative business. He set several precedents, creating the position of leader of the non–**Jacobite** opposition centered on the heirs to the throne (1717), and the post of minister for the House of Commons (1721). Unlike his predecessors at the treasury, Walpole did not move to the **House of Lords** but instead became a direct link between Commons and the king. He was the first minister to concentrate in his own hands the powers of leading the Commons, managing the country's finances, and dispensing the king's patronage.

Walpole first held office in the reign of **Queen Anne**, serving as War Secretary (1708–1710) and Treasurer of the **Navy** (1710–1711) while Whig leader in Commons. **George I**'s conviction that all **Tories** were Jacobites ensured Whig power in his reign. Walpole became First Lord of the Treasury and Chancellor of the Exchequer (1715), but not yet chief minister. In 1717 he established the **sinking fund**, in which were accumulated government revenue for reducing the national debt. At this point he had less influence at Court than did his chief ally and brother-in-law Charles **Townshend**, and Walpole resigned when the latter was dismissed from office (1717).

The collapse of the **South Sea Company** (1720) allowed Walpole to return to office as rescuer of investors and shield of George I's mistress, who was involved in the scandal. He was reappointed to head the treasury (1721) and continued to consolidate his power as his rivals died or resigned. He also enjoyed the trust and support of **Queen Caroline,** who used her influence on her husband, **George II**, to promote Walpole's policies. Walpole's control of Commons allowed parliaments to run their full 7 years, which encouraged political stability.

Walpole's brother Horatio (1678–1757) had none of his parliamentary skills but supported him with unswerving loyalty. Horatio's chief interest was **diplomacy**. While he was ambassador to **France** (1724–1730), he had an excellent working relationship with its first minister and helped maintain his brother's policy of cooperative Anglo–French **foreign relations**.

Sir Robert Walpole

Despite Sir Robert's usual command of a majority in Commons, the members could reject his authority, as when his 1733 **excise bill** was defeated. As the number of men desiring office and power increased and could not be accommodated, the **opposition** to his ministry grew louder and stronger. Walpole's distrust of able men, unpopular stand against **war** with Spain (1739), and the enmity of **Frederick, Prince of Wales** led to a declining majority in Commons. Fearing a greater loss of support, Walpole's colleagues urged him to resign, which he did in January 1742. Though then created Earl of Orford, he rarely attended or spoke in the Lords because of his poor health. Until his death, Walpole remained adviser to the king and to **Henry Pelham.**

Walpole's youngest son, **Horace Walpole**, the connoisseur and writer, believed his father had been betrayed by his Whig colleagues, and used his memoirs to damage their reputations through innuendoes and outright lies. Sir Robert needed no such defense. He was the consummate politician, a great parliamentarian and highly effective debater who respected the House of Commons. Only the inevitable waning of influence, combined with the strain of failing health and the loss of his wife, caused him to resign.

P.J. Kulisheck

Bibliography

Black, Jeremy. *Robert Walpole and the Nature of Politics in Early Eighteenth-Century Britain.* 1990.
Gerrard, Christine. *The Patriot Opposition to Walpole: Politics, Poetry, and National Myth, 1725–1742.* 1995.
Hill, Brian W. *Sir Robert Walpole: 'Sole and Prime Minister.'* 1989.
Plumb, J.H. *Sir Robert Walpole: The Making of a Statesman.* 1956.

———. *Sir Robert Walpole: The King's Minister.* 1960.
Rogers, Nicholas. *Whigs and Cities: Popular Politics in the Age of Walpole and Pitt.* 1990.
Sedgwick, Romney. *History of Parliament: The House of Commons, 1715–1754.* 2 vols. 1970.

See also Government, National; Party Politics; Pension and Place Bills; Political Thought; Prime Minister; Whigs and Whiggism

War and Military Engagements

In Hanoverian times the British **Army**, hampered by the public's unwillingness to maintain adequate forces during peacetime, often lost early engagements but prevailed in the end. Determined and increasingly scientific military leadership played an important part here and also in the successes of the Royal **Navy**. Naturally the strategic and tactical ideas of both services evolved in accordance with changing experiences, technologies, and global requirements.

The most characteristic instrument of 18th-century land war was the "Brown Bess" musket. In trained hands this weapon could be loaded and fired three or four times a minute, but its accuracy was limited to 50 yards. Musketry dictated that battles be fought at 40 to 200 yards, with massed volley fire to improve the chances of inflicting casualties; typically, only one musket ball in 400 hit an enemy. Socket bayonets, fixed to the weapons' muzzles, were more fearsome than deadly; when British troops charged with them, few opponents stood their ground. During the **French Revolutionary and Napoleonic Wars**, Napoleon introduced the tactic of attack by massed columns, preceded by an artillery barrage. **Wellington**, however, proved that after shielding his line from the artillery until the last moment, disciplined and steady line musket volleys could devastate and stop the massed column.

Soldiers rated personal courage high on the list of virtues, but the most successful British field commanders were those who, like Wellington, matched this with skills at organizing and coordinating all arms and forces, exploiting advantages of geography and terrain, and making prudent decisions. A commander who could maintain the British system of magazines, organized communications, and intact supply lines enjoyed a tremendous advantage over opponents attempting to "live off the land" or carry their supplies. The British system, though cumbersome, allowed flexibility of movement and maneuver, as well as providing greater ability to remain long in the field.

Battlefield factors such as communications (often limited) and lines of sight (often restricted by terrain, weather, and smoke) partially dictated tactics. Troops fought in close formations of lines and columns, which allowed for rapid movement and deployment, mutual support, and massed musketry fire. British infantry fought in a line formation two or three ranks deep, the fundamental unit being a company (approximately 50 men). In a "firing," every third company fired a volley while the other two loaded, giving continuous fire from each battalion (6 to 10 companies). Against cavalry, the line formed a four-sided, four-man-deep "battalion square." This, by wheels and turns, could rapidly maneuver over virtually any terrain except thick undergrowth.

Cavalry used the charge to break up enemy formations and pursue fleeing troops. Its other roles were to reconnoiter and harass the enemy, and to establish advanced posts, patrols, and scouts to protect against surprise attacks. Cavalry doctrine

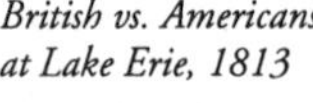
British vs. Americans at Lake Erie, 1813

alternated between favoring the pell-mell full gallop charge and the controlled, slow, deliberate attack. From frontier warfare in **North America** there evolved the light infantry concept, emphasizing agility, marksmanship, stealth, and the ability to operate in an extended line (or none at all) for skirmishing, sniping, and harassment. Grenadiers, originally designated to hurl small bombs (grenades) into an enemy's fortifications, remained the elite troops of each regiment long after their dangerous mission was abandoned. Grenadier and light infantry companies of each regiment were usually formed together into separate battalions for combat.

One of the earlier serious attempts to coordinate the armed services was made around 1760. After centuries of dispatching armies to campaign independently on the Continent, **William Pitt the Elder** instituted a radical change during the **Seven Years' War**, defining the army as the "spearpoint of the fleet." This new strategy emphasized using sea power to isolate outlying enemy strongpoints and colonial possessions, then following this up with troop landings to attack at weak points. After Pitt, small, seaborne British "expeditionary" forces continued to operate with larger Continental allied armies.

In naval warfare, superior seamanship was always Britain's prime advantage. Naval skills, honed by continuous sea duty, favored British arms in adverse weather, as did detailed knowledge of tides and other conditions, and efficient sailhandling and maneuvering. Tactically, the basic formation was the "line ahead" or "line of battle" configuration. A flag officer, in the lead or rear ship, could control his division's movements, with ships sailing in a single file, 120 yards apart. The advantages of the line included the ability to provide mutual support, avoidance of excessive exposure to concentrated enemy fire, a clear field of fire with little risk of hitting one's fellow ships, and adequate reloading time while passing between ships down the enemy's line. Disadvantages included the inability to concentrate fire on any portion of a tight enemy line, and a reduced scope for innovative tactical maneuvering. French doctrine emphasized firing at long range to demast and derig, then running; but running allowed a skilled British commander to break the French line and concentrate fire.

Discernment was the hallmark of great naval commanders such as **Anson**, **Hawke**, **Rodney**, and **Nelson**, the ability to recognize when the enemy had committed a tactical mistake or when he lacked battle discipline. Almost equally important was decisiveness, the ability to exploit the error rapidly—often by passing through the enemy's line, breaking up his formation, then concentrating fire and destroying him piecemeal.

Guns were typically fired simultaneously in a "broadside" while alongside the enemy. Marines, stationed in the masts and rigging, fired down on enemy gunners. Once an enemy ship surrendered or "struck its colours," a boarding party would take possession in the hope of preventing its sinking. A prize ship was valuable as an addition to the fleet or for sale on the commercial market.

British naval strategy had evolved by the late 18th century into five basic rules. First, the maintenance of a strong Western Squadron was understood to be the keystone of British naval strategy (after 1746); the Squadron guarded the western approaches to the Channel, prevented invasion, and countered French naval activity from Brest. Second, the purpose of the close blockade, perfected by Hawke, was to bottle up the enemy in port, interrupt his commerce, and allow the keeping of British **ships** at sea in all conditions and seasons. Third, the convoy system was to provide naval escorts and protection to massed groups of merchantmen against enemy warship attacks and privateering, and was to be supplemented by North Atlantic cruiser patrols. Fourth, the securing of forward base locations near the theater of operations was to give squadrons the ability to operate in distant waters with safe havens for resupply, repair, and refitting. And finally, it was recognized that the navy might transport and supply ground forces to strike at enemy weak points and colonial possessions.

Tactical doctrine was laid out in the various editions of the "Sailing and Fighting Instructions for His Majesty's Fleet" (first issued in 1673). These were mostly maneuvering instructions, but five tactical articles provided a common doctrine. Commanders issued Additional Fighting Instructions to account for their tactical preferences and local conditions, and might discard the existing Fighting Instructions altogether if necessary—a freedom that might often mean the difference between success and stalemate, as 18th-century commanders, including the great Nelson, increasingly discovered. The *Signal Book for Ships of War* (1799) replaced the tactical articles in the fighting instructions and, combined with the flag signaling system (1781), finally allowed commanders by the early 19th century to take full tactical control of their forces.

Stanley D.M. Carpenter

Bibliography

Barnett, Correlli. *Britain and Her Army, 1509–1970.* 1970.
Corbett, Julian S. *Some Principles of Maritime Strategy.* 1911.
Creswell, John. *British Admirals of the Eighteenth Century: Tactics in Battle.* 1972.
Gray, Colin S. *The Leverage of Sea Power.* 1992.
Hart, B.H.L. *The British Army in Warfare.* 1932.
Howard, Michael. *War in European History.* 1976.
Kennedy, Paul M. *The Rise and Fall of British Naval Mastery.* 1976.
Mahan, A.T. *The Influence of Sea Power upon History, 1660–1783.* 1984.
Marcus, G.J. *Heart of Oak: A Survey of British Sea Power in the Georgian Era.* 1975.
Rogers, H.C.B. *The British Army of the Eighteenth Century.* 1977.
Syrett, David, and R.L. DiNardo, eds. *The Commissioned Sea Officers of the Royal Navy, 1660–1815.* 1994.
Weigley, Russel F. *The Age of Battles.* 1991.

See also Education, Military; Weapons

War of 1812

After the **War of American Independence**, Anglo-American

Results of a 30-minute standoff, 1812

foreign relations were strained. Some problems stemmed from the war, including disputes over lost slave property, alleged British efforts to aid Indians trying to block trans–Appalachian settlement, and punitive restrictions on trade in the **West Indies.** Other problems were a result of the hostilities between Britain and **France** that continued during the **French Revolutionary and Napoleonic Wars** (1792–1815): the Americans resented Britain's efforts to discourage neutrals' trade with French-occupied Europe that would impair British economic warfare (enforced under the **Orders in Council**, 1807), and also the policy of impressing sailors (including Americans) into the British **Navy**. Some American politicians, "War Hawks," also saw war as a means to gain the economic independence that, in their view, had not come with political independence, and also as an opportunity to annex **Canada**. British concessions arrived too late to avert an American declaration of war (18 June 1812).

The war went badly for the United States. Invasions of Canada from Detroit, Niagara, and Lake Champlain failed miserably. Stalemate in 1813 broke down in 1814 as British redcoats regained control around Maine, burned the American capital in Washington, and descended on New Orleans. On advice from the **Duke of Wellington** the British government decided to press for a negotiated settlement. Talks at Ghent brought peace upon *status quo ante bellum* terms (24 December 1814). One effect of the war was to prolong antagonism between America and Britain; another, to strengthen Canadian national feeling.

David Sloan

Bibliography

Fowler, William M., Jr. *Jack Tars and Commodores.* 1984.
Horsman, Reginald. *The War of 1812.* 1969.
Lloyd, Alan. *The Scorching of Washington: The War of 1812.* 1975.
Rutland, Robert. *Madison's Alternatives: The Jeffersonian Republicans and the Coming of War, 1805–1812.* 1975.
Stagg, J.C.A. *Mr. Madison's War: Politics, Diplomacy, and Warfare in the Early Republic, 1783–1830.* 1983.
Watts, Steven. *The Republic Reborn: War and the Making of Liberal America, 1790–1820.* 1987.

See also War and Military Engagements

War of American Independence (1775–1783)

This conflict, sometimes called the American Revolutionary War, followed the failure of civilian authorities to stem the breakdown of relations between Britain and her **North American** colonies in the 1770s.

In April 1775, **General Thomas Gage** sent British troops to capture a colonial arms cache in Concord, Massachusetts. Their mission was accomplished but they were then driven back into Boston, a center of colonial resistance, and beseiged. Efforts to break the seige failed; British forces had to evacuate the town. The British government, throughout the war, would rely too heavily on information (often erroneous) from "loyalists" fleeing the colonies, and thus often had difficulty precisely understanding the conflict; but it now realized clearly that its task went beyond subduing small cliques of urban malcontents. Defining the struggle as a conventional war seemed more promising, since all rebel urban centers were seaport towns and, therefore, vulnerable to England's great military strength, the **navy**.

In June 1776 a force of 10,000 sailors and 32,000 troops, the largest land–sea operation in British history up to that time, invaded New York. While this force, under the command of **General William Howe** and his brother, Vice Admiral Richard Howe (1726–1799), failed to capture **George Washington**'s rebel army, it did force a full retreat south through New Jersey during the summer and fall. Had not Washington's daring winter attack across the Delaware River (26 December–6 January) succeeded in bolstering rebel morale, the war might have ended quickly.

In 1777 **General John Burgoyne** led an army south from **Canada** to join a force coming up the Hudson River, the goal being to control this crucial waterway and isolate the northern colonies. For reasons that have never been clear, General Howe instead moved his army south to occupy Philadelphia; Burgoyne, finding himself surrounded by rebel forces under General Horatio Gates (1728–1806) at **Saratoga**, surrendered his remaining army of 5,700 men (17 October).

France, which had been surreptitiously supporting the Americans, now entered into an open alliance (6 February 1778). This not only bolstered the military forces opposing Britain in North America but also created a war of many theaters, and, with the subsequent entry of Spain and the Netherlands, many enemies. As the conflicts dragged on, the war against the colonies became something of a sideshow.

Meanwhile the British government had gravitated toward an understanding of the war as one of pacification. This reconceptualization was instrumental in the decision to concentrate on the southern colonies, where loyalism was thought to be strongest, and to "roll up" the rebellion from that direction. To that end, the British first conquered Savannah (29 December 1779) and then Charleston (12 May 1780), capturing an army of 5,400 men in the worst defeat for the Americans in the entire war. Subsequently **General Charles Cornwallis** drove deep into the Carolinas, but finding himself unable to overcome the Fabian tactics of General Nathanael Greene (1742–1786), decided to remove his army north to Virginia and establish his headquarters at **Yorktown** (14 August 1781). A combined American–French army of nearly 17,000 men under Washington and Count Rochambeau (1725–1807) moved from New York (20 August) to besiege the British Army (28 September). Meanwhile a British fleet under Admiral Thomas Graves (1725–1802) had failed to dislodge the French fleet (Battle of the Capes, 5–10 September). Cornwallis, faced with a tightening siege and without hope of resupply, executed the surrender of Yorktown, turning over his 8,000 men (19 October).

While Britain's remaining 26,000 troops still controlled New York City, Charleston, Savannah, and Detroit, the political fallout from Yorktown effectively ended the war. **Lord North**'s response to the defeat was shock: "Oh God! It is the end!" **George III** contemplated abdication. North's administration, its failed military directorship under **Germain** and **Sandwich**, collapsed (20 March 1782). Negotiations beginning on 12 April resulted in the Preliminary Articles of Peace (30 November), by which Britain recognized the independence of the United States and ceded territory to the Mississippi River. These articles were incorporated into the general **Treaty of Paris** (20 January 1783), ending the European war.

David Sloan

Bibliography

Calhoon, Robert M. *The Loyalists in Revolutionary America, 1760–1781.* 1973.

De Conde, Alexander. "Historians, the War of American Independence, and the Persistence of the Exceptionalist Ideal." *International History Review.* Vol. 5, pp. 399–430.

Higginbotham, Don. *The War of American Independence: Military Attitudes, Policies, and Practice, 1763–1789.* 1971.

Hoffman, Ronald, and Peter J. Albert, eds. *Arms and Independence: The Military Character of the American Revolution.* 1984.

Kaplan, Roger. "The Hidden War: British Intelligence Operations during the American Revolution." *William and Mary Quarterly.* Vol. 47, pp. 115–138.

Mackesy, Piers. *The War for America, 1775–1783.* 1964.

Nelson, Paul David. "British Conduct of the American Revolutionary War: A Review of Interpretations." *Journal of American History.* Vol. 65, pp. 623–653.

Royster, Charles. *A Revolutionary People at War: The Continental Army and the American Character, 1775–1783.* 1979.

Shy, John. *A People Numerous and Armed: Reflections on the Military Struggle for American Independence.* Rev. ed., 1990.

See also American Revolution; Army; War and Military Engagements

War of Austrian Succession (1740–1748)

The Pragmatic Sanction (1713), signed by the Great Powers, permitted all Hapsburg territories to be inherited by the Princess Maria Theresa upon the death of her father the Hapsburg Emperor Charles VI (1685–1740). Violating this agreement, Frederick II of Prussia invaded Silesia (1740). In quick order, others, including Spain, **France**, Bavaria, and Saxony, disavowed the sanction. France coveted Austrian Belgium and Spain hoped for a revision of the Treaty of Utrecht (1713).

The war developed into a struggle between the houses of Bourbon and Hapsburg, with Prussia and Britain as significant participants also. Britain joined with Austria, Holland, and **Hanover**, while Prussia, France, Spain, and Bavaria fought on the other side. **George II** became the last British king to lead troops into battle (at Dettingen, 1743), as commander of a mixed Hanoverian and British auxiliary to the Austrian Army. In the Mediterranean, the British **Navy** sought to disrupt Spanish operations in northern Italy, leading to the inconclusive Battle of Toulon (1744) in which British and French ships engaged despite the absence of a formal state of war.

From 1744 to 1748 Britain and France were the chief combatants, though their battles were inconclusive. By late 1745 France had overrun Bohemia, seized Belgium, and won the Battle of Fontenoy, memorable for the ostentatious gallantry with which French officers invited the British to "shoot first." The French also supported the failed but disruptive **Forty-five**, the **Jacobite** rebellion in Britain. Overseas, the war went badly for France. A New England colonial force captured Louisburg at the mouth of the St. Lawrence; the Royal Navy effectively blockaded the **West Indies** and after two decisive engagements (1747) gained the upper hand at sea.

Fearing the loss of colonies and trade, France agreed to terms, resulting in the Treaty of Aix-la-Chapelle (1748). The treaty reestablished the prewar status quo, excepting Silesia, which Prussia retained. The peace proved to be merely an interlude in the continuing Anglo–French conflict.

Stanley D.M. Carpenter

Bibliography

Blair, Claude. *European and American Wars.* 1962.

Creswell, John. *British Admirals of the Eighteenth Century: Tactics in Battle.* 1972.

Fortescue, John. *History of the British Army.* 13 vols. Vol. 2. 1910.

Hufton, Olwen H. *Europe: Privilege and Protest, 1730–1789.* 1980.

Kennedy, Paul M. *The Rise and Fall of British Naval Mastery.* 1976.

See also Foreign Relations; War and Military Engagements

War of Jenkins' Ear (1739–1741)

Anglo–Spanish antagonism festered in the 1730s from growing British abuse of the strictly limited trading rights obtained from Spain in the Treaty of Utrecht (1713). British merchants, increasingly pursuing illegal **commerce** with Spain's colonies, pressed **Walpole's** government for a more aggressive stance toward Spain. The presumed sinking of several British merchant **ships** by the Spanish coast guard (1737), the suspension of the *asiento* (the British monopoly on the **slave trade**), the Spanish assertion of search and seizure rights against **smugglers**, and the propaganda campaign raised around the alleged mutilation of Captain Robert Jenkins, created public pressure for war.

Jenkins, master of the brig *Rebecca,* bound for **London** from Jamaica, had reputedly had his ear cut off and his ship plundered by the captain of a Spanish coast guard vessel near Havana on 9 April 1731. The case aroused some attention, which then subsided, then flared again when Jenkins testified before a committee of the **House of Commons** (1738), producing an artifact which he claimed to be the defunct organ of hearing. Despite evidence that he had lost it as **punishment** for theft in England, public indignation mounted. This, combined with the anti–Spanish campaign in the press, led to war (October 1739).

In the unsuccessful naval struggle that followed, Admiral Edward Vernon (1684–1757) captured Porto Bello (Panama) in November 1739, but the attack on Cartagena (Colombia) in early 1741 failed due to stout Spanish resistance, disease, and dissension between British **Army** and **Navy** commanders. Unsuccessful attempts to capture Santiago (Cuba) and raid the Florida coast resulted in heavy British casualties. Commodore **George Anson**, operating with a small squadron off Chile, raided coastal areas, then circumnavigated the globe in H.M.S. *Centurion* (1740–1744), capturing Spanish treasure along the way.

In America the war petered out into commercial raiding and attacks on Spanish trade, while in Europe Walpole's ineffectual policy of employing naval forces in the Mediterranean to prevent Spanish troop movement to Italy led to his government's fall (1742). All in all, the war cost Britain 20,000 casualties and 407 ships, primarily merchantmen, in exchange for little commercial or strategic gain. The Anglo–Spanish struggle and naval rivalry with **France** eventually helped bring Britain firmly into the broader **War of Austrian Succession** (1740–1748), allied with the Austrian Queen, Maria Theresa (1717–1780).

Stanley D.M. Carpenter

Bibliography

Barnett, Correlli. *Britain and Her Army, 1509–1970.* 1970.

Fortescue, John W. *History of the British Army.* 13 vols. Vol. 2. 1910.

Kennedy, Paul M. *The Rise and Fall of British Naval Mastery.* 1976.

Southworth, John. *The Age of Sails.* 1968.

See also War and Military Engagements

War of the Little Englishman (1820–1826)

What little opposition there was to agricultural **enclosures** in **Wales** largely occurred within the southwestern counties. Most of the trouble took place in the 1810s and 1820s at Mynydd Bach, the hilly land between Lampeter and Aberystwyth in Cardiganshire. Parliamentary acts of 1812 and 1815 authorized enclosure of 10,000 acres there, and from 1815, violence flared among the local peasantry intent upon defending their "rights" of commonage.

The "War of the Little Englishman" symbolized this defense of customary rights. In December 1819 Augustus Brackenbury, a young gentleman from Lincolnshire, purchased an allotment of 850 acres of the common earmarked for enclosure under the 1815 act. But it was on this particular tract that local inhabitants had been accustomed to cut peat. Such was the hostility to Brackenbury (doubtless augmented by his being a stranger) that no sooner did he erect a house than it was attacked in 1820, and again, when he rebuilt it, in 1821. After a lull of some years he erected another house, fortified with a moat, but this too was destroyed (1826). Soon afterward he sold out and left, dispirited. With magistrates powerless or reluctant to assert their authority, the bodyguards and troops defending Brackenbury's property were repeatedly defied by a mob which, sometimes disguised as women and wearing handkerchiefs over their faces, and viewing the enclosure commissioners as "Cannibals and Blood Suckers," successfully asserted and reasserted their "right" to cut peat.

D.W. Howell

Bibliography

Jones, D.J.V. "More Light on 'Rhyfel y Sais Bach.'" *Ceredigion.* Vol. 5, pp. 84–93.

———. *Before Rebecca.* 1973.

Williams, David. "'Rhyfel y Sais Bach,' an Enclosure Riot on Mynydd Bach." *Ceredigion.* Vol. 2, pp. 39–52.

See also Rockites and Rockism; Swing Riots; Welsh Agriculture; Whiteboys

War of Spanish Succession (1702–1713)

The death of Spain's King Charles II (1700) was the immediate cause of this war. Louis XIV of **France** (1638–1715) and the Holy Roman Emperor Leopold I (1640–1705), brothers-in-law of Charles, signed a treaty (1698) which arranged Spain's partition between them at his death. His will, however, stipulated that Spain and its empire would be ruled by Philip of Anjou, Louis's grandson. England's William III (*r.* 1689–1702), fearing a French-dominated Bourbon hegemony, arranged the Grand Alliance (1701), which included the Holy Roman Empire, the Dutch Netherlands, Portugal, Brandenburg, and Savoy. France allied with Spain and Bavaria in opposition.

The Alliance overwhelmed the French. Led by John Churchill (later **Duke of Marlborough**) and Prince Eugene of Savoy (1663–1736), it triumphed at Blenheim in Bavaria (1704), and Ramillies (1706), Oudenarde (1708), and Malplaquet (1709) in the Spanish Netherlands. Britain captured Gibraltar and, with the Dutch, undercut French maritime trade in the **West Indies** and the Mediterranean. Louis accepted terms; the treaties of Utrecht (1713) and Rastadt (1714) followed.

Britain emerged as the war's great winner. Spain lost its external territories in Europe, and although Philip remained on the Spanish throne as the first Bourbon king there (Philip V), it was established that no single person could rule both Spain and France. Britain obtained a strong position in the Mediterranean, North American concessions, overwhelming naval domination, and the *asiento* (the exclusive **slave trade** to Spanish America). The war preserved the changes made by the **Glorious Revolution** (1688–1689), heralded in Britain the increasing influence of merchant interests, and assured the **Hanoverian Succession** of **George I** (1714). Britain continued its rise as a colonial, commercial, and maritime power—a position it secured more fully at the end of the **Seven Years' War** (1763).

Stanley D.M. Carpenter

Bibliography

Barnett, Correlli. *Marlborough.* 1974.
Chandler, David. *Marlborough as Military Commander.* 1973.
Francis, A. David. *The First Peninsular War.* 1975.
Kennedy, Paul M. *The Rise and Fall of British Naval Mastery.* 1976.

See also Foreign Relations; War and Military Engagements

Warburton, William (1698–1779)

Warburton was a leading English churchman, theologian, literary scholar, and **letter** writer. In addition to numerous theological works, he produced the first edition of the works of **Alexander Pope** (1751) and a notorious edition of William Shakespeare (1747). Once famous and controversial, he is now often dismissed as an overbearing and wrongheaded eccentric who unfairly attacked many of the more progressive people and tendencies of his age, including **Wilkes**, J.-J. Rousseau (1712–1778), and **Wesley**; his *The Doctrine of Grace* (1762) was a strong attack on **Methodism**.

Warburton held numerous church posts, rising to become Bishop of Gloucester in 1759. His chief theological work, the unfinished *Divine Legation of Moses* (1738–1741), employed much curious lore in a paradoxical attack on **deism**. His own religious views were not entirely conventional, but he defended the orthodoxy of Pope's *Essay on Man* and became Pope's collaborator and literary executor.

As controversialist and editor, Warburton was ferocious and only partly successful. His *Divine Legation* pleased no one, but included **literary criticism** that often is original in substance and methodology. Despite his understandable attacks on the plagiarizing **Lewis Theobald**'s edition of Shakespeare, he outdid Theobald in irresponsible textual emendation; his own edition marked a low point in the editing of Shakespeare. His edition of Pope also tinkered with the text, but included commentary that is by turns enlightening and puzzling. **Robert Lowth** also convincingly attacked his scholarship in a controversy over the book of Job. His letters are readable, varied in style, and informative.

Bishop William Warburton

John Freehafer

Bibliography

Evans, A. *Warburton and the Warburtonians.* 1932.
Ryley, Robert. *William Warburton.* 1984.

See also Church of England; Shakespeare Industry

Warton Family

The Wartons were a remarkable literary family. Thomas Warton the elder (1688–1745) was a writer of occasional verse, Professor of **Poetry** at Oxford, and later master of the grammar school at Basingstoke. His first son, Joseph (1722–1800), a critic, poet, and **periodical** essayist, became Headmaster of Winchester. His second son, Thomas the younger (1728–1790), was also Professor of Poetry at Oxford, a poet, critic, editor, and historian of English poetry. He was created **Poet Laureate** in 1785.

The Wartons exercised their respective influences on literary taste and helped to make English poetry less formal and classical. For instance, the elder Warton's verse included some "runic" odes. Joseph Warton published *The Enthusiast* (1744), a blank-verse encomium on the scenic primitive and the **sublime.** In *Odes on Various Subjects* (1746) he announced that moralizing in verse had been "carried too far," and in the first volume of his important *Essay on the Genius and Writings of Pope* (1756) he judged **neoclassically** correct contemporary verse to be lacking in "transcendently sublime" and "pathetic" qualities, especially when compared with the more imaginative Elizabethan poetry. He brought out an edition of the works of **Alexander Pope** in 1797. His brother, Thomas

Thomas Warton the Younger, from a painting by J. Reynolds

Warton the younger, wrote minor verse and **biography**, but he is chiefly remembered for his three-volume history of English poetry (1774, 1778, 1781) down to the end of the Elizabethan age.

Joseph Warton has left a mark as a critic rather than a learned historian. He was one of those who cast off the predominant critical values of the time and provided a language for the acceptance of **Romanticism**. His brother Thomas, together with **Thomas Percy**, turned attention toward the beauties of English poetry and language in earlier times, and thus played a role in the growing interest in things **Gothic**, and the vogue of **antiquities and ruins**.

Ronald Rompkey

Bibliography

Partridge, Eric, ed. *The Three Wartons: A Choice of Their Verse.* 1927.

Vance, John A. *Joseph and Thomas Warton.* 1983a.

———. *Joseph and Thomas Warton: An Annotated Bibliography.* 1983b.

See also Literary Criticism

Washington, George (1732–1799)

"The Father of his Country" was the eldest of six children born to his father's second wife in rural Virginia. His great-grandfather had migrated to Virginia from Sulgrave (Northamptonshire) in 1657. By age 16, George had become a surveyor, operating mostly on lands near the western frontier. At age 19 (1751) he accompanied his ill step-brother Lawrence to the **West Indies** where he contracted the **smallpox** that would leave him marked for life. Lawrence soon died, and after an interval George inherited the family estate at Mount Vernon (1761) on the Potomac River.

By that time, Washington had already made a reputation as a soldier. In 1754, as Lieutenant-Colonel of a Virginia brigade, he accompanied a force sent by Virginia's governor and House of Burgesses into the west to push back the combined forces of Frenchmen and Indians who were encroaching into the Ohio Valley. The encounter of May 1754 marked the beginning of the **Seven Years' War** in North America. The following year, General Edward Braddock (1695–1755) arrived as Commander of British forces in **North America**, intending to drive the French out of their new position at Fort Duquesne. Washington accompanied his ill-fated wilderness expedition alongside 700 other provincial soldiers and some 1,400 British regulars. During the enemy ambush and slaughter of Braddock's forces (9 July 1755), Washington distinguished himself for bravery and levelheadedness, saving some of them from annihilation. Later he accompanied Brigadier-General John Forbes (1710–1759) in his capture of the fort (1758), which was then triumphantly renamed "Pitts-Bourgh" in honor of **Pitt the Elder**, directing war operations from **London**.

In the 1760s, Washington, greatly enriched by marriage as well as inheritance, entered politics, serving as burgess and Justice of the Peace in Fairfax County. His conduct, reading, interests, and religion resembled those of the English **gentry**. Though he owned **slaves**, he refused to sell them, declaring himself "principled against this kind of traffic in the human species." Like that other "Farmer George," his greatest love was farming (chiefly wheat and **tobacco**); he enjoyed cards, fox-hunting, **dancing**, and billiards, and insisted on the best **clothes** from London. In politics Washington remained on friendly terms with Virginia's governors, but in the latter 1760s became increasingly convinced that some military confrontation loomed. Though strongly opposed as late as 1774 to American independence, his attitude was that the colonists should not truckle to "our lordly masters" in Parliament. He participated in the first and second continental congresses (1774–1775) as a delegate from Virginia, and was put in charge of the new Continental Army in June of 1775.

During the new 7-year war that followed, Washington's greatest strengths were his energy, strong character, and persistence against heavy odds. His weaknesses, critics said, were excessive caution and reliance on his council of war, rather than on his own judgment. His greatest challenge lay simply in keeping an army in the field; American forces fluctuated between 5,000 and 18,000 men. The colonials disliked long enlistments and had a tendency to disappear at planting and harvest times. At the beginning, **General William Howe** forced the inexperienced Washington to retreat south from New York (1776), but the latter staged victories at Trenton and Princeton at year's end which kept the war alive. Howe captured Philadelphia the next summer, but the victory of the American General Horatio Gates (1728–1806) at **Saratoga** (October 1777) against **General Burgoyne** turned the tide and brought **France** into the struggle as an ally (1778). During the rough winter of 1777–1778 at Valley Forge (Pennsylvania), Washington's forces at last fused into a real army. The main battleground shifting south, Washington's greatest victory was the **Surrender of Yorktown** (1781), which effectively ended the struggle. Shaken to its core, the English government finally signed the **Treaty of Paris** (1783), granting independence.

Washington retired to Mount Vernon, but answered Virginia's call to attend the Constitutional Convention (1787). Elected to preside over debate, he was then overwhelmingly elected first President of the United States. During his two terms (1789–1797) he set his stamp upon the office, keeping it firmly republican yet lending it dignity, a general scope embracing all the new American states, and, in **foreign affairs**, impartiality and independence—a fact underlined in U.S. neutrality when war again broke out (1793) between Britain and America's former ally, France. When Washington died, he was buried at Mount Vernon, about 15 miles south of where the Washington Monument now stands in Washington, D.C.

Kim M. Gruenwald

Bibliography

Alden, John Richard. *George Washington: A Biography.* 1984.

Cunliffe, Marcus. *George Washington, Man and Monument.* 1958.

Flexner, James Thomas. *Washington, the Indispensable Man.* 1974.

Higginbotham, Don. *George Washington and the American Military Tradition.* 1985.

Longmore, Paul K. *The Invention of George Washington.* 1988.

See also American Revolution; War and Military Engagements; War of American Independence

Watercolor

In 1714, British watercolor painting was a minor tradition, used by professionals for maps and for military and architectural sketches, and by amateurs for the occasional drawing. By 1837, however, it rivaled oil painting as the most important genre in Britain; there were two exhibiting societies solely devoted to it in **London**, and many other venues, practitioners, and audiences elsewhere. This growth had much to do with the increasing British demand for and sophistication about art, a development attributable in part to foreign influences; but some conditions, such as the sheer number of amateur watercolorists, arose from circumstances peculiarly British.

Watercolor painting—the use of color pigments suspended in water rather than oil, and bound to the medium of support (generally paper, but sometimes ivory, cloth, or parchment) with the addition of some gum arabic—was not invented in Britain; however, it has become associated with the British. Nearly all cultures in all periods have found a place for watercolor among their art practices and media. In Europe, once the age of manuscript illumination had passed, watercolor was generally confined to the realm of the useful rather than the aesthetic, and used for designs and plans in the theater, for land surveys, military maps, and so on. The portability of watercolor also served it well (since water could be found easily anywhere, and did not slop and stain, the way oil did), making it a useful tool outside the studio; which is one reason why it became associated intimately with **landscape painting**.

Watercolor was widely practiced on the Continent in the 18th century but always considered a lesser medium than oil. In Britain, watercolor traditions derived primarily from Flemish artists, beginning with Anthony Van Dyke (1599–1641) and extending through Peter Tillemans (1684–1734). When Jonathan Richardson, Sr. (1665–1745) focused English taste on Italian art in the first decades of the 18th century, Italian drawing styles came to be appreciated and imitated. Prominent here was the tradition of drawing *vedutas,* views of Venice and of ancient Roman ruins, which were reproduced as etchings printed in sepia and black, and sold as souvenirs to foreign tourists. Gradually the practice grew up of coloring these with transparent watercolors, and by the 1750s several accomplished British artists regularly painted in watercolors, either in combination with their oil paintings or independently: Paul Sandby (1731–1809), called by some "the father of English watercolor"; Samuel Scott (*c.* 1702–1772); William Taverner (1703–1772); and Alexander Cozens (1717–1786).

By the 1750s, nearly all the technical possibilities of watercolor had been tried out. Pure watercolors without underdrawing had been created, and there were experiments with scratching-out and stopping-out (different ways to preserve the white of the paper from being tinted by a color wash, either by scratching the surface to reveal the white or by putting down egg white or other substances to stop the wash, then removing them). Huge topographical works were attempted, some as large as big oil landscapes, joining many sheets of paper; but more typically, watercolor topographies were limited to the size of the paper, whether folio or superfolio. Similar work existed on the Continent, from Holland to Italy, but only in England did watercolor develop into a mainstream tradition.

Three factors were responsible for this. First, the creation of institutions for the arts, which both professionalized artists

Emily Stapleton Pakenham, an amateur watercolorist

and created large and stable audiences for them, was a major accomplishment of Hanoverian Britain. However, the arts were not institutionalized along Continental lines. For example, the **Royal Academy of Arts** was never able to control access to resources and audiences as its French counterpart was; there were always competing groups. The Royal Society of the Arts played an important role in the 1760s and 1770s in encouraging draftsmen by holding exhibitions and competitions. Exhibiting societies such as the Society of Painters in Water-Colours (the Old Water-Colour Society), founded in 1804 to combat the Royal Academy's relative neglect of watercolor, the Associated Artists in Water-Colours (1808–1812), and the New Society of Painters in Water-Colours (founded in 1832) provided important forums for professional artists excluded from the Royal Academy (which did not admit watercolorists per se as members, though it regularly exhibited watercolors). And many sketching societies flourished at one point or another, in both London and the **provincial towns**.

Second, nearly every English watercolorist of note, with the major exception of **J.M.W. Turner**, supported himself by giving lessons and selling finished works (always cheaper than oils) to amateur pupils, providing steady, even substantial, incomes for the artists. No comparable group of amateur practitioners sustained oil painters. With the growing popularity of **travel and tourism** and with Britain's growing imperial ascendancy, amateurs were beginning to record scenes on nearly every corner of the globe. On the other hand, amateur production on the domestic front was increasingly becoming dominated by women, a tendency that left some disgruntled oil painters claiming that oil was a masculine and important (hence "professional") medium, whereas watercolor was effeminate. The later development of photography and of cheap color reproduction was to deal another blow to watercolor, but this occurred well into the Victorian period.

Third, with the growth of tourism in the 1770s, the chief watercolorists who visited the Continent—notably William Marlow (1740–1813), Francis Towne (1739–1816), John "Warwick" Smith (1749–1831), and J.R. Cozens (1752–1797)—came back with the ambition to give their work the same artistic seriousness that oil enjoyed. They could hope to realize this ambition because they knew they could have sustained careers as watercolorists, supported by teaching and also by the wide sale of aquatints (etchings resembling watercolors)—the first English book of aquatints was Sandby's *Twelve Views in South Wales* (1775). While they experimented with the techniques of the earlier generation, the essential step was conceptual. Thomas Girtin (1775–1802) and Turner, who trained themselves by copying Cozens's drawings in the home of Dr. Thomas Munro, an amateur, were his successors as the dominant figures at the turn of the century. Girtin, who showed remarkable abilities with glowing, transparent colors, died young; Turner, though equally skilled in oils, never abandoned watercolor and took it to heights of elaboration never before seen. The professionals who founded the Old Water-Colour Society just after Girtin's death, however, were the ones who most benefited from the success of watercolor: Francis Nicholson (1753–1844), John Glover (1767–1849), John Varley (1778–1842), Peter De Wint (1784–1849), and David Cox (1783–1859). Their styles and subjects (nearly all landscapes), enhanced by the **Romantic** spirit of the age and by the expressiveness and spontaneity peculiar to watercolor, dominated the scene for the remainder of the period.

Bruce Robertson

Bibliography

Clarke, Michael. *The Tempting Prospect: A Social History of English Watercolour.* 1978.
Hardie, Martin. *Water-Colour Painting in Britain.* 1966.
Wilton, Andrew. *British Watercolours, 1750 to 1850.* 1977.

See also Drawing; Engraving; Graphic Arts; Painting

Waterloo, Battle of (1815)

Napoleon's escape from Elba (26 February 1815) set in motion the "Hundred Days" which ended in his last defeat near Waterloo, a Belgian village (18 June). Hoping to destroy the combined Prussian and Anglo–Dutch forces, he mustered a 100,000-man veteran force and crossed the Belgian border. He soon encountered and fought the **Duke of Wellington**'s Anglo–Dutch force to a draw at Quatre Bras, and defeated the Prussians at Ligny (16 June).

Dividing his army, with one corps detached to defend against the Prussians (17 June), Napoleon faced Wellington's deployed forces on a ridge south of Brussels. Although rapidity of movement had always been the key to his successes, Napoleon delayed the assault to allow rain-soaked roads time to dry in order to deploy artillery; the plan called for a massive artillery bombardment, followed by a diversionary attack, then a main thrust to pierce the Allied center and open the road to Brussels.

All elements of surprise had been lost by 18 June. Napoleon's bombardment accomplished little because Wellington's troops were shielded by the crest of the ridge. The diversionary attack against the Allied right failed to draw off their reserves. The assault on the center faltered when confused orders created a broad front on which British artillery and cavalry inflicted massive casualties.

Wellington moved his main forces back over the ridge, where they formed battalion squares. Taking this as a retreat, Marshall Michel Ney (1769–1815), temporarily in command due to Napoleon's illness, charged with most of the French cavalry. Wet ground, the lack of infantry support, stout defense by the squares, and the loss of a third of the attackers as horses and riders tumbled into a deep, unseen ravine, doomed the French cavalry.

Late in the afternoon, though the French had captured a farmhouse on Wellington's left and set up guns that threatened to crumble the Allied center, Prussian advance units began arriving on Napoleon's right flank. In a final attempt to break Wellington's center, Napoleon committed his Imperial Guard. The steady British volley fire checked their advance, and they backed down the ridge. Their repulse, as well as the arrival of Prussian forces, caused panic in the French line.

Wellington at the Battle of Waterloo

Wellington's troops charged with bayonets against their disintegrating foes. The French army crumbled and fled, ending all hope of resurrecting the Napoleonic Empire. In Britain the battle was celebrated for many decades afterward as a confirmation of national greatness.

Stanley D.M. Carpenter

Bibliography

Chalfont, Lord, ed. *Waterloo: Battle of Three Armies.* 1980.
Chandler, David. *Napoleon.* 1973.
———. *Waterloo, the Hundred Days.* 1980.
Connelly, Owen. *Blundering to Glory: Napoleon's Military Campaigns.* 1987.
Howarth, David A. *Waterloo: Day of Battle.* 1968.
Keegan, J.D.P. "Waterloo," in Keegan's *Face of Battle.* 1976.

See also Army; War and Military Engagements

Watson, Richard (1737–1816)

Bishop Watson was born at Heversham, attended **Cambridge University** (B.A. 1757), and though he was offered at age 23 the curacy of Clermont, which would have brought him to the notice of the **Duke of Newcastle**, the main dispenser of high ecclesiastical **patronage**, Watson refused because he valued "independence above all prospects." At Cambridge he became Professor of Chemistry (1764), then of Divinity (1771), commenting that he hoped to reduce the study of divinity "into as narrow a compass as I could." His chemical lectures were well attended, and he wrote several scientific works, including a manual of *Chemical Essays* (1781).

At the university Watson was the contemporary of men like **William Paley** and **John Jebb**, and, though he shared their critical outlook, he felt called upon in his *Apology for Christianity* (1776) to respond to **Gibbon**'s adverse reflections on religion in the first volume of *The Decline and Fall of the Roman Empire* (1776), just as in 1796 he replied to **Paine** with *An Apology for the Bible,* frequently reprinted afterward. A liberal **Whig**, he supported relief for **dissent**, opposed **North**'s coercion of the Americans, and backed **Wyvill** in the early 1780s. Despite this, he became Bishop of Llandaff in 1782 (though he rarely visited his see, instead whiling away his time at **agricultural improvement** on his estate in Windermere). In later years he supported the conservative reaction against the **French Revolution** in his very popular *Address to the People of Great Britain* (1798), without giving up his strenuous opposition to the **slave trade**.

Donald W. Nichol

Bibliography

Brain, Timothy. "Richard Watson and the Debate on Toleration in the Late Eighteenth Century." *Price-Priestley Newsletter.* Vol. 2, pp. 4–26.
Watson, Richard. *Anecdotes of the Life of Richard Watson.* 1814.

See also Church of England

Watt, James (1736–1819)

Watt was a famous son of the **Scottish Enlightenment** who, through his development of the steam engine, contributed

James Watt

mightily to the early **Industrial Revolution**. He was born in Greenock in 1736. His father was a versatile merchant-cum-mathematical instrument-maker, and after schooling at the local grammar school he worked initially in his father's workshop before being sent to **Glasgow** and then **London** for further training in the craft.

By 1757 he had returned to Glasgow, where the friendship of Andrew Anderson, brother of **John Anderson**, Professor of Natural Philosophy, helped him secure an appointment as mathematical instrument-maker in the university. There **Joseph Black** encouraged him in his experiments on what was then called the "fire engine," beginning with the repair of a **Newcomen** model engine in 1764. Perceiving that this wasted energy and latent heat, Watt brilliantly remedied the problem by constructing a separate chamber for condensation (1765). In 1768 he built a small test engine in partnership with **John Roebuck** of **Carron Ironworks**, and in 1769 he **patented** it. Its further development was delayed because he spent much of the period 1766–1774 earning his living as a land surveyor, including advising on the routes of several Scottish **canals**.

In 1768 Watt had been introduced to **Matthew Boulton**, the **Birmingham** engineer who became his partner in the further exploitation of the steam engine after 1775. He moved to Birmingham and thereafter made rapid progress on technical improvements, though dividing his time by going to consult in Cornwall, where he supervised erection of steam pumping-engines in copper and tin mines. Some of his most important new inventions were: rotary motion, achieved by the sun-and-planet gear (1781); the oscillating or double-acting engine (1782); the parallel motion arrangement (1784); the centrifugal governor to control the speed of the engine (1788); and the pressure gauge (1790).

Watt's patent had been extended by Parliament in 1775, with the result that he and Boulton held virtually sole rights for 25 years and became wealthy men. They were elected to Fellowships of the **Royal Society** in 1785; Watt was also an eminent member of the **Lunar Society**. He bought an estate in Radnorshire, where he lived after his retirement in 1800. He was honored by his former employer, Glasgow University, which made him a Doctor of Law (1806); and by the French Academy of Sciences, which made him a foreign associate (1816).

Watt's inventions quickened the pace of industrialization as it affected major industries such as **coal mining** and **iron** and **textile** production, and they also influenced the development of new modes of **transport** in steam navigation and **railways**. It is estimated that there were over 1,000 steam engines in use in Britain by 1800.

Ian Donnachie

Bibliography

Robinson, E., and A.E. Musson. *James Watt and the Steam Revolution.* 1969.

Rolt, L.T.C. *James Watt.* 1962.

See also Science, Technology, and Invention; Steam Engines

Watt, Robert (*d.* 1794)

Watt is a shadowy figure associated with a revolutionary conspiracy hatched in **Edinburgh** after the demise of the Scottish Association of Friends of the People and the later sedition trials of 1793–1794. Watt had attended meetings of radical societies (including the Friends of the People) and apparently acted as a government informer until his services were dispensed with in 1793. After this he continued to associate with a small underground group that drew delegates from various surviving societies. Its Committee of Ways and Means, under his direction, planned an armed insurrection in the spring of 1794. Troops were to be won over; the workers mobilized in support; Edinburgh Castle, the post office, and banks seized; and a provisional government proclaimed. Similar plans were allegedly drawn up for **London** and **Dublin**.

The plot was discovered by early May 1794. Watt and an associate, David Downie, were tried for treason and sentenced to death; Downie was reprieved, but Watt was hanged and beheaded in October. The plot's discovery helped to justify the government's suspension of Habeas Corpus in May and its treason trials of **Hardy**, **Tooke**, and **Thelwall** later that year.

Ian Donnachie

Bibliography

McFarland, E.W. *Ireland and Scotland in the Age of Revolution: Planting the Green Bough.* 1994.

See also French Revolution; Muir, Thomas of Huntershill; Radicalism and Radical Politics

Watts, Isaac (1674–1748)

Watts, **Congregationalist** minister, one of the central figures of English hymn-writing and devotional literature, became a prototype for the pious Protestant of the Hanoverian period.

He was also an important literary figure, writing on philosophy, **theology**, **education**, and **poetry**. His prose works remained influential as university textbooks for many years after his death.

Educated at the **dissenting academy** at Stoke Newington, Watts became a pastor (1702) and continued his work writing hymns. In the *Horae Lyricae* (1706) and *Hymns* (1707) he experimented in the Pindaric and quasi-Miltonic manner, but his best hymns (and those that are still commonly sung) move back toward the conservative style of the **ballad** quatrain and the traditional metrical psalm. Some of his experiments, like the Sapphic ode "The Day of Judgment" and the choral ode "The Incomprehensible," work brilliantly. Hymns such as "When I Survey the Wondrous Cross" and "Our God, Our Help in Ages Past" have rightly become staples of Protestant church music.

Divine Songs (1715) and *Catechisms* (1730) were expressly for children. Watts, perhaps the inventor of this genre, explained in his preface to *Divine Songs* the importance of presenting children with the sublimities of Christianity in terms suited to their immature understandings. A great success, this book was imitated by **William Blake** and **Robert Southey**—and parodied by Lewis Carroll (1832–1898).

Watts wrote prose treatises on nearly every topic but science. He entered debate on the Trinity in several pieces, including "The Glory of Christ as God-Man Unveiled" (1746). Having worked his way dangerously close to complete Arianism and even **Unitarianism**, to the end of his life he prayed God's forgiveness for these unorthodox sallies. His two most important prose works are his *Logic* (1733), which became a university and school classic, and *Improvement of the Mind* (1741). A man of enormous intellectual energy, though sometimes inclined toward moral complacency, he was one of the great figures of contemporary religious culture.

Blanford Parker

Bibliography

Davies, Donald. *A Gathered Church*. 1980.
Davis, A.P. *Isaac Watts*. 1943.

See also Children's Literature; Dissenters; Music, Church; Sermons

Weapons

European firearms developed from the 14th century. The basic technique was to fashion a barrel by boring a long hole into wood or iron, leaving one end of the bore solid as a *breech* end from which the ignited gunpowder would explode the projectile in the opposite direction; a small touch-hole was drilled into the side of the breech for igniting the gunpowder. All early guns are called *muzzle-loaders* because powder and ball were dropped into the open end or muzzle before firing. Muzzle-loading was standard until the early 19th century.

The main changes that took place before the 19th century were in the method for igniting the powder at the touch-hole. The earliest guns were little more than long tubes with no trigger to pull, leaving the powder to be kindled by hand-applied fire. This left them so ineffective that crossbows and long bows continued to be equally useful well into the 17th century. But two improved weapons—the matchlock and the wheellock—were slowly revolutionizing thinking and, by developing the trigger and a small pan of powder at the touch-hole, preparing the way for the revolutionary *flintlock*. This prefigured the cocking hammer and protected powder of today's firearms. It featured a spring-hinged hammer that held a flint: When released from its cocked position by the trigger, the flint struck an iron arm, causing the arm to lift off the touch-hole pan and a shower of sparks to fall into the powder.

The Hanoverian period was the "flintlock era." The flintlock was fully developed and had become the standard military arm by 1690, and was not replaced until the mid-19th century. It was modified for various uses, and novel experiments were tried, involving breech-loading, revolving chambers, rifling, and percussion caps. Wooden ramrods were replaced by steel in the 1770s. But in general, the flintlock system of muzzle-loading and firing a solid round ball was used for military purposes, hunting, **dueling**, and even cannon for most of the era.

The standard Hanoverian military *musket* was the long flintlock musket, known more familiarly as the "Brown Bess," the "Kings Arms," or the "Tower Musket." Its nicknames came from its brown rustproof coating and its long use as a standard weapon by government troops. Equipped with a 46-inch barrel and weighing about 12 pounds, this was a very heavy, cumbersome implement. It had a large bore (.77 or .80 inches) so that British soldiers could use the smaller balls of their enemies, while the latter could not easily use the larger British ball. The British musket differed from most foreign ones in that its barrel was attached to the stock by pins, whereas bands around the barrel were used elsewhere. Around 1750 it was lightened and modified to make it more maneuverable: its barrel was shortened to 42 inches, its weight reduced to 11 pounds. The carbine model, used by mounted troops, was virtually the same weapon, though made lighter and more maneuverable by a shorter 31-inch barrel (modified several times between 1750 and 1775).

A famous subspecies of the flintlock was the *blunderbuss*, a large-bored weapon featuring a bell-shaped muzzle. The largest blunderbuss could fire 2-inch balls and be mounted on swivels to use as a small cannon from fortress walls or **ships'** rails. **Coaching** guards favored it because it scattered projectiles over a large area; they loaded it with nails and scrap iron for its "moral effect" on would-be robbers. But technological development produces its own tit-for-tat, and soon a shorter, pistol-size blunderbuss was also made (usually of brass); some **highwaymen** armed themselves with it.

Early Hanoverian hunting weapons were nothing but flintlock muskets, though sometimes with an extra barrel added. The "over and under" type of revolving two-barrel system became popular around 1750. By 1770, with bird-hunting in vogue, there was a great demand for a lighter sporting weapon. This spurred a reduction in weight, achieved by changing from a full-length wooden stock under the barrel to the now-familiar half stock. New methods of casting barrels allowed for a thinner barrel wall, and barrel lengths were also reduced, from 42 to 36 inches. The familiar side-by-side double-barreled weapon was created at about the same time, to allow two shots without reloading or changing barrel positions. The last major improvement to the hunting shotgun was incorporated by 1800: A method of ("choke") boring the barrel to make it narrower at the muzzle facilitated concentration of the shot pellets into a tighter and more deadly pattern.

The rifling of the barrel (inscribing its interior with spiral grooves) was first tried in the 1560s, but muzzle-loading, and problems with powder residue fouling the grooves, prevented this from catching on widely until after 1825. Its great advantages were heightened accuracy and longer range (the ball's new spin cut air-pressure drag); hence the *rifle* was especially popular for target-shooting and hunting. However, after just a few shots, the rifle had to be extensively cleaned for further use. On average, only one shot per minute could be accomplished, which in warfare could imperil a soldier's life. In fact, the only successful widespread military use of rifled muskets was by the Americans in the **War of American Independence**: Kentucky rifles were very effective for long-range sharpshooters. Kentucky riflemen would use a greased round leather patch with their ball; the patch helped clean the barrel each time it went into it, and supplied the tight fit needed to spin the round when fired. The expert backwoods American rifleman could fire three rounds a minute, the same rate as a regular flintlock user.

The British tried twice before the Victorian era to take up the rifled weapon, though with only limited success. In 1776, Patrick Ferguson successfully incorporated a breech-loading screw system with a four-groove rifled barrel. His 6-pound rifle was twice as fast in loading and firing as the British military standard, and accurate up to three times its distance. More remarkable still was its reliability in very wet conditions. Ferguson in fact solved most of the problems of rifled arms, and was allowed to form a company of men equipped with his weapon to use against the Americans. It performed well in the Battle of Brandywine Creek, but with his death (1780) the rifle was inexplicably boxed up and never used again. A few decades later the Baker Rifle was used by a new unit called the Rifle Brigade, but this muzzle-loading weapon fouled easily, and contemporary British military tactics still relied upon mass firepower at close range, rather than aimed fire or sharpshooting.

The *pistol* was a flintlock in all but length, shape of stock, and barrel. The standard "horse pistol" (for military use and travel protection) had a large bore and a 12-inch barrel (reduced to 8 inches in 1760). Simultaneously a new, specialized, dueling pistol was developed—light, well balanced, and increasingly accurate (accuracy was improved by a "sighting notch" added later). This had a 9- or 10-inch barrel of .5-inch bore and a half stock, and weighed about 3 pounds.

Many pistols, particularly Scottish models, were made of steel. In addition, pistols for maritime use were made with brass or gunsteel fittings and parts, to prevent rusting. Much experimentation took place concerning breech-loading methods and revolving chambers, but with no clear success until the 1820s. On some pistols of the latter 18th century, the hammer-and-lock mechanism was put into the center of the gun directly behind the barrel, as in modern pistols. This improved firing efficiency, but did not allow for aiming along the barrel. Another model in use was the pocket pistol. This was small, with a short barrel for fitting into pockets, skirts, or other small hiding places. It was used primarily as a travel weapon. One such small model, with a .5-inch bore, was made for use by the **Bow Street Runners** police service (1820).

At the opposite end of the scale were *cannons.* Early-18th-century cannons were chiefly very heavy, iron, molded, fixed, muzzle-loading pieces. Cannons with bored brass barrels, and the mounting of cannons on carriages for field use (as at Blenheim in 1704), were just appearing in the **army**. The mortar and the howitzer were short auxiliary cannons developed to fire in a high trajectory, lobbing balls into forts or castles; Woolwich became the first government-operated gun factory to produce these brass field guns (1717). Further dramatic changes occurred from 1750 as gunnery was updated to reflect new scientific understanding of flight trajectory. Experiments conducted on ball flights and travel arcs were published in 1742: a few years later, John Muller (1699–1784) designed a new system of lighter and more powerful ordnance, eliminating the heavy reinforcements of earlier cannons, shortening barrels, tapering the castings, and improving foundry techniques so as to allow thinner barrel walls without diminishing throwing power. The weight of British cannon after 1750 was reduced 50%. Muller published his *Treatise of Artillery* in 1768, outlining his ordnance system and in effect standardizing national artillery use for many years thereafter.

Then as now, many weapons developments were linked to innovations in **science, technology, and invention**. Another great advance occurred when the **Carron Company** produced a short-range cannon (1778) that provided much greater power with only half the powder then standard. This famous *carronade* gun, also known as "the smasher," was shorter and up to 60% lighter than contemporary naval cannons; hence it could be installed on upper decks and on smaller ships which formerly could not bear the weight of heavy weapons. The accuracy of all British cannons was again improved when better methods of boring barrels were introduced around 1800. At about the same time (1795), the human eyeing method of truing a bore was abandoned for the more accurate system of strings.

As to ammunition, the musket ball remained round and solid until the end of the Hanoverian period; the shaping of balls into cone-topped cartridges appeared with the breech-loading percussion rifles of the mid-19th century. Some artillery balls were small explosive devices. Such balls, called *shells,* were hollow and filled with gunpowder, which would be lit by a fuse just before the shell was fired from a mortar or howitzer. But around 1800 Rev. A.J. Forsyth, a dabbler in **chemicals**, perfected the use of fulminates to create a small charge that was impact-induced. This system was then ingeniously turned around to fire the ball. The result, replacing flints, was called the *percussion cap.* By 1816—too late to help in the war against Napoleon—small, brass, waterproof caps were replacing the venerable system of flints and powder pans. Civilian shooters were especially quick to convert their weapons, beginning in the 1820s. The army, relying on older tactics, was a little more reluctant; but by 1839 it had begun testing, and in 1842 it too accepted the new system and began converting all government flintlocks to percussion-locks. Conversion was relatively simple and cheap.

The chief weapons apart from firearms were the *bayonet* and *sword.* The bayonet had become a standard part of British military equipment by 1690 and was basically a blade on a socket handle, 21 inches long, which fit over the barrel of the flintlock. Its chief purpose was to defend against cavalry attacks while still allowing the gun to be fired; its introduction eliminated the need for the long pike, and also eliminated the sword as the ancient sidearm of foot soldiers. Officers, however, continued to carry swords, though long fencing and broad swords were slowly replaced by the "short sword" for officers and cavalry. The use of shooting weapons naturally reduced the value of swords because it diminished the frequency of close combat.

Roy S. Raby

Bibliography

Bowman, Hank Wieand. "The History of Small Firearms." *Antique Guns.* 1953.
Ellacott, S.E. *Guns.* 1955.
Hogg, O.F.G. *Artillery: Its Origin, Heyday and Decline.* 1970.
Patten, David. "Ferguson and His Rifle." *History Today.* Vol. 18, pp. 446–454.
Pollard, H.B.C. *A History of Firearms.* 1926.
Talbott, John E. "The Fall of the Carronade." *History Today.* Vol. 39, pp. 24–30.
Thatcher, Joseph. *Cast for War: A History of Muzzle-Loading Artillery.* 1985.
Treasures from the Tower of London: An Exhibition of Arms and Armour. Compiled by A.V.B. Norman and C.M. Wilson. 1983.

See also Blood Sports; Iron Industry; Navy; War and Military Engagements

Weaver, John (1673–1760)

Choreographer, **dance** theoretician, theatrical dancer, and social dancing master, Weaver spent most of his life teaching and writing in Shrewsbury. Between 1700 and 1736 he came to **London** for extended periods to design and perform dances for the **theater.**

Working within the tradition of the French noble style, Weaver **translated** French dance treatises and published books on dance history and the physiology of dance. His goals were to achieve the regulation of his art, the improvement of professional standards, and the growth of the status of dance as an art and as a social accomplishment. He was the first to stress the relevance of anatomical knowledge to dance instruction, as well as the importance of understanding the connections between the pulse of the music and movements of the dance.

Perhaps his greatest contribution was his innovative theatrical entertainments, in which the plot unfolded through dramatic action alone. In these works, Weaver sought breadth of expression within the academic style. Considered the first *ballets en action* and forerunners of English **pantomime,** they anticipated the reforms of Jean-Georges Noverre (1727–1810) and the much later expressive practices of Michel Fokine (1880–1942). For the comprehensiveness of his interests, new approaches to dance, and the thoroughness with which he explored them, Weaver must be considered a pioneer and major figure in British dance before the 20th century.

Kate Van Winkle Keller

Bibliography

Fletcher, Ifan Kyrle. *Famed for Dance: Essays on the Theory and Practice of Theatrical Dancing in England, 1660–1740.* 1960.
Marsh, Carol. "French Court Dance in England, 1706–1740: A Study of the Sources." Ph.D. diss. 1985.
Ralph, Richard. *The Life and Works of John Weaver.* 1985.

See also Dance; Minuet; Music, Dance

Weaving

See Spinning and Weaving

Webster, Alexander (1707–84)

The Rev. Dr. Webster, the son of the minister of Tolbooth Kirk, **Edinburgh,** became a minister himself, first at Culross and thereafter at his father's old charge. A strong supporter of the Hanoverian cause during the **Forty-five,** he was an establishment figure as well as a popular **Evangelical** preacher and an associate of many prominent Edinburgh intellectuals of the **Scottish Enlightenment.**

Webster is credited along with a colleague, the Rev. Dr. Robert Wallace (1697–1771)—himself something of a statistician—for the compilation in 1755 of the first unofficial census of **Scotland.** He involved the Scottish branch of the **Society for the Promotion of Christian Knowledge** in the Highlands and Islands in his scheme, threatening to withdraw **charity schools** if the clergy did not cooperate. He was also uniquely placed to press ministers elsewhere to comply with his queries because he was acting on behalf of the government; he was then Moderator of the General Assembly of the **Church of Scotland,** and was associated also with a scheme for the provision of annuities for widows and children of the clergy. The census, when it emerged, revealed the total **population** of Scotland in 1755 as 1,265,380 persons.

Webster's later interests included the planning of the Edinburgh New Town, dealing with the problems of the Highlands, and poor relief. He was a typical figure of the Scottish Enlightenment in his practical application to human problems of both **theology** and the new social sciences.

Ian Donnachie

Bibliography

Kyd, J.G. *Scottish Population Statistics.* 1952.

See also Statistical Account of Scotland

Wedgwood, Josiah (1730–1795)

Wedgwood, best known for a line of fine earthenware that captured contemporary **neoclassical** tastes, has been called "one of the great lesser men in history." Born in Burslem in Staffordshire, where a wide variety of clays supported the stoneware industry, he came from a family of small landowners who controlled a small pottery business. English products in the 1740s were losing ground to foreign imports, and Wedgwood, who went to the potter's wheel at age 10, grew up in an atmosphere of experimentation with a determination to succeed: "All things," he later wrote, "yield to experiment."

In 1753, his right leg having been amputated due to illness, he joined Thomas Whieldon (1719–1795), an excellent potter well known for "clouded ware" (ceramics treated with metal oxides to simulate tortoiseshell), and worked with him until 1759, when he inherited the pottery he called "Etruria." The romantic name gave no hint of his drive to establish an efficient **factory** that would assure high productivity with modern equipment, line assembly, and even **steam power** (instituted in 1782, the year Wedgwood developed a thermometer to check temperatures in the pottery furnace).

Wedgwood's products were marked by innovation in both technology and design. *Agateware* was made from contrasting clays kneaded together to produce a marbled effect; early pieces were generally painted in imitation of gilded bronze, but this technique was discontinued when domestic market tastes changed in the early 1770s. *Basaltware* provided two options: unpainted, it resembled the black Egyptian stone (and, not by coincidence, set off the arsenic-whitened hands of upper-class women); painted with red enamel, it recalled the Greek red-figure vases that were becoming popular. Porphyry was imitated with *terra cotta ware.*

The cream-colored *Queen's ware,* made for Queen Charlotte, earned Wedgwood Royal **patronage** in 1765 and was among his most popular products. Pieces of this lead-glazed stoneware, tough but not excessively hard (salt-glazing tending to erode silver spoons and forks), were often transfer-printed by the Liverpool firm of Sadler & Green, or sold unpainted to be enameled in independent workshops.

In 1775 the firm perfected the fine-grained *jasperware* now synonymous with "Wedgwood." Alive to its possibilities, Wedgwood employed young **John Flaxman** to produce the bas-reliefs on colored grounds that were reminiscent of ancient cameos. In addition to its beauty, jasperware was a shrewd industrial response to the increasingly classical tastes of the **aristocratic** buying public and, as such, an indication of the business acumen of Wedgwood and his cultured partner Thomas Bentley (who joined him in 1769). Sharp-eyed **entrepreneurs,** they both saw design development in terms of increased sales; and because their products could be, and were, quickly imitated by their competitors, were ever alert to persons and trends they might turn to financial advantage. Hence they advertised heavily, sought patronage and endorsements, held shows, urged artists to incorporate Wedgwood pieces in their work, and accepted difficult commissions for their publicity value (such as the 956-piece dinner set they made for Catherine the Great of Russia). To support these activities, they improved **transportation** to and from the factory, constructed warehouses and showrooms in **London, Bath, Liverpool,** and **Dublin,** and built a skilled international salesforce. By the 1770s, Wedgwood had transformed a small family business into a world enterprise. When **Arthur Young** visited Etruria some years later, he found 10,000 people at work making Wedgwood pottery.

A notable example of many pioneers of the **Industrial Revolution,** Wedgwood was paternalistic toward his workers, ensuring discipline and respect with punishments, rewards, education, amenities, and improved living conditions. He was an energetic improver of **turnpikes** and **canals** (the Trent-Mersey Canal for which he prominently agitated reduced freight costs for such things as clay, coal, lead ore, and salt from 10 pence to just over 1 penny per ton per mile). A liberal **humanitarian,** he pressed also for the founding of chapels and schools, denounced the **slave trade** (and perhaps his most memorable cameo is of a slave in chains with the inscription, "Am I not a man and a brother?"), saw the bright side of the **American** and **French revolutions,** and supported parliamentary reform and a very wide suffrage at home. He had many children, one of them, Susannah, becoming the mother of Charles Darwin (1809–1882). **Erasmus Darwin, Sir Joseph Banks,** and **Joseph Priestley** were among Wedgwood's friends. A modern historian (J.H. Plumb) wrote that "eighteenth century England bred few men of finer quality."

Reed Benhamou

Bibliography

Mankowitz, W., and R.G. Haggar. *Concise Encyclopedia of English Pottery & Porcelain.* 1957.

McKendrick, Neil, John Brewer, and J.H. Plumb. *The Birth of a Consumer Society: The Commercialization of Eighteenth-Century England.* 1982.

Meteyard, Eliza. *The Life of Josiah Wedgwood.* 1865–1866.

Tattersall, Bruce. *Stubbs and Wedgwood, Unique Alliance between Artist and Potter.* 1974.

Whiton, Sherrill. *Interior Design and Decoration.* 1974.

See also Spode Family

Wellesley (of Norragh), Marquess of (Richard Colley Wellesley) (1760–1842)

Wellesley served successively as Governor-General of India, British Foreign Secretary, and Lord-Lieutenant of **Ireland.** He expanded and consolidated British rule in India, and eased the way for **Roman Catholic** emancipation in Ireland.

Born in Ireland, he was the eldest son of the Earl of Mornington and the brother of the **Duke of Wellington.** He inherited his father's Irish titles in 1781, but from 1784 to 1797 Wellesley sat in the Westminster **House of Commons.** In 1793 he became a commissioner of the Board of Control for India; in 1797 he was made a marquess and appointed India's governor-general.

He pursued an aggressive policy of expansion in India, partly in order to remove French influence. He also sought to establish an Indian civil service college in Calcutta, a scheme which the **East India Company's** directors rejected. In 1802 Wellesley refused to implement the British government's order to restore to **France** its Indian territories. Although the resumption of **war** (1803) vindicated his position, the British cabinet recalled him under threat of impeachment in 1805.

This threat soon disappeared, and in 1809 Wellesley negotiated Britain's entry into the Peninsular War. He was Foreign Secretary in 1809–1812, and nearly became **Prime Minister** when he attempted to form a government in 1812. As Lord Lieutenant of Ireland (1821–1828, 1833–1834), he suppressed the **Whiteboys** and contended with **Daniel O'Connell**'s mass protests, but he also encouraged toleration of Roman Catholicism. His support of Catholic emancipation, and other differences, forced him out of office (1828) during his brother's premiership.

Wellesley spent his retirement in the shadow of his brother's glory, but his own accomplishments were numerous. His attempts to consolidate British rule in India and ameliorate it in Ireland foreshadowed the policies of the middle and latter 19th century.

A. Martin Wainwright

Bibliography

Butler, Iris. *The Eldest Brother: The Marquess of Wellesley, the Duke of Wellington's Eldest Brother.* 1973.

Malleson, G.B. *The Life of Marquess Wellesley.* 1985.

Renick, M.S. *Lord Wellesley and the Indian State.* 1987.

Roberts, Paul E. *India under Wellesley.* 1929.

Wellington, Duke of (Arthur Wellesley) (1769–1852)

Wellington, from a painting by T. Lawrence

Wellington (or Wellesley, as he was called until 1809), a younger son of the Earl of Mornington of the Irish peerage, was the greatest British general of the Hanoverian period and **Prime Minister** in 1828–1830. He was born in **Dublin**. When still in his teens he received an ensigncy in the 73rd **Highland Regiment** through family connections. He never joined the regiment but purchased a lieutenancy and successive appointments in several regiments (1787–1792). During this period he saw little active service and acted primarily as aide-de-camp to the lord-lieutenant of Ireland; like **Castlereagh**, also born in Dublin, he sat in the **Irish Parliament** (1790–1795).

As Lieutenant-Colonel, he commanded a battalion of the 33rd Regiment in **Frederick, Duke of York**'s disastrous Low Countries campaign (1794–1795) during the **French Revolutionary and Napoleonic Wars**. He proved tactically adept and assumed brigade command despite his relative inexperience. The campaign, he claimed, taught him "what one ought not to do."

Promoted to colonel, Wellington received a command in the campaign that toppled the last serious threat to British hegemony in **India** (led by Tippoo Sahib, the Sultan of Mysore, in 1797). He assumed command of all British forces in Mysore, where he organized a civil administration and built roads and fortifications. A rebellion in the Mahratta region of southern India faltered when he crushed the rebel forces at the Battle of Assaye (24 September 1803). His Indian service resulted in a Knighthood of the Bath (1804) as well as significant experience in military and civil administration, including engineering, supply, and diplomacy, all of which would aid his later endeavors.

Despite his civil obligations as Chief Secretary of Ireland (1807–1809), Wellington commanded the reserves in the Copenhagen expedition, which earned him promotion to Lieutenant-General. This period in his career strengthened his ability to manage multiple civil and military affairs simultaneously, a skill sharpened also by unusual self-discipline. He was known for his energetic hard work even at seemingly unimportant sinecures.

He resigned his civil offices and assumed command of the expedition to challenge French domination of the Iberian Peninsula (1809) following **Sir John Moore**'s defeat there. In his subsequent Peninsular Campaign (1809–1814), Wellington out-maneuvered and defeated numerically superior forces, prevented French occupation of Portugal, overturned French power in Spain, and invaded southern France across the Pyrenees. He deftly deployed his favorite tactic, the flank attack ("turning the position"), to overcome a numerically superior opponent. Initially elevated to the peerage as Viscount Wellington of Talavera (1809), he emerged from the campaign with a Knighthood of the Garter (1813) and the dukedom of Wellington (1814).

On Napoleon's return from his exile on Elba, Wellington, at the Congress of Vienna, signed the Treaty of Chaumont, creating the Quadruple Alliance against France. He took the field in Belgium as commander of all British, Hanoverian, and Dutch troops. Along with the Prussians, he defeated Napoleon at the **Battle of Waterloo** (18 June 1815), ending the Napoleonic Empire. Moved by the carnage, the Duke reportedly wept while hearing the casualty report. He then took the unprecedented step of ensuring that all troops, not merely senior officers, receive the Waterloo Medal. He commanded the Allied Occupation Army (1816–1818) and oversaw the settlement of claims against France and the peaceful restoration of the Bourbon monarchy.

In 1818 Wellington joined the cabinet as Master-General of the Ordnance. Politically he held decidedly antidemocratic views and soon became a leader of conservative **Tories.** On the death of the Duke of York he assumed the position of Commander-in-Chief of the Army (1827), but resigned to protest the liberal policies of **George Canning.** On Canning's death he formed his own government (1828).

Deep division within his cabinet between liberal and conservative Tories marked Wellington's tenure as Prime Minister. Opponents saw him as unable to control the cabinet, whereas even supporters characterized him as overbearing and abrupt. He could be flexible in the face of political reality, as in his reluctant support of **Catholic emancipation** despite his personal opposition to it. The need to avoid civil strife determined many of his positions. He took an uncompromising stand on parliamentary reform, deeming even modest change an attack on property and privilege as well as an incitement to mob violence. His speech (2 November 1830) opposing reform precipitated his fall, and the **Reform Act** was enacted despite his opposition.

Wellington continued in service in many positions, but most notably as Commander-in-Chief for Life (1842–1852). Tradition-bound to the end, he opposed formal military training (preferring instruction within each regiment), diminution of corporal **punishment**, and introduction of new weapons **technology** (such as the rifled musket). But he is justly considered a brilliant military commander and the principal architect of Napoleon's defeat.

Stanley D.M. Carpenter

Bibliography

Glover, Michael. *Wellington as Military Commander.* 1968.

Longford, Elizabeth. *Wellington: The Years of the Sword.* 1969.

———. *Wellington: Pillar of State.* 1972.

Thompson, Neville. *Wellington after Waterloo.* 1986.

See also Army; Government, National; Wellesley, Marquess of

Welsh Agriculture

Most cultivated open fields in the areas of Anglo–Norman settlement had been enclosed by around 1650. And, especially after the 1750s, **enclosure** of large areas of commons in lowland areas of **Wales** was being achieved either by common consent between landowners or by individual encroachment. Illegal encroachment upon upland wastes, too, by both squatters and larger landowners, had been going on for centuries, but quickened from the 1760s in response to rising **population** pressure. Thus the parliamentary enclosures after 1780 simply continued a trend.

Welsh agriculture was considerably behind English. Outside certain fertile lowland areas (such as along the coastal fringes and river valleys), Wales's hilly and upland terrain, together with the damp climate, required Welsh **farmers** to concentrate on producing store livestock for export by drivers to lusher English pastures, and also on the manufacture of butter and cheese; which, along with corn, was often shipped to neighboring centers such as **Bristol** and **Liverpool.** Corn (grain) production was essential, for before rail communication it was expensive to import it from outside; and farmers, moreover, held the typical peasant attitude that they should produce everything that was needed at home. Consequently, Wales's isolated, face-to-face farming neighborhoods were largely self-sufficient throughout the 18th century. Gold and silver were in short supply, and so barter, including payment in kind in produce such as barley, cheese, butter, and wool, predominated in exchange. In the remote western mountainous areas, tenants until the 1790s paid their rent in cattle.

Small farms of 50 to 100 acres, many containing fields belonging to neighboring holdings, were run mostly by family labor, with only small numbers of hired indoor **servants** and outdoor married **agricultural laborers.** Welsh farmers often survived only by dint of supplementary income from the sale of knitted stockings. Generally, they were slow to change their farming methods. They justified their stubborn attachment to old ways on the grounds that any improvements they made would prompt their landlord to raise their rent at the expiration of the lease (long leases for life were being replaced by shorter tenures over the course of the 18th century), that they could farm like their landlord if only they had his purse, and that if they adopted English fashions, their neighbors would laugh at them. Consequently, husbandry practices remained unimproved; above all, turnips remained a rarity in crop rotation until the mid-19th century, which necessitated the continuance of the wasteful summer fallowing. In this respect, Wales did not learn one of the important lessons of **agricultural improvement.**

Landlords were partly responsible for this backwardness. Taking advantage of improving economic conditions, many charged exorbitant rents from the 1760s. Moveover, rather than improving their estates by way of installing better farm buildings and drainage, they expended surplus capital for the purchase of more land. Nor, in the better market conditions of the late 18th century, did leases contain progressive husbandry clauses and provide compensation for unexhausted improvements.

Some landowners did attempt, especially from the late 18th century, to promote better farming by founding county **agricultural societies** and by growing clover, ryegrass, and turnips, and also by improving cattle breeds on their home farms. As a result, improvements did begin to occur, especially after around 1810 when farmers began to adopt the four-course system; but progress was significantly confined to those large tenants with capital.

D.W. Howell

Bibliography

Colyer, Richard J. *The Welsh Cattle Drovers.* 1976.
Davies, W. *A General View of the Agriculture and Domestic Economy of North Wales.* 1810.
———. *A General View of the Agriculture and Domestic Economy of South Wales.* 2 vols. 1814.
Howell, D.W. *Patriarchs and Parasites: The Gentry of South-West Wales in the Eighteenth Century.* 1986.
Owen, D.H., ed. *Settlement and Society in Wales.* 1989.
Reports to the Board of Agriculture on Welsh Counties. 1794.
Thirsk, J., ed. *Agrarian History of England and Wales.* Vol. 5: 1640–1750. 1984.

See also Agriculture; Irish Agriculture; Scottish Agriculture

Welsh Education

Prior to the 18th century, the grammar school was the main provider of education in Wales. The earliest known grammar school was established at Oswestry in 1407; expansion of such schools during the 16th century was linked to the anglicizing policies of successive Tudor governments. This expansion was not sustained in the following century, and Welsh grammar school education entered a trough from which it did not begin to emerge until the middle of the 19th century.

By the late 17th century, the educational focus had shifted to elementary schools that taught the Welsh language. Between 1677 and 1681 the "Welsh Trust," led by Thomas Gouge, established over 80 such schools, mainly in South Wales. Gouge also organized a large-scale distribution of religious books in the Welsh language, available free of charge to the poor.

The Welsh Trust laid foundations for the energetic work of the **Society for Promoting Christian Knowledge (SPCK)** during the 18th century. Between 1700 and 1740 the SPCK set up 96 schools, almost half of them in Carmarthen and Pembrokeshire. The SPCK did not advocate education in the Welsh language but was prepared to condone its use, notably in North Wales, where the distribution of religious tracts, **translated** into Welsh, had fired public interest.

Welsh education in this period owed a lot to the ideas and leadership of **Griffith Jones**, rector of Llanddowror. Jones realized that schools would have to circulate if they were to reach scattered rural communities. He also recognized that in the limited time available, a **circulating school** must concentrate on its prime task of teaching Welsh reading. By the middle of the 18th century, circulating schools were operating in every Welsh county and, in the process, stimulating Welsh cultural awareness. This was reflected in the foundation of the Society of Cymmrodoron in 1751. The society's promoters sought to promote the language and history of Wales, and their work laid the foundations for the revival of the Welsh eisteddfod (an annual assembly of Welsh poets and musicians) at Carmarthen in 1819.

The circulating schools movement was less active for a time after Griffith Jones's death (1761), but revived in the 1790s under a new inspirational leader, **Thomas Charles.** Charles was a Calvinist **Methodist** from Bala in North Wales; his leadership marks the beginning of a Methodist era in Welsh education. However, in general terms he wished to carry on the work and example of his Anglican predecessor, Jones. In 1787 Charles began to establish **Sunday schools** to supplement the religious and educational work of his day schools. His schools soon attracted parents as well as their children, and in 1811 Charles established adult Sunday schools in response to a growing demand for segregated education.

This expansion of day and Sunday school education increased the market for Bibles and prayer books. The British and Foreign Bible Society was established in 1804 to meet this need, both at home and abroad. Charles was a founding member of the society, and helped to ensure the publication of Bibles in the Welsh language. By the time of his death (1814), approximately 100,000 Welsh Bibles were in circulation.

The cultivation of literacy in the Welsh tongue by Jones and Charles undoubtedly helped to strengthen national cultural awareness, but the prime motive of both men was **Evangelical.** Learning to read Welsh was a means to the end of promoting biblical knowledge among the scattered Welsh population.

Lawrence Williams

Bibliography

Clement, Mary. *The S.P.C.K. and Wales, 1699–1740.* 1954.
Jenkins, D.E. *The Life of the Reverend Thomas Charles of Bala.* 1908.
Jones, Ieuan Gwynedd. *Pioneers of Welsh Education.* 1964.
Kelly, Thomas. *Griffith Jones, Llanddowror, Pioneer in Adult Education.* 1950.

See also Wales and Welsh Culture

Welsh Industry

This was the Cinderella of Hanoverian economic development, rising from humble inconsequentiality to predominance. **Wales** at the beginning of the 18th century, backward and sparsely populated, had a poorly developed industrial tradition. By the 1830s, south Wales was one of the world's chief industrial regions, and a smaller industrial district had been established in northeast Wales—though in central Wales, industry was in decline.

Woolen manufacture by rural outworking, supplemented by water-driven fulling mills, was widespread in 1714, and in north Wales it achieved some importance, with proto-industrial manufacturing districts emerging in Montgomeryshire, Merioneth, and Denbighshire. But until the late 18th century this manufacture remained in the thrall of the Shrewsbury Drapers Company, which dominated the area by economic power. At last the company's hold was broken by **Liverpool** merchants and a direct export trade. A boom began,

Thomas Brown, General Manager, Ebbw Vale Ironworks, South Wales

centered on Dolgellau (with its port at Barmouth), Llanidloes, and especially Newtown ("the **Leeds** of Wales"); there was some water-powered mechanization at these centers. The Merioneth industry, which produced a coarse cloth used by soldiers and **slaves**, was already in decline by 1820, and mid Wales, which manufactured a soft flannel, was beginning to show the first signs of crisis in the 1830s, the result of competition from other British **textile** districts. Ultimately, the Welsh woolen industry was the victim of the centralization of woolen manufacture in the West Riding.

Wales's greatest industries arose from metal processing. Copper smelting flourished around **Swansea** and became vertically integrated into large concerns by the end of the Hanoverian period (1837). There were four major smelting works there, and others lined the coast from Llanelli to Neath; 90% of British copper smelting was done in this area. The coalfield of northeast Wales also developed metal smelting, and the town of Flint accounted for 25% of British lead smelting by 1849.

Still more famous was Wales's **iron** manufacture. In 1700 this was small-scale, scattered, and localized. Rapid transformation came with the adoption of coke for smelting from the 1750s: the outcropping of coking **coal**, iron ore, and limestone at the northeastern rim of the south Wales coalfield gave the region a huge advantage. Early capital came largely from **merchants** with munitions contracts; later financing was generated by the reinvestment of profits. The demand for iron was so insatiable that it overcame the problems of labor supply and **transport** in a sparsely populated area, linked by indifferent **roads** to the coast some 25 miles and 500 feet in altitude away from the **mines**. Pack horses and then wagons (after road improvement) met early transport needs, while a speculative **canal** boom (1789–1793) more fully resolved transport difficulties; the major works were linked to the Glamorganshire and Monmouthshire Canals by means of descending **waggonways**. Skilled miners and ironworkers streamed in from the Midlands of England, and unskilled laborers came from the burgeoning **population** of rural Wales. In 1788 the area produced 8,000 tons of pig iron a year (18.3% of British production); by 1830 it was making 250,000 tons (41% of British output).

Dominating the central south Welsh upland, standing on the long and narrow strip at the heads of the valleys (approximately 18 × 3 miles), was **Merthyr Tydfil**, containing four major works. Cyfarthfa was in the early 19th century the world's largest and was only pushed aside by nearby Dowlais (which employed 5,000 people by 1840). Huge works like these were vertically integrated, and stockpiled their products during depressions; the smaller south Wales works, however, were driven into cut-throat competition in depressions because they lacked the capital to ride out economic storms.

Iron was also manufactured in north Wales, where **John Wilkinson** pioneered techniques of boring iron, which allowed specialization in the manufacture of cannon and of cylinders for the **steam engines** of **Boulton** and **Watt**. There was a boom in the period 1775–1825, but most furnaces were no longer in operation by the 1830s. **Tinplate** manufacture was a subsidiary of iron in south Wales. Innovations in that process were made by Sir John Hanbury (1664–1734) at Pontypool in the early 18th century, and the eastern part of the south Wales coalfield ruled British tinplate exports, leaving the domestic market for the Midlands producers. Welsh tinplate dominated world markets until the 1880s.

Neil Evans

Bibliography

Atkinson, Michael, and Colin Baber. *The South Wales Iron Industry, 1760–1880.* 1987.

Daunton, M.J. "The Dowlais Iron Company in the Iron Industry, 1800–1850." *Welsh History Review.* Vol. 6, pp. 16–45.

Dodd, A.H. *The Industrial Revolution in North Wales.* 1933.

Evans, Neil. "Two Paths to Economic Development: Wales and the North-East of England," in Pat Hudson, ed., *Regions and Industries: A Perspective on the Industrial Revolution in Britain.* 1989.

Jenkins, J. Geraint. *The Welsh Woollen Industry.* 1969.

John, A.H. *The Industrial Development of South Wales.* 1950.

Minchinton, W.E. *The British Tinplate Industry.* 1957.

See also Metallurgy and Metalworking; Welsh Mining

Welsh Mining

Wales abounds in varied mineral deposits, many of which were worked commercially in the 18th century. Lead has been mined in every Welsh county at some point in history; the Hanoverian workings were concentrated in Cardiganshire and western Montgomeryshire, and in northeast Wales. Mining expanded fitfully in the 18th century, was checked during the period 1793–1815, and in the early 19th century strengthened especially in northeast Wales. Gradually, deep mining displaced levels, with severe consequences for overall cost.

Copper came into prominence with the striking of the fabled lode on Parys Mountain in Anglesey (1768). The ore was low grade but easy to extract in great open casts. Welsh prices undercut Cornish copper producers, and by the 1790s the area controlled world copper prices. The central figure was **Thomas Williams** of Llanidan, who achieved his importance by refusing to be dominated by the smelters or the Cornish monopoly. He established his own smelting works in **Swansea**, North Wales, and Lancashire, and also developed **banking** and manufacturing interests. In 1801 the parish of Amlwch had a **population** of 4,977, mostly workers or dependents of his mines; the mines themselves employed some 1,200 people. But depletion of the best deposits was then just beginning. The area lost its price advantage and rapidly went into decline once shafts had to be sunk on the mountain. Other Welsh copper mines were small and scattered, but perhaps 400 people worked on the Great Orme mines in the 1840s before they were overtaken by the growth of Llandudno; Nantlle and Beddgelert were other centers of extraction.

Coal remained a subsidiary of other mineral industries for most of the period. There was a boom around Wrexham in the period 1760–1830, but this was mostly consumed in local **iron** furnaces. In 1840, almost half of south Wales' coal production of 4.5 million tons went to the iron industry. Copper smelting absorbed its share of coal, too. Sir Humphrey Mackworth (1657–1727) was important in developing the industry at Neath. In West Glamorgan, landowners dominated the coal industry. Innovations like the Savery and **Newcomen** engines allowed deeper shafts and longer levels to be used: by 1750, shafts of more than 80 fathoms and levels of up to 800 fathoms existed. Colliery **waggonways** were apparently used from the early 18th century.

Sale coal was well established around Swansea, where coal outcropped close to the coast, and Swansea dominated the west coast trade in the 18th century. In Gwent, **canals** were necessary to make the coal accessible. The Monmouthshire Canal Act (1797), which freed from **duty** that coal exported east of Flat Holme and Steep Holme in the Bristol Channel, gave Gwent an advantage. The coastwise coal trade was largely restricted to **Ireland** and the West Country, though some went to the Channel Islands, **France**, Spain, and Portugal. These markets were less lucrative than that of **London**, supplied mainly by the northeast of England. In the 1830s the first attempts to penetrate the London market were made, but Welsh coal mining did not really come into its own until the Victorian period.

Neil Evans

Bibliography

Cockshutt, E. "The Parys Mountain Copper Mines in the Island of Anglesey." *Archaelogica Cambrensis.* Vol. 114, pp. 87–111.

Harris, J.R. *The Copper King: A Biography of Thomas Williams of Llanidan.* 1964.

John, A.H. "Iron and Coal on a Glamorgan Estate, 1700–1740." *Economic History Review.* Vol. 13, pp. 93–103.

Lewis, W.J. *The Lead Industry in Wales.* 1969.

Moore, Donald, ed. *Wales in the Eighteenth Century.* 1976.

Morris, J.H., and L.J. Williams. *The South Wales Coal Industry, 1841–1875.* 1958.

Rees, Morgan. *The Industrial Archaeology of Wales.* 1969.

Rees, Williams. *Industry before the Industrial Revolution.* 2 vols. 1968.

Rowlands, John. *Copper Mountain.* 1966.

Trott C.D.J. "Coal Mining in the Borough of Neath in the Seventeenth and Early Eighteenth Centuries." *Morgannwg.* Vol. 13, pp. 93–103.

Williams, Christopher. "The Llandudno Copper Mines." *Transactions of the Caernarfonshire Historical Society.* Vol. 33, pp. 211–232.

See also Cardiff; Wales and Welsh Culture; Welsh Industry

Welsh Politics

Wales had gained regular parliamentary representation with an "Act of Union" in 1536. Each county had a single parliamentary seat (except Monmouthshire, which had two), and in addition, a **borough** seat representing all the boroughs in each county (except in Merioneth). Throughout the Hanoverian period, representation was somewhat less uneven than in England. The Welsh electorate totaled something over 20,000, varying from 400 in Anglesey to around 1,500 in populous counties like Glamorgan and Denbighshire.

Politics were at first dominated by the **Tories**, but after 1714 the **Whigs** during their growing ascendancy established "regional governors" in Wales. The central government aided them in elections, interfering in both the borough **franchise** and the entitlement of boroughs to representation in the contributory boroughs system. Such influence increased the number of government supporters from 8 in 1715 to 14 by 1734 as the local Tories were forced to adjust to the national distribution of power. Some, including a few great magnates, turned to **Jacobitism**, but despite exaggerated hopes (and fear of **riots**), there was little more than posturing in 1745.

Tory fortunes improved somewhat with the accession of **George III**. Contested elections declined, and seats were divided by formal treaty; 6 seats or so would be contested at a general election. Particular families established long-standing dominance over seats, something which reflected varying alterations in the fortunes of landowners as huge complexes of power emerged, often swallowing up smaller estates.

The rise of **Welsh industry** and of **radicalism** led to new political concerns in the latter 18th century. **Freemasons** and **dissenters** became linked in causes connected with the **Wilkes** phenomenon, the **War of American Independence**, and unrest in **Ireland**, but agitation was not significant until the 1790s, especially in the market towns. There were many attempts to harness contemporary food riots to radical politics. **Richard Price** and David Williams (1738–1816) were Welsh-born radicals who made their name on a wider stage but retained links and adherents in their home localities. Morgan John Rhys (1760–1804) established the first political **periodical** in Welsh with his *Cylchgrawn Cynmraeg* ([sic] 1793–1794), which, among other things, published French radical authors (Volney, for example) in **translation**. **Unitarianism** became especially active. Jac Glan Y Gors (1766–1821) published Welsh pamphlets, which advanced the ideas of **Paine**. William Jones, Llangadfan (1726–1795), was a radical admirer of Voltaire (1694–1778). Radicalism found an outlet in **emigration** to America in the 1790s, prompted partly by tall tales of Welsh Indian tribes on the headwaters of the Mississippi, and also by Morgan John Rhys's attempt to create a Welsh republican colony in Pennsylvania. But radical agitation charted a path for future Welsh politics, and the fact is noteworthy that the strongholds of Welsh Chartism 40 years later were almost all centers of radicalism in the 1790s.

There were serious food riots in 1795–1796, 1800–1801, and (of lesser magnitude) 1817–1818. Strikes, often violent, occurred after 1815; some of which were widespread, as in entire coalfield strikes in south Wales after 1816. "Scotch Cattle," a violent secret society that enforced solidarity during disputes, flourished in the Glamorgan–Monmouth border area (1822–1835) and formed the background to the later Chartist movement there. The North Wales coalfield also saw major conflicts, which culminated in the battle of Chirk Bridge (1831). The Hanoverian era ended with the bloody **Merthyr rising** and the Chartist insurrection at Newport (1839).

There was no coherent regional movement for parliamentary reform, though the English movement had an impact. Minor adjustments to Welsh representation were proposed in the parliamentary reform bills of 1831–1832. In the event, **Merthyr Tydfil** gained a seat. The more populous counties—Glamorgan, Denbighshire, and Carmarthen—gained extra seats, while the Glamorgan borough's seat was split into two, focusing on **Cardiff** and **Swansea**. Wales ended up with one member per 28,260 of **population**, only slightly below the English average of 27,709. This redistribution broke the landed class's monopoly of power in Wales, and henceforth some industrialists—**Sir Josiah John Guest**, for example—made their way into Parliament.

Neil Evans

Bibliography

Jenkins, Philip. *A History of Modern Wales, 1536–1990.* 1992.

Jones, David. *Before Rebecca: Popular Protest in Wales, 1790–1835.* 1973.

Thomas, Peter D.G. "Society, Government and Politics," in Donald Moore, ed., *Wales in the Eighteenth Century.* 1976.

Williams, Gwyn A. *The Search for Beulah Land: The Welsh and the Atlantic Revolution.* 1980.

Welsh Religious Revival

The Hanoverian period witnessed a major religious revival in **Wales**. Puritanism, late to arrive, had begun its career there only in the 1630s, and it remained a minority creed in 1714 despite the impact of **Quakerism** in mid Wales and a small but significant presence of **Baptists** and Independents (**Congregationalists**) on the trading routes across south Wales. These **dissenters**' central institution was the **Dissenting Academy** at Carmarthen; it was Wales's nearest approach to a university, and was attended by several future leaders of the **Methodist** revival.

The quickening in Welsh religious life was prepared by the established **Church of England**, notably in the creation of the **Society for Promoting Christian Knowledge (SPCK)**; 4 of its original 5 founders had Welsh connections. The SPCK provided schools in Welsh towns, and **libraries** for the education of the clergy. The **Rev. Griffith Jones**, dismayed at religious ignorance, began preaching out-of-doors after 1716 and attracted large crowds. But disciplinary pressures and his desire to produce more lasting converts led to a diversion of his efforts toward **circulating schools** in 1731. These peripatetic literacy classes, well suited to the scattered rural population, drew in adults and children; according to Jones, over 150,000 scholars were taught before 1760. If his figures are reliable (some historians doubt them), this was a literacy revolution on the scale of a contemporary Third World country.

The rise of Welsh Methodism is usually dated from the simultaneous "awakenings" of **Howel Harris** and **Daniel Rowland** (1735). These revivalists did not work in the intellectual vacuum that they liked to depict, but drew sustenance from the more general **religious revival** then at work. They benefited from contacts with English activists like **George Whitefield** and **Selina, Countess of Huntingdon**. The emotional preaching of the Methodists produced converts who were quickly organized into societies (*seiats*); separate meeting places for converts emerged as early as 1739. Harris and Rowland were joined (1738) by a third great Welsh evangelist, **William Williams, Pantycelyn**, the hymn-writer of the revival (his best-known piece is "Guide Me O thou Great Jehovah"), who set his **poetry** to the borrowed tunes of Welsh folk and love songs. Most early Methodist converts came from the families of the lesser **gentry**, **craftsmen**, and prosperous **farmers**; the majority were women. The movement offered a critique of the conspicuous consumption of the gentry and of the rumbustious popular culture of the time. Harris preached at race meetings, where elite and populace met; he attempted to inject them with a new seriousness. "I had a temptation to laughter last night," he confessed to his diary.

The early revival had its greatest impact in southwest Wales, where the church was particularly impoverished and weak. Methodist preaching was emotional, extempore, and marked by energetic audience participation, notorious among such groups as the "Holy Rollers" of Cardiganshire and the "Jumpers," whose inspiration sustained them well beyond ordinary levels of exhaustion. The penetration of North Wales proved more difficult. Methodism lacked a major leader there, and the church was in a less perilous condition. The breakthrough came with the efforts of **Thomas Charles** in Bala from the 1780s. His chief contribution was to introduce the **Sunday school**, which filled the gap left by the disappearance of the circulating schools after the money bequeathed them in the will of Bridget Bevan was expended in litigation in Chancery. The Methodists taught adults as well as children, boosting the drive to literacy. It was Charles who broke with the Anglican Church at last by ordaining Methodist ministers (1811), and he continued the characteristic emphasis on scriptural instruction by helping to found the British and Foreign Bible Society in 1804. By the time of his death (1814), Methodism and dissent (revivified by contact with it) together embraced some 15% of the Welsh **population**. This percentage mushroomed, so that by 1851, over half of the Welsh population attended a place of worship, 75% of which were nonconformist. Between 1800 and 1850, a new chapel was built every 8 days.

Neil Evans

Bibliography

Jenkins, Geraint H. *The Foundations of Modern Wales, 1642–1780.* 1987.

Jones, Ieuan Gwynedd. "Thomas Charles," in Faculty of Education, University College of Swansea, *Pioneers of Welsh Education.* 1964.

Williams, Glanmor. *Language, Religion and Nationality in Wales.* 1979.

See also Welsh Industry; Welsh Politics

Wesley, Charles (1707–1788)

Born in Lincolnshire, the younger brother of **John Wesley**, Charles was the poet of the family, composing the vast majority of the 8,900 hymns which appeared under the names of John and Charles Wesley. Although he always supported and encouraged his brother, he was less assertive on the religious question of "perfection." He disapproved when John began ordaining his own preachers, and vigorously objected to the idea that **Methodism** should ever withdraw from the **Church of England**.

Wesley's hymns touched on every aspect of spiritual life. He produced many to address contemporary topics. *Hymns for Times of Trouble and Persecution* (1744) prays for **King George II** and England as they are threatened by the French fleet; *Hymns on the Expected Invasion* (1759) celebrates the British victory over the French; *Hymns for the Nation* (1781) asks for forgiveness and peace between England and its recently emancipated colonies in America. Wesley's more straightforwardly religious hymns focus on liturgical celebrations of the Church of England, but include his own active and **Evangelical** passion. "Hark the Herald Angels Sing" is probably his best-known hymn. *Hymns on the Lord's Supper* (1745) contains 166 songs celebrating his belief that communion was the principal means of grace by which one could know the presence of the living Christ. Of special interest to Wesley was the importance of Christian fellowship ("All Praise to Our Redeeming Lord," No. 500, *1780 Hymnbook*), and the antipredestinarian assertion that all may be saved ("Let the Earth and Heaven Agree," No. 33; and "God's Universal Love," No. 121).

Charles Wesley

Wesley's **poetic** language was intentionally simple and direct because his audience was often the poor and unchurched, many of whom were uneducated. He fondly worked on many themes of Old Testament prophecy and New Testament fulfillment. Along with **Isaac Watts**, he is considered one of the greatest hymn-writers of the 18th century. His son, **Samuel Wesley**, was an accomplished musical composer.

Wight Martindale, Jr.

Bibliography

Baker, Frank. *Charles Wesley's Verse: An Introduction.* 1964.

Davie, Donald. *Purity of Diction in English Verse.* 1952.

———. *A Gathered Church.* 1978.

England, Martha W. "Blake and the Hymns of Charles Wesley." *Bulletin of the New York Public Library.* Vol. 70, pp. 7–26, 93–112, 153–168, 251–264.

Manning, Bernard Lord. *The Hymns of Wesley and Watts.* 1942.

Rogal, Samuel J. *John and Charles Wesley.* 1983.

Whaling, Frank. *John and Charles Wesley: Selected Prayers, Hymns, Journal Notes, Sermons, Letters and Treatises.* 1981.

Wesley, John (1703–1791)

Wesley, English preacher and founder of **Methodism**, was an indefatigable **Evangelist** whose zeal and industry, more than the efforts of any other man, altered the religious sensibility of the Hanoverian age.

Ordained a deacon in the **Church of England** in 1725, he became a minister on his graduation from Oxford 3 years later. While there, he and his younger brother **Charles Wesley** helped form a group known for its methodical study and devotion to religious duties; they were derisively referred to as the "Holy Club" or "Methodists." In 1735 the two brothers **traveled** to the colony of Georgia with **James Oglethorpe**;

John Wesley

John remained there for 2 years. Returning to England, John, after discovering Martin Luther's (1483–1546) commentaries on St. Paul's communications to the Galatians and the Romans, underwent an intense religious experience, which he described as a conversion. His message thereafter was that salvation could come only through faith alone in Christ. Officials of the Church of England soon grew wary of his **enthusiasm**, particularly after **George Whitefield**, having begun outdoor "field" preaching to the masses, urged Wesley to do the same. There are many stories told about Wesley's calm courage in the face of hostile mobs, and his ability to win rough men and women over with the eloquent sincerity of his religious appeals.

Although Wesley's reputation emerged from his effectiveness as a field preacher, he developed his religious and reform ideas of Methodism in his published writings, which included hymns, **sermons**, biographical and critical **tracts**, pedagogical and linguistic texts, political, historical, and medical works, and **essays** on **theology** and society. In 1739 he opened his first Methodist "band" in an old foundry in Moorfields, which for the next 40 years remained the center of Methodism in London. Other bands, modeled on the Moravians' preference for organizing small groups of people of the same sex and marital status, soon followed. Wesley formed these into larger societies known as circuits, and in 1744 the first Methodist Conference was held.

Wesley never intended to break from the established church. His rules, which he set forth in 1743, were specifically designed to avoid conflicts with it. He had hoped that Anglican officials would ordain his itinerant preachers, but when they refused, in 1784 he began to ordain his own preachers. By this date there were 356 Methodist chapels, many built up through the 250,000 miles Wesley rode and 40,000 sermons he preached during his remarkable lifetime. He remained within the church throughout his life, but afterward (in 1795) a definite break occurred, and within the next 20 years a variety of Methodist groups emerged.

Wesley's huge *Journal,* kept from 1735 to 1790, reveals him as a man of wide intellectual interests, many **humanitarian** concerns, and remarkable tolerance, considering the hostility he endured from those in the fashionable and literary worlds. It also reveals him as the leader of 18th-century **religious revivalism**, the head of a procession composed of tens of thousands of refugees from the Anglican establishment.

Samuel J. Rogal

Bibliography

Abelove, Henry. *The Evangelist of Desire: John Wesley and the Methodists.* 1990.

Brantley, Richard. *Locke, Wesley, and the Method of English Romanticism.* 1984.

Rogal, Samuel J. *John and Charles Wesley.* 1983.

Tuttle, R.G. *John Wesley, His Life and Theology.* 1979.

Wesley, Samuel (1766–1837)

Wesley was a musical genius at a time when Britain offered few opportunities for native composers. His organ voluntaries were valued, but his orchestral and choral works were unpublished and, until recently, almost unknown.

He was a nephew of **John Wesley** and the son of **Charles Wesley**. After a brief conversion to **Roman Catholicism** he seems to have become essentially agnostic but continued to compose Latin church music, most notably a motet for chorus and orchestra, *Confitebor tibi* (1799). He also contributed Anglican **church music, Methodist** hymn settings, organ voluntaries, piano music, songs, and partsongs. He was an early enthusiast for the music of Johann Sebastian Bach (1685–1750), and his letters are remarkable for their breadth of understanding and acerbic wit.

Nicholas Temperley

Bibliography

Routley, Erik. *The Musical Wesleys.* 1968.

Temperley, Nicholas. "Wesley Family," in Stanley Sadie, ed., *The New Grove Dictionary of Music and Musicians.* 1980.

Wesley, Eliza, ed. *The Wesley Bach Letters.* 1875; rpt. 1988. Intro. by Peter Williams.

See also London Pianoforte School

West, Benjamin (1738–1820)

West, a portraitist as well as a painter of historical and religious subjects, was a pioneer in **neoclassical, Romantic**, and modern **history painting**. Born to a **Quaker** family in Springfield, Pennsylvania, he supposedly was taught to paint by the Indians, though his early works were very awkward. He spent the years 1760–1763 in Italy, primarily in Rome, where he was influenced by various history painters. In 1763 he settled in **London**, where he spent the remainder of his life, becoming (in spite of his continuing loyalty to America) the favorite painter of **George III**, and eventually his official history painter.

West's earliest works, exhibited at the Society of Arts, were primarily of historical subjects—*Jacob Blessing the Sons of Joseph* (1766) and *Agrippina Landing at Brundisium with the Ashes of Germanicus* (1768). Both were indebted, in compo-

Benjamin West

sition and detail, to classical **sculpture**. West was a founder of the **Royal Academy** (1768), and succeeded Reynolds as president (1792); his works, including *The Death of General Wolfe* (1770)—often referred to as the first modern history painting in contemporary dress because the figures wear modern rather than antique costumes—were exhibited there from 1769 to 1819. Throughout his life, West, like his slightly less successful countryman John Singleton Copley (1738–1815), who also spent his later career in London, painted a wide variety of biblical, classical, historical, and literary subjects. Perhaps West's most famous painting is *Death on a Pale Horse* (1796), which incidentally was especially admired by the eccentric **William Beckford** who planned a revelation chamber of West's works at Fonthill Abbey. West never returned to America, but through contact with such American artists as Charles Wilson Peale (1741–1827), Gilbert Stuart (1755–1828), and Washington Allston (1779–1843) he influenced the evolution of American as well as British **painting**.

Thomas J. McCormick

Bibliography

Abrams, Ann U. *The Valiant Hero: Benjamin West and Grand Style History Painting.* 1985.

Cannon-Brookes, Peter. *The Painted Word: British History Painting, 1750–1830.* 1991.

Erffa, Helmut von, and Allen Staley. *The Paintings of Benjamin West.* 1986.

Meyer, Jerry D. "Benjamin West's Chapel of Revealed Religion, a Study in Eighteenth Century Protestant Religious Art." *Art Bulletin.* Vol. 62, pp. 247–265.

Mitchell, Charles. "Benjamin West's Death of General Wolfe and the Popular History Piece." *The Journal of the Warburg and Courtauld Institutes.* Vol. 7, pp. 20–33.

Paley, Morton D. *The Apocalyptic Sublime.* 1986.

Solkin, David. *Painting for Money: The Visual Arts and the Public Sphere in Eighteenth-Century England.* 1993.

West India Interest

This term refers to those who lobbied the British government on behalf of the white island colonists of the British **West Indies**. The lobby's chief concern was to protect a monopoly of the home **sugar** market against foreign competition. It included four subgroups: first, the island agents in **London** who had emerged as salaried lobbyists appointed by the island governments in the late 17th century (beginning with Barbados in 1671); second, the London **merchants** trading with the West Indies, whose lobbying activities date from the earliest periods of English settlement; third, the West India planters living in Britain, whose numbers grew during the period as more and more wealthy planters became absentees; and finally, the West India M.P.s, of whom there were some 50 or 60 by around 1770. Often these elements were to be found in one and the same person, as in the case of William Beckford (1709–1770), father of the writer by the same name, who, born in Jamaica and owning 22,000 acres there (he was Jamaica's largest landowner), became a London merchant of fabulous wealth, M.P., and Lord Mayor of London in the 1760s.

The West Indies, because of their great sugar wealth and key role in **overseas commerce**, have been described as the spoiled children of the **Empire**. Despite this, the lobbyists were sometimes internally divided over critical issues such as the **American Revolution** and even the **slave trade**. Its organization was relatively informal before 1763, owing to the close identification between the planters and the metropolis, and the conformity of their trade with the principles of the **navigation laws**. The interest group won some of its greatest political victories when it was thus loosely organized, for example the passage of the **Molasses Act** (1733) and the defeat of **Henry Pelham**'s proposed increase in sugar **duties** (1744). Many contemporaries believed that the acquisition of **Canada** in 1763 was due to the West Indians' jealous concern over their own holdings and profits, which led them to press for nonretention of the French sugar islands won in the **Seven Years' War**.

But this cozy relationship with the central government began to decline in the 1770s when the latter became less accessible, adopted colonial policy initiatives detrimental to the islands, and embarked on a **war** with America which had severe economic consequences for them. The interest group responded by formally organizing and embarking on public campaigns; the Society of West India Merchants and Plant-

West Indies

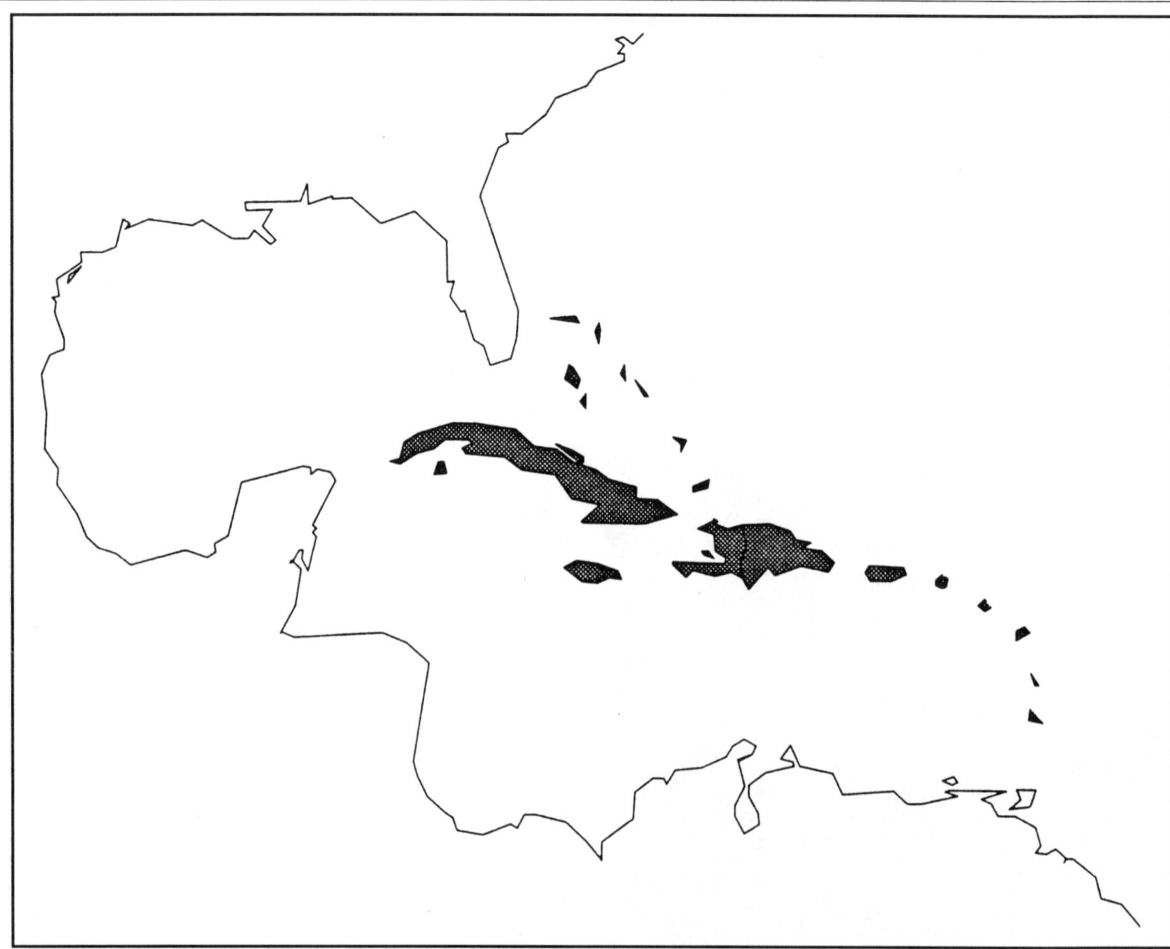

ers dates from the closing years of the **War of American Independence**. But thereafter the lobby was often on the defensive, opposing both the virtual closure of trade with the United States and the **antislavery movement**.

After 1815 the steady rise of free trade reduced the price of sugar by 50%, but in the 1820s the West India interest, formerly protected by differential **tariffs**, looked in vain for parliamentary supporters, having already alienated even the **East India Company** by its selfish insistence (from 1813) on sugar duties favoring its own products. It denounced the newly appointed Protectors of Slaves (created by pressure from the antislavery movement) as an outrage against property rights, attacked the supposed tyranny of the Colonial Office, and in the early 1830s vigorously opposed the **Reform Act**. (Many of its 56 parliamentary supporters now sat for rotten **boroughs** in the unreformed **Commons**.) After 1833, with Parliament reformed and all British slaves emancipated, it was no longer in existence.

Andrew J. O'Shaughnessy

Bibliography

Hall, Douglas. *A Brief History of the West India Committee.* 1971.

Higman, Barry. "The West India Interest in Parliament, 1807–1833." *Historical Studies.* Vol. 13, pp. 1–19.

Penson, Lillian M. "The London West India Interest in the Eighteenth Century." *English Historical Review.* Vol. 30, pp. 373–392.

———. *The Colonial Agents of the British West Indies.* 1924.

Sheridan, Ricard B. *Sugar and Slavery: An Economic History of the British West Indies, 1623–1775.* 1974.

Ward, J.R. *British West Indian Slavery, 1750–1834: The Process of Amelioration.* 1988.

West Indies

The West Indies, the islands of the Caribbean archipelago stretching from Cuba southeast to South America, received their name from Columbus who claimed them for Spain. But England, **France**, and Holland, drawn by accounts of their wealth, soon began to dispute Spanish ownership. The first English landing was in 1623, when Captain Thomas Warner reached St. Kitts. Britain's largest colony, Jamaica, slightly smaller than Wales, was captured (1655) by Admiral Sir William Penn (1621–1670), father of the founder of Pennsylvania. Soon a group of colonies, the British West Indies, existed, centered on the cultivation of **tobacco**. The Anglican religion was established in each, and government was similar to that of the Crown colonies of America, each island possessing a representative assembly.

In the 1660s, after a glut of tobacco on the London market, an alternative crop was found. The first pots of **sugar** reached England in 1673, and a "white revolution" followed. The Royal African Company was formed (1672) with a monopoly over slave traffic, and from this time forward, Jamaica became one of the biggest slave marts of the New World.

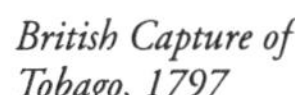
British Capture of Tobago, 1797

Around 1750 it was estimated that England's island possessions contained at least 230,000 Africans and 90,000 whites.

The booming success of sugar brought not only the large-scale importation of hundreds of thousands of Africans (who in fact were to initiate some 75 slave rebellions in British holdings before the end of slavery in 1833) but also an invasion of hordes of British adventurers, many of whom were well-heeled and well-connected back home. The result was that the West Indies became the favored child of the **Empire** in the 18th century, their small size greatly outweighed by their economic value and their clout in Parliament. Since they could not compete with rival French sugar, they relied on the **navigation laws** to protect their monopoly of the home market, and on the British **Navy** for security against neighboring European colonies. At the time of the **American Revolution**, total British **overseas commerce** with the 13 American colonies ran to the annual value of 2.8 million; whereas that with the "sugar islands" amounted to considerably more, some 3.4 million.

The islands' economic value dictated their military and strategic worth, and naturally the Caribbean remained the scene of imperial **war**, with the British often coming up as gainers. France, which in the early 18th century held a string of islands including Haiti (the richest), Guadeloupe, and Martinique, was forced in 1763 to cede Grenada, St. Vincent, Dominica, and Tobago. At the end of the Napoleonic wars, Britain regained Tobago from the Spanish, took Trinidad (about the size of Lancashire) from the Spanish also, and garnered St. Lucia from the French. By this time the British held more than a dozen colonies, with Jamaica in the Greater Antilles, then St. Kitts, Nevis, Montserrat, and Antigua in the Leeward Islands, and Barbados among the Windward Islands. More than 200,000 British military men died in this region before 1790, in attempts to extend the fortunes of Britain's slaveowners or to deplete those of her enemies, while perhaps another 100,000 British casualties resulted from similar efforts during the **French Revolutionary and Napoleonic Wars**.

The islands' economic value enhanced their political as well as military importance. For example, the terms of the **Peace of Paris** (1763) were greeted with considerable disapproval in **London** even though the treaty registered British acquisition of Canada and other North American possessions while returning conquered Guadeloupe, Martinique, St. Lucia, and Gorée to France. This choice had been approved, however, by the **West India interest**, a powerful lobby of West Indian sugar planters who did not want to compete with other, newly annexed sugar islands that would inevitably also be granted British colonial preferences and trading privileges. The same lobby favored **George Grenville**'s Sugar Act (1764), which, though it angered the American colonists, ensured a virtual monopoly of the American sugar market to British West Indian planters.

The two regions' economies were, however, partly interwoven in the so-called triangular trade, with both trading not only with Britain but with each other (the Americans traded flour, fish, and naval stores for Caribbean sugar and molasses); a fact that helps to explain the sympathy of some of the self-governing island colonies with the Americans in resisting the **Stamp Act** and the **Tea Act**. But their far greater dependence on the navy, as well as their specially privileged position in

British economics and politics, determined that they would stand with Britain in the **War of American Independence.**

In 1783 the West Indies remained among Britain's most valued imperial possessions. But they unknowingly faced a great decline over the next half century. The American war dislocated the triangular trade. Rival sugar planters emerged in the United States, in Cuba, and even in India under the control of the **East India Company.** Sugar beets, another competing crop, were developed in Europe. The rise from the 1820s of free trade and the concomitant decline of imperial protectionism damaged the islands' preferred status and prosperity. The planters became increasingly indebted to British merchants, at the same time watching their political power wane as they lost their bitter and selfish struggle against the **antislavery movement** that brought first the abolition of the **slave trade** (1807) and then (1833) complete emancipation of slaves throughout the **Empire.** The 18th-century literary portrayals of West Indians as *nouveux riches,* in the works of such artists as **Richard Cumberland** and **Samuel Foote,** thus gave way to the financially embarrassed fictional character of Sir Thomas Bertram in **Jane Austen**'s *Mansfield Park.* Yet, even after emancipation, planters persisted with sugar cultivation based on coercive labor.

Andrew J. O'Shaughnessy

Bibliography

Brathwaite, Edmund. *The Development of a Creole Society in Jamaica, 1770–1820.* 1971.

Craton, Michael. *Testing the Chains: Resistance to Slavery in the British West Indies.* 1982.

Duffy, Michael. *Soldiers, Sugar, and Seapower: The British Expeditions to the West Indies and the War against Revolutionary France.* 1987.

Dunn, Richard. *Sugar and Slaves: The Rise of the Planter Class in the English West Indies, 1624–1713.* 1972.

Higman, Barry W. *Slave Populations of the British Caribbean, 1807–1834.* 1984.

Morgan, Kenneth. *Bristol and the Atlantic Trade in the Eighteenth Century.* 1994.

Pares, Richard. *Merchants and Planters.* 1960.

Ragatz, Lowell J. *The Fall of the Planter Class in the British Caribbean, 1763–1833.* 1928.

Sheridan, Richard B. *Sugar and Slavery: An Economic History of the British West Indies, 1623–1775.* 1974.

Ward, J.R. *British West Indian Slavery, 1750–1834: The Process of Amelioration.* 1988.

Watts, David. *The West Indies: Patterns of Development, Culture and Environmental Change since 1492.* 1987.

Williams, Eric. *Capitalism and Slavery.* 1944.

See also Commerce, Overseas

Whately, Richard (1787–1863)

Prelate, reformer, writer, and (from 1831) Anglican Archbishop of **Dublin,** Whately involved himself in many contemporary projects. He published over 50 works on subjects ranging from logic and religion to education. A graduate of Oxford, he supported **Catholic emancipation** but reproved the Catholic revival in the Anglican church in his pamphlet "The Errors of Romanism Traced to Their Origin in Human Nature" (1830). After taking office as archbishop he headed a commission to establish a "united national education" providing **religious education** acceptable to both **Catholics** and Protestants in Irish schools, but the project failed amidst sectarian controversy. Whately was also interested in **penal reform** and political economy—under this heading he wrote, among other things, a well-received children's text called *Easy Lessons on Money Matters* (1837)—but educated Victorians perhaps knew him best as the linguist and philosopher whose "Elements of Logic" (1826) and "Elements of Rhetoric" (1828) became widely reprinted classics.

Laura B. Kennelly

Bibliography

Akenson, Donald H. *A Protestant in Purgatory: Richard Whately, Archbishop of Dublin.* 1981.

Rashid, S. "Richard Whately and the Struggle for Rational Christianity in the Mid-Nineteenth Century." *Historical Magazine of the Protestant Episcopal Church.* Vol. 47, pp. 293–331.

See also Children's Literature; Church of England

Whigs and Whiggism

The Whigs originated in the **opposition** to the succession of James II in the 1680s and took their name from enemies' epithets. In the Hanoverian era their leadership was anchored in some of the great families of the **aristocracy,** such as the **Cavendish family** (dukes of Devonshire), and the **Russell family** (dukes of Bedford); both dukedoms had been awarded in the 1690s in return for loyal services in the **Glorious Revolution.** In **Scotland,** the Campbell family (dukes of **Argyll**) were a mainstay of 18th-century Whig influence.

During most of the earlier Hanoverian period, the Whigs were a loose confederation of men with some beliefs in common, rather than a political party in the modern sense. In common their leaders shared the general admiration for the **Glorious Constitution,** supported the Protestant **Hanoverian Succession,** believed strongly in a constitutionally limited monarchy and the supremacy of Parliament, and favored wider **religious toleration.** These leaders, historically sensitive to the threat of Royal abuses of power, were usually more forward advocates of civil and political liberties than the **Tories.** Their wealth, power, urbanity, and coolness toward others' opinions led their inclination for somewhat lax manners and an underlying snobbishness, not always well concealed, against the German monarchs themselves. It is their detached, faintly bored, faintly amused, utterly self-confident faces that often stare out complacently from the canvases of **Reynolds, Gainsborough,** and **Romney.**

The first part of the Hanoverian age is known as that of the "Whig Ascendancy." **George I**'s conviction that all Tories were **Jacobites** led him to favor the Whigs in the 1715 general election and so begin their long dominance of office. Although the Whigs were tied to urban interests connected with **dissenters, merchants,** and bankers, their first great leader was a country gentleman, **Sir Robert Walpole.** His brilliant use of **patronage** installed Whigs in every level of government and the **Church of England** but also alienated those who received no rewards. Whig foreign policy was influenced by the monarchs' desire to protect **Hanover** and Walpole's determination to stay out of **wars** in order to keep the land **tax** low. His refusal to declare war on Spain until pressed by Parliament (1739) left him with only a slim majority after the 1741 general election, which forced his resignation.

George II after his accession (1727) continued to support the Whigs, and the Pelham brothers (**Henry Pelham** and the **Duke of Newcastle**) were able to form a ministry that took in many of Walpole's Whig opponents. The Jacobite rising of 1745 strengthened the Pelhams' position at home even while they were involved in a Continental war not settled until 1748. Their Whig opponents had grouped themselves around **Frederick, Prince of Wales,** but went over to the government after the prince's death in 1751.

The death of Henry Pelham in 1754 ended the brief period of Whig unity during which the Tories were marginalized. Newcastle, unable to settle on a Whig leader in **Commons,** finally struck a compromise with **William Pitt the Elder** which allowed them to prosecute the **Seven Years' War** successfully. Because the young **George III** had come to the throne (1760) determined to break the power of the Newcastle Whigs, the first half of his reign witnessed the continual dissolution and regrouping of alliances among Whig factions. While still united on principles, they lacked that agreement on policies which could make them a cohesive party.

Newcastle's successors the Rockingham Whigs, headed by the **Marquess of Rockingham,** led a successful attack on the influence of the Crown in the 1780s and helped to develop a respectable theory of opposition or what we might call **party politics.** But the Foxite Whigs who succeeded them, led by Charles James Fox of the **Fox family,** were no match for the revived Toryism of **William Pitt the Younger.** Fox's unrepentant francophilism was extremely damaging during the **French Revolution,** causing a split with old associates like **Edmund Burke** and resulting in the crossing over to Pitt of erstwhile Whig stalwarts like the **Duke of Portland** (1794).

Even after the death of both Pitt and Fox (1806), Whigs were kept from office by their unpopular support of **Catholic emancipation.** Though energized by progressive men like **Grey, Whitbread, Brougham,** and young **Lord John Russell,** and still socially and intellectually influential through such institutions as **Holland House** and the new *Edinburgh Review* edited by **Francis Jeffrey,** it was not until the 1820s that the Whigs were able to present a program of alternatives to Tory policies and draw on growing public demand for reform.

Now a true political party, they took their restoration to office in 1830 as a mandate for extensive change. The parliamentary **Reform Act** was, with much difficulty, steered through Parliament in 1832 by Grey and Russell. Other reform acts abolished slavery throughout the British **Empire** (1833), regulated **child labor** in factories (1833), and reorganized poor relief in the **New Poor Law** (1834). The **Melbourne** administration secured passage of acts reforming **municipal** government (1835), commuting the **tithe** to a cash payment (1836), and allowing civil registration of births, deaths, and marriages (1837). In the 1860s the Whigs relinquished their name and became part of the new Liberal party.

P.J. Kulisheck

Bibliography

Browning, Reed. *Political and Constitutional Ideas of the Court Whigs.* 1982.

Clark, J.C.D. *The Dynamics of Change: The Crisis of the 1750s and English Party Systems.* 1982.

Mitchell, Austin. *The Whigs in Opposition, 1815–1830.* 1967.

Mitchell, L.G. *Charles James Fox and the Disintegration of the Whig Party 1782–1794.* 1971.

O'Gorman, Frank. *The Rise of Party in England: The Rockingham Whigs, 1760–82.* 1975.

Roberts, Michael. *The Whig Party 1807–1812.* 1939, rpt. 1965.

See also Government, National; Tories and Toryism

Whiston, William (1667–1752)

Whiston, Anglican clergyman and mathematician, exemplified some of the peculiar combinations wrought by the rise of **science** in a culture still intensely religious. Born in Leicestershire, he was educated at Cambridge and received appointments as chaplain in Norwich (1694) and in the rectory at Lowestoft (1698). His ambitious *New Theory of the Earth, from Its Original to the Consummation of All Things* (1696), which concluded that the biblical stories concerning creation, the flood, and the end of the world by fire were based on known scientific precepts, received praise from both **Locke** and Sir Isaac Newton (1642–1727). In 1703 he succeeded Newton as Lucasian Professor of Mathematics at Cambridge, but was expelled in 1710 because of his growing Arian unorthodoxy.

Brave, imprudent, contentious, and interested in a remarkable variety of scientific as well as religious subjects, Whiston spent the remainder of his life attempting to restore what he regarded as "true" and "primitive" antitrinitarian Christianity, lecturing on astronomy, investigating **longitude,** and indulging various crotchets including his beliefs in touching for the king's evil, his conviction that the Tatars were the lost tribes of Israel, and his firm advocacy of clerical monogamy (immortalized by **Goldsmith** in *The Vicar of Wakefield*). Though himself a **freethinker,** Whiston's dislike of rationalistic religion made him an opponent of the views typified in **Benjamin Hoadly**'s rationalistic **Latitudinarianism.** His political views place him among the **commonwealthmen.**

Whiston published no fewer than 53 books and **tracts** on mathematics and religion. These included several thick studies of early Christian faith, *Historical Memoirs of the Life and Writings of Dr. Samuel Clarke* (1730), and a **translation** of the works of the Jewish historian Josephus (37?–*c.* 100), including notes and comments (1737), which was definitive well into the 19th century. Though already unorthodox in the extreme, in 1747 Whiston left the **Church of England** altogether and joined the General **Baptists**.

Samuel J. Rogal

Bibliography

Colligan, J.H. *The Arian Movement in England.* 1913.

Cross, F.L., and E.A. Livingstone, eds. *The Oxford Dictionary of the Christian Church.* 1983.

Ollard, S.L., and G. Cross, eds. *Dictionary of English Church History.* 1912.

See also Clarke, Samuel

Whitbread, Samuel (1758–1815)

Whitbread was a rich **Whig** politician known for his moderate political reformism, sympathy for the hardships of common people, and extended liberal and **humanitarian** interests. He was the son of the **brewer** Samuel Whitbread (1720–1796), a **dissenter** who purchased, besides his **London** industrial property, large estates in Bedfordshire and sat as M.P. for Bedford **borough** for most of the time from 1768 to his death, voting usually with the **Rockingham** and Foxite Whigs. The son was educated at Eton and Cambridge, married the sister of **Charles Grey**, and entered Parliament (1790). A founder of the **Society of the Friends of the People**, and a friend of **Fox**, he supported Grey's unsuccessful reform motions (1793, 1797) and remained a parliamentary liberal until his death, sometimes allying even with **Burdett** on the **radical** left of the Whigs. His position on the left wing may explain his omission from the one whiggish cabinet of the period, the **Ministry of all the Talents**.

Samuel Whitbread

Speaking often in **Commons**, Whitbread took the reformist line on such issues as wasteful military expenditure, abolition of the **slave trade**, national education (he was a prominent backer of **Joseph Lancaster**), expansion of religious and civil rights, and amelioration of the condition of the poor. If passed, his bill to permit magistrates to fix **wages** for **agricultural laborers** (1795, 1800) might have dealt more successfully with **poverty** than the **Speenhamland system**, which shifted the burden to taxpayers. His charges concerning naval department abuses led to the resignation of **Henry Dundas** as First Lord of the Admiralty (1805).

Detesting the war, Whitbread challenged the government regularly on its policies and its conduct of **foreign relations**. He cherished a certain admiration for Napoleon and urged peace with him in 1815 upon the latter's return from Elba; some writers have suggested that shock at the results of the **Battle of Waterloo** may even have hastened his **suicide** 3 weeks afterward.

Thomas D. Veve

Bibliography

Fulford, Roger. *Samuel Whitbread, 1764–1815: A Study in Opposition.* 1967.

Mitchell, Leslie G. *Charles James Fox and the Disintegration of the Whig Party, 1782–1794.* 1971.

Rapp, Dean. "Social Mobility in the Eighteenth Century: The Whitbreads of Bedfordshire, 1720–1815." *Economic History Review.* 2nd ser. Vol. 27, pp. 380–394.

Sack, James J. *The Grenvillites, 1801–1829: Party Politics and Factionalism in the Age of Pitt and Liverpool.* 1979.

White, Gilbert (1720–1793)

A naturalist and author of the fourth most frequently published book in the English language, White was born in the parsonage at Selborne in Hampshire, where his grandfather was vicar. He was educated at Basingstoke and Oriel College, Oxford, of which he became a Fellow in 1744. He served as curate in a number of rural parishes before becoming curate of Farringdon (a village near Selborne) from 1761 to 1784. He spent the final 10 years of his life as curate in Selborne, the parish with which his name is so closely linked.

Interested in natural history from boyhood, White began to keep a diary of events occurring in his garden, and later expanded this work into his *Naturalist's Journal.* He attended meetings of the **Royal Society** and Society of Antiquaries, meeting many scientists and naturalists of the day. But it was his correspondence with the traveler and naturalist **Thomas Pennant**, and the antiquary and naturalist Daines Barrington (1727–1800), that formed the basis of his famous book, *The Natural History and Antiquities of Selborne.* Although he made many new observations, he was more concerned with the relationships between creatures than with scientific systems, and his ability to convey a sense of place makes his writing remarkable. First published in 1788, his book has been edited and **translated** over 200 times, and serves as a monument to White's exact observations, meticulous recording, and precise descriptions.

C.J. Davey

Bibliography
Holt-White, R. *The Life and Letters of Gilbert White of Selborne.* 1901.
Rye, A. *Gilbert White and His Selborne.* 1970.
Scott, W.S. *White of Selborne.* 1950.
White, Gilbert. *The Natural History and Antiquities of Selborne.* 1976. Facsimile of the first edition.

See also Science, Technology, and Invention

Whiteboys

The Whiteboy movement originated in Tipperary toward the end of 1761. There, groups of men assembled at night to assert their traditional rights of free grazing by destroying ditches that had been constructed around local common land. They first called themselves "Levellers," but as they wore white shirts to enable easy recognition in the dark, they came to be known as *Buachailli Bana* or Whiteboys.

Opposition to the enclosure of common lands, access to which had eased the burden of increasing rents, remained a major concern of the movement, but it also agitated against oppressive **tithes**, rack-rents, and evictions. Tactics ranged from the sending of threatening letters to the destruction of property and violent attacks on individuals.

By 1762 the Whiteboys had spread through the counties of Kilkenny, Waterford, Limerick, and Cork. Although the accompanying wave of violence subsided by the following year, the authorities felt sufficiently threatened to introduce repressive measures. In 1765 the **Irish Parliament** passed an act to "prevent tumultuous risings," decreeing the death penalty for several Whiteboy activities. This failed to break the movement, however, as it had already become deeply embedded in local communities.

In the early 1770s, economic recession and poor harvests brought about a revival, particularly in Kilkenny. This was followed by a third major outbreak in late 1785, with people swearing an oath to obey Captain Right—hence the name **Rightboys** which was applied to them during this phase. Confusingly, in later decades the "Whiteboy" term continued to be used as a generic description of all types of agrarian protest in **Ireland**.

E.W. McFarland

Bibliography
Beames, M. *Peasants and Power: The Whiteboys Movement and Their Control in pre–Famine Ireland.* 1983.
Cornewall, Lewis G. *On Local Disturbances in Ireland.* 1836.
Donnelly, J.S. "The Whiteboy Movement, 1761–5." *Irish Historical Studies.* Vol. 21, pp. 20–54.
Williams, T.D., ed. *Secret Societies in Ireland.* 1973.

See also Irish Land Settlement; Ribbonmen and Ribbonism; Shanavests; Terry Alts

Whitefield, George (1714–1770)

Whitefield, a popular and dramatic Calvinist **Methodist** preacher, a major force in the 18th-century **religious revival**, pioneered open-air preaching (1739) to British and American congregations. He supported the Georgia colony and other philanthropic projects of his college friend **John Wesley**, established a preaching base in **Bristol**, and initiated the practice of calling preachers to conference.

A graduate of Oxford, he became a deacon in 1736. After preaching throughout England he spent 6 months in Georgia in 1738. In addition to bringing funds to support the colony that Wesley had helped organize, Whitefield also established schools and planned an orphanage there. He returned to England, was ordained in 1739, and then became a minister of Savannah; he made it a practice to **travel** back and forth between Georgia and England for the remainder of his life.

Whitefield began open-air preaching at Rose Green, near Bristol, in February 1739. This innovative approach, so influential for so many preachers later, gave him freedom from local church approval. His simple piety, legendary eloquence, and scripturally based **sermons** attracted large crowds of followers. At Stoke Newington, some 20,000 people heard his first sermon there, which emphasized the Calvinist doctrine of Election.

Whitefield died while on his seventh visit to **North America** in Newburyport, Massachusetts, after preaching despite poor health. Besides his Evangelical work he also founded Bethesda College (a home and school for orphans in Georgia) and numerous other schools. He created in 1740 *The Christian History,* a religious **periodical**, and wrote popular, though controversially frank, journals, criticized by Anglican authorities because they displayed his most privately held views. He preached over 18,000 sermons, some of which remain in print; these reveal his belief in the Evangelical doctrines of the necessity of the "new birth," his rejection of Arminianism, and his support of the doctrine of grace and of the fundamental inerrancy of Scripture. His works included *The Two First Parts of His Life* (1756). An energizing force in both English and American **Evangelicalism**, Whitefield is considered one of the founders of Methodism, although, like Wesley, he opposed any separation from the **Church of England**.

Laura B. Kennelly

Bibliography
Dallimore, Arnold A. *George Whitefield, the Life and Times of the Great Evangelist of the Eighteenth-Century Revival.* 1979.
Lambert, Frank. *"Pedlar in Divinity": George Whitefield and the Transatlantic Revival, 1737–1770.* 1994.
Stout, Harry S. *The Divine Dramatist: George Whitefield and the Rise of Modern Evangelicalism.* 1991.

See also Berridge, John; Huntingdon, Countess of

Wigs, Hair, and Hairdressing

The well-dressed person in Hanoverian Britain spent a considerable amount of time and money on hair. During most of the 18th century, every man who could afford a wig wore one,

A Macaroni, 1773

even farm hands and laborers. While beards and the display of natural hair were extremely rare, there were more than 200 wig styles for men alone, and wig-snatchers were almost as common as pickpockets. Women wore wigs less frequently than men, preferring to have their natural hair powdered, colored, or dressed in styles that ranged from simple rolls of curls to elaborate constructions imitating flower gardens or even battleships, depending on **fashion** and current social and political trends. When **George II** was crowned (1727), there were only a handful of hairdressers in **London**; by 1795 there were nearly 50,000 in Britain.

The *full-bottom* wig of the 17th century, consisting of long, flowing locks reaching to the middle of the chest, arrived at its apogee during the reign of **Queen Anne** and continued to be popular until around 1720. From that time on, men's wigs tended to become shorter, and natural colors were replaced by powder or bleach. Powder was applied with a bellows after the wig-wearer was suitably protected by a powdering jacket and paper mask or nose-bag. Affluent houses usually had a "wig closet" reserved for this purpose.

The type of wig worn often denoted a man's profession or social standing. Full-bottoms have been favored by the **legal profession** from the 17th century to the present day. **Merchants** and men of letters, who traditionally wore full-bottoms, took to wearing *tie-wigs* and *queue wigs* after 1720. These were highly stylized constructions in which the hair at the back of the neck was tied together by a black ribbon. **Army** officers and men would, for practical reasons, tie up the queues of their wigs in a black silk or taffeta bag, thus inventing the *bag wig,* which was later adopted by fashionable civilians as a dress wig. Men of the **clerical profession** preferred *bob wigs,* short, curly, or frizzed wigs without queues. The *scratch wig,* very popular with **artisans** and the lower classes, was casual, inexpensive, and resembled natural hair.

Natural hair became more popular toward the end of the 18th century, especially after a **tax** on hair-powdering was imposed in 1795. From 1810 to 1820, cropped natural styles such the *Titus* and the *Brutus* were in fashion. From 1810 to 1830 there was a reappearance of whiskers, and hair was worn long enough to show full curls.

Women's hairstyles tended to be very artificial at the end of the 17th century, consisting of high constructions of curls around *commodes* and *tours* worn directly above the forehead. The most extravagant coiffure of the early 18th century was the *Hanover cut,* which consisted of building the hair up over pads, then plastering down, powdering, and decorating it with gauze and ribbons. Until the 1750s, many women preferred to simply pull their hair toward the back of the head in a braid or twist, sometimes allowing curls to cascade over one shoulder on formal occasions. But then the natural look gave way to the use of ribbons, flowers, pearls, and decorative pins in hairstyles. Heavily influenced by French fashions promoted by Madame de Pompadour (*d.* 1764) and Marie Antoinette (1755–1793), women's hairstyles, and also those of the dandies derisively called "Macaronis," grew steadily taller and more artificial. In the 1770s and 1780s, egg-shaped coiffures that nearly reached the ceiling were often stuffed with cushions and wool, around which natural hair, stiffened with pomatum and powder, and sometimes supplemented with artificial hair, was stretched. Miniature ships or figurines were occasionally fastened into the female headdress, and feathers were very popular. Wig construction peaked at these heights, and indeed could not have been surpassed without innovations in **housebuilding** and **interior design**.

After the **French Revolution**, women wore decorated

headbands or bonnets over short, curly hair. Wigs were sometimes dyed to match the color of a dress. In the early part of the 19th century, various classical hairstyles, particularly the Roman and Grecian, were popular, the shift to natural hair marking a striking break with past practices. While wigs were increasingly stigmatized as old-fashioned, **hats** became more important as a medium of decorative display.

Deidre Dawson

Bibliography

Corson, Richard. *Fashions in Hair: The First Five Thousand Years.* 1988.

Woodforde, John. *The Strange Story of False Hair.* 1971.

See also Clothing; Clothing-Makers; Clothing Trade; Manners and Morals

Wilberforce, William (1759–1833)

Statesman and humanitarian, Wilberforce tirelessly worked to end the British **slave trade** and reform **manners and morals.** Born in Hull, he went, after a brief youthful flirtation with **Methodism** that alarmed his well-to-do family, to St. John's College, Cambridge, where he was known as a bright but indolent student who enjoyed entertaining. On coming of age he inherited enough money to allow him to take up politics. Standing for Hull, he was elected to the **House of Commons** in September 1780. There he often supported his Cambridge classmate and friend **William Pitt the Younger**. In 1797 he married Barbara Spooner; they had six children.

On a trip abroad (1784) with his family and former teacher **Isaac Milner**, Wilberforce studied **Philip Doddridge's** *The Rise and Progress of Religion* (1745) and the Greek Testament, and afterward announced his deep inward conversion to **Evangelicalism**. He now felt a compulsion to repair not only his own morals but those of his nation: England, he believed, was in deep moral crisis. His efforts included founding in 1787 the **Proclamation Society against Vice and Immorality**, unceasingly working in Parliament against the slave trade, and writing *A Practical View of the Prevailing Religious System of Professed Christians* (1797) to encourage Evangelical Christian action by shaming mere "nominal Christians" into more serious belief and conduct. The book became a best-seller and remained in print for many years.

Wilberforce's greatest work, that which gave him international moral stature, began in 1787 when he accepted Pitt's challenge to lead Parliament to abolish the slave trade in the colonies, a goal which he, **Thomas Clarkson**, and his associates in the **Clapham sect** had long sought. After years of struggle in and out of Parliament against planters, traders, and **merchants** who believed their economic welfare depended on slavery, Wilberforce and his **antislavery movement** successfully engineered Parliament's vote, 283 to 16, in February 1807 to declare the slave trade illegal. He lived to see the **Empire** abolish slavery in its domains in July 1833.

Wilberforce also helped to found the Evangelical *Christian Observer* (1801) and supported **Catholic emancipation** (despite his intense dislike of Catholicism), **Hannah More's**

William Wilberforce

schools, the Church **Missionary Society**, the Bible Society, the Society for Bettering the Condition of the Poor, the Indian Mission Society, and many other projects of contemporary **humanitarianism**. Many individuals successfully requested his aid and assistance. Though he often took highly independent political positions, viewing things by his own moral lights, he generally supported conservative positions on such matters as the **corn laws**, the **six acts**, and the **Reform Act** of 1832 (which at age 73 he thought "too radical"), while nevertheless taking the position of a humanitarian reformer on such issues as **factory acts** and **game laws**.

Laura B. Kennelly

Bibliography

Brown, F.K. *Fathers of the Victorians: The Age of Wilberforce.* 1961.

Cormack, Patrick. *Wilberforce: The Nation's Conscience.* 1983.

Cowie, Leonard W. *William Wilberforce, 1759–1833: A Bibliography.* 1992.

Furneaux, Robin. *William Wilberforce.* 1974.

Newsome, David. *The Wilberforces and Henry Manning: The Parting of Friends.* 1966.

Pollock, John C. *Wilberforce.* 1977.

Wilkes, John (1727–1797)

Wilkes, a member of the **House of Commons** known for his outrageous moral behavior and unrestrained political attacks, became a symbol of protest and a champion of political liberties largely as a result of governmental attempts to punish him for his political and moral improprieties. Historians date the development of modern British **radicalism** from his actions in the 1760s.

Wilkes was the son of a **Presbyterian** distiller. He married an heiress (1747), ran about **London** with other young men of **fashion**, joined the **Hell-Fire Club**, and entered Parliament (1757) as a supporter of **Pitt the Elder**. He first achieved notoriety in 1763 when he took over as owner and editor of the *North Briton* **newspaper**. Under him the journal, already provocative in tone, became even more violently antigovernment. In No. 45 of the paper Wilkes ridiculed the **Peace of Paris** as being against the best interests of England (contradicting what **George III** had claimed in a speech before Parliament), suggesting that the king's minister, **Bute**, had bribed Parliament to approve it, and, for good measure, hinting broadly that Bute was the lover of the king's mother. The inflammatory article resulted in Wilkes's arrest under a **general warrant** for seditious libel.

For the most part, general warrants had been used only in emergencies, and their use in this situation also raised the issue of the parliamentary privilege against arrest. Thus the resulting law cases made Wilkes a hero of English liberties. In the criminal case, he was released on the ground that an M.P. enjoyed a privilege against arrest for libel; in a civil suit filed by Wilkes, the general warrant was declared illegal for failure to name the persons to be arrested.

Pressing his luck, Wilkes then republished the offensive No. 45. The **House of Lords** countered by exposing an obscene *Essay on Woman* written by Wilkes and published privately, accusing him of an impious and obscene libel. Meanwhile the Commons, employing a different legal avenue, again formally charged him with seditious libel. Facing prosecution on both charges, he fled to **France**, after which he was expelled from the Commons and convicted *in absentia.*

He returned to England in 1768 and stood for election to Commons from Middlesex county. He was elected, but was nonetheless jailed, tried, convicted, and sentenced to 22

John Wilkes

months in **prison** and fined in the amount of £1,000 for the two libels outstanding against him, and was again expelled from Commons for his sins. Excited antigovernment demonstrations and organizations quickly took up his cause. A political association, the **Society for Supporters of the Bill of Rights**, was founded (July 1769) to provide him financial and political support. The government suddenly found itself besieged by a furious popular movement.

Rallying to "Wilkes and Liberty," Middlesex repeatedly reelected him in February, March, and April 1769, though he was still in prison and despite the Commons' equally regular expulsion of him. At last in May, Parliament named Wilkes' opponent to the seat. This raised another grave constitutional issue, whether or not Parliament could deprive an electorate of its right to choose its representative. The government finally conceded the right of electors to choose whomever they pleased, but also upheld the right of Commons to expel its own members.

What was most significant was the enormous popular excitement and unexpectedly effective political organization that surrounded these events, as Parliament, amidst **riots and popular disturbances**, became inundated with petitions from all around the country supporting Wilkes and decrying ministerial tyranny. Wilkes's supporters, led by **John Horne Tooke**, were actually more radical than he, but his confrontation with the government was the catalyst of a spreading popular reaction.

Prevented from taking his parliamentary seat, Wilkes was elected a London Alderman (1769), then Sheriff (1771), then Lord Mayor (1774). In the first capacity he defended London printers being sought for arrest on the charge of illegally publishing transcripts of parliamentary debates (1771). His intervention resulted in Parliament soon afterward abandoning its claims to prevent such publications—another important gain against an oligarchical government.

Wilkes again won election to Parliament in 1774 (from Middlesex), this time successfully taking his seat. In 1776 he became the first M.P. to propose parliamentary reform, calling for a revision of voting qualifications, a redistribution of parliamentary seats, and a drastic expansion of the electorate to include "the meanest mechanic, the poorest peasant and the day labourer." He strongly supported the Americans in their struggle with George III, and became a supporter of **Pitt the Younger** in the 1780s; but his greatest significance lay in his role both as propagandist and as first figurehead of the movement that ultimately brought about British democracy.

Frank M. Baglione

Bibliography

Christie, Ian. *Wilkes, Wyvill and Reform: The Parliamentary Reform Movement in British Politics, 1760–1785.* 1962.

Kronenberger, Louis. *The Extraordinary Mr. Wilkes: His Life and Times.* 1974.

Postgate, Raymond Williams. *"That Devil Wilkes."* 1956.

Rudé, George. *Wilkes and Liberty: A Social Study of 1763 to 1774.* 1983.

Sherrard, Owen Aubrey. *A Life of John Wilkes.* 1971.

Stevenson, John. *Popular Disturbances in England, 1700–1832.* 2nd ed., 1992.

See also Elections and the Franchise; Government, National

Wilkie, Sir David (1785–1841)

Wilkie rose to fame early in the 19th century as a **genre painter**, **portrait painter**, and **history painter**, and was a major figure in the Scottish cultural reawakening. Born in the hamlet of Cults, near Pitlessie (in Fife), the son of a minister, and showing great early talent in **drawing**, he was sent to study in **Edinburgh**, then **London**, where he quickly established a reputation on the basis of his crowded canvas portraying a festive event, *Pitlessie Fair* (1804). Here, as in *Blind Man's Buff* (1811) and *The Penny Wedding* (1818), the frank depiction of human behavior in a festive atmosphere is executed in a vigorous, anecdotal manner.

Social gatherings in humble dwellings, in scenes reminiscent of Dutch genre paintings of the 17th century, are the subject of *The Blind Fiddler* (1806) and *The Card Players* (1807–1808). A brilliant draftsman, Wilkie excelled in capturing the human form in motion. His psychological insight and human sympathy are also evident in many of his paintings, such as the *Chalmers-Bethune* portrait (1804), in which the attitude of each sitter is made evident by facial expression, and *The Letter of Introduction* (1813), inspired by 17th-century Dutch sources.

Wilkie's commitment to social realism did not always work to his professional advantage. In England his scenes of the simple joys of Scottish village life brought some ridicule by sophisticates; and when his **patriotism** and strong sense of social justice moved him to portray the misery of the Scottish peasantry in *Distraining for Rent* (1815), the painting was attacked as too political. Despite the fact that many critics favored history painting, Wilkie's first attempt at treating an historical subject, *Alfred Reprimanded by the Neatherd's Wife* (executed in 1806 and exhibited in 1812), received little praise. Notwithstanding, in 1816 he received a commission from the **Duke of Wellington** to commemorate the great victory over Napoleon at **Waterloo**. In *The Chelsea Pensioners Reading the Waterloo Dispatch,* the most successful painting of his career, Wilkie combined an historical subject with a genre scene by depicting the joyous celebration in England as news of Wellington's victory was announced. The painting caused almost equally joyous celebrations when it was exhibited in London in 1822, and had to be roped off to protect it from admirers.

On the death of Sir Henry Raeburn (1756–1823), Wilkie became king's limner for **Scotland**, and in 1830 he succeeded **Sir Thomas Lawrence** as painter in ordinary to **George IV**. During this time he produced several important history paintings, including *The Entrance of George IV at Holyrood House* (1830), *The Preaching of John Knox before the Lords of the Congregation* (1832), and a series of pictures on the Spanish War of Independence. In 1836 he was knighted by **William IV**. After 1837, his popularity waning, he embarked upon an extended trip to the Holy Land; he died on the return

David Wilkie

voyage. In 1842 **Turner** paid fine homage to Wilkie in his painting *Peace: Burial at Sea (The Death of Sir David Wilkie).*

Deidre Dawson

Bibliography

Cannon-Brookes, Peter. *The Painted Word: British History Painting, 1750–1830.* 1991.

Caw, Sir James Lewis. *Scottish Painting, Past and Present, 1620–1908.* 1908.

MacMillan, Duncan. *Painting in Scotland: The Golden Age.* 1986.

Sir David Wilkie of Scotland (1785–1841). North Carolina Museum of Art. 1987.

See also Painting

Wilkinson, John (1728–1808)

Wilkinson, the son of a small Cumberland farmer (Isaac Wilkinson, 1704–1784) who augmented his income by working as an iron-furnace overlooker, rose eventually to run a famous ironworks in the family name. An indefatigable "booster," he was one of the Hanoverian era's biggest promoters of the **iron industry**.

Wilkinson took advantage of the high demand for iron during the **Seven Years' War** to build the first coke-smelting furnace in the Black Country at Bradley (1757). He added a furnace at Willey near Brosely on the River Severn before entering into a partnership with his father at Bersham in north **Wales** (1762), later ousting his father and bringing in his brother William as manager. He perfected his father's blowing engine and in 1774 took out his famous **patent** for a method of boring cannon by holding the boring bar steady and rotating the casting. French concern at British superi-

"Iron John" Wilkinson

ority in arms production led certain Frenchmen to recruit his brother William to introduce the new technology to **France**.

Wilkinson, meanwhile, played a vital role in the development of the **steam engine** by using his casting and boring skills to produce components of quality required by **Matthew Boulton** and **James Watt**, and was the first to purchase a rotary-action steam engine. He enthusiastically promoted novel applications for iron, including its use for the world's first iron bridge at Coalbrookdale, for 40 miles of waterpipe for the city of Paris, and, in the face of great skepticism, for the first iron **ship**. In his later years, Boulton and Watt split with him on discovering that he had been secretly selling their engines, and he quarreled with his brother. On his death in 1808 his fortune was largely consumed by legal disputes among his legitimate and illegitimate descendants. In typically flamboyant fashion, "Iron John" arranged to be buried in an iron coffin.

R.D. Corrins

Bibliography

Chaloner, W.H. *People and Industries.* 1963.
Crouzet, François. *The First Industrialists.* 1985.
Dickinson, A.W. *John Wilkinson, Ironmaster.* 1914.

See also Entrepreneurs and Entrepreneurship; Metallurgy and Metalworking; Science, Technology, and Invention

William IV, King (1765–1837)

William, brother of **George IV**, was the third son of **George III** and Queen Charlotte (1744–1818). His father placed him in the **navy**. William saw action during the **War of American Independence** and was stationed in New York, still occupied by the British, where loyalists feted him. He gained a reputation as a stern but efficient commander, with an eye for the ladies when on land. He was created Duke of Clarence (1788) and retired from the navy (though 10 years later he was promoted to Admiral, without a command). He settled down with an actress, Dorothy Jordan (1762–1816), with whom he lived for more than 20 years and had 10 children.

This phase ended with the death of the prince regent's daughter, Princess Charlotte (1796–1817). No legitimate grandchildren of George III now remained living. William and his younger brother, Edward, Duke of Kent (1767–1820), were in effect commanded to produce an heir. William married Princess Adelaide of Saxe-Meiningen (1792–1846), but no heir issued. He himself became heir to the throne on the death of his elder brother, Frederick (1763–1827).

William IV succeeded in 1830, just as the campaign for parliamentary reform reached a peak. Friendly and popular, he was at pains to act in a constitutionally correct manner. He had a **Whig** government, but worked for compromise with the **opposition**. When this proved impossible, he granted his ministers' request for the dissolution of Parliament; this returned them with a majority sufficient to pass the first **Reform Act** (1832) through the **Commons**. More reluctantly, he had also agreed to create, if necessary, enough peers to swamp the **Tory** majority in the **House of Lords**. From then on, governments depended on Parliament rather than on the monarch's

King William IV

favor. At his death in 1837 William was succeeded by Victoria, daughter of his brother Edward.

Michael Fry

Bibliography

Fitzgerald, P. *The Life and Times of William IV.* 2 vols. 1884.

Ziegler, P. *William IV.* 1971.

See also Government, National

Williams, Edward (Iolo Morganwg) (1747–1826)

Iolo Morganwg (the bardic name of the stone mason Edward Williams), was a poet, antiquary, literary scholar, manuscript collector, accomplished forger, and a leading figure in the Welsh cultural revival of the late Hanoverian period. English was his first language, but he shared in the area's Cymricization. In his youth he wrote **Romantic** poems, far removed from the classical Welsh verse of the period, inspired instead by the carnal love poetry of Dafydd ap Gwilym (*fl.* 1334–1370). He worked in **London** in the 1770s and 1790s, and became a leading member of the Gwyneddigion Society, founded (1770) for the furtherance of Welsh culture.

In the 1790s William proclaimed himself the last surviving bard and keeper of the secret rites of the Bardic Order, maintaining that the Gorsedd (assembly) of Bards, which he saw as building on druidic traditions and ideas, had survived longest in his native Glamorgan. To further his purposes he launched a series of forgeries, both literary (his poems of Dafydd ap Gwilym deceived scholars for decades after his death) and of the Gorsedd of Bards (deceiving no one now, but still flourishing). The Gorsedd became an established part of the eisteddfod (congress of Welsh bards and musicians) at the Carmarthen meeting in 1819. His modern reputation is as a brilliant scholar and Romantic poet, and also as a political **radical** who dubbed himself "The Bard of Liberty." He was one of the founders of the **Unitarian** Association in south Wales (1802), and bitterly opposed the **Methodists** for their attacks on Welsh folk traditions.

Neil Evans

Bibliography

Honourable Society of Cymmrodorion. *The Dictionary of Welsh Biography.* 1959.

Morgan, Prys. *Iolo Morganwg.* 1975.

Stephens, Meic, ed. *The Oxford Companion to the Literature of Wales.* 1986.

Williams, Gruffydd John. *Iolo Morganwg.* This BBC radio lecture (Cardiff, 1963) is a short, posthumously published, English résumé of a lifetime's work, otherwise mainly published in Welsh.

See also Chatterton, Thomas; Macpherson, James; Wales and Welsh Culture

Williams, Thomas (1737–1802)

The "Copper King" typified the aggressive pioneer of the early **Industrial Revolution** in **Wales**. Beginning as a solicitor and businessman, he became involved in a major lawsuit concerning the ownership and revenues of Anglesey copper mines, and emerged (1778) as the managing partner in the Parys Mine Company. To fight the domination of the smelters' cartel, he founded smelting works in South Lancashire and **Swansea**, and a manufacturing plant in Flintshire. In the 1780s he perfected copper sheathing for **ships**, winning an important **East India Company** contract. Williams helped create a cartel agreement with the Cornish Metal Company, administering it from 1787, and dominating the copper trade until the later 1790s, when his influence declined because of falling ore output in Anglesey. His other business interests included **banking**, **chemicals**, **shipping**, and coin issue. Closely connected with the political life of Anglesey and Caernarvon, Williams was M.P. for Great Marlow in Buckinghamshire from 1790 to his death.

Theresa McDonald

Bibliography

Hamilton, Henry. *The English Brass and Copper Industries to 1800.* 1926.

Harris, John Raymond. *The Copper King.* 1964.

Thorne, R.G., ed. *History of Parliament: The House of Commons, 1790–1820.* Vol. 5. 1986.

See also Entrepreneurs and Entrepreneurship; Metallurgy and Metalworking; Welsh Industry; Welsh Mining

Williams, William, Pantycelyn (1717–1791)

A hymn-writer and **Methodist** evangelist, Pantycelyn was educated in an Independent (**Congregationalist**) academy. His conversion by **Howel Harris** at Talgarth (1737) deflected him from his original course of **medicine**. He became a curate (1740), but, refused a priest's orders (1743), devoted himself thereafter to itinerant preaching and overseeing Methodist societies. In the course of this he **traveled**, by his own estimate, 150,000 miles. His view was that conversion should come first, **theology** later. After the general rift of the late 1740s he became the main organizer of the Methodists, and the revival, which followed reunification in 1763, owed much to his work. He wrote more than a thousand hymns, a great deal of **poetry**, and also much Welsh prose concerned with developing the spiritual life. His 90-odd publications brought him a secure place in Welsh literature.

Neil Evans

Bibliography

Honourable Society of Cymmrodorion. *The Dictionary of Welsh Biography.* 1959.

Hughes, Glyn Tegai. *William Williams, Pantycelyn.* 1983.

Stephens, Meic, ed. *The Oxford Companion to the Literature of Wales.* 1986.

See also Welsh Religious Revival

John Wilson

Wilson, John ("Christopher North") (1785–1854)

Wilson, though a lawyer, poet, critic, and **Tory** Professor of Moral Philosophy at the University of Edinburgh (from 1820), is best known as the "Christopher North" of *Blackwood's Magazine.* The son of a wealthy manufacturer, he was born in **Paisley** and educated at Glasgow University and Magdalen College, Oxford, where he won the Newdigate Prize for Poetry (1806). He later settled at Elleray in the Lake District, where he wrote **poetry** and socialized with **Wordsworth**, **De Quincey**, **Coleridge**, and **Southey**. His *Isle of Palms* (1812) and *City of the Plague* (1816) evoked little interest despite favorable reviews by **Francis Jeffrey** in the *Edinburgh Review.*

Although he was a mediocre and derivative poet, Wilson's literary talents found better employment in his contributions to *Blackwood's Magazine* (from 1817), where he, with wit and irreverence, made his personal impact on the age in approximately 200 contributions. These included favorable reviews of poems by Wordsworth (Wilson was the most sympathetic major contemporary reviewer of the **Romantics**), **Lord Byron**, and Alfred, Lord Tennyson (1809–1892)—whom he heralded in 1832—and also **letters**, prose sketches, and the famous series of amusing dialogues titled "Noctes Ambrosianae" (1822–1835), which featured an "Ettrick Shepherd" based on **James Hogg**.

Alice D. Fasano

Bibliography

Swann, Elsie. *Christopher North.* 1934.
Wilson, John. *Specimens of British Critics.* 1846.
———. *Essays Critical and Imaginative.* 1856–1857.
———. *The Isle of Palms and Other Poems.* Ed. by Donald Reiman. 1978.

See also Lake School of Poetry; Literary Criticism; Periodicals

Wilson, Richard (1713–1782)

Wilson, the first of the great British **landscape painters**, was born in Penegoes, **Wales**. He received a classical education but turned to portraiture, studying under T. Wright (*fl.* 1750). An extended stay in Italy (Venice, Rome, and Naples) from 1750 to 1757 resulted in his turning to idyllic scenes of the Italian landscape, often with ruined buildings (*Temple of Minerva Medica* [*c.* 1754]), in emulation of the 17th-century French painters Claude Lorrain (1600–1682) and Gaspard Dughet (1615–1675). He returned to England in 1757 and continued to produce classical Italian landscapes, based on his sketches, for classically educated patrons. He also painted idyllic English and Welsh views (the masterpice *Snowdon,* for example [*c.* 1770]), views of country houses, and dramatic scenes of classical myths (*Destruction of Niobe's Children,* before 1766). His mastery of the effects of light, distance, air, and rugged terrain impressed and influenced later painters such as **Turner** and **Constable**, and helped strengthen British landscape painting in public esteem. Wilson was a founding member of the Society of Arts (1760) and of the **Royal Academy** (1768).

Thomas J. McCormick

Bibliography

Constable, W.G. *Richard Wilson.* 1953.
Ford, Brinsley. *Richard Wilson's Drawings.* 1951.
Hemingway, Andrew. *Landscape Imagery and Urban Culture in Early Nineteenth-Century Britain.* 1992.
Sulton, Denys, and Ann Clements. *An Italian Sketchbook by Richard Wilson R.A.* 2 vols. 1968.

See also Painting

Wit and Ridicule

During the early Hanoverian period, *wit* was a complex critical term, ranging in possible meanings from the idea of imaginative creativity down to that of a mere gift for clever persiflage. Wit at its noblest was a reliable guide to truth, implying discriminating judgment. Wit in this sense was a mental quality whose possession validated the writing of satire by the "wits" who used irony to expose incongruities between appearances and realities, and ridicule to correct and punish deviant behavior or attitudes.

But in *An Essay Concerning Human Understanding* (1690), **John Locke** had distinguished between judgment, which separated things that were apparently alike; and wit, which put ideas "together with quickness and variety, wherein can be found any resemblance or congruity, thereby to make up pleasant Pictures, and agreeable Visions in the Fancy." For Locke, wit and judgment were opposed, with wit too apt to lead away from truth to illusion.

These definitions lay at the center of a battle over the meaning and hence value of wit during the first third of the 18th century. **Jeremy Collier**'s *A Short View of the Immorality and Profaneness of the English Stage* (1698) and Sir Richard

Blackmore's (*c.* 1655–1729) *Satyr against Wit* (1700) built upon Locke by arguing that wit and ridicule (for them the two terms were virtually synonymous) ultimately threatened both church and state by bringing precious things into contempt. The alternative view was expressed by the Earl of Shaftesbury's (1671–1713) *Letter Concerning Enthusiasm* (1707) and his *Sensus Communis* (1709), which contended that ridicule and raillery were appropriate tests for truth; by **Joseph Addison**'s series of *Spectator* **essays** (1711), which distinguished false from true wit; by **Alexander Pope**'s *Essay on Criticism* (1711), which tried to uphold virtually all of wit's positive connotations; and by Anthony Collins's (1676–1729) *A Discourse Concerning Ridicule and Irony in Writing* (1729), which forcefully restated Shaftesbury's position that truth was better recognized when it could withstand the hard test of irony and ridicule.

The spirit of the age, however, was ultimately on the side of Locke, Collier, and Blackmore. Partly for economic reasons, partly for social and intellectual reasons, wit, particularly at social ranks inferior to the fashionable elite, was taking on connotations of heartlessness and intellectual artificiality by the 1760s and 1770s, the great heyday of literary and emotional **sensibility and sentimentalism**. Though there were countervailing tendencies—sensibility itself became a subject of ridicule, as did the galloping social pretentiousness fostered by economic prosperity—the status of wit declined during the late Hanoverian period just as did the status of **satire**, its typical literary form.

Vincent Carretta

Bibliography

Empson, William. "Wit in the *Essay on Criticism.*" *The Hudson Review.* Vol. 2, pp. 559–577.

Hooker, Edward Niles. "Pope on Wit: The *Essay on Criticism.*" *The Hudson Review.* Vol. 2, pp. 84–100.

Milburn, D. Judson. *The Age of Wit, 1650–1750.* 1966.

Sitter, John. *Arguments of Augustan Wit.* 1991.

Stave, Stuart. *The Amiable Humorist: A Study in the Comic Theory and Criticism of the Eighteenth and Early Nineteenth Centuries.* 1960.

See also Augustan; Satire

Witchcraft

The organized prosecution and persecution of witches peaked well before the Hanoverian period. In England the last legal execution of an alleged witch occurred, apparently, in 1685; in **Scotland**, in 1722. In England the last actual death sentence was handed down in 1712 (the accused was later reprieved), and the last recorded trial was held in 1717. The 1604 statute on witchcraft, which decreed the death penalty for doing harm through **supernatural** means or by consulting with wicked spirits, was repealed by Parliament in 1736. After this, witchcraft was treated by the authorities as merely a species of fraud.

But while nearly all educated opinion had rejected witchcraft as mere superstition by the early 18th century, belief in witches and informal community action against them persisted throughout the Hanoverian period, especially in rural areas. Fortunately the law intervened on behalf of the accused in at least some instances. In 1751, after a woman accused of witchcraft and her husband were murdered by a mob—they were probably the last people to suffer death on charges of witchcraft—one of the mob's ringleaders was hanged for murder.

The decline of belief in witchcraft is attributable to several causes rooted in the European **Enlightenment**: reaction against the 17th-century's history of excesses and persecution; the rise of **science** and the commensurate decline in superstition; the spread of literacy; and a loss, even among most religious people, of a belief in frequent supernatural intervention in everyday life.

It has been speculated also that changes in village life contributed to the decline. Those accused of witchcraft tended to be triply marginal: female, poor, and elderly. The accusations against them suggest that their supposed diabolical practices might have amounted to little more than hostile words and actions aimed at their superiors, people much more powerful than they. "Witches," often accused by neighbors who had refused them the kinds of charity expected in a small community, were punished for real or imagined acts of vengeance against these neighbors, themselves the original transgressors against the norms of communal life. But as the whole pattern of village life began breaking down under commercial pressures, and as alternative methods were found to deal with **poverty**, replacing to some extent the older code of communal mutual assistance, the environment that had given rise to the old witch hunts slipped away.

Kevin P. Mulcahy

Bibliography

Hole, Christina. *Witchcraft in England.* 1977.

Hutchinson, Francis. *Historical Essay Concerning Witchcraft.* 1718.

Levack, Brian P. *Articles on Witchcraft, Magic and Demonology: A Twelve Volume Anthology of Scholarly Articles.* 1992.

Thomas, Keith. *Religion and the Decline of Magic.* 1971.

Wolcot, John ("Peter Pindar") (1738–1819)

Although Wolcot held a medical degree and was a priest in Jamaica, it was as Peter Pindar, the author of topical, good-humored, **mock-heroic** verses, **fables**, and odes that he made his living, a rare accomplishment at the time. He introduced the young painter John Opie (1761–1807) to **London** in 1781 and satirized artists such as **Benjamin West** and Angelica Kauffmann (1741–1807) in *Lyric Odes to the Royal Academicians* (1738) and its sequels. Thereafter he gained his popularity by attacking whatever was socially, politically, or literarily current. By 1794 he was sufficiently successful to gain an annuity of £250 from a group of London **publishers**, but his popularity had waned by the time he died.

Pindar's major work, *The Lousiad* (1785–1795), five cantos of some 1,300 mock-heroic couplets (illustrated by **Tho-**

John Wolcot

mas Rowlandson), satirizes **George III**, who ordered his kitchen staff to shave their heads after he found a louse on his dinner plate. Pindar's satire of **Samuel Johnson**'s biographers, *Bozzi and Piozzi; or The British Biographies, a Town Eclogue* (1786), enjoyed 10 editions in 2 years. Without advocating an agenda of his own, Pindar attacked the foolishnesses of public persons to the delight of his common readers.

Peter A. Tasch

Bibliography

Vales, Robert L. *Peter Pindar (John Wolcot).* 1973.

Zall, R.M. *Peter Pindar's Poems.* 1972.

See also Satire

Wolfe, James (1727–1759)

Wolfe was the hero of the British capture of Quebec City (1759). Born into a military family, he received his first commission (1741), participated creditably in the **Duke of Cumberland**'s suppression of the **Forty-five** rebellion, and attained a lieutenant-colonelcy in the 20th Regiment of Foot. A fiery and audacious leader and strict disciplinarian, he had little taste for the administrative side of command. Noted for his severe treatment of both ordinary soldiers and officers, he nonetheless molded his regiment into one of the best in the **army**. While quartered in southern England (1754–1757) awaiting an anticipated French invasion he developed a system of battalion movements that became standard tactical doctrine for years after its publication (1766) as *Manoeuvres for a Battalion of Infantry.*

During the **Seven Years' War** Wolfe received a brigade command in the Canadian expedition under **Admiral Boscawen** and **General Amherst**. His leading role at the capture of Louisburg (1758) from the French earned him promotion to Major-General and made him **Pitt the Elder**'s choice to command the important expedition against Quebec. At Quebec City, rebuffed in a preliminary confrontation, Wolfe with characteristic audacity landed a force of 800 men who scaled the rugged, wooded cliffs above the city (13 September 1759), catching the French off guard. On the Plains of Abraham outside the city's walls the Marquis de Montcalm (1712–1759) mustered a force of 3,500 to oppose him. Wolfe's well-ordered troops closed to within 40 yards, then delivered a devastating musket volley and charged with bayonets, routing the French and capturing Quebec City.

Wolfe died of his wounds (as did Montcalm), but his troops, showing the positive effects of his system of training, had played a central role in the conquest of **Canada** for the **Empire**.

Stanley D.M. Carpenter

Bibliography

Fortescue, John W. *A History of the British Army.* 13 vols. Vol. 2. 1910.

Parkman, Francis. *Montcalm and Wolfe.* 1962.

Reilly, R. *The Rest to Fortune: The Life of Major-General James Wolfe.* 1960.

General James Wolfe

_________. *Wolfe of Quebec.* 1973.
Stacey, C.P. *Quebec, 1759: The Siege and the Battle.* 1959.

See also Quebec; War and Military Engagements

Wollstonecraft, Mary (1759–1797)

The self-educated daughter of a master weaver turned gentleman farmer, Wollstonecraft supported herself and her sisters by opening a school and by writing conduct books, **children's literature**, **translations**, reviews, **novels**, and polemical treatises on the rights of men and the rights of women. She is best known for her enduring feminist classic, *A Vindication of the Rights of Woman* (1792), although recently two of her other works have received serious critical attention: *Letters Written during a Short Residence in Sweden, Norway, and Denmark* (1796), an autobiographical account of an emotional as well as geographical journey; and *The Wrongs of Women, or Maria* (1797), a nearly finished novel of much power published posthumously by her widower, **William Godwin**.

Remarkable for her intellectual independence and protection of other women in an era when few were educated or self-supporting, she tried to protect her mother from domestic violence; helped her sister escape an unwanted **marriage**; established a school at Newington Green to support another sister and a poor friend, Fanny Blood; and later **traveled** alone to Portugal to be with Fanny at her lying-in. When Fanny died in childbirth, Wollstonecraft wrote, to raise money for Fanny's family, *Thoughts on the Education of Daughters* (1787), arguing for **women's education** and deploring how difficult it was for a woman to earn a living.

After working discontentedly as a **governess**, at which time she wrote *Mary, A Fiction* (1788), the story of her friendship with Blood, Wollstonecraft resolved to earn a living with her pen. Joseph Johnson (1738–1809), her **publisher**, provided her with room and board while she got started, and throughout her career gave her pecuniary and emotional support.

She wrote an unfinished philosophical tale, *The Cave of Fancy* (1787), sometimes compared with **Samuel Johnson**'s *Rasselas;* a children's book, *Original Stories from Real Life* (1788), illustrated by **William Blake**; and *The Female Reader* (1789), a book of extracts for young women published under the name of Mr. Cresswick. She taught herself French, German, Dutch, and Italian, and translated, among others, Necker, Lavater, Salzmann (who later translated her *Vindication of the Rights of Woman* into German), and Madame de Cambon. She also wrote book reviews and helped edit Joseph Johnson's new **periodical**, the *Analytic Review.* Her associates at this time included **Thomas Paine**, **Henry Fuseli**, Blake, Godwin, and **Thomas Holcroft**.

The **French Revolution** catalyzed Wollstonecraft's **radical** political thought and career. She wrote *A Vindication of the Rights of Man* (1790) to defend her friend **Richard Price**'s **sermon** supporting the revolution against **Edmund Burke**'s attack. Next she wrote *A Vindication of the Rights of Woman* (1792), in which she decried society's devaluation of women and exposed sexist attitudes in the Bible, **Milton**'s *Paradise Lost,*

Mary Wollstonecraft

Pope's *Moral Essays,* and Rousseau's *Émile.* **Mary Hays** commented at Wollstonecraft's death:

> In the cause of half the human race she stood forth, deprecating and exposing in a tone of impassioned eloquence, the various means and arts by which women had been forcibly subjected, flattered into imbecility and invariably held in bondage.

Traveling alone to **France** in December 1792, disillusioned by the revolution's violence and new tyrannies, she wrote *An Historical and Moral View of the Origin and Progress of the French Revolution* (1794), condemning revolutionary excesses and calling for a reform of consciousness. Her common-law liaison during this period with an American businessman, Gilbert Imlay, resulted in the birth of a daughter named Fanny after her girlhood friend. Imlay's teasing infidelity provoked several **suicide** attempts. Wollstonecraft's *Letters Written during a Short Residence in Sweden, Norway, and Denmark,* which influenced the English **Romantic** poets **Southey** and **Coleridge**, chronicled her melancholy meditations and experiences traveling with the baby while serving as Imlay's business agent.

After breaking definitively with Imlay, Wollstonecraft's renewed acquaintance with Godwin in 1796 ripened into love. Their circle at that time included Hays, Holcroft, John Opie (1761–1807), Amelia Alderson (1769–1853, later married to Opie), **Elizabeth Inchbald**, **Sarah Siddons**, and Eliza Fenwick (1766–1840). Although both she and Godwin had condemned the institution of **marriage**, they married quietly, while continuing in separate residences, when she became pregnant. In these months, Wollstonecraft worked on her novel, *The Wrongs of Women, or Maria,* which tells of a bourgeois woman incarcerated by her husband and abandoned by her rescuing lover, and of a working-class woman's struggle to stay alive in 18th-century **London**. Wollstonecraft died in 1797 of complications in childbirth; she was survived by Godwin and her two daughters.

Wollstonecraft has become an important influence for 20th-century feminists. Her independent and unconventional life—supporting herself, traveling alone, choosing her sexual partners—as well as her passionate women-centered texts, make her an exemplary cultural figure.

Ruth Perry

Bibliography

Detre, Jean. *A Most Extraordinary Pair: Mary Wollstonecraft and William Godwin.* 1975.

Flexner, Eleanor. *Mary Wollstonecraft: a Biography.* 1972.

Godwin, William. *Memoirs of Mary Wollstonecraft.* 1798.

Johnson, Claudia L. *Equivocal Beings: Politics, Gender, and Sentimentality in the 1790's—Wollstonecraft, Radcliffe, Burney, Austen.* 1995.

Kelly, Gary. *Women, Writing, and Revolution: 1790–1827.* 1993.

Sapiro, Virginia. *A Vindication of Political Virtue: The Political Theory of Mary Wollstonecraft.* 1992.

Todd, Janet, ed. *A Dictionary of British and American Women Writers 1660–1800.* 1985.

———. *A Wollstonecraft Anthology.* 1990.

Wardle, Ralph. *Mary Wollstonecraft, a Critical Biography.* 1951.

See also Shelley, Mary Wollstonecraft; Women in Literature

Women in Art

The number of women creating representational art grew dramatically under the Hanoverian kings, particularly late in the 18th century as the idea took hold that a refined woman should be able to draw, paint, dance, and play music. Still, the number of female professional artists remained quite small well into the 19th century, in part because the notion of amateurish "feminine accomplishments" undermined the seriousness of their claim to respect.

Although it was becoming less uncommon in 18th-century Britain for a woman to earn her living by teaching painting, real prominence as a master painter was unknown. The **Royal Academy of Arts**, when founded in 1768, did include two female artists among its 36 members—Angelica Kauffman (1741–1807) and Mary Moser (1744–1819)—both of whom were trained by their fathers. The two were not expected to attend academy meetings, however, and no other female members were appointed until the 20th century. The practice of appointing males exclusively was connected with another practice, one which prohibited women from studying nude figures; the lack of opportunity for such study prevented women from producing the **history paintings** that were most highly valued, and helps to explain their tendency to take up **portrait painting**, still life, and **landscape painting**. Even in the early 19th century, instruction for women in drawing and **painting** was elementary, aimed at preparing them either to be socially attractive upper-class ladies or to become **governesses**, competent only to instruct female children in the visual arts for the same dilettantish purposes. Representational painting by women was often considered a mere feminine activity like needlework, not to be taken seriously as art.

Kauffman was the exception. Even though she also did portraits, her important works were large history paintings of classical subjects, in a style she helped introduce in the late 1760s, when she moved to **London** from Italy. Among her commissioned works was a series of allegorical paintings that represent the stages of the artistic process, done on a ceiling of the Royal Academy in Burlington House, London. But unlike Kauffman, most other female painters worked in the less prestigious descriptive genres. Moser was a painter of flowers, usually on canvas, though she had a commission to paint a room of Queen Charlotte's estate at Frogmore. Other eminent painters of still life included Frances Byrne (1775–1837), who specialized in rendering flowers; and Mary Barret (1797–1825), whose paintings typically depicted birds, fish, and fruit.

Self-portraits and portraits of others were also popular among female artists because practice, once again, did not require training with nude models. Sarah Geddes Carpenter (1793–1872) was one of the most successful portrait painters, having had a portrait accepted for exhibition by the Royal Academy at age 21. Many women portraitists also did "miniatures," small portrait likenesses of others. Maria Hadfield Cosway (1758–1838) and her father helped to revive interest in miniature painting in the late 18th century. Cosway's portrait of *Georgiana, Duchess of Devonshire as Diana* (about 1782) is a highly dramatic representation of lady-as-goddess, who seems to be parting the clouds she is emerging from. Perhaps more typical of female portraitists was Frances Reynolds (1729–1807), whose painting of miniatures was discouraged and even **ridiculed** by her famous brother **Sir Joshua Reynolds**, whose household she managed for 25 years.

Pehaps the major obstacle to public success was the widespread belief that women's intellects were both different from and inferior to men's, and that women "naturally" preferred to work with detail, on a small scale, in media associated with domesticity. This helps to explain why **drawing** became an extremely fashionable activity for women around the mid-18th century, partly also as a result of technical advances allowing the production of "pastels," in chalk sticks known as "crayons"; of prints that one might study in the absence of live models or unique paintings; and of ready-to-use **watercolors**, which women soon took to with enthusiasm. Catherine Read (1740–1778) achieved a reputation as a professional artist excelling in the use of crayons as well as oils. A few female artists were recognized for their achievements in other "feminine" media: Lady Julia Calverly (1685–1736), for example, for an embroidered screen based on episodes from Virgil; and Mary Delaney (1700–1788) for her cut-out flowers on paper colored with India ink. Such work was generally considered a sign of refinement and domesticity, however, rather than of serious artistic achievement.

A distinctly unfashionable medium for women was **sculpture**, but Anne Seymour Damer (1749–1828) achieved considerable renown for her portrait statuary. She was named modeler in wax to Queen Charlotte in 1801, but also worked in clay, marble, and bronze. **Horace Walpole** particularly admired Damer's animal pieces, but more typical was her marble bust of *Elizabeth, Countess of Derby as Thalia* (1789).

Anne Steele (1717–1778), the talented **Baptist** hymnist, was an exception in her time, but women became ever more heavily involved in domestic music-making during the age of **George III** as pianos (introduced around 1760) became fashionable. Women had not formerly played string instruments (apart from the lute and guitar) or woodwinds to any great extent, but the advent of the piano marked a turning point, and the early 19th century witnessed a great influx of women into musical fields. Still, there were few women who earned money in music, beyond that received for giving lessons. Several female performing artists certainly did leave their marks on the partly representational arts of **opera**, **dance**, and **acting**. A rivalry between Italian sopranos Francesca Cuzzoni (1698–1770) and Faustina Bordoni (1700–1781) made **Handel's** *Admeto* (1727) one of the most popular operas of the 1720s and inspired the characters of Polly and Lucy in **John Gay's** *The Beggar's Opera* (1728), after Cuzzoni and Faustina had returned to Italy. The French ballerina Marie Sallé (1707–1756) came to London in 1734 to dance in **John Weaver's** "Silent Ballets of John Weaver," and subsequently became the first woman to choreograph her own performances; her rejection of traditional, restrictive costumes in favor of a Grecian-style muslin dress and loose hair for her 1736 *Pygmalion* was an important innovation in the history of dance and part of the general trend to more naturalistic movement in the 18th century. The stage performances of **Sarah Siddons** were critical to the success of many theatrical productions between 1782 and 1812. She was particularly known for her performance of great tragic Shakespearean roles.

Drawing of a young woman, 1814

In retrospect, despite hindrances to their training and limited professional opportunities, female artists of the Hanoverian period helped to negotiate the transition from an aristocratic canon of taste for works almost exclusively by males to a more broadly based, **middle-class** canon of more **sentimental** taste for works increasingly composed as well as performed by women.

James R. Aubrey

Bibliography

Barrell, John. *Painting and the Politics of Culture: New Essays on British Art, 1700–1850.* 1992.

Chadwick, Whitney. *Women, Art, and Society.* 1990.

Fine, Elsa Honig. *Women and Art: A History of Women Painters and Sculptors from the Renaissance to the Twentieth Century.* 1978.

Fiske, Roger. *English Theatre Music in the Eighteenth Century.* 1973.

Harris, Ann Sutherland, and Linda Nochlin. *Women Artists: 1550–1950.* 1977.

Petersen, Karen, and J.J. Wilson. *Women Artists: Recognition and Reappraisal from the Early Middle Ages to the Twentieth Century.* 1976.

Roworth, Wendy. *Angelica Kauffman: A Continental Artist in Georgian England.* 1993.

Solkin, David. *Painting for Money: The Visual Arts and the Public Sphere in Eighteenth-Century England.* 1993.

Yeldham, Charlotte. *Women Artists in Nineteenth-Century France and England: Their Art Education, Exhibition Opportunities and Membership of Exhibiting Societies and Academies, with an Assessment of the Subject Matter of Their Work and Summary Bibliographies.* 2 vols. 1984.

See also Dramatic Arts; Music; Music, Classical; Music Education; Women in Literature

Women in Literature

One of the main political and literary concerns of Hanoverian Britain was the question of identity—what it meant, how one defined it, how one compared one identity ("Englishness," for example) with others. For those considering the problem of women's identity, the issue was particularly difficult because of women's lack of definite control over many aspects of life. Possessing few rights to earn property or participate in interpreting the laws ruling their own conduct, women had, at best, a shifting notion of how to define themselves and their place within the changing social structure. Moreover, literary women were themselves unusual, and the enterprise of writing especially for women was also considered unusual (or worse). Not surprisingly, women writers represented their positions both by participating in and diverging from some of the standard literary practices accepted by male writers.

Women's concerns about British society were reflected not only in the sheer volume of their writing but in the enormous range of topics they tackled—from **manners**, female friendship, **women's education**, and debates over women's "true" place in society, to issues of social justice, slavery, **women's employment**, women's place in art, and the prevalence of **prostitution. Mary Astell**'s *A Serious Proposal to the Ladies* (1691, 1697) and *Some Reflections upon Marriage* (1700) set precedents for thinking about women's equality, especially about the quality of **marriage** and education for most women, which were to dominate much of contemporary women's literature. **Anne Finch**'s poems, published anonymously (1713), focused on themes of love and friendship, and show a concern for the position of women in general. Likewise, the works of Sarah Fyge Field Edgerton (1670–1723) provide examples of feminist polemic and of women's struggle against the tyranny of their lives.

Not many female writers were highborn, and with the growth of the literary marketplace and the commercialization of literary production, **middle-** and working-**class** women writers entered what was previously a closed sphere of activity. Writers such as **Mary Collier**, who was probably the first published working-class woman poet in England, called attention to problems of class in relation to female exploitation and subordination. Her text, *The Woman's Labour* (1739), angrily responded to **Stephen Duck**'s representation of female fieldworkers as irresponsible and weak (in *The Thresher's Labour* [1736]), and pointed to the troubles working women experienced to earn a decent living.

Collier, **Ann Yearsley** (*The Rural Lyre* [1796]), Mary Leapor (1722–1746), and Mary Barber (1690?–1757) marked an emerging pattern of working-class women's writing. **Sarah Fielding**'s *David Simple* (1749) articulated economic need as an impetus for women's writing. **Eliza Haywood** was forced to earn her own living after her separation from her husband, but her **novel** *Love in Excess; or The Fatal Enquiry* (1719–1720) became one of the most popular of its era. She also established the first **periodical** by and for women, the *Female Spectator* (1722–1746).

The list of female dramatists during the Hanoverian period is very long, and it would be extremely difficult to visualize the **London** theatrical world without the presence in it of such talented women—some of whom were not only playwrights but also actresses—as **Delarivière Manley, Charlotte Lennox, Frances Chamberlaine Sheridan, Elizabeth Inchbald, Hannah Cowley, Elizabeth Cooper, Joanna Baillie**, Sophia and Harriet **Lee**, and **Frances Brooke**. Female poets (**Felicia Hemans** and **Anna Seward**, for example) were less influential, though on the other hand, many of the foremost writers of **children's literature** were women, such as **Hannah More, Mary Lamb, Sarah Trimmer**, and **Mary Martha Sherwood.**

But the whole issue of female authorship concerned many of these women. The question turned on the propriety of their speaking from a public platform. Elizabeth Elstob (1683–1756), author of *Rudiments of Grammar for the English Saxon Tongue* (1715) may have had not only her unusual subject but herself in mind when she prefaced it with an "Apology for the Study of Northern Antiquities." **Lady Mary Wortley Montagu**'s famous **letters**, even though published posthumously, were another famous case in point. **Maria Edgeworth**'s *Letters for Literary Ladies* (1785), an exchange between a liberal father and his conservative friend on the subject of female authorship, offered a critique of the propriety of women writing.

One of the reasons for concern about female authorship came about as a result of Jean-Jacques Rousseau's (1712–1778) teachings, influential in Britain from the early 1760s on, which advocated separate spheres of male and female activity, confining the latter to things private and domestic. Although Rousseau's authority helped to edge British conceptions of women away from old Restoration stereotypes featuring a seductive but destructive Eve (needing to be controlled and regulated), he helped edge consciousness toward new mores depicting women as helpless dependents whose virtue rose from their weakness and need for masculine protection. These notions influenced many British writers, and ironically gave rise to certain literary conventions of women's writing such as the novel of manners, **Gothic fiction**, and the novel of social development for young women.

But strong-minded authors resisted many aspects of the new feminine stereotype. **Fanny Burney**'s *Evelina* (1778), most of **Jane Austen**'s novels, and the novels of **Ann Radcliffe** all exemplify ways in which female literary artists asserted their judgment and independence from these new claims. The same might be said of some of the novels of Sarah Fielding and **Clara Reeve**, and those of Edgeworth—one of the most influential novelists of the entire period.

The idea of the **bluestocking**, the intellectual woman, no matter how unpalatable to some traditionalists, survived past the heyday of **Elizabeth Montagu, Hester Chapone**, and their friends of the 1760s and 1770s. The 1790s, dominated by revolutionary ideas, raised still more insistently the question of **women's rights** in traditionally patriarchical societies. **Mary Wollstonecraft** stoutly asserted women's rights (focusing especially on the need for complete equality in education) in her political treatise *A Vindication of the Rights of Woman* (1792), a book that has ensured her place as one of the great feminist thinkers in British history. Her follower **Mary Hays** helped to keep heroic women in the public's eye with her six-volume *Female Biography* (1802), while on the other hand, conservative writers such as Trimmer, More, and Sherwood were among the most influential moral propagandists of the late Hanoverian era.

Revolution, however, could be literary no less than moral or political, and as a precursor to the "revolutionary" **Romantic poetry** offered in the ***Lyrical Ballads*** (1798), the poetry of Charlotte Smith (1749–1806) is especially noteworthy. Her *Elegiac Sonnets and Other Essays* (1784) demonstrates Romantic concerns with self-analysis. Also, though the journals of **Dorothy Wordsworth** have been treasured for what they reveal about her brother William, they are in fact important literary pieces of their own; unfortunately they also capture quite vividly the ways in which this creative woman's imagination was thwarted by contemporary constructs of femininity. But perhaps the most famous woman writer of the new age was **Mary Wollstonecraft Shelley**, whose *Frankenstein* (1818), one of the fictional classics of the age, roved commandingly through many of the central intellectual concerns of the era, exploring contradictions between **science** and nature, responsibility and desire, and again raising high the question of rights and autonomy for women.

Rajani Sudan

Bibliography

Brown, Laura. *Ends of Empire: Women and Ideology in Early Eighteenth-Century English Literature.* 1993.

Ferguson, Moira. *First Feminists: British Women Writers 1578–1799.* 1985.

Gilbert, Sandra, and Susan Gubar, eds. *The Norton Anthology of Literature by Women.* 1985.

Goreau, Angeline. *The Whole Duty of a Woman: Female Writers in Seventeenth Century England.* 1985.

Johnson, Claudia L. *Equivocal Beings: Politics, Gender, and Sentimentality in the 1790's—Wollstonecraft, Radcliffe, Burney, Austen.* 1995.

Kelly, Gary. *Women, Writing, and Revolution: 1790–1827.* 1993.

Koon, Helene, and Mary R. Mahl, eds. *The Female Spectator: English Women Writers before 1800.* 1977.

Landry, Donna. *The Muses of Resistance: Laboring-Class Women's Poetry in Britain, 1739–1796.* 1990.

McBurney, William H., ed. *Four before Richardson: Selected English Novels, 1720–1727.* 1963.

Morgan, Fidelis. *The Female Wits: Women Playwrights of the Restoration.* 1981.

Scheuermann, Mona. *Her Bread to Earn: Women, Money, & Society from Defoe to Austen.* 1994.

See also Women in Art

Women's Education

How women were educated, and the content of their education, varied widely in Hanoverian Britain. There was no system of schools or standardized expectations for them, and the traditional institutions—grammar schools, public schools, universities—were closed to them.

Female literacy, though it lagged behind male, rose to possibly 50% by the late 18th century. Most women in the middle and upper classes could read, but far fewer in the lower classes. The latter went to work at an early age and had little time or money to spare for education. **Charity schools** and **Sunday schools** provided minimal learning for some working-class females. The object of these schools, however, was primarily training in religion and in useful skills, rather than in academic subjects.

Anyone could start a school; nearly all for females were private, for-profit ventures. Such institutions were often short-lived; they lasted for the interest or necessity of the woman in charge. At the bottom level were the "dames' schools," which existed throughout Britain. The best dames' schools accepted children of both sexes, usually from age 4 to 7; they taught reading, simple arithmetic, some writing, and often some Scripture. Many, however, provided little more than basic daycare.

The usual girls' school was for youngsters age 10–16. A number of day schools and boarding schools for the daughters of the rich were established in the latter 18th century; some were run by French immigrants escaping the **French Revolution**. Such schools might cost a girl's family £50 a year plus extras, a very considerable sum, equivalent to more than the entire annual earnings of some poor village schoolmasters. Some of these schools gave excellent training in academic subjects, but others were finishing schools, concentrating on such accomplishments as **music**, **drawing**, **dancing**, and **manners**. Schools in **spas** and **seaside resorts** such as **Bath** and Brighton were particularly likely to emphasize social rather than academic skills. The same was true of schools for **middle-class** females (which, if boarding establishments, might be more likely to cost around £20 a year), though these attempted to inculcate domestic arts more suitable to establishing a bourgeois household, such as needlework and cookery.

Schools for females were widely criticized. Their sometimes excessive emphasis on accomplishments, and the giddiness and triviality which they were thought to encourage, brought strictures. Another complaint was that the lower-class girls who often attended such schools were apt to acquire in them ideas above their proper station—a notion, however insupportable in fact, which was often repeated in fictional and in nonfictional writings.

Nearly everyone believed that females should be educated at home. Certainly the best educated were those taught by parents, siblings, **governesses**, or **tutors**. When a tutor was employed for a family's sons, he often taught the daughters also. Tutors gave instruction most frequently in classical languages and mathematics. Governesses for older girls usually taught modern languages, literature, and subjects regarded as more suitable for females. The quality of education at home naturally depended on the interest and ability of the parents, and the choice of tutors and governesses. It could be excellent; it could be barely adequate.

Another issue was: Just what exactly should females be taught? The most conservative writers (usually men) believed that women's minds as well as their bodies were inferior; therefore, females were incapable of learning classical languages, mathematics, **science**, or other serious subjects. Other writers, including such women as **Hannah More**, believed that while women's minds were as capable as those of men, they did not need to have the same education. Since a woman's proper place was to be a wife and mother, masculine education would unsex her, deflect her from her path, and perhaps even imperil her soul. On the other hand, **radicals** such as **Mary Wollstonecraft** argued that since women's minds were as good as men's, they should have the same education. Until the late 19th century, however, such advocates were less influential than the simple luck of the draw in determining whether or not a female would even be helped to learn to read, much less to realize her greater intellectual capabilities.

Barbara Brandon Schnorrenberg

Bibliography

Hans, Nicholas. *New Trends in Education in the Eighteenth Century.* 1951.

Horn, Pamela. *Education in Rural England, 1800–1914.* 1978.

Kamm, Josephine. *Hope Deferred: Girls' Education in English History.* 1965.

Sanderson, Michael. *Education, Economic Change and Society in England 1780–1870.* 1983.

Schnorrenberg, Barbara Brandon. "Education for Women in Eighteenth Century England: An Annotated Bibliography." *Women & Literature.* Vol. 4, pp. 49–55.

See also Education, Elementary; Education, Secondary

Women's Employment

Women in the Hanoverian period worked in nearly every walk of life. The main exceptions lay among the clerical, legal, and medical professions, where they were ineligible for many jobs; and among many skilled **crafts**, where the rules of apprenticeship barred them from entry. Otherwise, women did what they could, while also bearing most of the burdens of housework and childcare. Though not many worked in heavy industry, they served as drawers on the great northern coalfield until around 1780 and were widely employed in metalworking, as one visitor to the Black Country noted in 1741 when he saw female nailers at their forges, like males "stript of their upper garment, and not overcharged with the latter, wielding the hammer with all the grace of the sex."

In 1714, Britain economically was still largely a collection of local entities. The making and distribution of most goods was on a small scale, for local use, in the system of **domestic production.** Women continued to work in **agriculture, textile** production, **metalworking**, the leather-goods trade, **brewing, retailing**, and so on, alongside their husbands, fathers, brothers, and sons. Some women were also independent **entrepreneurs**; Theodosia **Crowley**, for example, was the key figure for half a century in Europe's largest **iron** company. But as a more national economy developed in the mid-18th century, small-scale enterprises of the sort sometimes run by women began to give way to larger ones run by men. Local brewing of beer, for example, traditionally dominated by women, began to give way to more national commercial breweries run by males.

Agricultural **enclosures**, especially after 1760, deprived women as well as men of work; they did not always lose jobs, but the nature of their work changed. As cloth-making became mechanized, especially in the **cotton industry**, textile production became relocated in factories. Women had to choose to work factory hours as **factory workers**, or stay at home; combining domestic chores and production was no longer possible. The emphasis on the superiority of scientific reason and efficiency in production also affected employment for women. When science was applied to cheesemaking, for example—another traditional female occupation—women lost control of the industry and became hired hands.

Change was slower for those living in the country. There they continued to work in all agricultural jobs, cared for house and family, and did handwork to supplement the family income. Hand **spinning** (in which women greatly predominated) declined, but there remained such tasks as glove-making, knitting, straw-plaiting, and embroidery, which women performed on a piecework basis. Their pay rates were very poor. A publication of 1747 on **London**'s trades mentions only three apprenticeship-entered trades for women (milliners, staymakers, and mantua-makers), their **wages** (averaging around 7s. or 30p. a week) half those of men exercising equal skill in other trades (tailoring and painting).

The largest single area of employment available for women was domestic service. This increased in the Hanoverian period as men found other jobs and as expectations and assumptions of domestic comfort among the **middle classes** and upper classes changed. Since all the tasks of **servants** were performed by hand, more furniture, rugs, candles, and food, as well as higher standards of cleanliness, required more domestic workers.

The biggest decline in women's employment occurred among those who considered themselves, or had aspirations to be, middle class. Earlier, such women had participated in family enterprises and taken care of domestic chores. But as manufacturing, retailing, and other businesses were removed from the home, the idea of separate men's and women's work began to take hold. This was reinforced by **Evangelical** ideas of the patriarchal family and of woman's place in it. Another Evangelical concern was respectability. What was respectable work for women? It needed to be within the domestic sphere—a very narrow sphere of opportunity—and this is one reason why many single women became unpaid domestic drudges for their own families. Women could also become **governesses** or teachers in girls' schools, or paid companions. They could take positions as housekeepers or seamstresses, but these carried lower social status. To work or perform in public, with or without men, was not respectable. One occupation that women did adopt in considerable numbers was writing. This could be done at home, even anonymously, and could be profitable.

By the late 18th century a number of women writers had begun to comment bitterly on this situation. They saw various traditional female jobs such as midwifery and tailoring being usurped by men who claimed that they were more skillful, more educated, more scientific. **Mary Wollstonecraft** was but one author who argued that better **women's education** was the route to better jobs.

Part of the concern about jobs for females emerged from

"Gleaners Building a Bundle," by W.H. Pyne

worry over the apparently increasing number of single women who required some means of support. Not all such women could find husbands, neither did they all have families that could support them. How could they live respectably without some kind of employment? The problem was not resolved by 1837. In Victorian times, even men began to worry about "redundant" women.

Barbara Brandon Schnorrenberg

Bibliography

Berg, Maxine. *The Age of Manufactures: Industry, Innovation and Work in Britain, 1700–1820.* 1986.

Charles, Lindsey, and Lorna Duffin, eds. *Women and Work in Pre-Industrial England.* 1985.

Davidoff, Lenore, and Catherine Hall. *Family Fortunes: Men and Women of the English Middle Class, 1780–1850.* 1987.

Hill, Bridget. *Women, Work and Sexual Politics in Eighteenth-Century England.* 1989.

John, Angela V., ed. *Unequal Opportunities: Women's Employment in England, 1800–1918.* 1986.

Luddy, Maria. *Women and Philanthropy in Nineteenth-Century Ireland.* 1995.

McCurtain, Margaret, and Mary O'Dowd. *Women in Early Modern Ireland.* 1991.

Pinchbeck, Ivy. *Women Workers and the Industrial Revolution, 1750–1850.* 1930.

Scheuermann, Mona. *Her Bread to Earn: Women, Money, & Society from Defoe to Austen.* 1994.

See also Women's Rights

Women's Rights

In most accounts, **Mary Wollstonecraft** and her *Vindication of the Rights of Woman* (1792) mark the beginning of the women's rights movement. Wollstonecraft was, however, only one of several writers on women's rights in the Hanoverian period. These writers' main theme was the need for equality of education, which, they believed, would lead to more and better jobs for women. Political rights were not yet a major concern; economic opportunity was more important. Women's freedom, when it was thought of at all, was often thought of in relation to the question of whether a woman might choose to live unmarried. This freedom was also related to economic opportunity and to questions of **women's employment** because a single woman had to be able to support herself.

Mary Astell, in several very early publications, had made a persuasive argument for better **women's education** and for women's protection from bad marriages. Some decades later, *Woman Not Inferior to Man* (1739) and *Woman's Superior Excellence Over Man* (1740), published under the pseudonym Sophia, called for equality of education and contended that women were not innately inferior to men. **Catharine Macaulay**, in her *Letters on Education* (1790), repeated this position and called for reformed education for both sexes.

Wollstonecraft praised Macaulay's views, while she and other radical writers of the revolutionary era such as **Mary Hays** and Mary Anne Radcliffe (1746?–?) began looking at women's rights through the lens of contemporary thinking on the rights of man. Unfortunately, this association meant that women's causes would become generally discredited under the conservative political reaction of the early 19th century. Wollstonecraft and her sister reformers, though little read, were much maligned.

An exception to the reaction against women's rights was the *Appeal of One-Half of the Human Race, Women* (1825) by **William Thompson** and Anna Wheeler (1785–?), Anglo–Irish Owenite socialists who proposed political and marital equality for women. Socialists were the chief proponents of women's rights in the early 19th century. Their critical view of industrialization readied them to appreciate more clearly the new problems of women's work and **marriage**.

Meanwhile, the rights of women within marriage began to be raised by upper-class women. With the development of strict settlements and the substitution of the law of jointure for dower rights in the 18th century, lawyers and judges allowed husbands greater control over wives' property. Women had few ways to end bad marriages. **Evangelical** views of the patriarchal family were widely accepted. Some women began to question a completely male domination and definition of marriage. The writer and poet Caroline Norton (1808–1877) began a vigorous campaign for married women's rights in 1838.

Barbara Brandon Schnorrenberg

Bibliography

Browne, Alice. *The Eighteenth-Century Feminist Mind.* 1987.
Ferguson, Moira, ed. *First Feminists: British Women Writers, 1578–1799.* 1987.
McCurtain, Margaret, and Mary O'Dowd. *Women in Early Modern Ireland.* 1991.
Rogers, Katherine M. *Feminism in Eighteenth-Century England.* 1982.
Staves, Susan. *Married Women's Separate Property in England, 1660–1833.* 1990.
Taylor, Barbara. *Eve and the New Jerusalem: Socialism and Feminism in the Nineteenth Century.* 1983.
Thomis, Malcolm I., and Jennifer Grimmett. *Women in Protest, 1800–1850.* 1982.

See also Radicalism and Radical Politics; Women in Art; Women in Literature

Wood, William (1671–1730)

Wood is remembered today chiefly for the war of pamphlets and **satires** set off by his copper coinage. In 1722, Wood, of Wolverhampton, a prominent **iron** and copper manufacturer and mine lessee in the west of England, obtained a **patent** to coin copper halfpence and farthings for circulation in **Ireland** in the amount of £100,800. However, he obtained the patent under questionable circumstances (having paid for it some £10,000 through the king's mistress the Duchess of Kendal), the quantity of coin was much greater than what was required in Ireland, and its introduction involved what amounted to an Irish **tax** of some £6,000 or more a year. The Dublin Department of Revenue and the Irish House of Commons protested, believing that "Wood's Halfpence" would create an inflationary environment in Ireland while bringing Wood a profit of some £25,000. Local opposition was so great that the Privy Council suspended the coinage in March 1724.

A compromise to limit the total coinage to £40,000 was approved in July 1724, but protests continued and were strengthened by **Jonathan Swift**'s four famous "Drapier's Letters" (1724), denouncing the coinage and the "Irish slavery" it supposedly symbolized. Wood did not help matters by declaring that with the government's help he would cram his coppers down Irish throats. At length the Privy Council decided against resumption, and Wood's patent was canceled (1725). He was granted £8,000 a year for 8 years as compensation. Also in 1722 he gained a patent to manufacture coins for the American colonies, known as the "Rosa Americana" issue; but Wood was compelled to surrender this patent, too. There was one unequivocally happy episode in these otherwise dispiriting ventures into coinage: In 1723 he manufactured £500 worth of halfpence for the Isle of Man.

Theresa McDonald

Bibliography

Craig, Sir John. *The Mint: A History of the London Mint from A.D. 287 to 1948.* 1953.
Treadwell, J.M. "William Wood and the Company of Ironmasters of Great Britain." *Business History.* Vol. 16, pp. 97–112.

Woodforde, James (1740–1803)

Woodforde was an Anglican clergyman and diarist whose posthumously published *Diary of a Country Parson* (1924) earned him a reputation as the quintessential English parson of the Hanoverian period. He was not a distinguished man in his own day, neither was he in any way unconventional, but he was intelligent and observant. His diary, covering nearly every single day of the years 1759 through 1802, was an unpretentious portrayal of typical village life, with all its commonplaces and odd events.

Born at Ansford in Somerset, where his father was rector, Woodforde was educated at Oxford. After holding curacies in several towns in Somerset, he was (in 1774) presented to the rectory of Weston Longeville, Norfolk, where he remained until his death. He never married after proposing to Betsy White of Shepton Mallet, who broke the engagement to marry someone else the following year (1775). His niece, Nancy, lived with him during the last two decades of his life. His diary is one of the few books enabling the reader to step immediately into the everyday life of Hanoverian England.

Richard M. Riss

Bibliography

Beresford, John, ed. *The Diary of a Country Parson.* 1924.

Norwich, John Julius, and Ronald Blythe, eds. *A Country Parson.* 1985.
Winstanley, R.L. *The Ansford Diary of James Woodforde.* 1980.

See also Church of England; Clerical Profession

Woolen and Worsted Industries

Throughout the 18th century, the wool textile industry was the most important branch of British manufacturing in terms of output, exports, and employment; though it was rapidly overtaken by **cotton** thereafter. Cotton fibers proved more adaptable to mechanization than wool, the supply of raw cotton was more elastic, and cotton cloths came to be preferred for many uses because of their cheapness and versatility. Nevertheless, wool textiles remained a major industry, experiencing considerable innovation in products and processes, and important market growth.

Woolen cloth production, using indigenous wool, had been important from earliest times. Early manufacturing was scattered throughout the country, much of its output being consumed domestically or locally. Commercial production and export became increasingly important from the 16th century, when the existing broad and narrow woolens exports were supplemented by new draperies first introduced by Flemish weavers (early worsted mixes, unfulled and long-stapled): lighter in weight than traditional woolens, these were suitable for many European climates. Commercial expansion in the 17th and 18th centuries arose chiefly from extending **domestic production**, mostly on a putting-out basis, in rural and semi-rural areas which thereby became specialized in it, particularly in East Anglia, the West Country, and West Yorkshire. This countryside expansion occurred at the expense of older urban centers of production such as **York** because employers profited from the cheaper and more flexible underemployed and unapprenticed labor (especially of women and children) of the country.

Producers in the 18th century expanded their operations to satisfy not only growing European markets but also domestic and a burgeoning transatlantic trade as well. West Yorkshire grew to dominate all these markets with a variety of products, including fine woolens and worsted suitings, but particularly emphasized the cheaper, mass-produced end of the market. Yorkshire gained at the expense of East Anglia, which specialized in finer worsted paisleys and shawls, and the West Country, where the major product was finer woolens. Big West Country employers, contending with large bodies of skilled and organized domestic weavers and **London** wholesalers, proved less adaptable than the smaller Yorkshire masters. Most of these operated in family units, working their own raw material and selling their cloths weekly in the Cloth Halls of **Leeds**, Halifax, and Wakefield to Yorkshire merchants with direct overseas connections. By contrast, the worsted industry typically embraced larger putting-out concerns employing

Hargreaves' Spinning Jenny

domestic **spinners and weavers** on piece rates and marketing their own goods.

Yorkshire's share of national wool textile output during the 18th century grew from around 20% to around 60%, with approximately 80% exported. Yorkshire's dominance stemmed also from innovations in cloth finishing and in the use of water power in wool preparation (scribbling and carding). The concentration of spinning and weaving workers in mills also occurred with some giants, notably Benjamin Gott's Mill at Bean Ing, Leeds (established 1793), which was one of the largest in the world. Though most mills were small, introduction of water and later **steam** power in many processes increased the advantages of centralization, so that several businesses might come to share or rent space and power in a mill. Proximity to Lancashire and the technological innovations there in cotton manufacture promoted the early adoption of similar spinning and, later, weaving technologies in Yorkshire, first in (longer stapled) worsted, then in woolen manufacture. However, the greater frailty of woolen fibers meant that key cotton innovations typically lagged some 2 decades before finding successful application in woolens.

Pat Hudson

Bibliography

Heaton, H. *The Yorkshire Woollen and Worsted Industries from Earliest Times to the Industrial Revolution.* 2nd ed., 1965.

Hudson, Pat. *The Genesis of Industrial Capital: A Study of the West Riding Wool Textile Industry c.1750–1850.* 1986.

James, J. *History of the Worsted Manufacture in England from the Earliest Times.* 1857.

Kerridge, E. *Textile Manufactures in Early Modern England.* 1985.

Mann, J. de L. *The Cloth Industry of the West of England from 1640 to 1880.* 1971.

See also Factories and the Factory System; Industrial Revolution; Textile Industries

Wooler, Thomas (1786?–1853)

Wooler, like **Cobbett**, **Carlile**, **Wade**, and **Hone**, was a forceful journalistic critic of the repressive government of the late **Regency** period. Born in Yorkshire and trained as a printer, he moved to **London** and after 1800 edited and published several left-wing **periodicals**. In 1817 he began publishing his weekly periodical the *Black Dwarf* (1817–1824), which appealed to the discontented by **satirically** attacking the government's malicious and allegedly unconstitutional actions. This led to his arrest for seditious libel, but he was acquitted on a technicality.

However, like many others of the period, Wooler spent some time in **prison**. (He also criticized Cobbett for decamping to America in 1817 to escape such penalties.) A particular supporter of **Major John Cartwright**, he actively pursued parliamentary reform. His activities eventually caused his arrest and imprisonment for 18 months (1819–1820) on a trumped-up charge of seditious conspiracy. After the demise of the *Black Dwarf* (much imitated by other writers, including **Leigh Hunt**) he published another weekly, the *British Gazette*, in the late 1820s. He gave up politics after the passage of the **Reform Act**.

Thomas D. Veve

Bibliography

Baylen, Joseph O., and Norbert J. Gossman, eds. *Biographical Dictionary of Modern British Radicals.* Vol. 1. 1979.

Hone, J. Ann. *For the Cause of Truth: Radicalism in London, 1796–1821.* 1982.

Royle, Edward, and James Walvin. *English Radicals and Reformers, 1760–1848.* 1982.

Wickwar, William Hardy. *The Struggle for Freedom of the Press, 1819–1832.* 1928.

Wiener, Joel H. *The War of the Unstamped: The Movement to Repeal the British Newspaper Tax, 1830 to 1836.* 1969.

Maccoby, S. *English Radicalism, 1786–1832.* 1955.

See also Laws of Public Worship, Speech, and the Press; Radicalism and Radical Politics

Wordsworth, Dorothy (1771–1855)

Though she published almost nothing during her lifetime, Wordsworth is now regarded as a significant figure in English **Romantic** literature. She was born at Cockermouth in the Lake District, the daughter of an attorney who served as estate agent for the local landed magnate. After the early death of her parents she was raised apart from her four brothers. In 1794 she was reunited with her brother, **William Wordsworth**, and spent much of the remainder of her life with him

Dorothy Wordsworth

and his family. From 1829 she suffered increasingly from mental illness.

Wordsworth received the inadequate education typical for women of her class, and unlike her brothers had little chance to travel or mix in wider society. She did, however, have powerful natural feelings and was a close and sympathetic observer of people, especially of the poor. Considered an influence on her brother's **poetry**, she also conducted an extensive correspondence with his friends, wrote some poems and fiction of her own, and at various times kept a journal. These texts were published after her death, mainly to support the growing cultural and educational importance of William's version of Romanticism. But her writings are now seen to embody a woman's version of Romanticism—observing and celebrating the local, the particular, and the domestic with an intense subjective responsiveness and sympathy that offers an alternative to both her brother's poeticizing of these domains and also to conventionally "masculine" preoccupations with the public and political spheres.

Gary Kelly

Bibliography

Gittings, Robert, and Jo Manton. *Dorothy Wordsworth.* 1985.

Levin, Susan M. *Dorothy Wordsworth and Romanticism.* 1987.

Murphy, Peter T. *Poetry as an Occupation and an Art in Britain, 1760–1830.* 1993.

Wordsworth, Dorothy. *Journals of Dorothy Wordsworth.* Ed. Ernest de Selincourt. 2 vols. 1941, 1952.

———. *The Grasmere Journals.* Ed. Pamela Woof. 1991.

Wordsworth, Dorothy, and William Wordsworth. *The Letters of William and Dorothy Wordsworth.* Ed. Ernest de Selincourt. 1967–1982.

See also Lake School of Poetry; Women in Literature; Women's Education

Wordsworth, William (1770–1850)

Wordsworth is now widely regarded as one of the major English poets, yet he was a poet of his time in that he attempted to transcend the conflicts of the revolutionary 1790s. In many ways he was the central poetic figure of the Hanoverian period, a genius in his own right as well as a profoundly transitional writer bridging the pastoral **Augustan** age to the bustling Victorian civilization of the 19th century.

Wordsworth was born into the securely **middle-class** family of an attorney for the largest landowner in the Lake District, but his early life was overshadowed by the death of his parents and separation from his brothers and sister; he turned for consolation to nature and imaginative life. Eager to avoid a humdrum professional career, he left **Cambridge University** and, sympathizing with the **French Revolution**, **traveled** in France and Switzerland (1790). During a second visit to **France**, he fathered a daughter by a young Frenchwoman, Annette Vallon. By 1796, however, he had come to despair of the revolution. For inspiration he drew now on his

William Wordsworth

sister **Dorothy**'s love of nature, domestic life, and common humanity, and his own recollections of childhood in the Lake District.

His first long poems, *An Evening Walk* and *Descriptive Sketches* (both 1793), had been characteristic of the pre–**Romantic** literature of **sensibility**. In the mid-1790s, however, he tried combining both sensibility and his political sympathies in narrative poems such as "Guilt and Sorrow; or Incidents upon Salisbury Plain" and "The Ruined Cottage," rooted in local domestic life. He began a tragedy, *The Borderers*, set in common rather than noble or heroic life. He and his friend **Samuel Taylor Coleridge** planned a collection of shorter poems, ***Lyrical Ballads***, using popular forms of the street **ballad** but instilling a new "philosophical" reflectiveness into **sentimental** social sympathy, natural description, and **Gothic supernaturalism**. Wordsworth also composed fragments of blank-verse **autobiography** infused with **sublime** literariness by echoes from "classic" English poets such as Edmund Spenser (1552–1599) and **John Milton**. He then joined these fragments into a poem on the "growth of his mind" as a poet, reflecting on all his experiences since childhood. He labored at this majestic work over many years but it was published only after his death as *The Prelude* (1850).

Meanwhile, his domestic security and **poetic** reputation grew. In an enlarged edition of *Lyrical Ballads* (1800 and 1802) he gave a retrospective rationale for these "experimental" works; this prose "preface" became one of the best-known manifestos of Romantic literature. He settled in the Lake District with his sister, married a long-time family friend, Mary Hutchinson (1802), and finally received part of a family legacy. His major lyrics of these years appeared in *Poems, in Two Volumes* (1807). *The White Doe of Rylstone*, a major fictitious narrative incorporating elements of popular ballad culture, was published after some hesitation in 1815. In *The Excursion, Being a Portion of the Recluse* (1814), he gave notice of his plan to be the major philosophical poet of a postrevolutionary age, though the work was controversial and never completed. *Peter Bell* and *The Waggoner* (both 1819) did little for his reputation, and he was attacked as a political reactionary by **radical** poets such as **Percy Bysshe Shelley**.

But during the 1820s Wordsworth began reaching a wider readership and was admired by younger poets such as Alfred Tennyson (1809–1892). By the 1840s he was almost a national institution, receiving various state honors and the **Poet Laureateship** (1843). After his death, interest in his work again declined, until renewed by Matthew Arnold (1822–1888). In the early 20th century, scholars and critics revived interest in *The Prelude,* and after World War II made Wordsworth, his moral and social interests, and his refashioning of genre and style into central topics of high literary culture.

Gary Kelly

Bibliography

Chandler, James K. *Wordsworth's Second Nature: A Study of the Poetry and Politics.* 1984.
Gill, Stephen. *William Wordsworth: A Life.* 1989.
Hartman, Geoffrey H. *Wordsworth's Poetry 1787–1814.* 1964.
Jacobus, Mary. *Tradition and Experiment in Wordsworth's* Lyrical Ballads. 1976.
Johnston, Kenneth R. *Wordsworth and the Recluse.* 1984.
Roe, Nicholas. *Wordsworth and Coleridge: The Radical Years.* 1988.
Wordsworth, Jonathan. *The Music of Humanity.* 1969.
Wordsworth, William, and Dorothy Wordsworth. *The Letters of William and Dorothy Wordsworth.* Ed. Ernest de Selincourt. 1967–1982.

See also Lake School of Poetry

Wren, Sir Christopher (1631–1723)

Wren, the greatest English architect of the 17th century, had accomplished most of his important work before the Hanoverian period began, but his influence continued over 18th-century architects. His great achievement was to transform **London** after the Great Fire of 1666 by building the new St. Paul's Cathedral and 52 city churches in a baroque style based to a great extent on French and Italian precedents.

Wren, a member of the commission to repair old St. Paul's in 1663, was interrupted by its complete destruction in the Great Fire. His new plan for London, with long, angled boulevards and plazas at the intersections to replace the narrow, crooked streets, came to nothing, but his magnificent design for a new St. Paul's in the baroque style, centering on an enormous domed Greek cross with a long nave, was executed (1675–1710), as were the new and repaired city churches.

Wren was made Surveyor General of the King's Works in 1668, and Comptroller at Windsor in 1684. He was knighted

Sir Christopher Wren

in 1673. He served as President of the **Royal Society** from 1681 to 1683. In 1682–1689 he was involved in the building of the Chelsea Hospital, and in 1689–1702 in the enlargement of Hampton Court Palace for William and Mary. In 1696 he assumed from John Webb the building of the Greenwich Hospital, and was assisted in this by **Nicholas Hawksmoor**, who had also been involved with the city churches and work at Kensington Palace. Wren's baroque style was exaggerated by Hawksmoor and **Sir John Vanbrugh**, his chief Hanoverian successors. Later architectural theorists stressed his more conservative side to such a degree that he is considered by many to be the greatest English *Renaissance* architect.

Thomas J. McCormick

Bibliography

Beard, Geoffrey. *The Work of Christopher Wren.* 1982.
Colvin, H.M. *A Biographical Dictionary of English Architects 1660–1840.* 2nd ed., 1978.
Downes, Kerry. *The Architecture of Wren.* 1982.
Furst, Victor. *The Architecture of Sir Christopher Wren.* 1956.
Lang, Jane. *Rebuilding St. Paul's after the Great Fire.* 1956.
Sekler, Eduard. *Wren and His Place in European Architecture.* 1956.
Summerson, John. *Sir Christopher Wren.* 1953.
Whinney, Margaret. *Wren.* 1971.

See also Architects and Architecture

Wright of Derby, Joseph (1734–1797)

Wright, one of 18th-century England's greatest painters, was also a fascinated recorder of the progress of the **Industrial Revolution**. Though best known as a painter of industrial and scientific scenes, usually dramatically lit, he also produced excellent **portraits** and **landscapes** as well as subject pictures and literary paintings. His range excelled that of any other leading painter of his time.

Born in Derby, he trained in the **London** studio of the fashionable portrait painter Thomas Hudson (1701–1779) during the 1750s, became a leading portraitist, and exhibited at the Society of Artists in London from 1765 on. His most accomplished and famous works are *A Philosopher Lecturing on the Orrery* (1764–1766), *An Experiment on a Bird in the Air Pump* (1768), and *The Iron Forge* (1772). His pronounced interest in **science**, industry, and natural phenomena brought him the friendship and **patronage** of such Midland intellectuals and industrialists as **Erasmus Darwin** and **Josiah Wedgwood**, both members of the **Lunar Society**. His visit to Italy in 1773 resulted in dramatic moonlit Italian landscape paintings, including *Fireworks Display at the Castel Sant Angelo* (1775–1778), and a series of views of Mt. Vesuvius in eruption.

Wright then settled in **Bath**, hoping to become **Gainsborough**'s successor, but his portraits lacked Gainsborough's flattering elegance. He returned to Derby and continued his work, which now included dramatic landscapes of Matlock Tor and of **Richard Arkwright**'s cotton mill at night. He was named an associate of the **Royal Academy** (1781) and exhibited there from 1778 to 1794. Only in recent years has Wright's varied achievement been recognized.

Thomas J. McCormick

Bibliography

Barrell, John. *Painting and the Politics of Culture: New Essays on British Art, 1700–1850.* 1992.

Benrose, William. *The Life and Works of Joseph Wright, A.R.A., Commonly Called "Wright of Derby."* 1885.

Egerton, Judy. *Wright of Derby.* Exhibition catalogue, New York and London. 1990.

Nicolson, Benedict. *Joseph Wright of Derby: Painter of Light.* 2 vols., 1968.

Solkin, David. *Painting for Money: The Visual Arts and the Public Sphere in Eighteenth-Century England.* 1993.

See also Painting

Wyatt, James (1746–1813)

Wyatt is the best-known member of an architectural dynasty that began with his father Benjamin (1709–1772) and included such later architects as Lewis Wyatt, Sir Jeffry Wyattville, and Matthew Digby Wyatt (1820–1877). James was one of the leading and most prolific architects of his time, equally proficient in the **neoclassical** and **Gothic Revival** styles. Little is known of his early life, but he studied in Venice under the artist Antonio Visentini in the early 1760s, visited Rome, and returned to England in about 1768.

Wyatt's first building, the Pantheon, Oxford Street, London (1770–1772), based on the Roman prototype, established his reputation as a neoclassical architect and rival to **Robert Adam**. **Horace Walpole** described the Pantheon as "the most beautiful edifice in England." Later works in

Entrance Hall, Heveningham Hall, Suffolk

this style included Heaton Hall, Manchester (1772), with interiors by Biagio Rebecca (who also worked for Adam); the Radcliffe Observatory, Oxford (1776–1794); Heveningham Hall, Suffolk (1788–1799); and the mausoleum at Brocklesby Park, Lincolnshire (1787–1794), for Lord Yarborough. Wyatt's Gothic buildings are fewer in number but include Lee Priory, an experiment in Strawberry Hill Gothic (1782); Ashridge Park (1806–1813) for the earl of Bridgewater; and most notable of all, Fonthill Abbey (1795–1807) for the eccentric and colorful **William Beckford**. For Queen Charlotte at Frogmore House, Windsor (1792), he laid out gardens, created Gothic ruins, and designed the main house in a classical style.

Unfortunately, Wyatt is probably best known for his restorations of such cathedrals as Salisbury (1787–1793), Hereford (1788–1797), Lichfield (1788–1795), and Durham (1795–1796), which he attempted to make homogenous in style through a scheme that has earned him the title of "Wyatt the destroyer." His work at Westminster Abbey, to which he was named surveyor in 1776, was less extensive. He was elected to the **Royal Academy** (1785) and made a Fellow of the Society of Antiquaries (1796). Although he was disorganized in his practice (which resulted in numerous delays), he was one of the most successful architects of his time.

Thomas J. McCormick

Bibliography

Colvin, H.M. *A Biographical Dictionary of English Architects 1660–1840.* 2nd ed., 1978.

Dale, Anthony. *James Wyatt.* 1956.

Robinson, John Martin. *The Wyatts, an Architectural Dynasty.* 1979.

Summerson, John. *Architecture in Britain, 1530–1830.* 5th ed., 1970.

See also Architects and Architecture

Wyvill, Christopher (1740–1822)

An Anglican clergyman, Wyvill was an organizer of the Yorkshire Association in December 1779, and the most prominent figure in the **Association movement**. Association began as part of the **economical reform** movement seeking to curb government waste and corruption, but Wyvill directed it to political reform as well.

Educated at Cambridge, ordained in 1763, married to a wealthy cousin (1773), he involved himself in reformist politics. As a large landowner he represented the moderate radicalism of the **gentry** class, alarmed by high **taxation** and government extravagance. He was dedicated to the protection of property, but felt that the best way to safeguard its interests was through reform. Moderate measures would restore the people's faith in the British system and guard against more extreme radicalism.

The reforms proposed by Wyvill and the various county associations he headed in 1780 called for strict economy in government, annual elections, and the addition of 100 more county members to **Commons**, since county M.P.s were thought to be less susceptible to corruption than **borough** representatives. Though only the first of these proposals saw legislative enactment in economical reforms (1782), Wyvill remained a force in reform politics until 1785, working closely with the new young Prime Minister, **Pitt the Younger**, whom he strongly supported. Pitt's very modest and unsuccessful parliamentary reform bill of 1785 emerged from petitions initiated by Wyvill. Wyvill helped to start the **Proclamation Society against Vice and Immorality** (1787). In the 1790s he protested the government's anti–Jacobin measures and treason trials as more alarming than the threat they proposed to meet.

Frank M. Baglione

Bibliography

Baylen, Joseph O., and Norbert J. Gossman, eds. *Biographical Dictionary of Modern British Radicals.* Vol. 1. 1979.

Christie, Ian R. *Wilkes, Wyvill and Reform: The Parliamentary Reform Movement in British Politics, 1760–1785.* 1972.

Cone, Carl B. *The English Jacobins: Reformers in Late 18th Century England.* 1968.

Goodwin, Albert. *The Friends of Liberty: The English Democratic Movement in the Age of the French Revolution.* 1979.

Royle, Edward, and James Walvin. *English Radicals and Reformers, 1760–1848.* 1982.

See also Elections and the Franchise; Radicalism and Radical Politics

Yearsley, Ann Cromartie (1752–1806)

Yearsley, "Lactilla" in her poems, sold milk door-to-door in **Bristol** as her mother had. Marrying in 1774 and bearing six children in the next 10 years, she and her family came to the attention of **Hannah More**, the **Evangelical** writer, and **Elizabeth Montagu**, the "queen" of the **bluestockings**, when the family nearly starved to death during the winter of 1783–1784.

More gave Yearsley some basic spelling and grammar books, edited some of her **poetry**, and arranged for the publication of *Poems on Several Occasions* (1785). The first edition, a great success, initially earned £350; £250 came from later editions. Yearsley and More quarreled over More's attempt to put the earnings in a trust to which only she and Montagu had access. Yearsley published three more volumes of poems in her lifetime: *Poems on Various Subjects* (1787), *Stanzas of Woe* (1790), and *The Rural Lyre* (1796). She also opened a circulating **library** at Bristol Hot Wells in 1793 (unsuccessfully), possibly with the proceeds from her play, *Earl Goodwin* (1798); she also published a **novel**, *The Royal Captives* (1795).

Categorized in her own day as a plebeian poet (like **Stephen Duck** or **Mary Collier**), Yearsley is best known for her pre–**Romantic** "Clifton Hill" (1785), which locates her inspiration in the landscape where she lived and worked, and for her abolitionist "Poem on the Inhumanity of the **Slave Trade**" (1788).

Ruth Perry

Bibliography

Landry, Donna. *The Muses of Resistance.* 1990.

Todd, Janet. *A Dictionary of British and American Women Writers, 1660–1800.* 1985.

Tompkins, J.M.S. *The Polite Marriage.* 1938.

See also Women in Literature

York

The ancient city of York was in the 18th century the cultural capital of the north of England. As a city of trade it had been eclipsed by newer areas, but as a place of fashionable resort and as an administrative and ecclesiastical center, York continued to play a vital role in national life.

The **wool** trade that had brought prosperity to York in earlier centuries had shifted to the West Riding of Yorkshire by the beginning of the 18th century, and the town's **population** was stagnant. In 1801 it contained about 16,000 inhabitants. It nevertheless became in the Hanoverian period one of the most important **provincial towns** for the congregation of the polite and fashionable. This development was actively encouraged by the city's magistrates and other inhabitants, and stimulated by the relative cheapness of living in York.

The city undertook a vigorous civic investment in cultural amenities. **Townhouses** of the country **gentry** multiplied, as did the **retail** shops, circulating **libraries**, promenades, and other features of Georgian urban life. The York Assembly Rooms, built in 1736 to a design by **Lord Burlington**, were noted by contemporaries more for their Palladian purity than for their convenience, but their grandeur demonstrates the importance of the city in the social life of the propertied classes. York is perhaps the best example of a provincial capital that made a graceful transition into a center of commercialized leisure for which the 18th century is noted. Its revival as a center of manufacture as well as of consumption, however, awaited the age of the **railway**.

Daniel Statt

Bibliography

Borsay, Peter. *The English Urban Renaissance.* 1989.

Corfield, P.J. *The Impact of English Towns, 1700–1800.* 1982.

McInnes, Angus. *The English Town, 1660–1760.* 1980.

See also Cities and Urban Life

York, Duke of

See Frederick, Duke of York

York Buildings Company

Originally incorporated as a water-supply company in **London** in 1692, the York Buildings Company was acquired in 1719 by the syndicate involved in the flotation of the **Royal Exchange Assurance.** A quirk in its charter allowed the company to acquire the estates of **Jacobites** forfeited after the **Fifteen**, and to use the accompanying revenues as the basis of a life annuity scheme. Its shares soared during the **South Sea Bubble** (1720) but quickly collapsed afterward. In the following few years it attempted to recoup its fortunes by issuing annuities by way of lotteries, and developing industry (which mainly failed) on its Scottish estates.

In 1726, acquired by a group including the **Duke of Chandos**, the company extended its activities to include the development of a timber operation and ironworks on Speyside and a lead operation at Strontian in Ardnamurchan in the Scottish Highlands. The potential success of these activities led the directors of the fraudulent **Charitable Corporation** to speculate in the company's stock, but the optimism of both groups was excessive and the share price collapsed. The company became the subject of parliamentary investigations that found that irregularities had taken place since 1720.

By 1733 the company was virtually bankrupt, although the complications of bankruptcy procedures and innumerable lawsuits meant that it was not finally dissolved until 1829. The fact that its estates had increased in value meant that the descendants of its creditors were eventually paid. The company was unusual in that it had a diverse range of interests, including estate management, trade, and a range of industries, whereas other **joint-stock companies** in the Hanoverian period were usually confined to a single industry or trade.

A.J.G. Cummings

Bibliography

Cummings A.J.G. "Industry and Investment in the Eighteenth Century Highlands: The York Buildings Company of London," in A.J.G. Cummings and T.M. Devine, eds., *Industry, Business and Society in Scotland since 1700.* 1994.

Murray, David. *The York Buildings Company: A Chapter in Scotch History.* Rpt. 1973.

Scott, W.R. *The Constitution and Finance of English, Scottish and Irish Joint Stock Companies to 1720.* Vol. 3. Rpt. 1968.

Supple, Barry. *The Royal Exchange Assurance: A History of British Insurance, 1720–1970.* 1970.

Yorktown, Surrender of (1781)

Yorktown, a small **tobacco** port on the York River just off Chesapeake Bay, was the scene of the most fateful British military defeat of the Hanoverian age.

General Cornwallis, whose campaign in the Carolinas had failed to change the course of the war, determined to concentrate on Virginia from a coastal base that could be resupplied easily. He moved his army to Yorktown and on 14 August 1781 established posts there and on the opposite bank of the half-mile-wide York River at Gloucester. To counter this a combined American–French army of 15,000 under the command of **General Washington** moved south from New York to lay siege to the British forces, while the French fleet of Admiral François de Grasse established a blockade (30 August). When, after 5 days of intermittent naval action (5–9 September), the British fleet under Admiral Thomas Graves (1725–1802) failed to regain control of Yorktown's sea approaches, Cornwallis's position became increasingly untenable.

A desperate counterattack on 16 October failed to break the seige. Three days later (19 October), after determining that a plan to escape across the river stood no chance of success, Cornwallis surrendered his army of nearly 8,000 men (a quarter of the British strength in America), his band playing the old tune, "The World Turned Upside Down."

Even after this disaster the British still had 26,000 remaining troops in control of most of the American urban centers, including Savannah, Charleston, and New York. But Yorktown effectively ended the war, for news of the defeat dissolved the remaining prowar sentiment in Parliament, contributed to the collapse of the **North** ministry, and brought about negotiations ending the war in the **Treaty of Paris.**

David Sloan

Bibliography

Dull, Jonathan R. *The French Navy and the American Revolution: A Study in Arms and Diplomacy, 1774–1787.* 1975.

Lutnick, Solomon M. "The Defeat at Yorktown: A View from the British Press." *Virginia Magazine of History and Biography.* Vol. 72, pp. 471–478.

Sands, John O. *Yorktown's Captive Fleet.* 1983.

Wickwire, Franklin, and Mary Wickwire. *Cornwallis: The American Adventure.* 1970.

Willcox, William B. "The British Road to Yorktown: A Study in Divided Command." *American Historical Review.* Vol. 52, pp. 1–35.

See also Army; War of American Independence; War and Military Engagements

Young, Arthur (1741–1820)

Young was a prolific agricultural reporter whose writings greatly promoted **agricultural improvement.** Born in **London**, he began managing his own Essex farm in 1767, engaging in various experiments, which he described in *A Course of Experimental Agriculture* (1770). He also began **traveling** and recording his careful observations of farming techniques and economic conditions in his *Six Weeks Tour through the North of England* (1771), *Farmer's Tour through the East of England* (1771), *Six Weeks Tour through the Southern Counties of England and Wales* (1771), and *A Tour of Ireland* (1780). He founded and also wrote a good portion of the monthly **periodical** the *Annals of Agriculture* (1784–1815), which recorded farm statistics and discussed animal management; **George III** (under pen name) and **Jeremy Bentham** were among its contributors.

Appointed Secretary of the new Board of Agriculture (1793), Young was ideally situated to study and publicize

Arthur Young

improved agricultural practices. His studies covered many subject areas: fodder crops; dairy products; crop rotation; soil chemistry; and sheep, horse, pig, and cattle husbandry. He helped greatly to publicize agricultural improvements, lauding, for example, the stock-breeding efforts of **Robert Bakewell**; his endorsement of Bakewell's techniques greatly enhanced the stud fees that the latter was able to charge.

Young remains one of the greatest of all agricultural writers. Many of his works were **translated** into French, Russian, and German. He also wrote half a dozen **novels**, and during his travels in **France** became a warm admirer of J.-J. Rousseau (1712–1778). Young's *Travels in France* (1792), intended first as a discussion of farm techniques observed during a journey of 1787–1789, remains an excellent firsthand account of French country life on the eve of the **French Revolution**. In the late 1790s Young was drawn increasingly into the service of the **Evangelical** revival.

Thomas D. Veve

Bibliography

Dictionary of National Biography, s.v. "Young, Arthur."

Mingay, G.E., ed. *The Agricultural Revolution: Changes in Agriculture, 1650–1880.* 1977.

———. *The Agrarian History of England & Wales.* Vol. 6: 1750–1850. 1989.

Neeson, J.M. *Commoners: Common Right, Enclosure and Social Change in England, 1700–1820.* 1993.

Trow-Smith, Robert. *A History of British Livestock Husbandry, 1700–1900.* 1959.

See also Agriculture; Agricultural Societies

Young, Edward (1683–1765)

Of the **poetry**, tragedy, **literary criticism**, and homilies he published, first as Oxford don and town **wit** and later as Anglican divine, Young is principally remembered for his **satires** (1725–1728), *Conjectures on Original Composition* (1759), and *The Complaint; or, Night Thoughts* (1742–1746).

Like his father, a distinguished preacher, Young went from Winchester to Oxford, becoming a Fellow of All Souls in 1708 and receiving his doctorate in Civil Law in 1719. With support from **Richard Steele** and **Joseph Addison**, Young sought preferment through poetry, most significantly *The Force of Religion* (1714), a narrative of Lady Jane Grey's martyrdom; *A Letter to Mr. Tickell* (1719) on Addison's death; and *A Paraphrase on a Part of the Book of Job* (1719). His best and longest early composition, *A Poem on the Last Day* (1713), affecting the **sublime**, describes the resurrection and judgment of the dead, and the world's destruction.

With only his fellowship and pen for support, Young turned to tragedy in the inflated manner of heroic drama, producing *Busiris* (1719) and *The Revenge,* which ran for 9 nights in 1721. *The Brothers,* pulled from production in December 1724 when Young took holy orders, was produced in 1753.

Love of Fame the Universal Passion (1725–1728), seven satires with Horatian raillery punctuated with Juvenalian attacks on vice, broke new poetical ground, establishing Young as a major poet. Epigrammatic and antithetical in style, and characteristical and thematic in structure, these were the first formal verse satires to follow John Dryden's (1631–1700) precepts, and influenced **Alexander Pope**'s *Moral Epistles* (1731–1735). The satires resulted, through the offices of Young's friend **George Bubb Dodington**, in his receiving a **pension** of £200 (1726).

Capitalizing on his success, Young brought out a flurry

Edward Young

of publications, including *A Vindication of Providence; or True Estimate of Human Life* (1727), a discourse on the passions and other impediments to felicity; *Ocean* (1728) and *Imperium Pelagi* (1730), two odes praising English naval might and commerce; and *Two Epistles to Mr. Pope* (1730), mixing critical precepts with generalized attacks on the Dunces. In 1730 Young received the benefice of Welwyn, Hertfordshire, soon afterward marrying Lady Elizabeth Lee, a widow with three children, who bore him a son in 1732.

After the death of his step-daughter, wife, and son-in-law, and a severe illness, Young wrote *The Complaint; or, Night Thoughts on Life, Death, and Immortality.* Incorporating **graveyard poetry**, theodicy, elegy, homily, and cosmic voyage, the *Night Thoughts,* with roughly 9,750 lines of blank verse, begins as melancholic reflections on the poet's grief and moves to consolation, the reclamation of sinners, and a defense of Christian tenets. Although overextended, the poem passed through 100 editions by 1800, swept Germany and **France** soon after publication, and was **translated** into nearly all European languages.

Young remained an active man of letters, encouraged by friends like **Samuel Richardson**, who printed his works after 1744. In 1755 Young published *The Centaur Not Fabulous,* a satirical homily on licentiousness and irreligion. He revised, largely through deletions, works thought fit for posterity (1757). With Richardson's assistance he wrote *Conjectures on Original Composition* (1759), an enthusiastic celebration glancing critically at Pope, **Jonathan Swift**, and Addison, and ending with an account of Addison's pious death, thus linking literary with moral virtue. In 1761–1762, initially to console the widow of Admiral **Edward Boscawen**, he wrote *Resignation,* in which faith in providence is treated personally and joyfully, and contrasted with gloomy **freethinking**.

With **Evangelical** fervor, a luxuriant imagination, and musing self-reflexivity, Young repeatedly struck new directions and found imitators in England and on the Continent. Strong in imagination but weak in judgment, his idiosyncratic genius was recognized by contemporaries, even in anonymous works, for its original and often paradoxical thought and an expression marked by epigrammatic density, inventive diction, and copious metaphor and antithesis.

James E. May

Bibliography

Forster, Harold. *Edward Young: Poet of the 'Night Thoughts' (1683–1765).* 1986.

May, James. "A Bibliography of Secondary Materials for the Study of Edward Young, 1683–1765." *Bulletin of Bibliography.* Vol. 46, pp. 230–248.

Pettit, Henry. *A Bibliography of Young's 'Night Thoughts.' University of Colorado Studies,* Series in Language and Literature, No. 5. 1954; Rpt. 1973, 1977.

———, ed. *The Correspondence of Edward Young (1683–1765).* 1971.

Young, Edward. *The Complete Works of the Reverend Edward Young.* John Nichols, ed., with a biographical sketch by John Doran. 1854.

Younger, William (1733–1770)

Son of a successful **farmer**, William Younger turned from work as an excise man to become one of **Scotland**'s leading **brewers**, a move common in 18th-century Scotland. In 1749 his father provided capital to establish the Edinburgh Holyrood Abbey Brewery. Soon, Younger's "massive carts" were well established in the local markets of the Lothians and Berwickshire.

A shrewd **entrepreneur**, he was quick to take advantage of **transport** improvements to widen markets for his strong ales, employing **canal** shipments to **Glasgow** and **Paisley**, for example, and **coastal** transport from the Shetland Islands to **London** and the southeast of England. Younger's was one of the first of the large breweries to establish a chain of wholesale agencies, even one in **Dublin**. His products included strong ales and porter and, for trade within the **Empire**, the famous "India Pale Ales" and "Younger's Export Ales," specially brewed to withstand long sea passages. Younger bequeathed to his family a strong and vibrant business, and his sons continued to expand what was now the major brewing business of Scotland.

Patricia S. Collins

Bibliography

Donnachie, I. *A History of the Brewing Industry in Scotland.* 1979.

Keir, D. *The Younger Centuries: The Story of William Younger and Co. Ltd., 1749–1949.* 1951.

See also Brewing and Public Houses; Drink Industries; Drinking

Guide to Further Research on Britain in the Hanoverian Age

For additional information on any topic covered in this encyclopedia, be sure to consult the individual bibliographies appended to each article. What follows here is a listing of many of the most useful general tools for pursuing further research on the civilization of Hanoverian Britain.

A. Essential General Surveys

These texts, mostly volumes in prestigious series such as the *Oxford History of English Literature,* are valuable for the comprehensive detailed information they provide, as well as the excellent selected bibliographies they offer.

Black, Jeremy, ed. *British Politics and Society from Walpole to Pitt, 1742–1789.* 1990.

Boase, Thomas Sherrer Ross. *English Art, 1800–1870.* 1959.

Burke, Joseph T. *English Art, 1714–1800.* 1976.

Butt, John Everett. *The Mid-Eighteenth Century.* 1979. (English Literature.)

Dobrée, Bonamy. *English Literature in the Early Eighteenth Century, 1700–1740.* 1959.

Jack, Ian. *English Literature, 1815–1832.* 1963.

Johnstone, H. Diack, and Roger Fiske, eds. *The Eighteenth Century: Music in Britain.* 1990.

Langford, Paul. *A Polite and Commercial People: England 1727–1783.* 1989.

Lenman, Bruce. *The New History of Scotland: Integration and Enlightenment, 1746–1832.* 1992.

Mitchison, Rosalind. *The New History of Scotland: Lordship to Patronage, 1603–1745.* 1983.

Moody, T.W., and W.E. Vaughan, eds. *A New History of Ireland: Eighteenth-Century Ireland, 1691–1800.* 1986.

Porter, Roy. *English Society in the Eighteenth Century.* Rev. ed., 1990.

Renwick, William Lindsay. *English Literature, 1789–1815.* 1963.

Temperley, Nicholas, ed. *Music in Britain: The Romantic Age, 1800–1914.* 1988.

Vaughan, W.E., ed. *A New History of Ireland: Ireland under the Union, 1801–1870.* 1989.

Watson, John Steven. *The Reign of George III, 1760–1815.* 1960.

Williams, Basil. *The Whig Supremacy, 1714–1760.* 2nd ed., 1962.

Woodward, Llewellyn. *The Age of Reform, 1815–1870.* 2nd ed., 1962.

B. Current Bibliographies and Other Current Awareness Tools

Most of the following are ongoing bibliographies that are extremely useful for discovering recent research; however, they also have a long history and may readily be used for identifying older publications and sources. For journal articles these bibliographies may be amplified by using various standard indexes such as *Historical Abstracts, Part A: Modern History Abstracts, 1450–1914,* 1955– (an interdisciplinary subject and author index to several thousand periodicals and other published materials), and the *MLA, International Bibliography of Books and Articles on the Modern Languages and Literatures,* 1922–. Both selectively cover doctoral dissertations as well.

American Society for Eighteenth-Century Studies. *The Eighteenth Century, a Current Bibliography.* 1975–. Provides especially good coverage of literature, but also includes publications on history, science, philosophy, religion, and fine arts. For coverage of literature prior to 1975, see the antecedent of this bibliography, "English Literature, 1660–1800: A Current Bibliography." *Philological Quarterly.* 1922–. This extensive bibliography appeared as an annual feature from 1928 to 1975. Also, a cumulation of the annual bibliographies through 1970 may be found in *English Literature, 1660–1800: A Bibliography of Modern Studies.* 6 vols. 1950–1970.

"Annual Bibliography: British Labour History Publications." *Labour History Review.* 1990–. Formerly the *Society for the Study of Labour History Bulletin.* 1960–.

Annual Bibliography of Scottish Literature. 1969–.

H-ALBION (British and Irish History). An electronic discussion forum, available to anyone with access to electronic mail. Participants are serious scholars, ranging from graduate students to senior professors from the United States, the United Kingdom, Australia, and many other places. Information is exchanged on current research, bibliographies, book reviews, conference reports, and much more. To subscribe, send an e-mail message to **Listserv@h-net.msu.edu**. The message should read sub h-albion your first name surname school. If you have access to the INTERNET you may find out about other high-quality electronic discussion groups by connecting to **http://h-net2.msu.edu/about/lists.html**.

Historical Association (Great Britain). *Annual Bulletin of Historical Literature.* 1911–.

Isis: Current Bibliography of the History of Science and Its Cultural Influences. Currently published annually as a supplement to the journal *Isis,* 1913–. Its antecedent was the *Isis* feature, "Critical Bibliography," which was originally published within the journal. Several cumulations of this prestigious bibliography have been published: *Isis Cumulative Bibliography, 1913–1965,* 1971; *Isis Cumulative Bibliography, 1966–1975,* 1980; and *Isis Cumulative Bibliography, 1976–1985,* 1989.

"List of Articles on Scottish History, A." *Scottish Historical Review.* 1903–. Has appeared annually since 1960 and currently covers some 200 periodicals. Prior to 1960, a similar but less extensive bibliography was included on a regular basis.

"List of Publications on the Economic and Social History of Great Britain and Ireland." *Economic History Review.* 1927/28–. This annual feature has been ongoing since the first publication of the journal.

"Notes and Documents." *English Historical Review.* 1886–. The July issue has "notes" offering an overview of historical scholarship from a large number of periodical publications.

"Reviews." *Journal of British Studies.* 1961–. This feature often includes lengthy bibliographic review essays.

Royal Historical Society. *Annual Bibliography of British and Irish History.* 1975–.

Writings on British History. 1937–1986. In effect continued by the *Annual Bibliography of British and Irish History* (see immediately above).

Writings on Irish History. 1979–. From 1938 to 1978 this appeared in *Irish Historical Studies.* 1938–.

Year's Work in Scottish Literary and Linguistic Studies. 1984–. Prior to 1984 this was an annual supplement to the *Scottish Literary Journal.* 1974–.

C. Standard General Bibliographies and Selected Specialized Bibliographies

Auyong, Dorothy K., Dorothy Porter, and Roy Porter. *Consumption and Culture in the Seventeenth and Eighteenth Centuries: A Bibliography.* 1991.

Bibliographies of British Statesmen. 1989–.

Brown, Lucy M., and Ian R. Christie. *Bibliography of British History, 1789–1851.* 1977.

Chaloner, W.H., and R.C. Richardson, eds. *Bibliography of British Economic and Social History.* 2nd ed., 1984.

Creaton, Heather, ed. *Bibliography of Printed Works on London History to 1939.* 1994.

Frey, Linda, Marsha Frey, and Joanne Schneider (compilers and editors). *Women in Western European History, a Select Chronological, Geographical, and Topical Bibliography.* 1982–1984. 2 vols. *First Supplement.* 1986. An excellent selection of articles and books on every aspect of the history of women.

Gibson, Lawrence Henry. *A Bibliographical Guide to the History of the British Empire, 1748–1776.* 1968.

Innes, Joanna, and John Styles. "The Crime Wave: Recent Writing on Crime and Criminal Justice in Eighteenth-Century England." *Journal of British Studies.* Vol. 25, pp. 380–435.

Kanner, Barbara. *Women in English Social History, 1800–1914: A Guide to Research.* 3 vols. 1987–1990. Extensive coverage of primary and secondary sources.

Mullins, Edward Lindsay Carson. *A Guide to the Historical and Archaeological Publications of the Societies in England and Wales, 1901–1933.* 1968. Covers publications not included in *Writings on British History.*

Pargellis, Stanley, and D.J. Medley. *Bibliography of British History, the Eighteenth Century, 1714–1789.* 1951.

Pickering, Jennifer. *Music in the British Isles, 1700–1800: A Bibliography of Literature.* 1990.

Smith, Robert A. *Late Georgian and Regency England, 1760–1837.* 1984.

Soliday, Gerald L., ed. *History of the Family and Kinship: A Select International Bibliography.* 1980.

D. Doctoral Dissertations

Doctoral dissertations offer detailed analyses of topics often not treated elsewhere, and they also typically provide extensive bibliographies.

Bilboul, Roger, and Kent, Francis, eds. *Retrospective Index to Theses of Great Britain and Ireland, 1716–1950.* Vol 1: *Social Sciences and Humanities.* 1975. See also *Addenda.* 1977.

Comprehensive Dissertation Index. 1861–. Covers Canada and the United States. Most of the dissertations listed are abstracted in *Dissertation Abstracts International,* 1938–, which in recent years has provided somewhat limited coverage of Europe. Available in CD-ROM format.

Index to Theses Accepted for Higher Degrees in the Universities of Great Britain and Ireland. 1950–.

E. Guides to Primary Sources, Manuscripts, and Archives

See also the bibliographies listed above. Many list and describe primary sources.

Accessing English Literary Periodicals, a Guide to the Microfilm Collection. 1981. Lists and briefly describes 341 periodicals published in Britain between the 17th and late 19th centuries, which are available in a corresponding microfilm set owned by many large university libraries. Recently the first installment of a CD-ROM product, titled *Index to English Literary Periodicals, 1681–1941,* which corresponds to this microfilm set, was released by Computer Indexed Systems. This is the first general index to 18th-century articles ever produced.

Bond, Maurice F. *Guide to the Records of Parliament.* 1971. The best overall guide to parliamentary papers in their entirety. See also various specific guides below in this section.

British Library. Department of Manuscripts. *Index of Manuscripts in the British Library.* 1984. The first comprehensive index to the thirty-plus volumes, describing the manuscripts acquired by the British Library through 1949.

Cobbett's Parliamentary History of England, from the Norman Conquest in 1066 to the Year 1803. 36 vols. 1966. Essentially a recording of various accounts of Parliament before official records were kept of the debates and remarks on the floor of the House of Commons. Continued by *Hansard's Parliamentary Debates.* 1803–. For other records of the Commons, see listings below: (1) Cockton, and (2) Lambert.

Cockton, Peter, ed. *Subject Catalogue of the House of Commons Parliamentary Papers, 1801–1900.* 5 vols. 1988. The most thorough guide yet devised for discovering reports, testimony, and other papers outside parliamentary debates. (For these, see *Cobbett's,* above.)

EngSTC, the English Short Title Catalog (1473–1800). Formerly the *Eighteenth-Century Short Title Catalog,* a computer database, available through *RLIN (Research Libraries Information Network),* which includes titles printed in Great Britain and its colonies, and works in English printed anywhere else. The works themselves are being microfilmed as a set titled *The Eighteenth Century* (1982–).

Foster, Janet, and Julia Sheppard. *British Archives, a Guide to Archive Resources in the United Kingdom.* 3rd ed., 1995.

Great Britain. Public Records Office. *Guide to the Contents of the Public Records Office.* 3 vols. 1963–1969.

Great Britain. Royal Commission on Historical Manuscripts. *The Manuscript Papers of British Scientists, 1600–1940.* 1982.

Guide to the Early British Periodicals Collection on Microfilm, A. 1980. Lists and briefly describes over 160 periodicals, most of which were published during the 18th and 19th centuries. Includes periodicals dealing with the fine arts, science, philosophy, literature, and many other areas. The corresponding microfilm set is owned by many large university libraries.

Hamer, Philip M., ed. *A Guide to Archives and Manuscripts in the United States.* 1961. The standard guide to major archival repositories. Updated, but not superseded by the *Directory of Archives and Manuscript Repositories in the United States,* 1978, created through the auspices of the United States National Historical Publications and Records Commission.

Helferty, Seamus, and Raymond Refausse, eds. *Directory of Irish Archives.* 2nd ed., 1993.

Lambert, Sheila, ed. *House of Commons Sessional Papers of the Eighteenth Century: Introduction and Lists.* 2 vols. 1975. This serves as a guide and index to the largest single collection of Hanoverian parliamentary papers, totaling 145 volumes, published by Scholarly Resources in 1975. The sessional papers include all the reports and papers of the House of Commons, except the debates on the floor. (For these, see *Cobbett's,* above.)

Mullins, Edward Lindsay Carson. *Texts and Calendars: An Analytical Guide to Serial Publications.* 1958. Updated in 1983 as *Texts and Calendars II,* this describes and indexes a vast wealth of primary sources published through various British historical records societies.

Nineteenth Century Short Title Catalog. 1984–. Based on the holdings of the Bodleian Library, the British Library, the National Library of Scotland, and the libraries at Trinity College (Dublin), the universities of Cambridge and Newcastle, this project aims at producing the most extensive list of publications ever produced, covering the years 1801 through 1918. Series One covers 1801–1815; Series Two covers 1816–1870.

Repositories of Primary Sources. To a person who has access to the World Wide Web, this site has great value. It allows the user to connect to some 650 special collections or archives which to varying degrees describe their holdings. The United Kingdom is well represented. **http://www.uidaho.edu/special-collections/Other.Repositories.html** is the computer address.

Stevenson, David, and Wendy B. Stevenson. *Scottish Texts and Calendars, an Analytical Guide to Serial Publications.* 1987. Covers sources published by a number of private historical societies.

Times, The. London. *Tercentary Handlist of English and Welsh Newspapers, Magazines, and Reviews.* 1920. Covers periodicals published since 1620.

Williams, Judith Blow. *A Guide to the Printed Materials for English Social and Economic History, 1750–1850.* 2 vols. 1926.

F. Reference Works

The following list is highly selective. Hundreds of useful reference tools are available to aid the student of Hanoverian Britain. For a comprehensive guide, see the latest edition of *Walford's Guide to Reference Material.*

Aspinall, A.A., and E.A. Smith, eds. *English Historical Documents.* Vol. XI: *1782–1832.* 1959.

Black, Jeremy, and Roy Porter. *A Dictionary of Eighteenth Century World History.* 1994.

Burden, Michael, and Irena Cholij, eds. *Handbook for Studies in 18th-Century Music.* 3 vols. 1987–1993.

Cook, Chris. *British Historical Facts, 1688–1760.* 1988.

Cook, Chris, and John Stevenson. *The Longman Handbook of Modern British History, 1714–1987.* 2nd ed., 1988.

Crawford, Anne, et al., eds. *The Europa Biographical Dictionary of British Women.* 1983.

Dabundo, Laura, ed. *Encyclopedia of Romanticism: Culture in Britain, 1780s–1830s.* 1992.

Donnachie, Ian, and George Hewitt. *A Companion to Scottish History from the Reformation to the Present.* 1989.

Falkus, Malcolm E., and John Gillingham, eds. *Historical Atlas of Britain.* Rev. ed., 1987.

Fryde, E.B. *Handbook of British Chronology.* 3rd ed., 1986.

Horn, David B., and Mary Ransome, eds. *English Historical Documents.* Vol. X: *1714–1783.* 1957.

Mitchell, Brian. *British Historical Statistics.* 1988.

Newman, Peter R. *Companion to Irish History, 1603–1921.* 1991.

Paston, George. *Social Caricature in the Eighteenth Century.* 1905. Some 213 illustrations, including those of Gillray, Rowlandson, and Hogarth, and many others, along with commentary.

Rocque, John. *The A to Z of Georgian London* [1747]. 1982. Facsimile map with street index.

Weinreb, Ben, and Christopher Hibbert, eds. *The London Encyclopaedia.* Rev. ed., 1993.

Williams, E. Neville. *The Eighteenth-Century Constitution, 1688–1815, Documents and Commentary.* 1960.

Wrigley, E.A., and R.S. Schofield. *The Population History of England, 1541–1871.* 1981.

Wynn Jones, Michael. *The Cartoon History of Britain.* 1971. Covers from the 1720s and includes discussions of Hogarth and Gillray.

G. Biography

This list is very selective. For a comprehensive guide, see the latest edition of *Walford's Guide to Reference Material.*

Banks, Olive. *The Biographical Dictionary of British Feminists.* Vol. 1: *1800–1930.* 1985.

Baylen, Joseph O., and Norbert J. Gossman, eds. *Biographical Dictionary of Modern British Radicals.* Vol. 1: *1770–1830.* 1979.

Biographical Dictionary of Eminent Scotsmen, A. 5 vols. 1855. A new *Dictionary of Scottish Biography* is currently being prepared.

Boylan, Henry. *A Dictionary of Irish Biography.* 2nd ed., 1988. A six-volume work, in preparation by the Irish Royal Academy (forthcoming).

Colvin, Howard M. *A Biographical Dictionary of British Architects, 1600–1840.* 2nd ed., 1978.

Dictionary of National Biography. 1908–. A *New Dictionary of National Biography* is in progress.

Dictionary of Welsh Biography Down to 1940. 1959.

Gillispie, Charles Coulston, ed. *Dictionary of Scientific Biography.* 15 vols. and supplements. 1970–.

Gunnis, Rupert. *Dictionary of British Sculptors, 1660–1851.* New rev. ed., 1968.

Highfill, Philip H., Jr., Kalman A. Burnim, and Edward A. Langhans. *A Biographical Dictionary of Actors, Actresses, Musicians, Dancers, Managers & Other Stage Personnel in London, 1660–1800.* 16 vols. 1973–1993.

Namier, Lewis B., and John Brooke. *The House of Commons, 1754–1790.* 3 vols. 1964.

Sadie, Stanley, ed. *The New Grove Dictionary of Music and Musicians.* 20 vols. 1981.

Sedgwick, Romney, ed. *The House of Commons, 1715–1754.* 3 vols. 1970.

Thorne, R.G. *The House of Commons, 1790–1820.* 5 vols. 1986.

Treasure, Geoffrey. *Who's Who in British History.* Vol. 6: *Early Hanoverian Britain.* 1991a.

______. *Who's Who in British History.* Vol. 7: *Late Hanoverian Britain.* 1991b.

Turberville, Arthur Stanley. *English Men and Manners in the Eighteenth Century, an Illustrated Narrative.* 1926. Biographical sketches and anecdotes of people from many walks of life. Much of the information included would be very difficult to find elsewhere.

H. Periodicals

This selected list is by no means comprehensive. For fuller reference see Janet Fyfe (compiler), *History Journals and Serials, an Analytical Guide.* 1986. This offers excellent descriptions of 689 periodicals and periodical indexes. For a comprehensive guide to periodicals still being published, see *Ulrich's International Periodicals Directory.* 1932–.

Albion, a Quarterly Journal Concerned with British Studies. 1969/70–.

British Journal for the History of Science. 1962–.

Economic History Review, a Journal of Economic and Social History. 1927/28–.

Eighteenth-Century Fiction. 1988–.

Eighteenth-Century Life. 1974–. Covers art, language, science, and many other aspects of social and cultural history.

Eighteenth-Century Studies. 1967–. Embraces all disciplines including science, religion, literature, philosophy, history, music, and political science.

Eighteenth Century: Theory and Interpretation. 1979–. A continuation of *Studies in Burke and His Time* (1959–1979). Includes fine arts, literature, science, philosophy, as well as popular culture.

ELH: A Journal of English Literary History. 1934–.

English Historical Review. 1886–.

Enlightenment and Dissent. 1982–. Formerly the *Price-Priestly Newsletter.*

Historical Journal. 1958–. Continues the *Cambridge Historical Journal.* 1923–1957.

History. 1912–. The journal of the Historical Association.

Irish Economic and Social History. 1974–.

Irish Historical Studies. 1938–.

ISIS, an International Review Devoted to the History of Science and Its Cultural Influences. 1913–.

Journal of British Studies. 1961–.

Journal of Social History. 1967/68–.

Journal of the History of Ideas. 1940–.

Labour History Review. 1990–. Formerly *Society for the Study of Labour History Bulletin.*

Parliamentary History. 1982–.

Past & Present. 1952–.

Scottish Economic and Social History. 1981–.

Scottish Historical Review. 1903–.

Scottish Literary Journal. 1974–.

Social History. 1976–.

Studies in Romanticism. 1961–.

Contributors

Lisa Altomari
Bronxville, New York

David R. Anderson
Florida Atlantic University
Boca Raton, Florida

Constantinos Athanasopoulos
University of Glasgow
Glasgow, Scotland, U.K.

Rochelle R. Athey
Columbus, Ohio

James R. Aubrey
Metropolitan State College of Denver
Colorado Springs, Colorado

Frank Baglione
Tallahassee Community College
Tallahassee, Florida

Michael Bartholomew
Open University
Leeds, England, U.K.

Mahasveta Barua
University of Delaware
Newark, Delaware

James G. Basker
Barnard College
New York, New York

Richard D. Beards
Temple University
Philadelpha, Pennsylvania

Stephen C. Behrendt
University of Nebraska
Lincoln, Nebraska

Bruce Beiderwell
University of California
Los Angeles, California

G.T. Bell
Glasgow, Scotland, U.K.

Reed Benhamou
Indiana University
West Lafayette, Indiana

Betty T. Bennett
The American University
Washington, D.C.

Raymond Bentman
Temple University
Philadelphia, Pennsylvania

K.J.H. Berland
Penn State University, Shenango
Sharon, Pennsylvania

Richard W. Bevis
University of British Columbia
Vancouver, B.C., Canada

Bonita L. Billman
Georgetown University
Washington, D.C.

Jeremy Black
Exeter University
Exeter, England, U.K.

G. Kim Blank
University of Victoria
Victoria, B.C., Canada

Thomas F. Bonnell
Saint Mary's College
Notre Dame, Indiana

George Bretherton
Montclair State University
Upper Montclair, New Jersey

Janice Broder
Bloomsburg University
Bloomsburg, Pennsylvania

Leslie Ellen Brown
Alma College
Alma, Michigan

Michael Bruce
Goldsmiths College, University of London
London, England, U.K.

William J. Burling
Southwest Missouri State University
Cape Girardeau, Missouri

Jim Burton
Ilkley (Yorkshire), England, U.K.

John Butt
University of Strathclyde
Glasgow, Scotland, U.K.

Dominique Calapai
Malverne, New York

Raoul F. Camus
Queensborough Community College
Bayside, New York

Geoffrey Cantor
University of Leeds
Leeds, England, U.K.

Shawn E. Carleton
Temple University
Philadelphia, Pennsylvania

Stanley D.F. Carpenter
Florida State University
Tallahassee, Florida

Vincent Carretta
University of Maryland, College Park
College Park, Maryland

Timothy J.L. Chandler
Kent State University
Kent, Ohio

Brent Chesley
Aquinas College
Grand Rapids, Michigan

Peter Clapham
Edinburgh, Scotland, U.K.

George F. Clements
Cambridge, Massachusetts

Patricia Collins
University of Strathclyde
Glasgow, Scotland, U.K.

Kevin Cope
Louisiana State University
Baton Rouge, Louisiana

R.D. Corrins
Bell College of Technology
Hamilton, Scotland, U.K.

Taylor Corse
Arizona State University
Tempe, Arizona

Richard Cosgrove
University of Arizona
Tucson, Arizona

Jeffrey N. Cox
Texas A&M University
College Station, Texas

Lisa Plummer Crafton
West Georgia College
Carrollton, Georgia

L. Ben Crane
Temple University
Philadelphia, Pennsylvania

Louis Cullen
Trinity College
Dublin, Ireland

A.J.G. Cummings
University of Strathclyde
Glasgow, Scotland, U.K.

Kenneth Daley
Ohio University
Athens, Ohio

Richard H. Dammers
Illinois State University
Normal, Illinois

Marlies K. Danziger
Hunter College, CUNY
New York, New York

C.J. Davey
University of Dundee
Dundee, Scotland, U.K.

Deidre Dawson
Georgetown University
Washington, D.C.

Peter Diamond
University of Utah
Salt Lake City, Utah

Kathleen Dillon
Temple University
Philadelphia, Pennsylvania

Richard J. Dircks
St. John's University
Jamaica, New York

N. Merrill Distad
University of Alberta
Edmonton, Alberta, Canada

Ian Donnachie
Open University in Scotland
Edinburgh, Scotland, U.K.

J.A. Downie
Goldsmiths College, University of London
London, England, U.K.

Susan Bolet Egenolf
Texas A&M University
College Station, Texas

Ann W. Engar
University of Utah
Salt Lake City, Utah

William H. Epstein
University of Arizona
Tucson, Arizona

Timothy Erwin
University of Nevada, Las Vegas
Las Vegas, Nevada

Neil Evans
Coleg Harlech
Harlech, Wales, U.K.

Walter H. Evert
University of Pittsburgh
Pittsburgh, Pennsylvania

Chat Ewing
New York University
New York, New York

Carole Fabricant
University of California, Riverside
Riverside, California

David M. Fahey
Miami University
Oxford, Ohio

Alice D. Fasano
New York University
New York, New York

Richard Finlay
University of Strathclyde
Glasgow, Scotland, U.K.

Lauren Fitzgerald
Barnard College
New York, New York

Martin Fitzpatrick
University College of Wales
Aberystwyth, Wales, U.K.

W. Hamish Fraser
University of Strathclyde
Glasgow, Scotland, U.K.

John Freehafer
Temple University
Philadelphia, Pennsylvania

Valerie Frith
University of Toronto
Toronto, Canada

Jack Fruchtman, Jr.
Towson State University
Towson, Maryland

Michael Fry
Edinburgh, Scotland, U.K.

Carole Susan Fungaroli
University of Virginia
Charlottesville, Virginia

John Gascoigne
University of New South Wales
New South Wales, Australia

Marilyn Gaull
Temple University
Philadelphia, Pennsylvania

Mitchel Gerber
Southeast Missouri State University
Cape Girardeau, Missouri

Jane Girdham
Bowdoin College
Brunswick, Maine

Stuart Givens
Bowling Green State University
Bowling Green, Ohio

Samuel Lyndon Gladden
Texas A&M University
College Station, Texas

James Gray
Kentville, Nova Scotia, Canada

Isobel Grundy
University of Alberta
Edmonton, Alberta, Canada

Cynthia Guidici
University of North Texas
Denton, Texas

Phyllis J. Guskin
Powys, Wales, U.K.

H. George Hahn
Towson State University
Towson, Maryland

Donald Hassler
Kent State University
Kent, Ohio

Eric Heavner
Towson State University
Towson, Maryland

James Held
Temple University
Philadelphia, Pennsylvania

Mark C. Herman
Edison Community College
Fort Myers, Florida

Stephen Hicks
Bloomsburg University
Bloomsburg, Pennsylvania

C.E. Hivey
Glasgow, Scotland, U.K.

D.W. Howell
University College
Swansea, Wales, U.K.

Pat Hudson
University of Liverpool
Liverpool, England, U.K.

John A. Hutcheson, Jr.
Dalton College
Dalton, Georgia

Howard Irving
University of Alabama
Birmingham, Alabama

Sylvia Patterson Iskander
University of Southwestern Louisiana
Lafayette, Louisiana

Mary V. Jackson
City College, CUNY
New York, New York

T.V. Jackson
Silloth, England, U.K.

Elisabeth W. Joyce
Temple University
Philadelphia, Pennsylvania

John Kandl
New York University
New York, New York

Deborah Kaplan
George Mason University
Fairfax, Virginia

Tim Keirn
California State University, Long Beach
Long Beach, California

Kate Van Winkle Keller
Darnestown, Maryland

Gary Kelly
University of Alberta
Edmonton, Alberta, Canada

James Kelly
St. Patrick's College
Dublin, Ireland

William Kennefick
University of Dundee
Dundee, Scotland, U.K.

Laura B. Kennelly
University of North Texas
Denton, Texas

Carolyn Kephart
Nashville, Tennessee

Grace Rusk Kerr
Texas A&M University
College Station, Texas

Elise F. Knapp
Western Connecticut State University
Danbury, Connecticut

Greg Kucich
University of Notre Dame
Notre Dame, Indiana

P.J. Kulisheck
University of Minnesota
Minneapolis, Minnesota

J. Scott Lee
Temple University
Philadelphia, Pennsylvania

Beverly Lemire
University of New Brunswick
Fredericton, New Brunswick, Canada

Monica Letzring
Temple University
Philadelphia, Pennsylvania

David M. Levy
George Mason University
Fairfax, Virginia

Frederick M. Link
University of Nebraska
Lincoln, Nebraska

Roger D. Lund
LeMoyne College
Syracuse, New York

Joseph T. Malloy
Hamilton College
Clinton, New York

Elizabeth Wilkens Manus
New York, New York

Wight Martindale, Jr.
Temple University
Philadelphia, Pennsylvania

James E. May
Penn State University
University Park, Pennsylvania

Howard A. Mayer
University of Hartford
West Hartford, Connecticut

Michael McCahill
Brooks School
North Andover, Massachusetts

Anne Kapler McCallum
Ellenwood, Georgia

Thomas J. McCormick
Wheaton College
Brookline, Massachusetts

David McCracken
Washington University
St. Louis, Missouri

Theresa McDonald
Glasgow, Scotland, U.K.

E.W. McFarland
Glasgow Caledonian University
Glasgow, Scotland, U.K.

Barbara McGovern
Ohio State University, Mansfield
Mansfield, Ohio

Arthur McIvor
University of Strathclyde
Glasgow, Scotland, U.K.

Robert D. McJimsey
Colorado College
Colorado Springs, Colorado

David D. McKinney
Washington, D.C.

Lauren D. McKinney
Temple University
Philadelphia, Pennsylvania

Diane McManus
Temple University
Philadelphia, Pennsylvania

Joseph McMinn
University of Ulster at Jordanstown
Jordanstown, Northern Ireland, U.K.

Ann Messenger
Vancouver, B.C., Canada

Eve R. Meyer
Temple University
Havertown, Pennsylvania

David Mock
Tallahassee Community College
Tallahassee, Florida

Marjorie Morgan
Southern Illinois University
Carbondale, Illinois

William Edward Morris
University of Cincinnati
Cincinnati, Ohio

Laura Morrow
Louisiana State University, Shreveport
Shreveport, Louisiana

Timothy Morton
Princeton University
Princeton, New Jersey

Melissa M. Mowry
University of Delaware
Newark, Delaware

Kevin Mulcahy
Rutgers University
New Brunswick, New Jersey

Sterling E. Murray
West Chester University
West Chester, Pennsylvania

Wendy Jones Nakanishi
Shikoku Gakuin University
Zentsuji-Shi, Kagawa-Ken, Japan

Stanley D. Nash
Rutgers University
New Brunswick, New Jersey

Melvyn New
Temple University
Philadelphia, Pennsylvania

Gerald Newman
Kent State University
Kent, Ohio

Donald W. Nichol
Memorial University
St. John's, Newfoundland, Canada

Robin Nilon
Temple University
Philadelphia, Pennsylvania

David D. Nolta
College of the Holy Cross
Livonia, Michigan

Matthew S. Novak
California Polytechnic State University
San Luis Obispo, California

Michael Oberg
Syracuse University
Syracuse, New York

Glen A. Omans
Temple University
Philadelphia, Pennsylvania

Mary Margaret O'Reilly
Dublin, Ireland

Andrew J. O'Shaughnessy
University of Wisconsin
Oshkosh, Wisconsin

Robert M. Otten
Indiana University, Kokomo
Kokomo, Indiana

Blanford Parker
New York University
New York, New York

J.T. Parnell
Goldsmiths College, University of London
London, England, U.K.

Steve Patterson
Temple University
Philadelphia, Pennsylvania

Ruth Perry
Massachusetts Intitute of Technology
Cambridge, Massachusetts

Carl A. Peterson
Oberlin College
Oberlin, Ohio

Alexander Pettit
University of North Texas
Denton, Texas

Laura Pieringer
Temple University
Philadelphia, Pennsylvania

Mary Ann A. Powers
St. John's College
Sante Fe, New Mexico

Cathy Lynn Preston
University of Colorado
Boulder, Colorado

Roy S. Raby
Kent State University
Kent, Ohio

Richard N. Ramsey
Indiana University
Purdue University, Fort Wayne
Fort Wayne, Indiana

Ron Rarick
Ball State University
Muncie, Indiana

George F. Reed
West Chester University
West Chester, Pennsylvania

Joel Reed
Texas Tech University
Lubbock, Texas

Michael Reed
University of Loughborough
Loughborough, England, U.K.

Richard Riss
Drew University
Madison, New Jersey

Betty Rizzo
City College, CUNY
New York, New York

Bruce Robertson
University of California, Santa Barbara
Santa Barbara, California

Eric Robinson
University of Massachusetts, Boston
Boston, Massachusetts

Linda Smithey Robinson
Louisiana State University
Baton Rouge, Louisiana

Robb Robinson
Hull College
Hull, England, U.K.

Robert Gibson Robinson, III
Louisiana State University
Baton Rouge, Louisiana

Samuel Rogal
Illinois Valley Community College
Oglesby, Illinois

Pat Rogers
University of South Florida
Boca Raton, Florida

Ronald Rompkey
Memorial University of Newfoundland
St. John's, Newfoundland, Canada

Kimerly Rorschach
Swarthmore, Pennsylvania

Susan Rosa
University of Wisconsin, Milwaukee
Milwaukee, Wisconsin

John Rule
University of Southampton
Southampton, Hampshire, U.K.

Matthew Rusnak
University of Pennsylvania
Philadelphia, Pennsylvania

Janice Pence Ryan
Berryville, Virginia

Peter Sabor
Université Laval
Quebec, Canada

James J. Sack
University of Illinois at Chicago
Chicago, Illinois

Barbara Schnorrenberg
Birmingham, Alabama

Arthur F. Schrader
Southbridge, Massachusetts

Anne St.-John Scott
Kent State University
Kent, Ohio

Peter Seary
University of Toronto
Toronto, Ontario, Canada

Kim P. Sebaly
Kent State University
Kent, Ohio

John F. Sena
Ohio State University
Columbus, Ohio

Dan Shannon
DePauw University
Greencastle, Indiana

Richard B. Sher
New Jersey Institute of Technology
Newark, New Jersey

Kathryn Shevelow
University of California, San Diego
La Jolla, California

Geoffrey M. Sill
Rutgers University
Camden, New Jersey

David Sloan
University of Arkansas
Fayetteville, Arkansas

Robert Lance Snyder
West Georgia College
Carrollton, Georgia

Patricia Meyer Spacks
University of Virginia
Charlottesville, Virginia

David J. Starkey
University of Hull
Hull, England, U.K.

Daniel Statt
Auburn University, Montgomery
Montgomery, Alabama

Eugene Stelzig
SUNY Geneseo
Geneseo, New York

Joan K. Stemmler
Washington, D.C.

Carolyn Stevens
Kent State University
Kent, Ohio

J.C. Steward
University of California, Berkeley
Berkeley, California

Larry Stewart
University of Saskatchewan
Saskatoon, Saskatchewan, Canada

Damie Stillman
University of Delaware
Newark, Delaware

R.D. Stock
University of Nebraska
Lincoln, Nebraska

Michael F. Suarez, S.J.
Cambridge, Massachusetts

Rajani Sudan
Middlebury College
Middlebury, Vermont

Peter A. Tasch
Temple University
Philadelphia, Pennsylvania

Anya Taylor
John Jay College of Criminal Justice, CUNY
New York, New York

Nicholas Temperley
University of Illinois
Urbana, Illinois

Kenneth A. Thigpen
Penn State University
University Park, Pennsylvania

Anne Thompson
University of Minnesota
Minneapolis, Minnesota

Susan Thorne
Duke University
Durham, North Carolina

Mary Tiryak
Temple University
Philadelphia, Pennsylvania

Alma Topen
Scottish Brewing Archive
Glasgow, Scotland, U.K.

Neil L. Tranter
University of Stirling
Stirling, Scotland, U.K.

Lars E. Troide
McGill University
Montreal, Quebec, Canada

Linda Veronika Troost
Washington and Jefferson College
Washington, Pennsylvania

Randolph Trumbach
Baruch College, CUNY
New York, New York

Robert W. Uphaus
Michigan State University
East Lansing, Michigan

Simon Varey
University of California, Los Angeles
Los Angeles, California

Lawrence Venuti
Temple University
Philadelphia, Pennsylvania

Thomas D. Veve
Dalton College
Dalton, Georgia

A. Martin Wainwright
University of Akron
Akron, Ohio

Samantha Webb
Temple University
Philadelphia, Pennsylvania

Henry Weisser
Colorado State University
Fort Collins, Colorado

Arthur J. Weitzman
Northeastern University
Boston, Massachusetts

Christopher A. Whatley
University of Dundee
Dundee, Scotland, U.K.

Barbara Whitehead
DePauw University
Greencastle, Indiana

Jan Widmayer
Boise State University
Boise, Idaho

Mike Wiley
New York University
New York, New York

Lawrence Williams
University of Dundee
Dundee, Scotland, U.K.

Francis P. Wilson
Hofstra University
Hempstead, New York

K.R. Wood
Kent State University
Kent, Ohio

Paul B. Wood
University of Victoria
Victoria, British Columbia, Canada

R. Paul Yoder
University of Arkansas, Little Rock
Little Rock, Arkansas

John Roach Young
University of Strathclyde
Glasgow, Scotland, U.K.

Everett Zimmerman
University of California, Santa Barbara
Santa Barbara, California

Index

Principal entries are in **boldface** type. Illustrations are in *italics.*

B

C

D

G

H

I

J

K

L

N

O

P

Q

T

U

V

Y

Z